Vol. 13	Taber, et al., Employment Litigation in New York
Vols. 14-16	Kreindler, Rodriguez, et al., New York Law of Torts
Vols. 17-19	Field, Moskin, et al., New York and Delaware Business Organizations: Choice, Formation, Operation, Financing and Acquisitions
Vols. 20-25	Ostertag, Benson, et al., General Practice in New York
Vol. 26	Borchers, Markell, et al., New York State Administrative Procedure and Practice
Vol. A	Borges, et al., Enforcing Judgments and Collecting Debts in New York
Vols. B-C	Bensel, Frank, McKeon, et al., Personal Injury Practice in New York
Vols. D-E	Preminger, et al., Trusts and Estates Practice in New York
Vols. F-G	Finkelstein and Ferrara, Landlord and Tenant Practice in New York

This is Volume

25

of

WEST'S
NEW YORK PRACTICE
SERIES

West's New York Practice Series

Vol. 1	Walker, et al., New York Limited Liability Companies and Partnerships: A Guide to Law and Practice
Vols. 2-4	Haig, et al., Commercial Litigation in New York State Courts
Vol. 5	Barker and Alexander, Evidence in New York State and Federal Courts
Vol. 6	Greenberg, Marcus, et al., New York Criminal Law
Vol. 7	Marks, et al., New York Pretrial Criminal Procedure
Vol. 8	Davies, Stecich, Gold, et al., New York Civil Appellate Practice
Vol. 9	Ginsberg, Weinberg, et al., Environmental Law and Regulation in New York
Vol. 10	Sobie, et al., New York Family Court Practice
Vols. 11-12	Scheinkman, et al., New York Law of Domestic Relations

COORDINATED RESEARCH IN NEW YORK FROM WEST

New York Practice 2d
David D. Siegel

Handling the DWI Case in New York
Peter Gerstenzang

New York Elder Law Practice
Vincent J. Russo and Marvin Rachlin

WEST'S McKINNEY'S FORMS

Civil Practice Law and Rules

Uniform Commercial Code

Business Corporation Law

Matrimonial and Family Law

Real Property Practice

Estates and Surrogate Practice

Criminal Procedure Law

Not-For-Profit Corporation Law

Tax Practice and Procedure

Local Government Forms

Selected Consolidated Law Forms

McKinney's Consolidated Laws of New York Annotated

West's New York Legal Update

New York Digest

New York Law Finder

PAMPHLETS

New York Civil Practice Law and Rules

New York Sentence Charts

WESTLAW®

COORDINATED RESEARCH FROM WEST

WEST*Check*® and WESTMATE®

West CD–ROM Libraries™

To order any of these New York practice tools, call your West Representative or 1–800–328–9352.

NEED RESEARCH HELP?

If you have research questions concerning WESTLAW or West Publications, call West's Reference Attorneys at 1–800–733–2889.

GENERAL PRACTICE IN NEW YORK

By

ROBERT L. OSTERTAG
HON. JAMES D. BENSON

Sections 38.1 to End
TABLES and INDEX

ST. PAUL, MINN.
WEST GROUP
1998

GENERAL PRACTICE IN NEW YORK
FORMS ON DISK™

The **Forms on Disk**™ which accompany these volumes provide instant access to WordPerfect 5.1/5.2 versions of the forms included in *General Practice in New York*. These electronic forms will save you hours of time drafting legal documents. The electronic forms can be loaded into your word processing software and formatted to match the document style of your law firm. These electronic forms become templates for you to use over and over without having to retype them each time.

The forms in Volumes 20, 21, 22, 23, 24 and 25 that are included on the accompanying disks are marked with the following disk icon for easy identification. 💾

COPYRIGHT © 1998 By WEST GROUP
610 Opperman Drive
P.O. Box 64526
St. Paul, MN 55164–0526
1–800–328–9352

All rights reserved
Printed in the United States of America
ISBN 0–314–23146–3

TEXT IS PRINTED ON 10% POST CONSUMER RECYCLED PAPER

WESTLAW® ELECTRONIC RESEARCH GUIDE

Coordinating Legal Research with WESTLAW

The *New York Practice Series* is an essential aid to legal research. WESTLAW provides a vast, online library of over 8000 collections of documents and services that can supplement research begun in this publication, encompassing:

- Federal and state primary law (statutes, regulations, rules, and case law), including West's editorial enhancements, such as headnotes, Key Number classifications, annotations

- Secondary law resources (texts and treatises published by West Group and by other publishers, as well as law reviews)

- Legal news

- Directories of attorneys and experts

- Court records and filings

- Citators

Specialized topical subsets of these resources have been created for more than thirty areas of practice.

In addition to legal information, there are general news and reference databases and a broad array of specialized materials frequently useful in connection with legal matters, covering accounting, business, environment, ethics, finance, medicine, social and physical sciences.

This guide will focus on a few aspects of WESTLAW use to supplement research begun in this publication, and will direct you to additional sources of assistance.

Databases

A database is a collection of documents with some features in common. It may contain statutes, court decisions, administrative materials, commentaries, news or other information. Each database has a unique identifier, used in many WESTLAW commands to select a database of interest. For example, the database containing New York cases has the identifier NY-CS.

The WESTLAW Directory is a comprehensive list of databases with information about each database, including the types of documents each

WESTLAW ELECTRONIC RESEARCH GUIDE

contains. The first page of a standard or customized WESTLAW Directory is displayed upon signing on to WESTLAW, except when prior, saved research is resumed. To access the WESTLAW Directory at any time, enter DB.

Databases of potential interest in connection with your research include:

NY-AG	New York Attorney General Opinions
NYETH-EO	New York Ethics Opinions
NYETH-CS	Legal Ethics & Professional Responsibility - New York Cases
WLD-NY	West's Legal Directory - New York
LAWPRAC	The Legal Practice Database

For information as to currentness and search tips regarding any WESTLAW database, enter the SCOPE command SC followed by the database identifier (e.g., SC NY-CS). It is not necessary to include the identifier to obtain scope information about the currently selected database.

WESTLAW Highlights

Use of this publication may be supplemented through the WESTLAW Bulletin (WLB), the WESTLAW New York State Bulletin (WSB-NY) and various Topical Highlights. Highlights databases contain summaries of significant judicial, legislative and administrative developments and are updated daily; they are searchable both from an automatic list of recent documents and using general WESTLAW search methods for documents accumulated over time. The full text of any judicial decision may be retrieved by entering FIND.

Consult the WESTLAW Directory (enter DB) for a complete, current listing of highlights databases.

Retrieving a Specific Case

The FIND command can be used to quickly retrieve a case whose citation is known. For example:

FI 616 A.2d 1336

Updating Case Law Research

There are a variety of citator services on WESTLAW for use in updating research.

Insta-Cite® may be used to verify citations, find parallel citations, ascertain the history of a case, and see whether it remains valid law. References are also provided to secondary sources, such as Corpus Juris Secundum®, that cite the case. To view the Insta-Cite history of a displayed case, simply enter the command IC. To view the Insta-Cite history of a selected case, enter a command in this form:

IC 574 A.2d 502

Shepard's® Citations provides a comprehensive list of cases and publications that have cited a particular case, with explanatory analysis to indicate how the citing cases have treated the case, e.g., "followed," "explained." To view the Shepard's Citations about a displayed case, enter the command SH. Add a case citation, if necessary, as in the prior Insta-Cite example.

For the latest citing references, not yet incorporated in Shepard's Citations, use Shepard's PreView® (SP command) and QuickCite™ (QC command), in the same way.

To see a complete list of publications covered by any of the citator services, enter its service abbreviation (IC, SH, SP or QC) followed by PUBS. To ascertain the scope of coverage for any of the services, enter the SCOPE command (SC) followed by the appropriate service abbreviation. For the complete list of commands available in a citator service, enter its service abbreviation (IC, SH, SP or QC) followed by CMDS.

Retrieving Statutes, Court Rules and Regulations

Annotated and unannotated versions of the New York statutes are searchable on WESTLAW (identifiers NY-ST-ANN and NY-ST), as are New York court rules (NY-RULES) and New York Administrative Code (NY-ADC).

The United States Code and United States Code - Annotated are searchable databases on WESTLAW (identifiers USC and USCA, respectively), as are federal court rules (US-RULES) and regulations (CFR).

In addition, the FIND command may be used to retrieve specific provisions by citation, obviating the need for database selection or search. To FIND a desired document, enter FI, followed by the citation of the desired document, using the full name of the publication, or one of the abbreviated styles recognized by WESTLAW.

If WESTLAW does not recognize the style you enter, you may enter one of the following, using US, NY, or any other state code in place of XX:

FI XX-ST	Displays templates for codified statutes
FI XX-LEGIS	Displays templates for legislation
FI XX-RULES	Displays templates for rules
FI XX-ORDERS	Displays templates for court orders

Alternatively, entering FI followed by the publication's full name or an accepted abbreviation will normally display templates, useful jump possibilities, or helpful information necessary to complete the FIND process. For example:

FI USCA	Displays templates for United States Code - Annotated
FI FRAP	Displays templates for Federal Rules of Appellate Procedure
FI FRCP	Displays templates for Federal Rules of Civil Procedure
FI FRCRP	Displays templates for Federal Rules of Criminal Procedure
FI FRE	Displays templates for Federal Rules of Evidence
FI CFR	Displays templates for Code of Federal Regulations
FI FR	Displays templates for Federal Register

To view the complete list of FINDable documents and associated prescribed forms, enter FI PUBS.

Updating Research in re Statutes, Rules and Regulations

When viewing a statute, rule or regulation on WESTLAW after a search or FIND command, it is easy to update your research. A message will appear on the screen if relevant amendments, repeals or other new material are available through the UPDATE feature. Entering the UPDATE command will display such material.

Documents used to update New York statutes are also searchable in New York Legislative Service (NY-LEGIS). Those used to update rules are searchable in New York Orders (NY-ORDERS).

Documents used to update federal statutes, rules, and regulations are searchable in the United States Public Laws (US-PL), Federal Orders (US-ORDERS) and Federal Register (FR) databases, respectively.

When documents citing a statute, rule or regulation are of interest, Shepard's Citations on WESTLAW may be of assistance. That service covers federal constitutional provisions, statutes and administrative provisions, and corresponding materials from many states. The command SH PUBS displays a directory of publications which may be Shepardized on WESTLAW. Consult the WESTLAW manual for more information about citator services.

Using WESTLAW as a Citator

For research beyond the coverage of any citator service, go directly to the databases (cases, for example) containing citing documents and use standard WESTLAW search techniques to retrieve documents citing specific constitutional provisions, statutes, standard jury instructions or other authorities.

Fortunately, the specific portion of a citation is often reasonably distinctive, such as 22:636.1, 301.65, 401(k), 12-21-5, 12052. When it is, a search on that specific portion alone may retrieve applicable documents without any substantial number of inapplicable ones (unless the number happens to be coincidentally popular in another context).

Similarly, if the citation involves more than one number, such as 42 U.S.C.A. §1201, a search containing both numbers (e.g., 42 +5 1201) is likely to produce mostly desired information, even though the component numbers are common.

If necessary, the search may be limited in several ways:

A. Switch from a general database to one containing mostly cases within the subject area of the cite being researched;

B. Use a connector (&, /S, /P, etc.) to narrow the search to documents including terms which are highly likely to accompany the correct citation in the context of the issue being researched;

C. Include other citation information in the query. Because of the variety of citation formats used in documents, this option should be used primarily where other options prove insufficient. Below are illustrative queries for any database containing New York cases:

>N.Y.Const.! Const.! Constitution /s 6 VI +3 3

will retrieve cases citing the New York State Constitution, Art. 6, §3; and

>"Criminal Procedure Law" CPL /s 30.30

will retrieve cases citing Criminal Procedure Law §30.30.

Alternative Retrieval Methods

WIN® (WESTLAW Is Natural™) allows you to frame your issue in plain English to retrieve documents:

>Does new trial motion extend (toll) the time for filing (taking) appeal?

Alternatively, retrieval may be focused by use of the Terms and Connectors method:

>TO(30) /P DI(NEW +1 TRIAL /P EXTEND! EXTENSION TOLL! /P APPEAL)

In databases with Key Numbers, either of the above examples will identify Appeal and Error ⟠345.1 as a Key Number collecting headnotes relevant to this issue if there are pertinent cases.

Since the Key Numbers are affixed to points of law by trained specialists based on conceptual understanding of the case, relevant cases that were not retrieved by either of the language-dependent methods will often be found at a Key Number.

WESTLAW ELECTRONIC RESEARCH GUIDE

Similarly, citations in retrieved documents (to cases, statutes, rules, etc.) may suggest additional, fruitful research using other WESTLAW databases (e.g., annotated statutes, rules) or services (e.g., citator services).

Key Number Search

Frequently, case law research rapidly converges on a few topics, headings and Key Numbers within West's Key Number System that are likely to contain relevant cases. These may be discovered from known, relevant reported cases from any jurisdiction; Library References in West publications; browsing in a digest; or browsing the Key Number System on WESTLAW using the JUMP feature or the KEY command.

Once discovered, topics, subheadings or Key Numbers are useful as search terms (in databases containing reported cases) alone or with other search terms, to focus the search within a narrow range of potentially relevant material.

For example, to retrieve cases with at least one headnote classified to Appeal and Error ⟳345.1, sign on to a caselaw database and enter

    30k345.1   [use with other search terms, if desired]

The topic name (Appeal and Error) is replaced by its numerical equivalent (30) and the ⟳ by the letter k. A list of topics and their numerical equivalents is in the WESTLAW Reference Manual and is displayed in WESTLAW when the KEY command is entered.

Using JUMP

WESTLAW's JUMP feature allows you to move from one document to another or from one part of a document to another, then easily return to your original place, without losing your original result. Opportunities to move in this manner are marked in the text with a JUMP symbol (▶). Whenever you see the JUMP symbol, you may move to the place designated by the adjacent reference by using the Tab, arrow keys or mouse click to position the cursor on the JUMP symbol, then pressing Enter or clicking again with the mouse.

Within the text of a court opinion, JUMP arrows are adjacent to case cites and federal statute cites, and adjacent to parenthesized numbers marking discussions corresponding to headnotes.

On a screen containing the text of a headnote, the JUMP arrows allow movement to the corresponding discussion in the text of the opinion,

   ▶ (3)

and allow browsing West's Key Number System beginning at various heading levels:

- ▶ 30   APPEAL AND ERROR
- ▶ 30VII   Transfer of Cause
- ▶ 30VII(A)   Time of Taking Proceedings
- ▶ 30k343   Commencement of Period of Limitation
- ▶ 30k345.1 k.   Motion for new trial.

To return from a JUMP, enter GB (except for JUMPs between a headnote and the corresponding discussion in opinion, for which there is a matching number in parenthesis in both headnote and opinion). Returns from successive JUMPs (e.g., from case to cited case to case cited by cited case) without intervening returns may be accomplished by repeated entry of GB or by using the MAP command.

General Information

The information provided above illustrates some of the ways WESTLAW can complement research using this publication. However, this brief overview illustrates only some of the power of WESTLAW. The full range of WESTLAW search techniques is available to support your research.

Please consult the WESTLAW Reference Manual for additional information or assistance or call West's Reference Attorneys at 1-800-REF-ATTY (1-800-733-2889).

For information about subscribing to WESTLAW, please call 1-800-328-9352.

*

SUMMARY OF CONTENTS

Page

Volume 20

Chapter
1. Business Organizations: Corporations 2
2. Non-corporate Entities: Limited Liability Companies and Partnerships 253
3. Municipal Law 403
4. Administrative Law 468
5. Commercial Sales Contracts 594
6. Buying and Selling a Small Business 670

Volume 21

7. Consumer Law 2
8. Enforcement of Money Judgments 181
9. Bankruptcy 253
10. Mechanic's Liens 541
11. Mortgage Foreclosure 683
12. Purchase and Sale of Real Estate 792

Volume 22

13. Landlord–Tenant Law 2
14. Eminent Domain 108
15. Environmental Law 212
16. New York Land Use Law 296
17. New York Employment Law 467
18. Civil Rights Law 609
19. Immigration and Nationality Law—Permanent Residence Applications 733
20. Adoptions 857

Volume 23

21. Domestic Relations 2
22. Guardianship 162
23. Elder Law 329
24. Estate Planning 448
25. Probate and Estate Administration 545
26. Personal Injury 638

xv

SUMMARY OF CONTENTS

Chapter   **Page**

27. Products Liability 722

Volume 24

28. Legal Malpractice 2
29. Medical Malpractice 92
30. Damages 166
31. Insurance 251
32. Workers' Compensation 315
33. Local Criminal Court Practice 382
34. Social Security Disability Cases 452
35. Income Tax 551
36. Alcoholic Beverage Control Law 653
37. Civil Appellate Practice Before the Appellate Division and Other Intermediate Appellate Courts 738

Volume 25

38. Criminal Appellate Practice Before the Appellate Division and Other Intermediate Appelllate Courts 2
39. Civil and Criminal Appeals to the Court of Appeals 145

Table of Jury Instructions 235
Table of Forms 236
Table of Statutes iii
Table of Rules iii
Table of Cases iii
Index iii

TABLE OF CONTENTS

Volume 20

CHAPTER 1. BUSINESS ORGANIZATIONS: CORPORATIONS

Sec.
- 1.1 Scope Note.
- 1.2 Strategy.
- 1.3 Strategy Checklist.
- 1.4 Overview.
- 1.5 Definitions.
- 1.6 Formation of Corporations.
- 1.7 ——— Certificates; Notices.
- 1.8 ——— Corporate Seal.
- 1.9 ——— Corporate Purposes.
- 1.10 ——— ——— Upholding and Disregarding the Corporate Entity.
- 1.11 ——— ——— General Powers.
- 1.12 ——— ——— Defense of *Ultra Vires*.
- 1.13 ——— Corporate Name.
- 1.14 ——— ——— Reservation of Name.
- 1.15 ——— Service of Process.
- 1.16 ——— ——— Records and Certificates of Department of State.
- 1.17 ——— ——— Statutory Designation of Secretary of State as Agent for Service of Process.
- 1.18 ——— ——— Registered Agent for Service of Process.
- 1.19 ——— ——— Upon Unauthorized Foreign Corporation.
- 1.20 ——— Incorporators and Promoters.
- 1.21 ——— Certificate of Incorporation.
- 1.22 ——— Bylaws.
- 1.23 ——— Organization Meeting; Biennial Statement; Franchise Tax.
- 1.24 ——— Formation of Corporations Summary.
- 1.25 ——— Formation of Corporations Checklist.
- 1.26 Capital Structure.
- 1.27 ——— Authorized Shares.
- 1.28 ——— Preferred Shares in Series.
- 1.29 ——— Subscription for Shares.
- 1.30 ——— Consideration and Payment for Shares.
- 1.31 ——— Rights to Purchase Shares.
- 1.32 ——— Stated Capital.
- 1.33 ——— Corporate Bonds; Convertible Securities.
- 1.34 ——— Federal Income Taxation Aspects.
- 1.35 ——— Capital Structure Summary.
- 1.36 ——— Capital Structure Checklist.
- 1.37 Distributions.
- 1.38 ——— Dividends; Share Distributions and Changes.
- 1.39 ——— Purchase or Redemption of Shares.

TABLE OF CONTENTS

Sec.
1.40 ___ Federal Income Tax Aspects.
1.41 ___ Distributions Summary.
1.42 ___ Distributions Checklist.
1.43 Shareholders' Meetings and Agreements—Generally.
1.44 ___ Notice Requirements.
1.45 ___ Voting.
1.46 ___ Quorum Requirements.
1.47 ___ Agreements; Voting Trusts.
1.48 ___ Action Without a Meeting.
1.49 Shareholders' Meetings and Agreements Summary.
1.50 Shareholders' Meetings and Agreements Checklist.
1.51 Shareholders' Rights.
1.52 ___ Preemptive Rights.
1.53 ___ Inspection of Books and Records.
1.54 ___ Shareholders' Rights Summary.
1.55 ___ Shareholders' Rights Checklist.
1.56 Shareholders' Liabilities.
1.57 ___ Shareholders' Liabilities Summary.
1.58 ___ Shareholders' Liabilities Checklist.
1.59 Directors.
1.60 ___ Vacancies; New Directorships.
1.61 ___ Removal.
1.62 ___ Meetings.
1.63 ___ ___ Quorum and Voting Requirements.
1.64 ___ Executive Committee; Other Committees.
1.65 ___ Fiduciary Duties.
1.66 ___ Liabilities.
1.67 ___ Directors Summary.
1.68 ___ Directors Checklist.
1.69 Officers.
1.70 ___ Officers Summary.
1.71 ___ Officers Checklist.
1.72 Amendment of Certificate of Incorporation.
1.73 ___ Procedure.
1.74 ___ Class Vote.
1.75 ___ Certificate of Amendment.
1.76 ___ Certificate of Change.
1.77 ___ Restated Certificate of Incorporation.
1.78 ___ Reorganization Under Act of Congress.
1.79 Amendment of Certificate of Incorporation Summary.
1.80 Amendment of Certificate of Incorporation Checklist.
1.81 Business Combinations.
1.82 ___ Mergers and Consolidations.
1.83 ___ ___ Procedures.
1.84 ___ ___ Effect.
1.85 ___ Sale, Lease, Exchange, or Other Disposition of Assets.
1.86 ___ ___ Mortgage or Security Interest in Assets.
1.87 ___ ___ Guarantee Authorized by Shareholders.
1.88 ___ Share Exchanges.
1.89 ___ Takeover Bids.

TABLE OF CONTENTS

Sec.	
1.90	____ Right of Shareholder to Receive Payment for Shares.
1.91	____ Federal Income Taxation Aspects.
1.92	Business Combinations Summary.
1.93	Business Combinations Checklist.
1.94	Dissolution.
1.95	____ Non-judicial Dissolution.
1.96	____ ____ Authorization.
1.97	____ ____ Certificate of Dissolution.
1.98	____ ____ Notice to Creditors.
1.99	____ Judicial Dissolution.
1.100	____ ____ Attorney General's Action.
1.101	____ ____ Directors' Petition.
1.102	____ ____ Shareholders' Petition.
1.103	____ ____ Petition Upon Deadlock Among Directors or Shareholders and in Other Circumstances.
1.104	____ ____ Procedures.
1.105	____ ____ Preservation of Assets; Appointment of Receiver.
1.106	____ ____ Certain Transfers and Judgments Void; Injunction.
1.107	____ Liquidation Distributions.
1.108	____ ____ Federal Income Tax Aspects.
1.109	____ Dissolution Summary.
1.110	____ Dissolution Checklist.
1.111	Receivership.
1.112	Receivership—Summary.
1.113	____ Checklist.
1.114	Foreign Corporations.
1.115	____ Authorization to Do Business in New York.
1.116	____ Application for Authority.
1.117	____ ____ Effect of Filing.
1.118	____ Surrender of Authority.
1.119	____ Termination of Existence.
1.120	Foreign Corporations Summary.
1.121	Foreign Corporations Checklist.
1.122	Professional Service Corporations.
1.123	Professional Service Corporations Summary.
1.124	Professional Service Corporations Checklist.
1.125	Foreign Professional Service Corporations.
1.126	Foreign Professional Service Corporations Summary.
1.127	Foreign Professional Service Corporations Checklist.
1.128	Transactional Checklist—Generally.
1.129	____ Formation ("Birth").
1.130	____ Operation ("Growth").
1.131	____ Business Combinations ("Marriage").
1.132	____ Spin-offs and Split-offs ("Children" and "Divorce").
1.133	____ Repurchase of Shares ("Redemption").
1.134	____ Dissolution; Liquidation ("Death").
1.135	Procedural Checklist—Generally.
1.136	____ Notices.
1.137	____ Reservation of Corporate Name.
1.138	____ ____ Foreign Corporations.

TABLE OF CONTENTS

Sec.
1.139 ____ Mandatory and Permissive Provisions in Certificate of Incorporation.
1.140 ____ Incorporation.
1.141 ____ Filing Certificate of Incorporation.
1.142 ____ Bylaws.
1.143 ____ Organization Meetings.
1.144 ____ Share Certificate.
1.145 ____ Shareholder Approval Requirements.
1.146 ____ Shareholder's Right to Receive Payment for Shares.
1.147 ____ Close Corporations.
1.148 ____ Foreign Corporations.
1.149 Drafting Checklist.
1.150 Form—Application to Reserve Corporate Name.
1.151 ____ Certificate of Incorporation.
1.152 ____ Bylaws.
1.153 ____ Subscription Agreement.
1.154 ____ Certificate of Amendment.
1.155 ____ Certificate of Dissolution.

CHAPTER 2. NON-CORPORATE ENTITIES: LIMITED LIABILTY COMPANIES AND PARTNERSHIPS

2.1 Scope Note.
2.2 Strategy—Choice of Entity.
2.3 Tax Classification.
2.4 ____ Eagerly–Awaited Simplification.
2.5 ____ Former Corporate Characteristics Test.
2.6 ____ ____ Limited Liability.
2.7 ____ ____ Continuity of Life.
2.8 ____ ____ Free Transferability of Interests.
2.9 ____ ____ Centralized Management.
2.10 Partnership vs. LLC.
2.11 ____ Tax Implications.
2.12 ____ Liability.
2.13 ____ Flexibility.
2.14 Limited Liability Companies.
2.15 ____ Governing Law.
2.16 ____ Formation.
2.17 ____ ____ Articles of Organization.
2.18 ____ ____ Publication.
2.19 ____ ____ Operating Agreement.
2.20 ____ ____ Other Issues.
2.21 ____ Members.
2.22 ____ ____ Admission of New Members.
2.23 ____ ____ Liability.
2.24 ____ ____ One-member LLCs.
2.25 ____ Management.
2.26 ____ ____ Members vs. Managers.
2.27 ____ ____ Voting: Members.
2.28 ____ ____ Voting: Managers.

TABLE OF CONTENTS

Sec.	
2.29	_____ _____ Non-waivable Requirements.
2.30	_____ _____ Delegation of Responsibility.
2.31	_____ _____ Standard of Care.
2.32	_____ _____ Agency Authority.
2.33	_____ Assignment of Interests.
2.34	_____ _____ Default Rules.
2.35	_____ _____ Vote Required to Admit Assignee as Member.
2.36	_____ Dissolution.
2.37	_____ _____ Events.
2.38	_____ _____ Continuation of Business after Dissolution Event.
2.39	_____ _____ Winding Up.
2.40	_____ Conversions/Mergers.
2.41	_____ _____ Procedures.
2.42	_____ _____ Dissenters' Rights.
2.43	_____ PLLCs.
2.44	General Partnerships.
2.45	_____ Governing Law.
2.46	_____ Formation.
2.47	_____ _____ Agreement.
2.48	_____ _____ Business Certificate.
2.49	_____ _____ Publication.
2.50	_____ _____ Other Issues.
2.51	_____ Partners.
2.52	_____ _____ Admission of New Partners.
2.53	_____ _____ Liability.
2.54	_____ _____ Contribution Issues.
2.55	_____ Management.
2.56	_____ _____ Voting.
2.57	_____ _____ Non-waivable Requirements.
2.58	_____ _____ Delegation of Responsibility.
2.59	_____ _____ Standard of Care.
2.60	_____ _____ Agency Authority.
2.61	_____ Assignment of Interests.
2.62	_____ _____ Default Rules.
2.63	_____ _____ Vote Required to Admit New Partner.
2.64	_____ Dissolution.
2.65	_____ _____ Events.
2.66	_____ _____ Continuation of Business after Dissolution Event.
2.67	_____ _____ Winding Up.
2.68	_____ Conversions/Mergers.
2.69	_____ _____ Procedures.
2.70	_____ _____ Dissenters' Rights.
2.71	_____ Professional Organizations.
2.72	Limited Liability Partnerships.
2.73	_____ Governing Law.
2.74	_____ Comparison with General Partnerships.
2.75	_____ Formation/Registration.
2.76	_____ Other Issues.
2.77	Limited Partnerships.
2.78	_____ Governing Law.

TABLE OF CONTENTS

Sec.
2.79 ___ Formation.
2.80 ___ ___ Certificate of Limited Partnership.
2.81 ___ ___ Publication.
2.82 ___ ___ Agreement.
2.83 ___ ___ Other Issues.
2.84 ___ Partners.
2.85 ___ ___ Admission of New Partners.
2.86 ___ ___ Liability.
2.87 ___ Contribution Issues.
2.88 ___ Management.
2.89 ___ ___ Voting: General Partners.
2.90 ___ ___ Voting: Limited Partners.
2.91 ___ ___ Delegation of Responsibility.
2.92 ___ ___ Standard of Care.
2.93 ___ ___ Agency Authority.
2.94 ___ Assignment of Interests.
2.95 ___ ___ Default Rules.
2.96 ___ ___ Vote Required to Admit New Partner.
2.97 ___ Dissolution.
2.98 ___ ___ Events.
2.99 ___ ___ Continuation of Business after Dissolution Event.
2.100 ___ ___ Winding Up.
2.101 ___ Conversions/Mergers.
2.102 ___ ___ Procedures.
2.103 ___ ___ Dissenters' Rights.
2.104 ___ Professional Organizations.
2.105 Due Diligence Issues.
2.106 Securities Laws Issues.
2.107 Summary.
2.108 Chart Comparing New York Entities.
2.109 Drafting Checklist.
2.110 Forms.
2.111 ___ LLC Articles of Organization. 💾
2.112 ___ Operating Agreement: Member–Managed LLC. 💾
2.113 ___ Registration as LLP. 💾
2.114 ___ Certificate of Limited Partnership. 💾
2.115 ___ Limited Partnership Agreement. 💾

CHAPTER 3. MUNICIPAL LAW

3.1 Scope Note.
3.2 Strategy.
3.3 Municipal Corporations.
3.4 ___ Creation.
3.5 ___ Consolidation, Annexation and Dissolution.
3.6 ___ ___ Annexation Checklist.
3.7 Powers of Municipal Corporations.
3.8 ___ Governmental v. Proprietary Powers.
3.9 ___ Police Powers.
3.10 Legislative Enactments.

TABLE OF CONTENTS

Sec.
3.11	____ Resolutions.
3.12	____ Ordinances.
3.13	____ Rules and Regulations.
3.14	____ Local Laws.
3.15	____ Referendum Requirements.
3.16	Acquisition and Disposition of Property.
3.17	Officers and Employees.
3.18	____ Qualifications.
3.19	____ Terms.
3.20	____ Removal.
3.21	____ Collective Bargaining.
3.22	____ Conflicts of Interest.
3.23	____ ____ Checklist.
3.24	Contracts.
3.25	____ Competitive Bidding.
3.26	Municipal Finance.
3.27	____ Municipal Borrowing.
3.28	Public Meetings.
3.29	Access to Records.
3.30	Tort Claims Against Municipalities.
3.31	____ Checklist.
3.32	Challenges to Governmental Determinations.
3.33	Special Purpose Units of Government.
3.34	____ Industrial Development Agencies.
3.35	____ Public Authorities.
3.36	Forms.
3.37	____ Notice of Claim. 💾
3.38	____ Verified Complaint in Tort Action. 💾

CHAPTER 4. ADMINISTRATIVE LAW

4.1	Scope Note.
4.2	Strategy.
4.3	____ Checklist.
4.4	Procedural Due Process.
4.5	____ Individualized State Action.
4.6	____ Protected Interests.
4.7	____ The Process Due.
4.8	____ Summary.
4.9	____ Checklist.
4.10	Adjudicatory Proceedings.
4.11	____ Definition of an Adjudicatory Proceeding.
4.12	____ Notice.
4.13	____ Discovery.
4.14	____ Right to Counsel.
4.15	____ Evidence.
4.16	____ Cross-Examination and Witness Attendance.
4.17	____ Official Notice.
4.18	____ Statement of Decision and Decisional Record.
4.19	____ Burden of Proof.

TABLE OF CONTENTS

Sec.
4.20	___	Intervention.
4.21	___	Unreasonable Agency Delay.
4.22	___	Agency Duty to Decide Consistently.
4.23	___	Intra-agency Review.
4.24	___	Checking Agency Bias.
4.25	___	*Res Judicata* and Collateral Estoppel Effect.
4.26	___	Special Rules Applicable to Licensing Matters.
4.27	___	Special Issues in Handling Licensing Matters.
4.28	___ ___	Basic License Information.
4.29	___ ___	The Role of SAPA and SEQRA in the Licensing Process.
4.30	___ ___	Accuracy and Completeness in Applications.
4.31	___ ___	Opportunities to Expedite the Process.
4.32	___ ___	Opportunities for Variances from Standard Approaches.
4.33	___ ___	Renewal, Suspension and Revocation Issues.
4.34	___	Special Issues in Handling Enforcement Matters.
4.35	___ ___	Strategies to Minimize Violations.
4.36	___ ___	Agency Fact–Finding in the Pre-enforcement Phase.
4.37	___ ___	Agency Enforcement Options.
4.38	___ ___	The Settlement Process.
4.39	___ ___	The Hearing Process.
4.40	___ ___	Post–Hearing Issues.
4.41	___	Summary.
4.42	___	Checklist.
4.43	Administrative Rulemaking.	
4.44	___	Rulemaking Compared With Other Agency Action.
4.45	___	Rulemaking Notice.
4.46	___	Comments and Agency Assessment of Comments.
4.47	___	Agency Duty to Reveal Underlying Information.
4.48	___	Notice of Adoption and Effective Date of Rules.
4.49	___	Ancillary Documentation and the Role of GORR.
4.50	___	Rule Filing and Publication.
4.51	___	Declaratory Rulings Regarding Rules.
4.52	___	Overlapping State and Federal Rules.
4.53	___	Special Strategic Considerations in Handling Administrative Rulemaking Matters.
4.54	___ ___	Basic Sources of Information on Rulemaking.
4.55	___ ___	Participating in the Rulemaking Process.
4.56	___ ___	Special Issues in Negotiated Rulemakings.
4.57	___ ___	Special Issues in Emergency Rulemakings.
4.58	___ ___	Agency Guidance Documents.
4.59	___	Summary.
4.60	___	Checklist.
4.61	Agency Information–Gathering.	
4.62	___	Administrative Searches.
4.63	___	Administrative Subpoenas.
4.64	___	Reporting and Recordkeeping Requirements.
4.65	___	Summary.
4.66	___	Checklist.
4.67	Judicial Review.	
4.68	___	Delegation of Authority to Agencies.

TABLE OF CONTENTS

Sec.
4.69 ____ Standing to Seek Judicial Review.
4.70 ____ Ripeness.
4.71 ____ Final Order and Relief in the Nature of Prohibition.
4.72 ____ Exhaustion of Administrative Remedies.
4.73 ____ Primary Jurisdiction.
4.74 ____ Statutory Preclusion of Judicial Review.
4.75 ____ Article 78 and the Consolidation of the Common Law Prerogative Writs.
4.76 ____ Standards of Review.
4.77 ____ ____ Review of Agency Determinations of Law.
4.78 ____ ____ Review of Agency Determinations of Fact Under the Substantial Evidence Test.
4.79 ____ ____ Review of Agency Determinations of Fact Under the Arbitrary and Capricious Test.
4.80 ____ ____ Review of Administrative Rules.
4.81 ____ ____ Review of Administrative Discretion.
4.82 ____ Statutes of Limitation Applicable to Judicial Review of Agency Action.
4.83 ____ Venue in Article 78 Proceedings.
4.84 ____ Subject Matter Jurisdiction in Article 78 Proceedings.
4.85 ____ Summary.
4.86 ____ Checklist.
4.87 Forms.
4.88 ____ Notice of Appearance in Licensing or Permitting Matter.
4.89 ____ Notice for Discovery and Inspection in an Administrative Proceeding.
4.90 ____ Notice of Deposition in an Administrative Proceeding.
4.91 ____ Notice to Permit Entry Upon Real Property.

CHAPTER 5. COMMERCIAL SALES CONTRACTS

5.1 Scope Note.
5.2 Strategy.
5.3 Transactional Checklist—Breach of Contract.
5.4 Defining a Contract.
5.5 Governing Law.
5.6 ____ Freedom to Contract—Generally.
5.7 ____ ____ Presumption of Legality.
5.8 ____ ____ ____ Burden of Proof.
5.9 ____ ____ ____ Determining the Contract's Validity.
5.10 ____ ____ ____ Not All Illegal Contracts Are Unenforceable.
5.11 ____ Public Policy Issues.
5.12 ____ Unconscionability.
5.13 ____ ____ Elements.
5.14 ____ ____ Codification in UCC.
5.15 ____ Duty of Good Faith—Generally.
5.16 ____ ____ Codification in UCC.
5.17 The Written Contract—Statute of Frauds.
5.18 ____ ____ General Rules.
5.19 ____ ____ Formal Requirements.

XXV

TABLE OF CONTENTS

Sec.	
5.20	———— ———— Nature of the Writing.
5.21	———— Parol or Extrinsic Evidence.
5.22	———— Offer.
5.23	———— Acceptance.
5.24	———— ———— Additional Terms.
5.25	———— Indefiniteness.
5.26	———— Use of Open Terms.
5.27	Warranties.
5.28	———— Warranty of Title Against Infringement.
5.29	———— Express Warranty.
5.30	———— Implied Warranty of Merchantability.
5.31	———— Implied Warranty of Fitness for a Particular Purpose.
5.32	Assumption of the Risk of Loss.
5.33	———— In the Absence of Breach.
5.34	———— In the Event of a Breach.
5.35	Performance.
5.36	———— Buyer's Response to Tender of Delivery.
5.37	———— ———— Acceptance.
5.38	———— ———— Rejection.
5.39	———— ———— Revocation of Acceptance.
5.40	Breach of Contract.
5.41	———— Seller's Remedies.
5.42	———— ———— Action for the Price.
5.43	———— ———— Withholding the Goods and Stopping Delivery.
5.44	———— ———— Recovery of Goods Delivered.
5.45	———— ———— Resale.
5.46	———— ———— Damages for Non-acceptance or Repudiation.
5.47	———— Buyer's Remedies.
5.48	———— ———— Cover.
5.49	———— ———— Damages for Non-delivery.
5.50	———— ———— Damages for Breach Regarding Accepted Goods.
5.51	———— ———— Specific Performance or Replevin.
5.52	———— Liquidated Damages.
5.53	———— Mitigation of Damages.
5.54	Third-Party Interests.
5.55	———— Subsequent Buyers.
5.56	———— Other Creditors.
5.57	Drafting Checklists—Order of Goods for Resale by Buyer.
5.58	———— Verified Complaint On Account Stated for Goods, Services and Wares Delivered.
5.59	———— Plaintiff's Notice of Motion for Summary Judgment in Contract Action.
5.60	———— Affidavit of Officer of Plaintiff Company in Support of Summary Judgment Motion in Contract Action.
5.61	———— Notice of Petition for Order Staying Arbitration in Dispute Over Contract for Sale of Goods.
5.62	———— Petition for Order Staying Arbitration in Dispute Over Contract for Sale of Goods.
5.63	———— Affidavit in Opposition to Petition for Order Staying Arbitration in Dispute Over Contract for Sale of Goods.

TABLE OF CONTENTS

Sec.
5.64 ____ Answer to Petition for Order Staying Arbitration in Dispute Over Contract for Sale of Goods.
5.65 Forms—Order of Goods for Resale by Buyer. 💾
5.66 ____ Verified Complaint On Account Stated for Goods, Services and Wares Delivered. 💾
5.67 ____ Plaintiff's Notice of Motion for Summary Judgment in Contract Action. 💾
5.68 ____ Affidavit of Vice President of Plaintiff Purchaser in Support of Summary Judgment Motion in Contract Action. 💾
5.69 ____ Notice of Petition for Order Staying Arbitration in Dispute Over Contract for Sale of Goods. 💾
5.70 ____ Petition for Order Staying Arbitration in Dispute Over Contract for Sale of Goods. 💾
5.71 ____ Affidavit in Opposition to Petition for Order Staying Arbitration in Dispute Over Contract for Sale of Goods. 💾
5.72 ____ Answer to Petition for Order Staying Arbitration in Dispute Over Contract for Sale of Goods. 💾

CHAPTER 6. BUYING AND SELLING A SMALL BUSINESS

6.1 Scope Note.
6.2 Strategy: Representing the Buyer—Introduction.
6.3 ____ The Attorney's Role.
6.4 ____ Different Considerations Depending on the Type of Transaction.
6.5 ____ General Stages of the Transaction.
6.6 Representing the Buyer—Investigating the Business.
6.7 ____ Nature and Operation of Business.
6.8 ____ Geographic Location.
6.9 ____ The Negotiating Team.
6.10 ____ The Letter of Intent.
6.11 ____ Confidentiality Agreements.
6.12 ____ Drafting the Agreement.
6.13 Due Diligence Investigation.
6.14 ____ Legal Issues.
6.15 ____ ____ Organizational Documents.
6.16 ____ ____ Ownership Documents.
6.17 ____ ____ Existing Contracts.
6.18 ____ ____ Liens and Security Interests.
6.19 ____ ____ Corporate and Trade Names.
6.20 ____ ____ Real Estate.
6.21 ____ ____ Compliance With Law.
6.22 ____ ____ Litigation Investigation.
6.23 ____ Financial Issues—General Considerations.
6.24 ____ ____ Seller's Records From the Buyer's Position.
6.25 ____ ____ Buyer's Records From the Seller's Position.
6.26 ____ ____ Public Records.
6.27 ____ ____ Financial Statements.
6.28 ____ ____ The Need for Other Professionals.
6.29 ____ ____ Valuation of the Business.

TABLE OF CONTENTS

Sec.
6.30 ___ ___ Tax Returns.
6.31 Tax Issues for Buyer.
6.32 ___ Asset Purchase.
6.33 ___ ___ Allocation of Purchase Price.
6.34 ___ ___ Depreciation of Assets.
6.35 ___ ___ Land.
6.36 ___ ___ Good Will and Covenants Not to Compete.
6.37 ___ ___ Inventory.
6.38 ___ ___ Cash.
6.39 ___ ___ Supplies.
6.40 ___ ___ Patents, Franchises, Trademarks, Trade Names.
6.41 ___ Stock Purchase.
6.42 ___ ___ Basis of Stock.
6.43 ___ ___ Basis of Corporate Assets.
6.44 ___ ___ Election to Treat Stock Purchase as Asset Purchase.
6.45 ___ ___ Mergers, Consolidations, and Exchanges.
6.46 Structuring the Buyer's Transaction.
6.47 ___ Type of Payment.
6.48 ___ Assumption of Seller's Liabilities.
6.49 ___ Security to Seller.
6.50 ___ Notes.
6.51 ___ Escrow Arrangements and Agreements.
6.52 Drafting the Buyer's Asset Purchase Agreement.
6.53 ___ Identification of the Parties.
6.54 ___ Recitals.
6.55 ___ Assets and Property to Be Conveyed.
6.56 ___ Retained Assets of Seller.
6.57 ___ Purchase Price and Method of Payment.
6.58 ___ Closing.
6.59 ___ Representations, Warranties and Covenants of Seller.
6.60 ___ Representations, Warranties and Covenants of Buyer.
6.61 ___ Conduct of Business Prior to Closing.
6.62 ___ Indemnifications.
6.63 ___ Corporate or Other Name.
6.64 ___ ___ Notice to Customers and Suppliers.
6.65 ___ ___ UCC Bulk Sale Notices or Escrow Agreement in Lieu of UCC Bulk Sale Notice.
6.66 ___ ___ NYS Sales Tax and Bulk Sale Notification.
6.67 ___ ___ Covenant Not to Compete.
6.68 ___ Matters Respecting Real Property.
6.69 ___ Conditions Precedent to Purchaser's Obligations.
6.70 ___ Conditions Precedent to Seller's Obligations.
6.71 ___ Nature and Survival of Representations and Warranties.
6.72 ___ Non-disclosure Provisions.
6.73 ___ Miscellaneous Agreements Between Buyer and Seller.
6.74 ___ Documents to Be Delivered to Purchaser at Closing.
6.75 ___ Documents to Be Delivered to Seller at Closing.
6.76 ___ Notices, Severability and Other General Provisions.
6.77 ___ Documents to Be Prepared or Reviewed Prior to Closing.
6.78 Drafting the Buyer's Stock Purchase Agreement.

TABLE OF CONTENTS

Sec.	
6.79	____ Identification of the Parties.
6.80	____ Recitals.
6.81	____ Sale of Shares.
6.82	____ Purchase Price and Method of Payment.
6.83	____ Closing.
6.84	____ Representations, Warranties and Covenants of Seller.
6.85	____ Representations, Warranties and Covenants of Buyer.
6.86	____ Conduct of Business Prior to Closing.
6.87	____ Indemnifications.
6.88	____ Covenant Not to Compete.
6.89	____ Matters Respecting Real Property.
6.90	____ Nondisclosure Provisions.
6.91	____ Conditions Precedent to Purchaser's Obligations.
6.92	____ Conditions Precedent to Seller's Obligations.
6.93	____ Nature and Survival of Representations and Warranties.
6.94	____ Documents to Be Delivered to Purchaser at Closing.
6.95	____ Documents to Be Delivered to Seller at Closing.
6.96	____ Notices, Severability and Other General Provisions.
6.97	____ Documents to Be Prepared or Reviewed Prior to Closing.
6.98	Post–Contract and Pre-closing.
6.99	____ Bulk Sales Act—UCC Article 6.
6.100	____ NYS Sales Tax and Bulk Sale Notification.
6.101	____ Plant Closing Notice.
6.102	____ Environmental Searches and Testing.
6.103	____ Certificate of Good Standing.
6.104	____ Real Property Transfer Gains Tax.
6.105	Closing and Post–Closing.
6.106	Strategy: Representing the Seller—Introduction.
6.107	____ The Attorney's Role.
6.108	____ Different Considerations Depending on the Type of Transaction.
6.109	____ General Stages of the Transaction.
6.110	Representing the Seller—General Investigation.
6.111	____ Investigating the Buyer.
6.112	____ The Negotiating Team.
6.113	____ The Letter of Intent.
6.114	____ Confidentiality Agreements.
6.115	____ Drafting the Agreement.
6.116	Tax Issues for the Seller—General Overview.
6.117	____ Asset Sale.
6.118	____ ____ Allocation of Purchase Price.
6.119	____ ____ Depreciation Recapture.
6.120	____ ____ Capital Gains or Losses.
6.121	____ ____ Ordinary Income.
6.122	____ ____ Income to Corporation.
6.123	____ ____ Real Property Transfer Gains Tax.
6.124	____ ____ Covenant Not to Compete and Consulting Agreements.
6.125	____ Stock Sale—General Advantages.
6.126	____ ____ Capital Gain or Loss.
6.127	____ ____ No Concern for Income to a Corporate Entity.

TABLE OF CONTENTS

Sec.
- 6.128 ____ ____ Real Property Transfer Gains Tax.
- 6.129 ____ ____ Consulting and Non-compete Agreements.
- 6.130 ____ ____ I.R.C. § 1244 Stock and Qualified Small Business Stock.
- 6.131 ____ ____ Stock Transfer Tax.
- 6.132 ____ ____ Collapsible Corporation.
- 6.133 ____ ____ Mergers, Consolidations and Exchanges.
- 6.134 Structuring the Seller's Transaction—General Overview.
- 6.135 ____ Purchase Price and Payment Terms.
- 6.136 ____ Security to Seller.
- 6.137 ____ Notes.
- 6.138 ____ Escrow Arrangements.
- 6.139 Drafting the Seller's Asset Sale Agreement.
- 6.140 ____ Identification of the Parties.
- 6.141 ____ Recitals.
- 6.142 ____ Assets and Property to Be Conveyed.
- 6.143 ____ Assets Retained by Seller.
- 6.144 ____ Sale Price and Method of Payment.
- 6.145 ____ Closing.
- 6.146 ____ Representations, Warranties and Covenants of Buyer.
- 6.147 ____ Representations, Warranties and Covenants of Seller.
- 6.148 ____ Conduct of Business Prior to Closing.
- 6.149 ____ Indemnifications.
- 6.150 ____ Matters Respecting Real Property.
- 6.151 ____ Notice to Customers and Suppliers.
- 6.152 ____ Covenant Not to Compete and Consulting Agreements.
- 6.153 ____ UCC Bulk Sale Notices or Escrow Agreements in Lieu of UCC Bulk Sale Notice.
- 6.154 ____ New York State Sales Tax and Bulk Sale Notification.
- 6.155 ____ Nature and Survival of Representations and Warranties.
- 6.156 ____ Non-disclosure Provisions.
- 6.157 ____ Conditions Precedent to Seller's Obligations.
- 6.158 ____ Conditions Precedent to Buyer's Obligations.
- 6.159 ____ Documents to Be Delivered to Seller at Closing.
- 6.160 ____ Documents to Be Delivered to Buyer at Closing.
- 6.161 ____ Notices, Severability and Other General Provisions.
- 6.162 ____ Documents to Be Prepared or Reviewed Prior to Closing.
- 6.163 Drafting the Seller's Stock Sale Agreement.
- 6.164 ____ Identification of the Parties.
- 6.165 ____ Recitals.
- 6.166 ____ Sale of Shares.
- 6.167 ____ Sale Price and Method of Payment.
- 6.168 ____ Closing.
- 6.169 ____ Representations, Warranties and Covenants of Buyer.
- 6.170 ____ Representations, Warranties and Covenants of Seller.
- 6.171 ____ Conduct of Business Prior to Closing.
- 6.172 ____ Indemnifications.
- 6.173 ____ Matters Respecting Real Property.
- 6.174 ____ Non-disclosure Provisions.
- 6.175 ____ Covenants Not to Compete and Consulting Agreements.
- 6.176 ____ Notice to Customers and Suppliers.

TABLE OF CONTENTS

Sec.
6.177 ____ Conditions Precedent to Seller's Obligations.
6.178 ____ Conditions Precedent to Buyer's Obligations.
6.179 ____ Nature and Survival of Representations and Warranties.
6.180 ____ Documents to Be Delivered to Seller at Closing.
6.181 ____ Documents to Be Delivered to Buyer at Closing.
6.182 ____ Notices, Severability and Other General Provisions.
6.183 ____ Documents to Be Prepared or Reviewed Prior to Closing.
6.184 Post–contract and Pre-closing.
6.185 Closing and Post–Closing.
6.186 Forms.
6.187 ____ Asset Purchase and Sale Agreement. 💾
6.188 ____ Agreement of Purchase and Sale of Stock. 💾

Volume 21

CHAPTER 7. CONSUMER LAW

7.1 Scope Note.
7.2 Strategy—Generally.
7.3 ____ Automobile Sales Cases.
7.4 ____ Automobile Leasing Cases.
7.5 ____ Credit Reporting.
7.6 ____ Debt Collection.
7.7 ____ Deceptive Business Practices.
7.8 ____ Information to Obtain at Outset of Case.
7.9 Lemon Laws.
7.10 ____ New Cars.
7.11 ____ Used Cars.
7.12 ____ Arbitration or Plenary Action?
7.13 ____ Arbitration Procedure.
7.14 ____ ____ Preparation for the Hearing.
7.15 ____ ____ The Hearing.
7.16 ____ ____ Appeals and Confirmation Proceedings.
7.17 ____ ____ Scope of Review.
7.18 ____ Source Materials.
7.19 Automobile Leasing—Overview.
7.20 ____ Statutory Protection Overview.
7.21 ____ The Consumer Leasing Act.
7.22 ____ The Motor Vehicle Retail Leasing Act.
7.23 Motor Vehicle Installment Sales.
7.24 Repossession—Overview.
7.25 ____ Prevention and Avoidance.
7.26 ____ Defending Deficiency Claims.
7.27 Automobile Repairs.
7.28 Automobile Repair Shop Liens—Overview.
7.29 ____ Statutory Challenges.
7.30 Credit Reporting—Overview.
7.31 ____ Consumer Rights.
7.32 ____ Non-litigation Strategies.
7.33 ____ Litigating Credit Reporting Matters.

TABLE OF CONTENTS

Sec.	
7.34	Debt Collection—History and Overview.
7.35	___ Claims for Intentional Infliction of Emotional Distress.
7.36	___ Statutory Overview.
7.37	___ FDCPA—Contacts With Third Parties.
7.38	___ ___Contacts With a Debtor.
7.39	___ ___ Prohibited Tactics.
7.40	___ ___ Improper Omissions and Disclosures.
7.41	___ ___ Harassment or Abuse.
7.42	___ ___ Improper Demands.
7.43	___ ___ Judicial Enforcement.
7.44	___ State Law.
7.45	Deceptive Practices Act—Overview.
7.46	___ Elements of the Claim.
7.47	___ Types of Recovery Available.
7.48	Drafting Checklist—List of Essential Allegations.
7.49	Forms—Lemon Law Document Request Pursuant to 13 NYCRR § 300.9(a).
7.50	___ Notice of Petition to Vacate Lemon Law Arbitration Award Pursuant to CPLR Article 75.
7.51	___ Petition to Vacate Lemon Law Arbitration Award Pursuant to CPLR Article 75.
7.52	___ Complaint for Fraud, Breach of Warranties, Deceptive Business Practices, Used Car Lemon Law, Rescission and Revocation of Acceptance for Fraudulent Leasing Practices.
7.53	___ Answer and Third-party Complaint Alleging Fraud, Deceptive Practices, Breach of Warranty, and Federal Odometer Law Claims in Fraudulent Automobile Lease Case.
7.54	___ Answer to Complaint by Automobile Leasing Company for Deficiency Following Repossession, Alleging Commercially Unreasonable Resale and Deceptive Business Practices.
7.55	___ Affirmation in Opposition to Lessor's Motion for Summary Judgment and in Support of Lessee's Cross-motion for Summary Judgment Alleging Commercially Unreasonable Resale.
7.56	___ Notice of Rescission And/or Revocation of Acceptance and Demand for Restitution Pursuant to UCC 2–601 and 2–608.
7.57	___ Order to Show Cause in Proceeding under Lien Law § 201–a to Vacate Garageman's Lien.
7.58	___ Verified Petition in Proceeding under Lien Law § 201–a to Vacate Garageman's Lien.
7.59	___ Affirmation in Support of Petition in Proceeding under Lien Law § 201–a to Vacate Garageman's Lien.
7.60	___ Complaint Against Credit Reporting Agency Alleging Violations of the Fair Credit Reporting Act and the New York State Fair Credit Reporting Act and Deceptive Business Practices.
7.61	___ Stipulation of Settlement of Plaintiff's Lemon Law Claims Providing for Cancellation of Lease and Deletion of Any Derogatory Credit Information.

TABLE OF CONTENTS

Sec.
7.62 _____ Complaint Alleging Violations of the Fair Debt Collection Practices Act and the Deceptive Practices Act. 💾
7.63 _____ Order to Show Cause with Temporary Restraining Order, Seeking Preliminary Injunction in Action Alleging Fraud, Deceptive Business Practices and Breach of Warranties. 💾
7.64 _____ Affirmation in Support of Temporary Restraining Order and Preliminary Injunction in Action Alleging Fraud, Deceptive Business Practices and Breach of Warranties. 💾
7.65 _____ Complaint in Action Alleging Fraud, Deceptive Business Practices and Breach of Warranties. 💾

CHAPTER 8. ENFORCEMENT OF MONEY JUDGMENTS

8.1 Scope Note.
8.2 Strategy.
8.3 Judgments—Generally.
8.4 _____ Methods to Obtain.
8.5 Form of Judgment—Judgment–Roll.
8.6 _____ Interest.
8.7 _____ Fees, Costs and Disbursements.
8.8 _____ Entry.
8.9 _____ Transcript of Judgment.
8.10 Matters Affecting Judgment—Vacatur.
8.11 _____ Satisfaction By Payment or Otherwise.
8.12 _____ Assignment.
8.13 _____ Death of Judgment Debtor.
8.14 _____ Amendment or Correction.
8.15 Actions on Judgments.
8.16 Entry of a Foreign Judgment—Sister–State Judgments.
8.17 _____ Federal Court Judgments.
8.18 _____ Foreign Country Judgments.
8.19 Judgment Enforcement Against Property—Definition of Property.
8.20 _____ Exemptions.
8.21 _____ Property in the Possession of Others.
8.22 _____ Disclosure of Property.
8.23 _____ _____ Subpoenas.
8.24 Article 52 Enforcement Devices—Introduction.
8.25 _____ Restraining Notices—Nature and Use.
8.26 _____ _____ Formal Requirements.
8.27 _____ _____ Service and Punishment for Disobedience.
8.28 _____ Execution.
8.29 _____ _____ Property Execution With Regard to Personal Property.
8.30 _____ _____ _____ Sale, Distribution and Priority In Proceeds.
8.31 _____ _____ Property Execution With Regard to Real Property.
8.32 _____ _____ _____ Notice and Sale of Real Property.
8.33 _____ _____ _____ Distribution of Proceeds of Sale and Conveyance of Title.
8.34 _____ Income Execution.
8.35 _____ Installment Payment Order—Nature and Purpose.
8.36 _____ _____ Form of Application and Service.

TABLE OF CONTENTS

Sec.
8.37 ____ Receiver.
8.38 ____ ____ Application, Appointment and Extension.
8.39 ____ Turnover Orders For Property or Debts.
8.40 ____ ____ Turnover Against the Judgment Debtor.
8.41 ____ ____ Turnover Against A Garnishee.
8.42 ____ Contempt.
8.43 ____ Arrest of the Judgment Debtor.
8.44 Protective Orders.
8.45 Proceeding To Determine Adverse Claims.
8.46 Forms.
8.47 ____ Statement For Judgment (Default Judgment), Affidavit of Facts Constituting the Claim, the Default and the Amount Due.
8.48 ____ Affidavit of Confession of Judgment and Judgment by Confession.
8.49 ____ Notice to Judgment Debtor [or Obligor].
8.50 ____ Subpoena (*Duces Tecum*) To Take Deposition of Judgment Debtor With Restraining Notice.
8.51 ____ Subpoena (*Duces Tecum*) To Take Deposition of Witness With Restraining Notice.
8.52 ____ Information Subpoena.
8.53 ____ Restraining Notice to Judgment Debtor.
8.54 ____ Execution.
8.55 ____ Income Execution.
8.56 ____ Affirmation and Order To Show Cause To Punish Judgment Debtor—Witness For Contempt.

CHAPTER 9. BANKRUPTCY

9.1 Scope Note.
9.2 Strategy.
9.3 ____ Checklist for Representing a Debtor.
9.4 ____ Checklist for Representing a Creditor.
9.5 Governing Law.
9.6 Nature of Cases Under Each Chapter of the Bankruptcy Code.
9.7 Eligibility to File.
9.8 Commencement of a Case—Voluntary Cases.
9.9 ____ Involuntary Cases.
9.10 ____ ____ Procedure.
9.11 ____ Additional Requirements.
9.12 ____ First–Day Orders.
9.13 Joint Administration.
9.14 Substantive Consolidation.
9.15 Types of Proceedings in Cases Under the Bankruptcy Code.
9.16 ____ Adversary Proceedings.
9.17 ____ Contested Matters.
9.18 Jurisdiction of the Bankruptcy Court.
9.19 ____ Types of Jurisdiction.
9.20 ____ Case Ancillary to Foreign Proceedings.
9.21 Venue.
9.22 Withdrawal of Reference.

TABLE OF CONTENTS

Sec.
9.23   Abstention.
9.24   Removal.
9.25   Appeals—To District Court and Bankruptcy Appellate Panel From Bankruptcy Court.
9.26   ——— To Court of Appeals From District Court.
9.27   The Debtor in Possession.
9.28   ——— Rights, Powers and Duties.
9.29   Employment of Professionals.
9.30   ——— Compensation.
9.31   ——— ——— Fee Applications.
9.32   U.S. Trustee.
9.33   ——— Duties Owed by Debtors and Trustees.
9.34   Bankruptcy Trustee.
9.35   Mediators.
9.36   Creditors.
9.37   ——— Meeting of Creditors.
9.38   ——— ——— Scope of Examination.
9.39   Examinations Under Bankruptcy Rule 2004.
9.40   ——— Notice Requirements.
9.41   ——— Subpoena.
9.42   Right of Parties in Interest to Be Heard.
9.43   Statutory Committees.
9.44   ——— Function and Duties.
9.45   ——— Right to Bring Litigation.
9.46   ——— Fiduciary Duty.
9.47   ——— Removal of Members.
9.48   ——— Organizational Meeting.
9.49   Property of the Estate.
9.50   Automatic Stay.
9.51   ——— Exceptions.
9.52   ——— Obtaining Relief.
9.53   ——— ——— Strategy.
9.54   ——— ——— Hearing.
9.55   ——— ——— Single Asset Real Estate Debtor.
9.56   Adequate Protection.
9.57   ——— Types.
9.58   ——— Strategy.
9.59   ——— Objections and Hearing.
9.60   Use, Sale, or Lease of Property.
9.61   ——— Ordinary Course of Business.
9.62   ——— Outside Ordinary Course of Business.
9.63   ——— Sales Free and Clear of Liens.
9.64   ——— Appeals from Order Authorizing Sale.
9.65   Cash Collateral.
9.66   ——— Strategy.
9.67   ——— Hearing.
9.68   ——— Postpetition Proceeds.
9.69   ——— ——— Security Interests in Rents and Hotel Revenues.
9.70   Abandonment of Property.
9.71   Postpetition Financing.

TABLE OF CONTENTS

Sec.
- 9.72 ____ Hearing.
- 9.73 ____ Appeals From Order Authorizing.
- 9.74 Executory Contracts and Unexpired Leases.
- 9.75 ____ Strategy.
- 9.76 ____ Time for Assumption or Rejection.
- 9.77 ____ Nonresidential Real Property Leases.
- 9.78 ____ Assumption by the Debtor.
- 9.79 ____ Assumption and Assignment.
- 9.80 ____ Exceptions to Assumption and Assignment.
- 9.81 ____ Rejection by Debtor.
- 9.82 ____ Damages Arising From Rejection: Debtor as Tenant/Lessee.
- 9.83 ____ Calculation of Allowed Real Property Lease Rejection Damages.
- 9.84 ____ Debtor as Landlord/Lessor.
- 9.85 ____ Unexpired Personal Property Leases.
- 9.86 Collective Bargaining Agreements.
- 9.87 Retired Employees' Insurance Benefits.
- 9.88 ____ Procedure for Modifying.
- 9.89 Utility Services.
- 9.90 Claims Procedures.
- 9.91 ____ Filing Proofs of Claim or Interest.
- 9.92 ____ ____ Bar Dates.
- 9.93 ____ Late–Filed Proofs of Claim.
- 9.94 ____ Amendment of Proofs of Claim or Interest.
- 9.95 ____ Withdrawal of Claims.
- 9.96 ____ Allowance of, and Objections to, Claims or Interests.
- 9.97 ____ Compromise and Settlement of Claims.
- 9.98 ____ Allowance of Administrative Expense Claims.
- 9.99 ____ Secured Claims.
- 9.100 ____ ____ Bifurcation of Claims.
- 9.101 ____ ____ Avoidance of Liens.
- 9.102 ____ Interest on Claims and Charges Against Secured Claims.
- 9.103 ____ Valuation of Collateral.
- 9.104 ____ ____ Methods of Valuation.
- 9.105 ____ Reclamation Claims.
- 9.106 Priorities.
- 9.107 Subordination.
- 9.108 ____ Strategy.
- 9.109 Setoff.
- 9.110 ____ Strategy.
- 9.111 ____ Characteristics of Claims.
- 9.112 Recoupment.
- 9.113 The Avoiding Powers.
- 9.114 ____ Strategy.
- 9.115 ____ Strong Arm Powers.
- 9.116 ____ Avoidance of Certain Statutory Liens.
- 9.117 ____ Preferences.
- 9.118 ____ Exceptions to the Avoidance of Preferential Transfers.
- 9.119 ____ Fraudulent Conveyances.
- 9.120 ____ Liability of Transferee of Avoided Transfer.

TABLE OF CONTENTS

Sec.
- 9.121 ___ Statute of Limitations and Standing.
- 9.122 ___ Relation–Back Provision.
- 9.123 ___ Reclamation.
- 9.124 Return of Goods by Debtor.
- 9.125 Exemptions.
- 9.126 ___ Procedure.
- 9.127 ___ Objections.
- 9.128 ___ Lien Avoidance.
- 9.129 ___ Liens on Exempt Property.
- 9.130 Reaffirmation of Debts.
- 9.131 ___ Strategy.
- 9.132 Protection Against Discriminatory Treatment.
- 9.133 Tax Considerations.
- 9.134 Conversion and Dismissal of Cases Under Title 11.
- 9.135 Effect of Conversion.
- 9.136 Effect of Dismissal.
- 9.137 Closing and Reopening Cases.
- 9.138 Chapter 11—Appointment of a Trustee.
- 9.139 ___ Duties of a Trustee.
- 9.140 ___ Appointment of an Examiner.
- 9.141 ___ Duties of an Examiner.
- 9.142 ___ Exclusivity—Right to File a Plan.
- 9.143 ___ ___ Small Businesses.
- 9.144 ___ ___ Strategy: Representing a Debtor.
- 9.145 ___ ___ Strategy: Representing a Creditor.
- 9.146 ___ ___ Appealability of Orders.
- 9.147 ___ Plan.
- 9.148 ___ ___ Mandatory Provisions.
- 9.149 ___ ___ Discretionary Provisions.
- 9.150 ___ ___ Exemption from Securities Registration.
- 9.151 ___ ___ Retention of Jurisdiction by the Court.
- 9.152 ___ Classification of Claims.
- 9.153 ___ ___ Effect on Voting.
- 9.154 ___ ___ Substantially Similar Claims.
- 9.155 ___ ___ Convenience Class.
- 9.156 ___ Recourse and Nonrecourse Claims: The § 1111(b) Election.
- 9.157 ___ ___ Strategy.
- 9.158 ___ Impairment of Claims or Interests.
- 9.159 ___ ___ Rights Are Altered.
- 9.160 ___ ___ Defaults Are Not Cured.
- 9.161 ___ Disclosure and Solicitation.
- 9.162 ___ Acceptance of a Plan.
- 9.163 ___ Prepackaged and Prenegotiated Plans.
- 9.164 ___ Modification of a Plan.
- 9.165 ___ Confirmation.
- 9.166 ___ Cramdown.
- 9.167 ___ Effect of Confirmation.
- 9.168 ___ Discharge.
- 9.169 ___ ___ Limitations.
- 9.170 ___ ___ Release of Nondebtor.

TABLE OF CONTENTS

Sec.
9.171 ____ Channelling Injunctions: Asbestos–Related Cases.
9.172 ____ Plan Implementation.
9.173 ____ Small Business Reorganizations.
9.174 ____ Conversion or Dismissal of Cases.
9.175 ____ ____ Procedure.
9.176 ____ Closing and Reopening Cases.
9.177 Chapter 7—Overview.
9.178 ____ Commencement of a Case.
9.179 ____ Fees.
9.180 ____ Appointment of an Interim Trustee.
9.181 ____ Election of a Permanent Trustee.
9.182 ____ Duties of a Trustee.
9.183 ____ Employment of Professionals.
9.184 ____ Creditors' Committee.
9.185 ____ Protection Against Discriminatory Treatment.
9.186 ____ The Debtor's Statement of Intention.
9.187 ____ Exemptions.
9.188 ____ Redemption of Property.
9.189 ____ ____ Procedure.
9.190 ____ Reaffirmation of Debts.
9.191 ____ Abandonment of Property.
9.192 ____ Debtor's Surrender of Property and Records.
9.193 ____ Trustee's Turnover Powers.
9.194 ____ Liability of General Partners.
9.195 ____ Trustee's Operation of the Business.
9.196 ____ Executory Contracts.
9.197 ____ Adversary Proceedings to Avoid Liens and Transfers.
9.198 ____ ____ Statute of Limitations.
9.199 ____ Treatment of Certain Liens.
9.200 ____ Trustee's Sale of Assets.
9.201 ____ Disposition of Property Subject to the Interest of Another.
9.202 ____ Priorities.
9.203 ____ Special Tax Provisions.
9.204 ____ Discharge.
9.205 ____ ____ Exceptions to General Discharge of the Debtor.
9.206 ____ ____ Procedure for Objections to General Discharge of the Debtor.
9.207 ____ ____ Exceptions to Discharge of Particular Debts.
9.208 ____ ____ Procedure for Objections to Discharge of Particular Debts.
9.209 ____ Conversion or Dismissal of Cases.
9.210 ____ ____ Procedure.
9.211 ____ Closing and Reopening Cases.
9.212 Chapter 12—Overview.
9.213 ____ Rights and Powers of Debtor.
9.214 ____ Appointment of a Trustee.
9.215 ____ Duties of a Trustee.
9.216 ____ Automatic Stay.
9.217 ____ Property of the Estate.
9.218 ____ Sales Free of Interests.

TABLE OF CONTENTS

Sec.
- 9.219 ⎯⎯ Adequate Protection.
- 9.220 ⎯⎯ Exclusivity—Right to File a Plan.
- 9.221 ⎯⎯ Plan.
- 9.222 ⎯⎯ ⎯⎯ Mandatory Provisions.
- 9.223 ⎯⎯ ⎯⎯ Discretionary Provisions.
- 9.224 ⎯⎯ ⎯⎯ Modification.
- 9.225 ⎯⎯ ⎯⎯ Confirmation.
- 9.226 ⎯⎯ ⎯⎯ Confirmation: Objections.
- 9.227 ⎯⎯ Disbursements.
- 9.228 ⎯⎯ Effect of Confirmation.
- 9.229 ⎯⎯ Discharge.
- 9.230 ⎯⎯ Modification after Confirmation.
- 9.231 ⎯⎯ Special Tax Provisions.
- 9.232 ⎯⎯ Revocation of Confirmation Order.
- 9.233 ⎯⎯ Conversion or Dismissal of Cases.
- 9.234 ⎯⎯ ⎯⎯ Procedure.
- 9.235 ⎯⎯ Closing and Reopening Cases.
- 9.236 Chapter 13—Overview.
- 9.237 ⎯⎯ Eligibility.
- 9.238 ⎯⎯ Rights and Powers of Debtor.
- 9.239 ⎯⎯ Appointment of a Trustee.
- 9.240 ⎯⎯ Duties of a Trustee.
- 9.241 ⎯⎯ Automatic Stay.
- 9.242 ⎯⎯ ⎯⎯ Relief.
- 9.243 ⎯⎯ Property of the Estate.
- 9.244 ⎯⎯ ⎯⎯ Use, Sale, or Lease.
- 9.245 ⎯⎯ Exclusivity—Right to File a Plan.
- 9.246 ⎯⎯ Plan.
- 9.247 ⎯⎯ ⎯⎯ Mandatory Provisions.
- 9.248 ⎯⎯ ⎯⎯ Discretionary Provisions.
- 9.249 ⎯⎯ ⎯⎯ Discretionary Provisions: Debtor's Principal Residence.
- 9.250 ⎯⎯ ⎯⎯ Modification.
- 9.251 ⎯⎯ ⎯⎯ Confirmation.
- 9.252 ⎯⎯ ⎯⎯ Confirmation: Objections.
- 9.253 ⎯⎯ ⎯⎯ Confirmation: Effect.
- 9.254 ⎯⎯ Payments.
- 9.255 ⎯⎯ Discharge.
- 9.256 ⎯⎯ ⎯⎯ Exceptions.
- 9.257 ⎯⎯ ⎯⎯ Objections.
- 9.258 ⎯⎯ ⎯⎯ Revocation.
- 9.259 ⎯⎯ Postconfirmation Modification of a Plan.
- 9.260 ⎯⎯ Revocation of Confirmation Order.
- 9.261 ⎯⎯ Conversion or Dismissal of Cases.
- 9.262 ⎯⎯ ⎯⎯ Procedure.
- 9.263 ⎯⎯ Closing and Reopening Cases.
- 9.264 Procedural Checklist—Commencing a Voluntary Case.
- 9.265 ⎯⎯ Lists and Schedules to be Filed at the Commencement of a Case Under Chapter 7, 11, 12, or 13.
- 9.266 ⎯⎯ Commencing an Adversary Proceeding.
- 9.267 ⎯⎯ Commencing a Contested Matter.

TABLE OF CONTENTS

Sec.

9.268 ____ Appeal from an Interlocutory Judgment, Order, or Decree of a Bankruptcy Judge.
9.269 ____ Creditor's Motion to Request Relief from the Automatic Stay.
9.270 ____ Creditor's Motion to Obtain Adequate Protection.
9.271 ____ Debtor's Motion to Use, Sell, or Lease Property of the Estate.
9.272 ____ Debtor's Motion to Request Use of Cash Collateral.
9.273 ____ Cash Collateral Stipulation.
9.274 ____ Debtor's Motion to Obtain Postpetition Financing.
9.275 ____ Request to Assume, Reject, or Assign an Executory Contract or Unexpired Nonresidential Real Property Lease.
9.276 ____ Debtor's Motion to Reject or Modify a Collective Bargaining Agreement.
9.277 ____ Debtor's Motion to Obtain Approval of a Compromise and Settlement of a Claim.
9.278 ____ Claiming Exemptions.
9.279 ____ Debtor's Motion to Avoid a Judicial Lien or a Nonpossessory, Nonpurchase–Money Security Interest that Impairs Exempt Property.
9.280 ____ Debtor's Motion to Obtain Court Approval of a Reaffirmation Agreement.
9.281 ____ Debtor's Motion to Request an Extension of Exclusivity.
9.282 ____ Filing a Chapter 11 Plan and Disclosure Statement.
9.283 ____ Soliciting Acceptance of a Chapter 11 Plan.
9.284 ____ Filing a Chapter 12 or 13 Plan of Debt Adjustment.
9.285 ____ Objection to a Chapter 12 or 13 Plan.
9.286 ____ Debtor's Motion to Request Modification of a Chapter 12 or 13 Plan after Confirmation
9.287 Drafting Checklist—General Rules for all Motions, Applications, and Complaints.
9.288 ____ Complaint in an Adversary Proceeding.
9.289 ____ Motion for Leave to Appeal From an Interlocutory Judgment, Order, or Decree of a Bankruptcy Judge.
9.290 ____ Motion for a Stay of a Bankruptcy Court Judgment or Order Pending Appeal.
9.291 ____ Application of Debtor or Statutory Committee to Retain Professionals.
9.292 ____ Creditor's Motion to Request Relief From the Automatic Stay.
9.293 ____ Creditor's Motion to Obtain Adequate Protection.
9.294 ____ Debtor's Motion to Use, Sell, or Lease Property of the Estate.
9.295 ____ Debtor's Motion to Request Use of Cash Collateral.
9.296 ____ Cash Collateral Stipulation.
9.297 ____ Debtor's Motion to Obtain Postpetition Financing.
9.298 ____ Motion to Assume or Reject an Executory Contract or Unexpired Non-residential Real Property Lease.
9.299 ____ Debtor's Motion to Reject or Modify a Collective Bargaining Agreement (CBA).
9.300 ____ Debtor's Motion to Obtain Approval of a Compromise and Settlement of a Claim.

TABLE OF CONTENTS

Sec.
9.301 ___ Debtor's Motion to Avoid a Judicial Lien or a Nonpossessory, Nonpurchase–Money Security Interest that Impairs Exempt Property.
9.302 ___ Reaffirmation Agreement.
9.303 ___ Debtor's Motion for Approval of a Reaffirmation Agreement.
9.304 ___ Debtor's Motion to Request an Extension of Exclusivity.
9.305 Forms—Notice of Appearance and Demand for Service of Documents. 💾
9.306 ___ Contested Matter—Motion. 💾
9.307 ___ ___ Notice of Motion. 💾
9.308 ___ ___ Proposed Order. 💾
9.309 ___ Adversary Proceeding—Complaint. 💾
9.310 ___ Retention of Professionals—Application. 💾
9.311 ___ ___ Affidavit. 💾
9.312 ___ Plan Provision for Retention of Jurisdiction. 💾

CHAPTER 10. MECHANIC'S LIENS

10.1 Scope Note.
10.2 Strategy.
10.3 Nature of Mechanic's Lien.
10.4 Creation of Mechanic's Lien—Elements.
10.5 ___ ___ Protected Class.
10.6 ___ ___ Improvements to Real Property.
10.7 ___ ___ Consent or Request of Owner.
10.8 Extent of Lien—Ownership Interest at Time of Filing.
10.9 ___ Sale of Property.
10.10 ___ Insurance Proceeds.
10.11 ___ Amount.
10.12 ___ Loss of Profits.
10.13 Subcontractors and Materialmen—Derivative Rights.
10.14 ___ ___ Statutory Protections.
10.15 Procedure—Notice of Lien.
10.16 ___ ___ Contents.
10.17 ___ ___ Filing.
10.18 ___ ___ Service.
10.19 Amendment of Notice of Lien.
10.20 Lien for Private Improvements—Checklist.
10.21 Liens Under Contract for Public Improvements—Extent of Lien.
10.22 ___ Notice of Lien.
10.23 ___ Filing of Notice of Lien.
10.24 ___ Notice of Completion and Acceptance.
10.25 ___ Checklist.
10.26 Lien Priorities—Private Improvements—Parity of Mechanic's Liens.
10.27 ___ ___ Assignments of Contract Rights.
10.28 ___ ___ Building Loan Mortgages.
10.29 ___ ___ Contracts of Sale.
10.30 ___ ___ Seller's Mortgage.
10.31 ___ ___ Deeds.

XLI

TABLE OF CONTENTS

Sec.
10.32 ____ Contracts for Public Improvements.
10.33 Assignment of Liens.
10.34 Assignments of Contracts for Private Improvements and Orders to be Filed—Filing of Notice of Assignment.
10.35 ____ Contents of Notice of Assignment.
10.36 ____ Extension of Term of Notice of Assignment.
10.37 Assignment of Contracts and Orders for Public Improvements.
10.38 Duration of Lien for Private Improvements—Notice of Pendency.
10.39 ____ Extensions.
10.40 Duration of Lien Under Contract for a Public Improvement—Notice of Pendency.
10.41 ____ Extension of Lien.
10.42 Discharge of Lien for Private Improvement—Satisfaction of Lien.
10.43 ____ Expiration of Term.
10.44 ____ Termination of Notice of Pendency.
10.45 ____ Failure to Prosecute.
10.46 ____ Undertaking.
10.47 ____ Judgment.
10.48 ____ Defective Lien.
10.49 ____ Deposit of Money with County Clerk or Court.
10.50 Discharge of Lien for Public Improvement—Satisfaction of Lien.
10.51 ____ Expiration of Lien.
10.52 ____ Satisfaction of Judgment.
10.53 ____ Deposit of Money.
10.54 ____ Undertaking.
10.55 ____ Retention of Credit.
10.56 ____ Invalidity of Lien.
10.57 ____ Failure to Prosecute.
10.58 ____ Procedures.
10.59 Building Loan Contracts—Filing Requirements.
10.60 ____ Checklist.
10.61 Subordination of Liens—Agreement with Owner.
10.62 ____ ____ Postponement of Judgments.
10.63 Subordination of Liens to Subsequent Mortgage.
10.64 Subordination of Notices of *Lis Pendens*.
10.65 Discharge of Liens on Sale of Real Property.
10.66 Limitations on Waiver of Mechanic's Lien.
10.67 Effect of Filing of Notice of Lien on Right of Arbitration.
10.68 Bond to Discharge Liens—Effect of Bond.
10.69 ____ Requirements of Bond.
10.70 ____ Claim Against Bond.
10.71 ____ Notice of Claim.
10.72 ____ Action on Bond.
10.73 ____ Discharge of Liens and Notices of Claims.
10.74 Protecting the Owner—Itemized Statement.
10.75 ____ Lien Wilfully Exaggerated.
10.76 Repossession of Materials Not Used.
10.77 Enforcement of Mechanic's Liens—Courts.
10.78 ____ Courts of Record—Procedures.
10.79 ____ ____ Necessary Parties.

TABLE OF CONTENTS

Sec.
10.80 ____ ____ Actions in a Court Not of Record—Summons and Complaint.
10.81 ____ ____ Proceedings Upon Return of Summons.
10.82 ____ ____ Judgments and Transcripts.
10.83 ____ Costs and Disbursements.
10.84 ____ Effect of Failure to Establish Lien.
10.85 ____ Deposit of Money or Securities to Discharge Lien—Procedures.
10.86 ____ ____ Effect of Order.
10.87 ____ ____ Preference Over Contractors.
10.88 ____ ____ Delivery of Property in Lieu of Money.
10.89 ____ Deficiency Judgment.
10.90 ____ Vacating of Mechanic's Lien, Cancellation of Bond or Return of Deposit.
10.91 ____ Public Improvements.
10.92 ____ New Parties.
10.93 ____ Service of Answer on State or Public Corporation.
10.94 Trust Funds—Purpose.
10.95 ____ Creation.
10.96 ____ Contractors and Subcontractors.
10.97 ____ Beneficiaries.
10.98 Diversion of Trust Assets.
10.99 Notice of Lending.
10.100 Record Keeping Obligations.
10.101 Right of Beneficiaries to Examine Books or Records.
10.102 Action to Enforce Trust—Standing and Procedure.
10.103 ____ Remedies.
10.104 ____ Preferences.
10.105 Relief After Judgment on Obligation Constituting Trust Claim; Effect on Mechanic's Liens.
10.106 Misappropriation of Trust Funds.
10.107 Procedural Checklist.
10.108 Forms.
10.109 ____ Notice of Mechanic's Lien—General Form.
10.110 ____ Notice of Lien for Public Improvement.
10.111 ____ Form For Demand for Terms of Contract.
10.112 ____ Demand for Notice of Completion and Acceptance of Public Improvement.
10.113 ____ Petition to Amend Notice of Mechanic's Lien—Correct Name of Owner of Property.
10.114 ____ Assignment of Lien for Public Improvement.
10.115 ____ Assignment of Mechanic's Lien.
10.116 ____ Assignment of Moneys Due or to Become Due Under Public Improvement Contract.
10.117 ____ Affidavit for Continuance of Mechanic's Lien.
10.118 ____ Affidavit for Continuance of Lien for Public Improvement.
10.119 ____ Petition to Discharge Mechanic's Lien Where Notice of Lien Defective.
10.120 ____ Petition for Order Discharging Mechanic's Lien Upon Filing of Undertaking.

TABLE OF CONTENTS

Sec.
10.121 —— Undertaking to Discharge Mechanic's Lien.
10.122 —— Petition for Order Fixing Amount of Undertaking to Discharge Mechanic's Lien.
10.123 —— Approval by Lienors of Subordination of Mechanic's Liens to Trust Bond or Note and Mortgage.
10.124 —— Affidavit for Order Fixing Amount of Bond to Discharge All Mechanic's Liens.
10.125 —— Petition for Order Requiring Itemized Statement.
10.126 —— Notice of Application for Order Requiring Itemized Statement.
10.127 —— Demand for Itemized Statement.
10.128 —— Affidavit in Support of Application to Cancel Mechanic's Lien for Failure to Furnish Itemized Statement.
10.129 —— Notice Requiring Lienor to Commence Action to Enforce Mechanic's Lien.
10.130 —— Affidavit in Support of Application to Cancel Notice of Mechanic's Lien for Failure to Commence Action.
10.131 —— Notice Requiring Lienor to Commence Action to Enforce Lien for Public Improvement.
10.132 —— Affidavit in Support of Application to Cancel Notice of Lien for Public Improvement for Failure to Commence Action.
10.133 —— Complaint for Foreclosure of Lien for Public Improvement.
10.134 —— Complaint for Foreclosure of Mechanic's Lien—Contractor.
10.135 —— Defense and Counterclaim Based on Wilful Exaggeration of Mechanic's Lien.
10.136 —— Affidavit in Support of Motion to Consolidate Actions for Foreclosure of Mechanic's Liens.
10.137 —— Notice of Motion to Consolidate Actions to Foreclose Mechanic's Liens.
10.138 —— Acceptance of Offer to Pay Money Into Court in Discharge of Mechanic's Lien.
10.139 —— Offer to Pay Money Into Court in Discharge of Mechanic's Lien.
10.140 —— Judgment of Foreclosure and Sale—Mechanic's Lien.
10.141 —— Judgment of Foreclosure—Lien for Public Improvement—Where Lien Discharged and Fund Retained for Payment.
10.142 —— Affidavit in Support of Motion for Summary Judgment—Foreclosure of Lien for Public Improvement.
10.143 —— Demand for Verified Statement from Trustee.
10.144 —— Petition for Verified Statement from Trustee of Trust Funds.
10.145 —— Complaint by Subcontractor to Enforce Trust Against Funds Received by Contractor or Assignee of Contractor.
10.146 —— Complaint by Surety to Have Parties Declared Trustees of Subcontract Moneys and for Accounting.
10.147 —— Affidavit in Support of Motion to Determine if Class Action Can be Maintained—Action to Impress and Enforce Trust.

TABLE OF CONTENTS

CHAPTER 11. MORTGAGE FORECLOSURE

Sec.
11.1 Scope Note.
11.2 Strategy—Initial Client Interview.
11.3 ____ First Review of Loan Documents.
11.4 ____ Foreclosure Title Certificate.
11.5 New York Mortgage Foreclosure Law.
11.6 ____ Choice of Remedies: Foreclosure Action or Money Action.
11.7 ____ Partial Foreclosure Action.
11.8 ____ Non–Judicial Foreclosure.
11.9 Representing Subordinate Lienors.
11.10 Pre-commencement Procedure.
11.11 ____ Notice of Default.
11.12 ____ Notice of Acceleration.
11.13 ____ Foreclosure Title Certificate.
11.14 Determining the Necessary Defendants.
11.15 ____ The United States As a Necessary Defendant.
11.16 Starting the Foreclosure Action.
11.17 ____ Notice of Pendency of Action.
11.18 Summons.
11.19 ____ Venue.
11.20 Complaint.
11.21 ____ Allegations Regarding Parties.
11.22 ____ Allegations Regarding Loan, Note and Mortgage.
11.23 ____ References to Pertinent Terms of Note and Mortgage.
11.24 ____ Asserting Default(s).
11.25 ____ Reserving Right to Add Advances Made by Plaintiff to Indebtedness Secured by Mortgage.
11.26 ____ Allegation Regarding Subordinate Interest of Defendant(s).
11.27 ____ Whether There Has Been or is Pending Another Action Regarding the Mortgage Debt.
11.28 ____ Amendments.
11.29 Receivers.
11.30 ____ Considerations in Determining Whether to Seek Appointment of Receiver.
11.31 ____ *Ex Parte* Motion for Appointment of Receiver.
11.32 ____ Compensation.
11.33 ____ Opposing Appointment of Receiver.
11.34 ____ Discharging Receiver.
11.35 Defendant's Response.
11.36 ____ Motion to Dismiss Complaint.
11.37 ____ Answer and Defenses.
11.38 ____ Notice of Appearance and Waiver.
11.39 Obtaining Judgment.
11.40 ____ Motion for Judgment.
11.41 ____ Opposing Motion for Judgment.
11.42 Reference to Compute.
11.43 ____ Hearing Before Referee to Compute.
11.44 ____ Report of Referee to Compute.
11.45 ____ Motion to Confirm Referee's Computation Report and for Judgment of Foreclosure and Sale.

TABLE OF CONTENTS

Sec.
11.46 Judgment of Foreclosure and Sale.
11.47 Foreclosure Sale.
11.48 ____ Noticing and Advertising the Sale.
11.49 ____ Conducting the Sale.
11.50 ____ Vacating the Sale.
11.51 Referee's Deed, Other Closing Documents and Referee's Report of Sale.
11.52 Deficiency Judgment.
11.53 Surplus Money Proceedings.
11.54 Eviction of Tenants and Other Occupants After Foreclosure Sale.
11.55 Drafting Checklists.
11.56 ____ Notice of Default.
11.57 ____ Notice of Acceleration.
11.58 ____ Notice of Pendency of Action.
11.59 ____ Summons.
11.60 ____ Complaint.
11.61 ____ Order Appointing Receiver.
11.62 ____ Affidavit in Support of *Ex Parte* Application for Receiver.
11.63 ____ Notice of Motion for Summary Judgment and Related Relief.
11.64 ____ Affidavit of Regularity and in Support of Plaintiff's Motion for Summary Judgment and Related Relief.
11.65 ____ Judgment of Foreclosure and Sale.
11.66 ____ Notice of Sale.
11.67 ____ Terms and Memorandum of Sale.
11.68 Forms.
11.69 ____ Notice of Default. 💾
11.70 ____ Notice of Acceleration. 💾
11.71 ____ Notice of Pendency of Action. 💾
11.72 ____ Summons. 💾
11.73 ____ Verified Complaint for Foreclosure of Mortgage Affecting Single Family Residence. 💾
11.74 ____ Verified Complaint for Foreclosure of Mortgage Affecting Commercial, Multi–Unit Residential or Mixed Property. 💾
11.75 ____ Order Appointing Receiver. 💾
11.76 ____ Affidavit in Support of Motion for Appointment of Receiver. 💾
11.77 ____ Notice of Motion for Summary Judgment and Related Relief. 💾
11.78 ____ Affidavit of Regularity and in Support of Motion for Summary Judgment. 💾
11.79 ____ Judgment of Foreclosure and Sale. 💾
11.80 ____ Notice of Sale. 💾
11.81 ____ Terms and Memorandum of Sale. 💾

CHAPTER 12. PURCHASE AND SALE OF REAL ESTATE

12.1 Scope Note.
12.2 Strategy.
12.3 ____ Pre-contract Checklist.
12.4 Contract of Sale.

TABLE OF CONTENTS

Sec.
12.5 —— Preparation and Delivery
12.6 —— Recordation.
12.7 Residential Contract of Sale.
12.8 —— Parties.
12.9 —— Premises.
12.10 —— Personal Property.
12.11 —— Purchase Price and Method of Payment.
12.12 —— —— Down Payment.
12.13 —— —— Assumption of Existing Mortgage.
12.14 —— —— Purchase Money Mortgage.
12.15 —— —— Mortgage Contingency.
12.16 —— —— Acceptable Funds.
12.17 —— Permitted Exceptions.
12.18 —— Governmental Violations and Orders.
12.19 —— Seller's Representations.
12.20 —— Condition of Property.
12.21 —— Insurable and Marketable Title.
12.22 —— Closing, Deed and Title.
12.23 —— Closing Date and Place.
12.24 —— Conditions to Closing.
12.25 —— Deed Transfer and Recording Taxes.
12.26 —— Apportionments.
12.27 —— Allowance for Unpaid Taxes.
12.28 —— Title Examination; Seller's Inability to Convey; Limitation of Liability.
12.29 —— Defaults and Remedies.
12.30 —— Assignment.
12.31 —— Broker.
12.32 —— Risk of Loss.
12.33 Condominium Contract of Sale.
12.34 —— Comparisons to the Residential Contract of Sale.
12.35 —— Homeowner's Associations.
12.36 Contract of Sale for Office, Commercial and Multi-family Residential Premises.
12.37 Contract of Sale for Cooperative Apartment
12.38 —— Standard Form.
12.39 Contract of Sale for New Construction.
12.40 Title Insurance.
12.41 —— The Buyer's Obligation.
12.42 —— Role of the Title Insurer.
12.43 —— Duration and Cost.
12.44 —— Basic and Extended Coverage.
12.45 Title Insurance Policy.
12.46 —— Loan Policy Coverage.
12.47 —— New York Modifications of Loan Policy.
12.48 —— Owner's Policy Coverage.
12.49 —— New York Modifications of Owner's Policy.
12.50 —— Standard Exceptions.
12.51 —— Endorsements.
12.52 —— Exclusions.

TABLE OF CONTENTS

Sec.
12.53 Title Examination: Recording Title and the Torrens System.
12.54 ___ Objections to Be Disposed of Prior to Closing.
12.55 ___ ___ Checklist.
12.56 The Survey Map.
12.57 ___ What it May Disclose.
12.58 ___ Effect on Marketability of Title.
12.59 ___ ___ Where Contract Is Silent on the Matter of Survey.
12.60 ___ ___ Where Contract Subject to Any State of Facts an Accurate Survey May Show.
12.61 ___ ___ Where Contract Subject to Any State of Facts an Accurate Survey May Show Provided Same Does Not Render Title Unmarketable.
12.62 ___ ___ Where Contract Subject to Specific Encroachments or to Facts Shown on a Specific Survey.
12.63 ___ ___ Suggested Clause.
12.64 Marketability of Title.
12.65 ___ What Renders Title Unmarketable.
12.66 ___ ___ Encroachments Due to Adverse Possession.
12.67 ___ ___ Party Walls.
12.68 ___ Driveway Easements.
12.69 ___ Other Covenants and Restrictions.
12.70 ___ Reservations for Public Utilities.
12.71 ___ Land Abutting Bodies of Water and the Federal Navigational Servitude.
12.72 Closing of Title.
12.73 ___ Checklist.
12.74 ___ Recording Fees and Filings.
12.75 ___ Disclosure and Other Requirements.
12.76 ___ ___ Foreign Investors Real Property Tax.
12.77 ___ ___ Form 1099–S Federal Requirement for One to Four Family Residence.
12.78 ___ ___ Form 1099–S Federal Requirement for One to Four Family Residence—Checklist.
12.79 ___ ___ Cash Payments Received by Businesses in Excess of $10,000.
12.80 ___ ___ Lead Paint Hazards.
12.81 ___ ___ Agricultural Foreign Investment Disclosure Act.
12.82 ___ Payment of Taxes.
12.83 ___ ___ New York State Real Estate Transfer Tax and Mansion Tax.
12.84 ___ ___ Article 31–B—Real Property Transfer Gains Tax.
12.85 ___ ___ New York City Real Property Transfer Tax.
12.86 ___ ___ Cities of Mount Vernon and Yonkers.
12.87 ___ ___ Real Estate Investment Trusts.
12.88 ___ ___ Mortgage Recording Tax Outside New York City.
12.89 ___ ___ Mortgage Recording Tax Rate in New York City.
12.90 ___ Method of Payment.
12.91 ___ Other Required Forms and Information.
12.92 Forms.
12.93 ___ Residential Contract of Sale.

TABLE OF CONTENTS

Sec.
12.94 ___ Contract of Sale—Condominium Unit.
12.95 ___ ___ Office, Commercial and Multi–Family Residential Premises.
12.96 ___ ___ Cooperative Apartment.
12.97 ___ Durable General Power of Attorney. 💾
12.98 ___ Power of Attorney to Take Effect at a Later Time. 💾

Volume 22

CHAPTER 13. LANDLORD–TENANT LAW

13.1 Scope Note.
13.2 Strategy.
13.3 ___ Checklists.
13.4 Summary Proceedings.
13.5 ___ Venue and Jurisdiction.
13.6 ___ Service of Process.
13.7 ___ ___ Personal Delivery.
13.8 ___ ___ Substituted Service.
13.9 ___ ___ Conspicuous Place Service.
13.10 ___ ___ New York City Civil Court "Postcard Requirement."
13.11 Non-payment Proceedings.
13.12 ___ Rent Demands.
13.13 ___ Notice of Petition.
13.14 ___ ___ Form of Notice.
13.15 ___ ___ Content of Notice.
13.16 ___ ___ Defects in the Notice.
13.17 ___ The Petition.
13.18 ___ ___ Defects in the Petition.
13.19 ___ ___ Verification.
13.20 ___ ___ Defects in the Verification.
13.21 Responding to the Non-payment Petition.
13.22 ___ The Answer.
13.23 ___ The Motion to Dismiss.
13.24 ___ The RPAPL § 755 Motion to Stay.
13.25 Tenant Defenses to the Non-payment Proceeding.
13.26 ___ No Landlord Tenant Relationship.
13.27 ___ Tenant Out of Possession.
13.28 ___ Statutory Noncompliance.
13.29 ___ Illegal Rent.
13.30 ___ Actual Eviction.
13.31 ___ Constructive Eviction.
13.32 ___ Warranty of Habitability.
13.33 ___ Laches.
13.34 ___ Payment.
13.35 Holdover Proceedings.
13.36 ___ Predicate Notices.
13.37 ___ ___ Month-to-Month Tenants.
13.38 ___ ___ Illegal Use.
13.39 ___ ___ Rent–Controlled Tenants.

TABLE OF CONTENTS

Sec.
13.40 ___ ___ Rent–Stabilized Tenants.
13.41 ___ The Notice of Petition.
13.42 ___ ___ Defects in the Notice.
13.43 ___ Holdover Petition—Form and Content.
13.44 ___ ___ Defects in the Petition.
13.45 ___ ___ Verification and Verification Defects.
13.46 Responding to the Holdover Petition.
13.47 ___ The Answer.
13.48 ___ The Motion to Dismiss.
13.49 Tenant Defenses to the Holdover Proceeding.
13.50 ___ Acceptance of Rent After Expiration or Termination of Tenancy.
13.51 ___ Defective Predicate Notice.
13.52 ___ ___ Rent–Regulated Apartments.
13.53 ___ Waiver.
13.54 ___ Equitable Estoppel.
13.55 ___ Succession Rights to Rent–Regulated Apartments.
13.56 Counterclaims.
13.57 Bill of Particulars.
13.58 Discovery.
13.59 ___ Notice to Admit.
13.60 ___ Freedom of Information Law.
13.61 The Trial—Adjournments.
13.62 ___Amending Petition and Burden of Proof.
13.63 Stipulations—Overview.
13.64 ___ Non-payment Proceedings.
13.65 ___ Holdover Proceedings.
13.66 ___ Enforcement and Vacatur.
13.67 The Judgment and Warrant.
13.68 ___ Staying the Warrant in Non-payment Proceedings.
13.69 ___ Staying the Warrant in New York City Residential Holdover Proceedings.
13.70 Yellowstone Actions.
13.71 ___ Obtaining the Injunction.
13.72 Article 7–A Proceedings.
13.73 Rent Regulatory Proceedings.
13.74 ___ Rent Overcharge.
13.75 ___ Service Reduction.
13.76 ___ Major Capital Improvement Rent Increase.
13.77 Checklist of Essential Allegations.
13.78 ___ Petition Non-payment.
13.79 ___ Holdover Petition.
13.80 ___ Stipulation Settling Non-payment Proceeding.
13.81 ___ Stipulation Settling Holdover Proceeding.
13.82 Forms.
13.83 ___ Petition Non-payment. 💾
13.84 ___ Petition Holdover. 💾
13.85 ___ Individual Verification. 💾
13.86 ___ Corporate Officer Verification. 💾
13.87 ___ Partnership Verification. 💾

TABLE OF CONTENTS

Sec.
13.88 ____ Attorney Verification. 💾
13.89 ____ Stipulations. 💾
13.90 ____ ____ Settling Non-payment Proceeding. 💾
13.91 ____ ____ Settling Non-payment Proceeding With Final Judgment in Favor of Petitioner. 💾
13.92 ____ ____ Settling Holdover Proceeding Where Tenant Agrees to Cure Lease Violation. 💾
13.93 ____ ____ Settling Holdover Proceeding Where Tenant–Respondent Agrees to Vacate Premises. 💾

CHAPTER 14. EMINENT DOMAIN

14.1 Scope Note.
14.2 Strategies for Condemnors and Condemnees.
14.3 Exercise of the Power of Eminent Domain.
14.4 ____ The State as Condemnor.
14.5 ____ Other Public Entities as Condemnor.
14.6 ____ Private Entities.
14.7 Property Rights Subject to Acquisition.
14.8 ____ Real Property.
14.9 ____ Easements.
14.10 ____ Leases.
14.11 ____ Personal Property.
14.12 ____ Public Property/Priority of Taking.
14.13 ____ Excess Property.
14.14 *De Facto* Taking.
14.15 Public Use, Benefit or Purpose.
14.16 ____ Particular Uses.
14.17 ____ Incidental Private Benefit.
14.18 Just Compensation.
14.19 Summary.
14.20 The First Stage: The Condemnation Phase.
14.21 Public Hearing.
14.22 Exemptions From the Public Hearing Requirement.
14.23 ____ Overlap with Other Governmental Requirements.
14.24 ____ Overlap with Issuance of a Certificate of Environmental Compatibility and Public Need.
14.25 ____ Alternate Public Hearing.
14.26 ____ *De Minimis* Acquisition or Emergency Situation.
14.27 ____ Section 41.34 of the Mental Hygiene Law.
14.28 Notice.
14.29 Conduct of the Public Hearing and Requirement of a Record.
14.30 Determination and Findings.
14.31 ____ Publication of Synopsis.
14.32 ____ Interplay with SEQRA.
14.33 ____ Amendments for Field Conditions.
14.34 Judicial Review of Determination and Findings.
14.35 ____ Prerequisite Determination.
14.36 ____ Persons Entitled to Review.
14.37 ____ 30–Day Statute of Limitations.

TABLE OF CONTENTS

Sec.
14.38 ____ Scope of Review.
14.39 Summary.
14.40 The Second Stage—The "Offer and Negotiation" Phase.
14.41 ____ Pretaking Appraisals.
14.42 ____ Pretaking Discovery.
14.43 ____ Offer as Payment in Full.
14.44 ____ Advance Payment.
14.45 Use and Occupancy by Condemnee After Taking.
14.46 Summary.
14.47 The Third Stage—The Acquisition Phase.
14.48 ____ Court of Claims v. Supreme Court Jurisdiction.
14.49 ____ Statute of Limitations for Bringing an Acquisition Proceeding.
14.50 ____ ____ Acquisition in Stages.
14.51 ____ Acquisition Map.
14.52 Acquisition of Property—Court of Claims Jurisdiction.
14.53 ____ Condemnors Subject to Court of Claims Jurisdiction.
14.54 ____ Filing and Notice Requirements.
14.55 ____ Vesting of Title.
14.56 Acquisition of Property—Supreme Court Jurisdiction.
14.57 ____ Notice of Pendency.
14.58 ____ Petition in Condemnation.
14.59 ____ ____ Content.
14.60 ____ ____ Additional Content Rules for Certain Non-governmental Condemnors.
14.61 ____ Notice.
14.62 ____ ____ Certification of Names of Reputed Condemnees.
14.63 ____ Answer by Condemnee.
14.64 ____ ____ Defenses.
14.65 ____ Vesting of Title and Order of Condemnation.
14.66 Notice of Acquisition.
14.67 Immediate Entry.
14.68 Summary.
14.69 The Fourth Stage—The Compensation Phase.
14.70 ____ Court of Claims.
14.71 ____ ____ Time to File Claim.
14.72 ____ ____ Service.
14.73 ____ Supreme Court.
14.74 ____ ____ Time to File Claim.
14.75 ____ ____ Service.
14.76 Content of Claim.
14.77 Scope of Just Compensation.
14.78 ____ "Highest and Best Use."
14.79 ____ Total Taking.
14.80 ____ ____ Direct Damages.
14.81 ____ ____ Improvements.
14.82 ____ Partial Taking.
14.83 ____ Temporary Taking.
14.84 ____ ____ Easements.
14.85 Methods of Valuation to Determine Compensation.

LII

TABLE OF CONTENTS

Sec.
14.86 ____ Market Approach to Value.
14.87 ____ Income Approach to Value.
14.88 ____ Cost Approach to Value.
14.89 Specialty Property.
14.90 Effect of Environmental Contamination on Property Value.
14.91 Fixtures.
14.92 ____ Compensable Fixtures.
14.93 ____ Valuation of Fixtures.
14.94 Leasehold Interests.
14.95 ____ Valuation and Compensation.
14.96 Loss of Business and Goodwill.
14.97 Going Concern Value.
14.98 Moving and Relocation Expenses.
14.99 Conflicting Claims by Condemnees.
14.100 ____ Conflicting Claims to the Condemnor's Offer.
14.101 ____ Conflicting Claims to the Award.
14.102 The Trial on Compensation.
14.103 ____ Preference.
14.104 ____ Filing and Exchange of Appraisals.
14.105 ____ Expert Testimony.
14.106 ____ Viewing of the Property.
14.107 ____ Joint or Consolidated Trials.
14.108 ____ Interest.
14.109 Setoff for Indirect Benefit.
14.110 Incidental Expenses and Proration of Taxes.
14.111 Abandonment of Procedure by Condemnor.
14.112 Finding that Condemnor is Not Legally Authorized to Acquire the Property.
14.113 Finding Contrary to Claim by Condemnor That it Did Not Take Property.
14.114 Decision By the Court and Entry of Judgment.
14.115 Additional Allowances for Costs and Expenses.
14.116 Payment Pending Appeal.
14.117 Small Claims Proceedings.
14.118 Summary.
14.119 Procedural Checklist.
14.120 Forms—Demand on Condemnor to File Copy of Proceedings to Determine Need and Location of Public Project with Appellate Division for Purpose of Judicial Review.
14.121 ____ Petition for Review of Determination and Finding that Public Use, Benefit or Purpose Will be Served by Proposed Acquisition.
14.122 ____ Judgment of Appellate Division Rejecting the Determination and Finding that Public Use, Benefit or Purpose Will be Served by Proposed Acquisition.
14.123 ____ Complaint by Condemnee to Establish Fair and Reasonable Value for Temporary Use and Occupancy After Acquisition by Eminent Domain.

TABLE OF CONTENTS

Sec.

14.124 ____ Notice of Pendency of Proceeding in Supreme Court to Acquire Property by Eminent Domain and File Acquisition Map. 🖫

14.125 ____ Notice of Petition in Proceeding in Supreme Court to Acquire Property by Eminent Domain and File Acquisition Map. 🖫

14.126 ____ Petition in Proceeding in Supreme Court to Acquire Property by Eminent Domain and File Acquisition Map. 🖫

14.127 ____ Petition in Proceeding in Supreme Court to Acquire Property by Eminent Domain and File Acquisition Map—Petitioner Exempt from Compliance with Eminent Domain Procedure Law Article 2. 🖫

14.128 ____ Answer to Petition in Proceeding in Supreme Court to Acquire Property by Eminent Domain and File Acquisition Map. 🖫

14.129 ____ Order to Show Cause Why Condemnor Should Not be Permitted to Enter Immediately upon Real Property and Devote It Temporarily to Public Use Specified in Petition Upon Deposit of a Fixed Sum with the Court. 🖫

14.130 ____ Order to Show Cause Why Condemnor Should Not be Permitted to File Acquisition Maps or Enter upon Real Property. 🖫

14.131 ____ Order in Proceeding in Supreme Court to Acquire Property by Eminent Domain and File Acquisition Map. 🖫

14.132 ____ Notice of Acquisition by Eminent Domain Where Supreme Court Has Jurisdiction. 🖫

14.133 ____ Claim for Damages Arising from Acquisition by Eminent Domain—General Form. 🖫

14.134 ____ Judgment Awarding Compensation in Claim for Acquisition of Property by Eminent Domain. 🖫

14.135 ____ Notice of Motion for Additional Allowance to Condemnee for Expert Witnesses. 🖫

14.136 ____ Affidavit in Support of Motion for Additional Allowance to Condemnee for Expert Witnesses. 🖫

14.137 ____ Order Granting Additional Allowance to Condemnee for Expert Witnesses. 🖫

CHAPTER 15. ENVIRONMENTAL LAW

15.1 Scope Note.
15.2 Strategy.
15.3 State Environmental Quality Review Act.
15.4 ____ Determination of Significance.
15.5 ____ The Environmental Impact Statement and Findings Statement.
15.6 ____ Judicial Review.
15.7 ____ Checklist.
15.8 Water Pollution Control.
15.9 ____ SPDES Permit Program.
15.10 ____ Stormwater Discharges and Oil Spills.
15.11 ____ Enforcement.

TABLE OF CONTENTS

Sec.
15.12 ___ Strategy: Clean Water Act Citizen Suit Checklist.
15.13 Wetlands Protection.
15.14 ___ Strategy: Checklist.
15.15 ___ The Federal Scheme.
15.16 ___ New York Tidal and Freshwater Wetlands Law.
15.17 ___ Permit Procedure and Criteria.
15.18 ___ Penalties.
15.19 Air Pollution Control.
15.20 ___ The 1990 CAA Amendments.
15.21 ___ New York State Requirements.
15.22 ___ Enforcement.
15.23 Regulation of Solid and Hazardous Waste.
15.24 ___ New York Hazardous Waste Regulation.
15.25 ___ Enforcement.
15.26 Regulation of Underground Storage Tanks and Petroleum Storage Tanks—Federal Law.
15.27 ___ New York Law.
15.28 Regulation of Inactive Hazardous Waste Sites—CERCLA.
15.29 ___ CERCLA Section 107(a).
15.30 ___ Lender Liability, Contribution and Indemnification Under CERCLA.
15.31 ___ New York Law.
15.32 Relevant Common Law Doctrines—Nuisance.
15.33 Common Law Doctrines—Trespass.
15.34 Regulatory Takings.
15.35 Drafting Checklist—Clean Water Act Citizen Suit Notice Letter.
15.36 ___ Clean Water Act and Resource Conservation and Recovery Act Citizen Suit Notice Letter.
15.37 ___ Clean Water Act Complaint.
15.38 ___ Nuisance and Trespass Complaint.
15.39 ___ Oil Spill Complaint.
15.40 Forms—Clean Water Act Citizen Suit Notice Letter. 💾
15.41 ___ Clean Water Act and Resource Conservation and Recovery Act Citizen Suit Notice Letter. 💾
15.42 ___ Clean Water Act Complaint. 💾
15.43 ___ Nuisance and Trespass Complaint. 💾
15.44 ___ Oil Spill Complaint. 💾

CHAPTER 16. LAND USE LAW

16.1 Scope Note.
16.2 Strategy.
16.3 Local Land Use Law.
16.4 ___ Delegated Authority.
16.5 ___ Enabling Acts.
16.6 ___ ___ New York City.
16.7 ___·Home Rule Authority.
16.8 ___ ___ Flexibility.
16.9 ___ ___ Floating Zone.
16.10 ___ Summary.

TABLE OF CONTENTS

Sec.
16.11 Comprehensive Plan.
16.12 ____ Judicial Definition.
16.13 ____ Statutory Definition.
16.14 ____ Preparation and Adoption.
16.15 ____ Protects Zoning Against Challenge.
16.16 ____ Summary.
16.17 Substantive Limits—Illustrative Case.
16.18 ____ Substantive Due Process.
16.19 ____ Procedural Due Process.
16.20 ____ Equal Protection.
16.21 ____ *Ultra Vires*.
16.22 ____ Regulatory Takings.
16.23 ____ Vested Rights.
16.24 ____ Preemption.
16.25 ____ First Amendment.
16.26 ____ Summary.
16.27 Local Process.
16.28 ____ Structure of Local Regulations.
16.29 ____ Adoption.
16.30 ____ Amendment.
16.31 ____ Other Regulations/Official Map.
16.32 ____ Building Regulations and Permits.
16.33 ____ Summary.
16.34 Local Boards and Practices.
16.35 ____ Local Legislature.
16.36 ____ Planning Board.
16.37 ____ Zoning Board of Appeals.
16.38 ____ Freedom of Information.
16.39 ____ Open Meetings.
16.40 ____ Conflict of Interests.
16.41 ____ Summary.
16.42 Judicial Review.
16.43 ____ Procedures.
16.44 ____ Standards.
16.45 ____ ____ Local Legislature.
16.46 ____ ____ Zoning Board of Appeals.
16.47 ____ ____ Planning Board.
16.48 ____ Standing.
16.49 ____ Exhaustion.
16.50 ____ Remedies.
16.51 ____ Summary.
16.52 Local Environmental Review.
16.53 ____ Actions Subject to SEQRA.
16.54 ____ ____ Building Permits.
16.55 ____ ____ Variances.
16.56 ____ ____ Subdivisions.
16.57 ____ ____ Site Plans.
16.58 ____ ____ Rezoning.
16.59 ____ Summary.
16.60 Zoning Law—In General.

LVI

TABLE OF CONTENTS

Sec.
- 16.61 As of Right Use.
- 16.62 Nonconforming Use—Definition and Application.
- 16.63 ___ Changes.
- 16.64 ___ Reconstruction and Restoration.
- 16.65 ___ Enlargement, Alteration or Extension.
- 16.66 ___ Changes to Another Nonconforming Use.
- 16.67 ___ Termination.
- 16.68 ___ Abandonment.
- 16.69 ___ Amortization.
- 16.70 ___ Transfer of Ownership.
- 16.71 ___ Procedures.
- 16.72 ___ Summary.
- 16.73 Use Variance.
- 16.74 ___ Statutory Standard.
- 16.75 ___ ___ Reasonable Return.
- 16.76 ___ ___ Unique Hardship.
- 16.77 ___ ___ Protect Essential Neighborhood Character.
- 16.78 ___ ___ Self-Created Hardship.
- 16.79 ___ Minimum Variance Needed.
- 16.80 ___ Procedure.
- 16.81 ___ Summary.
- 16.82 Area Variance.
- 16.83 ___ Statutory Balancing Test.
- 16.84 ___ ___ Guiding Principles from Case Law.
- 16.85 ___ ___ Balancing Factors.
- 16.86 ___ Minimum Variance Needed.
- 16.87 ___ Procedure.
- 16.88 ___ Summary.
- 16.89 Conditions Imposed on Use and Area Variances.
- 16.90 Special Use Permits.
- 16.91 ___ Imposition and Use of Standards.
- 16.92 ___ Findings and Determination of Board.
- 16.93 ___ Limitation on Imposition of Conditions.
- 16.94 ___ Procedure.
- 16.95 ___ Summary.
- 16.96 Subdivision Approval.
- 16.97 ___ Procedure.
- 16.98 ___ ___ How Affected By SEQRA.
- 16.99 ___ Provision of Essential Services.
- 16.100 ___ Parkland.
- 16.101 ___ Decisions and Conditions.
- 16.102 ___ Summary.
- 16.103 Site Plans.
- 16.104 ___ Responsible Agency.
- 16.105 ___ ___ Procedure.
- 16.106 ___ ___ Standards for Review.
- 16.107 ___ ___ Conditions Imposed.
- 16.108 ___ Summary.
- 16.109 Particularized Actions.
- 16.110 ___ Spot Zoning.

TABLE OF CONTENTS

Sec.
16.111 ___ ___ Challenge Dismissed.
16.112 ___ ___ Challenge Successful.
16.113 ___ Rezoning.
16.114 ___ ___ Conditions.
16.115 ___ ___ Contract Zoning.
16.116 ___ ___ Development Agreements.
16.117 ___ Summary.
16.118 Special Regulations.
16.119 ___ Accessory Uses.
16.120 ___ Accessory Apartments.
16.121 ___ Home Offices.
16.122 ___ Definition of Family.
16.123 ___ Affordable Housing.
16.124 ___ Mobile Homes.
16.125 ___ Aesthetics.
16.126 ___ ___ Architectural Review.
16.127 ___ ___ Historic Preservation.
16.128 ___ Public Uses.
16.129 ___ ___ Public Utilities.
16.130 ___ ___ Cellular Transmission Facilities.
16.131 ___ ___ Religious Uses.
16.132 ___ Summary.
16.133 Forms—Environmental Assessment—Short Form.
16.134 ___ Environmental Assessment—Long Form.

CHAPTER 17. EMPLOYMENT LAW

17.1 Scope Note.
17.2 Strategy.
17.3 ___ Plaintiff's Counsel's Investigation.
17.4 ___ Defendant's Counsel's Investigation.
17.5 ___ Pre-litigation Settlement Process.
17.6 ___ Negotiating With Opposing Counsel.
17.7 ___ Alternative Dispute Resolution ("ADR").
17.8 ___ ___ Mediation.
17.9 ___ ___ Arbitration.
17.10 ___ Settlement and Severance Agreements.
17.11 ___ ___ Older Workers Benefit Protection Act ("OWBPA").
17.12 ___ ___ COBRA.
17.13 ___ ___ Pay.
17.14 ___ ___ Income Taxes.
17.15 ___ ___ Benefits.
17.16 ___ Other Severance Issues.
17.17 ___ Independent Contractor vs. Employee.
17.18 ___ Checklist: Initial Considerations for Plaintiff.
17.19 ___ Checklist: Terminating an Employee.
17.20 Causes of Action.
17.21 ___ Tort–Assault.
17.22 ___ ___ Battery.
17.23 ___ ___ Conspiracy.

LVIII

TABLE OF CONTENTS

Sec.
17.24 ___ ___ Conversion.
17.25 ___ ___ Defamation.
17.26 ___ ___ False Imprisonment; Malicious Prosecution.
17.27 ___ ___ Fraud, Negligent Misrepresentation and Fraudulent Inducement.
17.28 ___ ___ Intentional Infliction of Emotional Distress.
17.29 ___ ___ Interference with Business Relations.
17.30 ___ ___ Negligence.
17.31 ___ ___ *Prima Facie* Tort.
17.32 ___ ___ Wrongful Discharge.
17.33 ___ Contract.
17.34 ___ ___ Express Promises.
17.35 ___ ___ Implied Promises.
17.36 ___ ___ Estoppel.
17.37 Statutory Causes of Action—Age Discrimination.
17.38 ___ Anti-reprisal Provisions of Various Statutes.
17.39 ___ Arrest Records.
17.40 ___ Bankruptcy.
17.41 ___ Convictions.
17.42 ___ Credit Information.
17.43 ___ Disability.
17.44 ___ Equal Pay.
17.45 ___ Family and Medical Leave Act (FMLA).
17.46 ___ Health Plan Coverage (COBRA).
17.47 ___ Legal Off Duty Activities.
17.48 ___ Marital Status Discrimination.
17.49 ___ Discrimination on the Basis of Race, Color or National Origin.
17.50 ___ Pension Plans.
17.51 ___ Plant Closing, Mass Layoffs.
17.52 ___ Polygraphs.
17.53 ___ Public Employees.
17.54 ___ Pregnancy.
17.55 ___ Privacy.
17.56 ___ Religious Discrimination.
17.57 ___ Sex Discrimination, Harassment.
17.58 ___ Sexual Orientation Discrimination.
17.59 ___ Title VII, Burdens of Proof.
17.60 ___ Unemployment Insurance.
17.61 ___ Unionization, Rights Within Unions.
17.62 ___ Unsafe Workplace.
17.63 ___ Wages; Unpaid Compensation; Overtime.
17.64 ___ Whistleblowing/*Qui Tam*.
17.65 ___ Workers' Compensation.
17.66 Procedure—Anti-discrimination Agency Practice.
17.67 ___ Filing and Responding to Administrative Charges.
17.68 ___ Election of Remedies.
17.69 ___ Statutes of Limitations and Prerequisites to Private Lawsuits.
17.70 Private Lawsuits.

TABLE OF CONTENTS

Sec.
17.71 —— Discovery—General Considerations.
17.72 —— —— Plaintiff's Strategy.
17.73 —— Summary Judgment.
17.74 —— Trial.
17.75 —— Fee Application.
17.76 —— Post–Trial Motions and Appeal.
17.77 —— Checklist: Statutes of Limitations.
17.78 —— Checklist: Commencement of New York State Actions.
17.79 —— Checklist: Commencement of Federal Court Actions.
17.80 Miscellaneous Practice Issues—OFCCP/Glass Ceiling Audits.
17.81 —— Employment Policies and Handbooks.
17.82 Drafting the Complaint.
17.83 Drafting Checklist—Complaint.
17.84 Drafting the Answer.
17.85 Drafting Checklist—Answer
17.86 Forms—Client (Plaintiff) Intake Questionnaire.
17.87 —— Severance/Release Agreement.
17.88 —— Letter to EEOC Requesting "Mohasco" Waiver of State Processing.
17.89 —— Charge of Discrimination—New York State Division of Human Rights (Official Form).
17.90 —— Information Sheet—New York State Division of Human Rights (Official Form).
17.91 —— SDHR Information Sheet.
17.92 —— Charge of Discrimination—Equal Employment Opportunity Commission (Official Form).
17.93 —— Affidavit for a Charge of Discrimination—Equal Employment Opportunity Commission (Official Form).
17.94 —— EEOC Filing Cover Letter Requesting EEOC Processing of Dual–filed Charge.
17.95 —— Letter Requesting Administrative Convenience Dismissal from State or City Administrative Agency.
17.96 —— Pleadings—New York State Complaint.
17.97 —— —— New York State Answer.
17.98 —— —— Federal Complaint.
17.99 —— —— Federal Answer.

CHAPTER 18. CIVIL RIGHTS

18.1 Scope Note.
18.2 Strategy.
18.3 —— Checklist.
18.4 Overview of New York and Federal Civil Rights Provisions.
18.5 Jurisdiction over Civil Rights Actions.
18.6 New York Bill of Rights.
18.7 —— Overview.
18.8 —— Comparison With Federal Bill of Rights.
18.9 —— Search and Seizure.
18.10 —— —— Civil Liability.
18.11 —— —— Return of Seized Property.

TABLE OF CONTENTS

Sec.
18.12 ____ Rights of Persons Accused of Crimes.
18.13 ____ ____ Public Trial/Closure of Courtroom.
18.14 ____ ____ Exclusion of Public or Press.
18.15 ____ Rights of Jurors.
18.16 General Federal Civil Rights Provisions.
18.17 ____ 42 U.S.C.A. § 1981.
18.18 ____ 42 U.S.C.A. § 1983.
18.19 ____ Other Federal Civil Rights Provisions.
18.20 Police and Prosecutorial Misconduct.
18.21 ____ Excessive Force.
18.22 ____ False Arrest.
18.23 ____ False Imprisonment.
18.24 ____ Search and Seizure.
18.25 ____ Malicious Prosecution.
18.26 First Amendment.
18.27 ____ Freedom of Speech.
18.28 ____ Freedom of Religion.
18.29 Rights of Prisoners.
18.30 Defenses to Federal Actions.
18.31 ____ Absolute Immunity.
18.32 ____ Qualified Immunity.
18.33 ____ Eleventh Amendment.
18.34 ____ *Monell* and Its Progeny.
18.35 ____ *Respondeat Superior*.
18.36 ____ Abstention.
18.37 ____ *Res Judicata* and Collateral Estoppel.
18.38 ____ Statute of Limitations.
18.39 Housing.
18.40 ____ Prohibition Against Discrimination in Publicly Assisted Housing.
18.41 ____ ____ Owners and Lessors.
18.42 ____ ____ Real Estate Agents and Brokers.
18.43 ____ ____ Remedies for Discrimination.
18.44 ____ Prohibition Against Discrimination in Private Housing.
18.45 ____ ____ Owners and Lessors.
18.46 ____ ____ Real Estate Agents and Brokers.
18.47 ____ ____ Cooperatives.
18.48 ____ ____ Remedies for Discrimination.
18.49 ____ ____ ____ Administrative Proceedings.
18.50 ____ ____ ____ Actions in State and Federal Court.
18.51 ____ *Prima Facie* Case and Burden of Proof.
18.52 ____ Summary of Procedure for Filing an Administrative Claim and Challenging an SDHR Order.
18.53 Education.
18.54 Equal Rights in Places of Public Accommodation and Amusement.
18.55 ____ General Provisions.
18.56 ____ Private Clubs.
18.57 ____ Persons With Disabilities Accompanied by a Guide Dog, Hearing Dog or Service Dog.
18.58 ____ Remedies for Discrimination.

TABLE OF CONTENTS

Sec.
- 18.59 Employment Discrimination Provisions Exclusive to the New York Civil Rights Law.
- 18.60 ___ In General.
- 18.61 ___ Persons With Disabilities.
- 18.62 ___ Persons With Genetic Disorders.
- 18.63 Right of Privacy.
- 18.64 ___ Generally.
- 18.65 ___ Police Officers, Corrections Officers and Firefighters.
- 18.66 ___ Victims of Sex Offenses.
- 18.67 Changing One's Name.
- 18.68 ___ Procedure for Petition to Change Name.
- 18.69 ___ ___ Contents of Petition.
- 18.70 ___ ___ Special Procedures for Infants.
- 18.71 ___ Factors to Be Considered by the Court.
- 18.72 ___ Publication Requirement.
- 18.73 ___ Checklist.
- 18.74 Heart Balm Statute.
- 18.75 ___ Penalty for Bringing Action.
- 18.76 ___ Action for Return of Gifts Made in Contemplation of Marriage.
- 18.77 ___ ___ Procedure.
- 18.78 Miscellaneous Rights and Immunities.
- 18.79 ___ Frivolous Litigation.
- 18.80 ___ ___ Protection from SLAPP Suits.
- 18.81 ___ Libel and Slander.
- 18.82 ___ ___ Defenses.
- 18.83 ___ Breast Feeding.
- 18.84 ___ Suspension of Rights Due to Imprisonment.
- 18.85 ___ Shield Law.
- 18.86 ___ Performing Abortion.
- 18.87 ___ "Good Samaritan" Law Provisions.
- 18.88 Drafting Checklists.
- 18.89 ___ Framing the Federal Court § 1983 Complaint.
- 18.90 ___ Petition to Change One's Name.
- 18.91 Forms.
- 18.92 ___ Complaint for False Arrest, False Imprisonment and Malicious Prosecution.
- 18.93 ___ Complaint for Excessive Force.
- 18.94 ___ Complaint for Return of Seized Property.
- 18.95 ___ Complaint Against Landlord for Housing Discrimination.
- 18.96 ___ Complaint Against Cooperative for Discrimination.
- 18.97 ___ Notice of Commencement of Action for Discrimination.
- 18.98 ___ Complaint for Discrimination in Place of Public Accommodation.
- 18.99 ___ Petition to Change Name.

CHAPTER 19. IMMIGRATION AND NATIONALITY LAW —PERMANENT RESIDENCE APPLICATIONS

- 19.1 Scope Note.

TABLE OF CONTENTS

Sec.
19.2	Strategy.
19.3	___ Flowchart.
19.4	Overview of the U.S. Immigration System.
19.5	___ Numerical Limitations on Immigrant Selection.
19.6	___ Implementation: Foreign State Chargeability and Quota Allocation.
19.7	Family–Based Immigration.
19.8	___ Immediate Relative Categories.
19.9	___ Family Preference Categories.
19.10	___ Qualifying as a Relation.
19.11	___ ___ "Child" and "Parent" Issues.
19.12	___ ___ "Marriage" Issues.
19.13	___ Petitioning Procedures and Documentation.
19.14	___ ___ I–130 Petition.
19.15	___ Orphans and Amerasians.
19.16	___ Abused Spouse and Children.
19.17	Employment–Based Immigration.
19.18	___ First Employment Preference Applicants (Priority Workers).
19.19	___ ___ Extraordinary Ability Aliens.
19.20	___ ___ Outstanding Professors and Researchers.
19.21	___ ___ Managerial or Executive Intracompany Transferees.
19.22	___ Second Employment Preference Applicants.
19.23	___ ___ Exceptional Ability Aliens.
19.24	___ ___ Advanced Degree Professionals.
19.25	___ ___ The Role of "National Interest."
19.26	___ Third Employment Preference Applicants.
19.27	___ ___ Professional and Skilled Workers.
19.28	___ ___ Unskilled Workers.
19.29	___ I–140 Petition, Procedures and Documentation.
19.30	___ ___ Checklist.
19.31	___ Labor Certification.
19.32	___ ___ Procedures.
19.33	___ ___ Legal Issues.
19.34	___ ___ Job Description.
19.35	___ ___ Business Necessity.
19.36	___ ___ Recruitment.
19.37	___ ___ Approvals.
19.38	___ ___ Notices of Findings.
19.39	___ ___ Denials and Administrative Appeal.
19.40	___ Fourth Employment Preference Applicants.
19.41	___ ___ Religious Workers and Ministers.
19.42	___ Fifth Employment Preference Applicants (Immigrant Investors).
19.43	___ Petition Procedures and Requirements.
19.44	___ ___ Special Immigrant Investor Programs.
19.45	Special Categories.
19.46	___ The Diversity (Lottery) Program.
19.47	___ Registry.
19.48	___ Cancellation of Removal.
19.49	___ Legislatively Created Programs.

TABLE OF CONTENTS

Sec.
19.50 ____ Asylum and Refugee Status.
19.51 Applying for Permanent Residence.
19.52 ____ Exclusionary Grounds.
19.53 ____ Immigrant Visa Processing.
19.54 ____ ____ Framework of the Immigrant Visa Processing System.
19.55 ____ ____ Special Requirements, Public Law No. 103–317.
19.56 ____ ____ Checklist of Required Documents.
19.57 ____ Adjustment of Status.
19.58 ____ ____ General Requirements.
19.59 ____ ____ Special Provisions of Section 245(i).
19.60 ____ ____ Discretionary Factors.
19.61 ____ ____ Application Process.
19.62 ____ ____ Concurrent Filing of Petition and Adjustment of Status.
19.63 ____ ____ Completion of the Process.
19.64 ____ ____ Administrative and Judicial Review.
19.65 ____ ____ Checklist.
19.66 ____ Tactical Considerations.
19.67 ____ ____ Nonimmigrant Status as a Factor.
19.68 ____ ____ Immigrant Visa Processing Versus Adjustment of Status.
19.69 ____ ____ Flowchart.
19.70 The Green Card and its Limitations.
19.71 ____ Conditional Residence.
19.72 ____ ____ Marriage Cases, Removal of Condition.
19.73 ____ ____ Immigrant Investors, Removal of Condition.
19.74 ____ Unconditional Permanent Residence.
19.75 Forms.
19.76 ____ Form I–130.
19.77 ____ Form I–140.
19.78 ____ Form I–485.
19.79 ____ Form OF–230.

CHAPTER 20. ADOPTIONS

20.1 Scope Note.
20.2 Strategy.
20.3 ____ Checklist: Pre-adoption—Counsel for Parents.
20.4 ____ Checklist: Interview With Birth Mother.
20.5 Adoptions—Generally.
20.6 ____ Defined.
20.7 ____ Rationale.
20.8 ____ Judicial Construction of Statutes.
20.9 ____ Concurrent Jurisdiction.
20.10 ____ ____ Where to File Adoption Proceedings.
20.11 ____ Choice of Venue.
20.12 ____ Types.
20.13 ____ Effect of Adoption.
20.14 ____ Who May Adopt—Statutory Mandates.
20.15 ____ ____ Separated Persons.

TABLE OF CONTENTS

Sec.
20.16 ___ ___ Foster Parents: Preference to Adopt.
20.17 ___ ___ Second Parent Adoptions.
20.18 ___ ___ Unwed Putative Fathers.
20.19 ___ ___ Citizens and Aliens.
20.20 ___ ___ Age as a Factor.
20.21 ___ ___ Extended Family as Factor.
20.22 ___ ___ Adult Unmarried Person.
20.23 ___ Who May Be Adopted—In General.
20.24 ___ ___ Adult Adoptions.
20.25 ___ ___ Aliens.
20.26 ___ ___ Non-marital Children.
20.27 ___ ___ Interracial Adoptions.
20.28 ___ ___ Religion as a Factor.
20.29 ___ Consents Required—Statutory Mandate.
20.30 ___ ___ Rights of Unwed Fathers.
20.31 ___ ___ When Consent Not Required.
20.32 ___ ___ Notice of a Proposed Adoption.
20.33 ___ ___ Checklist of Fathers to Receive Notice of Adoption.
20.34 ___ Persons Excluded from Notice.
20.35 ___ Purpose of Notice.
20.36 ___ Procedure.
20.37 Private Placement Adoptions—In General.
20.38 ___ Terminating Parental Rights Based Upon Abandonment.
20.39 ___ Terminating Parental Rights Based Upon Mental Retardation.
20.40 ___ Dual Representation Prohibited.
20.41 ___ Independent Counsel.
20.42 ___ Permissible Dual Representation.
20.43 ___ Independent Representation of the Child.
20.44 ___ The Attorney's Fee.
20.45 ___ Locating an Infant for Adoption—The Attorney's Responsibility.
20.46 ___ Illegal Sale of Babies.
20.47 ___ Advertisement.
20.48 ___ Foreign Infants.
20.49 ___ Readoption of Foreign Infants.
20.50 ___ Native American Children.
20.51 ___ Residency Requirements.
20.52 ___ Permissible Payments by Adoptive Parents.
20.53 ___ Interstate Compact on the Placement of Children.
20.54 ___ Pre-certification of Adoptive Parents—In General.
20.55 ___ ___ Requirement of Pre-certification.
20.56 ___ ___ Procedure.
20.57 ___ ___ Checklist of Documents Needed for Certification.
20.58 ___ Hospital Procedures—Physical Transfer of Custody of the Infant to the Adoptive Parents.
20.59 ___ ___ Certification Procedures.
20.60 ___ Petition for Temporary Guardianship—Legislative Background.
20.61 ___ ___ Impact of Pre–placement Certification.

LXV

TABLE OF CONTENTS

Sec.
20.62 ____ Procedure Upon Filing Petition for Temporary Guardianship.
20.63 ____ Consent of Birth Parents.
20.64 ____ ____ Extra–Judicial Consent.
20.65 ____ ____ Judicial Consents.
20.66 ____ ____ Personal Appearances Required.
20.67 ____ ____ Step-Parent Adoptions.
20.68 ____ Foreign Born Children.
20.69 ____ Petition for Adoption.
20.70 ____ The Agreement of Adoption.
20.71 ____ Affidavit of Attorney Representing Adoptive Parents.
20.72 ____ Confidential Affidavit.
20.73 ____ Attorney's Affidavit of Financial Disclosure.
20.74 ____ Notification of Order of Adoption; Report of Adoption.
20.75 ____ Order of Adoption.
20.76 ____ Birth Mother's Affidavit Regarding Putative Father.
20.77 ____ Affidavit of Intermediary.
20.78 ____ Attorney's Affidavit Regarding Legal Fees.
20.79 ____ Affidavit of Explanation of Criminal Activity.
20.80 ____ Investigation by Disinterested Person.
20.81 ____ The Hearing.
20.82 ____ Certificate of Adoption.
20.83 ____ The New Birth Certificate.
20.84 ____ Checklist of Documents Required for Private Placement Adoption.
20.85 Agency Adoptions—Defined.
20.86 ____ Definition of "Authorized Agency."
20.87 ____ Venue.
20.88 ____ Child's Entry into the System.
20.89 ____ ____ Voluntary Transfer of Legal Custody of Children to the Authorized Agency.
20.90 ____ ____ Judicial Surrender.
20.91 ____ ____ Extra–Judicial Surrender.
20.92 ____ ____ Court Approval of Extra–Judicial Surrender.
20.93 ____ ____ Assigned Counsel.
20.94 ____ ____ Required Notice of Application.
20.95 ____ ____ Notification to Court.
20.96 ____ ____ Court Order.
20.97 ____ ____ Conditional Surrender.
20.98 ____ ____ Recording a Surrender.
20.99 ____ ____ Revocation of Surrender.
20.100 ____ ____ Proceedings Subsequent to Execution of Extra–Judicial Surrender.
20.101 ____ ____ Court Ordered Transfer of Children to Authorized Agency.
20.102 ____ Procedures.
20.103 ____ The Petition.
20.104 ____ The Agreement of Adoption.
20.105 ____ Verified Schedule.
20.106 ____ Affidavit of Financial Disclosure.
20.107 ____ Confidential Affidavit.

TABLE OF CONTENTS

Sec.
20.108 —— Marital Affidavit.
20.109 —— Child's Medical History.
20.110 —— Supplemental Affidavit.
20.111 —— Notification of Order of Adoption; Report of Adoption.
20.112 —— Doctor's Certificate of Health.
20.113 —— Authorization and Approval for Subsidized Adoption.
20.114 —— Adoption Homestudy.
20.115 —— Affidavit Identifying Party.
20.116 —— Order of Adoption.
20.117 —— Certificate of Adoption.
20.118 —— Abuse Clearance Form.
20.119 —— Unavailability of Abuse Clearance Form and Criminal Conviction Check.
20.120 —— Attorney's Affidavit of Legal Fees.
20.121 —— Checklist of Other Required Supporting Documentation.
20.122 —— The Adoption Hearing.
20.123 Post-adoption Issues—The Open Adoption.
20.124 —— Visitation With Siblings.
20.125 —— Sealing Adoption Records.
20.126 —— —— Constitutionality of Laws Relating to Sealing Records.
20.127 —— —— Good Cause for Unsealing Records.
20.128 —— —— —— Criminal Investigation and Probation Department.
20.129 —— —— —— Requirement of Medical Information.
20.130 —— —— —— Religion.
20.131 —— Abrogation of Order.
20.132 Checklist of Facts and Allegations to be Included in the Petition for a Private Placement Adoption.
20.133 Forms—Private Placement Adoptions—Petition for Certification as a Qualified Adoptive Parent. 💾
20.134 —— —— Petition for Temporary Guardianship. 💾
20.135 —— —— Judicial Consent of Natural Parent. 💾
20.136 —— —— Extra-Judicial Consent of Natural Parent. 💾
20.137 —— —— Petition for Adoption. 💾
20.138 —— —— Order of Adoption (Private Placement). 💾
20.139 —— Agency Adoptions—Petition for Adoption. 💾
20.140 —— —— Verified Schedule. 💾
20.141 —— —— Marital Affidavit. 💾
20.142 —— —— Marital Affidavit Dispensing With Consent of Spouse After Three Year Separation. 💾
20.143 —— —— Confidential Affidavit. 💾
20.144 —— —— Affidavit Pursuant to Section 111–a of the Domestic Relations Law. 💾
20.145 —— —— Agreement of Adoption and Consent. 💾
20.146 —— —— Affidavit Identifying Party. 💾
20.147 —— —— Affidavit of Financial Disclosure by Parents. 💾
20.148 —— —— Order of Adoption. 💾

Volume 23

CHAPTER 21. DOMESTIC RELATIONS

21.1 Scope Note.

TABLE OF CONTENTS

Sec.
21.2 Strategy.
21.3 Jurisdiction.
21.4 ___ Residence Requirements.
21.5 ___ Uniform Child Custody Jurisdiction Act.
21.6 Competency of the Court to Grant Relief.
21.7 ___ Equitable Distribution.
21.8 ___ Support.
21.9 ___ Custody and Visitation.
21.10 Jurisdiction Over the Defendant's Person or Property.
21.11 ___ Personal Jurisdiction.
21.12 ___ Long Arm Jurisdiction.
21.13 ___ *In Rem* Jurisdiction.
21.14 *Quasi in Rem* Jurisdiction.
21.15 Venue.
21.16 ___ Changing Venue.
21.17 Joinder, Consolidation and Joint Trials.
21.18 Grounds for Divorce.
21.19 ___ No Official No–Fault Ground.
21.20 ___ Cruel and Inhuman Treatment.
21.21 ___ ___ Defenses.
21.22 ___ Abandonment.
21.23 ___ ___ Defenses.
21.24 ___ ___ Effect of Separation Agreement.
21.25 ___ Imprisonment.
21.26 ___ Adultery.
21.27 ___ ___ Defenses.
21.28 ___ ___ Effect of Separation Agreement.
21.29 ___ Divorce Action Based Upon Living Apart Pursuant to Separation Decree or Judgment.
21.30 ___ Divorce Action Based Upon Living Apart Pursuant to Separation Agreement.
21.31 ___ Dual Divorce.
21.32 Effect of Sister State Divorce Judgment.
21.33 Equitable Distribution.
21.34 ___ When Available.
21.35 ___ Identification of Property.
21.36 ___ Characterization of Property.
21.37 ___ ___ Marital Property.
21.38 ___ ___ ___ Pensions.
21.39 ___ ___ ___ Professional Practices, Licenses, Degrees and Careers.
21.40 ___ ___ Separate Property.
21.41 ___ ___ ___ Increase in Value of Separate Property.
21.42 ___ Valuation Dates.
21.43 ___ Valuation Methods.
21.44 ___ Distribution Factors.
21.45 ___ Tax Considerations.
21.46 Maintenance.
21.47 ___ Legislative Factors.
21.48 ___ Effect of Fault.

TABLE OF CONTENTS

Sec.
21.49 ____ Current Trends.
21.50 ____ Payments Fixed by Agreement.
21.51 ____ Tax Consequences.
21.52 Child Support.
21.53 ____ Child Support Standards Act.
21.54 ____ ____ Where Statutory Percentages Are Unfair or Inappropriate.
21.55 ____ ____ Recent Trends.
21.56 ____ Effect of Agreement or Stipulation.
21.57 Health and Life Insurance.
21.58 Custody.
21.59 ____ Visitation.
21.60 ____ Relocation of Custodial Parent With the Child.
21.61 ____ Joint Custody.
21.62 ____ Proceedings in Which Custody Dispositions Are Available.
21.63 Financial Disclosure.
21.64 Disclosure on Matters Going to the Merits of the Case.
21.65 Net Worth Statement.
21.66 Statement of Proposed Disposition.
21.67 Findings of Fact and Conclusions of Law; Judgments.
21.68 Modification.
21.69 ____ Maintenance.
21.70 ____ Child Support.
21.71 ____ Custody.
21.72 Enforcement.
21.73 ____ Plenary Action to Enforce Agreement.
21.74 ____ Defenses.
21.75 Practice Considerations.
21.76 ____ Procedure for Attorneys in Domestic Relations Matters.
21.77 ____ Disciplinary Rules.
21.78 ____ Fee Arbitration Rules.
21.79 ____ Rules Regarding Case Management.
21.80 Procedural Checklist—Calendar Control.
21.81 Drafting Checklist—Retainer Agreements.
21.82 _____ Complaint in Action for Divorce.
21.83 _____ Statement of Proposed Disposition.
21.84 Forms.
21.85 ____ Retainer Agreement.
21.86 ____ Complaint for Divorce.
21.87 ____ Statement of Net Worth.
21.88 ____ Statement of Proposed Disposition.
21.89 ____ Findings of Fact and Conclusions of Law.
21.90 ____ Matrimonial Judgments.
21.91 ____ Referee's Report on Findings of Fact and Conclusions of Law.
21.92 ____ Matrimonial Judgment Entered Upon Referee's Report.

CHAPTER 22. GUARDIANSHIP

22.1 Scope Note.

TABLE OF CONTENTS

Sec.
22.2 Strategy.
22.3 Checklists.
22.4 Prior Law—Generally.
22.5 ____ Role of Committees and Conservators.
22.6 ____ Problems Encountered.
22.7 ____ Impact of *Matter of Grinker (Rose)*.
22.8 Legislative Purpose of Mental Hygiene Law Article 81.
22.9 Definitions.
22.10 Summary.
22.11 Power to Appoint Guardian—Generally.
22.12 ____ Elements.
22.13 ____ Incapacity.
22.14 ____ Primary Considerations.
22.15 ____ Jurisdiction.
22.16 ____ Venue.
22.17 ____ Standing to Commence Proceeding.
22.18 ____ Summary.
22.19 Proceeding to Appoint Guardian.
22.20 ____ Time and Method of Service of Notice.
22.21 ____ Persons Entitled to Notice.
22.22 ____ Notice Requirements.
22.23 ____ Petition.
22.24 ____ Summary.
22.25 Court Evaluator—Persons Eligible for Appointment.
22.26 ____ Duties.
22.27 ____ Compensation.
22.28 ____ Appointment of Counsel for the Alleged Incapacitated Person.
22.29 ____ Summary.
22.30 Hearing and Order—An Overview.
22.31 ____ Procedure.
22.32 ____ Presence of Person Alleged to be Incapacitated.
22.33 ____ Evidence.
22.34 ____ Findings of the Court.
22.35 ____ ____ Voluntary Appointment.
22.36 ____ ____ Personal Needs.
22.37 ____ ____ Property Management.
22.38 ____ Dispositional Alternatives.
22.39 ____ Award of Counsel Fees to Petitioner.
22.40 ____ Person to be Appointed Guardian.
22.41 ____ Priority and Criteria for Appointment.
22.42 ____ Requirement of Bond.
22.43 ____ Designation of Clerk and Issuance of Commission.
22.44 ____ Summary.
22.45 Role of Guardian—Overview.
22.46 ____ Duties.
22.47 ____ Powers; Property Management.
22.48 ____ Substituted Judgment.
22.49 ____ Petition for Authorization to Transfer Property.
22.50 ____ ____ Notice of Application.

TABLE OF CONTENTS

Sec.
22.51 ____ ____ Considerations of Court.
22.52 ____ ____ Granting Petition.
22.53 ____ Powers; Personal Needs.
22.54 ____ Effect of Appointment on Incapacitated Person.
22.55 ____ Summary.
22.56 Provisional Remedies.
22.57 ____ Temporary Guardian.
22.58 ____ Injunction and Temporary Restraining Orders.
22.59 ____ Notice of Pendency.
22.60 ____ Summary.
22.61 Compensation of Guardian.
22.62 Reports by Guardian.
22.63 ____ Initial Report.
22.64 ____ Annual Report.
22.65 ____ Examination; Court Examiners.
22.66 ____ Intermediate and Final Reports.
22.67 ____ Decree Upon Approving Accounts.
22.68 ____ Summary.
22.69 Removal, Discharge and Resignation of Guardian—Removal.
22.70 ____ Discharge or Modification of Powers.
22.71 ____ Resignation or Suspension of Powers.
22.72 ____ Vacancy in Office; Appointment of Interim and Successor Guardians.
22.73 ____ Standby Guardian.
22.74 ____ Summary.
22.75 Education Requirements—Generally.
22.76 ____ Guardian Training.
22.77 ____ Court Evaluator Training.
22.78 ____ Court Examiner Training.
22.79 ____ Compliance.
22.80 ____ Summary.
22.81 Proceedings to Discover Property Withheld.
22.82 ____ Petition and Supporting Papers.
22.83 ____ Grounds For Inquiry.
22.84 ____ Answer.
22.85 ____ Trial.
22.86 ____ Decree.
22.87 ____ Summary.
22.88 Drafting Checklists.
22.89 ____ Order to Show Cause.
22.90 ____ Petition.
22.91 ____ Court Evaluator's Report.
22.92 ____ Order and Judgment.
22.93 ____ Initial Report of the Guardian.
22.94 ____ Annual Report.
22.95 ____ Decree Approving Accounts.
22.96 ____ Petition on Proceeding to Discover Property Withheld.
22.97 Forms.
22.98 ____ Order to Show Cause.
22.99 ____ Petition.

TABLE OF CONTENTS

Sec.
22.100 ____ Court Evaluator's Report.
22.101 ____ Order and Judgment Appointing Guardian of the Person and Property.
22.102 ____ Oath and Designation of Guardian.
22.103 ____ Commission of Guardian.
22.104 ____ Initial Report of Guardian.
22.105 ____ Annual Report and Inventory of Guardian.
22.106 ____ Decree Upon Approving Accounts.
22.107 ____ Petition on Proceeding to Discover Property Withheld.

CHAPTER 23. ELDER LAW

23.1 Scope Note.
23.2 Strategy.
23.3 Ethical Considerations.
23.4 ____ Identifying the Client.
23.5 ____ Confidentiality.
23.6 ____ Diminished Capacity.
23.7 Social Security Benefits.
23.8 ____ Quarters of Coverage.
23.9 ____ Insured Status.
23.10 ____ Calculation of Benefits.
23.11 ____ Retirement Benefits.
23.12 ____ Benefits for Spouses, Survivors and Dependents.
23.13 ____ Reduction in Benefits Due to Earned Income.
23.14 ____ Overpayments and Underpayments.
23.15 ____ Administrative and Judicial Appeals.
23.16 ____ Representation by Attorneys.
23.17 Supplemental Security Income for the Elderly.
23.18 ____ Categorical Eligibility.
23.19 ____ Financial Eligibility.
23.20 ____ Benefit Calculation.
23.21 ____ Underpayments and Overpayments.
23.22 ____ Administrative and Judicial Appeals.
23.23 ____ Representation by Attorneys.
23.24 Retirement Income from Qualified Plans.
23.25 ____ Eligibility, Vesting and Accrual.
23.26 ____ Contribution Limitations.
23.27 ____ Payment of Benefits.
23.28 ____ Alienation and Assignment.
23.29 ____ Spousal Rights.
23.30 ____ Qualified Domestic Relations Orders.
23.31 ____ Waiver of Spousal Rights.
23.32 ____ Taxation of Contributions.
23.33 ____ Distributions.
23.34 ____ Termination or Merger.
23.35 ____ Appeals.
23.36 Railroad Retirement Benefits.
23.37 Benefits for Federal Employees.
23.38 ____ Federal Employees Retirement System ("FERS").

TABLE OF CONTENTS

Sec.
- 23.39 ____ Civil Service Retirement Act ("CSRA").
- 23.40 ____ Appeals.
- 23.41 Veterans' Benefits.
- 23.42 Medicare.
- 23.43 ____ Eligibility and Enrollment.
- 23.44 ____ Part A Benefits.
- 23.45 ____ ____ Hospital Services.
- 23.46 ____ ____ Skilled Nursing Facilities.
- 23.47 ____ ____ Home Health Care.
- 23.48 ____ ____ Hospice Care.
- 23.49 ____ Part B Supplementary Medical Insurance.
- 23.50 ____ ____ Deductibles and Coinsurance.
- 23.51 ____ ____ Assignment of Claims/Participating Physicians.
- 23.52 ____ ____ Limitations on Balance Billing.
- 23.53 ____ Administrative and Judicial Appeals.
- 23.54 ____ ____ Eligibility for Benefits.
- 23.55 ____ ____ Part A Fiscal Intermediary Decisions.
- 23.56 ____ ____ Part A Peer Review Organization Decisions.
- 23.57 ____ ____ Part B Determinations.
- 23.58 Supplemental Medical Insurance (Medigap Plans).
- 23.59 ____ Gaps in Medicare Coverage.
- 23.60 ____ Federal and State Regulation of the Industry.
- 23.61 ____ Ten Standard Plans.
- 23.62 ____ Criteria for Choosing the Right Plan.
- 23.63 Long Term Care Insurance.
- 23.64 ____ Regulation Under New York Law.
- 23.65 ____ Relationship to Medicaid Eligibility.
- 23.66 ____ The Partnership For Long Term Care/Robert Wood Johnson Program.
- 23.67 ____ Choosing a Policy.
- 23.68 ____ Tax Issues.
- 23.69 Medicaid.
- 23.70 ____ Covered Services.
- 23.71 ____ Basic Eligibility Requirements.
- 23.72 ____ Surplus Income Program for the "Medically Needy."
- 23.73 ____ Income.
- 23.74 ____ Resources.
- 23.75 ____ Exempt Resources.
- 23.76 ____ Transfer of Resources.
- 23.77 ____ Treatment of Trusts.
- 23.78 ____ ____ Self Settled Trusts.
- 23.79 ____ ____ Third Party Trusts.
- 23.80 ____ Spousal Budgeting: Protection of Resources and Income for the Community Spouse.
- 23.81 ____ Recoveries Against Estates.
- 23.82 ____ Liens.
- 23.83 ____ Administrative and Judicial Appeals.
- 23.84 Home Care Coverage.
- 23.85 ____ Medicare.
- 23.86 ____ Medicaid.

TABLE OF CONTENTS

Sec.
23.87 ____ Expanded In–Home Services for the Elderly Program ("EISEP").
23.88 ____ Private Insurance.
23.89 Hospital Patients Rights.
23.90 ____ Bill of Rights.
23.91 ____ Discharge Planning.
23.92 Nursing Home Resident Rights.
23.93 ____ Admission to a Facility.
23.94 ____ Bill of Rights.
23.95 ____ Financial Rights.
23.96 ____ Transfer and Discharge.
23.97 ____ Bed Hold Policy.
23.98 ____ Remedies for Violation of Rights or Improper Treatment.
23.99 Housing Issues.
23.100 ____ Real Property Tax Exemption.
23.101 ____ Real Property Tax Credit.
23.102 ____ Tax Assistance Loans.
23.103 ____ Home Repair Assistance.
23.104 ____ Reverse Mortgages and Home Equity Loans.
23.105 ____ Home Energy Assistance Program ("HEAP").
23.106 ____ Tenant Protections.
23.107 ____ Life Care Retirement Communities.
23.108 ____ Community Based Services.
23.109 Health Care Decision Making.
23.110 ____ Health Care Proxy.
23.111 ____ The Living Will.
23.112 ____ Do Not Resuscitate Orders.
23.113 ____ Physician Assisted Suicide.
23.114 Tax Issues.
23.115 ____ Additional Standard Deduction for the Aged and Blind.
23.116 ____ Incapacity.
23.117 ____ Sale of a Principal Residence.
23.118 ____ Medical Deductions.
23.119 Miscellaneous Programs.
23.120 ____ Elderly Pharmaceutical Insurance Coverage ("EPIC").
23.121 ____ Life Line Telephone Service.
23.122 Forms.
23.123 ____ Documentation Letter. 💾
23.124 ____ Consultation Letter. 💾
23.125 ____ Health Care Proxy Statutory Form. 💾
23.126 ____ Sample Living Will. 💾

CHAPTER 24. ESTATE PLANNING

24.1 Scope Note.
24.2 Strategy.
24.3 Wills.
24.4 ____ Execution Requirements.
24.5 ____ ____ Signature.
24.6 ____ ____ Publication.

TABLE OF CONTENTS

Sec.	
24.7	___ ___ Witnesses.
24.8	___ ___ Self Proving Affidavit.
24.9	___ Provisions—Personal Property Dispositions.
24.10	___ ___ Debts and Taxes.
24.11	___ ___ Real Property.
24.12	___ ___ Residuary Estate.
24.13	___ ___ Dispositions in Trust.
24.14	___ ___ Guardianships.
24.15	___ ___ Appointment of Executors and Trustees.
24.16	___ ___ Fiduciary Powers.
24.17	___ ___ Miscellaneous.
24.18	Federal Estate and Gift Taxes.
24.19	___ Rates.
24.20	New York State Estate and Gift Tax.
24.21	Estate Tax Planning—Utilizing the Unified Credit.
24.22	___ Utilizing the Marital Deduction.
24.23	___ Formula Clauses.
24.24	Generation Skipping Transfer Tax.
24.25	___ Taxable Termination.
24.26	___ Direct Skip.
24.27	___ Taxable Distribution.
24.28	___ Generation Assignment.
24.29	___ Multiple Skips.
24.30	___ Exemption.
24.31	___ "Reverse QTIP."
24.32	Charitable Bequests.
24.33	Planning With Certain Assets.
24.34	___ Life Insurance.
24.35	___ ___ Life Insurance Trusts.
24.36	___ ___ ___ "Crummey Powers."
24.37	___ Retirement Benefits.
24.38	___ Closely Held Business Interests.
24.39	___ ___ Buy-Sell Agreements.
24.40	___ ___ Liquidity Issues.
24.41	___ ___ Minority Discounts.
24.42	___ Farms and Business Real Property.
24.43	___ Installment Obligations.
24.44	Lifetime Planning.
24.45	___ Valuation of Gifts.
24.46	___ ___ Grantor Retained Trusts.
24.47	___ ___ Residence Trusts.
24.48	___ ___ ___ Income Tax Considerations.
24.49	___ Annual Gift Tax Exclusion.
24.50	___ ___ Section 2503(c) Trusts.
24.51	___ ___ Uniform Transfers to Minor's Act Accounts.
24.52	___ ___ Crummey Trusts.
24.53	___ ___ Family Limited Partnerships.
24.54	___ Charitable Remainder Trusts.
24.55	___ Charitable Lead Trusts.
24.56	Planning in Special Situations—Terminally Ill.

TABLE OF CONTENTS

Sec.

24.57	____ ____ Self-Canceling Installment Notes.
24.58	____ Non-citizen Spouses.
24.59	____ Multiple Marriages.
24.60	____ ____ Spousal Rights.
24.61	____ ____ ____ Joint Wills and Contracts to Make Wills.
24.62	____ ____ Long Term Care.
24.63	____ Separation.
24.64	____ Divorce.
24.65	____ ____ Death During Divorce Proceeding.
24.66	____ Unmarried Couples.
24.67	Postmortem Planning.
24.68	____ Disclaimers.
24.69	____ ____ Disclaimer Trusts.
24.70	____ ____ Creditor Avoidance.
24.71	____ ____ New York Statutory Requirements.
24.72	____ Partial QTIP Election.
24.73	____ Electing Alternate Valuation Date.
24.74	____ Allocation of Income and Expenses.
24.75	____ ____ U.S. Savings Bonds.
24.76	____ ____ Expenses.
24.77	____ Choosing the Fiscal Year of the Estate.
24.78	____ Electing to File Joint Return with Decedent's Spouse.
24.79	____ Waiving Commissions.
24.80	Probate Avoidance.
24.81	____ Revocable Trusts.
24.82	____ Totten Trusts.
24.83	____ Jointly Held Assets.
24.84	Asset Protection.
24.85	____ Statutory Exemptions.
24.86	____ Family Partnerships.
24.87	____ Domestic Trusts.
24.88	____ Foreign Trusts.
24.89	Powers of Attorney.
24.90	Advance Directives.
24.91	____ Health Care Proxy.
24.92	____ Living Will.
24.93	Ethical Considerations in Estate Planning.
24.94	____ Multiple Clients.
24.95	____ Attorney/Draftsman as Fiduciary or Beneficiary.
24.96	Forms
24.97	____ Estate Planner's Checklist.
24.98	____ Sample Information Request Letter.
24.99	____ Client Questionnaire.
24.100	____ "Durable" Power of Attorney Form.
24.101	____ Crummey Notice.
24.102	____ Spousal Conflicts Letter.

CHAPTER 25. PROBATE AND ESTATE ADMINISTRATION

25.1   Scope Note.

LXXVI

TABLE OF CONTENTS

Sec.
25.2 Explanation of Basic Legal Terms in Estate Practice.
25.3 Strategy.
25.4 Who May Commence the Estate of a Person Who Dies Without a Will.
25.5 Who Is Entitled to Letters of Administration.
25.6 Who May Commence the Estate of a Person Who Dies With a Will.
25.7 Documents Required on Application for Letters of Administration.
25.8 Who Must Be Cited on an Application for Letters of Administration.
25.9 When a Guardian *Ad Litem* Must be Appointed.
25.10 Denial or Revocation of Letters of Administration.
25.11 Letters of Temporary Administration.
25.12 Venue.
25.13 Duty of the Fiduciary to Expeditiously Seek Probate.
25.14 When a Beneficiary Should Petition for Probate.
25.15 When a Creditor Should Petition for Probate.
25.16 When a Person in Litigation with an Estate Should Petition for Probate.
25.17 Information to Be Gathered by Attorney.
25.18 Contents of Petition for Probate.
25.19 Documents Required to Accompany Probate Petition.
25.20 What to Do If Your Client Cannot Produce the Original Will.
25.21 Requirements and Procedure for Proving a Will Where the Original Is Lost.
25.22 How to Get a Will Admitted to Probate If None of the Witnesses to the Will are Available.
25.23 When a Court Must Appoint a Guardian *Ad Litem* in a Probate Proceeding.
25.24 Who May Oppose the Admission to Probate of a Will By Filing Objections.
25.25 When Objections Must Be Filed.
25.26 How to Start an Estate Administration Where There Will Be a Delay in Getting a Will Admitted to Probate.
25.27 Form of Objections to Probate.
25.28 Burden of Proof
25.29 Requirement of a Notice of Objections to Complete Jurisdiction in a Contested Probate.
25.30 Right to a Trial by Jury.
25.31 Right to Discovery in a Probate, Administration or Accounting Proceeding.
25.32 Who Is Entitled to Letters of Administration When a Person Dies Without a Will.
25.33 Procedures to Follow in Administering the Estate.
25.34 How to Force an Estate Administration to Be Completed—Compelling an Accounting.
25.35 Concluding an Estate Administration Without an Accounting Proceeding.
25.36 Obtaining a Decree Concluding the Estate Based on Filed Receipts and Releases.
25.37 Concluding an Estate by a Formal Judicial Accounting.

TABLE OF CONTENTS

Sec.
25.38 Objections to an Account.
25.39 Prosecuting Objections to an Account.
25.40 Claims Against an Estate by a Creditor.
25.41 Representing a Claimant Against an Estate.
25.42 Obtaining Information About Estate Assets and Recovering Estate Property.
25.43 How to Proceed When Your Client Has a Claim Against an Estate.
25.44 A Special Provision for an Estate Beneficiary Obtaining Funds for Education.
25.45 Who Is Entitled to Assets When Two or More Fiduciaries Are in Dispute.
25.46 Compensation of Executor and Administrator, When Payable.
25.47 Attorney's Fees.
25.48 Declining to Serve as an Executor or Trustee.
25.49 Renouncing an Inheritance.
25.50 Construction of a Will.
25.51 Forms.
25.52 ____ Probate Petition.
25.53 ____ Affidavit Proving Correct Copy of Will.
25.54 ____ Citation in Probate.
25.55 ____ Affidavit of Service of Citation.
25.56 ____ Affidavit of Mailing Notice of Application for Letters of Administration.
25.57 ____ Waiver and Consent.
25.58 ____ Notice of Probate.
25.59 ____ Deposition Affidavit of Subscribing Witness.
25.60 ____ Objections to Probate.
25.61 ____ Decree Granting Probate.
25.62 ____ Receipt and Release Agreement Concluding an Estate Without an Accounting Proceeding.
25.63 ____ Receipt and Release (Legacy).
25.64 ____ Petition to Judicially Settle Executor's Account.
25.65 ____ Citation to Executor to Show Cause Why Judicially Executor Should Not Account.
25.66 ____ Accounting Form.
25.67 ____ Petition for Letters of Administration or Limited Letters of Administration or Temporary Administration.
25.68 ____ Decree Appointing Administrator.
25.69 ____ Affidavit Asking Court to Fix Amount of Administrator's Bond.
25.70 ____ Waiver of Citation, Renunciation of Signer's Claim to Letters and Consent to Appointment of Administrator.
25.71 ____ Notice of Application for Letters of Administration.
25.72 ____ Citation That Can Be Adopted for Use in Any Proceeding.

CHAPTER 26. PERSONAL INJURY

26.1 Scope Note.
26.2 Strategy.

TABLE OF CONTENTS

Sec.
26.3	____	Client Interview.
26.4	____	Valuing the Case.
26.5	____	Skills and Ethics.
26.6	____	Retainer.
26.7	____ ____	Retainer Statement.
26.8	____	Expenses.
26.9		Investigation.
26.10	____	Premises Liability.
26.11	____	Medical Malpractice.
26.12	____ ____	Hospital.
26.13	____ ____	Dental and Podiatric Malpractice.
26.14	____	Products Liability.
26.15	____	Dog Bites.
26.16	____	Chemical Exposure.
26.17	____	Automobile Accidents.
26.18	____ ____	Police Report.
26.19	____ ____	Witness Statements.
26.20	____ ____	MV104.
26.21	____ ____	Application of No–Fault.
26.22	____ ____	Medical Records.
26.23	____ ____	Photographs.
26.24	____ ____	Insurance Policies and Coverage.
26.25		Claims Procedure for Automobile Accidents.
26.26	____	Filing Notice of Claim With the Motor Vehicle Accident Indemnity Corporation.
26.27	____ ____	Procedure for Cases in Which There Is No Insurance.
26.28	____ ____	Procedure for Cases in Which There Is No Insurance and the Identity of the Wrongdoer Is Not Ascertainable (Hit and Run).
26.29	____ ____	Procedure for Cases in Which Insurance Initially Is Believed to Exist, But There Is No Insurance After Later Disclaimer.
26.30	____ ____	Late Claims.
26.31		Theories of Liability.
26.32		Filing the Action.
26.33	____	When.
26.34	____	Where.
26.35	____	Potential Defendants.
26.36		The Summons and the Complaint.
26.37		The Answer.
26.38		Actions Against Municipal Corporations.
26.39	____	Notice of Claim.
26.40	____ ____	Content.
26.41		Actions Against the State.
26.42		Discovery—Generally.
26.43	____	Depositions.
26.44	____	Interrogatories.
26.45	____	Document Discovery and Inspection.
26.46	____	Bills of Particulars.
26.47	____	Demand for a Bill of Particulars.

LXXIX

TABLE OF CONTENTS

Sec.
26.48 Settlement.
26.49 Liens.
26.50 Alternative Dispute Resolution.
26.51 Trial Preparation: Introductory Note.
26.52 Trial.
26.53 ___ Subpoenas.
26.54 ___ Exhibits.
26.55 ___ *Voir Dire*.
26.56 Disbursement of Proceeds of Settlement or Recovery.
26.57 Drafting Checklists.
26.58 ___ Complaint.
26.59 ___ Answer.
26.60 ___ Demand for Bill of Particulars.
26.61 ___ Responses to Demand for Bill of Particulars.
26.62 Forms—Client's Retainer Agreement.
26.63 ___ Retainer Statement.
26.64 ___ Department of Motor Vehicles MV104 Form.
26.65 ___ Summons and Complaint.
26.66 ___ Amended Answer, Counterclaim and Cross Claim.
26.67 ___ Defendant's Demand for a Verified Bill of Particulars.
26.68 ___ Defendant's CPLR 3101 Demands.
26.69 ___ Plaintiff's Demand for a Verified Bill of Particulars.
26.70 ___ Plaintiff's CPLR 3101 Demands.
26.71 ___ Closing Statement.

CHAPTER 27. PRODUCTS LIABILITY

27.1 Scope Note.
27.2 Strategy.
27.3 Historical Overview.
27.4 Bases of a Products Liability Claim.
27.5 Theories of Liability.
27.6 ___ Manufacturing Defect or Mistake in the Manufacturing Process.
27.7 ___ Defective Design.
27.8 ___ ___ Burden of Proof.
27.9 ___ ___ Defense.
27.10 ___ Failure to Warn or Inadequate Warnings.
27.11 ___ ___ Burden of Proof.
27.12 ___ ___ Duty to Warn.
27.13 ___ ___ Adequacy of Warning.
27.14 ___ ___ Jury Question.
27.15 ___ ___ Informed Intermediary Defense.
27.16 ___ ___ Duty to Warn the Unusually Sensitive.
27.17 ___ ___ Non-Commercial Cases.
27.18 ___ Failure to Test.
27.19 ___ ___ FDA Approval.
27.20 ___ ___ Jury Question.
27.21 ___ ___ Preemption Defense.
27.22 Distributors' or Sellers' Liability.

TABLE OF CONTENTS

Sec.
27.23 ____ Sale Must Be Part of Ordinary Business.
27.24 ____ Service v. Sales.
27.25 ____ Medical Care Providers.
27.26 Successor Liability.
27.27 ____ Burden of Proof.
27.28 ____ Punitive Damages.
27.29 Liability of the Manufacturer of Component Parts.
27.30 Liability of the Manufacturer of the Complete Product.
27.31 Introducing Evidence of Post Accident Modification or Repairs.
27.32 Introducing Evidence of Other Incidents.
27.33 Effect of Destruction of the Product Upon Plaintiff's Ability to Prove a Defect.
27.34 Proof of Causation.
27.35 ____ Question for the Jury or Question for the Judge.
27.36 Foreseeability of Harm.
27.37 Discovery Issues.
27.38 ____ Confidentiality Orders or Stipulations.
27.39 Statute of Limitations.
27.40 Intervening Acts of Negligence—Plaintiff's Misuse of the Product.
27.41 ____ Alteration of the Product After it Has Left the Hands of the Manufacturer.
27.42 Preemption of Private Claims.
27.43 ____ Old Rule.
27.44 ____ New Rule.
27.45 ____ National Traffic & Motor Vehicle Safety Act and Its Savings Clause.
27.46 ____ Public Health Cigarette Labeling & Advertising Act of 1965 and the Public Health Cigarette Smoking Act of 1969—The *Cipollone* Decision.
27.47 ____ Federal Insecticide, Fungicide and Rodenticide Act (FIFRA) and Its Impact on Labeling Requirements.
27.48 ____ Medical Device Amendments to FDA Regulations.
27.49 ____ Limits on Preemption and Statutory Defenses.
27.50 ____ Validity of the Safety Standard or Regulatory Statute.
27.51 ____ Checklist.
27.52 Imposing Liability when the Manufacturer of a Fungible or Generic Product Is Unknown (Concert of Action/Market Share Liability).
27.53 Collateral Estoppel in Products Liability Cases.
27.54 Proof of Allegations Checklist.
27.55 Drafting Checklist—Complaint.
27.56 ____ Answer.
27.57 Forms—Products Liability Complaint.
27.58 ____ Products Liability Answer.

Volume 24

CHAPTER 28. LEGAL MALPRACTICE

28.1 Scope Note.

TABLE OF CONTENTS

Sec.
- 28.2 Strategy.
- 28.3 The Duty of Care.
- 28.4 ___ Specific Acts—Erroneous Advice.
- 28.5 ___ ___ Incompetent Tax Advice.
- 28.6 ___ ___ Proper Withdrawal.
- 28.7 ___ ___ Detecting Fraud.
- 28.8 ___ Causation.
- 28.9 ___ ___ The Doctrine of Compelled Settlement.
- 28.10 ___ Damages.
- 28.11 ___ Defenses—The Privity Rule.
- 28.12 ___ ___ Lawyer's Judgment Rule.
- 28.13 ___ ___ Statute of Limitations.
- 28.14 ___ ___ Continuous Representation Tolling Doctrine.
- 28.15 ___ ___ Extension by Estoppel.
- 28.16 ___ ___Standard Negligence Defenses of Lack of Foreseeability and Supervening Act.
- 28.17 ___ ___ Concealment of Malpractice Not a Separate Cause of Action.
- 28.18 ___ ___ Need for Consistent Positions.
- 28.19 The Duty of Loyalty.
- 28.20 ___ Conflict of Interest.
- 28.21 ___ Disqualification.
- 28.22 ___ Misappropriation of Client Funds.
- 28.23 Liability for Negligence of Independent Contractors.
- 28.24 Statutory Liability Under Judiciary Law § 487.
- 28.25 Vicarious Liability for Partner's Misdeeds.
- 28.26 Liability for Indemnity and Contribution.
- 28.27 Fee Disputes.
- 28.28 ___ Alternative Dispute Resolution.
- 28.29 ___ ___ Retainer Agreements Given Strict Scrutiny.
- 28.30 ___ ___ Arbitration Clause in Retainer Agreement May Waive Other Client Rights.
- 28.31 ___ Statutory Limitations.
- 28.32 ___ Account Stated.
- 28.33 ___ A Standard of Reasonableness.
- 28.34 Limited Liability Companies and Limited Liability Partnerships.
- 28.35 Lawyers Professional Liability Insurance.
- 28.36 ___ Extended Reporting Period.
- 28.37 ___ What Is a "Claim" and When Is It "Made"?
- 28.38 ___ Professional Capacity and Typical Exclusions.
- 28.39 ___ Limits, Deductibles and Defense.
- 28.40 ___ Notice of Claim and Notice of Occurrence.
- 28.41 ___ Cancellation.
- 28.42 ___ Innocent Partner Coverage.
- 28.43 ___ Application for Coverage and Rescission of Policy.
- 28.44 ___ Bad Faith.
- 28.45 ___ Cautions for Dissolving Law Firms.
- 28.46 Conclusion.
- 28.47 Drafting Checklist—Retainer Agreement.
- 28.48 ___ Malpractice Complaint Against Attorney.

TABLE OF CONTENTS

Sec.
28.49 ____ Answer to Malpractice Complaint on Behalf of Attorney.
28.50 Forms—Retainer Agreement With ADR Clause. 💾
28.51 ____ Retainer Agreement Without ADR Clause. 💾
28.52 ____ Complaint for Malpractice: Commercial Transaction. 💾
28.53 ____ Complaint for Malpractice: Personal Injury Action. 💾
28.54 ____ Answer: Commercial Transaction. 💾
28.55 ____ Answer: Personal Injury Action. 💾

CHAPTER 29. MEDICAL MALPRACTICE

29.1 Scope Note.
29.2 Strategy.
29.3 ____ Determining the Presence or Absence of Medical Malpractice.
29.4 ____ The Nature and Degree of Damages.
29.5 ____ Interviewing the Client.
29.6 ____ ____ History of the Current Condition.
29.7 ____ ____ Past Medical Conditions.
29.8 ____ ____ Current Medical Condition.
29.9 ____ ____ Miscellaneous Issues.
29.10 The Common Law Standards.
29.11 ____ The Standard of Care.
29.12 ____ ____ Hospitals' *Respondeat-Superior* Liability.
29.13 ____ ____ Hospitals' Direct Liability.
29.14 ____ Informed Consent.
29.15 ____ Health Maintenance Organizations.
29.16 ____ Expert Witnesses.
29.17 ____ Defenses in Medical Malpractice Cases.
29.18 Regulatory Standards.
29.19 ____ Qualifications of Nurse Midwives.
29.20 ____ Clinical Laboratories.
29.21 ____ Blood Banks.
29.22 ____ Testing for Phenylketonuria and Other Diseases and Conditions/Early Intervention Program.
29.23 ____ Hospitals.
29.24 Damages.
29.25 Procedure.
29.26 ____ Statutes of Limitation.
29.27 ____ Steps for Filing an Action.
29.28 ____ ____ Certificate of Merit.
29.29 ____ ____ Notice of Medical Malpractice Action.
29.30 ____ ____ Pre-calendar Conferences.
29.31 ____ Periodic Payment of Large Verdicts.
29.32 Hospital Operations and Medical Negligence—Credentialling of Physicians.
29.33 ____ Quality Assurance and Risk Management.
29.34 ____ Departmentalization of Services—Departmental Chairs.
29.35 Training and Education of Physicians.
29.36 ____ Medical School.
29.37 ____ PGY–1 (Internship).
29.38 ____ Residency.

TABLE OF CONTENTS

Sec.	
29.39	___ Fellowships.
29.40	___ Board Certification & Re-certification.
29.41	___ Associations, Societies, and Continuing Medical Education.
29.42	___ National Practitioner Data Bank.
29.43	Medical Literature.
29.44	___ Obtaining Medical Literature.
29.45	___ Sources.
29.46	___ Using Medical Literature to Evaluate a Case.
29.47	___ Preparing for Depositions.
29.48	___ Preparing for Trial.
29.49	___ Use of Treatises in State Court.
29.50	___ Use of Treatises in Federal Court.
29.51	Evaluating and Understanding Medical Records—Physician's Records.
29.52	___ Hospital Records.
29.53	___ ___ Informed Consent Forms.
29.54	___ ___ Progress Notes.
29.55	___ ___ Order Sheets.
29.56	___ ___ Consultation Records.
29.57	___ ___ Operative Records.
29.58	___ ___ Medication Records.
29.59	___ ___ Intake and Output Records.
29.60	___ ___ Radiographic Records.
29.61	___ ___ Obstetrical Records.
29.62	___ ___ ICU/CCU Records.
29.63	___ ___ Nurses' Notes.
29.64	Discovery.
29.65	___ Obtaining and Identifying Relevant Records.
29.66	___ ___ Physician's Records.
29.67	___ ___ Hospital Records.
29.68	___ ___ Billing Records.
29.69	___ ___ Pharmacy Records.
29.70	___ ___ Allied Health Provider Records.
29.71	___ ___ Workers' Compensation Claims File.
29.72	___ ___ Autopsy Report.
29.73	___ ___ Workers' Compensation Actions.
29.74	___ ___ Medical Malpractice Actions.
29.75	Trial Preparation.
29.76	Drafting Checklists.
29.77	___ Order to Show Cause to Obtain Medical Records.
29.78	___ Affirmation in Support of Order to Show Cause.
29.79	___ Certificate of Merit.
29.80	Forms
29.81	___ Order to Show Cause to Obtain Medical Records. 💾
29.82	___ Affirmation in Support of Order to Show Cause. 💾
29.83	___ Certificate of Merit. 💾

CHAPTER 30. DAMAGES

30.1	Scope Note.

LXXXIV

TABLE OF CONTENTS

Sec.
- 30.2 Strategy.
- 30.3 ____ Pretrial Stage.
- 30.4 ____ Trial Stage.
- 30.5 The Nature of Damages.
- 30.6 Compensatory Damages.
- 30.7 ____ Personal Injury.
- 30.8 ____ ____ Physical Pain and Suffering.
- 30.9 ____ ____ Mental or Emotional Pain and Suffering.
- 30.10 ____ ____ Loss of Earnings and Impairment of Future Earning Ability.
- 30.11 ____ ____ Aggravation of Pre-existing Injuries.
- 30.12 ____ Wrongful Death.
- 30.13 ____ ____ Damages Sustained Before Death.
- 30.14 ____ ____ Damages Sustained After Death.
- 30.15 ____ Loss of Consortium.
- 30.16 ____ Property Damage.
- 30.17 ____ ____ Real Property.
- 30.18 ____ Personal Property.
- 30.19 ____ Breach of Contract.
- 30.20 ____ ____ Contract Price and Actual Loss.
- 30.21 ____ ____ Delay in Performance.
- 30.22 ____ ____ Defective Performance.
- 30.23 ____ ____ Anticipatory Breach.
- 30.24 ____ ____ Damages Within the Contemplation of the Parties, and Loss of Profits.
- 30.25 ____ ____ Building and Construction.
- 30.26 ____ Minimizing and Mitigating Damages.
- 30.27 ____ ____ Contracts.
- 30.28 ____ ____ Personal Injury.
- 30.29 ____ Excessive or Inadequate Damages.
- 30.30 ____ ____ Specific Awards.
- 30.31 Punitive Damages.
- 30.32 ____ Intentional Torts.
- 30.33 ____ Negligence.
- 30.34 ____ Contract.
- 30.35 ____ Awards.
- 30.36 ____ Mitigation.
- 30.37 Nominal Damages.
- 30.38 Statutory Damages.
- 30.39 Liquidated Damages and Penalties.
- 30.40 Interest.
- 30.41 Attorney Fees.
- 30.42 ____ Statutory.
- 30.43 ____ Agreements and Miscellaneous.
- 30.44 Periodic Payment of Judgments.
- 30.45 Forms.
- 30.46 ____ *Ad Damnum* Clause in Ordinary Complaint.
- 30.47 ____ *Ad Damnum* Clause in Complaint in Medical or Dental Malpractice Action or in Action Against Municipal Government (Supreme Court).

TABLE OF CONTENTS

Sec.

30.48 —— Clauses in Complaint in Action Involving Automobile Accident. 💾
30.49 —— Request for Supplemental Demand for Relief in Medical or Dental Malpractice Action or Action Against Municipal Corporation. 💾
30.50 —— Defense of Culpable Conduct in Answer. 💾
30.51 —— Defense of Failure to Use Seat Belt Contained in Answer. 💾
30.52 —— Defense of Indemnification From Collateral Sources. 💾
30.53 —— Partial Defense; Mitigation of Damages. 💾
30.54 —— Partial Defense; Mitigation of Damages in Libel Action. 💾
30.55 —— Partial Defense; Inability to Convey Property. 💾
30.56 —— Notice of Motion to Amend Verdict (or Judgment) to Add Interest. 💾
30.57 —— Affidavit in Support of Motion to Amend Verdict (or Judgment) to Add Interest. 💾
30.58 —— Notice of Motion to Fix Date From Which Interest is to Be Computed. 💾
30.59 —— Affidavit in Support of Motion to Fix Date From Which Interest is to Be Computed. 💾
30.60 Pattern Jury Instructions.
30.61 —— Personal Injury—Subsequent Injury, Accident.
30.62 —— —— Loss of Earnings.
30.63 —— Damages—Personal Injury—Shock and Fright and Physical Consequences.
30.64 —— —— Aggravation of Injury.
30.65 —— Payment of Income Taxes on Damages for Personal Injury.
30.66 —— Reduction to Present Value.
30.67 —— Wrongful Death—Conscious Pain and Suffering.
30.68 —— Personal Injury—Collateral Sources—Itemized Verdict (CPLR 4111).
30.69 —— Damages—Property Without Market Value.
30.70 —— Damages—Property With Market Value.
30.71 —— Contracts—Damages—Generally.
30.72 —— —— Damages—Employment Contract.

CHAPTER 31. INSURANCE

31.1 Scope Note.
31.2 Strategy.
31.3 —— Checklist.
31.4 Sources of New York Insurance Law.
31.5 Third Parties Involved in the Placement and Administration of the Insurance Contract.
31.6 —— Insurance Brokers.
31.7 —— Insurance Agents.
31.8 Nature of Insurance.
31.9 Interpreting an Insurance Policy.
31.10 Notice.
31.11 The Cooperation Clause.

TABLE OF CONTENTS

Sec.
31.12	The Insurer's Duty to Defend.
31.13	____ Responding to a Request for a Defense.
31.14	____ Damages for Breach of the Duty.
31.15	Reservations of Rights By an Insurer.
31.16	Disclaiming/Denying Coverage.
31.17	The Insurer's Duty of Good Faith and Fair Dealing.
31.18	Rescission of Insurance Policies.
31.19	Reformation.
31.20	Lost Policies.
31.21	Nature of Relief.
31.22	Service of Process.
31.23	Pre-answer Security.
31.24	Arbitration Clauses.
31.25	Choice of Law.
31.26	Statutes of Limitation.
31.27	Burden of Proof.
31.28	Insolvent Insurers.
31.29	Subrogation.
31.30	Allocation of Losses Between Co-insurers.
31.31	Checklist of Essential Allegations.
31.32	Forms—Complaint By Policyholder for Declaratory Relief and Breach of Contract. 💾
31.33	____ Complaint By Insurer for Declaratory Relief. 💾
31.34	____ Complaint By Insurer for Rescission. 💾
31.35	____ Affirmative Defenses Asserted By Insurer in a Coverage Action. 💾

CHAPTER 32. WORKERS' COMPENSATION

32.1	Scope Note.
32.2	Strategy.
32.3	____ Employer's Counsel's Checklist.
32.4	____ Employee's Counsel's Checklist.
32.5	Introduction to The Workers' Compensation Law.
32.6	____ History and Theory.
32.7	____ ____ Workmen's Compensation Law of 1910.
32.8	____ ____ Constitutional Amendment.
32.9	____ ____ Workmen's Compensation Law of 1914.
32.10	____ ____ Statutory Changes.
32.11	Workers' Compensation Board.
32.12	Employer's Obligations and Methods of Coverage.
32.13	Compensable Injury.
32.14	Exclusive Remedy Doctrine.
32.15	____ Exceptions.
32.16	Pre-hearing Conference.
32.17	Hearings.
32.18	____ Statute of Limitations.
32.19	____ Burden of Proof, Presumptions and Defenses.
32.20	____ Conciliation Process.
32.21	Benefits.

TABLE OF CONTENTS

Sec.
32.22 ___ Classification of Disability.
32.23 ___ Wage Replacement.
32.24 ___ ___ Schedule vs. Non-schedule Awards.
32.25 ___ ___ Rehabilitation.
32.26 ___ ___ Industrially Disabled.
32.27 ___ ___ Special Disability Fund.
32.28 ___ Medical Benefits.
32.29 ___ Facial Disfigurement.
32.30 ___ Death Awards.
32.31 ___ ___ Funeral Expenses.
32.32 ___ Assignments, Liens and Lump-sum Settlements.
32.33 Board Review of Decisions, Orders and Awards.
32.34 Appeal to Court.
32.35 Reopening Closed Claims.
32.36 Discrimination.
32.37 Licensed Representative.
32.38 Attorney's Fees.
32.39 Posted Notice of Coverage.
32.40 Uninsured Employers' Fund.
32.41 Insurance Policy for Workers' Compensation.
32.42 State Insurance Fund.
32.43 Federal Workers' Compensation Laws and Benefits.
32.44 Disability Benefits Law.
32.45 ___ Employer's Obligations.
32.46 ___ Exempt Employees.
32.47 ___ Benefits and Employee Contribution.
32.48 ___ Special Fund.
32.49 ___ Employee Eligibility.
32.50 ___ Claim Filing.
32.51 ___ Pregnancy.
32.52 ___ End Note.
32.53 Forms.
32.54 ___ Workers' Compensation Board Employee's Claim For Compensation. (C–3 7–97)
32.55 ___ Workers' Compensation Board Employer's Report of Work-Related Accident/Occupational Disease. (C–2 10–97)
32.56 ___ Workers' Compensation Board Attending Doctor's Report and Carrier/Employer Billing. (C–4 3–97)
32.57 ___ Workers' Compensation Board Notice that Right to Compensation is Controverted. (C–7 2–97)
32.58 ___ Workers' Compensation Board Notice that Payment of Compensation for Disability has Been Stopped or Modified. (C–8/8.6 4–97)
32.59 ___ Notice and Proof of Claim for Disability Benefits. (DB–450 3–97)
32.60 ___ Notice of Total or Partial Rejection of Claim for Disability Benefits. (DB–451 3–97)

CHAPTER 33. LOCAL CRIMINAL COURT PRACTICE

33.1 Scope Note.

TABLE OF CONTENTS

Sec.
33.2	Strategy.
33.3	Overview of Local Criminal Court Process.
33.4	Police/Citizen Encounters.
33.5	___ Vehicle Stops.
33.6	___ The Parked Car.
33.7	___ Arrest Without Warrant.
33.8	Accusatory Instruments.
33.9	___ Information.
33.10	___ Simplified Information.
33.11	___ Prosecutor's Information.
33.12	___ Misdemeanor and Felony Complaints.
33.13	___ Supporting Depositions.
33.14	___ ___ Procedure.
33.15	___ ___ When Must They Be Provided?
33.16	___ ___ Who Must Be Served?
33.17	___ ___ Service of Request Must be Timely.
33.18	___ ___ Request By Attorney Requires Service on Counsel.
33.19	___ ___ Dismissal For Failure to Serve.
33.20	___ ___ Motion Must Be In Writing.
33.21	___ ___ Motion to Dismiss Must Be Timely.
33.22	___ ___ Factual Insufficiency Not Jurisdictional: Plea Waives Defect.
33.23	___ ___ Superseding Information Disallowed.
33.24	___ ___ People May File New Information Upon Dismissal of Supporting Deposition.
33.25	___ ___ Failure to Serve Not An Amendable Defect.
33.26	___ ___ Verification.
33.27	Probable Cause Hearing.
33.28	Plea Bargaining.
33.29	___ Plea Bargain Can Be Conditioned Upon Waiver of Right to Appeal.
33.30	___ Plea Bargaining—No Penalty for Asserting Right to Trial.
33.31	Pretrial Discovery.
33.32	___ Applicable to Simplified Informations.
33.33	___ Applicable to Traffic Infractions.
33.34	___ Subpoenas.
33.35	___ Demands to Produce/Bills of Particulars.
33.36	___ ___ Must Be Filed Within 30 Days.
33.37	___ ___ Response Within 15 Days.
33.38	___ ___ People's Failure to Comply With Time Limits.
33.39	___ *Brady* Material.
33.40	___ ___ Prosecutor Need Not Be Aware of Evidence.
33.41	___ ___ Timely Disclosure.
33.42	Evidence.
33.43	___ Motions to Suppress.
33.44	___ *Sandoval* Issues—Prior Convictions.
33.45	___ ___ Procedure.
33.46	___ ___ *Sandoval* Criteria.
33.47	___ ___ Defendant's Presence at *Sandoval* Hearing.
33.48	___ *Miranda*.

TABLE OF CONTENTS

Sec.
33.49 ___ ___ Applicable to Misdemeanor Traffic Offenses.
33.50 ___ ___ Stop and Frisk Does Not Constitute Custodial Interrogation.
33.51 ___ ___ Sobriety Checkpoint Stops Are Non-custodial.
33.52 ___ ___ Interrogation Defined.
33.53 ___ ___ Public Safety Exception.
33.54 ___ ___ Pedigree Exception.
33.55 ___ ___ Waiver Following Assertion of Right to Remain Silent.
33.56 ___ ___ Waiver Following Request for Counsel.
33.57 ___ Involuntary Statements.
33.58 ___ ___ May Not Be Used to Impeach.
33.59 ___ ___ Applicability of Harmless Error Doctrine.
33.60 ___ The Use of Defendant's Pre-arrest Silence.
33.61 ___ Corroboration of Admission or Confession Required.
33.62 Trial.
33.63 ___ Modes of Trial.
33.64 ___ Order of Jury Trial Proceedings.
33.65 ___ Order of Bench Trial Proceedings.
33.66 ___ Trial of Speeding Tickets.
33.67 ___ ___ Discovery.
33.68 ___ ___ People's *Prima Facie* Case.
33.69 ___ ___ When Not to Request a Supporting Deposition.
33.70 ___ ___ Speeding Trial Summary.
33.71 Speedy Trial Pursuant to CPL § 30.20.
33.72 ___ Application to Traffic Infractions.
33.73 ___ Criteria.
33.74 CPL § 30.30.
33.75 ___ Vehicle and Traffic Law Violations Generally Excluded.
33.76 ___ ___ Unless Combined With Felony, Misdemeanor or Violation.
33.77 ___ People's Readiness Rule.
33.78 ___ Requirements for An Assertion of Readiness.
33.79 ___ ___ Actual Readiness for Trial.
33.80 ___ Guilty Plea Waives CPL § 30.30 Motion.
33.81 ___ Burden of Proof.
33.82 ___ Commencement of Criminal Action—Appearance Tickets.
33.83 ___ Uniform Traffic Tickets.
33.84 ___ Excludable Time.
33.85 ___ ___ Motions.
33.86 ___ ___ Defective Accusatory Instrument.
33.87 ___ ___ Adjournments.
33.88 ___ ___ Delays by the Court.
33.89 ___ ___ Effect of Defendant's Unavailability.
33.90 ___ Post Readiness Delay.
33.91 Procedural Checklists.
33.92 ___ Notice of Motion to Dismiss For Failure to Serve a Timely Supporting Deposition/Attorney Affirmation in Support of Motion.
33.93 ___ Demand to Produce: Speeding Ticket.
33.94 Drafting Checklists.

TABLE OF CONTENTS

Sec.
33.95 ____ Notice of Motion to Dismiss For Failure to Serve a Timely Supporting Deposition.
33.96 ____ Attorney Affirmation in Support of Motion to Dismiss For Failure to Serve a Timely Supporting Deposition.
33.97 ____ Demand to Produce: Speeding Ticket.
33.98 Forms.
33.99 ____ Notice of Motion to Dismiss For Failure to Serve a Timely Supporting Deposition. 💾
33.100 ____ Attorney Affirmation in Support of Motion to Dismiss For Failure to Serve a Timely Supporting Deposition. 💾
33.101 ____ Demand to Produce: Speeding Ticket. 💾

CHAPTER 34. SOCIAL SECURITY DISABILITY CASES

34.1 Scope Note.
34.2 Strategy.
34.3 The Law of Disability.
34.4 ____ Statutory Definition of Disability.
34.5 ____ Judicial Definitions.
34.6 ____ Durational Requirements.
34.7 ____ Comparison to Workers' Compensation.
34.8 ____ Assessing Disability: The Sequential Evaluation.
34.9 ____ ____ Substantial Gainful Activity.
34.10 ____ ____ Severity.
34.11 ____ ____ Listings of Impairments.
34.12 ____ ____ Ability to Do Past Relevant Work.
34.13 ____ ____ Ability to Do Other Work.
34.14 ____ ____ Dispensing With Individualized Assessment.
34.15 Financial Consideration of The Two Federal Programs: Social Security Disability Insurance Benefits and Supplemental Security Income.
34.16 ____ Income.
34.17 ____ Assets.
34.18 ____ Amount of Benefits.
34.19 ____ SSI: Based on Financial Need.
34.20 ____ SSDIB: Based on FICA Withholding.
34.21 ____ Eligibility for Both SSI and SSDIB.
34.22 ____ Retroactivity of Benefits.
34.23 Administrative Procedure.
34.24 ____ Application.
34.25 ____ Reconsideration.
34.26 ____ Termination of Benefits.
34.27 ____ Administrative Hearing.
34.28 ____ Appeals Council.
34.29 ____ Federal District Court.
34.30 ____ Court of Appeals, Second Circuit.
34.31 Handling the Case—Generally.
34.32 ____ Initial Interview.
34.33 ____ Retainer Agreements.
34.34 ____ Social Security Administration's Records.

TABLE OF CONTENTS

Sec.
34.35	____ Medical Evidence.	
34.36	____ ____ Hospital Records.	
34.37	____ ____ Reports from Treating Physicians.	
34.38	____ Other Evidence.	
34.39	____ ____ Former Co-workers and Employers.	
34.40	____ ____ Family Members.	
34.41	____ Preparing for the Hearing.	
34.42	____ ____ Preparing the Claimant.	
34.43	____ ____ Other Witnesses or Documents.	
34.44	____ Conducting the Hearing.	
34.45	____ ____ Testimony of the Claimant.	
34.46	____ ____ Medical Advisors.	
34.47	____ ____ Vocational Experts.	
34.48	____ Post-hearing Evidence and Memoranda.	
34.49	Implementing Favorable Decisions.	
34.50	____ Collecting SSDIB Benefits.	
34.51	____ Collecting SSI Benefits.	
34.52	____ Collecting Fees.	
34.53	____ ____ Fee Applications.	
34.54	____ ____ Fee Agreements.	
34.55	Appealing Unfavorable Decisions.	
34.56	____ Strategic Considerations Regarding Unfavorable Decisions.	
34.57	____ Strategic Considerations Regarding Partially Favorable Decisions.	
34.58	Reopening Prior Applications.	
34.59	____ Reopening SSDIB.	
34.60	____ Reopening SSI.	
34.61	____ Review of Grants of Reopening.	
34.62	____ Review of Denials of Reopening.	
34.63	____ Court Decisions Requiring Reopening.	
34.64	____ Statutes and Regulations Requiring Reopening.	
34.65	Procedural Checklist.	
34.66	Checklists of Allegations—Medical Claims.	
34.67	____ Psychiatric Claims.	
34.68	Forms—Claimant Questionnaire. 💾	
34.69	____ Retainer Agreement. 💾	
34.70	____ Retainer Agreement: Concurrent Benefits. 💾	
34.71	____ Fee Agreement: Maximum Fee. 💾	
34.72	____ Request for Medical Records. 💾	
34.73	____ Medical Release. 💾	
34.74	____ Medical Questionnaire for Treating Physician. 💾	
34.75	____ Psychiatric Questionnaire. 💾	
34.76	____ Cover Letter to Treating Physician. 💾	
34.77	____ Thank-you Letter to Treating Physician. 💾	
34.78	____ Request for Appeals Council Review. 💾	

CHAPTER 35. INCOME TAX

35.1	Scope Note.
35.2	Strategy.

TABLE OF CONTENTS

Sec.
- 35.3 ____ Checklist.
- 35.4 Personal Income Tax.
- 35.5 ____ Computing Federal Adjusted Gross Income.
- 35.6 ____ Computing Federal Taxable Income.
- 35.7 ____ Definition of New York Taxable Income.
- 35.8 ____ Computing New York Adjusted Gross Income.
- 35.9 ____ Computing New York Taxable Income.
- 35.10 ____ New York Personal Exemptions.
- 35.11 ____ Itemized Deductions for Married Couple.
- 35.12 ____ Exclusion of Pension and Disability Distributions From New York Income.
- 35.13 ____ New York Minimum Tax.
- 35.14 ____ Definition of Residency.
- 35.15 ____ Burden of Proving Non-residency.
- 35.16 ____ Domicile and Change of Domicile.
- 35.17 ____ New York Income Tax on Non-resident Individuals.
- 35.18 ____ Checklist.
- 35.19 New York Corporate Franchise Tax.
- 35.20 ____ Comparison With Federal Taxation.
- 35.21 ____ Initial Tax on Corporate Capital Structure.
- 35.22 ____ Foreign Corporations.
- 35.23 ____ Corporations Subject to Tax.
- 35.24 ____ Corporations Exempt From Tax.
- 35.25 ____ Necessary Level of Activity.
- 35.26 ____ Calculation.
- 35.27 ____ Tax on Net Income Base.
- 35.28 ____ ____ Subtractions From Federal Taxable Income.
- 35.29 ____ Items From Subsidiaries.
- 35.30 ____ Tax on Capital Base.
- 35.31 ____ ____ Definition of Capital Base.
- 35.32 ____ ____ Exemption for Small Businesses.
- 35.33 ____ Minimum Taxable Income Base.
- 35.34 ____ Fixed Dollar Minimum Tax.
- 35.35 ____ Apportionment of Tax Bases to New York.
- 35.36 ____ ____ Business Allocation Percentage.
- 35.37 ____ ____ Investment Allocation Percentage.
- 35.38 ____ Definition of Subsidiary Capital.
- 35.39 ____ Franchise Tax Checklist.
- 35.40 Department of Taxation and Finance.
- 35.41 ____ Role of Office of the Counsel.
- 35.42 ____ Taxpayer Services Division.
- 35.43 ____ Office of Revenue and Information Management.
- 35.44 ____ Office of Tax Operations.
- 35.45 ____ ____ Audit Division.
- 35.46 ____ ____ Tax Compliance Division.
- 35.47 ____ ____ Revenue Opportunity Division.
- 35.48 ____ ____ Office of Tax Enforcement.
- 35.49 ____ ____ Division of Tax Appeals.
- 35.50 ____ Summary.
- 35.51 Filing Returns.

TABLE OF CONTENTS

Sec.
35.52 —— Where to File.
35.53 —— Keeping Records of Returns.
35.54 —— Extensions of Time for Filing.
35.55 —— Obtaining New York Tax Forms.
35.56 —— Filing Claims for Refund.
35.57 —— Time Limitations.
35.58 —— Where to File.
35.59 —— Special Refund Authority.
35.60 —— Claim Based on Federal Changes.
35.61 —— Petitions for Refund.
35.62 —— Judicial Review of Denied Refund Claims.
35.63 —— Checklist.
35.64 Statutes of Limitation.
35.65 —— General Statutes for Income Tax Assessment.
35.66 —— Effect.
35.67 —— Exceptions.
35.68 —— Request for Prompt Assessment.
35.69 —— Waiver.
35.70 Penalties.
35.71 —— Late Filing.
35.72 —— Late Payment.
35.73 —— Reasonable Cause.
35.74 —— Negligence.
35.75 —— Substantial Understatement.
35.76 —— Underpayment of Estimated Taxes.
35.77 —— —— Exceptions.
35.78 —— Fraud.
35.79 —— —— Elements.
35.80 —— —— Specific Determination Methods.
35.81 —— —— Common Cases.
35.82 —— —— Creative Methods of Proof.
35.83 —— Interest on Underpayment or Overpayment.
35.84 —— Checklist.
35.85 Audits and Appeals.
35.86 —— Audit Methods.
35.87 —— Taxpayer Bill of Rights.
35.88 —— Representation of Taxpayer.
35.89 —— Audit Results.
35.90 —— Bureau of Conciliation and Mediation Services.
35.91 —— —— Requesting a Conciliation Conference.
35.92 —— —— Conferences.
35.93 —— —— Conference Orders.
35.94 —— Petition to Division of Tax Appeals.
35.95 —— —— Referral to Bureau of Conciliation and Mediation Services.
35.96 —— —— Small Claims Hearings.
35.97 —— Summary.
35.98 —— Checklist.
35.99 Judicial Actions.
35.100 —— Appeal by Article 78 Proceeding.

TABLE OF CONTENTS

Sec.
35.101 __ __ Payment of Taxes.
35.102 __ __ Initiation.
35.103 __ __ Burden of Proof.
35.104 __ Declaratory Judgment Actions.
35.105 __ Appeal to New York Court of Appeals.
35.106 __ Summary.
35.107 __ Checklist.
35.108 Assessment and Collection of Tax.
35.109 __ Summary Assessment.
35.110 __ Deficiency Assessment.
35.111 __ Statute of Limitations.
35.112 __ Jeopardy Assessment.
35.113 __ Collection of Tax.
35.114 __ __ Lien.
35.115 __ __ Duration of Lien.
35.116 __ Collection by Levy or Warrant.
35.117 __ Installment Payment Agreements.
35.118 __ Offer in Compromise.
35.119 __ Bankruptcy as an Option.
35.120 __ Checklist.
35.121 Criminal Tax Provisions.
35.122 __ Failure to File Return.
35.123 __ False or Fraudulent Return.
35.124 __ Aiding or Assisting in False Return or Statement.
35.125 __ Failure to Pay Tax.
35.126 __ Failure to Properly Withhold Taxes.
35.127 Forms.
35.128 __ Power of Attorney to Represent an Individual.
35.129 __ Application for Automatic Extension of Time for Filing Return.
35.130 __ Application For Additional Extension of Time to File for Individuals.
35.131 __ Notice of Exception to Tax Tribunal.
35.132 __ Petition to Division of Tax Appeals.
35.133 __ Petition for Advisory Opinion.
35.134 __ Statement of Financial Condition.
35.135 __ Petition for Declaratory Ruling.
35.136 __ Request for Conciliation Conference.
35.137 __ Offer in Compromise.

CHAPTER 36. ALCOHOLIC BEVERAGE CONTROL LAW

36.1 Scope Note.
36.2 Strategy.
36.3 __ Checklist.
36.4 Historical Background of State and Federal Regulations.
36.5 Jurisdiction.
36.6 New York State Liquor Authority.
36.7 Licenses.
36.8 __ Retail Licenses.

TABLE OF CONTENTS

Sec.
- 36.9 ___ ___ On-Premises Licenses.
- 36.10 ___ ___ Off-Premises Licenses.
- 36.11 ___ Wholesale Licenses.
- 36.12 ___ Manufacturing Licenses.
- 36.13 ___ General Application Requirements.
- 36.14 ___ Special Qualifications for Licensees.
- 36.15 Permits.
- 36.16 ___ Temporary Permits.
- 36.17 ___ Other Permits.
- 36.18 Brand and/or Label Registration.
- 36.19 Penal and Tax Bonds.
- 36.20 Application Form (Retail) Reviewed.
- 36.21 ___ Lease Information.
- 36.22 ___ Applicant Information.
- 36.23 ___ Information Regarding Premises.
- 36.24 ___ Financial Information and Criminal Background.
- 36.25 ___ Community Notification.
- 36.26 ___ Landlord Information.
- 36.27 ___ Additional Requirements for On–Premises Consumption Licenses.
- 36.28 ___ ___ Neighborhood.
- 36.29 ___ ___ Premises Exterior.
- 36.30 ___ ___ Premises Interior.
- 36.31 ___ ___ Bars.
- 36.32 ___ ___ Kitchen.
- 36.33 ___ ___ Permits.
- 36.34 ___ ___ Hotel.
- 36.35 ___ Proposed Method of Operation.
- 36.36 ___ Additional Requirements for Off–Premises Liquor Store Applicants.
- 36.37 ___ Additional Requirements for Grocery Store Applicants.
- 36.38 ___ Liquidators Permit.
- 36.39 ___ Affidavit Requirements.
- 36.40 ___ Personal Questionnaire.
- 36.41 ___ On–Premises Liquor Applications 500 Foot Verification.
- 36.42 ___ Miscellaneous Requirements.
- 36.43 ___ Checklist.
- 36.44 Record–Keeping Requirements.
- 36.45 Reporting Changes.
- 36.46 ___ Application for Endorsement Certificate.
- 36.47 ___ Application for Approval of Corporate Change.
- 36.48 ___ Alteration of Premises.
- 36.49 ___ Removal of Premises.
- 36.50 ___ Financing and Method of Operation.
- 36.51 Renewals.
- 36.52 Trade Practices.
- 36.53 Enforcement.
- 36.54 Penalties.
- 36.55 ___ Revocation Order.
- 36.56 ___ Cancellation Order.

TABLE OF CONTENTS

Sec.
36.57 ____ Suspension Order.
36.58 ____ ____ Forthwith.
36.59 ____ ____ Deferred.
36.60 ____ ____ Combined Forthwith and Deferred Suspension.
36.61 ____ Letters of Warning.
36.62 ____ Suspension Proceedings.
36.63 ____ Revocation Notice of Pleading.
36.64 Pleadings and Procedure.
36.65 ____ Hearings.
36.66 ____ Judicial Review.
36.67 Forms.
36.68 ____ Application for Alcoholic Beverage Control Retail License.
36.69 ____ Application for Endorsement Certificate.
36.70 ____ Application for Approval of Corporate Change.
36.71 ____ Application for Permission to Make Alterations.
36.72 ____ Application for Wholesale License.
36.73 ____ Retail License and Filing Fee Schedule.

CHAPTER 37. CIVIL APPELLATE PRACTICE BEFORE THE APPELLATE DIVISION AND OTHER INTERMEDIATE APPELLATE COURTS

37.1 Scope Note.
37.2 Strategy.
37.3 Judiciary Structure.
37.4 Administration of the Appellate Division.
37.5 Administrative Powers of the Appellate Division.
37.6 ____ Admission, Removal and Disciplinary Jurisdiction.
37.7 ____ Administration of the Courts.
37.8 ____ Law Guardian Program.
37.9 ____ Mental Hygiene Legal Service Oversight.
37.10 ____ Assigned Counsel.
37.11 ____ Powers Relating to Appellate Term.
37.12 ____ Marshals.
37.13 An Overview of the Statutory Framework of the Appellate System and the Rules of the Court.
37.14 Appeals to the Appellate Division.
37.15 ____ Courts of Original Jurisdiction From Which Appeals Lie.
37.16 ____ ____ Supreme Court and County Court.
37.17 ____ ____ Court of Claims.
37.18 ____ ____ Surrogate's Court.
37.19 ____ ____ Family Court.
37.20 ____ Appeals From Other Appellate Courts.
37.21 ____ Who May Appeal.
37.22 ____ ____ Aggrieved Parties.
37.23 ____ ____ ____ Defaulters; Orders or Judgments on Consent.
37.24 ____ ____ ____ Intervenors.
37.25 ____ ____ ____ Substitution of Parties.
37.26 ____ ____ ____ Third Party Defendants.
37.27 ____ Scope of Review.

TABLE OF CONTENTS

Sec.
37.28 — — Questions of Law.
37.29 — — Questions of Fact and the Exercise of Discretion.
37.30 — — Limitations in Notice of Appeal or Brief.
37.31 — — Mootness.
37.32 — — Change in Law While Case Is Pending.
37.33 — Appeals as of Right.
37.34 — — Appeals From Final and Interlocutory Judgments.
37.35 — — Appeals From Orders.
37.36 — Appeals by Permission.
37.37 — Non-appealable Matters.
37.38 — Appealable Paper.
37.39 — Time for Taking the Appeal.
37.40 — — Appeal as of Right.
37.41 — — Appeal by Permission.
37.42 — — Cross-Appeal.
37.43 — — Extensions; Omissions.
37.44 — — Other Statutory Provisions.
37.45 — Notice of Appeal—Form and Content.
37.46 — — Service and Filing Requirements.
37.47 — Reargument; Subsequent Orders.
37.48 — Assignment of Counsel.
37.49 — Perfecting the Appeal.
37.50 — — Time.
37.51 — — Methods of Perfection.
37.52 — — Briefs.
37.53 — — Consolidation.
37.54 — What to File; Number of Copies.
37.55 — — First Department.
37.56 — — Second Department.
37.57 — — Third Department.
37.58 — — Fourth Department.
37.59 — Location; Transfer Plan.
37.60 — Calendars.
37.61 — Preferences.
37.62 — Oral Arguments.
37.63 — Disposition of the Appeal.
37.64 — — Affirmance.
37.65 — — Reversal or Modification.
37.66 — — Dismissal.
37.67 — — Costs and Disbursements; Attorneys' Fees.
37.68 — Post-disposition Proceedings.
37.69 — — Reargument.
37.70 — — Leave to Appeal to the Court of Appeals.
37.71 — — Enforcement.
37.72 — — Resettlement or Clarification.
37.73 — — *Certiorari* to the U.S. Supreme Court.
37.74 — Motion Practice—Generally.
37.75 — — First Department.
37.76 — — Second Department.
37.77 — — Third Department.

TABLE OF CONTENTS

Sec.		
37.78	____ ____	Fourth Department.
37.79	____ ____	Interim Relief.
37.80	____ ____	Stays.
37.81	____ ____	*Amicus Curiae*.
37.82	____ ____	Miscellaneous Motions.
37.83	____	Sanctions.
37.84	____	Preargument Conferences.
37.85	____	Unperfected Appeals.
37.86		Other Proceedings in the Appellate Division.
37.87	____	CPLR Article 78 Proceedings.
37.88	____	Writs of *Habeas Corpus*.
37.89	____	CPLR 5704 *Ex Parte* Order Review.
37.90	____	Miscellaneous Proceedings.
37.91		Appeals to Other Intermediate Courts.
37.92	____	Appeals from Justice Courts.
37.93	____ ____	Courts to Which Appeals Are Taken.
37.94	____ ____	Applicability of CPLR Article 55.
37.95	____ ____	Appeals as of Right and by Permission.
37.96	____ ____	Taking the Appeal: Settlement of Case and Return on Appeal.
37.97	____ ____	Perfection of Appeal.
37.98	____ ____	Costs on Appeal.
37.99	____ ____	Small Claims Review.
37.100	____ ____	Rule Governance by Administrative Board.
37.101	____	Appeals From City Courts.
37.102	____ ____	Courts to Which Appeals Are Taken.
37.103	____ ____	Applicability of CPLR Article 55.
37.104	____ ____	Appeals as of Right and by Permission.
37.105	____ ____	Taking the Appeal: Settlement of Case and Return on Appeal; Variations from CPLR.
37.106	____ ____	Perfection of Appeal.
37.107	____ ____	Costs on Appeal.
37.108	____ ____	Small Claims Review.
37.109	____	Appeals From District Courts.
37.110	____ ____	Court to Which Appeals Are Taken.
37.111	____ ____	Applicability of CPLR Article 55.
37.112	____ ____	Appeals as of Right and by Permission.
37.113	____ ____	Taking the Appeal: Settlement of Case and Return on Appeal.
37.114	____ ____	Perfecting the Appeal.
37.115	____ ____	Costs on Appeal.
37.116	____ ____	Small Claims Review.
37.117	____	Appeals from the Civil Court of the City of New York.
37.118	____ ____	Courts to Which Appeals Are Taken.
37.119	____ ____	Applicability of CPLR Article 55.
37.120	____ ____	Appeals as of Right and by Permission.
37.121	____ ____	Appeals to the Court of Appeals.
37.122	____ ____	Taking the Appeal: Settlement of Case and Return on Appeal; Variations From CPLR.
37.123	____ ____	Perfecting the Appeal.

TABLE OF CONTENTS

Sec.
37.124 ____ ____ Costs on Appeal.
37.125 ____ ____ Small Claims Review.
37.126 ____ Appeals from County Courts.
37.127 Procedural Checklist.
37.128 Forms.
37.129 ____ Notice of Appeal. 💾
37.130 ____ Notice of Motion for a Stay of Proceedings. 💾
37.131 ____ Order to Show Cause for a Stay of Proceedings. 💾
37.132 ____ Affirmation in Support of Motion or Order To Show Cause for a Stay of Proceedings. 💾
37.133 ____ Notice of Motion for a Preference to Expedite the Appeal. 💾
37.134 ____ Affirmation in Support of Motion for a Preference to Expedite the Appeal. 💾
37.135 ____ Notice of Motion to Enlarge Time for (Appellant to Perfect Appeal)(Respondent To File Brief). 💾
37.136 ____ Affirmation in Support of Motion to Enlarge Time for (Appellant to Perfect Appeal) (Respondent to File Brief). 💾
37.137 ____ Notice of Motion to Strike Matter *Dehors* the Record (Appendix)(Brief). 💾
37.138 ____ Affirmation in Support of Motion to Strike Matter *Dehors* the Record(Appendix)(Brief). 💾
37.139 ____ Notice of Motion for Reargument or Leave to Appeal to the Court of Appeals. 💾
37.140 ____ Affirmation in Support of Motion for Reargument or Leave to Appeal to the Court of Appeals. 💾

Volume 25

CHAPTER 38. CRIMINAL APPELLATE PRACTICE BEFORE THE APPELLATE DIVISION AND OTHER INTERMEDIATE APPELLATE COURTS

38.1 Scope Note.
38.2 Strategy.
38.3 Appeals to the Appellate Division—General Principles.
38.4 ____ Courts of Original Jurisdiction From Which Appeals Lie.
38.5 ____ Who May Appeal.
38.6 ____ ____ Status as Aggrieved by "Adverse" Determination.
38.7 ____ ____ Appeals by the Defendant From Superior Courts.
38.8 ____ ____ ____ As of Right.
38.9 ____ ____ ____ Appeals by Permission.
38.10 ____ ____ Appeals by the People.
38.11 ____ ____ Appeals from Orders Accepting or Sealing Grand Jury Reports; Appeals by Prosecutors; Appeals by Public Servants.
38.12 ____ Appeal Process—Appeals as of Right.
38.13 ____ ____ Appeals by Permission: Certificate Granting Leave.
38.14 ____ ____ Extensions of Time.
38.15 ____ ____ Stay of Judgment or Order.
38.16 ____ ____ Poor Person Relief and Assignment of Counsel.

TABLE OF CONTENTS

Sec.
38.17 ___ ___ Perfecting and Calendaring the Appeal.
38.18 ___ Scope of Review.
38.19 ___ ___ Questions of Law.
38.20 ___ ___ Questions of Fact; Weight of Evidence.
38.21 ___ ___ Interest of Justice/Discretion.
38.22 ___ ___ Change in Law While Case Pending.
38.23 ___ Disposition of Appeal.
38.24 ___ ___ Affirmance.
38.25 ___ ___ Modification.
38.26 ___ ___ Reversal.
38.27 ___ ___ Character of Order of Reversal or Modification: On the Law, On the Facts, in the Interest of Justice.
38.28 ___ ___ Corrective Action.
38.29 ___ Post-disposition Proceedings.
38.30 ___ ___ Responsibilities of Counsel.
38.31 ___ ___ Reargument.
38.32 ___ ___ Leave to Appeal.
38.33 ___ ___ *Certiorari* to U.S. Supreme Court.
38.34 ___ ___ *Coram Nobis*—Ineffective Assistance of Appellate Counsel.
38.35 ___ ___ Clarification/Resettlement.
38.36 ___ Motions in Connection With Appeals—Generally.
38.37 ___ ___ *Pro Se* Supplemental Brief.
38.38 ___ ___ *Anders* Brief.
38.39 ___ ___ Dismissal.
38.40 ___ ___ Reconstruction Hearing; Summary Reversal.
38.41 ___ ___ Death or Absence of a Defendant.
38.42 ___ ___ Assignment of New Counsel.
38.43 ___ ___ Expanding the Judgment Roll.
38.44 ___ ___ Briefs.
38.45 ___ ___ Withdrawal of Appeal.
38.46 Appeals to Intermediate Appellate Courts Other Than the Appellate Division.
38.47 ___ Appeals From Village Courts, Town Courts, City Courts and District Courts.
38.48 ___ Appeals From Criminal Court of the City of New York.
38.49 ___ ___ New York and Bronx County Branches.
38.50 ___ ___ Kings, Queens, Richmond County Branches.
38.51 ___ Orders, Sentences and Judgments Appealable.
38.52 ___ Taking the Appeal—Appeal as of Right.
38.53 ___ ___ Appeals by Permission.
38.54 ___ Stays Pending Appeal.
38.55 ___ Perfecting the Appeal.
38.56 ___ Determination of the Appeal.
38.57 Governance of the Appellate Term.
38.58 Original Application to County Court for Change of Venue.
38.59 Procedural Checklist for Appeals to Appellate Division.
38.60 Forms—Notice of Motion for a Stay of Execution of Judgment.

TABLE OF CONTENTS

Sec.
38.61 ____ Affirmation in Support of Motion for a Stay of Execution of Judgment. 💾
38.62 ____ Notice of Motion for an Extension of Time to Take an Appeal. 💾
38.63 ____ Affirmation in Support of Motion for an Extension of Time to Take an Appeal. 💾
38.64 Chart.

CHAPTER 39. CIVIL AND CRIMINAL APPEALS TO THE COURT OF APPEALS

39.1 Scope Note.
39.2 Strategy.
39.3 Civil Appeals.
39.4 ____ Finality.
39.5 ____ Non-appealable Orders.
39.6 ____ Appealable Paper.
39.7 ____ Scope of Review.
39.8 ____ Appeal as of Right.
39.9 ____ ____ Appellate Division Orders or Judgments.
39.10 ____ ____ Final Judgment of Court of Original Instance.
39.11 ____ ____ Judgment of Court of Original Instance to Review Prior Non-final Determination of the Appellate Division.
39.12 ____ Appeals by Permission of the Appellate Division or the Court of Appeals.
39.13 ____ ____ Judgment of Court of Original Instance to Review Prior Non-final Determination of the Appellate Division.
39.14 ____ ____ Final Order of the Appellate Division Determining the Action.
39.15 ____ ____ Non-final Appellate Division Orders in Proceedings by or Against Public Officers or Others.
39.16 ____ Appeals by Permission of the Appellate Division.
39.17 ____ Form, Content and Service of Motions for Leave to Appeal.
39.18 ____ ____ Motions Filed in the Appellate Division.
39.19 ____ ____ Motions Filed in the Court of Appeals.
39.20 ____ Time for Taking the Appeal or Moving for Leave to Appeal—Appeals as of Right.
39.21 ____ ____ Motions for Leave to Appeal.
39.22 ____ ____ Cross Appeals.
39.23 ____ ____ Extensions of Time.
39.24 ____ ____ Omissions.
39.25 ____ Notice of Appeal—Form and Content.
39.26 ____ The Jurisdictional Statement.
39.27 ____ Jurisdictional Inquiry.
39.28 ____ Perfecting and Readying the Appeal.
39.29 ____ ____ Full Briefing and Oral Argument.
39.30 ____ ____ *Sua Sponte* Merits Consideration ("SSM").
39.31 ____ Determination of the Appeal—*Remittitur*.
39.32 ____ Motion Practice.
39.33 ____ ____ Motion for a Stay.

TABLE OF CONTENTS

Sec.	
39.34	____ ____ Motion to File an *Amicus* Brief.
39.35	____ ____ Motion for Poor Person Relief.
39.36	____ ____ Motion for Reconsideration.
39.37	Criminal Appeals.
39.38	____ Definition of Criminal Case.
39.39	____ Orders and Judgments From Which Appeals May Be Taken.
39.40	____ By the Defendant in Death Penalty Cases.
39.41	____ By the Prosecution in Death Penalty Cases.
39.42	____ Intermediate Appellate Courts.
39.43	____ Additional Limitations on Appealability.
39.44	____ Appeals by Permission.
39.45	____ ____ Obligation of Intermediate Appellate Court Counsel.
39.46	____ ____ Who May Grant Leave to Appeal.
39.47	____ ____ Criminal Leave Application ("CLA") Practice.
39.48	____ ____ Stays and Continuation of Bail.
39.49	____ Appeals Practice.
39.50	____ Scope of Review.
39.51	____ Disposition of Appeal.
39.52	____ Motion Practice.
39.53	____ ____ Poor Person Relief and Assignment of Counsel.
39.54	____ ____ Extension of Time to Seek Leave to Appeal.
39.55	____ ____ Dismissal of Appeal.
39.56	____ ____ Withdrawal of Appeal.
39.57	____ ____ Reargument.
39.58	Other Proceedings in the Court of Appeals.
39.59	____ Review of Determinations of the Commission on Judicial Conduct.
39.60	____ Certified Questions From Other Courts.
39.61	____ Matters Regarding Admission of Attorneys and Licensing of Foreign Legal Consultants.
39.62	*Certiorari* to the Supreme Court of the United States.
39.63	Procedural Checklists.
39.64	____ Civil Appeals as of Right.
39.65	____ Civil Appeals by Permission of Court of Appeals.
39.66	____ Criminal Appeals by Leave of a Court of Appeals Judge.
39.67	____ Civil Appeals by Leave of the Appellate Division and Criminal Appeals by Leave of an Appellate Division Justice.
39.68	____ Appeals Selected for Expedited Review Pursuant to Rule 500.4
39.69	____ Appeals Tracked to Full Briefing and Oral Argument.
39.70	Drafting Checklists.
39.71	____ Notice of Appeal.
39.72	____ Rule 500.2 Jurisdictional Statement.
39.73	____ Motion for Leave to Appeal to Court of Appeals Filed in Court of Appeals.
39.74	____ Application for Leave to Appeal in Criminal Case Filed in Court of Appeals.
39.75	____ Appellant's Brief on the Merits.
39.76	____ Respondent's Brief on the Merits.

TABLE OF CONTENTS

Sec.
39.77 Forms—Notice of Appeal to Court of Appeals From Order of Appellate Division Finally Determining Action With Two Dissents on Question of Law.
39.78 ____ Notice of Appeal to Court of Appeals From Order of Appellate Division Finally Determining Action Where Construction of Constitution is Directly Involved.
39.79 ____ Notice of Appeal to Court of Appeals From Judgment of Supreme Court Where Constitutionality of Statute is Directly Involved.
39.80 ____ Notice of Appeal to Court of Appeals From Appellate Division Order of Reversal Granting New Trial With Stipulation for Judgment Absolute.
39.81 ____ Notice of Appeal to Court of Appeals From Judgment of Supreme Court to Review Prior Non-final Determination of Appellate Division.
39.82 ____ Rule 500.2 Jurisdictional Statement.
39.83 ____ Notice of Motion in Court of Appeals for Leave to Appeal to Court of Appeals From Order of Appellate Division.
39.84 ____ Affidavit in Support of Motion in Court of Appeals for Leave to Appeal to Court of Appeals From Order of Appellate Division.
39.85 ____ Notice of Motion in Court of Appeals for Reargument of Motion for Leave to Appeal.
39.86 ____ Notice of Motion in Court of Appeals for Leave to Appear *Amicus Curiae.*
39.87 ____ Notice of Motion to Dismiss Appeal as Untimely Taken.
39.88 ____ Affidavit in Support of Motion to Dismiss Appeal as Untimely Taken.
39.89 ____ CPLR 5531 Statement.
39.90 ____ Letter Seeking Leave to Appeal in Criminal Case.

	Page
Table of Jury Instructions	235
Table of Forms	236
Table of Statutes	iii
Table of Rules	iii
Table of Cases	iii
Index	iii

WEST'S NEW YORK PRACTICE SERIES
GENERAL PRACTICE IN NEW YORK

Volume 25

Chapter 38

CRIMINAL APPELLATE PRACTICE BEFORE THE APPELLATE DIVISION AND OTHER INTERMEDIATE APPELLLATE COURTS

by
The Honorable Albert M. Rosenblatt
Stuart M. Cohen
Martin H. Brownstein

Table of Sections

38.1	Scope Note.
38.2	Strategy.
38.3	Appeals to the Appellate Division—General Principles.
38.4	___ Courts of Original Jurisdiction From Which Appeals Lie.
38.5	___ Who May Appeal.
38.6	___ ___ Status as Aggrieved by "Adverse" Determination.
38.7	___ ___ Appeals by the Defendant From Superior Courts.
38.8	___ ___ ___ As of Right.
38.9	___ ___ ___ Appeals by Permission.
38.10	___ ___ Appeals by the People.
38.11	___ ___ Appeals from Orders Accepting or Sealing Grand Jury Reports; Appeals by Prosecutors; Appeals by Public Servants.
38.12	___ Appeal Process—Appeals as of Right.
38.13	___ ___ Appeals by Permission: Certificate Granting Leave.
38.14	___ ___ Extensions of Time.
38.15	___ ___ Stay of Judgment or Order.
38.16	___ ___ Poor Person Relief and Assignment of Counsel.
38.17	___ ___ Perfecting and Calendaring the Appeal.
38.18	___ Scope of Review.
38.19	___ ___ Questions of Law.
38.20	___ ___ Questions of Fact; Weight of Evidence.
38.21	___ ___ Interest of Justice/Discretion.
38.22	___ ___ Change in Law While Case Pending.
38.23	___ Disposition of Appeal.
38.24	___ ___ Affirmance.
38.25	___ ___ Modification.
38.26	___ ___ Reversal.

38.27 _____ _____ Character of Order of Reversal or Modification: On the Law, On the Facts, in the Interest of Justice.
38.28 _____ _____ Corrective Action.
38.29 _____ Post-disposition Proceedings.
38.30 _____ _____ Responsibilities of Counsel.
38.31 _____ _____ Reargument.
38.32 _____ _____ Leave to Appeal.
38.33 _____ _____ *Certiorari* to U.S. Supreme Court.
38.34 _____ _____ *Coram Nobis*—Ineffective Assistance of Appellate Counsel.
38.35 _____ _____ Clarification/Resettlement.
38.36 _____ Motions in Connection With Appeals—Generally.
38.37 _____ _____ *Pro Se* Supplemental Brief.
38.38 _____ _____ *Anders* Brief.
38.39 _____ _____ Dismissal.
38.40 _____ _____ Reconstruction Hearing; Summary Reversal.
38.41 _____ _____ Death or Absence of a Defendant.
38.42 _____ _____ Assignment of New Counsel.
38.43 _____ _____ Expanding the Judgment Roll.
38.44 _____ _____ Briefs.
38.45 _____ _____ Withdrawal of Appeal.
38.46 Appeals to Intermediate Appellate Courts Other Than the Appellate Division.
38.47 _____ Appeals From Village Courts, Town Courts, City Courts and District Courts.
38.48 _____ Appeals From Criminal Court of the City of New York.
38.49 _____ _____ New York and Bronx County Branches.
38.50 _____ _____ Kings, Queens, Richmond County Branches.
38.51 _____ Orders, Sentences and Judgments Appealable.
38.52 _____ Taking the Appeal—Appeal as of Right.
38.53 _____ _____ Appeals by Permission.
38.54 _____ Stays Pending Appeal.
38.55 _____ Perfecting the Appeal.
38.56 _____ Determination of the Appeal.
38.57 Governance of the Appellate Term.
38.58 Original Application to County Court for Change of Venue.
38.59 Procedural Checklist for Appeals to Appellate Division.
38.60 Forms—Notice of Motion for a Stay of Execution of Judgment. 💾
38.61 _____ Affirmation in Support of Motion for a Stay of Execution of Judgment. 💾
38.62 _____ Notice of Motion for an Extension of Time to Take an Appeal. 💾
38.63 _____ Affirmation in Support of Motion for an Extension of Time to Take an Appeal. 💾
38.64 Chart.

WESTLAW Electronic Research

See WESTLAW Electronic Research Guide preceding the Summary of Contents.

§ 38.1 Scope Note

This chapter discusses criminal appeals to the appellate division and other intermediate appellate courts.[1] The discussion begins with a review of the courts of original jurisdiction from which appeals to the appellate division lie.[2] Next, standing to appeal is analyzed.[3] The appeals process is reviewed, including the procedures required for appeals by permission of the court.[4]

The chapter addresses the scope of review of the appellate division,[5] as well as the possible dispositions of an appeal,[6] and post-dispositional proceedings.[7] Motions in connection with appeals in criminal cases are analyzed.[8] Also included are appeals to intermediate appellate courts other than the appellate division.[9] The chapter concludes with a practice checklist,[10] forms which are designed to guide the practitioner through this process,[11] and a chart.[12]

Civil appeals to the appellate division, as well as appeals to the Court of Appeals, are considered in other chapters. Civil appeals to the appellate division and to other intermediate appellate courts are addressed in Chapter 37. Civil and criminal appeals to the Court of Appeals are reviewed in Chapter 39.[13]

§ 38.2 Strategy

Criminal case appeals differ considerably from civil case appeals in a number of ways that are important to appellate counsel. To begin with, a great many criminal case appeals do not involve the question of financial expense, because an appreciable percentage of them involve indigent defendants whose cases are handled by public defenders, legal aid lawyers, and attorneys assigned at public expense. Similarly, a defendant who qualifies financially is entitled to a transcript of the proceedings at public expense.[1] Also bear in mind that a defendant may (with financial help from family or friends) be able to hire an appellate lawyer, and still be able to acquire a transcript at public expense if the defendant is indigent. Counsel should apply for that limited form of relief when appropriate.[2]

§ 38.1

1. Note that the chapter does not discuss the structure of the judiciary, the administrative powers of the appellate division, and the statutory framework of the appellate system and the rules of the appellate courts. See supra, §§ 37.3–37.13 for a full exposition of these important issues.
2. See infra, § 38.4.
3. See infra, §§ 38.5–38.11.
4. See infra, §§ 38.12–38.17.
5. See infra, §§ 38.18–38.22.
6. See infra, §§ 38.23–38.28.
7. See infra, §§ 38.29–38.35.
8. See infra, §§ 38.36–38.45.
9. See infra, §§ 38.46–38.58.
10. See infra, § 38.59.
11. See infra, §§ 38.60–38.63.
12. See infra, §§ 38.64.
13. See also, Marks, et al., New York Pretrial Criminal Procedure (West 1996); Greenberg, Marcus et al., New York Criminal Law (West 1996). See Chapter 33 "Local Criminal Court Practice," supra.

§ 38.2

1. See infra, § 38.16.
2. See id.

In non-indigent cases, the basic considerations parallel those of civil appeals (*i.e.*, cost-benefit analysis and the like),[3] but a chief difference between criminal and civil appeals deals with questions of appealability. In civil cases in New York State, the door to appellate review is open far wider than it is in federal practice or state criminal appellate practice. As we have seen in civil cases, there are so many opportunities to appeal at various stages along the way[4] that the cost-benefit analysis is pivotal. No such opportunities to appeal exist in the criminal appellate sphere. The vast majority of appeals by defendants are from judgments of conviction by plea or verdict.[5] A primary issue that appellate counsel must determine is whether the matter is appealable at all.[6]

In weighing the chances of success in criminal case appeals the practitioner must examine two paramount considerations that will often govern the outcome, notably "preservation" and "harmless error." These doctrines are employed with great frequency in criminal appeals. For that reason the practitioner, in identifying claims of error, should carefully review the record with an eye toward whether a claimed error has been preserved by adequate objection or protest.[7] If it has not been preserved, the appellate division may entertain the point nonetheless and should be asked to do so under the court's "interest of justice" powers[8] and the brief should be cast accordingly. Furthermore, there are instances in which an error is considered grave enough that a protest or objection is not necessary to preserve the point and counsel should be familiar with these exceptions.[9]

The same holds true for harmless error:[10] Counsel should be familiar with the hierarchy of errors under New York's decisional law. An error may be considered harmless or not, to the extent that the appellate court believes it to have affected the substantial rights of the appellant.[11] Counsel should discern whether the claimed error is of constitutional magnitude, in which case it will occasion reversal unless it is harmless beyond a reasonable doubt.[12] Counsel should also be aware of whether an error is considered so serious that it is not amenable to the harmless error doctrine at all. In such a case the question of prejudice to the defendant is irrelevant, and the appeal would be argued on the basis that automatic reversal is warranted.[13]

Attorneys should also be aware of the existence of any purported waiver of appeal. A great many guilty pleas are the product of negotiations, and the plea is agreed to by the court and the prosecutor on the condition that the defendant is foreclosed from appealing all or part of

3. *See supra*, § 37.2.
4. *See, e.g., supra*, §§ 37.33, 37.35, 37.36
5. *See infra*, § 38.8.
6. *See infra*, §§ 38.5 *et seq.*
7. *See infra*, § 38.19.
8. *See infra*, § 38.21.
9. *See infra*, § 38.19.
10. CPL § 470.05(1).
11. CPL § 470.05(1).
12. *See infra*, § 38.19.
13. *Id.*

what would otherwise be appealable. Counsel should determine the extent of the waiver, its integrity, and its validity. The waiver agreement, if valid, may extend to the right to appeal a negotiated sentence or an otherwise appealable adverse suppression order.[14]

In addition to these express waivers, appellate review will be denied to the defendant who has pleaded guilty and has thereby automatically forfeited the right to question the propriety of a host of rulings. We list them in Section 38.8 along with the exceptions. Counsel should know both before undertaking an appeal. A defendant's appellate attorney should also consider the prospect of appeal from a sentence only, and, when available, utilize the expedited review procedures that are detailed in Section 38.8.

One should also consider the unhappy possibility of a hollow victory for the defendant. A defendant's appellate counsel may succeed in identifying and overturning a favorable but defective guilty plea, only to find that the defendant would then face trial on the original, more serious charge, with commensurately greater exposure. Restoration to pre-plea status may thus turn out to be a disservice to the client.

§ 38.3 Appeals to the Appellate Division—General Principles

The United States Constitution does not guarantee a party's right to appeal; it is a matter left to the states.[1] In New York, criminal appeals are regulated by statute. They are governed by Criminal Procedure Law (hereinafter "CPL") Articles 450, 460, and 470.[2] Long established decisional law has held the right of appeal to be statutory, as the court stated in *People v. Reed*:[3]

> Appeal to the Appellate Division and to the Court of Appeals is entirely a matter of statute (*People v. Zerillo*, 200 N.Y. 443, 93 N.E. 1108). There is no constitutional right to an appeal from a judgment of conviction or of an acquittal or from any ruling of the trial judge. All appeal is a matter of legislative control. Review by the United States Supreme Court of a trial in a State court which deprived a defendant of the equal protection of the laws or of due process is not prevented by failure of the State Legislature to provide an appeal to higher State courts.

14. *See infra*, § 38.8.

§ 38.3
1. McKane v. Durston, 153 U.S. 684, 687, 14 S.Ct. 913, 914, 38 L.Ed. 867 (1894). *See* D.J. Meltzer, *State Court Forfeitures of Federal Rights*, 99 Harv.L.Rev. 1128, 1165 (1986).

2. CPL Article 450 relates to appealability, CPL Article 460 to the mode of taking appeals, and CPL Article 470 relates to determinations of appeals.

3. 276 N.Y. 5, 10, 11 N.E.2d 330, 332 (1937). *See also*, People v. Trezza, 128 N.Y. 529, 532, 28 N.E. 533, 534 (1891).

The New York State Constitution authorizes an appeal as of right to the Court of Appeals in a capital case,[4] and it sets up the apparatus for appellate jurisdiction including appeals to the appellate division.[5] The appellate scheme is, however, said to be "purely statutory."[6] Similar language has been employed as to the right of appeal in civil cases, holding it to be statutory only, to be given or taken away by the legislature.[7] The early cases did not include appellate review as integral to the scheme of "due process."[8] Later criminal cases, however, have spoken of a "fundamental" right to appeal a conviction[9] or an "absolute" right to do so.[10]

Given these varied expressions, the question may not be answered definitively, considering further that the Court of Appeals in *People v. Pollenz*[11] interpreted Article VI, Section 4(k) of the State Constitution as implicitly prohibiting the Legislature from restricting direct appeal (by the defendant to the appellate division) from a final judgment. The Court of Appeals left open the question of whether a defendant has a "due process" right to appellate division review of a conviction under Article I, § 6 of the State Constitution.[12] In sum, it is probably best to say that "the right to appeal depends on express [state] constitutional or statutory authorization."[13]

Because appeals to the appellate division from interlocutory orders are so freely available in civil cases in New York,[14] the general prohibition on interlocutory appeals in criminal cases is a major point of departure from civil appellate practice. Subject to some exceptions, this

---

4. N.Y. Constitution, Art. VI, § 3(b); In re Ryan, 306 N.Y. 11, 16, 114 N.E.2d 183, 185 (1953).

5. N.Y. Constitution, Art. VI, §§ 4, 5 (consider particularly Subdivision 4(k)).

6. *See* People v. Gersewitz, 294 N.Y. 163, 166, 61 N.E.2d 427, 428 (1945), cert. dismissed 326 U.S. 687, 66 S.Ct. 89, 90 L.Ed. 404 (1945); People v. Zerillo, 200 N.Y. 443, 446, 93 N.E. 1108, 1109. *See also*, State v. King, 36 N.Y.2d 59, 63, 364 N.Y.S.2d 879, 881, 324 N.E.2d 351, 353 (1975); People v. De Jesus, 54 N.Y.2d 447, 446 N.Y.S.2d 201, 430 N.E.2d 1254 (1981)(stating that in the absence of express statutory provisions there is no right of appeal in a criminal case in New York); and People v. Cousart, 58 N.Y.2d 62, 67, 458 N.Y.S.2d 507, 510, 444 N.E.2d 971, 974 (1982)(stating that the right to appeal a conviction rests not on common law grounds but on state statute).

7. *See, e.g.*, Croveno v. Atlantic Ave. R. Co. of Brooklyn, 150 N.Y. 225, 44 N.E. 968 (1896).

8. *See* People ex rel. Welch v. Bard, 209 N.Y. 304, 103 N.E. 140 (1913).

9. *See* People v. Montgomery, 24 N.Y.2d 130, 132, 299 N.Y.S.2d 156, 157, 247 N.E.2d 130, 131 (1969).

10. People v. Rivera, 39 N.Y.2d 519, 522, 384 N.Y.S.2d 726, 727, 349 N.E.2d 825, 826 (1976).

11. 67 N.Y.2d 264, 502 N.Y.S.2d 417, 493 N.E.2d 541 (1986).

12. 67 N.Y.2d 264, 268 note 3, 502 N.Y.S.2d 417, 419, note 3, 493 N.E.2d 541, 543, note 3 (1986).

13. Friedman v. State, 24 N.Y.2d 528, 535, 301 N.Y.S.2d 484, 486, 249 N.E.2d 369, 371 (1969), appeal dismissed 397 U.S. 317, 90 S.Ct. 1121, 25 L.Ed.2d 337 (1970).

14. Compare the federal practice in which such appeals are not authorized: Wilton v. Seven Falls Co., 515 U.S. 277, 115 S.Ct. 2137, 132 L.Ed.2d 214 (1995); Firestone Tire & Rubber Co. v. Risjord, 449 U.S. 368, 101 S.Ct. 669, 66 L.Ed.2d 571 (1981); Stringfellow v. Concerned Neighbors in Action, 480 U.S. 370, 107 S.Ct. 1177, 94 L.Ed.2d 389 (1987); 28 U.S.C.A. 1291.

prohibition in criminal cases has a long established statutory history.[15] Within the constitutional framework, the Legislature may expand or contract the jurisdiction of the appellate division, and with it the opportunity of a defendant to appeal from *non*-final orders.[16] Generally speaking, no separate appeal by the defendant lies from an *order* arising out of a "criminal proceeding" absent statutory authorization,[17] but the appeal from the final *judgment* will bring up the interlocutory order for review.[18]

There are exceptions to this rule under certain statutes.[19] CPL Article 450 is far more particular in enumerating the instances in which appeals may be taken than its civil counterpart.[20] Unlike CPLR 5701(a)(2)(iv) and (v), which contain catch-all provisions with generous allowances for appealability, CPL Article 450 strictly limits the types of orders and judgments that are appealable. It follows, therefore, that these statutes must be strictly construed.[21] It is important to distinguish a criminal case from a civil case, so as to be generally subject to the strictures of the CPL rather than the more permissive appealability provisions of the CPLR.

A criminal proceeding is defined in CPL § 1.20 as any proceeding "which ... (b) occurs in a criminal court and is related to a ... criminal action ... or ... involves a criminal investigation." But that is only the beginning of the inquiry.

Definitions are sometimes elusive, and when presented with hybrid cases the courts look to the "true nature of the proceeding" and to the relief sought, in order to determine whether the proceeding is criminal or civil.[22] Circumstances vary and the overlapping characteristics of the proceedings have generated a body of case law on the subject. For example, an appeal was dismissed as criminal in nature in a proceeding to compel a prosecutor to inquire of federal authorities as to eavesdropping surveillance.[23] An order directing a defendant to appear in a

15. In re Ryan, 306 N.Y. 11, 114 N.E.2d 183 (1953).

16. N.Y. Constitution, Art. VI, § 4(k). See also, People v. Farrell, 85 N.Y.2d 60, 623 N.Y.S.2d 550, 647 N.E.2d 762 (1995); People v. Pollenz, 67 N.Y.2d 264, 268, 502 N.Y.S.2d 417, 419, 493 N.E.2d 541, 543 (1986).

17. People v. Santos, 64 N.Y.2d 702, 485 N.Y.S.2d 524, 474 N.E.2d 1192 (1984).

18. People v. Gibbs, 21 A.D.2d 980, 243 N.Y.S.2d 492 (2d Dep't 1963); People v. Grubbs, 1 A.D.2d 1035, 152 N.Y.S.2d 46 (2d Dep't 1956), cert. denied 358 U.S. 854, 79 S.Ct. 84, 3 L.Ed.2d 88 (1958).

19. A provision in the new death penalty statute allows only the prosecution to appeal from a finding that the defendant is mentally retarded. CPL § 450.20(10). See also, CPL § 450.20 as to other appeals as of right by the prosecution, from non-final orders.

20. CPLR Art. 57.

21. People v. Zerillo, 200 N.Y. 443, 93 N.E. 1108 (1911).

22. Matter of Abrams, 62 N.Y.2d 183, 191, 476 N.Y.S.2d 494, 498, 465 N.E.2d 1, 5 (1984).

23. See, e.g., Santangello v. People, 38 N.Y.2d 536, 381 N.Y.S.2d 472, 344 N.E.2d 404 (1976).

line-up was also held to be criminal in nature and therefore not appealable to the appellate division.[24]

In *Cunningham v. Nadjari*,[25] an order denying *vacatur* of a grand jury subpoena in a criminal investigation was held appealable as a final order on the *civil* side.[26] A judgment that denies a motion to quash a subpoena issued to a third party by a criminal court in a criminal trial is appealable as a civil side order, but that rule does not apply in the absence of a written subpoena or a written motion to quash, and the appeal was dismissed in *People v. McDonald*.[27]

Another significant difference between civil and criminal appeals is the statutory distinction drawn between prosecution and defense appeals. Whereas under the CPLR the right to appeal does not depend on whether one is the defendant or plaintiff, it matters under the CPL. CPL Article 450 deals with who may appeal and the courts to which appeals are taken. CPL Article 460 deals with how to bring and perfect an appeal, and Article 470 deals with the determination of an appeal.

In a civil case the appellate division has broad powers of review concerning the arguments of a respondent urging affirmance.[28] The appellate division does not enjoy a similar power in criminal cases. The CPLR expressly permits consideration of "any non-final judgment or order ... including any which was adverse to the respondent on the appeal from the final judgment and which, if reversed, would entitle the respondent to prevail in whole or in part on that appeal ..."[29] The CPL, however, limits the appellate division's review to "any question of law or issue of fact involving error or defect in the criminal court proceedings *which may have adversely affected the appellant.*"[30]

There is also a difference in the origin of the court's interest of justice jurisdiction in civil and criminal cases. In criminal cases it is granted by statute[31] whereas in civil cases it springs from decisional law

24. Matter of Alphonso C. v. Morgenthau, 38 N.Y.2d 923, 382 N.Y.S.2d 980, 346 N.E.2d 819 (1976). *See also*, People v. Santos, 64 N.Y.2d 702, 485 N.Y.S.2d 524, 474 N.E.2d 1192 (1984); People v. Johnson, 103 A.D.2d 754, 477 N.Y.S.2d 225 (2d Dep't 1984)(differentiating between quashing subpoena before or after a criminal action is commenced); People v. Lincoln, 109 A.D.2d 1044, 487 N.Y.S.2d 164 (3d Dep't 1985)(appeal dismissed from order disqualifying defendant's attorney).

25. 39 N.Y.2d 314, 383 N.Y.S.2d 590, 347 N.E.2d 915 (1976).

26. *See also*, Matter of Abrams, 62 N.Y.2d 183, 191, 476 N.Y.S.2d 494, 498, 465 N.E.2d 1, 5 (1984)(orders issued by criminal term of supreme court denying motion to quash subpoena and to disqualify an attorney in Attorney General's investigation into illegal ticket sales held appealable, as civil in nature).

27. 199 A.D.2d 539, 606 N.Y.S.2d 252 (2d Dep't 1993), appeal denied 83 N.Y.2d 1005, 616 N.Y.S.2d 486, 640 N.E.2d 154 (1994).

28. *See* Parochial Bus Systems, Inc. v. Board of Educ. of City of New York, 60 N.Y.2d 539, 545–546, 470 N.Y.S.2d 564, 567, 458 N.E.2d 1241, 1244 (1983).

29. CPLR 5501(a)(1).

30. CPL § 470.15(1)(emphasis added); People v. Goodfriend, 64 N.Y.2d 695, 485 N.Y.S.2d 519, 474 N.E.2d 1187 (1984).

31. CPL § 470.15(3)(c).

§ 38.3   CRIMINAL APPELLATE PRACTICE   Ch. 38

as an inherent power of the court.[32]

Moreover, in criminal cases the appellate division has the authority to review a sentence, and if in its discretion it believes it to be excessive, it may impose a legally authorized lesser sentence.[33] In civil cases the appellate division does not directly reduce verdicts, so that there is no exact parallel. It does, however, have the power to order a new trial unless the parties stipulate to a lesser or greater amount.[34]

§ 38.4 Appeals to the Appellate Division—Courts of Original Jurisdiction From Which Appeals Lie

In criminal cases, the appellate division entertains appeals emanating only from the supreme and county courts. The supreme court has jurisdiction over criminal cases as a court of "original, unlimited, unqualified" jurisdiction in both criminal and civil cases.[1] At present, felony prosecutions in New York City are tried in supreme court with judges who are elected justices of the supreme court, or who are acting supreme court justices by way of administrative assignment from, most typically, the criminal court, the civil court, and the Court of Claims.[2]

The county court exists in every county outside of New York City, and among other things, hears criminal cases as a court of original jurisdiction. Its status as a court of original jurisdiction stems from the Constitution.[3] Most appeals to the appellate division from county courts are by defendants, upon judgments of conviction. CPL § 450.10 authorizes a defendant to take such an appeal from a "criminal court" (which includes supreme court and county court under CPL §§ 10.10 (1), (2)) to an intermediate appellate court (which includes the appellate division).[4] The routing provision is CPL § 450.60. Criminal case appeals from supreme court must go to the appellate division by virtue of CPL § 450.60(1); criminal case appeals from county court must go to the appellate division by virtue of CPL § 450.60(2).

The appellate division, however, has no jurisdiction to hear an appeal from a county court that served as an appellate court[5] reviewing a city court (or town or village court) judgment of conviction.[6] Any further

---

32. Gowdey v. Robbins, 3 App.Div. 353, 356, 38 N.Y.S. 280 (2d Dep't 1896). See supra, § 37.28.

33. CPL § 470.15(6)(b), 470.20(6).

34. See supra, §§ 37.29, 37.65.

§ 38.4

1. People v. Darling, 50 A.D.2d 1038, 377 N.Y.S.2d 718 (3d Dep't 1975); Vazquez v. Vazquez, 26 A.D.2d 701, 273 N.Y.S.2d 12 (2d Dep't 1966); N.Y. Const. Art. VI, § 7.

2. N.Y. Constitution, Art. VI, § 26.

3. N.Y. Constitution, Art. VI, § 11.

4. CPL § 1.20(22).

5. See CPL § 450.60(3).

6. People v. Catalfano, 228 App.Div. 112, 239 N.Y.S. 165 (4th Dep't 1930)(decided under earlier version of statute).

appeal from the county court may go only to the Court of Appeals, and only by permission of a judge of the Court of Appeals.[7]

Library References:

West's Key No. Digests, Criminal Law ⚖1022.

§ 38.5 Appeals to the Appellate Division—Who May Appeal

In New York every accusatory instrument, regardless of the person designated as the accuser, constitutes an accusation on behalf of the state, which is denominated as the *"plaintiff"* against a named person, known as the *"defendant."*[1] All prosecutions therefore are entitled *The People of the State of New York* against a designated *defendant*, regardless of whether the accusatory instrument is a superior court indictment,[2] a local criminal court information,[3] a prosecutor's information filed in a local criminal court,[4] a superior court information filed in a superior court,[5] a misdemeanor complaint filed in a local criminal court,[6] or a felony complaint filed with a local criminal court.[7]

The party appealing is designated the appellant.[8] The adverse party is the respondent.[9] Those designations, by Court Rule in the First and Second Departments, follow the designations of the parties in the action at the trial level, thus: Plaintiff–Respondent, Defendant–Appellant, as the case may be.[10] The Third and Fourth Departments also refer to appellants and respondents.[11]

The right of appeal by either the People or the defendant is governed by statute.[12] The ensuing discussions begin with an explanation of a prerequisite to an appeal, notably that the party seeking to appeal be "aggrieved" by an "adverse" determination.[13] Following that, the criminal appellate universe is divided into its two components, notably, appeals by the defendant[14] and appeals by the People,[15] followed by a discussion of appeals that relate to grand jury reports involving public servants.[16]

7. CPL § 460.20(2)(b).

§ 38.5

1. CPL § 1.20(1).
2. CPL § 1.20(3).
3. CPL §§ 1.20(2),(4).
4. CPL § 1.20(6).
5. CPL § 1.20(3–a).
6. CPL § 1.20(7).
7. CPL § 1.20(8).
8. CPLR 5511; CPL §§ 450.90, 460.10(1)(b),(c).
9. CPLR 5511; CPL §§ 450.90, 460.10(3).
10. See 22 NYCRR § 600.10(a)(5)(First Department); 22 NYCRR § 670.10(a)(3)(Second Department).
11. See 22 NYCRR §§ 800.8, 800.14(b)(Third Department); 22 NYCRR § 1000.3(c)(1)(Fourth Department).
12. CPL Arts. 450, 460, 470.
13. See infra, § 38.6.
14. See infra, §§ 38.7–38.9.
15. See infra, § 38.10.
16. See infra, § 38.11.

§ 38.5   CRIMINAL APPELLATE PRACTICE   Ch. 38

The format is designed to carry the practitioner through the various stages of the appeal, including taking the appeal, perfecting, and calendaring it.[17] The scope of appellate review is then considered,[18] followed by treatment of the various dispositions possible,[19] and the post-disposition proceedings.[20] Motion practice runs throughout the entire appellate practice, but for ease of application, sections on motion practice have been included.[21]

Library References:

West's Key No. Digests, Criminal Law ⟲1023.5.

§ 38.6   Appeals to the Appellate Division—Who May Appeal—Status as Aggrieved by "Adverse" Determination

To gain appellate review in a criminal case the appellant must be "aggrieved." Sometimes the word "adverse" is used (it has much the same meaning), as in CPL § 450.90, which speaks of the Court of Appeals review from "adverse or partially adverse" appellate division orders.[1] In *People v. Jackson*[2] the defendant's appeal was dismissed because the defendant, who wanted a dismissal, was not adversely affected by a reversal order directing a new trial. The concept is the same as in civil case appeals and is generally based on the principle that the overworked appellate machinery should not be switched on unless the appellant is aggrieved within the meaning of the statute as interpreted by decisional law.

The requirement that an appellant be aggrieved before appealing to the appellate division (or to any intermediate appellate court) is not an express statutory command. It has developed in decisional law based, no doubt, on the premise that an appeal from a determination that is not adverse would in essence be a request for an advisory opinion.[3] The rule that an appellant be aggrieved applies equally to the defendant and the People. Defendants' appeals or cross-appeals have been dismissed, for example, in *People v. Hansel*[4] and *People v. Hendry*,[5] where the defendants were not aggrieved by orders dismissing the indictments; and in *People v. Skinner*,[6] where the defendant's acquittal on the burglary count

---

17. *See infra*, §§ 38.12–38.17.
18. *See infra*, §§ 38.18–38.22.
19. *See infra*, §§ 38.23–38.28.
20. *See infra*, §§ 38.29–38.35.
21. *See infra*, §§ 38.36–38.45.

§ 38.6

1. *See, e.g.*, People v. Griminger, 71 N.Y.2d 635, 641, 529 N.Y.S.2d 55, 58, 524 N.E.2d 409, 412 (1988).
2. 80 N.Y.2d 112, 589 N.Y.S.2d 300, 602 N.E.2d 1116 (1992).

3. *See supra*, § 37.22 as to the same concept in civil case appeals.
4. 208 A.D.2d 1112, 617 N.Y.S.2d 542 (3d Dep't 1994).
5. 15 A.D.2d 784, 224 N.Y.S.2d 460 (2d Dep't 1962).
6. 200 A.D.2d 782, 606 N.Y.S.2d 792 (3d Dep't 1994), appeal denied 83 N.Y.2d 858, 612 N.Y.S.2d 390, 634 N.E.2d 991 (1994).

limited the appeal to challenges to the remaining charge. Note, however, that under *People v. Daghita*[7] a defendant is held to be aggrieved if one of the counts of a concurrent sentence is not sustained by the record, but the conviction on the other count is.

Similarly, appeals by the People have been dismissed owing to their non-aggrieved status. For example, in *People v. Skinner*[8] and in *People v. Strudwick*,[9] the People were not aggrieved by dismissals of indictments based on their motions. The condition of being aggrieved is a term of art with regard to appeals. The absence of a grievance will result in dismissal of the appeal or of so much of it as is not grievance based. There are, of course, other ways in which parties may or may not be "aggrieved." In common parlance, and often in legal parlance, the status of being aggrieved means something different from being aggrieved for appellate purposes. For example, in *People v. Mitchell*,[10] the court said that the defendant was not "aggrieved" by an allegedly unlawful search in that he lacked "standing" (*i.e.*, had no reasonable expectation of privacy) and affirmed the conviction. This was a determination made after review, and of course it did not result in dismissal of the defendant's appeal—as it would if he were not "aggrieved" in the appellate sense. In the appellate sense he was aggrieved aplenty: he was convicted and sentenced. But because of his lack of standing he had no constitutional grievance and his conviction was reviewed and affirmed.[11]

Library References:

West's Key No. Digests, Criminal Law ⚖1135.

§ 38.7 Appeals to the Appellate Division—Who May Appeal—Appeals by Defendant From Superior Courts

The following sections will detail, respectively, what judgments and orders may be appealed by the defendant, and by the People. In New York, the largest body of law in criminal cases relates to appeals from felony level trial courts (*i.e.*, county and supreme courts) to the appellate division. Because the appeals relate to two parties, and two parties only, (the defendant and the prosecution), the sections to follow begin with a treatment of defendants' appeals to the appellate division. Appeals by the People are discussed later.[1]

7. 276 App.Div. 20, 92 N.Y.S.2d 799 (3d Dep't 1949), modified 301 N.Y. 223, 93 N.E.2d 649 (1950).
8. 200 A.D.2d 782, 606 N.Y.S.2d 792 (3d Dep't 1994), appeal denied 83 N.Y.2d 858, 612 N.Y.S.2d 390, 634 N.E.2d 991 (1994).
9. People v. Strudwick, 170 A.D.2d 969, 565 N.Y.S.2d 944 (4th Dep't 1991).

10. People v. Mitchell, 75 A.D.2d 626, 426 N.Y.S.2d 833 (2d Dep't 1980).

11. *Id.*

§ 38.7

1. *See infra*, § 38.10.

§ 38.7   CRIMINAL APPELLATE PRACTICE   Ch. 38

Library References:
West's Key No. Digests, Criminal Law ⚖=1026.

§ 38.8   Appeals to the Appellate Division—Who May Appeal—Appeals by Defendant From Superior Courts—As of Right

An appeal "as of right" affords the convicted defendant an automatic appeal, with no need to seek permission of any judge or court. There are four instances in which a defendant may take an appeal as of right to the appellate division from a criminal court.[1]

Appeal From Judgment; Waiver by Defendant. The first of the appeals as of right is one from a *judgment* of conviction other than one including a sentence of death.[2]

CPL § 450.10(1) is a core appellate section of the CPL, and takes in the bulk of appellate business. It is not the last word—that belongs to the Court of Appeals—but in terms of volume and writing, the books are heaviest with appeals to the appellate division's four departments from judgments of conviction rendered upon trials or pleas in county court and supreme court. The appeal from the judgment of conviction[3] is the vehicle by which the defendant seeks and gains review of the sentence, as well as the other components of the judgment, including the verdict (from which no separate appeal lies)[4] and all of the preserved claims of error.[5] It is the judgment that is appealable; it is the event by which and the repository into which all otherwise non-appealable intermediate orders are gathered in for review. Phrases like "there is no appeal from this intermediate order but it may be brought up for review on appeal from the final judgment" are the essence of CPL § 450.10(1)'s purpose.

Until sentence is pronounced, there is no judgment and hence there may be no appeal.[6] The rendition of the judgment, *i.e.*, the imposition of the sentence, is the triggering event from which the time to take an appeal begins to run.[7]

Although the right to appeal the judgment (or the sentence)[8] is described in unconditional terms, those rights, like other rights, may be waived, or bargained away. The practice of negotiating appellate rights

---

§ 38.8

1. By criminal court, the Legislature means a court of original instance, notably, the supreme court and the county court. See CPL §§ 1.20(19), 10.10(1). Both are the only trial level courts designated in the CPL as superior courts. See CPL § 10.10(2).
2. CPL § 450.10(1).
3. CPL § 450.10.
4. People v. Berger, 1 A.D.2d 897, 149 N.Y.S.2d 480 (2d Dep't 1956).

5. As to the preservation requirement, see *infra*, § 38.19.
6. People v. Cioffi, 1 N.Y.2d 70, 150 N.Y.S.2d 192, 133 N.E.2d 703 (1956). See also, People ex rel. Emanuel v. McMann, 7 N.Y.2d 342, 344, 197 N.Y.S.2d 174, 175, 165 N.E.2d 187, 188 (1960).
7. See CPL § 460.10. See also *infra*, § 38.12.
8. See CPL § 450.10(2).

began with *People v. Williams*,[9] and *People v. Esajerre*,[10] in which the defendant and the prosecutor were permitted to stipulate (based typically on a guilty plea both sides found agreeable) that the defendant would forego the right to review of an adverse suppression order that would otherwise be reviewable on an appeal from a judgment of conviction, notwithstanding the guilty plea.[11] Under that practice, and with finality in mind, both sides agreed to the disposition, thereby rendering unassailable the suppression order that would otherwise be brought up for review on appeal from the judgment. Beginning in the mid–1970's this practice gained popularity and continued for several years until it broadened so as to put up for negotiation and waiver not only the defendant's adverse suppression order but the defendant's right to appeal the judgment or sentence itself. The Court of Appeals approved these wider waivers in *People v. Seaberg*.[12] It is now settled that a prosecutor may exact a waiver of defendant's right to appeal a judgment or sentence as a condition of offering a lesser plea,[13] and the same (of course) holds true for a waiver of a defendant's right to review of an adverse suppression order.[14]

A waiver of the right to appeal does not foreclose all review or inexorably lead to *dismissal* of the appeal. Even when there has been a purported waiver of appeal the defendant may raise, and the appellate division must review, a defendant's claim as to the sufficiency of the waiver in terms of its voluntariness and its underpinnings, including the knowing and intelligent waiver requirements.[15] Moreover, even though a valid waiver will foreclose review of most claims, there are exceptions, as when the defendant is raising a constitutional speedy trial claim[16] or when the waiver offends public policy.[17] Nor do such waivers foreclose review of a defendant's contention that he was denied effective assistance of counsel,[18] or a defendant's claim that the sentence was illegal.[19]

Similarly, a defendant does not waive his right to appeal the severity of his sentence when he was not made aware of its length prior to the

9. People v. Williams, 36 N.Y.2d 829, 370 N.Y.S.2d 904, 331 N.E.2d 684 (1975), cert. denied 423 U.S. 873, 96 S.Ct. 141, 46 L.Ed.2d 104 (1975).

10. 35 N.Y.2d 463, 363 N.Y.S.2d 931, 323 N.E.2d 175 (1974).

11. CPL § 710.70(2).

12. 74 N.Y.2d 1, 543 N.Y.S.2d 968, 541 N.E.2d 1022 (1989). *See also*, People v. Callahan, 80 N.Y.2d 273, 590 N.Y.S.2d 46, 604 N.E.2d 108 (1992).

13. People v. Sullivan, 223 A.D.2d 893, 636 N.Y.S.2d 221 (3d Dep't 1996); People v. Walker, 201 A.D.2d 896, 607 N.Y.S.2d 815 (4th Dep't 1994).

14. People v. Kirby, 216 A.D.2d 586, 628 N.Y.S.2d 567 (2d Dep't 1995); People v. Brewley, 211 A.D.2d 805, 621 N.Y.S.2d 922 (2d Dep't 1995).

15. People v. Callahan, 80 N.Y.2d 273, 590 N.Y.S.2d 46, 604 N.E.2d 108 (1992).

16. *Id.* at 281, 590 N.Y.S.2d at 50, 604 N.E.2d at 112.

17. *Id.* at 285, 590 N.Y.S.2d at 52, 604 N.E.2d at 114.

18. People v. Polanco, 216 A.D.2d 957, 629 N.Y.S.2d 583 (4th Dep't 1995).

19. People v. Cammarata, 216 A.D.2d 965, 629 N.Y.S.2d 716 (4th Dep't 1995); People v. White, 194 A.D.2d 1014, 600 N.Y.S.2d 642 (3d Dep't 1993).

§ 38.8 CRIMINAL APPELLATE PRACTICE Ch. 38

purported waiver,[20] or when the sentence was greater than negotiated, notwithstanding defendant's failing to appear at sentence after having been warned of the consequences.[21] In *People v. Evans*[22] the general waiver of appeal rights that the defendant executed did not effectively waive his right to claim on appeal that the amended sentence was unlawful as not being based on an updated presentence report.[23]

In the aftermath of *Callahan*[24] and *Seaberg*,[25] the appellate division has frequently affirmed judgments when it upheld waivers of the right to appeal the judgment of conviction and sentence.[26] Less frequently, the appellate division has found the waiver itself invalid,[27] but has long invoked the principle that a defendant who challenges the validity of the guilty plea but does not move to withdraw the guilty plea does not preserve a challenge to its sufficiency.[28] Most of the waivers follow guilty pleas,[29] but *Seaberg* goes further: even after a guilty verdict, the defendant and the prosecution may negotiate a lesser sentence in exchange for the defendant's waiving the right to appeal.[30]

While a notice of appeal may—and indeed should, to protect the client's rights—be filed on behalf of a defendant who has absconded, the appeal will be dismissed, inasmuch as the defendant will be unable to obey the mandate of the court if the judgment or sentence is affirmed.[31]

---

20. People v. Pickard, 216 A.D.2d 333, 627 N.Y.S.2d 988 (2d Dep't 1995); People v. Leach, 203 A.D.2d 484, 611 N.Y.S.2d 17 (2d Dep't 1994).

21. People v. Patterson, 211 A.D.2d 829, 621 N.Y.S.2d 672 (2d Dep't 1995).

22. 212 A.D.2d 628, 623 N.Y.S.2d 130 (2d Dep't 1995).

23. People v. Dorino, 200 A.D.2d 632, 606 N.Y.S.2d 741 (2d Dep't 1994) (citing CPL § 390.20(4)). See also, People v. Fisnar, 212 A.D.2d 628, 623 N.Y.S.2d 144 (2d Dep't 1995), appeal denied 85 N.Y.2d 972, 629 N.Y.S.2d 732, 653 N.E.2d 628 (1995).

24. 80 N.Y.2d 273, 590 N.Y.S.2d 46, 604 N.E.2d 108 (1992).

25. 74 N.Y.2d 1, 543 N.Y.S.2d 968, 541 N.E.2d 1022 (1989).

26. People v. Young, 221 A.D.2d 777, 634 N.Y.S.2d 409 (3d Dep't 1995); People v. Acevedo, 216 A.D.2d 476, 628 N.Y.S.2d 737 (2d Dep't 1995). See also, People v. Allen, 82 N.Y.2d 761, 763, 603 N.Y.S.2d 820, 821, 623 N.E.2d 1170, 1171 (1993)(defendant precluded from challenging severity of negotiated sentence).

27. People v. Dewberry, 223 A.D.2d 555, 636 N.Y.S.2d 1014 (2d Dep't 1996); People v. Rolon, 220 A.D.2d 543, 632 N.Y.S.2d 208 (2d Dep't 1995); People v. McCaskell, 206 A.D.2d 547, 615 N.Y.S.2d 55 (2d Dep't 1994); People v. Pressley, 202 A.D.2d 695, 610 N.Y.S.2d 828 (2d Dep't 1994); People v. Rendon, 208 A.D.2d 869, 618 N.Y.S.2d 554 (2d Dep't 1994); People v. Wright, 207 A.D.2d 566, 616 N.Y.S.2d 255 (2d Dep't 1994).

28. People v. Williams, 215 A.D.2d 1006, 626 N.Y.S.2d 346 (1st Dep't 1995); People v. Johnson, 214 A.D.2d 752, 625 N.Y.S.2d 944 (2d Dep't 1995), appeal denied 86 N.Y.2d 886, 635 N.Y.S.2d 952, 659 N.E.2d 775 (1995)(citing People v. Pellegrino, 60 N.Y.2d 636, 467 N.Y.S.2d 355, 454 N.E.2d 938 (1983)).

29. 74 N.Y.2d 1, 543 N.Y.S.2d 968, 541 N.E.2d 1022 (1989).

30. People v. Fields, 196 A.D.2d 550, 601 N.Y.S.2d 856 (2d Dep't 1993).

31. People v. Davis, 87 A.D.2d 578, 450 N.Y.S.2d 409 (2d Dep't 1982). See also, People v. Reyes, 214 A.D.2d 233, 632 N.Y.S.2d 123 (1st Dep't 1995)(holding that a defendant who absconds after pleading guilty may be sentenced when apprehended, with no loss of jurisdiction, notwithstanding the delay between the plea and the entry of the judgment of conviction upon sentencing).

If the defendant has been deported the appeal will be dismissed.[32] If the defendant returns to the state, counsel may move to vacate the order dismissing the appeal. If the defendant dies during the pendency of a direct appeal to the appellate division, the appeal abates.[33] It has been called "moot,"[34] but the correct disposition is "abatement."[35] On the other hand, a defendant is subject to the mootness doctrine when he challenges his sentence as harsh but has already served it.[36] Finally, as to appeals that raise no non-frivolous issues, a brief may be filed in accord with *Anders v. California*.[37]

Appeal From Sentence. The second category of a defendant's appeal as of right is set forth in CPL § 450.10(2), pursuant to which a convicted defendant has an appeal as of right from the *sentence* imposed. A sentence[38] means the imposition and entry of sentence upon a conviction. It is not the same as a judgment, which is comprised of a conviction *and* the sentence imposed thereon, and is completed by imposition and entry of the sentence.[39] A judgment is not complete and is not appealable until sentence is imposed. A sentence, however, is now separately appealable. Why? And why would a defendant appeal only a sentence? The defendant and the prosecutor may agree on a plea and sentence, leaving it for the court to either go along with it or, if unwilling, to let either side undo the guilty plea and be restored to pre-plea status.[40] In other instances the parties may agree on the plea only, leaving the sentence open to the court and possibly harsher than the defendant had hoped for or expected. In that event (or even if the defendant had agreed to the sentence) the defendant has a right[41] to have the appellate division review the sentence, and there have been instances in which the appellate division, as a matter of discretion in the interest of justice has reduced sentences imposed following guilty pleas.[42]

32. People v. Parmaklidis, 38 N.Y.2d 1005, 384 N.Y.S.2d 442, 348 N.E.2d 918 (1976); People v. Hernandez, 157 A.D.2d 854, 551 N.Y.S.2d 806 (2d Dep't 1990). *See also infra*, § 38.41.

33. People v. Mintz, 20 N.Y.2d 753, 283 N.Y.S.2d 120, 229 N.E.2d 712 (1967); People v. Baker, 221 A.D.2d 551, 635 N.Y.S.2d 481 (2d Dep't 1995); People v. Matteson, 75 N.Y.2d 745, 551 N.Y.S.2d 890, 551 N.E.2d 91 (1989).

34. People v. Coscia, 26 A.D.2d 649, 272 N.Y.S.2d 416 (2d Dep't 1966).

35. People v. Craig, 78 N.Y.2d 616, 623, 578 N.Y.S.2d 471, 473, 585 N.E.2d 783, 785 (1991). *See generally*, Abatement of State Criminal Case by Accused's Death Pending Appeal of Conviction, 80 A.L.R.4th 189.

36. People v. Mathison, 175 A.D.2d 966, 573 N.Y.S.2d 771 (3d Dep't 1991); People v. Ellsworth, 153 A.D.2d 965, 546 N.Y.S.2d 979 (3d Dep't 1989).

37. 386 U.S. 738, 87 S.Ct. 1396, 18 L.Ed.2d 493 (1967). *See infra*, § 38.38.

38. CPL § 1.20(14).

39. CPL § 1.20(15).

40. People v. Selikoff, 35 N.Y.2d 227, 360 N.Y.S.2d 623, 318 N.E.2d 784 (1974), cert. denied 419 U.S. 1122, 95 S.Ct. 806, 42 L.Ed.2d 822 (1975); People v. Farrar, 52 N.Y.2d 302, 437 N.Y.S.2d 961, 419 N.E.2d 864 (1981).

41. Waivable, as we have seen, but a right.

42. *See, e.g.*, People v. Johnson, 205 A.D.2d 344, 613 N.Y.S.2d 160 (1st Dep't 1994); People v. Hernandez, 143 A.D.2d 842, 533 N.Y.S.2d 488 (2d Dep't 1988); People v. Morales, 92 A.D.2d 575, 459 N.Y.S.2d 725 (2d Dep't 1983). By way of contrast, the People may appeal a sentence solely on the ground that it is invalid as a matter of law. People v. Cameron, 193 A.D.2d 752, 597

The Appellate Division, Second and Third Departments have, by rule, authorized a means of expedited review of sentences in certain instances. In the Second Department[43] when the only issue to be raised on appeal concerns the legality, propriety, or excessiveness of sentence, the appeal may be prosecuted by submitting a concise statement setting forth the reasons urged in support of the reversal or modification of the sentence. The statement must contain the information required by CPLR 5531 and 22 NYCRR § 670.10(d)(2)(viii) and a statement by counsel for the appellant that no other issues are asserted.

An appeal of this kind may be brought on as though it was a motion made in accordance with the provisions of 22 NYCRR § 670.5 and is placed on a special calendar for appeals submitted. The respondent must serve and file papers in opposition within 14 days after service of the motion papers.[44] The appellant is to submit the transcripts of sentence and the transcripts of the underlying plea or trial.[45] The parties are to file an original and four copies of their respective papers, including the necessary transcripts.[46]

The Third Department has a similar rule[47] when the sole question raised on appeal concerns the legality, propriety, or excessiveness of the sentence imposed. If so, the appeal may be heard upon a shortened record on appeal consisting of the notice of appeal, sentencing minutes, and minutes of the plea, if appellant pleaded guilty.[48] The record must be clearly labeled "Record on Appeal from Sentence," and must contain a statement pursuant to CPLR 5531 and is to be stipulated to or settled in the manner provided in 22 NYCRR § 800.7(b). The appeal shall be prosecuted in the manner provided for in the briefing schedule under 22 NYCRR § 800.14(b) and may be scheduled for oral argument or submission.[49] A copy of the presentence investigation report must be filed with the clerk.[50] In amending CPL § 450.10 in 1984[51] the Legislature endeavored, unsuccessfully, to eliminate "as of right" excessive sentence appeals that were based on sentences to which both sides had agreed. The statute[52] still includes those restrictions, but they were struck down by the Court of Appeals as an unconstitutional limitation on the power of the appellate division to review the "as of right" appeals from final judgments.[53] Accordingly Section 410.50(2) allows a challenge to a sentence, whether the sentence was agreed upon or not.

N.Y.S.2d 724 (2d Dep't 1993); People v. McGee, 186 A.D.2d 229, 587 N.Y.S.2d 1015 (2d Dep't 1992); People v. Ciccone, 91 A.D.2d 688, 457 N.Y.S.2d 328 (2d Dep't 1982).

43. 22 NYCRR § 670.12(c).
44. 22 NYCRR § 670.12(c)(1).
45. 22 NYCRR § 670.12(c)(2).
46. 22 NYCRR § 670.12(c)(2).
47. 22 NYCRR § 800.14(g).
48. 22 NYCRR § 800.14(g).
49. 22 NYCRR § 800.14(g).
50. 22 NYCRR § 800.14(g).
51. L. 1984, Ch. 671.
52. CPL §§ 450.10(1),(2).
53. People v. Pollenz, 67 N.Y.2d 264, 502 N.Y.S.2d 417, 493 N.E.2d 541 (1986); N.Y. Constitution, Art. VI, § 4(k). It is difficult to reconcile *Pollenz* with the case law holding that the right of appeal is statutory

Section 450.30(3) of the CPL further allows an appeal from the "sentence" as one from the original sentence or the resentence, with the proviso that if the defendant appeals from a resentence it will not authorize review of the judgment unless the defendant had filed a notice of appeal within 30 days following the judgment. When the defendant is resentenced, the original judgment is vacated and is supplanted by the later judgment from which an appeal lies.[54]

Pursuant to CPL § 450.10(2) there are a number of sentence challenges open to a defendant-appellant, as of right. The defendant may raise the claim that the sentence was illegal in the sense that is was beyond the statutory sentencing range, in which event the appellate division may remand for resentencing[55] or itself modify the sentence accordingly.[56]

In addition, the defendant-appellant may claim[57] that a sentence was unauthorized, owing to an erroneous determination that the defendant had a previous valid predicate conviction or convictions. If the defendant succeeds in this, the appellate division will vacate the sentence.[58] Also, the defendant may appeal upon a claim that when resentenced following a probation or conditional discharge violation, the original sentence was improperly revoked.[59] This is in contrast to the right of the People to appeal a defendant's sentence *solely* on the ground that it is invalid as a matter of law.[60]

Appeal From a Sentence Including a Criminal Forfeiture. The third category of defendants' appeals as of right to the appellate division is under CPL § 450.10(3). It is a little-used section and obviously contemplates a defendant's right to review of an order by which property was forfeited pursuant to Penal Law § 460.30, which involves enterprise corruption.[61]

only and not constitutionally-based. *See supra*, § 38.3.

54. People v. McKins, 76 A.D.2d 756, 429 N.Y.S.2d 338 (1st Dep't 1980).

55. People v. David, 102 A.D.2d 551, 477 N.Y.S.2d 384 (2d Dep't 1984), aff'd 65 N.Y.2d 809, 493 N.Y.S.2d 118, 482 N.E.2d 914 (1985); People v. Vergara, 102 A.D.2d 702, 476 N.Y.S.2d 332 (1st Dep't 1984); People v. Martinez, 213 A.D.2d 1072, 624 N.Y.S.2d 498 (4th Dep't 1995); People v. Frazier, 212 A.D.2d 976, 623 N.Y.S.2d 459 (4th Dep't 1995); People v. Keiffer, 207 A.D.2d 1022, 617 N.Y.S.2d 103 (4th Dep't 1994).

56. People v. Little, 108 A.D.2d 603, 484 N.Y.S.2d 831 (1st Dep't 1985); People v. Perez, 204 A.D.2d 662, 212 A.D.2d 814, 612 N.Y.S.2d 620 (2d Dep't 1994), appeal denied 84 N.Y.2d 871, 618 N.Y.S.2d 17, 642 N.E.2d 336 (1994); People v. Colon, 202 A.D.2d 710, 608 N.Y.S.2d 553 (3d Dep't 1994).

57. CPL §§ 450.10(2), 450.30(1).

58. People v. Hunter, 212 A.D.2d 731, 623 N.Y.S.2d 13 (2d Dep't 1995); People v. Johnson, 210 A.D.2d 257, 620 N.Y.S.2d 251 (2d Dep't 1994)(remanded for resentencing).

59. CPL § 450.30(1).

60. People v. Cameron, 193 A.D.2d 752, 597 N.Y.S.2d 724 (2d Dep't 1993); People v. McGee, 186 A.D.2d 229, 587 N.Y.S.2d 1015 (2d Dep't 1992); People v. Ciccone, 91 A.D.2d 688, 457 N.Y.S.2d 328 (2d Dep't 1982).

61. *See generally*, District Attorney of Kings County v. Iadarola, 164 Misc.2d 204, 623 N.Y.S.2d 999 (Sup.Ct., Kings County, 1995); Morgenthau v. Citisource, Inc., 68 N.Y.2d 211, 508 N.Y.S.2d 152, 500 N.E.2d 850 (1986).

§ 38.8   CRIMINAL APPELLATE PRACTICE   Ch. 38

Appeal From CPL Article 440 Orders Granting People's Application to Set Aside Sentence. The final category of defendants' appeals as of right to the appellate division is pursuant to CPL § 450.10(4). The section has not seen a great deal of use; it contemplates a successful CPL § 440.40 application by the People to set aside a sentence that is invalid as a matter of law.[62] If the People are successful at the trial level, resulting in an order setting aside the sentence, the defendant has an appeal as of right to the appellate division under CPL § 450.10(4).[63]

Miscellaneous Matters. There are a few proceedings for which defendants want and sometimes gain appellate recourse. They do not admit of easy classification in this format, and are collected here because they warrant treatment.

1. Bail. An application for bail pending trial (for instance, bail, recognizance, securing orders, and related matters) is covered in the securing order provisions of CPL Article 510. There is no provision in the CPL for either the defendant or the People to obtain direct appellate review of a bail order, whether by right or by permission. Hence, a bail order is not appealable[64] whether it denies bail[65] or denies a reduction in bail.[66] The matter is reviewable, however, by writ of *habeas corpus*.[67]

2. Habeas Corpus. A person may initiate a writ of *habeas corpus* in the appellate division,[68] as well as in other courts.[69] The classification of *habeas corpus* has had its share of exposition. CPL § 1.10(1)(a) provides that all criminal proceedings and all "appeals ... relating or attaching thereto" are governed exclusively by the Criminal Procedure Law. Even though a great many, if not most, *habeas corpus* writs arise in a criminal case context (most typically for release on bail or recognizance) the proceeding is classified by the Legislature as civil in nature and is governed by the provisions of CPLR Article 70.[70] A *habeas corpus* proceeding is denominated a "special proceeding" under CPLR 7001.[71]

---

62. *See infra,* § 38.10.

63. *See e.g.,* People v. Holley, 168 A.D.2d 992, 565 N.Y.S.2d 351 (4th Dep't 1990); People v. Barnes, 160 A.D.2d 342, 553 N.Y.S.2d 413 (1st Dep't 1990).

64. CPL §§ 450.10, 450.15.

65. People v. McCall, 16 A.D.2d 313, 228 N.Y.S.2d 52 (4th Dep't 1962).

66. People v. Ford, 40 A.D.2d 983, 338 N.Y.S.2d 381 (2d Dep't 1972).

67. People ex rel. Siegel on Behalf of Hudson v. Sielaff, 182 A.D.2d 389, 582 N.Y.S.2d 131 (1st Dep't 1992).

68. CPLR 7002(b)(2),(5); People ex rel. Lipman on Behalf of Castellano v. Mahoney, 219 A.D.2d 691, 631 N.Y.S.2d 537 (2d Dep't 1995).

69. CPLR 7002(b)(1),(3),(4),(5).

70. *See* People v. Gersewitz, 294 N.Y. 163, 168, 61 N.E.2d 427, 429 (1945), cert. dismissed 326 U.S. 687, 66 S.Ct. 89, 90 L.Ed. 404 (1945); Santangello v. People, 38 N.Y.2d 536, 538 note 1, 381 N.Y.S.2d 472, 473 note 1, 344 N.E.2d 404, 405 note 1 (1976) (referring to CPLR Article 70, misprinted as Article 7); People v. Farrell, 85 N.Y.2d 60, 67, 623 N.Y.S.2d 550, 553, 647 N.E.2d 762, 765 (1995).

71. *See also,* People ex rel. Robertson v. New York State Div. of Parole, 67 N.Y.2d 197, 201, 501 N.Y.S.2d 634, 636, 492 N.E.2d 762, 764 (1986); CPLR 103.

Because the purpose of the writ is to test the legality of detention[72] so that a successful petition would entitle the person detained or imprisoned to "immediate release,"[73] the writ may not be employed as a substitute for an appeal under a claim that would at best entitle the petitioner to a new trial.[74]

Because appeals in *habeas corpus* proceedings are civil in nature, it follows that the appellate procedures are governed not by the CPL appellate statutes, but by Article 55 *et seq.* of the CPLR.[75] A *habeas corpus* proceeding may get to the appellate division directly or on appeal. At the appellate division, the writ may be sustained and the bail reduced.[76] Similarly, the appellate division will dismiss the writ if it concludes that the bail set at *nisi prius* was not an improvident exercise of discretion and did not violate constitutional or statutory standards.[77] Moreover, if the appellate division concludes, on appeal, that the *nisi prius* bail setting or denial of bail was within the proper bounds of discretion, it will affirm the judgment by which the supreme court dismissed the writ.[78] However, on an appeal by the detention authorities (*i.e.*, an appeal brought on by the prosecutor from a judgment that sustained the writ and reduced bail), the appellate division will reverse the judgment and reinstate the arraigning court's original higher bail if it concludes that the *habeas corpus* court exceeded the narrow scope of the review powers available to it when it substituted its discretion for the arraignment court.[79]

---

72. People ex rel. Harrison v. Jackson, 298 N.Y. 219, 219, 82 N.E.2d 14, 15 (1948).

73. People ex rel. Brown v. New York State Div. of Parole, 70 N.Y.2d 391, 398, 521 N.Y.S.2d 657, 660, 516 N.E.2d 194, 197 (1987).

74. People ex rel. Hall on Behalf of Haralambou v. LeFevre, 60 N.Y.2d 579, 467 N.Y.S.2d 40, 454 N.E.2d 121 (1983); People ex rel. Robinson v. Scully, 122 A.D.2d 290, 505 N.Y.S.2d 193 (2d Dep't 1986).

75. *See, e.g.*, People ex rel. Fabre v. Warden, Brooklyn House of Detention, 34 N.Y.2d 566, 354 N.Y.S.2d 943, 310 N.E.2d 540 (1974)(CPLR 5520(a)); People v. Nettles, 30 N.Y.2d 841, 335 N.Y.S.2d 83, 286 N.E.2d 467 (1972)(CPLR 5513(a),(c)); People ex rel. Robertson v. Division of Parole; 67 N.Y.2d 197, 200, 501 N.Y.S.2d 634, 635, 492 N.E.2d 762, 763 (1986)(CPLR 5519(e)); State ex rel. White v. Supreme Court New York, 54 N.Y.2d 828, 443 N.Y.S.2d 725, 427 N.E.2d 1190 (1981)(CPLR 5513(b), 5602(a)); People ex rel. Frazier v. Fogg, 122 A.D.2d 377, 504 N.Y.S.2d 794 (3d Dep't 1986) (CPLR 5501); People ex rel. Cotton v. Rodriquez, 123 A.D.2d 338, 506 N.Y.S.2d 350 (2d Dep't 1986)(CPLR 5517(b)).

76. *See, e.g.*, People ex rel. Lipman on Behalf of Castellano v. Mahoney, 219 A.D.2d 691, 631 N.Y.S.2d 537 (2d Dep't 1995); People ex rel. Carbone on Behalf of Osorio v. Warden of Queens House of Detention, 219 A.D.2d 610, 631 N.Y.S.2d 528 (2d Dep't 1995).

77. People ex rel. Lester on Behalf of Geddes v. Warden, 218 A.D.2d 679, 630 N.Y.S.2d 932 (2d Dep't 1995).

78. People ex rel. Washor on Behalf of Lopez v. Freckelton, 187 A.D.2d 406, 590 N.Y.S.2d 203 (1st Dep't 1992); People ex rel. Washington v. Higgins, 207 A.D.2d 961, 617 N.Y.S.2d 670 (4th Dep't 1994); State ex rel. Capparelli v. McGrane, 189 A.D.2d 561, 592 N.Y.S.2d 15 (1st Dep't 1993), appeal denied 81 N.Y.2d 708, 598 N.Y.S.2d 767, 615 N.E.2d 224 (1993).

79. People ex rel. Brown v. Bednosky, 190 A.D.2d 836, 593 N.Y.S.2d 859 (2d Dep't 1993); People ex rel. Doyle v. Jacquin, 186 A.D.2d 235, 587 N.Y.S.2d 1019 (2d Dep't 1992).

3. Contempt.

3. Contempt. Contempt is a Penal Law crime, giving rise to a judgment of conviction,[80] or it may be a criminal contempt under Judiciary Law § 750. The question of whether the latter is reviewable by appeal or by Article 78 once occasioned nearly as much commentary as the age-old problem of the number of angels able to dance on a pin's head. Criminal contempt under the Judiciary Law differs from civil contempt in that the former has been described as a direct affront—an act of heightened willfulness—against the court, while a civil contempt is an offense primarily against a party.

Of course there is overlap, and it stands to reason that whenever a court finds X to be in civil contempt for disobeying an order to pay Y, there is an affront to the authority of the court as well as a disservice to Y. It is often difficult to draw the line between civil and criminal contempt; a single act or omission may straddle the categories, but a primary ingredient for the criminal contempt is said to be the level of willfulness associated with the conduct.[81] Consequently, punishment for a civil contempt is designed primarily to compensate a private litigant, while the punishment for a criminal contempt is meant to deter offensive conduct against the judiciary, and the state exacts the punishment in the form of an award (*i.e.*, a fine), if not incarceration.[82]

Is a contempt adjudication reviewable by appeal or by Article 78 in the nature of *certiorari*? Earlier case law did not provide an easy answer. To illustrate: no appeal lies from an order adjudging a person in criminal contempt; the proper method of review is by an Article 78 proceeding.[83] On the other hand, the proper practice for reviewing an order in a civil or a criminal contempt is by appeal.[84] The issue has been vexing enough to have occasioned back-to-back American Law Reports annotations totalling well over 200 pages.[85] There is a line of cases that have held that an *appeal* lies to review civil or criminal contempt judgments.[86]

---

80. NYPL §§ 215.50, 215.51, 215.60, 215.65, 215.66.

81. McCain v. Dinkins, 84 N.Y.2d 216, 639 N.E.2d 1132, 616 N.Y.S.2d 335 (1994), motion denied 84 N.Y.2d 846, 617 N.Y.S.2d 132, 641 N.E.2d 152 (1994).

82. State v. Unique Ideas, Inc., 44 N.Y.2d 345, 405 N.Y.S.2d 656, 376 N.E.2d 1301 (1978).

83. Cahn v. Vario, 32 A.D.2d 1035, 304 N.Y.S.2d 235 (2d Dep't 1969).

84. Eastern Concrete Steel Co. v. Bricklayers' & Mason Plasterers' International Union, Local No. 45 of Buffalo, 200 App. Div. 714, 717, 193 N.Y.S. 368, 369 (4th Dep't 1922).

85. Appealability of Contempt Adjudication or Conviction, 33 A.L.R.3d 448; Contempt—Review Other Than by Appeal, 33 A.L.R.3d 589.

86. People v. Diefendorf, 281 App.Div. 465, 468, 281 App.Div. 865, 119 N.Y.S.2d 469, 473 (1st Dep't 1953), aff'd 306 N.Y. 818, 118 N.E.2d 824 (1954)(settling the "confusion" theretofore existing); Wilwerth v. Levitt, 262 App.Div. 112, 28 N.Y.S.2d 257 (1st Dep't 1941)(refusal to answer questions at deposition); People v. Brayer, 6 A.D.2d 437, 179 N.Y.S.2d 248 (4th Dep't 1958), appeal denied 5 N.Y.2d 709, 180 N.Y.S.2d 1026, 154 N.E.2d 697 (1958), stay denied 5 N.Y.2d 861 (1959)(after a hearing); Alberti v. Dickens, 22 A.D.2d 770, 253 N.Y.S.2d 561 (1st Dep't 1964)(failure to respond to a grand jury subpoena).

Conversely, a number of cases have denied appealability of contempt orders.[87]

In *Cahn v. Vario*[88] the difference between appellate review and *certiorari* was said to turn on whether an adequate record was made (*i.e.*, a hearing), in which case an appeal of the contempt adjudication would be authorized.[89] This rationale appears to have emerged as the soundest principle of law. In *Matter of Ellman*,[90] the court held that a criminal contempt committed in the immediate view and presence of the court was punished summarily and therefore reviewable by Article 78 and not by appeal.[91]

4. Change of Venue. A motion for a change of venue may be made (and from all indications may be made only) at the appellate division.[92] The motion may be made by either the defendant or the prosecution. The statute speaks of "removal"[93] but is colloquially referred to as a change of venue.[94] CPL § 230.20 refers to superior court trials. For

---

87. Douglas v. Adel, 269 N.Y. 144, 199 N.E. 35 (1935) (committed in immediate view and presence of court); In re Teitelbaum, 84 App.Div. 351, 82 N.Y.S. 887 (1st Dep't 1903), mod. on other grounds 185 N.Y. 540, 77 N.E. 1183 (1906) (same; secreting the contract that was under investigation at trial); People v. Epps, 21 A.D.2d 650, 249 N.Y.S.2d 639 (1st Dep't 1964), cert. denied 379 U.S. 940, 85 S.Ct. 347, 13 L.Ed.2d 350 (1964)(in immediate view and presence of court); People v. Longo, 30 A.D.2d 828, 293 N.Y.S.2d 704 (2d Dep't 1968)(in presence of court).

88. 32 A.D.2d 564, 300 N.Y.S.2d 657 (2d Dep't 1969).

89. *See also*, People v. Sanders, 58 A.D.2d 525, 395 N.Y.S.2d 190 (1st Dep't 1977); People v. Clinton, 42 A.D.2d 815, 346 N.Y.S.2d 345 (3d Dep't 1973); People v. Zweig, 32 A.D.2d 569, 300 N.Y.S.2d 651 (2d Dep't 1969).

90. 117 A.D.2d 803, 499 N.Y.S.2d 431 (2d Dep't 1986).

91. *See also*, Brostoff v. Berkman, 79 N.Y.2d 938, 582 N.Y.S.2d 989, 591 N.E.2d 1175 (1992), cert. denied 506 U.S. 861, 113 S.Ct. 180, 121 L.Ed.2d 126 (1992); Williams v. Cornelius, 76 N.Y.2d 542, 561 N.Y.S.2d 701, 563 N.E.2d 15 (1990).

92. CPL § 230.20.

PRACTICE POINTER: Given that the motion should be made at the appellate division there is the matter of timing. The motion must be made within the time window fixed by CPL § 255.20. But if it is made before jury selection, the appellate division will likely deny the motion as premature with leave to renew and to await the actual *voir dire*. People v. Culhane, 33 N.Y.2d 90, 350 N.Y.S.2d 381, 305 N.E.2d 469 (1973), aff'd 45 N.Y.2d 757, 408 N.Y.S.2d 489, 380 N.E.2d 315 (1978), cert. denied 439 U.S. 1047, 99 S.Ct. 723, 58 L.Ed.2d 706 (1978). If the motion is not renewed in that manner the claim is lost; the appellate division will regard the claim as unpreserved. People v. Keefer, 197 A.D.2d 915, 602 N.Y.S.2d 268 (4th Dep't 1993), appeal denied 82 N.Y.2d 897, 610 N.Y.S.2d 164, 632 N.E.2d 474 (1993); People v. Bosket, 216 A.D.2d 791, 629 N.Y.S.2d 296 (3d Dep't 1995). The Court of Appeals will have no basis for review. See People v. Smith, 63 N.Y.2d 41, 479 N.Y.S.2d 706, 468 N.E.2d 879 (1984), cert. denied 469 U.S. 1227, 105 S.Ct. 1226, 84 L.Ed.2d 364 (1985). *See also*, People v. Pepper, 59 N.Y.2d 353, 465 N.Y.S.2d 850, 452 N.E.2d 1178 (1983).

93. CPL § 230.30(2).

94. Article 230 includes a once-related provision that contemplates the transfer of indictments between county court and supreme court. See CPL § 230.10. This was pursuant to rules that the Appellate Divisions in the Second, Third, and Fourth Departments were authorized to establish. Such rules were established by the Second Department, 22 NYCRR § 681.1(b); People v. Granatelli, 108 Misc.2d 1009, 438 N.Y.S.2d 707 (Sup.Ct., Suffolk County, 1981); and the Third Department, 22 NYCRR §§ 863.3, 1302.8(a),(b); People v. Taylor, 107 Misc.2d 183, 433 N.Y.S.2d 536 (Clinton County Ct.1980). They have, however, been rescinded, as have any such Fourth Department rules. CPL § 230.10. Transfers have been spoken of as recently as 1992, see People v. Ortiz, 202 A.D.2d

change of venue issues in local criminal courts, CPL § 170.15 is controlling.[95]

Although CPL § 230.20 authorizes the appellate division to grant a motion for a change of venue from one superior court to another, such motions have been made at the trial level and reviewed by the appellate division on appeal from the judgment.[96]

People v. Bloomfield,[97] however, suggests that the motion may be brought in the appellate division only. In practice, almost all such motions have been brought at the appellate division, at least for the past few decades. The protocol for such a motion is set forth in *People v. Parker*,[98] reminding the parties of the need for an adequate, transcribed record of *voir dire* minutes and the need to renew the motion based on the results of the *voir dire*. As the court put it:

> Proper procedure after denial of a motion for change of venue requires that a defendant attempt to select an impartial jury and that the proceedings be stenographically transcribed. At that time counsel could have attempted to establish by his questions and the answers to them that the extensive publicity made it impossible to select an impartial jury, if such was the fact, and upon said record the motion for change of venue could have been renewed and given proper consideration by the court.[99] An added factor for consideration would be whether or not the defendant exercised all of his allotted peremptory challenges in selecting a jury.

Difficult though they may be, such motions have been granted[100] but most decisions granting them are of older vintage.[101] Far more frequently they have been denied.[102]

860, 609 N.Y.S.2d 688 (3d Dep't 1994), appeal denied 83 N.Y.2d 970, 616 N.Y.S.2d 23, 639 N.E.2d 763 (1994), but the section is inoperative, and business is now conducted under 22 NYCRR § 200.14 upon authorization of the Chief Administrator of the courts.

95. See Chapter 33 "Local Criminal Court Practice," *supra. See also*, § 38.58.

96. People v. Higgins, 188 A.D.2d 839, 591 N.Y.S.2d 612 (3d Dep't 1992), appeal denied 81 N.Y.2d 972, 598 N.Y.S.2d 773, 615 N.E.2d 230 (1993).

97. 153 A.D.2d 987, 545 N.Y.S.2d 430 (3d Dep't 1989), appeal denied 74 N.Y.2d 947, 550 N.Y.S.2d 281, 549 N.E.2d 483 (1989).

98. 60 N.Y.2d 714, 468 N.Y.S.2d 870, 456 N.E.2d 811 (1983).

99. See CPL §§ 230.20(2), 255.50(3); People v. Shedrick, 83 A.D.2d 988, 443 N.Y.S.2d 716 (4th Dep't 1981), aff'd 66 N.Y.2d 1015, 499 N.Y.S.2d 388, 489 N.E.2d 1290 (1985).

100. See, e.g., People v. Boudin, 90 A.D.2d 253, 457 N.Y.S.2d 302 (2d Dep't 1982). See also, People v. Boudin, 95 A.D.2d 463, 467 N.Y.S.2d 261 (2d Dep't 1983); People v. Boudin, 97 A.D.2d 84, 469 N.Y.S.2d 89 (2d Dep't 1983)(for related appeals).

101. See, e.g., People v. Pratt, 27 A.D.2d 199, 278 N.Y.S.2d 89 (3d Dep't 1967); People v. Hill, 42 A.D.2d 679, 345 N.Y.S.2d 237 (4th Dep't 1973). *But see*, People v. Brensic, 136 A.D.2d 169, 526 N.Y.S.2d 968 (2d Dep't 1988).

102. See, e.g., People v. Parnes, 161 A.D.2d 615, 555 N.Y.S.2d 396 (2d Dep't 1990); People v. Ryan, 151 A.D.2d 528, 542 N.Y.S.2d 665 (2d Dep't 1989); People v. McClary, 150 A.D.2d 631, 541 N.Y.S.2d 503 (2d Dep't 1989); People v. Laezza, 143 A.D.2d 289, 532 N.Y.S.2d 178 (2d Dep't 1988); Prof. Preiser recounts the legislative innovations designed to simplify the process

There remains the question of review when the motion is denied. Considering that the appellate division is the court that denied the motion, its order would be considered the "law of the case" by the appellate division on review of the final judgment.[103]

5. Transfer or Removal of Cases: Family Court to Criminal Court. Pursuant to Family Court Act § 812 and following sections,[104] the family court and the criminal courts have concurrent jurisdiction over a number of offenses (harassment, some assaults, menacing, and others) between members of the same family or household under a broad definition that includes varied relationships.[105] The 1994 amendment[106] is entitled "The Family Protection and Domestic Violence Intervention Act of 1994." The legislation is designed to eliminate the 72–hour choice-of-forum rule contained in former CPL § 100.07 and sets forth new criteria for the issuance of arrest warrants. It also deals with orders of protection, criminal contempt, adjournments in contemplation of dismissal, child support, and domestic violence notice forms.[107]

Law enforcement authorities are charged with the obligation of furnishing the victim with written notice of his or her legal rights and remedies,[108] including the right to have a criminal complaint or a family court petition filed. Under Section 813, the family court (upon notice to the prosecutor and with the consent of the petitioner) may order the case into the appropriate criminal court at any time before a finding is made on the petition.[109] When a family court judge orders the case to criminal court pursuant to Section 813, the defendant (*i.e.*, the family court respondent) may take an appeal as of right to the appellate division challenging the order.[110] It has been held unnecessary for the family

by allowing the alternative of selecting jurors from a neighboring county in lieu of removal of the trial itself. Preiser, *Practice Commentary*, CPL § 230.20, p. 196; CPL § 230.20(2)(b). *See generally*, Pretrial Publicity in Criminal Case as Ground for Change of Venue, 33 A.L.R.3d 17.

103. People v. Knapp, 113 A.D.2d 154, 495 N.Y.S.2d 985 (3d Dep't 1985), appeal denied 67 N.Y.2d 945, 502 N.Y.S.2d 1038, 494 N.E.2d 123 (1986), cert. denied 479 U.S. 844, 107 S.Ct. 158, 93 L.Ed.2d 97 (1986); People v. Quartararo, 200 A.D.2d 160, 612 N.Y.S.2d 635 (2d Dep't 1994), appeal denied 84 N.Y.2d 939, 621 N.Y.S.2d 536, 645 N.E.2d 1236 (1994). *See also*, People v. Bosket, 216 A.D.2d 791, 629 N.Y.S.2d 296 (3d Dep't 1995).

104. L.1994, Ch.222.

105. Family Court Act § 812(1). *See also*, CPL §§ 100.07, 530.11, 140.10(4),(5), 530.12(14); Family Court Act §§ 846(b)(ii)(B),(C).

106. L. 1994, Ch. 222. *See also*, L. 1995, Ch. 440, adding aggravated harassment and L. 1995, Ch. 441 as to the exercise of jurisdiction beyond the state.

107. *See* Executive Memorandum, McKinney's Session Laws of New York, Sept. 1994, No. 6, p. A895. *See also*, Walker v. Walker, 86 N.Y.2d 624, 635 N.Y.S.2d 152, 658 N.E.2d 1025 (1995).

108. Family Court Act § 812(5); L. 1994, Ch. 224.

109. *See also*, Family Court Act § 846(b)(ii)(B),(C); Family Court Act § 1014.

110. People v. Johnson, 20 N.Y.2d 220, 223–224, 282 N.Y.S.2d 481, 482, 229 N.E.2d 180, 181 (1967); People v. Hopkins, 49 A.D.2d 682, 370 N.Y.S.2d 744 (4th Dep't 1975). It has also been suggested that a family court order *denying* transfer to "an appropriate criminal court," see Family Court Act § 1014, is subject to appellate division review, People v. Davis, 27 A.D.2d

§ 38.8   CRIMINAL APPELLATE PRACTICE   Ch. 38

court judge to conduct a hearing before ordering the case to a criminal court.[111] Also, under a Family Court Act § 1014 transfer, a defendant may appeal an order of transfer from family court to criminal court.[112]

A body of appellate law has developed relating to the mechanics of the transfer from family court to criminal court. If the case is to be transferred it is not only appropriate but obligatory that the respondent/defendant know about it so that he or she may take an appeal as of right challenging the transfer order.[113] A respondent/defendant who is not informed cannot be held to a waiver, unlike a person who was informed and fails to act until a judgment of conviction materializes in criminal court.[114] Having been informed, the respondent/defendant will not be able to challenge the criminal conviction collaterally if he or she fails to appeal the order of transfer.[115] If, however, the respondent/defendant is not informed of the transfer and thereby is denied the opportunity to timely appeal the transfer order, a judgment of conviction later rendered will be jurisdictionally defective, even if the defendant pleaded a guilty plea to the criminal court charges.[116]

If the order of transfer from family court to criminal court is properly made as an exercise of the family court's discretion, it will be upheld,[117] but if a case is inappropriately transferred, the appellate division will reverse the order and remit the case to the family court.[118] Only the offenses enumerated under Family Court Act § 812(1) are subject to transfer. An offense such as sodomy is not within the original jurisdiction of the family court,[119] nor is incest.[120] Both are prosecuted criminally.

In *People v. Kenyon*,[121] the family court concluded its proceeding with an order of disposition, following which the prosecutor commenced

299, 305, 278 N.Y.S.2d 750, 755 (1st Dep't 1967). *See also*, People v. Johnson, 20 N.Y.2d at 223–224, 282 N.Y.S.2d at 482, 229 N.E. at 181.

111. People v. Gemmill, 34 A.D.2d 177, 310 N.Y.S.2d 244 (3d Dep't 1970).

112. Matter of Easter, 71 A.D.2d 762, 419 N.Y.S.2d 327 (3d Dep't 1979)(there combined with judgment of conviction in county court).

113. People v. Bell, 41 A.D.2d 583, 340 N.Y.S.2d 194 (4th Dep't 1973).

114. People v. Brown, 80 A.D.2d 902, 437 N.Y.S.2d 22 (2d Dep't 1981).

115. People v. Isaacs, 43 A.D.2d 656, 349 N.Y.S.2d 844 (3d Dep't 1973); People v. Gemmill, 34 A.D.2d 177, 310 N.Y.S.2d 244 (3d Dep't 1970).

116. People v. Dupree, 67 A.D.2d 716, 412 N.Y.S.2d 424 (2d Dep't 1979), on remand 71 A.D.2d 860, 418 N.Y.S.2d 808 (2d Dep't 1979); People v. Hopkins, 49 A.D.2d 682, 370 N.Y.S.2d 744 (4th Dep't 1975).

117. *See, e.g.*, Appell v. Appell, 37 A.D.2d 966, 327 N.Y.S.2d 190 (2d Dep't 1971), aff'd 30 N.Y.2d 800, 334 N.Y.S.2d 900, 286 N.E.2d 276 (1972); People v. Brown, 80 A.D.2d 902, 437 N.Y.S.2d 22 (2d Dep't 1981).

118. *See, e.g.*, B. v. B., 32 A.D.2d 808, 303 N.Y.S.2d 216 (2d Dep't 1969); Librizzi v. Chisholm, 55 A.D.2d 954, 391 N.Y.S.2d 154 (2d Dep't 1977).

119. People v. Webb, 52 A.D.2d 8, 382 N.Y.S.2d 369 (3d Dep't 1976).

120. People v. Lewis, 29 N.Y.2d 923, 329 N.Y.S.2d 100, 279 N.E.2d 856 (1972).

121. 46 A.D.2d 409, 362 N.Y.S.2d 644 (4th Dep't 1975).

a criminal prosecution against the defendant for the same conduct. On appeal, the judgment of conviction was upheld.[122]

6. Transfer or Removal of Cases: Criminal Court to Family Court. The foregoing discussion relates to transfers from family court to criminal court—a condition that the respondent/defendant would more likely appeal than the prosecutor. The other side of the coin relates to removal from criminal court to family court. The constitutional basis for the removal of a case from a criminal court to the family court is found in Article VI, § 19(b) of the State Constitution.[123] The statutory basis for the removal of a juvenile case from a criminal court to family court is found in CPL § 725.05. If a juvenile offender case is to be transferred from a criminal court to family court, an "order of removal" is issued pursuant to CPL § 725.05 by the criminal court judge who directs the removal.[124] The order implements the mechanics for removal, which may take place at various stages, including the felony complaint stage,[125] the grand jury stage relative to transfer of juvenile cases to family court,[126] after arraignment on indictment,[127] upon the prosecutor's recommendation,[128] at the verdict stage,[129] and after verdict.

Under CPL § 725.10(2) the filing of an order of removal will generally have the effect of *permanently* divesting the criminal courts of jurisdiction.[130] The standards for removal to family court are set forth in CPL § 210.43(1)(a). Under the design of that statute, the prosecutor's consent is required before the most serious cases are transferred to family court.[131] In other instances[132] the prosecutor's consent is not required.[133] If the prosecutor refuses to consent, the defendant may appeal from the judgment of conviction in criminal court and raise the claim that the case should have been transferred.[134]

---

122. *See also*, People v. Roselle, 193 A.D.2d 56, 602 N.Y.S.2d 50 (2d Dep't 1993), aff'd, 84 N.Y.2d 350, 618 N.Y.S.2d 753, 643 N.E.2d 72 (1994). *See generally*, Appealability of Order Relating to Transfer, on Jurisdictional Grounds, of Case From one State Court to Another, 78 A.L.R.2d 1204.

123. *See also*, People v. Thompson, 70 A.D.2d 968, 417 N.Y.S.2d 125 (3d Dep't 1979); People v. DeJesus, 21 A.D.2d 236, 250 N.Y.S.2d 317 (4th Dep't 1964).

124. CPL § 725.05(9).

125. CPL § 180.75; CPL § 190.71.

126. CPL § 210.43.

127. CPL § 220.10.

128. CPL § 310.85.

129. CPL § 330.25.

130. Rodriguez v. Myerson, 69 A.D.2d 162, 418 N.Y.S.2d 936 (2d Dep't 1979); John G. v. Dubin, 89 A.D.2d 839, 452 N.Y.S.2d 907 (2d Dep't 1982); Rodriguez v. Grajales, 188 A.D.2d 474, 591 N.Y.S.2d 66 (2d Dep't 1992).

131. CPL § 210.43(1)(b). *See also*, Sobie, et al., *New York Family Court Practice* (West 1996).

132. CPL § 210.43(1)(a). *See also*, Sobie, et al., *New York Family Court Practice* (West 1996).

133. People v. Putland, 102 Misc.2d 517, 423 N.Y.S.2d 999 (Sup.Ct., Dutchess County, 1979), aff'd 105 A.D.2d 199, 482 N.Y.S.2d 882 (2d Dep't 1984); People v. Gregory C., 158 Misc.2d 872, 602 N.Y.S.2d 492 (Sup.Ct., Erie County, 1993). *See also*, Vega v. Bell, 47 N.Y.2d 543, 419 N.Y.S.2d 454, 393 N.E.2d 450 (1979).

134. Murphy v. Kelley, 116 A.D.2d 967, 498 N.Y.S.2d 537 (3d Dep't 1986)(appeal, not an Article 78 proceeding, is the method to review refusal to transfer case from criminal to family court). *But see*, John G. v. Dubin, 89 A.D.2d 839, 452 N.Y.S.2d 907 (2d

§ 38.8   CRIMINAL APPELLATE PRACTICE   Ch. 38

Section 1014(b) of the Family Court Act also authorizes a criminal court to transfer to the family court any criminal complaint charging facts amounting to abuse and neglect.[135] Conversely, Section 1014(a) authorizes the family court to transfer an abuse or neglect case to criminal court, or to refer it to the prosecutor.

As for the People, there is no provision in the CPL for their appeal from an order of removal from criminal court to family court.[136] The removal section, CPL § 725.05, does not authorize an appeal, nor is one granted to the People under CPL § 450.20. Research discloses no such appeal ever having been taken or attempted. In *Matter of Vega v. Bell*,[137] the appellate division held that the Legislature made a removal hearing a jurisdictional prerequisite to the grand jury's right to indict a juvenile offender, and that the removal hearing in the criminal court represents the only opportunity for a judicial determination on the issue of removal without the consent of the prosecutor. The appellate division nullified the indictment that the prosecutor acquired before the removal hearing, and ordered a removal hearing under CPL § 180.75(4). The Court of Appeals reversed the appellate division,[138] holding that in the adult criminal arena, such a hearing is not prerequisite to the assumption of jurisdiction by indictment, either on statutory or due process grounds. Following *Vega v. Bell*, the Legislature enacted L. 1979, Ch. 411, which provides that only a superior court may remove a case to family court over the prosecutor's objection, and which spells out the criteria for interest of justice dismissals.[139]

Appeals from Judgments Upon Guilty Pleas. A defendant may appeal a judgment of conviction as of right regardless of whether the judgment follows a jury verdict, a bench trial verdict,[140] or a guilty plea.[141] A judgment of conviction[142] may be based upon any of them, and the "as of right" appeal from the judgment does not distinguish among them. Practical considerations do. The guilty plea serves to foreclose review of numerous issues, some of which might otherwise be reviewable on appeal from a judgment that follows a verdict. Among the issues foreclos-

Dep't 1982) (Article 78 petition granted, so as to prevent the recall of the case from family court back to criminal court after it had been transferred to family court and was about to be reached for trial).

135. People v. Harrington, 131 Misc.2d 1017, 502 N.Y.S.2d 939 (Schoharie County Ct. 1986).

136. Before the enactment of CPL § 725.05, the County Court of Albany County dismissed an indictment for lack of jurisdiction in view of Family Court Act § 812. The appellate division corrected the determination by ordering the case trans-ferred to the family court on an appeal by the People from the order of dismissal. See People v. Thompson, 70 A.D.2d 968, 417 N.Y.S.2d 125 (3d Dep't 1979).

137. 67 A.D.2d 420, 415 N.Y.S.2d 424 (1st Dep't 1979).

138. Vega v. Bell, 47 N.Y.2d 543, 419 N.Y.S.2d 454, 393 N.E.2d 450 (1979).

139. L. 1979, Ch. 216; CPL § 210.40.

140. CPL § 1.20(12).

141. CPL § 1.20(10).

142. CPL § 1.20(13), 1.20(15).

ed by guilty plea, the following are the most prominent, considering that these claims have resulted in appellate decisional law:

—challenges to grand jury proceedings;[143]

—the sufficiency of evidence before the grand jury;[144]

—a claim that the court improperly denied defendant's motion to dismiss the indictment for lack of notice of the grand jury proceedings;[145]

—a claim of a denied right to testify before the grand jury;[146]

—challenges to instructions to the grand jury;[147]

—a claim as to the racial composition of the grand jury pool;[148]

—*ex post facto* claims relating to evidentiary matters;[149]

—a claim that the credibility of experts before the grand jury was impeached during subsequent judicial proceedings;[150]

—the factual specificity of an indictment;[151]

—objections to the form of the indictment;[152]

—the interpretation or application of a statute;[153]

—the denial of a severance motion[154] or a claim that defendant was forced to plead guilty because of its denial;[155]

—the denial of a motion for a separate trial;[156]

---

143. People v. Glenn, 220 A.D.2d 527, 632 N.Y.S.2d 188 (2d Dep't 1995); People v. Warf, 208 A.D.2d 874, 618 N.Y.S.2d 556 (2d Dep't 1994); People v. Nelson, 173 A.D.2d 205, 569 N.Y.S.2d 86 (1st Dep't 1991), appeal denied 78 N.Y.2d 956, 573 N.Y.S.2d 652, 578 N.E.2d 450 (1991); People v. Martin, 145 A.D.2d 440, 535 N.Y.S.2d 977 (2d Dep't 1988).

144. People v. Polanco, 216 A.D.2d 957, 629 N.Y.S.2d 693 (4th Dep't 1995); People v. Dunbar, 53 N.Y.2d 868, 440 N.Y.S.2d 613, 423 N.E.2d 36 (1981).

145. People v. Holt, 210 A.D.2d 994, 621 N.Y.S.2d 1003 (4th Dep't 1994).

146. People v. Dennis, 223 A.D.2d 814, 636 N.Y.S.2d 453 (3d Dep't 1996); People v. Torra, 191 A.D.2d 738, 594 N.Y.S.2d 419 (3d Dep't 1993), appeal denied 81 N.Y.2d 1021, 600 N.Y.S.2d 209, 616 N.E.2d 866 (1993); People v. Heady, 151 A.D.2d 844, 543 N.Y.S.2d 965 (3d Dep't 1989).

147. People v. Garcia, 216 A.D.2d 36, 627 N.Y.S.2d 666 (1st Dep't 1995).

148. People v. Self, 213 A.D.2d 998, 624 N.Y.S.2d 488 (4th Dep't 1995).

149. People v. Latzer, 71 N.Y.2d 920, 528 N.Y.S.2d 533, 523 N.E.2d 820 (1988).

150. People v. Maddox, 216 A.D.2d 329, 627 N.Y.S.2d 988 (2d Dep't 1995).

151. People v. Pollay, 145 A.D.2d 972, 538 N.Y.S.2d 714 (4th Dep't 1988).

152. People v. Iannone, 45 N.Y.2d 589, 412 N.Y.S.2d 110, 384 N.E.2d 656 (1978).

153. People v. Levin, 57 N.Y.2d 1008, 457 N.Y.S.2d 472, 443 N.E.2d 946 (1982), reconsideration denied 58 N.Y.2d 824, 459 N.Y.S.2d 1030, 445 N.E.2d 657 (1983), appeal denied 68 N.Y.2d 758, 506 N.Y.S.2d 1046, 497 N.E.2d 716 (1986).

154. People v. Grant, 140 A.D.2d 623, 528 N.Y.S.2d 993 (2d Dep't 1988); People v. Cotton, 219 A.D.2d 836, 632 N.Y.S.2d 35 (4th Dep't 1995); People v. Baez, 205 A.D.2d 695, 614 N.Y.S.2d 303 (2d Dep't 1994), appeal denied 84 N.Y.2d 822, 617 N.Y.S.2d 142, 641 N.E.2d 163 (1994).

155. People v. Welcome, 184 A.D.2d 916, 587 N.Y.S.2d 229 (3d Dep't 1992), appeal denied 80 N.Y.2d 935, 589 N.Y.S.2d 863, 603 N.E.2d 968 (1992).

156. People v. Smith, 41 A.D.2d 893, 342 N.Y.S.2d 513 (4th Dep't 1973).

—a motion to disqualify the prosecutor;[157] or the denial of a motion for a special prosecutor;[158]

—an adverse *Sandoval* ruling;[159]

—a claim of statutory previous prosecution;[160]

—a claim of statutory immunity,[161] or a claim of transactional immunity based on CPL § 190.45(2);[162]

—an adverse *Molineux* ruling;[163]

—a failure to provide a CPL § 710.30 notice;[164]

—a denial of a motion to file a late notice of intent pursuant to CPL § 250.10;[165]

—a claim that an improper foundation was laid regarding the accuracy of a blood alcohol test;[166]

—a claim of excessive pre-trial publicity;[167]

—a claim challenging probable cause for an arrest;[168]

—a claim that the court should have precluded certain evidence for violation of Penal Law § 450.10;[169]

—a claim of denial of a request to have an expert appointed and for an adjournment;[170]

—a Statute of Limitations claim;[171]

—a claim of selective prosecution;[172]

157. People v. Cole, 152 A.D.2d 851, 544 N.Y.S.2d 228 (3d Dep't 1989), appeal denied 74 N.Y.2d 895, 548 N.Y.S.2d 428, 547 N.E.2d 955 (1989); People v. Manzo, 99 A.D.2d 817, 472 N.Y.S.2d 151 (2d Dep't 1984).

158. People v. Sims, 217 A.D.2d 912, 629 N.Y.S.2d 923 (4th Dep't 1995).

159. People v. Johnson, 141 A.D.2d 848, 530 N.Y.S.2d 189 (2d Dep't 1988).

160. People v. Prescott, 66 N.Y.2d 216, 495 N.Y.S.2d 955, 486 N.E.2d 813 (1985), cert. denied 475 U.S. 1150, 106 S.Ct. 1804, 90 L.Ed.2d 349 (1986).

161. People v. Sobotker, 61 N.Y.2d 44, 471 N.Y.S.2d 78, 459 N.E.2d 187 (1984).

162. People v. Simpson, 213 A.D.2d 811, 624 N.Y.S.2d 970 (3d Dep't 1995), appeal denied 85 N.Y.2d 980, 629 N.Y.S.2d 740, 653 N.E.2d 636 (1995).

163. People v. Winchenbaugh, 120 A.D.2d 811, 501 N.Y.S.2d 929 (3d Dep't 1986).

164. People v. Taylor, 65 N.Y.2d 1, 489 N.Y.S.2d 152, 478 N.E.2d 755 (1985).

165. People v. DiDonato, 211 A.D.2d 842, 621 N.Y.S.2d 226 (3d Dep't 1995), aff'd 87 N.Y.2d 992, 642 N.Y.S.2d 616, 665 N.E.2d 186 (1996).

166. People v. Campbell, 73 N.Y.2d 481, 541 N.Y.S.2d 756, 539 N.E.2d 584 (1989).

167. People v. Taylor, 149 A.D.2d 984, 543 N.Y.S.2d 353 (4th Dep't 1989), appeal denied 74 N.Y.2d 747, 545 N.Y.S.2d 122, 543 N.E.2d 765 (1989).

168. Matter of Michael C., 215 A.D.2d 228, 626 N.Y.S.2d 774 (1st Dep't 1995).

169. People v. Williams, 214 A.D.2d 437, 625 N.Y.S.2d 42 (1st Dep't 1995), appeal denied 86 N.Y.2d 805, 632 N.Y.S.2d 518, 656 N.E.2d 617 (1995).

170. People v. Simcox, 219 A.D.2d 869, 631 N.Y.S.2d 956 (4th Dep't 1995).

171. People v. Dickson, 133 A.D.2d 492, 519 N.Y.S.2d 419 (3d Dep't 1987).

172. People v. Rodriguez, 55 N.Y.2d 776, 447 N.Y.S.2d 246, 431 N.E.2d 972 (1981).

—a claim of preindictment prosecutorial misconduct;[173]

—the statutory right to a speedy trial;[174]

—a factual basis for the particular lesser crime confessed;[175]

—a challenge to the arraignment proceedings;[176]

—the improper omission to file a bill of particulars;[177]

—the illegality of an arrest;[178]

—the lawfulness of a confession that was never challenged;[179]

—rulings on discovery motions;[180]

—a claim that a guilty plea was improperly conditioned on a waiver of defendant's constitutional right to a speedy trial. The defendant failed to preserve the claim by not moving to withdraw or vacate the plea;[181]

—the right to have counsel present at a psychiatric exam;[182]

—the denial of a motion to dismiss charges in the interest of justice;[183]

—an order denying an application for permission to make a late motion to suppress;[184] and

—claims under *Batson v. Kentucky*[185] as to discriminatory use of peremptory challenges.[186]

The reason for this is obvious. The guilty plea is designed to end

---

173. People v. Di Raffaele, 55 N.Y.2d 234, 448 N.Y.S.2d 448, 433 N.E.2d 513 (1982); People v. Gerber, 182 A.D.2d 252, 589 N.Y.S.2d 171 (2d Dep't 1992), appeal denied 80 N.Y.2d 1026, 592 N.Y.S.2d 676, 607 N.E.2d 823 (1992).

174. People v. Brisko, 219 A.D.2d 493, 631 N.Y.S.2d 516 (1st Dep't 1995); People v. O'Brien, 56 N.Y.2d 1009, 453 N.Y.S.2d 638, 439 N.E.2d 354 (1982).

175. People v. Crespo, 153 A.D.2d 573, 544 N.Y.S.2d 499 (2d Dep't 1989); People v. Hill, 220 A.D.2d 905, 632 N.Y.S.2d 691 (3d Dep't 1995).

176. People v. Meachem, 50 A.D.2d 953, 375 N.Y.S.2d 678 (3d Dep't 1975).

177. People v. Hendricks, 31 A.D.2d 982, 297 N.Y.S.2d 838 (1969).

178. People v. Grant, 16 N.Y.2d 722, 262 N.Y.S.2d 106, 209 N.E.2d 723 (1965), cert. denied 382 U.S. 975, 86 S.Ct. 541, 15 L.Ed.2d 466 (1966).

179. People v. Nicholson, 11 N.Y.2d 1067, 184 N.E.2d 190, 230 N.Y.S.2d 220 (1962), cert. denied 371 U.S. 929, 83 S.Ct. 300, 9 L.Ed.2d 237 (1962).

180. People v. Cusani, 153 A.D.2d 574, 544 N.Y.S.2d 499 (2d Dep't 1989).

181. People v. Gory, 220 A.D.2d 614, 633 N.Y.S.2d 970 (2d Dep't 1995)(citing People v. Pellegrino, 60 N.Y.2d 636, 467 N.Y.S.2d 355, 454 N.E.2d 938 (1983)).

182. People v. Reiblein, 200 A.D.2d 281, 613 N.Y.S.2d 789 (3d Dep't 1994), appeal denied 84 N.Y.2d 831, 617 N.Y.S.2d 151, 641 N.E.2d 172 (1994).

183. People v. Macy, 100 A.D.2d 557, 473 N.Y.S.2d 261 (2d Dep't 1984).

184. People v. Petgen, 55 N.Y.2d 529, 450 N.Y.S.2d 299, 435 N.E.2d 669 (1982).

185. 476 U.S. 79, 106 S.Ct. 1712, 90 L.Ed.2d 69 (1986).

186. People v. Green, 75 N.Y.2d 902, 554 N.Y.S.2d 821, 553 N.E.2d 1331 (1990), cert. denied 498 U.S. 860, 111 S.Ct. 165, 112 L.Ed.2d 130 (1990).

§ 38.8 CRIMINAL APPELLATE PRACTICE Ch. 38

litigation, "not as a gateway to further litigation."[187]

There are, however, a number of issues that do survive a guilty plea and are amenable to appellate review. Chief among them is the right of a defendant to seek review of an adverse suppression order on appeal from a judgment of conviction. It is expressly authorized by statute.[188] Other exceptions confirm the solemnity and finality of a guilty plea. It is only when the issue challenged on appeal goes to the jurisdiction of the court or to the very heart of the process that it may be raised notwithstanding a guilty plea.[189] The following issues or conditions have been held to survive guilty pleas:

—when the defendant is arguably incompetent to stand trial;[190] or is an amnesiac;[191]

—when the case raises other circumstances such as a challenge to the constitutionality of the statute under which a defendant was charged;[192]

—an attack upon an indictment that does not spell out criminality;[193]

—considerations involving constitutional (as opposed to statutory) speedy trial claims;[194]

—a joint representation claim;[195]

—constitutional double jeopardy issues;[196] and

—a prosecution based on knowingly false testimony.[197]

---

187. People v. Taylor, 65 N.Y.2d 1, 5, 489 N.Y.S.2d 152, 154, 478 N.E.2d 755, 757 (1985).

188. CPL § 710.70(2).

189. People v. Taylor, 65 N.Y.2d 1, 5, 489 N.Y.S.2d 152, 154, 478 N.E.2d 755, 757 (1985).

190. People v. Armlin, 37 N.Y.2d 167, 371 N.Y.S.2d 691, 332 N.E.2d 870 (1975); People v. Kennedy, 151 A.D.2d 831, 542 N.Y.S.2d 806 (3d Dep't 1989).

191. People v. Francabandera, 33 N.Y.2d 429, 434, note 2, 310 N.E.2d 292, 294, note 2, 354 N.Y.S.2d 609, 611, note 2 (1974). *See generally*, Amnesia as Affecting Capacity to Commit Crime or Stand Trial, 46 A.L.R.3d 544.

192. People v. Lee, 58 N.Y.2d 491, 462 N.Y.S.2d 417, 448 N.E.2d 1328 (1983). *See also*, People v. Whidden, 51 N.Y.2d 457, 434 N.Y.S.2d 936, 415 N.E.2d 927 (1980); People v. Di Raffaele, 55 N.Y.2d 234, 240–241, 448 N.Y.S.2d 448, 451, 433 N.E.2d 513, 516 (1982).

193. People v. Iannone, 45 N.Y.2d 589, 600, 412 N.Y.S.2d 110, 116, 384 N.E.2d 656, 661 (1978); People v. Case, 42 N.Y.2d 98, 396 N.Y.S.2d 841, 365 N.E.2d 872 (1977); People v. Koffroth, 2 N.Y.2d 807, 159 N.Y.S.2d 828, 140 N.E.2d 742 (1957).

194. People v. Blakley, 34 N.Y.2d 311, 357 N.Y.S.2d 459, 313 N.E.2d 763 (1974). *Cf.* People v. Rodriguez, 50 N.Y.2d 553, 429 N.Y.S.2d 631, 407 N.E.2d 475 (1980).

195. People v. Recupero, 73 N.Y.2d 877, 538 N.Y.S.2d 234, 535 N.E.2d 287 (1988).

196. Menna v. New York, 423 U.S. 61, 96 S.Ct. 241, 46 L.Ed.2d 195 (1975); People v. Prescott, 66 N.Y.2d 216, 495 N.Y.S.2d 955, 486 N.E.2d 813 (1985) cert. denied 475 U.S. 1150, 106 S.Ct. 1804, 90 L.Ed.2d 349 (1986); People v. Moore, 220 A.D.2d 621, 632 N.Y.S.2d 596 (2d Dep't 1995).

197. People v. Pelchat, 62 N.Y.2d 97, 476 N.Y.S.2d 79, 464 N.E.2d 447 (1984). *See also*, People v. Ortiz, 127 A.D.2d 305, 515 N.Y.S.2d 317 (3d Dep't 1987); Miller v. Angliker, 848 F.2d 1312 (2d Cir.1988), cert. denied 488 U.S. 890, 109 S.Ct. 224, 102 L.Ed.2d 214 (Brady claim).

In each of these instances a post-plea challenge is allowed because the proceedings have been essentially hollow, which is to say, lacking in jurisdiction, seriously befouled, or marked by the kind of governmental overreaching that renders them unpalatable. When the jurisdiction of the court is implicated, a guilty plea may be successfully challenged.[198] A defendant who pleads guilty and seeks to save an issue or issues for appellate review will be held to have forfeited the claim despite assurances by the prosecutor that the claim would survive the plea.[199] Conditional guilty pleas are disfavored, and no amount of prosecutorial assurance or consent will enable the defendant to gain appellate review of the issue.[200]

During the early stages of conditional plea jurisprudence, a defendant who was misled into the belief that a claim would, by prosecutorial consent, survive a guilty plea, was able to take back the plea when the appellate division rejected review.[201] In *People v. Thomas*,[202] the court agreed that as a matter of policy a plea conditioned on an ineffective attempt to preserve an issue for appellate review should be vacated.[203] After the prohibition against conditional pleas became better known, it hardened, and the later cases have not only foreclosed appellate review, but have refused to vacate the guilty pleas as well.[204]

198. People v. Trueluck, 219 A.D.2d 490, 631 N.Y.S.2d 164 (1st Dep't 1995), aff'd 88 N.Y.2d 546, 647 N.Y.S.2d 476, 670 N.E.2d 977 (1996)(waiver of indictment impermissible under CPL § 195.10 in class A felony complaint; plea to superior court information vacated); People v. Boston, 75 N.Y.2d 585, 555 N.Y.S.2d 27, 554 N.E.2d 64 (1990)(plea to superior court information after indictment violated CPL § 195.10); People v. Aponte, 212 A.D.2d 157, 629 N.Y.S.2d 773 (2d Dep't 1995)(court improperly raised defendant's guilty plea from manslaughter to murder owing to defendant's failure to cooperate with authorities as promised). *See also*, People v. Dupree, 67 A.D.2d 716, 412 N.Y.S.2d 424 (2d Dep't 1979), upon remand 71 A.D.2d 860, 418 N.Y.S.2d 808 (2d Dep't 1979); People v. Hopkins, 49 A.D.2d 682, 370 N.Y.S.2d 744 (4th Dep't 1975)(guilty pleas vacated; judgments of conviction were jurisdictionally defective when defendants' cases were transferred from family court to criminal court without sufficient notice to enable defendant to appeal transfer).

199. People v. Thomas, 53 N.Y.2d 338, 441 N.Y.S.2d 650, 424 N.E.2d 537 (1981).

200. PRACTICE POINTER AS TO CONDITIONAL GUILTY PLEAS: A defendant may not condition a guilty plea to preserve issues that do not *otherwise* survive a guilty plea. A defendant may, for example, believe that the trial court improperly denied a motion for a severance. An agreement to plead guilty and leave this claim open for appellate review will not work. For better or worse, a choice must be made between going to trial, and thus preserving the claim, or pleading guilty, and forfeiting it. The exception is CPL § 710.70(2) which expressly authorizes appellate review of a suppression ruling notwithstanding a guilty plea. People v. O'Brien, 84 A.D.2d 567, 568, 443 N.Y.S.2d 255, 257 (2d Dep't 1981), aff'd 56 N.Y.2d 1009, 453 N.Y.S.2d 638, 439 N.E.2d 354 (1982).

201. *See, e.g.*, People v. Jordan, 78 A.D.2d 878, 433 N.Y.S.2d 25 (2d Dep't 1980).

202. 53 N.Y.2d 338, 441 N.Y.S.2d 650, 424 N.E.2d 537 (1981).

203. *See also*, People v. Di Raffaele, 55 N.Y.2d 234, 240, 448 N.Y.S.2d 448, 451, 433 N.E.2d 513, 516 (1982).

204. *See* People v. O'Brien, 84 A.D.2d 567, 568, 443 N.Y.S.2d 255, 256 (2d Dep't 1981), aff'd, 56 N.Y.2d 1009, 453 N.Y.S.2d 638, 439 N.E.2d 354 (1982); People v. Campbell, 73 N.Y.2d 481, 486, 539 N.E.2d 584, 541 N.Y.S.2d 756, 758 (1989); People v. Hardy, 187 A.D.2d 810, 589 N.Y.S.2d 966 (3d Dep't 1992); People v. Levin, 119

§ 38.8 CRIMINAL APPELLATE PRACTICE Ch. 38

A guilty plea itself is not invulnerable to attack. A defendant who pleads guilty and even waives the right to appeal may still challenge the plea in terms of its voluntariness, or in terms of its integrity as knowingly and intelligently having been entered.[205] Although the courts have rejected such claims far more often than not, they have received more favorable reception in juvenile offender or youth cases,[206] particularly when there exists a violation of the parent notification requirements of Family Court Act § 341.2(3), as in *In re Kim F.*[207] Furthermore, a defendant who has pleaded guilty may raise the claim of ineffective assistance of counsel.[208]

As for the factual sufficiency of the plea, the defendant's failure to move to withdraw the plea[209] will foreclose challenge on appeal. Under *People v. Pellegrino*[210] and *People v. Lopez*[211] appellate challenges to guilty pleas have been rejected as unpreserved where defendants have failed to move to vacate or withdraw their pleas prior to sentencing, yet have asserted on appeal that the factual allocution underlying their pleas was insufficient or defective,[212] or devoid of an admission of guilt,[213] or improperly conditioned on a waiver of their constitutional right to a speedy trial[214] or, in a drug case, devoid of knowledge of the drug's weight.[215]

Although *Pellegrino* related to the preservation of claims as to the *sufficiency* of the allocution, courts have seemingly extended the *Pellegrino* preservation rule to claims of involuntariness of the guilty plea[216] and

A.D.2d 698, 699, 500 N.Y.S.2d 819, 820 (2d Dep't 1986), apeal denied, 68 N.Y.2d 758, 506 N.Y.S.2d 1046, 497 N.E.2d 716 (1986); Carney v. Feldstein, 193 A.D.2d 1016, 1019, 597 N.Y.S.2d 982, 983 (3d Dep't 1993)(Levine, J., concurring); People v. Simcox, 219 A.D.2d 869, 631 N.Y.S.2d 956 (4th Dep't 1995).

205. People v. Callahan, 80 N.Y.2d 273, 590 N.Y.S.2d 46, 604 N.E.2d 108 (1992).

206. *See, e.g.*, Matter of Melvin A., 216 A.D.2d 227, 628 N.Y.S.2d 698 (1st Dep't 1995); In re Gregory C., 202 A.D.2d 273, 608 N.Y.S.2d 655 (1st Dep't 1994).

207. In re Kim F., 109 A.D.2d 706, 487 N.Y.S.2d 31 (1st Dep't 1985). *See generally*, Family Court Act § 321.3(1)(as to the acceptance of a guilty plea); People v. Gina M.M., 40 N.Y.2d 595, 388 N.Y.S.2d 899, 357 N.E.2d 370 (1976).

208. People v. Seaberg, 74 N.Y.2d 1, 10–11, 543 N.Y.S.2d 968, 973, 541 N.E.2d 1022, 1027 (1989)(claim entertained but rejected in People v. Rosado, 199 A.D.2d 833, 606 N.Y.S.2d 368 (3d Dep't 1993), appeal denied 83 N.Y.2d 876, 613 N.Y.S.2d 136, 635 N.E.2d 305 (1994); People v. Ferguson, 192 A.D.2d 800, 596 N.Y.S.2d 533 (3d Dep't 1993), appeal denied 82 N.Y.2d 717, 602 N.Y.S.2d 814, 622 N.E.2d 315 (1993); People v. Polanco, 216 A.D.2d 957, 629 N.Y.S.2d 583 (4th Dep't 1995)).

209. CPL § 220.60.

210. 60 N.Y.2d 636, 467 N.Y.S.2d 355, 454 N.E.2d 938 (1983).

211. 71 N.Y.2d 662, 529 N.Y.S.2d 465, 525 N.E.2d 5 (1988).

212. People v. Brady, 220 A.D.2d 760, 633 N.Y.S.2d 983 (2d Dep't 1995).

213. People v. Johnson, 214 A.D.2d 752, 625 N.Y.S.2d 944 (2d Dep't 1995), appeal denied 86 N.Y.2d 736, 631 N.Y.S.2d 617, 655 N.E.2d 714 (1995).

214. People v. Gory, 220 A.D.2d 614, 633 N.Y.S.2d 970 (2d Dep't 1995).

215. People v. Hidalgo, 213 A.D.2d 493, 624 N.Y.S.2d 897 (2d Dep't 1995), appeal denied 85 N.Y.2d 974, 629 N.Y.S.2d 734, 653 N.E.2d 630 (1995); People v. Doyle, 222 A.D.2d 875, 635 N.Y.S.2d 718 (3d Dep't 1995).

216. People v. Outer, 197 A.D.2d 543, 602 N.Y.S.2d 215 (2d Dep't 1993), appeal

similar claims in which the defendant asserts that the plea was not entered knowingly and intelligently.[217] In *People v. Carbone*,[218] the appellate division affirmed the defendant's conviction based on his guilty plea, holding that his claim—that the court should have ordered a psychiatric examination—was not raised until after sentencing and was therefore unpreserved.[219] In the overwhelming majority of instances, however, the appellate division has gone on to examine such claims, pointing out the lack of preservation but then commenting on them "in any event." This seems an apt course, considering that under *People v. Callahan (DeSimone)*[220] a defendant who pleaded guilty may on appeal raise the issue of voluntariness and integrity of the waiver of a right to appeal.[221]

A defendant may challenge the harshness or severity of a sentence even though it was agreed upon as part of the guilty plea.[222] This is not to say that the defendant will easily prevail. The defendant's agreement to the plea and to the sentence, by way of negotiation, has been cited hundreds of times as a reason to affirm.[223] And of course a defendant may negotiate the sentence and then waive the right to appeal its severity, but not its legality.[224] If a defendant negotiates a plea that involves an illegal sentence, the court should offer the defendant an opportunity to withdraw the plea and, if the defendant refuses, impose a lawful sentence.[225]

denied 82 N.Y.2d 900, 610 N.Y.S.2d 167, 632 N.E.2d 477 (1993).

217. People v. Willsea, 221 A.D.2d 1019, 635 N.Y.S.2d 568 (4th Dep't 1995); People v. Velez, 202 A.D.2d 264, 609 N.Y.S.2d 783 (1st Dep't 1994), appeal denied 83 N.Y.2d 916, 614 N.Y.S.2d 398, 637 N.E.2d 289, appeal denied, 85 N.Y.2d 981, 629 N.Y.S.2d 741, 653 N.E.2d 637 (1995); People v. Martinez, 162 A.D.2d 274, 556 N.Y.S.2d 631 (1st Dep't 1990), appeal denied 76 N.Y.2d 860, 560 N.Y.S.2d 1000, 561 N.E.2d 900 (1990); People v. Tobie, 115 A.D.2d 321, 496 N.Y.S.2d 710 (4th Dep't 1985).

218. 159 A.D.2d 511, 552 N.Y.S.2d 380 (2d Dep't 1990), appeal denied 76 N.Y.2d 732, 558 N.Y.S.2d 894, 557 N.E.2d 1190 (1990).

219. *See also*, People v. Smith, 171 A.D.2d 1060, 569 N.Y.S.2d 243 (4th Dep't 1991), appeal denied 78 N.Y.2d 927, 573 N.Y.S.2d 479, 577 N.E.2d 1071 (1991).

220. People v. Callahan, 80 N.Y.2d 273, 590 N.Y.S.2d 46, 604 N.E.2d 108 (1992).

221. CAVEAT: The reports are replete with affirmances of convictions based upon guilty pleas wherein challenges to such pleas have been held unpreserved owing to the defendant's failure to move to withdraw or vacate the plea prior to sentencing. Although a voluntariness challenge to a guilty plea may be considered by the appellate division—at least in the interest of justice if unpreserved—it is far more efficacious to move, before sentencing, at the trial court level.

222. People v. Pollenz, 67 N.Y.2d 264, 502 N.Y.S.2d 417, 493 N.E.2d 541 (1986); N.Y. Constitution, Art. VI, § 4(k).

223. *See, e.g.*, People v. Kazepis, 101 A.D.2d 816, 475 N.Y.S.2d 351 (2d Dep't 1984); People v. Charlot, 203 A.D.2d 374, 612 N.Y.S.2d 908 (2d Dep't 1994), appeal denied 84 N.Y.2d 823, 617 N.Y.S.2d 143, 641 N.E.2d 164 (1994).

224. People v. Allen, 82 N.Y.2d 761, 603 N.Y.S.2d 820, 623 N.E.2d 1170 (1993).

225. *See generally*, People v. Bullard, 84 A.D.2d 845, 444 N.Y.S.2d 171 (2d Dep't 1981); People v. Stewart, 144 A.D.2d 601, 534 N.Y.S.2d 439 (2d Dep't 1988), appeal denied 73 N.Y.2d 896, 538 N.Y.S.2d 809, 535 N.E.2d 1349 (1989); People v. Tubbs, 157 A.D.2d 915, 550 N.Y.S.2d 441 (3d Dep't 1990), appeal denied 76 N.Y.2d 744, 558 N.Y.S.2d 906, 557 N.E.2d 1202 (1990); Plea Bargain—Illegal Sentence, 87 A.L.R.4th 384.

§ 38.8　　CRIMINAL APPELLATE PRACTICE　　Ch. 38

A guilty plea that was entered and induced by an unfulfilled promise must either be vacated or the promise honored.[226] When a guilty plea is made with a promise that the time will run concurrently with another conviction and the other conviction is reversed, the defendant will be allowed to withdraw the guilty plea.[227]

Library References:

West's Key No. Digests, Criminal Law ⊝1026.

§ 38.9　Appeals to the Appellate Division—Who May Appeal—Appeals by Defendant From Superior Courts—Appeals by Permission

Adverse Article 440 Determinations. Article 440 covers a species of collateral attack on a judgment or sentence and has taken on statutory status after having been developed under *coram nobis* case law beginning with the grandparenthood of *Matter of Lyons v. Goldstein*.[1] Article 440 relates to claims seeking *vacatur* for reasons that lie outside the record and are therefore not reviewable on direct appeal.

A defendant has no *right* to appeal an adverse CPL Article 440 order; he or she may do so by permission only.[2] The Legislature imposed this restriction to spare the appellate courts from having to entertain appeals—no matter how frivolous or successive—from denials of collateral attack applications.[3] Because an order denying collateral relief is an intermediate order, the Legislature could, and did, make such appeals dependent on appellate division leave.[4] This contrasts with the Legislature's inability to restrict appellate division review of final judgments of conviction.[5]

CPL § 450.15 is the sole "appeal by permission" section available to defendants. It *requires* a certificate granting leave by an appellate

---

226. *See, e.g.*, Santobello v. New York, 404 U.S. 257, 92 S.Ct. 495, 30 L.Ed.2d 427 (1971); People v. Selikoff, 35 N.Y.2d 227, 360 N.Y.S.2d 623, 318 N.E.2d 784 (1974), cert. denied 419 U.S. 1122, 95 S.Ct. 806, 42 L.Ed.2d 822 (1975). *See also*, People v. Rhodes, 199 A.D.2d 571, 604 N.Y.S.2d 349 (3d Dep't 1993); People v. Williams, 195 A.D.2d 1040, 600 N.Y.S.2d 529 (4th Dep't 1993); People v. John C., 184 A.D.2d 519, 584 N.Y.S.2d 320 (2d Dep't 1992); People v. Brien, 162 A.D.2d 1028, 559 N.Y.S.2d 195 (4th Dep't 1990).

227. *See, e.g.*, People v. Fuggazzatto, 62 N.Y.2d 862, 863, 477 N.Y.S.2d 619, 620, 466 N.E.2d 159, 160 (1984); People v. Clark, 45 N.Y.2d 432, 440, 408 N.Y.S.2d 463, 467, 380 N.E.2d 290, 294 (1978).

§ 38.9

1. Lyons v. Goldstein, 290 N.Y. 19, 47 N.E.2d 425 (1943).

2. CPL § 450.15(1).

3. *See* Preiser, *Practice Commentaries*, CPL § 450.15.

4. People v. Simmonds, 182 A.D.2d 650, 582 N.Y.S.2d 236 (2d Dep't 1992), appeal denied 80 N.Y.2d 910, 588 N.Y.S.2d 835, 602 N.E.2d 243 (1992). *See also*, People v. Ghee, 153 A.D.2d 954, 545 N.Y.S.2d 760 (2d Dep't 1989), appeal denied 76 N.Y.2d 735, 558 N.Y.S.2d 897, 557 N.E.2d 1193 (1990).

5. People v. Pollenz, 67 N.Y.2d 264, 502 N.Y.S.2d 417, 493 N.E.2d 541 (1986).

division justice, without which no appeal lies.[6] If no permission is obtained, the appellate division lacks jurisdiction and will dismiss the appeal.[7]

The so-called "440 applications"[8] generally cover what were formerly called *coram nobis* writs.[9] The writ itself is retained as a post-conviction remedy when all statutory doors are closed.[10] The writ is "subsumed" within CPL § 440.10 but the statute is not a mirror-like codification, having eight subsections that afford avenues of collateral attack upon a judgment.[11] Note also that this discussion is of Article 440 in the appellate context, which is to say, a defendant's appeal of an Article 440 denial. A CPL Article 440 application made before the trial court may never serve as a substitute for appeal.[12] It is, in a sense, the opposite of an appeal in that it takes in only those claims that are not revealed on the face of the record.[13]

The "permission to appeal" avenue takes in only those CPL Article 440 claims that are expressly listed under Sections 440.10 and 440.20. The Legislature, by enacting CPL § 440.10, attempted to cover many of the former *coram nobis* applications.[14] Section 440.10 does not, however, include any provision for relief to those who have not been advised of the right to appeal—the so called "*Montgomery* relief."[15] There is no such provision in CPL § 440.10 because "*Montgomery*" type relief does not contemplate *vacatur* of the judgment; CPL § 440.10, however, does. *Montgomery* relief involves an extension of the time to appeal and is now codified under CPL § 460.30, the extension section.[16]

CPL § 450.15(3) is a dead letter. It attempts to require leave for defense appeals from agreed upon sentences. But defendants have an

---

6. CPL § 460.15; People v. Kihm, 143 A.D.2d 199, 532 N.Y.S.2d 11 (2d Dep't 1988), appeal denied 72 N.Y.2d 958, 534 N.Y.S.2d 672, 531 N.E.2d 304 (1988).

7. People v. Harris, 107 A.D.2d 761, 484 N.Y.S.2d 127 (2d Dep't 1985); People v. Ramsey, 104 A.D.2d 388, 478 N.Y.S.2d 714 (2d Dep't 1984).

8. CPL Art. 440.

9. People v. Silverman, 3 N.Y.2d 200, 165 N.Y.S.2d 11, 144 N.E.2d 10 (1957); People v. Baxley, 84 N.Y.2d 208, 616 N.Y.S.2d 7, 639 N.E.2d 746 (1994).

10. See, e.g., People v. Bachert, 69 N.Y.2d 593, 516 N.Y.S.2d 623, 509 N.E.2d 318 (1987).

11. People v. Cooks, 67 N.Y.2d 100, 104 note 3, 500 N.Y.S.2d 503, 506, note 3, 491 N.E.2d 676, 679, note 3 (1986).

12. People v. Nettles, 30 N.Y.2d 841, 843, 335 N.Y.S.2d 83, 86, 286 N.E.2d 467 (1972); People v. Brown, 13 N.Y.2d 201, 204, 245 N.Y.S.2d 577, 578, 195 N.E.2d 293, 294 (1963), cert. denied 376 U.S. 972, 84 S.Ct. 1140, 12 L.Ed.2d 86 (1964).

13. People v. Angelakos, 70 N.Y.2d 670, 518 N.Y.S.2d 784, 512 N.E.2d 305 (1987); People v. Sadness, 300 N.Y. 69, 73, 89 N.E.2d 188, 190 (1949), cert. denied 338 U.S. 952, 70 S.Ct. 483, 94 L.Ed. 587 (1950).

14. People v. Session, 34 N.Y.2d 254, 255, 357 N.Y.S.2d 409, 410, 313 N.E.2d 728 (1974); People v. Corso, 40 N.Y.2d 578, 388 N.Y.S.2d 886, 357 N.E.2d 357 (1976).

15. People v. Montgomery, 24 N.Y.2d 130, 299 N.Y.S.2d 156, 247 N.E.2d 130 (1969).

16. See People v. Corso, 40 N.Y.2d 578, 388 N.Y.S.2d 886, 357 N.E.2d 357 (1976). See also, Harrington v. State Office of Court Admin., 94 A.D.2d 863, 463 N.Y.S.2d 586 (3d Dep't 1983), aff'd 62 N.Y.2d 626, 476 N.Y.S.2d 109, 464 N.E.2d 477 (1984).

appeal as of right, according to New York State Constitution Article VI, § 4(k)[17] and so the section is unenforceable.

Library References:
West's Key No. Digests, Criminal Law ⚖1072.

§ 38.10 Appeals to the Appellate Division—Who May Appeal—Appeals by the People

Dismissal of an Accusatory Instrument or a Count Thereof. CPL § 450.20 is the primary section for appeals by the People.[1] All appeals by the People are as of right; there are no appeals by permission. Under earlier law, and with concepts of symmetry apparently in mind, the Legislature provided that with certain exceptions an appeal could be taken by the People as of right in all cases in which the defendant could do so.[2] In revision, the drafters of the CPL (wisely) did not employ that parallelism. The criminal arena is not based on symmetry but on a proper balance between the state and the accused. A chief feature of the equation is the application of double jeopardy principles against the prosecution. The theme of double jeopardy runs through the body of decisional law interpreting the People's right to appeal. The People have no appeal from a judgment on the merits in favor of a defendant in a criminal case.[3]

If a court dismisses an accusatory instrument, *i.e.*, an indictment, information or complaint, or their subvarieties as defined by CPL § 1.20(1), on certain specified grounds, the People may appeal the dismissal order. This is true in all cases, including capital cases (L. 1995, Ch. 1). Pursuant to CPL § 450.20, there are a number of grounds upon which a court may dismiss an accusatory instrument. In the main, this section generates appeals from dismissals that occur before trial.[4]

The People's opportunities to appeal dismissals are governed by CPL § 450.20(1). The section allows the People to appeal only from orders of dismissal entered pursuant to certain specified statutory grounds. In the case of a dismissal of an information, the order of dismissal, to be appealable by the People, must have been entered pursuant to CPL

---

17. People v. Pollenz, 67 N.Y.2d 264, 502 N.Y.S.2d 417, 493 N.E.2d 541 (1986).

§ 38.10

1. The others are also addressed in this section: CPL § 450.40 (trial order of dismissal); CPL § 450.50 (suppression); and CPL § 450.55 (reduction of count of accusatory instrument).

2. CPL Art. 518 (repealed); People v. Moreli, 11 A.D.2d 437, 207 N.Y.S.2d 843 (3d Dep't 1960).

3. People v. Sabella, 42 A.D.2d 769, 346 N.Y.S.2d 757 (2d Dep't 1973), aff'd 35 N.Y.2d 158, 359 N.Y.S.2d 100, 316 N.E.2d 569 (1974); People v. Pantano, 46 A.D.2d 914, 363 N.Y.S.2d 16 (2d Dep't 1974).

4. People's appeals from trial orders of dismissal of accusatory instruments are codified under CPL § 450.40. *See also*, Marks, et al., *New York Pretrial Criminal Procedure* (West 1996).

§ 170.30 (local criminal court accusatory instruments)[5] or CPL § 170.50 (motion in superior court to dismiss prosecutor's information).

CPL § 170.30 covers, among other things, dismissals of informations based on facial insufficiency, immunity, double jeopardy, time-bars, speedy trial provisions, interest of justice, as well as jurisdictional and legal impediments.[6] CPL § 170.35 describes when an information or misdemeanor complaint is defective within the meaning of CPL § 170.30(1)(a).[7]

Most of the appellate case law under CPL § 450.20(1), however, relates to motions to dismiss indictments in superior court. Here, too, CPL § 450.20(1), in allowing the People to appeal from orders dismissing indictments or counts, is tailored to cover dismissals that are entered

---

5. *See generally*, Chapter 33 "Local Criminal Court Practice," *supra*.

6. CPL § 170.30:

Motion to dismiss information, simplified information, prosecutor's information or misdemeanor complaint

1. After arraignment upon an information, a simplified information, a prosecutor's information or a misdemeanor complaint, the local criminal court may, upon motion of the defendant, dismiss such instrument or any count thereof upon the ground that:

(a) It is *defective, within the meaning of section 170.35*; or

(b) The defendant has received *immunity* from prosecution for the offense charged, pursuant to sections 50.20 or 190.40; or

(c) The prosecution is barred by reason of a *previous prosecution*, pursuant to section 40.20; or

(d) The prosecution is *untimely*, pursuant to section 30.10; or

(e) The defendant has been denied the right to a *speedy trial*; or

(f) There exists some other *jurisdictional or legal impediment* to conviction of the defendant for the offense charged; or

(g) Dismissal is required in *furtherance of justice*, within the meaning of section 170.40. (Emphasis added).

7. CPL § 170.35:

Motion to dismiss information, simplified information, prosecutor's information or misdemeanor complaint; as defective

1. An information, a simplified information, a prosecutor's information or a misdemeanor complaint, or a count thereof, is *defective* within the meaning of paragraph (a) of subdivision one of section 170.30 when:

(a) *It is not sufficient on its face* pursuant to the requirements of section 100.40; provided that such an instrument or count may not be dismissed as defective, but must instead be amended, where the defect or irregularity is of a kind that may be cured by amendment and where the people move to so amend; or

(b) The allegations demonstrate that the court does not have *jurisdiction* of the offense charged, or

(c) The statute defining the offense charged is *unconstitutional* or otherwise invalid.

2. An information is also defective when it is filed in replacement of a misdemeanor complaint pursuant to section 170.65 but without satisfying the requirements stated therein.

3. A prosecutor's information is also defective when:

(a) It is filed at the direction of a grand jury, pursuant to section 190.70, and the offense or offenses charged are not among those authorized by such grand jury direction; or

(b) It is filed by the district attorney at his own instance, pursuant to subdivision two of section 100.50, and the factual allegations of the original information underlying it and any supporting depositions are not legally sufficient pursuant to CPL § 210.20. In light of *People v. Coppa*,[8] however, which allowed the People to appeal from an order of dismissal entered after their opening statement, CPL § 450.20(1) may be read to authorize an appeal by the People from any final order of dismissal so long as double jeopardy is not implicated. The list parallels the information dismissal list (*supra*) and covers, among other things, dismissals of indictments based on insufficiency of grand jury evidence, facial insufficiency, immunity, double jeopardy, time bars, speedy trial provisions, interest of justice, as well as jurisdictional and legal impediments.[9]

An indictment is "defective" under CPL § 210.25 when: (1) It does *not substantially conform to the requirements* stated in Article two hundred; provided that an indictment may not be dismissed as defective, but must instead be amended, where the defect or irregularity is of a kind that may be cured by amendment, pursuant to Section 200.70, and where the People move to so amend; or (2) the allegations demonstrate that the court does not have *jurisdiction* of the offense charged; or (3) the statute defining the offense charged is *unconstitutional* or otherwise invalid.[10]

CPL § 450.20 also contemplates appeals by the People from dismissals owing to defective grand jury proceedings, as when, under CPL § 210.35: (1) The grand jury was *illegally constituted*; or (2) the proceeding is conducted before *fewer than sixteen grand jurors*; or (3) *fewer than twelve grand jurors* concur in the finding of the indictment; or (4) the defendant is *not accorded an opportunity to appear and testify* before the grand jury in accordance with the provisions of Section 190.50; or (5) the proceeding otherwise *fails to conform to the requirements of Article one hundred ninety* to such degree that the integrity thereof is impaired and prejudice to the defendant may result.[11]

---

to support the charge in the prosecutor's information. (Emphasis added).

8. People v. Coppa, 45 N.Y.2d 244, 408 N.Y.S.2d 365, 380 N.E.2d 195 (1978).

9. CPL § 210.20 provides that:

1. After arraignment upon an indictment, the superior court may, upon motion of the defendant, dismiss such indictment or any count thereof upon the ground that:

(a) Such indictment or count is *defective, within the meaning of section 210.25*; or

(b) The evidence before the grand jury was *not legally sufficient* to establish the offense charged or any lesser included offense; or

(c) The *grand jury proceeding was defective*, within the meaning of section 210.35; or

(d) The defendant has *immunity* with respect to the offense charged, pursuant to section 50.20 or 190.40; or

(e) The prosecution is barred by reason of a *previous prosecution*, pursuant to section 40.20; or

(f) The prosecution is *untimely*, pursuant to section 30.10; or

(g) The defendant has been denied the right to a *speedy trial*; or

(h) There exists some other *jurisdictional or legal impediment* to conviction of the defendant for the offense charged; or

(i) Dismissal is required in the *interest of justice*, pursuant to section 210.40. (Emphasis added)

10. CPL § 210.25 (emphasis added).

11. CPL § 210.35 (emphasis added).

The possible grounds for Section 210.20 dismissals are extensive, and here we are less concerned with the substantive bases for the dismissal than with the procedural aspects of appellate review. When a court dismisses an accusatory instrument on a ground enumerated above, the intermediate appellate court (most frequently, the appellate division, upon a dismissal of an indictment in a county or supreme court case) may review the dismissal, and, if it finds the order of dismissal to have been erroneously made, it will reverse it and reinstate the accusatory instrument.[12] Of course it may affirm the dismissal.[13]

CPL § 450.20(1) authorizes a People's appeal not only when an accusatory instrument is dismissed, but also when a court dismisses one or more *counts* of the accusatory instrument.[14] In *People v. Moquin*,[15] the county court dismissed one count of an eight count indictment, leaving seven counts intact. The People appealed, and the appellate division reinstated the count. While the appeal was pending, however, the defendant pleaded guilty to what was left of the indictment (*i.e.*, the seven counts) over the objection of the People who were appealing the dismissal.[16] The People again appealed, seeking to vacate the defendant's guilty plea. The appellate division vacated the defendant's guilty plea,[17] but the Court of Appeals reversed the appellate division on double jeopardy grounds, holding that the defendant's guilty plea ended the matter.[18] The court noted[19] that although the People could not have acquired a stay, they could have "attempted to preserve their rights by requesting a presentencing adjournment pending disposition of their interlocutory appeal," citing CPL § 30.30(4)(a).

If the appellate division upholds the dismissal, the next question is whether the prosecution will be able to present the case to another grand jury. Sometimes the appellate division may modify the dismissal and

---

12. *See, e.g.*, People v. Forde, 153 A.D.2d 466, 552 N.Y.S.2d 113 (1st Dep't 1990)(evidence sufficient); People v. Field, 161 A.D.2d 660, 555 N.Y.S.2d 437 (2d Dep't 1990), appeal after remand 175 A.D.2d 291, 572 N.Y.S.2d 923 (1991)(dismissal in furtherance of justice, reversed); People v. Hernandez, 210 A.D.2d 504, 621 N.Y.S.2d 810 (2d Dep't 1994).

13. People v. Comer, 198 A.D.2d 874, 605 N.Y.S.2d 1006 (4th Dep't 1993).

14. *See, e.g.*, People v. Nugent, 194 A.D.2d 984, 598 N.Y.S.2d 861 (3d Dep't 1993)(counts reinstated, evidence sufficient); People v. Van Buren, 82 N.Y.2d 878, 609 N.Y.S.2d 170, 631 N.E.2d 112 (1993)(appellate division order which reversed county court order of dismissal of a count, in turn reversed by the Court of Appeals).

15. People v. Moquin, 142 A.D.2d 347, 536 N.Y.S.2d 561 (3d Dep't 1988), appeal after remand 153 A.D.2d 189, 550 N.Y.S.2d 490 (1990).

16. **PRACTICE POINTER:** In evaluating the People's appeal from the order of dismissal, the appellate division will consider only the grounds relied upon by the court in its dismissal. It may not consider alternate grounds raised by the defendant in arguing for the affirmance of the order dismissing the indictment. *See* CPL § 470.15(1); People v. Goodfriend, 64 N.Y.2d 695, 485 N.Y.S.2d 519, 474 N.E.2d 1187, (1984); People v. Vallone, 140 A.D.2d 729, 529 N.Y.S.2d 38 (2d Dep't 1988).

17. 153 A.D.2d 189, 550 N.Y.S.2d 490 (3d Dep't 1990).

18. People v. Moquin, 77 N.Y.2d 449, 568 N.Y.S.2d 710, 570 N.E.2d 1059 (1991).

19. *Id.* at 455, 568 N.Y.S.2d at 712, 570 N.E.2d at 1062.

authorize presentation to another grand jury,[20] but it may not do so if prosecution is legally barred.[21] CPL § 450.50, for example, precludes prosecution after an unsuccessful appeal by the People of a suppression order.[22] Moreover, the People have no right of appeal from an order denying presentation of a case to a grand jury.[23]

In addressing the People's appealability potential under CPL § 450.20, the courts have held fast to the doctrine that the People's right to appeal is statutory and must be strictly construed. In *People v. Rodriguez*,[24] the court, owing to the defendant's reliance on a proposed lesser plea, accepted the defendant's plea without the People's consent. The People's appeal was dismissed as not falling within any of the provisions of CPL § 450.20. Nor does a People's appeal—or anyone else's—lie from a decision[25] or order that does not dismiss the indictment but places the case on a reserve calendar.[26] If a court dismisses an indictment, there is no appeal until an order is entered. The refusal to issue an order can be reviewed in an Article 78 proceeding.[27]

There is no statutory provision for the People to appeal from an order granting discovery or inspection. However, an order granting inspection of the grand jury minutes is reviewable and will be successfully interdicted by way of an Article 78 proceeding in the nature of prohibition.[28] Mere non-reviewability by way of appeal is not a valid basis to employ a writ of prohibition,[29] but the appellate division has sustained the writ in instances of unauthorized discovery orders,[30] and in the case of an unauthorized trial order of dismissal, entered before any evidence is presented.[31]

The People may not appeal from a CPL § 190.85(2)(b) sealing of a grand jury report issued pursuant to CPL § 190.85(1)(c)[32] as opposed to

20. *See, e.g.*, People v. Golon, 174 A.D.2d 630, 571 N.Y.S.2d 98 (2d Dep't 1991); People v. Concepcion, 167 A.D.2d 413, 561 N.Y.S.2d 823 (2d Dep't 1990).

21. *See, e.g.*, People v. Ryan, 195 A.D.2d 1053, 601 N.Y.S.2d 895 (4th Dep't 1993).

22. People v. Chapman, 227 A.D.2d 665, 641 N.Y.S.2d 472 (3d Dep't 1996).

23. People v. Doe, 170 A.D.2d 690, 567 N.Y.S.2d 104 (2d Dep't 1991), appeal dismissed 77 N.Y.2d 956, 570 N.Y.S.2d 486, 573 N.E.2d 574 (1991).

24. 178 A.D.2d 1019, 578 N.Y.S.2d 774 (4th Dep't 1991).

25. People v. Crossland, 220 A.D.2d 764, 633 N.Y.S.2d 324 (2d Dep't 1995); People v. Austin, 208 A.D.2d 990, 618 N.Y.S.2d 115 (3d Dep't 1994).

26. People v. Herrara, 173 A.D.2d 850, 571 N.Y.S.2d 63 (2d Dep't 1991).

27. *Id*.

28. Jaffe v. Scheinman, 47 N.Y.2d 188, 417 N.Y.S.2d 241, 390 N.E.2d 1165 (1979); Proskin v. County Court of Albany County, 30 N.Y.2d 15, 330 N.Y.S.2d 44, 280 N.E.2d 875 (1972).

29. State v. King, 36 N.Y.2d 59, 62, 364 N.Y.S.2d 879, 880, 324 N.E.2d 351, 352 (1975).

30. *See, e.g.*, Hynes v. Cirigliano, 180 A.D.2d 659, 579 N.Y.S.2d 171 (2d Dep't 1992).

31. Holtzman v. Goldman, 71 N.Y.2d 564, 528 N.Y.S.2d 21, 523 N.E.2d 297 (1988).

32. In re Matter of Report, Grand Jury Exhibit 83A, 221 A.D.2d 541, 634 N.Y.S.2d 134 (2d Dep't 1995).

a CPL § 190.90 sealing.[33] The People are held strictly to timely appeal provisions.[34] There are no provisions for extending their time comparable to the defendant's.[35]

Reduction of a Count of an Indictment; Dismissal of an Indictment and Directing the Filing of a Prosecutor's Information. Often, evidence may not support a charge or count of an indictment, but a reasonable view of the evidence may support a lesser included offense. Juries sometimes say just that, following judges' instructions.[36]

In pretrial matters, however, judges are asked to review indictments for grand jury evidence sufficiency and may conclude that a count or counts are not supported by sufficient evidence.[37] Under earlier decisions the court was obliged to dismiss such a count even though the proof reasonably supported a lesser included offense.[38] The CPL was amended to add Section 210.20(1–a)[39] to allow the court to "reduce" the count accordingly[40] and to order the case into local criminal court upon a prosecutor's information if the proof supports only a petty offense. The amendment was held to be prospective only[41] and the *nisi prius* courts are now routinely addressing motions to "inspect and reduce" counts of indictments.[42] Having given these reduction powers to trial level courts, the Legislature accorded a corresponding right to the People to appeal from a reduction order and, if they prevail, to gain reinstatement of the count or counts.[43]

Orders Setting Aside a Verdict; Post–Verdict Trial Orders of Dismissal. Criminal Procedure Law §§ 450.20(2) and 450.20(3) authorize People's appeals from trial court orders setting aside verdicts. A trial court has the authority to set aside a verdict in a number of instances. One such instance relates to post-verdict trial orders of dismissal.[44] When a defendant moves for a trial order of dismissal ("T.O.D.") at the conclusion of the People's case or at the close of the evidence, the trial court may grant the order then and there, and dismiss the indictment or one of its counts based upon *legal* insufficiency (*i.e.*, failure to measure

33. Compare grand jury reports issued pursuant to CPL § 190.85(1)(a) and sealed pursuant to CPL § 190.85(5). *See infra generally*, § 38.11 as to grand jury reports.

34. People v. Castillo, 148 A.D.2d 463, 538 N.Y.S.2d 1009 (2d Dep't 1989).

35. People v. Voutsinas, 62 A.D.2d 465, 406 N.Y.S.2d 138 (3d Dep't 1978); CPL §§ 460.30, 460.10(1)(a).

36. CPL § 300.50.

37. CPL §§ 210.20, 210.30.

38. People v. Adorno, 112 A.D.2d 308, 491 N.Y.S.2d 755 (2d Dep't 1985), appeal denied 65 N.Y.2d 975, 494 N.Y.S.2d 1043, 484 N.E.2d 673 (1985).

39. L. 1990, Ch. 209.

40. *See* Preiser, *1990 Supplementary Practice Commentaries* CPL § 210.20, at p.9.

41. People v. Parmelee, 184 A.D.2d 534, 584 N.Y.S.2d 318 (2d Dep't 1992).

42. People v. Nunez, 157 Misc.2d 793, 598 N.Y.S.2d 917 (Sup.Ct., Queens County, 1993).

43. CPL § 450.20(1–a); People v. Smith, 182 A.D.2d 725, 582 N.Y.S.2d 454 (2d Dep't 1992); People v. Herndon, 176 A.D.2d 817, 575 N.Y.S.2d 141 (2d Dep't 1991).

44. CPL § 450.20(2).

§ 38.10

up to a "legal case") and thereby keep the case or part of it from the jury.[45] There are parallel provisions for trial of an information.[46] Or the court may take the preferred path, by reserving decision on the motion for a T.O.D., giving the case to the jury, and then ruling on the motion *after the verdict*. If the defendant is acquitted, that, of course, ends the matter, but if the defendant is found guilty, the court then rules on the T.O.D. motion. If the court grants the motion and orders the verdict set aside by dismissing the indictment or one of its counts, the People may appeal the order. That is the essence of CPL § 450.20(2). Courts are encouraged to reserve decision so as to rule on the T.O.D. motion *after* the verdict.[47] This will allow the case to go to the jury and thereby permit appellate review and possible reinstatement of the verdict after a trial court has set it aside, thus obviating double jeopardy problems.

If the court grants the T.O.D. before the verdict, the People will be stripped of the right to have the T.O.D. reviewed.[48] (Obviously, when the court dismisses an indictment or a count before the verdict, there is no verdict to set aside and the People's right to appeal a set-aside verdict under CPL § 450.20(2) becomes inoperative.) Nor may the People appeal a T.O.D. following a deadlocked jury.[49]

The post-verdict appeal by the People protocol of CPL § 450.20(2) satisfies double jeopardy concerns as long as the verdict is rendered as to any count or counts thereafter dismissed under a T.O.D. A verdict that had been set aside may be reinstated by the appellate court, if appropriate, with no occasion for any further fact-findings or renewal of proceedings. In adopting this protocol in CPL § 450.20,[50] the Legislature responded to a declaration of unconstitutionality of the predecessor statute[51] when the Court of Appeals struck down that statute on double jeopardy grounds, in *People v. Brown*.[52]

A trial order of dismissal, entered before evidence is presented, is unauthorized. Although the People may not appeal it, the order is reviewable under CPLR Article 78.[53]

The other section that authorizes Peoples' appeals from trial court orders setting aside verdicts is CPL § 450.20(3). That section becomes operative after a guilty verdict has been received, and the defendant, before sentencing, moves to set aside the verdict on any number of

45. CPL § 290.10(1)(a).
46. CPL § 360.40.
47. People v. Key, 45 N.Y.2d 111, 120, 408 N.Y.S.2d 16, 20, 379 N.E.2d 1147, 1151 (1978).
48. People v. Harding, 101 A.D.2d 221, 475 N.Y.S.2d 611 (3d Dep't 1984).
49. People v. Ainsworth, 145 A.D.2d 74, 537 N.Y.S.2d 798 (1st Dep't 1989), appeal withdrawn 74 N.Y.2d 894, 548 N.Y.S.2d 426, 547 N.E.2d 953 (1989).

50. L. 1983, Ch. 170.
51. L. 1970, Ch. 996.
52. 40 N.Y.2d 381, 386 N.Y.S.2d 848, 353 N.E.2d 811 (1976), cert. denied 433 U.S. 913, 97 S.Ct. 2986, 53 L.Ed.2d 1099 (1977).
53. Holtzman v. Goldman, 71 N.Y.2d 564, 528 N.Y.S.2d 21, 523 N.E.2d 297 (1988).

grounds under CPL § 330.30. When the ground is legal insufficiency, it is much the same as a motion for a trial order of dismissal that the court entertains after verdict. Other grounds for a motion to set aside a verdict include improper juror conduct,[54] newly discovered evidence,[55] and such grounds as would require an appellate court to reverse the judgment as a matter of law.[56]

If the court grants a CPL § 330.30 order[57] and sets aside or modifies the verdict in whole or in part, the People may appeal the order pursuant to CPL § 450.20(3),[58] and, if successful, gain reinstatement of the verdict.[59] When the indictment is reinstated by the appellate division, it will remit the matter to the trial court to impose sentence,[60] following which, on appeal by the defendant from what would then be a judgment of conviction, the appellate division will examine the *weight* of the evidence, having already examined and upheld its sufficiency.[61] It is important to bear in mind here that a trial court in a criminal case does not have the authority to set aside a verdict on the ground that it is against the weight of evidence. That is a question of fact, reviewable on appeal by the appellate division, but not by the trial court whose determination as to the evidence must relate only to its *legal* sufficiency, whether it be a bench trial[62] or a jury trial.[63]

Sentences (Legality). The People may appeal a sentence (other than one of death) to the appellate division so as to have it vacated or modified *if* it is legally invalid.[64] A major difference between sentence appeals by the People and those by the defendant is that the People may challenge only the sentence's legality, and may argue only that the sentence is invalid as a matter of law,[65] whereas the defendant may challenge the sentence on other grounds as well.[66]

54. CPL § 330.30(2).

55. CPL § 330.30(3).

56. CPL § 330.30(1).

57. CPL § 370.10 (as for informations).

58. People v. McDonald, 68 N.Y.2d 1, 7, 505 N.Y.S.2d 824, 827, 496 N.E.2d 844, 847 (1986), motion dismissed 69 N.Y.2d 724, 512 N.Y.S.2d 366, 504 N.E.2d 693 (1987).

59. People v. Painter, 221 A.D.2d 481, 633 N.Y.S.2d 547 (2d Dep't 1995)(order setting aside verdict on grounds of legal insufficiency reversed, verdict reinstated); People v. Copeland, 185 A.D.2d 280, 585 N.Y.S.2d 794 (2d Dep't 1992), appeal dismissed 80 N.Y.2d 902, 588 N.Y.S.2d 827, 602 N.E.2d 235 (1992)(order setting aside verdict on grounds of newly discovered evidence reversed, verdict reinstated).

60. People v. Carmody, 203 A.D.2d 298, 609 N.Y.S.2d 670 (2d Dep't 1994).

61. People v. Raucci, 202 A.D.2d 697, 609 N.Y.S.2d 333 (2d Dep't 1994).

62. People v. Carter, 63 N.Y.2d 530, 483 N.Y.S.2d 654, 473 N.E.2d 6 (1984).

63. People v. Jones, 188 A.D.2d 331, 591 N.Y.S.2d 159 (1st Dep't 1992), 188 A.D.2d 331, 591 N.Y.S.2d 159, appeal denied 81 N.Y.2d 888, 597 N.Y.S.2d 949, 613 N.E.2d 981 (1993); People v. D'Alessandro, 184 A.D.2d 114, 591 N.Y.S.2d 1001 (1st Dep't 1992), appeal denied 81 N.Y.2d 884, 597 N.Y.S.2d 945, 613 N.E.2d 977 (1993). Compare civil case (CPLR 4404(a)) powers of trial judge relative to setting aside a verdict as against the weight of evidence. *See supra*, § 37.65.

64. Anderson v. Kirk, 72 N.Y.2d 995, 534 N.Y.S.2d 369, 530 N.E.2d 1289 (1988); CPL § 450.20(4).

65. People v. Blanks, 62 A.D.2d 1021, 403 N.Y.S.2d 553 (2d Dep't 1978).

66. *See supra*, § 38.8.

§ 38.10   CRIMINAL APPELLATE PRACTICE   Ch. 38

Because the People's right to appeal a sentence is so narrowly based, it does not extend to their claim that the trial court acted improperly in imposing a sentence following the acceptance of a defendant's plea over the People's objection.[67] On the other hand, the People have been successful in overturning invalid sentences.[68] But when the appellate division has found the sentence merely to have been inappropriate, it would not vacate the sentence, considering that it was not invalid as a matter of law.[69] Similarly, the People have no right of appeal from an order lawfully modifying a condition of probation pursuant to CPL § 410.20.[70]

Orders Vacating Judgments. Pursuant to CPL § 440.10, if a court vacates a *judgment* of conviction (except one of death), the People may appeal the order of *vacatur* to the appellate division pursuant to CPL § 450.20(5).[71] When a court vacates a *sentence* (pursuant to CPL § 440.20) the People's appeal is authorized under CPL § 450.20(6). This, essentially, is the People's means of challenging a *nisi prius* grant of what used to be *coram nobis* relief that is now codified under CPL Article 440.

An order vacating a *judgment* pursuant to CPL § 440.10 may be based upon any of several grounds including, broadly speaking, a lack of jurisdiction, fraud, knowingly perjured testimony, constitutional deprivation, mental deficiency of the defendant, reversible *dehors* the record error, or newly discovered evidence. Each of these categories has its own set of standards and requirements that comprise the litigational content of CPL Article 440 applications.

Appeals of CPL § 440.10 Judgment Vacatur Orders. In this section of the work we will treat instances in which the People have appealed CPL § 440.10 judgment *vacatur* orders. By way of introduction, there is a long established body of decisional law dealing with the concept of post-conviction collateral attack on judgments. The cases are rooted in the idea that not all wrongs appear on the record, and that while review by direct appeal will ordinarily identify reversible record error there may be injustices, or claimed injustices, that have escaped the record but merit review. Within this early line of cases are those that

---

67. People v. Cosme, 80 N.Y.2d 790, 587 N.Y.S.2d 274, 599 N.E.2d 678 (1992).

68. *See, e.g.*, People v. Juliano, 207 A.D.2d 414, 615 N.Y.S.2d 460 (2d Dep't 1994), appeal denied 84 N.Y.2d 937, 621 N.Y.S.2d 534, 645 N.E.2d 1234 (1994) (defendant's predicate conviction established; sentence vacated); People v. Mastropietro, 198 A.D.2d 443, 604 N.Y.S.2d 149 (2d Dep't 1993)(trial court's finding of unconstitutionality of sentencing minima, reversed); People v. Hipp, 197 A.D.2d 590, 602 N.Y.S.2d 428 (2d Dep't 1993), appeal denied 82 N.Y.2d 896, 610 N.Y.S.2d 163, 632 N.E.2d 473 (1993) (sentence illegal under NYPL § 70.02(1)(a), reversed); People v. Cameron, 193 A.D.2d 752, 597 N.Y.S.2d 724 (2d Dep't 1993) (illegal minimum sentence, reversed).

69. People v. Washington, 175 A.D.2d 732, 573 N.Y.S.2d 180 (1st Dep't 1991), appeal denied 78 N.Y.2d 1082, 577 N.Y.S.2d 246, 583 N.E.2d 958 (1991).

70. People v. Cohen, 222 A.D.2d 447, 635 N.Y.S.2d 38 (2d Dep't 1995).

71. *See* this section as discussed below.

deal with the reasons for defendants' failure to take appeals, notably, the failure of counsel,[72] misconduct of prison officials,[73] insanity,[74] or ignorance.[75]

Recognizing that there ought to be a vehicle for review when for good and valid reasons the door to direct appellate review is closed, the courts had developed the writ of error *coram nobis*, now mostly (but not entirely) supplanted by CPL Article 440. The grounds for post-conviction collateral attacks on judgments reflect the evolution of the *coram nobis* writ, and its current statutory dimension under CPL § 440.10. Developments are best discerned by examining the Peoples' appeals from *nisi prius* CPL § 440.10 *vacaturs* to identify the arguments that trial level courts have accepted in entering orders vacating judgments of conviction, and how these orders of *vacatur* have fared at the appellate level.

Most of the CPL § 440.10 judgment *vacaturs* fall into several groupings, including claims of ineffective assistance of counsel, claims of guilty plea involuntariness or coercion, newly discovered evidence, and claims that the prosecution withheld material. The first subdivision, CPL § 440.10(1), relates to jurisdiction, and has not occasioned a great deal of appellate litigation. The *vacatur* of a judgment of conviction on jurisdictional grounds by way of collateral attack is a rare event. When it took place in *People v. Salvato*,[76] the appellate division reversed the order of *vacatur*, concluding that the language of the challenged indictment was adequate.

In the effective representation area, there have been several instances in which the People have appealed judgment *vacaturs* that were based on the trial court's conclusion that there was a denial of the right to effective representation. The People prevailed and gained reversals and reinstatements in *People v. Lane*[77] and in *People v. Appel*.[78] In *Appel*, the appellate division found no deprivation by an attorney who declined to go along with defendant's proposed perjury. In *People v. Tannenbaum*,[79] the appellate division remitted the matter for a hearing, and in *People v. Jones*[80] the appellate division affirmed the *vacatur*, owing to the attorney's conflict of interest.

A prosecutor's failure to disclose a cooperation agreement with a material witness amounts to a violation of a defendant's right to a fair

---

72. People v. Montgomery, 24 N.Y.2d 130, 299 N.Y.S.2d 156, 247 N.E.2d 130 (1969).

73. People v. Hairston, 10 N.Y.2d 92, 217 N.Y.S.2d 77, 176 N.E.2d 90 (1961).

74. People v. Hill, 8 N.Y.2d 935, 204 N.Y.S.2d 172, 168 N.E.2d 841 (1960).

75. People v. Adams, 12 N.Y.2d 417, 240 N.Y.S.2d 155, 190 N.E.2d 529 (1963).

76. 111 A.D.2d 773, 490 N.Y.S.2d 31 (2d Dep't 1985).

77. 93 A.D.2d 92, 460 N.Y.S.2d 926 (1st Dep't 1983), appeal denied 59 N.Y.2d 974, 466 N.Y.S.2d 1035, 453 N.E.2d 559 (1983).

78. 120 A.D.2d 319, 509 N.Y.S.2d 438 (3d Dep't 1986).

79. 173 A.D.2d 750, 570 N.Y.S.2d 625 (2d Dep't 1991).

80. 184 A.D.2d 405, 585 N.Y.S.2d 362 (1st Dep't 1992), appeal denied 80 N.Y.2d 905, 588 N.Y.S.2d 830, 602 N.E.2d 238 (1992).

§ 38.10   CRIMINAL APPELLATE PRACTICE   Ch. 38

trial.[81] In New York, it had been grounds for *coram nobis* relief[82] and would now be a proper basis for CPL § 440.10 relief. Based on *Giglio* grounds, CPL § 440.10 was invoked successfully by a defendant in *People v. Grice*.[83] The *vacatur* of his conviction was affirmed; the court characterized it as a *Brady* violation.[84]

In a number of instances, the People have appealed from judgment *vacaturs* that were based on claims of plea involuntariness. A claim of this kind is properly brought under CPL §§ 440.10(1)(b) or (f) or (h), but it must be bottomed on improper conduct not in the record.[85] If the assertion is reviewable with reference to the record, the *vacatur* will be reversed and conviction reinstated, inasmuch as the claim is cognizable on direct appeal.[86]

In other instances, Peoples' appeals have been successful in gaining reversals of *vacaturs* that were based on claims of plea involuntariness.[87] Newly discovered evidence has long been a claimed basis for a new trial,[88] and it is included within the statutory panoply under CPL § 440.10(1)(g). Trial courts have granted *vacaturs* in several such instances only to be reversed on People's appeals.[89] In *People v. Gurley*,[90] however, the appellate division affirmed the *vacatur*.

The most recent development under CPL § 440.10 involves claims under *People v. Rosario*[91] and *Brady v. Maryland*.[92] Considering that both cases involve obligations on the part of the People to turn over material to the defense, the question of timing arises. Section 440.10 comes into play when a *Rosario* or *Brady* issue arises after trial, beyond the point at

81. Giglio v. United States, 405 U.S. 150, 92 S.Ct. 763, 31 L.Ed.2d 104 (1972).

82. *See, e.g.*, People v. Savvides, 1 N.Y.2d 554, 154 N.Y.S.2d 885, 136 N.E.2d 853 (1956).

83. 188 A.D.2d 397, 591 N.Y.S.2d 380 (1st Dep't 1992), appeal denied 81 N.Y.2d 840, 595 N.Y.S.2d 739, 611 N.E.2d 778 (1993).

84. *See generally*, Brady v. Maryland, 373 U.S. 83, 83 S.Ct. 1194, 10 L.Ed.2d 215 (1963)(withholding or suppression of evidence by prosecution in criminal case as vitiating conviction).

85. People v. Cooks, 67 N.Y.2d 100, 500 N.Y.S.2d 503, 491 N.E.2d 676 (1986).

86. People v. Skinner, 154 A.D.2d 216, 552 N.Y.S.2d 932 (1st Dep't 1990), appeal denied 76 N.Y.2d 796, 559 N.Y.S.2d 1001, 559 N.E.2d 695 (1990); People v. Torres, 125 A.D.2d 252, 509 N.Y.S.2d 540 (1st Dep't 1986).

87. *See, e.g.*, People v. Harris, 198 A.D.2d 434, 604 N.Y.S.2d 824 (2d Dep't 1993); People v. Parker, 85 A.D.2d 565, 445 N.Y.S.2d 443 (1st Dep't 1981).

88. People v. Trezza, 128 N.Y. 529, 28 N.E. 533 (1891); People v. Kudon, 173 A.D. 342, 158 N.Y.S. 817 (3d Dep't 1916).

89. People v. Latella, 112 A.D.2d 321, 491 N.Y.S.2d 771 (2d Dep't 1985), appeal denied 65 N.Y.2d 983, 494 N.Y.S.2d 1052, 484 N.E.2d 682 (1985); People v. Balan, 107 A.D.2d 811, 484 N.Y.S.2d 648 (2d Dep't 1985).

90. 197 A.D.2d 534, 602 N.Y.S.2d 184 (2d Dep't 1993).

91. 9 N.Y.2d 286, 173 N.E.2d 881, 213 N.Y.S.2d 448 (1961), reargument denied, 9 N.Y.2d 908, 176 N.E.2d 111, 216 N.Y.S.2d 1025 (1961), cert. denied 368 U.S. 866, 82 S.Ct. 117, 7 L.Ed.2d 64 (1961), reargument denied 14 N.Y.2d 876, 200 N.E.2d 784, 252 N.Y.S.2d 1027 (1964), reargument denied 15 N.Y.2d 765, 257 N.Y.S.2d 1027, 205 N.E.2d 538 (1965)(a case so renowned deserves this expansive citation).

92. 373 U.S. 83, 83 S.Ct. 1194, 10 L.Ed.2d 215 (1963).

which a court can take appropriate, pre-verdict steps. Once the trial is over, and *Brady* or *Rosario* material comes to light, or when it is so alleged, the trial court must make a threshold determination as to whether the material qualifies as *Rosario* or *Brady* material, and, if so, what should follow from the prosecution's failure to have furnished it at the appropriate time. As for *Rosario* material, the CPL § 440.10 test is whether the defendant has been prejudiced by the People's failure to have turned it over when they should have.[93] This "prejudice" test, of course, contrasts with the rule applied on direct appeal, notably that harmless error does not apply; it is *per se* error.[94]

A showing of prejudice as a basis for CPL § 440.10 relief brings *Rosario* claims within the purview of CPL § 440.10(1)(f) which deals with "improper and prejudicial conduct."[95] Under the *Jackson* formulation a defendant bears the burden of showing prejudice, notably, "a reasonable possibility that the failure to disclose the *Rosario* material contributed to the verdict."

In a number of instances the People's appeals from *vacatur* orders have been successful, based on the appellate division's determination that the material withheld was not *Rosario* material.[96] When material has been found to be governed by *Rosario*, the appellate division has applied the *Jackson* "prejudice" test in a number of appeals by the People from *vacatur* orders. When the test has been met (imparting a reasonable possibility that the failure to disclose contributed to the verdict), trial court *vacatur* orders have been affirmed.[97] Conversely, when the test has not been met, as where the showing of prejudice is lacking and there is no reasonable possibility of a different outcome, *vacatur* orders have been reversed.[98] If on the basis of the record the appellate division is unable to assess the degree of prejudice (or the character of the data as *Rosario* material), it will remit the case to the

---

93. People v. Jackson, 78 N.Y.2d 638, 641, 578 N.Y.S.2d 483, 484, 585 N.E.2d 795, 796 (1991), on remand 154 Misc.2d 718, 593 N.Y.S.2d 410 (1992), aff'd 198 A.D.2d 301, 603 N.Y.S.2d 558 (1993).

94. People v. Jones, 70 N.Y.2d 547, 523 N.Y.S.2d 53, 517 N.E.2d 865 (1987); People v. Ranghelle, 69 N.Y.2d 56, 511 N.Y.S.2d 580, 503 N.E.2d 1011 (1986).

95. People v. Jackson, 78 N.Y.2d 638, 645, 578 N.Y.S.2d 483, 486, 585 N.E.2d 795, 798 (1991), on remand 154 Misc.2d 718, 593 N.Y.S.2d 410 (1992), aff'd 198 A.D.2d 301, 603 N.Y.S.2d 558 (1993). In People v. Machado, 90 N.Y.2d 187, 659 N.Y.S.2d 242, 681 N.E.2d 409 (1997), the Court of Appeals applied the "prejudice requirement" in a CPL § 440.10 motion that was made before the direct appeal was determined.

96. People v. White, 210 A.D.2d 447, 620 N.Y.S.2d 437 (2d Dep't 1994), appeal denied 85 N.Y.2d 916, 627 N.Y.S.2d 339, 650 N.E.2d 1341 (1995); People v. Kelly, 209 A.D.2d 436, 618 N.Y.S.2d 822 (2d Dep't 1994).

97. See, e.g., People v. Ramos, 201 A.D.2d 78, 614 N.Y.S.2d 977 (1st Dep't 1994); People v. Jackson, 198 A.D.2d 301, 603 N.Y.S.2d 558 (2d Dep't 1993), appeal denied 83 N.Y.2d 806, 611 N.Y.S.2d 142, 633 N.E.2d 497 (1994).

98. See, e.g., People v. Boyette, 201 A.D.2d 490, 607 N.Y.S.2d 402 (2d Dep't 1994), appeal denied 83 N.Y.2d 909, 614 N.Y.S.2d 391, 637 N.E.2d 282 (1994); People v. Stevens, 199 A.D.2d 441, 608 N.Y.S.2d 83 (2d Dep't 1993), appeal denied 83 N.Y.2d 877, 613 N.Y.S.2d 137, 635 N.E.2d 306 (1994).

§ 38.10   CRIMINAL APPELLATE PRACTICE   Ch. 38

trial court for a hearing.[99] The People's right to appeal the *vacatur* order does not carry with it the right to appeal from an order in which the trial court merely grants a hearing. That order is unappealable and the appeal will be dismissed.[100]

Brady differs from *Rosario* in that *Brady* requires the prosecutor to deliver "exculpatory" material to the defense, while *Rosario* is not so limited and obligates the prosecutor to turn over *any* material that falls within the rule, whether it is exculpatory to the defendant or not, so that the question of its utility or value to the defense is to be adjudged only by the defense.[101] In appeals in CPL § 440.10 settings, *Rosario* claims are often bound up with *Brady* claims—indeed there may be overlap. Appellate practitioners should be aware of the differences, and of the standard to be applied for *vacatur* of a conviction owing to a *Brady* claim. As to whether an item is *Brady* material at all, the test is whether the material is exculpatory (*i.e.*, favorable to the defense) material either as to guilt or punishment, or affecting the credibility of prosecution witnesses.[102] As for the obligation to disclose it, the good faith of the prosecutor is beside the point, and unavailing to the People.[103] Assuming there to have been a *Brady* violation, the standard for *vacatur* of the judgment is "whether the omitted evidence creates a reasonable doubt that did not otherwise exist."[104]

In setting forth this "reasonable doubt" standard in *Baxley*, the court referred to *People v. Vilardi*[105] which adds another wrinkle. In *Vilardi* the court laid down the following test: When the prosecutor was made aware by a *specific discovery request* that the defense considers the material important, the prosecutor's failure to disclose it will require *vacatur* under *Brady* if there is "a reasonable possibility that the exculpatory material contributed to the verdict." This formulation is identical to *Jackson*,[106] for *Rosario* violations. Further, "if there is a reasonable possibility that the undisclosed evidence might have led to a trial strategy that resulted in a different outcome," the *vacatur* of the

---

99. People v. Harden, 188 A.D.2d 426, 592 N.Y.S.2d 2 (1st Dep't 1992). *See also*, CPL § 440.30(5).

100. People v. Guastella, 26 A.D.2d 937, 275 N.Y.S.2d 804 (2d Dep't 1966); People v. Monahan, 21 A.D.2d 748, 250 N.Y.S.2d 241 (4th Dep't 1964).

101. People v. DaGata, 86 N.Y.2d 40, 629 N.Y.S.2d 186, 652 N.E.2d 932 (1995); People v. Flores, 84 N.Y.2d 184, 615 N.Y.S.2d 662, 639 N.E.2d 19 (1994); People v. Banch, 80 N.Y.2d 610, 593 N.Y.S.2d 491, 608 N.E.2d 1069 (1992).

102. People v. Novoa, 70 N.Y.2d 490, 496, 522 N.Y.S.2d 504, 507, 517 N.E.2d 219, 222 (1987).

103. People v. Baxley, 84 N.Y.2d 208, 213–214, 616 N.Y.S.2d 7, 9, 639 N.E.2d 746, 748 (1994).

104. People v. Baxley, 84 N.Y.2d 208, 214, 616 N.Y.S.2d 7, 10, 639 N.E.2d 746, 749 (1994).

105. 76 N.Y.2d 67, 556 N.Y.S.2d 518, 555 N.E.2d 915 (1990).

106. People v. Jackson, 78 N.Y.2d 638, 645, 578 N.Y.S.2d 483, 486, 585 N.E.2d 795, 798 (1991), on remand 154 Misc.2d 718, 593 N.Y.S.2d 410 (1992), aff'd 198 A.D.2d 301, 603 N.Y.S.2d 558 (1993).

conviction is required.[107]

In formulating the test under state constitutional law, in terms of "reasonable possibility" for "specific request" cases, the Court of Appeals has distanced itself from the federal test, which is less favorable to the defendant. Under federal law,[108] the prosecutor's failure to disclose favorable evidence is constitutional error only if the evidence is material in the sense that there is a reasonable *probability* that had the evidence been disclosed to the defense the result of the proceeding would have been different; that is to say, a *probability* sufficient to undermine confidence in the outcome.[109]

Reading *Vilardi* in connection with *Baxley*, the following lesson emerges: If the *Brady* violation is in the face of a "specific request," the reasonable possibility standard applies in CPL § 440.10 review. If it is merely a general request for *Brady* material, the standard is whether the omitted evidence created a reasonable doubt that did not otherwise exist.

Given this format, there have been Peoples' appeals from *vacaturs* of judgments based on *Brady* violations. In *People v. Scott*[110] the Court of Appeals applied the "reasonable possibility" test in sustaining the appellate division's reversal of the *vacatur*.[111]

Orders Setting Aside Sentences. Just as the People may appeal from a *vacatur* of a *judgment*, they may also appeal from an order in which a judge employs CPL § 440.20 to set aside a *sentence* at the defendant's behest. This authorization is found in CPL § 450.20(6). The proper grounds for a court to set aside a sentence under CPL § 440.20 are, essentially, that the sentence was unauthorized, illegally imposed, or otherwise invalid as a matter of law. Note also that the People are authorized to seek *vacatur* of a sentence that is "invalid as a matter of law"[112] and the defendant may appeal (pursuant to CPL § 450.10(4)) from a People's successful CPL § 440.40 motion.

These appeals by the People from CPL § 440.20 orders often relate to the defendant's status as a predicate felon, but there are other settings possible. In *People v. Argentine*,[113] the trial court employed CPL § 440.20 to set aside the defendant's sentence in order to restart the appeal time. The order was reversed as being outside the scope and purpose of CPL § 440.20. The section was held, however, to be an appropriate means of setting aside a sentence owing to a plea negotiation misunderstanding, as against the prosecutor's claim that under CPL

---

107. *Vilardi*, 76 N.Y.2d at 78, 536 N.Y.S.2d at 522, 555 N.E.2d at 919. *See also*, People v. Wright, 86 N.Y.2d 591, 635 N.Y.S.2d 136, 658 N.E.2d 1009 (1995).

108. United States. v. Bagley, 473 U.S. 667, 105 S.Ct. 3375, 87 L.Ed.2d 481 (1985).

109. *Bagley*, 473 U.S. at 682, 105 S.Ct. at 3383, 87 L.Ed.2d 481.

110. 88 N.Y.2d 888, 644 N.Y.S.2d 913, 667 N.E.2d 923 (1996).

111. *Id.*

112. CPL § 440.40. *See also*, People v. Askew, 66 A.D.2d 710, 411 N.Y.S.2d 569 (1st Dep't 1978).

113. 73 A.D.2d 649, 422 N.Y.S.2d 736 (2d Dep't 1979).

§ 430.10, a court may not interrupt or change a sentence once commenced.[114]

The People have been successful on appeal in upsetting CPL § 440.20 orders in which the trial court sought to correct a sentence that was lawful, but arguably excessive, inasmuch as the statute is a vehicle to correct unauthorized or illegal sentences only. If there is no such infirmity, an order setting it aside will be reversed.[115] Repudiating the People's argument on their appeal in *People v. Bligen*,[116] the appellate division held that CPL § 440.20 was properly employed to vacate a sentence that had been imposed without a hearing to determine whether the defendant's failure to appear for sentence was intentional.

The People's appeal was also unsuccessful in seeking to reverse a CPL § 440.20 order that the appellate division found to have been properly made, owing to the unconstitutionality of the defendant's predicate conviction.[117] But in *People v. Barton*,[118] the People gained a reversal of a CPL § 440.20 order based on the defendant's failure to challenge his predicate felony status.

Orders Denying People's 440.40 Motions to Set Aside Sentences. When it comes to illegal sentences,[119] the People have appellate rights that are the corollary of those of the defendant, but they are less than a mirror image. The defendant, as we have seen, has a right of direct appeal from a sentence on grounds of legal invalidity or harshness.[120] The People also have a right of direct appeal from a sentence,[121] but the grounds are limited to legal invalidity.[122]

Another avenue of attack upon illegal or invalid sentences, our present concern, is through CPL Article 440. The process begins with a motion to set aside the sentence as illegal. The defendant may do this by moving under CPL § 440.20 to set aside a sentence as illegal ("unauthorized, illegally imposed or otherwise invalid as a matter of law"). The People enjoy a parallel right by moving, under CPL § 440.40, to set aside a sentence on the ground that it is "invalid as a matter of law."[123] Each side has the right to appeal from adverse determinations.

114. People v. Turner, 47 A.D.2d 564, 363 N.Y.S.2d 638 (2d Dep't 1975).

115. People v. Ferguson, 119 A.D.2d 338, 507 N.Y.S.2d 622 (1st Dep't 1986), appeal denied 71 N.Y.2d 895, 527 N.Y.S.2d 1005, 523 N.E.2d 312 (1988).

116. 72 A.D.2d 678, 421 N.Y.S.2d 212 (1st Dep't 1979).

117. People v. Love, 129 A.D.2d 258, 517 N.Y.S.2d 649 (4th Dep't 1987), aff'd 71 N.Y.2d 711, 530 N.Y.S.2d 55, 525 N.E.2d 701 (1988).

118. 200 A.D.2d 888, 606 N.Y.S.2d 842 (3d Dep't 1994), appeal denied 83 N.Y.2d 849, 612 N.Y.S.2d 380, 634 N.E.2d 981 (1994).

119. When we speak of appeals from orders denying motions to set aside sentences, it contemplates sentences other than those of death. CPL § 450.20(7).

120. CPL §§ 450.10, 450.30(1). *See also supra*, § 38.8.

121. CPL § 450.20(4).

122. CPL § 450.30(2),(3). *See also supra*, § 38.10.

123. In practice this amounts to the same thing. A sentence that is unauthorized or invalid as a matter of law is one,

If the People are successful in their CPL § 440.40 motion resulting in the *vacatur* of the sentence, the defendant may appeal under CPL § 450.10(4).[124] Conversely, if the defense is successful in its CPL § 440.20 motion, the People may appeal pursuant to CPL § 450.20(6).

On the other hand, a defendant, unsuccessful in a CPL § 440.20 motion, may appeal (by permission only) pursuant to CPL § 450.15. The corollary right of the People is the section at hand and completes the round-robin: if the People's motion to set aside a sentence pursuant to CPL § 440.40 is denied, they may appeal the order as of right pursuant to CPL § 450.20(7).

CPL § 450.20(7) has its restrictions. The first is its time limitations. If the People are to invoke CPL § 440.40 successfully, their motion to set aside the sentence must be made in time for it to be granted before the expiration of a year after the entry of judgment. Put differently, a court may set aside the sentence "at any time not more than a year after the entry of judgment"[125] based upon the People's claim of legal invalidity. The time limit is inflexible and stands in contrast to the defendant's right of unlimited duration to move to set aside an illegal sentence under CPL § 440.20.[126]

The People's statutory right to seek *vacatur* of an invalid sentence under CPL § 440.40 must be read in connection with two well established principles. The first is the statutory prohibition against changing a sentence after it has begun. That statute, CPL § 430.10, provides that "(e)xcept as otherwise specifically authorized by law, when the court has imposed a sentence of imprisonment and such sentence is in accordance with law, such sentence may not be changed, suspended or interrupted once the term or period of the sentence has commenced."[127] The other principle is that a court has an inherent right to correct its own errors.[128]

Thus, there are three principles at work that bear on one another: (1) the CPL Article 440 statutory right to undo illegal or invalid sentences, as measured against; (2) the court's inherent corrective powers; and (3) the restrictions against changing sentences once commenced.

for example, that goes beyond the sentencing range. A sentence that is lawful (*i.e.*, within the sentencing range) might be illegally imposed if it is imposed too early. People ex rel. Hastings v. Hofstadter, 258 N.Y. 425, 436, 180 N.E. 106, 110 (1932)). It could also be illegal if imposed outside of the defendant's presence. People v. Stroman, 36 N.Y.2d 939, 373 N.Y.S.2d 548, 335 N.E.2d 853 (1975). But there is no need to split hairs. By and large, the terms have been used interchangeably, and the multiplicity of adjectives undoubtedly reflects the legislature's aim to cover every conceivable sentence infirmity.

124. *See supra*, § 38.8.

125. CPL § 440.40.

126. People v. Riggins, 164 A.D.2d 797, 559 N.Y.S.2d 535 (1st Dep't 1990); Campbell v. Pesce, 60 N.Y.2d 165, 168, 468 N.Y.S.2d 865, 866, 456 N.E.2d 806, 807 (1983).

127. *See generally*, People v. Yannicelli, 40 N.Y.2d 598, 389 N.Y.S.2d 290, 357 N.E.2d 947 (1976).

128. People ex rel. Hirschberg v. Orange County Court, 271 N.Y. 151, 156–157, 2 N.E.2d 521, 524 (1936); Bohlen v. Metropolitan El. Ry. Co., 121 N.Y. 546, 550, 24 N.E. 932, 934 (1890).

§ 38.10 CRIMINAL APPELLATE PRACTICE Ch. 38

As for the court's inherent powers to correct its errors, decisional law has developed the scope of those powers and has placed limitations upon them. A court is not free to simply go about correcting its own errors whenever and however it pleases.[129]

The error-correcting capacity of a criminal court is generally limited to clerical errors, or instances in which the court patently misspoke.[130] A correction that goes beyond the clerical is unauthorized.[131]

CPL § 430.10, which prohibits changing sentences once imprisonment has commenced, has a long statutory history,[132] and even before that was recognized as a judicial tenet: "I think it a safe rule to lay down, that a court of criminal jurisdiction may vacate or modify a judgment at the same term at which it is pronounced, and before the Sheriff has proceeded to execute it."[133]

CPL § 430.10 has been raised as a barrier against prosecution attempts to vacate (*i.e.*, change so as to increase or enhance) sentences. The attempts have been unsuccessful owing to the exclusion in CPL § 430.10 which itself suggests that the prohibition against change applies only to *legal* sentences.[134]

Given that the court has no inherent power to grant sentence *vacaturs* of consequence (unless, as we have seen, they are the result of clerical errors) we may concentrate on the scope of CPL § 440.40, which gives the prosecutor the statutory basis to have legally invalid sentences undone. To begin with, the statute accords the prosecutor the right to attack only the sentence, and not the underlying conviction. CPL § 440.40(5) itself states that an order entered granting the People's motion to set aside the sentence "does not affect the validity of the underlying conviction." As the court put it in *People v. Hardin*,[135] "we note that with respect to sentence, unlike the conviction, the People as

---

129. In the civil arena CPLR 5019 contemplates judicial error-correction even after judgment, but it is limited to mistakes, defects, or irregularities, providing that such correction does not affect the substantial right of a party.

130. People v. Wright, 56 N.Y.2d 613, 450 N.Y.S.2d 473, 435 N.E.2d 1088 (1982); People v. Minaya, 54 N.Y.2d 360, 445 N.Y.S.2d 690, 429 N.E.2d 1161 (1981), cert. denied 455 U.S. 1024, 102 S.Ct. 1725, 72 L.Ed.2d 144 (1982); Laveroni v. Rohl, 175 A.D.2d 163, 572 N.Y.S.2d 52 (2d Dep't 1991). It also has the power to vacate judgments obtained by fraud or misrepresentation. Lockett v. Juviler, 65 N.Y.2d 182, 490 N.Y.S.2d 764, 480 N.E.2d 378 (1985); Lyons v. Goldstein, 290 N.Y. 19, 47 N.E.2d 425 (1943).

131. People v. Thomas, 210 A.D.2d 443, 620 N.Y.S.2d 433 (2d Dep't 1994). *See also*, Kisloff on Behalf of Wilson v. Covington, 73 N.Y.2d 445, 541 N.Y.S.2d 737, 539 N.E.2d 565 (1989).

132. *See* Former Code Crim. Pro. § 482(3); former Penal Law § 2188; People ex rel. Paris v. Hunt, 201 App.Div. 573, 194 N.Y.S. 699 (3d Dep't 1922), aff'd, 234 N.Y. 558, 138 N.E. 445 (1922).

133. Miller v. Finkle, 1 Parker Cr. R. 374 (1853).

134. People v. Minaya, 54 N.Y.2d 360, 445 N.Y.S.2d 690, 429 N.E.2d 1161 (1981), cert. denied 455 U.S. 1024, 102 S.Ct. 1725, 72 L.Ed.2d 144 (1982); People v. Wright, 80 A.D.2d 624, 625, 436 N.Y.S.2d 68, 69 (2d Dep't 1981), aff'd 56 N.Y.2d 613, 450 N.Y.S.2d 473, 435 N.E.2d 1088 (1982).

135. 67 A.D.2d 12, 17, 414 N.Y.S.2d 320, 322 (1st Dep't 1979).

well as the defendant may move to set aside the sentence as invalid as a matter of law...." The Court of Appeals cited CPL § 440.40(5) to authorize *sentence vacatur* only,[136] so that even though the underlying plea was illegal (*i.e.*, in violation of the reduced plea provisions of CPL § 180.50(2)(b)(ii)), the People could not successfully invoke CPL § 440.40. The *Pesce* court held that the People have no statutory right to upset a plea, in contrast to a defendant who may challenge not only a sentence[137] but may seek to vacate a judgment (*i.e.*, including the plea) as well.[138] The inherent power of the court to correct clerical errors does not extend to the *vacatur* of a plea—however illegal it may have been—which was entered when the parties were laboring under a misimpression as to the grade of the crime to which the defendant pleaded guilty.[139] In *People v. Monereau*,[140] however, the appellate division held that the trial court was empowered to conform the defendant's plea to one of a less serious crime so that he would receive the same sentence that had been negotiated.

For the People, the real utility of CPL § 440.40 and its appellate enforcer, CPL § 450.20(7), comes about when the People move, in timely fashion, to upset a sentence as legally invalid, typically involving a predicate conviction. This most obvious basis of employment for the statute—in cases of recidivism—occurs in cases in which the court does not sentence the defendant in accordance with mandated predicate offender statutes. It is the same challenge that may be raised by the People on direct appeal under CPL § 450.20(4).[141]

CPL § 450.20(7) is also designed for less obvious settings, notably those in which the sentence is imposed and no one (except perhaps the defendant) realizes or remembers that the defendant is a predicate felon. It has come up in a number of ways. *People v. Barnes*[142] represents the epitome of CPL § 450.20(7) usage. The defendant concealed his status as a prior felon. He had, in effect, gained sentencing as a first felon by means of deceit and aliases. By the time the prosecution discovered it, several months had passed but they were within the one-year limitation and succeeded in having the sentence set aside as legally invalid.[143]

---

136. Campbell v. Pesce, 60 N.Y.S.2d 165, 168, 468 N.Y.S.2d 865, 866, 456 N.E.2d 806, 807 (1983).

137. CPL § 440.20.

138. CPL § 440.10.

139. Kisloff on Behalf of Wilson v. Covington, 73 N.Y.2d 445, 541 N.Y.S.2d 737, 539 N.E.2d 565 (1989). *See also*, People v. Moquin, 77 N.Y.2d 449, 568 N.Y.S.2d 710, 570 N.E.2d 1059 (1991).

140. 181 A.D.2d 918, 581 N.Y.S.2d 848 (2d Dep't 1992), appeal denied 79 N.Y.2d 1052, 584 N.Y.S.2d 1019, 596 N.E.2d 417 (1992).

141. *See, e.g.*, People v. Juliano, 207 A.D.2d 414, 615 N.Y.S.2d 460 (2d Dep't 1994), appeal denied 84 N.Y.2d 937, 621 N.Y.S.2d 534, 645 N.E.2d 1234 (1994); People v. Hipp, 197 A.D.2d 590, 602 N.Y.S.2d 428 (2d Dep't 1993), appeal denied 82 N.Y.2d 896, 610 N.Y.S.2d 163, 632 N.E.2d 473 (1993). *See supra*, § 38.10.

142. 160 A.D.2d 342, 553 N.Y.S.2d 413 (1st Dep't 1990).

143. *See also*, People v. Holley, 168 A.D.2d 992, 565 N.Y.S.2d 351 (4th Dep't 1990).

Another type of invalid sentence, vulnerable to *vacatur* upon the People's motion or appeal, is one that is imposed in violation of the People's rights under *People v. Farrar*.[144] Because the People have the right to negotiate sentences under *Ferrar*, a sentence imposed in violation of those rights was vacated.[145]

A sentence will be declared legally invalid and in violation of the mandatory repeat offender provisions of CPL § 400.21 when the court and the prosecutor are aware, or should be aware, of the defendant's predicate felony status, and did not invoke the mandatory sentencing provision.[146] In any case, CPL § 440.40 is a proper avenue for the People to set aside a sentence once the deadline for direct appeal passes.[147]

The statute has produced its share of irony. A defendant negotiated a sentence and then, after negotiating a shorter sentence, attacked its provisions and gained release on *habeas corpus*, only to be met with a motion to have the sentence vacated. He was resentenced in accordance with the parties' original intentions.[148]

Suppression Orders. CPL § 450.20(8) allows the People to appeal an order in which a court has suppressed evidence. There are several pre-conditions to such an appeal by the People.

First, the suppression *order* must have been made pursuant to CPL § 710.20.[149] That section covers a number of suppressible items of "evidence," (defined as tangible property or potential testimony) in the possession of, or available to, a prosecutor who may offer it in evidence.[150] Most of the suppression rulings relate to suppression of physical evidence, such as:

—tangible property, involving what are commonly called *Mapp*[151] hearings;[152]

—eavesdropping, recording, or video evidence;[153]

—statements of the defendant, involving what are known as "*Huntley*[154] hearings";[155]

144. 52 N.Y.2d 302, 437 N.Y.S.2d 961, 419 N.E.2d 864 (1981).

145. People v. Ciccone, 91 A.D.2d 688, 457 N.Y.S.2d 328 (2d Dep't 1982).

146. People v. Scarbrough, 66 N.Y.2d 673, 496 N.Y.S.2d 409, 487 N.E.2d 266 (1985). See also, People v. Gilchrist, 152 A.D.2d 923, 543 N.Y.S.2d 837 (4th Dep't 1989).

147. People v. Johnson, 215 A.D.2d 258, 626 N.Y.S.2d 775 (1st Dep't 1995), appeal denied 86 N.Y.2d 796, 632 N.Y.S.2d 510, 656 N.E.2d 609 (1995)(resentence affirmed; original sentence was in violation of NYPL § 70.08(2), (3)(c)). *But see*, Morgenthau v. Roberts, 47 A.D.2d 826, 366 N.Y.S.2d 20 (1st Dep't 1975).

148. People v. Herrington, 136 A.D.2d 871, 524 N.Y.S.2d 530 (3d Dep't 1988).

149. There is no appeal from a decision. See People v. Crossland, 220 A.D.2d 764, 633 N.Y.S.2d 324 (2d Dep't 1995).

150. CPL § 710.10(2).

151. Mapp v. Ohio, 367 U.S. 643, 81 S.Ct. 1684, 6 L.Ed.2d 1081 (1961). *See also*, Marks, *et al.*, *New York Pretrial Criminal Procedure* (West 1996).

152. CPL § 710.20(1).

153. CPL § 710.20(2).

154. People v. Huntley, 15 N.Y.2d 72, 255 N.Y.S.2d 838, 204 N.E.2d 179 (1965).

—derivative evidence of the above;[156]

—blood test evidence;[157]

—identification testimony under CPL § 710.20(6) tested at "*Wade*[158] hearings"; and

—pen register or trap device information.[159]

The threshold question for appealability is not whether the suppression order debilitated the People's proof or even destroyed it, but only whether the suppression order was based on one of the grounds enumerated above. If, for example, the court made a pretrial determination on evidentiary grounds by which it blocked the introduction of proof, the People could not appeal the determination, however disabling it might have been. Accordingly, a pretrial ruling by a court foreclosing the People from introducing evidence of the defendant's prior bad acts and "suppressing" a tape recording on the ground of inaudibility is not appealable.[160] In actuality the *Weaver* court foreclosed the use of the tape recording. It used the word "suppress," thus possibly exciting the People's appellate appetite, but it was not a suppression order of the type referred to under CPL § 710.20, which relates, by and large, to evidence subject to exclusionary rules that are dependent upon constitutional interpretations.

Second, the statute contemplates only pretrial suppression orders. If the order suppressing the evidence is entered after trial, the order will not be appealable.[161] The protocol for suppression motions contemplates pretrial hearings, so that the People's right to appeal does not interrupt a trial. If the order of suppression is entered after the trial starts, the People's right to appeal will be cut off and their appeal from the suppression order dismissed.[162]

Next, the order must be one of *suppression*; nothing else will do. The People may not appeal a preclusion order, no matter how destructive it is of their case. In *People v. Laing*,[163] the Court of Appeals held that there is a critical distinction between a suppression order under CPL § 710.20 and a preclusion order under CPL § 710.30. Only the former is appealable.[164]

155. CPL § 710.20(3).
156. CPL § 710.20(4).
157. CPL § 710.20(5).
158. United States v. Wade, 388 U.S. 218, 87 S.Ct. 1926, 18 L.Ed.2d 1149 (1967).
159. CPL § 710.20(7).
160. People v. Weaver, 177 A.D.2d 809, 576 N.Y.S.2d 424 (3d Dep't 1991).
161. CPL § 450.20(8).
162. People v. Garofalo, 71 A.D.2d 782, 419 N.Y.S.2d 784 (3d Dep't 1979), appeal dismissed 49 N.Y.2d 879, 427 N.Y.S.2d 990, 405 N.E.2d 233 (1980); People v. Austin, 208 A.D.2d 990, 618 N.Y.S.2d 115 (3d Dep't 1994).
163. 79 N.Y.2d 166, 581 N.Y.S.2d 149, 589 N.E.2d 372 (1992).
164. *See also*, People v. Austin, 208 A.D.2d 990, 618 N.Y.S.2d 115 (3d Dep't 1994); People v. Mabrey, 188 A.D.2d 1086, 592 N.Y.S.2d 1014 (4th Dep't 1992).

The proper remedy for a defendant is a motion to *preclude* if the People's CPL § 710.30 notice is lacking,[165] or inadequate,[166] or untimely.[167] There will be no waiver, however, if the defendant proceeds with the suppression motion after the motion to preclude is denied.[168]

Finally, in addition to the notice of appeal, the People must file a statement, pursuant to CPL § 450.50, asserting that:

> [T]he deprivation of the use of the evidence ordered suppressed has rendered the sum of the proof available to the People with respect to a criminal charge which has been filed with the court either (a) insufficient as a matter of law or (b) so weak in its entirety that any reasonable possibility of prosecuting such charge to a conviction has been effectively destroyed.

This is a legalistic way of saying that without the evidence the People cannot, or probably will not be able to, prevail. Once the evidence is suppressed and a CPL § 450.20(8) appeal is taken, the prosecution is halted unless and until the suppression order is reversed and vacated. The People may not, after affirmance of the suppression order, obtain a new indictment.[169] The courts need not question the People's certification, considering that the penalty is absolute and is itself a complete check on a prosecutor's overstating the need for the suppressed evidence.[170] The order must itself strip the People of the requisite proof; it may not be one of two successive orders.[171]

Forfeitures. CPL § 450.20(9) authorizes an appeal by the People from an order entered pursuant to Penal Law § 460.30 setting aside or modifying a *verdict* of forfeiture. This is a very specialized section that

---

165. People v. Chase, 85 N.Y.2d 493, 626 N.Y.S.2d 721, 650 N.E.2d 379 (1995); People v. Brunner, 209 A.D.2d 532, 619 N.Y.S.2d 90 (2d Dep't 1994).

166. People v. Lopez, 84 N.Y.2d 425, 618 N.Y.S.2d 879, 643 N.E.2d 501 (1994); People v. Sang, 212 A.D.2d 1024, 624 N.Y.S.2d 997 (4th Dep't 1995), appeal denied 86 N.Y.2d 740, 631 N.Y.S.2d 621, 655 N.E.2d 718 (1995).

167. People v. McMullin, 70 N.Y.2d 855, 523 N.Y.S.2d 455, 517 N.E.2d 1341 (1987); People v. O'Doherty, 70 N.Y.2d 479, 522 N.Y.S.2d 498, 517 N.E.2d 213 (1987).

CAVEAT: Pursuant to CPL § 710.30 the People are required to furnish a defendant with notice of their intention to offer CPL § 710.10(2) type evidence against a defendant.

168. People v. Merrill, 212 A.D.2d 987, 624 N.Y.S.2d 702 (4th Dep't 1995); People v. Bernier, 73 N.Y.2d 1006, 1008, 541 N.Y.S.2d 760, 761, 539 N.E.2d 588 (1989); People v. Dueno, 203 A.D.2d 476, 611 N.Y.S.2d 15 (2d Dep't 1994).

CAVEAT: If a defendant participates in a suppression hearing in the face of a defective CPL § 710.30 notice, the defendant will be held to have waived the right to preclude. *See* CPL § 710.30(3); People v. Bowman, 211 A.D.2d 590, 622 N.Y.S.2d 22 (1st Dep't 1995); People v. Linderberry, 222 A.D.2d 731, 634 N.Y.S.2d 571 (3d Dep't 1995); People v. Katowski, 204 A.D.2d 486, 611 N.Y.S.2d 907 (2d Dep't 1994), appeal denied 84 N.Y.2d 869, 618 N.Y.S.2d 14, 642 N.E.2d 333 (1994).

169. Forte v. Supreme Court of State of N.Y., 48 N.Y.2d 179, 422 N.Y.S.2d 26, 397 N.E.2d 717 (1979).

170. People v. Kates, 53 N.Y.2d 591, 597, 444 N.Y.S.2d 446, 449, 428 N.E.2d 852, 855 (1981).

171. People v. Voutsinas, 62 A.D.2d 465, 406 N.Y.S.2d 138 (3d Dep't 1978), appeal dismissed 47 N.Y.2d 798, 417 N.Y.S.2d 933, 391 N.E.2d 1014 (1979).

relates only to forfeiture verdicts in prosecutions for enterprise corruption.

Effective November 1, 1986, the Legislature passed the Organized Crime Control Act.[172] In doing so the Legislature created a new crime, entitled Enterprise Corruption[173] and a provision by which a person convicted of that crime may be subjected to a forfeiture of criminal enterprise property.[174] There have been prosecutions—relatively few—under Penal Law Article 460.[175] There are other forfeiture provisions that do not fall under CPL § 450.20(9), such as a civil proceeding under CPLR Article 13–A involving forfeitures for proceeds of crime.[176]

The right of the People to appeal under CPL § 450.20(9) relates only to Penal Law § 460.30 forfeitures. Pursuant to statutory criteria, a jury is authorized to render a verdict of forfeiture,[177] which the trial court is authorized to set aside (or limit or modify) if it is against the weight of the evidence or disproportionate.[178] If and when a court does so, the People may appeal. This is the essence of CPL § 450.20(9). Since its inception, there has been little forfeiture business generated under this statute, at least as far as reported cases are concerned, and no instances of appeals by the People from any orders (if indeed there have been any) of trial courts setting aside or otherwise disturbing jury forfeiture verdicts under Penal Law § 460.30.

Trial Orders of Dismissal. CPL § 450.40 expands upon the People's appeal from a trial order of dismissal. It interprets CPL § 450.20(2) as allowing an appeal from a trial order of dismissal in two instances: the first, upon the People's claim that the trial court's dismissal was improper in the face of legally sufficient evidence; and second, upon their claim that even though the evidence was concededly legally insufficient, it *would* have been legally sufficient had the trial court not excluded proof improperly by rejecting the People's CPL § 290.10(3) offer of proof.

Bear in mind that pre-verdict trial orders of dismissal are simply not appealable. Based on the decision of the Court of Appeals in *People v.*

---

172. NYPL Art. 460, L. 1986, Ch. 516. See also, legislative findings, NYPL § 460.00.

173. See Executive Memorandum, McKinney's Sessions Laws 1986, Vol. 2, p. 3175.

174. NYPL § 460.30.

175. See, e.g., People v. Moscatiello, 149 Misc.2d 752, 566 N.Y.S.2d 823 (Sup.Ct., N.Y. County, 1990); People v. Ali, 189 A.D.2d 770, 592 N.Y.S.2d 405 (2d Dep't 1993), appeal denied 81 N.Y.2d 881, 597 N.Y.S.2d 942, 613 N.E.2d 974 (1993); People v. Scarola, 186 A.D.2d 78, 588 N.Y.S.2d 154 (1st Dep't 1992), appeal denied 81 N.Y.2d 847, 595 N.Y.S.2d 746, 611 N.E.2d 785. See generally, Donnino, *Practice Commentaries*, NYPL § 460.30 at p.571.

176. See also, Hynes v. Iadarola, 221 A.D.2d 131, 645 N.Y.S.2d 69 (2d Dep't 1996); Public Health Law § 3388; Matter of Attorney General v. One Green 1993 Four Door Chrysler, 88 N.Y.2d 841, 644 N.Y.S.2d 682, 667 N.E.2d 332 (1996).

177. NYPL § 460.30(2)(b).

178. NYPL § 460.30(2)(c).

§ 38.10   CRIMINAL APPELLATE PRACTICE   Ch. 38

Brown[179] the Legislature amended CPL § 290.10 and CPL § 450.20(2) so as to limit the People's appeal of a trial order of dismissal to post-verdict dismissals, *i.e.*, those cases in which the trial order of dismissal was entered pursuant to CPL § 290.10(1)(b).[180]

The setting for the application of CPL § 450.40 would arise as follows: The defendant moves for a trial order of dismissal before verdict. If it is granted, the People may not appeal, which is why trial courts have been instructed to forbear from ruling on the motion until after the verdict.[181] If, after the verdict, the court grants the trial order of dismissal owing to a perceived legal insufficiency—a condition caused only by the trial court's erroneous exclusion of proof—the prospect of double jeopardy looms regarding any corrective action by an appellate court. In his learned discussion, Professor Preiser[182] aptly frames the issue, stating: "the question is whether an appellate court could within constitutional bounds reinstate the conviction or order a new trial." As for reinstating the conviction, the answer must be no. If the appellate court found the proof legally *sufficient* that would be different. It would reverse the trial judge's order of dismissal based upon a legal conclusion that the proof presented was adequate, *i.e.*, a legal case.

Double jeopardy will, however, act as a bar under the following sequence: (1) the appellate court reviews the post-verdict trial order of dismissal; (2) it agrees with the trial court that the proof was legally insufficient; (3) the excluded proof had been tendered to the trial court by way of offer of proof, on the record, outside of the jury's presence; (4) the appellate court, in accordance with CPL § 450.40(2) "treats the excluded evidentiary matter as it is summarized in the offer of proof as evidence constituting a part of the People's case"; (5) the appellate court concludes that the proof was improperly excluded; and (6) the appellate court concludes further that had the proof not been erroneously excluded, it would have supplied a legal (*i.e.*, legally sufficient) case. What now? For the appellate court to reinstate the verdict, it would have to patch in the excluded proof and then conclude that a jury would have believed it. The appellate court may not do that. It may not, in essence, supply evidence to bring the sufficiency level over the top by importing evidence that was excluded from jury consideration. The question of whether it may order a new trial has not yet been decided by any appellate court. There has been little if any litigation on the subject, considering that trial judges have honored the advice in *People v. Key*[183] by waiting until after the verdict before deciding a motion for a trial order of dismissal.

179. 40 N.Y.2d 381, 386 N.Y.S.2d 848, 353 N.E.2d 811 (1976), cert. denied 433 U.S. 913, 97 S.Ct. 2986, 53 L.Ed.2d 1099 (1977).

180. *See* Preiser, *Practice Commentaries*, CPL § 450.20, pp. 702–703.

181. People v. Key, 45 N.Y.2d 111, 115, 408 N.Y.S.2d 16, 18, 379 N.E.2d 1147, 1149 (1978).

182. *See* Preiser, *Practice Commentaries*, CPL § 450.20, pp. 702–703.

183. 45 N.Y.2d 111, 120, 408 N.Y.S.2d 16, 20, 379 N.E.2d 1147, 1151 (1978).

Mental Retardation. The reinstatement of the death penalty in New York has brought with it a new set of criminal appeals, most of which involve the Court of Appeals. CPL § 400.27(12)(e) permits a defendant who has been charged with or convicted of murder in the first degree to request a hearing to determine whether he or she is mentally retarded. The People may appeal as of right to the appellate division from an order finding that the defendant is mentally retarded.[184] A new uniform rule, applicable to all departments,[185] has been adopted to expedite the hearing and determination of such appeals.[186]

The rule was established by the appellate division following the December 20, 1995 authorization by the Court of Appeals,[187] effective *nunc pro tunc* as of December 5, 1995. The rule, 22 NYCRR Part 1100, reads as follows:

PART 1100

UNIFORM PROCEDURES FOR APPEALS FROM PRETRIAL FINDINGS OF MENTAL RETARDATION IN CAPITAL CASES

§ 1100.1 General

This Part shall govern the procedure for an expedited appeal by the People to the appellate division, pursuant to Criminal Procedure Law 400.27(12)(f) and 450.20(10), of an order by a superior court finding a defendant charged with Murder in the First Degree to be mentally retarded.

§ 1100.2 Procedure

(a) Upon filing the notice of appeal, the People shall give notice to the Appellate Division that an appeal is pending pursuant to Criminal Procedure Law 400.27(12)(f) and request that an expedited briefing schedule be set.

(b) The Appellate Division shall establish an expedited briefing schedule for the appeal. Briefs may be typewritten or reproduced. Both the People and the defendant shall file nine copies of a brief, and one copy of the brief shall be served on opposing counsel.

(c) The appeal may be taken on one original record, which shall include copies of the indictment, the motion papers, the minutes of, and all exhibits in, the hearing on mental retardation held in the superior court, the court's decision and order, and the notice of appeal.

---

184. CPL §§ 450.20(10), 400.27(12)(f).
185. 22 NYCRR Pt. 1100.
186. For orders and judgments appealable to the Court of Appeals in capital cases, *see infra*, §§ 39.40–39.41.
187. 22 NYCRR Pt. 540.

§ 38.10 CRIMINAL APPELLATE PRACTICE Ch. 38

(d) The Appellate Division shall give preference to the hearing of an appeal perfected pursuant to this Part and shall determine the appeal as expeditiously as possible.

§ 1100.3 Representation by Court—Assigned Counsel in the Appellate Division

In any appeal by the People from an order pursuant to this Part, the Appellate Division shall assign counsel to represent a defendant who is represented in the superior court by court-assigned counsel, and may direct that the court-assigned counsel in the superior court represent the defendant on appeal.

Library References:

West's Key No. Digests, Criminal Law ⟬1024.

§ 38.11 Appeals to the Appellate Division—Who May Appeal—Appeals From Orders Accepting or Sealing Grand Jury Reports; Appeals by Prosecutors; Appeals by Public Servants

CPL Article 450 relates to appeals in the context of criminal prosecutions, often in the context of grand jury indictments. Grand juries, however, do more than vote on criminal charges. Prosecutors and grand juries have long been in the business of rendering "reports" which do not amount to accusatory instruments in the statutory sense, but which, over the decades, have made various findings, condemnations, and observations in the name of the public interest. In some instances, reports of this type have been critical of named individuals who were stigmatized, but who had no statutory means of response.[1]

In 1961, the Court of Appeals wrote the landmark decision of *Matter of Wood v. Hughes*.[2] After reviewing the historical functions of the grand jury, the court concluded, by a 4–3 vote, that there was no legislative basis for grand jury reports that carry judicial pronouncements of condemnation with no safeguards to protect the individual named.

The Legislature responded promptly by enacting Section 253a of the former Code of Criminal Procedure, followed by the present statute, CPL § 190.85, which allows a grand jury to issue three types of reports. The first involves misconduct, nonfeasance, or neglect by a public servant as the basis for a recommendation of removal or disciplinary action.[3] It must be supported by the preponderance of evidence;[4] it must reveal that

---

§ 38.11

1. For a rich historical discussion on the subject, *see*, In re Wilcox, 153 Misc. 761, 276 N.Y.S. 117 (Sup.Ct., Monroe County, 1934).

2. 9 N.Y.2d 144, 212 N.Y.S.2d 33, 173 N.E.2d 21 (1961).

3. CPL § 190.85(1)(a).

4. CPL § 190.85(2)(a).

the named official was given a chance to testify.[5] Among other safeguards and provisions, it provides an opportunity for the named official to file an answer.[6] The purpose of the answer is to help the court determine whether to accept the report for filing. The answer may include additional facts that were not before the grand jury, so that the court may reconsider whether to accept the report for filing.[7] Pursuant to CPL § 190.85(5), the court may order a report of this type sealed if it is not satisfied that the procedural safeguards of CPL § 190.85(2) have been met. This type of report generates the most challenge and review.

The second type of report[8] is issued following an investigation of a public servant, and states that no misconduct or nonfeasance or neglect by the public servant has been found. Under this section, no report may be submitted to the court except upon the request of the public servant named.[9]

The third type of report does not relate to misconduct but proposes recommendations for legislative, executive, or administrative action in the public interest based upon stated findings.[10] The People have no right of appeal from an order sealing a CPL § 190.85(1)(c) report.[11]

Pursuant to CPL § 190.90 the People may appeal from a CPL § 190.85(5) sealing order within 10 days after service of a copy of the order and report upon each public servant named in the report.[12] The appeal is to the appellate division; the appellate division's procedural rules govern the appellate procedure. The Rules of the First, Second, and Third Departments are identical[13] and read as follows:

> The mode, time, and manner for perfecting an appeal from an order accepting a report of a grand jury pursuant to CPL 190.85(1)(a) or from an order sealing a report of a grand jury pursuant to CPL 190.85(5) shall be in accordance with the provisions of this Part governing appeals in criminal cases. Appeals from such order shall be preferred causes and may be added to the calendar by stipulation approved by the court or upon motion directed to the court. The record, briefs, and other papers on such an appeal shall be sealed and not available for public inspection

---

5. CPL § 190.85(2)(b).
6. CPL § 190.85(3).
7. Matter of Report of Special Grand Jury of Monroe County, 77 A.D.2d 199, 433 N.Y.S.2d 300 (4th Dep't 1980).
8. CPL § 190.85(1)(b).
9. CPL § 190.85(1)(b).
10. CPL § 190.85(1)(c).
11. Matter of Report of Grand Jury of Tompkins County Impaneled April 24, 1984, 110 A.D.2d 44, 493 N.Y.S.2d 648 (3d Dep't 1985); In Matter of Report, Grand Jury, Exhibit 83A of September/October 1993 Suffolk County Grand Jury IC, Term X, 221 A.D.2d 541, 634 N.Y.S.2d 134 (2d Dep't 1995). See generally, Matter of Report of August–September 1983 Grand Jury III, Term XI, Suffolk County, 103 A.D.2d 176, 479 N.Y.S.2d 226 (2d Dep't 1984).

12. Matter of Onondaga County District Attorney's Office to File a Sealed Grand Jury Report as a Public Record, 92 A.D.2d 32, 459 N.Y.S.2d 507 (4th Dep't 1983).

13. 22 NYCRR § 600.16 (First Department); 22 NYCRR § 670.14 (Second Department); 22 NYCRR § 800.15 (Third Department).

§ 38.11   CRIMINAL APPELLATE PRACTICE   Ch. 38

except as permitted by CPL 190.85(3). Unless otherwise directed by the court, oral argument will not be permitted.

The appellate division order determining the appeal is final, and, so far as evidentiary sufficiency is concerned, is unreviewable by the Court of Appeals.[14] That restriction, however, does not apply to considerations of the statute's constitutionality.[15]

In *In re Reports of April 30, 1979 Grand Jury*,[16] the appellate division held that the district attorney may not obtain an order authorizing the resubmission (to another grand jury) of evidence contained in a report that had been sealed. Although it is not clear that the *nisi prius* order denying re-submission was itself appealable, the Appellate Division, Third Department, entertained the appeal and made the point.

In order to prevail on an appeal from a sealing order, the People must show that the statutory procedural safeguards were followed. Thus, when the report is based upon insufficient evidence,[17] or when it did not relate to persons who were presently employed, or when it lacked a recommendation for removal or disciplinary action against someone who was presently employed, the report was ordered sealed.[18] Short of that it may be redacted *in part* owing to insufficient evidence.[19]

A report that blends misconduct[20] and governmental action has been sealed.[21] A report that contains a *specific* disciplinary recommendation has been held to be beyond the scope of the grand jury's power.[22]

In addition to authorizing a People's appeal from a sealing order, CPL § 190.90 also authorizes an appeal by any public servant named in a CPL § 190.85(1)(a) grand jury report that a court accepts. The order accepting the report is made pursuant to CPL § 190.85(2) and is appealable by the public servant pursuant to the procedures established

---

14. For Court of Appeals' scope of review, *see infra*, § 39.50. *See also*, CPL § 190.90(5); In re First Report of October 1972 Grand Jury of Supreme Court, Albany County, 34 N.Y.2d 915, 359 N.Y.S.2d 290, 316 N.E.2d 722 (1974); In Matter of Grand Jury of the County of Montgomery Empaneled on April 30, 1979, 57 N.Y.2d 924, 456 N.Y.S.2d 764, 442 N.E.2d 1275 (1982).

15. In re Second Report of November, 1968 Grand Jury of Erie County, 26 N.Y.2d 200, 309 N.Y.S.2d 297, 257 N.E.2d 859 (1970).

16. Matter of Reports of Grand Jury of Montgomery County Impaneled on April 30, 1979, 108 A.D.2d 482, 489 N.Y.S.2d 385 (3d Dep't 1985).

17. Matter of March 1975 Monroe County Grand Jury Report, 52 A.D.2d 745, 382 N.Y.S.2d 195 (4th Dep't 1976).

18. Matter of Reports of Grand Jury No. 1 of Monroe County Empaneled on Jan. 30, 1978 for the Feb., 1978 Term of County Court, 71 A.D.2d 1060, 420 N.Y.S.2d 946 (4th Dep't 1979).

19. In re First Report of Oct., 1972 Grand Jury of Supreme Court, Albany County, 44 A.D.2d 855, 354 N.Y.S.2d 966 (3d Dep't 1974). *See generally*, Validity and Construction of Statute Authorizing Grand Jury to Submit Report Concerning Public Servant's Noncriminal Misconduct, 63 A.L.R.3d 586, supp. § 5.

20. CPL § 190.85(1)(a).

21. Matter of Report of September 1975 Grand Jury of Supreme Court of St. Lawrence County, 55 A.D.2d 220, 390 N.Y.S.2d 251 (3d Dep't 1976).

22. In re Richard Roe Investigation of August 1973 Monroe County Grand Jury, 46 A.D.2d 723, 360 N.Y.S.2d 123 (4th Dep't 1974).

by the same appellate division rule that is set forth above, which governs appeals by either party.

A report will be ordered sealed when issued by a grand jury that has not been instructed as to the standard of proof necessary, or as to their options under the statute.[23] So too, if there have been irregularities in the voting procedures.[24] In *In re Onondaga County Dist. Attorney's Office*,[25] the appellate division held that after a public servant resigns voluntarily, a grand jury no longer may recommend removal.

§ 38.12 Appeals to the Appellate Division—Appeal Process—Appeals as of Right

A defendant seeking to appeal as of right to the appellate division must file with the clerk of the criminal court from which the appeal is taken two copies of a notice of appeal and must serve one copy upon the District Attorney.[1] If the appeal is from a judgment, sentence, or resentence, the notice must be served and filed within 30 days after the imposition of sentence.[2] The notice of appeal should recite the indictment number or superior court information number under which the conviction arose, the sentence or resentence that was imposed, the county of conviction, the date of sentence or resentence, and the court from which the appeal is taken (supreme or county).

It is important to list *each* indictment number or superior court information number under which the defendant was sentenced or resentenced. Each prosecution (*i.e.*, indictment) results in a separate conviction. That multiple indictments may have been joined for trial or plea, and sentence imposed on all at the same time, does not excuse this requirement that all numbers be listed. The failure to do so could require the defendant to later move for permission to amend the notice of appeal so as not to foreclose review of each conviction.

When the defendant seeks to appeal as of right from an order,[3] the time to serve and file the notice of appeal runs from the date of service upon the defendant of a copy of the order.[4] While the statute does not specify who must serve a copy of the order,[5] the Court of Appeals has held that service must be made by the prevailing party, *i.e.*, the district attorney.[6] The defendant must then file the notice of appeal in duplicate

---

23. Matter of Report of Special Grand Jury of Nassau County, New York, Panel 3, Second Term, 1982., 102 A.D.2d 871, 477 N.Y.S.2d 34 (2d Dep't 1984).

24. Matter of Report of Special Grand Jury of Monroe County, 77 A.D.2d 199, 433 N.Y.S.2d 300 (4th Dep't 1980).

25. 92 A.D.2d 32, 459 N.Y.S.2d 507 (4th Dep't 1983).

§ 38.12

1. CPL §§ 460.10(1)(a), (b).

2. CPL §§ 460.10(1)(a), (b).
3. CPL § 450.10(4).
4. CPL § 460.10(1)(a).
5. *Cf.* CPLR 5513.
6. People v. Washington, 86 N.Y.2d 853, 633 N.Y.S.2d 476, 657 N.E.2d 497 (1995). *Cf.* People v. Singleton, 72 N.Y.2d 845, 847, 531 N.Y.S.2d 798, 799, 527 N.E.2d 281, 282 (1988); People v. Coaye, 68 N.Y.2d 857, 858, 508 N.Y.S.2d 410, 410, 501 N.E.2d 18, 18 (1986).

with the clerk of the criminal court and serve a copy on the district attorney.

When an appeal is taken by the district attorney, the same 30-day period from service applies.[7] Again, service by the prevailing party, *i.e.*, the defendant, is required.[8] There are no provisions for extension.[9] In addition to filing the notice of appeal in duplicate, the district attorney must serve a copy on the defendant, or on the attorney who last appeared for the defendant in the court in which the order was entered.[10]

§ 38.13 Appeals to the Appellate Division—Appeal Process—Appeals by Permission: Certificate Granting Leave

There are no appeals by the People by permission; all appeals are as of right.[1]

A defendant seeking to appeal by permission from an order denying a motion pursuant to CPL §§ 440.10 or 440.20 must apply to the appellate division for a "certificate granting leave to appeal."[2] The "certificate" is an order of a justice granting permission to appeal and certifying that the case involves questions of law or fact that ought to be reviewed.[3] Only one leave application may be made for each order,[4] but if leave is denied, a motion to reargue, which would be referred to the same justice, may be made.

The application must be made within 30 days after the district attorney's service upon the defendant of a copy of the order.[5] If a certificate granting leave is issued, the defendant, within 15 days, must file the certificate and a written notice of appeal with the criminal court from which the order emanated.[6] It is possible that the appellate division, upon issuance of the certificate, will also deem the papers that accompanied the application to be the notice of appeal and to have been timely filed.

The rules of the First, Second and Fourth Departments require that the leave application be addressed to the court for assignment to a justice.[7] The Third Department allows the application to be addressed to a particular justice of the court.[8] The defendant should include with the application a copy of the order denying the CPL Article 440 motion and a

---

7. CPL § 460.10(1)(a).

8. People v. Washington, 86 N.Y.2d 853, 633 N.Y.S.2d 476, 657 N.E.2d 497 (1995).

9. People v. Marsh, 127 A.D.2d 945, 512 N.Y.S.2d 545 (3d Dep't 1987).

10. CPL § 460.10(1)(d).

§ 38.13

1. CPL § 450.20.
2. CPL § 450.15.

3. CPL § 460.15(1).

4. CPL § 460.15(2).

5. CPL § 460.10(4)(a); People v. Washington, 86 N.Y.2d 853, 633 N.Y.S.2d 476, 657 N.E.2d 497 (1995).

6. CPL § 460.10(4)(b).

7. 22 NYCRR §§ 600.8(d), 670.12(b), 1000.13(*o*).

8. 22 NYCRR § 800.3.

copy of any decision the court may have issued. If the motion is beyond the 30-day period, the defendant should set forth the reasons therefor.

Library References:

West's Key No. Digests, Criminal Law ⚖=1072.

§ 38.14 Appeals to the Appellate Division—Appeal Process—Extensions of Time

Unlike civil practice in which the CPLR, with limited exception,[1] makes no provision for extensions of time to take an appeal or to move for leave to appeal, the CPL expressly authorizes an application to be made after the 30-day period, but for the defendant only. The People are held to a strict 30-day limit.[2]

CPL § 460.30(1) authorizes a motion by a defendant for leave to take an appeal or move for permission to appeal up to one year after the time to do so as of right has expired. This is one year and 30 days from the imposition of sentence. Once that one-year period passes, the appellate court loses its jurisdiction to entertain the motion.[3]

The grounds upon which such a motion may be made are limited. The defendant must establish that the failure to act timely "resulted from (a) the improper conduct of a public servant or the improper conduct, death or disability of the defendant's attorney, or (b) the inability of the defendant and his attorney to have communicated in person or by mail, concerning whether an appeal should be taken, prior to the expiration of the time within which to take an appeal due to the defendant's incarceration in an institution and through no lack of due diligence or fault of the attorney or defendant."[4]

CPL § 460.30(2) sets forth the requirements of the motion. It must be made in writing, on notice, and must contain sworn allegations to support the claim. The motion may be granted or denied on the papers,[5] or the issues raised may be remitted to the criminal court to hear and report.[6] The addition of this provision to the CPL was to supersede the "*Montgomery*" resentence which had the effect of extending a defendant's time to take an appeal.[7]

§ 38.14

1. CPLR 5514(c).

2. People v. Marsh, 127 A.D.2d 945, 512 N.Y.S.2d 545 (3d Dep't 1987).

3. People v. Corso, 40 N.Y.2d 578, 388 N.Y.S.2d 886, 357 N.E.2d 357 (1976). *Cf.* People v. Thomas, 47 N.Y.2d 37, 416 N.Y.S.2d 573, 389 N.E.2d 1094 (1979)(the district attorney was estopped from asserting the time limit). *See infra*, §§ 38.62–38.63 for relevent forms.

4. CPL § 460.30(1); 22 NYCRR § 1000.13(i).

5. CPL §§ 460.30(3),(4).

6. CPL § 460.30(5).

7. *See* People v. Montgomery, 24 N.Y.2d 130, 299 N.Y.S.2d 156, 247 N.E.2d 130 (1969). *See supra*, § 38.9.

§ 38.15 Appeals to the Appellate Division—Appeal Process—Stay of Judgment or Order

An appeal by the defendant does not automatically stay enforcement of the judgment. After a notice of appeal is filed, the defendant may move to stay execution of judgment and for release on his or her own recognizance or on bail.[1] On an appeal to the appellate division from a judgment of the supreme court, the motion may be made to a justice of the appellate division or of the judicial district encompassing the county where the judgment was rendered.[2] On an appeal from a county court judgment, the motion may be made to a justice of the appellate division or of the judicial district encompassing the county where the judgment was rendered, or a judge of the county court.[3]

A motion for a stay may also be made by a defendant who has been granted permission to appeal from an order denying a CPL Article 440 motion.[4] A defendant who is granted a stay must bring the appeal on for argument or submission within 120 days after issuance of the order, or the stay will expire.[5] While the initial application is addressed to one justice, a request to extend the stay is addressed to a panel of the appellate division. A defendant who receives a class A felony sentence is not eligible for a stay of execution of judgment.[6] If that sentence is later modified and reduced, a motion for a stay will lie.[7]

An order of recognizance or bail may also be issued by an appellate division justice in limited circumstances before sentence is imposed. CPL § 530.45 covers a situation in which the defendant had been at liberty pursuant to an order of bail or recognizance during the criminal proceedings until conviction. At that time, the bail order may be revoked or bail raised to such an extent that it cannot be posted by the defendant, who stands to be remanded. As long as the conviction is not of a class A felony, a defendant so remanded may apply to a justice of the appellate division for a securing order for release upon his or her own recogni-

---

§ 38.15

1. CPL § 460.50(1); 22 NYCRR § 1000.13(c). See, infra, §§ 38.60–38.61 for relevant forms.

2. CPL § 460.50(2)(a).

3. CPL § 460.50(2)(b).

PRACTICE POINTER: A defendant who has filed a notice of appeal is permitted to make *only one* application for a stay. See CPL § 460.50(3). An application to the sentencing judge immediately after the imposition of sentence and before the notice of appeal is filed does not count. Thus, an application to a justice of the appellate division may be made after the notice of appeal is filed even though the prior application was denied by the sentencing judge. See Morgenthau v. Rosenberger, 86 N.Y.2d 826, 633 N.Y.S.2d 473, 657 N.E.2d 494 (1995).

4. CPL § 460.50(6).

5. CPL § 460.50(4).

6. CPL § 530.50.

7. People v. Vasquez, 88 A.D.2d 667, 450 N.Y.S.2d 606 (2d Dep't 1982).

zance, or for an order fixing bail, or reducing the bail set by the trial judge[8]

A defendant in whose favor such an order is issued must file a notice of appeal within 30 days after imposition of sentence, or the order will terminate and the defendant will have to surrender to the criminal court to commence serving the sentence.[9] The order will also terminate if the appeal is not brought on for argument or submission within 120 days after the notice of appeal is filed.[10] The order may be extended by the court.[11] Only one application for a securing order may be made.[12]

CPL § 510.20(2) sets forth the criteria to be considered on an application for recognizance or bail. Included are the defendant's prior criminal record, employment history, character and reputation, family ties, length of residence in the community, the nature of the evidence, and the likelihood that the judgment will be reversed.[13]

As previously noted,[14] the District Attorney may appeal as of right from an order reducing a count or counts of an indictment, or dismissing an indictment and directing the filing of a prosecutor's information.[15] Such an appeal stays the effect of the order,[16] but perfection thereof must be expedited.[17]

Library References:

West's Key No. Digests, Criminal Law ⚿1084.

§ 38.16 Appeals to the Appellate Division—Appeal Process—Poor Person Relief and Assignment of Counsel

Most criminal defendants who appeal to the appellate division are indigent and prosecute their appeals as poor persons. A defendant who moves successfully for permission to proceed in *forma pauperis*, will obtain an appellate division order directing that a copy of the transcripts be prepared at public expense and will have an attorney assigned to prosecute the appeal.[1]

A defendant seeking poor person relief and assignment of counsel should send the appellate court an affidavit to establish indigency. In practice, the clerks' offices have accepted letters from incarcerated

---

8. CPL §§ 530.45(1),(2).
9. CPL § 530.45(4).
10. CPL § 530.45(5).
11. CPL § 530.45(5).
12. CPL § 530.45(3).
13. CPL § 510.20(2). See Preiser, *Practice Commentaries*, CPL § 460.50, p. 794.
14. See supra, § 38.10.
15. CPL § 450.20(1–a).
16. CPL § 460.40(2); Preiser, *Practice Commentaries*, CPL § 460.40, p. 790.
17. 22 NYCRR §§ 600.8(e), 670.12(e), 800.14(h), 1000.7.

§ 38.16

1. CPL § 460.70(1); County Law Art. 18–B.

§ 38.16 CRIMINAL APPELLATE PRACTICE

defendants when the District Attorney does not contest the defendant's indigency.

In some instances, the family or friends of a defendant will raise funds to retain private counsel to prosecute the appeal, but the amount will not be sufficient to purchase the necessary transcripts. Retained counsel may then move for limited poor person relief to have the appellate division order production of a free copy of the transcripts.[2] There is no written rule relating to the contents of such a motion, but good practice dictates that the motion for that relief should establish the source of the funds used to pay the attorney and establish the defendant's indigency.

In the First Department, the attorney who represents the defendant in the supreme court, if a member of the Assigned Counsel Plan Appellate Panel, may, with the written consent of the defendant, apply to be assigned to the appeal.[3] The other three departments have no comparable rule.

When a poor person order is issued, two copies of the transcript will be prepared; one for the use of counsel and the other for the court file. An amendment to CPL § 460.70[4] does not affect the defendant's receipt of a free transcript, but will affect a defendant who pays for the transcript privately.

Library References:

West's Key No. Digests, Criminal Law ⚖1077.

§ 38.17 Appeals to the Appellate Division—Appeal Process—Perfecting and Calendaring the Appeal

Each department of the appellate division is authorized to establish the mode of, and time for, perfecting an appeal in a criminal action.[1] In the First Department, unless permission is granted to proceed on the original record, the appeal must be perfected on a full record or appendix.[2] All criminal appeals in the Second Department may be perfected on the original record.[3] An appendix is required in the Third Department, even if the defendant is granted permission to proceed as a poor person.[4] In the Fourth Department, the appeal may be prosecuted in any manner authorized for a civil appeal and if poor person relief is granted, the appeal may be prosecuted on the original record and an appendix.[5]

2. CPL § 460.70. Fullan v. Commissioner of Corrections, 891 F.2d 1007 (2d Cir. 1989), cert. denied 496 U.S. 942, 110 L.Ed.2d 675, 110 S.Ct. 3229 (1990).

3. 22 NYCRR § 600.8(g).

4. L. 1995, Ch. 83.

§ 38.17

1. CPL § 460.70(1).
2. 22 NYCRR § 600.8.
3. 22 NYCRR § 670.9(d)(1)(viii).
4. 22 NYCRR §§ 800.4(c), 800.14.
5. 22 NYCRR §§ 1000.3(c), 1000.4(e).

Ch. 38   PERFECTING AND CALENDARING APPEAL   § 38.17

The First Department. In the First Department, a criminal appeal must be brought on for argument within 120 days after the last day on which a notice of appeal must be filed, unless the time is enlarged by the court or a justice.[6] An application for an enlargement of time may be submitted to the court with an affidavit explaining the reason for the delay and stating whether execution of the judgment has been stayed and, if so, when.[7] When the court grants poor person relief to the defendant and orders production of the transcript, the time to perfect is enlarged until 120 days after the filing of the record. At the beginning of the brief for the defendant-appellant, counsel must state the details of the order or judgment appealed, the sentence, whether an application for a stay was made, and the result.[8] A program is in place to monitor assigned counsel.

An appeal from an order or judgment in a criminal action is classified as an enumerated appeal,[9] and is placed on the calendar in the same fashion as a civil appeal.[10] Counsel may have up to 15 minutes for oral argument.[11] On a People's appeal, the District Attorney is required to serve a copy of the brief on the defendant's appellate attorney within nine months after filing the notice of appeal.[12]

A dismissal calendar is compiled in May and October of each year for criminal appeals (or appeals involving writs of *habeas corpus*) not brought on for hearing within 18 months after the granting of poor person relief, with certain exceptions. The calendar is published in the New York Law Journal for five days, giving at least 15 days notice of the calendar call and of the opportunity to submit an affidavit. Notice is given to the defendant at the last available address, and to the attorney.[13] If the affidavit is not submitted, the appeal can be dismissed.[14]

The Second Department. In the Second Department, when no application has been made by a defendant-appellant for poor person relief within nine months after the date of the notice of appeal, the appeal is "deemed abandoned."[15] However, no provision is made for dismissal of such appeals. Internal procedures are in place to monitor the progress of assigned counsel.

Nine copies of the briefs must be filed in all criminal appeals.[16] The brief of a defendant-appellant must state in the beginning whether a stay has been granted, and its terms, whether there were codefendants

6. 22 NYCRR § 600.8(b).
7. 22 NYCRR § 600.8(c).
8. 22 NYCRR § 600.8(a)(2).
9. 22 NYCRR § 600.4(a)(7).
10. 22 NYCRR §§ 600.11(a), (b)(1)(i). See supra, § 37.60.
11. 22 NYCRR § 600.11(f). *See supra,* § 37.62.
12. 22 NYCRR § 600.8(f).
13. 22 NYCRR §§ 600.12(c)(2),(3),(4).
14. 22 NYCRR § 600.12(c)(4).
15. 22 NYCRR § 670.8(f).
16. 22 NYCRR § 670.8(a).

in the trial court and, if there were, the disposition as to the codefendants and the status of any appeal.[17]

In the Second Department, when the only issue raised is the legality, propriety or excessiveness of the sentence, the appeal may be prosecuted as a motion by filing five sets of motion papers, with the minutes of sentence and underlying plea or trial.[18] Under the rules of the Second Department, an attorney who files a brief on the defendant's behalf must also file proof that a copy of the brief has been mailed to the defendant at his or her last known address and, when an *Anders* brief is filed,[19] counsel must supply a copy of a letter advising the defendant of the right to apply to the court for permission to file a *pro se* supplemental brief.[20] An application to file such a brief must be made not later than 30 days after the attorney's brief is mailed to the defendant.[21]

Pursuant to Section 670.8(g) of the Second Department's rules, appeals by the People must be perfected within six months after the date of the notice of appeal, except that the period is three months on an appeal from an order pursuant to CPL § 450.20(1)(dismissal of an accusatory instrument or a count thereof in certain circumstances),[22] CPL § 450.20(1-a) (reduction of a count or counts of an indictment or dismissal of an indictment with a direction to file a prosecutor's information)[23] and CPL § 450.20(8) (an order suppressing evidence).[24] If the defendant's counsel was assigned in the trial court, that attorney is obligated to represent the defendant on the People's appeal, unless relieved by the appellate court.[25]

Calendaring is similar to civil appeals in the Second Department.[26] Criminal cases are generally heard in the order perfected, and in practice are given preference over civil appeals.[27] Argument of up to 30 minutes is allowed for appeals from judgments or orders made after a trial or hearing, up to 15 minutes on other matters, and no argument is allowed for sentence appeals.[28]

The Third Department. The Third Department rules require that appellant's counsel on a criminal appeal file a single copy of the record with seven copies of a brief and appendix within 60 days after the last day for filing a notice of appeal, unless the time is enlarged by order.[29] An enlargement may be sought by motion on notice supported by an affidavit setting forth the background of the case, the cause of the delay,

---

17. 22 NYCRR § 670.10(d)(2).
18. 22 NYCRR § 670.12(c).
19. Anders v. State of California, 386 U.S. 738, 87 S.Ct. 1396, 18 L.Ed.2d 493 (1967). See infra, § 38.38.
20. 22 NYCRR § 670.12(g).
21. 22 NYCRR § 670.12(h).
22. CPL § 450.20(1).
23. CPL § 450.20(1-a).
24. CPL § 450.20(8).
25. 22 NYCRR § 671.3(f).
26. *See supra*, § 37.60.
27. 22 NYCRR §§ 670.7, 670.12(a). *See supra*, § 37.60.
28. 22 NYCRR § 670.19.
29. 22 NYCRR § 800.14(b).

Ch. 38   PERFECTING AND CALENDARING APPEAL   § 38.17

and the date the brief and appendix is expected to be filed.[30] The perfected appeal will be scheduled for argument or submission at the next term of the court commencing more than 30 days after service and filing of the record, brief, and appendix, unless the respondent's time to serve and file has been extended.[31] When the only issue raised pertains to the sentence imposed, the appeal may be heard on a shortened record consisting of the notice of appeal, the minutes of sentence, and the minutes of plea (if defendant pleaded guilty).[32]

Up to 30 minutes of argument time is allowed on appeals from judgments.[33] As a practical matter, in most cases, only 10 minutes is allowed for each side. No argument is allowed when the only issue pertains to the sentence, except by leave of the court.[34]

On an appeal by the People from an order reducing a count in an indictment or dismissing an indictment and directing the filing of a prosecutor's information, an attorney assigned to represent the defendant in the trial court will continue that representation on the appeal, unless the court orders otherwise.[35]

The Fourth Department. Criminal appeals in the Fourth Department are generally governed by the rules applicable to civil appeals.[36] The court has established an Indigent Appeals Management Program to oversee and monitor the assigned counsel program.[37] An assigned counsel must file with the briefs a certified transcript of the trial or hearing, if any, a copy of the presentence report if relevant, a demand for exhibits when necessary, and one copy of an appendix consisting of the CPLR 5531 statement, a copy of the notice of appeal, a copy of the accusatory instrument and relevant exhibits, if practicable.[38] The appellant must also file the original stipulation to the record executed by the parties or their attorneys, or the original order settling the record.[39]

On or before the date an assigned counsel files a brief, a copy must be mailed to the defendant and counsel must file a writing with the court containing the date of mailing.[40] A defendant-appellant who is represented by assigned counsel and desires to file a *pro se* supplemental brief, must make an application within 35 days after counsel has mailed the brief to the defendant.[41]

After the appeal is perfected, the clerk issues a scheduling order specifying the term of court for which the appeal has been scheduled, and setting deadlines for filing respondent's and reply briefs.[42] Both

30. 22 NYCRR § 800.14(c).
31. 22 NYCRR § 800.14(b).
32. 22 NYCRR § 800.14(g).
33. 22 NYCRR § 800.10(c).
34. 22 NYCRR § 800.10(a).
35. 22 NYCRR § 800.14(h)(4).
36. 22 NYCRR §§ 1000.2(b), 1000.3.
37. 22 NYCRR Pt. 1021.
38. 22 NYCRR § 1000.3(c)(1).
39. 22 NYCRR § 1000.3(c)(1); 22 NYCRR § 1000.4(e).
40. 22 NYCRR § 1022.11(c).
41. 22 NYCRR § 1000.13(j).
42. 22 NYCRR § 1000.10(a).

parties are required to file 10 copies of their briefs.[43] The court determines the amount of argument time allowed.[44]

As in the Third Department, on an appeal by the People from an order reducing a count of an indictment or dismissing an indictment and directing the filing of a prosecutor's information, an attorney assigned by the trial court continues on the appeal unless otherwise ordered by the court.[45]

Special Rules. The First, Second and Third Departments have similar rules governing appeals from orders concerning grand jury reports.[46] Generally, they are prosecuted in any manner authorized for a criminal appeal, they are given preference, the record, briefs, etc., are sealed, and oral argument is not allowed except by permission of the court.

§ 38.18 Appeals to the Appellate Division—Scope of Review

The foregoing sections have related to appealability. The next concern once the appeal is before the court, is reviewability. Reviewability principles determine what questions the court may address and under what circumstances.

Library References:

West's Key No. Digests, Criminal Law ⚖1134.

§ 38.19 Appeals to the Appellate Division—Scope of Review—Questions of Law

The appellate division may consider and determine a question of law or an issue of fact involving an error or defect in the criminal court proceedings that may have adversely affected the appellant.[1] Issues of fact are discussed more fully below.[2]

For purposes of an appeal, a question of law is presented when a ruling or instruction is protested (*i.e.*, objected to) at the trial court level by the party asserting the error on appeal.[3] Subject to some exceptions discussed below, an appellate court will not review a claimed error unless it was preserved by a timely objection or protest. It must be timely in the sense that the court is told of the party's concern while the court still has the opportunity to act. The preservation doctrine, which has its

---

43. 22 NYCRR §§ 1000.3(c)(1), 1000.10(b).
44. 22 NYCRR § 1000.11(b).
45. 22 NYCRR § 1000.7(c).
46. CPL § 190.85(1)(a)(5); 22 NYCRR §§ 600.16, 670.14, 800.15. *See also supra*, § 38.11.

§ 38.19
1. CPL § 470.15(1).
2. *See infra*, § 38.20.
3. CPL § 470.05.

parallel in civil cases[4], is designed to provide an orderly process by which a party cues the trial court as to a request or claim of error so that the trial court may alter the ruling, adjust it, or deny the request. The point is that the trial court be alerted to the claim, so as to prohibit a party from allowing an error to pass into the record uncured, only to exploit it on appeal.[5]

There are exceptions to the preservation doctrine, which include a species of error considered so fundamental that preservation is unnecessary. As discussed in another section,[6] the appellate division has discretion to entertain an unpreserved claim of error in the interest of justice.[7] This earlier discussion analyzes the timeliness of an objection and the specificity and sufficiency of the objection in satisfying the preservation criteria.[8]

Exceptions. The Court of Appeals has carved out an exception to the preservation requirement. The exception applies when an improper event takes place at the trial level (be it a ruling or some procedure) that so affects "the organization of the court or the mode of proceedings proscribed by law" that protest is not necessary, and, if the error is extreme enough, even a consent or express waiver will not make it immune from appellate attack and reversal. Over the years the "organization of the court" standard has been widened to include certain constitutional and statutory claims.[9]

One of the earliest cases on the subject is *Cancemi v. People*[10] in which the Court of Appeals held, in 1858, that a defendant could not consent to being tried by a jury of less than twelve members. Seventy years later, in *People ex rel. Battista v. Christian*,[11] the Court of Appeals ruled that an information charging the defendant with an "infamous" crime was a nullity because the State Constitution provided that infamous crimes be prosecuted only by indictment, a requirement that a defendant could not waive.[12]

Fourteen years after *Battista*, the "organization" exception was again employed in *People v. Miles*,[13] and again in 1965 in *People v. McLucas*,[14] when the court held that the trial court's improper comment

4. See supra, § 37.28.

5. People v. Patterson, 39 N.Y.2d 288, 383 N.Y.S.2d 573, 347 N.E.2d 898 (1976), aff'd 432 U.S. 197, 97 S.Ct. 2319, 53 L.Ed.2d 281 (1977).

6. See infra, § 38.21.

7. CPL § 470.15(3)(c).

8. Given that an objection need not be followed by intoning the word "exception." See CPL § 470.05.

9. See also supra, § 37.28.

10. 18 N.Y. 128 (1858).

11. 249 N.Y. 314, 164 N.E. 111 (1928).

12. This was superseded by the waiver of indictment provisions of L. 1974, Ch. 467. See People v. Banville, 134 A.D.2d 116, 523 N.Y.S.2d 844 (2d Dep't 1988).

13. 289 N.Y. 360, 45 N.E.2d 910 (1942)(adding a count to an indictment by consent; conviction reversed).

14. 15 N.Y.2d 167, 256 N.Y.S.2d 799, 204 N.E.2d 846 (1965).

as to the defendant's failure to testify was reviewable, despite non-preservation, in that it involved the "deprivation of a fundamental constitutional right."[15]

In more recent years there has been increased expression to the concept of reviewing in the absence of preservation.[16] Beginning in 1985, with *People v. Ahmed*,[17] another series of cases further expanded the non-preservation concept. *Ahmed* involved the delegation by consent of judicial duties to the judge's law clerk during the judge's illness. The Court of Appeals held that the defendant's consent did not justify the process and reversed the conviction. *Ahmed* was followed by *People v. Mehmedi*[18] in which a violation of CPL § 310.30 (the absence of the defendant during supplemental jury instructions) was held to be an error of law mandating reversal in the absence of any protest, and by *People v. Coons*[19] in which reversal was based on an unobjected-to violation of the jury sequestration requirement.[20] The errors in *Ahmed*, *Mehmedi* and *Coons* were held to have affected "the organization of the court or the mode of proceedings prescribed by law" and therefore did not require preservation.

Following *Coons*, the preservation requirement was subordinated to the defendant's right to presence at *Sandoval* hearings[21] and at jury selection sidebars.[22] Preservation was also found unnecessary for review in *People v. O'Rama*,[23] which involved a violation of CPL § 310.30 requiring notification to counsel of the contents of a juror's note. In

---

15. *See also*, People v. Arthur, 22 N.Y.2d 325, 292 N.Y.S.2d 663, 239 N.E.2d 537 (1968)(same).

16. People v. Patterson, 39 N.Y.2d 288, 383 N.Y.S.2d 573, 347 N.E.2d 898 (1976) aff'd 432 U.S. 197, 97 S.Ct. 2319, 53 L.Ed.2d 281 (1977)(claim of improper distribution of burden of persuasion); People v. Ermo, 47 N.Y.2d 863, 419 N.Y.S.2d 65, 392 N.E.2d 1248 (1979)(violation of right to counsel unpreserved at trial level reviewable only because the appellate division predicated its reversal on it); People v. Dean, 47 N.Y.2d 967, 419 N.Y.S.2d 957, 393 N.E.2d 1030 (1979); People v. Samuels, 49 N.Y.2d 218, 424 N.Y.S.2d 892, 400 N.E.2d 1344 (1980)(claim of deprivation of right to counsel during police questioning raised for first time on appeal, reviewed by Court of Appeals even though appellate division had affirmed the conviction). *See also*, People v. Michael, 48 N.Y.2d 1, 420 N.Y.S.2d 371, 394 N.E.2d 1134 (1979)(double jeopardy claim raised for first time on appeal); People v. Carmine A., 53 N.Y.2d 816, 439 N.Y.S.2d 915, 422 N.E.2d 575 (1981)(right to counsel); People v. Kinchen, 60 N.Y.2d 772, 469 N.Y.S.2d 680, 457 N.E.2d 786 (1983)(deprivation of state constitutional right to counsel may be raised on appeal even though it was not preserved at the trial or suppression hearing); People v. Angelakos, 70 N.Y.2d 670, 518 N.Y.S.2d 784, 512 N.E.2d 305 (1987)(claim of ineffective assistance of counsel raised for the first time on collateral attack).

17. 66 N.Y.2d 307, 496 N.Y.S.2d 984, 487 N.E.2d 894 (1985).

18. 69 N.Y.2d 759, 513 N.Y.S.2d 100, 505 N.E.2d 610 (1987), motion denied 69 N.Y.2d 985, 516 N.Y.S.2d 1028, 509 N.E.2d 363 (1987).

19. 75 N.Y.2d 796, 552 N.Y.S.2d 94, 551 N.E.2d 587 (1990).

20. CPL § 310.10.

21. People v. Dokes, 79 N.Y.2d 656, 584 N.Y.S.2d 761, 595 N.E.2d 836 (1992).

22. People v. Antommarchi, 80 N.Y.2d 247, 590 N.Y.S.2d 33, 604 N.E.2d 95 (1992). *See also*, People v. Damiano, 87 N.Y.2d 477, 640 N.Y.S.2d 451, 663 N.E.2d 607 (1996).

23. 78 N.Y.2d 270, 574 N.Y.S.2d 159, 579 N.E.2d 189 (1991).

People v. Bayes,[24] the court held that the "organization of the court" standards were violated, and not subject to the preservation requirement, when the trial court allowed counsel to answer questions posed by the jury concerning the court's instructions. In *People v. Martinez*,[25] the court held that a verdict of guilty of an alleged lesser included crime that is non-existent is not subject to preservation requirement.

It was held in *People v. Fuller*[26] that preservation is not required to raise a claim of an illegal sentence. However, if the court was statutorily empowered to impose the sentence, an attack on the sentence at the appellate level requires an objection below even if couched in constitutional terms.[27]

The most recent decision of import, *People v. Smith*,[28] seems on the surface to depart from *Fuller*, tightening the preservation requirement, although *Fuller* is not mentioned. The uneven application of the preservation rule in the context of illegal sentences is discussed in *People v. Sullivan*[29] in which the claim was held unpreserved. *Smith* has been frequently cited for the proposition that the failure to preserve an argument relative to defendant's status as a predicate offender precludes review.[30] However, the failure to object below was held not to be a bar in *People v. Sellers*[31] where the sentence's illegality was apparent from the face of the record. In *Walker v. Walker*,[32] despite appellant's failure to object to consecutive jail terms for violations of orders of protection, the Court reached the issue because it involved a court's "essential" authority to incarcerate, citing *Fuller*. Also, in *People v. Morse*,[33] the Court entertained a challenge raised for the first time on appeal, as to the court's power to sentence.

24. 78 N.Y.2d 546, 577 N.Y.S.2d 585, 584 N.E.2d 643 (1991).

25. 81 N.Y.2d 810, 595 N.Y.S.2d 376, 611 N.E.2d 277 (1993).

26. 57 N.Y.2d 152, 156, 455 N.Y.S.2d 253, 254, 441 N.E.2d 563 (1982)(citing People v. Craig, 295 N.Y. 116, 120, 65 N.E.2d 192, 193 (1946)); People v. Bradner, 107 N.Y. 1, 4–5, 13 N.E. 87, 89 (1887). *See also*, People v. David, 65 N.Y.2d 809, 493 N.Y.S.2d 118, 482 N.E.2d 914 (1985)(prosecution may appeal illegal sentence despite its failure to object)).

27. People v. Ruz, 70 N.Y.2d 942, 524 N.Y.S.2d 668, 519 N.E.2d 614 (1988); People v. Lemon, 62 N.Y.2d 745, 476 N.Y.S.2d 824, 465 N.E.2d 363 (1984); People v. Sima–Rodriguez, 190 A.D.2d 596, 593 N.Y.S.2d 798 (1st Dep't 1993); People v. Charles, 168 A.D.2d 507, 562 N.Y.S.2d 748 (2d Dep't 1990).

28. 73 N.Y.2d 961, 540 N.Y.S.2d 987, 538 N.E.2d 339 (1989).

29. 153 A.D.2d 223, 550 N.Y.S.2d 358 (2d Dep't 1990).

30. *See, e.g.*, People v. Perez, 203 A.D.2d 123, 610 N.Y.S.2d 483 (1st Dep't 1994), appeal denied 83 N.Y.2d 970, 616 N.Y.S.2d 23, 639 N.E.2d 763 (1994); People v. Perez, 202 A.D.2d 695, 610 N.Y.S.2d 827 (2d Dep't 1994), appeal denied, 84 N.Y.2d 831, 617 N.Y.S.2d 151, 641 N.E.2d 172 (1994).

31. 222 A.D.2d 941, 635 N.Y.S.2d 773 (3d Dep't 1995).

32. 86 N.Y.2d 624, 635 N.Y.S.2d 152, 658 N.E.2d 1025 (1995).

33. 62 N.Y.2d 205, 476 N.Y.S.2d 505, 465 N.E.2d 12 (1984), appeal dismissed 469 U.S. 1186, 105 S.Ct. 951, 83 L.Ed.2d 959 (1985).

Smith[34] may be read to foreclose unpreserved predicate offender challenges that require hearings, as opposed to sentences that are obviously illegal on their face. At the very least, the appellate division may invoke its interest of justice powers so as not to abide an illegal sentence to which no challenge was made below.[35] A jurisdictional defect, as in the failure of an accusatory instrument to set forth sufficient allegations, is not waived by failure to raise the issue until after trial.[36]

Timeliness of Protest. As with marriage proposals, finding receivers in the end zone, trading in stocks, and catching airplanes, the timing of an objection is critical. The pertinent part of CPL § 470.05(2) reads as follows:

2. For purposes of appeal, a question of law with respect to a ruling or instruction of a criminal court during a trial or proceeding is presented when a protest thereto was registered, by the party claiming error, *at the time of such ruling or instruction or at any subsequent time when the court had an opportunity of effectively changing the same.*[37]

Timing is at the heart of preservation, for the obvious reason that a putative error can be cured by a judge who is given a cue. Without a timely objection the error will go uncorrected either because the party harmed made a strategic decision not to object (in which case any claim of error will be marked unpreserved for appeal[38]) or the party was not alert enough to act. Most failures of that kind do not rise to the level of ineffective representation of counsel, but if the point is serious enough and if the case calls for it, the appellate division's interest of justice jurisdiction exists for precisely this purpose.[39] There are countless instances in which the timing of an objection is critical, and some are discussed here to stress the importance of the concept and its recent application.

A defendant's claim that the court improperly precluded his expert from giving an opinion was held not preserved since the defendant made no offer of proof and failed to make known his position with respect to the court's ruling at a time when it could have been corrected.[40] Not all preservation pitfalls relate to objections during testimony. Sometimes problems relate to procedure, as where a defendant wants to challenge a

---

34. People v. Smith, 73 N.Y.2d 961, 540 N.Y.S.2d 987, 538 N.E.2d 339 (1989).

35. *See, e.g.*, People v. Bennett, 162 A.D.2d 694, 557 N.Y.S.2d 116 (2d Dep't 1990), appeal denied 76 N.Y.2d 1019, 565 N.Y.S.2d 769, 566 N.E.2d 1174 (1990).

36. People v. Alejandro, 70 N.Y.2d 133, 517 N.Y.S.2d 927, 511 N.E.2d 71 (1987). *See also*, William C. Donnino, *New York Court of Appeals on Criminal Law*, § 3.10.

37. Emphasis added.

38. People v. Pinchback, 187 A.D.2d 540, 589 N.Y.S.2d 600 (2d Dep't 1992), aff'd 82 N.Y.2d 857, 609 N.Y.S.2d 158, 631 N.E.2d 100 (1993); People v. Howell, 174 A.D.2d 356, 570 N.Y.S.2d 562 (1st Dep't 1991), appeal denied 78 N.Y.2d 1012, 575 N.Y.S.2d 820, 581 N.E.2d 1066 (1991).

39. CPL § 470.15(3)(c).

40. People v. Mejia, 221 A.D.2d 182, 633 N.Y.S.2d 157 (1st Dep't 1995).

verdict as repugnant. If the verdict is problematic and the defendant fails to object before the jury is discharged, the claim may be foreclosed on appeal.[41] Also, by failing to object to late disclosure on the grounds of *Rosario* and then by failing to seek a remedy for the violation, the defendant's claim will be held unpreserved.[42] In the absence of a sanction demand the *Rosario* issue will be held waived[43] or unpreserved.[44]

A claim will be held unpreserved for appeal when a defendant expresses satisfaction with a ruling. It is not necessary to voice an "exception" but a defendant who by more than mere silence acquiesces in a ruling will be blocked on appeal by the preservation bar. After a court gives curative instructions to which the defendant expresses no dissatisfaction, any appellate argument on the point will generally be held unpreserved.[45] In one case, the court struck testimony in response to a defendant's objection, and the defendant voiced no claim as to the inadequacy of the instructions to strike, and the claim was held unpreserved.[46]

Sufficiency of Protest. In order to preserve a point of error, it is usually necessary to raise a specific objection, urging the particular

---

41. People v. Satloff, 56 N.Y.2d 745, 452 N.Y.S.2d 12, 437 N.E.2d 271 (1982); People v. Benton, 196 A.D.2d 755, 601 N.Y.S.2d 918 (1st Dep't 1993), appeal denied 82 N.Y.2d 891, 610 N.Y.S.2d 158, 632 N.E.2d 468 (1993).

42. People v. Sutherland, 219 A.D.2d 523, 645 N.Y.S.2d 466 (1st Dep't 1995).

43. People v. Nieves, 205 A.D.2d 173, 617 N.Y.S.2d 751 (1st Dep't 1994), appeal granted 85 N.Y.2d 941, 627 N.Y.S.2d 1003, 651 N.E.2d 928 (1995).

44. People v. Capers, 198 A.D.2d 60, 603 N.Y.S.2d 14 (1st Dep't 1993), appeal denied 82 N.Y.2d 922, 610 N.Y.S.2d 174, 632 N.E.2d 484 (1994)(absence of a request for "specific relief").

PRACTICE POINTER: Not every failure to register immediate objection has been held fatal to preservation. There are common-sense exceptions. The rule was not rigidly applied against a defendant who did not immediately object to a prosecutor's *Sandoval* violation. He did not want to highlight the issue in front of the jury, but he made an appropriate protest at the first opportunity thereafter. People v. Butchino, 141 A.D.2d 986, 530 N.Y.S.2d 642 (3d Dep't 1988). *See also,* People v. Vasquez, 114 A.D.2d 589, 494 N.Y.S.2d 198 (3d Dep't 1985)(appellate division reversed because request to clarify was made when the court could have amended the jury charge). Nor was an objection to a trial judge's interference raised too late, inasmuch as a defendant is not obligated or expected to protest at the first sign of such conduct. *See* People v. Yut Wai Tom, 53 N.Y.2d 44, 439 N.Y.S.2d 896, 422 N.E.2d 556 (1981).

45. People v. Thomas, 200 A.D.2d 642, 606 N.Y.S.2d 742 (2d Dep't 1994), appeal denied 83 N.Y.2d 859, 612 N.Y.S.2d 391, 634 N.E.2d 992 (1994)(defendant expressed no dissatisfaction with prosecutor's *Batson* explanations); People v. Pope, 177 A.D.2d 658, 576 N.Y.S.2d 360 (2d Dep't 1991)(court sustained objection; defendant did not express dissatisfaction or seek mistrial); People v. Frye, 192 A.D.2d 412, 596 N.Y.S.2d 373 (1st Dep't 1993), appeal denied 82 N.Y.2d 894, 610 N.Y.S.2d 161, 632 N.E.2d 471 (1993)(defendant's acquiescence in court's failing to instruct jury to cease deliberations, held unpreserved). *See* People v. Sotelo, 176 A.D.2d 458, 574 N.Y.S.2d 360 (1st Dep't 1991), appeal denied, 80 N.Y.2d 838, 587 N.Y.S.2d 923, 600 N.E.2d 650 (1992)(on appeal defendant claimed that trial court's curative instruction was too late but claim was held unpreserved inasmuch as defendant also helped fashion the curative instruction).

46. People v. Orta, 198 A.D.2d 45, 603 N.Y.S.2d 305 (1st Dep't 1993), appeal denied 82 N.Y.2d 928, 610 N.Y.S.2d 180, 632 N.E.2d 490 (1994).

grounds.[47] In a number of instances, a general objection was held insufficient and the appellate court invoked the preservation doctrine.[48]

A defendant arguing on appeal that the evidence was legally insufficient must identify the claimed insufficiency to the trial court.[49] The need to preserve a "legal insufficiency" claim with particularity is underscored in *People v. Gray*.[50] There, Court of Appeals, drawing upon its holdings in *People v. Cona*[51] and *People v. Dekle*,[52] held that a general motion to dismiss at the close of the evidence was insufficient to preserve the issue of whether the prosecution proved, pursuant to *People v. Ryan*[53] that the defendant knew the weight of the drugs which he was alleged to have possessed. Thus, if a defendant has a particular argument on appeal as to why the conviction suffers from legal insufficiency, it may not be considered as a question of law unless that argument was made to the trial court with particularity.[54] The rule is the same for a bench trial: specificity is necessary for preserving a legal sufficiency claim.[55] Legal sufficiency is, of course, among the most critical considerations for

---

47. *See generally*, People v. Rivera, 73 N.Y.2d 941, 540 N.Y.S.2d 233, 537 N.E.2d 618 (1989); People v. Iannone, 45 N.Y.2d 589, 600, 412 N.Y.S.2d 110, 117, 384 N.E.2d 656 (1978).

48. *See, e.g.*, People v. Latta, 222 A.D.2d 303, 636 N.Y.S.2d 4 (1st Dep't 1995)(general objection to courtroom closure); People v. Jackson, 214 A.D.2d 475, 625 N.Y.S.2d 218 (1st Dep't 1995)(improperly questioning witness concerning her failure to come forward earlier); People v. Smaldone, 213 A.D.2d 685, 624 N.Y.S.2d 200 (2d Dep't 1995), appeal denied 86 N.Y.2d 784, 631 N.Y.S.2d 630, 655 N.E.2d 727 (1995)(objection to photograph); People v. West, 212 A.D.2d 651, 622 N.Y.S.2d 572 (1995), appeal denied 85 N.Y.2d 916, 627 N.Y.S.2d 339, 650 N.E.2d 1341 (1995)(questioning defendant as to his failure to tell the police that a friend of his committed the crime); People v. Watkins, 212 A.D.2d 357, 622 N.Y.S.2d 513 (1st Dep't 1995), appeal denied 85 N.Y.2d 981, 629 N.Y.S.2d 742, 653 N.E.2d 638 (1995)(claim of improper bolstering); People v. Michallow, 201 A.D.2d 915, 607 N.Y.S.2d 781 (4th Dep't 1994), appeal denied 83 N.Y.2d 874, 613 N.Y.S.2d 134, 635 N.E.2d 303 (1994)(testimony from victim about an uncharged act of harassment); People v. Piper, 201 A.D.2d 968, 610 N.Y.S.2d 912 (4th Dep't 1994), leave denied 83 N.Y.2d 1006, 616 N.Y.S.2d 487, 640 N.E.2d 155 (1994)(prosecution witness reading defendant's statement to the jury before it had been offered into evidence)).

CAVEAT: Being met with the preservation doctrine regarding legal sufficiency is a particularly distressing state of affairs. From a defendant's perspective a general, boilerplate statement as to legal insufficiency is an inept and ineffective way to preserve a legal sufficiency argument, and the courts have frequently said so. *See, e.g.*, People v. Williams, 221 A.D.2d 673, 634 N.Y.S.2d 493 (2d Dep't 1995); People v. Montero, 221 A.D.2d 570, 634 N.Y.S.2d 405 (2d Dep't 1995).

49. People v. Grant, 222 A.D.2d 607, 635 N.Y.S.2d 272 (2d Dep't 1995)(defendant's identity); People v. Caraballo, 221 A.D.2d 553, 634 N.Y.S.2d 135 (2d Dep't 1995)(geographical jurisdiction).

50. 86 N.Y.2d 10, 629 N.Y.S.2d 173, 652 N.E.2d 919 (1995), on remand 217 A.D.2d 430, 629 N.Y.S.2d 420 (1995).

51. 49 N.Y.2d 26, 33 note 2, 424 N.Y.S.2d 146, 149 note 2, 399 N.E.2d 1167, 1170 note 2 (1979).

52. 56 N.Y.2d 835, 452 N.Y.S.2d 568, 438 N.E.2d 101 (1982).

53. 82 N.Y.2d 497, 605 N.Y.S.2d 235, 626 N.E.2d 51 (1993). *See also*, People v. Lawrence, 85 N.Y.2d 1002, 630 N.Y.S.2d 963, 654 N.E.2d 1211 (1995), on remand 217 A.D.2d 902, 631 N.Y.S.2d 258 (1995).

54. People v. Bynum, 70 N.Y.2d 858, 523 N.Y.S.2d 492, 518 N.E.2d 4 (1987)(a general motion to dismiss at the close of the case is insufficient to preserve a claim regarding a particular element of the crime).

55. People v. Santos, 86 N.Y.2d 869, 635 N.Y.S.2d 168, 658 N.E.2d 1041 (1995).

appellate review, but it does not rise to the level of the "mode of proceedings" type exception to the preservation requirement.[56] In so holding the Court of Appeals disagreed with the interpretation of CPL § 470.15(4)(b) by which the appellate division in *People v. Kilpatrick*[57] held the section to be exempt from the preservation requirement. In making the point the court emphasized that any unpreserved error may be reviewed by the appellate division in its interest of justice jurisdiction.[58]

Sufficiency of Evidence. The standards for legal sufficiency versus weight of evidence in civil cases are discussed in the previous chapter.[59] A similar dichotomy applies in criminal cases. The appellate division is authorized to review a judgment of conviction in terms of its legal sufficiency.[60] Sometimes this is loosely referred to as having a "legal case" or a "*prima facie*" case.

When it comes to reversals on the ground of legal insufficiency, the appellate division and the Court of Appeals use precisely the same standard. That is, whether the evidence, viewed in the light most favorable to the People, could lead a rational trier of fact to conclude that the elements of the crime have been proven beyond a reasonable doubt.[61] A common example of legal insufficiency reversal is when the proof fails to establish an element of the crime. A defendant convicted of burglary will gain a reversal *on the law* if an appellate court concludes that an element of the crime, such as the defendant's lack of "license or privilege" to enter, was not established.[62]

Similarly, in *People v. Johnson*,[63] a forgery conviction was reversed "on the law" because the proof was legally insufficient to establish that the defendant's use of the name involved was unauthorized. Many

---

56. *See* discussion above in this Section under "Exceptions."

57. 143 A.D.2d 1, 531 N.Y.S.2d 262 (1st Dep't 1988).

58. People v. Gray, 86 N.Y.2d at 22, 629 N.Y.S.2d at 176, 652 N.E.2d 919 (1995).

59. *See supra*, §§ 37.28–37.29, 37.65.

60. CPL § 470.15(4)(b).

61. People v. Cabey, 85 N.Y.2d 417, 626 N.Y.S.2d 20, 649 N.E.2d 1164 (1995); People v. Contes, 60 N.Y.2d 620, 467 N.Y.S.2d 349, 454 N.E.2d 932 (1983).

62. People v. Watson, 163 A.D.2d 253, 558 N.Y.S.2d 537 (1st Dep't 1990), appeal denied 76 N.Y.2d 992, 563 N.Y.S.2d 781, 565 N.E.2d 530 (1990).

PRACTICE POINTER: This has nothing to do with preservation. The appellate division reversed the conviction in *Watson*, having reached the issue notwithstanding a lack of preservation. The court did not do so on interest of justice grounds, but on the ground that preservation was not required to raise a legal sufficiency claim, citing People v. Kilpatrick, 143 A.D.2d 1, 531 N.Y.S.2d 262 (1st Dep't 1988). Having been repudiated in 1995 in People v. Gray, 86 N.Y.2d 10, 629 N.Y.S.2d 173, 652 N.E.2d 919 (1995), the *Kilpatrick* rationale is no longer viable. The underlying point, however, is the same: If an element is lacking there is a legal insufficiency which will occasion reversal on the law under CPL § 470.15(3)(a) if preserved by proper articulation, or if unpreserved, it may be reversed by the appellate division in the interest of justice under CPL § 470.15(3)(c).

63. 96 A.D.2d 1083, 466 N.Y.S.2d 969 (2d Dep't 1983), aff'd 63 N.Y.2d 888, 483 N.Y.S.2d 201, 472 N.E.2d 1029 (1984).

§ 38.19　　　CRIMINAL APPELLATE PRACTICE　　　Ch. 38

examples can be cited. One can simply take any crime, remove an element from the proof, and the prosecution will be left with a legally insufficient case resulting in reversal on the law if the objection is preserved.[64]

The lack of proof of an element is a frequent source of reversals for legal insufficiency, but it is not the only one. If, discounting inadmissible proof, the quantum of proof to establish guilt beyond a reasonable doubt does not measure up to a legal case, a reversal on the law follows if properly preserved.[65] Similarly, if the testimony of an accomplice is not corroborated[66] the People's case will suffer from *legal* insufficiency.[67]

The same holds true when the People fail to corroborate the unsworn testimony of an infant upon whom the proof rests:[68] the evidence will be legally insufficient.[69] So too, CPL § 60.50 requires corroboration of a confession in order to constitute a legally sufficient case, under pain of dismissal.[70]

As is evident from all of these cases, if there is insufficient legal evidence, the indictment must be dismissed.[71] If, on the other hand, a trial court has committed reversible error but after subtracting improperly admitted evidence, there is enough evidence left to spell out a legally sufficient case the appellate court will reverse and order a new trial.[72]

The litany of cases referred to relating to legal insufficiency have a common theme: reversal on the law as prescribed by CPL § 470.15(4)(b), and dismissal of the indictment as prescribed by CPL § 470.20(2). There are no second chances here for the People. There can be no directive for

64. People v. Rivera, 82 N.Y.2d 695, 601 N.Y.S.2d 470, 619 N.E.2d 407 (1993)(possession of stolen property; element of possession lacking); People v. Capozzi, 133 A.D.2d 481, 519 N.Y.S.2d 210 (3d Dep't 1987)(malicious mischief, lack of causation); People v. Murray, 131 A.D.2d 885, 517 N.Y.S.2d 242 (2d Dep't 1987)(attempted murder); People v. Rockwell, 275 App.Div. 568, 90 N.Y.S.2d 281 (1st Dep't 1949)(lack of proof of false statements under former NYPL § 926–a); People v. Edwards, 147 A.D.2d 586, 537 N.Y.S.2d 879 (2d Dep't 1989), appeal denied 74 N.Y.2d 846, 546 N.Y.S.2d 1011, 546 N.E.2d 194 (1989)(evidence lacking of intent to use weapon unlawfully); People v. Guevara, 156 A.D.2d 379, 548 N.Y.S.2d 904 (2d Dep't 1989), appeal denied 75 N.Y.2d 868, 553 N.Y.S.2d 300, 552 N.E.2d 879 (1990)(failure to prove that defendant's possession of firearm did not take place in his "place of business"); People v. Cummings, 131 A.D.2d 865, 517 N.Y.S.2d 225 (2d Dep't 1987)(murder conviction, lack of intent); People v. Nieves, 135 A.D.2d 579, 522 N.Y.S.2d 166 (2d Dep't 1987)(murder, proof of accessorial conduct lacking); People v. Chapman, 137 A.D.2d 884, 524 N.Y.S.2d 863 (3d Dep't 1988)(arson conviction; lacking in requisite mental culpability to be convicted as accomplice).

65. *See, e.g.,* People v. Ardito, 58 N.Y.2d 842, 460 N.Y.S.2d 22, 446 N.E.2d 778 (1983).

66. CPL § 60.22.

67. People v. Moses, 63 N.Y.2d 299, 482 N.Y.S.2d 228, 472 N.E.2d 4 (1984); People v. Pynes, 170 A.D.2d 981, 566 N.Y.S.2d 143 (4th Dep't 1991).

68. CPL § 60.20(3).

69. People v. Badia, 163 A.D.2d 4, 558 N.Y.S.2d 500 (1st Dep't 1990).

70. People v. Ruckdeschel, 51 A.D.2d 861, 380 N.Y.S.2d 163 (4th Dep't 1976).

71. CPL § 470.20(2).

72. *See, e.g.,* People v. Weston, 92 A.D.2d 945, 460 N.Y.S.2d 633 (3d Dep't 1983); CPL § 470.20(1).

a new trial[73] in contrast to the numerous instances in which the proof was legally adequate, but reversible error occurred mandating a new trial.

The test for *legal sufficiency* is the same as it is in a civil case, namely, whether there is "any valid line of reasoning and permissible inferences that could lead a rational person to the conclusion reached by the jury on the basis of the evidence at trial." This is the same standard as in *Cohen v. Hallmark Cards*.[74] This standard differs from the appellate division's authority to examine whether, on the facts, the verdict is against the *weight of the evidence*,[75] which involves weighing conflicting inferences and testimony.

Abuse of Discretion and Improvident Exercise of Discretion. Considering that many actions of a criminal court are discretionary, practitioners who seek to appeal to the appellate division must consider whether and to what extent a criminal court's discretionary act is reviewable by the appellate division and whether, under existing standards, such discretionary actions might plausibly be overturned by the appellate division.

The appellate division "possesses the same discretionary power as the trial court and can, if so advised, substitute an exercise of discretion for that of Criminal Term even absent an abuse by the trial court."[76] Indeed, in reviewing a sentence for harshness, the appellate division may exercise its discretion without any deference to the sentencing court.[77]

Of course, the appellate division may, in a proper case, conclude that the trial court abused its discretion as a matter of law.[78] That is a legal, rather than a discretionary determination.[79] Because an "abuse of discre-

---

73. People v. Bleakley, 69 N.Y.2d 490, 494, 515 N.Y.S.2d 761, 763, 508 N.E.2d 672, 674 (1987).

74. 45 N.Y.2d 493, 410 N.Y.S.2d 282, 382 N.E.2d 1145 (1978). See People v. Bleakley, 69 N.Y.2d 490, 495, 515 N.Y.S.2d 761, 763, 508 N.E.2d 672, 673 (1987)(citing *Cohen*). See also supra, §§ 37.28, 37.29.

75. CPL § 470.15(5).

76. People v. Catten, 69 N.Y.2d 547, 516 N.Y.S.2d 186, 508 N.E.2d 920 (1987). For the comparable rule in civil cases, see supra, § 37.29.

CAVEAT: Some cases suggest that an *abuse* of discretion is needed to trigger appellate division action. See, e.g., People v. Ortiz, 224 A.D.2d 244, 638 N.Y.S.2d 9 (1st Dep't 1996); People v. Terry, 224 A.D.2d 202, 637 N.Y.S.2d 694 (1st Dep't 1996); People v. Simmons, 224 A.D.2d 229, 637 N.Y.S.2d 154 (1st Dep't 1996); People v. Crump, 197 A.D.2d 414, 602 N.Y.S.2d 394 (1st Dep't 1993), leave to appeal denied 82 N.Y.2d 893, 610 N.Y.S.2d 160, 632 N.E.2d 470 (1993); People v. Morin, 192 A.D.2d 791, 596 N.Y.S.2d 508 (3d Dep't 1993), leave to appeal denied 81 N.Y.2d 1077, 601 N.Y.S.2d 597, 619 N.E.2d 675 (1993). However, the correct rule is that there is no such limitation on the appellate division.

77. People v. Delgado, 80 N.Y.2d 780, 587 N.Y.S.2d 271, 599 N.E.2d 675 (1992). CPL § 470.15(6)(b). See infra, § 38.21.

78. People v. Brogdon, 213 A.D.2d 418, 623 N.Y.S.2d 332 (2d Dep't 1995); People v. James, 207 A.D.2d 564, 616 N.Y.S.2d 75 (2d Dep't 1994).

79. People v. Ocasio, 47 N.Y.2d 55, 416 N.Y.S.2d 581, 389 N.E.2d 1101 (1979).

§ 38.19 CRIMINAL APPELLATE PRACTICE Ch. 38

tion" creates an issue of law, any reversal by the appellate division based upon an abuse of discretion is necessarily a reversal on the law.[80]

If the Court of Appeals determines that the appellate division erred in reversing on the law based on the appellate division's conclusion that the trial court abused its discretion, the Court of Appeals may remit the case to the appellate division to determine whether, notwithstanding the absence of an abuse, the appellate division should substitute its own different discretionary determination for that of the trial court.[81]

When the appellate division substitutes an appropriate exercise of its discretion for that of the criminal court, its order of reversal or modification will not support an appeal to the Court of Appeals.[82] If, however, appellate division's discretion is exercised in such a way that the Court of Appeals determines that it constitutes an abuse of discretion *as a matter of law*, its determination would be reviewable by the Court of Appeals.[83] In *People v. Colon*,[84] the Court of Appeals held that a CPL § 210.40(1) dismissal of an indictment creates a question for its review as to whether the dismissal constitutes "an abuse of discretion as a matter of law." It should be stressed, however, that when it comes to discretionary sentence review, an appellate division abuse of discretion would be a virtual impossibility in the case of the reduction of a lawful sentence to another lawful, lesser sentence pursuant to CPL § 470.15(6)(b).[85]

---

80. People v. Bazalar, 211 A.D.2d 839, 621 N.Y.S.2d 224 (3d Dep't 1995), leave to appeal denied 85 N.Y.2d 969, 629 N.Y.S.2d 729, 653 N.E.2d 625 (1995); People v. Jones, 210 A.D.2d 904, 620 N.Y.S.2d 656 (4th Dep't 1994), aff'd 85 N.Y.2d 998, 630 N.Y.S.2d 961, 654 N.E.2d 1209 (1995)(which will support an appeal to, and review by, the Court of Appeals, provided leave to appeal is secured). *See also*, People v. Owens, 63 N.Y.2d 824, 482 N.Y.S.2d 250, 472 N.E.2d 26 (1984), on remand 108 A.D.2d 1014, 485 N.Y.S.2d 584 (1985); People v. Washington, 71 N.Y.2d 916, 528 N.Y.S.2d 531, 523 N.E.2d 818 (1988), on remand 145 A.D.2d 670, 536 N.Y.S.2d 812 (1988).

81. People v. Washington, 71 N.Y.2d 916, 918, 528 N.Y.S.2d 531, 532, 523 N.E.2d 818, 819 (1988), on remand 145 A.D.2d 670, 536 N.Y.S.2d 812 (1988).

82. CPL § 450.90(2)(a); People v. Baker, 64 N.Y.2d 1027, 489 N.Y.S.2d 56, 478 N.E.2d 197 (1985).

83. People v. Ocasio, 47 N.Y.2d 55, 60, 416 N.Y.S.2d 581, 583, 389 N.E.2d 1101, 1103 (1979).

84. 86 N.Y.2d 861, 635 N.Y.S.2d 165, 658 N.E.2d 1038 (1995).

85. People v. Thompson, 60 N.Y.2d 513, 521, 470 N.Y.S.2d 551, 555, 458 N.E.2d 1228, 1232 (1983).

PRACTICE POINTER: Determining whether an appellate division reversal is on the law—for instance, based on an abuse of discretion—is important. The appellate division is required to state whether its reversal is on the law, the facts, or as a matter of discretion, in the interest of justice, or any combination thereof, *see* CPL § 470.25(2)(a), but its characterization is not binding on the Court of Appeals, *see* CPL § 450.90(2)(a). Thus, counsel who can convince a justice or judge to whom an application for leave to appeal to the Court of Appeals has been addressed that a reversal, though stated to be other than on the law, actually is on the law, will at least be able to have the application considered on the merits rather than dismissed under CPL § 450.90(2)(a). Conversely, a potential Court of Appeals respondent who has benefitted from an appellate division reversal can protect that victory from the possibility of reversal in the Court of Appeals by convincing that judge or justice that the reversal—regardless of how the appellate division has described it—does not meet the criteria of CPL § 450.90(2)(a).

Harmless Error. Article 470 begins with the mandate that an appellate court "must determine an appeal without regard to technical errors or defects which do not affect the substantial rights of the parties."[86] Essentially this is the "harmless error" doctrine, the criminal law equivalent of CPLR 2002.

The doctrine is an acknowledgement that no trial is perfect and that if the defendant's guilt is so convincing as to be "overwhelming," some errors may be safely tolerated. It is axiomatic, however, that before the appellate courts will consider errors as harmless, they must first be satisfied that the proof of guilt is overwhelming.[87] If the defendant's guilt is "less than overwhelming," the doctrine of harmless error does not come into play.[88]

Even if the appellate court finds that the proof of defendant's guilt is overwhelming—thus satisfying the first prerequisite—the question of whether or not to affirm the conviction in the name of harmless error will vary with the character of the error. If the error involves a constitutional violation, the court must be satisfied, if it is to affirm the conviction, that the error was "harmless beyond a reasonable doubt," meaning that if there is a *"reasonable possibility"* that the error might have contributed to the defendant's conviction it is not harmless.[89] If there is such a possibility, the error may not be declared "harmless beyond a reasonable doubt" and reversal must follow.[90] Thus, an error of constitutional proportions must lead to reversal unless there is no reasonable *possibility* that the error might have contributed to the conviction.[91]

Obviously, not all trial errors are constitutional errors. A different test applies to non-constitutional errors. As governed by state law, the standard for non-constitutional harmless error is whether there is a "significant probability" that the jury would have acquitted the defendant had it not been for the error or errors. If so, there must be reversal. If not, the error or errors may be treated as harmless.[92]

86. CPL § 470.05(1).

87. People v. Crimmins, 36 N.Y.2d 230, 241, 367 N.Y.S.2d 213, 218, 326 N.E.2d 787, 792 (1975).

88. *See, e.g.*, People v. Creeden, 210 A.D.2d 422, 620 N.Y.S.2d 411 (2d Dep't 1994); People v. Dyer, 201 A.D.2d 498, 607 N.Y.S.2d 379 (2d Dep't 1994).

89. *See, e.g.*, People v. Crimmins, 36 N.Y.2d 230, 236, 367 N.Y.S.2d 213, 216, 326 N.E.2d 787, 790 (1975).

90. People v. Garofolo, 46 N.Y.2d 592, 604, 415 N.Y.S.2d 810, 816, 389 N.E.2d 123, 129 (1979).

91. Chapman v. California, 386 U.S. 18, 87 S.Ct. 824, 17 L.Ed.2d 705 (1967); Fahy v. State of Conn., 375 U.S. 85, 84 S.Ct. 229, 11 L.Ed.2d 171 (1963); People v. Ayala, 75 N.Y.2d 422, 554 N.Y.S.2d 412, 553 N.E.2d 960 (1990).

92. *See, e.g.*, People v. Mobley, 56 N.Y.2d 584, 450 N.Y.S.2d 302, 435 N.E.2d 672 (1982); People v. Johnson, 57 N.Y.2d

§ 38.19 CRIMINAL APPELLATE PRACTICE Ch. 38

In *People v. Martinez*,[93] a case involving an erroneous presumption charge, the Court of Appeals discussed whether to apply the harmless error analysis. The court stated that a harmless error evaluation is appropriate when the appeals court is presented with a problem of evaluating trial error and is able to assess the likelihood that the error may have contributed to the verdict. The doctrine, however, is inapplicable when it is impossible to tell whether the verdict was predicated on the illegally charged presumption or upon a finding of constructive possession irrespective of a presumption.[94] Thus, when it is impossible for a reviewing court to determine whether a guilty verdict was founded on an illegal theory, it may not review the evidence under a harmless error analysis: It may not, in effect, assume the jury's fact-finding function by concluding that the jury must have reached its result on some alternative legal ground.

The standards for harmless error are the same for the Court of Appeals and the appellate division. The Court of Appeals, however, sets the standards and occasions for their application, so that the correctness of a determination by the appellate division as to harmlessness raises a question of law reviewable by the Court of Appeals.[95]

The threshold question of the applicability of harmless error analysis must be answered before the *Crimmins* constitutional/nonconstitutional analysis begins. Some errors are not, as a matter of law, amenable to harmless error analysis. They mandate reversal *per se*. Thus, in those cases, upon appellate division review the question of prejudice to the defendant is irrelevant.

With that in mind, we turn to the case law, and to the instances in which harmless error, be it constitutional or nonconstitutional, may not be employed to affirm a conviction, irrespective of whether the defendant was prejudiced by the error:[96]

—cases in which a defendant was deprived of *Rosario*[97] material at

969, 457 N.Y.S.2d 230, 443 N.E.2d 478 (1982).

93. 83 N.Y.2d 26, 35, 607 N.Y.S.2d 610, 615, 628 N.E.2d 1320, 1325 (1993).

94. People v. Martinez, 83 N.Y.2d 26, 35, 607 N.Y.S.2d 610, 615, 628 N.E.2d 1320 (1993). *See also*, People v. Diaz, 19 N.Y.2d 547, 549–550, 281 N.Y.S.2d 53, 54, 227 N.E.2d 860, 861 (1967)(Court of Appeals reversed the appellate division's application of harmless error after the trial court incorrectly failed to charge that the testimony of an accomplice required corroboration); People v. Gallagher, 69 N.Y.2d 525, 530, 516 N.Y.S.2d 174, 176, 508 N.E.2d 909, 911 (1987); People v. Minarich, 46 N.Y.2d 970, 971, 415 N.Y.S.2d 825, 825, 389 N.E.2d 137, 137 (1979).

95. People v. Reddick, 65 N.Y.2d 835, 493 N.Y.S.2d 124, 482 N.E.2d 920 (1985).

96. Of course, these include a jurisdictionally defective accusatory instrument. *See, e.g.*, People v. Alejandro, 70 N.Y.2d 133, 517 N.Y.S.2d 927, 511 N.E.2d 71 (1987). Also included is a geographical jurisdictional failure. *See, e.g.*, People v. McLaughlin, 80 N.Y.2d 466, 471, 591 N.Y.S.2d 966, 968, 606 N.E.2d 1357, 1359 (1992). Neither has anything to do with the level of guilt proven, so we do not include these types of cases and others like them in the list to follow).

97. This is to be distinguished from a *Brady* violation which has been held amenable to harmless error analysis. *See, e.g.*,

trial;[98]

—denial of a defendant's access to counsel for an extended period of time after arraignment;[99]

—denial of effective assistance of counsel at trial;[100]

—furnishing a jury, over defense objection, with written excerpts from the charge;[101]

—furnishing the jury with a copy of the text of a pertinent statute without counsel's consent;[102]

—furnishing a verdict sheet, in the absence of consent, listing various counts of the indictment defining the elements of each count in statutory language;[103]

—furnishing a jury with a condensed version of the charge, over objection;[104]

—furnishing a jury, absent defendant's consent, with a verdict sheet that, in addition to listing the counts, lists some of the statutory elements of the counts;[105]

—the failure of the People, absent good cause, to serve a suppression notice within the proper time limit;[106]

People v. Steadman, 82 N.Y.2d 1, 603 N.Y.S.2d 382, 623 N.E.2d 509 (1993).

98. *See, e.g.*, People v. Young, 79 N.Y.2d 365, 370, 582 N.Y.S.2d 977, 980, 591 N.E.2d 1163 (1992); People v. Jones, 70 N.Y.2d 547, 523 N.Y.S.2d 53, 517 N.E.2d 865 (1987); People v. Ranghelle, 69 N.Y.2d 56, 511 N.Y.S.2d 580, 503 N.E.2d 1011 (1986).

99. Thirty days in the case of People v. Hilliard, 73 N.Y.2d 584, 542 N.Y.S.2d 507, 540 N.E.2d 702 (1989).

100. *See, e.g.*, Glasser v. United States, 315 U.S. 60, 62 S.Ct. 457, 86 L.Ed. 680 (1942); People v. Felder, 47 N.Y.2d 287, 418 N.Y.S.2d 295, 391 N.E.2d 1274 (1979)(being represented by "attorney" who had not been licensed). A contingent fee retainer, however, while unethical in a criminal case, does not mandate a *per se* reversal. *See, e.g.*, People v. Winkler, 71 N.Y.2d 592, 528 N.Y.S.2d 360, 523 N.E.2d 485 (1988). Also, the denial of counsel at the preliminary hearing stage is subject to harmless error analysis. *See, e.g.*, People v. Wicks, 76 N.Y.2d 128, 556 N.Y.S.2d 970, 556 N.E.2d 409 (1990). This is also true for the defendant's prosecution by a non-lawyer. *See also*, People v. Carter, 77 N.Y.2d 95, 564 N.Y.S.2d 992, 566 N.E.2d 119 (1990).

101. *See, e.g.*, People v. Owens, 69 N.Y.2d 585, 516 N.Y.S.2d 619, 509 N.E.2d 314 (1987).

102. *See* CPL § 310.30. *See also*, People v. Sanders, 70 N.Y.2d 837, 523 N.Y.S.2d 444, 517 N.E.2d 1330 (1987).

103. *See, e.g.*, People v. Nimmons, 72 N.Y.2d 830, 530 N.Y.S.2d 543, 526 N.E.2d 33 (1988). *See*, however, the 1996 amendment to CPLR § 310.20(2). L. 1996, Ch. 630 § 2.

104. *See, e.g.*, People v. Brooks, 70 N.Y.2d 896, 524 N.Y.S.2d 382, 519 N.E.2d 293 (1987).

105. *See, e.g.*, People v. Damiano, 87 N.Y.2d 477, 640 N.Y.S.2d 451, 663 N.E.2d 607 (1996); People v. Spivey, 81 N.Y.2d 356, 599 N.Y.S.2d 477, 615 N.E.2d 961 (1993); People v. Kelly, 76 N.Y.2d 1013, 565 N.Y.S.2d 754, 566 N.E.2d 1159 (1990); People v. Taylor, 76 N.Y.2d 873, 560 N.Y.S.2d 982, 561 N.E.2d 882 (1990). *See*, however, the 1996 amendment to CPLR § 310.20(2). L. 1996, Ch. 630 § 2.

106. *See, e.g.*, People v. Chase, 85 N.Y.2d 493, 626 N.Y.S.2d 721, 650 N.E.2d 379 (1995); People v. O'Doherty, 70 N.Y.2d 479, 522 N.Y.S.2d 498, 517 N.E.2d 213 (1987); People v. Lopez, 84 N.Y.2d 425, 618 N.Y.S.2d 879, 643 N.E.2d 501 (1994).

§ 38.19 CRIMINAL APPELLATE PRACTICE Ch. 38

—the failure to abide by the time requirements in wiretap statutes;[107]

—the denial of a request for a "no inference" charge pursuant to CPL § 300.10;[108]

—defendant's absence at side bar discussions with prospective jurors;[109]

—excessive questioning and intrusiveness of the trial judge;[110]

—violation of the right to an open, public trial;[111]

—a defendant's absence during the court's reinstructing the jury, even in the absence of an objection;[112]

—the erroneous denial of a motion to suppress evidence followed by a guilty plea;[113]

—a *Batson* violation;[114]

—summation excesses that reach "due process" proportions;[115]

—the denial of a defendant's right to receive preliminary hearing minutes[116] or prior trial minutes;[117]

---

107. People v. Capolongo, 85 N.Y.2d 151, 165–166, 623 N.Y.S.2d 778, 784, 647 N.E.2d 1286, 1291 (1995).

108. See, e.g., People v. Britt, 43 N.Y.2d 111, 400 N.Y.S.2d 785, 371 N.E.2d 504 (1977)(giving the no-inference charge unsolicited is subject, however, to harmless error analysis); People v. Koberstein, 66 N.Y.2d 989, 499 N.Y.S.2d 379, 489 N.E.2d 1281 (1985).

109. See, e.g., People v. Antommarchi, 80 N.Y.2d 247, 590 N.Y.S.2d 33, 604 N.E.2d 95 (1992). See also, People v. Sloan, 79 N.Y.2d 386, 583 N.Y.S.2d 176, 592 N.E.2d 784 (1992).

110. See, e.g., People v. Mees, 47 N.Y.2d 997, 420 N.Y.S.2d 214, 394 N.E.2d 283 (1979).

111. See, e.g., People v. Jones, 47 N.Y.2d 409, 418 N.Y.S.2d 359, 391 N.E.2d 1335 (1979), cert. denied 444 U.S. 946, 100 S.Ct. 307, 62 L.Ed.2d 315 (1979); People v. Kan, 78 N.Y.2d 54, 59, 571 N.Y.S.2d 436, 438, 574 N.E.2d 1042, 1044 (1991); Waller v. Georgia, 467 U.S. 39, 49–50, 104 S.Ct. 2210, 2217, 81 L.Ed.2d 31 (1984).

112. People v. Mehmedi, 69 N.Y.2d 759, 513 N.Y.S.2d 100, 505 N.E.2d 610 (1987). In People v. Mullen, 44 N.Y.2d 1, 403 N.Y.S.2d 470, 374 N.E.2d 369 (1978), however, the trial court's questioning of a juror in chambers, in defendant's absence, was held not reversible *per se*.

113. See, e.g., People v. Grant, 45 N.Y.2d 366, 408 N.Y.S.2d 429, 380 N.E.2d 257 (1978).

114. See, e.g., Rosa v. Peters, 36 F.3d 625, 634 (7th Cir.1994); Blair v. Armontrout, 976 F.2d 1130 (8th Cir.1992). See also, Vasquez v. Hillery, 474 U.S. 254, 106 S.Ct. 617, 88 L.Ed.2d 598(1986); People v. Jenkins, 75 N.Y.2d 550, 555 N.Y.S.2d 10, 554 N.E.2d 47 (1990).

115. See, e.g., People v. Williams, 46 N.Y.2d 1070, 416 N.Y.S.2d 792, 390 N.E.2d 299 (1979).

116. See, e.g., People v. Montgomery, 18 N.Y.2d 993, 278 N.Y.S.2d 226, 224 N.E.2d 730 (1966).

117. See, e.g., People v. Ballott, 20 N.Y.2d 600, 286 N.Y.S.2d 1, 233 N.E.2d 103 (1967). These cases did not mention harmless error analysis, but the court apparently considered such an analysis inappropriate and in People v. Zabrocky, 26 N.Y.2d 530, 311 N.Y.S.2d 892, 260 N.E.2d 529 (1970) the court expressly abjured any harmless error analysis in the case of a denial of

—a defective reasonable doubt instruction;[118]

—possible conflict of interest owing to joint representation, and insufficient inquiry by the trial court;[119]

—a trial judge's absence, and delegation of duties to his or her law clerk even upon consent;[120]

—a violation of constitutional double jeopardy provisions;[121]

—*ex parte* communication made by a clerk to deliberating jurors concerning the need to deliberate;[122]

—the improper discharge of a sworn juror;[123]

—defendant's absence at a *Sandoval* hearing;[124] and

—refusing prior disclosure to counsel of a jury's note seeking further instructions on a matter affecting the deliberative process.[125]

The cases cited above involve settings in which the harmless error analysis may not be applied. There are other instances in which the courts have undertaken a harmless error analysis, but have found that the error could not be classified as harmless, and therefore have reversed the convictions.

This occurred, for example, in *People v. Grega*,[126] *People v. Williams*,[127] *People v. Hudy*,[128] *People v. Owens*,[129] *People v. Sobieskoda*,[130] *People v. Knapp*,[131] *People v. Pitts*,[132] *People v. Eastman*,[133] *People v.*

pretrial suppression hearing minutes, citing *Montgomery* and *Ballott*.

118. Sullivan v. Louisiana, 508 U.S. 275, 113 S.Ct. 2078, 124 L.Ed.2d 182 (1993).

119. People v. Macerola, 47 N.Y.2d 257, 264, 417 N.Y.S.2d 908, 911, 391 N.E.2d 990 (1979).

120. *See, e.g.,* People v. Ahmed, 66 N.Y.2d 307, 496 N.Y.S.2d 984, 487 N.E.2d 894 (1985).

121. *See, e.g.,* People v. Mayo, 48 N.Y.2d 245, 422 N.Y.S.2d 361, 397 N.E.2d 1166 (1979).

122. *See, e.g.,* People v. Ciaccio, 47 N.Y.2d 431, 418 N.Y.S.2d 371, 391 N.E.2d 1347 (1979). *See also,* People v. Torres, 72 N.Y.2d 1007, 534 N.Y.S.2d 914, 531 N.E.2d 635 (1988)(trial justice directing court officer to tell jury, *ex parte*, to continue to deliberate).

123. *See, e.g.,* People v. Anderson, 70 N.Y.2d 729, 519 N.Y.S.2d 957, 514 N.E.2d 377 (1987).

124. *See, e.g.,* People v. Dokes, 79 N.Y.2d 656, 584 N.Y.S.2d 761, 595 N.E.2d 836 (1992); People v. Favor, 82 N.Y.2d 254, 267, 604 N.Y.S.2d 494, 501, 624 N.E.2d 631, 637 (1993).

125. People v. Cook, 85 N.Y.2d 928, 626 N.Y.S.2d 1000, 650 N.E.2d 847 (1995).

126. 72 N.Y.2d 489, 497, 534 N.Y.S.2d 647, 651, 531 N.E.2d 279 (1988)(variation between indictment and trial proof).

127. 56 N.Y.2d 236, 451 N.Y.S.2d 690, 436 N.E.2d 1292 (1982)(*Sandoval* failures).

128. 73 N.Y.2d 40, 58, 538 N.Y.S.2d 197, 207, 535 N.E.2d 250 (1988)(*ex post facto* issue).

129. 22 N.Y.2d 93, 98, 291 N.Y.S.2d 313, 317, 238 N.E.2d 715 (1968)(self-incrimination violation).

130. 235 N.Y. 411, 420, 139 N.E. 558, 561 (1923)(trial court's erroneous instructions).

131. 57 N.Y.2d 161, 455 N.Y.S.2d 539, 441 N.E.2d 1057 (1982)(right to counsel violation).

132. 71 N.Y.2d 923, 528 N.Y.S.2d 534, 523 N.E.2d 821 (1988)(*Cruz-Bruton* error).

133. 85 N.Y.2d 265, 276–278, 624 N.Y.S.2d 83, 89–90, 648 N.E.2d 459 (1995).

Johnson,[134] People v. Cintron,[135] People v. Taylor,[136] People v. Vasquez,[137] People v. Newball,[138] *and* People v. Steadman.[139]

In other cases errors that implicated constitutional rights were found to be harmless beyond a reasonable doubt.[140]

§ 38.20 Appeals to the Appellate Division—Scope of Review—Questions of Fact; Weight of Evidence

In addition to reviewing legal sufficiency and making other determinations of law pursuant to CPL § 470.15(4), the appellate division has not only the authority, but the obligation, to examine the evidence and determine whether a guilty verdict was, in whole or in part, "against the weight of the evidence."[1] This is a power of review in criminal cases that is unique to the intermediate appellate court;[2] it does not reside with courts either above or below. In this respect the criminal side is different from the civil. In a civil trial, the judge has the authority to set aside a verdict as against the weight of evidence pursuant to CPLR 4404.[3] In the criminal sphere, however, a *trial* judge has no power to set aside a guilty verdict as "against the weight of the evidence" or as a "matter of discretion in the interest of justice," whether it be a bench trial[4] or a jury trial.[5]

---

134. 80 N.Y.2d 798, 587 N.Y.S.2d 278, 599 N.E.2d 682 (1992)(erroneously received eyewitness testimony regarding line-up).

135. 75 N.Y.2d 249, 552 N.Y.S.2d 68, 551 N.E.2d 561 (1990)(insufficient basis for CPL art. 65 vulnerable witness procedures).

136. 80 N.Y.2d 1, 11, 586 N.Y.S.2d 545, 549, 598 N.E.2d 693 (1992)(erroneous admission of phone message).

137. 76 N.Y.2d 722, 725, 557 N.Y.S.2d 873, 874, 557 N.E.2d 109 (1990)(denial of request for missing witness charge).

138. 76 N.Y.2d 587, 592, 561 N.Y.S.2d 898, 901, 563 N.E.2d 269 (1990)(erroneous admission of prior identification testimony).

139. 82 N.Y.2d 1, 9, 603 N.Y.S.2d 382, 386, 623 N.E.2d 509 (1993)(*Brady* violation).

140. *See, e.g.*, People v. Smalls, 87 N.Y.2d 851, 638 N.Y.S.2d 609, 661 N.E.2d 1392 (1995)(*Sandstrom* error); People v. Wicks, 76 N.Y.2d 128, 556 N.Y.S.2d 970, 556 N.E.2d 409 (1990)(denial of counsel at preliminary hearing); People v. Hamlin, 71 N.Y.2d 750, 758, 530 N.Y.S.2d 74, 76, 525 N.E.2d 719 (1988)(*Bruton-Cruz* error); People v. Harris, 80 N.Y.2d 796, 587 N.Y.S.2d 277, 599 N.E.2d 681 (1992)(improper line-up identification testimony); People v. Moore, 71 N.Y.2d 684, 529 N.Y.S.2d 739, 525 N.E.2d 460 (1988)(permitting jurors to take part of the indictment into the jury room); People v. Tucker, 77 N.Y.2d 861, 568 N.Y.S.2d 342, 569 N.E.2d 1021 (1991)(juror's notes as to supplementary instructions in the jury room); People v. Basora, 75 N.Y.2d 992, 557 N.Y.S.2d 263, 556 N.E.2d 1070 (1990)(fifth amendment violation); People v. Kern, 75 N.Y.2d 638, 555 N.Y.S.2d 647, 554 N.E.2d 1235 (1990)(admission of statement made in the absence of counsel).

§ 38.20

1. *See* CPL § 470.15(5). *See also*, People v. Bleakley, 69 N.Y.2d 490, 515 N.Y.S.2d 761, 508 N.E.2d 672 (1987).

2. People v. Giles, 73 N.Y.2d 666, 667, 543 N.Y.S.2d 37, 38, 541 N.E.2d 37 (1989).

3. *See supra*, § 37.65.

4. People v. Carter, 63 N.Y.2d 530, 483 N.Y.S.2d 654, 473 N.E.2d 6 (1984).

5. People v. Colon, 65 N.Y.2d 888, 493 N.Y.S.2d 302, 482 N.E.2d 1218 (1985); People v. Jones, 188 A.D.2d 331, 591 N.Y.S.2d 159 (1st Dep't 1992), appeal denied 81 N.Y.2d 888, 597 N.Y.S.2d 949, 613 N.E.2d 981 (1993); People v. D'Alessandro, 184 A.D.2d 114, 591 N.Y.S.2d 1001 (1st Dep't

The appellate division's authority to weigh the evidence carries with it the power to take corrective action if and when it concludes that the verdict is against the weight of evidence. In earlier cases, that corrective action typically resulted in reversal and a new trial.[6] That was changed with the enactment of CPL § 470.20(5)[7] under which dismissal is mandated when the appellate division concludes that the verdict is against the weight of the evidence.

The test for whether the verdict is against the weight of evidence does not have the same body of exegesis that accompanies civil cases.[8] The most instructive case in point is *People v. Bleakley*,[9] which refers to *People ex rel. MacCracken v. Miller*,[10] and teaches that the appellate division must "weigh the relative probative force of conflicting testimony and the relative strength of conflicting inferences that may be drawn from the testimony."[11] Both before and after *Bleakley*, the appellate division has undertaken factual weight of the evidence analyses with resulting corrective action. Corrective action now requires reversal on the facts, and dismissal of the indictment.[12]

If the verdict is against the weight of the evidence as to all counts, the appellate division will reverse the entire conviction, but if it finds the verdict against the weight of evidence as to less than all the counts, it will reverse and dismiss the legally unsupported count or counts and affirm the rest.[13] The same factual review power, of course, exists when the appellate division hears an appeal from a bench trial verdict.[14]

The cases cited above all relate to reversals on the facts alone, in the context of judgments. The appellate division's same factual review powers exist in reviewing suppression rulings, and in a number of instances the court has reversed suppression orders "on the facts" so as to deny suppression.[15]

1992), appeal denied 81 N.Y.2d 884, 597 N.Y.S.2d 945, 613 N.E.2d 977 (1993).

6. *See, e.g.*, People v. Alexander, 206 App.Div. 780, 200 N.Y.S. 939 (2d Dep't 1923); People v. Sranko, 210 App.Div. 812, 205 N.Y.S. 944 (4th Dep't 1924); People v. Park, 238 App.Div. 29, 263 N.Y.S. 25 (4th Dep't 1933).

7. L. 1970, Ch. 996 (effective September 1, 1971).

8. *See supra*, § 37.65.

9. 69 N.Y.2d 490, 495, 515 N.Y.S.2d 761, 763, 508 N.E.2d 672, 674 (1987).

10. 291 N.Y. 55, 62, 50 N.E.2d 542, 545 (1943).

11. *See also*, People v. Acosta, 80 N.Y.2d 665, 672, 593 N.Y.S.2d 978, 981, 609 N.E.2d 518, 521 (1993).

12. *See, e.g.*, People v. Athanasopoulos, 206 A.D.2d 381, 614 N.Y.S.2d 61 (2d Dep't 1994); People v. Harry, 181 A.D.2d 694, 581 N.Y.S.2d 64 (2d Dep't 1992); People v. Roman, 160 A.D.2d 961, 554 N.Y.S.2d 684 (2d Dep't 1990), appeal denied 76 N.Y.2d 795, 559 N.Y.S.2d 1000, 559 N.E.2d 694 (1990); People v. Kennedy, 157 A.D.2d 856, 550 N.Y.S.2d 431 (2d Dep't 1990).

13. People v. Ruiz, 162 A.D.2d 350, 556 N.Y.S.2d 910 (1st Dep't 1990).

14. *See, e.g.*, People v. Van Akin, 197 A.D.2d 845, 602 N.Y.S.2d 450 (4th Dep't 1993); People v. Crudup, 100 A.D.2d 938, 474 N.Y.S.2d 827 (2d Dep't 1984).

15. *See, e.g.*, People v. Wilson, 147 A.D.2d 602, 537 N.Y.S.2d 897 (2d Dep't 1989); People v. Whitehead, 135 A.D.2d 997, 522 N.Y.S.2d 721 (3d Dep't 1987); People v. Castro, 80 A.D.2d 535, 436 N.Y.S.2d 22 (1st Dep't 1981), aff'd 53 N.Y.2d 1046, 442 N.Y.S.2d 500, 425 N.E.2d 888 (1981).

§ 38.20 CRIMINAL APPELLATE PRACTICE Ch. 38

Library References:
West's Key No. Digests, Criminal Law ⚖1158.

§ 38.21 Appeals to the Appellate Division—Scope of Review—Interest of Justice/Discretion

The Legislature has furnished the appellate division with statutory power to reverse or modify a judgment as a matter of discretion in the interest of justice.[1] This includes, but is not limited to, review of unpreserved error (*i.e.*, not duly protested under CPL § 470.05(2)) and the harshness or severity of an otherwise legal sentence.[2]

Although the interest of justice jurisdiction thus falls into the two main categories of unpreserved error and sentence severity, there is a third category of interest of justice jurisprudence. It is the highly unusual, but catch-all type authority that is invoked when something seems wrong and there is no other neatly defined pigeon hole available to prevent an injustice. This is covered, below, in this section under the heading of "Other Interest of Justice Applications."

Unpreserved Error. The most frequent application of the appellate division's interest of justice power is in the context of unpreserved error. Experienced practitioners know that the great majority of unpreserved errors will not be addressed by the appellate division. The reasons for preservation are so compelling[3] that it takes a potent issue to move the court to consider something that the appellant did not raise at the trial level. But issues have arisen that have prompted the appellate division to exercise its discretion in the interest of justice as a pure basis for reversal and dismissal. There are, of course, reversals based *on the facts* and the interest of justice—a sometimes thin line of discernment—and there are reversals *on the law* and in the interest of justice. But there have been reversals denominated purely "as a matter of discretion in the interest of justice" in which the appellate division has reached an issue notwithstanding what it explicitly held to be a lack of preservation and has reversed and dismissed solely in the interest of justice.[4]

In several other cases the appellate division has chosen not specifically to base its determination on a lack of preservation, but to couch its reversal in terms of interest of justice only.[5] In *People v. Fargher*,[6] the court found the point to have been preserved and went on to reverse and

---

§ 38.21

1. CPL § 470.15(3)(c).
2. CPL § 470.15(6)(b).
3. *See supra*, § 37.28.
4. People v. Wingate, 175 A.D.2d 191, 573 N.Y.S.2d 696 (2d Dep't 1991)(legal insufficiency); People v. Maldonado, 152 A.D.2d 707, 544 N.Y.S.2d 165 (2d Dep't 1989)(speedy trial denial).

5. People v. Prest, 105 A.D.2d 1078, 482 N.Y.S.2d 172 (4th Dep't 1984)(denial of right to testify before grand jury); People v. Smith, 120 A.D.2d 753, 503 N.Y.S.2d 72 (2d Dep't 1986)(failure of trial judge's recusal); People v. O'Connell, 133 A.D.2d 970, 521 N.Y.S.2d 121 (3d Dep't 1987)(speedy trial violation).
6. 112 A.D.2d 599, 492 N.Y.S.2d 123 (3d Dep't 1985).

dismiss in the interest of justice, owing to a violation of the interstate agreement on detainers. In a number of instances, the court's interest of justice dismissal has been mitigated by allowing prosecutors to represent their cases to other grand juries.[7]

Of course, an interest of justice reversal does not always occasion dismissal. The appellate division will consider the appropriate corrective action and will as often as not order a new trial, depending on the nature of the error. When the point involves an error of law that would warrant reversal and a new trial had the error been properly protested, the remedy will be the same—reversal and a new trial—if the appellate division reaches the error in its interest of justice jurisdiction. These unpreserved legal errors vary; sometimes they involve the court's improper charge to the jury,[8] but the reasons are diverse.[9]

In other instances the appellate division has decreed reversals as being both on the law and in the interest of justice, and in the order of reversal, has often accompanied the decretal language with the statement that the facts have been considered and found to have been established.[10] The reversals in the interest of justice typically involve errors of law decidedly or impliedly unpreserved.[11]

---

7. *See, e.g.*, People v. Roberts, 162 A.D.2d 729, 557 N.Y.S.2d 127 (2d Dep't 1990); People v. Banks, 193 A.D.2d 1051, 598 N.Y.S.2d 1014 (4th Dep't 1993), appeal dismissed 82 N.Y.2d 713, 602 N.Y.S.2d 810, 622 N.E.2d 311 (1993).

8. *See, e.g.*, People v. Perrotta, 121 A.D.2d 659, 504 N.Y.S.2d 51 (2d Dep't 1986); People v. Fuller, 108 A.D.2d 822, 485 N.Y.S.2d 298 (2d Dep't 1985).

9. *See, e.g.*, People v. Roberts, 203 A.D.2d 600, 611 N.Y.S.2d 214 (2d Dep't 1994)(Brady violation); People v. Kilstein, 174 A.D.2d 756, 571 N.Y.S.2d 781 (2d Dep't 1991), appeal denied, 78 N.Y.2d 1012, 575 N.Y.S.2d 820, 581 N.E.2d 1066 (1991) (ineffective counsel); People v. Dixon, 138 A.D.2d 929, 526 N.Y.S.2d 269 (4th Dep't 1988)(apparently unpreserved improper exclusion of evidence); People v. Jacobsen, 140 A.D.2d 938, 529 N.Y.S.2d 618 (4th Dep't 1988)(trial judge excessive intervention); People v. Ranum, 122 A.D.2d 959, 506 N.Y.S.2d 105 (2d Dep't 1986)(improper foundation for child's sworn testimony); People v. King, 112 A.D.2d 169, 491 N.Y.S.2d 66 (2d Dep't 1985)(apparently unpreserved prosecution summation excess).

10. The latter phrase has to do with the future of the case if it goes to the Court of Appeals. The Court of Appeals will act on the law only and may remit the case back to the appellate division as a last step for a review of the facts. *See, e.g.*, People v. Acosta, 80 N.Y.2d 665, 672, 593 N.Y.S.2d 978, 981, 609 N.E.2d 518, 521 (1993). When the appellate division indicates in its order that it has already reviewed the facts, this last step is obviated.

11. *See, e.g.*, People v. Rose, 223 A.D.2d 607, 637 N.Y.S.2d 172 (2d Dep't 1996)(improper unsworn testimony and jury charge error); People v. Moore, 193 A.D.2d 627, 597 N.Y.S.2d 444 (2d Dep't 1993)(restricted cross examination); People v. Robinson, 191 A.D.2d 595, 594 N.Y.S.2d 801 (2d Dep't 1993)(prosecutorial improprieties); People v. Pymm, 188 A.D.2d 561, 591 N.Y.S.2d 458 (2d Dep't 1992), appeal dismissed 81 N.Y.2d 1018, 600 N.Y.S.2d 206, 616 N.E.2d 863 (1993)(improper verdict sheet); People v. Barker, 183 A.D.2d 835, 584 N.Y.S.2d 79 (2d Dep't 1992) (premature discharge of sworn juror); People v. Morse, 182 A.D.2d 781, 582 N.Y.S.2d 776 (2d Dep't 1992)(prejudicial delay in responding to jury's question); People v. McCain, 177 A.D.2d 513, 576 N.Y.S.2d 146 (2d Dep't 1991)(embellishment of adverse inference charge); People v. Bryant, 170 A.D.2d 520, 566 N.Y.S.2d 83 (2d Dep't 1991), appeal dismissed 77 N.Y.2d 992, 571 N.Y.S.2d 918, 575 N.E.2d 404 (1991)(court's improper interjection during jury polling); People v. Baldelli, 152 A.D.2d 741, 544 N.Y.S.2d 193 (2d Dep't 1989)(improper bolstering); People v. Morgan, 145 A.D.2d 442, 535 N.Y.S.2d 97 (2d

§ 38.21   CRIMINAL APPELLATE PRACTICE   Ch. 38

The last grouping of cases have all dealt with legal error, with little or no factual involvement. In many of those cited, the appellate division has expressly found the facts adequate both as to weight and sufficiency.

Considering that a primary purpose of exercise of interest of justice jurisdiction is to address unpreserved errors of law, it is unusual for the appellate division to base reversal upon "the facts and in the interest of justice." In *People v. Jackson*[12] and in *People v. Albanese*,[13] the appellate division did so, but both cases had been remitted by the Court of Appeals to the appellate division for consideration of the "facts."

In *People v. Green*,[14] the appellate division reversed on the facts and, in the interest of justice, ordered a new trial. It acted under "the proper exercise of discretion under the facts disclosed," having found that the trial court should have granted an adjournment to the defense. It made no findings of fact and it is not unlikely that the court, today, would denominate it a reversal on the law in the interest of justice. Similarly, in *People v. Cartagena*,[15] the appellate division reversed on the facts and the law and ordered a new trial owing to the judge's coercive remarks. This too could just easily have been a reversal on the law in the interest of justice.[16] In *People v. Limoli*,[17] the appellate division reversed the defendant's conviction on the facts and in the interest of justice, ordering a new trial, so as to match the result in the co-defendant's case; and in *People v. Washington*,[18] the appellate division stressed the closeness of the factual issue in the case.

Although, as we have seen, interest of justice reversals generally mandate new trials, there are outright dismissals as well.[19] The same holds true for reversals that are based on "the facts and the interest of justice." Most will engender new trials, but when combined with a weight of the evidence shortcoming, the case will (and must) be dismissed.[20] Consider also *People v. Jones*[21] in which the appellate division concluded that the case was too weak to establish defendant's guilt beyond a reasonable doubt.

Dep't 1988)(inaudible tapes); People v. Woodhull, 105 A.D.2d 815, 481 N.Y.S.2d 749 (2d Dep't 1984)(*Molineux* violation).

12. 174 A.D.2d 552, 571 N.Y.S.2d 721 (1st Dep't 1991).

13. 29 A.D.2d 516, 285 N.Y.S.2d 179 (1st Dep't 1967).

14. 19 A.D.2d 749, 242 N.Y.S.2d 881 (2d Dep't 1963).

15. 78 A.D.2d 601, 432 N.Y.S.2d 176 (1st Dep't 1980).

16. *See, e.g.*, People v. Arce, 215 A.D.2d 277, 627 N.Y.S.2d 15 (1st Dep't 1995); People v. Bryant, 170 A.D.2d 520, 566 N.Y.S.2d 83 (2d Dep't 1991), appeal dismissed 77 N.Y.2d 992, 571 N.Y.S.2d 918, 575 N.E.2d 404 (1991).

17. 4 A.D.2d 1001, 169 N.Y.S.2d 483 (4th Dep't 1957).

18. 282 App.Div. 896, 125 N.Y.S.2d 231 (3d Dep't 1953).

19. *See, e.g.*, People v. Wingate, 175 A.D.2d 191, 573 N.Y.S.2d 696 (2d Dep't 1991); People v. Maldonado, 152 A.D.2d 707, 544 N.Y.S.2d 165 (2d Dep't 1989); People v. O'Connell, 133 A.D.2d 970, 521 N.Y.S.2d 121 (3d Dep't 1987).

20. People v. Jackson, 205 A.D.2d 639, 613 N.Y.S.2d 230 (2d Dep't 1994), appeal denied 84 N.Y.2d 827, 617 N.Y.S.2d 147, 641 N.E.2d 168 (1994).

21. 57 A.D.2d 905, 394 N.Y.S.2d 288 (2d Dep't 1977).

Other Interest of Justice Applications. The cases discussed above fall, for the most part, into clear categories. There is one area, however, that defies easy classification, and that is when the appellate division is not prepared to find the verdict legally insufficient or against the weight of evidence, but is so troubled by the prospect of an injustice—"a disturbing feeling" that an innocent person may have been convicted—that interest of justice jurisprudence is called upon to reverse the defendant's conviction. This is the essence of *People v. Kidd*.[22] Although it is infrequently called upon, *Kidd* has found an important and enduring place in the interest of justice scope of review. *In dictum*, it has been pointedly recognized by the Court of Appeals as a legitimate exercise of appellate division discretion,[23] and was otherwise mentioned by the court with no sign of disapproval.[24]

Kidd served as an example for a pure interest of justice dismissal in *People v. Mitchell*.[25] In *People v. Payne*,[26] *People v. Crudup*,[27] and *People v. Taylor*,[28] it was cited as a basis for dismissal on the law, the facts, and in the interest of justice.

Kidd was also employed as precedent for reversal and dismissal upon factual review in *People v. Roberts*,[29] *People v. Nickerson*,[30] *People v. Raffaele*,[31] and in *People v. Jackson*[32] to order a new trial. Cases citing *Kidd* may not have done so with exactitude, but that may be the very point of it. This small reservoir of interest of justice jurisdiction is not intended for exactitude, but for those rare occasions when it is a last resort to prevent injustice.

Excessive Sentences. The appellate division has the authority to take corrective action with regard to both lawful and unlawful sentences. If a sentence is unlawful—"unauthorized, illegally imposed, or otherwise invalid as a matter of law"[33]—the appellate division is empowered to take corrective action that involves a determination "on the law."[34] In evaluating an unlawful sentence claim, the appellate division does not

---

22. 76 A.D.2d 665, 431 N.Y.S.2d 542 (1st Dep't 1980), appeal dismissed 51 N.Y.2d 882, 434 N.Y.S.2d 1029, 414 N.E.2d 714 (1980).

23. People v. Carter, 63 N.Y.2d 530, 483 N.Y.S.2d 654, 473 N.E.2d 6 (1984).

24. People v. Bleakley, 69 N.Y.2d 490, 495, 515 N.Y.S.2d 761, 763, 508 N.E.2d 672 (1987); People v. Colon, 65 N.Y.2d 888, 493 N.Y.S.2d 302, 482 N.E.2d 1218 (1985).

25. 99 A.D.2d 609, 472 N.Y.S.2d 166 (3d Dep't 1984).

26. 149 A.D.2d 542, 540 N.Y.S.2d 256 (2d Dep't 1989).

27. 100 A.D.2d 938, 474 N.Y.S.2d 827 (2d Dep't 1984).

28. 98 A.D.2d 269, 470 N.Y.S.2d 153 (1st Dep't 1984).

29. 165 A.D.2d 598, 569 N.Y.S.2d 53 (1st Dep't 1991).

30. 175 A.D.2d 74, 573 N.Y.S.2d 169 (1st Dep't 1991).

31. 182 A.D.2d 783, 582 N.Y.S.2d 779 (2d Dep't 1992).

32. 205 A.D.2d 639, 613 N.Y.S.2d 230 (2d Dep't 1994).

33. CPL § 470.15(4)(c).

34. CPL §§ 470.15(3)(a), 470.15(4)(c).

undertake any exercise of discretion. It makes a purely legal determination as to whether the sentence was authorized, legal, and valid.[35]

If, however, a sentence is lawful, a defendant may still appeal the sentence to the appellate division and seek to have it reduced on the ground that it is unduly harsh or severe. The authority for the appellate division to entertain these appeals is found in CPL § 470.15(6)(b). The statute contemplates the exercise of discretion in the interest of justice.[36] It relates to lawfully imposed, authorized sentences that are legal in all respects and within the statutorily permissible range, but which merit reduction as an act of discretion on the part of the appellate division.[37]

A trial court must pronounce sentence upon a guilty verdict.[38] It is basic that a trial court is vested with discretion in imposing sentences.[39] In exercising its discretion, the trial court must give due consideration to the crime, the particular factual and individual circumstances, as well as considerations of societal protection, rehabilitation, and deterrence.[40] It is unavoidable, however, that there will be some variation—hopefully not too wide—among judges. The appellate division fulfills its function here so as to undertake its independent review to see that sentences do not go too far out of line, either individually or on the basis of similar cases. It is a long established power, pre-dating the statute, and was exercised originally under the inherent authority of the appellate division.[41] It was codified under former Code of Criminal Procedure § 543[42] which preceded the current statute.

Whether a particular sentence has been, or stands to be, reduced by the appellate division's discretion is an undertaking that falls outside this discussion. But it is fair to ask whether standards for the invocation of the appellate division's discretionary powers exist.[43] Of course, the

---

35. *See supra*, § 38.8 as to defendants' appeals from sentences, and § 38.10 as to appeals by the People from legally invalid sentences.

36. People v. Thompson, 60 N.Y.2d 513, 470 N.Y.S.2d 551, 458 N.E.2d 1228 (1983).

37. People v. Delgado, 80 N.Y.2d 780, 587 N.Y.S.2d 271, 599 N.E.2d 675 (1992).

38. CPL § 380.20.

39. Williams v. People of State of New York, 337 U.S. 241, 69 S.Ct. 1079, 93 L.Ed. 1337 (1949).

40. People v. Farrar, 52 N.Y.2d 302, 305–306, 437 N.Y.S.2d 961, 963, 419 N.E.2d 864, 866 (1981); People v. Golden, 41 A.D.2d 242, 342 N.Y.S.2d 309 (1st Dep't 1973); People v. Suitte, 90 A.D.2d 80, 455 N.Y.S.2d 675 (2d Dep't 1982).

41. People v. Miles, 173 App.Div. 179, 183–184, 158 N.Y.S. 819, 821 (3d Dep't 1916).

42. People v. Gittelson, 18 N.Y.2d 427, 276 N.Y.S.2d 596, 223 N.E.2d 14 (1966).

43. **PRACTICE POINTER:** The appellate division has often stated that it will not exercise its interest of justice discretionary review unless there is a "clear abuse of discretion or extraordinary circumstances." *See, e.g.,* People v. Charron, 198 A.D.2d 722, 604 N.Y.S.2d 311 (3d Dep't 1993), appeal denied 83 N.Y.2d 803, 611 N.Y.S.2d 139, 633 N.E.2d 494 (1994). The Court of Appeals, however, has made it clear that the appellate division is authorized to reduce sentences (when they are lawful, but overly harsh or severe) even in the absence of extraordinary circumstances or an abuse of discretion by the sentencing court. *See also,* People v. Delgado, 80 N.Y.2d 780, 587 N.Y.S.2d 271, 599 N.E.2d 675 (1992). Indeed, *Delgado* goes so far as to say that the appellate division may reduce sentences under CPL § 470.15(6)(b) "without deference to the sentencing court."

appellate division may reduce sentences and has done so when an "abuse of discretion" was found.[44]

In other instances, however, the appellate division has couched its affirmance upon its having found no "improvident exercise of discretion" on the part of the sentencing court[45] and has modified sentences it found to have been the product of an "improvident exercise of discretion."[46] Often, in recent instances, however, the appellate division has not characterized the trial court's sentence at all, but has simply acted in its interest of justice role by reducing the sentence as being "unduly harsh"[47] or "excessive"[48] or unduly "severe"[49] or "excessive to the extent indicated."[50]

More recently, and in accordance with *People v. Delgado*,[51] the appellate division, when affirming, has simply stated that it finds the sentence "neither harsh nor excessive."[52] *Delgado* is not an exercise in fussiness or semantics. It highlights the use of appellate division discretion in sentence review, which, technically but consequentially speaking, does not involve tests as to the trial court's "improvident exercise" or "abuse" of discretion. And it matters. Generally speaking, an "abuse of discretion" is a matter of law, subject to review by the Court of Appeals. Therefore, only if the action of a trial level court (or of the appellate division[53]) constitutes an abuse of discretion as a matter of law, will it pose an issue for review by the Court of Appeals, because the Court of Appeals is a court of law.

Although the authority of the appellate division is as broad as that of the trial court, the appellate division, in practice, will not substitute its discretion for that of the trial court unless it finds that court

---

44. *See, e.g.*, People v. Crump, 197 A.D.2d 414, 602 N.Y.S.2d 394 (1st Dep't 1993), appeal denied 82 N.Y.2d 893, 610 N.Y.S.2d 160, 632 N.E.2d 470 (1993); People v. Morin, 192 A.D.2d 791, 596 N.Y.S.2d 508 (3d Dep't 1993), appeal denied 81 N.Y.2d 1077, 601 N.Y.S.2d 597, 619 N.E.2d 675 (1993).

45. *See, e.g.*, People v. Sharlow, 185 A.D.2d 289, 585 N.Y.S.2d 799 (2d Dep't 1992), appeal denied 80 N.Y.2d 976, 591 N.Y.S.2d 146, 605 N.E.2d 882 (1992); People v. Roberts, 176 A.D.2d 903, 575 N.Y.S.2d 368 (2d Dep't 1991), appeal denied 79 N.Y.2d 923, 582 N.Y.S.2d 83, 590 N.E.2d 1211 (1992).

46. *See, e.g.*, People v. Castro, 111 A.D.2d 673, 491 N.Y.S.2d 268 (1st Dep't 1985), appeal denied 65 N.Y.2d 977, 494 N.Y.S.2d 1045, 484 N.E.2d 675 (1985); People v. Eisworth, 65 A.D.2d 960, 411 N.Y.S.2d 550 (4th Dep't 1978); People v. Snyder, 40 A.D.2d 754, 337 N.Y.S.2d 796 (4th Dep't 1972).

47. People v. Clarke, 222 A.D.2d 1035, 636 N.Y.S.2d 529 (4th Dep't 1995).

48. People v. Lentini, 221 A.D.2d 474, 633 N.Y.S.2d 569 (2d Dep't 1995).

49. People v. Cedeno, 219 A.D.2d 828, 632 N.Y.S.2d 1016 (4th Dep't 1995).

50. *See, e.g.*, People v. Pickard, 216 A.D.2d 333, 627 N.Y.S.2d 988 (2d Dep't 1995).

51. 80 N.Y.2d 780, 587 N.Y.S.2d 271, 599 N.E.2d 675 (1992).

52. *See, e.g.*, People v. Blake, 219 A.D.2d 730, 631 N.Y.S.2d 430 (2d Dep't 1995); People v. Jackson, 219 A.D.2d 676, 631 N.Y.S.2d 706 (2d Dep't 1995).

53. *See, e.g.*, People v. Rubicco, 30 N.Y.2d 897, 335 N.Y.S.2d 442, 286 N.E.2d 924 (1972).

improvidently exercised its discretion.[54] This itself is an act of discretion on the part of the appellate division. The question of whether that discretion is subject to review by the Court of Appeals is another matter. In *People v. Thompson*,[55] the Court of Appeals held that the question of whether "the appellate division abused its discretion when it found the sentence imposed in this case to be excessive, poses no question of law for this court to consider. It is well settled that any question as to whether an otherwise lawful sentence is harsh or severe in a particular case involves a type of discretion not reviewable by the Court of Appeals."[56]

The appellate division is not only the proper tribunal in which to raise the harshness or severity of a legal sentence, it is the *only* tribunal in which the claim may be made. The trial court may not normally change a lawful sentence,[57] and over the years the Court of Appeals has consistently rejected claims that a sentence was so harsh or excessive as to constitute an abuse of discretion as a matter of law.[58]

Library References:

West's Key No. Digests, Criminal Law ⚖1147–1155.

54. People v. Baker, 64 N.Y.2d 1027, 489 N.Y.S.2d 56, 478 N.E.2d 197 (1985).

55. 60 N.Y.2d 513, 521, 470 N.Y.S.2d 551, 555, 458 N.E.2d 1228, 1232 (1983).

56. People v. Thompson, 60 N.Y.2d 513, 521, 470 N.Y.S.2d 551, 555, 458 N.E.2d 1228, 1232 (citing People v. Rytel, 284 N.Y. 242, 30 N.E.2d 578 (1940); People v. Potskowski, 298 N.Y. 299, 303, 83 N.E.2d 125, 127 (1948)).

57. CPL § 430.10. *See, also, supra,* § 38.10, notes 127 and 132.

58. *See, e.g.,* People v. Goetz, 73 N.Y.2d 751, 536 N.Y.S.2d 45, 532 N.E.2d 1273 (1988); People v. Pedraza, 66 N.Y.2d 626, 495 N.Y.S.2d 30, 485 N.E.2d 237 (1985); People v. McCoy, 27 N.Y.2d 632, 313 N.Y.S.2d 762, 261 N.E.2d 668 (1970). *See also,* People v. Patterson, 59 N.Y.2d 794, 464 N.Y.S.2d 751, 451 N.E.2d 498 (1983); People v. Timmins, 33 N.Y.2d 887, 352 N.Y.S.2d 445, 307 N.E.2d 562 (1973); People v. Gianni, 33 N.Y.2d 547, 347 N.Y.S.2d 438, 301 N.E.2d 425 (1973); People v. Cohen, 32 N.Y.2d 942, 347 N.Y.S.2d 203, 300 N.E.2d 734 (1973); People v. Matarese, 307 N.Y. 752, 121 N.E.2d 553(1954); People v. Johnson, 252 N.Y. 387, 169 N.E. 619 (1930). Although the Court of Appeals has not entered the sentence-harshness arena, it has decided cases in which the sentences were excessive in the constitutional sense, as to whether a sentence constitutes cruel and unusual punishment under constitutional proscription. *See, e.g.,* People v. Thompson, 83 N.Y.2d 477, 611 N.Y.S.2d 470, 633 N.E.2d 1074 (1994); People v. Donovan, 59 N.Y.2d 834, 464 N.Y.S.2d 745, 451 N.E.2d 492 (1983). *See also,* People v. Broadie, 37 N.Y.2d 100, 371 N.Y.S.2d 471, 332 N.E.2d 338 (1975)(or unconstitutional vindictiveness under North Carolina v. Pearce, 395 U.S. 711, 89 S.Ct. 2072, 23 L.Ed.2d 656 (1969)). *See generally,* People v. Van Pelt, 76 N.Y.2d 156, 556 N.Y.S.2d 984, 556 N.E.2d 423 (1990); People v. Miller, 65 N.Y.2d 502, 493 N.Y.S.2d 96, 482 N.E.2d 892 (1985).

PRACTICE POINTER: Under People v. Thompson, 60 N.Y.2d 513, 521, 470 N.Y.S.2d 551, 555, 458 N.E.2d 1228, 1232 (1983), the power of the appellate division to exercise its interest of justice sentence modification is not subject to the rule in People v. Farrar, 52 N.Y.2d 302, 437 N.Y.S.2d 961, 419 N.E.2d 864 (1981) by which a *trial* court must afford the prosecutor an opportunity to withdraw consent to a plea when the trial judge finds the agreed upon sentence unpalatable. Thus, if the prosecutor and the defendant's attorney negotiate a plea with a certain stated expectation, the trial court is bound to honor the arrangement or allow the disappointed side the chance to have the plea withdrawn under *Farrar*. The appellate division, however, is not bound, and may reduce the sentence in its discretion without having to let the prosecutor withdraw the plea offer.

§ 38.22 Appeals to the Appellate Division—Scope of Review—Change in Law While Case Pending

When a change in statutory law occurs in criminal matters, the discussion focuses on the *ex post facto* clause of the United States Constitution,[1] and whether the defendant had "fair notice" that the conduct could result in criminal liability.[2] When a change is made in decisional law, whether to apply the change retroactively requires that the court consider the purpose of the new rule, the extent of reliance by law enforcement authorities on the old rule, and the effect application of the new rule would have on the administration of justice.[3]

Library References:
West's Key No. Digests, Criminal Law ⚖1181(2).

§ 38.23 Appeals to the Appellate Division—Disposition of Appeal

Upon an appeal to the appellate division from a judgment, sentence, or order, there are only three dispositional avenues open pursuant to CPL § 470.15(2): affirmance, reversal, or modification. Affirmance is obviously the most straightforward; it involves no "corrective action."[1] A reversal or modification must be based on a determination made upon the law or upon the facts, or as a matter of discretion in the interest of justice, or upon any two or three of them.[2]

§ 38.24 Appeals to the Appellate Division—Disposition of Appeal—Affirmance

An affirmance does not require an explanation or elaboration.[1] The appellate division is powerless to consider, as a basis for affirmance, any grounds not relied upon by *nisi prius*.[2] If, for example, a court dismisses

§ 38.22
1. U.S. Constitution Art. I, § 10.
2. Collins v. Youngblood, 497 U.S. 37, 110 S.Ct. 2715, 111 L.Ed.2d 30 (1990); People v. Hudy, 73 N.Y.2d 40, 48–49, 538 N.Y.S.2d 197, 201, 535 N.E.2d 250, 254 (1988); People v. Morse, 62 N.Y.2d 205, 217–218, 476 N.Y.S.2d 505, 511, 465 N.E.2d 12, 18 (1984).
3. *See* People v. Hill, 85 N.Y.2d 256, 262–263, 624 N.Y.S.2d 79, 82, 648 N.E.2d 455, 458 (1995); People v. Eastman, 85 N.Y.2d 265, 275–276, 624 N.Y.S.2d 83, 88, 648 N.E.2d 459, 464 (1995); People v. Favor, 82 N.Y.2d 254, 262, 604 N.Y.S.2d 494, 498, 624 N.E.2d 631 (1993); People v. Pepper, 53 N.Y.2d 213, 220–221, 440 N.Y.S.2d 889, 892, 423 N.E.2d 366, 369 (1981), cert. denied 454 U.S. 967, 102 S.Ct. 510, 70 L.Ed.2d 383 (1981).

§ 38.23
1. *See* CPL § 470.10(3).
2. *See* CPL § 470.15(3).

§ 38.24
1. CPL § 470.25(1).
2. In an *Anders* affirmance, (*see* Anders v. State of California, 386 U.S. 738, 87 S.Ct. 1396, 18 L.Ed.2d 493 (1967)), the court will also include the grant of the application by defendant-appellant's counsel for leave to withdraw. *See, e.g.*, People v. Toscano, 224 A.D.2d 558, 638 N.Y.S.2d 339 (2d Dep't 1996); People v. Ortiz, 224 A.D.2d 553, 638 N.Y.S.2d 341 (2d Dep't 1996).

§ 38.24 CRIMINAL APPELLATE PRACTICE Ch. 38

an indictment solely on the ground that the defendant was questioned improperly before the grand jury, the appellate division may not consider alternate arguments that the defendant seeks to propound to support the dismissal, (such as failure to instruct the grand jury properly).[3] Conversely, on a defendant's appeal, the appellate division will not consider for affirmance any alternate grounds that the People advance that had not been decided adversely to the defendant.[4]

Of course, an order of the appellate division, be it of affirmance, reversal, or modification, is the event that sets into motion the next stage that may be possible in appellate practice, *i.e.*, an appeal to the Court of Appeals. As for this step, the aggrieved party may seek permission to appeal by making an application pursuant to CPL § 460.20 for a certificate granting leave. It must be made within 30 days after service upon the appellant of a copy of the order sought to be appealed.[5]

Library References:

West's Key No. Digests, Criminal Law ⚖1182.

§ 38.25 Appeals to the Appellate Division—Disposition of Appeal—Modification

A modification of a judgment or order by the appellate division means that a part of the judgment or order is vacated and the remainder affirmed.[1] When modifying a sentence on grounds of harshness or excessiveness, the appellate division does not normally speak of *vacatur*, but "reduces" the sentence itself.[2] A modification, like a reversal, may be on the law, the facts, or as a matter of discretion in the interest of justice. It must be based on at least one of those determinations and may be based on any two, or on all three.[3]

Modifications on the Law. Modifications on the law include, but are not limited to, three types of determinations that are identified by statute.[4] The first contemplates a duly *protested* ruling or instruction of the court, at a trial resulting in a judgment, which deprived the defendant of a fair trial.[5] This contemplates modification by *vacatur*, and a

---

3. People v. Karp, 76 N.Y.2d 1006, 566 N.E.2d 1156, 565 N.Y.S.2d 751 (1990); People v. Goodfriend, 64 N.Y.2d 695, 474 N.E.2d 1187, 485 N.Y.S.2d 519 (1984); CPL § 470.15(1).
4. People v. Fields, 151 A.D.2d 598, 599, 542 N.Y.S.2d 356, 359 (2d Dep't 1989); People v. Powe, 146 A.D.2d 718, 537 N.Y.S.2d 208 (2d Dep't 1989), appeal denied 73 N.Y.2d 1020 (19), 541 N.Y.S.2d 774, 539 N.E.2d 602.
5. CPL § 460.10(5)(a). *See infra*, § 39.12 regarding leave to appeal to the Court of Appeals. For procedures in which a conviction is affirmed and the defendant has been out on bail. *See infra*, § 38.28.

§ 38.25

1. CPL § 470.10(2).
2. CPL § 470.20(6).
3. CPL § 470.15(3).
4. CPL § 470.15(4).
5. CPL § 470.15(4)(a).

new trial of the count or counts for which the defendant was convicted, but which were compromised by legal error that was preserved.[6]

The second type of modification set forth under CPL § 470.15(4) takes place when the evidence adduced at trial was not *legally* sufficient to establish the defendant's guilt.[7] This involves *dismissal* of only the legally insufficient count. Pursuant to CPL § 470.20(3), when the appellate division modifies a judgment after trial for legal insufficiency with respect to a count of which the defendant was convicted, it must and will dismiss the count determined to be legally unsupported and affirm the remainder of the judgment.[8] It will then either reduce the total sentence to that imposed by the criminal court upon the affirmed counts or it will remit the case to the criminal court for resentencing on those counts.[9]

If the trial adduced evidence insufficient to establish the defendant's guilt of a convicted count, but was legally sufficient to establish defendant's guilt of a *lesser* included offense, the court will modify the judgment by changing it (*i.e.*, reducing it) to one of conviction for the lesser offense.[10] If so, it will remit the case to the criminal court with a direction that the defendant be sentenced accordingly.[11] To illustrate: If a defendant is convicted of intentional murder and the appellate division concludes that there was legally insufficient evidence to justify the murder verdict, but that there was sufficient legal evidence to justify a first degree manslaughter verdict, the appellate division will modify, in effect, by reducing the conviction from murder to the lesser included offense of manslaughter first degree. Cases illustrative of this are *People v. Ortiz*,[12] and *People v. Lewis*.[13]

---

6. *See, e.g.*, People v. Corbitt, 221 A.D.2d 809, 633 N.Y.S.2d 865 (3d Dep't 1995); People v. Figueroa, 219 A.D.2d 667, 631 N.Y.S.2d 403 (2d Dep't 1995)(reversing and ordering new trial on third degree drug possession count); People v. Figueroa, 219 A.D.2d 667, 631 N.Y.S.2d 403 (2d Dep't 1995)(reversing and ordering new trial on robbery count). In People v. Vilardi, 150 A.D.2d 819, 542 N.Y.S.2d 238 (2d Dep't 1989), the court vacated the defendant's arson conviction count on the basis of a *Brady* violation, but affirmed as to the jointly tried counts that were not affected by the *Brady* violation. This same rationale applies to *Rosario* violations, in that it infects only the pertinent counts. *See* People v. Baghai–Kermani, 84 N.Y.2d 525, 620 N.Y.S.2d 313, 644 N.E.2d 1004 (1994). Many examples could be cited.

7. CPL §§ 470.15(2)(b),(4)(b).

8. *See, e.g.*, People v. Conto, 218 A.D.2d 665, 630 N.Y.S.2d 542 (1995)(evidence legally insufficient to support false filing count; count dismissed; remainder affirmed); People v. Santos, 210 A.D.2d 129, 620 N.Y.S.2d 62 (1st Dep't 1994), appeal withdrawn 85 N.Y.2d 942, 627 N.Y.S.2d 1004, 651 N.E.2d 929 (1995)(dismissing drug paraphernalia counts, and affirming the rest).

9. *See infra*, Chart in § 38.64.

10. CPL § 470.15(2)(a).

11. CPL § 470.20(4).

PRACTICE POINTER: After reducing the level of the crime, there is no point for remittal for resentencing if the defendant has already served the maximum sentence authorized under the lesser crime. *See, e.g.*, People v. Quinn, 186 A.D.2d 691, 588 N.Y.S.2d 646 (2d Dep't 1992).

12. 214 A.D.2d 451, 625 N.Y.S.2d 514 (1st Dep't 1995), appeal denied 86 N.Y.2d 739, 631 N.Y.S.2d 619, 655 N.E.2d 716 (1995) (reducing conviction from grand larceny third degree to fourth degree).

13. 213 A.D.2d 1065, 625 N.Y.S.2d 982 (4th Dep't 1995), appeal denied 86 N.Y.2d 782, 655 N.E.2d 725, 631 N.Y.S.2d 628

§ 38.25 CRIMINAL APPELLATE PRACTICE Ch. 38

The third statutory basis for modification on the law pertains to sentences that are unauthorized, illegally imposed, or otherwise invalid as a matter of law.[14] There are many ways in which a sentence may be unauthorized, illegally imposed, or invalid as a matter of law.[15] When it so concludes, the appellate division may modify and remit the case to the criminal court for resentence,[16] or it may itself reduce the sentence if it is illegally excessive.[17]

Modifications on the Facts. Modifications on the facts include, but are not limited to, a determination that a verdict of conviction resulting in a judgment was, in whole or in part, against the weight of the evidence.[18] When a conviction of a count of an indictment is against the weight of evidence, it calls for the dismissal of that count.[19] If other counts are valid, the appellate division will modify accordingly by affirming the valid counts. This is a modification on the facts, because a finding that a verdict on a count is against the weight of evidence is a factual determination.[20]

Modifications in the Interest of Justice. In addition to modifications on the law and modifications on the facts, the third variety of modification is *in the interest of justice*.[21] This relates to legal sentences that the appellate division, in its discretion, reduces as overly harsh or excessive, and it also relates to modifications based upon unpreserved error.[22]

Beyond the types of modifications set forth in the statute[23] and described above, there are other instances in which modifications on the law have been ordered that have fallen into no particular statutory cubby-hole. It has occurred, for example, in modifying a sentence on the law from consecutive to concurrent,[24] and by deleting the provisions in a judgment that directed payment of a surcharge.[25] Modifications have also

(1995)(reducing conviction for drug possession fifth degree to seventh degree).

14. CPL § 470.15(4)(c).

15. *See supra*, § 38.8.

16. People v. Giersz, 207 A.D.2d 843, 616 N.Y.S.2d 555 (2d Dep't 1994), appeal denied 84 N.Y.2d 1011, 622 N.Y.S.2d 922, 647 N.E.2d 128 (1994)(improper second felony offender sentence).

17. People v. Gadson, 190 A.D.2d 860, 593 N.Y.S.2d 875 (2d Dep't 1993), appeal denied 81 N.Y.2d 970, 598 N.Y.S.2d 772, 615 N.E.2d 229 (1993)(illegal one-year sentence); People v. Toledo, 204 A.D.2d 667, 614 N.Y.S.2d 238 (2d Dep't 1994), appeal denied 84 N.Y.2d 911, 621 N.Y.S.2d 528, 645 N.E.2d 1228 (1994)(illegal sentence range).

18. CPL § 470.15(5).

19. CPL § 470.20(5).

20. *See, e.g.*, People v. Ruiz, 162 A.D.2d 350, 556 N.Y.S.2d 910 (1st Dep't 1990)(criminal drug sale count dismissed against the weight of evidence); People v. Bobb, 207 A.D.2d 458, 615 N.Y.S.2d 764 (2d Dep't 1994), appeal denied 84 N.Y.2d 1009, 622 N.Y.S.2d 921, 647 N.E.2d 127 (1994)(reducing drug count on finding it was not supported by the weight of the evidence).

21. CPL § 470.15(3)(c).

22. CPL § 470.15(6)(a),(b); People v. Flores, 222 A.D.2d 450, 635 N.Y.S.2d 37 (2d Dep't 1995).

23. CPL § 470.15(4),(5).

24. People v. Racks, 221 A.D.2d 664, 635 N.Y.S.2d 501 (2d Dep't 1995).

25. People v. Richter, 223 A.D.2d 734, 637 N.Y.S.2d 206 (2d Dep't 1996).

taken place, for example, for the purpose of remitting a case to the trial court to impose sentence when none had been pronounced,[26] remanding for a restitution hearing[27] and remitting to the trial court to impose a sentence agreed upon or allow the defendant in the alternative, to withdraw his plea.[28]

Library References:

West's Key No. Digests, Criminal Law ⚖1184.

§ 38.26 Appeals to the Appellate Division—Disposition of Appeal—Reversal

Under the Criminal Procedure Law, reversal means *vacatur*. The term applies to judgments, sentences, and orders.[1] A reversal may be on the law, the facts, or as a matter of discretion in the interest of justice, or any combination of the three.[2] Before going into the various combinations and their import, it is useful to discuss the concepts of reversal generally.

By statute, reversals *on the law* include those based on rulings or instructions of the court, properly protested, that deprived the defendant of a fair trial.[3] This is a common variety of reversal and may involve any ruling that denied the defendant a fair trial.[4] It also covers all manner of jury instructions.[5] Under a law reversal of this kind there must be a new trial, as opposed to a dismissal.[6] A reversal on the law also includes those based on legal insufficiency of the proof.[7] A reversal based on legal insufficiency must result in a dismissal of the accusatory instrument.[8] Pursuant to CPL § 470.15(4)(c), a reversal on the law also takes place upon a finding that a sentence was *"unauthorized"*[9] or *"illegally im-*

---

26. People v. Burton, 214 A.D.2d 1037, 626 N.Y.S.2d 918 (4th Dep't 1995), appeal denied 86 N.Y.2d 840, 634 N.Y.S.2d 450, 658 N.E.2d 228 (1995).

27. People v. Alonzo, 155 A.D.2d 233, 546 N.Y.S.2d 617 (1st Dep't 1989); People v. La Manga Development Corp., 70 A.D.2d 541, 416 N.Y.S.2d 278 (1st Dep't 1979).

28. People v. Sitarski, 222 A.D.2d 1118, 636 N.Y.S.2d 533 (4th Dep't 1995); People v. Nelson, 216 A.D.2d 946, 629 N.Y.S.2d 705 (4th Dep't 1995).

§ 38.26

1. CPL § 470.10.
2. CPL § 470.15(3).
3. CPL § 470.15(4)(a).
4. People v. Bennett, 169 A.D.2d 369, 573 N.Y.S.2d 322 (3d Dep't 1991), aff'd 79 N.Y.2d 464, 583 N.Y.S.2d 825, 593 N.E.2d 279 (1992)(improper ruling by court as to defendant's freedom from self incrimination relative to pending unrelated criminal charge).

5. People v. Greene, 221 A.D.2d 559, 634 N.Y.S.2d 144 (2d Dep't 1995).

6. CPL § 470.20(1). *See infra*, Chart at § 38.64.

7. CPL § 470.15(4)(b). *See, e.g.*, People v. Rossey, 222 A.D.2d 710, 635 N.Y.S.2d 970 (2d Dep't 1995)(murder and weapons possession).

8. CPL § 470.20(2). *See infra*, Chart at § 38.64.

9. *See, e.g.*, People v. Jackson, 106 A.D.2d 93, 483 N.Y.S.2d 725 (2d Dep't 1984)(consecutive sentence unauthorized).

posed"[10] or was "*invalid as a matter of law.*"[11]

On occasion, and when not barred by double jeopardy provisions (*i.e.*, when reversal is not based on legal or factual insufficiency of the trial evidence), a reversal on the law may be accompanied by an authorization for the prosecutor to present the case to another grand jury. It happens when the defendant is convicted of only a lesser included count which is reversed. The defendant may not be retried on the higher count, but the prosecution may re-indict the defendant under the reversed count for which he was convicted. This is known as the "*Beslanovics*" procedure.[12]

To illustrate: Suppose the defendant is indicted and brought to trial on a manslaughter first degree charge. The jury is instructed that it may find the defendant guilty under that count or under a lesser included charge of manslaughter in the second degree. If the jury returns with a guilty verdict on the lesser charge of manslaughter second degree (under the manslaughter first degree count), it constitutes an acquittal and a double jeopardy bar as to the higher (manslaughter first degree) count.[13] If the appellate division then reverses the manslaughter second degree conviction for some legal error, there is nothing left to support the indictment.[14] How may the People proceed, considering that there is no double jeopardy bar to a retrial on the manslaughter second degree count, but there is no viable written accusatory instrument describing the lesser charge?

Beslanovics itself did not expressly state that in order to proceed the People either may or must present the charges to a new grand jury. For

---

10. *See, e.g.*, People v. Stroman, 36 N.Y.2d 939, 373 N.Y.S.2d 548, 335 N.E.2d 853 (1975)(sentence illegally imposed when defendant not in courtroom).

11. *See, e.g.*, People v. Blount, 49 A.D.2d 911, 373 N.Y.S.2d 402 (2d Dep't 1975)(sentenced under the wrong statute); People v. Kuyal, 155 A.D.2d 901, 547 N.Y.S.2d 731 (4th Dep't 1989), appeal denied 76 N.Y.2d 738, 558 N.Y.S.2d 900, 557 N.E.2d 1196 (1990) (People's appeal, sentence invalid as a matter of law, as defendant was a predicate offender). There is some nomenclature here. As we have seen, CPL § 470.15(4)(c) refers to sentences that are "*unauthorized, illegally imposed,* or otherwise *invalid as a matter of law*." The same three adjectives are found in CPL § 440.20 relative to collateral attacks by defendants on sentences. Each of the cases cited above uses one of the adjectives to describe the defectiveness of the sentence, but in truth, the cases have not kept separate the categories of "unauthorized" as opposed to "illegally imposed," as distinguished from "invalid as a matter of law." There is overlap at least, and the courts freely interchange the terms. It may be possible to make distinctions—for example, when defendant was not in court the sentence imposed may have been "authorized" in that it was within the permissible range, but was "illegally imposed" because he was not there—but this is an exercise in pedantry.

12. People v. Beslanovics, 57 N.Y.2d 726, 454 N.Y.S.2d 976, 440 N.E.2d 1322 (1982). *See infra*, § 38.28.

13. People v. Graham, 36 N.Y.2d 633, 635, 370 N.Y.S.2d 888, 891, 331 N.E.2d 673 (1975); People v. Ressler, 17 N.Y.2d 174, 269 N.Y.S.2d 414, 216 N.E.2d 582 (1966).

14. People v. Beslanovics, 57 N.Y.2d 726, 454 N.Y.S.2d 976, 440 N.E.2d 1322 (1982). *See also*, People v. Mayo, 48 N.Y.2d 245, 422 N.Y.S.2d 361, 397 N.E.2d 1166 (1979).

a time, there might have been some reason to believe that the People could simply proceed informally without getting a new indictment.[15] *Beslanovics*, was interpreted from the outset, however, as requiring re-presentation as a basis to proceed, and any question on this score was settled in *People v. Gonzalez*[16] in which the Court of Appeals stated that the proper procedure was re-presentation of the appropriate charges to another grand jury. The Beslanovics procedure of reversal and dismissal with leave to re-present to another grand jury has been followed routinely.[17]

A reversal on the *facts* includes one that is based on a determination that the verdict of conviction was, in whole or in part, against the weight of evidence.[18] A reversal on the facts, as against the weight of evidence,[19] mandates dismissal of the indictment.[20] This marks a statutory departure from prior law in which reversals on the facts resulted in new trials.[21]

The third type of reversal is one determined to be made "*as a matter of discretion in the interest of justice.*" It relates primarily to unpreserved errors;[22] and to reduction of legal sentences on grounds of undue harshness or severity.[23] But there are assorted other occasions when this ground is invoked.[24] If a conviction is reversed in the interest of justice,[25] a new trial is mandated when the reversal is based upon an (unpreserved) error or defect that either prejudiced or denied the defendant a fair trial.[26] Although there have been instances in which interest of justice reversals have resulted in orders of dismissal,[27] they were based on either the inadequacy of the proof (which more properly falls under a CPL § 470.20(2) reversal, requiring dismissal for legal insufficiency)[28] or

---

15. People v. Graham, 36 N.Y.2d 633, 370 N.Y.S.2d 888, 331 N.E.2d 673 (1975).

16. 61 N.Y.2d 633, 471 N.Y.S.2d 847, 459 N.E.2d 1285 (1983).

17. *See, e.g.*, People v. Simmons, 206 A.D.2d 550, 615 N.Y.S.2d 56 (2d Dep't 1994); People v. Patterson, 203 A.D.2d 597, 611 N.Y.S.2d 217 (2d Dep't 1994).

18. CPL § 470.15(5). *See, e.g.*, People v. Groce, 213 A.D.2d 363, 624 N.Y.S.2d 863 (2d Dep't 1995)(robbery); People v. Elliott, 209 A.D.2d 537, 619 N.Y.S.2d 68 (2d Dep't 1994)(sodomy).

19. CPL § 470.15(5).

20. CPL § 470.20(5). *See also, supra*, § 38.20.

21. *See, e.g.*, People v. Spadorcio, 247 App.Div. 862, 288 N.Y.S. 882 (4th Dep't 1936); People v. Smith, 234 App.Div. 728, 251 N.Y.S. 999 (4th Dep't 1931); People v. Alexander, 206 App.Div. 780, 200 N.Y.S. 939 (2d Dep't 1923).

22. CPL § 470.15(6)(a). *See supra*, § 38.21.

23. CPL § 470.15(6)(b). *See supra*, § 38.21.

24. *See supra*, § 38.21.

25. CPL § 470.15(6).

26. CPL § 470.20(1). *See. e.g.*, People v. Kilstein, 174 App.Div.2d 756, 571 N.Y.S.2d 781 (2d Dep't 1991), appeal denied 78 N.Y.2d 1012, 575 N.Y.S.2d 820, 581 N.E.2d 1066 (1991)(ineffective assistance of counsel); People v. Ranum, 122 A.D.2d 959, 506 N.Y.S.2d 105 (2d Dep't 1986)(improper foundation for child's sworn testimony). *See also supra*, § 38.21.

27. *See supra*, § 38.21.

28. *See, e.g.*, People v. Wingate, 175 A.D.2d 191, 573 N.Y.S.2d 696 (2d Dep't 1991); People v. Banks, 193 A.D.2d 1051, 598 N.Y.S.2d 1014 (4th Dep't 1993), appeal dismissed 82 N.Y.2d 713, 602 N.Y.S.2d 810, 622 N.E.2d 311 (1993).

as against the weight of the evidence[29] or other reasons that do not involve trial errors or defects.[30]

Library References:

West's Key No. Digests, Criminal Law ⚖1186.1.

§ 38.27 Appeals to the Appellate Division—Disposition of Appeal—Character of Order of Reversal or Modification: on the Law, on the Facts, in the Interest of Justice

When the appellate division reverses or modifies, the appellate division order must, and will, state the specific grounds of reversal or modification.[1] The body of intermediate appellate decisional law is replete with all manner of modification and reversal. Considering that there are three grounds (law, facts, and in interest of justice), there are seven possible combinations. Each carries implications for Court of Appeals appealability, but the crucial determination is made at the appellate division level.

Reversals and modifications may be and have been based upon:

—the law

—the facts

—the interest of justice

—the law and the facts

—the law and the interest of justice

—the facts and the interest of justice

—the law, the facts, and the interest of justice

Note that the Court of Appeals is not bound by the appellate division label and may look past it to discern whether the reversal or modification was made "on the law" alone, or on the law and such facts which, but for the determination of law, would not have led to reversal or modification.[2] The present CPL § 450.90(2)(a) has expanded the

---

29. See, e.g., People v. Bennett, 193 A.D.2d 808, 598 N.Y.S.2d 84 (2d Dep't 1993); People v. Levy, 179 A.D.2d 730, 578 N.Y.S.2d 637 (2d Dep't 1992).

30. See supra, § 38.21.

§ 38.27

1. CPL § 470.25(2)(b).

2. CPL § 450.90(2)(a). When first enacted, former CPL § 450.90(2)(a), provided that an appeal to the Court of Appeals could be taken only if the intermediate appellate court's order *expressly* stated the determination of reversal or modification to be *on the law* alone. If the intermediate appellate court described its order as being "on the law and the facts," the Court of Appeals could not look past the label even if it wanted to. See People v. Sullivan, 29 N.Y.2d 937, 329 N.Y.S.2d 325, 280 N.E.2d 98 (1972). If, however, the recital was "on the law," the Court of Appeals would look past an inapt label and reject an appeal that included an appreciable factual or interest of justice component. See also, People v. Woodruff, 27 N.Y.2d 801, 315 N.Y.S.2d 861, 264 N.E.2d 353 (1970); People v. Rainey, 27

Court of Appeals' authority to look past the label so as to find appealability no matter what the label says.[3]

Reversal or Modification on the Law. The most common reversals or modifications are those decided *"on the law."*[4] Subject to permission, and on the surface, a reversal "on the law" alone is the clearest illustration of appealability to the Court of Appeals. But, as we shall see, surfaces may sometimes be slippery.

In order to satisfy its jurisdictional threshold, the Court of Appeals must conclude, notwithstanding the label, that it was the determination on the law that was controlling, and that any consideration of the facts would *not* have led to reversal or modification.[5] In *People v. Christian*,[6] the Court of Appeals dismissed the People's appeal from an appellate division order even though it recited modification "on the law."[7] The court ruled that notwithstanding the law label, it was not the pure determination on the law that CPL § 450.90(2)(a) requires. The same was true in *People v. Bonilla–Lugo*,[8] in which the Court of Appeals dismissed a People's appeal from a reversal in which the appellate division reduced the degree of the crime.[9]

People v. Baker[10] provides a highly instructive explanation to a would be appellant. In that case, although the appellate division's order of reversal recited that it was "on the law," it is evident from its

N.Y.2d 748, 314 N.Y.S.2d 999, 263 N.E.2d 395 (1970)). *See also, infra*, § 39.42.

3. People v. Giles, 73 N.Y.2d 666, 543 N.Y.S.2d 37, 541 N.E.2d 37 (1989). "The first quality of a criminal investigator," said Sherlock Holmes, is to "see through a disguise." Arthur Conan Doyle, *The Hound of the Baskervilles, The Complete Sherlock Holmes* (Doubleday & Co., New York) p.750.

4. *See supra*, § 38.26.

5. CPL § 450.90(2). *See also, infra*, § 39.42.

PRACTICE POINTER: Consumers are always admonished to read labels carefully. In the appeals context, labels are not controlling, but there is no harm in asking the appellate division for an amendment of the label so as to have the order appear, at least on its face, to be appealable. Surely there can be no harm in it; at times applications have been successful in stripping the non-appealable components from the decretal label. *See, e.g.*, People v. Bell, 35 N.Y.2d 852, 363 N.Y.S.2d 89, 321 N.E.2d 880 (1974); People v. Kitt, 38 N.Y.2d 799, 381 N.Y.S.2d 872, 345 N.E.2d 343 (1975); Pliss v. Erie Railroad Co., 208 App.Div. 761, 202 N.Y.S. 947 (4th Dep't 1924); Langan v. First Trust & Deposit Company, 271 App. Div. 951, 68 N.Y.S.2d 448 (4th Dep't 1947), aff'd 296 N.Y. 951, 73 N.E.2d 264. Because of § 450.90(2)(a) and People v. Giles, 73 N.Y.2d 666, 543 N.Y.S.2d 37, 541 N.E.2d 37 (1989), it is no longer necessary, as it was under these older cases, to have the appellate division repeal the impeding surplusage. A positive word from the appellate division as to its intent would certainly not harm the chances of the would-be appellant. Indeed, in People v. Graham, 35 N.Y.2d 977, 365 N.Y.S.2d 527, 324 N.E.2d 885 (1975), the Court of Appeals asked the appellate division to clarify its modification order.

6. 85 N.Y.2d 965, 629 N.Y.S.2d 722, 653 N.E.2d 618 (1995).

7. People v. Christian, 209 A.D.2d 259, 618 N.Y.S.2d 711 (1st Dep't 1994).

8. 85 N.Y.2d 965, 629 N.Y.S.2d 721, 653 N.E.2d 618 (1995).

9. *See also*, People v. Blackwell, 85 N.Y.2d 851, 624 N.Y.S.2d 367, 648 N.E.2d 787 (1995).

10. 64 N.Y.2d 1027, 1028, 489 N.Y.S.2d 56, 56, 478 N.E.2d 197, 197 (1985).

memorandum that its order was made in the exercise of discretion and, therefore, did not satisfy the jurisdictional predicate of CPL § 450.90(2)(a).[11] Not only did it grant the People leave to resubmit to another Grand Jury, which CPL §§ 210.20(1)(i) and 210.20(4) authorize it to do "in its discretion" after dismissal pursuant to CPL § 210.40, but also it characterized the Trial Judge's denial of the Section 210.40 motion as an "improvident exercise of discretion," not as "an abuse of discretion as a matter of law." In so doing it substituted its discretion for the improvident discretionary denial of the Trial Judge, as it had the right to do, its authority being as broad as that of the trial court.[12]

Reversal or Modification on the Law and Facts. An appellate division reversal on *"the law and the facts"*[13] is not uncommon; it implies that factual evaluation played a part in the order of reversal. On its face it is jurisdictionally suspect in terms of further appealability. However, the phrase "on the law and the facts" may be interpreted as a determination that was essentially legal, in which the appellate division's factual review was incidental and jurisdictionally inconsequential.[14] In a number of cases, however, the Court of Appeals has treated the "law and facts" modification or reversal as foreclosing its jurisdiction, and has dismissed the appeals.[15]

Reversal or Modification on the Facts. Because most appellate division reversals or modifications *"on the facts"*[16] follow trials in which the appellate division has found the verdict, in whole or in part, against the weight of evidence,[17] a reversal or modification on the facts will not be appealable to the Court of Appeals unless the court concludes—and it is very unlikely—that the facts mean the law. It is almost like saying day means night, but research discloses that there have been such instances.[18] Almost without fail, however, a reversal or a modification on the

11. People v. Johnson, 47 N.Y.2d 124, 417 N.Y.S.2d 46, 390 N.E.2d 764 (1979); People v. Williams, 31 N.Y.2d 151, 335 N.Y.S.2d 271, 286 N.E.2d 715 (1972).

12. Matter of Von Bulow, 63 N.Y.2d 221, 225, 481 N.Y.S.2d 67, 69, 470 N.E.2d 866, 868 (1984); People v. Belge, 41 N.Y.2d 60, 390 N.Y.S.2d 867, 359 N.E.2d 377 (1976).

13. CPL §§ 470.15(3)(a),(b).

14. *See, e.g.,* People v. DeMarasse, 85 N.Y.2d 842, 623 N.Y.S.2d 845, 647 N.E.2d 1353 (1995)(People's appeal from dismissal of count); People v. Sanchez, 84 N.Y.2d 440, 618 N.Y.S.2d 887, 643 N.E.2d 509 (1994)(defendant's appeal from appellate division modification).

15. *See, e.g.,* People v. Hayden, 39 N.Y.2d 824, 385 N.Y.S.2d 767, 351 N.E.2d 434 (1976)(defendant's appeal from appellate division order reinstating charges); People v. Pendleton, 35 N.Y.2d 690, 361 N.Y.S.2d 160, 319 N.E.2d 422 (1974)(defendant's appeal from appellate division order reversing dismissal); People v. Barriera, 81 N.Y.2d 1040, 600 N.Y.S.2d 440, 616 N.E.2d 1102 (1993)(People's appeal from appellate division suppression grant).

16. CPL § 470.15(3)(b).

17. *See, e.g.,* People v. Athanasopoulos, 206 A.D.2d 381, 614 N.Y.S.2d 61 (2d Dep't 1994).

18. *See, e.g.,* People v. Castro, 53 N.Y.2d 1046, 442 N.Y.S.2d 500, 425 N.E.2d 888 (1981); People v. Zwickler, 16 N.Y.2d 1069, 266 N.Y.S.2d 140, 213 N.E.2d 467 (1965); People v. Scheinman, 295 N.Y. 142, 65 N.E.2d 750 (1946). *See also,* CPL § 450.90(2)(current version; as to appealability or legality of corrective action).

facts will not find its way to the Court of Appeals.[19]

Reversal or Modification in the Interest of Justice. Pursuant to CPL § 470.15(3)(c), a reversal or a modification made solely in the interest of justice (more formally, "As a matter of discretion in the interest of justice") is one that generally, but not always, involves either an unpreserved error or the reduction of a lawful sentence.[20] An appeal from an appellate division modification or reversal made solely in the interest of justice will no doubt be dismissed by the Court of Appeals.[21]

Reversal or Modification on the Law and in the Interest of Justice. A reversal or modification on the law and in the interest of justice is a hybrid type reversal or modification combining CPL §§ 470.15(3)(a) and (c). Such appellate division reversals do exist; some have been found to be appealable to the Court of Appeals.[22] Appeals from others have been dismissed for unappealability.[23]

On its face an *interest of justice* component in the reversal or modification order is a nonlegal determination,[24] and so an analysis of its underpinnings may come into play. In *People v. Johnson*,[25] the appellate division order of reversal originally recited that it was on the law and as a matter of discretion in the interests of justice. The appellant successfully moved the appellate division to amend the recital of the reversal order to state that it was on the law alone. But the triumph was short lived. The Court of Appeals dismissed the appeal, holding that the resettlement of the reversal order did not remove the discretionary aspect of the reversal, considering that the appellate division acted to correct unpreserved errors.

There have been some success stories, as where the appellate division order in *People v. Bell*[26] was resettled to state "on the law" only, and the appeal to the Court of Appeals was permitted.[27] *Bell* and *Kitt*

---

19. See, e.g., People v. Letterlough, 203 A.D.2d 589, 610 N.Y.S.2d 614 (2d Dep't 1994), appeal dismissed, 84 N.Y.2d 862, 618 N.Y.S.2d 4, 642 N.E.2d 323 (1994). See also, W. C. Donnino, *New York Court of Appeals on Criminal Law*, § 3.13.

20. CPL § 470.15(6). See generally supra, § 38.21.

21. See, e.g., People v. Gonzalez, 186 A.D.2d 12, 587 N.Y.S.2d 972 (1st Dep't 1992), appeal dismissed 81 N.Y.2d 879, 597 N.Y.S.2d 929, 613 N.E.2d 961 (1993).

22. See, e.g., People v. Gonzalez, 61 N.Y.2d 633, 471 N.Y.S.2d 847, 459 N.E.2d 1285 (1983)(People's appeal from appellate division dismissal); People v. Randazzo, 60 N.Y.2d 952, 471 N.Y.S.2d 52, 459 N.E.2d 161 (1983)(People's appeal from appellate term dismissal); People v. Rogers, 56 N.Y.2d 552, 449 N.Y.S.2d 961, 434 N.E.2d 1339 (1982)(People's appeal from appellate division reversal).

23. See, e.g., People v. Paige, 38 N.Y.2d 872, 382 N.Y.S.2d 742, 346 N.E.2d 543 (1976); People v. Fair, 27 N.Y.2d 814, 315 N.Y.S.2d 869, 264 N.E.2d 359 (1970); People v. Cooper, 25 N.Y.2d 928, 305 N.Y.S.2d 145, 252 N.E.2d 626 (1969).

24. People v. Mendola, 2 N.Y.2d 270, 274, 159 N.Y.S.2d 473, 475, 140 N.E.2d 353, 355 (1957).

25. 47 N.Y.2d 124, 417 N.Y.S.2d 46, 390 N.E.2d 764 (1979).

26. 35 N.Y.2d 852, 363 N.Y.S.2d 89, 321 N.E.2d 880 (1974).

27. See also, People v. Kitt, 38 N.Y.2d 799, 381 N.Y.S.2d 872, 345 N.E.2d 343 (1975).

§ 38.27   CRIMINAL APPELLATE PRACTICE   Ch. 38

were decided before the 1979 amendment to CPL § 450.90[28] which allowed the Court of Appeals to look past labels. Even so, these cases are still useful and instructive inasmuch as the CPL § 450.90 amendment was designed to accomplish the converse: to let the Court of Appeals address a question of law even though the appellate division reversal order, with the inclusion of a fact or interest of justice component, could superficially appear to be a barrier to review what might in reality be a question of law.

The Facts and the Interest of Justice. Reversals or modifications on the facts and in the interest of justice are the antithesis of reversals on the law.[29] On the face of it, an appeal based on the two non-law components would seem doomed to dismissal. It was, in *People v. Turcsik*.[30] But in three other instances the Court of Appeals has not dismissed. (There is no indication that anyone asked it to do so.)[31]

Reversal or Modification on the Law, the Facts, and in the Interest of Justice. This is the ultimate form of reversal or modification: the full catastrophe—everything but the kitchen sink. In practice, it poses the most difficulty in discerning the character of the determination—a consideration that bears on appealability. Such orders are far from unknown.[32] In a number of such instances the Court of Appeals has reached the merits despite the appellate division label.[33] In *People v. Woods*,[34] however, the Court of Appeals dismissed the appeal as one not involving a purely legal determination.

§ 38.28   Appeals to the Appellate Division—Disposition of Appeal—Corrective Action

Dismissal. When a judgment of conviction is reversed for legal insufficiency, the accusatory instrument must be dismissed.[1] When a judgment of conviction is modified by reversing counts for legal insufficiency, the unsupported counts must be dismissed.[2]

28. L. 1979, Ch. 651.

29. *See, e.g.*, People v. Jackson, 205 A.D.2d 639, 613 N.Y.S.2d 230 (2d Dep't 1994), appeal denied 84 N.Y.2d 827, 617 N.Y.S.2d 147, 641 N.E.2d 168 (1994).

30. 34 N.Y.2d 985, 360 N.Y.S.2d 414, 318 N.E.2d 605 (1974).

31. People v. Rubicco, 30 N.Y.2d 897, 335 N.Y.S.2d 442, 286 N.E.2d 924 (1972); People v. Lebovitz, 26 N.Y.2d 924, 310 N.Y.S.2d 321, 258 N.E.2d 723 (1970); People v. Letterio, 16 N.Y.2d 307, 266 N.Y.S.2d 368, 213 N.E.2d 670 (1965).

32. *See, e.g.*, People v. Williams, 212 A.D.2d 388, 622 N.Y.S.2d 275 (1st Dep't 1995); People v. Tolbert, 198 A.D.2d 132, 603 N.Y.S.2d 844 (1st Dep't 1993), appeal denied 83 N.Y.2d 811, 611 N.Y.S.2d 147, 633 N.E.2d 502 (1994).

33. People v. Perez, 74 N.Y.2d 637, 541 N.Y.S.2d 976, 539 N.E.2d 1104 (1989); People v. Natal, 66 N.Y.2d 802, 497 N.Y.S.2d 909, 488 N.E.2d 839 (1985); People v. Rivera, 71 N.Y.2d 705, 530 N.Y.S.2d 52, 525 N.E.2d 698 (1988).

34. 25 N.Y.2d 786, 303 N.Y.S.2d 531, 250 N.E.2d 588 (1969).

§ 38.28

1. CPL § 470.20(2); People v. Espino, 208 A.D.2d 556, 616 N.Y.S.2d 782 (2d Dep't 1994), appeal denied 84 N.Y.2d 1031, 623 N.Y.S.2d 187, 647 N.E.2d 459 (1995).

2. CPL § 470.20(3); People v. Miller, 174 A.D.2d 989, 572 N.Y.S.2d 149 (4th Dep't 1991), appeal denied 78 N.Y.2d 1078, 577 N.Y.S.2d 241, 583 N.E.2d 953 (1991).

Similarly, when a judgment of conviction is reversed because the verdict is against the weight of evidence, the accusatory instrument must be dismissed.[3] Correspondingly, when a judgment is modified upon a finding that one count (or more) is against the weight of evidence, any such count must be dismissed.[4]

New Trial. If a judgment is reversed because of a trial error that prejudiced the defendant or deprived the defendant of a fair trial, a dismissal is inappropriate. There must be a new trial[5] Similarly, if a count of an accusatory instrument is reversed owing to such legal error, a new trial for the reversed count or counts is mandated.[6] A judgment reversed in the interest of justice will be followed by a new trial,[7] inasmuch as this statute likens a reversal based on an unpreserved error to an error that, if preserved, would have led to reversal and a new trial.[8]

Following a reversal on the law based upon a trial error or defect that has prejudiced the defendant or deprived the defendant of a fair trial, the case must be remitted to the criminal court for a new trial.[9] When the appellate division reverses a conviction on the ground that the hearing court has erred in failing to grant a motion to suppress,[10] a question arises as to whether the reversal should result in a dismissal or a new trial. The analysis turns on whether there is enough unsuppressed evidence to make out a legally sufficient case[11] or not.[12]

Remittal. If a judgment is modified by reversing a count or counts for legal insufficiency, the appellate division may remit the case to the criminal court for resentencing upon the affirmed counts, or it may itself "reduce the total sentence to that imposed by the criminal court" on the affirmed counts,[13] which in essence affirms the sentences on the surviving counts. If a conviction is reduced by sustaining a lesser included crime, the court must remit the case to the criminal court for sentencing on the lesser crime.[14]

---

3. CPL § 470.20(5); People v. Roman, 160 A.D.2d 961, 554 N.Y.S.2d 684 (2d Dep't 1990), appeal denied 76 N.Y.2d 795, 559 N.Y.S.2d 1000, 559 N.E.2d 694 (1990).

4. CPL § 470.20(5); People v. Ruiz, 162 A.D.2d 350, 556 N.Y.S.2d 910 (1st Dep't 1990). *See also, infra,* Chart at § 38.64.

5. CPL § 470.20(1); People v. Bennett, 193 A.D.2d 808, 598 N.Y.S.2d 84 (2d Dep't 1993), aff'd 79 N.Y.2d 464, 583 N.Y.S.2d 825, 593 N.E.2d 279 (1992). *See also, infra,* Chart at § 38.64.

6. *See, e.g.,* People v. Almonte, 223 A.D.2d 593, 637 N.Y.S.2d 168 (2d Dep't 1996).

7. CPL § 470.20(1).

8. People v. LaPlanche, 193 A.D.2d 1062, 598 N.Y.S.2d 877 (4th Dep't 1993), appeal dismissed 82 N.Y.2d 756, 603 N.Y.S.2d 998, 624 N.E.2d 184 (1993).

9. CPL § 470.20(1). *See, e.g.,* People v. Johnson, 145 A.D.2d 932, 536 N.Y.S.2d 300 (4th Dep't 1988), appeal withdrawn 73 N.Y.2d 892, 538 N.Y.S.2d 805, 535 N.E.2d 1345 (1989).

10. CPL Art. 710.

11. *See* People v. Perkins, 189 A.D.2d 830, 592 N.Y.S.2d 752 (2d Dep't 1993).

12. *See* People v. Hernandez, 192 A.D.2d 620, 622, 596 N.Y.S.2d 123, 124 (2d Dep't 1993).

13. CPL § 470.20(3).

14. CPL § 470.20(4). *See, e.g.,* People v. Brantley, 186 A.D.2d 1036, 588 N.Y.S.2d 475 (4th Dep't 1992), appeal denied 81 N.Y.2d 785, 594 N.Y.S.2d 731, 610 N.E.2d 404 (1993).

§ 38.28   CRIMINAL APPELLATE PRACTICE   Ch. 38

The remittals described above are provided for by CPL § 470.20, the statute that deals with corrective action. Beyond those statutory remittals, there are a host of settings in which the appellate division may remit a case to a criminal court for further proceedings of one kind or another. Case law contains thousands of such instances, but some arise more frequently than others.[15] When the appellate division directs the suppression of evidence, a question may arise as to whether that grant should result in the dismissal of the indictment[16] or a new trial.[17] The answer is that it depends on whether the prosecution has enough remaining evidence to establish a legally sufficient case. In *People v. Perkins*,[18] the appellate division remitted the case to the trial court based on that possibility.

Abeyance. When the appellate division lacks information or evidence on a point that could influence the result, it will direct the trial court to furnish the information or evidence and will hold the appeal "in abeyance" until it receives the necessary data from the trial court. This may occur in any number of instances as when, for example, there is insufficient evidence in the record upon which to decide the defendant's speedy trial motion[19] or when there arises a question as to the accuracy of the clerk's minutes and verdict sheet.[20]

PRACTICE POINTER: When the appellate division reduces a conviction by sustaining only a lesser count, it follows that the conviction on the lesser count should serve to reduce the sentence. While the statute authorizes the appellate division to remit the case for resentencing for that purpose, see CPL § 470.20(4), the passage of time from verdict to reversal may, in some instances, be considerable. If the defendant has not been out on bail pending appeal, several months may have elapsed from verdict to reversal, so that the maximum authorized sentence for the lesser conviction may have actually been served. When this happens, counsel should point this out so that the appellate division would then be free to refrain from remitting for resentence, and indicate that the defendant has already served the maximum time. See People v. Quinn, 186 A.D.2d 691, 588 N.Y.S.2d 646 (2d Dep't 1992).

15. See, e.g., People v. Yant, 223 A.D.2d 747, 637 N.Y.S.2d 468 (2d Dep't 1996)(remittal for re-sentencing, owing to trial court's misapprehension regarding its discretion); People v. Tucker, 223 A.D.2d 424, 636 N.Y.S.2d 759 (1st Dep't 1996)(remitted for the defendant's surrender, pursuant to CPL 460.50(5)); People v. Manswell, 223 A.D.2d 561, 636 N.Y.S.2d 383 (2d Dep't 1996)(nature of particular peremptory challenges); People v. Hladky, 224 A.D.2d 545, 638 N.Y.S.2d 344 (2d Dep't 1996)(remittal for report on defendant's sentence, for purposes of clarification); People v. Shields, 205 A.D.2d 833, 613 N.Y.S.2d 281 (3d Dep't 1994)(for CPL § 440.10 hearing); People v. Bruce, 224 A.D.2d 438, 638 N.Y.S.2d 326 (2d Dep't 1996)(for *Rosario* documentation); People v. Goros, 224 A.D.2d 444, 638 N.Y.S.2d 107 (2d Dep't 1996)(for reconstruction hearing); People v. Jones, 213 A.D.2d 1049, 625 N.Y.S.2d 979 (4th Dep't 1995)(for a new *Wade* independent source hearing); People v. Shim, 218 A.D.2d 757, 630 N.Y.S.2d 510 (2d Dep't 1995)(for new *Huntley* hearing); People v. Richter, 223 A.D.2d 734, 637 N.Y.S.2d 206 (2d Dep't 1996)(to determine proper amount of restitution).

16. E.g., People v. Bouton, 50 N.Y.2d 130, 136, 428 N.Y.S.2d 218, 220, 405 N.E.2d 699 (1980); People v. Rossi, 80 N.Y.2d 952, 590 N.Y.S.2d 872, 605 N.E.2d 359 (1992).

17. People v. Gonzalez, 80 N.Y.2d 883, 587 N.Y.S.2d 607 600 N.E.2d 238 (1992).

18. 189 A.D.2d 830, 592 N.Y.S.2d 752 (2d Dep't 1993).

19. People v. Bryant, 139 A.D.2d 750, 527 N.Y.S.2d 500 (2d Dep't 1988).

20. People v. Molina, 203 A.D.2d 486, 610 N.Y.S.2d 589 (2d Dep't 1994).

When holding an appeal "in abeyance," the appellate division will either remit the case to the trial court with no stated time limit to report back[21] or it may direct the trial court to conduct the necessary proceedings within a specific time,[22] or "with all deliberate speed."[23] Although the procedure of holding an appeal in abeyance to await further information is not new, the illustrations of this practice have expanded, in connection with claims that arise out of a defendant's "right to presence" cases. In *People v. Antommarchi*,[24] the Court of Appeals held that the defendant has a right to be present during all questioning of prospective jurors. Following that holding, defense contentions began to arise on appeal as to the defendant's alleged absence when jurors were privately questioned during the *voir dire*. In a number of such instances, the appellate division has been unable to determine from the record whether the defendant was present or not because trial courts were often proceeding under pre-*Antommarchi* custom and thus not recording all of the juror interviews held at sidebar. When the record is silent on the point, the appellate division holds the appeal in abeyance and directs the trial court to conduct a hearing and to report to the appellate division as to whether the defendant was present or absent during the questioning of any prospective juror.[25]

The same process of holding an appeal in abeyance has taken place with regard to a defendant's right to be present at a hearing to determine the scope of cross-examination as to the defendant's prior crimes under *People v. Sandoval*.[26] This right to be present was the subject of a decision by the Court of Appeals in *People v. Dokes*.[27] Before *Dokes*, some courts had conducted *Sandoval* hearings in the defendant's absence. When the "right to presence" point was raised on appeal, the appellate division, unable to determine whether the defendant was present at the *Sandoval* hearing, has held the appeal in abeyance and has directed the trial court to make a determination and report accordingly.[28]

The appellate division may not, however, hold an appeal in abeyance for a post trial hearing to supply an independent source for already admitted in-court identification testimony in connection with a determination that the suppression court's ruling on the suggestiveness of the

---

21. *See, e.g.*, People v. Lloyd, 192 A.D.2d 411, 596 N.Y.S.2d 688 (1st Dep't 1993).

22. *See, e.g.*, People v. McMoore, 203 A.D.2d 612, 609 N.Y.S.2d 964 (3d Dep't 1994).

23. *See, e.g.*, People v. Farrell, 201 A.D.2d 665, 609 N.Y.S.2d 824 (2d Dep't 1994).

24. 80 N.Y.2d 247, 590 N.Y.S.2d 33, 604 N.E.2d 95 (1992).

25. *See, e.g.*, People v. Davis, 221 A.D.2d 557, 635 N.Y.S.2d 487 (2d Dep't 1995); People v. Patti, 216 A.D.2d 422, 628 N.Y.S.2d 525 (2d Dep't 1995).

26. 34 N.Y.2d 371, 357 N.Y.S.2d 849, 314 N.E.2d 413 (1974).

27. 79 N.Y.2d 656, 584 N.Y.S.2d 761, 595 N.E.2d 836 (1992).

28. *See, e.g.*, People v. Parchment, 203 A.D.2d 595, 612 N.Y.S.2d 939 (2d Dep't 1994); People v. Law, 202 A.D.2d 691, 610 N.Y.S.2d 834 (2d Dep't 1994).

identification was flawed.[29] But where there has been no determination at all the appellate division will hold the appeal in abeyance and direct the trial court to conduct a hearing on the admissibility of the identification.[30]

§ 38.29 Appeals to the Appellate Division—Post-disposition Proceedings

Following the disposition of a criminal appeal, the appellate division rules mandate that counsel advise the defendant of the possibility of seeking further review. The following sections discuss procedures that counsel is *mandated* to take, as well as motions that counsel *may* wish to pursue.

§ 38.30 Appeals to the Appellate Division—Post-disposition Proceedings—Responsibilities of Counsel

In the event the judgment of conviction (or order denying relief pursuant to CPL Article 440) is affirmed, the rules of each department require counsel, retained or assigned, to advise the defendant of the right to apply for permission to appeal to the Court of Appeals, the right to seek poor person relief if permission is granted, and to seek advice as to how the defendant might proceed. If the defendant so desires, counsel must make the motion for leave to appeal to the Court of Appeals.[1]

§ 38.31 Appeals to the Appellate Division—Post-disposition Proceedings—Reargument

A motion for reargument is not an enumerated additional responsibility of counsel, but is often made, by counsel or the defendant *pro se*. As with motions to reargue on the civil side, the movant must show that the appellate division overlooked or misapprehended the facts or law. Generally, the same provisions applicable to civil reargument motions apply.[1] Note, however, that the time to move for reargument in a criminal case in the Third Department is 60 days after service of a copy of the order with notice of entry.[2]

---

29. People v. Burts, 78 N.Y.2d 20, 571 N.Y.S.2d 418, 574 N.E.2d 1024 (1991).

30. People v. Williams, 182 A.D.2d 490, 582 N.Y.S.2d 406 (1st Dep't 1992), appeal denied 81 N.Y.2d 978, 598 N.Y.S.2d 780, 615 N.E.2d 237 (1993).

§ 38.30

1. 22 NYCRR §§ 606.5(b)(2), 671.4(a), 821.2(b), 1022.11(b).

§ 38.31

1. *See supra*, § 37.69.

2. 22 NYCRR § 800.14(f).

CAVEAT: A motion for reargument does not toll the time to move for leave to appeal to the Court of Appeals.

Library References:
West's Key No. Digests, Criminal Law ⚛1133.

§ 38.32 Appeals to the Appellate Division—Post-disposition Proceedings—Leave to Appeal

CPL § 460.20(2)(a) authorizes only a justice of the appellate division or judge of the Court of Appeals to grant leave to appeal to the Court of Appeals. While the statute allows the motion to be made to any appellate division justice, the Second and Fourth Departments, by rule, require that the motion be addressed to one of the justices on the panel that determined the appeal.[1] Only one motion may be made—there are no "second bites" as one may get on the civil side.[2]

The motion for leave to appeal must be made within 30 days after service upon the appellant of a copy of the order to be appealed.[3] The rules of each department provide that its order may be served pursuant to CPLR 2103.[4] CPLR 2103, *inter alia*, authorizes service upon an attorney.[5] As noted previously, each department also requires that counsel for an unsuccessful defendant advise the defendant of the right to move for leave to appeal to the Court of Appeals and to submit such a motion upon request.[6]

§ 38.33 Appeals to the Appellate Division—Post-disposition Proceedings—*Certiorari* to U.S. Supreme Court

The party aggrieved by the determination of the appeal and who has been denied leave to appeal to the Court of Appeals, may petition the United States Supreme Court for a writ of *certiorari*.[1]

§ 38.34 Appeals to the Appellate Division—Post-disposition Proceedings—*Coram Nobis*—Ineffective Assistance of Appellate Counsel

Prior to the enactment of CPL Article 440, a defendant seeking to attack a judgment of conviction commenced a *coram nobis* proceeding in order to gain review of issues that were outside the record and not reviewable on direct appeal.[1] Article 440 is essentially a codification of the *coram nobis* proceeding designed to embrace and standardize such

---

§ 38.32
1. 22 NYCRR §§ 670.6(d), 1000.13(p)(4)(iii).
2. People v. McCarthy, 250 N.Y. 358, 361, 165 N.E. 810, 811 (1929).
3. CPL § 460.10(5)(a).
4. 22 NYCRR §§ 600.8(h), 670.12(f), 800.14(i), 1000.17(c).
5. CPLR 2103(b).
6. See supra, § 38.30.

§ 38.33
1. See supra, § 37.73.

§ 38.34
1. Lyons v. Goldstein, 290 N.Y. 19, 47 N.E.2d 425 (1943).

post-judgment practice.[2] Article 440, however, does not cover every application that could conceivably have been brought under the writ, and so the writ has not been extinguished or supplanted totally by statute.

In modern practice, the writ of error *coram nobis* has found viability in a setting to which Article 440 does not speak, *i.e.*, as a vehicle to challenge the effectiveness of counsel on appeal.[3] Under *People v. Bachert*,[4] the application is brought directly in the appellate division. The defendant bears a heavy burden on the application.[5] The court will not second guess reasonable judgments of appellate counsel.[6] While the burden is not easily met, the appellate division will review the record and grant relief, such as a *de novo* appeal, where appropriate.[7] Note, that an order of the appellate division determining an application for *coram nobis* relief may not be appealed to the Court of Appeals by right or with permission.[8]

Library References:

West's Key No. Digests, Criminal Law ⚖=641.13(7).

§ 38.35 Appeals to the Appellate Division—Post-disposition Proceedings—Clarification/Resettlement

When necessary to seek this relief following determination of a criminal appeal, counsel should follow the motion practice discussed for civil cases.[1]

§ 38.36 Appeals to the Appellate Division—Motions in Connection With Appeals in Criminal Cases—Generally

The appellate division departments do not have special rules pertaining to predisposition motions in connection with criminal cases.[1] The most common motions in criminal cases in the appellate division are

2. *See* Preiser, *Practice Commentaries*, CPL § 440.10, pp. 423–424.

3. People v. Bachert, 69 N.Y.2d 593, 516 N.Y.S.2d 623, 509 N.E.2d 318 (1987).

4. 69 N.Y.2d 593, 516 N.Y.S.2d 623, 509 N.E.2d 318 (1987).

5. Jones v. Barnes, 463 U.S. 745, 103 S.Ct. 3308, 77 L.Ed.2d 987 (1983).

6. People v. Linden, 171 A.D.2d 694, 566 N.Y.S.2d 663 (2d Dep't 1991).

7. People v. Ballard, 214 A.D.2d 1050, 626 N.Y.S.2d 710 (4th Dep't 1995); People v. Hacker, 162 A.D.2d 815, 559 N.Y.S.2d 184 (3d Dep't 1990); People v. Johnson, 149 A.D.2d 534, 540 N.Y.S.2d 727 (2d Dep't 1989).

8. People v. Bachert, 69 N.Y.2d 593, 600, 516 N.Y.S.2d 623, 627, 509 N.E.2d 318, 322 (1987).

§ 38.35

1. *See supra*, §§ 37.74 *et seq.*

§ 38.36

1. For a discussion of motion practice, including return dates and service requirements, *see* this and successive sections.

motions to stay execution of a judgment and for poor person relief and the assignment of counsel.[2]

§ 38.37 Appeals to the Appellate Division—Motions in Connection With Appeals in Criminal Cases—*Pro Se* Supplemental Brief

An increasingly common application to the appellate division is the defendant's motion for permission to serve and file a *pro se* supplemental brief. Although a defendant represented by counsel, assigned or retained, does not have an absolute right to file a *pro se* brief,[1] the motions are often granted. The rules of the Second and Fourth Departments require that a defendant desiring to file a *pro se* brief submit the application within 30 and 35 days respectively after the attorney's brief is mailed to him or her and to set forth the issues the defendant proposes to raise.[2] When counsel sends a brief to the defendant, counsel should advise the defendant to make the application promptly and to set forth the issues that the defendant wants to raise. On such an application, the defendant may ask for a copy of the relevant transcripts. Otherwise, a copy is not prepared for, or made available to, the defendant. The First and Third Departments have no similar rules.

Library References:

West's Key No. Digests, Criminal Law ⚖1077.3.

§ 38.38 Appeals to the Appellate Division—Motions in Connection With Appeals in Criminal Cases—*Anders* Brief

When assigned counsel concludes that there are no nonfrivolous issues that could be raised on the appeal, counsel must so inform the defendant and solicit input from the defendant. The defendant may propose issues, but counsel is not obligated to argue them if he or she concludes that they are frivolous. There is a distinction between issues that counsel believes will not be successful and issues that are frivolous. It is not the function of counsel to judge the merits of an issue and whether it will lead to reversal; that is the function of the justices who hear the appeal. Thus, counsel should brief these issues which are arguable, even though they probably will not lead to reversal.

When there are no nonfrivolous issues, assigned counsel should file a brief pursuant to *Anders v. California*[1] reciting the facts in the record and concluding that the judgment should be affirmed and counsel

2. See supra, §§ 38.15, 38.16.

§ 38.37

1. People v. White, 73 N.Y.2d 468, 541 N.Y.S.2d 749, 539 N.E.2d 577 (1989).
2. 22 NYCRR §§ 670.12(h), 1000.13(j).

§ 38.38

1. 386 U.S. 738, 87 S.Ct. 1396, 18 L.Ed.2d 493 (1967). *See also*, 22 NYCRR §§ 1000.13(q), 1022.11(d).

§ 38.38   CRIMINAL APPELLATE PRACTICE   Ch. 38

relieved of further responsibility. In the brief, counsel is not obliged to discuss frivolous claims that the client wants to advance, but counsel will be proceeding inappropriately by undermining or disparaging issues proposed by the defendant.[2] If counsel believes that any of the defendant's claims are frivolous, counsel should so advise the defendant that the latter may apply to the appellate division for permission to file a *pro se* supplemental brief to raise the issues the defendant wants the appellate division to consider.[3] When an *Anders* brief[4] is submitted, the appellate division will independently review the record. If it agrees with counsel, the judgment will be affirmed and counsel will be relieved of the assignment and of the duty to seek leave to appeal to the Court of Appeals on the defendant's behalf. If the appellate division disagrees it may assign new counsel to brief the nonfrivolous issues or call for additional briefs.[5]

Library References:

West's Key No. Digests, Criminal Law ⟬1077.3.

§ 38.39   Appeals to the Appellate Division—Motions in Connection With Appeals in Criminal Cases—Dismissal

The appellate division, on its own motion or on motion of the respondent, may dismiss a criminal appeal on the ground of mootness, lack of jurisdiction to determine it, failure to prosecute, "or other substantial defect, irregularity or failure of action by the appellant with respect to the prosecution or perfection of such appeal."[1] An appellant who was the defendant below has rights under the statute. A notice of the motion must be served upon the defendant at the last known residence or place of incarceration, and upon the attorney, if any, who last appeared for the defendant.[2] If the defendant-appellant was represented by counsel in the trial court, but never had counsel in the appellate court, a motion to dismiss would have to be served upon the attorney who last appeared in the trial court. When an assigned counsel, in spite of diligent efforts, has been unable to communicate with the defendant counsel may move to dismiss the appeal as abandoned.[3] Under good practice, the motion should recite the efforts made to contact the

---

2. People v. Vasquez, 70 N.Y.2d 1, 509 N.E.2d 934, 516 N.Y.S.2d 921 (1987).

3. *See, e.g.*, 22 NYCRR § 670.12(g)(2).

4. *See also*, People v. Saunders, 52 A.D.2d 833, 384 N.Y.S.2d 161 (1st Dep't 1976); People v. Crawford, 71 A.D.2d 38, 421 N.Y.S.2d 485 (4th Dep't 1979).

5. People v. Casiano, 67 N.Y.2d 906, 501 N.Y.S.2d 808, 492 N.E.2d 1224 (1986); People v. Santiago, 222 A.D.2d 461, 635 N.Y.S.2d 525 (2d Dep't 1995).

§ 38.39

1. CPL § 470.60(1).
2. CPL § 470.60(2).
3. CPL § 470.60.

defendant, and it should be served on the defendant at the latter's last known address or place of incarceration.

Library References:

West's Key No. Digests, Criminal Law ⚖1131.

§ 38.40 Appeals to the Appellate Division—Motions in Connection With Appeals in Criminal Cases—Reconstruction Hearing; Summary Reversal

On occasion, counsel may not be able to secure the complete record for the appeal. The reasons may vary: lost or destroyed stenographic notes; a court reporter who has left the system and moved, or who has passed away, or for any number of reasons has failed to produce the minutes. Counsel's choices as to how to proceed without minutes may depend upon the reason for their absence. If the notes are lost or destroyed, a reconstruction hearing may be sought. If granted, witnesses could be presented to "reconstruct" the missing minutes; potential witnesses are the prosecutor, the defense counsel, the defendant, and the trial judge.[1]

There will be times that a reconstruction hearing is not possible. The defendant may move for summary reversal, but must show what issues could have been raised had the minutes been available.[2] In unusual cases involving unjustifiable delay, appellate attorneys have sought and obtained contempt adjudications against court reporters (resulting even in incarceration) to compel the production of minutes.[3]

Library References:

West's Key No. Digests, Criminal Law ⚖1110.

§ 38.41 Appeals to the Appellate Division—Motions in Connection With Appeals in Criminal Cases—Death or Absence of a Defendant

Upon the death of a defendant whose appeal has not been decided, the appeal abates and the case must be remitted to the trial court for

---

§ 38.40

1. *See, e.g.*, People v. King, 160 A.D.2d 531, 554 N.Y.S.2d 517 (1st Dept.1990), appeal denied 76 N.Y.2d 847, 560 N.Y.S.2d 132, 559 N.E.2d 1291 (1990).

2. *See, e.g.*, People v. Glass, 43 N.Y.2d 283, 401 N.Y.S.2d 189, 372 N.E.2d 24 (1977); People v. Gonzalez, 184 A.D.2d 525, 584 N.Y.S.2d 180 (2d Dep't 1992). If the reconstruction hearing is inadequate to protect a defendant's appellate rights, summary reversal will result. *See* People v. Hall, 200 A.D.2d 474, 608 N.Y.S.2d 403 (1st Dep't 1994).

3. *See* People v. Cameron, N.Y.L.J., 11/15/93, p. 28, col. 2, (2d Dep't) (adjudication that court reporter was guilty of criminal contempt); Today's News, N.Y.L.J., 12/12/93, p.1, col.2 (reporting the incarceration of the court reporter); People v. Cameron, 219 A.D.2d 662, 631 N.Y.S.2d 717 (2d Dep't 1995)(judgment of conviction reversed where court reporter could not transcribe the *voir dire* and reconstruction was not possible).

§ 38.41   CRIMINAL APPELLATE PRACTICE   Ch. 38

vacatur of the judgment.[1] Counsel will have to submit an appropriate motion to the appellate court, usually supported by a copy of the death certificate.[2] When a defendant is no longer within the jurisdiction so as to be available to obey the lawful mandate of the appellate court upon affirmance or modification of the judgment, the appeal will be dismissed. This will apply where the defendant has absconded,[3] or been deported.[4]

Library References:
West's Key No. Digests, Criminal Law ⟜1070.

§ 38.42 Appeals to the Appellate Division—Motions in Connection With Appeals in Criminal Cases—Assignment of New Counsel

An attorney who wants to be relieved of an assignment must move in the appellate court to have new counsel assigned. The motion should specify the reasons and be served on the defendant, as well as the district attorney. A disagreement with the defendant as to the issues to be briefed may not be sufficient; the final determination as to the issues lies with counsel. The defendant may timely request permission to file a supplemental brief. A conclusion that no nonfrivolous issues exist is also not sufficient to have counsel relieved on motion. The correct procedure is to submit a brief pursuant to *Anders v. California*.[1]

Library References:
West's Key No. Digests, Criminal Law ⟜1077.3.

§ 38.43 Appeals to the Appellate Division—Motions in Connection With Appeals in Criminal Cases—Expanding the Judgment Roll

The minutes usually prepared for an appeal pursuant to a poor person order include arraignment, pretrial hearings, jury *voir dire*, trial or plea, and sentence. When an attorney believes that additional minutes are necessary a motion must be made to expand the judgment roll. On such a motion, counsel should specify the dates requested and the basis for the motion. Often, it is to establish a claim that the People were not ready for trial within the statutory limits and that the defendant was denied his or her right to a speedy trial.[1]

§ 38.41

1. People v. Mintz, 20 N.Y.2d 753, 283 N.Y.S.2d 120, 229 N.E.2d 712 (1967); People v. Matteson, 75 N.Y.2d 745, 551 N.Y.S.2d 890, 551 N.E.2d 91 (1989).

2. *See supra*, § 38.8.

3. People v. Flemming, 104 A.D.2d 1048, 480 N.Y.S.2d 882 (2d Dep't 1984).

4. People v. Parmaklidis, 38 N.Y.2d 1005, 384 N.Y.S.2d 442, 348 N.E.2d 918 (1976).

§ 38.42

1. 386 U.S. 738, 87 S.Ct. 1396, 18 L.Ed.2d 493 (1967). *See also supra*, § 38.38.

§ 38.43

1. CPL § 30.30.

§ 38.44 Appeals to the Appellate Division—Motions in Connection With Appeals in Criminal Cases—Briefs

Many motions can be made with respect to counsel's briefs. Motions to extend the time to file should be promptly brought, in compliance with any local department rules that may apply.[1] When a respondent's brief is not filed within the time specified by court rules, the appellant may move to preclude. If counsel desires to file a brief in excess of the department's page limit, a request in compliance with the court's rules is necessary.[2] When the appeal raises a novel issue in the state or one of social significance, a group or person may wish to file an *amicus* brief.[3] One would expect appellate considerations under the death penalty statute to attract interested *amici*.

Library References:

West's Key No. Digests, Criminal Law ⇌1130.

§ 38.45 Appeals to the Appellate Division—Motions in Connection With Appeals in Criminal Cases—Withdrawal of Appeal

Many judgments result from negotiated pleas.[1] The defendant pleads guilty to a lesser crime than the top count of an indictment, and is sentenced to a lesser penalty than that which might have been imposed had the defendant been tried and convicted of the top count. Notices of appeal are often filed after such judgments, even if the defendant has waived the right to appeal. In fact, the rules of each department require that counsel advise a defendant of the right to appeal to the appellate division, and to file the notice at the defendant's request.[2] Counsel should secure a statement to that effect signed by the defendant. Sending the defendant a prepared statement which only needs to be signed is the easiest way of proceeding. That statement then forms the basis of a motion to withdraw the appeal. Counsel should check with the particular appellate division department to ascertain whether a formal motion is required where the defendant has signed an agreement to withdraw.

Library References:

West's Key No. Digests, Criminal Law ⇌1131.

§ 38.44

1. *See* 22 NYCRR §§ 600.8(c), 670.8(d), 800.14(c), 1000.13(h).
2. *See* 22 NYCRR §§ 600.10(d)(1)(i), 670.10(d)(1)(i), 800.8(a), 1000.4, 1000.13(r).
3. *See* 22 NYCRR § 1000.13(k).

§ 38.45

1. *See generally*, Chapter 33 "Local Criminal Practice," *supra*.
2. *See* 22 NYCRR §§ 606.5(b)(1), 671.3(a),(b), 821.2(a), 1022.11(a).

§ 38.46 Appeals to Intermediate Appellate Courts Other Than the Appellate Division

Most of the decisional law at the intermediate appellate level is generated by the supreme court, appellate division. There are, however, two other courts that serve as intermediate appellate courts: the appellate term of supreme court[1] and the county court.[2] These two courts are intermediate appellate courts in that they are interposed between the trial level local criminal courts, from which they hear appeals,[3] and the Court of Appeals.[4] Practice in these courts will briefly be described, and the relevant practice rules identified.[5]

§ 38.47 Appeals to Other Intermediate Appellate Courts—Appeals From Village Courts, Town Courts, City Courts, and District Courts.

The CPL speaks of "local criminal courts."[1] CPL § 10.10(3) in pertinent part defines a local criminal court as:

(a) A district court; or

(b) The New York City criminal court; or

(c) A city court; or

(d) A town court; or

(e) A village court.

CPL § 450.60 provides a road map, identifying the courts to which appeals from local criminal court orders, sentences, and judgments are taken. With respect to local criminal courts other than the New York City Criminal Court, the statute provides:

> 3. An appeal from a judgment, sentence or order of a local criminal court located outside of New York City must, except as otherwise provided in this subdivision, be taken to the county court of the county in which such judgment, sentence or order was entered.

If the appellate division of the second, third or fourth department has established an appellate term of the supreme court for its department, it may direct that appeals from such judgments, sentences and orders of such local criminal courts, or of particular

---

§ 38.46

1. N.Y. Constitution Art. VI, § 8.
2. N.Y. Constitution Art. VI, § 11(c).
3. CPL §§ 1.20, 450.60.
4. CPL § 450.90.
5. The authors gratefully acknowledge the assistance of the Hon. Fred L. Shapiro in providing a useful reference on this subject not generally available—his article, "Criminal Appeals from the Town and Village Justice Courts", *The Magistrate*, vol. XXIII, No. 3 (May–June 1983).

§ 38.47

1. CPL § 1.20(21).

classifications of such local criminal courts, be taken to such appellate term of the supreme court instead of to the county court; and in such case such an appeal must be so taken.[2]

The Third and Fourth Departments have not established appellate terms; therefore, all appeals from orders, sentences, and judgments of local criminal courts in those departments are taken to county courts within those departments.[3] The First Department has no local criminal court other than the New York City Criminal Court. Thus, only in the Second Department will counsel have to determine whether an appeal from a local criminal court is taken to the appellate term or to the county court. Fortunately, the answer is easy—an appeal from such court in the Second Department always is taken to the appellate term. The New York State Constitution provides:

> [a]s may be provided by law, an appellate term shall have jurisdiction to hear and determine appeals from the district court or a town, village or city court outside the city of New York.[4]

The law that "so provides" is CPL § 450.60(3), which delegates to the appellate division the designation of courts from which appeals shall be taken to the appellate term. The Rules of the Appellate Division, Second Department provide:

> (1) * * * that an appeal authorized by CPL 450.10 and 450.20 to be taken to intermediate courts shall be taken to the Appellate Term of the Supreme Court in and for the ninth and tenth judicial districts, hereinabove established, in accordance with its rules applicable thereto but not inconsistent with the applicable provisions of the CPL, where such appeal is from a judgment, sentence or order of a local criminal court and all classifications thereof (as defined and set forth in CPL 10.10) located in this department but outside New York City.[5]

The rules further provide:

> (2) In addition to, but not in limitation of the foregoing, such Appellate Term shall have jurisdiction to hear and determine all appeals
>
> (i) from the District Court of Nassau County, the District Court of Suffolk County and any other district court hereafter established in any county within the ninth judicial district, and
>
> (ii) from any town, village or city court within either the ninth judicial district or the tenth judicial district.[6]

2. CPL § 450.60.
3. CPL § 460.50(3).
4. N.Y. Constitution Art. VI, § 8(e).
5. 22 NYCRR § 730.1(d).
6. 22 NYCRR § 730.1(d).

§ 38.47 CRIMINAL APPELLATE PRACTICE Ch. 38

Thus, an appeal from a local criminal court outside New York City in the Second Department is taken to the appellate term for the Ninth and Tenth Judicial Districts.

§ 38.48 Appeals to Other Intermediate Appellate Courts—Appeals From Criminal Court of the City of New York

The City of New York lies within two of the state's four judicial departments. New York and Bronx counties comprise the entire First Department; Kings, Queens and Richmond Counties comprise part of the Second Department, which also embraces the counties within the Ninth and Tenth Judicial Districts, which lie outside New York City. The Criminal Court of the City of New York is a city-wide court with branches in each of the City's five counties.[1] It is a court of record.[2] The rules governing practice in the Criminal Court of the City of New York are promulgated by the Appellate Division, First and Second Departments.[3] The court has jurisdiction to try misdemeanors and offenses committed within the City of New York, except libel, and violations of the Administrative Code of the City of New York classified as misdemeanors.[4]

§ 38.49 Appeals to Other Intermediate Appellate Courts—Appeals From Criminal Court of the City of New York—New York and Bronx County Branches

The applicable rule of the First Department provides that the Appellate Term, First Department shall hear and determine all appeals from the Criminal Court of the City of New York in New York and Bronx counties.[1]

§ 38.50 Appeals to Other Intermediate Appellate Courts—Appeals From Criminal Court of the City of New York—Kings, Queens, Richmond County Branches

The applicable rule of the Second Department in pertinent part provides:

> The Appellate Division of the Supreme Court, Second Judicial Department ... does hereby ... (b) Direct that the Appellate Term of the Supreme Court in and for the second and eleventh judicial

§ 38.48
1. N.Y. Constitution Art. VI, §§ 1, 15.
2. Judiciary Law § 2(12).
3. New York City Criminal Court Act §§ 2(5), 21(1), 41(2).
4. New York City Criminal Court Act § 31.

§ 38.49
1. 22 NYCRR § 640.1.

districts, hereinabove established, shall have jurisdiction to hear and determine all appeals authorized by law to be taken: * * * (2) from a judgment, sentence or order of the Criminal Court of the City of New York in any of said counties.[1]

To summarize, by department, the courts to which appeals from local criminal courts are taken:

First Department:

> Appeal from: New York City Criminal Court, New York and Bronx Counties
>
> Taken to: Appellate Term, First Department

Second Department:

> Appeal from: New York City Criminal Court, Kings, Queens, and Richmond Counties
>
> Taken to: Appellate Term, Second Department (2d and 11th Districts)
>
> Appeal from: village, town, city, or district court[2]
>
> Taken to: Appellate Term, Second Department (9th and 10th Districts)

Third Department:

> Appeal from: village, town, or city court
>
> Taken to: county court

Fourth Department:

> Appeal from: village, town, or city court
>
> Taken to: county court

§ 38.51 Appeals to Other Intermediate Appellate Courts—Orders, Sentences, and Judgments Appealable

The same statutes that govern appealability to the Appellate Division[1] govern appealability of local criminal court orders, sentences, and judgments to the county court or appellate term. Permission of a justice or judge of the intermediate appellate court pursuant to CPL § 460.15 is required before an appeal may be taken from an order described in CPL § 450.15.[2]

§ 38.50

1. 22 NYCRR § 730.1(b)(2).
2. District courts exist only within the Second Department. They are found in Nassau County and part of Suffolk County.

§ 38.51

1. *See generally supra*, §§ 38.6–38.10.

2. That statute requires permission to appeal from an order denying a motion to vacate a judgment (other than one including a sentence of death) or to set aside a sentence (other than one of death) or to appeal from a sentence not otherwise appealable as of right.

§ 38.52 Appeals to Other Intermediate Appellate Courts—Taking the Appeal—Appeal as of Right

How an appeal in a criminal case is taken depends upon whether the proceedings below were transcribed. Initially, then, it must be determined whether in a given case the proceedings are deemed to have been transcribed. Clearly, when a stenographer has taken the minutes of the proceedings and has prepared transcripts, the proceedings are deemed to have been transcribed. But what if the proceedings were recorded on audio tape? There appears to be a split of authority, with one court holding in *dictum* that an appeal may *not* be taken by the method provided for cases in which the proceedings are not transcribed when the proceedings below were recorded on audio tape.[1] However, the weight of authority[2]—and the better view—is that the procedure for taking an appeal when the proceedings are not transcribed does apply even when an audio tape recording was made.[3]

Transcribed Proceedings. In a case in which the proceedings were transcribed, the appeal to county court or the appellate term is taken by filing two copies of a notice of appeal with the clerk of the court that issued the order, sentence, or judgment,[4] and serving upon the adverse party[5] one copy of the notice. The appeal must be taken within 30 days after imposition of sentence or service of a written order.[6] The clerk of the court in which the notice is filed is required to forward one copy to the court to which the appeal is taken.[7]

Untranscribed Proceedings. If the proceedings below were not transcribed, CPL § 460.10(3) provides two options for the preliminary steps toward taking an appeal. The first option is to file in the local criminal court, within 30 days after entry or imposition of the judgment, sentence or order being appealed, an affidavit of errors, setting forth the

---

§ 38.52

1. People v. Guernsey, 136 Misc.2d 791, 519 N.Y.S.2d 338 (Schoharie County Ct.1987).

2. People v. Knight, 116 Misc.2d 581, 455 N.Y.S.2d 971 (Broome County Ct.1982); People v. Deming, 80 Misc.2d 53, 362 N.Y.S.2d 804 (Albany County Ct.1974).

3. Although the tape or a transcript thereof is not considered a transcription by a court stenographer within the meaning of the statute for purposes of determining how the appeal is taken, a transcript of the tape may be submitted by the local criminal court to the intermediate appellate court as part of its return. People v. Robinson, 72 N.Y.2d 989, 534 N.Y.S.2d 367, 530 N.E.2d 1287 (1988).

4. If the court does not have a clerk, only one copy of the notice of appeal is filed with the judge of the local criminal court, and the other copy is filed with the clerk of the appellate court to which the appeal is being taken. CPL § 460.10(2).

5. If defendant is the appellant, the party that must be served is the district attorney of the county in which the court rendering the determination to be appealed is located. This is true even if the original prosecution was conducted by someone other than the district attorney or an assistant. CPL § 460.10(1)(b).

6. CPL § 460.10(1),(2).

7. CPL § 460.10(1), (2)(e).

alleged errors or defects upon which the appeal is based.[8] The second option is to file in the local criminal court and serve a notice of appeal within the 30 day time period. Within 30 days after the filing of the notice of appeal, appellant must file the affidavit of errors.[9]

Regardless of which preliminary option is chosen, appellant must, within three days after filing the affidavit of errors with the local criminal court, serve the adverse party.[10] It is only after the affidavit of errors is filed and served that the appeal is deemed to have been taken.[11]

Within 10 days after the appeal is taken, the local criminal court is required to file with the appellate court the affidavit of errors and the court's return. The local criminal court also must deliver a copy of its return, which provides the factual background for the evaluation of the contentions raised in the affidavit of errors, to each party or counsel.[12] Upon motion of the appellant, the appellate court may order the local criminal court to file a return or amended return if the local criminal court fails timely to file the return, or if it files a defective return.[13] If the local criminal court fails to comply with such order, the appellate court may deem the allegations in the affidavit of errors admitted.[14]

§ 38.53 Appeals to Other Intermediate Appellate Courts—Taking the Appeal—Appeals by Permission

The First Department rules require that an application for leave to appeal to the appellate term be addressed to the court for assignment to a justice of the appellate term.[1] The application must be in writing and on reasonable notice to the People. It must be made within 30 days after service upon the defendant of a copy of the order from which defendant seeks to appeal; it must set forth the questions of law or fact to be reviewed, and it must contain a statement as to whether or not any such application previously was made.[2] Although the rule does not require it, better practice dictates annexation of a copy of the order sought to be appealed and the court's written decision, if any, to the motion papers.

---

8. CPL § 460.10(3)(a)(i).
9. CPL § 460.10(3)(a)(ii).
10. CPL § 460.10(3)(b).
11. CPL § 460.10(3)(c).

CAVEAT: in a case in which the proceedings were not transcribed, the appeal is *not* deemed taken upon the service and filing of the notice of appeal. The timely filing and service of a notice of appeal merely gives the appellant 30 days to file an affidavit of errors, service of which must occur three days thereafter. Only then is the appeal deemed taken. People v. Proctor, 87 Misc.2d 893, 386 N.Y.S.2d 803 (Otsego County Ct.1976).

12. CPL § 460.10(3)(d).
13. CPL § 460.10(3)(e); People v. Rokahr, 141 Misc.2d 117, 532 N.Y.S.2d 710 (St. Lawrence County Ct.1988).
14. People v. Feldes, 73 N.Y.2d 661, 543 N.Y.S.2d 34, 541 N.E.2d 34 (1989).

§ 38.53

1. 22 NYCRR § 640.10(c).
2. 22 NYCRR § 640.10(c).

In the Second Department, the rules require that the application be in writing, and be filed in the office of the clerk of the appellate term with proof of service upon the prosecutor within 30 days after service upon the appellant of a copy of the order sought to be appealed.[3] The application must include the name and address of the applicant and the prosecutor, the docket or index number of the case, the questions of law or fact to be reviewed, a statement that no prior application for such certificate has been made, and a copy of the order sought to be reviewed and the decision of the court below, or a statement that no decision was rendered. The prosecutor's response, or statement that there is no opposition to the application, must be filed, with proof of service, within 15 days after service upon the prosecutor of the moving papers.[4]

The Uniform Rules for the Trial Courts and the rules of the Appellate Division in the Third and Fourth Departments do not have specific provisions dealing with application for leave to appeal to the county court. When seeking to appeal an order for which permission is required, such as a denial of a CPL Article 440 motion, counsel is advised to inquire of the clerk of that court for instructions.

Unlike an appeal from the intermediate appellate court to the Court of Appeals, which is deemed taken upon issuance of the certificate granting leave, an appeal by permission from a local criminal court is "taken"—and the clock marking the time within which that must be done stopped—by filing with the local criminal court the certificate granting leave to appeal together with a written notice of appeal, or, if the appeal is from a local criminal court in a case in which the underlying proceedings were not recorded by a court stenographer, by filing either (i) an affidavit of errors, or (ii) a notice of appeal.[5]

§ 38.54 Appeals to Other Intermediate Appellate Courts—Stays Pending Appeal

The statute applicable to stays pending appeal to the intermediate appellate courts is CPL § 460.50. The statute permits an authorized judge to issue an order staying or suspending the execution of the judgment pending the determination of the appeal, and either releasing the defendant on recognizance, or fixing bail pursuant to the provisions of Article 530 of the Criminal Procedure Law. The phase of the order staying or suspending execution of the judgment does not become effective unless and until the defendant is released, either on recogni-

---

3. 22 NYCRR §§ 731.10(c), 732.10(c).
4. 22 NYCRR §§ 731.10(c), 732.10(c).
5. CPL § 460.10(4)(b).

PRACTICE POINTER: No matter how the appeal is taken, a missed deadline by defendant (not the People) may in some cases be forgiven if a motion pursuant to CPL § 460.30 is made within a year after the expiration of the time for taking the appeal or seeking leave to appeal and if the failure to timely take the appeal or to seek leave was due to one of the circumstances listed in the statute. A more detailed discussion of CPL § 460.30 appears in the section on appeals to the appellate division, *see supra*, § 38.14.

zance or upon the posting of bail.[1] Which judges are authorized to issue such orders depends upon the courts from and to which the appeal is taken.

Appeal from New York City Criminal Court to Appellate Term. In the case of an appeal to the appellate term from a judgment or sentence of the New York City Criminal Court, the statute provides that an order granting a stay may be issued by a justice of the supreme court of the judicial district embracing the county in which the judgment was entered. Thus, one would not go to the appellate term initially for such a stay, and there is no provision in the rules of the appellate terms either of the First Department or of the Second and Eleventh Districts in the Second Department for applying there for an order granting a stay pending appeal to those courts.[2]

If within 120 days after the issuance of an order granting a stay, the appeal has not been brought to argument in or submitted to the appellate term, the stay terminates and the defendant must surrender to the criminal court in which the judgment was entered in order that execution of the judgment be commenced or resumed, unless the intermediate appellate court has extended the time for argument or submission of the appeal to a date beyond the specified period of 120 days, and, upon application of the defendant, expressly ordered that the operation of the order continue until the date of the determination of the appeal or some other designated future date or occurrence.[3]

Appeal from Village, Town, City, or District Courts to Appellate Term. In cases appealed to the appellate term from local criminal courts outside the City of New York, the Appellate Division, Second Department designates by 22 NYCRR § 732.12 the judges who may issue orders granting stays pursuant to CPL § 460.50(2)(d). The Rule provides:

> Upon application of a defendant, pursuant to section 460.50 of the Criminal Procedure Law, for an order staying or suspending the execution of the judgment pending the determination of an appeal taken to the Appellate Term, such order may be issued by a justice of the Appellate Term or a justice of the Supreme Court of the judicial district embracing the county in which the judgment was entered.

In practice, appellate term justices do not entertain bail applications in cases in which a sentence of incarceration has been imposed, although they have the power to do so. Such an application should be addressed to a supreme court justice in the district embracing the county in which the judgment was entered. An application for a stay not involving release from incarceration, such as one involving the payment of a fine, will be

§ 38.54
1. CPL § 460.50(1).
2. CPL § 460.50(2)(c).
3. CPL § 460.50(4).

entertained by a justice of the appellate term, though one also may seek such relief from a local supreme court justice.

Here, again, if within 120 days after the issuance of an order granting a stay, the appeal has not been brought to argument in or submitted to the appellate term, the stay terminates, and the defendant must surrender to the criminal court in which the judgment was rendered in order that execution of the judgment be commenced or resumed, unless the intermediate appellate court has extended the time for argument or submission of the appeal to a date beyond the specified period of 120 days, and, upon application of the defendant, it has expressly ordered that the operation of the order continue until the date of the determination of the appeal or some other designated future date or occurrence.[4]

Appeals to County Court. CPL § 460.50(2)(d) also delegates to the Appellate Division in the Third and Fourth Departments the power to designate judges who may issue orders granting stays pursuant to that section. The rules of those departments do not make any such designation; however, the Uniform Rules for the Trial Courts do. An order pursuant to CPL § 460.50 staying or suspending execution of a judgment may be issued by a judge of the county court to which the appeal has been taken or by a justice of the supreme court in the judicial district in which the local court is located. In the case of any appeal as of right from a judgment or sentence of a city court, such order also may be issued by a judge of such city court.[5] Such order will terminate if the appeal is not perfected within 120 days after the issuance of the order, unless the county judge has extended the 120-day period.[6]

§ 38.55 Appeals to Other Intermediate Appellate Courts—Perfecting the Appeal

Generally. An appeal to an intermediate appellate court is to be perfected according to the rules promulgated by the appellate division in each department.[1] Policies with respect to oral argument are left to each individual intermediate appellate court.[2] More detailed instructions are provided by CPL § 460.70(2) for perfecting the appeal in an action in which the proceedings below were not stenographically transcribed:

> After the local criminal court has, pursuant to paragraph (d) of subdivision three of [CPL] section 460.10, filed its return with the clerk of the appellate court and delivered a copy thereof to the appellant, the appellant must file with such clerk, and serve a copy thereof upon the respondent, a notice of argument, noticing the appeal for argument at the term of such appellate court immediately

---

4. CPL § 460.50(4).
5. 22 NYCRR § 200.31.
6. 22 NYCRR § 200.32.

§ 38.55
1. CPL § 460.70(1).
2. CPL § 460.80.

following the term being held at the time of the appellant's receipt of the return. Upon motion of the appellant, however, such appellate court may for good cause shown enlarge the time to a subsequent term, in which case the appellant must notice the appeal for argument at such subsequent term....

If the appellant does not file a notice of argument as provided in paragraph (a) or does not comply with all applicable court rules as provided in paragraph (b), the appellate court may, either upon motion of the respondent or upon its own motion, dismiss the appeal.[3]

In a case in which the minutes were stenographically transcribed, the second, unnumbered paragraph of subdivision 1 of CPL § 460.70 formerly required the preparation and settlement of two transcripts, one of which would be filed in the local criminal court by the court reporter. If the intermediate appellate court granted the defendant poor person relief, both transcripts would be filed with the criminal court and one would be made available to the defendant at public expense. In the case of a defendant-appellant not granted poor person relief, the court's transcript was still prepared at public expense, though the defendant would have to pay for his.[4]

The section was amended by Chapter 83 of the Laws of 1995, which changed the procedure in two phases. Under the first phase, pending a new contract between the court system and the court reporters' unions, two transcripts still must be prepared. If the defendant has not been granted poor person relief, the trial court's transcript is not charged to the defendant or to the state; it is provided free of charge. The defendant will have to pay for the defendant's transcript. If, however, the defendant has been granted poor person relief, the state pays for both transcripts, the court's and the defendant's.

Under the second phase, only a single transcript will be prepared. Its cost and the cost of any copies will be borne by the defendant, unless the defendant has been granted poor person relief, in which case the cost will be borne by the state.[5]

Appellate Term, First Department. The Rules of Practice for the Appellate Term, First Department, are set forth in 22 NYCRR Part 640. The rules provide that an appeal from the criminal court shall be heard on the original papers, certified by the clerk of the criminal court, a

---

3. This occurred in *People v. Landon*, 68 Misc.2d 809, 327 N.Y.S.2d 971 (Cortland County Ct.1971)(dismissal based on delay of four months from completion of preliminary appeal steps to filing of notice of argument).

4. *See* Harrington v. State of New York, Office of Court Administration, 94 A.D.2d 863, 463 N.Y.S.2d 586 (3d Dep't 1983), aff'd 62 N.Y.2d 626, 476 N.Y.S.2d 109, 464 N.E.2d 477 (1984)(noting the statute was "inartfully drawn"); Preiser, *Practice Commentary*, CPL § 460.70, p.808 (the provision "could stand some further legislative attention").

5. *See* Preiser, *Supplementary Practice Commentary*, CPL § 460.70, Supp. p. 85.

§ 38.55   CRIMINAL APPELLATE PRACTICE   Ch. 38

stenographic transcript of the minutes of the proceedings, certified by the judge before whom the action was tried, and five copies of the briefs.[6]

The appellant's brief must contain the statement required by CPLR 5531 and a statement setting forth whether the defendant is presently incarcerated or on bail, or if a fine was paid.[7] Briefs of all parties must display at the upper right corner of the cover the name of counsel arguing or submitting, and, at the upper left hand corner, the calendar number of the appeal.[8] If the brief does not specify that the appeal is to be argued, it shall be marked submitted without argument.[9] A party's main brief may not exceed 50 pages or a reply brief 20 pages without prior leave of a justice of the court, and briefs to which any matter is added or appended will not be accepted.[10]

Appellant is required to file the original record within 30 days after service of the notice of appeal. The appellant must then notice the appeal for argument or submission on a date within 120 days after the date of service of the notice of appeal. To do so, appellant must file, at least 53 days before the first day of the appointed term, the notice of argument and five copies of the appellant's brief, with proof of service of the notice, the brief and a copy of a transcript of the minutes of the proceeding. Respondent's brief (five copies, with proof of service of one) must be filed not later than 31 days prior to the first day of the term. Five copies of a reply brief, with proof of service of one copy, may be filed not later than 24 days prior to the first day of the appointed term.[11]

Not more than 15 minutes are allowed each side for argument, unless additional time is granted by the court. No matter will be accepted for filing after argument or submission of the appeal unless authorized by the court.[12] Motions for reargument must be made within 30 days after the date of the order determining the appeal.[13]

Appellate Terms, Second Department. The Second Department has two Appellate Terms, one for the Second and Eleventh Districts,[14] which hears appeals from the New York City Criminal Court, and one for the Ninth and Tenth Districts,[15] which hears appeals from village, town, city, and district courts. Each Appellate Term sits in various locations.[16]

6. 22 NYCRR § 640.3(a).
7. 22 NYCRR § 640.3(c).
8. 22 NYCRR § 640.5(a).
9. 22 NYCRR § 640.5(b).

CAVEAT: Indication on the brief alone will not ensure appellant's right to argue; a notice of argument also must be served and filed.

10. 22 NYCRR §§ 640.5(d),(e).
11. 22 NYCRR § 640.6(b)(1).
12. 22 NYCRR § 640.7(d).

13. 22 NYCRR § 640.9(a).

14. Composed of Richmond, Kings, and Queens Counties, all of which lie within New York City.

15. Composed of Rockland, Westchester, Putnam, Orange, and Dutchess Counties, and Nassau and Suffolk Counties on Long Island.

16. The Appellate Term for the Second and Eleventh Districts sits in Courtroom 1902 at 111 Livingston St., Brooklyn, and at the Courthouse at 88–11 Sutphin Boule-

The rules for the two appellate terms in the Second Department are virtually identical. Both provide that appeals in criminal matters are to be heard on the original papers, certified by the clerk of the court from which the appeal is taken, the court's return, if required by statute, and a stenographic transcript of the proceedings settled by the judge before whom the action was tried.[17] Briefs must conform to the provisions of CPLR 5528 and 5529. The calendar number of the appeal must appear at the upper left-hand corner of the cover page of each brief; each party's main brief also must specify, at the upper right-hand corner of the cover page, whether the appeal is to be argued or submitted, and the name of counsel arguing or submitting. The appellant's main brief also must include, at the beginning, the statement required by CPLR 5531, either the entire judgment or order appealed from, or its material provisions, including its date, the sentence imposed, if any, and a statement whether an order issued pursuant to CPL § 460.50 is outstanding, and, if so, the date of the order, the judge who issued it, and whether the appellant is free on bail or on recognizance.[18]

Criminal cases in which a duplicate notice of appeal or an affidavit of errors and the court's return have been transmitted to the clerk of the appellate term are placed on the court's general calendar.[19] An appeal on the general calendar, in which a record has been filed, may be assigned to an appointed term for argument or submission by filing a note of issue specifying the title of the appeal. The appellant must also file the judgment or order appealed from, its date, and the court from which the appeal has been taken, the names, addresses and telephone numbers of all counsel and the name, if known, of arguing counsel, and the identity of the party filing the note of issue. On or before the first Friday of any month, the appellant must file, with the note of issue, proof of service, an original and three copies of the appellant's brief with proof of service of one copy, blank, stamped post cards addressed to each party, and proof of service upon the respondent of one copy of a transcript of the minutes of all proceedings.

The original and three copies of the respondent's brief, with proof of service of one copy, must be filed on or before the third Friday of the month in which the note of issue is deemed filed. The original and three copies of a reply brief, with proof of service of one copy, shall be filed not later than the fourth Friday of the month in which the note of issue is

vard, Queens, and additional locations designated by the Chief Administrator of the Courts. The Appellate Term for the Ninth and Tenth Districts sits at the Nassau County Supreme Court Building and at the Courthouse at 140 Grand Street, White Plains in Westchester County, and at additional locations designated by the Chief Administrator of the Courts. The clerk's office for both Appellate Terms is located at 111 Livingston Street, Brooklyn, NY 11201. See generally, 22 NYCRR § 730.1.

17. 22 NYCRR § 731.1(b)(1).
18. 22 NYCRR §§ 731.2, 732.2.
19. 22 NYCRR §§ 731.4(a)(2), 732.4(a)(2).

§ 38.55   CRIMINAL APPELLATE PRACTICE   Ch. 38

deemed filed.[20] Counsel are notified by postcard of the term to which the appeal is assigned; that information also is published in the *New York Law Journal*.[21]

No more than 15 minutes are allowed for oral argument by each side, except by express permission of the court. If a party's main brief fails to set forth that the cause is to be argued, the appeal will be deemed submitted without argument as to that party.[22]

Except as provided by CPL § 460.70, and subject to the applicable provisions of CPL § 470.60, an appeal in a criminal case in which a note of issue was not filed within 90 days after the last day in which a notice of appeal was required to be filed may be dismissed, unless an extension or enlargement of time has been granted by the court. Appeals subject to dismissal for failure to timely file a note of issue are placed on a special day calendar, published in the *New York Law Journal*. Notice by postcard is sent to the appellant or counsel five days prior to publication.[23]

An application for an extension or enlargement of time or for adjournment of an appeal, whether on motion or by stipulation, must show good cause and include a statement by counsel setting forth the sentence imposed and whether the defendant is free on bail or on recognizance pursuant to an order issued pursuant to CPL § 460.50, and, if so, the date of such order and the name of the judge issuing it, and whether the court has previously granted any enlargement of time. An application for an extension of time for an appeal on the special day dismissal calendar[24] shall be filed at least two days before the day on which the appeal is scheduled to appear on the calendar.[25]

Motions for reargument, or to resettle an order, or to amend a decision must be made within 30 days after the appeal is decided. Upon good cause shown, the court may consider a late motion.[26]

County Courts. Subpart D of Part 200, 22 NYCRR, governs appeals to county courts. The rules are not comprehensive, and any interstices should be filled in by the clerk of the court or the judge's chambers. In all cases, when a notice of appeal is filed with a local criminal court, a copy shall be filed with the county clerk by the person filing with the local court.[27] After that, perfection of the appeal depends on whether the proceedings below were transcribed.

20. 22 NYCRR §§ 731.4(b), 732.4(b).
21. 22 NYCRR §§ 731.4(c), 732.4(c).
22. 22 NYCRR §§ 731.6(a), (b), 732.6(a), (b).
23. 22 NYCRR §§ 731.8(b), (c), 732.8(b), (c).
24. The clerk prepares the special day dismissal calendar for each term. It contains, with limited exceptions, criminal appeals in which a note of issue was not filed within 90 days after the last day in which a notice of appeal was required to be filed. 22 NYCRR §§ 731.8(c), 732.8(c).
25. 22 NYCRR §§ 731.9(b), 732.9(b).
26. 22 NYCRR §§ 731.11(a), 732.11(a).
27. 22 NYCRR § 200.33(a).

If they were (*i.e.*, if the appeal was taken pursuant to CPL § 460.10(2)), the local criminal court shall file with the clerk of the county court the notice of appeal, a transcript of the proceedings, a copy of the accusatory instrument, and any decisions on pretrial motions, and shall notify the appellant and the respondent. If the local criminal court does not file the required papers within 10 days after the transcript is filed with it, or if the transcript is defective, the county court may order the local criminal court to file it or shall order the parties to settle the transcript before the local criminal court.[28]

In all cases, within 20 days after the notice of appeal and transcript have been filed with the county court, or within 20 days after the affidavit of errors and the return of the lower court have been filed with the county court, the appellant must notice the appeal for the next term or special term of county court by filing with the judge of the county court, not less than 14 days prior to the date for which the appeal has been noticed, a brief and notice of argument[29] with proof of service of a copy of each upon the respondent. If the defendant is the appellant and the district attorney did not appear in the local criminal court, the defendant shall also file proof of service of a copy of the brief and notice of argument upon the district attorney.[30] The respondent's brief, or the district attorney's brief, if any, with proof of service of a copy upon appellant, must be filed with the judge of the county court within 12 days after service of appellant's brief.[31]

If the appellant does not timely perfect the appeal the county court may dismiss the appeal, upon the respondent's motion or upon its own motion.[32] An appellant may, upon motion for good cause shown, obtain an extension of time to perfect to a subsequent term or special term, in which case the appellant must notice the appeal for such subsequent term.[33]

§ 38.56 Appeals to Other Intermediate Appellate Courts—Determination of the Appeal

The same statutes that govern the determination of an appeal by the appellate division govern determinations by other intermediate appellate courts in criminal cases. CPL §§ 470.05, 470.10, 470.15, 470.20 and 470.25 are discussed in detail in the sections on criminal appeals to the appellate division.[1] A further appeal from either intermediate appellate court—the county court or the appellate term—to the Court of Appeals is available upon leave granted on application to a judge thereof. An appeal to the appellate division is not available. A judge of the county

---

28. 22 NYCRR § 200.33(a).
29. *See* CPL § 460.70(2).
30. 22 NYCRR § 200.33(b).
31. 22 NYCRR § 200.33(b).
32. 22 NYCRR § 200.33(c).
33. 22 NYCRR § 200.33(d).

§ 38.56
1. *See supra*, §§ 38.23–38.28.

court or a justice of the appellate term may not grant leave to appeal to the Court of Appeals.[2]

§ 38.57 Governance of the Appellate Term

The creation of appellate terms of supreme court is authorized by Article VI, § 8(a) of the New York State Constitution, which provides that the appellate division in each department may establish an appellate term in and for all or part of the department, which shall be composed of not less than three or more than five justices of the supreme court designated by the chief administrator of the courts with the approval of the presiding justice of the appellate division.[1] No more than three justices may sit in any action or proceeding. Two justices constitute a quorum and the concurrence of two is necessary to a decision.

§ 38.58 Original Application to County Court for Change of Venue

Applications for a change of venue in local criminal courts are governed by CPL § 170.15(3),[1] which provides:

> At any time within the period provided by section 255.20, where a defendant is arraigned upon an information, a simplified information, a prosecutor's information or a misdemeanor complaint pending in a city court, town court or a village court having trial jurisdiction thereof, a judge of the county court of the county in which such city court, town court or village court is located may, upon motion of the defendant or the people, order that the action be transferred for disposition from the court in which the matter is pending to another designated local criminal court of the county, upon the ground that disposition thereof within a reasonable time in the court from which removal is sought is unlikely owing to:
>
> (a) Death, disability or other incapacity or disqualification of all of the judges of such court; or
>
> (b) Inability of such court to form a jury in a case, in which the defendant is entitled to and has requested a jury trial.

Like its superior court counterpart,[2] a motion for a change of venue in a local criminal court case must be made within the time provided by CPL § 255.20. Unlike its superior court counterpart, CPL § 170.15(3) does not, by its terms, permit a transfer upon the ground that an

---

2. CPL § 460.20(2)(b).

2. CPL § 230.20.

§ 38.57
1. *See also,* 22 NYCRR § 1.1(f).

§ 38.58
1. This section is the local criminal court counterpart of CPL § 230.20, treated *supra* at §§ 38.8 note 92.

impartial trial cannot be had in the court in which the action is pending. Several courts have so held in denying motions asserting that ground.[3] The weight of authority, however, has construed the statute more broadly, and granted motions for changes of venue on the ground of local prejudice.[4]

Even in counties in which an appeal from a local criminal court would be taken to the appellate term, the motion for a change of venue is properly addressed to the county court.[5]

§ 38.59 Procedural Checklist for Appeals to Appellate Division

1. A judgment of conviction is appealable as of right. Since no fee is required, a notice of appeal should be served and filed promptly. (*See* § 38.12)

2. If the notice of appeal is not served and filed timely, a motion to take a late appeal may be made in the appellate division up to one year and thirty days after the imposition of sentence.[1] (*See* § 38.14)

3. When moving for leave to appeal from an order not appealable as of right, papers should include a copy of the order sought to be appealed and a copy of the papers submitted to the trial court. (*See* § 38.13)

4. When seeking a stay of execution of judgment pending the determination of the appeal, one may move before the trial court or a justice of the appellate division. Only one such application is allowed, so include all issues and bail criteria.[2] (*See* § 38.15) If you will be unable to perfect the appeal before the stay expires, move in a timely fashion for an extension.

5. The minutes of the trial court proceedings should be ordered promptly. If the defendant cannot afford to purchase the minutes, a motion should be made in the appellate court for poor person relief, which may also be accompanied by a request for assignment of counsel, if necessary. (*See* § 38.16)

6. Review the rules of the court to which the appeal is taken to determine time and filing requirements to perfect the appeal. (*See* § 38.17)

---

3. People v. Capuano, 68 Misc.2d 481, 327 N.Y.S.2d 17 (Monroe County Ct.1971)(noting that proper procedure is to move in local criminal court for recusal of the judge); People v. Smith, 93 Misc.2d 326, 402 N.Y.S.2d 766 (Rensselaer County Ct.1978).

4. *See, e.g.*, People v. Mundhenk, 141 Misc.2d 795, 534 N.Y.S.2d 843 (Rockland County Ct.1988); People v. Roberts, 95 Misc.2d 41, 406 N.Y.S.2d 432 (Tompkins County Ct.1978); People v. Kessler, 77 Misc.2d 640, 354 N.Y.S.2d 517 (Suffolk County Ct.1974).

5. *See* People v. Mundhenk, 141 Misc.2d 795, 534 N.Y.S.2d 843 (Rockland County Ct.1988); People v. Kessler, 77 Misc.2d 640, 354 N.Y.S.2d 517 (Suffolk County Ct.1974).

§ 38.59

1. CPL § 460.30.
2. CPL §§ 460.50, 510.30.

§ 38.59   CRIMINAL APPELLATE PRACTICE   Ch. 38

7. Prepare for oral argument by carefully reviewing the record of the trial and any pretrial hearings, and the brief of your adversary. The appellate advocate should anticipate questions and interruptions from the court. Do not expect to read or recite a prepared statement.

8. Check all the citations in the briefs for accuracy. Consider that the briefs may have been written weeks or even months before oral argument. Some decisions may have been affected by subsequent case law or legislative action.

9. Track the process to obtain the court's decision. You are required to notify your client of the decision and to request direction on whether to seek further review. (*See* §§ 38.30—38.33)

10. If the defendant so requests, counsel must timely move for leave to appeal. (*See* § 38.32)

11. In preparing the brief, be sure to discern whether a claimed error is adequately "preserved" (*i.e.*, protested; *see* § 38.19) and cast the brief accordingly. If the point is unpreserved, it is best to say so, and to call upon the court's interest of justice review powers. (*See* § 38.21)

§ 38.60   Forms—Notice of Motion for a Stay of Execution of Judgment

SUPREME COURT OF THE STATE OF NEW YORK
Appellate Division, _____ Department

_____
)
THE PEOPLE OF THE STATE   )
OF NEW YORK   )
) NOTICE OF MOTION FOR
        Plaintiff-respondent   ) A STAY OF EXECUTION
) OF JUDGMENT
        -against-   )
) Index No. _____
_____,   )
)
        Defendant-appellant.   )
_____)

PLEASE TAKE NOTICE that upon the annexed affirmation of [*Name*], dated _____, 19 __, the notice of appeal dated _____, 19 __, and upon all the pleadings and proceedings in this matter, the defendant-appellant will apply to Justice _____ of this Court at _____, New York, on _____, 19 __, at _____.M. for an order staying execution of the judgment appealed from and for such other relief as this Court considers appropriate.

PLEASE TAKE FURTHER NOTICE that, pursuant to CPLR 2214, opposing papers, if any, are to be served on movant's counsel no later than seven (7) days before the return date of this motion.

138

Ch. 38   AFFIRMATION IN SUPPORT OF MOTION   § 38.61

Dated: _____, New York
       _____, 19__

                                                  [*Print Name*]
                                                  Attorney for [*Party*]
                                                  [*Address*]
                                                  [*Telephone Number*]

To: Clerk, Supreme Court
    Appellate Division, _____
Department
    [*Address*]

    And To

[*Print Name*]
Attorney for [*Party*]
[*Address*]

§ 38.61 Forms—Affirmation in Support of Motion for a Stay of Execution of Judgment

SUPREME COURT OF THE STATE OF NEW YORK
Appellate Division, _____ Department

THE PEOPLE OF THE STATE OF NEW YORK	
Plaintiff-respondent	AFFIRMATION IN SUPPORT OF MOTION FOR A STAY OF EXECUTION OF JUDGMENT
-against-	
_____,	Index No. _____
Defendant-appellant.	

STATE OF NEW YORK)
)
COUNTY OF _____)

    I, [*Name of attorney*], am an attorney admitted to practice in the State of New York and make this affirmation under penalty of perjury pursuant to CPLR 2106.

    I am making this application on behalf of the defendant John Clay in support of this motion for an order staying execution of the judgment and releasing the defendant on reasonable bail or his or own recognizance.

§ 38.61   CRIMINAL APPELLATE PRACTICE   Ch. 38

[*In the next paragraph, briefly describe the nature of the criminal action, the procedural background of the case and the facts leading to the judgment appealed from*].

Annexed hereto as exhibit 1 is a copy of the notice of appeal.

[*State whether the defendant was free on bail or on his or her own recognizance during the course of the proceedings. If so, state the terms and whether the defendant made all court appearances*].

[*If appropriate*] The defendant was sentenced to a term of _____ and the time will be served unless this relief is granted.

[*If appropriate*] The defendant has had no prior criminal convictions.

We submit that this appeal is meritorious [*Establish merit to the appeal by setting forth the issues to be raised*].

The defendant's history and background reveals that his release on bail is warranted and appropriate [*Establish that the defendant is a good bail risk within the criteria set forth in CPL 510.30*].

No prior application for this relief has been sought since the notice of appeal has been filed.

WHEREFORE, the defendant requests that the court grant the relief we seek, along with costs, and such other relief as the court may deem appropriate.

_____[*Signature*]

§ 38.62   Forms—Notice of Motion for an Extension of Time to Take an Appeal

SUPREME COURT OF THE STATE OF NEW YORK
Appellate Division, _____ Department

THE PEOPLE OF THE STATE OF NEW YORK	)))
Plaintiff-respondent	) NOTICE OF MOTION FOR AN) EXTENSION OF TIME TO) TAKE AN APPEAL
-against-	))
_____,	) Index No. _____))
Defendant-appellant.	))

PLEASE TAKE NOTICE that upon the annexed affirmation of [*Name*], dated _____, 19 __, and upon all the proceedings in this matter, the defendant will apply to this Court at _____, New York, on

140

Ch. 38   AFFIRMATION IN SUPPORT OF MOTION   **§ 38.63**

_____, 19__, at _____.M. for an order extending the defendant's time to take an appeal and for such other relief as this Court considers appropriate.

PLEASE TAKE FURTHER NOTICE that, pursuant to CPLR 2214, opposing papers, if any, are to be served on movant's counsel no later than seven (7) days before the return date of this motion.

Dated: _____, New York
        _____, 19__

                                            [*Print Name*]
                                            Attorney for [*Party*]
                                            [*Address*]
                                            [*Telephone Number*]

To: Clerk, Supreme Court
    Appellate Division, _____
Department
    [*Address*]

    And To

    [*Print Name*]
    Attorney for [*Party*]
    [*Address*]

§ 38.63 Forms—Affirmation in Support of Motion for an Extension of Time to Take an Appeal

SUPREME COURT OF THE STATE OF NEW YORK
Appellate Division, _____ Department

THE PEOPLE OF THE STATE OF NEW YORK,	)))
Plaintiff-respondent	) AFFIRMATION IN SUPPORT OF) MOTION FOR AN EXTENSION) OF TIME TO TAKE AN APPEAL
-against-	)
_____,	) Index No. _____)
Defendant-appellant.	))

STATE OF NEW YORK)
)
COUNTY OF _____)

§ 38.63

I, [*Name of attorney*], am an attorney admitted to practice in the State of New York and make this affirmation under penalty of perjury pursuant to CPLR 2106.

I am making this application on behalf of the defendant Charles A. Milverton in support of this motion for an order extending the defendant's time to take an appeal.

[I*n the next paragraph, briefly describe the nature of the criminal action, the procedural background of the case and the facts leading to the judgment you wish to appeal from*].

[*If appropriate*] The defendant was sentenced to a term of _____ and the time will be served unless this relief is granted.

[*Establish that the sentence was imposed within one year and 30 days of the date of this application*].

Give a detailed statement of the reasons why a timely notice of appeal was not filed noting the specific issues enumerated in CPL 460.30(1): (a) improper conduct of a public servant, or improper conduct, death or disability of the defendant's attorney; (b) inability of the defendant and his or her attorney to have communicated, in person or by mail, concerning whether an appeal should be taken prior to the expiration of the time within which to take an appeal due to the defendant's incarceration, and through no lack of due diligence or fault of the defendant or the attorney.

No prior application for this relief has been sought.

WHEREFORE, the respondent requests that the court grant the relief we seek, along with costs, and such other relief as the court may deem appropriate.

_____ [*Signature*]

§ 38.64 Chart

Type of Reversal or Modification	On the Facts	On the Law	In the Interests of Justice (Discretion)	Basis for Reversal or Modification	Corrective Action	Illustrative Cases
Reversal of judgment after trial.		CPL § 470.20(1).		Trial error or defect (preserved) resulting in prejudice or deprivation of fair trial.	New trial. CPL § 470.20(1).	People v. Bennett, 169 A.D.2d 369 (3d Dep't 1991), aff'd 79 N.Y.2d 464 (1992); People v. Johnson, 145 A.D.2d 932 (4th Dep't 1988), appeal withdrawn 73 N.Y.2d 892 (1989).

CHART

Type of Reversal or Modification	On the Facts	On the Law	In the Interests of Justice (Discretion)	Basis for Reversal or Modification	Corrective Action	Illustrative Cases
Reversal of judgment after trial.			CPL § 470.20(1).	Trial error or defect (unpreserved) resulting in prejudice or deprivation of fair trial.	New trial. CPL § 470.20(1).	People v. La Planche, 193 A.D.2d 1062, (4th Dep't 1993) app. dismissed 82 N.Y.2d 756 (1993); People v. Tarantola, 178 A.D.2d 768 (3d Dep't 1991), app. denied 79 N.Y.2d 954 (1992).
Reversal of judgment after trial.		CPL § 470.20(2).		Legal insufficiency of one or more counts. CPL § 470.20(2).	Dismissal of accusatory instrument. CPL § 470.20(2).	People v. Espino, 208 A.D.2d 556 (2d Dep't 1994), app. denied 84 N.Y.2d 1031 (1995); People v. West, 195 A.D.2d 490 (2d Dep't 1993), app. denied 82 N.Y.2d 761 (1993).
Modification of judgment after trial.		CPL § 470.20(3).		Legal insufficiency of one or more counts. CPL § 470.20(3).	Dismissal of unsupported counts, affirmance of rest, and reduction of the total sentence, or remittal for resentence. CPL § 470.20(3).	People v. Miller, 174 A.D.2d 989 (4th Dep't 1991), app. denied 78 N.Y.2d 1078 (1991); People v. Zurak, 168 A.D.2d 196 (3d Dep't 1991), app. denied 79 N.Y.2d 834 (1991), cert. denied 504 U.S. 941 (4th Dep't 1992).
Modification of judgment after trial to reduce conviction to lesser included offense.			1	Proof supports lesser count, but not convicted.	Remittance to criminal court for sentencing.	People v. Brantley, 186 A.D.2d 1036 (4th Dep't 1992), app. denied 81 N.Y.2d 785 (1993); People v. Flores, 196 A.D.2d 882 (2d Dep't 1993), aff'd 84 N.Y.2d 957 (1994).
Reversal of judgment after trial as against the weight of the evidence.		CPL § 470.20(5).		Entire verdict against the weight of the evidence.	Dismissal of accusatory instrument. CPL § 470.20(5).	People v. Roman, 160 A.D.2d 961 (2d Dep't 1990), app. denied 76 N.Y.2d 795 (1990); People v. Barlow, 172 A.D.2d 546 (2d Dep't 1991).

§ 38.64

1. Modifications of this type are usually on the law (e.g., the two cited illustrations), but they may be on the law and the facts (e.g., People v. Scott, 93 A.D.2d 754, 461 N.Y.S.2d 309; People v. Sepulveda, 147 A.D.2d 720, 538 N.Y.S.2d 68, app. denied 74 N.Y.2d 669, 543 N.Y.S.2d 411, 541 N.E.2d 440; People v. Medina, 111 A.D.2d 653, 490 N.Y.S.2d 491, app. dismissed 67 N.Y.2d 644, 499 N.Y.S.2d 682, 490 N.E.2d 548), or even on the law, the facts, and the interest of justice (e.g., People v. Lyde, 98 A.D.2d 650, 469 N.Y.S.2d 716.)

§ 38.64 CRIMINAL APPELLATE PRACTICE Ch. 38

Type of Reversal or Modification	On the Facts	On the Law	In the Interests of Justice (Discretion)	Basis for Reversal or Modification	Corrective Action	Illustrative Cases
Modification of judgment after trial as to count or counts as against the weight of the evidence.		CPL § 470.20(5).		Count or counts against the weight of the evidence.	Dismissal of reversed count or counts. CPL § 470.20(5).	People v. Ruiz, 162 A.D.2d 350 (1st Dep't 1990); People v. Bastow, 217 A.D.2d 930, 630 N.Y.S.2d 432 (4th Dep't 1995), app. denied 86 N.Y.2d 872 (1995).
Modification of lawful sentence as unduly harsh or severe.			CPL § 470.20(6).	Harshness or severity.	Imposition of legally authorized lesser sentence. CPL § 470.20(6).	People v. Hodges, 173 A.D.2d 644 (2d Dep't 1991), app. denied 78 N.Y.2d 1011 (1991); People v. Gamble, 173 A.D.2d 555 (2d Dep't 1991) app. denied 78 N.Y.2d 1076 (1991).
Reversal of Sentence.			CPL § 470.20(6).	Harshness or severity.	Imposition of legally authorized lesser sentence. CPL § 470.20(6).	2

2. Although CPL § 470.20(6) speaks of "reversing a sentence" in the interest of justice on the ground that it is unduly harsh or severe, this happens rarely, if at all. It will happen routinely, however, on modification of a judgment, as also referred to in CPL § 470.20(6).

Chapter 39

CIVIL AND CRIMINAL APPEALS TO THE COURT OF APPEALS

by
Hon. Albert M. Rosenblatt
Stuart M. Cohen
Martin H. Brownstein

Table of Sections

39.1	Scope Note.
39.2	Strategy.
39.3	Civil Appeals.
39.4	____ Finality.
39.5	____ Non-appealable Orders.
39.6	____ Appealable Paper.
39.7	____ Scope of Review.
39.8	____ Appeal as of Right.
39.9	____ ____ Appellate Division Orders or Judgments.
39.10	____ ____ Final Judgment of Court of Original Instance.
39.11	____ ____ Judgment of Court of Original Instance to Review Prior Non-final Determination of the Appellate Division.
39.12	____ Appeals by Permission of the Appellate Division or the Court of Appeals.
39.13	____ ____ Judgment of Court of Original Instance to Review Prior Non-final Determination of the Appellate Division.
39.14	____ ____ Final Order of the Appellate Division Determining the Action.
39.15	____ ____ Non-final Appellate Division Orders in Proceedings by or Against Public Officers or Others.
39.16	____ Appeals by Permission of the Appellate Division.
39.17	____ Form, Content and Service of Motions for Leave to Appeal.
39.18	____ ____ Motions Filed in the Appellate Division.
39.19	____ ____ Motions Filed in the Court of Appeals.
39.20	____ Time for Taking the Appeal or Moving for Leave to Appeal—Appeals as of Right.
39.21	____ ____ Motions for Leave to Appeal.
39.22	____ ____ Cross Appeals.
39.23	____ ____ Extensions of Time.
39.24	____ ____ Omissions.
39.25	____ Notice of Appeal—Form and Content.

39.26	____ The Jurisdictional Statement.
39.27	____ Jurisdictional Inquiry.
39.28	____ Perfecting and Readying the Appeal.
39.29	____ ____ Full Briefing and Oral Argument.
39.30	____ ____ *Sua Sponte* Merits Consideration ("SSM").
39.31	____ Determination of the Appeal—*Remittitur*.
39.32	____ Motion Practice.
39.33	____ ____ Motion for a Stay.
39.34	____ ____ Motion to File an *Amicus* Brief.
39.35	____ ____ Motion for Poor Person Relief.
39.36	____ ____ Motion for Reconsideration.
39.37	Criminal Appeals.
39.38	____ Definition of Criminal Case.
39.39	____ Orders and Judgments From Which Appeals May Be Taken.
39.40	____ By the Defendant in Death Penalty Cases.
39.41	____ By the Prosecution in Death Penalty Cases.
39.42	____ Intermediate Appellate Courts.
39.43	____ Additional Limitations on Appealability.
39.44	____ Appeals by Permission.
39.45	____ ____ Obligation of Intermediate Appellate Court Counsel.
39.46	____ ____ Who May Grant Leave to Appeal.
39.47	____ ____ Criminal Leave Application ("CLA") Practice.
39.48	____ ____ Stays and Continuation of Bail.
39.49	____ Appeals Practice.
39.50	____ Scope of Review.
39.51	____ Disposition of Appeal.
39.52	____ Motion Practice.
39.53	____ ____ Poor Person Relief and Assignment of Counsel.
39.54	____ ____ Extension of Time to Seek Leave to Appeal.
39.55	____ ____ Dismissal of Appeal.
39.56	____ ____ Withdrawal of Appeal.
39.57	____ ____ Reargument.
39.58	Other Proceedings in the Court of Appeals.
39.59	____ Review of Determinations of the Commission on Judicial Conduct.
39.60	____ Certified Questions From Other Courts.
39.61	____ Matters Regarding Admission of Attorneys and Licensing of Foreign Legal Consultants.
39.62	*Certiorari* to the Supreme Court of the United States.
39.63	Procedural Checklists.
39.64	____ Civil Appeals as of Right.
39.65	____ Civil Appeals by Permission of Court of Appeals.
39.66	____ Criminal Appeals by Leave of a Court of Appeals Judge.
39.67	____ Civil Appeals by Leave of the Appellate Division and Criminal Appeals by Leave of an Appellate Division Justice.
39.68	____ Appeals Selected for Expedited Review Pursuant to Rule 500.4
39.69	____ Appeals Tracked to Full Briefing and Oral Argument.
39.70	Drafting Checklists.
39.71	____ Notice of Appeal.
39.72	____ Rule 500.2 Jurisdictional Statement.
39.73	____ Motion for Leave to Appeal to Court of Appeals Filed in Court of Appeals.

Ch. 39 **SCOPE NOTE** **§ 39.1**

39.74 ____ Application for Leave to Appeal in Criminal Case Filed in Court of Appeals.
39.75 ____ Appellant's Brief on the Merits.
39.76 ____ Respondent's Brief on the Merits.
39.77 Forms—Notice of Appeal to Court of Appeals From Order of Appellate Division Finally Determining Action With Two Dissents on Question of Law.
39.78 ____ Notice of Appeal to Court of Appeals From Order of Appellate Division Finally Determining Action Where Construction of Constitution is Directly Involved.
39.79 ____ Notice of Appeal to Court of Appeals From Judgment of Supreme Court Where Constitutionality of Statute is Directly Involved.
39.80 ____ Notice of Appeal to Court of Appeals From Appellate Division Order of Reversal Granting New Trial With Stipulation for Judgment Absolute.
39.81 ____ Notice of Appeal to Court of Appeals From Judgment of Supreme Court to Review Prior Non-final Determination of Appellate Division.
39.82 ____ Rule 500.2 Jurisdictional Statement.
39.83 ____ Notice of Motion in Court of Appeals for Leave to Appeal to Court of Appeals From Order of Appellate Division.
39.84 ____ Affidavit in Support of Motion in Court of Appeals for Leave to Appeal to Court of Appeals From Order of Appellate Division.
39.85 ____ Notice of Motion in Court of Appeals for Reargument of Motion for Leave to Appeal.
39.86 ____ Notice of Motion in Court of Appeals for Leave to Appear *Amicus Curiae*.
39.87 ____ Notice of Motion to Dismiss Appeal as Untimely Taken.
39.88 ____ Affidavit in Support of Motion to Dismiss Appeal as Untimely Taken.
39.89 ____ CPLR 5531 Statement.
39.90 ____ Letter Seeking Leave to Appeal in Criminal Case.

WESTLAW Electronic Research

See WESTLAW Electronic Research Guide preceding the Summary of Contents.

§ 39.1 Scope Note

This chapter is intended to provide the practitioner with the information and forms necessary to bring a civil or a criminal appeal to the Court of Appeals, as well as to introduce the reader to other proceedings that may be brought in the Court of Appeals. This chapter first discusses strategy for bringing an appeal.[1] Next, the discussion covers the basic considerations of finality,[2] non-appealable orders,[3] and the scope of

§ 39.1
1. See infra, § 39.2.
2. See infra, § 39.4.
3. See infra, § 39.5.

review.[4] Next considered are the types of orders and judgments from which appeals may be taken to the Court of Appeals as of right[5] and by permission.[6] In cases for which permission i.e., leave is required, those orders and judgments from which only the appellate division may grant leave are distinguished from those from which the appellate division or the Court of Appeals may grant leave.[7]

The requirements for motions made at the appellate division for leave to appeal to the Court of Appeals in civil cases are discussed in Section 37.70.[8] This chapter also explains the numerous requirements for motions for leave to appeal filed in the Court of Appeals,[9] and the time within which an appeal must be taken or motion for leave to appeal made.[10]

This chapter also follows the course of an appeal through the Court of Appeals and describes the various case-tracking options the Court of Appeals may employ, and what is expected of counsel under each.[11] The Court of Appeals' powers of review are distinguished from those of the appellate division, and its options in disposing of an appeal, and the ways in which it does so, also are described.[12] In addition, the chapter discusses a few of the most common motions filed in the Court of Appeals (other than for leave to appeal) in civil cases, and, where appropriate, practice pointers are given.[13]

Chapter 1 of the Laws of 1995 reinstated the death penalty in New York, and created several classes of appeals to the Court of Appeals in capital cases. Counsel should be aware of the basic provisions of the death penalty statute and to that end, where appropriate, various sections of the statute have been paraphrased and quoted.[14]

However, the portion of this chapter focusing on criminal cases concentrates mainly on appeals to the Court of Appeals in non-capital cases. All of these criminal, non-capital appeals are from orders of intermediate appellate courts, and all require the permission of either an appellate division justice or a Court of Appeals judge. The procedure for seeking permission from the latter is treated in this chapter.[15] The procedure in criminal cases for obtaining permission from a justice of the appellate division is treated in Chapter 38.[16]

4. See infra, § 39.7.
5. See infra, §§ 39.8—39.11.
6. See infra, §§ 39.12—39.16.
7. See infra, §§ 39.12—39.15 (appeals by permission of Court of Appeals or appellate division); see also, infra, § 39.16 (appeals by permission of appellate division).
8. See also, infra, § 39.18.
9. See infra, § 39.19.
10. See infra, §§ 39.20—39.24.
11. See infra, §§ 39.29—39.30.
12. See infra, § 39.7 (scope of review); see infra, § 39.31 (determination of appeal).
13. See infra, §§ 39.33—39.36.
14. See infra, §§ 39.40—39.41.
15. See infra, § 39.47.
16. See supra, § 38.32.

This chapter covers appealability of various types of determinations,[17] as well as the process for seeking stays of execution and release on bail.[18] The Court of Appeals' various appeals tracking options and the appropriate response by counsel handling the appeal are also covered,[19] as is the court's scope of review and disposition of appeals.[20] The most common motions filed in connection with non-capital cases are described, and practice pointers given, where applicable.[21]

Finally, this chapter deals with three types of proceedings other than appeals with which counsel may wish to be familiar—reviews of determinations of the Commission on Judicial Conduct, which are initial proceedings commenced in the Court of Appeals;[22] certified questions from other courts, wherein the Court of Appeals provides definitive statements of New York law when such statements would be determinative of appeals pending in the United States Supreme Court, United States Courts of Appeals, or state appellate courts of last resort;[23] and matters regarding the admission of attorneys and the licensing of foreign legal consultants.[24]

§ 39.2 Strategy

A client who has lost a first appeal in a civil case will undoubtedly want to know whether an appeal to the Court of Appeals may be taken. In order to advise the client intelligently, consider the following:

First, may the determination sought to be reviewed be appealed to the Court of Appeals as of right?[1] CPLR 5601 sets forth the circumstances in which an appeal as of right may be taken to the Court of Appeals.[2] In many cases, the application of CPLR 5601 forces counsel to consider whether the determination to be appealed "finally determines the action,"[3] because in many circumstances an appeal as of right will be available *only* if the court hearing the first appeal has entered an order that "finally determines an action."[4] Counsel also should be aware that any appeal as of right may be subject to a jurisdictional inquiry.[5] The cost of responding to such inquiry and the possibility that the Court of Appeals will dismiss the appeal for want of jurisdiction must both be figured into the decision as to whether to take the appeal.

Next, if the order or judgment sought to be reviewed is not appealable as of right, counsel then must determine by leave of which court the

---

17. See infra, §§ 39.39—39.43.
18. See infra, § 39.48.
19. See infra, § 39.49.
20. See infra, §§ 39.50—39.51.
21. See infra, §§ 39.52—39.57.
22. See infra, § 39.59.
23. See infra, § 39.60.
24. See infra, § 39.61.

§ 39.2
1. See infra, §§ 39.8—39.11.
2. CPLR 5601.
3. CPLR 5601(a),(b).
4. See infra, § 39.4.
5. See infra, § 39.27.

appeal may be taken.[6] If leave may be granted by either the appellate division or the Court of Appeals, counsel must determine whether to seek leave from the appellate division, and, if denied there, the Court of Appeals, or whether to skip the appellate division and seek leave directly and only from the Court of Appeals.[7] Counsel should also assess the chances of obtaining leave to appeal so that the client is not left with unreasonable expectations.

Before deciding whether to take an appeal or seek leave to appeal, counsel must also consider the scope of review of the Court of Appeals and whether the error believed to have been committed below may be reviewed by the Court of Appeals.[8] An affirmance with a comment from the court that the error alleged was not preserved, or was otherwise not reviewable, is not likely to please one's client.

Assuming an appealable determination presenting reviewable issues, counsel still must consider the cost of taking the appeal and how long the matter will take to be resolved. Familiarity with the number of copies of various documents required will permit counsel accurately to estimate printing or reproduction costs.[9] Knowing the time periods allowed for filing various papers similarly will help counsel estimate how long it will take for a motion or appeal to reach the Court of Appeals.[10] Familiarity with the court's expedited *sua sponte* merits procedure also is useful; in an appropriate case, counsel may request it in an effort to save the client time and money.[11]

Most criminal appeals involve indigents represented by assigned counsel in the intermediate appellate court. Such counsel need not consider whether to seek leave to take a further appeal; it is their obligation, as part of their assignment, to do so.[12] Counsel must ascertain, in any given case, whether the determination adverse to the client is appealable,[13] and, if so, by whose leave.[14] If there is a choice, counsel must determine whom to approach, since only one application is permitted.[15] If leave to appeal is granted, counsel should consider whether to seek assignment to represent the client in the Court of Appeals.[16]

Another function of the Court of Appeals is to review judicial punishments imposed by the State Commission on Judicial Conduct. If one's role is that of advising a judge or justice who has been sanctioned by the State Commission on Judicial Conduct, particularly one who has

6. See infra, §§ 39.12—39.16.
7. See infra, § 39.12.
8. See infra, § 39.7.
9. See infra, §§ 39.18, 39.19, 39.29.
10. See infra, §§ 39.20, 39.27, 39.29, 39.30, 39.31.
11. See infra, § 39.30.
12. See infra, § 39.45.
13. See infra, §§ 39.39—39.44.
14. See infra, § 39.46.
15. See infra, § 39.46.
16. See infra, § 39.53.

been meted a punishment less than removal, there are important strategic considerations. An important factor in evaluating whether to seek Court of Appeals review is that the court may impose a harsher sanction than that imposed by the Commission.[17]

Counsel litigating in other courts—especially federal courts exercising their diversity jurisdiction—may find a role for the Court of Appeals. Cases in other courts involving an unsettled question of New York law that is determinative of the action may want to consider whether the Court of Appeals will entertain a certified question.[18]

Finally, the Court of Appeals rules govern admission of attorneys. One seeking a waiver of these rules should be familiar with the requirements for such waiver petitions.[19]

§ 39.3 Civil Appeals

In addition to matters traditionally considered to be civil—for instance, contract or tort cases between private parties—the review of quasi-criminal matters is pursued in civil appeals. For example, appeals in proceedings involving commitment and retention orders are civil,[1] as are appeals in *habeas corpus* matters,[2] juvenile delinquency proceedings,[3] and proceedings to review prison disciplinary determinations.[4]

§ 39.4 Civil Appeals—Finality

Finality determines the issue of appealability to the Court of Appeals in most cases.[1] CPLR 5611 states that "[i]f the appellate division disposes of all the issues in the action its order shall be considered a final one." This seemingly simple definition has engendered volumes of com-

---

17. See infra, § 39.59.
18. See infra, § 39.60.
19. See infra, § 39.61.

§ 39.3
1. CPL §§ 330.20(21)(b),(c).
2. See e.g., People ex rel. Lazer (Palmieri) v. Warden, 79 N.Y.2d 839, 580 N.Y.S.2d 183, 588 N.E.2d 81 (1992)(appeal pursuant to CPLR 5601(a)).
3. See e.g., Matter of Jamar A., 86 N.Y.2d 387, 633 N.Y.S.2d 265, 657 N.E.2d 260 (1995)(appeal pursuant to CPLR 5601(a)).
4. See e.g., Matter of Abdur–Raheem v. Mann, 85 N.Y.2d 113, 623 N.Y.S.2d 758, 647 N.E.2d 1266 (1995)(appeal pursuant to CPLR 5601(a)(1)(i)).

§ 39.4
1. **PRACTICE POINTER:** The terms "final" and "appealable" are not synonymous. Non-final orders are appealable in many instances, including when the appellate division grants leave to appeal on a certified question, or by leave of the Court of Appeals when the order is entered in a proceeding pursuant to CPLR Article 78 and grants or affirms the grant of a new trial or hearing, or when the appellate division grants or affirms the grant of a new trial and the appellant stipulates to judgment absolute in the event of an affirmance. In other cases, the State Constitution limits the court's jurisdiction to appeals from final orders. N.Y. Constitution, Art. VI, § 3(a),(b). A nonappealable, non-final order may be reviewed on an appeal from a subsequent final order or judgment. See infra, § 39.7.

§ 39.4

mentary[2] and scores of rules applying to specific situations. This section explains the basic principles, and lists some common exceptions.

Finality is best thought of as a point along a temporal litigation continuum. Orders of intermediate appellate courts can be non-final for being either too early or too late. For instance, an order affirming the denial of a motion for summary judgment is too early to be final. The affirmance leaves the trial of the action pending, and thus is located too early on the continuum to constitute a final order. At the other end, an order denying a motion for reargument of an order affirming a judgment on the merits is non-final. Although, in a sense, it marks the "end" of the case, the truly final order is the one on which reargument might be sought. Thus, denials of reargument may be "post-final," but they are not "final" in the jurisdictional sense.[3]

Among the orders that occur too early to constitute final determinations are those that administer the course of litigation (*e.g.*, orders compelling disclosure and orders denying motions to dismiss) and those that dispose of motions for temporary or provisional relief. The common characteristic of these "too early" orders is that they result in the potential for substantial further activity in the case—such as a trial on the merits.[4] Those that are too late (*i.e.*, post-final) include orders dealing with enforcement of prior, final orders, orders determining motions to amend or vacate previous final orders and judgments, including those entered on default, and orders determining motions for leave to appeal.[5] Also, orders that leave further judicial or quasi-judicial action pending are non-final, even absent a remittal in the decretal portion of the order. Most commonly, such further action will consist of the calculation of damages or attorneys' fees.[6] An order that resolves only some claims asserted in an action also is non-final, leaving pending one or more claims, counterclaims, or cross-claims. To determine the finality of an order of an appellate court dismissing an appeal taken to it, the finality of the order appealed to the appellate court is examined.

There are exceptions of which the practitioner should be aware. First, an order that finally determines a separate special proceeding is

---

2. Among the most helpful of these are Karger, *Powers of the New York Court of Appeals*, Ch. 3 (3rd ed.); Scheinkman, *The Civil Jurisdiction of the New York Court of Appeals: The Rule and Role of Finality*, 54 St. John's L. Rev. 443 (1980), and Davies, Stecich, Gold, et al., *New York Civil Appellate Practice* (West 1996) § 3.11.

3. See *e.g.*, Greene v. Industrial Commissioner of New York, 17 N.Y.2d 728, 269 N.Y.S.2d 978, 216 N.E.2d 840 (1966)(order denying reargument is not "final").

4. See *e.g.*, Health Ins. Ass'n of America v. Harnett, 44 N.Y.2d 302, 405 N.Y.S.2d 634, 376 N.E.2d 1280 (1978)(order denying summary judgment not final because it leaves pending a trial on the merits).

5. See *e.g.*, Greene v. Industrial Commissioner of New York, 17 N.Y.2d 728, 269 N.Y.S.2d 978, 216 N.E.2d 840 (1966)(order denying leave to appeal is too late to be final).

6. See *e.g.*, Burke v. Crosson, 85 N.Y.2d 10, 623 N.Y.S.2d 524, 647 N.E.2d 736 (1995)(order requiring calculation of attorneys' fees is "nonfinal").

considered final.[7] Second, an order finally determining claims severed (expressly or impliedly) from the remaining unresolved claims may be considered final.[8] But, this "severance" situation must be distinguished from splitting items of relief which does not produce a final order.[9] Third, if all claims asserted by or against one or more parties are finally determined, then the order is "final" with regard to that party.[10] Fourth, the doctrine of irreparable injury may apply.[11] The Court of Appeals may entertain an appeal from a non-final order if the order directs an irrevocable change of position. Finally, if the remittal is simply for ministerial action, as opposed to judicial or quasi-judicial action, then the order is final.[12] In other words, if the disposition does not require any further exercise of judicial discretion, it is "final" in the jurisdictional sense. A determination granting all relief requested may be considered final, even if further non-ministerial action is contemplated.[13]

In *Whitfield v. City of New York*,[14] the Court of Appeals addressed the finality problems posed by appellate division orders that reverse a money judgment and grant a new trial unless a party stipulates to a new damages award. In *Whitfield*, the appellate division reversed the money judgment in favor of the plaintiff and granted a new trial on the issue of damages unless, within 20 days after service upon the plaintiff of a copy of the appellate division order with notice of entry, the plaintiff stipulated to reduce the award to a specified amount "and to the entry of an amended judgment accordingly." The appellate division order further provided that "[i]n the event that the plaintiff so stipulates, then the judgment, as so reduced and amended, is affirmed." The plaintiff subsequently stipulated to both the reduction and to the entry of an amended judgment, as provided for in the appellate division order, and the defendant City of New York sought leave to appeal from the appellate division order.

The Court of Appeals dismissed the motion for leave to appeal for non-finality of the appellate division order, noting that where the appellate division directs entry of an amended judgment and specifies that, in that event, the amended judgment is affirmed, the appellate division order is final only after the amended judgment is entered. The Court of

---

7. Karger, *Powers of the New York Court of Appeals* §§ 26–29 (3rd ed.).

8. *Cf.* Sontag v. Sontag, 66 N.Y.2d 554, 498 N.Y.S.2d 133, 488 N.E.2d 1245 (1986)(theories of relief not severable).

9. *See e.g.*, Burke v. Crosson, 85 N.Y.2d 10, 16–17, 623 N.Y.S.2d 524, 528, 647 N.E.2d 736, 740 (1995); Sontag v. Sontag, 66 N.Y.2d 554, 498 N.Y.S.2d 133, 488 N.E.2d 1245 (1986).

10. Karger, *Powers of the New York Court of Appeals* §§ 23–25 (3d ed.); We're Assoc. Co. v. Cohen, Stracher & Bloom, 65 N.Y.2d 148, 149, note 1, 490 N.Y.S.2d 743, 744, note 1, 480 N.E.2d 357, 358, note 1 (1985).

11. Karger, *Powers of the New York Court of Appeals* § 20 (3d ed.).

12. Karger, *Powers of the New York Court of Appeals* § 17 (3rd ed.).

13. *Id.* Matter of Inland Vale Farm Co. v. Stergianopoulos, 65 N.Y.2d 718, 719, note *, 492 N.Y.S.2d 7, 8, note *, 481 N.E.2d 547, 548, note * (1985).

14. ___ N.Y.2d ___, ___ N.Y.S.2d ___, ___ N.E.2d ___, 1997 WL 749429 (1997).

Appeals noted that the appellate division order in effect holds the appeal to that court in abeyance pending execution of an amended judgment. After such amended judgment is entered, the appellate division order affirms it and thus then becomes final.

In *Whitfield*, then, the motion for leave to appeal was premature, because the amended judgment had not yet been entered and thus could not have been affirmed by the appellate division order. After entry of such amended judgment and service of it upon the plaintiff with notice of entry, the appellate division order would become a final one affirming the amended judgment. After service of the then final appellate division order with notice of entry upon the plaintiff, the City presumably will have another chance to seek leave to appeal to the Court of Appeals.

Counsel encountering such a conditional order should not assume it fits the mold, however—slight variations in the language of the appellate division order may have drastic finality implications and may even determine what the appealable paper is, which, in turn, can have fatal timeliness consequences. In *Whitfield*, the Court of Appeals identified two variations on the order there before it.

The first alternative reverses and grants a new trial unless a party simply stipulates to a reduced or enhanced damages award. In that case, it is not the appellate division order, but the stipulation executed pursuant to it, that is the final paper from which leave to appeal must be sought or from which the appeal must be taken. Waiting for entry of a judgment upon the stipulation—if a stipulation is all the appellate division order requires—could result in an untimely appeal or motion for leave to appeal if taken after 30 days have passed after service of the stipulation with notice of entry (35 days if served by mail).

However, if the appellate division order is of the second alternative type, requiring both a stipulation to a different award and entry of an amended judgment pursuant thereto, but not then providing for affirmance of the amended judgment, it is the amended judgment entered pursuant to the stipulation that is the final paper.

Counsel aggrieved by a conditional appellate division order reversing a judgment and directing a new trial unless a party stipulates to a different damages award should read the order very carefully to determine into which of the variations the order falls. Counsel then should determine the final paper in the action, and whether it is appealable as of right or whether leave to appeal must be sought. Counsel must then take the appropriate action within the applicable period for taking an appeal or seeking leave to appeal.

Library References:

West's Key No. Digests, Appeal and Error ⚖︎66–84.

§ 39.5 Civil Appeals—Non-appealable Orders

In certain situations, the lack of finality will render an order non-appealable. Certain other orders, whether final or not, are inherently non-appealable. These are discussed in more detail in the chapter on civil appeals to the appellate division.[1] The most common are orders entered *ex parte*, orders entered on default,[2] orders denying reargument,[3] and orders by which the appellant is not aggrieved.[4]

Library References:

West's Key No. Digests, Appeal and Error ⚖85–122.

§ 39.6 Civil Appeals—Appealable Paper

An appeal may only be taken from an appealable paper. CPLR 5512(a) provides that "[i]f a timely appeal is taken from a judgment or order other than that specified ... and no prejudice results therefrom and the proper paper is furnished to the court to which the appeal is taken, the appeal shall be deemed taken from the proper judgment or order."[1] An order of the appellate division that disposes of all the issues in an action is final, and the appeal should be taken from it, not from any subsequent judgment or order entered pursuant to it.[2]

An appealable paper is defined as either the judgment or order of the court that originally heard the motion, or an order of an appellate court entered in the office of the clerk of the court.[3] An appeal or motion for leave to appeal from some paper other than a judgment or order will be dismissed.[4]

Library References:

West's Key No. Digests, Appeal and Error ⚖123.

§ 39.5

1. See supra, § 37.37.
2. CPLR 5511.
3. See e.g., Greene v. Industrial Commissioner of New York, 17 N.Y.2d 728, 269 N.Y.S.2d 978, 216 N.E.2d 840 (1966).
4. CPLR 5511; see also, Hecht v. City of New York, 60 N.Y.2d 57, 61, 467 N.Y.S.2d 187, 189, 454 N.E.2d 527, 529 (1983). When the appellate division orders a new trial on the amount or apportionment of damages unless plaintiff stipulates to a reduction or reapportionment, a plaintiff who so stipulates to avoid the new trial is not aggrieved by the appellate division order. See e.g., Sogg v. American Airlines, Inc., 83 N.Y.2d 846, 612 N.Y.S.2d 106, 634 N.E.2d 602 (1994). For examples of situations in which a party who stipulates to a reduction or increase in damages pursuant to a conditional appellate division order of reversal has been held not aggrieved by any part of such order, see Whitfield v. City of New York, ___ N.Y.2d ___, ___ N.Y.S.2d ___, ___ N.E.2d ___, 1997 WL 749429 (1997).

§ 39.6

1. CPLR 5512(a).
2. CPLR 5611; see also, supra, § 39.5.
3. CPLR 5512(a).
4. See e.g., Matter of Abdurrahman v. Berry, 73 N.Y.2d 806, 537 N.Y.S.2d 477, 534 N.E.2d 315 (1988)(dismissing appeal taken from a letter); Matter of Allah v. Scheinman, 61 N.Y.2d 755, 472 N.Y.S.2d 922, 460 N.E.2d 1357 (1984)(dismissing motion for leave to appeal from decision).

§ 39.7 Civil Appeals—Scope of Review

Generally. The Court of Appeals' appellate jurisdiction in civil cases is limited by Article VI, Section 3(a) of the State Constitution "to the review of questions of law except where ... the appellate division, on reversing or modifying a final or interlocutory judgment in an action or a final or interlocutory order in a special proceeding, finds new facts and a final judgment or a final order pursuant thereto is entered."[1]

Matters Not Reviewable. Certain questions thus are ordinarily *outside* the scope of Court of Appeals review. First, appellate division determinations as to whether the trial judge correctly decided a CPLR 4404(a) motion to set aside the verdict as contrary to the weight of the evidence ordinarily cannot be reviewed by the Court of Appeals.[2] Second, appellate division determinations of excessiveness or inadequacy of a jury verdict are beyond the Court of Appeals' jurisdiction.[3] Third, appellate division determinations reversing a judgment on the basis of unpreserved legal error are beyond the scope of Court of Appeals review.[4]

Matters Subject to Limited Review. In other cases, the Court of Appeals' review power is *limited*. Findings of fact affirmed by the appellate division are reviewable by the Court of Appeals only to determine if there is evidence in the record to support them.[5] Similarly, when the appellate division reverses or modifies and expressly or impliedly finds new facts, the Court of Appeals will determine which court's—the appellate division's or the trial court's—findings comport with the weight of the evidence.[6] Finally, if the matter is one in which the lower courts had discretion, the Court of Appeals will review that exercise of discretion only to determine whether it was abused.[7]

---

§ 39.7

1. *See also*, CPLR 5501(b). A proceeding to review a determination of the Commission on Judicial Conduct is not an appeal, but an original proceeding; accordingly, the court's scope of review is much broader. *See infra*, § 39.59.

2. *See e.g.*, Levo v. Greenwald, 66 N.Y.2d 962, 498 N.Y.S.2d 784, 489 N.E.2d 753 (1985); Gutin v. Frank Mascali & Sons, Inc., 11 N.Y.2d 97, 98–99, 226 N.Y.S.2d 434, 438, 181 N.E.2d 449, 453 (1962). This doctrine must be distinguished from the legal question of sufficiency of the evidence, which is reviewable. *See* Cohen v. Hallmark Cards, 45 N.Y.2d 493, 499, 410 N.Y.S.2d 282, 285, 382 N.E.2d 1145, 1147 (1978). For a fuller discussion of the sufficiency/weight of evidence distinction in connection with the appellate division's review powers, *see supra*, §§ 37.28–37.29, 37.65.

3. Zipprich v. Smith Trucking Co., 2 N.Y.2d 177, 180, 157 N.Y.S.2d 966, 967, 139 N.E.2d 146, 147 (1956).

4. Brown v. City of New York, 60 N.Y.2d 893, 894, 470 N.Y.S.2d 571, 572, 458 N.E.2d 1248, 1248 (1983).

5. Humphrey v. State of New York, 60 N.Y.2d 742, 743–744, 469 N.Y.S.2d 661, 662, 457 N.E.2d 767, 768 (1983).

6. *See e.g.*, Matter of Jaclyn P., 86 N.Y.2d 875, 876, 635 N.Y.S.2d 169, 170, 658 N.E.2d 1042, 1043 (1995), cert. denied sub nom. Papa v. Nassau County Dept. of Social Servs., ___ U.S. ___, 116 S.Ct. 816, 133 L.Ed.2d 760 (1996); Loughry v. Lincoln First Bank, N.A., 67 N.Y.2d 369, 380, 502 N.Y.S.2d 965, 971, 494 N.E.2d 70, 76 (1986).

7. *See e.g.*, Brady v. Ottaway Newspapers, 63 N.Y.2d 1031, 1032–1033, 484 N.Y.S.2d 798, 799, 473 N.E.2d 1172, 1173 (1984); Herrick v. Second Cuthouse, 64 N.Y.2d 692, 693, 485 N.Y.S.2d 518, 519, 474 N.E.2d 1186, 1187 (1984). While the Court of Appeals "will not, ordinarily, interfere with the appellate division's exercise of ...

Preservation. In order to present a question of law for Court of Appeals review, a ruling complained of must have been properly objected to.[8] If the appellate division decides—in the interest of justice—to review unpreserved error, notwithstanding the lack of a proper objection, the Court of Appeals generally may not review the error.[9]

Appellate courts generally will not consider legal arguments raised for the first time on appeal. The Court of Appeals may consider an argument raised at *nisi prius*, even if it was not asserted at the appellate division.[10] The court also may consider new arguments based on a change in the law while the appeal is pending,[11] as well as those that could not have been cured by factual showings or additional legal arguments, even had the arguments been presented below, such as questions of pure statutory construction.[12] The rule that legal issues must be raised in the trial court applies to constitutional questions,[13] subject to the very narrow exception that the Court of Appeals may examine a constitutional issue raised for the first time before it if grave policy concerns are implicated.[14]

Review of Administrative Agency Determination. In reviewing the determination of an administrative agency, the Court of Appeals must judge the propriety of the determination solely upon the grounds invoked by the agency. Arguments upon which the agency did not rely in reaching its determination may not be reviewed by the court.[15] Similarly, the court may not review arguments which were not raised by a party on administrative appeal.[16]

Scope of Review on Appeal from Final Determination. An appeal from a final determination below allows the aggrieved party a

---

discretion unless there has been an abuse of discretion as a matter of law[,] ... [w]here ... that court, in exercising its discretion, fails to take into account all the various factors entitled to consideration, it commits error of law reviewable by this court." Varkonyi v. S.A. Empresa De Viacao Airea Rio Grandense, 22 N.Y.2d 333, 337, 292 N.Y.S.2d 670, 673, 239 N.E.2d 542, 544 (1968).

8. *See* CPLR 4017, 4110–b, 5501(a)(3),(4); § 37.28, *supra*.

9. *See e.g.*, Brown v. City of New York, 60 N.Y.2d 893, 894, 470 N.Y.S.2d 571, 572, 458 N.E.2d 1248, 1249 (1983).

10. *See e.g.*, Telaro v. Telaro, 25 N.Y.2d 433, 436–439, 306 N.Y.S.2d 920, 921–22, 255 N.E.2d 158, 159–60 (1969). *See also*, *supra*, § 37.28.

11. *See e.g.*, Post v. 120 East End Ave. Corp., 62 N.Y.2d 19, 28–29, 475 N.Y.S.2d 821, 825, 464 N.E.2d 125, 129 (1984). *See* § 37.32, *supra*.

12. *See e.g.*, Telaro v. Telaro, 25 N.Y.2d 433, 436–39, 306 N.Y.S.2d 920, 921–22, 255 N.E.2d 158, 159–60 (1969); Richardson v. Fiedler Roofing, 67 N.Y.2d 246, 250, 502 N.Y.S.2d 125, 127, 493 N.E.2d 228, 230 (1986).

13. *See e.g.*, Matter of Barbara C., 64 N.Y.2d 866, 868, 487 N.Y.S.2d 549, 550, 476 N.E.2d 994, 995 (1985).

14. *See e.g.*, Massachusetts Nat. Bank v. Shinn, 163 N.Y. 360, 363, 57 N.E. 611, 612 (1900). As to the same concept at the appellate division level, *see supra*, § 37.28.

15. *See e.g.*, Matter of Klapak v. Blum, 65 N.Y.2d 670, 491 N.Y.S.2d 615, 481 N.E.2d 247 (1985).

16. *See e.g.*, Matter of Crowley v. O'Keefe, 74 N.Y.2d 780, 545 N.Y.S.2d 101, 543 N.E.2d 744 (1989). *See generally supra*, § 4.79.

§ 39.7 COURT OF APPEALS Ch. 39

review of interlocutory rulings that adversely affected the final determination. This is because CPLR 5501(a)(1) provides that an appeal from a final judgment brings up for review:

> any non-final judgment or order which necessarily affects the final judgment, including any which was adverse to the respondent on the appeal from the final judgment and which, if reversed, would entitle the respondent to prevail in whole or in part on that appeal, provided that such non-final judgment or order has not previously been reviewed by the court to which the appeal is taken.

In addition, CPLR 5501(b) provides in pertinent part that, on an appeal based on a subsequent final determination pursuant to CPLR 5601(d),[17] 5602(a)(1)(ii)[18] or 5602(b)(2)(ii),[19] "only the non-final determination of the appellate division shall be reviewed."

Harmless Error. Not every error determined by the court will result in reversal or modification. CPLR 2002 codifies this familiar harmless error rule: "An error in a ruling of the court shall be disregarded if a substantial right of a party is not prejudiced."[20] The test for harmless error is the same at the Court of Appeals and at the appellate division. Under this test, an error is harmless when there is no view of the evidence under which the appellant could have prevailed.[21] Thus, the burden is on the party asserting that the error is harmless to demonstrate that it did not affect the final disposition.[22]

Library References:

West's Key No. Digests, Appeal and Error ⚖︎836–1099(11).

§ 39.8 Civil Appeals—Appeal as of Right

CPLR 5601[1] prescribes the four jurisdictional classes of matters that may be appealed to the Court of Appeals as of right. These are commonly referred to as two-justice dissents,[2] constitutional grounds,[3] stipulations for judgment absolute,[4] and appeals based upon non-final determinations of the appellate division.[5] The following section describes the contours of each.

---

17. *See infra*, §§ 39.8, 39.9, 39.11.
18. *See infra*, § 39.13.
19. *See infra*, § 39.16.
20. *See* CPLR 2002.
21. *See e.g.*, Marine Midland Bank v. John E. Russo Produce Co., 50 N.Y.2d 31, 427 N.Y.S.2d 961, 405 N.E.2d 205 (1980). *See also, supra*, § 37.28.
22. *Id.*; *see also, supra*, § 37.28.

§ 39.8

1. **CAVEAT**: Prior to 1985, an appeal as of right could be taken from a final order of reversal or modification, or one containing a dissent on a question of law by a single justice. Since the amendments to CPLR 5601 (L.1985, Ch.300), this is no longer so.

2. *See* CPLR 5601(a).
3. *See* CPLR 5601(b).
4. *See* CPLR 5601(c).
5. *See* CPLR 5601(d).

§ 39.9 Civil Appeals—Appeal as of Right—Appellate Division Orders or Judgments

Final Order or Judgment on Two-Justice Dissent (CPLR 5601(a)). In order to take an appeal as of right in a civil case, based on a two-justice dissent at the appellate division, the following requirements must be met.[1] The action must have originated in supreme court, county court, surrogate's court, family court, the Court of Claims or an administrative agency. Also, the order or judgment must finally determine the action.[2] Although the statute speaks only of an appeal from an appellate division *order*, the Court of Appeals has held that the statute also permits an appeal from a *judgment* rendered by the appellate division.[3] The dissent must be on a question of law, meaning the question must be preserved. Thus, the doctrine does not apply to a question that dissenters would have reached in the interest of justice to review an unpreserved point.[4] Of course, the question must not be one of fact, such as whether a verdict was against the weight of the evidence or whether the damages awarded were inadequate or excessive.[5] Although the Court of Appeals has not yet so stated explicitly, it appears that the statute requires that both justices, if writing separately, be dissenting on the same question of law. Finally, the dissent must favor the position of the party appealing to the Court of Appeals.[6]

A Final Order or Judgment Based on Direct Involvement of a Substantial Constitutional Question (CPLR 5601(b)(1)). A second type of appeal as of right in a civil case is one based on the direct involvement of a substantial constitutional question. The following requirements must be met.[7] The order or judgment must finally determine

---

§ 39.9

1. *See generally*, Karger, *Powers of the New York Court of Appeals* § 33, (3rd ed.). Davies, Stecich, Gold, *et al.*, New York Civil Appellate Practice (West 1996).

2. *See* CPLR 5611; *see also, supra*, § 39.4.

3. *See e.g.*, Matter of Federal Deposit Insurance Corp. v. Commissioner of Taxation & Finance, 83 N.Y.2d 44, 48, 607 N.Y.S.2d 620, 622, 628 N.E.2d 1330, 1332 (1993).

4. *See* Merrill v. Albany Medical Center Hospital, 71 N.Y.2d 990, 991, 529 N.Y.S.2d 272, 272, 524 N.E.2d 873, 873 (1988). For a detailed treatment of the appellate division's "interest of justice" jurisdiction, *see supra*, § 37.28; Davies, Stecich, Gold, *et al.*, New York Civil Appellate Practice (West 1996).

5. *See e.g.*, Gillies Agency v. Filor, 32 N.Y.2d 759, 344 N.Y.S.2d 952, 298 N.E.2d 115 (1973)(if it is not clear whether the dissent rests on a disagreement in fact or in law, dissent is not on a question of law within the meaning of CPLR 5601(a)).

6. *See e.g.*, Donnelly v. Donnelly, 73 N.Y.2d 992, 540 N.Y.S.2d 1001, 538 N.E.2d 353 (1989).

7. Again, the statute speaks only of an appeal from an appellate division order, but the court has held it to apply to judgments rendered by that court, as well. *See e.g.*, Matter of Rochester Tel. Corp. v. Public Service Comm'n., 87 N.Y.2d 17, 637 N.Y.S.2d 333, 660 N.E.2d 1112 (1995); Matter of Henry v. Wetzler, 82 N.Y.2d 859, 861, 609 N.Y.S.2d 160, 160, 631 N.E.2d 102, 102 (1993), cert. denied 511 U.S. 1126, 114 S.Ct. 2133, 128 L.Ed.2d 863 (1994).

the action.[8] The constitutional question must be directly involved in the determination of the appellate division.[9] This means the constitutional question must have been raised in the courts below;[10] the appellate division also must have taken a view of the case that required it to pass upon the constitutional issue raised.[11]

The constitutional question raised must be "substantial,"[12] and may involve either the United States or the State Constitution.[13] After an appeal as of right has been taken, the court determines substantiality on a case by case basis.[14] Among the factors the Court of Appeals considers are the nature of the constitutional interest at stake, the novelty of the constitutional claim, whether the argument raised has merit, and whether a basis has been established for distinguishing a state (if asserted) from a federal constitutional claim.

Order Granting or Affirming Grant of New Trial or Hearing on Stipulation for Judgment Absolute (CPLR 5601(c)). A third type of appeal as of right also lies from an order granting or affirming the grant of a new trial on a stipulation for a judgment absolute.[15] This doctrine applies if the action originated in supreme court, county court, surrogate's court, family court, the Court of Claims or an administrative agency. The appellate division must have granted, or affirmed the grant of, a new—not an initial—trial or hearing.[16] The stipulation must be for judgment absolute, and must not be illusory, meaning the appellant must have an award to give up and must agree to give it all up in the event of an affirmance by the Court of Appeals.[17]

If the risk of losing everything instead of having to face a new trial were not enough of a deterrent, one contemplating an appeal pursuant

---

8. CPLR 5611; see also, supra, § 39.4.

9. See generally, Karger, *Powers of the New York Court of Appeals*, Ch. 7 (3rd ed.); Davies, Stecich, Gold, et al., *New York Civil Appellate Practice* (West 1996).

10. See e.g., Matter of Shannon B., 70 N.Y.2d 458, 462, 522 N.Y.S.2d 488, 490, 517 N.E.2d 203, 205 (1987).

11. See Board of Educ. of the Monroe–Woodbury Cent. School Dist. v. Wieder, 72 N.Y.2d 174, 182–83, 531 N.Y.S.2d 889, 893, 527 N.E.2d 767, 771 (1988).

12. See British Land (Maryland) v. Tax Appeals Tribunal, 85 N.Y.2d 139, 145, 623 N.Y.S.2d 772, 774, 647 N.E.2d 1280, 1282 (1995).

13. See Board of Educ. of the Monroe–Woodbury Central School Dist. v. Wieder, 72 N.Y.2d 174, 182, 531 N.Y.S.2d 889, 893, 527 N.E.2d 767, 771 (1988); CPLR 5601(b)(1).

14. For a description of the jurisdictional inquiry process to which many appeals taken on this ground are subject, see infra, § 39.27. Whether or not a jurisdictional inquiry is initiated, the Court of Appeals may examine its subject matter jurisdiction at any time.

15. See CPLR 5601(c).

CAVEAT: A leading commentator described the appeal by stipulation for judgment absolute as an "unusual and dangerous procedure" and "a perilous device whose potential is at best unpredictable." Siegel, Practice Commentary to CPLR § 5601, C5601:5. The risk-averse practitioner probably should proceed immediately from here to the next section; for those not convinced, the hazards such appeal entails are discussed in the text.

16. See CPLR 5601(c).

17. For a situation in which the court determined a stipulation for judgment absolute to be illusory, see Goldberg v. Elkom Corp., 36 N.Y.2d 914, 372 N.Y.S.2d 653, 334 N.E.2d 600 (1975).

to CPLR 5601(c) should also be aware that CPLR 5615 mandates an affirmance—and the appellant's consequent loss of all pursuant to the stipulation—if the appeal presents a question of fact, unless the appellate division opinion recites that questions of fact were not considered or that the appellate division has considered them and would not grant a new trial or hearing thereon.[18]

This unhappy fate befell the defendant-appellant in *Delizia v. Beavers*,[19] in which the trial court set aside, as against the weight of the evidence, a jury verdict in favor of the defendant in a personal injury action arising out of a collision at an intersection, and ordered a new trial pursuant to CPLR 4404. The jury had found the plaintiff "at fault."[20] The trial court found that the testimony of the defendant himself, as well as the testimony of the plaintiff and his witnesses, established the negligence of defendant in making a left turn in front of plaintiff's motorcycle.[21] The appellate division affirmed, holding that the trial court properly exercised its discretion since the jury could not have reached its conclusion on any fair interpretation of the evidence, noting that the record clearly established defendant's negligence and the plaintiff's freedom from contributory negligence.[22] The Court of Appeals affirmed without opinion and granted judgment absolute against the defendant, citing CPLR 5615.

The Court of Appeals may give the appellant an opportunity to withdraw an appeal on stipulation for judgment absolute involving a factual determination by the appellate division,[23] but the far better course is to avoid taking such a reckless appeal in the first place. By taking the appeal, the defendant may forfeit the opportunity to retry the matter.

Order of Appellate Division Which Finally Determines the Action, to Review Prior Non-final Determination of Appellate Division (CPLR (5601(d))). The fourth important class of mandatory appeal is that governed by CPLR 5601(d), which preserves an appeal as of right to review an order meeting all requirements for an appeal as of right under CPLR 5601(a) or 5601(b)(1) except for finality. Under CPLR 5601(d) the combination of a non-final order otherwise meeting the criteria for an appeal as of right with a later final determination provides all the elements of an appealable determination.[24] In other words, the "as of right" character of an appeal is not lost simply because the appeal is taken from a later final order itself not possessing the requirements for an appeal as of right. The appeal is taken from the final determina-

18. *See* CPLR 5615.
19. 34 N.Y.2d 902, 359 N.Y.S.2d 285, 316 N.E.2d 719 (1974).
20. 34 N.Y.2d at 902–03, 355 N.Y.S.2d at 285, 316 N.E.2d at 719.
21. 34 N.Y.2d at 903, 355 N.Y.S.2d at 285, 316 N.E.2d at 719.
22. 34 N.Y.2d at 903, 355 N.Y.S.2d at 285, 316 N.E.2d at 719.
23. *See e.g.*, Thrower v. Smith, 46 N.Y.2d 835, 414 N.Y.S.2d 124, 386 N.E.2d 1091 (1978).
24. *See* CPLR 5601(d).

tion, but review by the Court of Appeals in such case is limited to the prior non-final order. The error alleged with regard to the prior non-final order must necessarily affect the final determination from which the appeal is taken.[25] The CPLR 5601(d) appeal from a final determination of the appellate division is useful if review by the appellate division of a final trial court judgment following a non-final appellate division order is desired and that review produces an order not independently appealable as of right.[26] If appellate division review of the final judgment is not desired, a CPLR 5601(d) appeal may be taken directly from the final judgment to review the prior non-final appellate division order.[27]

Library References:

West's Key No. Digests, Appeal and Error ⇔1080.

§ 39.10 Civil Appeals—Appeals as of Right—Final Judgment of Court of Original Instance

Although an appeal to the Court of Appeals in a civil case typically is from an order of the appellate division, there are cases in which an appeal may be taken to the Court of Appeals from a judgment of the court of original instance, either after an earlier appeal to the appellate division, or, more rarely, as the first step of judicial review. We shall treat the latter case first. CPLR 5601(b)(2) provides:

> An appeal may be taken to the court of appeals as of right: . . . from a judgment of a court of record of original instance which finally determines an action where the only question involved on the appeal is the validity of a statutory provision of the state or of the United States under the constitution of the state or of the United States.

---

25. *See* CPLR 5501(b).

26. **PRACTICE POINTER:** If the final appellate division order *is* independently appealable as of right, the prior non-final order would be reviewable on the appeal therefrom pursuant to CPLR 5501(a). If the final appellate division order is *not* appealable as of right, review of both orders pursuant to CPLR 5501(a) would require the grant of a motion for leave to appeal. *See infra*, § 39.12.

27. *See infra*, § 39.11.

PRACTICE POINTER: A second appeal to the appellate division from a final judgment rendered after a non-final appellate division order may be worth taking in some instances. Assume the first order denying a motion to dismiss is affirmed, with two Justices dissenting. The defendant believes an appeal to the Court of Appeals (either by permission of the appellate division or as of right from a subsequent final judgment) has only a limited chance of resulting in reversal and dismissal of the complaint. In such a case, a second appeal to the appellate division from the final judgment for the plaintiff could be a worthwhile "hedge" for the defendant against losing the later 5601(d) appeal to the Court of Appeals. On the second appeal, the appellate division could review the amount of damages and anything occurring at the trial either relating to liability or damages. The right to eventual Court of Appeals review of the first order pursuant to CPLR 5601(d) and 5501(b) would not be forfeited by the taking of such an appeal to the appellate division, although the Court of Appeals review would, of course, have to await the outcome of the second appeal to the appellate division.

The requirements are strictly construed. The court issuing the judgment appealed from must be a court of record.[1] The judgment must finally determine the action.[2] The only question involved on the appeal must be the validity of a statutory provision of the State or United States under the Constitution of the State or of the United States. If it determines that other issues are present, the Court of Appeals will transfer the appeal to the appellate division.[3]

Library References:
West's Key No. Digests, Appeal and Error ⚖=358.

§ 39.11 Civil Appeals—Appeals as of Right—Judgment of Court of Original Instance to Review Prior Non–final Determination of the Appellate Division

This type of appeal from a determination of a court of original instance follows an appeal to the appellate division, which results in the issuance of a non-final order. A party aggrieved by such non-final appellate division order may not appeal to the Court of Appeals, unless the appellate division grants leave and certifies a question.[1] Therefore, the aggrieved party generally must proceed with the litigation until it is finalized by an order or judgment of the court of original instance. At that point, the order or judgment that imparts finality may be appealed directly to the Court of Appeals to secure review of the prior non-final appellate division order, if certain conditions are met.[2]

Under CPLR 5601(d), such a final judgment or order[3] may be appealed as of right to the Court of Appeals if the appellate division has made an order on a prior appeal which necessarily affects the judgment or order[4] and which meets the criteria of CPLR 5601(a) or CPLR 5601(b)(1) (two-justice dissent or direct involvement of a substantial constitutional question) for an appeal as of right but for the lack of finality in the appellate division's order. In other words, this is the

---

§ 39.10

1. See CPLR 5601(b)(2). For a definition of court of record, see also Judiciary Law § 2.

2. See supra, § 39.4.

3. See e.g., Town of Brookhaven v. State of New York, 70 N.Y.2d 999, 526 N.Y.S.2d 433, 521 N.E.2d 440 (1988); Matter of Morley v. Town of Oswegatchie, 70 N.Y.2d 925, 524 N.Y.S.2d 430, 519 N.E.2d 341 (1987); New York State Club Assn. v. City of New York, 67 N.Y.2d 717, 499 N.Y.S.2d 942, 490 N.E.2d 861 (1986).

§ 39.11

1. See infra, § 39.16.

2. Of course such determination may be appealed to the appellate division, which can review any matter taking place following the prior appeal to that court.

3. The determination from which the appeal is taken must itself finally determine the action. See e.g., Bartoo v. Buell, 84 N.Y.2d 885, 620 N.Y.S.2d 788, 644 N.E.2d 1344 (1994).

4. See e.g., Long v. Forest–Fehlhaber, 55 N.Y.2d 154, 158, note 5, 448 N.Y.S.2d 132, 133, note 5, 433 N.E.2d 115, 116, note 5 (1982).

analog of the doctrine discussed Section 39.9 under which a prior non-final appellate division determination that meets the criteria for an appeal as of right (but for finality) may be reviewed as of right from a later, final appellate division determination.

The practitioner contemplating taking this course of action should be aware of its limitations and of the other options that may exist. On such an appeal under CPLR 5601(d), the Court of Appeals may review only the prior non-final order of the appellate division.[5] Since simultaneous appeals to the appellate division and the Court of Appeals generally are not permitted,[6] one who takes such an appeal at this point, instead of appealing the final judgment to the appellate division, foregoes review of the judgment, or of anything transpiring from entry of the appellate division order to entry of the judgment.[7]

There are ways to avoid this problem. Instead of taking the appeal to the Court of Appeals, the aggrieved party may appeal the final judgment or order to the appellate division, obtain a second, final order from that court determining matters that arose after it issued its first order, and then appeal the second order to the Court of Appeals. Assuming the first order necessarily affects the second, the Court of Appeals will be able to review both.[8] If the second appellate division order is not appealable as of right pursuant to CPLR 5601(a) or 5601(b)(1) (either a two-justice dissent or direct involvement of a substantial constitutional question), the fact that the first order would have been appealable, but for the lack of finality, does not help if review of both orders is desired. In that case, leave to appeal must be sought, and the odds of leave being granted are, of course, low.[9] Consideration must also be given to the cost of the second appeal to the appellate division. However, if review only of the first order is desired, the CPLR 5601(d) appeal may be taken from the final appellate division order.[10]

In *Hirsch v. Lindor Realty Corp.*,[11] for example, the plaintiff sued for judgment declaring him the lawful owner of a certain consolidated mortgage on real property after the defendant allegedly defaulted in the making of payments due under an agreement granting defendant an option to purchase the mortgage. The supreme court rendered a judgment declaring the plaintiff the owner of the consolidated mortgage. The

---

5. CPLR 5501(b).

6. *See e.g.*, Parker v. Rogerson, 35 N.Y.2d 751, 753, 361 N.Y.S.2d 916, 917, 320 N.E.2d 650, 651 (1974). If different parties pursue different avenues of appeal, the appeal before the Court of Appeals will be allowed to continue despite the pendency of the other party's appeal before the appellate division. *See e.g.*, Defler Corp. v. Kleeman, 18 N.Y.2d 797, 275 N.Y.S.2d 384, 221 N.E.2d 914 (1966).

7. Hirsch v. Lindor Realty Corp., 63 N.Y.2d 878, 881, 483 N.Y.S.2d 196, 197, 472 N.E.2d 1024, 1025 (1984).

8. CPLR 5501(a).

9. *See infra*, § 39.13.

10. *See supra*, § 39.8; *see generally* First Westchester Nat'l Bank v. Olsen, 19 N.Y.2d 342, 280 N.Y.S.2d 117, 227 N.E.2d 24 (1967).

11. 63 N.Y.2d 878, 881, 483 N.Y.S.2d 196, 197, 472 N.E.2d 1024, 1025 (1984).

defendant appealed to the appellate division, which reversed and directed the defendant to tender payment within 30 days after entry of its order. If the defendant did so, the complaint would be dismissed; if it did not, the judgment would be affirmed. The appellate division further directed that, upon expiration of the 30 days, the prevailing party should move at special term in the supreme court for an order directing the entry of a final judgment.

The appellate division concluded that the parties, by their course of conduct, waived the established time periods; that only as to the final payment was time of the essence, and, in this instance, there was a timely tender of payment, which the plaintiff rejected. Since the plaintiff failed to prove a change in his position, the court concluded, equity may appropriately intervene to prevent a forfeiture. The defendant again tendered the sum and applied to the special term, which rendered a judgment dismissing the complaint.[12] The plaintiff appealed this final judgment to the Court of Appeals pursuant to CPLR 5601(d).[13]

In the Court of Appeals, the plaintiff took issue with the appellate division's conclusions regarding waiver of the time periods for all payments but the last, and the defendant's contention that he had timely tendered the last payment. The plaintiff also argued that defendant's tender pursuant to the appellate division's order was defective, a contention the Court of Appeals rejected as beyond its power to review:

> On this appeal taken pursuant to CPLR 5601 (subd. [d]), the only order before this court for review is the prior non-final order of the appellate division ... (see CPLR 5501, subd. [b]). Plaintiff argues that defendant's method of tender did not satisfy the condition set forth in the appellate division's order. As this involves circumstances occurring after entry of that non-final order, it is beyond the scope of this court's review (see CPLR 5501, subd. [b]; 5601, subd. [d]; *Matter of Board of Educ. v. Nyquist*, 31 N.Y.2d 468, 472, 341 N.Y.S.2d 441, 443, 293 N.E.2d 819). This was properly a matter to be presented to the Supreme Court when defendant applied for a final judgment in its favor pursuant to the appellate division's order. By choosing to appeal directly to this court from the Supreme Court judgment, plaintiff has waived review of the new matter (see *Parker v. Rogerson*, 35 N.Y.2d 751, 753, 361 N.Y.S.2d 916, 917, 320 N.E.2d 650; Siegel, Practice Commentaries, McKinney's Cons Laws of NY,

---

12. Though not relevant here, the Court of Appeals pointed out that the appellate division should have declared the parties' respective rights instead of dismissing the complaint. *See* Lanza v. Wagner, 11 N.Y.2d 317, 334, 229 N.Y.S.2d 380, 393, 183 N.E.2d 670 (1962), appeal dismissed 371 U.S. 74, 83 S.Ct. 177, 9 L.Ed.2d 163 (1962), cert. denied 371 U.S. 901, 83 S.Ct. 205, 9 L.Ed.2d 164 (1962).

13. At that time, an appeal as of right could be predicated on a unanimous reversal by the appellate division; now, a two-Justice dissent on a question of law in the appellant's favor or the direct involvement of a substantial constitutional question is required. CPLR 5601(a),(b)(1). *See supra*, §§ 39.8—39.9.

Book 7B, C5601:6, pp 499–500). Review of the merits of the Supreme Court's final judgment could have been obtained by taking an appeal to the appellate division.[14]

How one proceeds in these situations depends upon an individualized weighing of many factors, including, but not, limited to:

1. How likely is the Court of Appeals to reverse the prior non-final appellate division order?

2. How likely is it that a second appeal to the appellate division will produce an order also appealable as of right to the Court of Appeals? Bear in mind that an appeal raising only factual questions (such as the adequacy or excessiveness of a damages award) cannot produce a dissent on a question of law and therefore is unlikely to result in an order appealable as of right. On the other hand, an appeal based on legal issues may result in such an order, although a two-justice dissent on any question is rare. Consider also the possibility of direct involvement of a substantial constitutional question.

3. How important is the matter as to which appellate division review would be foregone? If a CPLR 5601(d) appeal is taken from the final judgment, is it worth foregoing review of matters that the appellate division could review?

4. How urgent, in terms of time and money, is a resolution of the issue or issues raised on the first appeal to the appellate division?

Library References:

West's Key No. Digests, Appeal and Error ⟲1082(1).

§ 39.12 Civil Appeals—Appeals by Permission of the Appellate Division or the Court of Appeals

The number of cases in which an appeal as of right may be taken is small in comparison to those requiring leave. Where the jurisdictional predicate for an appeal as of right is lacking, an appeal by permission may be available. Depending on the characteristics of the determination sought to be appealed, different avenues for seeking leave to appeal may exist. When the determination finally determines the action or proceeding, generally speaking, leave to appeal may be sought from the appellate division, and, if denied there, from the Court of Appeals.[1] If the appellant seeks leave first at the Court of Appeals, and that court denies leave, a second application at the appellate division is not available.[2] Whether an

---

14. Hirsch v. Lindor Realty Corp., 63 N.Y.2d 878, 881, 483 N.Y.S.2d 196, 197, 472 N.E.2d 1024, 1025 (1984).

§ 39.12
1. CPLR 5602(a).
2. CPLR 5602(a).

appellant should first seek leave from the appellate division (thus reserving a second bite at the apple), or only apply directly to the Court of Appeals, is strategic decision that requires a weighing of many factors.[3]

Library References:

West's Key No. Digests, Appeal and Error ⚖═366.

§ 39.13 Civil Appeals—Appeals by Permission of the Appellate Division or the Court of Appeals—Judgment of Court of Original Instance to Review Prior Non–final Determination of the Appellate Division

CPLR 5602(a)(1)(ii), like its as of right counterpart, CPLR 5601(d),[1] permits review of a non-final but otherwise appealable-by-permission appellate division determination after entry of a final judgment at *nisi prius*. In other words, if an appellate division determination would be—but for the lack of finality—eligible for an appeal by permission to the Court of Appeals, a later final determination at the trial level cures the lack of finality. The action must have originated in supreme court, county court, surrogate's court, family court, the Court of Claims, an administrative agency or an arbitration.[2] Though leave to appeal is sought, and, if granted, the appeal taken, from the final order or judgment, the Court of Appeals reviews only the prior non-final appellate division determination.[3]

Library References:

West's Key No. Digests, Appeal and Error ⚖═1082(1).

3. PRACTICE POINTER: The relative simplicity and low cost of the appellate division motion commends its use to situations in which time is of the essence—for example, if one has let most of the 30–day period for moving for leave slip by before deciding to seek leave, or if the motion need be made within five days after service with notice of entry of the order sought to be appealed in order to continue a stay in effect at the appellate division. *See* CPLR 5519(e). Moving first for leave to appeal at the appellate division, and then at the Court of Appeals, also will prolong the stay. If there is a single dissenter at the appellate division (two dissenters will produce an order appealable as of right), perhaps the dissenter can convince the others to let the Court of Appeals decide who is right.

On the other hand, the appellate division, more often than not, defers to the Court of Appeals in cases in which both courts have the power to grant leave. If there is a need for quick resolution, it may make sense to forego the motion at the appellate division and immediately seek leave at the Court of Appeals. Otherwise, prudence may argue for availing oneself, or one's client, of all possible avenues to secure a grant of leave to appeal.

§ 39.13

1. *See supra*, § 39.11.
2. CPLR 5602(a)(1).
3. CPLR 5501(b).

§ 39.14 Civil Appeals—Appeals by Permission of the Appellate Division or the Court of Appeals—Final Order of the Appellate Division Determining the Action

CPLR 5602(a)(1)(i) describes the most common type of appeal by permission—one from an order of the appellate division which finally determines an action and which is not appealable as of right.[1] Under this provision, the action must have originated in supreme court, county court, surrogate's court, family court, the Court of Claims, an administrative agency, or an arbitration, and the order sought to be appealed must finally determine the action or proceeding.[2]

Library References:

West's Key No. Digests, Appeal and Error ⚖=84(1)–84(5).

§ 39.15 Civil Appeals—Appeals by Permission of the Appellate Division or the Court of Appeals—Non-final Appellate Division Orders in Proceedings by or Against Public Officers or Others

CPLR 5602(a)(2) contains a specific provision governing appeals by permission to the Court of Appeals from non-final appellate division determinations in proceedings against public officers and boards. Often, of course, such proceedings are brought under Article 78 of the CPLR. While CPLR 5602(a)(2) describes a class of orders appealable to the Court of Appeals by leave of the appellate division or the Court of Appeals, it contains an exception that essentially swallows the rule. If a non-final order in such a proceeding[1] grants or affirms the grant of a new trial or hearing, only the Court of Appeals may grant leave.[2] In such case, the remittal for the new hearing must be to the public officer or board, not to a court.[3] Review by the appellate division in workers'

§ 39.14

1. See supra, §§ 39.8–39.11.

PRACTICE POINTER: The statute requires that the order not be appealable as of right. See CPLR 5602(a)(1)(i). If the appellant mistakenly seeks leave to appeal from an order appealable as of right, the Court of Appeals will deny the motion on the ground that an appeal lies as of right, but it will not dismiss the appeal provided the motion for leave to appeal was made within the time for taking the appeal. CPLR 5520(b). Appellant should then serve and file a notice of appeal, and proceed through the required steps described *infra* at §§ 39.25—39.30.

2. CPLR 5602(a)(1)(i). For a discussion of finality, *see supra*, § 39.4. *See also*, Davies, Stecich, Gold, *et al.*, *New York Civil Appellate Practice* (West 1996).

§ 39.15

1. By its terms, the statute applies only to proceedings, not actions. See CPLR 103(b); John T. Brady & Co. v. City of New York, 56 N.Y.2d 711, 451 N.Y.S.2d 735, 436 N.E.2d 1337 (1982).

2. CPLR 5602(a)(2).

3. Matter of Power Auth. v. Williams, 60 N.Y.2d 315, 323, 469 N.Y.S.2d 620, 624, 457 N.E.2d 726, 730 (1983).

compensation board cases is by appeal, not by CPLR Article 78 proceeding, so a non-final order resulting therefrom is not within the statute.[4]

Library References:
West's Key No. Digests, Appeal and Error ⌦93.

§ 39.16 Civil Appeals—Appeals by Permission of the Appellate Division

Generally, only the appellate division may grant leave to appeal to the Court of Appeals in two classes of cases: (1) those in which the appellate division has issued a non-final order (which has not been finalized by a later judgment),[1] and (2) those in which the action originated in the civil court of the City of New York, a city court, town court, village court, or district court.[2]

From Order of Appellate Division Which Does Not Finally Determine the Action (CPLR 5602(b)(2)). The first class—non-final appellate division determination—is covered by CPLR 5602(b)(1). The order referred to under this statute may arise from an action commenced in any court. In order to secure a grant of leave to appeal, the appellant must convince the appellate division that the issue involved cannot await final resolution of the action.[3] For example, a party affected by a pre-trial disclosure order could argue to the appellate division that the non-final order is one that could not be reviewed on an appeal from a subsequent final determination, because it might not be regarded by the Court of Appeals as necessarily affecting a subsequent final determination.[4] When the appellate division grants leave to appeal from a non-final appellate division order, its order must certify a question for determination by the Court of Appeals.[5]

The only types of non-final orders from which the appellate division cannot grant leave to appeal under CPLR 5602(b)(1) are those described in CPLR 5602(a)(2), CPLR 5602(b)(2)(iii), and CPLR 5601(c). Those are

---

4. *See generally*, Chapter 32 "Workers' Compensation" *supra*.

§ 39.16
1. CPLR 5602(b)(1).
2. CPLR 5602(b)(2). Town and village courts, among others, are referred to collectively in the Uniform Justice Court Act as justice courts. *See e.g.*, Uniform Justice Court Act § 102.
3. **PRACTICE POINTER:** Since, in the case of a non-final order, *only* the appellate division can grant leave, counsel who moves in that court for leave to appeal to the Court of Appeals, and who believes the order sought to be appealed is non-final, should be sure to assert non-finality as convincingly as possible, lest the appellate division mistakenly believe the Court of Appeals may grant leave to appeal if the appellate division denies the motion.

4. Kleinschmidt Div. of SCM Corp. v. Futuronics Corp., 38 N.Y.2d 910, 382 N.Y.S.2d 756, 346 N.E.2d 557 (1976); *but see* Poole v. Consolidated Rail Corp., 80 N.Y.2d 184, 590 N.Y.S.2d 1, 604 N.E.2d 63 (1992), cert. denied 510 U.S. 816, 114 S.Ct. 68, 126 L.Ed.2d 37 (1993), motion for reconsideration dismissed 82 N.Y.2d 921, 610 N.Y.S.2d 156, 632 N.E.2d 466 (1994)(order compelling disclosure of surveillance film reviewable on appeal from final judgment).

5. CPLR 5713.

orders granting or affirming the grant of a new trial or hearing. For appeals under the latter two sections, a stipulation for judgment absolute is required, and the appeal may or may not be as of right.[6]

From Final Judgment of a District Court, City Court, Town Court, Village Court or the Civil Court of the City of New York to Review Prior Order of Appellate Division. The second class comprises appeals from final judgments of district courts, city courts, town courts, village courts or the Civil Court of the City of New York[7] to review a prior order of the appellate division. This second class is defined by CPLR 5602(b)(2)(ii). This subparagraph complements CPLR 5602(a)(1)(ii), which permits either the Court of Appeals or the appellate division to grant leave to appeal to the Court of Appeals from a final judgment in an action originating in supreme court, county court, surrogate's court, family court, the Court of Claims, an administrative agency or an arbitration.[8] Again, the fundamental concept here is that a later final judgment at the trial level cures the lack of finality in the earlier appellate division determination. In actions originating in other courts, only the appellate division may grant leave to appeal.[9]

The type of judgment that may be appealed by leave of the appellate division pursuant to CPLR 5602(b)(2)(ii) is not appealable as of right pursuant to CPLR 5601(d) if the prior non-final appellate division order's appealability, but for the lack of finality, is based on a two-justice dissent. That is so because the subsidiary jurisdictional predicate, CPLR 5601(a), limits appeals on such dissents to orders in actions originating in supreme court, county court, surrogate's court, family court, the Court of Claims, or an administrative agency. A judgment in an action originating in one of the courts under this section is appealable as of right under CPLR 5601(d) if the prior non-final appellate division order's appealability, but for finality, is based on the direct involvement of a substantial constitutional question, since the subsidiary jurisdictional predicate, CPLR 5601(b)(1), does not limit constitutional question appeals to orders in actions arising out of the courts listed in CPLR 5601(a). Thus, before seeking leave to appeal from a final judgment pursuant to CPLR 5602(b)(2)(ii) in a case in which the prior non-final appellate division order directly involves a substantial constitutional

---

6. *Compare* CPLR 5601(c)(appeal as of right) *with* CPLR 5602(b)(2)(iii)(appeal only by permission of the appellate division).

7. The statute itself uses negative language, *i.e.*, "in an action originating in a court other than the supreme court, a county court, a surrogate's court, the family court, the court of claims or an administrative agency." Of course, what remains are those courts listed in the text.

8. *See supra*, § 39.10.

9. CPLR 5602(b)(2)(ii).

PRACTICE POINTER: Counsel seeking leave to appeal under CPLR 5602(b)(2)(ii) should be sure to note that, under the statute, only the appellate division may grant leave and that, if it denies the motion, the appellant may not seek leave to appeal from the Court of Appeals.

question, counsel always should consider whether an appeal as of right lies pursuant to CPLR 5601(d).[10]

From Final Appellate Division Order Not Appealable As of Right, In Action Originating in District Court, City Court, Town Court, Village Court or the Civil Court of the City of New York (CPLR 5602(b)(2)(i)). A final appellate division order in an action originating in district court, city court, town court, village court or the Civil Court of the City of New York only may be appealed as of right to the Court of Appeals if a substantial constitutional question is directly involved in the appellate division's determination.[11] In all other cases, even though the order finally determines the action, an appeal to the Court of Appeals may be taken only by leave of the appellate division.[12]

From Order of the Appellate Division Granting or Affirming the Granting of a New Trial or Hearing, Upon Stipulation for Judgment Absolute, in Action Originating in District Court, City Court, Town Court, or the Civil Court of the City of New York (CPLR 5602(b)(2)(ii)). For these courts, CPLR 5602(b)(2)(iii) is the counterpart to CPLR 5601(c), which permits an appeal as of right upon stipulation for judgment absolute in actions originating in several courts discussed above.[13] In actions originating in the courts that are discussed in this section, permission of the appellate division, in addition to the stipulation for judgment absolute, is required. Whether taken as of right or by permission, an appeal to the Court of Appeals on stipulation for judgment absolute is seldom worth the risk.[14]

Library References:

West's Key No. Digests, Appeal and Error ⚖=358.

§ 39.17 Civil Appeals—Form, Content and Service of Motions for Leave to Appeal

The requirements for motions for leave to appeal filed in the Court of Appeals are far different from the requirements for motions filed in the appellate division, for which each department has its own rules.

Library References:

West's Key No. Digests, Appeal and Error ⚖=361(.5)–361(5).

10. *See generally supra*, § 39.10.
11. CPLR 5601(b)(1).
12. CPLR 5602(b)(2)(i).
PRACTICE POINTER: When seeking leave to appeal from such an order, counsel should point out in the motion to the appellate division that even though the order is final, only the appellate division can grant leave to appeal to the Court of Appeals; because of the court in which the action originated, the Court of Appeals cannot grant leave to appeal after the appellate division declines to do so.

13. *See supra*, § 39.9.

14. *See id.* for a discussion of the risks of such an appeal.

§ 39.18 Civil Appeals—Form, Content and Service of Motions for Leave to Appeal—Motions Filed in the Appellate Division[1]

First Department. The applicable rule is 22 NYCRR § 600.14(b), which provides: "Applications for permission to appeal to the Court of Appeals shall be made in the manner and within the time prescribed by CPLR 5513(c) and 5516 and must be submitted without oral argument. The moving papers shall include a copy of the order of this court from which leave to appeal is requested, and shall set forth the questions of law to be reviewed by the Court of Appeals."

Second Department. 22 NYCRR § 670.6(c) provides: "Motions for leave to appeal to the Court of Appeals shall set forth the questions of law to be reviewed by the Court of Appeals and, where appropriate, the proposed questions of law decisive of the correctness of this court's determination or of any separable portion within it. A copy of this court's order shall be attached."

Third Department. In pertinent part, 22 NYCRR § 800.2(a) provides: "The moving papers on motions for permission to appeal to the Court of Appeals on certified questions shall state the questions proposed. A motion for permission to appeal to the Court of Appeals pursuant to CPLR 5602(a) shall be granted upon the approval of a majority of the justices comprising the panel assigned to consider the motion."

Fourth Department. 22 NYCRR § 1000.13(p) provides in pertinent part: "A motion for reargument of or leave to appeal to the Court of Appeals shall be made within 30 days of service of the order of this court with notice of entry.... An affidavit in support of a motion for leave to appeal ... shall briefly set forth the question of law sought to be reviewed ... and the reasons that the questions should be reviewed by the Court of Appeals. In a civil matter, a motion for leave to appeal to the Court of Appeals shall be determined by the panel of justices that determined the appeal."

Library References:

West's Key No. Digests, Appeal and Error ⚖358, 361(.5)–361(5).

§ 39.19 Civil Appeals—Form, Content and Service of Motions for Leave to Appeal—Motions Filed in the Court of Appeals

Section 500.11 of the Court of Appeals' rules of practice governs

---

§ 39.18

1. For a detailed treatment of this topic, see supra, §§ 37.74–37.78.

motions.[1] The particular requirements applicable to motions for leave to appeal are set forth in subdivision (d). Counsel must read it thoroughly, because several requirements of the court's rules are different from—and more onerous than—the rules for the lower courts regarding such matters.[2]

Return Date; Deadline for Filing. For all motions, eight days' notice must be given for personal service and 13 days' for service by mail. The return date must be an available motion day within the meaning of CPLR 5516. It must be a Monday (unless the Monday is a holiday, in which case the next day of the week that is not a holiday becomes the return date), whether or not the court is in session. Motions are submitted without oral argument. Papers in support of a motion must be filed no later than noon on the Friday immediately preceding the return date, and responding papers must be filed by the close of business on the return date. No adjournments—even by consent—are possible except as provided by CPLR 321(c) and 1022.[3] The court's rules do not contemplate a reply submission.[4]

Moving Papers. The particular requirements for motions for leave to appeal are more burdensome than for those filed at the appellate division.[5] Ten copies of moving (and responding) papers must be filed with the clerk, with proof of service of three copies on *each* other party, unless an affidavit of indigency is filed along with a single set of motion papers.[6] The moving papers must be a single document, bound on the left.[7] Following the notice of motion should be a statement of the questions presented for review, and the procedural history of the motion, including a showing of timeliness.[8] If there was a prior motion in the appellate division for leave to appeal to the Court of Appeals, the movant must demonstrate that the entire timeliness chain is intact, i.e., that the motion for leave to appeal filed at the appellate division was timely, and that the motion filed in the Court of Appeals is timely.[9] The movant must also establish subject matter jurisdiction by demonstrating that the order or judgment sought to be appealed is final (if the jurisdictional predicate is CPLR 5602(a)(1)(i) or (ii)), or that it falls within the class of non-final orders appealable by permission of the Court of Appeals under CPLR 5602(a)(2).[10] Lastly, the movant must present the reasons leave to appeal should be granted. The rule presents the following non-exclusive list of factors that may warrant a grant of leave to appeal:

§ 39.19

1. See 22 NYCRR § 500.11.
2. *See also*, Davies, Stecich, Gold, et al., New York Civil Appellate Practice (West 1996) § 15.3.
3. 22 NYCRR § 500.11(a).
4. 22 NYCRR § 500.11(c).
5. For sample forms, *see infra*, §§ 39.83—39.84.
6. 22 NYCRR § 500.11(d)(2).
7. 22 NYCRR § 500.11(d)(1).
8. 22 NYCRR § 500.11(d)(1)(iii); *see infra*, § 39.21.
9. 22 NYCRR § 500.11(d)(1)(iii); *see supra*, § 39.15.
10. 22 NYCRR § 500.11(d)(1)(iv).

- the questions presented are novel or of public importance;
- the decision below conflicts with prior decisions of the court; or
- the case presents an issue on which the departments of the appellate division have reached conflicting decisions.[11]

Along with 10 copies of the moving papers and proof of service of three copies on each other party, appellant must file copies of the briefs of all parties filed in the appellate division, and the record or appendix used in that court.[12]

Responding Papers. Ten copies of responding papers, each also in the form of a single document bound on the left, should "concisely present respondent's argument for dismissal or denial of the motion, with specific reference to movant's argument that the questions presented merit review." A respondent who chooses not to file responding papers must file with the clerk a copy of respondent's appellate division brief.[13]

Papers Filed by a Corporation. Motion papers filed by or on behalf of a corporation must list all parent companies, subsidiaries, and affiliates of the corporation.[14] The listing is to alert the judges of the Court of Appeals to possible reasons for recusal.

Orders to Show Cause. A motion may be brought on by order to show cause if there is a need for a return date sooner than the earliest permitted by the rules, or if there is a need for preliminary relief, such as a stay pending determination of a motion for a stay. The order to show cause should be presented to the clerk's office, which will assign the matter to a judge. The applicant should not contact a judge directly. Neither the court nor a single judge can grant any relief unless the court's jurisdiction has been invoked by the service and filing of a notice of appeal or by including a request for leave to appeal in the motion. A judge who determines the court is without subject matter jurisdiction to entertain the appeal or motion for leave to appeal may decline to sign the order to show cause.

In cases involving exigent circumstances, including matters in which relief is requested by order to show cause, matters involving election appeals, and the like, counsel should contact the clerk's office by telephone for instructions on how to proceed. The rules do not permit filing papers by facsimile, and the clerk's practice is to reject any papers so filed unless requested by the court or clerk. Counsel anticipating a need to file papers after hours should notify clerk's staff by telephone as far in advance as possible.

Filing Fee. The filing fee required in civil appeals[15] should not be filed with the motion papers. If the motion for leave to appeal is granted,

11. 22 NYCRR § 500.11(d)(1)(v).
12. 22 NYCRR § 500.11(d).
13. 22 NYCRR § 500.11(d)(2).
14. 22 NYCRR § 500.11(b).
15. CPLR 8022; 22 NYCRR § 500.14.

which will occur upon the concurrence of two judges,[16] the filing fee must be remitted, or entitlement to exemption therefrom established, when the appeal is perfected.[17]

Statistics. In 1996, 1309 motions for leave to appeal were filed with the Court of Appeals, which granted 126, denied 903 and dismissed 275 (usually for lack of finality, but sometimes for untimeliness or failure to comply with the requirements of the rules of practice). Five motions were withdrawn. The denial of a motion for leave to appeal is not the equivalent of an affirmance and has no precedential value.[18]

Library References:

West's Key No. Digests, Appeal and Error ⚖358, 361(.5)–361(5).

§ 39.20 Civil Appeals—Time for Taking the Appeal or Moving for Leave to Appeal—Appeals as of Right

Personal Service. The time within which an appeal as of right must be taken is 30 days from service with notice of entry upon appellant of a copy of the order or judgment appealed with written notice of its entry, except when the appellant has served a copy of the order or judgment with written notice of its entry, in which case the appeal must be taken within 30 days thereafter.[1]

Service by Mail. The time within which an appeal must be taken is extended by five days if the prevailing party serves the copy of the order or judgment with notice of entry by mail.[2] Mailing, in turn, means "the deposit of a paper enclosed in a first class postpaid wrapper, addressed to the address designated by a person for that purpose or, if none is designated, at that person's last known address, in a post office or official depository under the exclusive care and custody of the United States Postal Service within the state."[3] Service is complete upon mailing, not receipt, provided the requirements of the statutory definition are met.[4] If not (*e.g.*, if posted from out of state, or to the wrong address), service is not complete upon mailing.[5]

Service by Overnight Delivery. If the adverse party serves by overnight delivery,[6] the period within which the appeal must be taken is

---

16. CPLR 5602(a); 22 NYCRR § 500.11(d).
17. See infra, §§ 39.29–39.30.
18. Matter of Marchant v. Mead–Morrison Mfg. Co., 252 N.Y. 284, 169 N.E. 386 (1929), appeal dismissed 282 U.S. 808, 51 S.Ct. 104, 75 L.Ed. 725 (1930).

§ 39.20
1. CPLR 5513(a).

2. CPLR 2103(b)(2).
3. CPLR 2103(f).
4. CPLR 2103(b)(2).
5. *See e.g.*, Coonradt v. Averill Park Central School Dist., 73 A.D.2d 747, 422 N.Y.S.2d 544 (3d Dep't 1979).
6. For a definition, *see* CPLR 2103(b)(6).

extended by one day.[7] Service is complete upon deposit with the carrier prior to the latest time designated for overnight delivery, not upon receipt.[8]

Library References:

West's Key No. Digests, Appeal and Error ⚖︎337–357(2).

§ 39.21 Civil Appeals—Time for Taking the Appeal or Moving for Leave to Appeal—Motions for Leave to Appeal

The time within which a motion for leave to appeal must be made is 30 days from the operative event described below, depending on whether leave to appeal has first been sought at the appellate division.[1] If the initial motion for leave to appeal is made in the Court of Appeals, the 30 period begins to run from service of the order sought to be appealed with notice of entry, either upon or by the party seeking leave to appeal. The respective five-and one-day extensions for service by the adversary by mail and overnight delivery apply.[2]

If permission has already been denied by the court whose determination is sought to be reviewed, the 30–day period begins to run from service of such order of denial with notice of entry, either upon or by the party seeking leave to appeal.[3] Again, the respective five-and one-day extensions for service by the adversary by mail and overnight delivery apply.[4] As discussed in more detail above,[5] the rules of practice of the Court of Appeals require, on a motion filed at the court after denial by the appellate division of a motion for leave to appeal to the Court of Appeals, that the movant demonstrate that the entire timeliness chain is intact. Preserving the chain means that each link must be intact, *i.e.*, the motions at the appellate division and the Court of Appeals both must be timely.

Library References:

West's Key No. Digests, Appeal and Error ⚖︎358.

7. CPLR 2103(b)(6).
8. CPLR 2103(b)(6).

§ 39.21

1. CPLR 5513(b).
2. *See supra*, § 39.20.
3. **CAVEAT:** A common—and often fatal—mistake made by inexperienced appellate practitioners is, after losing at the appellate division, to seek reargument at that court, without including an alternative request for leave to appeal to the Court of Appeals. During the time the reargument motion is pending, the time to seek leave to appeal from the underlying appellate division order may expire. The order of the appellate division denying reargument is not appealable, and the door to the Court of Appeals may be closed. Therefore, the astute practitioner always includes an alternative request for leave to appeal to the Court of Appeals in the timely reargument motion filed at the appellate division, thus obtaining an additional 30 days from service with notice of entry of the appellate division order denying reargument or leave to appeal within which to move for leave to appeal in the Court of Appeals.

4. *See supra*, § 39.20.
5. *See supra*, § 39.19.

§ 39.22 Civil Appeals—Time for Taking the Appeal or Moving for Leave to Appeal—Cross Appeals

A party upon whom an adverse party has served a notice of appeal or motion for permission to appeal may take an appeal or move for permission to appeal within 10 days after such service or within the time provided by CPLR 5513 (a) or (b), whichever is longer, provided such appeal or motion is otherwise available.[1]

Library References:
West's Key No. Digests, Appeal and Error ⚖338(3).

§ 39.23 Civil Appeals—Time for Taking the Appeal or Moving for Leave to Appeal—Extensions of Time

Extensions of time for appeals to the appellate division are discussed in detail in Chapter 37.[1] The principles discussed there apply equally to appeals to the Court of Appeals. The important thing to bear in mind is that on the civil side, the time limits should be regarded as inviolate. This is in contrast to the situation in criminal cases, in which Criminal Procedure Law § 460.30 extends a measure of flexibility. In civil matters, the exclusive list of grounds for extensions includes:

a. appeals timely taken by the wrong method;[2]

b. the death or disability of the attorney for the aggrieved party before the expiration of the time to appeal or seek leave to appeal;[3] and

c. the occurrence of an event permitting the substitution of a party before expiration of the time to appeal or to seek leave to appeal.[4]

Library References:
West's Key No. Digests, Appeal and Error ⚖352.1–354.

§ 39.24 Civil Appeals—Time for Taking the Appeal or Moving for Leave to Appeal—Omissions

Although extensions of the time within which an appeal must be taken, or leave to appeal sought, are often not available, the law looks more generously on counsel who does something—even the wrong thing—to take the appeal within the time provided. Thus, if one timely

§ 39.22
1. CPLR 5513(c).

§ 39.23
1. See supra, § 37.43.

2. CPLR 5514(a). Note that the right to an extension is not absolute; the statute grants it "unless court to which appeal is sought to be taken orders otherwise."
3. CPLR 5514(b).
4. CPLR 1022.

serves or files a notice of appeal or a notice of motion for permission to appeal, but neglects through mistake or excusable neglect timely to do another required act (*i.e.*, file the papers served or serve the papers filed), the court from or to which the appeal is taken, or the court of original instance, may grant an extension of time for curing the omission.[1]

When permission is timely sought in a case in which an appeal as of right lies, the appellant is not punished for asking permission.[2] The Court of Appeals will deny leave upon the ground that an appeal lies as of right. Appellant then should serve and file a notice of appeal and proceed with preparation of the jurisdictional statement and appeal papers. A premature notice of appeal, or one that inaccurately describes the judgment or order appealed from, may be treated as valid by the Court of Appeals.

§ 39.25 Civil Appeals—Notice of Appeal—Form and Content[1]

The notice of appeal is a simple and straightforward document. It must state: (a) the identity of the party taking the appeal, (b) the judgment or order or specific part of the judgment or order appealed from (usually designated by court and date) and (c) the court to which the appeal is taken.[2] Good practice dictates reciting that the appeal is taken from all of the judgment or order, and each and every part thereof; appealing from only specified parts may limit the court's scope of review. The top of the caption should list the court of original instance, in whose clerk's office the notice will be filed. The parties should be designated plaintiff and defendant (or petitioner and respondent), and appellant (if taking the appeal) or respondent.[3]

Library References:
West's Key No. Digests, Appeal and Error ⚖︎416.1–430(2).

§ 39.26 Civil Appeals—The Jurisdictional Statement[1]

Rule 500.2 requires the appellant in the Court of Appeals to file two copies of a jurisdictional statement (or a "500.2 statement"), with proof of service of one copy upon every other party, within 10 days after taking an appeal.[2] The jurisdictional statement should be brief. The caption

§ 39.24
1. CPLR 5520(a).
2. CPLR 5520(b).

§ 39.25
1. For sample forms, *see infra*, §§ 39.77–39.81.
2. CPLR 5515(1).

3. CPLR 5511. In contrast to federal court practice, the statute does not use the term "appellee."

§ 39.26
1. For a sample form, *see infra*, § 39.82.
2. 22 NYCRR § 500.1 requires all filings, including jurisdictional statements, to be on 8-1/2 by 11 inch paper, with margins

should describe the litigation posture of the parties as they will appear in the Court of Appeals (appellant and respondent). The following information required by the rule should be set out in separately numbered paragraphs:

(1) the title of the case;

(2) the court from which the appeal is taken;

(3) the date of service and filing of the notice of appeal or the date of entry of the order granting leave to appeal;

(4) the date and type of service upon the appellant of the order or judgment appealed from, and its notice of entry; and

(5) the name and address of the attorney for the respondent.[3]

The following items should be attached as exhibits:

"(1) the dated notice of appeal, or the order granting leave to appeal;

(2) the order, judgment or determination appealed from;

(3) any other order brought up for review;

(4) the opinion or memorandum of the appellate division or other intermediate appellate court, or a statement of no opinion;

(5) the order, judgment or determination reviewed by the appellate division or other intermediate appellate court; and

(6) the formal or informal findings and conclusions upon which the order, judgment or determination was entered."[4]

A jurisdictional statement filed on behalf of a corporation should list all its parents, subsidiaries, and affiliates.[5]

Requests for extensions of time to perfect an appeal will not be entertained until appellant has filed a jurisdictional statement. Counsel perfecting an appeal without having first filed a jurisdictional statement risks having the appeal placed on a track that would not have required filing a full set of records or appendices and briefs. If the court does not learn of an appeal until more than 80 days after it is taken, the rules mandate dismissal.[6]

Review of the jurisdictional statement by staff attorneys helps the Clerk of the Court of Appeals determine how an appeal initially will be

conforming to CPLR 5529, bound or securely stapled on the left edge.
  3. 22 NYCRR § 500.2(a).
  4. 22 NYCRR § 500.2(b).
  5. 22 NYCRR § 500.1.
  6. 22 NYCRR § 500.9(a). Even if counsel does not file a Rule 500.2 statement, the court may know of the appeal if it granted leave, or if the notice of appeal was transmitted to it by the clerk of the court in which it was filed, as required by CPLR 5515(2). The only way counsel can be *sure* the court knows of an appeal, however, is to file the jurisdictional statement.

tracked. Counsel are notified by mail of the results of this review within a day or two after receipt of the jurisdictional statement.

The contents of the jurisdictional statements filed each week are summarized and published in many places, including the advance sheets of the Official New York Law Reports, West's New York Supplement, and the New York Law Journal. These "weekly filing digests" also are posted on the court's computerized bulletin board.[7] Counsel perusing the digests may find cases presenting the same issues as matters pending in their own offices, or learn of issues of concern to clients who might wish to seek leave to file briefs *amici curiae*.[8]

§ 39.27 Civil Appeals—Jurisdictional Inquiry[1]

Occasionally, an appeal will be dismissed for lack of "subject matter jurisdiction" of the appellate court. The phrase is encountered in the rules of practice of the Court of Appeals.[2] It also appears at the trial level, in the context of a motion to dismiss under CPLR 3211(a)(2) on the ground that "the court has not jurisdiction of the subject matter of the cause of action."

When the phrase is used in the appellate context it means, in effect, that the court will not take cognizance of the appeal because it is not authorized to do so. In a number of cases, appellants have argued that the Court of Appeals lacked subject matter jurisdiction because, for example, the order appealed from was not final.[3]

The Court of Appeals has not, however, frequently used the term in its decisions as to appealability, and the appellate division has scarcely used it at all, preferring to stay with the term "appealability." A decision, for example, is not appealable.[4] An appeal from a decision would lead to a dismissal, not a determination on the merits.[5] For

---

7. For more information on the court's computerized bulletin board system, which provides virtually instantaneous access to the court's decisions and other relevant information, see Cohen, New *York Court of Appeals Offers Instant Access to New Decisions*, 63 NYSBJ 50 (July–August 1991). For instructions on using the system, write the Clerk's Office at Court of Appeals Hall, 20 Eagle Street, Albany, New York 12207–1095.

8. See supra, § 37.81 and see infra, § 39.34.

§ 39.27

1. 22 NYCRR § 500.3. The rule provides:

This court may determine, sua sponte, whether it has subject matter jurisdiction and authority to review, based on the papers submitted in accordance with section 500.2 of this Part and on such other written submissions as may be sought.

2. 22 NYCRR §§ 500.3, 500.9(a), (b).

3. See e.g., Hooper Assocs. v. AGS Computers, 74 N.Y.2d 487, 489, 549 N.Y.S.2d 365, 366, 548 N.E.2d 903, 904 (1989); Matter of Sofair v. State Univ. of N.Y. Upstate Med. Center Coll. of Medicine, 44 N.Y.2d 475, 476, 406 N.Y.S.2d 276, 276, 377 N.E.2d 730, 731 (1978); Harcel Liqs. v. Evsam Parking, 48 N.Y.2d 503, 505, 423 N.Y.S.2d 873, 874, 399 N.E.2d 905, 906 (1979).

4. Sarfaty v. Rainbow Helicopters, 221 A.D.2d 618, 634 N.Y.S.2d 164 (2d Dep't 1995).

5. *See also, supra*, § 37.37.

Ch. 39   CIVIL APPEALS—JURISDICTIONAL INQUIRY   § 39.27

example, an appeal from a decision falls outside the subject matter jurisdiction of the Court of Appeals because the relevant statutes and constitutional provisions authorize appeals only from judgments, orders, or decrees. No action of the parties in the nature of consent or waiver can confer subject matter jurisdiction on the court[6] or vest it with authority to adjudge the matter.[7] On the other hand, it is incorrect to say that an unpreserved point falls outside the subject matter jurisdiction of an appellate court. The appellate division and appellate term may review it in the interest of justice (or decline to do so); the practice of the Court of Appeals has been not to dismiss an appeal on the civil side, but simply not to reach the unpreserved point.[8] The essential distinction is that errors of subject matter jurisdiction cannot be cured, while non-jurisdictional errors of appellate procedure occasionally can be cured.

The Court of Appeals treats mootness as a matter of subject matter jurisdiction,[9] because an appeal on a moot matter seeks a non-binding opinion.[10] In *Matter of Prospect v. Cohalan*,[11] non-justiciability doctrines such as mootness were explicitly connected with subject matter jurisdiction.

Sua sponte jurisdictional inquiries (known as "SSDs" for the *sua sponte* dismissals that sometimes result) apply only to civil appeals taken as of right pursuant to CPLR 5601 in which the Clerk of the Court of Appeals preliminarily determines whether the jurisdictional predicate for the appeal (as asserted in the jurisdictional statement) may be lacking. The parties are asked to comment on the jurisdictional issue, which the Court of Appeals immediately considers on its own motion.[12]

The clerk's letter initiating a *sua sponte* jurisdictional inquiry suspends the due dates for filing all appeal papers. Simultaneous responses, in letter form, are expected within 10 days after the date of the clerk's

---

6. See People ex rel. Harrison v. Jackson, 298 N.Y. 219, 234, 82 N.E.2d 14, 21 (1948) (Desmond, J., dissenting).

7. See Hunt v. Hunt, 72 N.Y. 217, 229 (1878).

8. See e.g., Snyder v. Wetzler, 84 N.Y.2d 941, 620 N.Y.S.2d 813, 644 N.E.2d 1369 (1994).

9. See e.g., Matter of Grand Jury Subpoenas for Locals 17, 135, 257 & 608 of United Brotherhood of Carpenters & Joiners, 72 N.Y.2d 307, 311, 532 N.Y.S.2d 722, 724, 528 N.E.2d 1195, 1197 (1988), cert. denied 488 U.S. 966, 109 S.Ct. 492, 102 L.Ed.2d 529 (1988).

10. See e.g., Cuomo v. Long Island Lighting Co., 71 N.Y.2d 349, 357, 525 N.Y.S.2d 828, 832, 520 N.E.2d 546, 550 (1988).

11. 65 N.Y.2d 867, 870, note 1, 493 N.Y.S.2d 293, 295, note 1, 482 N.E.2d 1209, 1211, note 1 (1985)(Titone, J., dissenting).

12. PRACTICE POINTER: The clerk's initiation of a jurisdictional inquiry is without prejudice to the respondent's moving to dismiss the appeal. Before considering filing a dismissal motion, a respondent with doubts regarding subject matter jurisdiction might consider waiting at least a week after the appellant files the jurisdictional statement to determine whether the clerk will initiate a *sua sponte* inquiry. The clerk does not initiate inquiries based on untimeliness; a respondent who desires dismissal of an appeal on that ground must move the court for it.

inquiry letter. Each party must send copies of its response to all other counsel in the case.

Completed submissions are referred to a court attorney for preparation of a written clerk's report analyzing the jurisdictional issue. The report is circulated to all the judges and conferenced by the court. If the court decides that it lacks jurisdiction, it will dismiss the appeal. Otherwise, counsel will be notified by letter from the clerk that the appeal will be retained without prejudice to the court's future examination of subject matter jurisdiction. Counsel also will be notified whether the appeal will be considered in the normal course after full briefing and oral argument,[13] or subject to a *sua sponte* merits determination pursuant to 22 NYCRR § 500.4,[14] and a schedule of filing dates for each side will be set.

An appellant unsure of whether the requirements for an appeal as of right will be met may take an appeal as of right and simultaneously move for leave to appeal.[15] In such case, the submissions with respect to each (jurisdictional statement and motion papers) should indicate that the other is simultaneously being filed; the court usually will take up the question of jurisdiction over the appeal as of right in connection with its consideration of the motion for leave to appeal, and the clerk will so notify the parties.

§ 39.28 Civil Appeals—Perfecting and Readying the Appeal[1]

After reviewing the jurisdictional statement, the clerk will notify the parties whether the appeal will be heard in the normal course of full briefing and oral argument[2] or on submissions pursuant to Section 500.4 of the rules of practice.[3]

§ 39.29 Civil Appeals—Perfecting and Readying the Appeal—Full Briefing and Oral Argument

Time for Filing. Full briefing and oral argument, with the filing deadlines provided by the rules, follows if the appellant receives a postcard or letter indicating the clerk's review and administrative approval of the jurisdictional statement. The rules allow the appellant 60 days to file the brief and record or appendix, with an automatic 20-day

---

13. See *infra*, § 39.29.

14. See *infra*, § 39.30.

15. Alternatively, CPLR 5514(a) permits the taking of an appeal as of right after denial or dismissal of a motion for leave to appeal, or moving for leave to appeal after dismissal of an appeal taken as of right, "unless the court to which the appeal is sought to be taken orders otherwise."

§ 39.28

1. As used here, the term "perfecting" means the filing of all appellant's initial papers (*i.e.*, record material and brief); the term "readying" refers to the filing of respondent's papers (*i.e.*, brief and appendix, if any).

2. See *infra*, § 39.29.

3. 22 NYCRR § 500.4; see *infra*, § 39.30.

extension if the papers are not filed within the initial 60–day period.[1] The respondent has 45 days after service of appellant's papers to file its brief and, if applicable, appendix, also with an automatic 20–day extension.[2] Appellant may serve and file a reply brief within 10 days after receipt of respondent's brief. No automatic extension is granted for the filing of a reply brief.[3]

After receipt of the 20–day extension notice, but before the expiration of the 20–day period, counsel may request of the clerk an extension of the 20–day period to a date certain.[4] Appellant's failure to file within the 20–day period (whether or not extended) will result in dismissal of the appeal.[5] Respondent's failure to file within the 20–day period (whether or not extended) will result in preclusion.[6] The discretionary extensions of time described above may be requested by telephone; no motion or written application is necessary. The clerk is more favorably inclined to grant extensions if the requesting party accurately represents that the opposing party does not object. The clerk's staff member granting the extension usually will ask the applicant to confirm the grant of the extension in writing, with a copy to each other party. Extensions for more than 30 days are not granted.

Alternatively, counsel may receive a letter specifying final due dates for papers, in which case no 20–day notice will issue. Even in such cases, extensions of the time for filing may nonetheless be available provided they are requested early enough and that good cause, along with the consent of all parties, is shown.

Appellant's and Respondent's Papers. The appellant may perfect the appeal by filing 20 copies of appellant's brief and 20 copies of the full record or 20 copies of an appendix supplemented by one full record, with proof of service of three copies on each other party to the appeal. In most civil cases, a filing fee of $250 must accompany the record or appendix.[7] The brief must include: (1) a statement showing that the Court of Appeals has jurisdiction over the appeal and to review the questions raised, with references to the record or appendix pages that demonstrate preservation; (2) a table of cases and authorities cited; and (3) on the cover, the name of counsel, the date the brief was completed, whether the appeal is to be argued and, if so, the time requested and name of arguing counsel. Where available, official citations must be given. A brief filed on behalf of a corporation must list all parent companies, affiliates and subsidiaries of such corporation.[8]

§ 39.29
1. 22 NYCRR § 500.9(a),(b).
2. 22 NYCRR §§ 500.7(a)(1), 500.9(c).
3. 22 NYCRR § 500.5(f).
4. 22 NYCRR § 500.9(b).
5. 22 NYCRR § 500.9(b).
6. 22 NYCRR § 500.9(c).
7. CPLR 8022(b); 22 NYCRR § 500.14(1).
8. 22 NYCRR § 500.5(d),(e).

§ 39.29

Full Record. A full record comprises each paper in the litigation folder, including transcripts, filed with the clerk of the court of original instance.[9] The format requirements of the CPLR[10] and the court's rules[11] must be observed. If a bound record was used in the intermediate appellate court, counsel may change the cover to reflect the status of the parties as they appear in the Court of Appeals and insert the additional papers (comprising the CPLR 5531 statement,[12] the notice of appeal or order granting leave to appeal to the Court of Appeals, the order being appealed to the Court of Appeals and any decision of the intermediate appellate court) to the back of the volume, add the certification or stipulation of correctness, continue the consecutive pagination, and adjust the table of contents to include the additional papers.

Appendix Method. The appendix is a volume of excerpted portions of the record to which the points raised in the brief relate.[13] The correctness of the appendix must be certified by its proponent or stipulated to.[14] The appendix method of perfecting an appeal may appropriately and economically be used when the record is substantial and the issues on appeal can be considered by reference to discrete parts of the whole. Conversely, the appendix method may not be appropriate for an appeal which requires the court to refer to most or all of the record on appeal, such as a case in which the sufficiency of the evidence is at issue. The appendix should permit a judge to review the case without resort to the record.

Given the difference in the scope of review in the appellate division and the Court of Appeals, it may be appropriate to use an appendix in the Court of Appeals, though a full record was used in the intermediate appellate court. If an appendix was used in the appellate division, the contents of the appendix filed in the Court of Appeals need not be as voluminous in all cases.

In addition to 20 copies of the appendix, one bound record used at the intermediate appellate level may be filed as is. If no reproduced record was used, the original file may be subpoenaed from the clerk of the trial court (usually the county clerk). Permission of the Court of Appeals to file the original record is not required. Appellant's brief should cite both to pages of the record and the appendix. The respondent may file a supplemental appendix, if so advised, along with its brief.[15]

---

9. CPLR 5526.
10. CPLR 5528, 5529.
11. 22 NYCRR § 500.1.
12. For a sample form, *see infra*, § 39.89.
13. *See generally* CPLR 5528.
14. 22 NYCRR § 500.5(b).

15. 22 NYCRR § 500.6(c). Although a respondent may move to strike an inadequate appendix, the Court prefers the filing of a supplemental appendix. A respondent who files a supplemental appendix may request an award of costs per CPLR 5528(e). *See* Court of Appeals Notice to the Bar, April 9, 1984.

Filing Fee; Exemptions. The clerk of an appellate court must collect a filing fee of $250.00, payable in advance, for each civil appeal.[16] In the Court of Appeals, the fee must be tendered by appellant, upon filing the record material, in the form of an attorney's personal check, certified check, cashier's check or money order payable to "State of New York, Court of Appeals," unless other payment arrangements have been made with the clerk.[17] Instead of the fee, an indigent appellant may tender a copy of an order entered by any court in the action granting that party poor person relief, with a sworn affidavit that the same financial circumstances obtain at the date of filing.[18] If no such order exists, relief from the filing fee may be sought in the Court of Appeals by motion.[19]

Respondent's Papers. The respondent's brief must contain: (1) a table of cases and authorities cited; (2) on the cover, the name of counsel, the date the brief was completed, whether the appeal is to be argued or submitted and (3) if argument is to be held, the time requested and name of arguing counsel. If available, official citations must be given. A brief filed on behalf of a corporation must list all parent companies, affiliates and subsidiaries of such corporation.[20]

Calendar Practice; Oral Argument. The Court of Appeals' day calendar of oral arguments is prepared by the clerk in consultation with a judge of the court. Written notification to counsel follows the calendar conference. The calendar is published in the New York Law Journal and is available on the court's computerized bulletin board.

Counsel may seek a calendaring preference by letter to the clerk, with copies to all other parties. Counsel must include the following information in the letter:

    (1) a statement of the nature of the case;

    (2) the jurisdictional predicate for appeal to the Court of Appeals;

    (3) the state of readiness of the appeal;

    (4) all relevant dates, such as the dates of the orders and judgments below, the notice of appeal or order granting leave, the dates of filing of briefs and papers on appeal; and

    (5) the reason why a calendar preference is needed and why it should be granted.[21]

Before being notified of the argument date, counsel may advise the clerk's office of specific days on which counsel will not be available, which will be considered when the appeal is being assigned a calendar

---

16. CPLR 8022(b).
17. 22 NYCRR § 500.14(1)(a).
18. 22 NYCRR § 500.14(1)(b).
19. 22 NYCRR § 500.11(f). *See infra,* § 39.35.
20. 22 NYCRR § 500.7(a)(1), (b).
21. 22 NYCRR § 500.8(b).

date. Once it has set an argument date for an appeal, the court rarely grants adjournments, even to another day within the same session. Requests for a calendar adjustment must be made by letter. Counsel should state in detail why the adjournment is necessary, and why submitting on the brief filed or having substitute counsel argue are not viable alternatives. The adversaries' consent may be helpful in obtaining an adjournment.

Approximately two weeks before the date of argument, copies of the calendar for the day on which their appeal is scheduled to be argued are sent to counsel. The calendar lists the arguing counsel and the time allotted for the oral presentation, which may differ from that requested.[22] Counsel may argue or submit as they choose. One counsel may choose to submit and the other argue. Split arguments in which two counsel argue on behalf of one party are not permitted.

After the Crier, attired in morning clothes, announces the entry of the court, the Chief Judge calls the first case. The Crier confirms readiness for the arguments to begin. At that point, counsel for the appellant traditionally begins with the introductory phrase: "May it please the Court." Appellant may request rebuttal time from the Chief Judge at the time of argument. Rebuttal time is deducted from the time allotted for argument.[23]

The lectern at which arguing counsel stands displays a white light, which the Crier turns on one minute before argument time expires, and a red light, which is lit when the time for argument has expired. Also affixed to the lectern is a photograph of the sitting bench, with the name of each judge printed below.

Each judge prepares independently for oral argument by reading the record or appendix and the briefs and by examining the main authorities cited. Since the court is familiar with the facts of each case, counsel should immediately address the legal issues. Frequent questions from the bench are the rule, rather than the exception; counsel therefore should spend preparation time in obtaining familiarity with—and ready access to—the record and the main authorities relied upon, rather than rehearsing a set speech.

All arguments are recorded on videotape. The tapes are available for viewing and purchase through the Government Law Center of the Albany Law School.[24]

22. The cover of the brief should indicate the argument time requested or that the appeal will be submitted without argument. If a time request does not appear on the brief, 10 minutes will be assigned. 22 NYCRR § 500.8(a).

23. 22 NYCRR § 500.8(a).

24. Inquiries may be addressed to:

Court of Appeals Videotape Archives
Government Law Center
Albany Law School
80 New Scotland Avenue
Albany, New York 12208–3494

Telephone (518) 445–2327.

Library References:
West's Key No. Digests, Appeal and Error ⊙=755–774, 824.

§ 39.30 Civil Appeals—Perfecting and Readying the Appeal—*Sua Sponte* Merits Consideration ("SSM")

Sua Sponte Merits Consideration ("SSM") is an alternative to the normal course of full briefing and oral argument, designed to save time and money by expediting the processing and determination of appropriate cases through the court. Instead of plenary briefing and oral argument, an SSM appeal may be decided on the record and briefs before the intermediate appellate court, supplemented by letter submissions of the parties.

The rule sets forth factors, the presence of which may subject a case to selection for SSM treatment:

(1) non-reviewable questions of discretion or affirmed findings of fact; (2) clear recent controlling precedent; (3) narrow issues of law not of overriding or statewide importance; (4) nonpreserved issues of law; or (5) other appropriate factors.[1]

A case may initially be selected for SSM by the court in granting leave to appeal in a civil case, by a judge of the court in granting leave to appeal in a criminal case, or by the clerk after staff review of the Rule 500.2 statement. In an appeal tentatively selected for SSM, after the jurisdictional statement is filed, a letter from the clerk directs appellant's counsel to perfect the appeal by filing three copies of the appellate division record and briefs, supplemented by three copies of a letter, with proof of service of one copy on all counsel (all parties already should have the appellate division records and briefs, which need not be re-served). Where applicable, the $250 filing fee must accompany appellant's filing. Three copies of the respondent's letter submission also must be filed, with proof of service of one copy.

Each party must respond to the clerk's SSM inquiry letter.[2] Appellant has 20 days from the date of the clerk's letter to file the required submissions.[3] Respondent has 15 days from receipt of appellant's submission.[4] Although the rule does not by its terms provide for appellant to file a reply, the court's policy is to permit appellant to file three copies of a reply to respondent's submission, with proof of service of one copy on each party, within 10 days after receipt of respondent's submission.

§ 39.30

1. 22 NYCRR § 500.4(b).
2. **CAVEAT:** 22 NYCRR § 500.4(f) provides for abandonment of all arguments in a party's appellate division brief not reserved in its letter submission. All of a party's appellate division brief, or specific numbered points thereof, may be reserved by reference, without verbatim repetition in the letter.
3. 22 NYCRR § 500.4(f).
4. 22 NYCRR § 500.4(f).

§ 39.30 COURT OF APPEALS Ch. 39

Consent or objection to SSM treatment should be indicated, but the author should not assume the case will be taken off SSM. Accordingly, the letter should address the merits as well.

If the appellant does not file the required papers within the initial 20–day period, or within such other period as the court may direct, the clerk will issue a demand that all required papers be filed within 20 days of the initial due date, unless the court, in setting a date certain for filing, has indicated that such date is final or that no 20–day notice will issue.[5] After appellant has received the 20–day notice, but before the expiration of the 20–day period, appellant may request of the clerk an extension of the 20–day period to a date certain. Failure to file within the 20–day period (whether or not extended) results in dismissal of the appeal.[6] Respondent's time to file is also subject to an automatic 20–day extension, where applicable, and failure on the part of respondent to file within the 20–day period (whether or not extended) will result in preclusion.[7] Appellant's reply filing is not subject to an automatic 20–day extension.

The discretionary extensions of time described above may be requested by telephone; no motion or written application is necessary. It helps to be able to represent truthfully that you have discussed the matter with your adversary, and that your adversary does not object. The clerk's staff member granting the extension usually will ask the applicant to confirm the grant of the extension in writing, with a copy to each other party. Extensions for more than 30 days generally are not granted.

After all submissions are received, a judge will prepare a report for the court on the propriety of expedited treatment of the appeal, and, if such treatment is recommended, a proposed resolution of the merits. A case selected for SSM and not restored to the normal course of full briefing and oral argument—as it may be at any time either administratively or at the court's direction if SSM treatment appears inappropriate—is conferenced and decided in the same manner as a normal course appeal. If a case is taken off SSM, the clerk notifies the parties and sets a new schedule for briefing and a date for oral argument.

§ 39.31 Civil Appeals—Determination of the Appeal— *Remittitur*

The court's adjudication is embodied in its *remittitur*, which is transmitted with the appeal papers to the court of original instance or to which the case was remitted, there to be proceeded upon according to law. Enforcement, including taxation of costs, is pursued in the court of

5. 22 NYCRR § 500.9(b). 6. 22 NYCRR § 500.9(b).
7. 22 NYCRR § 500.9(c).

original instance or to which the case is remitted.[1]

Permitted dispositions by the court include affirmance, reversal, or modification, in whole or in part, as to any party. The court may render a final determination or remit to another court for further proceedings.[2] The court may dismiss an appeal for lack of subject matter jurisdiction or failure to perfect the appeal, among other reasons.[3] If the appeal was taken by leave of the appellate division upon a certified question, the Court of Appeals must answer the question certified and direct entry of the appropriate judgment or order.[4]

The statute requires an appellate court to state its reasons for reversing or modifying a determination appealed to it.[5] It is the policy of the Court of Appeals to give a reason for its determination of all appeals.

When the court hands down decisions, all appeals and motions decided that day appear on a decision list. Next to the name of each matter is an entry, containing the court's disposition and indicating if there is a separate writing. Separate writings include opinions (signed or per curiam) and memoranda.

Library References:

West's Key No. Digests, Appeal and Error ⟿1100–1222.

§ 39.32 Civil Appeals—Motion Practice

Much of the Court of Appeals' rule relating to motions is discussed in the section of this chapter relating to motions for leave to appeal.[1] Motions other than for leave to appeal or for reargument (of either an appeal or a motion for leave to appeal) may be made on a single set of moving papers, with proof of service of one copy.[2] The requirements for specific motions are discussed below.

§ 39.33 Civil Appeals—Motion Practice—Motion for a Stay

Practitioners before the Court of Appeals should be familiar with CPLR 5519, which governs stays.[1] If a discretionary stay is desired, or if

§ 39.31
1. 22 NYCRR § 500.15.
2. CPLR 5522(a), 5613. The court generally will not grant affirmative relief to a nonappealing party and will not search a record and award such party summary judgment. Graubard Mollen Dannett & Horowitz v. Moskovitz, 86 N.Y.2d 112, 118, note 2, 629 N.Y.S.2d 1009, 1013, note 2, 653 N.E.2d 1179, 1182, note 2 (1995).
3. 22 NYCRR §§ 500.3, 500.9(a), (b).
4. CPLR 5614.
5. CPLR 5522(a).

§ 39.32
1. 22 NYCRR § 500.11; see supra, § 39.19.
2. 22 NYCRR § 500.11(g).

§ 39.33
1. See supra, § 37.80.

§ 39.33　　　　　COURT OF APPEALS　　　　　Ch. 39

one subject to a stay desires to have it vacated, the request is presented in the same way as any other motion.[2]

Library References:
West's Key No. Digests, Appeal and Error ⊙⇌476–481.

§ 39.34　Civil Appeals—Motion Practice—Motion to File an *Amicus* Brief[1]

A motion to file a brief *amicus curiae* should be made as far in advance as possible of the argument date of the appeal. A copy of the proposed brief should be included with the motion, if possible, and all parties to the appeal should be served. The court's rules require the following to secure a grant of *amicus* relief:

(1) a showing that the parties are not capable of a full and adequate presentation and that movants could remedy this deficiency;

(2) that movants would invite the court's attention to law or arguments which might otherwise escape its consideration; or

(3) that *amicus curiae* briefs would otherwise be of special assistance to the court.[2]

Amicus relief usually will be denied if the brief seeks to raise issues not before the courts below, or if the proposed *amicus* is a party to another, similar case before the Court of Appeals or another court. On appeals selected for expedited review pursuant to 22 NYCRR § 500.4, *amicus* relief may be sought by letter accompanied by the proposed submission, with copies served on all parties.

The court almost never permits an *amicus* to orally argue an appeal; one who wishes to assist the court as an *amicus*, even if requesting oral argument, should prepare a written submission, with the expectation

---

2. PRACTICE POINTER: In many cases, a motion for a stay is not necessary. CPLR 5519(e) provides for continuation of an existing stay (automatic or discretionary) for five days after service upon the appellant of the order with notice of entry if the judgment or order appealed from is affirmed or modified. If, within that five-day period, the appellant takes an appeal, or moves for leave to appeal, from the appellate court order, the stay will continue until five days after service with notice of entry of the order determining the appeal or motion. When a motion for leave to appeal is involved, the stay shall, if the motion is granted, continue until five days after the appeal is determined; if the motion is denied, it shall continue until five days after the movant is served with the order of denial with notice of its entry. Thus, the stay is designed to endure until the end of the matter—until the motion for leave to appeal is denied, which brings down the curtain, or until the Court of Appeals determines the appeal.

Counsel should not forego the opportunity to obtain a continuation of a stay when it is available. The court is not likely to grant a discretionary stay to a party that could have obtained one without its intervention.

§ 39.34

1. For a sample form, *see infra*, § 39.86. For sources of information on issues presented on cases recently filed in the Court of Appeals, *see supra*, § 39.26. For *amicus* motions at the appellate division, *see supra*, § 37.81. *See also*, Davies, Stecich, Gold, et al., New York Civil Appellate Practice (West 1996).

2. 22 NYCRR § 500.11(e).

that, at best, the request to appear *amicus* will be granted only to the extent of accepting the brief.

Library References:

West's Key No. Digests, Amicus Curiae ⚖1.

§ 39.35 Civil Appeals—Motion Practice—Motion for Poor Person Relief

Motions for assignment of counsel and relief from filing fees fall under the classification of "poor person relief." The financial information required by CPLR 1101 should be provided.[1] The court rarely waives its requirements for filing 20 copies of appellate papers, but, in cases in which the court assigns counsel, reimbursement from the Court of Appeals for printing costs up to a certain amount may be available.[2]

Library References:

West's Key No. Digests, Appeal and Error ⚖389.

§ 39.36 Civil Appeals—Motion Practice—Motion for Reconsideration[1]

Reconsideration or reargument must be sought no later than 30 days after the appeal or motion has been decided.[2] If seeking reargument of a motion, a single set of papers may be filed if that was the requirement on the original motion; otherwise, 10 copies must be filed with proof of service of three copies on each party.[3] New material normally may not be asserted on a motion for reargument; the motion should, however, state the ground upon which reargument is sought and the points claimed to have been overlooked or misapprehended by the court.[4] That the court "never" grants reargument is a misconception, though it does so very rarely.[5]

Library References:

West's Key No. Digests, Appeal and Error ⚖829–835(3).

§ 39.35

1. CPLR 1101(a) provides in pertinent part:

The moving party shall file an affidavit setting forth the amount and sources of his or her income and listing his or her property with its value; that he or she is unable to pay the costs, fees and expenses necessary to prosecute or defend the action or to maintain or respond to the appeal; the nature of the action; sufficient facts so that the merit of the contentions can be ascertained; and whether any other person is beneficially interested in any recovery sought and, if so, whether every such person is unable to pay such costs, fees and expenses.

2. 22 NYCRR § 500.10(c).

§ 39.36

1. For a sample form, *see infra*, § 39.85.

2. 22 NYCRR § 500.11(g)(3).

3. 22 NYCRR § 500.11(g)(1), (2).

4. 22 NYCRR § 500.11(g)(1), (3).

5. From 1993 through 1996, the court granted three motions for reargument of appeals, and eight motions for reargument of motions.

§ 39.37 Criminal Appeals

The principles governing criminal appeals to the Court of Appeals are found in the Criminal Procedure Law ("CPL"); the CPLR definitions of appealability as of right and by permission in civil cases do not apply to criminal cases. Indeed, there are no appeals to the Court of Appeals as of right in criminal cases, except in cases in which a sentence of death has been imposed.[1]

§ 39.38 Criminal Appeals—Definition of Criminal Case

No problem generally exists in distinguishing criminal from civil actions. The CPL applies to all "criminal actions and proceedings."[1] A "criminal action" is defined, in essence, as one commenced "with the filing of an accusatory instrument against a defendant in a criminal court,"[2] and a "criminal proceeding" is any proceeding which is "part of a criminal action."[3] The CPL also defines "criminal proceeding" as one which "occurs in a criminal court and is related to a prospective, pending or completed criminal action."[4] However, this latter definition is overinclusive, or at least subject to several exceptions. Appeals in proceedings involving commitment and retention orders are civil in nature,[5] as are bail forfeiture and remission proceedings.[6] Moreover, "quasi-criminal" proceedings, such as *habeas corpus* and those commenced pursuant to CPLR Article 78 in the nature of *mandamus*, prohibition and to review prison discipline, and the like are clearly civil, and leave to appeal from intermediate appellate court orders entered in these must be sought, or an appeal as of right taken, on the civil side.[7]

Library References:

West's Key No. Digests, Action ⟐18.

§ 39.39 Criminal Appeals—Orders and Judgments From Which Appeals May Be Taken

The primary focus of this portion of this chapter is upon appeals to the Court of Appeals from orders of intermediate appellate courts in non-capital cases.[1] However, appeals in capital cases merit discussion. Although the rules of practice for such appeals have not yet been

§ 39.37
1. See infra, §§ 39.39—39.42.

§ 39.38
1. CPL § 1.10(1)(a).
2. CPL § 1.20(16).
3. CPL § 1.20(18)(a).
4. CPL § 1.20(18)(b).
5. CPL § 330.20(21)(b), (c).
6. See e.g., People v. Schonfeld, 74 N.Y.2d 324, 327, 547 N.Y.S.2d 266, 267, 546 N.E.2d 395, 396 (1989).
7. See supra, § 39.3.

§ 39.39
1. See infra, § 39.42.

promulgated as of this writing, counsel should be aware of the statutory provisions for appeals in such cases.[2]

Library References:

West's Key No. Digests, Criminal Law ⚖1023.

§ 39.40 Criminal Appeals—By the Defendant in Death Penalty Cases

Criminal Procedure Law § 450.70 governs defense appeals in death penalty cases. It provides:

> An appeal directly to the court of appeals may be taken as of right by the defendant from the following judgment and orders of a superior court:
>
> 1. A judgment including a sentence of death;
>
> 2. An order denying a motion, made pursuant to section 440.10, to vacate a judgment including a sentence of death;
>
> 3. An order denying a motion, made pursuant to section 440.20, to set aside a sentence of death;
>
> 4. An order denying a motion, made pursuant to paragraph (d) of subdivision eleven of section 400.27, to set aside a sentence of death.

Library References:

West's Key No. Digests, Criminal Law ⚖1023(11).

§ 39.41 Criminal Appeals—By the Prosecution in Death Penalty Cases

Criminal Procedure Law § 450.80 governs appeals by the government in death cases. It provides:

> An appeal directly to the court of appeals may be taken as of right by the people from the following orders of a superior court:
>
> 1. An order, entered pursuant to section 440.10, vacating a judgment including a sentence of death;
>
> 2. An order, entered pursuant to section 440.20, setting aside a sentence of death;
>
> 3. An order, entered pursuant to paragraph (d) of subdivision eleven of section 400.27, setting aside a sentence of death;
>
> 4. An order, entered pursuant to subdivision twelve of section 400.27, setting aside a sentence of death.[1]

2. See infra, §§ 39.40—39.41.

§ 39.41

1. Counsel should be aware that some determinations in capital cases are appeal-

§ 39.41

Library References:
West's Key No. Digests, Criminal Law ⚖1024(9).

§ 39.42 Criminal Appeals—Intermediate Appellate Courts

Every appeal in a criminal case from an intermediate appellate court order requires a certificate granting leave to appeal pursuant to Criminal Procedure Law § 460.20. In addition, the order sought to be appealed must be adverse or partially adverse to the party seeking leave to appeal.[1] An intermediate appellate court order of *affirmance* is adverse to a party who was appellant in that court. An intermediate appellate court order of *reversal* is adverse to party who was respondent in that court, and an intermediate appellate court order of *modification* is partially adverse to each party. An intermediate appellate court order denying or granting a *motion* is not one of affirmance, reversal or modification, and therefore is not adverse to any party within the meaning of the statute.[2]

The order also must have been entered upon an appeal to the intermediate appellate court pursuant to Criminal Procedure Law §§ 450.10, 450.15 or 450.20.[3] Therefore, denials of "free standing" applications, such as for a writ of error *coram nobis* or for leave to appeal, are not appealable.

When the order of the intermediate appellate court is one of *reversal* or *modification*, Criminal Procedure Law § 450.90(2) additionally requires, as a predicate to appealability to the Court of Appeals, that the Court of Appeals conclude that the intermediate appellate court's determination of reversal or modification was "on the law alone or upon the law and such facts which, but for the determination of law, would not have led to reversal or modification"[4] or "[t]he appeal is based upon a contention that corrective action, as that term is defined in Section 470.10, taken or directed by the intermediate appellate court was illegal."[5] Examples of determinations held not to satisfy Criminal Procedure

able by the People to the appellate division. See CPL § 450.20; § 38.10, *supra*.

§ 39.42

1. CPL § 450.90(1). For exceptions to the "partially adverse" category of appealable orders, *see* People v. Griminger, 71 N.Y.2d 635, 641, 529 N.Y.S.2d 55, 58, 524 N.E.2d 409, 412 (1988), and cases cited therein.

2. CPL § 450.90(1). Accordingly, the court has held nonappealable an order of the appellate division denying a motion for an extension of time to take an appeal to that court, notwithstanding that language in CPL § 460.30(6) suggests such order may, at least in some circumstances, be appealable. *See* People v. Nealy, 82 N.Y.2d 773, 603 N.Y.S.2d 991, 624 N.E.2d 175 (1993).

3. CPL § 450.90(1).

4. CPL § 450.90(2)(a). When the intermediate appellate court reverses or modifies, as described above, the basis for its determination—whether it is on the law, on the facts, made as a matter of discretion in the interest of justice, or on a combination of any or all three—determines appealability to the Court of Appeals. For a full discussion of the dispositional options available to the appellate division or other intermediate appellate courts, *see supra*, § 38.27.

5. CPL § 450.90(2)(b).

Law § 450.90(2)(a), and hence not appealable to the Court of Appeals, include reversal on an unpreserved issue,[6] unless the issue is of the type that need not be preserved.

Also not appealable are determinations of modification or reversal based on resolutions of mixed questions of law and fact, or pure questions of fact, such as probable cause to search or arrest (but whether the correct standard was employed may be a question of law which will support an appeal), whether a verdict is contrary to the weight of the evidence (factual question; but whether verdict was supported by sufficient evidence is a question of law which will support an appeal), or whether there has been consent to questioning or search.[7] An order of an intermediate appellate court dismissing an appeal taken to it also is appealable, although it does not fit the above definitions.[8]

§ 39.43 Criminal Appeals—Additional Limitations on Appealability

Even if an intermediate appellate court order is appealable, an appeal or application for leave to appeal to the Court of Appeals will be dismissed if it appears that the defendant is not available to obey the mandate of the Court of Appeals in the event of an affirmance of the conviction[1] or the defendant dies, in which case the prosecution abates.[2]

Library References:
    West's Key No. Digests, Criminal Law ⚖1023.

§ 39.44 Criminal Appeals—Appeals by Permission

Having covered the types of determinations of intermediate appellate courts in non-capital cases that are appealable by permission,[1] we turn now to the process for seeking leave,[2] for seeking a stay of execution,[3] and for perfecting, readying, and arguing the appeal.[4]

---

6. *See e.g.*, People v. Dercole, 52 N.Y.2d 956, 437 N.Y.S.2d 966, 419 N.E.2d 869 (1981). For an example of a case in which an appeal was held to lie despite the appellate division's reversal on an unpreserved point, *see* People v. Cona, 49 N.Y.2d 26, 34, 424 N.Y.S.2d 146, 150, 399 N.E.2d 1167, 1171 (1979)(appellate division erroneously concluded as a matter of law that an issue was preserved despite a failure to object). The Court of Appeals held its power to review was limited to the correctness of the appellate division's preservation determination; remittal to the appellate division was required to give it an opportunity to reach the underlying merits issue as a matter of discretion in the interest of justice.

7. For a list of mixed questions, *see* People v. Harrison, 57 N.Y.2d 470, 457 N.Y.S.2d 199, 443 N.E.2d 447 (1982).

8. CPL § 470.60(3).

§ 39.43

1. *See* People v. Shaw, 72 N.Y.2d 838, 530 N.Y.S.2d 551, 526 N.E.2d 42 (1988), dismissal vacated 72 N.Y.2d 950, 533 N.Y.S.2d 55, 529 N.E.2d 423 (1988).

2. *See* People v. Parker, 71 N.Y.2d 887, 527 N.Y.S.2d 765, 522 N.E.2d 1063 (1988).

§ 39.44

1. *See supra*, § 39.42.
2. *See infra*, §§ 39.46—39.47.
3. *See infra*, § 39.48.
4. *See infra*, § 39.49.

§ 39.44   COURT OF APPEALS   Ch. 39

Library References:

West's Key No. Digests, Criminal Law ⇔1072.

§ 39.45   Criminal Appeals—Appeals by Permission—Obligation of Intermediate Appellate Court Counsel

The rules of practice of all four departments of the appellate division and the Court of Appeals require assigned or retained defense counsel in the appellate division to file a timely application for leave to appeal to the Court of Appeals upon the client's request in the event of the appellate division's affirmance or modification of the defendant's conviction.[1] Thus, even intermediate appellate court counsel who has no intention of pursuing an appeal to the Court of Appeals must be familiar with the procedure for timely filing a criminal leave application.

§ 39.46   Criminal Appeals—Appeals by Permission—Who May Grant Leave to Appeal

From an order of the appellate division (except one dismissing an appeal taken to it), an application for leave to appeal may be made to a judge of the Court of Appeals designated by the Chief Judge to hear the application[1] or to any justice of the appellate division of the department which entered the order sought to be appealed.[2] Only one application is permitted,[3] which is to say that if a justice of the appellate division denies leave to appeal, there is no second "bite at the apple," as there is in motions for leave to appeal from final orders in civil cases. From an order of any intermediate appellate court *other than* the appellate division, or from an order of the appellate division dismissing an appeal taken to that court, the appellant has no choice, and must apply to a judge of the Court of Appeals only, as designated by the Chief Judge, to

---

§ 39.45

1. 22 NYCRR § 606.5 (First Department); 22 NYCRR § 671.4 (Second Department); 22 NYCRR § 821.2 (Third Department); 22 NYCRR § 1022.11 (Fourth Department); and 22 NYCRR § 500.10 (Court of Appeals). Note that the appellate division rules, insofar as they apply to appeals in *habeas corpus* matters, have not all been updated to reflect that a single dissent is no longer a predicate for an appeal as of right in a civil case. See supra, §§ 39.8—39.9.

§ 39.46

1. CPL § 460.20(2)(a)(i).

2. CPL § 460.20(2)(a)(ii). The statute inexplicably fails to require that the justice have been on the panel that issued the order. The Rules of the Second (22 NYCRR § 670.6(d)) and Fourth (22 NYCRR § 1000.13(p)(4)(iii)) Departments do so require. The applicant may choose the justice, including a dissenter, if any. *See also supra*, § 38.32.

PRACTICE POINTER: Counsel, given a choice between applying to a Judge of the Court of Appeals or a justice of the appellate division, will usually go to a Judge of the Court of Appeals. When there has been a dissenter at the appellate division, however, counsel may direct the application to that justice, who, it is hoped, will seek vindication of the dissenting view in the higher court.

3. *See e.g.*, People v. McCarthy, 250 N.Y. 358, 361, 165 N.E. 810, 811 (1929).

hear the application.[4] Contrast this with the procedure for granting leave to appeal in civil cases, in which motions are addressed to the full court, and which, in the Court of Appeals, are granted upon the concurrence of two judges.

Library References:

West's Key No. Digests, Criminal Law ⚷1072.

§ 39.47 Criminal Appeals—Appeals by Permission—Criminal Leave Application ("CLA") Practice

Time to Seek Leave to Appeal. Normally, an application must be made (by mailing the letter seeking leave to appeal) within 30 days of service upon the appellant or counsel of a copy of the order sought to be appealed.[1] The time begins running upon service of the order by the prevailing party.[2]

Extensions of Time. If the deadline for applying for leave to appeal is missed by less than a year, relief by way of a motion for extension of time for making a criminal leave application may be available.[3] There is no parallel provision for civil appeals.

The motion must be addressed to the full court in compliance with the court's rules of practice.[4] The motion must be made within one year after the expiration of the 30-day period for making a criminal leave application, and must allege facts supporting one or more of the statutory grounds for granting an extension. These include that the failure to timely make the application resulted from the improper conduct of a public servant or the improper conduct, death or disability of the defendant's attorney, or the inability of the defendant and his attorney to communicate, in person or by mail, concerning whether an appeal should be taken, prior to the expiration of the time within which to apply for leave to appeal due to the defendant's incarceration in an institution

---

4. CPL § 460.20(2)(b). *See e.g.*, People v. Habel, 18 N.Y.2d 148, 272 N.Y.S.2d 357, 219 N.E.2d 183 (1966), appeal dismissed and cert. denied sub nom. Burkard v. New York, 388 U.S. 451, 87 S.Ct. 2104, 18 L.Ed.2d 1313 (1967)(dismissal of appeal to appellate division under former Code of Criminal Procedure).

§ 39.47

1. CPL § 460.10(5)(a). Notice of entry need not accompany the order, as in civil cases.

2. People v. Washington, 86 N.Y.2d 853, 854, 633 N.Y.S.2d 476, 476, 657 N.E.2d 497, 497 (1995).

CAVEAT: The service and filing of a motion for reargument or reconsideration in the appellate division does not suspend or toll the running of the 30-day period, and an order of that court denying reargument or reconsideration is not itself appealable to the Court of Appeals. However, the pendency of a reargument motion should be indicated in the application for leave to appeal, and the assigned judge should be informed as soon as counsel learns of its disposition.

3. CPL § 460.30.

4. 22 NYCRR § 500.11 governs motion practice; only one copy of the papers need be served and filed on a motion for an extension of time. 22 NYCRR § 500.11(f).

and through no lack of due diligence or fault of the attorney or defendant.[5]

A motion under Criminal Procedure Law § 460.30 is available only to a defendant, not to the People.[6] The same statute applies to appeals to the appellate division.[7]

Leave Applications to Appellate Division Justice.[8] An application for leave to appeal to the Court of Appeals addressed to an appellate division justice should comply with the applicable rules of practice. As noted above,[9] the rules of the four departments[10] permit the applicant to choose the justice to hear the application, unlike the rule of the Court of Appeals,[11] which does not allow the applicant to choose the judge.

Leave Applications to Court of Appeals Judge.[12] An application intended for a Court of Appeals judge should be in letter form, addressed to the Chief Judge and marked to the attention of the Clerk of the Court. Counsel may not request that a particular judge consider the application. A copy of the "leave letter" must be sent to opposing counsel or the adverse party (formal affidavit of service is not required).

The following should be enclosed with the application (papers will be returned when the application is decided if requested in the "leave letter"):

1. briefs filed by *all parties* in the intermediate appellate court;

2. the order of the intermediate appellate court sought to be appealed;

3. the opinion or decision of the intermediate appellate court, and any relevant writings of other courts in the case; and

4. the bound record or appendix, if available.[13]

The letter requesting leave to appeal should state:

1. that an application has *not* been made to a justice of the appellate division;

2. whether oral argument of the application is requested;

3. whether there are any codefendants, and, if there are, the status of their appeals;

---

5. CPL § 460.30(1).

6. CPL § 460.30(1); People v. Bender, 70 N.Y.2d 670, 518 N.Y.S.2d 962, 512 N.E.2d 545 (1987).

7. See supra, § 38.14.

8. For a discussion of practice and rules, see supra, § 38.32.

9. See supra, § 39.46.

10. The First Department has no specific rule concerning applications for leave to appeal to the Court of Appeals in criminal cases. Counsel seeking such relief from a justice of that court should consult the clerk before filing papers. The Rules of the other departments may be found at: 22 NYCRR § 670.6(d) (Second Department); 22 NYCRR § 800.3 (Third Department); and 22 NYCRR § 1000.13(p)(4)(iii) (Fourth Department).

11. 22 NYCRR § 500.10.

12. For a sample form, see infra, § 39.90.

13. 22 NYCRR § 500.10(a).

Ch. 39 CRIMINAL LEAVE APPLICATION § 39.47

    4. the incarceration or bail status of the defendant;

    5. a request for stay or continuation of bail, if applicable; and

    6. the issues sought to be raised on appeal to the Court of Appeals, and why such issues are reviewable and leaveworthy.[14]

Assuming an order is appealable, an application also should present issues that are reviewable.[15] The issues sought to be raised must be preserved for the Court of Appeals' review by appropriate objection or request or motion, as the case may be, in the trial court.

There are issues which are generally not reviewable in the Court of Appeals, even if preserved:

    1. the excessiveness of a lawful sentence;

    2. whether a verdict is contrary to the weight of the evidence (compare this with sufficiency of the evidence, which is a legal question); and

    3. determinations predicated upon a factual question or mixed question of law and fact.

If the issues presented are reviewable, the ones most likely to warrant a grant of leave to appeal are:

    1. those on which the departments of the appellate division have split;

    2. those presenting questions of statewide impact or first impression;

    3. those involving recent United States Supreme Court decisions and how they are to be applied in New York (such as whether New York should adopt a different rule under the State Constitution);

    4. those possibly erroneously determined in a published writing at the intermediate appellate court, which may mislead other courts, the bar or the public;

    5. those involving construction of new statutory schemes.

In 1996, 2,797 applications for leave to appeal in criminal cases were assigned to judges of the Court of Appeals. Only 53, or 1.8%, were granted.[16]

14. 22 NYCRR § 500.10(a).

15. For a more detailed discussion of the scope of review of the Court of Appeals in criminal cases, see infra, § 39.50.

16. PRACTICE POINTER: Counsel whose application for leave is successful and who wishes to continue his or her representation in the Court of Appeals must move to be assigned. See 22 NYCRR § 500.11; see infra, § 39.53. Assigned or retained counsel in the Court of Appeals should serve and file the jurisdictional statement within 10 days after the date of the certificate granting leave to appeal. See 22 NYCRR § 500.2; see supra, § 39.26.

§ 39.47

Reconsideration; Time for Seeking. A request for reconsideration of a decision on a criminal leave application must be filed with the Clerk of the Court, not sent directly to the chambers of the judge who ruled on the original application for leave to appeal. A letter request, with a copy mailed to opposing counsel or the adverse party, is sufficient. A new judge or *en banc* hearing may not be requested—the request will automatically be assigned to the judge who ruled on the original application.[17] The request must be made within 30 days of the date of decision on the original application (not the date of service of the certificate). A judge of the Court of Appeals may permit a reconsideration request to be made after expiration of the 30 day period, but only for compelling reasons.[18]

A reconsideration request should not assert arguments not raised on the original application. The request should only indicate the points the assigned judge may have overlooked or misapprehended on the original application.[19]

If an application for leave to appeal is granted, the matter becomes an appeal before the full court; the respondent may not request reconsideration by the judge who granted leave to appeal, who has no authority to rescind a certificate granting leave to appeal. Of course, the full court may dismiss the appeal, either on respondent's motion or *sua sponte*, for want of jurisdiction or if appellant fails to timely perfect.

§ 39.48 Criminal Appeals—Appeals by Permission—Stays and Continuation of Bail

In non-capital cases, the taking of an appeal by either party generally does not automatically stay the execution of any judgment, sentence or order of either a criminal court or an intermediate appellate court.[1]

Pursuant to Criminal Procedure Law § 460.60, a judge to whom a leave application has been assigned may, upon reasonable notice to the People and opportunity to be heard, order an interim stay of the judgment pending the determination of the application for leave to appeal, and, if that application is granted, stay or suspend execution of the judgment pending determination of the appeal itself, and either release the defendant on recognizance, continue bail previously determined, or fix bail pursuant to Criminal Procedure Law Article 530. An order releasing a defendant on recognizance or bail may not issue if the defendant has received a class A felony sentence.[2] If the application for

---

17. 22 NYCRR § 500.10(b).
18. 22 NYCRR § 500.10(b); 22 NYCRR § 500.11(g)(3).
19. 22 NYCRR §§ 500.10(b), 500.11(g)(3).

§ 39.48
1. CPL § 460.40(1). For the rare exception, involving a People's appeal from an order reducing a count or counts in an indictment, or dismissing an indictment, *see* CPL § 460.40(2).
2. CPL § 530.50.

leave to appeal is denied, the interim stay terminates upon the signing of the certificate denying leave. Only one application pursuant to Criminal Procedure Law § 460.60 is permitted between entry of the order sought to be appealed and determination of the appeal by the Court of Appeals.[3]

Any stay pursuant to Criminal Procedure Law § 460.60 terminates if the appeal is not argued within 120 days of the issuance of the certificate granting leave to appeal, unless the Court of Appeals, upon motion pursuant to 22 NYCRR § 500.11, extends the time for argument or submission beyond the specified period of 120 days *and*, upon application of the defendant, expressly orders that the stay continue until the determination of the appeal or some other designated future date or occurrence.[4]

§ 39.49 Criminal Appeals—Appeals Practice

In non-capital cases, once the appeal is taken (*i.e.*, once the certificate granting leave to appeal has issued), the appeal is handled exactly as a civil appeal,[1] with two exceptions—no filing fee is required, and, since there is no appeal as of right in a non-capital criminal case, the jurisdictional inquiry procedure does not apply.[2] In an appeal arising from a grant of leave to appeal by a justice of the appellate division where that court has reversed or modified the determination appealed to it, *sua sponte* merits procedure ("SSM") may be used to examine jurisdiction.[3] Counsel in such case should be prepared to address, in addition to the propriety of SSM tracking and their arguments on the merits, whether the appellate division order of reversal or modification has vested the court with subject matter jurisdiction under Criminal Procedure Law § 450.90(2)(a). A criminal case may be selected for SSM for any other appropriate reason, for example, the presence of non-reviewable issues, such as whether a sentence affirmed by the appellate division is excessive.[4]

Thus, in a criminal case, appellant's counsel should serve and file the jurisdictional statement and await the clerk's response. The appeal may be tracked to the normal course of full briefing and argument—with or without alternate due dates for filings set by the court—or it may be tracked on SSM. The appeal in a criminal case is perfected in the same way a civil appeal is perfected, but no filing fee is required. The calendaring and oral argument of criminal appeals is the same as civil appeals.

§ 39.50 Criminal Appeals—Scope of Review

Generally. Article VI, § 3(a) of the New York State Constitution provides in pertinent part:

3. CPL § 460.60(2).
4. CPL § 460.60(3).

§ 39.49
1. See supra, §§ 39.26—39.31.

2. See supra, § 39.27.
3. See supra, § 39.30.
4. See supra, § 39.30.

§ 39.50 COURT OF APPEALS Ch. 39

The jurisdiction of the court of appeals shall be limited to the review of questions of law except where the judgment is of death, or where the appellate division, on reversing or modifying a final or interlocutory judgment in an action or a final or interlocutory order in a special proceeding, finds new facts and a final judgment or a final order pursuant thereto is entered.

The Court of Appeals in non-capital criminal cases may only review questions of law. The constitutional power to review questions of fact when the appellate division finds new facts on reversing or modifying a judgment is not exercised on the criminal side because Criminal Procedure Law § 450.90(2)(a) precludes appeals to the Court of Appeals from such appellate division orders.[1]

Harmless Error.[2] Criminal Procedure Law § 470.05(1) codifies the harmless error rule that applies to review in criminal cases:

> An appellate court must determine an appeal without regard to technical errors or defects which do not affect the substantial rights of the parties.

This harmless error rule has further been refined in the cases, which distinguish between nonconstitutional and constitutional error, and which apply different standards. The court has recently summarized the rule as follows:

> Constitutional error is harmless only if it is harmless beyond a reasonable doubt. The court's review of a constitutional error is based on the entire record, and involves a determination of the "probable impact of [for example] the codefendant's admission[ ] on the 'minds of an average jury.' "[3]

Nonconstitutional error may be harmless if it satisfies two criteria: (1) that evidence of the defendant's guilt is overwhelming, and (2) that there is no significant *probability* (rather than only a rational *possibility*), that the defendant would have been acquitted had it not been for the error or errors.[4]

In certain types of cases, the court has declined to apply harmless error analysis. Violations of the *Rosario*[5] rule, for example, usually

---

§ 39.50

1. When the appellate division affirms, its order is appealable to the Court of Appeals, which may only review such affirmed findings to determine whether support for them exists in the record.

2. *See also, supra,* § 38.19.

3. People v. Eastman, 85 N.Y.2d 265, 276–77; 624 N.Y.S.2d 83, 89–90, 648 N.E.2d 459, 465–66 (1995)(citations omitted).

4. *See e.g.,* People v. Crimmins, 36 N.Y.2d 230, 243, 367 N.Y.S.2d 213, 223, 326 N.E.2d 787 (1975); *see also,* People v. Seit, 86 N.Y.2d 92, 100, 629 N.Y.S.2d 998, 1002, 653 N.E.2d 1168, 1172 (1995) (Bellacosa, J., dissenting (collecting recent cases)).

5. *See* People v. Rosario, 9 N.Y.2d 286, 213 N.Y.S.2d 448, 173 N.E.2d 881 (1961), cert. denied 368 U.S. 866, 82 S.Ct. 117, 7 L.Ed.2d 64 (1961).

mandate reversal if raised on direct appeal.[6] The court also has declined to apply harmless error analysis to a verdict that may have been based on an illegal theory, such as cases in which the jury was charged on an unlawful presumption.[7]

Preservation. Criminal Procedure Law § 470.05(2) provides:

> For purposes of appeal, a question of law with respect to a ruling or instruction of a criminal court during a trial or proceeding is presented when a protest thereto was registered, by the party claiming error, at the time of such ruling or instruction or at any subsequent time when the court had an opportunity of effectively changing the same. Such protest need not be in the form of an "exception" but is sufficient if the party made his position with respect to the ruling or instruction known to the court, or if in response to a protest by a party, the court expressly decided the question raised on appeal. In addition, a party who without success has either expressly or impliedly sought or requested a particular ruling or instruction, is deemed to have thereby protested the court's ultimate disposition of the matter or failure to rule or instruct accordingly sufficiently to raise a question of law with respect to such disposition or failure regardless of whether any actual protest thereto was registered.

Unlike the appellate division, which has the authority to review an unpreserved point in the exercise of its interest of justice jurisdiction,[8] review by the Court of Appeals is limited, in noncapital cases, to questions of law. This usually means that preservation, by appropriate objection, motion or request to charge, is required.[9] A limited exception is that a "defendant in a criminal case cannot waive, or even consent to, error that would effect the organization of the court or the mode of proceedings prescribed by law."[10] It is important to note that if a question was properly preserved in the trial court, the Court of Appeals

---

6. People v. Banch, 80 N.Y.2d 610, 615–16, 593 N.Y.S.2d 491, 493, 608 N.E.2d 1069, 1072 (1992)(listing exceptions to *per se* reversal rule).

7. People v. Martinez, 83 N.Y.2d 26, 35, 607 N.Y.S.2d 610, 615, 628 N.E.2d 1320, 1325 (1993), cert. denied 511 U.S. 1137, 114 S.Ct. 2153, 128 L.Ed.2d 880 (1994).

PRACTICE POINTER: In criminal cases, defense counsel always should anticipate that the prosecution will argue harmless error, at least as an alternative to a contention that any error alleged by defendant was not actually error. If the issue is one that is not amenable to harmless error analysis, defense counsel would do well to say so initially.

8. *See supra,* § 38.21.

9. *See e.g.,* People v. Gray, 86 N.Y.2d 10, 18–22, 629 N.Y.S.2d 173, 175–77, 652 N.E.2d 919, 921–23 (1995)(contention of insufficiency of proof of element of defendant's knowledge of weight of drugs in possession charge cannot be reviewed on appeal absent motion to dismiss based on that ground).

10. *See* People v. Patterson, 39 N.Y.2d 288, 295, 383 N.Y.S.2d 573, 577, 347 N.E.2d 898 (1976), aff'd 432 U.S. 197, 97 S.Ct. 2319, 53 L.Ed.2d 281 (1977). For a list of specific errors that the Court of Appeals can reach even absent preservation. *See* People v. Ahmed, 66 N.Y.2d 307, 310, 496 N.Y.S.2d 984, 985, 487 N.E.2d 894 (1985). For a full discussion of this principle and its history, *see supra,* § 38.19.

may reach it even though it was not argued in or passed upon by the intermediate appellate court.[11]

Matters Not Reviewable or Reviewable to Limited Extent. Certain questions are not reviewable in the Court of Appeals. The contention that a lawful sentence is excessive, which can be reached by the appellate division, is not reviewable in the Court of Appeals.[12] Affirmed or undisturbed findings of fact, or determinations of mixed questions of law and fact, are reviewable by the Court of Appeals only to the extent that the court may determine whether there is support for them in the record.[13] Exercises of discretion by lower courts are reviewable in the Court of Appeals only to determine whether that discretion was abused as a matter of law,[14] or whether the court failed to take into account all the factors entitled to consideration.[15]

Capital Cases. Counsel should be aware that the scope of review of the Court of Appeals on direct appeals from orders or judgments of criminal courts in capital cases is not limited, either by the Constitution or statute, to questions of law. The statute defining the court's scope of review and its obligations is Criminal Procedure Law § 470.30, which reads in pertinent part as follows:

1. Wherever appropriate, the rules set forth in sections 470.15 and 470.20, governing the consideration and determination by intermediate appellate courts of appeals thereto from judgments and orders of criminal courts, and prescribing their scope of review and the corrective action to be taken by them upon reversal or modification, apply equally to the consideration and determination by the court of appeals of appeals taken directly thereto, pursuant to sections 450.70 and 450.80, from judgments and orders of superior criminal courts.

2. Whenever a sentence of death is imposed, the judgment and sentence shall be reviewed on the record by the court of appeals. Review by the court of appeals pursuant to subdivision one of section 450.70 may not be waived.

3. With regard to the sentence, the court shall, in addition to exercising the powers and scope of review granted under subdivision one of this section, determine:

---

11. CPL § 470.35; People v. Colon, 71 N.Y.2d 410, 413, note 1, 526 N.Y.S.2d 932, 933, note 1, 521 N.E.2d 1075, 1076, note 1 (1988), cert. denied 487 U.S. 1239, 108 S.Ct. 2911, 101 L.Ed.2d 943 (1988).

12. See People v. Thompson, 60 N.Y.2d 513, 521, 470 N.Y.S.2d 551, 555, 458 N.E.2d 1228, 1232 (1983).

13. See e.g., People v. Harrison, 57 N.Y.2d 470, 478–479, 457 N.Y.S.2d 199, 203, 443 N.E.2d 447, 451 (1982)(collecting cases).

14. See People v. Baxley, 84 N.Y.2d 208, 213, 616 N.Y.S.2d 7, 9, 639 N.E.2d 746, 748 (1994).

15. See People v. Rickert, 58 N.Y.2d 122, 132, 459 N.Y.S.2d 734, 739, 446 N.E.2d 419, 423 (1983).

(a) whether the sentence of death was imposed under the influence of passion, prejudice, or any other arbitrary or legally impermissible factor including whether the imposition of the verdict or sentence was based upon the race of the defendant or a victim of the crime for which the defendant was convicted;

(b) whether the sentence of death is excessive or disproportionate to the penalty imposed in similar cases considering both the crime and the defendant. In conducting such review the court, upon request of the defendant, in addition to any other determination, shall review whether the sentence of death is excessive or disproportionate to the penalty imposed in similar cases by virtue of the race of the defendant or a victim of the crime for which the defendant was convicted; and

(c) whether the decision to impose the sentence of death was against the weight of the evidence.

4. The court shall include in its decision: (a) the aggravating and mitigating factors established in the record on appeal; and (b) those similar cases it took into consideration.

5. In addition to exercising any other corrective action pursuant to subdivision one of this section, the court, with regard to review of a sentence of death, shall be authorized to:

(a) affirm the sentence of death; or

(b) set the sentence aside and remand the case for resentencing pursuant to the procedures set forth in section 400.27 for a determination as to whether the defendant shall be sentenced to death, life imprisonment without parole or to a term of imprisonment for the class A–I felony of murder in the first degree other than a sentence of life imprisonment without parole; or

(c) set the sentence aside and remand the case for resentencing by the court for a determination as to whether the defendant shall be sentenced to life imprisonment without parole or to a term of imprisonment for the class A–I felony of murder in the first degree other than a sentence of life imprisonment without parole.

Library References:
West's Key No. Digests, Criminal Law ⟱1134.

§ 39.51 Criminal Appeals—Disposition of Appeal

Various statutes govern the disposition of an appeal by the Court of Appeals. The court must affirm, reverse, or modify the order appealed to it, or it may dismiss the appeal.[1] Upon reversing or modifying, the court must order the appropriate corrective action.[2] The court also must remit the case to the intermediate appellate court or to the court in which the judgment was rendered, to follow the direction of the Court of Appeals.[3]

§ 39.52 Criminal Appeals—Motion Practice

The Court of Appeals' rules of practice do not distinguish between motions in civil and criminal cases. Section 500.11 of the rules governs motion practice in criminal cases, and its dictates should be followed. The motion papers must comply with the format requirement that they be 8½ x 11 inches and bound on the left.[1] For most motions other than reargument of an appeal, only a single set of papers, with proof of service of one copy on each other party, need be filed.[2] The most common types of motions filed in connection with criminal appeals are discussed below briefly.

§ 39.53 Criminal Appeals—Motion Practice—Poor Person Relief and Assignment of Counsel

Continuation of counsel's assignment at the intermediate appellate court—and payment for services rendered—is not automatic, and must be sought by motion pursuant to Section 500.11 of the Court of Appeals' rules of practice.[1] The clerk's office will secure an original file for assigned counsel upon request. Waiver of the required number of copies of records or appendices and briefs rarely is granted, but reimbursement of reproduction costs to $350 may be available.[2]

Library References:

West's Key No. Digests, Criminal Law ⚖︎1077.

§ 39.54 Criminal Appeals—Motion Practice—Extension of Time to Seek Leave to Appeal

A motion for an extension of time to seek leave to appeal must be made within a year after expiration of the 30–day period for seeking leave to appeal; otherwise, the Court of Appeals has no authority to

§ 39.51

1. CPL §§ 470.10, 470.60. For a detailed discussion of the intermediate appellate court's dispositional options, see supra, §§ 38.23–38.28.

2. CPL § 470.10(3); see CPL § 470.40 for the range of permitted corrective action.

3. CPL §§ 470.40, 470.45.

§ 39.52

1. 22 NYCRR § 500.1.
2. 22 NYCRR § 500.11.

§ 39.53

1. 22 NYCRR § 500.11.
2. 22 NYCRR § 500.10(c). For such motions to the appellate division, see supra, § 38.16.

grant it and the motion will be dismissed.[1] The statutory grounds should be examined, and at least one of them asserted in the motion papers. When the Court of Appeals grants such a motion, it usually treats the motion papers as a timely leave application under Criminal Procedure Law § 460.20, and its order so provides.

Library References:
West's Key No. Digests, Criminal Law ⚷1071, 1072.

§ 39.55 Criminal Appeals—Motion Practice—Dismissal of Appeal[1]

While the Court of Appeals has authorized the clerk to enter an order dismissing an appeal if not timely perfected,[2] the procedure for *sua sponte* examination of subject matter jurisdiction is generally not employed in criminal cases.[3] Thus, counsel for respondent who is certain that subject matter jurisdiction is lacking, and who does not wish to respond to an appeal on the merits, should promptly move to dismiss the appeal. Similarly, counsel aware of the death of the defendant or of the defendant's inability to obey the mandate of the court in the event of an affirmance should notify the court, or move for dismissal, depending on which side counsel represents.

Library References:
West's Key No. Digests, Criminal Law ⚷1131.

§ 39.56 Criminal Appeals—Motion Practice—Withdrawal of Appeal

A criminal appeal may be withdrawn prior to argument or submission by filing with the clerk a stipulation signed by all counsel and by the defendant personally.[1] After argument or submission, permission of the court to withdraw or discontinue an appeal must be sought by motion.

Library References:
West's Key No. Digests, Criminal Law ⚷1131(1).

§ 39.57 Criminal Appeals—Motion Practice—Reargument

A motion for reargument or reconsideration of an appeal must be made on 10 copies of a brief or memorandum, with proof of service of

§ 39.54
1. CPL § 460.30(1); see supra, § 39.47. For such motions to the appellate division, see supra, § 38.14.

§ 39.55
1. See generally, CPL § 470.60.

2. 22 NYCRR § 500.9(a), (b).
3. See supra, § 39.27.

§ 39.56
1. 22 NYCRR § 500.16.

three copies upon each other party to the case.[1] The criteria for granting reargument are that the court may have overlooked or misapprehended a point raised in the original briefs or oral argument.[2] A reargument request ordinarily is not the appropriate forum for raising new points.[3] A notice of motion for reargument must be served no later than 30 days after the appeal was decided, *not* after service of the court's *remittitur*.[4] The court may, in its discretion, entertain late motions for reargument.

Library References:

West's Key No. Digests, Criminal Law ⚖︎1133.

§ 39.58 Other Proceedings in the Court of Appeals

In addition to its appellate jurisdiction, described above, the Court of Appeals may entertain original proceedings to review determinations of the State Commission on Judicial Conduct,[1] certified questions from other courts,[2] and applications for waivers of, or determinations it is required to render under, the Rules for Admission of Attorneys and Counselors at Law, and the Rules for the Licensing of Legal Consultants.[3]

§ 39.59 Other Proceedings in the Court of Appeals—Review of Determinations of the Commission on Judicial Conduct

Article VI, Section 22 of the State Constitution provides for a Commission on Judicial Conduct. It provides that the Commission:

> [S]hall receive, initiate, investigate and hear complaints with respect to the conduct, qualifications, fitness to perform or performance of official duties of any judge or justice of the unified court system, in the manner provided by law; and, in accordance with subdivision d of this section, may determine that a judge or justice be admonished, censured or removed from office for cause, including, but not limited to, misconduct in office, persistent failure to perform his duties, habitual intemperance, and conduct, on or off the bench, prejudicial to the administration of justice, or that a judge or justice be retired for mental or physical disability preventing the proper performance of his judicial duties.[1]

§ 39.57

1. 22 NYCRR § 500.11(g)(1), (3).
2. 22 NYCRR § 500.11(g)(1).
3. 22 NYCRR § 500.11(g)(3); *see* People v. Bachert, 69 N.Y.2d 593, 597, 516 N.Y.S.2d 623, 625, 509 N.E.2d 318, 320 (1987).
4. 22 NYCRR § 500.11(g)(3).

§ 39.58

1. *See infra*, § 39.59.
2. *See infra*, § 39.60.
3. *See infra*, § 39.61.

§ 39.59

1. Sections 23 and 24 of Article VI provide alternative means for removal of a judge by the Legislature and by impeachment, respectively.

Article 2–A of the Judiciary Law contains the corresponding statutory provisions.[2] Review of a commission determination is by way of an original review proceeding in the Court of Appeals pursuant to Part 530 of the court's rules of practice.[3] In addition to reviewing a determination of the Commission, the court may, in certain circumstances, suspend a judge.[4]

Review of a determination must be requested by way of a writing to the Court of Appeals within 30 days after receipt.[5] No jurisdictional statement should be filed.[6] The petitioner judge or justice seeking review must perfect the proceeding by filing 10 copies of the brief and record on review with proof of service of three copies within 30 days after the date of the written request for review;[7] if the papers are not filed within the 30–day period, a 20–day demand and automatic extension letter will issue.[8] Ten copies of respondent Commission's papers, with proof of service of three copies, must be filed within 30 days after service of petitioner's papers.[9] If respondent does not file within that time, a 20–day notice and automatic extension letter will issue.[10] The petitioner may file 10 copies of a reply brief, with proof of service of three copies, within 10 days after receipt of respondent commission's brief. Further discretionary extensions may be available to the petitioner and the respondent commission during the respective 20–day demand period pertaining to each. No 20–day demand or extension is applicable to the reply filing.[11]

The scope of review on a proceeding to review a determination of the commission is broader than the court's scope of review on an ordinary civil appeal;[12] the Constitution commands that the court "review the commission's findings of fact and conclusions of law on the record of the proceedings upon which the commission's determination was based."[13]

A request for reargument of the Court of Appeals' determination must be upon 10 copies of the motion papers served within 30 days after

---

2. Article 2–A also contains the apparently misplaced or misnumbered Section 40–a, which addresses the purchase by the court system of recycled products.

3. 22 NYCRR §§ 530.1—530.9; see N.Y. Constitution, Art. VI, § 22(a) and Judiciary Law § 44(7).

4. N.Y. Constitution, Art. VI, §§ 22(e), (f); Judiciary Law § 44(8).

5. N.Y. Constitution, Art. VI, § 22(a); Judiciary Law § 44(7).

6. 22 NYCRR § 530.2.

7. 22 NYCRR § 530.2. The appendix method may not be used except by order of the court granted upon motion.

8. 22 NYCRR § 530.6(a).

9. 22 NYCRR § 530.4.

10. 22 NYCRR § 530.6(b).

11. 22 NYCRR § 530.2.

12. See Matter of Greenfield, 76 N.Y.2d 293, 558 N.Y.S.2d 881, 557 N.E.2d 1177 (1990).

13. N.Y. Constitution, Art. VI, § 22(d).

CAVEAT: In determining whether to seek review of an adverse Commission determination, counsel should consider that "[t]he court of appeals may impose a less *or more* severe sanction prescribed by this section than the one determined by the commission, or impose no sanction." N.Y. Constitution, Art VI, § 22(d)(emphasis added); *see also*, Judiciary Law § 44(9). In Matter of Sims, 61 N.Y.2d 349, 474 N.Y.S.2d 270, 462 N.E.2d 370 (1984), the court rejected the sanction of censure determined by the Commission and imposed the sanction of removal.

the court has rendered its judgment or order; as with an appeal, a reargument motion is not the appropriate forum for the assertion of new points, except for extraordinary and compelling reasons.[14]

§ 39.60 Other Proceedings in the Court of Appeals—Certified Questions From Other Courts[1]

The Court of Appeals may, in its discretion, determine a question of New York law for which no controlling Court of Appeals precedent exists. Such question may be certified only by the United States Supreme Court, any United States Court of Appeals, or the court of last resort of any other state. The question or questions certified must be "determinative" of the matter pending before the certifying court.[2]

Upon receipt of the required papers, the Court of Appeals will, on its own motion, examine the merits presented by the certified question to determine whether to accept it and, if accepted, the review procedure to be followed.[3] When the Court of Appeals has determined the certified question, its determination is transmitted by the clerk to the certifying court.[4]

§ 39.61 Other Proceedings in the Court of Appeals—Matters Regarding Admission of Attorneys and Licensing of Foreign Legal Consultants

The Court of Appeals has statutory authority to promulgate by rule the qualifications for admission of attorneys and legal consultants.[1] Investigation and assessment of the character and fitness of individual applicants, and the actual admission of attorneys and legal consultants, is the province of the appellate division.[2] An applicant may not be admitted unless the appellate division determines that qualifications promulgated by the rules of the Court of Appeals have been met.[3] If the qualifications of the rules have not been met, the applicant may seek from the Court of Appeals a waiver of strict compliance. Similarly, an

---

14. 22 NYCRR § 530.7(b).

§ 39.60

1. *See generally*, Nessler, *Interjurisdictional Certification in New York*, N.Y.L.J., 3/23/94, p.1, col.1; Sorrentino & Broudy, *Certification of Questions of Law by the Second Circuit to the New York Court of Appeals*, 65 NYSBJ 8.

2. 22 NYCRR § 500.17(a); *see* Retail Software Services, Inc. v. Lashlee, 71 N.Y.2d 788, 530 N.Y.S.2d 91, 525 N.E.2d 737 (1988); N.Y. Constitution, Art. VI, § 3(a).

3. 22 NYCRR § 500.17(d). The review procedures available are full briefing and oral argument, *see supra*, § 39.29, and SSM review pursuant to 22 NYCRR § 500.4, *see supra*, § 39.30.

4. 22 NYCRR § 500.17(g).

§ 39.61

1. Judiciary Law § 53.

2. Judiciary Law §§ 53(6), 90. See also, *supra*, § 37.6.

3. Judiciary Law § 90(1). The rules of the Court of Appeals for the Admission of Attorneys and Counselors at Law are set forth in 22 NYCRR Pt. 520. The rules of the Court of Appeals for the Licensing of Legal Consultants are set forth at 22 NYCRR Pt. 521.

applicant for admission who is required to take the bar examination, but who is declared by the Board of Law Examiners ineligible to sit for the exam because the qualifications promulgated by the court's rules have not been met, may seek a waiver from the court to be permitted to take the bar exam.

The procedure for seeking a waiver is set forth in 22 NYCRR § 520.14 (attorneys) and 22 NYCRR § 521.7 (legal consultants), which identically require the filing of a verified petition (which may be in letter form, as long as it is verified in front of a notary) setting forth the applicant's name, age, and residence address, the facts relied upon and a prayer for relief. A copy of the petition should be filed with the original. The court may, in its discretion, grant a waiver and allow the applicant to be admitted or to take the bar exam "where strict compliance will cause undue hardship to the applicant."[4]

The procedure prescribed by 22 NYCRR § 520.14 also must be followed by an applicant seeking admission to the bar without examination who seeks to combine more than one job or type of service to satisfy the total five-year practice requirement in lieu of examination. This combination of service determination, required by 22 NYCRR § 520.10(a)(2)(i)(d), is not technically a waiver but is sought in the same way. The applicant seeking such determination should state in the petition, with specificity, the beginning and ending dates of each service sought to be aggregated, the duties performed in each service, and the location at which the duties were performed. Full details regarding admission and good standing should be given for all applicable jurisdictions. Generally, petitions seeking waivers of the number of law school residency weeks required[5] will not be considered until after the administration of the bar examination immediately prior to the one for which the waiver is sought.

§ 39.62 *Certiorari* to the Supreme Court of the United States

State remedies are exhausted when leave to appeal to the Court of Appeals is denied following an appellate division determination, or after the Court of Appeals hears and determines an appeal. The party aggrieved has a final avenue for potential review: a petition to the Supreme Court of the United States for a writ of *certiorari*.[1] The petition must be filed with the Clerk of the Supreme Court within 90 days after entry of the order denying leave to appeal to the Court of Appeals, or 90 days

4. 22 NYCRR §§ 520.14, 521.7.
5. 22 NYCRR § 520.3(d), (e).

§ 39.62

1. *See* Rules of the Supreme Court of the United States 10–14 (hereinafter "Rule").

§ 39.62   COURT OF APPEALS   Ch. 39

after entry of the *remittitur* of the Court of Appeals determining the appeal to that court.[2] The petition will be granted only upon a showing of "compelling reasons," which include (1) a claim that the New York Court of Appeals (a court of last resort) has decided an important federal question in a manner that conflicts with a decision of the court of last resort of another state or of a federal Court of Appeals, and (2) a claim that a state court (*e.g.*, the appellate division or the Court of Appeals) has decided an important question of federal law (a) that has not been, but should be, settled by the United States Supreme Court, or (b) in a way that conflicts with relevant decisions of the United States Supreme Court.[3]

The Rules of the United States Supreme Court detail the number of copies to be filed (40, unless the petitioner is a poor person),[4] the docketing fee ($300.00),[5] filing and service requirements,[6] and what the petition should contain (the questions presented, a list of the parties, a table of contents, etc.).[7]

The Supreme Court of the United States grants *certiorari* and hears arguments on only about one per cent of the cases filed each term. When a petition for a writ of *certiorari* is filed, the judge or justice of the court whose determination is being reviewed may grant a stay of enforcement or execution of the judgment.[8]

§ 39.63   Procedural Checklists

What follows are checklists of the important considerations in various kinds of appeals to the Court of Appeals. These checklists assume no special circumstances apply, such as poor person relief, or specified filing dates other than those provided by the rules.

§ 39.64   Procedural Checklists—Civil Appeals as of Right[1]

1. Serve one copy and file two copies of notice of appeal with proof of service in the office of the clerk of the court of original jurisdiction; pay filing fee. (For components of notice of appeal, *see* § 39.71. For sample forms, *see* §§ 39.77—39.81)

2. Appeal must be taken within 30 days after service with notice of entry of the order appealed from, with five days added from mailing if adversary serves by mail, or one day added from deposit with carrier if adversary serves by overnight delivery. (*See* § 39.20)

2. Rule 13(5).
3. Rule 10.
4. Rule 12(1).
5. Rule 38(a).
6. Rule 12(3), (4), (5), (6).

7. Rule 14.
8. 28 U.S.C.A. § 2101; Rule 23.

§ 39.64
1. *See supra*, §§ 39.8—39.15.

3. Within 10 days after taking the appeal, serve one copy of Rule 500.2 jurisdictional statement and file two copies with proof of service in office of the Clerk of the Court of Appeals.[2] (*See* § 39.26)

4. Await notification from clerk as to how the appeal will be tracked and when papers need be filed. (*See* §§ 39.28—39.30)

§ 39.65 Procedural Checklists—Civil Appeals by Permission of Court of Appeals (*See* §§ 39.12—39.15)

1. Timely serve three copies of the motion for leave to appeal and file 10 copies with proof of service with the Clerk of the Court of Appeals.[1] (*See* § 39.19)

2. The motion papers must be served within 30 days after service, with notice of entry, of the order sought to be appealed, or, if leave was sought at and denied by the appellate division, within 30 days after service, with notice of entry, of the appellate division order denying leave. (*See* § 39.21)

3. Moving papers must be filed by noon of the Friday preceding the return date.[2]

4. If leave to appeal is granted, within 10 days after the date of the order granting leave, serve one copy of the Rule 500.2 jurisdictional statement and file two copies with proof of service in the office of the Clerk of Court of Appeals.[3] (*See* § 39.26)

5. Await notification from the clerk as to how the appeal will be tracked and when papers need be filed. (*See* §§ 39.28–39.30)

§ 39.66 Procedural Checklists—Criminal Appeals by Leave of a Court of Appeals Judge (*See Generally* §§ 39.37—39.48)

1. Timely file the application for leave to appeal consisting of a letter seeking leave, the order and decision of the intermediate appellate court sought to be appealed, any written orders and decisions reviewed by the intermediate appellate court and briefs of all parties filed in the intermediate appellate court.[1] (*See* § 39.47)

2. For the components of a jurisdictional statement, *see infra*, § 39.72. For sample form, *see infra*, § 39.82.

3. For the components of a jurisdictional statement, *see infra*, § 39.72. For a sample form, *see infra*, § 39.89.

§ 39.65

1. For the components of a notice of motion and affirmation in support, *see infra*, § 39.73. For a sample form, *see infra*, § 39.83.

2. 22 NYCRR § 500.11(a).

§ 39.66

1. For the components of a letter seeking leave to appeal, *see infra*, § 39.74. For a sample form, *see infra*, § 39.90.

2. The application must be served within 30 days after service of the order sought to be appealed. (*See* § 39.47) If the deadline is missed, consider the possibility of a motion for extension of time to file pursuant to Criminal Procedure Law § 460.30. (*See* §§ 39.47, 39.54)

3. If leave to appeal is granted, within 10 days after date of order granting leave, serve one copy Rule 500.2 jurisdictional statement and file two copies with proof of service in the office of the Clerk of Court of Appeals.[2] (*See* § 39.26)

4. Await notification from the clerk as to how the appeal will be tracked and when papers need be filed. (*See* §§ 39.28–39.30)

§ 39.67 Procedural Checklists—Civil Appeals by Leave of the Appellate Division[1] and Criminal Appeals by Leave of an Appellate Division Justice[2]

1. Within 10 days after the date of an order or certificate granting leave, serve one copy of the Rule 500.2 jurisdictional statement and file two copies with proof of service in the office of the Clerk of the Court of Appeals.[3] (*See* § 39.26)

2. Await notification from the clerk as to how the appeal will be tracked and when papers need be filed. (*See* §§ 39.28–39.30)

§ 39.68 Procedural Checklists—Appeals Selected for Expedited Review Pursuant to Rule 500.4[1]

1. Timely file with the Clerk of the Court of Appeals three copies of the appellate division record and three copies of each brief filed by each party in that court. Remember to include the $250 filing fee for a civil appeal.[2]

2. Timely file with the Clerk of the Court of Appeals three copies of the appellant's submission on the merits, with proof of service of one copy. Remember to incorporate by reference any argument in the brief counsel wishes the court to consider.[3] (*See* § 39.30)

3. If counsel cannot file within the initial 20-day period, he or she should either file or obtain an extension within the automatic 20-day extension period.[4]

2. For the components of a jurisdictional statement, *see infra*, § 39.72. For a sample form, *see infra*, § 39.82.

§ 39.67

1. *See supra*, §§ 39.12—39.16.
2. *See supra*, § 39.46.
3. For the components of a jurisdictional statement, *see infra*, § 39.72. For a sample form, *see infra*, § 39.82.

§ 39.68

1. *See supra*, § 39.30.
2. 22 NYCRR § 500.14.
3. 22 NYCRR § 500.4(f).
4. 22 NYCRR § 500.9(b).

4. Counsel for the respondent should timely file with the Clerk of the Court of Appeals three copies of the respondent's submission on the merits, with proof of service of one copy. Remember to incorporate by reference any argument in the brief that the court should consider.[5]

5. If filing cannot be accomplished within 15 days after receipt of appellant's submission, be sure to either file or obtain an extension within the automatic 20-day extension period.[6]

6. If counsel for the appellant intends to file a reply, he or she should file three copies of the reply with proof of service, or obtain an extension for doing so, within 10 days after receiving the respondent's submission.[7]

§ 39.69 Procedural Checklists—Appeals Tracked to Full Briefing and Oral Argument[1]

1. Timely file with the Clerk of the Court of Appeals 20 copies of the record on appeal to the Court of Appeals, with proof of service of three copies, or one original record and 20 copies of an appendix, with proof of service of three copies.[2] Include the $250 filing fee for a civil appeal.[3]

2. Timely file with the Clerk of the Court of Appeals 20 copies of appellant's brief, with proof of service of three copies.[4]

3. If counsel cannot timely file within the initial 60-day period, be sure either to file or obtain an extension within the automatic 20-day extension period.[5]

4. Counsel for the respondent should timely file with the Clerk of the Court of Appeals 20 copies of respondent's brief with proof of service of three copies.[6]

5. If counsel cannot timely file within 45 days after receipt of the appellant's record material and brief, he or she should either file or obtain an extension within the automatic 20-day extension period.[7]

6. If counsel for the appellant intends to file a reply, he or she should file 20 copies, with proof of service of three, or obtain an extension for doing so, within 10 days after receiving the respondent's submission.

§ 39.70 Drafting Checklists

What follows are various drafting checklists. These are to help ensure that filed documents are complete.

5. 22 NYCRR § 500.4(f).
6. See 22 NYCRR § 500.4(f); 22 NYCRR § 500.9(c).
7. See 22 NYCRR § 500.4(f); 22 NYCRR § 500.9(c).

§ 39.69
1. See supra, § 39.29.

2. 22 NYCRR § 500.5(a).
3. 22 NYCRR § 500.14.
4. 22 NYCRR § 500.5(d).
5. 22 NYCRR § 500.9(b).
6. 22 NYCRR § 500.7(a)(1).
7. 22 NYCRR § 500.9(c).

§ 39.71 Drafting Checklists—Notice of Appeal[1]

1. Court in which notice is to be filed. (*See* § 39.25)
2. Caption or style of case. (*See id.*)
3. Identity of the party taking appeal.
4. Description of judgment or order appealed (by court and date), and what portion is being appealed (usually all and each and every part).
5. Identity of the court to which appeal is taken.
6. Proof of service.

§ 39.72 Drafting Checklists—Rule 500.2 Jurisdictional Statement[1]

1. Caption or style of case. (*See* § 39.26)
2. Identity of the court from which appeal is taken.
3. Date of service and filing of notice of appeal, or date of entry of order granting leave to appeal.
4. Date and type of service upon appellant of order or judgment appealed from, with notice of its entry.
5. Name and address of attorney for respondent.
6. Authority for the assertion that the court has jurisdiction to entertain the appeal and review the questions raised.
7. Point headings of issues likely to be raised.
8. Proof of service.

§ 39.73 Drafting Checklists—Motion for Leave to Appeal to Court of Appeals Filed in Court of Appeals[1]

1. Notice of motion—indicate court in which filed and caption or style of case. (*See* § 39.19)
2. Notice of motion—indicate return date (available Monday per CPLR 5516 or, if Monday is a holiday, first day after such Monday that is not a holiday). (*See id.*)
3. Notice of motion—indicate identity of the party seeking leave to appeal.

§ 39.71
1. See infra, §§ 39.77—39.81.

§ 39.72
1. See infra, § 39.82.

§ 39.73
1. See infra, §§ 39.83—39.84.

4. Notice of motion—indicate relief requested, identifying order or judgment sought to be appealed (by court and date) and what part is being sought to be appealed (usually each and every part).

5. Supporting papers—concise statement of questions presented for review.

6. Supporting papers—statement of procedural history of the case, including showing of timeliness of the motion.

7. Supporting papers—showing that the court has jurisdiction, including showing of finality or that the order is appealable pursuant to CPLR 5602(a)(2).

8. Supporting papers—argument demonstrating why the questions presented merit review, such as that they are novel or of public importance, or involve conflict with prior Court of Appeals decisions, or that there is a conflict among the departments of the appellate division, identifying with specific record references as to where the questions raised were presented and preserved.

9. Proof of service of three copies.

§ 39.74 Drafting Checklists—Application for Leave to Appeal in Criminal Case Filed in Court of Appeals[1]

1. Name of defendant. (See § 39.47)

2. Relief sought (leave to appeal, stay, etc.).

3. Applicant's incarceration status.

4. Whether there are co-defendants, and, if so, the status of their cases.

5. Statement that no application has been made to another judge or justice.

6. Whether oral argument is sought.

7. Issues presented for review and court's jurisdiction and capacity to review, including preservation (or rely on arguments in intermediate appellate court brief or reserve right to submit additional written argument).

8. Indicate service on adversary.

§ 39.75 Drafting Checklists—Appellant's Brief on the Merits

1. Cover—name and address of counsel. (See § 39.29)

2. Cover—indication whether appeal is to be argued or submitted; if to be argued, name of arguing counsel and time requested.

§ 39.74   1. See infra, § 39.90.

§ 39.75   COURT OF APPEALS   Ch. 39

3. Cover—identity of the court in which brief filed.

4. Cover—caption or style of case.

5. Cover—date brief was completed.

6. Body—statement showing the court has jurisdiction to entertain the appeal and to review the questions raised, including citations to the record or appendix to establish preservation.

7. Body—table of cases and authorities cited.

8. Body—table of contents.

9. Body—statement of facts.

10. Body—legal argument, divided by point headings.

11. Body—conclusion, stating relief requested.

12. Proof of service of three copies.

§ 39.76   Drafting Checklists—Respondent's Brief on the Merits

1. Cover—name and address of counsel. (*See* § 39.29)

2. Cover—indication whether appeal is to be argued or submitted; if to be argued, name of arguing counsel and time requested. (*See id.*)

3. Cover—court in which brief was filed.

4. Cover—caption or style of case.

5. Cover—date brief completed.

6. Body—table of cases and authorities cited.

7. Body—table of contents.

8. Body—statement of facts.

9. Body—legal argument, divided by point headings.

10. Body—conclusion, stating relief requested.

11. Proof of service of three copies.

§ 39.77   Forms—Notice of Appeal to Court of Appeals From Order of Appellate Division Finally Determining Action With Two Dissents on Question of Law

SUPREME COURT OF THE STATE OF NEW YORK
COUNTY OF _____

[*Add title of cause*]

                          NOTICE OF APPEAL
                          Index No. _____
                          [*Name of Assigned Judge*]

Ch. 39   NOTICE OF APPEAL TO COURT OF APPEALS § 39.78

SIRS:

PLEASE TAKE NOTICE that the above named defendant [*or plaintiff*] hereby appeals to the Court of Appeals from an order of the Appellate Division, _____ Department, entered in the office of the Clerk of the Appellate Division on _____, 19__, which order affirmed [*or reversed*] the judgment of the Supreme Court, _____ County, in favor of plaintiff [*or defendant*] and against the defendant [*or plaintiff*] in the sum of _____ ($_____) Dollars, entered in the office of the Clerk of _____ County on _____, 19__.

Two Justices of the Appellate Division, _____ Department, dissented on questions of law in favor of the defendant [*or plaintiff*] and would vote to reverse [*or affirm*] the judgment of the Supreme Court on the law.

PLEASE TAKE FURTHER NOTICE that the defendant [*or plaintiff*] appeals from each and every part of the order of the Appellate Division as well as from the whole thereof.

Dated, _____, 19__.

Yours, etc.

_____
Attorney for Defendant
[*or Plaintiff*]
[*P.O. Address*
Tel. No.]

To: Clerk of the County of
_____,

  –and–

_____
Attorney for Plaintiff
[*or Defendant*]
[*P.O. Address*
Tel. No.]

§ 39.78 Forms—Notice of Appeal to Court of Appeals From Order of Appellate Division Finally Determining Action Where Construction of Constitution is Directly Involved

SUPREME COURT OF THE STATE OF NEW YORK
COUNTY OF _____

[*Add title of cause*]

§ 39.78 COURT OF APPEALS Ch. 39

NOTICE OF APPEAL
Index No. _____
[*Name of Assigned Judge*]

SIRS:

PLEASE TAKE NOTICE that the above named _____, pursuant to CPLR 5601(b)(1), hereby appeals to the Court of Appeals from an order of the Appellate Division, _____ Department, entered in the office of the Clerk of the Appellate Division on _____, 19__. The order unanimously affirmed the judgment of the Supreme Court of _____ County entered in the office of the Clerk of _____ County on _____, 19__, and finally determines this action, in which there is directly involved the construction of the provisions of Article _____ Section _____, of the Constitution of the State of New York [*or the United States*], and _____ appeals from each and every part of that order of the Appellate Division as well as from the whole thereof.

Dated, _____, 19__.

_____
Attorney for [*Appellant*]
[*P.O. Address*
Tel. No.]

To: Clerk of the County of _____

_____
Attorney for [*Respondent*]
[*P.O. Address*
Tel. No.]

§ 39.79 **Forms—Notice of Appeal to Court of Appeals From Judgment of Supreme Court Where Constitutionality of Statute Is Directly Involved** 💾

SUPREME COURT OF THE STATE OF NEW YORK
COUNTY OF _____

[*Add title and cause*]

NOTICE OF APPEAL
Index No. _____

[*Name of Assigned Judge*]

220

Ch. 39   NOTICE OF APPEAL TO COURT OF APPEALS § 39.80

SIRS:

PLEASE TAKE NOTICE that the above named plaintiff, _____, pursuant to CPLR 5601(b)(2), hereby appeals to the Court of Appeals from the judgment entered herein in the office of the Clerk of the County of _____ on _____, 19__, wherein it is adjudged that Local Law No. _____ of 19__ of the City of _____ is constitutionally valid. The plaintiff appeals from each and every part of that judgment as well as from the whole thereof.

Dated, _____, 19___.

Yours, etc.,

_____
Attorney for Plaintiff
[P.O. Address
Tel. No.]

To: _____
Attorney for Defendant
[P.O. Address.
Tel. No.]

_____
Clerk, _____ County

§ 39.80 Forms—Notice of Appeal to Court of Appeals From Appellate Division Order of Reversal Granting New Trial With Stipulation for Judgment Absolute

SUPREME COURT OF THE STATE OF NEW YORK
COUNTY OF _____

_____, Plaintiff, -against- _____, Defendant.	))) NOTICE OF APPEAL TO) COURT OF APPEALS) WITH STIPULATION) FOR JUDGMENT ABSOLUTE)) Index No. _____) [Name of Assigned Judge]))

SIRS:

PLEASE TAKE NOTICE that pursuant to CPLR 5601(c), the above-named defendant hereby appeals to the Court of Appeals from the order of the Appellate Division, _____ Department, entered in the office of the Clerk of the Appellate Division on the _____ day of _____, 19__,

§ 39.80   COURT OF APPEALS   Ch. 39

which order (1) reversed a judgment of the Supreme Court, _____ County, entered in the office of the Clerk of the County of _____, on the _____ day of _____, 19__, in favor of the defendant; and (2) granted a new trial to _____, the above-named plaintiff.

    PLEASE TAKE FURTHER NOTICE, that the defendant stipulates that, upon affirmance, judgment absolute shall be entered against him.

Dated, _____, 19__.

Yours, etc.,

_____

& _____
Attorneys for Defendant
[*P.O. Address*
Tel. No.]

To: _____ & _____
Attorneys for Plaintiff
[*P.O. Address*
Tel. No.]

_____

Clerk, _____ County

§ 39.81   Forms—Notice of Appeal to Court of Appeals From Judgment of Supreme Court to Review Prior Non-final Determination of the Appellate Division 💾

SUPREME COURT OF THE STATE OF NEW YORK
COUNTY OF _____

[*Add title of cause*]

NOTICE OF APPEAL
Index No. _____
[*Name of Assigned Judge*]

SIRS:

    PLEASE TAKE NOTICE that pursuant to CPLR 5601(d) and (a), the above named defendant [*or plaintiff*] hereby appeals to the Court of Appeals from a judgment of the Supreme Court, _____ County, entered in the office of the Clerk of said court on _____, 19__, in favor of plaintiff [*or defendant*] and against the defendant [*or plaintiff*] in the sum of _____ ($_____) Dollars.

    The appeal brings up for review a prior non-final order of the Appellate Division, _____ Department, entered in the office of the Clerk of the Appellate Division on _____, 19__, in which two Justices

Ch. 39   RULE 500.2 JURISDICTIONAL STATEMENT   § **39.82**

dissented on a question of law in favor of defendant [*or plaintiff*], which necessarily affects the judgment, and which satisfies the requirements of CPLR 5601(a) except that of finality.

PLEASE TAKE FURTHER NOTICE that the defendant [*or plaintiff*] appeals from each and every part of the judgment of Supreme Court as well as from the whole thereof.

Dated, _____, 19__

Yours, etc.

_____
Attorney for Defendant
[*or Plaintiff*]
[*P.O. Address*
Tel. No.]

To: Clerk of the County of _____

   –and–

_____
Attorney for Plaintiff [*or Defendant*]
[*P.O. Address*
Tel. No.]

§ **39.82** Forms—Rule 500.2 Jurisdictional Statement

STATE OF NEW YORK
COURT OF APPEALS

THE PEOPLE OF THE STATE OF NEW YORK,	
Respondent,	_____ Co.
-against-	Indictment No. _____/9_
_____,	
Defendant-Appellant.	

APPELLANT'S JURISDICTIONAL STATEMENT
(RULE 500.2)

1. The title of the case appears in the above caption.

§ 39.82   COURT OF APPEALS   Ch. 39

2. The appeal is taken from an order of the Appellate Division of the Supreme Court of the State of New York, _____ Judicial Department.

3. The order granting leave to appeal is dated _____, 19___.

4. The order appealed from is dated _____, 19___.

5. The attorney for the Respondent is _____, District Attorney, _____ County, [P.O. Address, and Tel. No.].

Annexed hereto please find the following exhibits:

A-1. Certificate granting leave to appeal.

A-2. Order and decision of the Appellate Division appealed from.

A-3. Decision-order of Supreme Court, _____ County, reviewed by the Appellate Division.

The court has jurisdiction to entertain this appeal because a certificate granting leave to appeal was duly issued by an Associate Judge of this Court (_____, J.), pursuant to CPL § 460.20(1). The issue raised is a question of law, duly preserved by defendant's specific references in defendant's motions for a trial order of dismissal and to set aside the jury verdict (CPL § 470.05[2]). The issue raised, consisting solely of a question of law, is within this Court's scope of review as provided by CPL § 470.35(2).

The issue likely to be raised (reserving the right to raise additional issues in defendant's brief and at oral argument) is set forth in the following point:

DEFENDANT'S FALSE ALIBI WAS INSUFFICIENT AS A MATTER OF LAW TO SATISFY THE REQUIREMENT OF CPL § 60.22(1) THAT, FOR A CONVICTION TO REST ON THE TESTIMONY OF AN ACCOMPLICE, THERE MUST BE CORROBORATING EVIDENCE TENDING TO CONNECT THE DEFENDANT WITH THE COMMISSION OF THE OFFENSE.

Yours, etc.

_____

Attorney for Defendant–Appellant
[P.O. Address
Tel. No.]

To:

Office of the Clerk
Court of Appeals of the
State of New York
20 Eagle Street
Albany, New York 12207–1095

Ch. 39   NOTICE OF MOTION IN COURT OF APPEALS § 39.83

Hon. _____
District Attorney
_____ County
[*P.O. Address*
Tel. No.]

§ 39.83 Forms—Notice of Motion in Court of Appeals for Leave to Appeal to Court of Appeals From Order of Appellate Division

STATE OF NEW YORK
COURT OF APPEALS

_____
)
_____, Inc.,   )
)
    Plaintiff–Appellant,   )
)   NOTICE OF MOTION FOR
        -against-   )   LEAVE TO APPEAL
)
_____ Insurance Company,   )
)
    Defendant–Respondent.   )
_____)

SIRS:

PLEASE TAKE NOTICE, that upon the annexed affidavit of _____, sworn to the _____ day of _____, 19__, the briefs and record on appeal in the Appellate Division, _____ Department, from the order of the Supreme Court, _____ County, entered in the office of the Clerk of the County of _____ on _____, 19__, dismissing Plaintiff–Appellant's amended complaint, the notice of entry thereof, the unanimous order of the Appellate Division, _____ Department, affirming that order of _____, 19__, entered in the office of the Clerk of the Appellate Division, _____ Department, on _____, 19__, the notice of entry thereof, the order of the Appellate Division, _____ Department, entered in the office of the Clerk of the Appellate Division, _____ Department, on _____, 19__, denying the motion of the Plaintiff–Appellant for reargument or, in the alternative, for leave to appeal to the Court of Appeals from the order of unanimous affirmance, the notice of entry thereof, and the brief of the Plaintiff–Appellant submitted herewith, and upon all the proceedings heretofore had herein, the undersigned will move this Court at a stated term thereof, appointed to be held at the Court House of the Court of Appeals in the City of Albany, State of New York, on the _____ day of _____, 19__, for an order allowing an appeal to be taken by the Plaintiff–Appellant to this Court

§ 39.83   COURT OF APPEALS   Ch. 39

from the order of unanimous affirmance, pursuant to CPLR 5602(a)(1), and for such other and further relief as this court considers appropriate.

Dated: _____, N.Y.
_____, 19__

                         Yours, etc.,
                         _____
                         and _____
                         Attorneys for Plaintiff–Appellant,
                         [P.O. Address
                         Tel. No.]

To: _____ & _____, Esqs.,
     Attorneys for Defendant–
Respondent,
     [P.O. Address.
     Tel. No.]

§ 39.84 Forms—Affidavit in Support of Motion in Court of Appeals for Leave to Appeal to Court of Appeals From Order of Appellate Division

COURT OF APPEALS
OF THE STATE OF NEW YORK
_____
)
_____, Inc.,   )
)
     Plaintiff–Appellant,   )
) AFFIDAVIT IN SUPPORT
       -against-   ) OF MOTION FOR LEAVE
) TO APPEAL
_____ Insurance Company,)
)
     Defendant–Respondent.   )
_____)

STATE OF NEW YORK   )
) ss.:
COUNTY OF _____)

     1. I am a member of the firm of _____ and _____, the attorneys for the Plaintiff–Appellant in the above entitled action, and I am familiar with all the facts and circumstances, pleadings, and proceedings heretofore had herein.

     2. This is a motion, pursuant to CPLR 5602(a)(1), for leave to appeal to the Court of Appeals after refusal of the Appellate Division,

226

_____ Department, to grant reargument or, in the alternative, to grant leave to appeal to the Court of Appeals.

3. This is an action to recover moneys had and received, paid under mistake of fact.

4. The Plaintiff–Appellant commenced this action on _____, 19__, and served an amended complaint on _____, 19__. The Defendant–Respondent moved to dismiss, which motion was granted by order dated _____, 19__. The Plaintiff–Appellant then appealed from that order to the Appellate Division, _____ Department. By order of the Appellate Division, _____ Department, dated and filed _____, 19__, the order of dismissal at Special Term was unanimously affirmed without opinion. In affirming the dismissal of this action, that order finally determines this action. That order of unanimous affirmance was entered in the office of the Clerk of the County of _____ on _____, 19__, and a copy thereof with notice of entry was served on the attorneys for the Plaintiff–Appellant on _____, 19__.

5. By notice of motion served _____, 19__, and returnable before the Appellate Division, _____ Department, on _____, 19__, the Plaintiff–Appellant applied to that Court for an order granting reargument or, leave to appeal to the Court of Appeals from the order of unanimous affirmance. That motion was in all respects denied by the Appellate Division by order entered in the office of the Clerk of the Court on _____, 19__; a copy with notice of entry thereof was served upon the attorneys for the Plaintiff–Appellant on _____, 19__.

6. No opinion was handed down either at Special Term or in the Appellate Division herein on the motions or on the appeal.

7. Filed herewith are copies of the record of the appeal to the Appellate Division, _____ Department, each party's briefs on the appeal in the Appellate Division, its order of unanimous affirmance with notice of entry, and its order denying Plaintiff–Appellant's motion for reargument with notice of entry or, for leave to appeal to this Court.

8. [*It is significant that in the court below, the Defendant–Respondent cited Bergholm v. Peoria Life Insurance Company, 284 U.S. 489, 52 S.Ct. 230, 76 L.Ed. 416 (see Point VI of the accompanying brief) to support the view, accepted by the Appellate Division, that the waiver of disability clause created a condition precedent which prevents recovery by Plaintiff–Appellant here. This Court has not had the opportunity, heretofore, of ruling on the effect of these clauses for waiver of premiums on disability.*]

9. No previous motion has been made in this Court for permission to appeal to the Court of Appeals.

For reasons which appear in the brief hereto attached, deponent respectfully asks that leave to appeal to the Court of Appeals be granted,

§ 39.84   COURT OF APPEALS   Ch. 39

in accordance with the provisions of CPLR 5602(a)(1), in the interests of substantial justice.

                                   [*Signature*]

                                   [*Type name*]

[*Jurat*]

§ 39.85   Forms—Notice of Motion in Court of Appeals for Reargument of Motion for Leave to Appeal

COURT OF APPEALS
STATE OF NEW YORK

[*Add title of cause*]

                               NOTICE OF MOTION
                               FOR REARGUMENT OF
                               MOTION FOR
                               LEAVE TO APPEAL

SIRS:

     PLEASE TAKE NOTICE that upon the attached Brief of Appellant and the Order of the Court of Appeals entered on _____, 19__, denying Appellant permission to appeal to this Court from an order of the Appellate Division, the undersigned Appellant will move this Court on the _____ day of _____, 19__, for reargument of the motion by Appellant for leave to appeal to this court from an order of the Appellate Division, and upon such reargument, for an order granting such motion for permission to appeal upon the ground that the points specified in the brief appended hereto were overlooked or misapprehended, and for such other and further relief as may be just and proper.

     Dated: _____, New York,
              _____, 19__

                               Attorney for Appellant
                               [*P.O. Address*
                               Tel. No.]

To: _____, Esq.
     Attorney for Respondent
     [*P.O. Address*
     Tel. No.]

§ 39.86 Forms—Notice of Motion in Court of Appeals for Leave to Appear *Amicus Curiae*

COURT OF APPEALS
STATE OF NEW YORK

_____

_____, & _____,

Plaintiff–Respondents,

-against-

_____ & _____ d/b/a
_____ & _____,

Defendants–Appellants.
_____

NOTICE OF MOTION FOR LEAVE TO APPEAR *AMICUS CURIAE*

SIRS:

PLEASE TAKE NOTICE, that upon a copy of the proposed brief, the annexed affidavit of _____, sworn to the _____ day of _____, 19__, and upon all the pleadings and proceedings in this matter, the (plaintiffs) will apply to this Court on the _____ day of _____, 19__, for an order granting [*the Consulting Engineers Council and the New York Association of Consulting Engineers*], leave to appear *amicus curiae* in the above-entitled appeal, and for such other and further relief as this court considers appropriate.

Dated: _____, N.Y.
_____, 19__

Yours, etc.

_____ & _____
Attorneys for Movants
[*P.O. Address*
Tel. No.]

To: _____ & _____
Attorneys for Defendants–Appellants,
[*P.O. Address*
Tel. No.]

_____ & _____
Attorney for Plaintiffs–Respondents,
[*P.O. Address*
Tel. No.]

§ 39.87 Forms—Notice of Motion to Dismiss Appeal as Untimely Taken

[*Add title of appellate court and cause*]

                    NOTICE OF MOTION
                    TO DISMISS APPEAL
                    Index No. _____

SIRS:

    PLEASE TAKE NOTICE that upon the annexed affidavit of _____, sworn to on the _____ day of _____, 19__, the notice of appeal dated the _____ day of _____, 19__, and the judgment [*or order*] of the _____ Court entered in the office of the clerk of _____, on _____, 19__, the _____ respondent will apply to this Court on the _____ day of _____, 19__, for an order dismissing the appeal taken by the _____ appellant from the aforesaid judgment [*or order*] of the _____ Court, entered in the office of the clerk of _____ on _____, 19__, upon the ground that _____ appellant has not taken [*his or her*] appeal within the time limited by CPLR 5513, and for such other and further relief as this Court considers appropriate.

Dated, _____, 19__.

                    Yours, etc.

                    _____
                    Attorney for _____ Respondent
                    [*P.O. Address*
                    Tel. No.]

To: _____
    Attorney for _____
Appellant
    [*P.O. Address*
    Tel. No.]

§ 39.88 Forms—Affidavit in Support of Motion to Dismiss Appeal as Untimely Taken

[*Add title of appellate court and cause*]

                    AFFIDAVIT IN SUPPORT OF
                    MOTION
                    Index No. _____

STATE OF NEW YORK   )
) ss.:
COUNTY OF _____   )

Ch. 39   FORMS—CPLR 5531 STATEMENT   § 39.89

1. I am the attorney for the _____ respondent and am fully familiar with all the proceedings had herein.

2. On the _____ day of _____, 19__, an order was entered in the office of the clerk of _____, which order [*briefly describe*].

3. On the _____ day of _____, 19__, a copy of that order, together with written notice of entry, was personally served upon the attorney for the _____ appellant as more fully appears from the affidavit of _____ annexed hereto as Exhibit A.

4. On the _____ day of _____, 19__, the attorney for _____ appellant served a notice of appeal from the aforesaid order as more fully appears from the affidavit of _____, a clerk in my office, annexed hereto as Exhibit B. That notice of appeal is annexed hereto as Exhibit C.

5. The _____ appellant failed to serve the annexed notice of appeal within thirty days after personal service upon [*his or her*] attorney of a copy of the aforesaid judgment [*or order*] appealed from together with notice of entry thereof, as required by CPLR 5513 and 5515.

6. The _____ appellant failed to file the notice of appeal in the office of the clerk of _____, in accordance with the requirements of CPLR 5513 and 5515, as more fully appears from the certificate of the clerk annexed hereto as Exhibit D.

WHEREFORE it is respectfully requested that this Court grant an order dismissing the appeal of the _____ appellant as untimely taken, together with such other and further relief as this Court considers appropriate.

[*Signature*]

_____
[*Type Name*]

[*Jurat*]

§ 39.89   Forms—CPLR 5531 Statement

STATE OF NEW YORK
COURT OF APPEALS

_____

THE PEOPLE OF THE STATE   )
OF NEW YORK,   )
)
        Respondent,   )   _____ Co.
)
        -against-   )   Indictment No. _____/9__

231

§ 39.89　　　　COURT OF APPEALS　　　　Ch. 39

_____,　　)
　　　　　　　　　　　　　)
　　　　　　　　　　　　　)
　　　　Defendant-Appellant.　)
_____)

STATEMENT PURSUANT TO CPLR 5531

1. The indictment number of the case in the court below is ___/9__.

2. The full names of the original parties are as appear in the above caption, except that defendant was jointly tried with a codefendant, _____ _____, who is not a party to this appeal and was not a party to the prior appeal to the Appellate Division.

3. The action was commenced in the Supreme Court, _____ County.

4. The action was commenced by the filing of an indictment on _____, 199__.

5. The action is a criminal prosecution for murder in the second degree (two counts) and robbery in the second degree (reduced at trial to robbery in the third degree).

6. The appeal is from an order of the Appellate Division, _____ Department (_____, P.J., (or J.P.), _____, _____, _____, and _____, JJ.), entered _____, 199__, which reversed an order of Supreme Court, _____ County (_____, J.), entered _____, 199__.

7. The appeal is on the original record and a reproduced appendix.

§ 39.90　Forms—Letter Seeking Leave to Appeal in Criminal Case

　　　　　　　　　　　　　　Counsel for Defendant–Appellant
　　　　　　　　　　　　　　[*P.O. Address*
　　　　　　　　　　　　　　Tel. No.]

Chief Judge of the Court of Appeals
Court of Appeals Hall
20 Eagle Street
Albany, New York 12207-1095

　　Attention: Clerk of the Court

　　Re: People v. _____

Dear Chief Judge:

　　Pursuant to CPL § 460.20, defendant seeks leave to appeal to the Court of Appeals from an order of the Appellate Division, _____ Department, entered on _____, 199__ and served on defense counsel [*personally*][*by mail*] on _____, 199__, which affirmed a judgment of

232

[*County*][*Supreme*] Court, _____ County, rendered on _____, 199__, convicting defendant, upon a [*jury verdict*][*verdict following bench trial*][*guilty plea*] of robbery in the first degree [*or another crime or crimes*] and imposing sentence.

Defendant is incarcerated pursuant to the judgment and sentence. No stay is being sought. There were no codefendants. No application for this relief has been made to any other court, judge or justice. Oral argument of this application is not requested.

Enclosed please find the briefs filed by both parties in the Appellate Division, and the decision and order of that court sought to be appealed. The issues upon which leave is sought are set forth in defendant's Appellate Division brief, which contains a detailed discussion of those issues and how they have been preserved.

Kindly advise me of the Judge to whom this application is assigned, so that I may submit a more detailed argument in support.

Very truly yours,

_____
Counsel for Defendant–Appellant

cc: Hon. _____,
    District Attorney,

    _____,
    Defendant

*

TABLE OF JURY INSTRUCTIONS

Chapter 30. Damages

30.60 Pattern Jury Instructions.
30.61 ____ Personal Injury—Subsequent Injury—Accident.
30.62 ____ ____ Loss of Earnings.
30.63 ____ ____ Damages—Shock and Fright and Physical Consequences.
30.64 ____ ____ Aggravation of Injury.
30.65 ____ Payment of Income Taxes on Damages for Personal Injury.
30.66 ____ Reduction of Present Value.
30.67 ____ Wrongful Death—Conscious Pain and Suffering.
30.68 ____ Personal Injury—Collateral Sources—Itemized Verdict(CPLR 4111).
30.69 ____ Damages—Property With Market Value.
30.70 ____ ____ Property With Market Value.
30.71 ____ Contracts–Damages—General.
30.72 ____ ____ ____ Employment Contract.

TABLE OF FORMS

Chapter 1. Business Organizations: Corporations

1.150 Form—Application to Reserve Corporate Name.
1.151 ____ Certificate of Incorporation.
1.152 ____ Bylaws.
1.153 ____ Subscription Agreement.
1.154 ____ Certificate of Amendment.
1.155 ____ Certificate of Dissolution.

Chapter 2. Non-corporate Entities: Limited Liability Companies and Partnerships

2.110 Forms.
2.111 ____ LLC Articles of Organization.
2.112 ____ Operating Agreement: Member–Managed LLC.
2.113 ____ Registration as LLP.
2.114 ____ Certificate of Limited Partnership.
2.115 ____ Limited Partnership Agreement.

Chapter 3. Municipal Law

3.36 Forms.
3.37 ____ Notice of Claim.
3.38 ____ Verified Complaint in Tort Action.

Chapter 4. Administrative Law

4.87 Forms.
4.88 ____ Notice of Appearance in Licensing or Permitting Matter.
4.89 ____ Notice for Discovery and Inspection in an Administrative Proceeding.
4.90 ____ Notice of Deposition in an Administrative Proceeding.
4.91 ____ Notice to Permit Entry Upon Real Property.

Chapter 5. Commercial Sales Contracts

5.65 Forms—Order of Goods for Resale by Buyer.
5.66 ____ Verified Complaint On Account Stated for Goods, Services and Wares Delivered.
5.67 ____ Plaintiff's Notice of Motion for Summary Judgment in Contract Action.
5.68 ____ Affidavit of Vice President of Plaintiff Purchaser in Support of Summary Judgment Motion in Contract Action.
5.69 ____ Notice of Petition for Order Staying Arbitration in Dispute Over Contract for Sale of Goods.
5.70 ____ Petition for Order Staying Arbitration in Dispute Over Contract for Sale of Goods.
5.71 ____ Affidavit in Opposition to Petition for Order Staying Arbitration in Dispute Over Contract for Sale of Goods.

FORMS

5.72 ____ Answer to Petition for Order Staying Arbitration in Dispute Over Contract for Sale of Goods.

Chapter 6. Buying and Selling a Small Business

6.186 Forms.
6.187 ____ Asset Purchase and Sale Agreement.
6.188 ____ Agreement of Purchase and Sale of Stock.

Chapter 7. Consumer Law

7.49 Forms—Lemon Law Document Request Pursuant to 13 NYCRR § 300.9(a).
7.50 ____ Notice of Petition to Vacate Lemon Law Arbitration Award Pursuant to CPLR Article 75.
7.51 ____ Petition to Vacate Lemon Law Arbitration Award Pursuant to CPLR Article 75.
7.52 ____ Complaint for Fraud, Breach of Warranties, Deceptive Business Practices, Used Car Lemon Law, Rescission and Revocation of Acceptance for Fraudulent Leasing Practices.
7.53 ____ Answer and Third-party Complaint Alleging Fraud, Deceptive Practices, Breach of Warranty, and Federal Odometer Law Claims in Fraudulent Automobile Lease Case.
7.54 ____ Answer to Complaint by Automobile Leasing Company for Deficiency Following Repossession, Alleging Commercially Unreasonable Resale and Deceptive Business Practices.
7.55 ____ Affirmation in Opposition to Lessor's Motion for Summary Judgment and in Support of Lessee's Cross-motion for Summary Judgment Alleging Commercially Unreasonable Resale.
7.56 ____ Notice of Rescission And/or Revocation of Acceptance and Demand for Restitution Pursuant to UCC 2–601 and 2–608.
7.57 ____ Order to Show Cause in Proceeding under Lien Law § 201–a to Vacate Garageman's Lien.
7.58 ____ Verified Petition in Proceeding under Lien Law § 201–a to Vacate Garageman's Lien.
7.59 ____ Affirmation in Support of Petition in Proceeding under Lien Law § 201–a to Vacate Garageman's Lien.
7.60 ____ Complaint Against Credit Reporting Agency Alleging Violations of the Fair Credit Reporting Act and the New York State Fair Credit Reporting Act and Deceptive Business Practices.
7.61 ____ Stipulation of Settlement of Plaintiff's Lemon Law Claims Providing for Cancellation of Lease and Deletion of Any Derogatory Credit Information.
7.62 ____ Complaint Alleging Violations of the Fair Debt Collection Practices Act and the Deceptive Practices Act.
7.63 ____ Order to Show Cause with Temporary Restraining Order, Seeking Preliminary Injunction in Action Alleging Fraud, Deceptive Business Practices and Breach of Warranties.
7.64 ____ Affirmation in Support of Temporary Restraining Order and Preliminary Injunction in Action Alleging Fraud, Deceptive Business Practices and Breach of Warranties.
7.65 ____ Complaint in Action Alleging Fraud, Deceptive Business Practices and Breach of Warranties.

FORMS

Chapter 8. Enforcement of Money Judgments

8.46 Forms.
8.47 ____ Statement For Judgment (Default Judgment), Affidavit of Facts Constituting the Claim, the Default and the Amount Due.
8.48 ____ Affidavit of Confession of Judgment and Judgment by Confession.
8.49 ____ Notice to Judgment Debtor [or Obligor].
8.50 ____ Subpoena (*Duces Tecum*) To Take Deposition of Judgment Debtor With Restraining Notice.
8.51 ____ Subpoena (*Duces Tecum*) To Take Deposition of Witness With Restraining Notice.
8.52 ____ Information Subpoena.
8.53 ____ Restraining Notice to Judgment Debtor.
8.54 ____ Execution.
8.55 ____ Income Execution.
8.56 ____ Affirmation and Order To Show Cause To Punish Judgment Debtor—Witness For Contempt.

Chapter 9. Bankruptcy

9.305 Forms—Notice of Appearance and Demand for Service of Documents.
9.306 ____ Contested Matter—Motion.
9.307 ____ ____ Notice of Motion.
9.308 ____ ____ Proposed Order.
9.309 ____ Adversary Proceeding—Complaint.
9.310 ____ Retention of Professionals—Application.
9.311 ____ ____ Affidavit.
9.312 ____ Plan Provision for Retention of Jurisdiction.

Chapter 10. Mechanic's Liens

10.108 Forms.
10.109 ____ Notice of Mechanic's Lien—General Form.
10.110 ____ Notice of Lien for Public Improvement.
10.111 ____ Form for Demand for Terms of Contract.
10.112 ____ Demand for Notice of Completion and Acceptance of Public Improvement.
10.113 ____ Petition to Amend Notice of Mechanic's Lien—Correct Name of Owner of Property.
10.114 ____ Assignment of Lien for Public Improvement.
10.115 ____ Assignment of Mechanic's Lien.
10.116 ____ Assignment of Moneys Due or to Become Due Under Public Improvement Contract.
10.117 ____ Affidavit for Continuance of Mechanic's Lien.
10.118 ____ Affidavit for Continuance of Lien for Public Improvement.
10.119 ____ Petition to Discharge Mechanic's Lien Where Notice of Lien Defective.
10.120 ____ Petition for Order Discharging Mechanic's Lien Upon Filing of Undertaking.
10.121 ____ Undertaking to Discharge Mechanic's Lien.
10.122 ____ Petition for Order Fixing Amount of Undertaking to Discharge Mechanic's Lien.

FORMS

10.123 ____ Approval by Lienors of Subordination of Mechanic's Liens to Trust Bond or Note and Mortgage.
10.124 ____ Affidavit for Order Fixing Amount of Bond to Discharge All Mechanic's Liens.
10.125 ____ Petition for Order Requiring Itemized Statement.
10.126 ____ Notice of Application for Order Requiring Itemized Statement.
10.127 ____ Demand for Itemized Statement.
10.128 ____ Affidavit in Support of Application to Cancel Mechanic's Lien for Failure to Furnish Itemized Statement.
10.129 ____ Notice Requiring Lienor to Commence Action to Enforce Mechanic's Lien.
10.130 ____ Affidavit in Support of Application to Cancel Notice of Mechanic's Lien for Failure to Commence Action.
10.131 ____ Notice Requiring Lienor to Commence Action to Enforce Lien for Public Improvement.
10.132 ____ Affidavit in Support of Application to Cancel Notice of Lien for Public Improvement for Failure to Commence Action.
10.133 ____ Complaint for Foreclosure of Lien for Public Improvement.
10.134 ____ Complaint for Foreclosure of Mechanic's Lien—Contractor.
10.135 ____ Defense and Counterclaim Based on Wilful Exaggeration of Mechanic's Lien.
10.136 ____ Affidavit in Support of Motion to Consolidate Actions for Foreclosure of Mechanic's Liens.
10.137 ____ Notice of Motion to Consolidate Actions to Foreclose Mechanic's Liens.
10.138 ____ Acceptance of Offer to Pay Money Into Court in Discharge of Mechanic's Lien.
10.139 ____ Offer to Pay Money Into Court in Discharge of Mechanic's Lien.
10.140 ____ Judgment of Foreclosure and Sale—Mechanic's Lien.
10.141 ____ Judgment of Foreclosure—Lien for Public Improvement—Where Lien Discharged and Fund Retained for Payment.
10.142 ____ Affidavit in Support of Motion for Summary Judgment—Foreclosure of Lien for Public Improvement.
10.143 ____ Demand for Verified Statement from Trustee.
10.144 ____ Petition or Verified Statement from Trustee of Trust Funds.
10.145 ____ Complaint by Subcontractor to Enforce Trust Against Funds Received by Contractor or Assignee of Contractor.
10.146 ____ Complaint by Surety to Have Parties Declared Trustees of Subcontract Moneys and for Accounting.
10.147 ____ Affidavit in Support of Motion to Determine if Class Action Can be Maintained—Action to Impress and Enforce Trust.

Chapter 11. Mortgage Foreclosure

11.68 Forms.
11.69 ____ Notice of Default.
11.70 ____ Notice of Acceleration.
11.71 ____ Notice of Pendency of Action.
11.72 ____ Summons.
11.73 ____ Verified Complaint for Foreclosure of Mortgage Affecting Single Family Residence.

FORMS

11.74 ____ Verified Complaint for Foreclosure of Mortgage Affecting Commercial, Multi–Unit Residential or Mixed Property.
11.75 ____ Order Appointing Receiver.
11.76 ____ Affidavit in Support of Motion for Appointment of Receiver.
11.77 ____ Notice of Motion for Summary Judgment and Related Relief.
11.78 ____ Affidavit of Regularity and in Support of Motion for Summary Judgment.
11.79 ____ Judgment of Foreclosure and Sale.
11.80 ____ Notice of Sale.
11.81 ____ Terms and Memorandum of Sale.

Chapter 12. Purchase and Sale of Real Estate

12.92 Forms.
12.93 ____ Residential Contract of Sale.
12.94 ____ Contract of Sale—Condominium Unit.
12.95 ____ ____ Office, Commercial and Multi–Family Residential Premises.
12.96 ____ ____ Cooperative Apartment.
12.97 ____ Durable General Power of Attorney.
12.98 ____ Power of Attorney to Take Effect at a Later Time.

Chapter 13. Landlord–Tenant Law

13.82 Forms.
13.83 ____ Petition Non-payment.
13.84 ____ Petition Holdover.
13.85 ____ Individual Verification.
13.86 ____ Corporate Officer Verification.
13.87 ____ Partnership Verification.
13.88 ____ Attorney Verification.
13.89 ____ Stipulations.
13.90 ____ ____ Settling Non-payment Proceeding.
13.91 ____ ____ Settling Non-payment Proceeding with Final Judgment in Favor of Petitioner.
13.92 ____ ____ Settling Holdover Proceeding Where Tenant Agrees to Cure Lease Violation.
13.93 ____ ____ Settling Holdover Proceeding Where Tenant–Respondent Agrees to Vacate Premises.

Chapter 14. Eminent Domain

14.120 Forms—Demand on Condemnor to File Copy of Proceedings to Determine Need and Location of Public Project with Appellate Division for Purpose of Judicial Review.
14.121 ____ Petition for Review of Determination and Finding that Public Use, Benefit or Purpose Will be Served by Proposed Acquisition.
14.122 ____ Judgment of Appellate Division Rejecting the Determination and Finding that Public Use, Benefit or Purpose Will be Served by Proposed Acquisition.
14.123 ____ Complaint by Condemnee to Establish Fair and Reasonable Value for Temporary Use and Occupancy After Acquisition by Eminent Domain.
14.124 ____ Notice of Pendency of Proceeding in Supreme Court to Acquire Property by Eminent Domain and File Acquisition Map.

FORMS

14.125 _____ Notice of Petition in Proceeding in Supreme Court to Acquire Property by Eminent Domain and File Acquisition Map.
14.126 _____ Petition in Proceeding in Supreme Court to Acquire Property by Eminent Domain and File Acquisition Map.
14.127 _____ Petition in Proceeding in Supreme Court to Acquire Property by Eminent Domain and File Acquisition Map—Petitioner Exempt from Compliance with Eminent Domain Procedure Law Article 2.
14.128 _____ Answer to Petition in Proceeding in Supreme Court to Acquire Property by Eminent Domain and File Acquisition Map.
14.129 _____ Order to Show Cause Why Condemnor Should Not be Permitted to Enter Immediately upon Real Property and Devote It Temporarily to Public Use Specified in Petition upon Deposit of a Fixed Sum with the Court.
14.130 _____ Order to Show Cause Why Condemnor Should Not be Permitted to File Acquisition Maps or Enter upon Real Property.
14.131 _____ Order in Proceeding in Supreme Court to Acquire Property by Eminent Domain and File Acquisition Map.
14.132 _____ Notice of Acquisition by Eminent Domain Where Supreme Court Has Jurisdiction.
14.133 _____ Claim for Damages Arising from Acquisition by Eminent Domain—General Form.
14.134 _____ Judgment Awarding Compensation in Claim for Acquisition of Property by Eminent Domain.
14.135 _____ Notice of Motion for Additional Allowance to Condemnee for Expert Witnesses.
14.136 _____ Affidavit in Support of Motion for Additional Allowance to Condemnee for Expert Witnesses.
14.137 _____ Order Granting Additional Allowance to Condemnee for Expert Witnesses.

Chapter 15. Environmental Law

15.40 Forms—Clean Water Act Citizen Suit Notice Letter.
15.41 _____ Clean Water Act and Resource Conservation and Recovery Act Citizen Suit Notice Letter.
15.42 _____ Clean Water Act Complaint.
15.43 _____ Nuisance and Trespass Complaint.
15.44 _____ Oil Spill Complaint.

Chapter 16. Land Use Law

16.133 Forms—Environmental Assessment—Short Form.
16.134 _____ Environmental Assessment—Long Form.

Chapter 17. Employment Law

17.86 Forms—Client (Plaintiff) Intake Questionnaire.
17.87 _____ Severance/Release Agreement.
17.88 _____ Letter to EEOC Requesting "Mohasco" Waiver of State Processing.
17.89 _____ Charge of Discrimination—New York State Division of Human Rights (Official Form).
17.90 _____ Information Sheet—New York State Division of Human Rights (Official Form).
17.91 _____ SDHR Information Sheet.

FORMS

17.92 ____ Charge of Discrimination—Equal Employment Opportunity Commission (Official Form).
17.93 ____ Affidavit for a Charge of Discrimination—Equal Employment Opportunity Commission (Official Form).
17.94 ____ Equal Employment Opportunity Commission Filing Cover Letter Requesting Equal Employment Opportunity Commission Processing of Dual-filed Charge.
17.95 ____ Letter Requesting Administrative Convenience Dismissal from State or City Administrative Agency.
17.96 Pleadings—New York State Complaint.
17.97 ____ New York State Answer.
17.98 ____ ____ Federal Complaint.
17.99 ____ ____ Federal Answer.

Chapter 18. Civil Rights Law

18.91 Forms.
18.92 ____ Complaint for False Arrest, False Imprisonment and Malicious Prosecution.
18.93 ____ Complaint for Excessive Force.
18.94 ____ Complaint for Return of Seized Property.
18.95 ____ Complaint Against Landlord for Housing Discrimination.
18.96 ____ Complaint Against Cooperative for Discrimination.
18.97 ____ Notice of Commencement of Action for Discrimination.
18.98 ____ Complaint for Discrimination in Place of Public Accommodation.
18.99 ____ Petition to Change Name.

Chapter 19. Immigration and Nationality Law
Permanent Residence Applications

19.75 Forms.
19.76 ____ Form I–130.
19.77 ____ Form I–140.
19.78 ____ Form I–485.
19.79 ____ Form OF–230.

Chapter 20. Adoptions

20.133 Forms—Private Placement Adoptions—Petition for Certification as a Qualified Adoptive Parent.
20.134 ____ ____ Petition for Temporary Guardianship.
20.135 ____ ____ Judicial Consent of Natural Parent.
20.136 ____ ____ Extra-judicial Consent of Natural Parent.
20.137 ____ ____ Petition for Adoption.
20.138 ____ ____ Order of Adoption (Private Placement).
20.139 ____ Agency Adoptions—Petition for Adoption.
20.140 ____ ____ Verified Schedule.
20.141 ____ ____ Marital Affidavit.
20.142 ____ ____ Marital Affidavit Dispensing With Consent of Spouse After Three Year Separation.
20.143 ____ ____ Confidential Affidavit.
20.144 ____ ____ Affidavit Pursuant to Section 111–a of the Domestic Relations Law.
20.145 ____ ____ Agreement of Adoption and Consent.
20.146 ____ ____ Affidavit Identifying Party.

FORMS

20.147   ____ ____ Affidavit of Financial Disclosure by Parents.
20.148   ____ ____ Order of Adoption.

Chapter 21. Domestic Relations

21.84   Forms.
21.85   ____ Retainer Agreement.
21.86   ____ Complaint for Divorce.
21.87   ____ Statement of Net Worth.
21.88   ____ Statement of Proposed Disposition.
21.89   ____ Findings of Facts and Conclusions of Law.
21.90   ____ Matrimonial Judgments.
21.91   ____ Referee's Report on Findings of Fact and Conclusions of Law.
21.92   ____ Matrimonial Judgment Entered Upon Referee's Report.

Chapter 22. Guardianship

22.97   Forms.
22.98   ____ Order to Show Cause.
22.99   ____ Petition.
22.100   ____ Court Evaluator's Report.
22.101   ____ Order and Judgment Appointing Guardian of the Person and Property.
22.102   ____ Oath and Designation of Guardian.
22.103   ____ Commission of Guardian.
22.104   ____ Initial Report of Guardian.
22.105   ____ Annual Report and Inventory of Guardian.
22.106   ____ Decree Upon Approving Accounts.
22.107   ____ Petition on Proceeding to Discover Property Withheld.

Chapter 23. Elder Law

23.122   Forms.
23.123   ____ Documentation Letter.
23.124   ____ Consultation Letter.
23.125   ____ Health Care Proxy Statutory Form.
23.126   ____ Sample Living Will.

Chapter 24. Estate Planning

24.96   Forms
24.97   ____ Estate Planner's Checklist.
24.98   ____ Sample Information Request Letter.
24.99   ____ Client Questionnaire.
24.100   ____ "Durable" Power of Attorney Form.
24.101   ____ Crummey Notice.
24.102   ____ Spousal Conflicts Letter.

Chapter 25. Probate and Estate Administration

25.51   Forms.
25.52   ____ Probate Petition.
25.53   ____ Affidavit Proving Correct Copy of Will.
25.54   ____ Citation in Probate.
25.55   ____ Affidavit of Service of Citation.

FORMS

25.56 ____ Affidavit of Mailing Notice of Application for Letters of Administration.
25.57 ____ Waiver and Consent.
25.58 ____ Notice of Probate.
25.59 ____ Deposition Affidavit of Subscribing Witness.
25.60 ____ Objections to Probate.
25.61 ____ Decree Granting Probate.
25.62 ____ Receipt and Release Agreement Concluding an Estate Without an Accounting Proceeding.
25.63 ____ Receipt and Release (Legacy).
25.64 ____ Petition to Judicially Settle Executor's Account.
25.65 ____ Citation to Executor to Show Cause Why Executor Should Not Account.
25.66 ____ Accounting Form.
25.67 ____ Petition for Letters of Administration or Limited Letters of Administration or Temporary Administration.
25.68 ____ Decree Appointing Administrator.
25.69 ____ Affidavit Asking Court to Fix Amount of Administrator's Bond.
25.70 ____ Waiver of Citation, Renunciation of Signer's Claim to Letters and Consent to Appointment of Administrator.
25.71 ____ Notice of Application for Letters of Administration.
25.72 ____ Citation That Can Be Adopted for Use in Any Proceeding.

Chapter 26. Personal Injury

26.62 Forms—Client's Retainer Agreement.
26.63 ____ Retainer Statement.
26.64 ____ Department of Motor Vehicles MV104 Form.
26.65 ____ Summons and Complaint.
26.66 ____ Amended Answer, Counterclaim and Cross Claim.
26.67 ____ Defendant's Demand for a Verified Bill of Particulars.
26.68 ____ Defendant's CPLR 3101 Demands.
26.69 ____ Plaintiff's Demand for a Verified Bill of Particulars.
26.70 ____ Plaintiff's CPLR 3101 Demands.
26.71 ____ Closing Statement.

Chapter 27. Products Liability

27.57 Forms—Products Liability Complaint.
27.58 ____ Products Liability Answer.

Chapter 28. Legal Malpractice

28.50 Forms—Retainer Agreement With ADR Clause.
28.51 ____ Retainer Agreement Without ADR Clause.
28.52 ____ Complaint for Malpractice: Commercial Transaction.
28.53 ____ Complaint for Malpractice: Personal Injury Action.
28.54 ____ Answer: Commercial Transaction.
28.55 ____ Answer: Personal Injury Action.

Chapter 29. Medical Malpractice

29.80 Forms.
29.81 ____ Order to Show Cause to Obtain Medical Records.

FORMS

29.82 ____ Affirmation.
29.83 ____ Certificate of Merit.

Chapter 30. Damages

30.45 Forms.
30.46 ____ *Ad Damnum* Clause in Ordinary Complaint.
30.47 ____ *Ad Damnum* Clause in Complaint in Medical or Dental Malpractice Action or in Action Against Municipal Government (Supreme Court).
30.48 ____ Clauses in Complaint in Action Involving Automobile Accident.
30.49 ____ Request for Supplemental Demand for Relief in Medical or Dental Malpractice Action or Action Against Municipal Corporation.
30.50 ____ Defense of Culpable Conduct in Answer.
30.51 ____ Defense of Failure to Use Seat Belt Contained in Answer.
30.52 ____ Defense of Indemnification From Collateral Sources.
30.53 ____ Partial Defense; Mitigation of Damages.
30.54 ____ Partial Defense; Mitigation of Damages in Libel Action.
30.55 ____ Partial Defense; Inability to Convey Property.
30.56 ____ Notice of Motion to Amend Verdict (or Judgment) to Add Interest.
30.57 ____ Affidavit in Support of Motion to Amend Verdict (or Judgment) to Add Interest.
30.58 ____ Notice of Motion to Fix Date From Which Interest is to be Computed.
30.59 ____ Affidavit in Support of Motion to Fix Date from which Interest is to be Computed.

Chapter 31. Insurance

31.32 Form—Complaint By Policyholder for Declaratory Relief and Breach of Contract.
31.33 ____ Complaint By Insurer for Declaratory Relief.
31.34 ____ Complaint By Insurer for Rescission.
31.35 ____ Affirmative Defenses Asserted by Insurer In a Coverage Action.

Chapter 32. Workers' Compensation

32.53 Forms.
32.54 ____ Workers' Compensation Board Employee's Claim For Compensation. (C–3 3–97)
32.55 ____ Workers' Compensation Board Employer's Report of Work–Related Accident/Occupational Disease. (C–2 1–92)
32.56 ____ Workers' Compensation Board Attending Doctor's Report and Carrier/Employer Billing. (C–4 3–97)
32.57 ____ Workers' Compensation Board Notice that Right to Compensation is Controverted. (C–7 2–97)
32.58 ____ Workers' Compensation Board Notice that Payment of Compensation for Disability has Been Stopped or Modified. (C–8/8.6 1–97)
32.59 ____ Notice and Proof of Claim for Disability Benefits.(DB–450 3–97)
32.60 ____ Notice of Total or Partial Rejection of Claim for Disability Benefits. (DB–451 8–88)

Chapter 33. Local Criminal Court Practice

33.98 Forms.

FORMS

33.99   ____ Notice of Motion to Dismiss For Failure to Serve a Timely Supporting Deposition.
33.100   ____ Attorney Affirmation in Support of Motion to Dismiss For Failure to Serve a Timely Supporting Deposition
33.101   ____ Demand to Produce: Speeding Ticket.

Chapter 34. Social Security Disability Cases

34.68   Forms—Claimant Questionnaire.
34.69   ____ Retainer Agreement.
34.70   ____ Retainer Agreement: Concurrent Benefits.
34.71   ____ Fee Agreement: Maximum Fee.
34.72   ____ Request for Medical Records.
34.73   ____ Medical Release.
34.74   ____ Medical Questionnaire for Treating Physician.
34.75   ____ Psychiatric Questionnaire.
34.76   ____ Cover Letter to Treating Physician.
34.77   ____ Thank-you Letter to Treating Physician.
34.78   ____ Request for Appeals Council Review.

Chapter 35. Income Tax

35.127   Forms.
35.128   ____ Power of Attorney to Represent an Individual.
35.129   ____ Application for Automatic Extension of Time for Filing Return.
35.130   ____ Application for Additional Extension of Time to File for Individuals.
35.131   ____ Notice of Exception to Tax Tribunal.
35.132   ____ Petition to Division of Tax Appeals.
35.133   ____ Petition for Advisory Opinion.
35.134   ____ Statement of Financial Condition.
35.135   ____ Petition for Declaratory Ruling.
35.136   ____ Request for Conciliation Conference.
35.137   ____ Offer in Compromise.

Chapter 36. Alcoholic Beverage Control Law

36.67   Forms.
36.68   ____ Application for Alcoholic Beverage Control Retail License.
36.69   ____ Application for Endorsement Certificate.
36.70   ____ Application for Approval of Corporate Change.
36.71   ____ Application for Permission to Make Alterations.
36.72   ____ Application for Wholesale License.
36.73   ____ Retail License and Filing Fee Schedule.

Chapter 37. Civil Appellate Practice Before the Appellate Division and Other Intermediate Appellate Courts

37.128   Forms.
37.129   ____ Notice of Appeal.
37.130   ____ Notice of Motion for a Stay of Proceedings.
37.131   ____ Order to Show Cause for a Stay of Proceedings.
37.132   ____ Affirmation in Support of Motion or Order To Show Cause for a Stay of Proceedings.

FORMS

37.133 ___ Notice of Motion for a Preference to Expedite the Appeal.
37.134 ___ Affirmation in Support of Motion for a Preference to Expedite the Appeal.
37.135 ___ Notice of Motion to Enlarge Time for (Appellant to Perfect Appeal)(Respondent To File Brief).
37.136 ___ Affirmation in Support of Motion to Enlarge Time for (Appellant to Perfect Appeal) (Respondent to File Brief).
37.137 ___ Notice of Motion to Strike Matter Dehors the Record (Appendix)(Brief).
37.138 ___ Affirmation in Support of Motion to Strike Matter Dehors the Record (Appendix)(Brief).
37.139 ___ Notice of Motion for Reargument or Leave to Appeal to the Court of Appeals.
37.140 ___ Affirmation in Support of Motion for Reargument or Leave to Appeal to the Court of Appeals.

Chapter 38. Criminal Appellate Practice Before the Appellate Division and Other Intermediate Appellate Courts

38.60 Forms—Notice of Motion for a Stay of Execution of Judgment.
38.61 ___ Affirmation in Support of Motion for a Stay of Execution of Judgment.
38.62 ___ Notice of Motion for an Extension of Time to Take An Appeal.
38.63 ___ Affirmation in Support of Motion for an Extension of Time to Take an Appeal.

Chapter 39. Civil and Criminal Appeals to the Court of Appeals

39.77 Forms—Notice of Appeal to Court of Appeals From Order of Appellate Division Finally Determining Action With Two Dissents on Question of Law.
39.78 ___ Notice of Appeal to Court of Appeals From Order of Appellate Division Finally Determining Action Where Construction of Constitution is Directly Involved.
39.79 ___ Notice of Appeal to Court of Appeals From Judgment of Supreme Court Where Constitutionality of Statute is Directly Involved.
39.80 ___ Notice of Appeal to Court of Appeals From Appellate Division Order of Reversal Granting New Trial With Stipulation for Judgment Absolute.
39.81 ___ Notice of Appeal to Court of Appeals From Judgment of Supreme Court to Review Prior Non-final Determination of Appellate Division.
39.82 ___ Rule 500.2 Jurisdictional Statement.
39.83 ___ Notice of Motion in Court of Appeals for Leave to Appeal to Court of Appeals From Order of Appellate Division.
39.84 ___ Affidavit in Support of Motion in Court of Appeals for Leave to Appeal to Court of Appeals From Order of Appellate Division.
39.85 ___ Notice of Motion in Court of Appeals for Reargument of Motion for Leave to Appeal.
39.86 ___ Notice of Motion in Court of Appeals for Leave to Appear *Amicus Curiae*.
39.87 ___ Notice of Motion to Dismiss Appeal as Untimely Taken.
39.88 ___ Affidavit in Support of Motion to Dismiss Appeal as Untimely Taken.

FORMS

39.89 ____ CPLR 5531 Statement.
39.90 ____ Letter Seeking Leave to Appeal in Criminal Case.

TABLE OF STATUTES

NEW YORK, MCKINNEY'S CONSTITUTION

Art.	Sec.	This Work Note
I	9.18	
	9.18	2
	18.6	
I, § 1	18.7	
	18.8	1
	18.15	1
I, § 2	18.7	
	18.8	2
I, § 3	16.25	1
	18.7	
	18.8	3
	18.26	
	18.28	
I, § 4	18.7	
	18.8	
I, §§ 4—6	18.7	
I, § 5	18.7	
I, § 6	4.4	1
	16.18	1
	18.7	
	18.8	
	18.12	
	18.94	
	38.3	
I, § 7	16.22	1
	18.7	
I, § 7(a)	14.18	1
I, § 8	16.25	16
	18.7	
	18.8	
	18.26	
	18.27	6
	18.85	5
I, § 9	18.7	
	18.8	
I, § 11	16.20	1
	18.1	
	18.1	2
	18.5	
	18.7	
	18.8	8
	18.15	1
I, § 12	4.2	34
	4.62	
	17.55	
	18.5	
	18.7	
	18.8	
	18.9	1

NEW YORK, MCKINNEY'S CONSTITUTION

Art.	Sec.	This Work Note
I, § 12 (Cont'd)	18.9	
	18.10	
	18.92	
	18.94	
I, § 16	18.8	
I, § 17	18.7	
	18.8	
I, § 18	18.7	
	18.8	
	32.8	2
	32.13	4
	32.19	6
	32.19	7
I, § 19 (former)	32.8	2
III	9.18	4
	9.22	
III, § 1	16.4	1
	16.10	4
IV, § 8	4.50	9
	4.50	10
VI	37.3	
VI, § 1	37.3	
	38.48	1
VI, § 3	37.3	9
VI, § 3(a)	39.4	1
	39.7	
	39.50	
	39.60	2
VI, § 3(b)	38.3	4
	39.4	1
VI, § 3(b)(2)	37.121	
VI, § 4	37.3	
	37.3	2
	37.3	6
	38.3	5
VI, § 4(b)	37.3	8
	37.4	5
VI, § 4(c)	37.4	4
VI, § 4(f)	37.4	3
VI, § 4(g)	37.59	3
VI, § 4(i)	37.59	2
VI, § 4(k)	37.34	1
	38.3	
	38.3	16
	38.8	53
	38.8	222
	38.9	
VI, § 5	38.3	5
VI, § 6	37.3	1

249

TABLE OF STATUTES

NEW YORK, MCKINNEY'S CONSTITUTION

Art.	Sec.	This Work Note
VI, § 7	38.4	1
VI, § 8	37.3	4
	37.3	16
	37.5	5
	37.11	1
	37.16	2
	38.46	1
VI, § 8(a)	37.93	
	37.102	2
	38.57	
VI, § 8(e)	37.93	3
	37.110	1
	38.47	4
VI, § 9	14.4	5
	37.3	28
	37.17	1
VI, § 10	37.3	24
VI, § 11	37.3	16
	38.4	3
VI, § 11(a)	37.126	2
VI, § 11(b)	37.126	2
VI, § 11(c)	38.46	2
VI, § 12	37.3	27
VI, § 13	37.3	25
VI, § 15	37.3	18
	37.109	
	38.48	1
VI, § 16	37.3	19
VI, § 17	37.3	17
VI, § 19(b)	38.8	
VI, § 20(a)(c)	37.92	4
VI, § 22	37.91	10
	39.59	
VI, § 22(a)	39.59	3
	39.59	5
VI, § 22(d)	39.59	13
VI, § 22(e)	39.59	4
VI, § 22(f)	39.59	4
VI, § 23	39.59	1
VI, § 24	39.59	1
VI, § 26	38.4	2
VI, § 28	37.7	3
	37.91	9
	37.100	1
VI, § 30	37.4	6
VI, § 32	20.28	1
VII	3.26	
VIII	3.26	
VIII, § 1	3.16	14
	3.18	1
	3.34	6
VIII, § 2	3.19	1
	3.27	3
	3.27	5
VIII, § 4	3.27	18
	3.27	19
VIII, § 5(B)	3.27	20
VIII, § 5(C)	3.27	21

NEW YORK, MCKINNEY'S CONSTITUTION

Art.	Sec.	This Work Note
VIII, § 5(E)	3.27	20
VIII, § 10	3.26	7
IX	3.38	
	16.7	
	16.7	1
IX, § 1(e)	14.5	
	14.5	1
	14.13	1
IX, § 2(a)	3.3	7
	16.7	4
IX, § 2(b)(1)	16.7	4
IX, § 2(b)(2)	3.7	9
	3.14	2
	16.24	2
IX, § 2(c)	3.14	1
IX, § 2(c)(1)	16.7	2
IX, § 2(c)(10)	3.9	4
IX, § 3(a)(3)	16.24	1
IX, § 3(d)(1)	3.7	10
IX, § 3(d)(2)	3.3	6
IX, § 3(d)(4)	3.7	11
X, § 1	1.21	1
X, § 5	3.33	1
XIII, § 5	3.20	1
XIII, § 13	3.17	1
	3.20	1
XVI, § 5	35.12	3

NEW YORK, MCKINNEY'S STATUTES

Sec.	Sec.	This Work Note
51(c)	3.10	11

NEW YORK, MCKINNEY'S ABANDONED PROPERTY LAW

Sec.	Sec.	This Work Note
103(b)(i)	24.3	3

NEW YORK, MCKINNEY'S ALCOHOLIC BEVERAGE CONTROL LAW

Sec.	Sec.	This Work Note
Art. 8	36.4	4
2	36.5	4
	36.24	3
3	36.5	3
3(1)	36.5	1
3(13)	36.10	8
	36.37	1
3(14)	36.34	1
10	36.6	1
11	36.6	1
15	36.6	2
17	36.53	6

TABLE OF STATUTES

NEW YORK, MCKINNEY'S ALCOHOLIC BEVERAGE CONTROL LAW

Sec.	This Work Sec.	Note
17 (Cont'd)	36.57	1
17(3)	36.55	4
17(7)	36.53	1
51(4)	36.12	11
52	36.12	6
53	36.8	3
	36.9	1
	36.11	1
	36.11	2
	36.11	3
	36.11	9
	36.11	10
54	36.8	5
54(4)	36.10	7
	36.37	1
61	36.12	1
	36.12	2
	36.12	3
62	36.11	1
	36.11	3
63	36.8	4
	36.10	
	36.10	1
63(4)	36.10	2
63(6)	36.10	4
	36.36	1
64	36.8	1
	36.9	4
	36.25	3
64(2–a)	36.25	1
64(7)	36.4	9
64(7)(a)	36.9	8
	36.28	1
	36.28	2
64(7)(b)	36.9	6
	36.9	7
	36.41	1
64(7)(f)	36.9	7
	36.41	3
64–a	36.8	1
	36.9	4
64–a(7)	36.4	9
	36.28	1
64–a(7)(a)(i)	36.9	8
64–a(7)(a)(ii)	36.9	6
	36.41	1
64–a(7)(d)	36.9	7
	36.41	3
64–b	36.9	5
76	36.12	4
76–a	36.12	5
	36.12	7
76–b	36.12	10
76–b(6)	36.16	5
76–c(3)	36.12	9
76–c(4)	36.12	8
78	36.11	1
	36.11	3

NEW YORK, MCKINNEY'S ALCOHOLIC BEVERAGE CONTROL LAW

Sec.	This Work Sec.	Note
79	36.10	6
79(2)	36.14	12
81	36.8	2
	36.9	2
	36.9	3
	36.25	1
	36.25	2
	36.25	3
93	36.11	13
	36.17	1
93–a	36.17	5
94	36.11	14
	36.17	2
96	36.11	15
	36.17	3
97–a	36.16	1
	36.16	4
97–a(1)	36.16	2
97–a(2)	36.16	3
98	36.17	4
99–d(1)	36.48	1
	36.48	2
99–d(2)	36.47	1
99–g	36.17	6
100(1)	36.5	4
100(4)	36.31	1
	36.31	2
101	36.4	7
	36.52	2
101(1)(a)	36.21	3
	36.26	
	36.44	2
101(1)(c)	36.44	9
101–a	36.44	13
101–b	36.44	9
101–aa	36.44	11
102	36.26	1
103	36.44	8
103(7)	4.2	38
103.7	36.44	16
104	36.44	8
104(1)(a)	36.11	5
	36.11	7
	36.11	8
104(1)(a)(iv)	36.11	2
104(10)	4.2	38
104–a(4)	36.44	3
	36.44	4
105	6.8	2
105(3)	36.4	9
	36.10	3
	36.28	1
	36.28	2
105(15)	36.44	3
	36.44	4
	36.44	8
105(16)	36.4	7
	36.26	1

TABLE OF STATUTES

NEW YORK, MCKINNEY'S ALCOHOLIC BEVERAGE CONTROL LAW

Sec.	This Work Sec.	Note
105(16) (Cont'd)	36.52	2
105.1	36.21	1
105.10(a)	36.44	5
106	36.53	2
106(6)	36.53	3
106(12)	36.44	3
	36.44	4
	36.44	8
106(13)	36.4	7
	36.26	1
	36.52	2
106(16)	36.33	1
106.1	36.21	1
106.9	36.30	2
	36.30	3
107–a	36.18	1
	36.18	4
	36.44	6
107–a(4)	36.18	3
107–a(4)(b)	36.11	4
109(1–a)	36.51	1
110	36.50	1
110(1)(c)	36.9	12
110(2)	36.45	1
110(4)	36.39	1
111	36.49	2
112	36.19	1
	36.57	1
113	36.55	2
118	36.55	3
121	36.66	1
126	36.14	2
126(1)	36.14	9
126(3)	36.14	4
	36.14	5
126(5)	36.55	1
128	36.14	3
129	36.58	1

NEW YORK, MCKINNEY'S AGRICULTURE AND MARKETS LAW

Sec.	This Work Sec.	Note
Art. 25–AA	16.134	
27(10)	14.96	1
251–z–2	36.12	12
301	1.23	12
303	16.134	
304	16.134	
310	12.91	

NEW YORK, MCKINNEY'S ARTS AND CULTURAL AFFAIRS LAW

Sec.	This Work Sec.	Note
11.01.2	7.65	

NEW YORK, MCKINNEY'S ARTS AND CULTURAL AFFAIRS LAW

Sec.	This Work Sec.	Note
11.01.9	7.65	
11.01.20	7.65	
Art. 13	7.65	
Art. 13, Tit. C	7.65	
23.03(4)	2.81	2
57.07	1.7	13

NEW YORK, MCKINNEY'S BANKING LAW

Sec.	This Work Sec.	Note
6–a	23.102	
125	4.2	37
407	9.125	17
675	8.19	3
	24.83	1
	24.83	2
675(b)	21.37	

NEW YORK, MCKINNEY'S BUSINESS CORPORATION LAW

Sec.	This Work Sec.	Note
Art. 1	1.114	12
102	1.5	1
	1.32	5
102(a)(1)	1.5	2
102(a)(2)	1.5	3
102(a)(3)	1.5	4
102(a)(4)	1.5	5
102(a)(5)	1.5	6
102(a)(6)	1.5	7
	1.38	6
102(a)(7)	1.5	8
102(a)(7–a)	1.51	1
102(a)(8)	1.5	9
	1.10	4
102(a)(9)	1.5	10
102(a)(10)	1.5	11
	1.21	5
102(a)(11)	1.5	12
102(a)(12)	1.5	13
	1.72	
102(a)(12)(C)	1.38	30
103	1.5	1
104	1.7	4
	1.7	6
	1.21	5
	1.96	2
104(a)	1.7	6
104(b)	1.7	6
	1.23	11
104(c)	1.7	6
104(d)	1.7	5
	1.7	6
	1.20	1

252

TABLE OF STATUTES

NEW YORK, MCKINNEY'S BUSINESS CORPORATION LAW

Sec.	This Work Sec.	Note
104(e)	1.7	6
	1.7	8
	1.7	9
	1.7	10
	1.7	11
104(f)	1.7	12
	1.75	4
104(g)	1.7	13
	1.23	12
	1.104	22
104–A	1.7	14
104–A(c)	1.7	15
104–A(d)	1.21	2
	1.30	22
105	1.7	7
	1.20	1
106(a)	1.7	1
106(b)	1.7	2
	1.7	3
107	1.8	1
108	1.136	1
	1.136	2
	1.136	3
	1.136	4
108(a)	1.7	16
	1.7	17
108(b)	1.7	17
108(c)	1.7	18
109	1.12	5
	1.100	2
109(a)(1)	1.94	2
109(a)(2)	1.94	2
109(a)(5)	1.94	2
109(a)(6)	1.17	2
	1.114	6
109(b)	1.114	6
109(c)	1.17	2
	1.114	6
201	1.9	3
201(a)	1.9	1
	1.21	5
201(b)	1.9	2
	1.21	18
201(c)	1.9	2
201(d)	1.9	2
	1.21	18
	1.21	19
201(e)	1.9	2
	1.21	18
	1.21	22
202	1.11	3
	1.21	5
	1.21	17
202(a)	1.9	5
	1.11	1
	1.11	2
202(a)(10)	2.16	6
202(b)	1.9	6

NEW YORK, MCKINNEY'S BUSINESS CORPORATION LAW

Sec.	This Work Sec.	Note
203	1.12	
	1.12	6
	1.12	7
203(a)	1.12	2
203(a)(1)	1.12	3
203(a)(2)	1.12	4
203(a)(3)	1.12	5
Art. 3	1.114	12
301	1.13	
	1.13	1
	1.75	
	1.115	
	1.115	8
	2.79	8
301—306	1.21	5
301(a)	1.14	
301(a)(1)	1.13	1
	1.122	34
301(a)(2)	1.13	2
301(a)(2)—(a)(9)	1.115	
301(a)(3)	1.13	3
301(a)(4)	1.13	4
301(a)(5)(A)	1.13	5
301(a)(5)(B)	1.13	6
	1.21	18
301(a)(6)	1.13	7
	1.21	18
301(a)(7)	1.13	8
	1.21	18
301(a)(8)	1.13	11
301(a)(9)	1.13	12
301(a)(10)	1.13	9
	1.21	18
302	1.13	1
	1.115	
302(b)(3)	1.115	8
303	2.79	10
303(a)	1.14	
	1.14	1
	1.137	
303(a)(3)	1.138	1
303(a)(4)	1.138	2
303(a)(5)	1.138	3
303(b)	1.14	
	1.14	3
	1.137	
303(b)(1)	1.138	4
303(b)(2)	1.138	5
303(b)(3)	1.138	6
303(c)	1.14	4
	1.14	5
	1.14	6
	1.14	7
	1.14	8
	1.14	9
303(d)	1.14	10
	1.14	11
	1.14	12

253

TABLE OF STATUTES

NEW YORK, MCKINNEY'S BUSINESS CORPORATION LAW

Sec.	This Work Sec.	Note
303(e)	1.14	13
303(f)	1.14	13
304—307	1.15	1
	11.36	1
304(a)	1.17	1
304(b)	1.17	2
305(a)	1.18	2
305(b)	1.18	3
305(c)	1.18	4
	1.18	9
	1.18	10
305(d)	1.18	11
	1.18	12
306	1.7	
306(b)	1.117	8
	1.118	1
	1.119	1
307	1.7	
	1.19	
307(a)	1.19	2
	1.19	3
	1.19	4
307(b)	1.19	6
307(b)(2)	1.19	7
307(c)(1)	1.19	8
	1.19	9
307(c)(2)	1.19	10
	1.19	11
	1.19	12
	1.19	13
	1.19	14
307(d)	1.19	5
308	1.15	2
	1.16	1
	1.16	2
	1.16	3
401	1.20	1
	1.20	2
	1.147	2
	2.22	3
402	1.21	28
	1.147	3
	1.151	
402(a)	1.20	1
	1.21	1
	1.21	4
	1.21	14
402(a)(1)	1.21	5
402(a)(2)	1.9	1
	1.21	6
	1.21	9
	1.151	
402(a)(3)	1.21	7
402(a)(4)	1.21	8
	1.21	9
402(a)(6)	1.21	10
402(a)(7)	1.21	11
402(a)(8)	1.18	5

NEW YORK, MCKINNEY'S BUSINESS CORPORATION LAW

Sec.	This Work Sec.	Note
402(a)(8) (Cont'd)	1.21	12
402(a)(9)	1.21	13
402(b)	1.21	14
	1.21	15
	1.66	
	2.31	
402(b)(1)	1.21	16
402(b)(2)	1.21	16
402(c)	1.21	14
	1.21	17
403	1.7	
	1.21	26
404	1.20	1
	1.136	5
	1.147	5
404(a)	1.23	1
	1.23	2
	1.23	5
	1.23	6
	1.23	7
	1.23	8
404(b)	1.23	9
404(c)	1.23	10
405	1.21	19
	1.21	21
406	1.21	20
	1.21	21
407	1.21	21
408	1.23	
	1.23	12
408(1)	1.23	
	1.23	11
408(1)(c)	1.23	12
408(2)	1.23	13
408(3)	1.23	14
	1.23	15
408(4)	1.23	
	1.23	12
408(5)	1.23	12
409	1.23	12
409(1)	1.23	16
409(2)	1.23	17
	1.23	18
409(3)	1.23	19
501	1.21	5
	1.45	2
	1.51	3
	1.51	4
	1.51	6
	1.103	1
501(a)	1.27	1
	1.27	2
	1.32	3
	1.33	5
	1.51	5
501(b)	1.27	3
501(b)	1.32	3
501(b)	1.51	5

TABLE OF STATUTES

NEW YORK, MCKINNEY'S BUSINESS CORPORATION LAW		
		This Work
Sec.	Sec.	Note
501(c)	1.27	5
502	1.21	5
502(a)	1.28	1
502(b)	1.28	2
	1.32	3
502(c)	1.28	3
502(d)	1.28	4
	1.28	5
502(e)	1.21	
	1.28	3
503(a)	1.29	1
503(b)	1.20	5
	1.29	2
503(c)	1.29	3
503(d)	1.29	4
	1.29	5
	1.29	6
	1.29	7
	1.29	8
	1.29	9
503(e)	1.29	9
504	1.31	
	1.38	31
	1.56	7
	1.78	3
504(a)	1.30	
	1.30	1
	1.30	2
	1.34	44
	1.34	49
504(b)	1.30	3
504(c)	1.30	4
504(d)	1.30	5
	1.30	6
504(e)	1.30	7
504(f)	1.30	8
504(g)	1.30	9
	1.33	
504(h)	1.30	
	1.30	10
	1.144	4
504(i)	1.30	11
504(j)	1.30	11
505	1.31	
	1.31	10
505(a)(1)	1.31	1
505(a)(2)	1.27	4
505(a)(2)(i)	1.31	1
505(a)(2)(ii)	1.31	1
505(b)	1.31	2
505(c)	1.31	3
505(d)	1.31	5
	1.31	9
	1.31	10
	1.52	1
505(e)	1.30	
	1.31	
	1.31	6

NEW YORK, MCKINNEY'S BUSINESS CORPORATION LAW		
		This Work
Sec.	Sec.	Note
505(e) (Cont'd)	1.31	7
	1.136	6
	1.144	4
505(f)	1.30	
	1.31	8
505(g)	1.31	2
505(h)	1.31	4
505(i)	1.31	10
506	1.30	
506(a)	1.32	1
506(b)	1.32	2
	1.32	3
	1.32	4
506(c)	1.32	5
507	1.30	11
508(f)	1.136	6
508	1.30	17
	1.30	18
508(a)	1.30	17
	1.144	2
508(b)	1.30	21
	1.144	3
508(c)	1.30	19
	1.30	21
508(e)	1.30	21
508(f)	1.30	20
	1.30	21
509(a)	1.30	12
	1.30	16
509(b)	1.30	13
	1.30	16
509(c)	1.30	14
	1.30	15
509(d)	1.30	16
510	1.38	3
	1.38	6
	1.51	3
	1.66	
	1.136	8
510(a)	1.38	1
	1.38	10
	1.66	
510(b)	1.38	5
	1.38	10
	1.66	
510(c)	1.38	6
511(a)(4)	1.38	18
511	1.52	1
	1.136	8
511(a)	1.38	15
511(a)(1)	1.38	16
511(a)(2)	1.38	17
511(a)(3)	1.38	18
	1.48	3
	1.145	2
511(b)	1.38	19
511(c)	1.38	24
511(d)	1.38	20

255

TABLE OF STATUTES

NEW YORK, MCKINNEY'S BUSINESS CORPORATION LAW

Sec.	This Work Sec.	Note
511(e)	1.38	21
511(f)	1.32	5
	1.38	22
511(g)	1.32	5
	1.38	26
	1.38	28
512	1.21	5
	1.39	
	1.39	20
512(a)	1.39	15
512(b)	1.33	11
	1.39	
	1.39	16
	1.39	18
512(c)	1.39	20
512(d)	1.39	6
513	1.33	
	1.39	
	1.39	6
	1.44	3
	1.51	20
	1.66	
	1.122	22
	1.147	10
513(a)	1.39	1
	1.39	2
513(b)	1.39	4
	1.39	5
	1.39	20
	1.39	21
513(b)(3)	1.51	20
513(c)	1.39	13
513(e)	1.89	13
514	1.147	10
514(a)	1.39	7
514(b)	1.39	8
514(h)	1.144	5
515	1.39	21
	1.51	
	1.136	8
515(a)	1.39	22
515(b)	1.39	23
515(c)	1.39	24
515(d)	1.39	25
	1.39	26
515(e)	1.39	
516	1.32	5
	1.136	8
516(a)	1.38	29
	1.38	31
	1.38	34
516(b)	1.38	32
516(c)	1.38	33
	1.38	36
517	1.38	3
	1.136	8
518	1.52	
	1.59	

NEW YORK, MCKINNEY'S BUSINESS CORPORATION LAW

Sec.	This Work Sec.	Note
518(a)	1.33	1
	1.33	2
518(b)	1.33	3
	1.33	4
518(c)	1.33	5
	1.53	3
518(c)(1)	1.33	
519	1.31	10
	1.136	8
519(a)	1.33	6
519(b)	1.33	
	1.33	7
519(c)	1.33	
	1.33	8
519(c)(1)	1.33	8
519(c)(2)	1.33	10
519(c)(3)	1.33	11
519(d)	1.33	
	1.33	12
	1.33	13
519(e)	1.33	14
	1.33	15
520	1.38	22
	1.38	26
	1.38	36
	1.136	8
	1.136	9
539	1.147	12
601	1.147	4
601—605	1.136	10
601(a)	1.22	1
	1.22	2
	1.22	3
601(b)	1.22	4
602(a)	1.43	1
	1.43	2
	1.43	10
602(b)	1.43	3
602(c)	1.43	4
	1.43	5
602(d)	1.43	
603(a)	1.43	6
	1.43	7
	1.43	8
	1.43	9
	1.43	10
603(b)	1.43	12
604	1.52	
604(a)	1.43	13
	1.43	14
604(b)	1.43	15
	1.43	16
604(c)	1.43	17
605	1.43	
	1.45	
	1.51	26
	1.52	10
	6.15	1

TABLE OF STATUTES

NEW YORK, MCKINNEY'S BUSINESS CORPORATION LAW

Sec.	This Work Sec.	Note
605(a)	1.44	1
	1.44	2
	1.44	4
	1.44	5
	1.44	6
	1.44	7
	1.44	8
605(b)	1.44	9
	1.44	10
	1.44	11
606	1.44	12
	1.44	13
	1.136	11
607	1.45	34
	1.45	35
	1.45	36
	1.51	7
608	1.43	11
608(a)	1.46	1
	1.147	6
608(b)	1.46	2
608(c)	1.46	4
608(d)	1.46	5
609	1.45	
	1.147	9
609(a)	1.43	18
	1.45	18
	1.51	9
609(b)	1.45	19
	1.45	20
	1.45	26
	1.53	
609(c)	1.45	21
609(d)	1.45	21
609(e)	1.45	23
609(f)	1.45	
	1.45	21
	1.45	24
609(g)	1.45	25
	1.45	26
609(h)	1.45	27
	1.136	14
	1.144	6
609(i)	1.43	18
609(j)	1.43	18
610(a)	1.45	37
	1.45	40
610(b)	1.45	37
611	1.45	39
611(a)	1.45	
	1.45	38
	1.45	41
	1.45	42
611(b)	1.45	
	1.45	43
	1.45	44
611(c)	1.45	
	1.45	45

NEW YORK, MCKINNEY'S BUSINESS CORPORATION LAW

Sec.	This Work Sec.	Note
611(c) (Cont'd)	1.45	46
611(d)	1.45	47
612(a)	1.21	5
	1.45	1
612(b)	1.45	4
612(c)	1.45	8
	1.45	9
612(d)	1.45	10
612(e)	1.45	11
612(f)	1.45	12
612(g)	1.45	13
612(h)	1.45	
	1.45	14
	1.45	15
612(h)(3)	1.45	16
612(i)	1.45	17
613	1.21	5
	1.22	
	1.45	2
	1.51	6
	1.103	1
614	1.51	4
614—618	1.147	6
614(a)	1.45	29
614(b)	1.45	28
615	1.48	1
	12.55	16
615(a)	1.48	1
	1.48	3
	1.51	10
	2.27	8
615(b)	1.48	1
615(c)	1.7	
	1.23	10
	1.48	1
615(d)	1.48	1
615(e)	1.48	2
616	1.46	3
	1.136	10
	1.136	13
	1.147	12
616(a)(2)	1.45	3
616(b)	1.46	3
616(c)	1.45	3
	1.46	3
	1.144	7
617	1.21	5
	1.51	4
	1.51	6
	1.147	7
617(a)	1.45	5
617(b)	1.45	6
	1.45	7
618	1.45	32
	1.45	33
	1.51	6
619	1.43	18
	1.43	19

257

TABLE OF STATUTES

NEW YORK, MCKINNEY'S BUSINESS CORPORATION LAW

Sec.	This Work Sec.	Note
619 (Cont'd)	1.51	11
620	1.45	
	1.136	14
	1.147	9
	2.2	2
620(a)	1.45	24
	1.47	1
	1.147	13
620(b)	1.47	3
	1.52	3
	1.56	22
	1.59	
	1.144	8
	1.147	12
620(c)	1.47	4
	1.52	3
620(d)	1.47	5
620(d)(1)	1.46	5
620(d)(1)(A)(ii)	1.46	5
620(d)(2)	1.46	5
620(e)	1.46	5
	1.47	7
620(f)	1.47	8
	1.56	23
620(g)	1.47	9
	1.144	8
621	1.47	
	1.147	9
621(a)	1.45	24
	1.47	10
	1.47	11
	1.47	12
	1.144	9
621(b)	1.47	13
	1.47	14
621(c)	1.47	14
	1.47	15
	1.53	3
621(d)	1.47	16
	1.47	17
622	1.21	5
	1.51	6
	1.52	
	1.52	3
	1.136	7
622(a)	1.52	3
622(b)	1.52	
	1.52	1
622(b)(2)	1.52	3
622(c)	1.52	3
	1.521	
622(d)	1.52	2
	1.52	4
	1.52	5
	1.52	6
622(e)	1.52	8
622(f)	1.52	9
622(g)	1.52	10

NEW YORK, MCKINNEY'S BUSINESS CORPORATION LAW

Sec.	This Work Sec.	Note
622(g) (Cont'd)	1.52	11
	1.52	12
622(h)	1.52	13
	1.52	14
622(i)	1.52	7
	1.52	15
623	1.44	
	1.49	
	1.51	
	1.51	13
	1.51	18
	1.51	21
	1.51	26
	1.51	27
	1.72	
	1.83	18
	1.88	
	1.90	
	1.97	6
	1.114	12
	1.136	19
	1.152	
	6.15	2
623(a)	1.51	20
	1.51	23
	1.51	25
	1.51	26
	2.21	20
623(b)	1.51	27
	1.51	28
623(c)	1.51	29
	1.51	30
	1.90	
623(d)	1.51	36
	1.51	37
623(e)	1.51	39
	1.51	41
	1.51	42
	1.51	43
	1.51	44
	1.51	45
	1.51	46
	1.51	48
623(f)	1.51	31
	1.51	32
	1.51	33
	1.51	34
	1.51	35
	1.144	10
623(g)	1.51	
	1.51	49
	1.51	50
	1.51	51
	1.51	52
	1.51	53
	1.51	54
	1.51	55
	1.51	56

TABLE OF STATUTES

NEW YORK, MCKINNEY'S BUSINESS CORPORATION LAW

Sec.	This Work Sec.	Note
623(g) (Cont'd)	1.51	57
	1.51	58
	1.51	59
623(h)	1.51	60
	2.42	2
623(h)(1)	1.51	61
	1.51	62
623(h)(2)	1.51	63
	1.51	64
623(h)(3)	1.51	65
	1.51	66
	1.51	67
623(h)(4)	1.51	68
	1.51	69
	1.51	70
623(h)(5)	1.51	71
623(h)(6)	1.51	72
	1.51	73
623(h)(7)	1.51	74
	1.51	75
	1.51	76
623(h)(8)	1.51	77
623(i)	2.42	2
623(j)	1.51	78
	1.51	79
	1.51	80
	1.51	81
	1.51	82
	1.51	83
	2.42	2
623(k)	1.51	85
	2.42	2
623(L)	1.51	26
623(m)	1.51	23
624	1.47	
	1.47	14
	1.51	8
	1.53	
	1.53	3
	1.103	9
624(a)	1.53	1
	1.53	2
624(b)	1.53	
	1.53	3
	1.53	4
	1.53	6
	1.56	
624(c)	1.53	7
624(d)	1.53	8
624(e)	1.53	9
	1.53	10
624(f)	1.53	11
624(g)	1.53	12
625	1.51	1
	1.136	18
626	1.66	
	1.114	12
626(a)	1.51	12

NEW YORK, MCKINNEY'S BUSINESS CORPORATION LAW

Sec.	This Work Sec.	Note
626(a) (Cont'd)	1.51	86
626(b)	1.51	88
626(c)	1.51	89
626(d)	1.43	9
	1.51	91
	1.51	92
	1.51	93
626(e)	1.51	94
627	1.51	95
	1.51	96
	1.114	12
628	1.29	4
	1.51	7
	1.56	7
628(a)	1.56	3
	1.56	4
628(b)	1.56	5
	1.56	6
628(c)	1.56	7
	1.56	8
629	1.51	7
	1.56	9
630	1.10	2
	1.53	
	1.56	
	1.136	18
	1.147	12
	2.2	
	2.2	12
630(a)	1.53	3
	1.56	
	1.56	11
	1.56	12
	1.56	13
	1.56	14
630(b)	1.53	5
	1.56	
	1.56	15
	1.56	16
	1.56	17
630(c)	1.56	18
	1.56	19
	1.56	20
	1.56	21
Art. 7	1.59	5
Art. 7	1.66	
Art. 7	1.66	19
701	1.47	3
	1.59	3
	1.59	4
	1.147	7
	1.147	12
702	1.147	11
702(a)	1.59	
	1.59	5
	1.59	6
	1.59	7
	1.147	7

TABLE OF STATUTES

NEW YORK, MCKINNEY'S BUSINESS CORPORATION LAW

Sec.	This Work Sec.	Note
702(b)	1.59	8
703(a)	1.59	9
	1.59	11
703(b)	1.59	10
704	1.59	
	1.147	7
704(a)	1.23	1
	1.59	12
	1.59	13
	1.59	14
704(b)	1.23	1
	1.59	15
704(c)	1.59	16
705(a)	1.59	10
	1.60	
	1.60	1
	1.60	2
705(b)	1.60	
	1.60	3
705(c)	1.60	4
705(d)	1.60	5
706	1.147	7
706(a)	1.59	10
	1.61	1
	1.61	2
706(b)	1.61	3
706(c)	1.61	4
706(d)	1.61	5
	1.61	6
707	1.63	1
	1.63	2
707—709	1.147	11
708	1.152	
708(a)	1.62	1
708(b)	1.62	3
708(c)	1.62	4
	1.62	5
708(d)	1.62	2
	1.63	3
	1.65	10
709	1.60	2
	1.63	5
	1.136	13
709(a)	1.63	
709(a)(1)	1.63	1
709(a)(2)	1.62	2
	1.63	4
709(b)	1.63	5
709(b)(1)	1.63	5
709(b)(2)	1.63	5
709(c)	1.144	11
710	1.62	6
	1.62	7
711	1.136	12
711(a)	1.62	8
	1.62	9
711(b)	1.62	10
711(c)	1.62	11

NEW YORK, MCKINNEY'S BUSINESS CORPORATION LAW

Sec.	This Work Sec.	Note
711(d)	1.62	12
	1.62	13
712	1.64	2
	1.147	11
712(a)	1.64	1
	1.64	2
712(b)	1.64	3
712(c)	1.64	4
	1.64	5
713	1.65	8
	1.65	17
713(a)	1.65	
	1.65	9
	1.65	11
713(b)	1.65	12
713(c)	1.65	12
713(d)	1.65	13
713(e)	1.65	18
714	1.65	
	1.65	14
	1.66	
714		
714(a)	1.65	15
714(a)(2)	1.65	15
714(b)	1.65	16
715	1.147	8
715(a)	1.69	1
715(b)	1.46	3
	1.59	
	1.69	2
715(c)	1.69	3
715(d)	1.69	4
715(e)	1.69	5
	1.69	6
715(f)	1.69	13
715(g)	1.69	7
715(h)	1.69	8
	1.69	9
	1.69	10
	1.69	11
	1.69	12
716	1.46	3
	1.147	8
716(a)	1.69	14
	1.69	15
716(b)	1.69	16
	1.69	17
716(c)	1.69	18
	1.69	19
717	1.38	6
	1.64	
	1.65	6
717(a)	1.65	1
	1.65	2
	1.65	3
	1.66	
717(b)	1.65	
	1.65	4
	1.65	5

260

TABLE OF STATUTES

NEW YORK, MCKINNEY'S BUSINESS CORPORATION LAW

Sec.	This Work Sec.	Note
717(b) (Cont'd)	1.65	6
718(a)	1.59	17
	1.59	18
719	1.21	
	1.66	
	1.114	
719(a)	1.66	
	1.66	2
	1.66	13
719(a)(1)	1.38	6
	1.66	3
719(a)(2)	1.66	4
719(a)(3)	1.66	
	1.66	5
	1.101	2
719(a)(4)	1.66	
	1.66	6
719(b)	1.66	7
	1.66	8
	1.66	9
719(c)	1.66	10
719(d)	1.66	11
719(d)(1)	1.56	28
719(e)	1.66	12
719(f)	1.66	14
720	1.66	
	1.114	
720(a)	1.66	
720(a)(1)	1.66	16
720(a)(2)	1.66	17
720(a)(3)	1.66	18
720(b)	1.66	15
721	1.66	19
	1.66	25
721—725	1.69	20
721—727	1.114	12
722	1.66	
722(a)	1.66	19
722(b)	1.66	20
722(c)	1.66	21
	1.66	22
722(d)	1.66	22
723	1.66	
723(a)	1.66	
	1.66	23
723(b)	1.66	27
723(c)	1.66	
	1.66	37
724	1.66	26
	1.66	37
	1.136	16
724(a)	1.66	30
724(a)(1)	1.66	31
724(a)(2)	1.66	32
724(b)	1.66	33
	1.66	34
	1.66	35
724(c)	1.66	

NEW YORK, MCKINNEY'S BUSINESS CORPORATION LAW

Sec.	This Work Sec.	Note
724(c) (Cont'd)	1.66	36
725	1.66	37
	1.136	17
725(a)	1.66	
	1.66	40
725(b)	1.66	41
725(c)	1.66	
	1.66	42
	1.66	43
725(d)	1.66	43
725(e)	1.66	43
725(f)	1.66	49
726	1.69	21
726(a)	1.66	44
726(b)	1.66	45
726(c)	1.66	45
726(d)	1.66	47
726(e)	1.66	48
Art. 8	1.72	1
	1.73	
801	1.20	1
	1.72	
	1.72	10
	18.67	3
801(a)	1.72	1
801(b)	1.72	3
801(b)(7)—(12)	1.38	25
801(b)(10)	1.74	
801(b)(11)	1.72	
	1.72	10
	1.74	
801(b)(12)	1.51	24
	1.74	
801(c)	1.72	1
802	1.32	5
	1.38	35
	1.72	4
802(a)	1.38	25
	1.72	4
	1.72	10
802(b)	1.72	4
	1.72	10
803	1.38	35
803(a)	1.73	1
803(b)	1.76	1
803(c)	1.73	1
803(d)	1.73	3
804	1.83	6
	1.83	7
	1.83	8
	1.88	3
804(a)	1.74	1
	1.74	2
804(b)	1.74	3
805	1.18	7
	1.28	3
	1.31	2
	1.33	

TABLE OF STATUTES

NEW YORK, MCKINNEY'S BUSINESS CORPORATION LAW			NEW YORK, MCKINNEY'S BUSINESS CORPORATION LAW		
		This Work			This Work
Sec.	Sec.	Note	Sec.	Sec.	Note
805 (Cont'd)	1.39		Art. 9	1.83	1
	1.47	6		1.122	
805(a)	1.75		901	1.78	1
	1.75	1		1.83	14
805(b)	1.75	2	901—905	1.82	1
	1.75	3	901(a)(1)	1.83	1
805(c)	1.75	5	901(a)(2)	1.83	1
805–A	1.18	8		1.83	2
805–A(a)	1.76	2	901(b)	1.83	1
805–A(a)(1)	1.76	2	901(b)(1)	1.83	1
805–A(a)(2)	1.76	2	901(b)(2)	1.83	1
805–A(a)(3)	1.76	2	902	1.83	18
805–A(b)	1.76	2	902(a)	1.83	3
806	1.32	5	902(a)(1)	1.83	10
	1.44	3		1.83	18
	1.51	18	902(a)(2)	1.83	10
	1.52	1		1.83	18
806(a)	1.75	6	902(a)(4)	1.83	10
	1.75	7	903	1.83	6
806(b)	1.38	25		1.83	7
806(b)(1)	1.38	35		1.83	8
	1.72	5		1.83	17
	1.72	7		1.136	20
	1.72	8	903(a)	1.83	
806(b)(2)	1.72	9		1.83	4
806(b)(3)	1.38	35		1.83	5
	1.72	10		1.83	18
806(b)(4)	1.72	11	903(a)(2)	1.51	15
806(b)(5)	1.72	12		1.83	6
	1.72	13		1.83	7
806(b)(6)	1.51	20		1.83	8
	1.51	24	903(a)(2)(A)	1.83	6
	1.72	15		1.83	7
	1.90			1.83	8
807(a)	1.77	1	903(a)(2)(B)	1.83	6
	1.77	2		1.83	7
	1.77	3		1.83	8
807(b)	1.77	1	903(b)	1.83	9
807(c)	1.77	4		1.83	13
807(d)	1.77	5	904	1.83	17
807(e)	1.77	5	904(a)	1.83	10
807(f)	1.77	6	904(b)	1.83	10
808	1.44	3	905	1.51	
	1.72	6		1.78	1
	1.78	1		1.83	
	1.78	2		1.83	17
	1.78	4		1.83	18
	1.114	12		1.90	
808(a)	1.78	1	905(a)	1.83	11
808(b)	1.78	2	905(a)(1)	1.83	17
808(c)	1.78	2	905(a)(2)	1.83	17
808(d)	1.78	3	905(a)(4)	1.83	17
808(e)	1.78	3	905(b)	1.83	11
808(f)	1.78	2	905(c)	1.83	12
808(g)	1.78	2	905(c)(1)—(6)	1.83	12
808(h)	1.78	3	905(d)	1.83	12
	1.78	4	905(e)	1.83	13
808(i)	1.78	4	905(f)	1.83	11

TABLE OF STATUTES

NEW YORK, MCKINNEY'S BUSINESS CORPORATION LAW			NEW YORK, MCKINNEY'S BUSINESS CORPORATION LAW		
		This Work			This Work
Sec.	Sec.	Note	Sec.	Sec.	Note
906	1.21	5	910(a)(1)(C)	1.90	5
	1.84		910(a)(2)	1.90	6
	1.94	4	910(a)(3)	1.90	7
906(a)	1.84	2	911	1.86	1
906(b)(1)	1.84	3		1.86	2
906(b)(2)	1.84	4		12.55	16
906(b)(3)	1.84	5	912	1.31	1
906(b)(4)	1.84	6		1.39	
907	1.114	12		1.39	11
907(a)	1.83	14		1.39	12
907(b)	1.83	15		1.39	13
907(c)	1.51			1.88	1
	1.83	16		1.89	
	1.90			1.89	12
907(d)	1.83	17		1.89	14
907(e)(1)	1.83	18	912(a)(1)	1.89	11
907(e)(2)	1.51	23	912(a)(3)	1.89	11
	1.83	17	912(a)(4)	1.89	11
	1.83	18	912(a)(5)	1.81	2
907(f)	1.84	1		1.81	5
907(h)	1.83	18		1.89	13
	1.84	7	912(a)(5)(A)	1.83	1
	1.84	8	912(a)(5)(B)	1.85	5
908	1.87	1	912(a)(10)(A)	1.89	11
	1.87	2	912(b)	1.89	14
909	1.21	5	912(c)	1.89	14
	1.78	1	912(c)(3)	1.89	
	1.81	1	912(d)	1.31	1
	1.90			1.89	14
	1.97	6	913	1.51	
	1.122			1.78	1
	1.136	20		1.82	1
	6.15			1.88	
	6.31	1		1.88	1
	6.187			1.88	3
	12.22			1.88	9
	12.55	16		1.89	12
909(a)	1.85	2		1.90	
	1.85	3		1.136	20
909(a)(1)	1.51	16	913(a)(1)	1.88	1
909(a)(3)	1.85	1	913(a)(2)	1.88	1
	1.85	3		1.88	10
909(b)	1.85	2	913(a)(2)(A)	1.88	1
909(c)	1.85	2	913(a)(2)(B)	1.88	1
909(d)	1.85	5	913(b)	1.88	2
909(e)	1.85	5		1.88	10
909(f)	1.85	4		1.88	13
910	1.44	3	913(b)(1)	1.88	4
	1.51	18	913(b)(2)	1.88	4
	1.88		913(c)	1.51	14
	1.90	1		1.88	
	6.15			1.88	3
	6.15	3		1.88	10
910(a)	1.51	20	913(c)(1)	1.88	3
910(a)(1)(A)(i)	1.90	2	913(c)(2)(A)	1.88	3
910(a)(1)(A)(ii)	1.90	3	913(c)(2)(A)(ii)	1.88	3
910(a)(1)(A)(iii)	1.90	3	913(d)	1.88	4
910(a)(1)(B)	1.90	4		1.88	10

TABLE OF STATUTES

NEW YORK, MCKINNEY'S BUSINESS CORPORATION LAW			NEW YORK, MCKINNEY'S BUSINESS CORPORATION LAW		
		This Work			This Work
Sec.	Sec.	Note	Sec.	Sec.	Note
913(d) (Cont'd)	1.88	11	1005(a)(1) (Cont'd)	1.107	1
	1.88	13	1005(a)(2)	1.97	4
913(e)	1.88			1.97	5
	1.88	5		1.107	1
	1.88	6	1005(a)(3)	1.94	6
	1.88	7		1.107	2
	1.88	8	1005(a)(3)(A)	1.97	6
	1.88	10		1.146	2
913(f)	1.88	10	1005(a)(3)(B)	1.97	7
913(f)(1)	1.88	10	1005(b)	1.97	7
913(f)(2)	1.88	10	1005(c)	1.97	7
913(f)(3)	1.88	11		1.107	2
	1.88	13	1006	1.104	1
913(g)	1.51		1006(a)	1.97	8
	1.88		1006(a)(1)	1.97	9
	1.90		1006(a)(2)	1.97	10
913(g)(1)	1.88	12	1006(a)(3)	1.97	11
	1.88	13	1006(a)(4)	1.97	12
913(g)(2)	1.88	13	1006(b)	1.97	13
913(g)(3)	1.88	14	1007	1.97	
913(g)(4)	1.88	13		1.98	
913(h)	1.88	1		1.98	6
913(i)	1.88	1		1.98	9
913(i)(1)	1.88	1		1.104	1
913(i)(2)	1.88	9		1.111	23
913(i)(3)	1.88	9		1.136	23
Art. 10	1.66	5	1007(a)	1.98	1
	1.78	4		1.98	2
	1.85	5		1.98	3
	1.111	23		1.98	4
1001	1.51	17		1.98	5
	1.94	1		1.98	6
	1.96	1	1007(b)	1.98	6
	1.103	2		1.98	7
	1.122			1.98	9
	1.147	13	1007(c)	1.98	10
1001(a)	1.96	1		1.98	11
1001(b)	1.96	1	1007(d)	1.98	13
1002	1.96	1	1008	1.97	
	1.96	3		1.98	
	1.147	13		1.98	6
1002(a)	1.96	1		1.104	1
	1.96	2		1.136	23
1002(b)	1.96	3		1.136	24
1002(c)	1.96	3	1008(a)	1.95	4
	1.144	12		1.95	5
1003	1.96	2		1.95	6
	1.97	1	1008(a)(1)—(a)(11)	1.95	6
1003(a)	1.97	1	1008(a)(2)	1.98	2
1004	1.94	5		1.98	9
	1.95	1	1008(a)(3)	1.98	8
	1.97	1	1008(b)	1.95	6
	1.97	2	1008(c)(1)	1.95	6
1005	1.44	3	1008(c)(2)	1.95	6
	1.51	18	Art. 11	1.66	5
	1.51	20		1.104	1
	1.104	1		1.111	23
1005(a)(1)	1.97	3	1101	1.94	2

264

TABLE OF STATUTES

NEW YORK, MCKINNEY'S BUSINESS CORPORATION LAW

Sec.	This Work Sec.	Note
1101(a)(1)	1.100	1
1101(a)(2)	1.100	2
1101(b)	1.100	3
1101(c)	1.100	2
1102	1.94	3
	1.101	1
1102—1104	1.147	14
1103	1.51	19
	1.94	4
1103(a)	1.102	1
1103(b)	1.102	2
1103(c)	1.102	3
1104	1.51	19
	1.104	
1104(a)	1.103	2
	2.37	9
1104(a)(2)	1.43	9
1104(b)	1.103	2
1104(c)	1.43	3
	1.103	3
1104–a	1.103	
	1.103	6
	1.103	11
	1.104	
	1.147	12
	1.147	14
1104–a(a)	1.103	5
	1.103	7
1104–a(a)(1)	2.37	7
1104–a(a)(2)	2.37	8
1104–a(b)	1.103	8
1104–a(c)	1.103	10
1104–a(d)	1.103	8
1105	1.104	1
	1.104	2
1106	1.136	22
1106(a)	1.104	3
	1.104	4
1106(b)	1.104	5
1106(c)	1.104	6
	1.104	7
1106(d)	1.104	8
	1.104	9
1106(e)	1.104	10
1107	1.104	1
1108	1.104	11
1109	1.94	4
	1.104	12
	1.104	13
1110	1.104	14
	1.104	15
	1.104	16
	1.136	21
1111	1.147	14
1111(a)	1.104	17
1111(b)	1.104	18
	1.104	19
1111(b)(1)	1.94	5

NEW YORK, MCKINNEY'S BUSINESS CORPORATION LAW

Sec.	This Work Sec.	Note
1111(b)(2)	1.94	7
1111(c)	1.104	20
1111(d)	1.104	17
	1.104	21
1111(e)	1.104	22
1112	1.104	23
1113	1.94	6
	1.105	1
	1.105	2
1114	1.106	1
1115(a)(1)	1.106	2
1115(a)(2)	1.106	3
1115(a)(3)	1.106	4
1116	1.104	24
	1.104	25
1117(a)	1.104	1
1117(b)	1.104	1
1117(c)	1.104	1
1118	1.44	3
	1.103	
	1.103	11
	1.147	12
	1.147	14
1118(a)	1.103	11
	1.103	12
	1.103	13
	2.21	20
1118(b)	1.103	14
1118(c)(1)	1.103	15
1118(c)(2)	1.103	16
Art. 12	1.105	
1201	1.111	3
1202(a)(1)	1.111	1
	1.111	2
1202(a)(2)	1.111	3
1202(a)(3)	1.111	4
1202(a)(4)	1.111	
	1.111	5
1203	1.136	25
1203(a)	1.111	6
	1.111	7
1203(b)	1.111	8
	1.111	9
1204(a)(1)	1.111	10
1204(a)(2)	1.111	11
1205	1.111	13
1206(a)	1.111	14
1206(b)(1)	1.111	15
1206(b)(2)	1.111	16
1206(b)(3)	1.111	17
1206(b)(4)	1.111	19
1207	1.136	25
1207(a)(1)	1.111	20
	1.111	24
1207(a)(1)(A)	1.111	21
1207(a)(1)(B)	1.111	22
1207(a)(1)(C)	1.111	23
1207(a)(2)	1.111	26

TABLE OF STATUTES

NEW YORK, MCKINNEY'S BUSINESS CORPORATION LAW

Sec.	This Work Sec.	Note
1207(a)(2) (Cont'd)	1.111	27
	1.111	28
	1.111	29
1207(a)(3)	1.111	31
	1.111	32
	1.111	33
1208	1.111	25
1209	1.111	37
	1.136	25
1210	1.94	6
	1.111	30
1211	1.94	6
	1.111	34
	1.136	25
1212	1.111	35
1213	1.111	38
1213—1216	1.136	25
1214	1.111	39
1215	1.111	40
1216	1.111	36
1217	1.111	12
1217(a)	1.111	12
1217(b)	1.111	12
1217(c)	1.111	12
1218	1.111	41
Art. 13	1.5	
	1.83	17
	1.114	
	1.122	
1301	1.9	1
	1.115	9
	1.116	1
	1.138	5
	1.138	6
1301(a)	1.115	1
	1.115	2
1301(b)	1.115	3
	1.116	1
1301(c)	1.115	4
	1.115	5
1301(d)	1.13	1
	1.14	2
	1.115	6
	1.115	9
	1.117	8
	1.117	9
	1.118	1
	1.138	4
1303	1.115	10
	1.115	11
	1.115	12
	1.115	13
	1.115	14
	1.125	
1304	1.13	1
	1.116	1
	1.125	
1304(a)	1.116	1

NEW YORK, MCKINNEY'S BUSINESS CORPORATION LAW

Sec.	This Work Sec.	Note
1304(a)(7)	1.18	6
1304(b)	1.116	1
1305	1.116	1
	1.117	1
	1.117	2
1306	1.117	3
1307	1.117	3
1308	1.117	7
	1.117	8
1308(a)(7)	1.119	1
1309(a)	1.117	
	1.117	8
1309(b)	1.117	8
1309(c)	1.117	4
	1.117	5
	1.117	6
	1.117	8
1309–A	1.117	10
	1.119	1
1309–A(a)	1.117	9
1309–A(b)	1.117	9
	1.117	10
1309–A(c)	1.117	10
1310(a)	1.118	1
	1.118	3
1310(b)	1.118	1
1310(c)	1.118	2
1310(d)	1.118	3
1311	1.119	1
1312	1.114	7
	1.115	3
	11.36	3
1313	1.114	5
1314	1.114	6
1315(a)	1.114	8
1315(b)	1.114	8
1315(c)	1.114	8
1316	1.125	
	1.136	15
1316(a)	1.114	9
1316(b)	1.114	9
1316(c)	1.114	9
1316(d)	1.114	9
1316(e)	1.114	9
	1.114	13
1317	1.114	10
	1.125	
1317(a)(1)	1.114	13
1318	1.114	11
	1.114	13
1319	1.114	12
1319(a)(4)	1.114	13
1320	1.66	
	1.114	13
	1.125	
Art. 15	1.13	6
	1.122	
	1.122	1

TABLE OF STATUTES

NEW YORK, MCKINNEY'S BUSINESS CORPORATION LAW

Sec.	This Work Sec.	Note
Art. 15 (Cont'd)	1.122	37
Art. 15–A	1.13	6
	1.122	
	1.125	
	1.126	
1501	1.122	1
1501(b)	2.75	3
1503(a)	1.122	1
	1.122	2
	2.43	17
	2.43	18
1503(b)	1.122	3
1503(c)	1.122	3
1503(d)	1.122	4
1503(e)	1.122	4
1504(a)	1.122	5
1504(b)—(f)	1.122	6
1504(g)	1.122	6
1505(a)	1.122	7
	2.72	2
	2.76	5
1505(b)	1.122	8
1506	1.122	9
1507	1.122	10
	1.122	11
	1.122	12
1508	1.122	13
1509	1.122	14
	1.122	16
	1.122	17
	1.122	18
1510	1.122	
	1.122	21
	1.122	22
1510(a)	1.122	19
	1.122	20
	1.122	21
	1.122	22
1510(b)	1.122	23
1511	1.122	23
	1.122	24
	1.122	25
	1.122	26
	1.122	27
	1.122	28
	1.122	29
	1.122	30
	1.122	31
	1.144	13
1512(a)	1.122	32
	1.122	33
1512(b)	1.122	34
1513	1.122	35
	1.122	37
	1.122	41
	1.122	42
1514	1.122	43
	1.122	44

NEW YORK, MCKINNEY'S BUSINESS CORPORATION LAW

Sec.	This Work Sec.	Note
1516	1.122	36
	1.122	37
	1.122	38
	1.122	39
	1.122	40
1525	1.125	1
	1.125	2
1526(b)—(f)	1.125	3
1526(g)	1.125	4
1527(a)	1.125	6
	1.125	7
	1.125	8
1528	1.125	5
1529	1.125	9
	1.125	10
	1.125	11
1530	1.125	
1530(a)	1.125	12
1530(b)	1.125	12
1530(c)	1.125	12
	1.125	13
1531	1.125	13
1532(a)	1.125	14
1532(b)	1.125	15
	1.125	16
1532(c)	1.125	17
1533	1.125	2
Art. 16	1.89	
	1.89	1
	1.89	10
	1.89	20
1601(a)	1.89	2
1601(a)(1)—(a)(4)	1.89	2
1601(b)	1.89	2
1601(c)	1.89	2
1601(d)	1.89	4
1601(e)	1.89	3
1602	1.136	20
1602(a)	1.89	5
	1.89	6
	1.89	20
1602(b)	1.89	6
	1.89	7
1602(c)	1.89	8
1603	1.136	20
1603(a)	1.89	6
1603(b)	1.89	6
	1.89	20
1603(c)	1.89	6
1604(a)	1.89	18
1604(b)	1.89	19
	1.89	20
1605(a)	1.89	20
1605(b)	1.89	20
1605(c)	1.89	20
1606	1.89	4
1607	1.89	4
1608	1.89	4

TABLE OF STATUTES

NEW YORK, MCKINNEY'S BUSINESS CORPORATION LAW

Sec.	This Work Sec.	Note
1608 (Cont'd)	1.136	20
1609(a)	1.89	15
	1.89	16
1609(b)	1.89	17
1609(c)	1.89	15
1610	1.89	2
	1.89	10
1612	1.89	10
1613	1.89	21
	1.89	22

NEW YORK CITY CHARTER

Sec.	This Work Sec.	Note
192	16.6	6
	16.6	7
197–c	16.6	3
200	16.6	2
659	16.6	5
668	16.6	4
3020	16.6	10

NEW YORK CITY CIVIL COURT ACT

Sec.	This Work Sec.	Note
Art. 2	37.91	
	37.91	3
102	37.117	1
103	37.91	8
201	37.117	4
204	13.5	2
206	7.16	1
206(b)	7.51	
301(a)	7.58	
319	13.22	
401(c)	13.13	4
	13.41	4
1303(a)	13.22	12
	13.47	11
1303(c)	13.22	13
	13.47	12
1609	7.24	1
1612	37.5	6
	37.12	
	37.12	1
Art. 17	37.91	3
1701	37.118	
1702	37.120	
1703	37.119	2
	37.122	1
1704	37.122	4
	37.125	4
1707	37.121	
Art. 18	7.2	1
	37.91	3

NEW YORK CITY CIVIL COURT ACT

Sec.	This Work Sec.	Note
1801	7.27	14
	37.125	1
Art. 18–A	37.91	3
Art. 19	37.91	3
1907	37.124	1
1908(f)	37.124	1
1910(a)	37.124	1
1911(f)	37.122	3
Art. 21	37.91	3
2101(b)	37.122	2
2101(f)	37.122	2
2102	37.119	2
2103	37.91	5

NEW YORK CITY CRIMINAL COURT ACT

Sec.	This Work Sec.	Note
2(5)	38.48	3
21(1)	38.48	3
31	38.48	4
41(2)	38.48	3

NEW YORK, MCKINNEY'S CIVIL PRACTICE LAW

Sec.	This Work Sec.	Note
Art. 450	37.3	12
Art. 460	37.3	12
Art. 470	37.3	12

NEW YORK, MCKINNEY'S CIVIL PRACTICE LAW AND RULES

Sec.	This Work Sec.	Note
103	38.8	71
103(b)	39.15	1
103(c)	3.32	6
	16.45	2
105	8.24	2
105(b)	37.38	3
105(f)	7.39	7
105(i)	8.21	1
Art. 2	26.33	
	26.41	
201(e)	19.5	7
203(c)	18.38	2
203(f)	18.38	3
208	29.26	11
	29.26	12
210(b)	23.81	13
	28.14	7
211(b)	8.3	6
212(a)	12.66	5
213	7.47	4

TABLE OF STATUTES

NEW YORK, MCKINNEY'S CIVIL PRACTICE LAW AND RULES

Sec.	This Work Sec.	Note
213(1)	23.81	13
213(2)	28.13	
	31.26	
213(4)	11.36	2
	11.37	7
213(8)	9.119	1
214	27.39	
	27.39	1
214(6)	28.13	
	28.13	1
214–a	27.25	
	28.13	
	29.26	1
	29.26	4
214–b	27.39	
214–c	15.32	18
	15.32	19
	26.16	2
	27.39	
215	18.9	2
	18.20	1
	18.25	4
215(1)	18.11	5
215(3)	18.64	11
	18.81	6
	29.26	2
217	1.43	18
	4.2	
	4.2	41
	4.2	43
	4.3	
	4.82	
	4.82	2
	4.82	3
	4.82	5
	4.82	7
	4.86	
	16.43	4
	17.53	12
217(1)	23.83	16
Art. 3	1.19	
	7.54	
	11.36	1
301	17.82	6
	17.83	1
301(8)	26.37	1
302	1.19	1
	1.115	4
302(a)(4)	11.21	1
302(b)	21.12	
	21.12	1
	21.12	2
	21.12	3
	21.12	4
304	18.38	2
	21.11	
	26.32	2

NEW YORK, MCKINNEY'S CIVIL PRACTICE LAW AND RULES

Sec.	This Work Sec.	Note
304 (Cont'd)	28.23	2
305(b)	26.32	
	26.36	2
	26.32	4
306(d)	26.32	3
306–a	26.32	
306–a(b)	26.32	
306–b	26.32	
306–b(b)	17.78	2
307	26.41	14
308	8.32	4
	21.11	
	21.11	2
	25.19	
308—311	11.54	9
308(1)	21.11	
308(2)	21.11	
	22.20	4
308(3)	21.11	
308(4)	13.9	
	21.11	
	26.32	
308(5)	21.11	
	26.32	
	26.32	5
310(a)	13.7	2
310(b)	13.7	2
	13.7	3
311	1.18	1
	26.32	
311(a)	26.32	
311(a)(1)	13.7	1
311(a)(2)—(8)	13.7	1
311(b)	26.32	
312	35.102	3
314	21.11	4
315	21.11	
	21.11	5
318	1.18	1
	8.29	5
	21.11	
320	11.38	
321(b)	28.6	
321(c)	39.19	
325(b)	30.3	6
Art. 4	8.41	1
401	13.14	3
	13.14	4
402	13.14	1
403(b)	5.69	
	7.50	
403(c)	8.41	1
	8.42	15
	8.45	2
	35.102	3
404(a)	13.22	7
	13.23	2

269

TABLE OF STATUTES

NEW YORK, MCKINNEY'S CIVIL PRACTICE LAW AND RULES

Sec.	This Work Sec.	Note
404(a) (Cont'd)	13.23	4
	13.47	6
	13.48	2
	13.48	4
406	13.46	3
	13.48	1
408	13.58	1
	13.59	1
	13.23	1
410	13.62	1
411	8.41	1
503(a)	7.58	
	7.62	
	21.15	1
	21.15	2
	21.15	3
503(f)	7.39	7
504	26.34	1
506	4.83	
	4.85	
506(b)	4.63	11
	4.83	1
	4.84	2
	37.44	5
	37.87	16
506(b)(1)	37.86	1
	37.87	
	37.90	1
506(b)(2)	4.83	5
	37.87	16
506(b)(3)	37.87	16
506(b)(4)	37.87	16
507	11.19	1
	11.43	2
	21.15	
	21.15	4
510	21.16	
	21.16	1
510(2)	4.83	4
510(3)	4.83	4
601	21.17	
602	10.137	
	21.17	
	37.53	1
602(a)	21.17	2
603	37.37	
	37.37	32
Art. 9	7.47	5
	10.146	1
	10.147	
	10.147	1
	17.82	
908	10.102	
	10.103	
	10.146	1
	10.147	1
908(a)(1)	10.102	

NEW YORK, MCKINNEY'S CIVIL PRACTICE LAW AND RULES

Sec.	This Work Sec.	Note
1012(a)(1)	37.24	1
1012(a)(2)	37.24	2
1012(a)(3)	37.24	3
1012(b)	37.24	4
1013	37.22	11
	37.24	5
1015	8.13	1
	25.16	1
	37.25	1
1016	37.25	1
1021	8.13	1
	37.25	3
	37.25	4
	37.25	5
1022	37.25	2
	37.43	7
	39.19	
	39.23	4
1024	13.14	7
	13.17	5
	13.43	7
Art. 11	37.48	
1101	37.82	
	39.35	
1101(a)	39.35	1
1101(c)	37.46	6
	37.46	7
1102(c)	37.48	1
	37.51	39
1206	30.44	
Art. 13–A	38.10	
Art. 14	26.60	
	30.44	1
Art. 14–A	27.4	
	27.40	11
	30.28	
1401	28.26	
1411	26.37	
	26.66	
	27.4	3
Art. 16	26.37	3
	30.3	9
	30.44	1
1601	26.37	3
1602	26.58	
2002	37.28	
	38.19	
	39.7	
	39.7	20
2003	8.33	8
2004	37.43	1
2101(a)	13.14	1
	17.82	1
2101(b)	13.14	1
	17.82	1
2101(c)	13.14	2
	13.18	2

270

TABLE OF STATUTES

NEW YORK, MCKINNEY'S CIVIL PRACTICE LAW AND RULES

Sec.	This Work Sec.	Note
2101(d)	13.14	5
	17.82	
2103	8.42	
	38.32	
2103(b)	8.24	1
	38.32	5
2103(b)(2)	37.40	2
	37.41	5
	37.96	3
	39.20	2
	39.20	4
2103(b)(6)	37.40	2
	37.41	5
	37.96	3
	39.20	8
	39.20	6
	39.20	7
2103(e)	26.68	
	26.70	
2103(f)	39.20	3
2104	13.63	5
2105	37.51	
	37.51	12
2106	8.56	
	37.132	
	37.134	
	37.136	
	37.138	
	37.140	
	38.61	
	38.63	
2211	11.52	5
2214	37.76	
	37.77	
	37.78	
	37.130	
	37.133	
	37.135	
	37.137	
	37.139	
	38.60	
	38.62	
2214(b)	5.67	
	10.137	
	11.63	
	11.77	
	14.135	
	30.56	
	37.75	
2214(d)	37.41	9
2218	37.37	
2219(a)	37.37	38
	37.38	
	37.38	4
	37.38	6
	37.38	7
2303	8.23	5

NEW YORK, MCKINNEY'S CIVIL PRACTICE LAW AND RULES

Sec.	This Work Sec.	Note
2303 (Cont'd)	8.23	7
2304	4.63	11
2304, Comment 6	4.63	11
2305(a)	8.23	7
2308(a)	8.42	3
Art. 25	10.54	
Art. 30	26.46	
	26.67	
3001	3.32	
	16.50	11
	37.65	65
3002(e)	28.43	3
3004	28.43	3
3012	11.78	
3012(a)	11.35	
	26.36	1
	29.83	
3012(c)	11.35	
3012–a	26.11	2
	26.12	
	26.13	3
	29.16	7
	29.79	
3012–a(a)	29.28	1
	29.28	2
3012–a(a)(2)	26.11	7
	29.28	4
3012–a(a)(3)	29.28	5
3012–a(b)	29.28	3
3012–a(c)	29.16	8
	29.28	8
3012–a(e)	29.28	6
3012–a(f)	29.28	7
3013	17.82	
	17.82	11
	17.82	18
	26.36	3
3014	13.57	1
	17.82	1
	17.82	12
	17.82	19
	26.36	3
3015	17.82	3
3015(b)	13.17	3
	13.17	6
	13.43	4
	13.43	6
3015(d)	26.36	4
3015(e)	26.36	5
3016	17.82	15
	26.36	6
3016(a)	17.25	
3016(b)	17.27	
3016(f)	17.82	28
	30.3	7
3016(h)	17.78	1
	17.82	29

271

TABLE OF STATUTES

NEW YORK, MCKINNEY'S CIVIL PRACTICE LAW AND RULES

Sec.	This Work Sec.	Note
3017	17.82	20
	26.36	8
3017(a)	30.3	1
3017(b)	16.50	11
	31.21	
	31.21	1
3017(c)	3.38	
	26.36	9
	29.27	1
	29.27	2
	30.3	2
	30.3	3
	30.49	
3018	11.37	2
	29.17	4
	29.17	5
	29.17	6
3018(a)	17.84	
	17.84	3
	28.49	
3018(b)	5.8	1
	5.18	1
	17.84	
	17.84	4
	30.3	8
3019	17.84	6
3020	17.84	9
3020(a)	11.37	2
	13.19	1
	17.82	30
3020(b)	11.37	2
	17.82	31
3020(d)(1)	13.19	2
3020(d)(2)	13.19	3
3021	13.19	
3021	17.82	28
3024(b)	17.82	13
	17.84	2
3031	5.68	
3041	26.46	1
	30.3	12
3041—3044	26.46	
3042	26.46	2
3042(a)	26.47	1
	26.47	2
	26.47	3
3042(d)	26.46	3
3042	13.57	1
3043	26.60	1
3043(a)	30.3	
3043(b)	30.3	15
3045	30.3	16
Art. 31	4.90	
	22.31	14
	26.42	
	26.43	
3101	21.63	

NEW YORK, MCKINNEY'S CIVIL PRACTICE LAW AND RULES

Sec.	This Work Sec.	Note
3101 (Cont'd)	21.63	1
	26.42	2
	26.44	
	26.51	
	26.68	
	26.70	
3101(a)(4)	26.43	6
3101(d)	1.51	70
	26.42	5
	26.68	
	26.70	
	29.48	1
3101(d)(1)	30.4	3
3101(d)(1)(i)	21.63	
	21.79	
	26.42	7
	26.42	8
3101(d)(1)(iii)	26.42	10
3101(d)(2)	26.42	11
3101(e)	26.42	14
	26.68	
	26.70	
3101(f)	26.24	8
	26.42	15
	26.70	
3101(g)	26.68	
	26.70	
3102(c)	27.33	1
3104	8.44	4
3106	26.43	1
3106(a)	26.43	3
3106(d)	26.43	4
3106(f)	17.82	16
3107	26.43	2
	26.44	1
3110	8.23	
	26.43	12
3110(1)	26.43	7
3110(2)	26.43	8
	26.43	9
3110(3)	26.43	10
3111	26.43	14
3116(c)	26.43	16
3120	4.91	
	26.45	1
	26.68	
	26.70	
3120(a)(1)(i)	4.89	
3121	17.72	
	26.42	18
	30.3	
3121(b)	30.3	19
3122	26.44	4
	26.44	5
	26.45	1
3123	13.59	
3124	26.44	

TABLE OF STATUTES

NEW YORK, MCKINNEY'S CIVIL PRACTICE LAW AND RULES

Sec.	This Work Sec.	Note
3124 (Cont'd)	29.65	5
3126	21.65	
	26.46	3
3130	30.3	17
	30.3	18
3131	26.44	
3132	26.44	3
3201	8.4	11
3211	11.35	
	11.36	
	13.4	
	17.84	1
	37.28	
3211(a)	13.23	
	13.48	
	21.21	
	21.23	
	21.25	
	21.29	
	21.30	
	37.35	
3211(a)(1)	13.29	
3211(a)(2)	37.37	
	37.37	66
	39.27	
3211(a)(7)	7.54	
	11.77	
	11.78	
3211(a)(8)	7.53	
	26.32	7
3211(a)(10)	8.41	1
3211(b)	11.77	
	11.78	
3211(c)	37.37	
3211(d)	13.48	3
3211(e)	13.23	3
	26.32	8
3212	4.39	1
	5.59	
	5.60	
	5.67	
	11.1	
	11.39	
	11.41	
	11.77	
	11.78	
	26.30	4
	26.32	
3212(b)	11.78	
	37.65	67
3212(c)	37.37	
3213	8.4	
	8.4	8
	8.16	3
3215	11.39	
	11.40	
3215(a)	8.4	2

NEW YORK, MCKINNEY'S CIVIL PRACTICE LAW AND RULES

Sec.	This Work Sec.	Note
3215(b)	8.4	4
	8.4	5
3215(f)	8.4	3
3215(g)(3)	8.4	1
3215(g)(4)	8.4	1
3215(i)(1)	8.4	21
3218	8.4	10
3218(a)	8.4	11
	8.4	12
	8.4	18
3218(b)	8.4	14
3218(c)	8.4	15
3222	37.49	
	37.51	
	37.55	
3222(a)	37.51	44
	37.51	45
	37.51	48
	37.51	49
3222(b)(3)	37.51	45
3222(b)(4)	37.51	47
3222(b)(5)	37.51	47
3406(a)	29.29	1
3406(b)	29.30	
	29.30	1
	29.30	2
4017	37.28	15
	37.28	16
	39.7	8
4018	28.24	
4044(a)	37.65	29
	37.65	30
4101	17.96	1
4102	17.82	22
4102(a)	17.82	22
4102(e)	25.30	4
4109	17.74	1
	26.55	3
4110–b	39.7	8
4111	30.68	
4111(d)	29.24	4
	30.4	8
	30.4	9
	30.67	
4111(e)	30.4	8
	30.67	
4111(f)	30.4	8
	30.67	
4213	14.114	2
4213(b)	11.44	2
	37.29	
	37.29	10
	37.65	16
Art. 43	11.43	
4313	11.43	1
4318	11.43	3
4319	11.44	2

TABLE OF STATUTES

NEW YORK, MCKINNEY'S CIVIL PRACTICE LAW AND RULES

Sec.	This Work Sec.	Note
4401	37.37	38
	37.65	42
4401–a	29.14	5
	29.16	3
4404	17.76	1
	37.28	15
	37.29	
	37.65	
	37.65	23
	38.20	
	39.9	
4404(a)	37.29	2
	37.65	
	37.65	18
	38.10	63
	39.7	
Art. 45	30.4	
4502(a)	21.26	8
4511	37.29	
4511(a)	37.29	
	37.29	32
4511(b)	37.29	
	37.29	32
	37.29	36
4511(c)	37.29	
4518	30.4	
4518(a)	33.68	
4519	25.3	2
4532–a	30.4	
4533	30.4	
4533–a	30.4	
4533–a	30.4	5
4533–b	30.3	11
4540	8.16	5
4542	8.16	5
4544	7.29	5
	7.58	
	7.59	
4545	26.37	2
	26.66	
	30.3	10
	30.28	
	30.44	1
4545(a)	29.24	5
	30.28	1
4545(b)	30.28	1
4545(c)	30.28	1
	30.52	
4546	30.4	
	30.44	1
4546(3)	29.24	6
Art. 50–A	8.1	20
	29.31	
	29.31	1
	30.4	
	30.44	
	30.44	3

NEW YORK, MCKINNEY'S CIVIL PRACTICE LAW AND RULES

Sec.	This Work Sec.	Note
Art. 50–B	8.1	21
	30.4	
	30.44	
	30.44	3
5001	8.6	1
	8.6	4
	30.40	
5001(a)	30.40	2
	30.40	16
5001(b)	30.40	
5001(c)	8.6	2
	30.40	
	30.58	
5002	8.6	5
	30.40	
	30.40	8
	30.40	17
5003	8.6	6
	30.40	
	30.40	9
	30.40	17
5003–a	8.4	21
	26.48	
	30.4	11
5003–a(c)	30.4	13
5003–a(e)	26.48	4
	30.4	14
5003–a(g)	30.4	12
5004	8.6	3
	30.40	14
5011	8.3	2
	21.67	1
	37.38	2
	37.38	3
5012	8.3	1
5014	8.15	2
5014(1)	8.15	1
	8.31	7
5014(2)	8.15	4
5014(3)	8.15	5
5015	21.29	10
5015(a)	8.10	1
	8.10	2
5015(b)	8.10	3
5016	8.4	7
5016(a)	8.8	1
5016(d)	8.13	1
	8.13	2
5017(a)	8.5	1
5017(b)	8.5	2
5018	8.8	3
5018(a)	8.9	1
	8.9	3
5018(b)	8.17	1
	8.17	3
5019	38.10	129
5019(a)	8.14	3

274

TABLE OF STATUTES

NEW YORK, MCKINNEY'S CIVIL PRACTICE LAW AND RULES

Sec.	This Work Sec.	Note
5019(d)	8.12	2
5020(a)	8.11	2
5020(b)	8.11	2
5020(c)	8.11	4
	8.12	1
5020(d)	8.11	3
5020–a	8.11	5
	8.11	6
	8.11	7
5021(b)	8.11	4
5031	30.44	3
5031(a)	30.44	5
5031(b)	29.31	3
5031(c)	29.31	5
	30.44	7
5031(d)	29.31	6
5031(e)	30.44	
	30.44	2
	30.44	6
5031(f)	29.31	1
5035(a)	29.31	7
	29.31	8
5035(b)	29.31	9
5036	29.31	10
	29.31	11
5037	30.44	9
5038	29.31	12
	30.44	10
5041	30.44	3
5041(a)	30.44	5
5041(c)	30.44	7
5041(e)	30.44	
5041(e)	30.44	2
	30.44	6
5047	30.44	9
5048	30.44	10
5104	8.41	9
5106	8.37	5
Art. 52	7.24	
	7.28	6
	8.2	
	8.20	
	8.23	
	8.24	
	8.25	
	8.26	
	8.27	
	8.28	
	8.29	
	8.30	
	8.31	
	8.32	
	8.33	
	8.34	
	8.35	
	8.36	
	8.37	

NEW YORK, MCKINNEY'S CIVIL PRACTICE LAW AND RULES

Sec.	This Work Sec.	Note
Art. 52 (Cont'd)	8.38	
	8.39	
	8.40	
	8.41	
	8.42	
	8.43	
	8.44	
	21.72	
5201(a)	8.19	1
5201(b)	8.19	
5201(c)	8.21	2
5203(a)	8.15	1
	8.31	1
	11.53	5
5203(a)(2)	8.33	4
5203(b)	8.31	5
5205	7.24	2
	8.20	
	9.49	1
	9.125	7
5205(a)	8.20	4
5205(b)	8.20	5
5205(c)	8.20	6
5205(c)(2)	9.49	1
	24.85	2
5205(c)(3)	9.49	1
5205(d)	8.34	9
	24.85	2
5205(d)(2)	8.20	7
5205(e)	8.20	8
5205(f)	8.20	9
5205(g)	8.20	10
	8.20	11
5205(i)	8.20	12
5206	8.20	
	8.20	13
	9.125	9
	9.125	10
	9.128	6
5206(e)	8.33	2
5206(f)	8.20	14
5207	8.24	2
5208	8.13	3
	8.13	5
	8.24	3
5209	8.21	3
5210	8.42	1
5211	8.23	19
5221(a)	8.42	1
	8.45	
5221(a)(4)	8.38	1
5221(b)	8.23	6
5222	8.42	4
5222(a)	8.25	6
	8.25	7
	8.26	2
5222(b)	8.21	3

275

TABLE OF STATUTES

NEW YORK, MCKINNEY'S CIVIL PRACTICE LAW AND RULES

Sec.	This Work Sec.	Note
5222(b) (Cont'd)	8.25	
	8.25	7
	8.25	9
	8.25	11
	8.25	12
	8.26	
5222(d)	8.20	1
	8.20	3
	8.27	2
	8.27	3
5222(e)	8.20	2
	8.25	5
	8.29	1
5222(g)	8.25	10
5223	8.2	8
	8.23	1
	8.23	14
5224	8.23	
	8.23	3
5224(a)(3)	8.23	21
	8.23	22
5224(c)	8.23	4
	8.23	6
5224(d)	8.23	10
	8.23	11
5224(e)	8.23	12
5224(f)	8.23	13
5225	8.29	8
	8.29	9
	8.29	10
	8.39	1
5225(a)	8.40	1
	8.40	3
	8.40	4
	8.42	5
5225(b)	8.41	
	8.41	2
	8.41	3
	8.41	5
	8.41	6
	8.41	8
5225(c)	8.39	2
5226	8.35	3
	8.35	6
	8.36	1
5227	8.29	8
	8.29	9
	8.29	10
	8.39	3
	8.41	2
	8.41	3
	8.41	8
5228(a)	8.37	1
	8.38	1
	8.38	2
	8.38	5
	8.38	7

NEW YORK, MCKINNEY'S CIVIL PRACTICE LAW AND RULES

Sec.	This Work Sec.	Note
5228(a) (Cont'd)	8.38	8
5228(b)	8.38	3
5229	8.2	2
	8.22	1
5230	8.28	2
5230(a)	8.28	6
	8.28	7
	8.34	1
	11.6	8
5230(b)	8.28	4
5230(c)	8.28	11
	8.28	12
5230(e)	8.28	5
5231	8.28	3
	8.34	1
5231(a)	8.34	2
	8.34	3
5231(b)	8.34	11
	8.34	12
5231(c)(i)	8.34	8
5231(c)(ii)	8.34	10
5231(d)	8.34	4
	8.34	6
5231(e)	8.34	5
5231(f)	8.34	7
5231(g)	8.34	
5231(j)	8.34	13
	8.34	14
5232(a)	8.29	1
	8.29	4
	8.29	5
	8.29	6
	8.29	7
5232(b)	8.29	2
	8.29	3
5232(c)	8.20	2
	8.29	1
5233	11.1	15
5233(a)	8.30	1
	8.30	2
5233(b)	8.30	3
5233(c)	8.30	1
5233(d)	8.30	2
5234(a)	8.30	4
5234(b)	8.28	10
	8.30	5
	8.30	6
5234(c)	8.30	9
	8.30	10
	8.40	2
5235	8.31	2
	8.31	6
	11.6	8
5236	8.32	1
	11.1	15
5236(a)	8.31	3
	8.32	8

276

TABLE OF STATUTES

NEW YORK, MCKINNEY'S CIVIL PRACTICE LAW AND RULES

Sec.	This Work Sec.	Note
5236(b)	8.32	2
	8.32	3
	8.32	9
	11.6	8
5236(c)	8.32	4
	8.32	5
5236(d)	8.32	10
5236(e)	8.32	6
5236(f)	8.33	11
5236(g)	8.33	3
5236(g)(1)	8.32	7
5237	8.33	12
	8.33	13
5238	8.33	1
5239	8.41	3
	8.45	1
	8.45	2
	8.45	3
	8.45	4
	8.45	5
	8.45	6
5240	8.19	4
	8.23	2
	8.33	7
	8.35	
	8.44	1
	8.44	2
	8.44	3
	8.44	4
5241	21.72	
	21.72	2
5241(a)(8)	21.74	3
5241(e)	21.72	
	21.74	4
5242	21.72	
	21.72	3
5250	8.42	10
	8.42	11
	8.43	1
	8.43	2
	8.43	3
5251	8.23	20
	8.27	4
	8.40	5
	8.42	2
	8.42	6
5252(1)	8.34	16
5252(2)	8.34	17
5301(b)	8.18	2
5303	8.18	4
5304(a)	8.18	5
5304(b)	8.18	7
5305	8.18	6
5306	8.18	3
5309	8.18	1
5401	8.16	2
5401(a)	8.18	2

NEW YORK, MCKINNEY'S CIVIL PRACTICE LAW AND RULES

Sec.	This Work Sec.	Note
5402	8.18	2
5402(a)	8.16	7
5403	8.16	8
	8.16	9
5404(a)	8.16	10
5404(b)	8.16	10
5405	8.16	6
5408	8.16	1
Art. 55	37.3	11
	37.13	
	37.94	
	37.97	
	37.103	
	37.111	
	37.119	
	37.123	
et seq.	38.8	
5501	37.30	
	37.37	26
	38.8	75
5501(a)	37.85	4
	39.9	26
	39.11	8
5501(a)(1)	37.35	
	37.35	4
	37.37	
	37.127	3
	38.3	29
	39.7	
5501(a)(1)—(5)	37.35	
5501(a)(3)	37.28	16
	39.7	8
5501(a)(4)	37.28	16
	39.7	8
5501(b)	37.13	1
	39.7	
	39.7	1
	39.9	25
	39.9	27
	39.11	5
	39.13	3
5501(c)	30.29	
	37.13	2
	37.27	
	37.29	
	37.29	26
	37.65	61
5501(d)	37.13	3
5511	37.21	2
	37.22	1
	37.23	1
	37.37	14
	37.37	17
	38.5	8
	38.5	9
	39.5	2
	39.5	4

277

TABLE OF STATUTES

NEW YORK, MCKINNEY'S CIVIL PRACTICE LAW AND RULES

	This Work	
Sec.	Sec.	Note
5511 (Cont'd)	39.25	3
5512	37.38	1
5512(a)	39.6	
	39.6	1
	39.6	3
5513	8.3	8
	37.39	1
	37.43	
	37.69	
	38.12	5
	39.87	
	39.88	
5513(a)	35.105	6
	37.17	4
	37.40	1
	37.40	3
	37.46	
	37.96	2
	38.8	75
	39.20	1
	39.22	
5513(b)	37.41	2
	37.41	3
	37.41	4
	37.70	2
	37.95	9
	37.97	22
	37.97	24
	37.123	18
	38.8	75
	39.21	1
	39.22	
5513(c)	39.18	
	37.42	1
	38.8	75
	39.22	1
5514	37.39	1
5514(a)	37.43	4
	37.43	5
	39.23	2
	39.27	15
5514(b)	37.43	6
	39.23	3
5514(c)	37.43	1
	37.43	9
	37.127	1
	38.14	1
5515	39.88	
5515(1)	37.19	34
	37.45	1
	37.46	1
	39.25	2
5515(2)	39.26	6
5516	37.41	8
	37.70	5
	39.19	
	39.73	

NEW YORK, MCKINNEY'S CIVIL PRACTICE LAW AND RULES

	This Work	
Sec.	Sec.	Note
5517(a)	37.47	
	37.47	2
5517(b)	37.47	3
	38.8	75
5518	37.80	
	37.80	9
5519	8.3	9
	39.33	
5519(a)	37.80	
5519(a)(1)	37.80	
	37.80	1
5519(a)(2)	37.80	3
5519(a)(4)	37.80	4
5519(a)(5)	37.80	4
5519(a)(6)	37.80	4
5519(b)	37.80	5
5519(c)	37.80	
	37.80	6
	37.80	10
5519(e)	37.80	
	37.127	4
	38.8	75
	39.12	3
	39.33	2
5519(e)(i)	37.80	14
5519(f)	37.80	8
5519(g)	37.80	7
5520(a)	37.43	9
	37.127	2
	38.8	75
	39.24	1
5520(b)	39.14	1
	39.24	2
5520(c)	37.43	10
	37.45	4
5521(a)	37.61	
5521(b)	37.61	
	37.16	7
	37.19	
5522	37.27	1
	37.29	26
5522(a)	37.63	1
	37.65	1
	37.65	10
	39.31	2
	39.31	5
5523	37.65	
5525	37.51	10
	37.126	
5525(a)	37.51	
	37.51	2
5525(b)	37.51	
	37.68	1
5525(c)(1)	37.51	3
5525(c)(2)	37.51	4
5525(d)	37.51	
5526	37.49	

TABLE OF STATUTES

NEW YORK, MCKINNEY'S CIVIL PRACTICE LAW AND RULES

Sec.	This Work Sec.	Note
5526 (Cont'd)	37.51	
	37.51	8
	39.29	9
5527	37.49	
	37.51	
	37.51	35
	37.55	
	37.123	
5528	37.49	
	37.51	
	38.55	
	39.29	10
	39.29	13
5528(a)	37.51	
	37.52	
5528(a)—(c)	37.52	
5528(a)(5)	37.51	18
	37.51	20
5528(b)	37.51	
	37.51	21
	37.51	29
	37.52	24
5528(c)	37.51	
	37.52	26
5528(d)	37.51	22
5528(e)	37.52	
	39.29	15
5529	37.49	
	37.51	19
	37.123	
	38.55	
	39.26	2
	39.29	10
5529(a)	37.52	1
5529(a)(2)	37.52	2
5529(a)(3)	37.52	3
5529(b)	37.52	6
5529(d)	37.52	8
5529(e)	37.52	7
5530(a)	37.50	
5530(b)	37.50	
	37.51	
5530(c)	37.50	
5531	37.51	
	37.52	
	37.97	
	38.8	
	38.17	
	38.55	
	39.29	
	39.89	
5532	37.51	
	37.51	13
5601	39.2	
	39.2	2
	39.8	
	39.8	1

NEW YORK, MCKINNEY'S CIVIL PRACTICE LAW AND RULES

Sec.	This Work Sec.	Note
5601 (Cont'd)	39.9	15
	39.27	
5601(a)	35.105	2
	39.2	3
	39.3	2
	39.3	3
	39.8	2
	39.9	
	39.9	5
	39.11	
	39.11	13
	39.16	
	39.81	
5601(a)(1)(i)	39.3	4
5601(b)	35.105	3
	39.2	3
	39.8	3
5601(b)(1)	39.9	
	39.9	13
	39.11	
	39.11	13
	39.16	
	39.16	11
	39.78	
5601(b)(2)	37.121	
	39.10	
	39.10	1
	39.79	
5601(c)	35.105	4
	39.8	4
	39.9	
	39.9	15
	39.9	16
	39.16	
	39.16	6
	39.80	
5601(d)	35.105	5
	39.7	
	39.8	5
	39.9	
	39.9	24
	39.9	27
	39.11	
	39.13	
	39.16	
	39.81	
5602(a)	35.105	7
	38.8	75
	39.12	1
	39.12	2
	39.18	
	39.19	16
5602(a)(1)	39.13	2
	39.83	
	39.84	
5602(a)(1)(i)	37.70	6
	39.14	

279

TABLE OF STATUTES

NEW YORK, MCKINNEY'S CIVIL PRACTICE LAW AND RULES

Sec.	This Work Sec.	Note
5602(a)(1)(i) (Cont'd)	39.14	1
	39.14	2
	39.19	
5602(a)(1)(ii)	39.7	
	39.13	
	39.16	
	39.19	
5602(a)(2)	39.15	
	39.15	2
	39.16	
	39.19	
	39.73	
5602(b)(1)	39.16	
	39.16	1
5602(b)(2)	39.16	
	39.16	2
5602(b)(2)(i)	39.16	
	39.16	12
5602(b)(2)(ii)	39.7	
	39.16	
	39.16	9
5602(b)(2)(iii)	39.16	
	39.16	6
5611	37.34	3
	37.70	6
	39.4	
	39.6	2
	39.9	2
	39.9	8
5613	37.65	5
	39.31	2
5614	39.31	4
5615	39.9	
	39.9	18
Art. 57	37.3	11
	37.13	
	37.97	
	37.123	
	38.3	20
5701	37.15	1
	37.34	2
	37.95	
	37.126	3
5701(a)	18.31	7
	37.16	1
	37.33	1
	37.37	6
	37.95	
5701(a)(1)	37.33	3
	37.34	3
	37.38	1
5701(a)(2)	37.33	4
	37.35	
	37.35	2
	37.37	38
	37.37	39
	37.38	

NEW YORK, MCKINNEY'S CIVIL PRACTICE LAW AND RULES

Sec.	This Work Sec.	Note
5701(a)(2) (Cont'd)	37.38	1
	37.38	6
5701(a)(2)(i)—(vii)	37.35	
5701(a)(2)(iv)	37.35	
	38.3	
5701(a)(2)(v)	37.35	
	37.37	
	37.37	32
	38.3	
5701(a)(3)	37.33	4
	37.35	
	37.35	3
5701(b)	37.33	2
	37.36	
	37.37	
	37.37	5
	37.95	
5701(b)(1)	37.37	
5701(b)(1)—(3)	37.36	1
5701(b)(3)	37.37	47
5701(c)	37.16	1
	37.33	2
	37.36	
	37.36	2
	37.37	5
	37.37	39
	37.41	
	37.41	1
5702	37.16	4
	37.18	1
5703	37.3	15
	37.20	
5703(a)	37.20	1
	37.41	7
	37.97	21
5703(b)	37.20	
	37.20	2
	37.97	
	37.123	15
	37.123	16
5704	37.37	
	37.86	
	37.89	
	37.89	3
5704(a)	37.86	4
	37.89	
	37.89	1
	37.97	
5704(b)	37.97	
5711	37.18	1
	37.59	1
5712(b)	37.64	1
5712(c)	37.65	2
5712(c)(1)	37.65	4
5712(c)(2)	37.65	6
	37.65	7
5713	37.70	7

280

TABLE OF STATUTES

NEW YORK, MCKINNEY'S CIVIL PRACTICE LAW AND RULES

Sec.	This Work Sec.	Note
5713	39.16	5
Art. 60 et seq.	8.1	
Art. 62	8.1	
Arts. 62—65	37.35	1
Art. 63	7.12	
	7.47	5
	8.1	
6301	7.33	16
	7.63	
	7.64	
6311	7.63	
	7.64	
6313	7.33	16
Art. 64	8.1	
	8.37	
6401—6405	11.75	
6401(a)	8.37	4
6401(b)	11.31	7
6402—6405	8.38	6
6405	11.31	3
Art. 65	8.1	
6501	11.17	2
	11.54	
6511	11.17	3
6512	11.17	1
	11.17	3
6513	10.39	
	10.44	
	11.17	5
	11.17	7
6514	10.39	
	10.44	
	10.45	
6514(a)	11.17	9
6514(d)	11.17	8
	12.55	5
6514(e)	12.55	5
6515	12.55	6
Art. 70	22.20	4
	37.34	
	37.86	3
	38.8	
	38.8	70
7001	38.8	
7002(b)(1)	38.8	69
7002(b)(2)	37.88	1
	38.8	68
7002(b)(3)	38.8	69
7002(b)(4)	38.8	69
7002(b)(5)	37.88	2
	38.8	68
	38.8	69
7003(a)	37.37	
7003(b)	37.88	4
7004(c)	37.88	3
7010(b)	37.88	5
7011	37.34	6

NEW YORK, MCKINNEY'S CIVIL PRACTICE LAW AND RULES

Sec.	This Work Sec.	Note
7011 (Cont'd)	37.37	
Art. 71	7.24	5
	8.1	
	18.77	1
7202	8.11	4
7303(c)	31.24	5
Art. 75	7.13	5
	7.16	
	7.16	1
	7.16	6
	7.17	
	7.48	
	7.50	
	7.51	
	21.76	
	37.37	
7502(a)	5.69	
	7.51	
7503	7.14	
	28.29	1
	28.30	
	37.37	
	37.37	87
7503(b)	5.69	
7503(c)	5.61	1
	5.61	2
	5.61	3
	5.61	4
	5.71	
	5.72	
	31.24	6
7510	7.16	2
	31.24	10
7511(a)	7.16	1
7511(b)	7.17	1
	7.51	
7511(b)(iii)	7.51	
7511(c)	7.17	2
7511(d)	7.17	11
	7.51	
7514	7.16	3
Art. 78	3.29	
	3.32	
	3.32	6
	3.32	8
	3.32	12
	4.1	
	4.2	
	4.2	41
	4.63	
	4.70	4
	4.71	
	4.75	
	4.75	2
	4.75	20
	4.76	
	4.77	

TABLE OF STATUTES

	NEW YORK, MCKINNEY'S CIVIL PRACTICE LAW AND RULES			NEW YORK, MCKINNEY'S CIVIL PRACTICE LAW AND RULES	
		This Work			This Work
Sec.	Sec.	Note	Sec.	Sec.	Note
Art. 78 (Cont'd)	4.78		Art. 78 (Cont'd)	37.50	
	4.79			37.62	
	4.79	11		37.86	
	4.81			37.87	
	4.81	6		37.89	
	4.82			37.90	
	4.82	4		37.95	
	4.82	5		37.127	
	4.82	12		38.8	
	4.83			38.8	134
	4.84			38.10	
	4.85			39.4	1
	4.86			39.15	
	7.17			39.38	
	14.34		7801	3.32	11
	14.38			16.43	2
	14.39			16.49	1
	14.68			37.87	18
	15.6		7801 et seq.	16.43	1
	15.11		7802(a)	3.32	3
	16.43		7802(d)	37.87	3
	16.43	12	7803	3.32	5
	16.45			4.75	
	16.49			4.75	15
	16.49	1		4.85	
	16.50			23.83	15
	17.53		7803(1)	4.75	16
	17.55			4.77	1
	17.77			37.87	1
	17.78		7803(2)	4.75	17
	18.11			4.77	1
	18.28	3		37.87	2
	18.29		7803(3)	4.75	18
	18.37			4.77	1
	18.53			4.79	1
	18.53	6		4.81	2
	18.53	11		15.6	9
	18.53	12		37.87	
	20.118			37.87	15
	23.83			37.87	26
	35.62		7803(4)	4.75	19
	35.100			4.78	4
	35.100	2		37.37	62
	35.100	4		37.86	2
	35.100	5		37.87	
	35.101			37.87	15
	35.102			37.87	18
	35.103		7804	16.43	3
	35.107		7804(a)	35.102	1
	36.16		7804(b)	37.87	16
	36.66		7804(c)	35.102	2
	37.1			35.102	3
	37.32			37.87	7
	37.36			37.87	8
	37.37		7804(g)	4.84	3
	37.37	37		4.84	5
	37.44			4.84	6

TABLE OF STATUTES

NEW YORK, MCKINNEY'S CIVIL PRACTICE LAW AND RULES

Sec.	This Work Sec.	Note
7804(g) (Cont'd)	37.37	62
	37.87	17
7806	37.87	33
Art. 80	8.7	2
8001	8.7	2
	26.53	
8001(a)	8.23	7
8003(b)	11.51	
8004	8.7	2
	11.32	
8004(a)	11.30	2
	11.32	
8004(b)	11.30	3
	11.32	
8011	8.28	13
8012	8.7	2
	8.28	15
	8.28	16
	8.28	17
	8.28	18
8012(a)	8.28	14
8012(c)	8.28	19
8012(d)	8.28	14
8013	8.7	2
8016—8022	8.7	2
8021(b)(2)	1.13	17
8022	39.19	15
8022(a)	37.46	5
8022(b)	37.49	
	37.86	
	37.87	
	39.29	7
	39.29	16
Art. 81	8.7	4
8101	8.7	4
	37.87	36
8102	30.3	
8104	8.7	4
8106	8.7	4
8107	8.7	4
	37.18	3
	37.67	2
	37.67	9
8108	37.67	1
Art. 82	8.7	4
8201	8.7	4
	26.8	5
8201(1)—(3)	8.4	18
8202	8.7	4
8203	8.7	4
8203(a)	37.67	4
	37.87	37
	37.126	8
8203(b)	37.126	9
8204	8.7	4
Art. 83	30.1	19
8301	37.67	3

NEW YORK, MCKINNEY'S CIVIL PRACTICE LAW AND RULES

Sec.	This Work Sec.	Note
8301 (Cont'd)	37.67	5
8301(a)	1.19	6
	8.7	5
8301(a)(12)	1.19	6
	8.7	5
8302(d)	11.46	3
8303(a)	8.7	10
8303(a)(1)	11.46	4
8303(b)	8.7	11
8303–a	18.79	4
	18.80	3
	26.31	1
8401	8.7	6
	37.71	2
8402	8.7	7
	8.7	9
8403	8.7	8
8404	37.71	3
Art. 86	30.42	
	30.42	3
9801(1)	3.30	17

NEW YORK, MCKINNEY'S CIVIL RIGHTS LAW

Sec.	This Work Sec.	Note
Art. 2–A	18.47	1
2—15	18.6	
8	18.9	
	18.9	1
	18.92	
	18.94	
11	18.8	4
12	18.8	6
	18.12	
13	18.15	
18–a	18.41	
18–c	18.42	
	18.47	1
	18.97	1
18–c(1)	18.41	1
18–c(2)	18.41	1
18–c(3)	18.41	2
18–d	18.97	1
	18.43	
18–d(3)	18.43	1
18–e	18.40	1
19–a	18.47	
	18.47	1
	18.47	2
	18.96	
19–b	18.47	
	18.96	
40	18.54	
	18.54	2
	18.54	4

283

TABLE OF STATUTES

NEW YORK, MCKINNEY'S CIVIL RIGHTS LAW

Sec.	This Work Sec.	Note
40 (Cont'd)	18.97	1
	18.98	
40–a	18.60	
	18.60	1
	18.97	1
40–b	18.55	1
	18.60	
	18.97	1
40–c	18.50	4
	18.55	
	18.55	4
	18.97	
	18.97	1
	18.98	
40–d	18.55	7
	18.97	
	18.97	1
	18.98	
41	18.60	
	18.60	5
	18.60	6
	18.97	
	18.97	1
	18.98	
42	18.60	
	18.60	2
	18.97	1
43	18.60	
	18.60	3
	18.97	1
44	18.60	
	18.60	4
	18.60	5
44–a	18.60	5
47	18.57	2
	18.58	
47(1)	18.57	
47–a	18.58	
47–b	18.58	
47–c	18.58	
	18.61	1
48	18.62	1
48–a	18.62	1
48–b	18.62	2
Art. 5	18.1	
50	17.55	1
	18.63	
	18.63	6
	18.64	16
	30.30	11
	30.32	5
50–a	18.2	
	18.65	
	18.65	9
50–a(1)	18.65	
50–a(2)	18.65	1
50–a(3)	18.65	2
50–a(4)	18.65	10

NEW YORK, MCKINNEY'S CIVIL RIGHTS LAW

Sec.	This Work Sec.	Note
50–b	18.66	
50–b(1)	18.66	1
50–b(4)	18.66	3
50–c	18.66	
50–d	18.65	
50–d(3)	18.65	10
50–e	18.65	
50–e(4)	18.65	10
51	17.55	1
	18.63	
	18.63	6
	18.64	
	18.64	1
	18.64	16
	30.30	11
	30.32	5
Art. 6	18.67	
	18.88	
	18.99	
60	18.68	1
	18.68	3
	18.99	1
60—65	18.67	3
61	18.69	2
	18.69	3
	18.69	4
	18.73	1
	18.90	1
	18.99	4
	18.99	5
	18.99	6
	18.99	7
62	18.70	1
	18.70	2
	18.73	2
	18.99	2
63	18.71	1
	18.72	1
	18.73	3
64	18.70	
	18.70	5
	18.72	3
	18.72	4
	18.73	4
64–a	18.72	2
65(1)	18.67	2
65(2)	18.67	2
65(4)	18.67	1
Art. 7	18.1	
	18.78	
70	18.79	
	18.79	1
	18.79	3
70–a	18.80	
70–a(1)(b)	18.80	4
71	18.79	2
74	18.82	
75	18.82	

TABLE OF STATUTES

NEW YORK, MCKINNEY'S CIVIL RIGHTS LAW

Sec.	This Work Sec.	Note
75 (Cont'd)	18.82	4
76	18.82	
76-a(1)(a)	18.80	1
76-a(2)	18.80	4
77	18.81	
	18.81	1
78	18.82	
79(1)	18.84	1
79(2)	18.84	
	18.84	2
79(3)(b)	18.84	3
79-a(1)	18.84	
79-a(2)	18.84	
79-c	18.84	
79-d	18.84	5
79-e	18.83	1
79-f	18.87	
79-h	18.27	4
	18.85	
79-h(b)	18.85	2
79-h(c)	18.85	5
79-i	18.86	
79-k	18.87	4
Art. 8	18.1	
80-a	18.74	
	18.75	
80-b	18.76	1
81	18.75	
83	18.75	

NEW YORK, MCKINNEY'S CIVIL SERVICE LAW

Sec.	This Work Sec.	Note
35	17.53	
41(2)	17.53	2
42	17.53	3
	17.53	4
44	17.53	5
50(4)	17.53	6
75	17.53	
75-b	17.53	
	17.53	8
	17.64	
76	4.74	1
200	3.21	2
200 et seq.	17.53	13
	17.61	18
200—214	3.21	1
202	3.21	3
203	3.21	5
204(1)	3.21	6
204(2)	3.21	8
206	3.21	7
207	3.21	7

NEW YORK CODE OF CRIMINAL PROCEDURE

Sec.	This Work Sec.	Note
253a (former)	38.11	
482(3) (former)	38.10	132
543 (former)	38.21	

NEW YORK, MCKINNEY'S CORRECTION LAW

Sec.	This Work Sec.	Note
Art. 23-A	17.41	
21(10)	14.96	1
24	18.29	
701—703	36.14	8
752(2)	17.41	2

NEW YORK, MCKINNEY'S COUNTY LAW

Sec.	This Work Sec.	Note
Art. 5-A	3.33	2
Art. 5-B	3.33	7
Art. 5-D	3.33	8
Art. 7	3.26	1
Art. 18-B	20.44	3
	22.28	
	22.28	6
	22.28	19
	37.5	4
	38.16	1
52	3.30	17
100	3.15	5
101	3.15	10
101(2)	3.15	7
	3.15	8
	3.15	9
150	3.10	2
152	3.10	3
	3.28	1
153(2)	3.10	5
153(8)	3.10	4
200—235	3.7	4
215(3)	3.16	1
	3.16	5
215(4)	3.16	13
215(5)	3.16	13
	3.16	18
215(6)	3.16	15
215(8)	3.12	8
	3.16	19
215(11)	3.10	1
250	3.33	6
253(1)	3.33	3
256	3.33	4
264	3.13	2
355	3.26	2
356	3.26	2
359	3.26	3

TABLE OF STATUTES

NEW YORK, MCKINNEY'S COUNTY LAW

Sec.	This Work Sec.	Note
361	3.26	4
362(1)	3.26	5
363	3.26	6
400	3.17	2
400(4–a)	3.20	2
403	3.18	5
525(a)	8.8	2
722	37.10	
	37.37	
722–b	37.10	1
	37.37	

NEW YORK, MCKINNEY'S COURT OF CLAIMS ACT

Sec.	This Work Sec.	Note
8	3.30	3
	18.20	2
	26.41	1
8–b	18.23	7
9	18.20	2
10	26.41	3
10(2)	26.41	5
10(3)	26.41	12
10(6)	26.41	6
10(8)(a)	26.41	7
	26.41	8
11	26.41	11
17	26.43	11
17–a	26.41	9
24	37.15	3
	37.16	5
	37.17	2
	37.17	3
	37.29	12
25	37.17	4
	37.17	5
	37.46	4
26	37.17	6

NEW YORK, MCKINNEY'S CRIMINAL PROCEDURE LAW

Sec.	This Work Sec.	Note
1.10(1)(a)	38.8	
	39.38	1
1.20	38.3	
	38.46	3
1.20(1)	38.5	1
	38.10	
1.20(2)	38.5	3
1.20(3)	38.5	2
1.20(3–a)	38.5	5
1.20(4)	33.9	1
	33.9	2
	33.9	3

NEW YORK, MCKINNEY'S CRIMINAL PROCEDURE LAW

Sec.	This Work Sec.	Note
1.20(4) (Cont'd)	33.23	
	38.5	3
1.20(5)(a)	33.10	1
1.20(5)(b)	33.10	2
1.20(6)	33.11	1
	38.5	4
1.20(7)	38.5	6
1.20(8)	38.5	7
1.20(9)	33.17	10
1.20(10)	38.8	141
1.20(12)	38.8	140
1.20(13)	38.8	142
1.20(14)	38.8	38
1.20(15)	38.8	39
	38.8	142
1.20(16)	39.38	2
1.20(18)(a)	39.38	3
1.20(18)(b)	39.38	4
1.20(19)	38.8	1
1.20(21)	38.47	1
1.20(22)	38.4	4
1.20(24)	33.3	4
1.20(25)	33.3	6
1.20(39)	33.7	8
1.20(56)	33.23	
10.10(1)	38.4	
	38.8	1
10.10(2)	38.4	
	38.8	1
10.10(3)	33.3	2
	38.47	
10.30(1)	33.3	3
10.30(2)	33.3	5
Art. 18	37.99	
Art. 20	33.68	
20.20	33.68	9
20.50(2)	33.68	
30.20	33.71	
	33.71	1
	33.72	
	33.73	
30.30	33.71	
	33.74	
	33.75	
	33.76	
	33.77	
	33.78	
	33.79	
	33.80	
	33.81	
	33.82	
	33.83	
	33.84	
	33.85	
	33.86	
	33.87	
	33.88	
	33.89	

TABLE OF STATUTES

NEW YORK, MCKINNEY'S CRIMINAL PROCEDURE LAW

Sec.	This Work Sec.	Note
30.30 (Cont'd)	33.90	
	38.43	1
30.30(1)	33.74	
	33.74	1
30.30(2)	33.74	
	33.74	2
30.30(4)	33.84	
30.30(4)(a)	33.84	
	33.84	1
	38.10	
30.30(4)(b)	33.87	
30.30(4)(c)	33.89	
30.30(4)(c)(i)	33.89	1
30.30(4)(c)(ii)	33.89	2
30.30(5)(b)	33.82	
50.20	8.23	
	8.23	19
Art. 55	33.67	
60.10	37.13	4
60.20(3)	38.19	68
60.22	38.19	66
60.22(1)	39.82	
60.45	33.57	
60.45(2)(a)	33.57	3
60.50	33.61	
	33.61	1
	38.19	
Art. 65	38.19	135
70.10(2)	33.4	
	33.4	8
70.20	33.68	1
100.05	33.8	2
100.07	38.8	105
100.07 (former)	38.8	
100.10(1)	33.23	
100.10(2a)	33.23	
100.10(3)	33.11	3
	33.11	4
100.10(4)	33.12	1
	33.12	2
	33.12	4
100.10(5)	33.12	1
	33.12	3
	33.12	5
100.15	33.23	
100.15(3)	33.9	
	33.9	4
100.20	33.13	
	33.13	1
	33.92	1
	33.99	
100.25	33.17	
	33.17	3
	33.23	
	33.33	
	33.91	
	33.99	
100.25(2)	33.10	3

NEW YORK, MCKINNEY'S CRIMINAL PROCEDURE LAW

Sec.	This Work Sec.	Note
100.25(2) (Cont'd)	33.14	
	33.14	1
	33.14	2
	33.15	1
	33.15	2
	33.16	
	33.16	1
	33.17	
	33.17	1
	33.17	2
	33.17	6
	33.19	
	33.92	2
	33.92	3
	33.92	4
100.25(3)	33.17	5
100.30	33.26	
100.35	33.11	
	33.11	2
100.40	33.99	
100.40(1)	33.9	
100.40(1)(b)	33.9	5
100.40(1)(c)	33.9	5
100.40(2)	33.19	
	33.19	1
100.45(4)	33.33	
100.50	33.23	
130.10	33.83	
Art. 140	33.7	
140.10	33.7	
140.10(1)(a)	33.7	3
140.10(1)(b)	33.7	4
140.10(2)	33.7	9
	33.7	10
140.10(4)	38.8	105
140.10(5)	38.8	105
150.10	33.83	
	33.83	1
170.15	38.8	
170.15(3)	38.58	
170.30	33.99	
	38.10	
	38.10	6
170.30(1)(a)	33.19	
	38.10	
170.35	33.99	
	38.10	
	38.10	7
170.35(1)(a)	33.19	
170.50	38.10	
180.50(2)(b)(ii)	38.10	
180.75	38.8	125
180.75(4)	38.8	
190.45(2)	38.8	
190.71	38.8	125
190.85	38.11	
190.85(1)(a)	38.10	33
	38.11	

287

TABLE OF STATUTES

NEW YORK, MCKINNEY'S CRIMINAL PROCEDURE LAW

Sec.	This Work Sec.	Note
190.85(1)(a) (Cont'd)	38.11	3
	38.11	20
190.85(1)(a)(5)	38.17	46
190.85(1)(b)	38.11	8
	38.11	9
190.85(1)(c)	38.10	
	38.11	
	38.11	10
190.85(2)	38.11	
190.85(2)(a)	38.11	4
190.85(2)(b)	38.10	
	38.11	5
190.85(3)	38.11	6
190.85(5)	38.10	33
	38.11	
190.90	38.10	
	38.11	
190.90(5)	38.11	14
195.10	38.8	198
200.70	38.10	
200.70(2)(b)	33.25	1
200.95	33.35	
200.95(1)	33.35	1
200.95(1)(b)	33.35	
	33.35	3
200.95(2)	33.37	1
	33.37	2
200.95(3)	33.36	2
200.95(4)	33.37	1
200.95(5)	33.38	
	33.38	1
210.20	38.10	
	38.10	9
	38.10	37
210.20(1)(i)	38.27	
210.20(1–a)	38.10	
210.20(4)	38.27	
210.25	38.10	
	38.10	10
210.30	38.10	37
210.35	38.10	
	38.10	11
210.40	38.8	139
	38.27	
210.40(1)	38.19	
210.43	38.8	126
210.43(1)(a)	38.8	
	38.8	132
210.43(1)(b)	38.8	131
210.45	33.26	
210.45(4)(c)	33.81	2
220.10	38.8	127
220.60	38.8	209
Art. 230	38.8	94
230.10	38.8	94
	38.8	
	38.8	92
	38.58	1

NEW YORK, MCKINNEY'S CRIMINAL PROCEDURE LAW

Sec.	This Work Sec.	Note
230.10 (Cont'd)	38.58	2
230.20(2)	38.8	99
230.20(2)(b)	38.8	102
230.30(2)	38.8	93
Art. 240	33.34	
	33.35	
240.10(1)	33.35	
	33.35	2
	33.93	1
240.20	33.32	1
	33.33	
	33.67	
	33.101	
240.20(1)(h)	33.39	
	33.39	2
240.30	33.32	1
240.40	33.32	1
240.43	33.45	2
240.70	33.38	
	33.93	4
	33.93	5
240.70(1)	33.38	1
240.80	33.36	2
	33.93	2
240.80(2)	33.37	1
	33.93	3
240.80(3)	33.37	2
250.10	38.8	
255.20	38.8	92
	38.58	
255.20(1)	33.21	
	33.36	1
255.50(3)	38.8	99
260.30(1)—(7)	33.64	1
260.30(8)—(11)	33.64	2
270.15	37.13	
290.10	38.10	
290.10(1)	33.68	21
290.10(1)(a)	38.10	45
290.10(1)(b)	38.10	
290.10(3)	38.10	
300.10	38.19	
300.50	38.10	36
310.10	38.19	20
310.20(2)	38.19	103
	38.19	105
310.30	38.19	
	38.19	102
310.85	38.8	128
330.20(21)(b)	39.3	1
	39.38	5
330.20(21)(c)	39.3	1
	39.38	5
330.25	38.8	129
330.30	38.10	
330.30(1)	38.10	56
330.30(3)	38.10	55
340.40(2)	33.63	1

288

TABLE OF STATUTES

NEW YORK, MCKINNEY'S CRIMINAL PROCEDURE LAW

Sec.	This Work Sec.	Note
340.40(2) (Cont'd)	33.63	3
340.40(3)	33.63	2
350.10(3)(a)	33.65	1
	33.65	2
	33.65	3
	33.65	4
350.10(3)(b)	33.65	5
	33.65	6
	33.65	7
350.10(3)(c)	33.65	8
	33.65	9
	33.65	10
	33.65	11
350.10(3)(d)	33.65	12
360.05	33.64	1
360.40	38.10	46
370.10	38.10	57
380.20	38.21	38
390.20(4)	38.8	23
400.21	38.10	
400.27(12)(e)	38.10	
400.27(12)(f)	38.10	
	38.10	184
410.20	38.10	
430.10	38.10	
	38.21	57
Art. 440	38.8	
	38.9	
	38.9	8
	38.10	
	38.13	
	38.15	
	38.30	
	38.34	
	38.53	
440.10	38.9	
	38.10	
	38.10	95
	38.10	138
	38.13	
	38.28	15
440.10(1)	38.10	
440.10(1)(b)	38.10	
440.10(1)(f)	38.10	
440.10(1)(g)	38.10	
440.10(1)(h)	38.10	
440.20	38.9	
	38.10	
	38.10	137
	38.13	
	38.26	11
440.30(5)	38.10	99
440.40	38.8	
	38.10	
	38.10	112
	38.10	125
440.40(5)	38.10	
Art. 450	37.13	

NEW YORK, MCKINNEY'S CRIMINAL PROCEDURE LAW

Sec.	This Work Sec.	Note
Art. 450 (Cont'd)	38.3	
	38.3	2
	38.5	12
	38.11	
450.10	38.4	
	38.8	
	38.8	3
	38.8	64
	38.10	120
	39.42	
450.10(1)	38.8	
	38.8	2
	38.8	52
450.10(2)	38.8	
	38.8	8
	38.8	52
	38.8	57
450.10(3)	38.8	
450.10(4)	38.8	
	38.10	
	38.12	3
450.15	38.8	64
	38.9	
	38.10	
	38.13	2
	38.51	
	39.42	
450.15(1)	38.9	2
450.15(3)	38.9	
450.20	37.19	26
	38.3	19
	38.8	
	38.10	
	38.13	1
	39.41	1
	39.42	
450.20(1)	38.10	
	38.17	
	38.17	22
450.20(1-a)	38.10	43
	38.15	15
	38.17	
	38.17	23
450.20(2)		
	38.10	44
	38.10	54
450.20(3)	38.10	
450.20(4)	38.10	
	38.10	64
	38.10	121
450.20(5)	38.10	
450.20(6)	38.10	
450.20(7)	38.10	
	38.10	119
450.20(8)	38.10	
	38.10	161
	38.10	
	38.17	24

TABLE OF STATUTES

NEW YORK, MCKINNEY'S CRIMINAL PROCEDURE LAW

Sec.	This Work Sec.	Note
450.20(9)	38.10	
450.20(10)	38.3	19
	38.10	
	38.10	184
450.30(1)	38.8	57
	38.8	59
	38.10	120
450.30(2)	38.10	122
450.30(3)	38.8	
	38.10	122
450.40	38.10	
	38.10	1
	38.10	4
450.40(2)	38.10	
450.50	38.10	
	38.10	1
450.50(1)	37.19	26
450.55	38.10	1
450.60	38.4	
	38.46	3
	38.47	
	38.47	2
450.60(1)	38.4	
450.60(2)	38.4	
450.60(3)	38.4	5
	38.47	
450.70	39.40	
450.80	39.41	
450.90	38.5	8
	38.5	9
	38.6	
	38.27	
	38.46	4
450.90(1)	39.42	1
	39.42	2
	39.42	3
450.90(2)	38.27	5
	38.27	18
	39.42	
450.90(2)(a)	38.19	82
	38.19	85
	38.27	
	38.27	2
	39.42	
	39.42	4
	39.49	
	39.50	
450.90(2)(a) (former)	38.27	2
450.90(2)(b)	39.42	5
Art. 460	37.13	
	38.3	
	38.3	2
	38.5	12
460.10	38.8	7
460.10(1)	38.52	6
	38.52	7
460.10(1)(a)	38.10	35
	38.12	1

NEW YORK, MCKINNEY'S CRIMINAL PROCEDURE LAW

Sec.	This Work Sec.	Note
460.10(1)(a) (Cont'd)	38.12	2
	38.12	4
	38.12	7
460.10(1)(b)	38.5	8
	38.12	1
	38.12	2
	38.52	5
460.10(1)(c)	38.5	8
460.10(1)(d)	38.12	10
460.10(2)	38.52	4
	38.52	6
	38.55	
460.10(2)(e)	38.52	7
460.10(3)	38.5	9
	38.52	
460.10(3)(a)(i)	38.52	8
460.10(3)(a)(ii)	38.52	9
460.10(3)(b)	38.52	10
460.10(3)(c)	38.52	11
460.10(3)(d)	38.52	12
460.10(3)(e)	38.52	13
460.10(4)(a)	38.13	5
460.10(4)(b)	38.13	6
	38.53	5
460.10(5)(a)	38.24	5
	38.32	3
	39.47	1
460.15	38.9	6
	38.51	
460.15(1)	38.13	3
460.15(2)	38.13	4
460.20	38.24	
	39.42	
	39.54	
	39.90	
460.20(1)	39.82	
460.20(2)(a)	38.32	
460.20(2)(a)(i)	39.46	1
460.20(2)(a)(ii)	39.46	2
460.20(2)(b)	38.4	7
	38.56	2
	39.46	4
460.30	38.9	
	38.10	35
	38.53	5
	38.59	1
	39.23	
	39.47	
	39.47	3
	39.66	
460.30(1)	38.14	
	38.14	4
	38.63	
	39.47	5
	39.47	6
	39.54	1
460.30(2)	38.14	
460.30(3)	38.14	5

290

TABLE OF STATUTES

NEW YORK, MCKINNEY'S CRIMINAL PROCEDURE LAW

Sec.	This Work Sec.	Note
460.30(4)	38.14	5
460.30(5)	38.14	6
460.30(6)	39.42	2
460.40(1)	39.48	1
460.40(2)	38.15	16
	39.48	1
460.50	38.54	
	38.55	
	38.59	2
460.50(1)	38.15	1
	38.54	1
460.50(2)(a)	38.15	2
460.50(2)(b)	38.15	3
460.50(2)(c)	38.54	2
460.50(2)(d)	38.54	
460.50(3)	38.15	3
	38.47	3
460.50(4)	38.15	5
	38.54	3
	38.54	4
460.50(5)	38.28	15
460.50(6)	38.15	4
460.60	39.48	
460.60(2)	39.48	3
460.60(3)	39.48	4
460.70	38.16	
	38.16	2
	38.55	
	38.55	4
460.70(1)	38.16	1
	38.17	1
	38.55	
	38.55	1
460.70(2)	38.55	
	38.55	29
460.80	38.55	2
Art. 470	37.13	
	38.3	
	38.3	2
	38.5	12
	38.19	
470.05	38.19	3
	38.19	8
	38.56	
470.05(1)	38.2	10
	38.2	11
	38.19	86
	39.50	
470.05(2)	38.19	
	38.21	
	39.50	
	39.82	
470.10	38.26	1
	38.56	
	39.51	1
470.10(2)	38.25	1
470.10(3)	38.23	1
	39.51	2

NEW YORK, MCKINNEY'S CRIMINAL PROCEDURE LAW

Sec.	This Work Sec.	Note
470.15	38.56	
470.15(1)	38.3	30
	38.10	16
	38.19	1
	38.24	3
470.15(2)	38.23	
470.15(2)(a)	38.25	10
470.15(2)(b)	38.25	7
470.15(3)	38.23	2
	38.25	3
	38.26	2
470.15(3)(a)	38.19	62
	38.21	34
	38.27	
	38.27	13
470.15(3)(b)	38.27	13
	38.27	16
470.15(3)(c)	37.28	13
	38.3	31
	38.19	7
	38.19	39
	38.19	62
	38.21	1
	38.25	21
	38.27	
470.15(4)	38.20	
	38.25	
	38.25	4
	38.25	23
470.15(4)(a)	38.25	5
	38.26	3
470.15(4)(b)	38.19	
	38.19	60
	38.25	7
	38.26	7
470.15(4)(c)	38.21	33
	38.21	34
	38.25	14
	38.26	
	38.26	11
470.15(5)	38.19	75
	38.20	1
	38.25	18
	38.25	23
	38.26	18
	38.26	19
470.15(6)	38.26	25
	38.27	20
470.15(6)(a)	38.25	22
	38.26	22
470.15(6)(b)	38.3	33
	38.19	
	38.19	77
	38.21	
	38.21	2
	38.21	43
	38.25	22
	38.26	23

TABLE OF STATUTES

NEW YORK, MCKINNEY'S CRIMINAL PROCEDURE LAW

Sec.	This Work Sec.	Note
470.20	38.28	
	38.56	
470.20(1)	38.19	72
	38.26	6
	38.26	26
	38.28	5
	38.28	7
	38.28	9
470.20(2)	38.19	
	38.19	71
	38.26	
	38.26	8
	38.28	1
470.20(3)	38.25	
	38.28	2
	38.28	13
470.20(4)	38.25	11
	38.28	14
470.20(5)	38.20	
	38.25	19
	38.26	20
	38.28	3
	38.28	4
470.20(6)	38.3	33
	38.25	2
	38.64	2
470.25	38.56	
470.25(1)	38.24	1
470.25(2)(a)	38.19	85
470.25(2)(b)	38.27	1
470.30	39.50	
470.35	39.50	11
470.35(2)	39.82	
470.40	39.51	2
	39.51	3
470.45	39.51	3
470.60	38.39	3
	38.55	
	39.51	1
	39.55	1
470.60(1)	38.39	1
470.60(2)	38.39	2
470.60(3)	39.42	8
Art. 510	38.8	
510.20(2)	38.15	
	38.15	13
510.30	38.59	2
	38.61	
Art. 518 (repealed)	38.10	2
Art. 530	38.54	
	39.48	
530.11	38.8	105
530.12(14)	38.8	105
530.45	38.15	
530.45(1)	38.15	8
530.45(2)	38.15	8
530.45(3)	38.15	12
530.45(4)	38.15	9

NEW YORK, MCKINNEY'S CRIMINAL PROCEDURE LAW

Sec.	This Work Sec.	Note
530.45(5)	38.15	10
	38.15	11
530.50	38.15	6
	39.48	2
Art. 710	33.27	1
	38.28	10
710.10(2)	38.10	150
	38.10	167
710.20	38.10	
710.20(1)	38.10	152
710.20(2)	38.10	153
710.20(3)	38.10	155
710.20(4)	38.10	156
710.20(5)	38.10	157
710.20(6)	38.10	
710.20(7)	38.10	159
710.30	33.68	
	38.8	
	38.10	
	38.10	167
	38.10	168
710.30(3)	38.10	168
710.60(1)	33.43	
	33.43	1
	33.43	2
710.60(2)	33.43	4
710.60(2)—(4)	33.43	3
710.60(3)	33.43	5
710.60(4)	33.43	6
710.70(2)	38.8	11
	38.8	188
	38.8	200
725.05	38.8	
	38.8	136
725.05(9)	38.8	124
725.10(2)	38.8	

NEW YORK, MCKINNEY'S DEBTOR AND CREDITOR LAW

Sec.	This Work Sec.	Note
Art. 10	9.115	7
3	1.101	2
150	12.55	
150.4	9.129	3
270—281	24.84	2
270 et seq.	8.21	
	8.41	4
282	9.49	1
	9.125	13
	24.85	2
283(1)	9.125	8
	9.128	3
283(2)	9.125	11
284	9.125	3

TABLE OF STATUTES

NEW YORK, MCKINNEY'S DOMESTIC RELATIONS LAW

Sec.	This Work Sec.	Note
Art. 7	20.6	
	20.80	
Art. 75	21.5	
11(1)	21.82	
15	18.67	2
32	24.62	1
75–d	21.5	
75–d(1)	21.5	1
75–d(1)(c)	21.6	
75–d(1)(d)	21.6	
75–d(2)	21.5	2
75–d(3)	21.5	3
75–h(1)	21.5	5
75–i(1)	21.5	6
81	24.14	1
109—117	20.5	
110	20.1	2
	20.1	3
	20.1	20
	20.6	
	20.6	1
	20.8	
	20.14	
	20.14	1
	20.15	1
	20.17	
	20.18	
	20.20	
	20.22	
	20.23	
	20.24	
	20.26	1
	20.36	1
	20.108	1
	20.142	
111	20.29	
	20.32	
	20.123	1
	20.137	
	20.138	
	20.148	
111 (proposed)	20.35	
111(1)	20.24	
111(1)(a)	20.43	1
111(1)(b)	20.42	2
111(1)(d)	20.42	3
111(1)(e)	20.29	1
	20.30	
111(1)(e)(i)	20.30	
111(1)(f)	20.145	
111(2)	20.31	
111(2)(a)	20.38	1
	20.42	5
	20.43	6
	20.67	1
111(2)(d)	20.39	
111(2)(e)	20.31	5
111(3)	20.42	3

NEW YORK, MCKINNEY'S DOMESTIC RELATIONS LAW

Sec.	This Work Sec.	Note
111(3) (Cont'd)	20.137	
	20.139	
111(4)	20.24	
	20.24	1
111(6)(d)	20.67	2
111–a	20.32	1
	20.33	
	20.34	
	20.35	
	20.76	
	20.76	1
	20.137	
	20.139	
	20.140	
	20.144	
111–a(1)	20.139	
111–a(2)	20.42	3
111–a(3)	20.35	1
111–a(4)	20.35	5
111–a(6)	20.35	6
111–a(7)	20.35	7
111–b	20.9	1
112	20.103	1
	20.137	
	20.138	
	20.139	
	20.148	
112 et seq.	20.37	4
112(2)	20.103	2
	20.103	3
	20.107	1
	20.119	1
112(2)(b)	20.104	1
	20.145	
112(2–a)	20.103	3
112(3)	20.105	
	20.109	1
	20.139	
	20.140	
112(5)	20.109	1
112(7)	20.114	1
	20.119	1
113	20.1	23
	20.19	
	20.28	
	20.28	1
	20.28	5
	20.87	1
	20.104	2
	20.122	1
	20.145	
	20.148	
113(3)	20.114	1
114	18.67	3
	20.1	26
	20.1	27
	20.1	28
	20.75	2

293

TABLE OF STATUTES

NEW YORK, MCKINNEY'S DOMESTIC RELATIONS LAW			NEW YORK, MCKINNEY'S DOMESTIC RELATIONS LAW		
		This Work			This Work
Sec.	Sec.	Note	Sec.	Sec.	Note
114 (Cont'd)	20.81		115–c	20.60	
	20.122	1		20.61	
	20.125			20.62	1
	20.126			20.62	3
	20.127			20.69	1
	20.128			20.134	
	20.131		115–d	20.1	12
	20.138			20.55	
	20.148			20.56	
114(1)	20.83	1		20.56	1
	20.116	3		20.61	
	20.117	1		20.62	
115	20.1	8		20.80	
	20.19			20.133	
	20.37	2	115–d(1)(d)	20.55	
	20.51		115–d(2)	20.55	
	20.52		115–d(4)	20.133	
	20.59	1	115–d(6)	20.56	6
	20.133			20.133	
	20.135		115–d(8)	20.56	8
	20.136		116	20.75	2
	20.137			20.138	
115(1)(b)	20.54	1	116(2)	20.60	
	20.56	9		20.69	4
115(2)	20.1	18		20.80	1
	20.11			20.80	3
	20.69	3	116(3)	20.80	2
115(8)	20.2	1	116(3)(a)—(f)	20.80	
	20.3	3	116(4)	20.81	1
	20.52	1	117	20.8	
	20.78			20.13	2
	20.78	1		20.17	
115(12)	20.137			25.52	
115–a	20.1	21		25.67	
	20.25		117(1)(c)	20.116	2
	20.48	3	140	21.89	
	20.53	9		21.90	
	20.68			21.91	
	20.68	2	140(1–b)(f)	21.89	
115–a(1)	20.25	1		21.91	
115–a(7)	20.68	2		21.92	
115–a(8)	20.49		170	21.18	
115–b	20.1	5		21.20	
	20.1	4	170(1)	21.20	1
	20.63	1	170(2)	21.22	1
	20.64			21.24	1
	20.134		170(3)	21.25	1
	20.135		170(4)	21.26	1
	20.136			21.26	2
115–b(2)	20.65		170(5)	21.29	1
115–b(3)	20.64	1		21.31	
	20.66		170(6)	21.30	
	20.137			21.30	1
115–b(3)(b)(iv)	20.64	2		21.30	4
115–b(4)(a)(v)	20.64			21.31	
115–b(6)	20.43	5	171	21.21	
115–b(7)	20.42	4		21.27	1
	20.43	4	171(3)	21.26	

TABLE OF STATUTES

NEW YORK, MCKINNEY'S DOMESTIC RELATIONS LAW

Sec.	This Work Sec.	Note
200	21.19	1
	21.29	
	21.29	2
203	21.29	
210	21.21	
	21.21	1
	21.23	
	21.25	
	21.26	
210(a)	21.23	1
	21.30	10
211	21.11	1
	21.37	6
230	21.4	
	21.4	1
	21.4	2
	21.14	
	21.89	
	21.91	
232	21.11	
	21.11	2
232(a)(1)	21.11	7
232(a)(2)(a)	21.11	7
232(a)(2)(b)	21.11	3
	21.11	8
233	8.1	
	21.13	
	21.13	1
234	21.44	3
236	21.72	
	21.79	
236(A)	21.20	
236(A)	21.48	
236(B)	21.33	1
	21.49	
236(B)(1)(a)	21.46	7
236(B)(1)(c)	21.36	
	21.37	1
	21.37	3
236(B)(1)(d)	21.40	
236(B)(1)(d)(1—4)	21.36	
	21.37	2
236(B)(1)(d)(3)	21.41	
236(B)(2)	21.34	
	21.34	1
236(B)(3)	21.2	9
	21.30	
	21.30	2
	21.34	
	21.40	
236(B)(4)	21.65	1
	21.65	3
	21.65	6
	21.80	1
	21.80	2
236(B)(4)(b)	21.42	
236(B)(5)	21.7	
	21.14	2

NEW YORK, MCKINNEY'S DOMESTIC RELATIONS LAW

Sec.	This Work Sec.	Note
236(B)(5) (Cont'd)	21.34	
	21.89	
	21.91	
236(B)(5)(a)	21.34	
	21.34	2
	21.34	5
236(B)(5)(d)	21.44	
236(B)(5)(d)(1—10)	21.89	
	21.91	
236(B)(5)(f)	21.44	3
236(B)(5)(h)	21.44	
236(B)(6)	21.46	
	21.47	
	21.48	
	21.89	
	21.91	
236(B)(6)(a)	21.46	
	21.47	1
236(B)(6)(a)(1—10)	21.89	
	21.91	
236(B)(6)(b)	21.46	6
236(B)(7)	21.53	
236(B)(8)(a)	21.57	
	21.57	1
236(B)(9)(a)	21.72	1
	21.72	10
236(B)(9)(b)	21.68	
	21.69	1
	21.69	3
	21.69	7
	21.69	10
	21.70	1
237	30.42	
237(c)	21.79	
238	21.79	
240	21.53	
	21.59	
	21.62	
	21.70	
	21.71	
	21.72	
	30.42	
240(1)	21.52	
	21.52	1
	21.57	
	21.58	
	21.58	1
	21.59	3
	21.62	
	21.70	3
	21.70	6
	21.71	1
	21.72	11
240(1–b)	21.8	
	21.53	
	21.53	3
	21.89	
	21.91	

TABLE OF STATUTES

NEW YORK, MCKINNEY'S DOMESTIC RELATIONS LAW

Sec.	This Work Sec.	Note
240(1–b) (Cont'd)	21.92	
240(1–b)(b)(2)	21.53	3
240(1–b)(b)(3)	21.53	12
240(1–b)(b)(5)(i)	21.53	4
240(1–b)(b)(5)(ii)	21.53	5
240(1–b)(b)(5)(iii)	21.53	6
240(1–b)(b)(5)(iv)	21.53	7
240(1–b)(b)(5)(v)	21.53	8
240(1–b)(b)(5)(vi)	21.53	9
240(1–b)(b)(5)(vii)	21.53	11
240(1–b)(c)(2)	21.53	2
240(1–b)(c)(3)	21.53	18
240(1–b)(c)(4)	21.53	13
240(1–b)(c)(5)	21.53	15
240(1–b)(c)(6)	21.53	14
240(1–b)(c)(7)	21.53	16
240(1–b)(d)	21.53	17
240(1–b)(e)	21.53	10
240(1–b)(f)	21.53	18
	21.54	1
	21.54	3
	21.70	
	21.89	
	21.90	
	21.91	
	21.92	
240(1–b)(g)	21.54	4
	21.54	5
240(1–b)(h)	21.56	1
	21.56	2
	21.89	
	21.91	
240(1–b)(L)	21.70	4
	21.70	5
240(2)	21.72	9
240(2)(a)	21.72	10
240(2)(b)	21.72	12
	21.72	13
240(2)(c)	21.70	7
240(4)	21.70	
	21.70	8
	21.70	9
	21.70	10
240–a	18.67	2
243	21.72	5
	21.72	6
244	21.69	
	21.69	4
	21.74	1
	21.74	2
244–a	21.72	14
244–b	21.72	7
244–c	21.72	8
245	21.72	4
253	21.44	
253(2)	21.82	
271	30.42	

NEW YORK, MCKINNEY'S EDUCATION LAW

Sec.	This Work Sec.	Note
Tit. VIII	1.122	
	1.122	1
	1.125	
	1.125	1
	2.73	
	2.75	3
Art. 145	1.122	
224	1.13	1
378(5)	12.73	7
401	16.128	5
407	16.128	5
408	16.128	5
524	9.125	19
3020–a	17.53	7
4404	18.53	5
6201	18.53	9
6221	18.53	9
6509 et seq.	29.74	6
6510	4.1	1
	37.90	
6513	1.9	1
6612(4)(d)	1.9	1
6815	27.13	12
7009	1.9	1
7200—7209	12.56	6
7203	12.56	1
7208(e)	12.56	7
7209	1.9	1
	1.13	1
7209(6)	1.122	37
7302	1.13	1
7307	1.9	1
7307(4)	1.122	37

NEW YORK, MCKINNEY'S ELECTION LAW

Sec.	This Work Sec.	Note
16–108	37.90	
16–116	37.51	41
	37.61	1

NEW YORK, MCKINNEY'S EMERGENCY HOUSING RENT CONTROL ACT

Sec.	This Work Sec.	Note
5	13.39	

NEW YORK, MCKINNEY'S EMINENT DOMAIN PROCEDURE LAW

Sec.	This Work Sec.	Note
101	14.1	6
	14.1	8

TABLE OF STATUTES

		NEW YORK, MCKINNEY'S EMINENT DOMAIN PROCEDURE LAW		
Sec.	Sec.	This Work Note		
101 (Cont'd)	14.1	10		
	14.21	1		
	14.40	2		
101 et seq.	14.1	1		
103	14.8			
103(C)	14.99	1		
103(G)	14.15	7		
104	14.1	3		
Art. 2	14.1			
	14.23			
	14.32	2		
	14.34			
	14.34	2		
	14.35			
	14.36			
	14.38			
	14.39			
	14.59	6		
	14.64			
	14.68			
	14.120			
	14.126			
	14.127			
201	14.21	2		
	14.21	4		
	14.21	5		
	14.30			
	14.121			
	14.126			
202	14.28			
	14.121			
	14.126			
202(C)	14.28			
203	14.29			
	14.29	1		
	14.29	4		
204	14.34			
	14.34	1		
	14.121			
	14.126			
204(A)	14.30	1		
	14.30	3		
	14.31	1		
	14.34			
204(B)	14.30	2		
	14.34			
205	14.33	1		
206	14.22			
	14.34			
	14.127			
	14.127	1		
206(A)	14.23			
	14.23	2		
206(B)	14.24			
206(C)	14.25	2		
206(D)	14.26	1		
	14.26	6		
206(E)	14.27	1		

Sec.	Sec.	This Work Note
207	14.34	
	14.36	
	14.38	
	14.120	
	14.122	
	37.90	
207(A)	14.34	
	14.34	3
	14.36	
	14.37	1
	14.120	1
	14.121	1
207(B)	14.34	
	14.34	2
207(C)	14.38	
	14.38	3
	14.122	1
208	14.34	
Art. 3	14.1	
	14.115	
301	14.40	1
	14.41	
	14.113	
302	14.41	1
	14.42	1
	14.43	
304	14.44	
304(A)	14.43	
304(A)(1)	14.43	3
304(A)(2)	14.43	4
304(A)(3)	14.43	5
304(A)(4)	14.44	4
304(C)	14.44	7
304(D)	14.44	8
	14.100	3
304(E)	14.44	8
304(E)(1)	14.100	2
304(H)	14.44	2
305(A)	14.45	2
305(B)	14.45	3
	14.123	1
305(C)	14.45	2
Art. 4	14.1	
	14.37	3
	14.47	
	14.51	
401(A)	14.48	1
	14.49	
401(D)	14.49	5
402(A)	14.52	
	14.53	1
402(A)(1)	14.51	1
	14.54	
402(A)(2)	14.54	
402(A)(3)	14.54	2
	14.55	1
402(B)	14.48	2
	14.56	

297

TABLE OF STATUTES

NEW YORK, MCKINNEY'S EMINENT DOMAIN PROCEDURE LAW

Sec.	This Work Sec.	Note
402(B) (Cont'd)	14.56	2
	14.126	1
	14.127	1
402(B)(1)	14.57	1
	14.124	1
402(B)(2)	14.61	
	14.61	1
	14.125	1
402(B)(2)(a)	14.61	4
402(B)(2)(b)	14.61	5
402(B)(3)	14.58	
402(B)(3)(c)	14.59	5
402(B)(3)(f)	14.60	1
402(B)(4)	14.63	1
	14.128	1
402(B)(5)	14.65	
	14.130	
	14.130	1
	14.131	1
402(B)(6)	14.67	
	14.129	
	14.129	1
	14.130	
402(C)	14.50	2
403	14.62	
	14.66	
404	14.67	2
Art. 5	14.1	
	14.115	
	14.117	
501(A)	14.4	1
	14.108	4
502(A)(1)	14.66	2
502(A)(2)	14.66	3
502(A)(3)	14.66	4
502(B)	14.4	2
	14.66	5
	14.132	1
503	14.127	
503(A)	14.44	
	14.70	2
	14.71	3
	14.72	1
503(B)	14.73	2
	14.74	2
	14.75	1
504	14.76	
	14.133	1
505(A)	14.101	
505(B)	14.101	1
505(C)	14.101	2
508	14.104	1
510	14.106	1
511(A)	14.107	1
	14.107	2
511(B)	14.107	3
512	14.114	
	14.114	2

NEW YORK, MCKINNEY'S EMINENT DOMAIN PROCEDURE LAW

Sec.	This Work Sec.	Note
513	14.114	
	14.134	1
514	14.108	
514(A)	14.108	1
	14.108	3
514(B)	14.108	7
514(C)	14.116	1
Art. 6	14.117	
601(A)	14.117	1
601(B)	14.117	3
602	14.117	6
603	14.117	4
604	14.117	5
701	14.43	2
	14.115	
	14.135	1
	14.136	
	14.136	1
	14.137	
	14.137	1
	14.138	
	14.110	
702(A)(3)	14.110	1
702(B)	14.111	1
	14.112	2
702(C)	14.113	2
703	14.1	4
707	14.1	5
708	14.11	

NEW YORK, MCKINNEY'S ENERGY LAW

Sec.	This Work Sec.	Note
6–106	37.90	
18–113	37.90	

NEW YORK, MCKINNEY'S ESTATES, POWERS AND TRUSTS LAW

Sec.	This Work Sec.	Note
1–2.8	24.10	2
1–2.16	24.10	3
1–2.19	22.49	4
2–1.6	24.17	
2–1.8	24.10	7
	25.66	
2–1.11	22.3	
	22.47	
	24.71	
	25.49	
2–1.11(b)(2)	24.71	1
	24.71	2
2–1.11(c)	24.71	3
	25.49	2

TABLE OF STATUTES

NEW YORK, MCKINNEY'S ESTATES, POWERS AND TRUSTS LAW

Sec.	This Work Sec.	Note
2-1.11(d)	25.49	1
2-1.12	24.10	
3-2.1	24.4	2
	25.21	
	25.28	5
3-2.1(a)(1)	24.5	2
3-2.1(a)(1)(B)	24.5	1
3-2.1(a)(1)(C)	24.5	2
3-2.1(a)(2)	24.7	1
3-2.1(a)(3)	24.6	1
	24.7	3
3-2.1(a)(4)	24.7	2
	24.7	3
3-2.1(c)(4)	25.28	2
3-2.2	24.4	1
3-3.2(a)	24.7	4
3-3.2(a)(3)	24.7	5
3-3.3	25.17	2
3-3.4	24.12	1
3-3.5	24.66	6
3-4.1	24.63	3
Art. 4	24.3	2
4-1.1	22.23	4
	24.3	4
	25.2	2
	25.4	
	25.19	
	25.52	
	25.67	
4-1.1(d)	20.116	2
4-1.2	25.4	3
	25.52	
	25.67	
4-1.2(a)(2)	25.4	
4-1.4	25.3	7
	25.4	2
5-1.1	22.47	13
5-1.1-A	22.47	13
	24.22	7
	24.60	
	24.60	3
	24.60	4
	24.60	9
5-1.1-A(e)(1)	24.60	
	24.60	
5-1.1-A(e)(2)	24.60	10
5-1.1-A(e)(3)(A)	24.60	6
5-1.1-A(e)(3)(C)	24.60	6
5-1.1-A(e)(3)(D)	24.60	7
5-1.1-A(e)(3)(E)	24.60	8
5-1.2	24.63	1
	24.63	3
5-1.2(a)(3)	25.3	5
	25.4	1
5-1.2(a)(5)	25.3	7
	25.4	1
5-1.2(a)(6)	25.3	7
	25.4	1
5-1.4	24.63	3
	24.64	

NEW YORK, MCKINNEY'S ESTATES, POWERS AND TRUSTS LAW

Sec.	This Work Sec.	Note
5-1.4 (Cont'd)	24.64	1
5-3.1	24.60	
5-3.1(a)	24.60	5
5-3.3 (repealed)	24.32	1
5-4.1 et seq.	22.15	5
5-4.3	30.12	3
	30.12	4
	30.40	
5-4.4	25.52	
	25.67	
6-2.2(a)	24.83	1
6-2.2(b)	24.83	6
6-2.2(c)	12.37	4
	24.83	5
7-1.1	24.81	1
7-1.5(a)	24.87	2
7-1.12	23.79	2
7-1.13	24.30	7
	24.72	4
7-1.17	24.81	2
7-1.18	24.81	8
7-3.1	23.78	2
	24.87	1
7-4.8	24.17	1
7-5.2	24.82	2
7-6.1—7-6.24	24.51	
7-6.11	24.51	2
7-6.20(a)	24.51	2
9-1.7	24.85	2
10-10.7	1.45	
	12.55	13
Art. 11	25.33	
11-1.1	12.55	8
	24.16	
11-1.1(b)(9)	24.17	2
11-1.2(a)	24.76	2
11-3.3	30.12	1
12-1.2	24.10	4
12-1.3	24.10	4
	24.10	5

NEW YORK, MCKINNEY'S ENVIRONMENTAL CONSERVATION LAW

Sec.	This Work Sec.	Note
3-0301	4.55	2
3-0301(2)(a)	4.46	3
3-0305(1)	14.16	2
3-0305(10)	14.96	1
Art. 8	4.29	6
	14.38	
	14.38	2
	16.52	
	16.52	1
	16.59	
	16.134	
Art. 8, Tit. 6, Pt. 617	16.80	5

299

TABLE OF STATUTES

NEW YORK, MCKINNEY'S ENVIRONMENTAL CONSERVATION LAW

Sec.	This Work Sec.	Note
Art. 8, Tit. 6, Pt. 617 (Cont'd)	16.87	9
8–0101	15.3	5
8–0101 et seq.	14.32	1
	15.3	1
8–0101 to 8–0117	4.29	6
8.0101—8.0117	16.29	8
8–0103	15.3	5
8–0103(6)	16.56	4
8–0103(7)	15.3	9
8–0103(8)	16.52	1
8–0103(9)	15.3	3
8–0105	4.29	9
8–0105(1)	15.3	12
8–0105(2)	15.3	12
8–0105(3)	15.3	12
	16.52	1
8–0105(4)	15.3	13
8–0105(5)	15.3	14
8–0109	4.29	7
	16.98	2
8–0109(1)	15.3	10
	16.52	7
8–0109(2)	15.3	2
	15.4	9
	15.4	13
	15.5	1
	15.5	3
	15.7	7
8–0109(2)(a)—(i)	15.5	2
8–0109(4)	15.4	1
	15.5	4
	15.5	7
8–0109(5)	15.5	8
8–0109(8)	15.5	12
8–0111(6)	15.4	10
Tit. 9	15.24	
Art. 15	16.134	
17–0105(2)	15.8	13
17–0105(16)	15.8	8
17–0105(17)	15.8	7
17–0801	15.8	4
17–0801 et seq.	15.8	4
17–0803	15.8	6
	15.8	12
	15.9	1
17–0805(1)	15.9	6
17–0805(1)(b)	15.9	7
	15.9	13
17–0805(2)	15.9	6
17–0808	15.10	2
17–0809	15.9	3
17–0809(3)	15.9	12
17–0817(1)	15.9	11
17–0817(3)	15.9	11
17–0817(4)	15.9	13
17–1001	15.27	2
Art. 19	15.21	
	15.22	

NEW YORK, MCKINNEY'S ENVIRONMENTAL CONSERVATION LAW

Sec.	This Work Sec.	Note
19–0107(2)	15.21	1
19–0303(4)	15.21	8
19–0304	15.22	2
19–0311	15.21	6
19–0311(2)(a)	15.21	7
19–0315	15.21	9
19–0317	15.21	9
19–0319	15.21	9
19–0703	15.22	6
Art. 24	15.16	6
	16.134	
24–0101 et seq.	15.13	3
	15.16	3
24–0107	15.16	6
24–0107(1)	15.14	6
	15.16	4
	15.16	1
24–1509	16.4	5
	16.31	3
Art. 25	16.134	
25–0101 et seq.	15.13	3
	15.16	2
25–0103(1)	15.14	10
	15.16	4
Art. 27	15.23	
27–0303(7)	15.23	4
27–0305	15.23	8
27–0701(2)	15.23	9
27–0707	15.23	8
27–0711	15.23	1
27–0900	15.24	4
27–0905	15.24	5
27–13	15.31	
27–1301(1)	15.31	3
27–1313(3)(a)	15.31	2
33–1001(1)	27.47	11
40–0111	15.27	2
Art. 70	15.17	
70–0119	15.9	8
	15.9	9
Art. 71	15.11	
	15.11	2
	15.22	
	15.32	
71–0301	15.25	24
71–0307	4.37	1
71–1927	15.11	3
71–1929(1)	15.11	1
71–1931	15.11	4
71–1933	15.11	5
71–2103	15.22	1
	15.22	2
71–2105	15.22	4
71–2107	15.22	5
71–2113	15.22	2
71–2113(2)	15.22	4
71–2115	15.22	3
71–2303	15.18	1

TABLE OF STATUTES

NEW YORK, MCKINNEY'S ENVIRONMENTAL CONSERVATION LAW

Sec.	This Work Sec.	Note
71–2303 (Cont'd)	15.18	2
71–2703(1)	15.25	19
71–2703(2)	15.25	20
71–2703(3)	15.25	20
71–2705	15.25	21
	15.25	22
71–2707	15.25	23
71–2709	15.25	23

NEW YORK, MCKINNEY'S EXECUTIVE LAW

Sec.	This Work Sec.	Note
Art. 15	17.89	
	18.1	
	18.4	1
Art. 19–AA	16.124	2
Art. 39	4.27	5
	4.27	6
	4.49	20
63(12)	7.45	
96(11)	1.23	12
96–a	12.74	8
101–a	4.44	3
101–a(1)(b)	4.44	4
102	4.44	3
	4.48	6
102(1)(a)	4.48	7
145—149	4.50	11
290 et seq.	17.96	
292(5)	17.37	
292(9)	18.54	4
	18.98	
295(7)	18.49	6
	18.52	7
296	17.38	
	17.41	3
	17.82	22
	17.95	
	17.98	2
	18.57	2
	30.9	27
296(1)(a)	17.49	7
	17.57	
296(1)(d)	17.48	2
	17.49	8
296(2)(a)	18.54	3
	18.58	1
	18.98	
296(2)(b)	18.54	3
296(2–a)	18.41	3
	18.41	4
	18.47	2
296(3–a)(d) et seq.	17.37	7
296(3–b)	18.46	4
296(4)	18.53	3
296(5)	18.95	

NEW YORK, MCKINNEY'S EXECUTIVE LAW

Sec.	This Work Sec.	Note
296(5)(a)	18.45	1
	18.45	2
	18.50	2
	18.50	4
	18.95	
	18.96	
296(5)(a)(2)	18.96	
296(5)(b)	18.45	3
296(5)(c)(1)	18.46	1
296(5)(c)(2)	18.46	3
296(6)	17.82	5
296(10)(c)	17.56	4
296(11)	17.56	8
296(14)	18.57	2
	18.58	
296(15)	17.41	
	17.41	1
296(16)	17.39	1
296(18)	18.47	3
296.1(a)	17.43	5
	17.48	1
296.3–a(a)	17.37	
297(1)	18.52	2
297(2)(b)	18.52	3
	18.52	4
297(4)(a)	18.49	7
	18.49	8
	18.52	8
297(4)(a)(i)	18.49	5
	18.52	6
297(4)(a)(ii)	18.49	5
297(4)(c)	18.49	9
	18.49	11
	18.52	9
	18.52	10
297(4)(c) et seq.	17.39	2
297(5)	18.49	1
	18.52	1
297(6)	18.49	3
297(9)	17.67	3
	17.68	
	17.68	1
	17.94	
	17.95	
	18.48	1
	18.50	
298	18.49	12
	18.49	13
	18.52	11
	18.52	12
	37.51	40
298(2)(a)	18.49	2
298(2)(b)	18.49	2
298(3)(a)	18.49	4
	18.52	5
313	37.90	
377	16.4	3
	16.32	2

301

TABLE OF STATUTES

NEW YORK, MCKINNEY'S EXECUTIVE LAW

Sec.	This Work Sec.	Note
378(5)	12.91	2
481(7)	4.49	13
541(2)(e)—(2)(h)	23.87	1
547 et seq.	23.120	1
547–a(1)	23.120	11
547–a(2)	23.120	12
547–b(1)	23.120	2
547–b(2)	23.120	2
547–b(2)(a)	23.120	8
547–b(2)(b)	23.120	8
547–b(3)	23.120	3
	23.120	4
547–g(2)	23.120	5
547–g(3)	23.120	6
547–g(4)	23.120	7
547–h(2)	23.120	9
547–h(4)	23.120	10
629	37.90	
800—820	16.4	4
	16.24	3
828(1)(b)	14.1	3
878	4.26	11
878(1)	4.26	12
878(4)	4.26	12
878(6)	4.26	12

NEW YORK, MCKINNEY'S FAMILY COURT ACT

Sec.	This Work Sec.	Note
116(g)	20.28	5
243	37.5	2
	37.8	
	37.8	1
249	20.43	2
	37.8	1
254	37.19	36
254–A	37.19	36
262	20.65	
	20.93	1
	37.48	3
	20.135	
	20.136	
262(a)	37.19	
Art. 3	37.19	
	37.19	21
	37.19	46
	37.61	
301.2(12)	37.19	36
321.3(1)	38.8	207
330.2(9)	37.19	
341.2(3)	38.8	
352.2	37.19	11
354.2	37.19	59
365.1(1)	37.19	22
365.1(2)	37.19	25
365.2	37.19	23

NEW YORK, MCKINNEY'S FAMILY COURT ACT

Sec.	This Work Sec.	Note
365.3(1)	37.19	33
365.3(2)	37.19	37
365.3(3)	37.19	37
384	37.19	
Art. 4	37.19	3
412	21.8	
	21.8	3
	21.8	4
413	21.8	
	21.8	3
	21.8	5
413(13)	21.70	
438	30.42	
439	37.19	
464	21.79	
467(a)	21.9	2
	21.62	1
	21.71	
467(b)	21.71	
Art. 5	37.19	4
	37.19	14
Art. 6	20.101	1
	37.19	5
Art. 6, Pt. 1	37.19	
	37.19	48
	37.61	
Art. 6, Pt. 3	37.19	
641	20.9	1
Art. 7	37.19	
	37.19	1
	37.19	2
	37.19	47
	37.61	
760	37.19	59
Art. 8	37.19	
	37.19	6
812	38.8	
	38.8	136
812(1)	38.8	
	38.8	105
812(5)	38.8	108
813	37.19	15
	38.8	
841	37.19	11
846(b)(ii)(B)	38.8	105
	38.8	109
846(b)(ii)(C)	38.8	105
	38.8	109
Art. 10	37.19	
	37.19	7
	37.61	
Art. 10, Pt. 2	37.19	
Art. 10, Pt. 8	37.19	
1012(f)	18.28	6
1014	38.8	
	38.8	109
	38.8	110
1014(a)	38.8	

302

TABLE OF STATUTES

NEW YORK, MCKINNEY'S FAMILY COURT ACT

Sec.	This Work Sec.	Note
1014(b)	38.8	
1017	20.21	1
1028	37.29	35
1045	37.19	11
1052	20.88	2
1052-b	37.19	59
1055	20.21	1
	20.88	2
1111	37.15	2
	37.16	7
1112	37.19	12
	37.19	13
	37.19	20
	37.37	42
	37.37	46
1112(a)	37.19	9
	37.19	10
	37.19	17
	37.19	18
	37.19	45
	37.41	6
1112(b)	37.19	39
1113	37.19	32
	37.46	4
1114(b)	37.19	40
	37.19	41
1114(c)	37.19	38
1114(d)	37.19	43
1115	37.19	33
1115(a)	37.19	35
	37.46	3
1115(b)	37.19	34
1116	37.19	50
	37.51	40
1118	37.19	8
1120	37.48	3
1120(a)	37.19	
	37.19	63
1120(b)	37.19	60
1121(2)	37.19	59
1121(3)	37.19	59
1121(6)	37.19	58

NEW YORK, MCKINNEY'S GENERAL BUSINESS LAW

Sec.	This Work Sec.	Note
Art. 22	7.64	
Art. 22-A	7.1	8
	7.1	31
	7.44	10
	7.45	
	7.45	1
	7.52	
	7.53	
	7.54	
	7.56	

NEW YORK, MCKINNEY'S GENERAL BUSINESS LAW

Sec.	This Work Sec.	Note
Art. 22-A (Cont'd)	7.60	
	7.62	
	7.63	
	7.64	
	7.65	
Art. 23	1.89	20
Art. 25	7.31	2
	7.60	
Art. 29-H	7.44	1
	7.44	10
	7.62	
Art. 36-C	12.12	2
130	1.9	6
	1.115	9
	2.79	11
130(1)(a)	2.48	1
	2.48	2
	6.15	5
	6.19	1
130(1)(b)	1.13	17
	6.19	2
130(3)	2.48	2
130(4)	2.48	2
130(5)(b)	1.13	17
130(6)	2.48	5
130(8)	2.48	4
130(9)	2.48	3
	2.48	5
132	2.46	16
135	1.13	1
138	1.13	1
139	1.13	1
198-a	7.1	1
	7.3	3
	7.9	1
	7.16	7
	7.22	21
	7.26	17
	7.50	
	7.51	
198-a(a)(1)	7.10	6
198-a(a)(2)	7.10	3
	7.10	10
198-a(a)(4)	7.15	11
198-a(b)(1)	7.10	10
	7.10	11
	7.10	14
198-a(b)(2)	7.10	14
198-a(c)(1)	7.10	2
	7.15	12
	7.51	
198-a(c)(2)	7.4	2
198-a(c)(3)	7.51	
198-a(c)(3)(i)	7.10	15
	7.10	17
198-a(c)(3)(ii)	7.10	15
198-a(d)(1)	7.10	12
	7.10	16

303

TABLE OF STATUTES

NEW YORK, MCKINNEY'S GENERAL BUSINESS LAW

Sec.	This Work Sec.	Note
198–a(d)(1) (Cont'd)	7.51	
198–a(d)(2)	7.10	13
	7.51	
198–a(g)	7.12	2
	7.12	6
198–a(h)	7.16	5
198–a(j)	7.10	2
	7.12	2
198–a(k)	7.12	5
	7.15	2
	7.51	
198–a(L)	7.12	3
	7.14	5
	7.16	4
	7.17	
	7.17	8
	7.51	
198–a(n)	7.10	8
198–b	7.1	1
	7.9	2
	7.9	7
	7.22	21
	7.26	17
	7.52	
	7.56	
198–b et seq.	7.11	1
	7.61	
198–b(a)(1)	7.11	7
	7.52	
198–b(a)(2)	7.11	2
	7.52	
198–b(a)(3)	7.11	5
	7.52	
198–b(b)	7.11	8
198–b(b)(1)	7.52	
198–b(b)(2)	7.11	10
	7.11	15
	7.52	
198–b(b)(4)	7.11	11
	7.11	12
198–b(c)	7.10	15
198–b(c)(1)	7.4	2
	7.11	16
	7.52	
198–b(c)(1)(a)	7.10	17
198–b(c)(2)(a)	7.10	16
	7.11	13
198–b(c)(2)(b)	7.11	14
198–b(c)(3)	7.11	9
198–b(d)(1)	7.52	
198–b(d)(3)	7.11	4
	7.11	6
198–b(e)	7.52	
198–b(f)(1)	7.12	2
198–b(f)(2)	7.10	2
198–b(f)(3)	7.12	5
	7.12	6
198–b(f)(5)	7.10	2

NEW YORK, MCKINNEY'S GENERAL BUSINESS LAW

Sec.	This Work Sec.	Note
198–b(f)(5) (Cont'd)	7.12	2
	7.12	3
	7.16	4
	7.52	
349	7.3	2
	7.7	2
	7.7	3
	7.22	
	7.22	43
	7.22	45
	7.23	26
	7.25	2
	7.26	
	7.27	14
	7.44	10
	7.45	3
	7.47	10
	7.64	
	30.42	
349 et seq.	7.45	1
349(a)	7.45	
349(b)	7.47	1
349(c)	7.47	1
349(g)	7.45	
	7.47	8
349(h)	7.7	5
	7.7	6
	7.46	1
	7.46	2
	7.46	7
	7.46	9
	7.47	2
	7.52	
	7.53	
	7.54	
	7.60	
	7.62	
	7.64	
	7.65	
350	7.3	1
	7.7	4
	7.7	6
	7.45	2
350 et seq.	7.7	2
352	2.106	
352—359–h	1.20	3
	1.26	9
352–e	2.106	
	12.34	
	12.35	
352–e(1)	2.106	3
352–e(1)(a)	2.106	4
360(a—iii)	6.19	3
380	7.3	8
	7.33	16
380 et seq.	7.31	2
	7.33	12
380–a(b)	7.60	

TABLE OF STATUTES

NEW YORK, MCKINNEY'S GENERAL BUSINESS LAW

Sec.	This Work Sec.	Note
380–a(c)(1)	7.60	
380–a(e)	7.60	
380–b	7.31	6
380–b(b)	17.42	1
380–d(c)	7.32	2
380–f	7.31	8
	7.33	3
	7.60	
380–f(a)	7.33	16
380–f(b)(3)	7.31	9
380–f(c)	7.31	9
	7.33	4
380–i(a)	7.32	1
	7.33	15
380–j(a)(3)	7.33	
	7.33	14
	7.33	16
	7.60	
380–j(e)	7.31	7
	7.33	2
	7.60	
380–j(f)(1)—(2)	7.31	5
380–l	7.33	6
	7.60	
380–l(c)	7.60	
380–m	7.33	5
380–m(b)	7.60	
380–n	7.33	6
380–o	7.31	6
395–b	17.55	7
397	18.63	4
600 et seq.	7.36	3
600(1)	7.36	4
600(3)	7.36	10
600.1	7.62	
600.2	7.62	
600.3	7.62	
601	7.36	9
	7.36	10
	7.44	2
601(1)	7.44	4
601(2)	7.44	5
601(3)	7.38	1
	7.38	3
601(4)	7.38	2
601(5)	7.32	6
	7.44	6
601(6)	7.44	3
	7.56	
601(7)	7.44	7
601(8)	7.44	8
601(9)	7.44	4
601.2	7.62	
601.3	7.62	
601.8	7.62	
601.9	7.62	
602(2)	7.44	9
778–a	12.12	3

NEW YORK, MCKINNEY'S GENERAL BUSINESS LAW

Sec.	This Work Sec.	Note
778–a (Cont'd)	12.12	4

NEW YORK, MCKINNEY'S GENERAL CITY LAW

Sec.	This Work Sec.	Note
Art. 5–A	16.6	
17(13)	16.96	7
	16.96	8
20	3.7	4
	16.7	2
	16.125	3
20(24)	16.5	2
	16.5	6
20(25)	16.5	6
	16.5	8
	16.11	2
	16.11	13
	16.15	5
	16.17	10
20–f	16.8	4
26	16.31	6
	16.31	7
27(1)	16.36	1
	16.36	3
27(3)	16.36	2
27(13)	16.36	7
27(14)	16.36	9
27–a	16.8	4
	16.36	5
	16.36	6
	16.43	6
	16.103	1
27–a(1)	16.103	5
	16.103	6
27–a(2)	16.36	5
	16.104	1
27–a(2)(a)	16.103	7
	16.103	8
	16.103	9
	16.104	5
	16.105	14
	16.106	4
27–a(3)	16.87	6
27–a(4)	16.107	1
27–a(5)	16.104	6
27–a(6)(a)	16.107	6
27–a(6)(b)	16.107	7
27–a(6)(c)	16.107	8
	16.107	9
27–a(7)	16.43	10
	16.105	15
27–a(8)	16.105	2
	16.105	3
	16.105	4
	16.105	5
	16.105	6

TABLE OF STATUTES

NEW YORK, MCKINNEY'S GENERAL CITY LAW			NEW YORK, MCKINNEY'S GENERAL CITY LAW		
Sec.	This Work Sec.	Note	Sec.	This Work Sec.	Note
27–a(8) (Cont'd)	16.105	7	32(5)(h)	16.97	5
	16.105	10		16.97	6
	16.105	12	32(6)	16.97	11
	16.105	13	32(6)(b)	16.97	7
27–a(13)	16.103	1	32(6)(d)	16.97	12
27–b	16.8	4	32(8)	16.97	10
	16.43	8	32(9)	16.43	10
	16.90	2		16.97	8
27–b(1)	16.90	2	32(10)	16.97	13
27–b(2)	16.36	5	32(11)	16.97	9
	16.90	3	33	16.96	5
27–b(4)	16.90	7	33(1)	16.96	4
	16.93	1		16.99	2
27–b(6)	16.43	10	33(2)	16.99	3
	16.90	9		16.99	4
	16.94	1	33(4)	16.99	5
27–b(7)	16.90	9		16.100	1
27–b(8)	16.94	2		16.100	2
27–b(12)	16.90	2		16.100	4
28–a	16.5	7		16.100	6
	16.31	6	33(6)	16.87	6
28–a(2)(b)	16.13	2	33(7)	16.101	8
28–a(2)(c)	16.13	2	33(8)	16.99	7
28–a(2)(h)	16.13	2	35	12.55	9
	16.13	4	38	16.43	7
28–a(3)(a)	16.13	1	38–a	12.65	9
28–a(3)(b)	16.13	5	81(1)	16.37	1
28–a(3)(c)	16.14	2		16.37	2
28–a(4)(b)	16.13	3	81(2)	16.37	3
28–a(4)(h)	16.13	3	81–a	16.80	6
28–a(5)	16.14	1		16.87	10
	16.14	2	81–a(1)	16.39	4
	16.14	4	81–a(4)	16.37	6
28–a(6)(b)	16.14	6		16.37	7
	16.14	7		16.37	8
28–a(7)	16.11	14	81–a(5)	16.37	9
	16.14	3		16.37	10
28–a(7)(b)	16.14	5	81–a(7)	16.37	11
28–a(8)	16.14	8	81–a(8)	16.37	12
28–a(11)	16.13	6	81–a(9)	16.43	10
28–a(12)	16.13	4	81–a(11)	16.37	13
32(1)	16.96	1	81–b	16.8	4
	16.96	6		16.37	4
32(5)(b)	16.98	1		16.37	5
32(5)(c)	16.98	4		16.73	1
	16.98	5		16.74	2
32(5)(d)	16.98	6	81–b(1)(a)	16.73	2
32(5)(d)(i)	16.97	1	81–b(1)(b)	16.82	1
32(5)(d)(ii)	16.97	2		16.83	1
	16.98	8	81–b(3)	16.87	6
32(5)(d)(iv)	16.97	4	81–b(3)(a)	16.73	3
	16.101	2		16.73	6
32(5)(e)	16.98	7	81–b(3)(b)	16.73	7
32(5)(e)(i)	16.97	1		16.73	8
32(5)(e)(ii)	16.97	2		16.75	5
32(5)(e)(iv)	16.97	4	81–b(3)(b)(i)	16.75	1
32(5)(g)	16.43	10		16.75	6
	16.97	3	81–b(3)(b)(ii)	16.76	1

TABLE OF STATUTES

NEW YORK, MCKINNEY'S GENERAL CITY LAW

Sec.	This Work Sec.	Note
81–b(3)(b)(iii)	16.77	2
81–b(3)(b)(iv)	16.78	1
	16.78	3
81–b(3)(c)	16.73	13
	16.79	1
	16.89	1
81–b(4)(b)	16.83	2
	16.84	7
81–b(4)(c)	16.86	1
	16.89	1
81–b(5)	16.79	4
	16.86	2
	16.89	3
81–c	16.43	5
	16.43	9
81–d	16.8	4
81–e	16.6	1
83	16.30	1
	16.30	4
	16.109	2
	16.113	1
	16.113	2
	16.113	3
83(1)	16.113	3
83(2)	16.30	2
83(2)(a)—(c)	16.113	11
83–a	16.23	2
83–a(2)	16.23	3

NEW YORK, MCKINNEY'S GENERAL CONSTRUCTION LAW

Sec.	This Work Sec.	Note
37–a	21.40	
41	3.10	6
65(a)	3.3	1
65(b)	3.3	2
66(2)	3.3	3
66(3)	3.33	14

NEW YORK, MCKINNEY'S GENERAL MUNICIPAL LAW

Sec.	This Work Sec.	Note
Art. 5–A	3.25	
Art. 12–F	16.31	4
Art. 15	3.3	5
Art. 17	3.5	3
Art. 18	3.22	
	3.22	14
	16.40	1
Art. 18–A	3.34	
Art. 19–A	3.33	15
2	3.3	3
	18.87	3

NEW YORK, MCKINNEY'S GENERAL MUNICIPAL LAW

Sec.	This Work Sec.	Note
3–a	30.40	14
10	3.26	8
10(3)	3.26	9
11	3.26	8
20(5)	16.29	6
35	12.57	3
50	26.38	1
50–c(1)	3.30	17
50–e	3.30	
	3.30	25
	3.31	2
	18.65	
	26.40	
	26.41	
50–e et seq.	26.12	2
50–e(1)(a)	3.30	17
	3.30	27
	18.9	2
	18.11	5
	18.20	2
	26.39	1
	26.39	2
50–e(2)	3.30	18
	3.30	21
	26.40	1
	26.40	2
50–e(3)	3.30	19
50–e(3)(a)	3.30	22
	26.40	3
50–e(3)(c)	3.30	23
	26.40	5
50–e(3)(d)	3.30	23
	26.40	6
	26.40	7
50–e(5)	3.30	20
	3.30	25
	3.30	26
	3.37	
	18.11	5
50–e(5)	26.40	8
	26.40	9
	26.40	10
50–e(6)	3.30	24
50–h	26.40	4
	26.40	11
	26.40	12
50–i	26.40	13
50–i(1)	3.31	3
50–i(1)(c)	18.9	2
	18.11	5
51	3.32	
	3.32	13
	3.32	16
	3.35	5
	3.35	6
71–a	18.87	3
72–g	3.16	16
74	3.16	2

307

TABLE OF STATUTES

NEW YORK, MCKINNEY'S GENERAL MUNICIPAL LAW

Sec.	This Work Sec.	Note
96–a	16.126	4
	16.126	5
	16.127	1
	16.127	3
100—109–b	3.25	1
101	3.25	12
103	3.24	6
	3.25	
	3.25	2
103(1)	3.25	2
	3.25	11
	3.25	13
103(2)	3.25	
103(3)	3.25	11
103(4)	3.25	5
103(5)	3.10	6
103(6)	3.25	6
104	3.25	7
104–b	3.25	10
	3.27	2
109–b(1)(b)	3.27	4
109–b(2)(f)	3.27	6
119aa	16.127	2
119bb	16.127	2
119cc	16.127	2
119dd	16.127	2
119dd(2)	16.127	4
205–a	30.38	
239–m	16.4	4
	16.14	7
	16.29	10
	16.30	3
	16.94	
	16.97	
	16.105	11
	16.113	9
239–n	16.105	13
502(2)	3.3	5
507(2)	3.16	20
700 et seq.	3.5	3
701(1)	3.5	3
703	3.6	2
703(1)	3.5	4
	3.6	1
703(2)	3.5	5
703(3)	3.5	5
	3.5	6
704	3.6	4
704(1)	3.5	7
	3.5	8
	3.5	9
	3.5	10
	3.5	11
	3.5	12
	3.6	3
704(2)	3.5	13
704(3)	3.5	14
705(1)	3.5	15

NEW YORK, MCKINNEY'S GENERAL MUNICIPAL LAW

Sec.	This Work Sec.	Note
711(1)	3.5	16
711(4)	3.5	17
712	37.90	
712(1)	3.5	18
712(6)	3.5	19
712(7)	3.5	20
712(8)	3.5	21
712(9)	3.5	22
712(10)	3.5	23
713(1)	3.5	26
	3.15	11
800—809	3.22	1
800(2)	3.22	5
	3.22	6
	3.22	7
	3.23	
800(3)	3.23	
800(4)	3.23	
800(5)	3.23	
	16.40	2
801	3.22	3
	3.22	4
	3.22	8
	3.23	
	16.40	3
802	3.22	8
	3.23	
803	3.22	9
804	3.22	10
	3.23	1
805	3.22	11
	3.23	1
805–a	3.22	12
806	3.22	13
	3.22	14
809	16.40	6
852	3.34	5
854(14)	3.34	7
856(1)(a)	3.34	2
856(2)	3.34	1
	3.34	3
856(4)	3.34	4
858(15)	3.34	14
864	3.34	8
864(1)	3.34	12
870	3.34	13
874(1)	3.34	14
874(2)	3.34	9
980–c	3.33	16
980–l	3.33	17

NEW YORK, MCKINNEY'S GENERAL OBLIGATIONS LAW

Sec.	This Work Sec.	Note
3–101	12.73	2
3–501	12.8	4

TABLE OF STATUTES

NEW YORK, MCKINNEY'S GENERAL OBLIGATIONS LAW

Sec.	This Work Sec.	Note
Art. 5, Tit. 15	12.97	
Art. 5, Tit. 15	12.98	
5–15	24.100	
5–327	7.23	26
	7.26	
	7.52	
	7.53	
5–327(1)(a)	7.52	
5–327(1)(d)	7.52	
5–327(2)	7.52	
	7.53	
5–501	12.73	4
5–501 et seq.	11.37	11
5–517	11.37	11
5–521	11.37	11
5–701	5.18	
	17.34	14
5–701(10)	6.20	6
5–703	12.41	1
5–703(2)	12.4	1
5–703(4)	12.4	1
5–1311	6.68	
	6.68	6
	6.150	
	6.150	5
	6.187	
	12.20	
	12.32	1
5–1311(1)(a)	6.68	6
	6.150	5
5–1501	12.8	5
	12.8	7
	22.21	
	24.89	3
5–1501 et seq.	12.8	2
	22.26	6
	22.41	7
	22.53	13
	22.54	4
5–1501.1	24.89	4
5–1502A—5–1503	12.97	
5–1502A—5–1503	24.100	
5–1502A—5–1506	12.98	
5–1503	12.98	
	12.97	
	24.100	
5–1505	12.8	6
	22.21	4
	22.53	13
5–1506	12.8	6
	22.21	4
	24.89	7
5–1601	22.21	
	22.53	13
5–1601 (repealed)	22.21	4
5–1602	22.21	
5–1602 (repealed)	22.21	4
7–101 et seq.	12.26	1

NEW YORK, MCKINNEY'S GENERAL OBLIGATIONS LAW

Sec.	This Work Sec.	Note
7–401	7.23	27
	7.26	
	7.26	2
	7.26	3
7–401(1)	7.23	18
7–401(2)	7.23	18
9–401—9–410	12.74	8
11–100	30.38	
	30.38	5
15–108	26.35	2
	30.44	1
15–109	27.58	
17–105	11.37	7

NEW YORK, MCKINNEY'S HEALTH INSURANCE ACCOUNTABILITY AND PORTABILITY ACT

Sec.	This Work Sec.	Note
217	22.48	11

NEW YORK, MCKINNEY'S HIGHWAY LAW

Sec.	This Work Sec.	Note
29(8)	14.96	1
271	16.24	13

NEW YORK CITY HUMAN RIGHTS LAW

Sec.	This Work Sec.	Note
8–107(3)(a)	17.56	7
8–107(3)(b)	17.56	7

NEW YORK, MCKINNEY'S INSURANCE LAW

Sec.	This Work Sec.	Note
50–h	26.48	2
403	28.43	2
1101 et seq.	31.22	4
1101—1116	31.4	9
1101(a)(1)	31.8	3
1110	10.120	
1117(g)(1)	23.68	4
1213	31.4	10
	31.22	
1213(b)(1)	31.22	5
1213(c)(1)	31.23	
	31.23	1
1216	1.66	43
2101	31.6	1
2101—2178	31.4	9

TABLE OF STATUTES

NEW YORK, MCKINNEY'S INSURANCE LAW

Sec.	This Work Sec.	Note
2102	31.5	1
2108(c)	31.4	9
2120	31.7	4
2401 et seq.	7.47	10
2401—2610	31.4	6
2601	7.47	10
3105	31.18	1
	31.18	2
3211(d)	31.26	6
3212	9.125	12
3216(d)(1)(K)	31.26	4
3221(m)	17.12	2
	17.46	
	17.46	3
3229	23.66	2
3231	23.60	11
	23.60	12
3231(b)	23.60	13
3231(c)	23.60	13
3404	31.26	5
3407(a)	31.4	8
	31.11	
	31.11	7
3420	31.16	1
3420(a)(3)	28.40	1
3420(a)(4)	28.40	2
3420(d)	31.4	7
	31.16	1
3420(f)(1)	26.24	15
3420(f)(2)	26.24	10
3420(f)(2)	26.24	12
3420(f)(2)	26.24	14
3420(j)	32.41	9
3425	32.41	10
3426(b)	28.41	1
3426(c)	28.41	2
5102	26.67	
5102(a)	26.36	7
	26.60	
	30.3	
	30.48	
5102(a)(2)	26.24	1
5102(d)	26.17	1
	26.22	1
	26.36	7
	26.58	
	26.60	
	26.65	
	26.66	
	30.3	
	30.48	
5104	26.60	
5105	31.24	1
Art. 52	26.24	
5201(b)	26.24	7
5202(b)	26.24	5
5208(a)	26.28	
	26.28	1

NEW YORK, MCKINNEY'S INSURANCE LAW

Sec.	This Work Sec.	Note
5208(a)(1)	26.30	
5208(a)(1)(A)—(C)	26.28	2
5208(a)(3)(A)(i)—(iii)	26.27	1
	26.29	1
5208(a)(3)(B)	26.29	2
5208(b)	26.30	
5208(b)(1)	26.30	1
5208(b)(2)(A)	26.30	2
5208(b)(2)(B)	26.30	2
5208(b)(2)(C)	26.30	2
5208(c)	26.30	3
5209	26.30	6
5213(a)	26.30	5
5217	26.28	6
5218	26.30	7
	26.30	9
Art. 74	32.42	4
7401 et seq.	31.28	1
7401—7434	31.4	11
7417—7418	31.28	3
7419	31.28	6
7428	31.28	8
7432	31.28	
	31.28	8

NEW YORK, MCKINNEY'S JUDICIARY LAW

Sec.	This Work Sec.	Note
Art. 2–A	39.59	
	39.59	2
Art. 4	37.3	10
Art. 7–A	37.7	
	37.91	9
Art. 7–A (former)	37.7	
2	10.78	1
2(10)	37.121	2
2(11)	37.121	2
2(12)	37.121	1
	38.48	2
4	3.29	3
21	37.4	5
25	37.91	11
27(b)	8.3	7
35	20.64	
	20.65	
	20.135	
	20.136	
	37.10	1
35(1)(a)	37.48	4
35–a	11.75	
40–a	39.59	2
44(7)	39.59	3
	39.59	5
44(8)	39.59	4
44(9)	39.59	13
53	39.61	1

310

TABLE OF STATUTES

NEW YORK, MCKINNEY'S JUDICIARY LAW

Sec.	This Work Sec.	Note
53(6)	37.6	6
	39.61	2
70	37.3	6
71	37.4	3
75	37.4	
85	37.7	5
86	37.7	5
90	37.5	1
	37.6	
	37.6	1
	39.61	2
90(1)	39.61	3
91	37.4	7
93 et seq.	37.4	9
101	37.11	1
102—108	37.7	5
115	37.4	2
140	37.3	7
210(a)	37.100	1
255–c	8.9	
431 et seq.	37.4	8
464	1.122	4
	1.125	
466	1.122	4
	1.125	
467	1.122	4
	1.125	
474	26.6	1
474–a(2)	26.6	5
	28.31	2
476	18.75	
	18.79	4
476–a	37.6	
	37.6	8
478	37.6	
	37.6	7
484	37.6	
487	28.1	
	28.24	
	28.24	1
	28.24	2
	28.24	9
	30.38	
	30.38	4
489	7.39	7
497	12.12	
509	37.90	
522	37.7	5
750	8.42	7
	38.8	
750 et seq.	8.23	
753	8.42	8
755	37.19	62
756	8.42	9
	8.42	10
	8.42	11
761	8.42	13
770	8.42	16

NEW YORK, MCKINNEY'S JUDICIARY LAW

Sec.	This Work Sec.	Note
770 (Cont'd)	8.42	17
	8.42	20
773	8.42	21
	8.42	22
	8.42	23
	8.42	24
	8.42	25

NEW YORK, MCKINNEY'S LABOR LAW

Sec.	This Work Sec.	Note
130—144	17.63	
131(3)	32.12	
	32.12	
132(3)	32.12	
191–a(d)	30.38	1
191–c	30.38	1
193	17.13	5
194	17.44	3
198(1–a)	17.13	4
	17.34	
	17.63	1
	30.39	
198–c	17.63	1
200 et seq.	17.62	3
205–d	17.47	
215	17.38	
	17.62	3
220	37.90	
220–b	37.90	
511	17.60	1
527(1)	17.60	3
590(4)	17.60	4
590(5)	17.60	4
593(1)	17.60	9
593(3)	17.60	10
596(1)	17.60	6
597(1)	17.60	7
601(3)	17.60	5
620(1)	17.60	8
624	37.44	7
652	17.63	14
657	17.63	14
	37.44	
676	37.44	
700 et seq.	17.61	17
716	37.90	
740	17.32	
	17.64	
	17.64	1
	17.64	2
	17.64	3
740(7)	17.64	
807(9)	37.61	1

TABLE OF STATUTES

NEW YORK, MCKINNEY'S LEGISLATIVE LAW

Sec.	This Work Sec.	Note
Art. 2	14.59	
87(1)	4.55	14
388	26.18	2

NEW YORK, MCKINNEY'S LIEN LAW

Sec.	This Work Sec.	Note
Art. 2	10.123	
Art. 3–A	10.1	
	10.94	
	10.146	
	10.147	
	11.9	
Art. 4	10.1	
	10.142	
Art. 5	10.1	
Art. 6	10.1	
Art. 7	10.1	
Arts. 8—9	10.1	
2	10.6	
	10.20	1
2(4)	10.20	2
	10.20	3
2(7)	10.21	2
2(9)	10.4	1
	10.5	3
2(10)	10.4	2
	10.5	4
2(11)	10.4	3
2(12)	10.4	4
	10.5	6
2(13)	12.45	8
	12.47	1
2(14)	12.45	8
3	10.4	
	10.4	5
	10.7	1
	10.20	4
	10.21	
	10.11	1
4(1)	10.8	
	10.9	
4(2)	10.8	1
	10.8	2
4(3)	10.8	1
	10.8	2
4–a	10.10	
5	10.21	
	10.21	1
	10.21	3
	10.21	7
	10.25	1
	10.25	2
	10.25	3
6	10.1	
7	10.14	
	10.14	4

NEW YORK, MCKINNEY'S LIEN LAW

Sec.	This Work Sec.	Note
8	10.14	1
	10.14	2
	10.14	3
	10.20	11
	10.68	
	10.111	
9	10.16	
	10.20	6
	10.48	
	10.119	
9(7)	10.16	1
	10.16	3
	10.20	7
	10.109	
10	10.17	
	10.17	3
	10.20	5
	10.20	8
	10.48	
	10.70	3
	12.45	8
10(1)	10.17	6
	10.17	7
	10.17	11
	10.17	12
	10.17	17
	10.17	15
10(2)	10.17	16
11	10.18	1
	10.18	4
	10.18	6
	10.20	9
	10.20	10
11–a	10.24	
	10.24	2
	10.25	10
	10.112	
11–a(2)	10.24	3
	10.24	4
11–a(3)	10.24	5
11–a(4)	10.24	6
11–b	10.18	7
	10.18	8
	10.18	9
	10.18	10
	10.18	11
	10.18	12
11–c	10.23	
	10.25	8
	10.25	9
12	10.21	
	10.22	
	10.23	1
	10.23	2
	10.23	3
	10.25	4
	10.25	5
	10.25	6
	10.25	7

TABLE OF STATUTES

NEW YORK, MCKINNEY'S LIEN LAW

Sec.	This Work Sec.	Note
12 (Cont'd)	10.56	
12–a	10.19	
12–a(1)	10.19	1
12–a(2)	10.19	4
	10.19	6
13	10.26	
	10.60	
	10.87	
	11.9	2
	11.9	7
	12.22	
	12.73	5
13(1)	10.8	3
	10.26	1
	10.26	2
	10.26	3
	10.26	5
13(1–a)	10.27	
13(2)	10.28	1
13(3)	10.28	
	10.28	2
	10.28	4
	10.29	1
	10.59	2
	12.45	8
	12.47	1
13(4)	10.30	1
13(5)	10.14	
	10.31	1
	10.31	2
	12.45	8
	12.47	1
13(6)	10.36	3
14	10.33	
	10.33	1
	10.33	2
	10.33	3
15	10.34	
15(1)	10.34	1
	10.34	2
	10.34	3
15(2)	10.35	1
	10.35	2
15(3)	10.36	1
15(4)	10.36	2
16	10.37	
	10.37	1
	10.37	2
17	10.38	1
	10.39	
	10.39	1
	10.39	2
	10.39	3
	10.43	
	10.72	1
18	10.40	1
	10.41	
	10.41	1
	10.41	2

NEW YORK, MCKINNEY'S LIEN LAW

Sec.	This Work Sec.	Note
18 (Cont'd)	10.51	
	10.54	
19	10.42	
	10.45	
	10.50	
	10.121	
19(1)	10.42	1
19(2)	10.43	2
19(4)	10.46	1
	10.46	3
	10.46	4
	10.46	5
	10.54	
19(5)	10.47	1
19(6)	10.48	1
	10.48	4
	10.48	5
20	10.49	
	10.49	1
	10.49	2
	10.49	3
	10.50	1
	10.85	
20(2)	10.51	2
21	10.50	
21(1)	10.50	2
21(2)	10.51	1
21(3)	10.52	1
21(3–a)	10.53	2
21(4)	10.53	1
21(5)	10.54	
	10.54	1
21(6)	10.55	1
	10.141	
21(6–a)	10.55	2
21(7)	10.56	1
	10.56	2
21(8)	10.57	1
21–a	10.19	3
	10.58	1
	10.131	
	10.132	
22	10.28	
	10.59	
	10.59	1
	10.60	1
	11.9	3
	11.41	
	12.45	8
	12.47	1
	12.73	5
23	10.16	2
25	10.32	
	10.87	
	10.116	
25(1)	10.32	1
25(4)	10.32	1
25(5)	10.37	3
26	10.61	

313

TABLE OF STATUTES

NEW YORK, MCKINNEY'S LIEN LAW

Sec.	This Work Sec.	Note
26 (Cont'd)	10.61	1
	10.63	
	10.64	
	10.65	
	10.123	
28	10.62	
	10.62	1
	10.64	
	10.65	
29	10.63	
	10.63	1
	10.63	2
	10.63	3
	10.64	
	10.65	
31	10.64	1
	10.65	
	10.65	1
	10.65	2
33	10.61	
	10.61	3
	10.62	
	10.63	
34	10.66	
	10.66	1
35	10.67	1
37	10.124	
37(1)	10.68	1
37(2)	10.68	2
37(3)	10.69	1
37(4)	10.68	4
37(5)	10.70	1
37(6)	10.71	1
37(8)	10.72	4
37(9)	10.72	2
	10.72	3
	10.73	
37(10)	10.70	4
37(11)	10.73	1
37(12)	10.73	2
	10.74	1
38	10.75	1
	10.125	
	10.126	
	10.127	
	10.128	
	10.135	
39	10.135	
39–a	10.75	4
	10.135	
39–c	10.76	1
41	10.77	1
42	10.77	2
43	10.78	2
	10.78	3
	10.137	
44	10.92	
44(1)	10.79	1
44(2)	10.79	2

NEW YORK, MCKINNEY'S LIEN LAW

Sec.	This Work Sec.	Note
44(3)	10.79	3
44(4)	10.79	4
44(6)	10.79	5
	10.79	7
44–a	10.79	6
	11.14	3
45	10.79	8
	10.79	9
46	10.80	1
47	10.80	2
	10.83	
48	10.81	1
49	10.81	2
50	10.81	3
51	10.82	1
	10.82	2
53	10.83	1
	10.83	2
54	10.84	1
55	10.85	
	10.85	1
	10.85	2
	10.86	1
	10.86	2
	10.86	3
	10.86	4
	10.138	
	10.139	
56	10.26	4
	10.87	2
	10.87	3
	10.87	4
57	10.88	1
59	10.89	1
	10.90	1
	10.90	2
	10.90	3
	10.129	
	10.130	
60	10.91	1
	10.91	3
	10.92	1
61	10.1	
62	10.72	
	10.92	
	10.92	2
	10.92	3
	10.92	4
	10.92	5
63	10.93	1
64	10.84	1
70(1)	10.94	4
70(3)	10.95	1
70(5)	10.95	2
70(6)	10.96	1
71	10.36	3
	10.116	
71(1)	10.97	1
71(2)	10.97	3

TABLE OF STATUTES

NEW YORK, MCKINNEY'S LIEN LAW

Sec.	This Work Sec.	Note
71(3)(a)	10.97	2
71(4)	10.97	4
71(7)	10.96	2
71–a	10.36	3
	10.95	2
	12.12	1
72	10.98	1
73	10.99	2
73(3)(a)	10.99	3
73(3)(c)	10.99	4
73(4)	10.99	5
74	10.94	5
75	10.100	1
	10.100	2
	10.100	3
	10.100	4
75(4)	10.100	5
76	10.101	1
	10.101	2
	10.101	3
	10.101	4
	10.101	5
	10.101	6
	10.143	
	10.143	1
	10.144	
76(5)	10.144	
77	10.104	1
77(1)	10.102	3
	10.103	1
77(3)(a)	10.103	2
77(3)(b)	10.103	3
77(4)	10.103	4
77(5)	10.103	5
77(6)	10.102	1
77(7)	10.103	6
78	10.105	1
78—79	10.105	2
79	10.105	3
79–a	10.106	
79–a(1)	10.106	1
	10.106	2
79–a(2)	10.106	3
79–a(3)	10.106	4
184	7.28	
	7.28	2
	7.58	
	7.59	
184(1)	7.28	3
	7.28	8
184(4)	7.28	4
200	7.28	5
201	7.28	10
	7.28	11
	7.28	16
	7.28	17
	7.29	
	7.29	5
	7.57	

NEW YORK, MCKINNEY'S LIEN LAW

Sec.	This Work Sec.	Note
201 (Cont'd)	7.58	
	7.59	
201(1)	7.28	12
201(2)	7.28	13
201(3)	7.28	14
201(4)	7.28	15
201–a	7.1	5
	7.29	
	7.29	2
	7.29	3
	7.29	4
	7.29	5
	7.29	7
	7.57	
	7.58	
	7.59	

NEW YORK, MCKINNEY'S LIMITED LIABILITY COMPANY LAW

Sec.	This Work Sec.	Note
102(d)	2.37	10
102(e)	2.16	2
102(O)	2.7	7
	2.8	
	2.17	9
	2.22	4
102(q)	2.21	1
102(r)	2.21	3
	2.21	2
102(v)	2.40	1
102(w)	2.21	1
	2.40	1
201	2.16	1
	2.16	5
202	2.16	6
202(c)	12.55	21
202(e)	2.16	7
	2.16	8
	2.105	7
202(k)	2.17	5
203	2.111	
203(a)	2.16	10
	2.22	3
203(b)	2.16	11
	2.22	3
203(c)	2.22	
	2.24	1
	2.105	
203(d)	2.16	9
204	2.16	4
204(a)	2.17	1
205	2.16	
	2.79	10
206	2.17	2
206(a)(6)	2.9	
	2.9	9
206(a)(7)	2.6	7

315

TABLE OF STATUTES

NEW YORK, MCKINNEY'S LIMITED LIABILITY COMPANY LAW

Sec.	This Work Sec.	Note
206(c)	2.18	1
	2.18	2
	2.18	3
	2.18	4
	2.18	5
	2.41	11
207(a)	2.22	3
207(d)	2.105	4
210(a)(1)	2.17	12
210(a)(2)	2.17	13
210(b)	2.17	14
211	2.17	
211(a)	2.17	8
211(e)	2.17	11
212	2.23	6
213(a)	2.17	9
213(b)	2.17	10
301(e)	2.20	3
401 et seq.	2.106	11
401(a)	2.9	9
	2.26	1
	2.26	3
401(b)(i)	2.26	4
402(a)	2.34	6
402(b)	2.27	
402(c)	2.27	6
402(c)(3)	2.19	6
402(e)	2.27	
	2.29	1
402(f)	2.27	5
403	2.27	1
404(a)	2.27	3
404(b)	2.27	4
405(a)	2.27	2
407(a)	2.19	6
	2.27	8
408(a)	2.30	1
408(b)	2.28	4
	2.28	6
408(c)	2.28	8
409	2.26	
	2.31	
409(a)	2.17	4
	2.26	3
	2.31	
	2.31	1
409(b)	2.31	2
409(c)	2.31	3
410	2.28	1
411	2.21	13
	2.105	10
411(a)	2.28	9
411(b)	2.28	9
	2.28	10
412(a)	2.9	
	2.9	11
	2.17	3
	2.32	1

NEW YORK, MCKINNEY'S LIMITED LIABILITY COMPANY LAW

Sec.	This Work Sec.	Note
412(b)	2.32	
	2.32	2
	2.45	7
412(b)(1)	2.9	
413	2.28	2
414	2.28	12
415	2.28	11
416	2.28	13
417(a)	2.17	5
	2.19	1
	2.31	4
417(a)(iii)	2.9	10
417(b)	2.19	5
	2.27	
417(c)	2.19	1
418(a)	2.9	10
	2.27	9
	2.28	7
	2.30	1
419(b)	2.28	3
420	2.16	6
	2.17	5
	2.31	5
501	1.30	3
	2.21	9
502	2.35	
502(a)	2.21	10
	2.23	10
	2.23	11
502(b)	2.23	12
503	2.21	11
	2.27	
504	2.21	11
508	2.12	1
	2.35	
508(a)	2.21	
	2.23	
	2.23	7
	2.23	8
508(b)	2.21	
509	2.21	20
601	2.21	4
	12.55	21
602(a)	2.22	
602(a)(1)	2.22	1
	2.105	4
602(a)(2)	2.22	1
	2.22	2
602(b)(1)	2.22	5
603	2.21	25
	2.21	26
	2.34	1
	2.43	
603(a)	2.8	10
	2.21	3
	2.33	1
603(a)(1)	2.8	
603(a)(2)	2.8	

316

TABLE OF STATUTES

NEW YORK, MCKINNEY'S LIMITED LIABILITY COMPANY LAW

Sec.	This Work Sec.	Note
603(a)(2) (Cont'd)	2.34	1
603(a)(3)	2.8	
	2.34	2
603(a)(4)	2.8	
	2.34	4
	2.34	5
603(b)	2.21	5
	2.21	8
603(c)	2.35	2
604	2.21	25
	2.21	26
604(a)	2.8	
	2.35	1
604(b)	2.35	3
	2.35	4
605	2.35	5
606	2.21	14
	2.21	15
	2.21	16
	2.21	18
	2.21	19
	2.21	21
	2.35	
607	2.8	11
	2.21	24
608	2.8	10
	2.21	28
	2.21	27
	2.34	1
609(a)	2.6	11
	2.23	1
	2.23	2
	2.23	3
	2.43	13
609(b)	2.2	13
	2.6	7
	2.6	12
	2.23	16
610	2.21	29
611	2.21	12
	2.23	4
701(a)	2.7	7
	2.37	2
701(b)	2.7	7
	2.37	2
701(c)	2.7	7
	2.37	2
701(d)	2.7	7
	2.21	23
	2.37	10
	2.38	1
	2.38	2
701(e)	2.7	7
	2.37	2
702	2.37	
703(a)	2.39	1
	2.39	2
703(b)	2.39	1

NEW YORK, MCKINNEY'S LIMITED LIABILITY COMPANY LAW

Sec.	This Work Sec.	Note
703(b) (Cont'd)	2.39	3
704(a)	2.39	4
704(b)	2.39	5
704(c)	2.39	5
705(a)	2.39	6
705(a)(1)—(4)	2.39	8
705(b)	2.39	7
802(a)	2.105	5
	2.105	6
802(b)	2.18	1
803	2.34	1
1001(b)	2.40	1
	2.42	3
1002(b)	2.41	1
1002(c)	2.29	2
	2.41	1
	2.41	3
1002(f)	2.42	1
1003(a)	2.41	4
	2.41	5
1003(b)	2.41	6
1004(a)	2.41	7
1004(c)	2.41	8
1004(d)	2.41	8
1005(b)	2.42	2
1006	2.41	9
	2.101	
1006(c)	2.69	1
1006(d)	2.41	10
1006(f)	2.41	11
1006(g)	2.41	11
1101(f)	2.17	7
1102(a)	2.20	1
	2.20	2
1102(a)(2)	2.105	8
1102(b)	2.20	1
Art. XII	2.43	
1201 et seq.	28.34	1
1201(b)	2.75	3
1203—1206	37.90	
1203(a)	2.16	3
	2.43	1
	2.43	2
	2.43	3
1203(c)	2.43	6
1204(a)	2.43	4
1204(e)	2.43	5
1205	28.34	3
1205(a)	2.6	7
	2.43	
	2.43	13
1207(c)	2.43	
1209	2.43	9
1210	2.43	12
1210(a)	2.43	10
	2.43	11
1211	2.43	
1211(c)	2.43	7

317

TABLE OF STATUTES

NEW YORK, MCKINNEY'S LIMITED LIABILITY COMPANY LAW

Sec.	This Work Sec.	Note
1213	2.43	8
	2.43	13
1301(c)	2.75	3
1302	2.43	14
1304	2.43	16
1306	2.43	14
	2.43	15
1306(d)	2.43	16
1308–a	37.90	

NEW YORK, MCKINNEY'S LIMITED LIABILITY PARTNERSHIP LAW

Sec.	This Work Sec.	Note
Art. 8	12.55	
Art. 8A	12.55	

NEW YORK, MCKINNEY'S LOCAL FINANCE LAW

Sec.	This Work Sec.	Note
10.00	3.27	17
11.00	3.27	
20.00(a)	3.27	1
20.00(d)	3.27	2
21.00	3.27	12
21.00(b)	3.27	3
22.10(c)	3.27	3
23.00	3.27	10
24.00(a)(1)	3.27	14
24.00(g)	3.27	16
25.00(b)	3.27	15
25.00(d)	3.27	16
28.00	3.27	11
29.00	3.27	13
33.00(a)	3.10	6
	3.27	23
36.00(a)	3.16	7
51.00(8)	3.27	5
85.90	37.44	13
123.00	3.27	21
124.10	3.27	20
162.00	3.27	8
167.00	37.44	3
	37.44	4

NEW YORK, MCKINNEY'S MENTAL HYGIENE LAW

Sec.	This Work Sec.	Note
1.03	22.16	3
	22.17	6
	22.21	6
	22.25	9

NEW YORK, MCKINNEY'S MENTAL HYGIENE LAW

Sec.	This Work Sec.	Note
1.03 (Cont'd)	22.28	13
	22.64	14
	22.66	11
Art. 9	17.26	
	22.53	5
	22.53	11
9.35	37.80	18
Art.15	22.53	11
19.03	22.16	4
	22.17	7
	22.21	7
	22.25	10
	22.28	14
	22.64	15
	22.66	12
Art. 21	22.53	12
47.01	37.5	3
	37.9	
	37.9	2
	37.9	3
Art. 77	12.55	
	22.1	
	22.6	8
	22.27	
Art. 77 (former)	22.1	
	22.1	1
	22.4	
	22.6	1
	22.7	
	22.7	6
	22.8	
	22.8	4
	22.10	1
	22.12	
	22.13	
	22.13	8
	22.15	1
	22.15	4
	22.21	
	22.28	
	22.59	
	22.61	
	22.64	
	22.65	
	22.66	
	22.69	
	22.71	
Art. 77 (repealed)	22.10	
77.01 et seq. (former)	22.4	11
	22.4	12
77.04 (former)	22.4	22
	22.5	13
77.07(d) (former)	22.39	2
77.10	22.6	8
77.19 (former)	22.4	17
	22.4	18
	22.4	23
	22.5	6

TABLE OF STATUTES

NEW YORK, MCKINNEY'S MENTAL HYGIENE LAW

Sec.	This Work Sec.	Note
77.19 (former) (Cont'd)	22.5	7
	22.5	8
	22.6	6
	22.7	3
	22.53	7
77.25(a) (former)	22.4	14
77.29 (former)	22.5	9
	22.5	10
Art. 78	12.55	
	22.1	
	22.4	
	22.5	
	22.6	8
	22.8	
	22.12	
Art. 78 (former)	22.1	1
	22.7	
	22.7	6
	22.8	4
	22.10	1
	22.13	
	22.15	1
	22.21	
	22.28	
	22.53	7
	22.59	
	22.61	
	22.64	
	22.65	
	22.66	
Art. 78 (repealed)	22.10	
78.01 (former)	22.5	1
78.01 et seq.	22.4	4
78.02 (former)	22.4	22
	22.5	12
78.15 (former)	22.5	2
	22.5	3
78.15(a) (former)	22.5	3
78.23 (former)	22.5	5
Art. 81	22.1	
	22.2	
	22.3	
	22.4	2
	22.7	8
	22.8	
	22.8	4
	22.9	
	22.10	
	22.11	
	22.12	
	22.13	3
	22.16	
	22.17	
	22.18	
	22.20	4
	22.26	
	22.27	
	22.27	1

NEW YORK, MCKINNEY'S MENTAL HYGIENE LAW

Sec.	This Work Sec.	Note
Art. 81 (Cont'd)	22.28	
	22.28	22
	22.30	
	22.31	
	22.31	10
	22.32	
	22.33	
	22.38	
	22.38	17
	22.39	
	22.40	
	22.40	3
	22.41	
	22.45	
	22.46	5
	22.47	
	22.47	4
	22.47	12
	22.49	
	22.53	5
	22.53	13
	22.54	
	22.54	2
	22.54	5
	22.55	
	22.56	
	22.57	
	22.58	
	22.59	
	22.61	1
	22.63	
	22.64	
	22.65	
	22.66	
	22.68	
	22.69	
	22.70	
	22.70	5
	22.70	6
	22.72	
	22.73	
	22.75	
	22.79	
	22.80	
	22.88	
	22.92	
	22.97	
	22.98	
	22.99	
	23.76	
	23.109	1
Art. 81 (former)	22.6	2
81.01	22.8	
81.01 (former)	22.8	4
81.02	22.8	6
	22.11	
	22.11	1
	22.12	5

TABLE OF STATUTES

NEW YORK, MCKINNEY'S MENTAL HYGIENE LAW			NEW YORK, MCKINNEY'S MENTAL HYGIENE LAW		
Sec.	This Work Sec.	Note	Sec.	This Work Sec.	Note
81.02 (Cont'd)	22.14		81.07(d)(2)(i) (Cont'd)	22.20	6
81.02(a)	22.11	2	81.07(d)(2)(ii)	22.20	9
	22.12	2	81.07(d)(2)(iii)	22.20	11
81.02(b)	22.11	3	81.07(e)	22.20	12
	22.12		81.08	22.19	1
	22.13	2		22.24	1
81.02(c)	22.11	4		22.90	
	22.14		81.08(a)	22.23	
81.02(d)	22.11	4	81.09	22.91	
	22.14	1		22.99	
81.03	22.9		81.09(a)	22.25	2
81.03(e)	22.12	4	81.09(b)(1)	22.25	6
81.04	22.15			22.25	8
	22.15	1	81.09(b)(2)	22.25	13
81.04(b)	22.15		81.09(b)(3)	22.25	
	22.15	3	81.09(c)	22.26	
	22.15	6	81.09(d)	22.2	10
	22.16			22.26	
81.05	22.15	6		22.26	16
81.05(a)	22.16	2	81.09(e)	22.26	
	22.16	7		22.26	19
	22.16	8	81.09(f)	22.27	
	22.16	9		22.27	2
81.05(b)	22.16	12	81.10	22.25	
	22.16	13		22.26	
81.06(a)	22.17	2		22.28	
81.06(a)(6)	22.17	5		22.28	1
81.07	22.19			22.28	3
	22.21	4		22.28	6
	22.22		81.10(a)	22.28	4
	22.22	2	81.10(b)	22.28	5
	22.24		81.10(c)	22.28	
	22.89		81.10(d)	22.28	12
81.07(a)	22.19	3	81.10(e)	22.28	
	22.20	2	81.10(f)	22.28	
	22.20	3		22.28	17
	22.22	5		22.28	18
	22.31			22.28	20
81.07(b)	22.19	3	81.10(g)	22.28	22
	22.22		81.11	22.32	
81.07(c)	22.19	2		22.73	
	22.22			22.89	
	22.24	2	81.11(a)	22.31	1
	22.24	3	81.11(b)	22.31	3
	22.89		81.11(c)	22.30	3
	22.98	2		22.32	
81.07(d)	22.19	4	81.11(d)	22.32	14
	22.22		81.11(e)	22.30	4
	22.24	4		22.32	16
81.07(d)(1)	22.20			22.44	2
	22.21		81.11(f)	22.31	5
	22.21	2	81.12(a)	22.30	5
	22.50			22.30	6
	22.58			22.33	1
	22.63			22.44	3
81.07(d)(1)(i)	22.79	2		22.44	4
81.07(d)(2)	22.20		81.12(b)	22.30	7
81.07(d)(2)(i)	22.20	5		22.33	

TABLE OF STATUTES

NEW YORK, MCKINNEY'S MENTAL HYGIENE LAW

Sec.	This Work Sec.	Note
81.12(b) (Cont'd)	22.33	5
	22.33	8
	22.44	5
81.13	22.30	2
	22.31	6
	22.31	8
	22.31	10
81.14	22.31	12
81.14(a)	22.31	11
81.14(b)	22.31	14
81.14(c)	22.31	
81.14(d)	22.31	15
81.15	22.1	4
	22.3	
	22.30	8
	22.34	
	22.44	6
	22.53	
	22.92	
81.15(a)	22.35	1
81.15(b)	22.36	1
81.15(c)	22.37	1
81.16	22.8	7
	22.30	9
	22.38	
	22.44	7
	22.45	3
	22.55	3
	22.92	
81.16(a)	22.38	4
81.16(b)	22.38	
	22.38	5
	22.38	6
81.16(c)	22.30	10
	22.44	8
81.16(c)(1)	22.38	12
81.16(c)(2)	22.38	16
81.16(c)(3)	22.38	
	22.38	17
	22.64	
	22.66	
	22.67	
	22.69	
	22.70	
	22.70	6
81.16(d)	22.38	18
81.16(e)	22.38	21
	22.101	
81.16(f)	22.30	11
	22.39	
	22.39	1
	22.39	2
	22.44	9
81.17	22.26	
	22.30	12
	22.40	1
	22.41	
	22.44	10

NEW YORK, MCKINNEY'S MENTAL HYGIENE LAW

Sec.	This Work Sec.	Note
81.18	22.15	
	22.40	3
81.19	22.40	
81.19(a)	22.30	13
	22.44	11
81.19(a)(1)	22.40	
81.19(a)(2)	22.40	
	22.40	8
81.19(a)(3)	22.40	9
81.19(b)	22.41	3
81.19(c)	22.26	
	22.41	4
81.19(d)	22.30	14
	22.41	
	22.44	12
81.19(e)	22.41	14
81.19(f)	22.41	15
81.20	22.3	9
	22.3	10
	22.46	
81.20(a)(1)	22.46	7
81.20(a)(2)	22.46	2
81.20(a)(3)	22.46	3
81.20(a)(4)	22.46	8
	22.62	1
81.20(a)(5)	22.46	5
	22.101	14
81.20(a)(6)	22.46	9
81.20(a)(6)(vi)	22.59	
81.20(a)(7)	22.46	12
81.21	22.3	4
	22.3	11
	22.23	2
	22.37	
	22.47	
	22.48	
	22.92	
	22.99	3
81.21(a)	22.1	6
	22.47	
	22.47	6
	22.47	7
	22.54	2
81.21(a)(6)	22.48	13
	22.49	1
81.21(b)	22.49	
81.21(c)	22.50	2
81.21(d)	22.51	
81.21(e)	22.52	1
81.21(f)	22.49	6
81.22	22.3	3
	22.3	12
	22.23	1
	22.53	
	22.53	3
	22.92	
	22.99	2
	23.109	1

TABLE OF STATUTES

NEW YORK, MCKINNEY'S MENTAL HYGIENE LAW

Sec.	This Work Sec.	Note
81.22(a)	22.53	
81.22(a)(9)	22.53	
81.22(b)	22.53	
81.22(b)(2)	22.53	5
	22.54	4
81.23	22.3	
	22.3	5
	22.23	
	22.28	
	22.43	
	22.90	
	22.99	
81.23(a)	22.1	7
	22.56	1
	22.57	
	22.60	1
	22.60	2
81.23(a)(1)	22.57	4
81.23(a)(2)	22.57	5
81.23(a)(3)	22.57	6
81.23(a)(4)	22.57	7
81.23(b)	22.1	8
	22.56	2
	22.58	
	22.60	4
81.23(b)(1)	22.58	1
	22.58	2
81.23(b)(2)	22.58	3
	22.58	4
81.23(b)(3)	22.58	5
81.23(b)(4)	22.58	6
81.23(b)(5)	22.58	7
81.24	22.1	9
	22.56	
	22.59	1
	22.60	5
81.25	22.30	15
	22.44	13
	22.57	
81.25(a)	22.42	1
	22.43	2
81.25(b)	22.42	3
81.25(c)	22.42	8
81.25(d)	22.42	7
81.26	22.30	16
	22.43	
	22.65	4
	22.65	9
	22.101	
81.27	22.30	17
	22.31	9
	22.43	5
81.28	22.68	1
81.28(a)	22.61	1
	22.61	3
81.28(b)	22.61	7
81.29	22.54	
81.29(a)	22.1	5

NEW YORK, MCKINNEY'S MENTAL HYGIENE LAW

Sec.	This Work Sec.	Note
81.29(a) (Cont'd)	22.45	6
	22.54	1
	22.55	6
81.29(b)	22.45	7
	22.54	2
	22.55	7
81.29(c)	22.45	8
	22.54	3
	22.55	8
81.29(d)	22.54	5
81.29(e)	22.54	7
81.30	22.1	10
	22.3	13
	22.3	14
	22.46	
	22.62	
	22.68	2
	22.93	
	22.104	
81.30(a)	22.63	3
	22.63	6
	22.68	4
81.30(b)	22.63	8
	22.68	4
81.30(c)	22.63	13
	22.63	14
81.30(d)	22.63	17
81.31	22.1	11
	22.3	15
	22.46	
	22.62	
	22.68	3
	22.94	
	22.105	
81.31(a)	22.64	1
	22.68	5
	22.101	
81.31(b)	22.64	6
	22.68	6
	22.101	
81.31(b)(10)	22.101	
81.31(c)	22.64	13
	22.64	18
	22.68	7
81.31(d)	22.64	12
	22.64	19
81.31(e)	22.64	
	22.64	23
81.32	22.65	3
	22.78	
	37.90	
81.32(a)	22.68	9
81.32(a)(1)	22.65	1
81.32(a)(2)	22.65	2
81.32(b)	22.65	
	22.68	8
81.32(c)	22.68	10
	22.69	2

322

TABLE OF STATUTES

NEW YORK, MCKINNEY'S MENTAL HYGIENE LAW

Sec.	This Work Sec.	Note
81.32(c)(1)	22.65	5
81.32(c)(2)	22.65	8
81.32(d)	22.68	11
81.32(d)(1)	22.65	10
81.32(d)(2)	22.65	13
81.32(e)	22.65	14
81.32(f)	22.65	15
81.33	22.66	1
81.33(a)	22.66	3
	22.68	12
81.33(b)	22.66	5
	22.68	13
81.33(c)	22.66	7
81.33(d)	22.66	9
81.33(e)	22.66	10
81.33(f)	22.66	15
81.34	22.68	14
	22.95	
81.34(a)	22.67	3
81.34(b)	22.67	1
81.34(c)	22.67	4
81.34(d)	22.67	6
81.35	22.69	
	22.69	8
	22.69	9
	22.74	1
	22.74	3
	22.70	
81.36	22.74	4
81.36(a)	22.70	3
81.36(b)	22.70	5
81.36(c)	22.70	7
81.36(d)	22.70	9
81.36(e)	22.70	11
81.37	22.71	
	22.74	5
81.37(a)	22.71	2
81.37(b)	22.71	3
81.38(a)	22.72	1
	22.72	5
	22.74	6
81.38(b)	22.73	
	22.74	2
	22.74	7
	22.74	8
81.39	22.1	12
	22.75	
	22.75	2
	22.76	7
	22.80	1
	22.104	
81.39(a)	22.76	1
81.39(b)	22.76	6
81.39(c)	22.75	2
	22.76	7
	22.80	4
81.40	22.1	13
	22.75	

NEW YORK, MCKINNEY'S MENTAL HYGIENE LAW

Sec.	This Work Sec.	Note
81.40 (Cont'd)	22.77	
	22.80	2
81.40(a)	22.77	1
81.40(b)	22.77	5
81.40(c)	22.75	2
	22.77	6
	22.80	4
81.41	22.1	14
	22.75	
	22.80	3
81.41(a)	22.78	1
81.41(b)	22.78	2
81.41(c)	22.75	2
	22.78	5
	22.80	4
81.42	22.79	
81.42(a)	22.79	3
	22.80	5
81.42(b)	22.79	4
	22.80	6
81.44	22.87	1
	22.96	
81.44(a)	22.81	2
	22.82	1
	22.83	1
	22.83	2
81.44(b)	22.84	1
	22.85	1
	22.86	2
	22.87	2
141.34	16.24	6
	16.128	12

NEW YORK, MCKINNEY'S MILITARY LAW

Sec.	This Work Sec.	Note
300 et seq.	13.14	8

NEW YORK, MCKINNEY'S MULTIPLE DWELLING LAW

Sec.	This Work Sec.	Note
4(7)	13.17	14
	13.43	15
301	13.28	
302	13.28	
	13.28	6
	13.28	13
302(1)(b)	13.28	
302–a	13.28	
302–a(1)	13.28	1
302–a(2)	13.28	1
302–a(3)(c)	13.28	2
325	13.17	14
	13.28	

TABLE OF STATUTES

NEW YORK, MCKINNEY'S MULTIPLE DWELLING LAW

Sec.	This Work Sec.	Note
325 (Cont'd)	13.43	15
325(2)	13.28	3
358	37.90	

NEW YORK, MCKINNEY'S MUNICIPAL HOME RULE LAW

Sec.	This Work Sec.	Note
10	16.7	2
	16.24	10
	16.125	3
10(1)(i)	3.16	1
10(1)(ii)(a)(1)	3.17	3
	3.18	3
	3.20	4
10(1)(ii)(d)	16.7	2
10(1)(ii)(d)(3)	3.14	9
	16.24	10
10(1)(ii)(e)	16.7	2
10(1)(ii)(e)(3)	3.14	9
	16.24	10
10(2)	3.14	12
	16.7	2
11	3.14	11
20	3.11	4
	16.29	6
	16.113	4
20(3)	3.14	14
20(4)	3.14	15
	3.14	16
	3.14	17
20(5)	3.14	18
	16.29	9
22	16.24	10
23(1)	3.15	5
24(2)	3.15	4
27(3)	3.10	12
51	3.14	13

NEW YORK, MCKINNEY'S NAVIGATION LAW

Sec.	This Work Sec.	Note
172(8)	15.10	8
172(15)	15.27	3
173	15.10	8
174	15.27	22
174(4)	15.27	23
175	15.10	9
	15.27	25
176	15.10	9
	15.27	26
181	15.33	4
	15.44	
181(1)	15.27	26

NEW YORK, MCKINNEY'S NAVIGATION LAW

Sec.	This Work Sec.	Note
181(1) (Cont'd)	15.44	
181(5)	15.27	27
	15.44	

NEW YORK, MCKINNEY'S NOT-FOR-PROFIT CORPORATION LAW

Sec.	This Work Sec.	Note
114	37.44	14
201	12.55	23
	12.55	24
210	12.55	22
504	12.55	22
509	12.55	22
510	12.55	22
	12.55	23
511	12.55	22
1412	1.13	6

NEW YORK, MCKINNEY'S PARTNERSHIP LAW

Sec.	This Work Sec.	Note
Art. 8	2.78	
	2.86	
Art. 8A	2.2	
	2.45	
	2.78	
2	2.73	2
	2.75	3
3(1)	2.60	2
4(3)	2.45	9
10	2.46	3
10(1)	2.46	2
	2.79	6
11	2.46	3
	2.46	11
11(2)	2.46	3
12(1)	2.51	3
12(2)	2.51	4
20	2.9	
	2.45	6
	2.45	8
20(1)	2.51	17
	2.55	2
	2.60	1
	2.60	3
20(2)	2.60	4
20(3)	2.60	4
	2.60	5
	2.60	6
20(4)	2.60	2
21(1)	2.60	3
23	2.60	7
	2.60	8

TABLE OF STATUTES

NEW YORK, MCKINNEY'S PARTNERSHIP LAW

Sec.	This Work Sec.	Note
24	2.45	4
	2.53	1
	2.53	2
25	2.45	4
	2.53	1
	2.53	4
26	2.2	7
	2.2	10
	2.51	14
	2.72	1
	2.74	
26(a)	2.6	3
	2.45	5
26(a)(1)	2.45	4
	2.53	1
	2.53	4
26(a)(2)	2.45	3
	2.53	5
26(b)	2.6	5
	2.72	3
	2.74	2
	2.74	3
	2.74	4
26(c)	2.2	11
	2.6	4
	2.72	3
	2.74	2
	2.74	4
26(d)	2.74	
	2.74	5
27	2.47	8
27(1)	2.53	7
	2.53	8
	2.53	9
28	2.52	2
	2.52	3
40	2.13	4
	2.84	4
40(1)	2.50	4
	2.51	11
	2.51	14
	2.51	18
	2.51	29
	2.54	2
40(2)	2.51	20
	2.54	1
40(3)	2.51	19
40(4)	2.51	18
	2.51	29
40(5)	2.50	4
	2.51	15
	2.51	16
	2.55	1
	2.88	1
	2.89	1
	2.89	2
	2.89	6
40(6)	2.54	1

NEW YORK, MCKINNEY'S PARTNERSHIP LAW

Sec.	This Work Sec.	Note
40(7)	2.8	
	2.52	1
	2.63	1
	2.63	2
	2.69	3
40(8)	2.56	1
	2.56	2
	2.69	3
	2.75	4
41	2.50	5
	2.50	6
42	2.57	1
	2.59	
	2.59	1
	2.59	8
43	2.45	9
	2.59	
	2.59	1
	2.92	1
43(1)	2.57	2
	2.59	5
44	2.57	3
	2.59	
	2.59	1
45(1)	2.66	5
45(2)	2.66	6
50	2.51	2
51(1)	2.51	5
51(2)	2.51	6
51(2)(b)	2.51	7
51(2)(c)	2.51	8
51(2)(d)	2.51	9
52	2.51	10
53	2.46	12
	2.51	10
53(1)	2.61	1
	2.61	2
	2.62	1
53(2)	2.62	2
54	2.51	13
54(1)	2.51	13
60	2.7	
	2.64	1
	2.65	
61	2.51	28
	2.64	3
62	2.7	
	2.51	27
	2.64	2
	2.65	3
62(1)(b)	2.51	25
62(1)(d)	2.51	24
62(2)	2.51	25
62(4)	2.51	23
62(5)	2.51	22
63	2.37	3
	2.64	2
63(1)(a)	2.65	6

325

TABLE OF STATUTES

NEW YORK, MCKINNEY'S PARTNERSHIP LAW		
Sec.	This Work Sec.	Note
63(1)(b)—(f)	2.65	7
63(1)(e)	2.37	6
	2.98	4
	2.51	15
63(2)	2.51	15
	2.65	8
66(1)	2.65	9
66(1)(b)	2.65	9
66(3)(b)	2.65	10
66(3)(c)	2.65	10
67(1)	2.65	11
	2.51	29
69(2)	2.65	4
	2.66	3
69(2)(a)	2.51	26
	2.51	29
69(2)(b)	2.64	3
69(2)(c)	2.51	26
69(2)(c)(II)	2.66	7
	2.66	8
71	2.67	
71(d)	2.67	3
72	2.64	3
	2.66	4
72(1)	2.65	5
	2.66	1
72(2)	2.66	1
72(3)	2.66	1
72(5)	2.66	3
72(6)	2.66	2
73	2.66	9
74	2.67	1
75	2.67	2
80	2.46	14
82	2.46	15
	2.46	16
121–80(c)	12.55	18
121–101(b)	2.84	7
121–101(f)	2.84	1
121–101(g)	2.84	1
121–101(h)	2.2	8
	2.79	6
121–101(L)	2.79	2
121–101(m)	2.84	3
121–101(n)	2.84	1
121–102(a)	2.79	8
121–102(a)(2)	2.79	7
121–102(b)	2.79	11
121–103(a)	2.79	10
121–106(a)	2.83	1
	2.83	2
121–106(b)	2.83	3
121–107	2.79	5
121–108	2.84	15
121–110(a)	2.79	2
	2.82	9
121–110(b)	2.79	2
	2.82	1
	2.82	10

NEW YORK, MCKINNEY'S PARTNERSHIP LAW		
Sec.	This Work Sec.	Note
121–110(c)	2.82	4
	2.82	11
	2.82	12
121–201	2.78	3
	2.114	
121–201(a)	2.79	1
	2.80	2
121–201(b)	2.79	3
121–201(c)	2.81	2
	2.81	3
	2.81	4
	2.81	5
	2.81	6
	2.81	7
121–202(a)	2.78	4
121–202(b)	2.80	5
121–202(c)	2.80	
	2.80	9
121–202(d)	2.80	6
121–203	2.100	
121–203(b)	2.100	7
121–203(c)	2.100	7
121–204	2.80	
121–204(a)(1)	2.80	1
121–204(a)(2)	2.80	8
121–205(a)	2.80	13
121–205(b)	2.82	13
121–207	2.86	2
121–207(a)(1)	2.80	7
	2.80	10
	2.80	11
121–207(a)(2)	2.80	7
	2.80	12
121–301(a)	2.85	1
121–301(b)(1)	2.85	2
	2.90	1
121–302	2.82	4
121–302(a)	2.90	2
121–302(b)	2.90	3
121–303	2.13	3
	2.78	7
121–303(a)	2.2	8
	2.2	9
	2.12	4
	2.77	1
	2.78	5
	2.78	6
	2.82	10
	2.86	3
	2.86	4
121–303(b)	2.2	9
	2.86	
	2.86	5
	2.86	6
	2.86	7
	2.88	
121–303(b)(1)	2.91	1
121–303(c)	2.2	9

326

TABLE OF STATUTES

NEW YORK, MCKINNEY'S PARTNERSHIP LAW			NEW YORK, MCKINNEY'S PARTNERSHIP LAW		
		This Work			This Work
Sec.	Sec.	Note	Sec.	Sec.	Note
121–303(c) (Cont'd)	2.86	5	121–603 (Cont'd)	2.84	16
	2.86	6		2.84	17
	2.86	7		2.84	18
	2.86	8		2.84	24
121–303(d)	2.2	9		2.90	1
	2.79	9	121–604	2.84	22
	2.86	10		2.84	23
121–303(e)	2.2	9	121–607	2.84	
	2.86	9		2.96	
121–304	2.86	14	121–607(a)	2.84	14
121–304(a)	2.86	15		2.86	
121–304(b)	2.82	10	121–607(b)	2.12	4
	2.86	16		2.86	13
121–401	2.85	3	121–607(c)	2.86	13
	2.90	1	121–701	2.84	2
	2.96	1	121–702	2.8	
121–402	2.84	21		2.82	7
121–403	2.84	4		2.84	20
	2.93	1		2.94	1
121–403(a)	2.45	7	121–702(a)(1)	2.95	1
	2.82	6	121–702(a)(2)	2.95	3
	2.84	4		2.95	4
	2.88	1	121–702(a)(3)	2.95	2
	2.89	1	121–702(a)(4)	2.34	4
	2.89	2		2.95	6
121–403(b)	2.82	6		2.95	7
	2.84	5	121–702(b)	2.84	6
	2.86	1	121–702(c)	2.95	5
	2.91	2	121–703	2.21	24
121–403(c)	2.82	6		2.21	25
	2.84	4		2.21	26
	2.91	3		2.84	26
	2.92	1		2.84	27
121–404	2.84	8	121–704	2.8	
121–405	2.82	4		2.94	1
	2.89	3	121–704(a)	2.90	1
121–405(a)	2.89	4		2.96	2
	2.89	5	121–704(b)	2.96	3
	2.89	7		2.96	4
121–405(b)	2.89	6	121–705	2.94	1
121–501	2.84	7	121–705(a)	2.96	6
121–502	2.12	4	121–705(b)	2.96	4
121–502(a)	2.84	9		2.96	5
121–502(b)	2.84	10	121–706	2.21	27
	2.86	11		2.21	28
	2.86	12	121–801	2.80	
	2.90	1		2.97	1
121–502(c)	2.84	11		2.98	2
121–503	2.82	5	121–801(d)	2.99	1
	2.84	12		2.99	2
	2.84	13	121–802	2.98	4
121–504	2.82	5	121–803(a)	2.100	1
	2.84	12	121–803(b)	2.100	2
	2.84	13	121–804(a)	2.100	3
121–602	2.84	19	121–804(b)	2.100	4
	2.84	24	121–804(c)	2.100	5
121–603	2.21	16	121–901	2.105	6
	2.21	17	121–902	2.105	5

TABLE OF STATUTES

NEW YORK, MCKINNEY'S PARTNERSHIP LAW

Sec.	This Work Sec.	Note
121–902(a)	2.79	12
121–904	2.105	5
121–907	2.79	13
121–1001	2.84	28
	2.84	29
121–1002	2.84	29
121–1003	2.84	29
121–1004	2.84	29
121–1101	2.40	1
	2.101	1
121–1102	2.82	8
121–1102(a)	2.102	1
	2.102	2
	2.102	3
121–1102(b)	2.103	1
121–1102(c)	2.103	2
121–1102(d)	2.103	3
121–1103	2.102	4
121–1104	2.102	6
121–1105	2.103	3
121–1106	2.101	1
121–1201	2.78	1
	2.78	2
121–1202	2.78	1
	2.78	2
121–1300(f)	2.81	5
121–1500	2.7	
	2.72	1
121–1500(a)	2.73	2
	2.75	2
	2.75	5
	2.75	9
	2.75	10
	2.75	11
	2.113	
121–1500(a)(1)	2.75	4
121–1500(b)	2.75	7
121–1500(c)	2.75	8
121–1500(d)	2.73	1
	2.74	1
	2.75	8
	2.75	12
	2.75	14
121–1500(e)	2.75	8
121–1500(f)	2.75	17
	2.75	18
121–1500(g)	2.75	15
	2.75	16
121–1500(j)	2.75	
121–1500(m)	2.73	4
	2.75	19
121–1500(p)	2.75	20
121–1500(q)	2.75	1
121–1501	2.75	6
121–5000(d)	2.72	6
Art. 280	1.9	1
	2.72	5

NEW YORK, MCKINNEY'S PENAL LAW

Sec.	This Work Sec.	Note
Tit. H	20.2	6
Tit. O	20.2	6
10.00(1)	33.7	2
10.00(2)	33.7	8
	33.75	
10.00(3)	33.7	8
10.00(6)	33.7	5
	12.55	20
21	12.55	20
	18.97	1
	12.55	19
26(a)(1)	28.25	2
70.02(1)(a)	38.10	68
70.08(2)(3)(c)	38.10	147
98	12.55	17
111	24.86	2
120.15(1)	23.113	1
120.30	23.113	1
125.15(3)	23.113	1
130.00(2)	21.26	
130.20(3)	21.26	
130.35	20.34	
Art. 175	4.30	1
175.30	4.30	1
175.35	4.30	1
185.05(2)	7.25	11
190.40	11.37	11
190.42	11.37	11
190.50	7.62	
215.50	38.8	80
215.51	38.8	80
215.60	38.8	80
215.65	38.8	80
215.66	38.8	80
240.26	18.55	3
240.30(2)	18.27	
240.30(3)	18.55	
	18.55	5
240.31	18.55	
	18.55	6
240.35(1)	18.27	7
245.01	18.83	1
250.05	17.55	8
	17.55	8
450.10	38.8	
Art. 460	38.10	
	38.10	172
460.00	38.10	172
460.30	38.8	
	38.10	
	38.10	174
460.30(2)(b)	38.10	177
460.30(2)(c)	38.10	178
926–a (former)	38.19	64
2188 (former)	38.10	132

NEW YORK, MCKINNEY'S PERSONAL PROPERTY LAW

Sec.	This Work Sec.	Note
Art. 9	7.1	2

TABLE OF STATUTES

NEW YORK, MCKINNEY'S PERSONAL PROPERTY LAW

Sec.	This Work Sec.	Note
Art. 9 (Cont'd)	7.3	4
	7.3	12
	7.21	7
	7.22	20
	7.26	14
Art. 9–A	7.1	3
	7.19	1
	7.26	8
301—316	7.22	2
	7.23	1
	7.24	6
301(4)	7.23	3
	7.23	4
301(5)	7.24	4
302(1)	7.23	6
302(2)(c)	7.23	8
302(7)	7.23	21
	7.23	22
	7.23	26
302(9)	7.23	10
302(13)(a)	7.23	12
	7.25	7
	7.26	
302(13)(b)	7.23	13
302(13)(c)	7.23	14
	7.24	5
	7.25	9
302(13)(d)	7.23	15
302(13)(e)	7.23	16
302(13)(f)	7.23	17
302(13)(g)	7.23	18
	7.26	3
302(13)(h)	7.23	19
305(2)—(3)	7.23	23
307(1)	7.23	24
307(2)	7.23	25
	7.23	26
307(3)	7.23	26
314	7.23	20
316	7.22	24
	7.23	7
	7.23	18
	7.23	27
	7.26	2
330 et seq.	7.22	1
331(7)	7.22	31
331(11)	7.22	12
333	7.22	6
335	7.22	17
335(1)	7.22	18
335(2)	7.22	19
336	7.20	2
	7.22	10
336(3)	7.22	11
337(1)	7.22	4
337(2)	7.22	5
337(3)	7.22	7
337(5)(a)	7.22	9

NEW YORK, MCKINNEY'S PERSONAL PROPERTY LAW

Sec.	This Work Sec.	Note
337(5)(b)	7.22	12
337(5)(g)	7.22	13
337(5)(h)	7.22	14
337(5)(i)	7.22	25
	7.22	26
337(10)	7.22	22
337(14)(a)—(i)	7.22	42
	7.22	45
339	7.22	27
	7.26	8
341	7.22	15
	7.22	32
342	7.22	16
343	7.22	34
343(1)(a)	7.22	35
343(2)(a)	7.22	36
343(2)(e)—(5)	7.22	37
346(1)	7.22	38
346(2)	7.22	39
346(3)	7.22	40
346(4)	7.22	41
346(5)	7.22	41
346(5)(a)	7.22	41
346(6)	7.22	43
	7.22	45
346(6)(a)	7.22	43
346(7)	7.22	43
346(9)	7.22	45
351	7.22	46
401–422	7.23	2
401(6)	7.24	4
403(2)(d)	7.24	5
403(2)(d)	7.25	9
403(4)	7.25	7
	7.26	
	7.26	3
422	7.26	5

NEW YORK, MCKINNEY'S PRIVATE HOUSING FINANCE LAW

Sec.	This Work Sec.	Note
87	37.44	

NEW YORK, MCKINNEY'S PUBLIC AUTHORITIES LAW

Sec.	This Work Sec.	Note
1123(1)	3.35	7
	3.35	8
1209–a	12.55	3
2500 et seq.	3.35	9

TABLE OF STATUTES

NEW YORK, MCKINNEY'S PUBLIC HEALTH LAW

Sec.	This Work Sec.	Note
17	29.65	1
	34.36	1
	34.36	2
18	29.65	1
18(2)(e)	29.74	2
18(3)(d)	29.74	3
19	23.52	2
Art. 2, Tit. II–A	1.122	4
	1.125	
230–c	37.90	
1350(1)	4.62	2
2164	18.28	5
2164(9)	18.28	5
2504	22.9	
2782	17.55	16
2782(2)(b)	29.65	3
Art. 28	1.9	2
	1.21	22
2801	22.16	6
	22.17	9
	22.21	9
	22.25	12
	22.28	7
	22.28	16
	22.53	9
	22.64	17
	22.66	14
2801–d	23.98	
	23.98	1
2801–d(2)	23.98	3
	23.98	4
2801–d(3)	23.98	6
2801–d(4)	23.98	7
2801–d(5)	23.98	5
2801–d(6)	23.98	8
2801–d(10)(b)	23.98	7
2803(3)(f)	23.95	9
2803–c	23.92	1
	29.65	2
2803–c(1)(d)	23.95	1
2803–c(3)	23.94	2
2803–c(3)(b)	23.94	9
2803–c(3)(h)	23.94	13
	23.94	14
	23.94	15
2803–d	23.98	9
2805	29.13	3
2805–d	29.14	
	29.17	1
	29.17	2
	29.17	3
2805–l	29.74	5
2806	37.44	
2806(6)(e)	37.61	1
Art. 29–B	23.112	
Art. 29–C	22.12	7
	23.110	
2905	22.21	

NEW YORK, MCKINNEY'S PUBLIC HEALTH LAW

Sec.	This Work Sec.	Note
2960—2979	23.112	1
2962	23.112	2
2963	23.112	3
2964.2(a)	23.112	4
2964.2(b)	23.112	5
2964.2(c)	23.112	6
2965	22.26	7
	22.41	8
	22.53	14
	22.54	4
	22.63	11
2965.1(a)	23.112	7
2965.2	23.112	8
2965.3(a)	23.112	9
2965.3(c)	23.112	10
2965.5	23.112	12
2966	23.112	11
2969	23.112	13
2970	23.112	14
2976	23.112	11
2977	23.112	15
2977.10	23.112	16
2980—2994	23.110	1
2980(8)	24.91	1
2981	22.21	
	22.26	8
	22.41	9
	22.53	15
	22.54	4
	22.63	12
2981(2)(a)	24.91	2
2981(3)(a)	23.110	7
2981(5)	24.91	2
2981.1(a)	23.110	3
2981.1(b)	23.110	4
2981.2(a)	23.110	5
2981.3(a)—(c)	23.110	7
2981.3(d)	23.110	6
2981.5(c)	23.125	7
2981.5(d)	23.125	2
2981.6	23.125	
	23.125	6
2982(2)	24.91	3
2982.1	23.110	14
2982.2	23.110	15
2982.2(b)	24.91	4
2982.3	23.110	16
2982.4	23.110	17
2983.1	23.110	8
	23.110	9
2983.3	23.110	10
2983.5	23.110	11
2983.7	23.110	12
2984.2	23.110	18
2984.3	23.110	18
2984.4	23.110	18
2985	23.110	13
2986	23.110	19

TABLE OF STATUTES

NEW YORK, MCKINNEY'S PUBLIC HEALTH LAW

Sec.	This Work Sec.	Note
2990	23.110	20
3388	38.10	176
3608	37.44	
3610	37.44	
3620	37.44	
4008	37.44	
4100–a(4)	20.84	
4138(1)(c)	20.83	2
4410(1)	29.15	1
Art. 46	23.107	
4601 et seq.	23.107	1
4601(8)	23.107	2
	23.107	4
4601(9)	23.107	2

NEW YORK, MCKINNEY'S PUBLIC HOUSING LAW

Sec.	This Work Sec.	Note
14(4)	13.55	

NEW YORK, MCKINNEY'S PUBLIC OFFICERS LAW

Sec.	This Work Sec.	Note
Art. 6	7.8	2
	16.38	2
Art. 7	16.39	1
3(1)	3.18	2
5	3.19	6
10	3.18	1
10(2)	3.18	2
10(3)	3.18	2
11	3.18	5
36	3.20	
	3.20	2
	3.20	7
	37.90	
84 et seq.	3.29	2
	4.2	27
	4.13	3
	4.35	2
	4.38	4
	17.55	11
84—90	13.60	1
86(3)	3.29	3
	16.38	3
86(4)	3.29	5
	16.38	4
87(1)(b)	3.29	8
87(1)(b)(iii)	3.29	19
87(2)	3.29	9
87(3)	3.29	6
89	17.55	12
89(1)(a)	3.28	25

NEW YORK, MCKINNEY'S PUBLIC OFFICERS LAW

Sec.	This Work Sec.	Note
89(3)	3.29	6
	3.29	11
	3.29	12
	3.29	14
89(4)(a)	3.29	15
	3.29	16
89(4)(b)	3.29	17
89(4)(c)	3.29	18
91 et seq.	17.55	13
95—106	16.38	1
100–111	3.28	4
102(1)	3.28	7
102(2)	3.28	6
102(2)	16.39	2
102(3)	3.28	8
103(a)	3.28	5
	3.28	15
104(1)	3.28	11
104(2)	3.28	12
104(3)	3.28	13
105(1)	3.28	
	3.28	16
	3.28	17
106(1)	3.28	18
106(2)	3.28	18
106(3)	3.28	20
107(1)	3.28	23
	3.28	22
107(2)	3.28	24
108(1)	16.39	3
109	3.28	26

NEW YORK, MCKINNEY'S PUBLIC SERVICE LAW

Sec.	This Work Sec.	Note
Art. VII	14.24	
	14.127	
Art. VIII	14.24	
112	37.90	
112(1)	37.90	14
	37.90	15
120	14.126	
121	14.24	1
128	37.90	
148	37.90	
170	37.90	

NEW YORK, MCKINNEY'S RAILROAD LAW

Sec.	This Work Sec.	Note
9	37.90	
16	37.44	
32	37.90	12

TABLE OF STATUTES

NEW YORK, MCKINNEY'S RAILROAD LAW

Sec.	This Work Sec.	Note
91	37.44	
93–a	37.44	
93–b	37.44	
174—176	37.90	12
180	37.90	12
185	37.90	
202	37.90	12
223	37.90	12

NEW YORK, MCKINNEY'S RAPID TRANSIT LAW

Sec.	This Work Sec.	Note
80	37.90	12

NEW YORK, MCKINNEY'S REAL PROPERTY LAW

Sec.	This Work Sec.	Note
Art. 9	12.53	
Art. 9–B	12.34	
	12.34	2
Art. 12	12.53	
	12.53	3
122	37.61	1
231(1)	13.38	1
232–a	13.37	
	13.37	1
	13.37	2
	13.51	13
232–b	13.37	
232–c	13.50	5
233	16.124	7
234	13.2	
	13.64	2
	30.42	
235–a	13.34	
235–b	13.32	
	13.75	
235–b(2)	13.32	2
	13.64	4
235–b(3)(a)	13.32	11
235–b(3)(b)	13.32	14
235–e	13.34	1
235–f	18.45	4
251	12.41	2
254(10)	11.3	2
	11.31	
258	11.12	1
274–a	12.13	1
	12.15	2
275	12.88	
	12.89	6
280	23.104	
	23.104	3

NEW YORK, MCKINNEY'S REAL PROPERTY LAW

Sec.	This Work Sec.	Note
280(1)(a)	23.104	5
280(1)(b)	23.104	6
280(1)(c)	23.104	6
280(2)(g)	23.104	8
280(3)(a)	23.104	9
280(7)	23.104	10
280(8)	23.104	7
280–a	23.104	
	23.104	3
280–a(1)(a)	23.104	5
280–a(1)(b)	23.104	6
280–a(1)(c)	23.104	6
280–a(2)(j)	23.104	8
280–a(3)(b)	23.104	9
280–a(7)	23.104	10
280–a(8)	23.104	7
281	12.88	
	12.89	
290	11.53	
	12.45	6
290 et seq.	12.41	3
	12.41	4
290(3)	11.54	
290(4)	12.74	2
291	11.2	1
	11.9	2
	11.13	3
	11.53	
	12.53	2
	12.53	4
294	10.29	
	12.8	2
294(1)	12.6	1
294(2)	12.6	2
294(3)	12.6	3
294(4)	12.6	4
294(5)	12.6	5
	12.55	11
294(6)	12.6	7
294(8)(a)	12.6	6
317	11.2	1
326	12.8	2
333 et seq.	12.9	2
333(1–e)(ii)(8)(b)	16.28	7
	16.96	9
334	12.56	7
339—3aa	11.9	10
339–z	11.9	10
375	12.56	8
377	37.90	
381	12.53	8
396	12.53	9
400	12.53	
406	12.53	6
407	12.53	10
414	12.53	11
418	12.53	12
419	12.53	13

TABLE OF STATUTES

NEW YORK, MCKINNEY'S REAL PROPERTY LAW

Sec.	This Work Sec.	Note
423	12.53	14
426 to 429	12.53	
441–c	18.46	5
	18.50	5
441–h	18.46	5

NEW YORK, MCKINNEY'S REAL PROPERTY TAX LAW

Sec.	This Work Sec.	Note
467	23.100	
467(1)	23.100	8
467(1)(a)	23.100	1
467(1)(b)	23.100	7
467(3)(a)	23.100	7
467(3)(b)	23.100	4
467(3)(c)	23.100	2
467(3)(d)	23.100	3
467(4)	23.100	9
467(6)(a)	23.100	10
467(6)(b)	23.100	10
467(6)(c)	23.100	10
467(9)	23.100	5
467–b	23.106	1
503(1)(a)	12.9	2
503(1)(b)	12.9	2
744	37.44	

NEW YORK, MCKINNEY'S REAL PROPERTY ACTIONS & PROCEEDINGS LAW

Sec.	This Work Sec.	Note
71	37.44	12
202	11.21	
202–a	11.21	
221	11.8	
	11.54	
231	11.48	
231(2)(a)	11.48	1
	11.48	3
	11.50	
231(2)(b)	11.48	
231(3)	11.48	
	11.50	
231(4)	11.49	1
231(6)	11.50	
501—551	12.66	1
511	12.66	5
Art. 7	11.8	
	10.108	
Art. 7–A	13.72	
	13.26	1
701(1)	13.5	
701(2)	13.5	1

NEW YORK, MCKINNEY'S REAL PROPERTY ACTIONS & PROCEEDINGS LAW

Sec.	This Work Sec.	Note
711	13.35	2
711(1)	13.35	1
	13.50	
	13.50	4
711(2)	13.12	
	13.17	10
	13.26	1
711(5)	13.38	
713	13.35	
	13.35	3
	13.36	
713(5)	11.8	
	11.54	
713(11)	13.36	
721	13.35	
	13.43	3
	13.61	
721(1)	13.17	2
721(9)	13.26	1
731(1)	13.13	1
	13.13	2
	13.13	3
	13.41	1
	13.41	2
	13.41	3
731(2)	13.15	4
	13.15	7
	13.15	8
	13.15	10
	13.41	5
	13.41	6
731(3)	13.15	6
731(4)	13.15	6
732	13.15	
	13.22	
	13.22	1
	13.23	
	13.47	1
732(1)	13.15	5
732(2)	13.15	2
	13.15	5
	13.22	5
732(3)	13.7	6
	13.15	2
	13.15	3
	13.22	6
733(1)	13.15	9
	13.41	8
735	11.54	
	11.54	9
	13.6	
	13.9	
	13.23	
	13.47	
	13.48	
	13.51	13
735(1)	13.6	

333

TABLE OF STATUTES

NEW YORK, MCKINNEY'S REAL PROPERTY ACTIONS & PROCEEDINGS LAW

Sec.	This Work Sec.	Note
735(1) (Cont'd)	13.8	1
735(1)(a)	13.9	5
735(1)(b)	13.8	6
	13.9	7
735(2)	13.7	5
735(2)(a)	13.7	4
735(2)(b)	13.8	7
	13.9	8
741	13.16	2
	13.17	
	13.19	
	13.19	1
	13.45	
	13.88	
741(1)	13.17	1
	13.43	2
741(2)	13.17	4
	13.43	5
741(3)	13.17	7
	13.43	8
741(4)	13.17	9
	13.43	10
	13.43	11
741(5)	13.15	11
	13.17	17
	13.41	7
	13.43	18
	13.43	19
743	13.15	
	13.22	
	13.22	1
	13.22	2
	13.22	8
	13.41	9
	13.47	
	13.47	1
	13.47	2
	13.47	4
	13.47	5
	13.47	7
	13.56	1
745	13.22	9
	13.47	8
745(1)	13.61	
	13.61	1
	13.62	1
745(2)	13.61	
	13.61	2
745(2)(a)	13.3	
747(1)	13.67	1
749(1)	13.67	2
749(2)	13.67	4
751(1)	13.11	1
	13.68	
	13.68	1
751(4)	13.35	
753	13.35	5

NEW YORK, MCKINNEY'S REAL PROPERTY ACTIONS & PROCEEDINGS LAW

Sec.	This Work Sec.	Note
753 (Cont'd)	13.69	
753(1)	13.69	
753(3)	13.69	4
753(4)	13.35	4
	13.69	
753(5)	13.69	5
755	13.3	
	13.21	
	13.21	5
	13.24	
755(1)(a)	13.24	1
	13.24	2
755(1)(b)	13.24	1
	13.24	3
755(2)	13.24	4
755(3)	13.24	5
769et seq.	13.72	1
769(1)	13.72	3
770(1)	13.72	2
770(2)	13.72	4
778	13.26	1
853	13.35	3
	30.31	2
	30.38	8
881	12.55	1
1064	37.80	18
Art. 13	11.5	
	11.8	
	11.75	
1301	11.5	1
	11.6	
	11.6	1
	11.6	7
	11.7	
	11.27	
1301(1)	11.6	4
1301(3)	11.36	
	11.52	1
1311	11.9	1
1311(3)	11.14	1
1321	11.1	
	11.38	
	11.39	
	11.40	
1321(1)	11.42	1
1325(1)	11.31	1
1325(3)	11.31	
	11.61	
1325(3)	11.75	
1331	11.40	1
	11.9	4
1351(2)	11.7	
1351(3)	11.53	
1354	11.9	4
	11.53	
1354(1)	11.53	
1354(1)—(3)	11.53	

334

TABLE OF STATUTES

NEW YORK, MCKINNEY'S REAL PROPERTY ACTIONS & PROCEEDINGS LAW

Sec.	This Work Sec.	Note
1354(2)	11.53	
1354(3)	11.53	
1354(4)	11.53	
1355(1)	11.51	
1355(2)	11.51	
	11.53	
1361	11.53	
1361(1)	11.53	
	11.53	3
1361(2)	11.53	
	11.53	3
1361(3)	11.53	
	11.53	3
1371	10.89	
	11.5	2
	11.46	
	11.52	
	11.65	
	11.73	
	11.79	
1371(1)	11.52	
1371(2)	11.51	
	11.52	
1371(4)	11.52	
Art. 14	11.8	
	11.8	2
1401 et seq.	11.8	2
Art. 15	12.55	7
1503	11.1	14
1521	11.1	13
1521(2)(b)	11.1	13
1921	37.90	
2001	12.69	
	12.69	4

NEW YORK, MCKINNEY'S RELIGIOUS CORPORATION LAW

Sec.	This Work Sec.	Note
2–b	12.55	22
12	12.55	22

NEW YORK RENT CONTROL LAW

Sec.	This Work Sec.	Note
21	13.55	
36	13.61	

NEW YORK RENT STABILIZATION CODE

Sec.	This Work Sec.	Note
2525.1	13.12	12

NEW YORK, MCKINNEY'S RETIREMENT AND SOCIAL SECURITY LAW

Sec.	This Work Sec.	Note
110	9.125	18
410	9.125	15

NEW YORK, MCKINNEY'S SECOND CLASS CITIES LAW

Sec.	This Work Sec.	Note
3(1)	3.16	1
30	16.125	3
35	3.12	6
133	3.13	2
138–a	37.44	
244	3.30	17

NEW YORK, MCKINNEY'S SOCIAL SERVICES LAW

Sec.	This Work Sec.	Note
Art. 6, Tit. 6	20.133	
Art. 9–B	22.21	
	22.26	
Art. 9–B, Tit. 3	22.40	
2	22.16	5
	22.17	8
	22.21	8
	22.25	11
	22.28	15
	22.64	16
	22.66	13
22	23.83	1
	37.90	
22(9)(c)	37.90	7
39	20.86	1
101	23.74	3
104–b	23.82	4
	26.49	2
104–b(2)	26.49	3
104–b(3)	26.49	4
111–g	21.70	
	21.72	
111–h(12)	21.70	
111–i	21.89	
	21.90	
	21.91	
	21.92	
141(6)	23.75	4
143–b	13.61	
209(6)(a)	23.75	4
358–a	37.19	
	37.61	
358–a(11)	20.124	
363–a	23.69	2
365–a	23.86	2
366(1)(a)(1)—(4)	23.71	1
366(1)(a)(5)	23.71	2

TABLE OF STATUTES

NEW YORK, MCKINNEY'S SOCIAL SERVICES LAW

Sec.	This Work Sec.	Note
366(2)	23.71	4
	23.71	5
	23.75	2
366(2)(a)(1)	23.75	5
	23.81	6
366(2)(a)(3)	23.75	3
366(2)(a)(10)(ii)(A)	23.71	6
366(2)(b)	23.74	2
366(2)(b)(1)	23.73	4
366(2)(b)(2)(i)	23.78	5
366(2)(b)(2)(iii)	23.78	6
366(2)(b)(2)(iv)	23.78	7
366(2)(b)(2)(v)	23.78	7
366(2)(b)(3)	23.72	1
366(3)(a)	23.80	3
366(3)(b)(iii)	23.74	3
366(5)(c)(3)(i)	23.76	11
366(5)(d)(1)(i)	23.74	2
366(5)(d)(1)(v)	23.74	2
366(5)(d)(1)(vi)	23.76	14
	23.76	17
	23.78	4
366(5)(d)(1)(vii)—(x)	23.76	8
366(5)(d)(3)	23.76	1
	23.76	7
	23.76	9
	23.76	14
366(5)(d)(3)(ii)	23.76	10
366(5)(d)(3)(ii)(D)	23.78	6
	23.78	7
	23.78	8
	23.79	1
366(5)(d)(3)(iii)	23.76	13
366(5)(d)(4)	23.76	2
	23.76	3
366(5)(d)(5)	23.76	21
	23.76	22
	23.76	23
366–c	23.80	5
366–c(2)(c)	23.80	8
366–c(2)(d)	23.80	10
366–c(2)(g)	23.80	14
366–c(2)(h)	23.80	15
366–c(3)	24.62	2
366–c(3)(b)	23.80	18
366–c(5)(a)	23.80	6
	23.80	9
366–c(5)(b)	24.62	3
366–c(7)	23.80	7
366–c(7)(c)	23.80	11
	23.80	21
366–c(8)(b)	23.80	16
366–c(8)(c)	23.80	12
	23.80	13
367–f	23.66	2
367–j	23.86	4
367–k	23.86	4
367–l	23.86	4

NEW YORK, MCKINNEY'S SOCIAL SERVICES LAW

Sec.	This Work Sec.	Note
369(2)(a)(i)	23.82	1
369(2)(a)(ii)	23.75	7
	23.82	3
	23.82	6
	23.82	7
369(2)(a)(ii)(C)	23.82	8
369(2)(b)(i)(A)	23.82	10
369(2)(b)(i)(B)	23.81	4
369(2)(b)(ii)	23.81	8
369(2)(b)(iii)	23.81	10
369(2)(c)	23.82	2
369(3)	23.79	3
369(6)	23.81	5
371	20.68	2
371(10)	20.68	2
	20.86	1
371(10)(b)	20.45	4
	20.86	1
371(10)(c)	20.25	1
	20.86	1
371(12)	20.45	4
372(3)	20.90	1
	20.98	1
372(4)	20.90	1
	20.98	1
372–c	20.33	
	20.144	
373(7)	20.28	5
373–a	20.109	1
374	20.1	17
	20.45	
	20.45	2
	20.77	
374(2)	20.45	
	20.45	4
	20.46	1
	20.77	1
374(6)	20.1	9
	20.1	10
	20.1	29
	20.3	1
	20.3	2
	20.37	3
	20.40	
	20.40	1
	20.44	
	20.45	
	20.52	2
	20.85	1
	20.106	1
	20.147	
374–a	20.1	19
	20.2	3
	20.3	
	20.53	1
	20.53	3
	20.137	
	20.139	

TABLE OF STATUTES

NEW YORK, MCKINNEY'S SOCIAL SERVICES LAW

Sec.	This Work Sec.	Note
382	20.45	
	20.137	
383(3)	20.16	
383(5)(b)	20.91	3
383-b(3)(b)	20.90	5
383-c	20.1	25
	20.89	1
	20.97	
	20.97	1
383-c(2)	20.91	
383-c(3)	20.90	1
	20.96	
383-c(4)	20.91	1
383-c(4)(a)	20.91	2
383-c(4)(b)	20.92	1
383-c(4)(c)	20.92	3
383-c(4)(d)	20.94	1
383-c(4)(e)	20.95	1
383-c(4)(f)	20.96	1
383-c(5)	20.90	2
	20.90	4
383-c(5)(b)(ii)	20.91	4
383-c(5)(b)(iii)	20.91	5
383-c(5)(b)(iv)	20.91	6
383-c(5)(e)	20.90	1
383-c(6)	20.96	2
383-c(6)(a)	20.99	1
383-c(6)(b)	20.99	2
	20.100	4
383-c(6)(c)	20.100	3
383-c(7)	20.92	5
383-c(8)(b)	20.100	1
383-c(9)	20.99	3
384	20.88	1
	20.140	
	37.18	
384(b)	20.1	7
	20.1	18
	20.11	1
384(c)	20.1	6
384-a(1-a)	20.124	
384-a(2)(e)	37.19	
384-b	20.31	4
	20.33	
	20.76	
	20.87	2
	20.87	3
	20.89	2
	20.92	4
	20.144	
	37.18	
	37.19	
	37.61	
384-b(3)(d)	20.101	1
384-b(3)(g)	20.50	5
384-b(4)	20.101	1
384-b(4)(c)	20.39	3
384-b(6)(a)	20.39	

NEW YORK, MCKINNEY'S SOCIAL SERVICES LAW

Sec.	This Work Sec.	Note
384-b(6)(b)	20.39	
384-b(6-a)	20.31	4
384-b(6-b)	20.31	4
384-b(10)	20.87	4
384-c	20.94	
389	20.1	17
	20.45	1
	20.45	2
392	37.19	
	37.61	
398	37.90	
412	20.55	1
	20.133	
	20.137	
	20.138	
	20.139	
	20.148	
422(4)	20.118	4
422(8)(a)	20.118	2
422(8)(b)	20.118	2
412(12)	20.118	1
	20.132	
424-a	20.118	1
450	20.113	3
450—458	20.2	4
451	20.113	1
453	20.113	1
454	20.113	3
461-b	37.44	

NEW YORK, MCKINNEY'S STATE ADMINISTRATIVE PROCEDURE ACT

Sec.	This Work Sec.	Note
102(1)	4.2	3
	4.2	8
	4.2	9
	4.3	
	4.4	2
	4.5	
	4.24	10
	4.42	
	4.60	
102(2)	4.2	6
	4.5	7
	4.44	4
102(2)(a)(ii)	4.24	10
	4.49	3
102(2)(b)	4.50	1
	4.50	7
	4.60	
102(2)(b)(ii)	4.50	5
102(2)(b)(iv)	4.50	2
102(2)(b)(xi)	4.50	14
102(3)	4.1	2
	4.2	5

337

TABLE OF STATUTES

NEW YORK, MCKINNEY'S STATE ADMINISTRATIVE PROCEDURE ACT

Sec.	This Work Sec.	Note
102(3) (Cont'd)	4.2	13
	4.3	
	4.4	
	4.8	1
	4.10	2
	4.11	
	4.11	1
	4.42	
	4.75	8
	4.78	2
	4.78	11
	4.79	3
102(4)	4.1	5
	4.2	15
	4.11	3
	4.27	2
102(5)	4.2	16
	4.11	4
102(9)	4.45	19
	4.60	
Art. 2	4.1	
	4.45	
201—206	4.3	
	4.44	2
201–a	4.49	19
	4.55	9
202	4.45	
	4.45	11
	4.48	
202(1)	4.2	23
	4.2	24
202(1)(a)	4.46	1
	4.55	1
202(1)(a)(i)	4.45	5
	4.45	6
	4.46	5
202(1)(a)(ii)	4.45	7
	4.46	6
202(1)(c)	4.45	8
202(1)(f)	4.45	
	4.60	
202(1)(f)(v)	4.55	3
202(1)(f)(vi)	4.55	5
	4.55	6
202(1)(f)(vii)	4.55	5
	4.55	7
202(1)(f)(viii)	4.55	4
202(2)	4.45	13
202(2)(a)(ii)	4.45	14
202(3)(b)	4.45	15
202(3)(d)	4.60	
202(4–a)	4.45	16
	4.45	17
	4.45	18
	4.60	1
202(5)	4.46	7
202(5)(a)	4.48	1

NEW YORK, MCKINNEY'S STATE ADMINISTRATIVE PROCEDURE ACT

Sec.	This Work Sec.	Note
202(5)(b)	4.55	11
202(5)(c)	4.48	4
202(6)	4.2	28
	4.2	29
	4.2	30
	4.57	
	4.57	1
202(6)(a)(i)	4.57	5
202(6)(d)	4.48	4
202(6)(d)(i)	4.57	3
202(6)(e)	4.57	6
	4.57	7
202(6–a)(c)	4.45	8
	4.54	
	4.54	3
	4.54	4
202(8)	4.45	12
202–a	4.55	6
	4.60	
202–a(1)	4.49	1
202–a(2)	4.49	4
202–a(2)(b)	4.2	27
202–a(3)	4.49	2
202–a(3)(b)	4.47	3
	4.47	4
202–a(4)(a)	4.49	4
202–a(5)	4.49	4
202–a(5)(a)	4.49	4
202–a(5)(b)	4.49	4
202–a(5)(d)	4.49	4
202–a(6)(ii)	4.49	4
202–b	4.49	5
	4.55	7
	4.60	
202–b(1)	4.49	6
	4.49	7
202–b(2)	4.49	9
202–b(3)	4.49	8
202–b(4)	4.49	8
202–b(6)	4.49	10
202–b(7)	4.49	8
202–bb	4.49	11
	4.60	
202–bb(2)	4.49	16
202–bb(2)(b)	4.49	15
202–bb(2)(b)	4.55	8
202–bb(3)	4.49	17
202–bb(4)	4.49	12
	4.49	14
202–bb(7)	4.49	18
202–c	4.49	
	4.49	25
202–c(4)	4.49	21
	4.55	12
202–c(5)	4.49	22
202–c(6)	4.49	22
	4.49	23

338

TABLE OF STATUTES

NEW YORK, MCKINNEY'S STATE ADMINISTRATIVE PROCEDURE ACT

Sec.	This Work Sec.	Note
202–c(7)	4.49	23
	4.55	13
202–c(8)	4.49	23
202–c(10)	4.49	21
203	4.48	
203(1)	4.48	7
204	4.51	1
	4.51	7
	4.60	
204(1)	4.51	2
	4.51	3
204(2)(a)	4.51	4
204(2)(b)	4.51	7
204(2)(c)	4.51	6
206	4.52	1
	4.60	
206(2)	4.52	2
	4.52	3
206(3)	4.52	4
206(4)	4.52	5
	4.52	6
206(5)	4.52	7
Art. 3	4.2	
	4.2	14
	4.4	
	4.10	
	4.41	
	4.42	
	4.44	
	4.87	
301	4.12	
	4.12	8
	4.42	
301(1)	4.21	1
	4.21	2
301(2)	4.4	4
	4.12	1
	4.42	
	4.74	1
301(2)(a)	4.12	2
301(2)(b)	4.12	3
301(2)(c)	4.12	4
301(2)(d)	4.12	5
301(2)(e)	4.12	6
301—307	4.1	3
	4.2	12
	4.2	19
	4.3	
	4.4	3
	4.8	1
	4.10	3
302	4.18	
302(1)(a)	4.18	1
302(1)(b)	4.18	2
302(1)(c)	4.18	3
302(1)(d)	4.18	4
302(1)(e)	4.18	5

NEW YORK, MCKINNEY'S STATE ADMINISTRATIVE PROCEDURE ACT

Sec.	This Work Sec.	Note
302(1)(f)	4.18	6
302(1)(g)	4.18	7
302(2)	4.18	8
302(3)	4.18	9
303	4.24	2
	4.24	3
	4.42	
304(2)	4.16	
	4.16	4
	4.42	
305	4.2	20
	4.13	
	4.13	1
305(1)	4.2	22
306	4.57	7
306(1)	4.15	1
	4.16	1
	4.19	1
	4.19	4
	4.39	6
306(3)	4.4	4
	4.16	1
	4.42	2
306(4)	4.17	1
	4.17	2
	4.17	3
307	4.24	10
307(1)	4.18	10
	4.18	12
307(2)	4.2	26
	4.24	8
	4.24	9
307(3)	4.22	3
	4.42	
Art. 4, § 2	36.51	2
401	4.1	6
	4.3	
	4.13	
	4.27	2
	4.33	
	4.42	
401(1)	4.2	17
	4.11	5
	4.26	2
401(2)	4.2	18
	4.11	7
	4.26	3
	4.26	4
	4.29	1
	4.33	
	4.33	1
401(3)	4.2	18
	4.11	7
	4.26	5
	4.26	6
	4.26	7
	4.29	4

TABLE OF STATUTES

NEW YORK, MCKINNEY'S STATE ADMINISTRATIVE PROCEDURE ACT

Sec.	This Work Sec.	Note
401(3) (Cont'd)	4.29	5
	4.33	
	4.33	5
401(4)	4.2	18
	4.2	21
	4.11	7
	4.13	7
	4.26	8
	4.26	9
	4.26	10
	4.29	2
	4.29	3
	4.33	4
	4.42	1
501	4.14	
	4.14	1
	4.14	2
	4.42	

NEW YORK, MCKINNEY'S STATE FINANCE LAW

Sec.	This Work Sec.	Note
97–t	28.22	1
137	10.133	

NEW YORK, MCKINNEY'S STATUTE OF LOCAL GOVERNMENTS LAW

Art.	This Work Sec.	Note
2—11	16.24	1
10	16.7	7
10(6)	16.7	5
10(7)	16.7	6

NEW YORK, MCKINNEY'S SURROGATE'S COURT PROCEDURE ACT

Sec.	This Work Sec.	Note
102	25.31	1
103(42)	22.90	
	22.99	
205	25.12	1
206	25.12	6
209(3)	25.12	5
262	20.64	
Art. 3	25.52	
303	25.38	3
306(1)(d)	25.47	7
	25.47	9
307	25.29	
	25.38	4
307(2)(a)	25.19	7

NEW YORK, MCKINNEY'S SURROGATE'S COURT PROCEDURE ACT

Sec.	This Work Sec.	Note
307(2)(b)	25.19	9
308	25.19	14
309	25.19	10
309(2)(d)	25.19	7
402	25.9	
402(2)	25.23	1
403(1)	25.9	1
403(1)(a)(i)	25.9	1
403(1)(a)(ii)	25.9	1
403(2)	25.9	
403–a	37.90	
403–a(1)	20.36	4
405	25.23	3
	25.23	4
407	20.65	
	20.135	
	20.136	
	37.18	
407(1)(b)	37.18	13
502	25.30	
502(2)(a)	25.30	1
	25.30	2
502(2)(b)	25.30	
502(5)(b)	25.30	
707	25.8	
	25.10	
	25.14	
	25.31	
	25.32	
707(1)	24.15	2
707(1)(e)	25.13	2
707(2)	24.15	2
711	25.8	
	25.10	
	25.14	
	25.31	
	25.32	
718	25.10	
719	25.10	
806	24.15	3
901(1)	25.14	
902	25.11	
902(2)(b)	25.14	2
903	25.11	1
1001	25.5	
	25.10	
	25.32	
1001(1)(a)—(1)(e)	25.32	
1001(1)(f)(ii)	25.32	
Art. 11	37.18	
	37.18	9
1124	37.18	10
1128	37.90	
Art. 12	37.18	
	37.18	9
1218	37.18	10
1401	25.20	
	25.20	1

340

TABLE OF STATUTES

NEW YORK, MCKINNEY'S SURROGATE'S COURT PROCEDURE ACT

Sec.	This Work Sec.	Note
1401 (Cont'd)	25.20	2
	25.20	3
	25.20	4
	25.20	5
	25.21	3
1402	25.6	1
1402(2)	25.18	
1403(1)	24.66	5
	24.8	1
	25.25	
	25.25	1
	25.31	
1404(1)	25.31	2
	25.31	3
1404(4)	25.31	4
1405	24.8	1
	25.22	5
1405(1)	25.22	3
1405(4)	25.22	4
1406	25.22	
	25.59	
1407	25.21	
1407(2)	25.21	5
1407(3)	25.21	2
1409	25.19	
	25.58	
1410	25.24	
	25.24	1
	25.24	2
	25.25	
1411	25.29	
	25.29	10
1411(1)(a)	25.29	1
1411(1)(b)(i)	25.29	2
1411(1)(b)(ii)	25.29	3
	25.29	6
1411(1)(b)(iii)	25.29	4
1411(1)(c)(i)	25.29	5
1411(1)(c)(ii)	25.29	7
1411(1)(c)(iii)	25.29	7
	25.29	8
1411(2)	25.29	9
1412	25.13	1
	25.26	
1412(1)	25.26	1
	25.26	2
	25.26	3
1412(2)(a)	25.26	4
	25.26	5
	25.26	6
1412(2)(b)	25.26	7
	25.26	8
1417	25.48	1
1418	25.2	4
1420	25.50	
	25.50	2
1420(1)	25.50	4
1420(4)	25.50	3

NEW YORK, MCKINNEY'S SURROGATE'S COURT PROCEDURE ACT

Sec.	This Work Sec.	Note
Art. 16	12.55	14
	25.2	5
Art. 17	22.8	4
Art. 17–A	22.8	4
	22.73	
	22.73	1
	23.112	8
1719	22.3	
	22.64	9
	22.94	
	22.105	
1725	20.60	
	20.134	
1725(1)	20.62	2
	20.137	
1725(2)(d)	20.69	2
1725(3)(c)	20.62	4
1725(5)	20.62	5
	20.69	1
1801	25.40	
1802	23.81	12
	25.40	
1805	25.66	
1809	23.81	13
2102	25.43	
2102(1)	25.43	1
2102(5)	25.44	
	25.44	1
2102(6)	25.45	
2103	25.42	
2103(5)	25.42	1
2110	25.41	1
	25.47	1
2202	25.35	
	25.66	
2203	25.36	
2205	23.81	13
2206	25.34	
2209	25.37	
2210	25.37	
	25.38	1
	25.41	
	25.65	
2220	24.17	2
2301	25.6	2
2301(5)	25.42	2
2303(5)	37.18	8
2303(6)	37.18	8
2304(1)(a)	37.18	4
2304(1)(b)	37.18	5
2304(2)	37.18	7
2304(3)	37.18	6
2307	22.61	1
	24.15	
	25.46	
2307(1)	25.46	8
	25.47	1
2307(2)	25.46	1

341

TABLE OF STATUTES

NEW YORK, MCKINNEY'S SURROGATE'S COURT PROCEDURE ACT

Sec.	This Work Sec.	Note
2307(5)	25.46	3
	25.46	4
2307(6)	25.46	2
2307A	24.95	
	24.95	3
2309	22.61	
	22.61	1
	22.101	
2310	25.46	
2310(5)	25.46	7
2311	25.46	
2402	24.80	2
2402(10)	25.38	5
2701	37.15	4
	37.16	6
	37.18	
	37.18	1
	37.46	4
2701(1)	37.18	2
	37.30	1

NEW YORK, MCKINNEY'S TAX LAW

Sec.	This Work Sec.	Note
Art. 11	12.25	
Art. 31	6.187	
	12.25	
Art. 31–B	12.24	2
	12.25	
	12.84	
Art. 37, Pt. II	35.121	
123.21	35.118	1
170	35.40	1
170(3–a)(b)	35.91	1
170.1	35.49	1
170.3	35.89	1
	35.90	2
170.3–a(e)	35.93	1
171.15	35.118	3
171.18–a	35.118	1
180	1.21	3
	1.30	22
	1.74	2
180.1	35.21	1
	35.21	2
	35.21	3
181(1)	35.22	1
	35.22	2
181(2)	35.22	3
203	1.100	2
203–a	1.94	4
	1.100	2
208(1)	35.23	1
208(5)	35.37	1
208(6)	35.37	2
208(9)	35.27	1
208(9)(a)	35.28	

NEW YORK, MCKINNEY'S TAX LAW

Sec.	This Work Sec.	Note
208(9)(a)(2)	35.28	2
208(9)(a)(3)	35.28	3
208(9)(a)(5)	35.28	4
208(9)(a)(6)	35.28	5
208(9)(b)	35.27	
208(9)(b)(1)	35.27	2
208(9)(b)(2)	35.27	3
208(9)(b)(3)	35.27	4
	35.27	5
208(9)(b)(4)	35.27	6
208(9)(f)	35.28	6
208.3	35.38	1
208.7	35.31	2
208.8–B(a)(4)	35.33	2
208.8–B(b)	35.33	3
208.9	35.20	
	35.20	1
208.9(a)(1)	35.29	1
208.9(b)(6)	35.29	2
209	1.23	20
209(1)	35.25	1
	35.25	2
209(3)	35.23	5
209(9)(a)(1)	35.28	1
209–A	35.26	2
210	1.23	20
210(1)	35.19	1
	35.26	1
	35.30	1
210(1)(c)	35.32	1
	35.33	1
210(1)(d)(1)(D)	35.34	1
210(3)	35.19	2
210(3)(a)	35.19	3
210(3)(b)	35.19	4
	35.37	3
250 et seq.	12.25	2
253	12.88	3
	12.89	1
253(1–a)	12.88	10
	12.89	9
253(1–a)(a)	12.88	4
	12.88	5
	12.89	2
	12.89	4
	12.91	1
253(1–a)(b)	12.88	5
	12.88	6
	12.89	4
	12.89	5
253(2)(a)	12.88	8
	12.89	7
253(2)(a)	12.91	
253–a	12.89	3
253–b	12.88	
	12.89	
	12.89	8
253–b(1–a)	12.88	9
258	11.13	3

TABLE OF STATUTES

NEW YORK, MCKINNEY'S TAX LAW

Sec.	This Work Sec.	Note
258 (Cont'd)	11.22	2
270	1.30	23
	6.131	1
270(2)	6.131	2
270–e	1.30	23
272(1)	6.131	4
280–a	1.30	23
	6.131	3
290	35.24	4
420	36.5	3
428	36.44	15
440(7)	6.104	2
	6.123	2
	6.128	2
601	35.11	3
	35.11	5
602(b)	35.13	1
605.5(b)	35.14	1
606(e)	23.101	1
606(e)(1)(A)	23.101	4
606(e)(1)(G)	23.101	6
606(e)(7)(A)	23.101	2
606(e)(7)(C)	23.101	5
606(e)(7)(D)	23.101	7
606(e)(7)(G)	23.101	3
606(e)(9)	23.101	9
611	35.7	2
	35.7	8
612	35.7	1
	35.7	8
	35.8	1
612(a)(1)	35.8	2
612(a)(2)	35.8	3
612(a)(3)	35.8	4
612(a)(4)	35.8	5
612(a)(5)	35.8	6
612(c)(3)	35.8	7
	35.12	1
	35.12	2
	35.12	4
612(c)(3)(i)	35.12	3
612(c)(31)	23.68	1
	23.68	2
614	35.51	2
615	35.9	1
	35.11	2
615(c)(1)	35.7	3
616	35.7	5
	35.10	1
620	35.7	6
	35.11	4
622	35.13	2
631	35.7	9
	35.10	2
	35.17	1
631(a)(1)	35.17	3
631(a)(2)	35.17	4
631(a)(3)	35.17	5
631(b)	2.11	4

NEW YORK, MCKINNEY'S TAX LAW

Sec.	This Work Sec.	Note
631(b)(1)	35.17	6
631(b)(2)	35.17	7
631(b)(3)	35.17	8
631(b)(6)	35.17	9
638	35.7	10
638(a)	35.7	11
657	35.54	2
	35.54	3
658(c)(3)	2.74	7
659	35.67	4
	35.85	1
	35.110	4
660(a)	35.24	5
681	35.108	1
681(a)	35.110	1
681(c)	35.110	2
681(d)	35.110	3
681(e)	35.110	4
682	35.108	1
682(a)	35.109	1
683	35.56	1
683(a)	35.65	1
	35.111	1
683(c)	35.67	1
	35.111	3
683(c)(1)	35.67	2
683(c)(3)	35.67	5
683(c)(6)	35.68	1
683(d)	35.67	6
685	2.23	
	2.23	13
	35.54	4
685(a)(1)	35.71	1
	35.71	2
685(a)(2)	35.72	1
685(b)(1)	35.74	1
685(b)(2)	35.74	2
685(c)	35.76	1
685(d)(4)	35.77	1
	35.77	2
685(e)(1)	35.78	1
685(e)(2)	35.78	1
685(e)(3)	35.78	2
685(g)	2.23	13
685(n)	2.23	14
685(p)	35.75	1
687	35.56	3
687(a)	35.56	2
	35.57	1
687(c)	35.60	1
688	35.83	2
689(b)	35.112	6
689(c)	35.61	1
689(e)	35.86	4
690	35.62	1
690(c)	35.101	1
	35.101	2
	35.101	3
692	35.101	2

343

TABLE OF STATUTES

NEW YORK, MCKINNEY'S TAX LAW

Sec.	This Work Sec.	Note
692 (Cont'd)	35.101	3
692(c)	35.112	9
	35.116	1
692(f)	35.116	1
694	35.108	1
694(a)	35.112	1
	35.112	3
694(b)	35.112	5
694(h)	35.112	7
697(d)	35.59	1
697(j)	35.76	
	35.83	1
952	24.20	1
	24.21	
954	24.20	1
955(f)	24.20	3
956	24.20	1
960	24.20	2
1090	35.101	3
1090(c)	35.101	2
1092	35.101	3
1092(b)	35.113	2
1092(c)	35.112	9
	35.113	3
1092(j)(3)	35.115	1
	35.115	2
1105	6.66	1
1116(a)(1)	3.34	15
1131	2.23	13
1131(L)	2.23	15
1141	6.66	2
	6.100	1
	6.138	2
	6.154	1
	6.184	4
1141(c)	6.66	4
	6.66	5
	6.154	2
	6.154	3
	6.184	5
	6.184	6
1147(b)	6.66	5
	6.100	2
	6.154	3
	6.184	6
1201	12.85	
1201(b)(xi)	12.87	4
1230(b)	12.86	2
1304-c	2.74	8
1400-1421	11.51	
1440-1449(c) (repealed)	11.51	
1401	12.83	
1402	12.83	2
	12.83	4
1402(a)	12.83	5
	12.83	11
1402(b)	12.87	
1402(b)(2)(A)	12.87	1
	12.87	3

NEW YORK, MCKINNEY'S TAX LAW

Sec.	This Work Sec.	Note
1402(b)(2)(B)	12.87	2
1402(b)(2)(B)(i)	12.87	3
1402(b)(2)(B)(ii)	12.87	3
1402(b)(3)	12.87	3
1402(f)	12.83	6
1402-a	11.51	4
1410	12.85	4
1440	6.104	1
1440 et seq.	6.35	1
	6.123	1
	6.128	1
1440(2)	6.104	4
	6.123	4
	6.128	4
1440(7)	6.104	5
	6.123	5
	6.128	5
1447(3)(a)	6.66	6
1801—1810	35.121	1
1801(a)	35.51	1
	35.122	1
1802	35.122	3
1804(a)	35.123	1
	35.123	4
1804(b)	35.123	2
1804(c)	35.123	3
1805(a)	35.123	1
1806(a)	35.126	1
1806(b)	35.126	1
1807(a)	35.124	1
1808(b)	35.124	2
1810	35.125	1
2006(7)	35.100	1
2012	35.96	1
2016	35.62	2
	35.99	1
	35.100	2
	35.100	3
	35.100	5
	35.100	6
	37.90	
2018	35.94	4
3000	35.87	1
3006(a)	35.86	3
3006(b)	35.86	2
3006(c)	35.88	1

NEW YORK, MCKINNEY'S TOWN LAW

Sec.	This Work Sec.	Note
Art. 8	3.26	1
Art. 12	3.33	2
Art. 12-A	3.33	2
Art. 12-C	3.33	2
20	3.17	2
23	3.18	2
24	3.19	2
	3.20	5

TABLE OF STATUTES

NEW YORK, MCKINNEY'S TOWN LAW

Sec.	This Work Sec.	Note
25	3.18	5
60	3.10	2
62	3.10	3
	3.28	1
	3.28	14
63	3.10	4
	3.10	5
64	3.7	4
64(2)	3.15	4
	3.16	1
	3.16	17
64(2-a)	3.16	1
64(6)	3.24	4
65-a	3.30	13
	3.31	1
67	3.30	17
79-a	3.5	27
79-b et seq.	3.5	1
79-d	3.5	2
81(3)	3.16	6
81(4)	3.16	6
91	3.15	7
	3.15	8
	3.15	9
	3.15	10
104	3.26	2
	3.33	13
107	3.26	2
107(3)	16.24	13
108	3.26	3
109(3)	3.26	4
112	3.26	6
117	3.26	5
130	3.10	1
	3.12	5
	3.12	7
	16.125	3
130(7)	12.65	9
131	3.13	4
133	3.12	5
138	16.32	1
	16.32	2
170 et seq.	3.33	11
174	3.33	12
184	3.33	12
190	3.33	3
	3.33	9
	16.18	13
	16.18	14
209-b	3.33	3
209-e(3)	3.33	5
209-q	3.33	3
220(3)	3.16	6
220(4)	3.16	6
261	16.5	1
	16.5	8
261-a(1)(d)	16.8	4
261-b(1)(e)	16.8	4
262	16.5	5

NEW YORK, MCKINNEY'S TOWN LAW

Sec.	This Work Sec.	Note
263	16.11	1
	16.11	13
	16.17	10
264	16.29	5
	16.29	6
	16.29	6
265	16.30	1
	16.30	4
	16.109	2
	16.113	1
	16.113	2
265(1)	16.30	2
265(1)(a)—(c)	16.113	11
265-a	16.23	2
265-a(2)	16.23	3
266	16.29	1
	16.29	2
266(2)	16.29	3
	16.29	4
267	16.73	1
267(1)	16.8	4
267(1)(a)	16.73	2
267(1)(b)	16.82	1
	16.83	1
267(2)	16.37	1
	16.37	2
267(3)	16.37	3
267(5)	16.127	
267-a	16.80	6
	16.87	10
267-a(1)	16.39	4
267-a(4)	16.37	6
	16.37	7
	16.37	8
267-a(5)	16.37	9
	16.37	10
267-a(7)	16.37	11
267-a(8)	16.37	12
267-a(9)	16.43	10
267-a(11)	16.37	13
267-b	16.37	4
	16.37	5
	16.74	2
267-b(2)	16.78	3
267-b(2)(a)	16.73	3
	16.73	6
267-b(2)(b)	16.73	7
	16.73	8
	16.75	5
267-b(2)(b)(1)	16.75	1
	16.75	6
267-b(2)(b)(2)	16.76	1
267-b(2)(b)(3)	16.77	2
267-b(2)(b)(4)	16.78	1
267-b(2)(c)	16.73	13
	16.79	1
	16.89	1
267-b(3)(b)	16.83	2
	16.84	7

TABLE OF STATUTES

NEW YORK, MCKINNEY'S TOWN LAW

Sec.	This Work Sec.	Note
267–b(3)(c)	16.86	1
	16.89	1
267–b(4)	16.78	3
	16.79	4
	16.86	2
	16.89	3
267–c	16.43	5
	16.43	9
268	16.50	13
270	16.31	6
	16.31	7
271(1)	16.36	1
	16.36	3
271(3)	16.36	2
271(13)	16.36	7
	16.96	7
	16.96	8
271(14)	16.36	9
272–a	16.5	7
	16.31	6
272–a(1)(b)	16.13	2
272–a(1)(c)	16.13	2
272–a(1)(h)	16.13	2
	16.13	4
272–a(2)(a)	16.13	1
272–a(2)(b)	16.13	5
272–a(2)(c)	16.14	2
272–a(3)(b)	16.13	3
272–a(3)(h)	16.13	3
272–a(4)	16.14	1
	16.14	2
	16.14	4
272–a(5)(b)	16.14	6
	16.14	7
272–a(6)	16.14	3
272–a(6)(b)	16.14	5
272–a(7)	16.11	14
	16.14	8
272–a(10)	16.13	6
272–a(11)	16.13	4
274–a	16.36	5
	16.36	6
	16.43	6
	16.103	1
274–a(1)	16.8	4
	16.103	5
	16.103	6
274–a(2)	16.36	5
	16.104	1
274–a(2)(a)	16.103	7
	16.103	8
	16.103	9
	16.104	5
	16.105	14
	16.106	4
274–a(3)	16.87	6
274–a(4)	16.107	1
274–a(5)	16.104	6
274–a(6)(a)	16.107	6

NEW YORK, MCKINNEY'S TOWN LAW

Sec.	This Work Sec.	Note
274–a(6)(b)	16.107	7
274–a(6)(c)	16.107	8
	16.107	9
274–a(7)	16.43	10
	16.105	15
274–a(8)	16.105	2
	16.105	3
	16.105	4
	16.105	5
	16.105	6
	16.105	10
	16.105	12
	16.105	13
274–b	16.43	8
274–b(1)	16.8	4
	16.90	2
274–b(2)	16.36	5
	16.90	3
274–b(3)	16.87	6
274–b(4)	16.90	7
	16.93	1
274–b(6)	16.43	10
	16.90	9
	16.94	1
274–b(7)	16.90	9
274–b(8)	16.94	2
276	16.52	6
276(1)	16.96	1
	16.96	6
276(5)(b)	16.98	1
276(5)(c)	16.98	4
	16.98	5
276(5)(d)	16.98	6
276(5)(d)(i)	16.97	1
276(5)(d)(ii)	16.97	2
	16.98	8
276(5)(d)(iv)	16.97	4
	16.101	2
276(5)(e)	16.98	7
276(5)(e)(i)	16.97	1
276(5)(e)(ii)	16.97	2
276(5)(e)(iv)	16.97	4
276(5)(g)	16.43	10
	16.97	3
276(5)(h)	16.97	5
	16.97	6
276(6)	16.97	11
276(6)(b)	16.97	7
276(6)(d)	16.97	12
276(8)	16.97	10
276(9)	16.43	10
	16.97	8
276(10)	16.97	13
276(11)	16.97	9
277	16.96	5
277(1)	16.96	4
	16.99	2
277(2)	16.99	3
	16.99	4

346

TABLE OF STATUTES

NEW YORK, MCKINNEY'S TOWN LAW

Sec.	This Work Sec.	Note
277(4)	16.99	5
	16.100	1
	16.100	6
	16.100	2
	16.100	4
277(6)	16.87	6
277(7)	16.101	8
277(9)	16.99	7
277(10)	16.99	8
279	12.55	9
282	16.43	7

NEW YORK, MCKINNEY'S TRANSPORTATION LAW

Sec.	This Work Sec.	Note
18	14.1	3
226	37.44	

NEW YORK, MCKINNEY'S UNCONSOLIDATED LAWS

Sec.	This Work Sec.	Note
8	12.56	2
934	9.125	16
8581 et seq.	13.2	7
8585	13.39	
8585(2)(a)	23.106	2
8621 et seq.	13.2	3
	13.52	2
8632	13.74	2

NEW YORK, MCKINNEY'S UNIFORM COMMERCIAL CODE

Sec.	This Work Sec.	Note
1–103	5.5	
1–201(3)	5.4	2
1–201(11)	5.4	2
1–201(23)	5.43	2
1–201(37)	7.24	3
	7.26	7
1–203	5.15	1
	5.16	
	5.16	1
1–203, Comment	5.16	2
	5.16	4
	5.16	5
	5.16	6
1–205	5.21	
	5.21	2
1–208	7.25	6
Art. 2	5.1	

NEW YORK, MCKINNEY'S UNIFORM COMMERCIAL CODE

Sec.	This Work Sec.	Note
Art. 2 (Cont'd)	5.5	
	5.5	4
	5.17	
	5.27	
	5.33	
	5.40	
	5.50	
	5.52	
	5.54	
	5.56	
	7.1	11
	7.21	7
2–103	5.16	
2–103(b)	5.16	3
2–105(1)	5.17	1
2–105, Comment	5.17	1
2–201	5.18	
	5.19	
	5.20	
	5.20	7
	5.23	4
2–201(1)	5.17	
	5.17	2
	5.17	3
	5.17	4
	5.19	1
2–201(2)	5.19	4
2–201(3)(a)	5.18	
2–201(3)(b)	5.18	
2–201(3)(c)	5.18	2
2–201, Comment	5.17	
2–201, Comment 1	5.17	5
	5.19	2
	5.20	1
2–202	5.21	
	5.21	1
	5.21	8
2–203	5.20	1
2–204	5.17	
	5.26	10
2–204(1)	5.17	1
	5.25	
2–204(2)	5.25	1
2–204(3)	5.25	
2–204, Comment 1	5.25	3
2–205	5.22	3
2–206	5.22	
	5.23	1
	5.57	1
2–206(1)(a)	5.22	1
2–206(1)(b)	5.22	2
2–206(2)	5.22	3
2–206, Comment 1	5.23	2
2–207	5.24	
2–207(1)	5.24	1
2–207(3)	5.24	4
2–207, Comment 1	5.24	2
2–208	5.21	

347

TABLE OF STATUTES

NEW YORK, MCKINNEY'S UNIFORM COMMERCIAL CODE

Sec.	This Work Sec.	Note
2–208 (Cont'd)	5.21	7
2–208, Comment 2	5.21	6
2–301	5.35	
	5.36	1
2–302	5.14	
	5.14	1
	7.65	
2–302(1)	5.14	
	5.14	2
2–302(2)	5.14	
	5.14	4
2–302, Comment 1	5.14	3
	5.14	6
2–305	5.26	1
	5.26	12
2–305(1)	5.26	
2–305(3)	5.26	2
2–305(4)	5.26	3
2–308	5.26	13
2–308(a)	5.26	4
2–308, Comment 2	5.26	5
2–309	5.26	
2–309(1)	5.26	6
2–309(2)	5.26	7
2–309(3)	5.26	8
2–311	5.26	
	5.26	11
	5.26	14
2–311, Comment 1	5.26	9
2–312	5.27	1
	5.28	
2–312—2–315	5.57	2
2–312(2)	5.28	2
2–312(3)	5.28	3
2–312, Comment 5	5.28	2
2–313	5.27	2
	7.53	
	7.65	
2–313(1)	5.29	
	5.29	1
2–314	5.27	3
	5.30	1
	7.9	3
	7.65	
2–314(2)(c)	27.3	
2–315	5.27	4
	5.31	1
	7.9	4
	7.65	
2–316	5.31	
	5.31	4
2–316(2)	5.30	2
2–316(3)	5.31	6
2–318	7.53	
2–319(1)(a)	5.35	
2–320	5.35	8
2–327	5.33	7
2–401	5.32	

NEW YORK, MCKINNEY'S UNIFORM COMMERCIAL CODE

Sec.	This Work Sec.	Note
2–401 (Cont'd)	5.32	3
2–401, Comment	5.32	
2–402	5.54	
2–402(1)	5.54	1
	5.56	1
2–402(2)	5.56	2
	5.56	3
2–402(3)	5.56	4
2–402(3)(a)	5.54	2
2–403	5.54	
	5.55	1
2–403(1)	5.44	5
	5.55	
2–403(2)	5.55	
2–502	5.3	15
2–502(1)	5.43	2
2–503	5.35	
2–503(1)	5.35	2
2–503(2)	5.35	3
2–503(3)	5.35	3
2–503(4)	5.35	4
2–503(4)(b)	5.33	4
2–503(5)	5.35	5
2–504	5.35	
	5.35	6
	5.42	4
2–504, Comment 1	5.35	7
2–505	5.33	1
2–507(1)	5.35	1
2–508(1)	5.34	
	5.34	2
2–508(2)	5.34	
	5.34	3
2–508(3)	5.34	
2–509	5.32	
	5.32	1
	5.33	
2–509(1)(a)	5.42	5
2–509(2)	5.33	
2–509(3)	5.33	6
	12.32	2
2–509(4)	5.33	7
2–509, Comment	5.33	
2–509, Comment 3	5.33	3
2–509, Comment 4	5.33	5
2–510	5.32	
	5.33	8
	5.34	1
2–510(2)	5.34	4
2–510(3)	5.34	5
2–601	5.36	
	5.36	2
	7.9	5
	7.25	
	7.25	11
	7.26	
	7.32	6
	7.56	

348

TABLE OF STATUTES

NEW YORK, MCKINNEY'S UNIFORM COMMERCIAL CODE

Sec.	This Work Sec.	Note
2–601(a)	5.3	2
2–601(b)	5.3	1
2–601(c)	5.3	3
2–601, Comment	5.36	
2–601, Comment 1	5.36	4
2–602	5.3	4
2–602(1)	5.38	1
2–602(2)	5.38	
2–602(2)(b)	5.3	7
2–603	5.38	
	5.53	
2–603(1)	5.3	8
	5.3	9
	5.38	4
	5.38	5
	5.53	1
	5.53	2
2–603(2)	5.38	6
	5.53	3
2–603(3)	5.38	7
	5.53	4
2–604	5.3	10
	5.38	
	5.53	
2–604, Comment	5.38	8
	5.53	6
2–606(1)	5.37	1
2–606, Comment 3	5.37	4
2–607	5.3	18
2–607(1)	5.40	1
2–607(2)	5.40	
	5.50	1
2–607(3)	5.40	4
2–607(3)(a)	5.50	2
2–607(3)(b)	5.40	4
2–607(4)	5.40	5
	5.50	3
2–607(5)(a)	5.40	6
2–607(5)(b)	5.40	7
2–607, Comment 1	5.40	2
2–608	5.39	4
	5.40	3
	7.9	6
	7.25	
	7.25	11
	7.26	
	7.32	6
	7.56	
2–608(1)	5.39	1
2–608(1)(a)	5.3	5
2–608(1)(b)	5.3	6
2–608(2)	5.39	2
2–608(3)	5.39	2
2–608, Comment 1	5.39	3
2–609(1)	5.43	7
2–612	5.36	
	5.36	5
2–612(2)	5.36	6

NEW YORK, MCKINNEY'S UNIFORM COMMERCIAL CODE

Sec.	This Work Sec.	Note
2–612(3)	5.36	
	5.36	7
2–612, Comment 6	5.36	8
2–702	9.105	1
	9.105	2
2–702(1)	5.65	
2–702(2)	5.44	
	5.44	3
2–702(3)	5.44	4
	5.44	5
	9.105	6
2–703	5.3	17
	5.3	18
	5.3	19
	5.3	20
	5.41	
	5.43	1
2–703(a)	5.3	21
2–703(b)	5.3	22
2–703(d)	5.3	23
2–703(e)	5.3	25
	5.3	26
2–703(f)	5.3	27
2–704	5.41	
	5.53	
2–704(1)(a)	5.45	6
2–704(2)	5.3	24
	5.45	7
2–704, Comment	5.41	1
2–704, Comment 2	5.45	9
	5.53	7
2–705	5.3	22
2–705(1)	5.43	3
2–705(2)	5.43	5
2–705(3)(a)	5.43	4
2–706	5.3	23
	5.41	2
	5.45	
	5.52	
2–706(1)	5.45	1
2–706(2)	5.45	8
2–706(5)	5.45	2
2–706(6)	5.45	3
2–708	5.3	25
	5.41	3
	5.42	3
	5.45	4
2–708(1)	5.46	3
2–708(2)	5.41	3
	5.46	4
2–709	5.3	26
	5.42	
2–709(1)(a)	5.42	2
	5.42	6
2–709(1)(b)	5.42	7
	5.45	5
2–709(2)	5.42	8
2–709(3)	5.42	3

349

TABLE OF STATUTES

NEW YORK, MCKINNEY'S UNIFORM COMMERCIAL CODE

Sec.	This Work Sec.	Note
2-709, Comment	5.41	4
2-709, Comment 2	5.41	4
2-710	5.41	2
	5.41	3
	5.45	1
	5.46	2
2-711	5.47	
2-711(1)	5.3	11
	5.3	12
2-711(1)(a)	5.3	13
2-711(1)(b)	5.3	14
	5.49	1
2-711(2)(a)	5.3	15
2-711(2)(b)	5.3	16
2-711(3)	5.38	
	7.56	
2-712(1)	5.3	13
	5.48	1
2-712(2)	5.48	2
2-712(3)	5.48	6
2-712, Comment	5.47	1
2-712, Comment 1	5.47	1
2-712, Comment 3	5.47	1
2-713	5.3	14
	5.47	2
	5.48	
	5.49	
2-713(1)	5.47	2
	5.49	5
2-713(2)	5.49	6
2-713, Comment 5	5.49	2
2-714	5.50	
2-714(1)	5.50	4
2-714(2)	5.50	5
2-714(3)	5.50	8
2-715	5.47	1
	5.47	2
	5.49	4
	5.50	8
2-715(1)	5.48	3
2-715(2)(a)	5.48	4
2-715(2)(b)	5.48	5
2-716	5.3	16
	5.47	3
	5.51	
2-716(1)	5.51	1
2-716(2)	5.51	2
2-716(3)	5.48	7
	5.51	4
2-716, Comment	5.50	
2-716, Comment 2	5.51	3
2-717	5.50	10
2-718	5.36	9
	5.52	
2-718(1)	5.52	
2-718(2)	5.52	
	5.52	2
2-718(3)	5.52	4

NEW YORK, MCKINNEY'S UNIFORM COMMERCIAL CODE

Sec.	This Work Sec.	Note
2-718(4)	5.52	5
	5.52	6
2-718, Comment 2	5.52	3
2-719	5.36	10
	5.52	
2-719(2)	5.52	8
2-719(3)	5.52	9
2-719, Comment	5.52	7
2-719, Comment 1	5.52	7
2-723	5.46	1
	5.49	
2-723(1)	5.49	3
2-723(2)	5.49	3
	5.49	6
2-723(3)	5.49	3
	5.49	6
2-724	5.49	3
Art. 2-A	7.20	3
	7.22	
	7.22	46
3-503(2)(a)	9.118	3
5-604	5.53	5
Art. 6	6.31	
	6.65	
	6.99	
	6.99	1
	6.153	
	6.184	
6-102	6.65	1
	6.153	1
	6.184	8
6-104	6.65	2
	6.65	3
	6.153	2
	6.153	3
	6.184	9
6-105	6.65	6
6-107	6.65	4
	6.65	5
	6.153	4
	6.153	5
	6.184	11
6-111	6.65	6
	6.153	6
	6.184	13
Art. 8	1.30	21
8-102	2.21	
	2.84	
8-102(1)(a)	2.21	6
8-102(1)(b)	2.21	7
8-102(3)	1.53	3
8-105	1.30	21
8-107	1.30	21
8-204	1.21	24
	1.30	21
	1.144	14
	1.147	15
8-301(1)	6.82	3

350

TABLE OF STATUTES

NEW YORK, MCKINNEY'S UNIFORM COMMERCIAL CODE

Sec.	This Work Sec.	Note
8–301(1) (Cont'd)	6.167	2
8–405	1.30	21
Art. 9	5.44	
	5.54	
	5.56	
	7.3	9
	7.21	5
	7.21	6
	7.21	7
	7.26	
	7.26	8
9–201	7.26	3
9–203(1)	6.167	2
9–301(2)	9.115	3
9–501 et seq.	11.1	16
9–503	5.44	1
	7.25	8
	7.56	
9–503 to 9–506	7.24	
9–504	7.26	
9–504(2)	7.26	5
9–504(3)	7.22	28
	7.26	
	7.26	6
	7.54	
	7.55	
9–505(2)	7.54	
9–506	7.26	3
9–507	7.26	
	7.56	
9–507(1)	7.25	4
9–507(2)	7.26	6

NEW YORK, MCKINNEY'S UNIFORM CITY COURT ACT

Sec.	This Work Sec.	Note
102	37.101	1
Art. 2	37.91	
	37.91	3
202	37.101	2
204	13.5	3
Art. 17	37.91	3
1701	37.102	1
1702	37.104	
1703	37.103	1
	37.105	1
1704	37.113	4
1704(a)	37.105	5
1705	37.105	6
1706	37.103	2
Art. 18	7.2	1
	37.91	3
1807	37.108	1
Art. 18–A	37.91	3
1807–A(a)	37.108	2
Art. 19	37.91	3

NEW YORK, MCKINNEY'S UNIFORM CITY COURT ACT

Sec.	This Work Sec.	Note
1907	37.107	1
	37.115	1
1908(f)	37.107	1
	37.115	1
1910(a)	37.107	1
	37.115	1
1911(a)(6)	37.105	3
2012	37.91	6
Art. 21	37.91	3
2101(f)	37.105	2
2102	37.103	1
2103	37.91	5
2104(e)	37.101	
2300(b)	37.101	1

NEW YORK, MCKINNEY'S UNIFORM DISTRICT COURT ACT

Sec.	This Work Sec.	Note
Art. 2	37.91	
	37.91	3
103(e)	37.91	7
201	37.109	3
204	13.5	5
Art. 17	37.91	3
1701	37.110	1
1702	37.112	
1703	37.111	1
	37.113	1
1704	37.113	4
1705	37.113	5
1706	37.111	2
Art. 18	7.2	1
	37.91	3
1801	37.116	1
1807	37.116	2
	37.116	3
	37.125	2
Art. 18–A	37.91	3
1807–A(a)	37.116	4
	37.125	3
Art. 19	37.91	3
1911(a)(4)	37.113	3
Art. 21	37.91	3
2102	37.111	1
2103	37.91	5

NEW YORK, MCKINNEY'S UNIFORM DISTRICT, CITY AND JUSTICE ACT

Sec.	This Work Sec.	Note
1705	37.122	5
1706	37.119	3
2102(d)	37.113	2

351

TABLE OF STATUTES

NEW YORK, MCKINNEY'S UNIFORM JUSTICE COURT ACT

Sec.	This Work Sec.	Note
102	37.92	1
	39.16	2
Art. 2	37.91	
	37.91	3
202	37.92	6
204	13.5	4
Art. 17	37.91	3
1701	37.93	1
	37.93	5
1702	37.104	
1702(a)(1)	37.95	3
1702(a)(2)(iv)	37.95	4
1702(a)(2)(v)	37.95	4
1702(b)	37.95	
1702(c)	37.95	7
1702(d)	37.95	
1703	37.94	2
	37.96	2
1704	37.97	1
1704(a)	37.96	
	37.96	7
	37.97	9
1704(b)	37.96	8
	37.97	9
1704(c)	37.96	9
1705	37.96	12
1706	37.94	3
Art. 18	7.2	1
	37.91	3
1801	37.99	1
1807	37.99	2
Art. 18-A	37.91	3
Art. 19	37.91	3
1907	37.98	2
1908(f)	37.98	2
1910(a)	37.98	1
1911(a)(5)	37.96	6
Art. 21	37.91	3
2101(f)	37.92	5
	37.96	5
	37.105	2
	37.113	2
2102	37.94	2
2103	37.100	1
2300	37.92	
	37.92	3
2300(b)(1)	37.92	1
2300(b)(1)(ii)	37.92	2

NEW YORK, MCKINNEY'S VEHICLE AND TRAFFIC LAW

Sec.	This Work Sec.	Note
Art. 12-A	7.27	1
155	33.7	8
	33.33	
	33.33	1

NEW YORK, MCKINNEY'S VEHICLE AND TRAFFIC LAW

Sec.	This Work Sec.	Note
155 (Cont'd)	33.66	
	33.68	
159	33.68	
	33.68	6
319(1)	26.25	2
398	7.27	14
	7.28	1
398 et seq.	7.1	4
398-a	7.27	4
398-c	7.27	2
398-d	7.27	3
398-d(1)	7.27	5
	7.27	6
	7.27	7
398-d(2)	7.27	8
	7.28	
398-e(1)(g)	7.27	9
398-e(1)(h)	7.27	10
398-e(1)(i)	7.27	11
398-e(1)(j)	7.27	12
398-e(1)(k)	7.27	13
398-e(3)	7.27	14
398-e(3)(e)	7.27	14
401(4)	33.68	
	33.68	2
415-a(5)(a)	4.62	11
417	7.52	
	7.56	
417-a	7.14	3
425	7.26	1
1180	33.68	
1180(a)	33.68	
1180(b)	33.68	
1180(c)	33.68	
1180(d)	33.68	
1180(e)	33.68	
1180(f)	33.68	
1192(1)	33.8	
1192(2)	33.22	
1194(1)(a)	33.7	
	33.7	6
	33.7	7
1640	3.10	1
	3.13	1
1650	3.13	1
1660	3.13	1
1808	37.80	18

NEW YORK, MCKINNEY'S VILLAGE LAW

Sec.	This Work Sec.	Note
1-102(1)	3.16	1
Art. 2	3.4	
	4.44	
2-202(1)	3.4	4
2-204	3.4	5
2-212	3.4	6

TABLE OF STATUTES

NEW YORK, MCKINNEY'S VILLAGE LAW

Sec.	This Work Sec.	Note
3–300	3.18	2
3–301	3.17	2
3–302(1)	3.28	3
3–302(2)	3.28	2
3–302(3)	3.19	2
3–306	3.18	5
4–400(1)(I)	3.24	4
4–401(1)(a)	3.10	2
4–412	16.125	3
4–412(1)	3.7	4
	3.9	4
4–412(2)	3.10	4
	3.10	5
4–412(3)	3.7	4
Art. 5	3.26	1
5–502	3.26	2
5–506	3.26	2
5–508(3)	3.26	3
5–508(4)	3.26	4
5–520(2)	3.26	5
5–520(4)	3.26	6
6–628	3.30	13
	3.31	1
6–632	12.65	9
7–700	16.5	3
	16.9	2
7–701(1)(d)	16.8	4
7–702	16.5	4
7–703(1)(c)	16.8	4
7–704	16.5	8
	16.9	6
	16.11	1
	16.11	13
	16.17	10
7–706	16.29	5
	16.29	6
7–708	16.30	1
	16.30	4
	16.109	2
	16.113	1
	16.113	2
7–708(1)	16.30	2
7–708(1)—(3)	16.113	11
7–708(2)	16.23	2
7–708(2)(b)	16.23	3
7–710	16.29	1
	16.29	2
7–710(2)	16.29	3
	16.29	4
7–712	16.73	1
7–712(1)	16.8	4
7–712(1)(a)	16.73	2
7–712(1)(b)	16.82	1
	16.83	1
7–712(2)	16.37	1
	16.37	2
7–712(2)(b)	16.75	5
7–712(2)(b)(1)	16.75	6
7–712(2)(b)(2)	16.76	1

NEW YORK, MCKINNEY'S VILLAGE LAW

Sec.	This Work Sec.	Note
7–712(2)(b)(3)	16.77	2
7–712(2)(b)(4)	16.78	1
7–712(3)	16.37	3
7–712–a	16.80	6
	16.87	10
7–712–a(1)	16.39	4
7–712–a(4)	16.37	6
	16.37	7
	16.37	8
7–712–a(5)	16.37	9
	16.37	10
7–712–a(7)	16.37	11
7–712–a(8)	16.37	12
7–712–a(9)	16.43	10
7–712–a(11)	16.37	13
7–712–b	16.37	4
	16.37	5
	16.74	2
7–712–b(2)	16.130	1
7–712–b(2)(a)	16.73	3
	16.73	6
7–712–b(2)(b)	16.73	7
	16.73	8
7–712–b(2)(b)(1)	16.75	1
7–712–b(2)(b)(4)	16.78	3
7–712–b(2)(c)	16.73	13
	16.79	1
	16.89	1
7–712–b(3)(b)	16.83	2
	16.84	7
7–712–b(3)(c)	16.86	1
	16.89	1
7–712–b(4)	16.79	4
	16.86	2
	16.89	3
7–712–c	16.43	5
	16.43	9
7–712–c(1)	4.2	42
7–714	16.50	13
7–718(1)	16.36	1
	16.36	3
7–718(3)	16.36	2
7–718(13)	16.36	7
	16.96	7
	16.96	8
7–718(14)	16.36	9
7–722	16.5	7
	16.31	6
7–722(1)(b)	16.13	2
7–722(1)(c)	16.13	2
7–722(1)(h)	16.13	2
	16.13	4
7–722(2)(a)	16.13	1
7–722(2)(b)	16.13	5
7–722(2)(c)	16.14	2
7–722(3)(b)	16.13	3
7–722(3)(h)	16.13	3
7–722(4)	16.14	1
	16.14	2

TABLE OF STATUTES

NEW YORK, MCKINNEY'S VILLAGE LAW

Sec.	This Work Sec.	Note
7–722(4)(b)	16.14	4
7–722(5)(b)	16.14	6
	16.14	7
7–722(6)	16.14	3
7–722(6)(b)	16.14	5
7–722(7)	16.11	14
	16.14	8
7–722(10)	16.13	6
7–722(11)	16.13	4
7–724	16.31	6
	16.31	7
7–725(b)(6)	16.43	10
7–725–a	16.36	5
	16.36	6
	16.43	6
	16.103	1
7–725–a(1)	16.8	4
	16.103	5
	16.103	6
7–725–a(2)	16.36	5
	16.104	1
7–725–a(2)(a)	16.103	7
	16.103	8
	16.103	9
	16.104	5
	16.105	14
	16.106	4
7–725–a(3)	16.87	6
7–725–a(4)	16.107	1
7–725–a(5)	16.104	6
7–725–a(6)(a)	16.107	6
7–725–a(6)(b)	16.107	7
7–725–a(6)(c)	16.107	8
	16.107	9
7–725–a(7)	16.43	10
	16.105	2
	16.105	3
	16.105	4
	16.105	5
	16.105	6
	16.105	15
7–725–a(8)	16.105	10
	16.105	12
	16.105	13
7–725–b	16.43	8
7–725–b(1)	16.8	4
	16.90	2
7–725–b(2)	16.90	3
	16.36	5
7–725–b(3)	16.87	6
	16.90	7
7–725–b(4)	16.90	7
	16.93	1
7–725–b(6)	16.90	9
	16.94	1
7–725–b(7)	16.90	9
7–725–b(8)	16.94	2
7–728(1)	16.96	1
	16.96	6
7–728(5)(b)	16.98	1
7–728(5)(c)	16.98	4

NEW YORK, MCKINNEY'S VILLAGE LAW

Sec.	This Work Sec.	Note
7–728(5)(c)	16.98	5
7–728(5)(d)	16.98	6
7–728(5)(d)(i)	16.97	1
7–728(5)(d)(ii)	16.97	2
	16.98	8
7–728(5)(d)(iv)	16.97	4
	16.101	2
7–728(5)(e)	16.98	7
7–728(5)(e)(i)	16.97	1
7–728(5)(e)(ii)	16.97	2
7–728(5)(e)(iv)	16.97	4
7–728(5)(g)	16.43	10
	16.97	3
7–728(5)(h)	16.97	5
	16.97	6
7–728(6)	16.97	11
7–728(6)(b)	16.97	7
7–728(6)(d)	16.97	12
7–728(8)	16.97	10
7–728(9)	16.43	10
	16.97	8
7–728(10)	16.97	13
7–728(11)	16.97	9
7–730	16.96	5
7–730(1)	16.96	4
	16.99	2
7–730(2)	16.99	3
	16.99	4
7–730(4)	16.99	5
	16.100	1
	16.100	6
	16.100	2
	16.100	4
7–730(6)	16.87	6
7–730(7)	16.101	8
7–730(9)	16.99	7
7–730(10)	16.99	8
7–734	12.55	9
7–740	16.43	7
9–902	3.15	10
9–902(1)	3.15	7
	3.15	8
	3.15	9
10–1002	3.13	2
11–1116	3.13	2
Art. 17	3.4	3
18–1806	3.5	1
	3.5	2
18–1824	3.15	11
19–1900(1)	3.5	28
19–1902	3.5	29
20–2000	3.10	1
	3.12	
	3.13	3

NEW YORK, MCKINNEY'S WORKERS' COMPENSATION LAW

Sec.	This Work Sec.	Note
Art. 6	32.42	1

TABLE OF STATUTES

NEW YORK, MCKINNEY'S WORKERS' COMPENSATION LAW

Sec.	Sec.	This Work Note
Art. 6–A	32.42	3
Art. 9	32.3	
	32.39	2
	32.44	
1	32.10	1
2(4)	32.12	13
	32.12	14
	32.12	15
	32.12	16
	32.12	26
2(7)	17.65	1
	32.13	3
3	32.12	11
	32.41	
3(1)	32.12	9
	32.12	10
	32.12	12
	32.12	21
	32.12	24
3(2)	17.65	7
	32.10	2
	32.19	
3(30)	32.10	2
10	32.2	1
	32.3	
	32.12	1
	32.12	25
	32.15	1
	32.18	1
	32.19	6
	32.19	7
10(1)	17.65	1
	32.12	2
	32.13	4
	32.13	5
11	29.73	1
	32.14	2
	32.14	3
	32.15	1
	32.15	3
12	32.4	1
	32.28	2
13	32.21	1
	32.28	1
	32.28	4
	32.28	8
	32.39	4
	32.39	6
13(a)	32.28	5
	32.28	6
13(a)(4)	32.28	
13–g(1)	32.28	7
14(4–a)	29.73	3
15	29.73	1
	29.73	3
	32.21	2
	32.22	1
	32.23	2

NEW YORK, MCKINNEY'S WORKERS' COMPENSATION LAW

Sec.	Sec.	This Work Note
15 (Cont'd)	32.23	3
	32.24	2
	32.24	3
	32.24	4
	32.24	5
15(1)	29.73	3
	32.25	
15(2)	29.73	3
15(3)	29.73	3
15(3)(a)—(q)	32.24	1
15(3)(t)	32.21	3
	32.29	1
	32.29	2
	32.29	3
15(3)(v)	32.25	1
15(5)	29.73	3
15(5–b)	32.32	2
	32.32	3
	32.32	4
	32.32	5
	32.32	6
	32.35	1
15(8)	32.27	2
	32.27	8
15(8)(i)	32.27	9
16	32.21	5
	32.21	6
	32.30	1
	32.30	2
	32.30	3
	32.30	4
	32.30	5
	32.30	6
	32.30	7
	32.31	1
16(1)	32.31	2
18	17.65	9
	32.13	
	32.13	1
	32.17	10
	32.18	
	32.18	1
	32.18	2
	32.18	3
	32.18	4
	32.18	5
	32.18	6
	32.19	
	32.39	3
	32.41	
19	32.28	
	32.32	4
20	32.17	3
	32.17	7
21	32.18	8
	32.19	1
21(1)	17.65	5
21(5)	32.17	9

355

TABLE OF STATUTES

NEW YORK, MCKINNEY'S WORKERS' COMPENSATION LAW			NEW YORK, MCKINNEY'S WORKERS' COMPENSATION LAW		
	This Work			This Work	
Sec.	Sec.	Note	Sec.	Sec.	Note
22	32.35	3	33	9.125	20
23	32.17	11		32.21	4
	32.33	1		32.32	1
	32.33	3	37—49	17.65	7
	32.33	5	47	32.19	9
	32.33	7		32.19	10
	32.34	1		32.19	11
	37.44	7	49bb	32.18	15
	37.44	8	50	32.12	6
24	32.2	7	50(3)	32.12	7
	32.38	1		32.12	8
	32.38	2	51	32.39	1
	32.38	3	53	32.42	2
24–a	32.37	1	54	32.41	8
	32.37	3	54(5)	32.41	5
25	32.17	4	76—105a	32.12	4
	32.17	5	81	32.42	6
	32.17	6	82(2)	32.42	9
25(2–a)	32.16	2	113	32.12	22
	32.16	3		32.12	23
	32.16	4		32.43	2
	32.16	5	115	32.18	16
	32.16	6	120	17.65	11
	32.16	8		32.36	1
	32.16	9		32.36	2
	32.16	10		32.36	3
	32.16	11		32.36	4
	32.16	12		32.36	5
25(2–b)	32.20	1		32.36	6
	32.20	2		32.36	7
25(2–b)(e)	32.20	1		32.36	8
25(2–b)(h)	32.20	4	123	32.17	8
25(2–h)(g)	32.20	3		32.33	2
25(4)	32.3	1		32.35	
26–a	32.40	1		32.35	2
	32.40	3		32.35	4
28	17.65	10		32.35	5
	32.13		140	32.11	1
	32.17	10		32.11	3
	32.18	9		32.33	4
	32.18	10	142(2)	32.11	5
	32.18	11		32.11	6
	32.18	12	146	32.11	2
	32.18	13	150	32.11	4
	32.39	5		32.12	3
	32.54			32.17	1
29	26.48	1	151	32.34	2
	26.49			32.40	2
	32.4		200 et seq.	32.2	8
	32.4	2	200—242	32.44	1
	32.4	3	201(5)	32.46	1
	32.32	8	201(6)	32.46	1
29(1)	17.65	2	201(9)(A)	32.47	4
	32.15	6		32.51	1
31	32.41	1	201(13)	32.47	1
	32.47	2	202	32.45	1
32	32.32	1	203	32.48	1
	32.32	7		32.49	1

356

TABLE OF STATUTES

NEW YORK, MCKINNEY'S WORKERS' COMPENSATION LAW

Sec.	This Work Sec.	Note
203 (Cont'd)	32.49	2
205(1)	32.47	1
205(2)	32.49	4
205(5)	32.44	2
206	32.44	2
206(2)	32.52	1
207	32.48	2
209	32.47	3
211(3)	32.45	2
211(4)	32.45	3
	32.45	5
211(5)	32.45	5
212	32.46	2
213	32.12	1
	32.48	3
217	32.49	5
217(1)	32.50	1
	32.50	2
217(6)	32.50	3
217(6)—221	32.50	5
218	9.125	20
221	32.50	4
229	32.39	1

NEW YORK LAWS

Year	This Work Sec.	Note
1922, c. 490, § 120	37.44	10
1922, c. 490, § 127-f	37.44	10
1933, c. 606	24.66	1
1939, c. 860	37.3	29
1946, c. 274, § 1	13.2	7
1959, c. 578	32.40	1
1962, c. 686	37.3	26
1962, c. 693	37.3	22
1963, c. 565	37.3	23
1964, c. 497	37.3	20
1964, c. 946	3.22	1
1964, c. 946, § 1	3.22	2
1966, c. 898	37.3	21
1966, c. 953	37.3	27
1967, c. 392	3.21	1
1970, c. 494	20.28	6
1970, c. 996	37.13	6
	38.10	51
	38.20	7
1972, c. 251	22.4	10
1973, c. 974	3.12	9
1974, c. 297	22.4	22
1974, c. 576, § 4	13.2	3
1974, c. 578	3.29	1
1974, c. 579	3.29	1
1974, c. 580	3.29	1
1974, c. 623	22.4	23
	22.6	6
1975, c. 756, § 21	1.13	7
1977, c. 933	3.29	2

NEW YORK LAWS

Year	This Work Sec.	Note
1978, c. 156	37.7	1
1979, c. 216	38.8	139
1979, c. 411	38.8	
1979, c. 651	38.27	28
1980, c. 281	21.33	
1981, c. 461	24.32	1
1983, c. 170	38.10	50
1984, c. 671	38.8	51
1985, c. 789	37.9	1
1986, c. 516	38.10	172
1986, c. 682	37.29	26
1986, c. 884, § 4	21.46	3
1986, c. 884, § 5	21.46	3
1987, c. 422	32.37	4
1988, c. 397, § 7	37.92	3
1988, c. 577	20.60	1
1989, c. 364	32.25	2
	32.25	3
1989, c. 567	21.53	1
1989, c. 700	20.54	1
1989, c. 700, § 3	20.61	1
1990, c. 209	38.10	39
1992, c. 216	26.32	1
1992, c. 698	22.1	3
	22.8	2
	22.10	3
1992, c. 698, § 3	22.8	10
1992, c. 698, § 4	22.8	11
1993, c. 208, § 14(4)	16.89	14
1994, c. 222	38.8	104
	38.8	106
1994, c. 224	38.8	108
1994, c. 419	22.21	4
1995, c. 1	38.10	
	39.1	
1995, c. 81	23.68	1
1995, c. 83	38.16	4
	38.55	
1995, c. 300	39.8	1
1995, c. 440	38.8	106
1995, c. 441	38.8	106
1995, c. 466	26.41	10
1995, c. 628	4.52	8
1995, c. 648	4.18	11
1996, c. 67	33.17	2
	33.17	5
1996, c. 89	12.88	9
	12.89	10
1996, c. 214	37.46	2
1996, c. 227	12.53	5
1996, c. 309	11.51	
	12.87	5
1996, c. 309, §§ 171–180	12.84	2
1996, c. 404	1.89	12
1996, c. 490	12.88	10
	12.89	9
1996, c. 499	12.8	7
1996, c. 606, § 3	26.32	6
1996, c. 630, § 2	38.19	103

TABLE OF STATUTES

NEW YORK LAWS

Year	Sec.	Note
1996, c. 630, § 2 (Cont'd)	38.19	105
1996, c. 835	32.15	8
	32.27	12
1997, c. 116	13.2	
1997, c. 116, § 1	13.61	
1997, c. 116, §§ 31 to 34	13.74	
1997, c. 389	24.1	3
	24.20	3
	24.21	
1997, c. 461	37.19	32

NEW YORK EXECUTIVE ORDER

No.	Sec.	Note
2	4.43	2
20	4.26	13
	4.28	2
	4.31	2
	4.49	
	4.49	26
91	16.6	8
131	4.18	13
	4.23	2
	4.24	8
	4.24	9
	4.24	10
156	4.56	1

DELAWARE CODE

Tit.	Sec.	Note
8, § 141(a)	1.46	3
8, § 142	1.69	1
8, § 152	1.30	1
8, § 153	1.30	1
8, § 156	1.30	1
8, § 220(c)	1.53	7
8, § 228	1.48	3
8, § 342	1.46	3
8, § 350	1.46	3
8, § 354	1.46	3

UNITED STATES

UNITED STATES CONSTITUTION

Art.	Sec.	Note
I, § 5	18.8	
I, § 8, cl. 4	9.5	1
I, § 9	18.8	
I, § 10	38.22	1
III	9.18	
III, § 2, cl. 3	18.8	2
IV	21.32	

UNITED STATES CONSTITUTION

Art.	Sec.	Note
IV, § 1	18.37	9
IV, § 2, cl. 1	18.8	1
Amend.		
1	16.25	
	16.25	1
	16.125	3
	17.55	
	17.64	
	18.1	
	18.8	
	18.8	3
	18.8	7
	18.26	
	18.26	1
	18.26	6
	18.27	
	18.27	2
	18.28	
	18.28	3
	18.55	4
	18.56	1
	18.80	5
	18.82	6
4	4.1	
	4.2	
	17.55	
	18.8	
	18.9	
	18.9	1
	18.9	3
	18.10	
	18.21	
	18.21	3
	18.22	
	18.92	
	18.93	
5	4.1	
	4.2	
	4.63	
	4.64	
	4.64	5
	4.65	
	14.18	1
	15.34	
	15.34	1
	16.18	
	16.18	1
	16.19	
	16.22	
	16.22	1
	18.8	
	18.8	1
	18.8	6
	18.92	
	38.19	140
6	18.8	
	18.8	2
	18.8	6
	33.56	
7	18.8	2

TABLE OF STATUTES

UNITED STATES CONSTITUTION

Amend.	This Work Sec.	Note
8	18.29	2
11	9.18	2
	18.2	
	18.30	
	18.33	
	18.33	1
14	4.6	1
	9.18	2
	15.34	
	15.34	1
	16.18	1
	16.20	
	16.20	1
	16.22	1
	18.8	
	18.8	1
	18.8	6
	18.8	8
	18.9	
	18.26	6
	18.29	2
	18.56	1
	18.92	
	18.93	
	18.94	
21, § 1 et seq.	36.4	2
	36.4	3

UNITED STATES CODE ANNOTATED

5 U.S.C.A.—Government Organization and Employees

Sec.	This Work Sec.	Note
Art. 19, Tit. 5	15.21	6
103(d)	4.48	5
504	23.16	8
	23.23	4
552	17.55	10
552(a)(1)(D)	4.50	12
552a	17.55	14
553	4.50	12
729	9.125	24
2265	9.125	24
2301	17.38	
2302	17.38	
7101 et seq.	17.61	3
7102	17.38	
7116	17.38	
7701(g)(1)	23.40	3
7703(b)(1)	23.40	4
8101	32.43	1
8331 et seq.	23.37	1
	23.39	1
8336(d)	23.39	2
8337(a)	23.39	5
8338(a)	23.39	3
8341	23.39	4

UNITED STATES CODE ANNOTATED

5 U.S.C.A.—Government Organization and Employees

Sec.	This Work Sec.	Note
8347(d)(2)	23.40	2
8401 et seq.	23.37	2
8403	23.38	1
8423	23.38	1
8461	23.38	1
8901 et seq.	23.38	7

6 U.S.C.A.—Surety Bonds

Sec.	This Work Sec.	Note
1983	18.53	
	18.53	11

7 U.S.C.A.—Agriculture

Sec.	This Work Sec.	Note
135 et seq.	27.47	2
302—304	6.40	2
3501—3508	12.81	1

8 U.S.C.A.—Aliens and Nationality

Sec.	This Work Sec.	Note
155(i)	19.59	
1101 et seq.	19.1	7
1101(a)(15)	19.1	1
	19.2	2
1101(a)(15)(B)	19.67	1
1101(a)(15)(F)	19.67	2
1101(a)(15)(H)	19.67	3
1101(a)(15)(L)	19.67	4
1101(a)(20)	19.4	1
1101(a)(27)(C)—		
(A)(27)(J)	19.17	1
1101(a)(32)	19.24	1
1101(a)(33)	19.74	2
1101(a)(42)(A)	19.50	
1101(a)(43)	19.48	1
1101(b)	19.11	1
	19.12	1
1101(b)(1)	19.68	6
1101(b)(1)(A)	19.11	
1101(b)(1)(B)	19.11	8
1101(b)(1)(C)	19.11	5
	19.11	22
1101(b)(1)(D)	19.11	20
1101(b)(1)(E)	19.11	14
1101(b)(1)(F)	19.15	2
	19.15	3
	19.15	12
1101(b)(2)	19.10	13
	19.11	19
1103	19.1	8
1105a(a)	19.57	3

TABLE OF STATUTES

UNITED STATES CODE ANNOTATED
8 U.S.C.A.—Aliens and Nationality

Sec.	This Work Sec.	Note
1151	19.16	5
	19.58	
1151—1156	19.4	
	19.4	14
1151(a)	19.9	1
1151(a)(1)	19.4	7
1151(a)(2)	19.4	8
1151(a)(3)	19.4	9
1151(b)	19.8	4
1151(b)(2)(A)(i)	19.4	6
	19.8	1
	19.8	2
	19.12	5
1151(b)(2)(A)(ii)	19.8	3
1151(b)(2)(B)	19.8	3
1151(c)	19.5	1
1151(c)(1)(B)(ii)	19.5	3
1151(d)	19.5	5
1151(e)	19.5	7
1152(b)	19.6	2
1152(b)(1)	19.6	3
1152(b)(2)	19.6	3
1152(b)(3)	19.6	4
1153	19.20	
1153(a)	19.4	7
1153(a)(1)	19.9	2
1153(a)(3)	19.9	4
	19.9	5
1153(a)(3)(B)	19.9	4
1153(a)(4)	19.9	3
	19.9	6
1153(b)	19.4	8
	19.17	
1153(b)(1)	19.18	1
1153(b)(1)(B)	19.20	2
1153(b)(1)(C)	19.21	1
1153(b)(2)(A)	19.22	1
1153(b)(2)(B)	19.22	2
	19.25	1
1153(b)(3)	19.28	1
1153(b)(3)(A)	19.26	1
1153(b)(4)	19.40	1
1153(b)(5)	19.42	1
	19.43	1
1153(c)	19.4	9
	19.46	1
1153(c)(2)	19.46	3
1153(d)	19.6	9
	19.68	6
1154	19.16	5
1154(a)(1)(A)(iii)(I)	19.16	1
	19.16	7
1154(a)(1)(A)(iii)(II)	19.16	1
1154(h)	19.72	35
1155	19.9	7
1157	19.4	
	19.50	3
1158	19.4	

UNITED STATES CODE ANNOTATED
8 U.S.C.A.—Aliens and Nationality

Sec.	This Work Sec.	Note
1158 (Cont'd)	19.50	
	19.50	3
1158(a)	19.50	5
1159	19.4	10
1160	19.71	3
1181(a)	19.51	1
	19.74	
1181(a)(6)(A)	19.59	2
1182	19.2	4
	19.59	3
	19.70	3
1182(a)	19.1	2
1182(a)(1)	19.52	1
1182(a)(1)(A)(ii)	19.54	4
1182(a)(2)	19.1	16
	19.51	5
	19.52	3
1182(a)(2)(A)(ii)	19.52	5
1182(a)(2)(B)	19.52	4
	19.55	1
1182(a)(2)(C)	19.52	6
1182(a)(2)(D)	19.52	6
1182(a)(2)(E)	19.52	6
1182(a)(3)(A)	19.52	8
1182(a)(3)(B)	19.52	8
1182(a)(3)(C)	19.52	9
1182(a)(3)(D)	19.52	10
1182(a)(3)(E)	19.52	11
1182(a)(4)	19.52	12
1182(a)(5)	19.52	13
1182(a)(5)(A) (former)	19.31	1
1182(a)(5)(C)	19.26	3
1182(a)(6)	19.52	14
1182(a)(7)	19.52	15
	19.70	4
1182(a)(8)	19.52	16
1182(a)(9)	19.52	14
	19.52	17
1182(g)	19.52	2
1182(h)	19.52	7
1182(O)	19.55	1
1184(b)	19.67	8
	19.67	9
1186(c)(1)	19.73	6
1186a	19.16	5
	19.43	6
	19.71	1
	19.72	1
1186a(b)	19.8	7
1186a(b)(1)	19.72	13
1186a(b)(1)(A)(i)	19.72	10
1186a(b)(1)(A)(ii)	19.72	11
1186a(b)(1)(B)	19.72	12
1186a(b)(2)	19.72	30
1186a(c)(1)	19.72	16
1186a(c)(2)	19.72	18
1186a(c)(3)(B)	19.72	23
1186a(c)(4)(C)	19.16	4

360

TABLE OF STATUTES

UNITED STATES CODE ANNOTATED
8 U.S.C.A.—Aliens and Nationality

Sec.	This Work Sec.	Note
1186a(d)(2)	19.72	19
1186a(d)(2)(A)	19.72	9
1186a(e)	19.72	4
1186a(g)(1)(C)	19.72	2
1186b	19.43	1
	19.43	5
	19.71	2
1186b(a)(1)	19.73	1
1186b(d)(3)	19.73	5
1201	19.53	1
1201(d)	19.54	4
1203	19.74	9
1224	19.63	2
	19.65	3
1250A(b)	19.48	2
1251	19.1	2
	19.2	4
	19.70	2
1251(a)(1)	19.52	
1251(a)(1)(A)	19.52	18
1251(a)(2)	19.1	16
1252	19.52	19
1252(a)(2)(B)	19.48	5
1254	19.2	4
	19.16	5
1254(a)	19.48	3
1255	19.4	10
	19.14	16
	19.51	2
	19.57	1
	19.60	1
	19.63	
	19.68	1
1255(a)	19.58	1
	19.61	3
1255(c)	19.51	3
	19.57	4
	19.58	4
1255(d)	19.58	5
1255(e)	19.58	7
1255(i)	19.51	4
	19.57	5
	19.59	2
1255a	19.71	3
1256(a)	19.47	7
1256(b)	19.47	8
1259	19.4	12
	19.47	
1304(e)	19.74	5
1324(a)	19.1	3
1324a	17.49	5
	19.1	17
1324b	17.49	5
	19.1	17
	19.70	1
1324b(a)(1)	17.49	6
1325(b)	19.72	31
1329	19.57	3

UNITED STATES CODE ANNOTATED
8 U.S.C.A.—Aliens and Nationality

Sec.	This Work Sec.	Note
1361	19.4	4
	19.10	2
1401—1489	19.1	4
1421—1433	19.70	5
1447	18.67	3
1454	18.67	3
2245	19.16	5

9 U.S.C.A.—Arbitration

Sec.	This Work Sec.	Note
1 et seq.	31.24	2

11 U.S.C.A.—Bankruptcy

Sec.	This Work Sec.	Note
Ch. 1	9.6	
	9.6	1
101	1.5	7
	9.6	6
101 et seq.	1.78	1
101—1330	9.1	1
	9.5	2
101(5)	9.36	2
	9.50	2
101(8)	9.209	9
	9.216	1
	9.241	1
101(14)	9.140	4
	9.311	
101(14)(A)	9.29	8
101(14)(B)	9.29	9
101(14)(C)	9.29	10
101(14)(D)	9.29	11
101(14)(E)	9.29	12
101(16)	9.36	4
101(17)	9.36	4
101(18)	9.212	4
101(19)	9.212	5
101(21)	9.212	3
101(23)	9.20	1
101(24)	9.20	2
101(27)	9.132	3
101(30)	9.236	1
101(31)	9.29	8
	9.107	13
	9.117	6
	9.165	20
	9.205	7
101(32)	1.10	4
	9.117	4
	9.119	4
101(36)	9.128	2
101(41)	9.7	2
	9.43	11
	9.43	12

TABLE OF STATUTES

UNITED STATES CODE ANNOTATED
11 U.S.C.A.—Bankruptcy

Sec.	This Work Sec.	Note
101(51)	9.128	2
101(51B)	9.55	1
	9.7	9
101(51C)	9.43	4
	9.173	2
101(53)	9.128	2
101(54)	9.117	1
	9.205	2
102	9.6	
	9.15	1
102(1)(A)	9.15	1
102(1)(B)(i)	9.15	1
102(1)(B)(ii)	9.15	1
103	9.6	
105	9.151	
105(a)	9.12	
	9.18	
	9.18	4
	9.35	
	9.151	1
	9.174	11
	9.312	
105(d)	9.18	
106	9.18	2
108	9.8	5
109	9.7	
	9.7	8
	9.8	1
	9.20	
109(a)	9.7	1
109(c)(3)	9.7	8
109(e)	9.237	1
109(f)	9.212	2
109(g)	9.7	7
	9.177	5
Ch. 3	9.6	
301	9.8	2
	9.8	3
	9.43	1
	9.264	1
	9.264	2
303	9.9	4
303(a)	9.9	1
	9.174	13
303(b)	9.9	2
303(f)	9.10	4
303(h)	9.10	9
	9.43	1
303(i)	9.2	9
304	9.20	4
304(a)	9.20	3
305	9.19	1
307	9.42	4
321	9.138	3
322	9.138	3
	9.214	
	9.239	
323	9.138	3

UNITED STATES CODE ANNOTATED
11 U.S.C.A.—Bankruptcy

Sec.	This Work Sec.	Note
324	9.138	3
325	9.138	3
326	9.138	3
327	9.12	
	9.30	
	9.98	1
	9.291	
	9.291	1
327(a)	9.29	
	9.29	3
	9.29	17
	9.43	14
	9.310	
327(c)	9.29	16
327(d)	9.30	
327(e)	9.29	
	9.29	15
328	9.29	16
	9.98	1
328(a)	9.30	1
	9.30	2
	9.311	
328(b)	9.30	4
328(c)	9.29	19
	9.30	3
329	9.311	
330	9.31	1
	9.31	9
	9.98	1
	9.312	
330(a)	9.98	
330(a)(1)	9.31	1
	9.31	4
330(a)(3)(A)	9.31	5
330(a)(3)(B)	9.31	6
330(a)(3)(C)	9.31	7
330(a)(3)(D)	9.31	8
330(a)(3)(E)	9.31	9
330(a)(4)(A)	9.31	9
330(a)(4)(B)	9.31	9
331	9.31	2
	9.312	
341	9.37	1
	9.127	
	9.169	
	9.181	
	9.181	4
	9.264	
341(a)	9.37	
	9.92	
	9.184	
	9.207	3
341(b)	9.37	1
341(c)	9.37	3
343	9.38	1
	9.41	2
345	9.139	2
346	9.133	

362

TABLE OF STATUTES

UNITED STATES CODE ANNOTATED
11 U.S.C.A.—Bankruptcy

Sec.	Sec.	This Work Note
346 (Cont'd)	9.231	
	9.312	
346(a)	9.133	1
346(b)(1)	9.133	2
346(b)(1)	9.133	3
346(c)(1)	9.133	4
346(f)	9.133	5
348	9.210	
	9.234	
	9.262	
348(a)	9.135	
	9.135	1
	9.135	2
348(c)	9.135	5
348(d)	9.135	7
348(e)	9.27	6
348(f)(1)	9.135	8
348(f)(2)	9.135	8
349(a)	9.136	1
349(b)	9.136	2
350(a)	9.137	1
	9.176	1
	9.211	1
	9.235	1
	9.263	1
350(a)(1)	9.138	2
350(a)(2)	9.138	3
350(b)	9.137	2
	9.176	2
	9.211	2
	9.235	2
	9.263	2
361	9.56	1
	9.57	1
	9.218	
362	9.2	8
	9.8	4
	9.25	
	9.53	
	9.106	
	9.243	1
	9.269	
	11.2	2
362(a)	9.50	
	9.50	1
	9.50	2
	9.51	
362(a)(4)	9.69	4
362(a)(7)	9.109	3
362(b)	9.51	
	9.51	1
362(c)	9.244	
	9.294	3
362(d)	9.52	6
	9.53	2
	9.244	
	9.269	
	9.270	

UNITED STATES CODE ANNOTATED
11 U.S.C.A.—Bankruptcy

Sec.	Sec.	This Work Note
362(d) (Cont'd)	9.293	1
362(d)—(g)	9.292	1
362(d)(1)	9.52	2
	9.52	5
	9.292	4
362(d)(2)	9.52	3
	9.53	4
	9.292	6
362(d)(2)(B)	9.53	10
362(d)(3)	9.7	9
	9.55	3
362(e)	9.53	13
	9.54	2
362(f)	9.54	3
362(g)	9.292	7
363	9.10	4
	9.25	
	9.25	11
	9.53	
	9.60	
	9.69	
	9.106	
	9.156	
	9.195	
	9.200	
	9.218	2
	9.244	1
	9.271	
	9.271	1
	9.272	1
	9.273	1
	9.294	1
363(a)	9.63	4
	9.65	1
363(b)	9.12	
	9.103	
	9.156	
	9.218	
	9.238	1
	9.244	
	9.295	
363(b)(1)	9.62	1
	9.62	1
363(c)	9.63	4
	9.218	
363(c)(1)	9.60	3
	9.65	3
363(c)(2)	9.53	
	9.65	5
	9.69	9
	9.99	
363(c)(2)(A)	9.65	5
	9.273	
363(c)(2)(B)	9.272	
	9.295	1
	9.296	1
363(c)(3)	9.67	2
	9.295	

363

TABLE OF STATUTES

UNITED STATES CODE ANNOTATED
11 U.S.C.A.—Bankruptcy

Sec.	This Work Sec.	Note
363(d)	9.238	1
363(e)	9.53	
	9.62	3
	9.66	
	9.238	1
	9.244	
	9.270	
	9.293	1
363(f)	9.63	2
	9.200	5
	9.218	
	9.238	1
	9.244	
	9.271	3
	9.294	
363(g)	9.63	3
363(h)	9.16	
	9.63	3
	24.85	3
363(k)	9.156	4
363(L)	9.238	1
	9.244	
363(m)	9.25	11
	9.64	
	9.64	1
363(n)	9.60	2
364	9.2	5
	9.3	
	9.25	
	9.53	
	9.71	
	9.103	
	9.163	4
	9.274	
	9.274	1
	9.297	1
	9.297	2
364(a)	9.71	3
364(b)	9.71	5
364(c)	9.71	6
	9.71	9
364(c)(1)	9.106	3
364(d)	9.71	7
	9.106	
364(d)(1)(B)	9.71	8
364(e)	9.73	1
	9.73	2
365	9.74	
	9.74	3
	9.78	
	9.85	
	9.86	
	9.86	2
	9.149	
	9.149	2
	9.163	3
	9.223	
	9.248	

UNITED STATES CODE ANNOTATED
11 U.S.C.A.—Bankruptcy

Sec.	This Work Sec.	Note
365 (Cont'd)	9.275	
	9.275	2
	9.298	1
365(a)	9.82	1
365(b)(1)	9.79	3
365(b)(2)	9.275	4
365(c)	9.80	1
	9.80	2
365(d)	9.135	
365(d)(1)	9.76	1
	9.196	3
365(d)(2)	9.76	2
	9.275	3
365(d)(3)	9.75	
	9.77	2
365(d)(4)	9.77	1
	9.196	3
365(d)(10)	9.85	1
365(e)(1)	9.74	4
365(f)	9.79	1
365(f)(2)	9.79	4
365(g)(1)	9.82	1
365(h)	9.84	1
365(h)(1)	9.84	4
365(h)(1)(A)(i)	9.84	5
365(h)(1)(A)(ii)	9.84	2
365(h)(1)(D)	9.84	3
365(k)	9.79	5
365(n)	9.74	1
366	9.89	
	9.89	2
366(b)	9.89	2
	9.89	3
	9.89	4
Ch. 5	9.6	
501	9.91	
	9.91	6
	9.101	
	9.202	
501(b)	9.91	10
501(c)	9.91	12
501(d)	9.91	13
	9.91	14
	9.91	15
	9.91	16
	9.91	17
	9.91	18
502	9.96	3
	9.111	
	9.163	5
	9.255	
502(a)	9.96	1
502(b)	9.111	3
502(b)(2)	9.102	1
502(b)(5)	9.101	
502(b)(6)	9.75	1
	9.83	
	9.83	1

364

TABLE OF STATUTES

	UNITED STATES CODE ANNOTATED 11 U.S.C.A.—Bankruptcy			UNITED STATES CODE ANNOTATED 11 U.S.C.A.—Bankruptcy	
		This Work			This Work
Sec.	Sec.	Note	Sec.	Sec.	Note
502(b)(7)	9.81	3	506(b) (Cont'd)	9.107	24
	9.88		506(c)	9.66	
502(b)(9)	9.91	10		9.69	
	9.93			9.102	
	9.93	3		9.102	8
	9.93	5	506(d)	9.101	
502(c)	9.3			9.182	10
	9.163	8	506(d)(2)	9.101	4
502(d)(1)	9.113	1	507	1.98	12
502(e)	9.91	13		9.106	
502(e)	9.101			9.177	3
502(f)	9.91	14		9.202	
	9.106	6		9.202	2
	9.135	7		9.222	
502(g)	9.91	15		9.222	2
	9.135	7		9.247	
502(h)	9.91	16		9.247	2
	9.91	17	507(a)(1)	9.106	5
502(i)	9.91	18		9.148	2
	9.135	7		9.165	10
503	9.30			9.199	
503(a)	9.98	10	507(a)(2)	9.106	6
503(b)	9.31	10		9.148	3
	9.71			9.165	11
	9.98	4		9.199	
	9.105		507(a)(3)	9.106	8
	9.106	5		9.165	13
	9.135			9.199	
	9.312		507(a)(4)	9.106	9
503(b)(1)	9.71			9.165	14
	9.107	21		9.199	
503(b)(1)(A)	9.98	1	507(a)(5)	9.106	10
503(b)(2)	9.98	9		9.165	15
503(b)(3)(A)	9.98	5		9.199	
503(b)(3)(D)	9.43	10	507(a)(6)	9.106	11
	9.98	6		9.165	16
503(b)(3)(F)	9.98	7		9.199	
503(b)(4)	9.98	8	507(a)(7)	9.106	12
504	9.30	5		9.148	4
	9.30	6		9.199	
	9.311		507(a)(7)(E)	9.107	21
505	9.312		507(a)(8)	9.106	13
506	1.98	13		9.135	7
	9.101	4	507(a)(9)	9.106	14
506(a)	9.100		507(b)	9.53	
	9.100	1		9.53	3
	9.100	2		9.71	
	9.101			9.71	9
	9.103	2		9.106	
	9.104	2		9.106	4
	9.109		509(c)	9.107	1
	9.156		510(a)	9.107	3
	9.156	2	510(b)	9.107	6
	9.251	3		9.107	7
506(b)	9.53	4		9.107	8
	9.58	1	510(c)	9.107	10
	9.102	7		9.107	21
	9.103		521	9.265	1

365

TABLE OF STATUTES

UNITED STATES CODE ANNOTATED
11 U.S.C.A.—Bankruptcy

Sec.	This Work Sec.	Note
521 (Cont'd)	9.265	2
	9.265	3
521(1)	9.91	
	9.139	7
	9.174	
	9.209	
	9.261	7
521(2)	9.265	10
521(2)(A)	9.186	
	9.186	6
	9.186	11
521(2)(B)	9.186	7
	9.189	2
521(2)(C)	9.186	10
521(4)	9.192	1
522	9.69	
	9.128	5
522(a)(2)	9.128	5
522(b)	9.63	3
	9.125	2
522(b)(2)(A)	9.125	
522(b)(2)(B)	9.125	30
522(c)	9.111	10
	9.129	5
522(c)(2)	9.129	2
522(d)	9.125	
	24.85	
522(e)	9.125	31
522(f)	9.128	
	9.128	1
	9.128	2
	9.128	3
	9.279	1
	9.301	1
522(f)(1)	9.125	32
522(f)(2)	9.128	5
522(f)(2)(B)	9.128	5
522(f)(2)(C)	9.128	4
522(g)	9.125	34
522(g)(1)(A)	9.129	6
522(g)(1)(B)	9.129	7
522(h)	9.125	33
522(L)	9.125	6
	9.126	2
	9.126	3
	9.126	4
	9.278	1
	9.278	3
522(m)	9.125	4
523	9.3	3
	9.168	2
	9.169	
	9.169	1
	9.169	6
	9.204	1
	9.207	
	9.207	1
	9.208	

UNITED STATES CODE ANNOTATED
11 U.S.C.A.—Bankruptcy

Sec.	This Work Sec.	Note
523 (Cont'd)	9.229	6
	9.255	3
	9.309	
	9.310	
523(a)	9.207	
	9.208	
	9.229	
	9.256	
	9.256	6
	9.256	7
	9.309	
523(a)(2)	9.207	4
	9.208	
523(a)(2)(A)	9.208	3
	9.255	4
	9.309	2
523(a)(2)(B)	9.208	3
	9.255	5
523(a)(2)(C)	9.255	6
523(a)(3)	9.207	
523(a)(4)	9.207	4
	9.208	
	9.255	7
523(a)(6)	9.207	4
	9.208	
	9.255	8
523(a)(15)	9.169	7
	9.208	
523(b)	9.207	
523(c)	9.169	
	9.207	
	9.229	6
	9.257	
	9.257	2
523(c)(1)	9.208	
	9.208	4
	9.208	5
523(c)(2)	9.208	5
524	9.130	
	9.130	2
	9.168	
	9.204	1
	9.206	7
	9.229	
	9.229	1
524(a)(1)	9.168	3
524(a)(2)	9.168	4
524(c)	9.130	
	9.130	1
	9.130	2
	9.130	4
	9.190	1
	9.208	2
	9.280	
	9.302	
	9.302	1
	9.303	1
524(c)(1)	9.130	5

TABLE OF STATUTES

UNITED STATES CODE ANNOTATED
11 U.S.C.A.—Bankruptcy

Sec.	This Work Sec.	Note
524(c)(1) (Cont'd)	9.208	9
	9.280	2
524(c)(2)(A)	9.130	6
	9.302	2
524(c)(2)(B)	9.130	7
	9.302	3
524(c)(3)	9.130	9
524(c)(4)	9.130	12
524(c)(6)	9.130	11
524(d)	9.130	1
	9.130	2
	9.130	10
	9.130	11
	9.190	1
	9.280	
524(e)	9.170	
	9.170	1
524(f)	9.131	2
524(g)	9.171	
524(g)(1)(B)	9.171	1
524(g)(2)(B)(ii)(V)	9.171	2
525	9.132	
	9.168	
	9.168	5
	9.185	1
	17.40	1
525(a)	9.132	1
	9.132	4
525(b)	9.132	5
525(c)	9.132	6
525(c)(2)	9.132	6
541	9.217	
	9.243	
541(a)	9.49	1
	9.49	4
	9.49	5
541(a)(3)	9.49	3
541(a)(6)	9.49	4
541(c)(2)	9.49	1
542	9.193	
542(a)	9.193	1
	9.193	4
542(b)	9.193	2
	9.193	3
544	9.69	
	9.115	
	9.121	1
	9.122	
	9.122	1
	9.129	
	9.129	4
544—545	9.182	10
544(a)	9.123	
544(a)(1)	9.115	1
544(a)(2)	9.115	4
544(a)(3)	9.115	5
544(b)	9.115	6
	9.119	

UNITED STATES CODE ANNOTATED
11 U.S.C.A.—Bankruptcy

Sec.	This Work Sec.	Note
544(b) (Cont'd)	9.119	1
545	9.69	
	9.116	1
	9.118	
	9.121	1
	9.122	
	9.122	1
	9.123	
	9.129	
	9.129	4
545(3)	9.116	2
545(4)	9.116	2
546(a)	9.121	1
	9.194	2
	9.198	
	9.198	1
	9.198	2
546(b)(1)	9.115	2
	9.122	
	9.122	1
546(b)(2)	9.122	2
546(c)	9.105	
	9.105	3
	9.105	5
	9.123	1
	9.123	2
	9.198	
	9.198	2
546(c)(1)	9.105	4
546(c)(2)	9.105	5
546(g)	9.124	1
547	9.18	2
	9.69	
	9.117	1
	9.121	1
	9.123	
	9.129	
	9.129	4
547—549	9.182	10
547(a)	9.118	10
547(a)(2)	9.118	2
547(b)	9.117	1
	9.309	2
547(b)(1)	9.117	2
547(b)(2)	9.117	3
547(b)(3)	9.117	4
547(b)(4)	9.2	8
547(b)(4)(A)	9.117	5
547(b)(4)(B)	9.117	6
547(b)(5)	9.117	7
547(c)	9.117	1
	9.118	1
547(c)(1)	9.118	3
547(c)(2)(A)	9.118	5
547(c)(2)(B)	9.118	6
547(c)(2)(C)	9.118	7
547(c)(3)	9.118	8
547(c)(4)	9.118	9

367

TABLE OF STATUTES

UNITED STATES CODE ANNOTATED
11 U.S.C.A.—Bankruptcy

Sec.	This Work Sec.	Note
547(c)(5)	9.118	11
547(c)(6)	9.118	12
547(c)(7)	9.118	13
547(c)(8)	9.118	14
547(e)(2)	9.117	1
547(e)(3)	9.117	1
547(f)	9.117	4
548	8.33	10
	9.28	4
	9.69	
	9.119	
	9.121	1
	9.121	3
	9.129	
	9.129	4
	9.163	10
548(a)	9.119	1
	9.309	2
548(a)(1)	9.119	2
548(a)(2)	9.119	3
	9.119	5
548(b)	9.309	2
549	9.122	
	9.122	1
	9.123	
	9.129	
	9.129	4
550(a)	9.120	1
	9.121	3
550(b)	9.120	2
550(c)	9.120	5
550(e)(1)	9.120	4
550(e)(2)	9.120	3
550(f)	9.120	1
552	9.69	
552(a)	9.68	1
552(b)	9.68	2
	9.294	2
552(b)(1)	9.69	12
552(b)(2)	9.69	6
553	9.91	17
	9.109	1
	9.110	1
	9.111	1
	9.121	1
	9.193	
553(a)(2)(A)	9.111	6
553(a)(2)(B)	9.111	7
553(a)(3)	9.111	9
553(b)	9.111	11
553(c)	9.111	8
554	9.70	
	9.70	1
	9.70	5
	9.188	
	9.191	
554(a)	9.70	2
554(b)	9.70	4

UNITED STATES CODE ANNOTATED
11 U.S.C.A.—Bankruptcy

Sec.	This Work Sec.	Note
Ch. 7	9.1	
	9.2	6
	9.3	
	9.3	2
	9.3	3
	9.4	
	9.4	2
	9.6	
	9.6	1
	9.7	
	9.7	6
	9.8	
	9.9	
	9.10	
	9.10	6
	9.27	
	9.28	
	9.28	4
	9.31	
	9.32	
	9.33	
	9.34	
	9.34	1
	9.37	
	9.42	
	9.43	1
	9.43	3
	9.49	
	9.60	
	9.62	
	9.62	1
	9.63	
	9.63	3
	9.70	
	9.71	
	9.76	
	9.77	
	9.91	
	9.92	
	9.93	
	9.99	
	9.101	
	9.101	8
	9.113	
	9.117	
	9.121	
	9.125	
	9.129	4
	9.130	
	9.130	2
	9.131	3
	9.134	
	9.134	1
	9.135	
	9.135	2
	9.135	8
	9.138	
	9.138	8

TABLE OF STATUTES

UNITED STATES CODE ANNOTATED
11 U.S.C.A.—Bankruptcy

Sec.	This Work Sec.	Note
Ch. 7 (Cont'd)	9.139	
	9.160	
	9.161	
	9.165	
	9.169	
	9.174	
	9.174	2
	9.175	
	9.177	
	9.177	1
	9.177	2
	9.178	
	9.179	
	9.180	
	9.181	
	9.182	
	9.183	
	9.184	
	9.185	
	9.186	
	9.187	
	9.188	
	9.189	
	9.190	
	9.191	
	9.192	
	9.193	
	9.194	
	9.195	
	9.196	
	9.197	
	9.197	1
	9.198	
	9.198	1
	9.199	
	9.200	
	9.200	1
	9.200	6
	9.201	
	9.202	
	9.202	1
	9.203	
	9.204	
	9.204	2
	9.205	
	9.206	
	9.207	
	9.207	1
	9.207	2
	9.207	3
	9.208	
	9.208	2
	9.208	5
	9.209	
	9.209	9
	9.210	
	9.210	1
	9.211	

UNITED STATES CODE ANNOTATED
11 U.S.C.A.—Bankruptcy

Sec.	This Work Sec.	Note
Ch. 7 (Cont'd)	9.215	
	9.216	
	9.217	
	9.218	
	9.220	
	9.225	
	9.229	
	9.229	6
	9.231	
	9.232	
	9.233	
	9.234	
	9.236	
	9.241	
	9.244	
	9.251	
	9.251	3
	9.255	
	9.260	
	9.261	
	9.261	7
	9.262	
	9.264	
	9.264	8
	9.265	
	9.291	
Ch. 7, subch. III	9.177	1
Ch. 7, subch. IV	9.177	1
701	9.34	1
701(a)(1)	9.180	2
702	9.138	8
	9.181	3
	9.198	
	9.198	1
702(a)	9.181	3
702(d)	9.181	4
704	9.182	
	9.200	2
704(1)	9.182	2
	9.215	1
704(2)	9.139	2
704(3)	9.182	3
704(4)	9.182	4
	9.215	2
704(5)	9.139	3
	9.182	5
704(6)	9.182	7
704(7)	9.139	4
704(8)	9.33	9
	9.139	5
	9.182	6
	9.215	3
704(9)	9.139	6
705	9.4	2
705(a)	9.184	3
705(b)	9.184	4
706	9.134	1
	9.233	

369

TABLE OF STATUTES

UNITED STATES CODE ANNOTATED
11 U.S.C.A.—Bankruptcy

Sec.	This Work Sec.	Note
706 (Cont'd)	9.261	
706(a)	9.209	2
	9.209	4
706(b)	9.209	5
706(c)	9.209	6
706(d)	9.209	7
707(a)	9.209	8
707(a)(3)	9.209	8
707(b)	9.3	3
	9.209	9
	9.209	10
	9.210	
	9.210	2
721	9.195	1
722	9.188	
	9.188	2
723	9.194	
	9.194	1
	9.194	2
723(a)	9.194	
	9.194	1
723(c)	9.203	3
724(a)	9.129	
	9.129	4
	9.199	2
724(b)	9.199	3
	9.199	4
725	9.177	3
	9.182	11
	9.201	1
726	9.177	3
	9.182	11
	9.184	3
	9.202	
726(a)(1)	9.93	
	9.202	3
726(a)(2)	9.181	3
	9.184	
726(a)(2)(C)	9.202	4
726(a)(2)(C)(i)	9.93	5
726(a)(2)(C)(ii)	9.93	6
	9.93	10
726(a)(3)	9.181	3
726(a)(4)	9.181	3
726(b)	9.202	5
	9.202	6
727	9.3	3
	9.130	
	9.204	1
	9.208	
	9.280	
727(a)	9.169	
	9.204	
	9.205	
	9.206	
	9.207	
727(a)(1)	9.3	2
	9.177	2

UNITED STATES CODE ANNOTATED
11 U.S.C.A.—Bankruptcy

Sec.	This Work Sec.	Note
727(a)(1) (Cont'd)	9.205	1
727(a)(2)	9.205	2
727(a)(3)	9.205	3
727(a)(4)	9.205	4
727(a)(5)	9.205	5
727(a)(6)	9.205	6
727(a)(7)	9.205	7
727(a)(8)	9.205	8
727(a)(9)	9.205	9
727(a)(10)	9.205	10
	9.206	
727(b)	9.204	
	9.207	
727(c)(1)	9.206	1
727(c)(2)	9.206	2
727(d)	9.206	3
727(e)	9.206	3
728(a)	9.203	1
728(b)	9.203	2
728(c)	9.203	3
752(a)	9.181	3
766(h)	9.181	3
766(i)	9.181	3
Ch. 9	9.6	
	9.7	8
	9.16	
Ch. 11	9.1	
	9.2	
	9.2	6
	9.3	
	9.3	2
	9.3	4
	9.4	2
	9.6	
	9.7	
	9.7	3
	9.7	6
	9.7	9
	9.8	
	9.9	
	9.10	
	9.10	6
	9.11	
	9.16	
	9.19	8
	9.27	
	9.28	
	9.29	
	9.31	
	9.33	
	9.34	
	9.34	2
	9.37	
	9.42	
	9.42	1
	9.43	
	9.43	1
	9.43	13

TABLE OF STATUTES

	UNITED STATES CODE ANNOTATED 11 U.S.C.A.—Bankruptcy			UNITED STATES CODE ANNOTATED 11 U.S.C.A.—Bankruptcy	
Sec.	This Work Sec.	Note	Sec.	This Work Sec.	Note
Ch. 11 (Cont'd)	9.44		Ch. 11 (Cont'd)	9.148	4
	9.46			9.148	8
	9.48			9.149	
	9.49			9.149	3
	9.53	4		9.149	4
	9.56	5		9.150	
	9.60			9.151	
	9.62	1		9.152	
	9.63			9.153	
	9.63	3		9.154	
	9.70			9.155	
	9.71			9.156	
	9.72	2		9.157	
	9.75	1		9.158	
	9.76			9.158	3
	9.77			9.158	5
	9.91			9.159	
	9.92			9.160	
	9.93			9.160	2
	9.98			9.161	
	9.99			9.162	
	9.100	2		9.162	10
	9.101			9.163	
	9.101	4		9.164	
	9.101	6		9.165	
	9.101	8		9.166	
	9.102			9.167	
	9.103			9.168	
	9.104	3		9.169	
	9.106	7		9.170	
	9.107			9.171	
	9.107	22		9.172	
	9.108			9.173	
	9.113			9.174	
	9.114			9.174	2
	9.121			9.174	13
	9.124			9.175	
	9.125			9.176	
	9.130			9.177	
	9.130	2		9.178	
	9.130	11		9.191	
	9.133			9.198	1
	9.133	5		9.203	1
	9.134			9.205	
	9.134	1		9.207	1
	9.135			9.209	
	9.135	2		9.210	
	9.138			9.210	1
	9.139			9.213	
	9.140			9.213	1
	9.141			9.217	
	9.142			9.217	1
	9.143			9.218	
	9.144			9.222	2
	9.145			9.223	4
	9.146			9.223	6
	9.147			9.229	6
	9.148			9.234	

TABLE OF STATUTES

UNITED STATES CODE ANNOTATED 11 U.S.C.A.—Bankruptcy			UNITED STATES CODE ANNOTATED 11 U.S.C.A.—Bankruptcy		
		This Work			This Work
Sec.	Sec.	Note	Sec.	Sec.	Note
Ch. 11 (Cont'd)	9.236		1104	9.34	2
	9.240			9.198	1
	9.241			9.265	3
	9.248	1	1104(b)	9.138	8
	9.251	3	1104(b)(2)	9.140	2
	9.255		1104(c)	9.140	1
	9.258		1104(c)(2)	9.140	2
	9.261		1104(d)	9.138	7
	9.261	1		9.140	5
	9.261	6	1105	9.138	9
	9.262		1106(a)(1)	9.139	2
	9.264			9.139	3
	9.265			9.139	4
	9.275	2		9.139	5
	9.280			9.139	6
	9.282		1106(a)(2)	9.91	
	9.283			9.139	7
	9.291			9.265	2
	9.304	1	1106(a)(3)	9.139	8
	9.306			9.141	1
	9.309		1106(a)(4)	9.139	9
	9.310			9.141	2
	9.311		1106(a)(5)	9.139	10
	9.312		1106(a)(6)	9.139	11
1101	9.27	5	1106(a)(7)	9.139	12
	9.121	1	1106(b)	9.141	1
1101(1)	9.27	1		9.141	2
1101(2)	9.172			9.141	3
1102	9.4	2	1107(a)	9.27	5
	9.43	6		9.28	1
	9.43	12		9.306	
	9.44		1107(b)	9.311	
	9.48		1108	9.28	5
	9.306			9.138	6
1102(a)	9.43	14		9.306	
1102(a)(1)	9.43	1	1109(b)	9.42	
	9.43	8		9.42	1
	9.47	1		9.44	7
	9.48			9.305	
	9.48	1	1111(a)	9.91	5
1102(a)(2)	9.43	10	1111(b)	9.100	2
1102(a)(3)	9.43	5		9.156	
	9.48	1		9.156	1
	9.173	3		9.157	
1102(b)(1)	9.43	2		9.157	5
	9.43	12	1111(b)(1)(A)(i)	9.156	7
1102(c) (repealed)	9.47		1111(b)(1)(A)(ii)	9.156	3
1103	9.48		1111(b)(1)(B)	9.156	8
	9.291		1111(b)(2)	9.156	
1103(a)	9.29	4		9.157	
	9.48	2	1112	9.3	2
1103(b)	9.48	3		9.6	1
	9.48	4		9.134	1
1103(c)(1)	9.44	2		9.233	
1103(c)(2)	9.44	3		9.261	
1103(c)(3)	9.44	4	1112(a)	9.174	
1103(c)(4)	9.44	5		9.174	1
1103(c)(5)	9.44	6		9.174	3

TABLE OF STATUTES

UNITED STATES CODE ANNOTATED
11 U.S.C.A.—Bankruptcy

Sec.	This Work Sec.	Note
1112(b)	9.174	
	9.174	5
	9.174	11
1112(c)	9.174	2
1112(d)	9.174	13
1112(e)	9.174	12
	9.261	7
1112(f)	9.174	4
1113	9.86	
	9.87	
	9.163	6
	9.276	1
	9.276	2
	9.299	1
1113(b)(1)(A)	9.86	5
1113(b)(1)(B)	9.86	6
1113(b)(2)	9.86	8
	9.276	4
1113(c)	9.86	9
	9.86	10
1113(c)(1)	9.299	2
1113(c)(2)	9.299	3
1113(c)(3)	9.299	4
1113(e)	9.86	13
1114	9.87	
	9.87	3
	9.163	7
	9.291	
1114(a)	9.165	25
1114(e)(1)(B)	9.165	25
1114(g)	9.87	4
	9.165	25
1114(h)	9.87	5
1114(j)	9.88	3
1114(k)(2)	9.88	2
1121	9.2	4
	9.282	
1121—1125	9.282	1
1121(a)	9.142	1
1121(b)	9.142	1
	9.306	
	9.308	
1121(c)	9.142	2
	9.308	
1121(c)(3)	9.142	1
	9.306	
	9.308	
1121(d)	9.142	3
	9.146	
	9.281	
	9.281	1
	9.304	
	9.304	1
	9.306	
	9.307	
	9.308	
1121(e)	9.173	
	9.173	1

UNITED STATES CODE ANNOTATED
11 U.S.C.A.—Bankruptcy

Sec.	This Work Sec.	Note
1121(e)(1)	9.143	1
1121(e)(2)	9.143	2
1121(e)(3)	9.143	3
	9.143	4
1121(e)(3)(B)	9.304	1
1122	9.153	
	9.164	
	9.282	
1122(a)	9.107	3
	9.152	
	9.152	1
	9.154	
	9.154	1
1122(b)	9.155	
	9.155	1
1123	9.147	1
	9.164	
	9.282	
1123(a)	9.147	
	9.147	1
1123(a)(1)	9.148	1
1123(a)(2)	9.148	
	9.148	5
	9.158	5
1123(a)(3)	9.148	7
1123(a)(4)	9.148	8
	9.152	2
1123(a)(5)	9.148	9
1123(a)(6)	9.148	10
1123(a)(7)	9.148	11
1123(b)	9.147	
1123(b)(1)	9.149	1
1123(b)(2)	9.76	3
	9.149	2
1123(b)(3)	9.149	3
1123(b)(4)	9.6	1
	9.149	4
1123(b)(5)	9.101	6
	9.149	5
	9.223	4
1124	9.103	
	9.158	
	9.158	3
	9.159	
	9.160	
1124(1)	9.159	1
1124(2)	9.160	2
1124(2)(B)	9.160	4
1124(3)	9.160	
	9.160	6
1124(3) (repealed)	9.160	5
1125	9.161	
	9.161	2
	9.164	
	9.282	
1125(a)	9.163	
1125(a)(1)	9.161	
	9.161	4

373

TABLE OF STATUTES

UNITED STATES CODE ANNOTATED
11 U.S.C.A.—Bankruptcy

Sec.	This Work Sec.	Note
1125(b)	9.161	9
	9.161	11
	9.283	3
1125(c)	9.161	13
1125(d)	9.161	5
1125(f)	9.173	
1125(f)(3)	9.161	13
	9.173	4
1126	9.162	
	9.163	2
	9.283	1
1126(a)	9.153	2
1126(b)	9.163	1
	9.163	2
	9.282	
1126(c)	9.153	3
	9.162	2
	9.162	3
	9.162	9
1126(d)	9.153	3
	9.162	4
	9.162	9
1126(e)	9.162	
	9.162	8
	9.162	10
1126(f)	9.153	2
	9.158	1
	9.162	12
1126(g)	9.153	2
	9.162	13
1127	9.164	
	9.283	4
1127(a)	9.164	
	9.164	1
	9.164	3
1127(b)	9.164	
	9.164	6
1127(c)	9.164	2
1127(d)	9.164	4
1129	9.154	
1129(a)	9.42	3
	9.165	
	9.166	
	9.166	2
1129(a)(1)	9.148	
	9.153	6
	9.158	5
	9.165	1
1129(a)(2)	9.165	2
1129(a)(3)	9.165	3
1129(a)(4)	9.165	4
1129(a)(5)	9.165	5
1129(a)(6)	9.165	6
1129(a)(7)	9.160	
1129(a)(7)(A)	9.165	7
1129(a)(7)(B)	9.156	5
1129(a)(8)	9.157	3
	9.165	8

UNITED STATES CODE ANNOTATED
11 U.S.C.A.—Bankruptcy

Sec.	This Work Sec.	Note
1129(a)(8) (Cont'd)	9.166	1
1129(a)(9)(A)	9.165	12
1129(a)(9)(B)(i)	9.165	17
1129(a)(9)(B)(ii)	9.165	18
1129(a)(9)(C)	9.165	19
1129(a)(10)	9.153	4
	9.158	2
	9.165	20
1129(a)(11)	9.165	22
1129(a)(12)	9.165	24
	9.165	26
1129(b)	9.160	
	9.165	
	9.166	
1129(b)(1)	9.107	5
	9.157	3
	9.158	2
	9.166	3
1129(b)(2)	9.107	4
	9.166	
	9.166	6
	9.166	7
1129(b)(2)(A)(i)(II)	9.156	5
1129(b)(2)(A)(iii)	9.166	9
1129(b)(2)(B)(ii)	9.166	11
1141	9.167	
	9.280	
1141(a)	9.167	1
1141(b)	9.167	3
1141(c)	9.101	4
	9.167	4
1141(d)	9.91	10
	9.168	
1141(d)(1)(A)	9.168	1
1141(d)(2)	9.169	1
1141(d)(3)	9.3	2
	9.3	3
	9.169	3
1141(d)(3)(C)	9.177	2
1142	9.148	
	9.151	
	9.151	2
	9.312	
1142(a)	9.148	12
1145	9.150	
	9.150	1
1146	9.312	
1146(c)	9.3	
	9.294	
Ch. 12	9.1	
	9.2	
	9.2	6
	9.3	
	9.6	
	9.7	
	9.7	6
	9.8	
	9.16	

TABLE OF STATUTES

UNITED STATES CODE ANNOTATED
11 U.S.C.A.—Bankruptcy

Sec.	This Work Sec.	Note
Ch. 12 (Cont'd)	9.27	
	9.28	
	9.31	
	9.31	9
	9.32	
	9.33	
	9.34	
	9.34	3
	9.37	
	9.42	
	9.43	1
	9.43	3
	9.49	
	9.60	
	9.63	
	9.63	3
	9.70	
	9.71	
	9.76	
	9.77	
	9.91	
	9.92	
	9.93	
	9.99	
	9.103	
	9.104	3
	9.107	
	9.113	
	9.121	
	9.125	
	9.130	
	9.130	2
	9.134	
	9.134	1
	9.135	
	9.135	2
	9.138	8
	9.139	
	9.169	
	9.174	
	9.174	13
	9.175	
	9.191	
	9.203	1
	9.205	
	9.207	1
	9.209	
	9.209	6
	9.210	
	9.212	
	9.212	1
	9.213	
	9.214	
	9.214	1
	9.215	
	9.216	
	9.217	
	9.217	1

UNITED STATES CODE ANNOTATED
11 U.S.C.A.—Bankruptcy

Sec.	This Work Sec.	Note
Ch. 12 (Cont'd)	9.217	2
	9.218	
	9.220	
	9.220	1
	9.221	
	9.222	
	9.222	2
	9.223	
	9.223	4
	9.224	
	9.224	2
	9.225	
	9.226	
	9.227	
	9.228	
	9.229	
	9.229	6
	9.230	
	9.230	1
	9.231	
	9.232	
	9.233	
	9.234	
	9.234	
	9.235	
	9.236	
	9.240	1
	9.241	
	9.243	
	9.245	1
	9.247	
	9.248	5
	9.251	3
	9.261	
	9.262	
	9.264	
	9.265	
	9.275	2
	9.284	
	9.284	1
	9.285	
	9.285	1
	9.286	
	9.286	1
	9.291	
1201	9.25	
	9.216	
	9.216	1
1201(a)	9.216	3
1201(b)	9.216	1
1201(c)	9.216	4
1201(d)	9.216	5
1202	9.34	3
	9.214	1
1202(b)(1)	9.215	1
	9.215	2
	9.215	3
1202(b)(2)	9.215	7

375

TABLE OF STATUTES

UNITED STATES CODE ANNOTATED
11 U.S.C.A.—Bankruptcy

Sec.	This Work Sec.	Note
1202(b)(3)	9.215	4
1202(b)(3)(D)	9.215	5
	9.240	2
1202(b)(4)	9.215	6
1202(b)(5)	9.215	
1203	9.27	5
	9.28	1
	9.213	1
	9.214	3
1204	9.214	4
	9.217	
1205(a)	9.219	1
1205(b)	9.219	3
1206	9.63	3
	9.218	
	9.218	3
1207	9.49	6
	9.217	
1207(a)	9.217	2
1207(b)	9.217	3
1208	9.134	1
	9.261	
1208(a)	9.233	1
1208(b)	9.233	2
1208(c)	9.233	3
1208(c)(3)	9.220	4
1208(d)	9.220	5
	9.233	4
1221	9.2	3
	9.217	1
	9.220	1
	9.220	3
	9.284	2
1221—1222	9.284	1
1222	9.221	
	9.224	
1222(a)	9.222	3
	9.230	2
1222(b)	9.223	1
	9.223	8
	9.230	2
1222(b)(1)	9.223	2
	9.223	3
1222(b)(2)	9.223	4
1222(b)(4)	9.223	6
1222(b)(5)	9.229	
1222(b)(6)	9.76	3
1222(b)(10)	9.229	
1222(c)	9.223	9
	9.226	
	9.226	2
1222(d)	9.223	5
1223	9.286	1
1223(a)	9.224	1
1223(c)	9.224	2
	9.230	2
1224	9.217	1
	9.225	1

UNITED STATES CODE ANNOTATED
11 U.S.C.A.—Bankruptcy

Sec.	This Work Sec.	Note
1224 (Cont'd)	9.225	2
1225(a)	9.225	4
	9.230	2
1225(a)(5)	9.223	
1225(b)(1)	9.226	3
1225(b)(2)	9.226	4
1225(c)	9.226	5
1226	9.227	1
1227(a)	9.228	2
1227(b)	9.228	3
1227(c)	9.228	4
1228	9.229	
	9.280	
1228(a)	9.229	2
1228(a)(1)	9.229	6
1228(a)(2)	9.229	6
1228(b)	9.229	4
1228(c)	9.91	10
	9.229	6
1228(d)	9.229	7
1229	9.232	
	9.286	
1229(a)	9.230	1
1229(b)(1)	9.230	2
1229(c)	9.230	3
1230	9.232	1
1230(b)	9.232	2
1231(a)	9.231	1
1231(b)	9.231	2
1231(c)	9.231	3
1231(d)	9.231	4
Ch. 13	9.1	
	9.2	
	9.2	6
	9.3	
	9.6	
	9.6	3
	9.6	4
	9.6	5
	9.7	
	9.7	6
	9.8	
	9.16	
	9.27	
	9.28	
	9.28	4
	9.31	
	9.31	9
	9.32	
	9.33	
	9.34	
	9.34	3
	9.37	
	9.42	
	9.43	1
	9.43	3
	9.49	
	9.60	

TABLE OF STATUTES

UNITED STATES CODE ANNOTATED 11 U.S.C.A.—Bankruptcy			UNITED STATES CODE ANNOTATED 11 U.S.C.A.—Bankruptcy		
Sec.	This Work Sec.	Note	Sec.	This Work Sec.	Note
Ch. 13 (Cont'd)	9.63		Ch. 13 (Cont'd)	9.247	
	9.63	3		9.248	
	9.70			9.249	
	9.71			9.249	6
	9.76			9.250	
	9.77			9.251	
	9.91			9.251	2
	9.92			9.251	3
	9.93			9.252	
	9.99			9.253	
	9.101			9.254	
	9.101	6		9.255	
	9.103			9.256	
	9.104	3		9.257	
	9.107			9.259	3
	9.113			9.261	
	9.121			9.261	1
	9.125			9.262	
	9.130			9.263	
	9.130	2		9.264	
	9.134			9.264	8
	9.134	1		9.265	
	9.135			9.275	2
	9.135	2		9.284	
	9.135	8		9.284	1
	9.138	8		9.285	
	9.139			9.285	1
	9.160	2		9.286	
	9.167	4		9.286	1
	9.174			9.291	
	9.174	13		11.37	6
	9.175		1301	9.25	
	9.191			9.241	2
	9.205		1301(a)	9.241	3
	9.207	1	1301(a)(1)	9.241	5
	9.207	2	1301(b)	9.241	5
	9.208	2	1301(c)	9.242	1
	9.209		1302	9.34	3
	9.209	6		9.239	1
	9.209	9	1302(b)	9.240	1
	9.210		1302(b)(2)	9.240	2
	9.214	1	1302(b)(4)	9.240	3
	9.217	2	1303	9.28	2
	9.223	4		9.238	1
	9.223	5		9.240	2
	9.230	1		9.244	
	9.234			9.244	1
	9.236			9.244	3
	9.237		1304	9.27	5
	9.238			9.28	2
	9.239		1304(a)	9.237	2
	9.240	1	1304(b)	9.237	2
	9.242		1304(c)	9.237	2
	9.243		1305	9.248	
	9.244		1305(b)	9.248	7
	9.245		1306	9.49	6
	9.245	1	1306(a)	9.217	2
	9.246			9.243	1

377

TABLE OF STATUTES

UNITED STATES CODE ANNOTATED
11 U.S.C.A.—Bankruptcy

Sec.	This Work Sec.	Note
1307	9.134	1
	9.260	
1307(a)	9.261	1
1307(b)	9.261	2
	9.261	3
1307(c)	9.261	4
	9.261	7
1307(c)(9)	9.261	7
1307(d)	9.261	8
1307(e)	9.261	5
1321	9.2	3
	9.245	1
	9.284	3
1321—1322	9.284	1
1322	9.246	
	9.250	
1322(a)(1)	9.247	1
1322(a)(2)	9.247	3
1322(a)(3)	9.247	4
1322(b)	9.249	5
1322(b)(1)	9.248	1
	9.248	2
1322(b)(2)	9.6	5
	9.101	6
	9.223	4
	9.248	
	9.248	3
	9.249	
1322(b)(3)	9.248	4
1322(b)(4)	9.248	5
1322(b)(5)	9.248	6
	9.249	
	9.256	
1322(b)(6)	9.248	7
1322(b)(7)	9.76	3
	9.248	8
1322(b)(8)	9.248	9
1322(b)(9)	9.248	10
1322(b)(10)	9.248	11
1322(c)	9.6	4
1322(c)(1)	9.249	7
1322(c)(2)	9.249	13
1322(d)	9.248	12
	9.249	5
	9.249	
1322(e)	9.249	
	9.249	10
1323	9.250	2
	9.286	1
1323(a)	9.250	1
1324	9.251	1
1325(a)	9.251	4
1325(a)(3)	9.255	2
	9.255	8
1325(a)(4)	9.251	2
1325(a)(5)	9.249	
1325(a)(5)(B)	9.251	3
1325(a)(5)(B)(ii)	9.250	9
1325(b)	9.252	2

UNITED STATES CODE ANNOTATED
11 U.S.C.A.—Bankruptcy

Sec.	This Work Sec.	Note
1325(c)	9.252	3
1326(a)(1)	9.254	1
1326(a)(2)	9.254	2
1326(c)	9.254	3
1327	9.253	3
1327(a)	9.253	1
1327(b)	9.253	2
1328	9.280	
1328(a)	9.255	1
	9.255	3
	9.256	3
1328(b)	9.256	5
	9.257	
1328(c)	9.256	6
	9.258	1
	9.91	10
1328(c)(1)	9.249	6
1328(d)	9.256	4
1329	9.286	
1329(a)	9.259	1
1329(b)(1)	9.259	2
1329(c)	9.259	3
1330	9.260	2
1330(a)	9.260	1
1330(b)	9.260	3
7004	9.309	
7004(a)	9.310	

12 U.S.C.A.—Banks and Banking

Sec.	This Work Sec.	Note
7512	15.20	3

15 U.S.C.A.—Commerce and Trade

Sec.	This Work Sec.	Note
45(a)(1)	7.45	4
77b(1)	2.106	2
78 et seq.	1.39	17
78a et seq.	1.89	14
78l	1.31	1
	1.46	3
78n(d)	1.89	9
79et seq.	1.78	1
80a–1 et seq.	1.39	16
	1.56	10
	1.103	6
1011 et seq.	31.4	5
1334	27.46	7
1334(b)	27.46	3
	27.46	4
1397(c)	27.45	1
1397(k)	27.45	4
1601 et seq.	7.3	5
	7.21	1
	7.21	7

378

TABLE OF STATUTES

UNITED STATES CODE ANNOTATED
15 U.S.C.A.—Commerce and Trade

Sec.	This Work Sec.	Note
1601 et seq. (Cont'd)	7.23	2
	7.24	7
	7.26	15
	7.36	2
1637	7.23	26
1640(a)(1)	7.21	12
1640(a)(2)(A)(ii)	7.21	13
1640(a)(3)	7.21	14
1667	7.20	4
	7.22	8
1667(1)	7.21	2
	7.21	3
	7.21	4
	7.21	8
1667(c)	7.21	14
1667b(b)	7.22	30
1667d(a)	7.21	9
1674	17.38	
1681	7.3	8
1681 et seq.	7.1	6
	7.31	1
	7.60	
	8.2	1
1681(d)	7.60	
1681(f)	7.60	
1681(p)	7.60	
1681a et seq.	17.42	2
1681a(c)	7.60	
1681b	7.30	
	7.31	6
1681b(2)	7.31	6
1681b(3)(E)	7.31	6
1681c	7.31	5
1681c(a)(1)	7.31	5
1681c(a)(2)—(6)	7.31	5
1681c(b)	7.31	5
1681e(a)	7.31	5
1681e(b)	7.31	7
	7.31	12
	7.33	2
	7.60	
1681i	7.31	12
	7.32	
1681i(a)	7.31	8
	7.33	3
	7.60	
1681i(b)	7.33	
1681i(b)—(c)	7.31	9
	7.33	4
1681i(d)	7.31	9
1681j	7.32	2
1681m(a)	7.32	1
1681n	7.31	6
	7.33	6
	7.60	
1681o	7.31	6
	7.33	5
	7.60	

UNITED STATES CODE ANNOTATED
15 U.S.C.A.—Commerce and Trade

Sec.	This Work Sec.	Note
1681p	7.33	6
1681q	7.31	6
1681t	7.33	13
1692 et seq.	7.1	7
	7.3	7
	7.6	1
	7.25	2
	7.26	16
	7.36	1
	7.62	
	8.2	1
1692a(3)	7.62	
1692a(5)	7.36	4
	7.62	
1692a(6)	7.36	5
	7.36	6
	7.36	8
	7.62	
1692a(6)(F)	7.36	10
1692a(7)	7.37	2
1692b	7.37	2
	7.37	3
1692b(6)	7.38	7
	7.38	10
1692c	7.6	4
1692c(a)(1)	7.38	4
	7.38	5
1692c(a)(2)	7.38	7
	7.38	8
1692c(a)(3)	7.38	6
1692c(b)	7.37	1
	7.38	10
	7.40	4
1692c(c)	7.6	3
	7.38	8
	7.38	10
	7.62	
1692d	7.41	1
	7.62	
1692d(1)	7.41	2
1692d(2)	7.41	3
1692d(4)	7.41	7
1692d(5)	7.41	4
1692d(6)	7.39	2
	7.41	5
1692e	7.39	1
1692e(1)	7.39	2
1692e(2)	7.42	2
1692e(2)(A)	7.39	6
	7.62	
1692e(2)(B)	7.62	
1692e(3)	7.39	2
	7.39	5
1692e(4)	7.25	11
	7.41	6
1692e(5)	7.25	11
	7.39	7
	7.42	2

379

TABLE OF STATUTES

UNITED STATES CODE ANNOTATED
15 U.S.C.A.—Commerce and Trade

Sec.	This Work Sec.	Note
1692e(5) (Cont'd)	7.62	
1692e(6)(A)—(B)	7.41	8
1692e(8)	7.32	6
	7.40	4
	7.62	
1692e(9)	7.39	4
	7.62	
1692e(10)	7.25	11
	7.62	
1692e(11)	7.40	1
	7.62	
1692e(13)	7.62	
1692e(14)	7.39	2
	7.39	3
1692f(1)	7.42	2
	7.43	
	7.62	
1692f(2)—(3)	7.42	1
1692f(5)	7.42	3
1692f(7)—(8)	7.40	3
1692f(8)	7.40	2
1692g	7.6	1
	7.38	10
1692g(a)	7.38	9
1692g(b)	7.38	10
	7.40	4
1692i(a)(2)	7.39	7
1692k	7.62	
1692k(a)	7.43	2
1692k(a)(1)	7.62	
1692k(a)(2)(A)	7.62	
1692k(a)(3)	7.62	
1692k(c)	7.43	3
1692k(d)	7.43	1
1692m(g)	7.43	2
1693e(10)	7.62	
1861i(a)	7.31	
1901	7.3	6
	7.12	4
1980 et seq.	7.53	
1981—1991	7.3	6
	7.12	4
1985(2)	17.38	
1988(b)	7.53	
1989(a)(1)	7.53	
2622	17.38	
2681 et seq.	12.80	1

17 U.S.C.A.—Copyrights

Sec.	This Work Sec.	Note
106A	12.1	7
301(b)(3)	18.63	7

18 U.S.C.A.—Crimes and Criminal Procedure

Sec.	This Work Sec.	Note
706	1.13	1

UNITED STATES CODE ANNOTATED
18 U.S.C.A.—Crimes and Criminal Procedure

Sec.	This Work Sec.	Note
2510—2520	17.55	6
2511	30.38	
2520	30.38	

20 U.S.C.A.—Education

Sec.	This Work Sec.	Note
1400 et seq.	18.53	5
1415	18.53	5
1415(e)(2)	18.53	6
1415(f)	18.53	5
1681—1688	18.53	
3608	17.38	

21 U.S.C.A.—Food and Drugs

Sec.	This Work Sec.	Note
352	27.13	12
360 et seq.	27.48	2

22 U.S.C.A.—Foreign Relations and Intercourse

Sec.	This Work Sec.	Note
4060	9.125	21

25 U.S.C.A.—Indians

Sec.	This Work Sec.	Note
1901—1963	20.50	
	20.50	3
	20.69	5
	20.69	6
	20.137	
	20.139	
1911(a)	20.50	4
1912(f)	20.50	6
1915	20.50	7

26 U.S.C.A.—Internal Revenue Code

Sec.	This Work Sec.	Note
Chs. 11—13	24.1	
1	1.2	15
1 et seq.	24.1	2
1(e)	24.74	3
1(g)	24.50	3
1(h)	1.108	1
	6.117	1
	35.6	7
11	1.2	15
11(b)	1.81	1

380

TABLE OF STATUTES

UNITED STATES CODE ANNOTATED
26 U.S.C.A.—Internal Revenue Code

Sec.	Sec.	This Work Note
56	35.33	
57	35.13	
	35.33	
58	35.33	
61	1.30	3
	1.34	28
	24.79	1
61(a)(1)	1.34	28
61(a)(3)	1.34	27
62	35.5	1
62(a)(1)	35.5	2
62(a)(2)	35.5	3
62(a)(3)	35.5	4
62(a)(4)	35.5	5
62(a)(6)	35.5	6
62(a)(7)	35.5	6
62(a)(10)	35.5	7
62(a)(15)	35.5	8
63	35.6	1
63(b)	23.115	2
63(c)(3)	23.115	3
	23.115	4
63(c)(4)	23.115	5
63(c)(5)	23.115	6
	23.116	7
63(f)	23.115	3
	23.115	4
63(f)(1)	23.115	3
	23.115	4
63(f)(4)	23.115	3
	23.115	4
67	35.6	6
71(a)	21.51	1
71(b)(1)(B)	21.51	2
78	35.20	
	35.24	
	35.28	
78(c)(3)	35.24	
83	1.30	3
	1.34	28
	1.34	64
	1.34	65
83(b)	1.34	68
83(h)	1.34	69
103	3.27	7
	3.34	10
104(a)(2)	17.14	
	17.14	1
121	23.117	
	23.117	3
	24.48	2
	24.48	5
121(a)	23.117	2
	23.117	4
121(b)(3)	23.117	1
141—150	3.34	10
148	3.27	9
151	23.115	1

UNITED STATES CODE ANNOTATED
26 U.S.C.A.—Internal Revenue Code

Sec.	Sec.	This Work Note
151 (Cont'd)	23.118	3
152	23.118	3
152(c)	23.118	3
162	1.2	
	1.9	1
	35.6	6
162(a)	1.21	26
162(a)(1)	1.40	18
163	1.2	
	24.57	5
	35.6	4
163(a)	1.34	
	1.40	7
163(d)	1.40	7
163(e)	1.40	7
164	1.34	
	35.6	2
	35.6	4
165	1.34	
165(f)	1.108	1
165(g)	1.34	51
	1.108	1
165(g)(2)	1.34	50
167	1.9	1
	6.34	1
	6.119	1
167—168	6.34	4
170	35.6	5
170(b)(1)(A)(ii)	24.49	
170(c)	24.32	3
170(f)(2)(A)	24.32	5
170(f)(2)(B)	24.55	1
	24.55	2
	24.55	3
171	1.34	72
171(b)(1)	1.34	72
174	1.34	
179	6.34	5
	6.40	
	6.57	2
195	1.34	
	1.34	15
195(a)	1.21	26
	1.34	9
195(b)	1.34	10
195(b)(2)	1.34	11
195(c)(1)	1.34	14
195(c)(1)(A)	1.34	12
195(c)(1)(B)	1.34	13
195(c)(2)(A)	1.34	15
195(c)(2)(B)	1.34	16
195(d)(1)	1.34	10
195(d)(2)	1.34	10
197	6.36	
	6.36	2
	6.40	
212	1.9	1
	35.6	6

TABLE OF STATUTES

UNITED STATES CODE ANNOTATED
26 U.S.C.A.—Internal Revenue Code

Sec.	Sec.	This Work Note
213	23.118	
	23.118	1
	23.118	3
	35.6	3
213(a)	24.76	2
213(a)(1)(C)	23.118	3
213(c)	24.76	1
213(d)	24.49	
213(d)(i)	23.68	7
216	12.77	
217	35.5	
219(a)	23.32	2
248	1.30	11
	1.34	
	1.34	15
248(a)	1.21	26
	1.34	2
248(b)	1.34	4
248(c)	1.34	3
249	1.34	72
267	2.40	3
269	1.81	1
269A(a)	1.34	25
269A(b)(1)	1.34	22
	1.34	23
269A(b)(2)	1.34	24
280A	24.47	
	24.47	5
301	1.40	
	1.40	9
	1.74	2
301(c)(1)	1.40	1
301(c)(2)	1.40	2
301(c)(3)	1.40	3
302(a)	1.40	11
302(b)	1.40	
	1.40	15
302(c)(2)	1.40	11
302(d)	1.40	12
303	24.97	
303(a)	1.40	11
	24.40	7
303(b)	24.40	7
304(a)	1.40	11
305	1.40	9
305(a)	1.34	61
	1.40	4
305(b)	1.40	4
	1.40	8
305(c)	1.40	9
	1.74	2
305(d)	1.34	61
306(a)	1.40	11
307	1.40	10
311(a)	1.40	5
311(b)	1.40	6
316(a)	1.40	1
318(a)	1.40	11

UNITED STATES CODE ANNOTATED
26 U.S.C.A.—Internal Revenue Code

Sec.	Sec.	This Work Note
331	1.108	1
	2.40	4
332	1.108	3
334(a)	1.108	1
334(b)	1.108	5
336(a)	1.108	2
336(a)	2.40	3
336(d)	2.40	3
337	1.108	5
338	6.41	
	6.44	
	6.44	1
338(b)(5)	6.33	2
	6.118	2
338(g)	6.44	2
341	6.132	
	6.132	1
351	1.34	
	1.34	27
	1.34	28
	1.34	47
351(a)	1.34	
	1.34	49
351(b)	1.34	33
	1.34	34
	1.34	35
351(c)	1.34	32
351(d)	1.34	28
354	1.91	4
	6.45	1
	6.45	3
	6.133	1
355	1.91	4
	6.45	1
	6.133	1
356	1.91	4
357(a)	1.34	36
357(b)	1.34	37
357(c)	1.34	37
358(a)(1)(A)(i)—(ii)	1.34	38
358(a)(1)(B)	1.34	39
358(a)(2)	1.34	40
358(d)	1.34	38
361	6.45	1
	6.45	4
	6.133	1
362	1.34	43
362(a)(1)	1.34	46
	1.34	47
368	1.78	1
	6.45	
	6.45	1
	6.133	
	6.133	1
368(a)	6.45	
	6.133	
368(a)(1)	1.122	36
368(a)(1)(A)	1.91	1

TABLE OF STATUTES

UNITED STATES CODE ANNOTATED
26 U.S.C.A.—Internal Revenue Code

Sec.	This Work Sec.	Note
368(a)(1)(B)	1.91	2
368(a)(1)(C)	1.91	3
368(a)(1)(D)	1.91	4
368(a)(1)(E)	1.74	2
	1.91	5
368(a)(1)(F)	1.91	6
368(a)(1)(G)	1.78	3
	1.91	7
368(a)(2)(B)	1.91	3
368(a)(2)(B)(iii)	1.91	3
368(a)(2)(C)	1.91	1
	1.91	2
	1.91	3
368(a)(2)(D)	1.91	1
368(a)(2)(E)	1.91	1
368(c)	1.34	29
	1.34	30
	1.88	1
	1.91	2
385	1.26	4
385(b)	1.40	8
401	8.20	6
	9.49	1
401 et seq.	23.24	1
	24.37	1
401(a)	9.49	1
401(a)(9)	23.27	1
401(a)(9)(B)(iii)	24.37	9
402(a)(1)	23.32	1
	23.33	1
402(q)(1)	23.26	1
408	23.33	1
408(d)(3)	24.37	3
414	23.28	1
422	1.34	63
	1.34	70
441(f)	24.77	1
453	6.119	3
	6.135	2
	24.43	1
	24.57	4
454(a)	24.75	1
482	1.34	21
501	12.88	6
	12.89	5
501(c)(3)	19.41	
	19.41	1
531—533	1.2	16
533(a)	1.9	1
533(b)	1.9	1
537	1.2	16
541	1.122	5
541—547	1.122	5
543(a)	1.122	5
543(a)(6)	1.122	5
543(a)(7)	1.122	5
642(c)(2)	24.54	6
642(g)	24.76	2

UNITED STATES CODE ANNOTATED
26 U.S.C.A.—Internal Revenue Code

Sec.	This Work Sec.	Note
643	24.74	2
663(a)	24.11	1
664(d)(1)(A)	24.54	2
664(d)(2)(A)	24.54	4
671	24.46	5
	24.55	3
671—677	24.48	1
674	24.81	2
674(a)	23.117	3
676	24.81	2
677	24.81	2
691	24.37	
	24.43	3
691(a)	24.74	1
691(a)(2)	24.43	4
691(a)(5)	24.43	4
691(c)	24.37	2
701 et seq.	6.42	2
708(b)(1)(B)	2.11	10
709	1.34	15
721	2.11	6
	2.40	2
722	2.11	
743	6.41	
	6.41	2
752	2.11	
752(b)	2.11	7
754	2.112	
	6.41	
	6.41	2
856	12.87	
861(a)(5)	12.76	2
871(a)	19.2	3
871(b)	19.2	3
897	12.76	2
	19.2	3
911	19.74	4
951—958	1.34	30
1001(a)	1.108	1
1001(a)—(c)	1.34	27
1001(c)	1.34	
	1.34	28
	1.108	1
1012	1.34	45
	1.34	47
1014	1.34	
	24.40	8
	24.73	4
1014(e)	24.83	4
1031	6.4	
	6.45	
	6.45	2
	6.45	6
	6.133	
1031(a)(2)(A)	6.45	11
1032	1.34	28
	1.34	41
	1.34	42

TABLE OF STATUTES

UNITED STATES CODE ANNOTATED
26 U.S.C.A.—Internal Revenue Code

Sec.	This Work Sec.	Note
1032(a)	1.40	16
1034	12.77	
	24.47	
1034(a)	23.117	3
1034(a)(2)	24.40	9
1041(a)	21.45	2
1041(b)(1)	21.45	3
1041(b)(2)	21.45	4
1041(c)	21.45	5
1060	6.33	
	6.34	3
	6.118	
	6.118	2
	6.121	
1201 et seq.	6.120	1
1202	6.130	4
1202(a)	1.34	52
1211	6.130	1
	35.5	4
1212	35.5	4
1221	1.9	1
	1.34	40
	6.120	3
1222(10)	1.108	1
1222(11)	1.108	1
1223(1)	1.34	40
1223(2)	1.34	43
1223(11)	24.48	4
1231	1.9	1
	1.34	40
	6.120	
	6.120	2
1244	1.34	52
	6.130	2
	6.130	3
	35.32	
1245	6.119	2
1250	6.119	2
1253(d)(1)	6.40	1
1271—1288	1.34	72
1272	1.34	74
1274(d)(1)	24.46	
1311—1314	35.57	
1361	1.2	21
1361—1363	1.34	53
1361 et seq.	6.42	1
1361(b)(1)(A)	2.2	5
1361(b)(1)(D)	1.2	26
1361(b)(2)	2.2	4
1361(c)(4)	1.2	27
1361(d)	2.2	4
1374	2.40	3
	6.122	1
1401	2.23	9
1402(a)	2.23	9
1402(a)(13)	2.23	9
1445	12.76	
1446	12.76	2

UNITED STATES CODE ANNOTATED
26 U.S.C.A.—Internal Revenue Code

Sec.	This Work Sec.	Note
1504	1.88	1
1504(a)(2)	1.108	4
1561	1.81	1
2001	24.18	1
	24.19	1
2001(b)	24.18	3
2001(c)(2)	24.19	2
2010	24.18	2
	24.21	1
2010(a)	24.18	5
2011	24.19	3
	24.23	1
	24.44	3
2013	24.22	13
2031	24.73	1
2032(a)	24.73	2
2032(c)	24.73	3
2032A	24.42	1
	24.97	
2032A(b)(1)(C)	24.42	4
2032A(b)(2)	24.42	2
2032A(e)	24.42	3
2033A	24.38	1
2035(c)	24.44	2
	24.56	3
2035(d)	24.56	1
2035(d)(2)	24.34	2
	24.35	2
2036	24.81	3
2036(a)	24.21	3
2038	24.81	3
2040	24.83	4
2041	24.21	3
	24.25	5
2041(b)	24.35	3
2041(b)(1)(A)	24.89	5
2041(b)(2)	24.89	5
2042	24.34	1
2053(a)(2)	24.79	2
2055	24.32	
2055(a)	24.32	3
2055(e)(2)(B)	24.55	1
2056	24.97	
2056(a)	24.22	3
	24.37	4
2056(b)	24.22	3
	24.22	4
	24.72	2
2056(b)(3)	24.22	9
2056(b)(5)	24.22	10
2056(b)(6)	24.22	8
2056(b)(7)	24.22	5
2056(b)(7)(B)(i)(II)	24.37	8
2056(b)(7)(B)(ii)(I)	24.37	8
2056(d)	24.22	1
	24.58	3
2056(d)(2)	24.58	4
2056A(a)	24.58	5

384

TABLE OF STATUTES

UNITED STATES CODE ANNOTATED
26 U.S.C.A.—Internal Revenue Code

Sec.	This Work Sec.	Note
2056A(b)	24.58	6
2056A(b)(3)	24.58	7
2056A(b)(12)	24.58	8
2207A	24.10	
2501(a)	19.2	3
2502	24.18	1
	24.19	1
2503(b)	24.36	1
	24.49	1
2503(b)(2)	24.49	1
2503(c)	24.50	
	24.50	6
	24.51	
	24.97	
2503(c)(1)	24.50	1
2503(c)(2)	24.50	2
2503(e)	24.49	
2503(e)(2)(b)	23.118	3
2505	24.18	2
	24.21	1
2505(a)	24.18	5
2512	24.46	3
2513(a)	24.49	1
2514(c)	24.69	2
2518	24.71	
	24.71	1
2518(a)	24.68	1
2518(b)	24.68	
	24.68	3
2518(c)	24.68	4
2522(c)(2)(B)	24.55	1
2523(i)	24.22	1
	24.49	3
	24.58	2
2572	24.32	6
2603(a)(1)	24.27	3
2603(a)(2)	24.25	2
2603(a)(3)	24.26	3
2611	24.24	3
2612	24.24	3
2612(a)(1)	24.25	3
2612(b)	24.27	1
2612(c)	24.26	1
	24.28	3
2613	24.24	3
2613(a)	24.25	1
2613(b)	24.25	1
2631(a)	24.30	2
2631(c)	24.30	1
2641(a)	24.30	5
2641(a)(1)	24.24	2
2642(a)	24.30	6
2642(b)	24.30	3
2642(c)	24.24	3
2651(b)	24.28	1
2651(c)	24.28	2
2651(d)	24.28	4
	24.28	5

UNITED STATES CODE ANNOTATED
26 U.S.C.A.—Internal Revenue Code

Sec.	This Work Sec.	Note
2651(e)	24.28	3
2652(a)(2)	24.30	4
2652(a)(3)	24.31	1
2652(c)	24.25	6
	24.26	2
2653	24.29	1
2701	24.41	2
2702	24.46	3
2702(a)(1)	24.46	3
2702(c)(2)	24.46	3
2702(e)	24.46	3
2703	24.39	
	24.41	2
2704	24.41	2
2704(c)(2)	24.46	3
4974(a)	24.37	7
4975	6.188	
4980A(d)(5)	24.37	6
4980B	17.12	1
5081	36.4	12
5091	36.4	12
5111	36.4	12
	36.11	19
5121	36.4	12
6012(a)	23.114	1
6012(b)(1)	24.78	1
6013	24.78	1
6013(a)	35.11	1
6039(c)	12.76	2
6039C	12.76	1
6045(c)	12.77	
6050I	12.79	1
6166	24.97	
6166(a)(1)	24.40	1
6166(a)(2)	24.40	2
6166(a)(3)	24.40	3
6166(b)(6)	24.40	1
6166(j)	24.40	3
6166(j)(2)	24.40	5
6231(a)(7)	2.112	
6652(g)	12.76	2
6662	2.4	
6672	2.23	
	2.23	13
6672(a)	2.23	13
6721	12.77	
6722	12.77	
6723	12.77	
6851	35.112	2
	35.112	4
6861	35.112	4
7203	12.77	
	35.122	2
7206	12.77	
7207	12.77	
7520	24.46	
	24.46	2
	24.46	5

385

TABLE OF STATUTES

UNITED STATES CODE ANNOTATED
26 U.S.C.A.—Internal Revenue Code

Sec.	This Work Sec.	Note
7520 (Cont'd)	24.46	6
	24.47	
7701	2.4	
	19.2	3
7701(b)	19.74	3
7702B	23.68	6
	23.68	8
	23.118	
7702B(e)(10)	23.118	7
7702B(g)	23.68	10
7702B(g)(3)	23.68	9
7704	2.2	
	2.4	1

27 U.S.C.A.—Intoxicating Liquors

Sec.	This Work Sec.	Note
201—219a	36.4	5
203	36.4	11

28 U.S.C.A.—Judiciary and Judicial Procedure

Sec.	This Work Sec.	Note
Ch. 123	9.106	
	9.209	
	9.227	
	9.233	
	9.251	
151	9.19	
157	9.18	2
	9.288	2
	9.310	
157(a)	9.19	
	9.309	
157(b)	9.310	
157(b)(1)	9.19	
157(b)(2)	9.308	
157(b)(2)(A)	9.309	
157(b)(2)(E)	9.309	
157(b)(2)(O)	9.309	
157(b)(5)	9.19	8
157(c)	9.19	
157(c)(1)	9.19	5
157(c)(2)	9.19	3
	9.19	5
157(d)	9.22	
	9.22	5
	9.22	7
157(e)	9.18	6
158(a)	9.25	1
	9.289	
	9.289	1
158(a)(2)	9.146	1
158(b)	9.25	2
158(b)(1)	9.25	3

UNITED STATES CODE ANNOTATED
28 U.S.C.A.—Judiciary and Judicial Procedure

Sec.	This Work Sec.	Note
158(c)	9.25	2
	9.25	8
158(d)	9.26	
	9.26	1
349(a)	9.137	2
586	9.32	1
	9.33	1
586(a)(1)	9.180	
586(a)(3)(A)	9.29	2
586(a)(3)(H)	9.29	2
586(e)	9.214	1
	9.240	1
1291	18.31	7
	38.3	14
1292(b)	9.26	
	9.26	3
1331	15.42	
	18.89	
	18.92	
	18.93	
1334	9.24	
	9.308	
	9.309	
	9.310	
1334(a)	9.19	
1334(b)	9.19	
	9.19	8
1334(c)	9.19	4
	9.23	1
	9.23	2
1334(c)(2)	9.23	
1334(d)	9.23	3
1343	18.92	
	18.93	
1361	34.29	
1367(a)	18.19	8
1367(c)(1)	18.19	8
1391(b)	7.60	
	18.89	1
1391(b)(2)	18.92	
	18.93	
1408	9.21	1
1409	9.19	1
	9.21	3
1409(a)	9.309	
1412	9.21	4
1452	9.16	
	9.24	1
1601 et seq.	31.23	7
1738	18.37	9
1746	9.264	
1870	17.74	1
1875	17.38	
1914	9.266	2
	17.79	2
1914(a)	9.16	3
	9.17	8

386

TABLE OF STATUTES

UNITED STATES CODE ANNOTATED
28 U.S.C.A.—Judiciary and Judicial Procedure

Sec.	This Work Sec.	Note
1927	18.79	4
1930	9.16	3
	9.17	8
	9.165	
	9.179	
	9.266	
	9.267	
1930(a)	9.2	6
	9.7	6
	9.10	1
	9.176	2
	9.210	1
	9.211	2
	9.235	2
	9.261	1
	9.263	2
	9.264	11
1930(a)(6)	9.2	6
	9.33	
	9.33	6
	9.33	7
1962	8.17	1
1963	8.17	2
2001 et seq.	8.1	18
2075	9.5	5
2101	37.73	9
	39.62	8
2201(a)	31.21	2
2410	11.15	
2410(b)	11.15	
	11.15	1
2410(c)	11.8	4
	11.15	2
2412	23.16	8
	23.23	4
	23.41	19
2412(d)(1)(A)	23.16	8

29 U.S.C.A.—Labor

Sec.	This Work Sec.	Note
11(3)	17.62	2
141 et seq.	1.89	6
151 et seq.	17.61	1
157	17.61	4
158	17.38	
	17.61	
	17.61	9
158(a)	17.61	7
158(b)	17.61	8
160	17.61	10
160(f)	17.61	11
185	17.61	12
201 et seq.	1.89	6
206	17.63	9
206 et seq.	18.59	2

UNITED STATES CODE ANNOTATED
29 U.S.C.A.—Labor

Sec.	This Work Sec.	Note
206(d)	17.44	1
206(d)(1)	17.44	2
207(a)(1)	17.63	3
212	17.63	10
213(1)	17.63	4
215	17.38	
215(a)(3)	17.38	
	17.63	13
216	17.63	11
216(b)	17.82	10
255(a)	17.63	12
301(a)	17.77	
411(a)(1)	17.61	14
411(a)(2)	17.61	15
	17.75	1
501(a)	17.61	16
501(b)	17.79	1
	17.82	34
502	17.82	26
502(h)	17.50	6
	17.79	4
510	17.82	27
621 et seq.	17.37	
	18.59	3
623	17.38	
623(f)	17.37	3
626(f)	17.10	1
651 et seq.	1.89	6
	17.62	1
660	17.38	
794	17.43	3
	18.19	
	18.19	5
1001 et seq.	1.89	6
	17.50	1
	23.24	1
	24.85	1
1052(a)(1)(A)	23.25	1
1053(9)	23.25	3
1054(b)	23.25	4
1055	23.29	1
1055(c)(2)(A)	23.31	1
1055(e)(2)	23.29	2
1055(f)(1)	23.29	3
1056	23.28	1
1056(d)(3)	23.30	1
1104(a)(1)	17.50	3
1132	23.35	2
1132(a)(1)	17.50	3
1132(g)	23.35	3
1133	23.35	1
1140	17.38	
	17.50	2
1141	17.38	
1161—1168	17.12	1
1161(b)	17.46	1
1163	17.46	2
1165	17.12	3

387

TABLE OF STATUTES

UNITED STATES CODE ANNOTATED
29 U.S.C.A.—Labor

Sec.	This Work Sec.	Note
1166	17.12	3
1321(b)	23.34	2
1322	23.34	2
1322a	23.34	2
1344	23.34	1
1431	23.34	2
1855	17.38	
2001 et seq.	17.38	
2006(d)(1)	17.52	1
2101 et seq.	6.101	1
	6.184	2
2102 et seq.	17.51	1
2601 et seq.	17.45	1
2612(a)(1)(D)	17.45	2
2612(b)	17.45	3
2615	17.38	

30 U.S.C.A.—Mineral Lands and Mining

Sec.	This Work Sec.	Note
801 et seq.	32.43	1
815	17.38	
820(b)	17.38	
901 et seq.	32.43	1
1201	17.38	
1293	17.38	

31 U.S.C.A.—Money and Finance

Sec.	This Work Sec.	Note
3729	17.64	
3729(a)(1)	17.64	7
3729(b)(1)	17.64	9
3729(b)(2)	17.64	10
3729(b)(3)	17.64	11
3730	17.38	
3730(b)(1)	17.64	12
	17.64	14
3730(b)(4)(B)	17.64	
3730(c)(1)	17.64	15
3730(d)(1)	17.64	16
3730(d)(2)	17.64	17
9303	9.139	2

33 U.S.C.A.—Navigation and Navigable Waters

Sec.	This Work Sec.	Note
901 et seq.	32.43	1
901—950	32.12	22
916	9.125	25
948(a)	17.38	
1251	15.41	
1251 et seq.	15.8	1
	15.40	

UNITED STATES CODE ANNOTATED
33 U.S.C.A.—Navigation and Navigable Waters

Sec.	This Work Sec.	Note
1251 et seq. (Cont'd)	15.42	
1311	15.9	1
	15.9	4
	15.37	1
	15.41	
1311(a)	15.42	
1312	15.9	4
1313(d)	15.9	12
1316	15.9	4
1317	15.9	4
1318(b)	15.9	6
1319	15.15	15
1319(g)	15.12	
	15.37	
	15.42	
1319(g)(2)	15.15	15
1319(g)(6)(A)	15.11	16
1321(b)(2)(A)	15.29	11
1341	15.15	11
1342	15.8	2
	15.42	
1342(a)	15.41	
1342(b)	15.8	3
	15.9	15
1342(d)(2)	15.8	5
1342(O)	15.9	12
1342(p)	15.10	1
1344(a)	15.13	3
	15.15	1
1344(c)	15.13	1
	15.15	9
1344(f)(1)	15.14	2
	15.15	8
1362(5)	15.42	
1362(6)	15.8	7
	15.41	
	15.42	
1362(7)	15.8	13
	15.41	
	15.42	
1362(14)	15.8	8
	15.41	
	15.42	
1365	15.12	1
	15.15	16
	15.41	
1365(a)	15.40	
	15.42	
1365(a)(1)	15.11	7
1365(a)(2)	15.11	7
1365(b)	15.40	
	15.42	
1365(b)(1)(A)	15.11	13
1365(b)(1)(B)	15.11	14
	15.12	3
1365(d)	15.42	
1367	17.38	

388

TABLE OF STATUTES

UNITED STATES CODE ANNOTATED
36 U.S.C.A.—Patriotic Societies and Observances

Sec.	This Work Sec.	Note
27	1.13	1
48	1.13	1
67–p	1.13	

38 U.S.C.A.—Veterans' Benefits

Sec.	This Work Sec.	Note
101 et seq.	23.41	2
101(2)	23.41	3
114	23.41	6
770(g)	9.125	27
1101 et seq.	23.41	2
1110	23.41	4
1114	23.41	5
1155	23.41	5
1310—1315	23.41	7
1501	23.41	8
1502	23.41	8
1521	23.41	8
	23.41	9
1522	23.41	8
1541	23.41	10
1710	23.41	11
1710(a)(2)(F)	23.41	12
3101	9.125	27
	9.125	28
5904	23.41	19
7263	23.41	19

42 U.S.C.A.—The Public Health and Welfare

Sec.	This Work Sec.	Note
71 et seq.	23.7	1
300f to 300j	15.8	13
300j–9	17.38	
300bb–1	17.12	1
401	23.7	3
401 et seq.	34.3	2
401—433	34.3	3
402(a)(1)	23.9	1
402(b)(1)(G)	23.12	4
	23.12	5
402(b)(1)(H)	23.12	4
	23.12	5
402(b)(1)(J)	23.12	4
	23.12	5
402(b)(2)	23.12	3
	23.12	6
402(c)(2)	23.12	6
402(d)	23.12	11
402(e)(1)(B)	23.12	9
402(e)(2)(A)	23.12	8
402(e)(3)	23.12	10
402(f)(1)(B)	23.12	9

42 U.S.C.A.—The Public Health and Welfare

Sec.	This Work Sec.	Note
402(f)(4)	23.12	10
402(h)	23.12	12
402(i)	23.12	13
402(q)	23.11	3
402(w)	23.11	4
403(b)	23.13	1
403(f)(3)	23.13	1
404(a)(1)	23.14	1
404(a)(1)(A)	23.13	1
	23.14	4
404(a)(1)(B)	23.14	3
404(b)	23.14	6
405	23.15	1
405(c)	23.10	2
405(g)	23.15	13
	23.15	14
	34.29	
	34.29	1
	34.29	2
	34.29	4
	34.29	5
	34.29	6
	34.29	7
406(a)	34.33	1
	34.52	3
406(a)(1)	23.16	1
	23.16	3
406(a)(2)	23.16	6
406(a)(2)(A)	34.54	1
406(a)(3)(A)	34.33	3
	34.54	2
	34.54	3
	34.54	4
406(a)(4)(A)	34.53	1
406(b)	23.16	5
407(a)	34.52	5
410	23.8	1
412(e)	23.12	7
412(f)	23.12	7
413(a)(2)(A)(ii)	23.8	3
413(d)(1)	23.8	2
414(a)	23.9	2
415	23.10	1
416	34.6	2
416(d)	23.12	4
	23.12	5
416(e)	23.12	11
416(h)(1)	23.12	1
416(i)(1)(A)	34.6	1
	34.6	3
416(*l*)(1)	23.11	1
418(n)	23.43	4
421(i)(1)	34.26	1
421(i)(2)	34.26	1
423	34.6	2
423(c)(2)(A)	34.6	3
423(d)(1)(A)	34.4	1

389

TABLE OF STATUTES

UNITED STATES CODE ANNOTATED
42 U.S.C.A.—The Public Health and Welfare

Sec.	This Work Sec.	Note
423(d)(1)(A) (Cont'd)	34.6	1
	34.6	3
	34.8	1
423(d)(2)	34.4	5
423(d)(2)(A)	34.8	2
	34.8	3
	34.14	1
423(d)(2)(B)	34.10	10
423(d)(3)	34.4	4
423(g)	34.26	10
426	23.11	4
426(a)	23.43	9
	23.43	6
	23.43	8
426(b)	23.43	3
426–1(a)(2)	23.43	5
1320a–7b	23.76	
1320a–7b(a)	23.76	
1320A–7b(a)(6)	23.76	
1320c et seq.	23.56	1
1320c–3	23.56	2
1320c–3(a)(3)(A)	23.56	3
1320c–4	23.56	6
1365(d)	15.42	
1381—1383d	34.3	3
1381—1385	23.17	1
1382(a)(1)	23.19	1
1382(a)(1)(B)	23.19	10
1382(a)(2)(B)	23.19	11
1382(a)(3)(A)	23.19	11
1382(a)(3)(B)	23.19	10
1382(e)(1)(E)	23.73	8
1382(e)(1)(G)	23.73	8
1382a(a)(1)	23.19	13
1382a(a)(1)(A)	23.20	2
1382a(a)(2)	23.19	14
1382a(a)(2)(A)	23.19	3
	23.19	15
	23.20	2
1382a(a)(2)(A)(i)	23.19	15
1382a(b)(2)(A)	23.19	16
1382a(b)(3)(A)	23.19	18
1382a(b)(3)(B)	23.19	19
1382a(b)(4)	23.19	17
1382a(b)(13)	23.19	15
1382b(a)	23.19	8
1382b(a)(1)	23.19	2
1382b(a)(2)(A)	23.19	4
1382b(a)(2)(B)	23.19	5
1382b(a)(3)	23.19	7
1382b(a)(7)	23.19	9
1382b(b)(1)	23.19	12
1382b(d)	23.19	6
1382c(a)(1)(A)	23.18	1
1382c(a)(1)(B)(1)	23.18	3
1382c(a)(3)(A)	34.4	1
	34.6	4

UNITED STATES CODE ANNOTATED
42 U.S.C.A.—The Public Health and Welfare

Sec.	This Work Sec.	Note
1382c(a)(3)(B)	34.4	5
1382c(f)	23.19	20
1382f	23.20	2
1383	34.19	1
1383(b)(1)(A)	23.21	2
	23.21	3
1383(b)(1)(B)	23.21	6
1383(b)(1)(B)(ii)	23.21	4
1383(c)	23.22	2
1383(c)(3)	23.22	7
1383(d)(2)(A)	23.23	2
1395 et seq.	29.13	3
1395 et seq.	23.42	1
1395(e)(1)(A)	23.43	17
1395a(a)(2)(E)	23.43	14
1395c	23.42	4
	23.43	1
	23.43	2
	23.44	1
1395d	23.42	4
1395d(a)(2)(A)	23.46	5
1395d(a)(4)	23.48	6
1395d(d)	23.48	6
1395d(d)(1)	23.48	3
	23.48	4
1395e	23.46	7
1395e(a)(1)	23.45	4
1395e(a)(1)(A)	23.45	5
1395e(a)(1)(B)	23.45	7
1395f(a)	23.44	2
1395f(a)(1)	23.55	1
1395f(a)(2)(C)	23.47	2
	23.47	5
	23.85	1
	23.85	4
1395f(a)(8)	23.47	2
	23.85	1
1395h	23.55	2
1395i–2(a)	23.43	15
1395i–3(c)	23.92	2
	23.94	1
1395i–3(c)(1)(A)(i)	23.94	4
	23.94	5
	23.94	6
1395i–3(c)(1)(A)(ii)	23.94	13
	23.94	14
	23.94	15
1395i–3(c)(1)(A)(iii)	23.94	9
1395i–3(c)(1)(A)(iv)	23.94	11
	23.94	12
1395i–3(c)(1)(A)(vi)	23.94	20
1395i–3(c)(1)(A)(vii)	23.94	22
	23.94	23
1395i–3(c)(1)(B)	23.94	3
1395i–3(c)(1)(B)(iii)	23.95	4
1395i–3(c)(2)(A)	23.96	2
1395i–3(c)(2)(B)(i)(I)	23.96	3

TABLE OF STATUTES

UNITED STATES CODE ANNOTATED
42 U.S.C.A.—The Public Health and Welfare

Sec.	This Work Sec.	Note
1395i–3(c)(2)(B)(ii)	23.96	4
1395i–3(c)(2)(D)	23.97	1
1395i–3(c)(4)	23.93	4
1395i–3(c)(5)(A)(i)	23.93	6
1395i–3(c)(5)(A)(ii)	23.93	7
1395i–3(c)(6)	23.95	2
1395i–3(c)(6)(B)	23.95	3
1395j	23.42	5
1395k	23.42	5
	23.49	2
1395l	23.50	2
1395l(b)	23.50	1
1395n(a)(2)(F)	23.47	2
	23.85	1
1395p(e)	23.43	13
1395r	23.46	1
1395u	23.51	4
1395u(b)(3)(C)	23.57	2
1395u(h)	23.51	1
1395w–4	23.50	3
	23.52	1
1395w–4(g)(4)	23.51	2
1395x(a)	23.45	2
1395x(b)	23.45	1
1395x(b)(4)	23.45	1
1395x(b)(5)	23.45	1
1395x(l)	23.46	2
1395x(m)	23.47	1
1395x(dd)(1)	23.48	2
1395x(dd)(2)(A)(ii)	23.48	2
1395x(dd)(3)(A)	23.48	1
1395y(a)	23.49	1
1395y(a)(9)	23.46	3
	23.46	4
1395cc(a)(1)	23.44	2
1395cc(a)(1)(A)	23.46	7
1395cc(a)(1)(M)	23.91	6
	23.91	7
1395dd(s)	23.60	7
1395ff	23.55	4
1395ff(b)	23.54	2
	23.55	7
1395ff(b)(2)	23.55	13
1395ff(b)(2)(A)	23.55	8
1395ff(b)(2)(B)	23.55	9
1395ss et seq.	23.60	1
1395ss(d)(3)	23.60	10
1395ss(p)(2)	23.60	3
	23.61	1
1395ss(p)(9)	23.60	4
1395ss(q)	23.60	5
	23.60	6
1395ss(r)	23.60	9
1395ww(d)	23.91	1
1395ww(e)	23.91	1
1396 et seq.	23.69	1
1396a(a)(3)	23.83	1

UNITED STATES CODE ANNOTATED
42 U.S.C.A.—The Public Health and Welfare

Sec.	This Work Sec.	Note
1396a(a)(10)(E)	23.43	18
1396a(a)(17)	23.65	1
	23.80	2
1396a(o)	23.73	8
1396a(r)(1)	23.73	9
1396d(p)	23.43	18
1396p(a)(1)(A)	23.82	1
1396p(a)(1)(B)	23.75	7
	23.82	3
1396p(a)(1)(B)(ii)	23.82	6
1396p(a)(2)	23.82	7
1396p(a)(2)(C)	23.82	8
1396p(a)(3)	23.82	6
1396p(a)(17)	23.75	1
1396p(b)	23.81	1
	23.81	2
	23.81	3
1396p(b)(1)(A)	23.82	10
1396p(c)	23.76	
	23.76	1
1396p(c)(1)(A)	23.76	6
1396p(c)(1)(A) (former)	23.76	15
1396p(c)(1)(B)	23.76	17
	23.78	4
1396p(c)(1)(C)(i)	23.76	8
1396p(c)(1)(D)	23.76	3
1396p(c)(1)(E)(i)	23.76	2
1396p(c)(2)(A)	23.76	11
1396p(c)(2)(B)	23.76	10
1396p(c)(2)(B)(iv)	23.78	6
	23.79	1
1396p(c)(2)(C)	23.76	13
1396p(c)(3)	23.76	21
	23.76	22
	23.76	23
1396p(d)(2)(A)	23.77	1
1396p(d)(3)(A)(i)	23.78	1
1396p(d)(3)(B)	23.78	5
1396p(d)(4)	23.78	6
1396p(d)(4)(A)	23.78	7
1396p(d)(4)(C)	23.78	8
1396r(b)(3)(F)	23.93	13
1396r(c)	23.92	2
	23.94	1
1396r(c)(1)(A)(i)	23.94	4
	23.94	5
	23.94	6
1396r(c)(1)(A)(ii)	23.94	13
	23.94	14
	23.94	15
1396r(c)(1)(A)(iii)	23.94	9
1396r(c)(1)(A)(iv)	23.94	11
	23.94	12
1396r(c)(1)(A)(vi)	23.94	20
1396r(c)(1)(A)(vii)	23.94	22
	23.94	23
1396r(c)(1)(B)	23.94	3

TABLE OF STATUTES

UNITED STATES CODE ANNOTATED
42 U.S.C.A.—The Public Health and Welfare

Sec.	This Work Sec.	Note
1396r(c)(1)(B)(iii)	23.95	5
1396r(c)(1)(B)(iv)	23.95	4
1396r(c)(2)(A)	23.96	2
1396r(c)(2)(B)(i)(I)	23.96	3
1396r(c)(2)(B)(ii)	23.96	4
1396r(c)(2)(D)	23.97	1
1396r(c)(2)(D)(iii)	23.97	6
1396r(c)(4)(A)	23.93	4
1396r(c)(5)(A)(i)	23.93	6
1396r(c)(5)(A)(ii)	23.93	7
1396r(c)(5)(A)(iii)	23.93	8
1396r(c)(6)	23.95	2
1396r(c)(6)(B)	23.95	3
1396r–5	23.80	5
1396r–5(b)(1)	23.80	18
1396r–5(c)(1)(A)	23.80	8
1396r–5(c)(1)(B)	23.80	7
1396r–5(c)(2)	23.80	9
1396r–5(d)(2)	23.80	14
1396r–5(e)	23.80	21
1396r–5(e)(1)	23.80	11
1396r–5(e)(2)(B)	23.80	16
1396r–5(e)(2)(C)	23.80	12
1396r–5(f)(1)	23.80	6
1396r–5(f)(2)	23.80	10
1717	9.125	22
1981	17.49	
	17.49	3
	17.77	
	17.82	5
	18.2	
	18.16	
	18.17	
	18.17	1
	18.17	5
	18.43	
	18.50	
	18.50	2
	18.50	4
	18.53	
	18.96	
	18.98	
1981 et seq.	18.1	4
	18.2	6
	18.4	2
1981(c)	18.17	4
1981a(b)(1)	17.82	24
1981a(b)(3)	17.82	23
1982	18.43	
	18.50	
	18.50	2
	18.50	4
	18.96	
1983	17.55	
	17.64	5
	17.77	
	17.82	24

UNITED STATES CODE ANNOTATED
42 U.S.C.A.—The Public Health and Welfare

Sec.	This Work Sec.	Note
1983 (Cont'd)	18.2	4
	18.5	
	18.9	
	18.9	2
	18.16	
	18.16	1
	18.17	
	18.17	5
	18.18	
	18.18	4
	18.18	8
	18.18	10
	18.19	2
	18.20	
	18.20	1
	18.20	2
	18.21	
	18.22	
	18.22	2
	18.23	
	18.23	5
	18.25	
	18.25	3
	18.25	4
	18.29	
	18.33	4
	18.34	
	18.34	3
	18.35	
	18.37	
	18.38	
	18.38	2
	18.38	7
	18.43	
	18.53	
	18.53	1
	18.53	5
	18.88	
	18.89	
	18.89	1
	18.92	
	18.92	2
	18.93	
	18.93	4
	18.94	
	18.94	3
1985	17.77	
	17.82	24
	18.19	
1985(3)	17.23	4
	18.19	1
	18.19	2
1986	18.19	
	18.19	4
1988	18.2	
	18.50	2
	18.92	

392

TABLE OF STATUTES

UNITED STATES CODE ANNOTATED
42 U.S.C.A.—The Public Health and Welfare

Sec.	This Work Sec.	Note
1988 (Cont'd)	18.93	
	18.94	
	18.96	
	18.98	
	28.33	
	30.42	10
1997(d)	17.38	
2000 et seq.	18.4	2
2000a	18.98	
2000a et seq.	18.54	3
	18.58	2
	18.98	
2000a(a)	18.54	3
2000a–3(c)	18.58	2
	18.98	
2000d et seq.	18.40	2
2000e et seq.	17.98	
	18.59	1
2000e(k)	17.54	1
2000e–1	17.56	8
2000e–2	17.49	1
	17.56	
2000e–2(e)(1)	17.59	6
2000e–2(k)	17.59	10
2000e–3	17.38	
2000e–3(a)	17.59	
2000e–j	17.56	2
2000bb–2	18.28	2
2000bb et seq.	18.28	2
3601	18.40	2
3601 et seq.	18.40	2
	18.43	
3601—3631	18.50	2
3604	18.42	
3604(a)	18.41	
	18.45	1
	18.46	1
	18.95	
	18.96	
3604(a)—(d)	18.50	4
3604(b)	18.95	
	18.96	
3604(c)	18.46	3
3604(d)	18.46	1
3604(e)	18.46	4
3604(f)(2)(A)	18.41	6
3604(f)(3)(B)	18.41	7
	18.47	3
3610	18.49	
3610(e)	18.49	17
3610(f)	18.49	17
3612(i)	18.49	18
3612(O)	18.49	17
3613(a)	18.50	
	18.95	
3613(a)(1)(A)	18.2	
	18.50	2

UNITED STATES CODE ANNOTATED
42 U.S.C.A.—The Public Health and Welfare

Sec.	This Work Sec.	Note
3613(c)(2)	18.2	7
	18.50	2
	18.95	
	18.96	
3617	18.50	4
3631	18.43	3
4321	15.3	4
4331	15.3	5
4332	15.3	5
4332(2)	15.3	6
4332(2)(c)	15.4	13
4852d	12.80	3
5403(d)	16.124	4
5851	17.38	
6901 et seq.	15.23	2
	15.41	
6903(5)	15.23	5
6903(27)	15.23	3
6904	15.23	1
6921	15.29	11
6925	15.23	12
6926(b)	15.24	2
6928(a)	15.25	2
6928(d)(1)—(7)	15.25	3
6945	15.23	7
	15.41	
6946	15.23	7
6972	17.38	
6972(a)(1)(A)	15.25	12
	15.41	
6972(a)(1)(B)	15.25	13
	15.41	
6972(b)(1)(A)	15.25	16
6972(b)(1)(B)	15.25	18
6973(a)	15.25	4
6991—699li	15.26	1
6991(h)	15.30	5
6991a	15.26	3
6991a(a)(3)	15.26	6
6991b	15.26	3
6991b(c)	15.26	8
6991b(e)	15.26	7
7401	17.38	
7407(a)—(c)	15.19	5
7408	15.19	2
7408(a)(1)	15.19	2
7409(b)	15.19	4
7410(a)(1)	15.19	7
7410(a)(2)	15.19	8
7410(k)	15.19	9
7411(a)(1)	15.19	11
7411(b)(1)(A)	15.19	10
7412	15.20	4
7412(b)	15.20	5
7412(b)(3)	15.20	5
7412(c)	15.20	5
7412(c)(2)	15.20	6

393

TABLE OF STATUTES

UNITED STATES CODE ANNOTATED
42 U.S.C.A.—The Public Health and Welfare

Sec.	This Work Sec.	Note
7412(d)(3)(A)	15.20	6
7412(d)(3)(B)	15.20	6
7470—7479	15.19	16
7471	15.19	17
7501—7515	15.19	12
7502(c)(5)	15.19	13
7503(a)(1)	15.19	15
7503(a)(2)	15.19	14
7511	15.20	3
7512(b)	15.20	3
7604(a)(1)	15.22	7
7604(a)(2)	15.22	8
7604(a)(3)	15.22	8
7604(b)(1)(A)	15.22	13
7604(b)(1)(B)	15.22	13
7622	17.38	
7661	15.21	5
8621 et seq.	23.105	4
9007(n)	15.30	5
9601 et seq.	11.6	9
	15.28	2
9601(2)(E)—(G)	15.30	5
9601(9)	15.29	10
9601(14)	15.29	11
9601(20)(A)	15.30	2
9601(22)	15.29	13
9601(23)	15.28	5
9601(24)	15.28	5
9601(35)	15.29	19
9601(35)(A)	15.29	21
	15.29	22
9605(a)	15.28	6
9606	15.29	5
	15.32	13
9606(a)	15.28	8
9606(b)(1)	15.29	5
9607	15.29	2
	15.29	3
9607(a)	15.29	8
	15.32	13
9607(a)(1)	15.30	10
9607(b)	15.29	16
9607(b)(3)	15.29	18
9607(c)(3)	15.29	5
9610	17.38	
9611	15.28	4
	15.28	7
9613(f)(1)	15.30	6
	15.30	8
	15.30	7
9613(f)(2)	15.30	9
9620(h)	6.20	2
11101	29.13	3
11131(a)	29.42	3
11132(a)	29.42	1
11133(a)	29.42	2
11133(a)(1)(C)	29.42	4

UNITED STATES CODE ANNOTATED
42 U.S.C.A.—The Public Health and Welfare

Sec.	This Work Sec.	Note
11135(a)	29.32	1
	29.32	3
	29.42	5
12101 et seq.	6.8	1
	18.2	
	18.62	3
12101—12117 et seq.	17.43	1
12112(b)(5)(A)	17.43	2
	17.43	9
12112(b)(5)(B)	17.43	2
12131 et seq.	18.19	
	18.58	3
12203(a)	17.38	
13981	18.53	

43 U.S.C.A.—Public Lands

Sec.	This Work Sec.	Note
175	9.125	29

45 U.S.C.A.—Railroads

Sec.	This Work Sec.	Note
51 et seq.	32.43	1
60	17.38	
228(L)	9.125	26
231	23.36	1
231 et seq.	23.36	
231(a)(c)	23.36	2
231g	23.36	6
231k	23.36	3
441	17.38	

46 U.S.C.A.—Shipping

Sec.	This Work Sec.	Note
601	9.125	23
1506	17.38	

49 U.S.C.A.—Transportation

Sec.	This Work Sec.	Note
30161	27.50	3

50 U.S.C.A.—War and National Defense

Sec.	This Work Sec.	Note
520(1)	13.14	8

STATUTES AT LARGE

Year	This Work Sec.	Note
1922, Sept. 21, c. 370, 42 Stat. 1007	32.43	1

TABLE OF STATUTES

STATUTES AT LARGE

Year	This Work Sec.	Note
1940, Oct. 14, c. 876, § 328(b), 54 Stat. 1152	19.47	1
1948, June 25, c. 718, 62 Stat. 1009	19.50	2
1950, June 15, c. 262, 64 Stat. 219	19.50	2
1953, Aug. 7, c. 336, 67 Stat. 400	19.50	2
1956, Aug. 1, c. 836, 70 Stat. 815	34.6	2
1965, July 30, P.L. 89–97, § 303(a), 79 Stat. 367	34.6	3
1965, Oct. 20, P.L. 89–272, 79 Stat. 992	15.23	2
1965, Oct. 20, P.L. 89–272, § 9001, 79 Stat. ___	15.26	3
1968, May 29, P.L. 90–321, 81 Stat. 146	7.30	5
1976, Nov. 21, P.L. 94–578, 90 Stat. 2743	12.57	4
1979, Sept. 27, P.L. 96–70, § 3201(a), 93 Stat. 496	19.40	3
1979, Sept. 27, P.L. 96–70, § 3201(c), 93 Stat. 496	19.40	3
1980, Mar. 17, P.L. 96–212, 94 Stat. 102	19.50	2
1982, Oct. 22, P.L. 97–359, 96 Stat. 1716	19.15	
1984, July 18, P.L. 98–369, 98 Stat. 494	21.45	1
1984, Oct. 9, P.L. 98–460, 98 Stat. 1794	34.10 34.64	10
1984, Nov. 8, P.L. 98–616, 98 Stat. 3268	15.23	2
1984, Nov. 8, P.L. 98–616, § 601(a), 98 Stat. 3277	15.26	3
1986, Oct. 17, P.L. 99–499, 100 Stat. 1613	15.28	2

STATUTES AT LARGE

Year	This Work Sec.	Note
1986, Oct. 22, P.L. 99–514, § 1433(c), 100 Stat. 2731	24.24	1
1986, Oct. 27, P.L. 99–554, § 302(f), 100 Stat. 3124	9.212	6
1986, Nov. 5, P.L. 99–601, 100 Stat. 3356	19.11	13
1986, Nov. 10, P.L. 99–639, § 2(a), 100 Stat. 3537	19.71 19.72	1 9
1986, Nov. 10, P.L. 99–639, § 5(d), 100 Stat. 3543	19.72	35
1987, Dec. 22, P.L. 100–203, 101 Stat. 1330	23.92	2
1989, Nov. 21, P.L. 101–162, 103 Stat. 955	9.269	
1990, Nov. 5, P.L. 101–508, § 11602(e)(1)(A)(ii), 104 Stat. 1388–500	24.30	2
1990, Nov. 5, P.L. 101–509, 104 Stat. 1397	19.49	1
1990, Nov. 28, P.L. 101–649, 104 Stat. 4978	19.12	5
1991, Dec. 12, P.L. 102–232, 105 Stat. 1733	19.25	1
1992, Oct. 6, P.L. 102–395, § 610, 106 Stat. 1874	19.5	
1993, Aug. 6, P.L. 103–65, § 1, 107 Stat. 311	9.212	6
1994, Aug. 15, P.L. 103–296, 108 Stat. 1465	34.3	6
1994, Aug. 26, P.L. 103–317, 108 Stat. 1732	19.51 19.55	4
1994, Aug. 26, P.L. 103–317, § 506(b), 108 Stat. 1765	19.57	5
1994, Sept. 13, P.L. 103–322, 108 Stat. 1902	19.16	5

TABLE OF STATUTES

STATUTES AT LARGE

Year	This Work Sec.	Note
1994, Sept. 13, P.L. 103–322,		
§ 40701, 108 Stat. 1953	19.8	12
1994, Oct. 22, P.L. 103–394,		
108 Stat. 4106	9.5	3
1994, Oct. 25, P.L. 103–416,		
§ 214, 108 Stat. 4308	19.41	3
1994, Oct. 25, P.L. 103–416,		
108 Stat. 4311	19.48	1
1995, Nov. 15, P.L. 104–51,		
109 Stat. 467	19.10	13
	19.11	1
	19.11	12
	19.15	9
1996, Sept. 30, P.L. 104–208,		
110 Stat. 3009	19.48	1
	19.55	1
	19.57	3
	19.64	5
1996, Sept. 30, P.L. 104–208,		
§ 305(b), 110 Stat. 3009	19.50	3
1996, Sept. 30, P.L. 104–208,		
§§ 2501—2505, 110 Stat. 3009	15.30	5

POPULAR NAME ACTS

ATOMIC ENERGY ACT OF 1946

Sec.	This Work Sec.	Note
189	4.10	5

BANKRUPTCY ACT

Sec.	This Work Sec.	Note
16 (former)	9.170	

BANKRUPTCY REFORM ACT

Sec.	This Work Sec.	Note
213(d)	9.160	

CIVIL RIGHTS ACT OF 1964

Sec.	This Work Sec.	Note
Tit. II	18.54	3
	18.58	
Tit. VI	18.53	5
Tit. VII	17.37	
	17.43	
	17.48	
	17.49	
	17.56	
	17.57	
	17.58	
	17.59	
	17.59	1
	17.59	5
	17.59	7
	17.65	
	17.67	
	17.67	2
	17.67	3
	17.67	4
	17.82	5
	17.82	23
	17.82	24
	17.87	
	17.88	
	17.89	
	17.98	2
	18.5	2
	18.17	
	18.59	
Tit. VIII	18.43	

CIVIL RIGHTS ACT OF 1991

Sec.	This Work Sec.	Note
107(b)(3)(B)(i)	17.59	2
107(b)(3)(B)(ii)	17.59	2

CLEAN AIR ACT

Sec.	This Work Sec.	Note
Tit. V	15.20	
304	15.22	

CLEAN WATER ACT

Sec.	This Work Sec.	Note
301	15.9	
	15.41	
306	15.9	4
307	15.9	4
309(g)	15.11	
	15.11	18
402	15.8	
402(a)	15.41	
404	15.13	

396

TABLE OF STATUTES

CLEAN WATER ACT

Sec.	This Work Sec.	Note
404 (Cont'd)	15.14	
	15.15	
	15.15	15
502(6)	15.41	
502(7)	15.41	
502(14)	15.41	
505	15.11	
	15.11	11
	15.41	

COMPREHENSIVE ENVIRONMENTAL RESPONSE, COMPENSATION AND LIABILITY ACT

Sec.	This Work Sec.	Note
101(35)	15.29	
102	15.29	11
106	15.29	
	15.29	5
	15.30	
107	15.30	
107(a)	15.29	
	15.29	2
	15.29	3
	15.30	
	15.30	6
	15.30	7
113(f)(1)	15.30	
113(f)(2)	15.30	

EDUCATION AMENDMENTS OF 1972

Sec.	This Work Sec.	Note
Tit. IX	18.53	

EMPLOYEE RETIREMENT INCOME SECURITY ACT

Sec.	This Work Sec.	Note
Tit. VII	17.54	
3(1)	6.188	
	17.50	5
3(2)	6.188	
3(3)	6.188	
406	6.188	
501(a)(1)(B)	17.50	
502	17.50	3
502(i)	6.188	
510	17.15	1
	17.50	

FEDERAL TRADE COMMISSION ACT

Sec.	This Work Sec.	Note
5	7.45	

FEDERAL TRADE COMMISSION ACT

Sec.	This Work Sec.	Note
5 (Cont'd)	7.45	4

HIGHER EDUCATION ACT

Sec.	This Work Sec.	Note
Tit. IV, Pt. B	9.132	6
Tit. IV, Pt. D	9.132	6
Tit. IV, Pt. E	9.132	6

HOUSING AND COMMUNITY DEVELOPMENT ACT

Sec.	This Work Sec.	Note
Tit. IV	16.124	3

IMMIGRATION AND NATIONALITY ACT

Sec.	This Work Sec.	Note
101	19.12	5
101(a)(15)	19.1	1
	19.2	2
101(a)(15)(B)	19.67	1
101(a)(15)(F)	19.67	2
101(a)(15)(H)	19.67	3
101(a)(15)(L)	19.67	4
101(a)(20)	19.4	1
101(a)(27)(C)—(J)	19.17	1
101(a)(32)	19.24	1
101(a)(33)	19.74	2
101(a)(42)(A)	19.50	
101(a)(43)	19.48	1
101(b)	19.11	1
	19.12	1
101(b)(1)	19.68	6
101(b)(1)(A)	19.11	
101(b)(1)(B)	19.11	8
101(b)(1)(C)	19.11	5
	19.11	22
101(b)(1)(D)	19.11	20
101(b)(1)(E)	19.11	14
101(b)(1)(F)	19.15	2
	19.15	3
	19.15	12
101(b)(2)	19.11	19
	19.10	13
103	19.1	8
106(a)	19.57	3
201—206	19.4	
201(a)(1)	19.4	7
201(a)(2)	19.4	8
201(a)(3)	19.4	9
201(b)	19.8	4
	19.58	
201(b)(2)(A)(i)	19.4	6
	19.8	2

TABLE OF STATUTES

IMMIGRATION AND NATIONALITY ACT			IMMIGRATION AND NATIONALITY ACT		
		This Work			This Work
Sec.	Sec.	Note	Sec.	Sec.	Note
201(b)(2)(A)(i) (Cont'd)	19.8	1	212(a)(2)	19.1	16
	19.12	5		19.51	5
201(b)(2)(A)(ii)	19.8	3		19.52	3
201(b)(2)(B)	19.8	3	212(a)(2)(A)(ii)	19.52	5
201(c)	19.5	1	212(a)(2)(B)	19.52	4
201(c)(1)(B)(ii)	19.5	3		19.55	1
201(d)	19.5	5	212(a)(2)(C)	19.52	6
202(b)	19.6	2	212(a)(2)(D)	19.52	6
202(b)(1)	19.6	3	212(a)(2)(E)	19.52	6
202(b)(2)	19.6	3	212(a)(3)(A)	19.52	8
202(b)(3)	19.6	4	212(a)(3)(B)	19.52	8
203(a)	19.4	7	212(a)(3)(C)	19.52	9
	19.9	1	212(a)(3)(D)	19.52	10
203(a)(1)	19.9	2	212(a)(3)(E)	19.52	11
203(a)(2)(A)	19.9	4	212(a)(4)	19.52	12
203(a)(2)(B)	19.9	4	212(a)(5)	19.52	13
203(a)(3)	19.9	5	212(a)(5)(A)	19.31	1
203(a)(4)	19.9	3	212(a)(5)(C)	19.26	3
	19.9	6	212(a)(6)	19.52	14
203(b)	19.4	8	212(a)(6)(A)	19.59	2
	19.17		212(a)(7)	19.52	15
203(b)(1)	19.18	1		19.70	4
203(b)(1)(B)	19.20		212(a)(8)	19.52	16
	19.20	2	212(a)(9)	19.52	14
203(b)(1)(C)	19.21	1		19.52	17
203(b)(2)(A)	19.22	1	212(a)(14) (former)	19.31	1
203(b)(2)(B)	19.22	2	212(g)	19.52	2
	19.25	1	212(h)	19.52	7
203(b)(3)(A)	19.26	2	212(O)	19.55	1
	19.26	1	214(b)	19.67	8
203(b)(3)(B)	19.28	1		19.67	9
203(b)(4)	19.40	1	216	19.43	6
203(b)(5)	19.42	1		19.71	1
	19.43	1		19.72	1
203(c)	19.4	9	216(b)	19.8	7
	19.46	1	216(b)(1)	19.72	13
203(c)(2)	19.46	3	216(b)(1)(A)(i)	19.72	10
203(d)	19.6	9	216(b)(1)(A)(ii)	19.72	11
	19.68	6	216(b)(1)(B)	19.72	12
204(a)(1)(A)(iii)(I)	19.16	7	216(b)(2)	19.72	30
204(h)	19.72	35	216(c)(1)	19.72	16
205	19.9	7	216(c)(2)	19.72	18
207	19.4		216(c)(3)(B)	19.72	23
	19.50	3	216(c)(4)(C)	19.16	4
208	19.4		216(d)(2)	19.72	19
	19.50		216(d)(2)(A)	19.72	9
	19.50	3	216(e)	19.72	4
208(a)	19.50	5	216(g)(1)(C)	19.72	2
209	19.4	10	216A	19.43	1
210	19.71	3		19.43	5
211(a)	19.51	1		19.71	2
211(a)(7)	19.74		216A(a)(1)	19.73	1
212	19.2	4	216A(c)(1)	19.73	6
	19.59	3	216A(d)(3)	19.73	5
	19.70	3	221	19.53	1
212(a)	19.1	2	221(d)	19.54	4
212(a)(1)	19.52	1	223	19.74	9
212(a)(1)(A)	19.52	18	234	19.63	2
212(a)(1)(A)(ii)	19.54	4		19.65	3

398

TABLE OF STATUTES

IMMIGRATION AND NATIONALITY ACT

Sec.	This Work Sec.	Note
237(a)	19.52	
237(a)(2)	19.1	16
238	19.52	19
239	19.52	19
240	19.1	2
240A	19.1	2
	19.2	4
240A(b)	19.48	2
240A(b)(2)	19.16	3
241	19.70	2
242(a)(2)(B)	19.48	5
	19.57	3
	19.64	5
244	19.2	4
244(a)	19.48	3
245	19.4	10
	19.14	
	19.51	2
	19.57	1
	19.60	1
	19.63	
245(a)	19.58	1
	19.61	3
245(c)	19.51	3
	19.57	4
	19.58	4
245(d)	19.58	5
245(e)	19.58	7
245(i)	19.51	4
	19.57	5
	19.59	
	19.59	2
	19.68	1
245A	19.71	3
246(a)	19.47	7
246(b)	19.47	8
249	19.47	
264(e)	19.74	5
274A	19.1	3
	19.1	17
274B	19.1	17
	19.70	1
275(b)	19.72	31
279	19.57	3
291	19.4	4
	19.10	2
301	19.59	1
301—357	19.1	4
310—322	19.70	5

NATIONAL LABOR RELATIONS ACT

Sec.	This Work Sec.	Note
7	17.61	
8	17.61	
8(a)	17.61	

OCCUPATIONAL SAFETY & HEALTH ACT

Sec.	This Work Sec.	Note
11(c)	17.62	

PUBLIC HEALTH CIGARETTE LABELING AND ADVERTISING ACT OF 1965

Sec.	This Work Sec.	Note
4	27.46	2
5	27.46	

PUBLIC HEALTH CIGARETTE SMOKING ACT OF 1969

Sec.	This Work Sec.	Note
5	27.46	
5(b)	27.46	

REHABILITATION ACT

Sec.	This Work Sec.	Note
504	17.43	

RESOURCE CONSERVATION AND RECOVERY ACT

Sec.	This Work Sec.	Note
3001	15.29	11
3005	15.23	12
3006(b)	15.24	2
4005	15.41	
6991a(a)(1)	15.26	5
7002(a)(1)(A)	15.25	
	15.41	
7002(a)(1)(B)	15.25	
	15.41	
7003	15.25	

REVISED MODEL BUSINESS CORPORATION ACT

Sec.	This Work Sec.	Note
1.24	1.20	1
1.29	1.20	1
1.40(22)	1.53	3
2.01, Comment	1.20	1
2.04, Comment	1.21	28
6.01	1.32	1
6.03	1.32	1
6.21	1.32	1
6.21(b)	1.30	1
6.21(e)	1.30	1
6.22(b)	1.56	24
	1.56	26
7.21(b)	1.45	4
7.21, Comment 3	1.45	4

TABLE OF STATUTES

REVISED MODEL BUSINESS CORPORATION ACT

Sec.	This Work Sec.	Note
7.23, Comment	1.53	3
7.40	1.51	88
7.40(d)	1.51	95
7.40, Comment 1.h	1.51	95
8.25(f)	1.64	5
8.25, Comment	1.64	5
8.30(a)	1.66	12
8.30, Comment	1.66	12
8.31, Comment	1.65	8
8.40, Comment	1.69	1
8.50—8.56	1.66	27
8.51(e)	1.66	21
8.51, Comment 1	1.66	21
8.51, Comment 5	1.66	21
8.52	1.66	23
8.53	1.66	37
8.58, Comment	1.66	19
13.02(a)	1.51	20
13.02(a)(4)	1.51	24
13.02, Comment 1(4)	1.51	24
13.02, Comment 2	1.51	47
14.30(3)	1.101	2
15.01	1.115	3
15.04	1.117	4
16.02(c)	1.53	7

SECURITIES ACT OF 1933

Sec.	This Work Sec.	Note
2(1)	2.106	

SECURITIES EXCHANGE ACT OF 1934

Sec.	This Work Sec.	Note
12	1.31	1
	1.46	3
	1.89	14
14(d)	1.89	

SOCIAL SECURITY ACT

Sec.	This Work Sec.	Note
Tit. XVII	30.28	2

TAXPAYER RELIEF ACT

Sec.	This Work Sec.	Note
311(a)	35.6	7
	6.117	1
311(d)	35.6	7
311(e)	6.117	1

VIOLENCE AGAINST WOMEN ACT

Sec.	This Work Sec.	Note
40302	18.53	

TABLE OF RULES

OFFICIAL COMPILATION OF CODES, RULES AND REGULATIONS OF THE STATE OF NEW YORK

Tit.	This Work Sec.	Note
1, Pt. 370	16.134	
5, § 664.7(a)(2)	15.17	5
6, § 200.10	15.21	3
6, § 200.10(d)	15.21	4
6, § 211.2	15.32	1
6, Pt. 218	15.21	10
6, Pt. 325	27.47	11
6, Pt. 360	15.23	
6, § 360.2	15.23	10
	15.23	11
6, § 360.3	15.23	11
6, § 360.4	15.23	11
6, § 360.5	15.23	11
6, § 360.6	15.23	11
6, § 360.11	15.23	11
6, Pt. 364	15.24	
6, § 370.2(164)	15.24	11
	15.24	14
6, § 371.1(f)(7)	15.24	13
6, § 371.1(f)(7)(ii)	15.24	13
6, Pt. 372	15.24	5
6, Pt. 373	15.24	
6, § 373–1.1(b)	15.24	18
6, § 373–1.1(d)(1)(i)	15.24	20
6, § 373–1.1(d)(1)(ii)	15.24	19
6, § 373–1.1(e)	15.24	19
6, § 375–1.3(n)	15.31	13
6, § 375–1.4(c)	15.31	5
6, § 375–1.5(c)(2)	15.31	14
6, § 375–1.8	15.31	6
6, § 375–1.8(a)(1)	15.31	4
6, § 375–1.9	15.31	10
6, § 375–1.10(b)	15.31	12
6, § 375–1.10(d)	15.31	15
6, § 372.2(a)(2)	15.24	6
6, § 372.2(a)(3)	15.24	7
6, § 372.2(a)(8)(iii)	15.24	14
	15.24	15
6, § 372.2(a)(8)(iii)(a)	15.24	15
6, § 372.2(a)(8)(iv)	15.24	19
6, § 372.2(a)(8)(v)	15.24	16
6, § 372.2(b)	15.24	8
	15.24	10
6, § 372.2(c)	15.24	9
6, § 372.3	15.24	17
6, Pt. 375	15.31	
6, Pt. 597	15.27	2
6, § 600.5	15.15	13

OFFICIAL COMPILATION OF CODES, RULES AND REGULATIONS OF THE STATE OF NEW YORK

Tit.	This Work Sec.	Note
6, § 608.7	15.15	12
6, Pt. 610	15.27	22
6, § 610.2(j)	15.27	23
6, § 610.4(a)	15.27	23
6, § 610.4(a)(4)	15.27	24
6, § 612.1(b)(21)	15.27	3
6, § 612.1(c)(9)	15.27	9
6, § 612.1(c)(13)	15.27	10
6, § 612.2(a)(1)	15.27	4
	15.27	5
6, § 612.2(a)(2)	15.27	6
6, § 612.2(b)	15.27	7
6, § 612.3(a)	15.27	8
6, § 612.4	15.27	9
6, § 613.3(c)	15.27	11
6, § 613.3(d)	15.27	12
6, § 613.4	15.27	13
6, § 613.5	15.27	13
6, § 613.5(a)(1)(v)	15.27	14
6, § 613.5(a)(2)	15.27	15
6, § 613.6	15.27	16
6, § 613.8	15.27	25
6, § 613.9	15.27	17
6, § 613.9(c)	15.27	18
6, § 614.2	15.27	19
6, § 614.6	15.27	20
6, § 614.8	15.27	21
6, Pt. 617	15.4	
	16.52	2
	16.98	2
	16.98	3
	16.134	
6, § 617.1(b)	16.52	1
6, § 617.2	16.80	4
	16.87	8
6, § 617.2(a)	16.53	2
6, § 617.2(ai)	15.4	4
6, § 617.2(ak)	15.4	4
	15.4	8
6, § 617.2(b)	15.4	3
	15.7	1
	15.7	2
	16.53	1
6, § 617.2(c)	4.29	12
6, § 617.2(k)	16.53	2
6, § 617.2(p)	15.5	11
6, § 617.2(u)	15.4	9
	15.4	10

TABLE OF RULES

OFFICIAL COMPILATION OF CODES, RULES AND REGULATIONS OF THE STATE OF NEW YORK

Tit.	Sec.	This Work Note
6, § 617.2(y)	4.29	11
6, § 617.3	4.29	9
6, § 617.3(a)	4.29	8
6, § 617.3(g)	15.6	28
6, § 617.4	15.4	5
	15.7	5
	16.53	5
6, § 617.4(a)(1)	15.4	6
	16.53	8
6, § 617.4(b)(5)	16.53	6
	16.53	7
6, § 617.4(b)(6)	16.53	7
6, § 617.5	16.53	3
	16.53	4
6, § 617.5(12)	16.55	1
6, § 617.5(13)	16.55	1
6, § 617.5(a)	15.4	7
6, § 617.6	4.29	10
	15.4	1
	15.7	3
	15.7	4
	16.133	
6, § 617.6(a)(1)(i)	15.4	7
6, § 617.6(a)(2)	15.4	16
6, § 617.6(a)(3)	15.4	16
6, § 617.6(b)(1)	15.4	12
6, § 617.6(b)(2)	15.4	11
6, § 617.6(b)(2)(i)	15.4	12
6, § 617.6(d)(2)	15.4	20
6, § 617.6(g)	4.29	11
6, § 617.7	15.7	5
	16.53	9
6, § 617.7(a)	15.4	8
	15.7	6
	16.52	3
	16.52	4
6, § 617.7(b)	15.4	18
	15.7	8
6, § 617.7(b)(8)	15.5	3
6, § 617.7(c)	15.4	17
6, § 617.7(d)	15.4	19
6, § 617.7(d)(1)	15.7	9
6, § 617.7(d)(1)(i)	15.4	19
6, § 617.7(e)	15.4	20
6, § 617.8	4.29	13
	15.7	11
6, § 617.8(a)	15.5	5
6, § 617.9	4.29	16
6, § 617.9(a)(3)	15.5	7
	15.7	12
6, § 617.9(a)(4)	15.5	8
	15.7	13
6, § 617.9(a)(6)	15.5	9
	15.7	14
	15.7	15
6, § 617.9(b)	15.5	2
	15.7	10

OFFICIAL COMPILATION OF CODES, RULES AND REGULATIONS OF THE STATE OF NEW YORK

Tit.	Sec.	This Work Note
6, § 617.10(b)	4.29	12
6, § 617.10(f)	4.29	15
6, § 617.11	15.7	16
6, § 617.11(a)	15.5	10
6, § 617.11(d)	15.5	12
6, § 617.12	16.133	
6, § 617.12(c)	15.5	7
6, § 617.12(d)	15.5	7
6, § 617.14(f)	4.29	14
6, § 617.20	15.4	14
	15.4	15
6, § 617.21	4.29	11
6, Pt. 621	15.16	7
	15.17	9
	15.21	6
6, § 621.14	15.9	8
6, § 621.3(b)(2)	4.32	1
6, § 622.8(c)	4.39	2
6, Pt. 624	15.16	7
	15.17	9
6, § 624et seq.	4.10	8
6, § 624.7	4.13	2
6, § 624.10	4.24	10
6, § 625.5	4.19	2
6, Pt. 661	15.16	2
6, § 661.4	15.14	12
6, § 661.4(b)	15.17	6
6, § 661.4(h)	15.14	10
	15.17	4
6, § 661.5	15.14	11
	15.14	13
	15.17	7
6, § 661.6	15.17	8
6, § 661.15(b)	15.17	5
6, Pt. 662	15.16	3
	15.16	7
6, § 662.1(k)	15.14	5
	15.16	8
6, § 662.2(a)	15.16	7
6, § 662.4(a)	15.16	9
6, Pt. 663	15.16	3
	15.16	7
	15.17	
	15.17	1
6, § 663.4	15.14	7
	15.14	9
	15.16	12
	15.17	2
	15.17	3
6, § 663.5	15.14	8
6, § 663.5(e)	15.16	11
6, Pt. 665	15.16	1
	15.17	1
6, Pt. 754	15.9	5
6, § 754.5(k)	15.9	14
8, Pt. 14	16.128	5
8, § 60.4(a)	29.36	2

TABLE OF RULES

OFFICIAL COMPILATION OF CODES, RULES AND REGULATIONS OF THE STATE OF NEW YORK

Tit.	Sec.	This Work Note
8, Pt. 155	16.128	5
9, § 4.131	4.18	13
	4.23	2
	4.24	8
	4.24	9
9, § 4.156	4.56	1
9, § 5.2	4.43	2
9, § 46.1	36.47	3
9, § 48.4(a)	36.29	2
9, § 48.4(b)(1)	36.29	3
9, § 48.4(d)(2)	36.9	9
	36.9	10
	36.9	11
	36.30	1
9, § 53.1(j)	36.39	1
	36.53	5
9, § 53.1(m)	36.53	3
9, § 53.1(q)	36.53	3
9, § 54.1(b)	36.62	1
9, § 54.2(a)	36.64	1
	36.65	1
9, § 54.2(b)	36.64	2
	36.64	3
9, § 54.3(c)	36.65	3
9, § 54.3(h)	36.65	3
9, § 54.4	36.65	3
9, § 54.4(g)	36.65	4
	36.65	5
9, § 54.6	36.65	6
9, § 54.6(b)	36.56	1
9, § 63.1(c)	36.11	11
9, Pt. 64	36.44	8
9, Pt. 65	36.18	2
	36.44	9
9, § 65.2	36.11	12
9, Pt. 68	36.44	10
	36.44	14
9, § 68.6	36.44	12
9, Pt. 69	36.44	7
9, §§ 81.1—81.7	36.19	1
	36.19	3
	36.19	4
9, § 253.1(j)	36.53	4
9, § 465.3(a)(4)	17.82	7
9, § 465.5(d)(1)	17.68	2
9, § 465.5(d)(2)(vi)	17.68	3
9, Pts. 2100—2109	13.2	8
9, Pt. 2104	13.39	
9, §§ 2104.1 to 2104.9	13.39	
9, § 2104.6(d)	13.55	
9, Pt. 2200 et seq.	13.52	
9, Pts. 2200—2210	13.2	6
9, Pt. 2204	13.39	
9, § 2204.2	13.39	2
9, § 2204.2—2204.9	13.39	1
9, § 2204.2(a)(1)	13.39	7
9, § 2204.2(a)(2)	13.39	3

OFFICIAL COMPILATION OF CODES, RULES AND REGULATIONS OF THE STATE OF NEW YORK

Tit.	Sec.	This Work Note
9, § 2204.2(a)(3)	13.39	4
9, § 2204.2(a)(4)	13.39	5
9, § 2204.2(a)(6)	13.39	9
9, § 2204.3(a)	13.39	2
	13.39	11
9, § 2204.3(b)	13.39	2
9, § 2204.3(c)	13.39	11
9, § 2204.3(d)(1)	13.39	6
9, § 2204.3(d)(2)	13.39	8
9, § 2204.6(d)	13.55	
9, § 2205.1	13.12	12
9, § 2422.4	13.76	1
9, Pts. 2500—2510	13.2	4
9, § 2500.2(n)	13.55	
9, § 2503.4	13.74	4
9, § 2503.5(d)	13.55	
9, § 2503.5(e)	13.55	
9, Pt. 2504	13.40	
9, §§ 2504.1 to 2504.4	13.40	
9, Pts. 2520—2530	13.2	2
9, § 2520.6(p)	13.43	12
9, § 2520.6(q)	13.43	12
9, § 2523.4	13.75	1
9, § 2523.5(b)	13.55	
9, Pt. 2524	13.40	
9, §§ 2524.1 to 2524.5	13.40	
9, § 2524.2(b)	13.40	1
	13.52	1
9, § 2524.2(c)(1)	13.40	5
9, § 2524.2(c)(2)	13.40	3
	13.40	10
	13.40	14
	13.52	11
9, § 2524.2(c)(3)	13.40	14
9, § 2524.2(d)	13.40	16
9, § 2524.3	13.40	
9, § 2524.3(a)	13.40	2
9, § 2524.3(b)	13.40	6
9, § 2524.3(c)	13.40	7
9, § 2524.3(d)	13.40	8
9, § 2524.3(f)	13.40	4
9, § 2524.3(h)	13.40	9
9, § 2524.4	13.40	
9, § 2524.4(a)	13.40	12
9, § 2524.4(a)(2)	13.43	12
9, § 2524.4(b)	13.40	13
9, § 2524.4(c)	13.40	11
	13.40	15
9, § 2524.5	13.40	
9, § 2526.1	13.74	2
	13.74	3
9, § 2526.1(a)(1)	30.38	
9, § 2527.3(a)	13.73	1
9, § 2527.4	13.73	2
	13.73	3
9, § 2527.5	13.73	4
9, § 2527.6	13.73	5

403

TABLE OF RULES

OFFICIAL COMPILATION OF CODES, RULES AND REGULATIONS OF THE STATE OF NEW YORK

Tit.	This Work Sec.	Note
9, § 2529.1 et seq.	13.73	6
9, § 6654.1 et seq.	23.87	1
9, § 6654.6(a)	23.87	12
9, § 6654.6(a)(2)	23.87	13
9, § 6654.6(b)(2)	23.87	12
9, § 6654.6(b)(2)(ii)	23.87	11
9, § 6654.6(b)(2)(iii)	23.87	12
9, § 6654.6(c)(2)	23.87	12
9, § 6654.11	23.87	9
9, § 6654.15(a)(1)	23.87	2
9, § 6654.15(a)(2)	23.87	3
9, § 6654.15(a)(3)	23.87	4
9, § 6654.15(a)(4)	23.87	5
9, § 6654.16	23.87	7
9, § 6654.17(e)	23.87	6
9, § 6654.17(f)	23.87	6
9, § 6654.18	23.87	8
9, § 6654.19	23.87	10
9, Pt. 8600	4.31	2
9, § 8600.1(a)	4.31	3
9, § 8600.4(c)	4.31	4
9, § 8600.4(f)	4.31	5
9, Pt. 8800	4.51	7
9, Pt. 9600	23.120	1
9, § 9630.1	23.120	14
9, § 9720 et seq.	23.120	15
9, § 9977 et seq.	4.10	8
Tit. 10	29.51	
10, Pt. 20	29.19	1
10, § 50–3.4(a)	29.74	3
10, § 50–3.4(b)	29.74	3
10, § 52.22(d)(6)(x)	23.88	2
10, § 52.22(d)(6)(x)(4)	23.88	4
10, Subpt. 58–1	29.20	1
	29.20	2
	29.20	3
10, Subpt. 58–2	29.21	1
10, Pt. 69	29.22	2
10, § 85.6	23.91	11
10, § 400.12	23.93	17
10, § 400.13	23.93	17
10, § 400.21(b)(3)	24.92	1
10, Pt. 405	29.13	2
	29.23	1
10, § 405.2	29.23	4
10, § 405.2(e)(2)	29.23	3
10, § 405.2(e)(3)	29.32	2
10, § 405.2(e)(8)	29.32	5
10, § 405.6	29.33	1
10, § 405.6(b)(7)	29.33	2
10, § 405.7	23.89	2
10, § 405.7(a)(1)	23.90	1
10, § 405.7(a)(2)	23.90	1
10, § 405.7(a)(3)	23.90	2
10, § 405.7(a)(5)	23.90	3
10, § 405.7(a)(5)—(a)(7)	23.90	6
10, § 405.7(a)(6)	23.90	3

OFFICIAL COMPILATION OF CODES, RULES AND REGULATIONS OF THE STATE OF NEW YORK

Tit.	This Work Sec.	Note
10, § 405.7(a)(7)	23.90	4
10, § 405.7(b)(1)	23.90	6
10, § 405.7(b)(2)	23.90	7
10, § 405.7(b)(3)	23.90	8
10, § 405.7(b)(5)	23.90	8
10, § 405.7(b)(6)	23.90	9
	23.90	10
10, § 405.7(b)(7)	23.90	11
10, § 405.7(b)(8)	23.90	13
10, § 405.7(b)(9)	23.90	14
10, § 405.7(b)(10)	23.90	11
	23.90	16
10, § 405.7(b)(11)	23.90	15
10, § 405.7(b)(12)	23.90	18
10, § 405.7(b)(13)	23.90	18
10, § 405.7(b)(15)	23.90	19
10, § 405.7(b)(16)	23.90	19
10, § 405.7(b)(18)	23.90	17
10, § 405.7(b)(19)	23.90	21
10, § 405.7(b)(21)	23.90	12
10, § 405.7(b)(23)	23.90	22
10, § 405.7(b)(24)	23.90	20
10, § 405.7(c)	23.90	5
10, § 405.9	23.89	3
10, § 405.9(b)(2)	23.90	7
10, § 405.9(b)(14)	23.91	4
10, § 405.9(b)(14)(i)	23.91	5
	23.91	6
	23.91	7
10, § 405.9(b)(14)(ii)	23.91	5
	23.91	10
10, § 405.9(f)	23.91	10
10, § 405.9(f)(1)	23.91	3
	23.91	13
10, § 405.9(f)(3)(viii)	23.91	12
10, § 405.9(g)(3)(i)	23.91	14
10, § 405.9(g)(3)(ii)	23.91	15
10, § 405.9(g)(4)(i)	23.91	18
	23.91	19
10, § 405.9(g)(4)(ii)	23.91	16
10, § 405.9(g)(6)	23.91	17
10, § 405.9(g)(9)(i)	23.91	4
	23.91	5
10, § 405.9(g)(9)(ii)	23.91	5
10, § 405.10	29.51	1
	29.52	1
10, § 405.13	29.34	1
10, § 405.21	29.34	2
10, Pt. 415 et seq.	23.92	1
10, § 415.3	23.94	2
10, § 415.3(a)(2)	23.94	3
10, § 415.3(b)(1)	23.93	7
10, § 415.3(b)(2)	23.93	8
10, § 415.3(b)(3)	23.93	6
10, § 415.3(b)(4)	23.93	6
10, § 415.3(b)(5)	23.93	4
10, § 415.3(b)(6)	23.93	7

TABLE OF RULES

OFFICIAL COMPILATION OF CODES, RULES AND REGULATIONS OF THE STATE OF NEW YORK

Tit.	Sec.	This Work Note
10, § 415.3(c)(1)(ii)	23.94	20
10, § 415.3(c)(2)(b)	23.94	7
10, § 415.3(c)(2)(ii)(a)	23.96	1
10, § 415.3(d)	23.94	9
	23.94	12
10, § 415.3(e)(1)(i)	23.94	5
	23.95	6
10, § 415.3(e)(1)(iii)	23.94	4
10, § 415.3(e)(1)(iv)	23.94	5
	23.95	6
10, § 415.3(e)(1)(v)	23.94	5
	23.94	6
10, § 415.3(f)(2)	23.94	10
10, § 415.3(f)(3)	23.94	8
10, § 415.3(g)(1)	23.95	1
10, § 415.3(g)(2)(i)	23.95	5
10, § 415.3(g)(2)(iii)	23.95	4
10, § 415.3(h)	23.96	1
10, § 415.3(h)(1)	23.96	2
	23.96	5
10, § 415.3(h)(1)(iii)	23.96	3
10, § 415.3(h)(1)(iv)	23.96	4
10, § 415.3(h)(1)(v)(a)	23.96	5
10, § 415.3(h)(2)	23.96	5
10, § 415.3(h)(2)(i)	23.96	6
10, § 415.3(h)(2)(iii)	23.96	7
10, § 415.3(h)(2)(v)	23.96	8
10, § 415.3(h)(3)	23.96	9
10, § 415.3(h)(4)(i)	23.97	1
10, § 415.3(h)(4)(iii)	23.97	6
10, § 415.3(h)(5)	23.93	4
10, § 415.4	23.94	13
	23.94	14
10, § 415.4(a)(2)(ii)	23.94	18
10, § 415.4(a)(2)(iii)	23.94	16
10, § 415.4(a)(3)(ii)	23.94	17
10, § 415.4(a)(3)(iii)	23.94	19
10, § 415.4(a)(6)	23.94	15
10, § 415.4	23.94	15
10, § 415.5(c)	23.94	22
	23.94	23
10, § 415.5(c)(3)	23.94	24
10, § 415.5(c)(4)	23.94	24
10, § 415.11(e)	23.93	13
10, § 415.26(b)(6)	23.94	20
10, § 415.26(b)(6)(iii)	23.94	21
10, § 415.26(h)(5)	23.95	3
10, § 415.26(h)(5)(vi)	23.95	6
10, § 415.26(i)(1)(i)	23.93	15
10, § 415.26(i)(1)(iii)	23.93	16
10, § 415.26(i)(1)(v)	23.93	5
10, § 415.26(i)(1)(vi)	23.95	7
10, § 415.26(i)(1)(x)	23.93	11
10, § 415.26(i)(1)(xi)	23.93	12
10, § 505.9(f)	23.93	2
10, § 700.5(b)(3)	24.92	1
10, Pt. 900	23.107	1

OFFICIAL COMPILATION OF CODES, RULES AND REGULATIONS OF THE STATE OF NEW YORK

Tit.	Sec.	This Work Note
11, Pt. 39	23.66	2
11, § 39.3(b)(1)	23.66	3
	23.66	4
11, § 39.3(b)(2)	23.66	5
11, § 39.3(b)(2)(i)	23.66	5
11, § 39.3(b)(2)(ii)	23.66	5
	23.66	7
11, § 39.3(b)(2)(iii)	23.66	6
11, § 39.3(b)(3)	23.66	8
	23.66	9
11, § 39.3(b)(5)	23.66	11
11, § 39.3(b)(9)	23.66	12
11, § 39.39(b)(4)	23.66	10
11, § 52.1	23.60	2
11, § 52.11	23.60	2
11, § 52.12	23.64	1
11, § 52.12(a)	23.64	2
11, § 52.12(a)(1)(i)	23.64	3
11, § 52.12(a)(1)(ii)	23.64	3
11, § 52.12(a)(2)(i)	23.64	3
11, § 52.12(a)(2)(ii)	23.64	3
11, § 52.12(a)(3)(i)	23.64	3
11, § 52.12(a)(3)(ii)	23.64	3
11, § 52.12(b)	23.64	4
11, § 52.13	23.64	1
	23.64	4
11, § 52.16	23.60	2
	23.64	1
11, § 52.16(j)	23.64	4
11, § 52.17	23.60	2
	23.64	1
11, § 52.18	23.60	2
	23.64	1
11, § 52.22	23.60	2
	23.61	2
11, § 52.22(b)(1)	23.60	5
11, § 52.22(b)(3)	23.60	7
11, § 52.22(c)(1)	23.60	5
	23.60	6
11, § 52.22(d)	23.60	3
	23.60	4
11, § 52.22(f)(5)	23.60	10
11, § 52.25	23.64	1
11, § 52.25(b)(1)	23.64	10
11, § 52.25(b)(2)(i)	23.64	6
	23.67	2
11, § 52.25(b)(2)(ii)	23.64	5
	23.67	2
11, § 52.25(b)(2)(iii)	23.67	2
11, § 52.25(b)(2)(iv)	23.67	2
11, § 52.25(c)(1)(i)	23.64	7
11, § 52.25(c)(1)(ii)	23.64	8
11, § 52.25(c)(1)(iii)	23.64	9
11, § 52.25(c)(3)	23.64	11
11, § 52.25(c)(7)	23.64	12
11, § 52.29	23.64	1
11, § 52.63	23.60	2

TABLE OF RULES

OFFICIAL COMPILATION OF CODES, RULES AND REGULATIONS OF THE STATE OF NEW YORK

Tit.	Sec.	This Work Note
11, § 52.63 (Cont'd)	23.61	4
11, § 52.65	23.64	1
11, Pt. 60–2	26.24	13
11, Pt. 65(11)	26.21	2
11, § 71.0 et seq.	28.39	2
11, § 71.3(b)	28.39	6
	28.39	7
11, § 71.3(d)	28.39	3
	28.39	4
	28.39	5
11, § 71.3(e)	28.39	4
	28.39	6
	28.39	7
11, § 73.0 et seq.	28.35	1
	28.36	1
11, § 73.1(b)	28.35	6
11, § 73.2(n)	28.36	4
11, § 73.3	28.36	3
11, § 73.3(b)	28.35	6
11, § 73.3(e)(1)	28.36	6
11, § 73.3(e)(2)	28.36	10
11, § 73.3(e)(3)	28.36	8
11, § 73.3(f)	28.36	7
11, § 73.3(k)	28.36	5
11, § 73.3(m)	28.45	2
11, § 73.3(n)(1)	28.36	9
11, § 360.4	23.60	13
11, § 421.16(p)(1)	20.2	6
12, Pt. 300	32.34	4
12, § 300.2	32.28	10
12, § 300.5	32.27	11
12, § 300.9	32.17	17
12, § 300.13(a)	32.17	12
12, § 300.13(b)	32.17	13
12, § 300.13(c)	32.17	14
12, § 300.13(e)	32.17	15
12, § 300.13(g)	32.17	16
12, § 300.17	32.4	4
12, § 300.17(c)(1)	32.38	7
	32.38	8
12, § 300.17(c)(2)	32.38	9
12, § 300.17(c)(3)	32.38	9
12, § 300.17(d)	32.38	4
12, Pt. 302	32.37	2
12, § 325–1.18	32.19	8
	32.28	11
12, § 325–1.21	32.28	12
12, § 360.1	32.45	4
12, Pt. 425	32.53	1
13, Pt. 300 et seq.	7.12	5
	7.51	
13, § 300 et seq.	7.50	
13, § 300.4	7.51	
13, § 300.4(c)	7.13	3
	7.51	
13, § 300.4(f)	7.13	4
13, § 300.4(g)	7.13	4

OFFICIAL COMPILATION OF CODES, RULES AND REGULATIONS OF THE STATE OF NEW YORK

Tit.	Sec.	This Work Note
13, § 300.4(e)	7.13	4
13, § 300.6(e)	7.15	1
13, § 300.7(b)	7.13	2
13, § 300.7(e)	7.15	3
13, § 300.8	7.15	4
13, § 300.9	7.14	
	7.51	
13, § 300.9(a)	7.49	
13, § 300.9(b)	7.49	
13, § 300.9(c)	7.14	7
13, § 300.12	7.15	6
13, § 300.12(c)	7.15	8
13, § 300.12(d)	7.15	7
13, § 300.12(f)	7.14	9
13, § 300.16(a)	7.15	10
15, § 124 et seq.	4.10	8
15, § 124.5(b)(3)	4.15	5
15, § 124.5(c)	4.15	5
18, § 311.4(a)(1)	23.76	11
18, § 350–4.4(c)(2)(iv)(b)	23.76	3
18, § 350–7.2	23.82	5
18, § 358–2.4	23.83	4
18, § 358–2.13	23.83	9
18, § 358–3.1	23.83	1
18, § 358–3.3(a)	23.83	1
18, § 358–3.4(e)	23.83	6
18, § 358–3.6(a)(1)	23.83	5
18, § 358–3.6(a)(3)	23.83	5
18, § 358–3.8	23.83	4
18, § 358–3.9	23.83	6
18, § 358–5.3	23.83	8
18, § 358–5.6	23.83	9
18, § 358–5.9(b)	23.83	12
18, § 358–5.9(c)	23.83	11
18, § 358–6.1	23.83	13
18, § 358–6.3	23.83	14
18, Pt. 360	23.69	2
18, § 360–1.4(f)	23.75	5
18, § 360–1.4(h)	23.74	3
18, § 360–2.3(c)	23.71	3
18, § 360–2.5	23.83	1
18, § 360–2.7	23.83	1
18, § 360–2.8	23.83	2
18, § 360–2.9	23.83	3
18, § 360–3.3(a)	23.71	1
18, § 360–3.3(b)	23.71	2
18, § 360–3.7	23.83	7
18, § 360–4.1(b)	23.73	4
18, § 360–4.2(a)	23.80	1
18, § 360–4.2(b)	23.71	4
	23.71	5
	23.75	2
18, § 360–4.3(a)(3)	23.80	2
18, § 360–4.3(b)	23.73	1
	23.73	2
18, § 360–4.3(d)	23.73	3
18, § 360–4.3(e)	23.73	11

TABLE OF RULES

OFFICIAL COMPILATION OF CODES, RULES AND REGULATIONS OF THE STATE OF NEW YORK

Tit.	Sec.	This Work Note
18, § 360–4.3(f)(1)	23.80	2
	23.80	3
18, § 360–4.4(a)(1)	23.74	1
18, § 360–4.4(b)	23.74	3
18, § 360–4.4(c)	23.76	1
18, § 360–4.4(c)(1)	23.76	15
18, § 360–4.4(c)(2)(i)(b)	23.76	8
18, § 360–4.4(c)(2)(i)(c)	23.76	14
	23.76	17
	23.78	4
18, § 360–4.4(c)(2)(ii)	23.76	7
	23.76	9
	23.76	14
18, § 360–4.4(c)(2)(iii)(a)	23.76	12
18, § 360–4.4(c)(2)(iii)(b)	23.76	11
18, § 360–4.4(c)(2)(iii)(c)	23.76	10
18, § 360–4.4(c)(2)(iii)(c)(1)(iv)	23.78	6
18, § 360–4.4(c)(2)(iii)(c)(iv)	23.79	1
18, § 360–4.4(c)(2)(iii)(d)	23.76	13
18, § 360–4.4(c)(2)(iv)	23.76	2
18, § 360–4.4(d)	23.76	21
	23.76	22
	23.76	23
18, § 360–4.5(b)	23.78	6
18, § 360–4.5(b)(1)(ii)	23.78	5
18, § 360–4.5(b)(2)(i)	23.78	1
18, § 360–4.5(b)(5)(i)(a)	23.78	7
18, § 360–4.5(b)(5)(i)(b)	23.78	8
18, § 360–4.5(b)(5)(iii)	23.78	7
18, § 360–4.5(d)	23.78	2
18, § 360–4.6(a)	23.73	4
18, § 360–4.6(a)(1)(xxi)	23.73	10
18, § 360–4.6(a)(2)(ii)	23.73	9
18, § 360–4.6(a)(2)(iii)	23.73	5
18, § 360–4.6(a)(2)(vii)	23.73	6
18, § 360–4.6(a)(2)(xvii)	23.73	7
18, § 360–4.6(a)(2)(xxii)	23.73	9
18, § 360–4.6(a)(2)(xix)	23.73	8
18, § 360–4.6(b)(1)	23.75	3
18, § 360–4.6(b)(2)	23.75	5
18, § 360–4.6(b)(2)(iv)	23.75	8
18, § 360–4.6(b)(2)(v)	23.73	8
	23.75	10
18, § 360–4.6(b)(2)(viii)	23.75	8
18, § 360–4.6(b)(6)	23.75	9
18, § 360–4.6(b)(ii)	23.75	3
18, § 360–4.7(a)(1)	23.75	5
	23.81	6
18, § 360–4.8(c)	23.72	1
18, § 360–4.8(c)(1)	23.72	3
18, § 360–4.8(c)(4)	23.72	4
18, § 360–4.9(a)(1)	23.71	6
18, § 360–4.10	23.80	5

OFFICIAL COMPILATION OF CODES, RULES AND REGULATIONS OF THE STATE OF NEW YORK

Tit.	Sec.	This Work Note
18, § 360–4.10(a)(3)	23.80	14
18, § 360–4.10(a)(4)	23.80	10
18, § 360–4.10(a)(8)	23.80	15
18, § 360–4.10(a)(10)	23.80	16
18, § 360–4.10(b)(2)(i)	23.80	18
18, § 360–4.10(b)(2)(ii)	23.80	18
18, § 360–4.10(b)(4)(i)	23.71	6
18, § 360–4.10(b)(5)	23.80	19
	23.80	20
18, § 360–4.10(b)(6)	23.80	16
18, § 360–4.10(c)(1)	23.80	7
18, § 360–4.10(c)(1)(i)	23.80	7
18, § 360–4.10(c)(1)(iii)	23.80	11
18, § 360–4.10(c)(2)	23.80	6
	23.80	9
18, § 360–4.10(c)(7)	23.80	12
	23.80	13
18, § 360–4.10(c)(iii)	23.80	21
18, § 360–5.6(b)(8)	23.83	10
18, § 360–5.7(d)	23.83	10
18, § 360–7.7	23.43	18
18, § 360–7.8	23.43	18
18, § 360–7.11	23.75	7
18, § 360–7.11(5)	23.82	5
18, § 360–7.11(a)(1)	23.82	1
18, § 360–7.11(a)(2)	23.82	2
18, § 360–7.11(a)(3)	23.82	3
18, § 360–7.11(a)(3)(i)	23.82	6
18, § 360–7.11(a)(3)(ii)	23.82	7
	23.82	8
18, § 360–7.11(b)(1)(ii)	23.82	10
18, § 360–7.11(b)(2)	23.81	8
18, § 360–7.11(b)(3)	23.81	10
18, § 360–7.11(b)(4)	23.79	3
18, §§ 393.1—393.5	23.105	1
18, § 393.4(3)	23.105	3
18, § 393.4(d)	23.105	8
18, § 393.5	23.105	7
18, § 421.16(h)(2)	20.17	7
18, Pts. 505—510	23.70	1
18, § 505.9(d)	23.97	3
	23.97	6
18, § 505.9(d)(5)(i)(b)	23.97	4
	23.97	5
18, § 505.14	23.86	2
18, § 505.14(a)(1)	23.86	2
18, § 505.14(a)(3)	23.86	5
18, § 505.14(a)(6)(i)(a)	23.86	2
18, § 505.14(a)(6)(ii)(a)	23.86	2
18, § 505.14(a)(6)(ii)(b)(1)	23.86	4
18, § 505.14(a)(6)(iii)(c)(1)	23.86	4
18, § 505.14(b)(3)(i)(a)(3)	23.86	3
18, § 505.14(b)(3)(vi)	23.86	4
18, § 505.14(b)(4)(i)(c)	23.86	5

407

TABLE OF RULES

OFFICIAL COMPILATION OF CODES, RULES AND REGULATIONS OF THE STATE OF NEW YORK

Tit.	Sec.	This Work Note
18, 505.20(b)(1)	23.91	20
18, 505.20(b)(3)(i)	23.91	21
18, 505.20(b)(3)(iii)	23.91	22
	23.91	23
18, 505.20(b)(6)	23.91	24
19, § 260.1	4.45	3
19, § 260.2	4.45	3
19, § 260.3	4.45	9
19, § 264.1	4.51	6
20, § 1–2.2(c)	35.23	6
20, § 1–2.3(c)	35.23	1
20, § 1–3.2(a)(1)	35.25	2
20, § 1–3.4(b)(6)	35.24	1
	35.24	2
	35.24	3
20, § 3–2.2(b)	35.27	1
20, § 3–4.2	35.37	1
20, § 105.20(a)	35.14	2
	35.14	3
20, § 105.20(c)	35.14	4
20, § 132.4	35.12	2
20, § 135.1	35.17	2
20, § 440.1(h)	6.131	1
20, Pt. 537	6.66	5
	6.154	3
	6.184	6
20, § 537.1(a)(1)	6.66	4
	6.154	2
	6.184	5
20, Pt. 572	12.83	3
20, Pt. 575(6)	12.83	3
20, § 575.1(d)(6)	12.83	10
20, § 575.11	12.83	7
20, § 575.11(2)	12.83	8
	12.83	9
20, § 575.11(15)	12.83	10
20, Pt. 666	12.83	3
20, Pt. 2394	35.112	8
20, § 4000.3(a)	35.91	3
20, § 4000.4	35.90	1
20, § 4000.5	35.92	1
20, § 4000.6	35.92	2
20, § 5000.1	35.118	2
20, § 5000.6(b)	35.118	6
21B, § 4401.2(a)	3.29	13
Tit. 22	21.75	1
22, §§ 1.0—40.2	37.13	9
22, § 1.1(f)	38.57	1
22, Pt. 36	11.31	12
	22.25	2
	22.25	5
	22.27	1
	22.27	4
	22.28	17
	22.61	1
	22.75	1
	22.98	

OFFICIAL COMPILATION OF CODES, RULES AND REGULATIONS OF THE STATE OF NEW YORK

Tit.	Sec.	This Work Note
22, Pt. 36 (Cont'd)	22.98	6
	22.100	4
22, § 36.1	22.100	4
22, § 36.1(d)	22.98	
22, § 36.3	22.98	
22, § 36.3(a)	22.100	2
	22.100	3
22, § 36.4	22.27	4
	22.28	18
	22.61	1
22, Pt. 130	18.80	3
	37.83	
	37.83	1
22, § 130–1.1 et seq.	18.75	
	18.75	1
	18.79	4
22, § 130–1.1(a)	37.83	2
22, § 130–1.1(c)	37.83	
22, § 130–1.1(d)	37.83	3
	37.83	5
22, § 130–1.2	37.83	4
22, Pt. 136	21.78	
	21.78	1
22, § 136.1	21.78	2
22, § 136.2	21.78	3
22, § 136.3	21.78	4
22, § 136.4	21.78	5
22, § 136.5	21.78	6
	21.78	7
22, Pt. 200	38.55	
22, § 200.14	38.8	94
22, § 200.31	38.54	5
22, § 200.32	38.54	6
22, § 200.33(a)	38.55	27
	38.55	28
22, § 200.33(b)	38.55	30
22, § 200.33(c)	38.55	32
22, § 200.33(d)	38.55	33
22, Pt. 202	37.38	9
	37.126	1
22, § 202.3	26.51	1
22, § 202.5	17.82	2
22, § 202.12	37.38	10
22, § 202.12(d)	37.38	11
22, § 202.16	21.63	
	21.63	3
	21.75	1
	21.76	2
	21.79	
	21.79	1
	21.80	
	21.88	
22, § 202.16(a)	21.79	1
	21.79	3
22, § 202.16(b)	21.79	4
22, § 202.16(c)(1)	21.65	5
	21.79	5

TABLE OF RULES

OFFICIAL COMPILATION OF CODES, RULES AND REGULATIONS OF THE STATE OF NEW YORK

Tit.	This Work Sec.	Note
22, § 202.16(c)(1) (Cont'd)	21.80	4
	21.80	5
22, § 202.16(c)(2)	21.79	6
22, § 202.16(c)(3)	21.79	7
	21.80	7
22, § 202.16(d)	21.79	8
	21.80	8
	21.80	9
22, § 202.16(e)	21.65	4
	21.79	9
	21.79	10
22, § 202.16(f)(1)	21.79	11
	21.79	12
	21.79	13
	21.80	3
	21.80	10
22, § 202.16(f)(2)	21.63	4
	21.79	14
	21.80	11
22, § 202.16(f)(3)	21.79	16
	21.79	17
	21.79	18
	21.79	19
	21.79	20
	21.79	21
	21.80	12
	21.80	13
22, § 202.16(g)	21.63	6
	21.63	7
	21.79	22
	21.79	23
	21.80	14
	21.80	15
22, § 202.16(h)	21.66	1
	21.79	24
	21.80	16
	21.80	17
	21.88	
22, § 202.16(h) (proposed)	21.83	
22, § 202.16(i)	21.79	25
22, § 202.16(j)	21.79	26
22, § 202.16(k)(1)	21.79	15
22, § 202.16(k)(2)	21.79	15
22, § 202.16(k)(3)	21.79	15
22, § 202.16(k)(4)	21.79	15
22, § 202.16(k)(5)	21.79	15
22, § 202.16(k)(6)	21.79	15
22, § 202.16(k)(7)	21.79	15
22, § 202.16(L)	21.79	27
22, § 202.17	30.3	
22, § 202.21	17.82	22
	30.3	20
22, § 202.21(e)	30.3	
	30.3	21
22, § 202.33	26.55	2
22, § 202.46(b)	8.4	6

OFFICIAL COMPILATION OF CODES, RULES AND REGULATIONS OF THE STATE OF NEW YORK

Tit.	This Work Sec.	Note
22, § 202.48	8.4	9
	8.14	5
22, § 202.50	21.67	2
	21.67	3
	21.89	1
	21.90	1
	21.91	1
	21.92	1
22, § 202.54	22.21	10
	22.66	15
22, § 202.55(a)	37.97	2
	37.97	3
22, § 202.55(b)	37.97	4
22, § 202.55(c)	37.97	5
	37.97	6
22, §§ 202.59—202.61	14.102	1
	14.104	2
22, § 202.59(g)(2)	14.104	6
22, § 202.59(g)(ii)	14.104	4
22, § 202.59(h)	14.105	3
22, § 202.60(g)(3)		6
22, § 202.60(h)	14.105	3
22, § 202.61	14.105	5
22, § 205.51	20.50	3
	20.69	5
22, § 205.52 et seq.	20.5	
22, § 205.53	20.1	14
	20.1	15
	20.1	16
	20.1	22
	20.1	24
22, §§ 205.53—205.55	20.1	8
	20.9	2
	20.36	2
22, § 205.53(b)(2)	20.146	
22, § 205.53(b)(8)	20.106	1
	20.147	
22, § 205.58(c)	20.56	2
	20.56	3
22, Pt. 206	26.41	2
22, § 206.5(a)	26.41	13
22, § 206.6	26.41	11
22, § 206.12	26.41	15
22, § 206.18	14.114	4
22, § 206.21	14.102	1
	14.104	2
22, § 206.21(b)	14.104	3
	14.104	7
22, § 206.21(d)	14.104	4
22, § 206.21(f)	14.105	4
22, § 206.21(h)	14.105	3
22, § 207.7(c)	25.55	
22, § 207.16(b)	25.52	
	25.67	
22, § 207.19(c)	25.52	
22, § 207.19(g)	25.52	
	25.67	

TABLE OF RULES

OFFICIAL COMPILATION OF CODES, RULES AND REGULATIONS OF THE STATE OF NEW YORK

Tit.	This Work Sec.	Note
22, § 207.50	25.52	
	25.67	
22, §§ 207.54—207.58	20.1	8
	20.9	2
	20.36	2
22, § 207.54 et seq.	20.5	
22, § 207.55	20.108	1
	20.120	1
	20.121	1
	20.146	
22, § 207.55(b)(2)	20.71	1
	20.115	1
22, § 207.55(b)(6)	20.75	1
22, § 207.55(b)(7)	20.73	1
22, § 207.55(b)(8)(vi)	20.52	4
22, § 207.58	20.69	1
22, § 207.58(1)	20.62	5
22, § 207.58(2)	20.62	4
22, § 207.60	25.52	
	25.67	
22, § 207.61(c)	20.56	2
	20.56	3
22, Pt. 208	37.117	3
	37.119	2
22, § 208.2	37.117	2
22, § 208.37	8.24	1
22, § 208.38(a)	37.122	1
22, § 208.39	8.23	6
22, § 208.42(b)	13.41	11
22, § 208.42(c)	13.41	11
22, § 208.42(d)	13.15	1
	13.15	12
	13.22	4
22, § 208.42(i)	13.10	
	13.10	1
22, § 208.42g	13.17	14
	13.43	15
22, Pt. 210	37.101	1
	37.103	1
22, § 210.37	8.24	1
22, § 210.38(a)	37.105	1
22, § 210.39	8.23	6
22, § 210.42(b)	13.15	13
	13.41	12
22, § 210.42(c)	13.15	13
	13.41	12
22, Pt. 212	37.109	1
	37.111	1
22, § 212.2(a)	37.109	2
22, § 212.37	8.24	1
22, § 212.38(a)	37.113	1
22, § 212.39	8.23	6
22, § 212.42(b)	13.15	14
	13.41	13
22, § 212.42(c)	13.15	14
	13.41	13
22, Pt. 214	37.92	1

OFFICIAL COMPILATION OF CODES, RULES AND REGULATIONS OF THE STATE OF NEW YORK

Tit.	This Work Sec.	Note
22, Pt. 214 (Cont'd)	37.94	2
	37.100	2
22, § 214.8(a)	37.96	4
22, Pt. 216	22.31	12
22, § 216.1	22.31	12
	27.38	6
22, § 321.2	39.45	1
22, § 500.1	39.26	2
	39.26	5
	39.29	11
	39.52	1
22, § 500.2	39.26	6
	39.47	16
	39.66	
	39.67	
	39.82	
22, § 500.2(a)	39.26	3
22, § 500.2(b)	39.26	4
22, § 500.3	37.37	65
	39.27	1
	39.31	3
22, § 500.3(a)	39.27	2
22, § 500.4	39.27	
	39.28	
	39.28	3
	39.34	
	39.60	3
22, § 500.4(b)	39.30	1
22, § 500.4(f)	39.30	2
	39.30	3
	39.30	4
	39.68	3
	39.68	5
	39.68	6
	39.68	7
22, § 500.5(a)	39.69	2
22, § 500.5(b)	39.29	14
22, § 500.5(d)	39.29	8
	39.69	4
22, § 500.5(e)	39.29	8
22, § 500.5(f)	39.29	3
22, § 500.6(c)	39.29	15
22, § 500.7(a)(1)	39.29	2
	39.29	20
	39.69	6
22, § 500.7(b)	39.29	20
22, § 500.8(a)	39.29	22
	39.29	23
22, § 500.8(b)	39.29	21
22, § 500.9(a)	39.26	6
	39.29	1
	39.31	3
	39.55	2
22, § 500.9(a)(b)	37.37	65
22, § 500.9(b)	39.27	2
	39.29	1
	39.29	4

TABLE OF RULES

OFFICIAL COMPILATION OF CODES, RULES AND REGULATIONS OF THE STATE OF NEW YORK

Tit.	Sec.	This Work Note
22, § 500.9(6) (Cont'd)	39.29	5
	39.30	5
	39.30	6
	39.31	3
	39.55	2
	39.68	4
	39.69	5
22, § 500.9(c)	39.29	2
	39.29	6
	39.30	7
	39.68	6
	39.68	7
	39.69	7
22, § 500.10	39.45	1
	39.47	11
22, § 500.10(a)	39.47	13
	39.47	14
22, § 500.10(b)	39.47	17
	39.47	18
	39.47	19
22, § 500.10(c)	39.35	2
	39.53	2
22, § 500.11	39.19	
	39.19	1
	39.32	1
	39.47	4
	39.47	16
	39.48	
	39.52	
	39.52	2
	39.53	
	39.53	1
22, § 500.11(a)	39.19	3
	39.65	2
22, § 500.11(b)	39.19	14
22, § 500.11(c)	39.19	4
22, § 500.11(d)	39.19	12
	39.19	16
22, § 500.11(d)(1)	39.19	7
22, § 500.11(d)(1)(iii)	39.19	8
	39.19	9
22, § 500.11(d)(1)(iv)	39.19	10
22, § 500.11(d)(1)(v)	39.19	11
22, § 500.11(d)(2)	39.19	6
	39.19	13
22, § 500.11(e)	39.34	2
22, § 500.11(f)	39.29	19
	39.47	4
22, § 500.11(g)	39.32	2
22, § 500.11(g)(1)	39.36	3
	39.36	4
	39.57	1
	39.57	2
22, § 500.11(g)(2)	39.36	3
22, § 500.11(g)(3)	39.36	2
	39.36	4
	39.47	18

OFFICIAL COMPILATION OF CODES, RULES AND REGULATIONS OF THE STATE OF NEW YORK

Tit.	Sec.	This Work Note
22, § 500.11(g)(3) (Cont'd)	39.47	19
	39.57	1
	39.57	3
	39.57	4
22, § 500.14	39.19	15
	39.68	2
	39.69	3
22, § 500.14(1)	39.29	7
22, § 500.14(1)(a)	39.29	17
22, § 500.14(1)(b)	39.29	18
22, § 500.15	39.31	1
22, § 500.16	39.56	1
22, § 500.17(a)	39.60	2
22, § 500.17(d)	39.60	3
22, § 500.17(g)	39.60	4
22, Pt. 520	39.61	3
22, § 520.3(d)	39.61	5
22, § 520.3(e)	39.61	5
22, § 520.10(a)(2)(i)(d)	39.61	
22, § 520.14	39.61	
	39.61	4
22, Pt. 521	39.61	3
22, § 521.1	37.6	6
22, § 521.7	39.61	
	39.61	4
22, § 530.2	39.59	6
	39.59	7
	39.59	11
22, § 530.4	39.59	9
22, § 530.6(a)	39.59	8
22, § 530.6(b)	39.59	10
22, § 530.7(b)	39.59	14
22, §§ 530.1—530.9	39.59	3
22, Pt. 540	38.10	187
22, Pt. 600	37.13	
22, § 600.2(a)(1)	37.75	1
	37.79	1
22, § 600.2(a)(2)	37.75	2
22, § 600.2(a)(3)	37.75	3
22, § 600.2(a)(4)	37.75	4
22, § 600.2(a)(5)	37.75	4
	37.75	5
22, § 600.2(a)(6)	37.75	6
22, § 600.2(a)(7)	37.79	2
22, § 600.2(b)	37.87	9
22, § 600.2(d)	37.87	10
22, § 600.3(a)	37.41	10
22, § 600.3(b)	37.41	10
22, § 600.3(b)(2)	37.41	12
22, § 600.4	37.60	2
	37.62	1
22, § 600.4(a)	37.62	2
22, § 600.4(a)(7)	38.17	9
22, § 600.4(b)	37.62	3
22, § 600.5	37.19	53
	37.55	4
22, § 600.5(a)	37.51	23

411

TABLE OF RULES

OFFICIAL COMPILATION OF CODES, RULES AND REGULATIONS OF THE STATE OF NEW YORK

Tit.	Sec.	This Work Note
22, § 600.5(a)(1)	37.50	5
22, § 600.5(a)(3)	37.51	24
22, § 600.5(b)	37.51	36
	37.55	1
22, § 600.5(b)(2)	37.50	5
22, § 600.5(c)	37.19	54
	37.50	4
	37.51	11
	37.55	1
	37.60	3
22, § 600.5(d)	37.50	4
22, § 600.5(f)	37.51	5
22, § 600.6	37.19	52
	37.51	40
	37.55	3
22, § 600.7(a)	37.51	46
	37.55	2
22, § 600.7(b)	37.87	29
	37.87	30
22, § 600.8	38.17	2
22, § 600.8(a)(2)	38.17	8
22, § 600.8(b)	38.17	6
22, § 600.8(c)	38.17	7
	38.44	1
22, § 600.8(d)	38.13	7
22, § 600.8(e)	38.15	17
22, § 600.8(f)	38.17	12
22, § 600.8(g)	38.16	3
22, § 600.8(h)	38.32	4
22, § 600.9	37.51	42
22, § 600.10	37.52	9
22, § 600.10(a)	37.51	11
22, § 600.10(a)(5)	38.5	10
22, § 600.10(a)(11)	37.52	7
22, § 600.10(b)	37.51	11
22, § 600.10(c)	37.51	23
22, § 600.10(c)(1)	37.51	27
22, § 600.10(d)	37.52	17
22, § 600.10(d)(1)(i)	37.52	10
	37.52	11
	37.52	13
	37.52	15
	38.44	2
22, § 600.10(d)(1)(iii)	37.52	21
22, § 600.10(d)(2)(v)	37.52	19
22, § 600.10(d)(2)(vi)	37.52	22
22, § 600.10(d)(3)	37.52	25
22, § 600.10(d)(4)	37.52	27
22, § 600.10(e)	37.51	16
	37.51	32
	37.52	4
22, § 600.11(a)	38.17	10
22, § 600.11(a)(3)	37.50	2
22, § 600.11(b)(1)(i)	38.17	10
	37.60	1
22, § 600.11(b)(2)	37.19	54
	37.55	1

OFFICIAL COMPILATION OF CODES, RULES AND REGULATIONS OF THE STATE OF NEW YORK

Tit.	Sec.	This Work Note
22, § 600.11(b)(2) (Cont'd)	37.60	3
22, § 600.11(c)	37.60	4
22, § 600.11(d)	37.51	50
	37.60	5
22, § 600.11(f)	38.17	11
22, § 600.11(f)(1)	37.62	4
22, § 600.11(f)(2)	37.62	4
22, § 600.11(f)(3)	37.62	4
22, § 600.11(g)	37.60	6
22, § 600.12(a)	37.61	2
22, § 600.12(a)(2)	37.61	3
22, § 600.12(c)(1)	37.85	1
22, § 600.12(c)(2)	38.17	13
22, § 600.12(c)(3)	37.85	2
	38.17	13
22, § 600.12(c)(4)	37.85	2
	38.17	13
	38.17	14
22, § 600.14(a)	37.69	1
	37.69	2
	37.70	3
22, § 600.14(b)	39.18	
22, § 600.16	38.11	13
	38.17	46
22, § 600.17	37.19	37
	37.45	6
	37.84	1
22, § 600.17(a)	37.45	5
22, § 600.17(b)	37.84	2
22, § 600.17(h)	37.83	7
22, Pt. 602	37.6	2
22, Pt. 603	37.6	2
22, § 603.7	26.7	1
22, § 603.7(e)	26.6	3
22, § 603.7(e)(2)	26.6	
	26.6	1
	26.6	2
22, § 603.7(e)(3)	26.6	
	26.6	1
22, § 603.18	26.6	4
22, § 603.23	20.78	4
22, Pt. 604	37.6	2
22, Pt. 605	37.6	2
22, Pt. 606	37.10	2
22, § 606.5	39.45	1
22, § 606.5(b)(1)	38.45	2
22, § 606.5(b)(2)	38.30	1
22, Pt. 610	37.6	5
22, Pt. 611 et seq.	37.8	1
22, Pt. 612	37.10	2
22, Pt. 622	37.9	4
22, Pt. 635	37.12	2
22, Pt. 640	37.3	5
	37.11	2
	37.93	2
	38.55	
22, § 640.1	37.118	1

412

TABLE OF RULES

OFFICIAL COMPILATION OF CODES, RULES AND REGULATIONS OF THE STATE OF NEW YORK

Tit.	Sec.	This Work Note
22, § 640.1 (Cont'd)	38.49	1
22, § 640.2(a)	37.123	1
	37.123	11
22, § 640.2(b)	37.125	5
22, § 640.2(c)	37.123	2
22, § 640.2(d)	37.123	3
22, § 640.3(a)	38.55	6
22, § 640.3(c)	38.55	7
22, § 640.5(a)	37.123	4
	38.55	8
22, § 640.5(b)	37.123	4
	38.55	9
22, § 640.5(c)	37.123	6
22, § 640.5(d)	38.55	10
22, § 640.5(e)	38.55	10
22, § 640.6(a)	37.123	7
22, § 640.6(a)(3)(i)	37.123	8
22, § 640.6(a)(3)(ii)	37.123	9
22, § 640.6(a)(3)(iii)	37.123	10
22, § 640.6(b)(1)	38.55	11
22, § 640.7(a)	37.123	12
22, § 640.7(b)	37.123	12
22, § 640.7(d)	37.123	5
	38.55	12
22, § 640.8(a)	37.123	19
22, § 640.8(b)	37.123	19
22, § 640.9(a)	37.123	14
	38.55	13
22, § 640.9(b)(1)	37.123	16
22, § 640.9(b)(2)	37.123	17
22, § 640.10(c)	38.53	1
	38.53	2
22, Pt. 670	37.13	
	37.51	7
22, § 670.2(a)(1)	37.51	46
22, § 670.2(a)(6)	37.51	54
22, § 670.2(d)	37.76	6
22, § 670.2(e)	37.51	17
	37.51	33
	37.52	5
22, § 670.2(g)	37.83	
	37.83	8
22, § 670.3	37.45	8
22, § 670.3(a)	37.19	37
	37.84	3
22, § 670.3(c)	37.87	32
22, § 670.3(e)	37.87	12
22, § 670.4	37.45	9
	37.84	1
22, § 670.4(b)	37.83	9
22, § 670.5	38.8	
22, § 670.5(a)	37.76	1
	37.76	3
	37.76	4
	37.87	11
22, § 670.5(b)	37.76	2
	37.76	4

OFFICIAL COMPILATION OF CODES, RULES AND REGULATIONS OF THE STATE OF NEW YORK

Tit.	Sec.	This Work Note
22, § 670.5(b) (Cont'd)	37.87	11
22, § 670.5(d)	37.76	5
22, § 670.5(e)	37.79	2
	37.89	3
22, § 670.6(a)	37.69	1
	37.69	2
	37.69	3
	37.72	1
22, § 670.6(b)	37.97	24
22, § 670.6(b)(1)	37.41	14
22, § 670.6(b)(2)	37.41	15
22, § 670.6(c)	37.70	3
	39.18	
22, § 670.6(d)	38.32	1
	39.46	2
	39.47	10
22, § 670.7	37.60	7
	38.17	27
22, § 670.7(b)	37.61	2
22, § 670.7(b)(2)	37.61	3
22, § 670.7(c)	37.53	2
22, § 670.8(a)	37.19	55
	37.60	8
	38.17	16
22, § 670.8(b)	37.60	9
22, § 670.8(c)	37.51	50
	37.60	10
22, § 670.8(c)(1)	37.51	53
22, § 670.8(c)(2)	37.51	55
22, § 670.8(d)	38.44	1
22, § 670.8(e)	37.50	3
22, § 670.8(f)	38.17	15
22, § 670.8(g)	38.17	
22, § 670.8(h)	37.85	3
22, § 670.9(a)	37.51	11
	37.56	1
22, § 670.9(b)	37.51	23
22, § 670.9(b)(3)	37.51	24
22, § 670.9(b)(4)	37.56	1
22, § 670.9(c)	37.51	37
	37.56	1
22, § 670.9(d)(1)(iii)	37.51	42
22, § 670.9(d)(1)(viii)	38.17	3
22, § 670.10	37.52	9
22, § 670.10(a)	37.51	11
	37.52	17
22, § 670.10(a)(2)	37.51	15
22, § 670.10(a)(3)	38.5	10
22, § 670.10(a)(5)	37.51	15
22, § 670.10(b)	37.51	11
22, § 670.10(c)	37.37	96
	37.51	23
22, § 670.10(d)	37.52	17
22, § 670.10(d)(1)(i)	37.52	10
	37.52	11
	37.52	13
	37.52	15

TABLE OF RULES

OFFICIAL COMPILATION OF CODES, RULES AND REGULATIONS OF THE STATE OF NEW YORK

Tit.	Sec.	This Work Note
22, § 670.10(d)(1)(i) (Cont'd)	38.44	2
22, § 670.10(d)(1)(ii)	37.62	10
22, § 670.10(d)(1)(iii)	37.52	21
22, § 670.10(d)(2)	38.17	17
22, § 670.10(d)(2)(i)	37.52	20
22, § 670.10(d)(2)(vi)	37.52	23
22, § 670.10(d)(2)(viii)	38.8	
22, § 670.10(d)(3)	37.52	25
22, § 670.10(d)(4)	37.52	27
22, § 670.10(d)(ii)	37.51	40
22, § 670.10(e)	37.24	4
22, § 670.11	37.81	1
22, § 670.11(b)	37.81	2
22, § 670.12(a)	38.17	27
22, § 670.12(b)	38.13	7
22, § 670.12(c)	38.8	43
	38.17	18
22, § 670.12(c)(1)	38.8	44
22, § 670.12(c)(2)	38.8	45
	38.8	46
22, § 670.12(e)	38.15	17
22, § 670.12(f)	38.32	4
22, § 670.12(g)	38.17	20
22, § 670.12(g)(2)	38.38	3
22, § 670.12(h)	38.17	21
	38.37	2
22, § 670.14	38.11	13
	38.17	46
22, § 670.16	37.87	29
22, § 670.18	37.90	5
	37.90	8
	37.90	9
	37.90	10
	37.90	11
22, § 670.19	38.17	28
22, § 670.19(a)	37.51	46
22, § 670.19(a)(4)	37.51	45
22, § 670.20(a)	37.62	5
22, § 670.20(b)	37.62	6
22, § 670.20(c)	37.62	7
	37.62	8
22, § 670.20(d)	37.62	12
22, § 670.20(e)	37.62	9
22, § 670.20(f)	37.62	11
22, § 670.21(a)	37.71	
22, § 671.3(a)	38.45	2
22, § 671.3(b)	38.45	2
22, § 671.3(f)	38.17	25
22, § 671.4	39.45	1
22, § 671.4(a)	38.30	1
22, § 671.10	37.19	61
22, Pt. 678	37.10	2
22, Pt. 679 et seq.	37.8	1
22, § 681.1(b)	38.8	94
22, Pt. 690	37.6	2
22, Pt. 691	37.6	2
22, § 691.20	26.7	1

OFFICIAL COMPILATION OF CODES, RULES AND REGULATIONS OF THE STATE OF NEW YORK

Tit.	Sec.	This Work Note
22, § 691.20(e)	26.6	3
22, § 691.20(e)(2)	26.6	1
	26.6	2
22, § 691.20(e)(3)	26.6	1
22, § 691.23	20.78	4
22, Pt. 692	37.6	5
22, Pt. 694	37.9	4
22, Pt. 700	37.6	2
22, Pt. 730	37.3	5
	37.93	2
22, Pts. 730—732	37.11	2
22, § 730.1	38.55	16
22, § 730.1(a)(1)	37.118	1
22, § 730.1(b)(1)	37.118	1
22, § 730.1(b)(2)	38.50	1
22, § 730.1(c)	37.16	3
	37.93	4
	37.126	5
22, § 730.1(d)	37.16	3
	38.47	5
	38.47	6
22, § 730.1(d)(2)(ii)	37.93	4
22, § 730.1(d)(2)(iii)	37.102	3
	37.126	5
22, Pt. 731	37.123	
22, § 731.1(b)(1)	38.55	17
22, § 731.2	38.55	18
22, § 731.4(a)(2)	38.55	19
22, § 731.4(b)	38.55	20
22, § 731.4(c)	38.55	21
22, § 731.6(a)	38.55	22
22, § 731.6(b)	38.55	22
22, § 731.8(b)	38.55	23
22, § 731.8(c)	38.55	23
	38.55	24
22, § 731.9(b)	38.55	25
22, § 731.10(c)	38.53	3
	38.53	4
22, § 731.11(a)	38.55	26
22, Pt. 732	37.97	
	37.123	
22, § 732.1(a)	37.97	8
	37.126	7
22, § 732.2	38.55	18
22, § 732.2(a)	37.97	13
	37.97	14
22, § 732.2(b)	37.97	14
22, § 732.4(a)(1)	37.97	10
22, § 732.4(a)(2)	38.55	19
22, § 732.4(b)	37.97	11
	38.55	20
22, § 732.4(c)	37.97	12
	38.55	21
22, § 732.4(d)	37.97	17
22, § 732.6(a)	37.97	15
	37.97	16
	38.55	22

414

TABLE OF RULES

OFFICIAL COMPILATION OF CODES, RULES AND REGULATIONS OF THE STATE OF NEW YORK

Tit.	Sec.	This Work Note
22, § 732.6(b)	37.97	16
	38.55	22
22, § 732.7	37.97	25
22, § 732.8(a)	37.97	18
22, § 732.8(b)	38.55	23
22, § 732.8(c)	38.55	23
	38.55	24
22, § 732.9(b)	38.55	25
22, § 732.10	37.95	8
22, § 732.10(a)	37.95	9
22, § 732.10(c)	38.53	3
	38.53	4
22, § 732.11(a)	37.97	20
	38.55	26
22, § 732.11(b)	37.97	22
22, § 732.11(d)	37.97	23
22, § 732.12	38.54	
22, Pt. 800	37.13	
22, Pt. 800 et seq.	32.34	3
22, Pt. 800(c)	35.99	1
22, § 800.2(a)	37.69	1
	37.70	3
	37.77	1
	37.77	2
	37.77	3
	39.18	
22, § 800.2(b)	37.87	13
22, § 800.2(c)	37.90	2
	37.90	3
	37.90	4
	37.90	5
	37.90	6
22, § 800.2(d)	37.79	2
22, § 800.3	37.41	16
	38.13	8
	39.47	10
22, § 800.4(a)	37.57	1
22, § 800.4(b)	37.51	23
	37.51	24
	37.51	25
22, § 800.4(c)	37.57	2
	38.17	4
22, § 800.4(d)	37.51	36
22, § 800.5	37.51	11
22, § 800.5(a)	37.51	14
22, § 800.6	37.51	11
22, § 800.6(a)	37.51	6
22, § 800.7	37.51	11
22, § 800.7(b)	37.51	26
	38.8	
22, § 800.8	37.52	9
	38.5	11
22, § 800.8(a)	37.52	10
	37.52	11
	37.52	12
	37.52	14
	37.52	16

OFFICIAL COMPILATION OF CODES, RULES AND REGULATIONS OF THE STATE OF NEW YORK

Tit.	Sec.	This Work Note
22, § 800.8(a) (Cont'd)	37.52	17
	38.44	2
22, § 800.8(b)	37.51	23
22, § 800.8(c)	37.51	28
22, § 800.9(a)	37.19	56
	37.50	6
	37.57	1
22, § 800.9(b)	37.60	12
22, § 800.9(c)	37.60	13
22, § 800.9(e)	37.51	51
	37.60	14
22, § 800.10(a)	37.62	14
	38.17	34
22, § 800.10(a)(5)	37.62	15
22, § 800.10(b)	37.62	17
22, § 800.10(c)	37.62	13
	37.62	16
	38.17	33
22, § 800.11	37.60	11
	37.60	15
22, § 800.12	37.50	2
22, § 800.13	37.51	40
	37.57	3
22, § 800.14	38.17	4
22, § 800.14(b)	38.5	11
	38.8	
	38.17	29
	38.17	31
22, § 800.14(c)	38.17	30
	38.44	1
22, § 800.14(f)	38.31	2
22, § 800.14(g)	38.8	47
	38.8	49
	38.8	50
	38.17	32
22, § 800.14(h)	38.15	17
22, § 800.14(h)(4)	38.17	35
22, § 800.14(i)	38.32	4
22, § 800.15	38.11	13
	38.17	46
22, § 800.16	37.51	42
	37.57	4
22, § 800.17	37.44	9
22, § 800.18	37.44	9
22, § 800.19	37.87	29
	37.87	31
22, § 800.20	37.57	5
22, § 800.21	37.51	46
22, § 800.24(a)	37.84	4
22, § 800.24(b)	37.84	1
22, § 800.24–a	37.45	10
22, § 800.24–a(a)	37.45	11
22, § 800.24–a(c)	37.45	13
22, § 800.24–b(a)	37.45	12
22, § 800.24–b(b)	37.83	11
22, Pt. 805	37.6	2
22, Pt. 805.4	37.6	5

415

TABLE OF RULES

OFFICIAL COMPILATION OF CODES, RULES AND REGULATIONS OF THE STATE OF NEW YORK

Tit.	Sec.	This Work Note
22, Pt. 806	37.6	2
22, § 806.13	26.6	3
22, § 806.13(b)	26.6	1
	26.6	2
22, § 806.13(c)	26.6	1
22, § 806.14	20.78	4
22, § 821.2(a)	38.45	2
22, § 821.2(b)	38.30	1
22, Pt. 822	37.10	2
22, Pt. 823	37.9	4
22, Pt. 835	37.8	1
22, § 863.3	38.8	94
22, Pt. 1000	37.13	
	37.51	7
22, § 1000.1	37.58	16
22, § 1000.2	37.51	52
22, § 1000.2(a)(1)	37.69	1
22, § 1000.2(b)	37.50	6
	38.17	36
22, § 1000.2(d)	37.58	18
22, § 1000.2(e)	37.58	19
22, § 1000.2(f)	37.58	20
22, § 1000.3	38.17	36
22, § 1000.3(b)	37.19	57
	37.58	1
	37.58	2
22, § 1000.3(c)	38.17	5
22, § 1000.3(c)(1)	38.5	11
	38.17	38
	38.17	39
	38.17	45
22, § 1000.3(c)(2)	37.51	40
22, § 1000.3(c)(12)	37.19	57
22, § 1000.3(d)	37.58	1
22, § 1000.3(d)(2)	37.51	37
22, § 1000.4	37.51	11
	38.44	2
22, § 1000.4(a)(3)	37.51	
22, § 1000.4(a)(3)(iii)	37.51	
22, § 1000.4(b)(1)	37.53	
22, § 1000.4(b)(2)	37.53	
22, § 1000.4(c)	37.51	35
	37.51	37
22, § 1000.4(d)	37.51	23
22, § 1000.4(d)(2)(ii)	37.51	29
22, § 1000.4(d)(3)	37.51	
22, § 1000.4(e)	38.17	5
	38.17	39
22, § 1000.4(f)	37.52	9
22, § 1000.4(f)(3)	37.52	
22, § 1000.4(f)(5)	37.52	
22, § 1000.4(f)(6)	37.52	
	37.52	17
	37.52	25
22, § 1000.5(c)	37.51	24
22, § 1000.5(e)	37.58	3
22, § 1000.5(i)	37.51	42

OFFICIAL COMPILATION OF CODES, RULES AND REGULATIONS OF THE STATE OF NEW YORK

Tit.	Sec.	This Work Note
22, § 1000.5(i) (Cont'd)	37.58	3
22, § 1000.5(j)	37.58	3
22, § 1000.6	37.51	46
	37.58	1
22, § 1000.6(d)	37.58	2
22, § 1000.7(e)	38.17	45
22, § 1000.7(L)		17
22, § 1000.8	37.58	2
	37.87	
22, § 1000.8(b)	37.50	
22, § 1000.9	37.87	14
22, § 1000.10(a)	37.58	17
	38.17	42
22, § 1000.10(b)	37.58	18
	38.17	44
	38.17	45
22, § 1000.10(c)	37.60	21
22, § 1000.10(e)	37.60	22
22, § 1000.11(a)	37.62	18
22, § 1000.11(b)	37.62	19
	37.62	20
22, § 1000.11(c)	37.62	20
	37.62	21
22, § 1000.12 (repealed)	37.45	7
	37.83	10
22, § 1000.12(a)	37.50	6
22, § 1000.12(b)	37.50	2
	37.85	
22, § 1000.13(a)	37.78	1
	37.41	17
22, § 1000.13(a)(4)(iii)	37.78	3
22, § 1000.13(b)(1)	37.79	2
22, § 1000.13(b)(2)	37.89	3
22, § 1000.13(c)	38.15	1
22, § 1000.13(c—q)	37.78	2
22, § 1000.13(e)	37.50	7
22, § 1000.13(h)	38.44	1
22, § 1000.13(j)	38.17	41
	38.37	2
22, § 1000.13(k)	37.81	
	37.81	1
	37.81	2
	38.44	3
22, § 1000.13(I)	38.14	4
22, § 1000.13(O)	38.13	7
22, § 1000.13(p)	39.18	
22, § 1000.13(p)(1)	37.69	3
22, § 1000.13(p)(4)	37.70	3
22, § 1000.13(p)(4)(iii)	38.32	1
	39.46	2
	39.47	10
22, § 1000.13(q)	38.38	1
22, § 1000.13(r)	38.44	2
22, § 1000.15	37.58	3
22, § 1000.16	37.83	12
22, § 1000.17(c)	38.32	4
22, § 1000.19	37.62	20

TABLE OF RULES

OFFICIAL COMPILATION OF CODES, RULES AND REGULATIONS OF THE STATE OF NEW YORK

Tit.	Sec.	This Work Note
22, § 1000.19 (Cont'd)	37.62	22
22, Pt. 1021	37.10	2
	38.17	37
22, Pt. 1022	37.6	2
22, § 1022.2	26.7	1
22, § 1022.11	39.45	1
22, § 1022.11(a)	38.45	2
22, § 1022.11(b)	38.30	1
22, § 1022.11(c)	38.17	40
22, § 1022.11(d)	38.38	1
22, § 1022.31	26.6	3
22, § 1022.31(b)	26.6	1
	26.6	2
22, § 1022.31(c)	26.6	1
22, § 1022.33	20.78	4
22, Pt. 1023	37.9	4
22, § 1026.4	26.52	2
22, Pt. 1029	37.6	5
22, Pt. 1032 et seq.	37.8	1
22, Pt. 1100	38.10	
	38.10	185
22, § 1200.3	21.75	1
	21.77	1
	21.77	4
22, § 1200.10–a	21.75	1
	21.77	1
22, § 1200.11	21.75	1
	21.77	1
	21.77	2
	21.77	3
22, § 1200.11(c)(2)(B)	21.77	2
22, § 1200.11(c)(2)(C)	21.77	2
22, § 1200.11(e)	21.77	2
22, § 1200.20	28.20	1
22, § 1200.21	28.21	14
22, § 1200.24	28.20	1
22, § 1200.27	28.21	3
22, § 1302.8(a)	38.8	94
22, § 1302.8(b)	38.8	94
22, Pt. 1400	21.75	1
	21.76	
	21.76	1
	21.76	2
	21.77	
22, § 1400.1	21.76	2
22, § 1400.2	21.76	
	21.76	3
22, § 1400.3	21.65	5
	21.76	5
	21.77	
	21.80	4
	21.80	5
	21.80	6
	21.81	
22, § 1400.4	21.76	6
	21.77	
22, § 1400.5	21.76	7

OFFICIAL COMPILATION OF CODES, RULES AND REGULATIONS OF THE STATE OF NEW YORK

Tit.	Sec.	This Work Note
22, § 1400.5 (Cont'd)	21.77	
22, § 1400.6	21.76	8
	21.76	9
	21.80	7
22, § 1400.7	21.76	10
	21.77	

NEW YORK CITY ADMINISTRATIVE CODE

Sec.	Sec.	This Work Note
Ch. 3	17.61	19
Ch. 21	11.51	3
7–701 et seq.	15.32	1
8–101 et seq.	18.49	15
8–102(5)	17.17	1
8–102(16)(a)	17.43	8
8–102(18)	18.47	3
8–107(1)	17.37	10
	17.56	6
8–107(1)(a)	17.48	4
	17.49	10
8–107(2)	17.56	6
	17.58	
8–107(3)	18.41	5
8–107(5)	18.47	3
8–107(9)	17.56	8
8–107(12)	17.56	8
8–107(14)	17.49	11
8–107(15)	18.47	3
8–107(15)(a)	17.43	10
8–107(17)(a)	17.59	10
8–107(17)(a)(2)	17.59	11
8–107(19)	17.38	
8–107(21)	17.49	11
8–113(a)	17.68	2
8–113(c)	17.68	6
8–123	18.49	16
8–502	30.32	6
8–502(a)	17.68	1
8–502(c)	17.69	2
	17.78	3
	17.79	4
8–502(e)	17.69	1
8–602	17.57	
11–602.1	1.23	20
11–1712(c)(31)	23.68	3
11–2102	11.51	3
	12.85	
11–2104	12.85	3
11–2105(g)	12.73	6
11–2106	12.85	1
11–2106(8)	12.85	5
11–2601	12.89	3
14–140	18.11	2
	18.11	3

417

TABLE OF RULES

NEW YORK CITY ADMINISTRATIVE CODE

Sec.	This Work Sec.	Note
14–140 (Cont'd)	18.94	
14–140(e)	18.11	2
14–140(f)	18.11	6
17–151 et seq.	12.55	2
Tit. 20, Ch. 2, subch. 11, § B20–264et seq.	7.65	
25–301 et seq.	16.6	9
26–401et seq.	13.2	5
26–403(a)(2)	13.39	10
26–403(a)(10)	13.39	10
26–408	13.39	1
26–408(b)(4)	13.39	1
26–408(b)(5)	13.39	1
26–413	13.74	2
26–501et seq.	13.2	1
26–514	13.75	
	13.75	1
26–516(a)	13.74	3
26–516(a)(2)(i)	13.74	4
Tit. 27, Ch. 1, Subch. 17, Art. 6	12.91	2
27–2009.1	13.53	6
27–2099(c)	11.51	
27–2107(b)	13.17	15
	13.43	16
692h–6.0(a)	12.65	9

LOCAL RULES OF THE U.S. DISTRICT COURT FOR SOUTHERN AND EASTERN DISTRICT OF NEW YORK

Rule	This Work Sec.	Note
1(b)	17.82	33

LOCAL BANKRUPTCY RULES FOR THE SOUTHERN DISTRICT OF NEW YORK

Rule	This Work Sec.	Note
9013–1(b)	9.287	1
	9.306	
	9.310	

UNIFORM CIVIL RULES FOR THE SUPERME COURT

Rule	This Work Sec.	Note
202.52(a)	11.75	
202.52(b)	11.75	

DISCIPLINARY RULES OF THE NEW YORK CODE OF PROFESSIONAL RESPONSIBILITY

Sec.	This Work Sec.	Note
1–102(a)(5)	4.35	3

DISCIPLINARY RULES OF THE NEW YORK CODE OF PROFESSIONAL RESPONSIBILITY

Sec.	This Work Sec.	Note
1–102(a)(7)	4.35	3
2–105(A)	23.1	8
2–105(B)	23.1	8
2–107	26.6	4
	26.62	
2–109(A)(1)	18.80	3
3–103	2.43	2
4–101(C)(2)—(5)	23.5	1
5–101	28.20	1
5–102	28.21	
5–105	28.20	1
5–105(A)	23.4	6
	24.94	1
5–105(B)	23.4	6
	24.94	1
5–105(C)	23.4	9
	24.94	1
5–107	2.43	2
5–107(A)	23.4	4
5–107(B)	23.4	4
6–101(A)	26.5	1
6–101(A)(1)	26.5	2
7–101	23.4	1
7–101(B)(2)	23.4	10
7–102	18.80	3
7–102(A)(7)	23.4	10
7–102(B)	23.5	1
7–104(a)(1)	17.72	3

ETHICAL CONSIDERATIONS OF THE NEW YORK CODE OF PROFESSIONAL RESPONSIBILITY

EC	This Work Sec.	Note
2–22	26.5	2
2–23	28.28	3
4–1—4–7	23.5	1
5–1	23.4	2
5–1et seq.	28.20	1
5–5	24.95	6
5–6	24.95	1
6–3	26.5	2
5–14	23.4	5
5–15	23.4	5
5–16	23.4	9
5–17	23.4	7
	23.4	8
5–19	23.4	8
5–21	23.4	2
5–22	23.4	3
5–23	23.4	3
7–11	23.6	1
7–12	23.6	2
	23.6	3
7–18	23.4	13

418

TABLE OF RULES

FEDERAL RULES OF CIVIL PROCEDURE

Rule	Sec.	Note
4(d)	17.79	
4(d)(1)—(6)	9.266	
8	17.82	17
	17.84	
8(a)	17.82	
	34.29	
8(c)	17.84	
8(e)(1)	17.84	
11	7.30	
	9.107	24
	9.287	
	17.82	
	18.79	4
	18.89	3
12	9.10	
12(a)	17.84	8
12(b)	17.84	7
12(b)(6)	17.84	1
12(c)	34.29	3
	17.84	
13	17.84	
15(c)(3)(B)	18.38	3
16	17.74	
23	17.82	10
23(a)	17.82	9
23(b)(2)	17.82	9
26(a)	17.72	
26(a)(2)	29.16	10
	29.48	2
35	17.72	
	17.72	6
35(a)	17.72	
38(b)	17.82	
45	9.41	1
50	17.76	1
54(d)(1)	1.19	6
59	17.76	1
60(b)	9.137	2
	9.176	2
	9.211	2
	9.235	2
	9.263	2
62	9.25	
62(a)	9.25	
64	31.23	5

FEDERAL RULES OF EVIDENCE

Rule	Sec.	Note
403	17.74	
501	18.85	7
609(a)(2)	29.9	2
702	17.74	
	27.35	
	27.35	4
803(18)	29.50	
	29.50	1

FEDERAL RULES OF APPELLATE PROCEDURE

Rule	Sec.	Note
4(a)(1)	34.30	1

UNITED STATES SUPREME COURT RULES

Rule	Sec.	Note
10	37.73	4
	39.62	3
10—14	37.73	1
	39.62	1
12(1)	37.73	5
	39.62	4
12(3)	37.73	7
	39.62	6
12(4)	37.73	7
	39.62	6
12(5)	37.73	7
	39.62	6
12(6)	37.73	7
	39.62	6
13(1)	37.73	2
13(5)	37.73	3
	39.62	2
14	37.73	8
	39.62	7
23	37.73	9
	39.62	8
38(a)	37.73	6
	39.62	5

FEDERAL RULES OF BANKRUPTCY PROCEDURE

Rule	Sec.	Note
Ch. 13	9.259	
	9.260	
Pt. VII	9.16	4
	9.16	2
	9.17	
	9.17	7
	9.70	5
	9.113	
	9.169	
	9.232	1
	9.257	
	9.266	1
	9.288	1
Pt. VIII	9.25	1
	9.26	1
Pt. IX	9.113	
1002	9.264	1
1002(a)	9.8	2
	9.264	2
1002(b)	9.264	5
1003(b)	9.10	7

TABLE OF RULES

FEDERAL RULES OF BANKRUPTCY PROCEDURE

Rule	Sec.	Note
1004	9.264	1
1005	9.264	1
1006	9.179	1
	9.264	1
	9.264	10
1006(b)	9.7	6
	9.264	13
1006(b)(1)	9.179	1
1006(b)(3)	9.179	1
1007	9.126	
	9.126	2
	9.265	1
	9.265	2
	9.278	
1007(a)(1)	9.265	4
1007(a)(2)	9.265	5
1007(a)(3)	9.265	6
1007(a)(4)	9.11	3
1007(c)	9.11	3
	9.265	11
	9.265	12
	9.278	1
1007(d)	9.265	8
1008	9.11	2
	9.264	1
	9.264	9
1009	9.278	4
1009(a)	9.11	4
1009(b)	9.186	9
1010	9.10	2
1011(b)	9.10	3
	9.10	5
1013(b)	9.10	5
1015	9.13	1
1017	9.209	1
1017(d)	9.175	
	9.176	1
	9.210	
	9.210	1
	9.234	
	9.234	1
	9.262	
	9.262	1
1019	9.135	2
	9.175	
	9.210	
	9.234	
	9.262	
1019(3)	9.176	3
	9.176	4
	9.210	3
	9.234	3
	9.262	3
1020	9.173	1
2002	9.15	1
	9.17	7
	9.169	
	9.200	

FEDERAL RULES OF BANKRUPTCY PROCEDURE

Rule	Sec.	Note
1003(b) (Cont'd)	9.200	6
	9.206	
	9.266	1
	9.267	1
	9.277	2
	9.282	
	9.284	
	9.305	
2002(a)	9.200	
2002(a)(2)	9.271	2
2002(a)(4)	9.176	2
2002(a)(5)	9.210	2
	9.234	2
	9.262	2
2002(b)	9.283	2
2002(b)(1)	9.282	5
2002(c)(1)	9.271	2
2002(e)	9.207	3
2002(f)	9.264	14
	9.264	16
2002(i)	9.36	3
	9.271	2
2002(k)	9.271	2
2002(m)	9.200	8
2003	9.37	1
2003(a)	9.264	15
	9.37	2
2004	9.39	
	9.39	3
	9.40	
	9.40	2
	9.40	3
	9.41	
2004(b)	9.39	1
2004(c)	9.41	1
	9.41	2
2014	9.12	1
	9.29	
	9.98	1
2014(a)	9.29	
	9.29	17
	9.291	2
	9.311	
2014(b)	9.29	6
2015(a)(1)	9.33	3
2015(a)(2)	9.33	4
2015(a)(3)	9.33	9
2015(a)(4)	9.33	5
2015(a)(5)	9.33	8
2015(b)	9.33	3
	9.33	4
	9.33	5
	9.33	9
2015(c)	9.33	4
2015(c)(1)	9.33	3
	9.33	5
	9.33	9
2015(d)	9.33	10

420

TABLE OF RULES

FEDERAL RULES OF BANKRUPTCY PROCEDURE

Rule	Sec.	Note
2016	9.31	
	9.98	1
2016(a)	9.31	3
2016(b)	9.311	
2018(a)	9.42	1
	9.42	2
2018(b)	9.42	5
2018(d)	9.42	6
3001(a)	9.91	1
3001(b)	9.91	11
3001(c)	9.91	2
3001(d)	9.91	2
3001(e)	9.91	1
3001(f)	9.91	8
3002	9.207	3
3002(a)	9.91	6
3002(c)	9.92	2
	9.92	3
	9.93	
	9.93	9
3002(c)(3)	9.92	4
3002(c)(4)	9.92	5
	9.149	2
3002(c)(5)	9.92	6
3002(c)(6)	9.93	6
	9.93	10
3003(b)(1)	9.91	5
3003(c)(2)	9.91	6
3003(c)(3)	9.92	1
	9.92	3
	9.92	4
	9.92	5
	9.163	9
3003(c)(4)	9.91	7
3004	9.91	12
3005	9.91	10
3006	9.95	1
3007	9.96	4
3012	9.103	1
3013	9.284	1
3014	9.156	10
3015	9.224	1
	9.224	2
	9.284	1
	9.286	1
3015(a)	9.220	2
	9.284	2
3015(b)	9.245	1
	9.284	3
3015(c)	9.284	4
3015(d)	9.284	5
3015(e)	9.284	6
3015(f)	9.226	6
	9.226	7
	9.252	4
	9.252	5
	9.285	1
3015(g)	9.230	4

FEDERAL RULES OF BANKRUPTCY PROCEDURE

Rule	Sec.	Note
3015(g) (Cont'd)	9.259	3
	9.286	
3016	9.282	
	9.282	1
	9.283	1
3016(b)	9.282	2
3016(c)	9.161	1
	9.161	2
	9.282	3
3017	9.161	3
	9.161	13
	9.162	
3017(a)	9.282	4
	9.282	6
3017(d)	9.161	
3017(e)	9.161	15
3018	9.162	5
3018(a)	9.96	5
	9.162	6
	9.162	14
	9.283	4
3018(b)	9.163	2
3018(c)	9.162	7
3019	9.164	
	9.283	4
	9.286	1
3020(b)(1)	9.166	
3020(b)(2)	9.166	14
4001	9.53	
	9.271	1
	9.272	
	9.273	1
	9.274	
	9.292	1
	9.294	1
	9.295	1
	9.296	1
	9.297	1
4001(a)	9.269	
4001(a)(1)	9.66	
4001(a)(2)	9.54	3
4001(b)	9.272	1
	9.272	2
4001(b)(1)	9.272	3
4001(b)(2)	9.67	1
	9.67	3
4001(c)	9.274	1
	9.297	3
4001(c)(1)	9.274	2
4001(c)(2)	9.72	1
	9.72	2
	9.295	
4001(d)	9.270	
	9.273	
	9.273	1
	9.274	1
	9.293	1
4001(d)(1)	9.269	3

421

TABLE OF RULES

FEDERAL RULES OF BANKRUPTCY PROCEDURE

Rule	This Work Sec.	Note
4001(d)(1) (Cont'd)	9.270	2
	9.273	2
4001(d)(2)	9.59	1
	9.273	3
4001(d)(3)	9.59	2
4003(a)	9.126	2
	9.126	3
	9.278	1
	9.278	3
4003(b)	9.127	2
	9.127	3
4003(c)	9.127	4
	9.127	5
4003(d)	9.128	7
4004	9.130	11
	9.206	5
	9.208	5
4004(a)	9.169	11
	9.206	6
4004(b)	9.206	5
4004(c)	9.206	7
	9.208	8
4004(d)	9.206	4
4005	9.208	5
4007	9.208	2
	9.208	5
	9.229	6
4007(a)	9.208	2
	9.257	1
4007(b)	9.208	6
	9.257	2
4007(c)	9.169	8
	9.169	9
	9.208	4
	9.264	16
4007(d)	9.257	3
	9.257	4
	9.264	16
4007(e)	9.208	1
	9.257	5
4008	9.130	11
	9.280	
	9.280	2
	9.280	3
	9.302	1
	9.303	1
5003	9.208	
5005	9.91	3
	9.264	1
	9.265	2
5010	9.137	1
	9.176	2
	9.235	2
	9.263	2
5011	9.23	2
5011(a)	9.22	3
6004	9.200	
	9.271	

FEDERAL RULES OF BANKRUPTCY PROCEDURE

Rule	This Work Sec.	Note
6004 (Cont'd)	9.271	1
	9.271	2
	9.294	1
6004(b)	9.271	5
6004(c)	9.271	4
6004(d)	9.271	6
	9.271	7
6004(f)	9.62	2
6004(f)(1)	9.62	1
6006	9.275	
	9.275	2
	9.298	1
6006(b)	9.275	3
6006(c)	9.275	7
6007(a)	9.70	2
	9.70	3
	9.189	1
	9.189	3
6007(b)	9.70	4
7001	9.271	1
	9.288	1
	9.294	1
7001(1)	9.70	5
7001(4)	9.206	4
7001(5)	9.260	4
7001(6)	9.208	1
7001(8)	9.107	
7002	9.16	4
	9.266	1
7004	9.10	2
	9.266	
	9.266	1
	9.267	
	9.309	
7004(h)	9.272	3
	9.273	2
7007(b)(1)	9.287	2
	9.287	3
7062	9.25	
7087	9.21	4
8001(a)	9.25	4
8001(b)	9.268	2
8002(a)	9.25	4
	9.268	2
8002(c)	9.25	5
8003	9.25	
	9.268	
8003(a)	9.25	6
	9.289	1
8005	9.25	10
	9.290	1
8007(c)	9.290	1
8008	9.25	
	9.268	
8008(d)	9.266	3
	9.267	4
	9.269	4
	9.270	3

TABLE OF RULES

FEDERAL RULES OF BANKRUPTCY PROCEDURE

Rule	This Work Sec.	Note
8008(d) (Cont'd)	9.271	8
	9.272	4
	9.273	4
	9.274	3
	9.275	8
	9.276	5
	9.277	3
	9.279	3
	9.280	4
	9.281	4
	9.284	7
	9.285	3
	9.286	3
8013	9.25	9
8015(f)	9.285	2
9006	9.8	5
	9.15	1
	9.17	7
	9.200	6
	9.206	5
	9.210	2
	9.266	1
	9.267	1
9006(b)(1)	9.92	3
	9.93	7
	9.93	8
9006(b)(3)	9.93	9
9007	9.305	
9009	9.5	4
9010	9.305	
9011	9.107	24
	9.131	3
9013	9.17	7
	9.175	
	9.210	
	9.234	
	9.262	
	9.279	
	9.292	2
9014	9.17	
	9.17	7
	9.23	2
	9.70	
	9.70	5
	9.128	
	9.128	8
	9.175	
	9.189	
	9.189	1
	9.210	
	9.224	2
	9.230	
	9.234	
	9.262	
	9.267	1
	9.267	3
	9.269	
	9.271	

FEDERAL RULES OF BANKRUPTCY PROCEDURE

Rule	This Work Sec.	Note
9014 (Cont'd)	9.272	
	9.274	
	9.275	
	9.276	1
	9.279	
	9.280	
	9.281	
	9.285	
	9.295	1
	9.296	1
	9.297	1
	9.298	1
	9.301	1
	9.304	1
9016	9.41	1
9017	9.5	7
9019	9.97	1
	9.277	
	9.277	2
	9.300	1
9020	9.18	4
9020(a)	9.18	4
9020(b)	9.18	4
9021	9.208	
9024	9.137	2
	9.176	2
	9.211	2
	9.235	2
	9.263	2
9027(a)(2)	9.24	

EXECUTIVE ORDERS

No.	This Work Sec.	Note
11246, § 202(1)	17.60	1

TEMPORARY TREASURY REGULATIONS

Sec.	This Work Sec.	Note
14a.422A–1	1.34	71

PROPOSED TREASURY REGULATIONS

Sec.	This Work Sec.	Note
1.401(a)(9)–1	24.37	8
	24.37	9
25.2518–2	24.68	4

TREASURY REGULATIONS

Sec.	This Work Sec.	Note
1.61–2	1.40	19
1.61–12(c)(2)	1.34	73

423

TABLE OF RULES

TREASURY REGULATIONS			TREASURY REGULATIONS		
		This Work			This Work
Sec.	Sec.	Note	Sec.	Sec.	Note
1.83–1(a)	1.34	64	1.958–1	1.34	30
1.83–1 to 1.83–7	1.34	66	1.958–2	1.34	30
1.83–7(a)	1.34	62	1.1031(a)–1(a)(2)	6.45	7
	1.34	64		6.45	8
	1.34	65	1.1031(a)–1(b)	6.45	7
1.163–37(b)	1.34	75		6.45	8
1.167–1.168	6.34	4	1.1031(a)–2(b)(2)	6.45	9
1.167(a)–1	6.34	1	1.1060–1T	6.33	2
	6.119	1		6.118	2
1.167(a)–6	6.40	1	1.1060–1T(h)	6.33	2
1.171–1	1.34	72		6.118	2
1.213–1(d)	24.76	1	1.1272–1	1.34	74
1.213–1(e)(1)(v)	23.118	2	1.1402–1(a)(2)	2.23	9
1.248–1(a)(3)	1.21	26	1.6012–3(a)(9)	24.81	4
	1.34	7	1.7520–3(b)(3)	24.57	1
	1.34	8	4.954–1	1.34	30
1.248–1(b)	1.34	6	20.2031–2(h)	24.39	1
1.248–1(b)(2)	1.34	5	20.2042–1(a)	24.34	1
1.301–1(j)	1.40	17	20.2042–1(c)(2)	24.34	3
1.302–2(b)	1.40	13	20.2053–3(b)	24.79	2
1.302–3(b)	1.40	14	20.2056(b)–5(a)	24.22	10
1.305(c)	1.40	12	20.2056(b)–5(f)(5)	24.22	6
1.305–1 to 1.305–8	1.40	9		24.22	7
1.305–4(b)	1.40	9	20.2056(b)–7(b)	24.72	3
1.305–5(d)	1.40	9	20.2056(b)–7(b)(2)(ii)(b)	24.72	4
1.305–7(a)	1.40	9	20.2056(b)–7(b)(4)	24.22	5
1.305–7(c)	1.74	2	20.2056A–2(a)	24.58	5
1.307–1	1.40	10	20.2056A–2T(d)	24.58	5
1.307–1(b)	1.40	10	20.2056A–5(c)(1)	24.58	7
1.307–2	1.40	10	20.7520–3(b)(3)	24.57	1
1.351–1(a)(1)	1.34	30	25.2503–3(a)	24.49	2
1.351–1(a)(1)(ii)	1.34	28	25.2503–6(b)(3)	24.49	4
1.351–1(a)(2)	1.34	28	25.2511–1(h)(1)	24.83	3
1.351–1(b)(1)	1.34	44	25.2511–2(c)	24.61	3
1.368–2(e)	1.74	2	25.2512–5	24.46	1
1.401(a)–20	24.60	11	25.2513–2	24.49	1
1.409(a)(9)–1	24.37	9	25.2518–1(b)	24.68	2
1.532–1(a)(1)	1.2	16	25.2518–1(d)	24.68	2
1.533–1(a)(1)	1.2	16	25.2518–2(e)(2)	24.69	3
1.537–1(a)	1.2	16	25.2702–2(b)(2)	24.46	6
1.537–1(b)	1.2	16		24.46	7
1.543–1(b)(8)(ii)	1.122	5	25.2702–3(b)	24.46	4
1.671–4(b)(1)	24.81	5	25.2702–3(e)	24.46	5
1.691(a)–2(a)	24.74	1	25.2702–5(a)	24.47	1
1.691(a)–4	24.43	3	25.2702–5(b)(1)	24.48	
1.704–1(b)	2.2	6	25.2702–5(c)	24.47	6
1.704–1(b)(2)	2.13	1	25.2702–5(c)(5)(ii)	24.47	2
	2.13	2	25.2702–5(c)(8)	24.47	3
1.704–1(b)(2)(iv)	2.112		25.2702–5(c)(9)	24.48	
	2.115		25.2703–1(b)(3)	24.39	3
1.752–3(a)(2)	2.11	8	25.7520–3(b)(3)	24.57	1
1.761–2	2.4	3	26.2612–1(b)(1)(i)	24.25	4
1.951–1	1.34	30	26.2613–1(f), Ex. 12	24.27	2
1.952–1	1.34	30	26.2632–1(a)	24.30	3
1.954–1	1.34	30	26.2652–1(a)(1)	24.25	5
1.954–2	1.34	30	301.7701–1	2.4	
1.954–4	1.34	30	301.7701–1 to 301.7701–		
1.957–1	1.34	30	3	1.34	60
1.957–4	1.34	30	301.7701–2	2.4	

424

TABLE OF RULES

TREASURY REGULATIONS

Sec.	This Work Sec.	Note
301.7701–2 (Cont'd)	2.5	
	35.23	3
301.7701–2(a)	1.34	54
	1.34	59
	2.4	2
301.7701–2(a) (former)	2.6	6
301.7701–2(b)	1.2	10
	1.34	55
301.7701–2(b)(1) (former)	2.7	
	2.7	6
301.7701–2(b)(2) (former)	2.7	3
	2.7	4
301.7701–2(b)(3) (former)	2.7	
	2.7	1
301.7701–2(c)	1.2	11
	1.34	56
301.7701–2(c)(1) (former)	2.9	1
	2.9	2
301.7701–2(c)(3) (former)	2.9	3
301.7701–2(c)(4) (former)	2.9	4
	2.9	6
	2.9	8
301.7701–2(d)	1.2	12
	1.34	57
301.7701–2(d) (former)	2.6	1
	2.6	10
301.7701–2(d)(1)	1.34	60
301.7701–2(d)(2)	1.34	60
301.7701–2(e)	1.2	13
	1.34	58
301.7701–2(e)(1) (former)	2.8	1
301.7701–2(e)(2) (former)	2.8	13
301.7701–3	2.4	
301.7701–3(b)	2.4	2
	2.4	3
301.7701–3(c)(1)(iv)	2.4	4
301.7701–3(f)(2)	2.4	5

CODE OF FEDERAL REGULATIONS

Tit.	This Work Sec.	Note
5, Pt. 831 et seq.	23.37	1
	23.39	1
5, § 831.109	23.40	1
5, § 831.502	23.39	5
5, § 831.504	23.39	2
5, § 831.604	23.39	4
5, § 831.701(c)	23.39	3
5, Pts. 841—843	23.37	2
5, § 841.503	23.38	2

CODE OF FEDERAL REGULATIONS

Tit.	This Work Sec.	Note
5, §§ 842.601—842.615	23.38	3
5, § 843.201	23.38	4
5, § 843.202	23.38	4
5, §§ 843.301—843.312	23.38	5
5, §§ 843.401—843.411	23.38	6
5, § 843.501—843.504	23.38	6
5, § 890.101 et seq.	23.38	7
7, Pt. 781	12.81	1
Tit. 8	19.1	9
8, § 2.1	19.1	9
8, §§ 3.1—3.41	19.1	10
8, § 3.1(b)	19.11	23
8, § 3.1(b)(2)	19.64	4
8, § 3.3	19.14	15
8, § 103.1(f)	19.19	5
8, § 103.1(f)(3)(E)(iii)	19.1	21
	19.19	5
8, § 103.2(b)(4)	19.10	1
8, § 103.3	19.1	21
8, § 103.5	19.64	2
8, § 204.1(a)	19.14	10
8, § 204.1(c)	19.6	7
8, § 204.1(d)	19.6	7
8, § 204.1(e)	19.6	7
8, § 204.1(e)(1)	19.14	2
8, § 204.1(e)(2)	19.14	4
8, § 204.1(e)(3)	19.14	5
	19.14	6
8, § 204.1(f)(2)	19.10	1
8, § 204.1(f)(3)	19.10	4
8, § 204.1(g)	19.10	
8, § 204.1(g)(1)(ii)	19.10	5
8, § 204.1(g)(1)(vii)	19.10	8
8, § 204.1(g)(2)	19.10	3
	19.10	6
8, § 204.2	19.10	
8, § 204.2(a)(1)(i)	19.10	9
	19.72	33
8, § 204.2(a)(1)(i)(A)(2)	19.72	34
8, § 204.2(a)(1)(ii)	19.10	9
	19.72	32
8, § 204.2(a)(2)	19.10	
8, § 204.2(b)	19.14	7
8, § 204.2(b)(1)	19.12	13
	19.14	8
8, § 204.2(b)(2)	19.14	9
8, § 204.2(c)(1)	19.14	1
8, § 204.2(c)(2)(i)	19.10	10
8, § 204.2(c)(2)(iii)	19.10	11
	19.10	13
8, § 204.2(c)(2)(iv)	19.10	15
8, § 204.2(c)(2)(vii)	19.10	16
8, § 204.2(e)	19.10	18
8, § 204.2(f)(2)(i)	19.10	19
8, § 204.2(f)(2)(ii)	19.10	19
8, § 204.3(b)	19.15	7
	19.15	9
	19.15	11
8, § 204.3(c)(1)(vi)	19.15	13

425

TABLE OF RULES

CODE OF FEDERAL REGULATIONS

Tit.	Sec.	This Work Note
8, § 204.3(d)(1)(iv)(B)(2)	19.15	5
8, § 204.3(d)(1)(iv)(B)(3)	19.15	12
8, § 204.3(d)(1)(v)(B)(2)	19.15	4
8, § 204.4(a)	19.15	14
8, § 204.4(f)(1)(ii)(C)	19.15	15
8, § 204.5(c)	19.20	1
8, § 204.5(d)	19.6	8
8, § 204.5(g)(1)	19.65	5
8, § 204.5(h)(2)	19.19	1
8, § 204.5(h)(3)	19.19	2
	19.19	3
8, § 204.5(h)(4)	19.19	4
8, § 204.5(i)(1)	19.20	1
8, § 204.5(i)(2)	19.20	3
8, § 204.5(i)(3)(i)	19.20	4
8, § 204.5(j)(2)	19.21	5
	19.21	7
	19.21	11
8, § 204.5(j)(3)(i)	19.21	2
8, § 204.5(j)(4)	19.21	3
8, § 204.5(k)(3)(ii)	19.23	1
8, § 204.5(k)(4)	19.23	2
8, § 204.5(L)(2)	19.27	1
	19.27	3
8, § 204.5(L)(4)	19.27	5
8, § 204.5(m)(1)	19.41	1
	19.41	3
8, § 204.5(m)(2)	19.41	2
8, § 204.5(m)(3)(i)(A)	19.41	4
8, § 204.5(m)(3)(i)(B)	19.41	5
8, § 204.5(m)(3)(ii)(A)	19.41	6
8, § 204.5(m)(3)(ii)(B)	19.41	7
8, § 204.5(m)(3)(ii)(C)	19.41	8
8, § 204.5(m)(4)	19.41	9
8, § 204.6(a)	19.43	8
8, § 204.6(b)	19.43	8
8, § 204.6(c)	19.43	8
8, § 204.6(e)	19.43	3
	19.44	2
8, § 204.6(j)(1)	19.43	2
8, § 204.6(j)(2)	19.43	2
8, § 204.6(j)(5)	19.43	4
8, § 211.1	19.70	4
	19.74	2
8, § 211.1(b)	19.74	6
8, § 214.2(f)(5)	19.67	5
8, § 214.2(f)(10)	19.67	5
8, § 214.2(h)(13)(iii)	19.67	6
8, § 214.2(L)(1)(ii)(C)	19.21	8
8, § 214.2(L)(1)(ii)(G)	19.21	11
8, § 214.2(L)(1)(ii)(G)(2)	19.21	10
8, § 214.2(L)(1)(ii)(H)	19.21	11
8, § 214.2(L)(1)(ii)(K)	19.21	4
	19.21	6
8, § 214.2(L)(1)(ii)(L)	19.21	4
	19.21	6
8, § 214.2(L)(12)(i)	19.67	7
8, § 216.2	19.72	9
8, § 216.2(b)	19.72	3

CODE OF FEDERAL REGULATIONS

Tit.	Sec.	This Work Note
8, § 216.3	19.73	11
8, § 216.3(a)	19.72	5
	19.72	14
	19.72	15
	19.73	7
8, § 216.4	19.72	16
8, § 216.4(a)(2)	19.72	6
	19.72	7
	19.72	36
8, § 216.4(a)(6)	19.72	18
8, § 216.4(c)	19.72	24
8, § 216.4(d)(1)	19.72	28
8, § 216.4(d)(2)	19.72	24
	19.72	29
	19.72	30
8, § 216.5	19.72	16
	19.72	25
8, § 216.5(d)	19.72	27
8, § 216.5(e)(3)	19.72	26
8, § 216.5(f)	19.72	28
	19.72	29
8, § 216.6(a)(2)	19.73	2
8, § 216.6(a)(4)	19.43	7
	19.73	3
8, § 216.6(a)(5)	19.73	8
8, § 216.6(b)(1)	19.73	4
8, § 216.6(c)(1)	19.73	9
8, § 216.6(c)(2)	19.73	10
8, Pt. 217	19.58	3
8, § 223.1	19.74	9
8, § 242.17	19.57	2
	19.58	8
8, Pt. 245	19.1	25
8, § 245.2(a)(1)	19.61	4
	19.64	3
8, § 245.2(a)(2)	19.62	2
8, § 245.2(a)(4)(ii)	19.63	4
8, § 245.2(a)(5)	19.64	1
8, § 245.6	19.61	5
8, § 264.1(g)	19.74	7
8, § 274a.2(b)(1)(v)(A)(5)	19.4	3
8, § 299.1	19.75	1
12, § 213 et seq.	7.21	10
12, § 213.4(g)(12)	7.22	29
12, § 226.5 et seq.	7.23	26
15, § 325.2(b)(2)(ii)	15.15	13
16, Pt. 703	7.12	1
20, Pts. 200—266	23.36	
20, § 200.3	23.36	
20, § 216.20	23.36	2
20, § 260.3	23.36	4
20, § 260.5	23.36	5
20, § 262.12	23.36	7
20, Pt. 266	23.36	3
20, Pt. 404	34.3	5
20, Pt. 404 et seq.	23.7	1
20, Pt. 404, Subpt. P	34.11	2
	34.11	5

TABLE OF RULES

CODE OF FEDERAL REGULATIONS

Tit.	Sec.	This Work Note
20, Pt. 404, Subpt. P (Cont'd)	34.11	7
	34.13	2
	34.13	4
	34.13	6
	34.13	7
	34.13	8
	34.13	9
	34.13	10
	34.13	11
	34.13	12
	34.13	13
	34.13	14
	34.13	15
	34.13	17
	34.13	18
	34.47	5
	34.67	2
	34.67	3
	34.67	4
	34.67	5
	34.67	6
	34.67	7
20, § 404.110	34.15	2
20, § 404.110(b)	23.9	2
20, § 404.130	34.16	1
20, § 404.143	23.8	2
20, § 404.143(a)	23.8	3
20, § 404.204 et seq.	23.10	1
20, § 404.312	23.11	3
20, § 404.313	23.11	4
20, § 404.313(a)(2)	23.11	2
20, § 404.330	34.20	1
20, § 404.331	23.12	4
	23.12	5
20, § 404.333	23.12	3
20, § 404.335	23.12	7
20, § 404.335(c)	23.12	9
20, § 404.335(e)	23.12	10
20, §§ 404.345—404.436	23.12	1
20, § 404.350	34.20	1
20, § 404.350 et seq.	23.12	11
20, § 404.370 et seq.	23.12	12
20, § 404.390	23.12	13
20, §§ 404.410—404.413	23.11	3
20, § 404.415	23.13	1
20, § 404.434	23.13	1
20, § 404.502	23.13	1
	23.14	4
20, § 404.506	23.14	6
20, §§ 404.506—404.512	23.14	6
20, §§ 404.603—404.623	34.24	
20, § 404.603(b)	34.24	6
20, § 404.610	34.24	10
20, § 404.614(a)	34.24	1
	34.24	3
20, § 404.615	34.24	11
20, § 404.615(b)	34.24	12
20, § 404.615(c)	34.24	12
20, § 404.615(d)	34.24	12

CODE OF FEDERAL REGULATIONS

Tit.	Sec.	This Work Note
20, § 404.701(a)	23.54	2
20, § 404.802 et seq.	23.10	2
20, § 404.901	34.25	3
20, § 404.902	23.14	5
20, § 404.902(j)	23.14	2
20, § 404.902(k)(1)	23.14	2
20, § 404.907	23.15	2
20, § 404.907 et seq.	23.15	1
20, § 404.908(a)	34.25	1
20, § 404.909	23.15	3
20, § 404.909(a)(1)	34.25	2
20, § 404.909(b)	34.25	4
20, § 404.911	34.25	4
20, § 404.913	23.15	4
20, § 404.913(a)	34.25	8
20, § 404.913(b)	34.25	9
20, § 404.922	23.15	5
20, § 404.929	23.15	6
	23.15	8
20, § 404.930	23.15	6
	23.15	7
20, § 404.933	23.15	7
20, § 404.933(b)(1)	34.27	1
20, § 404.944	34.27	9
20, § 404.948	34.2	1
	34.27	7
20, § 404.949	34.27	4
	34.39	1
	34.40	1
20, § 404.950	23.15	8
20, § 404.950(c)	34.39	1
	34.40	1
20, § 404.950(d)(1)	34.36	3
20, § 404.950(d)(2)	34.36	4
20, § 404.950(e)	34.27	6
20, § 404.951	34.42	1
20, § 404.953(a)	34.49	1
20, § 404.967	23.15	9
	23.15	12
20, § 404.968	23.15	9
	23.55	11
20, § 404.968(a)	34.55	2
20, § 404.969	23.15	10
	34.28	2
	34.28	13
20, § 404.970	23.15	11
20, § 404.970(b)	34.28	5
20, § 404.974	34.28	4
20, § 404.975	34.55	3
20, § 404.976(c)	23.55	12
	34.28	6
20, § 404.979	34.28	8
	34.28	9
	34.57	1
20, § 404.981	23.15	13
	23.15	14
	34.28	7
20, § 404.983	34.28	10
20, § 404.984(b)	34.28	11

427

TABLE OF RULES

CODE OF FEDERAL REGULATIONS

Tit.	Sec.	Note
20, § 404.987(a)	34.58	1
	34.58	3
20, § 404.987(b)	34.59	1
20, § 404.988(a)	34.59	2
20, § 404.988(b)	34.59	3
20, § 404.988(c)	34.59	4
20, § 404.989(a)(1)	34.59	3
20, § 404.989(a)(3)	34.59	3
20, § 404.989(b)	34.59	5
20, § 404.1205	23.19	10
	23.19	11
20, § 404.1505(a)	34.6	1
	34.6	5
20, § 404.1508	34.66	2
20, § 404.1509	34.66	3
	34.67	8
20, § 404.1510	34.9	5
20, § 404.1513(b)	34.66	5
20, § 404.1513(e)	34.37	4
20, § 404.1519	34.25	7
20, § 404.1519a–t	34.25	
20, § 404.1520(b)	34.9	1
20, § 404.1520(d)	34.11	3
20, § 404.1520(e)	34.12	2
20, § 404.1520(f)(1)	34.13	1
	34.47	2
20, § 404.1521	34.10	1
20, § 404.1521(b)(3)	34.67	9
20, § 404.1521(b)(5)	34.67	9
20, § 404.1523	34.10	12
20, § 404.1525(a)	34.11	1
20, § 404.1525(b)(1)	34.11	8
20, § 404.1525(c)	34.66	7
20, § 404.1526(a)	34.11	11
	34.11	12
	34.11	17
20, § 404.1526(b)	34.11	13
	34.66	8
20, § 404.1527(d)(2)	34.66	4
20, § 404.1529(a)	34.66	6
20, § 404.1545	34.12	1
20, § 404.1545(a)	34.66	9
20, § 404.1564(b)(2)	34.13	16
20, § 404.1564(b)(3)	34.13	5
20, § 404.1566(a)	34.47	4
20, § 404.1566(e)	34.47	8
	34.47	14
20, § 404.1569	34.13	3
20, § 404.1571	34.9	15
20, § 404.1572	34.9	4
20, § 404.1572(a)	34.9	14
20, § 404.1572(b)	34.9	2
20, § 404.1572(c)	34.9	3
20, § 404.1574(a)(1)	34.9	18
20, § 404.1574(a)(3)	34.9	27
20, § 404.1574(b)(2)	34.9	10
20, § 404.1574(b)(2)(i)	34.9	11
20, § 404.1574(b)(2)(vii)	34.9	12
20, § 404.1574(b)(3)	34.9	7

CODE OF FEDERAL REGULATIONS

Tit.	Sec.	Note
20, § 404.1574(b)(3)(i)	34.9	8
20, § 404.1574(b)(3)(vii)	34.9	9
20, § 404.1574(b)(4)(vii)	34.9	28
20, § 404.1574(b)(6)	34.9	13
20, § 404.1575(a)	34.9	22
	34.9	23
20, § 404.1575(a)(1)	34.9	24
20, § 404.1575(a)(2)	34.9	25
20, § 404.1594(a)	34.26	3
20, § 404.1597(a)	34.26	4
20, § 404.1597a(f)	34.26	5
	34.26	6
20, § 404.1597a(h)(2)(i)	34.26	7
20, § 404.1705	23.16	1
	34.27	4
20, § 404.1707	23.16	2
20, § 404.1710	23.16	2
20, § 404.1720	23.16	3
20, § 404.1720(b)	34.33	4
20, § 404.1720(b)(2)	34.33	2
	34.53	2
20, § 404.1720(b)(4)	23.16	4
20, § 404.1725(a)	34.53	3
20, § 404.1725(b)(2)	23.16	7
20, § 404.1730(b)	23.16	5
	34.52	1
20, § 404.1730(b)(2)	23.16	4
20, Pt. 416	23.17	1
	34.3	5
20, § 416.202	23.19	1
20, § 416.202(a)	23.18	1
20, § 416.202(b)	23.18	3
20, §§ 416.305—416.36	34.24	
20, § 416.310	34.24	10
20, § 416.310(b)	34.24	1
	34.24	3
20, § 416.335	34.24	7
20, § 416.350	34.24	9
20, § 416.438	23.21	3
20, § 416.535	23.21	2
	23.21	3
20, § 416.536	23.21	2
20, § 416.537	23.21	3
20, §§ 416.538—416.543	23.21	2
20, §§ 416.550—416.556	23.21	7
20, § 416.570	23.21	3
20, § 416.571	23.21	4
	23.21	6
20, § 416.708	23.21	1
20, §§ 416.801—416.806	23.18	2
20, § 416.905(a)	34.6	1
	34.6	5
20, § 416.908	34.66	2
20, § 416.909	34.66	3
	34.67	8
20, § 416.910	34.9	5
20, § 416.913(b)	34.66	5
20, § 416.913(e)	34.37	4
20, § 416.919	34.25	7

428

TABLE OF RULES

CODE OF FEDERAL REGULATIONS

Tit.	Sec.	This Work Note
20, § 416.919a–t	34.25	
20, § 416.920(b)	34.9	1
20, § 416.920(d)	34.11	3
20, § 416.920(e)	34.12	2
20, § 416.920(f)(1)	34.13	1
	34.47	2
20, § 416.921	34.10	1
20, § 416.921(b)(3)	34.67	9
20, § 416.921(b)(5)	34.67	9
20, § 416.923	34.10	12
20, § 416.925(a)	34.11	1
20, § 416.925(b)(1)	34.11	8
20, § 416.925(c)	34.66	7
20, § 416.926(a)	34.11	11
	34.11	12
	34.11	17
20, § 416.926(b)	34.11	13
	34.66	8
20, § 416.927(d)(2)	34.66	4
20, § 416.929(a)	34.66	6
20, § 416.945	34.12	1
20, § 416.945(a)	34.66	9
20, § 416.964(b)(2)	34.13	16
20, § 416.964(b)(3)	34.13	5
20, § 416.966(a)	34.47	4
20, § 416.966(e)	34.47	14
	34.47	8
20, § 416.969	34.13	3
20, § 416.971	34.9	15
20, § 416.972	34.9	4
20, § 416.972(a)	34.9	14
20, § 416.972(b)	34.9	2
20, § 416.972(c)	34.9	3
20, § 416.974(a)(1)	34.9	18
20, § 416.974(a)(3)	34.9	27
20, § 416.974(b)(2)	34.9	10
20, § 416.974(b)(2)(i)	34.9	11
20, § 416.974(b)(2)(vii)	34.9	12
20, § 416.974(b)(3)	34.9	7
20, § 416.974(b)(3)(i)	34.9	8
20, § 416.974(b)(3)(vii)	34.9	9
20, § 416.974(b)(4)(vii)	34.9	28
20, § 416.974(b)(6)	34.9	13
20, § 416.975(a)	34.9	22
	34.9	23
20, § 416.975(a)(1)	34.9	24
20, § 416.975(a)(2)	34.9	25
20, § 416.1110	23.19	13
20, § 416.1112(c)(2)	23.19	19
20, § 416.1112(c)(5)	23.19	17
20, § 416.1112(c)(7)	23.19	17
20, § 416.1120	23.19	14
20, § 416.1121	23.19	14
20, § 416.1121(h)	23.19	15
20, § 416.1124(c)(6)	23.19	18
20, § 416.1124(c)(12)	23.19	16
20, § 416.1130 et seq.	23.19	15
20, § 416.1131	23.19	15
20, § 416.1132	23.19	15

CODE OF FEDERAL REGULATIONS

Tit.	Sec.	This Work Note
20, § 416.1157	23.19	15
20, § 416.1201(b)	34.17	2
20, §§ 416.1202– 416.1204	23.19	20
20, § 416.1205(c)	34.17	1
20, § 416.1212	23.19	2
20, § 416.1212(b)	34.17	4
20, § 416.1212(c)	23.19	2
20, § 416.1216(b)	23.19	3
20, § 416.1218	23.19	4
20, § 416.1218(b)	34.17	5
20, § 416.1218(b)(2)	34.17	6
20, § 416.1220 et seq.	23.19	7
20, § 416.1230	23.19	8
20, § 416.1231(a)	23.19	5
20, § 416.1231(b)	23.19	6
20, § 416.1231(b)(1)	34.17	3
20, § 416.1233	23.19	9
20, § 416.1246	23.19	12
20, § 416.1336(b)	23.22	4
20, § 416.1401	34.25	3
20, § 416.1408(a)	34.25	1
20, § 416.1409	23.22	3
20, § 416.1409(a)	34.25	2
20, § 416.1409(b)	34.25	4
20, § 416.1411	34.25	4
20, § 416.1413	23.22	3
20, § 416.1413(a)	34.25	8
20, § 416.1413(b)	34.25	10
20, § 416.1413(c)	34.25	10
20, § 416.1413(d)	34.25	9
20, § 416.1429 et seq.	23.22	5
20, § 416.1431b	34.26	9
20, § 416.1433	23.22	5
20, § 416.1433(b)	34.27	1
20, § 416.1444	34.27	9
20, § 416.1448	34.2	1
	34.27	7
20, § 416.1449	34.27	4
	34.39	1
	34.40	1
20, § 416.1450(c)	34.39	1
	34.40	1
20, § 416.1450(d)(1)	34.36	3
20, § 416.1450(d)(2)	34.36	4
20, § 416.1450(e)	34.27	6
20, § 416.1451	34.42	1
20, § 416.1453(a)	34.49	1
20, §§ 416.1467– 416.1468	23.22	6
20, § 416.1468(a)	34.55	2
20, § 416.1469	34.28	2
	34.28	13
20, § 416.1470(b)	34.28	5
20, § 416.1474	34.28	4
20, § 416.1475	34.55	3
20, § 416.1476(c)	34.28	6
20, § 416.1479	34.28	8
	34.28	9

TABLE OF RULES

CODE OF FEDERAL REGULATIONS

Tit.	Sec.	This Work Note
20, § 416.1479 (Cont'd)	34.57	1
20, § 416.1481	34.28	7
20, § 416.1481 et seq.	23.22	7
20, § 416.1483	34.28	10
20, § 416.1484(b)	34.28	11
20, § 416.1487(a)	34.58	1
	34.58	3
20, § 416.1488(a)	34.60	1
20, § 416.1488(a)(1)	34.59	3
	34.60	2
20, § 416.1488(b)	34.59	3
	34.60	2
20, § 416.1488(b)(3)	34.59	3
	34.60	2
20, § 416.1488(c)	34.60	4
20, § 416.1489(b)	34.59	5
	34.60	3
20, § 416.1505	34.27	4
20, § 416.1520	23.23	3
20, § 416.1520 et seq.	23.23	2
20, § 416.1520(b)(2)	34.33	4
20, § 416.1525	23.23	3
20, § 416.1525(a)	34.52	3
	34.53	3
20, § 416.1600 et seq.	23.18	3
20, § 422.206(b)(1)	34.3	8
20, § 422.416	34.34	1
20, § 541.2(e)(2)	17.63	6
20, § 541.3(a)—(c)	17.63	7
20, § 541.5(a)	17.63	8
20, § 541.103	17.63	5
20, Pt. 655	19.1	13
20, Pt. 656	19.1	14
20, § 656.20(g)	19.32	4
20, § 656.21(a)	19.32	2
20, § 656.21(a)—(h)	19.1	15
20, § 656.21(b)(2)(ii)	19.35	6
20, § 656.21(b)(2)(iii)	19.35	6
20, § 656.21(b)(5)	19.33	3
20, § 656.21(j)(2)	19.32	5
20, § 656.25(b)	19.37	1
20, § 656.25(c)	19.38	1
20, § 656.25(c)(3)	19.38	5
20, § 656.25(d)	19.38	1
20, § 656.25(g)	19.38	3
20, § 656.26(a)	19.38	3
20, § 656.26(b)	19.39	1
20, § 656.27(c)	19.39	2
20, § 656.28	19.37	1
Tit. 22	19.1	26
22, Pt. 40	19.1	11
22, § 40.1(a)	19.6	6
22, § 40.104	19.55	2
22, Pt. 41	19.1	11
22, Pt. 42	19.1	11
22, § 42.12(a)	19.6	2
22, § 42.12(b)	19.6	3
22, § 42.12(c)	19.6	3
22, § 42.12(d)	19.6	4

CODE OF FEDERAL REGULATIONS

Tit.	Sec.	This Work Note
22, § 42.12(e)	19.6	5
22, § 42.53(a)	19.6	7
22, § 42.53(d)	19.6	10
22, § 42.61	19.53	3
	19.53	4
22, § 42.62	19.54	5
22, § 42.65(c)	19.68	4
22, § 42.66	19.54	4
22, § 42.72(a)	19.54	10
22, § 42.81(b)	19.54	11
22, § 42.81(c)	19.54	12
22, § 42.81(d)	19.54	13
22, Pt. 514	19.1	12
24, Pt. 35	12.80	2
26, § 1.401–6	23.34	1
26, § 1.401(a)–20(Q27)	23.31	2
26, § 1.1041–1T	21.45	6
	21.45	7
26, § 1.6045–4 et seq.	12.77	1
26, § 1.6045–4(b)(2)	12.77	2
26, § 1–6050I–1(c)(1) et seq.	12.79	1
26, Pt. 301	36.4	6
26, Pt. 601	36.4	6
27, § 1.20	36.4	11
	36.11	17
27, § 1.21	36.4	11
	36.11	17
27, § 1.22	36.4	11
27, Pts. 19–25	36.4	6
27, § 24.106	36.12	15
27, Pt. 170	36.4	6
27, Pt. 194	36.4	6
27, Pt. 197	36.4	6
27, Pts. 250–252	36.4	6
29, § 404.971	34.28	12
29, § 416.1471	34.28	12
29, §§ 541.1—541.3	17.63	4
29, § 639.3	17.51	4
29, § 825.114(a)	17.45	2
29, § 860.120(f) (1)(iv)(B)(1)—(7)	23.25	2
29, § 1606.1 et seq.	17.49	2
29, § 2510.3–2(b)	17.50	5
33, § 323.2(a) (1)(iii)	15.15	7
33, § 323.2(d)	15.15	7
33, § 325.2(b) (2)(ii)	15.15	14
33, § 328.3	15.14	1
	15.15	2
	15.15	3
33, § 328.3(b)	15.15	5
33, Pt. 330	15.15	9
33, § 330.1	15.14	4
33, § 330.1(e)	15.14	3
	15.15	10
33, § 330.4(c)	15.15	9
33, Pt. 620 et seq.	15.13	1
38, Pt. IV	23.41	5
38, § 3.1 et seq.	23.41	2

TABLE OF RULES

CODE OF FEDERAL REGULATIONS

Tit.	Sec.	This Work Note
38, § 3.1(d)	23.41	3
38, § 3.4	23.41	4
38, § 3.274	23.41	8
38, § 3.275	23.41	8
38, § 14.629	23.41	19
38, § 17.47	23.41	12
38, § 17.47(a) (1)—(a)(5)	23.41	11
38, § 17.48	23.41	12
38, § 17.48(e)(1)	23.41	13
	23.41	14
38, § 17.51	23.41	15
38, §§ 19.26—19.29	23.41	21
38, § 20.302	23.41	20
38, § 20.302(b)	23.41	22
38, § 20.700	23.41	23
38, § 20.1000	23.41	24
38, § 38.1600	23.41	16
40, Pt. 50	15.19	3
40, Pt. 51	15.19	9
	15.19	17
40, § 52.21	15.21	4
40, § 52.1682	15.19	6
40, Pt. 54	15.22	13
40, Pt. 60	15.19	11
	15.21	3
40, Pt. 61	15.21	3
40, Pt. 74	12.80	2
40, § 81.333	15.19	12
	15.20	3
40, Pt. 116	15.29	11
40, § 122.26 (b)(14)	15.10	3
40, § 122.26(b) (14)(x)	15.10	5
40, § 122.48	15.9	14
40, Pt. 135	15.42	
40, Pt. 135, Subpt. A	15.11	13
40, § 135.2	15.12	2
	15.35	3
	15.40	1
	15.41	1
40, § 135.3	15.35	1
	15.35	2
40, Pt. 241	15.23	7
40, Pt. 254	15.25	16
	15.40	1
	15.41	1
40, § 254.2	15.36	4
40, § 254.3	15.36	1
	15.36	2
40, § 254.3(b)	15.36	3
40, Pt. 256	15.23	7
40, Pt. 261	15.29	11
40, § 261.2	15.23	3
40, § 261.5	15.24	12
40, § 261.5(g)(3)	15.24	13
40, §§ 261.20—261.24	15.23	6
40, § 261.30	15.23	6
40, § 262.11	15.24	6
	15.24	13
40, § 262.12(c)	15.24	10

CODE OF FEDERAL REGULATIONS

Tit.	Sec.	This Work Note
40, § 262.20	15.24	5
40, § 262.34(d)	15.24	14
40, § 262.34(d)	15.24	15
40, Pt. 280	15.26	10
40, § 280.10	15.26	4
40, § 280.12	15.26	4
40, § 280.20	15.26	7
40, § 280.21	15.26	9
40, § 280.22	15.26	5
40, § 280.40	15.26	8
40, § 280.41	15.26	8
40, § 280.42	15.26	7
40, Pt. 300	15.28	6
40, Pts. 300 et seq.	15.29	8
40, § 300.430	15.31	15
40, Pt. 302	15.26	2
42, Pts. 405—424	23.42	1
42, § 405.702	23.55	3
42, § 405.711	23.55	4
42, § 405.712	23.55	4
42, § 405.715	23.55	5
42, § 405.720	23.55	7
42, § 405.720(d)	23.55	8
42, § 405.722	23.55	7
	23.55	11
42, § 405.724	23.55	11
42, § 405.730	23.55	13
42, § 405.740(a)(3)	23.55	9
42, § 405.803	23.57	1
42, § 405.804	23.57	2
42, § 405.807(b)	23.57	4
42, § 405.807(c)	23.57	3
42, § 405.815	23.57	4
42, § 405.821	23.57	4
42, § 405.823	23.57	5
	23.57	6
	23.57	7
	23.57	8
42, § 406.5(a)	23.43	1
	23.43	2
42, § 406.5(b)	23.43	15
42, § 406.6(a)	23.43	6
42, § 406.6(d)(4)	23.43	8
	23.43	9
42, § 406.10(a)	23.43	6
42, § 406.10(b)(1)	23.43	7
42, § 406.12(a)(1)	23.43	3
42, § 406.13	23.43	5
42, § 406.13(b)	23.43	5
42, § 406.13(e)	23.43	5
42, § 406.15	23.43	4
42, § 406.20	23.43	15
42, § 406.21(c)(1)	23.43	13
42, § 406.21(c)(3)	23.43	14
42, § 406.32	23.43	16
42, § 407.14(a)(1)	23.43	10
42, § 407.17	23.49	3
42, § 407.17(a)	23.43	1
	23.43	2

431

TABLE OF RULES

CODE OF FEDERAL REGULATIONS

Tit.	Sec.	This Work Note
42, § 407.25(a)(1)	23.43	11
42, § 407.25(a)(2)—(a)(5)	23.43	12
42, § 407.25(b)(1)	23.43	14
42, § 407.40	23.43	18
42, § 408.4(a)(1)	23.43	17
42, § 408.20(c)	23.43	17
42, §§ 409.10—409.16	23.45	1
42, § 409.12(b)	23.59	7
42, §§ 409.30—409.33	23.46	2
42, § 409.31	23.46	2
42, § 409.32(b)	23.46	4
42, § 409.33(d)	23.46	4
42, § 409.42	23.47	2
	23.47	5
	23.85	1
	23.85	4
42, § 409.60(a)	23.45	2
42, § 409.61(a)(2)	23.45	6
42, § 409.61(b)	23.46	5
	23.46	7
42, § 409.61(d)	23.47	6
	23.47	7
	23.85	5
42, §§ 410.1—410.105	23.42	5
42, § 410.152(b)(1)	23.50	2
42, § 410.160(f)	23.50	1
42, § 411.15	23.49	1
42, § 414.48(b)	23.52	1
42, § 418.3	23.48	2
42, § 418.21(a)	23.48	3
	23.48	4
42, § 418.24(a)	23.48	5
42, § 418.24(b)(2)	23.48	6
42, § 418.24(d)(2)	23.48	6
42, § 418.28	23.48	6
42, § 418.204(b)	23.48	8
42, § 418.400(a)	23.48	8
42, § 418.400(b)	23.48	8
42, § 424.51	23.55	1
42, § 424.55	23.51	1
	23.51	4
42, § 466.70	23.56	2
42, § 466.70 et seq.	23.56	1
42, § 466.78(b)(3)	23.91	6
42, § 466.78(b)(3)	23.91	7
42, § 466.78(b)(4)	23.56	5
42, § 466.83	23.56	3
42, § 466.94	23.56	3
	23.91	5
42, § 466.94(a)(1)	23.56	4
42, § 473.12(a)(2)	23.56	10
42, § 473.12(a)(3)	23.56	11
42, § 473.18	23.56	6
42, § 473.20(c)	23.56	7
42, § 473.32	23.56	9
42, § 482.43(b)(3)	23.91	9
42, § 482.43(c)	23.91	8
42, § 482.102(b)(1)	23.93	14

CODE OF FEDERAL REGULATIONS

Tit.	Sec.	This Work Note
42, Pt. 483	23.92	2
42, § 483.10	23.94	1
42, § 483.10(b)(1)	23.94	3
42, § 483.10(b)(2)(i)	23.94	11
42, § 483.10(b)(6)	23.95	4
42, § 483.10(c)	23.95	2
	23.95	3
42, § 483.10(c)(8)	23.95	6
42, § 483.10(e)	23.94	9
	23.94	11
	23.94	12
42, § 483.10(f)	23.94	20
42, § 483.12(a)(1)	23.96	1
42, § 483.12(a)(2)	23.96	2
42, § 483.12(a)(4)	23.96	3
42, § 483.12(a)(5)	23.96	4
42, § 483.12(a)(6)(iv)	23.96	5
42, § 483.12(b)(1)(i)	23.97	1
42, § 483.12(b)(3)	23.97	6
42, § 483.12(d)(1)(i)	23.93	6
42, § 483.12(d)(1)(ii)	23.93	6
42, § 483.12(d)(2)	23.93	7
42, § 483.13(a)	23.94	13
	23.94	14
	23.94	15
42, § 483.13(b)	23.94	13
	23.94	14
	23.94	15
42, § 483.13(d)(3)	23.93	8
42, § 483.15(c)	23.94	22
	23.94	23
42, § 483.15(c)(3)	23.94	24
42, § 483.15(c)(4)	23.94	24
42, § 483.102(a)	23.93	13
42, § 485.10(b)(5)	23.95	5
42, §§ 489.20—489.34	23.46	7
47, § 25.104	16.125	16
48, § 9.403(b)	17.80	1
49, § 260.10	15.24	11

FEDERAL REGISTER

Vol.	Sec.	This Work Note
49, p. 171	21.45	6
	21.45	7
51, p. 57583	19.65	2
52, p. 11217	19.33	1
55, p. 20767–71	19.19	5
56, p. 60897	19.21	2
	19.21	5
	19.23	3
	19.25	2
	19.27	1
	19.27	2
56, p. 60900	19.23	3
	19.25	2
56, p. 60907	19.21	2
	19.21	5
56, p. 60908	19.27	1

TABLE OF RULES

FEDERAL REGISTER

Vol.	Sec.	This Work Note
59, p. 39952	19.53	5
61, p. 13061–79	19.16	5
61, p. 55346	23.8	2
	23.13	1
61, p. 56060	19.61	1
	19.61	5
62, p. 2442	23.41	9
	23.41	10
62, p. 10112	23.41	6
	23.41	7

REVENUE PROCEDURES

Rev.Proc.	Sec.	This Work Note
77–37	1.34	28
87–56	6.45	10
89–12	1.34	60
91–13	1.34	60
92–33	2.8	2
92–87	1.34	60
92–88	2.6	
94–46	1.34	60
	2.8	
95–10	1.34	60
	2.6	
	2.7	
	2.7	11
95–10, § 5.01(1)	2.7	10
95–10, § 5.01(2)	2.7	
95–10, § 5.01(4)	2.7	8
95–10, § 5.02(2)	2.8	
95–10, § 5.02(3)	2.8	
95–10, § 5.02(4)	2.8	
95–10, § 5.03(1)	2.9	
95–10, § 5.04	2.6	

REVENUE RULINGS

Rev.Rul.	Sec.	This Work Note
55–335	24.32	2
58–301	17.14	3
59–60	6.29	1
	21.43	12
	24.39	1
68–49	24.11	1
68–145	24.75	2
68–554	24.22	11
70–140	1.34	30
72–333	24.22	11
74–252	17.14	3
75–44	17.14	3
75–128	24.22	11
77–357	24.76	2
77–454	24.46	5
79–522	1.34	30
84–52	2.40	2
85–45	23.117	2
86–72	24.57	3
	24.57	7

REVENUE RULINGS

Rev.Rul.	Sec.	This Work Note
89–89	24.37	6
93–5	2.7	2
93–12	24.41	1
	24.45	2
93–38	2.7	1
94–43	2.2	5
95–10	35.23	3

PRIVATE LETTER RULINGS

Sec.	Sec.	This Work Note
931035	24.37	5
9026036	24.48	3
9210019	2.7	11
	2.8	10
9237020	24.37	11
	24.54	8
9253013	2.8	10
9306008	2.8	3
9321035	24.37	7
9350013	2.8	4
9415007	24.53	2
9436005	24.45	3
9537005	24.37	5
9544038	24.37	5
	24.37	9
9704029	24.37	7
9719006	24.45	3
9735003	24.45	3

SOCIAL SECURITY RULINGS

Rul.	Sec.	This Work Note
82–55	34.10	6
	34.10	9
83–12	34.47	10
	34.47	11
	34.47	15
83–19	34.11	14
84–25	34.9	19
	34.9	20
	34.9	21
85–15	34.47	11
85–28	34.10	5
	34.10	7
	34.10	8
91–5p	34.64	

MODEL RULES OF PROFESSIONAL CONDUCT

Rule	Sec.	This Work Note
1.1	26.5	1
1.6, Comment	23.5	2
1.7	23.4	4
	23.4	9
1.7, Comment	23.4	1
	23.4	8

433

TABLE OF RULES

MODEL RULES OF PROFESSIONAL CONDUCT

Rule	This Work Sec.	Note
1.8(f)	23.4	4
1.14	23.6	1
	23.6	2

MODEL RULES OF PROFESSIONAL CONDUCT

Rule	This Work Sec.	Note
1.14(b)	23.6	5
1.14(d)	23.6	5
1.14, Comment	23.5	2

TABLE OF CASES

A

Abajian, People v., 142 Misc.2d 250, 537 N.Y.S.2d 449 (N.Y.Just.Ct.1989)—**§ 33.25, n. 1.**

Abar v. Freightliner Corp., 208 A.D.2d 999, 617 N.Y.S.2d 209 (N.Y.A.D. 3 Dept. 1994)—**§ 27.34; § 27.34, n. 10.**

Abbott House v. Village of Tarrytown, 34 A.D.2d 821, 312 N.Y.S.2d 841 (N.Y.A.D. 2 Dept.1970)—**§ 16.50, n. 9.**

Abbott Laboratories v. Gardner, 387 U.S. 136, 87 S.Ct. 1507, 18 L.Ed.2d 681 (1967)—**§ 4.70, n. 2.**

Abbott Manor Nursing Home, People v., 112 A.D.2d 40, 490 N.Y.S.2d 411 (N.Y.A.D. 4 Dept.1985)—**§ 11.32, n. 4.**

Abco Bus Co., Inc. v. Macchiarola, 437 N.Y.S.2d 967, 419 N.E.2d 870 (N.Y. 1981)—**§ 3.25, n. 14.**

Abdur-Raheem v. Mann, 623 N.Y.S.2d 758, 647 N.E.2d 1266 (N.Y.1995)—**§ 4.15, n. 5; § 39.3, n. 4.**

Abdurrahman v. Berry, 537 N.Y.S.2d 477, 534 N.E.2d 315 (N.Y.1988)—**§ 39.6, n. 4.**

Abedi, People v., 156 Misc.2d 904, 595 N.Y.S.2d 1011 (N.Y.Sup.1993)—**§ 4.30, n. 2.**

Abel v. Bonfanti, 625 F.Supp. 263 (S.D.N.Y. 1985)—**§ 17.55, n. 6.**

Abel v. Monteleone, 39 A.D.2d 741, 332 N.Y.S.2d 859 (N.Y.A.D. 2 Dept.1972)—**§ 37.37, n. 37.**

Abe Schild Stone Corp. v. Apostle, 41 Misc.2d 732, 246 N.Y.S.2d 446 (N.Y.Sup. 1964)—**§ 10.14, n. 5.**

Aborn v. Aborn, 196 A.D.2d 561, 601 N.Y.S.2d 339 (N.Y.A.D. 2 Dept.1993)—**§ 21.43, n. 18.**

Abrahami v. UPC Const. Co., Inc., 224 A.D.2d 231, 638 N.Y.S.2d 11 (N.Y.A.D. 1 Dept.1996)—**§ 17.27, n. 2.**

Abraham L., Matter of, 53 A.D.2d 669, 385 N.Y.S.2d 103 (N.Y.A.D. 2 Dept.1976)—**§ 20.123, n. 3.**

Abrahams v. New York State Tax Com'n, 131 Misc.2d 594, 500 N.Y.S.2d 965 (N.Y.Sup.1986)—**§ 8.19, n. 8.**

Abrahante, People v., N.Y.L.J., 4/9/90, p.32, col.3 (N.Y.C.Crim.Ct.)—**§ 33.90, n. 4.**

Abramowitz v. New York University Dental Center, College of Dentistry, 110 A.D.2d 343, 494 N.Y.S.2d 721 (N.Y.A.D. 2 Dept. 1985)—**§ 5.11, n. 8, 9.**

Abrams, Matter of, 476 N.Y.S.2d 494, 465 N.E.2d 1 (N.Y.1984)—**§ 38.3, n. 22, 26.**

Abrams v. Allen, 297 N.Y. 52, 74 N.E.2d 305 (N.Y.1947)—**§ 1.66, n. 12.**

Abrams v. Thruway Food Market & Shopping Center, Inc., 147 A.D.2d 143, 541 N.Y.S.2d 856 (N.Y.A.D. 2 Dept.1989)—**§ 4.63, n. 2, 5.**

Abramson v. Abramson, 55 A.D.2d 519, 388 N.Y.S.2d 619 (N.Y.A.D. 1 Dept.1976)—**§ 28.16; § 28.16, n. 4.**

Abreu v. Ferrer, 198 A.D.2d 150, 603 N.Y.S.2d 485 (N.Y.A.D. 1 Dept.1993)—**§ 37.28, n. 11.**

Abudayeh v. Fair Plan Ins. Co., 105 A.D.2d 764, 481 N.Y.S.2d 711 (N.Y.A.D. 2 Dept. 1984)—**§ 31.11, n. 3.**

Academy Mews, Inc. v. Kane, 143 A.D.2d 960, 533 N.Y.S.2d 620 (N.Y.A.D. 2 Dept. 1988)—**§ 16.127, n. 14.**

Acequia, Inc., In re, 787 F.2d 1352 (9th Cir.1986)—**§ 9.148, n. 10; § 9.159, n. 4.**

Aceto Agr. Chemicals Corp., United States v., 872 F.2d 1373 (8th Cir.1989)—**§ 15.25, n. 6.**

Acevedo v. Acevedo, 200 A.D.2d 567, 606 N.Y.S.2d 307 (N.Y.A.D. 2 Dept.1994)—**§ 21.58, n. 2.**

Acevedo, People v., 216 A.D.2d 476, 628 N.Y.S.2d 737 (N.Y.A.D. 2 Dept.1995)—**§ 38.8, n. 26.**

Ace Wire & Cable Co., Inc. v. Aetna Cas. & Sur. Co., 469 N.Y.S.2d 655, 457 N.E.2d 761 (N.Y.1983)—**§ 31.9, n. 4.**

Ackerman v. Price Waterhouse, 156 Misc.2d 865, 591 N.Y.S.2d 936 (N.Y.Co.Ct. 1992)—**§ 28.5, n. 4.**

Ackerman v. Price Waterhouse, N.Y.L.J., 5/13/97, p.25, col.6 (Sup.Ct., N.Y.County)—**§ 28.13, n. 1.**

ACLI Government Securities, Inc. v. Rhoades, 813 F.Supp. 255 (S.D.N.Y. 1993)—**§ 2.46, n. 7.**

Acme Realty Co. v. Schinasi, 215 N.Y. 495, 109 N.E. 577 (N.Y.1915)—**§ 12.65, n. 7.**

Acosta, People v., 593 N.Y.S.2d 978, 609 N.E.2d 518 (N.Y.1993)—**§ 38.20, n. 11; § 38.21, n. 10.**

Acosta v. Wollett, 447 N.Y.S.2d 241, 431 N.E.2d 966 (N.Y.1981)—**§ 4.78, n. 9.**

TABLE OF CASES

Acoustic Chemical Corp. v. Gottlob, 22 Misc.2d 438, 197 N.Y.S.2d 225 (N.Y.Sup. 1960)—§ **30.5, n. 13.**

Acquafredda, Matter of, 189 A.D.2d 504, 596 N.Y.S.2d 839 (N.Y.A.D. 2 Dept. 1993)—§ **30.12, n. 6, 10.**

Acquisition of Real Property by Fulton County, Matter of, 136 A.D.2d 115, 525 N.Y.S.2d 948 (N.Y.A.D. 3 Dept.1988)—§ **14.24, n. 2.**

Acquisition of Real Property by Niagara Mohawk Power Corp., Matter of, 114 A.D.2d 542, 494 N.Y.S.2d 157 (N.Y.A.D. 3 Dept.1985)—§ **14.85, n. 7.**

Adamo Properties Inc. v. Almanzar, N.Y.L.J., 1/11/95, p.31, col.6, 23 HCR 27 (Civ.Ct., Kings County, 1995)—§ **13.12, n. 7.**

Adams v. Brant, 130 A.D.2d 957, 516 N.Y.S.2d 147 (N.Y.A.D. 4 Dept.1987)—§ **37.19, n. 14.**

Adams v. Clark, 239 N.Y. 403, 146 N.E. 642 (N.Y.1925)—§ **17.27, n. 4.**

Adams v. Nadel, 124 N.Y.S.2d 427 (N.Y.Sup.1953)—§ **20.8; § 20.8, n. 2.**

Adams, People v., 240 N.Y.S.2d 155, 190 N.E.2d 529 (N.Y.1963)—§ **38.10, n. 75.**

Adana Mortg. Bankers, Inc., In re, 14 B.R. 29 (Bkrtcy.N.D.Ga.1981)—§ **9.161, n. 10.**

Addesso v. Belting Associates, Inc., 128 A.D.2d 489, 512 N.Y.S.2d 416 (N.Y.A.D. 2 Dept.1987)—§ **37.37, n. 33.**

Adebahr v. 3840 Orloff Ave. Corp., 106 A.D.2d 770, 483 N.Y.S.2d 803 (N.Y.A.D. 3 Dept.1984)—§ **32.41, n. 6.**

Adirondack Ry. Co., People v., 160 N.Y. 225, 54 N.E. 689 (N.Y.1899)—§ **14.12, n. 2.**

Adler v. Deegan, 251 N.Y. 467, 167 N.E. 705 (N.Y.1929)—§ **3.14; § 3.14, n. 4.**

Adler v. Forham Co., 171 N.Y.S. 49 (N.Y.Sup.App.Term 1918)—§ **30.25, n. 2.**

Adler v. Pilot Industries, 57 N.Y.S.2d 539 (N.Y.Sup.1945)—§ **30.26, n. 2.**

Adolf Gobel, Inc., In re, 89 F.2d 171 (2nd Cir.1937)—§ **9.52, n. 7; § 9.53, n. 8.**

Adoption of A. by K.S., Matter of, 158 Misc.2d 760, 601 N.Y.S.2d 762 (N.Y.Fam.Ct.1993)—§ **20.37, n. 4; § 20.68, n. 3; § 20.85, n. 2.**

Adoption of Anonymous, In re, 46 Misc.2d 928, 261 N.Y.S.2d 439 (N.Y.Fam.Ct. 1965)—§ **20.45; § 20.45, n. 3, 10.**

Adoption of Anonymous, Matter of, 131 Misc.2d 666, 501 N.Y.S.2d 240 (N.Y.Sur. 1986)—§ **20.52, n. 3.**

Adoption of Anthony, Matter of, 113 Misc.2d 26, 448 N.Y.S.2d 377 (N.Y.Fam. Ct.1982)—§ **20.124; § 20.124, n. 1.**

Adoption of Baby Boy, Matter of, 147 Misc.2d 873, 556 N.Y.S.2d 463 (N.Y.Sur. 1990)—§ **20.45, n. 10.**

Adoption of Baby Boy, Matter of, 146 Misc.2d 896, 552 N.Y.S.2d 1005 (N.Y.Fam.Ct.1990)—§ **20.52, n. 5.**

Adoption of Baby Boy M.G., Matter of, 135 Misc.2d 252, 515 N.Y.S.2d 198 (N.Y.Sur. 1987)—§ **20.45; § 20.45, n. 11, 12; § 20.46; § 20.46, n. 2, 3; § 20.47; § 20.47, n. 1; § 20.53; § 20.53, n. 5; § 20.77; § 20.77, n. 3.**

Adoption of Baby Girl R, Matter of, 105 A.D.2d 575, 481 N.Y.S.2d 516 (N.Y.A.D. 3 Dept.1984)—§ **37.28, n. 27.**

Adoption of Black, In re, 57 Misc.2d 890, 293 N.Y.S.2d 797 (N.Y.Sur.1968)—§ **20.43, n. 3.**

Adoption of Caitlin, Matter of, 163 Misc.2d 999, 622 N.Y.S.2d 835 (N.Y.Fam.Ct. 1994)—§ **20.17, n. 7.**

Adoption of Calynn, M.G., Matter of, 137 Misc.2d 1005, 523 N.Y.S.2d 729 (N.Y.Sur.1987)—§ **20.2, n. 3; § 20.53; § 20.53, n. 6, 7.**

Adoption of Dafina T.G., Matter of, 161 Misc.2d 106, 613 N.Y.S.2d 329 (N.Y.Sur. 1994)—§ **20.49; § 20.49, n. 1.**

Adoption of Danielle, Matter of, 88 Misc.2d 78, 387 N.Y.S.2d 48 (N.Y.Sur.1976)—§ **20.51, n. 3.**

Adoption of Doe, Matter of, 161 Misc.2d 935, 615 N.Y.S.2d 823 (N.Y.Fam.Ct. 1994)—§ **20.56, n. 7.**

Adoption of D.S., Matter of, 160 Misc.2d 331, 609 N.Y.S.2d 139 (N.Y.Sur.1994)—§ **20.116; § 20.116, n. 1.**

Adoption of Earl B. and Willie A., Matter of, 119 Misc.2d 515, 463 N.Y.S.2d 724 (N.Y.Fam.Ct.1983)—§ **20.9, n. 3.**

Adoption of Evan, Matter of, 153 Misc.2d 844, 583 N.Y.S.2d 997 (N.Y.Sur.1992)—§ **20.17; § 20.17, n. 2.**

Adoption of E. W. C., Matter of, 89 Misc.2d 64, 389 N.Y.S.2d 743 (N.Y.Sur.1976)—§ **20.1, n. 11, 18; § 20.7; § 20.7, n. 2; § 20.11; § 20.11, n. 2; § 20.45; § 20.45, n. 8; § 20.51; § 20.51, n. 1, 2.**

Adoption of Female F. D., Matter of, 105 Misc.2d 866, 433 N.Y.S.2d 318 (N.Y.Sur. 1980)—§ **20.10, n. 2, 3.**

Adoption of Hope, Matter of, 150 Misc.2d 319, 571 N.Y.S.2d 182 (N.Y.Fam.Ct. 1991)—§ **20.17; § 20.17, n. 1.**

Adoption of Jarrett, Matter of, 224 A.D.2d 1029, 637 N.Y.S.2d 912 (N.Y.A.D. 4 Dept.1996)—§ **20.66; § 20.66, n. 1.**

Adoption of Jessica XX, Matter of, 446 N.Y.S.2d 20, 430 N.E.2d 896 (N.Y. 1981)—§ **20.35, n. 3, 8.**

Adoption of Jon K., Matter of, 141 Misc.2d 949, 535 N.Y.S.2d 660 (N.Y.Fam.Ct.

TABLE OF CASES

1988)—§ 20.2, n. 3; § 20.53; § 20.53, n. 4.

Adoption of J.O.T., Matter of, 120 Misc.2d 817, 466 N.Y.S.2d 636 (N.Y.Fam.Ct. 1983)—§ 18.67, n. 3.

Adoption of Male Infant A., Matter of, 150 Misc.2d 893, 578 N.Y.S.2d 988 (N.Y.Fam.Ct.1991)—§ 20.2, n. 3.

Adoption of Malpica-Orsini, In re, 370 N.Y.S.2d 511, 331 N.E.2d 486 (N.Y. 1975)—§ 20.5, n. 1; § 20.42, n. 1.

Adoption of Maria S., Matter of, 145 Misc.2d 99, 545 N.Y.S.2d 676 (N.Y.Fam. Ct.1989)—§ 20.67, n. 6.

Adoption of Mark L. Jr., Matter of, 172 A.D.2d 158, 567 N.Y.S.2d 697 (N.Y.A.D. 1 Dept.1991)—§ 20.31, n. 3.

Adoption of Maxwell, In re, 176 N.Y.S.2d 281, 151 N.E.2d 848 (N.Y.1958)— § 20.28; § 20.28, n. 3.

Adoption of Minor, In re, 130 Misc. 793, 226 N.Y.S. 445 (N.Y.Sur.1927)—§ 20.19, n. 1.

Adoption of Pyung B., In re, 83 Misc.2d 794, 371 N.Y.S.2d 993 (N.Y.Fam.Ct. 1975)—§ 20.25, n. 2.

Adoption of Raana Beth N., In re, 78 Misc.2d 105, 355 N.Y.S.2d 956 (N.Y.Sur. 1974)—§ 20.123; § 20.123, n. 2.

Adoption of Randi Q, Matter of, 214 A.D.2d 784, 624 N.Y.S.2d 474 (N.Y.A.D. 3 Dept. 1995)—§ 20.38; § 20.38, n. 3.

Adoption of Robert Paul P., Matter of, 481 N.Y.S.2d 652, 471 N.E.2d 424 (N.Y. 1984)—§ 20.7, n. 1; § 20.8, n. 1; § 20.13, n. 2; § 20.24; § 20.24, n. 2, 4.

Adoption of Samuel, Matter of, 167 A.D.2d 909, 562 N.Y.S.2d 278 (N.Y.A.D. 4 Dept. 1990)—§ 20.41; § 20.41, n. 2; § 20.45; § 20.45, n. 7; § 20.46, n. 1; § 20.77; § 20.77, n. 2.

Adoption of Vincent, Matter of, 158 Misc.2d 942, 602 N.Y.S.2d 303 (N.Y.Fam.Ct. 1993)—§ 20.120; § 20.120, n. 2.

Adoption of X, Matter of, 84 Misc.2d 770, 376 N.Y.S.2d 825 (N.Y.Sur.1975)— § 20.31, n. 2.

Adoption on Proceeding of Jose L., Matter of, 126 Misc.2d 612, 483 N.Y.S.2d 929 (N.Y.Fam.Ct.1984)—§ 20.45; § 20.45, n. 5; § 20.106, n. 3.

Adorno, People v., 112 A.D.2d 308, 491 N.Y.S.2d 755 (N.Y.A.D. 2 Dept.1985)— § 38.10, n. 38.

Adult Anonymous II, In re, 88 A.D.2d 30, 452 N.Y.S.2d 198 (N.Y.A.D. 1 Dept. 1982)—§ 20.24; § 20.24, n. 3.

Adventist Living Centers, Inc., Matter of, 52 F.3d 159 (7th Cir.1995)—§ 9.105, n. 5.

Adventurers Whitestone Corp. v. City of New York, 489 N.Y.S.2d 896, 479 N.E.2d 241 (N.Y.1985)—§ 14.108, n. 8, 9.

A.E. (TX), Matter of, 4 I & N Dec. 405 (BIA 1951)—§ 19.12, n. 11.

Aetna Cas. & Sur. Co. v. Lanza, 70 A.D.2d 508, 415 N.Y.S.2d 859 (N.Y.A.D. 1 Dept. 1979)—§ 31.10, n. 12.

Aetna Casualty & Surety Co. v. LTV Steel Co. (In re Chateaugay Corp.), 94 F.3d 772 (2nd Cir.1996)—§ 9.111, n. 1.

Aetna Cas. & Sur. Co. v. Scirica, 170 A.D.2d 448, 565 N.Y.S.2d 557 (N.Y.A.D. 2 Dept. 1991)—§ 37.28, n. 30.

Aetna Cas. & Sur. Co. v. Smith, 100 A.D.2d 751, 474 N.Y.S.2d 17 (N.Y.A.D. 1 Dept. 1984)—§ 26.28, n. 7.

Aetna Life and Cas. Co. v. Nelson, 501 N.Y.S.2d 313, 492 N.E.2d 386 (N.Y. 1986)—§ 26.49, n. 1.

Affiliated Credit Adjustors, Inc. v. Carlucci & Legum, 139 A.D.2d 611, 527 N.Y.S.2d 426 (N.Y.A.D. 2 Dept.1988)—§ 28.17, n. 3.

Afftrex, Ltd. v. General Elec. Co., 161 A.D.2d 855, 555 N.Y.S.2d 903 (N.Y.A.D. 3 Dept.1990)—§ 17.25, n. 2.

AG Consultants Grain Div., Inc., In re, 77 B.R. 665 (Bkrtcy.N.D.Ind.1987)— § 9.154, n. 4.

Agent Orange Product Liability Litigation, In re, 611 F.Supp. 1223 (E.D.N.Y. 1985)—§ 17.74, n. 3.

Agent Orange Product Liability Litigation, In re, 597 F.Supp. 740 (E.D.N.Y.1984)— § 27.35, n. 14.

Agins v. City of Tiburon, 447 U.S. 255, 100 S.Ct. 2138, 65 L.Ed.2d 106 (1980)— § 16.22; § 16.22, n. 8.

A.G. Ship Maintenance Corp. v. Lezak, 511 N.Y.S.2d 216, 503 N.E.2d 681 (N.Y. 1986)—§ 8.7, n. 3; § 13.64, n. 2.

Agugliaro v. Brooks Bros., Inc., 802 F.Supp. 956 (S.D.N.Y.1992)—§ 17.29, n. 5, 11.

Aharanwa v. Trustees of Columbia University in City of New York, 163 A.D.2d 8, 557 N.Y.S.2d 76 (N.Y.A.D. 1 Dept. 1990)—§ 17.34, n. 6.

Ahearn v. Zoning Bd. of Appeals of Town of Shawangunk, Ulster County, 158 A.D.2d 801, 551 N.Y.S.2d 392 (N.Y.A.D. 3 Dept. 1990)—§ 16.8, n. 9.

Ahmad v. Getty Petroleum Corp., 217 A.D.2d 600, 629 N.Y.S.2d 779 (N.Y.A.D. 2 Dept.1995)—§ 37.37, n. 93.

Ahmadi v. Government Employees Ins. Co. (GEICO), 204 A.D.2d 374, 612 N.Y.S.2d 50 (N.Y.A.D. 2 Dept.1994)—§ 30.34, n. 5.

Ahmed, People v., 496 N.Y.S.2d 984, 487 N.E.2d 894 (N.Y.1985)—§ 38.19; § 38.19, n. 17, 120; § 39.50, n. 10.

TABLE OF CASES

Aho, Matter of, 383 N.Y.S.2d 285, 347 N.E.2d 647 (N.Y.1976)—§ **37.34, n. 4;** § **37.35, n. 12;** § **37.37, n. 79;** § **37.47, n. 1.**

A.H. Robins Co., Inc., In re, 880 F.2d 694 (4th Cir.1989)—§ **9.170, n. 6.**

Aim Rent A Car, Inc. v. Zoning Bd. of Appeals of Village of Montebello, 156 A.D.2d 323, 548 N.Y.S.2d 275 (N.Y.A.D. 2 Dept.1989)—§ **16.119, n. 3, 4.**

Ainsworth, People v., 145 A.D.2d 74, 537 N.Y.S.2d 798 (N.Y.A.D. 1 Dept.1989)—§ **38.10, n. 49.**

A & J Buyers, Inc. v. Johnson, Drake & Piper, Inc., 303 N.Y.S.2d 841, 250 N.E.2d 845 (N.Y.1969)—§ **10.5, n. 5.**

A. J. J., Matter of, 108 Misc.2d 657, 438 N.Y.S.2d 444 (N.Y.Sur.1981)—§ **20.18, n. 1;** § **20.26, n. 1.**

Akpan v. Koch, 555 N.Y.S.2d 16, 554 N.E.2d 53 (N.Y.1990)—§ **15.6, n. 15.**

Akullian, Matter of Estate of, 167 A.D.2d 596, 563 N.Y.S.2d 223 (N.Y.A.D. 3 Dept. 1990)—§ **23.82, n. 1.**

Akzo Coatings, Inc. v. Aigner Corp., 30 F.3d 761 (7th Cir.1994)—§ **15.30, n. 7.**

Alabama v. Pugh, 438 U.S. 781, 98 S.Ct. 3057, 57 L.Ed.2d 1114 (1978)—§ **18.33, n. 2.**

Alanthus Corp. v. Travelers Ins. Co., 92 A.D.2d 830, 460 N.Y.S.2d 549 (N.Y.A.D. 1 Dept.1983)—§ **17.27, n. 1.**

Albanese, People v., 29 A.D.2d 516, 285 N.Y.S.2d 179 (N.Y.A.D. 1 Dept.1967)—§ **38.21;** § **38.21, n. 13.**

Albany Area Builders Ass'n v. Town of Guilderland, 547 N.Y.S.2d 627, 546 N.E.2d 920 (N.Y.1989)—§ **16.24;** § **16.24, n. 9, 11.**

Albany, City of v. Helsby, 328 N.Y.S.2d 658, 278 N.E.2d 898 (N.Y.1972)—§ **3.21, n. 4.**

Albany Community Development Agency v. Abdelgader, 205 A.D.2d 905, 613 N.Y.S.2d 473 (N.Y.A.D. 3 Dept.1994)—§ **14.94, n. 1.**

Albany Indus. Development Agency, City of v. Degraff–Moffly/General Contractors, Inc., 164 A.D.2d 20, 562 N.Y.S.2d 821 (N.Y.A.D. 3 Dept.1990)—§ **10.17, n. 8.**

Albenda (Gonzalez), Matter of, N.Y.L.J., 1/3/92, p.27, col.5 (Sup.Ct., Kings County)—§ **22.81, n. 2;** § **22.86, n. 1.**

Alberi v. Rossi, 108 A.D.2d 833, 485 N.Y.S.2d 337 (N.Y.A.D. 2 Dept.1985)—§ **37.37, n. 40.**

Albert v. Carovano, 851 F.2d 561 (2nd Cir. 1988)—§ **18.53, n. 1.**

Albert v. Salzman, 41 A.D.2d 501, 344 N.Y.S.2d 457 (N.Y.A.D. 1 Dept.1973)—§ **1.51, n. 88.**

Alberti v. Dickens, 22 A.D.2d 770, 253 N.Y.S.2d 561 (N.Y.A.D. 1 Dept.1964)—§ **38.8, n. 86.**

Albertina Realty Co. v. Rosbro Realty Corporation, 258 N.Y. 472, 180 N.E. 176 (N.Y.1932)—§ **11.12, n. 1.**

Albert J. Schiff Associates, Inc. v. Flack, 435 N.Y.S.2d 972, 417 N.E.2d 84 (N.Y. 1980)—§ **31.13, n. 9.**

Albion Indus. Center v. Town of Albion (Orleans County), 62 A.D.2d 478, 405 N.Y.S.2d 521 (N.Y.A.D. 4 Dept.1978)—§ **3.25, n. 3.**

Albright v. Oliver, 510 U.S. 266, 114 S.Ct. 807, 127 L.Ed.2d 114 (1994)—§ **18.22, n. 3.**

Alcan Aluminum Corp., United States v., 990 F.2d 711 (2nd Cir.1993)—§ **15.29, n. 15.**

Alcan Aluminum Corp., United States v., 964 F.2d 252 (3rd Cir.1992)—§ **15.29, n. 15.**

Alden v. Time Warner, Inc., 1995 WL 679238 (S.D.N.Y.1995)—§ **17.72, n. 7.**

Aldrich v. Pattison, 107 A.D.2d 258, 486 N.Y.S.2d 23 (N.Y.A.D. 2 Dept.1985)—§ **15.6, n. 20.**

Alejandro, People v., 517 N.Y.S.2d 927, 511 N.E.2d 71 (N.Y.1987)—§ **33.9;** § **33.9, n. 6;** § **38.19, n. 36, 96.**

Alert Holdings Inc., In re, 157 B.R. 753 (Bkrtcy.S.D.N.Y.1993)—§ **9.31, n. 10.**

Alexander v. Choate, 469 U.S. 287, 105 S.Ct. 712, 83 L.Ed.2d 661 (1985)—§ **18.19, n. 5.**

Alexander v. Donohoe, 143 N.Y. 203, 38 N.E. 263 (N.Y.1894)—§ **1.51, n. 87.**

Alexander, People v., 206 A.D. 780, 200 N.Y.S. 939 (N.Y.A.D. 2 Dept.1923)—§ **38.20, n. 6;** § **38.26, n. 21.**

Alexander's Dept. Stores v. Ohrbach's, Inc., 269 A.D. 321, 56 N.Y.S.2d 173 (N.Y.A.D. 1 Dept.1945)—§ **30.5, n. 6;** § **30.24, n. 6.**

Alexandra C., Matter of, 157 Misc.2d 262, 596 N.Y.S.2d 958 (N.Y.Fam.Ct.1993)—§ **20.90, n. 3;** § **20.97;** § **20.97, n. 3.**

Alford v. Niagara Mohawk Power Corp., 115 A.D.2d 924, 496 N.Y.S.2d 820 (N.Y.A.D. 3 Dept.1985)—§ **30.26, n. 1.**

Alfred P. Sloan Foundation, Inc. v. Atlas, 42 Misc.2d 603, 248 N.Y.S.2d 524 (N.Y.Sup. 1964)—§ **1.10, n. 7.**

Ali v. I.N.S., 661 F.Supp. 1234 (D.Mass. 1986)—§ **19.14;** § **19.14, n. 18.**

Ali, People v., 189 A.D.2d 770, 592 N.Y.S.2d 405 (N.Y.A.D. 2 Dept.1993)—§ **38.10, n. 175.**

Alison VV, Matter of, 211 A.D.2d 988, 621 N.Y.S.2d 739 (N.Y.A.D. 3 Dept.1995)—§ **20.2, n. 6;** § **20.22, n. 1;** § **20.79;** § **20.79, n. 1.**

TABLE OF CASES

Al–Jundi v. Estate of Rockefeller, 885 F.2d 1060 (2nd Cir.1989)—§ **18.35, n. 2.**

All City Ins. Co. v. Pioneer Ins. Co., 194 A.D.2d 424, 599 N.Y.S.2d 245 (N.Y.A.D. 1 Dept.1993)—§ **31.16, n. 7.**

Allegheny Intern., Inc., In re, 954 F.2d 167 (3rd Cir.1992)—§ **9.96, n. 2.**

Allegheny Intern., Inc., In re, 118 B.R. 282 (Bkrtcy.W.D.Pa.1990)—§ **9.162, n. 10.**

Allegheny Intern., Inc., In re, 100 B.R. 241 (Bkrtcy.W.D.Pa.1988)—§ **9.46, n. 1.**

Allen v. Blum, 85 A.D.2d 228, 448 N.Y.S.2d 163 (N.Y.A.D. 1 Dept.1982)—§ **37.30;** § **37.30, n. 7.**

Allen v. Crowell–Collier Pub. Co., 288 N.Y.S.2d 449, 235 N.E.2d 430 (N.Y. 1968)—§ **26.42, n. 3.**

Allen v. Hattrick, 87 A.D.2d 575, 447 N.Y.S.2d 741 (N.Y.A.D. 2 Dept.1982)— § **16.89, n. 7.**

Allen v. Howe, 621 N.Y.S.2d 287, 645 N.E.2d 720 (N.Y.1994)—§ **4.76, n. 2.**

Allen v. McCurry, 449 U.S. 90, 101 S.Ct. 411, 66 L.Ed.2d 308 (1980)—§ **18.37, n. 2.**

Allen, People v., 603 N.Y.S.2d 820, 623 N.E.2d 1170 (N.Y.1993)—§ **38.8, n. 26, 224.**

Allen, People v., N.Y.L.J., 7/29/94, p.25, col. 3 (North Hills Vill.Ct.)—§ **33.32, n. 21** § **33.33, n. 3.**

Allen v. Town of North Hempstead, 103 A.D.2d 144, 478 N.Y.S.2d 919 (N.Y.A.D. 2 Dept.1984)—§ **16.120, n. 8;** § **16.123, n. 7.**

Alliance of American Insurers v. Cuomo, 854 F.2d 591 (2nd Cir.1988)—§ **31.21, n. 4.**

Allied Chemical, an Operating Unit of Allied Corp. v. Niagara Mohawk Power Corp., 532 N.Y.S.2d 230, 528 N.E.2d 153 (N.Y.1988)—§ **4.25, n. 1, 2;** § **4.51, n. 3.**

Allied Corp. v. Town of Camillus, 590 N.Y.S.2d 417, 604 N.E.2d 1348 (N.Y. 1992)—§ **14.85, n. 1;** § **14.86, n. 2;** § **14.88, n. 4;** § **14.89, n. 4;** § **14.90, n. 3.**

Allied Semi–Conductors Intern., Ltd. v. Pulsar Components Intern., Inc., 907 F.Supp. 618 (E.D.N.Y.1995)—§ **5.48, n. 2.**

Allied 31st Ave. Corp. v. City of New York, 23 A.D.2d 678, 257 N.Y.S.2d 652 (N.Y.A.D. 2 Dept.1965)—§ **37.47, n. 4.**

Allison v. Roslyn Plaza, Ltd., 86 Misc.2d 849, 385 N.Y.S.2d 454 (N.Y.Sup.1976)— § **11.34, n. 1.**

Allocco v. Rainone, 73 N.Y.S.2d 330 (N.Y.Sup.1947)—§ **8.14, n. 5.**

Alls, People v., 608 N.Y.S.2d 139, 629 N.E.2d 1018 (N.Y.1993)—§ **33.49, n. 4.**

All Seasons Resorts, Inc. v. Abrams, 506 N.Y.S.2d 10, 497 N.E.2d 33 (N.Y.1986)— § **2.106, n. 9.**

Allstate Ins. Co. v. Foschio, 93 A.D.2d 328, 462 N.Y.S.2d 44 (N.Y.A.D. 2 Dept. 1983)—§ **7.27, n. 14;** § **7.46, n. 7.**

Allstate Ins. Co. v. Furman, 84 A.D.2d 29, 445 N.Y.S.2d 236 (N.Y.A.D. 2 Dept. 1981)—§ **31.10, n. 1.**

Allstate Ins. Co. v. Gross, 317 N.Y.S.2d 309, 265 N.E.2d 736 (N.Y.1970)—§ **31.15, n. 10.**

Allstate Ins. Co. v. McGouey, 42 A.D.2d 730, 346 N.Y.S.2d 115 (N.Y.A.D. 2 Dept. 1973)—§ **26.28, n. 5.**

Allstate Ins. Co. v. Patrylo, 144 A.D.2d 243, 533 N.Y.S.2d 436 (N.Y.A.D. 1 Dept. 1988)—§ **31.10, n. 17.**

Allstate Ins. Co. v. Ramirez, 208 A.D.2d 828, 618 N.Y.S.2d 396 (N.Y.A.D. 2 Dept. 1994)—§ **37.28, n. 18.**

Allstate Ins. Co. v. Stewart, 329 N.Y.S.2d 102, 279 N.E.2d 858 (N.Y.1972)—§ **4.82, n. 8.**

Allstate Ins. Co. v. Tax Com'n, 502 N.Y.S.2d 1004, 494 N.E.2d 109 (N.Y. 1986)—§ **35.104, n. 2.**

Alma Soc. Inc. v. Mellon, 601 F.2d 1225 (2nd Cir.1979)—§ **20.126, n. 1;** § **20.130, n. 1.**

Almonte, People v., 223 A.D.2d 593, 637 N.Y.S.2d 168 (N.Y.A.D. 2 Dept.1996)— § **38.28, n. 6.**

Aloe v. Dassler, 278 A.D. 975, 106 N.Y.S.2d 24 (N.Y.A.D. 2 Dept.1951)—§ **16.91, n. 3.**

Alonzo, People v., 155 A.D.2d 233, 546 N.Y.S.2d 617 (N.Y.A.D. 1 Dept.1989)— § **38.25, n. 27.**

Alphonso C. v. Morgenthau, 382 N.Y.S.2d 980, 346 N.E.2d 819 (N.Y.1976)—§ **38.3, n. 24.**

Alscot Investing Corp. v. Incorporated Village of Rockville Centre, 488 N.Y.S.2d 629, 477 N.E.2d 1083 (N.Y.1985)— § **37.32, n. 5.**

Altamore v. Friedman, 193 A.D.2d 240, 602 N.Y.S.2d 894 (N.Y.A.D. 2 Dept.1993)— § **28.30;** § **28.30, n. 2, 4.**

Aluminum Co. of America, United States v., 824 F.Supp. 640 (E.D.Tex.1993)—§ **4.38, n. 2.**

Alva v. Hurley, Fox, Selig, Caprari & Kelleher, 156 Misc.2d 550, 593 N.Y.S.2d 728 (N.Y.Sup.1993)—§ **28.3, n. 1;** § **28.10;** § **28.10, n. 1.**

Alvarado, Matter of, 166 A.D.2d 932, 560 N.Y.S.2d 586 (N.Y.A.D. 4 Dept.1990)— § **18.71, n. 3.**

Alvarado v. State, Dept. of State, Div. of State Athletic Com'n, 110 A.D.2d 583,

TABLE OF CASES

488 N.Y.S.2d 177 (N.Y.A.D. 1 Dept. 1985)—§ **4.12, n. 11.**
Alvarez v. Immigration and Naturalization Service, 539 F.2d 1220 (9th Cir.1976)—§ **19.74, n. 1.**
Alvaro Inc. v. Chow, 221 A.D.2d 752, 633 N.Y.S.2d 643 (N.Y.A.D. 3 Dept.1995)—§ **10.11, n. 2.**
Alverson v. State Div. of Human Rights on Complaints of Grey, 181 A.D.2d 1019, 581 N.Y.S.2d 953 (N.Y.A.D. 4 Dept. 1992)—§ **18.46, n. 1; § 18.49, n. 12.**
Alyeska Pipeline Service Co. v. Wilderness Society, 421 U.S. 240, 95 S.Ct. 1612, 44 L.Ed.2d 141 (1975)—§ **37.67, n. 12.**
Amanda, Matter of, 197 A.D.2d 923, 602 N.Y.S.2d 461 (N.Y.A.D. 4 Dept.1993)—§ **20.43, n. 6.**
Amann v. Caccese, 223 A.D.2d 663, 637 N.Y.S.2d 217 (N.Y.A.D. 2 Dept.1996)—§ **21.16, n. 1.**
Ambassador Group, Inc. Litigation, In re, 830 F.Supp. 147 (E.D.N.Y.1993)—§ **28.37, n. 1.**
Amco Development, Inc. v. Zoning Bd. of Appeals of Town of Perinton, 185 A.D.2d 637, 586 N.Y.S.2d 50 (N.Y.A.D. 4 Dept. 1992)—§ **16.78, n. 4.**
Amdar Co. v. Hahalis, 145 Misc.2d 987, 554 N.Y.S.2d 759 (N.Y.Sup.App.Term 1990)—§ **13.56, n. 6.**
Amer v. Bay Terrace Co-op. Section II, Inc., 142 A.D.2d 704, 531 N.Y.S.2d 33 (N.Y.A.D. 2 Dept.1988)—§ **1.27, n. 5.**
American Airlines, Inc. v. Rolex Realty Co., Inc., 165 A.D.2d 701, 560 N.Y.S.2d 146 (N.Y.A.D. 1 Dept.1990)—§ **13.71; § 13.71, n. 2.**
American Aniline Products v. D. Nagase & Co., 187 A.D. 555, 176 N.Y.S. 114 (N.Y.A.D. 1 Dept.1919)—§ **5.32, n. 2.**
American Auto. Plan, Inc. v. Corcoran, 166 A.D.2d 215, 560 N.Y.S.2d 435 (N.Y.A.D. 1 Dept.1990)—§ **4.15, n. 3.**
American Body Armor & Equipment, Inc., In re, 155 B.R. 588 (M.D.Fla.1993)—§ **9.22, n. 6.**
American Cigar Lighter Co., In re, 77 Misc. 643, 138 N.Y.S. 455 (N.Y.Sup.1912)—§ **1.13, n. 13.**
American Cities Co. v. Stevenson, 187 Misc. 107, 60 N.Y.S.2d 685 (N.Y.Sup.1946)—§ **8.14, n. 4.**
American Community Servs., Inc. v. Wright Marketing Inc. (In re American Community Services, Inc.), 86 B.R. 681 (D.Utah 1988)—§ **9.22, n. 8.**
American Consumer Industries, Inc. v. City of New York, 28 A.D.2d 38, 281 N.Y.S.2d 467 (N.Y.A.D. 1 Dept.1967)—§ **3.9, n. 1.**

American Express Travel Related Services v. Hashemi (In re Hashemi), 104 F.3d 1122 (9th Cir.1996)—§ **9.208, n. 3.**
American Fibre Chair Seat Corp., In re, 241 A.D. 532, 272 N.Y.S. 206 (N.Y.A.D. 2 Dept.1934)—§ **1.43, n. 22.**
American Friends of Society of St. Pius, Inc. v. Schwab, 69 A.D.2d 646, 417 N.Y.S.2d 991 (N.Y.A.D. 2 Dept.1979)—§ **16.25, n. 3.**
American Healthcare Management, Inc., Matter of, 900 F.2d 827 (5th Cir.1990)—§ **9.77, n. 1.**
American Home Assur. Co. v. Fremont Indem. Co., 745 F.Supp. 974 (S.D.N.Y. 1990)—§ **31.18, n. 6.**
American Home Assur. Co. v. Hartford Ins. Co., 74 A.D.2d 224, 427 N.Y.S.2d 26 (N.Y.A.D. 1 Dept.1980)—§ **31.2, n. 14.**
American Home Assur. Co. v. International Ins. Co., 661 N.Y.S.2d 584, 684 N.E.2d 14 (N.Y.1997)—§ **31.10, n. 4, 5; § 31.12, n. 1.**
American Home Assur. Co. v. International Ins. Co., 219 A.D.2d 143, 641 N.Y.S.2d 241 (N.Y.A.D. 1 Dept.1996)—§ **28.40, n. 3.**
American Home Assur. Co. v. Joseph, 213 A.D.2d 633, 624 N.Y.S.2d 250 (N.Y.A.D. 2 Dept.1995)—§ **37.28, n. 19; § 37.37, n. 88.**
American Home Assurance Co. v. Morris J. Eisen, P.C., N.Y.L.J., 9/4/92, p.22, col.2 (Sup.Ct., N.Y. County, 1992)—§ **28.43; § 28.43, n. 4, 5, 9.**
American Home Products Corp. v. Liberty Mut. Ins. Co., 748 F.2d 760 (2nd Cir. 1984)—§ **31.9, n. 7.**
American Home Products Corp. v. Liberty Mut. Ins. Co., 565 F.Supp. 1485 (S.D.N.Y.1983)—§ **31.2, n. 7.**
American Ins. Co. v. Messinger, 401 N.Y.S.2d 36, 371 N.E.2d 798 (N.Y. 1977)—§ **31.24, n. 12.**
American List Corp. v. United States News and World Report, Inc., 550 N.Y.S.2d 590, 549 N.E.2d 1161 (N.Y.1989)—§ **30.6, n. 1, 4; § 30.23, n. 2.**
American Min. Congress v. United States Army Corps of Engineers, 951 F.Supp. 267 (D.D.C.1997)—§ **15.15, n. 7.**
American Motorists Ins. Co. v. Salvatore, 102 A.D.2d 342, 476 N.Y.S.2d 897 (N.Y.A.D. 1 Dept.1984)—§ **31.6, n. 13.**
American Solar King Corp., In re, 90 B.R. 808 (Bkrtcy.W.D.Tex.1988)—§ **9.158, n. 4.**
American Tel. and Tel. Co. v. Salesian Soc., Inc., 77 A.D.2d 706, 430 N.Y.S.2d 408 (N.Y.A.D. 3 Dept.1980)—§ **14.129, n. 2.**

TABLE OF CASES

Ames v. Ames, 212 A.D.2d 653, 622 N.Y.S.2d 774 (N.Y.A.D. 2 Dept.1995)—§ 21.55, n. 7.

Ames v. City of New York, 177 A.D.2d 528, 575 N.Y.S.2d 917 (N.Y.A.D. 2 Dept. 1991)—§ 30.9, n. 5.

Ames v. Johnston, 169 A.D.2d 84, 571 N.Y.S.2d 831 (N.Y.A.D. 3 Dept.1991)—§ 16.56, n. 5.

Ames Dept. Stores, Inc., In re, 115 B.R. 34 (Bkrtcy.S.D.N.Y.1990)—§ 9.72, n. 2.

A. M. Knitwear Corp. v. All America Export-Import Corp., 390 N.Y.S.2d 832, 359 N.E.2d 342 (N.Y.1976)—§ 5.33, n. 2.

Ammann v. Ammann, 209 A.D.2d 1032, 619 N.Y.S.2d 469 (N.Y.A.D. 4 Dept.1994)—§ 37.29, n. 11.

Amodio v. Amodio, 516 N.Y.S.2d 923, 509 N.E.2d 936 (N.Y.1987)—§ **21.43**; § 21.43, n. 8.

AMR Services Corp. v. New York State Div. of Human Rights, 214 A.D.2d 665, 625 N.Y.S.2d 583 (N.Y.A.D. 2 Dept.1995)—§ 17.68, n. 5.

Amsterdam Nursing Home Corp. v. Commissioner of New York State Dept. of Health, 192 A.D.2d 945, 596 N.Y.S.2d 877 (N.Y.A.D. 3 Dept.1993)—§ 4.72, n. 7.

Amsterdam Sav. Bank v. Amsterdam Pharmaceutical Development Corp., 106 A.D.2d 797, 484 N.Y.S.2d 217 (N.Y.A.D. 3 Dept.1984)—§ 11.52, n. 6.

Amusement Business Underwriters, a Div. of Bingham & Bingham, Inc. v. American Intern. Group, Inc., 498 N.Y.S.2d 760, 489 N.E.2d 729 (N.Y.1985)—§ 31.9, n. 7.

Anastas v. American Savings (In re Anastas), 94 F.3d 1280 (9th Cir.1996)—§ 9.208, n. 3.

Ancott Realty, Inc. v. Gramercy Stuyvesant Independent Democrats, 127 Misc.2d 490, 486 N.Y.S.2d 672 (N.Y.City Civ.Ct. 1985)—§ 13.9, n. 2.

Anders v. Segall, 124 A.D.2d 1029, 508 N.Y.S.2d 765 (N.Y.A.D. 4 Dept.1986)—§ 37.29, n. 25.

Anders v. State of Cal., 386 U.S. 738, 87 S.Ct. 1396, 18 L.Ed.2d 493 (1967)—§ 38.8; § 38.8, n. 37; § 38.17, n. 19; § 38.24, n. 2; § 38.38; § 38.38, n. 1; § 38.42; § 38.42, n. 1.

Anderson, Matter of, 16 I & N Dec. 596 (BIA 1978)—§ 19.48, n. 4.

Anderson v. Carney, 161 A.D.2d 1002, 557 N.Y.S.2d 575 (N.Y.A.D. 3 Dept.1990)—§ 30.15, n. 7.

Anderson v. Creighton, 483 U.S. 635, 107 S.Ct. 3034, 97 L.Ed.2d 523 (1987)—§ 18.32, n. 1.

Anderson v. Eli Lilly & Co., 158 A.D.2d 91, 557 N.Y.S.2d 981 (N.Y.A.D. 3 Dept. 1990)—§ **30.15, n. 1.**

Anderson v. John L. Hayes Const. Co., 243 N.Y. 140, 153 N.E. 28 (N.Y.1926)—§ 10.21, n. 4.

Anderson v. Kirk, 534 N.Y.S.2d 369, 530 N.E.2d 1289 (N.Y.1988)—§ **38.10, n. 64.**

Anderson v. National Fuel Gas Supply Corp., 105 A.D.2d 1097, 482 N.Y.S.2d 644 (N.Y.A.D. 4 Dept.1984)—§ **14.26, n. 4.**

Anderson, People v., 519 N.Y.S.2d 957, 514 N.E.2d 377 (N.Y.1987)—§ **38.19, n. 123.**

Anderson, People v., 498 N.Y.S.2d 119, 488 N.E.2d 1231 (N.Y.1985)—§ **33.90;** § **33.90, n. 1, 5.**

Anderson, People v., 396 N.Y.S.2d 625, 364 N.E.2d 1318 (N.Y.1977)—§ **33.57, n. 1, 7.**

Anderson v. Stephen M. Donis, D.P.M.P.C., 150 A.D.2d 414, 541 N.Y.S.2d 25 (N.Y.A.D. 2 Dept.1989)—§ 30.29, n. 2; § 37.29, n. 15.

Andres R., In re, 216 A.D.2d 145, 629 N.Y.S.2d 7 (N.Y.A.D. 1 Dept.1995)—§ 20.20; § 20.20, n. 1.

Andrews, In re, 80 F.3d 906 (4th Cir. 1996)—§ 9.49, n. 4.

Andrulonis v. United States, 724 F.Supp. 1421 (N.D.N.Y.1989)—§ 27.17; § **27.17, n. 1.**

Angelakos, People v., 518 N.Y.S.2d 784, 512 N.E.2d 305 (N.Y.1987)—§ **38.9, n. 13;** § **38.19, n. 16.**

Angeloff v. Angeloff, 453 N.Y.S.2d 630, 439 N.E.2d 346 (N.Y.1982)—§ **21.30, n. 12.**

Anna W. v. Bane, 863 F.Supp. 125 (W.D.N.Y.1993)—§ **23.75, n. 6.**

Annunziata v. Colasanti, 126 A.D.2d 75, 512 N.Y.S.2d 381 (N.Y.A.D. 1 Dept. 1987)—§ **37.65, n. 54.**

Anonymous, Matter of, 153 Misc.2d 893, 582 N.Y.S.2d 941 (N.Y.City Civ.Ct. 1992)—§ 18.69, n. 1, 4; § 18.90, n. 1.

Anonymous v. Anonymous, 108 Misc.2d 1098, 439 N.Y.S.2d 255 (N.Y.Sup. 1981)—§ **20.45, n. 10.**

Anonymous v. Anonymous, 57 A.D.2d 938, 395 N.Y.S.2d 103 (N.Y.A.D. 2 Dept. 1977)—§ **21.31, n. 4.**

Anonymous v. Anonymous, 166 Misc. 861, 2 N.Y.S.2d 663 (N.Y.Sup.1938)—§ **21.26, n. 5;** § **21.27, n. 2.**

Anonymous, Application of, 155 Misc.2d 241, 587 N.Y.S.2d 548 (N.Y.City Civ.Ct. 1992)—§ **18.69, n. 1, 4;** § **18.90, n. 1.**

Anonymous' Adoption, Matter of, 177 Misc. 683, 31 N.Y.S.2d 595 (N.Y.Sur.1941)—§ **20.6, n. 1;** § **20.23, n. 1.**

TABLE OF CASES

Anonymous, R.A., Matter of, N.Y.L.J., 9/28/93, p.27, col.2 (Surr.Ct., Nassau County)—§ **22.15, n. 6**; § **22.38, n. 4.**

Anthony v. Interform Corp., 96 F.3d 692 (3rd Cir.1996)—§ **9.81, n. 3.**

Anthony Marino Const. Corp. v. INA Underwriters Ins. Co., 513 N.Y.S.2d 379, 505 N.E.2d 944 (N.Y.1987)—§ **31.11, n. 8.**

Antico Mfg. Co., Inc., In re, 31 B.R. 103 (Bkrtcy.E.D.N.Y.1983)—§ **9.71, n. 11.**

Antillean Holding Co., Inc. v. Lindley, 76 Misc.2d 1044, 352 N.Y.S.2d 557 (N.Y.City Civ.Ct.1973)—§ **13.33, n. 5;** § **13.58, n. 3.**

Antoian v. Antoian, 215 A.D.2d 421, 626 N.Y.S.2d 535 (N.Y.A.D. 2 Dept.1995)—§ **21.37, n. 7.**

Antoine, Matter of, 207 A.D.2d 829, 616 N.Y.S.2d 635 (N.Y.A.D. 2 Dept.1994)—§ **20.119;** § **20.119, n. 1.**

Antoine v. Byers & Anderson, Inc., 508 U.S. 429, 113 S.Ct. 2167, 124 L.Ed.2d 391 (1993)—§ **18.31, n. 2.**

Antommarchi, People v., 590 N.Y.S.2d 33, 604 N.E.2d 95 (N.Y.1992)—§ **18.12, n. 2;** § **38.19, n. 22, 109;** § **38.28;** § **38.28, n. 24.**

AOV Industries, Inc., In re, 792 F.2d 1140, 253 U.S.App.D.C. 186 (D.C.Cir.1986)—§ **9.148, n. 8;** § **9.170, n. 3.**

Apel, Matter of, 96 Misc.2d 839, 409 N.Y.S.2d 928 (N.Y.Fam.Ct.1978)—§ **20.43, n. 8, 9.**

Apex Oil Co. v. Vanguard Oil & Service Co. Inc., 760 F.2d 417 (2nd Cir.1985)—§ **5.20, n. 5.**

Aponte, People v., 212 A.D.2d 157, 629 N.Y.S.2d 773 (N.Y.A.D. 2 Dept.1995)—§ **38.8, n. 198.**

Apostolou v. Mutual of Omaha Ins. Co., 72 A.D.2d 781, 421 N.Y.S.2d 600 (N.Y.A.D. 2 Dept.1979)—§ **31.21, n. 7.**

Appel, People v., 120 A.D.2d 319, 509 N.Y.S.2d 438 (N.Y.A.D. 3 Dept.1986)—§ **38.10;** § **38.10, n. 78.**

Appell v. Appell, 37 A.D.2d 966, 327 N.Y.S.2d 190 (N.Y.A.D. 2 Dept.1971)—§ **38.8, n. 117.**

Applegate Property, Ltd., In re, 133 B.R. 827 (Bkrtcy.W.D.Tex.1991)—§ **9.162, n. 10;** § **9.165, n. 20.**

Appleton v. City of New York, 219 N.Y. 150, 114 N.E. 73 (N.Y.1916)—§ **12.57, n. 3.**

Application by Bon Neuve Realty Corp., Matter of, 196 A.D.2d 694, 601 N.Y.S.2d 491 (N.Y.A.D. 1 Dept.1993)—§ **1.21, n. 23.**

Application of (see name of party)

Applications of Greenfield, 66 Misc.2d 733, 322 N.Y.S.2d 276 (N.Y.City Civ.Ct. 1970)—§ **18.71, n. 5.**

Application to Quash Subpoena to Nat. Broadcasting Co., Inc. v. Graco Children Products, Inc., 79 F.3d 346 (2nd Cir. 1996)—§ **18.85, n. 8.**

AP Propane, Inc. v. Sperbeck, 157 A.D.2d 27, 555 N.Y.S.2d 211 (N.Y.A.D. 3 Dept. 1990)—§ **30.39, n. 10.**

Approved Properties, Inc. v. City of New York, 52 Misc.2d 956, 277 N.Y.S.2d 236 (N.Y.Sup.1966)—§ **12.20, n. 2.**

Apuzzo, Matter of, N.Y.L.J., 9/14/95, p.32, col.3—§ **25.43, n. 2.**

Aragon v. A & L Refrigeration Corp., 209 A.D.2d 268, 618 N.Y.S.2d 345 (N.Y.A.D. 1 Dept.1994)—§ **37.28, n. 12.**

Arai, Matter of, 13 I & N Dec. 494, 496 (BIA 1970)—§ **19.60, n. 2.**

Arce, People v., 215 A.D.2d 277, 627 N.Y.S.2d 15 (N.Y.A.D. 1 Dept.1995)—§ **38.21, n. 16.**

Ardito, People v., 460 N.Y.S.2d 22, 446 N.E.2d 778 (N.Y.1983)—§ **38.19, n. 65.**

Arena v. Manganello, 31 A.D.2d 540, 295 N.Y.S.2d 170 (N.Y.A.D. 2 Dept.1968)—§ **37.25, n. 6.**

Arett Sales Corp. v. Island Garden Center Queens, Inc., 25 A.D.2d 546, 267 N.Y.S.2d 623 (N.Y.A.D. 2 Dept.1966)—§ **26.43, n. 15.**

Argentine, People v., 73 A.D.2d 649, 422 N.Y.S.2d 736 (N.Y.A.D. 2 Dept.1979)—§ **38.10;** § **38.10, n. 113.**

Arimento v. McCall, 211 A.D.2d 958, 621 N.Y.S.2d 409 (N.Y.A.D. 3 Dept.1995)—§ **4.19, n. 2.**

Arizona v. Fulminante, 499 U.S. 279, 111 S.Ct. 1246, 113 L.Ed.2d 302 (1991)—§ **33.57, n. 7;** § **33.59, n. 1, 2.**

Arkansas Leasing Co. v. Furag, N.Y.L.J., 6/16/93, p.29, col.5 (Civ.Ct., Queens County, 1993)—§ **13.9, n. 1**

Arkansas–Platte & Gulf Partnership v. Van Waters & Rogers, Inc., 959 F.2d 158 (10th Cir.1992)—§ **27.44, n. 1;** § **27.47, n. 4.**

Arlen of Nanuet, Inc. v. State, 310 N.Y.S.2d 465, 258 N.E.2d 890 (N.Y.1970)—§ **14.95, n. 1.**

Arlinghaus v. Ritenour, 622 F.2d 629 (2nd Cir.1980)—§ **17.23, n. 1.**

Armenia v. Luther, 152 A.D.2d 928, 543 N.Y.S.2d 832 (N.Y.A.D. 4 Dept.1989)—§ **16.128, n. 2.**

Armlin, People v., 371 N.Y.S.2d 691, 332 N.E.2d 870 (N.Y.1975)—§ **38.8, n. 190.**

Armstrong v. Grimes, 70 Misc.2d 549, 334 N.Y.S.2d 558 (N.Y.Fam.Ct.1972)—§ **24.14, n. 2.**

Armstrong v. United States, 364 U.S. 40, 80 S.Ct. 1563, 4 L.Ed.2d 1554 (1960)—§ **16.109, n. 4.**

TABLE OF CASES

Armstrong Properties, Inc. v. Glasso, 141 A.D.2d 687, 529 N.Y.S.2d 572 (N.Y.A.D. 2 Dept.1988)—§ **12.29, n. 5.**

Arred Enterprises Corp. v. Indemnity Ins. Co. of North America, 108 A.D.2d 624, 485 N.Y.S.2d 80 (N.Y.A.D. 1 Dept. 1985)—§ **8.10, n. 5, 6.**

Arrington v. New York Times Co., 449 N.Y.S.2d 941, 434 N.E.2d 1319 (N.Y. 1982)—§ **18.63, n. 6.**

Arroyo v. City of New York, 171 A.D.2d 541, 567 N.Y.S.2d 257 (N.Y.A.D. 1 Dept. 1991)—§ **37.29; § 37.29, n. 23.**

Arroyo v. New York City Health and Hospitals Corp., 163 A.D.2d 9, 558 N.Y.S.2d 8 (N.Y.A.D. 1 Dept.1990)—§ **30.9, n. 42.**

Arroyo by Arroyo v. City of New York, 185 A.D.2d 829, 587 N.Y.S.2d 851 (N.Y.A.D. 2 Dept.1992)—§ **37.37, n. 83.**

Art & Co., Inc., In re, 179 B.R. 757 (Bkrtcy. D.Mass.1995)—§ **9.181, n. 4; § 9.198, n. 1.**

Arteaga v. State, 532 N.Y.S.2d 57, 527 N.E.2d 1194 (N.Y.1988)—§ **18.31, n. 3.**

Arther v. Backster, 24 A.D.2d 940, 265 N.Y.S.2d 579 (N.Y.A.D. 1 Dept.1965)—§ **37.35, n. 9.**

Arthur, People v., 292 N.Y.S.2d 663, 239 N.E.2d 537 (N.Y.1968)—§ **33.56, n. 3; § 38.19, n. 15.**

Arvantides v. Arvantides, 489 N.Y.S.2d 58, 478 N.E.2d 199 (N.Y.1985)—§ **21.39, n. 1.**

Arzente, Matter of Mary, N.Y.L.J., 9/8/95, p.30, col.1 (Surr.Ct., Queens County)—§ **30.12, n. 6.**

Asen Bros. & Brook v. Leventhal, 444 N.Y.S.2d 58, 428 N.E.2d 390 (N.Y. 1981)—§ **4.79, n. 9.**

Ashland Management Inc. v. Janien, 604 N.Y.S.2d 912, 624 N.E.2d 1007 (N.Y. 1993)—§ **30.24, n. 2.**

Asian Americans for Equality v. Koch, 531 N.Y.S.2d 782, 527 N.E.2d 265 (N.Y. 1988)—§ **16.123, n. 5, 12.**

Askew, People v., 66 A.D.2d 710, 411 N.Y.S.2d 569 (N.Y.A.D. 1 Dept.1978)—§ **38.10, n. 112.**

Askew v. Rigler, 130 F.R.D. 26 (S.D.N.Y. 1990)—§ **18.65, n. 7, 8.**

Aspen Industries, Inc. v. Marine Midland Bank, 439 N.Y.S.2d 316, 421 N.E.2d 808 (N.Y.1981)—§ **8.25, n. 1.**

A.S. Rampell, Inc. v. Hyster Co., 165 N.Y.S.2d 475, 144 N.E.2d 371 (N.Y. 1957)—§ **17.29, n. 17.**

Associated Press v. Bell, 517 N.Y.S.2d 444, 510 N.E.2d 313 (N.Y.1987)—§ **18.14, n. 2.**

Associates Capital Services Corp. of New Jersey v. Fairway Private Cars, Inc., 590 F.Supp. 10 (E.D.N.Y.1982)—§ **7.46, n. 9.**

Associates Commercial Corp. v. Rash, ___ U.S. ___, 117 S.Ct. 1879, 138 L.Ed.2d 148 (1997)—§ **9.251, n. 3.**

Associates Commercial Corp. v. Rash (Matter of Rash), 90 F.3d 1036 (5th Cir. 1996)—§ **9.104, n. 3.**

Association Center Ltd. Partnership, In re, 87 B.R. 142 (Bkrtcy.W.D.Wash.1988)—§ **9.69, n. 5.**

Association for Preservation of Freedom of Choice, Inc. v. Simon, 11 A.D.2d 927, 206 N.Y.S.2d 532 (N.Y.A.D. 1 Dept. 1960)—§ **37.89, n. 7.**

Association for Retarded Citizens, Petition of, 94 A.D.2d 958, 464 N.Y.S.2d 84 (N.Y.A.D. 4 Dept.1983)—§ **22.69, n. 7.**

Association of Surrogate and Supreme Court Reporters Within City of New York v. Bartlett, 388 N.Y.S.2d 882, 357 N.E.2d 353 (N.Y.1976)—§ **4.75, n. 4.**

Ast v. State, 123 Misc.2d 200, 474 N.Y.S.2d 174 (N.Y.Ct.Cl.1984)—§ **18.87, n. 3.**

Astoria Federal Sav. and Loan Ass'n v. Rambalakos, 49 A.D.2d 715, 372 N.Y.S.2d 689 (N.Y.A.D. 2 Dept.1975)—§ **8.6, n. 4.**

Aswad v. City School Dist. of City of Binghamton, 74 A.D.2d 972, 425 N.Y.S.2d 896 (N.Y.A.D. 3 Dept.1980)—§ **14.23, n. 4.**

Atembe, Matter of, 19 I & N Dec. 427 (BIA 1986)—§ **19.11, n. 13.**

Athanasopoulos, People v., 206 A.D.2d 381, 614 N.Y.S.2d 61 (N.Y.A.D. 2 Dept. 1994)—§ **38.20, n. 12; § 38.27, n. 17.**

Atherton v. 21 East 92nd Street Corp., 149 A.D.2d 354, 539 N.Y.S.2d 933 (N.Y.A.D. 1 Dept.1989)—§ **30.9, n. 21.**

ATI, Inc. v. Ruder & Finn, Inc., 398 N.Y.S.2d 864, 368 N.E.2d 1230 (N.Y. 1977)—§ **17.31, n. 3.**

Atkins v. Bowen, 690 F.Supp. 383 (E.D.Pa. 1988)—§ **34.6, n. 6.**

Atkins v. Guest, 201 A.D.2d 411, 607 N.Y.S.2d 655 (N.Y.A.D. 1 Dept.1994)—§ **4.63, n. 5.**

Atkins v. Parker, 472 U.S. 115, 105 S.Ct. 2520, 86 L.Ed.2d 81 (1985)—§ **4.5, n. 5.**

Atkinson v. Trehan, 70 Misc.2d 612, 334 N.Y.S.2d 291 (N.Y.City Civ.Ct.1972)—§ **13.58, n. 2.**

Atlantic Cement Co. v. St. Lawrence Cement Co., 22 A.D.2d 228, 254 N.Y.S.2d 676 (N.Y.A.D. 3 Dept.1964)—§ **10.5, n. 1.**

Atlantic Cement Co., Inc. v. Fidelity & Cas. Co. of New York, 91 A.D.2d 412, 459 N.Y.S.2d 425 (N.Y.A.D. 1 Dept.1983)—§ **37.65, n. 53.**

Atlantic States Legal Foundation, Inc. v. Eastman Kodak Co., 12 F.3d 353 (2nd

TABLE OF CASES

Cir.1993)—§ **4.30;** § **4.30, n. 3;** § **15.9;** § **15.9, n. 15;** § **15.11, n. 9.**

Atlantic States Legal Foundation, Inc. v. Eastman Kodak Co., 933 F.2d 124 (2nd Cir.1991)—§ **15.11, n. 12.**

Atlantic Westerly Co. v. De Almeida, 117 Misc.2d 1047, 461 N.Y.S.2d 143 (N.Y.Sup.App.Term 1982)—§ **13.17, n. 18;** § **13.44, n. 6.**

Atlas Realty of East Meadow, Inc. v. Ostrofsky, 56 Misc.2d 787, 289 N.Y.S.2d 784 (N.Y.Sup.1967)—§ **12.29, n. 9;** § **12.64, n. 9.**

Atlas Tile and Marble Works, Inc. and Atamco Inc., Application of, 191 A.D.2d 247, 595 N.Y.S.2d 10 (N.Y.A.D. 1 Dept. 1993)—§ **10.16, n. 9.**

AT & T v. Zoning Bd. of Appeals of Town of Ramapo, 213 A.D.2d 479, 623 N.Y.S.2d 628 (N.Y.A.D. 2 Dept.1995)—§ **37.28, n. 30.**

Attie, People v., 131 Misc.2d 921, 502 N.Y.S.2d 342 (N.Y.City Ct.1986)—§ **33.72, n. 1.**

Attorney General of State of N.Y. v. One Green 1993 Four Door Chrysler, 644 N.Y.S.2d 682, 667 N.E.2d 332 (N.Y. 1996)—§ **38.10, n. 176.**

Attridge v. Pembroke, 235 A.D. 101, 256 N.Y.S. 257 (N.Y.A.D. 4 Dept.1932)—§ **5.11, n. 1, 6.**

Aucello v. Moylan, 60 Misc.2d 1094, 304 N.Y.S.2d 765 (N.Y.Sup.1969)—§ **16.8, n. 10.**

Aucello, People v., 146 Misc.2d 417, 558 N.Y.S.2d 436 (N.Y.Sup.App.Term 1990)—§ **33.25, n. 1.**

Auerbach v. Bennett, 419 N.Y.S.2d 920, 393 N.E.2d 994 (N.Y.1979)—§ **1.66, n. 12;** § **37.24, n. 3.**

Augustine v. Town of Brant, 249 N.Y. 198, 163 N.E. 732 (N.Y.1928)—§ **3.30, n. 12.**

Auld v. Estridge, 86 Misc.2d 895, 382 N.Y.S.2d 897 (N.Y.Sup.1976)—§ **2.45, n. 9.**

Aurrichio v. Rinaldi, 56 Misc.2d 663, 289 N.Y.S.2d 808 (N.Y.Sup.1968)—§ **12.15, n. 4.**

Austin v. Austin, 204 A.D.2d 316, 614 N.Y.S.2d 142 (N.Y.A.D. 2 Dept.1994)—§ **37.19, n. 31.**

Austin v. BankAmerica Service Corp., 419 F.Supp. 730 (N.D.Ga.1974)—§ **7.31, n. 10.**

Austin v. Board of Higher Ed. of City of New York, 186 N.Y.S.2d 1, 158 N.E.2d 681 (N.Y.1959)—§ **4.82, n. 13.**

Austin v. Hudson River R. Co., 25 N.Y. 334 (N.Y.1862)—§ **30.17, n. 6.**

Austin v. Metropolitan St. Ry. Co., 108 A.D. 249, 95 N.Y.S. 740 (N.Y.A.D. 1 Dept. 1905)—§ **30.14, n. 9.**

Austin, People v., 208 A.D.2d 990, 618 N.Y.S.2d 115 (N.Y.A.D. 3 Dept.1994)—§ **38.10, n. 25, 162, 164.**

Auten v. Auten, 308 N.Y. 155, 124 N.E.2d 99 (N.Y.1954)—§ **31.25, n. 2.**

Avco Financial Service of New York Inc., State v., 429 N.Y.S.2d 181, 406 N.E.2d 1075 (N.Y.1980)—§ **5.12, n. 2;** § **5.13, n. 4;** § **5.14, n. 3, 5.**

Avery, Matter of, 93 A.D.2d 886, 461 N.Y.S.2d 734 (N.Y.A.D. 2 Dept.1983)—§ **22.16, n. 1.**

Avis Rent-A-Car System, Inc. v. Franklin, 82 Misc.2d 66, 366 N.Y.S.2d 83 (N.Y.Sup.1975)—§ **7.26, n. 9;** § **7.55.**

Avondale Industries, Inc. v. Travelers Indem. Co., 774 F.Supp. 1416 (S.D.N.Y. 1991)—§ **31.25, n. 5.**

Avoyelles Sportsmen's League, Inc. v. Marsh, 715 F.2d 897 (5th Cir.1983)—§ **15.8, n. 9.**

A.W. Cowen & Bros., In re, 11 F.2d 692 (2nd Cir.1926)—§ **5.31, n. 2.**

Awwal, Matter of, 19 I & N Dec. 617 (BIA 1988)—§ **19.11, n. 11.**

Axelrad v. 77 Park Ave. Corp., 225 A.D. 557, 234 N.Y.S. 27 (N.Y.A.D. 1 Dept. 1929)—§ **37.30;** § **37.30, n. 3.**

Ayala, People v., 554 N.Y.S.2d 412, 553 N.E.2d 960 (N.Y.1990)—§ **38.19, n. 91.**

Ayala v. Speckard, 89 F.3d 91 (2nd Cir. 1996)—§ **18.13, n. 1.**

Ayers v. Coughlin, 780 F.2d 205 (2nd Cir. 1985)—§ **18.35, n. 2.**

Ayers v. Johnson & Johnson, 117 Wash.2d 747, 818 P.2d 1337 (Wash.1991)—§ **27.12;** § **27.12, n. 6;** § **27.16, n. 1.**

B

B., Application of, 81 Misc.2d 284, 366 N.Y.S.2d 98 (N.Y.Co.Ct.1975)—§ **18.71, n. 4.**

B. v. B., 32 A.D.2d 808, 303 N.Y.S.2d 216 (N.Y.A.D. 2 Dept.1969)—§ **38.8, n. 118.**

Baader v. Town Bd. of Town of Aurelius, 171 A.D.2d 1046, 568 N.Y.S.2d 991 (N.Y.A.D. 4 Dept.1991)—§ **16.113, n. 11.**

Babcock v. Dean, 140 Misc. 800, 252 N.Y.S. 419 (N.Y.Co.Ct.1931)—§ **13.26, n. 4.**

Babcock v. Jackson, 240 N.Y.S.2d 743, 191 N.E.2d 279 (N.Y.1963)—§ **31.25, n. 2.**

Babigian v. Evans, 104 Misc.2d 136, 427 N.Y.S.2d 688 (N.Y.Sup.1980)—§ **3.29, n. 7.**

Baby Girl, Matter of, 206 A.D.2d 932, 615 N.Y.S.2d 800 (N.Y.A.D. 4 Dept.1994)—§ **20.30, n. 5.**

TABLE OF CASES

Baby Girl S., Matter of, 208 A.D.2d 930, 617 N.Y.S.2d 539 (N.Y.A.D. 2 Dept. 1994)—§ **20.35, n. 4.**

Babylon Associates v. Suffolk County, 101 A.D.2d 207, 475 N.Y.S.2d 869 (N.Y.A.D. 2 Dept.1984)—§ **30.39, n. 11.**

Bachert, People v., 516 N.Y.S.2d 623, 509 N.E.2d 318 (N.Y.1987)—§ **38.9, n. 10;** § **38.34;** § **38.34, n. 3, 4, 8;** § **39.57, n. 3.**

Bachman v. State Div. of Human Rights, 104 A.D.2d 111, 481 N.Y.S.2d 858 (N.Y.A.D. 1 Dept.1984)—§ **18.49, n. 14.**

Badaracco v. Commissioner, 464 U.S. 386, 104 S.Ct. 756, 78 L.Ed.2d 549 (1984)— § **35.67, n. 3.**

Badia, People v., 163 A.D.2d 4, 558 N.Y.S.2d 500 (N.Y.A.D. 1 Dept.1990)— § **38.19, n. 69.**

Baecher v. Baecher, 95 A.D.2d 841, 464 N.Y.S.2d 199 (N.Y.A.D. 2 Dept.1983)— § **37.37, n. 18.**

Baer v. Broder, 86 A.D.2d 881, 447 N.Y.S.2d 538 (N.Y.A.D. 2 Dept.1982)—§ **28.11, n. 4.**

Baer v. Town of Brookhaven, 540 N.Y.S.2d 234, 537 N.E.2d 619 (N.Y.1989)— § **16.122;** § **16.122, n. 7.**

Baez v. Bane, 220 A.D.2d 166, 633 N.Y.S.2d 765 (N.Y.A.D. 1 Dept.1995)—§ **30.42, n. 5.**

Baez, People v., 205 A.D.2d 695, 614 N.Y.S.2d 303 (N.Y.A.D. 2 Dept.1994)— § **38.8, n. 154.**

Baghai-Kermani, People v., 620 N.Y.S.2d 313, 644 N.E.2d 1004 (N.Y.1994)— § **38.25, n. 6.**

Baginski v. Lysiak, 154 Misc.2d 275, 594 N.Y.S.2d 99 (N.Y.Sup.App.Term 1992)— § **13.50, n. 6.**

Bagley, United States v., 473 U.S. 667, 105 S.Ct. 3375, 87 L.Ed.2d 481 (1985)— § **33.39, n. 4;** § **38.10, n. 108.**

Baiko v. Baiko, 141 A.D.2d 635, 530 N.Y.S.2d 7 (N.Y.A.D. 2 Dept.1988)— § **37.19, n. 51.**

Bailey, Estate of, 147 Misc.2d 46, 554 N.Y.S.2d 791 (N.Y.Sur.1990)—§ **23.81, n. 13.**

Bailey v. Morgan, 95 A.D.2d 883, 463 N.Y.S.2d 882 (N.Y.A.D. 3 Dept.1983)— § **30.20, n. 3.**

Bailin (Geiger), Mater of, N.Y.L.J., 5/19/95, p.36, col.4 (Sup.Ct., Rockland County)— § **22.34, n. 2;** § **22.101, n. 1.**

Baird, Matter of, 167 Misc.2d 526, 634 N.Y.S.2d 971 (N.Y.Sup.1995)—§ **22.21, n. 6;** § **22.48, n. 11, 12.**

Baker, Application of, 87 Misc.2d 592, 386 N.Y.S.2d 313 (N.Y.Sup.1976)—§ **3.20, n. 3.**

Baker v. McCollan, 443 U.S. 137, 99 S.Ct. 2689, 61 L.Ed.2d 433 (1979)—§ **18.18, n. 2.**

Baker, People v., 221 A.D.2d 551, 635 N.Y.S.2d 481 (N.Y.A.D. 2 Dept.1995)— § **38.8, n. 33.**

Baker, People v., 489 N.Y.S.2d 56, 478 N.E.2d 197 (N.Y.1985)—§ **38.19, n. 82;** § **38.21, n. 54;** § **38.27;** § **38.27, n. 10.**

Baker v. Polsinelli, 177 A.D.2d 844, 576 N.Y.S.2d 460 (N.Y.A.D. 3 Dept.1991)— § **16.121, n. 3.**

Baker v. St. Agnes Hospital, 70 A.D.2d 400, 421 N.Y.S.2d 81 (N.Y.A.D. 2 Dept. 1979)—§ **27.13;** § **27.13, n. 1, 4, 5.**

Baker v. Wight, 158 A.D.2d 293, 550 N.Y.S.2d 701 (N.Y.A.D. 1 Dept.1990)— § **37.37, n. 34.**

Baker & Getty Financial Services, Inc., In re, 974 F.2d 712 (6th Cir.1992)— § **9.107, n. 11.**

Balan, People v., 107 A.D.2d 811, 484 N.Y.S.2d 648 (N.Y.A.D. 2 Dept.1985)— § **38.10, n. 89.**

Balber-Strauss v. Markowitz (In re Frankel), 192 B.R. 623 (Bkrtcy.S.D.N.Y. 1996)—§ **9.18, n. 4.**

Baldelli, People v., 152 A.D.2d 741, 544 N.Y.S.2d 193 (N.Y.A.D. 2 Dept.1989)— § **38.21, n. 11.**

Baleno by Baleno v. Jacuzzi Research, Inc., 93 A.D.2d 982, 461 N.Y.S.2d 659 (N.Y.A.D. 4 Dept.1983)—§ **27.37, n. 3, 4.**

Ballard, People v., 214 A.D.2d 1050, 626 N.Y.S.2d 710 (N.Y.A.D. 4 Dept.1995)— § **38.34, n. 7.**

Ball Memorial Hosp., Inc. v. Mutual Hosp. Ins., Inc., 784 F.2d 1325 (7th Cir. 1986)—§ **27.38, n. 3.**

Ballott, People v., 286 N.Y.S.2d 1, 233 N.E.2d 103 (N.Y.1967)—§ **38.19, n. 117.**

Balodis v. Fallwood Park Homes, Inc., 54 Misc.2d 936, 283 N.Y.S.2d 497 (N.Y.Sup. 1967)—§ **16.89, n. 13.**

Balsam v. Axelrod, 102 Misc.2d 1000, 424 N.Y.S.2d 814 (N.Y.Sup.1979)—§ **12.5, n. 3.**

Baltimore Gas and Elec. Co. v. Natural Resources Defense Council, Inc., 462 U.S. 87, 103 S.Ct. 2246, 76 L.Ed.2d 437 (1983)—§ **15.3, n. 7.**

B. Altman & Co. v. City of White Plains, 456 N.Y.S.2d 755, 442 N.E.2d 1266 (N.Y. 1982)—§ **14.85, n. 6.**

Ba Mar, Inc. v. County of Rockland, 164 A.D.2d 605, 566 N.Y.S.2d 298 (N.Y.A.D. 2 Dept.1991)—§ **16.124, n. 9.**

Banch, People v., 593 N.Y.S.2d 491, 608 N.E.2d 1069 (N.Y.1992)—§ **38.10, n. 101;** § **39.50, n. 6.**

TABLE OF CASES

Bankers Commercial Corp. v. Mittleman, 21 Misc.2d 1096, 198 N.Y.S.2d 184 (N.Y.Sup.1960)—§ **7.59.**

Bankers Federal Sav. Bank FSB v. Off West Broadway Developers, 224 A.D.2d 376, 638 N.Y.S.2d 72 (N.Y.A.D. 1 Dept. 1996)—§ **11.30, n. 5.**

Bankers Trust v. Jackson, 99 Misc.2d 225, 415 N.Y.S.2d 731 (N.Y.City Civ.Ct. 1979)—§ **13.61; § 13.61, n. 3.**

Bankers Trust Co. v. State Dept. of Audit and Control, 28 A.D.2d 272, 284 N.Y.S.2d 594 (N.Y.A.D. 3 Dept.1967)— § **8.24, n. 2.**

Bankers Trust Co. of Western New York v. Zecher, 103 Misc.2d 777, 426 N.Y.S.2d 960 (N.Y.Sup.1980)—§ **1.21, n. 27.**

Bank Leumi Trust Co. of New York v. Liggett, 115 A.D.2d 378, 496 N.Y.S.2d 14 (N.Y.A.D. 1 Dept.1985)—§ **8.33, n. 5.**

Bank Leumi Trust Co. of New York v. Taylor–Cishahayo, 147 Misc.2d 685, 556 N.Y.S.2d 211 (N.Y.City Civ.Ct.1990)— § **8.42, n. 11.**

Bank of New York v. Forlini, 220 A.D.2d 377, 631 N.Y.S.2d 440 (N.Y.A.D. 2 Dept. 1995)—§ **37.65, n. 75.**

Bank of New York Co., Inc. v. Irving Bank Corp., 142 Misc.2d 145, 536 N.Y.S.2d 923 (N.Y.Sup.1988)—§ **1.27, n. 5.**

Bank of Nova Scotia v. Cartwright & Goodwin, Inc., 160 Misc.2d 856, 611 N.Y.S.2d 770 (N.Y.City Civ.Ct.1994)—§ **13.27, n. 1.**

Banks, People v., 193 A.D.2d 1051, 598 N.Y.S.2d 1014 (N.Y.A.D. 4 Dept.1993)— § **38.21, n. 7; § 38.26, n. 28.**

Banville, People v., 134 A.D.2d 116, 523 N.Y.S.2d 844 (N.Y.A.D. 2 Dept.1988)— § **38.19, n. 12.**

Bapp v. Bowen, 802 F.2d 601 (2nd Cir. 1986)—§ **34.47, n. 6, 13.**

Barash v. Pennsylvania Terminal Real Estate Corp., 308 N.Y.S.2d 649, 256 N.E.2d 707 (N.Y.1970)—§ **13.30, n. 1; § 13.31; § 13.31, n. 3.**

Barasky v. Huttner, 210 A.D.2d 367, 620 N.Y.S.2d 121 (N.Y.A.D. 2 Dept.1994)— § **12.65, n. 2.**

Barbara C., Matter of, 487 N.Y.S.2d 549, 476 N.E.2d 994 (N.Y.1985)—§ **39.7, n. 13.**

Barbera v. Smith, 836 F.2d 96 (2nd Cir. 1987)—§ **18.35, n. 1.**

Barbro Realty Co. v. Newburger, 53 A.D.2d 34, 385 N.Y.S.2d 68 (N.Y.A.D. 1 Dept. 1976)—§ **2.52, n. 3.**

Barco Auto Leasing Corp. v. Atlas Co., 165 A.D.2d 851, 560 N.Y.S.2d 314 (N.Y.A.D. 2 Dept.1990)—§ **7.55.**

Bard, People ex rel. Welch v., 209 N.Y. 304, 103 N.E. 140 (N.Y.1913)—§ **38.3, n. 8.**

Bardol's Will, In re, 253 A.D. 498, 254 A.D. 647, 4 N.Y.S.2d 795 (N.Y.A.D. 4 Dept. 1938)—§ **37.30, n. 5.**

Bargaintown, D. C., Inc. v. Bellefonte Ins. Co., 442 N.Y.S.2d 975, 426 N.E.2d 469 (N.Y.1981)—§ **31.26, n. 10.**

Bark v. Immigration and Naturalization Service, 511 F.2d 1200 (9th Cir.1975)— § **19.12, n. 6.**

Barker, People v., 183 A.D.2d 835, 584 N.Y.S.2d 79 (N.Y.A.D. 2 Dept.1992)— § **38.21, n. 11.**

Barnes v. P & C Food Markets, Inc., 132 A.D.2d 921, 518 N.Y.S.2d 478 (N.Y.A.D. 4 Dept.1987)—§ **26.42, n. 10.**

Barnes, People v., 160 A.D.2d 342, 553 N.Y.S.2d 413 (N.Y.A.D. 1 Dept.1990)— § **38.8, n. 63; § 38.10; § 38.10, n. 142.**

Barnhard v. Barnhard, 179 A.D.2d 715, 578 N.Y.S.2d 615 (N.Y.A.D. 2 Dept.1992)— § **2.53, n. 3.**

Barnhill v. Johnson, 503 U.S. 393, 112 S.Ct. 1386, 118 L.Ed.2d 39 (1992)—§ **9.117, n. 1.**

Baron v. Jeffer, 98 A.D.2d 810, 469 N.Y.S.2d 815 (N.Y.A.D. 2 Dept.1983)— § **30.9, n. 36.**

Baron, People v., 107 Misc.2d 59, 438 N.Y.S.2d 425 (N.Y.Sup.1980)—§ **33.23, n. 3.**

Barracato v. Camp Bauman Buses, Inc., 217 A.D.2d 677, 630 N.Y.S.2d 261 (N.Y.A.D. 2 Dept.1995)—§ **37.28, n. 39.**

Barrett v. United States, 798 F.2d 565 (2nd Cir.1986)—§ **18.31, n. 1.**

Barrientos v. Sulit, 133 Misc.2d 1061, 509 N.Y.S.2d 288 (N.Y.City Ct.1986)— § **5.31, n. 8.**

Barriera, People v., 600 N.Y.S.2d 440, 616 N.E.2d 1102 (N.Y.1993)—§ **38.27, n. 15.**

Barron v. Getnick, 107 A.D.2d 1017, 486 N.Y.S.2d 528 (N.Y.A.D. 4 Dept.1985)— § **16.4, n. 9.**

Barron v. Topliffe, 229 A.D. 217, 241 N.Y.S. 605 (N.Y.A.D. 1 Dept.1930)—§ **30.28, n. 18.**

Barrow v. Wethersfield Police Dept., 66 F.3d 466 (2nd Cir.1995)—§ **18.38, n. 3.**

Barry v. Chefales, 185 A.D.2d 842, 586 N.Y.S.2d 989 (N.Y.A.D. 2 Dept.1992)— § **21.59, n. 4.**

Barry v. Manglass, 55 A.D.2d 1, 389 N.Y.S.2d 870 (N.Y.A.D. 2 Dept.1976)— § **27.31; § 27.31, n. 2.**

Barsky, Application of, 165 Misc.2d 175, 627 N.Y.S.2d 903 (N.Y.Sup.1995)— § **22.54, n. 6, 8.**

Bartel, Will of, 214 A.D.2d 476, 625 N.Y.S.2d 519 (N.Y.A.D. 1 Dept.1995)— § **25.31, n. 7.**

446

TABLE OF CASES

Bartel v. Shugrue (In re Ionosphere Clubs, Inc.), 171 B.R. 18 (S.D.N.Y.1994)—**§ 9.18, n. 4.**

Barth v. Barth, Sullivan & Lancaster, 179 A.D.2d 1049, 579 N.Y.S.2d 283 (N.Y.A.D. 4 Dept.1992)—**§ 28.13, n. 9.**

Bartlett, by Bartlett v. General Elec. Co., 90 A.D.2d 183, 457 N.Y.S.2d 628 (N.Y.A.D. 3 Dept.1982)—**§ 27.13; § 27.13, n. 17.**

Bartolone v. Jeckovich, 103 A.D.2d 632, 481 N.Y.S.2d 545 (N.Y.A.D. 4 Dept.1984)—**§ 30.11, n. 4.**

Barton, People v., 200 A.D.2d 888, 606 N.Y.S.2d 842 (N.Y.A.D. 3 Dept.1994)—**§ 38.10; § 38.10, n. 118.**

Bartoo v. Buell, 620 N.Y.S.2d 788, 644 N.E.2d 1344 (N.Y.1994)—**§ 39.11, n. 3.**

Barzack Realty Co. v. Joseph Legatti & Son, Inc., 114 Misc.2d 245, 450 N.Y.S.2d 983 (N.Y.City Civ.Ct.1982)—**§ 13.43, n. 19.**

Basile Stable, Inc. v. Vonderwell, 203 A.D.2d 223, 612 N.Y.S.2d 883 (N.Y.A.D. 2 Dept.1994)—**§ 37.37, n. 49.**

Basora, People v., 557 N.Y.S.2d 263, 556 N.E.2d 1070 (N.Y.1990)—**§ 38.19, n. 140.**

Bassett v. American Meter Co., 20 A.D.2d 956, 249 N.Y.S.2d 815 (N.Y.A.D. 4 Dept. 1964)—**§ 2.59, n. 4.**

Batavia, City of v. Bolas, 174 A.D.2d 993, 573 N.Y.S.2d 8 (N.Y.A.D. 4 Dept.1991)—**§ 14.82, n. 2.**

Bath Beach Health Spa of Park Slope, Inc. v. Bennett, 176 A.D.2d 874, 575 N.Y.S.2d 344 (N.Y.A.D. 2 Dept.1991)—**§ 16.75, n. 2.**

Bath Gaslight Co. v. Claffy, 151 N.Y. 24, 45 N.E. 390 (N.Y.1896)—**§ 1.12, n. 1.**

Batson v. Kentucky, 476 U.S. 79, 106 S.Ct. 1712, 90 L.Ed.2d 69 (1986)—**§ 17.74, n. 1; § 18.15, n. 9; § 38.8; § 38.8, n. 185.**

Battaglia v. Sisters of Charity Hosp., 124 A.D.2d 987, 508 N.Y.S.2d 802 (N.Y.A.D. 4 Dept.1986)—**§ 17.34, n. 6.**

Battalla v. State, 219 N.Y.S.2d 34, 176 N.E.2d 729 (N.Y.1961)—**§ 30.9, n. 3.**

Battista, People ex rel. v. Christian, 249 N.Y. 314, 164 N.E. 111 (N.Y.1928)—**§ 38.19; § 38.19, n. 11.**

Bauer v. Raymark Industries, Inc., 849 F.2d 790 (2nd Cir.1988)—**§ 27.52, n. 1.**

Bauer's Estate, Matter of, 96 Misc.2d 40, 408 N.Y.S.2d 649 (N.Y.Sup.1978)—**§ 22.4, n. 19, 20.**

Baughman v. Bradford Coal Co., Inc., 592 F.2d 215 (3rd Cir.1979)—**§ 15.11, n. 15.**

Baum v. State, 156 A.D.2d 927, 548 N.Y.S.2d 819 (N.Y.A.D. 4 Dept.1989)—**§ 37.29, n. 12.**

Bautista, Matter of, 17 I & N Dec. 122 (I.D. 2731, BIA 1979)—**§ 19.8, n. 11.**

Baxley, People v., 616 N.Y.S.2d 7, 639 N.E.2d 746 (N.Y.1994)—**§ 38.9, n. 9; § 38.10, n. 103, 104; § 39.50, n. 14.**

Baxter v. Orans, 63 A.D.2d 875, 405 N.Y.S.2d 470 (N.Y.A.D. 1 Dept.1978)—**§ 26.42, n. 4.**

Bayes, People v., 577 N.Y.S.2d 585, 584 N.E.2d 643 (N.Y.1991)—**§ 38.19; § 38.19, n. 24.**

Bayswater Health Related Facility v. Karagheuzoff, 373 N.Y.S.2d 49, 335 N.E.2d 282 (N.Y.1975)—**§ 37.28, n. 31.**

Bayswater Realty & Capital Corp. v. Planning Bd. of Town of Lewisboro, 560 N.Y.S.2d 623, 560 N.E.2d 1300 (N.Y. 1990)—**§ 16.100, n. 4, 5.**

Bazak Intern. Corp. v. Mast Industries, Inc., 538 N.Y.S.2d 503, 535 N.E.2d 633 (N.Y.1989)—**§ 5.20, n. 4.**

Bazalar, People v., 211 A.D.2d 839, 621 N.Y.S.2d 224 (N.Y.A.D. 3 Dept.1995)—**§ 38.19, n. 80.**

Bazant v. Bazant, 80 A.D.2d 310, 439 N.Y.S.2d 521 (N.Y.A.D. 4 Dept.1981)—**§ 21.22, n. 2.**

B & B West 164th Street Corp., In re, 147 B.R. 832 (Bkrtcy.E.D.N.Y.1992)—**§ 9.160, n. 4.**

Beach v. Shanley, 476 N.Y.S.2d 765, 465 N.E.2d 304 (N.Y.1984)—**§ 18.85; § 18.85, n. 1.**

Beacon Const. Co., Inc. v. Matco Elec. Co., Inc., 521 F.2d 392 (2nd Cir.1975)—**§ 10.17, n. 1; § 10.18, n. 2.**

Beasley, People v., 592 N.Y.S.2d 644, 607 N.E.2d 791 (N.Y.1992)—**§ 33.47, n. 2.**

Beattie, People v., 587 N.Y.S.2d 585, 600 N.E.2d 216 (N.Y.1992)—**§ 33.22; § 33.22, n. 1.**

Beauchamp v. Riverbay Corp., 156 A.D.2d 172, 548 N.Y.S.2d 215 (N.Y.A.D. 1 Dept. 1989)—**§ 26.42, n. 12.**

Beaumont v. American Can Co., 215 A.D.2d 249, 626 N.Y.S.2d 201 (N.Y.A.D. 1 Dept. 1995)—**§ 1.27, n. 5.**

Beaumont v. American Can Co., 160 A.D.2d 174, 553 N.Y.S.2d 145 (N.Y.A.D. 1 Dept. 1990)—**§ 1.27, n. 5.**

Beck v. City of New York, 133 Misc.2d 265, 507 N.Y.S.2d 129 (N.Y.Sup.1986)—**§ 18.11, n. 5.**

Beck v. Moishe's Moving and Storage, Inc., 167 Misc.2d 960, 641 N.Y.S.2d 517 (N.Y.Sup.1995)—**§ 30.34, n. 3.**

Becker v. City of New York, 159 N.Y.S.2d 174, 140 N.E.2d 262 (N.Y.1957)—**§ 3.30, n. 11.**

Becker v. Ginsberg, 23 A.D.2d 916, 258 N.Y.S.2d 886 (N.Y.A.D. 3 Dept.1965)—**§ 30.7, n. 1.**

TABLE OF CASES

Becker v. Huss Co., Inc., 402 N.Y.S.2d 980, 373 N.E.2d 1205 (N.Y.1978)—§ **37.32, n. 1.**

Becker v. Julien, Blitz & Schlesinger, P. C., 95 Misc.2d 64, 406 N.Y.S.2d 412 (N.Y.Sup.1977)—§ **28.9;** § **28.9, n. 2, 6.**

Becker v. Optical Radiation Corp., 66 F.3d 18 (2nd Cir.1995)—§ **27.48, n. 3.**

Becker v. Schwartz, 413 N.Y.S.2d 895, 386 N.E.2d 807 (N.Y.1978)—§ **29.11, n. 8.**

Beckerman v. Sands, 364 F.Supp. 1197 (S.D.N.Y.1973)—§ **2.46, n. 4.**

Beckhusen v. E. P. Lawson Co., 214 N.Y.S.2d 342, 174 N.E.2d 327 (N.Y. 1961)—§ **27.36, n. 1.**

Becknell & Crace Coal Co., Inc., In re, 761 F.2d 319 (6th Cir.1985)—§ **9.74, n. 1.**

Bedford, Town of v. Village of Mount Kisco, 351 N.Y.S.2d 129, 306 N.E.2d 155 (N.Y. 1973)—§ **16.12;** § **16.12, n. 3, 22;** § **16.111, n. 4;** § **16.113, n. 7.**

Bednosky, People ex rel. Brown v., 190 A.D.2d 836, 593 N.Y.S.2d 859 (N.Y.A.D. 2 Dept.1993)—§ **38.8, n. 79.**

Beer Garden, Inc. v. New York State Liquor Authority, 582 N.Y.S.2d 65, 590 N.E.2d 1193 (N.Y.1992)—§ **4.33, n. 3.**

Beezley & California Land Title (In re Beezley), 994 F.2d 1433 (9th Cir.1993)—§ **9.207, n. 4.**

Behar, Application of, 779 F.Supp. 273 (S.D.N.Y.1991)—§ **18.85, n. 6.**

Behrens v. Behrens, 143 A.D.2d 617, 532 N.Y.S.2d 893 (N.Y.A.D. 2 Dept.1988)—§ **21.43, n. 19.**

Beker Industries Corp., In re, 58 B.R. 725 (Bkrtcy.S.D.N.Y.1986)—§ **9.71, n. 11.**

Beker Industries Corp., In re, 55 B.R. 945 (Bkrtcy.S.D.N.Y.1985)—§ **9.43, n. 9.**

Belandres v. Belandres, 58 A.D.2d 63, 395 N.Y.S.2d 458 (N.Y.A.D. 1 Dept.1977)—§ **21.31, n. 3.**

Belanger, In re, 962 F.2d 345 (4th Cir. 1992)—§ **9.186, n. 11.**

Belanoff v. Grayson, 98 A.D.2d 353, 471 N.Y.S.2d 91 (N.Y.A.D. 1 Dept.1984)—§ **17.48, n. 2.**

Belco Petroleum Corp. v. AIG Oil Rig, Inc., 164 A.D.2d 583, 565 N.Y.S.2d 776 (N.Y.A.D. 1 Dept.1991)—§ **31.17, n. 19.**

Belge, People v., 390 N.Y.S.2d 867, 359 N.E.2d 377 (N.Y.1976)—§ **38.27, n. 12.**

Belgian Overseas Securities Corp. v. Howell Kessler Co., 88 A.D.2d 559, 450 N.Y.S.2d 493 (N.Y.A.D. 1 Dept.1982)—§ **2.54, n. 3.**

Belinson v. Sewer Dist. No. 16 of Town of Amherst, 65 A.D.2d 912, 410 N.Y.S.2d 469 (N.Y.A.D. 4 Dept.1978)—§ **3.33, n. 10.**

Bell v. Bell, 116 A.D.2d 97, 500 N.Y.S.2d 387 (N.Y.A.D. 3 Dept.1986)—§ **18.70, n. 4.**

Bell v. Duncan, N.Y.L.J., 1/4/95, p.31, col.2, 23 HCR 2 (Civ.Ct., N.Y. County)—§ **24.28, n. 24.**

Bell, People v., 538 N.Y.S.2d 754, 535 N.E.2d 1294 (N.Y.1989)—§ **35.122, n. 1.**

Bell, People v., 363 N.Y.S.2d 89, 321 N.E.2d 880 (N.Y.1974)—§ **38.27;** § **38.27, n. 5, 26.**

Bell, People v., 41 A.D.2d 583, 340 N.Y.S.2d 194 (N.Y.A.D. 4 Dept.1973)—§ **37.19, n. 16;** § **38.8, n. 113.**

Bell v. Shopwell, Inc., 119 A.D.2d 715, 501 N.Y.S.2d 129 (N.Y.A.D. 2 Dept.1986)—§ **30.28, n. 16.**

Belle Harbor Realty Corp. v. Kerr, 364 N.Y.S.2d 160, 323 N.E.2d 697 (N.Y. 1974)—§ **3.9, n. 9.**

Belle Terre, Village of v. Boraas, 416 U.S. 1, 94 S.Ct. 1536, 39 L.Ed.2d 797 (1974)—§ **16.122;** § **16.122, n. 1.**

Bellevue Place Associates, In re, 171 B.R. 615 (Bkrtcy.N.D.Ill.1994)—§ **9.29, n. 18.**

Bell-Tronics Communications, Inc. v. Winkler, 178 A.D.2d 455, 577 N.Y.S.2d 126 (N.Y.A.D. 2 Dept.1991)—§ **5.46, n. 3.**

Belmont Owners Corp. v. Murphy, 153 Misc.2d 444, 590 N.Y.S.2d 659 (N.Y.Sup. App.Term 1992)—§ **13.69, n. 2, 3.**

Benedor Corp. v. Conejo Enter., Inc. (In re Conejo Enterprises, Inc.), 96 F.3d 346 (9th Cir.1996)—§ **9.19, n. 2.**

Bender, People v., 518 N.Y.S.2d 962, 512 N.E.2d 545 (N.Y.1987)—§ **39.47, n. 6.**

Beneficial Discount Co. of New York, Inc. v. Spike, 91 Misc.2d 733, 398 N.Y.S.2d 651 (N.Y.Sup.1977)—§ **8.6, n. 6.**

Benjamin v. Diamond (Matter of Mobile Steel Co.), 563 F.2d 692 (5th Cir.1977)—§ **9.107, n. 11, 17.**

Ben Heller, Inc. v. St. Paul Fire & Marine Ins. Co., 107 Misc.2d 687, 435 N.Y.S.2d 669 (N.Y.Sup.1981)—§ **31.6, n. 6.**

Benintendi v. Kenton Hotel, 294 N.Y. 112, 60 N.E.2d 829 (N.Y.1945)—§ **1.45, n. 3;** § **1.63, n. 4.**

Benitez, Matter of, 165 A.D.2d 924, 560 N.Y.S.2d 366 (N.Y.A.D. 3 Dept.1990)—§ **17.60, n. 11.**

Benlian v. Vartabedian, 91 Misc.2d 968, 398 N.Y.S.2d 984 (N.Y.City Civ.Ct.1977)—§ **8.38, n. 4.**

Bennett, In re, 185 B.R. 4 (Bkrtcy.E.D.N.Y. 1995)—§ **9.49, n. 1.**

Bennett v. Cruz, 168 A.D.2d 307, 562 N.Y.S.2d 638 (N.Y.A.D. 1 Dept.1990)—§ **30.30, n. 18.**

Bennett, People v., 193 A.D.2d 808, 598 N.Y.S.2d 84 (N.Y.A.D. 2 Dept.1993)—§ **38.26, n. 29;** § **38.28, n. 5.**

TABLE OF CASES

Bennett, People v., 169 A.D.2d 369, 573 N.Y.S.2d 322 (N.Y.A.D. 3 Dept.1991)—**§ 38.26, n. 4.**

Bennett, People v., 162 A.D.2d 694, 557 N.Y.S.2d 116 (N.Y.A.D. 2 Dept.1990)—**§ 38.19, n. 35.**

Bennett, People v., 524 N.Y.S.2d 378, 519 N.E.2d 289 (N.Y.1987)—**§ 33.49, n. 4; § 33.50, n. 2.**

Bennett v. Van Syckel, 18 N.Y. 481 (N.Y. 1859)—**§ 37.37, n. 92.**

Bennett Bros. v. Bracewood Realty No. 1, Inc., 23 A.D.2d 498, 256 N.Y.S.2d 308 (N.Y.A.D. 2 Dept.1965)—**§ 10.19, n. 5.**

Benson v. Boston Old Colony Ins. Co., 134 A.D.2d 214, 521 N.Y.S.2d 14 (N.Y.A.D. 1 Dept.1987)—**§ 31.26, n. 2.**

Benson v. Dean, 232 N.Y. 52, 133 N.E. 125 (N.Y.1921)—**§ 29.11, n. 3.**

Bentley, Matter of, 12 B.R. 528 (Bkrtcy. S.D.N.Y.1981)—**§ 13.26, n. 5.**

Bentley v. Great Lakes Collection Bureau, 6 F.3d 60 (2nd Cir.1993)—**§ 7.43; § 7.43, n. 5.**

Benton, People v., 196 A.D.2d 755, 601 N.Y.S.2d 918 (N.Y.A.D. 1 Dept.1993)—**§ 38.19, n. 41.**

Bereck v. Meyer, 222 A.D.2d 243, 635 N.Y.S.2d 15 (N.Y.A.D. 1 Dept.1995)—**§ 2.46, n. 7.**

Berenhaus v. Ward, 522 N.Y.S.2d 478, 517 N.E.2d 193 (N.Y.1987)—**§ 4.76, n. 3; § 4.78, n. 7; § 4.81, n. 5.**

Berenson v. Town of New Castle, 67 A.D.2d 506, 415 N.Y.S.2d 669 (N.Y.A.D. 2 Dept. 1979)—**§ 16.50, n. 7.**

Berenson v. Town of New Castle, 378 N.Y.S.2d 672, 341 N.E.2d 236 (N.Y. 1975)—**§ 16.113, n. 5; § 16.123; § 16.123, n. 1.**

Berg v. New York Soc. for Relief of the Ruptured and Crippled, 154 N.Y.S.2d 455, 136 N.E.2d 523 (N.Y.1956)—**§ 29.21, n. 2.**

Berger v. Estate of Berger, 203 A.D.2d 502, 611 N.Y.S.2d 246 (N.Y.A.D. 2 Dept. 1994)—**§ 21.30, n. 6.**

Berger v. Manhattan Life Ins. Co., 805 F.Supp. 1097 (S.D.N.Y.1992)—**§ 31.18, n. 2.**

Berger, People v., 1 A.D.2d 897, 149 N.Y.S.2d 480 (N.Y.A.D. 2 Dept.1956)—**§ 38.8, n. 4.**

Bergholm v. Peoria Life Ins. Co. of Peoria, Ill., 284 U.S. 489, 52 S.Ct. 230, 76 L.Ed. 416 (1932)—**§ 39.84.**

Beritely (Luberoff), Matter of, N.Y.L.J., 12/8/95, p. 37, col. 3 (Sup.Ct., Suffolk County)—**§ 22.28, n. 8; § 22.71, n. 3.**

Berkeley Associates Co. v. Camlakides, 173 A.D.2d 193, 569 N.Y.S.2d 629 (N.Y.A.D. 1 Dept.1991)—**§ 13.52, n. 5.**

Berkemer v. McCarty, 468 U.S. 420, 104 S.Ct. 3138, 82 L.Ed.2d 317 (1984)—**§ 33.49, n. 1.**

Berkey v. Third Ave. Ry. Co., 244 N.Y. 84, 155 N.E. 58 (N.Y.1926)—**§ 2.23, n. 18.**

Berkowitz, People v., 428 N.Y.S.2d 927, 406 N.E.2d 783 (N.Y.1980)—**§ 33.81, n. 1.**

Berlin v. Herbert, 48 Misc.2d 393, 265 N.Y.S.2d 25 (N.Y.Dist.Ct.1965)—**§ 8.19, n. 5.**

Berman v. Parker, 348 U.S. 26, 75 S.Ct. 98, 99 L.Ed. 27 (1954)—**§ 16.125, n. 1.**

Bermudez, People v., 98 Misc.2d 704, 414 N.Y.S.2d 645 (N.Y.Sup.1979)—**§ 33.46, n. 2.**

Bernard v. Block, 176 A.D.2d 843, 575 N.Y.S.2d 506 (N.Y.A.D. 2 Dept.1991)—**§ 37.65, n. 40.**

Bernard v. United States, 25 F.3d 98 (2nd Cir.1994)—**§ 18.25, n. 1.**

Bernardine v. City of New York, 294 N.Y. 361, 62 N.E.2d 604 (N.Y.1945)—**§ 3.30, n. 4; § 37.65, n. 11.**

Bernier, People v., 541 N.Y.S.2d 760, 539 N.E.2d 588 (N.Y.1989)—**§ 38.10, n. 168.**

Bernstein v. Board of Appeals, Village of Matinecock, 60 Misc.2d 470, 302 N.Y.S.2d 141 (N.Y.Sup.1969)—**§ 16.93, n. 2, 3.**

Bernstein v. 1995 Associates, 217 A.D.2d 512, 630 N.Y.S.2d 68 (N.Y.A.D. 1 Dept. 1995)—**§ 17.69, n. 3.**

Bernstein v. Oppenheim & Co., P.C., 160 A.D.2d 428, 554 N.Y.S.2d 487 (N.Y.A.D. 1 Dept.1990)—**§ 28.9, n. 10; § 28.12; § 28.12, n. 2, 3.**

Bert v. Port Authority of New York and New Jersey, 166 A.D.2d 351, 561 N.Y.S.2d 416 (N.Y.A.D. 1 Dept.1990)—**§ 30.30, n. 10.**

Bertolo, People v., 490 N.Y.S.2d 475, 480 N.E.2d 61 (N.Y.1985)—**§ 33.56, n. 3.**

Besen v. State, 17 Misc.2d 119, 185 N.Y.S.2d 495 (N.Y.Ct.Cl.1959)—**§ 14.109, n. 2.**

Beslanovics, People v., 454 N.Y.S.2d 976, 440 N.E.2d 1322 (N.Y.1982)—**§ 38.26, n. 12, 14.**

Beslity v. Manhattan Honda, a Div. of Dah Chong Hong Trading Corp., 120 Misc.2d 848, 467 N.Y.S.2d 471 (N.Y.Sup.App. Term 1983)—**§ 7.47, n. 5.**

Besser v. K. L. T. Associates, Inc., 42 A.D.2d 725, 345 N.Y.S.2d 659 (N.Y.A.D. 2 Dept.1973)—**§ 12.5, n. 3.**

Best Products Co., Inc., In re, 173 B.R. 862 (Bkrtcy.S.D.N.Y.1994)—**§ 9.31, n. 10.**

Best Products Co., Inc., In re, 140 B.R. 353 (Bkrtcy.S.D.N.Y.1992)—**§ 9.93, n. 1.**

Best Products Co., Inc., In re, 138 B.R. 155 (Bkrtcy.S.D.N.Y.1992)—**§ 9.56, n. 5.**

TABLE OF CASES

Betances v. Hexreed Industries, Inc., 141 A.D.2d 945, 530 N.Y.S.2d 622 (N.Y.A.D. 3 Dept.1988)—§ **32.41, n. 7.**

Betcher v. Rademacher, 35 Misc.2d 693, 230 N.Y.S.2d 535 (N.Y.Sup.1962)—§ **11.9, n. 7.**

Beth Israel Medical Center (Farbstein), Matter of, 163 Misc.2d 26, 619 N.Y.S.2d 239 (N.Y.Sup.1994)—§ **22.53, n. 5, 11.**

Bettencourt v. Board of Registration In Medicine of Com. of Mass., 904 F.2d 772 (1st Cir.1990)—§ **18.31, n. 2.**

Better Home Imp. Corp. v. Forovus Realty Corp., 235 N.Y.S.2d 209 (N.Y.Sup. 1962)—§ **10.3, n. 3.**

Beutler v. Maynard, 80 A.D.2d 982, 437 N.Y.S.2d 463 (N.Y.A.D. 4 Dept.1981)—§ **12.69, n. 3.**

Beverley v. Choices Women's Medical Center, Inc., 579 N.Y.S.2d 637, 587 N.E.2d 275 (N.Y.1991)—§ **30.30, n. 11.**

Beyer v. Burns, 150 Misc.2d 10, 567 N.Y.S.2d 599 (N.Y.Sup.1991)—§ **16.110, n. 3.**

B.F. Goodrich v. Betkoski, 99 F.3d 505 (2nd Cir.1996)—§ **9.63, n. 1.**

B.F. Goodrich Co. v. Murtha, 958 F.2d 1192 (2nd Cir.1992)—§ **15.24, n. 3; § 15.29, n. 3.**

BFP v. Resolution Trust Corp., 511 U.S. 531, 114 S.Ct. 1757, 128 L.Ed.2d 556 (1994)—§ **9.119, n. 3.**

Bibeau v. Village Clerk of Village of Tuxedo Park, 145 A.D.2d 478, 535 N.Y.S.2d 106 (N.Y.A.D. 2 Dept.1988)—§ **37.32, n. 5.**

Bichler v. Eli Lilly and Co., 450 N.Y.S.2d 776, 436 N.E.2d 182 (N.Y.1982)—§ **27.52; § 27.52, n. 6; § 27.53; § 27.53, n. 5.**

Bichler v. Eli Lilly and Co., 79 A.D.2d 317, 436 N.Y.S.2d 625 (N.Y.A.D. 1 Dept. 1981)—§ **27.5, n. 8; § 27.18, n. 2; § 27.19; § 27.19, n. 2.**

Bici, People v., 211 A.D.2d 804, 621 N.Y.S.2d 666 (N.Y.A.D. 2 Dept.1995)—§ **18.12, n. 3.**

Bielich v. Winters, 95 A.D.2d 750, 464 N.Y.S.2d 189 (N.Y.A.D. 1 Dept.1983)—§ **30.10, n. 13.**

Bigelow v. Virginia, 421 U.S. 809, 95 S.Ct. 2222, 44 L.Ed.2d 600 (1975)—§ **16.25, n. 9.**

Bihn v. Wavecrest Apartments Corp., 222 A.D.2d 640, 636 N.Y.S.2d 663 (N.Y.A.D. 2 Dept.1995)—§ **37.37, n. 42.**

Bikowicz v. La Bombard, 212 A.D.2d 866, 622 N.Y.S.2d 358 (N.Y.A.D. 3 Dept. 1995)—§ **37.65, n. 48.**

Bill v. Bill, 214 A.D.2d 84, 631 N.Y.S.2d 699 (N.Y.A.D. 2 Dept.1995)—§ **21.56, n. 1.**

Billiar v. Minnesota Min. and Mfg. Co., 623 F.2d 240 (2nd Cir.1980)—§ **27.10, n. 3; § 27.14, n. 2, 5.**

Bilzerian, United States v., 926 F.2d 1285 (2nd Cir.1991)—§ **27.42, n. 1.**

Bi-Metallic Inv. Co. v. State Bd. of Equalization, 239 U.S. 441, 36 S.Ct. 141, 60 L.Ed. 372 (1915)—§ **4.5, n. 3.**

Binderman v. Kazdan, 145 Misc.2d 628, 547 N.Y.S.2d 984 (N.Y.City Civ.Ct.1989)—§ **30.9, n. 25.**

Bing, People v., 559 N.Y.S.2d 474, 558 N.E.2d 1011 (N.Y.1990)—§ **33.56; § 33.56, n. 7.**

Bing v. Thunig, 163 N.Y.S.2d 3, 143 N.E.2d 3 (N.Y.1957)—§ **29.12, n. 1, 2.**

Bingham v. Town of Greenburgh, 30 Misc.2d 64, 218 N.Y.S.2d 888 (N.Y.Sup. 1961)—§ **3.24, n. 15.**

Binghamton, City of v. Gartell, 275 A.D. 457, 90 N.Y.S.2d 556 (N.Y.A.D. 3 Dept. 1949)—§ **16.68, n. 1, 2.**

Binghamton GHS Employees Federal Credit Union v. State Div. of Human Rights, 563 N.Y.S.2d 385, 564 N.E.2d 1051 (N.Y. 1990)—§ **17.54, n. 6.**

Birchwood Towers No. 2 Associates v. Schwartz, 98 A.D.2d 699, 469 N.Y.S.2d 94 (N.Y.A.D. 2 Dept.1983)—§ **13.16, n. 2; § 13.18, n. 1.**

Bird v. Penn Cent. Co., 341 F.Supp. 291 (E.D.Pa.1972)—§ **28.43, n. 2.**

Bird v. Shearson Lehman/American Exp., Inc., 926 F.2d 116 (2nd Cir.1991)—§ **17.9, n. 1.**

Birger v. Tuner, 104 Misc.2d 63, 427 N.Y.S.2d 904 (N.Y.City Civ.Ct.1980)—§ **5.11, n. 7.**

Birnbaum, Estate of v. White, 136 A.D.2d 965, 525 N.Y.S.2d 82 (N.Y.A.D. 4 Dept. 1988)—§ **14.38; § 14.38, n. 8.**

Bischoff, Estate of v. Commssioner, 69 T.C. 32 (U.S.Tax Ct.1977)—§ **24.39, n. 1.**

Bishop v. Bostick, 141 A.D.2d 487, 529 N.Y.S.2d 116 (N.Y.A.D. 2 Dept.1988)—§ **30.5, n. 2; § 30.31, n. 3, 4.**

Bissonette v. National Biscuit Co., 100 F.2d 1003 (2nd Cir.1939)—§ **30.10, n. 16.**

Bivens v. Six Unknown Named Agents of Federal Bureau of Narcotics, 403 U.S. 388, 91 S.Ct. 1999, 29 L.Ed.2d 619 (1971)—§ **18.18, n. 4.**

B-K of Kansas, Inc., In re, 69 B.R. 812 (Bkrtcy.D.Kan.1987)—§ **9.74, n. 3.**

Black v. Board of Appeals of Inc. Village of Westbury, 33 A.D.2d 916, 308 N.Y.S.2d 302 (N.Y.A.D. 2 Dept.1969)—§ **16.50, n. 1.**

Black v. Summers, 151 A.D.2d 863, 542 N.Y.S.2d 837 (N.Y.A.D. 3 Dept.1989)—§ **16.101, n. 5.**

TABLE OF CASES

Blackburn v. Johnson Chemical Co., Inc., 128 Misc.2d 623, 490 N.Y.S.2d 452 (N.Y.Sup.1985)—§ **27.24, n. 5.**

Blackburn v. State of Ala., 361 U.S. 199, 80 S.Ct. 274, 4 L.Ed.2d 242 (1960)— § **33.57, n. 1.**

Black & Geddes, Inc., In re, 35 B.R. 827 (Bkrtcy.S.D.N.Y.1983)—§ **9.198, n. 1.**

Blackgold Realty Corp. v. Milne, 512 N.Y.S.2d 25, 504 N.E.2d 392 (N.Y. 1987)—§ **13.28, n. 5.**

Blackwell, People v., 624 N.Y.S.2d 367, 648 N.E.2d 787 (N.Y.1995)—§ **38.27, n. 9.**

Blair v. Armontrout, 976 F.2d 1130 (8th Cir.1992)—§ **38.19, n. 114.**

Blair v. CBS Inc., 662 F.Supp. 947 (S.D.N.Y. 1987)—§ **17.34, n. 3, 9.**

Blair v. Five Points Shopping Plaza, Inc., 51 A.D.2d 167, 379 N.Y.S.2d 532 (N.Y.A.D. 3 Dept.1976)—§ **37.99, n. 2.**

Blake v. Gardino, 35 A.D.2d 1022, 315 N.Y.S.2d 973 (N.Y.A.D. 3 Dept.1970)— § **26.10, n. 4.**

Blake, People v., 219 A.D.2d 730, 631 N.Y.S.2d 430 (N.Y.A.D. 2 Dept.1995)— § **38.21, n. 52.**

Blakley, People v., 357 N.Y.S.2d 459, 313 N.E.2d 763 (N.Y.1974)—§ **38.8, n. 194.**

Blank v. Schafrann, 206 A.D.2d 771, 615 N.Y.S.2d 107 (N.Y.A.D. 3 Dept.1994)— § **37.46, n. 2.**

Blanks, People v., 62 A.D.2d 1021, 403 N.Y.S.2d 553 (N.Y.A.D. 2 Dept.1978)— § **38.10, n. 65.**

Blasy, Matter of, 170 A.D.2d 451, 566 N.Y.S.2d 526 (N.Y.A.D. 2 Dept.1991)— § **37.85, n. 5.**

Blauner v. Blauner, 60 A.D.2d 215, 400 N.Y.S.2d 335 (N.Y.A.D. 1 Dept.1977)— § **21.31, n. 2.**

Blaustein v. Lazar Borck & Mensch, 161 A.D.2d 507, 555 N.Y.S.2d 776 (N.Y.A.D. 1 Dept.1990)—§ **2.45, n. 1.**

Bleakley, People v., 515 N.Y.S.2d 761, 508 N.E.2d 672 (N.Y.1987)—§ **38.19, n. 73, 74;** § **38.20;** § **38.20, n. 1, 9;** § **38.21, n. 24.**

Blesedell v. Mobil Oil Co., 708 F.Supp. 1408 (S.D.N.Y.1989)—§ **18.38, n. 8.**

Blickstein v. Blickstein, 99 A.D.2d 287, 472 N.Y.S.2d 110 (N.Y.A.D. 2 Dept.1984)— § **21.44;** § **21.44, n. 10;** § **21.48;** § **21.48, n. 1;** § **21.64, n. 1.**

Bligen, People v., 72 A.D.2d 678, 421 N.Y.S.2d 212 (N.Y.A.D. 1 Dept.1979)— § **38.10;** § **38.10, n. 116.**

Blinn Wholesale Drug Co., Inc., In re, 164 B.R. 440 (Bkrtcy.E.D.N.Y.1994)—§ **5.44, n. 5.**

Blissett v. Coughlin, 66 F.3d 531 (2nd Cir. 1995)—§ **18.32, n. 1.**

Blitman Const. Corp. v. Insurance Co. of North America, 498 N.Y.S.2d 349, 489 N.E.2d 236 (N.Y.1985)—§ **31.15, n. 7.**

Block v. Ambach, 540 N.Y.S.2d 6, 537 N.E.2d 181 (N.Y.1989)—§ **4.12, n. 8.**

Block Shim Development Company–Irving, In re, 118 B.R. 450 (N.D.Tex.1990)— § **9.160, n. 4.**

Bloom v. City of New York, 202 A.D.2d 465, 609 N.Y.S.2d 45 (N.Y.A.D. 2 Dept. 1994)—§ **30.14, n. 8.**

Bloomfield, People v., 153 A.D.2d 987, 545 N.Y.S.2d 430 (N.Y.A.D. 3 Dept.1989)— § **38.8;** § **38.8, n. 97.**

Bloomingdale v. Bloomingdale, 107 Misc. 646, 177 N.Y.S. 873 (N.Y.Sup.1919)— § **1.21, n. 23.**

Blount, People v., 49 A.D.2d 911, 373 N.Y.S.2d 402 (N.Y.A.D. 2 Dept.1975)— § **38.26, n. 11.**

Blue v. Koren, 72 F.3d 1075 (2nd Cir. 1995)—§ **18.32, n. 14.**

Blue v. Whalen, 57 A.D.2d 240, 394 N.Y.S.2d 290 (N.Y.A.D. 3 Dept.1977)— § **23.93, n. 4.**

Blueberry Investors Co. v. Ilana Realty Inc., 184 A.D.2d 906, 585 N.Y.S.2d 564 (N.Y.A.D. 3 Dept.1992)—§ **11.37, n. 5.**

Blum v. Schlegel, 150 F.R.D. 42 (W.D.N.Y. 1993)—§ **18.85, n. 6.**

Blunt, People v., 162 A.D.2d 86, 561 N.Y.S.2d 90 (N.Y.A.D. 2 Dept.1990)— § **18.15, n. 3.**

B. Milligan Contracting Inc. v. Andrew R. Mancini Associates Inc., 174 A.D.2d 136, 578 N.Y.S.2d 931 (N.Y.A.D. 3 Dept. 1992)—§ **5.50, n. 4.**

Board of Ed. of City of Buffalo v. City of Buffalo, 32 A.D.2d 98, 302 N.Y.S.2d 71 (N.Y.A.D. 4 Dept.1969)—§ **16.128, n. 5.**

Board of Ed. of City of New York v. Nyquist, 341 N.Y.S.2d 441, 293 N.E.2d 819 (N.Y.1973)—§ **39.11.**

Board of Ed. of Union Free School Dist. No. 3 of Town of Huntington v. Associated Teachers of Huntington, Inc., 331 N.Y.S.2d 17, 282 N.E.2d 109 (N.Y. 1972)—§ **3.21, n. 9, 10.**

Board of Ed. of Yonkers City School Dist. v. Yonkers Federation of Teachers, 386 N.Y.S.2d 657, 353 N.E.2d 569 (N.Y. 1976)—§ **3.21, n. 11.**

Board of Educ. of Monroe–Woodbury Cent. School Dist. v. Wieder, 531 N.Y.S.2d 889, 527 N.E.2d 767 (N.Y.1988)—§ **39.9, n. 11, 13.**

Board of Educ. of Ramapo Cent. School Dist. (Ramapo Teachers' Ass'n), Matter of, 200 A.D.2d 62, 611 N.Y.S.2d 962 (N.Y.A.D. 3 Dept.1994)—§ **37.28, n. 33.**

TABLE OF CASES

Board of Higher Ed. of City of New York v. Carter, 250 N.Y.S.2d 33, 199 N.E.2d 141 (N.Y.1964)—§ **18.60, n. 4.**

Board of Regents of State Colleges v. Roth, 408 U.S. 564, 92 S.Ct. 2701, 33 L.Ed.2d 548 (1972)—§ **4.6, n. 6.**

Board of Visitors—Marcy Psychiatric Center v. Coughlin, 466 N.Y.S.2d 668, 453 N.E.2d 1085 (N.Y.1983)—§ **4.79, n. 8.**

Bobandal Realties, Inc. v. Worthington, 21 A.D.2d 784, 250 N.Y.S.2d 575 (N.Y.A.D. 2 Dept.1964)—§ **16.64, n. 1, 2.**

Bobb, People v., 207 A.D.2d 458, 615 N.Y.S.2d 764 (N.Y.A.D. 2 Dept.1994)—§ **38.25, n. 20.**

Bobinski, United States v., 244 F.2d 299 (2nd Cir.1957)—§ **14.81, n. 6, 7.**

Bodnar Industries, Inc. v. State, 19 Misc.2d 720, 187 N.Y.S.2d 359 (N.Y.Ct.Cl. 1959)—§ **14.95, n. 9.**

Boecher v. Borth, 51 A.D.2d 598, 377 N.Y.S.2d 781 (N.Y.A.D. 3 Dept.1976)—§ **12.64, n. 1.**

Boerner's Will, In re, 58 Misc.2d 144, 294 N.Y.S.2d 725 (N.Y.Sur.1968)—§ **24.9, n. 2.**

Bohlen v. Metropolitan Elev. Ry. Co., 121 N.Y. 546, 24 N.E. 932 (N.Y.1890)—§ **38.10, n. 128.**

Bolden, People v., 597 N.Y.S.2d 270, 613 N.E.2d 145 (N.Y.1993)—§ **33.89, n. 3, 4.**

Boll v. Sharp & Dohme, 281 A.D. 568, 121 N.Y.S.2d 20 (N.Y.A.D. 1 Dept.1953)—§ **5.11, n. 10.**

Bolling, People v., 157 A.D.2d 733, 550 N.Y.S.2d 27 (N.Y.A.D. 2 Dept.1990)—§ **33.41; § 33.41, n. 2.**

Bolm v. Triumph Corp., 71 A.D.2d 429, 422 N.Y.S.2d 969 (N.Y.A.D. 4 Dept.1979)—§ **27.7, n. 4, 5; § 27.32; § 27.32, n. 5; § 27.37, n. 4.**

Bolm v. Triumph Corp., 350 N.Y.S.2d 644, 305 N.E.2d 769 (N.Y.1973)—§ **27.5, n. 10.**

Bolsenbroek v. Tully & Di Napoli, Inc., 12 A.D.2d 376, 212 N.Y.S.2d 323 (N.Y.A.D. 1 Dept.1961)—§ **28.16, n. 5.**

Boltax v. Joy Day Camp, 499 N.Y.S.2d 660, 490 N.E.2d 527 (N.Y.1986)—§ **27.12, n. 4; § 28.16, n. 6.**

Bomze v. Jaybee Photo Suppliers, Inc., 117 Misc.2d 957, 460 N.Y.S.2d 862 (N.Y.Sup. App.Term 1983)—§ **13.56, n. 3.**

Bonacorsa v. Van Lindt, 528 N.Y.S.2d 519, 523 N.E.2d 806 (N.Y.1988)—§ **17.41, n. 3.**

Bon–Air Estates, Inc. v. Building Inspector of Town of Ramapo, 31 A.D.2d 502, 298 N.Y.S.2d 763 (N.Y.A.D. 2 Dept.1969)—§ **3.9, n. 3.**

Bonavisa v. Motor Vehicle Acc. Indemnification Corp., 21 Misc.2d 963, 198 N.Y.S.2d 332 (N.Y.Sup.1960)—§ **26.30, n. 8.**

Bonde v. General Sec. Ins. Co. of Canada, 55 Misc.2d 588, 285 N.Y.S.2d 675 (N.Y.Sup.1967)—§ **8.3, n. 5.**

Bondi, People v., 104 Misc.2d 627, 429 N.Y.S.2d 146 (N.Y.Town Ct.1980)—§ **15.16, n. 6.**

Bonesteel, Matter of, 175 A.D.2d 361, 571 N.Y.S.2d 961 (N.Y.A.D. 3 Dept.1991)—§ **22.31, n. 1.**

Bonilla–Lugo, People v., 629 N.Y.S.2d 721, 653 N.E.2d 618 (N.Y.1995)—§ **38.27; § 38.27, n. 8.**

Bonner Mall Partnership, In re, 2 F.3d 899 (9th Cir.1993)—§ **9.166, n. 11.**

Bon Temps Agency Ltd. v. Greenfield, 184 A.D.2d 280, 584 N.Y.S.2d 824 (N.Y.A.D. 1 Dept.1992)—§ **17.63, n. 2.**

Booden, People v., 513 N.Y.S.2d 87, 505 N.E.2d 598 (N.Y.1987)—§ **33.61; § 33.61, n. 2.**

Boodrow, In re, 192 B.R. 57 (Bkrtcy. N.D.N.Y.1995)—§ **9.186, n. 11.**

Booker, People v., 145 A.D.2d 564, 536 N.Y.S.2d 118 (N.Y.A.D. 2 Dept.1988)—§ **33.45, n. 5.**

Bookhout v. Levitt, 403 N.Y.S.2d 200, 374 N.E.2d 111 (N.Y.1978)—§ **3.17, n. 10.**

Boomer v. Atlantic Cement Co., 309 N.Y.S.2d 312, 257 N.E.2d 870 (N.Y. 1970)—§ **15.32; § 15.32, n. 23.**

Booth v. Spuyten Duyvil Rolling Mill Co., 60 N.Y. 487 (N.Y.1875)—§ **30.24, n. 5.**

Boothe v. TRW Credit Data, 557 F.Supp. 66 (S.D.N.Y.1982)—§ **7.31, n. 6; § 7.33, n. 11.**

Borchardt v. New York Life Ins. Co., 102 A.D.2d 465, 477 N.Y.S.2d 167 (N.Y.A.D. 1 Dept.1984)—§ **31.18, n. 14.**

Bord v. Brindisi, 49 A.D.2d 695, 370 N.Y.S.2d 766 (N.Y.A.D. 4 Dept.1975)—§ **12.64, n. 12, 14.**

Bordell v. General Elec. Co., 208 A.D.2d 219, 622 N.Y.S.2d 1001 (N.Y.A.D. 3 Dept.1995)—§ **17.64, n. 3.**

Boreali v. Axelrod, 523 N.Y.S.2d 464, 517 N.E.2d 1350 (N.Y.1987)—§ **4.68; § 4.68, n. 3, 4; § 4.76, n. 1; § 4.80, n. 1; § 37.13, n. 8.**

Borgia v. City of New York, 237 N.Y.S.2d 319, 187 N.E.2d 777 (N.Y.1962)—§ **18.38, n. 7; § 28.14, n. 1; § 37.29, n. 16.**

Borg–Warner Corp. v. Insurance Co. of North America, 174 A.D.2d 24, 577 N.Y.S.2d 953 (N.Y.A.D. 3 Dept.1992)—§ **31.2, n. 6.**

Borkowski v. Valley Cent. School Dist., 63 F.3d 131 (2nd Cir.1995)—§ **17.43, n. 4.**

TABLE OF CASES

Borntrager v. Delaware County, 76 A.D.2d 969, 428 N.Y.S.2d 766 (N.Y.A.D. 3 Dept. 1980)—§ 14.14, n. 5.

Boryszewski v. Brydges, 372 N.Y.S.2d 623, 334 N.E.2d 579 (N.Y.1975)—§ 4.69, n. 9.

Bosket, People v., 216 A.D.2d 791, 629 N.Y.S.2d 296 (N.Y.A.D. 3 Dept.1995)—§ 38.8, n. 92, 103.

Boston, People v., 555 N.Y.S.2d 27, 554 N.E.2d 64 (N.Y.1990)—§ 38.8, n. 198.

Boston Post Road Ltd. Partnership, Matter of, 145 B.R. 745 (Bkrtcy.D.Conn.1992)—§ 9.154, n. 3.

Boston Post Road Ltd. Partnership v. FDIC (In re Boston Post Road Ltd. Partnership), 21 F.3d 477 (2nd Cir.1994)—§ 9.157, n. 4; § 9.166, n. 12.

Boudin, People v., 97 A.D.2d 84, 469 N.Y.S.2d 89 (N.Y.A.D. 2 Dept.1983)—§ 38.8, n. 100.

Boudin, People v., 95 A.D.2d 463, 467 N.Y.S.2d 261 (N.Y.A.D. 2 Dept.1983)—§ 38.8, n. 100.

Boudin, People v., 90 A.D.2d 253, 457 N.Y.S.2d 302 (N.Y.A.D. 2 Dept.1982)—§ 38.8, n. 100.

Boulder Apartments, Inc., Application of, 14 Misc.2d 287, 155 N.Y.S.2d 520 (N.Y.Sup. 1956)—§ 10.19, n. 5.

Boulukos v. Chresafes, 20 Misc.2d 673, 187 N.Y.S.2d 141 (N.Y.Sup.1959)—§ 11.37, n. 7.

Bouton, People v., 428 N.Y.S.2d 218, 405 N.E.2d 699 (N.Y.1980)—§ 38.28, n. 16.

Bovsun v. Sanperi, 473 N.Y.S.2d 357, 461 N.E.2d 843 (N.Y.1984)—§ 30.9, n. 1, 2, 43.

Bowen v. City of New York, 476 U.S. 467, 106 S.Ct. 2022, 90 L.Ed.2d 462 (1986)—§ 34.5, n. 1, 2.

Bowen v. Galbreath, 485 U.S. 74, 108 S.Ct. 892, 99 L.Ed.2d 68 (1988)—§ 34.52, n. 2.

Bowen v. Yuckert, 482 U.S. 137, 107 S.Ct. 2287, 96 L.Ed.2d 119 (1987)—§ 34.10; § 34.10, n. 2, 3, 4; § 34.14, n. 3, 4.

Bowers, Matter of Guardianship of, 164 Misc.2d 298, 624 N.Y.S.2d 750 (N.Y.Sur. 1995)—§ 22.15, n. 6, 7.

Bowery Savings Bank v. Giannattasio, N.Y.L.J., 5/10/95, p.25, col.3 (Sup.Ct., Suffolk County)—§ 11.54, n. 8.

Bowles v. Errico, 163 A.D.2d 771, 558 N.Y.S.2d 734 (N.Y.A.D. 3 Dept.1990)—§ 1.10, n. 19.

Bowman, People v., 211 A.D.2d 590, 622 N.Y.S.2d 22 (N.Y.A.D. 1 Dept.1995)—§ 38.10, n. 168.

Boyar's Realty Corp. v. Queens–Nassau Auto Sales Corp., N.Y.L.J., 4/17/91, p.25, col.4, 19 HCR 228A (Civ.Ct., Kings County)—§ 13.28; § 13.28, n. 14.

Boyajian v. Casey, 52 A.D.2d 1014, 383 N.Y.S.2d 714 (N.Y.A.D. 3 Dept.1976)—§ 12.9, n. 8.

Boyce Thompson Institute for Plant Research, Inc. v. Insurance Co. of North America, 751 F.Supp. 1137 (S.D.N.Y. 1990)—§ 31.20, n. 2.

Boyd v. Constantine, 597 N.Y.S.2d 605, 613 N.E.2d 511 (N.Y.1993)—§ 4.62, n. 14.

Boyd v. Jarvis, 74 A.D.2d 937, 426 N.Y.S.2d 142 (N.Y.A.D. 3 Dept.1980)—§ 11.6, n. 2.

Boyd, Will of, 161 Misc.2d 191, 613 N.Y.S.2d 330 (N.Y.Sur.1994)—§ 24.60, n. 2.

Boyette, People v., 201 A.D.2d 490, 607 N.Y.S.2d 402 (N.Y.A.D. 2 Dept.1994)—§ 38.10, n. 98.

Boyle v. Kelley, 396 N.Y.S.2d 834, 365 N.E.2d 866 (N.Y.1977)—§ 18.11, n. 4.

Boyle, United States v., 469 U.S. 241, 105 S.Ct. 687, 83 L.Ed.2d 622 (1985)—§ 28.5, n. 3.

Bozer v. Higgins, 204 A.D.2d 979, 613 N.Y.S.2d 312 (N.Y.A.D. 4 Dept.1994)—§ 18.10, n. 13.

Bracker v. Cohen, 204 A.D.2d 115, 612 N.Y.S.2d 113 (N.Y.A.D. 1 Dept.1994)—§ 17.68, n. 7.

Bradford v. Weber, 138 A.D.2d 860, 525 N.Y.S.2d 968 (N.Y.A.D. 3 Dept.1988)—§ 17.29, n. 4.

Bradley v. Consolidated Edison Co. of New York, Inc., 657 F.Supp. 197 (S.D.N.Y. 1987)—§ 17.28, n. 4.

Bradner, People v., 107 N.Y. 1, 13 N.E. 87 (N.Y.1887)—§ 38.19, n. 26.

Brady v. Brady, 486 N.Y.S.2d 891, 476 N.E.2d 290 (N.Y.1985)—§ 21.20; § 21.20, n. 10.

Brady v. Maryland, 373 U.S. 83, 83 S.Ct. 1194, 10 L.Ed.2d 215 (1963)—§ 33.39; § 33.39, n. 1; § 38.10; § 38.10, n. 84, 92.

Brady v. Ottaway Newspapers, Inc., 484 N.Y.S.2d 798, 473 N.E.2d 1172 (N.Y. 1984)—§ 18.82, n. 5; § 37.29, n. 47; § 39.7, n. 7.

Brady v. Ottaway Newspapers, Inc., 97 A.D.2d 451, 467 N.Y.S.2d 417 (N.Y.A.D. 2 Dept.1983)—§ 37.22; § 37.22, n. 8.

Brady, People v., 220 A.D.2d 760, 633 N.Y.S.2d 983 (N.Y.A.D. 2 Dept.1995)—§ 38.8, n. 212.

Brady's Will, In re, 273 A.D. 968, 77 N.Y.S.2d 916 (N.Y.A.D. 4 Dept.1948)—§ 25.31, n. 6.

Braiman v. Braiman, 407 N.Y.S.2d 449, 378 N.E.2d 1019 (N.Y.1978)—§ 21.61; § 21.61, n. 2.

TABLE OF CASES

Bralus Corporation v. Berger, 307 N.Y. 626, 120 N.E.2d 829 (N.Y.1954)—§ **10.5, n. 2.**

Branchinelli, People v., 146 Misc.2d 73, 545 N.Y.S.2d 914 (N.Y.Dist.Ct.1989)—§ **33.25, n. 1.**

Braniff Airways, Inc. v. Midwest Corp., 873 F.2d 805 (5th Cir.1989)—§ **9.117, n. 1.**

Brannigan v. Dubuque, 199 A.D.2d 851, 606 N.Y.S.2d 401 (N.Y.A.D. 3 Dept.1993)—§ **37.23, n. 1.**

Brantley, People v., 186 A.D.2d 1036, 588 N.Y.S.2d 475 (N.Y.A.D. 4 Dept.1992)—§ **38.28, n. 14.**

Braswell v. United States, 487 U.S. 99, 108 S.Ct. 2284, 101 L.Ed.2d 98 (1988)—§ **4.63, n. 10.**

Braun v. Ahmed, 127 A.D.2d 418, 515 N.Y.S.2d 473 (N.Y.A.D. 2 Dept.1987)—§ **30.4, n. 7.**

Braun v. Roux Distributing Co., 312 S.W.2d 758 (Mo.1958)—§ **27.20, n. 3.**

Braunstein v. Jason Tarantella, Inc., 87 A.D.2d 203, 450 N.Y.S.2d 862 (N.Y.A.D. 2 Dept.1982)—§ **5.7, n. 7.**

Bravo v. Terstiege, 196 A.D.2d 473, 601 N.Y.S.2d 129 (N.Y.A.D. 2 Dept.1993)—§ **37.28, n. 5.**

Brawer v. Pinkins, N.Y.L.J., 6/12/95, p.3, col.1—§ **21.7, n. 2.**

Bray v. Alexandria Women's Health Clinic, 506 U.S. 263, 113 S.Ct. 753, 122 L.Ed.2d 34 (1993)—§ **18.19, n. 1.**

Bray v. Cox, 379 N.Y.S.2d 803, 342 N.E.2d 575 (N.Y.1976)—§ **37.85, n. 5.**

Brayer, People v., 6 A.D.2d 437, 179 N.Y.S.2d 248 (N.Y.A.D. 4 Dept.1958)—§ **38.8, n. 86.**

Braynard v. Morgan, 50 A.D.2d 810, 376 N.Y.S.2d 575 (N.Y.A.D. 2 Dept.1975)—§ **26.42, n. 16.**

Brearton v. De Witt, 252 N.Y. 495, 170 N.E. 119 (N.Y.1930)—§ **5.7, n. 5; § 5.8, n. 1.**

Brecher v. Laikin, 430 F.Supp. 103 (S.D.N.Y.1977)—§ **5.52, n. 1.**

Breed v. Insurance Co. of North America, 413 N.Y.S.2d 352, 385 N.E.2d 1280 (N.Y. 1978)—§ **13.63, n. 6; § 31.9, n. 1.**

Brensic, People v., 136 A.D.2d 169, 526 N.Y.S.2d 968 (N.Y.A.D. 2 Dept.1988)—§ **38.8, n. 101.**

Brent v. Hoch, 25 Misc.2d 1062, 205 N.Y.S.2d 66 (N.Y.Sup.1960)—§ **14.21, n. 3.**

Brentrup v. Culkin, 167 Misc.2d 211, 639 N.Y.S.2d 247 (N.Y.Sup.1996)—§ **21.52, n. 1.**

Bretton v. Mutual of Omaha Ins. Co., 110 A.D.2d 46, 492 N.Y.S.2d 760 (N.Y.A.D. 1 Dept.1985)—§ **31.9, n. 2.**

Brewer v. Jamaica Hospital, 73 A.D.2d 851, 423 N.Y.S.2d 188 (N.Y.A.D. 1 Dept. 1980)—§ **26.45, n. 2.**

Brewley, People v., 211 A.D.2d 805, 621 N.Y.S.2d 922 (N.Y.A.D. 2 Dept.1995)—§ **38.8, n. 14.**

Brickel, Estate of, N.Y.L.J., 1/13/94, p.26, col.5 (Surr.Ct., N.Y. County)—§ **23.81, n. 13.**

Bridges v. Eastman Kodak Co., 850 F.Supp. 216 (S.D.N.Y.1994)—§ **17.72, n. 6.**

Bridges v. Eastman Kodak Co., 822 F.Supp. 1020 (S.D.N.Y.1993)—§ **17.57, n. 2.**

Bridges v. 725 Riverside Drive, Inc., 119 A.D.2d 789, 501 N.Y.S.2d 414 (N.Y.A.D. 2 Dept.1986)—§ **28.24, n. 2.**

Brien, People v., 162 A.D.2d 1028, 559 N.Y.S.2d 195 (N.Y.A.D. 4 Dept.1990)—§ **38.8, n. 226.**

Brierley, Petition of, 145 B.R. 151 (Bkrtcy. S.D.N.Y.1992)—§ **9.20, n. 4, 5.**

Bright's Estate v. United States, 658 F.2d 999 (5th Cir.1981)—§ **24.56, n. 4.**

Brignoli v. Balch, Hardy & Scheinman, Inc., 126 F.R.D. 462 (S.D.N.Y.1989)—§ **28.24, n. 2.**

Brinks, Inc. v. Commercial Union Ins. Co., 217 A.D.2d 620, 629 N.Y.S.2d 777 (N.Y.A.D. 2 Dept.1995)—§ **37.37, n. 88.**

Briscoe v. LaHue, 460 U.S. 325, 103 S.Ct. 1108, 75 L.Ed.2d 96 (1983)—§ **18.31, n. 2.**

Brisko, People v., 219 A.D.2d 493, 631 N.Y.S.2d 516 (N.Y.A.D. 1 Dept.1995)—§ **38.8, n. 174.**

Bristol, Litynski, Wojcik, P.C. v. Town of Queensbury, 166 A.D.2d 772, 562 N.Y.S.2d 976 (N.Y.A.D. 3 Dept.1990)—§ **27.38, n. 2.**

British Land (Maryland), Inc. v. Tax Appeals Tribunal of State of N.Y., 623 N.Y.S.2d 772, 647 N.E.2d 1280 (N.Y. 1995)—§ **39.9, n. 12.**

Britt, People v., 400 N.Y.S.2d 785, 371 N.E.2d 504 (N.Y.1977)—§ **38.19, n. 108.**

Britt v. United States Army Corps of Engineers, 769 F.2d 84 (2nd Cir.1985)—§ **15.3, n. 8.**

Broad v. Conway, 675 F.Supp. 768 (N.D.N.Y.1987)—§ **28.9; § 28.9, n. 11.**

Broadie, People v., 371 N.Y.S.2d 471, 332 N.E.2d 338 (N.Y.1975)—§ **38.21, n. 58.**

Broadway Photoplay Co. v. World Film Corporation, 225 N.Y. 104, 121 N.E. 756 (N.Y.1919)—§ **30.5, n. 8, 10.**

Broadway–Spring St. Corp. v. Jack Berens Export Corp., 12 Misc.2d 460, 171 N.Y.S.2d 342 (N.Y.Mun.Ct.1958)—§ **13.30, n. 4.**

Brock v. Merrell Dow Pharmaceuticals, Inc., 874 F.2d 307 (5th Cir.1989)—§ **27.35, n. 15.**

TABLE OF CASES

Brocros Realty Corp. v. David Perry Photography, N.Y.L.J. 4/19/95, p.27, col. 1, 23 HCR 210 (Civ. Ct. N.Y. County)— § 13.57, n. 3.
Brodsky v. Brodsky, 214 A.D.2d 599, 624 N.Y.S.2d 960 (N.Y.A.D. 2 Dept.1995)— § 37.30, n. 10.
Brodsky v. Zagata, 165 Misc.2d 510, 629 N.Y.S.2d 373 (N.Y.Sup.1995)—§ 4.57, n. 4; § 4.69, n. 5.
Brody, Matter of, N.Y.L.J. 4/8/74, p. 394 (Surr.Ct., Bronx County)—§ 25.28, n. 3.
Brogdon, People v., 213 A.D.2d 418, 623 N.Y.S.2d 332 (N.Y.A.D. 2 Dept.1995)— § 38.19, n. 78.
Brokaw v. Duffy, 165 N.Y. 391, 59 N.E. 196 (N.Y.1901)—§ 12.58, n. 1.
Bronx River Expressway in City of New York, Application of, 278 A.D. 813, 104 N.Y.S.2d 554 (N.Y.A.D. 1 Dept.1951)— § 14.95, n. 2.
Bronxville Palmer, Limited v. State, 36 A.D.2d 10, 318 N.Y.S.2d 57 (N.Y.A.D. 3 Dept.1971)—§ 14.82, n. 3.
Bronxville, Village of v. Francis, 1 A.D.2d 236, 150 N.Y.S.2d 906 (N.Y.A.D. 2 Dept. 1956)—§ 16.84, n. 2.
Brookhaven Aggregates, Ltd., State v., 121 A.D.2d 440, 503 N.Y.S.2d 413 (N.Y.A.D. 2 Dept.1986)—§ 15.25, n. 24.
Brookhaven, N.Y., Town of v. State, 526 N.Y.S.2d 433, 521 N.E.2d 440 (N.Y. 1988)—§ 39.10, n. 3.
Brookhaven, Town of v. Gold, 89 A.D.2d 963, 454 N.Y.S.2d 111 (N.Y.A.D. 2 Dept. 1982)—§ 14.82, n. 12.
Brookhaven, Town of v. Spadaro, 204 A.D.2d 533, 612 N.Y.S.2d 175 (N.Y.A.D. 2 Dept.1994)—§ 16.119, n. 12.
Brooklyn Bureau of Social Service v. Transamerica Ins. Co., 28 A.D.2d 841, 281 N.Y.S.2d 708 (N.Y.A.D. 1 Dept.1967)— § 26.44, n. 6.
Brooklyn Elevated R. Co. v. Flynn, 33 N.Y.S. 974 (N.Y.Sup.1895)—§ 14.109, n. 4.
Brooklyn Law School v. Aetna Cas. and Sur. Co., 849 F.2d 788 (2nd Cir.1988)— § 31.12, n. 8.
Brooklyn Park Com'rs v. Armstrong, 45 N.Y. 234 (N.Y.1871)—§ 3.16, n. 9.
Brooklyn Union Gas Co. v. New York State Human Rights Appeal Bd., 390 N.Y.S.2d 884, 359 N.E.2d 393 (N.Y.1976)— § 17.54, n. 6.
Brook Plaza Ophthalmology Associates, P.C. v. Fink, Weinberger, Fredman, Berman & Lowell, P.C., 173 A.D.2d 170, 569 N.Y.S.2d 25 (N.Y.A.D. 1 Dept.1991)— § 28.12; § 28.12, n. 3, 9; § 28.29; § 28.29, n. 9.

Brooks, People v., 524 N.Y.S.2d 382, 519 N.E.2d 293 (N.Y.1987)—§ 38.19, n. 104.
Broome County, Matter of, 133 A.D.2d 984, 521 N.Y.S.2d 134 (N.Y.A.D. 3 Dept. 1987)—§ 14.86, n. 6.
Broome County v. Vincent J. Smith, Inc., 78 Misc.2d 889, 358 N.Y.S.2d 998 (N.Y.Sup.1974)—§ 28.14, n. 4.
Broome County Farmers' Fire Relief Ass'n v. New York State Electric & Gas Corp., 239 A.D. 304, 268 N.Y.S. 131 (N.Y.A.D. 3 Dept.1933)—§ 37.13, n. 7.
Brostoff v. Berkman, 582 N.Y.S.2d 989, 591 N.E.2d 1175 (N.Y.1992)—§ 38.8, n. 91.
Brothers, People v., 429 N.Y.S.2d 558, 407 N.E.2d 405 (N.Y.1980)—§ 33.90, n. 6.
Brotherton v. Celotex Corp., 202 N.J.Super. 148, 493 A.2d 1337 (N.J.Super.L.1985)— § 27.28; § 27.28, n. 2.
Broughton v. State, 373 N.Y.S.2d 87, 335 N.E.2d 310 (N.Y.1975)—§ 17.26, n. 1; § 18.22, n. 2; § 18.23, n. 1.
Brous v. Planning Bd. of Village of Southampton, 191 A.D.2d 553, 594 N.Y.S.2d 816 (N.Y.A.D. 2 Dept.1993)—§ 16.85, n. 10; § 16.101, n. 4.
Brousal v. Schmukler, 154 A.D.2d 494, 546 N.Y.S.2d 120 (N.Y.A.D. 2 Dept.1989)— § 37.28, n. 26.
Broward Nat. Bank of Fort Lauderdale v. Starzec, 30 A.D.2d 603, 290 N.Y.S.2d 112 (N.Y.A.D. 3 Dept.1968)—§ 11.52, n. 8.
Brown, In re, 163 B.R. 596 (Bkrtcy.N.D.Fla. 1993)—§ 9.264, n. 6.
Brown v. Albany Citizens Council on Alcoholism, Inc., 199 A.D.2d 904, 605 N.Y.S.2d 577 (N.Y.A.D. 3 Dept.1993)— § 17.25, n. 9.
Brown v. Albert Einstein College of Medicine of Yeshiva University, 172 A.D.2d 197, 568 N.Y.S.2d 61 (N.Y.A.D. 1 Dept. 1991)—§ 18.53, n. 3.
Brown v. Board of Trustees of Town of Hamptonburg, School Dist. No. 4, 303 N.Y. 484, 104 N.E.2d 866 (N.Y.1952)— § 3.7, n. 7; § 3.30, n. 1.
Brown v. Braun, 659 N.Y.S.2d 301 (N.Y.A.D. 2 Dept.1997)—§ 37.87, n. 3.
Brown v. City of New York, 470 N.Y.S.2d 571, 458 N.E.2d 1248 (N.Y.1983)— § 39.7, n. 4, 9.
Brown v. Daytop Village, Inc., 161 Misc.2d 248, 613 N.Y.S.2d 1021 (N.Y.Sup. 1994)—§ 18.55, n. 8.
Brown v. Farmers' Loan & Trust Co., 117 N.Y. 266, 22 N.E. 952 (N.Y.1889)— § 5.18, n. 2.
Brown v. Halperin, N.Y.L.J., 7/6/94, p.31, col.6 (Sup.Ct., Queens County)— § 13.55, n. 2.

TABLE OF CASES

Brown v. Lockwood, 76 A.D.2d 721, 432 N.Y.S.2d 186 (N.Y.A.D. 2 Dept.1980)—§ **17.27, n. 4.**

Brown v. Micheletti, 97 A.D.2d 529, 468 N.Y.S.2d 160 (N.Y.A.D. 2 Dept.1983)—§ **37.37, n. 37, 38.**

Brown v. Pennsylvania State Employees Credit Union, 851 F.2d 81 (3rd Cir. 1988)—§ **9.131, n. 1.**

Brown, People v., 157 A.D.2d 790, 550 N.Y.S.2d 389 (N.Y.A.D. 2 Dept.1990)—§ **33.30, n. 1.**

Brown, People v., 80 A.D.2d 902, 437 N.Y.S.2d 22 (N.Y.A.D. 2 Dept.1981)—§ **38.8, n. 114, 117.**

Brown, People v., 386 N.Y.S.2d 848, 353 N.E.2d 811 (N.Y.1976)—§ **38.10;** § **38.10, n. 52, 179.**

Brown, People v., 245 N.Y.S.2d 577, 195 N.E.2d 293 (N.Y.1963)—§ **38.9, n. 12;** § **38.10.**

Brown, People ex rel. v. Bednosky, 190 A.D.2d 836, 593 N.Y.S.2d 859 (N.Y.A.D. 2 Dept.1993)—§ **38.8, n. 79.**

Brown, People ex rel. v. New York State Div. of Parole, 521 N.Y.S.2d 657, 516 N.E.2d 194 (N.Y.1987)—§ **38.8, n. 73.**

Brown v. Poritzky, 332 N.Y.S.2d 872, 283 N.E.2d 751 (N.Y.1972)—§ **31.7, n. 6.**

Brown v. Ramsay (In re Ragar), 3 F.3d 1174 (8th Cir.1993)—§ **9.18, n. 4.**

Brown v. Samalin & Bock, P.C., 168 A.D.2d 531, 563 N.Y.S.2d 426 (N.Y.A.D. 2 Dept. 1990)—§ **28.10;** § **28.10, n. 4.**

Brown v. Samalin & Bock, P.C., 155 A.D.2d 407, 547 N.Y.S.2d 80 (N.Y.A.D. 2 Dept. 1989)—§ **28.10, n. 12;** § **28.17, n. 3;** § **28.24, n. 5.**

Brown v. State, 652 N.Y.S.2d 223, 674 N.E.2d 1129 (N.Y.1996)—§ **18.5;** § **18.5, n. 3, 4.**

Brown v. United States Fidelity & Guaranty Co., 46 A.D.2d 97, 361 N.Y.S.2d 232 (N.Y.A.D. 3 Dept.1974)—§ **31.14, n. 2.**

Brown v. United States Vanadium Corp., 198 A.D.2d 863, 604 N.Y.S.2d 432 (N.Y.A.D. 4 Dept.1993)—§ **37.45, n. 2.**

Brown v. Weir, 95 A.D. 78, 88 N.Y.S. 479 (N.Y.A.D. 2 Dept.1904)—§ **30.26, n. 7.**

Brown Bros. Elec. Contractors, Inc. v. Beam Const. Corp., 393 N.Y.S.2d 350, 361 N.E.2d 999 (N.Y.1977)—§ **17.35, n. 1.**

Brownell, Matter of, 112 Misc.2d 719, 447 N.Y.S.2d 591 (N.Y.Co.Ct.1981)—§ **22.69, n. 3.**

Brownstone, Matter of, 191 A.D.2d 167, 594 N.Y.S.2d 31 (N.Y.A.D. 1 Dept.1993)—§ **22.31, n. 12.**

Brownstone Publishers, Inc. v. New York City Dept. of Bldgs., 166 A.D.2d 294, 560 N.Y.S.2d 642 (N.Y.A.D. 1 Dept.1990)—§ **3.29, n. 7.**

Brownstone School and Daycare Center v. Lenihan, N.Y.L.J., 5/5/92, p.23, col.3, 20 HCR 255 (Civ.Ct., N.Y.County)—§ **13.28, n. 11.**

B & R Textile Corp. v. Domino Textiles Inc., 77 A.D.2d 539, 430 N.Y.S.2d 89 (N.Y.A.D. 1 Dept.1980)—§ **5.19, n. 3;** § **5.20, n. 2.**

Bruce, People v., 224 A.D.2d 438, 638 N.Y.S.2d 326 (N.Y.A.D. 2 Dept.1996)—§ **38.28, n. 15.**

Brucia v. Planning Bd. of Town of Huntington, 157 A.D.2d 657, 549 N.Y.S.2d 757 (N.Y.A.D. 2 Dept.1990)—§ **16.101, n. 7.**

Bruck v. Meatto Trucking Corp., 20 A.D.2d 521, 245 N.Y.S.2d 232 (N.Y.A.D. 1 Dept. 1963)—§ **30.13, n. 3.**

Brudnicki v. General Elec. Co., 535 F.Supp. 84 (N.D.Ill.1982)—§ **17.27, n. 3.**

Brum v. City of Niagara Falls, 145 A.D.2d 928, 535 N.Y.S.2d 856 (N.Y.A.D. 4 Dept. 1988)—§ **5.7, n. 4.**

Brumbaugh v. CEJJ, Inc., 152 A.D.2d 69, 547 N.Y.S.2d 699 (N.Y.A.D. 3 Dept. 1989)—§ **27.24, n. 6.**

Brunner, People v., 209 A.D.2d 532, 619 N.Y.S.2d 90 (N.Y.A.D. 2 Dept.1994)—§ **38.10, n. 165.**

Bruno v. Guerra, 146 Misc.2d 206, 549 N.Y.S.2d 925 (N.Y.Sup.1990)—§ **18.76, n. 8.**

Brunson v. Wendover Funding (In re Brunson), 201 B.R. 351 (Bkrtcy.W.D.N.Y. 1996)—§ **9.248, n. 3.**

Brusco v. Braun, 621 N.Y.S.2d 291, 645 N.E.2d 724 (N.Y.1994)—§ **13.7, n. 6.**

Brusco v. Miller, 167 Misc.2d 54, 639 N.Y.S.2d 246 (N.Y.Sup.App.Term 1995)—§ **13.12, n. 11;** § **13.16, n. 2;** § **13.18, n. 1.**

Bryant, People v., 170 A.D.2d 520, 566 N.Y.S.2d 83 (N.Y.A.D. 2 Dept.1991)—§ **38.21, n. 11, 16.**

Bryant, People v., 139 A.D.2d 750, 527 N.Y.S.2d 500 (N.Y.A.D. 2 Dept.1988)—§ **38.28, n. 19.**

Bryant v. TRW, Inc., 487 F.Supp. 1234 (E.D.Mich.1980)—§ **7.31, n. 11.**

Bryant Ave. Tenants' Ass'n v. Koch, 620 N.Y.S.2d 825, 644 N.E.2d 1381 (N.Y. 1994)—§ **13.76, n. 3.**

Bryson Properties, XVIII, In re, 961 F.2d 496 (4th Cir.1992)—§ **9.154, n. 3.**

Brzonkala v. Virginia Polytechnic and State University, 935 F.Supp. 779 (W.D.Va. 1996)—§ **18.53, n. 8.**

B.S., Matter of, 6 I & N Dec. 305 (A.G. 1955)—§ **19.8, n. 9.**

B. T. Productions, Inc. v. Barr, 405 N.Y.S.2d 9, 376 N.E.2d 171 (N.Y.1978)—§ **4.62, n. 5.**

TABLE OF CASES

BT/SAP Pool C Associates v. Coltex Loop Central Three Partners, 203 B.R. 527 (S.D.N.Y.1996)—§ **9.166, n. 11.**
Buchardt, In re, 114 B.R. 362 (Bkrtcy. N.D.N.Y.1990)—§ **8.15, n. 2.**
Buckaloo v. Johnson, 122 Cal.Rptr. 745, 537 P.2d 865 (Cal.1975)—§ **17.29, n. 12.**
Buckley v. Buckley, 142 Misc.2d 560, 537 N.Y.S.2d 943 (N.Y.Sup.1989)—§ **21.30, n. 8.**
Buckley v. Fitzsimmons, 509 U.S. 259, 113 S.Ct. 2606, 125 L.Ed.2d 209 (1993)—§ **18.31, n. 3.**
Buckner for Benefit of Buckner, Matter of, 157 Misc.2d 23, 595 N.Y.S.2d 862 (N.Y.Sur.1993)—§ **22.40, n. 2, 4; § 22.47, n. 12.**
Buffalo Broadcasting Co. Inc. v. New York State Dept. of Correctional Services, 174 A.D.2d 212, 578 N.Y.S.2d 928 (N.Y.A.D. 3 Dept.1992)—§ **3.29, n. 9.**
Buffalo, City of v. J. W. Clement Co., 321 N.Y.S.2d 345, 269 N.E.2d 895 (N.Y. 1971)—§ **14.93, n. 1, 2.**
Buffalo News, Inc. v. Buffalo Enterprise Development Corp., 619 N.Y.S.2d 695, 644 N.E.2d 277 (N.Y.1994)—§ **3.29, n. 4.**
Buffalo Urban Renewal Agency, City of v. Lane Bryant Queens, Inc., 90 A.D.2d 976, 456 N.Y.S.2d 568 (N.Y.A.D. 4 Dept 1982)—§ **13.51, n. 8.**
Buffalo Urban Renewal Agency, City of v. Moreton, 100 A.D.2d 20, 473 N.Y.S.2d 278 (N.Y.A.D. 4 Dept.1984)—§ **14.25, n. 2; § 14.34, n. 4; § 14.64, n. 4; § 14.65, n. 1.**
Buffolino v. Long Island Sav. Bank, FSB, 126 A.D.2d 508, 510 N.Y.S.2d 628 (N.Y.A.D. 2 Dept.1987)—§ **17.25, n. 1; § 17.28, n. 4.**
Bulk Farms, Inc. v. Martin, 963 F.2d 1286 (9th Cir.1992)—§ **19.33, n. 2.**
Bulkin v. Western Kraft East, Inc., 422 F.Supp. 437 (E.D.Pa.1976)—§ **17.30, n. 1.**
Bullard, People v., 84 A.D.2d 845, 444 N.Y.S.2d 171 (N.Y.A.D. 2 Dept.1981)—§ **38.8, n. 225.**
Bullis v. State, 51 Misc.2d 448, 273 N.Y.S.2d 392 (N.Y.Ct.Cl.1966)—§ **14.92, n. 2.**
Bumpurs v. New York City Housing Authority, 139 A.D.2d 438, 527 N.Y.S.2d 217 (N.Y.A.D. 1 Dept.1988)—§ **30.14, n. 2, 4.**
Bunge Corp. v. Manufacturers Hanover Trust Co., 65 Misc.2d 829, 318 N.Y.S.2d 819 (N.Y.Sup.1971)—§ **5.8, n. 2.**
Burdick v. Bryant, 111 Misc.2d 756, 444 N.Y.S.2d 997 (N.Y.Sup.1981)—§ **16.127, n. 13.**

Burford v. Sun Oil Co., 319 U.S. 315, 63 S.Ct. 1098, 87 L.Ed. 1424 (1943)—§ **18.36; § 18.36, n. 6.**
Burger v. Litton Industries, Inc., 1995 WL 363741 (S.D.N.Y.1995)—§ **17.72, n. 6.**
Burgos v. Hopkins, 14 F.3d 787 (2nd Cir. 1994)—§ **18.37, n. 3.**
Burke, Matter of, 82 A.D.2d 260, 441 N.Y.S.2d 542 (N.Y.A.D. 2 Dept.1981)—§ **25.28, n. 6.**
Burke v. Crosson, 623 N.Y.S.2d 524, 647 N.E.2d 736 (N.Y.1995)—§ **39.4, n. 6, 9.**
Burke v. Crosson, 191 A.D.2d 998, 595 N.Y.S.2d 274 (N.Y.A.D. 4 Dept.1993)—§ **28.33; § 28.33, n. 4.**
Burke v. Denison, 203 A.D.2d 642, 609 N.Y.S.2d 959 (N.Y.A.D. 3 Dept.1994)—§ **16.92, n. 3.**
Burke v. Yudelson, 81 Misc.2d 870, 368 N.Y.S.2d 779 (N.Y.Sup.1975)—§ **3.29, n. 10.**
Burke, Kuipers & Mahoney v. Dallas Dispatch Co., 253 A.D. 206, 1 N.Y.S.2d 674 (N.Y.A.D. 1 Dept.1938)—§ **30.37, n. 7.**
Burnette, People v., 160 Misc.2d 1005, 612 N.Y.S.2d 774 (N.Y.Sup.1994)—§ **33.34, n. 2.**
Burns v. Burns, 618 N.Y.S.2d 761, 643 N.E.2d 80 (N.Y.1994)—§ **21.38; § 21.38, n. 3; § 21.43; § 21.43, n. 6, 7, 10.**
Burns, Estate of, 130 Misc.2d 317, 496 N.Y.S.2d 921 (N.Y.Sur.1985)—§ **25.16, n. 3.**
Burns v. Reed, 500 U.S. 478, 111 S.Ct. 1934, 114 L.Ed.2d 547 (1991)—§ **18.31, n. 3.**
Burns Jackson Miller Summit & Spitzer v. Lindner, 88 A.D.2d 50, 452 N.Y.S.2d 80 (N.Y.A.D. 2 Dept.1982)—§ **17.23, n. 3.**
Burstein, Matter of Estate of, 160 Misc.2d 900, 611 N.Y.S.2d 739 (N.Y.Sur.1994)—§ **23.81, n. 8.**
Burton, People v., 214 A.D.2d 1037, 626 N.Y.S.2d 918 (N.Y.A.D. 4 Dept.1995)—§ **38.25, n. 26.**
Burton, People v., 189 A.D.2d 532, 597 N.Y.S.2d 488 (N.Y.A.D. 3 Dept.1993)—§ **3.29, n. 3; § 18.66, n. 2.**
Burts, People v., 571 N.Y.S.2d 418, 574 N.E.2d 1024 (N.Y.1991)—§ **38.28, n. 29.**
Bush v. Dolan, 149 A.D.2d 799, 540 N.Y.S.2d 21 (N.Y.A.D. 3 Dept.1989)—§ **29.12, n. 4.**
Bush v. St. Clare's Hosp., 602 N.Y.S.2d 324, 621 N.E.2d 691 (N.Y.1993)—§ **17.30, n. 4.**
Busick, Matter of, 831 F.2d 745 (7th Cir. 1987)—§ **9.10, n. 8.**
Business and Community Coalition to Save Brownsville v. New York City Dept. of Environmental Protection, 173 A.D.2d

TABLE OF CASES

586, 570 N.Y.S.2d 169 (N.Y.A.D. 2 Dept. 1991)—§ **15.6, n. 14.**
Business Envelope Mfrs., Inc. v. Williams, 40 A.D.2d 597, 336 N.Y.S.2d 62 (N.Y.A.D. 1 Dept.1972)—§ **26.43, n. 5.**
Butchino, People v., 141 A.D.2d 986, 530 N.Y.S.2d 642 (N.Y.A.D. 3 Dept.1988)—§ **38.19, n. 44.**
Butler v. Brown, 180 A.D.2d 406, 579 N.Y.S.2d 79 (N.Y.A.D. 1 Dept.1992)—§ **30.40, n. 7.**
Butler v. Castro, 896 F.2d 698 (2nd Cir. 1990)—§ **18.11, n. 1;** § **18.94.**
Butler v. L. Sonneborn Sons, Inc., 296 F.2d 623 (2nd Cir.1961)—§ **27.36;** § **27.36, n. 2, 5.**
Butner v. United States, 440 U.S. 48, 99 S.Ct. 914, 59 L.Ed.2d 136 (1979)—§ **9.49, n. 2.**
Buttonwood Partners, Ltd., In re, 111 B.R. 57 (Bkrtcy.S.D.N.Y.1990)—§ **9.166, n. 5.**
Butz v. Economou, 438 U.S. 478, 98 S.Ct. 2894, 57 L.Ed.2d 895 (1978)—§ **18.31, n. 5.**
Bynum, People v., 523 N.Y.S.2d 492, 518 N.E.2d 4 (N.Y.1987)—§ **38.19, n. 54.**
Byrne on behalf of Pine Grove Beach Ass'n v. New York State Office of Parks, Recreation & Historic Preservation, 101 A.D.2d 701, 476 N.Y.S.2d 42 (N.Y.A.D. 4 Dept.1984)—§ **14.15, n. 1.**

C

Caban v. Mohammed, 441 U.S. 380, 99 S.Ct. 1760, 60 L.Ed.2d 297 (1979)—§ **20.30;** § **20.30, n. 2.**
Cabbad v. Melendez, 81 A.D.2d 626, 438 N.Y.S.2d 120 (N.Y.A.D. 2 Dept.1981)—§ **13.66, n. 2.**
Cabey, People v., 626 N.Y.S.2d 20, 649 N.E.2d 1164 (N.Y.1995)—§ **38.19, n. 61.**
Cabrera v. Jakabovitz, 24 F.3d 372 (2nd Cir.1994)—§ **18.45, n. 6;** § **18.46, n. 2;** § **18.51, n. 2.**
Cadin Const. Corp. v. Adam Jay Associates, 86 Misc.2d 407, 382 N.Y.S.2d 671 (N.Y.Sup.1976)—§ **10.94, n. 3.**
Cadwallader v. State, 210 A.D.2d 885, 621 N.Y.S.2d 1013 (N.Y.A.D. 4 Dept.1994)—§ **37.28, n. 23.**
Cafaro v. Pedersen, 123 A.D.2d 860, 507 N.Y.S.2d 645 (N.Y.A.D. 2 Dept.1986)—§ **4.24, n. 7.**
Cagney v. Blaikie, 219 A.D.2d 483, 631 N.Y.S.2d 514 (N.Y.A.D. 1 Dept.1995)—§ **30.30, n. 2.**
Cahill, People ex rel. Hoefle v., 188 N.Y. 489, 81 N.E. 453 (N.Y.1907)—§ **3.17, n. 6.**
Cahill v. Rosa, 651 N.Y.S.2d 344, 674 N.E.2d 274 (N.Y.1996)—§ **18.54, n. 4.**
Cahn v. Town of Huntington, 328 N.Y.S.2d 672, 278 N.E.2d 908 (N.Y.1972)—§ **3.7, n. 6.**
Cahn v. Vario, 32 A.D.2d 1035, 304 N.Y.S.2d 235 (N.Y.A.D. 2 Dept.1969)—§ **38.8, n. 83.**
Cahn v. Vario, 32 A.D.2d 564, 300 N.Y.S.2d 657 (N.Y.A.D. 2 Dept.1969)—§ **38.8;** § **38.8, n. 88.**
Caiado v. Bischoff, 140 Misc.2d 1014, 532 N.Y.S.2d 213 (N.Y.City Ct.1988)—§ **13.51, n. 6.**
Caira v. Bell Bay Properties, Inc., 143 A.D.2d 870, 533 N.Y.S.2d 550 (N.Y.A.D. 2 Dept.1988)—§ **12.29, n. 5.**
Calamari v. Grace, 98 A.D.2d 74, 469 N.Y.S.2d 942 (N.Y.A.D. 2 Dept.1983)—§ **28.11, n. 4.**
Calandro v. Bowen, 697 F.Supp. 423 (D.Wyo.1988)—§ **34.6, n. 8.**
Calcagni Const. Co., Inc. v. Zoning Bd. of Appeals, Town and Village of Harrison, 56 A.D.2d 845, 392 N.Y.S.2d 86 (N.Y.A.D. 2 Dept.1977)—§ **16.66, n. 3.**
Calder v. Planned Community Living, Inc., 1995 WL 456400 (S.D.N.Y.1995)—§ **17.23, n. 4;** § **17.29, n. 11;** § **17.30, n. 5;** § **17.32, n. 5;** § **17.35, n. 10.**
Caldor, Inc. NY, In re, 193 B.R. 165 (Bkrtcy.S.D.N.Y.1996)—§ **9.29, n. 5, 13, 14, 16;** § **9.48, n. 4.**
Caldwell v. Caldwell, 298 N.Y. 146, 81 N.E.2d 60 (N.Y.1948)—§ **21.3, n. 1.**
Caldwell v. Village of Island Park, 304 N.Y. 268, 107 N.E.2d 441 (N.Y.1952)—§ **3.30, n. 9.**
Califano v. Sanders, 430 U.S. 99, 97 S.Ct. 980, 51 L.Ed.2d 192 (1977)—§ **34.62, n. 1.**
California v. Greenwood, 486 U.S. 35, 108 S.Ct. 1625, 100 L.Ed.2d 30 (1988)—§ **18.9, n. 3.**
Callahan, In re, 158 B.R. 898 (Bkrtcy. W.D.N.Y.1993)—§ **9.249, n. 6, 9.**
Callahan, Matter of, 155 A.D.2d 454, 547 N.Y.S.2d 113 (N.Y.A.D. 2 Dept.1989)—§ **24.94, n. 4.**
Callahan, People v., 590 N.Y.S.2d 46, 604 N.E.2d 108 (N.Y.1992)—§ **37.37, n. 72;** § **38.8;** § **38.8, n. 12, 15, 24, 205, 220.**
Callan v. State, 134 A.D.2d 882, 521 N.Y.S.2d 923 (N.Y.A.D. 4 Dept.1987)—§ **30.30, n. 7.**
Camara v. Municipal Court of City and County of San Francisco, 387 U.S. 523, 87 S.Ct. 1727, 18 L.Ed.2d 930 (1967)—§ **4.62, n. 4.**
Camarda v. Danziger, Bangser & Weiss, 167 A.D.2d 152, 561 N.Y.S.2d 233 (N.Y.A.D. 1 Dept.1990)—§ **28.12;** § **28.12, n. 13.**

TABLE OF CASES

Camarella v. East Irondequoit Central School Bd., 356 N.Y.S.2d 553, 313 N.E.2d 29 (N.Y.1974)—§ **37.67, n. 7.**

Cameron, People v., 219 A.D.2d 662, 631 N.Y.S.2d 717 (N.Y.A.D. 2 Dept.1995)—§ **38.40, n. 3.**

Cameron, People v., 193 A.D.2d 752, 597 N.Y.S.2d 724 (N.Y.A.D. 2 Dept.1993)—§ **38.8, n. 42, 60;** § **38.10, n. 68.**

Cameron, People v., N.Y.L.J., 11/15/93, p. 28, col. 2, 2d Dep't.—§ **38.40, n. 3.**

Camilla, Matter of, 163 Misc.2d 272, 620 N.Y.S.2d 897 (N.Y.Fam.Ct.1994)—§ **20.7, n. 3;** § **20.17, n. 5;** § **20.21, n. 1.**

Camillo v. Geer, 185 A.D.2d 192, 587 N.Y.S.2d 306 (N.Y.A.D. 1 Dept.1992)—§ **30.31, n. 11.**

Cammarata, People v., 216 A.D.2d 965, 629 N.Y.S.2d 716 (N.Y.A.D. 4 Dept.1995)—§ **38.8, n. 19.**

Cammarota v. Bella Vista Development Corp., 88 A.D.2d 703, 451 N.Y.S.2d 309 (N.Y.A.D. 3 Dept.1982)—§ **13.26, n. 1;** § **37.20, n. 3.**

Campaign For Fiscal Equity, Inc. v. Marino, 638 N.Y.S.2d 591, 661 N.E.2d 1372 (N.Y. 1995)—§ **37.31;** § **37.31, n. 6.**

Campbell v. City of N.Y., 244 N.Y. 317, 155 N.E. 628 (N.Y.1927)—§ **3.32, n. 18.**

Campbell, People v., 541 N.Y.S.2d 756, 539 N.E.2d 584 (N.Y.1989)—§ **38.8, n. 166, 204.**

Campbell v. Pesce, 468 N.Y.S.2d 865, 456 N.E.2d 806 (N.Y.1983)—§ **38.10, n. 126, 136.**

Campbell v. WABC Towing Corp., 78 Misc.2d 671, 356 N.Y.S.2d 455 (N.Y.Sup. 1974)—§ **7.28, n. 8;** § **7.59.**

Camperlino and Fatti Builders, Inc. v. Dimovich Const. Corp., 198 A.D.2d 803, 604 N.Y.S.2d 389 (N.Y.A.D. 4 Dept. 1993)—§ **12.29, n. 10.**

Campo Corp. v. Feinberg, 279 A.D. 302, 110 N.Y.S.2d 250 (N.Y.A.D. 3 Dept.1952)—§ **4.20, n. 2.**

Campos–Serrano, United States v., 404 U.S. 293, 92 S.Ct. 471, 30 L.Ed.2d 457 (1971)—§ **19.4, n. 2.**

Canadian Industrial Alcohol Co. v. Dunbar Molasses Co., 258 N.Y. 194, 179 N.E. 383 (N.Y.1932)—§ **30.27, n. 5.**

Canavan v. Steenburg, 170 A.D.2d 858, 566 N.Y.S.2d 960 (N.Y.A.D. 3 Dept.1991)—§ **28.12;** § **28.12, n. 11.**

Cancemi v. People, 18 N.Y. 128 (N.Y. 1858)—§ **38.19;** § **38.19, n. 10.**

Cannon v. Murphy, 196 A.D.2d 498, 600 N.Y.S.2d 965 (N.Y.A.D. 2 Dept.1993)—§ **16.18, n. 20;** § **16.58;** § **16.58, n. 3;** § **16.112;** § **16.112, n. 1.**

Canosa v. Abadir, 221 A.D.2d 579, 635 N.Y.S.2d 490 (N.Y.A.D. 2 Dept.1995)—§ **37.37, n. 79.**

Canron Corp. v. City of New York, 652 N.Y.S.2d 211, 674 N.E.2d 1117 (N.Y. 1996)—§ **10.98, n. 3.**

Canton, Ohio, City of v. Harris, 489 U.S. 378, 109 S.Ct. 1197, 103 L.Ed.2d 412 (1989)—§ **18.34, n. 4.**

Cantor, People v., 365 N.Y.S.2d 509, 324 N.E.2d 872 (N.Y.1975)—§ **33.4, n. 1.**

Capdevilla v. Capdevilla, 149 A.D.2d 312, 539 N.Y.S.2d 365 (N.Y.A.D. 1 Dept. 1989)—§ **21.4, n. 5.**

Capers, People v., 198 A.D.2d 60, 603 N.Y.S.2d 14 (N.Y.A.D. 1 Dept.1993)—§ **38.19, n. 44.**

Capicchioni v. Morrissey, 205 A.D.2d 959, 613 N.Y.S.2d 499 (N.Y.A.D. 3 Dept. 1994)—§ **37.28, n. 10.**

Capital Newspapers Div. of Hearst Corp. v. Burns, 109 A.D.2d 92, 490 N.Y.S.2d 651 (N.Y.A.D. 3 Dept.1985)—§ **18.65, n. 5.**

Capital Resources Corp. v. Doe, 154 Misc.2d 864, 586 N.Y.S.2d 706 (N.Y.City Civ.Ct. 1992)—§ **13.18, n. 7.**

Capital Telephone Co., Inc. v. Pattersonville Telephone Co., Inc., 451 N.Y.S.2d 11, 436 N.E.2d 461 (N.Y.1982)—§ **4.73, n. 3.**

Caplan v. Winslett, 218 A.D.2d 148, 637 N.Y.S.2d 967 (N.Y.A.D. 1 Dept.1996)—§ **18.82, n. 3.**

Caplin v. Caplin, 33 A.D.2d 908, 307 N.Y.S.2d 486 (N.Y.A.D. 2 Dept.1970)—§ **37.35, n. 6.**

Capolongo, People v., 623 N.Y.S.2d 778, 647 N.E.2d 1286 (N.Y.1995)—§ **38.19, n. 107.**

Capozzi, People v., 133 A.D.2d 481, 519 N.Y.S.2d 210 (N.Y.A.D. 3 Dept.1987)—§ **38.19, n. 64.**

Capparelli, State ex rel. v. McGrane, 189 A.D.2d 561, 592 N.Y.S.2d 15 (N.Y.A.D. 1 Dept.1993)—§ **38.8, n. 78.**

Cappiello v. Cappiello, 495 N.Y.S.2d 318, 485 N.E.2d 983 (N.Y.1985)—§ **21.40, n. 9.**

Cappiello v. Ragen Precision Industries, Inc., 192 N.J.Super. 523, 471 A.2d 432 (N.J.Super.A.D.1984)—§ **17.29, n. 3.**

Caprara v. Chrysler Corp., 436 N.Y.S.2d 251, 417 N.E.2d 545 (N.Y.1981)—§ **27.9, n. 3;** § **27.11, n. 2;** § **27.31, n. 1;** § **27.34, n. 3;** § **29.16, n. 1.**

Capuano (State Report Title: People, Application of v. Capuano), 68 Misc.2d 481, 327 N.Y.S.2d 17 (N.Y.Sup.1971)—§ **38.58, n. 3.**

Caraballo, People v., 221 A.D.2d 553, 634 N.Y.S.2d 135 (N.Y.A.D. 2 Dept.1995)—§ **38.19, n. 49.**

TABLE OF CASES

Carat Diamond Corp. v. Underwriters at Lloyd's, London, 123 A.D.2d 544, 506 N.Y.S.2d 708 (N.Y.A.D. 1 Dept.1986)—§ 31.26, n. 9.

Carballo by Tersigni, Matter of, 137 Misc.2d 553, 521 N.Y.S.2d 375 (N.Y.Fam.Ct. 1987)—§ 20.78; § 20.78, n. 3.

Carbone, People v., 159 A.D.2d 511, 552 N.Y.S.2d 380 (N.Y.A.D. 2 Dept.1990)—§ 38.8; § 38.8, n. 218.

Carbone on Behalf of Osorio, People ex rel. v. Warden of Queens House of Detention, 219 A.D.2d 610, 631 N.Y.S.2d 528 (N.Y.A.D. 2 Dept.1995)—§ 38.8, n. 76.

Carcone v. Gordon Heating & Air Conditioning Co., Inc., 212 A.D.2d 1017, 623 N.Y.S.2d 679 (N.Y.A.D. 4 Dept.1995)—§ 5.50, n. 9.

Cardinale v. Golinello, 401 N.Y.S.2d 191, 372 N.E.2d 26 (N.Y.1977)—§ 28.21; § 28.21, n. 10.

Cardinal Industries, Inc., In re, 109 B.R. 755 (Bkrtcy.S.D.Ohio 1990)—§ 9.138, n. 1.

Carey v. Oswego County Legislature, 91 A.D.2d 62, 458 N.Y.S.2d 283 (N.Y.A.D. 3 Dept.1983)—§ 3.14, n. 6.

Carey v. Piphus, 435 U.S. 247, 98 S.Ct. 1042, 55 L.Ed.2d 252 (1978)—§ 18.18, n. 12.

Caristo Const. Corp. v. Diners Financial Corp., 289 N.Y.S.2d 175, 236 N.E.2d 461 (N.Y.1968)—§ 10.94, n. 1.

Carjef Realty Corp. v. Straker, N.Y.L.J., 2/18/83, p.13, col.5, 11 HCR 10 (App. Term, 2d Dep't)—§ 13.18, n. 14.

Carlin v. Equitable Life Assur. Soc. of United States, 440 N.Y.S.2d 926, 423 N.E.2d 403 (N.Y.1981)—§ 31.26, n. 1.

Carll v. Oakley, 97 N.Y. 633 (N.Y.1884)—§ 37.37, n. 92.

Carlson, People v., 222 A.D. 54, 225 N.Y.S. 149 (N.Y.A.D. 4 Dept.1927)—§ 8.23, n. 19.

Carlucci v. Piper Aircraft Corp., 102 F.R.D. 472 (S.D.Fla.1984)—§ 27.33; § 27.33, n. 6.

Carman v. European American Bank & Trust Co., 576 N.Y.S.2d 90, 581 N.E.2d 1345 (N.Y.1991)—§ 12.55, n. 12.

Carmania Corp., N.V., In re, 154 B.R. 160 (S.D.N.Y.1993)—§ 9.69, n. 8.

Carmel, Town of v. Meadowbrook Nat. Bank of Nassau County, 15 Misc.2d 789, 182 N.Y.S.2d 465 (N.Y.Sup.1959)—§ 16.66, n. 1.

Carmel, Town of v. Suburban Outdoor Advertising Co., Inc., 127 A.D.2d 204, 514 N.Y.S.2d 387 (N.Y.A.D. 2 Dept.1987)—§ 16.25, n. 12, 13.

Carmine v. Murphy, 285 N.Y. 413, 35 N.E.2d 19 (N.Y.1941)—§ 5.7, n. 6.

Carmine A., People v., 439 N.Y.S.2d 915, 422 N.E.2d 575 (N.Y.1981)—§ 38.19, n. 16.

Carmody, People v., 203 A.D.2d 298, 609 N.Y.S.2d 670 (N.Y.A.D. 2 Dept.1994)—§ 38.10, n. 60.

Carnat Realty, Inc. v. Town of Islip, 34 A.D.2d 780, 311 N.Y.S.2d 239 (N.Y.A.D. 2 Dept.1970)—§ 16.110, n. 3.

Carney v. Carney, 202 A.D.2d 907, 609 N.Y.S.2d 425 (N.Y.A.D. 3 Dept.1994)—§ 21.38, n. 6.

Carney v. Feldstein, 193 A.D.2d 1016, 597 N.Y.S.2d 982 (N.Y.A.D. 3 Dept.1993)—§ 38.8, n. 204.

Carney v. Memorial Hosp. and Nursing Home of Greene County, 485 N.Y.S.2d 984, 475 N.E.2d 451 (N.Y.1985)—§ 17.25, n. 7.

Carola v. Grogan, 102 A.D.2d 934, 477 N.Y.S.2d 525 (N.Y.A.D. 3 Dept.1984)—§ 2.65, n. 1.

Carolco Television, Inc. v. National Broadcasting (In re De Laurentiis Entertainment Group Inc.), 963 F.2d 1269 (9th Cir.1992)—§ 9.111, n. 5.

Caroline, Matter of, 218 A.D.2d 388, 638 N.Y.S.2d 997 (N.Y.A.D. 4 Dept.1996)—§ 20.39; § 20.39, n. 1.

Carp v. Marcus, 112 A.D.2d 546, 491 N.Y.S.2d 484 (N.Y.A.D. 3 Dept.1985)—§ 13.32, n. 9.

Carparelli Bros., Inc. v. State, 150 Misc.2d 720, 570 N.Y.S.2d 266 (N.Y.Sup.1991)—§ 14.1, n. 3.

Carr v. Axelrod, 798 F.Supp. 168 (S.D.N.Y. 1992)—§ 18.36, n. 5.

Carr v. Integon General Ins. Corp., 185 A.D.2d 831, 586 N.Y.S.2d 986 (N.Y.A.D. 2 Dept.1992)—§ 37.65, n. 70.

Carriage Court Inn, Inc. v. Rains, 138 Misc.2d 444, 524 N.Y.S.2d 647 (N.Y.City Civ.Ct.1988)—§ 13.51, n. 5; § 13.52, n. 7.

Carrols Equities Corp. v. Villnave, 57 A.D.2d 1044, 395 N.Y.S.2d 800 (N.Y.A.D. 4 Dept.1977)—§ 30.26, n. 9.

Cartagena, People v., 78 A.D.2d 601, 432 N.Y.S.2d 176 (N.Y.A.D. 1 Dept.1980)—§ 38.21; § 38.21, n. 15.

Carter, People v., 564 N.Y.S.2d 992, 566 N.E.2d 119 (N.Y.1990)—§ 38.19, n. 100.

Carter, People v., 483 N.Y.S.2d 654, 473 N.E.2d 6 (N.Y.1984)—§ 38.10, n. 62; § 38.20, n. 4; § 38.21, n. 23.

Carter v. Willert Home Products, Inc., 714 S.W.2d 506 (Mo.1986)—§ 17.25, n. 8.

Carucci v. Dulan, 24 A.D.2d 529, 261 N.Y.S.2d 677 (N.Y.A.D. 4 Dept.1965)—§ 3.25, n. 15.

TABLE OF CASES

Caruso v. Ward, 146 A.D.2d 22, 539 N.Y.S.2d 313 (N.Y.A.D. 1 Dept.1989)—§ 13.63, n. 2.

Cary v. Fisher, 101 A.D.2d 924, 475 N.Y.S.2d 628 (N.Y.A.D. 3 Dept.1984)—§ 28.10, n. 11, 12.

Case, People v., 396 N.Y.S.2d 841, 365 N.E.2d 872 (N.Y.1977)—§ 38.8, n. 193.

Casella v. Equifax Credit Information Services, 56 F.3d 469 (2nd Cir.1995)—§ 7.33; § 7.33, n. 7.

Casella v. Stumpf, 29 Misc.2d 460, 217 N.Y.S.2d 709 (N.Y.Sup.1961)—§ 16.124, n. 12.

Caselli v. Messina, 148 Misc.2d 671, 567 N.Y.S.2d 972 (N.Y.Sup.App.Term 1990)—§ 12.58, n. 1.

Casey v. Woodruff, 49 N.Y.S.2d 625 (N.Y.Sup.1944)—§ 1.66, n. 12.

Cashin v. City of New Rochelle, 256 N.Y. 190, 176 N.E. 138 (N.Y.1931)—§ 30.16, n. 1.

Casiano, People v., 501 N.Y.S.2d 808, 492 N.E.2d 1224 (N.Y.1986)—§ 38.38, n. 5.

Cassano v. Cassano, 628 N.Y.S.2d 10, 651 N.E.2d 878 (N.Y.1995)—§ 21.55; § 21.55, n. 3.

Cassano v. Cassano, 203 A.D.2d 563, 612 N.Y.S.2d 160 (N.Y.A.D. 2 Dept.1994)—§ 21.55, n. 10.

Cassas, People v., 622 N.Y.S.2d 228, 646 N.E.2d 449 (N.Y.1995)—§ 33.60, n. 2.

Cassia Corp. v. North Hills Holding Corp., 281 A.D. 709, 118 N.Y.S.2d 220 (N.Y.A.D. 2 Dept.1952)—§ 11.52, n. 3.

Castillo v. Carver Federal Sav. and Loan Ass'n, 125 A.D.2d 287, 508 N.Y.S.2d 574 (N.Y.A.D. 2 Dept.1986)—§ 11.30, n. 5.

Castillo, People v., 148 A.D.2d 463, 538 N.Y.S.2d 1009 (N.Y.A.D. 2 Dept.1989)—§ 38.10, n. 34.

Castle Associates v. Schwartz, 63 A.D.2d 481, 407 N.Y.S.2d 717 (N.Y.A.D. 2 Dept. 1978)—§ 12.66, n. 5.

Castle Hill Houses, Borough of Bronx, City of New York, In re, 113 N.Y.S.2d 417 (N.Y.Sup.1950)—§ 14.83, n. 3.

Castle Properties Co. v. Ackerson, 163 A.D.2d 785, 558 N.Y.S.2d 334 (N.Y.A.D. 3 Dept.1990)—§ 16.107, n. 3, 5.

Castore v. Breite, 167 A.D.2d 799, 563 N.Y.S.2d 361 (N.Y.A.D. 3 Dept.1990)—§ 16.65, n. 2.

Castro, People v., 111 A.D.2d 673, 491 N.Y.S.2d 268 (N.Y.A.D. 1 Dept.1985)—§ 38.21, n. 46.

Castro, People v., 442 N.Y.S.2d 500, 425 N.E.2d 888 (N.Y.1981)—§ 38.27, n. 18.

Castro, People v., 80 A.D.2d 535, 436 N.Y.S.2d 22 (N.Y.A.D. 1 Dept.1981)—§ 38.20, n. 15.

Catalfano, People v., 228 A.D. 112, 239 N.Y.S. 165 (N.Y.A.D. 4 Dept.1930)—§ 38.4, n. 6.

Catania v. Lippman, 98 A.D.2d 826, 470 N.Y.S.2d 487 (N.Y.A.D. 3 Dept.1983)—§ 28.21; § 28.21, n. 12; § 28.26, n. 4.

Catholic Charities of Roman Catholic Diocese of Syracuse v. Zoning Bd. of Appeals of City of Norwich, 187 A.D.2d 903, 590 N.Y.S.2d 918 (N.Y.A.D. 3 Dept. 1992)—§ 16.131, n. 12.

Cathy v. Prober, 195 A.D.2d 999, 600 N.Y.S.2d 561 (N.Y.A.D. 4 Dept.1993)—§ 3.20, n. 5.

Catten, People v., 516 N.Y.S.2d 186, 508 N.E.2d 920 (N.Y.1987)—§ 38.19, n. 76.

Catterson, Matter of, 215 A.D.2d 653, 628 N.Y.S.2d 502 (N.Y.A.D. 2 Dept.1995)—§ 37.37; § 37.37, n. 85.

Caussade, People v., 162 A.D.2d 4, 560 N.Y.S.2d 648 (N.Y.A.D. 2 Dept.1990)—§ 33.78, n. 3; § 33.79, n. 2.

Cavaretta v. Cavaretta, 127 A.D.2d 1002, 512 N.Y.S.2d 945 (N.Y.A.D. 4 Dept. 1987)—§ 21.38, n. 2.

Cave v. Zoning Bd. of Appeals of Village of Fredonia, 49 A.D.2d 228, 373 N.Y.S.2d 932 (N.Y.A.D. 4 Dept.1975)—§ 16.63, n. 1.

Cawley v. City of Port Jervis, 753 F.Supp. 128 (S.D.N.Y.1990)—§ 16.125, n. 18.

Cawley v. SCM Corp., 534 N.Y.S.2d 344, 530 N.E.2d 1264 (N.Y.1988)—§ 1.27, n. 5.

Cayuga County v. McHugh, 176 N.Y.S.2d 643, 152 N.E.2d 73 (N.Y.1958)—§ 3.7, n. 8.

C.B. Foods, Inc. v. Quarex Co., 204 A.D.2d 504, 611 N.Y.S.2d 915 (N.Y.A.D. 2 Dept. 1994)—§ 37.37, n. 40.

C.B.H. Properties, Inc. v. Rose, 205 A.D.2d 686, 613 N.Y.S.2d 913 (N.Y.A.D. 2 Dept. 1994)—§ 16.92, n. 4.

C.B. Strain & Son, Inc. v. J. Baranello & Sons, 90 A.D.2d 924, 457 N.Y.S.2d 925 (N.Y.A.D. 3 Dept.1982)—§ 10.13, n. 1, 2.

CECOS Intern., Inc. v. Jorling, 895 F.2d 66 (2nd Cir.1990)—§ 18.36, n. 4.

Cedeno, People v., 219 A.D.2d 828, 632 N.Y.S.2d 1016 (N.Y.A.D. 4 Dept.1995)—§ 38.21, n. 49.

Celeste Court Apartments, Inc., Matter of, 47 B.R. 470 (D.Del.1985)—§ 9.160, n. 3.

Cellular Information Systems, Inc., In re, 171 B.R. 926 (Bkrtcy.S.D.N.Y.1994)—§ 9.166, n. 7.

Cellular Telephone Co. v. Meyer, 200 A.D.2d 743, 607 N.Y.S.2d 81 (N.Y.A.D. 2 Dept.1994)—§ 16.130, n. 5.

TABLE OF CASES

Cellular Telephone Co. v. Rosenberg, 604 N.Y.S.2d 895, 624 N.E.2d 990 (N.Y. 1993)—§ **16.130**; § **16.130, n. 1.**

Cellular Telephone Company v. Town-Village of Harrison, (Sup.Ct., Westchester County, Justice Cowhey) N.Y.L.J., 11/30/95, p.35, col.3—§ **16.130, n. 7, 8.**

Cellular Telephone Co. v. Village of Tarrytown, 209 A.D.2d 57, 624 N.Y.S.2d 170 (N.Y.A.D. 2 Dept.1995)—§ **16.130, n. 6.**

Celotex Corp. v. Edwards, 514 U.S. 300, 115 S.Ct. 1493, 131 L.Ed.2d 403 (1995)—§ **9.18, n. 3;** § **9.19, n. 6.**

Cen-Pen Corp. v. Hanson, 58 F.3d 89 (4th Cir.1995)—§ **9.167, n. 4.**

Centerbank v. D'Assaro, 158 Misc.2d 92, 600 N.Y.S.2d 1015 (N.Y.Sup.1993)—§ **11.12, n. 1.**

Centereach Rentals Inc. v. Town of Huntington, 150 Misc.2d 462, 574 N.Y.S.2d 636 (N.Y.Dist.Ct.1991)—§ **3.24, n. 13.**

Central Budget Corp. v. Garrett, 48 A.D.2d 825, 368 N.Y.S.2d 268 (N.Y.A.D. 2 Dept. 1975)—§ **7.26, n. 9.**

Central General Hosp. v. Bramex Ltd., 174 A.D.2d 556, 570 N.Y.S.2d 670 (N.Y.A.D. 2 Dept.1991)—§ **31.6, n. 7.**

Central Hudson Gas & Elec. Corp. v. Newman, 35 A.D.2d 989, 317 N.Y.S.2d 887 (N.Y.A.D. 2 Dept.1970)—§ **37.37, n. 75.**

Central Hudson Gas & Elec. Corp. v. Public Service Commission of New York, 447 U.S. 557, 100 S.Ct. 2343, 65 L.Ed.2d 341 (1980)—§ **16.25, n. 10.**

Central School Dist. No. 1 of Towns of Ontario, et al., Wayne County v. Rochester Gas & Elec. Corp., 61 Misc.2d 846, 306 N.Y.S.2d 765 (N.Y.Sup.1970)—§ **3.32, n. 15.**

Central Trust Co., Rochester v. Alcon Developers, Inc., 93 Misc.2d 686, 403 N.Y.S.2d 396 (N.Y.Sup.1978)—§ **11.50, n. 6.**

Central Trust Co., Rochester v. Goldman, 70 A.D.2d 767, 417 N.Y.S.2d 359 (N.Y.A.D. 4 Dept.1979)—§ **30.41, n. 1.**

Central Trust Co., Rochester v. Mann's Restaurants, 166 Misc. 381, 2 N.Y.S.2d 447 (N.Y.Sup.1938)—§ **36.4, n. 8.**

Century Apartments Assocs. v. Merritt, N.Y.L.J., 6/24/85, p.6, col.1 (App.Term, 1st Dep't)—§ **13.58, n. 7.**

Century Apartments, Inc. v. Yalkowsky, 106 Misc.2d 762, 435 N.Y.S.2d 627 (N.Y.City Civ.Ct.1980)—§ **13.32, n. 3, 6.**

Century Brass Prods., Inc. v. UAW Local 1604 (In re Century Brass Products, Inc.), 795 F.2d 265 (2nd Cir.1986)—§ **9.86, n. 5, 14.**

Century Circuit, Inc. v. Ott, 65 Misc.2d 250, 317 N.Y.S.2d 468 (N.Y.Sup.1970)—§ **16.111, n. 3, 6.**

Century Realty (A Div. of Century 21, Inc.) v. Grass, 117 Misc.2d 224, 457 N.Y.S.2d 731 (N.Y.City Civ.Ct.1982)—§ **13.18, n. 5.**

Cerf v. Diener, 210 N.Y. 156, 104 N.E. 126 (N.Y.1914)—§ **12.64, n. 2.**

C.F.C. Realty Corp. v. Empire Fire and Marine Ins. Co., 110 A.D.2d 508, 487 N.Y.S.2d 47 (N.Y.A.D. 1 Dept.1985)—§ **31.11, n. 8.**

CF Holding Corp., Matter of, 164 B.R. 799 (Bkrtcy.D.Conn.1994)—§ **9.29, n. 14.**

Chachkers, Application of, 159 Misc.2d 912, 606 N.Y.S.2d 959 (N.Y.Sup.1993)—§ **22.26, n. 2;** § **22.27, n. 1;** § **22.31, n. 2;** § **22.39, n. 6.**

Chachra v. Katharine Gibbs School Inc., 828 F.Supp. 176 (E.D.N.Y.1993)—§ **17.68, n. 5.**

Chae Chan Ping v. United States, 130 U.S. 581, 9 S.Ct. 623, 32 L.Ed. 1068 (1889)—§ **19.1, n. 5.**

Chaffin, Matter of, 816 F.2d 1070 (5th Cir. 1987)—§ **9.207, n. 2.**

Chaitovitz v. Lewis, 222 A.D.2d 392, 634 N.Y.S.2d 727 (N.Y.A.D. 2 Dept.1995)—§ **37.22, n. 1.**

Chalasani, In re, 92 F.3d 1300 (2nd Cir. 1996)—§ **9.127, n. 2.**

Chalfonte Realty Corp. v. Streator, Inc., 142 Misc.2d 501, 537 N.Y.S.2d 980 (N.Y.City Civ.Ct.1989)—§ **13.15, n. 15;** § **13.16, n. 1, 6;** § **13.41, n. 14.**

Chamberlain v. Bissell Inc., 547 F.Supp. 1067 (W.D.Mich.1982)—§ **17.30, n. 1.**

Chambers, 17 I & N Dec. 117 (I.D. 2730, BIA 1979)—§ **19.8, n. 10.**

Chambers v. Capital Cities/ABC, 851 F.Supp. 543 (S.D.N.Y.1994)—§ **17.68, n. 7.**

Chambers v. Glens Falls Ins. Co., 41 Misc.2d 727, 245 N.Y.S.2d 863 (N.Y.Sup. 1964)—§ **31.26, n. 9.**

Chambers' Will, In re, 169 Misc. 124, 7 N.Y.S.2d 250 (N.Y.Sur.1938)—§ **8.37, n. 6.**

Champagne v. State Farm Mut. Auto. Ins. Co., 185 A.D.2d 835, 586 N.Y.S.2d 813 (N.Y.A.D. 2 Dept.1992)—§ **30.15, n. 5.**

Chan v. Bell, 464 F.Supp. 125 (D.D.C. 1978)—§ **19.12, n. 6.**

Chan v. City of New York, 1 F.3d 96 (2nd Cir.1993)—§ **18.18, n. 5.**

Chan v. Immigration & Naturalization Service, 610 F.2d 651 (9th Cir.1979)—§ **19.48, n. 4.**

Chandler v. Coughlin, 131 Misc.2d 442, 500 N.Y.S.2d 628 (N.Y.Sup.1986)—§ **4.2, n. 41;** § **4.82, n. 5.**

Chang v. General Acc. Ins. Co. of America, 193 A.D.2d 521, 598 N.Y.S.2d 178

TABLE OF CASES

(N.Y.A.D. 1 Dept.1993)—§ **31.9, n. 16;** § **31.18, n. 17.**
Chang v. New York City Health and Hospitals Corp., 82 A.D.2d 764, 440 N.Y.S.2d 211 (N.Y.A.D. 1 Dept.1981)—§ **30.15, n. 10.**
Chanler v. Manocherian, 151 A.D.2d 432, 543 N.Y.S.2d 671 (N.Y.A.D. 1 Dept. 1989)—§ **37.29, n. 34.**
Channel Home Centers, Inc., In re, 989 F.2d 682 (3rd Cir.1993)—§ **9.77, n. 1.**
Channel Master Corp. v. Aluminium Limited Sales, Inc., 176 N.Y.S.2d 259, 151 N.E.2d 833 (N.Y.1958)—§ **17.27, n. 1.**
Chao v. Chang, 192 A.D.2d 649, 597 N.Y.S.2d 81 (N.Y.A.D. 2 Dept.1993)—§ **37.29, n. 8;** § **37.65, n. 11.**
Chapel v. Mitchell, 618 N.Y.S.2d 626, 642 N.E.2d 1082 (N.Y.1994)—§ **30.43, n. 3;** § **37.67, n. 11.**
Chaloupka v. Nassau Travel Center, N.Y.L.J., 2/1/80, p.13, col.5 (Appellate Term, Ninth and Tenth Judicial Districts)—§ **37.99, n. 3.**
Chapman v. California, 386 U.S. 18, 87 S.Ct. 824, 17 L.Ed.2d 705 (1967)—§ **38.19, n. 91.**
Chapman v. Houston Welfare Rights Organization, 441 U.S. 600, 99 S.Ct. 1905, 60 L.Ed.2d 508 (1979)—§ **18.16, n. 2.**
Chapman, People v., 227 A.D.2d 665, 641 N.Y.S.2d 472 (N.Y.A.D. 3 Dept.1996)—§ **38.10, n. 22.**
Chapman, People v., 137 A.D.2d 884, 524 N.Y.S.2d 863 (N.Y.A.D. 3 Dept.1988)—§ **38.19, n. 64.**
Charlebois v. J.M. Weller Associates, Inc., 535 N.Y.S.2d 356, 531 N.E.2d 1288 (N.Y. 1988)—§ **5.10, n. 4.**
Charles v. Diamond, 392 N.Y.S.2d 594, 360 N.E.2d 1295 (N.Y.1977)—§ **3.10, n. 8.**
Charles, People v., 168 A.D.2d 507, 562 N.Y.S.2d 748 (N.Y.A.D. 2 Dept.1990)—§ **38.19, n. 27.**
Charles A. Field Delivery Service, Inc., Matter of, 498 N.Y.S.2d 111, 488 N.E.2d 1223 (N.Y.1985)—§ **4.22, n. 1;** § **37.44, n. 15.**
Charles C. Kellogg & Sons Co. v. DeLia, 173 Misc. 156, 17 N.Y.S.2d 330 (N.Y.Sup. 1940)—§ **10.3, n. 2.**
Charlot, People v., 203 A.D.2d 374, 612 N.Y.S.2d 908 (N.Y.A.D. 2 Dept.1994)—§ **38.8, n. 223.**
Charlton v. United States Fire Ins. Co., 165 Misc.2d 90, 627 N.Y.S.2d 221 (N.Y.Sup. 1995)—§ **31.15, n. 6.**
Charnille, Matter of, 206 A.D.2d 423, 613 N.Y.S.2d 946 (N.Y.A.D. 2 Dept.1994)—§ **20.56;** § **20.56, n. 5.**

Charron, People v., 198 A.D.2d 722, 604 N.Y.S.2d 311 (N.Y.A.D. 3 Dept.1993)—§ **38.21, n. 43.**
Charter Co., In re, 50 B.R. 57 (Bkrtcy. W.D.Tex.1985)—§ **9.42, n. 1.**
Charter Land Development Corp. v. Hartmann, 170 A.D.2d 600, 566 N.Y.S.2d 375 (N.Y.A.D. 2 Dept.1991)—§ **16.50, n. 6.**
Chase, People v., 626 N.Y.S.2d 721, 650 N.E.2d 379 (N.Y.1995)—§ **38.10, n. 165;** § **38.19, n. 106.**
Chase Manhattan Bank, N.A. v. State, 103 A.D.2d 211, 479 N.Y.S.2d 983 (N.Y.A.D. 2 Dept.1984)—§ **14.86, n. 5.**
Chase Manhattan Bank (Nat. Ass'n) v. 264 Water Street Associates, 174 A.D.2d 504, 571 N.Y.S.2d 281 (N.Y.A.D. 1 Dept. 1991)—§ **1.10, n. 14.**
Chas. H. Sells, Inc. v. Chance Hills Joint Venture, 163 Misc.2d 814, 622 N.Y.S.2d 422 (N.Y.Sup.1995)—§ **10.5, n. 2;** § **10.6, n. 1.**
Chasin v. Chasin, 182 A.D.2d 862, 582 N.Y.S.2d 512 (N.Y.A.D. 3 Dept.1992)—§ **21.55, n. 3.**
Chas. S. Higgins Co. v. Higgins Soap Co., 144 N.Y. 462, 39 N.E. 490 (N.Y.1895)—§ **1.13, n. 19.**
Chassin v. Helaire Nursing Agency, Inc., 211 A.D.2d 581, 621 N.Y.S.2d 611 (N.Y.A.D. 1 Dept.1995)—§ **4.63, n. 5.**
Chateaugay Corp., In re, 10 F.3d 944 (2nd Cir.1993)—§ **9.25, n. 11.**
Chateaugay Corp., In re, 155 B.R. 625 (Bkrtcy.S.D.N.Y.1993)—§ **9.154, n. 4.**
Chatham, Village of v. Board of Fire Com'rs of Delmar Fire Dist., 90 A.D.2d 860, 456 N.Y.S.2d 494 (N.Y.A.D. 3 Dept.1982)—§ **5.31, n. 3.**
Chattman v. Bennett, 57 A.D.2d 618, 393 N.Y.S.2d 768 (N.Y.A.D. 2 Dept.1977)—§ **20.129;** § **20.129, n. 1.**
Chavez v. Nevell Mgmt. Co., 69 Misc.2d 718, 330 N.Y.S.2d 890 (N.Y.City Civ.Ct. 1972)—§ **13.14, n. 7.**
Chazon v. Parkway Medical Group, 168 A.D.2d 660, 563 N.Y.S.2d 488 (N.Y.A.D. 2 Dept.1990)—§ **37.29, n. 20.**
Cheche, People v., 151 Misc.2d 15, 571 N.Y.S.2d 992 (N.Y.Co.Ct.1991)—§ **18.85, n. 5.**
Checho v. State Tax Com'n of State, 111 A.D.2d 470, 488 N.Y.S.2d 859 (N.Y.A.D. 3 Dept.1985)—§ **35.80, n. 1.**
Chemical Bank v. Columbia Asphalt Corp., 70 A.D.2d 925, 417 N.Y.S.2d 756 (N.Y.A.D. 2 Dept.1979)—§ **11.54, n. 7.**
Chemical Bank v. Flaherty, 121 Misc.2d 509, 468 N.Y.S.2d 315 (N.Y.City Civ.Ct. 1983)—§ **8.27, n. 2.**

TABLE OF CASES

Chemical Specialties Mfrs. Ass'n v. Jorling, 626 N.Y.S.2d 1, 649 N.E.2d 1145 (N.Y. 1995)—§ **4.80, n. 7.**

Chennault, People v., 285 N.Y.S.2d 289, 232 N.E.2d 324 (N.Y.1967)—§ **33.57, n. 4.**

Chenu v. Board of Trustees, Police Pension Fund, Article No. 1, 12 A.D.2d 422, 212 N.Y.S.2d 818 (N.Y.A.D. 1 Dept.1961)—§ **21.32, n. 5.**

Cherilyn P., Matter of, 192 A.D.2d 1084, 596 N.Y.S.2d 233 (N.Y.A.D. 4 Dept. 1993)—§ **37.23, n. 2.**

Cherniakova (Kolischer), Matter of, N.Y.L.J., 7/10/92, p.21, col.4 (Sup.Ct., N.Y. County)—§ **22.26, n. 14.**

Chess, People v., 149 Misc.2d 430, 565 N.Y.S.2d 416 (N.Y.Just.Ct.1991)—§ **33.17; § 33.17, n. 7.**

Chester Civic Imp. Ass'n, Inc. v. New York Transit Authority, 122 A.D.2d 715, 505 N.Y.S.2d 638 (N.Y.A.D. 1 Dept.1986)—§ **4.69, n. 11.**

Chiaramonte v. Immigration and Naturalization Service, 626 F.2d 1093 (2nd Cir. 1980)—§ **19.48, n. 4.**

Chiarello v. Harold Sylvan, P.C., 161 A.D.2d 948, 557 N.Y.S.2d 517 (N.Y.A.D. 3 Dept. 1990)—§ **28.24, n. 4.**

Chicago, B. & Q.R. Co. v. City of Chicago, 166 U.S. 226, 17 S.Ct. 581, 41 L.Ed. 979 (1897)—§ **16.22, n. 1.**

Child World, Inc. v. Service Merchandise Co. (In re Child World, Inc.), 173 B.R. 473 (Bkrtcy.S.D.N.Y.1994)—§ **9.117, n. 3.**

Chilton, People v., 516 N.Y.S.2d 633, 509 N.E.2d 327 (N.Y.1987)—§ **33.5; § 33.5, n. 1.**

Chin v. Bowen, 833 F.2d 21 (2nd Cir. 1987)—§ **18.18, n. 4.**

Chinatown Apartments, Inc. v. Chu Cho Lam, 433 N.Y.S.2d 86, 412 N.E.2d 1312 (N.Y.1980)—§ **13.51, n. 3.**

Chinese Staff and Workers Ass'n v. City of New York, 509 N.Y.S.2d 499, 502 N.E.2d 176 (N.Y.1986)—§ **15.6, n. 21; § 16.52, n. 5.**

Chinichian, In re, 784 F.2d 1440 (9th Cir. 1986)—§ **9.81, n. 2.**

Chirico v. Office of Vocational and Educational Services for Individuals with Disabilities (VESID), 211 A.D.2d 258, 627 N.Y.S.2d 815 (N.Y.A.D. 3 Dept. 1995)—§ **37.87, n. 35.**

C.H.L.C. Realty Corp. v. Gottlieb, N.Y.L.J., 10/19/88, p.28, col.4, 16 HCR 376 (App. Term, 2d Dep't)—§ **13.33, n. 6.**

Chmiel, Matter of Will of, 164 Misc.2d 854, 626 N.Y.S.2d 681 (N.Y.Sur.1995)—§ **24.63, n. 4.**

Christ v. Lake Erie Distributors, Inc., 51 Misc.2d 811, 273 N.Y.S.2d 878 (N.Y.Sup. 1966)—§ **1.43, n. 18.**

Christal v. Petry, 275 A.D. 550, 90 N.Y.S.2d 620 (N.Y.A.D. 1 Dept.1949)—§ **2.46, n. 11.**

Christian, People v., 629 N.Y.S.2d 722, 653 N.E.2d 618 (N.Y.1995)—§ **38.27; § 38.27, n. 6.**

Christian, People v., 209 A.D.2d 259, 618 N.Y.S.2d 711 (N.Y.A.D. 1 Dept.1994)—§ **38.27, n. 7.**

Christian, People ex rel. Battista v., 249 N.Y. 314, 164 N.E. 111 (N.Y.1928)—§ **38.19; § 38.19, n. 11.**

Christiania General Ins. Corp. of New York v. Great American Ins. Co., 979 F.2d 268 (2nd Cir.1992)—§ **31.18, n. 1.**

Christina A., Matter of, 216 A.D.2d 928, 629 N.Y.S.2d 553 (N.Y.A.D. 4 Dept.1995)—§ **37.29, n. 35.**

Christine M., Matter of, 157 Misc.2d 4, 595 N.Y.S.2d 606 (N.Y.Fam.Ct.1992)—§ **18.28, n. 5, 6.**

Christman v. Bailey, 38 A.D.2d 773, 327 N.Y.S.2d 966 (N.Y.A.D. 3 Dept.1972)—§ **30.15, n. 16.**

Christman v. Filer, 167 A.D.2d 819, 562 N.Y.S.2d 311 (N.Y.A.D. 4 Dept.1990)—§ **5.31, n. 7.**

Christopher v. Great Atlantic & Pacific Tea Co., Inc., 564 N.Y.S.2d 715, 565 N.E.2d 1266 (N.Y.1990)—§ **37.29, n. 26.**

Christopher S., People v., 126 Misc.2d 594, 483 N.Y.S.2d 609 (N.Y.City Crim.Ct. 1984)—§ **33.51; § 33.51, n. 1.**

Chrysler Credit Corp. v. Smith, N.Y.L.J. (4/1/93), p.27, col. 1 (Civ.Ct.Kings Co.)—§ **7.55.**

Chrysler Motors Corp. v. Schachner, 166 A.D.2d 683, 561 N.Y.S.2d 595 (N.Y.A.D. 2 Dept.1990)—§ **7.17, n. 4.**

Church v. Town of Islip, 203 N.Y.S.2d 866, 168 N.E.2d 680 (N.Y.1960)—§ **16.8, n. 7; § 16.114, n. 1; § 16.115; § 16.115, n. 3.**

Church of St. Paul and St. Andrew v. Barwick, 505 N.Y.S.2d 24, 496 N.E.2d 183 (N.Y.1986)—§ **4.70, n. 3, 5.**

Ciaccio v. Housman, 97 Misc.2d 367, 411 N.Y.S.2d 524 (N.Y.Sup.1978)—§ **29.49, n. 1.**

Ciaccio, People v., 418 N.Y.S.2d 371, 391 N.E.2d 1347 (N.Y.1979)—§ **38.19, n. 122.**

Cicciarelli, People v., 145 A.D.2d 938, 536 N.Y.S.2d 310 (N.Y.A.D. 4 Dept.1988)—§ **33.55, n. 2.**

Ciccone, People v., 91 A.D.2d 688, 457 N.Y.S.2d 328 (N.Y.A.D. 2 Dept.1982)—§ **38.8, n. 42, 60; § 38.10, n. 145.**

TABLE OF CASES

Cicorelli v. Capobianco, 89 A.D.2d 842, 90 A.D.2d 524, 453 N.Y.S.2d 21 (N.Y.A.D. 2 Dept.1982)—§ **28.4; § 28.4, n. 3.**

Ciervo, Matter of, 124 A.D.2d 583, 507 N.Y.S.2d 868 (N.Y.A.D. 2 Dept.1986)— **§ 24.89, n. 2.**

Cinerama, Inc. v. Equitable Life Assur. Soc. of United States, 38 A.D.2d 698, 328 N.Y.S.2d 160 (N.Y.A.D. 1 Dept.1972)— **§ 37.35, n. 5.**

Cintron, People v., 552 N.Y.S.2d 68, 551 N.E.2d 561 (N.Y.1990)—§ **38.19; § 38.19, n. 135.**

Cintron v. Tony Royal Quality Used Cars, Inc., 132 Misc.2d 75, 503 N.Y.S.2d 230 (N.Y.City Civ.Ct.1986)—§ **30.34, n. 3.**

Ciofalo v. Vic Tanney Gyms, Inc., 220 N.Y.S.2d 962, 177 N.E.2d 925 (N.Y. 1961)—**§ 5.11, n. 8, 10.**

Cioffi, People v., 150 N.Y.S.2d 192, 133 N.E.2d 703 (N.Y.1956)—§ **38.8, n. 6.**

Cipollone v. Liggett Group, Inc., 505 U.S. 504, 112 S.Ct. 2608, 120 L.Ed.2d 407 (1992)—§ **27.45; § 27.45, n. 5; § 27.46; § 27.46, n. 1, 6; § 27.51, n. 2.**

Ciraolo v. Melville Court Associates, 221 A.D.2d 582, 634 N.Y.S.2d 205 (N.Y.A.D. 2 Dept.1995)—§ **37.22, n. 2; § 37.26, n. 2.**

Citibank, N.A. v. Easha (In re Eashai), 87 F.3d 1082 (9th Cir.1996)—§ **9.208, n. 3.**

Citibank, N.A. v. Plapinger, 495 N.Y.S.2d 309, 485 N.E.2d 974 (N.Y.1985)— **§ 12.20, n. 1.**

Citicorp Intern. Trading Co., Inc. v. Western Oil & Refining Co., Inc., 790 F.Supp. 428 (S.D.N.Y.1992)—§ **1.10, n. 11.**

Cities Service Oil Co. v. City of New York, 180 N.Y.S.2d 769, 154 N.E.2d 814 (N.Y. 1958)—§ **14.14, n. 2.**

Citizens Bank of Maryland v. Strumpf, 516 U.S. 16, 116 S.Ct. 286, 133 L.Ed.2d 258 (1995)—§ **9.109, n. 3.**

City Bank Farmers Trust Co. v. Cannon, 265 A.D. 863, 38 N.Y.S.2d 245 (N.Y.A.D. 2 Dept.1942)—§ **8.3, n. 3.**

City Council of City of Mechanicville v. Town Bd. of Town of Halfmoon, 318 N.Y.S.2d 307, 267 N.E.2d 96 (N.Y. 1971)—§ **3.5, n. 25.**

City of (see name of city)

City Partners Ltd.-BMG v. Jamaica Savings Bank, N.Y.L.J., 1/3/79, p.13, col.2 (Sup. Ct., Nassau County)—§ **11.31, n. 2.**

City School Dist. of City of Elmira v. New York State Public Employment Relations Bd., 144 A.D.2d 35, 536 N.Y.S.2d 214 (N.Y.A.D. 3 Dept.1988)—§ **4.84, n. 9.**

City School Dist. of City of Kingston v. Vasilevich, 61 A.D.2d 276, 402 N.Y.S.2d 865 (N.Y.A.D. 3 Dept.1978)—§ **14.83, n. 2.**

City Streets Realty Corp. v. Jan Jay Const. Enterprises Corp., 88 A.D.2d 558, 450 N.Y.S.2d 492 (N.Y.A.D. 1 Dept.1982)— **§ 11.12, n. 1; § 11.33, n. 1.**

City University of New York v. Finalco, Inc., 93 A.D.2d 792, 461 N.Y.S.2d 830 (N.Y.A.D. 1 Dept.1983)—§ **5.25, n. 4.**

Civic Ass'n at Roslyn Country Club, Inc. v. Levitt and Sons Inc., 143 A.D.2d 385, 532 N.Y.S.2d 559 (N.Y.A.D. 2 Dept. 1988)—§ **37.37, n. 55.**

Civil Service Emp. Ass'n, City of v. City of Troy, 36 A.D.2d 145, 319 N.Y.S.2d 106 (N.Y.A.D. 3 Dept.1971)—§ **3.11, n. 2.**

CJOGS Associates v. Harris, 151 A.D.2d 571, 542 N.Y.S.2d 679 (N.Y.A.D. 2 Dept. 1989)—§ **14.14, n. 2.**

Clahar, Mztter of, 18 I & N Dec. 1 (BIA 1981)—§ **19.11, n. 7.**

Claiman, Matter of, 169 Misc.2d 881, 646 N.Y.S.2d 940 (N.Y.Sup.1996)—§ **22.11, n. 2; § 22.31, n. 5.**

Claim of Eilers, 213 A.D.2d 955, 624 N.Y.S.2d 307 (N.Y.A.D. 3 Dept.1995)— **§ 37.44, n. 15.**

Claim of Weinstein, 207 A.D.2d 942, 616 N.Y.S.2d 561 (N.Y.A.D. 3 Dept.1994)— **§ 37.44, n. 15.**

Claremont Acquisition Corp. v. General Motors (In re Claremont Acquisition Corp., Inc.), 113 F.3d 1029 (9th Cir.1997)— **§ 9.248, n. 4.**

Clark, In re, 1995 WL 495951 (N.D.Ill. 1995)—§ **9.174, n. 11.**

Clark v. Bendix Corp., 42 A.D.2d 727, 345 N.Y.S.2d 662 (N.Y.A.D. 2 Dept.1973)— **§ 27.29, n. 1.**

Clark v. Board of Zoning Appeals of Town of Hempstead, 301 N.Y. 86, 92 N.E.2d 903 (N.Y.1950)—§ **16.76, n. 4; § 16.78, n. 2.**

Clark v. Dodge, 269 N.Y. 410, 199 N.E. 641 (N.Y.1936)—§ **1.47, n. 3.**

Clark v. Fuller, 136 Misc. 151, 239 N.Y.S. 269 (N.Y.Sup.1930)—§ **11.14, n. 2.**

Clark, People v., 408 N.Y.S.2d 463, 380 N.E.2d 290 (N.Y.1978)—§ **38.8, n. 227.**

Clarke, Matter of, 18 I & N Dec. 369 (BIA 1983)—§ **19.11, n. 3.**

Clarke v. Frank, 960 F.2d 1146 (2nd Cir. 1992)—§ **18.37, n. 1.**

Clarke, People v., 222 A.D.2d 1035, 636 N.Y.S.2d 529 (N.Y.A.D. 4 Dept.1995)— **§ 38.21, n. 47.**

Clarke v. Shepard, 188 Misc. 588, 68 N.Y.S.2d 707 (N.Y.Sup.1947)—§ **13.37, n. 5.**

Clark Oil and Trading Co. v. Haberbush (In re Sahuaro Petroleum & Asphalt Co.),

TABLE OF CASES

170 B.R. 689 (C.D.Cal.1994)—§ **9.198, n. 1.**
Clark Pipe and Supply Co., Inc., Matter of, 893 F.2d 693 (5th Cir.1990)—§ **9.107, n. 15.**
Clark–Robinson Corp. v. Jet Enterprises, Inc., 159 N.Y.S.2d 214 (N.Y.Sup.1957)—§ **11.37, n. 9.**
Clarkson v. Coughlin, 898 F.Supp. 1019 (S.D.N.Y.1995)—§ **18.19, n. 7.**
Clary, People v., 438 N.Y.S.2d 298, 420 N.E.2d 96 (N.Y.1981)—§ **33.80, n. 1.**
Claude H. v. County of Oneida, 214 A.D.2d 964, 626 N.Y.S.2d 933 (N.Y.A.D. 4 Dept. 1995)—§ **18.31, n. 3.**
Clayton v. Automobile Workers, 451 U.S. 679, 101 S.Ct. 2088, 68 L.Ed.2d 538 (1981)—§ **17.61, n. 13.**
Clay, Town of v. Helsby, 45 A.D.2d 292, 357 N.Y.S.2d 291 (N.Y.A.D. 4 Dept.1974)—§ **3.21, n. 8.**
Clearview Concrete Products Corp. v. S. Charles Gherardi, Inc., 88 A.D.2d 461, 453 N.Y.S.2d 750 (N.Y.A.D. 2 Dept. 1982)—§ **30.37, n. 9.**
Cleg Co. v. Henry Moss & Co., 64 N.Y.S.2d 99 (N.Y.Sup.1946)—§ **10.16, n. 7.**
Clemens, Matter of, 200 Misc. 772, 104 N.Y.S.2d 720 (N.Y.Sup.1951)—§ **10.19, n. 16.**
Clemente, United States v., 640 F.2d 1069 (2nd Cir.1981)—§ **29.9, n. 3.**
Clements v. Nassau County, 835 F.2d 1000 (2nd Cir.1987)—§ **18.53, n. 1.**
Clemons Management Corp. v. Quick Quality Copies, Inc., 164 Misc.2d 144, 623 N.Y.S.2d 498 (N.Y.City Civ.Ct.1995)—§ **13.12, n. 11.**
Clerk v. Clerk, 132 A.D.2d 456, 133 A.D.2d 328, 517 N.Y.S.2d 512 (N.Y.A.D. 1 Dept. 1987)—§ **21.37, n. 5.**
Clermont v. Clermont, 198 A.D.2d 631, 603 N.Y.S.2d 923 (N.Y.A.D. 3 Dept.1993)—§ **5.13, n. 1.**
Clients' Sec. Fund of State v. Grandeau, 530 N.Y.S.2d 775, 526 N.E.2d 270 (N.Y. 1988)—§ **2.53, n. 4; § 28.22; § 28.22, n. 2; § 28.25; § 28.25, n. 2.**
Clifford v. Clifford Rental Management, Inc., 198 A.D.2d 790, 604 N.Y.S.2d 380 (N.Y.A.D. 4 Dept.1993)—§ **30.37, n. 5.**
Cliffstar Corp. v. Riverbend Products, Inc., 750 F.Supp. 81 (W.D.N.Y.1990)—§ **5.50, n. 9.**
Clifton Steel Corp. v. General Elec. Co., 80 A.D.2d 715, 437 N.Y.S.2d 735 (N.Y.A.D. 3 Dept.1981)—§ **10.19, n. 9.**
Clifton Steel Corp. v. General Elec. Co., 80 A.D.2d 714, 437 N.Y.S.2d 734 (N.Y.A.D. 3 Dept.1981)—§ **5.9, n. 5.**
Clifton Steel Corp. v. Monroe County Public Works Dept., 74 A.D.2d 715, 425 N.Y.S.2d 672 (N.Y.A.D. 4 Dept.1980)—§ **26.44, n. 2.**
Clinton, Estate of, 157 Misc.2d 506, 597 N.Y.S.2d 900 (N.Y.Sur.1993)—§ **28.31; § 28.31, n. 1.**
Clinton, People v., 42 A.D.2d 815, 346 N.Y.S.2d 345 (N.Y.A.D. 3 Dept.1973)—§ **38.8, n. 89.**
Clinton v. Summers, 144 A.D.2d 145, 534 N.Y.S.2d 473 (N.Y.A.D. 3 Dept.1988)—§ **16.107, n. 2.**
Clinton, Town of v. Dumais, 69 A.D.2d 836, 415 N.Y.S.2d 81 (N.Y.A.D. 2 Dept. 1979)—§ **16.43, n. 12.**
Clio Realty Corp. v. Heflam Bldg. Corp., 227 A.D. 439, 238 N.Y.S. 127 (N.Y.A.D. 2 Dept.1929)—§ **10.61, n. 2.**
Clomon v. Jackson, 988 F.2d 1314 (2nd Cir.1993)—§ **7.36, n. 7; § 7.43; § 7.43, n. 4.**
Club St. Agnello Abate of Amsterdam, New York, Inc. v. State, 68 A.D.2d 264, 417 N.Y.S.2d 21 (N.Y.A.D. 3 Dept.1979)—§ **14.88, n. 3.**
Clute, People v., 47 Misc.2d 1005, 263 N.Y.S.2d 826 (N.Y.Co.Ct.1965)—§ **16.124, n. 13.**
CNA Ins. Co. v. Rauso, 213 A.D.2d 712, 624 N.Y.S.2d 454 (N.Y.A.D. 2 Dept.1995)—§ **37.30, n. 10.**
Coalition Against Lincoln West, Inc. v. City of New York, 94 A.D.2d 483, 465 N.Y.S.2d 170 (N.Y.A.D. 1 Dept.1983)—§ **15.6, n. 15.**
Coalition for a Liveable West Side, Inc. v. New York City Dept. of Environmental Protection, 830 F.Supp. 194 (S.D.N.Y. 1993)—§ **15.11, n. 17.**
Coan v. Bernier (In re Bernier), 176 B.R. 976 (Bkrtcy.D.Conn.1995)—§ **9.194, n. 1.**
Coastal Equities, Inc., In re, 33 B.R. 898 (Bkrtcy.S.D.Cal.1983)—§ **9.149, n. 4.**
Coastal Fishermen's Ass'n v. New York City Dept. of Sanitation, 772 F.Supp. 162 (S.D.N.Y.1991)—§ **15.11, n. 18.**
Coaye, People v., 508 N.Y.S.2d 410, 501 N.E.2d 18 (N.Y.1986)—§ **38.12, n. 6.**
Coca–Cola Bottling Co. of New York, Inc. v. New York City Board of Estimate, 536 N.Y.S.2d 33, 532 N.E.2d 1261 (N.Y. 1988)—§ **15.4, n. 9.**
Codling v. Paglia, 345 N.Y.S.2d 461, 298 N.E.2d 622 (N.Y.1973)—§ **27.4; § 27.4, n. 1, 4; § 27.34; § 27.34, n. 1, 6, 8.**
Coffed's Estate, Matter of, 88 Misc.2d 610, 388 N.Y.S.2d 552 (N.Y.Sur.1976)—§ **24.64, n. 2.**
Cohalan v. Johnson Elec. Const. Corp., 105 A.D.2d 770, 481 N.Y.S.2d 714 (N.Y.A.D. 2 Dept.1984)—§ **37.37, n. 84; § 37.38, n. 13.**

TABLE OF CASES

Cohen v. Ambach, 112 A.D.2d 497, 490 N.Y.S.2d 908 (N.Y.A.D. 3 Dept.1985)— § 4.17, n. 4.

Cohen v. Bayside Federal Sav. & Loan Ass'n, 62 Misc.2d 738, 309 N.Y.S.2d 980 (N.Y.Sup.1970)—§ 18.76, n. 2.

Cohen v. Beneficial Indus. Loan Corp., 337 U.S. 541, 69 S.Ct. 1221, 93 L.Ed. 1528 (1949)—§ 18.31, n. 7.

Cohen v. Biernoff, 84 A.D.2d 802, 444 N.Y.S.2d 152 (N.Y.A.D. 2 Dept.1981)— § 2.46, n. 6.

Cohen v. Hahn, 155 A.D.2d 969, 547 N.Y.S.2d 780 (N.Y.A.D. 4 Dept.1989)— § 16.46, n. 1.

Cohen v. Hallmark Cards, Inc., 410 N.Y.S.2d 282, 382 N.E.2d 1145 (N.Y. 1978)—§ 37.29, n. 1, 3; § 37.65; § 37.65, n. 19, 21, 22; § 38.19; § 38.19, n. 74; § 39.7, n. 2.

Cohen v. Herbal Concepts, Inc., 482 N.Y.S.2d 457, 472 N.E.2d 307 (N.Y. 1984)—§ 18.64, n. 1, 7, 8.

Cohen v. Lipsig, 92 A.D.2d 536, 459 N.Y.S.2d 98 (N.Y.A.D. 2 Dept.1983)— § 28.9, n. 10; § 28.23, n. 8.

Cohen v. Lord, Day & Lord, 551 N.Y.S.2d 157, 550 N.E.2d 410 (N.Y.1989)—§ 6.67, n. 2; § 6.88, n. 2.

Cohen v. 120 Owners Corp., 205 A.D.2d 394, 613 N.Y.S.2d 615 (N.Y.A.D. 1 Dept. 1994)—§ 1.27, n. 5.

Cohen, People v., 665 N.Y.S.2d 30, 687 N.E.2d 1313 (N.Y.1997)—§ 33.56; § 33.56, n. 8.

Cohen, People v., 222 A.D.2d 447, 635 N.Y.S.2d 38 (N.Y.A.D. 2 Dept.1995)— § 38.10, n. 70.

Cohen, People v., 131 Misc.2d 898, 502 N.Y.S.2d 123 (N.Y.City Ct.1986)— § 33.32, n. 2; § 33.33, n. 3.

Cohen, People v., 347 N.Y.S.2d 203, 300 N.E.2d 734 (N.Y.1973)—§ 38.21, n. 58.

Cohen v. State, 51 A.D.2d 494, 382 N.Y.S.2d 128 (N.Y.A.D. 3 Dept.1976)—§ 37.30, n. 8.

Cohen v. The Drexel Burnham Lambert Group (In re Drexel Burnham Lambert Group, Inc.), 138 B.R. 687 (Bkrtcy. S.D.N.Y.1992)—§ 9.74, n. 1.

Cohen v. Varig Airlines, S.A. Empresa de Viacao Aerea Rio Grandense, 85 Misc.2d 653, 380 N.Y.S.2d 450 (N.Y.City Civ.Ct. 1975)—§ 30.18, n. 10.

Cole v. Lawas, 116 A.D.2d 936, 498 N.Y.S.2d 512 (N.Y.A.D. 3 Dept.1986)— § 30.39, n. 6.

Cole, People v., 152 A.D.2d 851, 544 N.Y.S.2d 228 (N.Y.A.D. 3 Dept.1989)— § 38.8, n. 157.

Cole, People v., 540 N.Y.S.2d 984, 538 N.E.2d 336 (N.Y.1989)—§ 33.81, n. 2.

Coleman, People v., 142 A.D.2d 586, 530 N.Y.S.2d 242 (N.Y.A.D. 2 Dept.1988)— § 33.52, n. 2.

Coleman v. Wagner College, 429 F.2d 1120 (2nd Cir.1970)—§ 18.53, n. 1.

Colin, Matter of, 44 B.R. 806 (Bkrtcy. S.D.N.Y.1984)—§ 9.107, n. 20.

Coliniatis v. Dimas, 848 F.Supp. 462 (S.D.N.Y.1994)—§ 18.82, n. 6.

Collard v. Village of Flower Hill, 439 N.Y.S.2d 326, 421 N.E.2d 818 (N.Y. 1981)—§ 16.109, n. 3; § 16.114, n. 2.

Colletti v. Credit Bureau Services, Inc., 644 F.2d 1148 (5th Cir.1981)—§ 7.31, n. 10.

Collins v. A & R Pizzeria, 223 A.D.2d 572, 636 N.Y.S.2d 398 (N.Y.A.D. 2 Dept. 1996)—§ 37.28, n. 34.

Collins v. Greater New York Sav. Bank, 194 A.D.2d 514, 598 N.Y.S.2d 544 (N.Y.A.D. 2 Dept.1993)—§ 26.42, n. 6.

Collins v. Lonergan, 198 A.D.2d 349, 603 N.Y.S.2d 330 (N.Y.A.D. 2 Dept.1993)— § 16.119, n. 8.

Collins v. McWilliams, 185 A.D. 712, 173 N.Y.S. 850 (N.Y.A.D. 1 Dept.1919)— § 37.35, n. 8.

Collins v. Willcox, Inc., 158 Misc.2d 54, 600 N.Y.S.2d 884 (N.Y.Sup.1992)—§ 17.28; § 17.28, n. 1, 5.

Collins v. Youngblood, 497 U.S. 37, 110 S.Ct. 2715, 111 L.Ed.2d 30 (1990)— § 38.22, n. 2.

Colon v. Aetna Life and Cas. Ins. Co., 494 N.Y.S.2d 688, 484 N.E.2d 1040 (N.Y. 1985)—§ 31.12, n. 6.

Colon v. Coughlin, 58 F.3d 865 (2nd Cir. 1995)—§ 18.37, n. 7, 8.

Colon, People v., 635 N.Y.S.2d 165, 658 N.E.2d 1038 (N.Y.1995)—§ 38.19; § 38.19, n. 84.

Colon, People v., 202 A.D.2d 710, 608 N.Y.S.2d 553 (N.Y.A.D. 3 Dept.1994)— § 38.8, n. 56.

Colon, People v., 526 N.Y.S.2d 932, 521 N.E.2d 1075 (N.Y.1988)—§ 39.50, n. 11.

Colon, People v., 493 N.Y.S.2d 302, 482 N.E.2d 1218 (N.Y.1985)—§ 38.20, n. 5; § 38.21, n. 24.

Colon v. State, 209 A.D.2d 842, 620 N.Y.S.2d 1015 (N.Y.A.D. 3 Dept.1994)— § 37.29, n. 33.

Colon v. Tompkins Square Neighbors, Inc., 289 F.Supp. 104 (S.D.N.Y.1968)— § 18.43, n. 2.

Colonial Diversified, Inc. v. Assured Holding Corp., 71 A.D.2d 1011, 420 N.Y.S.2d 419 (N.Y.A.D. 2 Dept.1979)—§ 12.16, n. 1.

Colonial Penn Ins. Co. v. Culley, 144 A.D.2d 363, 534 N.Y.S.2d 876 (N.Y.A.D. 2 Dept. 1988)—§ 37.37, n. 24.

TABLE OF CASES

Colorado & Eastern R. Co., United States v., 50 F.3d 1530 (10th Cir.1995)— § 15.30, n. 7.

Colpan Realty Corp. v. Great Am. Ins. Co., 83 Misc.2d 730, 373 N.Y.S.2d 802 (N.Y.Sup.1975)—§ 28.14, n. 4.

Columbia Cas. Co. v. Bristol–Myers Squibb Co., 215 A.D.2d 91, 635 N.Y.S.2d 173 (N.Y.A.D. 1 Dept.1995)—§ 31.22, n. 3.

Columbia, County of v. Continental Ins. Co., 612 N.Y.S.2d 345, 634 N.E.2d 946 (N.Y.1994)—§ 31.2, n. 1.

Comband Technologies, Inc., In re, 69 F.3d 532 (4th Cir.1995)—§ 9.102, n. 9.

Combustion Engineering, Inc. v. Travelers Indem. Co., 75 A.D.2d 777, 428 N.Y.S.2d 235 (N.Y.A.D. 1 Dept.1980)—§ 31.21, n. 3.

Combustion Equipment Associates, Inc., In re, 67 B.R. 709 (S.D.N.Y.1986)—§ 9.22, n. 4.

Comeaux v. Brown & Williamson Tobacco Co., 915 F.2d 1264 (9th Cir.1990)— § 17.42, n. 4.

Comer, People v., 198 A.D.2d 874, 605 N.Y.S.2d 1006 (N.Y.A.D. 4 Dept.1993)— § 38.10, n. 13.

Commack, People v., 194 A.D.2d 619, 599 N.Y.S.2d 56 (N.Y.A.D. 2 Dept.1993)— § 33.85, n. 2.

Commander Oil Corp. v. Advance Food Service Equipment, 991 F.2d 49 (2nd Cir. 1993)—§ 15.30, n. 10.

Commerce and Industry Ins. Co. v. Nester, 660 N.Y.S.2d 366, 682 N.E.2d 967 (N.Y. 1997)—§ 37.37, n. 90.

Commerce Bank v. Mountain View Village, Inc., 5 F.3d 34 (3rd Cir.1993)—§ 9.66, n. 4.

Commercial Union Ins. Co. v. International Flavors & Fragrances, Inc., 822 F.2d 267 (2nd Cir.1987)—§ 28.40, n. 2; § 31.10, n. 7; § 31.13, n. 2.

Commissioner v. ___ (see opposing party)

Commissioner of Cayuga County (Bessie C.), Matter of, 225 A.D.2d 1027, 639 N.Y.S.2d 234 (N.Y.A.D. 4 Dept.1996)— § 22.41, n. 13.

Commissioner of Social Services of City of New York on Behalf of Tabitha McC., Matter of, 202 A.D.2d 502, 610 N.Y.S.2d 793 (N.Y.A.D. 2 Dept.1994)—§ 37.37, n. 16.

Commissioner of Social Services of City of New York (Tyrique P.), Matter of, 216 A.D.2d 387, 629 N.Y.S.2d 47 (N.Y.A.D. 2 Dept.1995)—§ 37.19, n. 67.

Commissioner of Social Services on Behalf of Michael W. v. Susan W., 221 A.D.2d 627, 635 N.Y.S.2d 498 (N.Y.A.D. 2 Dept. 1995)—§ 37.37, n. 81.

Commissioners of State Ins. Fund v. Low, 285 A.D. 525, 138 N.Y.S.2d 437 (N.Y.A.D. 3 Dept.1955)—§ 32.42, n. 7.

Committee of Equity Security Holders v. Lionel Corp. (In re Lionel Corp.), 722 F.2d 1063 (2nd Cir.1983)—§ 9.62, n. 4.

Commodity Futures Trading Com'n v. Weintraub, 471 U.S. 343, 105 S.Ct. 1986, 85 L.Ed.2d 372 (1985)—§ 9.28, n. 6; § 9.139, n. 1.

Commoss v. Pearson, 190 A.D. 699, 180 N.Y.S. 482 (N.Y.A.D. 1 Dept.1920)— § 5.9, n. 3.

Community Housing Imp. Program, Inc. v. New York State Div. of Housing and Community Renewal, 175 A.D.2d 905, 573 N.Y.S.2d 522 (N.Y.A.D. 2 Dept. 1991)—§ 4.70, n. 4.

Community Resource Center for Developmentally Disabled, Inc. v. City of Yonkers, 140 Misc.2d 1018, 532 N.Y.S.2d 332 (N.Y.Sup.1988)—§ 16.24, n. 7; § 16.128, n. 13.

Comstock v. Wilson, 257 N.Y. 231, 177 N.E. 431 (N.Y.1931)—§ 30.9, n. 18.

Cona, People v., 424 N.Y.S.2d 146, 399 N.E.2d 1167 (N.Y.1979)—§ 38.19; § 38.19, n. 51; § 39.42, n. 6.

Concepcion, People v., 167 A.D.2d 413, 561 N.Y.S.2d 823 (N.Y.A.D. 2 Dept.1990)— § 38.10, n. 20.

Concerned Area Residents for Environment v. Southview Farm, 34 F.3d 114 (2nd Cir.1994)—§ 15.8, n. 10.

Concerned Citizens of Westbury v. Board of Appeals of Incorporated Village of Westbury, 173 A.D.2d 615, 570 N.Y.S.2d 314 (N.Y.A.D. 2 Dept.1991)—§ 16.55; § 16.55, n. 2.

Concordia Collegiate Institute v. Miller, 301 N.Y. 189, 93 N.E.2d 632 (N.Y.1950)— § 16.91, n. 1.

Concord Square Apartments of Wood County, Ltd., In re, 174 B.R. 71 (Bkrtcy. S.D.Ohio 1994)—§ 9.162, n. 3.

Concord Village Management Co. v. Rubin, 101 Misc.2d 625, 421 N.Y.S.2d 811 (N.Y.Dist.Ct.1979)—§ 13.32, n. 12.

Concrete Const. Systems, Inc. v. Jensen, 65 A.D.2d 918, 410 N.Y.S.2d 460 (N.Y.A.D. 4 Dept.1978)—§ 1.23, n. 4.

Condon, Matter of, 118 Misc.2d 544, 461 N.Y.S.2d 181 (N.Y.Sur.1983)—§ 22.15, n. 4.

Confederation Life Ins. Co. v. Beau Rivage Ltd., 126 B.R. 632 (N.D.Ga.1991)— § 9.102, n. 4.

Conforti & Eisele, Inc. v. William J. Scully, Inc., 98 A.D.2d 646, 469 N.Y.S.2d 400 (N.Y.A.D. 1 Dept.1983)—§ 37.38, n. 5.

Conklin v. Central New York Telephone & Telegraph Co., 130 A.D. 308, 114 N.Y.S.

TABLE OF CASES

190 (N.Y.A.D. 3 Dept.1909)—§ **30.14, n. 17.**

Conley v. Bowen, 859 F.2d 261 (2nd Cir. 1988)—§ **34.9, n. 16.**

Conley v. Town of Brookhaven Zoning Bd. of Appeals, 386 N.Y.S.2d 681, 353 N.E.2d 594 (N.Y.1976)—§ **16.84, n. 4.**

Conmar Builders, Inc. v. Board of Appeals of Inc. Village of Upper Brookville, 43 Misc.2d 577, 251 N.Y.S.2d 521 (N.Y.Sup. 1964)—§ **16.93, n. 4, 5.**

Connecticut Coastal Fishermen's Ass'n v. Remington Arms Co., Inc., 989 F.2d 1305 (2nd Cir.1993)—§ **15.23, n. 6.**

Connecticut Nat. Bank v. Germain, 503 U.S. 249, 112 S.Ct. 1146, 117 L.Ed.2d 391 (1992)—§ **9.26, n. 2.**

Conner v. Conner, 97 A.D.2d 88, 468 N.Y.S.2d 482 (N.Y.A.D. 2 Dept.1983)—§ **21.39, n. 6.**

Conservation Chemical Co., United States v., 628 F.Supp. 391 (W.D.Mo.1985)—§ **15.30, n. 8.**

Consolation Nursing Home, Inc. v. Commissioner of New York State Dept. of Health, 624 N.Y.S.2d 563, 648 N.E.2d 1326 (N.Y.1995)—§ **4.80, n. 6; § 37.87, n. 24.**

Consolidated Edison Co. of New York, Inc., Matter of, 143 A.D.2d 1012, 533 N.Y.S.2d 591 (N.Y.A.D. 2 Dept.1988)—§ **14.64, n. 5; § 14.130, n. 2.**

Consolidated Edison Co. of New York, Inc. v. Hoffman, 403 N.Y.S.2d 193, 374 N.E.2d 105 (N.Y.1978)—§ **16.129; § 16.129, n. 5; § 16.130; § 16.130, n. 3.**

Consolidated Edison Co. of New York, Inc. v. Neptune Associates, 190 A.D.2d 669, 593 N.Y.S.2d 259 (N.Y.A.D. 2 Dept. 1993)—§ **14.78, n. 4.**

Consolidated Edison Co. of New York, Inc. v. State Human Rights Appeal Bd., 65 A.D.2d 546, 409 N.Y.S.2d 141 (N.Y.A.D. 2 Dept.1978)—§ **17.82, n. 7.**

Consolidated Edison Co. of New York, Inc. v. Town of Red Hook, 468 N.Y.S.2d 596, 456 N.E.2d 487 (N.Y.1983)—§ **3.14, n. 8.**

Consolidated Edison Co. of N.Y. v. Village of Briarcliff Manor, 208 Misc. 295, 144 N.Y.S.2d 379 (N.Y.Sup.1955)—§ **16.128, n. 6.**

Consolidated Motor Inns, Matter of, 666 F.2d 189 (5th Cir.1982)—§ **9.170, n. 2.**

Consolidated Rail Corp. v. Industrial Scrap Processing Corp., 97 A.D.2d 532, 468 N.Y.S.2d 164 (N.Y.A.D. 2 Dept.1983)—§ **37.67, n. 8.**

Constantine v. Leto, 157 A.D.2d 376, 557 N.Y.S.2d 611 (N.Y.A.D. 3 Dept.1990)—§ **33.34, n. 2.**

Consumers Distributing Co., Ltd. v. Pelham Gourmet Deli, N.Y.L.J., 10/3/88, p.25, col.3, 16 HCR 363 (App. Term, 2d Dep't)—§ **13.18, n. 4.**

Contelmo's Sand & Gravel, Inc. v. J & J Milano, Inc., 96 A.D.2d 1090, 467 N.Y.S.2d 55 (N.Y.A.D. 2 Dept.1983)—§ **10.16, n. 8.**

Contemporary Mission, Inc. v. United States Postal Service, 648 F.2d 97 (2nd Cir.1981)—§ **18.18, n. 6; § 18.35, n. 2.**

Contes, People v., 467 N.Y.S.2d 349, 454 N.E.2d 932 (N.Y.1983)—§ **38.19, n. 61.**

Continental Bldg. Co., Inc. v. Town of North Salem, 211 A.D.2d 88, 625 N.Y.S.2d 700 (N.Y.A.D. 3 Dept.1995)—§ **16.123, n. 6, 9.**

Continental Cas. Co. v. Aetna Cas. and Sur. Co., 823 F.2d 708 (2nd Cir.1987)—§ **31.30, n. 2.**

Continental Cas. Co. v. Rapid–American Corp., 593 N.Y.S.2d 966, 609 N.E.2d 506 (N.Y.1993)—§ **28.39, n. 8, 9; § 31.9, n. 10.**

Continental Cas. Co. v. Rapid–American Corp., 177 A.D.2d 61, 581 N.Y.S.2d 669 (N.Y.A.D. 1 Dept.1992)—§ **31.30, n. 3.**

Continental Cas. Co. v. Stronghold Ins. Co., Ltd., 866 F.Supp. 143 (S.D.N.Y.1994)—§ **31.26, n. 2.**

Continental Grain, Matter of, 14 I & N Dec. 140 (D.D.1972)—§ **19.21, n. 2.**

Continental Holdings, Inc., In re, 170 B.R. 919 (Bkrtcy.N.D.Ohio 1994)—§ **9.174, n. 11.**

Contini by Contini v. Hyundai Motor Co., 876 F.Supp. 540 (S.D.N.Y.1995)—§ **27.50; § 27.50, n. 1; § 27.51, n. 7.**

Conto, People v., 218 A.D.2d 665, 630 N.Y.S.2d 542 (N.Y.A.D. 2 Dept.1995)—§ **38.25, n. 8.**

Contreras–Sotelo, Matter of, 12 I & N Dec. 596 (BIA 1967)—§ **19.47, n. 5.**

Conway v. Brooklyn Union Gas Co., 189 A.D.2d 851, 592 N.Y.S.2d 782 (N.Y.A.D. 2 Dept.1993)—§ **30.9, n. 19.**

Conway v. Samet, 59 Misc.2d 666, 300 N.Y.S.2d 243 (N.Y.Sup.1969)—§ **1.21, n. 28.**

Conway's Estate, In re, 74 Misc.2d 909, 346 N.Y.S.2d 682 (N.Y.Sur.1973)—§ **20.75, n. 4.**

Cook, Matter of, 133 A.D.2d 823, 520 N.Y.S.2d 400 (N.Y.A.D. 2 Dept.1987)—§ **22.47, n. 11; § 22.69, n. 4.**

Cook, People v., 626 N.Y.S.2d 1000, 650 N.E.2d 847 (N.Y.1995)—§ **38.19, n. 125.**

Cook v. State, 105 Misc.2d 1040, 430 N.Y.S.2d 507 (N.Y.Ct.Cl.1980)—§ **14.104, n. 5.**

TABLE OF CASES

Cooke v. Laidlaw, Adams & Peck, Inc., 126 A.D.2d 453, 510 N.Y.S.2d 597 (N.Y.A.D. 1 Dept.1987)—§ **28.21;** § **28.21, n. 11.**

Cooks, People v., 500 N.Y.S.2d 503, 491 N.E.2d 676 (N.Y.1986)—§ **38.9, n. 11;** § **38.10, n. 85.**

Cooley v. Carter-Wallace Inc., 102 A.D.2d 642, 478 N.Y.S.2d 375 (N.Y.A.D. 4 Dept. 1984)—§ **27.14;** § **27.14, n. 1.**

Cooley v. Lobdell, 153 N.Y. 596, 47 N.E. 783 (N.Y.1897)—§ **12.4, n. 2;** § **12.9, n. 1.**

Coolite Corp. v. American Cyanamid Co., 52 A.D.2d 486, 384 N.Y.S.2d 808 (N.Y.A.D. 1 Dept.1976)—§ **17.27, n. 5.**

Coonradt v. Averill Park Central School Dist., 73 A.D.2d 747, 422 N.Y.S.2d 544 (N.Y.A.D. 3 Dept.1979)—§ **39.20, n. 5.**

Coons, People v., 552 N.Y.S.2d 94, 551 N.E.2d 587 (N.Y.1990)—§ **38.19;** § **38.19, n. 19.**

Cooper v. Ateliers de la Motobecane, S.A., 456 N.Y.S.2d 728, 442 N.E.2d 1239 (N.Y. 1982)—§ **31.24, n. 3.**

Cooper v. Manufacturers Hanover Trust Co., 185 A.D.2d 150, 586 N.Y.S.2d 6 (N.Y.A.D. 1 Dept.1992)—§ **17.34, n. 11.**

Cooper, People v., 305 N.Y.S.2d 145, 252 N.E.2d 626 (N.Y.1969)—§ **38.27, n. 23.**

Cooperman, Matter of, 611 N.Y.S.2d 465, 633 N.E.2d 1069 (N.Y.1994)—§ **28.19;** § **28.19, n. 1, 11;** § **28.29, n. 3;** § **28.47, n. 1.**

Coopersmith v. Gold, 172 A.D.2d 982, 568 N.Y.S.2d 250 (N.Y.A.D. 3 Dept.1991)—§ **28.17, n. 5.**

Copart Industries, Inc. v. Consolidated Edison Co. of New York, Inc., 394 N.Y.S.2d 169, 362 N.E.2d 968 (N.Y.1977)—§ **15.32, n. 2, 3, 4, 5, 6;** § **15.33, n. 1.**

Copeland v. Bowen, 861 F.2d 536 (9th Cir. 1988)—§ **34.47, n. 20.**

Copeland, People v., 185 A.D.2d 280, 585 N.Y.S.2d 794 (N.Y.A.D. 2 Dept.1992)—§ **38.10, n. 59.**

Coppa, People v., 408 N.Y.S.2d 365, 380 N.E.2d 195 (N.Y.1978)—§ **38.10;** § **38.10, n. 8.**

Coppola v. Fredstrom, 45 A.D.2d 857, 358 N.Y.S.2d 538 (N.Y.A.D. 2 Dept.1974)—§ **12.4, n. 3.**

Corbett v. Sherwood, 84 A.D.2d 571, 443 N.Y.S.2d 443 (N.Y.A.D. 2 Dept.1981)—§ **18.87, n. 1.**

Corbin-Kellogg Agency v. Tasker, 248 A.D. 58, 289 N.Y.S. 156 (N.Y.A.D. 3 Dept. 1936)—§ **10.62, n. 2.**

Corbitt, People v., 221 A.D.2d 809, 633 N.Y.S.2d 865 (N.Y.A.D. 3 Dept.1995)—§ **38.25, n. 6.**

Corcoran v. Ardra Ins. Co., Ltd., 566 N.Y.S.2d 575, 567 N.E.2d 969 (N.Y. 1990)—§ **31.28, n. 10.**

Cordero v. Corbisiero, 587 N.Y.S.2d 266, 599 N.E.2d 670 (N.Y.1992)—§ **4.45, n. 2.**

Cordero, People v., N.Y.L.J., 4/21/94, p.25, col.4 (N.Y.C.Crim.Ct.)—§ **33.81, n. 2.**

Core Joint Concrete Pipe Corp. v. Paino Bros., 247 A.D. 746, 285 N.Y.S. 706 (N.Y.A.D. 2 Dept.1936)—§ **10.19, n. 11.**

Corey L. v. Martin L., 408 N.Y.S.2d 439, 380 N.E.2d 266 (N.Y.1978)—§ **20.43, n. 6.**

Corina Associates, Inc. v. McManus, Longe, Brockwehl, Inc., 39 A.D.2d 613, 330 N.Y.S.2d 847 (N.Y.A.D. 3 Dept.1972)—§ **10.19, n. 12.**

Corletta v. Oliveri, 169 Misc.2d 1, 641 N.Y.S.2d 498 (N.Y.Sup.1996)—§ **21.75;** § **21.75, n. 2.**

Cornell v. Cornell, 196 N.Y.S.2d 98, 164 N.E.2d 395 (N.Y.1959)—§ **24.65, n. 1, 4.**

Cornell v. T. V. Development Corp., 268 N.Y.S.2d 29, 215 N.E.2d 349 (N.Y. 1966)—§ **30.22, n. 1;** § **30.27, n. 2.**

Cornell University v. Bagnardi, 510 N.Y.S.2d 861, 503 N.E.2d 509 (N.Y. 1986)—§ **16.25, n. 5.**

Cornwell v. Safeco Ins. Co. of America, 42 A.D.2d 127, 346 N.Y.S.2d 59 (N.Y.A.D. 4 Dept.1973)—§ **31.17, n. 5.**

Coronet Capital Co. v. Spodek, 202 A.D.2d 20, 615 N.Y.S.2d 351 (N.Y.A.D. 1 Dept. 1994)—§ **11.32, n. 4.**

Correll v. Correll, 109 N.Y.S.2d 531 (N.Y.Sup.1951)—§ **8.3, n. 3.**

Corsel v. Corsel, 133 A.D.2d 604, 519 N.Y.S.2d 710 (N.Y.A.D. 2 Dept.1987)—§ **21.64, n. 1.**

Corso, People v., 388 N.Y.S.2d 886, 357 N.E.2d 357 (N.Y.1976)—§ **38.9, n. 14, 16;** § **38.14, n. 3.**

Cortez, Matter of, 16 I & N Dec. 289 (BIA 1977)—§ **19.11, n. 4.**

Cortlandt Nursing Home v. Axelrod, 495 N.Y.S.2d 927, 486 N.E.2d 785 (N.Y. 1985)—§ **4.21, n. 2.**

Corva v. United Services Auto. Ass'n, 108 A.D.2d 631, 485 N.Y.S.2d 264 (N.Y.A.D. 1 Dept.1985)—§ **28.26;** § **28.26, n. 6.**

Corwin, People ex rel. v. Walter, 68 N.Y. 403 (N.Y.1877)—§ **37.31, n. 1.**

Cory Michael F., Matter of, 124 A.D.2d 992, 508 N.Y.S.2d 798 (N.Y.A.D. 4 Dept. 1986)—§ **20.35, n. 7.**

Coscia, People v., 26 A.D.2d 649, 272 N.Y.S.2d 416 (N.Y.A.D. 2 Dept.1966)—§ **38.8, n. 34.**

Cosentino v. Kelly, 926 F.Supp. 391 (S.D.N.Y.1996)—§ **18.13, n. 3.**

Cosme, People v., 587 N.Y.S.2d 274, 599 N.E.2d 678 (N.Y.1992)—§ **38.10, n. 67.**

Cosmopolitan Aviation Corp. v. New York State Dept. of Transportation (In re

TABLE OF CASES

Cosmopolitan Aviation Corp.), 763 F.2d 507 (2nd Cir.1985)—§ **9.25, n. 7.**
Costa v. District Nursing Ass'n of Northern Westchester, Inc., 175 A.D.2d 274, 572 N.Y.S.2d 727 (N.Y.A.D. 2 Dept.1991)—§ **12.29, n. 3.**
Costanza v. City of New York, 147 Misc.2d 94, 553 N.Y.S.2d 616 (N.Y.City Civ.Ct. 1990)—§ **30.28, n. 7.**
Cotgreave v. Public Adm'r of Imperial County, 91 A.D.2d 600, 456 N.Y.S.2d 432 (N.Y.A.D. 2 Dept.1982)—§ **37.37, n. 27.**
Cotilletta v. Tepedino, 151 Misc.2d 660, 573 N.Y.S.2d 396 (N.Y.Sup.1991)—§ **30.13, n. 6.**
Cotton, People v., 219 A.D.2d 836, 632 N.Y.S.2d 35 (N.Y.A.D. 4 Dept.1995)—§ **38.8, n. 154.**
Cotton, People ex rel. v. Rodriquez, 123 A.D.2d 338, 506 N.Y.S.2d 350 (N.Y.A.D. 2 Dept.1986)—§ **38.8, n. 75.**
Coulter v. Barber, 214 A.D.2d 195, 632 N.Y.S.2d 270 (N.Y.A.D. 3 Dept.1995)—§ **30.42, n. 13.**
Council of Commuter Organizations v. Metropolitan Transp. Authority, 683 F.2d 663 (2nd Cir.1982)—§ **15.22, n. 10.**
Country Sam Inc. v. Bennett, 192 A.D.2d 448, 597 N.Y.S.2d 13 (N.Y.A.D. 1 Dept. 1993)—§ **16.65, n. 1.**
Counts v. Commissioner, 42 T.C. 755 (Tax Ct.1964)—§ **23.118, n. 2.**
County Nat. Bank v. Vogt, 28 A.D.2d 793, 280 N.Y.S.2d 1016 (N.Y.A.D. 3 Dept. 1967)—§ **8.4, n. 17.**
County of (see name of county)
Cousart, People v., 458 N.Y.S.2d 507, 444 N.E.2d 971 (N.Y.1982)—§ **38.3, n. 6.**
Coutant v. Town of Poughkeepsie, 69 A.D.2d 506, 419 N.Y.S.2d 148 (N.Y.A.D. 2 Dept.1979)—§ **3.15, n. 6; § 16.113, n. 7, 8.**
Cover v. Cohen, 473 N.Y.S.2d 378, 461 N.E.2d 864 (N.Y.1984)—§ **27.10, n. 5; § 27.14, n. 3; § 27.22, n. 1.**
Cowan v. Kern, 394 N.Y.S.2d 579, 363 N.E.2d 305 (N.Y.1977)—§ **16.44, n. 2, 3.**
Cox v. Leahy, 209 A.D. 313, 204 N.Y.S. 741 (N.Y.A.D. 3 Dept.1924)—§ **1.38, n. 8.**
Coxsackie, Town of v. Dernier, 105 A.D.2d 966, 482 N.Y.S.2d 106 (N.Y.A.D. 3 Dept. 1984)—§ **14.26, n. 3; § 14.38, n. 10; § 14.64, n. 4.**
CPH Intern., Inc. v. Phoenix Assur. Co. of New York, 1994 WL 259810 (S.D.N.Y. 1994)—§ **31.8, n. 4.**
Crabtree v. Elizabeth Arden Sales Corporation, 305 N.Y. 48, 110 N.E.2d 551 (N.Y. 1953)—§ **17.34; § 17.34, n. 14, 15.**
Craig, People v., 578 N.Y.S.2d 471, 585 N.E.2d 783 (N.Y.1991)—§ **38.8, n. 35.**

Craig, People v., 295 N.Y. 116, 65 N.E.2d 192 (N.Y.1946)—§ **38.19, n. 26.**
Craig v. Pierce, 231 A.D. 159, 246 N.Y.S. 573 (N.Y.A.D. 1 Dept.1930)—§ **31.6, n. 12.**
Cram v. Town of Geneva, 190 A.D.2d 1028, 593 N.Y.S.2d 651 (N.Y.A.D. 4 Dept. 1993)—§ **16.113, n. 14; § 16.114, n. 5.**
Cramer, Inc., In re, 105 B.R. 433 (Bkrtcy. W.D.Tenn.1989)—§ **9.142, n. 4.**
Crandall's Estate, In re, 196 N.Y. 127, 89 N.E. 578 (N.Y.1909)—§ **24.65, n. 1.**
Cranston v. Oxford Resources Corp., 173 A.D.2d 757, 571 N.Y.S.2d 733 (N.Y.A.D. 2 Dept.1991)—§ **30.10, n. 3.**
Crater Club, Inc. v. Adirondack Park Agency, 86 A.D.2d 714, 446 N.Y.S.2d 565 (N.Y.A.D. 3 Dept.1982)—§ **37.29, n. 29.**
Crawford v. Investors Planning Corp., 21 A.D.2d 888, 251 N.Y.S.2d 723 (N.Y.A.D. 2 Dept.1964)—§ **26.42, n. 20.**
Crawford v. McCarthy, 159 N.Y. 514, 54 N.E. 277 (N.Y.1899)—§ **24.10, n. 2.**
Crawford v. Merrill Lynch, Pierce, Fenner & Smith, Inc., 361 N.Y.S.2d 140, 319 N.E.2d 408 (N.Y.1974)—§ **37.28, n. 5, 35.**
Crawford, People v., 71 A.D.2d 38, 421 N.Y.S.2d 485 (N.Y.A.D. 4 Dept.1979)—§ **38.38, n. 4.**
Creative Living, Inc. v. Steinhauser, 78 Misc.2d 29, 355 N.Y.S.2d 897 (N.Y.Sup. 1974)—§ **12.64, n. 7.**
Credit Alliance Corp. v. Arthur Andersen & Co., 493 N.Y.S.2d 435, 483 N.E.2d 110 (N.Y.1985)—§ **28.11, n. 5.**
Credit Car Leasing Corp. v. DeCresenzo, 138 Misc.2d 726, 525 N.Y.S.2d 492 (N.Y.City Civ.Ct.1988)—§ **7.21, n. 5; § 7.26, n. 8, 9; § 7.55.**
Credit Lyonnais v. Getty Square Associates, 876 F.Supp. 517 (S.D.N.Y.1995)—§ **9.66, n. 4.**
Creeden, People v., 210 A.D.2d 422, 620 N.Y.S.2d 411 (N.Y.A.D. 2 Dept.1994)—§ **38.19, n. 88.**
Crepeau v. Zoning Bd. of Appeals of Village of Cambridge, 195 A.D.2d 919, 600 N.Y.S.2d 821 (N.Y.A.D. 3 Dept.1993)—§ **16.55; § 16.55, n. 3.**
Crescent Mfg. Co., In re, 122 B.R. 979 (Bkrtcy.N.D.Ohio 1990)—§ **9.142, n. 5.**
Crespo v. Harris, 484 F.Supp. 1167 (S.D.N.Y.1980)—§ **34.5, n. 5.**
Crespo, People v., 153 A.D.2d 573, 544 N.Y.S.2d 499 (N.Y.A.D. 2 Dept.1989)—§ **38.8, n. 175.**
Cresswell v. Sullivan & Cromwell, 771 F.Supp. 580 (S.D.N.Y.1991)—§ **28.24, n. 2, 5.**
Criado v. ITT Corp., 1993 WL 322837 (S.D.N.Y.1993)—§ **17.34; § 17.34, n. 8.**

TABLE OF CASES

Cricchio v. Pennisi, 660 N.Y.S.2d 679, 683 N.E.2d 301 (N.Y.1997)—§ **23.82, n. 2.**

Crimmins, People v., 367 N.Y.S.2d 213, 326 N.E.2d 787 (N.Y.1975)—§ **38.19, n. 87, 89; § 39.50, n. 4.**

Crippen's Estate, In re, 32 Misc.2d 1019, 224 N.Y.S.2d 116 (N.Y.Sur.1961)—§ **25.46, n. 5.**

Criscione v. City of Albany Bd. of Zoning Appeals, 185 A.D.2d 420, 585 N.Y.S.2d 821 (N.Y.A.D. 3 Dept.1992)—§ **16.121, n. 2.**

Criscuola v. Power Authority of State of New York, 602 N.Y.S.2d 588, 621 N.E.2d 1195 (N.Y.1993)—§ **14.82, n. 11.**

Crisona v. Macaluso, 33 A.D.2d 569, 305 N.Y.S.2d 441 (N.Y.A.D. 2 Dept.1969)—§ **11.49, n. 3.**

Crist v. Art Metal Works, 230 A.D. 114, 243 N.Y.S. 496 (N.Y.A.D. 1 Dept.1930)—§ **27.40, n. 7.**

Cronin v. Aetna Life Ins. Co., 46 F.3d 196 (2nd Cir.1995)—§ **17.37, n. 1.**

Cronin v. Cronin, 131 Misc.2d 879, 502 N.Y.S.2d 368 (N.Y.Sup.1986)—§ **21.39, n. 2.**

Cronin v. Scott, 78 A.D.2d 745, 432 N.Y.S.2d 656 (N.Y.A.D. 3 Dept.1980)—§ **28.11, n. 4, 12.**

Cronk v. State, 100 Misc.2d 680, 420 N.Y.S.2d 113 (N.Y.Ct.Cl.1979)—§ **14.104, n. 5.**

Cropper Co., Inc., Matter of, 35 B.R. 625 (Bkrtcy.M.D.Ga.1983)—§ **9.65, n. 2.**

Cross v. Cross, 146 A.D.2d 302, 541 N.Y.S.2d 202 (N.Y.A.D. 1 Dept.1989)—§ **24.66, n. 2.**

Crossland, People v., 220 A.D.2d 764, 633 N.Y.S.2d 324 (N.Y.A.D. 2 Dept.1995)—§ **38.10, n. 25, 149.**

Crosson v. Mielcarek, 27 A.D.2d 690, 276 N.Y.S.2d 910 (N.Y.A.D. 4 Dept.1967)—§ **12.4, n. 3.**

Crossroads Apartments Associates v. LeBoo, 152 Misc.2d 830, 578 N.Y.S.2d 1004 (N.Y.City Ct.1991)—§ **13.22, n. 11; § 13.47, n. 10.**

Crossroads Recreation, Inc. v. Broz, 172 N.Y.S.2d 129, 149 N.E.2d 65 (N.Y.1958)—§ **16.75, n. 4, 7.**

Cross Westchester Development Corp. v. Sleepy Hollow Motor Court, Inc., 222 A.D.2d 644, 636 N.Y.S.2d 372 (N.Y.A.D. 2 Dept.1995)—§ **37.37; § 37.37, n. 95; § 37.51, n. 31.**

Crouch v. Gutman, 134 N.Y. 45, 31 N.E. 271 (N.Y.1892)—§ **30.25, n. 4.**

Crounse v. Curtis, 193 A.D.2d 844, 597 N.Y.S.2d 521 (N.Y.A.D. 3 Dept.1993)—§ **37.65, n. 48.**

Croveno v. Atlantic Ave. R. Co. of Brooklyn, 150 N.Y. 225, 44 N.E. 968 (N.Y.1896)—§ **38.3, n. 7.**

Crowley v. O'Keefe, 545 N.Y.S.2d 101, 543 N.E.2d 744 (N.Y.1989)—§ **39.7, n. 16.**

Crown Publishers, Inc. v. Tully, 96 A.D.2d 990, 466 N.Y.S.2d 822 (N.Y.A.D. 3 Dept. 1983)—§ **37.87, n. 22.**

Crowthers McCall Pattern, Inc., In re, 120 B.R. 279 (Bkrtcy.S.D.N.Y.1990)—§ **9.97, n. 3.**

Crudup, People v., 100 A.D.2d 938, 474 N.Y.S.2d 827 (N.Y.A.D. 2 Dept.1984)—§ **38.20, n. 14; § 38.21; § 38.21, n. 27.**

Crump, People v., 197 A.D.2d 414, 602 N.Y.S.2d 394 (N.Y.A.D. 1 Dept.1993)—§ **38.19, n. 76; § 38.21, n. 44.**

Cruz v. City of New York, 201 A.D.2d 606, 607 N.Y.S.2d 969 (N.Y.A.D. 2 Dept. 1994)—§ **37.65, n. 63.**

Cruz v. Latin News Impacto Newspaper, 216 A.D.2d 50, 627 N.Y.S.2d 388 (N.Y.A.D. 1 Dept.1995)—§ **18.64, n. 6.**

Cruz v. Sullivan, 912 F.2d 8 (2nd Cir. 1990)—§ **34.27, n. 9; § 34.35, n. 1; § 34.44, n. 1.**

Cruzan by Cruzan v. Director, Missouri Dept. of Health, 497 U.S. 261, 110 S.Ct. 2841, 111 L.Ed.2d 224 (1990)—§ **23.109; § 23.109, n. 5; § 24.90, n. 1.**

C.S. Associates, In re, 29 F.3d 903 (3rd Cir.1994)—§ **9.102, n. 9.**

C. Schmidt & Sons, Inc. v. New York State Liquor Authority, 73 A.D.2d 399, 426 N.Y.S.2d 482 (N.Y.A.D. 1 Dept.1980)—§ **36.45, n. 2.**

C-TC 9th Avenue Partnership, In re, 113 F.3d 1304 (2nd Cir.1997)—§ **9.3, n. 4; § 9.4, n. 4; § 9.7, n. 3, 9.**

Cuban Cigar Brands N. V. v. Upmann Intern., Inc., 457 F.Supp. 1090 (S.D.N.Y. 1978)—§ **28.34, n. 1.**

Culhane, People v., 350 N.Y.S.2d 381, 305 N.E.2d 469 (N.Y.1973)—§ **38.8, n. 92.**

Cull, People v., 218 N.Y.S.2d 38, 176 N.E.2d 495 (N.Y.1961)—§ **4.1, n. 7; § 4.44, n. 7; § 4.50; § 4.50, n. 13.**

Cullen v. Margiotta, 811 F.2d 698 (2nd Cir. 1987)—§ **18.38, n. 4.**

Cully Realty, Inc., People v., 109 Misc.2d 169, 442 N.Y.S.2d 847 (N.Y.Sup.App. Term 1981)—§ **16.121, n. 7.**

Cummings, People v., 131 A.D.2d 865, 517 N.Y.S.2d 225 (N.Y.A.D. 2 Dept.1987)—§ **38.19, n. 64.**

Cunard S.S. Co. Ltd. v. Salen Reefer Services AB, 773 F.2d 452 (2nd Cir.1985)—§ **9.20, n. 4.**

Cundill v. Lewis, 245 N.Y. 383, 157 N.E. 502 (N.Y.1927)—§ **5.35, n. 4.**

Cunha, United States v., 209 F.2d 326 (1st Cir.1954)—§ **19.16, n. 8.**

TABLE OF CASES

Cunliffe v. Monroe County, 63 Misc.2d 62, 312 N.Y.S.2d 879 (N.Y.Sup.1970)—§ **14.14, n. 14.**
Cunningham v. Nadjari, 383 N.Y.S.2d 590, 347 N.E.2d 915 (N.Y.1976)—§ **38.3;** § **38.3, n. 25.**
Cunningham, People v., 424 N.Y.S.2d 421, 400 N.E.2d 360 (N.Y.1980)—§ **33.56, n. 1, 4.**
Cunningham v. Planning Bd. and Bd. of Appeals of Town of Brighton, 157 N.Y.S.2d 698 (N.Y.Sup.1956)—§ **16.50, n. 2.**
Cunnison v. Richardson Greenshields Securities Inc., 107 A.D.2d 50, 485 N.Y.S.2d 272 (N.Y.A.D. 1 Dept.1985)—§ **17.36, n. 6, 7.**
Cuomo v. Long Island Lighting Co., 525 N.Y.S.2d 828, 520 N.E.2d 546 (N.Y. 1988)—§ **37.37, n. 73;** § **39.27, n. 10.**
Curiale v. Ardra Ins. Co., Ltd., 644 N.Y.S.2d 663, 667 N.E.2d 313 (N.Y.1996)—§ **30.6, n. 6;** § **31.23, n. 3.**
Curiale v. Ardra Ins. Co., Ltd., 189 A.D.2d 217, 595 N.Y.S.2d 186 (N.Y.A.D. 1 Dept. 1993)—§ **31.23, n. 10.**
Curiano v. Suozzi, 480 N.Y.S.2d 466, 469 N.E.2d 1324 (N.Y.1984)—§ **17.31, n. 1.**
Curran v. City of Rochester, 50 A.D.2d 1059, 376 N.Y.S.2d 284 (N.Y.A.D. 4 Dept.1975)—§ **37.43, n. 1.**
Curtin v. Campbell Distributing Co., Inc., 151 A.D.2d 861, 542 N.Y.S.2d 836 (N.Y.A.D. 3 Dept.1989)—§ **28.16, n. 6.**
Curtis, In re, 40 B.R. 795 (Bkrtcy.D.Utah 1984)—§ **9.52, n. 6.**
Curtis v. Eide, 19 A.D.2d 507, 244 N.Y.S.2d 330 (N.Y.A.D. 1 Dept.1963)—§ **3.4, n. 1.**
Curtiss–Wright Corp. v. Town of East Hampton, 82 A.D.2d 551, 442 N.Y.S.2d 125 (N.Y.A.D. 2 Dept.1981)—§ **16.22, n. 15.**
Cusani, People v., 153 A.D.2d 574, 544 N.Y.S.2d 499 (N.Y.A.D. 2 Dept.1989)—§ **38.8, n. 180.**
Custody of Rebecca B., Matter of, 204 A.D.2d 57, 611 N.Y.S.2d 831 (N.Y.A.D. 1 Dept.1994)—§ **21.58, n. 2;** § **21.71, n. 2.**
Cutler v. Weinberger, 516 F.2d 1282 (2nd Cir.1975)—§ **34.43, n. 1.**

D

D., Matter of, 8 I & N Dec. 628 (Reg'l Comm'r 1960)—§ **19.15, n. 8.**
DaGata, People v., 629 N.Y.S.2d 186, 652 N.E.2d 932 (N.Y.1995)—§ **38.10, n. 101.**
Daghita, People v., 276 A.D. 20, 92 N.Y.S.2d 799 (N.Y.A.D. 3 Dept.1949)—§ **38.6;** § **38.6, n. 7.**
Dague v. City of Burlington, 935 F.2d 1343 (2nd Cir.1991)—§ **15.8, n. 9;** § **15.25, n. 7.**
Dahlberg v. Becker, 748 F.2d 85 (2nd Cir. 1984)—§ **18.18, n. 1.**
Daily Gazette Co., Inc. v. Town of Cobleskill, 111 Misc.2d 303, 444 N.Y.S.2d 44 (N.Y.Sup.1981)—§ **16.39, n. 9.**
Dairylea Cooperative, Inc. v. Walkley, 377 N.Y.S.2d 451, 339 N.E.2d 865 (N.Y. 1975)—§ **4.20, n. 1;** § **4.69, n. 1.**
Dale P., Matter of, 189 A.D.2d 325, 595 N.Y.S.2d 970 (N.Y.A.D. 2 Dept.1993)—§ **20.120;** § **20.120, n. 3.**
D'Alessandro, People v., 184 A.D.2d 114, 591 N.Y.S.2d 1001 (N.Y.A.D. 1 Dept. 1992)—§ **38.10, n. 63;** § **38.20, n. 5.**
Dalton v. Union Bank of Switzerland, 134 A.D.2d 174, 520 N.Y.S.2d 764 (N.Y.A.D. 1 Dept.1987)—§ **17.27, n. 3, 10;** § **17.31, n. 2;** § **17.36, n. 8.**
Damato v. Damato, 215 A.D.2d 348, 626 N.Y.S.2d 221 (N.Y.A.D. 2 Dept.1995)—§ **21.46, n. 4.**
Damiano v. Damiano, 94 A.D.2d 132, 463 N.Y.S.2d 477 (N.Y.A.D. 2 Dept.1983)—§ **21.38, n. 2.**
Damiano, People v., 640 N.Y.S.2d 451, 663 N.E.2d 607 (N.Y.1996)—§ **38.19, n. 22, 105.**
Dana, In re, 86 N.Y.2d 651, 636 N.Y.S.2d 716, 660 N.E.2d 397 (1995)—§ **20.5. n. 3;** § **20.8;** § **20.17;** § **20.17, n. 3, 4;** § **20.97;** § **20.97, n. 2.**
Danahy v. Meese, 84 A.D.2d 670, 446 N.Y.S.2d 611 (N.Y.A.D. 4 Dept.1981)—§ **17.23, n. 3.**
Danann Realty Corp. v. Harris, 184 N.Y.S.2d 599, 157 N.E.2d 597 (N.Y. 1959)—§ **12.20, n. 1.**
Danielenko v. Kinney Rent A Car, Inc., 455 N.Y.S.2d 555, 441 N.E.2d 1073 (N.Y. 1982)—§ **28.16, n. 1.**
Daniel Goldreyer, Ltd. v. Van de Wetering, 217 A.D.2d 434, 630 N.Y.S.2d 18 (N.Y.A.D. 1 Dept.1995)—§ **18.82, n. 1.**
Daniels, Matter of, 162 Misc.2d 840, 618 N.Y.S.2d 499 (N.Y.Sup.1994)—§ **22.48, n. 1, 11;** § **23.76, n. 20.**
Daniels, Matter of, N.Y.L.J., 11/7/94, p.34, col.4 (Sup.Ct., Suffolk County)—§ **22.47, n. 10;** § **22.48, n. 6, 7, 9, 11, 12.**
Daniels v. Williams, 474 U.S. 327, 106 S.Ct. 662, 88 L.Ed.2d 662 (1986)—§ **18.18, n. 7.**
Dante v. 310 Associates, 121 A.D.2d 332, 503 N.Y.S.2d 786 (N.Y.A.D. 1 Dept. 1986)—§ **13.33, n. 1.**
D'Antoni v. Goff, 52 A.D.2d 973, 383 N.Y.S.2d 117 (N.Y.A.D. 3 Dept.1976)—§ **12.9, n. 9.**

TABLE OF CASES

Darcy v. Zoning Bd. of Appeals of City of Rochester, 185 A.D.2d 624, 586 N.Y.S.2d 44 (N.Y.A.D. 4 Dept.1992)—§ **16.68, n. 4.**

Darla E v. Barry F, 222 A.D.2d 857, 635 N.Y.S.2d 715 (N.Y.A.D. 3 Dept.1995)—§ **37.37, n. 42, 47.**

Darling, People v., 50 A.D.2d 1038, 377 N.Y.S.2d 718 (N.Y.A.D. 3 Dept.1975)—§ **38.4, n. 1.**

Darlington v. City of Ithaca, Bd. of Zoning Appeals, 202 A.D.2d 831, 609 N.Y.S.2d 378 (N.Y.A.D. 3 Dept.1994)—§ **16.48, n. 11.**

Darob Holding Co. v. House of Pile Fabrics, Inc., 62 Misc.2d 899, 310 N.Y.S.2d 418 (N.Y.City Civ.Ct.1970)—§ **13.27, n. 2.**

DaRonco, Matter of, 167 Misc.2d 140, 638 N.Y.S.2d 275 (N.Y.Sup.1995)—§ **22.48, n. 11.**

Darwin v. Catherwood, 30 A.D.2d 996, 294 N.Y.S.2d 82 (N.Y.A.D. 3 Dept.1968)—§ **37.44, n. 15.**

Da Silva, Matter of, 15 I & N Dec. 778 (BIA 1976)—§ **19.12, n. 9.**

Da Silva v. Musso, 560 N.Y.S.2d 109, 559 N.E.2d 1268 (N.Y.1990)—§ **37.65, n. 76, 77, 78.**

Da Silva v. Time Inc., 908 F.Supp. 184 (S.D.N.Y.1995)—§ **18.64, n. 3.**

Daubert v. Merrell Dow Pharmaceuticals, Inc., 509 U.S. 579, 113 S.Ct. 2786, 125 L.Ed.2d 469 (1993)—§ **17.74; § 17.74, n. 4; § 27.35; § 27.35, n. 3.**

Daum v. Meade, 65 Misc.2d 572, 318 N.Y.S.2d 199 (N.Y.Sup.1971)—§ **16.12, n. 1.**

Daus v. Gunderman & Sons, 283 N.Y. 459, 28 N.E.2d 914 (N.Y.1940)—§ **32.19, n. 4.**

David, People v., 493 N.Y.S.2d 118, 482 N.E.2d 914 (N.Y.1985)—§ **38.19, n. 26.**

David, People v., 102 A.D.2d 551, 477 N.Y.S.2d 384 (N.Y.A.D. 2 Dept.1984)—§ **38.8, n. 55.**

Davidoff v. Davidoff, 93 A.D.2d 805, 460 N.Y.S.2d 603 (N.Y.A.D. 2 Dept.1983)—§ **21.29, n. 8.**

Davidovich v. Welton (In re Davidovich), 901 F.2d 1533 (10th Cir.1990)—§ **9.111, n. 4.**

Davidson v. Cannon, 474 U.S. 344, 106 S.Ct. 668, 88 L.Ed.2d 677 (1986)—§ **18.18, n. 7.**

Davidson v. Capuano, 792 F.2d 275 (2nd Cir.1986)—§ **18.37, n. 8.**

David T., Matter of, 555 N.Y.S.2d 675, 554 N.E.2d 1263 (N.Y.1990)—§ **33.9, n. 8.**

Davila v. New York Hosp., 1995 WL 115598 (S.D.N.Y.1995)—§ **17.82, n. 22.**

Davis, In re, 169 B.R. 285 (E.D.N.Y.1994)—§ **9.119, n. 3.**

Davis v. Davis, 128 A.D.2d 470, 513 N.Y.S.2d 405 (N.Y.A.D. 1 Dept.1987)—§ **21.37, n. 4.**

Davis v. Davis, 95 A.D.2d 674, 463 N.Y.S.2d 462 (N.Y.A.D. 1 Dept.1983)—§ **31.19, n. 4.**

Davis v. Dunnet, 239 N.Y. 338, 146 N.E. 620 (N.Y.1925)—§ **12.8, n. 2.**

Davis v. Home Ins. Co., 1995 WL 380133 (S.D.N.Y.1995)—§ **28.39, n. 10.**

Davis, People v., 221 A.D.2d 557, 635 N.Y.S.2d 487 (N.Y.A.D. 2 Dept.1995)—§ **38.28, n. 25.**

Davis, People v., 598 N.Y.S.2d 156, 614 N.E.2d 719 (N.Y.1993)—§ **33.39, n. 7.**

Davis, People v., 168 A.D.2d 218, 562 N.Y.S.2d 104 (N.Y.A.D. 1 Dept.1990)—§ **33.46, n. 2.**

Davis, People v., 554 N.Y.S.2d 460, 553 N.E.2d 1008 (N.Y.1990)—§ **33.56, n. 6.**

Davis, People v., 473 N.Y.S.2d 146, 461 N.E.2d 283 (N.Y.1984)—§ **33.60, n. 2.**

Davis, People v., 87 A.D.2d 578, 450 N.Y.S.2d 409 (N.Y.A.D. 2 Dept.1982)—§ **38.8, n. 31.**

Davis, People v., 27 A.D.2d 299, 278 N.Y.S.2d 750 (N.Y.A.D. 1 Dept.1967)—§ **38.8, n. 110.**

Davis v. Sapa, 107 A.D.2d 1005, 484 N.Y.S.2d 568 (N.Y.A.D. 3 Dept.1985)—§ **13.63, n. 2.**

Davis v. Scherer, 468 U.S. 183, 104 S.Ct. 3012, 82 L.Ed.2d 139 (1984)—§ **18.32, n. 1.**

Davis v. Travelers Ins. Companies, 105 Misc.2d 582, 432 N.Y.S.2d 592 (N.Y.Sup. 1980)—§ **24.64, n. 4.**

Davis' Estate, Matter of, 456 N.Y.S.2d 716, 442 N.E.2d 1227 (N.Y.1982)—§ **23.81, n. 4.**

Dawson v. Dawson, 152 A.D.2d 717, 544 N.Y.S.2d 172 (N.Y.A.D. 2 Dept.1989)—§ **21.38, n. 8; § 21.43, n. 4.**

Dawson, People ex rel. v. Knox, 231 A.D. 490, 247 N.Y.S. 731 (N.Y.A.D. 3 Dept. 1931)—§ **3.17, n. 7, 8.**

Day v. Morgenthau, 909 F.2d 75 (2nd Cir. 1990)—§ **18.31, n. 3; § 18.38, n. 1.**

Dayton Beach Park No. 1 Corp. v. National Union Fire Ins. Co., 175 A.D.2d 854, 573 N.Y.S.2d 700 (N.Y.A.D. 2 Dept.1991)—§ **28.39, n. 9.**

D. C. G. Trucking Corp. v. Zurich Ins. Co., 81 A.D.2d 990, 440 N.Y.S.2d 74 (N.Y.A.D. 3 Dept.1981)—§ **31.10, n. 18.**

D.C. Leathers, Inc. v. Gelmart Industries, Inc., 125 A.D.2d 738, 509 N.Y.S.2d 161 (N.Y.A.D. 3 Dept.1986)—§ **5.38, n. 3.**

Deal v. Meenan Oil Co., 153 A.D.2d 665, 544 N.Y.S.2d 672 (N.Y.A.D. 2 Dept. 1989)—§ **37.29, n. 40.**

TABLE OF CASES

Deal v. Spears, 980 F.2d 1153 (8th Cir. 1992)—§ **17.55, n. 6.**

Dean v. Dean, 214 A.D.2d 786, 624 N.Y.S.2d 666 (N.Y.A.D. 3 Dept.1995)—§ **21.52, n. 2.**

Dean, People v., 542 N.Y.S.2d 512, 540 N.E.2d 707 (N.Y.1989)—§ **33.21; § 33.21, n. 1.**

Dean, People v., 419 N.Y.S.2d 957, 393 N.E.2d 1030 (N.Y.1979)—§ **38.19, n. 16.**

Deane v. Dunbar, 777 F.2d 871 (2nd Cir. 1985)—§ **18.32, n. 1.**

DeAngelis v. Lutheran Medical Center, 84 A.D.2d 17, 445 N.Y.S.2d 188 (N.Y.A.D. 2 Dept.1981)—§ **30.15, n. 11.**

Dean S., Matter of, 185 A.D.2d 324, 586 N.Y.S.2d 276 (N.Y.A.D. 2 Dept.1992)—§ **37.19, n. 24.**

Dearborn Process Service, Inc., In re, 149 B.R. 872 (Bkrtcy.N.D.Ill.1993)—§ **9.264, n. 6.**

Deats v. Carpenter, 61 A.D.2d 320, 403 N.Y.S.2d 128 (N.Y.A.D. 3 Dept.1978)—§ **3.20, n. 8.**

DeBellis v. Commissioner of Educ. of State of N.Y., 95 A.D.2d 907, 464 N.Y.S.2d 259 (N.Y.A.D. 3 Dept.1983)—§ **37.28, n. 18.**

DeBellis v. Luney, 128 A.D.2d 778, 513 N.Y.S.2d 478 (N.Y.A.D. 2 Dept.1987)—§ **16.43, n. 11.**

DeBellis v. New York City Property Clerk, 580 N.Y.S.2d 157, 588 N.E.2d 55 (N.Y. 1992)—§ **18.11, n. 4.**

DeBonis v. State, 37 A.D.2d 878, 325 N.Y.S.2d 215 (N.Y.A.D. 3 Dept.1971)—§ **18.20, n. 2.**

De Bour, People v., 386 N.Y.S.2d 375, 352 N.E.2d 562 (N.Y.1976)—§ **33.4; § 33.4, n. 2, 7; § 33.6; § 33.6, n. 2.**

De Cillis Auto Service Center, Inc. v. New York State Dept. of Motor Vehicles, 212 A.D.2d 700, 622 N.Y.S.2d 787 (N.Y.A.D. 2 Dept.1995)—§ **7.27, n. 15.**

Decker v. Amalgamated Mutual Casualty Insurance Company, 365 N.Y.S.2d 172, 324 N.E.2d 552 (N.Y.1974)—§ **28.44, n. 1.**

Dedvukaj v. Madonado, 115 Misc.2d 211, 453 N.Y.S.2d 965 (N.Y.City Civ.Ct. 1982)—§ **13.33, n. 7.**

Deeb v. Johnson, 170 A.D.2d 865, 566 N.Y.S.2d 688 (N.Y.A.D. 3 Dept.1991)—§ **28.11; § 28.11, n. 1.**

Deem v. Bane, 159 Misc.2d 461, 605 N.Y.S.2d 191 (N.Y.Sup.1993)—§ **4.22, n. 3.**

Defense Services, Inc., In re, 104 B.R. 481 (Bkrtcy.S.D.Fla.1989)—§ **9.111, n. 2.**

De Feo, People v., 77 Misc.2d 523, 355 N.Y.S.2d 905 (N.Y.Sup.App.Term 1974)—§ **33.19, n. 2; § 33.100.**

De Filippis v. Kirchner, 217 A.D.2d 145, 636 N.Y.S.2d 134 (N.Y.A.D. 3 Dept.1995)—§ **20.66, n. 1.**

DeGeorge, People v., 543 N.Y.S.2d 11, 541 N.E.2d 11 (N.Y.1989)—§ **33.60, n. 1.**

Deitch v. Shamash, 56 Misc.2d 875, 290 N.Y.S.2d 137 (N.Y.City Civ.Ct.1968)—§ **12.32, n. 3.**

Deitsch Textiles, Inc. v. New York Property Ins. Underwriting Ass'n, 479 N.Y.S.2d 487, 468 N.E.2d 669 (N.Y.1984)—§ **31.18, n. 18.**

DeJesus, Application of, 44 Misc.2d 833, 254 N.Y.S.2d 23 (N.Y.City Civ.Ct. 1964)—§ **18.70, n. 2.**

DeJesus v. Cat Auto Tech Corp., 161 Misc.2d 723, 615 N.Y.S.2d 236 (N.Y.City Civ.Ct.1994)—§ **5.38, n. 2.**

De Jesus, People v., 446 N.Y.S.2d 201, 430 N.E.2d 1254 (N.Y.1981)—§ **38.3, n. 6.**

DeJesus, People v., 21 A.D.2d 236, 250 N.Y.S.2d 317 (N.Y.A.D. 4 Dept.1964)—§ **38.8, n. 123.**

DeJong v. Mandelbaum, 122 A.D.2d 772, 505 N.Y.S.2d 659 (N.Y.A.D. 2 Dept. 1986)—§ **12.65, n. 5.**

Dekle, People v., 452 N.Y.S.2d 568, 438 N.E.2d 101 (N.Y.1982)—§ **38.19; § 38.19, n. 52.**

De Lancey v. Piepgras, 138 N.Y. 26, 33 N.E. 822 (N.Y.1893)—§ **37.28, n. 2.**

Delaware v. Prouse, 440 U.S. 648, 99 S.Ct. 1391, 59 L.Ed.2d 660 (1979)—§ **33.5; § 33.5, n. 3.**

Delbridge v. United States, 89 F.Supp. 845 (E.D.Mich.1950)—§ **24.32, n. 2.**

Delchi Carrier SpA v. Rotorex Corp., 71 F.3d 1024 (2nd Cir.1995)—§ **5.50, n. 7.**

Del Cid v. Beloit Corp., 901 F.Supp. 539 (E.D.N.Y.1995)—§ **27.36; § 27.36, n. 7; § 27.40; § 27.40, n. 3.**

Del Conte, Matter of , 10 I & N Dec. 761 (Dist.Dir.1964)—§ **19.15, n. 10.**

DelCostello v. Teamsters, 462 U.S. 151, 103 S.Ct. 2281, 76 L.Ed.2d 476 (1983)—§ **17.61, n. 13.**

Delegated Properties, Limited v. Lewis, 36 A.D.2d 766, 321 N.Y.S.2d 234 (N.Y.A.D. 2 Dept.1971)—§ **12.29, n. 6.**

De Leon v. Secretary of Health and Human Services, 734 F.2d 930 (2nd Cir.1984)—§ **34.47, n. 17.**

Delgado, People v., 587 N.Y.S.2d 271, 599 N.E.2d 675 (N.Y.1992)—§ **38.19, n. 77; § 38.21; § 38.21, n. 37, 43, 51.**

Del Galdo v. Del Galdo, 51 A.D.2d 741, 379 N.Y.S.2d 479 (N.Y.A.D. 2 Dept.1976)—§ **21.23, n. 4.**

Delio v. Westchester County Medical Center, 129 A.D.2d 1, 516 N.Y.S.2d 677 (N.Y.A.D. 2 Dept.1987)—§ **22.54, n. 8.**

TABLE OF CASES

Delightful Music Ltd. v. Taylor (In re Taylor), 913 F.2d 102 (3rd Cir.1990)— § 9.80, n. 1.

Delizia v. Beavers, 359 N.Y.S.2d 285, 316 N.E.2d 719 (N.Y.1974)—§ 39.9; § 39.9, n. 19.

Delloiaco v. City of New York, 174 A.D.2d 705, 571 N.Y.S.2d 555 (N.Y.A.D. 2 Dept. 1991)—§ 37.38, n. 13.

DeLong v. Erie County, 89 A.D.2d 376, 455 N.Y.S.2d 887 (N.Y.A.D. 4 Dept.1982)— § 30.14, n. 3.

De Long Corp. v. Morrison–Knudsen Co., 251 N.Y.S.2d 657, 200 N.E.2d 557 (N.Y. 1964)—§ 8.6, n. 1.

DeLong Corp. v. Morrison–Knudsen Co., 20 A.D.2d 104, 244 N.Y.S.2d 859 (N.Y.A.D. 1 Dept.1963)—§ 30.40, n. 6.

Delorey, Matter of, 141 A.D.2d 540, 529 N.Y.S.2d 153 (N.Y.A.D. 2 Dept.1988)— § 25.22, n. 2.

De Los Santos v. I. N. S., 690 F.2d 56 (2nd Cir.1982)—§ 19.11, n. 6.

Delsack v. Cumella, 189 A.D.2d 640, 593 N.Y.S.2d 2 (N.Y.A.D. 1 Dept.1993)— § 12.15, n. 2.

Delta Petroleum (P.R.), Ltd., In re, 193 B.R. 99 (D.Puerto Rico 1996)—§ 9.139, n. 1.

De Luca, Matter of, N.Y.L.J., 12/14/93, p.27, col.3 (Sup.Ct., Nassau County)—§ 22.48, n. 11; § 23.76, n. 11, 20; § 23.81, n. 11.

Delulio v. 320–57 Corp., 99 A.D.2d 253, 472 N.Y.S.2d 379 (N.Y.A.D. 1 Dept.1984)— § 8.6, n. 4.

Del Vecchio v. Del Vecchio, 131 A.D.2d 536, 516 N.Y.S.2d 700 (N.Y.A.D. 2 Dept. 1987)—§ 21.43, n. 2.

Del Vecchio v. Lalla, 136 A.D.2d 820, 523 N.Y.S.2d 654 (N.Y.A.D. 3 Dept.1988)— § 16.119, n. 1, 5.

Delzotti v. American LaFrance, 179 A.D.2d 497, 579 N.Y.S.2d 33 (N.Y.A.D. 1 Dept. 1992)—§ 27.30; § 27.30, n. 1.

DeMarasse, People v., 623 N.Y.S.2d 845, 647 N.E.2d 1353 (N.Y.1995)—§ 38.27, n. 14.

De Marinis v. De Marinis, 74 A.D.2d 815, 425 N.Y.S.2d 361 (N.Y.A.D. 2 Dept. 1980)—§ 21.31, n. 1.

de Mello v. 79th Street Tenants Corp., 136 Misc.2d 73, 517 N.Y.S.2d 892 (N.Y.City Civ.Ct.1987)—§ 1.27, n. 5.

Demenus v. Sylvester, 146 A.D.2d 668, 537 N.Y.S.2d 43 (N.Y.A.D. 2 Dept.1989)— § 37.65, n. 71.

De Milio v. Borghard, 448 N.Y.S.2d 441, 433 N.E.2d 506 (N.Y.1982)—§ 4.75, n. 6; § 4.82, n. 10.

Deming, People v., 80 Misc.2d 53, 362 N.Y.S.2d 804 (N.Y.Co.Ct.1974)—§ 38.52, n. 2.

Demis v. Demis, 168 A.D.2d 840, 564 N.Y.S.2d 515 (N.Y.A.D. 3 Dept.1990)— § 21.63, n. 8.

Demov, Morris, Levin & Shein v. Glantz, 444 N.Y.S.2d 55, 428 N.E.2d 387 (N.Y. 1981)—§ 28.19, n. 11.

Dempsey v. Methodist Hosp., 159 A.D.2d 541, 552 N.Y.S.2d 406 (N.Y.A.D. 2 Dept. 1990)—§ 37.28, n. 45.

Denburg v. Parker Chapin Flattau & Klimpl, 604 N.Y.S.2d 900, 624 N.E.2d 995 (N.Y.1993)—§ 6.67, n. 2; § 6.88, n. 2.

Deni v. Air Niagara, 190 A.D.2d 1011, 594 N.Y.S.2d 468 (N.Y.A.D. 4 Dept.1993)— § 28.11; § 28.11, n. 4, 11.

Dennis, People v., 223 A.D.2d 814, 636 N.Y.S.2d 453 (N.Y.A.D. 3 Dept.1996)— § 38.8, n. 146.

Denniston's Crossing, Inc. v. State, 76 A.D.2d 988, 429 N.Y.S.2d 304 (N.Y.A.D. 3 Dept.1980)—§ 14.85, n. 8.

Den Norske Ameriekalinje Actiesselskabet v. Sun Printing & Publishing Ass'n, 226 N.Y. 1, 122 N.E. 463 (N.Y.1919)— § 30.26, n. 6.

Denny v. Ford Motor Co., 639 N.Y.S.2d 250, 662 N.E.2d 730 (N.Y.1995)—§ 27.3; § 27.3, n. 15; § 27.5, n. 1, 3; § 27.39, n. 4.

Dental Soc. of State v. Carey, 474 N.Y.S.2d 262, 462 N.E.2d 362 (N.Y.1984)—§ 4.69, n. 4, 6.

Denti, People v., 44 A.D.2d 44, 353 N.Y.S.2d 10 (N.Y.A.D. 1 Dept.1974)—§ 37.65, n. 10.

Denton v. Grumbach, 2 A.D.2d 420, 157 N.Y.S.2d 91 (N.Y.A.D. 3 Dept.1956)— § 8.19, n. 3.

De Oteris v. Mario, 185 Misc. 1029, 60 N.Y.S.2d 674 (N.Y.Sup.1945)—§ 21.17, n. 1.

Department of Economic Development v. Arthur Andersen & Co. (USA), 683 F.Supp. 1463 (S.D.N.Y.1988)—§ 2.106, n. 10.

Department of Environmental Protection of City of New York v. Department of Environmental Conservation of State, 120 A.D.2d 166, 508 N.Y.S.2d 643 (N.Y.A.D. 3 Dept.1986)—§ 4.79, n. 10.

Department of Housing Preservation and Development of City of New York v. Greenpoint Sav. Bank, 169 Misc.2d 61, 646 N.Y.S.2d 601 (N.Y.City Civ.Ct. 1995)—§ 11.30, n. 1.

Department of Social Services on Behalf of Valerie M. v. Victor A.R., 120 A.D.2d 526, 501 N.Y.S.2d 725 (N.Y.A.D. 2 Dept. 1986)—§ 37.19, n. 14.

DePascale v. Delco Appliance Division, General Motors Corp., 27 A.D.2d 602, 275

TABLE OF CASES

N.Y.S.2d 635 (N.Y.A.D. 3 Dept.1966)—§ **32.17, n. 3.**

De Puccio v. Motor Vehicle Acc. Indemnification Corp., 30 A.D.2d 1015, 294 N.Y.S.2d 113 (N.Y.A.D. 3 Dept.1968)—§ **26.28, n. 4.**

Dercole, People v., 437 N.Y.S.2d 966, 419 N.E.2d 869 (N.Y.1981)—§ **39.42, n. 6.**

Derdiarian v. Felix Contracting Corp., 434 N.Y.S.2d 166, 414 N.E.2d 666 (N.Y. 1980)—§ **27.40; § 27.40, n. 1.**

De Rosa v. Michelman, P.C., 184 A.D.2d 490, 584 N.Y.S.2d 202 (N.Y.A.D. 2 Dept. 1992)—§ **28.10, n. 9.**

Desa v. City of New York, 188 A.D.2d 313, 590 N.Y.S.2d 483 (N.Y.A.D. 1 Dept. 1992)—§ **37.29, n. 17.**

De Sena v. Board of Zoning Appeals of Inc. Village of Hempstead, 408 N.Y.S.2d 14, 379 N.E.2d 1144 (N.Y.1978)—§ **16.125, n. 4, 5.**

DeSeno, In re, 17 F.3d 642 (3rd Cir.1994)—§ **9.160, n. 2.**

DeShaney v. Winnebago County Dept. of Social Services, 489 U.S. 189, 109 S.Ct. 998, 103 L.Ed.2d 249 (1989)—§ **18.34; § 18.34, n. 5.**

Deso v. London & Lancashire Indem. Co. of America, 164 N.Y.S.2d 689, 143 N.E.2d 889 (N.Y.1957)—§ **31.10, n. 9.**

de St. Aubin v. Flacke, 505 N.Y.S.2d 859, 496 N.E.2d 879 (N.Y.1986)—§ **14.14, n. 9; § 15.34, n. 13; § 16.22, n. 16.**

De Stefano v. Immerman, 188 A.D.2d 448, 591 N.Y.S.2d 47 (N.Y.A.D. 2 Dept. 1992)—§ **29.11, n. 1.**

De Stefano v. Village of Port Chester, 211 A.D.2d 716, 622 N.Y.S.2d 75 (N.Y.A.D. 2 Dept.1995)—§ **37.87, n. 34.**

DeVita, Matter of, N.Y.L.J., 2/17/95, p.33, col.5 (Sup.Ct., Suffolk County)—§ **22.48, n. 13.**

Detwiler v. Bristol–Myers Squibb Co., 884 F.Supp. 117 (S.D.N.Y.1995)—§ **27.25; § 27.25, n. 1.**

Detzel, In re, 134 A.D.2d 205, 521 N.Y.S.2d 6 (N.Y.A.D. 1 Dept.1987)—§ **22.6, n. 8, 10.**

Deutsch Relays, Inc. v. New York State Dept. of Environmental Conservation, 179 A.D.2d 756, 579 N.Y.S.2d 128 (N.Y.A.D. 2 Dept.1992)—§ **15.11, n. 2.**

Devine, Will of, 130 Misc.2d 933, 498 N.Y.S.2d 280 (N.Y.Sur.1986)—§ **25.31, n. 1.**

DeVita, Matter of, N.Y.L.J., 2/17/95, p.33, col.5 (Sup.Ct., Suffolk County)—§ **22.39, n. 1.**

De Vito v. City of Troy, 72 A.D.2d 866, 421 N.Y.S.2d 719 (N.Y.A.D. 3 Dept.1979)—§ **14.31, n. 3.**

Devorah Leah B., Matter of, 152 A.D.2d 566, 543 N.Y.S.2d 495 (N.Y.A.D. 2 Dept. 1989)—§ **20.31, n. 1.**

Devyr v. Schaefer, 55 N.Y. 446 (N.Y.1874)—§ **12.66, n. 2.**

Dewberry, People v., 223 A.D.2d 555, 636 N.Y.S.2d 1014 (N.Y.A.D. 2 Dept.1996)—§ **38.8, n. 27.**

Dewsnup v. Timm, 502 U.S. 410, 112 S.Ct. 773, 116 L.Ed.2d 903 (1992)—§ **9.101; § 9.101, n. 1, 2, 5; § 9.197, n. 1.**

Dexter v. Town Bd. of Town of Gates, 365 N.Y.S.2d 506, 324 N.E.2d 870 (N.Y. 1975)—§ **16.8, n. 2; § 16.89, n. 10, 12; § 16.90, n. 8; § 16.112, n. 2; § 16.114, n. 4.**

D & F Const. Inc., Matter of, 865 F.2d 673 (5th Cir.1989)—§ **9.166, n. 7.**

Diamond Central, Inc. v. Gilbert, 13 A.D.2d 931, 216 N.Y.S.2d 609 (N.Y.A.D. 1 Dept. 1961)—§ **12.29, n. 11.**

Diaz, People v., 281 N.Y.S.2d 53, 227 N.E.2d 860 (N.Y.1967)—§ **38.19, n. 94.**

Diaz v. Shalala, 59 F.3d 307 (2nd Cir. 1995)—§ **34.37, n. 5; § 34.48, n. 2.**

DiBlasi v. Aetna Life and Cas. Ins. Co., 147 A.D.2d 93, 542 N.Y.S.2d 187 (N.Y.A.D. 2 Dept.1989)—§ **28.44, n. 1; § 31.17, n. 9.**

DiBlasi v. Caldara, 123 A.D.2d 738, 507 N.Y.S.2d 209 (N.Y.A.D. 2 Dept.1986)—§ **37.51, n. 31.**

Dickens v. Director of Finance of City of New York, 45 Misc.2d 882, 258 N.Y.S.2d 211 (N.Y.Sup.1965)—§ **8.35, n. 3.**

Dickens v. Ernesto, 330 N.Y.S.2d 346, 281 N.E.2d 153 (N.Y.1972)—§ **20.28; § 20.28, n. 2.**

Dickerson v. Kaplan, 763 F.Supp. 694 (E.D.N.Y.1990)—§ **17.34, n. 16.**

Dickman v. City of New York, 25 A.D.2d 931, 270 N.Y.S.2d 304 (N.Y.A.D. 3 Dept. 1966)—§ **32.38, n. 5.**

Dickson v. Ferullo, 96 A.D.2d 745, 465 N.Y.S.2d 328 (N.Y.A.D. 4 Dept.1983)—§ **8.27, n. 4.**

Dickson, People v., 133 A.D.2d 492, 519 N.Y.S.2d 419 (N.Y.A.D. 3 Dept.1987)—§ **38.8, n. 171.**

Dicocco v. Capital Area Community Health Plan, Inc., 159 A.D.2d 119, 559 N.Y.S.2d 395 (N.Y.A.D. 3 Dept.1990)—§ **17.34, n. 6, 9.**

Dicocco v. Capital Area Community Health Plan, Inc., 135 A.D.2d 308, 525 N.Y.S.2d 417 (N.Y.A.D. 3 Dept.1988)—§ **17.34, n. 6.**

DiDomenico Packaging Corp. v. Nails Again, Inc., 139 Misc.2d 525, 527 N.Y.S.2d 676 (N.Y.City Civ.Ct.1988)—§ **5.37, n. 5.**

TABLE OF CASES

DiDominici v. Parmet, 118 A.D.2d 618, 499 N.Y.S.2d 768 (N.Y.A.D. 2 Dept.1986)—§ **18.79, n. 1.**

DiDonato, People v., 211 A.D.2d 842, 621 N.Y.S.2d 226 (N.Y.A.D. 3 Dept.1995)—§ **38.8, n. 165.**

Dieckhaus Stationers of King of Prussia, Inc., In re, 73 B.R. 969 (Bkrtcy.E.D.Pa. 1987)—§ **9.174, n. 3.**

Diefendorf, People v., 281 A.D. 465, 281 A.D. 865, 119 N.Y.S.2d 469 (N.Y.A.D. 1 Dept.1953)—§ **38.8, n. 86.**

Diemer v. Diemer, 203 N.Y.S.2d 829, 168 N.E.2d 654 (N.Y.1960)—§ **21.22;** § **21.22, n. 7.**

Dieppa, People v., 158 Misc.2d 584, 601 N.Y.S.2d 786 (N.Y.Sup.1993)—§ **18.55, n. 7.**

Dietzel v. City of New York, 218 N.Y. 270, 112 N.E. 720 (N.Y.1916)—§ **30.17, n. 1.**

DiFigola v. Horatio Arms, Inc., 189 A.D.2d 724, 593 N.Y.S.2d 9 (N.Y.A.D. 1 Dept. 1993)—§ **37.28, n. 24, 35.**

Di Gerlando v. Second Ave. R. Corporation, 155 Misc. 168, 278 N.Y.S. 797 (N.Y.Sup. 1935)—§ **30.8, n. 5.**

Di Gilio v. William J. Burns Intern. Detective Agency, 46 A.D.2d 650, 359 N.Y.S.2d 688 (N.Y.A.D. 2 Dept.1974)—§ **17.21, n. 2.**

Dignan v. Dignan, 156 A.D.2d 995, 549 N.Y.S.2d 539 (N.Y.A.D. 4 Dept.1989)—§ **21.43, n. 9.**

DiJurico, Estate of, 134 Misc.2d 263, 510 N.Y.S.2d 465 (N.Y.Sur.1987)—§ **25.6, n. 3.**

Dillenbeck v. Bailey, 32 A.D.2d 735, 301 N.Y.S.2d 900 (N.Y.A.D. 4 Dept.1969)—§ **37.37, n. 32.**

Dillenbeck v. Hess, 539 N.Y.S.2d 707, 536 N.E.2d 1126 (N.Y.1989)—§ **26.42, n. 17.**

Dillon v. Anderson, 43 N.Y. 231 (N.Y. 1870)—§ **30.27, n. 1, 4.**

Dillon v. Dean, 158 A.D.2d 579, 551 N.Y.S.2d 547 (N.Y.A.D. 2 Dept.1990)—§ **28.19;** § **28.19, n. 5.**

DiMarco v. Supermarkets General Corp., 137 A.D.2d 651, 524 N.Y.S.2d 743 (N.Y.A.D. 2 Dept.1988)—§ **30.9, n. 45.**

Dimas v. Motor Vehicle Acc. Indemnification Corp., 18 A.D.2d 761, 235 N.Y.S.2d 461 (N.Y.A.D. 4 Dept.1962)—§ **26.28, n. 3.**

DiMatteo v. North Tonawanda Auto Wash, Inc., 101 A.D.2d 692, 476 N.Y.S.2d 40 (N.Y.A.D. 4 Dept.1984)—§ **11.37, n. 9.**

Dime Sav. Bank of New York v. Glavey, 214 A.D.2d 419, 625 N.Y.S.2d 181 (N.Y.A.D. 1 Dept.1995)—§ **11.12, n. 2.**

Dime Sav. Bank of New York, F.S.B. v. Levy, 161 Misc.2d 480, 615 N.Y.S.2d 218 (N.Y.Sup.1994)—§ **11.9, n. 10.**

Dime Sav. Bank of New York, FSB v. Roberts, 167 A.D.2d 674, 563 N.Y.S.2d 253 (N.Y.A.D. 3 Dept.1990)—§ **11.53, n. 8.**

Diocese of Rochester v. Planning Bd. of Town of Brighton, 154 N.Y.S.2d 849, 136 N.E.2d 827 (N.Y.1956)—§ **16.91, n. 7;** § **16.131, n. 1, 5, 6.**

DiPaolo v. DiPaolo, 223 A.D.2d 589, 637 N.Y.S.2d 167 (N.Y.A.D. 2 Dept.1996)—§ **37.19, n. 14.**

DiPippo v. Prudential Ins. Co. of America, 88 A.D.2d 631, 450 N.Y.S.2d 237 (N.Y.A.D. 2 Dept.1982)—§ **31.27, n. 6.**

DiPrima v. DiPrima, 111 A.D.2d 901, 490 N.Y.S.2d 607 (N.Y.A.D. 2 Dept.1985)—§ **28.24, n. 5, 8.**

DiPrisco v. 2556 Boston Road Food Corp., 129 A.D.2d 411, 513 N.Y.S.2d 683 (N.Y.A.D. 1 Dept.1987)—§ **30.8, n. 12.**

Di Raffaele, People v., 448 N.Y.S.2d 448, 433 N.E.2d 513 (N.Y.1982)—§ **38.8, n. 173, 192, 203.**

Director of Assigned Counsel Plan of City of New York, Matter of, 638 N.Y.S.2d 415, 661 N.E.2d 988 (N.Y.1995)—§ **37.37, n. 76.**

Dirschel v. Speck, 1994 WL 330262 (S.D.N.Y.1994)—§ **17.69, n. 3.**

Disenhouse Associates v. Mazzaferro, 135 Misc.2d 1135, 519 N.Y.S.2d 119 (N.Y.City Civ.Ct.1987)—§ **13.18, n. 21.**

Di Siena, Matter of Estate of, 178 A.D.2d 720, 576 N.Y.S.2d 952 (N.Y.A.D. 3 Dept. 1991)—§ **25.50, n. 5.**

Display Printers, Inc. v. Globe Albums, Inc., 24 Misc.2d 331, 200 N.Y.S.2d 453 (N.Y.Mun.Ct.1959)—§ **5.39, n. 4.**

Di Stasi v. Nationwide Mut. Ins. Co., 132 A.D.2d 305, 522 N.Y.S.2d 340 (N.Y.A.D. 3 Dept.1987)—§ **26.24, n. 18.**

District Attorney of Kings County v. Iadarola, 164 Misc.2d 204, 623 N.Y.S.2d 999 (N.Y.Sup.1995)—§ **38.8, n. 61.**

Division of Triple T Service, Inc. v. Mobil Oil Corp., 60 Misc.2d 720, 304 N.Y.S.2d 191 (N.Y.Sup.1969)—§ **5.21, n. 7.**

Dixon v. Heckler, 589 F.Supp. 1494 (S.D.N.Y.1984)—§ **34.63;** § **34.63, n. 3.**

Dixon v. Motor Vehicle Acc. Indemnification Corp., 56 A.D.2d 650, 391 N.Y.S.2d 898 (N.Y.A.D. 2 Dept.1977)—§ **26.28, n. 3.**

Dixon v. Pacific Mutual Life Insurance Company, 268 F.2d 812 (2nd Cir.1959)—§ **31.19, n. 3.**

Dixon, People v., 138 A.D.2d 929, 526 N.Y.S.2d 269 (N.Y.A.D. 4 Dept.1988)—§ **38.21, n. 9.**

Dodge v. Richmond, 10 A.D.2d 4, 196 N.Y.S.2d 477 (N.Y.A.D. 1 Dept.1960)—§ **5.7, n. 1, 3.**

TABLE OF CASES

Dodge, Estate of v. Commissioner, T.C. Memo. 1961-346 (Tax Ct.1961)—§ **23.118, n. 2, 4, 5.**

Dodson v. Planning Bd. of Town of Highlands, 163 A.D.2d 804, 558 N.Y.S.2d 1012 (N.Y.A.D. 3 Dept.1990)—§ **16.106, n. 6.**

Doe, In re, 58 F.3d 494 (9th Cir.1995)—§ **9.111, n. 1.**

Doe v. Axelrod, 527 N.Y.S.2d 368, 522 N.E.2d 444 (N.Y.1988)—§ **4.71, n. 2, 5, 9;** § **4.75, n. 14.**

Doe v. Axelrod, 123 A.D.2d 21, 510 N.Y.S.2d 92 (N.Y.A.D. 1 Dept.1986)—§ **4.13, n. 5.**

Doe v. City of New York, 15 F.3d 264 (2nd Cir.1994)—§ **17.55, n. 17;** § **18.63, n. 6.**

Doe v. Doe, 929 F.Supp. 608 (D.Conn. 1996)—§ **18.53, n. 8.**

Doe, People v., 170 A.D.2d 690, 567 N.Y.S.2d 104 (N.Y.A.D. 2 Dept.1991)—§ **38.10, n. 23.**

Doe v. Phillips, 81 F.3d 1204 (2nd Cir. 1996)—§ **18.31, n. 3.**

Doe v. Roe, 190 A.D.2d 463, 599 N.Y.S.2d 350 (N.Y.A.D. 4 Dept.1993)—§ **29.65, n. 4.**

Doe v. Roe, 155 Misc.2d 392, 588 N.Y.S.2d 236 (N.Y.Sup.1992)—§ **29.65, n. 4.**

Doe v. Roe, 93 Misc.2d 201, 400 N.Y.S.2d 668 (N.Y.Sup.1977)—§ **30.31, n. 13.**

Doe v. Roe, 37 A.D.2d 433, 326 N.Y.S.2d 421 (N.Y.A.D. 2 Dept.1971)—§ **20.13, n. 1.**

Doe v. State, 189 A.D.2d 199, 595 N.Y.S.2d 592 (N.Y.A.D. 4 Dept.1993)—§ **30.10, n. 7.**

Dokes, People v., 584 N.Y.S.2d 761, 595 N.E.2d 836 (N.Y.1992)—§ **33.47, n. 1;** § **38.19, n. 21, 124;** § **38.28;** § **38.28, n. 27.**

Dolan v. City of Tigard, 512 U.S. 374, 114 S.Ct. 2309, 129 L.Ed.2d 304 (1994)—§ **16.22, n. 17.**

Dolan, United States v., 120 F.3d 856 (8th Cir.1997)—§ **9.205, n. 4.**

Dole v. Dow Chemical Co., 331 N.Y.S.2d 382, 282 N.E.2d 288 (N.Y.1972)—§ **32.15;** § **32.15, n. 5.**

Dolin v. Passero–Scardetta Associates, 110 A.D.2d 1051, 489 N.Y.S.2d 21 (N.Y.A.D. 4 Dept.1985)—§ **37.37, n. 92.**

Dollar v. Long Mfg., N. C., Inc., 561 F.2d 613 (5th Cir.1977)—§ **27.37;** § **27.37, n. 10.**

Dollar Dry Dock Bank v. Piping Rock Builders, Inc., 181 A.D.2d 709, 581 N.Y.S.2d 361 (N.Y.A.D. 2 Dept.1992)—§ **11.6, n. 7;** § **11.19, n. 2.**

Dolphin v. Marocik, 222 A.D.2d 549, 635 N.Y.S.2d 84 (N.Y.A.D. 2 Dept.1995)—§ **37.37, n. 94;** § **37.66, n. 2.**

Domagalski v. Springfield Fire & Marine Ins. Co., 218 A.D. 187, 218 N.Y.S. 164 (N.Y.A.D. 4 Dept.1926)—§ **31.18, n. 19.**

Dominguez v. Manhattan and Bronx Surface Transit Operating Authority, 415 N.Y.S.2d 634, 388 N.E.2d 1221 (N.Y. 1979)—§ **37.28, n. 2.**

Domus Realty Corp. v. 3440 Realty Co., 179 Misc. 749, 40 N.Y.S.2d 69 (N.Y.Sup. 1943)—§ **11.37, n. 9.**

Donaloio v. State, 99 A.D.2d 335, 472 N.Y.S.2d 946 (N.Y.A.D. 3 Dept.1984)—§ **14.82, n. 1.**

Donato v. Baltrusaitis, 56 Misc.2d 935, 290 N.Y.S.2d 659 (N.Y.Sup.1958)—§ **12.15, n. 5.**

Dondi v. Jones, 386 N.Y.S.2d 4, 351 N.E.2d 650 (N.Y.1976)—§ **4.71, n. 8.**

Done Holding Co. v. State, 144 A.D.2d 528, 534 N.Y.S.2d 406 (N.Y.A.D. 2 Dept. 1988)—§ **14.109, n. 1.**

Donnelly v. Bauder, 217 A.D. 59, 216 N.Y.S. 437 (N.Y.A.D. 4 Dept.1926)—§ **5.8, n. 5.**

Donnelly v. Donnelly, 540 N.Y.S.2d 1001, 538 N.E.2d 353 (N.Y.1989)—§ **39.9, n. 6.**

Donohoe v. Goldner, 168 A.D.2d 412, 562 N.Y.S.2d 538 (N.Y.A.D. 2 Dept.1990)—§ **37.29, n. 17.**

Donohue v. Donohue, 222 A.D.2d 646, 636 N.Y.S.2d 104 (N.Y.A.D. 2 Dept.1995)—§ **21.22, n. 6.**

Donovan v. Dewey, 452 U.S. 594, 101 S.Ct. 2534, 69 L.Ed.2d 262 (1981)—§ **4.62, n. 7.**

Donovan, People v., 464 N.Y.S.2d 745, 451 N.E.2d 492 (N.Y.1983)—§ **38.21, n. 58.**

Dontas v. City of New York, 183 A.D.2d 868, 584 N.Y.S.2d 134 (N.Y.A.D. 2 Dept. 1992)—§ **30.14, n. 13, 14.**

Dooley v. Skodnek, 138 A.D.2d 102, 529 N.Y.S.2d 569 (N.Y.A.D. 2 Dept.1988)—§ **30.15;** § **30.15, n. 3.**

Dorfman v. Chu, 148 A.D.2d 917, 539 N.Y.S.2d 549 (N.Y.A.D. 3 Dept.1989)—§ **35.126, n. 1.**

Dorfman v. Leidner, 563 N.Y.S.2d 723, 565 N.E.2d 472 (N.Y.1990)—§ **37.32, n. 1.**

Dorino, People v., 200 A.D.2d 632, 606 N.Y.S.2d 741 (N.Y.A.D. 2 Dept.1994)—§ **38.8, n. 23.**

Dorsey v. Honda Motor Co. Ltd., 655 F.2d 650 (5th Cir.1981)—§ **27.43, n. 1, 4.**

Dorsey v. Stuyvesant Town Corp., 299 N.Y. 512, 87 N.E.2d 541 (N.Y.1949)—§ **18.1, n. 3.**

Dory v. Ryan, 25 F.3d 81 (2nd Cir.1994)—§ **18.31, n. 3.**

Douglas v. Adel, 269 N.Y. 144, 199 N.E. 35 (N.Y.1935)—§ **38.8, n. 87.**

TABLE OF CASES

Douglas, People v., 205 A.D.2d 280, 617 N.Y.S.2d 733 (N.Y.A.D. 1 Dept.1994)—**§ 37.29, n. 43; § 37.65, n. 10.**

Douglaston and Little Neck Coalition v. Sexton, 145 A.D.2d 480, 535 N.Y.S.2d 634 (N.Y.A.D. 2 Dept.1988)—**§ 15.6, n. 2.**

Douglaston Civic Ass'n, Application of v. Board of Standards and Appeals of City of N.Y., 278 A.D. 659, 102 N.Y.S.2d 582 (N.Y.A.D. 2 Dept.1951)—**§ 16.89, n. 15.**

Douglaston Civic Ass'n, Inc. v. Klein, 435 N.Y.S.2d 705, 416 N.E.2d 1040 (N.Y. 1980)—**§ 16.76, n. 3.**

Dow Corning Corp., In re, 212 B.R. 258 (E.D.Mich.1997)—**§ 9.47, n. 1.**

Dow Corning Corp., In re, 86 F.3d 482 (6th Cir.1996)—**§ 9.19, n. 8.**

Dowly v. State, 190 Misc. 16, 68 N.Y.S.2d 573 (N.Y.Ct.Cl.1947)—**§ 30.8, n. 4.**

Doxsee, People ex rel. Swan v., 136 A.D. 400, 120 N.Y.S. 962 (N.Y.A.D. 2 Dept. 1910)—**§ 3.16, n. 8.**

Doyle, Matter of, N.Y.L.J., 2/14/90, p.22, col. 5—**§ 25.24, n. 3, 4.**

Doyle, People v., 222 A.D.2d 875, 635 N.Y.S.2d 718 (N.Y.A.D. 3 Dept.1995)—**§ 38.8, n. 215.**

Doyle, People ex rel. v. Jacquin, 186 A.D.2d 235, 587 N.Y.S.2d 1019 (N.Y.A.D. 2 Dept.1992)—**§ 38.8, n. 79.**

Drachman Structurals, Inc. v. Anthony Rivara Contracting Co., Inc., 78 Misc.2d 486, 356 N.Y.S.2d 974 (N.Y.Sup.1974)—**§ 10.18, n. 6; § 10.26, n. 4.**

Drago v. Buonagurio, 61 A.D.2d 282, 402 N.Y.S.2d 250 (N.Y.A.D. 3 Dept.1978)—**§ 28.11, n. 12.**

Drexel Burnham Lambert Group, Inc., In re, 138 B.R. 723 (Bkrtcy.S.D.N.Y. 1992)—**§ 9.149, n. 3; § 9.158, n. 5; § 9.170, n. 6.**

Drexel Burnham Lambert Group, Inc., In re, 118 B.R. 209 (Bkrtcy.S.D.N.Y. 1990)—**§ 9.47, n. 1.**

Drexel Burnham Lambert Group Inc., In re, 113 B.R. 830 (Bkrtcy.S.D.N.Y.1990)—**§ 9.112, n. 5.**

Drexel Burnham Lambert Group Inc., In re, 112 B.R. 584 (Bkrtcy.S.D.N.Y.1990)—**§ 9.39, n. 3.**

Drexel Burnham Lambert Group, Inc. v. Vigilant Ins. Co., 130 B.R. 405 (S.D.N.Y. 1991)—**§ 9.22, n. 1.**

Dreyer and Traub v. Rubinstein, 191 A.D.2d 236, 594 N.Y.S.2d 257 (N.Y.A.D. 1 Dept.1993)—**§ 28.32; § 28.32, n. 1.**

Dreyfus Special Income Fund, Inc. v. State Tax Com'n, 532 N.Y.S.2d 356, 528 N.E.2d 509 (N.Y.1988)—**§ 35.20, n. 1.**

Driscoll, Matter of, N.Y.L.J., 10/22/93, p.30, col.4 (Sup.Ct., Nassau County)—**§ 22.47, n. 14; § 22.48, n. 1, 11, 12; § 23.76, n. 20.**

Drouin v. Ridge Lumber, Inc., 209 A.D.2d 957, 619 N.Y.S.2d 433 (N.Y.A.D. 4 Dept. 1994)—**§ 15.33, n. 4.**

Drummond v. Drummond, 205 A.D.2d 847, 613 N.Y.S.2d 717 (N.Y.A.D. 3 Dept. 1994)—**§ 21.71, n. 2.**

Duane Jones Co. v. Burke, 306 N.Y. 172, 117 N.E.2d 237 (N.Y.1954)—**§ 30.5, n. 12.**

Dubin, Matter of Estate of, 166 Misc.2d 971, 636 N.Y.S.2d 991 (N.Y.Sur.1995)—**§ 25.46, n. 6.**

Du Bois v. Community Hosp. of Schoharie County, Inc., 150 A.D.2d 893, 540 N.Y.S.2d 917 (N.Y.A.D. 3 Dept.1989)—**§ 30.14, n. 10.**

Dubowsky v. Goldsmith, 202 A.D. 818, 195 N.Y.S. 67 (N.Y.A.D. 2 Dept.1922)—**§ 13.58, n. 3.**

Du Bray, Matter of Estate of, 132 A.D.2d 914, 518 N.Y.S.2d 245 (N.Y.A.D. 3 Dept. 1987)—**§ 25.31, n. 6.**

Duell v. Condon, 200 A.D.2d 549, 606 N.Y.S.2d 690 (N.Y.A.D. 1 Dept.1994)—**§ 30.42, n. 8.**

Dueno, People v., 203 A.D.2d 476, 611 N.Y.S.2d 15 (N.Y.A.D. 2 Dept.1994)—**§ 38.10, n. 168.**

Duggan v. Bowen, 691 F.Supp. 1487 (D.D.C. 1988)—**§ 23.47, n. 3; § 23.85, n. 2.**

Dugue v. Dugue, 172 A.D.2d 974, 568 N.Y.S.2d 244 (N.Y.A.D. 3 Dept.1991)—**§ 21.37, n. 10.**

Duke, Matter of, 79 F.3d 43 (7th Cir. 1996)—**§ 9.131, n. 1.**

Duke, Matter of, 640 N.Y.S.2d 446, 663 N.E.2d 602 (N.Y.1996)—**§ 25.10, n. 1, 2.**

Duke v. Fargo, 172 A.D. 746, 158 N.Y.S. 1009 (N.Y.A.D. 2 Dept.1916)—**§ 37.29, n. 14.**

Dukes v. 800 Grand Concourse Owners, Inc., 198 A.D.2d 13, 603 N.Y.S.2d 138 (N.Y.A.D. 1 Dept.1993)—**§ 37.28, n. 6.**

Dulber v. Dulber, 37 A.D.2d 566, 322 N.Y.S.2d 862 (N.Y.A.D. 2 Dept.1971)—**§ 37.35, n. 7.**

Dumas, People v., 506 N.Y.S.2d 319, 497 N.E.2d 686 (N.Y.1986)—**§ 33.10, n. 4.**

Dunaway v. New York, 442 U.S. 200, 99 S.Ct. 2248, 60 L.Ed.2d 824 (1979)—**§ 33.27; § 33.27, n. 2.**

Dunbar, People v., 440 N.Y.S.2d 613, 423 N.E.2d 36 (N.Y.1981)—**§ 38.8, n. 144.**

Dune Deck Owners Corp., In re, 175 B.R. 839 (Bkrtcy.S.D.N.Y.1995)—**§ 9.162, n. 10.**

Dunham v. Hilco Const. Co., Inc., 654 N.Y.S.2d 335, 676 N.E.2d 1178 (N.Y. 1996)—**§ 37.2, n. 9; § 37.65, n. 69.**

TABLE OF CASES

Dunham v. Williams, 37 N.Y. 251 (N.Y. 1867)—§ **12.57, n. 3.**

Dunn v. Dunn, 224 A.D.2d 888, 638 N.Y.S.2d 238 (N.Y.A.D. 3 Dept.1996)—§ **21.37, n. 10.**

Dunn v. Fishbein, 123 A.D.2d 659, 507 N.Y.S.2d 29 (N.Y.A.D. 2 Dept.1986)—§ **18.45, n. 1.**

Dunn v. Moss, 193 A.D.2d 983, 598 N.Y.S.2d 350 (N.Y.A.D. 3 Dept.1993)—§ **37.29, n. 22.**

Dunn v. Town of Warwick, 146 A.D.2d 601, 537 N.Y.S.2d 174 (N.Y.A.D. 2 Dept. 1989)—§ **16.128, n. 1.**

Dunne v. Harnett, 92 Misc.2d 48, 399 N.Y.S.2d 562 (N.Y.Sup.1977)—§ **3.32, n. 2.**

DuPont v. Brady, 646 F.Supp. 1067 (S.D.N.Y.1986)—§ **28.12; § 28.12, n. 15; § 28.18, n. 3.**

Dupree, People v., 67 A.D.2d 716, 412 N.Y.S.2d 424 (N.Y.A.D. 2 Dept.1979)—§ **38.8, n. 116, 198.**

Durant v. Abendroth, 97 N.Y. 132 (N.Y. 1884)—§ **37.67, n. 10.**

Dur–Bar Realty Co. v. City of Utica, 57 A.D.2d 51, 394 N.Y.S.2d 913 (N.Y.A.D. 4 Dept.1977)—§ **16.15; § 16.15, n. 1; § 16.61, n. 2.**

Durepo v. Flower City Television Corp., 147 A.D.2d 934, 537 N.Y.S.2d 391 (N.Y.A.D. 4 Dept.1989)—§ **30.9, n. 39.**

Durham v. Barker Chemical Corp., 151 A.D.2d 887, 543 N.Y.S.2d 182 (N.Y.A.D. 3 Dept.1989)—§ **26.48, n. 1.**

Durham Temporaries, Inc. v. New York State Tax Com'n, 132 A.D.2d 843, 517 N.Y.S.2d 630 (N.Y.A.D. 3 Dept.1987)—§ **37.37, n. 47.**

Durkin v. Peluso, 184 A.D.2d 940, 585 N.Y.S.2d 137 (N.Y.A.D. 3 Dept.1992)—§ **37.65, n. 37.**

Durkin v. Shea, 957 F.Supp. 1360 (S.D.N.Y. 1997)—§ **28.13, n. 1.**

DuSesoi v. United Refining Co., 540 F.Supp. 1260 (W.D.Pa.1982)—§ **17.27, n. 3.**

Dusing, People v., 181 N.Y.S.2d 493, 155 N.E.2d 393 (N.Y.1959)—§ **33.68; § 33.68, n. 13, 15.**

Dutchess & C.C.R. Co. v. Mabbett, 58 N.Y. 397 (N.Y.1874)—§ **1.21, n. 13.**

Dwares v. City of New York, 985 F.2d 94 (2nd Cir.1993)—§ **18.18, n. 1; § 18.34, n. 3.**

D & W Realty Corp., In re, 156 B.R. 140 (Bkrtcy.S.D.N.Y.1993)—§ **9.157, n. 4.**

Dyer, People v., 201 A.D.2d 498, 607 N.Y.S.2d 379 (N.Y.A.D. 2 Dept.1994)—§ **38.19, n. 88.**

E

EAD Metallurgical, Inc. v. Aetna Cas. & Sur. Co., 905 F.2d 8 (2nd Cir.1990)—§ **31.10, n. 7.**

Eagle Bus Mfg., Inc., In re, 134 B.R. 584 (Bkrtcy.S.D.Tex.1991)—§ **9.148, n. 4, 8.**

Eagle Star Ins. Co. of America v. Behar, 140 A.D.2d 664, 528 N.Y.S.2d 1019 (N.Y.A.D. 2 Dept.1988)—§ **37.37; § 37.37, n. 21.**

Eagleston v. Guido, 41 F.3d 865 (2nd Cir. 1994)—§ **18.22, n. 4.**

Easter, Matter of, 71 A.D.2d 762, 419 N.Y.S.2d 327 (N.Y.A.D. 3 Dept.1979)—§ **38.8, n. 112.**

Eastern Concrete Steel Co. v. Bricklayers' & Mason Plasterers' International Union, Local No. 45, of Buffalo, 200 A.D. 714, 193 N.Y.S. 368 (N.Y.A.D. 4 Dept. 1922)—§ **38.8, n. 84.**

East Europe Domestic Intern. Sales Corp. v. Island Creek Coal Sales Co., 572 F.Supp. 702 (S.D.N.Y.1983)—§ **5.20, n. 3.**

East Haven Associates Inc. v. Gurian, 64 Misc.2d 276, 313 N.Y.S.2d 927 (N.Y.City Civ.Ct.1970)—§ **13.31; § 13.31, n. 5.**

Eastland v. United States Servicemen's Fund, 421 U.S. 491, 95 S.Ct. 1813, 44 L.Ed.2d 324 (1975)—§ **18.31, n. 4.**

Eastman, People v., 624 N.Y.S.2d 83, 648 N.E.2d 459 (N.Y.1995)—§ **38.19; § 38.19, n. 133; § 38.22, n. 3; § 39.50, n. 3.**

East Ramapo Cent. School Dist. v. Orangetown–Monsey Hebrew School, 141 A.D.2d 693, 529 N.Y.S.2d 576 (N.Y.A.D. 2 Dept.1988)—§ **28.16, n. 5.**

Eastrich Multiple Investor Fund, L.P. v. Citiwide Development Associates, 218 A.D.2d 43, 637 N.Y.S.2d 712 (N.Y.A.D. 1 Dept.1996)—§ **11.32, n. 4.**

East Thirteenth Street Community Ass'n v. New York State Urban Development Corp., 617 N.Y.S.2d 706, 641 N.E.2d 1368 (N.Y.1994)—§ **14.29, n. 3; § 14.36; § 14.36, n. 2; § 14.38, n. 14.**

Eccleston, In re, 70 B.R. 210 (Bkrtcy. N.D.N.Y.1986)—§ **9.130, n. 5.**

Edelman v. Jordan, 415 U.S. 651, 94 S.Ct. 1347, 39 L.Ed.2d 662 (1974)—§ **18.33, n. 1.**

Eden Park Health Services, Inc. v. Whalen, 73 A.D.2d 993, 424 N.Y.S.2d 33 (N.Y.A.D. 3 Dept.1980)—§ **4.12, n. 7.**

Edmead v. McGuire, 114 A.D.2d 758, 494 N.Y.S.2d 712 (N.Y.A.D. 1 Dept.1985)—§ **4.2, n. 44; § 4.82, n. 11.**

Edmonson v. Leesville Concrete Co., Inc., 500 U.S. 614, 111 S.Ct. 2077, 114 L.Ed.2d 660 (1991)—§ **18.15, n. 5.**

TABLE OF CASES

Edward Franz F., Matter of, 186 A.D.2d 256, 588 N.Y.S.2d 331 (N.Y.A.D. 2 Dept. 1992)—§ **20.67, n. 5.**

Edwards, In re, 50 B.R. 933 (Bkrtcy. S.D.N.Y.1985)—§ **9.209, n. 9.**

Edwards, People v., 147 A.D.2d 586, 537 N.Y.S.2d 879 (N.Y.A.D. 2 Dept.1989)—§ **38.19, n. 64.**

E.E.O.C. v. Doremus & Co., 921 F.Supp. 1048 (S.D.N.Y.1995)—§ **17.37, n. 1.**

E.F. Curialle & Co. v. Kenray Realty Corp., 25 Misc.2d 745, 202 N.Y.S.2d 677 (N.Y.Sup.1960)—§ **10.13, n. 4.**

Eggert v. Town Bd. of Town of Westfield, 217 A.D.2d 975, 630 N.Y.S.2d 179 (N.Y.A.D. 4 Dept.1995)—§ **16.58;** § **16.58, n. 1.**

Ehrhart v. Secretary of Health and Human Services, 969 F.2d 534 (7th Cir.1992)—§ **34.47, n. 19.**

E.I. Du Pont de Nemours & Co. v. White, 8 F.2d 5 (3rd Cir.1925)—§ **27.32;** § **27.32, n. 4.**

Eight Associates v. Hynes, 492 N.Y.S.2d 15, 481 N.E.2d 555 (N.Y.1985)—§ **13.9, n. 4.**

Eighth Ave. Coach Corporation v. City of New York, 286 N.Y. 84, 35 N.E.2d 907 (N.Y.1941)—§ **14.11, n. 1.**

840 West End Avenue Assocs. v. Zurkowski, N.Y.L.J., 2/28/91, p.24, col.4 (App. Term, 1st Dep't)—§ **13.18, n. 23.**

81 Franklin Co. v. Ginaccini, 160 A.D.2d 558, 554 N.Y.S.2d 207 (N.Y.A.D. 1 Dept. 1990)—§ **13.30, n. 5.**

Einach's Estate, In re, 1 Misc.2d 537, 146 N.Y.S.2d 240 (N.Y.Sur.1955)—§ **10.3, n. 1.**

Eisele v. Malone, 2 A.D.2d 550, 157 N.Y.S.2d 155 (N.Y.A.D. 1 Dept.1956)—§ **26.11, n. 5.**

Eisenthal v. Wittlock, 198 A.D.2d 395, 603 N.Y.S.2d 586 (N.Y.A.D. 2 Dept.1993)—§ **12.61, n. 4.**

Eisworth, People v., 65 A.D.2d 960, 411 N.Y.S.2d 550 (N.Y.A.D. 4 Dept.1978)—§ **38.21, n. 46.**

EJG Corp. v. New York State Liquor Authority, 213 A.D.2d 924, 624 N.Y.S.2d 68 (N.Y.A.D. 3 Dept.1995)—§ **4.15, n. 2.**

Ekeland v. Bowen, 899 F.2d 719 (8th Cir. 1990)—§ **34.47, n. 22.**

Elaine W. v. Joint Diseases North General Hosp., Inc., 597 N.Y.S.2d 617, 613 N.E.2d 523 (N.Y.1993)—§ **17.54, n. 7;** § **18.55, n. 8.**

E. Landau Industries, Inc. v. 385 McLean Corp., 58 Misc.2d 725, 296 N.Y.S.2d 707 (N.Y.Sup.1969)—§ **11.30, n. 5.**

Elbaum by Elbaum v. Grace Plaza of Great Neck, Inc., 148 A.D.2d 244, 544 N.Y.S.2d 840 (N.Y.A.D. 2 Dept.1989)—§ **22.54, n. 8;** § **23.109, n. 6.**

Elianne M., Matter of, 184 A.D.2d 98, 592 N.Y.S.2d 296 (N.Y.A.D. 1 Dept.1992)—§ **20.28;** § **20.28, n. 7.**

Elias, Schewel and Schwartz, Application of, 55 A.D.2d 448, 390 N.Y.S.2d 739 (N.Y.A.D. 4 Dept.1977)—§ **25.33, n. 1.**

Elichar Realty Corp. v. Town of Eastchester, 150 A.D.2d 444, 541 N.Y.S.2d 53 (N.Y.A.D. 2 Dept.1989)—§ **16.121, n. 2.**

Elizabeth Broome Realty Corp. v. China Printing Co., Inc., 157 Misc.2d 572, 598 N.Y.S.2d 138 (N.Y.City Civ.Ct.1993)—§ **13.28;** § **13.28, n. 13.**

Elkins v. Moreno, 435 U.S. 647, 98 S.Ct. 1338, 55 L.Ed.2d 614 (1978)—§ **19.60, n. 1.**

Elkus v. Elkus, 169 A.D.2d 134, 572 N.Y.S.2d 901 (N.Y.A.D. 1 Dept.1991)—§ **21.39;** § **21.39, n. 14.**

Elle v. Neenan, 68 Misc.2d 725, 327 N.Y.S.2d 706 (N.Y.Sup.1972)—§ **16.50, n. 3.**

Eller Bros., Inc., In re, 53 B.R. 10 (Bkrtcy. M.D.Tenn.1985)—§ **9.159, n. 3.**

Ellingsworth v. City of Watertown, 113 A.D.2d 1013, 494 N.Y.S.2d 587 (N.Y.A.D. 4 Dept.1985)—§ **37.20, n. 5.**

Ellinwood, In re, 206 B.R. 300 (Bkrtcy. W.D.N.Y.1997)—§ **9.52, n. 6.**

Elliott, People v., 209 A.D.2d 537, 619 N.Y.S.2d 68 (N.Y.A.D. 2 Dept.1994)—§ **38.26, n. 18.**

Ellis, People v., 459 N.Y.S.2d 25, 445 N.E.2d 201 (N.Y.1982)—§ **33.56, n. 5.**

Ellman, Matter of, 117 A.D.2d 803, 499 N.Y.S.2d 431 (N.Y.A.D. 2 Dept.1986)—§ **38.8;** § **38.8, n. 90.**

Ellsasser, Estate of v. Commssioner, 61 T.C. 241 (U.S.Tax Ct.1973)—§ **2.23, n. 9.**

Ellsworth, People v., 153 A.D.2d 965, 546 N.Y.S.2d 979 (N.Y.A.D. 3 Dept.1989)—§ **38.8, n. 36.**

Elmira, City of v. Larry Walter, Inc., 563 N.Y.S.2d 45, 564 N.E.2d 655 (N.Y. 1990)—§ **30.39, n. 12.**

Elmira, City of v. Larry Walter, Inc., 150 A.D.2d 129, 546 N.Y.S.2d 183 (N.Y.A.D. 3 Dept.1989)—§ **8.7, n. 1.**

Elmira, City of v. Larry Walter, Inc., 111 A.D.2d 553, 489 N.Y.S.2d 424 (N.Y.A.D. 3 Dept.1985)—§ **37.37, n. 37.**

Elmore v. Shell Oil Co., 733 F.Supp. 544 (E.D.N.Y.1988)—§ **17.25, n. 12.**

Elmsmere Associates v. Gladstone, 153 A.D.2d 501, 153 A.D.2d 821, 545 N.Y.S.2d 136 (N.Y.A.D. 1 Dept.1989)—§ **2.59, n. 6.**

TABLE OF CASES

Ely–Cruikshank Co., Inc. v. Bank of Montreal, 185 A.D.2d 182, 585 N.Y.S.2d 765 (N.Y.A.D. 1 Dept.1992)—§ **30.5, n. 4.**

Emanuel, People ex rel. v. McMann, 197 N.Y.S.2d 174, 165 N.E.2d 187 (N.Y. 1960)—§ **38.8, n. 6.**

Emanuele v. Emanuele, 218 A.D.2d 726, 630 N.Y.S.2d 558 (N.Y.A.D. 2 Dept. 1995)—§ **21.22, n. 1.**

Emanuel Law Outlines, Inc. v. Multi–State Legal Studies, Inc., 899 F.Supp. 1081 (S.D.N.Y.1995)—§ **5.42, n. 7.**

Emblem v. Juras, 112 A.D.2d 134, 491 N.Y.S.2d 382 (N.Y.A.D. 2 Dept.1985)— § **37.28, n. 18.**

Emerald Painting, Inc. v. PPG Industries, Inc., 99 A.D.2d 891, 472 N.Y.S.2d 485 (N.Y.A.D. 3 Dept.1984)—§ **5.31, n. 3.**

Eminon Acoustical Contractors Corp. v. Richkill Associates, Inc., 89 Misc.2d 992, 392 N.Y.S.2d 1007 (N.Y.Sup.1977)— § **10.94, n. 3.**

Emons Industries, Inc., In re, 50 B.R. 692 (Bkrtcy.S.D.N.Y.1985)—§ **9.43, n. 9.**

Empire Produce Co. v. Ring, 225 A.D. 6, 232 N.Y.S. 82 (N.Y.A.D. 4 Dept.1928)— § **8.14, n. 2.**

Employers Commercial Union Ins. Co. v. Firemen's Fund Ins. Co., 412 N.Y.S.2d 121, 384 N.E.2d 668 (N.Y.1978)— § **31.20, n. 5.**

Employers Ins. of Wausau v. Duplan Corp., 899 F.Supp. 1112 (S.D.N.Y.1995)— § **31.25, n. 3.**

Employers Mut. Cas. Co. v. Key Pharmaceuticals, 75 F.3d 815 (2nd Cir.1996)— § **31.14, n. 1.**

Emray Realty Corp. v. Edwards, 11 Misc.2d 889, 172 N.Y.S.2d 609 (N.Y.Sup.1958)— § **13.62, n. 3.**

Emslie, In re, 102 F. 291 (2nd Cir.1900)— § **10.16, n. 6.**

Eng v. Coughlin, 858 F.2d 889 (2nd Cir. 1988)—§ **18.32, n. 3.**

England, People v., N.Y.L.J., 3/27/81, p.13, col.1—§ **33.74, n. 3.**

English, People v., 110 Misc.2d 139, 441 N.Y.S.2d 928 (N.Y.Sup.1981)—§ **35.80, n. 5.**

Enslein v. Hudson & Manhattan R. Co., 8 Misc.2d 87, 165 N.Y.S.2d 630 (N.Y.Sup. 1957)—§ **30.11, n. 7.**

Entertainment Partners Group, Inc. v. Davis, 155 Misc.2d 894, 590 N.Y.S.2d 979 (N.Y.Sup.1992)—§ **18.80, n. 3.**

Envirodyne Industries, Inc., In re, 161 B.R. 440 (Bkrtcy.N.D.Ill.1993)—§ **9.108, n. 1.**

Envirodyne Industries, Inc., Matter of, 79 F.3d 579 (7th Cir.1996)—§ **9.107, n. 22.**

E.P.A. v. City of Green Forest, Ark., 921 F.2d 1394 (8th Cir.1990)—§ **15.11, n. 12.**

Epps, People v., 21 A.D.2d 650, 249 N.Y.S.2d 639 (N.Y.A.D. 1 Dept.1964)— § **38.8, n. 87.**

E. P. Reynolds, Inc. v. Nager Elec. Co., 268 N.Y.S.2d 15, 215 N.E.2d 339 (N.Y. 1966)—§ **37.51, n. 30.**

Epstein v. Official Committee of Unsecured Creditors of Estate of Piper Aircraft Corp., 58 F.3d 1573 (11th Cir.1995)— § **9.169, n. 5.**

Equal Employment Opportunity Commission v. Enterprise Ass'n Steamfitters Local No. 638 of U. A., 542 F.2d 579 (2nd Cir.1976)—§ **17.84, n. 5.**

Equitable Life Ins. Co. v. Atlanta-Stewart Partners (In re Atlanta–Stewart Partners), 193 B.R. 79 (Bkrtcy.N.D.Ga. 1996)—§ **9.160, n. 6.**

Equitable Lumber Corp. v. IPA Land Development Corp., 381 N.Y.S.2d 459, 344 N.E.2d 391 (N.Y.1976)—§ **5.12, n. 4, 5, 6.**

Erie County Dept. of Social Services (Cheryl P.) v. Theodore D., 217 A.D.2d 997, 630 N.Y.S.2d 822 (N.Y.A.D. 4 Dept.1995)— § **37.37, n. 47.**

Erie County Dept. of Social Services on Behalf of Deborah A.R. v. Felix M.C., 209 A.D.2d 1031, 619 N.Y.S.2d 1019 (N.Y.A.D. 4 Dept.1994)—§ **37.19, n. 28.**

Ermo, People v., 419 N.Y.S.2d 65, 392 N.E.2d 1248 (N.Y.1979)—§ **38.19, n. 16.**

Esajerre, People v., 363 N.Y.S.2d 931, 323 N.E.2d 175 (N.Y.1974)—§ **38.8;** § **38.8, n. 10.**

Eschbach v. Eschbach, 451 N.Y.S.2d 658, 436 N.E.2d 1260 (N.Y.1982)—§ **21.58, n. 2.**

Escher, Estate of, 94 Misc.2d 952, 407 N.Y.S.2d 106 (N.Y.Sur.1978)—§ **23.79, n. 2.**

Eshun v. New York State Dept. of Social Services, 652 F.Supp. 455 (S.D.N.Y. 1987)—§ **18.33, n. 4.**

Esner v. Janiszewski, 180 A.D.2d 991, 580 N.Y.S.2d 551 (N.Y.A.D. 3 Dept.1992)— § **37.28, n. 44.**

Espino, In re, 806 F.2d 1001 (11th Cir. 1986)—§ **9.205, n. 4.**

Espino, People v., 208 A.D.2d 556, 616 N.Y.S.2d 782 (N.Y.A.D. 2 Dept.1994)— § **38.28, n. 1.**

Esselte Pendaflex Corp. v. Incorporated Village of Garden City, 216 A.D.2d 519, 629 N.Y.S.2d 59 (N.Y.A.D. 2 Dept.1995)— § **16.44, n. 1.**

Essex Cryogenics Industries Inc., 14 I & N Dec. 196, 197 (Dep. Assoc. Comm. 1972)—§ **19.14, n. 1.**

Estabrook v. Chamberlain, 240 A.D. 899, 267 N.Y.S. 425 (N.Y.A.D. 2 Dept.1933)— § **16.29, n. 7.**

TABLE OF CASES

Estate of (see name of party)
Estin v. Estin, 334 U.S. 541, 68 S.Ct. 1213, 92 L.Ed. 1561 (1948)—§ **21.14, n. 1.**
Ettinger v. Clayton, 282 A.D. 876, 124 N.Y.S.2d 469 (N.Y.A.D.1953)—§ **8.35, n. 8.**
Ettman v. Equitable Life Assur. Soc. of United States, 6 A.D.2d 697, 174 N.Y.S.2d 553 (N.Y.A.D. 2 Dept.1958)—§ **17.27, n. 13.**
Euclid, Ohio, Village of v. Ambler Realty Co., 272 U.S. 365, 47 S.Ct. 114, 71 L.Ed. 303 (1926)—§ **16.18;** § **16.18, n. 2;** § **16.22, n. 6, 15.**
Evans v. Bellevue Hospital, N.Y.L.J., 7/14/93, p. 11, col. 1 (Sup.Ct., N.Y. County)—§ **24.93, n. 2.**
Evans v. Ithaca Urban Renewal Agency, 205 A.D.2d 844, 613 N.Y.S.2d 446 (N.Y.A.D. 3 Dept.1994)—§ **17.34, n. 6.**
Evans, People v., 212 A.D.2d 628, 623 N.Y.S.2d 130 (N.Y.A.D. 2 Dept.1995)—§ **38.8;** § **38.8, n. 22.**
Evans v. S. J. Groves & Sons Co., 315 F.2d 335 (2nd Cir.1963)—§ **30.11, n. 3.**
Evanston Ins. Co. v. GAB Business Services, Inc., 132 A.D.2d 180, 521 N.Y.S.2d 692 (N.Y.A.D. 1 Dept.1987)—§ **28.37, n. 1.**
Evelyn P., Matter of, 135 A.D.2d 716, 522 N.Y.S.2d 617 (N.Y.A.D. 2 Dept.1987)—§ **22.6, n. 8, 10;** § **22.31, n. 13.**
Eveready Ins. Co. v. Levine, 145 A.D.2d 526, 536 N.Y.S.2d 87 (N.Y.A.D. 2 Dept. 1988)—§ **31.10, n. 11.**
Everhart v. Johnston, 30 A.D.2d 608, 290 N.Y.S.2d 348 (N.Y.A.D. 3 Dept.1968)—§ **16.75, n. 2.**
Evvtex Co., Inc. v. Hartley Cooper Associates Ltd., 911 F.Supp. 732 (S.D.N.Y. 1996)—§ **31.6, n. 2.**
Ewing v. N.L.R.B., 861 F.2d 353 (2nd Cir. 1988)—§ **17.61, n. 2.**
Exeter Mfg. Co., In re, 254 A.D. 496, 5 N.Y.S.2d 438 (N.Y.A.D. 1 Dept.1938)—§ **5.18, n. 1.**

Ex parte (see name of party)
Exxon Corp. v. Board of Standards and Appeals of City of New York, 151 A.D.2d 438, 542 N.Y.S.2d 639 (N.Y.A.D. 1 Dept. 1989)—§ **16.119, n. 7.**
Exxon Corp. v. Gallelli, 192 A.D.2d 706, 597 N.Y.S.2d 139 (N.Y.A.D. 2 Dept.1993)—§ **16.106, n. 8.**
Ezagui v. Dow Chemical Corp., 598 F.2d 727 (2nd Cir.1979)—§ **27.10, n. 6;** § **27.13, n. 13.**

F

Fabian v. Motor Vehicle Acc. Indemnification Corp., 111 A.D.2d 366, 489 N.Y.S.2d 581 (N.Y.A.D. 2 Dept.1985)—§ **31.16, n. 13.**
Fabre, People ex rel. v. Warden, Brooklyn House of Detention, 354 N.Y.S.2d 943, 310 N.E.2d 540 (N.Y.1974)—§ **38.8, n. 75.**
Facci v. General Elec. Co., 192 A.D.2d 991, 596 N.Y.S.2d 928 (N.Y.A.D. 3 Dept. 1993)—§ **37.28, n. 40.**
Facet Industries, Inc. v. Wright, 477 N.Y.S.2d 316, 465 N.E.2d 1252 (N.Y. 1984)—§ **31.27, n. 2.**
Factor v. Commissioner, 281 F.2d 100 (9th Cir.1960)—§ **1.34, n. 19.**
Fafard v. Ajamian, 60 A.D.2d 853, 400 N.Y.S.2d 856 (N.Y.A.D. 2 Dept.1978)—§ **30.28, n. 11.**
Fahy v. State of Conn., 375 U.S. 85, 84 S.Ct. 229, 11 L.Ed.2d 171 (1963)—§ **38.19, n. 91.**
Faiola v. Jac Towers Apartments, Inc., 147 Misc.2d 630, 558 N.Y.S.2d 478 (N.Y.Sup. 1990)—§ **18.47, n. 2.**
Fair, People v., 315 N.Y.S.2d 869, 264 N.E.2d 359 (N.Y.1970)—§ **38.27, n. 23.**
Fairbairn's Estate, Matter of, 56 A.D.2d 259, 392 N.Y.S.2d 152 (N.Y.A.D. 4 Dept. 1977)—§ **22.48, n. 1.**
Fairchild Aircraft Corp., In re, 184 B.R. 910 (Bkrtcy.W.D.Tex.1995)—§ **9.169, n. 5.**
Fairley v. Fairley, 75 A.D.2d 975, 428 N.Y.S.2d 530 (N.Y.A.D. 3 Dept.1980)—§ **21.30, n. 9.**
Falbaum v. Pomerantz, 891 F.Supp. 986 (S.D.N.Y.1995)—§ **17.68, n. 8.**
Fales v. State, 108 Misc.2d 636, 438 N.Y.S.2d 449 (N.Y.Ct.Cl.1981)—§ **22.15, n. 1.**
Fanning v. Belle Terre Estates, Inc., 152 A.D. 718, 137 N.Y.S. 595 (N.Y.A.D. 2 Dept.1912)—§ **10.16, n. 6.**
Fanta–Sea Swim Center, Inc. v. Rabin, 113 A.D.2d 1011, 494 N.Y.S.2d 568 (N.Y.A.D. 4 Dept.1985)—§ **31.7, n. 5.**
Fargher, People v., 112 A.D.2d 599, 492 N.Y.S.2d 123 (N.Y.A.D. 3 Dept.1985)—§ **38.21;** § **38.21, n. 6.**
Farkas v. Saary, 191 A.D.2d 178, 594 N.Y.S.2d 195 (N.Y.A.D. 1 Dept.1993)—§ **29.16, n. 5.**
Farley v. Promovision Video Displays Corp., 198 A.D.2d 122, 603 N.Y.S.2d 476 (N.Y.A.D. 1 Dept.1993)—§ **28.32, n. 3.**
Farmer v. Farmer, 109 Misc.2d 137, 439 N.Y.S.2d 584 (N.Y.Sup.1981)—§ **21.58, n. 2.**
Farm Family Mut. Ins. Co. v. Nass, 121 A.D.2d 498, 503 N.Y.S.2d 820 (N.Y.A.D. 2 Dept.1986)—§ **31.22, n. 5.**
Farrar, People v., 437 N.Y.S.2d 961, 419 N.E.2d 864 (N.Y.1981)—§ **38.8, n. 40;**

TABLE OF CASES

§ 38.10; § 38.10, n. 144; § 38.21, n. 40, 58.
Farrell, People v., 623 N.Y.S.2d 550, 647 N.E.2d 762 (N.Y.1995)—§ 38.3, n. 16; § 38.8, n. 70.
Farrell, People v., 201 A.D.2d 665, 609 N.Y.S.2d 824 (N.Y.A.D. 2 Dept.1994)—§ 38.28, n. 23.
Farrington v. Pinckney, 150 N.Y.S.2d 585, 133 N.E.2d 817 (N.Y.1956)—§ 3.7, n. 10.
Faruque, Matter of, 10 I & N Dec. 561 (BIA 1964)—§ 19.12, n. 2.
Fasano v. Board of County Com'rs of Washington County, 264 Or. 574, 507 P.2d 23 (Or.1973)—§ 16.12, n. 12.
F. A. Straus & Co. v. Canadian Pac. R. Co., 254 N.Y. 407, 173 N.E. 564 (N.Y.1930)—§ 5.11, n. 3.
Fata, In re, 22 A.D.2d 116, 254 N.Y.S.2d 289 (N.Y.A.D. 1 Dept.1964)—§ 28.25, n. 1.
Fattizzi, People v., 98 Misc.2d 288, 413 N.Y.S.2d 804 (N.Y.Sup.1978)—§ 33.20, n. 1.
Faulk v. Aware, Inc., 35 Misc.2d 302, 35 Misc.2d 315, 35 Misc.2d 317, 231 N.Y.S.2d 270 (N.Y.Sup.1962)—§ 30.10; § 30.10, n. 4.
Faust v. Luke, 80 Misc.2d 953, 364 N.Y.S.2d 344 (N.Y.City Civ.Ct.1975)—§ 31.29, n. 2.
Favier by Favier v. Winick, 151 Misc.2d 910, 583 N.Y.S.2d 907 (N.Y.Sup.1992)—§ 30.28, n. 13, 14.
Favor, People v., 604 N.Y.S.2d 494, 624 N.E.2d 631 (N.Y.1993)—§ 38.19, n. 124; § 38.22, n. 3.
Fay v. Waldron, 3 N.Y.S. 894 (N.Y.Sup. 1889)—§ 2.50, n. 2.
F.D.I.C. v. Commissioner of Taxation and Finance, 607 N.Y.S.2d 620, 628 N.E.2d 1330 (N.Y.1993)—§ 39.9, n. 3.
Feathers v. Walter S. Kozdranski, Inc., 129 A.D.2d 975, 514 N.Y.S.2d 838 (N.Y.A.D. 4 Dept.1987)—§ 37.29, n. 15.
Featherworks Corp., In re, 25 B.R. 634 (Bkrtcy.E.D.N.Y.1982)—§ 9.165, n. 20.
Febesh v. Elcejay Inn Corp., 157 A.D.2d 102, 555 N.Y.S.2d 46 (N.Y.A.D. 1 Dept. 1990)—§ 37.65, n. 39.
Fe Bland v. Two Trees Management Co., 498 N.Y.S.2d 336, 489 N.E.2d 223 (N.Y. 1985)—§ 1.27, n. 5.
Fe Bland v. Two Trees Management Co., 125 Misc.2d 111, 479 N.Y.S.2d 123 (N.Y.Sup.1984)—§ 1.27, n. 5.
Federal Deposit Ins. Corp. v. Richman, 98 A.D.2d 790, 470 N.Y.S.2d 19 (N.Y.A.D. 2 Dept.1983)—§ 8.17, n. 3.
Federal Deposit Ins. Corp. v. Salesmen Unlimited Agency Corp., 101 A.D.2d 876, 475 N.Y.S.2d 1020 (N.Y.A.D. 2 Dept. 1984)—§ 37.37, n. 50.
Federal Deposit Ins. Corp. v. Shea & Gould, 1997 WL 401822 (S.D.N.Y.1997)—§ 28.13, n. 1; § 28.25, n. 2.
Federal Home Loan Mortg. Corp. v. Dutch Lane Associates, 810 F.Supp. 86 (S.D.N.Y.1992)—§ 11.48, n. 6.
Federal Home Loan Mortg. Corp. v. Dutch Lane Associates, 775 F.Supp. 133 (S.D.N.Y.1991)—§ 11.30, n. 4.
Federal Ins. Co. v. Arthur Andersen & Co., 553 N.Y.S.2d 291, 552 N.E.2d 870 (N.Y. 1990)—§ 31.29, n. 3.
Federal Nat. Mortg. Ass'n v. Levine–Rodriguez, 153 Misc.2d 8, 579 N.Y.S.2d 975 (N.Y.Sup.1991)—§ 11.2, n. 1; § 11.22, n. 1.
Federal Nat. Mortg. Ass'n v. Miller, 123 Misc.2d 431, 473 N.Y.S.2d 743 (N.Y.Sup. 1984)—§ 11.37, n. 6.
Federal Nat. Mortg. Assoc. v. Graham, 67 Misc.2d 735, 324 N.Y.S.2d 827 (N.Y.Sup. 1971)—§ 11.54, n. 10.
Federated Dept. Stores, Inc., Matter of, 1991 WL 79143 (Bkrtcy.S.D.Ohio 1991)—§ 9.46, n. 1.
Federated Group, Inc., In re, 107 F.3d 730 (9th Cir.1997)—§ 9.9, n. 2.
Federation of Puerto Rican Organizations of Brownsville, Inc. v. Howe, 157 B.R. 206 (E.D.N.Y.1993)—§ 9.18, n. 4.
Fedmet Trading Corp. v. Ekco Intern. Trade Corp., 151 Misc.2d 927, 574 N.Y.S.2d 122 (N.Y.Sup.1991)—§ 5.50, n. 6.
Fehlhaber Corp. v. O'Hara, 53 A.D.2d 746, 384 N.Y.S.2d 270 (N.Y.A.D. 3 Dept. 1976)—§ 14.44, n. 6.
Fehlhaber Corp. v. State, 69 A.D.2d 362, 419 N.Y.S.2d 773 (N.Y.A.D. 3 Dept. 1979)—§ 30.5, n. 3.
Feit & Drexler, Inc., In re, 760 F.2d 406 (2nd Cir.1985)—§ 9.54, n. 4.
Felder v. Casey, 487 U.S. 131, 108 S.Ct. 2302, 101 L.Ed.2d 123 (1988)—§ 18.2, n. 4; § 18.5, n. 1; § 18.9, n. 2; § 18.20, n. 2.
Felder, People v., 418 N.Y.S.2d 295, 391 N.E.2d 1274 (N.Y.1979)—§ 38.19, n. 100.
Feldes, People v., 543 N.Y.S.2d 34, 541 N.E.2d 34 (N.Y.1989)—§ 38.52, n. 14.
Feldman v. Board of Ed., Chappaqua Central School Dist., 55 A.D.2d 619, 389 N.Y.S.2d 409 (N.Y.A.D. 2 Dept.1976)—§ 37.67, n. 8.
Feliberty v. Damon, 531 N.Y.S.2d 778, 527 N.E.2d 261 (N.Y.1988)—§ 31.12, n. 3.
Felicie, Inc. v. Leibovitz, 67 A.D.2d 656, 412 N.Y.S.2d 625 (N.Y.A.D. 1 Dept.1979)—§ 5.18, n. 1.

TABLE OF CASES

Fell v. Fell, 213 A.D.2d 374, 623 N.Y.S.2d 315 (N.Y.A.D. 2 Dept.1995)—§ **37.28, n. 29.**

Female D., Matter of, 83 A.D.2d 933, 442 N.Y.S.2d 575 (N.Y.A.D. 2 Dept.1981)—§ **20.43, n. 3.**

Female R., Matter of, 202 A.D.2d 672, 609 N.Y.S.2d 295 (N.Y.A.D. 2 Dept.1994)—§ **20.90, n. 5.**

Fenton, Town of v. New York State Dept. of Environmental Conservation, 117 A.D.2d 920, 498 N.Y.S.2d 923 (N.Y.A.D. 3 Dept.1986)—§ **4.82, n. 17.**

Ferber v. Schultz, 104 Misc.2d 1009, 429 N.Y.S.2d 861 (N.Y.City Civ.Ct.1980)—§ **28.30, n. 7.**

Ferebee v. Chevron Chemical Co., 736 F.2d 1529, 237 U.S.App.D.C. 164 (D.C.Cir. 1984)—§ **27.47;** § **27.47, n. 1.**

Ferguson, People v., 192 A.D.2d 800, 596 N.Y.S.2d 533 (N.Y.A.D. 3 Dept.1993)—§ **38.8, n. 208.**

Ferguson, People v., 119 A.D.2d 338, 507 N.Y.S.2d 622 (N.Y.A.D. 1 Dept.1986)—§ **38.10, n. 115.**

Ferman v. Board of Appeals, Incorporated Village of Sea Cliff, Nassau County, 69 A.D.2d 882, 415 N.Y.S.2d 469 (N.Y.A.D. 2 Dept.1979)—§ **16.92, n. 1.**

Fernandez v. Arturi, 208 A.D.2d 923, 618 N.Y.S.2d 79 (N.Y.A.D. 2 Dept.1994)—§ **37.19, n. 19.**

Fern, Inc. v. Adjmi, 197 A.D.2d 444, 602 N.Y.S.2d 615 (N.Y.A.D. 1 Dept.1993)—§ **1.10, n. 13.**

Ferrara v. Bernstein, 597 N.Y.S.2d 636, 613 N.E.2d 542 (N.Y.1993)—§ **30.9, n. 7, 16.**

Ferrara v. Galluchio, 176 N.Y.S.2d 996, 152 N.E.2d 249 (N.Y.1958)—§ **30.9;** § **30.9, n. 9.**

Ferrari v. Town of Penfield Planning Bd., 181 A.D.2d 149, 585 N.Y.S.2d 925 (N.Y.A.D. 4 Dept.1992)—§ **16.105, n. 11.**

Ferraro v. Koncal Associates, 97 A.D.2d 429, 467 N.Y.S.2d 284 (N.Y.A.D. 2 Dept. 1983)—§ **27.33, n. 5.**

Ferraro v. New York Telephone Co., 94 A.D.2d 784, 463 N.Y.S.2d 31 (N.Y.A.D. 2 Dept.1983)—§ **26.43, n. 13.**

Ferrin v. Department of Correctional Services, 523 N.Y.S.2d 485, 517 N.E.2d 1370 (N.Y.1987)—§ **18.84, n. 4.**

F.F. Proctor Troy Properties Co. v. Dugan Store, 191 A.D. 685, 181 N.Y.S. 786 (N.Y.A.D. 3 Dept.1920)—§ **5.11, n. 7.**

FGL & L Property Corp. v. City of Rye, 495 N.Y.S.2d 321, 485 N.E.2d 986 (N.Y. 1985)—§ **16.4, n. 8;** § **16.127, n. 11, 12.**

Fiacco, People v., 146 Misc.2d 330, 549 N.Y.S.2d 901 (N.Y.City Ct.1989)—§ **33.75, n. 5.**

Fialkowski v. Gilroy, 200 A.D.2d 668, 607 N.Y.S.2d 50 (N.Y.A.D. 2 Dept.1994)—§ **21.58, n. 2.**

Fiallo v. Bell, 430 U.S. 787, 97 S.Ct. 1473, 52 L.Ed.2d 50 (1977)—§ **19.11, n. 21.**

Fichtner v. Town of Babylon, 24 Misc.2d 56, 203 N.Y.S.2d 533 (N.Y.Sup.1960)—§ **3.30, n. 28.**

Fidler v. Sullivan, 93 A.D.2d 964, 463 N.Y.S.2d 279 (N.Y.A.D. 3 Dept.1983)—§ **28.3, n. 1, 7.**

Field v. Mans, 516 U.S. 59, 116 S.Ct. 437, 133 L.Ed.2d 351 (1995)—§ **9.208, n. 3.**

Field, People v., 161 A.D.2d 660, 555 N.Y.S.2d 437 (N.Y.A.D. 2 Dept.1990)—§ **38.10, n. 12.**

Fielding v. Drew, 94 A.D.2d 687, 463 N.Y.S.2d 15 (N.Y.A.D. 1 Dept.1983)—§ **11.6, n. 5.**

Fields v. City University of New York, 216 A.D.2d 87, 628 N.Y.S.2d 76 (N.Y.A.D. 1 Dept.1995)—§ **30.30, n. 24.**

Fields, People v., 196 A.D.2d 550, 601 N.Y.S.2d 856 (N.Y.A.D. 2 Dept.1993)—§ **38.8, n. 30.**

Fields, People v., 151 A.D.2d 598, 542 N.Y.S.2d 356 (N.Y.A.D. 2 Dept.1989)—§ **38.24, n. 4.**

50 Court Street Associates v. Mendelson and Mendelson, 151 Misc.2d 87, 572 N.Y.S.2d 997 (N.Y.City Civ.Ct.1991)—§ **13.8, n. 4.**

50 E. 78th Corp. v. Jire, N.Y.L.J., 12/2/91, p.25, col.1, 19 HCR 695 (App. Term, 1st Dep't)—§ **13.28, n. 10.**

55 Motor Ave. Co. v. Liberty Indus. Finishing Corp., 1994 WL 241104 (E.D.N.Y. 1994)—§ **15.30, n. 11.**

Fifty States Management Corp. v. Pioneer Auto Parks, Inc., 415 N.Y.S.2d 800, 389 N.E.2d 113 (N.Y.1979)—§ **5.52, n. 3.**

Figgie Intern., Inc. v. Town of Huntington, 203 A.D.2d 416, 610 N.Y.S.2d 563 (N.Y.A.D. 2 Dept.1994)—§ **16.105, n. 7;** § **16.106, n. 12.**

Figter Ltd. v. Teachers Ins. & Annuity Asso. (In re Figter Ltd.), 118 F.3d 635 (9th Cir.1997)—§ **9.162, n. 3.**

Figueira, In re, 163 B.R. 192 (Bkrtcy. D.Kan.1993)—§ **9.192, n. 1.**

Figueroa, People v., 219 A.D.2d 667, 631 N.Y.S.2d 403 (N.Y.A.D. 2 Dept.1995)—§ **38.25, n. 6.**

Filali v. Gronowicz, N.Y.L.J., 11/19/85, p.7, col.1, 13 HCR 375 (App. Term, 1st Dep't)—§ **13.58, n. 8.**

Filipiak's Estate, In re, 66 Misc.2d 742, 321 N.Y.S.2d 973 (N.Y.Sur.1971)—§ **25.39, n. 2.**

Filmways Communications of Syracuse, Inc. v. Douglas, 106 A.D.2d 185, 484

TABLE OF CASES

N.Y.S.2d 738 (N.Y.A.D. 4 Dept.1985)—§ **16.54, n. 2.**

Financial Guaranty Insurance Co. v. Drexel Burnham Lambert, Inc., N.Y.L.J., 4/12/90—§ **28.11, n. 8.**

Financial Security Assurance v. T–H New Orleans Ltd. Partnership, 116 F.3d 790 (5th Cir.1997)—§ **9.102, n. 6;** § **9.103, n. 2.**

Fine v. Bellefonte Underwriters Ins. Co., 758 F.2d 50 (2nd Cir.1985)—§ **31.18, n. 18.**

Fineman v. Callahan, 222 A.D. 752, 225 N.Y.S. 401 (N.Y.A.D. 2 Dept.1927)—§ **12.62, n. 3.**

Finger v. Levenson, 163 A.D.2d 477, 558 N.Y.S.2d 163 (N.Y.A.D. 2 Dept.1990)—§ **16.79, n. 3;** § **16.86, n. 2.**

Finger v. Omni Publications Intern., Ltd., 564 N.Y.S.2d 1014, 566 N.E.2d 141 (N.Y. 1990)—§ **18.64, n. 5.**

Fink v. Cole, 150 N.Y.S.2d 175, 133 N.E.2d 691 (N.Y.1956)—§ **4.79, n. 11.**

Fink v. Lefkowitz, 419 N.Y.S.2d 467, 393 N.E.2d 463 (N.Y.1979)—§ **3.29, n. 8.**

Finkelstein's Estate, In re, 40 Misc.2d 910, 245 N.Y.S.2d 225 (N.Y.Sur.1963)—§ **2.51, n. 10.**

Finley v. Park Ten Associates, 83 A.D.2d 537, 441 N.Y.S.2d 475 (N.Y.A.D. 1 Dept. 1981)—§ **13.35, n. 4.**

Finnan v. L.F. Rothschild & Co., Inc., 726 F.Supp. 460 (S.D.N.Y.1989)—§ **17.51, n. 3.**

Finnegan v. Fountain, 915 F.2d 817 (2nd Cir.1990)—§ **18.21, n. 3.**

Finn's Liquor Shop, Inc. v. State Liquor Authority, 301 N.Y.S.2d 584, 249 N.E.2d 440 (N.Y.1969)—§ **4.62, n. 13.**

Finocchio v. Finocchio, 162 A.D.2d 1044, 556 N.Y.S.2d 1007 (N.Y.A.D. 4 Dept. 1990)—§ **21.43, n. 20.**

Fiore v. Fiore, 415 N.Y.S.2d 826, 389 N.E.2d 138 (N.Y.1979)—§ **13.63, n. 4.**

Fiore v. Oakwood Plaza Shopping Center, Inc., 578 N.Y.S.2d 115, 585 N.E.2d 364 (N.Y.1991)—§ **8.16, n. 2.**

Fiore v. Zoning Bd. of Appeals of Town of Southeast, 288 N.Y.S.2d 62, 235 N.E.2d 121 (N.Y.1968)—§ **16.77, n. 6.**

Firedoor Corp. of America v. Reliance Elec. Co., Haughton Elevator Division, 56 A.D.2d 523, 391 N.Y.S.2d 414 (N.Y.A.D. 1 Dept.1977)—§ **37.47, n. 4.**

Fireman's Ins. Co. of Newark, New Jersey v. Wheeler, 165 A.D.2d 141, 566 N.Y.S.2d 692 (N.Y.A.D. 3 Dept.1991)—§ **31.29, n. 2, 16.**

Firester v. Lipson, 50 Misc.2d 527, 270 N.Y.S.2d 844 (N.Y.Sup.1966)—§ **30.32, n. 2.**

Firestone v. Firestone, 44 A.D.2d 671, 354 N.Y.S.2d 645 (N.Y.A.D. 1 Dept.1974)—§ **37.19, n. 14.**

Firestone Tire & Rubber Co. v. Risjord, 449 U.S. 368, 101 S.Ct. 669, 66 L.Ed.2d 571 (1981)—§ **38.3, n. 14.**

First American Bank of New York (FAB) v. Century Glove, Inc., 81 B.R. 274 (D.Del. 1988)—§ **9.283, n. 3.**

First and Farmers Bank of Somerset, Inc. v. Henderson, 763 S.W.2d 137 (Ky.App. 1988)—§ **7.25, n. 8.**

First Bank & Trust Co. of Corning v. State, 184 A.D.2d 1034, 585 N.Y.S.2d 261 (N.Y.A.D. 4 Dept.1992)—§ **14.115;** § **14.115, n. 8.**

First Broadcasting Corp. v. City of Syracuse, 78 A.D.2d 490, 435 N.Y.S.2d 194 (N.Y.A.D. 4 Dept.1981)—§ **14.3, n. 1, 2;** § **14.15, n. 5.**

First Coinvestors, Inc. v. Coppola, 88 Misc.2d 495, 388 N.Y.S.2d 833 (N.Y.Dist. Ct.1976)—§ **5.35, n. 2.**

First English Evangelical Lutheran Church of Glendale v. Los Angeles County, Cal., 482 U.S. 304, 107 S.Ct. 2378, 96 L.Ed.2d 250 (1987)—§ **16.22, n. 4.**

First Federal Sav. and Loan Ass'n of Rochester v. Brown, 78 A.D.2d 119, 434 N.Y.S.2d 306 (N.Y.A.D. 4 Dept.1980)—§ **11.53, n. 4.**

First Federal Sav. & Loan Ass'n of Rochester v. Brown, 86 A.D.2d 963, 448 N.Y.S.2d 302 (N.Y.A.D. 4 Dept.1982)—§ **11.53, n. 9.**

First Federal Sav. & Loan Ass'n of Rochester v. Dietz Intern. Public Adjusters, Inc., 143 A.D.2d 45, 531 N.Y.S.2d 801 (N.Y.A.D. 1 Dept.1988)—§ **28.8, n. 10.**

First Fidelity Bank NA v. Jason Realty, L.P. (In re Jason Realty, L.P.), 59 F.3d 423 (3rd Cir.1995)—§ **9.66, n. 4.**

First Meridian Planning Corp., People v., 201 A.D.2d 145, 614 N.Y.S.2d 811 (N.Y.A.D. 3 Dept.1994)—§ **2.106, n. 9.**

First Nat. Bank v. Fourth Nat. Bank, 77 N.Y. 320 (N.Y.1879)—§ **30.28, n. 6.**

First Nat. Bank of Olathe, Kan. v. Pontow, 111 F.3d 604 (8th Cir.1997)—§ **9.208, n. 3.**

First Nat. City Bank v. Wall St. Leasing Corp., 80 Misc.2d 707, 363 N.Y.S.2d 699 (N.Y.City Civ.Ct.1974)—§ **13.27, n. 3.**

First Nat. Stores, Inc. v. Yellowstone Shopping Center, Inc., 290 N.Y.S.2d 721, 237 N.E.2d 868 (N.Y.1968)—§ **13.70;** § **13.70, n. 2.**

First Report of October 1972 Grand Jury of Supreme Court, Albany County, In re, 359 N.Y.S.2d 290, 316 N.E.2d 722 (N.Y. 1974)—§ **38.11, n. 14.**

TABLE OF CASES

First Report of Oct., 1972 Grand Jury of Supreme Court, Albany County, In re, 44 A.D.2d 855, 354 N.Y.S.2d 966 (N.Y.A.D. 3 Dept.1974)—§ **38.11, n. 19.**

First RepublicBank Corp., In re, 95 B.R. 58 (Bkrtcy.N.D.Tex.1988)—§ **9.43, n. 14.**

First Sterling Corp. v. Zurkowski, 142 Misc.2d 978, 542 N.Y.S.2d 899 (N.Y.Sup. App.Term 1989)—§ **13.39, n. 10.**

First Truck Lines, Inc., In re, 48 F.3d 210 (6th Cir.1995)—§ **9.107, n. 21.**

First Westchester Nat. Bank v. Olsen, 280 N.Y.S.2d 117, 227 N.E.2d 24 (N.Y. 1967)—§ **39.11, n. 10.**

Fisch v. Chason, 99 Misc.2d 1089, 418 N.Y.S.2d 495 (N.Y.City Civ.Ct.1979)—§ **13.19, n. 1.**

Fischer v. Homes for Homeless, Inc., 1994 WL 319166 (S.D.N.Y.1994)—§ **17.64, n. 5.**

Fischer v. Maloney, 402 N.Y.S.2d 991, 373 N.E.2d 1215 (N.Y.1978)—§ **17.28, n. 1;** § **18.79, n. 1;** § **28.10, n. 6, 7.**

Fischer, People v., 159 A.D.2d 953, 552 N.Y.S.2d 787 (N.Y.A.D. 4 Dept.1990)—§ **33.55, n. 2.**

Fish v. Anstey Const. Co., 71 Misc. 2, 130 N.Y.S. 927 (N.Y.Sup.1911)—§ **10.19, n. 14.**

Fisher, Matter of, 147 Misc.2d 329, 552 N.Y.S.2d 807 (N.Y.Sup.1989)—§ **22.4, n. 1, 5, 7, 8, 13, 14, 17;** § **22.6, n. 7, 8;** § **22.33, n. 1.**

Fisher v. Biderman, 154 A.D.2d 155, 552 N.Y.S.2d 221 (N.Y.A.D. 1 Dept.1990)—§ **3.32, n. 21.**

Fisher v. City of Mechanicville, 225 N.Y. 210, 121 N.E. 764 (N.Y.1919)—§ **3.17, n. 5.**

Fisher v. New York City Dept. of Housing (In re Pan Trading Corp., S.A.), 125 B.R. 869 (Bkrtcy.S.D.N.Y.1991)—§ **9.117, n. 3.**

Fisher v. Schenck, 39 A.D.2d 813, 332 N.Y.S.2d 477 (N.Y.A.D. 3 Dept.1972)—§ **37.37, n. 76, 86.**

Fisher v. Vassar College, 114 F.3d 1332 (2nd Cir.1997)—§ **17.59, n. 5.**

Fishman v. Town of Islip, 20 Misc.2d 180, 189 N.Y.S.2d 979 (N.Y.Sup.1959)—§ **3.16, n. 7.**

Fisnar, People v., 212 A.D.2d 628, 623 N.Y.S.2d 144 (N.Y.A.D. 2 Dept.1995)—§ **38.8, n. 23.**

Fitzgerald, In re, 20 B.R. 27 (Bkrtcy. N.D.N.Y.1982)—§ **9.188, n. 6.**

Fitzgerald v. Bertram (Matter of Killian Const. Co., Inc.), 24 B.R. 848 (Bkrtcy.D.Idaho 1982)—§ **9.180, n. 3.**

Fitzner v. Beach, 174 A.D.2d 798, 571 N.Y.S.2d 119 (N.Y.A.D. 3 Dept.1991)—§ **16.101, n. 3, 6.**

Fitzpatrick v. American Honda Motor Co., Inc., 571 N.Y.S.2d 672, 575 N.E.2d 90 (N.Y.1991)—§ **31.12, n. 2.**

Fitzpatrick v. Bank of New York, 125 Misc.2d 1069, 480 N.Y.S.2d 864 (N.Y.City Civ.Ct.1984)—§ **7.26, n. 9.**

Fitzpatrick v. Bank of New York, 124 Misc.2d 732, 480 N.Y.S.2d 157 (N.Y.Sup. App.Term 1983)—§ **7.55.**

Fitzsimmons v. City of Brooklyn, 102 N.Y. 536, 7 N.E. 787 (N.Y.1886)—§ **3.17, n. 10.**

599 Consumer Electronics, Inc., In re, 195 B.R. 244 (S.D.N.Y.1996)—§ **9.14, n. 1.**

524 West End Ave. v. Rawak, 125 Misc. 862, 212 N.Y.S. 287 (N.Y.Sup.1925)—§ **13.30, n. 4.**

Flagg, People ex rel. Smith v., 17 N.Y. 584 (N.Y.1857)—§ **3.25, n. 8.**

Flamm v. Noble, 296 N.Y. 262, 72 N.E.2d 886 (N.Y.1947)—§ **30.40, n. 18.**

Flansburg v. Merritt Meridian Const. Corp. Inc., 191 A.D.2d 756, 594 N.Y.S.2d 421 (N.Y.A.D. 3 Dept.1993)—§ **30.30, n. 23.**

Flecha v. Seybold Mach. Co., 146 A.D.2d 515, 536 N.Y.S.2d 455 (N.Y.A.D. 1 Dept. 1989)—§ **27.27, n. 1.**

Fleck v. Fleck, 6 Misc.2d 202, 163 N.Y.S.2d 218 (N.Y.Sup.1957)—§ **21.26, n. 9.**

Fleck v. Perla, 40 A.D.2d 1069, 339 N.Y.S.2d 246 (N.Y.A.D. 4 Dept.1972)—§ **10.99, n. 1.**

Fleet Bank NH v. Royall, 218 A.D.2d 727, 630 N.Y.S.2d 559 (N.Y.A.D. 2 Dept. 1995)—§ **2.53, n. 7, 8, 9.**

Fleet Factors Corp., United States v., 901 F.2d 1550 (11th Cir.1990)—§ **11.6, n. 9;** § **15.30;** § **15.30, n. 3.**

Fleitz v. Fleitz, 223 A.D.2d 946, 636 N.Y.S.2d 911 (N.Y.A.D. 3 Dept.1996)—§ **21.42, n. 1;** § **21.49;** § **21.49, n. 4.**

Fleitz v. Fleitz, 200 A.D.2d 874, 606 N.Y.S.2d 825 (N.Y.A.D. 3 Dept.1994)—§ **21.40, n. 5.**

Flemming, People v., 104 A.D.2d 1048, 480 N.Y.S.2d 882 (N.Y.A.D. 2 Dept.1984)—§ **38.41, n. 3.**

Fletcher v. Kidder, Peabody & Co., Inc., 184 A.D.2d 359, 584 N.Y.S.2d 838 (N.Y.A.D. 1 Dept.1992)—§ **17.9, n. 1.**

Flick Lumber Co., Inc. v. Breton Industries, Inc., 223 A.D.2d 779, 636 N.Y.S.2d 169 (N.Y.A.D. 3 Dept.1996)—§ **5.50, n. 9.**

Flynn v. New York Life Ins. Co., N.Y.L.J. 10/24/96, p.31, col.3 (Sup.Ct., Suffolk County)—§ **32.15, n. 9.**

Florence, Matter of, 140 Misc.2d 393, 530 N.Y.S.2d 981 (N.Y.Sur.1988)—§ **22.48, n. 1, 3.**

Florence v. Goldberg, 404 N.Y.S.2d 583, 375 N.E.2d 763 (N.Y.1978)—§ **3.30, n. 6.**

TABLE OF CASES

Flores v. City of New York, 207 A.D.2d 302, 615 N.Y.S.2d 400 (N.Y.A.D. 1 Dept. 1994)—§ **18.65, n. 3.**

Flores v. Las Americas Communications, Inc., 218 A.D.2d 595, 630 N.Y.S.2d 502 (N.Y.A.D. 1 Dept.1995)—§ **30.43, n. 1.**

Flores, People v., 222 A.D.2d 450, 635 N.Y.S.2d 37 (N.Y.A.D. 2 Dept.1995)—§ **38.25, n. 22.**

Flores, People v., 615 N.Y.S.2d 662, 639 N.E.2d 19 (N.Y.1994)—§ **38.10, n. 101.**

Florsz v. Ogruk, 184 A.D.2d 546, 585 N.Y.S.2d 220 (N.Y.A.D. 2 Dept.1992)—§ **30.28, n. 15.**

Flynn, In re, 143 B.R. 798 (Bkrtcy.D.R.I. 1992)—§ **9.131, n. 1.**

Flynn v. City of New York, 103 A.D.2d 98, 478 N.Y.S.2d 666 (N.Y.A.D. 2 Dept. 1984)—§ **3.30, n. 10.**
W8

Flynn v. New York Life Ins. Co., N.Y.L.J., 10/24/96, p.31, col.3 (Sup.Ct.,Suffolk County)—§ **32.15, n. 10.**

Foertsch v. Foertsch, 187 A.D.2d 635, 591 N.Y.S.2d 785 (N.Y.A.D. 2 Dept.1992)—§ **37.37, n. 12.**

Fogarty v. Secretary of Health and Human Services, 690 F.Supp. 166 (W.D.N.Y. 1988)—§ **34.9, n. 6, 26.**

Fogg, People ex rel. Frazier v., 122 A.D.2d 377, 504 N.Y.S.2d 794 (N.Y.A.D. 3 Dept. 1986)—§ **38.8, n. 75.**

Foglesong v. Commissioner, T.C. Memo. 1976-294 (U.S.Tax Ct.1976)—§ **1.34, n. 20.**

Foley, Matter of, 140 A.D.2d 892, 528 N.Y.S.2d 709 (N.Y.A.D. 3 Dept.1988)—§ **22.20, n. 4.**

Foley v. Pittsburgh–Des Moines Co., 363 Pa. 1, 68 A.2d 517 (Pa.1949)—§ **27.20, n. 3.**

Fonda v. Paulsen, 46 A.D.2d 540, 363 N.Y.S.2d 841 (N.Y.A.D. 3 Dept.1975)—§ **28.14, n. 1.**

Fonda Mfg. Corp. v. Lincoln Laminating Corp., 72 A.D.2d 522, 420 N.Y.S.2d 904 (N.Y.A.D. 1 Dept.1979)—§ **37.35, n. 10.**

Fontecchio v. Esposito, 108 A.D.2d 780, 485 N.Y.S.2d 113 (N.Y.A.D. 2 Dept.1985)—§ **26.15, n. 1.**

Fontheim v. Third Ave. Ry. Co., 257 A.D. 147, 12 N.Y.S.2d 90 (N.Y.A.D. 1 Dept. 1939)—§ **30.12, n. 7, 8.**

Foos v. Bausch and Lomb Inc., 181 A.D.2d 951, 581 N.Y.S.2d 458 (N.Y.A.D. 3 Dept. 1992)—§ **32.27, n. 3.**

Ford v. Union Bank (In re San Joaquin Roast Beef), 7 F.3d 1413 (9th Cir. 1993)—§ **9.198, n. 1.**

Ford, People v., 40 A.D.2d 983, 338 N.Y.S.2d 381 (N.Y.A.D. 2 Dept.1972)—§ **38.8, n. 66.**

Forde, People v., 153 A.D.2d 466, 552 N.Y.S.2d 113 (N.Y.A.D. 1 Dept.1990)—§ **38.10, n. 12.**

Fordham Manor Reformed Church, People ex rel. v. Walsh, 244 N.Y. 280, 155 N.E. 575 (N.Y.1927)—§ **16.73, n. 4; § 16.74, n. 1.**

Ford Motor Credit Co. v. Dobbins, 35 F.3d 860 (4th Cir.1994)—§ **9.53, n. 4.**

Ford Motor Credit Co. v. Hickey Ford Sales, Inc., 476 N.Y.S.2d 791, 465 N.E.2d 330 (N.Y.1984)—§ **30.9, n. 40.**

Foremost Ins. Co. Grand Rapids, Michigan v. Facultative Group, Inc., 80 A.D.2d 598, 436 N.Y.S.2d 40 (N.Y.A.D. 2 Dept. 1981)—§ **8.23, n. 15.**

Forest Hills Assoc. v. N.Y. State Div. of Housing & Community Renewal, N.Y.L.J., 9/7/95, p.30, col.2 (Sup.Ct., Queens County)—§ **30.38, n. 7.**

Fornaby v. Feriola, 18 A.D.2d 215, 239 N.Y.S.2d 185 (N.Y.A.D. 2 Dept.1963)—§ **16.106, n. 3.**

Forrester v. White, 484 U.S. 219, 108 S.Ct. 538, 98 L.Ed.2d 555 (1988)—§ **18.31, n. 2.**

Forrest Hills Associates, Ltd., In re, 18 B.R. 104 (Bkrtcy.D.Del.1982)—§ **9.158, n. 7.**

Forte v. Supreme Court of State of N. Y., 422 N.Y.S.2d 26, 397 N.E.2d 717 (N.Y. 1979)—§ **38.10, n. 169.**

Forth by Forth v. McQuire, 193 A.D.2d 1146, 600 N.Y.S.2d 646 (N.Y.A.D. 4 Dept.1993)—§ **37.25, n. 6.**

Fort Worth Campbell & Associates, Inc., In re, 182 B.R. 748 (Bkrtcy.N.D.Tex. 1995)—§ **9.181, n. 4.**

40 Clinton Street Associates v. Dolgin, 126 Misc.2d 373, 481 N.Y.S.2d 960 (N.Y.City Civ.Ct.1984)—§ **13.28, n. 6, 7.**

Fosmire v. Nicoleau, 551 N.Y.S.2d 876, 551 N.E.2d 77 (N.Y.1990)—§ **23.109, n. 3.**

Foster v. Moses Ludington Hosp., 223 A.D.2d 905, 636 N.Y.S.2d 220 (N.Y.A.D. 3 Dept.1996)—§ **37.65, n. 75.**

487 Elmwood, Inc. v. Hassett, 107 A.D.2d 285, 486 N.Y.S.2d 113 (N.Y.A.D. 4 Dept. 1985)—§ **13.30, n. 3.**

401 East 72nd St. Realty Co. v. Ebling Realty Co., 222 A.D. 388, 226 N.Y.S. 58 (N.Y.A.D. 1 Dept.1928)—§ **12.62, n. 1.**

417 East Realty Associates v. Ryan, 110 Misc.2d 607, 442 N.Y.S.2d 880 (N.Y.City Civ.Ct.1981)—§ **13.8, n. 5; § 13.9, n. 6.**

425 Realty Co. v. Herrera, 146 Misc.2d 790, 559 N.Y.S.2d 442 (N.Y.Sup.App.Term 1990)—§ **18.45, n. 4.**

4M Club, Inc. v. Andrews, 11 A.D.2d 720, 204 N.Y.S.2d 610 (N.Y.A.D. 2 Dept. 1960)—§ **16.91, n. 5.**

Four Star Holding Co. v. Alex Furs, Inc., 153 Misc.2d 447, 590 N.Y.S.2d 667

TABLE OF CASES

(N.Y.Sup.App.Term 1992)—§ **13.12, n. 3.**

Foust v. Munson S.S. Lines, 299 U.S. 77, 57 S.Ct. 90, 81 L.Ed. 49 (1936)—§ **9.52, n. 6, 7;** § **9.53, n. 8.**

Fowler v. Town of Ticonderoga, 131 A.D.2d 919, 516 N.Y.S.2d 368 (N.Y.A.D. 3 Dept. 1987)—§ **30.9, n. 22.**

Fox v. Ashland Oil, Inc., 134 A.D.2d 850, 521 N.Y.S.2d 594 (N.Y.A.D. 4 Dept. 1987)—§ **5.9, n. 5.**

Fox v. Coughlin, 893 F.2d 475 (2nd Cir. 1990)—§ **18.32, n. 2.**

Fox-Knapp, Inc. v. Employers Mut. Cas. Co., 725 F.Supp. 706 (S.D.N.Y.1989)—§ **31.26, n. 10.**

Francabandera, People v., 354 N.Y.S.2d 609, 310 N.E.2d 292 (N.Y.1974)—§ **38.8, n. 191.**

Frances G. v. Vincent G., 530 N.Y.S.2d 93, 525 N.E.2d 739 (N.Y.1988)—§ **37.65, n. 50, 51.**

Frane, Estate of v. Commissioner, 98 T.C. No. 26, 98 T.C. 341 (U.S.Tax Ct.1992)—§ **24.57, n. 7.**

Frank, Matter of, 39 B.R. 166 (Bkrtcy. E.D.N.Y.1984)—§ **8.33, n. 10.**

Frank v. Mandel, 107 N.Y.S. 116 (N.Y.Sup. App.Term 1907)—§ **30.22, n. 3.**

Frank B. Hall and Co. of New York, Inc. v. Orient Overseas Associates, 65 A.D.2d 424, 411 N.Y.S.2d 233 (N.Y.A.D. 1 Dept. 1978)—§ **28.29, n. 12.**

Frank Boufford Co. v. Lomenzo, 38 A.D.2d 986, 329 N.Y.S.2d 644 (N.Y.A.D. 3 Dept. 1972)—§ **1.13, n. 16.**

Frank Buttermark Plumbing and Heating Corp. v. Sagarese, 119 A.D.2d 540, 500 N.Y.S.2d 551 (N.Y.A.D. 2 Dept.1986)—§ **11.50, n. 5.**

Frankel v. Foreman & Clark, 33 F.2d 83 (2nd Cir.1929)—§ **5.37, n. 5.**

Frankel v. Frankel, 111 A.D.2d 447, 488 N.Y.S.2d 825 (N.Y.A.D. 3 Dept.1985)—§ **8.42, n. 7.**

Frankel v. Manufacturers Hanover Trust Co., 106 A.D.2d 542, 483 N.Y.S.2d 67 (N.Y.A.D. 2 Dept.1984)—§ **37.43, n. 10.**

Frank, Estate of v. Commissioner, T.C. Memo. 1995-132 (U.S.Tax Ct.1995)—§ **24.56, n. 4.**

Frank Gilbert Paper Co. v. Prankard, 195 N.Y.S. 638 (N.Y.Sup.1922)—§ **1.38, n. 8.**

Frankl v. Motor Vehicle Acc. Indemnification Corp., 53 A.D.2d 614, 384 N.Y.S.2d 20 (N.Y.A.D. 2 Dept.1976)—§ **26.30, n. 9.**

Franklin Nat. Bank v. DeGiacomo, 44 Misc.2d 518, 253 N.Y.S.2d 819 (N.Y.Sup. 1964)—§ **11.49, n. 3;** § **11.50, n. 3.**

Franklin Research & Development Corp. v. Swift Elec. Supply Co., 236 F.Supp. 992 (S.D.N.Y.1964)—§ **5.19, n. 3.**

Frazier, People v., 212 A.D.2d 976, 623 N.Y.S.2d 459 (N.Y.A.D. 4 Dept.1995)—§ **38.8, n. 55.**

Frazier, People ex rel. v. Fogg, 122 A.D.2d 377, 504 N.Y.S.2d 794 (N.Y.A.D. 3 Dept. 1986)—§ **38.8, n. 75.**

Freckelton, People ex rel. Washor on Behalf of Lopez v., 187 A.D.2d 406, 590 N.Y.S.2d 203 (N.Y.A.D. 1 Dept.1992)—§ **38.8, n. 78.**

Freddolino v. Village of Warwick Zoning Bd. of Appeals, 192 A.D.2d 839, 596 N.Y.S.2d 490 (N.Y.A.D. 3 Dept.1993)—§ **4.25, n. 2.**

Freeman, In re, 86 F.3d 478 (6th Cir. 1996)—§ **9.252, n. 2.**

Freeman, Matter of, 11 I & N Dec. 482 (BIA 1966)—§ **19.12, n. 2.**

Freeman v. Freeman, 119 Misc.2d 775, 464 N.Y.S.2d 676 (N.Y.Sup.1983)—§ **8.39, n. 3.**

Freeman v. Seligson, 405 F.2d 1326, 132 U.S.App.D.C. 56 (D.C.Cir.1968)—§ **9.39, n. 2;** § **9.40, n. 3.**

Freeman's Estate, In re, 355 N.Y.S.2d 336, 311 N.E.2d 480 (N.Y.1974)—§ **25.47, n. 6.**

Freiberger v. State, 33 A.D.2d 619, 304 N.Y.S.2d 782 (N.Y.A.D. 3 Dept.1969)—§ **14.78, n. 5.**

Freitag, Matter of, 123 Misc.2d 266, 473 N.Y.S.2d 334 (N.Y.Sur.1984)—§ **25.42, n. 2.**

Fremar Bldg. Corp. v. Sand, 104 A.D.2d 1025, 480 N.Y.S.2d 945 (N.Y.A.D. 2 Dept.1984)—§ **10.19, n. 10.**

Fremont-Rockland Sewage Corp. v. Bock, 79 A.D.2d 768, 435 N.Y.S.2d 61 (N.Y.A.D. 3 Dept.1980)—§ **14.17, n. 2.**

Freyer v. Freyer, 138 Misc.2d 158, 524 N.Y.S.2d 147 (N.Y.Sup.1987)—§ **21.39, n. 2.**

Friedlander v. Doherty, 851 F.Supp. 515 (N.D.N.Y.1994)—§ **9.111, n. 5.**

Friedman, Matter of, 64 A.D.2d 70, 407 N.Y.S.2d 999 (N.Y.A.D. 2 Dept.1978)—§ **5.13, n. 9;** § **5.15, n. 2.**

Friedman v. Gerax Realty Associates, 100 Misc.2d 820, 420 N.Y.S.2d 247 (N.Y.Sup. 1979)—§ **11.31, n. 2.**

Friedman v. Medtronic, Inc., 42 A.D.2d 185, 345 N.Y.S.2d 637 (N.Y.A.D. 2 Dept. 1973)—§ **5.29, n. 2.**

Friedman v. State, 301 N.Y.S.2d 484, 249 N.E.2d 369 (N.Y.1969)—§ **38.3, n. 13.**

Friendly Ice Cream Corp. v. Barrett, 106 A.D.2d 748, 483 N.Y.S.2d 782 (N.Y.A.D. 3 Dept.1984)—§ **16.46, n. 2;** § **16.85, n. 1.**

TABLE OF CASES

Friends of the Earth v. Consolidated Rail Corp., 768 F.2d 57 (2nd Cir.1985)—§ 15.11, n. 15.

Friends of Woodstock, Inc. v. Town of Woodstock Planning Bd., 152 A.D.2d 876, 543 N.Y.S.2d 1007 (N.Y.A.D. 3 Dept.1989)—§ 16.48, n. 10.

Fritz v. Fritz, 88 A.D.2d 778, 451 N.Y.S.2d 519 (N.Y.A.D. 4 Dept.1982)—§ 21.21, n. 2.

Fritz on Behalf of Tice v. Murray, 195 A.D.2d 1088, 601 N.Y.S.2d 894 (N.Y.A.D. 4 Dept.1993)—§ 37.37, n. 42.

Frohmann's Will, In re, 205 Misc. 913, 133 N.Y.S.2d 239 (N.Y.Sur.1954)—§ 24.9, n. 3.

Frommann, In re, 153 B.R. 113 (Bkrtcy. E.D.N.Y.1993)—§ 9.205, n. 3.

Frycek v. Corning Inc., 171 Misc.2d 220, 654 N.Y.S.2d 264 (N.Y.Sup.1997)—§ 32.15, n. 10.

Frye, People v., 192 A.D.2d 412, 596 N.Y.S.2d 373 (N.Y.A.D. 1 Dept.1993)—§ 38.19, n. 45.

Frye v. United States, 293 F. 1013 (D.C.Cir. 1923)—§ 27.35, n. 6.

Ft. Greene Assets v. Fields, N.Y.L.J. 10/26/94, p. 32, col. 6, 22 HCR 615 (Civ. Ct. Kings County)—§ 13.57, n. 2.

Ft. Holding Corp. v. Otero, 157 Misc.2d 834, 598 N.Y.S.2d 908 (N.Y.City Civ.Ct. 1993)—§ 13.20, n. 1, 3.

Fucci v. Fucci, 166 A.D.2d 551, 560 N.Y.S.2d 833 (N.Y.A.D. 2 Dept.1990)—§ 21.63, n. 8.

Fuchs v. Fuchs, 216 A.D.2d 648, 628 N.Y.S.2d 193 (N.Y.A.D. 3 Dept.1995)—§ 21.20, n. 3.

Fuentes v. Shevin, 407 U.S. 67, 92 S.Ct. 1983, 32 L.Ed.2d 556 (1972)—§ 11.8; § 11.8, n. 3.

Fugardi v. Angus, 216 A.D.2d 85, 628 N.Y.S.2d 77 (N.Y.A.D. 1 Dept.1995)—§ 18.49, n. 16.

Fuggazzatto, People v., 477 N.Y.S.2d 619, 466 N.E.2d 159 (N.Y.1984)—§ 38.8, n. 227.

Fuhst v. Foley, 410 N.Y.S.2d 56, 382 N.E.2d 756 (N.Y.1978)—§ 16.84, n. 5.

Fuji, Matter of, 12 I & N Dec. 495 (Dist.Dir. 1967)—§ 19.11, n. 18.

Fulghum Const. Corp., In re, 872 F.2d 739 (6th Cir.1989)—§ 9.118, n. 6.

Fullan v. Commissioner of Corrections of State of N.Y., 891 F.2d 1007 (2nd Cir. 1989)—§ 38.16; § 38.16, n. 2.

Fuller, People v., 155 Misc.2d 812, 590 N.Y.S.2d 159 (N.Y.City Crim.Ct.1992)—§ 18.55, n. 7.

Fuller, People v., 108 A.D.2d 822, 485 N.Y.S.2d 298 (N.Y.A.D. 2 Dept.1985)—§ 38.21, n. 8.

Fuller, People v., 455 N.Y.S.2d 253, 441 N.E.2d 563 (N.Y.1982)—§ 38.19; § 38.19, n. 26.

Fulling v. Palumbo, 286 N.Y.S.2d 249, 233 N.E.2d 272 (N.Y.1967)—§ 16.84, n. 3; § 16.85, n. 3, 9.

Furber, People v., 5 Misc.2d 614, 133 N.Y.S.2d 101 (N.Y.Co.Ct.1954)—§ 33.68, n. 11.

Furlow, In re, 70 B.R. 973 (Bkrtcy.E.D.Pa. 1987)—§ 9.148, n. 8.

Furrer, Matter of, N.Y.L.J., 2/22/96, p. 35, col. 2 (Sup.Ct., Suffolk County)—§ 22.48, n. 13

Future Energy Corp., In re, 83 B.R. 470 (Bkrtcy.S.D.Ohio 1988)—§ 9.165, n. 20.

Futuronics Corp. v. Arutt, Machamie & Benjamin (Matter of Futuronics Corp.), 655 F.2d 463 (2nd Cir.1981)—§ 9.12, n. 1.

F.W. Myers & Co., Inc. v. Owsley & Sons, Inc., 192 A.D.2d 927, 597 N.Y.S.2d 178 (N.Y.A.D. 3 Dept.1993)—§ 37.23, n. 3.

G

Gabrelian v. Gabrelian, 108 A.D.2d 445, 489 N.Y.S.2d 914 (N.Y.A.D. 2 Dept.1985)—§ 10.78, n. 1.

Gaden v. Gaden, 323 N.Y.S.2d 955, 272 N.E.2d 471 (N.Y.1971)—§ 18.76, n. 1.

Gadson, People v., 190 A.D.2d 860, 593 N.Y.S.2d 875 (N.Y.A.D. 2 Dept.1993)—§ 38.25, n. 17.

Gaebel, People v., 2 Misc.2d 458, 153 N.Y.S.2d 102 (N.Y.Co.Ct.1956)—§ 33.68, n. 11.

Gager v. White, 442 N.Y.S.2d 463, 425 N.E.2d 851 (N.Y.1981)—§ 37.32, n. 2.

Gagliano v. Immigration and Naturalization Service, 353 F.2d 922 (2nd Cir.1965)—§ 19.48, n. 4.

Gagliardo v. Clemente, 180 A.D.2d 551, 580 N.Y.S.2d 278 (N.Y.A.D. 1 Dept.1992)—§ 18.76, n. 4.

Gajeway, Matter of Estate of, 159 A.D.2d 837, 553 N.Y.S.2d 64 (N.Y.A.D. 3 Dept. 1990)—§ 25.39, n. 3.

Galieta v. Young Men's Christian Ass'n of City of Schenectady, 32 A.D.2d 711, 300 N.Y.S.2d 170 (N.Y.A.D. 3 Dept.1969)—§ 27.32, n. 8.

Gallagher v. Ashland Oil, Inc., 183 A.D.2d 1033, 583 N.Y.S.2d 624 (N.Y.A.D. 3 Dept.1992)—§ 17.35, n. 2.

Gallagher v. Lambert, 549 N.Y.S.2d 945, 549 N.E.2d 136 (N.Y.1989)—§ 17.35, n. 8.

Gallagher, People v., 516 N.Y.S.2d 174, 508 N.E.2d 909 (N.Y.1987)—§ 38.19, n. 94.

TABLE OF CASES

Gallo v. Prudential Residential Services, Ltd. Partnership, 22 F.3d 1219 (2nd Cir. 1994)—§ **17.59, n. 5;** § **17.73, n. 3.**

Gallo v. Supermarkets General Corp., 112 A.D.2d 345, 491 N.Y.S.2d 796 (N.Y.A.D. 2 Dept.1985)—§ **30.8, n. 2.**

Gambill v. Bowen, 823 F.2d 1009 (6th Cir. 1987)—§ **34.11, n. 6.**

Gamer v. Secretary of Health and Human Services, 815 F.2d 1275 (9th Cir.1987)—§ **34.47, n. 18.**

Gannett Co., Inc. v. De Pasquale, 401 N.Y.S.2d 756, 372 N.E.2d 544 (N.Y. 1977)—§ **18.14, n. 1.**

Gant v. Wallingford Bd. of Educ., 69 F.3d 669 (2nd Cir.1995)—§ **18.53, n. 1.**

Gantos, Inc., In re, 176 B.R. 793 (Bkrtcy. W.D.Mich.1995)—§ **9.83, n. 2.**

Garay, Application of, 136 Misc.2d 233, 518 N.Y.S.2d 723 (N.Y.Sur.1987)—§ **20.42, n. 1.**

Garbow, Application of, 155 Misc.2d 1001, 591 N.Y.S.2d 754 (N.Y.Sur.1992)—§ **22.47, n. 12;** § **22.48, n. 3, 4, 5, 6, 13.**

Garcia, Matter of, 16 I & N Dec. 623 (BIA 1978)—§ **19.12, n. 2.**

Garcia v. Director, N.Y.L.J., 1/17/97, p.26, col.2 (Sup.Ct., N.Y. County)—§ **28.13, n. 1.**

Garcia v. Montefiore Medical Center, 209 A.D.2d 208, 617 N.Y.S.2d 775 (N.Y.A.D. 1 Dept.1994)—§ **37.37, n. 57.**

Garcia, People v., 216 A.D.2d 36, 627 N.Y.S.2d 666 (N.Y.A.D. 1 Dept.1995)—§ **38.8, n. 147.**

Garcia–Rodriguez, Matter of, 16 I & N Dec. 438 (BIA 1978)—§ **19.11, n. 16.**

Gardiner, Estate of, 144 Misc.2d 797, 545 N.Y.S.2d 466 (N.Y.Sur.1989)—§ **20.51, n. 3.**

Gardiner, Town of v. Stanley Orchards, Inc., 105 Misc.2d 460, 432 N.Y.S.2d 335 (N.Y.Sup.1980)—§ **16.124, n. 13.**

Gardner v. Toilet Goods Ass'n, 387 U.S. 167, 87 S.Ct. 1526, 18 L.Ed.2d 704 (1967)—§ **4.70, n. 2.**

Garland v. Titan West Associates, 147 A.D.2d 304, 543 N.Y.S.2d 56 (N.Y.A.D. 1 Dept.1989)—§ **13.70, n. 4.**

Garofalo, People v., 71 A.D.2d 782, 419 N.Y.S.2d 784 (N.Y.A.D. 3 Dept.1979)—§ **38.10, n. 162.**

Garofolo, People v., 415 N.Y.S.2d 810, 389 N.E.2d 123 (N.Y.1979)—§ **38.19, n. 90.**

Garr, Matter of Will of, 192 A.D.2d 396, 596 N.Y.S.2d 53 (N.Y.A.D. 1 Dept.1993)—§ **24.66, n. 2.**

Garrison Fuel Oil of Long Island, Inc. v. Grippo, 127 Misc.2d 275, 486 N.Y.S.2d 136 (N.Y.Co.Ct.1985)—§ **8.42, n. 18.**

Garson v. Hendlin, 141 A.D.2d 55, 532 N.Y.S.2d 776 (N.Y.A.D. 2 Dept.1988)—§ **18.82, n. 5.**

Garvey v. Long Island R. Co., 159 N.Y. 323, 54 N.E. 57 (N.Y.1899)—§ **14.14, n. 14.**

Garvin v. Garvin, 176 A.D.2d 318, 574 N.Y.S.2d 760 (N.Y.A.D. 2 Dept.1991)—§ **21.58, n. 2.**

Gasda Ltd. v. Adduci, 179 A.D.2d 173, 582 N.Y.S.2d 525 (N.Y.A.D. 3 Dept.1992)—§ **4.46, n. 2.**

Gaskell, Matter of, N.Y.L.J., 3/1/94, p.27, col.2 (Sup.Ct., Suffolk County)—§ **22.53, n. 5.**

Gastel v. Bridges, 110 A.D.2d 146, 493 N.Y.S.2d 674 (N.Y.A.D. 4 Dept.1985)—§ **37.20, n. 4.**

Gastwirth v. Rosenberg, 117 A.D.2d 706, 499 N.Y.S.2d 95 (N.Y.A.D. 2 Dept. 1986)—§ **30.15, n. 8.**

Gates Engineering Co., Inc., Matter of, 104 B.R. 653 (Bkrtcy.D.Del.1989)—§ **9.43, n. 13.**

Gatling, People v., N.Y.L.J., 4/15/94, p. 27, col. 1 (Sup.Ct., Crim. Term, N.Y. County)—§ **33.79, n. 2.**

Gaynor v. Rockefeller, 256 N.Y.S.2d 584, 204 N.E.2d 627 (N.Y.1965)—§ **3.32, n. 14.**

Gayton v. Palmateer, 163 A.D.2d 780, 558 N.Y.S.2d 744 (N.Y.A.D. 3 Dept.1990)—§ **30.30, n. 20.**

Gazza v. New York State Dept. of Environmental Conservation, 159 Misc.2d 591, 605 N.Y.S.2d 642 (N.Y.Sup.1993)—§ **15.34, n. 17, 18.**

GBJ Corp. v. Sequa Corp., 804 F.Supp. 564 (S.D.N.Y.1992)—§ **2.106, n. 10.**

GCI, Inc., Matter of, 131 B.R. 685 (Bkrtcy. N.D.Ind.1991)—§ **9.86, n. 7.**

Geberth v. Augustine, 143 A.D.2d 910, 533 N.Y.S.2d 504 (N.Y.A.D. 2 Dept.1988)—§ **37.44, n. 11, 15.**

Gehl, United States v., 852 F.Supp. 1150 (N.D.N.Y.1994)—§ **4.45, n. 12;** § **4.82, n. 9.**

Geismar v. Abraham & Strauss, 109 Misc.2d 495, 439 N.Y.S.2d 1005 (N.Y.Dist.Ct.1981)—§ **7.7, n. 2;** § **7.22, n. 45;** § **7.46, n. 1;** § **7.64.**

Gelbard v. Esses, 96 A.D.2d 573, 465 N.Y.S.2d 264 (N.Y.A.D. 2 Dept.1983)—§ **8.41, n. 6.**

Gelder Medical Group v. Webber, 394 N.Y.S.2d 867, 363 N.E.2d 573 (N.Y. 1977)—§ **2.51, n. 1;** § **5.15, n. 1.**

Gelezewski, Matter of , N.Y.L.J., 11/17/93, p.30, col.2 (Sup.Ct., Nassau County)—§ **22.27, n. 1;** § **22.28, n. 18;** § **22.32;** § **22.32, n. 3.**

Geller v. Markham, 635 F.2d 1027 (2nd Cir.1980)—§ **17.37, n. 2.**

TABLE OF CASES

Gemmill, People v., 34 A.D.2d 177, 310 N.Y.S.2d 244 (N.Y.A.D. 3 Dept.1970)—**§ 38.8, n. 111, 115.**

General Acc. Ins. Co. v. David C. Smith & Associates, Inc., 184 A.D.2d 616, 584 N.Y.S.2d 900 (N.Y.A.D. 2 Dept.1992)—**§ 31.7, n. 5.**

General Acc. Ins. Group v. Cirucci, 414 N.Y.S.2d 512, 387 N.E.2d 223 (N.Y. 1979)—**§ 31.16, n. 12.**

General Elec. Co. v. Rabin, 177 A.D.2d 354, 576 N.Y.S.2d 116 (N.Y.A.D. 1 Dept. 1991)—**§ 37.37, n. 54.**

General Electric Credit Corp. v. Levin & Weintraub (In re Flagstaff Foodservice Corp.), 739 F.2d 73 (2nd Cir.1984)—**§ 9.71, n. 9; § 9.102, n. 9.**

General Homes Corp., In re, 134 B.R. 853 (Bkrtcy.S.D.Tex.1991)—**§ 9.148, n. 8.**

General Motors Acceptance Corp. v. Dykes (In re Dykes), 10 F.3d 184 (3rd Cir. 1993)—**§ 9.25, n. 7.**

General Motors Acceptance Corp. v. Jones, 999 F.2d 63 (3rd Cir.1993)—**§ 9.166, n. 8.**

General Motors Acceptance Corp. v. Valenti (In re Valenti), 105 F.3d 55 (2nd Cir. 1997)—**§ 9.166, n. 8; § 9.251, n. 3.**

General Motors Corporation–Delco Products Div. v. Rosa, 604 N.Y.S.2d 14, 624 N.E.2d 142 (N.Y.1993)—**§ 4.24, n. 5.**

General Oil Distributors, Inc., In re, 42 B.R. 402 (Bkrtcy.E.D.N.Y.1984)—**§ 9.138, n. 1.**

Genesco Entertainment, a Div. of Lymutt Industries, Inc. v. Koch, 593 F.Supp. 743 (S.D.N.Y.1984)—**§ 7.46, n. 11.**

Genesee Hospital v. State Division of Human Rights, 431 N.Y.S.2d 523, 409 N.E.2d 995 (N.Y.1980)—**§ 17.56, n. 5.**

Genesis Assembly of God v. Davies, 208 A.D.2d 627, 617 N.Y.S.2d 202 (N.Y.A.D. 2 Dept.1994)—**§ 16.25, n. 6.**

Gentile v. County of Suffolk, 926 F.2d 142 (2nd Cir.1991)—**§ 18.25, n. 6.**

Gentile v. Kim, 101 A.D.2d 939, 475 N.Y.S.2d 631 (N.Y.A.D. 3 Dept.1984)—**§ 12.64, n. 13.**

George Larkin Trucking Co. v. Lisbon Tire Mart, Inc., 210 A.D.2d 899, 620 N.Y.S.2d 654 (N.Y.A.D. 4 Dept.1994)—**§ 27.34; § 27.34, n. 14.**

George Muhlstock & Co. v. American Home Assur. Co., 117 A.D.2d 117, 502 N.Y.S.2d 174 (N.Y.A.D. 1 Dept.1986)—**§ 28.39, n. 10.**

Georgia v. McCollum, 505 U.S. 42, 112 S.Ct. 2348, 120 L.Ed.2d 33 (1992)—**§ 18.15, n. 2.**

Geraldine Rose W., Matter of, 196 A.D.2d 313, 609 N.Y.S.2d 324 (N.Y.A.D. 2 Dept. 1994)—**§ 37.23, n. 1; § 37.37, n. 30.**

Gerard Lollo & Sons, Inc. v. Stern, 168 A.D.2d 606, 563 N.Y.S.2d 442 (N.Y.A.D. 2 Dept.1990)—**§ 28.18; § 28.18, n. 1.**

Gerber, People v., 182 A.D.2d 252, 589 N.Y.S.2d 171 (N.Y.A.D. 2 Dept.1992)—**§ 38.8, n. 173.**

Gerloff, People v., 145 Misc.2d 683, 547 N.Y.S.2d 544 (N.Y.Just.Ct.1989)—**§ 33.23, n. 3.**

Germain v. Connecticut Nat. Bank, 988 F.2d 1323 (2nd Cir.1993)—**§ 9.19, n. 2.**

Gernatt Asphalt Products, Inc. v. Town of Sardinia, 208 A.D.2d 139, 622 N.Y.S.2d 395 (N.Y.A.D. 4 Dept.1995)—**§ 16.39, n. 6, 8.**

Gersewitz, People v., 294 N.Y. 163, 61 N.E.2d 427 (N.Y.1945)—**§ 38.3, n. 6; § 38.8, n. 70.**

Gershowitz v. Gershowitz, 112 A.D.2d 67, 491 N.Y.S.2d 356 (N.Y.A.D. 1 Dept. 1985)—**§ 18.67, n. 2.**

Gersten v. Levin, 150 Misc.2d 594, 577 N.Y.S.2d 580 (N.Y.Sup.1991)—**§ 30.40, n. 4.**

Gerzof v. Sweeney, 264 N.Y.S.2d 376, 211 N.E.2d 826 (N.Y.1965)—**§ 3.25, n. 16.**

Getty Oil Co. v. State, 33 A.D.2d 705, 304 N.Y.S.2d 701 (N.Y.A.D. 3 Dept.1969)—**§ 14.95, n. 3.**

Gewirtz v. Wenig, N.Y.L.J., 8/9/91, p.22, col.4 (Sup.Ct., N.Y. County)—**§ 28.8; § 28.8, n. 3, 4.**

G–Fours, Inc. v. Miele, 496 F.2d 809 (2nd Cir.1974)—**§ 8.23, n. 18.**

G & G Shops, Inc. v. New York City Loft Bd., 193 A.D.2d 405, 597 N.Y.S.2d 65 (N.Y.A.D. 1 Dept.1993)—**§ 4.84, n. 7, 8.**

Ghee, People v., 153 A.D.2d 954, 545 N.Y.S.2d 760 (N.Y.A.D. 2 Dept.1989)—**§ 38.9, n. 4.**

GHR Companies, Inc., In re, 43 B.R. 165 (Bkrtcy.D.Mass.1984)—**§ 9.140, n. 2.**

GHR Energy Corp., In re, 35 B.R. 534 (Bkrtcy.D.Mass.1983)—**§ 9.40, n. 2.**

Gianni, People v., 347 N.Y.S.2d 438, 301 N.E.2d 425 (N.Y.1973)—**§ 38.21, n. 58.**

Giannini v. Stuart, 6 A.D.2d 418, 178 N.Y.S.2d 709 (N.Y.A.D. 1 Dept.1958)—**§ 13.18, n. 20; § 13.44, n. 4.**

Gibbons v. O'Reilly, 44 Misc.2d 353, 253 N.Y.S.2d 731 (N.Y.Sup.1964)—**§ 16.125, n. 3.**

Gibbs v. Hawaiian Eugenia Corp., 966 F.2d 101 (2nd Cir.1992)—**§ 31.29, n. 4.**

Gibbs, People v., 21 A.D.2d 980, 243 N.Y.S.2d 492 (N.Y.A.D. 2 Dept.1963)—**§ 38.3, n. 18.**

Gibeau v. Nellis, 18 F.3d 107 (2nd Cir. 1994)—**§ 18.18, n. 10.**

Giblin v. Murphy, 536 N.Y.S.2d 54, 532 N.E.2d 1282 (N.Y.1988)—**§ 17.27, n. 16.**

TABLE OF CASES

Gibouleau v. Society of Women Engineers, 127 A.D.2d 740, 511 N.Y.S.2d 932 (N.Y.A.D. 2 Dept.1987)—§ **17.34, n. 6.**

Gibson Group, Inc. v. J.D. Irving (In re Gibson Group, Inc.), 66 F.3d 1436 (6th Cir.1995)—§ **9.121, n. 2.**

Gielski v. State, 3 Misc.2d 578, 155 N.Y.S.2d 863 (N.Y.Ct.Cl.1956)—§ **27.20, n. 3.**

Gielskie v. State, 216 N.Y.S.2d 85, 175 N.E.2d 455 (N.Y.1961)—§ **27.20, n. 3.**

Giersz, People v., 207 A.D.2d 843, 616 N.Y.S.2d 555 (N.Y.A.D. 2 Dept.1994)—§ **38.25, n. 16.**

Gifford v. Harley, 62 A.D.2d 5, 404 N.Y.S.2d 405 (N.Y.A.D. 3 Dept.1978)—§ **28.11, n. 4.**

Giggles Restaurant, Inc., Matter of, 103 B.R. 549 (Bkrtcy.D.N.J.1989)—§ **9.264, n. 6.**

Giglio v. United States, 405 U.S. 150, 92 S.Ct. 763, 31 L.Ed.2d 104 (1972)—§ **38.10, n. 81.**

Gigliotti v. Wrape, 156 A.D.2d 946, 549 N.Y.S.2d 243 (N.Y.A.D. 4 Dept.1989)—§ **37.29, n. 25.**

Gilberg v. Barbieri, 441 N.Y.S.2d 49, 423 N.E.2d 807 (N.Y.1981)—§ **27.53, n. 2.**

Gilbert, In re, 104 B.R. 206 (Bkrtcy. W.D.Mo.1989)—§ **9.162, n. 3.**

Gilbert Frank Corp. v. Federal Ins. Co., 525 N.Y.S.2d 793, 520 N.E.2d 512 (N.Y. 1988)—§ **31.26, n. 15.**

Gilchrest House v. Guaranteed Title & Mortg. Co., 277 A.D. 788, 97 N.Y.S.2d 226 (N.Y.A.D. 2 Dept.1950)—§ **12.64, n. 6.**

Gilchrist, People v., 152 A.D.2d 923, 543 N.Y.S.2d 837 (N.Y.A.D. 4 Dept.1989)—§ **38.10, n. 146.**

Giles, People v., 543 N.Y.S.2d 37, 541 N.E.2d 37 (N.Y.1989)—§ **38.20, n. 2;** § **38.27, n. 3, 5.**

Giles v. State of Md., 386 U.S. 66, 87 S.Ct. 793, 17 L.Ed.2d 737 (1967)—§ **33.39, n. 3.**

Gill v. Montgomery Ward & Co., 284 A.D. 36, 129 N.Y.S.2d 288 (N.Y.A.D. 3 Dept. 1954)—§ **30.28, n. 18;** § **30.36, n. 3.**

Gill v. Mooney, 824 F.2d 192 (2nd Cir. 1987)—§ **18.35, n. 1.**

Gillespie, Estate of, 145 Misc.2d 542, 547 N.Y.S.2d 531 (N.Y.Sur.1989)—§ **25.47, n. 5.**

Gillespie v. Great Atlantic & Pacific Tea Co. and O'Neil, 288 N.Y.S.2d 907, 235 N.E.2d 911 (N.Y.1968)—§ **30.40, n. 5.**

Gillies Agency, Inc. v. Filor, 344 N.Y.S.2d 952, 298 N.E.2d 115 (N.Y.1973)—§ **39.9, n. 5.**

Gillings v. Fernan, 204 A.D.2d 450, 612 N.Y.S.2d 49 (N.Y.A.D. 2 Dept.1994)—§ **16.85, n. 10.**

Gillman v. Chase Manhattan Bank, N.A., 537 N.Y.S.2d 787, 534 N.E.2d 824 (N.Y. 1988)—§ **5.12, n. 1;** § **5.13, n. 2, 3, 5.**

Gilmer v. Interstate/Johnson Lane Corp., 500 U.S. 20, 111 S.Ct. 1647, 114 L.Ed.2d 26 (1991)—§ **17.9, n. 1.**

Gilmore v. Beyer, 46 A.D.2d 208, 361 N.Y.S.2d 739 (N.Y.A.D. 3 Dept.1974)—§ **16.63, n. 2.**

Gimbel v. Waldman, 193 Misc. 758, 84 N.Y.S.2d 888 (N.Y.Sup.1948)—§ **28.4;** § **28.4, n. 5.**

Gimprich v. Board of Education of City of New York, 306 N.Y. 401, 118 N.E.2d 578 (N.Y.1954)—§ **3.32, n. 9.**

Gina M. M., People v., 388 N.Y.S.2d 899, 357 N.E.2d 370 (N.Y.1976)—§ **38.8, n. 207.**

Ginsberg v. Fairfield-Noble Corp., 81 A.D.2d 318, 440 N.Y.S.2d 222 (N.Y.A.D. 1 Dept.1981)—§ **17.36, n. 8.**

Gintell v. Coleman, 136 A.D.2d 515, 523 N.Y.S.2d 830 (N.Y.A.D. 1 Dept.1988)—§ **37.38, n. 12.**

Giorgio, In re, 862 F.2d 933 (1st Cir.1988)—§ **9.107, n. 11.**

Gittelson, People v., 276 N.Y.S.2d 596, 223 N.E.2d 14 (N.Y.1966)—§ **38.21, n. 42.**

Gittens v. Lefevre, 891 F.2d 38 (2nd Cir. 1989)—§ **18.32, n. 2.**

Giuffrida v. Panasonic Indus. Co., 200 A.D.2d 713, 607 N.Y.S.2d 72 (N.Y.A.D. 2 Dept.1994)—§ **27.22, n. 1.**

Gizzi v. State Farm Mut. Ins. Co., 56 A.D.2d 973, 393 N.Y.S.2d 107 (N.Y.A.D. 3 Dept.1977)—§ **28.40, n. 3.**

Gladstone, In re, 16 A.D.2d 512, 229 N.Y.S.2d 663 (N.Y.A.D. 1 Dept.1962)—§ **28.25, n. 1.**

Glamm v. Allen, 453 N.Y.S.2d 674, 439 N.E.2d 390 (N.Y.1982)—§ **28.14;** § **28.14, n. 2, 7, 16.**

Glasberg v. Glasberg, 162 A.D.2d 586, 556 N.Y.S.2d 772 (N.Y.A.D. 2 Dept.1990)—§ **21.38, n. 9.**

Glaser, In re, 49 B.R. 1015 (S.D.N.Y. 1985)—§ **9.205, n. 2.**

Glass, People v., 401 N.Y.S.2d 189, 372 N.E.2d 24 (N.Y.1977)—§ **38.40, n. 2.**

Glasser v. United States, 315 U.S. 60, 62 S.Ct. 457, 86 L.Ed. 680 (1942)—§ **38.19, n. 100.**

Glassman v. Hyder, 28 A.D.2d 974, 283 N.Y.S.2d 419 (N.Y.A.D. 1 Dept.1967)—§ **8.19, n. 9.**

Glazer v. Glazer, 190 A.D.2d 951, 593 N.Y.S.2d 905 (N.Y.A.D. 3 Dept.1993)—§ **21.40, n. 7.**

TABLE OF CASES

Gleason v. Callanan Industries Inc., 203 A.D.2d 750, 610 N.Y.S.2d 671 (N.Y.A.D. 3 Dept.1994)—§ **30.9, n. 37, 38.**

Gleason v. Gleason, 308 N.Y.S.2d 347, 256 N.E.2d 513 (N.Y.1970)—§ **21.29, n. 3, 4.**

Gleason v. Holman Contract Warehousing, Inc., 170 Misc.2d 668, 649 N.Y.S.2d 647 (N.Y.Sup.1996)—§ **32.15, n. 10.**

Gleason v. McBride, 715 F.Supp. 59 (S.D.N.Y.1988)—§ **18.38, n. 8.**

Gleason v. Temple Hill Associates, 159 A.D.2d 682, 553 N.Y.S.2d 430 (N.Y.A.D. 2 Dept.1990)—§ **31.7, n. 8.**

Gleason, United States v., 265 F.Supp. 880 (S.D.N.Y.1967)—§ **33.39, n. 3.**

Gleckman v. Kaplan, 215 A.D.2d 527, 215 A.D.2d 529, 626 N.Y.S.2d 549 (N.Y.A.D. 2 Dept.1995)—§ **21.22, n. 4.**

Glendora v. Gannett Suburban Newspapers, 201 A.D.2d 620, 608 N.Y.S.2d 239 (N.Y.A.D. 2 Dept.1994)—§ **18.82, n. 1.**

Glener, Matter of, 202 A.D.2d 503, 609 N.Y.S.2d 26 (N.Y.A.D. 2 Dept.1994)—§ **22.70, n. 2.**

Glen Head—Glenwood Landing Civic Council, Inc. v. Town of Oyster Bay, 88 A.D.2d 484, 453 N.Y.S.2d 732 (N.Y.A.D. 2 Dept.1982)—§ **15.6, n. 13.**

Glenn, People v., 220 A.D.2d 527, 632 N.Y.S.2d 188 (N.Y.A.D. 2 Dept.1995)—§ **38.8, n. 143.**

Glensder Textile Co. v. Commissioner, 46 B.T.A. 176 (B.T.A.1942)—§ **2.9, n. 5.**

Glenwood TV, Inc. v. Ratner, 103 A.D.2d 322, 480 N.Y.S.2d 98 (N.Y.A.D. 2 Dept. 1984)—§ **4.64, n. 1, 5.**

Glick v. Summer, 213 A.D.2d 403, 623 N.Y.S.2d 323 (N.Y.A.D. 2 Dept.1995)—§ **16.120, n. 4.**

Gobhai v. KLM Royal Dutch Airlines, 85 A.D.2d 566, 445 N.Y.S.2d 445 (N.Y.A.D. 1 Dept.1981)—§ **27.23; § 27.23, n. 3.**

God Kundalini Isa Allah v. Scheinman, 472 N.Y.S.2d 922, 460 N.E.2d 1357 (N.Y. 1984)—§ **39.6, n. 4.**

Goetz, In re, 175 B.R. 743 (Bkrtcy.C.D.Cal. 1994)—§ **9.198, n. 1.**

Goetz v. Kunstler, 164 Misc.2d 557, 625 N.Y.S.2d 447 (N.Y.Sup.1995)—§ **18.8, n. 7; § 18.27, n. 2; § 18.82, n. 7.**

Goetz, People v., 536 N.Y.S.2d 45, 532 N.E.2d 1273 (N.Y.1988)—§ **38.21, n. 58.**

Gold v. Vanden Brul, 28 Misc.2d 644, 211 N.Y.S.2d 757 (N.Y.Sup.1961)—§ **11.12, n. 1.**

Goldberg v. American Home Assur. Co., 80 A.D.2d 409, 439 N.Y.S.2d 2 (N.Y.A.D. 1 Dept.1981)—§ **28.39, n. 1; § 31.12, n. 5.**

Goldberg v. Bosworth, 29 Misc.2d 1057, 215 N.Y.S.2d 849 (N.Y.Sup.1961)—§ **28.14, n. 2.**

Goldberg v. Elkom Co., Inc., 372 N.Y.S.2d 653, 334 N.E.2d 600 (N.Y.1975)—§ **39.9, n. 17.**

Goldberg v. Kelly, 397 U.S. 254, 90 S.Ct. 1011, 25 L.Ed.2d 287 (1970)—§ **4.5, n. 4; § 4.6, n. 7; § 4.7, n. 3; § 34.26, n. 11.**

Goldberg v. Kollsman Instrument Corp., 240 N.Y.S.2d 592, 191 N.E.2d 81 (N.Y. 1963)—§ **27.3, n. 11; § 27.5, n. 1, 3.**

Goldberg v. Lumber Mutual Casualty Ins. Co., of New York, 297 N.Y. 148, 77 N.E.2d 131 (N.Y.1948)—§ **31.15, n. 6.**

Goldblatt v. Town of Hempstead, N. Y., 369 U.S. 590, 82 S.Ct. 987, 8 L.Ed.2d 130 (1962)—§ **16.18, n. 3.**

Golden, People v., 41 A.D.2d 242, 342 N.Y.S.2d 309 (N.Y.A.D. 1 Dept.1973)—§ **38.21, n. 40.**

Golden v. Planning Bd. of Town of Ramapo, 334 N.Y.S.2d 138, 285 N.E.2d 291 (N.Y. 1972)—§ **16.96, n. 2; § 16.99, n. 1.**

Golden v. Ramapo Imp. Corp., 78 A.D.2d 648, 432 N.Y.S.2d 238 (N.Y.A.D. 2 Dept. 1980)—§ **11.7, n. 1.**

Golden v. Steam Heat, Inc., 216 A.D.2d 440, 628 N.Y.S.2d 375 (N.Y.A.D. 2 Dept. 1995)—§ **16.48, n. 6.**

Golden v. Worldvision Enterprises, Inc., 133 A.D.2d 50, 519 N.Y.S.2d 1 (N.Y.A.D. 1 Dept.1987)—§ **17.34, n. 10.**

Golden Arrow Films, Inc. v. Standard Club of California, Inc., 38 A.D.2d 813, 328 N.Y.S.2d 901 (N.Y.A.D. 1 Dept.1972)—§ **13.63, n. 5.**

Golden Distributors, Ltd., In re, 134 B.R. 770 (Bkrtcy.S.D.N.Y.1991)—§ **1.10, n. 19.**

Golden State Bottling Co., Inc. v. N.L.R.B., 414 U.S. 168, 94 S.Ct. 414, 38 L.Ed.2d 388 (1973)—§ **6.17, n. 3.**

Golden Triangle Associates v. Town Bd. of Town of Amherst, 185 A.D.2d 617, 585 N.Y.S.2d 895 (N.Y.A.D. 4 Dept.1992)—§ **15.6, n. 14.**

Goldfarb, Matter of, 160 Misc.2d 1036, 612 N.Y.S.2d 788 (N.Y.Sup.1994)—§ **22.2, n. 9; § 22.22, n. 14; § 22.26, n. 15, 17; § 22.33, n. 3, 4.**

Goldfarb v. Goldfarb, 86 A.D.2d 459, 450 N.Y.S.2d 212 (N.Y.A.D. 2 Dept.1982)—§ **5.9, n. 1.**

Gold Fields American Corp. v. Aetna Cas. and Sur. Co., 173 Misc.2d 901, 661 N.Y.S.2d 948 (N.Y.Sup.1997)—§ **31.20, n. 3.**

Goldheart Intern. Ltd. v. Vulcan Const. Corp., 124 A.D.2d 507, 508 N.Y.S.2d 182 (N.Y.A.D. 1 Dept.1986)—§ **37.38, n. 12.**

Goldman v. McCord, 120 Misc.2d 754, 466 N.Y.S.2d 584 (N.Y.City Civ.Ct.1983)—§ **13.21, n. 3; § 13.46, n. 3.**

TABLE OF CASES

Goldowitz v. Henry Kupfer & Co., 80 Misc. 487, 141 N.Y.S. 531 (N.Y.Sup.1913)—§ 5.20, n. 6.

Goldsmith v. Howmedica, Inc., 500 N.Y.S.2d 640, 491 N.E.2d 1097 (N.Y. 1986)—§ 29.26, n. 10.

Goldsmith, People v., 110 Misc.2d 528, 442 N.Y.S.2d 760 (N.Y.Vill.Ct.1981)—§ 33.68; § 33.68, n. 4.

Goldstein v. Perez, 133 Misc.2d 303, 506 N.Y.S.2d 999 (N.Y.City Civ.Ct.1986)—§ 13.18, n. 15.

Goldstein v. Rosenthal, 56 Misc.2d 311, 288 N.Y.S.2d 503 (N.Y.City Civ.Ct.1968)—§ 18.76, n. 5.

Golf v. New York State Dept. of Social Services, 221 A.D.2d 997, 634 N.Y.S.2d 581 (N.Y.A.D. 4 Dept.1995)—§ 23.80, n. 13.

Golino v. City of New Haven, 950 F.2d 864 (2nd Cir.1991)—§ 18.22, n. 4.

Golisano v. Town Bd. of Town of Macedon, 31 A.D.2d 85, 296 N.Y.S.2d 623 (N.Y.A.D. 4 Dept.1968)—§ 16.19, n. 11.

Golon, People v., 174 A.D.2d 630, 571 N.Y.S.2d 98 (N.Y.A.D. 2 Dept.1991)—§ 38.10, n. 20.

Golsen v. Commssioner, 54 T.C. 742 (U.S.Tax Ct.1970)—§ 24.57, n. 7.

Golub v. Frank, 493 N.Y.S.2d 451, 483 N.E.2d 126 (N.Y.1985)—§ 13.40, n. 15; § 13.52, n. 10.

Golub v. Golub, 139 Misc.2d 440, 527 N.Y.S.2d 946 (N.Y.Sup.1988)—§ 21.39; § 21.39, n. 12.

Gombert v. New York Cent. & H.R.R. Co., 195 N.Y. 273, 88 N.E. 382 (N.Y.1909)—§ 30.10, n. 15.

Gomez v. City of New York, 215 A.D.2d 353, 625 N.Y.S.2d 646 (N.Y.A.D. 2 Dept. 1995)—§ 37.28, n. 42.

Gomprecht v. Gomprecht, 629 N.Y.S.2d 190, 652 N.E.2d 936 (N.Y.1995)—§ 23.80, n. 17.

Gonzalez v. AMR Services Corp., 68 F.3d 1529 (2nd Cir.1995)—§ 17.51, n. 2.

Gonzalez v. New York City Housing Authority, 569 N.Y.S.2d 915, 572 N.E.2d 598 (N.Y.1991)—§ 30.14, n. 5.

Gonzalez, People v., 186 A.D.2d 12, 587 N.Y.S.2d 972 (N.Y.A.D. 1 Dept.1992)—§ 38.27, n. 21.

Gonzalez, People v., 587 N.Y.S.2d 607, 600 N.E.2d 238 (N.Y.1992)—§ 38.28, n. 17.

Gonzalez, People v., 184 A.D.2d 525, 584 N.Y.S.2d 180 (N.Y.A.D. 2 Dept.1992)—§ 38.40, n. 2.

Gonzalez, People v., 116 A.D.2d 735, 497 N.Y.S.2d 778 (N.Y.A.D. 2 Dept.1986)—§ 33.81, n. 2.

Gonzalez, People v., 471 N.Y.S.2d 847, 459 N.E.2d 1285 (N.Y.1983)—§ 38.26; § 38.26, n. 16; § 38.27, n. 22.

Goodfriend, People v., 485 N.Y.S.2d 519, 474 N.E.2d 1187 (N.Y.1984)—§ 38.3, n. 30; § 38.10, n. 16; § 38.24, n. 3.

Good Humor Corporation v. City of New York, 290 N.Y. 312, 49 N.E.2d 153 (N.Y. 1943)—§ 3.10, n. 9.

Goodman, People v., 338 N.Y.S.2d 97, 290 N.E.2d 139 (N.Y.1972)—§ 3.9, n. 5.

Goodrich v. John Hancock Mut. Life Ins. Co. of Boston, Mass., 17 A.D.2d 271, 234 N.Y.S.2d 587 (N.Y.A.D. 3 Dept.1962)—§ 37.28, n. 20.

Goodrich Silvertown Stores of B.F. Goodrich Co. v. Valentine, 10 N.Y.S.2d 447 (N.Y.Co.Ct.1939)—§ 7.59.

Goodridge v. Harvey Group, Inc., 778 F.Supp. 115 (S.D.N.Y.1991)—§ 17.27, n. 11.

Goodson Todman Enterprises, Ltd. v. Town Bd. of Milan, 151 A.D.2d 642, 542 N.Y.S.2d 373 (N.Y.A.D. 2 Dept.1989)—§ 3.28, n. 9.

Goodstein, United States v., 883 F.2d 1362 (7th Cir.1989)—§ 9.200, n. 7.

Gordon, Matter of, N.Y.L.J., 11/22/94, p.33, col.4 (Sup.Ct., Rockland County)—§ 22.53, n. 5.

Gordon, Matter of, 162 Misc.2d 697, 619 N.Y.S.2d 235 (N.Y.Sup.1994)—§ 22.13, n. 6; § 22.53, n. 11.

Gordon v. Elliman, 280 A.D. 655, 116 N.Y.S.2d 671 (N.Y.A.D. 1 Dept.1952)—§ 1.38, n. 11.

Gordon v. Marrone, 155 Misc.2d 726, 590 N.Y.S.2d 649 (N.Y.Sup.1992)—§ 18.80, n. 2.

Gordon v. Nationwide Mut. Ins. Co., 334 N.Y.S.2d 601, 285 N.E.2d 849 (N.Y. 1972)—§ 28.44, n. 1; § 31.17, n. 1.

Gordon v. Town of Huntington, 230 N.Y.S.2d 619 (N.Y.Sup.1962)—§ 14.14, n. 7.

Gordon v. Zoning Bd. of Appeals of Town of Clarkstown, 126 Misc.2d 75, 481 N.Y.S.2d 275 (N.Y.Sup.1984)—§ 16.89, n. 7.

Gorieb v. Fox, 274 U.S. 603, 47 S.Ct. 675, 71 L.Ed. 1228 (1927)—§ 16.22, n. 6.

Goros, People v., 224 A.D.2d 444, 638 N.Y.S.2d 107 (N.Y.A.D. 2 Dept.1996)—§ 38.28, n. 15.

Gorrill v. Icelandair/Flugleidir, 761 F.2d 847 (2nd Cir.1985)—§ 17.34, n. 2.

Gory, People v., 220 A.D.2d 614, 633 N.Y.S.2d 970 (N.Y.A.D. 2 Dept.1995)—§ 38.8, n. 181, 214.

Goss v. Lopez, 419 U.S. 565, 95 S.Ct. 729, 42 L.Ed.2d 725 (1975)—§ 18.53, n. 9.

TABLE OF CASES

Gottlieb v. Board of Appeals of City of Rye, 139 A.D.2d 617, 527 N.Y.S.2d 258 (N.Y.A.D. 2 Dept.1988)—§ **16.125, n. 15.**

Gottlieb v. Kenneth D. Laub & Co., Inc., 605 N.Y.S.2d 213, 626 N.E.2d 29 (N.Y. 1993)—§ **30.39, n. 13.**

Gould v. Community Health Plan of Suffolk, Inc., 99 A.D.2d 479, 470 N.Y.S.2d 415 (N.Y.A.D. 2 Dept.1984)—§ **17.23, n. 1.**

Gould v. McBride, 36 A.D.2d 706, 319 N.Y.S.2d 125 (N.Y.A.D. 1 Dept.1971)—§ **11.37, n. 5.**

Gould v. Pollack, 68 Misc.2d 670, 327 N.Y.S.2d 808 (N.Y.City Civ.Ct.1971)—§ **13.43, n. 11.**

Government Emp. Ins. Co. v. Elman, 40 A.D.2d 994, 338 N.Y.S.2d 666 (N.Y.A.D. 2 Dept.1972)—§ **31.10, n. 9.**

Government Employees Ins. Co. v. Cusi, 163 A.D.2d 918, 558 N.Y.S.2d 430 (N.Y.A.D. 4 Dept.1990)—§ **31.16, n. 14.**

Gowdey v. Robbins, 3 A.D. 353, 38 N.Y.S. 280 (N.Y.A.D. 2 Dept.1896)—§ **37.28, n. 15; § 38.3, n. 32.**

Grace v. Nappa, 415 N.Y.S.2d 793, 389 N.E.2d 107 (N.Y.1979)—§ **12.13, n. 2.**

Grace v. State Tax Commission, 375 N.Y.S.2d 1027, 338 N.E.2d 330 (N.Y. 1975)—§ **35.103, n. 1.**

Grace Plaza of Great Neck, Inc. v. Elbaum, 603 N.Y.S.2d 386, 623 N.E.2d 513 (N.Y. 1993)—§ **22.54, n. 8; § 24.90, n. 2.**

Grady, Matter of, N.Y.L.J., 4/21/95, p.25, col.5 (Sup.Ct., N.Y. County)—§ **22.39, n. 4.**

Graf v. Hope Bldg. Corp., 254 N.Y. 1, 171 N.E. 884 (N.Y.1930)—§ **11.37, n. 10.**

Grago v. Robertson, 49 A.D.2d 645, 370 N.Y.S.2d 255 (N.Y.A.D. 3 Dept.1975)—§ **28.14, n. 4.**

Graham v. Connor, 490 U.S. 386, 109 S.Ct. 1865, 104 L.Ed.2d 443 (1989)—§ **18.21; § 18.21, n. 1.**

Graham v. Dim-Rosy United StatesA. Corp., 128 A.D.2d 417, 512 N.Y.S.2d 700 (N.Y.A.D. 1 Dept.1987)—§ **17.29, n. 8.**

Graham, People v., 370 N.Y.S.2d 888, 331 N.E.2d 673 (N.Y.1975)—§ **38.26, n. 13, 15.**

Graham, People v., 365 N.Y.S.2d 527, 324 N.E.2d 885 (N.Y.1975)—§ **38.27, n. 5.**

Gramatan Home Investors Corp. v. Lopez, 414 N.Y.S.2d 308, 386 N.E.2d 1328 (N.Y. 1979)—§ **8.3, n. 4.**

Gramercy Equities Corp. v. Dumont, 534 N.Y.S.2d 908, 531 N.E.2d 629 (N.Y. 1988)—§ **2.46, n. 2.**

Gramford Realty Corp. v. Valentin, 71 Misc.2d 784, 337 N.Y.S.2d 160 (N.Y.City Civ.Ct.1972)—§ **13.33; § 13.33, n. 3.**

Granatelli, People v., 108 Misc.2d 1009, 438 N.Y.S.2d 707 (N.Y.Sup.1981)—§ **38.8, n. 94.**

Grand Jury Subpoena Duces Tecum Dated Dec. 14, 1984, Y., M.D., P.C. v. Kuriansky, 513 N.Y.S.2d 359, 505 N.E.2d 925 (N.Y.1987)—§ **4.2, n. 39; § 4.64, n. 5.**

Grand Jury Subpoenas Duces Tecum, Matter of, 58 A.D.2d 1, 395 N.Y.S.2d 645 (N.Y.A.D. 1 Dept.1977)—§ **20.128; § 20.128, n. 1.**

Grand Jury Subpoenas for Locals 17, 135, 257 and 608 of the United Broth. of Carpenters and Joiners of America, AFL-CIO, Matter of, 532 N.Y.S.2d 722, 528 N.E.2d 1195 (N.Y.1988)—§ **37.31, n. 3; § 37.37, n. 73; § 39.27, n. 9.**

Grand Jury Subpoenas to Maguire, In re, 161 Misc.2d 960, 615 N.Y.S.2d 848 (N.Y.Co.Ct.1994)—§ **18.85, n. 5.**

Grand Liberte Co-op., Inc. v. Bilhaud, 126 Misc.2d 961, 487 N.Y.S.2d 250 (N.Y.Sup. App.Term 1984)—§ **13.11, n. 4; § 13.36, n. 2.**

Grando v. Town of Islip, 172 A.D.2d 663, 568 N.Y.S.2d 635 (N.Y.A.D. 2 Dept. 1991)—§ **16.125, n. 13.**

Granser v. Box Tree South Ltd., 164 Misc.2d 191, 623 N.Y.S.2d 977 (N.Y.Sup. 1994)—§ **17.64, n. 3.**

Grant, In re, 160 B.R. 839 (Bkrtcy.S.D.Cal. 1993)—§ **9.207, n. 4.**

Grant v. DCA Food Industries, Inc., 124 A.D.2d 909, 508 N.Y.S.2d 327 (N.Y.A.D. 3 Dept.1986)—§ **17.27, n. 3.**

Grant v. Martinez, 973 F.2d 96 (2nd Cir. 1992)—§ **17.75, n. 3.**

Grant, People v., 222 A.D.2d 607, 635 N.Y.S.2d 272 (N.Y.A.D. 2 Dept.1995)—§ **38.19, n. 49.**

Grant, People v., 140 A.D.2d 623, 528 N.Y.S.2d 993 (N.Y.A.D. 2 Dept.1988)—§ **38.8, n. 154.**

Grant, People v., 408 N.Y.S.2d 429, 380 N.E.2d 257 (N.Y.1978)—§ **38.19, n. 113.**

Grant, People v., 262 N.Y.S.2d 106, 209 N.E.2d 723 (N.Y.1965)—§ **38.8, n. 178.**

Grant-Howard Associates v. General Housewares Corp., 482 N.Y.S.2d 225, 472 N.E.2d 1 (N.Y.1984)—§ **27.26, n. 1, 8.**

Graphic Arts Mut. Ins. Co. (Leno on Behalf of Leno), Matter of, 214 A.D.2d 976, 626 N.Y.S.2d 916 (N.Y.A.D. 4 Dept.1995)—§ **31.24, n. 5.**

Grassi v. Ulrich, 641 N.Y.S.2d 588, 664 N.E.2d 499 (N.Y.1996)—§ **37.65, n. 31.**

Grasso v. Country-Wide Ins. Co., 132 A.D.2d 451, 517 N.Y.S.2d 150 (N.Y.A.D. 1 Dept.1987)—§ **31.14, n. 1.**

Graubard Mollen Dannett & Horowitz v. Moskovitz, 629 N.Y.S.2d 1009, 653

TABLE OF CASES

N.E.2d 1179 (N.Y.1995)—§ **6.67, n. 2;** § **6.88, n. 2;** § **17.27, n. 12;** § **39.31, n. 2.**

Gray, People v., 629 N.Y.S.2d 173, 652 N.E.2d 919 (N.Y.1995)—§ **37.37, n. 70;** § **38.19;** § **38.19, n. 50, 62;** § **39.50, n. 9.**

Gray v. Ward, 74 Misc.2d 50, 343 N.Y.S.2d 749 (N.Y.Sup.1973)—§ **16.119, n. 2, 6;** § **16.120, n. 4;** § **16.121, n. 1.**

Grayson v. Irvmar Realty Corp., 7 A.D.2d 436, 184 N.Y.S.2d 33 (N.Y.A.D. 1 Dept. 1959)—§ **30.9;** § **30.9, n. 10;** § **30.10;** § **30.10, n. 2.**

Grcic v. City of New York, 139 A.D.2d 621, 527 N.Y.S.2d 263 (N.Y.A.D. 2 Dept. 1988)—§ **30.13, n. 8.**

Greater New York Sav. Bank v. Travelers Ins. Co., 173 A.D.2d 521, 570 N.Y.S.2d 122 (N.Y.A.D. 2 Dept.1991)—§ **31.15, n. 9.**

Greatsinger, Matter of Estate of, 501 N.Y.S.2d 623, 492 N.E.2d 751 (N.Y. 1986)—§ **25.16, n. 2;** § **25.50, n. 1.**

Greaves v. Public Service Mut. Ins. Co., 181 N.Y.S.2d 489, 155 N.E.2d 390 (N.Y. 1959)—§ **31.9, n. 13.**

Greco, Matter of, 99 A.D.2d 810, 472 N.Y.S.2d 140 (N.Y.A.D. 2 Dept.1984)—§ **3.20, n. 8.**

Green v. Gray, 237 N.Y.S.2d 788 (N.Y.Sup. App.Term 1963)—§ **13.27, n. 6.**

Green v. Le Beau, 281 A.D. 836, 118 N.Y.S.2d 585 (N.Y.A.D. 2 Dept.1953)—§ **2.46, n. 9.**

Green v. Leibowitz, 118 A.D.2d 756, 500 N.Y.S.2d 146 (N.Y.A.D. 2 Dept.1986)—§ **28.10;** § **28.10, n. 7.**

Green, People v., 148 Misc.2d 666, 561 N.Y.S.2d 130 (N.Y.Co.Ct.1990)—§ **18.15, n. 4.**

Green, People v., 554 N.Y.S.2d 821, 553 N.E.2d 1331 (N.Y.1990)—§ **38.8, n. 186.**

Green, People v., 19 A.D.2d 749, 242 N.Y.S.2d 881 (N.Y.A.D. 2 Dept.1963)—§ **38.21;** § **38.21, n. 14.**

Green, People ex rel. Ryan v., 58 N.Y. 295 (N.Y.1874)—§ **3.18, n. 6, 7.**

Green v. Wells Fargo Alarm Service, a Div. of Baker Protective Services, Inc., 192 A.D.2d 463, 596 N.Y.S.2d 412 (N.Y.A.D. 1 Dept.1993)—§ **17.41, n. 3.**

Green Bus Lines, In re, 166 Misc. 800, 2 N.Y.S.2d 556 (N.Y.Sup.1937)—§ **1.43, n. 23.**

Greene, Estates of, N.Y.L.J., 3/1/93, p.29, col.4 (Surr.Ct., Bronx County)—§ **23.81, n. 13.**

Greene v. Greene, 451 N.Y.S.2d 46, 436 N.E.2d 496 (N.Y.1982)—§ **28.14;** § **28.14, n. 5;** § **28.19, n. 1;** § **28.29;** § **28.29, n. 4.**

Greene v. Industrial Comr., 269 N.Y.S.2d 978, 216 N.E.2d 840 (N.Y.1966)—§ **39.4, n. 3, 5;** § **39.5, n. 3.**

Greene v. Johnson, 121 A.D.2d 632, 503 N.Y.S.2d 656 (N.Y.A.D. 2 Dept.1986)—§ **16.47, n. 7.**

Greene v. Payne, Wood and Littlejohn, 197 A.D.2d 664, 602 N.Y.S.2d 883 (N.Y.A.D. 2 Dept.1993)—§ **28.3;** § **28.3, n. 6.**

Greene, People v., 221 A.D.2d 559, 634 N.Y.S.2d 144 (N.Y.A.D. 2 Dept.1995)—§ **38.26, n. 5.**

Greene v. Town Bd. of Town of Warrensburg, 90 A.D.2d 916, 456 N.Y.S.2d 873 (N.Y.A.D. 3 Dept.1982)—§ **3.15, n. 2.**

Greenfield, Matter of, 558 N.Y.S.2d 881, 557 N.E.2d 1177 (N.Y.1990)—§ **39.59, n. 12.**

Green Point Sav. Bank v. Board of Zoning Appeals of Town of Hempstead, 281 N.Y. 534, 24 N.E.2d 319 (N.Y.1939)—§ **16.91, n. 4.**

Green Point Savings Bank v. Leselrod, N.Y.L.J., 7/31/91, p.25, col.3 (Sup.Ct., Suffolk County)—§ **11.54, n. 8.**

Greenspan v. Commercial Ins. Co. of Newark, New Jersey, 57 A.D.2d 387, 395 N.Y.S.2d 519 (N.Y.A.D. 3 Dept.1977)—§ **30.31, n. 6.**

Greenstone v. Klar, 69 N.Y.S.2d 548 (N.Y.Sup.1947)—§ **2.46, n. 8.**

Greentree at Murray Hill Condominium v. Good Shepherd Episcopal Church, 146 Misc.2d 500, 550 N.Y.S.2d 981 (N.Y.Sup. 1989)—§ **16.119, n. 9;** § **16.131, n. 4, 10.**

Greenwald v. Greenwald, 164 A.D.2d 706, 565 N.Y.S.2d 494 (N.Y.A.D. 1 Dept. 1991)—§ **21.42, n. 5;** § **21.68, n. 1.**

Greenwaldt, People v., 103 A.D.2d 933, 479 N.Y.S.2d 781 (N.Y.A.D. 3 Dept.1984)—§ **33.79, n. 2.**

Greenwich Associates v. Metropolitan Transp. Authority, 152 A.D.2d 216, 548 N.Y.S.2d 190 (N.Y.A.D. 1 Dept.1989)—§ **14.28, n. 1;** § **14.38, n. 5.**

Greenwich Citizens Committee, Inc. v. Counties of Warren and Washington Indus. Development Agency, 77 F.3d 26 (2nd Cir.1996)—§ **18.80, n. 5.**

Grega, People v., 534 N.Y.S.2d 647, 531 N.E.2d 279 (N.Y.1988)—§ **38.19;** § **38.19, n. 126.**

Gregory C., In re, 202 A.D.2d 273, 608 N.Y.S.2d 655 (N.Y.A.D. 1 Dept.1994)—§ **38.8, n. 206.**

Gregory C., People v., 158 Misc.2d 872, 602 N.Y.S.2d 492 (N.Y.Sup.1993)—§ **38.8, n. 133.**

Gregory S, Matter of, 85 Misc.2d 846, 380 N.Y.S.2d 620 (N.Y.Fam.Ct.1976)—§ **18.28, n. 6.**

TABLE OF CASES

Grenier v. Grenier, 210 A.D.2d 557, 620 N.Y.S.2d 139 (N.Y.A.D. 3 Dept.1994)— § 21.38, n. 5; § 21.49, n. 6.

Greschler v. Greschler, 434 N.Y.S.2d 194, 414 N.E.2d 694 (N.Y.1980)— § 8.16, n. 4; § 21.32, n. 1.

Greyhound Corp. v. Commercial Cas. Ins. Co., 259 A.D. 317, 19 N.Y.S.2d 239 (N.Y.A.D. 1 Dept.1940)— § 17.29, n. 4.

Greystone III Joint Venture, Matter of, 995 F.2d 1274 (5th Cir.1991)— § 9.154, n. 3; § 9.166, n. 12.

Grice, People v., 188 A.D.2d 397, 591 N.Y.S.2d 380 (N.Y.A.D. 1 Dept.1992)— § 38.10; § 38.10, n. 83.

Griffen, People v., 141 Misc.2d 627, 533 N.Y.S.2d 807 (N.Y.City Crim.Ct.1988)— § 33.83; § 33.83, n. 3.

Griffin v. Breckenridge, 403 U.S. 88, 91 S.Ct. 1790, 29 L.Ed.2d 338 (1971)— § 18.19, n. 1.

Griffin v. Coughlin, 649 N.Y.S.2d 903, 673 N.E.2d 98 (N.Y.1996)— § 18.28, n. 3; § 18.29, n. 1.

Griffith v. Oles (Matter of Hipp, Inc.), 895 F.2d 1503 (5th Cir.1990)— § 9.18, n. 4.

Griggs v. Duke Power Co., 401 U.S. 424, 91 S.Ct. 849, 28 L.Ed.2d 158 (1971)— § 17.59, n. 9.

Grillo, People v., 176 A.D.2d 346, 574 N.Y.S.2d 583 (N.Y.A.D. 2 Dept.1991)— § 33.57, n. 3, 4.

Grimaldi v. Shop Rite Big V, 90 A.D.2d 608, 456 N.Y.S.2d 176 (N.Y.A.D. 3 Dept. 1982)— § 32.19, n. 2.

Griminger, People v., 529 N.Y.S.2d 55, 524 N.E.2d 409 (N.Y.1988)— § 38.6, n. 1; § 39.42, n. 1.

Grimpel v. Hochman, 74 Misc.2d 39, 343 N.Y.S.2d 507 (N.Y.City Civ.Ct.1972)— § 10.75, n. 5.

Grimson v. I.N.S., 1993 WL 792443 (N.D.Ill.1993)— § 19.19; § 19.19, n. 8, 9.

Grinker, Matter of, 570 N.Y.S.2d 448, 573 N.E.2d 536 (N.Y.1991)— § 22.1; § 22.1, n. 2; § 22.4, n. 23; § 22.6; § 22.6, n. 11; § 22.7; § 22.7, n. 2; § 22.10; § 22.10, n. 2; § 22.13; § 22.13, n. 4, 7, 8; § 22.38; § 22.38, n. 2; § 22.53; § 22.53, n. 7.

Grisi v. Shainswit, 119 A.D.2d 418, 507 N.Y.S.2d 155 (N.Y.A.D. 1 Dept.1986)— § 37.87, n. 4.

Groce, People v., 213 A.D.2d 363, 624 N.Y.S.2d 863 (N.Y.A.D. 2 Dept.1995)— § 38.26, n. 18.

Groden v. Random House, Inc., 61 F.3d 1045 (2nd Cir.1995)— § 18.63, n. 2; § 18.64, n. 16.

Gross, Matter of, 127 A.D.2d 658, 511 N.Y.S.2d 885 (N.Y.A.D. 2 Dept.1987)— § 22.47, n. 15.

Gross, Matter of, 127 A.D.2d 658, 511 N.Y.S.2d 1018 (N.Y.A.D. 2 Dept.1987)— § 22.47, n. 15.

Gross, Matter of, 102 Misc.2d 1073, 425 N.Y.S.2d 220 (N.Y.City Fam.Ct.1980)— § 20.67, n. 9.

Gross v. Kurk, 224 A.D.2d 582, 639 N.Y.S.2d 711 (N.Y.A.D. 2 Dept.1996)— § 37.22, n. 1.

Gross v. New York City Alcoholic Beverage Control Bd., 200 N.Y.S.2d 12, 166 N.E.2d 818 (N.Y.1960)— § 4.45, n. 1.

Gross v. New York Times Co., 603 N.Y.S.2d 813, 623 N.E.2d 1163 (N.Y.1993)— § 18.82, n. 6.

Gross, People v., 127 A.D.2d 892, 512 N.Y.S.2d 254 (N.Y.A.D. 3 Dept.1987)— § 33.52, n. 2.

Gross v. Perales, 532 N.Y.S.2d 68, 527 N.E.2d 1205 (N.Y.1988)— § 4.10, n. 6; § 4.79, n. 2.

Gross v. Sweet, 424 N.Y.S.2d 365, 400 N.E.2d 306 (N.Y.1979)— § 5.11, n. 8, 9, 12.

Gross' Estate, In re, 79 Misc.2d 204, 359 N.Y.S.2d 484 (N.Y.Sur.1974)— § 25.38, n. 3.

Grossman v. Kralik, 217 A.D.2d 625, 629 N.Y.S.2d 467 (N.Y.A.D. 2 Dept.1995)— § 4.15, n. 5.

Grossman v. Planning Bd. of Town of Colonie, 126 A.D.2d 887, 510 N.Y.S.2d 929 (N.Y.A.D. 3 Dept.1987)— § 16.106, n. 9.

Grosso, In re, 9 B.R. 815 (Bkrtcy.N.D.N.Y. 1981)— § 10.94, n. 2.

Group House of Port Washington, Inc. v. Town of North Hempstead, 408 N.Y.S.2d 377, 380 N.E.2d 207 (N.Y. 1978)— § 16.122, n. 14.

Grova v. Bottge, 73 A.D.2d 763, 423 N.Y.S.2d 297 (N.Y.A.D. 3 Dept.1979)— § 32.41, n. 3.

Grove Street Realty, Inc. v. Testa, 100 Misc.2d 278, 418 N.Y.S.2d 858 (N.Y.City Ct.1979)— § 13.16, n. 3, 4.

Grubbs, People v., 1 A.D.2d 1035, 152 N.Y.S.2d 46 (N.Y.A.D. 2 Dept.1956)— § 38.3, n. 18.

Gruen v. Chase, 215 A.D.2d 481, 626 N.Y.S.2d 261 (N.Y.A.D. 2 Dept.1995)— § 4.14, n. 2.

Grullon v. City of New York, 222 A.D.2d 257, 635 N.Y.S.2d 24 (N.Y.A.D. 1 Dept. 1995)— § 18.20, n. 2.

Guadagnolo v. Town of Mamaroneck Bd. of Appeals, 52 A.D.2d 902, 383 N.Y.S.2d 377 (N.Y.A.D. 2 Dept.1976)— § 16.77, n. 7.

Guarantee Ins. Co. v. City of Long Beach, 106 A.D.2d 428, 482 N.Y.S.2d 522 (N.Y.A.D. 2 Dept.1984)— § 31.17, n. 8.

499

TABLE OF CASES

Guaranty Trust Co. v. Meer, 114 Misc. 327, 187 N.Y.S. 288 (N.Y.Sup.1921)—§ **30.5, n. 7.**

Guardian Life Ins. Co. v. Bohlinger, 308 N.Y. 174, 124 N.E.2d 110 (N.Y.1954)—§ **4.74, n. 2.**

Guardian Life Ins. Co. of America v. Handel, 190 A.D.2d 57, 596 N.Y.S.2d 804 (N.Y.A.D. 1 Dept.1993)—§ **28.24, n. 6.**

Guardian Loan Co., Inc. v. Early, 419 N.Y.S.2d 56, 392 N.E.2d 1240 (N.Y. 1979)—§ **8.33, n. 9; § 11.50, n. 4.**

Guardianship of (see name of party)

Guard-Life Corp. v. S. Parker Hardware Mfg. Corp., 428 N.Y.S.2d 628, 406 N.E.2d 445 (N.Y.1980)—§ **17.29, n. 2.**

Guariglia, United States v., 962 F.2d 160 (2nd Cir.1992)—§ **9.18, n. 4.**

Guarneri v. Korea News, Inc., 214 A.D.2d 649, 625 N.Y.S.2d 291 (N.Y.A.D. 2 Dept. 1995)—§ **18.27, n. 5.**

Guarnier v. Guarnier, 155 A.D.2d 744, 547 N.Y.S.2d 455 (N.Y.A.D. 3 Dept.1989)—§ **21.61, n. 4.**

Guastella, People v., 26 A.D.2d 937, 275 N.Y.S.2d 804 (N.Y.A.D. 2 Dept.1966)—§ **38.10, n. 100.**

Guenther Pub. Corp. v. Lomenzo, 29 A.D.2d 708, 286 N.Y.S.2d 497 (N.Y.A.D. 3 Dept. 1968)—§ **1.13, n. 14.**

Guernsey, People v., 136 Misc.2d 791, 519 N.Y.S.2d 338 (N.Y.Co.Ct.1987)—§ **38.52, n. 1.**

Guerra by Guerra v. Fernandez, 149 Misc.2d 25, 562 N.Y.S.2d 1020 (N.Y.Sup. 1990)—§ **26.24, n. 10.**

Guevara, People v., 156 A.D.2d 379, 548 N.Y.S.2d 904 (N.Y.A.D. 2 Dept.1989)—§ **38.19, n. 64.**

Guggenheimer v. Ginzburg, 401 N.Y.S.2d 182, 372 N.E.2d 17 (N.Y.1977)—§ **7.7, n. 2; § 7.22, n. 45; § 7.46, n. 4.**

Guidi's Will, In re, 259 A.D. 652, 20 N.Y.S.2d 240 (N.Y.A.D. 1 Dept.1940)—§ **25.28, n. 8.**

Guild v. Herrick, 51 N.Y.S.2d 326 (N.Y.Sup. 1944)—§ **2.53, n. 2.**

Guimond v. Trans Union Credit Information Co., 45 F.3d 1329 (9th Cir.1995)—§ **7.33; § 7.33, n. 8.**

Gullo v. Califano, 609 F.2d 649 (2nd Cir. 1979)—§ **34.48, n. 1.**

Gundlach v. Gundlach, 223 A.D.2d 942, 636 N.Y.S.2d 914 (N.Y.A.D. 3 Dept.1996)—§ **21.37, n. 12.**

Gurley, People v., 197 A.D.2d 534, 602 N.Y.S.2d 184 (N.Y.A.D. 2 Dept.1993)—§ **38.10; § 38.10, n. 90.**

Gurnee v. Aetna Life and Cas. Co., 448 N.Y.S.2d 145, 433 N.E.2d 128 (N.Y. 1982)—§ **37.32, n. 2.**

Gus Russell, Inc. v. Commissioner, 36 T.C. 965 (Tax Ct.1961)—§ **1.34, n. 48.**

Guterman v. RGA Accessories, Inc., 196 A.D.2d 785, 602 N.Y.S.2d 116 (N.Y.A.D. 1 Dept.1993)—§ **17.34, n. 13.**

Gutheil v. City of New York, 119 A.D. 20, 103 N.Y.S. 972 (N.Y.A.D. 2 Dept.1907)—§ **3.17, n. 11.**

Gutin v. Frank Mascali & Sons, Inc., 226 N.Y.S.2d 434, 181 N.E.2d 449 (N.Y. 1962)—§ **39.7, n. 2.**

Guzman v. American Life Ins. Co. of New York, 156 A.D.2d 332, 548 N.Y.S.2d 284 (N.Y.A.D. 2 Dept.1989)—§ **31.27, n. 5.**

Guzman v. Scully, 80 F.3d 772 (2nd Cir. 1996)—§ **18.13, n. 3.**

Gwaltney of Smithfield, Ltd. v. Chesapeake Bay Foundation, Inc., 484 U.S. 49, 108 S.Ct. 376, 98 L.Ed.2d 306 (1987)—§ **15.11; § 15.11, n. 10; § 15.22; § 15.22, n. 9.**

G. Warhit Real Estate, Inc. v. Krauss, 127 Misc.2d 845, 487 N.Y.S.2d 484 (N.Y.Dist. Ct.1985)—§ **13.54, n. 3.**

H

Haar v. Daly, 232 A.D. 423, 250 N.Y.S. 59 (N.Y.A.D. 2 Dept.1931)—§ **12.64, n. 7.**

Haas v. Reiser, 201 Misc. 234, 105 N.Y.S.2d 98 (N.Y.Sup.1951)—§ **8.35, n. 6.**

Haas Tobacco Co. v. American Fidelity Co., 226 N.Y. 343, 123 N.E. 755 (N.Y.1919)—§ **31.10, n. 9.**

Habel, People v., 272 N.Y.S.2d 357, 219 N.E.2d 183 (N.Y.1966)—§ **39.46, n. 4.**

Haberkorn v. Da Silva, 210 N.Y.S.2d 391 (N.Y.Sup.1960)—§ **11.37, n. 7.**

Hablin Realty Corp. v. McCain, 123 Misc.2d 777, 478 N.Y.S.2d 224 (N.Y.Sup.App. Term 1984)—§ **13.20, n. 2, 6.**

Hacker, People v., 162 A.D.2d 815, 559 N.Y.S.2d 184 (N.Y.A.D. 3 Dept.1990)—§ **38.34, n. 7.**

Haddad v. Salzman, 188 A.D.2d 515, 591 N.Y.S.2d 193 (N.Y.A.D. 2 Dept.1992)—§ **16.49, n. 4.**

Hafer v. Melo, 502 U.S. 21, 112 S.Ct. 358, 116 L.Ed.2d 301 (1991)—§ **18.18, n. 8.**

Hafner v. Guerlain, Inc., 34 A.D.2d 162, 310 N.Y.S.2d 141 (N.Y.A.D. 1 Dept.1970)—§ **30.31, n. 9.**

Hagel, In re, 184 B.R. 793 (9th Cir.1995)—§ **9.252, n. 2.**

Hager v. Union Carbide Corp., 106 A.D.2d 348, 483 N.Y.S.2d 261 (N.Y.A.D. 1 Dept. 1984)—§ **17.34, n. 5; § 17.36, n. 8.**

Hairston, People v., 217 N.Y.S.2d 77, 176 N.E.2d 90 (N.Y.1961)—§ **38.10, n. 73.**

TABLE OF CASES

Hakes v. State, 599 N.Y.S.2d 498, 615 N.E.2d 982 (N.Y.1993)—§ **14.115; § 14.115, n. 10.**

Haley v. Continental Cas. Co., 749 F.Supp. 560 (D.Vt.1990)—§ **28.43, n. 12.**

HAL, Inc. v. United States (In re HAL, Inc.), 196 B.R. 159 (9th Cir.1996)—§ **9.111, n. 1.**

Hall v. Cole, 412 U.S. 1, 93 S.Ct. 1943, 36 L.Ed.2d 702 (1973)—§ **17.75, n. 1.**

Hall, People v., 200 A.D.2d 474, 608 N.Y.S.2d 403 (N.Y.A.D. 1 Dept.1994)—§ **38.40, n. 2.**

Hall, People v., 49 N.Y.S.2d 309 (N.Y.Co.Ct. 1944)—§ **21.26, n. 6.**

Hall, United States ex rel. v. Schwartzman, 887 F.Supp. 60 (E.D.N.Y.1995)—§ **34.34, n. 2.**

Hall & Co., Inc. v. Steiner and Mondore, 147 A.D.2d 225, 543 N.Y.S.2d 190 (N.Y.A.D. 3 Dept.1989)—§ **28.14, n. 14.**

Halleran v. City of New York, 132 Misc. 73, 228 N.Y.S. 116 (N.Y.Sup.1928)—§ **16.116, n. 1.**

Halligan, Application of, 46 A.D.2d 170, 361 N.Y.S.2d 458 (N.Y.A.D. 4 Dept.1974)—§ **37.89, n. 6.**

Hall on Behalf of Haralambou, People ex rel. v. LeFevre, 467 N.Y.S.2d 40, 454 N.E.2d 121 (N.Y.1983)—§ **38.8, n. 74.**

Halloran v. Virginia Chemicals Inc., 393 N.Y.S.2d 341, 361 N.E.2d 991 (N.Y. 1977)—§ **27.34, n. 3.**

Hallstrom v. Tillamook County, 493 U.S. 20, 110 S.Ct. 304, 107 L.Ed.2d 237 (1989)—§ **15.11, n. 13; § 15.25, n. 17.**

Halperin v. Kissinger, 807 F.2d 180, 257 U.S.App.D.C. 35 (D.C.Cir.1986)—§ **18.32, n. 13.**

Halperin v. Salvan, 117 A.D.2d 544, 499 N.Y.S.2d 55 (N.Y.A.D. 1 Dept.1986)—§ **30.9, n. 30; § 30.32, n. 1.**

Halpern v. State Furniture Co., 186 Misc. 551, 61 N.Y.S.2d 618 (N.Y.Sup.1946)—§ **13.20, n. 4.**

Halpin v. Prudential Ins. Co. of America, 425 N.Y.S.2d 48, 401 N.E.2d 171 (N.Y. 1979)—§ **31.17, n. 21.**

Halvorsen v. Ford Motor Co., 132 A.D.2d 57, 522 N.Y.S.2d 272 (N.Y.A.D. 3 Dept. 1987)—§ **29.16, n. 6; § 30.30, n. 26.**

Hambleton v. Commssioner, 60 T.C. 558 (U.S.Tax Ct.1973)—§ **24.61, n. 3.**

Hameed, People v., 644 N.Y.S.2d 466, 666 N.E.2d 1339 (N.Y.1996)—§ **18.15, n. 9.**

Hamilton, People v., 415 N.Y.S.2d 208, 388 N.E.2d 345 (N.Y.1979)—§ **33.77; § 33.77, n. 1.**

Hamilton v. Wein, 132 Misc.2d 1023, 506 N.Y.S.2d 387 (N.Y.Sup.1986)—§ **26.42, n. 9.**

Hamlin, People v., 530 N.Y.S.2d 74, 525 N.E.2d 719 (N.Y.1988)—§ **38.19, n. 140.**

Hammond v. Econo-Car of North Shore, Inc., 71 Misc.2d 546, 336 N.Y.S.2d 493 (N.Y.Sup.1972)—§ **8.19, n. 6.**

Hammond's Estate, In re, 2 A.D.2d 160, 154 N.Y.S.2d 820 (N.Y.A.D. 2 Dept. 1956)—§ **24.3, n. 3.**

Hammons, Application of, 164 Misc.2d 609, 625 N.Y.S.2d 408 (N.Y.Sup.1995)—§ **22.8, n. 1; § 22.12, n. 1.**

Hammons (McCarthy), Matter of, 168 Misc.2d 874, 645 N.Y.S.2d 392 (N.Y.Sup. 1996)—§ **22.20, n. 5, 6.**

Hammons (Perreau), Matter of, N.Y.L.J., 7/7/95, p.29, col.3 (Sup.Ct., N.Y. County)—§ **22.12, n. 4.**

Hampton v. Guare, 195 A.D.2d 366, 600 N.Y.S.2d 57 (N.Y.A.D. 1 Dept.1993)—§ **18.64, n. 20.**

Han, Kwan, People v., N.Y.L.J., 8/14/95 p. 31, col. 2 (Crim.Ct.,Bronx County, 1995)—§ **33.82, n. 1.**

Handzel v. Handzel, 59 A.D.2d 810, 399 N.Y.S.2d 79 (N.Y.A.D. 3 Dept.1977)—§ **24.65, n. 3.**

Hankerson v. Harris, 636 F.2d 893 (2nd Cir.1980)—§ **34.43, n. 1.**

Hanlin v. Mitchelson, 623 F.Supp. 452 (S.D.N.Y.1985)—§ **28.12; § 28.12, n. 4.**

Hann, Matter of, 18 I & N Dec. 196 (BIA 1982—§ **19.12, n. 7.**

Hanna v. Mitchell, 202 A.D. 504, 196 N.Y.S. 43 (N.Y.A.D. 1 Dept.1922)—§ **37.4, n. 6.**

Hannon Real Estate Co., Inc. v. 1006 McKinley Parkway Inc., 133 A.D.2d 548, 519 N.Y.S.2d 986 (N.Y.A.D. 4 Dept. 1987)—§ **37.20, n. 5.**

Hanover Ins. Co. v. Suffolk Overhead Door Co., Inc., 207 A.D.2d 428, 615 N.Y.S.2d 742 (N.Y.A.D. 2 Dept.1994)—§ **31.16, n. 3; § 37.2, n. 8.**

Hansel, People v., 208 A.D.2d 1112, 617 N.Y.S.2d 542 (N.Y.A.D. 3 Dept.1994)—§ **38.6; § 38.6, n. 4.**

Hanson v. First Bank of South Dakota, N.A., 828 F.2d 1310 (8th Cir.1987)—§ **9.154, n. 3.**

Hanvey v. Awan, N.Y.L.J., 7/13/94, p. 29, col. 4 (Sup.Ct., Kings County)—§ **30.15, n. 6.**

Harar Realty Corp. v. Michlin & Hill, Inc., 86 A.D.2d 182, 449 N.Y.S.2d 213 (N.Y.A.D. 1 Dept.1982)—§ **30.16, n. 2, 3.**

Harbison v. City of Buffalo, 176 N.Y.S.2d 598, 152 N.E.2d 42 (N.Y.1958)—§ **16.69, n. 1.**

Harcel Liquors, Inc. v. Evsam Parking, Inc., 423 N.Y.S.2d 873, 399 N.E.2d 905 (N.Y. 1979)—§ **37.37, n. 67; § 39.27, n. 3.**

TABLE OF CASES

Hardele Realty Corp. v. State, 125 A.D.2d 543, 509 N.Y.S.2d 621 (N.Y.A.D. 2 Dept. 1986)—§ **14.86, n. 4.**

Harden, People v., 188 A.D.2d 426, 592 N.Y.S.2d 2 (N.Y.A.D. 1 Dept.1992)—§ **38.10, n. 99.**

Harder v. Arthur F. McGinn, Jr., P.C., 89 A.D.2d 732, 454 N.Y.S.2d 42 (N.Y.A.D. 3 Dept.1982)—§ **28.11, n. 4.**

Hardin, People v., 67 A.D.2d 12, 414 N.Y.S.2d 320 (N.Y.A.D. 1 Dept.1979)—§ **38.10;** § **38.10, n. 135.**

Harding, People v., 101 A.D.2d 221, 475 N.Y.S.2d 611 (N.Y.A.D. 3 Dept.1984)—§ **38.10, n. 48.**

Hardware, In re, 189 B.R. 273 (Bkrtcy. E.D.N.Y.1995)—§ **9.249, n. 6, 9.**

Hardy, People v., 187 A.D.2d 810, 589 N.Y.S.2d 966 (N.Y.A.D. 3 Dept.1992)—§ **38.8, n. 204.**

Har Enterprises v. Town of Brookhaven, 549 N.Y.S.2d 638, 548 N.E.2d 1289 (N.Y. 1989)—§ **15.6, n. 8.**

Hargrave v. Presher, 221 A.D.2d 677, 632 N.Y.S.2d 886 (N.Y.A.D. 3 Dept.1995)—§ **37.37, n. 27.**

Hargro, People v., 144 A.D.2d 971, 534 N.Y.S.2d 274 (N.Y.A.D. 4 Dept.1988)—§ **33.79, n. 2.**

Harlem Gaslight Co. v. City of New York, 33 N.Y. 309 (N.Y.1865)—§ **3.25, n. 9.**

Harlem River Consumers Co-op., Inc. v. State Tax Commission, 44 A.D.2d 738, 354 N.Y.S.2d 472 (N.Y.A.D. 3 Dept. 1974)—§ **35.102, n. 1.**

Harlem River Houses II, Borough of Manhattan, City of New York, In re, 22 A.D.2d 882, 254 N.Y.S.2d 647 (N.Y.A.D. 1 Dept.1964)—§ **14.93, n. 3.**

Harlow v. Fitzgerald, 457 U.S. 800, 102 S.Ct. 2727, 73 L.Ed.2d 396 (1982)—§ **18.32, n. 1.**

Harman v. Fairview Associates, 302 N.Y.S.2d 791, 250 N.E.2d 209 (N.Y. 1969)—§ **10.97, n. 4;** § **10.102, n. 5, 6.**

Harmon v. Harmon, 173 A.D.2d 98, 578 N.Y.S.2d 897 (N.Y.A.D. 1 Dept.1992)—§ **21.55, n. 3.**

Harner v. Schecter, 105 A.D.2d 932, 482 N.Y.S.2d 124 (N.Y.A.D. 3 Dept.1984)—§ **10.7, n. 5, 6.**

Harriet R., Matter of, 224 A.D.2d 625, 639 N.Y.S.2d 390 (N.Y.A.D. 2 Dept.1996)—§ **22.33, n. 4.**

Harrington, Application of, 127 A.D.2d 468, 511 N.Y.S.2d 26 (N.Y.A.D. 1 Dept. 1987)—§ **22.53, n. 6.**

Harrington, People v., 131 Misc.2d 1017, 502 N.Y.S.2d 939 (N.Y.Co.Ct.1986)—§ **38.8, n. 135.**

Harrington v. State Office of Court Admin., 94 A.D.2d 863, 463 N.Y.S.2d 586 (N.Y.A.D. 3 Dept.1983)—§ **38.9, n. 16;** § **38.55, n. 4.**

Harris v. Codd, 408 N.Y.S.2d 501, 380 N.E.2d 327 (N.Y.1978)—§ **4.33, n. 3.**

Harris v. Forklift Systems, Inc., 510 U.S. 17, 114 S.Ct. 367, 126 L.Ed.2d 295 (1993)—§ **17.57, n. 3.**

Harris v. Harris, 35 A.D.2d 894, 315 N.Y.S.2d 773 (N.Y.A.D. 3 Dept.1970)—§ **21.29, n. 9;** § **21.30, n. 11.**

Harris v. Hirsh, 161 A.D.2d 452, 555 N.Y.S.2d 735 (N.Y.A.D. 1 Dept.1990)—§ **17.25, n. 9.**

Harris v. Lederfine, 196 Misc. 410, 92 N.Y.S.2d 645 (N.Y.Sup.1949)—§ **1.56, n. 11.**

Harris v. New York, 401 U.S. 222, 91 S.Ct. 643, 28 L.Ed.2d 1 (1971)—§ **33.58.**

Harris, People v., 198 A.D.2d 434, 604 N.Y.S.2d 824 (N.Y.A.D. 2 Dept.1993)—§ **38.10, n. 87.**

Harris, People v., 587 N.Y.S.2d 277, 599 N.E.2d 681 (N.Y.1992)—§ **38.19, n. 140.**

Harris, People v., 107 A.D.2d 761, 484 N.Y.S.2d 127 (N.Y.A.D. 2 Dept.1985)—§ **38.9, n. 7.**

Harris, People ex rel. v. Scully, 114 A.D.2d 919, 495 N.Y.S.2d 660 (N.Y.A.D. 2 Dept. 1985)—§ **37.34, n. 6.**

Harris v. Village of Dobbs Ferry, 208 A.D. 853, 204 N.Y.S. 325 (N.Y.A.D. 2 Dept. 1924)—§ **16.12, n. 11.**

Harris v. Ware, 142 A.D.2d 666, 531 N.Y.S.2d 18 (N.Y.A.D. 2 Dept.1988)—§ **37.25, n. 7.**

Harris Corp., People v., 104 A.D.2d 130, 483 N.Y.S.2d 442 (N.Y.A.D. 3 Dept.1984)—§ **4.45, n. 12.**

Harrison v. Harrison, 199 A.D.2d 1091, 607 N.Y.S.2d 204 (N.Y.A.D. 4 Dept.1993)—§ **37.65, n. 55.**

Harrison, People v., 457 N.Y.S.2d 199, 443 N.E.2d 447 (N.Y.1982)—§ **39.42, n. 7;** § **39.50, n. 13.**

Harrison, People ex rel. v. Jackson, 298 N.Y. 219, 82 N.E.2d 14 (N.Y.1948)—§ **37.37, n. 69;** § **38.8, n. 72;** § **39.27, n. 6.**

Harrison Orthodox Minyan, Inc. v. Town Bd. of Harrison, 159 A.D.2d 572, 552 N.Y.S.2d 434 (N.Y.A.D. 2 Dept.1990)—§ **16.131, n. 3.**

Harry, People v., 181 A.D.2d 694, 581 N.Y.S.2d 64 (N.Y.A.D. 2 Dept.1992)—§ **38.20, n. 12.**

Harry Kolomick Contractors, Inc. v. Shelter Rock Estates, Inc., 172 A.D.2d 492, 567 N.Y.S.2d 845 (N.Y.A.D. 2 Dept.1991)—§ **5.46, n. 2.**

Harry R. Defler Corp. v. Kleeman, 275 N.Y.S.2d 384, 221 N.E.2d 914 (N.Y. 1966)—§ **39.11, n. 6.**

TABLE OF CASES

Hart v. Allstate Ins. Co., 201 A.D.2d 621, 608 N.Y.S.2d 241 (N.Y.A.D. 2 Dept. 1994)—§ **7.46, n. 10.**

Hart v. Moore, 155 Misc.2d 203, 587 N.Y.S.2d 477 (N.Y.Sup.1992)—§ **7.46, n. 8.**

Hart Envtl. Mgmt. Corp. v. Sanshoe Worldwide Corp. (In re Sanshoe Worldwide Corp.), 993 F.2d 300 (2nd Cir.1993)—§ **9.74, n. 3.**

Hartford Acc. & Indem. Co. v. CNA Ins. Companies, 99 A.D.2d 310, 472 N.Y.S.2d 342 (N.Y.A.D. 1 Dept.1984)—§ **31.29, n. 3.**

Hartford Acc. & Indem. Co. v. Oles, 152 Misc. 876, 274 N.Y.S. 349 (N.Y.Sup. 1934)—§ **2.47, n. 4.**

Hartford Fire Ins. Co. v. Advocate, 576 N.Y.S.2d 80, 581 N.E.2d 1335 (N.Y. 1991)—§ **31.29, n. 1.**

Hartford Fire Ins. Co. v. Albertson, 59 Misc.2d 207, 298 N.Y.S.2d 321 (N.Y.Co. Ct.1969)—§ **7.28, n. 8;** § **7.59.**

Hartford Ins. Co. v. Nassau County, 416 N.Y.S.2d 539, 389 N.E.2d 1061 (N.Y. 1979)—§ **31.16, n. 5.**

Hartford Ins. Group v. Mello, 81 A.D.2d 577, 437 N.Y.S.2d 433 (N.Y.A.D. 2 Dept. 1981)—§ **31.13, n. 10.**

Hartman v. Bell, 137 A.D.2d 585, 524 N.Y.S.2d 477 (N.Y.A.D. 2 Dept.1988)—§ **5.11, n. 2.**

Hartog v. Hartog, 623 N.Y.S.2d 537, 647 N.E.2d 749 (N.Y.1995)—§ **21.37, n. 7;** § **21.41;** § **21.41, n. 5;** § **21.49;** § **21.49, n. 1;** § **21.57;** § **21.57, n. 2.**

Hartshorn v. Chaddock, 135 N.Y. 116, 31 N.E. 997 (N.Y.1892)—§ **30.16, n. 3;** § **30.17, n. 2.**

Hartwich v. American Transit Ins. Co., 167 A.D.2d 788, 563 N.Y.S.2d 345 (N.Y.A.D. 3 Dept.1990)—§ **28.6;** § **28.6, n. 1.**

Harvey v. Mazal American Partners, 179 A.D.2d 1, 581 N.Y.S.2d 748 (N.Y.A.D. 1 Dept.1992)—§ **30.15, n. 14.**

Harvey v. Mazal American Partners, 581 N.Y.S.2d 639, 590 N.E.2d 224 (N.Y. 1992)—§ **30.15, n. 14;** § **30.29, n. 4;** § **37.29, n. 26.**

Harvey v. NYRAC, Inc., 813 F.Supp. 206 (E.D.N.Y.1993)—§ **18.17, n. 2;** § **18.55, n. 7.**

Hasani B., In re, 195 A.D.2d 404, 600 N.Y.S.2d 694 (N.Y.A.D. 1 Dept.1993)—§ **20.113, n. 2.**

Hassan, Matter of, 16 I & N Dec. 16 (BIA 1976)—§ **19.12, n. 4.**

Hassett v. BancOhio Nat'l Bank (In re CIS Corp.), 172 B.R. 748 (S.D.N.Y.1994)—§ **9.19, n. 2.**

Hastings,, People ex rel. v. Hofstadter, 258 N.Y. 425, 180 N.E. 106 (N.Y.1932)—§ **38.10, n. 123.**

Hatch, In re, 199 A.D.2d 765, 605 N.Y.S.2d 428 (N.Y.A.D. 3 Dept.1993)—§ **20.124, n. 2.**

Hausladen, In re, 146 B.R. 557 (Bkrtcy. D.Minn.1992)—§ **9.93, n. 2.**

Haven Associates v. Donro Realty Corp., 121 A.D.2d 504, 503 N.Y.S.2d 826 (N.Y.A.D. 2 Dept.1986)—§ **30.10, n. 1.**

Haverstraw Park, Inc. v. Runcible Properties Corporation, 347 N.Y.S.2d 585, 301 N.E.2d 553 (N.Y.1973)—§ **37.43, n. 1.**

Haverstraw, Town of, State v., 219 A.D.2d 64, 641 N.Y.S.2d 879 (N.Y.A.D. 2 Dept. 1996)—§ **37.80, n. 2.**

Hayden, People v., 385 N.Y.S.2d 767, 351 N.E.2d 434 (N.Y.1976)—§ **38.27, n. 15.**

Haydock v. Haydock, 222 A.D.2d 554, 634 N.Y.S.2d 766 (N.Y.A.D. 2 Dept.1995)—§ **21.20, n. 3.**

Hayes' Will, In re, 263 N.Y. 219, 188 N.E. 716 (N.Y.1934)—§ **37.28, n. 4.**

Hazen Paper Co. v. Biggins, 507 U.S. 604, 113 S.Ct. 1701, 123 L.Ed.2d 338 (1993)—§ **17.37, n. 4.**

Hazzard v. Moraitis, 172 A.D.2d 753, 569 N.Y.S.2d 140 (N.Y.A.D. 2 Dept.1991)—§ **16.120, n. 8.**

Heady, People v., 151 A.D.2d 844, 543 N.Y.S.2d 965 (N.Y.A.D. 3 Dept.1989)—§ **38.8, n. 146.**

Heagney v. European American Bank, 122 F.R.D. 125 (E.D.N.Y.1988)—§ **17.82, n. 10.**

Health Ins. Ass'n of America v. Harnett, 405 N.Y.S.2d 634, 376 N.E.2d 1280 (N.Y. 1978)—§ **39.4, n. 4.**

Hearst Corp. v. Clyne, 431 N.Y.S.2d 400, 409 N.E.2d 876 (N.Y.1980)—§ **37.31;** § **37.31, n. 5.**

Hecht v. City of New York, 467 N.Y.S.2d 187, 454 N.E.2d 527 (N.Y.1983)—§ **37.65, n. 60, 68;** § **39.5, n. 4.**

Hecht v. Monaghan, 307 N.Y. 461, 121 N.E.2d 421 (N.Y.1954)—§ **4.16, n. 2.**

Hecht v. New York State Teachers' Retirement System, 138 Misc.2d 198, 523 N.Y.S.2d 742 (N.Y.Sup.1987)—§ **4.83, n. 3.**

Heck v. Humphrey, 512 U.S. 477, 114 S.Ct. 2364, 129 L.Ed.2d 383 (1994)—§ **18.18, n. 10;** § **18.23;** § **18.23, n. 4.**

Heckler v. Campbell, 461 U.S. 458, 103 S.Ct. 1952, 76 L.Ed.2d 66 (1983)—§ **34.4, n. 3;** § **34.8, n. 4, 5;** § **34.14, n. 3;** § **34.44, n. 2;** § **34.47, n. 2, 6.**

Heckler v. Day, 467 U.S. 104, 104 S.Ct. 2249, 81 L.Ed.2d 88 (1984)—§ **34.5, n. 2.**

TABLE OF CASES

Hedges, Matter of, 100 A.D.2d 586, 473 N.Y.S.2d 529 (N.Y.A.D. 2 Dept.1984)—§ 25.28, n. 4.

Hehl v. Gross, 35 A.D.2d 570, 313 N.Y.S.2d 422 (N.Y.A.D. 2 Dept.1970)—§ 3.10, n. 13.

Heidelmark, People v., 214 A.D.2d 767, 624 N.Y.S.2d 656 (N.Y.A.D. 3 Dept.1995)—§ 37.29, n. 43.

Heights v. United States Elec. Tool Co., 138 A.D.2d 369, 525 N.Y.S.2d 653 (N.Y.A.D. 2 Dept.1988)—§ 27.27, n. 2.

Heine v. Colton, Hartnick, Yamin & Sheresky, 786 F.Supp. 360 (S.D.N.Y.1992)—§ 28.25; § 28.25, n. 4.

Heintz v. Brown, 592 N.Y.S.2d 652, 607 N.E.2d 799 (N.Y.1992)—§ 4.79, n. 9.

Heintz v. Jenkins, 514 U.S. 291, 115 S.Ct. 1489, 131 L.Ed.2d 395 (1995)—§ 7.36, n. 7; § 7.43, n. 7, 8.

Heiser v. Union Cent. Life Ins. Co., 1995 WL 355612 (N.D.N.Y.1995)—§ 31.15, n. 5.

Heldman on Behalf of T.H. v. Sobol, 962 F.2d 148 (2nd Cir.1992)—§ 18.53, n. 6.

Helfer v. Amos, 198 A.D.2d 887, 606 N.Y.S.2d 1023 (N.Y.A.D. 4 Dept.1993)—§ 37.28, n. 33.

Heller (Ratner), Matter of, N.Y.L.J., 7/28/95, p.24, col.5 (Sup.Ct., Kings County)—§ 22.48, n. 8, 9, 10, 11; § 22.49, n. 4; § 22.51, n. 3, 6; § 22.52, n. 2, 3; § 23.76, n. 20.

Heller v. Champion Intern. Corp., 891 F.2d 432 (2nd Cir.1989)—§ 17.3, n. 4; § 17.55, n. 9.

Heller v. Chu, 111 A.D.2d 1007, 490 N.Y.S.2d 326 (N.Y.A.D. 3 Dept.1985)—§ 4.21, n. 5.

Heller v. Encore of Hicksville, Inc., 76 A.D.2d 917, 429 N.Y.S.2d 258 (N.Y.A.D. 2 Dept.1980)—§ 27.12; § 27.12, n. 2.

Heller v. Ingber, 134 A.D.2d 733, 521 N.Y.S.2d 554 (N.Y.A.D. 3 Dept.1987)—§ 30.35, n. 4.

Heller v. State, 180 A.D.2d 299, 585 N.Y.S.2d 579 (N.Y.A.D. 3 Dept.1992)—§ 14.110, n. 2.

Helmsley v. Cohen, 56 A.D.2d 519, 391 N.Y.S.2d 522 (N.Y.A.D. 1 Dept.1977)—§ 2.12, n. 3.

Helvering v. ____(see opposing party)

Hempstead General Hosp. v. Pennsylvania Nat. Mut. Cas. Ins. Co., 155 A.D.2d 542, 547 N.Y.S.2d 582 (N.Y.A.D. 2 Dept. 1989)—§ 37.37, n. 48.

Hempstead (Malibu Associates, Inc.), Matter of Town of, 453 N.Y.S.2d 642, 439 N.E.2d 357 (N.Y.1982)—§ 14.81, n. 3.

Hempstead, Village of v. SRA Realty Corp., 160 Misc.2d 819, 611 N.Y.S.2d 441 (N.Y.Sup.1994)—§ 16.125, n. 6.

Henaghan v. Dicuia, 98 A.D.2d 742, 469 N.Y.S.2d 446 (N.Y.A.D. 2 Dept.1983)—§ 30.9, n. 29.

Henderberg, In re, 108 B.R. 407 (Bkrtcy. N.D.N.Y.1989)—§ 9.167, n. 2.

Henderson, Matter of, 590 N.Y.S.2d 836, 605 N.E.2d 323 (N.Y.1992)—§ 24.95, n. 7.

Hendricks, People v., 31 A.D.2d 982, 297 N.Y.S.2d 838 (N.Y.A.D. 3 Dept.1969)—§ 38.8, n. 177.

Hendricks v. Stark, 37 N.Y. 106 (N.Y. 1867)—§ 12.67; § 12.67, n. 2.

Hendry, People v., 15 A.D.2d 784, 224 N.Y.S.2d 460 (N.Y.A.D. 2 Dept.1962)—§ 38.6; § 38.6, n. 5.

Henn v. Perales, 186 A.D.2d 740, 588 N.Y.S.2d 653 (N.Y.A.D. 2 Dept.1992)—§ 4.50, n. 3, 12.

Hennekens v. State Tax Com'n of State of N.Y., 114 A.D.2d 599, 494 N.Y.S.2d 208 (N.Y.A.D. 3 Dept.1985)—§ 35.80, n. 1.

Henrietta Bldg. Supplies, Inc. v. Rogers, 117 Misc.2d 843, 459 N.Y.S.2d 372 (N.Y.Sup.1983)—§ 11.2, n. 1; § 11.22, n. 1.

Henrietta, Town of v. Department of Environmental Conservation of New York, 76 A.D.2d 215, 430 N.Y.S.2d 440 (N.Y.A.D. 4 Dept.1980)—§ 15.3, n. 11.

Henry v. Green, 126 Misc.2d 360, 481 N.Y.S.2d 940 (N.Y.City Ct.1984)—§ 13.26, n. 2.

Henry v. Wetzler, 609 N.Y.S.2d 160, 631 N.E.2d 102 (N.Y.1993)—§ 39.9, n. 7.

Henry v. Wilson, 85 A.D.2d 885, 446 N.Y.S.2d 730 (N.Y.A.D. 4 Dept.1981)—§ 4.78, n. 10.

Henry Hof, Inc. v. Noll, 273 A.D. 361, 77 N.Y.S.2d 484 (N.Y.A.D. 1 Dept.1948)—§ 30.37, n. 6.

Henry Modell & Co., Inc. v. City of New York, 159 A.D.2d 354, 552 N.Y.S.2d 632 (N.Y.A.D. 1 Dept.1990)—§ 4.6, n. 8.

Henschke v. New York Hospital–Cornell Medical Center, 821 F.Supp. 166 (S.D.N.Y.1993)—§ 17.67, n. 1.

Hensley v. Eckerhart, 461 U.S. 424, 103 S.Ct. 1933, 76 L.Ed.2d 40 (1983)—§ 17.75, n. 3.

Henson v. CSC Credit Services, 29 F.3d 280 (7th Cir.1994)—§ 7.31, n. 11.

Herbert v. City of New York, 126 A.D.2d 404, 510 N.Y.S.2d 112 (N.Y.A.D. 1 Dept. 1987)—§ 37.38, n. 12.

Herlihy v. Metropolitan Museum of Art, 214 A.D.2d 250, 633 N.Y.S.2d 106 (N.Y.A.D. 1 Dept.1995)—§ 17.29, n. 15.

Herman v. Siegmund, 69 A.D.2d 871, 415 N.Y.S.2d 681 (N.Y.A.D. 2 Dept.1979)—§ 8.45, n. 1.

TABLE OF CASES

Hernandez, Matter of, 19 I & N Dec. 14 (BIA 1983)—§ **19.10, n. 12.**
Hernandez, Matter of, 17 I & N Dec. 7 (BIA 1979)—§ **19.11, n. 25.**
Hernandez, People v., 210 A.D.2d 504, 621 N.Y.S.2d 810 (N.Y.A.D. 2 Dept.1994)—§ **38.10, n. 12.**
Hernandez, People v., 192 A.D.2d 620, 596 N.Y.S.2d 123 (N.Y.A.D. 2 Dept.1993)—§ **38.28, n. 12.**
Hernandez, People v., 157 A.D.2d 854, 551 N.Y.S.2d 806 (N.Y.A.D. 2 Dept.1990)—§ **38.8, n. 32.**
Hernandez, People v., 143 A.D.2d 842, 533 N.Y.S.2d 488 (N.Y.A.D. 2 Dept.1988)—§ **38.8, n. 42.**
Herndon, People v., 176 A.D.2d 817, 575 N.Y.S.2d 141 (N.Y.A.D. 2 Dept.1991)—§ **38.10, n. 43.**
Herold v. East Coast Scaffolding, Inc., 208 A.D.2d 592, 617 N.Y.S.2d 197 (N.Y.A.D. 2 Dept.1994)—§ **31.10, n. 10.**
Herrara, People v., 173 A.D.2d 850, 571 N.Y.S.2d 63 (N.Y.A.D. 2 Dept.1991)—§ **38.10, n. 26, 27.**
Herrick v. Second Cuthouse, Ltd., 485 N.Y.S.2d 518, 474 N.E.2d 1186 (N.Y. 1984)—§ **39.7, n. 7.**
Herrington, People v., 136 A.D.2d 871, 524 N.Y.S.2d 530 (N.Y.A.D. 3 Dept.1988)—§ **38.10, n. 148.**
Herrmann v. Moore, 576 F.2d 453 (2nd Cir.1978)—§ **18.19, n. 3.**
Hertz Corp. v. Attorney General of State, 136 Misc.2d 420, 518 N.Y.S.2d 704 (N.Y.Sup.1987)—§ **5.12, n. 3.**
Hessen v. Hessen, 353 N.Y.S.2d 421, 308 N.E.2d 891 (N.Y.1974)—§ **21.20; § 21.20, n. 4.**
Heumann, Matter of, N.Y.L.J., 11/17/93, p.29, col.6 (Sup.Ct., Kings County)—§ **22.8, n. 9; § 22.32, n. 9; § 22.38, n. 4.**
Hewitt v. Helms, 459 U.S. 460, 103 S.Ct. 864, 74 L.Ed.2d 675 (1983)—§ **4.6, n. 4, 9.**
Heyman v. Steich, 134 A.D. 176, 114 N.Y.S. 603 (N.Y.Sup.1908)—§ **12.62, n. 4.**
Hezekiah v. Williams, 100 Misc.2d 807, 420 N.Y.S.2d 161 (N.Y.City Civ.Ct.1979)—§ **30.8, n. 9, 10.**
H.H., Matter of, 6 I & N Dec. 278 (BIA 1954)—§ **19.12, n. 10.**
Hickey v. James R. Hanna, Inc., 48 A.D.2d 349, 369 N.Y.S.2d 851 (N.Y.A.D. 3 Dept. 1975)—§ **32.18, n. 14.**
Hickey v. Planning Bd. of Town of Kent, 173 A.D.2d 1086, 571 N.Y.S.2d 105 (N.Y.A.D. 3 Dept.1991)—§ **16.97, n. 12.**
Hickox v. Griffin, 298 N.Y. 365, 83 N.E.2d 836 (N.Y.1949)—§ **16.76, n. 2.**
Hidalgo v. Bowen, 822 F.2d 294 (2nd Cir. 1987)—§ **34.46, n. 2, 4, 5.**

Hidalgo, People v., 213 A.D.2d 493, 624 N.Y.S.2d 897 (N.Y.A.D. 2 Dept.1995)—§ **38.8, n. 215.**
Higgins (England), Matter of, N.Y.L.J., 10/6/95, p.27, col.2 (Sup.Ct., N.Y. County)—§ **22.2, n. 9; § 22.26, n. 16, 18; § 22.33, n. 4.**
Higgins, People v., 188 A.D.2d 839, 591 N.Y.S.2d 612 (N.Y.A.D. 3 Dept.1992)—§ **38.8, n. 96.**
Higgins, People ex rel. Washington v., 207 A.D.2d 961, 617 N.Y.S.2d 670 (N.Y.A.D. 4 Dept.1994)—§ **38.8, n. 78.**
High v. AMR Services Corp., 1995 WL 362419 (E.D.N.Y.1995)—§ **17.68, n. 2.**
High Fashions Hair Cutters v. Commercial Union Ins. Co., 145 A.D.2d 465, 535 N.Y.S.2d 425 (N.Y.A.D. 2 Dept.1988)—§ **31.11, n. 5.**
Higley, People v., 55 Misc.2d 460, 285 N.Y.S.2d 467 (N.Y.Sp.Sess.1967)—§ **33.68, n. 13.**
Hildreth, In re, 28 A.D.2d 290, 284 N.Y.S.2d 755 (N.Y.A.D. 1 Dept.1967)—§ **8.42, n. 19.**
Hill v. City of New York, 45 F.3d 653 (2nd Cir.1995)—§ **18.31, n. 3.**
Hill, People v., 220 A.D.2d 905, 632 N.Y.S.2d 691 (N.Y.A.D. 3 Dept.1995)—§ **38.8, n. 175.**
Hill, People v., 624 N.Y.S.2d 79, 648 N.E.2d 455 (N.Y.1995)—§ **38.22, n. 3.**
Hill, People v., 42 A.D.2d 679, 345 N.Y.S.2d 237 (N.Y.A.D. 4 Dept.1973)—§ **38.8, n. 101.**
Hill, People v., 204 N.Y.S.2d 172, 168 N.E.2d 841 (N.Y.1960)—§ **38.10, n. 74.**
Hill v. St. Clare's Hosp., 499 N.Y.S.2d 904, 490 N.E.2d 823 (N.Y.1986)—§ **29.12, n. 2; § 30.11, n. 10.**
Hill v. Sullivan, 125 F.R.D. 86 (S.D.N.Y. 1989)—§ **34.63; § 34.63, n. 8.**
Hill v. Thompson, 475 N.Y.S.2d 373, 463 N.E.2d 1225 (N.Y.1984)—§ **32.12, n. 17, 18.**
Hilliard, People v., 542 N.Y.S.2d 507, 540 N.E.2d 702 (N.Y.1989)—§ **38.19, n. 99.**
Hillis Motors, Inc. v. Hawaii Auto. Dealers' Ass'n, 997 F.2d 581 (9th Cir.1993)—§ **9.148, n. 10.**
Hills Stores Co., In re, 137 B.R. 4 (Bkrtcy. S.D.N.Y.1992)—§ **9.47, n. 1.**
Hilton Hotels Corp. v. Commissioner of Finance of City of New York, 219 A.D.2d 470, 632 N.Y.S.2d 56 (N.Y.A.D. 1 Dept. 1995)—§ **37.32, n. 2.**
Hilzenradt v. Breindel, 139 N.Y.S.2d 688 (N.Y.Co.Ct.1955)—§ **10.19, n. 13.**
Hind v. Willich, 127 Misc. 355, 216 N.Y.S. 155 (N.Y.Sup.1926)—§ **5.36, n. 3.**
Hinton, People v., 334 N.Y.S.2d 885, 286 N.E.2d 265 (N.Y.1972)—§ **18.13, n. 2.**

TABLE OF CASES

Hinton v. State Farm Mut. Auto. Ins. Co., 741 S.W.2d 696 (Mo.App. W.D.1987)—§ **7.25, n. 8.**

Hipp, People v., 197 A.D.2d 590, 602 N.Y.S.2d 428 (N.Y.A.D. 2 Dept.1993)—§ **38.10, n. 68, 141.**

Hirent Realty Corp. v. Mosley, 64 Misc.2d 1011, 317 N.Y.S.2d 592 (N.Y.City Civ.Ct. 1970)—§ **13.20, n. 1.**

Hirsch v. Hirsch, 142 A.D.2d 138, 534 N.Y.S.2d 681 (N.Y.A.D. 2 Dept.1988)—§ **21.8, n. 7.**

Hirsch v. Lindor Realty Corp., 483 N.Y.S.2d 196, 472 N.E.2d 1024 (N.Y.1984)—§ **39.11; § 39.11, n. 7, 11, 14.**

Hirsch v. Weisman, 189 A.D.2d 643, 592 N.Y.S.2d 337 (N.Y.A.D. 1 Dept.1993)—§ **28.11; § 28.11, n. 14; § 28.23; § 28.23, n. 8.**

Hirschberg, People ex rel. v. Orange County Court, 271 N.Y. 151, 2 N.E.2d 521 (N.Y. 1936)—§ **38.10, n. 128.**

Hispano Americano Advertising, Inc. v. Dryer, 112 Misc.2d 936, 448 N.Y.S.2d 128 (N.Y.1982)—§ **13.26, n. 3.**

Hitter v. Rubin, 208 A.D.2d 480, 617 N.Y.S.2d 730 (N.Y.A.D. 1 Dept.1994)—§ **18.51, n. 3.**

Hizington v. Eldred Refining Co. of New York, 235 A.D. 486, 257 N.Y.S. 464 (N.Y.A.D. 4 Dept.1932)—§ **5.7, n. 10.**

Hladky, People v., 224 A.D.2d 545, 638 N.Y.S.2d 344 (N.Y.A.D. 2 Dept.1996)—§ **38.28, n. 15.**

HMB Acquisition Corp., Inc. v. F & K Supply, Inc., 209 A.D.2d 412, 618 N.Y.S.2d 422 (N.Y.A.D. 2 Dept.1994)—§ **10.18, n. 3.**

H./M. Children, Matter of, 217 A.D.2d 164, 634 N.Y.S.2d 675 (N.Y.A.D. 1 Dept. 1995)—§ **20.53, n. 2.**

Hobson, People v., 384 N.Y.S.2d 419, 348 N.E.2d 894 (N.Y.1976)—§ **33.56, n. 3.**

Hochstein v. United States, 900 F.2d 543 (2nd Cir.1990)—§ **2.23, n. 13.**

Hodes v. Axelrod, 520 N.Y.S.2d 933, 515 N.E.2d 612 (N.Y.1987)—§ **4.33, n. 3.**

Hodes, United States v., 355 F.2d 746 (2nd Cir.1966)—§ **8.17, n. 1.**

Hodges v. City of New York, 195 A.D.2d 269, 599 N.Y.S.2d 586 (N.Y.A.D. 1 Dept. 1993)—§ **30.30, n. 15.**

Hoefle, People ex rel. v. Cahill, 188 N.Y. 489, 81 N.E. 453 (N.Y.1907)—§ **3.17, n. 6.**

Hoelzer v. Blum, 93 A.D.2d 605, 462 N.Y.S.2d 684 (N.Y.A.D. 2 Dept.1983)—§ **23.79, n. 2.**

Hoemke v. New York Blood Center, 912 F.2d 550 (2nd Cir.1990)—§ **29.21, n. 3.**

Hoffman v. Domenico Bus Service, Inc., 183 A.D.2d 807, 584 N.Y.S.2d 122 (N.Y.A.D. 2 Dept.1992)—§ **30.5, n. 17.**

Hoffman v. Harris, 269 N.Y.S.2d 119, 216 N.E.2d 326 (N.Y.1966)—§ **16.82, n. 2, 3.**

Hofstadter, People ex rel. Hastings, v., 258 N.Y. 425, 180 N.E. 106 (N.Y.1932)—§ **38.10, n. 123.**

Hogan v. State, 41 A.D.2d 428, 343 N.Y.S.2d 884 (N.Y.A.D. 3 Dept.1973)—§ **14.109, n. 3.**

Holcomb v. Daily News, 412 N.Y.S.2d 118, 384 N.E.2d 665 (N.Y.1978)—§ **32.5, n. 1; § 32.12, n. 19.**

Holder, In re, 182 B.R. 770 (Bkrtcy. M.D.Tenn.1995)—§ **9.109, n. 1.**

Holland v. Edwards, 282 A.D. 353, 122 N.Y.S.2d 721 (N.Y.A.D. 1 Dept.1953)—§ **17.49, n. 10.**

Holland v. St. Paul Mercury Ins. Co., 135 So.2d 145 (La.App. 1 Cir.1961)—§ **27.20, n. 3.**

Holley, People v., 168 A.D.2d 992, 565 N.Y.S.2d 351 (N.Y.A.D. 4 Dept.1990)—§ **38.8, n. 63; § 38.10, n. 143.**

Hollman, People v., 581 N.Y.S.2d 619, 590 N.E.2d 204 (N.Y.1992)—§ **33.4; § 33.4, n. 3.**

Holmberg, Matter of, 206 A.D.2d 479, 614 N.Y.S.2d 751 (N.Y.A.D. 2 Dept.1994)—§ **25.40, n. 2.**

Holmes & Murphy, Inc. v. Bush, 6 A.D.2d 200, 176 N.Y.S.2d 183 (N.Y.A.D. 4 Dept. 1958)—§ **16.91, n. 7.**

Holmes Protection of New York, Inc. v. Provident Loan Soc. of New York, 179 A.D.2d 400, 577 N.Y.S.2d 850 (N.Y.A.D. 1 Dept.1992)—§ **7.46, n. 11.**

Holt v. Fleischman, 75 A.D. 593, 78 N.Y.S. 647 (N.Y.A.D. 1 Dept.1902)—§ **12.69, n. 1.**

Holt, People v., 210 A.D.2d 994, 621 N.Y.S.2d 1003 (N.Y.A.D. 4 Dept.1994)—§ **38.8, n. 145.**

Holt v. Tioga County, 452 N.Y.S.2d 383, 437 N.E.2d 1140 (N.Y.1982)—§ **26.10, n. 3.**

Holthaus v. Zoning Bd. of Appeals of Town of Kent, 209 A.D.2d 698, 619 N.Y.S.2d 160 (N.Y.A.D. 2 Dept.1994)—§ **16.89, n. 15.**

Holtkamp, Matter of, 669 F.2d 505 (7th Cir.1982)—§ **9.52, n. 7; § 9.53, n. 8.**

Holtzman v. Goldman, 528 N.Y.S.2d 21, 523 N.E.2d 297 (N.Y.1988)—§ **4.71, n. 6; § 37.87, n. 5; § 38.10, n. 31, 53.**

Holy Sepulchre Cemetery v. Board of Appeals of Town of Greece, Monroe County, 271 A.D. 33, 60 N.Y.S.2d 750 (N.Y.A.D. 4 Dept.1946)—§ **16.77, n. 4.**

TABLE OF CASES

Holy Sepulchre Cemetery v. Town of Greece, 191 Misc. 241, 79 N.Y.S.2d 683 (N.Y.Sup.1947)—§ **16.104, n. 3.**

Holy Spirit Ass'n for Unification of World Christianity v. Rosenfeld, 91 A.D.2d 190, 458 N.Y.S.2d 920 (N.Y.A.D. 2 Dept. 1983)—§ **16.25, n. 2.**

Holywell Corp. v. Smith, 503 U.S. 47, 112 S.Ct. 1021, 117 L.Ed.2d 196 (1992)—§ **9.133, n. 5.**

Home Federal Sav. & Loan Ass'n v. Four Star Heights, Inc., 70 Misc.2d 118, 333 N.Y.S.2d 334 (N.Y.Sup.1971)—§ **10.17, n. 2.**

Home Ins. Co. v. American Home Products Corp., 902 F.2d 1111 (2nd Cir.1990)—§ **31.2, n. 13.**

Home Ins. Co. v. American Home Products Corp., 551 N.Y.S.2d 481, 550 N.E.2d 930 (N.Y.1990)—§ **30.32, n. 3; § 31.4, n. 4.**

Home Ins. Co. v. American Home Products Corp., 873 F.2d 520 (2nd Cir.1989)—§ **31.4, n. 3.**

Home Ins. Co. v. Dunn, 963 F.2d 1023 (7th Cir.1992)—§ **28.43, n. 9.**

Homer v. State, 36 A.D.2d 333, 320 N.Y.S.2d 349 (N.Y.A.D. 3 Dept.1971)—§ **14.104, n. 8.**

H. O. M. E. S. v. New York State Urban Development Corp., 69 A.D.2d 222, 418 N.Y.S.2d 827 (N.Y.A.D. 4 Dept.1979)—§ **15.6, n. 15, 16.**

Honey Dippers Septic Tank Services, Inc. v. Landi, 198 A.D.2d 402, 604 N.Y.S.2d 128 (N.Y.A.D. 2 Dept.1993)—§ **4.72, n. 3.**

Hooker Chemicals & Plastics Corp., United States v., 90 F.R.D. 421 (W.D.N.Y. 1981)—§ **27.38, n. 5.**

Hooper Associates, Ltd. v. AGS Computers, Inc., 549 N.Y.S.2d 365, 548 N.E.2d 903 (N.Y.1989)—§ **30.39, n. 15; § 37.37, n. 67; § 37.67, n. 12; § 39.27, n. 3.**

Hope v. Cortines, 872 F.Supp. 14 (E.D.N.Y. 1995)—§ **18.53, n. 5.**

Hopkins, In re Estate of, 214 Ill.App.3d 427, 158 Ill.Dec. 436, 574 N.E.2d 230 (Ill. App. 2 Dist.1991)—§ **24.60, n. 11.**

Hopkins, People v., 49 A.D.2d 682, 370 N.Y.S.2d 744 (N.Y.A.D. 4 Dept.1975)—§ **37.19, n. 16; § 38.8, n. 110, 116, 198.**

Hopkins v. Players' Three, Inc., 99 A.D.2d 912, 472 N.Y.S.2d 519 (N.Y.A.D. 3 Dept. 1984)—§ **17.65, n. 4.**

Horgan v. New York State Div. of Human Rights on Behalf of O'Connor, 194 A.D.2d 674, 599 N.Y.S.2d 99 (N.Y.A.D. 2 Dept.1993)—§ **30.30, n. 12.**

Horizon Roofing & Sheetmetal Inc. v. City of Glens Falls, 205 A.D.2d 916, 613 N.Y.S.2d 464 (N.Y.A.D. 3 Dept.1994)—§ **37.37, n. 60.**

Hornfeld v. Gaare, 130 A.D.2d 398, 515 N.Y.S.2d 258 (N.Y.A.D. 1 Dept.1987)—§ **13.28, n. 11.**

Horowitz Bros. & Margareten v. Margareten, 489 N.Y.S.2d 53, 478 N.E.2d 194 (N.Y.1985)—§ **37.67, n. 6.**

Horst, Helvering v., 311 U.S. 112, 61 S.Ct. 144, 85 L.Ed. 75 (1940)—§ **1.34, n. 20.**

Horton, In re, 149 B.R. 49 (Bkrtcy.S.D.N.Y. 1992)—§ **9.206, n. 5.**

Hoskins, Matter of, 102 F.3d 311 (7th Cir. 1996)—§ **9.251, n. 3.**

Hospital Ass'n of New York State v. Axelrod, 164 A.D.2d 518, 565 N.Y.S.2d 243 (N.Y.A.D. 3 Dept.1990)—§ **4.70, n. 5.**

Hotel Dorset Co. v. Trust for Cultural Resources of City of New York, 413 N.Y.S.2d 357, 385 N.E.2d 1284 (N.Y. 1978)—§ **3.7, n. 11.**

Houbigant, Inc. v. ACB Mercantile, Inc. (In re Houbigant, Inc.), 190 B.R. 185 (Bkrtcy.S.D.N.Y.1995)—§ **9.91, n. 1.**

House of Fabrics, Inc., In re, 27 Bank.Ct. Dec. 742 (Bkrtcy.C.D.Cal.1995)—§ **9.47, n. 2.**

Houston v. TRW Information Services, Inc., 707 F.Supp. 689 (S.D.N.Y.1989)—§ **7.31, n. 11.**

Howard v. Handler Bros. & Winell, 279 A.D. 72, 107 N.Y.S.2d 749 (N.Y.A.D. 1 Dept.1951)—§ **5.11, n. 11.**

Howard v. Lecher, 397 N.Y.S.2d 363, 366 N.E.2d 64 (N.Y.1977)—§ **29.11; § 29.11, n. 9, 10.**

Howard v. National Westminister Bank, U.S.A. (In re Howard), 184 B.R. 644 (Bkrtcy.E.D.N.Y.1995)—§ **9.101, n. 8.**

Howard v. Poseidon Pools, Inc., 534 N.Y.S.2d 360, 530 N.E.2d 1280 (N.Y. 1988)—§ **27.12, n. 4.**

Howard v. Wyman, 322 N.Y.S.2d 683, 271 N.E.2d 528 (N.Y.1971)—§ **35.2, n. 1; § 35.103, n. 1.**

Howard Fuel v. Lloyd's Underwriters, 588 F.Supp. 1103 (S.D.N.Y.1984)—§ **31.6, n. 3.**

Howard Stores Corp. v. Foremost Ins. Co., 82 A.D.2d 398, 441 N.Y.S.2d 674 (N.Y.A.D. 1 Dept.1981)—§ **30.26, n. 8.**

Howdy Jones Const. Co., Inc. v. Parklaw Realty, Inc., 76 A.D.2d 1018, 429 N.Y.S.2d 768 (N.Y.A.D. 3 Dept.1980)—§ **10.75, n. 2.**

Howe v. Ampil, 185 A.D.2d 520, 585 N.Y.S.2d 869 (N.Y.A.D. 3 Dept.1992)—§ **28.17, n. 5.**

Howe, People v., 450 N.Y.S.2d 477, 435 N.E.2d 1092 (N.Y.1982)—§ **33.80, n. 1.**

Howell v. New York Post Co., Inc., 596 N.Y.S.2d 350, 612 N.E.2d 699 (N.Y. 1993)—§ **18.63, n. 1.**

TABLE OF CASES

Howell, People v., 158 Misc.2d 653, 601 N.Y.S.2d 778 (N.Y.City Crim.Ct.1993)—§ 33.10, n. 4.
Howell, People v., 174 A.D.2d 356, 570 N.Y.S.2d 562 (N.Y.A.D. 1 Dept.1991)—§ 38.19, n. 38.
Howes v. Peckham Road Corp., 270 N.Y.S.2d 213, 217 N.E.2d 37 (N.Y. 1966)—§ 30.27; § 30.27, n. 7.
Hoxsie v. Zoning Bd. of Appeals of City of Saratoga Springs, 129 Misc.2d 493, 493 N.Y.S.2d 535 (N.Y.Sup.1985)—§ 16.48, n. 7.
H.R. Moch Co. v. Rensselaer Water Co., 247 N.Y. 160, 159 N.E. 896 (N.Y.1928)—§ 3.30, n. 8.
Hubbard v. Town of Sand Lake, 211 A.D.2d 1005, 622 N.Y.S.2d 126 (N.Y.A.D. 3 Dept.1995)—§ 14.32, n. 2.
Hubbard–Hall Chemical Co. v. Silverman, 340 F.2d 402 (1st Cir.1965)—§ 27.43, n. 1.
Hubbell v. Trans World Life Ins. Co. of New York, 430 N.Y.S.2d 589, 408 N.E.2d 918 (N.Y.1980)—§ 30.31, n. 2.
Huber v. Marine Midland Bank, 51 F.3d 5 (2nd Cir.1995)—§ 9.18, n. 4.
Hudson Motor Partnership v. Crest Leasing Enterprises Inc. and Metro Auto Leasing Inc., N.Y.L.J., 3/3/94, p.1 col.3 (E.D.N.Y.)—§ 17.35, n. 12.
Hudson, People v., 167 A.D.2d 950, 561 N.Y.S.2d 1014 (N.Y.A.D. 4 Dept.1990)—§ 33.87, n. 4.
Hudson River Sloop Clearwater, Inc. v. Consolidated Rail Corp., 591 F.Supp. 345 (N.D.N.Y.1984)—§ 15.11, n. 19.
Hudson River Sloop Clearwater, Inc. v. Cuomo, N.Y.L.J., 8/10/93, p.22, col.3, Justice Glen (Sup.Ct., N.Y.County)—§ 28.21; § 28.21, n. 6, 7, 8.
Hudson River Yards Corp. v. Tillotson, 144 N.Y.S.2d 183 (N.Y.Sup.1955)—§ 11.37, n. 4.
Hudson View Properties v. Weiss, 463 N.Y.S.2d 428, 450 N.E.2d 234 (N.Y. 1983)—§ 18.45, n. 4.
Hudy, People v., 538 N.Y.S.2d 197, 535 N.E.2d 250 (N.Y.1988)—§ 38.19; § 38.19, n. 128; § 38.22, n. 2.
Huffman, People v., 473 N.Y.S.2d 945, 462 N.E.2d 122 (N.Y.1984)—§ 33.52, n. 2.
Huggins v. Castle Estates, Inc., 44 A.D.2d 25, 352 N.Y.S.2d 719 (N.Y.A.D. 4 Dept. 1974)—§ 12.9, n. 3.
Hughes v. New York Hospital–Cornell Medical Center, 195 A.D.2d 442, 600 N.Y.S.2d 145 (N.Y.A.D. 2 Dept.1993)—§ 30.9, n. 11.
Hughes by Hughes v. Physicians Hosp., 149 Misc.2d 661, 566 N.Y.S.2d 496 (N.Y.Sup. 1991)—§ 22.4, n. 1, 7.

Hulme v. Patchogue Motors, Inc., 168 A.D.2d 425, 562 N.Y.S.2d 549 (N.Y.A.D. 2 Dept.1990)—§ 37.65, n. 59.
Hults, People v., 557 N.Y.S.2d 270, 556 N.E.2d 1077 (N.Y.1990)—§ 33.58, n. 1.
Humbert v. State, 278 A.D. 1041, 107 N.Y.S.2d 507 (N.Y.A.D.1951)—§ 14.97, n. 1.
Humphrey v. State, 469 N.Y.S.2d 661, 457 N.E.2d 767 (N.Y.1983)—§ 39.7, n. 5.
Hunley v. Commissioner, T.C. Memo. 1966-066 (Tax Ct.1966)—§ 1.34, n. 61.
Hunt v. Hunt, 72 N.Y. 217 (N.Y.1878)—§ 37.37, n. 69; § 39.27, n. 7.
Hunt, People ex rel. Paris v., 201 A.D. 573, 194 N.Y.S. 699 (N.Y.A.D. 3 Dept.1922)—§ 38.10, n. 132.
Hunt v. Sharp, 626 N.Y.S.2d 57, 649 N.E.2d 1201 (N.Y.1995)—§ 37.67, n. 11.
Hunt v. State, 117 A.D.2d 1005, 499 N.Y.S.2d 294 (N.Y.A.D. 4 Dept.1986)—§ 30.37, n. 2.
Hunt v. Werner Spitz Const. Co., Inc., 99 A.D.2d 671, 472 N.Y.S.2d 46 (N.Y.A.D. 4 Dept.1984)—§ 37.65, n. 52.
Hunter v. Board of Directors of Grymes Hill Owners Corp., 204 A.D.2d 395, 614 N.Y.S.2d 182 (N.Y.A.D. 2 Dept.1994)—§ 18.47, n. 2.
Hunter v. Bryant, 502 U.S. 224, 112 S.Ct. 534, 116 L.Ed.2d 589 (1991)—§ 18.32, n. 6, 9.
Hunter v. Ford Motor Co., 37 A.D.2d 335, 325 N.Y.S.2d 469 (N.Y.A.D. 3 Dept. 1971)—§ 27.34, n. 5.
Hunter v. New York, O. & W. Ry. Co., 116 N.Y. 615, 23 N.E. 9 (N.Y.1889)—§ 37.29; § 37.29, n. 28, 42.
Hunter v. Payne, 113 Misc. 385, 184 N.Y.S. 433 (N.Y.Sup.1920)—§ 5.43, n. 6.
Hunter, People v., 212 A.D.2d 731, 623 N.Y.S.2d 13 (N.Y.A.D. 2 Dept.1995)—§ 38.8, n. 58.
Huntington, Town of v. New York State Div. of Human Rights, 604 N.Y.S.2d 541, 624 N.E.2d 678 (N.Y.1993)—§ 4.71, n. 9; § 4.75, n. 2.
Huntington, Town of v. Schwartz' Estate, 63 Misc.2d 836, 313 N.Y.S.2d 918 (N.Y.Dist.Ct.1970)—§ 16.125, n. 3.
Huntley, People v., 255 N.Y.S.2d 838, 204 N.E.2d 179 (N.Y.1965)—§ 33.27, n. 5; § 33.57, n. 4; § 38.10, n. 154.
Hunt Ltd. v. Lifschultz Fast Freight, Inc., 889 F.2d 1274 (2nd Cir.1989)—§ 31.9, n. 8.
Huot v. Dworman, 13 Misc.2d 104, 173 N.Y.S.2d 58 (N.Y.Sup.1958)—§ 8.8, n. 4; § 8.14, n. 6.
Hurd Bros. v. H.R. Day Const. Co., 146 Misc. 103, 261 N.Y.S. 90 (N.Y.Sup. 1932)—§ 10.12, n. 2.

TABLE OF CASES

Hurlbutt, Estate of v. A.J. Cerasaro, Inc., 120 A.D.2d 792, 501 N.Y.S.2d 526 (N.Y.A.D. 3 Dept.1986)—§ 32.19, n. 3.
Hurwitz v. Sher, 982 F.2d 778 (2nd Cir. 1992)—§ 23.31, n. 1.
Hurwitz v. Sher, 789 F.Supp. 134 (S.D.N.Y. 1992)—§ 24.60, n. 11.
Hurwitz v. United States, 884 F.2d 684 (2nd Cir.1989)—§ 18.63, n. 6.
Hust, People v., 74 Misc.2d 887, 346 N.Y.S.2d 303 (N.Y.Co.Ct.1973)— § 33.100.
Hustis v. City of White Plains, 201 N.Y.S.2d 909 (N.Y.Sup.1960)—§ 16.66, n. 2.
Hutchinson v. Curtiss, 45 Misc. 484, 92 N.Y.S. 70 (N.Y.Sup.1904)—§ 1.38, n. 7.
Hutton, People v., 88 N.Y.2d 363, 645 N.Y.S.2d 759, 668 N.E.2d 879 (1996)— § 18.12, n. 2.
Huzar v. State, 156 Misc.2d 370, 590 N.Y.S.2d 1000 (N.Y.Ct.Cl.1992)— § 17.28, n. 4.
Hyatt Legal Services, Matter of, 97 A.D.2d 983, 468 N.Y.S.2d 778 (N.Y.A.D. 4 Dept. 1983)—§ 37.6, n. 8.
Hymowitz v. Eli Lilly and Co., 541 N.Y.S.2d 941, 539 N.E.2d 1069 (N.Y.1989)— § 27.52, n. 1, 2.
Hynes v. Cirigliano, 180 A.D.2d 659, 579 N.Y.S.2d 171 (N.Y.A.D. 2 Dept.1992)— § 37.87; § 37.87, n. 6; § 38.10, n. 30.
Hynes v. Commssioner, 74 T.C. 1266 (U.S.Tax Ct.1980)—§ 2.7, n. 1.
Hynes v. Iadarola, 221 A.D.2d 131, 645 N.Y.S.2d 69 (N.Y.A.D. 2 Dept.1996)— § 38.10, n. 176.

I

Iannelli Bros., Inc. v. Muscarella, 30 A.D.2d 698, 291 N.Y.S.2d 851 (N.Y.A.D. 2 Dept. 1968)—§ 12.29, n. 8.
Iannone, People v., 412 N.Y.S.2d 110, 384 N.E.2d 656 (N.Y.1978)—§ 38.8, n. 152, 193; § 38.19, n. 47.
Iannone v. Zoning Bd. of Appeals of Village of Wappingers Falls, 161 A.D.2d 1101, 557 N.Y.S.2d 659 (N.Y.A.D. 3 Dept. 1990)—§ 16.85, n. 1.
Iappini, In re, 192 B.R. 8 (Bkrtcy.D.Mass. 1995)—§ 9.131, n. 3.
Iazzetti v. City of New York, 216 A.D.2d 214, 628 N.Y.S.2d 112 (N.Y.A.D. 1 Dept. 1995)—§ 30.28, n. 3.
Ideal Mut. Ins. Co., In re, 9 A.D.2d 60, 190 N.Y.S.2d 895 (N.Y.A.D. 1 Dept.1959)— § 1.43, n. 24.
Idylwoods Associates v. Mader Capital, Inc., 915 F.Supp. 1290 (W.D.N.Y.1996)— § 15.30, n. 7.

Igbara Realty Corp. v. New York Property Ins. Underwriting Ass'n, 481 N.Y.S.2d 60, 470 N.E.2d 858 (N.Y.1984)—§ 31.11, n. 8.
I. H. P. Corp. v. 210 Central Park South Corp., 16 A.D.2d 461, 228 N.Y.S.2d 883 (N.Y.A.D. 1 Dept.1962)—§ 30.35, n. 1.
Ilemar Corp. v. Krochmal, 58 A.D.2d 853, 396 N.Y.S.2d 676 (N.Y.A.D. 2 Dept. 1977)—§ 12.64, n. 11, 12.
ILMS Realty Ass'n v. Madden, 174 A.D.2d 603, 571 N.Y.S.2d 310 (N.Y.A.D. 2 Dept. 1991)—§ 8.4, n. 13.
Imbler v. Pachtman, 424 U.S. 409, 96 S.Ct. 984, 47 L.Ed.2d 128 (1976)—§ 18.31, n. 3.
Immigration and Naturalization Service v. Wang, 450 U.S. 139, 101 S.Ct. 1027, 67 L.Ed.2d 123 (1981)—§ 19.48, n. 4.
Immuno AG. v. Moor-Jankowski, 566 N.Y.S.2d 906, 567 N.E.2d 1270 (N.Y. 1991)—§ 18.27, n. 2; § 18.81, n. 5; § 18.82, n. 6.
Impastato v. Hellman Enterprises, Inc., 147 A.D.2d 788, 537 N.Y.S.2d 659 (N.Y.A.D. 3 Dept.1989)—§ 18.55, n. 2.
Imperial Plumbing & Heating Corp. v. Stratford Development Corp., 26 Misc.2d 815, 208 N.Y.S.2d 174 (N.Y.Sup.1960)— § 10.102, n. 2.
INA Underwriters Ins. Co. v. D.H. Forde & Co., P.C., 630 F.Supp. 76 (W.D.N.Y. 1985)—§ 28.43, n. 2, 7.
Incorporated Village of Atlantic Beach v. Gavalas, 599 N.Y.S.2d 218, 615 N.E.2d 608 (N.Y.1993)—§ 16.54, n. 3.
Incorporated Village of Freeport v. Association for Help of Retarded Children, 94 Misc.2d 1048, 406 N.Y.S.2d 221 (N.Y.Sup.1977)—§ 16.122, n. 13.
Incorporated Village of Great Neck Plaza v. Nassau County Rent Guidelines Bd., 69 A.D.2d 528, 418 N.Y.S.2d 796 (N.Y.A.D. 2 Dept.1979)—§ 4.2, n. 4.
Incorporated Village of Hempstead v. Carlson, 129 Misc.2d 537, 493 N.Y.S.2d 280 (N.Y.Sup.1985)—§ 16.25, n. 11.
Incorporated Village of Old Field v. Introne, 104 Misc.2d 122, 430 N.Y.S.2d 192 (N.Y.Sup.1980)—§ 16.24, n. 8; § 16.128, n. 14.
Incorporated Village of Patchogue v. Simon, 112 A.D.2d 374, 491 N.Y.S.2d 827 (N.Y.A.D. 2 Dept.1985)—§ 14.34, n. 2.
Incorporated Village of Williston Park v. Argano, 197 A.D.2d 670, 602 N.Y.S.2d 878 (N.Y.A.D. 2 Dept.1993)—§ 16.50, n. 13.
Index Const. Corp. v. City of New York, 103 Misc.2d 16, 425 N.Y.S.2d 249 (N.Y.City Civ.Ct.1980)—§ 13.18, n. 8.

TABLE OF CASES

Industralease Automated & Scientific Equipment Corp. v. R.M.E. Enterprises, Inc., 58 A.D.2d 482, 396 N.Y.S.2d 427 (N.Y.A.D. 2 Dept.1977)—§ **5.13, n. 7.**

Industrial Liaison Committee of Niagara Falls Area Chamber of Commerce v. Williams, 531 N.Y.S.2d 791, 527 N.E.2d 274 (N.Y.1988)—§ **4.47, n. 1; § 4.77, n. 2.**

Ingalls Iron Works Co. v. Fehlhaber Corp., 337 F.Supp. 1085 (S.D.N.Y.1972)—§ **10.105, n. 4.**

Ingber v. State, 187 A.D.2d 826, 590 N.Y.S.2d 145 (N.Y.A.D. 3 Dept.1992)—§ **14.82, n. 7.**

Ingle v. Glamore Motor Sales, Inc., 538 N.Y.S.2d 771, 535 N.E.2d 1311 (N.Y. 1989)—§ **17.29; § 17.29, n. 6, 16.**

Ingle, People v., 369 N.Y.S.2d 67, 330 N.E.2d 39 (N.Y.1975)—§ **33.5; § 33.5, n. 2, 6.**

Ingram & Greene, Inc. v. Wynne, 47 Misc.2d 200, 262 N.Y.S.2d 663 (N.Y.Sup. 1965)—§ **10.7, n. 4.**

Inland Vale Farm Co. v. Stergianopoulos, 492 N.Y.S.2d 7, 481 N.E.2d 547 (N.Y. 1985)—§ **37.37, n. 72; § 39.4, n. 12.**

In Matter of Grand Jury of the County of Montgomery Empaneled on April 30, 1979, 456 N.Y.S.2d 764, 442 N.E.2d 1275 (N.Y.1982)—§ **38.11, n. 14.**

In re (see name of party)

I.N.S. v. Cardoza–Fonseca, 480 U.S. 421, 107 S.Ct. 1207, 94 L.Ed.2d 434 (1987)—§ **19.50, n. 4.**

I.N.S. v. Rios–Pineda, 471 U.S. 444, 105 S.Ct. 2098, 85 L.Ed.2d 452 (1985)—§ **19.48, n. 4.**

Insurance Co. of Ireland, Ltd. v. Mead Reinsurance Corp., 1994 WL 605987 (S.D.N.Y.1994)—§ **31.20, n. 4.**

Integrated Resources, Inc., In re, 147 B.R. 650 (S.D.N.Y.1992)—§ **9.62, n. 4.**

Integrated Resources, Inc. v. Ameritrust Co. Nat. Assoc. (In re Integrated Resources, Inc.), 157 B.R. 66 (S.D.N.Y.1993)—§ **9.94, n. 1; § 9.112, n. 3.**

Interboro Mut. Indem. Ins. Co. v. Rivas, 205 A.D.2d 536, 613 N.Y.S.2d 191 (N.Y.A.D. 2 Dept.1994)—§ **31.16, n. 10.**

Interco Inc., Matter of, 137 B.R. 999 (Bkrtcy.E.D.Mo.1992)—§ **9.145, n. 1.**

Interglobal Travel Service, Inc., Matter of, 156 A.D.2d 849, 549 N.Y.S.2d 849 (N.Y.A.D. 3 Dept.1989)—§ **17.60, n. 2.**

International Aircraft Trading Co. v. Manufacturers Trust Co., 297 N.Y. 285, 79 N.E.2d 249 (N.Y.1948)—§ **2.23, n. 18.**

International Business Machines Corp. v. Murphy & O'Connell, 204 A.D.2d 236, 612 N.Y.S.2d 143 (N.Y.A.D. 1 Dept. 1994)—§ **37.83, n. 6.**

International Paper Co. v. Continental Cas. Co., 361 N.Y.S.2d 873, 320 N.E.2d 619 (N.Y.1974)—§ **31.12, n. 7; § 31.27, n. 2.**

International Paper Credit Corp. v. Columbia Wax Products Co., Inc., 102 Misc.2d 738, 424 N.Y.S.2d 827 (N.Y.Sup.1980)—§ **7.26, n. 9.**

International Ribbon Mills, Ltd. v. Arjan Ribbons, Inc., 365 N.Y.S.2d 808, 325 N.E.2d 137 (N.Y.1975)—§ **8.28, n. 12.**

International Salt Co. v. State, 125 Misc.2d 939, 480 N.Y.S.2d 983 (N.Y.Ct.Cl. 1984)—§ **14.106, n. 2.**

Interpool Ltd. v. Patterson, 890 F.Supp. 259 (S.D.N.Y.1995)—§ **9.119, n. 3.**

Interstate Commerce Commission v. Louisville & N.R. Co., 227 U.S. 88, 33 S.Ct. 185, 57 L.Ed. 431 (1913)—§ **4.5, n. 8.**

Investors Ins. Co. of America v. Dorinco Reinsurance Co., 917 F.2d 100 (2nd Cir. 1990)—§ **31.9, n. 12.**

Irni v. Williams, 146 Misc.2d 894, 553 N.Y.S.2d 70 (N.Y.City Civ.Ct.1990)—§ **37.91; § 37.91, n. 4.**

Iroff v. Iroff, 125 A.D.2d 197, 509 N.Y.S.2d 316 (N.Y.A.D. 1 Dept.1986)—§ **21.11, n. 6.**

Iron–Oak Supply Corp., In re, 169 B.R. 414 (Bkrtcy.E.D.Cal.1994)—§ **9.83, n. 2.**

Irv–Ceil Realty Corp. v. State, 43 A.D.2d 775, 350 N.Y.S.2d 784 (N.Y.A.D. 3 Dept. 1973)—§ **14.95, n. 4.**

Irvmor Corp. v. Rodewald, 253 N.Y. 472, 171 N.E. 747 (N.Y.1930)—§ **12.4, n. 2.**

Isaacs, People v., 43 A.D.2d 656, 349 N.Y.S.2d 844 (N.Y.A.D. 3 Dept.1973)—§ **38.8, n. 115.**

Islamic Soc. of Westchester and Rockland, Inc. v. Foley, 96 A.D.2d 536, 464 N.Y.S.2d 844 (N.Y.A.D. 2 Dept.1983)—§ **16.25, n. 7, 8; § 16.131, n. 2.**

Islip, Matter of Town of, 426 N.Y.S.2d 220, 402 N.E.2d 1123 (N.Y.1980)—§ **14.86, n. 8.**

Islip, Town of v. Caviglia, 542 N.Y.S.2d 139, 540 N.E.2d 215 (N.Y.1989)—§ **16.25; § 16.25, n. 14.**

Islip, Town of v. Cuomo, 147 A.D.2d 56, 541 N.Y.S.2d 829 (N.Y.A.D. 2 Dept.1989)—§ **16.24, n. 14.**

Islip, Town of v. P.B.S. Marina, Inc., 133 A.D.2d 81, 518 N.Y.S.2d 427 (N.Y.A.D. 2 Dept.1987)—§ **16.68, n. 3.**

Issa v. Reliance Ins. Co. of New York, 683 F.Supp. 82 (S.D.N.Y.1988)—§ **31.26, n. 15.**

I. Tanenbaum Son & Co. v. Brooklyn Furniture Co., 229 A.D. 469, 242 N.Y.S. 381 (N.Y.A.D. 1 Dept.1930)—§ **5.7, n. 9.**

ITT Commercial Finance Corp. v. Kallmeyer & Sons Truck Tire Service Inc., 156

TABLE OF CASES

Misc.2d 505, 593 N.Y.S.2d 951 (N.Y.Sup. 1993)—**§ 7.28, n. 9.**
Ivancic v. Olmstead, 497 N.Y.S.2d 326, 488 N.E.2d 72 (N.Y.1985)—**§ 15.33, n. 3.**
Ives v. South Buffalo Ry. Co., 201 N.Y. 271, 94 N.E. 431 (N.Y.1911)—**§ 32.7, n. 1.**

J

J & Y, Matter of, 3 I & N Dec. 657 (BIA 1949)—**§ 19.11, n. 26.**
Jack Parker Const. Corp. v. Williams, 35 A.D.2d 839, 317 N.Y.S.2d 911 (N.Y.A.D. 2 Dept.1970)—**§ 37.37, n. 36, 37.**
Jackson v. Firestone Tire & Rubber Co., 779 F.2d 1047 (5th Cir.1986)—**§ 27.37, n. 8.**
Jackson v. Jackson, 206 A.D.2d 966, 616 N.Y.S.2d 285 (N.Y.A.D. 4 Dept.1994)—**§ 37.30, n. 4.**
Jackson v. Melvey, 56 A.D.2d 836, 392 N.Y.S.2d 312 (N.Y.A.D. 2 Dept.1977)—**§ 27.34; § 27.34, n. 4.**
Jackson v. New York City Housing Authority, 88 Misc.2d 121, 387 N.Y.S.2d 38 (N.Y.Sup.App.Term 1976)—**§ 13.16, n. 2; § 13.18, n. 1.**
Jackson v. New York State Urban Development Corp., 503 N.Y.S.2d 298, 494 N.E.2d 429 (N.Y.1986)—**§ 14.21, n. 6; § 14.29, n. 2; § 14.38, n. 4; § 15.3, n. 9; § 15.6, n. 9; § 16.52, n. 8.**
Jackson, People v., 219 A.D.2d 676, 631 N.Y.S.2d 706 (N.Y.A.D. 2 Dept.1995)—**§ 38.21, n. 52.**
Jackson, People v., 214 A.D.2d 475, 625 N.Y.S.2d 218 (N.Y.A.D. 1 Dept.1995)—**§ 38.19, n. 48.**
Jackson, People v., 205 A.D.2d 639, 613 N.Y.S.2d 230 (N.Y.A.D. 2 Dept.1994)—**§ 38.21; § 38.21, n. 20, 32; § 38.27, n. 29.**
Jackson, People v., 198 A.D.2d 301, 603 N.Y.S.2d 558 (N.Y.A.D. 2 Dept.1993)—**§ 38.10, n. 97.**
Jackson, People v., 589 N.Y.S.2d 300, 602 N.E.2d 1116 (N.Y.1992)—**§ 38.6; § 38.6, n. 2.**
Jackson, People v., 154 Misc.2d 718, 593 N.Y.S.2d 410 (N.Y.Sup.1992)—**§ 33.40; § 33.40, n. 1.**
Jackson, People v., 578 N.Y.S.2d 483, 585 N.E.2d 795 (N.Y.1991)—**§ 38.10, n. 93, 95, 106.**
Jackson, People v., 174 A.D.2d 552, 571 N.Y.S.2d 721 (N.Y.A.D. 1 Dept.1991)—**§ 38.21; § 38.21, n. 12.**
Jackson, People v., 106 A.D.2d 93, 483 N.Y.S.2d 725 (N.Y.A.D. 2 Dept.1984)—**§ 38.26, n. 9.**

Jackson, People ex rel. Harrison v., 298 N.Y. 219, 82 N.E.2d 14 (N.Y.1948)—**§ 37.37, n. 69; § 38.8, n. 72; § 39.27, n. 6.**
Jackson v. State, 213 N.Y. 34, 106 N.E. 758 (N.Y.1914)—**§ 14.81, n. 1; § 14.91, n. 1, 2.**
Jaclyn P., Matter of, 635 N.Y.S.2d 169, 658 N.E.2d 1042 (N.Y.1995)—**§ 39.7, n. 6.**
Jacob, Matter of, 636 N.Y.S.2d 716, 660 N.E.2d 397 (N.Y.1995)—**§ 20.5, n. 3; § 20.8; § 20.8, n. 3; § 20.17; § 20.17, n. 6; § 20.39; § 20.39, n. 2; § 20.97; § 20.97, n. 2.**
Jacobe, In re, 116 B.R. 463 (Bkrtcy.E.D.Va. 1990)—**§ 9.205, n. 7.**
Jacobs v. Larry Biscornet, Inc., 155 A.D.2d 644, 548 N.Y.S.2d 235 (N.Y.A.D. 2 Dept. 1989)—**§ 37.65, n. 56.**
Jacobsen v. Overseas Tankship Corp., 11 F.R.D. 97 (E.D.N.Y.1950)—**§ 28.11, n. 4.**
Jacobsen, People v., 140 A.D.2d 938, 529 N.Y.S.2d 618 (N.Y.A.D. 4 Dept.1988)—**§ 38.21, n. 9.**
Jacobson v. AEG Capital Corp., 50 F.3d 1493 (9th Cir.1995)—**§ 9.161, n. 7.**
Jacobson v. State Tax Com'n, 129 A.D.2d 880, 514 N.Y.S.2d 145 (N.Y.A.D. 3 Dept. 1987)—**§ 35.100, n. 9.**
Jacob & Youngs v. Kent, 230 N.Y. 239, 129 N.E. 889 (N.Y.1921)—**§ 30.22, n. 2; § 30.25, n. 10.**
Jacquin, People ex rel. Doyle v., 186 A.D.2d 235, 587 N.Y.S.2d 1019 (N.Y.A.D. 2 Dept.1992)—**§ 38.8, n. 79.**
Jaffe v. Scheinman, 417 N.Y.S.2d 241, 390 N.E.2d 1165 (N.Y.1979)—**§ 38.10, n. 28.**
Jaked v. Torncello, 201 A.D.2d 819, 609 N.Y.S.2d 682 (N.Y.A.D. 3 Dept.1994)—**§ 30.30, n. 13.**
Jakubowski v. Lengen, 86 A.D.2d 398, 450 N.Y.S.2d 612 (N.Y.A.D. 4 Dept.1982)—**§ 26.42, n. 21.**
Jamaica Sav. Bank v. Florizal Realty Corp., 95 Misc.2d 654, 407 N.Y.S.2d 1016 (N.Y.Sup.1978)—**§ 11.29, n. 2.**
Jamaica Sav. Bank v. Henry, 112 A.D.2d 920, 492 N.Y.S.2d 437 (N.Y.A.D. 2 Dept. 1985)—**§ 11.6, n. 4.**
Jamar A., Matter of, 633 N.Y.S.2d 265, 657 N.E.2d 260 (N.Y.1995)—**§ 39.3, n. 3.**
James v. Gannett Co., Inc., 386 N.Y.S.2d 871, 353 N.E.2d 834 (N.Y.1976)—**§ 18.81, n. 1.**
James, People v., 207 A.D.2d 564, 616 N.Y.S.2d 75 (N.Y.A.D. 2 Dept.1994)—**§ 38.19, n. 78.**
James v. Powell, 279 N.Y.S.2d 10, 225 N.E.2d 741 (N.Y.1967)—**§ 37.23, n. 5.**
James v. Saltsman, 99 A.D.2d 797, 472 N.Y.S.2d 129 (N.Y.A.D. 2 Dept.1984)—**§ 30.9, n. 31, 34.**

TABLE OF CASES

James AA, Matter of, 188 A.D.2d 60, 594 N.Y.S.2d 430 (N.Y.A.D. 3 Dept.1993)— § **22.39, n. 2.**

James A. Phillips, Inc., In re, 29 B.R. 391 (S.D.N.Y.1983)—§ **10.17, n. 10.**

Jamesway Corp., In re, 202 B.R. 697 (Bkrtcy.S.D.N.Y.1996)—§ **9.75, n. 1.**

Janczak, Matter of, 167 Misc.2d 766, 634 N.Y.S.2d 1020 (N.Y.Sup.1995)—§ **22.38, n. 6.**

Jandreau v. LaVigne, 170 A.D.2d 861, 566 N.Y.S.2d 683 (N.Y.A.D. 3 Dept.1991)— § **7.10, n. 15, 17; § 7.15, n. 9.**

Jane PP v. Paul QQ, 483 N.Y.S.2d 1007, 473 N.E.2d 257 (N.Y.1984)—§ **37.19, n. 14.**

Janes, Matter of Will of, 139 Misc.2d 179, 527 N.Y.S.2d 707 (N.Y.Sur.1988)— § **25.30, n. 3.**

Janetka v. Dabe, 892 F.2d 187 (2nd Cir. 1989)—§ **18.25, n. 2.**

Janiak v. Planning Bd. of Town of Greenville, 159 A.D.2d 574, 552 N.Y.S.2d 436 (N.Y.A.D. 2 Dept.1990)—§ **16.106, n. 5; § 16.107, n. 4.**

Janiak v. Town of Greenville, 203 A.D.2d 329, 610 N.Y.S.2d 286 (N.Y.A.D. 2 Dept. 1994)—§ **16.50, n. 8.**

Jason v. Chusid, 578 N.Y.S.2d 867, 586 N.E.2d 50 (N.Y.1991)—§ **37.83, n. 6.**

Jasopersaud v. Rho, 169 A.D.2d 184, 572 N.Y.S.2d 700 (N.Y.A.D. 2 Dept.1991)— § **26.42, n. 9.**

Javarone, In re, 181 B.R. 151 (Bkrtcy. N.D.N.Y.1995)—§ **9.249, n. 5.**

Javid v. Scott, 913 F.Supp. 223 (S.D.N.Y. 1996)—§ **18.34, n. 3; § 18.93, n. 1, 4.**

Jay v. Jay, 67 Misc.2d 371, 323 N.Y.S.2d 387 (N.Y.Sup.1971)—§ **21.31, n. 1.**

Jayne Estates, Inc. v. Raynor, 293 N.Y.S.2d 75, 239 N.E.2d 713 (N.Y.1968)—§ **16.76, n. 3.**

Jayson v. Jayson, 54 A.D.2d 687, 387 N.Y.S.2d 274 (N.Y.A.D. 2 Dept.1976)— § **24.65, n. 2.**

J. Baranello & Sons v. Hausmann Industries, Inc., 571 F.Supp. 333 (E.D.N.Y. 1983)—§ **5.24, n. 3; § 5.25, n. 4.**

J. Crew Group, Inc. v. Griffin, 1990 WL 193918 (S.D.N.Y.1990)—§ **17.25, n. 13.**

J.E.B. v. Alabama ex rel. T.B., 511 U.S. 127, 114 S.Ct. 1419, 128 L.Ed.2d 89 (1994)— § **18.15, n. 6.**

Jefferds v. Ellis, 127 Misc.2d 477, 486 N.Y.S.2d 649 (N.Y.Sup.1985)—§ **7.24, n. 5.**

Jefferson Ins. Co. of New York v. Glens Falls Ins. Co., 88 A.D.2d 925, 450 N.Y.S.2d 888 (N.Y.A.D. 2 Dept.1982)— § **31.30, n. 1.**

Jeffries v. Harleston, 52 F.3d 9 (2nd Cir. 1995)—§ **17.55, n. 5.**

Jefpaul Garage Corp. v. Presbyterian Hosp. in City of New York, 474 N.Y.S.2d 458, 462 N.E.2d 1176 (N.Y.1984)—§ **13.53, n. 2.**

Jemison v. Citizens' Sav. Bank, 122 N.Y. 135, 25 N.E. 264 (N.Y.1890)—§ **1.12, n. 1, 6.**

Jenelle P, Matter of, 220 A.D.2d 853, 632 N.Y.S.2d 245 (N.Y.A.D. 3 Dept.1995)— § **20.131, n. 1.**

Jenkins v. Etlinger, 447 N.Y.S.2d 696, 432 N.E.2d 589 (N.Y.1982)—§ **30.5, n. 5; § 30.37, n. 3.**

Jenkins, People v., 555 N.Y.S.2d 10, 554 N.E.2d 47 (N.Y.1990)—§ **38.19, n. 114.**

Jennifer Lauren D., Matter of, 110 A.D.2d 699, 487 N.Y.S.2d 817 (N.Y.A.D. 2 Dept. 1985)—§ **20.67; § 20.67, n. 3.**

Jennings v. Baumann, 214 A.D. 361, 212 N.Y.S. 334 (N.Y.A.D. 2 Dept.1925)— § **12.65, n. 8.**

Jensen v. General Elec. Co., 603 N.Y.S.2d 420, 623 N.E.2d 547 (N.Y.1993)— § **15.32, n. 19.**

Jensen v. Southern Pac. Co., 215 N.Y. 514, 109 N.E. 600 (N.Y.1915)—§ **32.8, n. 1; § 32.9, n. 1.**

Jeppson, In re, 66 B.R. 269 (Bkrtcy.D.Utah 1986)—§ **9.158, n. 6.**

Jeras v. East Mfg. Corp., 168 A.D.2d 889, 566 N.Y.S.2d 418 (N.Y.A.D. 4 Dept. 1990)—§ **1.10, n. 19.**

Jermoo's Inc., Matter of, 38 B.R. 197 (Bkrtcy.W.D.Wis.1984)—§ **9.45, n. 2.**

Jerome E., In re, 187 A.D.2d 85, 593 N.Y.S.2d 205 (N.Y.A.D. 1 Dept.1993)— § **20.90, n. 6; § 20.93, n. 2.**

Jervis Corp. v. Secretary of State, 43 Misc.2d 185, 250 N.Y.S.2d 544 (N.Y.Sup. 1964)—§ **1.13, n. 2, 14.**

Jet Setting Service Corp. v. Toomey, 91 A.D.2d 431, 459 N.Y.S.2d 751 (N.Y.A.D. 1 Dept.1983)—§ **31.6, n. 3.**

Jett v. Dallas Independent School Dist., 491 U.S. 701, 109 S.Ct. 2702, 105 L.Ed.2d 598 (1989)—§ **18.17; § 18.17, n. 3.**

Jewell–Rung Agency, Inc. v. Haddad Organization, Ltd., 814 F.Supp. 337 (S.D.N.Y.1993)—§ **5.48, n. 6.**

Jewett v. Luau–Nyack Corp., 338 N.Y.S.2d 874, 291 N.E.2d 123 (N.Y.1972)—§ **3.11, n. 1; § 3.12, n. 1.**

Jewish Home and Infirmary of Rochester, New York, Inc. v. Commissioner of New York State Dept. of Health, 616 N.Y.S.2d 458, 640 N.E.2d 125 (N.Y. 1994)—§ **4.44, n. 7.**

Jewish Memorial Hospital v. Whalen, 418 N.Y.S.2d 318, 391 N.E.2d 1296 (N.Y. 1979)—§ **4.44, n. 7.**

TABLE OF CASES

Jewish Press, Inc. v. Willner, 190 A.D.2d 841, 594 N.Y.S.2d 51 (N.Y.A.D. 2 Dept. 1993)—§ **30.27, n. 9.**

Jews for Jesus, Inc. v. Jewish Community Relations Council of New York, Inc., 968 F.2d 286 (2nd Cir.1992)—§ **18.54, n. 1.**

Jillson v. Vermont Log Bldgs., Inc., 857 F.Supp. 985 (D.Mass.1994)—§ **27.49; § 27.49, n. 5; § 27.51, n. 3.**

Jiminez v. Southridge Co-op., Section I, Inc., 626 F.Supp. 732 (E.D.N.Y.1985)—§ **18.50, n. 1.**

J.M. Braun Builders, Inc. v. Maryland Cas. Co., 152 A.D.2d 963, 544 N.Y.S.2d 528 (N.Y.A.D. 4 Dept.1989)—§ **31.17, n. 2.**

Jo Ann Homes at Bellmore, Inc. v. Dworetz, 302 N.Y.S.2d 799, 250 N.E.2d 214 (N.Y. 1969)—§ **11.37, n. 8.**

Jobin v. Boryla (In re M & L Business Mach. Co., Inc.), 75 F.3d 586 (10th Cir. 1996)—§ **9.198, n. 1.**

Joblon v. Solow, 1997 WL 158357 (S.D.N.Y. 1997)—§ **32.15, n. 10.**

Jocar Realty Co., Inc. v. Rukavina, 130 Misc.2d 1009, 498 N.Y.S.2d 244 (N.Y.City Civ.Ct.1985)—§ **13.18, n. 12, 14; § 13.28, n. 4.**

Joffe v. Rubenstein, 24 A.D.2d 752, 263 N.Y.S.2d 867 (N.Y.A.D. 1 Dept.1965)—§ **28.11, n. 4.**

John C., People v., 184 A.D.2d 519, 584 N.Y.S.2d 320 (N.Y.A.D. 2 Dept.1992)—§ **38.8, n. 226.**

John E. Rosasco Creameries v. Cohen, 276 N.Y. 274, 11 N.E.2d 908 (N.Y.1937)—§ **5.10, n. 1, 2, 3.**

John F. Kennedy Memorial Hospital v. Heston, 58 N.J. 576, 279 A.2d 670 (N.J. 1971)—§ **29.14, n. 7.**

John G. v. Dubin, 89 A.D.2d 839, 452 N.Y.S.2d 907 (N.Y.A.D. 2 Dept.1982)—§ **38.8, n. 130, 134.**

John Grace & Co., Inc. v. State University Const. Fund, 404 N.Y.S.2d 316, 375 N.E.2d 377 (N.Y.1978)—§ **14.4, n. 6.**

John Grace & Co., Inc. v. Tunstead, Schechter & Torre, 186 A.D.2d 15, 588 N.Y.S.2d 262 (N.Y.A.D. 1 Dept.1992)—§ **28.30; § 28.30, n. 1.**

John Hancock Property and Cas. Ins. Co. v. Universale Reinsurance Co., Ltd., 147 F.R.D. 40 (S.D.N.Y.1993)—§ **31.23, n. 10.**

John H. Black Co. v. Surdam Holding Corp., 140 Misc. 113, 250 N.Y.S. 17 (N.Y.Sup.1931)—§ **10.12, n. 3.**

John Johnson Const. Co. v. State, 211 A.D. 512, 207 N.Y.S. 570 (N.Y.A.D. 4 Dept. 1925)—§ **30.25, n. 7.**

John P., Matter of, 74 A.D.2d 403, 427 N.Y.S.2d 447 (N.Y.A.D. 2 Dept.1980)—§ **37.24, n. 4.**

Johns–Manville Corp., In re, 68 B.R. 155 (S.D.N.Y.1986)—§ **9.43, n. 9.**

Johns–Manville Corp., In re, 60 B.R. 612 (Bkrtcy.S.D.N.Y.1986)—§ **9.61, n. 1, 2, 3.**

Johns–Manville Corp., In re, 60 B.R. 842 (S.D.N.Y.1986)—§ **9.46, n. 2.**

Johns–Manville Corp., In re, 42 B.R. 362 (S.D.N.Y.1984)—§ **9.39, n. 3; § 9.40, n. 3.**

Johns–Manville Corp., Matter of, 68 B.R. 618 (Bkrtcy.S.D.N.Y.1986)—§ **9.165, n. 23; § 9.166, n. 13.**

Johnson, In re, 148 B.R. 532 (Bkrtcy. N.D.Ill.1992)—§ **9.130, n. 3.**

Johnson v. Anderson, 258 N.Y.S.2d 846, 206 N.E.2d 869 (N.Y.1965)—§ **37.40, n. 3.**

Johnson v. Hallam Enterprises Ltd., 208 A.D.2d 1110, 617 N.Y.S.2d 405 (N.Y.A.D. 3 Dept.1994)—§ **37.65, n. 40.**

Johnson v. Home State Bank, 501 U.S. 78, 111 S.Ct. 2150, 115 L.Ed.2d 66 (1991)—§ **9.129, n. 2.**

Johnson v. International Harvester Co. of America, 237 A.D. 778, 263 N.Y.S. 262 (N.Y.A.D. 3 Dept.1933)—§ **37.35, n. 13.**

Johnson v. Johnson, 167 A.D.2d 954, 561 N.Y.S.2d 1018 (N.Y.A.D. 4 Dept.1990)—§ **21.22, n. 3.**

Johnson v. Johnson Chemical Co., Inc., 183 A.D.2d 64, 588 N.Y.S.2d 607 (N.Y.A.D. 2 Dept.1992)—§ **27.11, n. 3; § 27.13, n. 3.**

Johnson v. Jones, 515 U.S. 304, 115 S.Ct. 2151, 132 L.Ed.2d 238 (1995)—§ **18.32, n. 1.**

Johnson v. Oval Pharmacy, 165 A.D.2d 587, 569 N.Y.S.2d 49 (N.Y.A.D. 1 Dept. 1991)—§ **37.65, n. 43.**

Johnson, People v., 215 A.D.2d 258, 626 N.Y.S.2d 775 (N.Y.A.D. 1 Dept.1995)—§ **38.10, n. 147.**

Johnson, People v., 214 A.D.2d 752, 625 N.Y.S.2d 944 (N.Y.A.D. 2 Dept.1995)—§ **38.8, n. 28, 213.**

Johnson, People v., 210 A.D.2d 257, 620 N.Y.S.2d 251 (N.Y.A.D. 2 Dept.1994)—§ **38.8, n. 58.**

Johnson, People v., 205 A.D.2d 344, 613 N.Y.S.2d 160 (N.Y.A.D. 1 Dept.1994)—§ **38.8, n. 42.**

Johnson, People v., 587 N.Y.S.2d 278, 599 N.E.2d 682 (N.Y.1992)—§ **38.19; § 38.19, n. 134.**

Johnson, People v., 149 A.D.2d 534, 540 N.Y.S.2d 727 (N.Y.A.D. 2 Dept.1989)—§ **38.34, n. 7.**

Johnson, People v., 145 A.D.2d 932, 536 N.Y.S.2d 300 (N.Y.A.D. 4 Dept.1988)—§ **38.28, n. 9.**

Johnson, People v., 141 A.D.2d 848, 530 N.Y.S.2d 189 (N.Y.A.D. 2 Dept.1988)—§ **38.8, n. 159.**

TABLE OF CASES

Johnson, People v., 103 A.D.2d 754, 477 N.Y.S.2d 225 (N.Y.A.D. 2 Dept.1984)—§ **38.3, n. 24.**
Johnson, People v., 96 A.D.2d 1083, 466 N.Y.S.2d 969 (N.Y.A.D. 2 Dept.1983)—§ **38.19, n. 63.**
Johnson, People v., 457 N.Y.S.2d 230, 443 N.E.2d 478 (N.Y.1982)—§ **38.19, n. 92.**
Johnson, People v., 417 N.Y.S.2d 46, 390 N.E.2d 764 (N.Y.1979)—§ **38.27, n. 11, 25.**
Johnson, People v., 282 N.Y.S.2d 481, 229 N.E.2d 180 (N.Y.1967)—§ **38.8, n. 110.**
Johnson, People v., 252 N.Y. 387, 169 N.E. 619 (N.Y.1930)—§ **38.19;** § **38.21, n. 58;** § **38.27.**
Johnson v. Secretary of Health and Human Services, 794 F.2d 1106 (6th Cir.1986)—§ **34.11, n. 9.**
Johnson v. Space Saver Corp., 172 Misc.2d 147, 656 N.Y.S.2d 715 (N.Y.Sup.1997)—§ **32.15, n. 9.**
Johnson v. State, 72 A.D.2d 487, 426 N.Y.S.2d 98 (N.Y.A.D. 3 Dept.1980)—§ **14.44, n. 2.**
Johnson and Smith (Dot E.W.), N.Y.L.J., 3/26/97, p. 32, col. 6 (Sup.Ct., Suffolk County)—§ **22.54, n. 5.**
Johnson City, Matter of Village of, 215 A.D.2d 917, 626 N.Y.S.2d 869 (N.Y.A.D. 3 Dept.1995)—§ **14.86, n. 5.**
Johnston v. Fargo, 184 N.Y. 379, 77 N.E. 388 (N.Y.1906)—§ **5.11, n. 5.**
Johnstown, N.Y., City of v. Bankers Standard Ins. Co., 877 F.2d 1146 (2nd Cir. 1989)—§ **31.8, n. 2.**
John T. Brady & Co. v. City of New York, 451 N.Y.S.2d 735, 436 N.E.2d 1337 (N.Y. 1982)—§ **39.15, n. 1.**
John W. S. v. Jeanne F. S., 48 A.D.2d 30, 367 N.Y.S.2d 814 (N.Y.A.D. 2 Dept. 1975)—§ **21.31, n. 1.**
John XX, Matter of, 226 A.D.2d 79, 652 N.Y.S.2d 329 (N.Y.A.D. 3 Dept.1996)—§ **22.48, n. 11.**
Joint Diseases North General Hosp., Matter of, 148 A.D.2d 873, 539 N.Y.S.2d 511 (N.Y.A.D. 3 Dept.1989)—§ **37.89, n. 5.**
Joint Eastern and Southern Dist. Asbestos Litigation, In re, 827 F.Supp. 1014 (S.D.N.Y.1993)—§ **27.35, n. 13.**
Joint Eastern and Southern Dist. Asbestos Litigation, In re, 758 F.Supp. 199 (S.D.N.Y.1991)—§ **27.35, n. 11.**
Joint Eastern & Southern Dist. Asbestos Litigation, In re, 52 F.3d 1124 (2nd Cir. 1995)—§ **27.35;** § **27.35, n. 9.**
Joint Eastern & Southern Dist. Asbestos Litigation, In re, 964 F.2d 92 (2nd Cir. 1992)—§ **27.35, n. 12.**
Joint Queensview Housing Enterprise, Inc. v. Balogh, 174 A.D.2d 605, 571 N.Y.S.2d 312 (N.Y.A.D. 2 Dept.1991)—§ **37.37, n. 8.**
Jolis v. Jolis, 111 Misc.2d 965, 446 N.Y.S.2d 138 (N.Y.Sup.1981)—§ **21.40, n. 10.**
Jones v. Barnes, 463 U.S. 745, 103 S.Ct. 3308, 77 L.Ed.2d 987 (1983)—§ **38.34, n. 5.**
Jones v. Dunkirk Radiator Corp., 21 F.3d 18 (2nd Cir.1994)—§ **17.34, n. 13.**
Jones v. Inter–County Imaging Centers, 889 F.Supp. 741 (S.D.N.Y.1995)—§ **18.62, n. 3.**
Jones v. Knowlton, 199 A.D.2d 871, 606 N.Y.S.2d 355 (N.Y.A.D. 3 Dept.1993)—§ **8.32, n. 3.**
Jones v. Palermo, 105 Misc.2d 405, 432 N.Y.S.2d 288 (N.Y.Sup.1980)—§ **2.51, n. 12.**
Jones, People v., 88 N.Y.2d 172, 643 N.Y.S.2d 949, 666 N.E.2d 542 (1996)—§ 18.15, n. 9.
Jones, People v., 213 A.D.2d 1049, 625 N.Y.S.2d 979 (N.Y.A.D. 4 Dept.1995)—§ **38.28, n. 15.**
Jones, People v., 210 A.D.2d 904, 620 N.Y.S.2d 656 (N.Y.A.D. 4 Dept.1994)—§ **38.19, n. 80.**
Jones, People v., 188 A.D.2d 331, 591 N.Y.S.2d 159 (N.Y.A.D. 1 Dept.1992)—§ **38.10, n. 63;** § **38.20, n. 5.**
Jones, People v., 184 A.D.2d 405, 585 N.Y.S.2d 362 (N.Y.A.D. 1 Dept.1992)—§ **38.10;** § **38.10, n. 80.**
Jones, People v., 523 N.Y.S.2d 53, 517 N.E.2d 865 (N.Y.1987)—§ **38.10, n. 94;** § **38.19, n. 98.**
Jones, People v., 105 A.D.2d 179, 483 N.Y.S.2d 345 (N.Y.A.D. 2 Dept.1984)—§ **33.85, n. 2.**
Jones, People v., 81 A.D.2d 22, 440 N.Y.S.2d 248 (N.Y.A.D. 2 Dept.1981)—§ **37.28, n. 17.**
Jones, People v., 418 N.Y.S.2d 359, 391 N.E.2d 1335 (N.Y.1979)—§ **18.13, n. 2;** § **38.19, n. 111.**
Jones, People v., 57 A.D.2d 905, 394 N.Y.S.2d 288 (N.Y.A.D. 2 Dept.1977)—§ **38.21;** § **38.21, n. 21.**
Jones v. Smith, 489 N.Y.S.2d 50, 478 N.E.2d 191 (N.Y.1985)—§ **4.50, n. 6.**
Jones v. Utilities Painting Corp., 198 A.D.2d 268, 603 N.Y.S.2d 546 (N.Y.A.D. 2 Dept.1993)—§ **37.29, n. 40.**
Jordan, People v., 78 A.D.2d 878, 433 N.Y.S.2d 25 (N.Y.A.D. 2 Dept.1980)—§ **38.8, n. 201.**
Joseph C. Spiess Co., In re, 145 B.R. 597 (Bkrtcy.N.D.Ill.1992)—§ **9.82, n. 1.**
Joseph Michael D., Matter of, 138 A.D.2d 974, 526 N.Y.S.2d 305 (N.Y.A.D. 4 Dept. 1988)—§ **20.67, n. 5.**

TABLE OF CASES

Josephson v. Caral Real Estate Co., 200 N.Y.S.2d 1016 (N.Y.Sup.1960)—§ **11.37, n. 9.**

Josephson v. New York World-Telegram Corp., 179 Misc. 786, 38 N.Y.S.2d 986 (N.Y.Sup.1942)—§ **30.26, n. 4.**

Jospe (Grala), Matter of, N.Y.L.J., 1/30/95, p.30, col.2 (Sup.Ct., Nassau County)—§ **22.46, n. 5; § 22.53, n. 10.**

J.P.M. Properties, Inc. v. Town of Oyster Bay, 204 A.D.2d 722, 612 N.Y.S.2d 634 (N.Y.A.D. 2 Dept.1994)—§ **16.91, n. 6.**

J & R Esposito Builders, Inc. v. Coffman, 183 A.D.2d 828, 584 N.Y.S.2d 73 (N.Y.A.D. 2 Dept.1992)—§ **16.106, n. 7.**

Juan P.H.C., Matter of, 130 Misc.2d 387, 496 N.Y.S.2d 630 (N.Y.Sur.1985)—§ **20.106, n. 2, 3.**

Judd v. Wolfe, 78 F.3d 110 (3rd Cir.1996)—§ **9.207, n. 4.**

Juliano, People v., 207 A.D.2d 414, 615 N.Y.S.2d 460 (N.Y.A.D. 2 Dept.1994)—§ **38.10, n. 68, 141.**

Jump v. Jump, 69 A.D.2d 947, 415 N.Y.S.2d 499 (N.Y.A.D. 3 Dept.1979)—§ **37.65, n. 47.**

June v. Laris, 205 A.D.2d 166, 618 N.Y.S.2d 138 (N.Y.A.D. 3 Dept.1994)—§ **27.47, n. 5.**

J.W. Van Cott & Son v. Gallon, 163 Misc. 914, 298 N.Y.S. 67 (N.Y.Co.Ct.1937)—§ **10.14, n. 5.**

K

Kacer (Osohowsky), Matter of, N.Y.L.J., 11/1/94, p.33, col.1 (Sup.Ct., Suffolk County)—§ **22.48, n. 13.**

Kaczmarek v. Conroy, 218 A.D.2d 97, 635 N.Y.S.2d 310 (N.Y.A.D. 3 Dept.1995)—§ **18.31, n. 5.**

Kahn v. Crames, 92 A.D.2d 634, 459 N.Y.S.2d 941 (N.Y.A.D. 3 Dept.1983)—§ **28.11, n. 12.**

Kahn v. Kahn, 801 F.Supp. 1237 (S.D.N.Y. 1992)—§ **21.32, n. 1.**

Kahn v. Kahn, 401 N.Y.S.2d 47, 371 N.E.2d 809 (N.Y.1977)—§ **24.64, n. 5.**

Kahn v. Lumbermens Mut. Cas. Co., 293 F.Supp. 985 (E.D.N.Y.1968)—§ **31.15, n. 8.**

Kaiser's Estate, In re, 198 Misc. 582, 100 N.Y.S.2d 218 (N.Y.Sur.1950)—§ **30.12; § 30.12, n. 5.**

Kajtazi v. Kajtazi, 488 F.Supp. 15 (E.D.N.Y. 1978)—§ **30.9, n. 32.**

Kalenak, Matter of Will of, 182 A.D.2d 1124, 583 N.Y.S.2d 332 (N.Y.A.D. 4 Dept.1992)—§ **25.21, n. 4.**

Kalfin v. United States Olympic Committee, 209 A.D.2d 279, 618 N.Y.S.2d 724 (N.Y.A.D. 1 Dept.1994)—§ **17.34, n. 16.**

Kalian, In re, 169 B.R. 503 (Bkrtcy.D.R.I. 1994)—§ **9.102, n. 4.**

Kalikow Properties v. Modny, N.Y.L.J., 5/2/78, p.5, col.1, (App. Term, 1st Dep't)—§ **13.32, n. 7.**

Kalisch-Jarcho, Inc. v. City of New York, 461 N.Y.S.2d 746, 448 N.E.2d 413 (N.Y. 1983)—§ **5.15, n. 1.**

Kallenberg v. Beth Israel Hospital, 45 A.D.2d 177, 357 N.Y.S.2d 508 (N.Y.A.D. 1 Dept.1974)—§ **27.35; § 27.35, n. 1.**

Kallins v. Kallins, 170 A.D.2d 436, 565 N.Y.S.2d 227 (N.Y.A.D. 2 Dept.1991)—§ **21.42, n. 5.**

Kalt Lumber Co. v. Sterner, 121 Misc. 505, 201 N.Y.S. 567 (N.Y.Sup.1923)—§ **10.13, n. 3.**

Kamakazi Music Corp. v. Robbins Music Corp., 534 F.Supp. 57 (S.D.N.Y.1981)—§ **5.21, n. 5.**

Kamhi v. Planning Bd. of Town of Yorktown, 465 N.Y.S.2d 865, 452 N.E.2d 1193 (N.Y.1983)—§ **16.4, n. 7; § 16.100, n. 3.**

Kamhi v. Town of Yorktown, 548 N.Y.S.2d 144, 547 N.E.2d 346 (N.Y.1989)—§ **16.24, n. 10.**

Kamin v. American Exp. Co., 86 Misc.2d 809, 383 N.Y.S.2d 807 (N.Y.Sup.1976)—§ **1.38, n. 12.**

Kaminski v. United Parcel Service, 120 A.D.2d 409, 501 N.Y.S.2d 871 (N.Y.A.D. 1 Dept.1986)—§ **17.26, n. 1; § 17.28; § 17.28, n. 3; § 17.29; § 17.29, n. 7.**

Kamyr, Inc. v. St. Paul Surplus Lines Ins. Co., 152 A.D.2d 62, 547 N.Y.S.2d 964 (N.Y.A.D. 3 Dept.1989)—§ **31.6, n. 2.**

Kanbar v. Quad Cinema Corp., 151 Misc.2d 439, 581 N.Y.S.2d 260 (N.Y.Sup.App. Term 1991)—§ **8.42, n. 21.**

Kane, Matter of, 15 I & N Dec. 258 (BIA 1975)—§ **19.74, n. 8.**

Kane v. Johns-Manville Corp. (In re John-Manville Corp.), 843 F.2d 636 (2nd Cir. 1988)—§ **9.25, n. 7.**

Kanopke v. Village of Freeport, 121 A.D.2d 690, 503 N.Y.S.2d 1012 (N.Y.A.D. 2 Dept.1986)—§ **3.30, n. 16.**

Kan, People v., 571 N.Y.S.2d 436, 574 N.E.2d 1042 (N.Y.1991)—§ **38.19, n. 111.**

Kaplan v. Bergmann, 122 A.D. 876, 107 N.Y.S. 423 (N.Y.A.D. 2 Dept.1907)—§ **12.60, n. 3.**

Kaplan v. Long Island University, 116 A.D.2d 508, 497 N.Y.S.2d 378 (N.Y.A.D. 1 Dept.1986)—§ **17.82, n. 22.**

TABLE OF CASES

Kaplan v. Meskin, 108 A.D.2d 787, 485 N.Y.S.2d 117 (N.Y.A.D. 2 Dept.1985)—§ 20.9, n. 4.

Kaplan's Estate, In re, 49 Misc.2d 335, 267 N.Y.S.2d 345 (N.Y.Sur.1966)—§ 25.31, n. 11; § 25.39, n. 1.

Karas v. Wasserman, 91 A.D.2d 812, 458 N.Y.S.2d 280 (N.Y.A.D. 3 Dept.1982)—§ 11.37, n. 9.

Karasik v. Karasik, 172 A.D.2d 294, 568 N.Y.S.2d 384 (N.Y.A.D. 1 Dept.1991)—§ 21.17, n. 2.

Karen v. Cane, 152 Misc.2d 639, 578 N.Y.S.2d 85 (N.Y.City Civ.Ct.1991)—§ 5.42, n. 1, 7.

Karen BB, Matter of, 216 A.D.2d 754, 628 N.Y.S.2d 431 (N.Y.A.D. 3 Dept.1995)—§ 37.29, n. 38.

Karibian v. Columbia University, 14 F.3d 773 (2nd Cir.1994)—§ 17.57, n. 3, 5.

Karmali v. I.N.S., 707 F.2d 408 (9th Cir. 1983)—§ 19.21, n. 2.

Karp, People v., 565 N.Y.S.2d 751, 566 N.E.2d 1156 (N.Y.1990)—§ 38.24, n. 3.

Kase, People v., 76 A.D.2d 532, 431 N.Y.S.2d 531 (N.Y.A.D. 1 Dept.1980)—§ 4.30, n. 2.

Kasper v. Town of Brookhaven, 142 A.D.2d 213, 535 N.Y.S.2d 621 (N.Y.A.D. 2 Dept. 1988)—§ 16.120, n. 2, 7.

Kass v. Club Mart of America, Inc., 160 A.D.2d 1148, 554 N.Y.S.2d 357 (N.Y.A.D. 3 Dept.1990)—§ 32.27, n. 6.

Kaste v. Hartford Acc. & Indem. Co., 5 A.D.2d 203, 170 N.Y.S.2d 614 (N.Y.A.D. 1 Dept.1958)—§ 31.12, n. 4.

Kaszubowski v. State, 112 A.D.2d 742, 492 N.Y.S.2d 237 (N.Y.A.D. 4 Dept.1985)—§ 14.82, n. 1.

Kates, People v., 444 N.Y.S.2d 446, 428 N.E.2d 852 (N.Y.1981)—§ 38.10, n. 170.

Kathleen Foley, Inc. v. Gulf Oil Corp., 12 A.D.2d 644, 208 N.Y.S.2d 781 (N.Y.A.D. 2 Dept.1960)—§ 30.35, n. 5.

Katonah Realties, Inc. v. Wasserman, 98 Misc.2d 630, 414 N.Y.S.2d 234 (N.Y.City Civ.Ct.1978)—§ 13.19, n. 2.

Kator (Elefant), Matter of, 164 Misc.2d 265, 624 N.Y.S.2d 348 (N.Y.Sup.1995)—§ 22.38, n. 17; § 22.70, n. 2, 6.

Katowski, People v., 204 A.D.2d 486, 611 N.Y.S.2d 907 (N.Y.A.D. 2 Dept.1994)—§ 38.10, n. 168.

Katsaros v. Cody, 568 F.Supp. 360 (E.D.N.Y.1983)—§ 17.50, n. 3.

Katz, Matter of, 2 Misc.2d 325, 143 N.Y.S.2d 282 (N.Y.Sup.1955)—§ 1.43, n. 26.

Katz v. Katz, 68 A.D.2d 536, 418 N.Y.S.2d 99 (N.Y.A.D. 2 Dept.1979)—§ 37.23, n. 5.

Katz v. N.Y. Tint Taxi Corp., 213 A.D.2d 599, 624 N.Y.S.2d 65 (N.Y.A.D. 2 Dept. 1995)—§ 1.10, n. 9.

Katz v. State, 10 A.D.2d 164, 198 N.Y.S.2d 463 (N.Y.A.D. 3 Dept.1960)—§ 14.105, n. 2.

Katz v. Zuckermann, 126 Misc.2d 135, 481 N.Y.S.2d 271 (N.Y.Sup.1984)—§ 5.7, n. 8.

Katz, Estate of v. Commissioner, T.C. Memo. 1968-171 (Tax Ct.1968)—§ 24.41, n. 2.

Kauffman v. State, 43 A.D.2d 1004, 353 N.Y.S.2d 61 (N.Y.A.D. 3 Dept.1974)—§ 14.84, n. 2.

Kaufman, In re, 114 Misc.2d 1078, 453 N.Y.S.2d 304 (N.Y.Sup.1982)—§ 22.17, n. 4; § 22.71, n. 2.

Kaufman v. Eli Lilly and Co., 492 N.Y.S.2d 584, 482 N.E.2d 63 (N.Y.1985)—§ 27.53, n. 1.

Kaufman v. Public Serv. (In re Public Service Co. of New Hampshire), 43 F.3d 763 (1st Cir.1995)—§ 9.161, n. 7.

Kaufman v. State, 57 A.D.2d 1025, 395 N.Y.S.2d 513 (N.Y.A.D. 3 Dept.1977)—§ 14.81, n. 3.

Kavanaugh v. Nussbaum, 129 A.D.2d 559, 514 N.Y.S.2d 55 (N.Y.A.D. 2 Dept. 1987)—§ 30.10, n. 6.

Kavares v. Motor Vehicle Acc. Indemnification Corp., 29 A.D.2d 68, 285 N.Y.S.2d 983 (N.Y.A.D. 1 Dept.1967)—§ 8.6, n. 1.

Kay v. Sussel, 22 Misc.2d 627, 199 N.Y.S.2d 180 (N.Y.Sup.1960)—§ 17.29, n. 4.

Kaye v. Artmatic Corp., 214 A.D.2d 473, 625 N.Y.S.2d 216 (N.Y.A.D. 1 Dept. 1995)—§ 30.38, n. 2.

Kaye v. Whalen, 56 A.D.2d 111, 391 N.Y.S.2d 712 (N.Y.A.D. 3 Dept.1977)—§ 23.93, n. 4.

Kazepis, People v., 101 A.D.2d 816, 475 N.Y.S.2d 351 (N.Y.A.D. 2 Dept.1984)—§ 38.8, n. 223.

Kazlow & Kazlow v. Zaslow., 60 A.D.2d 907, 401 N.Y.S.2d 997 (N.Y.A.D. 2 Dept. 1978)—§ 37.67, n. 8.

Kazmi v. Kazmi, 201 A.D.2d 857, 608 N.Y.S.2d 535 (N.Y.A.D. 3 Dept.1994)—§ 21.58, n. 2.

Kearney Hotel Partners, In re, 92 B.R. 95 (Bkrtcy.S.D.N.Y.1988)—§ 9.69, n. 10.

Keefer, People v., 197 A.D.2d 915, 602 N.Y.S.2d 268 (N.Y.A.D. 4 Dept.1993)—§ 38.8, n. 92.

Keenan v. Brooklyn City R. Co., 145 N.Y. 348, 40 N.E. 15 (N.Y.1895)—§ 30.14, n. 15.

Keeton v. Hustler Magazine, Inc., 465 U.S. 770, 104 S.Ct. 1473, 79 L.Ed.2d 790 (1984)—§ 31.23, n. 5.

TABLE OF CASES

Keiffer, People v., 207 A.D.2d 1022, 617 N.Y.S.2d 103 (N.Y.A.D. 4 Dept.1994)—§ 38.8, n. 55.

Kel-Car Associates, Ltd. v. Adduci, 176 A.D.2d 942, 575 N.Y.S.2d 554 (N.Y.A.D. 2 Dept.1991)—§ 7.27, n. 15.

Keleher v. American Airlines, Inc., 132 A.D.2d 949, 518 N.Y.S.2d 276 (N.Y.A.D. 4 Dept.1987)—§ 17.32, n. 4.

Keller v. Lee, 1997 WL 218435 (S.D.N.Y. 1997)—§ 28.13, n. 1.

Keller v. Morgan, 149 A.D.2d 801, 539 N.Y.S.2d 589 (N.Y.A.D. 3 Dept.1989)—§ 16.40, n. 4.

Kelley v. E.P.A., 15 F.3d 1100, 304 U.S.App. D.C. 369 (D.C.Cir.1994)—§ 15.30, n. 4.

Kelley v. McGee, 457 N.Y.S.2d 434, 443 N.E.2d 908 (N.Y.1982)—§ 3.14, n. 5.

Kelley for and on Behalf of People of State of Mich. v. United States, 618 F.Supp. 1103 (W.D.Mich.1985)—§ 15.8, n. 13.

Kelly, People v., 209 A.D.2d 436, 618 N.Y.S.2d 822 (N.Y.A.D. 2 Dept.1994)—§ 38.10, n. 96.

Kelly, People v., 565 N.Y.S.2d 754, 566 N.E.2d 1159 (N.Y.1990)—§ 38.19, n. 105.

Kelly, People v., 478 N.Y.S.2d 834, 467 N.E.2d 498 (N.Y.1984)—§ 33.39, n. 9.

Kemp v. Zoning Bd. of Appeals of Village of Wappingers Falls, 216 A.D.2d 466, 628 N.Y.S.2d 187 (N.Y.A.D. 2 Dept.1995)—§ 16.48, n. 8.

Kemp & Beatley, Inc., Matter of, 484 N.Y.S.2d 799, 473 N.E.2d 1173 (N.Y. 1984)—§ 1.103, n. 8.

Kenai Corp., In re, 136 B.R. 59 (S.D.N.Y. 1992)—§ 28.38, n. 2.

Kendzia, People v., 486 N.Y.S.2d 888, 476 N.E.2d 287 (N.Y.1985)—§ 33.78, n. 1.

Kennedy, People v., 157 A.D.2d 856, 550 N.Y.S.2d 431 (N.Y.A.D. 2 Dept.1990)—§ 38.20, n. 12.

Kennedy, People v., 151 A.D.2d 831, 542 N.Y.S.2d 806 (N.Y.A.D. 3 Dept.1989)—§ 38.8, n. 190.

Kennis v. Sherwood, 82 A.D.2d 847, 439 N.Y.S.2d 962 (N.Y.A.D. 2 Dept.1981)—§ 8.41, n. 1.

Kent v. Quicksilver Min. Co., 78 N.Y. 159 (N.Y.1879)—§ 1.12, n. 8.

Kenyon, People v., 46 A.D.2d 409, 362 N.Y.S.2d 644 (N.Y.A.D. 4 Dept.1975)—§ 38.8; § 38.8, n. 121.

Keogh v. Breed, Abbott & Morgan, 224 A.D.2d 180, 637 N.Y.S.2d 124 (N.Y.A.D. 1 Dept.1996)—§ 6.67, n. 2; § 6.88, n. 2.

Kern, Matter of, 165 Misc.2d 108, 627 N.Y.S.2d 257 (N.Y.Sup.1995)—§ 22.39, n. 2; § 22.41, n. 7, 13; § 22.53, n. 13.

Kern v. News Syndicate Co., 20 A.D.2d 528, 244 N.Y.S.2d 665 (N.Y.A.D. 1 Dept. 1963)—§ 30.35, n. 3.

Kern, People v., 555 N.Y.S.2d 647, 554 N.E.2d 1235 (N.Y.1990)—§ 18.15, n. 2; § 38.19, n. 140.

Kessler v. Kessler, 212 A.D.2d 1038, 623 N.Y.S.2d 435 (N.Y.A.D. 4 Dept.1995)—§ 21.43, n. 15.

Kessler, People v., 77 Misc.2d 640, 354 N.Y.S.2d 517 (N.Y.Co.Ct.1974)—§ 38.58, n. 4, 5.

Kessler v. Rae, 40 A.D.2d 708, 336 N.Y.S.2d 680 (N.Y.A.D. 2 Dept.1972)—§ 12.29, n. 11.

Kessler v. Town of Niskayuna, 774 F.Supp. 711 (N.D.N.Y.1991)—§ 16.125, n. 17.

Keta, People v., 583 N.Y.S.2d 920, 593 N.E.2d 1328 (N.Y.1992)—§ 4.2, n. 36; § 4.62; § 4.62, n. 3, 10.

Key, People v., 408 N.Y.S.2d 16, 379 N.E.2d 1147 (N.Y.1978)—§ 33.21; § 33.21, n. 3; § 33.24; § 33.24, n. 1, 3; § 38.10; § 38.10, n. 47, 181, 183.

Key Bank of New York v. Becker, 646 N.Y.S.2d 656, 669 N.E.2d 814 (N.Y. 1996)—§ 13.26, n. 6.

Keydata Corp., In re, 12 B.R. 156 (1st Cir. BAP (Mass.) 1981)—§ 9.89, n. 2.

Keystone Bituminous Coal Ass'n v. DeBenedictis, 480 U.S. 470, 107 S.Ct. 1232, 94 L.Ed.2d 472 (1987)—§ 16.22, n. 4.

Keystone Hardware Corporation v. Tague, 246 N.Y. 79, 158 N.E. 27 (N.Y.1927)—§ 12.10, n. 1.

KFJ Realty Co. v. Second Ave. Boutique, N.Y.L.J., 6/5/91, p.23, col.4, 19 HCR 348 (Civ.Ct., N.Y. County)—§ 13.20, n. 3.

Khalil v. Marion, 200 A.D.2d 500, 606 N.Y.S.2d 652 (N.Y.A.D. 1 Dept.1994)—§ 30.30, n. 6.

Khan v. Galvin, 206 A.D.2d 776, 615 N.Y.S.2d 111 (N.Y.A.D. 3 Dept.1994)—§ 37.28, n. 44.

Kidd, People v., 76 A.D.2d 665, 431 N.Y.S.2d 542 (N.Y.A.D. 1 Dept.1980)—§ 38.21; § 38.21, n. 22.

Kier v. Sullivan, 888 F.2d 244 (2nd Cir. 1989)—§ 34.11, n. 15, 16.

Kiernan Equipment Corp. v. Centre Lighting Fixture Mfg. Co., 20 A.D.2d 895, 248 N.Y.S.2d 961 (N.Y.A.D. 2 Dept.1964)—§ 10.19, n. 15.

Kihm, People v., 143 A.D.2d 199, 532 N.Y.S.2d 11 (N.Y.A.D. 2 Dept.1988)—§ 38.9, n. 6.

Kilpatrick, People v., 143 A.D.2d 1, 531 N.Y.S.2d 262 (N.Y.A.D. 1 Dept.1988)—§ 38.19; § 38.19, n. 57, 62.

Kilstein, People v., 174 A.D.2d 756, 571 N.Y.S.2d 781 (N.Y.A.D. 2 Dept.1991)—§ 38.21, n. 9; § 38.26, n. 26.

TABLE OF CASES

Kim v. Kim, 215 A.D.2d 356, 626 N.Y.S.2d 217 (N.Y.A.D. 2 Dept.1995)—§ **21.46, n. 6.**

Kim F., In re, 109 A.D.2d 706, 487 N.Y.S.2d 31 (N.Y.A.D. 1 Dept.1985)—§ **38.8, n. 207.**

Kincaid v. Simmons, 66 A.D.2d 428, 414 N.Y.S.2d 407 (N.Y.A.D. 4 Dept.1979)—§ **31.8, n. 1.**

Kinchen, People v., 469 N.Y.S.2d 680, 457 N.E.2d 786 (N.Y.1983)—§ **38.19, n. 16.**

King v. Chmielewski, 556 N.Y.S.2d 996, 556 N.E.2d 435 (N.Y.1990)—§ **16.105, n. 13.**

King v. Collagen Corp., 983 F.2d 1130 (1st Cir.1993)—§ **27.21, n. 1; § 27.48;** § **27.48, n. 1.**

King v. Conde, 121 F.R.D. 180 (E.D.N.Y. 1988)—§ **18.2, n. 8; § 18.65, n. 6.**

King, People v., 160 A.D.2d 531, 554 N.Y.S.2d 517 (N.Y.A.D. 1 Dept.1990)—§ **38.40, n. 1.**

King, People v., 112 A.D.2d 169, 491 N.Y.S.2d 66 (N.Y.A.D. 2 Dept.1985)—§ **38.21, n. 9.**

King, People v., 352 N.Y.S.2d 935, 308 N.E.2d 451 (N.Y.1973)—§ **37.13, n. 7.**

King, State v., 364 N.Y.S.2d 879, 324 N.E.2d 351 (N.Y.1975)—§ **38.3, n. 6;** § **38.10, n. 29.**

King v. State Farm Mut. Auto. Ins. Co., 218 A.D.2d 863, 630 N.Y.S.2d 397 (N.Y.A.D. 3 Dept.1995)—§ **31.11, n. 11.**

King v. Tanner, 142 Misc.2d 1004, 539 N.Y.S.2d 617 (N.Y.Sup.1989)—§ **18.82, n. 7.**

King Service, Inc., State v., 167 A.D.2d 777, 563 N.Y.S.2d 331 (N.Y.A.D. 3 Dept. 1990)—§ **37.30, n. 5.**

Kingston Trust Co. v. State, 57 Misc.2d 55, 291 N.Y.S.2d 208 (N.Y.Sup.1968)—§ **10.21, n. 5.**

Kinnard, People v., 479 N.Y.S.2d 2, 467 N.E.2d 886 (N.Y.1984)—§ **33.55;** § **33.55, n. 1.**

Kinney v. Massachusetts Bonding & Insurance Co., 210 A.D. 285, 206 N.Y.S. 163 (N.Y.A.D. 3 Dept.1924)—§ **30.25, n. 3.**

Kirby, People v., 216 A.D.2d 586, 628 N.Y.S.2d 567 (N.Y.A.D. 2 Dept.1995)—§ **38.8, n. 1.**

Kirkaldy v. Hertz Corp., 221 A.D.2d 599, 634 N.Y.S.2d 177 (N.Y.A.D. 2 Dept. 1995)—§ **37.37, n. 94.**

Kirkwall Corp. v. Sessa, 422 N.Y.S.2d 368, 397 N.E.2d 1172 (N.Y.1979)—§ **12.65, n. 3.**

Kirkwall Corp. v. Sessa, 60 A.D.2d 563, 400 N.Y.S.2d 349 (N.Y.A.D. 1 Dept.1977)—§ **12.58, n. 1.**

Kirschenbaum v. M-T-S Franchise Corp., 77 Misc.2d 1012, 355 N.Y.S.2d 256 (N.Y.City Civ.Ct.1974)—§ **13.51, n. 9, 10.**

Kish v. Board of Educ. of City of New York, 559 N.Y.S.2d 687, 558 N.E.2d 1159 (N.Y. 1990)—§ **30.10, n. 8; § 30.28, n. 9.**

Kisloff on Behalf of Wilson v. Covington, 541 N.Y.S.2d 737, 539 N.E.2d 565 (N.Y. 1989)—§ **38.10, n. 131, 139.**

Kitsalis, Matter of, 11 I & N Dec. 613 (BIA 1966)—§ **19.8, n. 6.**

Kitt, People v., 381 N.Y.S.2d 872, 345 N.E.2d 343 (N.Y.1975)—§ **38.27, n. 5, 27.**

Kittinger v. Churchill, 161 Misc. 3, 292 N.Y.S. 35 (N.Y.Sup.1936)—§ **1.5, n. 4.**

Klapak v. Blum, 491 N.Y.S.2d 615, 481 N.E.2d 247 (N.Y.1985)—§ **39.7, n. 15.**

Klapper, Matter of, N.Y.L.J., 8/9/94, p.26, col.1 (Sup.Ct., Kings County)—§ **22.46, n. 11; § 22.47, n. 4, 9; § 22.48, n. 4, 10, 11; § 22.49, n. 2, 5; § 22.51, n. 3, 5;** § **22.52, n. 2, 3; § 23.76, n. 20.**

Klapper v. Shapiro, 154 Misc.2d 459, 586 N.Y.S.2d 846 (N.Y.Sup.1992)—§ **7.31, n. 6.**

Kleeman v. Rheingold, 598 N.Y.S.2d 149, 614 N.E.2d 712 (N.Y.1993)—§ **28.23;** § **28.23, n. 1, 4.**

Kleeman v. Rheingold, 185 A.D.2d 118, 585 N.Y.S.2d 733 (N.Y.A.D. 1 Dept.1992)—§ **28.23, n. 3.**

Kleet Lumber Co., Inc., Matter of, 197 A.D.2d 576, 602 N.Y.S.2d 663 (N.Y.A.D. 2 Dept.1993)—§ **10.16, n. 4.**

Klein, Matter of, 145 A.D.2d 145, 538 N.Y.S.2d 274 (N.Y.A.D. 2 Dept.1989)—§ **22.40, n. 7.**

Klein v. Civale T Trovato (In re Lionel Corp.), 29 F.3d 88 (2nd Cir.1994)—§ **9.122, n. 1.**

Klein v. Hoffman, 15 A.D.2d 899, 225 N.Y.S.2d 628 (N.Y.A.D. 1 Dept.1962)—§ **28.16, n. 3.**

Klein v. Klein, 112 N.Y.S.2d 546 (N.Y.Sup. 1952)—§ **24.84, n. 3.**

Klein v. Sobol, 167 A.D.2d 625, 562 N.Y.S.2d 856 (N.Y.A.D. 3 Dept.1990)—§ **37.87, n. 21.**

Kleindienst v. Mandel, 408 U.S. 753, 92 S.Ct. 2576, 33 L.Ed.2d 683 (1972)—§ **19.54, n. 14.**

Kleinschmidt Divisions of SCM Corp. v. Futuronics Corp., 382 N.Y.S.2d 756, 346 N.E.2d 557 (N.Y.1976)—§ **39.16, n. 4.**

Kleppe v. Sierra Club, 427 U.S. 390, 96 S.Ct. 2718, 49 L.Ed.2d 576 (1976)—§ **15.3, n. 8.**

Klepper, People v., 302 N.Y.S.2d 555, 250 N.E.2d 51 (N.Y.1969)—§ **33.68, n. 3.**

Klette v. Klette, 167 A.D.2d 197, 561 N.Y.S.2d 580 (N.Y.A.D. 1 Dept.1990)—§ **21.12, n. 2.**

TABLE OF CASES

Kliegl Bros. Universal Elec. Stage Lighting Co., Inc., In re, 189 B.R. 874 (Bkrtcy. E.D.N.Y.1995)—§ **9.29, n. 16.**

Klimek v. Town of Ghent, Columbia County, 71 A.D.2d 359, 423 N.Y.S.2d 517 (N.Y.A.D. 3 Dept.1979)—§ **3.30, n. 14.**

Klingaman v. Miller, 168 A.D.2d 856, 564 N.Y.S.2d 526 (N.Y.A.D. 3 Dept.1990)—§ **16.121, n. 4.**

Klinick v. 66 East 80 Realty Corp., 15 Misc.2d 911, 185 N.Y.S.2d 1009 (N.Y.Sup.1959)—§ **30.5, n. 4.**

Klotz v. Klotz, 176 A.D.2d 661, 575 N.Y.S.2d 663 (N.Y.A.D. 1 Dept.1991)—§ **22.17, n. 3.**

Knapp v. Brown, 45 N.Y. 207 (N.Y.1871)—§ **37.37, n. 92.**

Knapp v. Fasbender, 109 N.Y.S.2d 294 (N.Y.Sup.1951)—§ **3.15, n. 12.**

Knapp, People v., 113 A.D.2d 154, 495 N.Y.S.2d 985 (N.Y.A.D. 3 Dept.1985)—§ **38.8, n. 103.**

Knapp, People v., 455 N.Y.S.2d 539, 441 N.E.2d 1057 (N.Y.1982)—§ **38.19;** § **38.19, n. 131.**

Knickerbocker Agency, Inc. v. Holz, 173 N.Y.S.2d 602, 149 N.E.2d 885 (N.Y. 1958)—§ **31.28, n. 5.**

Knight v. McClean, 148 A.D.2d 421, 538 N.Y.S.2d 576 (N.Y.A.D. 2 Dept.1989)—§ **12.29, n. 5.**

Knight, People v., 534 N.Y.S.2d 353, 530 N.E.2d 1273 (N.Y.1988)—§ **33.68;** § **33.68, n. 17, 18.**

Knight, People v., 116 Misc.2d 581, 455 N.Y.S.2d 971 (N.Y.Co.Ct.1982)—§ **38.52, n. 2.**

Knights, People v., 124 A.D.2d 935, 508 N.Y.S.2d 679 (N.Y.A.D. 3 Dept.1986)—§ **33.57, n. 5.**

Knobloch v. Royal Globe Ins. Co., 381 N.Y.S.2d 433, 344 N.E.2d 364 (N.Y. 1976)—§ **28.44, n. 1;** § **31.17, n. 6.**

Knox, People ex rel. Dawson v., 231 A.D. 490, 247 N.Y.S. 731 (N.Y.A.D. 3 Dept. 1931)—§ **3.17, n. 7, 8.**

Knudsen v. Quebecor Printing (USA) Inc., 792 F.Supp. 234 (S.D.N.Y.1992)—§ **17.34, n. 3;** § **17.35, n. 9.**

Koagel v. Ryan Homes, Inc., 167 A.D.2d 822, 562 N.Y.S.2d 312 (N.Y.A.D. 4 Dept. 1990)—§ **31.18, n. 27.**

Koberstein, People v., 499 N.Y.S.2d 379, 489 N.E.2d 1281 (N.Y.1985)—§ **38.19, n. 108.**

Kock, Matter of, 20 B.R. 453 (Bkrtcy.D.Neb. 1982)—§ **9.205, n. 2.**

Koelbl v. Whalen, 63 A.D.2d 408, 406 N.Y.S.2d 621 (N.Y.A.D. 3 Dept.1978)—§ **4.18, n. 16.**

Koffroth, People v., 159 N.Y.S.2d 828, 140 N.E.2d 742 (N.Y.1957)—§ **38.8, n. 193.**

Kohler v. Ford Motor Credit Co., Inc., 93 A.D.2d 205, 462 N.Y.S.2d 297 (N.Y.A.D. 3 Dept.1983)—§ **7.26, n. 10.**

Kohl Indus. Park Co. v. Rockland County, 710 F.2d 895 (2nd Cir.1983)—§ **14.7, n. 1.**

Kolar v. Kolar, 133 Misc.2d 995, 509 N.Y.S.2d 245 (N.Y.Fam.Ct.1986)—§ **21.7, n. 3.**

Koncelik v. Planning Bd. of Town of East Hampton, 188 A.D.2d 469, 590 N.Y.S.2d 900 (N.Y.A.D. 2 Dept.1992)—§ **16.99, n. 6.**

Konigsberg v. Coughlin, 200 A.D.2d 848, 608 N.Y.S.2d 883 (N.Y.A.D. 3 Dept. 1994)—§ **37.37, n. 82.**

Koopmans v. Farm Credit Services of Mid-America, ACA, 102 F.3d 874 (7th Cir. 1996)—§ **9.166, n. 8.**

Kordonsky v. Andrst, 172 A.D.2d 497, 568 N.Y.S.2d 117 (N.Y.A.D. 2 Dept.1991)—§ **30.13, n. 12.**

Koreag, Controle et Revision S.A., In re, 961 F.2d 341 (2nd Cir.1992)—§ **5.44, n. 2.**

Korkala, People v., 99 A.D.2d 161, 472 N.Y.S.2d 310 (N.Y.A.D. 1 Dept.1984)—§ **18.85, n. 2.**

Korn v. Gulotta, 534 N.Y.S.2d 108, 530 N.E.2d 816 (N.Y.1988)—§ **3.32, n. 20.**

Korobkin v. Chalek, 13 A.D.2d 704, 214 N.Y.S.2d 63 (N.Y.A.D. 2 Dept.1961)—§ **37.37, n. 53.**

Koropoulos v. Credit Bureau, Inc., 734 F.2d 37, 236 U.S.App.D.C. 136 (D.C.Cir. 1984)—§ **7.31, n. 11.**

Kosches v. Nichols, 68 Misc.2d 795, 327 N.Y.S.2d 968 (N.Y.City Civ.Ct.1971)—§ **7.24, n. 5.**

Kosinski v. Consolidated Rail Corp., 195 A.D.2d 964, 601 N.Y.S.2d 754 (N.Y.A.D. 4 Dept.1993)—§ **37.29, n. 15.**

Kostaras v. United Airlines, Inc., 650 F.Supp. 576 (S.D.N.Y.1986)—§ **17.31;** § **17.31, n. 5.**

Koston v. Town of Newburgh, 45 Misc.2d 382, 256 N.Y.S.2d 837 (N.Y.Sup.1965)—§ **16.124, n. 10.**

Koump v. Smith, 303 N.Y.S.2d 858, 250 N.E.2d 857 (N.Y.1969)—§ **26.42, n. 17.**

Kouril v. Bowen, 912 F.2d 971 (8th Cir. 1990)—§ **34.5, n. 6.**

Kovacs v. Briarcliffe School, Inc., 208 A.D.2d 686, 617 N.Y.S.2d 804 (N.Y.A.D. 2 Dept.1994)—§ **17.25, n. 4.**

Kovarsky v. Housing and Development Administration of City of New York, 335 N.Y.S.2d 383, 286 N.E.2d 882 (N.Y. 1972)—§ **3.32, n. 6.**

Kover v. Kover, 328 N.Y.S.2d 641, 278 N.E.2d 886 (N.Y.1972)—§ **37.65, n. 14.**

TABLE OF CASES

Kowalchyk v. Wade Lupe Const. Co., 151 A.D.2d 927, 543 N.Y.S.2d 200 (N.Y.A.D. 3 Dept.1989)—§ **32.26, n. 1.**

Kozlowski v. City of Amsterdam, 111 A.D.2d 476, 488 N.Y.S.2d 862 (N.Y.A.D. 3 Dept.1985)—§ **37.65;** § **37.65, n. 58.**

Kozlowski v. Kozlowski, 221 A.D.2d 322, 633 N.Y.S.2d 523 (N.Y.A.D. 2 Dept. 1995)—§ **21.44, n. 14.**

Kraizberg v. Shankey, 167 A.D.2d 370, 561 N.Y.S.2d 600 (N.Y.A.D. 2 Dept.1990)— § **16.18;** § **16.18, n. 11, 24.**

Kramer, In re, 128 B.R. 707 (Bkrtcy. E.D.N.Y.1991)—§ **9.49, n. 1.**

Kramer v. Belfi, 106 A.D.2d 615, 482 N.Y.S.2d 898 (N.Y.A.D. 2 Dept.1984)— § **28.11, n. 4.**

Kramer, Levin, Nessen, Kamin & Frankel v. International 800 Telecom Corp., 190 A.D.2d 538, 593 N.Y.S.2d 211 (N.Y.A.D. 1 Dept.1993)—§ **28.33;** § **28.33, n. 2.**

Kraus v. Brandstetter, 167 A.D.2d 445, 562 N.Y.S.2d 127 (N.Y.A.D. 2 Dept.1990)— § **17.25;** § **17.25, n. 1, 3.**

Kraus v. New Rochelle Hosp. Medical Center, 216 A.D.2d 360, 628 N.Y.S.2d 360 (N.Y.A.D. 2 Dept.1995)—§ **17.32, n. 4.**

Kravetz v. Plenge, 84 A.D.2d 422, 446 N.Y.S.2d 807 (N.Y.A.D. 4 Dept.1982)— § **16.110, n. 4, 6;** § **16.111, n. 6.**

Kreindler & Kreindler, United States ex rel. v. United Technologies Corp., 985 F.2d 1148 (2nd Cir.1993)—§ **17.64, n. 13.**

Kreiss, In re, 46 B.R. 164 (Bkrtcy.E.D.N.Y. 1985)—§ **9.40, n. 2.**

Kreloff, In re, 65 Misc.2d 692, 319 N.Y.S.2d 51 (N.Y.Sup.1971)—§ **8.37, n. 3.**

Kremer v. Chemical Const. Corp., 456 U.S. 461, 102 S.Ct. 1883, 72 L.Ed.2d 262 (1982)—§ **18.37, n. 9.**

Kremer v. Kremer, 150 A.D.2d 759, 542 N.Y.S.2d 24 (N.Y.A.D. 2 Dept.1989)— § **37.65, n. 74.**

Kreshover v. Berger, 135 A.D. 27, 119 N.Y.S. 737 (N.Y.A.D. 1 Dept.1909)— § **12.62, n. 2.**

Krimko, People v., 145 Misc.2d 822, 548 N.Y.S.2d 615 (N.Y.Vill.Ct.1989)— § **16.125, n. 18.**

Krishnasastry, Matter of, N.Y.L.J., 8/25/95, p. 31, col. 1 (Sup.Ct., Nassau County)— § **22.27, n.1;** § **22.28, n. 20, 21..**

Kristin O., Matter of, 220 A.D.2d 670, 633 N.Y.S.2d 52 (N.Y.A.D. 2 Dept.1995)— § **20.38;** § **20.38, n. 4.**

Kritzik v. Gallman, 41 A.D.2d 994, 344 N.Y.S.2d 107 (N.Y.A.D. 3 Dept.1973)— § **35.15, n. 1.**

Kroh v. T.R.M. Mfg. (In re Conco Bldg. Supplies, Inc.), 102 B.R. 190 (9th Cir. BAP (Cal.) 1989)—§ **9.181, n. 4.**

Kronold v. City of New York, 186 N.Y. 40, 78 N.E. 572 (N.Y.1906)—§ **30.10;** § **30.10, n. 14.**

Kronos, Inc. v. AVX Corp., 595 N.Y.S.2d 931, 612 N.E.2d 289 (N.Y.1993)— § **30.37, n. 4.**

Krouner v. Koplovitz, 175 A.D.2d 531, 572 N.Y.S.2d 959 (N.Y.A.D. 3 Dept.1991)— § **28.24, n. 3.**

Kucinski v. Rish, 108 Misc.2d 188, 437 N.Y.S.2d 250 (N.Y.Sup.1981)—§ **30.11, n. 8.**

Kudon, People v., 173 A.D. 342, 158 N.Y.S. 817 (N.Y.A.D. 3 Dept.1916)—§ **38.10, n. 88.**

Kuhn v. Kuhn, 129 A.D.2d 967, 514 N.Y.S.2d 284 (N.Y.A.D. 4 Dept.1987)— § **37.38, n. 5, 6.**

Kumble v. Windsor Plaza Co., 161 A.D.2d 259, 555 N.Y.S.2d 290 (N.Y.A.D. 1 Dept. 1990)—§ **37.30, n. 9.**

Kuppersmith v. Perales, 145 A.D.2d 1005, 535 N.Y.S.2d 510 (N.Y.A.D. 1 Dept. 1988)—§ **23.86, n. 3.**

Kurnyk, Matter of, 109 Misc.2d 1019, 441 N.Y.S.2d 328 (N.Y.Sup.1981)—§ **22.5, n. 7, 8;** § **22.48, n. 2;** § **22.49, n. 3;** § **22.51, n. 2.**

Kurzius, Inc. v. Village of Upper Brookville, 434 N.Y.S.2d 180, 414 N.E.2d 680 (N.Y. 1980)—§ **16.123, n. 8, 10.**

Kush by Marszalek v. City of Buffalo, 462 N.Y.S.2d 831, 449 N.E.2d 725 (N.Y. 1983)—§ **28.16, n. 6.**

Kustka, Matter of, 163 Misc.2d 694, 622 N.Y.S.2d 208 (N.Y.Sup.1994)—§ **22.8, n. 8;** § **22.12, n. 1;** § **22.33, n. 4;** § **22.38, n. 7;** § **22.47, n. 3.**

Kuwahara v. Bowen, 677 F.Supp. 553 (N.D.Ill.1988)—§ **34.47, n. 9.**

Kuyal, People v., 155 A.D.2d 901, 547 N.Y.S.2d 731 (N.Y.A.D. 4 Dept.1989)— § **38.26, n. 11.**

Kwok, Matter of, 14 I & N Dec. 127 (BIA 1972)—§ **19.11, n. 17.**

Kwong v. Eng, 183 A.D.2d 558, 583 N.Y.S.2d 457 (N.Y.A.D. 1 Dept.1992)— § **13.12, n. 9.**

Kwong v. Eng, 147 Misc.2d 750, 557 N.Y.S.2d 1019 (N.Y.City Civ.Ct.1990)— § **13.12, n. 4.**

Kyle v. Kyle, 156 A.D.2d 508, 548 N.Y.S.2d 781 (N.Y.A.D. 2 Dept.1989)—§ **21.39, n. 9.**

Kyritsis v. Fenny, 66 Misc.2d 329, 320 N.Y.S.2d 702 (N.Y.Sup.1971)—§ **16.124, n. 1, 6.**

L

Laba v. Carey, 327 N.Y.S.2d 613, 277 N.E.2d 641 (N.Y.1971)—§ **12.61;** § **12.61, n. 1;** § **12.64, n. 10.**

TABLE OF CASES

Labate v. Plotkin, 195 A.D.2d 444, 600 N.Y.S.2d 144 (N.Y.A.D. 2 Dept.1993)— § **29.43, n. 1.**

LaBombardi v. LaBombardi, 220 A.D.2d 642, 632 N.Y.S.2d 829 (N.Y.A.D. 2 Dept. 1995)— § **21.53, n. 11, 15.**

La Bounty v. Coughlin, 153 A.D.2d 981, 545 N.Y.S.2d 425 (N.Y.A.D. 3 Dept.1989)— § **4.19, n. 3.**

LaBow v. LaBow, 466 N.Y.S.2d 304, 453 N.E.2d 533 (N.Y.1983)— § **21.71, n. 2.**

La Brake v. Enzien, 167 A.D.2d 709, 562 N.Y.S.2d 1009 (N.Y.A.D. 3 Dept.1990)— § **28.15**; § **28.15, n. 6**; § **28.17**; § **28.17, n. 1.**

Lacaille v. Feldman, 44 Misc.2d 370, 253 N.Y.S.2d 937 (N.Y.Sup.1964)— § **11.9, n. 6.**

Lac D'Amiante du Quebec, Ltee v. American Home Assur. Co., 864 F.2d 1033 (3rd Cir.1988)— § **31.28, n. 4.**

Lachanski v. Craig, 141 A.D.2d 995, 530 N.Y.S.2d 648 (N.Y.A.D. 3 Dept.1988)— § **37.65, n. 47.**

Lachover v. C & A Builders, Inc., 199 A.D.2d 658, 604 N.Y.S.2d 982 (N.Y.A.D. 3 Dept.1993)— § **37.44, n. 15.**

Lackner v. Abrams, 160 Misc. 424, 289 N.Y.S. 1031 (N.Y.Sup.1936)— § **8.35, n. 4.**

Lacks v. Lacks, 390 N.Y.S.2d 875, 359 N.E.2d 384 (N.Y.1976)— § **21.4**; § **21.4, n. 3, 4.**

La Dirot Associates v. Smith, 169 A.D.2d 896, 564 N.Y.S.2d 620 (N.Y.A.D. 3 Dept. 1991)— § **16.78, n. 5.**

Laezza, People v., 143 A.D.2d 289, 532 N.Y.S.2d 178 (N.Y.A.D. 2 Dept.1988)— § **38.8, n. 102.**

Lagano v. Chrysler Corp., 957 F.Supp. 36 (E.D.N.Y.1997)— § **32.15, n. 10.**

Laing, People v., 581 N.Y.S.2d 149, 589 N.E.2d 372 (N.Y.1992)— § **38.10**; § **38.10, n. 163.**

Laino, People v., 218 N.Y.S.2d 647, 176 N.E.2d 571 (N.Y.1961)— § **35.80, n. 2.**

Lake v. Lake, 192 A.D.2d 751, 596 N.Y.S.2d 171 (N.Y.A.D. 3 Dept.1993)— § **21.60, n. 2.**

Lake George Steamboat Co. v. Blais, 330 N.Y.S.2d 336, 281 N.E.2d 147 (N.Y. 1972)— § **3.16, n. 8.**

Lakeland Water Dist. v. Onondaga County Water Authority, 301 N.Y.S.2d 1, 248 N.E.2d 855 (N.Y.1969)— § **4.82, n. 4.**

Laks v. Division of Taxation of Dept. of Taxation and Finance of State, 183 A.D.2d 316, 590 N.Y.S.2d 958 (N.Y.A.D. 4 Dept.1992)— § **2.23, n. 13.**

Lama Holding Co. v. Shearman & Sterling, 758 F.Supp. 159 (S.D.N.Y.1991)— § **28.12**; § **28.12, n. 14.**

La Manga Development Corp., People v., 70 A.D.2d 541, 416 N.Y.S.2d 278 (N.Y.A.D. 1 Dept.1979)— § **38.25, n. 27.**

Lambert v. Genesee Hosp., 10 F.3d 46 (2nd Cir.1993)— § **18.38, n. 8.**

Lamb's Chapel v. Center Moriches Union Free School Dist., 508 U.S. 384, 113 S.Ct. 2141, 124 L.Ed.2d 352 (1993)— § **18.28**; § **18.28, n. 10.**

La Mendola v. Butler, 179 A.D.2d 862, 578 N.Y.S.2d 280 (N.Y.A.D. 3 Dept.1992)— § **17.65, n. 8.**

Lamming v. Galusha, 30 N.Y.S. 767 (N.Y.Sup.1894)— § **1.21, n. 27.**

LaMontagne v. E.I. Du Pont De Nemours & Co., Inc., 41 F.3d 846 (2nd Cir.1994)— § **27.21, n. 1.**

Lamport v. Smedley, 213 N.Y. 82, 106 N.E. 922 (N.Y.1914)— § **37.29**; § **37.29, n. 7.**

Lana Estates, Inc. v. National Energy Reduction Corp., 123 Misc.2d 324, 473 N.Y.S.2d 912 (N.Y.City Civ.Ct.1984)— § **13.6, n. 1, 2**; § **13.18, n. 27**; § **13.22, n. 10**; § **13.47, n. 9**; § **13.56, n. 3.**

Lancaster Silo & Block Co. v. Northern Propane Gas Co., 75 A.D.2d 55, 427 N.Y.S.2d 1009 (N.Y.A.D. 4 Dept.1980)— § **27.11, n. 1**; § **27.12, n. 3**; § **27.37, n. 4.**

Lancellotti v. Howard, 155 A.D.2d 588, 547 N.Y.S.2d 654 (N.Y.A.D. 2 Dept.1989)— § **28.10, n. 9**; § **30.9, n. 12.**

Landahl v. Chrysler Corp., 144 A.D.2d 926, 534 N.Y.S.2d 245 (N.Y.A.D. 4 Dept. 1988)— § **27.34, n. 5.**

Landau v. Landau, 214 A.D.2d 541, 625 N.Y.S.2d 239 (N.Y.A.D. 2 Dept.1995)— § **21.55, n. 6.**

Landes v. Town of North Hempstead, 284 N.Y.S.2d 441, 231 N.E.2d 120 (N.Y. 1967)— § **3.18, n. 4.**

Landesman v. Board of Regents of State of N.Y., 94 A.D.2d 827, 463 N.Y.S.2d 118 (N.Y.A.D. 3 Dept.1983)— § **4.11, n. 2.**

Land for Farmington Access Road of the Town of Farmington, Ontario County, Matter of, 156 A.D.2d 936, 549 N.Y.S.2d 236 (N.Y.A.D. 4 Dept.1989)— § **14.37, n. 3.**

Landmark Ins. Co. v. Beau Rivage Restaurant, Inc., 121 A.D.2d 98, 509 N.Y.S.2d 819 (N.Y.A.D. 2 Dept.1986)— § **26.42, n. 11.**

Landon, People v., 68 Misc.2d 809, 327 N.Y.S.2d 971 (N.Y.Co.Ct.1971)— § **38.55, n. 3.**

Landsing Diversified Properties - II v. First National Bank and Trust Co. (In re Western Real Estate Fund, Inc.), 922 F.2d 592 (10th Cir.1990)— § **9.170, n. 2.**

Lane v. Chantilly Corp., 251 N.Y. 435, 167 N.E. 578 (N.Y.1929)— § **12.60, n. 2.**

TABLE OF CASES

Lane, People v., 93 A.D.2d 92, 460 N.Y.S.2d 926 (N.Y.A.D. 1 Dept.1983)—§ **38.10**; § **38.10, n. 77.**

Langan v. First Trust & Deposit Company, 271 A.D. 951, 68 N.Y.S.2d 448 (N.Y.A.D. 4 Dept.1947)—§ **38.27, n. 5.**

Langenkamp v. Culp, 498 U.S. 42, 111 S.Ct. 330, 112 L.Ed.2d 343 (1990)—§ **9.19, n. 2.**

Langston, People v., 167 Misc.2d 400, 641 N.Y.S.2d 513 (N.Y.Sup.1996)—§ **18.15, n. 7.**

Lanier v. Bowdoin, 282 N.Y. 32, 24 N.E.2d 732 (N.Y.1939)—§ **2.47, n. 2.**

Lansford v. Lansford, 96 A.D.2d 832, 465 N.Y.S.2d 583 (N.Y.A.D. 2 Dept.1983)—§ **21.32, n. 7.**

Lanza v. Wagner, 229 N.Y.S.2d 380, 183 N.E.2d 670 (N.Y.1962)—§ **3.19, n. 5;** § **37.65, n. 66;** § **39.11, n. 12.**

LaPenta v. General Acc. Fire & Life Assur. Corp., 62 A.D.2d 1145, 404 N.Y.S.2d 182 (N.Y.A.D. 4 Dept.1978)—§ **31.20, n. 5.**

Lapidus v. New York City Chapter of the New York State Ass'n For Retarded Children, Inc., 118 A.D.2d 122, 504 N.Y.S.2d 629 (N.Y.A.D. 1 Dept.1986)—§ **17.28, n. 4;** § **17.34, n. 6.**

LaPlanche, People v., 193 A.D.2d 1062, 598 N.Y.S.2d 877 (N.Y.A.D. 4 Dept.1993)—§ **38.28, n. 8.**

LaPorta v. LaPorta, 216 A.D.2d 365, 628 N.Y.S.2d 364 (N.Y.A.D. 2 Dept.1995)—§ **21.54, n. 2;** § **21.55, n. 6.**

Laprease v. Raymours Furniture Co., 315 F.Supp. 716 (N.D.N.Y.1970)—§ **7.24, n. 5.**

Larkin Co. v. Schwab, 242 N.Y. 330, 151 N.E. 637 (N.Y.1926)—§ **16.91, n. 4, 5;** § **16.104, n. 4.**

La Rocca v. Lane, 376 N.Y.S.2d 93, 338 N.E.2d 606 (N.Y.1975)—§ **4.71, n. 4;** § **18.28;** § **18.28, n. 8.**

Larsen v. Roanoke Intern. Agency, 1988 WL 75018 (S.D.N.Y.1988)—§ **31.8, n. 2.**

Larson v. Commssioner, 66 T.C. 159 (U.S.Tax Ct.1976)—§ **2.8, n. 5.**

Lasa Corp., Application of, 27 Misc.2d 495, 203 N.Y.S.2d 731 (N.Y.Sup.1960)—§ **10.90, n. 4.**

LaScala v. D'Angelo, 104 A.D.2d 930, 480 N.Y.S.2d 546 (N.Y.A.D. 2 Dept.1984)—§ **37.67, n. 6.**

Latanowich, In re, 207 B.R. 326 (Bkrtcy. D.Mass.1997)—§ **9.131, n. 3.**

Latella, People v., 112 A.D.2d 321, 491 N.Y.S.2d 771 (N.Y.A.D. 2 Dept.1985)—§ **38.10, n. 89.**

Latham Four Partnership v. SSI Medical Services, Inc., 182 A.D.2d 880, 581 N.Y.S.2d 891 (N.Y.A.D. 3 Dept.1992)—§ **37.20, n. 6.**

Latta, People v., 222 A.D.2d 303, 636 N.Y.S.2d 4 (N.Y.A.D. 1 Dept.1995)—§ **38.19, n. 48.**

Latzer, People v., 528 N.Y.S.2d 533, 523 N.E.2d 820 (N.Y.1988)—§ **38.8, n. 149.**

Laughlin, United States v., 10 F.3d 961 (2nd Cir.1993)—§ **15.25, n. 3.**

Laurenzano v. Laurenzano, 208 A.D.2d 808, 617 N.Y.S.2d 859 (N.Y.A.D. 2 Dept. 1994)—§ **37.83, n. 6.**

Lauria v. New York City Dept. of Environmental Protection, 152 Misc.2d 543, 577 N.Y.S.2d 764 (N.Y.City Civ.Ct.1991)—§ **30.29, n. 5.**

Laurie Marie M. v. Jeffrey T.M., 159 A.D.2d 52, 559 N.Y.S.2d 336 (N.Y.A.D. 2 Dept. 1990)—§ **17.22, n. 1.**

Lavanant v. General Acc. Ins. Co. of America, 212 A.D.2d 450, 622 N.Y.S.2d 726 (N.Y.A.D. 1 Dept.1995)—§ **28.3, n. 1.**

Lavane v. Lavane, 201 A.D.2d 623, 608 N.Y.S.2d 475 (N.Y.A.D. 2 Dept.1994)—§ **21.60, n. 2.**

Lavar C., Matter of, 185 A.D.2d 36, 592 N.Y.S.2d 535 (N.Y.A.D. 4 Dept.1992)—§ **37.22;** § **37.22, n. 9.**

Lavecchia, Matter of, 170 Misc.2d 211, 650 N.Y.S.2d 955 (N.Y.Sup.1996)—§ **22.8, n. 4.**

Laveroni v. Rohl, 175 A.D.2d 163, 572 N.Y.S.2d 52 (N.Y.A.D. 2 Dept.1991)—§ **38.10, n. 130.**

Law, People v., 202 A.D.2d 691, 610 N.Y.S.2d 834 (N.Y.A.D. 2 Dept.1994)—§ **38.28, n. 28.**

Law, People ex rel. Standard Oil Co. of New York v., 237 N.Y. 142, 142 N.E. 446 (N.Y.1923)—§ **35.20, n. 1.**

Lawless v. O'Brien, 222 A.D.2d 657, 636 N.Y.S.2d 92 (N.Y.A.D. 2 Dept.1995)—§ **37.37, n. 11.**

Lawrence v. Adduci, 183 A.D.2d 1009, 583 N.Y.S.2d 663 (N.Y.A.D. 3 Dept.1992)—§ **37.87, n. 21.**

Lawrence v. M.G. Ellis Agency, Inc., 138 A.D.2d 980, 526 N.Y.S.2d 308 (N.Y.A.D. 4 Dept.1988)—§ **37.43, n. 9.**

Lawrence, People v., 630 N.Y.S.2d 963, 654 N.E.2d 1211 (N.Y.1995)—§ **38.19, n. 53.**

Lawrence v. Weinstein, 181 A.D.2d 888, 582 N.Y.S.2d 25 (N.Y.A.D. 2 Dept.1992)—§ **37.87, n. 21.**

Lawrence Paperboard Corp., In re, 52 B.R. 907 (Bkrtcy.D.Mass.1985)—§ **9.105, n. 7.**

Lawrence School Corp. v. Lewis, 174 A.D.2d 42, 578 N.Y.S.2d 627 (N.Y.A.D. 2 Dept. 1992)—§ **16.119, n. 10;** § **16.128, n. 3.**

Lawson v. Lawson, 79 A.D.2d 787, 435 N.Y.S.2d 84 (N.Y.A.D. 3 Dept.1980)—§ **37.30, n. 6.**

TABLE OF CASES

Layer v. City of Buffalo, 274 N.Y. 135, 8 N.E.2d 307 (N.Y.1937)—§ **3.8, n. 5.**

Lazer Elec. Corp. v. Cecchi, 1997 WL 311925 (S.D.N.Y.1997)—§ **28.24, n. 5.**

Lazer on Behalf of Palmieri, People ex rel. v. Warden, New York County Men's House of Detention, 580 N.Y.S.2d 183, 588 N.E.2d 81 (N.Y.1992)—§ **39.3, n. 2.**

Lazich v. Lazich, 189 A.D.2d 750, 592 N.Y.S.2d 415 (N.Y.A.D. 2 Dept.1993)—§ **37.29, n. 46.**

Lazich v. Vittoria & Parker, 189 A.D.2d 753, 592 N.Y.S.2d 418 (N.Y.A.D. 2 Dept. 1993)—§ **28.24; § 28.24, n. 7; § 30.9, n. 35.**

Le, Matter of, 168 Misc.2d 384, 637 N.Y.S.2d 614 (N.Y.Sup.1995)—§ **22.15, n. 2.**

Leach, People v., 203 A.D.2d 484, 611 N.Y.S.2d 17 (N.Y.A.D. 2 Dept.1994)—§ **38.8, n. 20.**

Leahy v. Federal Exp. Corp., 609 F.Supp. 668 (E.D.N.Y.1985)—§ **17.21; § 17.21, n. 3; § 17.26, n. 1.**

Leamy v. Berkshire Life Ins. Co., 383 N.Y.S.2d 564, 347 N.E.2d 889 (N.Y. 1976)—§ **31.18, n. 8.**

Leasco Corp. v. Taussig, 473 F.2d 777 (2nd Cir.1972)—§ **17.27, n. 14.**

Leasco Data Processing Equipment Corp. v. Atlas Shirt Co., 66 Misc.2d 1089, 323 N.Y.S.2d 13 (N.Y.City Civ.Ct.1971)—§ **7.55.**

Leathem v. Research Foundation of City University of New York, 658 F.Supp. 651 (S.D.N.Y.1987)—§ **17.34, n. 3.**

Leatherman v. Tarrant County Narcotics Intelligence and Coordination Unit, 507 U.S. 163, 113 S.Ct. 1160, 122 L.Ed.2d 517 (1993)—§ **18.34, n. 3.**

LeBovici, Matter of, 135 A.D.2d 635, 522 N.Y.S.2d 214 (N.Y.A.D. 2 Dept.1987)—§ **22.46, n. 10.**

Lebovitz, People v., 310 N.Y.S.2d 321, 258 N.E.2d 723 (N.Y.1970)—§ **38.27, n. 31.**

Leder v. Dry Dock Savings Institution, 8 N.Y.S.2d 68 (N.Y.City Ct.1938)—§ **12.64; § 12.64, n. 15.**

Lederer's Will, In re, 4 A.D.2d 623, 168 N.Y.S.2d 343 (N.Y.A.D. 1 Dept.1957)—§ **25.50, n. 5.**

Ledogar v. Giordano, 122 A.D.2d 834, 505 N.Y.S.2d 899 (N.Y.A.D. 2 Dept.1986)—§ **29.16, n. 2; § 30.10, n. 6; § 37.65, n. 35.**

Lee v. Aetna Casualty & Surety Co., 178 F.2d 750 (2nd Cir.1949)—§ **31.12, n. 9.**

Lee v. Bank of New York, 144 A.D.2d 543, 534 N.Y.S.2d 409 (N.Y.A.D. 2 Dept. 1988)—§ **30.8, n. 7.**

Lee v. Caric, 125 A.D.2d 453, 509 N.Y.S.2d 383 (N.Y.A.D. 2 Dept.1986)—§ **5.7, n. 2.**

Lee, People v., 462 N.Y.S.2d 417, 448 N.E.2d 1328 (N.Y.1983)—§ **38.8, n. 192.**

Lee v. Wright, 108 A.D.2d 678, 485 N.Y.S.2d 543 (N.Y.A.D. 1 Dept.1985)—§ **13.53, n. 2, 5.**

Lee County Nat. Bank v. Nelson, 761 S.W.2d 851 (Tex.App.-Beaumont 1988)—§ **7.25, n. 8.**

Leeds Peninsula Pharmacy, Inc. v. American Nat. Fire Ins. Co., 125 A.D.2d 551, 509 N.Y.S.2d 627 (N.Y.A.D. 2 Dept. 1986)—§ **31.29, n. 11.**

Leeling v. Smith (In re Leeling), 129 B.R. 637 (Bkrtcy.D.Colo.1991)—§ **9.193, n. 4.**

Leemon v. Wicke, 216 A.D.2d 272, 627 N.Y.S.2d 761 (N.Y.A.D. 2 Dept.1995)—§ **18.76, n. 3.**

Lee TT. v. Dowling, 642 N.Y.S.2d 181, 664 N.E.2d 1243 (N.Y.1996)—§ **20.118; § 20.118, n. 3.**

LeFevre, People ex rel. Hall on Behalf of Haralambou v., 467 N.Y.S.2d 40, 454 N.E.2d 121 (N.Y.1983)—§ **38.8, n. 74.**

LeFrak v. Commissioner, T.C. Memo. 1993-526 (U.S.Tax Ct.1993)—§ **24.41, n. 2.**

Legal Aid Soc. of Orange County v. Crosson, 784 F.Supp. 1127 (S.D.N.Y.1992)—§ **18.10, n. 13.**

Legal Aid Soc. of Schenectady County, Inc. v. City of Schenectady, 78 A.D.2d 933, 433 N.Y.S.2d 234 (N.Y.A.D. 3 Dept. 1980)—§ **14.28, n. 2.**

Legal Aid Soc. of Sullivan County, Inc. v. Scheinman, 439 N.Y.S.2d 882, 422 N.E.2d 542 (N.Y.1981)—§ **4.75, n. 3.**

Lehr v. Robertson, 463 U.S. 248, 103 S.Ct. 2985, 77 L.Ed.2d 614 (1983)—§ **20.35, n. 3.**

Leibert v. Clapp, 247 N.Y.S.2d 102, 196 N.E.2d 540 (N.Y.1963)—§ **1.101, n. 2.**

Leibring v. Planning Bd. of Town of Newfane, 144 A.D.2d 903, 147 A.D.2d 984, 534 N.Y.S.2d 236 (N.Y.A.D. 4 Dept. 1988)—§ **16.47, n. 6.**

Leicht v. Town of Newburgh Water Dist., 213 A.D.2d 604, 624 N.Y.S.2d 506 (N.Y.A.D. 2 Dept.1995)—§ **30.27, n. 10.**

Leichter v. Barber, 120 A.D.2d 776, 501 N.Y.S.2d 925 (N.Y.A.D. 3 Dept.1986)—§ **4.50, n. 12.**

Leighty v. Brunn, 125 A.D.2d 648, 510 N.Y.S.2d 174 (N.Y.A.D. 2 Dept.1986)—§ **30.6, n. 5.**

Leiva, Matter of, 170 Misc.2d 361, 650 N.Y.S.2d 949 (N.Y.Sup.1996)—§ **22.2, n. 1.**

Lemelle v. Universal Mfg. Corp., 18 F.3d 1268 (5th Cir.1994)—§ **9.169, n. 5.**

Lemir Realty Corp. v. Larkin, 8 A.D.2d 970, 190 N.Y.S.2d 952 (N.Y.A.D. 2 Dept. 1959)—§ **16.92, n. 2.**

TABLE OF CASES

Le Mistral, Inc. v. Columbia Broadcasting System, 61 A.D.2d 491, 402 N.Y.S.2d 815 (N.Y.A.D. 1 Dept.1978)—**§ 30.32, n. 4.**

Lemke v. Lemke, 100 A.D.2d 735, 473 N.Y.S.2d 646 (N.Y.A.D. 4 Dept.1984)—**§ 21.64, n. 2.**

Lemon, People v., 476 N.Y.S.2d 824, 465 N.E.2d 363 (N.Y.1984)—**§ 38.19, n. 27.**

Lencrif Realty Corporation v. Cappelen, 247 N.Y. 566, 161 N.E. 184 (N.Y.1928)—**§ 12.65, n. 8.**

Lenczycki v. Lenczycki, 152 A.D.2d 621, 543 N.Y.S.2d 724 (N.Y.A.D. 2 Dept.1989)—**§ 21.61, n. 5.**

Lenkay Sani Products Corp. v. Benitez, 47 A.D.2d 524, 362 N.Y.S.2d 572 (N.Y.A.D. 2 Dept.1975)—**§ 5.40, n. 3.**

Lennon v. Miller, 66 F.3d 416 (2nd Cir. 1995)—**§ 18.21, n. 2; § 18.22, n. 1; § 18.32, n. 4.**

Lennox, People v., 94 Misc.2d 730, 405 N.Y.S.2d 581 (N.Y.Just.Ct.1978)—**§ 33.26, n. 1.**

Lentini, People v., 221 A.D.2d 474, 633 N.Y.S.2d 569 (N.Y.A.D. 2 Dept.1995)—**§ 38.21, n. 48.**

Lentini Bros. Moving & Storage Co., Inc. v. New York Property Ins. Underwriting Ass'n, 440 N.Y.S.2d 174, 422 N.E.2d 819 (N.Y.1981)—**§ 31.11, n. 11.**

Leonard v. Kinney Systems, Inc., 199 A.D.2d 470, 605 N.Y.S.2d 762 (N.Y.A.D. 2 Dept.1993)—**§ 30.28, n. 17.**

Leonard v. Wargon, 55 N.Y.S.2d 626 (N.Y.Sup.1945)—**§ 8.23, n. 1, 17.**

Leone v. Leewood Service Station, Inc., 212 A.D.2d 669, 624 N.Y.S.2d 610 (N.Y.A.D. 2 Dept.1995)—**§ 15.33, n. 4.**

Leonedas Realty Corp. v. Brodowsky, 115 Misc.2d 88, 454 N.Y.S.2d 183 (N.Y.City Civ.Ct.1982)—**§ 18.50, n. 3.**

Leon's Collision Shop, Inc. v. Adduci, 167 A.D.2d 986, 562 N.Y.S.2d 316 (N.Y.A.D. 4 Dept.1990)—**§ 7.27, n. 15.**

Lerand Corporation v. Meltzer, 267 N.Y. 343, 196 N.E. 283 (N.Y.1935)—**§ 12.4, n. 2.**

Lesch v. Lesch, 201 A.D.2d 900, 608 N.Y.S.2d 39 (N.Y.A.D. 4 Dept.1994)—**§ 21.43, n. 1.**

Leslie v. Lorillard, 110 N.Y. 519, 18 N.E. 363 (N.Y.1888)—**§ 1.12, n. 1.**

Leslie Fay Companies, Inc., In re, 181 B.R. 156 (Bkrtcy.S.D.N.Y.1995)—**§ 9.19, n. 2.**

Leslie Fay Companies, Inc., In re, 175 B.R. 525 (Bkrtcy.S.D.N.Y.1994)—**§ 9.29, n. 14, 19.**

Leslie Fay Companies, Inc., In re, 168 B.R. 294 (Bkrtcy.S.D.N.Y.1994)—**§ 9.86, n. 12.**

Lesman v. Lesman, 88 A.D.2d 153, 452 N.Y.S.2d 935 (N.Y.A.D. 4 Dept.1982)—**§ 21.35, n. 7.**

Lesocovich v. 180 Madison Ave. Corp., 165 A.D.2d 963, 561 N.Y.S.2d 851 (N.Y.A.D. 3 Dept.1990)—**§ 30.15, n. 1.**

Lester (Geddes), People ex rel. v. Warden, 218 A.D.2d 679, 630 N.Y.S.2d 932 (N.Y.A.D. 2 Dept.1995)—**§ 38.8, n. 77.**

Letterio, People v., 266 N.Y.S.2d 368, 213 N.E.2d 670 (N.Y.1965)—**§ 38.27, n. 31.**

Letterlough, People v., 203 A.D.2d 589, 610 N.Y.S.2d 614 (N.Y.A.D. 2 Dept.1994)—**§ 38.27, n. 19.**

Levada v. Board of Zoning Appeals of Incorporated Village of Freeport, 199 A.D.2d 504, 605 N.Y.S.2d 397 (N.Y.A.D. 2 Dept. 1993)—**§ 16.50, n. 5.**

Levandusky v. One Fifth Ave. Apartment Corp., 554 N.Y.S.2d 807, 553 N.E.2d 1317 (N.Y.1990)—**§ 18.47, n. 2.**

Levesque v. Sharpe, 106 Misc.2d 432, 430 N.Y.S.2d 482 (N.Y.City Ct.1980)—**§ 13.44, n. 5.**

Levin v. Murawski, 462 N.Y.S.2d 836, 449 N.E.2d 730 (N.Y.1983)—**§ 4.2, n. 32; § 4.63, n. 2, 4.**

Levin, People v., 119 A.D.2d 698, 500 N.Y.S.2d 819 (N.Y.A.D. 2 Dept.1986)—**§ 38.8, n. 204.**

Levin, People v., 457 N.Y.S.2d 472, 443 N.E.2d 946 (N.Y.1982)—**§ 38.8, n. 153.**

Levine v. Board of Educ. of City of New York, 173 A.D.2d 619, 570 N.Y.S.2d 200 (N.Y.A.D. 2 Dept.1991)—**§ 4.72, n. 6.**

Levine v. Ehrenberg, N.Y.L.J., 6/11/73, p.18, col.2 (App. Term, 1st Dep't)—**§ 13.32, n. 8.**

Levine v. Graphic Scanning Corp., 87 A.D.2d 755, 448 N.Y.S.2d 692 (N.Y.A.D. 1 Dept.1982)—**§ 28.11, n. 4.**

Levine v. Korman, 185 A.D.2d 323, 586 N.Y.S.2d 620 (N.Y.A.D. 2 Dept.1992)—**§ 16.125, n. 12.**

Levine v. Murray Hill Manor Co., 143 A.D.2d 298, 532 N.Y.S.2d 130 (N.Y.A.D. 1 Dept.1988)—**§ 2.92, n. 3.**

Levine, Petition of, 137 A.D.2d 394, 529 N.Y.S.2d 301 (N.Y.A.D. 1 Dept.1988)—**§ 22.61, n. 6.**

Levine v. Town Bd. of Carmel, 34 A.D.2d 796, 311 N.Y.S.2d 691 (N.Y.A.D. 2 Dept. 1970)—**§ 16.50, n. 10.**

Levine v. Town of Oyster Bay, 26 A.D.2d 583, 272 N.Y.S.2d 171 (N.Y.A.D. 2 Dept. 1966)—**§ 16.112, n. 3; § 16.114, n. 6.**

Levine v. Whalen, 384 N.Y.S.2d 721, 349 N.E.2d 820 (N.Y.1976)—**§ 4.68, n. 2.**

Levit v. Ingersoll Rand Financial Corp., 874 F.2d 1186 (7th Cir.1989)—**§ 9.120, n. 5.**

Levo v. Greenwald, 498 N.Y.S.2d 784, 489 N.E.2d 753 (N.Y.1985)—**§ 39.7, n. 2.**

TABLE OF CASES

Levy v. Bronx County Carting Co., 172 A.D.2d 356, 568 N.Y.S.2d 774 (N.Y.A.D. 1 Dept.1991)—§ **30.31, n. 12.**

Levy v. Levy, 185 A.D.2d 15, 592 N.Y.S.2d 480 (N.Y.A.D. 3 Dept.1993)—§ **21.12, n. 2.**

Levy, People v., 179 A.D.2d 730, 578 N.Y.S.2d 637 (N.Y.A.D. 2 Dept.1992)—§ **38.26, n. 29.**

Levy's Estate, In re, 19 A.D.2d 413, 244 N.Y.S.2d 22 (N.Y.A.D. 1 Dept.1963)—§ **28.19; § 28.19, n. 9.**

Lewis v. Equitable Life Assur. Soc. of the United States, 389 N.W.2d 876 (Minn. 1986)—§ **17.25, n. 11.**

Lewis v. Garber, N.Y.L.J., 2/11/92, p.21, col.2 (App.Term, 1st Dep't)—§ **13.64, n. 3; § 13.65, n. 4.**

Lewis v. Levick, 99 A.D.2d 659, 472 N.Y.S.2d 235 (N.Y.A.D. 4 Dept.1984)—§ **13.22, n. 11; § 13.47, n. 10.**

Lewis, People v., 213 A.D.2d 1065, 625 N.Y.S.2d 982 (N.Y.A.D. 4 Dept.1995)—§ **38.25; § 38.25, n. 13.**

Lewis, People v., 329 N.Y.S.2d 100, 279 N.E.2d 856 (N.Y.1972)—§ **38.8, n. 120.**

Lewis, People v., 245 N.Y.S.2d 1, 194 N.E.2d 831 (N.Y.1963)—§ **33.68, n. 10.**

Lewis, People v., 4 Misc.2d 735, 158 N.Y.S.2d 37 (N.Y.Co.Ct.1957)—§ **33.68; § 33.68, n. 5.**

Lewis v. Permut, 66 Misc.2d 127, 320 N.Y.S.2d 408 (N.Y.City Civ.Ct.1971)—§ **18.76, n. 6.**

Lex–56th Corp. v. Morgan, 24 Misc.2d 48, 203 N.Y.S.2d 59 (N.Y.Mun.Ct.1960)—§ **13.27, n. 7.**

L. Fatato, Inc. v. Decrescente Distributing Co., Inc., 86 A.D.2d 600, 446 N.Y.S.2d 120 (N.Y.A.D. 2 Dept.1982)—§ **5.18, n. 2.**

Liberman v. Gallman, 396 N.Y.S.2d 159, 364 N.E.2d 823 (N.Y.1977)—§ **35.103, n. 1.**

Liberman v. Gelstein, 590 N.Y.S.2d 857, 605 N.E.2d 344 (N.Y.1992)—§ **17.25, n. 9; § 18.81, n. 2.**

Librizzi v. Chisholm, 55 A.D.2d 954, 391 N.Y.S.2d 154 (N.Y.A.D. 2 Dept.1977)—§ **38.8, n. 118.**

Licensing by Paolo, Inc. v. Sinatra (In re Paolo Gucci), 105 F.3d 837 (2nd Cir. 1997)—§ **9.64, n. 1.**

Lichtenstein, Matter of Application of, 223 A.D.2d 309, 646 N.Y.S.2d 94 (N.Y.A.D. 1 Dept.1996)—§ **22.28, n. 7.**

Lieb v. Lieb, 53 A.D.2d 67, 385 N.Y.S.2d 569 (N.Y.A.D. 2 Dept.1976)—§ **21.12, n. 2.**

Lieberman v. Templar Motor Co., 236 N.Y. 139, 140 N.E. 222 (N.Y.1923)—§ **30.19, n. 2.**

Liff v. Schildkrout, 427 N.Y.S.2d 746, 404 N.E.2d 1288 (N.Y.1980)—§ **30.15, n. 9.**

Lightfoot v. Union Carbide Corp., 1994 WL 184670 (S.D.N.Y.1994)—§ **17.69, n. 3.**

Lighthouse Shores, Inc. v. Town of Islip, 390 N.Y.S.2d 827, 359 N.E.2d 337 (N.Y. 1976)—§ **3.10, n. 7.**

Lighton v. Madison–Onondaga Mut. Fire Ins. Co., 106 A.D.2d 892, 483 N.Y.S.2d 515 (N.Y.A.D. 4 Dept.1984)—§ **31.18, n. 10.**

Lilley, In re, 185 B.R. 489 (E.D.Pa.1995)—§ **9.207, n. 2.**

Limoli, People v., 4 A.D.2d 1001, 169 N.Y.S.2d 483 (N.Y.A.D. 4 Dept.1957)—§ **38.21; § 38.21, n. 17.**

Lin v. McDonnell Douglas Corp., 574 F.Supp. 1407 (S.D.N.Y.1983)—§ **30.13, n. 10.**

Lincoln v. Austic, 60 A.D.2d 487, 401 N.Y.S.2d 1020 (N.Y.A.D. 3 Dept.1978)—§ **37.22; § 37.22, n. 6.**

Lincoln, People v., 109 A.D.2d 1044, 487 N.Y.S.2d 164 (N.Y.A.D. 3 Dept.1985)—§ **38.3, n. 24.**

Lincoln First Bank, N.A. v. Polishuk, 86 A.D.2d 652, 446 N.Y.S.2d 399 (N.Y.A.D. 2 Dept.1982)—§ **11.54, n. 3, 4.**

Lind v. Lind, 203 A.D.2d 696, 610 N.Y.S.2d 347 (N.Y.A.D. 3 Dept.1994)—§ **13.26, n. 4.**

Lind v. Lind, 89 A.D.2d 518, 452 N.Y.S.2d 204 (N.Y.A.D. 1 Dept.1982)—§ **21.22, n. 5.**

Linda Ann A., Matter of, 126 Misc.2d 43, 480 N.Y.S.2d 996 (N.Y.Sup.1984)—§ **18.71, n. 4.**

Linda F. M., Matter of, 437 N.Y.S.2d 283, 418 N.E.2d 1302 (N.Y.1981)—§ **20.127, n. 1.**

Lindale National Bank v. Artzt (In re Artzt), 145 B.R. 866 (Bkrtcy.E.D.Tex. 1992)—§ **9.130, n. 3.**

Linden, People v., 171 A.D.2d 694, 566 N.Y.S.2d 663 (N.Y.A.D. 2 Dept.1991)—§ **38.34, n. 6.**

Linderberry, People v., 222 A.D.2d 731, 634 N.Y.S.2d 571 (N.Y.A.D. 3 Dept.1995)—§ **38.10, n. 168.**

Lindsay v. Ortho Pharmaceutical Corp., 637 F.2d 87 (2nd Cir.1980)—§ **27.13; § 27.13, n. 14; § 27.15, n. 1.**

Lindsey v. A.H. Robins Co., Inc., 91 A.D.2d 150, 458 N.Y.S.2d 602 (N.Y.A.D. 2 Dept. 1983)—§ **27.39, n. 2.**

Liotta, People v., 580 N.Y.S.2d 184, 588 N.E.2d 82 (N.Y.1992)—§ **33.87, n. 5.**

Lipinski v. Skinner, 781 F.Supp. 131 (N.D.N.Y.1991)—§ **18.85, n. 3.**

Lipkis v. Gilmour, 158 Misc.2d 609, 606 N.Y.S.2d 503 (N.Y.Sup.App.Term 1993)—§ **13.22, n. 3; § 13.47, n. 3.**

TABLE OF CASES

Lipkis v. Pikus, 96 Misc.2d 581, 409 N.Y.S.2d 598 (N.Y.City Civ.Ct.1978)—§ **13.28, n. 9.**

Lipman on Behalf of Castellano, People ex rel. v. Mahoney, 219 A.D.2d 691, 631 N.Y.S.2d 537 (N.Y.A.D. 2 Dept.1995)—§ **38.8, n. 68, 76.**

Lippes v. Bradley, 203 A.D.2d 959, 612 N.Y.S.2d 719 (N.Y.A.D. 4 Dept.1994)—§ **12.65, n. 5.**

Lippman v. Lippman, 192 A.D.2d 1060, 596 N.Y.S.2d 241 (N.Y.A.D. 4 Dept.1993)—§ **21.30, n. 7.**

Lippman v. New York Water Service Corp., 25 Misc.2d 267, 205 N.Y.S.2d 541 (N.Y.Sup.1960)—§ **1.38, n. 14.**

Lipton v. Lipton, N.Y.L.J., 4/11/89, p.25, col.6, (2d Dep't, April 5, 1989)—§ **37.71, n. 4.**

Liquidation of Union Indem. Ins. Co. of New York, Matter of, 200 A.D.2d 99, 611 N.Y.S.2d 506 (N.Y.A.D. 1 Dept.1994)—§ **28.43, n. 5; § 31.28, n. 6.**

Lisa W., Matter of, 159 Misc.2d 359, 604 N.Y.S.2d 474 (N.Y.Fam.Ct.1993)—§ **20.65, n. 2.**

Lischynsky v. Lischynsky, 120 A.D.2d 824, 501 N.Y.S.2d 938 (N.Y.A.D. 3 Dept. 1986)—§ **21.37, n. 8, 11.**

Lisle, Matter of, N.Y.L.J., 8/9/94, p.27, col.4 (Surr.Ct., Nassau County)—§ **22.15, n. 6; § 22.15, n.7; § 22.32, n. 11; § 22.47, n. 8, 14; § 22.75, n. 2; § 22.76, n. 7; § 22.77, n. 2, 5; § 22.78, n. 4, 5.**

Liss v. Manuel, 58 Misc.2d 614, 296 N.Y.S.2d 627 (N.Y.City Civ.Ct.1968)—§ **5.8, n. 4.**

Litman v. Litman, 93 A.D.2d 695, 463 N.Y.S.2d 24 (N.Y.A.D. 2 Dept.1983)—§ **21.35; § 21.35, n. 5.**

Little, People v., 108 A.D.2d 603, 484 N.Y.S.2d 831 (N.Y.A.D. 1 Dept.1985)—§ **38.8, n. 56.**

Little v. Young, 299 N.Y. 699, 87 N.E.2d 74 (N.Y.1949)—§ **16.91, n. 2.**

Little Creek Dev Co. v. Commonwealth Mortgage Corp. (Matter of Little Creek Development Co.), 779 F.2d 1068 (5th Cir.1986)—§ **9.7, n. 9.**

Little Joseph Realty, Inc. v. Town of Babylon, 395 N.Y.S.2d 428, 363 N.E.2d 1163 (N.Y.1977)—§ **3.8, n. 6; § 15.32, n. 22.**

Little Neck Community Ass'n v. Working Organization for Retarded Children, 52 A.D.2d 90, 383 N.Y.S.2d 364 (N.Y.A.D. 2 Dept.1976)—§ **16.122, n. 12.**

Little Reb Auto Corp. v. New York State Dept. of Motor Vehicles, 93 A.D.2d 821, 460 N.Y.S.2d 618 (N.Y.A.D. 2 Dept. 1983)—§ **7.27, n. 15.**

Litz v. Town Bd. of Guilderland, 197 A.D.2d 825, 602 N.Y.S.2d 966 (N.Y.A.D. 3 Dept. 1993)—§ **16.113, n. 4.**

Livant v. Livant, 18 A.D.2d 383, 239 N.Y.S.2d 608 (N.Y.A.D. 1 Dept.1963)—§ **37.28, n. 2.**

Livigne v. D'Agostino Supermarkets, Inc., 207 A.D.2d 776, 616 N.Y.S.2d 515 (N.Y.A.D. 2 Dept.1994)—§ **30.43, n. 2.**

Livreri, Matter of, N.Y.L.J., 2/23/96, p. 30, col. 3 (Sup.Ct., Suffolk County)—§ **22.47, n. 6, 7.**

Lloyd, People v., 192 A.D.2d 411, 596 N.Y.S.2d 688 (N.Y.A.D. 1 Dept.1993)—§ **38.28, n. 21.**

Lloyd Capital Corp. v. Pat Henchar, Inc., 589 N.Y.S.2d 396, 603 N.E.2d 246 (N.Y. 1992)—§ **5.7, n. 1; § 5.10, n. 1, 2, 3, 4.**

L & M Realty v. Village of Millbrook Planning Bd., 207 A.D.2d 346, 615 N.Y.S.2d 434 (N.Y.A.D. 2 Dept.1994)—§ **16.120, n. 6.**

LNC Investments, Inc. v. First Fidelity Bank, Nat. Ass'n, New Jersey, 1995 WL 231322 (S.D.N.Y.1995)—§ **9.102, n. 5.**

L. N. Scott Co., Inc., In re, 13 B.R. 387 (Bkrtcy.E.D.Pa.1981)—§ **9.149, n. 4.**

Loadholt v. Funaway Tours of N.J. Inc., N.Y.L.J., 4/18/1994, p.28, col. 5 (Sup.Ct., N.Y. County)—§ **30.30, n. 21.**

Lo Biondo v. D'Auria, 45 A.D.2d 735, 356 N.Y.S.2d 679 (N.Y.A.D. 2 Dept.1974)—§ **12.5, n. 1.**

Loblaw v. Employers' Liability Assur. Corp., Ltd., 456 N.Y.S.2d 40, 442 N.E.2d 438 (N.Y.1982)—§ **31.4, n. 2.**

Loblaw, Inc. v. Employers' Liability Assur. Corp., 85 A.D.2d 880, 446 N.Y.S.2d 743 (N.Y.A.D. 4 Dept.1981)—§ **31.9, n. 14.**

Lo Bue, Commissioner v., 351 U.S. 243, 76 S.Ct. 800, 100 L.Ed. 1142 (1956)—§ **1.34, n. 61.**

Loccisano, Matter of, N.Y.L.J., 8/28/96, p. 27, col. 6 (Sup.Ct., Suffolk County)—§ **22.40, n. 1.**

Lochner v. Surles, 149 Misc.2d 243, 564 N.Y.S.2d 673 (N.Y.Sup.1990)—§ **17.55, n. 15.**

Locicero, Matter of, 11 I & N Dec.805 (BIA 1966)—§ **19.47, n. 7.**

Lockett v. Juviler, 490 N.Y.S.2d 764, 480 N.E.2d 378 (N.Y.1985)—§ **38.10, n. 130.**

Lockley v. Robie, 276 A.D. 291, 94 N.Y.S.2d 335 (N.Y.A.D. 4 Dept.1950)—§ **1.38, n. 13.**

Lockwood, In re, 14 B.R. 374 (Bkrtcy. E.D.N.Y.1981)—§ **9.107, n. 23.**

Loeb v. Teitelbaum, 112 Misc.2d 1039, 448 N.Y.S.2d 391 (N.Y.City Civ.Ct.1982)—§ **30.40, n. 3.**

TABLE OF CASES

Loeb v. Teitelbaum, 77 A.D.2d 92, 432 N.Y.S.2d 487 (N.Y.A.D. 2 Dept.1980)— § 18.25, n. 1, 5.

Loew v. McNeill, 170 Misc. 647, 10 N.Y.S.2d 658 (N.Y.Sup.1939)—§ 3.19, n. 3.

Lo Gerfo v. Lo Gerfo, 30 A.D.2d 156, 290 N.Y.S.2d 1005 (N.Y.A.D. 2 Dept.1968)— § 37.51, n. 30.

Logue v. Young, 94 A.D.2d 827, 463 N.Y.S.2d 120 (N.Y.A.D. 3 Dept.1983)— § 11.12, n. 1.

Lolik v. Big V Supermarkets, Inc., 631 N.Y.S.2d 122, 655 N.E.2d 163 (N.Y. 1995)—§ 37.65; § 37.65, n. 25, 31.

Lomas Mortg., Inc. v. Louis, 82 F.3d 1 (1st Cir.1996)—§ 9.248, n. 3.

Lombardoni v. Boccaccio, 121 A.D.2d 828, 504 N.Y.S.2d 260 (N.Y.A.D. 3 Dept. 1986)—§ 18.31, n. 2.

Londoner v. City and County of Denver, 210 U.S. 373, 28 S.Ct. 708, 52 L.Ed. 1103 (1908)—§ 4.5, n. 2.

London Terrace Gardens v. Stevens, 159 Misc.2d 542, 605 N.Y.S.2d 814 (N.Y.City Civ.Ct.1993)—§ 13.12, n. 12.

London Typographers, Inc. v. Sava, 628 F.Supp. 570 (S.D.N.Y.1986)—§ 19.33, n. 4.

Long v. Beneficial Finance Co. of New York, 39 A.D.2d 11, 330 N.Y.S.2d 664 (N.Y.A.D. 4 Dept.1972)—§ 7.35; § 7.35, n. 1.

Long v. Forest-Fehlhaber, 448 N.Y.S.2d 132, 433 N.E.2d 115 (N.Y.1982)— § 39.11, n. 4.

Longines-Wittnauer Watch Co. v. Barnes & Reinecke, Inc., 261 N.Y.S.2d 8, 209 N.E.2d 68 (N.Y.1965)—§ 37.32, n. 1.

Long Island Bank v. Knight, 122 Misc.2d 878, 473 N.Y.S.2d 901 (N.Y.Sup.App. Term 1983)—§ 7.26, n. 9.

Long Island Lighting Co. v. Griffin, 272 A.D. 551, 74 N.Y.S.2d 348 (N.Y.A.D. 2 Dept.1947)—§ 16.129, n. 4.

Long Island Lighting Co. v. Steel Derrick Barge FSC 99, 725 F.2d 839 (2nd Cir. 1984)—§ 31.6, n. 8.

Long Island Pine Barrens Soc., Inc. v. Planning Bd. of Town of Brookhaven, 591 N.Y.S.2d 982, 606 N.E.2d 1373 (N.Y. 1992)—§ 15.6, n. 24, 25.

Long Island Pine Barrens Soc., Inc. v. Planning Bd. of Town of Brookhaven, 578 N.Y.S.2d 466, 585 N.E.2d 778 (N.Y. 1991)—§ 15.6; § 15.6, n. 1, 4.

Long Island R. Co. v. Long Island Lighting Co., 103 A.D.2d 156, 479 N.Y.S.2d 355 (N.Y.A.D. 2 Dept.1984)—§ 14.4; § 14.4, n. 8, 9; § 14.12, n. 1; § 14.38, n. 7.

Long Island Trust Co. v. Porta Aluminum, Inc., 63 A.D.2d 670, 404 N.Y.S.2d 682 (N.Y.A.D. 2 Dept.1978)—§ 7.26, n. 9; § 7.55.

Long Island Trust Co. v. Williams, 133 Misc.2d 746, 507 N.Y.S.2d 993 (N.Y.City Civ.Ct.1986)—§ 7.55.

Long Meadow Associates v. City of Glen Cove, 171 A.D.2d 731, 567 N.Y.S.2d 287 (N.Y.A.D. 2 Dept.1991)—§ 3.25, n. 4.

Longo, People v., 30 A.D.2d 828, 293 N.Y.S.2d 704 (N.Y.A.D. 2 Dept.1968)— § 38.8, n. 87.

Long Park v. Trenton-New Brunswick Theatres Co., 297 N.Y. 174, 77 N.E.2d 633 (N.Y.1948)—§ 1.47, n. 3.

Loomis v. Civetta Corinno Const. Corp., 444 N.Y.S.2d 571, 429 N.E.2d 90 (N.Y. 1981)—§ 17.82, n. 21; § 30.3; § 30.3, n. 4.

Loper v. New York City Police Dept., 999 F.2d 699 (2nd Cir.1993)—§ 18.27, n. 7.

Loper v. O'Rourke, 86 Misc.2d 441, 382 N.Y.S.2d 663 (N.Y.Dist.Ct.1976)— § 12.15, n. 6.

Lopes v. Cunnane Development, N.Y.L.J, 3/10/97, p.32, col.2 (Sup.Ct., Westchester County)—§ 32.15, n. 10.

Lopez, People v., 618 N.Y.S.2d 879, 643 N.E.2d 501 (N.Y.1994)—§ 38.10, n. 166; § 38.19, n. 106.

Lopez, People v., 529 N.Y.S.2d 465, 525 N.E.2d 5 (N.Y.1988)—§ 38.8; § 38.8, n. 211.

Lopez v. Precision Papers, Inc., 107 A.D.2d 667, 484 N.Y.S.2d 585 (N.Y.A.D. 2 Dept. 1985)—§ 27.41; § 27.41, n. 5.

Lopez v. Secretary of Dept. of Health and Human Services, 728 F.2d 148 (2nd Cir. 1984)—§ 34.27, n. 5; § 34.44, n. 2.

Lopez, United States v., 514 U.S. 549, 115 S.Ct. 1624, 131 L.Ed.2d 626 (1995)— § 18.33, n. 1.

Lord v. Lord, 124 A.D.2d 930, 508 N.Y.S.2d 676 (N.Y.A.D. 3 Dept.1986)—§ 21.37, n. 8; § 21.42, n. 4.

Lord v. Thomas, 64 N.Y. 107 (N.Y.1876)— § 30.27, n. 4.

Lord v. Yonkers Fuel Gas Co., 99 N.Y. 547, 2 N.E. 909 (N.Y.1885)—§ 1.11, n. 3.

Lorenzato, In re, 147 B.R. 346 (Bkrtcy. S.D.N.Y.1992)—§ 9.205, n. 5.

Lorenzo v. Rivera, 132 Misc.2d 591, 504 N.Y.S.2d 955 (N.Y.City Civ.Ct.1986)— § 13.17, n. 13; § 13.18, n. 29; § 13.43, n. 14.

Loretto v. Teleprompter Manhattan CATV Corp., 459 N.Y.S.2d 743, 446 N.E.2d 428 (N.Y.1983)—§ 14.1, n. 3.

Lorkowski v. J.C. Pitman Co., Inc., 177 A.D.2d 1021, 578 N.Y.S.2d 40 (N.Y.A.D. 4 Dept.1991)—§ 1.10, n. 19.

TABLE OF CASES

Los-Green, Inc. v. Weber, 156 A.D.2d 994, 548 N.Y.S.2d 832 (N.Y.A.D. 4 Dept. 1989)—§ **16.113, n. 13.**

Lotz, People v., 145 A.D.2d 900, 536 N.Y.S.2d 281 (N.Y.A.D. 4 Dept.1988)—§ **33.46, n. 2.**

Loucks v. State, 83 A.D.2d 761, 444 N.Y.S.2d 784 (N.Y.A.D. 4 Dept.1981)—§ **14.81, n. 2.**

Loughlin v. City of New York, 186 A.D.2d 176, 587 N.Y.S.2d 732 (N.Y.A.D. 2 Dept. 1992)—§ **30.30, n. 21.**

Loughry v. Lincoln First Bank, N.A., 502 N.Y.S.2d 965, 494 N.E.2d 70 (N.Y. 1986)—§ **17.25, n. 10; § 17.30; § 17.30, n. 2; § 39.7, n. 6.**

Louis v. Ward, 444 F.Supp. 1107 (S.D.N.Y. 1978)—§ **18.35, n. 2.**

Louise Paris Ltd. v. Those Certain Underwriters at Lloyds, 192 A.D.2d 356, 595 N.Y.S.2d 776 (N.Y.A.D. 1 Dept.1993)—§ **31.24, n. 4.**

Louis Harris and Associates, Inc. v. deLeon, 622 N.Y.S.2d 217, 646 N.E.2d 438 (N.Y. 1994)—§ **4.21, n. 4.**

Louisiana World Exposition v. Federal Ins. Co., 858 F.2d 233 (5th Cir.1988)—§ **9.44, n. 7.**

Loury (Loury), Matter of, N.Y.L.J., 9/23/93, p.26, col.2 (Sup.Ct., Kings County)—§ **22.14, n. 2; § 22.40, n. 7; § 22.41, n. 13; § 22.47, n. 4; § 22.53, n. 2.**

Love, People v., 129 A.D.2d 258, 517 N.Y.S.2d 649 (N.Y.A.D. 4 Dept.1987)—§ **38.10, n. 117.**

Love v. State, 577 N.Y.S.2d 359, 583 N.E.2d 1296 (N.Y.1991)—§ **30.40, n. 13.**

Lovelace v. Ametek, Inc., 111 A.D.2d 953, 490 N.Y.S.2d 49 (N.Y.A.D. 3 Dept. 1985)—§ **27.41; § 27.41, n. 2.**

Lovett, People ex rel. v. Randall, 151 N.Y. 497, 45 N.E. 841 (N.Y.1897)—§ **3.19, n. 3.**

Lovick, Matter of Estate of, 201 A.D.2d 736, 608 N.Y.S.2d 310 (N.Y.A.D. 2 Dept. 1994)—§ **21.32, n. 1.**

Lovisa Const. Co., Inc. v. Facilities Development Corp., 148 A.D.2d 913, 539 N.Y.S.2d 541 (N.Y.A.D. 3 Dept.1989)—§ **37.29, n. 46.**

Low v. Peach, 179 A.D.2d 1094, 579 N.Y.S.2d 506 (N.Y.A.D. 4 Dept.1992)—§ **37.37, n. 91.**

Lowe v. Lowe, 211 A.D.2d 595, 622 N.Y.S.2d 26 (N.Y.A.D. 1 Dept.1995)—§ **21.51, n. 3.**

Lowe v. Quinn, 318 N.Y.S.2d 467, 267 N.E.2d 251 (N.Y.1971)—§ **18.76, n. 2.**

Lowery, People v., 88 N.Y.2d 172, 643 N.Y.S.2d 949, 666 N.E.2d 542 (1996)—§ **18.15, n. 9.**

Lowrance v. Achtyl, 20 F.3d 529 (2nd Cir. 1994)—§ **4.6, n. 9.**

Lowy v. Bay Terrace Co-op, Section VIII, Inc., 698 F.Supp. 1058 (E.D.N.Y.1988)—§ **1.27, n. 5.**

L.R. Dean, Inc. v. International Energy Resources, Inc., 213 A.D.2d 455, 623 N.Y.S.2d 624 (N.Y.A.D. 2 Dept.1995)—§ **8.4, n. 16.**

LTV Corp. v. Aetna Casualty & Surety (In re Chateaugay Corp.), 167 B.R. 776 (S.D.N.Y.1994)—§ **9.170, n. 6.**

Lubeck Realty, Inc. v. Flintkote Co., 170 A.D.2d 800, 565 N.Y.S.2d 922 (N.Y.A.D. 3 Dept.1991)—§ **37.65, n. 45.**

Lucas v. Earl, 281 U.S. 111, 50 S.Ct. 241, 74 L.Ed. 731 (1930)—§ **1.34, n. 20.**

Lucas v. South Carolina Coastal Council, 505 U.S. 1003, 112 S.Ct. 2886, 120 L.Ed.2d 798 (1992)—§ **15.34; § 15.34, n. 1, 3; § 16.22, n. 7, 11.**

Lucas v. State, 44 A.D.2d 633, 353 N.Y.S.2d 831 (N.Y.A.D. 3 Dept.1974)—§ **14.14, n. 15.**

Luciano v. Fanberg Realty Co., 102 A.D.2d 94, 475 N.Y.S.2d 854 (N.Y.A.D. 1 Dept. 1984)—§ **3.30, n. 25.**

Lucy-Turner v. Builders Bonds Ltd., 160 A.D.2d 484, 554 N.Y.S.2d 148 (N.Y.A.D. 1 Dept.1990)—§ **17.34, n. 13.**

Lugar v. Edmondson Oil Co., Inc., 457 U.S. 922, 102 S.Ct. 2744, 73 L.Ed.2d 482 (1982)—§ **18.18, n. 5.**

Lugo v. AIG Life Ins. Co., 852 F.Supp. 187 (S.D.N.Y.1994)—§ **31.15, n. 2.**

Lugo by Lopez v. LJN Toys, Ltd., 146 A.D.2d 168, 539 N.Y.S.2d 922 (N.Y.A.D. 1 Dept.1989)—§ **27.40, n. 8.**

Lugo, People v., N.Y.L.J., 1/10/94, p.25, col.3 (N.Y.C.Crim.Ct.)—§ **33.76, n. 1.**

Luk Lamellen U. Kupplungbau GmbH v. Lerner, 166 A.D.2d 505, 560 N.Y.S.2d 787 (N.Y.A.D. 2 Dept.1990)—§ **28.14; § 28.14, n. 10.**

Lula XX, Matter of, 224 A.D.2d 742, 637 N.Y.S.2d 234 (N.Y.A.D. 3 Dept.1996)—§ **22.41, n. 13.**

Lumber Exchange Bldg. Ltd. Partnership, In re, 968 F.2d 647 (8th Cir.1992)—§ **9.154, n. 3.**

Lund v. Town Bd. of Town of Philipstown, 162 A.D.2d 798, 557 N.Y.S.2d 712 (N.Y.A.D. 3 Dept.1990)—§ **16.85, n. 1.**

Lundgren v. Curiale, 836 F.Supp. 165 (S.D.N.Y.1993)—§ **17.64, n. 6.**

Lunding v. New York Tax Appeals Tribunal, 1998 WL 17105 (1998)—§ **35.18, n. 9.**

Lundquist v. Security Pacific Automotive Financial Services Corp., 993 F.2d 11 (2nd Cir.1993)—§ **7.21, n. 11.**

TABLE OF CASES

Luniewski v. Zeitlin, 188 A.D.2d 642, 591 N.Y.S.2d 524 (N.Y.A.D. 2 Dept.1992)—§ **28.3, n. 1.**

Luria Bros. & Co., Inc. v. Alliance Assur. Co., Ltd., 780 F.2d 1082 (2nd Cir. 1986)—§ **28.38, n. 2;** § **31.15, n. 4.**

Lusenskas v. Axelrod, 183 A.D.2d 244, 592 N.Y.S.2d 685 (N.Y.A.D. 1 Dept.1992)—§ **30.38, n. 3.**

Lutheran Church In America v. City of New York, 359 N.Y.S.2d 7, 316 N.E.2d 305 (N.Y.1974)—§ **16.127, n. 10.**

Lutheran Church in America v. City of New York, 27 A.D.2d 237, 278 N.Y.S.2d 1 (N.Y.A.D. 1 Dept.1967)—§ **4.2, n. 41;** § **4.82, n. 5.**

Lutzken v. City of Rochester, 7 A.D.2d 498, 184 N.Y.S.2d 483 (N.Y.A.D. 4 Dept. 1959)—§ **3.24, n. 2.**

Lutz' Will, In re, 202 Misc. 903, 112 N.Y.S.2d 640 (N.Y.Sur.1952)—§ **2.51, n. 9.**

L.W.C. Agency, Inc. v. St. Paul Fire and Marine Ins. Co., 125 A.D.2d 371, 509 N.Y.S.2d 97 (N.Y.A.D. 2 Dept.1986)—§ **17.29, n. 1.**

Lycee Francais De New York, Application of, 26 Misc.2d 374, 204 N.Y.S.2d 490 (N.Y.Sup.1960)—§ **10.15, n. 1.**

Lyde, People v., 98 A.D.2d 650, 469 N.Y.S.2d 716 (N.Y.A.D. 1 Dept.1983)—§ **38.64, n. 1.**

Lynch III Properties Corp., In re, 125 B.R. 857 (Bkrtcy.E.D.N.Y.1991)—§ **10.59, n. 3.**

Lyons v. Donnelly, 204 A.D.2d 696, 612 N.Y.S.2d 246 (N.Y.A.D. 2 Dept.1994)—§ **28.13, n. 9.**

Lyons v. Goldstein, 290 N.Y. 19, 47 N.E.2d 425 (N.Y.1943)—§ **38.9;** § **38.9, n. 1;** § **38.10, n. 130;** § **38.34, n. 1.**

Lyons v. Legal Aid Soc., 68 F.3d 1512 (2nd Cir.1995)—§ **17.43, n. 2.**

Lyons, People ex rel. Siegel v., 201 A.D. 530, 194 N.Y.S. 484 (N.Y.A.D. 1 Dept. 1922)—§ **1.21, n. 9.**

M

M, Matter of, I & N Dec. 118 (BIA 1959)—§ **19.11, n. 15.**

Mabrey, People v., 188 A.D.2d 1086, 592 N.Y.S.2d 1014 (N.Y.A.D. 4 Dept.1992)—§ **38.10, n. 164.**

MacArthur Co. v. Johns–Manville Corp., 837 F.2d 89 (2nd Cir.1988)—§ **9.170, n. 6.**

Macchio v. Planning Bd. of Town of East Hampton, 152 Misc.2d 622, 578 N.Y.S.2d 355 (N.Y.Sup.1991)—§ **16.125, n. 11.**

MacCracken, People ex rel. v. Miller, 291 N.Y. 55, 50 N.E.2d 542 (N.Y.1943)—§ **38.20;** § **38.20, n. 10.**

MacDonald v. Carpenter & Pelton, Inc., 31 A.D.2d 952, 298 N.Y.S.2d 780 (N.Y.A.D. 2 Dept.1969)—§ **31.6, n. 5.**

Macerola, People v., 417 N.Y.S.2d 908, 391 N.E.2d 990 (N.Y.1979)—§ **38.19, n. 119.**

MacGregor v. Watts, 254 A.D. 904, 5 N.Y.S.2d 525 (N.Y.A.D. 2 Dept.1938)—§ **30.18, n. 7, 8.**

Machado, People v., 659 N.Y.S.2d 242, 681 N.E.2d 409 (N.Y.1997)—§ **38.10, n. 95.**

Machinery Rental, Inc. v. Herpel (Matter of Multiponics, Inc.), 622 F.2d 709 (5th Cir. 1980)—§ **9.107, n. 16.**

Mack v. Mack, 130 A.D.2d 632, 515 N.Y.S.2d 560 (N.Y.A.D. 2 Dept.1987)—§ **37.23, n. 5.**

Mack Financial Corp. v. Knoud, 98 A.D.2d 713, 469 N.Y.S.2d 116 (N.Y.A.D. 2 Dept. 1983)—§ **7.26, n. 9.**

Mackston v. State, 126 A.D.2d 710, 510 N.Y.S.2d 912 (N.Y.A.D. 2 Dept.1987)—§ **37.29, n. 30, 40.**

Macmillan, Inc. v. Federal Ins. Co., 764 F.Supp. 38 (S.D.N.Y.1991)—§ **31.21, n. 5.**

MacNair v. Salamon, 199 A.D.2d 170, 606 N.Y.S.2d 152 (N.Y.A.D. 1 Dept.1993)—§ **37.65, n. 53.**

MacPherson v. Buick Motor Co., 217 N.Y. 382, 111 N.E. 1050 (N.Y.1916)—§ **27.3;** § **27.3, n. 8.**

Macy, People v., 100 A.D.2d 557, 473 N.Y.S.2d 261 (N.Y.A.D. 2 Dept.1984)—§ **38.8, n. 183.**

Madany v. Smith, 696 F.2d 1008, 225 U.S.App.D.C. 53 (D.C.Cir.1983)—§ **19.33, n. 4.**

Maddox, People v., 216 A.D.2d 329, 627 N.Y.S.2d 988 (N.Y.A.D. 2 Dept.1995)—§ **38.8, n. 150.**

Madison Hotel Associates, Matter of, 749 F.2d 410 (7th Cir.1984)—§ **9.160, n. 2.**

Maffei v. Kolaeton Industry, Inc., 164 Misc.2d 547, 626 N.Y.S.2d 391 (N.Y.Sup. 1995)—§ **17.58, n. 3.**

Mahal, Matter of, 12 I & N Dec. 409 (BIA 1967)—§ **19.11, n. 2.**

Maher, Matter of, 207 A.D.2d 133, 621 N.Y.S.2d 617 (N.Y.A.D. 2 Dept.1994)—§ **22.8, n. 4, 5;** § **22.12, n. 1, 5;** § **22.13, n. 1, 8;** § **22.14, n. 5;** § **22.32;** § **22.32, n. 4, 5, 12;** § **22.33, n. 1;** § **22.38, n. 4.**

Maher, Matter of, N.Y.L.J., 9/7/93, p.24, col.6 (Sup.Ct., Kings County)—§ **22.14, n. 3.**

Mahlmann, In re, 149 B.R. 866 (N.D.Ill. 1993)—§ **9.22, n. 7.**

TABLE OF CASES

Mahoney v. Mahoney, 131 A.D.2d 822, 517 N.Y.S.2d 184 (N.Y.A.D. 2 Dept.1987)—§ 21.32, n. 6.

Mahoney v. O'Shea Funeral Homes, Inc., 408 N.Y.S.2d 470, 380 N.E.2d 297 (N.Y. 1978)—§ 16.110, n. 5, 7; § 16.111, n. 5.

Mahoney, People ex rel. Lipman on Behalf of Castellano v., 219 A.D.2d 691, 631 N.Y.S.2d 537 (N.Y.A.D. 2 Dept.1995)—§ 38.8, n. 68, 76.

Mahoney v. Temporary Com'n of Investigation of State of N.Y., 165 A.D.2d 233, 565 N.Y.S.2d 870 (N.Y.A.D. 3 Dept. 1991)—§ 17.31, n. 3.

Maiore v. City of Buffalo, 78 A.D.2d 979, 433 N.Y.S.2d 674 (N.Y.A.D. 4 Dept. 1980)—§ 37.28, n. 26.

Mair Realty Corp. v. Siegel, 34 A.D.2d 735, 310 N.Y.S.2d 680 (N.Y.A.D. 2 Dept. 1970)—§ 16.128, n. 7.

Maitrejean v. Levon Properties Corp., 87 A.D.2d 605, 448 N.Y.S.2d 46 (N.Y.A.D. 2 Dept.1982)—§ 30.31, n. 10.

Majauskas v. Majauskas, 474 N.Y.S.2d 699, 463 N.E.2d 15 (N.Y.1984)—§ 21.35; § 21.35, n. 3; § 21.38; § 21.38, n. 1; § 21.42, n. 2; § 21.43, n. 5.

Majchrzak v. Zawadski, 275 A.D. 1066, 92 N.Y.S.2d 193 (N.Y.A.D. 4 Dept.1949)—§ 37.3, n. 15.

Majer v. Metropolitan Trans. Authority, 1990 WL 212928 (S.D.N.Y.1990)—§ 17.32, n. 4.

Majer v. Schmidt, 169 A.D.2d 501, 564 N.Y.S.2d 722 (N.Y.A.D. 1 Dept.1991)—§ 28.22; § 28.22, n. 4.

Majewski v. Broadalbin-Perth Cent. School Dist., 169 Misc.2d 429, 653 N.Y.S.2d 822 (N.Y.Sup.1996)—§ 32.15, n. 9.

Mako, Inc., In re, 102 B.R. 809 (Bkrtcy. E.D.Okla.1988)—§ 9.138, n. 1.

Malacarne v. City of Yonkers Parking Authority, 391 N.Y.S.2d 402, 359 N.E.2d 992 (N.Y.1976)—§ 32.19, n. 2.

Malamut v. Sassower, P.C., 171 A.D.2d 780, 567 N.Y.S.2d 499 (N.Y.A.D. 2 Dept. 1991)—§ 28.19, n. 1.

Maldini v. Ambro, 369 N.Y.S.2d 385, 330 N.E.2d 403 (N.Y.1975)—§ 16.8, n. 6; § 16.120, n. 7.

Maldonado, People v., 152 A.D.2d 707, 544 N.Y.S.2d 165 (N.Y.A.D. 2 Dept.1989)—§ 38.21, n. 4, 19.

Maldonado v. WABC Towing Corp., 121 A.D.2d 517, 504 N.Y.S.2d 21 (N.Y.A.D. 2 Dept.1986)—§ 30.15, n. 12.

Maldonado De Vasquez v. Ilchert, 614 F.Supp. 538 (N.D.Cal.1985)—§ 19.48, n. 4.

Male Infant B., Matter of, 96 A.D.2d 1055, 466 N.Y.S.2d 482 (N.Y.A.D. 2 Dept. 1983)—§ 20.44; § 20.44, n. 2; § 20.46, n. 1; § 20.78; § 20.78, n. 2; § 37.89, n. 6.

Mallan v. Samowich, 94 A.D.2d 249, 464 N.Y.S.2d 122 (N.Y.A.D. 1 Dept.1983)—§ 8.4, n. 19; § 8.16, n. 2.

Malley v. Briggs, 475 U.S. 335, 106 S.Ct. 1092, 89 L.Ed.2d 271 (1986)—§ 18.32, n. 4.

Maloney v. Rincon, 153 Misc.2d 162, 581 N.Y.S.2d 120 (N.Y.City Civ.Ct.1992)—§ 7.29; § 7.29, n. 6.

Malverne, Matter of Village of, 70 A.D.2d 920, 418 N.Y.S.2d 93 (N.Y.A.D. 2 Dept. 1979)—§ 14.26, n. 7.

Mancini v. Mancini, 216 A.D.2d 535, 628 N.Y.S.2d 803 (N.Y.A.D. 2 Dept.1995)—§ 21.34, n. 3.

Mancini v. Mormile, 229 A.D.2d 542, 645 N.Y.S.2d 837 (N.Y.A.D. 2 Dept.1996)—§ 37.19, n. 32.

Mancini-Ciolo, Inc. v. Scaramellino, 118 A.D.2d 761, 500 N.Y.S.2d 276 (N.Y.A.D. 2 Dept.1986)—§ 12.29, n. 2.

Mancuso v. Russo, 132 A.D.2d 533, 517 N.Y.S.2d 539 (N.Y.A.D. 2 Dept.1987)—§ 18.76, n. 7.

Mandel v. Brooklyn Nat. League Baseball Club, 179 Misc. 27, 37 N.Y.S.2d 152 (N.Y.Sup.1942)—§ 18.55, n. 2.

Mandel v. Liebman, 303 N.Y. 88, 100 N.E.2d 149 (N.Y.1951)—§ 5.12, n. 1.

Mandigo, People v., 176 A.D.2d 386, 574 N.Y.S.2d 92 (N.Y.A.D. 3 Dept.1991)—§ 33.45, n. 5.

Manekas v. Allied Discount Co., 6 Misc.2d 1079, 166 N.Y.S.2d 366 (N.Y.Sup. 1957)—§ 30.32, n. 4.

Mangan v. Terminal Transp. System, 157 Misc. 627, 284 N.Y.S. 183 (N.Y.Sup. 1935)—§ 2.23, n. 18.

Mangno v. Mangno, 206 A.D.2d 936, 615 N.Y.S.2d 181 (N.Y.A.D. 4 Dept.1994)—§ 28.15; § 28.15, n. 7.

Manhattan and Bronx Surface Transit Operating Authority v. New York State Executive Dept., 220 A.D.2d 668, 632 N.Y.S.2d 642 (N.Y.A.D. 2 Dept.1995)—§ 37.87, n. 28.

Manhattan Bldg. Co. v. Commissioner, 27 T.C. 1032 (Tax Ct.1957)—§ 1.34, n. 30.

Manhattan Embassy Co. v. Embassy Parking Corp., 164 Misc.2d 977, 627 N.Y.S.2d 245 (N.Y.City Civ.Ct.1995)—§ 13.8, n. 3.

Manhattan Life Ins. Co. v. Wall Investing Corporation, 131 Misc. 363, 226 N.Y.S. 717 (N.Y.Sup.1928)—§ 12.18, n. 1.

Manhattan Mansions v. Moe's Pizza, 149 Misc.2d 43, 561 N.Y.S.2d 331 (N.Y.City Civ.Ct.1990)—§ 13.31, n. 7.

Manhattan Pizza Hut, Inc. v. New York State Human Rights Appeal Bd., 434

TABLE OF CASES

N.Y.S.2d 961, 415 N.E.2d 950 (N.Y. 1980)—§ **17.48, n. 3.**

Manhattan Theatre Club, Inc. v. Bohemian Benev. and Literary Ass'n of City of New York, 102 A.D.2d 788, 478 N.Y.S.2d 274 (N.Y.A.D. 1 Dept.1984)—§ **12.5, n. 3.**

Manley v. Pandick Press, Inc., 72 A.D.2d 452, 424 N.Y.S.2d 902 (N.Y.A.D. 1 Dept. 1980)—§ **17.29, n. 4.**

Manniello v. Dea, 92 A.D.2d 426, 461 N.Y.S.2d 582 (N.Y.A.D. 3 Dept.1983)—§ **30.25, n. 1.**

Manning v. Manning, 97 A.D.2d 910, 470 N.Y.S.2d 744 (N.Y.A.D. 3 Dept.1983)—§ **13.63, n. 5.**

Manno v. Manno, 224 A.D.2d 395, 637 N.Y.S.2d 743 (N.Y.A.D. 2 Dept.1996)—§ **21.55, n. 5; § 21.69, n. 1; § 21.72, n. 6.**

Manocherian v. Lenox Hill Hosp., 618 N.Y.S.2d 857, 643 N.E.2d 479 (N.Y. 1994)—§ **15.34, n. 12.**

Manor Inv. Co., Inc. v. F.W. Woolworth, Inc., 159 Cal.App.3d 586, 206 Cal.Rptr. 37 (Cal.App. 1 Dist.1984)—§ **17.29, n. 2.**

Manson v. Curtis, 223 N.Y. 313, 119 N.E. 559 (N.Y.1918)—§ **1.47, n. 3.**

Mansour v. Abrams, 120 A.D.2d 933, 502 N.Y.S.2d 877 (N.Y.A.D. 4 Dept.1986)—§ **17.29, n. 10.**

Manswell, People v., 223 A.D.2d 561, 636 N.Y.S.2d 383 (N.Y.A.D. 2 Dept.1996)—§ **38.28, n. 15.**

Mante v. Mante, 34 A.D.2d 134, 309 N.Y.S.2d 944 (N.Y.A.D. 2 Dept.1970)—§ **21.21, n. 3.**

Manuel S. (Renee M.), Matter of, 216 A.D.2d 569, 628 N.Y.S.2d 578 (N.Y.A.D. 2 Dept.1995)—§ **37.37, n. 17.**

Manufacturers Hanover Trust Co. v. 400 Garden City Associates, 150 Misc.2d 247, 568 N.Y.S.2d 505 (N.Y.Sup.1991)—§ **11.6, n. 2.**

Manufacturers Hanover Trust Co. v. Goldstein, 25 A.D.2d 405, 270 N.Y.S.2d 261 (N.Y.A.D. 1 Dept.1966)—§ **7.55.**

Manufacturers Nat. Bank v. Auto Specialities Mfg. (In re Auto Specialties Mfg. Co.), 18 F.3d 358 (6th Cir.1994)—§ **9.107, n. 24.**

Manufacturers Trust Co. v. Stehle, 1 A.D.2d 471, 151 N.Y.S.2d 384 (N.Y.A.D. 1 Dept. 1956)—§ **7.28, n. 7; § 7.59.**

Manville Corp. v. The Equity Security Holders Committee (In re Johns–Manville Corp.), 801 F.2d 60 (2nd Cir.1986)—§ **9.28, n. 6.**

Many v. Village of Sharon Springs Bd. of Trustees, 218 A.D.2d 845, 629 N.Y.S.2d 868 (N.Y.A.D. 3 Dept.1995)—§ **16.48, n. 3.**

Manzo, People v., 99 A.D.2d 817, 472 N.Y.S.2d 151 (N.Y.A.D. 2 Dept.1984)—§ **38.8, n. 157.**

Map Intern., Inc., In re, 105 B.R. 5 (Bkrtcy. E.D.Pa.1989)—§ **9.43, n. 15; § 9.46, n. 1.**

Mapp v. Ohio, 367 U.S. 643, 81 S.Ct. 1684, 6 L.Ed.2d 1081 (1961)—§ **33.27, n. 6; § 38.10, n. 151.**

Marc v. Pinkard, 133 Misc. 83, 230 N.Y.S. 765 (N.Y.Mun.Ct.1928)—§ **8.9, n. 3.**

Marchant v. Mead–Morrison Mfg. Co., 252 N.Y. 284, 169 N.E. 386 (N.Y.1929)—§ **39.19, n. 18.**

Marchetti v. United States, 390 U.S. 39, 88 S.Ct. 697, 19 L.Ed.2d 889 (1968)—§ **4.64, n. 5.**

Marchione v. State, 194 A.D.2d 851, 598 N.Y.S.2d 592 (N.Y.A.D. 3 Dept.1993)—§ **29.14, n. 4.**

March 1975 Monroe County Grand Jury Report, Matter of, 52 A.D.2d 745, 382 N.Y.S.2d 195 (N.Y.A.D. 4 Dept.1976)—§ **38.11, n. 17.**

Marcus, In re, 45 B.R. 338 (S.D.N.Y.1984)—§ **9.205, n. 2.**

Marcus v. Bowen, 696 F.Supp. 364 (N.D.Ill. 1988)—§ **34.14, n. 2.**

Marcus v. Marcus, 135 A.D.2d 216, 525 N.Y.S.2d 238 (N.Y.A.D. 2 Dept.1988)—§ **21.39, n. 3; § 21.43; § 21.43, n. 17.**

Marder's Nurseries, Inc. v. Hopping, 171 A.D.2d 63, 573 N.Y.S.2d 990 (N.Y.A.D. 2 Dept.1991)—§ **12.4, n. 2.**

Margolies v. Lawrence, 67 Misc.2d 468, 324 N.Y.S.2d 418 (N.Y.City Civ.Ct.1971)—§ **13.17, n. 12; § 13.18, n. 28; § 13.43, n. 13.**

Margulis v. Teichman, 125 Misc.2d 729, 479 N.Y.S.2d 953 (N.Y.Sur.1984)—§ **24.61, n. 3.**

Maria E v. Anthony E, 125 Misc.2d 933, 481 N.Y.S.2d 227 (N.Y.Fam.Ct.1984)—§ **18.68, n. 2.**

Maria Elizabeth A., In re, 219 A.D.2d 503, 631 N.Y.S.2d 334 (N.Y.A.D. 1 Dept. 1995)—§ **20.21; § 20.21, n. 2.**

Marill Alarm Systems, Inc., In re, 100 B.R. 606 (Bkrtcy.S.D.Fla.1989)—§ **9.174, n. 3.**

Marine Bank v. Weaver, 455 U.S. 551, 102 S.Ct. 1220, 71 L.Ed.2d 409 (1982)—§ **2.106, n. 10.**

Marine Management, Inc. v. Seco Management, Inc., 176 A.D.2d 252, 574 N.Y.S.2d 207 (N.Y.A.D. 2 Dept.1991)—§ **8.6, n. 4.**

Marine Midland Bank v. John E. Russo Produce Co., Inc., 427 N.Y.S.2d 961, 405 N.E.2d 205 (N.Y.1980)—§ **37.28, n. 43; § 39.7, n. 21.**

TABLE OF CASES

Marine Midland Bank v. Marcal Enterprises, Inc., 91 Misc.2d 810, 398 N.Y.S.2d 782 (N.Y.Co.Ct.1977)—§ **11.15, n. 3.**

Marine Midland Bank–Central v. Watkins, 89 Misc.2d 949, 392 N.Y.S.2d 819 (N.Y.Sup.1977)—§ **7.26, n. 9.**

Marine Midland Bank, N.A. v. Mitchell, 100 A.D.2d 733, 473 N.Y.S.2d 664 (N.Y.A.D. 4 Dept.1984)—§ **11.37, n. 4.**

Marine Midland Bank, N.A. v. New York State Div. of Human Rights, 552 N.Y.S.2d 65, 551 N.E.2d 558 (N.Y. 1989)—§ **17.68, n. 5.**

Marine Midland Trust Co. of Western New York v. Halik, 28 A.D.2d 1077, 285 N.Y.S.2d 136 (N.Y.A.D. 4 Dept.1967)—§ **5.28, n. 1.**

Marino Industries Corp. v. Kahn Lumber & Millwork Co., Inc., 70 A.D.2d 629, 416 N.Y.S.2d 642 (N.Y.A.D. 2 Dept.1979)—§ **17.29, n. 13.**

Markel v. Spencer, 5 A.D.2d 400, 171 N.Y.S.2d 770 (N.Y.A.D. 4 Dept.1958)—§ **27.34, n. 3.**

Market Square Inn, Inc., In re, 163 B.R. 64 (Bkrtcy.W.D.Pa.1994)—§ **9.170, n. 4.**

Markowitz v. New York Racing Assn., N.Y.L.J., 1/9/86, p.14, col.3 (Appellate Term Second and Eleventh Judicial Districts)—§ **37.99, n. 3.**

Markowitz v. Town Bd. of Town of Oyster Bay, 200 A.D.2d 673, 606 N.Y.S.2d 705 (N.Y.A.D. 2 Dept.1994)—§ **16.91, n. 8.**

Marks Polarized Corp. v. Solinger & Gordon, 124 Misc.2d 266, 476 N.Y.S.2d 743 (N.Y.Sup.1984)—§ **28.4, n. 2.**

Markus, In re Estate of, 188 A.D.2d 361, 591 N.Y.S.2d 35 (N.Y.A.D. 1 Dept. 1992)—§ **24.12, n. 1.**

Marmol, Matter of, 168 Misc.2d 845, 640 N.Y.S.2d 969 (N.Y.Sup.1996)—§ **22.8, n. 4.**

Mar Oil, S.A. v. Morrissey, 982 F.2d 830 (2nd Cir.1993)—§ **28.30, n. 2.**

Maroth v. Maroth, 64 N.Y.S.2d 260 (N.Y.Sup.1946)—§ **21.26, n. 10.**

Marr v. Forrest, 208 A.D.2d 908, 617 N.Y.S.2d 881 (N.Y.A.D. 2 Dept.1994)—§ **30.15, n. 13.**

Marriott v. Shaw, 151 Misc.2d 938, 574 N.Y.S.2d 477 (N.Y.City Civ.Ct.1991)—§ **13.33, n. 7.**

Mars Associates, Inc. v. Facilities Development Corp., 124 A.D.2d 291, 508 N.Y.S.2d 87 (N.Y.A.D. 3 Dept.1986)—§ **30.39, n. 9.**

Mars Associates, Inc. v. New York City Educational Const. Fund, 126 A.D.2d 178, 513 N.Y.S.2d 125 (N.Y.A.D. 1 Dept. 1987)—§ **37.37, n. 35.**

Marsch v. Marsch, (In re Marsch) 36 F.3d 825 (9th Cir.1994)—§ **9.7, n. 9.**

Marsh v. Peckham, 245 A.D. 14, 280 N.Y.S. 44 (N.Y.A.D. 4 Dept.1935)—§ **37.96, n. 11.**

Marsh, People v., 127 A.D.2d 945, 512 N.Y.S.2d 545 (N.Y.A.D. 3 Dept.1987)—§ **38.12, n. 9;** § **38.14, n. 2.**

Marshak v. Green, 746 F.2d 927 (2nd Cir. 1984)—§ **8.19, n. 10.**

Marshack v. Mesa Valley Farms (In re Ridge II), 158 B.R. 1016 (Bkrtcy. C.D.Cal.1993)—§ **9.194, n. 1.**

Marshall v. Barlow's, Inc., 436 U.S. 307, 98 S.Ct. 1816, 56 L.Ed.2d 305 (1978)—§ **4.62, n. 8.**

Marshall v. Town of Pittsford, 105 A.D.2d 1140, 482 N.Y.S.2d 619 (N.Y.A.D. 4 Dept.1984)—§ **14.26, n. 5.**

Marshall v. Village of Wappingers Falls, 28 A.D.2d 542, 279 N.Y.S.2d 654 (N.Y.A.D. 2 Dept.1967)—§ **16.15, n. 8;** § **16.61, n. 2.**

Martin v. City of Albany, 396 N.Y.S.2d 612, 364 N.E.2d 1304 (N.Y.1977)—§ **18.25, n. 1.**

Martin v. Hacker, 607 N.Y.S.2d 598, 628 N.E.2d 1308 (N.Y.1993)—§ **27.13;** § **27.13, n. 10;** § **27.14, n. 3, 4;** § **27.15, n. 3.**

Martin v. Herzog, 228 N.Y. 164, 126 N.E. 814 (N.Y.1920)—§ **27.43, n. 3.**

Martin v. New York State Dept. of Mental Hygiene, 588 F.2d 371 (2nd Cir.1978)—§ **18.18, n. 6;** § **18.35, n. 2.**

Martin, People v., 145 A.D.2d 440, 535 N.Y.S.2d 977 (N.Y.A.D. 2 Dept.1988)—§ **38.8, n. 143.**

Martin, People v., 175 N.Y. 315, 67 N.E. 589 (N.Y.1903)—§ **5.9, n. 5.**

Martinez v. Blum, 624 F.2d 1 (2nd Cir. 1980)—§ **4.19, n. 2.**

Martinez v. CPC Intern. Inc., 88 A.D.2d 656, 450 N.Y.S.2d 528 (N.Y.A.D. 2 Dept. 1982)—§ **26.42, n. 4.**

Martinez v. Gouverneur Gardens Housing Corp., 184 A.D.2d 264, 585 N.Y.S.2d 23 (N.Y.A.D. 1 Dept.1992)—§ **27.40, n. 5.**

Martinez, People v., 213 A.D.2d 1072, 624 N.Y.S.2d 498 (N.Y.A.D. 4 Dept.1995)—§ **38.8, n. 55.**

Martinez, People v., 607 N.Y.S.2d 610, 628 N.E.2d 1320 (N.Y.1993)—§ **38.19;** § **38.19, n. 93, 94;** § **39.50, n. 7.**

Martinez, People v., 604 N.Y.S.2d 932, 624 N.E.2d 1027 (N.Y.1993)—§ **37.29, n. 44.**

Martinez, People v., 595 N.Y.S.2d 376, 611 N.E.2d 277 (N.Y.1993)—§ **38.19;** § **38.19, n. 25.**

Martinez, People v., 162 A.D.2d 274, 556 N.Y.S.2d 631 (N.Y.A.D. 1 Dept.1990)—§ **38.8, n. 217.**

TABLE OF CASES

Martino v. Assco Assocs (In re SSS Enterprises, Inc.), 145 B.R. 915 (Bkrtcy. N.D.Ill.1992)—§ **9.198, n. 1.**

Martin-Trigona, In re, 760 F.2d 1334 (2nd Cir.1985)—§ **9.264, n. 6.**

Martonik v. Heckler, 773 F.2d 236 (8th Cir.1985)—§ **34.6, n. 7.**

Marvex Processing & Finishing Corp. v. Allendale Mut. Ins. Co., 91 Misc.2d 683, 398 N.Y.S.2d 464 (N.Y.Sup.1977)— § **30.34, n. 4.**

Marx v. Akers, 644 N.Y.S.2d 121, 666 N.E.2d 1034 (N.Y.1996)—§ **1.51, n. 90.**

Maryland Cas. Co. v. Pacific Coal & Oil Co., 312 U.S. 270, 61 S.Ct. 510, 85 L.Ed. 826 (1941)—§ **31.21, n. 4.**

Maryland Cas. Co. v. W.R. Grace & Co., 794 F.Supp. 1206 (S.D.N.Y.1991)—§ **31.27, n. 1.**

Maryland Casualty Co. v. Board of Water Com'rs of City of Dunkirk, 66 F.2d 730 (2nd Cir.1933)—§ **10.21, n. 8.**

Mary M. v. Clark, 100 A.D.2d 41, 473 N.Y.S.2d 843 (N.Y.A.D. 3 Dept.1984)— § **4.11, n. 2;** § **4.14, n. 2.**

Maryon v. Maryon, 60 A.D.2d 623, 400 N.Y.S.2d 160 (N.Y.A.D. 2 Dept.1977)— § **21.23, n. 5.**

Mascaro v. State, 46 A.D.2d 941, 362 N.Y.S.2d 78 (N.Y.A.D. 3 Dept.1974)— § **26.10, n. 6.**

Masi v. Iwanski, 136 A.D.2d 609, 523 N.Y.S.2d 588 (N.Y.A.D. 2 Dept.1988)— § **12.24, n. 1.**

Mason By and Through Mason v. Schenectady City School Dist., 879 F.Supp. 215 (N.D.N.Y.1993)—§ **18.53, n. 5, 6.**

Mason Tenders Dist. Council Pension Fund v. Messera, 958 F.Supp. 869 (S.D.N.Y. 1997)—§ **28.13, n. 1;** § **28.14, n. 10.**

Maspeth Bowl Inc. v. P.M.P. Partnership, N.Y.L.J., 9/16/88, p.22, col.2, 16 HCR 335 (Civ.Ct., Queens County)—§ **13.9, n. 3.**

Mass v. Leinker, 46 A.D.2d 383, 362 N.Y.S.2d 552 (N.Y.A.D. 2 Dept.1975)— § **37.65, n. 64.**

Massa v. Wanamaker Academy of Beauty Culture, 80 N.Y.S.2d 923 (N.Y.City Ct.1948)—§ **1.12, n. 9.**

Massachusetts Mut. Life Ins. Co. v. Avon Associates, Inc., 83 Misc.2d 829, 373 N.Y.S.2d 464 (N.Y.Sup.1975)—§ **11.31, n. 2.**

Massachusetts Mutual Life Ins. Co. v. Columbus Broadway Marble Corp. (In re Columbus Broadway Marble Corp.), 84 B.R. 322 (Bkrtcy.E.D.N.Y.1988)—§ **9.52, n. 6.**

Massachusetts Nat. Bank v. Shinn, 163 N.Y. 360, 57 N.E. 611 (N.Y.1900)— § **39.7, n. 14.**

Massena, Town of v. Niagara Mohawk Power Corp., 410 N.Y.S.2d 276, 382 N.E.2d 1139 (N.Y.1978)—§ **37.35, n. 15.**

Mast, Matter of, 79 B.R. 981 (Bkrtcy. W.D.Mich.1987)—§ **9.28, n. 4.**

Masten v. Baldauf, 147 A.D.2d 566, 537 N.Y.S.2d 860 (N.Y.A.D. 2 Dept.1989)— § **16.47, n. 5.**

Master Billiard Co., Inc. v. Rose, 194 A.D.2d 607, 599 N.Y.S.2d 68 (N.Y.A.D. 2 Dept. 1993)—§ **16.92, n. 4.**

Master Mortg. Inv. Fund, Inc., In re, 168 B.R. 930 (Bkrtcy.W.D.Mo.1994)— § **9.170, n. 3.**

Mastrobuono v. Shearson Lehman Hutton, Inc., 514 U.S. 52, 115 S.Ct. 1212, 131 L.Ed.2d 76 (1995)—§ **17.9, n. 2.**

Mastropietro, People v., 198 A.D.2d 443, 604 N.Y.S.2d 149 (N.Y.A.D. 2 Dept. 1993)—§ **38.10, n. 68.**

Matarese, People v., 307 N.Y. 752, 121 N.E.2d 553 (N.Y.1954)—§ **38.21, n. 58.**

Matco Products, Inc. v. Boston Old Colony Ins. Co., 104 A.D.2d 793, 480 N.Y.S.2d 134 (N.Y.A.D. 2 Dept.1984)—§ **31.6, n. 3.**

Materna v. ZCWK Associates, N.Y.L.J., 2/13/97, p.31, col.1 (Sup.Ct., Kings County)—§ **32.15, n. 9, 10.**

Matherson v. Marchello, 100 A.D.2d 233, 473 N.Y.S.2d 998 (N.Y.A.D. 2 Dept. 1984)—§ **18.81, n. 2.**

Mathews v. Eldridge, 424 U.S. 319, 96 S.Ct. 893, 47 L.Ed.2d 18 (1976)—§ **4.7, n. 4.**

Mathison, People v., 175 A.D.2d 966, 573 N.Y.S.2d 771 (N.Y.A.D. 3 Dept.1991)— § **38.8, n. 36.**

Mathurin v. Jackson, N.Y.L.J., 12/12/90, p.23, col.2, 18 HCR 592 (Civ.Ct., N.Y. County)—§ **13.28, n. 6, 7.**

Matie v. Sealed Air Corp., __ A.D.2d __, 665 N.Y.S.2d 360 (4th Dep't 1997)— § **32.15, n. 10.**

Matott v. Ward, 423 N.Y.S.2d 645, 399 N.E.2d 532 (N.Y.1979)—§ **29.16, n. 1.**

Mattei, Matter of, 169 Misc.2d 989, 647 N.Y.S.2d 415 (N.Y.Sup.1996)—§ **22.47, n. 13;** § **22.48, n. 11, 12.**

Matter of (see name of party)

Matteson v. Herkimer County, 94 A.D.2d 950, 464 N.Y.S.2d 75 (N.Y.A.D. 4 Dept. 1983)—§ **14.26, n. 2.**

Matteson, People v., 551 N.Y.S.2d 890, 551 N.E.2d 91 (N.Y.1989)—§ **38.8, n. 33;** § **38.41, n. 1.**

Matthews, People v., 506 N.Y.S.2d 149, 497 N.E.2d 287 (N.Y.1986)—§ **33.45;** § **33.45, n. 4.**

Matthews v. Rosene, 739 F.2d 249 (7th Cir. 1984)—§ **9.52, n. 6.**

TABLE OF CASES

Mattivi v. South African Marine Corp., Huguenot, 618 F.2d 163 (2nd Cir.1980)—§ **27.35, n. 24.**

Matt Petroleum Corporation, 1994 WL 370385 (N.Y. Tax App. Trib.)—§ **35.118, n. 4, 5.**

Maturo v. National Graphics, Inc., 722 F.Supp. 916 (D.Conn.1989)—§ **17.84, n. 5.**

Maul v. Fitzgerald, 78 A.D.2d 706, 432 N.Y.S.2d 282 (N.Y.A.D. 3 Dept.1980)—§ **23.79, n. 2.**

Maurizzio v. Lumbermens Mut. Cas. Co., 540 N.Y.S.2d 982, 538 N.E.2d 334 (N.Y. 1989)—§ **26.24, n. 16.**

Max Sugarman Funeral Home, Inc. v. A.D.B. Investors, 926 F.2d 1248 (1st Cir. 1991)—§ **9.119, n. 2.**

Maxwell v. Maxwell, 88 Misc.2d 535, 389 N.Y.S.2d 84 (N.Y.Sup.1976)—§ **21.64, n. 2.**

Maxwell v. N.W. Ayer, Inc., 159 Misc.2d 454, 605 N.Y.S.2d 174 (N.Y.Sup.1993)—§ **18.64, n. 4.**

Maxwell v. Simons, 77 Misc.2d 184, 353 N.Y.S.2d 589 (N.Y.City Civ.Ct.1973)—§ **13.33, n. 4.**

Maxwell Z, Matter of, N.Y.L.J., 10/1/96, p. 27, col. 3 (Sup.Ct., Suffolk County)—§ **22.54, n. 8.**

May v. Flowers, 106 A.D.2d 873, 483 N.Y.S.2d 551 (N.Y.A.D. 4 Dept.1984)—§ **2.37, n. 4.**

Maycumber v. Wolfe, 10 Misc.2d 464, 171 N.Y.S.2d 44 (N.Y.Sup.1958)—§ **10.11, n. 2.**

Mayfair Leather Products v. Piedmont Fire Ins. Co., 105 N.Y.S.2d 802 (N.Y.Sup. 1951)—§ **31.18, n. 20.**

Mayo, People v., 422 N.Y.S.2d 361, 397 N.E.2d 1166 (N.Y.1979)—§ **38.19, n. 121;** § **38.26, n. 14.**

Mayor of Village of Mount Kisco v. Supervisor of Town of Bedford, 408 N.Y.S.2d 414, 380 N.E.2d 243 (N.Y.1978)—§ **3.5, n. 24.**

Mays v. New York City Police Dept., 701 F.Supp. 80 (S.D.N.Y.1988)—§ **17.59, n. 8.**

Mazur v. Mazur, 207 A.D.2d 61, 621 N.Y.S.2d 981 (N.Y.A.D. 4 Dept.1994)—§ **37.89, n. 4.**

Mazzara v. Town of Pittsford, 34 A.D.2d 90, 310 N.Y.S.2d 865 (N.Y.A.D. 4 Dept. 1970)—§ **16.112, n. 2.**

Mazzeo, Matter of Estate of, 95 A.D.2d 91, 466 N.Y.S.2d 759 (N.Y.A.D. 3 Dept. 1983)—§ **20.75, n. 4.**

Mazzochetti v. Cassarino, 49 A.D.2d 695, 370 N.Y.S.2d 765 (N.Y.A.D. 4 Dept. 1975)—§ **12.4, n. 3.**

M & B Plumbing & Heating Co., Inc. v. Cammarota, 103 A.D.2d 879, 477 N.Y.S.2d 901 (N.Y.A.D. 3 Dept.1984)—§ **10.7, n. 2.**

McAlpine v. McAlpine, 143 Misc.2d 30, 539 N.Y.S.2d 680 (N.Y.Sup.1989)—§ **21.39, n. 9.**

McBarnette v. Sobol, 610 N.Y.S.2d 460, 632 N.E.2d 866 (N.Y.1994)—§ **4.13, n. 6.**

McBride v. McBride, 222 A.D.2d 563, 635 N.Y.S.2d 298 (N.Y.A.D. 2 Dept.1995)—§ **21.53, n. 8.**

McBride v. Town of Forestburgh, 54 A.D.2d 396, 388 N.Y.S.2d 940 (N.Y.A.D. 3 Dept. 1976)—§ **16.15, n. 11, 12.**

McCabe v. Hoffman, 138 A.D.2d 287, 526 N.Y.S.2d 93 (N.Y.A.D. 1 Dept.1988)—§ **1.27, n. 5.**

McCabe v. Voorhis, 243 N.Y. 401, 153 N.E. 849 (N.Y.1926)—§ **3.15, n. 1.**

McCahill v. New York Transp. Co., 201 N.Y. 221, 94 N.E. 616 (N.Y.1911)—§ **30.11, n. 5.**

McCain v. Dinkins, 616 N.Y.S.2d 335, 639 N.E.2d 1132 (N.Y.1994)—§ **38.8, n. 81.**

McCain, People v., 177 A.D.2d 513, 576 N.Y.S.2d 146 (N.Y.A.D. 2 Dept.1991)—§ **38.21, n. 11.**

McCall, People v., 16 A.D.2d 313, 228 N.Y.S.2d 52 (N.Y.A.D. 4 Dept.1962)—§ **38.8, n. 65.**

McCarter v. Crawford, 245 N.Y. 43, 156 N.E. 90 (N.Y.1927)—§ **12.60, n. 1.**

McCarthy, People v., 250 N.Y. 358, 165 N.E. 810 (N.Y.1929)—§ **38.32, n. 2;** § **39.46, n. 3.**

McCaskell, People v., 206 A.D.2d 547, 615 N.Y.S.2d 55 (N.Y.A.D. 2 Dept.1994)—§ **38.8, n. 27.**

McClary v. O'Hare, 786 F.2d 83 (2nd Cir. 1986)—§ **18.33, n. 4.**

McClary, People v., 150 A.D.2d 631, 541 N.Y.S.2d 503 (N.Y.A.D. 2 Dept.1989)—§ **38.8, n. 102.**

McClelland v. Climax Hosiery Mills, 252 N.Y. 347, 169 N.E. 605 (N.Y.1930)—§ **37.23, n. 4.**

McClendon v. Rosetti, 369 F.Supp. 1391 (S.D.N.Y.1974)—§ **18.11, n. 1.**

McClendon v. Rosetti, 460 F.2d 111 (2nd Cir.1972)—§ **18.94.**

McCole v. City of New York, 221 A.D.2d 605, 634 N.Y.S.2d 183 (N.Y.A.D. 2 Dept. 1995)—§ **37.37, n. 78.**

McConnell v. Commonwealth Pictures Corp., 199 N.Y.S.2d 483, 166 N.E.2d 494 (N.Y.1960)—§ **5.8, n. 3.**

McCoy, People v., 313 N.Y.S.2d 762, 261 N.E.2d 668 (N.Y.1970)—§ **38.21, n. 58.**

McCrory v. Henderson, 82 F.3d 1243 (2nd Cir.1996)—§ **18.15, n. 10.**

TABLE OF CASES

McCullough v. Certain Teed Products Corp., 70 A.D.2d 771, 417 N.Y.S.2d 353 (N.Y.A.D. 4 Dept.1979)—§ **17.31, n. 3.**

McCuskey v. Central Trailer Services, Ltd., 37 F.3d 1329 (8th Cir.1994)—§ **9.198, n. 1.**

McDermott v. City of New York, 428 N.Y.S.2d 643, 406 N.E.2d 460 (N.Y. 1980)—§ **28.26; § 28.26, n. 1.**

McDermott v. Torre, 452 N.Y.S.2d 351, 437 N.E.2d 1108 (N.Y.1982)—§ **18.38, n. 7.**

McDonald v. Metropolitan St. Ry. Co., 167 N.Y. 66, 60 N.E. 282 (N.Y.1901)—§ **37.65, n. 32.**

McDonald v. North Shore Yacht Sales, Inc., 134 Misc.2d 910, 513 N.Y.S.2d 590 (N.Y.Sup.1987)—§ **7.46, n. 1; § 7.47, n. 5; § 7.64.**

McDonald v. Northside Sav. Bank, 184 A.D.2d 426, 585 N.Y.S.2d 389 (N.Y.A.D. 1 Dept.1992)—§ **30.30, n. 17.**

McDonald, People v., 199 A.D.2d 539, 606 N.Y.S.2d 252 (N.Y.A.D. 2 Dept.1993)—§ **38.3; § 38.3, n. 27.**

McDonald, People v., 505 N.Y.S.2d 824, 496 N.E.2d 844 (N.Y.1986)—§ **37.37, n. 71; § 38.10, n. 58.**

McDonald v. Santa Fe Trail Transp. Co., 427 U.S. 273, 96 S.Ct. 2574, 49 L.Ed.2d 493 (1976)—§ **18.17, n. 1.**

McDonald v. Secretary of Health and Human Services, 795 F.2d 1118 (1st Cir. 1986)—§ **34.10, n. 9.**

McDonald v. State, 397 N.Y.S.2d 990, 366 N.E.2d 1344 (N.Y.1977)—§ **14.82, n. 2.**

McDonald's Corp. v. Rose, 111 A.D.2d 850, 490 N.Y.S.2d 588 (N.Y.A.D. 2 Dept. 1985)—§ **16.47, n. 4.**

McDonnell Douglas Corp. v. Green, 411 U.S. 792, 93 S.Ct. 1817, 36 L.Ed.2d 668 (1973)—§ **17.59; § 17.59, n. 3.**

McDougald v. Garber, 538 N.Y.S.2d 937, 536 N.E.2d 372 (N.Y.1989)—§ **28.10, n. 10.**

McDowell v. Dart, 201 A.D.2d 895, 607 N.Y.S.2d 755 (N.Y.A.D. 4 Dept.1994)—§ **17.25, n. 6.**

McEniry v. Landi, 620 N.Y.S.2d 328, 644 N.E.2d 1019 (N.Y.1994)—§ **17.43, n. 6.**

McFadden v. Haritatos, 86 A.D.2d 761, 448 N.Y.S.2d 79 (N.Y.A.D. 4 Dept.1982)—§ **27.13, n. 6; § 27.14, n. 2.**

McFarland v. McFarland, 221 A.D.2d 983, 634 N.Y.S.2d 290 (N.Y.A.D. 4 Dept. 1995)—§ **21.53, n. 5.**

McFarlane v. City of Niagara Falls, 247 N.Y. 340, 160 N.E. 391 (N.Y.1928)—§ **15.32, n. 11.**

McGaffin v. Family & Children's Service of Albany, Inc., 6 Misc.2d 776, 164 N.Y.S.2d 444 (N.Y.Sup.1957)—§ **20.100, n. 2.**

McGarrity v. McGarrity, 211 A.D.2d 669, 622 N.Y.S.2d 521 (N.Y.A.D. 2 Dept. 1995)—§ **21.37, n. 12; § 21.49, n. 6.**

McGee, People v., 186 A.D.2d 229, 587 N.Y.S.2d 1015 (N.Y.A.D. 2 Dept.1992)—§ **38.8, n. 42, 60.**

McGettrick, People v., 139 Misc.2d 403, 528 N.Y.S.2d 758 (N.Y.City Ct.1988)—§ **33.32, n. 2; § 33.33, n. 3.**

McGloine v. Dominy, 233 N.Y.S.2d 161 (N.Y.City Ct.1962)—§ **13.37, n. 7.**

McGoldrick v. Whitney M. Young, Jr. Health Center, Inc., 135 Misc.2d 200, 514 N.Y.S.2d 872 (N.Y.Sup.1987)—§ **26.42, n. 9.**

McGowan v. McGowan, 142 A.D.2d 355, 535 N.Y.S.2d 990 (N.Y.A.D. 2 Dept. 1988)—§ **21.39; § 21.39, n. 8.**

McGrane, State ex rel. Capparelli v., 189 A.D.2d 561, 592 N.Y.S.2d 15 (N.Y.A.D. 1 Dept.1993)—§ **38.8, n. 78.**

McGreevy v. Simon, 220 A.D.2d 713, 633 N.Y.S.2d 177 (N.Y.A.D. 2 Dept.1995)—§ **37.28, n. 31; § 37.37, n. 15.**

McIlwain v. Korbean Intern. Inv. Corp., 896 F.Supp. 1373 (S.D.N.Y.1995)—§ **17.69, n. 3.**

McIntyre v. New York Central Railroad Co., 37 N.Y.286 (1867)—§ **30.14, n. 1.**

McKane v. Durston, 153 U.S. 684, 14 S.Ct. 913, 38 L.Ed. 867 (1894)—§ **38.3, n. 1.**

McKee, Matter of, 17 I & N Dec. 332 (BIA 1980)—§ **19.12, n. 3.**

McKenna, People v., 556 N.Y.S.2d 514, 555 N.E.2d 911 (N.Y.1990)—§ **33.90, n. 4.**

McKeon v. Sears, Roebuck and Co., 190 A.D.2d 577, 593 N.Y.S.2d 519 (N.Y.A.D. 1 Dept.1993)—§ **27.37, n. 7.**

McKinney v. State, 111 Misc.2d 382, 444 N.Y.S.2d 386 (N.Y.Ct.Cl.1981)—§ **18.65, n. 9.**

McKins, People v., 76 A.D.2d 756, 429 N.Y.S.2d 338 (N.Y.1980)—§ **38.8, n. 54.**

McLamb, United States v., 5 F.3d 69 (4th Cir.1993)—§ **11.6, n. 9.**

McLane v. McLane, 209 A.D.2d 1001, 619 N.Y.S.2d 899 (N.Y.A.D. 4 Dept.1994)—§ **21.49, n. 6.**

McLane's Estate, In re, 90 Misc.2d 1067, 398 N.Y.S.2d 460 (N.Y.Sur.1976)—§ **23.81, n. 7.**

McLaughlin v. Mine Safety Appliances Co., 226 N.Y.S.2d 407, 181 N.E.2d 430 (N.Y. 1962)—§ **27.10, n. 3.**

McLaughlin, People v., 591 N.Y.S.2d 966, 606 N.E.2d 1357 (N.Y.1992)—§ **33.68, n. 9; § 38.19, n. 96.**

McLaurin v. Ryder Truck Rental, 123 A.D.2d 671, 507 N.Y.S.2d 41 (N.Y.A.D. 2 Dept.1986)—§ **30.28, n. 4.**

McLean Industries, Inc., In re, 184 B.R. 10 (Bkrtcy.S.D.N.Y.1995)—§ **9.113, n. 1.**

TABLE OF CASES

McLean Industries, Inc., In re, 87 B.R. 830 (Bkrtcy.S.D.N.Y.1987)—§ **9.142, n. 5;** § **9.306.**
McLean Industries, Inc., In re, 70 B.R. 852 (Bkrtcy.S.D.N.Y.1987)—§ **9.47, n. 2.**
McLucas, People v., 256 N.Y.S.2d 799, 204 N.E.2d 846 (N.Y.1965)—§ **38.19;** § **38.19, n. 14.**
McMahan v. McMahan, 100 A.D.2d 826, 474 N.Y.S.2d 974 (N.Y.A.D. 1 Dept. 1984)—§ **21.64, n. 1.**
McMains v. McMains, 258 N.Y.S.2d 93, 206 N.E.2d 185 (N.Y.1965)—§ **21.69;** § **21.69, n. 5.**
McMann, People ex rel. Emanuel v., 197 N.Y.S.2d 174, 165 N.E.2d 187 (N.Y. 1960)—§ **38.8, n. 6.**
McManus, Matter of, 83 A.D.2d 553, 440 N.Y.S.2d 954 (N.Y.A.D. 2 Dept.1981)—§ **5.23, n. 4.**
McMinn v. Town of Oyster Bay, 498 N.Y.S.2d 128, 488 N.E.2d 1240 (N.Y. 1985)—§ **16.18;** § **16.18, n. 4, 23;** § **16.122;** § **16.122, n. 5.**
McMoore, People v., 203 A.D.2d 612, 609 N.Y.S.2d 964 (N.Y.A.D. 3 Dept.1994)—§ **38.28, n. 22.**
McMorrow v. Trimper, 149 A.D.2d 971, 540 N.Y.S.2d 106 (N.Y.A.D. 4 Dept.1989)—§ **37.65, n. 44.**
McMullen, Matter of, 166 Misc.2d 117, 632 N.Y.S.2d 401 (N.Y.Sup.1995)—§ **22.48, n. 13.**
McMullen, Matter of, 19 I & N Dec. 90 (BIA 1984)—§ **19.50, n. 6.**
McMullin v. Pelham Bay Riding, Inc., 190 A.D.2d 529, 593 N.Y.S.2d 27 (N.Y.A.D. 1 Dept.1993)—§ **1.10, n. 19.**
McMullin, People v., 523 N.Y.S.2d 455, 517 N.E.2d 1341 (N.Y.1987)—§ **38.10, n. 167.**
McNab, Matter of Estate of, 163 A.D.2d 790, 558 N.Y.S.2d 751 (N.Y.A.D. 3 Dept. 1990)—§ **25.50, n. 1.**
McNabb v. MacAndrews & Forbes Group, Inc., 1991 WL 284104 (S.D.N.Y.1991)—§ **17.25, n. 14.**
McNeill, People ex rel. Tatra v., 19 A.D.2d 845, 244 N.Y.S.2d 463 (N.Y.A.D. 2 Dept. 1963)—§ **37.34, n. 6.**
MCorp Financial, Inc., In re, 137 B.R. 219 (Bkrtcy.S.D.Tex.1992)—§ **9.148, n. 8.**
McPhee v. Chilton Corp., 468 F.Supp. 494 (D.Conn.1978)—§ **7.31, n. 12.**
McPherson v. Schade, 149 N.Y. 16, 43 N.E. 527 (N.Y.1896)—§ **12.9, n. 4;** § **12.59;** § **12.59, n. 1.**
McQuade v. Stoneham, 263 N.Y. 323, 189 N.E. 234 (N.Y.1934)—§ **1.47, n. 3.**
McQuillan v. Kenyon & Kenyon, 220 A.D.2d 395, 631 N.Y.S.2d 884 (N.Y.A.D. 2 Dept. 1995)—§ **2.65, n. 1.**

McSparron v. McSparron, 639 N.Y.S.2d 265, 662 N.E.2d 745 (N.Y.1995)—§ **21.39;** § **21.39, n. 4;** § **21.42;** § **21.42, n. 7;** § **21.43;** § **21.43, n. 16, 21;** § **37.30, n. 4;** § **37.45, n. 2.**
Meachem, People v., 50 A.D.2d 953, 375 N.Y.S.2d 678 (N.Y.A.D. 3 Dept.1975)—§ **38.8, n. 176.**
Meachum v. Outdoor World Corp., 235 A.D.2d 462, 652 N.Y.S.2d 749 (N.Y.A.D. 2 Dept.1997)—§ **7.47, n. 7.**
Mead v. Warner Pruyn Division, Finch Pruyn Sales, Inc., 57 A.D.2d 340, 394 N.Y.S.2d 483 (N.Y.A.D. 3 Dept.1977)—§ **27.22, n. 1.**
Mecca v. Connelly, 150 A.D.2d 353, 543 N.Y.S.2d 317 (N.Y.A.D. 2 Dept.1989)—§ **37.37, n. 26.**
Mechanick v. Conradi, 139 A.D.2d 857, 527 N.Y.S.2d 586 (N.Y.A.D. 3 Dept.1988)—§ **29.16, n. 6.**
Mediators, Inc. v. Manney (In re Mediators, Inc.), 105 F.3d 822 (2nd Cir.1997)—§ **9.42, n. 1;** § **9.45, n. 2.**
Mediators, Inc. v. Money (Matter of Mediators, Inc.), 190 B.R. 515 (S.D.N.Y. 1995)—§ **9.198, n. 2.**
Medical Facilities, Inc. v. Pryke, 476 N.Y.S.2d 532, 465 N.E.2d 39 (N.Y. 1984)—§ **31.26, n. 12.**
Medical Malpractice Ins. Assoc. v. Hirsch (In re Lavigne), 114 F.3d 379 (2nd Cir. 1997)—§ **9.62, n. 1.**
Medical Malpractice Ins. Ass'n v. Superintendent of Ins. of State of N.Y., 537 N.Y.S.2d 1, 533 N.E.2d 1030 (N.Y. 1988)—§ **4.77, n. 3;** § **37.29, n. 31.**
Medical Soc. v. State Dept. of Health, 189 A.D.2d 453, 596 N.Y.S.2d 477 (N.Y.A.D. 3 Dept.1993)—§ **23.52, n. 2.**
Medical Soc. of State of N.Y. v. Cuomo, 777 F.Supp. 1157 (S.D.N.Y.1991)—§ **23.52, n. 2.**
Medina, People v., 111 A.D.2d 653, 490 N.Y.S.2d 491 (N.Y.A.D. 1 Dept.1985)—§ **38.64, n. 1.**
Medi–Physics Inc. v. Community Hospital of Rockland County, 105 Misc.2d 574, 432 N.Y.S.2d 594 (N.Y.Co.Ct.1980)—§ **8.25, n. 5.**
Medtronic, Inc. v. Lohr, ___ U.S. ___, 116 S.Ct. 2240, 135 L.Ed.2d 700 (1996)—§ **27.48;** § **27.48, n. 4.**
Meehan v. Newman Imp. Corporation, 262 N.Y. 682, 188 N.E. 119 (N.Y.1933)—§ **12.60, n. 3.**
Meehan v. State, 95 Misc.2d 678, 408 N.Y.S.2d 652 (N.Y.Ct.Cl.1978)—§ **15.33, n. 4.**
Mees, People v., 420 N.Y.S.2d 214, 394 N.E.2d 283 (N.Y.1979)—§ **38.19, n. 110.**

TABLE OF CASES

Meghrig v. KFC Western, Inc., ___ U.S. ___, 116 S.Ct. 1251, 134 L.Ed.2d 121 (1996)—§ **15.25, n. 14, 15.**

Mehmedi, People v., 513 N.Y.S.2d 100, 505 N.E.2d 610 (N.Y.1987)—§ **38.19;** § **38.19, n. 18, 112.**

Meichsner v. Valentine Gardens Co-op., Inc., 137 A.D.2d 797, 525 N.Y.S.2d 345 (N.Y.A.D. 2 Dept.1988)—§ **1.27, n. 5.**

Meierdiercks, People v., 505 N.Y.S.2d 51, 496 N.E.2d 210 (N.Y.1986)—§ **33.87, n. 2.**

Meiselman v. Allstate Ins. Co., 197 A.D.2d 561, 602 N.Y.S.2d 659 (N.Y.A.D. 2 Dept. 1993)—§ **8.6, n. 6.**

Mejia, People v., 221 A.D.2d 182, 633 N.Y.S.2d 157 (N.Y.A.D. 1 Dept.1995)— § **38.19, n. 40.**

Melancon v. Melancon, 204 A.D.2d 1061, 613 N.Y.S.2d 65 (N.Y.A.D. 4 Dept. 1994)—§ **21.58, n. 2.**

Melkonyan v. Sullivan, 501 U.S. 89, 111 S.Ct. 2157, 115 L.Ed.2d 78 (1991)— § **34.29, n. 7.**

Mellon Bank, N.A. v. The Official Committee of Unsecured Creditors of R.M.L., Inc. (In re R.M.L., Inc.), 92 F.3d 139 (3rd Cir.1996)—§ **9.119, n. 3.**

Melniker v. Grae, 82 A.D.2d 798, 439 N.Y.S.2d 409 (N.Y.A.D. 2 Dept.1981)— § **10.16, n. 5.**

Melnyk v. Adria Laboratories, a Div. of Erbamont Inc., 799 F.Supp. 301 (W.D.N.Y.1992)—§ **17.34, n. 3.**

Meloff v. New York Life Ins. Co., 51 F.3d 372 (2nd Cir.1995)—§ **17.73, n. 1.**

Melrose Ave. in Borough of the Bronx, In re, 234 N.Y. 48, 136 N.E. 235 (N.Y. 1922)—§ **24.3, n. 3.**

Melroy Realty Corp. v. Siegel, 60 Misc.2d 383, 303 N.Y.S.2d 198 (N.Y.City Civ.Ct. 1969)—§ **13.50;** § **13.50, n. 2.**

Melvin, People v., 188 A.D.2d 555, 591 N.Y.S.2d 454 (N.Y.A.D. 2 Dept.1992)— § **33.53, n. 2.**

Melvin A., Matter of, 216 A.D.2d 227, 628 N.Y.S.2d 698 (N.Y.A.D. 1 Dept.1995)— § **38.8, n. 206.**

Memphis Community School Dist. v. Stachura, 477 U.S. 299, 106 S.Ct. 2537, 91 L.Ed.2d 249 (1986)—§ **18.18, n. 11.**

Mendel v. Pittsburgh Plate Glass Co., 305 N.Y.S.2d 490, 253 N.E.2d 207 (N.Y. 1969)—§ **27.3;** § **27.3, n. 12;** § **27.39, n. 4.**

Mendelowitz v. Xerox Corp., 169 A.D.2d 300, 573 N.Y.S.2d 548 (N.Y.A.D. 1 Dept. 1991)—§ **27.37;** § **27.37, n. 6.**

Mendelson, Application of, 151 Misc.2d 367, 572 N.Y.S.2d 1014 (N.Y.City Civ.Ct. 1991)—§ **18.67, n. 5.**

Mendola, People v., 159 N.Y.S.2d 473, 140 N.E.2d 353 (N.Y.1957)—§ **38.27, n. 24.**

Mendoza, In re, 16 B.R. 990 (Bkrtcy. S.D.Cal.1982)—§ **9.205, n. 8.**

Mendoza, People v., 211 A.D.2d 493, 621 N.Y.S.2d 553 (N.Y.A.D. 1 Dept.1995)— § **18.10, n. 2.**

Mendoza, People v., 604 N.Y.S.2d 922, 624 N.E.2d 1017 (N.Y.1993)—§ **33.43;** § **33.43, n. 7.**

Mendoza v. Schlossman, 87 A.D.2d 606, 448 N.Y.S.2d 45 (N.Y.A.D. 2 Dept.1982)— § **28.3, n. 1.**

Mendoza v. SSC & B Lintas, New York, 799 F.Supp. 1502 (S.D.N.Y.1992)—§ **17.25, n. 14.**

Menga v. Raquet, 150 A.D.2d 434, 541 N.Y.S.2d 43 (N.Y.A.D. 2 Dept.1989)— § **30.30, n. 22.**

Menges v. Board of County Com'rs of Jackson County, 44 Or.App. 603, 606 P.2d 681 (Or.App.1980)—§ **16.12, n. 12.**

Menna v. New York, 423 U.S. 61, 96 S.Ct. 241, 46 L.Ed.2d 195 (1975)—§ **38.8, n. 196.**

Mente v. Wenzel, 192 A.D.2d 862, 596 N.Y.S.2d 520 (N.Y.A.D. 3 Dept.1993)— § **8.42, n. 11.**

Merced v. City of New York, 142 Misc.2d 442, 534 N.Y.S.2d 60 (N.Y.Sup.1987)— § **30.13, n. 9.**

Mercedes-Benz of North America, Inc. v. Yoon, Matter of, N.Y.L.J., 4/26/94, p.21, col.5 (Sup.Ct., N.Y.County)—§ **7.10, n. 9;** § **7.14, n. 5;** § **7.20, n. 1.**

Mercurio, People v., 93 Misc.2d 1126, 404 N.Y.S.2d 252 (N.Y.Dist.Ct.1978)— § **33.100.**

Mercy Hosp. of Watertown v. New York State Dept. of Social Services, 171 B.R. 490 (N.D.N.Y.1994)—§ **9.112, n. 3.**

Meritor Sav. Bank, FSB v. Vinson, 477 U.S. 57, 106 S.Ct. 2399, 91 L.Ed.2d 49 (1986)—§ **17.57, n. 1.**

Meriwether v. Garrett, 102 U.S. 472, 12 Otto 472, 26 L.Ed. 197 (1880)—§ **3.16, n. 9.**

Merrill, People v., 212 A.D.2d 987, 624 N.Y.S.2d 702 (N.Y.A.D. 4 Dept.1995)— § **38.10, n. 168.**

Merrill by Merrill v. Albany Medical Center Hosp., 529 N.Y.S.2d 272, 524 N.E.2d 873 (N.Y.1988)—§ **39.9, n. 4.**

Merrimack Valley Oil Co., Inc., In re, 32 B.R. 485 (Bkrtcy.D.Mass.1983)— § **9.165, n. 23.**

Merritt v. Ramos, 167 Misc.2d 269, 639 N.Y.S.2d 643 (N.Y.City Civ.Ct.1995)— § **30.35, n. 2.**

Merritt Hill Vineyards Inc. v. Windy Heights Vineyard, Inc., 472 N.Y.S.2d

TABLE OF CASES

592, 460 N.E.2d 1077 (N.Y.1984)—§ 37.2, n. 8; § 37.65, n. 69.
Mertz, People v., 506 N.Y.S.2d 290, 497 N.E.2d 657 (N.Y.1986)—§ 33.68; § 33.68, n. 22.
Mesick v. State, 118 A.D.2d 214, 504 N.Y.S.2d 279 (N.Y.A.D. 3 Dept.1986)—§ 37.65, n. 12.
Messina v. Basso, 170 A.D.2d 656, 567 N.Y.S.2d 77 (N.Y.A.D. 2 Dept.1991)—§ 37.28, n. 9.
Metchick v. Bidermann Industries Corp., 1995 WL 106139 (S.D.N.Y.1993)—§ 17.25, n. 14.
Metflex Corp. v. Klafter, 123 A.D.2d 845, 507 N.Y.S.2d 460 (N.Y.A.D. 2 Dept. 1986)—§ 2.53, n. 3.
Methe v. General Elec. Co., 169 A.D.2d 864, 564 N.Y.S.2d 593 (N.Y.A.D. 3 Dept. 1991)—§ 17.35, n. 2.
Metivier v. Sarandrea, 154 Misc.2d 355, 585 N.Y.S.2d 291 (N.Y.Sup.1992)—§ 10.17, n. 5.
Metpath Inc. v. Birmingham Fire Ins. Co. of Pennsylvania, 86 A.D.2d 407, 449 N.Y.S.2d 986 (N.Y.A.D. 1 Dept.1982)—§ 31.5, n. 4.
Metropolitan Life Ins. Co. v. Carroll, 43 Misc.2d 639, 251 N.Y.S.2d 693 (N.Y.Sup. App.Term 1964)—§ 13.21; § 13.21, n. 4; § 13.46; § 13.46, n. 4.
Metropolitan Transp. Authority v. Cosmopolitan Aviation Corp., 99 A.D.2d 767, 471 N.Y.S.2d 872 (N.Y.A.D. 2 Dept. 1984)—§ 13.51; § 13.51, n. 15.
Metropolitan Transp. Authority v. Pinelawn Cemetery, 135 A.D.2d 686, 522 N.Y.S.2d 586 (N.Y.A.D. 2 Dept.1987)—§ 14.64, n. 1.
Metropolitan Transp. Authority v. Pizzuti, 156 A.D.2d 546, 549 N.Y.S.2d 52 (N.Y.A.D. 2 Dept.1989)—§ 14.71, n. 1.
Metropolitan Waste Management Corp. v. Town of Hempstead, 135 Misc.2d 548, 515 N.Y.S.2d 956 (N.Y.Sup.1987)—§ 3.32, n. 15.
Metz v. Great Atlantic & Pacific Tea Co., 30 Misc.2d 258, 215 N.Y.S.2d 175 (N.Y.Sup. 1961)—§ 30.10, n. 10.
Metzeler v. Bouchard (In re Metzeler), 66 B.R. 977 (Bkrtcy.S.D.N.Y.1986)—§ 9.198, n. 2.
Meyers Industries, 281 NLRB No. 118, 281 NLRB 882 (N.L.R.B.1986)—§ 17.61, n. 2.
Meyers Industries, 268 NLRB No. 73, 268 NLRB 493 (N.L.R.B.1984)—§ 17.61, n. 2.
M. F. Hickey Co. v. Port of New York Authority, 23 A.D.2d 739, 258 N.Y.S.2d 129 (N.Y.A.D. 1 Dept.1965)—§ 8.19, n. 2.

MHG Enterprises Inc. v. City of New York, 91 Misc.2d 842, 399 N.Y.S.2d 837 (N.Y.Sup.1977)—§ 14.81, n. 8, 9.
Miano v. AC & R Advertising, Inc., 148 F.R.D. 68 (S.D.N.Y.1993)—§ 17.3, n. 4.
Micallef v. Miehle Co., Division of Miehle–Goss Dexter, Inc., 384 N.Y.S.2d 115, 348 N.E.2d 571 (N.Y.1976)—§ 27.5, n. 5; § 27.8, n. 1.
Miccio, People v., 155 Misc.2d 697, 589 N.Y.S.2d 762 (N.Y.City Crim.Ct.1992)—§ 18.55, n. 4.
Michael, People v., 420 N.Y.S.2d 371, 394 N.E.2d 1134 (N.Y.1979)—§ 38.19, n. 16.
Michael C., Matter of, 215 A.D.2d 228, 626 N.Y.S.2d 774 (N.Y.A.D. 1 Dept.1995)—§ 38.8, n. 168.
Michael Chad M., Matter of, 143 A.D.2d 189, 531 N.Y.S.2d 637 (N.Y.A.D. 2 Dept. 1988)—§ 20.67; § 20.67, n. 7.
Michael JJ, Matter of, 200 A.D.2d 80, 613 N.Y.S.2d 715 (N.Y.A.D. 3 Dept.1994)—§ 20.56, n. 4.
Michalek, People v., 138 Misc.2d 1, 521 N.Y.S.2d 609 (N.Y.City Crim.Ct.1987)—§ 33.75; § 33.75, n. 1.
Michallow, People v., 201 A.D.2d 915, 607 N.Y.S.2d 781 (N.Y.A.D. 4 Dept.1994)—§ 38.19, n. 48.
Michel v. Federated Dept. Stores, Inc. (In re Federated Dept. Stores, Inc.), 44 F.3d 1310 (6th Cir.1995)—§ 9.12, n. 1.
Michelle W. v. Forrest James P., 218 A.D.2d 175, 637 N.Y.S.2d 538 (N.Y.A.D. 4 Dept. 1996)—§ 37.19, n. 65.
Michelman, People v., 93 Misc.2d 297, 403 N.Y.S.2d 417 (N.Y.Sup.1978)—§ 20.45; § 20.45, n. 9; § 20.46, n. 3.
Michelson, In re, 141 B.R. 715 (Bkrtcy. E.D.Cal.1992)—§ 9.161, n. 5.
Mickel v. State, 77 A.D.2d 794, 430 N.Y.S.2d 741 (N.Y.A.D. 4 Dept.1980)—§ 14.14, n. 11.
Middlesex County Ethics Committee v. Garden State Bar Ass'n, 457 U.S. 423, 102 S.Ct. 2515, 73 L.Ed.2d 116 (1982)—§ 18.36, n. 4.
Middleton v. Whitridge, 213 N.Y. 499, 108 N.E. 192 (N.Y.1915)—§ 37.29, n. 3.
Midland–Ross Corp. v. Sunbeam Equipment Corp., 316 F.Supp. 171 (W.D.Pa.1970)—§ 27.38, n. 4.
Midlantic Nat. Bank v. New Jersey Dept. of Environmental Protection, 474 U.S. 494, 106 S.Ct. 755, 88 L.Ed.2d 859 (1986)—§ 9.70, n. 1.
M.I.F. Securities Co. v. R.C. Stamm & Co., 94 A.D.2d 211, 463 N.Y.S.2d 771 (N.Y.A.D. 1 Dept.1983)—§ 2.46, n. 7.
Mighty Midgets, Inc. v. Centennial Ins. Co., 416 N.Y.S.2d 559, 389 N.E.2d 1080 (N.Y. 1979)—§ 31.14, n. 1.

TABLE OF CASES

Mignott v. Sears, Roebuck & Co., 101 A.D.2d 731, 475 N.Y.S.2d 44 (N.Y.A.D. 1 Dept.1984)—§ **37.37, n. 33.**

Migra v. Warren City School Dist. Bd. of Educ., 465 U.S. 75, 104 S.Ct. 892, 79 L.Ed.2d 56 (1984)—§ **18.37, n. 9.**

Mikes, United States ex rel. v. Straus, 853 F.Supp. 115 (S.D.N.Y.1994)—§ **17.64, n. 4.**

Mikes, United States ex rel. v. Straus, 846 F.Supp. 21 (S.D.N.Y.1994)—§ **17.64, n. 4.**

Milbrandt v. A.P. Green Refractories Co., 580 N.Y.S.2d 147, 588 N.E.2d 45 (N.Y. 1992)—§ **30.40; § 30.40, n. 10.**

Miles, People v., 289 N.Y. 360, 45 N.E.2d 910 (N.Y.1942)—§ **38.19; § 38.19, n. 13.**

Miles, People v., 173 A.D. 179, 158 N.Y.S. 819 (N.Y.A.D. 3 Dept.1916)—§ **38.21, n. 41.**

Milkovich v. Lorain Journal Co., 497 U.S. 1, 110 S.Ct. 2695, 111 L.Ed.2d 1 (1990)—§ **18.82, n. 6.**

Miller, Matter of, 220 A.D.2d 591, 632 N.Y.S.2d 817 (N.Y.A.D. 2 Dept.1995)—§ **25.22, n. 2.**

Miller, Matter of, 162 Misc.2d 527, 617 N.Y.S.2d 1024 (N.Y.City Civ.Ct.1994)—§ **18.71, n. 3.**

Miller v. Angliker, 848 F.2d 1312 (2nd Cir. 1988)—§ **38.8, n. 197.**

Miller v. Beaugrand, 169 A.D.2d 537, 564 N.Y.S.2d 390 (N.Y.A.D. 1 Dept.1991)—§ **30.30, n. 27.**

Miller v. City of New York, 255 N.Y.S.2d 78, 203 N.E.2d 478 (N.Y.1964)—§ **3.16, n. 10.**

Miller v. Finkle (N.Y.Gen.Tr 1853)—§ **38.10, n. 133.**

Miller v. Messina, 150 A.D.2d 535, 541 N.Y.S.2d 121 (N.Y.A.D. 2 Dept.1989)—§ **16.125, n. 15.**

Miller, People v., 174 A.D.2d 989, 572 N.Y.S.2d 149 (N.Y.A.D. 4 Dept.1991)—§ **38.28, n. 2.**

Miller, People v., 493 N.Y.S.2d 96, 482 N.E.2d 892 (N.Y.1985)—§ **38.21, n. 58.**

Miller, People v., 300 N.Y.S.2d 584, 248 N.E.2d 441 (N.Y.1969)—§ **33.68, n. 3.**

Miller, People ex rel. MacCracken v., 291 N.Y. 55, 50 N.E.2d 542 (N.Y.1943)—§ **38.20; § 38.20, n. 10.**

Miller v. Perini Corp. (In re A.J. Lane & Co., Inc.), 164 B.R. 409 (Bkrtcy.D.Mass. 1994)—§ **9.118, n. 6.**

Miller v. Rivard, 180 A.D.2d 331, 585 N.Y.S.2d 523 (N.Y.A.D. 3 Dept.1992)—§ **29.11, n. 8.**

Miller v. Schloss, 218 N.Y. 400, 113 N.E. 337 (N.Y.1916)—§ **17.33; § 17.33, n. 1.**

Miller v. Southold Town, 190 A.D.2d 672, 593 N.Y.S.2d 74 (N.Y.A.D. 2 Dept. 1993)—§ **16.44, n. 6.**

Miller v. Valley Forge Village, 403 N.Y.S.2d 207, 374 N.E.2d 118 (N.Y.1978)—§ **16.124, n. 8, 9.**

Miller Brewing Co. v. State Div. of Human Rights, 498 N.Y.S.2d 776, 489 N.E.2d 745 (N.Y.1985)—§ **17.59, n. 1.**

Mills v. Pappas, 174 A.D.2d 780, 570 N.Y.S.2d 726 (N.Y.A.D. 3 Dept.1991)—§ **28.3, n. 1.**

Mills v. Sweeney, 219 N.Y. 213, 114 N.E. 65 (N.Y.1916)—§ **3.15, n. 2.**

Mil–Pine Plaza, Inc. v. State, 72 A.D.2d 460, 424 N.Y.S.2d 937 (N.Y.A.D. 4 Dept. 1980)—§ **14.87, n. 1.**

Miltland Raleigh–Durham v. Myers, 807 F.Supp. 1025 (S.D.N.Y.1992)—§ **2.59, n. 7.**

Minarich, People v., 415 N.Y.S.2d 825, 389 N.E.2d 137 (N.Y.1979)—§ **38.19, n. 94.**

Minarovich v. Sobala, 121 A.D.2d 701, 504 N.Y.S.2d 143 (N.Y.A.D. 2 Dept.1986)—§ **21.69, n. 8.**

Minaya, People v., 445 N.Y.S.2d 690, 429 N.E.2d 1161 (N.Y.1981)—§ **38.10, n. 130, 134.**

Mincey v. Arizona, 437 U.S. 385, 98 S.Ct. 2408, 57 L.Ed.2d 290 (1978)—§ **33.58.**

Mindel v. Village of Thomaston, 150 A.D.2d 653, 541 N.Y.S.2d 526 (N.Y.A.D. 2 Dept. 1989)—§ **4.72, n. 3.**

Miner v. City of Glens Falls, 999 F.2d 655 (2nd Cir.1993)—§ **18.18, n. 10.**

Miner v. Walden, 101 Misc.2d 814, 422 N.Y.S.2d 335 (N.Y.Sup.1979)—§ **28.29; § 28.29, n. 6.**

Minges, Matter of, 602 F.2d 38 (2nd Cir. 1979)—§ **9.78, n. 1; § 9.81, n. 1.**

Minick v. Park, 217 A.D.2d 489, 629 N.Y.S.2d 754 (N.Y.A.D. 1 Dept.1995)—§ **30.42, n. 7.**

Minister, Elders and Deacons of Reformed Protestant Dutch Church of City of New York v. 198 Broadway, Inc., 559 N.Y.S.2d 866, 559 N.E.2d 429 (N.Y. 1990)—§ **37.83, n. 6.**

Minjak Co. v. Randolph, 140 A.D.2d 245, 528 N.Y.S.2d 554 (N.Y.A.D. 1 Dept. 1988)—§ **13.31; § 13.31, n. 1, 6.**

Minnick v. Mississippi, 498 U.S. 146, 111 S.Ct. 486, 112 L.Ed.2d 489 (1990)—§ **33.56, n. 2.**

Minotti v. Lensink, 798 F.2d 607 (2nd Cir. 1986)—§ **18.33, n. 5.**

Minsky v. Tully, 78 A.D.2d 955, 433 N.Y.S.2d 276 (N.Y.A.D. 3 Dept.1980)—§ **35.16, n. 4.**

Minton Group, Inc., In re, 43 B.R. 705 (Bkrtcy.S.D.N.Y.1984)—§ **9.205, n. 6.**

TABLE OF CASES

Mintz v. Banks, N.Y.L.J., 6/2/76, p.13, col.6 (App. Term, 2d Dep't)—§ **13.18, n. 18.**

Mintz, People v., 283 N.Y.S.2d 120, 229 N.E.2d 712 (N.Y.1967)—§ **38.8, n. 33;** § **38.41, n. 1.**

Mirand v. City of New York, 614 N.Y.S.2d 372, 637 N.E.2d 263 (N.Y.1994)—§ **37.29, n. 2.**

Miranda v. Arizona, 384 U.S. 436, 86 S.Ct. 1602, 16 L.Ed.2d 694 (1966)—§ **33.48, n. 1;** § **33.58.**

Mirchel v. RMJ Securities Corp., 205 A.D.2d 388, 613 N.Y.S.2d 876 (N.Y.A.D. 1 Dept.1994)—§ **17.34;** § **17.34, n. 16, 19.**

Mireille J. v. Ernst F.J., 220 A.D.2d 503, 632 N.Y.S.2d 162 (N.Y.A.D. 2 Dept. 1995)—§ **37.19, n. 30.**

Mireles v. Waco, 502 U.S. 9, 112 S.Ct. 286, 116 L.Ed.2d 9 (1991)—§ **18.31, n. 2.**

Mirsky's Estate, In re, 81 Misc.2d 9, 365 N.Y.S.2d 122 (N.Y.Sur.1975)—§ **25.30, n. 4.**

Missan v. Schoenfeld, 95 A.D.2d 198, 465 N.Y.S.2d 706 (N.Y.A.D. 1 Dept.1983)—§ **2.46, n. 9.**

Mission of Immaculate Virgin v. Cronin, 143 N.Y. 524, 38 N.E. 964 (N.Y.1894)—§ **12.68, n. 3.**

Mississippi Band of Choctaw Indians v. Holyfield, 490 U.S. 30, 109 S.Ct. 1597, 104 L.Ed.2d 29 (1989)—§ **20.50, n. 2.**

Misuis, People v., 419 N.Y.S.2d 961, 393 N.E.2d 1034 (N.Y.1979)—§ **33.27;** § **33.27, n. 9.**

Mitchell v. Bane, 218 A.D.2d 537, 630 N.Y.S.2d 495 (N.Y.A.D. 1 Dept.1995)—§ **30.42, n. 6.**

Mitchell v. Board of Educ. of Garden City Union Free School Dist., 113 A.D.2d 924, 493 N.Y.S.2d 826 (N.Y.A.D. 2 Dept. 1985)—§ **3.28, n. 21.**

Mitchell v. Ford Motor Credit Co., 688 P.2d 42 (Okla.1984)—§ **7.25, n. 8.**

Mitchell v. Forest City Printing Co., 107 Misc. 709 (N.Y.Sup.1916)—§ **1.43, n. 27.**

Mitchell v. Forsyth, 472 U.S. 511, 105 S.Ct. 2806, 86 L.Ed.2d 411 (1985)—§ **18.31, n. 7;** § **18.32, n. 6.**

Mitchell v. Lindstrom, 12 A.D.2d 813, 209 N.Y.S.2d 923 (N.Y.A.D. 2 Dept.1961)—§ **37.26, n. 1.**

Mitchell, People v., 99 A.D.2d 609, 472 N.Y.S.2d 166 (N.Y.A.D. 3 Dept.1984)—§ **38.21;** § **38.21, n. 25.**

Mitchell, People v., 75 A.D.2d 626, 426 N.Y.S.2d 833 (N.Y.A.D. 2 Dept.1980)—§ **38.6;** § **38.6, n. 10, 11.**

Mitchill v. Lath, 247 N.Y. 377, 160 N.E. 646 (N.Y.1928)—§ **5.21, n. 8.**

Mitran v. Williamson, 21 Misc.2d 106, 197 N.Y.S.2d 689 (N.Y.Sup.1960)—§ **30.9, n. 33.**

Mittco, Inc., In re, 44 B.R. 35 (Bkrtcy. E.D.Wis.1984)—§ **9.39, n. 3.**

Mitzner v. Mitzner, 209 A.D.2d 487, 619 N.Y.S.2d 51 (N.Y.A.D. 2 Dept.1994)—§ **21.44, n. 6.**

Mize v. State Division of Human Rights, 38 A.D.2d 278, 328 N.Y.S.2d 983 (N.Y.A.D. 4 Dept.1972)—§ **17.44, n. 4, 7.**

Mizugami v. Sharin West Overseas, Inc., 183 A.D.2d 962, 583 N.Y.S.2d 577 (N.Y.A.D. 3 Dept.1992)—§ **37.28, n. 25.**

M.M.E. Power Enterprises, Inc., Matter of, 205 A.D.2d 631, 613 N.Y.S.2d 266 (N.Y.A.D. 2 Dept.1994)—§ **10.16, n. 9.**

M & M Partnership v. Sweenor, 210 A.D.2d 575, 619 N.Y.S.2d 802 (N.Y.A.D. 3 Dept. 1994)—§ **16.101, n. 1.**

Mobay Corp. v. Allied-Signal, Inc., 761 F.Supp. 345 (D.N.J.1991)—§ **15.30, n. 12.**

Mobile Home Owners Protective Ass'n v. Town of Chatham, 33 A.D.2d 78, 305 N.Y.S.2d 334 (N.Y.A.D. 3 Dept.1969)—§ **16.124, n. 13.**

Mobil Oil Corp. v. Syracuse Indus. Development Agency, 559 N.Y.S.2d 947, 559 N.E.2d 641 (N.Y.1990)—§ **15.6;** § **15.6, n. 7.**

Mobley, People v., 450 N.Y.S.2d 302, 435 N.E.2d 672 (N.Y.1982)—§ **38.19, n. 92.**

Mock v. LaGuardia Hospital-Hip Hosp., Inc., 117 A.D.2d 721, 498 N.Y.S.2d 446 (N.Y.A.D. 2 Dept.1986)—§ **17.25, n. 9.**

Model Imperial Supply Co., Inc. v. Westwind Cosmetics, Inc., 829 F.Supp. 35 (E.D.N.Y.1993)—§ **5.50, n. 7.**

Modjeska Sign Studios, Inc. v. Berle, 402 N.Y.S.2d 359, 373 N.E.2d 255 (N.Y. 1977)—§ **16.69, n. 2.**

Modu Craft, Inc. v. Liberatore, 89 A.D.2d 776, 453 N.Y.S.2d 488 (N.Y.A.D. 4 Dept. 1982)—§ **5.17, n. 6.**

Moed, Matter of, 1995 WL 46982, (N.Y. Tax App.)—§ **35.15, n. 1.**

Moehlenbrock v. Parke, Davis & Co., 141 Minn. 154, 169 N.W. 541 (Minn.1918)—§ **27.20, n. 3.**

Moffitt v. Town of Brookfield, 950 F.2d 880 (2nd Cir.1991)—§ **18.35, n. 1.**

Mohasco Corp. v. Silver, 447 U.S. 807, 100 S.Ct. 2486, 65 L.Ed.2d 532 (1980)—§ **17.88.**

Mojica v. City of New York, 199 A.D.2d 250, 604 N.Y.S.2d 235 (N.Y.A.D. 2 Dept. 1993)—§ **37.29, n. 21.**

Molina, People v., 203 A.D.2d 486, 610 N.Y.S.2d 589 (N.Y.A.D. 2 Dept.1994)—§ **38.28, n. 20.**

TABLE OF CASES

Molinelli v. Tucker, 901 F.2d 13 (2nd Cir. 1990)—§ **18.32, n. 7.**
Moller v. North Shore University Hosp., 12 F.3d 13 (2nd Cir.1993)—§ **30.11, n. 9.**
Monaco v. Lincoln Sav. Bank, 1995 WL 66643 (S.D.N.Y.1995)—§ **17.69, n. 3.**
Monahan, People v., 21 A.D.2d 748, 250 N.Y.S.2d 241 (N.Y.A.D. 4 Dept.1964)—§ **38.10, n. 100.**
Monclavo, People v., 643 N.Y.S.2d 470, 666 N.E.2d 175 (N.Y.1996)—§ **18.12, n. 1.**
Monell v. Department of Social Services of City of New York, 436 U.S. 658, 98 S.Ct. 2018, 56 L.Ed.2d 611 (1978)—§ **18.34;** § **18.34, n. 1.**
Monereau, People v., 181 A.D.2d 918, 581 N.Y.S.2d 848 (N.Y.A.D. 2 Dept.1992)—§ **38.10;** § **38.10, n. 140.**
Monnin, Matter of Estate of, 221 A.D.2d 1033, 635 N.Y.S.2d 405 (N.Y.A.D. 4 Dept.1995)—§ **37.37, n. 7.**
Monroe v. Leonard, 62 Misc.2d 463, 308 N.Y.S.2d 933 (N.Y.City Civ.Ct.1969)—§ **30.30, n. 1.**
Monroe County v. Morgan, 83 A.D.2d 777, 443 N.Y.S.2d 467 (N.Y.A.D. 4 Dept. 1981)—§ **14.23, n. 3.**
Monroe Well Service, Inc., In re, 80 B.R. 324 (Bkrtcy.E.D.Pa.1987)—§ **9.148, n. 8;** § **9.170, n. 5.**
Monser v. State, 96 A.D.2d 702, 466 N.Y.S.2d 780 (N.Y.A.D. 3 Dept.1983)—§ **14.82, n. 9.**
Montauk Imp., Inc. v. Proccacino, 394 N.Y.S.2d 619, 363 N.E.2d 344 (N.Y. 1977)—§ **4.18, n. 14.**
Montero, People v., 221 A.D.2d 570, 634 N.Y.S.2d 405 (N.Y.A.D. 2 Dept.1995)—§ **38.19, n. 48.**
Montey Corp. v. Maletta (In re Maletta), 159 B.R. 108 (Bkrtcy.D.Conn.1993)—§ **9.181, n. 2.**
Montgomery, People v., 299 N.Y.S.2d 156, 247 N.E.2d 130 (N.Y.1969)—§ **38.3, n. 9;** § **38.9, n. 15;** § **38.10, n. 72;** § **38.14, n. 7.**
Montgomery, People v., 278 N.Y.S.2d 226, 224 N.E.2d 730 (N.Y.1966)—§ **38.19, n. 116.**
Montgomery Court Apartments of Ingham County, Ltd., In re, 141 B.R. 324 (Bkrtcy.S.D.Ohio 1992)—§ **9.157, n. 5.**
Moody Hill Farms, Inc. v. Zoning Bd. of Appeals of Town of North East, 199 A.D.2d 954, 605 N.Y.S.2d 560 (N.Y.A.D. 3 Dept.1993)—§ **16.119, n. 11.**
Moon v. New York State Dept. of Social Services, 207 A.D.2d 103, 621 N.Y.S.2d 164 (N.Y.A.D. 3 Dept.1995)—§ **4.63, n. 3.**

Mooney v. Nationwide Mut. Ins. Co., 172 A.D.2d 144, 577 N.Y.S.2d 506 (N.Y.A.D. 3 Dept.1991)—§ **30.27, n. 8.**
Mooney, People v., 560 N.Y.S.2d 115, 559 N.E.2d 1274 (N.Y.1990)—§ **17.74, n. 5.**
Moore v. Aegon Reinsurance Co. of America, 196 A.D.2d 250, 608 N.Y.S.2d 166 (N.Y.A.D. 1 Dept.1994)—§ **31.23, n. 8.**
Moore v. Commissioner, T.C. Memo. 1991-546 (U.S.Tax Ct.1991)—§ **24.41, n. 2.**
Moore v. City of East Cleveland, Ohio, 431 U.S. 494, 97 S.Ct. 1932, 52 L.Ed.2d 531 (1977)—§ **16.122, n. 3.**
Moore v. Constantine, 191 A.D.2d 769, 594 N.Y.S.2d 395 (N.Y.A.D. 3 Dept.1993)—§ **18.10, n. 6.**
Moore v. Metropolitan St. Ry. Co., 84 A.D. 613, 82 N.Y.S. 778 (N.Y.A.D. 2 Dept. 1903)—§ **30.18, n. 6.**
Moore v. New York Cotton Exchange, 270 U.S. 593, 46 S.Ct. 367, 70 L.Ed. 750 (1926)—§ **9.112, n. 2.**
Moore, People v., 220 A.D.2d 621, 632 N.Y.S.2d 596 (N.Y.A.D. 2 Dept.1995)—§ **38.8, n. 196.**
Moore, People v., 193 A.D.2d 627, 597 N.Y.S.2d 444 (N.Y.A.D. 2 Dept.1993)—§ **38.21, n. 11.**
Moore, People v., 168 A.D.2d 463, 562 N.Y.S.2d 582 (N.Y.A.D. 2 Dept.1990)—§ **33.55, n. 2.**
Moore, People v., 529 N.Y.S.2d 739, 525 N.E.2d 460 (N.Y.1988)—§ **38.19, n. 140.**
Moore v. Sims, 442 U.S. 415, 99 S.Ct. 2371, 60 L.Ed.2d 994 (1979)—§ **18.36, n. 4.**
Moore v. State Div. of Human Rights of State of N.Y., 154 A.D.2d 823, 546 N.Y.S.2d 487 (N.Y.A.D. 3 Dept.1989)—§ **18.49, n. 10.**
Moore–McCormack Lines, Inc v. Maryland Cas Co, 181 F.Supp. 854 (S.D.N.Y. 1959)—§ **31.2, n. 5.**
Moorhead, People v., 473 N.Y.S.2d 967, 462 N.E.2d 144 (N.Y.1984)—§ **33.85, n. 1.**
Moquin, People v., 568 N.Y.S.2d 710, 570 N.E.2d 1059 (N.Y.1991)—§ **38.10, n. 18, 139.**
Moquin, People v., 153 A.D.2d 189, 550 N.Y.S.2d 490 (N.Y.A.D. 3 Dept.1990)—§ **38.10, n. 17.**
Moquin, People v., 142 A.D.2d 347, 536 N.Y.S.2d 561 (N.Y.A.D. 3 Dept.1988)—§ **38.10;** § **38.10, n. 15.**
Morales (Morales), Matter of, N.Y.L.J., 7/28/95, p. 25, col. 1 (Sup.Ct., Kings County)—§ **22.48, n. 13.**
Morales v. Gross, 230 A.D.2d 7, 657 N.Y.S.2d 711 (N.Y.A.D. 2 Dept.1997)—§ **32.15, n. 9, 10.**
Morales, People v., 494 N.Y.S.2d 95, 484 N.E.2d 124 (N.Y.1985)—§ **33.50;** § **33.50, n. 1.**

TABLE OF CASES

Morales, People v., 92 A.D.2d 575, 459 N.Y.S.2d 725 (N.Y.A.D. 2 Dept.1983)—§ 38.8, n. 42.

Morawetz' Will, In re, 35 Misc.2d 762, 231 N.Y.S.2d 1000 (N.Y.Sur.1962)—§ 24.9, n. 2.

Moreli, People v., 11 A.D.2d 437, 207 N.Y.S.2d 843 (N.Y.A.D. 3 Dept.1960)—§ 38.10, n. 2.

Morell v. Balasubramanian, 520 N.Y.S.2d 530, 514 N.E.2d 1101 (N.Y.1987)—§ 26.41, n. 14.

Moreno v. City of New York, 515 N.Y.S.2d 733, 508 N.E.2d 645 (N.Y.1987)—§ 18.11, n. 1, 5.

Moretti, Application of, 159 Misc.2d 654, 606 N.Y.S.2d 543 (N.Y.Sup.1993)—§ 22.48, n. 1, 13; § 22.49, n. 1.

Morfesis v. Sobol, 172 A.D.2d 897, 567 N.Y.S.2d 954 (N.Y.A.D. 3 Dept.1991)—§ 29.49, n. 2.

Morgan v. American Risk Management, Inc., 1990 WL 106837 (S.D.N.Y.1990)—§ 31.23, n. 3, 11.

Morgan, People v., 145 A.D.2d 442, 535 N.Y.S.2d 97 (N.Y.A.D. 2 Dept.1988)—§ 38.21, n. 11.

Morgenthau v. Citisource, Inc., 508 N.Y.S.2d 152, 500 N.E.2d 850 (N.Y. 1986)—§ 38.8, n. 61.

Morgenthau v. Roberts, 47 A.D.2d 826, 366 N.Y.S.2d 20 (N.Y.A.D. 1 Dept.1975)—§ 38.10, n. 147.

Morgenthau v. Rosenberger, 633 N.Y.S.2d 473, 657 N.E.2d 494 (N.Y.1995)—§ 38.15, n. 3.

Moriarty v. Planning Bd. of Village of Sloatsburg, 119 A.D.2d 188, 506 N.Y.S.2d 184 (N.Y.A.D. 2 Dept.1986)—§ 16.12, n. 20; § 16.17, n. 11; § 16.21; § 16.21, n. 2; § 16.106, n. 10.

Morimando v. Morimando, 145 A.D.2d 609, 536 N.Y.S.2d 701 (N.Y.A.D. 2 Dept. 1988)—§ 21.39, n. 9.

Morin v. Foster, 408 N.Y.S.2d 387, 380 N.E.2d 217 (N.Y.1978)—§ 3.8, n. 6; § 3.16, n. 4; § 3.24, n. 10.

Morin, People v., 192 A.D.2d 791, 596 N.Y.S.2d 508 (N.Y.A.D. 3 Dept.1993)—§ 38.19, n. 76; § 38.21, n. 44.

Morley v. Arricale, 495 N.Y.S.2d 966, 486 N.E.2d 824 (N.Y.1985)—§ 4.79, n. 7.

Morley v. Town of Oswegatchie, 524 N.Y.S.2d 430, 519 N.E.2d 341 (N.Y. 1987)—§ 39.10, n. 3.

Morris v. Clements, 228 A.D.2d 990, 644 N.Y.S.2d 850 (N.Y.A.D. 3 Dept.1996)—§ 26.42, n. 9.

Morris v. Snappy Car Rental, Inc., 614 N.Y.S.2d 362, 637 N.E.2d 253 (N.Y. 1994)—§ 5.12, n. 5, 6.

Morris v. United Parcel Service, 134 A.D.2d 840, 521 N.Y.S.2d 591 (N.Y.A.D. 4 Dept. 1987)—§ 17.65, n. 3.

Morrison, Matter of, 147 Misc.2d 657, 559 N.Y.S.2d 448 (N.Y.Sup.1990)—§ 22.5, n. 11.

Morrison, Application of, 7 A.D.2d 42, 180 N.Y.S.2d 760 (N.Y.A.D. 1 Dept.1958)—§ 1.43, n. 25.

Morrissey v. Sobol, 176 A.D.2d 1147, 575 N.Y.S.2d 960 (N.Y.A.D. 3 Dept.1991)—§ 4.81, n. 1.

Morschauser v. American News Co., 6 A.D.2d 1028, 178 N.Y.S.2d 279 (N.Y.A.D. 1 Dept.1958)—§ 17.33, n. 5.

Morse, People v., 182 A.D.2d 781, 582 N.Y.S.2d 776 (N.Y.A.D. 2 Dept.1992)—§ 38.21, n. 11.

Morse, People v., 476 N.Y.S.2d 505, 465 N.E.2d 12 (N.Y.1984)—§ 38.19; § 38.19, n. 33; § 38.22, n. 2.

Morse v. Swank, Inc., 459 F.Supp. 660 (S.D.N.Y.1978)—§ 17.27, n. 5.

Morse v. University of Vermont, 973 F.2d 122 (2nd Cir.1992)—§ 18.19, n. 6; § 18.53, n. 4.

Mortgagee Affiliates, Inc. v. Jerder Realty Corp., 62 A.D.2d 591, 406 N.Y.S.2d 326 (N.Y.A.D. 2 Dept.1978)—§ 37.37, n. 94.

Moscatiello, People v., 149 Misc.2d 752, 566 N.Y.S.2d 823 (N.Y.Sup.1990)—§ 38.10, n. 175.

Moses, People v., 482 N.Y.S.2d 228, 472 N.E.2d 4 (N.Y.1984)—§ 38.19, n. 67.

Moskowitz v. Simms, N.Y.L.J., 4/28/75, p.18, col. (App. Term, 2d Dep't)—§ 13.33, n. 11.

Mosser v. Darrow, 341 U.S. 267, 71 S.Ct. 680, 95 L.Ed. 927 (1951)—§ 9.139, n. 1.

Mosseri v. Zimmerman & Zimmerman, 114 A.D.2d 338, 494 N.Y.S.2d 327 (N.Y.A.D. 1 Dept.1985)—§ 28.10, n. 12.

Moss, Estate of v. Commssioner, 74 T.C. 1239 (U.S.Tax Ct.1980)—§ 24.57, n. 3.

Motor Vehicle Acc. Indemnification Corp. v. Eisenberg, 271 N.Y.S.2d 641, 218 N.E.2d 524 (N.Y.1966)—§ 26.28, n. 8.

Motor Vehicle Mfrs. Ass'n of United States, Inc. v. Jorling, 152 Misc.2d 405, 577 N.Y.S.2d 346 (N.Y.Sup.1991)—§ 4.45, n. 19.

Motor Vehicle Mfrs. Ass'n of United States, Inc. v. New York State Dept. of Environmental Conservation, 17 F.3d 521 (2nd Cir.1994)—§ 15.21, n. 11.

Motor Vehicle Mfrs. Ass'n of United States, Inc. v. State, 551 N.Y.S.2d 470, 550 N.E.2d 919 (N.Y.1990)—§ 4.68; § 4.68, n. 7; § 7.17, n. 6.

Motor Vehicle Mfrs. Ass'n of United States, Inc. v. State, 146 A.D.2d 212, 540

TABLE OF CASES

N.Y.S.2d 888 (N.Y.A.D. 3 Dept.1989)—§ **7.17, n. 3.**
Motsiff v. State, 32 A.D.2d 729, 301 N.Y.S.2d 786 (N.Y.A.D. 4 Dept.1969)—§ **14.95, n. 5.**
Motyka v. City of Amsterdam, 256 N.Y.S.2d 595, 204 N.E.2d 635 (N.Y.1965)—§ **3.30, n. 5.**
Mountain View Coach Lines, Inc. v. Storms, 102 A.D.2d 663, 476 N.Y.S.2d 918 (N.Y.A.D. 2 Dept.1984)—§ **37.3, n. 14.**
Mount St. Mary's Hospital of Niagara Falls v. Catherwood, 311 N.Y.S.2d 863, 260 N.E.2d 508 (N.Y.1970)—§ **4.68, n. 5;** § **4.74, n. 2;** § **7.17, n. 4, 7.**
Mount's Will, In re, 185 N.Y. 162, 77 N.E. 999 (N.Y.1906)—§ **25.50, n. 6.**
Mount Vernon, City of v. Mount Vernon Housing Authority, 235 A.D.2d 516, 652 N.Y.S.2d 771 (N.Y.A.D. 2 Dept.1997)—§ **37.30, n. 7.**
Mount Vernon Fire Ins. Co. v. Mott, 179 A.D.2d 626, 578 N.Y.S.2d 231 (N.Y.A.D. 2 Dept.1992)—§ **31.21, n. 6.**
Mount Vernon Housing Authority v. Jordan, 120 Misc.2d 670, 466 N.Y.S.2d 546 (N.Y.City Ct.1982)—§ **4.2, n. 4.**
Mowrer, Matter of, 17 I & N Dec. 613 (BIA 1981)—§ **19.11, n. 9.**
Mozzochi v. Borden, 959 F.2d 1174 (2nd Cir.1992)—§ **18.32, n. 3.**
Mrs. C. v. Wheaton, 916 F.2d 69 (2nd Cir. 1990)—§ **18.53, n. 5.**
Mrs. W. v. Tirozzi, 832 F.2d 748 (2nd Cir. 1987)—§ **18.53, n. 5.**
Mrvica v. Esperdy, 376 U.S. 560, 84 S.Ct. 833, 11 L.Ed.2d 911 (1964)—§ **19.47, n. 4.**
MSG Pomp Corp. v. Doe, 185 A.D.2d 798, 586 N.Y.S.2d 965 (N.Y.A.D. 1 Dept. 1992)—§ **13.16, n. 2;** § **13.18, n. 22;** § **13.44, n. 4.**
M. S. R. Associates Ltd. v. Consolidated Mut. Ins. Co., 58 A.D.2d 858, 396 N.Y.S.2d 684 (N.Y.A.D. 2 Dept.1977)—§ **30.34, n. 2.**
Mt. Nebo Baptist Church of NY v. Myers, N.Y.L.J., 4/10/79, p.10, col.5 (App. Term, 1st Dep't)—§ **13.33, n. 6.**
Muccini's Estate, Matter of, 118 Misc.2d 38, 460 N.Y.S.2d 680 (N.Y.Sur.1983)—§ **28.29, n. 3.**
Muchard v. Wilmet, 84 Misc.2d 949, 378 N.Y.S.2d 332 (N.Y.Sup.1976)—§ **11.50, n. 3.**
Mudge, Rose, Guthrie, Alexander & Ferdon v. Penguin Air Conditioning Corp., 221 A.D.2d 243, 633 N.Y.S.2d 493 (N.Y.A.D. 1 Dept.1995)—§ **37.37, n. 14.**
Muhlker v. Ruppert, 124 N.Y. 627, 26 N.E. 313 (N.Y.1891)—§ **12.9, n. 5.**

Mulder v. Donaldson, Lufkin & Jenrette, 208 A.D.2d 301, 623 N.Y.S.2d 560 (N.Y.A.D. 1 Dept.1995)—§ **17.33, n. 3;** § **17.35, n. 11, 13.**
Mullen v. Axelrod, 549 N.Y.S.2d 953, 549 N.E.2d 144 (N.Y.1989)—§ **37.25, n. 7.**
Mullen, People v., 403 N.Y.S.2d 470, 374 N.E.2d 369 (N.Y.1978)—§ **38.19, n. 112.**
Mullen v. United States, 696 F.2d 470 (6th Cir.1983)—§ **9.112, n. 4.**
Muller v. Muller, 221 A.D.2d 635, 634 N.Y.S.2d 190 (N.Y.A.D. 2 Dept.1995)—§ **37.19, n. 66.**
Mulligan, People v., 139 Misc.2d 1034, 530 N.Y.S.2d 434 (N.Y.Sup.1988)—§ **33.74, n. 3.**
Mullins v. 510 East 86th Street Owners, Inc., 126 Misc.2d 758, 483 N.Y.S.2d 631 (N.Y.City Civ.Ct.1984)—§ **1.27, n. 5.**
Mullins v. Pfizer, Inc., 23 F.3d 663 (2nd Cir.1994)—§ **17.50, n. 3.**
Multi–Group III Ltd. Partnership, In re, 99 B.R. 5 (Bkrtcy.D.Ariz.1989)—§ **9.69, n. 5.**
Mumford v. McKay, 8 Wend. 442 (N.Y.Sup. 1832)—§ **2.37, n. 5.**
Mundhenk, People v., 141 Misc.2d 795, 534 N.Y.S.2d 843 (N.Y.Co.Ct.1988)—§ **38.58, n. 4, 5.**
Munoz v. City of New York, 271 N.Y.S.2d 645, 218 N.E.2d 527 (N.Y.1966)—§ **18.25, n. 2.**
Munroe v. 344 East 76th Realty Corp., 113 Misc.2d 155, 448 N.Y.S.2d 388 (N.Y.Sup. 1982)—§ **18.45, n. 4.**
Munzer v. St. Paul Fire and Marine Ins. Co., 145 A.D.2d 193, 538 N.Y.S.2d 633 (N.Y.A.D. 3 Dept.1989)—§ **31.27, n. 1.**
Murel Holding Corp., In re, 75 F.2d 941 (2nd Cir.1935)—§ **9.57, n. 1.**
Murphy v. American Home Products Corp., 136 A.D.2d 229, 527 N.Y.S.2d 1 (N.Y.A.D. 1 Dept.1988)—§ **17.37, n. 8.**
Murphy v. American Home Products Corp., 461 N.Y.S.2d 232, 448 N.E.2d 86 (N.Y. 1983)—§ **17.28;** § **17.28, n. 2;** § **17.31;** § **17.31, n. 4;** § **17.32, n. 1, 6;** § **17.33, n. 3;** § **17.35, n. 5;** § **17.69, n. 1;** § **30.9, n. 28.**
Murphy v. John Hofman Co., 177 A.D. 380, 163 N.Y.S. 932 (N.Y.A.D. 3 Dept.1917)—§ **30.28, n. 5.**
Murphy v. Kelley, 116 A.D.2d 967, 498 N.Y.S.2d 537 (N.Y.A.D. 3 Dept.1986)—§ **38.8, n. 134.**
Murphy v. Lynn, 53 F.3d 547 (2nd Cir. 1995)—§ **18.25, n. 4;** § **18.38, n. 5.**
Murphy v. Murphy, 109 A.D.2d 965, 486 N.Y.S.2d 457 (N.Y.A.D. 3 Dept.1985)—§ **18.74, n. 1.**
Murphy v. Relaxation Plus Commodore, Ltd., 83 Misc.2d 838, 373 N.Y.S.2d 793

TABLE OF CASES

(N.Y.Sup.App.Term 1975)—§ **13.38, n. 1.**

Murphy v. 253 Garth Tenants Corp., 579 F.Supp. 1150 (S.D.N.Y.1983)—§ **18.50, n. 2.**

Murphy v. Wack, 186 A.D.2d 427, 588 N.Y.S.2d 555 (N.Y.A.D. 1 Dept.1992)—§ **37.37, n. 25.**

Murphy-Artale v. Artale, 219 A.D.2d 587, 632 N.Y.S.2d 19 (N.Y.A.D. 2 Dept. 1995)—§ **21.53, n. 4.**

Murphy, Estate of v. Commissioner, T.C. Memo. 1990-472 (U.S.Tax Ct.1990)—§ **24.56, n. 4.**

Murray v. Narwood, 192 N.Y. 172, 84 N.E. 958 (N.Y.1908)—§ **5.8, n. 4.**

Murray v. National Broadcasting Co., Inc., 217 A.D.2d 651, 629 N.Y.S.2d 802 (N.Y.A.D. 2 Dept.1995)—§ **37.65, n. 66.**

Murray v. New York University College of Dentistry, 57 F.3d 243 (2nd Cir.1995)—§ **18.53, n. 7.**

Murray, People v., 131 A.D.2d 885, 517 N.Y.S.2d 242 (N.Y.A.D. 2 Dept.1987)—§ **38.19, n. 64.**

Murray v. Robin, 108 A.D.2d 903, 485 N.Y.S.2d 788 (N.Y.A.D. 2 Dept.1985)—§ **37.28, n. 28.**

Murriello v. Crapotta, 51 A.D.2d 381, 382 N.Y.S.2d 513 (N.Y.A.D. 2 Dept.1976)—§ **29.26, n. 4.**

Murtha v. New York Homeopathic Medical College and Flower Hospital, 228 N.Y. 183, 126 N.E. 722 (N.Y.1920)—§ **3.30, n. 2.**

Musco v. Conte, 22 A.D.2d 121, 254 N.Y.S.2d 589 (N.Y.A.D. 2 Dept.1964)—§ **28.26, n. 2.**

Mutual Ben. Life Ins. Co. v. JMR Electronics Corp., 848 F.2d 30 (2nd Cir.1988)—§ **31.18, n. 3.**

M. Viaggio & Sons, Inc. v. City of New York, 114 A.D.2d 939, 495 N.Y.S.2d 680 (N.Y.A.D. 2 Dept.1985)—§ **30.39, n. 4, 5.**

MXP Realty Corp. v. Angrisani, 152 Misc.2d 458, 576 N.Y.S.2d 754 (N.Y.Sup.1991)—§ **10.19, n. 3.**

Mycak v. Honeywell, Inc., 953 F.2d 798 (2nd Cir.1992)—§ **17.34, n. 7.**

Myers, Smith & Granady, Inc. v. New York Property Ins. Underwriting Ass'n, 201 A.D.2d 312, 607 N.Y.S.2d 288 (N.Y.A.D. 1 Dept.1994)—§ **31.26, n. 9.**

Mykap Realty Corp. v. Goodman, 5 A.D.2d 780, 169 N.Y.S.2d 956 (N.Y.A.D. 2 Dept. 1958)—§ **11.54, n. 5.**

Mylott v. Sisca, 168 A.D.2d 852, 564 N.Y.S.2d 523 (N.Y.A.D. 3 Dept.1990)—§ **12.66; § 12.66, n. 6.**

Myrick v. Freuhauf Corp., 13 F.3d 1516 (11th Cir.1994)—§ **27.45, n. 3; § 27.51, n. 1.**

Myrick v. Freuhauf Corp., 795 F.Supp. 1139 (N.D.Ga.1992)—§ **27.45; § 27.45, n. 2.**

Myzal v. Mecca, 28 A.D.2d 1022, 283 N.Y.S.2d 785 (N.Y.A.D. 3 Dept.1967)—§ **8.10, n. 4.**

N

Nadel v. Brillo Mfg. Co., 123 Misc. 952, 206 N.Y.S. 631 (N.Y.Sup.1924)—§ **1.12, n. 8.**

Nadel v. Manhattan Life Ins. Co., 211 A.D.2d 900, 621 N.Y.S.2d 180 (N.Y.A.D. 3 Dept.1995)—§ **31.18, n. 11.**

Nagin v. Long Island Sav. Bank, 94 A.D.2d 710, 462 N.Y.S.2d 69 (N.Y.A.D. 2 Dept. 1983)—§ **37.43, n. 8.**

Nagy v. Riblet Products Corp., 79 F.3d 572 (7th Cir.1996)—§ **9.87, n. 1.**

N. A. Kerson Co., Inc. v. Shayne, Dachs, Weiss, Kolbrenner, Levy and Moe Levine, 59 A.D.2d 551, 397 N.Y.S.2d 142 (N.Y.A.D. 2 Dept.1977)—§ **28.9; § 28.9, n. 1, 3.**

Nanuet Nat. Bank v. Eckerson Terrace, Inc., 417 N.Y.S.2d 901, 391 N.E.2d 983 (N.Y.1979)—§ **10.59, n. 3.**

Napoli v. Domnitch, 18 A.D.2d 707, 236 N.Y.S.2d 549 (N.Y.A.D. 2 Dept.1962)—§ **2.51, n. 26.**

Napolitano v. Branks, 128 A.D.2d 686, 513 N.Y.S.2d 185 (N.Y.A.D. 2 Dept.1987)—§ **30.6, n. 7.**

Nappi, People v., 272 N.Y.S.2d 347, 219 N.E.2d 176 (N.Y.1966)—§ **33.68, n. 10.**

Nasello v. Motor Vehicle Acc. Indemnification Corp., 30 A.D.2d 1041, 294 N.Y.S.2d 851 (N.Y.A.D. 4 Dept.1968)—§ **26.26, n. 2.**

Nassau, Matter of County of, 149 A.D.2d 701, 540 N.Y.S.2d 496 (N.Y.A.D. 2 Dept. 1989)—§ **14.93, n. 1, 2.**

Nassau, Matter of County of, 148 A.D.2d 533, 538 N.Y.S.2d 865 (N.Y.A.D. 2 Dept. 1989)—§ **14.84, n. 2.**

Nassau, Matter of County of, 144 A.D.2d 364, 533 N.Y.S.2d 781 (N.Y.A.D. 2 Dept. 1988)—§ **14.82, n. 4.**

Nassau, Matter of County of v. Incorporated Village of Roslyn, N.Y.L.J., 10/17/94, p.33, col.4—§ **37.71; § 37.71, n. 5.**

Nassau, Matter of County of v. Incorporated Village of Roslyn, N.Y.L.J., 12/16/94, p.34, col.3—§ **37.71, n. 6.**

Nassau County v. South Farmingdale Water Dist., 62 A.D.2d 380, 405 N.Y.S.2d 742 (N.Y.A.D. 2 Dept.1978)—§ **3.8, n. 2.**

TABLE OF CASES

Nassau Ins. Co. v. Guarascio, 82 A.D.2d 505, 442 N.Y.S.2d 83 (N.Y.A.D. 2 Dept. 1981)—§ **31.8, n. 1.**
Nassau Trust Co. v. Montrose Concrete Products Corp., 451 N.Y.S.2d 663, 436 N.E.2d 1265 (N.Y.1982)—§ **17.36, n. 1.**
Natal, People v., 497 N.Y.S.2d 909, 488 N.E.2d 839 (N.Y.1985)—§ **38.27, n. 33.**
Nate B. & Frances Spingold Foundation v. Wallin, Simon, Black and Co., 184 A.D.2d 464, 585 N.Y.S.2d 416 (N.Y.A.D. 1 Dept.1992)—§ **2.53, n. 6.**
National Conversion Corp. v. Cedar Bldg. Corp., 298 N.Y.S.2d 499, 246 N.E.2d 351 (N.Y.1969)—§ **30.5, n. 16.**
National Fuel Gas Supply Corp. v. Cunningham Natural Gas Corp., 191 A.D.2d 1003, 595 N.Y.S.2d 275 (N.Y.A.D. 4 Dept.1993)—§ **14.115, n. 9.**
National Life Ins. Co. v. Frank B. Hall & Co. of New York, Inc., 503 N.Y.S.2d 318, 494 N.E.2d 449 (N.Y.1986)—§ **28.14, n. 13.**
National Microsales Corp. v. Chase Manhattan Bank, N.A., 761 F.Supp. 304 (S.D.N.Y.1991)—§ **5.46, n. 4.**
National Recovery Systems v. Mazzei, 123 Misc.2d 780, 475 N.Y.S.2d 208 (N.Y.Sup. 1984)—§ **5.8, n. 1; § 5.11, n. 6.**
National Sur. Corp. v. R.H. Macy & Co., Inc., 116 Misc.2d 780, 455 N.Y.S.2d 1007 (N.Y.Sup.1982)—§ **8.34, n. 7.**
National Telecanvass Associates, Ltd. v. Smith, 98 A.D.2d 796, 470 N.Y.S.2d 22 (N.Y.A.D. 2 Dept.1983)—§ **30.39, n. 7.**
National Union Fire Ins. Co. v. Ranger Ins. Co., 190 A.D.2d 395, 599 N.Y.S.2d 347 (N.Y.A.D. 4 Dept.1993)—§ **31.29, n. 17.**
National Union Fire Ins. Co. of Pittsburgh, Pennsylvania v. Town of Huntington, 215 A.D.2d 544, 627 N.Y.S.2d 698 (N.Y.A.D. 2 Dept.1995)—§ **37.28, n. 31.**
National Westminster Bank USA v. Weksel, 124 A.D.2d 144, 511 N.Y.S.2d 626 (N.Y.A.D. 1 Dept.1987)—§ **28.11, n. 4.**
Nationwide Mut. Ins. Co. v. Darden, 503 U.S. 318, 112 S.Ct. 1344, 117 L.Ed.2d 581 (1992)—§ **17.17, n. 1.**
Nationwide Mut. Ins. Co. v. Rothbart, 220 A.D.2d 509, 632 N.Y.S.2d 481 (N.Y.A.D. 2 Dept.1995)—§ **37.37, n. 90.**
Natoli v. Sullivan, 159 Misc.2d 681, 606 N.Y.S.2d 504 (N.Y.Sup.1993)—§ **30.38, n. 6.**
Naujokas v. H. Frank Carey High School, 33 A.D.2d 703, 306 N.Y.S.2d 195 (N.Y.A.D. 2 Dept.1969)—§ **30.3, n. 5.**
Navaretta v. Group Health Inc., 191 A.D.2d 953, 595 N.Y.S.2d 839 (N.Y.A.D. 3 Dept. 1993)—§ **17.27; § 17.27, n. 7.**

Navarro v. Federal Paper Bd. Co., Inc., 185 A.D.2d 590, 586 N.Y.S.2d 381 (N.Y.A.D. 3 Dept.1992)—§ **17.28, n. 4.**
Nazito v. Holton, 96 A.D.2d 550, 465 N.Y.S.2d 62 (N.Y.A.D. 2 Dept.1983)—§ **37.38, n. 8.**
Neal v. Riverside Service, 75 A.D.2d 932, 427 N.Y.S.2d 520 (N.Y.A.D. 3 Dept. 1980)—§ **32.11, n. 7.**
Nealy, People v., 603 N.Y.S.2d 991, 624 N.E.2d 175 (N.Y.1993)—§ **39.42, n. 2.**
Nebbia v. People of New York, 291 U.S. 502, 54 S.Ct. 505, 78 L.Ed. 940 (1934)—§ **3.9, n. 2.**
NECA Ins. Ltd. v. National Union Fire Ins. Co. of Pittsburgh, Pa., 595 F.Supp. 955 (S.D.N.Y.1984)—§ **31.22, n. 3.**
Nectow v. City of Cambridge, 277 U.S. 183, 48 S.Ct. 447, 72 L.Ed. 842 (1928)—§ **16.22, n. 6.**
Neddermeyer v. Town of Ontario Planning Bd., 155 A.D.2d 908, 548 N.Y.S.2d 951 (N.Y.A.D. 4 Dept.1989)—§ **16.25, n. 4; § 16.131, n. 3.**
Nehorayoff v. Nehorayoff, 108 Misc.2d 311, 437 N.Y.S.2d 584 (N.Y.Sup.1981)—§ **21.40, n. 1.**
Nehrbas v. Village of Lloyd Harbor, 159 N.Y.S.2d 145, 140 N.E.2d 241 (N.Y. 1957)—§ **3.8, n. 6.**
Neil Plumbing & Heating Const. Corp. v. Providence Washington Ins. Co., 125 A.D.2d 295, 508 N.Y.S.2d 580 (N.Y.A.D. 2 Dept.1986)—§ **31.7, n. 9.**
Nell v. Nell, 166 A.D.2d 154, 560 N.Y.S.2d 426 (N.Y.A.D. 1 Dept.1990)—§ **21.40; § 21.40, n. 2.**
Nelsen v. Rampone, 31 A.D.2d 933, 299 N.Y.S.2d 18 (N.Y.A.D. 2 Dept.1969)—§ **37.51, n. 30.**
Nelson, In re, 173 A.D.2d 995, 569 N.Y.S.2d 513 (N.Y.A.D. 3 Dept.1991)—§ **17.60, n. 9.**
Nelson v. Bowen, 882 F.2d 45 (2nd Cir. 1989)—§ **34.46, n. 7; § 34.47, n. 7, 12, 23.**
Nelson v. Coughlin, 115 A.D.2d 131, 495 N.Y.S.2d 528 (N.Y.A.D. 3 Dept.1985)—§ **18.37, n. 8.**
Nelson v. Heckler, 712 F.2d 346 (8th Cir. 1983)—§ **34.46, n. 6.**
Nelson, People v., 216 A.D.2d 946, 629 N.Y.S.2d 705 (N.Y.A.D. 4 Dept.1995)—§ **38.25, n. 28.**
Nelson, People v., 173 A.D.2d 205, 569 N.Y.S.2d 86 (N.Y.A.D. 1 Dept.1991)—§ **38.8, n. 143.**
Nelson v. Schrank, 273 A.D. 72, 75 N.Y.S.2d 761 (N.Y.A.D. 2 Dept.1947)—§ **10.17, n. 9.**

TABLE OF CASES

Nelson's Will, In re, 105 Misc.2d 747, 433 N.Y.S.2d 314 (N.Y.Sur.1980)—§ **25.39, n. 2.**

Neptune Associates, Inc. v. Consolidated Edison Co. of New York, Inc., 125 A.D.2d 473, 509 N.Y.S.2d 574 (N.Y.A.D. 2 Dept.1986)—§ **14.38, n. 9.**

Nereida S., Matter of, 454 N.Y.S.2d 61, 439 N.E.2d 870 (N.Y.1982)—§ **20.39, n. 3.**

Netbai v. New York State Elec. and Gas Corp., 162 A.D.2d 862, 559 N.Y.S.2d 186 (N.Y.A.D. 3 Dept.1990)—§ **37.37, n. 47.**

Netfa P., Matter of, 115 A.D.2d 390, 496 N.Y.S.2d 21 (N.Y.A.D. 1 Dept.1985)— § **20.21, n. 2.**

Netherby Ltd. v. G.V. Licensing, Inc., 1994 WL 463007 (S.D.N.Y.1994)—§ **31.19, n. 2.**

Nettles, People v., 335 N.Y.S.2d 83, 286 N.E.2d 467 (N.Y.1972)—§ **38.8, n. 75;** § **38.9, n. 12.**

Neuman v. Pike, 591 F.2d 191 (2nd Cir. 1979)—§ **28.29, n. 11.**

Neumerski v. Califano, 513 F.Supp. 1011 (E.D.Pa.1981)—§ **34.9, n. 3.**

Neuwirth v. Blue Cross & Blue Shield of Greater New York, 476 N.Y.S.2d 814, 465 N.E.2d 353 (N.Y.1984)—§ **31.27, n. 2.**

Nevada v. Hall, 440 U.S. 410, 99 S.Ct. 1182, 59 L.Ed.2d 416 (1979)—§ **18.33, n. 1.**

Nevarez, People v., 142 Misc.2d 1064, 539 N.Y.S.2d 645 (N.Y.City Crim.Ct.1989)— § **33.90, n. 4.**

Neverla, In re, 194 B.R. 547 (Bkrtcy. W.D.N.Y.1996)—§ **9.249, n. 9.**

Newball, People v., 561 N.Y.S.2d 898, 563 N.E.2d 269 (N.Y.1990)—§ **38.19;** § **38.19, n. 138.**

Newberns, People v., 65 A.D.2d 533, 409 N.Y.S.2d 401 (N.Y.A.D. 1 Dept.1978)— § **37.37, n. 64.**

Newbery Corp. v. Fireman's Fund Ins. Co., 95 F.3d 1392 (9th Cir.1996)—§ **9.112, n. 2.**

Newbrand v. City of Yonkers, 285 N.Y. 164, 33 N.E.2d 75 (N.Y.1941)—§ **4.75, n. 1.**

Newburger, Loeb & Co., Inc. v. Gross, 563 F.2d 1057 (2nd Cir.1977)—§ **2.59, n. 2.**

Newcomb's Estate, In re, 192 N.Y. 238, 84 N.E. 950 (N.Y.1908)—§ **35.16, n. 2.**

New England Marine Services, Inc., In re, 174 B.R. 391 (Bkrtcy.E.D.N.Y.1994)— § **31.5, n. 2.**

New Era Homes Corporation v. Forster, 299 N.Y. 303, 86 N.E.2d 757 (N.Y. 1949)—§ **30.25, n. 6.**

New Jersey v. T.L.O., 469 U.S. 325, 105 S.Ct. 733, 83 L.Ed.2d 720 (1985)— § **18.9, n. 3;** § **18.10;** § **18.10, n. 9.**

New Life Fellowship, Inc. v. City of Cortland, 175 A.D.2d 343, 572 N.Y.S.2d 421 (N.Y.A.D. 3 Dept.1991)—§ **14.28, n. 3.**

Newmark v. Weingrad, 43 A.D.2d 983, 352 N.Y.S.2d 660 (N.Y.A.D. 2 Dept.1974)— § **12.64, n. 9.**

Newport, City of v. Fact Concerts, Inc., 453 U.S. 247, 101 S.Ct. 2748, 69 L.Ed.2d 616 (1981)—§ **18.34, n. 3.**

Newport News Shipbuilding and Dry Dock Co. v. E.E.O.C., 462 U.S. 669, 103 S.Ct. 2622, 77 L.Ed.2d 89 (1983)—§ **17.54, n. 3.**

New Rochelle, City of v. O. Mueller, Inc., 191 A.D.2d 435, 594 N.Y.S.2d 301 (N.Y.A.D. 2 Dept.1993)—§ **14.37, n. 3;** § **14.64, n. 2.**

New Valley Corp., In re, 168 B.R. 73 (Bkrtcy.D.N.J.1994)—§ **9.43, n. 13;** § **9.160, n. 6.**

New Windsor, Town of v. Tesa Tuck, Inc., 919 F.Supp. 662 (S.D.N.Y.1996)— § **15.30, n. 7.**

New York, Matter of City of, 98 A.D.2d 166, 471 N.Y.S.2d 105 (N.Y.A.D. 2 Dept. 1983)—§ **14.86, n. 1, 5.**

New York, Matter of City of, 73 A.D.2d 646, 422 N.Y.S.2d 742 (N.Y.A.D. 2 Dept. 1979)—§ **37.37, n. 44.**

New York v. Burger, 482 U.S. 691, 107 S.Ct. 2636, 96 L.Ed.2d 601 (1987)— § **4.62, n. 9, 11.**

New York v. Fermenta ASC Corp., 166 Misc.2d 524, 630 N.Y.S.2d 884 (N.Y.Sup. 1995)—§ **15.33, n. 2.**

New York v. Fermenta ASC Corp., 162 Misc.2d 288, 616 N.Y.S.2d 702 (N.Y.Sup. 1994)—§ **15.33, n. 3.**

New York v. Monarch Chemicals, Inc., 90 A.D.2d 907, 456 N.Y.S.2d 867 (N.Y.A.D. 3 Dept.1982)—§ **15.32, n. 9.**

New York v. Quarles, 467 U.S. 649, 104 S.Ct. 2626, 81 L.Ed.2d 550 (1984)— § **33.53;** § **33.53, n. 1.**

New York v. Wal–Mart Stores, Inc., 207 A.D.2d 150, 621 N.Y.S.2d 158 (N.Y.A.D. 3 Dept.1995)—§ **17.47, n. 1.**

New York Cent. & H.R.R. Co. v. City of Buffalo, 200 N.Y. 113, 93 N.E. 520 (N.Y. 1910)—§ **14.12;** § **14.12, n. 3.**

New York Cent. & H.R.R. Co. v. Metropolitan Gaslight Co., 63 N.Y. 326 (N.Y. 1875)—§ **14.11, n. 1.**

New York Cent. Mut. Fire Ins. Co. v. Nichols, 192 A.D.2d 1131, 596 N.Y.S.2d 621 (N.Y.A.D. 4 Dept.1993)—§ **31.24, n. 9.**

New York City Dept. of Correction v. White, 163 A.D.2d 250, 558 N.Y.S.2d 71 (N.Y.A.D. 1 Dept.1990)—§ **30.9, n. 27.**

New York City Dept. of Environmental Protection v. New York City Civil Service

TABLE OF CASES

Com'n, 574 N.Y.S.2d 664, 579 N.E.2d 1385 (N.Y.1991)—§ **4.74, n. 3, 4.**

New York City Health and Hospitals Corp. v. McBarnette, 616 N.Y.S.2d 1, 639 N.E.2d 740 (N.Y.1994)—§ **4.2, n. 41;** § **4.75, n. 5, 6;** § **4.82;** § **4.82, n. 5, 6.**

New York City Housing Authority v. Torres, 61 A.D.2d 681, 403 N.Y.S.2d 527 (N.Y.A.D. 1 Dept.1978)—§ **13.68;** § **13.68, n. 2.**

New York, City of v. Betancourt, 79 Misc.2d 907, 362 N.Y.S.2d 728 (N.Y.Sup.App. Term 1974)—§ **13.33, n. 11.**

New York, City of v. Betancourt, 79 Misc.2d 146, 359 N.Y.S.2d 707 (N.Y.City Civ.Ct. 1974)—§ **13.33, n. 2.**

New York, City of v. Brown, 119 Misc.2d 1054, 465 N.Y.S.2d 388 (N.Y.City Civ.Ct. 1982)—§ **13.20, n. 2.**

New York, City of v. Chemical Waste Disposal Corp., 836 F.Supp. 968 (E.D.N.Y. 1993)—§ **15.28, n. 2;** § **15.29, n. 4.**

New York, City of v. Cole, 422 N.Y.S.2d 367, 397 N.E.2d 1171 (N.Y.1979)— § **17.43, n. 7.**

New York, City of v. Exxon Corp., 744 F.Supp. 474 (S.D.N.Y.1990)—§ **15.28, n. 3.**

New York, City of v. Exxon Corp., 697 F.Supp. 677 (S.D.N.Y.1988)—§ **15.29, n. 9.**

New York, City of v. Exxon Corp., 633 F.Supp. 609 (S.D.N.Y.1986)—§ **15.28, n. 5.**

New York, City of v. Fillmore Real Estate, Ltd., 665 F.Supp. 178 (E.D.N.Y.1987)— § **18.50, n. 4.**

New York, City of v. Heckler, 578 F.Supp. 1109 (E.D.N.Y.1984)—§ **34.63;** § **34.63, n. 5.**

New York, City of v. Midmanhattan Realty Corp., 119 Misc.2d 968, 464 N.Y.S.2d 938 (N.Y.Sup.1983)—§ **8.39, n. 3.**

New York, City of v. Mortel, 156 Misc.2d 305, 592 N.Y.S.2d 912 (N.Y.City Civ.Ct. 1992)—§ **13.17, n. 8;** § **13.43, n. 9.**

New York, City of v. New York State Dept. of Health, 164 Misc.2d 247, 623 N.Y.S.2d 491 (N.Y.Sup.1995)—§ **4.51, n. 5.**

New York, City of v. Rogers, 165 Misc.2d 240, 629 N.Y.S.2d 628 (N.Y.City Civ.Ct. 1995)—§ **13.44, n. 3.**

New York, City of v. Schoeck, 294 N.Y. 559, 63 N.E.2d 104 (N.Y.1945)—§ **3.32, n. 10.**

New York, City of v. 17 Vista Associates, 618 N.Y.S.2d 249, 642 N.E.2d 606 (N.Y. 1994)—§ **16.115, n. 2;** § **16.116;** § **16.116, n. 3.**

New York, City of v. Torres, 164 Misc.2d 1037, 631 N.Y.S.2d 208 (N.Y.Sup.App. Term 1995)—§ **13.44, n. 4.**

New York, City of v. Wall Street Racquet Club, Inc., 136 Misc.2d 405, 518 N.Y.S.2d 737 (N.Y.City Civ.Ct.1987)— § **13.8, n. 2.**

New York City Transit Authority, Matter of, 160 A.D.2d 705, 553 N.Y.S.2d 785 (N.Y.A.D. 2 Dept.1990)—§ **14.115, n. 4.**

New York City Transit Authority v. New York State Dept. of Labor, 211 A.D.2d 432, 621 N.Y.S.2d 312 (N.Y.A.D. 1 Dept. 1995)—§ **4.78, n. 8.**

New York, College Point Indus. Park Urban Renewal Project II, City of v. G & C Amusements, Inc., 449 N.Y.S.2d 671, 434 N.E.2d 1038 (N.Y.1982)—§ **14.95, n. 7, 8.**

New York, College Point Indus. Park, Urban Renewal Project II, City of v. Reiss, 449 N.Y.S.2d 18, 433 N.E.2d 1266 (N.Y. 1982)—§ **14.85, n. 6.**

New York (Franklin Record Center, Inc.), Matter of City of, 463 N.Y.S.2d 168, 449 N.E.2d 1246 (N.Y.1983)—§ **14.78, n. 1.**

New York Gaslight Club, Inc. v. Carey, 447 U.S. 54, 100 S.Ct. 2024, 64 L.Ed.2d 723 (1980)—§ **17.91.**

New York Investors v. Manhattan Beach Bathing Parks Corp., 229 A.D. 593, 243 N.Y.S. 548 (N.Y.A.D. 2 Dept.1930)— § **12.64, n. 8.**

New York, L. & W. Ry. Co., In re, 35 Hun. 220 (N.Y.Gen.Tr 1885)—§ **1.21, n. 13.**

New York, People ex rel. v. Nichols, 79 N.Y. 582 (N.Y.1880)—§ **37.7, n. 2.**

New York Post Corp. v. Moses, 219 N.Y.S.2d 7, 176 N.E.2d 709 (N.Y.1961)— § **3.35, n. 5.**

New York Public Interest Research Group, Inc., by Wathen v. Williams, 127 A.D.2d 512, 511 N.Y.S.2d 864 (N.Y.A.D. 1 Dept. 1987)—§ **4.24, n. 7.**

New York, South Bronx Neighborhood Development Plan (Bronxchester–Third Taking), Application of City of, 88 A.D.2d 537, 450 N.Y.S.2d 197 (N.Y.A.D. 1 Dept.1982)—§ **14.85, n. 7.**

New York State Ass'n for Retarded Children, Inc. v. Carey, 711 F.2d 1136 (2nd Cir.1983)—§ **17.75, n. 2.**

New York State Ass'n of Counties v. Axelrod, 213 A.D.2d 18, 629 N.Y.S.2d 335 (N.Y.A.D. 3 Dept.1995)—§ **37.80, n. 16.**

New York State Ass'n of Counties v. Axelrod, 573 N.Y.S.2d 25, 577 N.E.2d 16 (N.Y.1991)—§ **4.80;** § **4.80, n. 4;** § **4.82, n. 9.**

New York State Ass'n of Realtors, Inc. v. Shaffer, 27 F.3d 834 (2nd Cir.1994)— § **18.46, n. 5.**

New York State Bd. of Parole, People ex rel. Piccarillo v., 421 N.Y.S.2d 842, 397 N.E.2d 354 (N.Y.1979)—§ **4.62, n. 15.**

TABLE OF CASES

New York State Builders Ass'n, Inc. v. State, 98 Misc.2d 1045, 414 N.Y.S.2d 956 (N.Y.Sup.1979)—§ **4.69, n. 10.**

New York State Club Ass'n, Inc. v. City of New York, 487 U.S. 1, 108 S.Ct. 2225, 101 L.Ed.2d 1 (1988)—§ **18.56, n. 1.**

New York State Club Ass'n, Inc. v. City of New York, 499 N.Y.S.2d 942, 490 N.E.2d 861 (N.Y.1986)—§ **39.10, n. 3.**

New York State Com'n on Government Integrity v. Congel, 142 Misc.2d 9, 535 N.Y.S.2d 880 (N.Y.Sup.1988)—§ **4.63, n. 1, 7.**

New York State Com'n on Judicial Conduct v. Doe, 471 N.Y.S.2d 557, 459 N.E.2d 850 (N.Y.1984)—§ **4.63, n. 6.**

New York State Dept. of Taxation and Finance v. Tax Appeals Tribunal, 151 Misc.2d 326, 573 N.Y.S.2d 140 (N.Y.Sup. 1991)—§ **35.49, n. 1; § 35.100, n. 5.**

New York State Div. of Parole, People ex rel. Brown v., 521 N.Y.S.2d 657, 516 N.E.2d 194 (N.Y.1987)—§ **38.8, n. 73.**

New York State Div. of Parole, People ex rel. Pilotti v., 201 A.D.2d 376, 607 N.Y.S.2d 343 (N.Y.A.D. 1 Dept.1994)—§ **37.37, n. 63.**

New York State Div. of Parole, People ex rel. Robertson v., 501 N.Y.S.2d 634, 492 N.E.2d 762 (N.Y.1986)—§ **38.8, n. 71, 75.**

New York State Elec. & Gas Corp. v. Karas, 119 Misc.2d 373, 463 N.Y.S.2d 138 (N.Y.Sup.1983)—§ **14.60, n. 2.**

New York State Elec. & Gas Corp. v. Karas, 85 A.D.2d 758, 445 N.Y.S.2d 279 (N.Y.A.D. 3 Dept.1981)—§ **14.127, n. 2.**

New York State Elec. & Gas Corp. v. McCabe, 32 Misc.2d 898, 224 N.Y.S.2d 527 (N.Y.Sup.1961)—§ **16.128, n. 6.**

New York State Medical Transporters Ass'n, Inc. v. Perales, 564 N.Y.S.2d 1007, 566 N.E.2d 134 (N.Y.1990)—§ **4.51, n. 8; § 5.7, n. 1.**

New York State Mortg. Loan Enforcement and Admin. Corp. v. North Town Phase II Houses, Inc., 191 A.D.2d 151, 594 N.Y.S.2d 183 (N.Y.A.D. 1 Dept.1993)—§ **11.37, n. 7.**

New York State Nat. Organization for Women v. Terry, 886 F.2d 1339 (2nd Cir.1989)—§ **9.18, n. 4.**

New York State Silicone Breast Implant Litigation, N.Y.L.J., 6/1/95, p.27, col.2 (Sup.Ct., New York County)—§ **27.28; § 27.28, n. 1.**

New York, State of v. AMRO Realty Corp., 936 F.2d 1420 (2nd Cir.1991)—§ **31.15, n. 3.**

New York, State of v. Blank, 820 F.Supp. 697 (N.D.N.Y.1993)—§ **31.20, n. 1.**

New York, State of v. Lashins Arcade Co., 91 F.3d 353 (2nd Cir.1996)—§ **15.29, n. 17.**

New York, State of v. Shore Realty Corp., 759 F.2d 1032 (2nd Cir.1985)—§ **15.32, n. 11, 13.**

New York, State of v. Sullivan, 906 F.2d 910 (2nd Cir.1990)—§ **34.63; § 34.63, n. 6.**

New York State Pesticide Coalition, Inc. v. Jorling, 874 F.2d 115 (2nd Cir.1989)—§ **27.47; § 27.47, n. 10; § 27.51, n. 4.**

New York State Thruway Authority v. John Civetta Const. Corp., 62 A.D.2d 530, 405 N.Y.S.2d 778 (N.Y.A.D. 3 Dept.1978)—§ **30.17, n. 4.**

New York State Urban Development Corp. v. Vanderlex Merchandise Co., Inc., 98 Misc.2d 264, 413 N.Y.S.2d 982 (N.Y.Sup. 1979)—§ **14.1, n. 2; § 14.15, n. 6.**

New York Tel. Co. v. Town of North Hempstead, 395 N.Y.S.2d 143, 363 N.E.2d 694 (N.Y.1977)—§ **3.9, n. 8.**

New York Times Co. v. Rothwax, 143 A.D.2d 592, 533 N.Y.S.2d 73 (N.Y.A.D. 1 Dept.1988)—§ **18.14, n. 1.**

New York Times Co. v. Sullivan, 376 U.S. 254, 84 S.Ct. 710, 11 L.Ed.2d 686 (1964)—§ **18.81; § 18.81, n. 4, 7.**

New York Trap Rock Corp., In re, 42 F.3d 747 (2nd Cir.1994)—§ **9.60, n. 2.**

New York Trap Rock Corp., In re, 126 B.R. 19 (Bkrtcy.S.D.N.Y.1991)—§ **9.87, n. 1.**

New York Trap Rock Corporation v. Town of Clarkstown, 299 N.Y. 77, 85 N.E.2d 873 (N.Y.1949)—§ **3.7, n. 5.**

New York Typographical Union No. 6 v. Maxwell Newspapers (In re Maxwell Newspapers, Inc.), 981 F.2d 85 (2nd Cir. 1992)—§ **9.86, n. 9.**

New York University v. Continental Ins. Co., 639 N.Y.S.2d 283, 662 N.E.2d 763 (N.Y.1995)—§ **7.46, n. 9; § 30.34, n. 3; § 31.17, n. 20.**

New York University v. Farkas, 121 Misc.2d 643, 468 N.Y.S.2d 808 (N.Y.City Civ.Ct.1983)—§ **13.58; § 13.58, n. 4, 6.**

New York University v. Whalen, 413 N.Y.S.2d 637, 386 N.E.2d 245 (N.Y. 1978)—§ **16.39, n. 7.**

New York Water Service Corp. v. City of New York, 4 A.D.2d 209, 163 N.Y.S.2d 538 (N.Y.A.D. 1 Dept.1957)—§ **30.19, n. 1; § 30.24, n. 4.**

New York Yellow Cab Co. Sales Agency v. Laurel Garage, 219 A.D. 329, 219 N.Y.S. 671 (N.Y.A.D. 1 Dept.1927)—§ **7.59.**

Niagara Frontier Transp. Authority v. Encon Underwriting Agency, Inc., 185 A.D.2d 642, 586 N.Y.S.2d 53 (N.Y.A.D. 4 Dept.1992)—§ **31.26, n. 1.**

TABLE OF CASES

Niagara Mohawk Power Corp. v. Olin, 138 A.D.2d 940, 526 N.Y.S.2d 278 (N.Y.A.D. 4 Dept.1988)—§ **14.82, n. 4.**

Niagara Venture v. Sicoli & Massaro, Inc., 565 N.Y.S.2d 449, 566 N.E.2d 648 (N.Y. 1990)—§ **10.8, n. 2;** § **10.9, n. 1, 2.**

Nicastro v. Park, 113 A.D.2d 129, 495 N.Y.S.2d 184 (N.Y.A.D. 2 Dept.1985)—§ **37.65, n. 33.**

Nice v. Combustion Engineering, Inc., 193 A.D.2d 1088, 599 N.Y.S.2d 205 (N.Y.A.D. 4 Dept.1993)—§ **17.34, n. 6.**

Nicholas v. Kahn, 416 N.Y.S.2d 565, 389 N.E.2d 1086 (N.Y.1979)—§ **4.53, n. 1;** § **4.68, n. 1, 2.**

Nichols, People ex rel. New York v., 79 N.Y. 582 (N.Y.1880)—§ **37.7, n. 2.**

Nicholson, Matter of, 180 A.D.2d 685, 580 N.Y.S.2d 65 (N.Y.A.D. 2 Dept.1992)—§ **21.32, n. 6.**

Nicholson, People v., 230 N.Y.S.2d 220, 184 N.E.2d 190 (N.Y.1962)—§ **38.8, n. 179.**

Nicholson v. State Commission on Judicial Conduct, 431 N.Y.S.2d 340, 409 N.E.2d 818 (N.Y.1980)—§ **4.71, n. 10.**

Nickerson, People v., 175 A.D.2d 74, 573 N.Y.S.2d 169 (N.Y.A.D. 1 Dept.1991)—§ **38.21;** § **38.21, n. 30.**

Nicolla v. Fasulo, 161 A.D.2d 966, 557 N.Y.S.2d 539 (N.Y.A.D. 3 Dept.1990)—§ **29.11, n. 15.**

Niemann v. Whalen, 911 F.Supp. 656 (S.D.N.Y.1996)—§ **18.92, n. 1.**

Niesig v. Team I, 559 N.Y.S.2d 493, 558 N.E.2d 1030 (N.Y.1990)—§ **17.72, n. 4.**

Nieves, People v., 205 A.D.2d 173, 617 N.Y.S.2d 751 (N.Y.A.D. 1 Dept.1994)—§ **38.19, n. 43.**

Nieves, People v., 135 A.D.2d 579, 522 N.Y.S.2d 166 (N.Y.A.D. 2 Dept.1987)—§ **38.19, n. 64.**

Nimmons, People v., 530 N.Y.S.2d 543, 526 N.E.2d 33 (N.Y.1988)—§ **38.19, n. 103.**

Nina M, Matter of, 220 A.D.2d 869, 632 N.Y.S.2d 242 (N.Y.A.D. 3 Dept.1995)—§ **20.131;** § **20.131, n. 1.**

Nineteen New York Properties Ltd. Partnership v. 535 5th Operating Inc., 211 A.D.2d 411, 621 N.Y.S.2d 42 (N.Y.A.D. 1 Dept.1995)—§ **30.42, n. 9.**

9281 Shore Road Owners Corp. v. Seminole Realty Co. (In re 9281 Shore Road Owners Corp.), 187 B.R. 837 (E.D.N.Y. 1995)—§ **9.7, n. 9;** § **9.107, n. 12.**

99 Realty Co. v. Wall Street Transcript Corp., 160 Misc.2d 850, 611 N.Y.S.2d 767 (N.Y.City Civ.Ct.1994)—§ **30.42, n. 2.**

Nipkow & Kobelt, Inc., Parliament Textile Div. v. North River Ins. Co., 673 F.Supp. 1185 (S.D.N.Y.1987)—§ **31.15, n. 8;** § **31.18, n. 16.**

Nite Lite Inns, In re, 17 B.R. 367 (Bkrtcy. S.D.Cal.1982)—§ **9.165, n. 23.**

Nitis v. Goldenthal, 128 A.D.2d 687, 513 N.Y.S.2d 186 (N.Y.A.D. 2 Dept.1987)—§ **28.3, n. 1.**

Nitti v. Credit Bureau of Rochester, Inc., 84 Misc.2d 277, 375 N.Y.S.2d 817 (N.Y.Sup. 1975)—§ **7.33, n. 6.**

Nixon (Corey), Matter of, N.Y.L.J., 6/4/96, p. 36, col. 6 (Sup.Ct., Suffolk County)—§ **22.20, n. 4.**

N.L.R.B. v. Better Bldg. Supply Corp., 837 F.2d 377 (9th Cir.1988)—§ **9.205, n. 1.**

N.L.R.B. v. Bildisco and Bildisco, 465 U.S. 513, 104 S.Ct. 1188, 79 L.Ed.2d 482 (1984)—§ **9.27, n. 2, 3;** § **9.74, n. 1;** § **9.78, n. 1;** § **9.81, n. 1.**

N.L.R.B. v. City Disposal Systems Inc., 465 U.S. 822, 104 S.Ct. 1505, 79 L.Ed.2d 839 (1984)—§ **17.61, n. 5, 6.**

Nobelman v. American Sav. Bank, 508 U.S. 324, 113 S.Ct. 2106, 124 L.Ed.2d 228 (1993)—§ **9.101, n. 6;** § **9.249, n. 1.**

Noble, In re, 182 B.R. 854 (Bkrtcy. W.D.Wash.1995)—§ **9.130, n. 6.**

Noble v. Creative Technical Services, Inc., 126 A.D.2d 611, 511 N.Y.S.2d 51 (N.Y.A.D. 2 Dept.1987)—§ **17.23, n. 1;** § **17.25, n. 6.**

Nojaim Bros., Inc. v. CNA Ins. Companies, 113 A.D.2d 109, 115 A.D.2d 354, 496 N.Y.S.2d 113 (N.Y.A.D. 4 Dept.1985)—§ **31.7, n. 7.**

Nolan v. Nolan, 215 A.D.2d 795, 626 N.Y.S.2d 568 (N.Y.A.D. 3 Dept.1995)—§ **21.44, n. 3;** § **21.55, n. 9.**

Nolan v. Nolan, 107 A.D.2d 190, 486 N.Y.S.2d 415 (N.Y.A.D. 3 Dept.1985)—§ **21.48, n. 2.**

Nolan v. United States (In re Nolan), 205 B.R. 885 (Bkrtcy.M.D.Tenn.1997)—§ **9.207, n. 2.**

Noland, United States v., 517 U.S. 535, 116 S.Ct. 1524, 134 L.Ed.2d 748 (1996)—§ **9.107, n. 21.**

Nolden v. Van Dyke Seed (In re Gold Coast Seed Co.), 751 F.2d 1118 (9th Cir. 1985)—§ **9.117, n. 3.**

Nollan v. California Coastal Com'n, 483 U.S. 825, 107 S.Ct. 3141, 97 L.Ed.2d 677 (1987)—§ **16.22, n. 4, 17.**

Nones v. Security Title & Guaranty Co., 4 Misc.2d 1057, 162 N.Y.S.2d 761 (N.Y.Sup.1956)—§ **28.24, n. 2.**

Normal Realty Co. v. Rios, 109 Misc.2d 555, 440 N.Y.S.2d 442 (N.Y.City Civ.Ct. 1981)—§ **13.18, n. 16.**

Norplant Contraceptive Products Liability Litigation, In re, 886 F.Supp. 586 (E.D.Tex.1995)—§ **27.18, n. 3.**

Norsal Industries, Inc., In re, 147 B.R. 85 (Bkrtcy.E.D.N.Y.1992)—§ **9.89, n. 3.**

TABLE OF CASES

North American Dealer Group, Inc., In re, 62 B.R. 423 (Bkrtcy.E.D.N.Y.1986)— § **9.198, n. 1.**

North Am. Holding Corp. v. Murdock, 6 A.D.2d 596, 180 N.Y.S.2d 436 (N.Y.A.D. 1 Dept.1958)—§ **37.37, n. 59.**

North and South Rivers Watershed Ass'n, Inc. v. Town of Scituate, 949 F.2d 552 (1st Cir.1991)—§ **15.11, n. 17.**

North Carolina v. Pearce, 395 U.S. 711, 89 S.Ct. 2072, 23 L.Ed.2d 656 (1969)— § **38.21, n. 58.**

Northeast Doran, Inc. v. Key Bank of Maine, 15 F.3d 1 (1st Cir.1994)—§ **11.6, n. 9.**

Northeastern Pharmaceutical & Chemical Co., Inc., United States v., 810 F.2d 726 (8th Cir.1986)—§ **15.25, n. 11.**

Northeastern Stud Welding Corp. v. Webster, 211 A.D.2d 889, 621 N.Y.S.2d 170 (N.Y.A.D. 3 Dept.1995)—§ **37.87, n. 34.**

Northeast Parent & Child Soc., Inc. v. City of Schenectady Indus. Development Agency, 114 A.D.2d 741, 494 N.Y.S.2d 503 (N.Y.A.D. 3 Dept.1985)—§ **14.15, n. 6.**

Northern Pipeline Const. Co. v. Marathon Pipe Line Co., 458 U.S. 50, 102 S.Ct. 2858, 73 L.Ed.2d 598 (1982)—§ **9.18, n. 2.**

Northern Trust Bank of Florida/Sarasota N.A. v. Coleman, 632 F.Supp. 648 (S.D.N.Y.1986)—§ **28.24, n. 9.**

Northern Westchester Professional Park Associates v. Town of Bedford, 470 N.Y.S.2d 350, 458 N.E.2d 809 (N.Y. 1983)—§ **15.34, n. 13;** § **37.29, n. 6;** § **37.65, n. 9.**

North Hempstead, Town of v. Bonner, 77 A.D.2d 567, 429 N.Y.S.2d 739 (N.Y.A.D. 2 Dept.1980)—§ **12.66, n. 4.**

Northport Marina Associates, In re, 136 B.R. 911 (Bkrtcy.E.D.N.Y.1992)—§ **9.69, n. 3.**

North River Ins. Co. v. Huff, 628 F.Supp. 1129 (D.Kan.1985)—§ **28.43, n. 12.**

North Shore Beach Property Owners Ass'n v. Town of Brookhaven, 115 N.Y.S.2d 670 (N.Y.Sup.1952)—§ **16.50, n. 12.**

North Shore Bottling Co. v. C. Schmidt & Sons, Inc., 292 N.Y.S.2d 86, 239 N.E.2d 189 (N.Y.1968)—§ **17.27, n. 3.**

North Shore Equities, Inc. v. Fritts, 81 A.D.2d 985, 440 N.Y.S.2d 84 (N.Y.A.D. 3 Dept.1981)—§ **16.90, n. 6;** § **16.106, n. 2.**

North Shore Steak House, Inc. v. Board of Appeals of Incorporated Village of Thomaston, 331 N.Y.S.2d 645, 282 N.E.2d 606 (N.Y.1972)—§ **16.90, n. 5.**

North Shore University Hosp. v. Rosa, 633 N.Y.S.2d 462, 657 N.E.2d 483 (N.Y. 1995)—§ **18.55, n. 8;** § **37.87, n. 20.**

North Syracuse First Baptist Church v. Village of North Syracuse, N.Y., 136 A.D.2d 942, 524 N.Y.S.2d 894 (N.Y.A.D. 4 Dept. 1988)—§ **16.25, n. 7.**

Northwestern Nat. Ins. Co. v. Kansa General Ins. Co., Ltd., 1992 WL 36708 (S.D.N.Y.1992)—§ **31.23, n. 6.**

Norton, People v., 135 A.D.2d 984, 522 N.Y.S.2d 958 (N.Y.A.D. 3 Dept.1987)— § **33.52, n. 2.**

Nostas Assocs. v. Costich (In re Klein Sleep Products, Inc.), 78 F.3d 18 (2nd Cir. 1996)—§ **9.75, n. 1.**

Nottingham v. Nottingham, 209 A.D. 459, 204 N.Y.S. 750 (N.Y.A.D. 4 Dept.1924)— § **21.26, n. 10.**

Novak v. Callahan (Matter of GAC Corp.), 681 F.2d 1295 (11th Cir.1982)—§ **9.107, n. 20.**

Novak v. Town of Poughkeepsie, 63 Misc.2d 385, 311 N.Y.S.2d 393 (N.Y.Sup.1970)— § **3.7, n. 12.**

Novoa, People v., 522 N.Y.S.2d 504, 517 N.E.2d 219 (N.Y.1987)—§ **38.10, n. 102.**

Novogorodskaya, Matter of, 104 Misc.2d 1006, 429 N.Y.S.2d 387 (N.Y.City Civ.Ct. 1980)—§ **18.67, n. 4.**

Nuccio, People v., 571 N.Y.S.2d 693, 575 N.E.2d 111 (N.Y.1991)—§ **33.19;** § **33.19, n. 2;** § **33.24;** § **33.24, n. 2, 4.**

Nugent, People v., 194 A.D.2d 984, 598 N.Y.S.2d 861 (N.Y.A.D. 3 Dept.1993)— § **38.10, n. 14.**

Numano v. Vicario, 165 Misc.2d 457, 632 N.Y.S.2d 926 (N.Y.Sup.App.Term 1995)—§ **13.52, n. 6.**

Nunez, People v., 157 Misc.2d 793, 598 N.Y.S.2d 917 (N.Y.Sup.1993)—§ **38.10, n. 42.**

Nutting v. Ford Motor Co., 180 A.D.2d 122, 584 N.Y.S.2d 653 (N.Y.A.D. 3 Dept. 1992)—§ **27.23;** § **27.23, n. 5.**

Nyack Hosp. v. Government Employees Ins. Co., 139 A.D.2d 515, 526 N.Y.S.2d 614 (N.Y.A.D. 2 Dept.1988)—§ **31.24, n. 9.**

NYS Tax Commission v. Jenkins, 1983 WL 21009 (Sup.Ct., Albany County)— § **35.114, n. 2.**

O

Oak Point Indus. Park, Inc. v. Massachusetts Bay Ins. Co., 143 A.D.2d 79, 531 N.Y.S.2d 329 (N.Y.A.D. 2 Dept.1988)— § **31.18, n. 23.**

Oakwood Island Yacht Club, Inc. v. Board of Appeals of City of New Rochelle, 32

TABLE OF CASES

Misc.2d 677, 223 N.Y.S.2d 907 (N.Y.Sup. 1961)—§ **16.93, n. 4.**
Oates v. Oates, 33 A.D.2d 133, 306 N.Y.S.2d 108 (N.Y.A.D. 1 Dept.1969)—§ **8.23, n. 2.**
O'Brien v. City of Syracuse, 445 N.Y.S.2d 687, 429 N.E.2d 1158 (N.Y.1981)—§ **8.3, n. 5.**
O'Brien v. City of Syracuse, 54 A.D.2d 186, 388 N.Y.S.2d 866 (N.Y.A.D. 4 Dept. 1976)—§ **14.14, n. 11.**
O'Brien v. O'Brien, 498 N.Y.S.2d 743, 489 N.E.2d 712 (N.Y.1985)—§ **21.35;** § **21.35, n. 1, 6, 8;** § **21.39;** § **21.39, n. 2, 7;** § **21.43, n. 15;** § **21.44;** § **21.44, n. 11, 12.**
O'Brien, People v., 453 N.Y.S.2d 638, 439 N.E.2d 354 (N.Y.1982)—§ **33.80, n. 1;** § **38.8, n. 174.**
O'Brien, People v., 84 A.D.2d 567, 443 N.Y.S.2d 255 (N.Y.A.D. 2 Dept.1981)—§ **38.8, n. 200, 204.**
O'Brien v. Vassar Bros. Hosp., 207 A.D.2d 169, 622 N.Y.S.2d 284 (N.Y.A.D. 2 Dept. 1995)—§ **37.29, n. 45;** § **37.65, n. 14.**
O'Brien's Trust, In re, 28 A.D.2d 1040, 283 N.Y.S.2d 926 (N.Y.A.D. 3 Dept.1967)—§ **25.16, n. 2.**
O'Bryan v. Commissioner, T.C. Memo. 1991-593 (U.S.Tax Ct.1991)—§ **1.34, n. 26.**
Ocasio, People v., 416 N.Y.S.2d 581, 389 N.E.2d 1101 (N.Y.1979)—§ **38.19, n. 79, 83.**
Oceana Apts. v. Spielman, 164 Misc.2d 98, 623 N.Y.S.2d 724 (N.Y.City Civ.Ct. 1995)—§ **13.17, n. 15;** § **13.18, n. 13;** § **13.43, n. 16.**
Ocean Gate Associates Starrett Systems, Inc. v. Dopico, 109 Misc.2d 774, 441 N.Y.S.2d 34 (N.Y.City Civ.Ct.1981)—§ **18.45, n. 5.**
Ocean Rock Associates v. Cruz, 66 A.D.2d 878, 411 N.Y.S.2d 663 (N.Y.A.D. 2 Dept. 1978)—§ **13.32, n. 5.**
Oceanside Enterprises, Inc. v. Capobianco, 146 A.D.2d 685, 537 N.Y.S.2d 190 (N.Y.A.D. 2 Dept.1989)—§ **18.79, n. 1.**
O'Connell, People v., 133 A.D.2d 970, 521 N.Y.S.2d 121 (N.Y.A.D. 3 Dept.1987)—§ **38.21, n. 5, 19.**
O'Connell, United States v., 890 F.2d 563 (1st Cir.1989)—§ **17.64, n. 8.**
O'Connor v. 11 West 30th Street Rest. Corp., 1995 WL 354904 (S.D.N.Y. 1995)—§ **18.58, n. 2.**
O'Connor v. Ortega, 480 U.S. 709, 107 S.Ct. 1492, 94 L.Ed.2d 714 (1987)—§ **17.55, n. 2;** § **18.10, n. 1.**
Odell v. Dalrymple, 156 A.D.2d 967, 549 N.Y.S.2d 260 (N.Y.A.D. 4 Dept.1989)—§ **30.15, n. 7.**

Odette Realty Co. v. DiBianco, 170 A.D.2d 299, 565 N.Y.S.2d 815 (N.Y.A.D. 1 Dept. 1991)—§ **2.51, n. 27.**
Odiat, People v., 609 N.Y.S.2d 166, 631 N.E.2d 108 (N.Y.1993)—§ **33.47;** § **33.47, n. 3, 4.**
O'Doherty, People v., 522 N.Y.S.2d 498, 517 N.E.2d 213 (N.Y.1987)—§ **38.10, n. 167;** § **38.19, n. 106.**
O'Doherty v. Postal Telegraph–Cable Co., 134 A.D. 298, 118 N.Y.S. 871 (N.Y.A.D. 2 Dept.1909)—§ **30.14, n. 1.**
Odom v. Columbia University, 906 F.Supp. 188 (S.D.N.Y.1995)—§ **18.53, n. 2.**
Odom v. G.D. Searle & Co., 979 F.2d 1001 (4th Cir.1992)—§ **27.18, n. 1.**
O'Donnell v. NPS Corp., 133 A.D.2d 73, 518 N.Y.S.2d 418 (N.Y.A.D. 2 Dept.1987)—§ **17.32, n. 2.**
O'Dowd v. American Sur. Co. of N.Y., 165 N.Y.S.2d 458, 144 N.E.2d 359 (N.Y. 1957)—§ **31.13, n. 9.**
Oelsner v. State, 495 N.Y.S.2d 359, 485 N.E.2d 1024 (N.Y.1985)—§ **26.11, n. 4.**
O'Fennell Corp. v. O'Fennell's of Pine Hill Inc., 195 A.D.2d 904, 601 N.Y.S.2d 32 (N.Y.A.D. 3 Dept.1993)—§ **37.20, n. 3.**
Official Committee of Manville Forest Prods. Corp. v. Manville Forest Prods. Corp. (In re Manville Forest Products Corp.), 60 B.R. 403 (S.D.N.Y.1986)—§ **9.158, n. 3.**
Official Committee of Unsecured Creditors v. Vardi Stonhouse (In re Faleck & Margolies, Inc.), 153 B.R. 123 (S.D.N.Y. 1993)—§ **9.118, n. 4, 6.**
Ogden Corp. v. Travelers Indem. Co., 924 F.2d 39 (2nd Cir.1991)—§ **31.12, n. 8.**
Ogden Corp. v. Travelers Indem. Co., 739 F.Supp. 796 (S.D.N.Y.1989)—§ **31.16, n. 2.**
Ogdensburg Sav. and Loan Ass'n v. Moore, 100 A.D.2d 679, 473 N.Y.S.2d 877 (N.Y.A.D. 3 Dept.1984)—§ **11.52, n. 8.**
O'Gilvie v. United States, ___ U.S. ___, 117 S.Ct. 452, 136 L.Ed.2d 454 (1996)—§ **30.33, n. 4.**
Ohanian v. Avis Rent A Car System, Inc., 779 F.2d 101 (2nd Cir.1985)—§ **17.34;** § **17.34, n. 12.**
O'Hayer v. de St. Aubin, 30 A.D.2d 419, 293 N.Y.S.2d 147 (N.Y.A.D. 2 Dept.1968)—§ **24.16, n. 1.**
O'Hear on Behalf of Rodriguez, Matter of, 219 A.D.2d 720, 631 N.Y.S.2d 743 (N.Y.A.D. 2 Dept.1995)—§ **22.14, n. 5.**
Ohio Agr. Commodity Depositors Fund v. Mahern, ___ U.S. ___, 116 S.Ct. 1411, 134 L.Ed.2d 537 (1996)—§ **9.18, n. 4.**
Ohio Bureau of Employment Services v. Hodory, 431 U.S. 471, 97 S.Ct. 1898, 52 L.Ed.2d 513 (1977)—§ **18.36, n. 8.**

TABLE OF CASES

Ohio Civil Rights Com'n v. Dayton Christian Schools, Inc., 477 U.S. 619, 106 S.Ct. 2718, 91 L.Ed.2d 512 (1986)—§ 18.36, n. 4.

O'Keefe v. Niagara Mohawk Power Corp., 714 F.Supp. 622 (N.D.N.Y.1989)—§ 17.31, n. 3.

O'Keefe v. O'Keefe, 216 A.D.2d 549, 628 N.Y.S.2d 766 (N.Y.A.D. 2 Dept.1995)—§ 21.49, n. 3.

O'Keeffe, Estate of v. Commissioner, T.C. Memo. 1992-210 (U.S.Tax Ct.1992)—§ 24.41, n. 2.

Old Country Burgers Co., Inc. v. Town Bd. of Town of Oyster Bay, 160 A.D.2d 805, 553 N.Y.S.2d 843 (N.Y.A.D. 2 Dept. 1990)—§ 16.93, n. 3.

Old Dock Associates v. Sullivan, 150 A.D.2d 695, 541 N.Y.S.2d 569 (N.Y.A.D. 2 Dept. 1989)—§ 16.105, n. 11.

Old Farm Road, Inc. v. Town of New Castle, 311 N.Y.S.2d 500, 259 N.E.2d 920 (N.Y.1970)—§ 16.126; § 16.126, n. 3, 6.

Olim v. Wakinekona, 461 U.S. 238, 103 S.Ct. 1741, 75 L.Ed.2d 813 (1983)—§ 18.18, n. 3.

Olin Corp. v. Insurance Co. of North America, 966 F.2d 718 (2nd Cir.1992)—§ 31.10, n. 15.

Olin Corp. v. Insurance Co. of North America, 743 F.Supp. 1044 (S.D.N.Y.1990)—§ 31.10, n. 4.

Oliva v. Heller, 839 F.2d 37 (2nd Cir. 1988)—§ 18.31, n. 2.

Olivo v. Olivo, 604 N.Y.S.2d 23, 624 N.E.2d 151 (N.Y.1993)—§ 21.38; § 21.38, n. 10.

Olsen, People v., 292 N.Y.S.2d 420, 239 N.E.2d 354 (N.Y.1968)—§ 33.68; § 33.68, n. 12, 13.

Olson v. Dougherty, 128 A.D.2d 920, 512 N.Y.S.2d 730 (N.Y.A.D. 3 Dept.1987)—§ 37.65, n. 48.

Olson v. Smithtown Medical Specialists, P.C., 197 A.D.2d 564, 602 N.Y.S.2d 649 (N.Y.A.D. 2 Dept.1993)—§ 2.46, n. 11.

Ombony & Dain v. Jones, 19 N.Y. 234 (N.Y. 1859)—§ 10.7, n. 3.

185 East 85th St. v. Gravanis, N.Y.L.J., 1/21/81, p.6, col.2 (App. Term, 1st Dep't)—§ 13.51, n. 2.

150 East 73rd Street Corp. v. Wehringer, N.Y.L.J., 4/17/75, p.2, col.4 (App. Term, 1st Dep't 1975)—§ 13.6, n. 1, 2.

119-121 East 97th Street Corp. v. New York City Comm'n on Human Rights, 220 A.D.2d 79, 642 N.Y.S.2d 638 (N.Y.A.D. 1 Dept.1996)—§ 18.49, n. 16.

117 East 24th Street Associates v. Karr, 95 A.D.2d 735, 464 N.Y.S.2d 473 (N.Y.A.D. 1 Dept.1983)—§ 17.23, n. 1.

160 Chambers St. Realty Corp. v. Register of City of New York, 226 A.D.2d 606, 641 N.Y.S.2d 351 (N.Y.A.D. 2 Dept. 1996)—§ 12.4, n. 2; § 12.11, n. 1.

125 Bar Corp. v. State Liquor Authority, 299 N.Y.S.2d 194, 247 N.E.2d 157 (N.Y. 1969)—§ 37.87, n. 22.

121 Realty v. Gonzalez, N.Y.L.J., 11/11/91, p.26, col.5 (App.Term, 1st Dep't)—§ 13.66, n. 3.

O'Neill v. City of New York, 160 Misc.2d 1086, 612 N.Y.S.2d 303 (N.Y.City Civ.Ct. 1994)—§ 18.15, n. 10.

O'Neill v. Krzeminski, 839 F.2d 9 (2nd Cir. 1988)—§ 18.21, n. 3.

O'Neill v. Oakgrove Const., Inc., 528 N.Y.S.2d 1, 523 N.E.2d 277 (N.Y.1988)—§ 18.6; § 18.6, n. 1; § 18.8, n. 7; § 18.27; § 18.27, n. 1; § 18.85, n. 4, 5.

O'Neill v. Van Tassel, 137 N.Y. 297, 33 N.E. 314 (N.Y.1893)—§ 12.67; § 12.67, n. 1.

1460 Grand Concourse Assoc. v. Martinez, N.Y.L.J., 5/6/94, p.29, col.1, 22 HCR 269 (App. Term, 1st Dep't)—§ 13.64, n. 5.

1180 Anderson Ave. Realty Corp. v. Mina Equities Corp., 95 A.D.2d 169, 465 N.Y.S.2d 511 (N.Y.A.D. 1 Dept.1983)—§ 11.30, n. 4.

1777 Penfield Road Corp. v. Morrison–Vega, 116 A.D.2d 1035, 498 N.Y.S.2d 653 (N.Y.A.D. 4 Dept.1986)—§ 16.27, n. 1.

1616 Second Ave. Restaurant Corp. v. State Liquor Authority, 207 A.D.2d 721, 617 N.Y.S.2d 156 (N.Y.A.D. 1 Dept.1994)—§ 30.42, n. 11.

1616 Second Ave. Restaurant, Inc. v. New York State Liquor Authority, 551 N.Y.S.2d 461, 550 N.E.2d 910 (N.Y. 1990)—§ 4.24, n. 6.

1303 Webster Ave. Realty Corp. v. Great American Surplus Lines Ins. Co., 481 N.Y.S.2d 322, 471 N.E.2d 135 (N.Y. 1984)—§ 31.26, n. 1.

1202 Realty Assoc. v. Evans, 126 Misc.2d 99, 481 N.Y.S.2d 208 (N.Y.City Civ.Ct. 1984)—§ 13.22, n. 10; § 13.47, n. 9.

Onondaga County v. Sargent, 92 A.D.2d 743, 461 N.Y.S.2d 84 (N.Y.A.D. 4 Dept. 1983)—§ 14.7, n. 1; § 14.9, n. 2; § 14.14, n. 6.

Onondaga County District Attorney's Office to File a Sealed Grand Jury Report as a Public Record, Matter of, 92 A.D.2d 32, 459 N.Y.S.2d 507 (N.Y.A.D. 4 Dept. 1983)—§ 38.11; § 38.11, n. 12, 25.

Onorati v. Testco Inc., 204 A.D.2d 876, 612 N.Y.S.2d 473 (N.Y.A.D. 3 Dept.1994)—§ 10.19, n. 18.

Opera v. Hyva, Inc., 86 A.D.2d 373, 450 N.Y.S.2d 615 (N.Y.A.D. 4 Dept.1982)—§ 27.6, n. 1; § 27.37, n. 4.

Oppenheim v. Spike, 107 Misc.2d 55, 437 N.Y.S.2d 826 (N.Y.Sup.App.Term 1980)—§ 13.50, n. 1.

TABLE OF CASES

Oppenheim & Co., P.C. v. Bernstein, 198 A.D.2d 163, 604 N.Y.S.2d 62 (N.Y.A.D. 1 Dept.1993)—§ **28.8, n. 2.**

O'Quinn v. New York University Medical Center, 163 F.R.D. 226 (S.D.N.Y.1995)— § **17.72, n. 6.**

Oram v. Capone, 206 A.D.2d 839, 615 N.Y.S.2d 799 (N.Y.A.D. 4 Dept.1994)— § **37.28, n. 21.**

O'Rama, People v., 574 N.Y.S.2d 159, 579 N.E.2d 189 (N.Y.1991)—§ **38.19;** § **38.19, n. 23.**

Orange County Court, People ex rel. Hirschberg v., 271 N.Y. 151, 2 N.E.2d 521 (N.Y.1936)—§ **38.10, n. 128.**

Orange County Publications, Division of Ottaway Newspapers, Inc. v. Council of City of Newburgh, 60 A.D.2d 409, 401 N.Y.S.2d 84 (N.Y.A.D. 2 Dept.1978)— § **3.28, n. 10.**

Orange Environment, Inc. v. County of Orange, 860 F.Supp. 1003 (S.D.N.Y. 1994)—§ **15.11, n. 17.**

Orange & Rockland Utilities, Inc. v. New England Petroleum Corp., 60 A.D.2d 233, 400 N.Y.S.2d 79 (N.Y.A.D. 1 Dept. 1977)—§ **30.19, n. 3.**

Orangetown, Town of v. Magee, 643 N.Y.S.2d 21, 665 N.E.2d 1061 (N.Y. 1996)—§ **18.34, n. 3.**

Orangetown, Town of v. Magee, 216 A.D.2d 343, 631 N.Y.S.2d 41 (N.Y.A.D. 2 Dept. 1995)—§ **37.80, n. 15.**

Orangetown, Town of v. Magee, 156 Misc.2d 881, 594 N.Y.S.2d 951 (N.Y.Sup. 1992)—§ **16.18, n. 14.**

O'Reilly v. Citibank, N.A., 198 A.D.2d 270, 603 N.Y.S.2d 572 (N.Y.A.D. 2 Dept. 1993)—§ **17.32, n. 2;** § **17.34, n. 5.**

O'Reilly v. Executone of Albany, Inc., 121 A.D.2d 772, 503 N.Y.S.2d 185 (N.Y.A.D. 3 Dept.1986)—§ **17.28;** § **17.28, n. 6.**

Oreiro v. Board of Appeals of City of White Plains, 204 A.D.2d 964, 612 N.Y.S.2d 509 (N.Y.A.D. 3 Dept.1994)—§ **16.66, n. 3.**

Orelli v. Ambro, 394 N.Y.S.2d 636, 363 N.E.2d 360 (N.Y.1977)—§ **3.16, n. 15.**

Organek v. State, 151 Misc.2d 78, 573 N.Y.S.2d 116 (N.Y.Ct.Cl.1991)—§ **14.14, n. 15.**

Origlia, People v., 138 Misc.2d 286, 524 N.Y.S.2d 163 (N.Y.City Ct.1988)— § **33.19, n. 2;** § **33.23;** § **33.23, n. 1.**

Orion Pictures Corp., In re, 4 F.3d 1095 (2nd Cir.1993)—§ **9.22, n. 9;** § **9.74, n. 3.**

Orix Credit Alliance, Inc. v. Delta Resources, Inc. (In re Delta Resources, Inc.), 54 F.3d 722 (11th Cir.1995)— § **9.102, n. 10.**

Orlando F., Matter of, 386 N.Y.S.2d 64, 351 N.E.2d 711 (N.Y.1976)—§ **20.43, n. 8, 9.**

Orlick v. Granit Hotel and Country Club, 331 N.Y.S.2d 651, 282 N.E.2d 610 (N.Y. 1972)—§ **27.32;** § **27.32, n. 1.**

Orta, People v., 198 A.D.2d 45, 603 N.Y.S.2d 305 (N.Y.A.D. 1 Dept.1993)— § **38.19, n. 46.**

Ortiz, People v., 224 A.D.2d 553, 638 N.Y.S.2d 341 (N.Y.A.D. 2 Dept.1996)— § **38.24, n. 2.**

Ortiz, People v., 224 A.D.2d 244, 638 N.Y.S.2d 9 (N.Y.A.D. 1 Dept.1996)— § **38.19, n. 76.**

Ortiz, People v., 214 A.D.2d 451, 625 N.Y.S.2d 514 (N.Y.A.D. 1 Dept.1995)— § **38.25;** § **38.25, n. 12.**

Ortiz, People v., 202 A.D.2d 860, 609 N.Y.S.2d 688 (N.Y.A.D. 3 Dept.1994)— § **38.8, n. 94.**

Ortiz, People v., 127 A.D.2d 305, 515 N.Y.S.2d 317 (N.Y.A.D. 3 Dept.1987)— § **38.8, n. 197.**

Osborn v. Planning Bd. of Town of Colonie, 146 A.D.2d 838, 536 N.Y.S.2d 244 (N.Y.A.D. 3 Dept.1989)—§ **16.121, n. 6.**

Osiecki v. Town of Huntington, 170 A.D.2d 490, 565 N.Y.S.2d 564 (N.Y.A.D. 2 Dept. 1991)—§ **16.20;** § **16.20, n. 3.**

Osinoff v. Queens Apartments, Inc., 10 Misc.2d 762, 173 N.Y.S.2d 225 (N.Y.Sup. 1958)—§ **10.59, n. 4.**

Osohowsky by Kacer v. Romaniello, 201 A.D.2d 473, 607 N.Y.S.2d 396 (N.Y.A.D. 2 Dept.1994)—§ **31.5, n. 5.**

Ossining Union Free School Dist. v. Anderson LaRocca Anderson, 541 N.Y.S.2d 335, 539 N.E.2d 91 (N.Y. 1989)—§ **28.11, n. 7.**

Ostrer v. Aronwald, 567 F.2d 551 (2nd Cir. 1977)—§ **18.19, n. 2.**

Oswald v. Allen, 417 F.2d 43 (2nd Cir. 1969)—§ **5.19, n. 3.**

Oswego Laborers' Local 214 Pension Fund v. Marine Midland Bank, N.A., 623 N.Y.S.2d 529, 647 N.E.2d 741 (N.Y. 1995)—§ **7.45, n. 4;** § **7.46, n. 3.**

Otero Mills, Inc., In re, 31 B.R. 185 (Bkrtcy. D.N.M.1983)—§ **9.158, n. 7.**

Otis v. Bausch & Lomb Inc., 143 A.D.2d 649, 532 N.Y.S.2d 933 (N.Y.A.D. 2 Dept. 1988)—§ **27.33;** § **27.33, n. 8.**

Otis Elevator Co. v. Heggie Realty Co., Inc., 107 Misc.2d 67, 437 N.Y.S.2d 832 (N.Y.Sup.App.Term 1980)—§ **13.54, n. 1.**

O'Toole v. Greenberg, 488 N.Y.S.2d 143, 477 N.E.2d 445 (N.Y.1985)—§ **29.11;** § **29.11, n. 11.**

Otsego 2000, Inc. v. Planning Bd. of Town of Otsego, 171 A.D.2d 258, 575 N.Y.S.2d

TABLE OF CASES

584 (N.Y.A.D. 3 Dept.1991)—§ **16.48, n. 9.**
Ottaviani v. State University of New York at New Paltz, 679 F.Supp. 288 (S.D.N.Y. 1988)—§ **17.59, n. 7.**
Ottaviano, Matter of, 68 B.R. 238 (Bkrtcy. D.Conn.1986)—§ **9.28, n. 4.**
Otte v. Manufactures Hanover Commercial Corp. (In re Texlon Corp.), 596 F.2d 1092 (2nd Cir.1979)—§ **9.71, n. 10, 11.**
Otto v. Otto, 150 A.D.2d 57, 545 N.Y.S.2d 321 (N.Y.A.D. 2 Dept.1989)—§ **37.65, n. 75.**
Otto v. Steinhilber, 282 N.Y. 71, 24 N.E.2d 851 (N.Y.1939)—§ **16.73, n. 4; § 16.74, n. 3.**
Outer, People v., 197 A.D.2d 543, 602 N.Y.S.2d 215 (N.Y.A.D. 2 Dept.1993)—§ **38.8, n. 216.**
Outin, Matter of, 14 I & N Dec. 6 (BIA 1972)—§ **19.47, n. 3.**
Overhill Bldg. Co. v. Delany, 322 N.Y.S.2d 696, 271 N.E.2d 537 (N.Y.1971)—§ **3.32, n. 6.**
Owasco River Ry., Inc. v. State, 181 A.D.2d 665, 580 N.Y.S.2d 466 (N.Y.A.D. 2 Dept. 1992)—§ **14.101, n. 1.**
Owego Properties v. Campfield, 182 A.D.2d 1058, 583 N.Y.S.2d 37 (N.Y.A.D. 3 Dept. 1992)—§ **13.51, n. 12.**
Owens v. Okure, 488 U.S. 235, 109 S.Ct. 573, 102 L.Ed.2d 594 (1989)—§ **18.38, n. 1.**
Owens, People v., 516 N.Y.S.2d 619, 509 N.E.2d 314 (N.Y.1987)—§ **38.19, n. 101.**
Owens, People v., 482 N.Y.S.2d 250, 472 N.E.2d 26 (N.Y.1984)—§ **38.19, n. 80.**
Owens, People v., 291 N.Y.S.2d 313, 238 N.E.2d 715 (N.Y.1968)—§ **38.19; § 38.19, n. 129.**
Owl Wet Wash Laundry Co. v. Karish, 188 N.Y.S. 782 (N.Y.Sup.App.Term 1921)—§ **7.28, n. 9.**
O. W. Siebert Co., Inc. v. Kramer, 107 Misc.2d 520, 435 N.Y.S.2d 476 (N.Y.Sup. 1980)—§ **12.65, n. 6.**
Oysterman's Bank & Trust Co. v. Weeks, 35 A.D.2d 580, 313 N.Y.S.2d 535 (N.Y.A.D. 2 Dept.1970)—§ **8.13, n. 4.**

P

P & A Bros., Inc. v. City of New York Dept. of Parks & Recreation, 184 A.D.2d 267, 585 N.Y.S.2d 335 (N.Y.A.D. 1 Dept. 1992)—§ **13.35, n. 3.**
Pace College v. City Commission on Human Rights, 377 N.Y.S.2d 471, 339 N.E.2d 880 (N.Y.1975)—§ **17.59, n. 1.**
Pacheco v. Board of Educ. of City of New York, 219 A.D.2d 625, 631 N.Y.S.2d 400 (N.Y.A.D. 2 Dept.1995)—§ **37.65, n. 45.**
Pacific Ins. Co. v. State Farm Mut. Auto. Ins. Co., 150 A.D.2d 455, 541 N.Y.S.2d 65 (N.Y.A.D. 2 Dept.1989)—§ **31.26, n. 7.**
Pacifico v. Pacifico, 101 A.D.2d 709, 475 N.Y.S.2d 952 (N.Y.A.D. 4 Dept.1984)—§ **21.48, n. 2.**
Pacific Salmon Unlimited v. New York State Dept. of Environmental Conservation, 208 A.D.2d 241, 622 N.Y.S.2d 820 (N.Y.A.D. 3 Dept.1995)—§ **4.49, n. 24.**
Paco Corp. v. Vigliarola, 611 F.Supp. 923 (E.D.N.Y.1985)—§ **7.26, n. 10.**
Pacor, Inc. v. Higgins, 743 F.2d 984 (3rd Cir.1984)—§ **9.19, n. 6, 7.**
Padilla v. New York City Transit Authority, 184 A.D.2d 760, 585 N.Y.S.2d 491 (N.Y.A.D. 2 Dept.1992)—§ **28.13, n. 9.**
Pagan, People v., 211 A.D.2d 532, 622 N.Y.S.2d 9 (N.Y.A.D. 1 Dept.1995)—§ **33.57, n. 3.**
Pagano v. Smith, 201 A.D.2d 632, 608 N.Y.S.2d 268 (N.Y.A.D. 2 Dept.1994)—§ **11.6, n. 2.**
Pagnerre, Matter of, 13 I & N Dec. 668 (BIA 1971)—§ **19.11, n. 10.**
Pagnerre, Matter of, 12 I & N Dec. 688 (BIA 1977)—§ **19.10, n. 14.**
Paige, People v., 382 N.Y.S.2d 742, 346 N.E.2d 543 (N.Y.1976)—§ **38.27, n. 23.**
Painter, People v., 221 A.D.2d 481, 633 N.Y.S.2d 547 (N.Y.A.D. 2 Dept.1995)—§ **38.10, n. 59.**
PAK Realty Associates v. RE/MAX Universal, Inc., 157 Misc.2d 985, 599 N.Y.S.2d 399 (N.Y.City Civ.Ct.1993)—§ **13.12, n. 1.**
Palega's Estate, In re, 208 Misc. 966, 145 N.Y.S.2d 271 (N.Y.Sur.1955)—§ **2.46, n. 13.**
Paley v. Brust, 21 A.D.2d 758, 250 N.Y.S.2d 356 (N.Y.A.D. 1 Dept.1964)—§ **30.8, n. 3.**
Palin v. Palin, 213 A.D.2d 707, 624 N.Y.S.2d 630 (N.Y.A.D. 2 Dept.1995)—§ **21.20; § 21.20, n. 6; § 21.26, n. 7.**
Palma v. Palma, 101 A.D.2d 812, 474 N.Y.S.2d 990 (N.Y.A.D. 2 Dept.1984)—§ **37.37, n. 48.**
Palmer v. Palmer, 223 A.D.2d 944, 637 N.Y.S.2d 225 (N.Y.A.D. 3 Dept.1996)—§ **21.61, n. 4.**
Palmieri v. Long Island Jewish Medical Center, 221 A.D.2d 511, 635 N.Y.S.2d 483 (N.Y.A.D. 2 Dept.1995)—§ **37.29, n. 24.**
Palsgraf v. Long Island R. Co., 248 N.Y. 339, 162 N.E. 99 (N.Y.1928)—§ **28.16, n. 2.**

TABLE OF CASES

Pamela Equities Corp. v. Louis Frey Co., Inc., 120 Misc.2d 281, 465 N.Y.S.2d 659 (N.Y.City Civ.Ct.1983)—§ **13.58**; § **13.58, n. 5.**

Pan Am Corp. v. Delta Air Lines, Inc., 175 B.R. 438 (S.D.N.Y.1994)—§ **9.107, n. 19.**

Pan American World Airways, Inc. v. New York State Human Rights Appeal Bd., 475 N.Y.S.2d 256, 463 N.E.2d 597 (N.Y. 1984)—§ **17.68, n. 2.**

Panossian v. Panossian, 201 A.D.2d 983, 607 N.Y.S.2d 840 (N.Y.A.D. 4 Dept. 1994)—§ **21.55, n. 3.**

Pantano, People v., 46 A.D.2d 914, 363 N.Y.S.2d 16 (N.Y.A.D. 2 Dept.1974)— § **38.10, n. 3.**

Paolini v. Paolini, 99 A.D.2d 742, 471 N.Y.S.2d 647 (N.Y.A.D. 2 Dept.1984)— § **37.29, n. 10;** § **37.65, n. 17.**

Papa v. City of New York, 194 A.D.2d 527, 598 N.Y.S.2d 558 (N.Y.A.D. 2 Dept. 1993)—§ **37.29, n. 18.**

Papacostopulos v. Morrelli, 122 Misc.2d 938, 472 N.Y.S.2d 284 (N.Y.City Civ.Ct. 1984)—§ **13.17, n. 16;** § **13.18, n. 11, 20;** § **13.43, n. 17.**

Papaioannou v. Lukas, 170 A.D.2d 289, 566 N.Y.S.2d 16 (N.Y.A.D. 1 Dept.1991)— § **28.4;** § **28.4, n. 8.**

Paparella v. Paparella, 74 A.D.2d 106, 426 N.Y.S.2d 610 (N.Y.A.D. 4 Dept.1980)— § **21.12, n. 2.**

Papas v. Upjohn Co., 926 F.2d 1019 (11th Cir.1991)—§ **27.44, n. 1;** § **27.47, n. 4.**

Pappas v. Air France, 652 F.Supp. 198 (E.D.N.Y.1986)—§ **17.25, n. 8, 10.**

Parchment, People v., 203 A.D.2d 595, 612 N.Y.S.2d 939 (N.Y.A.D. 2 Dept.1994)— § **38.28, n. 28.**

Parente v. Drozd, 171 A.D.2d 847, 567 N.Y.S.2d 534 (N.Y.A.D. 2 Dept.1991)— § **6.67, n. 4.**

Parilli v. Brooklyn City R.R., 236 A.D. 577, 260 N.Y.S. 60 (N.Y.A.D. 2 Dept.1932)— § **30.18, n. 5.**

Paris, People ex rel. v. Hunt, 201 A.D. 573, 194 N.Y.S. 699 (N.Y.A.D. 3 Dept.1922)— § **38.10, n. 132.**

Paris v. United States, 381 F.Supp. 597 (N.D.Ohio 1974)—§ **24.32, n. 1.**

Paris v. Waterman S.S. Corp., 218 A.D.2d 561, 630 N.Y.S.2d 716 (N.Y.A.D. 1 Dept. 1995)—§ **30.31, n. 12.**

Parisi v. Moore, 37 A.D.2d 783, 325 N.Y.S.2d 378 (N.Y.A.D. 2 Dept.1971)— § **37.37, n. 23, 37.**

Parkchester Apartments Co. v. Metropolitan Retail Recovery, Inc., N.Y.L.J., 11/23/94, p.27, col.4, 22 HCR 666 (Civ. Ct., Bronx County)—§ **13.31;** § **13.31, n. 8.**

Park, People v., 238 A.D. 29, 263 N.Y.S. 25 (N.Y.A.D. 4 Dept.1933)—§ **38.20, n. 6.**

Park East Corp. v. Whalen, 381 N.Y.S.2d 819, 345 N.E.2d 289 (N.Y.1976)— § **37.43, n. 5.**

Parker v. Paton Associates Inc. of Amsterdam, 128 Misc.2d 871, 491 N.Y.S.2d 550 (N.Y.City Ct.1985)—§ **13.16, n. 5.**

Parker, People v., 527 N.Y.S.2d 765, 522 N.E.2d 1063 (N.Y.1988)—§ **39.43, n. 2.**

Parker, People v., 468 N.Y.S.2d 870, 456 N.E.2d 811 (N.Y.1983)—§ **38.8;** § **38.8, n. 98.**

Parker, People v., 85 A.D.2d 565, 445 N.Y.S.2d 443 (N.Y.A.D. 1 Dept.1981)— § **38.10, n. 87.**

Parker v. Rogerson, 361 N.Y.S.2d 916, 320 N.E.2d 650 (N.Y.1974)—§ **39.11;** § **39.11, n. 6.**

Parker v. Town of Gardiner Planning Bd., 184 A.D.2d 937, 585 N.Y.S.2d 571 (N.Y.A.D. 3 Dept.1992)—§ **16.40, n. 5.**

Parker Montana Co., In re, 47 B.R. 419 (D.Mont.1985)—§ **9.107, n. 24.**

Park St. (Lido Boulevard) Vicinity of Bay Lane, Town of Hempstead, In re, 67 Misc.2d 1065, 325 N.Y.S.2d 555 (N.Y.Sup.1971)—§ **14.78, n. 2.**

Park Summit Realty Corp. v. Frank, 107 Misc.2d 318, 434 N.Y.S.2d 73 (N.Y.Sup. App.Term 1980)—§ **13.11, n. 5;** § **13.36, n. 2.**

Parksville Mobile Modular, Inc. v. Fabricant, 73 A.D.2d 595, 422 N.Y.S.2d 710 (N.Y.A.D. 2 Dept.1979)—§ **28.3, n. 1;** § **28.12, n. 5.**

Park West Management Corp. v. Mitchell, 418 N.Y.S.2d 310, 391 N.E.2d 1288 (N.Y. 1979)—§ **13.32, n. 1.**

Parlato v. Chrysler Corp., 170 A.D.2d 442, 565 N.Y.S.2d 230 (N.Y.A.D. 2 Dept. 1991)—§ **7.10, n. 9;** § **7.20, n. 1.**

Parmaklidis, People v., 384 N.Y.S.2d 442, 348 N.E.2d 918 (N.Y.1976)—§ **38.8, n. 32;** § **38.41, n. 4.**

Parmelee, People v., 184 A.D.2d 534, 584 N.Y.S.2d 318 (N.Y.A.D. 2 Dept.1992)— § **38.10, n. 41.**

Parmisani v. Grasso, 218 A.D.2d 870, 629 N.Y.S.2d 865 (N.Y.A.D. 3 Dept.1995)— § **28.3, n. 1.**

Parnes, Matter of, N.Y.L.J., 11/2/94, p.32, col.2 (Sup.Ct., Kings County)—§ **22.48, n. 11;** § **23.76, n. 20;** § **23.80, n. 9.**

Parnes, Matter of, N.Y.L.J., 4/7/95, p. 33, col. 5 (Sup.Ct.,Kings County)—§ **22.48, n. 11;** § **23.76, n. 20.**

Parnes, People v., 161 A.D.2d 615, 555 N.Y.S.2d 396 (N.Y.A.D. 2 Dept.1990)— § **38.8, n. 102.**

Parochial Bus Systems, Inc. v. Board of Educ. of City of New York, 470 N.Y.S.2d

TABLE OF CASES

564, 458 N.E.2d 1241 (N.Y.1983)—§ 37.22, n. 1, 5; § 37.28; § 37.28, n. 32, 33; § 37.35, n. 15; § 38.3, n. 28.

Paroff v. Muss, 171 A.D.2d 782, 567 N.Y.S.2d 502 (N.Y.A.D. 2 Dept.1991)—§ 13.64, n. 2.

Parris, People v., 580 N.Y.S.2d 167, 588 N.E.2d 65 (N.Y.1992)—§ 33.82, n. 2.

Parrish v. Parrish, 213 A.D.2d 928, 623 N.Y.S.2d 955 (N.Y.A.D. 3 Dept.1995)—§ 21.38; § 21.38, n. 4.

Parry v. Pyramid Crossgates Co., 158 A.D.2d 787, 551 N.Y.S.2d 77 (N.Y.A.D. 3 Dept.1990)—§ 27.37, n. 1.

Partridge, Matter of, 141 Misc.2d 159, 532 N.Y.S.2d 814 (N.Y.Sur.1988)—§ 25.31, n. 6.

Parvi v. City of Kingston, 394 N.Y.S.2d 161, 362 N.E.2d 960 (N.Y.1977)—§ 17.26, n. 1.

Pascarella v. Pascarella, 210 A.D.2d 915, 621 N.Y.S.2d 821 (N.Y.A.D. 4 Dept. 1994)—§ 21.20, n. 2; § 21.22; § 21.22, n. 8; § 21.23, n. 5.

Pasch v. Katz Media Corp., 1995 WL 469710 (S.D.N.Y.1995)—§ 17.47, n. 1; § 17.48, n. 1.

Pasner (Tenenbaum), Matter of, N.Y.L.J., 7/14/95, p.29, col.1 (Sup.Ct., Kings County)—§ 22.40, n. 1, 7; § 22.41, n. 2, 5, 13.

Pasquale v. Pasquale, 210 A.D.2d 387, 620 N.Y.S.2d 95 (N.Y.A.D. 2 Dept.1994)—§ 21.30, n. 6.

Passalacqua v. Skop, 142 A.D.2d 723, 531 N.Y.S.2d 304 (N.Y.A.D. 2 Dept.1988)—§ 30.30, n. 8.

Passaretti v. State, 37 A.D.2d 1021, 325 N.Y.S.2d 707 (N.Y.A.D. 3 Dept.1971)—§ 14.81, n. 4.

Passeri v. Katzenstein, 183 A.D.2d 817, 586 N.Y.S.2d 523 (N.Y.A.D. 2 Dept.1992)—§ 18.76, n. 6.

Passuello, Matter of Estate of, 169 A.D.2d 1007, 565 N.Y.S.2d 281 (N.Y.A.D. 3 Dept.1991)—§ 25.21, n. 1.

Patchogue Nursing Center v. New York State Dept. of Health, 189 A.D.2d 1054, 592 N.Y.S.2d 900 (N.Y.A.D. 3 Dept. 1993)—§ 4.72, n. 2.

Patel v. Albany Medical Center Hospital, 101 Misc.2d 457, 421 N.Y.S.2d 182 (N.Y.Sup.1979)—§ 30.33, n. 3.

Pat Hartly, Inc. v. American Reciprocal Insurers, 43 Misc.2d 153, 21 A.D.2d 761, 250 N.Y.S.2d 351 (N.Y.A.D. 1 Dept. 1964)—§ 30.18, n. 2.

Patricia Ann W., Matter of, 89 Misc.2d 368, 392 N.Y.S.2d 180 (N.Y.Fam.Ct.1977)—§ 20.124, n. 2.

Patrizio v. Patrizio, 96 A.D.2d 1149, 464 N.Y.S.2d 320 (N.Y.A.D. 4 Dept.1983)—§ 37.29, n. 10; § 37.65, n. 17.

Patten v. State, 99 A.D.2d 922, 473 N.Y.S.2d 47 (N.Y.A.D. 3 Dept.1984)—§ 14.54, n. 1.

Patten of New York Corp. v. Geoffrion, 193 A.D.2d 1007, 598 N.Y.S.2d 355 (N.Y.A.D. 3 Dept.1993)—§ 12.64, n. 11; § 12.65, n. 10.

Patterson v. Commissioner, T.C. Memo. 1966-239 (Tax Ct.1966)—§ 1.10, n. 19; § 1.34, n. 18.

Patterson, People v., 211 A.D.2d 829, 621 N.Y.S.2d 672 (N.Y.A.D. 2 Dept.1995)—§ 38.8, n. 21.

Patterson, People v., 203 A.D.2d 597, 611 N.Y.S.2d 217 (N.Y.A.D. 2 Dept.1994)—§ 38.26, n. 17.

Patterson, People v., 106 A.D.2d 520, 483 N.Y.S.2d 55 (N.Y.A.D. 2 Dept.1984)—§ 33.30, n. 1.

Patterson, People v., 464 N.Y.S.2d 751, 451 N.E.2d 498 (N.Y.1983)—§ 38.21, n. 58.

Patterson, People v., 383 N.Y.S.2d 573, 347 N.E.2d 898 (N.Y.1976)—§ 38.19, n. 5, 16; § 39.50, n. 10.

Patterson v. Shumate, 504 U.S. 753, 112 S.Ct. 2242, 119 L.Ed.2d 519 (1992)—§ 9.49, n. 1.

Patti, People v., 216 A.D.2d 422, 628 N.Y.S.2d 525 (N.Y.A.D. 2 Dept.1995)—§ 38.28, n. 25.

Paul v. Boschenstein, 105 A.D.2d 248, 482 N.Y.S.2d 870 (N.Y.A.D. 2 Dept.1984)—§ 29.11, n. 15.

Paul v. Davis, 424 U.S. 693, 96 S.Ct. 1155, 47 L.Ed.2d 405 (1976)—§ 4.6, n. 5.

Paulemon v. Tobin, 30 F.3d 307 (2nd Cir. 1994)—§ 7.43; § 7.43, n. 6.

Pavia v. State Farm Mut. Auto. Ins. Co., 605 N.Y.S.2d 208, 626 N.E.2d 24 (N.Y. 1993)—§ 31.17, n. 1.

Pavlovic, Matter of, 17 I & N Dec. 407 (BIA 1980)—§ 19.11, n. 25.

Pavlovic v. Pavlovic, 124 A.D.2d 732, 508 N.Y.S.2d 234 (N.Y.A.D. 2 Dept.1986)—§ 20.67, n. 8.

Payn, People ex rel. United States Grand Lodge of Order of Brith Abraham v., 161 N.Y. 229, 55 N.E. 849 (N.Y.1900)—§ 1.13, n. 2.

Payne v. A.O. Smith Corp., 627 F.Supp. 226 (S.D.Ohio 1985)—§ 27.42, n. 1.

Payne, People v., 643 N.Y.S.2d 949, 666 N.E.2d 542 (N.Y.1996)—§ 18.15, n. 9.

Payne, People v., 149 A.D.2d 542, 540 N.Y.S.2d 256 (N.Y.A.D. 2 Dept.1989)—§ 38.21; § 38.21, n. 26.

Payne's Estate, In re, 12 A.D.2d 940, 210 N.Y.S.2d 925 (N.Y.A.D. 2 Dept.1961)—§ 30.13, n. 4.

TABLE OF CASES

P & D Cards and Gifts, Inc. v. Matejka, 150 A.D.2d 660, 541 N.Y.S.2d 533 (N.Y.A.D. 2 Dept.1989)—§ **13.53, n. 1.**

Pearson v. Pearson, 108 A.D.2d 402, 489 N.Y.S.2d 332 (N.Y.A.D. 2 Dept.1985)—§ **21.7, n. 3.**

Pearson v. Shoemaker, 25 Misc.2d 591, 202 N.Y.S.2d 779 (N.Y.Sup.1960)—§ **16.89, n. 5, 9; § 16.93, n. 4, 5, 6.**

Peart v. T. D. Bross Line Const. Co., 45 A.D.2d 801, 357 N.Y.S.2d 53 (N.Y.A.D. 3 Dept.1974)—§ **24.66, n. 2.**

Pebble Cove Homeowners' Ass'n, Inc. v. Fidelity New York FSB, 153 A.D.2d 843, 545 N.Y.S.2d 362 (N.Y.A.D. 2 Dept. 1989)—§ **1.10, n. 19.**

Peck v. Ernst Bros., Inc., 81 A.D.2d 940, 439 N.Y.S.2d 515 (N.Y.A.D. 3 Dept. 1981)—§ **37.43, n. 9.**

Peck v. Sony Music Corp., 1995 WL 505653 (S.D.N.Y.1995)—§ **17.56, n. 1.**

Peck v. Tired Iron Transport, Inc., 209 A.D.2d 979, 620 N.Y.S.2d 199 (N.Y.A.D. 4 Dept.1994)—§ **37.29, n. 25; § 37.65, n. 62.**

Pecoraro v. Board of Educ. of Van Corlaer Elementary School, 201 A.D.2d 769, 607 N.Y.S.2d 185 (N.Y.A.D. 3 Dept.1994)—§ **37.37, n. 31.**

Pedersen v. Manitowoc Co., 306 N.Y.S.2d 903, 255 N.E.2d 146 (N.Y.1969)—§ **2.53, n. 2.**

Pedraza, People v., 495 N.Y.S.2d 30, 485 N.E.2d 237 (N.Y.1985)—§ **38.21, n. 58.**

Pedro Abich, Inc., In re, 165 B.R. 5 (D.Puerto Rico 1994)—§ **9.174, n. 11.**

Peebler v. Reno, 965 F.Supp. 28 (D.Or. 1997)—§ **23.76, n. 5.**

Pelchat, People v., 476 N.Y.S.2d 79, 464 N.E.2d 447 (N.Y.1984)—§ **38.8, n. 197.**

Pelham Esplanade, Inc. v. Board of Trustees of Village of Pelham Manor, 563 N.Y.S.2d 759, 565 N.E.2d 508 (N.Y. 1990)—§ **16.64, n. 2.**

Pell v. Board of Ed. of Union Free School Dist. No. 1 of Towns of Scarsdale and Mamaroneck, Westchester County, 356 N.Y.S.2d 833, 313 N.E.2d 321 (N.Y. 1974)—§ **4.2, n. 46; § 4.40, n. 2; § 4.76, n. 4; § 4.79; § 4.79, n. 4; § 4.81; § 4.81, n. 1, 3; § 17.53, n. 10; § 37.87, n. 19, 24, 25, 27.**

Pellegrino, People v., 467 N.Y.S.2d 355, 454 N.E.2d 938 (N.Y.1983)—§ **38.8; § 38.8, n. 28, 181, 210.**

Peloquin v. Arsenault, 162 Misc.2d 306, 616 N.Y.S.2d 716 (N.Y.Sup.1994)—§ **3.28, n. 21.**

Pelow, People v., 299 N.Y.S.2d 185, 247 N.E.2d 150 (N.Y.1969)—§ **37.28, n. 36.**

Pena v. New York City Transit Authority, 185 A.D.2d 794, 587 N.Y.S.2d 331 (N.Y.A.D. 1 Dept.1992)—§ **37.65, n. 34.**

Pendleton, People v., 361 N.Y.S.2d 160, 319 N.E.2d 422 (N.Y.1974)—§ **38.27, n. 15.**

Penn Central Transp. Co. v. City of New York, 397 N.Y.S.2d 914, 366 N.E.2d 1271 (N.Y.1977)—§ **16.127; § 16.127, n. 5, 8, 9.**

Penn Cent. Transp. Co. v. City of New York, 438 U.S. 104, 98 S.Ct. 2646, 57 L.Ed.2d 631 (1978)—§ **16.22, n. 3; § 16.127, n. 6, 7.**

Penn–Dixie Industries, Inc., In re, 32 B.R. 173 (Bkrtcy.S.D.N.Y.1983)—§ **9.167, n. 2.**

Pennhurst State School & Hosp. v. Halderman, 465 U.S. 89, 104 S.Ct. 900, 79 L.Ed.2d 67 (1984)—§ **18.33, n. 2.**

Pennsylvania Coal Co. v. Mahon, 260 U.S. 393, 43 S.Ct. 158, 67 L.Ed. 322 (1922)—§ **15.34; § 15.34, n. 2; § 16.22, n. 2.**

Pennsylvania Dept. of Public Welfare v. Davenport, 495 U.S. 552, 110 S.Ct. 2126, 109 L.Ed.2d 588 (1990)—§ **9.255, n. 9.**

Pennsylvania General Ins. Co. v. Austin Powder Co., 510 N.Y.S.2d 67, 502 N.E.2d 982 (N.Y.1986)—§ **31.29, n. 6; § 37.22, n. 5.**

Penny Arcade, Inc. v. Town Bd. of Town of Oyster Bay, 75 A.D.2d 620, 427 N.Y.S.2d 52 (N.Y.A.D. 2 Dept.1980)—§ **16.8, n. 8.**

Pennzoil Co. v. Texaco, Inc., 481 U.S. 1, 107 S.Ct. 1519, 95 L.Ed.2d 1 (1987)—§ **18.36, n. 4.**

Penrod, Matter of, 50 F.3d 459 (7th Cir. 1995)—§ **9.101, n. 4; § 9.167, n. 4.**

People v. ——(see opposing party)

People by Koppell v. Empyre Inground Pools Inc., 227 A.D.2d 731, 642 N.Y.S.2d 344 (N.Y.A.D. 3 Dept.1996)—§ **7.46, n. 11; § 7.47, n. 7.**

People by Lefkowitz v. Volkswagen of America, Inc., 47 A.D.2d 868, 366 N.Y.S.2d 157 (N.Y.A.D. 1 Dept.1975)—§ **7.46, n. 5.**

People by Vacco v. Mid Hudson Medical Group, P.C., 877 F.Supp. 143 (S.D.N.Y. 1995)—§ **18.19, n. 8.**

People ex rel. v. ——(see opposing party and relator)

People of State of N.Y. by Abrams v. Merlino, 694 F.Supp. 1101 (S.D.N.Y.1988)—§ **18.50, n. 4.**

Peoples Commercial Bank v. Jerry Greene Distributing, Inc., 149 A.D.2d 774, 539 N.Y.S.2d 569 (N.Y.A.D. 3 Dept.1989)—§ **37.28, n. 19.**

Peoples Sav. Bank of Yonkers v. County Dollar Corp., 43 A.D.2d 327, 351 N.Y.S.2d 157 (N.Y.A.D. 2 Dept.1974)—§ **37.65, n. 69.**

TABLE OF CASES

Pepe v. Miller & Miller Consulting Actuaries, Inc., 221 A.D.2d 545, 634 N.Y.S.2d 490 (N.Y.A.D. 2 Dept.1995)—§ **13.17, n. 10.**

Pepper v. Litton, 308 U.S. 295, 60 S.Ct. 238, 84 L.Ed. 281 (1939)—§ **9.107, n. 10.**

Pepper, People v., 465 N.Y.S.2d 850, 452 N.E.2d 1178 (N.Y.1983)—§ **38.8, n. 92.**

Pepper, People v., 440 N.Y.S.2d 889, 423 N.E.2d 366 (N.Y.1981)—§ **38.22, n. 3.**

Perazone v. Sears, Roebuck and Co., 128 A.D.2d 15, 515 N.Y.S.2d 908 (N.Y.A.D. 3 Dept.1987)—§ **27.24; § 27.24, n. 1.**

Pereira v. Lehigh Savings Bank (In re Artha Management, Inc.), 174 B.R. 671 (Bkrtcy.S.D.N.Y.1994)—§ **9.117, n. 3.**

Perez v. Campbell, 402 U.S. 637, 91 S.Ct. 1704, 29 L.Ed.2d 233 (1971)—§ **9.132, n. 1.**

Perez v. One Clark Street Housing Corp., 108 A.D.2d 844, 485 N.Y.S.2d 346 (N.Y.A.D. 2 Dept.1985)—§ **1.10, n. 18.**

Perez, People v., 204 A.D.2d 662, 212 A.D.2d 814, 612 N.Y.S.2d 620 (N.Y.A.D. 2 Dept.1994)—§ **38.8, n. 56.**

Perez, People v., 203 A.D.2d 123, 610 N.Y.S.2d 483 (N.Y.A.D. 1 Dept.1994)—§ **38.19, n. 30.**

Perez, People v., 202 A.D.2d 695, 610 N.Y.S.2d 827 (N.Y.A.D. 2 Dept.1994)—§ **38.19, n. 30.**

Perez, People v., 167 A.D.2d 308, 562 N.Y.S.2d 53 (N.Y.A.D. 1 Dept.1990)—§ **33.53, n. 2.**

Perez, People v., 541 N.Y.S.2d 976, 539 N.E.2d 1104 (N.Y.1989)—§ **38.27, n. 33.**

Pergament Home Centers, Inc. v. Net Realty Holding Trust, 171 A.D.2d 736, 567 N.Y.S.2d 292 (N.Y.A.D. 2 Dept.1991)—§ **13.71; § 13.71, n. 3.**

Perino v. St. Vincent's Medical Center of Staten Island, 132 Misc.2d 20, 502 N.Y.S.2d 921 (N.Y.Sup.1986)—§ **18.57, n. 1.**

Perkins, People v., 189 A.D.2d 830, 592 N.Y.S.2d 752 (N.Y.A.D. 2 Dept.1993)—§ **38.28; § 38.28, n. 11, 18.**

Perla v. New York Daily News, Inc., 123 A.D.2d 349, 506 N.Y.S.2d 361 (N.Y.A.D. 2 Dept.1986)—§ **30.28, n. 12.**

Perlman, People v., 89 Misc.2d 973, 392 N.Y.S.2d 985 (N.Y.Dist.Ct.1977)—§ **33.68, n. 14.**

Perrotta v. City of New York, 498 N.Y.S.2d 368, 489 N.E.2d 255 (N.Y.1985)—§ **4.33, n. 3.**

Perrotta, People v., 121 A.D.2d 659, 504 N.Y.S.2d 51 (N.Y.A.D. 2 Dept.1986)—§ **38.21, n. 8.**

Perry v. Klein, 198 A.D.2d 576, 603 N.Y.S.2d 227 (N.Y.A.D. 3 Dept.1993)—§ **28.8, n. 1.**

Perry, People v., 639 N.Y.S.2d 307, 662 N.E.2d 787 (N.Y.1996)—§ **33.17; § 33.17, n. 8.**

Perry v. Sindermann, 408 U.S. 593, 92 S.Ct. 2694, 33 L.Ed.2d 570 (1972)—§ **4.6, n. 8, 9.**

Perryman, In re, 111 B.R. 227 (Bkrtcy. E.D.Ark.1990)—§ **9.130, n. 6.**

Persing v. Coughlin, 214 A.D.2d 145, 632 N.Y.S.2d 366 (N.Y.A.D. 4 Dept.1995)—§ **37.28, n. 5; § 37.29, n. 41.**

Persky, In re, 893 F.2d 15 (2nd Cir.1989)—§ **24.85, n. 3.**

Pester Refining Co. v. Ethyl Corp., 964 F.2d 842 (8th Cir.1992)—§ **9.105, n. 6, 8.**

Peterson, Matter of, N.Y.L.J., 1/15/97, p. 26, col. 4 (Sup.Ct., N.Y. County)—§ **22.12, n. 6.**

Petersen v. Owens, 186 A.D.2d 1029, 588 N.Y.S.2d 677 (N.Y.A.D. 4 Dept.1992)—§ **30.14, n. 11, 12.**

Peterson v. Williams, 85 F.3d 39 (2nd Cir. 1996)—§ **18.13, n. 4.**

Petgen, People v., 450 N.Y.S.2d 299, 435 N.E.2d 669 (N.Y.1982)—§ **38.8, n. 184.**

Petition of (see name of party)

Petito v. Piffath, 623 N.Y.S.2d 520, 647 N.E.2d 732 (N.Y.1994)—§ **11.37, n. 7.**

Petramale v. Laborers Intern. Union of North America, 736 F.2d 13 (2nd Cir. 1984)—§ **17.61, n. 15.**

Petroleum Products Antitrust Litigation, In re, 680 F.2d 5 (2nd Cir.1982)—§ **18.85, n. 7.**

Petryszyn v. Di Fulvio, 185 A.D.2d 405, 585 N.Y.S.2d 808 (N.Y.A.D. 3 Dept.1992)—§ **37.28, n. 8.**

Petterson v. Pattberg, 248 N.Y. 86, 161 N.E. 428 (N.Y.1928)—§ **5.23, n. 3.**

Pfohl v. Wipperman, 354 N.Y.S.2d 951, 310 N.E.2d 546 (N.Y.1974)—§ **37.28, n. 3.**

Phelps v. A. R. Gundry, Inc., 23 A.D.2d 960, 261 N.Y.S.2d 194 (N.Y.A.D. 4 Dept. 1965)—§ **30.40, n. 3.**

Phelps v. Phelps, 199 A.D.2d 608, 604 N.Y.S.2d 339 (N.Y.A.D. 3 Dept.1993)—§ **21.43, n. 18.**

Philbrook v. Ansonia Bd. of Educ., 925 F.2d 47 (2nd Cir.1991)—§ **17.56, n. 1.**

Philippeaux v. North Central Bronx Hosp., 871 F.Supp. 640 (S.D.N.Y.1994)—§ **18.17, n. 5.**

Philips Consumer Electronics Co. v. Arrow Carrier Corp., 785 F.Supp. 436 (S.D.N.Y. 1992)—§ **30.18, n. 4.**

Phillip v. Gallant, 62 N.Y. 256 (N.Y.1875)—§ **30.25, n. 9.**

Phillips v. Sun Oil Co., 307 N.Y. 328, 121 N.E.2d 249 (N.Y.1954)—§ **15.33, n. 3.**

TABLE OF CASES

Philpott v. Essex County Welfare Bd., 409 U.S. 413, 93 S.Ct. 590, 34 L.Ed.2d 608 (1973)—§ **34.52, n. 4.**

Phinpathya v. Immigration and Naturalization Service, 673 F.2d 1013 (9th Cir. 1981)—§ **19.48, n. 4.**

Phoenix Home Life Mut. Ins. Co. v. Brown, 857 F.Supp. 7 (W.D.N.Y.1994)—§ **31.7, n. 5.**

Phoenix Mut. Life Ins. Co. v. Conway, 229 N.Y.S.2d 740, 183 N.E.2d 754 (N.Y. 1962)—§ **37.65, n. 14.**

Piazza v. Sutherland, 53 Misc.2d 726, 279 N.Y.S.2d 640 (N.Y.Sup.1967)—§ **12.9, n. 8.**

Piccarillo, People ex rel. v. New York State Bd. of Parole, 421 N.Y.S.2d 842, 397 N.E.2d 354 (N.Y.1979)—§ **4.62, n. 15.**

Piccinich v. Grace Lines, Inc., 62 A.D.2d 974, 404 N.Y.S.2d 351 (N.Y.A.D. 1 Dept. 1978)—§ **30.9, n. 23.**

Pickard, People v., 216 A.D.2d 333, 627 N.Y.S.2d 988 (N.Y.A.D. 2 Dept.1995)— § **38.8, n. 20;** § **38.21, n. 50.**

Picker, Estate of, 103 Misc.2d 594, 426 N.Y.S.2d 688 (N.Y.Sur.1980)—§ **25.46, n. 9, 10.**

Pickerell v. Town of Huntington, 219 A.D.2d 24, 641 N.Y.S.2d 887 (N.Y.A.D. 2 Dept.1996)—§ **37.80, n. 2.**

Pickwick Intern., Inc. v. Tomato Music Co., Ltd., 119 Misc.2d 227, 462 N.Y.S.2d 781 (N.Y.Sup.1983)—§ **8.16, n. 10.**

Pierson v. Ray, 386 U.S. 547, 87 S.Ct. 1213, 18 L.Ed.2d 288 (1967)—§ **18.31, n. 2.**

Pietra v. State, 530 N.Y.S.2d 510, 526 N.E.2d 1 (N.Y.1988)—§ **18.31, n. 3.**

Pigler by Reed v. Adam, Meldrum & Anderson Co., 195 A.D.2d 1011, 602 N.Y.S.2d 572 (N.Y.A.D. 4 Dept.1993)— § **37.20, n. 6.**

Pihlman v. Connery, 111 N.Y.S. 654 (N.Y.Sup.App.Term 1908)—§ **30.5, n. 11.**

Pike v. Honsinger, 155 N.Y. 201, 49 N.E. 760 (N.Y.1898)—§ **29.1, n. 1.**

Pilotti, People ex rel. v. New York State Div. of Parole, 201 A.D.2d 376, 607 N.Y.S.2d 343 (N.Y.A.D. 1 Dept.1994)— § **37.37, n. 63.**

Pinaud v. County of Suffolk, 52 F.3d 1139 (2nd Cir.1995)—§ **18.20, n. 3;** § **18.38, n. 6.**

Pinchback, People v., 187 A.D.2d 540, 589 N.Y.S.2d 600 (N.Y.A.D. 2 Dept.1992)— § **38.19, n. 38.**

Pineda, Matter of, N.Y.L.J., 5/28/97, p. 26, col. 3 (Sup.Ct., N.Y. County)—§ **22.61, n. 1.**

Pinner v. Schmidt, 805 F.2d 1258 (5th Cir. 1986)—§ **7.31, n. 11.**

Pioneer Inv. Services Co. v. Brunswick Associates Ltd. Partnership, 507 U.S. 380, 113 S.Ct. 1489, 123 L.Ed.2d 74 (1993)— § **9.93, n. 7, 8.**

Piotrowski v. Town of Glenville, 101 A.D.2d 654, 475 N.Y.S.2d 511 (N.Y.A.D. 3 Dept. 1984)—§ **14.34, n. 4.**

Piper, People v., 201 A.D.2d 968, 610 N.Y.S.2d 912 (N.Y.A.D. 4 Dept.1994)— § **38.19, n. 48.**

Pirre v. Printing Developments, Inc., 468 F.Supp. 1028 (S.D.N.Y.1979)—§ **17.25, n. 7.**

Pisano v. Tupper, 188 A.D.2d 991, 591 N.Y.S.2d 888 (N.Y.A.D. 3 Dept.1992)— § **8.33, n. 9.**

Pitts, People v., 528 N.Y.S.2d 534, 523 N.E.2d 821 (N.Y.1988)—§ **38.19;** § **38.19, n. 132.**

Pittsford, Town of v. Sweeney, 34 Misc.2d 436, 228 N.Y.S.2d 518 (N.Y.Sup.1962)— § **14.84, n. 1.**

Pius v. Bletsch, 524 N.Y.S.2d 395, 519 N.E.2d 306 (N.Y.1987)—§ **16.54;** § **16.54, n. 1.**

Pizzi v. Muccia, 127 A.D.2d 338, 515 N.Y.S.2d 341 (N.Y.A.D. 3 Dept.1987)— § **26.42, n. 13.**

Place v. Hack, 34 Misc.2d 777, 230 N.Y.S.2d 583 (N.Y.Sup.1962)—§ **16.15, n. 16.**

Plander v. Rappalyea, N.Y.L.J., 10/20/72, at p.18, col.4 (2d Dep't)—§ **11.54, n. 11.**

Planned Consumer Marketing, Inc. v. Coats & Clark, Inc., 127 A.D.2d 355, 513 N.Y.S.2d 417 (N.Y.A.D. 1 Dept.1987)— § **2.23, n. 18.**

Planned Parenthood of Dutchess–Ulster, Inc. v. Steinhaus, 60 F.3d 122 (2nd Cir. 1995)—§ **18.36, n. 8.**

Plastiros v. Idell (In re Sequoia Auto Brokers Ltd., Inc.), 827 F.2d 1281 (9th Cir. 1987)—§ **9.18, n. 4.**

Plaza Health Laboratories, Inc., United States v., 3 F.3d 643 (2nd Cir.1993)— § **15.8, n. 11.**

Pleasant East Associates v. Cabrera, 125 Misc.2d 877, 480 N.Y.S.2d 693 (N.Y.City Civ.Ct.1984)—§ **13.32, n. 10.**

Pleasant Valley Home Const., Ltd. v. Van Wagner, 395 N.Y.S.2d 631, 363 N.E.2d 1376 (N.Y.1977)—§ **16.124, n. 13.**

P & L Group, Inc. v. Garfinkel, 150 A.D.2d 663, 541 N.Y.S.2d 535 (N.Y.A.D. 2 Dept. 1989)—§ **17.63, n. 2.**

Pliss v. Erie Railroad Co., 208 A.D. 761, 202 N.Y.S. 947 (N.Y.A.D. 4 Dept.1924)— § **38.27, n. 5.**

Plotkin v. New York City Health and Hospitals Corp., 221 A.D.2d 425, 633 N.Y.S.2d 585 (N.Y.A.D. 2 Dept.1995)—§ **37.29, n. 24.**

TABLE OF CASES

Plumbing, Heating, Piping & Air Conditioning Contractors Ass'n, Inc., v. New York State Thruway Authority, 185 N.Y.S.2d 534, 158 N.E.2d 238 (N.Y.1959)—§ **3.35, n. 5, 6.**

Pluto's Retreat, Inc. v. Granito, 80 A.D.2d 899, 437 N.Y.S.2d 112 (N.Y.A.D. 2 Dept. 1981)—§ **16.92, n. 1.**

Pneuman v. Pneuman, 33 A.D.2d 646, 305 N.Y.S.2d 272 (N.Y.A.D. 4 Dept.1969)—§ **21.32, n. 2.**

Pocantico Water-Works Co. v. Bird, 130 N.Y. 249, 29 N.E. 246 (N.Y.1891)—§ **14.12, n. 6.**

Pocchia v. Motahedeh, 154 A.D.2d 662, 547 N.Y.S.2d 249 (N.Y.A.D. 2 Dept.1989)—§ **37.37, n. 27.**

Podolsky v. Narnoc Corp., 196 A.D.2d 593, 601 N.Y.S.2d 320 (N.Y.A.D. 2 Dept. 1993)—§ **10.18, n. 5.**

Poirier v. City of Schenectady, 624 N.Y.S.2d 555, 648 N.E.2d 1318 (N.Y.1995)—§ **3.30, n. 15.**

Poklitar v. CBS, Inc., 652 F.Supp. 1023 (S.D.N.Y.1987)—§ **17.34, n. 3.**

Pokoik v. Department of Health Services of County of Suffolk, 220 A.D.2d 13, 641 N.Y.S.2d 881 (N.Y.A.D. 2 Dept.1996)—§ **37.80, n. 2.**

Pokoik v. Silsdorf, 390 N.Y.S.2d 49, 358 N.E.2d 874 (N.Y.1976)—§ **16.19; § 16.19, n. 3; § 37.32, n. 6.**

Polanco, People v., 216 A.D.2d 957, 629 N.Y.S.2d 693 (N.Y.A.D. 4 Dept.1995)—§ **38.8, n. 144.**

Polanco, People v., 216 A.D.2d 957, 629 N.Y.S.2d 583 (N.Y.A.D. 4 Dept.1995)—§ **38.8, n. 18, 208.**

Polish Nat. Alliance of Brooklyn, United StatesA. v. White Eagle Hall Co., Inc., 98 A.D.2d 400, 470 N.Y.S.2d 642 (N.Y.A.D. 2 Dept.1983)—§ **11.50, n. 4.**

Pollack, Matter of, N.Y.L.J., 9/27/96, p. 31, col. 1 (Sup.Ct., Nassau County)—§ **22.27, n. 1.**

Pollak v. State, 394 N.Y.S.2d 617, 363 N.E.2d 342 (N.Y.1977)—§ **12.65, n. 2.**

Pollard v. State, 173 A.D.2d 906, 569 N.Y.S.2d 770 (N.Y.A.D. 3 Dept.1991)—§ **37.29, n. 13.**

Pollay, People v., 145 A.D.2d 972, 538 N.Y.S.2d 714 (N.Y.A.D. 4 Dept.1988)—§ **38.8, n. 151.**

Pollenz, People v., 502 N.Y.S.2d 417, 493 N.E.2d 541 (N.Y.1986)—§ **38.3; § 38.3, n. 11, 12, 16; § 38.8, n. 53, 222; § 38.9, n. 5, 17.**

Pollock v. Holsa Corp., 98 A.D.2d 265, 470 N.Y.S.2d 151 (N.Y.A.D. 1 Dept.1984)—§ **30.9, n. 17.**

Polo Park Civic Ass'n v. Kiernan, 133 A.D.2d 116, 518 N.Y.S.2d 652 (N.Y.A.D. 2 Dept.1987)—§ **3.32, n. 9.**

Polytherm Industries, Inc., In re, 33 B.R. 823 (W.D.Wis.1983)—§ **9.148, n. 6; § 9.158, n. 5.**

Pompey, Town of v. Parker, 53 A.D.2d 125, 385 N.Y.S.2d 959 (N.Y.A.D. 4 Dept. 1976)—§ **16.123, n. 13.**

Pondexter, People v., 88 N.Y.2d 363, 645 N.Y.S.2d 759, 668 N.E.2d 879 (1996)—§ **18.12, n. 2.**

Poole v. Consolidated Rail Corp., 590 N.Y.S.2d 1, 604 N.E.2d 63 (N.Y.1992)—§ **39.16, n. 4.**

Pope, People v., 177 A.D.2d 658, 576 N.Y.S.2d 360 (N.Y.A.D. 2 Dept.1991)—§ **38.19, n. 45.**

Poplar v. Bourjois, Inc., 298 N.Y. 62, 80 N.E.2d 334 (N.Y.1948)—§ **27.36, n. 1.**

Porianda v. Amelkin, 115 A.D.2d 650, 496 N.Y.S.2d 487 (N.Y.A.D. 2 Dept.1985)—§ **16.119, n. 13.**

Port Clyde Foods, Inc. v. Holiday Syrups, Inc., 563 F.Supp. 893 (S.D.N.Y.1982)—§ **31.6, n. 4.**

Portee v. Hastava, 853 F.Supp. 597 (E.D.N.Y.1994)—§ **18.49, n. 10.**

Porter v. LSB Industries, Inc., 192 A.D.2d 205, 600 N.Y.S.2d 867 (N.Y.A.D. 4 Dept. 1993)—§ **1.10, n. 19.**

Porter v. Shapiro, 124 A.D.2d 794, 508 N.Y.S.2d 516 (N.Y.A.D. 2 Dept.1986)—§ **30.3; § 30.3, n. 14.**

Portfolio v. Rubin, 233 N.Y. 439, 135 N.E. 843 (N.Y.1922)—§ **5.39, n. 4.**

Posner v. United States Fidelity & Guaranty Co., 33 Misc.2d 653, 226 N.Y.S.2d 1011 (N.Y.Sup.1962)—§ **5.7, n. 5.**

Posr v. Doherty, 944 F.2d 91 (2nd Cir. 1991)—§ **18.22, n. 2.**

Post v. 120 East End Ave. Corp., 475 N.Y.S.2d 821, 464 N.E.2d 125 (N.Y. 1984)—§ **13.69, n. 1; § 13.70, n. 4; § 39.7, n. 11.**

Post v. Reynolds, 101 Misc.2d 504, 421 N.Y.S.2d 320 (N.Y.City Civ.Ct.1979)—§ **13.17, n. 16; § 13.43, n. 17.**

Potskowski, People v., 298 N.Y. 299, 83 N.E.2d 125 (N.Y.1948)—§ **38.21, n. 56.**

Potts' Estate, In re, 213 A.D. 59, 209 N.Y.S. 655 (N.Y.A.D. 4 Dept.1925)—§ **25.39, n. 3.**

Poughkeepsie, City of v. Black, 130 A.D.2d 541, 515 N.Y.S.2d 275 (N.Y.A.D. 2 Dept. 1987)—§ **13.63, n. 3.**

Poughkeepsie Sav. Bank, FSB v. R.S. Paralegal & Recovery Services, Inc., 160 A.D.2d 857, 554 N.Y.S.2d 290 (N.Y.A.D. 2 Dept.1990)—§ **8.26, n. 3.**

TABLE OF CASES

Powe, People v., 146 A.D.2d 718, 537 N.Y.S.2d 208 (N.Y.A.D. 2 Dept.1989)—§ **38.24, n. 4.**

Power Authority v. Westinghouse Elec. Corp., 117 A.D.2d 336, 502 N.Y.S.2d 420 (N.Y.A.D. 1 Dept.1986)—§ **31.10, n. 3.**

Power Authority of State v. Williams, 469 N.Y.S.2d 620, 457 N.E.2d 726 (N.Y. 1983)—§ **39.15, n. 3.**

Powers v. General Acc. Ins. Co. of America, 109 A.D.2d 830, 486 N.Y.S.2d 764 (N.Y.A.D. 2 Dept.1985)—§ **26.24, n. 3.**

Powers v. Manhattan Ry. Co., 120 N.Y. 178, 24 N.E. 295 (N.Y.1890)—§ **30.33, n. 1.**

PPM America, Inc. v. Marriott Corp., 152 F.R.D. 32 (S.D.N.Y.1993)—§ **18.85, n. 7.**

Pratt, People v., 27 A.D.2d 199, 278 N.Y.S.2d 89 (N.Y.A.D. 3 Dept.1967)—§ **38.8, n. 101.**

Precision Steel Shearing, Inc. v. Fremont, Financial Corp. (In re Visual Industries, Inc.), 57 F.3d 321 (3rd Cir.1995)—§ **9.102, n. 9.**

Pregent, People v., 142 Misc.2d 344, 537 N.Y.S.2d 424 (N.Y.City Ct.1988)—§ **33.75; § 33.75, n. 3.**

Presbyterian Hospital in the City of New York (Helen Early), Matter of, N.Y.L.J., 7/2/93, p.22, col.2 (Sup.Ct., N.Y. County)—§ **22.8, n. 1, 4; § 22.14, n. 3.**

Prescott, People v., 495 N.Y.S.2d 955, 486 N.E.2d 813 (N.Y.1985)—§ **38.8, n. 160, 196.**

President, etc. of Village of Sing Sing, People ex rel. Seward v., 54 A.D. 555, 66 N.Y.S. 1094 (N.Y.A.D. 2 Dept.1900)—§ **3.20, n. 5.**

Presidential Fairfield, Inc. v. Holman, 98 Misc.2d 1095, 415 N.Y.S.2d 348 (N.Y.City Civ.Ct.1979)—§ **13.17, n. 18; § 13.44, n. 6.**

Press v. Monroe County, 431 N.Y.S.2d 394, 409 N.E.2d 870 (N.Y.1980)—§ **4.2, n. 41; § 4.82, n. 5, 7.**

Pressley, People v., 202 A.D.2d 695, 610 N.Y.S.2d 828 (N.Y.A.D. 2 Dept.1994)—§ **38.8, n. 27.**

Prest, People v., 105 A.D.2d 1078, 482 N.Y.S.2d 172 (N.Y.A.D. 4 Dept.1984)—§ **38.21, n. 5.**

Preston v. Preston, 165 Misc.2d 151, 627 N.Y.S.2d 518 (N.Y.Sup.1995)—§ **21.20, n. 5.**

Preston v. Secretary of Health and Human Services, 854 F.2d 815 (6th Cir.1988)—§ **34.9, n. 19.**

Price v. Brown Group, Inc., 206 A.D.2d 195, 619 N.Y.S.2d 414 (N.Y.A.D. 4 Dept. 1994)—§ **31.22, n. 3.**

Price v. Gurney, 324 U.S. 100, 65 S.Ct. 513, 89 L.Ed. 776 (1945)—§ **9.264, n. 6.**

Price v. Price, 511 N.Y.S.2d 219, 503 N.E.2d 684 (N.Y.1986)—§ **21.41; § 21.41, n. 1.**

Price, United States v., 688 F.2d 204 (3rd Cir.1982)—§ **15.25, n. 7.**

Prince's Estate, In re, 36 A.D.2d 946, 321 N.Y.S.2d 798 (N.Y.A.D. 1 Dept.1971)—§ **25.3, n. 9.**

Prior Aviation Service, Inc. v. State, 100 Misc.2d 237, 418 N.Y.S.2d 872 (N.Y.Ct. Cl.1979)—§ **18.87, n. 2.**

Prisoners' Legal Services of New York v. New York State Dept. of Correctional Services, 538 N.Y.S.2d 190, 535 N.E.2d 243 (N.Y.1988)—§ **18.65, n. 5.**

Pritchard Services (NY) Inc. v. First Winthrop Properties, Inc., 172 A.D.2d 394, 568 N.Y.S.2d 775 (N.Y.A.D. 1 Dept. 1991)—§ **1.10, n. 15.**

Procario v. Procario, 164 Misc.2d 79, 623 N.Y.S.2d 971 (N.Y.Sup.1994)—§ **21.39; § 21.39, n. 10.**

Process Plants Corp. v. Beneficial National Life Ins. Co., 53 A.D.2d 214, 385 N.Y.S.2d 308 (N.Y.A.D. 1 Dept.1976)—§ **31.18, n. 7.**

Proctor, People v., 87 Misc.2d 893, 386 N.Y.S.2d 803 (N.Y.Co.Ct.1976)—§ **38.52, n. 11.**

Progressive Cas. Ins. Co. v. C.A. Reaseguradora Nacional De Venezuela, 991 F.2d 42 (2nd Cir.1993)—§ **31.24, n. 4.**

Propoco, Inc. v. Birnbaum, 157 A.D.2d 774, 550 N.Y.S.2d 901 (N.Y.A.D. 2 Dept. 1990)—§ **30.39, n. 8.**

Propstra v. United States, 680 F.2d 1248 (9th Cir.1982)—§ **24.41, n. 2.**

Proskin v. County Court of Albany County, 330 N.Y.S.2d 44, 280 N.E.2d 875 (N.Y. 1972)—§ **38.10, n. 28.**

Proskin v. Donovan, 150 A.D.2d 937, 541 N.Y.S.2d 628 (N.Y.A.D. 3 Dept.1989)—§ **16.125, n. 10.**

Prospect v. Cohalan, 493 N.Y.S.2d 293, 482 N.E.2d 1209 (N.Y.1985)—§ **37.37; § 37.37, n. 74; § 39.27; § 39.27, n. 11.**

Prote Contracting Co., Inc. v. Board of Educ. of City of New York, 132 A.D.2d 538, 517 N.Y.S.2d 425 (N.Y.A.D. 2 Dept. 1987)—§ **28.29, n. 14.**

Protective Committee for Independent Stockholders of TMT Trailer Ferry, Inc. v. Anderson, 390 U.S. 414, 88 S.Ct. 1157, 20 L.Ed.2d 1 (1968)—§ **9.97, n. 2, 4.**

Province of Meribah Soc. of Mary, Inc. v. Village of Muttontown, 148 A.D.2d 512, 538 N.Y.S.2d 850 (N.Y.A.D. 2 Dept. 1989)—§ **16.131, n. 3.**

Provost v. Provost, 82 A.D.2d 995, 440 N.Y.S.2d 89 (N.Y.A.D. 3 Dept.1981)—§ **37.19, n. 14.**

TABLE OF CASES

Prozeralik v. Capital Cities Communications, Inc., 605 N.Y.S.2d 218, 626 N.E.2d 34 (N.Y.1993)—§ **18.81, n. 4; § 30.31, n. 8.**

Prudence v. Town of Ithaca Zoning Bd. of Appeals, 195 A.D.2d 662, 599 N.Y.S.2d 749 (N.Y.A.D. 3 Dept.1993)—§ **16.66, n. 4.**

Prudential Ins. Co. of America v. Dewey, Ballantine, Bushby, Palmer & Wood, 590 N.Y.S.2d 831, 605 N.E.2d 318 (N.Y. 1992)—§ **28.8; § 28.8, n. 6; § 28.11; § 28.11, n. 6, 10.**

Prudential Lines, Inc., In re, 170 B.R. 222 (S.D.N.Y.1994)—§ **31.9, n. 10.**

Prudential Property & Cas. Ins. Co. v. Carleton, 145 A.D.2d 492, 535 N.Y.S.2d 738 (N.Y.A.D. 2 Dept.1988)—§ **31.24, n. 11.**

Prudential Property & Cas. Ins. Co. v. Godfrey, 169 A.D.2d 1035, 565 N.Y.S.2d 315 (N.Y.A.D. 3 Dept.1991)—§ **28.39, n. 1.**

Prudential Property & Cas. Ins. Co. (Mathieu), Matter of, 213 A.D.2d 408, 623 N.Y.S.2d 336 (N.Y.A.D. 2 Dept.1995)—§ **31.16, n. 11.**

Pruitt, In re, 72 B.R. 436 (Bkrtcy.E.D.N.Y. 1987)—§ **9.28, n. 4.**

Pruitt v. Cheney, 963 F.2d 1160 (9th Cir. 1991)—§ **17.58, n. 1.**

Prunty v. YMCA of Lockport, Inc., 206 A.D.2d 911, 616 N.Y.S.2d 117 (N.Y.A.D. 4 Dept.1994)—§ **30.29; § 30.29, n. 9.**

P.S. Auctions, Inc. v. Exchange Mut. Ins. Co., 105 A.D.2d 473, 480 N.Y.S.2d 610 (N.Y.A.D. 3 Dept.1984)—§ **31.10, n. 17.**

P.T. & L. Const. Co., Inc. v. State, 179 A.D.2d 850, 578 N.Y.S.2d 921 (N.Y.A.D. 3 Dept.1992)—§ **37.29, n. 13.**

Public Interest Research Group of New Jersey, Inc. v. GAF Corp., 770 F.Supp. 943 (D.N.J.1991)—§ **15.11, n. 18.**

Public Interest Research Group of New Jersey, Inc. v. Rice, 774 F.Supp. 317 (D.N.J. 1991)—§ **4.38, n. 2.**

Public Service Co. of New Hampshire, In re, 88 B.R. 521 (Bkrtcy.D.N.H.1988)—§ **9.142, n. 5.**

Public Service Mut. Ins. Co. v. Goldfarb, 442 N.Y.S.2d 422, 425 N.E.2d 810 (N.Y. 1981)—§ **28.38, n. 1; § 28.39, n. 1; § 31.4, n. 4.**

Pugliese (Nicolais), Matter of, N.Y.L.J., 7/28/97, p. 30, col. 5 (Sup.Ct., Queens County)—§ **22.48, n. 11.**

Purolator Products Corp. v. Allied–Signal, Inc., 772 F.Supp. 124 (W.D.N.Y.1991)—§ **15.30, n. 11.**

Putcha v. Beattie, 129 A.D.2d 918, 514 N.Y.S.2d 559 (N.Y.A.D. 3 Dept.1987)—§ **16.50, n. 8.**

Putland, People v., 102 Misc.2d 517, 423 N.Y.S.2d 999 (N.Y.Co.Ct.1979)—§ **38.8, n. 133.**

Putnam v. Stout, 381 N.Y.S.2d 848, 345 N.E.2d 319 (N.Y.1976)—§ **26.10, n. 5.**

Putnam Armonk, Inc. v. Town of Southeast, 52 A.D.2d 10, 382 N.Y.S.2d 538 (N.Y.A.D. 2 Dept.1976)—§ **16.23, n. 5.**

Putnam's Will, In re, 257 N.Y. 140, 177 N.E. 399 (N.Y.1931)—§ **24.95, n. 4; § 25.22, n. 2.**

PVM Oil Futures, Inc. v. Banque Paribas, 161 A.D.2d 220, 554 N.Y.S.2d 606 (N.Y.A.D. 1 Dept.1990)—§ **17.27, n. 5.**

Pyle by Straub v. United States, 766 F.2d 1141 (7th Cir.1985)—§ **24.61, n. 3.**

Pymm, People v., 188 A.D.2d 561, 591 N.Y.S.2d 458 (N.Y.A.D. 2 Dept.1992)—§ **38.21, n. 11.**

Pynes, People v., 170 A.D.2d 981, 566 N.Y.S.2d 143 (N.Y.A.D. 4 Dept.1991)—§ **38.19, n. 67.**

Pyramid Co. of Auburn v. Chu, 177 A.D.2d 970, 577 N.Y.S.2d 1015 (N.Y.A.D. 4 Dept.1991)—§ **4.72, n. 3.**

Q

Quackenboss v. Globe & Rutgers Fire Ins. Co., 177 N.Y. 71, 69 N.E. 223 (N.Y. 1903)—§ **1.8, n. 2.**

Quaglia v. Village of Munsey Park, 54 A.D.2d 434, 389 N.Y.S.2d 616 (N.Y.A.D. 2 Dept.1976)—§ **3.11, n. 6; § 3.12, n. 2.**

Quail Ridge Associates v. Chemical Bank, 162 A.D.2d 917, 558 N.Y.S.2d 655 (N.Y.A.D. 3 Dept.1990)—§ **7.46, n. 11.**

Quantum Heating Services Inc. v. Austern, 100 A.D.2d 843, 474 N.Y.S.2d 81 (N.Y.A.D. 2 Dept.1984)—§ **8.42, n. 14.**

Quarant v. Ferrara, 111 Misc.2d 1042, 445 N.Y.S.2d 885 (N.Y.Sup.1981)—§ **8.31, n. 4.**

Quaranta v. Quaranta, 212 A.D.2d 683, 622 N.Y.S.2d 778 (N.Y.A.D. 2 Dept.1995)—§ **21.50, n. 2.**

Quaratino v. Tiffany & Co., 71 F.3d 58 (2nd Cir.1995)—§ **17.54, n. 2; § 17.59, n. 5; § 17.73, n. 3.**

Quartararo v. Catterson, 917 F.Supp. 919 (E.D.N.Y.1996)—§ **18.31, n. 5.**

Quartararo, People v., 200 A.D.2d 160, 612 N.Y.S.2d 635 (N.Y.A.D. 2 Dept.1994)—§ **38.8, n. 103.**

Quern v. Jordan, 440 U.S. 332, 99 S.Ct. 1139, 59 L.Ed.2d 358 (1979)—§ **18.33, n. 2.**

Quinn, People v., 186 A.D.2d 691, 588 N.Y.S.2d 646 (N.Y.A.D. 2 Dept.1992)—§ **38.25, n. 11; § 38.28, n. 14.**

TABLE OF CASES

Quintana v. Ciba-Geigy Corp., 1997 WL 160308 (S.D.N.Y.1997)—§ **32.15, n. 10.**
Quintel Corp., N.V. v. Citibank, N.A., 589 F.Supp. 1235 (S.D.N.Y.1984)—§ **28.11, n. 4, 12.**
Quirk, Estate of v. Commissioner, 928 F.2d 751 (6th Cir.1991)—§ **2.51, n. 21.**

R

Racks, People v., 221 A.D.2d 664, 635 N.Y.S.2d 501 (N.Y.A.D. 2 Dept.1995)—§ **38.25, n. 24.**
Radford by Radford v. Sheridan Products, Inc., 181 A.D.2d 667, 581 N.Y.S.2d 683 (N.Y.A.D. 2 Dept.1992)—§ **37.37, n. 20, 36.**
Raffaele, People v., 182 A.D.2d 783, 582 N.Y.S.2d 779 (N.Y.A.D. 2 Dept.1992)—§ **38.21;** § **38.21, n. 31.**
Ragen, United States ex rel. Weber v., 176 F.2d 579 (7th Cir.1949)—§ **37.28, n. 36.**
Ragusa, People v., 44 Misc.2d 940, 255 N.Y.S.2d 269 (N.Y.Co.Ct.1964)—§ **33.26, n. 1.**
Raguso v. Ferreira, 60 N.Y.S.2d 418 (N.Y.Sup.1946)—§ **13.26, n. 4.**
Rahabi v. Morrison, 81 A.D.2d 434, 440 N.Y.S.2d 941 (N.Y.A.D. 2 Dept.1981)—§ **12.69, n. 2.**
Railroad Commission of Tex. v. Pullman Co., 312 U.S. 496, 61 S.Ct. 643, 85 L.Ed. 971 (1941)—§ **18.36;** § **18.36, n. 1, 7.**
Raimon v. City of Ithaca, 157 A.D.2d 999, 550 N.Y.S.2d 479 (N.Y.A.D. 3 Dept. 1990)—§ **3.30, n. 10.**
Rainbow v. Albert Elia Bldg. Co., Inc., 79 A.D.2d 287, 436 N.Y.S.2d 480 (N.Y.A.D. 4 Dept.1981)—§ **27.9, n. 1.**
Rainbow v. Albert Elia Bldg. Co., Inc., 49 A.D.2d 250, 373 N.Y.S.2d 928 (N.Y.A.D. 4 Dept.1975)—§ **27.14, n. 5.**
Rainbow v. Swisher, 531 N.Y.S.2d 775, 527 N.E.2d 258 (N.Y.1988)—§ **21.69, n. 6, 9;** § **21.73, n. 1.**
Rainbow Venture Associates, L.P. v. Parc Vendome Associates, Ltd., 221 A.D.2d 164, 633 N.Y.S.2d 478 (N.Y.A.D. 1 Dept. 1995)—§ **11.6, n. 2, 7.**
Rainey, People v., 314 N.Y.S.2d 999, 263 N.E.2d 395 (N.Y.1970)—§ **38.27, n. 2.**
Raja, People v., 77 A.D.2d 322, 433 N.Y.S.2d 200 (N.Y.A.D. 2 Dept.1980)—§ **4.23, n. 3.**
Rajala v. Allied Corp., 919 F.2d 610 (10th Cir.1990)—§ **5.40, n. 4.**
Raji v. Bank Sepah-Iran, 139 Misc.2d 1026, 529 N.Y.S.2d 420 (N.Y.Sup.1988)—§ **8.23, n. 16.**

Rake v. Wade, 508 U.S. 464, 113 S.Ct. 2187, 124 L.Ed.2d 424 (1993)—§ **9.223, n. 5;** § **9.249, n. 11.**
Rakich v. Lawes, 186 A.D.2d 932, 589 N.Y.S.2d 617 (N.Y.A.D. 3 Dept.1992)—§ **37.28, n. 41.**
Rakowski v. Irmisch, 46 A.D.2d 826, 361 N.Y.S.2d 68 (N.Y.A.D. 3 Dept.1974)—§ **26.42, n. 19.**
Rambersed, People v., 170 Misc.2d 923, 649 N.Y.S.2d 640 (N.Y.Sup.1996)—§ **18.15, n. 8.**
Ramgoolam, People v., N.Y.L.J., 1/2/92, p. 24, col. 2 (Sup.Ct., Kings County)—§ **33.34, n. 2.**
Ramirez v. St. Luke's Hosp. Center, 188 A.D.2d 419, 591 N.Y.S.2d 836 (N.Y.A.D. 1 Dept.1992)—§ **29.26, n. 14.**
Ramos, People v., 201 A.D.2d 78, 614 N.Y.S.2d 977 (N.Y.A.D. 1 Dept.1994)—§ **38.10, n. 97.**
Ramsey, People v., 104 A.D.2d 388, 478 N.Y.S.2d 714 (N.Y.A.D. 2 Dept.1984)—§ **38.9, n. 7.**
Rand v. Hearst Corp., 31 A.D.2d 406, 298 N.Y.S.2d 405 (N.Y.A.D. 1 Dept.1969)—§ **18.64, n. 18.**
Randall v. Bailey, 23 N.Y.S.2d 173 (N.Y.Sup.1940)—§ **1.38, n. 6.**
Randall, People ex rel. Lovett v., 151 N.Y. 497, 45 N.E. 841 (N.Y.1897)—§ **3.19, n. 3.**
Randall Co. v. Alan Lobel Photography, Inc., 120 Misc.2d 112, 465 N.Y.S.2d 489 (N.Y.City Civ.Ct.1983)—§ **13.56, n. 4.**
Randall-Smith, Inc. v. 43rd St. Estates Corp., 268 N.Y.S.2d 306, 215 N.E.2d 494 (N.Y.1966)—§ **30.19, n. 4.**
Randazzo, People v., 471 N.Y.S.2d 52, 459 N.E.2d 161 (N.Y.1983)—§ **38.27, n. 22.**
Randolph v. City of New York, 514 N.Y.S.2d 705, 507 N.E.2d 298 (N.Y.1987)—§ **37.29, n. 4.**
Randolph v. Town of Brookhaven, 375 N.Y.S.2d 315, 337 N.E.2d 763 (N.Y. 1975)—§ **16.12, n. 2;** § **16.15, n. 15.**
Ranellucci v. New York Cent. R. Co., 282 A.D. 789, 122 N.Y.S.2d 432 (N.Y.A.D. 3 Dept.1953)—§ **32.28, n. 9.**
Ranghelle, People v., 511 N.Y.S.2d 580, 503 N.E.2d 1011 (N.Y.1986)—§ **38.10, n. 94;** § **38.19, n. 98.**
Ranum, People v., 122 A.D.2d 959, 506 N.Y.S.2d 105 (N.Y.A.D. 2 Dept.1986)—§ **38.21, n. 9;** § **38.26, n. 26.**
Raphael v. Shapiro, 154 Misc.2d 920, 587 N.Y.S.2d 68 (N.Y.Sup.1992)—§ **28.19;** § **28.19, n. 7.**
Rapoport v. 55 Perry Co., 50 A.D.2d 54, 376 N.Y.S.2d 147 (N.Y.A.D. 1 Dept.1975)—§ **2.52, n. 1.**

TABLE OF CASES

Rappaport v. Phil Gottlieb–Sattler, Inc., 280 A.D. 424, 114 N.Y.S.2d 221 (N.Y.A.D. 1 Dept.1952)—§ **5.11, n. 11.**

Raquel Marie X., Matter of, 173 A.D.2d 709, 570 N.Y.S.2d 604 (N.Y.A.D. 2 Dept. 1991)—§ **20.30, n. 4.**

Raquel Marie X., Matter of, 559 N.Y.S.2d 855, 559 N.E.2d 418 (N.Y.1990)—§ **20.3; § 20.29, n. 1; § 20.30; § 20.30, n. 3, 4; § 20.35, n. 2; § 20.76, n. 1.**

Raschel v. Rish, 110 A.D.2d 1067, 488 N.Y.S.2d 923 (N.Y.A.D. 4 Dept.1985)—§ **29.32, n. 4.**

Rau v. Rau, 78 A.D.2d 617, 434 N.Y.S.2d 336 (N.Y.A.D. 1 Dept.1980)—§ **22.31, n. 2.**

Raucci v. City School Dist. of City of Mechanicville, 203 A.D.2d 714, 610 N.Y.S.2d 653 (N.Y.A.D. 3 Dept.1994)—§ **37.65, n. 47.**

Raucci, People v., 202 A.D.2d 697, 609 N.Y.S.2d 333 (N.Y.A.D. 2 Dept.1994)—§ **38.10, n. 61.**

Rauenstein v. New York, L. & W. Ry. Co., 120 N.Y. 661, 24 N.E. 1020 (N.Y.1890)—§ **30.17, n. 5.**

Rauh's Estate, In re, 156 N.Y.S.2d 862 (N.Y.Sur.1952)—§ **25.31, n. 5, 6.**

Ravine Point Corporation v. Kott, 254 N.Y. 580, 173 N.E. 875 (N.Y.1930)—§ **12.65, n. 7.**

Rawstorne v. Maguire, 265 N.Y. 204, 192 N.E. 294 (N.Y.1934)—§ **35.16, n. 1.**

Ray v. Alad Corp., 136 Cal.Rptr. 574, 560 P.2d 3 (Cal.1977)—§ **27.26, n. 4.**

Ray v. Ray, 62 Misc.2d 652, 309 N.Y.S.2d 53 (N.Y.Sup.1970)—§ **21.21, n. 2.**

Raymond Corp. v. Coopers & Lybrand, 105 A.D.2d 926, 482 N.Y.S.2d 377 (N.Y.A.D. 3 Dept.1984)—§ **17.23, n. 2.**

Raysor v. Port Authority of New York and New Jersey, 768 F.2d 34 (2nd Cir. 1985)—§ **18.22, n. 2.**

Read v. Dickson, 150 A.D.2d 543, 541 N.Y.S.2d 126 (N.Y.A.D. 2 Dept.1989)—§ **37.65, n. 72.**

REA Holding Corp., Matter of, 8 B.R. 75 (Bkrtcy.S.D.N.Y.1980)—§ **9.46, n. 1.**

Reale v. International Business Machines Corp., 34 A.D.2d 936, 311 N.Y.S.2d 767 (N.Y.A.D. 1 Dept.1970)—§ **17.29, n. 2.**

Realty Associates Securities Corp., In re, 53 F.Supp. 1010 (E.D.N.Y.1943)—§ **9.155, n. 2.**

Recupero, People v., 538 N.Y.S.2d 234, 535 N.E.2d 287 (N.Y.1988)—§ **38.8, n. 195.**

Reddick, People v., 493 N.Y.S.2d 124, 482 N.E.2d 920 (N.Y.1985)—§ **38.19, n. 95.**

Redmond v. Scaduto, N.Y.L.J. 2/18/83, p.26, col.4 (Civ.Ct., Kings County)—§ **13.18, n. 14.**

Redwing Carriers, Inc. v. Saraland Apartments, 94 F.3d 1489 (11th Cir.1996)—§ **15.30, n. 7.**

Reece, People v., 204 A.D.2d 495, 612 N.Y.S.2d 61 (N.Y.A.D. 2 Dept.1994)—§ **18.13, n. 1.**

Reed v. Board of Standards and Appeals of City of New York, 255 N.Y. 126, 174 N.E. 301 (N.Y.1931)—§ **16.77, n. 3.**

Reed v. McCord, 160 N.Y. 330, 54 N.E. 737 (N.Y.1899)—§ **37.28, n. 3.**

Reed, People v., 276 N.Y. 5, 11 N.E.2d 330 (N.Y.1937)—§ **38.3, n. 3.**

Re, Estate of v. Kornstein Veisz & Wexler, 958 F.Supp. 907 (S.D.N.Y.1997)—§ **28.13, n. 1.**

Regan v. Lanze, 387 N.Y.S.2d 79, 354 N.E.2d 818 (N.Y.1976)—§ **12.64, n. 3.**

Reiblein, People v., 200 A.D.2d 281, 613 N.Y.S.2d 789 (N.Y.A.D. 3 Dept.1994)—§ **38.8, n. 182.**

Reich, Matter of, 94 Misc.2d 319, 404 N.Y.S.2d 781 (N.Y.Sup.1978)—§ **22.61, n. 6.**

Reichel v. Government Employees Ins. Co., 499 N.Y.S.2d 385, 489 N.E.2d 1287 (N.Y. 1985)—§ **26.24, n. 19.**

Reichelt v. Emhart Corp., 921 F.2d 425 (2nd Cir.1990)—§ **17.50, n. 4.**

Reid, Matter of, 1994 WL 725872 (N.Y. Tax App.)—§ **35.15, n. 1.**

Reid v. Axelrod, 164 A.D.2d 973, 559 N.Y.S.2d 417 (N.Y.A.D. 4 Dept.1990)—§ **4.21, n. 4.**

Reid by Reid v. County of Nassau, 215 A.D.2d 466, 627 N.Y.S.2d 396 (N.Y.A.D. 2 Dept.1995)—§ **30.30; § 30.30, n. 25.**

Reifenstein v. Allstate Ins. Co., 92 A.D.2d 715, 461 N.Y.S.2d 104 (N.Y.A.D. 4 Dept. 1983)—§ **30.34, n. 1.**

Reilly v. Reid, 407 N.Y.S.2d 645, 379 N.E.2d 172 (N.Y.1978)—§ **8.3, n. 5.**

Reilly's Will, In re, 139 Misc. 732, 249 N.Y.S. 152 (N.Y.Sur.1931)—§ **25.28, n. 7.**

Reinfeld v. 325 West End Corp., 43 A.D.2d 671, 350 N.Y.S.2d 140 (N.Y.A.D. 1 Dept. 1973)—§ **37.43, n. 1.**

Reinforced Paper Bottle Corp., People v., 176 Misc. 268, 27 N.Y.S.2d 14 (N.Y.Sup. 1941)—§ **8.3, n. 3.**

Reisman v. Independence Realty Corp., 195 Misc. 260, 89 N.Y.S.2d 763 (N.Y.Sup. 1949)—§ **8.3, n. 6.**

Rejent v. Liberation Publications, Inc., 197 A.D.2d 240, 611 N.Y.S.2d 866 (N.Y.A.D. 1 Dept.1994)—§ **18.81, n. 1.**

Reliable Drug Stores, Inc., Matter of, 70 F.3d 948 (7th Cir.1995)—§ **9.105, n. 5, 8.**

TABLE OF CASES

Rella v. McMahon, 169 A.D.2d 555, 564 N.Y.S.2d 409 (N.Y.A.D. 1 Dept.1991)—§ 2.46, n. 9.

Remanco, Inc. v. Wexler, 98 Misc.2d 955, 415 N.Y.S.2d 179 (N.Y.City Ct.1979)—§ 13.18, n. 2.

Rembert v. Perales, 187 A.D.2d 784, 589 N.Y.S.2d 649 (N.Y.A.D. 3 Dept.1992)—§ 4.33, n. 3.

Renaud, People v., 145 A.D.2d 367, 535 N.Y.S.2d 985 (N.Y.A.D. 1 Dept.1988)—§ 28.12, n. 8; § 13.28, n. 8.

Rendon, People v., 208 A.D.2d 869, 618 N.Y.S.2d 554 (N.Y.A.D. 2 Dept.1994)—§ 38.8, n. 27.

Rensselaer & S.R. Co. v. Davis, 43 N.Y. 137 (N.Y.1870)—§ 14.6, n. 1, 2.

Renton, City of v. Playtime Theatres, Inc., 475 U.S. 41, 106 S.Ct. 925, 89 L.Ed.2d 29 (1986)—§ 16.25, n. 15.

Rent Stabilization Ass'n of New York City, Inc. v. Higgins, 608 N.Y.S.2d 930, 630 N.E.2d 626 (N.Y.1993)—§ 15.34, n. 15, 16.

Reorganized CF & I Fabricators of Utah, Inc., United States v., 518 U.S. 213, 116 S.Ct. 2106, 135 L.Ed.2d 506 (1996)—§ 9.107, n. 21.

Report, Grand Jury, Exhibit 83A of September/October 1993 Suffolk County Grand Jury IC, Term X, Matter of, 221 A.D.2d 541, 634 N.Y.S.2d 134 (N.Y.A.D. 2 Dept. 1995)—§ 38.10, n. 32; § 38.11, n. 11.

Report of August–September 1983 Grand Jury III, Term XI, Suffolk County, Matter of, 103 A.D.2d 176, 479 N.Y.S.2d 226 (N.Y.A.D. 2 Dept.1984)—§ 38.11, n. 11.

Report of Grand Jury of Tompkins County Impaneled April 24, 1984, Matter of, 110 A.D.2d 44, 493 N.Y.S.2d 648 (N.Y.A.D. 3 Dept.1985)—§ 38.11, n. 11.

Report of September 1975 Grand Jury of Supreme Court of St. Lawrence County, Matter of, 55 A.D.2d 220, 390 N.Y.S.2d 251 (N.Y.A.D. 3 Dept.1976)—§ 38.11, n. 21.

Report of Special Grand Jury of Monroe County, Matter of, 77 A.D.2d 199, 433 N.Y.S.2d 300 (N.Y.A.D. 4 Dept.1980)—§ 38.11, n. 7, 24.

Report of Special Grand Jury of Nassau County, New York, Panel 3, Second Term, 1982., Matter of, 102 A.D.2d 871, 477 N.Y.S.2d 34 (N.Y.A.D. 2 Dept. 1984)—§ 38.11, n. 23.

Reports of Grand Jury No. 1 of Monroe County Empaneled on Jan. 30, 1978 for the Feb., 1978 Term of County Court, Matter of, 71 A.D.2d 1060, 420 N.Y.S.2d 946 (N.Y.A.D. 4 Dept.1979)—§ 38.11, n. 18.

Reports of Grand Jury of Montgomery County Impaneled on April 30, 1979, Matter of, 108 A.D.2d 482, 489 N.Y.S.2d 385 (N.Y.A.D. 3 Dept.1985)—§ 38.11, n. 16.

Republic Bank v. Getzoff (In re Getzoff), 180 B.R. 572 (9th Cir.1995)—§ 9.130, n. 3.

Republic Ins. Co. v. Atlantica Ins. Co., Ltd., 1994 WL 163705 (S.D.N.Y.1994)—§ 31.23, n. 2.

Republic Reader's Service, Inc., In re, 81 B.R. 422 (Bkrtcy.S.D.Tex.1987)—§ 9.23, n. 2.

Republic Supply Co. v. Shoaf, 815 F.2d 1046 (5th Cir.1987)—§ 9.167, n. 2.

Resolution Trust Corp. v. Best Prods. Co. (In re Best Products Co., Inc.), 177 B.R. 791 (S.D.N.Y.1995)—§ 9.25, n. 11.

Resolution Trust Corp. v. Polmar Realty, Inc., 780 F.Supp. 177 (S.D.N.Y.1991)—§ 11.6, n. 9.

Resolution Trust Corp. v. Preferred Entity Advancements, Inc., 157 Misc.2d 683, 598 N.Y.S.2d 437 (N.Y.Sup.1993)—§ 11.32, n. 3.

Resorts Intern., Inc., In re, 145 B.R. 412 (Bkrtcy.D.N.J.1990)—§ 9.170, n. 3, 4.

Resorts International, Inc. v. Lowenschuss (In re Lowenschuss), 67 F.3d 1394 (9th Cir.1995)—§ 9.170, n. 2.

Ressler, People v., 269 N.Y.S.2d 414, 216 N.E.2d 582 (N.Y.1966)—§ 38.26, n. 13.

Retail Software Services, Inc. v. Lashlee, 530 N.Y.S.2d 91, 525 N.E.2d 737 (N.Y. 1988)—§ 39.60, n. 2.

Revco D.S., Inc., In re, 901 F.2d 1359 (6th Cir.1990)—§ 9.73, n. 1.

Revco D.S., Inc., In re, 898 F.2d 498 (6th Cir.1990)—§ 9.140, n. 2.

Rex Realty of Connecticut, Inc. v. Broderick, 215 A.D.2d 664, 628 N.Y.S.2d 500 (N.Y.A.D. 2 Dept.1995)—§ 16.106, n. 7.

Reyes v. New York City Housing Authority, 221 A.D.2d 240, 634 N.Y.S.2d 2 (N.Y.A.D. 1 Dept.1995)—§ 37.37, n. 7.

Reyes, People v., 214 A.D.2d 233, 632 N.Y.S.2d 123 (N.Y.A.D. 1 Dept.1995)—§ 38.8, n. 31.

Reyes v. Talley Motors, Inc., N.Y.L.J., 8/20/92, p.23, col.8 (Sup.Ct., N.Y. County)—§ 7.16, n. 4; § 7.16, n. 6, 8.

Reynolds, Matter of Estate of, 214 A.D.2d 944, 626 N.Y.S.2d 603 (N.Y.A.D. 4 Dept. 1995)—§ 24.60, n. 1.

Reynolds v. Merit Oil of New York, Inc., 167 A.D.2d 521, 562 N.Y.S.2d 195 (N.Y.A.D. 2 Dept.1990)—§ 30.15, n. 15; § 30.30, n. 16.

R.G. Group, Inc. v. Horn & Hardart Co., 751 F.2d 69 (2nd Cir.1984)—§ 17.36, n. 5.

TABLE OF CASES

Rhinebeck Bicycle Shop, Inc. v. Sterling Ins. Co., 151 A.D.2d 122, 546 N.Y.S.2d 499 (N.Y.A.D. 3 Dept.1989)—§ **31.9, n. 3.**

Rhoades, Matter of Estate of, 160 Misc.2d 262, 607 N.Y.S.2d 893 (N.Y.Sup.1994)—§ **24.60, n. 3.**

Rhode Island v. Innis, 446 U.S. 291, 100 S.Ct. 1682, 64 L.Ed.2d 297 (1980)—§ **33.52; § 33.52, n. 1.**

Rhodes, In re Estate of, 148 Misc.2d 744, 561 N.Y.S.2d 344 (N.Y.Sur.1990)—§ **23.82, n. 1.**

Rhodes v. Astro–Pac, Inc., 51 A.D.2d 656, 378 N.Y.S.2d 195 (N.Y.A.D. 4 Dept. 1976)—§ **12.65, n. 4; § 12.68, n. 1.**

Rhodes, People v., 199 A.D.2d 571, 604 N.Y.S.2d 349 (N.Y.A.D. 3 Dept.1993)—§ **38.8, n. 226.**

R. Hoe & Co., In re, 14 Misc.2d 500, 137 N.Y.S.2d 142 (N.Y.Sup.1954)—§ **1.43, n. 25.**

Ricarte Angel C., In re, 220 A.D.2d 514, 632 N.Y.S.2d 222 (N.Y.A.D. 2 Dept.1995)—§ **20.38, n. 5.**

Ricciuti v. New York City Transit Authority, 941 F.2d 119 (2nd Cir.1991)—§ **18.34, n. 3.**

Rich v. Mottek, 226 N.Y.S.2d 428, 181 N.E.2d 445 (N.Y.1962)—§ **24.61, n. 3.**

Rich, People v., 8 Misc.2d 148, 167 N.Y.S.2d 244 (N.Y.Co.Ct.1957)—§ **33.68, n. 7, 8.**

Rich v. Rich, 126 Misc.2d 536, 483 N.Y.S.2d 150 (N.Y.Sup.1984)—§ **21.40, n. 5.**

Richard Buick, Inc., In re, 126 B.R. 840 (Bkrtcy.E.D.Pa.1991)—§ **9.154, n. 4.**

Richard Roe Investigation of August 1973 Monroe County Grand Jury, In re, 46 A.D.2d 723, 360 N.Y.S.2d 123 (N.Y.A.D. 4 Dept.1974)—§ **38.11, n. 22.**

Richardson v. Fiedler Roofing, Inc., 502 N.Y.S.2d 125, 493 N.E.2d 228 (N.Y. 1986)—§ **17.65, n. 6; § 37.28, n. 25; § 39.7, n. 12.**

Richardson v. Selsky, 5 F.3d 616 (2nd Cir. 1993)—§ **18.32, n. 1.**

Richlands Medical Ass'n v. Commissioner, T.C. Memo. 1990-660 (U.S.Tax Ct.1990)—§ **2.6, n. 10.**

Richman, Matter of, 164 Misc.2d 403, 625 N.Y.S.2d 443 (N.Y.Sup.1995)—§ **22.32, n. 9.**

Richter, People v., 223 A.D.2d 734, 637 N.Y.S.2d 206 (N.Y.A.D. 2 Dept.1996)—§ **38.25, n. 25; § 38.28, n. 15.**

Rickert, People v., 459 N.Y.S.2d 734, 446 N.E.2d 419 (N.Y.1983)—§ **39.50, n. 15.**

Ricky AA, Matter of, 146 A.D.2d 433, 541 N.Y.S.2d 264 (N.Y.A.D. 3 Dept.1989)—§ **20.65; § 20.65, n. 3.**

Riddell Sports Inc. v. Brooks, 872 F.Supp. 73 (S.D.N.Y.1995)—§ **17.31, n. 1.**

Riddle v. Memorial Hospital, 43 A.D.2d 750, 349 N.Y.S.2d 855 (N.Y.A.D. 3 Dept. 1973)—§ **30.9, n. 6.**

Rider v. State, 192 A.D.2d 983, 596 N.Y.S.2d 900 (N.Y.A.D. 3 Dept.1993)—§ **14.82, n. 7.**

Riemenschneider v. Motor Vehicle Acc. Indemnification Corp., 285 N.Y.S.2d 593, 232 N.E.2d 630 (N.Y.1967)—§ **26.28, n. 5.**

Riggins, People v., 164 A.D.2d 797, 559 N.Y.S.2d 535 (N.Y.A.D. 1 Dept.1990)—§ **38.10, n. 126.**

RIHGA Intern. United StatesA., Inc. v. New York State Liquor Authority, 620 N.Y.S.2d 784, 644 N.E.2d 1340 (N.Y. 1994)—§ **36.4, n. 8; § 36.21, n. 3; § 36.26, n. 2, 3, 4; § 36.44, n. 2.**

Rinaldi v. Holt, Rinehart & Winston, Inc., 397 N.Y.S.2d 943, 366 N.E.2d 1299 (N.Y. 1977)—§ **18.82, n. 7.**

Rinaldo v. McCormick, 139 A.D.2d 874, 527 N.Y.S.2d 601 (N.Y.A.D. 3 Dept.1988)—§ **31.7, n. 5.**

Ringers' Dutchocs, Inc. v. S. S. S. L. 180, 494 F.2d 678 (2nd Cir.1974)—§ **31.23, n. 2.**

Riodizio, Inc., In re, 204 B.R. 417 (Bkrtcy. S.D.N.Y.1997)—§ **9.74, n. 1.**

Riordan v. Nationwide Mut. Fire Ins. Co., 977 F.2d 47 (2nd Cir.1992)—§ **7.47; § 7.47, n. 9.**

Risbano v. 3rd & 60th Associates, 200 A.D.2d 658, 606 N.Y.S.2d 335 (N.Y.A.D. 2 Dept.1994)—§ **12.20, n. 1.**

Ritzel v. Blum, 81 A.D.2d 1029, 440 N.Y.S.2d 428 (N.Y.A.D. 4 Dept.1981)—§ **4.12, n. 9.**

Rivera v. Blum, 98 Misc.2d 1002, 420 N.Y.S.2d 304 (N.Y.Sup.1978)—§ **8.4, n. 20.**

Rivera, People v., 195 A.D.2d 389, 600 N.Y.S.2d 248 (N.Y.A.D. 1 Dept.1993)—§ **18.13, n. 2.**

Rivera, People v., 601 N.Y.S.2d 470, 619 N.E.2d 407 (N.Y.1993)—§ **38.19, n. 64.**

Rivera, People v., 540 N.Y.S.2d 233, 537 N.E.2d 618 (N.Y.1989)—§ **38.19, n. 47.**

Rivera, People v., 530 N.Y.S.2d 52, 525 N.E.2d 698 (N.Y.1988)—§ **38.27, n. 33.**

Rivera, People v., 72 A.D.2d 922, 422 N.Y.S.2d 211 (N.Y.A.D. 4 Dept.1979)—§ **33.85, n. 2.**

Rivera, People v., 384 N.Y.S.2d 726, 349 N.E.2d 825 (N.Y.1976)—§ **38.3, n. 10.**

Rivera v. Schweiker, 717 F.2d 719 (2nd Cir.1983)—§ **34.46, n. 7.**

Rivera v. W. & R. Service Station, Inc., 34 A.D.2d 115, 309 N.Y.S.2d 274 (N.Y.A.D. 1 Dept.1970)—§ **37.28, n. 14.**

TABLE OF CASES

Rivers, Matter of, 17 I & N Dec. 419 (I.D. 2802, BIA 1980—§ **19.8, n. 8; § 19.11, n. 5.**

Rivers v. Corron, 160 Misc.2d 968, 608 N.Y.S.2d 977 (N.Y.Sup.1993)—§ **16.124, n. 4.**

Rivers v. Katz, 504 N.Y.S.2d 74, 495 N.E.2d 337 (N.Y.1986)—§ **18.28, n. 4; § 22.13; § 22.13, n. 4, 5; § 22.53, n. 5.**

Riverside Bayview Homes, Inc., United States v., 474 U.S. 121, 106 S.Ct. 455, 88 L.Ed.2d 419 (1985)—§ **15.15, n. 5.**

Riverside, City of v. Rivera, 477 U.S. 561, 106 S.Ct. 2686, 91 L.Ed.2d 466 (1986)—§ **17.75, n. 3.**

Riviera Congress Associates v. Yassky, 277 N.Y.S.2d 386, 223 N.E.2d 876 (N.Y. 1966)—§ **2.45, n. 2.**

Rizika v. Potter, 72 N.Y.S.2d 372 (N.Y.Sup. 1947)—§ **2.46, n. 1.**

Rizk v. Cohen, 538 N.Y.S.2d 229, 535 N.E.2d 282 (N.Y.1989)—§ **28.15; § 28.15, n. 4.**

Rizzo, People v., 386 N.Y.S.2d 878, 353 N.E.2d 841 (N.Y.1976)—§ **4.62, n. 1.**

Robb v. New York Joint Bd., Amalgamated Clothing Workers of America, 506 F.2d 1246 (2nd Cir.1974)—§ **9.25, n. 9.**

Roberson v. Ammons, 477 So.2d 957 (Ala. 1985)—§ **7.25, n. 8.**

Roberson v. Rochester Folding Box Co., 171 N.Y. 538, 64 N.E. 442 (N.Y.1902)—§ **18.63, n. 5.**

Robert Hunt Co. v. S & R Coachworks, Inc., 215 A.D.2d 361, 625 N.Y.S.2d 662 (N.Y.A.D. 2 Dept.1995)—§ **5.37, n. 3.**

Robert Lee Realty Co. v. Village of Spring Valley, 474 N.Y.S.2d 475, 462 N.E.2d 1193 (N.Y.1984)—§ **16.91, n. 8.**

Robert R. Scott Corp. v. D. Kwitman & Son, Inc., 3 Misc.2d 812, 146 N.Y.S.2d 518 (N.Y.Sup.1955)—§ **5.36, n. 3.**

Roberts v. Conde Nast Publications, 286 A.D. 729, 146 N.Y.S.2d 493 (N.Y.A.D. 1 Dept.1955)—§ **30.36, n. 1, 2.**

Roberts v. Heckler, 783 F.2d 110 (8th Cir. 1985)—§ **34.47, n. 19, 21.**

Roberts, People v., 203 A.D.2d 600, 611 N.Y.S.2d 214 (N.Y.A.D. 2 Dept.1994)—§ **33.41; § 33.41, n. 1; § 38.21, n. 9.**

Roberts, People v., 176 A.D.2d 903, 575 N.Y.S.2d 368 (N.Y.A.D. 2 Dept.1991)—§ **38.21, n. 45.**

Roberts, People v., 165 A.D.2d 598, 569 N.Y.S.2d 53 (N.Y.A.D. 1 Dept.1991)—§ **38.21; § 38.21, n. 29.**

Roberts, People v., 162 A.D.2d 729, 557 N.Y.S.2d 127 (N.Y.A.D. 2 Dept.1990)—§ **38.21, n. 7.**

Roberts, People v., 152 A.D.2d 678, 544 N.Y.S.2d 157 (N.Y.A.D. 2 Dept.1989)—§ **33.29, n. 2.**

Roberts, People v., 95 Misc.2d 41, 406 N.Y.S.2d 432 (N.Y.Co.Ct.1978)—§ **38.58, n. 4.**

Roberts v. United States Jaycees, 468 U.S. 609, 104 S.Ct. 3244, 82 L.Ed.2d 462 (1984)—§ **17.55, n. 5.**

Robertson, People ex rel. v. New York State Div. of Parole, 501 N.Y.S.2d 634, 492 N.E.2d 762 (N.Y.1986)—§ **38.8, n. 71, 75.**

Robertson v. Zimmermann, 268 N.Y. 52, 196 N.E. 740 (N.Y.1935)—§ **3.35, n. 3.**

Robins v. Max Mara, USA, Inc., 923 F.Supp. 460 (S.D.N.Y.1996)—§ **17.69, n. 3.**

Robinson, Application of, 74 Misc.2d 63, 344 N.Y.S.2d 147 (N.Y.City Civ.Ct. 1972)—§ **18.70, n. 4.**

Robinson v. Jacksonville Shipyards, Inc., 760 F.Supp. 1486 (M.D.Fla.1991)—§ **17.74, n. 6.**

Robinson, People v., 191 A.D.2d 595, 594 N.Y.S.2d 801 (N.Y.A.D. 2 Dept.1993)—§ **38.21, n. 11.**

Robinson, People v., 143 Misc.2d 163, 539 N.Y.S.2d 852 (N.Y.Sup.1989)—§ **33.79, n. 2.**

Robinson, People v., 534 N.Y.S.2d 367, 530 N.E.2d 1287 (N.Y.1988)—§ **38.52, n. 3.**

Robinson, People ex rel. v. Scully, 122 A.D.2d 290, 505 N.Y.S.2d 193 (N.Y.A.D. 2 Dept.1986)—§ **38.8, n. 74.**

Robinson v. Reed–Prentice Division of Package Machinery Co., 426 N.Y.S.2d 717, 403 N.E.2d 440 (N.Y.1980)—§ **27.6, n. 2; § 27.10, n. 6; § 27.41, n. 1.**

Robinson v. 12 Lofts Realty, Inc., 610 F.2d 1032 (2nd Cir.1979)—§ **18.50, n. 2.**

Robison v. Lockridge, 230 A.D. 389, 244 N.Y.S. 663 (N.Y.A.D. 4 Dept.1930)—§ **30.8, n. 1.**

Robison v. Via, 821 F.2d 913 (2nd Cir. 1987)—§ **18.32; § 18.32, n. 10.**

Robison v. von Langendorff, 221 A.D.2d 189, 633 N.Y.S.2d 303 (N.Y.A.D. 1 Dept. 1995)—§ **25.47, n. 4; § 30.41, n. 2.**

Roblin Industries, Inc., In re, 78 F.3d 30 (2nd Cir.1996)—§ **9.117, n. 4; § 9.118, n. 7.**

Roblin Industries, Inc., In re, 52 B.R. 241 (Bkrtcy.W.D.N.Y.1985)—§ **9.71, n. 11.**

Rob Tess Restaurant Corp. v. New York State Liquor Authority, 427 N.Y.S.2d 936, 405 N.E.2d 181 (N.Y.1980)—§ **37.87, n. 28.**

Rocanova v. Equitable Life Assur. Soc. of United States, 612 N.Y.S.2d 339, 634 N.E.2d 940 (N.Y.1994)—§ **8.6, n. 4; § 17.27, n. 15; § 30.34, n. 6; § 31.17, n. 18.**

Rocco, Petition of, 161 Misc.2d 760, 615 N.Y.S.2d 260 (N.Y.Sup.1994)—§ **22.2, n. 12; § 22.28, n. 18; § 22.39, n. 5.**

TABLE OF CASES

Rochester, Matter of City of, 533 N.Y.S.2d 702, 530 N.E.2d 202 (N.Y.1988)—§ **3.8, n. 8;** § **16.128;** § **16.128, n. 9.**

Rochester, City of v. Macauley–Fien Milling Co., 199 N.Y. 207, 92 N.E. 641 (N.Y. 1910)—§ **37.29, n. 27.**

Rochester, City of v. S. C. Toth, Inc., 59 A.D.2d 1020, 399 N.Y.S.2d 755 (N.Y.A.D. 4 Dept.1977)—§ **14.81, n. 5.**

Rochester Gas & Elec. Corp. v. Monroe County, 115 A.D.2d 1012, 497 N.Y.S.2d 1017 (N.Y.A.D. 4 Dept.1985)—§ **37.20, n. 4.**

Rochester General Hosp., Application of, 158 Misc.2d 522, 601 N.Y.S.2d 375 (N.Y.Sup.1993)—§ **22.13, n. 3;** § **22.17, n. 5;** § **22.25, n. 4;** § **22.28, n. 6, 22;** § **22.32, n. 11;** § **22.53, n. 7, 13.**

Rochester Telephone Corp. v. Public Service Com'n of State of N.Y., 637 N.Y.S.2d 333, 660 N.E.2d 1112 (N.Y.1995)—§ **39.9, n. 7.**

Rochester Telephone Corp. v. Village of Fairport, 84 A.D.2d 455, 446 N.Y.S.2d 823 (N.Y.A.D. 4 Dept.1982)—§ **16.125, n. 9.**

Rochester Urban Renewal Agency, Application of, 110 A.D.2d 1086, 489 N.Y.S.2d 436 (N.Y.A.D. 4 Dept.1985)—§ **37.30, n. 4.**

Rochester Urban Renewal Agency v. Lee, 83 A.D.2d 770, 443 N.Y.S.2d 479 (N.Y.A.D. 4 Dept.1981)—§ **14.78, n. 3, 4.**

Rochester Urban Renewal Agency v. Willsea Works, 422 N.Y.S.2d 59, 397 N.E.2d 749 (N.Y.1979)—§ **14.86, n. 2, 3;** § **14.89, n. 6.**

Rochler v. Rochler, 215 A.D.2d 831, 626 N.Y.S.2d 312 (N.Y.A.D. 3 Dept.1995)—§ **21.55, n. 1.**

Rockefeller v. Moront, 601 N.Y.S.2d 86, 618 N.E.2d 119 (N.Y.1993)—§ **29.26, n. 11.**

Rockefeller v. Nickerson, 36 Misc.2d 869, 233 N.Y.S.2d 314 (N.Y.Sup.1962)—§ **20.27, n. 1.**

Rock Hill Sewerage Disposal Corp. v. Town of Thompson, 27 A.D.2d 626, 276 N.Y.S.2d 188 (N.Y.A.D. 3 Dept.1966)—§ **4.2, n. 41;** § **4.82, n. 5.**

Rockland County Sewer Dist. No. 1 v. J. & J. Dodge, Inc., 213 A.D.2d 409, 635 N.Y.S.2d 233 (N.Y.A.D. 2 Dept.1995)—§ **14.23, n. 4;** § **14.26, n. 2;** § **14.34, n. 7.**

Rockland (Kohl Indus. Park Co.), Matter of County of, 147 A.D.2d 478, 537 N.Y.S.2d 309 (N.Y.A.D. 2 Dept.1989)—§ **14.82, n. 10.**

Rockland Psychiatric Center v. Virginia G., 166 Misc.2d 659, 634 N.Y.S.2d 648 (N.Y.Sup.1995)—§ **18.28, n. 4.**

Rockwell, People v., 275 A.D. 568, 90 N.Y.S.2d 281 (N.Y.A.D. 1 Dept.1949)—§ **38.19, n. 64.**

Rocon Mfg., Inc. v. Ferraro, 199 A.D.2d 999, 605 N.Y.S.2d 591 (N.Y.A.D. 4 Dept. 1993)—§ **31.9, n. 3.**

Rodgers v. Lenox Hill Hosp., 211 A.D.2d 248, 626 N.Y.S.2d 137 (N.Y.A.D. 1 Dept. 1995)—§ **17.64, n. 3.**

Rodgers v. Village of Tarrytown, 302 N.Y. 115, 96 N.E.2d 731 (N.Y.1951)—§ **16.4, n. 10;** § **16.8, n. 5;** § **16.9;** § **16.9, n. 1, 2;** § **16.15, n. 13;** § **16.18, n. 3, 17;** § **16.110, n. 2, 8;** § **16.111, n. 2, 7;** § **16.112, n. 3.**

Rodman v. State, 109 A.D.2d 737, 485 N.Y.S.2d 842 (N.Y.A.D. 2 Dept.1985)—§ **14.86, n. 7.**

Rodney, People v., 624 N.Y.S.2d 95, 648 N.E.2d 471 (N.Y.1995)—§ **33.54, n. 2.**

Rodrigues v. City of New York, 193 A.D.2d 79, 602 N.Y.S.2d 337 (N.Y.A.D. 1 Dept. 1993)—§ **18.31, n. 7.**

Rodriguez v. City of New York, 72 F.3d 1051 (2nd Cir.1995)—§ **18.32, n. 1.**

Rodriguez v. Grajales, 188 A.D.2d 474, 591 N.Y.S.2d 66 (N.Y.A.D. 2 Dept.1992)—§ **38.8, n. 130.**

Rodriguez v. Manhattan Medical Group, P.C., 155 A.D.2d 114, 552 N.Y.S.2d 947 (N.Y.A.D. 1 Dept.1990)—§ **29.26, n. 10.**

Rodriguez v. Myerson, 69 A.D.2d 162, 418 N.Y.S.2d 936 (N.Y.A.D. 2 Dept.1979)—§ **38.8, n. 130.**

Rodriguez v. New York City Housing Authority, 209 A.D.2d 260, 618 N.Y.S.2d 352 (N.Y.A.D. 1 Dept.1994)—§ **27.42, n. 1.**

Rodriguez v. New York City Transit Authority, 151 Misc.2d 1027, 574 N.Y.S.2d 505 (N.Y.Sup.1991)—§ **30.29;** § **30.29, n. 7.**

Rodriguez, People v., 178 A.D.2d 1019, 578 N.Y.S.2d 774 (N.Y.A.D. 4 Dept.1991)—§ **38.10;** § **38.10, n. 24.**

Rodriguez, People v., 447 N.Y.S.2d 246, 431 N.E.2d 972 (N.Y.1981)—§ **38.8, n. 172.**

Rodriguez, People v., 429 N.Y.S.2d 631, 407 N.E.2d 475 (N.Y.1980)—§ **38.8, n. 194.**

Rodriguez v. Yosi Trucking, 151 A.D.2d 556, 542 N.Y.S.2d 335 (N.Y.A.D. 2 Dept. 1989)—§ **37.26, n. 1.**

Rodriguez–Barajas v. I.N.S., 992 F.2d 94 (7th Cir.1993)—§ **19.47, n. 3.**

Rodriques v. McCluskey, 156 A.D.2d 369, 548 N.Y.S.2d 323 (N.Y.A.D. 2 Dept. 1989)—§ **16.45, n. 3;** § **16.113, n. 2.**

Rodriquez, People ex rel. Cotton v., 123 A.D.2d 338, 506 N.Y.S.2d 350 (N.Y.A.D. 2 Dept.1986)—§ **38.8, n. 75.**

Roe v. Strong, 119 N.Y. 316, 23 N.E. 743 (N.Y.1890)—§ **12.68, n. 3.**

TABLE OF CASES

Roese's Will, In re, 36 Misc.2d 643, 232 N.Y.S.2d 592 (N.Y.Sur.1962)—§ **25.47, n. 8.**

Rogers v. Di Christina, 195 A.D.2d 1061, 600 N.Y.S.2d 402 (N.Y.A.D. 4 Dept. 1993)—§ **37.65, n. 46.**

Rogers v. O'Brien, 153 N.Y. 357, 47 N.E. 456 (N.Y.1897)—§ **3.32, n. 17.**

Rogers, People v., 449 N.Y.S.2d 961, 434 N.E.2d 1339 (N.Y.1982)—§ **38.27, n. 22.**

Rogers, People v., 422 N.Y.S.2d 18, 397 N.E.2d 709 (N.Y.1979)—§ **33.54, n. 1.**

Rogers v. Village of Port Chester, 234 N.Y. 182, 137 N.E. 19 (N.Y.1922)—§ **3.30, n. 28.**

Roginsky v. Richardson-Merrell, Inc., 378 F.2d 832 (2nd Cir.1967)—§ **27.5, n. 7;** § **27.18, n. 7.**

Rohnke v. National Broadcasting Co., Inc., 186 A.D.2d 436, 588 N.Y.S.2d 564 (N.Y.A.D. 1 Dept.1992)—§ **17.25, n. 1.**

Rohring v. City of Niagara Falls, 614 N.Y.S.2d 714, 638 N.E.2d 62 (N.Y. 1994)—§ **30.44, n. 8.**

Rokahr, People v., 141 Misc.2d 117, 532 N.Y.S.2d 710 (N.Y.Co.Ct.1988)—§ **38.52, n. 13.**

Roland v. Sunmark Industries, 127 A.D.2d 894, 511 N.Y.S.2d 972 (N.Y.A.D. 3 Dept. 1987)—§ **32.27, n. 13.**

Roldan v. Allstate Ins. Co., 149 A.D.2d 20, 544 N.Y.S.2d 359 (N.Y.A.D. 2 Dept. 1989)—§ **31.17, n. 11.**

Rolon, People v., 220 A.D.2d 543, 632 N.Y.S.2d 208 (N.Y.A.D. 2 Dept.1995)— § **38.8, n. 27.**

Roman, People v., 160 A.D.2d 961, 554 N.Y.S.2d 684 (N.Y.A.D. 2 Dept.1990)— § **38.20, n. 12;** § **38.28, n. 3.**

Roman Catholic Diocese of Albany v. New York State Dept. of Health, 109 A.D.2d 140, 490 N.Y.S.2d 636 (N.Y.A.D. 3 Dept. 1985)—§ **4.50;** § **4.50, n. 15.**

Romanian American Interests, Inc. v. Scher, 94 A.D.2d 549, 464 N.Y.S.2d 821 (N.Y.A.D. 2 Dept.1983)—§ **28.18, n. 4.**

Romano, Application of, 109 Misc.2d 99, 438 N.Y.S.2d 967 (N.Y.Sur.1981)— § **20.126, n. 1.**

Romeike v. Romeike, 251 F. 273 (2nd Cir. 1918)—§ **1.13, n. 20.**

Romeike v. Romeike, 179 A.D. 712, 167 N.Y.S. 235 (N.Y.A.D. 1 Dept.1917)— § **1.13, n. 20.**

Ron Pair Enterprises, Inc., United States v., 489 U.S. 235, 109 S.Ct. 1026, 103 L.Ed.2d 290 (1989)—§ **9.102, n. 6.**

Roper v. Recore, 222 A.D.2d 911, 635 N.Y.S.2d 755 (N.Y.A.D. 3 Dept.1995)— § **37.37, n. 80.**

Rosa, People v., 492 N.Y.S.2d 542, 482 N.E.2d 21 (N.Y.1985)—§ **33.57, n. 6.**

Rosa v. Peters, 36 F.3d 625 (7th Cir.1994)— § **38.19, n. 114.**

Rosado, People v., 199 A.D.2d 833, 606 N.Y.S.2d 368 (N.Y.A.D. 3 Dept.1993)— § **38.8, n. 208.**

Rosario, People v., 213 N.Y.S.2d 448, 173 N.E.2d 881 (N.Y.1961)—§ **38.10;** § **38.10, n. 91;** § **39.50, n. 5.**

Rose, People v., 223 A.D.2d 607, 637 N.Y.S.2d 172 (N.Y.A.D. 2 Dept.1996)— § **38.21, n. 11.**

Rose v. Rose, 167 Misc.2d 562, 637 N.Y.S.2d 1002 (N.Y.Sup.1995)—§ **21.30, n. 4.**

Rose v. Spa Realty Associates, 60 A.D.2d 937, 400 N.Y.S.2d 919 (N.Y.A.D. 3 Dept. 1978)—§ **12.64, n. 11.**

Rose v. State, 298 N.Y.S.2d 968, 246 N.E.2d 735 (N.Y.1969)—§ **14.93, n. 4.**

Rosecrans, Matter of, 144 A.D.2d 214, 534 N.Y.S.2d 528 (N.Y.A.D. 3 Dept.1988)— § **22.61, n. 2.**

Roselle, People v., 193 A.D.2d 56, 602 N.Y.S.2d 50 (N.Y.A.D. 2 Dept.1993)— § **38.8, n. 122.**

Rose Marie M., Matter of, 94 A.D.2d 734, 462 N.Y.S.2d 483 (N.Y.A.D. 2 Dept. 1983)—§ **20.67, n. 10.**

Rosen v. First Manhattan Bank, 202 A.D.2d 864, 609 N.Y.S.2d 436 (N.Y.A.D. 3 Dept. 1994)—§ **32.19, n. 5.**

Rosen v. Rosen, 161 Misc.2d 795, 614 N.Y.S.2d 1018 (N.Y.Sup.1994)—§ **21.79, n. 9.**

Rosen v. Sterling Symphony, 193 Misc. 12, 84 N.Y.S.2d 755 (N.Y.City Ct.1948)— § **30.30, n. 3.**

Rosen & Bardunias v. County of Westchester, 158 A.D.2d 679, 552 N.Y.S.2d 134 (N.Y.A.D. 2 Dept.1990)—§ **18.31, n. 3.**

Rosenbaum v. Lefrak Corp., 80 A.D.2d 337, 438 N.Y.S.2d 794 (N.Y.A.D. 1 Dept. 1981)—§ **37.30, n. 8.**

Rosenbaum v. Rosenbaum, 56 Misc.2d 221, 288 N.Y.S.2d 285 (N.Y.Sup.1968)— § **21.24, n. 3.**

Rosenberg's Will, In re, 14 A.D.2d 879, 221 N.Y.S.2d 401 (N.Y.A.D. 2 Dept.1961)— § **37.37, n. 52.**

Rosenman & Colin, Petition of, 850 F.2d 57 (2nd Cir.1988)—§ **28.30, n. 2.**

Rosenthal v. Hartnett, 367 N.Y.S.2d 247, 326 N.E.2d 811 (N.Y.1975)—§ **4.68;** § **4.68, n. 6.**

Rosen Trust v. Rosen, 53 A.D.2d 342, 386 N.Y.S.2d 491 (N.Y.A.D. 4 Dept.1976)— § **11.44, n. 2.**

Roseton Hills Sewage-Works Corp. v. Leitman, 69 A.D.2d 834, 414 N.Y.S.2d 928 (N.Y.A.D. 2 Dept.1979)—§ **14.43, n. 1.**

Rosgro Realty Co. v. Braynen, 70 Misc.2d 808, 334 N.Y.S.2d 962 (N.Y.Sup.App. Term 1972)—§ **13.18, n. 18.**

TABLE OF CASES

Rosiny v. Schmidt, 185 A.D.2d 727, 587 N.Y.S.2d 929 (N.Y.A.D. 1 Dept.1992)—§ **5.13, n. 2.**

Rosner v. Paley, 492 N.Y.S.2d 13, 481 N.E.2d 553 (N.Y.1985)—§ **28.26;** § **28.26, n. 5.**

Ross v. Disare, 500 F.Supp. 928 (S.D.N.Y. 1977)—§ **18.53, n. 10.**

Ross v. Manhattan Chelsea Associates, 194 A.D.2d 332, 598 N.Y.S.2d 502 (N.Y.A.D. 1 Dept.1993)—§ **27.42, n. 1.**

Ross v. Pawtucket Mut. Ins. Co., 246 N.Y.S.2d 213, 195 N.E.2d 892 (N.Y. 1963)—§ **31.29, n. 7.**

Ross v. Wilson, 308 N.Y. 605, 127 N.E.2d 697 (N.Y.1955)—§ **3.16, n. 15.**

Rossey, People v., 222 A.D.2d 710, 635 N.Y.S.2d 970 (N.Y.A.D. 2 Dept.1995)—§ **38.26, n. 7.**

Rossi v. Boehner, 116 A.D.2d 636, 498 N.Y.S.2d 318 (N.Y.A.D. 2 Dept.1986)—§ **28.11, n. 4.**

Rossi v. Kelly, 96 A.D.2d 451, 465 N.Y.S.2d 1 (N.Y.A.D. 1 Dept.1983)—§ **17.29, n. 3.**

Rossi, People v., 590 N.Y.S.2d 872, 605 N.E.2d 359 (N.Y.1992)—§ **38.28, n. 16.**

Rossi, People v., 154 Misc.2d 616, 587 N.Y.S.2d 511 (N.Y.Just.Ct.1992)—§ **33.18;** § **33.18, n. 1.**

Rostlee Associates, Ltd. v. Amelkin, 121 A.D.2d 725, 503 N.Y.S.2d 902 (N.Y.A.D. 2 Dept.1986)—§ **16.77, n. 5.**

Rothko's Estate, In re, 77 Misc.2d 168, 352 N.Y.S.2d 574 (N.Y.Sur.1974)—§ **24.9, n. 3.**

Rothschild v. Grottenthaler, 907 F.2d 286 (2nd Cir.1990)—§ **18.19, n. 6;** § **18.53, n. 4.**

Rothschild, People v., 361 N.Y.S.2d 901, 320 N.E.2d 639 (N.Y.1974)—§ **33.60, n. 2.**

Rothstein v. Tennessee Gas Pipeline Co., 204 A.D.2d 39, 616 N.Y.S.2d 902 (N.Y.A.D. 2 Dept.1994)—§ **37.32, n. 1.**

Rotondo v. Reeves, 192 A.D.2d 1086, 596 N.Y.S.2d 272 (N.Y.A.D. 4 Dept.1993)—§ **37.30, n. 4;** § **37.80, n. 2.**

Rouson, Application of, 119 Misc.2d 1069, 465 N.Y.S.2d 155 (N.Y.Co.Ct.1983)—§ **18.67, n. 5.**

Rowe v. Board of Educ. of Chatham Cent. School Dist., 120 A.D.2d 850, 502 N.Y.S.2d 294 (N.Y.A.D. 3 Dept.1986)—§ **37.65, n. 47.**

Rowe v. Great Atlantic & Pac. Tea Co., Inc., 412 N.Y.S.2d 827, 385 N.E.2d 566 (N.Y. 1978)—§ **5.6, n. 2.**

Roy, Application of, 164 Misc.2d 146, 623 N.Y.S.2d 995 (N.Y.Sup.1995)—§ **22.39, n. 1, 4.**

Roy (Lepkowski), Matter of, N.Y.L.J., 10/31/94, p.34, col.3 (Sup.Ct., Suffolk County)—§ **22.78, n. 3.**

Royal v. Brooklyn Union Gas Co., 122 A.D.2d 132, 504 N.Y.S.2d 519 (N.Y.A.D. 2 Dept.1986)—§ **37.45, n. 2.**

Royal Composing Room, Inc., In re, 62 B.R. 403 (Bkrtcy.S.D.N.Y.1986)—§ **9.86, n. 15.**

Roy's Will, In re, 9 Misc.2d 991, 174 N.Y.S.2d 119 (N.Y.Sur.1957)—§ **24.14, n. 3.**

RSP Realty Assocs. v. Paege, N.Y.L.J., 8/14/92, p.21, col.4, 20 HCR 491 (App. Term, 1st Dep't)—§ **13.55, n. 6.**

RTC v. Swedeland Dev. Group, Inc. (In re Swedeland Development Group, Inc.), 16 F.3d 552 (3rd Cir.1994)—§ **9.73, n. 2.**

Rubenfeld, People v., 254 N.Y. 245, 172 N.E. 485 (N.Y.1930)—§ **15.32, n. 8.**

Rubenstein v. Benedictine Hosp., 790 F.Supp. 396 (N.D.N.Y.1992)—§ **17.21, n. 1;** § **17.22, n. 2;** § **17.26, n. 2.**

Rubicco, People v., 335 N.Y.S.2d 442, 286 N.E.2d 924 (N.Y.1972)—§ **38.21, n. 53;** § **38.27, n. 31.**

Rubin, In re, 12 B.R. 436 (Bkrtcy.S.D.N.Y. 1981)—§ **9.205, n. 2.**

Rubin v. Manufacturers Hanover Trust Co., 661 F.2d 979 (2nd Cir.1981)—§ **9.117, n. 4.**

Ruckdeschel, People v., 51 A.D.2d 861, 380 N.Y.S.2d 163 (N.Y.A.D. 4 Dept.1976)—§ **38.19, n. 70.**

Rudow v. City of New York, 822 F.2d 324 (2nd Cir.1987)—§ **18.31, n. 5.**

Rudow v. New York City Com'n on Human Rights, 123 Misc.2d 709, 474 N.Y.S.2d 1005 (N.Y.Sup.1984)—§ **17.57, n. 4, 6.**

Ruffino v. Isadore Rosen and Sons, 142 A.D.2d 177, 535 N.Y.S.2d 488 (N.Y.A.D. 3 Dept.1988)—§ **32.27, n. 10.**

Ruggiero v. Krzeminski, 928 F.2d 558 (2nd Cir.1991)—§ **18.10, n. 12.**

Ruginski v. I.N.S., 942 F.2d 13 (1st Cir. 1991)—§ **19.57, n. 3.**

Ruhm v. C. P. Craska, Inc., 59 A.D.2d 1016, 399 N.Y.S.2d 749 (N.Y.A.D. 4 Dept. 1977)—§ **16.63, n. 2.**

Ruiz, People v., 162 A.D.2d 350, 556 N.Y.S.2d 910 (N.Y.A.D. 1 Dept.1990)—§ **38.20, n. 13;** § **38.25, n. 20;** § **38.28, n. 4.**

Rumph, People v., 190 A.D.2d 698, 593 N.Y.S.2d 530 (N.Y.A.D. 2 Dept.1993)—§ **37.65, n. 10.**

Runcie v. Central Hanover Bank & Trust Co., 6 N.Y.S.2d 625 (N.Y.Sup.1938)—§ **1.12, n. 9.**

Runcie v. Corn Exchange Bank Trust Co., 6 N.Y.S.2d 616 (N.Y.Sup.1938)—§ **1.12, n. 9.**

Rundell's Estate, In re, 41 A.D.2d 995, 344 N.Y.S.2d 6 (N.Y.A.D. 3 Dept.1973)—§ **23.81, n. 7.**

TABLE OF CASES

Rundlett, In re, 153 B.R. 126 (S.D.N.Y. 1993)—§ **9.10, n. 6.**
Runkle v. Commissioner, 39 B.T.A. 458 (B.T.A.1939)—§ **1.34, n. 40.**
Ruotolo v. State, 609 N.Y.S.2d 148, 631 N.E.2d 90 (N.Y.1994)—§ **37.32, n. 1.**
Ruotolo v. State, 187 A.D.2d 160, 593 N.Y.S.2d 198 (N.Y.A.D. 1 Dept.1993)—§ **37.37, n. 9.**
Rupp (Stollmeyer), Matter of, N.Y.L.J., 1/14/94, p.28, col.3 (Sup.Ct., Suffolk County)—§ **22.21, n. 3.**
Rushing v. Commercial Cas. Ins. Co., 251 N.Y. 302, 167 N.E. 450 (N.Y.1929)—§ **31.10, n. 9.**
Rusoff v. Engel, 89 A.D.2d 587, 452 N.Y.S.2d 250 (N.Y.A.D. 2 Dept.1982)—§ **12.66, n. 3.**
Russell v. Smith, 68 F.3d 33 (2nd Cir. 1995)—§ **18.25, n. 2, 4.**
Russell v. Societe Anonyme Des Etablissements Aeroxon, 268 N.Y. 173, 197 N.E. 185 (N.Y.1935)—§ **5.9, n. 4.**
Russo v. Huntington Town House, Inc., 184 A.D.2d 627, 584 N.Y.S.2d 883 (N.Y.A.D. 2 Dept.1992)—§ **18.64, n. 11.**
Russo v. Port Authority of New York and New Jersey, 98 A.D.2d 618, 469 N.Y.S.2d 359 (N.Y.A.D. 1 Dept.1983)—§ **30.30, n. 5.**
Russo v. State of N. Y., 672 F.2d 1014 (2nd Cir.1982)—§ **18.25, n. 1.**
Russo v. Waller, 171 Misc.2d 707, 655 N.Y.S.2d 313 (N.Y.Sup.1997)—§ **28.13, n. 1.**
Rutan v. Republican Party of Illinois, 497 U.S. 62, 110 S.Ct. 2729, 111 L.Ed.2d 52 (1990)—§ **17.55, n. 5.**
Ruz, People v., 524 N.Y.S.2d 668, 519 N.E.2d 614 (N.Y.1988)—§ **38.19, n. 27.**
Ruzicka v. Rager, 305 N.Y. 191, 111 N.E.2d 878 (N.Y.1953)—§ **37.4, n. 5.**
Ryan, In re, 306 N.Y. 11, 114 N.E.2d 183 (N.Y.1953)—§ **38.3, n. 4, 15.**
Ryan v. New York City Health and Hospitals Corp., 220 A.D.2d 734, 633 N.Y.S.2d 500 (N.Y.A.D. 2 Dept.1995)—§ **37.28, n. 37; § 37.29, n. 21.**
Ryan v. New York State Thruway Authority, 889 F.Supp. 70 (N.D.N.Y.1995)—§ **17.68, n. 4, 5.**
Ryan v. New York Telephone Co., 478 N.Y.S.2d 823, 467 N.E.2d 487 (N.Y.1984)—§ **4.25, n. 2; § 18.37, n. 4, 7.**
Ryan, People v., 605 N.Y.S.2d 235, 626 N.E.2d 51 (N.Y.1993)—§ **38.19; § 38.19, n. 53.**
Ryan, People v., 195 A.D.2d 1053, 601 N.Y.S.2d 895 (N.Y.A.D. 4 Dept.1993)—§ **38.10, n. 21.**
Ryan, People v., 151 A.D.2d 528, 542 N.Y.S.2d 665 (N.Y.A.D. 2 Dept.1989)—§ **38.8, n. 102.**
Ryan, People ex rel. v. Green, 58 N.Y. 295 (N.Y.1874)—§ **3.18, n. 6, 7.**
Ryan v. Ryan, 123 A.D.2d 679, 506 N.Y.S.2d 977 (N.Y.A.D. 2 Dept.1986)—§ **21.40; § 21.40, n. 3.**
Rye v. Branca, N.Y.L.J., 4/28/94 (Sup.Ct.,Westchester County)—§ **15.5, n. 4.**
Rye Town/King Civic Ass'n v. Town of Rye, 82 A.D.2d 474, 442 N.Y.S.2d 67 (N.Y.A.D. 2 Dept.1981)—§ **15.6, n. 11, 12.**
Rymkevitch v. State, 42 Misc.2d 1021, 249 N.Y.S.2d 514 (N.Y.Ct.Cl.1964)—§ **14.82, n. 6.**
Rytel, People v., 284 N.Y. 242, 30 N.E.2d 578 (N.Y.1940)—§ **38.21, n. 56.**

S

Saada v. Master Apts. Inc., 152 Misc.2d 861, 579 N.Y.S.2d 536 (N.Y.Sup.1991)—§ **13.71, n. 5.**
Sabatino v. Denison, 203 A.D.2d 781, 610 N.Y.S.2d 383 (N.Y.A.D. 3 Dept.1994)—§ **16.89, n. 6.**
Sabella, People v., 42 A.D.2d 769, 346 N.Y.S.2d 757 (N.Y.A.D. 2 Dept.1973)—§ **38.10, n. 3.**
Sabetay v. Sterling Drug, Inc., 514 N.Y.S.2d 209, 506 N.E.2d 919 (N.Y.1987)—§ **17.32, n. 1, 6; § 17.33, n. 3; § 17.34; § 17.34, n. 4; § 17.35, n. 1, 5.**
Sabin–Goldberg v. Horn, 179 A.D.2d 462, 578 N.Y.S.2d 187 (N.Y.A.D. 1 Dept. 1992)—§ **17.82, n. 14; § 17.84, n. 2.**
Sablosky v. Edward S. Gordon Co., Inc., 538 N.Y.S.2d 513, 535 N.E.2d 643 (N.Y. 1989)—§ **5.13, n. 6.**
Sabo v. Delman, 164 N.Y.S.2d 714, 143 N.E.2d 906 (N.Y.1957)—§ **17.27, n. 11.**
Sabol v. People, 203 A.D.2d 369, 610 N.Y.S.2d 93 (N.Y.A.D. 2 Dept.1994)—§ **37.37, n. 56.**
Sabrina D. v. Thomas W., 110 Misc.2d 796, 443 N.Y.S.2d 111 (N.Y.City Fam.Ct. 1981)—§ **8.16, n. 2.**
Sacred Heart Hosp. of Norristown, In re, 182 B.R. 413 (Bkrtcy.E.D.Pa.1995)—§ **9.159, n. 2.**
Sadigur v. State, 173 Misc. 645, 18 N.Y.S.2d 356 (N.Y.Ct.Cl.1940)—§ **32.42, n. 8.**
Sadness, People v., 300 N.Y. 69, 89 N.E.2d 188 (N.Y.1949)—§ **38.9, n. 13.**
Sadow v. Poskin Realty Corp., 63 Misc.2d 499, 312 N.Y.S.2d 901 (N.Y.Sup.1970)—§ **11.53, n. 6.**

TABLE OF CASES

Safari Motor Coaches, Inc. v. Corwin, 162 Misc.2d 449, 617 N.Y.S.2d 289 (N.Y.Sup. 1994)—§ **7.10, n. 7.**

Safe Flight Instrument Corp. v. Atlantic Aviation Corp., 205 A.D.2d 747, 613 N.Y.S.2d 681 (N.Y.A.D. 2 Dept.1994)— § **5.15, n. 1; § 37.37, n. 19.**

Sagan v. Sagan, 438 N.Y.S.2d 782, 420 N.E.2d 974 (N.Y.1981)—§ **21.30, n. 3.**

Sage v. Fairchild–Swearingen Corp., 523 N.Y.S.2d 418, 517 N.E.2d 1304 (N.Y. 1987)—§ **27.4, n. 4.**

Saidel v. Village of Tupper Lake, 254 A.D. 22, 4 N.Y.S.2d 814 (N.Y.A.D. 3 Dept. 1938)—§ **3.9, n. 7.**

Saint Calle v. Prudential Ins. Co. of America, 815 F.Supp. 679 (S.D.N.Y.1993)— § **31.18, n. 1.**

Saint Francis College v. Al–Khazraji, 481 U.S. 604, 107 S.Ct. 2022, 95 L.Ed.2d 582 (1987)—§ **17.49, n. 4; § 18.17, n. 1.**

Saint Peter's School, In re, 16 B.R. 404 (Bkrtcy.S.D.N.Y.1982)—§ **9.160, n. 3.**

Sainz v. New York City Health and Hospitals Corp., 106 A.D.2d 500, 483 N.Y.S.2d 37 (N.Y.A.D. 2 Dept.1984)—§ **37.37, n. 42.**

Sakaris by Sakaris, Application of, 160 Misc.2d 657, 610 N.Y.S.2d 1007 (N.Y.City Civ.Ct.1993)—§ **18.70, n. 3.**

Saks & Co. v. Continental Ins. Co., 295 N.Y.S.2d 668, 242 N.E.2d 833 (N.Y. 1968)—§ **31.18, n. 17.**

Salerno v. D'Alessandro, 213 A.D.2d 391, 623 N.Y.S.2d 305 (N.Y.A.D. 2 Dept. 1995)—§ **12.20, n. 1.**

Salesian Soc., Inc. v. Village of Ellenville, 121 A.D.2d 823, 505 N.Y.S.2d 197 (N.Y.A.D. 3 Dept.1986)—§ **14.105, n. 3.**

Saletta v. Allegheny Ludlum Steel Corp., 62 A.D.2d 360, 404 N.Y.S.2d 896 (N.Y.A.D. 3 Dept.1978)—§ **32.27, n. 3.**

Salles v. Manhattan and Bronx Surface Transit Operating Authority, 224 A.D.2d 334, 638 N.Y.S.2d 451 (N.Y.A.D. 1 Dept. 1996)—§ **37.65, n. 36.**

Salling v. Bowen, 641 F.Supp. 1046 (W.D.Va.1986)—§ **34.27, n. 8.**

Salomon v. Salomon, 102 Misc.2d 427, 423 N.Y.S.2d 605 (N.Y.Sup.1979)—§ **21.26, n. 3.**

Salt Creek Freightways, In re, 47 B.R. 835 (Bkrtcy.D.Wyo.1985)—§ **9.86, n. 14.**

Salter v. Columbia Concerts, 191 Misc. 479, 77 N.Y.S.2d 703 (N.Y.Sup.1948)—§ **1.51, n. 88.**

Saltzman v. Friedman, 226 A.D.2d 245, 641 N.Y.S.2d 31 (N.Y.A.D. 1 Dept.1996)— § **37.19, n. 14.**

Salvan v. 127 Management Corp., 101 A.D.2d 721, 475 N.Y.S.2d 30 (N.Y.A.D. 1 Dept.1984)—§ **13.32, n. 4.**

Salvati v. Salvati, 221 A.D.2d 541, 633 N.Y.S.2d 819 (N.Y.A.D. 2 Dept.1995)— § **21.71, n. 2.**

Salvato, People v., 111 A.D.2d 773, 490 N.Y.S.2d 31 (N.Y.A.D. 2 Dept.1985)— § **38.10; § 38.10, n. 76.**

Salvo Realty Corp. v. Rosenkrantz, 34 A.D.2d 1021, 312 N.Y.S.2d 787 (N.Y.A.D. 2 Dept.1970)—§ **11.50, n. 2.**

Salz, In re, 80 A.D.2d 769, 436 N.Y.S.2d 713 (N.Y.A.D. 1 Dept.1981)—§ **22.48, n. 4.**

Salzhandler v. Caputo, 316 F.2d 445 (2nd Cir.1963)—§ **17.61, n. 15.**

Samovar of Russia Jewelry Antique Corp. v. Generali the General Ins. Co. of Trieste and Venice, 102 A.D.2d 279, 476 N.Y.S.2d 869 (N.Y.A.D. 1 Dept.1984)— § **31.17, n. 21.**

Sampson, In re, 65 Misc.2d 658, 317 N.Y.S.2d 641 (N.Y.Fam.Ct.1970)— § **18.28, n. 5.**

Samuels v. Air Transport Local 504, 992 F.2d 12 (2nd Cir.1993)—§ **27.35, n. 19, 29.**

Samuels, People v., 424 N.Y.S.2d 892, 400 N.E.2d 1344 (N.Y.1980)—§ **38.19, n. 16.**

Samuels & Co., Inc., Matter of, 526 F.2d 1238 (5th Cir.1976)—§ **9.105, n. 6.**

Samuelson, Matter of, 110 A.D.2d 187, 493 N.Y.S.2d 784 (N.Y.A.D. 2 Dept.1985)— § **23.81, n. 8.**

Sanchez, Matter of, 16 I & N Dec. 671 (BIA 1979)—§ **19.12, n. 25.**

Sanchez, People v., 618 N.Y.S.2d 887, 643 N.E.2d 509 (N.Y.1994)—§ **38.27, n. 14.**

Sanchez v. Sirmons, 121 Misc.2d 249, 467 N.Y.S.2d 757 (N.Y.Sup.1983)—§ **28.29; § 28.29, n. 7.**

Sanders, People v., 523 N.Y.S.2d 444, 517 N.E.2d 1330 (N.Y.1987)—§ **38.19, n. 102.**

Sanders, People v., 58 A.D.2d 525, 395 N.Y.S.2d 190 (N.Y.A.D. 1 Dept.1977)— § **38.8, n. 89.**

Sanders v. Quikstak, Inc., 889 F.Supp. 128 (S.D.N.Y.1995)—§ **27.29, n. 1.**

Sanders v. Rosen, 159 Misc.2d 563, 605 N.Y.S.2d 805 (N.Y.Sup.1993)—§ **18.74, n. 1.**

Sanders v. Winship, 456 N.Y.S.2d 720, 442 N.E.2d 1231 (N.Y.1982)—§ **18.47, n. 2.**

Sandin v. Conner, 515 U.S. 472, 115 S.Ct. 2293, 132 L.Ed.2d 418 (1995)—§ **4.6, n. 4, 9.**

Sandler v. Fishman, 157 A.D.2d 708, 549 N.Y.S.2d 808 (N.Y.A.D. 2 Dept.1990)— § **2.59, n. 7.**

Sandoval, People v., 357 N.Y.S.2d 849, 314 N.E.2d 413 (N.Y.1974)—§ **33.1, n. 2; § 33.44; § 33.44, n. 1; § 33.46, n. 1; § 38.28; § 38.28, n. 26.**

TABLE OF CASES

San Filippo v. United States Trust Co. of New York, Inc., 737 F.2d 246 (2nd Cir. 1984)—§ **18.18, n. 6**; § **18.35, n. 2**.

Sang, People v., 212 A.D.2d 1024, 624 N.Y.S.2d 997 (N.Y.A.D. 4 Dept.1995)—§ **38.10, n. 166**.

San Marco Const. Corp. v. Gillert, 15 Misc.2d 208, 178 N.Y.S.2d 137 (N.Y.Sup. 1958)—§ **10.19, n. 8**.

Santangello v. People, 381 N.Y.S.2d 472, 344 N.E.2d 404 (N.Y.1976)—§ **38.3, n. 23**; § **38.8, n. 70**.

Santiago v. New York State Dept. of Correctional Services, 945 F.2d 25 (2nd Cir. 1991)—§ **18.33, n. 2**.

Santiago, People v., 222 A.D.2d 461, 635 N.Y.S.2d 525 (N.Y.A.D. 2 Dept.1995)—§ **38.38, n. 5**.

Santobello v. New York, 404 U.S. 257, 92 S.Ct. 495, 30 L.Ed.2d 427 (1971)—§ **38.8, n. 226**.

Santos, People v., 635 N.Y.S.2d 168, 658 N.E.2d 1041 (N.Y.1995)—§ **38.19, n. 55**.

Santos, People v., 210 A.D.2d 129, 620 N.Y.S.2d 62 (N.Y.A.D. 1 Dept.1994)—§ **38.25, n. 8**.

Santos, People v., 485 N.Y.S.2d 524, 474 N.E.2d 1192 (N.Y.1984)—§ **38.3, n. 17, 24**.

Santosky v. Kramer, 455 U.S. 745, 102 S.Ct. 1388, 71 L.Ed.2d 599 (1982)—§ **4.6, n. 3**.

Santulli v. Englert, Reilly & McHugh, P.C., 579 N.Y.S.2d 324, 586 N.E.2d 1014 (N.Y. 1992)—§ **28.13**; § **28.13, n. 2**; § **28.14**; § **28.14, n. 15**.

Santy v. Santy, 207 A.D.2d 535, 616 N.Y.S.2d 92 (N.Y.A.D. 2 Dept.1994)—§ **21.55, n. 2**.

Sanusi, United States v., 813 F.Supp. 149 (E.D.N.Y.1992)—§ **18.85, n. 9**.

Sanzone v. City of Rome, 170 A.D.2d 977, 565 N.Y.S.2d 666 (N.Y.A.D. 4 Dept. 1991)—§ **16.125, n. 7**.

Saphier, Matter of, 167 Misc.2d 130, 637 N.Y.S.2d 630 (N.Y.Sup.1995)—§ **22.70, n. 2**.

Sapir v. Green Forest Lumber Ltd. (In re Ajayem Lumber Corp.), 145 B.R. 813 (Bkrtcy.S.D.N.Y.1992)—§ **9.118, n. 6**.

Sapp v. Gleason, 187 A.D.2d 599, 590 N.Y.S.2d 119 (N.Y.A.D. 2 Dept.1992)—§ **37.44, n. 11**.

Saracione v. Oliver Const. Co., 87 A.D.2d 926, 450 N.Y.S.2d 63 (N.Y.A.D. 3 Dept. 1982)—§ **32.41, n. 4**.

Saraf v. Vacanti, 223 A.D.2d 836, 636 N.Y.S.2d 189 (N.Y.A.D. 3 Dept.1996)—§ **37.22, n. 1**; § **37.37, n. 17**.

Sarafian v. Sarafian, 140 A.D.2d 801, 528 N.Y.S.2d 192 (N.Y.A.D. 3 Dept.1988)—§ **21.37, n. 9**.

Sarah K., Matter of, 496 N.Y.S.2d 384, 487 N.E.2d 241 (N.Y.1985)—§ **20.64**; § **20.64, n. 4**.

Sarfaty v. Rainbow Helicopters, Inc., 221 A.D.2d 618, 634 N.Y.S.2d 164 (N.Y.A.D. 2 Dept.1995)—§ **37.37, n. 22, 68**; § **39.27, n. 4**.

Sasso v. Osgood, 633 N.Y.S.2d 259, 657 N.E.2d 254 (N.Y.1995)—§ **16.85**; § **16.85, n. 4**.

Sassower, In re, 76 B.R. 957 (Bkrtcy. S.D.N.Y.1987)—§ **9.252, n. 2**.

Satchell v. Dilworth, 745 F.2d 781 (2nd Cir.1984)—§ **18.31, n. 6**.

Satloff, People v., 452 N.Y.S.2d 12, 437 N.E.2d 271 (N.Y.1982)—§ **38.19, n. 41**.

Sauer v. Sauer, 91 A.D.2d 1166, 459 N.Y.S.2d 131 (N.Y.A.D. 4 Dept.1983)—§ **21.40, n. 7**.

Saumell v. New York Racing Ass'n, Inc., 460 N.Y.S.2d 763, 447 N.E.2d 706 (N.Y. 1983)—§ **4.26, n. 7**.

Saunders v. Big Bros., Inc., 115 Misc.2d 845, 454 N.Y.S.2d 787 (N.Y.City Civ.Ct. 1982)—§ **17.35, n. 2**.

Saunders, People v., 52 A.D.2d 833, 384 N.Y.S.2d 161 (N.Y.A.D. 1 Dept.1976)—§ **38.38, n. 4**.

Saunderson, Matter of, N.Y.L.J., 4/12/94, p.26, col.6 (Sup.Ct., Suffolk County)—§ **22.12, n. 7**.

Savage v. Pacific Gas and Elec. Co., 26 Cal.Rptr.2d 305 (Cal.App. 1 Dist.1993)—§ **17.29, n. 2**.

Saveland Park Holding Corporation v. Wieland, 350 U.S. 841, 76 S.Ct. 81, 100 L.Ed. 750 (1955)—§ **16.126**; § **16.126, n. 2**.

Save Pine Bush, Inc. v. City of Albany, 518 N.Y.S.2d 943, 512 N.E.2d 526 (N.Y. 1987)—§ **15.6**; § **15.6, n. 5, 21, 22, 23**; § **16.45, n. 1, 4, 5**.

Save the Pine Bush, Inc. v. Common Council of City of Albany, 188 A.D.2d 969, 591 N.Y.S.2d 897 (N.Y.A.D. 3 Dept. 1992)—§ **15.34, n. 18**.

Save The Pine Bush, Inc. v. Planning Bd. of Town of Guilderland, 217 A.D.2d 767, 629 N.Y.S.2d 124 (N.Y.A.D. 3 Dept. 1995)—§ **16.56**; § **16.56, n. 1**.

Savvides, People v., 154 N.Y.S.2d 885, 136 N.E.2d 853 (N.Y.1956)—§ **38.10, n. 82**.

Sawyer v. Dreis & Krump Mfg. Co., 502 N.Y.S.2d 696, 493 N.E.2d 920 (N.Y. 1986)—§ **27.32, n. 7**.

Sayville Federal Sav. and Loan Ass'n v. Schons, 17 Misc.2d 54, 183 N.Y.S.2d 106 (N.Y.Co.Ct.1958)—§ **11.14, n. 2**.

Scaduto v. Restaurant Associates Industries, Inc., 180 A.D.2d 458, 579 N.Y.S.2d 381 (N.Y.A.D. 1 Dept.1992)—§ **17.32, n. 4**.

TABLE OF CASES

Scalone v. Phelps Memorial Hosp. Center, 184 A.D.2d 65, 591 N.Y.S.2d 419 (N.Y.A.D. 2 Dept.1992)—§ **30.28, n. 2.**

Scandale v. New York Tel. Co., 55 A.D.2d 761, 390 N.Y.S.2d 465 (N.Y.A.D. 3 Dept. 1976)—§ **32.38, n. 6.**

Scarano v. Board of Regents of University, 57 A.D.2d 991, 394 N.Y.S.2d 322 (N.Y.A.D. 3 Dept.1977)—§ **12.56, n. 8.**

Scarbrough, People v., 496 N.Y.S.2d 409, 487 N.E.2d 266 (N.Y.1985)—§ **38.10, n. 146.**

Scaringe v. Holstein, 103 A.D.2d 880, 477 N.Y.S.2d 903 (N.Y.A.D. 3 Dept.1984)— § **5.29, n. 2.**

Scarola, People v., 186 A.D.2d 78, 588 N.Y.S.2d 154 (N.Y.A.D. 1 Dept.1992)— § **38.10, n. 175.**

Scarpetta, People ex rel. v. Spence–Chapin Adoption Service, 321 N.Y.S.2d 65, 269 N.E.2d 787 (N.Y.1971)—§ **20.64; § 20.64, n. 3.**

Scarsdale Pub. Co.-The Colonial Press v. Carter, 63 Misc. 271, 116 N.Y.S. 731 (N.Y.Sup.1909)—§ **1.21, n. 5.**

Scerbo v. Robinson, 63 A.D.2d 1096, 406 N.Y.S.2d 370 (N.Y.A.D. 3 Dept.1978)— § **12.29, n. 7.**

Schabe v. Hampton Bays Union Free School Dist., 103 A.D.2d 418, 480 N.Y.S.2d 328 (N.Y.A.D. 2 Dept.1984)—§ **37.37, n. 37.**

Schachner v. Perales, 624 N.Y.S.2d 558, 648 N.E.2d 1321 (N.Y.1995)—§ **23.80, n. 17.**

Schaible v. Kane, 150 A.D.2d 668, 541 N.Y.S.2d 541 (N.Y.A.D. 2 Dept.1989)— § **37.65, n. 63.**

Schamber Chemical Co. v. Ross & Kominsky Plumbing & Heating Co., 259 A.D. 784, 18 N.Y.S.2d 368 (N.Y.A.D. 4 Dept. 1940)—§ **37.35, n. 11.**

Schare v. Welsbach Elec. Corp., 138 A.D.2d 477, 526 N.Y.S.2d 25 (N.Y.A.D. 2 Dept. 1988)—§ **30.30, n. 14.**

Schauer v. Joyce, 444 N.Y.S.2d 564, 429 N.E.2d 83 (N.Y.1981)—§ **28.21, n. 13; § 28.26; § 28.26, n. 3.**

Scheeler v. Buffalo Wire Works Co., 50 Misc.2d 158, 269 N.Y.S.2d 897 (N.Y.Sup. 1966)—§ **1.43, n. 18.**

Scheibe v. Zaro, 199 A.D. 807, 192 N.Y.S. 433 (N.Y.A.D. 1 Dept.1922)—§ **30.20, n. 1.**

Scheiber (Zahodnick), Matter of, N.Y.L.J., 10/18/93, p.38, col.5 (Sup.Ct., Nassau County)—§ **22.47, n. 14; § 22.48, n. 5, 6, 7, 8, 9, 10; § 22.49, n. 5; § 22.51, n. 1, 4, 5, 6; § 22.52, n. 4.**

Scheinman, People v., 295 N.Y. 142, 65 N.E.2d 750 (N.Y.1946)—§ **38.27, n. 18.**

Schenck v. Coordinated Coverage Corp., 50 A.D.2d 50, 376 N.Y.S.2d 131 (N.Y.A.D. 1 Dept.1975)—§ **31.28, n. 6.**

Schenck v. State Tax Com'n, 112 A.D.2d 517, 490 N.Y.S.2d 922 (N.Y.A.D. 3 Dept. 1985)—§ **35.102, n. 4.**

Schenectady Chemicals, Inc., State v., 103 A.D.2d 33, 479 N.Y.S.2d 1010 (N.Y.A.D. 3 Dept.1984)—§ **15.32, n. 14.**

Schenectady, City of v. Flacke, 100 A.D.2d 349, 475 N.Y.S.2d 506 (N.Y.A.D. 3 Dept. 1984)—§ **14.34, n. 6.**

Schenectady Homes Corp. v. Greenside Painting Corp., 37 N.Y.S.2d 53 (N.Y.Co. Ct.1942)—§ **10.12, n. 1; § 10.75, n. 3.**

Schenley Industries, Inc. v. State Liquor Authority, 25 A.D.2d 285, 268 N.Y.S.2d 848 (N.Y.A.D. 1 Dept.1966)—§ **36.4, n. 8; § 36.24, n. 4.**

Scherbyn v. Wayne–Finger Lakes Bd. of Co-op. Educational Services, 570 N.Y.S.2d 474, 573 N.E.2d 562 (N.Y.1991)—§ **4.79, n. 12; § 17.53, n. 11.**

Scherling v. Texaco Int'l Trade (In re Transpacific Carriers Corp.), 50 B.R. 649 (Bkrtcy.S.D.N.Y.1985)—§ **9.117, n. 3.**

Schiaroli v. Village of Ellenville, 111 A.D.2d 947, 490 N.Y.S.2d 43 (N.Y.A.D. 3 Dept. 1985)—§ **18.87, n. 3.**

Schiavone v. Fortune, 477 U.S. 21, 106 S.Ct. 2379, 91 L.Ed.2d 18 (1986)— § **18.38, n. 3.**

Schicchi v. J.A. Green Const. Corp., 100 A.D.2d 509, 472 N.Y.S.2d 718 (N.Y.A.D. 2 Dept.1984)—§ **37.38, n. 5.**

Schiff v. Loomer, 23 A.D.2d 481, 255 N.Y.S.2d 482 (N.Y.A.D. 1 Dept.1965)— § **37.67, n. 7.**

Schiffman, Estate of, 105 Misc.2d 1029, 430 N.Y.S.2d 229 (N.Y.Sur.1980)—§ **24.70, n. 2.**

Schimenti v. Whitman & Ransom, 208 A.D.2d 470, 617 N.Y.S.2d 742 (N.Y.A.D. 1 Dept.1994)—§ **28.7; § 28.7, n. 1.**

Schine v. Schine, 335 N.Y.S.2d 58, 286 N.E.2d 449 (N.Y.1972)—§ **21.22, n. 5.**

Schisler v. Bowen, 851 F.2d 43 (2nd Cir. 1988)—§ **34.46, n. 5; § 34.63, n. 4.**

Schisler v. Heckler, 787 F.2d 76 (2nd Cir. 1986)—§ **34.63; § 34.63, n. 4.**

Schisler v. Sullivan, 3 F.3d 563 (2nd Cir. 1993)—§ **34.37, n. 1; § 34.63, n. 4.**

Schlachet v. Schlachet, 84 Misc.2d 782, 378 N.Y.S.2d 308 (N.Y.Sup.1976)—§ **21.26, n. 4; § 21.28, n. 1, 2.**

Schlesinger v. Sanford Main Shopping Center, Inc., 37 Misc.2d 840, 237 N.Y.S.2d 190 (N.Y.Sup.1962)—§ **12.45, n. 6.**

Schliessman v. Anderson, 31 A.D.2d 367, 298 N.Y.S.2d 646 (N.Y.A.D. 2 Dept. 1969)—§ **37.29, n. 18.**

Schloendorff v. Society of New York Hospital, 211 N.Y. 125, 105 N.E. 92 (N.Y. 1914)—§ **23.109, n. 2; § 24.90, n. 1; § 29.14, n. 1.**

TABLE OF CASES

Schlossberg v. State of Maryland (In re Creative Goldsmiths of Washington, D.C., Inc.), 119 F.3d 1140 (4th Cir. 1997)—§ **9.18, n. 2.**

Schlosser v. Michaelis, 18 A.D.2d 940, 238 N.Y.S.2d 433 (N.Y.A.D. 2 Dept.1963)— § **16.89, n. 11.**

Schlosser, People v., 129 Misc.2d 690, 493 N.Y.S.2d 750 (N.Y.Dist.Ct.1985)— § **33.16; § 33.16, n. 2, 4.**

Schlude v. Northeast Cent. School Dist., 892 F.Supp. 560 (S.D.N.Y.1995)— § **18.53, n. 5.**

Schmidt, In re, 64 B.R. 226 (Bkrtcy.S.D.Ind. 1986)—§ **9.130, n. 8.**

Schmidt, Matter of, 97 A.D.2d 244, 468 N.Y.S.2d 663 (N.Y.A.D. 2 Dept.1983)— § **1.43, n. 20, 28.**

Schmidt's Wholesale, Inc. v. Miller & Lehman Const., Inc., 173 A.D.2d 1004, 569 N.Y.S.2d 836 (N.Y.A.D. 3 Dept.1991)— § **11.37, n. 7.**

Schneider v. Brenner, 134 Misc. 449, 235 N.Y.S. 55 (N.Y.Sup.1929)—§ **2.59, n. 9.**

Schneider's Estate, In re, 198 Misc. 1017, 96 N.Y.S.2d 652 (N.Y.Sur.1950)— § **25.46, n. 10.**

Schonfeld, People v., 547 N.Y.S.2d 266, 546 N.E.2d 395 (N.Y.1989)—§ **39.38, n. 6.**

Schoonmaker Homes—John Steinberg, Inc. v. Village of Maybrook, 178 A.D.2d 722, 576 N.Y.S.2d 954 (N.Y.A.D. 3 Dept. 1991)—§ **16.23, n. 4.**

Schrader, People v., 162 Misc.2d 789, 617 N.Y.S.2d 429 (N.Y.City Crim.Ct.1994)— § **18.27, n. 7.**

Schreck v. Wyman, 39 A.D.2d 809, 332 N.Y.S.2d 482 (N.Y.A.D. 3 Dept.1972)— § **37.36, n. 3.**

Schreiber v. State, 452 N.Y.S.2d 16, 437 N.E.2d 275 (N.Y.1982)—§ **14.82, n. 10.**

Schreier v. Albrecht, 126 Misc.2d 336, 482 N.Y.S.2d 674 (N.Y.City Civ.Ct.1984)— § **13.18, n. 25; § 13.43, n. 12; § 13.44, n. 1.**

Schubart v. Hotel Astor, 168 Misc. 431, 5 N.Y.S.2d 203 (N.Y.Sup.1938)—§ **27.36, n. 1.**

Schubtex, Inc. v. Allen Snyder, Inc., 424 N.Y.S.2d 133, 399 N.E.2d 1154 (N.Y. 1979)—§ **5.21; § 5.21, n. 4.**

Schuler v. Birnbaum, 62 A.D.2d 461, 405 N.Y.S.2d 351 (N.Y.A.D. 4 Dept.1978)— § **2.54, n. 3.**

Schultheis, Matter of, N.Y.L.J., 3/17/89, p.26, col.3—§ **25.24, n. 5.**

Schulz v. State, 599 N.Y.S.2d 469, 615 N.E.2d 953 (N.Y.1993)—§ **4.69, n. 9.**

Schulz v. State, 175 A.D.2d 356, 572 N.Y.S.2d 434 (N.Y.A.D. 3 Dept.1991)— § **37.83, n. 6.**

Schulze, Matter of, N.Y.L.J., 9/3/96, p. 30, col. 1 (Surr.Ct., N.Y. County)—§ **22.47, n. 8.**

Schumacher v. Richards Shear Co., Inc., 464 N.Y.S.2d 437, 451 N.E.2d 195 (N.Y. 1983)—§ **27.26, n. 2, 4.**

Schunk, Matter of, 136 A.D.2d 904, 524 N.Y.S.2d 925 (N.Y.A.D. 4 Dept.1988)— § **22.69, n. 4.**

Schuster v. City of New York, 180 N.Y.S.2d 265, 154 N.E.2d 534 (N.Y.1958)—§ **3.30, n. 7.**

Schuttinger, People v., 143 Misc.2d 1032, 542 N.Y.S.2d 927 (N.Y.Dist.Ct.1989)— § **33.16, n. 5.**

Schuykill Fuel Corp. v. B. & C. Nieberg Realty Corp., 250 N.Y. 304, 165 N.E. 456 (N.Y.1929)—§ **8.3, n. 5.**

Schwadron v. Freund, 69 Misc.2d 342, 329 N.Y.S.2d 945 (N.Y.Sup.1972)—§ **10.98, n. 2; § 10.100, n. 5.**

Schwartfigure v. Hartnett, 610 N.Y.S.2d 125, 632 N.E.2d 434 (N.Y.1994)—§ **4.50, n. 4, 6.**

Schwartz, Matter of Estate of, 130 Misc.2d 786, 497 N.Y.S.2d 834 (N.Y.Sur.1986)— § **25.31, n. 8.**

Schwartz v. Abt, N.Y.L.J., 5/4/78, p.5, col.4 (App. Term, 1st Dep't)—§ **13.33, n. 6.**

Schwartz v. Certified Management Corp., 117 A.D.2d 521, 498 N.Y.S.2d 135 (N.Y.A.D. 1 Dept.1986)—§ **13.8, n. 5; § 13.9, n. 6.**

Schwartz v. Crozier, 169 A.D.2d 1003, 565 N.Y.S.2d 567 (N.Y.A.D. 3 Dept.1991)— § **30.18, n. 1.**

Schwartz v. Goldberg, 58 Misc.2d 308, 295 N.Y.S.2d 245 (N.Y.Sup.1968)—§ **8.35, n. 5.**

Schwartz v. Greenfield, Stein and Weisinger, 90 Misc.2d 882, 396 N.Y.S.2d 582 (N.Y.Sup.1977)—§ **28.11, n. 13.**

Schwartz v. Heyden Newport Chemical Corp., 237 N.Y.S.2d 714, 188 N.E.2d 142 (N.Y.1963)—§ **27.39, n. 2.**

Schwartz v. Horn, 338 N.Y.S.2d 613, 290 N.E.2d 816 (N.Y.1972)—§ **24.61, n. 3.**

Schwartz v. New York City Housing Authority, 219 A.D.2d 47, 641 N.Y.S.2d 885 (N.Y.A.D. 2 Dept.1996)—§ **37.80, n. 2.**

Schwartz v. Public Adm'r of Bronx County, 298 N.Y.S.2d 955, 246 N.E.2d 725 (N.Y. 1969)—§ **18.37, n. 5.**

Schwartz v. United States (In re Schwartz), 954 F.2d 569 (9th Cir.1992)—§ **9.52, n. 6.**

Schwartz v. Weiss–Newell, 87 Misc.2d 558, 386 N.Y.S.2d 191 (N.Y.City Civ.Ct. 1976)—§ **13.12, n. 5.**

Schwartzman, United States ex rel. Hall v., 887 F.Supp. 60 (E.D.N.Y.1995)— § **34.34, n. 2.**

TABLE OF CASES

Schwarzenbach v. Oneonta Light & Power Co., 144 A.D. 884, 129 N.Y.S. 384 (N.Y.A.D. 3 Dept.1911)—§ **15.32, n. 21.**

Schweitzer, In re, 19 B.R. 860 (Bkrtcy. E.D.N.Y.1982)—§ **9.188, n. 2, 6.**

Schweitzer v. State Tax Commission, 106 Misc.2d 658, 434 N.Y.S.2d 876 (N.Y.Sup. 1980)—§ **35.100, n. 8.**

Sciolino v. Ryan, 81 A.D.2d 475, 440 N.Y.S.2d 795 (N.Y.A.D. 4 Dept.1981)—§ **16.39, n. 5.**

Scioto Valley Mortg. Co., In re, 88 B.R. 168 (Bkrtcy.S.D.Ohio 1988)—§ **9.161, n. 8.**

Scopas, People v., 227 N.Y.S.2d 5, 181 N.E.2d 754 (N.Y.1962)—§ **20.45, n. 10.**

Scott v. Dixon, 720 F.2d 1542 (11th Cir. 1983)—§ **18.31, n. 2.**

Scott, People v., 644 N.Y.S.2d 913, 667 N.E.2d 923 (N.Y.1996)—§ **38.10; § 38.10, n. 110, 111.**

Scott, People v., 212 A.D.2d 477, 623 N.Y.S.2d 212 (N.Y.A.D. 1 Dept.1995)—§ **18.65, n. 3.**

Scott, People v., 93 A.D.2d 754, 461 N.Y.S.2d 309 (N.Y.A.D. 1 Dept.1983)—§ **38.64, n. 1.**

Scuccimarra, Matter of, 69 A.D.2d 157, 418 N.Y.S.2d 132 (N.Y.A.D. 2 Dept.1979)—§ **28.24, n. 2.**

Scully, People ex rel. Harris v., 114 A.D.2d 919, 495 N.Y.S.2d 660 (N.Y.A.D. 2 Dept. 1985)—§ **37.34, n. 6.**

Scully, People ex rel. Robinson v., 122 A.D.2d 290, 505 N.Y.S.2d 193 (N.Y.A.D. 2 Dept.1986)—§ **38.8, n. 74.**

S & D Maintenance Co., Inc. v. Goldin, 844 F.2d 962 (2nd Cir.1988)—§ **4.6, n. 8.**

Seaberg, People v., 543 N.Y.S.2d 968, 541 N.E.2d 1022 (N.Y.1989)—§ **33.29; § 33.29, n. 1; § 38.8; § 38.8, n. 12, 25, 29, 208.**

Seaboard Sur. Co. v. Gillette Co., 486 N.Y.S.2d 873, 476 N.E.2d 272 (N.Y. 1984)—§ **31.12, n. 9.**

Seaescape Cruises, Ltd., In re, 131 B.R. 241 (Bkrtcy.S.D.Fla.1991)—§ **9.43, n. 15.**

Seagrave Corp. v. Vista Resources, Inc., 696 F.2d 227 (2nd Cir.1982)—§ **2.106, n. 12, 13.**

Sean B. W., Matter of, 86 Misc.2d 16, 381 N.Y.S.2d 656 (N.Y.Sur.1976)—§ **20.36; § 20.36, n. 3.**

Sean Y. v. John Y., 62 A.D.2d 426, 405 N.Y.S.2d 148 (N.Y.A.D. 3 Dept.1978)—§ **20.42, n. 1.**

Sears, Roebuck & Co. v. Enco Associates, Inc., 401 N.Y.S.2d 767, 372 N.E.2d 555 (N.Y.1977)—§ **28.13; § 28.13, n. 5, 6.**

Sears, Roebuck & Co. v. Galloway, 195 A.D.2d 825, 600 N.Y.S.2d 773 (N.Y.A.D. 3 Dept.1993)—§ **5.37, n. 5.**

Seatrain Lines, Inc., Matter of, 13 B.R. 980 (Bkrtcy.S.D.N.Y.1981)—§ **9.29, n. 1.**

Seawall Associates v. City of New York, 544 N.Y.S.2d 542, 542 N.E.2d 1059 (N.Y. 1989)—§ **15.34; § 15.34, n. 10, 11; § 16.22, n. 10.**

S.E.C. v. W.J. Howey Co., 328 U.S. 293, 66 S.Ct. 1100, 90 L.Ed. 1244 (1946)—§ **2.106; § 2.106, n. 5.**

Second Report of November, 1968 Grand Jury of Erie County, In re, 309 N.Y.S.2d 297, 257 N.E.2d 859 (N.Y.1970)—§ **38.11, n. 15.**

Security Mut. Ins. Co. of New York v. Acker-Fitzsimons Corp., 340 N.Y.S.2d 902, 293 N.E.2d 76 (N.Y.1972)—§ **28.40, n. 2; § 31.10, n. 2.**

Security Trust Co. of Rochester v. Thomas, 59 A.D.2d 242, 399 N.Y.S.2d 511 (N.Y.A.D. 4 Dept.1977)—§ **7.55.**

See v. City of Seattle, 387 U.S. 541, 87 S.Ct. 1737, 18 L.Ed.2d 943 (1967)—§ **4.2, n. 35; § 4.62, n. 4.**

Seelig v. Koehler, 556 N.Y.S.2d 832, 556 N.E.2d 125 (N.Y.1990)—§ **17.55, n. 3.**

Sega v. State, 469 N.Y.S.2d 51, 456 N.E.2d 1174 (N.Y.1983)—§ **37.28, n. 24, 34.**

Segal v. Zoning Bd. of Appeals of Town of Bethel, 191 A.D.2d 873, 594 N.Y.S.2d 459 (N.Y.A.D. 3 Dept.1993)—§ **16.46, n. 3.**

Seggio v. Town of West Seneca, 145 A.D.2d 956, 536 N.Y.S.2d 328 (N.Y.A.D. 4 Dept. 1988)—§ **16.113, n. 6.**

Sehr, Matter of, 169 Misc.2d 543, 646 N.Y.S.2d 937 (N.Y.Sur.1996)—§ **22.61, n. 1.**

Seif v. City of Long Beach, 286 N.Y. 382, 36 N.E.2d 630 (N.Y.1941)—§ **3.7, n. 15; § 3.24, n. 12.**

Seigel v. Neary, 38 Misc. 297, 77 N.Y.S. 854 (N.Y.Sup.1902)—§ **13.30, n. 4.**

Seit, People v., 629 N.Y.S.2d 998, 653 N.E.2d 1168 (N.Y.1995)—§ **39.50, n. 4.**

Seitz v. Department of Fire, City of Syracuse, 55 A.D.2d 829, 390 N.Y.S.2d 308 (N.Y.A.D. 4 Dept.1976)—§ **30.11, n. 1, 2.**

Seitz v. Drogheo, 287 N.Y.S.2d 29, 234 N.E.2d 209 (N.Y.1967)—§ **21.3, n. 1.**

Self, People v., 213 A.D.2d 998, 624 N.Y.S.2d 488 (N.Y.A.D. 4 Dept.1995)—§ **38.8, n. 148.**

Selikoff, People v., 360 N.Y.S.2d 623, 318 N.E.2d 784 (N.Y.1974)—§ **38.8, n. 40, 226.**

Selleck v. Board of Ed. of Central School Dist. No. 1 of Towns of Jay, Keene, Chesterfield, Wilmington, Essex County, 276 A.D. 263, 94 N.Y.S.2d 318 (N.Y.A.D. 3 Dept.1949)—§ **29.16, n. 4.**

TABLE OF CASES

Sellers, People v., 222 A.D.2d 941, 635 N.Y.S.2d 773 (N.Y.A.D. 3 Dept.1995)—§ 38.19; § 38.19, n. 31.

Seminole Housing Corp. v. M & M Garages, Inc., 78 Misc.2d 755, 359 N.Y.S.2d 711 (N.Y.City Civ.Ct.1974)—§ 13.37, n. 6.

Seminole Tribe of Florida v. Florida, 517 U.S. 44, 116 S.Ct. 1114, 134 L.Ed.2d 252 (1996)—§ 9.18, n. 2; § 18.33, n. 1.

Seneca Knitting Mills Corp. v. Wilkes, 120 A.D.2d 955, 502 N.Y.S.2d 844 (N.Y.A.D. 4 Dept.1986)—§ 17.28, n. 4.

Senftner v. Kleinhans, 80 Misc. 519, 141 N.Y.S. 533 (N.Y.Sup.1913)—§ 28.30, n. 2.

S.E. Nichols, Inc. v. American Shopping Centers, Inc., 115 A.D.2d 856, 495 N.Y.S.2d 810 (N.Y.A.D. 3 Dept.1985)—§ 13.71, n. 5.

Senzamici v. Young, 174 A.D.2d 831, 570 N.Y.S.2d 760 (N.Y.A.D. 3 Dept.1991)—§ 12.5, n. 3.

Septuagenarian v. Septuagenarian, 126 Misc.2d 699, 483 N.Y.S.2d 932 (N.Y.Fam.Ct.1984)—§ 23.80, n. 10.

Sepulveda, People v., 147 A.D.2d 720, 538 N.Y.S.2d 68 (N.Y.A.D. 2 Dept.1989)—§ 38.64, n. 1.

Seronde, Matter of, 99 Misc.2d 485, 416 N.Y.S.2d 716 (N.Y.Sup.1979)—§ 22.4, n. 6; § 22.15, n. 2.

Serota v. Town Bd. of Town of Oyster Bay, 191 A.D.2d 700, 595 N.Y.S.2d 525 (N.Y.A.D. 2 Dept.1993)—§ 16.91, n. 9.

Servatius v. Town of Verona, 112 A.D.2d 706, 491 N.Y.S.2d 879 (N.Y.A.D. 4 Dept. 1985)—§ 16.124, n. 11.

Servidone Const. Corp. v. Security Ins. Co. of Hartford, 488 N.Y.S.2d 139, 477 N.E.2d 441 (N.Y.1985)—§ 31.2, n. 4.

Servidori v. Mahoney, 129 A.D.2d 944, 515 N.Y.S.2d 328 (N.Y.A.D. 3 Dept.1987)—§ 31.29, n. 9.

S.E.S. Importers, Inc. v. Pappalardo, 442 N.Y.S.2d 453, 425 N.E.2d 841 (N.Y. 1981)—§ 12.29, n. 1.

Session, People v., 357 N.Y.S.2d 409, 313 N.E.2d 728 (N.Y.1974)—§ 38.9, n. 14.

Severin v. Rouse, 134 Misc.2d 940, 513 N.Y.S.2d 928 (N.Y.City Civ.Ct.1987)—§ 13.12, n. 6.

Seward, People ex rel. v. President, etc., of Village of Sing Sing, 54 A.D. 555, 66 N.Y.S. 1094 (N.Y.A.D. 2 Dept.1900)—§ 3.20, n. 5.

Sewell v. Singh, 160 A.D.2d 592, 554 N.Y.S.2d 236 (N.Y.A.D. 1 Dept.1990)—§ 30.3, n. 22.

Seyfried v. Greenspan, 92 A.D.2d 563, 459 N.Y.S.2d 316 (N.Y.A.D. 2 Dept.1983)—§ 17.27, n. 13.

S. G. Phillips Contructors, Inc. v. City of Burlington (In re S.G. Phillips Constructors, Inc.), 45 F.3d 702 (2nd Cir.1995)—§ 9.19, n. 2.

Shaare Tefila Congregation v. Cobb, 481 U.S. 615, 107 S.Ct. 2019, 95 L.Ed.2d 594 (1987)—§ 17.49, n. 4.

Shabazz v. Coughlin, 852 F.2d 697 (2nd Cir.1988)—§ 18.32, n. 5.

Shabazz v. State of New York Workers' Compensation Bd., 133 A.D.2d 285, 518 N.Y.S.2d 363 (N.Y.A.D. 3 Dept.1987)—§ 37.37, n. 77.

Shack, People v., 634 N.Y.S.2d 660, 658 N.E.2d 706 (N.Y.1995)—§ 18.27, n. 6.

Shahar v. Bowers, 114 F.3d 1097 (11th Cir. 1997)—§ 17.58, n. 1.

Shaida W., Matter of, 626 N.Y.S.2d 35, 649 N.E.2d 1179 (N.Y.1995)—§ 37.19, n. 64; § 37.29, n. 39.

Shailam, In re, 144 B.R. 626 (Bkrtcy. N.D.N.Y.1992)—§ 1.10, n. 12.

Shaitelman v. Phoenix Mut. Life Ins. Co., 517 F.Supp. 21 (S.D.N.Y.1980)—§ 17.27, n. 3; § 17.31, n. 3.

Shalala v. Schaefer, 509 U.S. 292, 113 S.Ct. 2625, 125 L.Ed.2d 239 (1993)—§ 34.29, n. 7.

Shamberg Marwell Cherneff & Hocherman, P.C. v. Laufer, 193 A.D.2d 664, 597 N.Y.S.2d 471 (N.Y.A.D. 2 Dept.1993)—§ 28.32, n. 3.

Shamsky v. Garan, Inc., 167 Misc.2d 149, 632 N.Y.S.2d 930 (N.Y.Sup.1995)—§ 18.63, n. 7; § 18.64, n. 13.

Shanahan v. Shanahan, 92 A.D.2d 566, 459 N.Y.S.2d 319 (N.Y.A.D. 2 Dept.1983)—§ 13.63, n. 5.

Shannon B., Matter of, 522 N.Y.S.2d 488, 517 N.E.2d 203 (N.Y.1987)—§ 39.9, n. 10.

Shante D. by Ada D. v. City of New York, 190 A.D.2d 356, 598 N.Y.S.2d 475 (N.Y.A.D. 1 Dept.1993)—§ 37.65, n. 44.

Shape, Inc., In re, 138 B.R. 334 (Bkrtcy. D.Me.1992)—§ 9.198, n. 2.

Shapiro v. American Home Assur. Co., 584 F.Supp. 1245 (D.C.Mass.1984)—§ 28.43; § 28.43, n. 2, 6.

Shapiro v. Cadman Towers, Inc., 51 F.3d 328 (2nd Cir.1995)—§ 18.47, n. 3.

Shapiro v. New York City Police Dept. (License Div.), 157 Misc.2d 28, 595 N.Y.S.2d 864 (N.Y.Sup.1993)—§ 4.84, n. 7.

Shapiro v. United States, 335 U.S. 1, 68 S.Ct. 1375, 92 L.Ed. 1787 (1948)—§ 4.64, n. 5.

Shapiro & Saybrook Mfg. Co. (Matter of Saybrook Mfg. Co., Inc.), 963 F.2d 1490 (11th Cir.1992)—§ 9.71, n. 11.

TABLE OF CASES

Sharlow, People v., 185 A.D.2d 289, 585 N.Y.S.2d 799 (N.Y.A.D. 2 Dept.1992)—§ 38.21, n. 45.

Sharma v. Sobol, 188 A.D.2d 833, 591 N.Y.S.2d 572 (N.Y.A.D. 3 Dept.1992)—§ 4.21, n. 2.

Sharon Steel Corp., In re, 871 F.2d 1217 (3rd Cir.1989)—§ 9.138, n. 5.

Sharon Steel Corp., In re, 78 B.R. 762 (Bkrtcy.W.D.Pa.1987)—§ 9.142, n. 5.

Sharrock v. Dell Buick–Cadillac, Inc., 408 N.Y.S.2d 39, 379 N.E.2d 1169 (N.Y. 1978)—§ 4.4, n. 2; § 7.29, n. 1.

Shattuc Cable Corp., In re, 138 B.R. 557 (Bkrtcy.N.D.Ill.1992)—§ 9.105, n. 7.

Shaw, People v., 530 N.Y.S.2d 551, 526 N.E.2d 42 (N.Y.1988)—§ 39.43, n. 1.

Shawn P., Matter of, 187 A.D.2d 432, 589 N.Y.S.2d 565 (N.Y.A.D. 2 Dept.1992)—§ 20.67; § 20.67, n. 4.

Shay v. Mitchell, 50 A.D.2d 404, 378 N.Y.S.2d 334 (N.Y.A.D. 4 Dept.1976)—§ 12.9, n. 9.

Shea v. McCarthy, 953 F.2d 29 (2nd Cir. 1992)—§ 17.61, n. 13.

Shecora's Estate, In re, 201 N.Y.S.2d 191 (N.Y.Sur.1960)—§ 30.12, n. 11.

Shedlinsky v. Budweiser Brewing Co., 163 N.Y. 437, 57 N.E. 620 (N.Y.1900)—§ 5.7, n. 4.

Shedrick, People v., 83 A.D.2d 988, 443 N.Y.S.2d 716 (N.Y.A.D. 4 Dept.1981)—§ 38.8, n. 99.

Sheehan v. Plotkin, N.Y.L.J., 9/8/95, p.29, col. 4 (Sup.Ct., Kings County)—§ 30.29; § 30.29, n. 6.

Sheffield Commercial Corp. v. Clemente, 792 F.2d 282 (2nd Cir.1986)—§ 7.21, n. 5; § 7.26, n. 8.

Sheik v. Sheik, 187 A.D.2d 572, 591 N.Y.S.2d 334 (N.Y.A.D. 2 Dept.1992)—§ 37.37, n. 39, 84.

Sheil v. Sheil, 29 A.D.2d 950, 289 N.Y.S.2d 86 (N.Y.A.D. 2 Dept.1968)—§ 30.42, n. 1.

Sheinwald v. Doldo, 143 A.D.2d 129, 531 N.Y.S.2d 588 (N.Y.A.D. 2 Dept.1988)—§ 30.30, n. 9.

Sheldon v. Town of Highlands, 539 N.Y.S.2d 722, 536 N.E.2d 1141 (N.Y. 1989)—§ 4.5, n. 6.

Sheldon Terrace, Inc. v. Schneider, 18 Misc.2d 456, 193 N.Y.S.2d 484 (N.Y.Sup. App.Term 1959)—§ 13.27, n. 6, 7.

Shelter Resources Corp., In re, 35 B.R. 304 (Bkrtcy.N.D.Ohio 1983)—§ 9.140, n. 2.

Shepard v. Spring Hollow at Sagaponack, 87 A.D.2d 126, 450 N.Y.S.2d 547 (N.Y.A.D. 2 Dept.1982)—§ 12.29, n. 1.

Shepardson by Shepardson v. Town of Schodack, 613 N.Y.S.2d 850, 636 N.E.2d 1383 (N.Y.1994)—§ 3.30, n. 14.

Sherbak v. Doughty, 72 A.D.2d 548, 420 N.Y.S.2d 724 (N.Y.A.D. 2 Dept.1979)—§ 28.10, n. 7.

Sher–Del Foods, Inc., In re, 186 B.R. 358 (Bkrtcy.W.D.N.Y.1995)—§ 9.195, n. 2.

Sheridan Const. Corp., Application of, 22 A.D.2d 390, 256 N.Y.S.2d 210 (N.Y.A.D. 4 Dept.1965)—§ 37.30, n. 5.

Sheriff's Dept. v. State Div. of Human Rights, 129 A.D.2d 789, 514 N.Y.S.2d 779 (N.Y.A.D. 2 Dept.1987)—§ 17.39, n. 2.

Shermack v. Board of Regents of University of New York, 64 A.D.2d 798, 407 N.Y.S.2d 926 (N.Y.A.D. 3 Dept.1978)—§ 4.18, n. 15.

Sherman v. Frazier, 84 A.D.2d 401, 446 N.Y.S.2d 372 (N.Y.A.D. 2 Dept.1982)—§ 16.120, n. 9.

Sherman v. M. Lowenstein & Sons, Inc., 28 A.D.2d 922, 282 N.Y.S.2d 142 (N.Y.A.D. 2 Dept.1967)—§ 27.40, n. 9; § 27.43, n. 1.

Sherrer v. Sherrer, 334 U.S. 343, 68 S.Ct. 1087, 92 L.Ed. 1429 (1948)—§ 21.32, n. 3.

Sherri v. National Surety Co. of New York, 243 N.Y. 266, 153 N.E. 70 (N.Y.1926)—§ 31.20, n. 5.

Sherwood Group, Inc. v. Dornbush, Mensch, Mandelstam & Silverman, 191 A.D.2d 292, 594 N.Y.S.2d 766 (N.Y.A.D. 1 Dept.1993)—§ 28.8; § 28.8, n. 1.

Shields v. Gross, 461 N.Y.S.2d 254, 448 N.E.2d 108 (N.Y.1983)—§ 18.63, n. 5.

Shields, People v., 205 A.D.2d 833, 613 N.Y.S.2d 281 (N.Y.A.D. 3 Dept.1994)—§ 38.28, n. 15.

Shim, People v., 218 A.D.2d 757, 630 N.Y.S.2d 510 (N.Y.A.D. 2 Dept.1995)—§ 38.28, n. 15.

Shine, Julianelle, Karp, Bozelko & Karazin, P.C. v. Rubens, 192 A.D.2d 345, 596 N.Y.S.2d 20 (N.Y.A.D. 1 Dept.1993)—§ 8.16, n. 9.

Shiner v. Board of Estimate of City of New York, 95 A.D.2d 831, 463 N.Y.S.2d 872 (N.Y.A.D. 2 Dept.1983)—§ 16.75, n. 8.

Shipley, Application of, 26 Misc.2d 204, 205 N.Y.S.2d 581 (N.Y.Sup.1960)—§ 18.67, n. 1.

Shirdel, Matter of, 19 I & N Dec. 33, 1 Immig.Rptr. B1-12 (BIA 1984)—§ 19.50, n. 5.

Shoenfeld v. Shoenfeld, 168 A.D.2d 674, 563 N.Y.S.2d 500 (N.Y.A.D. 2 Dept.1990)—§ 21.43, n. 18.

Sholz Buick, Inc. v. Melton, 92 A.D.2d 871, 459 N.Y.S.2d 829 (N.Y.A.D. 2 Dept. 1983)—§ 7.27, n. 15.

TABLE OF CASES

Shore Haven Motor Inn, Inc., In re, 124 B.R. 617 (Bkrtcy.S.D.Fla.1991)—§ **9.69, n. 10.**

Shultis v. Woodstock Land Development Associates, 195 A.D.2d 677, 599 N.Y.S.2d 340 (N.Y.A.D. 3 Dept.1993)— § **11.43, n. 4.**

Sicari, In re, 187 B.R. 861 (Bkrtcy.S.D.N.Y. 1994)—§ **9.205, n. 4.**

Sichol v. Crocker, 177 A.D.2d 842, 576 N.Y.S.2d 457 (N.Y.A.D. 3 Dept.1991)— § **11.37, n. 7.**

Siderpali, S.P.A. v. Judal Industries, Inc., 833 F.Supp. 1023 (S.D.N.Y.1993)— § **5.43, n. 5.**

Siegel v. Kentucky Fried Chicken of Long Island, Inc., 108 A.D.2d 218, 488 N.Y.S.2d 744 (N.Y.A.D. 2 Dept.1985)— § **13.12, n. 8;** § **13.51;** § **13.51, n. 11.**

Siegel v. Kranis, 29 A.D.2d 477, 288 N.Y.S.2d 831 (N.Y.A.D. 2 Dept.1968)— § **28.14, n. 4.**

Siegel, People ex rel. v. Lyons, 201 A.D. 530, 194 N.Y.S. 484 (N.Y.A.D. 1 Dept. 1922)—§ **1.21, n. 9.**

Siegel v. Siegel, 197 A.D.2d 569, 602 N.Y.S.2d 421 (N.Y.A.D. 2 Dept.1993)— § **21.73, n. 2.**

Siegel, on Behalf of Hudson, People ex rel. v. Sielaff, 182 A.D.2d 389, 582 N.Y.S.2d 131 (N.Y.A.D. 1 Dept.1992)—§ **38.8, n. 67.**

Siegert v. Gilley, 500 U.S. 226, 111 S.Ct. 1789, 114 L.Ed.2d 277 (1991)—§ **4.6, n. 5;** § **18.32, n. 1.**

Siegert v. Luney, 111 A.D.2d 854, 491 N.Y.S.2d 15 (N.Y.A.D. 2 Dept.1985)— § **16.131, n. 11.**

Sielaff, People ex rel. Siegel, on Behalf of Hudson v., 182 A.D.2d 389, 582 N.Y.S.2d 131 (N.Y.A.D. 1 Dept.1992)—§ **38.8, n. 67.**

Siemens & Halske Gmbh. v. Gres, 77 Misc.2d 745, 354 N.Y.S.2d 762 (N.Y.Sup. 1973)—§ **8.23, n. 17.**

Sierra Club v. SCM Corp., 572 F.Supp. 828 (W.D.N.Y.1983)—§ **15.11, n. 19.**

Sierra Club v. Simkins Industries, Inc., 847 F.2d 1109 (4th Cir.1988)—§ **4.38, n. 2.**

Sievers v. City of New York, Dept. of Bldgs., 146 A.D.2d 473, 536 N.Y.S.2d 441 (N.Y.A.D. 1 Dept.1989)—§ **16.49, n. 6.**

Siewert v. Loudonville Elementary School, 210 A.D.2d 568, 620 N.Y.S.2d 149 (N.Y.A.D. 3 Dept.1994)—§ **37.37, n. 28.**

Silberman v. Faber Piano Co., 190 N.Y.S. 629 (N.Y.Sup.1921)—§ **30.5, n. 7.**

Silberman v. Georges, 91 A.D.2d 520, 456 N.Y.S.2d 395 (N.Y.A.D. 1 Dept.1982)— § **37.28, n. 2.**

Silpin Plumbing Corp. v. A Builders Corp., 190 Misc. 598, 75 N.Y.S.2d 681 (N.Y.Sup.1947)—§ **10.89, n. 2.**

Silver v. Equitable Life Assur. Soc. of United States, 168 A.D.2d 367, 563 N.Y.S.2d 78 (N.Y.A.D. 1 Dept.1990)—§ **18.55, n. 7.**

Silver v. Moe's Pizza, Inc., 121 A.D.2d 376, 503 N.Y.S.2d 86 (N.Y.A.D. 2 Dept. 1986)—§ **13.28;** § **13.28, n. 15.**

Silver v. Mohasco Corp., 94 A.D.2d 820, 462 N.Y.S.2d 917 (N.Y.A.D. 3 Dept.1983)— § **17.27, n. 10.**

Silverberg, Matter of, 81 A.D.2d 640, 438 N.Y.S.2d 143 (N.Y.A.D. 2 Dept.1981)— § **2.51, n. 28.**

Silverman v. New York University School of Law, 193 A.D.2d 411, 597 N.Y.S.2d 314 (N.Y.A.D. 1 Dept.1993)—§ **18.53, n. 11.**

Silverman, People v., 165 N.Y.S.2d 11, 144 N.E.2d 10 (N.Y.1957)—§ **38.9, n. 9.**

Silverman's Estate, In re, 43 Misc.2d 909, 252 N.Y.S.2d 587 (N.Y.Sur.1964)— § **24.61, n. 2.**

Silverman's Will, In re, 144 Misc. 675, 259 N.Y.S. 272 (N.Y.Sur.1932)—§ **25.38, n. 2.**

Silverstein, Matter of, 121 A.D.2d 728, 504 N.Y.S.2d 62 (N.Y.A.D. 2 Dept.1986)— § **22.69, n. 8, 9.**

Silverstein v. Harmonie Club of City of New York, 173 A.D.2d 378, 569 N.Y.S.2d 965 (N.Y.A.D. 1 Dept.1991)—§ **37.65, n. 49, 64.**

Sima–Rodriguez, People v., 190 A.D.2d 596, 593 N.Y.S.2d 798 (N.Y.A.D. 1 Dept. 1993)—§ **38.19, n. 27.**

Simblest v. Maynard, 427 F.2d 1 (2nd Cir. 1970)—§ **27.35, n. 29.**

Simcox, People v., 219 A.D.2d 869, 631 N.Y.S.2d 956 (N.Y.A.D. 4 Dept.1995)— § **38.8, n. 170, 204.**

Simcuski v. Saeli, 406 N.Y.S.2d 259, 377 N.E.2d 713 (N.Y.1978)—§ **27.25;** § **27.25, n. 2;** § **28.15;** § **28.15, n. 1, 6.**

Simkowitz v. Stewart, N.Y.L.J. 1/30/90, p.21, col.5, 18 HCR 41 (App. Term, 1st Dep't)—§ **13.66, n. 3.**

Simmonds, People v., 182 A.D.2d 650, 582 N.Y.S.2d 236 (N.Y.A.D. 2 Dept.1992)— § **38.9, n. 4.**

Simmons, People v., 224 A.D.2d 229, 637 N.Y.S.2d 154 (N.Y.A.D. 1 Dept.1996)— § **38.19, n. 76.**

Simmons, People v., 206 A.D.2d 550, 615 N.Y.S.2d 56 (N.Y.A.D. 2 Dept.1994)— § **38.26, n. 17.**

Simon v. Board of Appeals on Zoning of City of New Rochelle, 208 A.D.2d 931, 618 N.Y.S.2d 729 (N.Y.A.D. 2 Dept. 1994)—§ **16.121, n. 8.**

TABLE OF CASES

Simon v. Indursky, 211 A.D.2d 404, 630 N.Y.S.2d 2 (N.Y.A.D. 1 Dept.1995)—§ 37.28, n. 43.

Simon v. Massapequa General Hosp., 167 A.D.2d 533, 562 N.Y.S.2d 948 (N.Y.A.D. 2 Dept.1990)—§ 37.37, n. 43.

Simpkins v. Bellevue Hosp., 832 F.Supp. 69 (S.D.N.Y.1993)—§ 18.34, n. 3.

Simpson, People v., 213 A.D.2d 811, 624 N.Y.S.2d 970 (N.Y.A.D. 3 Dept.1995)—§ 38.8, n. 162.

Simpson v. Wolansky, 380 N.Y.S.2d 630, 343 N.E.2d 274 (N.Y.1975)—§ 4.18, n. 9; § 4.75, n. 11; § 4.78, n. 10, 12.

Sims, Matter of, 474 N.Y.S.2d 270, 462 N.E.2d 370 (N.Y.1984)—§ 39.59, n. 13.

Sims, People v., 217 A.D.2d 912, 629 N.Y.S.2d 923 (N.Y.A.D. 4 Dept.1995)—§ 38.8, n. 158.

Sinclair Refining Co. v. State, 279 A.D. 692, 107 N.Y.S.2d 934 (N.Y.A.D. 3 Dept. 1951)—§ 14.98, n. 2.

Sindell v. Abbott Laboratories, 163 Cal. Rptr. 132, 607 P.2d 924 (Cal.1980)—§ 27.52, n. 4.

Singer v. Fulton County Sheriff, 63 F.3d 110 (2nd Cir.1995)—§ 18.18, n. 5; § 18.25, n. 3, 4.

Singer v. Whitman & Ransom, 83 A.D.2d 862, 442 N.Y.S.2d 26 (N.Y.A.D. 2 Dept. 1981)—§ 28.11, n. 12.

Singer Mfg. Co. v. Granite Spring Water Co., 66 Misc. 595, 123 N.Y.S. 1088 (N.Y.Sup.1910)—§ 1.115, n. 3.

Singleton v. City of New York, 632 F.2d 185 (2nd Cir.1980)—§ 18.38, n. 5, 6.

Singleton, People v., 531 N.Y.S.2d 798, 527 N.E.2d 281 (N.Y.1988)—§ 38.12, n. 6.

Sinha v. Ambach, 91 A.D.2d 703, 457 N.Y.S.2d 603 (N.Y.A.D. 3 Dept.1982)—§ 4.13, n. 4.

Sinistaj, People v., 501 N.Y.S.2d 793, 492 N.E.2d 1209 (N.Y.1986)—§ 33.86, n. 1.

Sinon v. Zoning Bd. of Appeals of Town of Shelter Island, 117 A.D.2d 606, 497 N.Y.S.2d 952 (N.Y.A.D. 2 Dept.1986)—§ 16.119, n. 11.

Siriano v. Beth Israel Hosp. Center, 161 Misc.2d 512, 614 N.Y.S.2d 700 (N.Y.Sup. 1994)—§ 18.15, n. 11.

Sitarski, People v., 222 A.D.2d 1118, 636 N.Y.S.2d 533 (N.Y.A.D. 4 Dept.1995)—§ 38.25, n. 28.

Sivel v. Readers Digest, Inc., 677 F.Supp. 183 (S.D.N.Y.1988)—§ 17.27, n. 10; § 17.34; § 17.34, n. 17.

680 Fifth Ave. Assocs. v. The Mutual Benefit Life Ins. Co. (In re 680 Fifth Ave. Associates), 29 F.3d 95 (2nd Cir.1994)—§ 9.156, n. 1.

680 Fifth Ave. Associates, In re, 156 B.R. 726 (Bkrtcy.S.D.N.Y.1993)—§ 9.101, n. 8.

641 Ave. of Americas Ltd. Partnership v. 641 Associates, Ltd., 189 B.R. 583 (S.D.N.Y.1995)—§ 9.66, n. 4; § 9.69, n. 3.

600 West 115th Street Corp. v. Von Gutfeld, 589 N.Y.S.2d 825, 603 N.E.2d 930 (N.Y.1992)—§ 18.82, n. 3.

6–8 Pelham Parkway Corp. v. Rusciano & Son Corp., 170 A.D.2d 497, 565 N.Y.S.2d 843 (N.Y.A.D. 2 Dept.1991)—§ 16.116, n. 6.

61 West 62nd Owners Corp. v. Harkness Apartment Owners Corp., 173 A.D.2d 372, 570 N.Y.S.2d 8 (N.Y.A.D. 1 Dept. 1991)—§ 13.51, n. 14.

67 Liquor Shop v. O'Connell, 273 A.D. 68, 75 N.Y.S.2d 411 (N.Y.A.D. 1 Dept. 1947)—§ 36.62, n. 2.

S. & J. Pharmacies, Inc. v. Axelrod, 91 A.D.2d 1131, 458 N.Y.S.2d 728 (N.Y.A.D. 3 Dept.1983)—§ 4.12, n. 10.

Skelly v. Visiting Nurse Ass'n of Capital Region Inc., 210 A.D.2d 683, 619 N.Y.S.2d 879 (N.Y.A.D. 3 Dept.1994)—§ 17.34, n. 6, 11.

Skinner, Matter of, 171 Misc.2d 551, 655 N.Y.S.2d 311 (N.Y.Sup.1997)—§ 22.61, n. 1.

Skinner, People v., 200 A.D.2d 782, 606 N.Y.S.2d 792 (N.Y.A.D. 3 Dept.1994)—§ 38.6; § 38.6, n. 6, 8.

Skinner, People v., 154 A.D.2d 216, 552 N.Y.S.2d 932 (N.Y.A.D. 1 Dept.1990)—§ 38.6; § 38.10, n. 86.

Skinner v. Smith, 134 N.Y. 240, 31 N.E. 911 (N.Y.1892)—§ 1.12, n. 8.

Sklarin v. Sklarin, 86 A.D.2d 606, 447 N.Y.S.2d 681 (N.Y.A.D. 2 Dept.1982)—§ 37.37, n. 48.

Sky Acres Aviation Services, Inc. v. Styles Aviation, Inc., 210 A.D.2d 393, 620 N.Y.S.2d 442 (N.Y.A.D. 2 Dept.1994)—§ 5.31, n. 6.

Skywark v. Isaacson, 202 B.R. 557 (S.D.N.Y.1996)—§ 28.12, n. 12.

Slagsvol v. Schneck, 213 A.D.2d 537, 624 N.Y.S.2d 182 (N.Y.A.D. 2 Dept.1995)—§ 21.50, n. 1.

Slamow v. Del Col, 584 N.Y.S.2d 424, 594 N.E.2d 918 (N.Y.1992)—§ 28.29, n. 13.

Slank v. Sam Dell's Dodge Corp., 46 A.D.2d 445, 363 N.Y.S.2d 138 (N.Y.A.D. 4 Dept. 1975)—§ 7.28, n. 7; § 7.59.

Slankard v. Chahinian, 204 A.D.2d 529, 611 N.Y.S.2d 300 (N.Y.A.D. 2 Dept.1994)—§ 21.55, n. 3.

Slater, In re, 8 A.D.2d 169, 186 N.Y.S.2d 558 (N.Y.A.D. 1 Dept.1959)—§ 20.45, n. 10.

TABLE OF CASES

Slavin v. Berlin, 172 A.D.2d 514, 568 N.Y.S.2d 334 (N.Y.A.D. 2 Dept.1991)—§ **37.37, n. 26.**

Sleasman v. Sherwood, 212 A.D.2d 868, 622 N.Y.S.2d 360 (N.Y.A.D. 3 Dept.1995)—§ **37.29, n. 37.**

Sloan, People v., 583 N.Y.S.2d 176, 592 N.E.2d 784 (N.Y.1992)—§ **38.19, n. 109.**

Sloan v. Pinafore Homes Inc., 34 A.D.2d 681, 310 N.Y.S.2d 731 (N.Y.A.D. 2 Dept. 1970)—§ **12.29, n. 4.**

Sloan v. United States, 31 F.2d 902 (8th Cir.1929)—§ **19.16, n. 8.**

Slominski v. Codd, 83 Misc.2d 260, 372 N.Y.S.2d 294 (N.Y.Sup.1975)—§ **4.81, n. 6.**

Smaldone, People v., 213 A.D.2d 685, 624 N.Y.S.2d 200 (N.Y.A.D. 2 Dept.1995)—§ **38.19, n. 48.**

Small v. Moss, 279 N.Y. 288, 18 N.E.2d 281 (N.Y.1938)—§ **16.91, n. 2, 7.**

Smalls, People v., 638 N.Y.S.2d 609, 661 N.E.2d 1392 (N.Y.1995)—§ **38.19, n. 140.**

Smallwood-El v. Coughlin, 589 F.Supp. 692 (S.D.N.Y.1984)—§ **18.18, n. 3.**

Smerling v. Smerling, 177 A.D.2d 429, 576 N.Y.S.2d 271 (N.Y.A.D. 1 Dept.1991)—§ **21.42, n. 6.**

Smiley, In re, 369 N.Y.S.2d 87, 330 N.E.2d 53 (N.Y.1975)—§ **37.48, n. 2.**

Smith, In re, 190 B.R. 753 (Bkrtcy.E.D.N.Y. 1996)—§ **9.198, n. 2.**

Smith, In re, 77 B.R. 496 (Bkrtcy.E.D.Pa. 1987)—§ **9.174, n. 7, 8.**

Smith v. Boscov's Dept. Store, 192 A.D.2d 949, 596 N.Y.S.2d 575 (N.Y.A.D. 3 Dept. 1993)—§ **28.33; § 28.33, n. 6.**

Smith v. Coughlin, 748 F.2d 783 (2nd Cir. 1984)—§ **18.18, n. 12.**

Smith v. D.A. Schulte, Inc., 280 A.D. 913, 116 N.Y.S.2d 212 (N.Y.A.D. 1 Dept. 1952)—§ **30.5, n. 14.**

Smith v. Fishkill Health-Related Center, Inc., 169 A.D.2d 309, 572 N.Y.S.2d 762 (N.Y.A.D. 3 Dept.1991)—§ **29.11, n. 6.**

Smith v. Hooker Chemical & Plastics Corp., 517 N.Y.S.2d 938, 511 N.E.2d 81 (N.Y. 1987)—§ **37.23, n. 2.**

Smith v. Hub Mfg. Inc., 634 F.Supp. 1505 (N.D.N.Y.1986)—§ **27.10, n. 1.**

Smith v. Jansen, 85 Misc.2d 81, 379 N.Y.S.2d 254 (N.Y.Sup.1975)—§ **3.17, n. 4; § 3.19, n. 5.**

Smith v. Long Island Jewish-Hillside Medical Center, 118 A.D.2d 553, 499 N.Y.S.2d 167 (N.Y.A.D. 2 Dept.1986)—§ **18.64, n. 9.**

Smith v. New York State Elec. and Gas Corp., 155 A.D.2d 850, 548 N.Y.S.2d 117 (N.Y.A.D. 3 Dept.1989)—§ **17.33, n. 5.**

Smith v. Peerless Glass Co., 259 N.Y. 292, 181 N.E. 576 (N.Y.1932)—§ **27.29, n. 1.**

Smith, People v., 601 N.Y.S.2d 466, 619 N.E.2d 403 (N.Y.1993)—§ **33.78, n. 3; § 33.88, n. 1.**

Smith, People v., 182 A.D.2d 725, 582 N.Y.S.2d 454 (N.Y.A.D. 2 Dept.1992)—§ **38.10, n. 43.**

Smith, People v., 171 A.D.2d 1060, 569 N.Y.S.2d 243 (N.Y.A.D. 4 Dept.1991)—§ **38.8, n. 219.**

Smith, People v., 540 N.Y.S.2d 987, 538 N.E.2d 339 (N.Y.1989)—§ **38.19, n. 28, 34.**

Smith, People v., 120 A.D.2d 753, 503 N.Y.S.2d 72 (N.Y.A.D. 2 Dept.1986)—§ **38.21, n. 5.**

Smith, People v., 479 N.Y.S.2d 706, 468 N.E.2d 879 (N.Y.1984)—§ **38.8, n. 92.**

Smith, People v., 86 A.D.2d 251, 450 N.Y.S.2d 57 (N.Y.A.D. 3 Dept.1982)—§ **4.4, n. 2.**

Smith, People v., 62 A.D.2d 1043, 404 N.Y.S.2d 48 (N.Y.A.D. 2 Dept.1978)—§ **37.29, n. 40.**

Smith, People v., 93 Misc.2d 326, 402 N.Y.S.2d 766 (N.Y.Co.Ct.1978)—§ **38.58, n. 3.**

Smith, People v., 41 A.D.2d 893, 342 N.Y.S.2d 513 (N.Y.A.D. 4 Dept.1973)—§ **38.8, n. 156.**

Smith, People v., 234 A.D. 728, 251 N.Y.S. 999 (N.Y.A.D. 4 Dept.1931)—§ **38.19; § 38.26, n. 21.**

Smith, People ex rel. v. Flagg, 17 N.Y. 584 (N.Y.1857)—§ **3.25, n. 8.**

Smith v. Putnam, 145 A.D.2d 383, 535 N.Y.S.2d 725 (N.Y.A.D. 1 Dept.1988)—§ **30.39, n. 3.**

Smith v. Russell Sage College, 445 N.Y.S.2d 68, 429 N.E.2d 746 (N.Y.1981)—§ **8.3, n. 5; § 18.37, n. 10.**

Smith v. Slocum, 71 A.D.2d 1058, 420 N.Y.S.2d 814 (N.Y.A.D. 4 Dept.1979)—§ **12.9, n. 7.**

Smith v. Stark, 499 N.Y.S.2d 922, 490 N.E.2d 841 (N.Y.1986)—§ **28.16, n. 6.**

Smith v. State, 65 Misc. 376, 118 N.Y.S. 780 (N.Y.Sup.1909)—§ **10.91, n. 2.**

Smith v. The Affinity Group (In re Morgan), 145 B.R. 760 (Bkrtcy.N.D.N.Y. 1992)—§ **9.49, n. 1.**

Smith v. Town of Warwick, 71 A.D.2d 618, 418 N.Y.S.2d 141 (N.Y.A.D. 2 Dept. 1979)—§ **12.9, n. 7.**

Smith v. Van Gorkom, 488 A.2d 858 (Del. Supr.1985)—§ **1.66, n. 12.**

Smithback v. Sullivan, 899 F.2d 698 (7th Cir.1990)—§ **34.24, n. 2.**

Smith, Estate of v. Commssioner, 79 T.C. 313 (U.S.Tax Ct.1982)—§ **23.118, n. 3.**

TABLE OF CASES

Smithline v. Monica, 1987 WL 14296 (N.Y.City Ct.1987)—§ **13.32, n. 13.**

Smith's Estate, In re, 243 A.D. 348, 276 N.Y.S. 646 (N.Y.A.D. 4 Dept.1935)—§ **24.63, n. 2.**

Snay v. Wood, 50 A.D.2d 651, 374 N.Y.S.2d 809 (N.Y.A.D. 3 Dept.1975)—§ **12.9, n. 8.**

Snell v. Remington Paper Co., 102 A.D. 138, 92 N.Y.S. 343 (N.Y.A.D. 4 Dept.1905)—§ **30.27, n. 6.**

Snell v. Timmerman, 67 A.D.2d 1096, 415 N.Y.S.2d 152 (N.Y.A.D. 4 Dept.1979)—§ **11.48, n. 6.**

Snow v. Snow, 209 A.D.2d 399, 618 N.Y.S.2d 442 (N.Y.A.D. 2 Dept.1994)—§ **21.63, n. 2.**

Snyder, Matter of, 56 B.R. 1007 (N.D.Ind. 1986)—§ **9.161, n. 10.**

Snyder v. Bio-Lab, Inc., 94 Misc.2d 816, 405 N.Y.S.2d 596 (N.Y.Sup.1978)—§ **30.18, n. 3.**

Snyder v. Parke, Davis & Co., 56 A.D.2d 536, 391 N.Y.S.2d 579 (N.Y.A.D. 1 Dept. 1977)—§ **27.38, n. 1, 3.**

Snyder, People v., 40 A.D.2d 754, 337 N.Y.S.2d 796 (N.Y.A.D. 4 Dept.1972)—§ **38.21, n. 46.**

Snyder v. Wetzler, 620 N.Y.S.2d 813, 644 N.E.2d 1369 (N.Y.1994)—§ **37.37, n. 70;** § **39.27, n. 8.**

Soares v. Brockton Credit Union (In re Soares), 107 F.3d 969 (1st Cir.1997)—§ **9.52, n. 6.**

Soares v. State of Conn., 8 F.3d 917 (2nd Cir.1993)—§ **18.32, n. 5.**

Sobania v. Secretary of Health & Human Services, 879 F.2d 441 (8th Cir.1989)—§ **34.47, n. 21.**

Sobieskoda, People v., 235 N.Y. 411, 139 N.E. 558 (N.Y.1923)—§ **38.19;** § **38.19, n. 130.**

Sobotker, People v., 471 N.Y.S.2d 78, 459 N.E.2d 187 (N.Y.1984)—§ **38.8, n. 161.**

Sobotker, People v., 402 N.Y.S.2d 993, 373 N.E.2d 1218 (N.Y.1978)—§ **33.5;** § **33.5, n. 4;** § **33.6, n. 1.**

Sochor v. International Business Machines Corp., 469 N.Y.S.2d 591, 457 N.E.2d 696 (N.Y.1983)—§ **8.19, n. 9.**

Societa Mutuo Soccorso San Rocco Fra I Cittadini De Palo Colle Bari, In re, 255 A.D. 815, 7 N.Y.S.2d 337 (N.Y.A.D. 2 Dept.1938)—§ **1.43, n. 21.**

Societe Generale v. Charles & Co. Acquisition, Inc., 157 Misc.2d 643, 597 N.Y.S.2d 1004 (N.Y.Sup.1993)—§ **11.9, n. 8, 10.**

Society for Ethical Culture in City of New York v. Spatt, 434 N.Y.S.2d 932, 415 N.E.2d 922 (N.Y.1980)—§ **16.127, n. 10.**

Society of New York Hosp. v. Del Vecchio, 518 N.Y.S.2d 781, 512 N.E.2d 302 (N.Y. 1987)—§ **16.113, n. 3.**

Society of New York Hospital v. Burstein, 22 A.D.2d 768, 253 N.Y.S.2d 753 (N.Y.A.D. 1 Dept.1964)—§ **37.27, n. 1.**

Society of New York Hospital v. Johnson, 180 N.Y.S.2d 287, 154 N.E.2d 550 (N.Y. 1958)—§ **14.4, n. 13.**

Society of Plastics Industry, Inc. v. County of Suffolk, 570 N.Y.S.2d 778, 573 N.E.2d 1034 (N.Y.1991)—§ **4.69, n. 5, 8;** § **15.6, n. 8;** § **16.48, n. 4, 12.**

Sofair v. State University of New York Upstate Medical Center College of Medicine, 406 N.Y.S.2d 276, 377 N.E.2d 730 (N.Y.1978)—§ **37.37, n. 67;** § **39.27, n. 3.**

Sogg v. American Airlines, Inc., 612 N.Y.S.2d 106, 634 N.E.2d 602 (N.Y. 1994)—§ **39.5, n. 4.**

Sogg v. American Airlines, Inc., 193 A.D.2d 153, 603 N.Y.S.2d 21 (N.Y.A.D. 1 Dept. 1993)—§ **37.28, n. 6.**

Sohn v. Calderon, 579 N.Y.S.2d 940, 587 N.E.2d 807 (N.Y.1991)—§ **4.73, n. 2.**

Sohns v. Little Prince Productions, Ltd., 791 F.Supp. 88 (S.D.N.Y.1992)—§ **28.3, n. 2.**

Soho Community Council v. New York State Liquor Authority, N.Y.L.J., 1/28/97 p.25, col.6 (Sup.Ct., N.Y. County)—§ **36.9, n. 7.**

Solack Estates, Inc. v. Goodman, 102 Misc.2d 504, 425 N.Y.S.2d 906 (N.Y.Sup. App.Term 1979)—§ **13.12, n. 6;** § **13.66, n. 4.**

Solnick v. Whalen, 425 N.Y.S.2d 68, 401 N.E.2d 190 (N.Y.1980)—§ **3.32, n. 8.**

Solomon, In re, 67 F.3d 1128 (4th Cir. 1995)—§ **9.252, n. 2;** § **9.255, n. 8.**

Solomon, People v., 124 Misc.2d 33, 475 N.Y.S.2d 749 (N.Y.Dist.Ct.1984)—§ **33.75, n. 2;** § **33.83;** § **33.83, n. 2.**

Solomon v. Stroler, 82 A.D.2d 756, 440 N.Y.S.2d 200 (N.Y.A.D. 1 Dept.1981)—§ **30.5, n. 15.**

Solow v. Bethlehem Steel Corp., 204 A.D.2d 227, 612 N.Y.S.2d 402 (N.Y.A.D. 1 Dept. 1994)—§ **8.24, n. 1.**

Solow v. City of New York, 49 A.D.2d 414, 375 N.Y.S.2d 356 (N.Y.A.D. 1 Dept. 1975)—§ **16.110, n. 1.**

Solow v. City of New York, 25 A.D.2d 442, 266 N.Y.S.2d 823 (N.Y.A.D. 2 Dept. 1966)—§ **3.7, n. 14.**

Solow v. W.R. Grace & Co., 610 N.Y.S.2d 128, 632 N.E.2d 437 (N.Y.1994)—§ **28.21, n. 5.**

Solow v. W.R. Grace & Co., 193 A.D.2d 459, 597 N.Y.S.2d 361 (N.Y.A.D. 1 Dept. 1993)—§ **28.21;** § **28.21, n. 1, 2, 8.**

TABLE OF CASES

Soma Realty Co. v. Romeo, 31 Misc.2d 20, 220 N.Y.S.2d 752 (N.Y.Sup.1961)—§ 12.67; § 12.67, n. 3.

Sommer v. Kaufman, 59 A.D.2d 843, 399 N.Y.S.2d 7 (N.Y.A.D. 1 Dept.1977)—§ 17.29, n. 14.

Sommer v. Sommer, 176 A.D.2d 1022, 575 N.Y.S.2d 178 (N.Y.A.D. 3 Dept.1991)—§ 21.43, n. 13; § 21.44, n. 13.

Sonkin Associates, Inc. v. Columbian Mut. Life Ins. Co., 150 A.D.2d 764, 541 N.Y.S.2d 611 (N.Y.A.D. 2 Dept.1989)—§ 31.18, n. 5.

Sonnax Industries Inc. v. Tri Component Products Corp. (In re Sonnax Industries, Inc.), 907 F.2d 1280 (2nd Cir.1990)—§ 9.52, n. 6; § 9.53, n. 9.

Sontag v. Sontag, 498 N.Y.S.2d 133, 488 N.E.2d 1245 (N.Y.1986)—§ 39.4, n. 8, 9.

Sorel v. Iacobucci, 221 A.D.2d 852, 633 N.Y.S.2d 688 (N.Y.A.D. 3 Dept.1995)—§ 37.29, n. 38; § 37.65, n. 48.

Sotelo, People v., 176 A.D.2d 458, 574 N.Y.S.2d 360 (N.Y.A.D. 1 Dept.1991)—§ 38.19, n. 45.

Soto v. Brooklyn Correctional Facility, 80 F.3d 34 (2nd Cir.1996)—§ 18.38, n. 3.

Soto v. Montanez, 201 A.D.2d 876, 608 N.Y.S.2d 37 (N.Y.A.D. 4 Dept.1994)—§ 37.37, n. 23, 37; § 37.43, n. 10.

Soto v. Soto, 216 A.D.2d 455, 628 N.Y.S.2d 391 (N.Y.A.D. 2 Dept.1995)—§ 21.20, n. 5.

Soto v. State Farm Ins. Co., 613 N.Y.S.2d 352, 635 N.E.2d 1222 (N.Y.1994)—§ 30.34, n. 7; § 31.17, n. 7.

Soucy v. Greyhound Corp., 27 A.D.2d 112, 276 N.Y.S.2d 173 (N.Y.A.D. 3 Dept.1967)—§ 30.33, n. 2.

Soules v. United States Dept. of Housing and Urban Development, 967 F.2d 817 (2nd Cir.1992)—§ 18.49, n. 18.

Southcroft Co. v. Konopko, 128 Misc.2d 179, 488 N.Y.S.2d 1011 (N.Y.City Civ.Ct.1985)—§ 13.18, n. 19.

South-Eastern Underwriters Ass'n, United States v., 322 U.S. 533, 64 S.Ct. 1162, 88 L.Ed. 1440 (1944)—§ 31.24, n. 2.

South Ferry Bldg. Co. v. 44 Wall Street Fund, Inc., 142 Misc.2d 54, 535 N.Y.S.2d 685 (N.Y.City Civ.Ct.1988)—§ 13.27, n. 1.

South Gwinnett Venture v. Pruitt, 491 F.2d 5 (5th Cir.1974)—§ 16.18, n. 26.

South Street Seaport Limited Partnership & Burger Boys (In re Burger Boys, Inc.), 94 F.3d 755 (2nd Cir.1996)—§ 9.77, n. 1.

Southwest Oil Co. of Jourdanton, Inc., In re, 84 B.R. 448 (Bkrtcy.W.D.Tex.1987)—§ 9.142, n. 5.

Spadaccini v. Dolan, 63 A.D.2d 110, 407 N.Y.S.2d 840 (N.Y.A.D. 1 Dept.1978)—§ 30.13, n. 7; § 30.14, n. 18.

Spadanuta v. Incorporated Village of Rockville Centre, 20 A.D.2d 799, 248 N.Y.S.2d 405 (N.Y.A.D. 2 Dept.1964)—§ 3.32, n. 19.

Spadorcio, People v., 247 A.D. 862, 288 N.Y.S. 882 (N.Y.A.D. 4 Dept.1936)—§ 38.26, n. 21.

Spahn v. Julian Messner, Inc., 286 N.Y.S.2d 832, 233 N.E.2d 840 (N.Y.1967)—§ 18.64, n. 23.

Sparacino v. Pawtucket Mut. Ins. Co., 50 F.3d 141 (2nd Cir.1995)—§ 31.10, n. 7.

Spatz v. Wide World Travel Service Inc., 70 A.D.2d 835, 418 N.Y.S.2d 19 (N.Y.A.D. 1 Dept.1979)—§ 26.43, n. 13.

Spears v. Berle, 422 N.Y.S.2d 636, 397 N.E.2d 1304 (N.Y.1979)—§ 14.14, n. 4; § 14.38, n. 12.

Specialty Equipment Companies, Inc., Matter of, 3 F.3d 1043 (7th Cir.1993)—§ 9.170, n. 4.

Spectrum Systems Intern. Corp. v. Chemical Bank, 575 N.Y.S.2d 809, 581 N.E.2d 1055 (N.Y.1991)—§ 26.42, n. 1.

Speed v. Avis Rent-A-Car, 172 A.D.2d 267, 568 N.Y.S.2d 90 (N.Y.A.D. 1 Dept.1991)—§ 27.34; § 27.34, n. 7.

Spellman, Commissioner v., N.Y.L.J., 2/11/97, p.26, col.3 (Sup.Ct., New York County)—§ 23.80, n. 4.

Spence-Chapin Adoption Service, People ex rel. Scarpetta v., 321 N.Y.S.2d 65, 269 N.E.2d 787 (N.Y.1971)—§ 20.64; § 20.64, n. 3.

Spencer v. Faulkner, 65 Misc.2d 298, 317 N.Y.S.2d 374 (N.Y.City Civ.Ct.1971)—§ 13.37, n. 3.

Sperling, People v., 165 Misc.2d 1024, 631 N.Y.S.2d 221 (N.Y.Dist.Ct.1995)—§ 33.17, n. 4.

Spicer v. Holihan, 158 A.D.2d 459, 550 N.Y.S.2d 943 (N.Y.A.D. 2 Dept.1990)—§ 16.68, n. 5.

Spiegel v. Metropolitan Life Ins. Co., 188 N.Y.S.2d 486, 160 N.E.2d 40 (N.Y.1959)—§ 31.6, n. 10.

Spiegel, Inc. v. F.T.C., 540 F.2d 287 (7th Cir.1976)—§ 7.39, n. 7.

Spiegelman, People v., 142 Misc.2d 617, 537 N.Y.S.2d 964 (N.Y.Vill.Ct.1989)—§ 33.16; § 33.16, n. 3.

Spillman v. City of Rochester, 132 A.D.2d 1008, 518 N.Y.S.2d 475 (N.Y.A.D. 4 Dept.1987)—§ 37.80, n. 2.

Spingarn, Matter of, 164 Misc.2d 891, 626 N.Y.S.2d 650 (N.Y.Sup.1995)—§ 22.39, n. 1, 3.

Spitz v. Lesser, 302 N.Y. 490, 99 N.E.2d 540 (N.Y.1951)—§ 30.20, n. 2.

TABLE OF CASES

Spivey, People v., 599 N.Y.S.2d 477, 615 N.E.2d 961 (N.Y.1993)—§ **38.19, n. 105.**

Spodek v. New York State Com'r of Taxation and Finance, 628 N.Y.S.2d 256, 651 N.E.2d 1275 (N.Y.1995)—§ **37.90, n. 3.**

Sporza v. German Sav. Bank, 192 N.Y. 8, 84 N.E. 406 (N.Y.1908)—§ **22.4, n. 6.**

Spose v. Ragu Foods, Inc., 142 Misc.2d 366, 537 N.Y.S.2d 739 (N.Y.Sup.1989)— § **30.10, n. 9.**

Springs v. James, 137 A.D. 110, 121 N.Y.S. 1054 (N.Y.A.D. 1 Dept.1910)—§ **5.8, n. 4.**

Spring Valley, In re Village of, 189 Misc. 324, 71 N.Y.S.2d 848 (N.Y.1947)—§ **3.3, n. 8; § 3.4, n. 7.**

Sprinzen, Matter of, 415 N.Y.S.2d 974, 389 N.E.2d 456 (N.Y.1979)—§ **5.11, n. 4.**

Sranko, People v., 210 A.D. 812, 205 N.Y.S. 944 (N.Y.A.D. 4 Dept.1924)—§ **38.20, n. 6.**

SRW Associates v. Bellport Beach Property Owners, 129 A.D.2d 328, 517 N.Y.S.2d 741 (N.Y.A.D. 2 Dept.1987)—§ **17.29, n. 1.**

Staatsburg Water Co. v. Staatsburg Fire Dist., 531 N.Y.S.2d 876, 527 N.E.2d 754 (N.Y.1988)—§ **4.25, n. 2; § 4.73, n. 1.**

Stackhouse by Stackhouse v. New York City Health and Hospitals Corp., 179 A.D.2d 357, 577 N.Y.S.2d 833 (N.Y.A.D. 1 Dept. 1992)—§ **37.29, n. 19.**

Stafford v. Village of Sands Point, 200 Misc. 57, 102 N.Y.S.2d 910 (N.Y.Sup.1951)— § **16.120, n. 3.**

St. Agatha Home for Children, People v., 416 N.Y.S.2d 577, 389 N.E.2d 1098 (N.Y. 1979)—§ **16.24, n. 5; § 16.128, n. 11.**

St. Agnes Cemetery v. State, 163 N.Y.S.2d 655, 143 N.E.2d 377 (N.Y.1957)— § **14.96, n. 2.**

Staiano, Matter of, 160 Misc.2d 494, 609 N.Y.S.2d 1021 (N.Y.Sup.1994)—§ **22.19, n. 1; § 22.20, n. 8.**

Staiano, Matter of, N.Y.L.J., 5/13/94 p.36, col.4 (Sup.Ct., Suffolk County)—§ **22.34, n. 7.**

Standard Acc. Ins. Co. v. Newman, 2 Misc.2d 348, 47 N.Y.S.2d 804 (N.Y.Sup. 1944)—§ **30.12, n. 7, 8.**

Standard Oil Co. of New York v. Central Dredging Co., 225 A.D. 407, 233 N.Y.S. 279 (N.Y.A.D. 3 Dept.1929)—§ **30.21, n. 1.**

Standard Oil Co. of New York, People ex rel. v. Law, 237 N.Y. 142, 142 N.E. 446 (N.Y.1923)—§ **35.20, n. 1.**

Stanford v. Union Labor Life Ins. Co., 74 Misc.2d 781, 345 N.Y.S.2d 928 (N.Y.Sup. 1973)—§ **24.64, n. 4.**

Stanley, In re, 185 B.R. 417 (Bkrtcy. D.Conn.1995)—§ **9.162, n. 10.**

Stanley v. Illinois, 405 U.S. 645, 92 S.Ct. 1208, 31 L.Ed.2d 551 (1972)—§ **20.30; § 20.30, n. 1.**

Stanton v. United States, 512 F.2d 13 (3rd Cir.1975)—§ **1.34, n. 30.**

Stark, Matter of, 174 A.D.2d 746, 571 N.Y.S.2d 772 (N.Y.A.D. 2 Dept.1991)— § **22.27, n. 3.**

Star Plaza, Inc. v. State, 79 A.D.2d 746, 434 N.Y.S.2d 804 (N.Y.A.D. 3 Dept.1980)— § **14.87, n. 1.**

Starr L.B., Matter of, 130 Misc.2d 599, 497 N.Y.S.2d 597 (N.Y.Fam.Ct.1985)— § **20.38, n. 5.**

State v. ____(see opposing party)

State by Abrams v. Ford Motor Co., 549 N.Y.S.2d 368, 548 N.E.2d 906 (N.Y. 1989)—§ **7.10, n. 18.**

State by Lefkowitz v. Colorado State Christian College of Church of Inner Power, Inc., 76 Misc.2d 50, 346 N.Y.S.2d 482 (N.Y.Sup.1973)—§ **7.45, n. 4; § 7.46, n. 7.**

State Division of Human Rights v. Carnation Co., 397 N.Y.S.2d 781, 366 N.E.2d 869 (N.Y.1977)—§ **17.56, n. 5.**

State Division of Human Rights v. Kilian Mfg. Corp., 360 N.Y.S.2d 603, 318 N.E.2d 770 (N.Y.1974)—§ **17.59, n. 9.**

State Div. of Human Rights v. Muia, 176 A.D.2d 1142, 575 N.Y.S.2d 957 (N.Y.A.D. 3 Dept.1991)—§ **18.49, n. 10.**

State Div. of Human Rights on Complaint of Maymi v. Sorrento Cheese Co., Inc., 115 A.D.2d 323, 495 N.Y.S.2d 865 (N.Y.A.D. 4 Dept.1985)—§ **17.41, n. 3.**

State ex rel. v. ____(see opposing party and relator)

State Farm Ins. Co. v. Brosnan, 220 A.D.2d 599, 632 N.Y.S.2d 628 (N.Y.A.D. 2 Dept. 1995)—§ **31.16, n. 6.**

State Farm Mut. Auto. Ins. Co. v. Isler, 38 A.D.2d 966, 331 N.Y.S.2d 547 (N.Y.A.D. 2 Dept.1972)—§ **26.24, n. 11.**

State Farm Mut. Auto. Ins. Co. v. Romero, 109 A.D.2d 786, 486 N.Y.S.2d 297 (N.Y.A.D. 2 Dept.1985)—§ **26.25, n. 1.**

State Farm Mut. Auto. Ins. Co. v. Taglianetti, 122 A.D.2d 40, 504 N.Y.S.2d 476 (N.Y.A.D. 2 Dept.1986)—§ **26.24, n. 11.**

State Farm Mut. Ins. Co. v. Donath, 164 A.D.2d 889, 559 N.Y.S.2d 567 (N.Y.A.D. 2 Dept.1990)—§ **26.24, n. 11.**

State of (see name of state)

State Tax Commission v. Shor, 400 N.Y.S.2d 805, 371 N.E.2d 523 (N.Y. 1977)—§ **8.19, n. 7; § 12.37; § 12.37, n. 2.**

Stathatos v. Arnold Bernstein S S Corp, 87 F.Supp. 1007 (S.D.N.Y.1950)—§ **31.24, n. 8.**

TABLE OF CASES

Statler v. George A. Ray Mfg. Co., 195 N.Y. 478, 88 N.E. 1063 (N.Y.1909)—§ **27.3; § 27.3, n. 3.**

Steadman, People v., 603 N.Y.S.2d 382, 623 N.E.2d 509 (N.Y.1993)—§ **38.19; § 38.19, n. 97, 139.**

Steer Inn Realty Corp. v. Bowen, 52 Misc.2d 963, 277 N.Y.S.2d 231 (N.Y.Dist. Ct.1967)—§ **13.58, n. 3.**

Steigerwald v. Dean Witter Reynolds, Inc., 107 A.D.2d 1026, 486 N.Y.S.2d 516 (N.Y.A.D. 4 Dept.1985)—§ **17.27, n. 8.**

Stein v. American Mortg. Banking, Ltd., 216 A.D.2d 458, 628 N.Y.S.2d 162 (N.Y.A.D. 2 Dept.1995)—§ **11.43, n. 4.**

Stein v. Nellen Development Corp., 123 Misc.2d 268, 473 N.Y.S.2d 331 (N.Y.Sup. 1984)—§ **11.6, n. 3.**

Stein v. Yonkers Contracting, ___ A.D.2d ___, 664 N.Y.S.2d 332 (2d Dept 1997)—§ **32.15, n. 10.**

Steinberg, In re, 121 A.D.2d 872, 503 N.Y.S.2d 795 (N.Y.A.D. 1 Dept.1986)—§ **22.32; § 22.32, n. 7, 8.**

Steinberg v. Monasch, 85 A.D.2d 403, 448 N.Y.S.2d 200 (N.Y.A.D. 1 Dept.1982)—§ **30.31, n. 2.**

Steinberg's Estate, In re, 208 Misc. 135, 143 N.Y.S.2d 341 (N.Y.Sur.1955)—§ **25.46, n. 10.**

Steinhilber v. Alphonse, 508 N.Y.S.2d 901, 501 N.E.2d 550 (N.Y.1986)—§ **18.27, n. 5.**

Steitz v. Gifford, 280 N.Y. 15, 19 N.E.2d 661 (N.Y.1939)—§ **30.6, n. 3.**

Stempler, Application of, 110 Misc.2d 174, 441 N.Y.S.2d 800 (N.Y.Sup.1981)—§ **18.71, n. 2.**

Stempler v. Stempler, 200 A.D.2d 733, 607 N.Y.S.2d 111 (N.Y.A.D. 2 Dept.1994)—§ **21.69, n. 2; § 21.70, n. 2.**

Stephanie L. v. Benjamin L., 158 Misc.2d 665, 602 N.Y.S.2d 80 (N.Y.Sup.1993)—§ **18.27, n. 8.**

Stephan Joseph S., Matter of, 158 A.D.2d 524, 551 N.Y.S.2d 289 (N.Y.A.D. 2 Dept. 1990)—§ **20.31, n. 1; § 20.75, n. 3.**

Stephens v. American Home Assur. Co., 811 F.Supp. 937 (S.D.N.Y.1993)—§ **31.18, n. 1.**

Stephens Industries, Inc. v. McClung, 789 F.2d 386 (6th Cir.1986)—§ **9.62, n. 4.**

Sterling Products Corporation v. Sterling Products, 43 F.Supp. 548 (S.D.N.Y. 1942)—§ **1.13, n. 16.**

Stern v. Delphi Internet Services Corp., 165 Misc.2d 21, 626 N.Y.S.2d 694 (N.Y.Sup. 1995)—§ **18.64, n. 16.**

Stern v. Morgenthau, 476 N.Y.S.2d 810, 465 N.E.2d 349 (N.Y.1984)—§ **4.63, n. 8.**

Sternaman v. Metropolitan Life Ins. Co., 170 N.Y. 13, 62 N.E. 763 (N.Y.1902)—§ **5.6, n. 3, 4.**

Sternberg v. Foreign Cars of New Paltz, Inc., 140 A.D.2d 822, 528 N.Y.S.2d 209 (N.Y.A.D. 3 Dept.1988)—§ **37.65; § 37.65, n. 57.**

Sternberg v. Gardstein, 120 A.D.2d 93, 508 N.Y.S.2d 14 (N.Y.A.D. 2 Dept.1986)—§ **29.26, n. 11.**

Sternheim v. Silver Bell of Roslyn, Inc., 66 Misc.2d 726, 321 N.Y.S.2d 965 (N.Y.City Civ.Ct.1971)—§ **5.21; § 5.21, n. 3.**

Stevens v. Episcopal Church History Co., 140 A.D. 570, 125 N.Y.S. 573 (N.Y.A.D. 1 Dept.1910)—§ **1.21, n. 28.**

Stevens v. Halstead, 181 A.D. 198, 168 N.Y.S. 142 (N.Y.A.D. 2 Dept.1917)—§ **20.5, n. 2.**

Stevens, People v., 199 A.D.2d 441, 608 N.Y.S.2d 83 (N.Y.A.D. 2 Dept.1993)—§ **38.10, n. 98.**

Stevens v. Smolka, 11 A.D.2d 896, 202 N.Y.S.2d 783 (N.Y.A.D. 4 Dept.1960)—§ **16.124, n. 12.**

Stevens v. Town of Huntington, 283 N.Y.S.2d 16, 229 N.E.2d 591 (N.Y. 1967)—§ **16.85, n. 9.**

Steward, People v., 646 N.Y.S.2d 974, 670 N.E.2d 214 (N.Y.1996)—§ **33.56, n. 7.**

Stewart v. Credit Bureau, Inc., 734 F.2d 47, 236 U.S.App.D.C. 146 (D.C.Cir.1984)—§ **7.33; § 7.33, n. 9.**

Stewart v. Jackson & Nash, 976 F.2d 86 (2nd Cir.1992)—§ **17.27; § 17.27, n. 1, 9.**

Stewart, People v., 144 A.D.2d 601, 534 N.Y.S.2d 439 (N.Y.A.D. 2 Dept.1988)—§ **38.8, n. 225.**

Stewart v. Stewart, 118 A.D.2d 455, 499 N.Y.S.2d 945 (N.Y.A.D. 1 Dept.1986)—§ **37.22, n. 10.**

Stewart Infra-Red Commissary of Massachusetts, Inc. v. Coomey, 661 F.2d 1 (1st Cir.1981)—§ **19.33, n. 4.**

S. T. Grand, Inc. v. City of New York, 344 N.Y.S.2d 938, 298 N.E.2d 105 (N.Y. 1973)—§ **3.25, n. 16, 17.**

Stieberger v. Heckler, 615 F.Supp. 1315 (S.D.N.Y.1985)—§ **34.28, n. 14; § 34.63; § 34.63, n. 2.**

Stieberger v. Sullivan, 801 F.Supp. 1079 (S.D.N.Y.1992)—§ **34.3, n. 10.**

Stier v. Don Mar Operating Co., 33 A.D.2d 816, 305 N.Y.S.2d 397 (N.Y.A.D. 3 Dept. 1969)—§ **11.54, n. 11.**

Stier v. President Hotel, Inc., 28 A.D.2d 795, 281 N.Y.S.2d 140 (N.Y.A.D. 3 Dept. 1967)—§ **13.17, n. 11; § 13.18, n. 26, 27; § 13.44, n. 2.**

TABLE OF CASES

Stile v. City of New York, 172 A.D.2d 743, 569 N.Y.S.2d 129 (N.Y.A.D. 2 Dept. 1991)—§ 18.25, n. 2.

Stipo v. Town of North Castle, 205 A.D.2d 608, 613 N.Y.S.2d 407 (N.Y.A.D. 2 Dept. 1994)—§ 18.9, n. 2.

St. Lawrence County Deputy Sheriffs, Local 2390, Council 82, AFSCME, AFL–CIO on Behalf of Bonno (County of St. Lawrence), Matter of, 213 A.D.2d 875, 623 N.Y.S.2d 661 (N.Y.A.D. 3 Dept.1995)—§ 31.24, n. 9.

St. Louis County Bank v. United States, 674 F.2d 1207 (8th Cir.1982)—§ 24.39, n. 1.

St. Louis Globe–Democrat, Inc., In re, 63 B.R. 131 (Bkrtcy.E.D.Mo.1985)—§ 9.138, n. 1.

St. Luke's–Roosevelt Hosp. Center, Matter of, 653 N.Y.S.2d 257, 675 N.E.2d 1209 (N.Y.1996)—§ 22.28, n. 6, 12, 19.

St. Luke's–Roosevelt Hosp. Center, Application of, 159 Misc.2d 932, 607 N.Y.S.2d 574 (N.Y.Sup.1993)—§ 22.28, n. 6, 11.

St. Mary's Honor Center v. Hicks, 509 U.S. 502, 113 S.Ct. 2742, 125 L.Ed.2d 407 (1993)—§ 17.59, n. 4; § 17.73, n. 2.

STN Enterprises, In re, 779 F.2d 901 (2nd Cir.1985)—§ 9.45, n. 2; § 9.121, n. 2.

Stokes v. United States, Immigration and Naturalization Service, 393 F.Supp. 24 (S.D.N.Y.1975)—§ 19.14, n. 12, 13, 14.

Stoll v. Gottlieb, 305 U.S. 165, 59 S.Ct. 134, 83 L.Ed. 104 (1938)—§ 9.167, n. 2.

Stolz v. Board of Regents of University, 4 A.D.2d 361, 165 N.Y.S.2d 179 (N.Y.A.D. 3 Dept.1957)—§ 37.87, n. 27.

Stone v. Freeman, 298 N.Y. 268, 82 N.E.2d 571 (N.Y.1948)—§ 5.7, n. 7.

Stone v. McGowan, 157 A.D.2d 882, 550 N.Y.S.2d 153 (N.Y.A.D. 3 Dept.1990)—§ 16.49, n. 3.

Stonewall Ins. Co. v. Asbestos Claims Management Corp., 73 F.3d 1178 (2nd Cir. 1995)—§ 31.8, n. 5.

St. Onge v. Donovan, 527 N.Y.S.2d 721, 522 N.E.2d 1019 (N.Y.1988)—§ 16.46, n. 1; § 16.89, n. 2, 4, 9; § 16.90, n. 8.

Storar, Matter of, 438 N.Y.S.2d 266, 420 N.E.2d 64 (N.Y.1981)—§ 22.54, n. 8; § 23.109, n. 3.

Storch's Estate, In re, 53 N.Y.S.2d 409 (N.Y.Sur.1945)—§ 36.4, n. 8; § 36.24, n. 4.

Stork Restaurant v. Boland, 282 N.Y. 256, 26 N.E.2d 247 (N.Y.1940)—§ 4.75, n. 7; § 4.78; § 4.78, n. 5.

Storyk v. Secretary of Health, Ed., and Welfare, 462 F.Supp. 152 (S.D.N.Y.1978)—§ 34.9, n. 17.

Stout, Application of, 1 A.D.2d 901, 149 N.Y.S.2d 897 (N.Y.A.D. 2 Dept.1956)—§ 25.50, n. 6.

Stover, People v., 240 N.Y.S.2d 734, 191 N.E.2d 272 (N.Y.1963)—§ **16.125**; § 16.125, n. 2.

St. Paul Fire & Marine Ins. Co. v. United States Fidelity & Guaranty Co., 404 N.Y.S.2d 552, 375 N.E.2d 733 (N.Y. 1978)—§ 28.44, n. 1; § 31.17, n. 14.

Stranahan v. New York State Tax Commission, 68 A.D.2d 250, 416 N.Y.S.2d 836 (N.Y.A.D. 3 Dept.1979)—§ 35.15, n. 1.

Strang v. Strang, 222 A.D.2d 975, 635 N.Y.S.2d 786 (N.Y.A.D. 3 Dept.1995)—§ 21.44, n. 1.

Stratton Group, Ltd. v. Sprayregen, 466 F.Supp. 1180 (S.D.N.Y.1979)—§ 28.11, n. 4.

Straus, United States ex rel. Mikes v., 853 F.Supp. 115 (S.D.N.Y.1994)—§ 17.64, n. 4.

Straus, United States ex rel. Mikes v., 846 F.Supp. 21 (S.D.N.Y.1994)—§ 17.64, n. 4.

Strausberg, Matter of Guardianship of, 92 Misc.2d 620, 400 N.Y.S.2d 1013 (N.Y.Fam.Ct.1977)—§ 20.39, n. 3.

Strelov v. Hertz Corp., 171 A.D.2d 420, 566 N.Y.S.2d 646 (N.Y.A.D. 1 Dept.1991)—§ 27.33; § 27.33, n. 2.

Stribula v. Wien, 107 Misc.2d 114, 438 N.Y.S.2d 52 (N.Y.Sup.App.Term 1980)—§ 13.51, n. 4.

Strickland, People v., 169 A.D.2d 9, 570 N.Y.S.2d 712 (N.Y.A.D. 3 Dept.1991)—§ 33.53, n. 2.

Stringfellow v. Concerned Neighbors in Action, 480 U.S. 370, 107 S.Ct. 1177, 94 L.Ed.2d 389 (1987)—§ 38.3, n. 14.

Stringile v. Rothman, 142 A.D.2d 637, 530 N.Y.S.2d 838 (N.Y.A.D. 2 Dept.1988)—§ 37.65, n. 38, 41.

Stroman, People v., 373 N.Y.S.2d 548, 335 N.E.2d 853 (N.Y.1975)—§ 38.10, n. 123; § 38.26, n. 10.

Stroock & Stroock & Lavan v. Beltramini, 157 A.D.2d 590, 550 N.Y.S.2d 337 (N.Y.A.D. 1 Dept.1990)—§ 28.12, n. 5.

Strough v. Conley, 257 A.D. 1057, 13 N.Y.S.2d 606 (N.Y.A.D. 3 Dept.1939)—§ 30.24, n. 1.

Strough v. Conley, 164 Misc. 248, 298 N.Y.S. 516 (N.Y.Sup.1937)—§ 30.19, n. 5.

Strudwick, People v., 170 A.D.2d 969, 565 N.Y.S.2d 944 (N.Y.A.D. 4 Dept.1991)—§ 38.6; § 38.6, n. 9.

Stuart v. D & D Associates, 160 A.D.2d 547, 554 N.Y.S.2d 197 (N.Y.A.D. 1 Dept. 1990)—§ 13.71; § 13.71, n. 1.

TABLE OF CASES

Stuart v. Koch (In re Koch), 109 F.3d 1285 (8th Cir.1997)—§ **9.209, n. 9**; § **9.252, n. 2.**

Stuhler v. State, 127 Misc.2d 390, 485 N.Y.S.2d 957 (N.Y.Sup.1985)—§ **8.41, n. 6.**

Sturges Mfg. Co. v. Utica Mut. Ins. Co., 371 N.Y.S.2d 444, 332 N.E.2d 319 (N.Y. 1975)—§ **31.12, n. 9.**

Sturman v. Polito, 161 Misc. 536, 291 N.Y.S. 621 (N.Y.City Ct.1936)—§ **7.24, n. 5.**

St. Vincent's Hosp. and Medical Center of New York v. New York State Div. of Housing and Community Renewal, 109 A.D.2d 711, 487 N.Y.S.2d 36 (N.Y.A.D. 1 Dept.1985)—§ **32.27, n. 7.**

Suderov v. Ogle, 149 Misc.2d 906, 574 N.Y.S.2d 249 (N.Y.Sup.App.Term 1991)—§ **13.26, n. 6.**

Suderov v. Robyn Industries, Inc., 130 Misc.2d 339, 496 N.Y.S.2d 618 (N.Y.City Ct.1985)—§ **13.20, n. 5.**

Suffolk County, Matter of, 419 N.Y.S.2d 52, 392 N.E.2d 1236 (N.Y.1979)—§ **14.88, n. 1**; § **14.89, n. 1**; § **14.92, n. 1.**

Suffolk County Federal Sav. & Loan Ass'n v. Geiger, 57 Misc.2d 184, 291 N.Y.S.2d 982 (N.Y.Sup.1968)—§ **12.45, n. 9.**

Suffolk Housing Services v. Town of Brookhaven, 517 N.Y.S.2d 924, 511 N.E.2d 67 (N.Y.1987)—§ **16.123, n. 5, 11.**

Suffolk Outdoor Advertising Co., Inc. v. Hulse, 402 N.Y.S.2d 368, 373 N.E.2d 263 (N.Y.1977)—§ **16.125, n. 3.**

Suffolk Sports Center, Inc. v. Belli Const. Corp., 212 A.D.2d 241, 628 N.Y.S.2d 952 (N.Y.A.D. 2 Dept.1995)—§ **30.31, n. 5.**

Suitte, People v., 90 A.D.2d 80, 455 N.Y.S.2d 675 (N.Y.A.D. 2 Dept.1982)—§ **38.21, n. 40.**

Sukljian v. Charles Ross & Son Co., Inc., 511 N.Y.S.2d 821, 503 N.E.2d 1358 (N.Y. 1986)—§ **27.4, n. 4**; § **27.23**; § **27.23, n. 1, 2**; § **27.24, n. 7.**

Suleiman, Estate of, 130 Misc.2d 336, 496 N.Y.S.2d 919 (N.Y.Sur.1985)—§ **28.29**; § **28.29, n. 2.**

Sullivan, In re, 31 B.R. 125 (Bkrtcy. N.D.N.Y.1983)—§ **8.25, n. 1.**

Sullivan, In re, 26 B.R. 677 (Bkrtcy. W.D.N.Y.1982)—§ **9.154, n. 2**; § **9.156, n. 6.**

Sullivan, Matter of, 167 Misc.2d 534, 635 N.Y.S.2d 437 (N.Y.Sup.1995)—§ **18.85, n. 5.**

Sullivan v. Hudson, 490 U.S. 877, 109 S.Ct. 2248, 104 L.Ed.2d 941 (1989)—§ **34.29, n. 8.**

Sullivan v. Locastro, 178 A.D.2d 523, 577 N.Y.S.2d 631 (N.Y.A.D. 2 Dept.1991)—§ **30.10, n. 5.**

Sullivan v. Louisiana, 508 U.S. 275, 113 S.Ct. 2078, 124 L.Ed.2d 182 (1993)—§ **38.19, n. 118.**

Sullivan, People v., 223 A.D.2d 893, 636 N.Y.S.2d 221 (N.Y.A.D. 3 Dept.1996)—§ **38.8, n. 13.**

Sullivan, People v., 153 A.D.2d 223, 550 N.Y.S.2d 358 (N.Y.A.D. 2 Dept.1990)—§ **38.19**; § **38.19, n. 29.**

Sullivan, People v., 329 N.Y.S.2d 325, 280 N.E.2d 98 (N.Y.1972)—§ **38.27, n. 2.**

Sullivan v. Town Bd. of Town of Riverhead, 102 A.D.2d 113, 476 N.Y.S.2d 578 (N.Y.A.D. 2 Dept.1984)—§ **16.124, n. 13.**

Sullivan v. Zebley, 493 U.S. 521, 110 S.Ct. 885, 107 L.Ed.2d 967 (1990)—§ **34.3, n. 9**; § **34.4, n. 2**; § **34.11, n. 1, 4**; § **34.63**; § **34.63, n. 7.**

Sulner v. General Acc. Fire and Life Assur. Corp., Ltd., 122 Misc.2d 597, 471 N.Y.S.2d 794 (N.Y.Sup.1984)—§ **7.46, n. 9.**

Sulzberger, Matter of, 159 Misc.2d 236, 603 N.Y.S.2d 656 (N.Y.Sup.1993)—§ **22.8, n. 4**; § **22.25, n. 4**; § **22.28, n. 2, 6, 22**; § **22.40, n. 3**; § **22.77, n. 1.**

Sumitomo Marine & Fire Ins. Co., Ltd.-United States Branch v. Cologne Reinsurance Co. of America, 552 N.Y.S.2d 891, 552 N.E.2d 139 (N.Y.1990)—§ **28.43, n. 12.**

Summer v. Summer, 630 N.Y.S.2d 970, 654 N.E.2d 1218 (N.Y.1995)—§ **21.49, n. 3.**

Summit School v. Neugent, 82 A.D.2d 463, 442 N.Y.S.2d 73 (N.Y.A.D. 2 Dept. 1981)—§ **16.89, n. 11**; § **16.128, n. 5.**

Sun Beach Real Estate Development Corp. v. Anderson, 479 N.Y.S.2d 341, 468 N.E.2d 296 (N.Y.1984)—§ **16.52, n. 6.**

Sun Beach Real Estate Development Corp. v. Anderson, 98 A.D.2d 367, 469 N.Y.S.2d 964 (N.Y.A.D. 2 Dept.1983)—§ **16.105, n. 9.**

Sunbright Fashions, Inc. v. Greater New York Mut. Ins. Co., 34 A.D.2d 235, 310 N.Y.S.2d 760 (N.Y.A.D. 1 Dept.1970)—§ **31.18, n. 16.**

Sun-Brite Car Wash, Inc. v. Board of Zoning and Appeals of Town of North Hempstead, 515 N.Y.S.2d 418, 508 N.E.2d 130 (N.Y.1987)—§ **16.48, n. 1.**

Sun Co., Inc. (R & M) v. City of Syracuse Indus. Development Agency, 209 A.D.2d 34, 625 N.Y.S.2d 371 (N.Y.A.D. 4 Dept. 1995)—§ **16.116**; § **16.116, n. 5.**

Sun Co. Inc. (R & M) v. City of Syracuse Indus. Development Agency, 197 A.D.2d 912, 602 N.Y.S.2d 456 (N.Y.A.D. 4 Dept. 1993)—§ **14.35, n. 4**; § **14.67, n. 3.**

Sunkyong America, Inc. v. Beta Sound of Music Corp., 199 A.D.2d 100, 605

TABLE OF CASES

N.Y.S.2d 62 (N.Y.A.D. 1 Dept.1993)—§ **5.37, n. 7.**

Sunrise Federal Sav. & Loan Ass'n v. West Park Ave. Corp., 47 Misc.2d 940, 263 N.Y.S.2d 529 (N.Y.Sup.1965)—§ **11.32, n. 2.**

Sunrise Properties, Inc. v. Jamestown Urban Renewal Agency, 206 A.D.2d 913, 614 N.Y.S.2d 841 (N.Y.A.D. 4 Dept. 1994)—§ **14.17, n. 1; § 14.38, n. 7.**

Sun Ship, Inc. v. Pennsylvania, 447 U.S. 715, 100 S.Ct. 2432, 65 L.Ed.2d 458 (1980)—§ **32.12, n. 22.**

Support Ministries For Persons With Aids, Inc. v. Village of Waterford, N.Y., 799 F.Supp. 272 (N.D.N.Y.1992)—§ **18.19, n. 8.**

Supreme Court New York, State ex rel. White v., 443 N.Y.S.2d 725, 427 N.E.2d 1190 (N.Y.1981)—§ **38.8, n. 75.**

Susan M. v. New York Law School, 557 N.Y.S.2d 297, 556 N.E.2d 1104 (N.Y. 1990)—§ **18.53, n. 12.**

Susquehanna Valley Cent. School Dist. at Conklin v. Susquehanna Valley Teachers' Ass'n, 376 N.Y.S.2d 427, 339 N.E.2d 132 (N.Y.1975)—§ **3.21, n. 11.**

Sutherland v. Elpower Corp., 923 F.2d 1285 (8th Cir.1991)—§ **27.40, n. 6.**

Sutherland, People v., 219 A.D.2d 523, 645 N.Y.S.2d 466 (N.Y.A.D. 1 Dept.1995)—§ **38.19, n. 42.**

Suydam's Estate, In re, 139 Misc. 845, 248 N.Y.S. 431 (N.Y.Sur.1925)—§ **25.50, n. 6.**

Svaigsen v. City of New York, 203 A.D.2d 32, 609 N.Y.S.2d 894 (N.Y.A.D. 1 Dept. 1994)—§ **18.2, n. 4; § 18.5, n. 1.**

Swan v. Mutual Reserve Fund Life Ass'n, 155 N.Y. 9, 49 N.E. 258 (N.Y.1898)—§ **37.28, n. 2.**

Swan, People ex rel. v. Doxsee, 136 A.D. 400, 120 N.Y.S. 962 (N.Y.A.D. 2 Dept. 1910)—§ **3.16, n. 8.**

Sweatland v. Park Corp., 181 A.D.2d 243, 587 N.Y.S.2d 54 (N.Y.A.D. 4 Dept. 1992)—§ **27.26; § 27.26, n. 6.**

Sweeney, In re, 113 B.R. 359 (Bkrtcy. N.D.Ohio 1990)—§ **17.40, n. 2.**

Swerdloff v. Mobil Oil Corp., 74 A.D.2d 258, 427 N.Y.S.2d 266 (N.Y.A.D. 2 Dept. 1980)—§ **17.36, n. 3, 4.**

Swett, Will of, 52 A.D.2d 330, 383 N.Y.S.2d 770 (N.Y.A.D. 4 Dept.1976)—§ **25.50, n. 5.**

Swick v. New York State and Local Employees' Retirement System, 213 A.D.2d 934, 623 N.Y.S.2d 960 (N.Y.A.D. 3 Dept. 1995)—§ **4.15, n. 2.**

Swinton v. W.J. Bush & Co., 199 Misc. 321, 102 N.Y.S.2d 994 (N.Y.Sup.1951)—§ **1.38, n. 12.**

Swiss Credit Bank v. International Bank, Limited, 23 Misc.2d 572, 200 N.Y.S.2d 828 (N.Y.Sup.1960)—§ **30.5, n. 9.**

Swoager v. Credit Bureau of Greater St. Petersburg, Fla., 608 F.Supp. 972 (M.D.Fla.1985)—§ **7.31, n. 11.**

Sydelman v. Marici, 56 A.D.2d 866, 392 N.Y.S.2d 333 (N.Y.A.D. 2 Dept.1977)—§ **12.65, n. 6.**

Sylvan Beach, N.Y., Village of v. Travelers Indem. Co., 55 F.3d 114 (2nd Cir. 1995)—§ **31.12, n. 10.**

Syracuse Aggregate Corp. v. Weise, 434 N.Y.S.2d 150, 414 N.E.2d 651 (N.Y. 1980)—§ **16.65, n. 3.**

Syracuse, City of v. State, 121 Misc.2d 8, 467 N.Y.S.2d 159 (N.Y.Ct.Cl.1983)—§ **14.44, n. 9.**

Syracuse Television, Inc. v. Channel 9, Syracuse, Inc., 51 Misc.2d 188, 273 N.Y.S.2d 16 (N.Y.Sup.1966)—§ **1.66, n. 12.**

Syracuse United Neighbors v. City of Syracuse, 80 A.D.2d 984, 437 N.Y.S.2d 466 (N.Y.A.D. 4 Dept.1981)—§ **3.28, n. 9.**

Szuchy v. Hillside Coal & Iron Co., 150 N.Y. 219, 44 N.E. 974 (N.Y.1896)—§ **37.28, n. 3.**

T

T-, Matter of, 8 I & N Dec. 529 (BIA 1960)—§ **19.12, n. 9.**

Taber, Matter of, 96 A.D.2d 890, 466 N.Y.S.2d 50 (N.Y.A.D. 2 Dept.1983)—§ **25.34, n. 1.**

Taddeo, In re, 685 F.2d 24 (2nd Cir.1982)—§ **9.160, n. 2; § 9.248, n. 4; § 9.249, n. 3, 4.**

Taffi v. United States (In re Taffi), 96 F.3d 1190 (9th Cir.1996)—§ **9.251, n. 3.**

Taft v. Shaffer Trucking, Inc., 52 A.D.2d 255, 383 N.Y.S.2d 744 (N.Y.A.D. 4 Dept. 1976)—§ **28.26, n. 5.**

Tagawa, Matter of, 13 I & N Dec. 13 (D.D. 1967)—§ **19.23, n. 4.**

Tagliasacchi v. Tagliasacchi, 83 A.D.2d 963, 443 N.Y.S.2d 17 (N.Y.A.D. 2 Dept. 1981)—§ **21.24, n. 2.**

Tankoos-Yarmon Hotels, Inc. v. Smith, 58 Misc.2d 1072, 299 N.Y.S.2d 937 (N.Y.Sup.App.Term 1968)—§ **13.56, n. 2.**

Tannenbaum, People v., 173 A.D.2d 750, 570 N.Y.S.2d 625 (N.Y.A.D. 2 Dept. 1991)—§ **38.10; § 38.10, n. 79.**

Tanners Realty Corp. v. Ruggerio, 111 A.D.2d 974, 490 N.Y.S.2d 73 (N.Y.A.D. 3 Dept.1985)—§ **12.65, n. 11.**

Taranovich, People v., 373 N.Y.S.2d 79, 335 N.E.2d 303 (N.Y.1975)—§ **33.73; § 33.73, n. 1, 2.**

TABLE OF CASES

Tarasoff v. Regents of University of California, 131 Cal.Rptr. 14, 551 P.2d 334 (Cal. 1976)—§ **29.11, n. 5.**

Tara X, Matter of, N.Y.L.J., 9/18/96, p. 27, col. 1 (Sup.Ct., Suffolk County)—§ **22.2, n. 9;** § **22.26, n. 15, 17;** § **22.33, n. 3, 4, 6.**

Tartan Oil Corp. v. Board of Zoning Appeals of Town of Brookhaven, 213 A.D.2d 486, 623 N.Y.S.2d 902 (N.Y.A.D. 2 Dept.1995)—§ **16.63, n. 2.**

Tatra, People ex rel. v. McNeill, 19 A.D.2d 845, 244 N.Y.S.2d 463 (N.Y.A.D. 2 Dept. 1963)—§ **37.34, n. 6.**

Taylor, In re, 3 F.3d 1512 (11th Cir.1993)—§ **9.186, n. 11.**

Taylor v. Freeland & Kronz, 503 U.S. 638, 112 S.Ct. 1644, 118 L.Ed.2d 280 (1992)—§ **9.127, n. 2.**

Taylor v. Incorporated Village of Head of the Harbor, 104 A.D.2d 642, 480 N.Y.S.2d 21 (N.Y.A.D. 2 Dept.1984)—§ **16.110, n. 1.**

Taylor v. Kinsella, 742 F.2d 709 (2nd Cir. 1984)—§ **31.2, n. 5.**

Taylor, People v., 586 N.Y.S.2d 545, 598 N.E.2d 693 (N.Y.1992)—§ **38.19;** § **38.19, n. 136.**

Taylor, People v., 560 N.Y.S.2d 982, 561 N.E.2d 882 (N.Y.1990)—§ **38.19, n. 105.**

Taylor, People v., 149 A.D.2d 984, 543 N.Y.S.2d 353 (N.Y.A.D. 4 Dept.1989)—§ **38.8, n. 167.**

Taylor, People v., 489 N.Y.S.2d 152, 478 N.E.2d 755 (N.Y.1985)—§ **38.8, n. 164, 187, 189.**

Taylor, People v., 98 A.D.2d 269, 470 N.Y.S.2d 153 (N.Y.A.D. 1 Dept.1984)—§ **38.21;** § **38.21, n. 28.**

Taylor, People v., 107 Misc.2d 183, 433 N.Y.S.2d 536 (N.Y.Co.Ct.1980)—§ **38.8, n. 94.**

Taylor v. State, 200 A.D.2d 273, 613 N.Y.S.2d 743 (N.Y.A.D. 3 Dept.1994)—§ **14.115, n. 7.**

TBS Enterprises, Inc. v. Grobe, 114 A.D.2d 445, 494 N.Y.S.2d 716 (N.Y.A.D. 2 Dept. 1985)—§ **11.6, n. 1.**

Teachers College v. Wolterding, 77 Misc.2d 81, 351 N.Y.S.2d 587 (N.Y.Sup.App. Term 1974)—§ **13.18, n. 3, 7.**

Teachers Ins. and Annuity Ass'n of America v. City of New York, 603 N.Y.S.2d 399, 623 N.E.2d 526 (N.Y.1993)—§ **4.77, n. 2, 3.**

Teachers Ins. and Annuity Ass'n of America v. Rogers, 41 A.D.2d 1020, 343 N.Y.S.2d 956 (N.Y.A.D. 4 Dept.1973)—§ **24.64, n. 4.**

Tebbutt v. Virostek, 493 N.Y.S.2d 1010, 483 N.E.2d 1142 (N.Y.1985)—§ **30.9, n. 14, 15.**

Tebeje, People v., 161 Misc.2d 440, 613 N.Y.S.2d 577 (N.Y.City Crim.Ct.1994)—§ **33.78, n. 3.**

Ted A. Petras Furs, Inc., In re, 172 B.R. 170 (Bkrtcy.E.D.N.Y.1994)—§ **9.198, n. 1.**

Teitelbaum, In re, 84 A.D. 351, 82 N.Y.S. 887 (N.Y.A.D. 1 Dept.1903)—§ **38.8, n. 87.**

Teitelbaum Holdings, Ltd. v. Gold, 421 N.Y.S.2d 556, 396 N.E.2d 1029 (N.Y. 1979)—§ **13.63, n. 3.**

Telaro v. Telaro, 306 N.Y.S.2d 920, 255 N.E.2d 158 (N.Y.1969)—§ **37.28, n. 22;** § **39.7, n. 10, 12.**

Telemark Const., Inc. v. Greenberg, 205 A.D.2d 438, 613 N.Y.S.2d 900 (N.Y.A.D. 1 Dept.1994)—§ **5.7, n. 2.**

Teltronics Services, Inc., Matter of, 29 B.R. 139 (Bkrtcy.E.D.N.Y.1983)—§ **9.107, n. 15.**

Temkin v. Karagheuzoff, 357 N.Y.S.2d 470, 313 N.E.2d 770 (N.Y.1974)—§ **37.32, n. 5.**

Tenants Committee of 425 East 86th St. (Electricity Matter) v. Joy, 58 A.D.2d 797, 397 N.Y.S.2d 383 (N.Y.A.D. 1 Dept. 1977)—§ **37.37, n. 58, 59.**

Tennant v. Farm Bureau Mut. Auto. Ins. Co., 286 A.D. 117, 141 N.Y.S.2d 449 (N.Y.A.D. 4 Dept.1955)—§ **31.10, n. 1.**

Tennant v. Schweiker, 682 F.2d 707 (8th Cir.1982)—§ **34.47, n. 17.**

Tepperman (Bloom), Matter of, N.Y.L.J., 9/12/95, p. 30, col. 2 (Sup.Ct., Nassau County)—§ **22.70, n. 2.**

Terrell v. Meisenhelder, 143 Misc. 911, 257 N.Y.S. 625 (N.Y.Co.Ct.1932)—§ **10.17, n. 4.**

Terry v. Ohio, 392 U.S. 1, 88 S.Ct. 1868, 20 L.Ed.2d 889 (1968)—§ **18.10, n. 8.**

Terry, People v., 224 A.D.2d 202, 637 N.Y.S.2d 694 (N.Y.A.D. 1 Dept.1996)—§ **38.19, n. 76.**

Terry D., Matter of, 601 N.Y.S.2d 452, 619 N.E.2d 389 (N.Y.1993)—§ **33.33, n. 3;** § **33.34, n. 1.**

Tesoro Petroleum Corp. v. Holborn Oil Co., Ltd., 118 A.D.2d 506, 500 N.Y.S.2d 118 (N.Y.A.D. 1 Dept.1986)—§ **1.10, n. 17.**

Tessy Plastics Corp. v. State Div. of Human Rights, 62 A.D.2d 36, 403 N.Y.S.2d 946 (N.Y.A.D. 4 Dept.1978)—§ **37.28, n. 20.**

Tevaha, People v., 620 N.Y.S.2d 786, 644 N.E.2d 1342 (N.Y.1994)—§ **37.37, n. 70.**

Texaco Inc., In re, 84 B.R. 911 (S.D.N.Y. 1988)—§ **9.22, n. 2.**

Texaco Inc., In re, 81 B.R. 806 (Bkrtcy. S.D.N.Y.1988)—§ **9.148, n. 10.**

Texaco Inc., In re, 79 B.R. 560 (Bkrtcy. S.D.N.Y.1987)—§ **9.43, n. 7;** § **9.47, n. 2.**

TABLE OF CASES

Texaco Inc., In re, 76 B.R. 322 (Bkrtcy. S.D.N.Y.1987)—§ **9.142, n. 5.**

Texaco Inc. v. Sanders (In re Texaco Inc.), 182 B.R. 937 (Bkrtcy.S.D.N.Y.1995)— § **9.169, n. 4.**

Texas Dept. of Community Affairs v. Burdine, 450 U.S. 248, 101 S.Ct. 1089, 67 L.Ed.2d 207 (1981)—§ **18.51;** § **18.51, n. 1.**

Texas Sheet Metals, Inc., In re, 90 B.R. 260 (Bkrtcy.S.D.Tex.1988)—§ **9.86, n. 10.**

Theil v. Radetzky, 254 A.D. 604, 2 N.Y.S.2d 867 (N.Y.A.D. 3 Dept.1938)—§ **37.28, n. 3.**

Thenebe v. Ansonia Associates, 226 A.D.2d 211, 640 N.Y.S.2d 552 (N.Y.A.D. 1 Dept. 1996)—§ **37.65, n. 75.**

Theresa S. v. Karel S., 120 Misc.2d 395, 466 N.Y.S.2d 216 (N.Y.Fam.Ct.1983)— § **21.7, n. 3.**

The Thomas Tracy, 24 F.2d 372 (2nd Cir. 1928)—§ **18.51, n. 3.**

Thill, People v., 438 N.Y.S.2d 297, 420 N.E.2d 95 (N.Y.1981)—§ **33.80, n. 1.**

Thinking Machs. Corp. v. Mellon Fin Service (In re Thinking Machines Corp.), 67 F.3d 1021 (1st Cir.1995)—§ **9.82, n. 1.**

32 Beechwood Corp. v. Fisher, 281 N.Y.S.2d 843, 228 N.E.2d 823 (N.Y.1967)— § **30.39, n. 14.**

30 West 15th Street Owners Corp. v. Travelers Ins. Co., 165 A.D.2d 731, 563 N.Y.S.2d 784 (N.Y.A.D. 1 Dept.1990)— § **28.35, n. 6;** § **28.39, n. 10.**

Thomaier v. Hoffman Chevrolet, Inc., 64 A.D.2d 492, 410 N.Y.S.2d 645 (N.Y.A.D. 2 Dept.1978)—§ **5.24, n. 4.**

Thomas v. Brookins, 175 A.D.2d 619, 572 N.Y.S.2d 557 (N.Y.A.D. 4 Dept.1991)— § **16.47, n. 1, 2.**

Thomas v. Coughlin, 194 A.D.2d 281, 606 N.Y.S.2d 378 (N.Y.A.D. 3 Dept.1993)— § **30.42, n. 4.**

Thomas v. June, 194 A.D.2d 842, 598 N.Y.S.2d 615 (N.Y.A.D. 3 Dept.1993)— § **16.114, n. 3.**

Thomas, People v., 210 A.D.2d 443, 620 N.Y.S.2d 433 (N.Y.A.D. 2 Dept.1994)— § **38.10, n. 131.**

Thomas, People v., 200 A.D.2d 642, 606 N.Y.S.2d 742 (N.Y.A.D. 2 Dept.1994)— § **38.19, n. 45.**

Thomas, People v., 441 N.Y.S.2d 650, 424 N.E.2d 537 (N.Y.1981)—§ **38.8;** § **38.8, n. 199, 202.**

Thomas, People v., 416 N.Y.S.2d 573, 389 N.E.2d 1094 (N.Y.1979)—§ **38.14, n. 3.**

Thomas v. Supermarkets General Corp., 154 Misc.2d 828, 586 N.Y.S.2d 454 (N.Y.Sup.1992)—§ **30.9, n. 46.**

Thomas v. Town of Bedford, 230 N.Y.S.2d 684, 184 N.E.2d 285 (N.Y.1962)— § **16.111, n. 1.**

Thomas v. Winchester, 6 N.Y. 397 (N.Y. 1852)—§ **27.3;** § **27.3, n. 1.**

Thomas J. Lipton, Inc. v. Liberty Mut. Ins. Co., 357 N.Y.S.2d 705, 314 N.E.2d 37 (N.Y.1974)—§ **31.9, n. 6.**

Thompson v. Hofstatter, 265 N.Y. 54, 191 N.E. 772 (N.Y.1934)—§ **3.17, n. 5.**

Thompson, People v., 611 N.Y.S.2d 470, 633 N.E.2d 1074 (N.Y.1994)—§ **38.21, n. 58.**

Thompson, People v., 470 N.Y.S.2d 551, 458 N.E.2d 1228 (N.Y.1983)—§ **38.19, n. 85;** § **38.21, n. 36, 55, 56, 58;** § **39.50, n. 12.**

Thompson, People v., 70 A.D.2d 968, 417 N.Y.S.2d 125 (N.Y.A.D. 3 Dept.1979)— § **38.8, n. 123, 136;** § **38.21.**

Thompson v. San Antonio Retail Merchants Ass'n, 682 F.2d 509 (5th Cir.1982)— § **7.31, n. 11.**

Thorne, In re, 240 N.Y. 444, 148 N.E. 630 (N.Y.1925)—§ **24.14, n. 2.**

Thorne v. City of El Segundo, 726 F.2d 459 (9th Cir.1983)—§ **17.55, n. 4.**

Thornton v. Heckler, 609 F.Supp. 1185 (E.D.N.Y.1985)—§ **34.47, n. 16.**

Thorpe, People v., 160 Misc.2d 558, 613 N.Y.S.2d 795 (N.Y.Sup.App.Term 1994)—§ **33.72, n. 1.**

Thourot v. Delahaye Import. Co., 69 Misc. 351, 125 N.Y.S. 827 (N.Y.Sup.1910)— § **7.28, n. 9.**

Thrasher v. United States Liability Ins. Co., 278 N.Y.S.2d 793, 225 N.E.2d 503 (N.Y. 1967)—§ **31.11, n. 6.**

354 East 66th Street Realty Corp., In re, 177 B.R. 776 (Bkrtcy.E.D.N.Y.1995)— § **9.102, n. 1.**

353 Realty Corp. v. Disla, 81 Misc.2d 68, 364 N.Y.S.2d 676 (N.Y.City Civ.Ct. 1974)—§ **13.18, n. 17.**

352 West 15th St. Assoc. v. Tietz, N.Y.L.J., 9/21/89, p.22, col.3, 17 HCR 353 (App. Term, 1st Dep't)—§ **13.33, n. 11.**

300 Gramatan Ave. Associates v. State Division of Human Rights, 408 N.Y.S.2d 54, 379 N.E.2d 1183 (N.Y.1978)—§ **4.15, n. 4;** § **37.87, n. 20.**

319 West 48 St. Realty Corp. v. Slenis, 117 Misc.2d 259, 458 N.Y.S.2d 153 (N.Y.City Civ.Ct.1982)—§ **13.22, n. 13;** § **13.47, n. 12.**

375 Park Ave. Associates, Inc., In re, 182 B.R. 690 (Bkrtcy.S.D.N.Y.1995)—§ **5.45, n. 3.**

379 Madison Ave. v. Stuyvesant Co., 242 A.D. 567, 275 N.Y.S. 953 (N.Y.A.D. 1 Dept.1934)—§ **5.6, n. 1.**

TABLE OF CASES

300 West Realty Co. v. Wood, 69 Misc.2d 580, 330 N.Y.S.2d 524 (N.Y.City Civ.Ct. 1971)—§ **13.18, n. 4.**

3 Lafayette Ave. Corp. v. Comptroller of State of N.Y., 186 A.D.2d 301, 587 N.Y.S.2d 456 (N.Y.A.D. 3 Dept.1992)— § **14.44, n. 5.**

Thrower v. Smith, 414 N.Y.S.2d 124, 386 N.E.2d 1091 (N.Y.1978)—§ **39.9, n. 23.**

Thumser, People v., 148 Misc.2d 472, 567 N.Y.S.2d 571 (N.Y.Sup.App.Term 1990)—§ **33.16, n. 5.**

Thurber Lumber Co., Inc. v. N.F.B. Development Corp., 215 A.D.2d 551, 626 N.Y.S.2d 841 (N.Y.A.D. 2 Dept.1995)— § **10.8, n. 2.**

Tiana Queen Motel, Inc., In re, 749 F.2d 146 (2nd Cir.1984)—§ **9.174, n. 6.**

Tidball v. Tidball, 108 A.D.2d 957, 484 N.Y.S.2d 945 (N.Y.A.D. 3 Dept.1985)— § **37.47, n. 5.**

Tien's Estate, In re, 72 Misc.2d 650, 340 N.Y.S.2d 249 (N.Y.Sur.1973)—§ **25.19, n. 5.**

Tierney v. Black Bros. Co., 852 F.Supp. 994 (M.D.Fla.1994)—§ **27.49;** § **27.49, n. 1;** § **27.51, n. 6.**

Tigr Restaurant, Inc. v. Rouse S.I. Shopping Center, Inc., 79 B.R. 954 (E.D.N.Y. 1987)—§ **9.77, n. 1.**

Tilles Inv. Co. v. Town of Huntington, 547 N.Y.S.2d 835, 547 N.E.2d 90 (N.Y. 1989)—§ **16.15, n. 17, 18.**

Tillow v. Daystrom Corp., 273 A.D. 1045, 78 N.Y.S.2d 720 (N.Y.A.D. 3 Dept.1948)— § **30.28, n. 10.**

Timal v. Kiamzon, 164 Misc.2d 159, 623 N.Y.S.2d 1016 (N.Y.Sup.1995)—§ **10.68, n. 3.**

Timbers of Inwood Forest Assocs., Ltd. (In re Timbers of Inwood Forest Associates, Ltd.), 793 F.2d 1380 (5th Cir.1986)— § **9.58, n. 2.**

Time, Inc. v. Hill, 385 U.S. 374, 87 S.Ct. 534, 17 L.Ed.2d 456 (1967)—§ **18.64; **§ **18.64, n. 21.**

Times Circle East, Inc. v. Edward Isaacs & Co. (In re Times Circle East, Inc.), 1995 WL 489551 (S.D.N.Y.1995)—§ **9.22, n. 9.**

Timme v. Steinfeld, 214 A.D. 611, 213 N.Y.S. 110 (N.Y.A.D. 1 Dept.1925)— § **5.26, n. 6.**

Timmins, People v., 352 N.Y.S.2d 445, 307 N.E.2d 562 (N.Y.1973)—§ **38.21, n. 58.**

Ting, Matter of, 11 I & N Dec. 849 (BIA 1966)—§ **19.47, n. 3.**

Tingling v. Secretary of Health and Human Services, 575 F.Supp. 905 (S.D.N.Y. 1983)—§ **34.11, n. 9.**

Tinnerholm v. Parke, Davis & Co., 411 F.2d 48 (2nd Cir.1969)—§ **27.5, n. 1.**

Tinnerholm v. Parke Davis & Co., 285 F.Supp. 432 (S.D.N.Y.1968)—§ **27.18;** § **27.18, n. 4.**

Tipon v. Appeals Bd. of Administrative Adjudication Bureau, 52 A.D.2d 1065, 384 N.Y.S.2d 324 (N.Y.A.D. 4 Dept.1976)— § **4.84, n. 4.**

Tirado v. Bowen, 842 F.2d 595 (2nd Cir. 1988)—§ **34.30, n. 2.**

Tischler v. Dimenna, 160 Misc.2d 525, 609 N.Y.S.2d 1002 (N.Y.Sup.1994)—§ **30.9, n. 8.**

Titan Sports, Inc. v. Comics World Corp., 870 F.2d 85 (2nd Cir.1989)—§ **18.64, n. 3.**

Titus St. Paul Property Owners Ass'n v. Board of Zoning Appeals of Town of Irondequoit, 205 Misc. 1083, 132 N.Y.S.2d 148 (N.Y.Sup.1954)—§ **16.89, n. 8.**

TKU–Queens Corp., Inc. v. Mabel Food Corp., 90 Misc.2d 48, 393 N.Y.S.2d 272 (N.Y.City Civ.Ct.1977)—§ **13.66;** § **13.66, n. 1.**

T & N PLC v. Fred S. James & Co. of New York, Inc., 29 F.3d 57 (2nd Cir.1994)— § **31.6, n. 9.**

Tobey T., Matter of, 204 A.D.2d 1067, 614 N.Y.S.2d 350 (N.Y.A.D. 4 Dept.1994)— § **37.37, n. 29.**

Tobie, People v., 115 A.D.2d 321, 496 N.Y.S.2d 710 (N.Y.A.D. 4 Dept.1985)— § **38.8, n. 217.**

Tobin v. Grossman, 30 A.D.2d 229, 291 N.Y.S.2d 227 (N.Y.A.D. 3 Dept.1968)— § **30.9, n. 47.**

Today's News, N.Y.L.J., 12/12/93, p.1, col.2—§ **38.40, n. 3.**

Todd v. Associated Credit Bureau Services, Inc., 451 F.Supp. 447 (E.D.Pa.1977)— § **7.31, n. 10.**

Todd v. Bankers Life & Cas. Co., 135 A.D.2d 1066, 523 N.Y.S.2d 206 (N.Y.A.D. 3 Dept.1987)—§ **31.10, n. 14.**

Todd, People v., 209 A.D.2d 652, 619 N.Y.S.2d 121 (N.Y.A.D. 2 Dept.1994)— § **18.12, n. 3.**

Toilet Goods Ass'n, Inc. v. Gardner, 387 U.S. 158, 87 S.Ct. 1520, 18 L.Ed.2d 697 (1967)—§ **4.70, n. 2.**

Tolbert, People v., 198 A.D.2d 132, 603 N.Y.S.2d 844 (N.Y.A.D. 1 Dept.1993)— § **38.27, n. 32.**

Toledo, People v., 204 A.D.2d 667, 614 N.Y.S.2d 238 (N.Y.A.D. 2 Dept.1994)— § **38.25, n. 17.**

Toliver v. Sullivan County, 841 F.2d 41 (2nd Cir.1988)—§ **18.38, n. 2.**

Tomka v. Seiler Corp., 66 F.3d 1295 (2nd Cir.1995)—§ **17.4, n. 1;** § **17.82, n. 5;** § **17.98, n. 2.**

TABLE OF CASES

Tom Sawyer Motor Inns, Inc. v. Chemung County Sewer Dist. No. 1, 33 A.D.2d 720, 305 N.Y.S.2d 408 (N.Y.A.D. 3 Dept. 1969)—§ **3.33, n. 10.**

Torelli v. City of New York, 176 A.D.2d 119, 574 N.Y.S.2d 5 (N.Y.A.D. 1 Dept.1991)— § **30.13, n. 11.**

Torgesen v. Schultz, 192 N.Y. 156, 84 N.E. 956 (N.Y.1908)—§ **27.3, n. 5.**

Tornheim, In re, 181 B.R. 161 (Bkrtcy. S.D.N.Y.1995)—§ **9.174, n. 10.**

Torra, People v., 191 A.D.2d 738, 594 N.Y.S.2d 419 (N.Y.A.D. 3 Dept.1993)— § **38.8, n. 146.**

Torres, People v., 534 N.Y.S.2d 914, 531 N.E.2d 635 (N.Y.1988)—§ **38.19, n. 122.**

Torres, People v., 125 A.D.2d 252, 509 N.Y.S.2d 540 (N.Y.A.D. 1 Dept.1986)— § **38.10, n. 86.**

Torrogrossa v. Towmotor Co., 405 N.Y.S.2d 448, 376 N.E.2d 920 (N.Y.1978)—§ **27.5, n. 6; § 27.10, n. 6; § 27.14, n. 4.**

Toscano, People v., 224 A.D.2d 558, 638 N.Y.S.2d 339 (N.Y.A.D. 2 Dept.1996)— § **38.24, n. 2.**

Toth v. Community Hospital at Glen Cove, 292 N.Y.S.2d 440, 239 N.E.2d 368 (N.Y. 1968)—§ **29.11, n. 2.**

Totten, In re, 179 N.Y. 112, 71 N.E. 748 (N.Y.1904)—§ **24.82, n. 1.**

Towner v. Towner, 225 A.D.2d 614, 639 N.Y.S.2d 133 (N.Y.A.D. 2 Dept.1996)— § **21.30, n. 12.**

Townley v. Heckler, 748 F.2d 109 (2nd Cir. 1984)—§ **34.48, n. 1.**

Town of (see name of town)

T.P.K. Const. Corp. v. Southern American Ins. Co., 739 F.Supp. 213 (S.D.N.Y. 1990)—§ **31.23, n. 4.**

Trach v. Trach, 162 A.D.2d 678, 557 N.Y.S.2d 112 (N.Y.A.D. 2 Dept.1990)— § **21.63, n. 5.**

Trade Creditors v. L.J. Hooker Corp. (In re Hooker Investments, Inc.), 188 B.R. 117 (S.D.N.Y.1995)—§ **9.31, n. 10.**

Trainer's Inc., In re, 17 B.R. 246 (Bkrtcy. E.D.Pa.1982)—§ **9.142, n. 4.**

Trainor v. Hernandez, 431 U.S. 434, 97 S.Ct. 1911, 52 L.Ed.2d 486 (1977)— § **18.36, n. 4.**

Transamerica Interway, Inc. v. Commercial Union Assur. Co. of South Africa, Ltd., 97 F.R.D. 419 (S.D.N.Y.1983)—§ **31.5, n. 2.**

Transit Cas. Co., Matter of, 580 N.Y.S.2d 140, 588 N.E.2d 38 (N.Y.1992)—§ **31.28, n. 2.**

Trans World Airlines, Inc. v. Hardison, 432 U.S. 63, 97 S.Ct. 2264, 53 L.Ed.2d 113 (1977)—§ **17.56, n. 3.**

Trautz v. Weisman, 819 F.Supp. 282 (S.D.N.Y.1993)—§ **18.19, n. 1.**

Traveler Real Estate, Inc. v. Cain, 160 A.D.2d 1214, 555 N.Y.S.2d 217 (N.Y.A.D. 3 Dept.1990)—§ **16.65, n. 4.**

Travelers Indem. Co. v. Crown Cork & Seal Co., Inc., 865 F.Supp. 1083 (S.D.N.Y. 1994)—§ **31.2, n. 17.**

Travelers Ins. Co. v. Buffalo Reinsurance Co. (S.D.N.Y.1990)—§ **31.2, n. 3.**

Travelers Ins. Co. (Magyar), Matter of, 217 A.D.2d 954, 629 N.Y.S.2d 900 (N.Y.A.D. 4 Dept.1995)—§ **37.37, n. 89.**

Traynor on Behalf of Schirmer v. Sears, 161 A.D.2d 1123, 556 N.Y.S.2d 501 (N.Y.A.D. 4 Dept.1990)—§ **37.65, n. 15.**

Trefoil Capital Corp. v. Creed Taylor, Inc., 121 A.D.2d 874, 504 N.Y.S.2d 112 (N.Y.A.D. 1 Dept.1986)—§ **37.65, n. 76, 78.**

Trepasso, People v., 197 A.D.2d 891, 602 N.Y.S.2d 291 (N.Y.A.D. 4 Dept.1993)— § **33.80, n. 2.**

Trezza, People v., 128 N.Y. 529, 28 N.E. 533 (N.Y.1891)—§ **38.3, n. 3; § 38.10, n. 88.**

Triangle Inn, Inc. v. Lo Grande, 124 A.D.2d 737, 508 N.Y.S.2d 240 (N.Y.A.D. 2 Dept. 1986)—§ **37.32, n. 7.**

Triborough Bridge and Tunnel Authority v. Wimpfheimer, 163 Misc.2d 412, 620 N.Y.S.2d 914 (N.Y.City Civ.Ct.1994)— § **13.14, n. 6.**

Tribune Co. v. Abiola, 66 F.3d 12 (2nd Cir.1995)—§ **18.36, n. 6.**

Tri Cities Indus. Park v. Department of Environmental Conservation, 76 A.D.2d 232, 430 N.Y.S.2d 411 (N.Y.A.D. 3 Dept. 1980)—§ **15.16, n. 6.**

Tri City Roofers, Inc. v. Northeastern Indus. Park, 473 N.Y.S.2d 161, 461 N.E.2d 298 (N.Y.1984)—§ **8.12, n. 2.**

Tri–County Taxpayers Ass'n, Inc. v. Town Bd. of Town of Queensbury, 447 N.Y.S.2d 699, 432 N.E.2d 592 (N.Y. 1982)—§ **3.27, n. 22; § 15.6, n. 11, 12.**

Trietley v. Board of Ed. of City of Buffalo, 65 A.D.2d 1, 409 N.Y.S.2d 912 (N.Y.A.D. 4 Dept.1978)—§ **18.28; § 18.28, n. 9.**

Trihedron Intern. Assur., Ltd. v. Superior Court (Weber), 218 Cal.App.3d 934, 267 Cal.Rptr. 418 (Cal.App. 4 Dist.1990)— § **31.23, n. 3.**

Trimboli v. Scarpaci Funeral Home, Inc., 37 A.D.2d 386, 326 N.Y.S.2d 227 (N.Y.A.D. 2 Dept.1971)—§ **37.37, n. 37.**

Triple Cities Const. Co. v. Maryland Cas. Co., 176 N.Y.S.2d 292, 151 N.E.2d 856 (N.Y.1958)—§ **31.26, n. 14.**

Tripoli v. Tripoli, 83 A.D.2d 764, 443 N.Y.S.2d 488 (N.Y.A.D. 4 Dept.1981)— § **37.65, n. 37.**

Tri–State Sol–Aire, Corp. v. United States Fidelity & Guar. Co., 198 A.D.2d 494,

TABLE OF CASES

604 N.Y.S.2d 576 (N.Y.A.D. 2 Dept. 1993)—§ **37.29, n. 9.**

Trombetta v. Conkling, 187 A.D.2d 213, 593 N.Y.S.2d 670 (N.Y.A.D. 4 Dept.1993)—§ **30.9, n. 44.**

Tropea v. Tropea, 642 N.Y.S.2d 575, 665 N.E.2d 145 (N.Y.1996)—§ **21.60, n. 3.**

Trotman v. Palisades Interstate Park Commission, 557 F.2d 35 (2nd Cir.1977)—§ **18.33, n. 1.**

Troy v. Santry, 151 Misc. 791, 272 N.Y.S. 320 (N.Y.Sup.1934)—§ **3.32, n. 4.**

Truck Rent-A-Center, Inc. v. Puritan Farms 2nd, Inc., 393 N.Y.S.2d 365, 361 N.E.2d 1015 (N.Y.1977)—§ **7.55; § 30.39, n. 1, 2.**

Trueluck, People v., 219 A.D.2d 490, 631 N.Y.S.2d 164 (N.Y.A.D. 1 Dept.1995)—§ **38.8, n. 198.**

Trustees of C.I. Mtge. Group v. NYILR Ltd., N.Y.L.J., 12/8/78, p.6, col.3 (App. Term, 1st Dep't)—§ **13.33, n.6.**

Trustees of Columbia University of Gwathmey Siegel & Assocs. Architects, N.Y.L.J., 9/28/93, p.22, col.5, (Sup.Ct., N.Y. County)—§ **28.21; § 28.21, n. 9.**

Tsomis v. Benenson, 23 A.D.2d 654, 257 N.Y.S.2d 894 (N.Y.A.D. 1 Dept.1965)—§ **37.52, n. 28; § 37.67, n. 6.**

T.S.P. Industries, Inc., In re, 120 B.R. 107 (Bkrtcy.N.D.Ill.1990)—§ **9.174, n. 3.**

Tubbs, People v., 157 A.D.2d 915, 550 N.Y.S.2d 441 (N.Y.A.D. 3 Dept.1990)—§ **38.8, n. 225.**

Tuck v. Tuck, 251 N.Y.S.2d 653, 200 N.E.2d 554 (N.Y.1964)—§ **18.74, n. 1.**

Tucker v. Elimelech, 184 A.D.2d 636, 584 N.Y.S.2d 895 (N.Y.A.D. 2 Dept.1992)—§ **37.28, n. 7.**

Tucker, People v., 223 A.D.2d 424, 636 N.Y.S.2d 759 (N.Y.A.D. 1 Dept.1996)—§ **38.28, n. 15.**

Tucker, People v., 568 N.Y.S.2d 342, 569 N.E.2d 1021 (N.Y.1991)—§ **38.19, n. 140.**

Tucker Freight Lines, Inc., In re, 62 B.R. 213 (Bkrtcy.W.D.Mich.1986)—§ **9.46, n. 2.**

Tulloch v. Coughlin, 50 F.3d 114 (2nd Cir. 1995)—§ **18.31, n. 5.**

Tunney, Will of, 101 Misc.2d 1058, 422 N.Y.S.2d 622 (N.Y.Sur.1979)—§ **24.14, n. 2.**

Turcsik, People v., 360 N.Y.S.2d 414, 318 N.E.2d 605 (N.Y.1974)—§ **38.27; § 38.27, n. 30.**

Turner, In re, 59 F.3d 1041 (10th Cir. 1995)—§ **9.111, n. 1.**

Turner, In re, 724 F.2d 338 (2nd Cir. 1983)—§ **9.19, n. 6.**

Turner v. Bituminous Cas. Co., 397 Mich. 406, 244 N.W.2d 873 (Mich.1976)—§ **27.26, n. 3.**

Turner v. Halliburton Co., 240 Kan. 1, 722 P.2d 1106 (Kan.1986)—§ **17.25, n. 8.**

Turner v. Meierdiercks, 106 A.D.2d 445, 482 N.Y.S.2d 538 (N.Y.A.D. 2 Dept. 1984)—§ **11.52, n. 7.**

Turner, People v., 47 A.D.2d 564, 363 N.Y.S.2d 638 (N.Y.A.D. 2 Dept.1975)—§ **38.10, n. 114.**

Turner's Estate, In re, 179 Misc. 217, 38 N.Y.S.2d 769 (N.Y.Sur.1942)—§ **8.35, n. 8.**

Turrisi v. Ponderosa Inc., 179 A.D.2d 956, 578 N.Y.S.2d 724 (N.Y.A.D. 3 Dept. 1992)—§ **37.22, n. 7.**

29/35 Realty Associates v. 35th Street New York Yarn Center, Inc., 181 A.D.2d 540, 581 N.Y.S.2d 43 (N.Y.A.D. 1 Dept. 1992)—§ **1.10, n. 19.**

TWI Intern., Inc. v. Vanguard Oil and Service Co., 162 B.R. 672 (S.D.N.Y.1994)—§ **9.29, n. 13, 14.**

Twin Lakes Farms Associates v. Town Clerk of Town of Bedford, 215 A.D.2d 667, 628 N.Y.S.2d 310 (N.Y.A.D. 2 Dept. 1995)—§ **16.98, n. 1.**

Two Guys From Harrison–NY v. S.F.R. Realty Associates, 186 A.D.2d 186, 587 N.Y.S.2d 962 (N.Y.A.D. 2 Dept.1992)—§ **37.35, n. 5.**

200 East 74 Corporation v. Dallas, N.Y.L.J., 3/15/95, p.26, col.5 (Civ.Ct., N.Y. County)—§ **13.12, n. 12.**

251 East 119th Street Tenants Assoc. v. Torres, 125 Misc.2d 279, 479 N.Y.S.2d 466 (N.Y.City Civ.Ct.1984)—§ **13.17, n. 16; § 13.18, n. 18; § 13.43, n. 17.**

245 Associates, LLC, In re, 188 B.R. 743 (Bkrtcy.S.D.N.Y.1995)—§ **9.29, n. 17.**

269 Associates v. Yerkes, 113 Misc.2d 450, 449 N.Y.S.2d 593 (N.Y.City Civ.Ct. 1982)—§ **13.33, n. 9, 10; § 13.54, n. 2.**

232 Broadway Corp. v. Calvert Ins. Co., 149 A.D.2d 694, 540 N.Y.S.2d 324 (N.Y.A.D. 2 Dept.1989)—§ **37.65, n. 72.**

232 Broadway Corp. v. New York Property Ins. Underwriting Ass'n, 206 A.D.2d 419, 615 N.Y.S.2d 42 (N.Y.A.D. 2 Dept. 1994)—§ **31.11, n. 2.**

222 Liberty Associates, In re, 108 B.R. 971 (Bkrtcy.E.D.Pa.1990)—§ **9.156, n. 5; § 9.157, n. 5.**

2657 East 68th Street Corp. v. Bergen Beach Yacht Club, 161 Misc.2d 1031, 615 N.Y.S.2d 858 (N.Y.City Civ.Ct. 1994)—§ **13.50, n. 3.**

2312–2316 Realty Corp. v. Font, 140 Misc.2d 901, 531 N.Y.S.2d 727 (N.Y.City Civ.Ct.1988)—§ **13.38, n. 1.**

TABLE OF CASES

221 E. 10th St., Inc. v. Walker, N.Y.L.J. 6/30/93, p. 21, col. 5, 21 HCR 348 (App. Term 1st Dep't)—§ **13.57, n. 3.**

Tymon v. Linoki, 23 A.D.2d 663, 256 N.Y.S.2d 862 (N.Y.A.D. 2 Dept.1965)— § **37.22; § 37.22, n. 3, 4.**

U

Uah–Braendly Hydro Associates v. RKDK Associates, 138 A.D.2d 493, 526 N.Y.S.2d 122 (N.Y.A.D. 2 Dept.1988)— § **14.64, n. 6.**

Udell v. Haas, 288 N.Y.S.2d 888, 235 N.E.2d 897 (N.Y.1968)—§ **16.11, n. 3; § 16.12; § 16.12, n. 4, 5; § 16.17; § 16.17, n. 9; § 16.20; § 16.20, n. 1; § 16.109, n. 1.**

Udzinski, People v., 146 A.D.2d 245, 541 N.Y.S.2d 9 (N.Y.A.D. 2 Dept.1989)— § **37.28, n. 17.**

Ugarriza v. Schmieder, 414 N.Y.S.2d 304, 386 N.E.2d 1324 (N.Y.1979)—§ **27.14, n. 2.**

Ulrich v. Veterans Admin. Hosp., 853 F.2d 1078 (2nd Cir.1988)—§ **18.38, n. 7.**

Ultrashmere House, Ltd. v. 38 Town Associates, 123 Misc.2d 102, 473 N.Y.S.2d 120 (N.Y.Sup.1984)—§ **13.56, n. 4.**

Ulysse v. Nelsk Taxi, Inc., 135 A.D.2d 528, 522 N.Y.S.2d 162 (N.Y.A.D. 2 Dept. 1987)—§ **28.16, n. 6.**

Unanue v. Unanue, 141 A.D.2d 31, 532 N.Y.S.2d 769 (N.Y.A.D. 2 Dept.1988)— § **21.4, n. 5.**

Underhill v. Royal, 769 F.2d 1426 (9th Cir. 1985)—§ **9.170, n. 2.**

Unido R., Matter of, 109 Misc.2d 1031, 441 N.Y.S.2d 325 (N.Y.Fam.Ct.1981)— § **20.38, n. 5.**

Uniformed Firefighters Ass'n v. City of New York, 428 N.Y.S.2d 197, 405 N.E.2d 679 (N.Y.1980)—§ **3.14, n. 7.**

Unigard Sec. Ins. Co., Inc. v. North River Ins. Co., 584 N.Y.S.2d 290, 594 N.E.2d 571 (N.Y.1992)—§ **28.40, n. 3; § 31.10, n. 1.**

Unigard Sec. Ins. Co., Inc. v. North River Ins. Co., 949 F.2d 630 (2nd Cir.1991)— § **31.4, n. 3.**

Unigard Sec. Ins. Co., Inc. v. North River Ins. Co., 762 F.Supp. 566 (S.D.N.Y. 1991)—§ **31.8, n. 7.**

Unimax Corp. v. Tax Appeals Tribunal of State of N.Y., 581 N.Y.S.2d 135, 589 N.E.2d 358 (N.Y.1992)—§ **4.76, n. 5; § 4.80, n. 3.**

Union Bank v. Wolas, 502 U.S. 151, 112 S.Ct. 527, 116 L.Ed.2d 514 (1991)— § **9.118, n. 7.**

Union Carbide Corp. v. Newboles, 686 F.2d 593 (7th Cir.1982)—§ **9.170, n. 2.**

Union Meeting Partners, In re, 178 B.R. 664 (Bkrtcy.E.D.Pa.1995)—§ **9.102, n. 4.**

Union Savings Bank v. Augie/Restivo Banking Co., Ltd. (In re Augie/Restivo Baking Co., Ltd.), 860 F.2d 515 (2nd Cir.1988)— § **9.14, n. 1.**

Unique Ideas, Inc., State v., 405 N.Y.S.2d 656, 376 N.E.2d 1301 (N.Y.1978)— § **38.8, n. 82.**

Unitarian Universalist Church of Central Nassau v. Shorten, 63 Misc.2d 978, 314 N.Y.S.2d 66 (N.Y.Sup.1970)—§ **16.24, n. 5; § 16.128, n. 11.**

United Auto., Aerospace and Agr. Implement Workers of America, UAW v. Johnson Controls, Inc., 499 U.S. 187, 111 S.Ct. 1196, 113 L.Ed.2d 158 (1991)—§ **17.54, n. 4.**

United Calendar Mfg. Corp. v. Huang, 94 A.D.2d 176, 463 N.Y.S.2d 497 (N.Y.A.D. 2 Dept.1983)—§ **5.7, n. 7; § 5.11, n. 2.**

United Community Ins. Co. v. Mucatel, 127 Misc.2d 1045, 487 N.Y.S.2d 959 (N.Y.Sup.1985)—§ **26.24, n. 17.**

United Housing Foundation, Inc. v. Forman, 421 U.S. 837, 95 S.Ct. 2051, 44 L.Ed.2d 621 (1975)—§ **2.106; § 2.106, n. 8.**

United Press Intern., Inc., In re, 60 B.R. 265 (Bkrtcy.D.Dist.Col.1986)—§ **9.142, n. 4.**

United Sav. Ass'n of Texas v. Timbers of Inwood Forest Associates, Ltd., 484 U.S. 365, 108 S.Ct. 626, 98 L.Ed.2d 740 (1988)—§ **9.58, n. 2; § 9.102, n. 3.**

United Services Auto. Ass'n v. United States, 285 F.Supp. 854 (S.D.N.Y. 1968)—§ **31.29, n. 8.**

United States v. ____(see opposing party)

United States ex rel. v. ____(see opposing party and relator)

United States Fidelity and Guar. Co. v. U.S. Underwriters Ins. Co., 194 A.D.2d 1028, 599 N.Y.S.2d 654 (N.Y.A.D. 3 Dept. 1993)—§ **31.12, n. 11.**

United States Fidelity & Guar. Co. v. Annunziata, 501 N.Y.S.2d 790, 492 N.E.2d 1206 (N.Y.1986)—§ **31.9, n. 5.**

United States Fire Ins. Co. v. General Reinsurance Corp., 949 F.2d 569 (2nd Cir. 1991)—§ **31.9, n. 9.**

United States Grand Lodge of Order of Brith Abraham, People ex rel. v. Payn, 161 N.Y. 229, 55 N.E. 849 (N.Y.1900)— § **1.13, n. 2.**

United States Power Squadrons v. State Human Rights Appeal Bd., 465 N.Y.S.2d

TABLE OF CASES

871, 452 N.E.2d 1199 (N.Y.1983)—§ **18.54, n. 4;** § **18.56, n. 1.**

United States Truck Co., Inc., Matter of, 42 B.R. 790 (Bkrtcy.E.D.Mich.1984)—§ **9.154, n. 4.**

United States Underwriters Ins. Co. v. Congregation B'Nai Israel, 900 F.Supp. 641 (E.D.N.Y.1995)—§ **31.16, n. 10.**

United Technologies Corp. v. Browning-Ferris Industries, Inc., 33 F.3d 96 (1st Cir.1994)—§ **15.30, n. 7.**

United Technologies Corp., United States ex rel. Kreindler & Kreindler v., 985 F.2d 1148 (2nd Cir.1993)—§ **17.64, n. 13.**

United Veterans Mut. Housing No. 2 Corp. v. New York City Com'n on Human Rights, 207 A.D.2d 551, 616 N.Y.S.2d 84 (N.Y.A.D. 2 Dept.1994)—§ **18.47, n. 3.**

Universal Empire Industries, Inc. v. State, 149 Misc.2d 773, 566 N.Y.S.2d 442 (N.Y.Ct.Cl.1990)—§ **14.93, n. 2.**

University of Tennessee v. Elliott, 478 U.S. 788, 106 S.Ct. 3220, 92 L.Ed.2d 635 (1986)—§ **18.37, n. 6.**

Upholsterers' Intern. Union Pension Fund v. Artistic Furniture of Pontiac, 920 F.2d 1323 (7th Cir.1990)—§ **6.17, n. 2.**

Upjohn's Will, In re, 304 N.Y. 366, 107 N.E.2d 492 (N.Y.1952)—§ **20.116, n. 2.**

Upper Nyack, Village of v. Christian and Missionary Alliance, 143 Misc.2d 414, 540 N.Y.S.2d 125 (N.Y.Sup.1988)—§ **5.7, n. 1;** § **5.11, n. 5.**

Upstate Builders Supply Corp., Application of, 63 Misc.2d 35, 310 N.Y.S.2d 862 (N.Y.Sup.1970)—§ **10.19, n. 7, 17.**

Urbach v. Krouner, 213 A.D.2d 833, 623 N.Y.S.2d 380 (N.Y.A.D. 3 Dept.1995)—§ **21.55, n. 8.**

Urdang, Matter of, 194 A.D.2d 615, 599 N.Y.S.2d 60 (N.Y.A.D. 2 Dept.1993)—§ **25.12, n. 4.**

Urquhart v. New York City Transit Authority, 221 A.D.2d 336, 633 N.Y.S.2d 206 (N.Y.A.D. 2 Dept.1995)—§ **37.29, n. 24;** § **37.65, n. 62.**

USAA Cas. Ins. Co. v. Brown, 206 A.D.2d 470, 614 N.Y.S.2d 571 (N.Y.A.D. 2 Dept. 1994)—§ **31.29, n. 8.**

U.S. Brass & Cooper Co. v. Caplan (In re Century Brass Products, Inc), 22 F.3d 37 (2nd Cir.1984)—§ **9.121, n. 1;** § **9.198, n. 1.**

Utica Mut. Ins. Co. v. Gruzlewski, 217 A.D.2d 903, 630 N.Y.S.2d 826 (N.Y.A.D. 4 Dept.1995)—§ **31.11, n. 4.**

Uvalde Asphalt Paving Co. v. City of New York, 196 A.D. 740, 188 N.Y.S. 304 (N.Y.A.D. 1 Dept.1921)—§ **30.25, n. 8.**

Uzwij v. Robins, 133 A.D.2d 695, 519 N.Y.S.2d 866 (N.Y.A.D. 2 Dept.1987)—§ **4.72, n. 8.**

V

Vaca v. Sipes, 386 U.S. 171, 87 S.Ct. 903, 17 L.Ed.2d 842 (1967)—§ **17.61, n. 12.**

Vaccaro v. Jorling, 151 A.D.2d 34, 546 N.Y.S.2d 470 (N.Y.A.D. 3 Dept.1989)—§ **14.36, n. 1.**

Vaccaro v. Vaccaro, 98 Misc.2d 406, 413 N.Y.S.2d 875 (N.Y.Sup.1979)—§ **21.64, n. 2.**

Vacco v. Quill, ___ U.S. ___, 117 S.Ct. 2293, 138 L.Ed.2d 834 (1997)—§ **23.113;** § **23.113, n. 2.**

Valatie, Village of v. Smith, 610 N.Y.S.2d 941, 632 N.E.2d 1264 (N.Y.1994)—§ **16.70;** § **16.70, n. 1, 2.**

Valentino v. State, 44 A.D.2d 338, 355 N.Y.S.2d 212 (N.Y.A.D. 3 Dept.1974)—§ **37.28, n. 20.**

Valet v. American Motors Inc., 105 A.D.2d 645, 481 N.Y.S.2d 364 (N.Y.A.D. 1 Dept. 1984)—§ **27.37, n. 2.**

Valley Nat. Bank of Long Island v. Levy, 45 A.D.2d 771, 356 N.Y.S.2d 1003 (N.Y.A.D. 2 Dept.1974)—§ **11.53, n. 7.**

Valley Realty Development Co., Inc. v. Town of Tully, 187 A.D.2d 963, 590 N.Y.S.2d 375 (N.Y.A.D. 4 Dept.1992)—§ **16.58;** § **16.58, n. 5;** § **16.113, n. 10.**

Vallone, Application of, 92 A.D.2d 799, 460 N.Y.S.2d 44 (N.Y.A.D. 1 Dept.1983)—§ **1.43, n. 23.**

Vallone, People v., 140 A.D.2d 729, 529 N.Y.S.2d 38 (N.Y.A.D. 2 Dept.1988)—§ **38.10, n. 16.**

Valloni v. Crisona, 170 A.D.2d 596, 566 N.Y.S.2d 372 (N.Y.A.D. 2 Dept.1991)—§ **30.40, n. 15.**

Valmonte v. Bane, 18 F.3d 992 (2nd Cir. 1994)—§ **4.4, n. 5;** § **4.6, n. 5.**

Van Akin, People v., 197 A.D.2d 845, 602 N.Y.S.2d 450 (N.Y.A.D. 4 Dept.1993)—§ **38.20, n. 14.**

Van Buren, People v., 609 N.Y.S.2d 170, 631 N.E.2d 112 (N.Y.1993)—§ **38.10, n. 14.**

Van Cleef Realty, Inc. v. New York State Div. of Human Rights, 216 A.D.2d 306, 627 N.Y.S.2d 744 (N.Y.A.D. 2 Dept. 1995)—§ **18.46, n. 1;** § **18.49, n. 10.**

Vanderbilt v. Vanderbilt, 153 N.Y.S.2d 1, 135 N.E.2d 553 (N.Y.1956)—§ **21.14;** § **21.14, n. 1.**

Van Ess v. Van Ess, 100 A.D.2d 848, 474 N.Y.S.2d 90 (N.Y.A.D. 2 Dept.1984)—§ **21.64, n. 1.**

TABLE OF CASES

Vanguard Commercial Leasing Corp. v. Dayanzadeh, 147 A.D.2d 557, 538 N.Y.S.2d 492 (N.Y.A.D. 2 Dept.1989)—§ 7.55.

Vanguard Diversified, Inc., In re, 31 B.R. 364 (Bkrtcy.E.D.N.Y.1983)—§ 9.71, n. 11.

VanIderstine v. Lane Pipe Corp., 89 A.D.2d 459, 455 N.Y.S.2d 450 (N.Y.A.D. 4 Dept. 1982)—§ 27.24, n. 3.

Vanneck v. Vanneck, 427 N.Y.S.2d 735, 404 N.E.2d 1278 (N.Y.1980)—§ 21.5; § 21.5, n. 4.

Van Patten v. Buyce, 37 A.D.2d 448, 326 N.Y.S.2d 197 (N.Y.A.D. 3 Dept.1971)—§ 30.9, n. 20.

Van Pelt, People v., 556 N.Y.S.2d 984, 556 N.E.2d 423 (N.Y.1990)—§ 38.21, n. 58.

Vantage Petroleum Corp., In re, 34 B.R. 650 (Bkrtcy.E.D.N.Y.1983)—§ 9.39, n. 3.

Varela, Matter of, 13 I & N Dec. 453 (BIA 1970)—§ 19.12, n. 12.

Varela v. Investors Ins. Holding Corp., 598 N.Y.S.2d 761, 615 N.E.2d 218 (N.Y. 1993)—§ 7.44, n. 9.

Vargas, People v., 645 N.Y.S.2d 759, 668 N.E.2d 879 (N.Y.1996)—§ 18.12, n. 2.

Vargas v. Sullivan, 898 F.2d 293 (2nd Cir. 1990)—§ 34.44, n. 3; § 34.46, n. 1, 3.

Vargulik, People v., 130 A.D.2d 530, 515 N.Y.S.2d 111 (N.Y.A.D. 2 Dept.1987)—§ 33.39, n. 9.

Varkonyi v. S. A. Empresa De Viacao Airea Rio Grandense (Varig), 292 N.Y.S.2d 670, 239 N.E.2d 542 (N.Y.1968)—§ 39.7, n. 7.

Vasquez v. Hillery, 474 U.S. 254, 106 S.Ct. 617, 88 L.Ed.2d 598 (1986)—§ 38.19, n. 114.

Vasquez, People v., 200 A.D.2d 344, 613 N.Y.S.2d 595 (N.Y.A.D. 1 Dept.1994)—§ 33.43, n. 11.

Vasquez, People v., 557 N.Y.S.2d 873, 557 N.E.2d 109 (N.Y.1990)—§ 38.19; § 38.19, n. 137.

Vasquez, People v., 516 N.Y.S.2d 921, 509 N.E.2d 934 (N.Y.1987)—§ 38.38, n. 2.

Vasquez, People v., 133 Misc.2d 963, 509 N.Y.S.2d 458 (N.Y.Sup.1986)—§ 33.74, n. 3.

Vasquez, People v., 114 A.D.2d 589, 494 N.Y.S.2d 198 (N.Y.A.D. 3 Dept.1985)—§ 38.19, n. 44.

Vasquez, People v., 88 A.D.2d 667, 450 N.Y.S.2d 606 (N.Y.A.D. 2 Dept.1982)—§ 38.15, n. 7.

Vassura v. Taylor, 117 A.D.2d 798, 499 N.Y.S.2d 120 (N.Y.A.D. 2 Dept.1986)—§ 30.29, n. 8.

Vaughan v. Commonwealth Land Title Ins. Co., 133 A.D.2d 626, 519 N.Y.S.2d 734 (N.Y.A.D. 2 Dept.1987)—§ 12.9, n. 5.

Vaughn v. Mobil Oil Corp., 708 F.Supp. 595 (S.D.N.Y.1989)—§ 17.37, n. 6.

Vaughan v. Resolution Trust Corp. (In re Lease-Sea, Inc.), 140 B.R. 182 (Bkrtcy. N.D.Ohio 1992)—§ 9.111, n. 2.

Vaughter, In re, 109 B.R. 229 (Bkrtcy. W.D.Tex.1989)—§ 17.40, n. 2.

Vazquez v. Vazquez, 26 A.D.2d 701, 273 N.Y.S.2d 12 (N.Y.A.D. 2 Dept.1966)—§ 38.4, n. 1.

Vecchio, In re, 20 F.3d 555 (2nd Cir.1994)—§ 9.93, n. 4.

Vector East Realty Corp. v. Abrams, 89 A.D.2d 453, 455 N.Y.S.2d 773 (N.Y.A.D. 1 Dept.1982)—§ 4.2, n. 14; § 4.11, n. 2.

Vega v. Bell, 419 N.Y.S.2d 454, 393 N.E.2d 450 (N.Y.1979)—§ 38.8, n. 133, 138.

Vega v. Bell, 67 A.D.2d 420, 415 N.Y.S.2d 424 (N.Y.A.D. 1 Dept.1979)—§ 38.8; § 38.8, n. 137.

Vega v. Commissioner, T.C. Memo. 1996-144 (U.S.Tax Ct.1996)—§ 24.36, n. 2.

Velez v. Craine & Clark Lumber Corp., 350 N.Y.S.2d 617, 305 N.E.2d 750 (N.Y. 1973)—§ 27.5, n. 3.

Velez, People v., 202 A.D.2d 264, 609 N.Y.S.2d 783 (N.Y.A.D. 1 Dept.1994)—§ 38.8, n. 217.

Vella v. Equitable Life Assur. Soc. of United States, 887 F.2d 388 (2nd Cir.1989)—§ 31.18, n. 2.

Velsicol Chemical Corp. v. Enenco, Inc., 9 F.3d 524 (6th Cir.1993)—§ 15.30, n. 7.

Vergara, People v., 102 A.D.2d 702, 476 N.Y.S.2d 332 (N.Y.A.D. 1 Dept.1984)—§ 38.8, n. 55.

Vermont Com'r of Banking and Ins. v. Welbilt Corp., 133 A.D.2d 396, 519 N.Y.S.2d 390 (N.Y.A.D. 2 Dept.1987)—§ 31.17, n. 12.

Vermont Real Estate Inv. Trust, In re, 20 B.R. 33 (Bkrtcy.D.Vt.1982)—§ 9.43, n. 15.

Vermont Yankee Nuclear Power Corp. v. Natural Resources Defense Council, Inc., 435 U.S. 519, 98 S.Ct. 1197, 55 L.Ed.2d 460 (1978)—§ 15.3, n. 7.

Verna v. O'Brien, 78 Misc.2d 288, 356 N.Y.S.2d 929 (N.Y.Sup.1974)—§ 11.36, n. 4; § 11.37, n. 7.

Vernes v. Phillips, 266 N.Y. 298, 194 N.E. 762 (N.Y.1935)—§ 28.11, n. 12.

Vescur, People v., 134 Misc.2d 574, 511 N.Y.S.2d 997 (N.Y.City Crim.Ct.1987)—§ 33.82, n. 1.

Vezza v. Bauman, 192 A.D.2d 712, 597 N.Y.S.2d 418 (N.Y.A.D. 2 Dept.1993)—§ 16.45, n. 2.

TABLE OF CASES

Victoria Station Inc., In re, 875 F.2d 1380 (9th Cir.1989)—§ **9.77, n. 1.**

Victorson v. Bock Laundry Mach. Co., 373 N.Y.S.2d 39, 335 N.E.2d 275 (N.Y. 1975)—§ **27.3, n. 14; § 27.5, n. 2; § 27.39; § 27.39, n. 3.**

Victrix S.S. Co., S.A. v. Salen Dry Cargo A.B., 825 F.2d 709 (2nd Cir.1987)—§ **9.20, n. 4.**

Vienna Park Properties, In re, 976 F.2d 106 (2nd Cir.1992)—§ **9.69, n. 2, 8.**

Viken, People v., 161 Misc.2d 217, 613 N.Y.S.2d 824 (N.Y.City Crim.Ct.1994)—§ **33.78, n. 3.**

Vilardi, People v., 556 N.Y.S.2d 518, 555 N.E.2d 915 (N.Y.1990)—§ **33.39, n. 6, 7; § 38.10; § 38.10, n. 105.**

Vilardi, People v., 150 A.D.2d 819, 542 N.Y.S.2d 238 (N.Y.A.D. 2 Dept.1989)—§ **38.25, n. 6.**

Vilardi v. Roth, 192 A.D.2d 662, 597 N.Y.S.2d 86 (N.Y.A.D. 2 Dept.1993)—§ **16.84, n. 8.**

Vilas v. City of Manila, 220 U.S. 345, 31 S.Ct. 416, 55 L.Ed. 491 (1911)—§ **3.3, n. 4.**

Villa v. Marciano, 167 A.D.2d 828, 561 N.Y.S.2d 938 (N.Y.A.D. 4 Dept.1990)—§ **30.9, n. 13.**

Villa Charlotte Bronte, Inc. v. Commercial Union Ins. Co., 487 N.Y.S.2d 314, 476 N.E.2d 640 (N.Y.1985)—§ **31.12, n. 6.**

Village Bd. of Trustees of Village of Malone v. Zoning Bd. of Appeals of Village of Malone, 164 A.D.2d 24, 562 N.Y.S.2d 973 (N.Y.A.D. 3 Dept.1990)—§ **16.124, n. 5.**

Village of (see name of village)

Villanueva v. Muniz, 136 A.D.2d 546, 523 N.Y.S.2d 167 (N.Y.A.D. 2 Dept.1988)—§ **26.30, n. 9.**

Villas of Forest Hills Co. v. Lumberger, 128 A.D.2d 701, 513 N.Y.S.2d 116 (N.Y.A.D. 2 Dept.1987)—§ **13.18, n. 18.**

Villella v. Waikem Motors, Inc., 45 Ohio St.3d 36, 543 N.E.2d 464 (Ohio 1989)—§ **7.25, n. 8.**

Vinnie Montes Waste System, Inc. v. Town of Oyster Bay, 150 Misc.2d 109, 567 N.Y.S.2d 335 (N.Y.Sup.1991)—§ **15.34, n. 19.**

Virginia Elec. & Power Co. v. Caldor, Incorporated–New York, 117 F.3d 646 (2nd Cir.1997)—§ **9.89, n. 2.**

Virginia State Bd. of Pharmacy v. Virginia Citizens Consumer Council, Inc., 425 U.S. 748, 96 S.Ct. 1817, 48 L.Ed.2d 346 (1976)—§ **16.25, n. 9.**

Virtual Network Services Corp., Matter of, 902 F.2d 1246 (7th Cir.1990)—§ **9.107, n. 20.**

Virtuoso v. Aetna Cas. and Sur. Co., 134 A.D.2d 252, 520 N.Y.S.2d 439 (N.Y.A.D. 2 Dept.1987)—§ **31.10, n. 15.**

Viscardi v. Lerner, 125 A.D.2d 662, 510 N.Y.S.2d 183 (N.Y.A.D. 2 Dept.1986)—§ **28.11, n. 4.**

Vitale v. City Const. Management Co., Inc., 172 A.D.2d 326, 568 N.Y.S.2d 399 (N.Y.A.D. 1 Dept.1991)—§ **28.6, n. 3.**

Vitale v. City of New York, 183 A.D.2d 502, 583 N.Y.S.2d 445 (N.Y.A.D. 1 Dept. 1992)—§ **8.37, n. 3.**

Vitkauskas v. Tynedale Shipping Co., Ltd., 416 F.Supp. 990 (S.D.N.Y.1976)—§ **30.9, n. 24.**

Vitreous Steel Products Co., Matter of, 911 F.2d 1223 (7th Cir.1990)—§ **9.107, n. 23.**

Viuker v. Allstate Ins. Co., 70 A.D.2d 295, 420 N.Y.S.2d 926 (N.Y.A.D. 2 Dept. 1979)—§ **31.27, n. 3.**

Vizcaino, Matter of, 19 Int.Dec. 3061 (BIA 1988)—§ **19.11, n. 24.**

Voelckers v. Guelli, 460 N.Y.S.2d 8, 446 N.E.2d 764 (N.Y.1983)—§ **3.32, n. 8.**

Vogel v. Luitwieler, 5 N.Y.S. 154 (N.Y.Sup. 1889)—§ **10.15, n. 1.**

Vogel v. New York State Dept. of Taxation and Finance, 98 Misc.2d 222, 413 N.Y.S.2d 862 (N.Y.Sup.1979)—§ **2.23, n. 13.**

Volkell v. Volkell, 102 A.D.2d 889, 477 N.Y.S.2d 60 (N.Y.A.D. 2 Dept.1984)—§ **21.21, n. 2.**

Volvo North America Corp. v. DePaola, 156 A.D.2d 40, 554 N.Y.S.2d 835 (N.Y.A.D. 1 Dept.1990)—§ **7.10, n. 2.**

Von Bulow, Matter of, 481 N.Y.S.2d 67, 470 N.E.2d 866 (N.Y.1984)—§ **38.27, n. 12.**

Von Bulow, Matter of, 122 Misc.2d 129, 470 N.Y.S.2d 72 (N.Y.Sup.1983)—§ **22.31, n. 1.**

von Bulow by Auersperg v. von Bulow, 811 F.2d 136 (2nd Cir.1987)—§ **18.85, n. 7.**

Voorheesville Rod and Gun Club, Inc. v. E.W. Tompkins Co., Inc., 606 N.Y.S.2d 132, 626 N.E.2d 917 (N.Y.1993)—§ **12.64, n. 3; § 12.65, n. 1.**

Voorhis v. State, 107 Misc.2d 956, 436 N.Y.S.2d 187 (N.Y.Ct.Cl.1981)—§ **14.55, n. 2.**

Voss v. Black & Decker Mfg. Co., 463 N.Y.S.2d 398, 450 N.E.2d 204 (N.Y. 1983)—§ **27.7, n. 1, 2, 3; § 27.9, n. 2.**

Voss v. Multifilm Corp. of America, 112 A.D.2d 216, 491 N.Y.S.2d 434 (N.Y.A.D. 2 Dept.1985)—§ **11.52, n. 6.**

Voulgarelis v. Voulgarelis, 634 N.Y.S.2d 447, 658 N.E.2d 225 (N.Y.1995)—§ **37.66, n. 1.**

TABLE OF CASES

Voulgarelis v. Voulgarelis, 210 A.D.2d 398, 620 N.Y.S.2d 983 (N.Y.A.D. 2 Dept. 1994)—§ **37.37, n. 29.**
Voutsinas, People v., 62 A.D.2d 465, 406 N.Y.S.2d 138 (N.Y.A.D. 3 Dept.1978)—§ **38.10, n. 35, 171.**
Vowteras v. Argo Compressor Service Corp., 83 A.D.2d 834, 441 N.Y.S.2d 562 (N.Y.A.D. 2 Dept.1981)—§ **1.38, n. 6.**
Vrooman v. Village of Middleville, 106 Misc.2d 945, 436 N.Y.S.2d 662 (N.Y.Sup. 1981)—§ **5.8, n. 1.**
Vulpis, United States v., 967 F.2d 734 (2nd Cir.1992)—§ **8.37, n. 2.**
V. Zappala & Co., Inc. v. Pyramid Co. of Glens Falls, 81 A.D.2d 983, 439 N.Y.S.2d 765 (N.Y.A.D. 3 Dept.1981)—§ **5.37, n. 6.**

W

W, Matter of, 4 I & N Dec. 209 (BIA 1955)—§ **19.12, n. 10.**
Wachsberger v. Michalis, 19 Misc.2d 909, 191 N.Y.S.2d 621 (N.Y.Sup.1959)—§ **16.84, n. 1.**
Wachtler v. County of Herkimer, 35 F.3d 77 (2nd Cir.1994)—§ **18.22, n. 4.**
Wade v. Citibank, N.A., 118 A.D.2d 648, 122 A.D.2d 625, 500 N.Y.S.2d 7 (N.Y.A.D. 2 Dept.1986)—§ **1.10, n. 16.**
Wade, United States v., 388 U.S. 218, 87 S.Ct. 1926, 18 L.Ed.2d 1149 (1967)—§ **38.10, n. 158.**
Wade Lupe Const. Co., Inc., Application of, 134 Misc.2d 738, 512 N.Y.S.2d 338 (N.Y.Sup.1987)—§ **10.21, n. 6.**
Wagner, Matter of, 107 A.D.2d 60, 485 N.Y.S.2d 278 (N.Y.A.D. 1 Dept.1985)—§ **35.80, n. 4.**
Wagner v. Mittendorf, 232 N.Y. 481, 134 N.E. 539 (N.Y.1922)—§ **30.11, n. 6.**
Wagner Seed Co. v. Daggett, 800 F.2d 310 (2nd Cir.1986)—§ **15.29, n. 6.**
Wais, Matter of, 119 Misc.2d 911, 464 N.Y.S.2d 634 (N.Y.Sup.1983)—§ **22.17, n. 3.**
Wakefield v. Northern Telecom, Inc., 813 F.2d 535 (2nd Cir.1987)—§ **17.33, n. 4;** § **17.35, n. 7.**
Wakefield v. Northern Telecom, Inc., 769 F.2d 109 (2nd Cir.1985)—§ **17.33, n. 4;** § **17.35, n. 6.**
Walbern Press, Inc. v. C.V. Communications, Inc., 212 A.D.2d 460, 622 N.Y.S.2d 951 (N.Y.A.D. 1 Dept.1995)—§ **5.40, n. 3.**
Walczyk v. Chresfield, 52 A.D.2d 601, 382 N.Y.S.2d 274 (N.Y.A.D. 2 Dept.1976)—§ **37.65, n. 48.**

Waldman's Estate, In re, 1 A.D.2d 980, 151 N.Y.S.2d 389 (N.Y.A.D. 2 Dept.1956)—§ **37.37, n. 51.**
Waldo v. Schmidt, 200 N.Y. 199, 93 N.E. 477 (N.Y.1910)—§ **37.3, n. 13.**
Waldorf v. Coffey, 5 Misc.2d 80, 159 N.Y.S.2d 852 (N.Y.Sup.1957)—§ **14.14, n. 7.**
Waldo's Inc. v. Village of Johnson City, 544 N.Y.S.2d 809, 543 N.E.2d 74 (N.Y. 1989)—§ **14.38, n. 11.**
Waldo's, Inc. v. Village of Johnson City, 141 A.D.2d 194, 534 N.Y.S.2d 723 (N.Y.A.D. 3 Dept.1988)—§ **14.17, n. 1.**
Waldron v. Ball Corp., 210 A.D.2d 611, 619 N.Y.S.2d 841 (N.Y.A.D. 3 Dept.1994)—§ **18.63, n. 2.**
Walker v. City of New York, 974 F.2d 293 (2nd Cir.1992)—§ **18.25, n. 6.**
Walker v. General Motors Corp., Pontiac Motor Div., 160 Misc.2d 903, 611 N.Y.S.2d 741 (N.Y.City Civ.Ct.1994)—§ **7.17;** § **7.17, n. 9, 10.**
Walker v. General Motors Corp., Pontiac Motor Div., 159 Misc.2d 651, 606 N.Y.S.2d 125 (N.Y.City Civ.Ct.1993)—§ **7.10, n. 15, 17;** § **7.15, n. 9;** § **7.17, n. 3, 7.**
Walker, People v., 201 A.D.2d 896, 607 N.Y.S.2d 815 (N.Y.A.D. 4 Dept.1994)—§ **38.8, n. 13.**
Walker v. Sheldon, 223 N.Y.S.2d 488, 179 N.E.2d 497 (N.Y.1961)—§ **28.44, n. 1;** § **30.31, n. 7.**
Walker v. Walker, 635 N.Y.S.2d 152, 658 N.E.2d 1025 (N.Y.1995)—§ **38.8, n. 107;** § **38.19;** § **38.19, n. 32.**
Walkovszky v. Carlton, 276 N.Y.S.2d 585, 223 N.E.2d 6 (N.Y.1966)—§ **2.23, n. 18.**
Wallace v. Parks Corp., 212 A.D.2d 132, 629 N.Y.S.2d 570 (N.Y.A.D. 4 Dept.1995)—§ **27.51, n. 3.**
Wallace v. Universal Ins. Inc., 227 N.Y.S.2d 999 (N.Y.Sup.1962)—§ **31.27, n. 4.**
Waller v. Georgia, 467 U.S. 39, 104 S.Ct. 2210, 81 L.Ed.2d 31 (1984)—§ **18.13, n. 3;** § **38.19, n. 111.**
Wallfor, Inc. v. Eaton, 127 A.D.2d 838, 512 N.Y.S.2d 228 (N.Y.A.D. 2 Dept.1987)—§ **37.37, n. 47.**
Walls, In re, 17 B.R. 701 (Bkrtcy.S.D.W.Va. 1982)—§ **9.28, n. 4.**
Wallschlaeger v. Schweiker, 705 F.2d 191 (7th Cir.1983)—§ **34.23, n. 1.**
Walsam Fifth Ave. Development Co. v. Lions Gate Capital Corp., 163 Misc.2d 1071, 623 N.Y.S.2d 94 (N.Y.City Civ.Ct. 1995)—§ **13.62, n. 2.**
Walsh v. Lincoln Sav. Bank, FSB, 1995 WL 66639 (S.D.N.Y.1995)—§ **17.69, n. 3.**
Walsh, People v., 500 N.Y.S.2d 96, 490 N.E.2d 1222 (N.Y.1986)—§ **35.125, n. 1.**

TABLE OF CASES

Walsh, People ex rel. Fordham Manor Reformed Church v., 244 N.Y. 280, 155 N.E. 575 (N.Y.1927)—§ **16.73, n. 4;** § **16.74, n. 1.**
Walsh v. Walsh, 227 A.D.2d 497, 643 N.Y.S.2d 137 (N.Y.A.D. 2 Dept.1996)—§ **37.19, n. 30.**
Walter v. Doe, 93 Misc.2d 286, 402 N.Y.S.2d 723 (N.Y.City Civ.Ct.1978)—§ **28.11, n. 12.**
Walter v. Hangen, 71 A.D. 40, 75 N.Y.S. 683 (N.Y.A.D. 1 Dept.1902)—§ **30.25, n. 5.**
Walter, People ex rel. Corwin v., 68 N.Y. 403 (N.Y.1877)—§ **37.31, n. 1.**
Walters v. Fullwood, 675 F.Supp. 155 (S.D.N.Y.1987)—§ **5.11, n. 3.**
Walters v. Geheran, 192 N.Y.S.2d 23 (N.Y.Sup.1959)—§ **30.37, n. 1.**
Walters v. National Ass'n of Radiation Survivors, 473 U.S. 305, 105 S.Ct. 3180, 87 L.Ed.2d 220 (1985)—§ **4.14, n. 2.**
Walther's Will, In re, 188 N.Y.S.2d 168, 159 N.E.2d 665 (N.Y.1959)—§ **25.28, n. 6.**
Walton v. Town of Brookhaven, 41 Misc.2d 798, 246 N.Y.S.2d 985 (N.Y.Sup.1964)—§ **16.50, n. 4.**
Walus v. Millington, 49 Misc.2d 104, 266 N.Y.S.2d 833 (N.Y.Sup.1966)—§ **16.18;** § **16.18, n. 16, 25.**
Wambat Realty Corp. v. State, 393 N.Y.S.2d 949, 362 N.E.2d 581 (N.Y.1977)—§ **16.24, n. 4.**
Wamsley v. Atlas S.S. Co., 50 A.D. 199, 63 N.Y.S. 761 (N.Y.A.D. 1 Dept.1900)—§ **30.18, n. 9.**
Wanamaker v. Columbian Rope Co., 713 F.Supp. 533 (N.D.N.Y.1989)—§ **30.9, n. 26.**
Wanamaker v. Pietraszek, 107 A.D.2d 1020, 486 N.Y.S.2d 523 (N.Y.A.D. 4 Dept. 1985)—§ **30.10, n. 11.**
Wand v. Saleh, 218 A.D.2d 647, 630 N.Y.S.2d 367 (N.Y.A.D. 2 Dept.1995)—§ **11.6, n. 2.**
Wang v. Wang, 87 Misc.2d 980, 386 N.Y.S.2d 922 (N.Y.Sup.1976)—§ **21.29, n. 6.**
Wappingers Cent. School Dist. v. Public Employment Relations Bd. of State of N.Y., 215 A.D.2d 669, 627 N.Y.S.2d 701 (N.Y.A.D. 2 Dept.1995)—§ **37.37;** § **37.37, n. 61.**
Ward v. Bennett, 214 A.D.2d 741, 625 N.Y.S.2d 609 (N.Y.A.D. 2 Dept.1995)—§ **14.14, n. 5.**
Ward v. Corbally, Gartland & Rappleyea, 207 A.D.2d 342, 615 N.Y.S.2d 430 (N.Y.A.D. 2 Dept.1994)—§ **31.16, n. 4.**
Ward, United States v., 448 U.S. 242, 100 S.Ct. 2636, 65 L.Ed.2d 742 (1980)—§ **4.38, n. 2.**

Warden, People ex rel. Lester (Geddes) v., 218 A.D.2d 679, 630 N.Y.S.2d 932 (N.Y.A.D. 2 Dept.1995)—§ **38.8, n. 77.**
Warden, Brooklyn House of Detention, People ex rel. Fabre v., 354 N.Y.S.2d 943, 310 N.E.2d 540 (N.Y.1974)—§ **38.8, n. 75.**
Warden, New York County Men's House of Detention, People ex rel. Lazer on Behalf of Palmieri v., 580 N.Y.S.2d 183, 588 N.E.2d 81 (N.Y.1992)—§ **39.3, n. 2.**
Warden of Queens House of Detention, People ex rel. Carbone on Behalf of Osorio v., 219 A.D.2d 610, 631 N.Y.S.2d 528 (N.Y.A.D. 2 Dept.1995)—§ **38.8, n. 76.**
Ward La France Truck Corp. v. City of New York, 7 Misc.2d 739, 160 N.Y.S.2d 679 (N.Y.Sup.1957)—§ **3.25, n. 14.**
Ware v. Ware, 193 A.D.2d 684, 598 N.Y.S.2d 532 (N.Y.A.D. 2 Dept.1993)—§ **37.22, n. 5.**
Warf, People v., 208 A.D.2d 874, 618 N.Y.S.2d 556 (N.Y.A.D. 2 Dept.1994)—§ **38.8, n. 143.**
Wargold, Matter of, 152 Misc.2d 172, 575 N.Y.S.2d 230 (N.Y.Sur.1991)—§ **22.28, n. 10;** § **22.33, n. 1.**
Waring v. Burke Steel Co., 69 N.Y.S.2d 399 (N.Y.Sup.1947)—§ **10.15, n. 1.**
Warms' Estate, In re, 140 N.Y.S.2d 169 (N.Y.Sur.1955)—§ **24.76, n. 3.**
Warmus, People v., 148 Misc.2d 374, 561 N.Y.S.2d 111 (N.Y.Co.Ct.1990)—§ **7.31, n. 6.**
Warner v. American Fluoride Corp., 204 A.D.2d 1, 616 N.Y.S.2d 534 (N.Y.A.D. 2 Dept.1994)—§ **27.44, n. 1;** § **27.47, n. 4.**
Warren v. Dwyer, 906 F.2d 70 (2nd Cir. 1990)—§ **18.32, n. 8.**
Warrin v. Haverty, 149 A.D. 564, 133 N.Y.S. 959 (N.Y.A.D. 1 Dept.1912)—§ **13.27, n. 1.**
Warsawer v. Burghard, 234 A.D. 346, 254 N.Y.S. 749 (N.Y.A.D. 1 Dept.1932)—§ **12.31, n. 1.**
Warshawsky, Matter of, N.Y.L.J., 1/9/95, p.30, col.4 (Sup.Ct., Kings County)—§ **22.70, n. 1, 10.**
Washington, Matter of, 216 A.D.2d 781, 628 N.Y.S.2d 837 (N.Y.A.D. 3 Dept.1995)—§ **18.67, n. 5.**
Washington v. Glucksberg, ___ U.S. ___, 117 S.Ct. 2258, 138 L.Ed.2d 772 (1997)—§ **23.113;** § **23.113, n. 3.**
Washington, People v., 633 N.Y.S.2d 476, 657 N.E.2d 497 (N.Y.1995)—§ **38.12, n. 6, 8;** § **38.13, n. 5;** § **39.47, n. 2.**
Washington, People v., 175 A.D.2d 732, 573 N.Y.S.2d 180 (N.Y.A.D. 1 Dept.1991)—§ **38.10, n. 69.**

TABLE OF CASES

Washington, People v., 528 N.Y.S.2d 531, 523 N.E.2d 818 (N.Y.1988)—§ **37.29, n. 48; § 38.19, n. 80, 81.**

Washington, People v., 433 N.Y.S.2d 745, 413 N.E.2d 1159 (N.Y.1980)—§ **33.58.**

Washington, People v., 282 A.D. 896, 125 N.Y.S.2d 231 (N.Y.A.D. 3 Dept.1953)—§ **38.21; § 38.21, n. 18.**

Washington, People ex rel. v. Higgins, 207 A.D.2d 961, 617 N.Y.S.2d 670 (N.Y.A.D. 4 Dept.1994)—§ **38.8, n. 78.**

Washington County Cease, Inc. v. Persico, 120 Misc.2d 207, 465 N.Y.S.2d 965 (N.Y.Sup.1983)—§ **16.128, n. 8.**

Washington-St. Tammany Elec. Co-op., Inc., In re, 97 B.R. 852 (E.D.La.1989)—§ **9.142, n. 5.**

Washor on Behalf of Lopez, People ex rel. v. Freckelton, 187 A.D.2d 406, 590 N.Y.S.2d 203 (N.Y.A.D. 1 Dept.1992)—§ **38.8, n. 78.**

Wasserman v. Wong, 181 A.D.2d 672, 581 N.Y.S.2d 221 (N.Y.A.D. 2 Dept.1992)—§ **37.65, n. 35, 63.**

Waste Industries, Inc., United States v., 734 F.2d 159 (4th Cir.1984)—§ **15.25, n. 10.**

Watergate II Apartments v. Buffalo Sewer Authority, 412 N.Y.S.2d 821, 385 N.E.2d 560 (N.Y.1978)—§ **4.72, n. 3, 4; § 37.38, n. 6.**

Waterloo Stock Car Raceway, Inc., State v., 96 Misc.2d 350, 409 N.Y.S.2d 40 (N.Y.Sup.1978)—§ **15.32, n. 7, 8.**

Waterman Steamship Corp. v. Aguiar (In re Waterman S.S. Corp.), 157 B.R. 220 (S.D.N.Y.1993)—§ **9.169, n. 5.**

Waters v. Churchill, 511 U.S. 661, 114 S.Ct. 1878, 128 L.Ed.2d 686 (1994)—§ **17.55, n. 5.**

Waterside Associates v. New York State Dept. of Environmental Conservation, 534 N.Y.S.2d 915, 531 N.E.2d 636 (N.Y. 1988)—§ **4.82, n. 14.**

Watkins v. Commercial Stevedoring Co., 216 A.D. 234, 214 N.Y.S. 634 (N.Y.A.D. 1 Dept.1926)—§ **37.28, n. 1.**

Watkins, People v., 212 A.D.2d 357, 622 N.Y.S.2d 513 (N.Y.A.D. 1 Dept.1995)—§ **38.19, n. 48.**

Watson, People v., 163 A.D.2d 253, 558 N.Y.S.2d 537 (N.Y.A.D. 1 Dept.1990)—§ **38.19, n. 62.**

Watts' Estate, Matter of, 49 A.D.2d 961, 373 N.Y.S.2d 898 (N.Y.A.D. 3 Dept. 1975)—§ **25.6, n. 3.**

Waxman, Matter of, 96 A.D.2d 906, 466 N.Y.S.2d 85 (N.Y.A.D. 2 Dept.1983)—§ **22.33, n. 1.**

Weaver, People v., 177 A.D.2d 809, 576 N.Y.S.2d 424 (N.Y.A.D. 3 Dept.1991)—§ **38.10, n. 160.**

Weaver, People v., 429 N.Y.S.2d 399, 406 N.E.2d 1335 (N.Y.1980)—§ **33.57, n. 5.**

Webb, In re, 157 B.R. 614 (Bkrtcy.N.D.Ohio 1993)—§ **9.206, n. 5.**

Webb, People v., 52 A.D.2d 8, 382 N.Y.S.2d 369 (N.Y.A.D. 3 Dept.1976)—§ **38.8, n. 119.**

Webber's Will, In re, 187 Misc. 674, 64 N.Y.S.2d 281 (N.Y.Sur.1946)—§ **22.5, n. 4; § 25.12, n. 3.**

Webb, Town of v. Sisters Realty North Corp., 168 A.D.2d 896, 566 N.Y.S.2d 109 (N.Y.A.D. 4 Dept.1990)—§ **14.59, n. 5.**

Weber v. Bridgman, 113 N.Y. 600, 21 N.E. 985 (N.Y.1889)—§ **12.8, n. 4.**

Weber v. Dell, 804 F.2d 796 (2nd Cir. 1986)—§ **18.32, n. 5.**

Weber, United States ex rel. v. Ragen, 176 F.2d 579 (7th Cir.1949)—§ **37.28, n. 36.**

Weber v. Weber, 213 A.D.2d 1021, 624 N.Y.S.2d 323 (N.Y.A.D. 4 Dept.1995)—§ **1.63, n. 4.**

W.E. Blume, Inc. v. Postal Tel. Cable Co., 265 A.D. 1062, 39 N.Y.S.2d 539 (N.Y.A.D. 2 Dept.1943)—§ **10.13, n. 5.**

Wechter v. Wechter, 50 A.D.2d 826, 376 N.Y.S.2d 180 (N.Y.A.D. 2 Dept.1975)—§ **21.29, n. 5.**

Weckstein v. Breitbart, 111 A.D.2d 6, 488 N.Y.S.2d 665 (N.Y.A.D. 1 Dept.1985)—§ **37.29, n. 5.**

Wedtech Corp. v. Federal Ins. Co., 740 F.Supp. 214 (S.D.N.Y.1990)—§ **28.43, n. 4, 8.**

Wegman v. Dairylea Co-op., Inc., 50 A.D.2d 108, 376 N.Y.S.2d 728 (N.Y.A.D. 4 Dept. 1975)—§ **17.31, n. 3.**

Wegman v. Wegman, 123 A.D.2d 220, 509 N.Y.S.2d 342 (N.Y.A.D. 2 Dept.1986)—§ **21.42, n. 3.**

Wegmans Food Markets, Inc. v. Department of Taxation and Finance of the State of New York, 126 Misc.2d 144, 481 N.Y.S.2d 298 (N.Y.Sup.1984)—§ **3.34, n. 15.**

Whitehead, Matter of, N.Y.L.J., 5/30/95, p. 34, col. 1 (Sup.Ct., Suffolk County)—§ **22.40, n. 3.**

Weichert v. Shea, 186 A.D.2d 992, 588 N.Y.S.2d 454 (N.Y.A.D. 4 Dept.1992)—§ **37.83, n. 6.**

Weicker v. Weicker, 290 N.Y.S.2d 732, 237 N.E.2d 876 (N.Y.1968)—§ **18.74, n. 1.**

Weicker v. Weicker, 26 A.D.2d 39, 270 N.Y.S.2d 640 (N.Y.A.D. 1 Dept.1966)—§ **37.37, n. 41.**

Weiler v. Cranny, 215 A.D.2d 752, 627 N.Y.S.2d 956 (N.Y.A.D. 2 Dept.1995)—§ **37.37, n. 10.**

Weinbaum v. Cuomo, 219 A.D.2d 554, 631 N.Y.S.2d 825 (N.Y.A.D. 1 Dept.1995)—§ **18.53, n. 9.**

TABLE OF CASES

Weinberg v. Hertz Corp., 516 N.Y.S.2d 652, 509 N.E.2d 347 (N.Y.1987)—§ **7.47, n. 6.**

Weinberg v. Transamerica Ins. Co., 477 N.Y.S.2d 99, 465 N.E.2d 819 (N.Y. 1984)—§ **26.49, n. 5; § 31.29, n. 10.**

Weinberger v. Semenenko, 36 N.Y.S.2d 396 (N.Y.Sup.1942)—§ **1.38, n. 9.**

Weiner v. Lenox Hill Hosp., 193 A.D.2d 380, 597 N.Y.S.2d 58 (N.Y.A.D. 1 Dept. 1993)—§ **30.14, n. 6.**

Weiner v. McGraw-Hill, Inc., 457 N.Y.S.2d 193, 443 N.E.2d 441 (N.Y.1982)— § **17.33, n. 3; § 17.34; § 17.34, n. 1.**

Weingarten v. Town of Lewisboro, 569 N.Y.S.2d 599, 572 N.E.2d 40 (N.Y. 1991)—§ **16.49, n. 2.**

Weinman v. Hamilton Properties Corp. (In re Hamilton), 186 B.R. 991 (Bkrtcy. D.Colo.1995)—§ **9.180, n. 3.**

Weinreich v. Sandhaus, 850 F.Supp. 1169 (S.D.N.Y.1994)—§ **1.10, n. 10.**

Weinreich v. Weinreich, 184 A.D.2d 505, 585 N.Y.S.2d 770 (N.Y.A.D. 2 Dept. 1992)—§ **8.42, n. 11.**

Weinstock v. Hammond, 270 N.Y. 64, 200 N.E. 581 (N.Y.1936)—§ **3.32, n. 12.**

Weinstock's Estate, Matter of, 386 N.Y.S.2d 1, 351 N.E.2d 647 (N.Y.1976)—§ **24.95, n. 2.**

Weiss v. Manfredi, 616 N.Y.S.2d 325, 639 N.E.2d 1122 (N.Y.1994)—§ **28.11; § 28.11, n. 3.**

Weiss v. Shapolsky, 161 A.D.2d 707, 555 N.Y.S.2d 843 (N.Y.A.D. 2 Dept.1990)— § **12.20, n. 1.**

Weiss v. Weiss, 206 A.D.2d 741, 615 N.Y.S.2d 468 (N.Y.A.D. 3 Dept.1994)— § **6.67, n. 4.**

Weiss v. Weiss, 436 N.Y.S.2d 862, 418 N.E.2d 377 (N.Y.1981)—§ **21.59, n. 1, 2; § 21.60, n. 1.**

Weitz, In re, 11 A.D.2d 76, 202 N.Y.S.2d 393 (N.Y.A.D. 1 Dept.1960)—§ **28.25, n. 1.**

Welch v. Dura-Wound, Inc., 894 F.Supp. 76 (N.D.N.Y.1995)—§ **27.23, n. 4.**

Welch v. Law, 121 A.D.2d 808, 504 N.Y.S.2d 790 (N.Y.A.D. 3 Dept.1986)—§ **16.84, n. 6.**

Welch v. Mr. Christmas Inc., 454 N.Y.S.2d 971, 440 N.E.2d 1317 (N.Y.1982)— § **18.64, n. 10, 14.**

Welch, People ex rel. v. Bard, 209 N.Y. 304, 103 N.E. 140 (N.Y.1913)—§ **38.3, n. 8.**

Welcome, People v., 184 A.D.2d 916, 587 N.Y.S.2d 229 (N.Y.A.D. 3 Dept.1992)— § **38.8, n. 155.**

Wellman v. Wellman, 933 F.2d 215 (4th Cir.1991)—§ **9.121, n. 2, 3.**

Wells v. Town of Salina, 119 N.Y. 280, 23 N.E. 870 (N.Y.1890)—§ **3.7, n. 3; § 3.9, n. 3.**

Wells Fargo Alarm Services v. Consumers Distributing Ltd., 150 A.D.2d 372, 543 N.Y.S.2d 299 (N.Y.A.D. 2 Dept.1989)— § **37.65, n. 73.**

Wells' Will, In re, 36 A.D.2d 471, 321 N.Y.S.2d 200 (N.Y.A.D. 4 Dept.1971)— § **2.46, n. 5.**

Weltman v. Independence Sav. Bank, 1990 WL 96087 (S.D.N.Y.1990)—§ **9.52, n. 6.**

Wendell v. Supermarkets General Corp., 189 A.D.2d 1063, 592 N.Y.S.2d 895 (N.Y.A.D. 3 Dept.1993)—§ **30.30, n. 21; § 37.29, n. 22.**

WEOK Broadcasting Corp. v. Planning Bd. of Town of Lloyd, 583 N.Y.S.2d 170, 592 N.E.2d 778 (N.Y.1992)—§ **16.57; § 16.57, n. 1; § 16.105, n. 8; § 16.125, n. 8.**

We're Associates Co. v. Cohen, Stracher & Bloom, P.C., 490 N.Y.S.2d 743, 480 N.E.2d 357 (N.Y.1985)—§ **1.122, n. 7; § 39.4, n. 10.**

Werfel v. Agresta, 44 A.D.2d 610, 354 N.Y.S.2d 143 (N.Y.A.D. 2 Dept.1974)— § **37.37, n. 76.**

Werle v. Rumsey, 278 N.Y. 186, 15 N.E.2d 572 (N.Y.1938)—§ **28.4, n. 1.**

Wern v. D'Alessandro, 219 A.D.2d 646, 631 N.Y.S.2d 425 (N.Y.A.D. 2 Dept.1995)— § **37.28, n. 38.**

Werner v. Katal Country Club, 234 A.D.2d 659, 650 N.Y.S.2d 866 (N.Y.A.D. 3 Dept. 1996)—§ **28.24, n. 5.**

Wernham v. Moore, 121 A.D.2d 297, 504 N.Y.S.2d 3 (N.Y.A.D. 1 Dept.1986)— § **17.34, n. 6.**

Wesley L., Matter of, 72 A.D.2d 137, 423 N.Y.S.2d 482 (N.Y.A.D. 1 Dept.1980)— § **20.43, n. 7.**

Wesser v. House of Good Shepherd, 37 A.D.2d 1005, 325 N.Y.S.2d 594 (N.Y.A.D. 3 Dept.1971)—§ **32.18, n. 7.**

Wesson v. Dullzell, 15 A.D.2d 744, 223 N.Y.S.2d 876 (N.Y.A.D. 1 Dept.1962)— § **37.37, n. 91.**

West v. Masso, N.Y.L.J., 2/28/90, p.23, col.1, 18 HCR 101 (Civ.Ct., N.Y. County)— § **13.17, n. 12; § 13.18, n. 28; § 13.43, n. 13.**

West, People v., 212 A.D.2d 651, 622 N.Y.S.2d 572 (N.Y.A.D. 2 Dept.1995)— § **38.19, n. 48.**

West v. West, 213 A.D.2d 1025, 625 N.Y.S.2d 116 (N.Y.A.D. 4 Dept.1995)— § **21.39, n. 11.**

West Ave., New York City, In re, 27 A.D.2d 539, 275 N.Y.S.2d 119 (N.Y.A.D. 2 Dept. 1966)—§ **14.93, n. 5.**

TABLE OF CASES

Westbury, Village of v. Department of Transp., 550 N.Y.S.2d 604, 549 N.E.2d 1175 (N.Y.1989)—**§ 15.6, n. 26, 27.**

Westchester County Medical Center on Behalf of O'Connor, Matter of, 534 N.Y.S.2d 886, 531 N.E.2d 607 (N.Y. 1988)—**§ 22.54, n. 8; § 23.109, n. 4; § 23.111, n. 3; § 24.92, n. 1.**

Westchester Reform Temple v. Brown, 293 N.Y.S.2d 297, 239 N.E.2d 891 (N.Y. 1968)—**§ 16.131, n. 8, 9.**

Westchester Resco Co., L.P. v. New England Reinsurance Corp., 818 F.2d 2 (2nd Cir.1987)—**§ 31.9, n. 13.**

Westchester Resco Co., L.P. v. New England Reinsurance Corp., 648 F.Supp. 842 (S.D.N.Y.1986)—**§ 31.19, n. 1.**

Westchester Structures, Inc., In re, 181 B.R. 730 (Bkrtcy.S.D.N.Y.1995)—**§ 10.102, n. 4.**

West Chicago, Ill., City of v. United States Nuclear Regulatory Com'n, 701 F.2d 632 (7th Cir.1983)—**§ 4.10, n. 5.**

West Coast Video Enterprises, Inc., In re, 174 B.R. 906 (Bkrtcy.E.D.Pa.1994)—**§ 9.170, n. 4.**

Westergreen, People v., 168 A.D.2d 395, 562 N.Y.S.2d 703 (N.Y.A.D. 1 Dept.1990)—**§ 33.52, n. 2.**

West–Fair Elec. Contractors v. Aetna Cas. & Sur. Co., 638 N.Y.S.2d 394, 661 N.E.2d 967 (N.Y.1995)—**§ 10.3, n. 4.**

West Harlem Pork Center, Ltd. v. Empire Nat. Bank, 60 A.D.2d 859, 400 N.Y.S.2d 859 (N.Y.A.D. 2 Dept.1978)—**§ 8.25, n. 4.**

Weston, People v., 92 A.D.2d 945, 460 N.Y.S.2d 633 (N.Y.A.D. 3 Dept.1983)—**§ 38.19, n. 72.**

Westover, In re Will of, 145 Misc.2d 469, 546 N.Y.S.2d 937 (N.Y.Sur.1989)—**§ 25.28, n. 1.**

Westwood Pharmaceuticals, Inc. v. National Fuel Gas Distribution Corp., 964 F.2d 85 (2nd Cir.1992)—**§ 15.29, n. 20.**

Wetzler v. O'Brien, 81 A.D.2d 517, 437 N.Y.S.2d 343 (N.Y.A.D. 1 Dept.1981)—**§ 12.56, n. 12.**

WFB Telecommunications, Inc. v. NYNEX Corp., 188 A.D.2d 257, 590 N.Y.S.2d 460 (N.Y.A.D. 1 Dept.1992)—**§ 17.29, n. 4.**

WFDR, Inc., In re, 10 B.R. 109 (Bkrtcy. N.D.Ga.1981)—**§ 9.149, n. 4.**

Whalen v. Gerzof, 154 A.D.2d 843, 546 N.Y.S.2d 705 (N.Y.A.D. 3 Dept.1989)—**§ 2.46, n. 12.**

Whalen v. Slocum, 84 A.D.2d 956, 446 N.Y.S.2d 727 (N.Y.A.D. 4 Dept.1981)—**§ 4.24, n. 4.**

Wheeler Technology, Inc., In re, 139 B.R. 235 (9th Cir.BAP (Wash.) 1992)—**§ 9.47, n. 1.**

Whelan v. Pitts, 150 A.D.2d 380, 540 N.Y.S.2d 536 (N.Y.A.D. 2 Dept.1989)—**§ 3.20, n. 6.**

Whetstone v. Immigration and Naturalization Service, 561 F.2d 1303 (9th Cir. 1977)—**§ 19.12, n. 6.**

Whidden, People v., 434 N.Y.S.2d 936, 415 N.E.2d 927 (N.Y.1980)—**§ 38.8, n. 192.**

White v. City of New York, 37 A.D.2d 603, 322 N.Y.S.2d 920 (N.Y.A.D. 2 Dept. 1971)—**§ 30.14, n. 16.**

White v. Guarente, 401 N.Y.S.2d 474, 372 N.E.2d 315 (N.Y.1977)—**§ 17.27, n. 6; § 28.11, n. 5.**

White v. Long, 626 N.Y.S.2d 989, 650 N.E.2d 836 (N.Y.1995)—**§ 15.27, n. 27.**

White, People v., 210 A.D.2d 447, 620 N.Y.S.2d 437 (N.Y.A.D. 2 Dept.1994)—**§ 38.10, n. 96.**

White, People v., 194 A.D.2d 1014, 600 N.Y.S.2d 642 (N.Y.A.D. 3 Dept.1993)—**§ 38.8, n. 19.**

White, People v., 541 N.Y.S.2d 749, 539 N.E.2d 577 (N.Y.1989)—**§ 28.12, n. 7; § 38.37, n. 1.**

White v. Secretary of Health and Human Services, 910 F.2d 64 (2nd Cir.1990)—**§ 34.47, n. 3.**

White, State ex rel. v. Supreme Court New York, 443 N.Y.S.2d 725, 427 N.E.2d 1190 (N.Y.1981)—**§ 38.8, n. 75.**

White v. White, 204 A.D.2d 825, 611 N.Y.S.2d 951 (N.Y.A.D. 3 Dept.1994)—**§ 21.39, n. 3.**

White by White v. City of New York, 598 N.Y.S.2d 759, 615 N.E.2d 216 (N.Y. 1993)—**§ 31.10, n. 13.**

White Devon Farm v. Stahl, 88 Misc.2d 961, 389 N.Y.S.2d 724 (N.Y.Sup.1976)—**§ 5.39, n. 2.**

Whiteford Plastics Co. v. Chase National Bank of New York City, 179 F.2d 582 (2nd Cir.1950)—**§ 9.121, n. 3.**

Whiteford's Estate, In re, 61 Misc.2d 402, 306 N.Y.S.2d 32 (N.Y.Sur.1969)—**§ 24.63, n. 5.**

Whitehall, Estate of v. State, 174 A.D.2d 707, 573 N.Y.S.2d 871 (N.Y.A.D. 2 Dept. 1991)—**§ 14.114, n. 1.**

Whitehall Tenants Corp. v. Estate of Olnick, 213 A.D.2d 200, 623 N.Y.S.2d 585 (N.Y.A.D. 1 Dept.1995)—**§ 37.65, n. 43.**

Whitehead, Matter of, 169 Misc.2d 554, 642 N.Y.S.2d 979 (N.Y.Sup.1996)—**§ 22.39, n. 1; § 22.40, n. 3.**

Whitehead, Matter of, N.Y.L.J., 5/30/95, p. 34, col. 1 (Sup.Ct., Suffolk County)—**§ 22.25, n. 4.**

Whitehead, People v., 135 A.D.2d 997, 522 N.Y.S.2d 721 (N.Y.A.D. 3 Dept.1987)—**§ 38.20, n. 15.**

TABLE OF CASES

Whitemarsh Industries, Inc. v. Sears Roebuck and Co., 192 A.D.2d 331, 595 N.Y.S.2d 763 (N.Y.A.D. 1 Dept.1993)—§ **5.19, n. 5.**

White Motor Credit Corp., In re, 27 B.R. 554 (N.D.Ohio 1982)—§ **9.43, n. 9.**

White Plains, City of v. Ferraioli, 357 N.Y.S.2d 449, 313 N.E.2d 756 (N.Y. 1974)—§ **16.122; § 16.122, n. 11.**

Whitfield v. City of New York, 1997 WL 749429 (N.Y.1997)—§ **39.4; § 39.4, n. 14; § 39.5, n. 4.**

Whiting v. Town of Pittsford, 105 A.D.2d 1141, 482 N.Y.S.2d 1015 (N.Y.A.D. 4 Dept.1984)—§ **14.128, n. 2.**

Whiting Pools, Inc., United States v., 462 U.S. 198, 103 S.Ct. 2309, 76 L.Ed.2d 515 (1983)—§ **9.49, n. 1.**

Whitler Contracting Corp., Inc. v. City of New York, 161 A.D.2d 484, 555 N.Y.S.2d 748 (N.Y.A.D. 1 Dept.1990)—§ **37.28, n. 30.**

Wick v. Gozigian, 85 A.D.2d 805, 445 N.Y.S.2d 643 (N.Y.A.D. 3 Dept.1981)—§ **23.79, n. 2.**

Wicks, People v., 556 N.Y.S.2d 970, 556 N.E.2d 409 (N.Y.1990)—§ **38.19, n. 100, 140.**

Wieder v. Chemical Bank, 202 A.D.2d 168, 608 N.Y.S.2d 195 (N.Y.A.D. 1 Dept. 1994)—§ **17.25, n. 12.**

Wieder v. Skala, 593 N.Y.S.2d 752, 609 N.E.2d 105 (N.Y.1992)—§ **17.32, n. 1; § 17.33; § 17.33, n. 2; § 17.35; § 17.35, n. 10.**

Wiegand v. Berger, 151 A.D.2d 343, 542 N.Y.S.2d 598 (N.Y.A.D. 1 Dept.1989)—§ **29.26, n. 11.**

Wiehe v. Town of Babylon, 169 A.D.2d 728, 564 N.Y.S.2d 193 (N.Y.A.D. 2 Dept. 1991)—§ **16.44, n. 4.**

Wiercinski v. Wiercinski, 116 A.D.2d 789, 497 N.Y.S.2d 179 (N.Y.A.D. 3 Dept. 1986)—§ **21.38, n. 7.**

Wierzbieniec's Estate, Matter of, 93 A.D.2d 978, 461 N.Y.S.2d 653 (N.Y.A.D. 4 Dept. 1983)—§ **24.61, n. 2.**

Wiggin v. Gordon, 115 Misc.2d 1071, 455 N.Y.S.2d 205 (N.Y.City Civ.Ct.1982)—§ **28.24, n. 2.**

Wiggins, Matter of Estate of, 200 A.D.2d 813, 606 N.Y.S.2d 423 (N.Y.A.D. 3 Dept. 1994)—§ **25.47, n. 2, 3.**

Wiggins, People v., 197 A.D.2d 802, 603 N.Y.S.2d 81 (N.Y.A.D. 3 Dept.1993)—§ **33.87, n. 3.**

Wiggins v. Town of Somers, 173 N.Y.S.2d 579, 149 N.E.2d 869 (N.Y.1958)—§ **3.9, n. 5; § 3.10, n. 7.**

Wiktorowicz v. Kimberly-Clark Corp., 99 A.D.2d 903, 472 N.Y.S.2d 505 (N.Y.A.D. 3 Dept.1984)—§ **32.19, n. 4.**

Wilcher, Matter of, 56 B.R. 428 (Bkrtcy. N.D.Ill.1985)—§ **9.39, n. 3.**

Wilcox, In re, 153 Misc. 761, 276 N.Y.S. 117 (N.Y.Sup.1934)—§ **38.11, n. 1.**

Wilczak v. Ruda & Capozzi, Inc., 203 A.D.2d 944, 611 N.Y.S.2d 73 (N.Y.A.D. 4 Dept.1994)—§ **31.16, n. 9.**

Wildcat Const. Co., Inc., In re, 57 B.R. 981 (Bkrtcy.D.Vt.1986)—§ **9.54, n. 4.**

Wilder v. Thomas, 854 F.2d 605 (2nd Cir. 1988)—§ **15.22, n. 11.**

Wildman, Estate of v. Commissioner, T.C. Memo. 1989-667 (U.S.Tax Ct.1989)—§ **24.41, n. 2.**

Wilen v. Harridge House Associates, 94 A.D.2d 123, 463 N.Y.S.2d 453 (N.Y.A.D. 1 Dept.1983)—§ **13.69, n. 2, 3.**

Wilhelm, In re, 101 B.R. 120 (Bkrtcy. W.D.Mo.1989)—§ **9.159, n. 5.**

Wilkes v. Wilkes, 212 A.D.2d 719, 622 N.Y.S.2d 608 (N.Y.A.D. 2 Dept.1995)—§ **37.37, n. 63.**

Wilkin v. Dana R. Pickup & Co., 74 Misc.2d 1025, 347 N.Y.S.2d 122 (N.Y.Sup. 1973)—§ **28.14, n. 4.**

Wilkins v. Wilkins, 85 Misc.2d 985, 382 N.Y.S.2d 240 (N.Y.Sup.1976)—§ **21.29, n. 7.**

Will v. Michigan Dept. of State Police, 491 U.S. 58, 109 S.Ct. 2304, 105 L.Ed.2d 45 (1989)—§ **18.18, n. 8; § 18.33, n. 4.**

Willard v. Mercer, 83 A.D.2d 656, 442 N.Y.S.2d 200 (N.Y.A.D. 3 Dept.1981)—§ **12.64, n. 12.**

Willard Van Dyke Productions, Inc. v. Eastman Kodak Co., 239 N.Y.S.2d 337, 189 N.E.2d 693 (N.Y.1963)—§ **5.11, n. 8, 10.**

Willets v. Schnell, 261 N.Y.S.2d 888, 209 N.E.2d 547 (N.Y.1965)—§ **16.124, n. 11.**

William J. Kline & Son, Inc. v. State, 35 A.D.2d 465, 317 N.Y.S.2d 401 (N.Y.A.D. 3 Dept.1971)—§ **14.93, n. 5.**

William P. Pahl Equipment Corp. v. Kassis, 182 A.D.2d 22, 588 N.Y.S.2d 8 (N.Y.A.D. 1 Dept.1992)—§ **31.19, n. 2.**

Williams, In re, 188 B.R. 331 (E.D.N.Y. 1995)—§ **9.10, n. 6.**

Williams v. American Home Assur. Co., 97 A.D.2d 707, 468 N.Y.S.2d 341 (N.Y.A.D. 1 Dept.1983)—§ **31.11, n. 2.**

Williams v. Associated Mut. Ins. Co., 211 A.D.2d 865, 621 N.Y.S.2d 206 (N.Y.A.D. 3 Dept.1995)—§ **31.14, n. 1.**

Williams v. Bright, 167 Misc.2d 312, 632 N.Y.S.2d 760 (N.Y.Sup.1995)—§ **18.28; § 18.28, n. 1.**

Williams v. City of New York, 169 A.D.2d 713, 564 N.Y.S.2d 464 (N.Y.A.D. 2 Dept. 1991)—§ **30.13, n. 5.**

Williams v. Cornelius, 561 N.Y.S.2d 701, 563 N.E.2d 15 (N.Y.1990)—§ **38.8, n. 91.**

TABLE OF CASES

Williams v. Forbes, 157 A.D.2d 837, 550 N.Y.S.2d 903 (N.Y.A.D. 2 Dept.1990)—§ 37.46, n. 2.

Williams v. Metropolitan Distribution, 213 A.D.2d 852, 623 N.Y.S.2d 657 (N.Y.A.D. 3 Dept.1995)—§ 32.19, n. 5.

Williams, People v., 221 A.D.2d 673, 634 N.Y.S.2d 493 (N.Y.A.D. 2 Dept.1995)—§ 38.19, n. 48.

Williams, People v., 215 A.D.2d 1006, 626 N.Y.S.2d 346 (N.Y.A.D. 1 Dept.1995)—§ 38.8, n. 28.

Williams, People v., 214 A.D.2d 437, 625 N.Y.S.2d 42 (N.Y.A.D. 1 Dept.1995)—§ 38.8, n. 169.

Williams, People v., 212 A.D.2d 388, 622 N.Y.S.2d 275 (N.Y.A.D. 1 Dept.1995)—§ 38.27, n. 32.

Williams, People v., 195 A.D.2d 1040, 600 N.Y.S.2d 529 (N.Y.A.D. 4 Dept.1993)—§ 38.8, n. 226.

Williams, People v., 182 A.D.2d 490, 582 N.Y.S.2d 406 (N.Y.A.D. 1 Dept.1992)—§ 38.28, n. 30.

Williams, People v., 146 Misc.2d 866, 553 N.Y.S.2d 584 (N.Y.Sup.1990)—§ 33.79, n. 2.

Williams, People v., 451 N.Y.S.2d 690, 436 N.E.2d 1292 (N.Y.1982)—§ 38.19; § 38.19, n. 127.

Williams, People v., 416 N.Y.S.2d 792, 390 N.E.2d 299 (N.Y.1979)—§ 38.19, n. 115.

Williams, People v., 370 N.Y.S.2d 904, 331 N.E.2d 684 (N.Y.1975)—§ 38.8, n. 9.

Williams, People v., 335 N.Y.S.2d 271, 286 N.E.2d 715 (N.Y.1972)—§ 38.8; § 38.27, n. 11.

Williams v. People of State of N.Y., 337 U.S. 241, 69 S.Ct. 1079, 93 L.Ed. 1337 (1949)—§ 38.21, n. 39.

Williams v. Smith, 781 F.2d 319 (2nd Cir. 1986)—§ 18.35, n. 1.

Williams v. State, 90 A.D.2d 882, 456 N.Y.S.2d 528 (N.Y.A.D. 3 Dept.1982)—§ 14.82, n. 8.

Williams v. State of N. C., 325 U.S. 226, 65 S.Ct. 1092, 89 L.Ed. 1577 (1945)—§ 8.16, n. 4.

Williams v. State of North Carolina, 317 U.S. 287, 63 S.Ct. 207, 87 L.Ed. 279 (1942)—§ 21.32, n. 4.

Williams v. Town of Oyster Bay, 343 N.Y.S.2d 118, 295 N.E.2d 788 (N.Y. 1973)—§ 16.75, n. 2.

Williamsburg Candy & Tobacco, Inc. v. State, 106 Misc.2d 728, 435 N.Y.S.2d 252 (N.Y.Ct.Cl.1981)—§ 14.1, n. 15.

Williamsburgh Savings Bank v. McLeod, N.Y.L.J., 10/24/79, p.15, col.3 (Sup.Ct., Queens County)—§ 11.50, n. 1.

Williams on Behalf of Williams v. Bowen, 859 F.2d 255 (2nd Cir.1988)—§ 34.5, n. 3, 4; § 34.11, n. 10.

Willis v. Willis, 107 A.D.2d 867, 484 N.Y.S.2d 309 (N.Y.A.D. 3 Dept.1985)—§ 21.42, n. 2.

Will of (see name of party)

Willsea, People v., 221 A.D.2d 1019, 635 N.Y.S.2d 568 (N.Y.A.D. 4 Dept.1995)—§ 38.8, n. 217.

Wills Motors, Inc., In re, 133 B.R. 303 (Bkrtcy.S.D.N.Y.1991)—§ 9.80, n. 1.

Wilmot v. State, 344 N.Y.S.2d 350, 297 N.E.2d 90 (N.Y.1973)—§ 14.18, n. 2.

Wilson v. DeAngelis, 161 A.D.2d 709, 555 N.Y.S.2d 846 (N.Y.A.D. 2 Dept.1990)—§ 37.28, n. 4.

Wilson v. Econom, 56 Misc.2d 272, 288 N.Y.S.2d 381 (N.Y.Sup.1968)—§ 28.14, n. 4.

Wilson v. Huffman (Matter of Missionary Baptist Foundation of America, Inc.), 712 F.2d 206 (5th Cir.1983)—§ 9.107, n. 12, 24.

Wilson, People v., 631 N.Y.S.2d 127, 655 N.E.2d 168 (N.Y.1995)—§ 33.79, n. 1.

Wilson, People v., 88 N.Y.2d 363, 645 N.Y.S.2d 759, 668 N.E.2d 879 (1996)—§ 18.12, n. 2.

Wilson, People v., 147 A.D.2d 602, 537 N.Y.S.2d 897 (N.Y.A.D. 2 Dept.1989)—§ 38.20, n. 15.

Wilson v. Town of Islip, 179 A.D.2d 763, 578 N.Y.S.2d 642 (N.Y.A.D. 2 Dept. 1992)—§ 3.29, n. 9.

Wilson v. Wilson, 101 A.D.2d 536, 476 N.Y.S.2d 120 (N.Y.A.D. 1 Dept.1984)—§ 21.48, n. 2.

Wilton v. Seven Falls Co., 515 U.S. 277, 115 S.Ct. 2137, 132 L.Ed.2d 214 (1995)—§ 38.3, n. 14.

Wiltwyck School for Boys, Inc. v. Hill, 227 N.Y.S.2d 655, 182 N.E.2d 268 (N.Y. 1962)—§ 16.128, n. 5.

Wilwerth v. Levitt, 262 A.D. 112, 28 N.Y.S.2d 257 (N.Y.A.D. 1 Dept.1941)—§ 38.8, n. 86.

Winchenbaugh, People v., 120 A.D.2d 811, 501 N.Y.S.2d 929 (N.Y.A.D. 3 Dept. 1986)—§ 38.8, n. 163.

Wineburgh v. State, 20 A.D.2d 961, 249 N.Y.S.2d 763 (N.Y.A.D. 4 Dept.1964)—§ 14.82, n. 5.

Wing v. Coyne, 129 A.D.2d 213, 517 N.Y.S.2d 576 (N.Y.A.D. 3 Dept.1987)—§ 15.6, n. 2.

Wingate, Matter of, 169 Misc.2d 701, 647 N.Y.S.2d 433 (N.Y.Sup.1996)—§ 22.38, n. 6; § 22.54, n. 4.

Wingate, People v., 175 A.D.2d 191, 573 N.Y.S.2d 696 (N.Y.A.D. 2 Dept.1991)—§ 38.21, n. 4, 19; § 38.26, n. 28.

TABLE OF CASES

Wingerter v. State, 460 N.Y.S.2d 20, 446 N.E.2d 776 (N.Y.1983)—§ **30.12, n. 9.**
Winkelmann v. Excelsior Ins. Co., 626 N.Y.S.2d 994, 650 N.E.2d 841 (N.Y. 1995)—§ **31.29, n. 1.**
Winkler, People v., 528 N.Y.S.2d 360, 523 N.E.2d 485 (N.Y.1988)—§ **38.19, n. 100.**
Winnie v. O'Brien, 171 A.D.2d 997, 567 N.Y.S.2d 943 (N.Y.A.D. 3 Dept.1991)— § **16.121, n. 5.**
Winstead v. Uniondale Union Free School Dist., 201 A.D.2d 721, 608 N.Y.S.2d 487 (N.Y.A.D. 2 Dept.1994)—§ **31.10, n. 14.**
Winther v. Railroad Maintenance Corp., 169 A.D.2d 591, 564 N.Y.S.2d 744 (N.Y.A.D. 1 Dept.1991)—§ **30.30, n. 19.**
Winthrop Gardens, Inc. v. Goodwin, 58 A.D.2d 764, 396 N.Y.S.2d 400 (N.Y.A.D. 1 Dept.1977)—§ **4.2, n. 25;** § **4.57, n. 7.**
Winthrop Old Farm Nurseries v. New Bedford Ins. for Savs. (In re Winthrop Old Farm Nurseries, Inc.), 50 F.3d 72 (1st Cir.1995)—§ **9.251, n. 3.**
Wirth v. Malter, 11 A.D.2d 614, 201 N.Y.S.2d 528 (N.Y.A.D. 3 Dept.1960)— § **8.35, n. 4.**
Wisconsin Public Intervenor v. Mortier, 501 U.S. 597, 111 S.Ct. 2476, 115 L.Ed.2d 532 (1991)—§ **27.47;** § **27.47, n. 7;** § **27.51, n. 5.**
Wise, People v., 141 Misc.2d 409, 532 N.Y.S.2d 833 (N.Y.Dist.Ct.1988)— § **33.76, n. 2.**
Wise, People v., 413 N.Y.S.2d 334, 385 N.E.2d 1262 (N.Y.1978)—§ **33.27;** § **33.27, n. 7.**
Wiseman v. American Motors Sales Corp., 103 A.D.2d 230, 479 N.Y.S.2d 528 (N.Y.A.D. 2 Dept.1984)—§ **27.37, n. 5.**
Witcher v. Children's Television Workshop, 187 A.D.2d 292, 589 N.Y.S.2d 454 (N.Y.A.D. 1 Dept.1992)—§ **17.26, n. 3.**
Witherspoon, People v., 498 N.Y.S.2d 789, 489 N.E.2d 758 (N.Y.1985)—§ **33.57, n. 6.**
Withrow v. Larkin, 421 U.S. 35, 95 S.Ct. 1456, 43 L.Ed.2d 712 (1975)—§ **4.24, n. 1.**
Witkowski v. Blaskiewicz, 162 Misc.2d 66, 615 N.Y.S.2d 640 (N.Y.City Civ.Ct. 1994)—§ **18.76, n. 3.**
Witt, In re, 60 B.R. 556 (Bkrtcy.N.D.Iowa 1986)—§ **9.159, n. 6.**
Witten, Application of, 78 Misc.2d 162, 355 N.Y.S.2d 533 (N.Y.Sup.1974)—§ **22.40, n. 3.**
Wittner v. IDS Ins. Co. of New York, 96 A.D.2d 1053, 466 N.Y.S.2d 480 (N.Y.A.D. 2 Dept.1983)—§ **31.18, n. 14.**
Wohn v. County of Suffolk, 211 A.D.2d 761, 621 N.Y.S.2d 392 (N.Y.A.D. 2 Dept. 1995)—§ **37.37, n. 19.**

Woicik v. Woicik, 66 Misc.2d 357, 321 N.Y.S.2d 5 (N.Y.Sup.1971)—§ **21.21, n. 2.**
Wojcik v. Aluminum Co. of America, 18 Misc.2d 740, 183 N.Y.S.2d 351 (N.Y.Sup. 1959)—§ **29.11, n. 4.**
Wolf v. Weinstein, 372 U.S. 633, 83 S.Ct. 969, 10 L.Ed.2d 33 (1963)—§ **9.28, n. 6.**
Wolfe v. Frankel, N.Y.L.J., 10/3/79, p.6, col.1 (App. Term, 1st Dep't.)—§ **13.51, n. 1.**
Wolfe v. Sibley, Lindsay & Curr Co., 369 N.Y.S.2d 637, 330 N.E.2d 603 (N.Y. 1975)—§ **32.13, n. 2.**
Wolfgruber v. Upjohn Co., 72 A.D.2d 59, 423 N.Y.S.2d 95 (N.Y.A.D. 4 Dept. 1979)—§ **27.13, n. 2;** § **27.15, n. 1.**
Wolf Partnership v. Manheit (In re Ames Dept. Stores, Inc.), 173 B.R. 80 (Bkrtcy. S.D.N.Y.1994)—§ **9.83, n. 2.**
Wolfson v. Rosenthal, 210 A.D.2d 47, 619 N.Y.S.2d 43 (N.Y.A.D. 1 Dept.1994)— § **2.70, n. 1.**
Wollaber v. State, 80 A.D.2d 706, 437 N.Y.S.2d 748 (N.Y.A.D. 3 Dept.1981)— § **14.82, n. 7.**
Wolowitz, State v., 96 A.D.2d 47, 468 N.Y.S.2d 131 (N.Y.A.D. 2 Dept.1983)— § **5.13, n. 1, 8;** § **5.14, n. 5;** § **37.32, n. 1.**
Wolstencroft v. Sassower, 124 A.D.2d 582, 507 N.Y.S.2d 728 (N.Y.A.D. 2 Dept. 1986)—§ **28.9, n. 10.**
Wood v. Hughes, 212 N.Y.S.2d 33, 173 N.E.2d 21 (N.Y.1961)—§ **38.11;** § **38.11, n. 2.**
Wood v. Mitchell, 117 N.Y. 439, 22 N.E. 1125 (N.Y.1889)—§ **8.4, n. 13.**
Wood v. Peabody Intern. Corp., 187 A.D.2d 824, 589 N.Y.S.2d 960 (N.Y.A.D. 3 Dept. 1992)—§ **27.12, n. 1.**
Wood, People v., 115 A.D.2d 834, 495 N.Y.S.2d 794 (N.Y.A.D. 3 Dept.1985)— § **33.81, n. 1.**
Wood v. Town of Whitehall, 120 Misc. 124, 197 N.Y.S. 789 (N.Y.Sup.1923)—§ **3.18, n. 10.**
Wood v. Wood (Matter of Wood), 825 F.2d 90 (5th Cir.1987)—§ **9.19, n. 4.**
Woodhull, People v., 105 A.D.2d 815, 481 N.Y.S.2d 749 (N.Y.A.D. 2 Dept.1984)— § **38.21, n. 11.**
Woodring v. Board of Ed. of Manhasset Union Free School Dist., 79 A.D.2d 1022, 435 N.Y.S.2d 52 (N.Y.A.D. 2 Dept. 1981)—§ **30.10, n. 12.**
Woodruff, People v., 315 N.Y.S.2d 861, 264 N.E.2d 353 (N.Y.1970)—§ **38.27, n. 2.**
Woods v. Candela, 47 F.3d 545 (2nd Cir. 1995)—§ **18.23, n. 5.**

TABLE OF CASES

Woods v. City Nat. Bank & Trust Co. of Chicago, 312 U.S. 262, 61 S.Ct. 493, 85 L.Ed. 820 (1941)—§ **9.46, n. 2.**

Woods, People v., 303 N.Y.S.2d 531, 250 N.E.2d 588 (N.Y.1969)—§ **38.27; § 38.27, n. 34.**

Woolf v. Hamburger, 129 A.D. 883, 114 N.Y.S. 186 (N.Y.A.D. 1 Dept.1909)—§ **30.27, n. 3.**

Workman v. Bolen, 67 Misc.2d 957, 326 N.Y.S.2d 811 (N.Y.Co.Ct.1971)—§ **37.96, n. 10.**

Workmen's Benefit Fund of United States, In re, 265 A.D. 176, 38 N.Y.S.2d 429 (N.Y.A.D. 1 Dept.1942)—§ **1.43, n. 28.**

Workmen's Compensation Fund, In re, 224 N.Y. 13, 119 N.E. 1027 (N.Y.1918)—§ **37.31, n. 4.**

Worley, People v., 498 N.Y.S.2d 116, 488 N.E.2d 1228 (N.Y.1985)—§ **33.85, n. 1; § 33.87; § 33.87, n. 1.**

Worm v. American Cyanamid Co., 970 F.2d 1301 (4th Cir.1992)—§ **27.44, n. 1; § 27.47, n. 4.**

Woroski v. Nashua Corp., 31 F.3d 105 (2nd Cir.1994)—§ **17.73, n. 4.**

Wright v. Carter Products, Inc., 244 F.2d 53 (2nd Cir.1957)—§ **27.16; § 27.16, n. 2.**

Wright v. Guarinello, 165 Misc.2d 720, 635 N.Y.S.2d 995 (N.Y.Sup.1995)—§ **17.25, n. 12.**

Wright, People v., 635 N.Y.S.2d 136, 658 N.E.2d 1009 (N.Y.1995)—§ **38.10, n. 107.**

Wright, People v., 207 A.D.2d 566, 616 N.Y.S.2d 255 (N.Y.A.D. 2 Dept.1994)—§ **38.8, n. 27.**

Wright, People v., 450 N.Y.S.2d 473, 435 N.E.2d 1088 (N.Y.1982)—§ **38.10, n. 130.**

Wright, People v., 80 A.D.2d 624, 436 N.Y.S.2d 68 (N.Y.A.D. 2 Dept.1981)—§ **38.10, n. 134.**

Wright v. Smith, 21 F.3d 496 (2nd Cir. 1994)—§ **18.18, n. 9.**

W.T. Grant Co., In re, 699 F.2d 599 (2nd Cir.1983)—§ **9.97, n. 2; § 9.107, n. 18.**

W. T. Grant Co., Matter of, 4 B.R. 53 (Bkrtcy.S.D.N.Y.1980)—§ **9.107, n. 14.**

Wulfsohn v. Burden, 241 N.Y. 288, 150 N.E. 120 (N.Y.1925)—§ **3.9, n. 6.**

Wyatt v. Armstrong, 186 Misc. 216, 59 N.Y.S.2d 502 (N.Y.Sup.1945)—§ **1.43, n. 18, 24.**

Wyche v. New Amsterdam Garage Corp., 82 Misc.2d 956, 371 N.Y.S.2d 754 (N.Y.City Civ.Ct.1975)—§ **7.28, n. 7.**

X

XAR Corp. v. Di Donato, 76 A.D.2d 972, 429 N.Y.S.2d 59 (N.Y.A.D. 3 Dept.1980)—§ **12.57, n. 1.**

Y

Yachthaven Restaurant, Inc., In re, 103 B.R. 68 (Bkrtcy.E.D.N.Y.1989)—§ **9.80, n. 1.**

Yadkin Valley Bank v. Northwestern Bank (In re Hutchinson), 132 B.R. 827 (Bkrtcy.M.D.N.C.1991)—§ **9.200, n. 5.**

Yager v. Arlen Realty & Development Corp., 95 A.D.2d 853, 464 N.Y.S.2d 214 (N.Y.A.D. 2 Dept.1983)—§ **27.34, n. 2.**

Yakubiv, People v., N.Y.L.J., 8/24/94, pp.25, 26, col.6 (Sup.Ct., Kings County)—§ **33.81, n. 1.**

Yanni v. Bruce Brandwen Productions, Inc., 160 Misc.2d 109, 609 N.Y.S.2d 759 (N.Y.City Civ.Ct.1994)—§ **13.56, n. 5.**

Yannicelli, People v., 389 N.Y.S.2d 290, 357 N.E.2d 947 (N.Y.1976)—§ **38.10, n. 127.**

Yant, People v., 223 A.D.2d 747, 637 N.Y.S.2d 468 (N.Y.A.D. 2 Dept.1996)—§ **38.28, n. 15.**

Yaphank Development Co., Inc. v. County of Suffolk, 203 A.D.2d 280, 609 N.Y.S.2d 346 (N.Y.A.D. 2 Dept.1994)—§ **14.118, n. 1.**

Yaretsky v. Blum, 456 F.Supp. 653 (S.D.N.Y.1978)—§ **4.50, n. 4.**

Yaron v. Yaron, 84 Misc.2d 644, 378 N.Y.S.2d 285 (N.Y.Sup.1975)—§ **21.22, n. 5.**

Yates v. Dow Chemical Co., 68 A.D.2d 907, 414 N.Y.S.2d 200 (N.Y.A.D. 2 Dept. 1979)—§ **27.29, n. 1.**

Yeh v. Seakan, 119 Misc.2d 681, 464 N.Y.S.2d 627 (N.Y.Sup.1983)—§ **8.28, n. 8.**

Yellow Creek Hunting Club, Inc. v. Todd Supply, Inc., 145 A.D.2d 679, 535 N.Y.S.2d 222 (N.Y.A.D. 3 Dept.1988)—§ **8.33, n. 6.**

Yeshiva & Mesivta Toras Chaim v. Rose, 136 A.D.2d 710, 523 N.Y.S.2d 907 (N.Y.A.D. 2 Dept.1988)—§ **16.131, n. 13.**

Ying Jing Gan v. City of New York, 996 F.2d 522 (2nd Cir.1993)—§ **18.33, n. 3.**

Ying Lung Corp. v. Medrano, 123 Misc.2d 1074, 475 N.Y.S.2d 772 (N.Y.City Civ.Ct. 1984)—§ **13.28; § 13.28, n. 12.**

Yiouti Restaurant, Inc. v. Sotiriou, 151 A.D.2d 744, 542 N.Y.S.2d 767 (N.Y.A.D. 2 Dept.1989)—§ **28.5; § 28.5, n. 1.**

Yonkers By Green, City of v. Hvizd, 93 A.D.2d 887, 461 N.Y.S.2d 408 (N.Y.A.D. 2 Dept.1983)—§ **14.26, n. 7.**

Yonkers by Kelly, City of v. A. & J. Cianciulli, Inc., 117 N.Y.S.2d 792 (N.Y.Sup. 1952)—§ **14.83, n. 4.**

Yonkers Hamilton Sanitarium Inc., In re, 34 B.R. 385 (S.D.N.Y.1983)—§ **9.112, n. 5.**

TABLE OF CASES

Yonkers Motors Corp., People v., 126 Misc.2d 141, 481 N.Y.S.2d 591 (N.Y.City Ct.1984)—§ **33.19, n. 2.**

York v. McGuire, 480 N.Y.S.2d 320, 469 N.E.2d 838 (N.Y.1984)—§ **17.53, n. 9.**

York v. McGuire, 99 A.D.2d 1023, 473 N.Y.S.2d 815 (N.Y.A.D. 1 Dept.1984)—§ **4.79, n. 11.**

Yorktown, Town of v. New York State Dept. of Mental Hygiene, 92 A.D.2d 897, 459 N.Y.S.2d 891 (N.Y.A.D. 2 Dept.1983)—§ **15.6, n. 3.**

Young, Ex parte, 209 U.S. 123, 28 S.Ct. 441, 52 L.Ed. 714 (1908)—§ **18.33, n. 5.**

Young, Matter of, 11 I & N Dec. 38 (BIA 1965)—§ **19.47, n. 5.**

Young v. Continental Worsteds (In re Wingspread Corp.), 120 B.R. 8 (Bkrtcy. S.D.N.Y.1990)—§ **9.117, n. 1.**

Young v. Elmira Transit Mix, Inc., 52 A.D.2d 202, 383 N.Y.S.2d 729 (N.Y.A.D. 4 Dept.1976)—§ **27.10, n. 3; § 27.14, n. 5.**

Young v. Kalow, 214 A.D.2d 559, 625 N.Y.S.2d 231 (N.Y.A.D. 2 Dept.1995)—§ **37.29, n. 46.**

Young v. Morse, 92 A.D.2d 706, 460 N.Y.S.2d 388 (N.Y.A.D. 3 Dept.1983)—§ **37.37, n. 45.**

Young v. New York City Transit Authority, 903 F.2d 146 (2nd Cir.1990)—§ **18.27, n. 7.**

Young, People v., 221 A.D.2d 777, 634 N.Y.S.2d 409 (N.Y.A.D. 3 Dept.1995)—§ **38.8, n. 26.**

Young, People v., 582 N.Y.S.2d 977, 591 N.E.2d 1163 (N.Y.1992)—§ **38.19, n. 98.**

Young v. Selsky, 41 F.3d 47 (2nd Cir. 1994)—§ **18.31, n. 5.**

Young v. Torelli, 135 A.D.2d 813, 522 N.Y.S.2d 918 (N.Y.A.D. 2 Dept.1987)—§ **8.23, n. 16.**

Younger v. Harris, 401 U.S. 37, 91 S.Ct. 746, 27 L.Ed.2d 669 (1971)—§ **18.36; § 18.36, n. 2.**

Young Men's Christian Ass'n v. Rochester Pure Waters Dist., 372 N.Y.S.2d 633, 334 N.E.2d 586 (N.Y.1975)—§ **4.72, n. 1.**

Younker v. Younker, 42 A.D.2d 534, 344 N.Y.S.2d 758 (N.Y.A.D. 1 Dept.1973)—§ **22.41, n. 11.**

Yukl, People v., 307 N.Y.S.2d 857, 256 N.E.2d 172 (N.Y.1969)—§ **33.7, n. 1.**

Yurika Foods Corp. v. United Parcel Services (In re Yurika Foods Corp.), 888 F.2d 42 (6th Cir.1989)—§ **9.118, n. 6.**

Yusuf v. Vassar College, 35 F.3d 709 (2nd Cir.1994)—§ **18.53, n. 7.**

Yut Wai Tom, People v., 439 N.Y.S.2d 896, 422 N.E.2d 556 (N.Y.1981)—§ **38.19, n. 44.**

Z

Zabrocky, People v., 311 N.Y.S.2d 892, 260 N.E.2d 529 (N.Y.1970)—§ **38.19, n. 117.**

Zagami v. Zagami, 173 A.D.2d 698, 571 N.Y.S.2d 1011 (N.Y.A.D. 2 Dept.1991)—§ **37.37, n. 13.**

Zagoreos v. Conklin, 109 A.D.2d 281, 491 N.Y.S.2d 358 (N.Y.A.D. 2 Dept.1985)—§ **16.129, n. 7.**

Zagorsky, People v., 73 Misc.2d 420, 341 N.Y.S.2d 791 (N.Y.Co.Ct.1973)—§ **33.16, n. 5; § 33.75, n. 2; § 33.100.**

Zahn v. Board of Public Works of City of Los Angeles, 274 U.S. 325, 47 S.Ct. 594, 71 L.Ed. 1074 (1927)—§ **16.22, n. 6.**

Zaicek, In re, 29 B.R. 31 (Bkrtcy.W.D.Ky. 1983)—§ **9.188, n. 1.**

Zaleski v. Zaleski, 128 A.D.2d 865, 513 N.Y.S.2d 784 (N.Y.A.D. 2 Dept.1987)—§ **21.60, n. 2.**

Zambito v. Zambito, 171 A.D.2d 918, 566 N.Y.S.2d 789 (N.Y.A.D. 3 Dept.1991)—§ **21.30, n. 9.**

Zamzok v. 650 Park Ave. Corp., 167 A.D.2d 252, 561 N.Y.S.2d 752 (N.Y.A.D. 1 Dept. 1990)—§ **13.31, n. 2.**

Zanesville, Ohio, City of v. Mohawk Data Sciences Corp., 97 A.D.2d 64, 468 N.Y.S.2d 271 (N.Y.A.D. 4 Dept.1983)—§ **3.24, n. 5.**

Zappone v. Home Ins. Co., 447 N.Y.S.2d 911, 432 N.E.2d 783 (N.Y.1982)—§ **31.16, n. 2.**

Zarin v. Reid & Priest, 184 A.D.2d 385, 585 N.Y.S.2d 379 (N.Y.A.D. 1 Dept.1992)—§ **28.3; § 28.3, n. 1, 4; § 28.12, n. 5.**

Zaro v. Coughlin, 195 A.D.2d 1003, 601 N.Y.S.2d 744 (N.Y.A.D. 4 Dept.1993)—§ **37.28, n. 27.**

Zarriello, Matter of, N.Y.L.J., 1/25/95, p.32, col.5 (Sup.Ct., Rockland County)—§ **22.34, n. 2; § 22.101, n. 1.**

Zdeb, Matter of, 215 A.D.2d 803, 626 N.Y.S.2d 298 (N.Y.A.D. 3 Dept.1995)—§ **22.40, n. 7.**

Zegman v. State, 99 Misc.2d 473, 416 N.Y.S.2d 505 (N.Y.Ct.Cl.1979)—§ **30.8; § 30.8, n. 11.**

Zeifman v. Board of Trustees of Inc. Village of Great Neck, 40 Misc.2d 130, 242 N.Y.S.2d 738 (N.Y.Sup.1963)—§ **16.90, n. 4; § 16.92, n. 2.**

Zelnik v. Zelnik, 169 A.D.2d 317, 573 N.Y.S.2d 261 (N.Y.A.D. 1 Dept.1991)—§ **21.30; § 21.30, n. 5, 7; § 21.40, n. 4; § 21.42, n. 5.**

Zemo Leasing Corp. v. Bank of New York, 158 Misc.2d 991, 602 N.Y.S.2d 503 (N.Y.Sup.1993)—§ **8.25, n. 10.**

TABLE OF CASES

Zenila Realty Corp. v. Masterandrea, 123 Misc.2d 1, 472 N.Y.S.2d 980 (N.Y.City Civ.Ct.1984)—§ **13.12**; § **13.12, n. 2, 10.**

Zenkel v. Oneida County Creameries Co., 104 Misc. 251, 171 N.Y.S. 676 (N.Y.Sup. 1918)—§ **27.32, n. 3.**

Zerillo, People v., 200 N.Y. 443, 93 N.E. 1108 (N.Y.1911)—§ **38.3, n. 6, 21.**

Ziegler, Matter of, 157 Misc.2d 423, 596 N.Y.S.2d 963 (N.Y.Sur.1993)—§ **25.31, n. 10.**

Zimet v. New York State Liquor Authority, 27 A.D.2d 558, 276 N.Y.S.2d 79 (N.Y.A.D. 2 Dept.1966)—§ **4.20, n. 2.**

Zimmer v. Chemung County Performing Arts, Inc., 493 N.Y.S.2d 102, 482 N.E.2d 898 (N.Y.1985)—§ **37.65, n. 53.**

Zinke, People v., 556 N.Y.S.2d 11, 555 N.E.2d 263 (N.Y.1990)—§ **2.51, n. 6.**

Zipprich v. Smith Trucking Co., 157 N.Y.S.2d 966, 139 N.E.2d 146 (N.Y. 1956)—§ **39.7, n. 3.**

Zirinsky v. Violet Mills, Inc., 152 Misc.2d 538, 578 N.Y.S.2d 88 (N.Y.City Civ.Ct. 1991)—§ **13.16, n. 7;** § **13.18, n. 6;** § **13.20, n. 6.**

Zirn v. Bradley, 270 A.D. 829, 60 N.Y.S.2d 114 (N.Y.A.D. 2 Dept.1946)—§ **30.26, n. 3.**

Zises v. Zises, 210 A.D.2d 170, 620 N.Y.S.2d 959 (N.Y.A.D. 1 Dept.1994)—§ **37.28, n. 29.**

Zolg v. Kelly (In re Kelly), 841 F.2d 908 (9th Cir.1988)—§ **9.209, n. 9.**

Zubli v. Community Mainstreaming Associates, Inc., 102 Misc.2d 320, 423 N.Y.S.2d 982 (N.Y.Sup.1979)—§ **16.24, n. 8;** § **16.128, n. 14.**

Zunino v. Mahoney, 204 A.D.2d 469, 614 N.Y.S.2d 161 (N.Y.A.D. 2 Dept.1994)—§ **37.19, n. 29.**

Zurat v. Town of Stockport, 142 A.D.2d 1, 534 N.Y.S.2d 777 (N.Y.A.D. 3 Dept. 1988)—§ **18.9, n. 2.**

Zurich Ins. Co. v. Shearson Lehman Hutton, Inc., 618 N.Y.S.2d 609, 642 N.E.2d 1065 (N.Y.1994)—§ **31.25, n. 3.**

Zurkow's Estate, In re, 74 Misc.2d 736, 345 N.Y.S.2d 436 (N.Y.Sur.1973)—§ **24.95, n. 5.**

Zweig, People v., 32 A.D.2d 569, 300 N.Y.S.2d 651 (N.Y.A.D. 2 Dept.1969)—§ **38.8, n. 89.**

Zwickler, People v., 266 N.Y.S.2d 140, 213 N.E.2d 467 (N.Y.1965)—§ **38.27, n. 18.**

Zwitzer v. Zoning Bd. of Appeals of Town of Canandaigua, 144 A.D.2d 1023, 534 N.Y.S.2d 298 (N.Y.A.D. 4 Dept.1988)—§ **16.125, n. 14.**

INDEX

ABORTIONS
Discrimination against person refusing to perform abortion prohibited, § 18.86

ABSTENTION
Federal civil rights law, defenses, § 18.36

ACCIDENTS
Motor Vehicle Accidents, generally, this index
Notice, insurance, § 31.10
Products liability, post-accident modification or repairs, § 27.31
Workers' compensation,
    Employer's report of work-related accident/occupational disease, form, § 32.55

ACCOUNTANTS
Bankruptcy, § 9.29
Small business, purchase or sale,
    Buyer, representation of, § 6.9
    Due diligence investigation, financial review, § 6.27

ACCOUNTS AND ACCOUNTING
Gift taxes, federal,
    Annual gift tax exclusion,
        Uniform Transfers to Minor's Act accounts, § 24.51
Guardianships,
    Decrees approving accounts, § 22.67
        Checklists, § 22.95
        Forms, § 22.106
Probate and estate administration,
    Compelling an accounting, § 25.34
    Concluding administration without accounting proceeding, § 25.35
    Discovery, § 25.31
    Form, § 25.66
    Formal judicial accounting, concluding estate by, § 25.37
    Objections, § 25.38
        Prosecuting objections to, § 25.39

ACCUSATORY INSTRUMENTS
    Generally, § 33.8 et seq.
Complaints, § 33.12
Dismissal of accusatory instrument,
    Appeal by the people to appellate division, criminal, § 38.10
Information, § 33.9
    Prosecutor's information, § 33.11
        Appeal by the people, § 38.10
    Re-filing upon dismissal of supporting deposition not constituting double jeopardy, § 33.24
    Reduction in count in indictment,
        Appeal by the people, § 38.10
    Simplified information, § 33.10
        Pretrial discovery, § 33.32
        Superseding information disallowed, § 33.23
Speedy trial,
    CPL § 30.30 excludable time, defective accusatory instruments, § 33.86

INDEX

ACCUSATORY INSTRUMENTS—Continued
Supporting depositions, § 33.13 et seq.
  Attorney affirmation in support of motion,
    Drafting checklists, § 33.96
    Form, § 33.100
    Procedural checklists, § 33.92
  Drafting checklists, § 33.94
    Notice of motion to dismiss for failure to serve a timely supporting deposition, § 33.95
  Factual insufficiency not jurisdictional defect, § 33.22
  Forms, § 33.98
  Guilty plea waiving defects, § 33.22
  Notice of motion to dismiss for failure to serve a timely supporting deposition,
    Attorney affirmation in support of motion,
      Drafting checklists, § 33.96
      Form, § 33.100
      Procedural checklists, § 33.92
    Form, § 33.99
  Procedural checklists, § 33.91
    Notice of motion to dismiss for failure to serve a timely supporting deposition, § 33.92
  Procedure, § 33.14
  Re-filing of information upon dismissal of supporting deposition, § 33.24
  Service of process,
    Dismissal for failure to serve, § 33.19
      Not amendable defect, § 33.25
    Motion to dismiss,
      Timeliness, § 33.21
      Writing requirement, § 33.20
    Request by attorney requiring service on counsel, § 33.18
    Requirements, § 33.15
    Timing, § 33.17
    Who must be served, § 33.16
  Speeding, when not to request, § 33.69
Verification, § 33.26

ACTIONS
  See also specific action, this index
Bankruptcy, generally, this index
Commencement,
  Bankruptcy, generally, this index
  Checklist, § 17.78
  Civil rights,
    Public accommodations and amusement, equal rights in places of,
      Notice of commencement of action for discrimination, form, § 18.97
  Foreclosure, § 11.16
    Lis Pendens, § 11.17
    Notice of pendency of action, § 11.17
      Drafting checklist, § 11.58
  Speedy trial,
    CPL § 30.30, commencement of criminal action, § 33.82
Complaints, generally, this index
Court of appeals,
  Civil appeals. Court of Appeals, generally, this index
  Criminal appeals. Court of Appeals, generally, this index
Dismissal of Actions, generally, this index
Eminent Domain, generally, this index
Enforcement of Money Judgments, generally, this index
Environmental Law, generally, this index
Federal court,
  Commencement, § 17.79
  Responsive pleadings, § 17.79
  Service of process, § 17.79

INDEX

ACTIONS—Continued
Foreclosure, generally, this index
Limitation of Actions, generally, this index
Local Land Use Law, generally, this index
Mechanic's Liens, generally, this index
Medical Malpractice, generally, this index
State Environmental Quality Review Act (SEQRA), generally, this index
"Yellowstone" actions,
    New York Landlord-Tenant Law, § 13.70
        Obtaining injunction, § 13.71

ADJUDICATORY PROCEEDINGS
Administrative Law and Proceedings, this index

ADMINISTRATIVE LAW AND PROCEEDINGS
    Generally, § 4.1 et seq.
Adjudicatory proceedings, § 4.10
    Agency,
        Checking agency bias, § 4.24
        Delay, unreasonable, § 4.21
        Duty to decide consistently, § 4.22
        Intra-agency review, § 4.23
    Burden of proof, § 4.19
    Checklist, § 4.42
    Collateral estoppel, § 4.25
    Cross-examination, § 4.16
    Decisional record, § 4.18
    Defined, § 4.11
    Discovery, § 4.13
    Enforcement matters,
        Issues in handling, § 4.34
            Enforcement options of agency, § 4.37
            Fact-finding by agency in pre-enforcement phase, § 4.36
            Hearing process, § 4.39
                Post-hearing issues, § 4.40
            Settlement process, § 4.38
            Violations, strategies to minimize, § 4.35
    Evidence, § 4.15
    Intervention, § 4.20
    Licensing matters,
        Issues in handling, § 4.27
            Applications, accuracy and completedness, § 4.30
            Basic license information, § 4.28
            Expediting process, § 4.31
            Renewal, suspension and revocation issues, § 4.33
            SAPA and SEQRA, role in licensing process, § 4.29
            Standard approaches, varying from, § 4.32
        Notice of appearance in licensing or permitting matter, forms, § 4.88
        Rules applicable to, § 4.26
    Notice, § 4.12
        Official notice, § 4.17
    Res judicata, § 4.25
    Right to counsel, § 4.14
    Statement of decision, § 4.18
    Summary, § 4.41
    Witness attendance, § 4.16
Administrative Procedures Act,
    Alcoholic beverage license, hearing and review, § 36.2
Agency information gathering, § 4.61
    Checklist, § 4.66
    Reporting and recordkeeping requirements, § 4.64
    Searches, administrative, § 4.62
    Subpoenas, administrative, § 4.63

INDEX

ADMINISTRATIVE LAW AND PROCEEDINGS—Continued
Agency information gathering—Continued
    Summary, § 4.65
Checklists, this index
Court of appeals,
    Civil appeals, scope of review, § 39.7
Forms, § 4.87 et seq.
Judicial review, § 4.67
    Administrative remedies, exhaustion of, § 4.72
    Article 78 and consolidation of common law prerogative writs, § 4.75
    Article 78 proceedings,
        Subject matter jurisdiction, § 4.84
        Venue, § 4.83
    Checklist, § 4.86
    Delegation of authority to agencies, § 4.68
    Final order, § 4.70
    Jurisdiction, primary, § 4.73
    Limitation of actions, § 4.82
    Relief in the nature of prohibition, § 4.71
    Ripeness, § 4.70
    Standards of review, § 4.76
        Administrative discretion, review of, § 4.81
        Administrative rules, review of, § 4.80
        Agency determinations of fact, review of,
            Arbitrary and capricious test, § 4.79
            Substantial evidence test, § 4.78
        Agency determinations of law, review of, § 4.77
    Standing to seek, § 4.69
    Statutory preclusion of, § 4.74
    Summary, § 4.85
Notice,
    Adjudicatory proceedings, § 4.12
    Appearance in licensing or permitting matter, forms, § 4.88
    Deposition in administrative proceeding, forms, § 4.90
    Discovery and inspection in administrative proceeding, forms, § 4.89
    Official notice, adjudicatory proceedings, § 4.17
    Permit entry upon real property, forms, § 4.91
    Rulemaking, § 4.45
        Notice of adoption, § 4.48
Procedural due process,
    Checklists, § 4.9
    Individualized state action, § 4.5
    Process due, § 4.7
    Protected interests, § 4.6
    Summary, § 4.8
Rulemaking, § 4.43
    Adoption, notice of, § 4.48
    Ancillary documentation, § 4.49
    Checklist, § 4.60
    Comments and agency assessment of comments, § 4.46
    Declaratory rulings, § 4.51
    Effective date of rules, § 4.48
    Filing of rule, § 4.50
    GORR, role, § 4.49
    Information, underlying,
        Agency duty to reveal, § 4.47
    Notice, § 4.45
    Other agency action, compared with, § 4.44
    Publication, § 4.50
    State and federal rules, overlapping, § 4.52
    Strategic considerations in handling rulemaking matters, § 4.53
        Emergency rulemakings, special issues, § 4.57

INDEX

ADMINISTRATIVE LAW AND PROCEEDINGS—Continued
Rulemaking—Continued
    Strategic considerations in handling rulemaking matters—Continued
        Guidance documents, § 4.58
        Information sources on rulemaking, § 4.54
        Negotiated rulemakings, special issues, § 4.56
        Participation in rulemaking process, § 4.55
    Summary, § 4.59
Scope, § 4.1
Strategy, § 4.2
    Checklist, § 4.3

ADMINISTRATORS
Probate and Estate Administration, generally, this index

ADOPTION
    Generally, § 20.1 et seq.
Abrogation of order, § 20.131
Abuse clearance form, §§ 20.2, 20.118
    Unavailability, § 20.119
Adult adoptions, §§ 20.23, 20.24
Affidavits required, § 20.36
    Affidavit of no appeal, § 20.2
    Attorney fees, §§ 20.78, 20.120
    Birth mother's affidavit regarding putative father, form, § 20.144
    Confidential affidavit, § 20.107
        Form, § 20.143
    Financial disclosure, § 20.106
        Form, § 20.147
    Identification of parties, § 20.115
        Form, § 20.146
    Marital affidavit, § 20.108
        Dispensing with consent of spouse, form, § 20.142
        Form, § 20.141
    Payments made to birth parents, § 20.52
    Supplemental affidavit, § 20.110
Age as factor, § 20.20
Agreement of adoption,
    Filing, § 20.2
    Form, § 20.145
    Signatories, § 20.104
Alien orphans, § 20.25
Attorney fees, § 20.3
Authorized agency, defined, § 20.86
Background check, § 20.119
Biological father, by, § 20.18
Birth mother,
    Attorney fees, § 20.2
    Background information, § 20.4
    Medical expenses, § 20.3
    Medical insurance, § 20.4
    Permissible payments to, § 20.52
Certificate of adoption, §§ 20.117, 20.122
Certification as qualified adoptive parents, § 20.3
Certified birth certificate,
    Filing, § 20.2
Citizenship rights of adopted child, § 20.19
Commencement of proceedings,
    Jurisdiction, § 20.102
    Notice to birth parents, § 20.100
Conflict of interest,
    Dual representation by attorney, § 20.120
Consent of adoption, § 20.29

INDEX

ADOPTION—Continued
Consent of adoption—Continued
    Father, § 20.3
    Form, § 20.145
    Relinquishment, § 20.31
Contested,
    Guardian ad litem, appointment, §§ 20.36, 20.43
    Jurisdiction, § 20.10
Criminal conviction check, § 20.119
Custody of child to agency, § 20.101
Definitions, §§ 20.6, 20.85
Doctor's certificate of health, § 20.112
Documents required, § 20.121
Dual representation, §§ 20.2, 20.3
Extended family as factor, § 20.21
Family-based immigration,
    Amerasians, § 19.15
    Orphans, § 19.15
Family court, jurisdiction, § 20.9
Fingerprint check, § 20.2
Foster parents, by, § 20.16
Handicapped children, subsidized adoptions, § 20.113
Hearings, §§ 20.2, 20.36, 20.122
History of adoption laws, § 20.5
Home study report, § 20.114
Indian Child Welfare Act, § 20.50
Interracial adoptions, § 20.27
Interstate Compact Act, § 20.3
Interview of prospective adoptive parents, § 20.2
Intestate succession, § 20.13
Judicial construction of statutes, § 20.8
Jurisdiction, §§ 20.101, 20.102
    Concurrent, §§ 20.9, 20.10
Legal rights of parties, § 20.13
Married couples, by, § 20.14
Medical history of child, § 20.109
Medical records of natural parents, availability to child, § 20.129
New birth certificates, § 20.111
Non-marital children, § 20.26
Noncitizens, by, § 20.19
Notice of proposed adoption, § 20.32
    Exclusions, § 20.34
    Fathers' right to, §§ 20.33, 20.35
Open adoption, § 20.123
Order of adoption, § 20.111
    Filing, § 20.2
    Form, § 20.148
    Notification, § 20.111
    Signing of order, § 20.116
    Vacating order, § 20.131
Petition,
    Filing, §§ 20.2, 20.36, 20.103
    Form, § 20.139
Post-adoption issues, § 20.124 et seq.
Pre-certification procedures, § 20.3
Private, § 20.12
    Abuse clearance form, §§ 20.55, 20.56
    Adult adoptions, § 20.42
    Advertisements, § 20.47
    Advertising by adoptive parents, § 20.2
    Affidavits required,
        Attorney's affidavit, § 20.71

INDEX

ADOPTION—Continued
Private—Continued
    Affidavits required—Continued
        Attorney's affidavit of financial disclosure, § 20.73
        Birth mother's affidavit regarding putative father, § 20.76
        Explanation of criminal activity, § 20.79
        Intermediary's affidavit, § 20.77
    Agreement of adoption, § 20.70
    Attorney fees, §§ 20.2, 20.41, 20.44
        Affidavits, § 20.78
    Background check of prospective parents, §§ 20.56, 20.57
        Affidavit of explanation of criminal activity, § 20.79
    Certificate of adoption, § 20.82
    Certification as qualified adoptive parents, § 20.56
        Waiver, § 20.56
    Compensation for arranging, § 20.45
    Confidential affidavit, § 20.72
    Consent of birth parents, §§ 20.37, 20.63
        Abandonment, § 20.67
        Extra-judicial consent, § 20.64
            Form, § 20.136
        Judicial consent, § 20.65
            Form, § 20.135
        Personal appearances required, § 20.66
        Revocation, § 20.64
    Documents required, § 20.84
    Dual representation, §§ 20.2, 20.40, 20.42
    Escrow accounts, § 20.2
    Fingerprint card required, §§ 20.55, 20.57
    Foreign born children,
        Non-quota immigrant status, § 20.68
        Pre-certification of adoptive parents, § 20.68
    Foreign born infants, § 20.48
        Readoption, § 20.49
    Hearing, § 20.81
    Hospital procedures, § 20.58
        Order of certification, § 20.59
    Illegal sale of children, §§ 20.46, 20.78
    Independent counsel for birth mother, § 20.41
    Independent counsel for child, § 20.43
    Interstate Compact Act, § 20.53
    Jurisdiction, § 20.2
    Letters of reference, § 20.84
    Locating infants for adoption, § 20.45
    Medical certification of child, § 20.84
    Medical certification of parents, § 20.84
    Native American children, §§ 20.50, 20.69
    New birth certificates, §§ 20.74, 20.83
    Notification of order of adoption, § 20.74
    Order of adoption, §§ 20.75, 20.81
        Form, § 20.138
    Order of certification as qualified adoptive parents, § 20.57
    Order of investigation by disinterested person, § 20.80
    Parental rights terminated,
        Abandonment, § 20.38
        Mental retardation, § 20.39
    Payments to birth parents, § 20.52
    Petition for adoption, § 20.2
        Drafting, § 20.132
        Filing, §§ 20.56, 20.69
        Form, § 20.137
    Petition for certification as qualified adoptive parents, §§ 20.56, 20.57

INDEX

ADOPTION—Continued
Private—Continued
    Petition for certification as qualified adoptive parents—Continued
        Form, § 20.133
    Pre-certification of adoptive parents, § 20.54
        Petition for certification as qualified adoptive parent, § 20.55
    Pre-placement investigation, §§ 20.55, 20.56, 20.57
    Putative father, hearing on consent issue, § 20.76
    Releasing infant from hospital, § 20.58
    Report of adoption, § 20.74
    Residency requirements of adoptive parents, § 20.51
    Resumes of adoptive parents, § 20.2
    Step-parent adoptions, §§ 20.42, 20.56, 20.67
    Temporary guardianship, § 20.60
        Application, § 20.61
        Filing of petition, § 20.62
            Form, § 20.134
        Order of, § 20.62
    Venue, § 20.2
Purpose, § 20.7
Recording placement of child, § 20.100
Religion as factor, § 20.28
Report of adoption, § 20.111
    Private adoption, § 20.74
Rights of unwed fathers, § 20.30
Sealing adoption records, § 20.125
    Constitutionality, § 20.126
    Good cause for unsealing records, § 20.127
        Religious identity crisis, § 20.130
Second parents, § 20.17
Separated adults, by, §§ 20.14, 20.15
Single adult, by, §§ 20.14, 20.22
Social Services Law, § 20.45
Subpoena of records by grand jury, § 20.128
Subsidized adoptions, § 20.2
    Authorization, § 20.113
Surrogate's court, jurisdiction, § 20.9
Termination of parental rights,
    Affidavits required, § 20.92
    Assigned counsel for indigent parents, § 20.93
    Conditional surrender, §§ 20.90, 20.97
    Court approval of surrender, § 20.92
    Court order approving or disapproving surrender, § 20.96
    Extra-judicial surrender, § 20.91
        Notice, § 20.94
    Judicial surrender, § 20.90
    Neglect or abuse, § 20.101
    Recording of surrender, § 20.98
    Revocation of surrender, §§ 20.91, 20.99
        Notification to court, § 20.95
    Right to visitation, § 20.97
Transfer of custody of children to agency, § 20.89
Unmarried couples, by, § 20.17
Venue, § 20.11
    Foster parents, § 20.87
Verified schedule, § 20.105
    Form, § 20.140
Visitation rights,
    Natural parents, § 20.123
    Siblings, § 20.124

ADVANCE DIRECTIVES
    Generally, § 24.90

INDEX

ADVANCE DIRECTIVES—Continued
Do not resuscitate orders, health care decision making, § 23.112
Durable power of attorney, form, § 24.100
Living Wills, generally, this index

ADVERSE POSSESSION
Real property, marketability of title,
    Encroachments due to adverse possession, § 12.66
    Title examinations, checklist of objections to be disposed of prior to closing, § 12.55
    Title insurance policy, standard exemptions, § 12.50

AFFIDAVITS
Adoption proceedings, § 20.36
    Affidavit identifying parties, § 20.115
        Form, § 20.146
    Attorney fees, § 20.120
    Attorney's affidavit, § 20.71
    Attorney's affidavit of financial disclosure, § 20.73
    Birth mother's affidavit regarding putative father, § 20.76
        Form, § 20.144
    Confidential affidavit, §§ 20.72, 20.107
        Form, § 20.143
    Financial disclosure affidavit, § 20.106
    Financial disclosure by parents,
        Form, § 20.147
    Intermediary's affidavit, § 20.77
    Marital affidavit, § 20.108
        Dispensing with consent of spouse,
            Form, § 20.142
        Form, § 20.141
    Payments made to birth parents, § 20.52
    Supplemental affidavit, § 20.110
    Surrender of parental rights, § 20.92
Alcoholic beverage control, retail licenses, § 36.39
Bankruptcy,
    Professionals, employment of, form, § 9.310
Commercial sales contract,
    Drafting checklists,
        Petition for order staying arbitration in dispute over contract for sale of goods,
            Affidavit in opposition to petition, § 5.63
            Form, § 5.71
        Plaintiff's notice of motion for summary judgment,
            Affidavit in support by officer of plaintiff company, § 5.60
                Form, § 5.68
Court of appeals,
    Appeal as of right, time for taking,
        Notice of motion to dismiss appeal as untimely taken,
            Affidavit in support, form, § 39.88
    Cross appeals, time for taking,
        Notice of motion to dismiss appeal as untimely taken,
            Affidavit in support, form, § 39.88
    Leave to appeal,
        Motions filed in court of appeals,
            Notice of motion for leave to appeal from order of appellate division,
                Affidavit in support, form, § 39.84
        Time for taking appeal,
            Notice of motion to dismiss appeal as untimely taken,
                Affidavit in support, form, § 39.88
    Perfecting the appeal, time for filing,
        Notice of motion to dismiss appeal as untimely taken,
            Affidavit in support, form, § 39.88
Damages,
    Interest,

INDEX

AFFIDAVITS—Continued
Damages—Continued
  Interest—Continued
    Notice of motion to amend verdict to add interest, form,
      Affidavit in support, § 30.57
    Notice of motion to fix date from which interest is computed, form,
      Affidavit in support, § 30.59
Default judgments,
  Enforcement of money judgments,
    Affidavit of facts constituting claim, form, § 8.47
Eminent domain,
  Just compensation trial,
    Expert witnesses,
      Affidavit in support of motion for additional allowance to condemnee for expert witnesses, form, § 14.136
Enforcement of money judgments,
  Confession of judgment,
    Affidavit of confession, form, § 8.48
  Default judgment,
    Affidavit of facts constituting claim, form, § 8.47
Equal Employment Opportunity Commission,
  Charge of discrimination, form, § 17.93
Expert witnesses,
  Eminent domain,
    Just compensation trial,
      Affidavit in support of motion for additional allowance to condemnee for expert witnesses, form, § 14.136
Foreclosure,
  Mortgages,
    Receivers, appointment,
      Affidavit in support of motion for appointment of receiver,
        Ex parte motion, § 11.62
        Form, § 11.76
    Summary judgment,
      Affidavit of regularity and in support of motion,
        Drafting checklist, § 11.64
        Form, § 11.78
Interest,
  Damages,
    Notice of motion to amend verdict to add interest, form,
      Affidavit in support, § 30.57
    Notice of motion to fix date from which interest is computed, form,
      Affidavit in support, § 30.59
Mechanic's liens,
  Affidavit for continuance, form, § 10.117
  Bond to discharge liens,
    Discharge of liens and notices of claims,
      Affidavit for order fixing amount of bond, form, § 10.124
  Enforcement,
    Affidavit in support of application to cancel notice of mechanic's lien for failure to commence action, form, § 10.130
    Affidavit in support of motion to determine if class action can be maintained, § 10.147
    Foreclosure of mechanic's lien,
      Affidavit in support of motion to consolidate actions, form, § 10.136
    Public improvements,
      Affidavit in support of application to cancel notice of mechanic's lien for failure to commence action, form, § 10.132
  Protecting the owner,
    Itemized statement,
      Affidavit in support of application to cancel mechanic's lien for failure to furnish itemized statement, form, § 10.128

INDEX

AFFIDAVITS—Continued
Mechanic's liens—Continued
  Public improvements,
    Affidavit for continuance, form, § 10.118
    Enforcement,
      Affidavit in support of application to cancel notice of mechanic's lien for failure to commence action, form, § 10.132
    Foreclosure of lien,
      Affidavit in support of motion for summary judgment, form, § 10.142
Motor vehicle accident insurance,
  Notice of claim, § 26.27 et seq.
Notice,
  Commercial sales contract, drafting checklists,
    Plaintiff's notice of motion for summary judgment,
      Affidavit in support by officer of plaintiff company, § 5.60
      Form, § 5.68
  Damages,
    Interest,
      Notice of motion to amend verdict to add interest, form,
        Affidavit in support, § 30.57
      Notice of motion to fix date from which interest is computed, form,
        Affidavit in support, § 30.59
  Interest,
    Damages,
      Notice of motion to amend verdict to add interest, form,
        Affidavit in support, § 30.57
      Notice of motion to fix date from which interest is computed, form,
        Affidavit in support, § 30.59
  Mechanic's liens,
    Bond to discharge liens,
      Discharge of liens and notices of claims,
        Affidavit for order fixing amount of bond, form, § 10.124
    Enforcement,
      Affidavit in support of application to cancel notice of mechanic's lien for failure to commence action, form, §§ 10.130, 10.132
Probate and estate administration,
  Administrators, asking court to fix amount of bond, § 25.69
  Application for letters of administration, mailing notice of,
    Forms, § 25.56
  Deposition affidavit of subscribing witness, forms, § 25.59
  Service of citation, form, § 25.55
  Wills, proving correct copy of,
    Forms, § 25.53
Self-proving affidavits,
  Wills, execution requirements, § 24.8
Service of process, form, § 26.65
Summary judgments,
  Mechanic's liens,
    Public improvements, foreclosure of lien,
      Affidavit in support of motion for summary judgment, form, § 10.142
  Mortgage foreclosure,
    Affidavit of regularity and in support of motion,
      Drafting checklist, § 11.64

AFFIRMATIVE ACTION
Office of Federal Contract Compliance Programs,
  Federal contractors review, § 17.80

AFFIRMATIVE DEFENSES
Arbitration, § 26.37
Bankruptcy, § 26.37
Collateral estoppel, § 26.37
Commercial sales contract, governing law,

INDEX

AFFIRMATIVE DEFENSES—Continued
Commercial sales contract—Continued
    Freedom to contract, presumption of legality, § 5.8
Employment cases, § 17.83
Fraud, § 26.37
Insurance,
    Affirmative defenses asserted by insurer in coverage action, forms, § 31.35
Limitation of actions, § 26.37
Personal injury cases, § 26.59
    Form, § 26.66
Release, § 26.37
Res judicata, § 26.37
Statute of frauds, § 26.37

AGE DISCRIMINATION IN EMPLOYMENT ACT
Antireprisal provisions, § 17.38
Older Workers Benefit Protection Act,
    Amends ADEA, § 17.11
Provisions of statute, § 17.37

AGENCIES
Administrative Law and Proceedings, generally, this index

AGENTS AND AGENCY
Authority, management,
    Limited liability companies, § 2.32
    Limited partnerships, § 2.93
    Partnerships, § 2.60
Insurance,
    Third parties involved in placement/administration of insurance contract, § 31.7
Real Estate Agents and Brokers
Workers' compensation,
    Licensed representatives, § 32.37
        Fees, § 32.38

AGREEMENTS
Adoption, generally, this index
Attorney Fees, generally, this index
Bankruptcy, generally, this index
Breach of Contract, generally, this index
Child Custody, generally, this index
Child Support, generally, this index
Collective Bargaining, this index
Commercial Sales Contract, generally, this index
Corporations, generally, this index
Definitions, § 5.4
Divorce, generally, this index
Employment Law, generally, this index
Limited Liability Companies, generally, this index
Limited Partnerships, generally, this index
Mechanic's Liens, generally, this index
Municipal Corporations, generally, this index
Partnerships, generally, this index
Real Property, generally, this index
Small Business, Purchase or Sale, generally, this index
Social Security, generally, this index
Spousal Support, generally, this index
Statute of Frauds, generally, this index

AGRICULTURAL FOREIGN INVESTMENT DISCLOSURE ACT
Real property sale,
    Closing of title, disclosure, § 12.81

INDEX

AIDS
Disclosure restrictions, § 17.55

AIR POLLUTION CONTROL
Environmental Law, this index

ALCOHOLIC BEVERAGE CONTROL
    Generally, § 36.1 et seq.
Bars, licensing, § 36.31
Beer,
    Drug stores, license to sell, §§ 36.8, 36.10
    Grocery stores, license to sell, §§ 36.8, 36.10
Bowling alleys, license for sale of beer, wine and spirits, § 36.9
Brewers license, § 36.12
Catering licenses, § 36.9
Club liquor licenses, § 36.9
Discos, license for sale of beer, wine and spirits, § 36.9
Distillers licenses, § 36.12
Excise tax, § 36.44
Federal permits, § 36.4
Five hundred foot rule, §§ 36.2, 36.3
    Hearing, § 36.9
    Retail licenses, § 36.41
Hotel license for sale of beer, wine and spirits, §§ 36.9, 36.34
Legislative history, § 36.4
Licensed premises, lease, § 36.2
Licenses,
    Applications, §§ 36.2, 36.20 et seq.
        Fees, form, § 36.73
        Form, § 36.67
        Requirements, § 36.13
    Approval of corporate change, § 36.47
        Form, § 36.70
    Background check of applicant, § 36.4
    Brewers, § 36.12
    Cancellation, § 36.56
        Judicial review, § 36.66
    Citizenship of applicant, § 36.3
    Criminal record of applicant, § 36.4
    Distillers, § 36.12
    Eating place beer license, § 36.9
    Financing and method of operation, § 36.50
    Fingerprint cards, § 36.14
    Grocery beer license, § 36.3
    Hotel, § 36.34
    Lease for premises, §§ 36.2, 36.3
    Location of premises, § 36.3
    Manufacturing, §§ 36.3, 36.4, 36.12
        Brand and label registration, § 36.18
        Federal approval, § 36.12
        Tax bonds, § 36.19
    Off-premises, §§ 36.3, 36.4, 36.8, 36.10
        Credit provisions, § 36.44
    On-premises, §§ 36.3, 36.4, 36.8
        Certificate of occupancy, § 36.9
        Credit provisions, § 36.44
        Malt beverages, wine and spirits, § 36.9
        Restroom facilities requirements, § 36.9
    Package stores, § 36.8
    Penalties, § 36.54 et seq.
        Letters of warning, § 36.61
    Pending violations, § 36.3
    Prohibitions, § 36.2

INDEX

ALCOHOLIC BEVERAGE CONTROL—Continued
Licenses—Continued
    Refusal to issue, judicial review, § 36.66
    Renewals, § 36.51
    Reporting changes of facts, § 36.45 et seq.
    Restaurant wine license, § 36.9
    Restrictions, § 36.14
    Retail licenses, §§ 36.3, 36.8 et seq., 36.20 et seq.
    Revocation, §§ 36.53, 36.55
        Judicial review, § 36.66
        Notice of pleading, § 36.63
    Source of client's funding, § 36.3
    Suspension, §§ 36.53, 36.57, 36.58
        Deferred, §§ 36.59, 36.60
        Judicial review, § 36.66
        Notice of pleading and hearing, §§ 36.62, 36.64, 36.65
        Proceedings, § 36.62
        Rights of licensee, § 36.62
    Tied-house relationships prohibited, §§ 36.14, 36.26
    Trade practices, § 36.52
    Violations, § 36.53
    Wholesale license, §§ 36.3, 36.4, 36.11
        Application,
            Form, § 36.72
        Brand and label registration, § 36.18
        Federal approval, § 36.11
        Invoices, § 36.44
        Removal of premises, § 36.49
        Tax bonds, § 36.19
    Winery, § 36.12
Liquor Authority,
    Full Board of Commissioners, § 36.6
    Investigative powers, § 36.53
    Jurisdiction, § 36.5 et seq.
    Licensing bureau, § 36.2
    Permits, issuance, § 36.15 et seq.
Malt beverages, license to sell, § 36.9
Manufacturing license, § 36.12
    Brand and label registration, § 36.18
    Federal approval, § 36.12
    Record keeping requirements, § 36.44
    Tax bonds, § 36.19
Package stores,
    200 foot rule, § 36.10
    Credit provisions, § 36.44
    Licenses, §§ 36.10, 36.36
Penalties for violations, § 36.54 et seq.
    Letters of warning, § 36.61
Permits, § 36.15
    Auction, § 36.44
    Board of Health, § 36.33
    Cabaret, § 36.35
    Caterer's, § 36.17
    Fees, § 36.42
    Liquidator's, § 36.38
    Solicitor's, § 36.17
    Temporary, § 36.16
    Trucking, § 36.17
    Warehouse, § 36.17
    Wholesalers to obtain, § 36.11
    Wine auction, § 36.17
Proof of payment, § 36.44

INDEX

ALCOHOLIC BEVERAGE CONTROL—Continued
Record-keeping requirements, § 36.44
Restaurants, § 36.2
    Wine license, § 36.9
Retail licenses, §§ 36.8 et seq., 36.20
    200 foot rule, § 36.28
    500 foot rule, § 36.41
    Affidavits required, § 36.39
    Alteration of premises, § 36.48
        Form, § 36.71
    Applicant information, § 36.22
    Application form checklist, § 36.43
    Applications, § 36.20 et seq.
    Bars, § 36.31
    Board of Health permits, § 36.33
    Criminal background of applicants, §§ 36.24, 36.40
    Employees required, § 36.35
    Endorsement certificate, § 36.46
        Form, § 36.69
    Entertainment, § 36.35
    Fees, § 36.42
        Schedule, form, § 36.73
    Financial information of applicants, §§ 36.24, 36.40, 36.42
    Fingerprint cards, § 36.42
    Grocery stores, § 36.37
    Holding Corporation Stipulation form, § 36.24
    Kitchens, § 36.32
    Landlord information, § 36.26
    Lease information, § 36.21
    Live music or dancing, § 36.35
    Neighborhood characteristics, § 36.28
    Notification to community board, § 36.25
    Personal questionnaire, § 36.40
    Pool tables, § 36.33
    Premises information, §§ 36.23, 36.42
        Exterior, § 36.29
        Interior, § 36.30
    Removal of premises, § 36.49
    Renewals, § 36.51
    Service regulations, § 36.52
Sales slips, § 36.44
Spirits, license to sell, § 36.9
Tax stamp, § 36.4
Two hundred foot rule, §§ 36.3, 36.9
Violations, § 36.53
Wholesale license, § 36.11
    Brand and label registration, § 36.18
    Federal approval, § 36.11
    Record keeping requirements, § 36.44
    Tax bonds, § 36.19
Wine,
    Auction permit, § 36.17
    Drug stores, license to sell, § 36.10
    Grocery and drug stores, license to sell, § 36.8
    Grocery stores, license to sell, § 36.10
    License to sell, § 36.9
Winery licenses, § 36.12

ALIENATION
Retirement income from qualified plans, § 23.28

ALIMONY
Spousal Support, generally, this index

INDEX

ALTERNATIVE DISPUTE RESOLUTION (ADR)
Employment discrimination, § 17.7
Employment law, negotiation, § 17.7
Fee disputes, § 28.28 et seq.

AMERASIANS
Family-based immigration, § 19.15

AMERICANS WITH DISABILITIES ACT
Antireprisal provisions, § 17.38
Employment law, prohibitions against discrimination, § 17.43
Federal civil rights law, education, § 18.53

ANNEXATION
Municipal corporations, § 3.5
    Checklist, § 3.6

ANNULMENT OF MARRIAGE
Distribution of property, § 21.7
Judgments, form, § 21.90

ANSWER
Damages,
    Defense of culpable conduct, form, § 30.50
    Defense of failure to use seat belt, form, § 30.51
    Strategy, § 30.3
Eminent domain,
    Supreme court jurisdiction,
        Answer by condemnee, § 14.63
        Defenses, § 14.64
Guardianships,
    Proceedings to recover property withheld, § 22.84
Holdover proceedings, § 13.47
Mechanic's liens, enforcement,
    Service of answer on state or public corporation, § 10.93
Medical malpractice cases, § 26.59
Mortgage foreclosure, § 11.37
Motor vehicle accident cases, § 26.59
Non-payment proceedings, § 13.22
Personal injury cases,
    Affirmative defenses, form, § 26.66
    Complaints, § 26.37
        Affirmative defenses, § 26.59
            Bills of particulars, § 26.60
Products liability, § 27.56
    Form, § 27.58

APPEALS
Administrative and judicial appeals,
    Employment-based immigration. labor certification denial, § 19.39
    Medicaid, § 23.83
    Medicare, § 23.53
        Benefits, eligibility, § 23.54
        Part A fiscal intermediary decisions, § 23.55
        Part A peer review organization decisions, § 23.56
        Part B determinations, § 23.57
    Social security benefits, § 23.15
    Supplemental security income for the elderly, § 23.22
Appellate Division, Civil Appellate Practice Before, generally, this index; Appellate Division, Criminal Appellate Practice Before, generally, this index
Arbitration awards, lemon law cases, §§ 7.16, 7.17
Bankruptcy, this index
Civil,
    Civil, generally. Appellate Division, Civil Appellate Practice Before, this index

INDEX

APPEALS—Continued
Civil—Continued
    Court of Appeals, generally, this index
    Intermediate Appellate Courts, generally, this index
Court of Appeals, generally, this index
Criminal,
    City courts, § 38.47
    Court of Appeals, generally, this index
    Appellate Division, Criminal Appellate Practice Before, generally, this index
    Criminal court of New York City, § 38.48
        Kings, Queens, and Richmond county branches, § 38.50
        New York and Bronx county branches, § 38.49
        Stay pending appeal, appeal from New York City criminal court to appellate term, § 38.54
    District courts, § 38.47
    Intermediate Appellate Courts, generally, this index
Discrimination cases, § 17.76
Eminent domain, § 14.2
    Just compensation, payment pending appeal, § 14.116
Federal employees benefits, elder law, § 23.40
Intermediate Appellate Courts, generally, this index
Lemon law, § 7.48
Retirement income from qualified plans, § 23.35
Disability cases, generally. Social Security, this index
Unemployment insurance, § 17.60
Village courts, § 38.47
Waiver,
    Plea bargaining, conditioning on basis of waiver, § 33.29
Workers' compensation, § 32.34
Zoning board of appeals, local land use law, § 16.37

APPELLATE DIVISION, CIVIL APPELLATE PRACTICE BEFORE
Abandonment of appeal. Failure to prosecute, generally, post
Abeyance, holding appeal in, § 37.65
Abide the event, costs to, § 37.67
Abuse and neglect proceedings,
    Appeals in family court proceedings, § 37.19 (n. 7)
Abuse of discretion. Discretion, generally, post
Academic or moot issues, §§ 37.31, 37.37
Action on submitted facts, § 37.51
    See also Perfecting appeal, at Methods of, post
Additur and remittitur,
    Jury trials, § 37.29
    Non-jury trials, § 37.65
Administration of appellate division, § 37.4
Administrative Board, rulemaking powers, § 39.100
Administrative powers of appellate division, § 37.5 et seq.
    Administration of courts, § 37.7
    Admission, removal and disciplinary jurisdiction, § 37.6
    Appellate Term oversight, § 37.11
    Assigned counsel, § 37.10
    Attorney admission and disciplinary proceedings, § 37.6
    Court system administration, § 37.7
    Law guardian program, § 37.8
    Legal consultants, § 37.6
    Marshals, § 37.12
    Mental hygiene legal service oversight, § 37.9
    Powers relating to appellate term, § 37.11
Administrative regulations, standard of review, § 37.87 (n. 24)
Advisory opinions, § 37.31
Affirmance,
    Alternate grounds for, by non-aggrieved party, § 37.28
    Disposition of appeal, § 37.64

INDEX

APPELLATE DIVISION, CIVIL APPELLATE PRACTICE BEFORE—Continued
Aggrieved parties, § 37.21 et seq.
    Consent judgments and orders, § 37.23
    Criteria for capacity to appeal (civil), § 37.22
    Death of party, § 37.25
    Defaulters or consenters, capacity to appeal (civil), § 37.23
    Intervenors as, § 37.24
    Non-aggrieved party's alternate grounds for affirmance, § 37.28
    Non-parties, appeal by (civil), § 37.22
    Required status for appealability (civil), §§ 37.21, 37.22, 37.28, 37.37
    Stipulation in excessive or inadequate verdict challenge, § 37.29
    Substitution of parties, § 37.25
    Successful party's status as, § 37.28
    Third party defendants, § 37.26
Agreed statement in lieu of facts, § 37.51
    See also Perfecting appeal, at Methods of, post
Agreed statement in lieu of record, § 37.51
    See also Perfecting appeal, at Methods of, post
Amendment, complaint, reviewability, § 37.36
    Of order of appellate division, § 37.72
Amicus briefs, § 37.81
Appeal, notice of. Notice of appeal, generally, post
Appealability
    See also specific headings
    Aggrieved status required, § 37.22
    By right or permission, to appellate division, § 37.19
    Defaulters, § 37.21
    Distinguished from reviewability, § 37.2
    Ex parte orders, § 37.90
    Intervenors, § 37.21
    Proceedings in various trial level courts, to appellate division, §§ 37.17, 37.18
Appealable paper, § 37.38
Appeals, § 37.14
    See also specific headings
    Civil, § 37.1 et seq.
    Criminal, § 38.1 et seq.
Appeals as of right, § 37.33 et seq.
    Court of appeals, judgment of court of original instance to review prior non-final determination of appellate division, § 39.11
    Final judgments, § 37.34
    Interlocutory judgments, § 37.34
    Orders, § 37.35
    Time for taking appeal, § 37.40
Appeals by permission, §§ 37.36, 39.16
    Civil court of New York City, § 37.120
    Court of appeals, § 39.12
        Final order of appellate division determining action, § 39.14
        Judgment of court of original instance to review prior non-final determination of appellate division, § 39.13
        Non-final order of appellate division in proceedings by or against public officers, § 39.15
    Time for taking appeal, § 37.41
Appeals from other appellate courts, § 37.20
Appeals to other intermediate courts, § 37.91 et seq.
Appellate Term,
    Administration by appellate division, § 37.11
    Appeals from county court to (civil cases), § 37.126
    Appeals from justice courts to, §§ 37.93, 37.95
    Appeals to appellate division from, §§ 37.20, 37.97
    Constitutional basis, §§ 37.31, 37.93
    Costs on appeal, § 37.98
    Establishment of, §§ 37.16, 37.93

INDEX

APPELLATE DIVISION, CIVIL APPELLATE PRACTICE BEFORE—Continued
Appellate Term—Continued
    Perfection of appeal from justice courts, §§ 37.96, 37.97
    Permission by, from justice court orders, § 37.95
    Permission to appeal determination of, § 37.41
Appendix, joint, § 37.51
Appendix method, perfecting appeal, § 37.51
Apportionment of fault or liability, § 37.65
Arbitrary and capricious,
    Article 78 proceedings, standard, § 37.87
Arbitration,
    Stay of appeals relating to, § 37.37
    Waiver, and dismissal of appeal by participation in, § 37.37 (n. 92)
Argument of appeal, § 37.62
Article 78 Proceedings,
    Annulment or confirmation in, § 37.88
    Commenced in appellate division, § 37.87
    Costs to prevailing party, § 37.88
    Direct review by appellate division of certain agency determinations, § 37.44
    Non-final (interim or interlocutory) orders in, § 37.36
    Penalty, review of, § 37.87
    Prosecution of transferred, §§ 37.50, 37.88
    Remitting to administrative agency, appealability, §§ 37.37, 37.88
    "Shocking to one's sense of fairness" standard, § 37.87
    Standards of review, § 37.87
    Time limitations on transferred proceedings, § 37.49
    Transfer of, § 37.87
    Venue, § 37.87
Assigned counsel,
    Appellate division provisions, civil, § 37.10
    Assigned counsel plan, § 37.10
    Civil cases, generally, § 37.48
    Family court appeals, § 37.19
    Habeas corpus, § 37.48
    Rules regulating conduct and discipline, § 37.6
    Surrogate's court appeals, § 37.18
Assignment of counsel. Assigned counsel, generally, ante
Attorney General,
    Intervention by, § 37.24
    Notice to, in appeal involving statute's constitutionality, § 37.24
    Service of notice upon, in constitutional challenge to statute, § 37.24
Attorneys,
    Admission to practice, disciplinary and grievance proceedings, § 37.6
    Assigned counsel, generally, ante
Attorneys' fees,
    Family Court appeals, § 37.19
    On appeal, § 37.67
    Sanctions, including, § 37.83
    Surrogate's court appeals, § 37.18
Automatic stays,
    In connection with appeal, § 37.80
Bail, review in habeas corpus proceedings, § 37.88
Bench trials, scope of review, §§ 37.29, 37.65
Bifurcation orders, appealability, § 37.37
Bond,
    Appeals by public administrators, § 37.18
Briefs
    See also Perfecting appeal, generally, post
    Amicus, § 37.81
    Appellant's, § 37.52
    Appellate term, § 37.97
    Departmental variations, § 37.52

INDEX

APPELLATE DIVISION, CIVIL APPELLATE PRACTICE BEFORE—Continued
Briefs—Continued
    Family court appeals, § 37.19
    Form and content, § 37.52
    Limitations of, as affecting review, § 37.30
    Perfecting appeal, filing of, § 37.52
    Reply, § 37.52
    Respondent's, § 37.52
    Sanctions relative to, § 37.52
Calendars,
    Calendar conference orders, appealability, § 37.38 (n. 12-13)
    Calendar practices, by department, § 37.60
    Dismissal, § 37.85
    Publication of, § 37.85
"C.A.M.P." (Civil Appeals Management Program), § 37.84
Capacity to appeal (civil), § 37.21
    See also Aggrieved parties, generally, ante
Censure, attorneys. Attorneys, ante
Certification of appellate division justices, § 37.4
Certiorari to U.S. Supreme Court, § 37.73
Change in law when case pending, § 37.32
Character and fitness, attorneys. Attorneys, ante
Chief administrator of the courts, §§ 37.7, 37.91
City courts,
    Appeals as of right, § 37.104
    Appeals by permission, § 37.104
    Appeals from, § 37.101 et seq.
    Constitutional basis, § 37.3
    Courts to which appeals are taken, § 37.102
    Settlement of record and return, § 37.105
    Small claims review, § 37.108
    Uniform City Court Act, § 37.101
Civil Appeals Management Program (C.A.M.P.), § 37.84
Civil Court of New York City, § 37.117 et seq.
    Appeals as of right and by permission, § 37.120
    Appeals from, §§ 37.117, 37.118
    Appeals to the Court of Appeals, § 37.121
    Constitutional basis, § 37.3
    Costs on appeal, § 37.124
    Courts to which appeals are taken, § 37.118
    CPLR applicability, § 37.119
    Jurisdiction, § 37.117
    Perfection of appeal, § 37.123
    Settlement of record and return, § 37.122
    Small claims review, § 37.125
Civil Practice Law and Rules. CPLR, generally, post
Clarification of order of appellate division, § 37.72
Clerks (appellate division), appointment of, § 37.4
Collateral estoppel,
    Effect on aggrieved status, § 37.22
Commission on judicial conduct, § 37.91
Committee,
    Costs on appeal, § 37.18
Complaint, amendment, reviewability, § 37.36
Concurrent appeals, Second Department, § 37.51
Condensed format transcript, Second Department, § 37.51
Conditional relief by appellate division, § 37.65
Conferences, preargument settlement, § 37.84
Consent, order on, as not aggrieved, §§ 37.23, 37.37
Conservator,
    Costs on appeal, § 37.18
Consolidation of appeals, § 37.53

INDEX

APPELLATE DIVISION, CIVIL APPELLATE PRACTICE BEFORE—Continued
Constitution, New York State,
    Judicial structure, § 37.3
    Rulemaking powers of the appellate division, § 37.5 et seq.
Constitutionality or constitutional issues,
    Orders, appealable as of right, § 37.35
    Preservation doctrine as to, § 37.28
    Raised initially on appeal, § 37.28
    Statutes, intervention by attorney general, § 37.24
Consultants, § 37.7
Contempt,
    Before appellate division, § 37.71
Corrective action,
    By appellate division, generally (civil), § 37.65
    Jury and non-jury cases, § 37.29
    Remand or remittance, § 37.65
    Restitution, § 37.65
    Reversal or modification, § 37.65
Costs and disbursements,
    Abide the event, § 37.67
    Acceptance of as waiver of appeal, § 37.37
    Article 78 proceedings, § 37.88
    Attorneys' fees, § 37.67
    Award, on appeal, § 37.67
    Bill of costs, § 37.77
    Enforcing judgment for, on appeal, § 37.71
    On appeal from city courts, § 37.107
    On appeal to appellate division, § 37.67
    On appeal to appellate term or county court, §§ 37.98, 37.107
    Surrogate's court appeals, § 37.18
Counsel. Attorneys, generally, ante
    Assignment of. Assigned counsel, generally, ante
    Fees. Attorneys' fees, generally, ante
County court,
    Appeals to appellate division, civil case judgments and orders, § 37.16
    Appeals to appellate division, civil cases from county court as intermediate appellate court, §§ 37.20, 37.126
    Appeals to, from justice courts or city courts, §§ 37.20, 37.93, 37.97
    Constitutional basis, § 37.3
    Costs on appeal to, § 37.98
    Jurisdiction, § 37.126
    Perfection of appeal from justice courts, § 37.96
Court acts,
    Court of Claims Act, § 37.3
    Family Court Act, § 37.3
    Surrogate's Court Act, § 37.3
    Uniform City Court Act, § 37.3
    Uniform District Court Act, § 37.3
    Uniform Justice Court Act, § 37.3
Court of appeals,
    Leave to appeal to, § 37.70
    Review of questions of law, §§ 37.3, 37.70
    Stay of proceedings on appeal to, § 37.80
Court of claims,
    Appeals to appellate division from civil case judgments and orders, § 37.17
    Applicability of CPLR to appeals, § 37.17
    Constitutional basis, § 37.3
    Governing practice, § 37.3
    jurisdiction, § 37.17
    Notice of appeal, timing, § 37.17
Court of Claims Act, § 37.3
Courts of original jurisdiction from which appeals lie, § 37.15

INDEX

APPELLATE DIVISION, CIVIL APPELLATE PRACTICE BEFORE—Continued
Courts of original jurisdiction from which appeals lie—Continued
    County courts, § 37.16
    Court of claims, § 37.17
    Family court, § 37.19
        Advisements, § 37.19
        Appeal as of right, § 37.19
        Appeal by permission, § 37.19
        Appeals by law guardians, § 37.19
        Assignment of counsel, § 37.19
        Child support, § 37.19
        Duties of counsel, § 37.19
        Juvenile delinquency, § 37.19
        Notice of appeal, § 37.19
        Papers on appeal, § 37.19
        Preferences, § 37.19
        Stays, § 37.19
        Time to appeal, § 37.19
    Supreme court, § 37.16
    Surrogate's court, § 37.18
CPLR,
    Application of, to appeals from city courts, § 37.103
    Application of, to appeals from district courts, § 37.111
    Application of, to appeals from justice courts, § 37.94
    Comparison with Uniform Justice Court Act, § 37.95
    CPLR 5704 ex parte order review, § 37.89
    CPLR Article 78 proceedings, § 37.87
Criminal Court of the City of New York,
    Constitutional basis, § 37.3
Cross-appeals,
    Bar by stipulation, § 37.29
    Inability to, as non-aggrieved, § 37.28
    Perfecting the appeal, § 37.51
    Sequence of briefs, § 37.51
    Time limits, § 37.42
Curative powers of appellate division in notices. Omissions and errors, generally, post
Custody,
    Stays, in appeals, § 37.19
Damages, increase or reduction of. Excessive or inadequate recovery, generally, post
Death,
    Party, substitution of, following, § 37.25
Decision and order combined, appealability of, § 37.37
Decisions, non-appealability, §§ 37.37, 37.37 (n. 5), 37.37 (n. 68)
Declaratory relief, by appellate division, § 37.65
Decrees,
    Appeals to appellate division from surrogate's court, §§ 37.18, 37.30
Default or defaulter,
    Appealability, §§ 37.21, 37.23, 37.37
Dehors-the-record, matters, § 37.28
Departments,
    Appellate division, structure, § 37.3
    Filing requirements, perfection of appeals, § 37.55 et seq.
Deviates materially, as standard for verdict review, § 37.29
Disability retirement of judge, by appellate division, § 37.91
Disbarment, attorneys. Attorneys, generally, ante
Disbursements,
    Award, on appeal, § 37.67
Disciplinary proceedings. Attorneys, generally, ante
Discovery, appealability of order deferring until after in camera inspection, § 37.37
Discretion,
    Abuse of as compared with improvident exercise of and substitution of, § 37.29
    Abuse of in article 78 proceedings, § 37.87

INDEX

APPELLATE DIVISION, CIVIL APPELLATE PRACTICE BEFORE—Continued
Discretionary stays,
    In connection with appeals, § 37.80
Dismissal calendar, § 37.85
Dismissal of appeal, § 37.66
    By county court, § 37.97
    Calendar as to, § 37.85
    Consequences of, § 37.85
    Failure to obtain permission, for, § 37.37
    Failure to perfect or prosecute, for, §§ 37.37, 37.66, 37.85
    Failure to substitute party, for, § 37.25
    Lack of subject matter jurisdiction, § 37.37
    Miscellaneous grounds for, § 37.37
    Non-appealability, for, § 37.37
    Of order, owing to superseding order or final judgment, § 37.37
Dismissal of complaint,
    Legally insufficient evidence, § 37.65 et seq.
Disposition of appeal, § 37.63 et seq.
    Affirmance, § 37.64
    Attorney fees, § 37.67
    Conditional relief, § 37.65
    Corrective action, § 37.65
    Costs and disbursements, § 37.67
    Declaratory relief, § 37.65
    Dismissal, § 37.66
    Modification, § 37.65
    Reargument, appeal, grounds for, § 37.69
    Restitution, § 37.65
    Reversal, § 37.65
    Sufficiency of evidence, § 37.65
    Summary judgment, § 37.65
    Weight of evidence, § 37.65
District courts, § 37.109 et seq.
    Appeals by right or permission, § 37.112
    Appeals from, § 37.109
    Constitutional basis, § 37.3
    Costs on appeal from, § 37.115
    Courts to which appeals are taken, § 37.110
    CPLR applicability, § 37.111
    Perfecting the appeal, § 37.114
    Settlement of record and return, § 37.114
    Small claims review, § 37.116
Districts,
    Judicial structure, § 37.3
Election law appeals, on original record, § 37.51
Enumerated and nonenumerated appeals, § 37.62
Error, harmless, in civil appeals, § 37.28
Errors and omissions. Omissions and errors, generally, post
Evidence,
    Rules of, civil applicable to criminal, § 37.13
    Sufficiency of evidence (civil), generally, post
    Weight of evidence of verdict, generally, post
Ex parte orders,
    Appealability, § 37.90
    Dismissal of appeal from, § 37.37
    Review of under CPLR 5704, §§ 37.37, 37.89
Examinations before trial,
    Appealability of orders relating to, § 37.37 (n. 42-43)
Excessive or inadequate recovery, §§ 37.29, 37.65
    Powers of appellate division, in jury trials, § 37.29
    Powers of appellate division, in non-jury trials, § 37.65
Executor,

INDEX

APPELLATE DIVISION, CIVIL APPELLATE PRACTICE BEFORE—Continued
Executor—Continued
    Costs on appeal, § 37.18
Extensions of time to file notices, § 37.43
Fact, findings of,
    Affirmance of, § 37.65
    By appellate division, §§ 37.29, 37.64, 37.65
    Deference by appellate division to, § 37.29
    Remit for, §§ 37.29, 37.65 (n. 16)
Fact, questions of,
    As opposed to questions of law, § 37.29
    Jury versus non-jury trials, § 37.29
    Resolution of by appellate division, § 37.22
    Scope of review, § 37.29
Facts, modification on the, § 37.65 et seq.
Facts, reversal on the, § 37.65 et seq.
Failure to prosecute
    See also Dismissal calendar, ante; Dismissal of appeal, generally, ante; Perfection of appeal, generally, post
    As basis for dismissal of appeal, § 37.37
    Consequences of, § 37.85
Family court,
    Appeals as of right or by permission, § 37.19
    Appeals from criminal court transfer orders, § 37.19
    Appeals from various family court proceedings, § 37.19
    Appeals to appellate division from orders and judgments, generally, § 37.19
    Appellate counsel, advisements, § 37.19
    Applicability of CPLR to appeals, § 37.19
    Assignment of counsel, indigency, § 37.19
    Attorney fees on appeal, § 37.19
    Constitutional basis, § 37.3
    Family Court Act governing practice, § 37.3
    Filiation order, § 37.19
    Finality, § 37.19
    Jurisdiction, § 37.19
    Juvenile delinquency proceedings, § 37.19
    Law guardian program, § 37.8
    Law guardians, on appeal, § 37.19
    Papers on appeal, § 37.19
    Preferences in appeals, § 37.19
    Presentment agency, appeal by, § 37.19
    Stays of appeal, § 37.19
    Support proceedings, § 37.19
    Timeliness, notice, and service provisions for appeals, § 37.19
Fault, apportionment of, § 37.65
Federal law, binding effect of, § 37.3
Filiation order appeal, §§ 37.19, 37.37 (n. 47)
Filing, § 37.54 et seq.
    Filing fee, § 37.46 (n. 5)
    First Department, § 37.55
    Fourth Department, § 37.58
    Notice of appeal, § 37.46
    Number of copies, § 37.54
    Requirements, perfecting appeal, § 37.54 et seq.
    Second Department, § 37.56
    Third Department, § 37.57
    What to file, § 37.54
Final judgments. Judgments, post
Findings of fact. Fact, findings of, generally, ante
Forms, § 37.128 et seq.
Frivolous appeals, sanctions for, § 37.83
Full record,

INDEX

APPELLATE DIVISION, CIVIL APPELLATE PRACTICE BEFORE—Continued
Full record—Continued
    Method of perfection, § 37.51
Fundamental error, § 37.28
Governance of term, § 38.57
Grievance procedure, attorneys. Attorneys, generally, ante
Guardian,
    Costs on appeal, § 37.18
Guardian ad litem,
    Costs on appeal, § 37.18
Habeas corpus proceedings,
    Assignment of counsel, § 37.48
    Bail review in, § 37.88
    Initiated in appellate division, § 37.88
    Non-final or interim orders in, §§ 37.34, 37.37
Harmless error in civil appeals, § 37.28
Hear and Report, directive to,
    Appealability, § 37.37
    Corrective action, § 37.65
Hearing, appealability of order directing, § 37.37
Hearing examiners,
    Review of determinations by, § 37.19
Improvident exercise of discretion. Discretion, generally, ante
Inaccuracies in notice, etc.. Omissions and errors, generally, post
Inadequate recovery. Excessive or inadequate recovery, generally, ante
Incompetency of party, substitution upon, § 37.25
Increase of damages award. Excessive or inadequate recovery, generally, ante
Indigent parties,
    Assignment of attorneys, surrogate's court appeals, § 37.18
    Civil appeals, generally, § 37.48
    Exemption from filing fee, § 37.46
    Family court appeals, § 37.19
    Habeas corpus proceedings, § 37.48
    Mentally ill persons, proceedings, § 37.48
    Original record, use of, § 37.51
    Service requirements by, § 37.46
Injunction, preliminary. Preliminary injunction, generally, post
Insufficiency of evidence as a matter of law, § 37.65
Insurance carrier,
    Stay of judgment or order by posting undertaking, § 37.80
Interest of justice jurisdiction,
    Grounds for exercise of, § 37.28
    History of, § 37.28
    Relative to motions, § 37.28
    When preservation lacking, § 37.28
Interim relief,
    Appellate motion practice, § 37.79
    Ex parte orders, § 37.89
Interlocutory judgments,
    Appeals as of right, from, §§ 37.34, 37.38
Interlocutory orders
    See also Orders, at Non-final, post
    Appealability in,
        Article 78 proceedings, § 37.37
        Habeas corpus proceedings, § 37.37
    Appeals from, as of right, § 37.35
    Appeals from, by permission, § 37.36
    Appeals from, (criminal), prohibited, § 38.3
    Non-appealable, § 37.37
Intermediate appellate courts,
    Other than appellate division, § 37.91
        See also Appellate Term, generally, ante; County court, generally, ante

INDEX

APPELLATE DIVISION, CIVIL APPELLATE PRACTICE BEFORE—Continued
Intermediate orders. Interlocutory orders, generally, ante
Intervenors and intervention,
    As aggrieved, § 37.24
    Attorney general, § 37.24
    Capacity to appeal (civil), § 37.21
    Civil appeal, as of right or by permission, § 37.24
    Discretion of court, § 37.24
Joint appendix or record, § 37.51
    See also Perfecting appeal, at Methods of, post
    Compelling of, § 37.51
    In cross appeals, § 37.51
    Relative to agreed statement in lieu of record, § 37.51
Judgments, § 37.38
    Absolute, when stipulation is required, §§ 37.41, 37.97
    Appeals to appellate division,
        County court, from, § 37.16
        Court of claims, § 37.17
        Supreme court, § 37.16
    Defined, § 37.38
    Entry of, post-appeal, § 37.71
    Final,
        Appeals as of right from, § 37.34
        Matters reviewable under, § 37.35
    For costs, § 37.71
    Grant of, on the law, on appellate review, § 37.65
    Interlocutory judgments, appeals as of right, from, §§ 37.34, 37.38
    Law, on the,
        Appellate review, § 37.65
    Matters not reviewable under, § 37.36
    Non-final, as reviewable under final, § 37.35
    Notwithstanding verdict,
        Judgment on appeal for defendant, notwithstanding verdict for plaintiff, § 37.65
        Judgment on appeal for plaintiff, notwithstanding verdict for defendant, § 37.65
    Service of, by prevailing party or aggrieved party, §§ 37.40, 37.41
Judicial hearing officer, appealability of orders directing, § 37.37
Judicial notice, § 37.29
    harmless error, § 37.29
    Mandatory versus permissive, § 37.29
    Preservation of issue, § 37.29
Judiciary,
    Counties, § 37.3
    Departments, appellate division, § 37.3
    Districts, judicial, § 37.3
    Structure, § 37.3
Jurisdiction,
    As affected by time limits to take appeal, §§ 37.39, 37.43 (n. 1)
    Flexibility of appellate division in treatment of notices or omissions, § 37.43
    Subject matter,
        As related to mootness, § 37.31
        Dismissal for lack of, § 37.37
Jury, appellate review of verdict,
    Sufficiency of evidence, § 37.65
    Weight of evidence, § 37.65
Justice courts
    See also Town courts, generally, post; Village courts, generally, post
    Appeals from, §§ 37.93, 37.96
    Appeals from, as of right and by permission, § 37.95
    Appellate term, § 37.93
    Appellate term, appeals to, § 37.97
    Applicability of CPLR on appeals from, § 37.95
    Costs on appeal, § 37.98

INDEX

APPELLATE DIVISION, CIVIL APPELLATE PRACTICE BEFORE—Continued
Justice courts—Continued
    County court, § 37.93
        Appeals from, § 37.98
    Courts to which appeals are taken, § 37.93
    CPLR Article 55, applicability, § 37.94
    Filing fee in appeals from, § 37.96
    Jurisdiction, § 37.92
    Notice of appeal, § 37.96
    Perfecting the appeal, § 37.97
    Return on appeal, § 37.96
    Rule governance by administrative board, § 37.100
    Settlement of case, § 37.96
    Small claims review, § 37.99
    Taking the appeal, § 37.96
    Uniform Justice Court Act, § 37.92
Justice, interest of. Interest of justice jurisdiction, generally, ante
Justices, appellate division,
    Certification of, § 37.4
    Grant permission to appeal by, § 37.41
    Quorum, § 37.4
    Requirements, § 37.4
    Residency requirement, § 37.4
Justiciability or non-justiciability, as related to subject matter jurisdiction, § 37.37
Juvenile delinquency,
    Advisements, duties of counsel as to, § 37.19
    Appeals involving, § 37.19
    Preferences, on appeal, § 37.19
    Quasi-criminal nature, § 37.19
Labor law, special provisions for appeal under certain sections, § 37.44
Law, change in,
    When case pending, § 37.32
Law guardian,
    Appeal by, § 37.19
    Continuation of assignment on appeal, § 37.19 (n. 60)
    Program, § 37.9
    Stay application, on family court appeal, § 37.19
Law, questions of,
    As opposed to questions of fact, § 37.29
    Raised initially on appeal, § 37.28
    Scope of review, § 37.28
Law, reversal on the, § 37.65
Law students, appearances by, § 37.6
Leave to appeal to court of appeals, motion for, in appellate division, § 37.70
Legal consultants, Department rules, § 37.6
Liability, apportionment of, relative to appellate division powers, § 37.65
Limitations in brief, § 37.30
Limitations in notice of appeal, §§ 37.30, 37.45
Location, § 37.59
Mandamus. Article 78 Proceedings, generally, ante
Marshals,
    Administration by appellate division, § 37.12
Matrimonial actions, inapplicability of "action submitted facts", § 37.51
Matters dehors the record, § 37.28
    Notice of motion to strike,
        Affirmation in support, form, § 37.138
        Form, § 37.137
Memorandum decisions, unappealability of, § 37.37
Mental hygiene legal service,
    Appellate division oversight and rules, § 37.9
Mentally ill persons,
    Assignment of counsel, § 37.48

INDEX

APPELLATE DIVISION, CIVIL APPELLATE PRACTICE BEFORE—Continued

Merits,
    Orders involving some part of, as appealable as of right, § 37.35
Miscellaneous proceedings in appellate division, § 37.87 et seq.
Misdescriptions. Omissions and errors, generally, post
Modifications, in disposition of appeal, § 37.65
    Statement by appellate division of reasons for, § 37.65
Moot or academic issues, §§ 37.31, 37.37
Motion practice, §§ 37.74, 37.82
    Amicus curiae, § 37.81
    First Department, § 37.75
    Second Department, § 37.76
    Third Department, § 37.77
    Fourth Department, § 37.78
    Interim relief, § 37.79
    Miscellaneous motions, § 37.82
    Stays, § 37.80
        Notice of motion for stay in proceedings,
            Affirmation in support, form, § 37.132
            Form, § 37.130
        Order to show cause for stay of proceedings,
            Affirmation in support, form, § 37.132
            Form, § 37.131
Mount Vernon, special provision relating to, § 37.44
Municipalities and school districts, special provisions, § 37.40
Neglect and abuse proceedings,
    Appeals in family court proceedings, § 37.19 (n. 7)
New trial,
    Appeal from order denying or granting, § 37.35
    Grant by appellate division based on verdict against weight of evidence, § 37.65
New York Citiy Civil Court Act, governing practice, § 37.3
New York State Constitution. Constitution, New York State, generally, ante
New York State Reports, § 37.4
Newspaper, official daily, § 37.4
Non-appealable matters, § 37.37
    Dismissal for lack of subject matter jurisdiction, § 37.37
Non-final order, appeals to court of appeals, § 37.70
Non-jury trial, scope of review, §§ 37.29, 37.65
Non-moving party,
    Grant of summary judgment to, §§ 37.2, 37.65
Non-party, appeal by, as aggrieved, § 37.22
Notice,
    Lack of. Ex parte orders, generally, ante
    Order determining motion made without, § 37.38
Notice, judicial. Judicial notice, generally, ante
Notice of appeal,
    Appeals from justice courts, § 37.96
    Comprehensiveness of, as delimiting issues, §§ 37.30, 37.45
    Departmental requirements, § 37.45
    Family court, § 37.19
    Filing, § 37.46
    Form, § 37.129
    Form and content, § 37.45
    Limitations in, §§ 37.30, 37.45
    Scope of review, § 37.30
    Service and filing, § 37.46
    Time for filing. Time or time limits, civil appeals, generally, post
Notice of entry,
    Service by prevailing party on appeal of order with, § 37.71
    Service by prevailing party or aggrieved party at nisi pruis of order with, §§ 37.40, 37.41, 37.71
Notice of motion to enlarge time to perfect appeal,

INDEX

APPELLATE DIVISION, CIVIL APPELLATE PRACTICE BEFORE—Continued
Notice of motion to enlarge time to perfect appeal—Continued
    Affirmation in support, form, § 37.136
    Form, § 37.135
Omissions and errors,
    Flexibility of appellate division in treatment of, §§ 37.43, 37.44 (n. 4)
    Harmless error in civil appeals, § 37.28
Oral arguments, § 37.62
Orders,
    Appealable by permission or right. Permission or right, appeals by, generally, post
    Appeals to appellate division from,
        As of right, § 37.35
        County court, from, § 37.16
        Court of claims, from, § 37.17
        Supreme court, from, § 37.16
    Clarification of, post-appeal, § 37.72
    Defined, § 37.38
    Entry of, post-appellate disposition, § 37.71
    Ex parte orders. Ex parte orders, generally, ante
    Non-final,
        Article 78 proceedings, § 37.36
        Reviewable under final judgments, §§ 37.35, 37.47
    Not reviewable under final judgment, illustrations, § 37.35
    Preliminary conference orders, appealability, § 37.37
    Resettlement, post-appeal, § 37.72
    Service of, by prevailing party or by aggrieved party, §§ 37.31, 37.40, 37.41
    Subsequent orders, as affecting appeal, § 37.47
    Types of, as appealable as of right, § 37.35
Original proceedings in appellate division,
    Article 78 proceedings, § 37.87
    Habeas corpus, § 37.88
    Listed, § 37.90
Original record, method of perfecting appeal, § 37.51
Other proceedings, § 37.86 et seq.
Parental rights or parental custody,
    Advisements, duties of counsel as to, § 37.19
    Preferences, on appeals from termination of, by reason of permanent neglect, § 37.19
    Termination, family court, § 37.19
Paternity,
    Filiation order appeal, §§ 37.19, 37.37 (n. 47)
Perfecting appeal, § 37.50
    Actions on submitted facts, § 37.51
    Agreed statement in lieu of record, § 37.51
    Appeals from justice courts, § 37.97
    Appendix method, § 37.51
    Article 78 transferred proceedings, § 37.50
    Briefs, contents, form, requirements, § 37.52
    City courts, appeals from, § 37.105 et seq.
    Consolidation of appeals, § 37.53
    Copies required, § 37.54 et seq.
    Cross appeals, § 37.51
    Department variations, § 37.50 et seq.
    Failure, as basis for dismissal, §§ 37.37, 37.66, 37.85
    Filing requirements,
        Fees, § 37.49
        Number of copies, per department,
            First Department, § 37.55
            Second Department, § 37.56
            Third Department, § 37.57
            Fourth Department, § 37.58
    Full record, § 37.51
    Justice courts, appeals from, § 37.96

INDEX

APPELLATE DIVISION, CIVIL APPELLATE PRACTICE BEFORE—Continued
Perfecting appeal—Continued
    Methods of (full record, agreed statement, in lieu of record, original record, action on submitted facts), § 37.51
    Notice of motion to enlarge time to perfect appeal,
        Affirmation in support,
            Form, § 37.136
        Form, § 37.135
    Original record, § 37.51
    Record, filing of, § 37.50 et seq.
    Record, format, § 37.51
    Time requirements, § 37.50
    Unperfected appeals, § 37.85
Permission or right, appeals by,
    Appeal from appellate term to appellate division, § 37.20
    As of right, to appellate division,
        Final and interlocutory judgments, from, § 37.34
        Orders, from, § 37.35
    By permission, to appellate division, § 37.36
        Who may grant permission, § 37.37
    City courts, from, § 37.103
    Department rules regulating permission, § 37.41
    District courts, from, § 37.111
    Failure to obtain permission, § 37.37
    Family court appeals to appellate division, § 37.19
        Permission (leave), § 37.41
    Grant of permission, application for,
        Appeal to appellate division, § 37.41
        Appeals from appellate term, § 37.41
        Appeals from family courts, § 37.41
        Appeals from justice courts, § 37.95
        Formalities of motion papers, § 37.41
    Justice court, appeals from, § 37.95
    Motions for permission, timing of notice, § 37.41
    Refusal of permission, consequences, § 37.36
    Time for taking appeal,
        Permission, by, § 37.41
        Right, by, § 37.40
Persons in need of supervision,
    Advisement by counsel, § 37.19
    Preferences on appeal, § 37.19
Poor persons. Indigent parties, generally, ante
Post judgment appellate proceedings,
    Certiorari to U.S. Supreme Court, § 37.73
    Clarification, § 37.72
    Contempt, § 37.71
    Enforcement, § 37.71
    Entry of judgment or order, § 37.71
    Judgment for costs, § 37.71
    Leave to appeal to court of appeals, § 37.70
    Reargument, § 37.69
        Notice of motion for argument or leave to appeal to court of appeals,
            Affirmation in support, form, § 37.140
            Form, § 37.139
    Resettlement or clarification of order, § 37.72
Preargument conference,
    First and Second Department, §§ 37.83, 37.84
    Second Department, § 37.45
Preargument statement in First Department, § 37.46
Preference, trial, reviewability on appeal, § 37.36
Preferences on appeal, § 37.61
    Family court proceedings, § 37.19

INDEX

APPELLATE DIVISION, CIVIL APPELLATE PRACTICE BEFORE—Continued
Preferences on appeal—Continued
    Minors, cases involving (civil), § 37.19
    Notice of motion for preference to expedite appeal,
        Affirmation in support, form, § 37.134
        Form, § 37.133
    Persons in need of supervision, § 37.19
Preliminary conference orders, appealability, § 37.37
Preliminary injunction,
    By appellate division, pending appeal, § 37.80
    Review on final judgment of order granting, § 37.36
Prematurity of notice, § 37.43
    See also Omissions and errors, generally, ante
Preservation (civil appeals), § 37.28
    Constitutional issues, as to, § 37.28
    Face of the record, matters appearing on, § 37.28
    Interest of justice, § 37.28
    Motions, as related to, § 37.28
Presiding justice, appointment of, § 37.4
Printed record, dispensing with, § 37.51 (n. 40)
Private Housing Finance Law,
    Variant statutory appellate requirements, § 37.44
Procedural checklist, § 37.127
Prosecute, failure to
    See also Dismissal of appeal, ante
    As basis for dismissal of appeal, § 37.37
    Consequences of, § 37.85
Provisional remedies, appeals relating to, § 37.35
Public administrators,
    Appeals by, § 37.18
    Stays in appeals by, § 37.18
Public Health Law,
    Certain appeals to Third Department, § 37.44
Questions of fact. Fact, questions of, generally, ante
Questions of law. Law, questions of, generally, ante
Quorum,
    Justices of appellate division, § 37.4
RADI (Request for Appellate Division Intervention), §§ 37.45, 37.84, 37.88
Railroad law,
    Variant statutory appellate requirements, § 37.44
Raised for first time on appeal versus unpreserved, § 37.28
Real Property Tax Law,
    Variant statutory appellate requirements, § 37.44
Reargument and renewal motions,
    Appealability, § 37.37 (n. 7-12)
    Denial of renewal motion, as affecting appealability of original order, § 37.47
    Grant of, as affecting appeal from original order, § 37.47
    Grant of, as appealable paper, § 37.37
    Of appeal itself, § 37.69
Record and papers on appeal
    See also Perfecting appeal, generally, ante
    Appeals from family court, § 37.19
    Appendix method, § 37.51
    Filing. Perfecting appeal, generally, ante
    Format of records, § 37.51
    Full record, § 37.51
    Original, method of perfecting appeal, § 37.51
    Settlement of,
        Appeals to appellate division, § 37.50
        City court appeals, § 37.105
        Justice court appeals, § 37.96
Reduction of damages award. Excessive or inadequate recovery, generally, ante

INDEX

APPELLATE DIVISION, CIVIL APPELLATE PRACTICE BEFORE—Continued
Reference, orders of,
  Appealability, § 37.37
Remand or remittance, corrective action, § 37.65
Remedial,
  Law, change in, when case pending, § 37.32
Renewal motions. Reargument and renewal motions, generally, ante
Reply brief, § 37.52
  See also Briefs, generally, ante
Request for appellate division intervention, §§ 37.45, 37.84, 37.88
Resettlement
  See also Record and papers on appeal, ante
  Decretal paragraphs in judgment, § 37.37
  Motion, before appellate division, § 37.72
  Order granting, as affecting appeal from original order, § 37.47
Restitution, upon reversal or modification, § 37.65
Retirement, by appellate division, of judge under disability, § 37.91
Return,
  On appeal from city court, § 37.105
  On appeal from justice court, § 37.96
  To appellate term, § 37.97
Reversal of judgment, order, or decree, § 37.65
  Based on ground not raised below, § 37.28
  On law or facts, § 37.65 et seq.
  Statement by appellate division of reasons for, § 37.65
Review (civil case appeals),
  Court of appeals, as contrasted with, § 37.3
  Final judgments, matters included, § 37.35
  Mixed questions of law and fact, § 37.29
  Questions of fact, § 37.29
  Questions of law, § 37.28
  Reviewability, as distinguished from appealability, § 37.2
  Scope of, § 37.28
    Fact questions, § 37.29
    Legal sufficiency of evidence, § 37.28
    Weight of evidence, §§ 37.29, 37.65
Right, civil appeals as of. Permission or right, appeals by, generally, ante
Right to counsel, § 37.48
Rules,
  Attorneys' conduct, § 37.6
  Chief judge's, § 37.13
  Compilation of, § 37.13
  Department of appellate division, § 37.13
  Disciplinary, § 37.6
  Extent of authority of judiciary, § 37.13
  Legal consultants, § 37.6
  Motion practice of appellate division departments, § 37.74 et seq.
  Rule making power, § 37.4
Rules of court, § 37.13
Sanctions,
  For noncompliance with requirements for briefs, § 37.52
  For various failures, § 37.83
  In connection with frivolous appeals, § 37.83
Scope of review
  See also Review, ante
  Abuse of discretion, § 37.29
  Change of law while case is pending, § 37.32
  Discretion, § 37.29
  Excessive or inadequate recovery, § 37.29
  Harmless error, § 37.28
  Improvident exercise of discretion, § 37.29
  Judicial notice, § 37.29

640

INDEX

APPELLATE DIVISION, CIVIL APPELLATE PRACTICE BEFORE—Continued
Scope of review—Continued
    Limitations in notice of appeal or brief, § 37.30
    Matters dehors the record, § 37.28
    Mootness, § 37.31
    Notice of appeal, § 37.30
    Preservation of issues for review, § 37.28
    Questions of fact, § 37.29
    Questions of law, § 37.28
    Substitution of discretion, § 37.29
Searching the record,
    Grant of summary judgment to non-moving party, §§ 37.2 (n. 8), 37.65
Second class cities law,
    Variant statutory appellate requirements, § 37.44
Separate trial (order granting or denying bifurcation), § 37.37
Separately state and number, appealability of order granting or denying motion to, § 37.37
Service and filing requirements,
    Notice of appeal, § 37.46
Setting aside of verdict, §§ 37.29, 37.65
Shock the conscience standard in monetary verdicts, § 37.29
Small claims review,
    City courts, § 37.108
    District courts, § 37.116
    Justice courts, § 37.99
Standing to appeal. Aggrieved parties, generally, ante
Stare decisis, § 37.3
Statutory framework, § 37.13
Stays,
    Appeals by public administrator, § 37.18
    Automatic, § 37.80
    By appellate division, § 37.80 et seq.
    Certiorari application, § 37.74
    Discretionary, § 37.80
    Expiration of, § 37.80
    Family court proceedings, § 37.19
    Insurance carriers, § 37.80
    Notice of motion for stay of proceedings,
        Affirmation in support, form, § 37.132
        Form, § 37.130
    Order to show cause for stay of proceedings,
        Affirmation in support, form, § 37.132
        Form, § 37.131
    Scope of, § 37.80
    Undertaking, in conjunction with, § 37.80
    Vacatur or modification of, § 37.80
Stipulation,
    Aggrievement, affecting lack of, § 37.37
    By party, relative to apportionment of fault, § 37.65
    By party, relative to excessive or inadequate recovery, § 37.29
Strategy, § 37.2
Striking scandalous or prejudicial matter, appealability of order upon, § 37.37
Sua sponte orders, appealability, § 37.37 (n. 39)
Subsequent orders, as affecting appeal, § 37.47
Substantial evidence,
    Standard in Article 78 proceedings, § 37.87
Substantial right,
    Orders affecting, as appealable as of right, §§ 37.35, 37.37
Substituted parties or substitution of parties,
    Capacity to appeal, § 37.21
    Death of party, § 37.25
    Extension of time, §§ 37.25, 37.43
    Incompetency of party, § 37.25

INDEX

APPELLATE DIVISION, CIVIL APPELLATE PRACTICE BEFORE—Continued
Substitution of discretion, § 37.29
Sufficiency of evidence (civil),
    As questions of law, § 37.28
    Compared with weight of evidence, § 37.65
Summary judgment on appeal,
    Searching the record, §§ 37.2, 37.65
Support proceedings,
    Appeals relative to, § 37.19
Supreme court,
    Appeals to appellate division, civil judgments and orders, § 37.16
    Lack of appellate jurisdiction, § 37.3
Sur-reply briefs, prohibition against, § 37.52
Surrogate's court,
    Appeals to appellate division from orders, decrees, and judgments, § 37.18
    Applicability of CPLR to appeals, § 37.18
    Assigned counsel on appeal, § 37.18
    Attorneys' fees on appeal, § 37.18
    Constitutional basis, § 37.3
    Costs on appeal, § 37.18
    Counsel fees on appeal, § 37.18
    Governing practice, § 37.3
Suspension of attorneys. Attorneys, generally, ante
Temporary order of custody (Family court), § 37.19
Temporary order of support (Family court), § 37.19
Temporary restraining order by appellate division
    See also Stays, generally, ante
    Granting, modifying, or limiting, pending appeal, § 37.80
Termination of parental rights. Parental rights or parental custody, ante
Third Department, appellate division,
    Appeals taken to, from certain proceedings, § 37.44
    Proceedings required to be commenced in, § 37.90
Third-party defendants,
    As aggrieved, § 37.28
    Capacity or standing to appeal, §§ 37.21, 37.26
Time or time limits, civil appeals,
    Administrative agency variations, § 37.44
    Appeal as of right, § 37.40
    Appeal by permission, § 37.41
    Appeal, notice of,
        City court, appeal from, § 37.104
        County court, appeal from, § 37.40
        Court of claims, appeal from, § 37.17
        Family court, appeal from, § 37.19
        Justice court, appeal from, § 37.95
        Supreme court, appeal from, § 37.40
        Surrogate's court, appeal from, § 37.18
    Cross appeals, § 37.42
    Extensions and omissions, § 37.43
    Labor law, § 37.44
    Municipalities and school districts, special provisions, § 37.44
    Omissions, § 37.43
    Other statutory provisions, § 37.44
    Substitution of parties, effect on, § 37.25
    Thirty-day period, computation of, §§ 37.40, 37.41
    Workers' compensation, § 37.44
Town courts, constitutional basis, § 37.3
Transcripts, appeals from orders relating to, § 37.35
    Perfection of appeal, § 37.51 et seq.
    Settlement of, § 37.51
Transfer of cases from one department to another, § 37.59
Transportation law,

INDEX

APPELLATE DIVISION, CIVIL APPELLATE PRACTICE BEFORE—Continued
Transportation law—Continued
    Variant statutory appellate requirements, § 37.44
Trial rulings, appealability, § 37.37
Undertaking,
    To stay judgment or order, § 37.80
Unemployment Insurance Appeal Board,
    Appeals to Third Department, § 37.44
Uniform City Court Act,
    Governing practice, § 37.3
Uniform court acts, generally, § 37.91
    See also specific headings
Uniform District Court Act,
    Governing practice, § 37.3
Uniform Justice Court Act,
    Appeals to appellate term, § 37.92
    Comparison with CPLR, § 37.95
    Costs on appeal, § 37.98
    Governing practice, § 37.3
    Preparation of record, § 37.96
    Small claims review, § 37.99
Unperfected appeals, § 37.85
Unpreserved. Preservation (civil appeals), generally, ante
Venue, change of, reviewability, § 37.36
Verdict,
    As against weight of evidence, §§ 37.29, 37.65
    As excessive or inadequate in jury trials, § 37.29
    As excessive or inadequate in non-jury trials, § 37.65
    As insufficient, legally, § 37.65
    Excessive or inadequate recovery, generally, ante
    Judgment for defendant, notwithstanding, § 37.65 (n. 42)
    Judgment for plaintiff, notwithstanding, § 37.65 (n. 51)
    Non-appealability, § 37.37
    Setting aside, on appellate review, §§ 37.29, 37.65
Village courts,
    Constitutional bases, § 37.3
Weight of evidence of verdict,
    As question of fact on civil appeal, § 37.29
    Compared with sufficiency of evidence, § 37.65
    Contrary to, on appellate review, § 37.29
    Test for, § 37.65
Who may appeal, § 37.21 et seq.
    Aggrieved parties, § 37.22
        Consent judgments and orders, § 37.23
        Death of party, § 37.25
        Defaulters, § 37.23
        Intervenors, § 37.24
        Substitution of parties, § 37.25
        Third party defendants, § 37.26
Withdrawal,
    Of appeal, as basis for dismissal, § 37.37
Workers' Compensation Board,
    Appeals to Third Department, § 37.44

APPELLATE DIVISION, CRIMINAL APPELLATE PRACTICE BEFORE
    Generally, § 38.1 et seq.
Aggrieved parties, § 38.5
    Aggrieved status as prerequisite to appeal, § 38.6
    Defendant, appeals by, § 38.5
        County court, § 38.7
        Supreme court, § 38.7
    People, appeals by, § 38.5
Appeal as of right, §§ 38.8, 38.12

INDEX

APPELLATE DIVISION, CRIMINAL APPELLATE PRACTICE BEFORE—Continued
Appeal as of right—Continued
    Appeal from CPL Article 440 orders granting people's application to set aside sentence, § 38.8
    Appeal from judgment of conviction, § 38.8
    Appeal from judgment upon guilty plea, § 38.8
        Adverse suppression order appealable following guilty plea, § 38.8
        Conditional guilty pleas disfavored, § 38.8
        Constitutional challenges not waiverable, § 38.8
        Constitutional speedy trial challenges not waiverable, § 38.8
        Double jeopardy claims, § 38.8
        Incompetency to stand trial not waiverable, § 38.8
        Indictment not spelling out criminality, § 38.8
        Ineffective assistance of counsel, § 38.8
        Joint representation claims, § 38.8
        Prosecution based on knowingly false testimony, § 38.8
        Vacation of guilty pleas, § 38.8
        Violation of parental notification requirement in juvenile cases, § 38.8
        Voluntariness of guilty plea, § 38.8
        Waiver of most issues on appeal, § 38.8
    Appeal from sentence, § 38.8
    Appeal from sentence including criminal forfeiture, § 38.8
    Appeal process, § 38.12
    Capital cases, § 38.3
    CPL # 440.40,
        Application by people to set aside sentence as invalid as matter of law, § 38.8
    CPL § 450.10, § 38.8
    CPL Article 450,
        Interlocutory appeals prohibited, § 38.3
    CPL Article 460,
        How to bring and perfect appeal, § 38.3
    CPL Article 470,
        Determination of appeal, § 38.3
    CPL Article 510,
        Denial of bail not appealable by right or permission, § 38.8
    CPLR Article 55,
        Habeas corpus proceedings, § 38.8
    CPLR Article 70,
        Habeas corpus proceedings, § 38.8
    Notice of appeal, filing, § 38.12
    Penal Law § 460.30, enterprise corruption, § 38.8
    Plea bargaining, waiver of appeal, § 38.8
    Waiver, § 38.8
Appeal by permission, § 38.9
    Adverse CPL Article 440 determinations, § 38.9
    Certificate granting leave, § 38.13
    Collateral attack, § 38.9
    Coram nobis writs, CPL Article 440 applications formerly known as, § 38.9
    CPL § 450.15, § 38.9
    Montgomery relief, § 38.9
        CPL § 460.30, § 38.9
        Extension of time to appeal, § 38.9
    Vacatur for reasons outside record, § 38.9
Appeal by the people, § 38.10
    Blood test evidence, suppression, § 38.10
    Brady material, § 38.10
    Coram nobis writs, § 38.10
    CPL § 440.10 judgment vacatur orders, § 38.10
    CPL § 450.20, § 38.10
    Dismissal of accusatory instrument, § 38.10
    Dismissal of complaint, § 38.10
    Dismissal of indictment, § 38.10

INDEX

APPELLATE DIVISION, CRIMINAL APPELLATE PRACTICE BEFORE—Continued
Appeal by the people—Continued
    Dismissal of information, § 38.10
        CPL § 170.30, § 38.10
        CPL § 170.50, § 38.10
    Dismissal of local criminal court accusatory instruments, § 38.10
    Dismissal owing to defective grand jury proceedings, § 38.10
    Double jeopardy issues, § 38.10
    Eavesdropping, recording or video evidence, suppression, § 38.10
    Forfeitures, § 38.10
    Huntley hearings, § 38.10
    Jackson "prejudice" test, § 38.10
    Mapp hearings, suppression, § 38.10
    Orders denying people's 440.40 motions to set aside sentences, § 38.10
    Orders setting aside sentences, § 38.10
    Orders setting aside verdicts, § 38.10
    Orders vacating judgments, § 38.10
    Pen register and trap device information, suppression, § 38.10
    Post-conviction collateral attack, § 38.10
    Post-verdict trial orders of dismissal, § 38.10
    Prosecutors information, § 38.10
    Reduction of count in indictment, § 38.10
    Rosario material, § 38.10
    Sentences, legality, § 38.10
    Suppression orders, § 38.10
    Trial orders of dismissal, § 38.10
    Wade identification hearings, § 38.10
Appeals by defendants to superior courts, § 38.7
Assignment of counsel, § 38.16
    First Department, Assigned Counsel Plan Appellate Panel, § 38.16
    Motion for assignment of new counsel, § 38.42
    Responsibilities, § 38.29
Bail,
    CPL Article 510, denial of bail not appealable by right or permission, § 38.8
    Criteria, § 38.15
    Denial not appealable, § 38.8
"Beslanovics" procedure, § 38.26
Calendaring appeal, § 38.17
    First Department, § 38.17
    Second Department, § 38.17
    Third Department, § 38.17
    Fourth Department, § 38.17
Certiorari to U.S. Supreme Court, § 38.33
Change of venue, § 38.8
    CPL § 170.15, § 38.8
    CPL § 230.20, § 38.8
    Criminal court to family court, § 38.8
        Abuse and neglect, § 38.8
        CPL § 210.43(1)(a), § 38.8
        Family Court Act § 1014(b), § 38.8
    Family court to criminal court, § 38.8
        Abuse and neglect, § 38.8
        Family Court Act §1014(a), § 38.8
        Prosecutor's consent required, § 38.8
        Referral to prosecutor, § 38.8
    Family Protection and Domestic Violence Intervention Act of 1994, § 38.8
    Juvenile case from criminal court to family court, § 38.8
        CPL § 725.05, § 38.8
    Removal hearing,
        CPL § 180.75(4), § 38.8
    Transfer or removal of cases, § 38.8
Chart, § 38.64

INDEX

APPELLATE DIVISION, CRIMINAL APPELLATE PRACTICE BEFORE—Continued
Civil appellate practice distinguished, § 38.3
Contempt, § 38.8
    Article 78 proceedings, § 38.8
    Civil contempt compared, § 38.8
    Judiciary Law 750, § 38.8
    Penal Law crime, § 38.8
County courts,
    Appeals, from, § 38.4
    Appeals, to, § 38.46
Courts of original jurisdiction from which appeals lie, § 38.4
    County court, § 38.4
    Supreme court, § 38.4
Death penalty and mentally retardation, § 38.10
Disposition of appeal, § 38.23 et seq.
    Abatement due to death of defendant, § 38.8
    Abeyance, § 38.28
    Affirmance, § 38.24
    Appeal to court of appeals, application for permission and certificate granting leave, § 38.24
    "Beslanovics" procedure, § 38.26
    Corrective action, § 38.28
    CPL § 450.30(3), § 38.8
    CPL § 460.20, § 38.24
    CPL § 470.15(2), § 38.23
    CPL # 470.15(3)(a),
        Reversal or modification on the law or in interest of justice, § 38.27
    CPL # 470.15(3)(c),
        Reversal or modification on the law or in interest of justice, § 38.27
    CPL # 470.20,
        Remittal, § 38.28
    Dismissal, § 38.28
        Absconding defendant, § 38.8
        Deportation of defendant, § 38.8
        Frivolous appeals, Anders brief, § 38.8
        Vacation of dismissal upon defendant's return to state, § 38.8
    Modification, § 38.25
        Interest of justice, §§ 38.25, 38.27
        On the facts, §§ 38.25, 38.27
        On the facts and in the interest of justice, §§ 38.25, 38.27
        On the law, §§ 38.25, 38.27
        On the law and facts, §§ 38.25, 38.27
        On the law and in the interest of justice, §§ 38.25, 38.27
        On the law, facts and in the interest of justice, §§ 38.25, 38.27
        Second Department, § 38.8
        Third Department, § 38.8
    Mootness,
        Defendant serving complete sentence, § 38.8
    New trial, § 38.28
    Reduction of verdict, § 38.3
    Remittal, § 38.28
    Resentencing, § 38.8
    Reversal, § 38.26
        "Beslanovics" procedure, § 38.26
        Interest of justice, §§ 38.26, 38.27
            CPL § 470.15(3)(c), §§ 38.26, 38.27
        On the facts, §§ 38.26, 38.27
        On the facts and in the interest of justice, §§ 38.26, 38.27
        On the law, §§ 38.26, 38.27
        On the law and facts, §§ 38.26, 38.27
        On the law and in the interest of justice, §§ 38.26, 38.27
        On the law, facts and in the interest of justice, §§ 38.26, 38.27

INDEX

APPELLATE DIVISION, CRIMINAL APPELLATE PRACTICE BEFORE—Continued
Disposition of appeal—Continued
  Reversal—Continued
    Retrial following, reindictment, § 38.26
      Second Department, § 38.8
      Third Department, § 38.8
Due process right to appeal, § 38.3
Extensions of time, § 38.14
  CPL § 460.30(1), § 38.14
Forfeitures,
  CPL Article 450, § 38.10
  CPLR Article 13-A, § 38.10
  Organized Crime Control Act, § 38.10
General principles, § 38.3
Grand jury,
  CPL § 190.85, § 38.11
  Sealing order, § 38.11
Guilty pleas, waiver of appeal, § 38.8
Habeas corpus, § 38.8
  CPLR Article 55, § 38.8
  CPLR Article 70, § 38.8
Interest of justice, jurisdiction, § 38.3
Interlocutory orders, appeals from prohibited, § 38.3
Mental retardation in capital cases,
  CPL § 400.27(12)(e), § 38.10
Motions, § 38.36 et seq.
  Abatement of appeal upon death of defendant, § 38.41
  Anders brief, § 38.38
  Assignment of new counsel, § 38.42
  Briefs, § 38.44
    Amicus briefs, § 38.44
    Motion to exclude untimely filed brief, § 38.44
    Pro se supplemental brief,
      Second Department, time limits, § 38.37
      Fourth Department, time limits, § 38.37
  Death or absence of defendant, § 38.41
  Dismissal, § 38.39
    Defendant absent from jurisdiction, § 38.41
    Notice, § 38.39
  Expanding the judgment roll, § 38.43
  Extension of time, § 38.14
    Notice of motion for extension of time to take appeal,
      Affirmation in support, form, § 38.63
      Form, § 38.62
  Frivolous appeals, § 38.38
  Notice of motion for extension of time to take appeal,
    Affirmation in support, form, § 38.63
    Form, § 38.62
  Poor person relief, § 38.16
  Pro se supplemental brief, § 38.37
    Second Department, time limits, § 38.37
    Fourth Department, time limits, § 38.37
  Reconstruction hearing, § 38.40
  Stay of execution of judgment, § 38.15
    Affirmation in support, form, § 38.61
    Form, § 38.60
  Summary reversal, § 38.40
  Withdrawal of appeal, § 38.45
Orders accepting or sealing grand jury reports, § 38.11
Perfecting the appeal, § 38.17
  First, § 38.17
  Second, § 38.17

INDEX

APPELLATE DIVISION, CRIMINAL APPELLATE PRACTICE BEFORE—Continued
Perfecting the appeal—Continued
    Third, § 38.17
    (d)Fourth, § 38.17
Poor person relief, § 38.16
Post-disposition proceedings, § 38.29 et seq.
    Certiorari to U.S. Supreme Court, § 38.33
    Clarification, § 38.35
    Coram nobis proceedings, § 38.34
    CPL # 460.20(2)(a),
        Leave to appeal, § 38.32
    CPL Article 440,
        Coram nobis proceedings, § 38.34
    CPLR 2103,
        Service of leave to appeal, § 38.32
    Ineffective assistance of counsel, § 38.34
    Leave to appeal, § 38.32
        Service, CPLR 2103, § 38.32
    Reargument, § 38.31
        Third Department, time limits for filing of motion, § 38.31
    Resettlement, § 38.35
    Responsibilities of counsel, § 38.30
Procedural checklist, § 38.59
Prosecutors, § 38.11
Public servants, § 38.11
Scope, § 38.1
Scope of review, § 38.18 et seq.
    Abuse of discretion, §§ 38.19, 38.21
    Change in law while case pending, § 38.22
    CPL § 470.15(4), § 38.20
    CPL § 470.15(6)(b), § 38.21
    Discretion, § 38.21
    Ex post facto clause, § 38.22
    Excessive sentences, § 38.21
    Harmless error, § 38.19
    Improvident exercise of discretion, § 38.19
    Interest of justice, § 38.21
    Other interest of justice applications,
        Abuse of discretion, § 38.21
        CPL § 470.15(6)(b), § 38.21
        Excessive sentences, § 38.21
    Preservation doctrine, § 38.19
        CPL § 470.05(2), § 38.19
    Questions of fact, § 38.20
        CPL § 470.15(4), § 38.20
    Questions of law, § 38.19
        Organization of court exception, § 38.19
    Reasonable possibility of error standard, § 38.19
    Sufficiency of evidence, § 38.19
    Sufficiency of protest, § 38.19
    Timeliness of objection, § 38.19
        CPL § 470.05(2), § 38.19
    Unpreserved error, § 38.21
    Weight of evidence, § 38.20
Status as aggrieved by adverse order, § 38.6
Stay of judgment or order, § 38.15
Strategy, § 38.2
Supreme court,
    Appeals, from, § 38.4
    Appeals, to, § 38.46
Verdict,
    Reduction, authority of court, § 38.3

INDEX

APPELLATE DIVISION, CRIMINAL APPELLATE PRACTICE BEFORE—Continued
Who may appeal, § 38.5 et seq.
  Aggrieved parties, § 38.5
    Aggrieved status as prerequisite to appeal, § 38.6
    Defendant, appeals by, § 38.5
      County court, § 38.7
      Supreme court, § 38.7
    People, appeals by, § 38.5
  Appeal as of right, §§ 38.8, 38.12
    Appeal from CPL Article 440 orders granting people's application to set aside sentence, § 38.8
    Appeal from judgment of conviction, § 38.8
    Appeal from judgment upon guilty plea, § 38.8
      Adverse suppression order appealable following guilty plea, § 38.8
      Conditional guilty pleas disfavored, § 38.8
      Constitutional challenges not waiverable, § 38.8
      Constitutional speedy trial challenges not waiverable, § 38.8
      Double jeopardy claims, § 38.8
      Incompetency to stand trial not waiverable, § 38.8
      Indictment not spelling out criminality, § 38.8
      Ineffective assistance of counsel, § 38.8
      Joint representation claims, § 38.8
      Prosecution based on knowingly false testimony, § 38.8
      Vacation of guilty pleas, § 38.8
      Violation of parental notification requirement in juvenile cases, § 38.8
      Voluntariness of guilty plea, § 38.8
      Waiver of most issues on appeal, § 38.8
    Appeal from sentence, § 38.8
    Appeal from sentence including criminal forfeiture, § 38.8
    Appeal process, § 38.12
    Capital cases, § 38.3
    CPL # 440.40,
      Application by people to set aside sentence as invalid as matter of law, § 38.8
    CPL § 450.10, § 38.8
    CPL Article 450,
      Interlocutory appeals prohibited, § 38.3
    CPL Article 460,
      How to bring and perfect appeal, § 38.3
    CPL Article 470,
      Determination of appeal, § 38.3
    CPL Article 510,
      Denial of bail not appealable by right or permission, § 38.8
    CPLR Article 55,
      Habeas corpus proceedings, § 38.8
    CPLR Article 70,
      Habeas corpus proceedings, § 38.8
    Notice of appeal, filing, § 38.12
    Penal Law § 460.30, enterprise corruption, § 38.8
    Plea bargaining, waiver of appeal, § 38.8
    Waiver, § 38.8
  Appeal by permission, § 38.9
    Adverse CPL Article 440 determinations, § 38.9
    Certificate granting leave, § 38.13
    Collateral attack, § 38.9
    Coram nobis writs, CPL Article 440 applications formerly known as, § 38.9
    CPL § 450.15, § 38.9
    Montgomery relief, § 38.9
      CPL § 460.30, § 38.9
        Extension of time to appeal, § 38.9
    Vacatur for reasons outside record, § 38.9
  Appeal by the people, § 38.10
    Blood test evidence, suppression, § 38.10

INDEX

APPELLATE DIVISION, CRIMINAL APPELLATE PRACTICE BEFORE—Continued
Who may appeal—Continued
    Appeal by the people—Continued
        Brady material, § 38.10
        Coram nobis writs, § 38.10
        CPL § 440.10 judgment vacatur orders, § 38.10
        CPL § 450.20, § 38.10
        Dismissal of accusatory instrument, § 38.10
        Dismissal of complaint, § 38.10
        Dismissal of indictment, § 38.10
        Dismissal of information, § 38.10
            CPL § 170.30, § 38.10
            CPL § 170.50, § 38.10
        Dismissal of local criminal court accusatory instruments, § 38.10
        Dismissal owing to defective grand jury proceedings, § 38.10
        Double jeopardy issues, § 38.10
        Eavesdropping, recording or video evidence, suppression, § 38.10
        Forfeitures, § 38.10
        Huntley hearings, § 38.10
        Jackson "prejudice" test, § 38.10
        Mapp hearings, suppression, § 38.10
        Orders denying people's 440.40 motions to set aside sentences, § 38.10
        Orders setting aside sentences, § 38.10
        Orders setting aside verdicts, § 38.10
        Orders vacating judgments, § 38.10
        Pen register and trap device information, suppression, § 38.10
        Post-conviction collateral attack, § 38.10
        Post-verdict trial orders of dismissal, § 38.10
        Prosecutors information, § 38.10
        Reduction of count in indictment, § 38.10
        Rosario material, § 38.10
        Sentences, legality, § 38.10
        Suppression orders, § 38.10
        Trial orders of dismissal, § 38.10
        Wade identification hearings, § 38.10
    Appeals by defendants to superior courts, § 38.7
    Death penalty and mentally retardation, § 38.10
    Forfeitures,
        CPL Article 450, § 38.10
        CPLR Article 13-A, § 38.10
        Organized Crime Control Act, § 38.10
    Mental retardation in capital cases,
        CPL § 400.27(12)(e), § 38.10
    Orders accepting or sealing grand jury reports, § 38.11
    Prosecutors, § 38.11
    Public servants, § 38.11
    Status as aggrieved by adverse order, § 38.6

APPELLATE TERM
Administration by appellate division, § 37.11
Appeals as of right,
    City courts, §§ 37.102, 37.104
    Civil Court of New York City, §§ 37.118, 37.120
    District courts, § 37.112
    Justice courts, §§ 37.93, 37.95
Appeals by permission,
    City courts, §§ 37.102, 37.104
    Civil Court of New York City, §§ 37.118, 37.120
    District courts, § 37.112
    Justice courts, §§ 37.93, 37.95
Appeals from county court to (civil cases), § 37.126
Appeals from justice courts to, §§ 37.93, 37.95
Appeals to appellate division from, §§ 37.20, 37.97

INDEX

APPELLATE TERM—Continued
Constitutional basis, §§ 37.31, 37.93
Costs on appeal, § 37.98
Criminal court of New York City, from, § 38.54
Establishment of, §§ 37.16, 37.93
Local criminal courts, from, § 38.47
    Stays, § 38.54
Perfection of appeal from justice courts, §§ 37.96, 37.97
Permission by, from justice court orders, § 37.95
Permission to appeal determination of, § 37.41

APPRAISERS AND APPRAISALS
Bankruptcy, § 9.29
Eminent domain,
    Just compensation trial, filing and exchange of, § 14.104
    Pretaking appraisals, offer and negotiation, § 14.41
Small business, purchase or sale,
    Buyer, representation of, § 6.9
    Due diligence investigation,
        Financial review, § 6.28
            Valuation of business, § 6.29

ARBITRATION
Affirmative defense, § 26.37
Employment disputes, § 17.9
Insurance clauses, § 31.24
Legal malpractice cases, § 28.29
    Fee disputes, § 28.30
Lemon law, §§ 7.3, 7.12, 7.48
    Appeals, §§ 7.16, 7.17
    Awards, § 7.15
    Burden of proof, § 7.15
    Hearing, §§ 7.14, 7.15
    Notice of petition to vacate award, § 7.50
    Petition to vacate award, § 7.51
    Procedures, § 7.13
Matrimonial cases, fee disputes, §§ 21.76, 21.78
Mechanic's liens, filing notice of lien, effect, § 10.67
Motor vehicle accidents, §§ 26.24, 26.30
Personal injury cases, § 26.50
    Arbitrators, § 26.50
    Binding, § 26.50
Stay of appeals relating to, § 37.37
Waiver, and dismissal of appeal by participation in, § 37.62

ARREST
Employment law, denial of job or entitlements, § 17.39
Local criminal courts, police/citizen encounters, § 33.4
Police and prosecutorial misconduct, § 18.20 et seq.
    Excessive force, § 18.21
        Complaint, form, § 18.93
    False arrest, § 18.22
        Complaint, form, § 18.92
    False imprisonment, § 18.23
        Complaint, form, § 18.92
Police/citizen encounters, § 33.7
Warrantless arrest, § 33.7
    Petty offenses, § 33.7
    Traffic infractions, § 33.7

ARTICLE 78 PROCEEDINGS
Annulment or confirmation in, § 37.88
Appellate division, civil, § 37.87
Costs to prevailing party, § 37.88

INDEX

ARTICLE 78 PROCEEDINGS—Continued
Direct review by appellate division of certain agency determinations, § 37.44
Federal civil rights law, collateral estoppel inapplicable, § 18.37
Local land use law, judicial review, §§ 16.43, 16.45
    Writ of certiorari, § 16.50
Municipal corporations, § 3.32
Non-final (interim or interlocutory) orders in, § 37.36
Penalty, review of, § 37.87
Prosecution of transferred, §§ 37.50, 37.88
Remitting to administrative agency, appealability, §§ 37.37, 37.88
"Shocking to one's sense of fairness" standard, § 37.87
Standards of review, § 37.87
Time limitations on transferred proceedings, § 37.49
Transfer of, § 37.87
Venue, § 37.87

ARTICLES OF ORGANIZATION
Limited liability companies, § 2.17

ASBESTOS
Asbestos School Hazard Detection and Control Act,
    Antireprisal provisions, § 17.38
Bankruptcy, Chapter 11,
    Asbestos-related cases, channeling injunctions, § 9.171

ASBESTOS SCHOOL HAZARD DETECTION AND CONTROL ACT
Antireprisal provisions, § 17.38

ASSET SALES
Small business, purchase or sale,
    Tax issues. Small Business, Purchase or Sale, this index

ASSETS
Jointly held assets, probate avoidance, § 24.83
Planning with certain assets, generally. Estate Planning, this index
Probate and estate administration,
    Fiduciaries, two or more in dispute,
        Entitlement to assets, § 25.45
    Information about, obtaining, § 25.42
    Jointly held assets,
        Avoidance of probate, § 24.83
Protection, § 24.84
    Domestic trusts, § 24.87
    Family partnerships, § 24.86
    Foreign trusts, § 24.88
    Statutory exemptions, § 24.85

ASSIGNMENT
Enforcement of money judgments, § 8.12
Generation skipping transfer taxes, § 24.28
Interests. Assignment of Interests, generally, this index
Medicare part B supplementary medical insurance, § 23.51
Residential contract of sale, § 12.30
Retirement income from qualified plans, § 23.28
Workers' compensation benefits, § 32.32

ASSIGNMENT OF INTERESTS
Limited liability companies, § 2.33
    Default rules, § 2.34
    Vote required to admit assignee as member, § 2.35
Limited partnerships, § 2.94
    Default rules, § 2.95
    New partners, vote required to admit, § 2.96
Partnerships, § 2.61
    Default rules, § 2.62

INDEX

ASSIGNMENT OF INTERESTS—Continued
Partnerships—Continued
    Vote required to admit new partner, § 2.63

ASSUMPTION OF RISK
Generally, § 30.38

ASSUMPTION OF RISK OF LOSS
Commercial Sales Contract, this index

ATTORNEY FEES
Adoptions, § 20.3
    Affidavits, § 20.120
Appellate division, civil,
    Disposition of appeal, § 37.67
Damages, § 30.41 et seq.
    Agreements, § 30.43
    Statutes, § 30.42
Debt collection lawsuits, § 7.43
Deceptive Practices Act, § 7.47
Deceptive trade practices, § 7.62
    Motor vehicle sales, § 7.3
Discrimination cases, § 17.75
Employment law,
    Discharge of employee, § 17.16
Enforcement of money judgments, § 8.7
Fair credit reporting violations, § 7.62
Fair Debt Collection Practice Act, § 7.48
Family court appeals, § 37.19
Fee disputes, § 28.27 et seq.
    Action for an account stated, § 28.32
    Reasonableness standard, § 28.33
Guardianships, awarding to petitioner, § 22.39
Lemon law, §§ 7.12, 7.48
Matrimonial cases, § 21.79
    Fee disputes, § 28.27 et seq.
Motor Vehicle Retail Leasing Act, §§ 7.22, 7.48
Motor vehicle sales, false advertising, § 7.7
New York Fair Credit Reporting Act, §§ 7.48, 7.60
On appeal, § 37.67
Personal injury cases, § 26.6
Private adoptions, §§ 20.2, 20.41, 20.44
    Affidavits, § 20.78
Probate and estate administration, § 25.47
Sanctions, including, § 37.83
Social security disability cases,
    Collecting, § 34.52
        Fee agreements, § 34.54
            Maximum fee, form, § 34.71
        Fee applications, § 34.53
Surrogate's court appeals, § 37.18
Wage claims, § 17.63
Workers' compensation, § 32.38

ATTORNEY GENERAL
Arbitration, lemon law cases, § 7.12
Bureau of Consumer Fraud and Protection, powers and duties, § 7.2
Consumer protection, powers and duties, § 7.2
Corporations,
    Foreign, § 1.115
    Judicial dissolution, § 1.100
Intervention by, § 37.24
Notice to, in appeal involving statute's constitutionality, § 37.24
Personal injury claim against state, notice of claim, § 26.41
Service upon,

INDEX

ATTORNEY GENERAL—Continued
Service upon—Continued
    Eminent domain action, just compensation, § 14.72
    Notice, in constitutional challenge to statute, § 37.24

ATTORNEYS
Appellate division, civil appellate practice before,
    Admission, removal and disciplinary jurisdiction, § 37.6
Assignment of new counsel,
    Appellate division, civil appellate practice before,
        Appellate division provisions, civil, § 37.10
        Assigned counsel plan, § 37.10
        Civil cases, generally, § 37.48
        Family court appeals, § 37.19
        Habeas corpus, § 37.48
        Rules regulating conduct and discipline, § 37.6
        Surrogate's court appeals, § 37.18
    Appellate division, criminal appellate practice before,
        Motions, § 38.42
Bankruptcy, § 9.29
Court of appeals,
    Admission of attorneys and licensing of foreign legal consultants, § 39.61
Disciplinary Rules,
    Matrimonial cases, § 21.77
Eminent domain, role, § 14.2
Ethical considerations, estate planning,
    Beneficiary, as, § 24.95
    Fiduciaries, as, § 24.95
Family court,
    Duties of counsel, § 37.19
Fees. Attorney Fees, generally, this index
Ineffective assistance of counsel,
    Appellate division, criminal,
        Post-disposition proceedings, § 38.34
Matrimonial cases, § 21.2
    Conduct of attorneys, § 21.75
    Procedures, § 21.76
    Rules of Court, § 21.76
Prosecutorial misconduct, § 18.20 et seq.
    Malicious prosecution, § 18.25
Representation of claimants,
    Social security benefits, § 23.16
    Supplemental security income for the elderly, § 23.23
Responsibilities of counsel,
    Appellate division, criminal,
        Post-disposition proceedings, § 38.30
Right to Counsel, generally, this index

AUCTIONS
Wine, permits, § 36.44

AUDITS
Income tax, state, § 35.85
    Audit methods, § 35.86
    Checklist, § 35.98
    Conciliation and mediation services bureau, § 35.90
        Conciliation conferences, § 35.92
            Orders, § 35.93
            Requesting, § 35.91
    Petitions to division of tax appeals, § 35.94
        Referrals to bureau of conciliation and mediation services, § 35.95
        Small claims hearings, § 35.96
    Results of audit, § 35.89

INDEX

AUDITS—Continued
Income tax—Continued
   Summary, § 35.97
   Taxpayer bill of rights, § 35.87
   Taxpayer representation, § 35.88
Small business, purchase or sale,
   Due diligence investigation,
     Financial review, audited statements, § 6.28
Taxation and finance department, audit division, § 35.45

BAIL
Continuation,
   Criminal leave application "CLA",
     Court of appeals,
       Appeal by permission, § 39.48
Denial, not appealable, § 38.8
Review in habeas corpus proceedings, § 37.88

BANKRUPTCY
   Generally, § 9.1 et seq.
Abandonment of property, § 9.70
Abstention, § 9.23
Adequate protection, § 9.56
   Chapter 12, § 9.219
   Creditor's deficiency claim, superpriority, § 9.71
   Creditor's motion,
     Drafting checklist, § 9.293
     Procedural checklist, § 9.270
   Hearings, § 9.59
   "Indubitable equivalent" method, § 9.57
   Objections, § 9.59
   Postpetition financing, § 9.71
   Strategy, § 9.58
   Types, § 9.57
Advantages and disadvantages, § 9.2
Adversary proceedings, §§ 9.15, 9.16
   Complaint,
     Drafting checklist, § 9.288
     Form, § 9.309
   Liens and transfers, to avoid, § 9.197
     Limitation of actions, § 9.198
   Procedural checklist, § 9.266
Affirmative defense, § 26.37
Appeals,
   Chapter 11,
     Exclusivity, appealability of orders, § 9.146
   Interlocutory judgment, order or decree,
     Procedural checklist, § 9.268
   Motion for leave to appeal from interlocutory judgment, order or decree, drafting checklist, § 9.289
   Motion for stay pending appeal, drafting checklist, § 9.290
   Postpetition financing, appeals from orders authorizing, § 9.73
   To court of appeals from district court, § 9.26
   To district court and bankruptcy appellate panel from bankruptcy court, § 9.25
   Use, sale or lease of property,
     Appeals from order authorizing sale, § 9.64
"Arising in" proceedings, § 9.19
"Arising under" proceedings, § 9.19
Automatic stay, § 9.50
   Chapter 12, § 9.216
   Chapter 13, § 9.241
   Exceptions, § 9.51
   Relief, obtaining, § 9.52

INDEX

BANKRUPTCY—Continued
Automatic stay—Continued
  Relief—Continued
    Chapter 13, § 9.242
    Creditor's motion,
      Drafting checklist, § 9.292
      Procedural checklist, § 9.269
    Hearings, § 9.54
    Single asset real estate debtor, § 9.55
    Strategy, § 9.53
  Setoff, limitations, § 9.109
Avoiding powers, § 9.113
  Constructive fraud, § 9.119
  Fraudulent conveyances, §§ 9.113, 9.115, 9.119
  Intentional fraud, § 9.119
  Liability of transferee of avoided transfer, § 9.120
  Limitation of actions, § 9.121
  New York Fraudulent Conveyances Statute, § 9.115
  Preferences, § 9.117
    Alimony, maintenance and child support, exception, § 9.118
    Contemporaneous exchange for new value, exception, § 9.118
    Exceptions, § 9.118
    Individual debtor's consumer debt, exception, § 9.118
    Ordinary course of business, exception, § 9.118
    Purchase money security interest in newly acquired property, exception, § 9.118
    Security interest in inventory or receivables, exception, § 9.118
    Subsequent new value, exception, § 9.118
    Unavoidable statutory liens, exception, § 9.118
  Reclamation, § 9.123
  Relation-back provision, § 9.122
  Standing, § 9.121
  Statutory liens, § 9.116
  Strategy, § 9.114
  Strong arm powers, § 9.115
Bankruptcy Code, § 9.5
Bankruptcy Reform Act of 1994, § 9.5
Cash collateral, § 9.65
  Debtor's motion to use,
    Drafting checklist, § 9.295
      Cash collateral stipulation, § 9.296
    Procedural checklist, § 9.272
      Cash collateral stipulation, § 9.273
  Hearings, § 9.67
  Postpetition proceeds, § 9.68
    Security interests in rents and hotel revenues, § 9.69
  Restraining orders, § 9.66
  Stipulations, § 9.66
  Strategy, § 9.66
Chapter 1,
  Nature of cases, § 9.6
Chapter 3,
  Nature of cases, § 9.6
Chapter 5,
  Nature of cases, § 9.6
Chapter 7,
  Abandonment of property, § 9.191
  Adversary proceedings to avoid liens and transfers, § 9.197
    Limitation of actions, § 9.198
  Closing, § 9.211
  Commencement, § 9.178
    Procedural checklist, § 9.265
  Conduct in bankruptcy case of an insider,

INDEX

BANKRUPTCY—Continued
Chapter 7—Continued
  Conduct in bankruptcy case of an insider—Continued
    Exceptions to general discharge of debtor, § 9.205
  Conversion, § 9.209
    Procedure, § 9.210
  Creditors' committee, § 9.184
  Debtor's statement of intention, § 9.186
  Destruction or falsification of records,
    Exceptions to general discharge of debtor, § 9.205
  Discharge, § 9.204
    Exceptions to discharge of particular debts, § 9.207
    Exceptions to general discharge, § 9.205
    Objections to discharge of particular debts, procedure, § 9.208
    Objections to general discharge, procedure, § 9.206
  Dismissal, § 9.209
    Procedure, § 9.210
  Disposition of property subject to interest of another, § 9.201
  Employment of professionals, § 9.183
  Executory contracts, § 9.196
  Exemptions, § 9.187
  False oath, account, or claim,
    Exceptions to general discharge of debtor, § 9.205
  Fees, § 9.179
  Filing fees, § 9.179
  Fraud, exceptions to general discharge of debtor, § 9.205
  General partners, liability, § 9.194
  Interim trustee, appointment, § 9.180
  Loss or deficiency of assets, failure to explain,
    Exceptions to general discharge of debtor, § 9.205
  Nature of cases, § 9.6
  Overview, § 9.177
  Permanent trustee,
    Duties, § 9.182
    Election, § 9.181
    Operation of business by trustee, § 9.195
    Sale of assets, § 9.200
    Turnover powers, § 9.193
  Prior Chapter 7 or 11 discharge,
    Exceptions to general discharge of debtor, § 9.205
  Prior Chapter 12 or 13 discharge,
    Exceptions to general discharge of debtor, § 9.205
  Priorities, § 9.202
  Protection against discriminatory treatment, § 9.185
  Reaffirmation of debts, § 9.190
    Debtor's motion to obtain court approval of reaffirmation agreement,
      Drafting checklist, § 9.302
      Procedural checklist, § 9.280
  Redemption of property, § 9.188
    Procedure, § 9.189
  Refusal to obey court order,
    Exceptions to general discharge of debtor, § 9.205
  Reopening, § 9.211
  Sale of assets, § 9.200
  Surrender of property and records, § 9.192
  Tax considerations, § 9.203
  Treatment of certain liens, § 9.199
  Written waiver of discharge,
    Exceptions to general discharge of debtor, § 9.205
Chapter 9,
  Nature of cases, § 9.6
Chapter 11,

INDEX

BANKRUPTCY—Continued
Chapter 11—Continued
  Absolute priority rule, § 9.166
  Acceptance of plan, § 9.162
  Asbestos-related cases, § 9.171
  Channeling injunctions, § 9.171
  Classification of claims, § 9.152
    Convenience class, § 9.155
    Effect on voting, § 9.153
    Substantially similar claims, § 9.154
  Closing, § 9.176
  Commencement, procedural checklist, § 9.265
  Confirmation, § 9.165
    Effect, § 9.167
  Conversion, § 9.174
  "Cram down", § 9.166
  Discharge, § 9.168
    Limitations, § 9.169
    Release of nondebtor, § 9.170
  Disclosure statement, § 9.161
    Filing plan and disclosure statement, procedural checklist, § 9.282
  Dismissal, § 9.174
    Procedure, § 9.175
  Examiner,
    Appointment, § 9.140
    Duties, § 9.141
  Exclusivity,
    Appealability of orders, § 9.146
    Debtor's motion to request an extension of exclusivity,
      Drafting checklist, § 9.304
      Procedural checklist, § 9.281
    Right to file a plan, § 9.142
    Small businesses, § 9.143
    Strategy, § 9.144
      Creditor, representation of, § 9.145
      Debtor, representation of, § 9.144
  Fair and equitable test, § 9.166
  Impairment of claims or interests, § 9.158
    Alteration of rights, § 9.159
    Debtor's motion to avoid judicial lien or nonpossessory, nonpurchase-money security interest,
      Drafting checklist, § 9.301
      Procedural checklist, § 9.279
    Defaults not cured, § 9.160
  "Indubitable equivalent", § 9.166
  Modification of plan, § 9.164
  Nature of cases, § 9.6
  Plan of reorganization, §§ 9.142, 9.147
    Discretionary provisions, § 9.149
    Exemption from securities registration, § 9.150
    Filing plan and disclosure statement, procedural checklist, § 9.282
    Implementation, § 9.172
    Jurisdiction, retention of, § 9.151
    Limited safe harbor exemption, § 9.150
    Mandatory provisions, § 9.148
    Soliciting acceptance of plan, procedural checklist, § 9.283
  Prepackaged and prenegotiated plans, § 9.163
  Recourse and nonrecourse claims,
    Section 1111(b) election, § 9.156
      Strategy, § 9.157
  Reopening, § 9.176
  Small business reorganizations, § 9.173

INDEX

BANKRUPTCY—Continued
Chapter 11—Continued
    Solicitation, § 9.161
    Statutory creditors committee, § 9.43 et seq.
    Trustees,
        Appointment, § 9.138
        Duties, § 9.139
Chapter 12,
    Adequate protection, § 9.219
    Automatic stay, § 9.216
    Closing, § 9.235
    Commencement, procedural checklist, § 9.265
    Conversion, § 9.233
        Procedure, § 9.234
    Debtor, rights and powers, § 9.213
    Disbursements, § 9.227
    Discharge, § 9.228
    Dismissal, § 9.233
        Procedure, § 9.234
    Exclusivity, § 9.220
        Debtor's motion to request an extension of exclusivity, procedural checklist, § 9.281
    Family farmer defined, § 9.212
    Nature of cases, § 9.6
    Overview, § 9.212
    Plan, § 9.221
        Confirmation, § 9.225
            Effect, § 9.227
            Modification following, § 9.230
                Procedural checklist, § 9.286
            Objections, § 9.226
                Procedural checklist, § 9.285
            Revocation of confirmation order, § 9.232
        Discretionary provisions, § 9.223
        Exclusive right to file, § 9.220
        Filing, procedural checklist, § 9.284
        Hearings, § 9.225
        Mandatory provisions, § 9.222
        Modification, § 9.224
            Confirmation, following, § 9.230
    Property of estate, § 9.217
        Sale free of interests, § 9.218
    Reopening, § 9.235
    Tax considerations, § 9.231
    Trustees,
        Appointment, § 9.214
        Duties, § 9.215
Chapter 13,
    Automatic stay, § 9.241
        Relief, § 9.242
    Closing, § 9.263
    Commencement, procedural checklist, § 9.265
    Conversion, § 9.261
        Procedure, § 9.262
    Debtor, rights and powers, § 9.238
    Discharge, § 9.255
        Exceptions, § 9.256
        Objections, § 9.257
        Revocation, § 9.258
    Dismissal, § 9.261
        Procedure, § 9.262
    Eligibility, § 9.237
    Exclusivity, § 9.245

INDEX

BANKRUPTCY—Continued
Chapter 13—Continued
  Exclusivity—Continued
    Debtor's motion to request an extension of exclusivity, procedural checklist, § 9.281
  Nature of cases, § 9.6
  Overview, § 9.236
  Payments, § 9.254
  Plan, § 9.246
    Confirmation, § 9.251
      Effect, § 9.253
      Modification following, § 9.259
        Procedural checklist, § 9.286
      Objections, § 9.252
        Procedural checklist, § 9.285
      Revocation of confirmation order, § 9.260
    Discretionary provisions, § 9.248
      Debtor's principal residence, § 9.249
    Exclusive right to file, § 9.245
    Filing, procedural checklist, § 9.284
    Mandatory provisions, § 9.247
    Modification, § 9.250
      Confirmation, following, § 9.259
  Property of estate, § 9.243
    Use, sale or lease, § 9.244
  Reopening, § 9.263
  Trustees,
    Appointment, § 9.239
    Duties, § 9.240
  Use, sale or lease of property, § 9.244
Claims procedures, § 9.90 et seq.
  Allowance of claim or interest, § 9.96
    Administrative expense claim, § 9.98
  Bar dates, § 9.92
  Compromise, § 9.97
    Debtor's motion to obtain approval of compromise,
      Drafting checklist, § 9.300
      Procedural checklist, § 9.277
  Forced sale value, § 9.104
  Going concern value, § 9.104
  Liquidation value, § 9.104
  Objections to claim or interest, § 9.96
  Proofs of claim or interest,
    Allowance of claim or interest, § 9.96
    Amendment, § 9.94
    Bar dates, § 9.92
    Debtor's schedules, § 9.91
    Filing, § 9.91
    Late filing, § 9.93
    Objections to, § 9.96
    Withdrawal of claims, notice, § 9.95
  Reclamation claims, § 9.105
  Reorganization value, § 9.104
  Retail value, § 9.104
  Secured claims, § 9.99
    Avoidance of liens, § 9.101
    Bifurcation of claims, § 9.100
    Interest on claims and charges against, § 9.102
    "Lien stripping", § 9.101
    "Lost opportunity costs", § 9.102
    Oversecured creditors, § 9.102
    Undersecured creditors, § 9.102
  Settlement, § 9.97

INDEX

BANKRUPTCY—Continued
Claims procedures—Continued
  Settlement—Continued
    Debtor's motion to obtain approval of settlement,
      Drafting checklist, § 9.300
      Procedural checklist, § 9.277
  Valuation of collateral, § 9.103
    Methods of valuation, § 9.104
  Wholesale value, § 9.104
  Withdrawal of claims, notice, § 9.95
Closing, § 9.137
Collective bargaining agreements, § 9.86
  Debtor's motion to reject or modify,
    Drafting checklist, § 9.299
    Procedural checklist, § 9.276
Commencement,
  Additional requirements, § 9.11
  Chapter 7, § 9.178
  First-day orders, § 9.12
  Involuntary case, § 9.9
    Procedure, § 9.10
  Procedural checklist, § 9.264
  Voluntary case, § 9.8
Contested matters, §§ 9.15, 9.17
  Motion, form, § 9.306
  Notice of motion, form, § 9.307
  Procedural checklist, § 9.267
  Proposed order, form, § 9.308
Conversion, § 9.134
  Effect, § 9.135
Core proceedings, § 9.19
Creditors, § 9.36
  Meeting of creditors, § 9.37
    Scope of examination, § 9.38
  Representation, checklist, § 9.4
  Statutory creditors committee, § 9.43 et seq.
Debtor,
  Chapter 12, rights and powers, § 9.213
  Chapter 13, rights and powers, § 9.238
  Debtor's schedules,
    Claims procedures, filing of proofs of claim or interest, § 9.91
  Executory contracts and unexpired leases,
    Assumption, § 9.78
    Debtor as landlord/lessor, § 9.84
    Rejection, § 9.81
      Damages arising from rejection, § 9.82
        Calculation of allowed real property lease rejection damages, § 9.83
      Debtor as tenant/lessee, § 9.82
  Preferences, avoiding powers,
    Individual debtor's consumer debt, exception, § 9.118
  Representation of, checklist, § 9.3
  Return of goods by debtor, § 9.124 et seq.
  Subordination, co-debtor claims, § 9.107
Debtor in possession, § 9.27
  Employment of professionals, § 9.29
  Rights, powers and duties, § 9.28
Discharge,
  Chapter 7, § 9.204
    Exceptions to general discharge, § 9.205
Dismissal, § 9.134
  Effect, § 9.136
Eligibility to file, § 9.7

INDEX

BANKRUPTCY—Continued
Employment law, denial of job or entitlements, § 17.40
Examinations under Bankruptcy Rule 2004, § 9.39
 Notice, § 9.40
 Subpoenas, § 9.41
Executory contracts and unexpired leases, § 9.74
 Assignment, § 9.79
  Exceptions, § 9.80
  Request to assign, procedural checklist, § 9.275
 Assumption, § 9.79
  Debtor, by, § 9.78
  Exceptions, § 9.80
  Request to assume,
   Drafting checklist, § 9.298
   Procedural checklist, § 9.275
  Time for, § 9.76
 Chapter 7, § 9.196
 Debtor as landlord/lessor, § 9.84
 Nonresidential real property leases, § 9.77
 Rejection, § 9.81
  Damages arising from, § 9.82
   Calculation of allowed real property lease rejection damages, § 9.83
   Section 502(b)(6) worksheet, § 9.83
  Request to reject,
   Drafting checklist, § 9.298
   Procedural checklist, § 9.275
  Time for, § 9.76
 Strategy, § 9.75
 Unexpired personal property leases, § 9.85
Exemptions,
 Chapter 7, § 9.187
 Chapter 11 plan of reorganization,
  Limited safe harbor, § 9.150
  Securities registration, from, § 9.150
 Claiming exemptions, procedural checklist, § 9.278
 Return of goods by debtor, § 9.125
  Liens, avoiding, § 9.128
   Liens on exempt property, § 9.129
  Objections, § 9.127
  Procedure, § 9.126
Federal Rules of Bankruptcy Procedure, § 9.5
Fraud,
 Avoiding powers,
  Constructive fraud, § 9.119
  Fraudulent conveyances, §§ 9.113, 9.115, 9.119
  Intentional fraud, § 9.119
  New York Fraudulent Conveyances Statute, § 9.115
 Chapter 7,
  Exception to general discharge of debtor, § 9.205
 Statutory creditors committee,
  Fraudulent conveyance action against third party, § 9.45
Governing law, § 9.5
Income tax, state,
 Collection of tax, filing for, § 35.119
Joint administration, § 9.13
Jurisdiction, § 9.18
 Case ancillary to foreign proceedings, § 9.20
 Retention of,
  Chapter 11 plan of reorganization, § 9.151
   Form, § 9.312
 Types, § 9.19
Liens,

INDEX

BANKRUPTCY—Continued
Liens—Continued
    Avoiding,
        Adversary proceedings to avoid liens and transfers, § 9.197
            Chapter 7, § 9.197
                Limitation of actions, § 9.198
            Limitation of actions, § 9.198
        Claims procedures, secured claims, § 9.101
            "Lien stripping", § 9.101
        Debtor's motion to avoid judicial lien or nonpossessory, nonpurchase-money security interest,
            Drafting checklist, § 9.301
            Procedural checklist, § 9.279
        Preferences,
            Unavoidable statutory liens, exception, § 9.118
        Return of goods by debtor,
            Exemptions, § 9.128
                Liens on exempt property, § 9.129
        Statutory liens, § 9.116
    Chapter 7,
        Adversary proceedings to avoid liens and transfers, § 9.197
            Limitation of actions, § 9.198
        Treatment of certain liens, § 9.199
    Use, sale or lease of property,
        Sales free and clear of liens, § 9.63
Mediators, § 9.35
Meeting of creditors, § 9.37
    Scope of examination, § 9.38
Motions, applications and complaints, drafting checklist, § 9.287
Nature of cases, § 9.6
Non-core proceedings, § 9.19
Notice of appearance, form, § 9.305
Postpetition financing, § 9.71
    Appeals from orders authorizing, § 9.73
    Debtor's motion to obtain,
        Drafting checklist, § 9.297
        Procedural checklist, § 9.274
    "Forward cross-collateralization", § 9.71
    Hearings, § 9.72
Priorities, § 9.106
    Chapter 7, § 9.202
    Creditor's deficiency claim, superpriority, § 9.71
Professionals, employment of, § 9.29
    Affidavit, form, § 9.310
    Application to retain,
        Drafting checklist, § 9.291
        Form, § 9.310
    Chapter 7, § 9.183
    Compensation, § 9.30
        Fee applications, § 9.31
    Conflicts of interest, § 9.29
Property of estate, § 9.49
    Chapter 12, § 9.217
        Sale free of interests, § 9.218
    Chapter 13, § 9.243
Protection against discriminatory treatment,
    Chapter 7, § 9.185
    Chapter 11, § 9.132
Reaffirmation of debts, § 9.130
    Debtor's motion to obtain court approval of reaffirmation agreement,
        Drafting checklist, § 9.303
        Procedural checklist, § 9.280

INDEX

BANKRUPTCY—Continued
Reaffirmation of debts—Continued
    Strategy, § 9.131
Recoupment, § 9.112
"Related to" proceedings, § 9.19
Removal, § 9.24
Reopening, § 9.137
Retired employees' insurance benefits, § 9.87
    Modification, procedure, § 9.88
Return of goods by debtor, § 9.124 et seq.
    Exemptions, § 9.125
        Lien avoidance, § 9.128
        Liens on exempt property, § 9.129
        Objections, § 9.127
        Procedure, § 9.126
Right of parties in interest to be heard, § 9.42
Scope, § 9.1
Service demand, form, § 9.305
Setoff, § 9.109
    Automatic stay limitations, § 9.109
    Characteristics of claims, § 9.111
    Strategy, § 9.110
Standing, subordination, § 9.107
Statutory creditors committee, § 9.43
    Application to retain professionals, drafting checklist, § 9.291
    Appointment, § 9.44
    Fiduciary duties, § 9.46
    Fraudulent conveyance action against third party, § 9.45
    Function and duties, § 9.44
    Organizational meeting, § 9.48
    Preference action against third party, § 9.45
    Removal of members, § 9.47
    Right to bring litigation, § 9.45
Strategy, § 9.2
Subordination, § 9.107
    Burden of proof, § 9.108
    Co-debtor claims, § 9.107
    Consensual subordination agreements, § 9.107
    Equitable subordination, § 9.107
    Inequitable conduct requirement not absolute, § 9.107
    Misconduct, § 9.107
    Rescission claims, § 9.107
    Standing, § 9.107
    Strategy, § 9.108
Substantive consolidation, § 9.14
Tax considerations, § 9.133
    Chapter 7, § 9.203
    Chapter 12, § 9.231
Trustees, § 9.34
    Appointment,
        Chapter 7, § 9.180
        Chapter 11, § 9.138
        Chapter 12, § 9.214
        Chapter 13, § 9.239
    Chapter 7,
        Interim trustee,
            Appointment, § 9.180
            Duties, § 9.182
        Operation of business by trustee, § 9.195
        Permanent trustee,
            Duties, § 9.182
            Election, § 9.181

INDEX

BANKRUPTCY—Continued
Trustees—Continued
  Chapter 7—Continued
    Sale of assets, § 9.200
    Turnover powers, § 9.193
  Chapter 11,
    Appointment, § 9.138
    Duties, § 9.139
  Duties,
    Chapter 7, § 9.182
    Chapter 11, § 9.139
    Chapter 12, § 9.215
    Chapter 13, § 9.240
  U.S. trustee, § 9.32
    Duties owed by debtors and trustees, § 9.33
    Inventory of property, § 9.33
    Notice of case, § 9.33
    Periodic reports, § 9.33
    Quarterly fees, § 9.33
    Record keeping, § 9.33
    Transmission of records, § 9.33
Use, sale or lease of property, § 9.60
  Appeals from order authorizing sale, § 9.64
  Chapter 12, sale free of interests, § 9.218
  Chapter 13, § 9.244
  Creditor's expectation test, § 9.61
  Debtor's motion,
    Drafting checklist, § 9.294
    Procedural checklist, § 9.271
  "Good faith" purchaser, protection, § 9.64
  Horizontal test, § 9.61
  Industry-wide test, § 9.61
  Ordinary course of business, § 9.61
  Outside ordinary course of business, § 9.62
  Sales free and clear of liens, § 9.63
  Vertical test, § 9.61
Utility services, § 9.89
Venue, § 9.21
Withdrawal of reference, § 9.22

BARBER SHOPS
Public accommodations and amusement, equal rights in places of, § 18.54

BARS
Alcoholic beverage control, retail licenses, § 36.31

BEER
Brewers license, § 36.12
Drug stores, license to sell, §§ 36.8, 36.10
Grocery stores, license to sell, §§ 36.8, 36.10

BENCH TRIALS
  Generally, §§ 33.63, 33.65
Scope of review, §§ 37.29, 37.65

BENEFICIARIES
Attorney/draftsman as,
  Ethical considerations, estate planning, § 24.95
Insurance, generally, this index
Mechanic's liens,
  Trust funds, § 10.97
    Right to examine books or records, § 10.101
Motor Vehicle Insurance, generally, this index
Probate and Estate Administration, generally, this index

665

INDEX

BENEFICIARIES—Continued
Supplemental Medical Insurance (Medigap plans), generally, this index
Title insurance. Purchase and sale, generally. Real Property, this index

BENEFITS
Social Security, generally, this index
Workers' Compensation, this index

BETTER BUSINESS BUREAU
Consumer protection cases, § 7.8

BILL OF RIGHTS
Hospital patient rights, § 23.90
Nursing homes resident's rights, § 23.94
Taxpayer bill of rights,
    Income tax, state, § 35.87

BILLING
Balance billing, limitations,
    Medicare part B supplementary medical insurance, § 23.52

BILLS OF PARTICULARS
Damages, strategy, § 30.3
Liquor license suspensions, § 36.62
New York Landlord-Tenant Law, § 13.57
Personal injury cases, §§ 26.46, 26.47
    Contents, § 26.60
    Form, §§ 26.67, 26.69
    Responses, § 26.61
Pretrial discovery, § 33.35 et seq.
    Filing,
        Response time, § 33.37
        Time limits, § 33.36
    People's failure to comply with time limits, § 33.38

BLIND PERSONS
Handicapped Persons, this index
Taxation, additional standard deduction for the aged and blind, § 23.115

BLOOD BANKS
Medical malpractice, regulatory standards, § 29.21

BLUE SKY LAWS
Issues, § 2.106

BOARD OF HEALTH
Alcoholic beverage control, permits, § 36.33

BONDS
Appeals by public administrators, § 37.18
Guardianships, § 22.42
Mechanic's Liens, generally, this index
U.S. savings bonds,
    Postmortem planning, allocation of income and expenses, § 24.75

BOWLING ALLEYS
License for sale of beer, wine and spirits, § 36.9

BRADY MATERIAL
Appeal by the people,
    Appellate division, criminal, § 38.10
Pretrial discovery, § 33.39 et seq.
    Prosecutor need not be aware of evidence, § 33.40
    Timely disclosure, § 33.41

BREACH OF CONTRACT
Commercial sales contract, § 5.40

INDEX

BREACH OF CONTRACT—Continued
Commercial sales contract—Continued
    Buyer's remedies, § 5.47
        Acceptance of non-conforming goods, damages, § 5.50
        Cover, § 5.48
        Non-delivery, damages, § 5.49
        Purchase of goods in substitution, § 5.48
        Replevin, § 5.51
        Specific performance, § 5.51
    Limitation of damages, § 5.52
    Liquidated damages, § 5.52
    Mitigation of damages, § 5.53
    Seller's remedies, § 5.41
        Action for price, § 5.42
        Non-acceptance or repudiation, damages, § 5.46
        Recovery of goods delivered, § 5.44
        Resale, § 5.45
        Right of reclamation, § 5.44
        Withholding goods and stopping delivery, § 5.43
    Transactional checklist, § 5.3
Enforcement of money judgments, interest, § 8.6
Insurance, § 31.21
    Complaint by policyholder for declaratory relief and breach of contract, forms, § 31.32
    Duty to defend, damages, § 31.14
Limitation of actions, § 17.77

BROKERS
Insurance,
    Third parties involved in placement/administration of insurance contract, § 31.6
Real Estate Agents and Brokers, generally, this index

BURDEN OF PROOF
Administrative law, adjudicatory proceedings, § 4.19
Bankruptcy, subordination, § 9.108
Commercial sales contract, presumption of legality, § 5.8
Damages, § 30.5
Employment law, discrimination, § 17.59
Family-based immigration, § 19.10
Federal civil rights law, housing, § 18.51
Holdover proceedings, § 13.62
Housing discrimination, § 18.51
Income tax, state,
    Appeal by Article 78 proceeding, § 35.103
Insurance, § 31.27
Lemon law, arbitration, § 7.15
New York landlord-tenant law, trial, § 13.62
Non-payment proceedings, § 13.62
Probate and estate administration, objections, § 25.28
Products liability,
    Defective design, § 27.8
    Failure to warn, § 27.11
    Successor liability, § 27.27
Speedy trial, CPL § 30.30, § 33.81
Workers' compensation hearings, § 32.19

BUREAU OF ALCOHOL, TOBACCO AND FIREARMS
Permits for manufacturing, importing or wholesaling of alcoholic beverages, §§ 36.4, 36.11
Tax stamp, alcoholic beverages, § 36.4

BUSINESS CERTIFICATES
Partnerships, formation, § 2.48

BUSINESS REAL PROPERTY
Estate planning with certain assets, § 24.42

INDEX

BUY-SELL AGREEMENTS
Estate Planning, generally, this index
Probate and Estate Administration, generally, this index
Small Business, Purchase or Sale, generally, this index

CAPACITY
Diminished capacity,
    Elder law, ethical considerations, § 23.6

CAPITAL GAINS
Corporate Franchise Tax, State, generally, this index
Elder Law, generally, this index
Estate Planning, generally, this index
Foreign Investors Real Property Tax Act, § 12.76
Generation Skipping Transfer Taxes, generally, this index
Gift Taxes, Federal, generally, this index
Gift Taxes, State, generally, this index
Income Tax, Federal, generally, this index
Income Tax, State, generally, this index
Probate and Estate Administration, generally, this index
Real Property, Taxation, generally, this index
Real Property Transfer Gains Tax, generally, this index
Small Business, Purchase or Sale, generally, this index
Taxation, generally, this index

CAPITAL PUNISHMENT
Death Penalty, generally, this index

CERCLA
Comprehensive Environmental Response, Compensation and Liability Act(CERCLA), generally, this index

CHARITABLE BEQUESTS
Estate planning, § 24.32

CHECKLISTS
Administrative law and proceedings,
    Adjudicatory proceedings, § 4.42
    Agency information gathering, § 4.66
    Rulemaking, § 4.60
    Strategy, § 4.3
Corporate franchise tax, state, § 35.39
Estate planning, § 24.97
Guardianships, §§ 22.3, 22.88 et seq.
    Annual report, § 22.94
    Court evaluators,
        Duties, § 22.3(c)
        Report, § 22.91
    Decree approving account, § 22.95
    Functional evaluation of abilities of alleged incapacitated person, § 22.3(a)
    Guardian,
        Powers and duties,
            Personal needs, §§ 22.3(f), 22.3(h)
            Property management, §§ 22.3(e), 22.3(g)
        Reports,
            Annual reports, requirements, § 22.3(j)
            Initial reports, requirements, § 22.3(i)
        Selection, criteria, § 22.3(d)
    Initial report of guardian, § 22.93
    Order and judgment, § 22.92
    Order to show cause, § 22.89
    Petitions, § 22.90
        Allegations, required, § 22.3(b)
        Proceedings to recover property withheld, § 22.96

INDEX

CHECKLISTS—Continued
Guardianships—Continued
    Reports, initial, § 22.93
Income tax, state,
    Assessment and collection of tax, § 35.120
    Audits and appeals, § 35.98
    Judicial review, § 35.107
    Penalties, § 35.84
    Personal income tax, § 35.18
    Returns, filing, § 35.63
    Strategy, § 35.3
Insurance,
    Allegations, essential, § 31.31
    Strategy, § 31.3
Judicial review,
    Administrative law, § 4.86
Non-corporate entities, § 2.109
Procedural due process, administrative law, § 4.9
Social security disability cases. Disability cases. Social Security, this index
Workers' Compensation, this index

CHILD CUSTODY
Best interests of child, §§ 21.58, 21.60
    Modification of judgments, § 21.71
Case management rules, § 21.79
Domestic violence considerations, § 21.58
Expert witnesses, reports, § 21.79
Factors for consideration, § 21.58
Family Court Act, § 21.71
Joint or shared custody, § 21.58
    Voluntary or imposed, § 21.61
Judgments,
    Enforcement, § 21.72
    Form, § 21.90
Jurisdiction, §§ 21.5, 21.6, 21.9, 21.62
Modification of judgments, change in circumstances, § 21.71
Preference of child, § 21.58
Primary caretaker, § 21.58
Relocation of custodial parent, visitation arrangements, § 21.60
Schedule for discovery, § 21.79
Siblings, § 21.58
Statement of agreement, § 21.66
Statement of proposed disposition, § 21.83
"Tender years" presumption, § 21.58
Visitation arrangements, § 21.59
    Grandparents, § 21.59
    Judgments, form, § 21.90
    Jurisdiction, § 21.9
    Relocation of custodial parent, § 21.60
    Statement of agreement, § 21.66

CHILD SUPPORT
    Generally, § 21.52
Agreement, § 21.56
Bankruptcy preferences, exception, § 9.118
Case management rules, § 21.79
Family court,
    Appeals to appellate division, civil, § 37.19
Findings of fact and conclusions of law, form, § 21.89
Guidelines, § 21.53 et seq.
Health and life insurance, § 21.57
Judgments, form, § 21.90
    USC-113, § 21.67

669

INDEX

CHILD SUPPORT—Continued
Jurisdiction, § 21.8
Modification of judgments, § 21.68
    Change in circumstances, § 21.70
Motions, § 21.79
Parental income, § 21.53
Private school education, § 21.55
Schedule for discovery, § 21.79
Standards Act, §§ 21.53 et seq., 21.70
Statement of proposed disposition, § 21.83
Statutory factors, § 21.54
    Deviation from, § 21.55
Stipulation, § 21.56
Unjust or inappropriate obligations, § 21.54

CHOICE OF LAW
Insurance, § 31.25

CITY COURTS
Appeals, §§ 37.101 et seq., 38.47
    Appeals as of right, § 37.104
    Appeals by permission, § 37.104
    Appeals from, § 37.101 et seq.
    Constitutional basis, § 37.3
    Costs on appeal, § 37.107
    Courts to which appeals are taken, § 37.102
    CPLR Article 55, applicability, § 37.103
    Perfecting the appeal, § 37.106
    Return on appeal, § 37.105
    Settlement of record and return, § 37.105
    Small claims review, § 37.108
    Stay pending appeal,
        Appeal from city court to appellate term, § 38.54
        Notice of motion for stay of proceedings,
            Affirmation in support, form, § 37.132
            Form, § 37.130
        Order to show cause for stay of proceedings,
            Affirmation in support, form, § 37.132
            Form, § 37.131
    Taking the appeal, § 37.105
    Uniform City Court Act, § 37.101

CIVIL COURT OF NEW YORK CITY
Appeals, § 37.117 et seq.
    Appeals as of right, § 37.120
    Appeals by permission, § 37.120
    Appeals from, §§ 37.117, 37.118
    Appeals to court of appeals, § 37.121
    Constitutional basis, § 37.3
    Costs on appeal, § 37.124
    Courts to which appeals are taken, § 37.118
    CPLR Article 55, applicability, § 37.119
    Jurisdiction, § 37.117
    New York City Civil Court Act, § 37.117
    Perfecting the appeal, § 37.123
    Return on appeal, § 37.122
    Settlement of record and return, § 37.122
    Small claims review, § 37.125
    Taking the appeal, § 37.122

CIVIL RIGHTS
    Generally, § 18.1 et seq.
Abortions, performing,
    Discrimination against person refusing to perform abortion prohibited, § 18.86

INDEX

CIVIL RIGHTS—Continued
Employment discrimination, § 18.59 et seq.
  Age discrimination in Employment Act, § 18.59
  Equal Pay Act, § 18.59
  General provisions, § 18.60
  Handicapped persons, § 18.61
  Persons with genetic disorders, § 18.62
  Title VII of Civil Rights Act of 1964, § 18.59
Federal civil rights law, § 18.16 et seq.
  20 U.S.C.A. Sections 1681-88,
    Education, § 18.53
  42 U.S.C.A. Section 13981,
    Education, § 18.53
  42 U.S.C.A. Section 1981, § 18.17
    Housing discrimination,
      Private housing, § 18.50
      Publicly assisted housing, § 18.43
  42 U.S.C.A. Section 1982,
    Housing discrimination,
      Private housing, § 18.50
      Publicly assisted housing, § 18.43
  42 U.S.C.A. Section 1983, § 18.18
    Acting under color of state law, § 18.18
    Complaint,
      Drafting checklist, § 18.89
    Education, § 18.53
    Housing discrimination,
      Publicly assisted housing, § 18.43
    Limitation of actions, § 18.38
    Police and prosecutorial misconduct,
      Excessive force, § 18.21
        Complaint, form, § 18.93
      False arrest, § 18.22
        Complaint, form, § 18.92
      Malicious prosecution, § 18.25
    Prisoners' rights, § 18.29
      Suspension due to imprisonment, § 18.84
    Respondeat superior doctrine inapplicable, § 18.18
    State action, § 18.18
  42 U.S.C.A. Section 1985(3), § 18.19
  42 U.S.C.A. Section 1986, § 18.19
  42 U.S.C.A. Section 3601, § 18.43
    Housing discrimination,
      Publicly assisted housing, § 18.43
  Americans with Disabilities Act,
    Education, § 18.53
  Antireprisal provisions, § 17.38
  Breast feeding, § 18.83
  Defenses, § 18.30 et seq.
    Absolute immunity, § 18.31
    Abstention, § 18.36
    "Burford" abstention, § 18.36
    Collateral estoppel, § 18.37
    Eleventh Amendment, § 18.33
    Limitation of actions, § 18.38
    "Monell v. New York City Dept of Social Services", § 18.34
    "Pullman" abstention, § 18.36
    Qualified immunity, § 18.32
    Res judicata, § 18.37
    Respondeat superior doctrine, § 18.35
    "Younger" abstention, § 18.36
  Education, § 18.53

INDEX

CIVIL RIGHTS—Continued
Federal civil rights law—Continued
  Employment law, § 17.49
  First Amendment, § 18.26 et seq.
    Freedom of religion, § 18.28
      Refusal of medical treatment, § 18.28
    Freedom of speech, § 18.27
    Libel, § 18.27
    Slander, § 18.27
  Handicapped persons, discrimination prohibited, § 18.19
  Housing, § 18.39 et seq.
    Burden of proof, § 18.51
    Complaint, form, § 18.95
    Prima facie case, § 18.51
    Private housing, § 18.44 et seq.
      Cooperatives, § 18.47
        Complaint, form, § 18.96
      New York Human Rights Law, § 18.44
      Owners and lessors, § 18.45
        Complaint, form, § 18.95
      Real estate agents and brokers, § 18.46
      Remedies, § 18.48
        Actions in state and federal court, § 18.50
        Administrative proceedings, § 18.49
        New York City Commission on Human Rights, § 18.49
        New York State Division of Human Rights (SDHR), § 18.49
        Secretary of Housing and Urban Development, § 18.49
    Procedure for challenging an SDHR order, summary, § 18.52
    Procedure for filing administrative claim, summary, § 18.52
    Publicly assisted housing, § 18.40
      42 U.S.C.A. Section 1981, § 18.43
      42 U.S.C.A. Section 1982, § 18.43
      42 U.S.C.A. Section 3601, § 18.43
      Civil Rights Act of 1968, Title VIII, § 18.43
      Complaint, form, § 18.95
      Fair Housing Act, § 18.43
      New York City Administrative Code, § 18.41
      New York Civil Rights Law, Section 18-a, § 18.41
      New York Human Rights Law, § 18.41
      Owners and lessors, § 18.41
        Complaint, form, § 18.95
      Real estate agents and brokers, § 18.42
      Remedies, § 18.43
  Individuals with Disabilities Education Act (IDEA),
    Education, § 18.53
  Libel, §§ 18.27, 18.81
    Defenses, § 18.82
  Municipal corporations, applicability, § 18.17
  New York Human Rights Law, education, § 18.53
  Prisoners' rights, § 18.29
    Suspension due to imprisonment, § 18.84
  Rehabilitation Act, education, § 18.53
  Rehabilitation Act section 504, § 18.19
  Sex discrimination, education, § 18.53
  Slander, §§ 18.27, 18.81
    Defenses, § 18.82
  Title IX of Education Amendments of 1972, education, § 18.53
  Violence Against Women Act, education, § 18.53
Forms, § 18.91 et seq.
Frivolous litigation, § 18.79
  Protection from Strategic Lawsuit Against Public Participation (SLAPP) suits, § 18.80
"Good samaritan" law, § 18.87

INDEX

CIVIL RIGHTS—Continued
Handicapped persons,
    Americans with Disabilities Act, education, § 17.38
    Antireprisal provisions, § 17.38
    Discrimination prohibited, § 18.19
    Individuals with Disabilities Act (IDEA), education, § 17.38
    Public accommodations and amusement, equal rights in places of,
        Accompanied by guide dog, hearing dog or service dog, § 18.57
"Heart balm" statute, § 18.74 et seq.
    Action for return of gifts made in contemplation of marriage, § 18.76
        Procedure, § 18.77
    Penalty for bringing action, § 18.75
Jurisdiction, § 18.5
Miscellaneous rights and immunities, § 18.78 et seq.
    "Good samaritan" law, § 18.87
Name, changing, § 18.67 et seq.
    Checklist, § 18.73
    Factors considered by court, § 18.71
    Procedure for petition to change name, § 18.68
        Contents of petition, § 18.69
        Drafting checklist, § 18.90
        Petition for name change, form, § 18.99
        Special procedures for infants, § 18.70
    Publication requirements, § 18.72
New York Bill of Rights, § 18.6
    Federal Bill of Rights compared, § 18.8
    Overview, § 18.7
    Rights of jurors, § 18.15
    Rights of persons accused of crimes, § 18.12
        Closure of courtroom, § 18.13
        Exclusion of public or press, § 18.14
        Gag order, § 18.14
        Public trial, § 18.13
    Search and seizure, § 18.9
        Civil liability, § 18.10
        Expectation of privacy, § 18.10
        Return of seized property, § 18.11
            Complaint, form, § 18.94
News media,
    Shield law, § 18.85
Overview, § 18.4
Police and prosecutorial misconduct, § 18.20 et seq.
    Excessive force, § 18.21
        Complaint, form, § 18.93
    False arrest, § 18.22
        Complaint, form, § 18.92
    False imprisonment, § 18.23
        Complaint, form, § 18.92
    Malicious prosecution, § 18.25
    Search and seizure, § 18.24
Prisoners' rights, § 18.29
    Suspension due to imprisonment, § 18.84
Privacy,
    Expectation of privacy, search and seizure, § 18.10
    Invasion of privacy, § 18.63
    Right to, § 18.63 et seq.
        Corrections officers, § 18.65
        Firefighters, § 18.65
        General provisions, § 18.64
        "Incidental use" exception, § 18.64
        "Newsworthy" exception, § 18.64
        Police officers, § 18.65

INDEX

CIVIL RIGHTS—Continued
Privacy—Continued
  Right to—Continued
    Victims of sex offenses, § 18.66
Public accommodations and amusement, equal rights in places of, § 18.54
  Complaint, form, § 18.98
  General provisions, § 18.55
  Handicapped persons accompanied by guide dog, hearing dog or service dog, § 18.57
  Human Rights Law, §§ 18.54, 18.58
  Notice of commencement of action for discrimination, form, § 18.97
  Private clubs, § 18.56
  Remedies, § 18.58
  Title II of Civil Rights Act of 1964, § 18.58
Scope, § 18.1
Strategy, § 18.2
  Checklist, § 18.3

CIVIL RIGHTS ACT
Antireprisal provisions, § 17.38
Employment law, § 17.49

CIVIL RIGHTS OF INSTITUTIONALIZED PERSONS ACT
Antireprisal provisions, § 17.38

CIVIL SERVICE REFORM ACT
Antireprisal provisions, § 17.38

CIVIL SERVICE RETIREMENT ACT (CSRA)
Federal employees benefits,
  Elder law, § 23.39

CLASS ACTIONS
Deceptive Practices Act, § 7.47
Discrimination claims, §§ 17.59, 17.82

CLEAN AIR ACT (CAA)
Air pollution control, § 15.19
  1990 CAA amendments, § 15.20
Antireprisal provisions, § 17.38

CLEAN WATER ACT (CWA)
Environmental Law, this index

CLIENTS
Information sheet,
  New York State Division of Human Rights, form, §§ 17.90, 17.91
Intake questionnaire, form, § 17.86

CLINICAL LABORATORIES
Medical malpractice, regulatory standards, § 29.20

CLOSELY HELD BUSINESSES
Estate planning with certain assets, § 24.38
  Buy-sell agreements, § 24.39
  Liquidity issues, § 24.40
  Minority discounts, § 24.41

COBRA
Employment law, rights of employee to health insurance, §§ 17.12, 17.46

COINSURANCE
Insurance, generally, this index

COLLATERAL ESTOPPEL
Adjudicatory proceedings, administrative law, § 4.25
Affirmative defense, § 26.37
Effect on aggrieved status, § 37.22

INDEX

COLLATERAL ESTOPPEL—Continued
Federal civil rights law,
    Article 78 proceedings, inapplicable to, § 18.37
    Defenses, § 18.37
Products liability, § 27.53

COLLECTION AGENCIES
Complaints,
    Attorney fees, § 7.62
    Deceptive trade practices, § 7.62
    Fair credit reporting violations, § 7.62
Consumer protection, § 7.2
Debt Collection Procedures Act, § 7.36
Fair Debt Collection Practices Act, §§ 7.3, 7.36, 7.48
    Compliance, § 7.6
    Limitations, § 7.37
False or misleading representations, §§ 7.39, 7.48
Harassment of consumer, § 7.41
History of abuses, § 7.34
Intentional infliction of emotional distress claim, §§ 7.35, 7.48
Lawsuits,
    Attorney fees, § 7.43
    Damages, § 7.43
Motor vehicle sales,
    Compliance with Fair Debt Collection Practices Act, § 7.6
    Consumer protection, § 7.3
Prohibited activities, §§ 7.38, 7.40, 7.42

COLLECTIVE BARGAINING
Agreements,
    Bankruptcy, § 9.86
        Debtor's motion to reject or modify, procedural checklist, § 9.276
    Municipal corporations, officers and employees, § 3.21
Discrimination prohibited, § 17.61
Labor-Management Relationship Act, § 17.61
Taylor Law, § 17.53

COLLEGES
Universities and Colleges, generally, this index

COMMERCIAL SALES CONTRACT
    Generally, § 5.1 et seq.
Acceptance, § 5.23
    Additional terms, § 5.24
Assumption of risk of loss, § 5.32
    In absence of breach, § 5.33
    In event of breach, § 5.34
Breach, § 5.40
    Buyer's remedies, § 5.47
        Acceptance of non-conforming goods, damages, § 5.50
        Cover, § 5.48
        Non-delivery, damages, § 5.49
        Purchase of goods in substitution, § 5.48
        Replevin, § 5.51
        Specific performance, § 5.51
    Limitation of damages, § 5.52
    Liquidated damages, § 5.52
    Mitigation of damages, § 5.53
    Seller's remedies, § 5.41
        Action for price, § 5.42
        Non-acceptance or repudiation, damages, § 5.46
        Recovery of goods delivered, § 5.44
        Resale, § 5.45
        Right of reclamation, § 5.44

INDEX

COMMERCIAL SALES CONTRACT—Continued
Breach—Continued
  Seller's remedies—Continued
    Withholding goods and stopping delivery, § 5.43
  Transactional checklist, § 5.3
Drafting checklists,
  Order of goods for resale by buyer, § 5.57
    Form, § 5.65
  Petition for order staying arbitration in dispute over contract for sale of goods, § 5.62
    Affidavit in opposition to partition, § 5.63
    Answer to petition, § 5.64
    Notice of petition, § 5.61
  Plaintiff's notice of motion for summary judgment, § 5.59
    Affidavit in support by officer of plaintiff company, § 5.60
      Form, § 5.68
    Form, § 5.67
  Verified complaint on account stated for goods, services and wares delivered, § 5.58
    Form, § 5.66
Governing law, § 5.5
  Freedom to contract, § 5.6
    Presumption of legality, § 5.7
      Affirmative defense, § 5.8
      Burden of proof, § 5.8
      Enforcement of illegal contracts, § 5.10
      Validity of contract, determination, § 5.9
  Good faith, § 5.15
    Uniform Commercial Code, § 5.16
  Public policy, § 5.11
  Unconscionability, § 5.12
    Elements, § 5.13
    Uniform Commercial Code, § 5.14
Indefiniteness, § 5.25
Offer, § 5.22
Performance, § 5.35
  Buyer's response to tender of delivery, § 5.36
    Acceptance, § 5.37
    Rejection, § 5.38
    Revocation of acceptance, § 5.39
  Tender of delivery, § 5.35
Petition for order staying arbitration in dispute over contract for sale of goods,
  Affidavit in opposition to petition,
    Drafting checklists, § 5.63
    Form, § 5.71
  Answer to petition,
    Drafting checklists, § 5.64
    Form, § 5.72
  Drafting checklists, § 5.62
  Form, § 5.70
  Notice of petition,
    Drafting checklists, § 5.61
    Form, § 5.69
Scope, § 5.1
Statute of Frauds, § 5.17
  Course of dealing, § 5.21
  Course of performance, § 5.21
  Formal requirements, § 5.19
  Nature of writing, § 5.20
  Parol or extrinsic evidence, § 5.21
  Rules, § 5.18
Strategy, § 5.2
Third-party interests, § 5.54
  Other creditors, § 5.56

INDEX

COMMERCIAL SALES CONTRACT—Continued
Third-party interests—Continued
    Subsequent buyers, § 5.55
Uniform Commercial Code, § 5.5
Use of open terms, § 5.26
Warranties, § 5.27
    "As is" clauses, § 5.31
    Express warranties, § 5.29
    Implied warranty of fitness for particular purpose, § 5.31
    Implied warranty of merchantability, § 5.30
    Warranty of title against infringement, § 5.28

COMMISSIONS
Executors,
    Waiving, postmortem planning, § 24.79

COMPENSATION
Court evaluators,
    Guardianships, § 22.27
Guardians, § 22.61
Probate and estate administration,
    Administrators, § 25.46
    Executors, § 25.46
Workers' Compensation, generally, this index

COMPLAINTS
Accusatory instruments, § 33.12
    See also Accusatory Instruments, generally, this index
Alternative pleadings, § 17.82
Amendment, reviewability, § 37.36
Answers,
    Caption, § 17.83
    Drafting checklist, § 17.85
    Employment law,
        Form, § 17.97
Bankruptcy,
    Adversary proceedings,
        Drafting checklist, § 9.288
        Form, § 9.309
    Motions, applications and complaints,
        Drafting checklist, § 9.287
Breach of warranties, § 7.52
    Defenses, § 7.53
Captions, § 17.82
Cause of action denomination, § 17.82
Civil rights,
    New York Bill of Rights,
        Search and seizure, return of seized property, form, § 18.94
    Public accommodations and amusement, equal rights in places of, form, § 18.98
Clean Water Act (CWA),
    Drafting checklist, § 15.37
    Form, § 15.42
    Oil spills,
        Drafting checklist, § 15.39
        Form, § 15.44
Commercial sales contract,
    Drafting checklists,
        Verified complaint on account stated for goods, services and wares delivered, § 5.58
        Form, § 5.66
Damages,
    Ad damnum clause, form, § 30.46
        Medical or dental malpractice action, § 30.47
        Municipal corporation, action against, § 30.47

INDEX

COMPLAINTS—Continued
Damages—Continued
    Motor vehicle accidents, form, § 30.48
    Strategy, § 30.3
Deceptive trade practices, § 7.65
    Attorney fees, § 7.62
    Defenses, § 7.53
    Motor vehicle leasing company, § 7.52
        Defenses, § 7.54
Demand for relief, § 17.82
Discrimination,
    New York State Division of Human Rights, form, § 17.89
Divorce, § 26.36
Drafting, § 17.82
    Checklist, § 17.83
Employment law,
    Discharge of employee, form, § 17.96
Fair debt collection practice violations, attorney fees, § 7.62
Federal civil rights law,
    42 U.S.C.A. Section 1983,
        Drafting checklist, § 18.89
        Police and prosecutorial misconduct,
            False arrest, form, § 18.92
            False imprisonment, form, § 18.92
            Malicious prosecution, form, § 18.92
    Housing,
        Private housing,
            Cooperatives, form, § 18.96
            Owners and lessors, form, § 18.95
        Publicly assisted housing,
            Form, § 18.95
            Owners and lessors, form, § 18.95
Federal court,
    Answers, form, § 17.99
    Captions, § 17.82
    Drafting, § 17.82
    Employment law, form, § 17.98
    Jurisdictional statement, § 17.82
    Jury trial demand, form, § 17.98
    Separate count pleading, § 17.82
    Signature block, § 17.82
Felony, § 33.12
Filing, § 17.78
Fraud, §§ 7.65, 26.36
    Motor vehicle leasing, § 7.52
        Defenses, § 7.53
Jurisdictional statement, § 17.82
Jury demand, § 17.82
Legal malpractice, § 28.48
    Form, §§ 28.52, 28.53
Lemon law, § 7.52
Libel and slander, § 26.36
Local criminal courts, § 33.12
Mechanic's liens,
    Enforcement,
        Courts not of record, § 10.80
        Foreclosure of mechanic's lien,
            Complaint of contractor, form, § 10.134
    Trust funds,
        Subcontractor to enforce trust against funds received by contractor or assignee,
            form, § 10.145

INDEX

COMPLAINTS—Continued
Mechanic's liens—Continued
    Trust funds—Continued
        Surety to have parties declared trustees of subcontract moneys and for accounting, form, § 10.146
Medical malpractice, §§ 26.36, 26.58
Misdemeanor, § 33.12
Mortgages, generally. Foreclosure, this index
New York City Human Rights Law, service of process, § 17.78
Nuisance,
    Drafting checklist, § 15.38
    Form, § 15.43
Personal injury, §§ 26.36, 26.58
    Form, § 26.65
Pleading with particularity, § 17.82
Preparation, § 17.78
Products liability, § 27.55
    Form, § 27.57
Sale of goods, § 26.36
Service of process, § 17.78
Signature block, § 17.82
Third-party,
    Fraudulent motor vehicle leasing case, defenses, § 7.53
Trespass,
    Drafting checklist, § 15.38
    Form, § 15.43
Verification, § 17.82

COMPREHENSIVE ENVIRONMENTAL RESPONSE, COMPENSATION AND LIABILITY ACT (CERCLA)
Hazardous substance trust fund, § 15.28
Hazardous waste regulation, § 15.25
Inactive hazardous waste sites, § 15.28
    Contribution, § 15.30
    Indemnification, § 15.30
    Innocent landowner exception, § 15.29
    Lender liability, § 15.30
    Section 107(a), § 15.29
    Strict liability, § 15.29
    Third party defense, § 15.29
Small business, purchase or sale,
    Due diligence investigation, legal review, § 6.20
Solid waste regulation, § 15.25
Superfund, also known as, § 15.28

CONCILIATION AND MEDIATION SERVICES BUREAU
Income tax, state,
    Audits and appeals, § 35.90
        Conciliation conferences, § 35.92
            Orders, § 35.93
            Requesting, § 35.91

CONFESSIONS
Corroboration of admission or confession required, § 33.61
Involuntary statements. Statements, generally, this index
Traffic offenses, speeding, § 33.68

CONFIDENTIALITY
Adoption,
    Confidential affidavit, §§ 20.72, 20.107
        Form, § 20.143
Discovery,
    Products liability, confidentiality orders or stipulations, § 27.38
Elder law, ethical considerations, § 23.5

INDEX

CONFIDENTIALITY—Continued
Employment law, discharge of employee, § 17.16
Small business, purchase or sale,
    Confidentiality agreements,
        Buyer, representation of, § 6.11
        Seller, representation of, § 6.114
Stipulations,
    Trade secrets, discovery in products liability cases, § 27.38

CONFLICT OF INTEREST
Adoption proceedings, § 20.41
    Dual representation by attorney, §§ 20.2, 20.3, 20.40, 20.120
Bankruptcy,
    Professionals, employment of, § 9.29
Elder law, ethical considerations, § 23.4
Employment-based immigration,
    Labor certification, § 19.33
Legal malpractice cases, §§ 28.20, 28.21
Local land use law, § 16.40
Multiple representation, employment cases, § 17.4
Municipal corporations, officers and employees, § 3.22
    Checklist, § 3.23

CONSENT
Order on, as not aggrieved, §§ 37.23, 37.37
Probate and estate administration, forms, § 25.57

CONSORTIUM
Complaint for loss of, form, § 26.65

CONSPIRACY
Employment cases, § 17.23

CONSPIRACY TO OBSTRUCT JUSTICE ACT
Antireprisal provisions, § 17.38

CONSTITUTIONALITY
Court of appeals, civil appeals,
    Appeal as of right,
        Direct involvement of substantial constitutional question, § 39.9
            Notice of appeal from order of appellate division, form, § 39.78
    Notice of appeal,
        Final determination of action where constitutionality of statute involved, form, § 39.79
Local land use law,
    Judicial review standard, § 16.45
Municipal corporations,
    Legislative enactments, constitutionality presumed, § 3.10
Orders, appealable as of right, § 37.35
Preservation doctrine as to, § 37.28
Raised initially on appeal, § 37.28
Sealing adoption records, § 20.126
Statutes, intervention by attorney general, § 37.24

CONSUMER CREDIT PROTECTION ACT
Antireprisal provisions, § 17.38

CONSUMER LEASING ACT
    Generally, § 7.21 et seq.
Limitation of actions, § 7.48

CONSUMER PROTECTION
Attorney general, powers and duties, § 7.2
Better Business Bureau reports, § 7.8
Collection agencies, § 7.2

INDEX

CONSUMER PROTECTION—Continued
Deceptive Practices Act, generally, this index
Deceptive trade practices, § 7.2
Department of Consumer Affairs, powers and duties, § 7.2
Fair Credit Reporting Act, § 7.31
Federal Reserve Board, § 7.2
Federal Trade Commission, powers and duties, § 7.2
Freedom of Information Law requests, § 7.8
Interstate Commerce Commission, § 7.2
Motor Vehicle Repair Shop Registration Act, § 7.27
Motor Vehicle Retail Leasing Act, § 7.22
Motor Vehicle Sales, generally, this index
New York Fair Credit Reporting Act, § 7.31
Small claims court, § 7.2

CONTEMPT
Appellate division,
    Civil,
        Post-disposition proceedings, § 37.71
    Criminal, § 38.8
Enforcement of Money Judgments, generally, this index

CONTRACTS
Breach of Contract, generally, this index
Commercial Sales Contract, generally, this index
Definitions, § 5.4
Employment Law, generally, this index
Mechanic's Liens, generally, this index
Municipal Corporations, this index
Real Property, generally, this index
Small Business, Purchase or Sale, generally, this index
Statute of Frauds, generally, this index

CONVERSIONS
Limited liability companies, § 2.40
    Dissenters' rights, § 2.42
    Procedures, § 2.41
Limited partnerships, § 2.101
    Dissenters rights, § 2.103
    Procedures, § 2.102
Partnerships, § 2.68
    Dissenters' rights, § 2.70
    Procedures, § 2.69

CONVICTIONS
Employment law, denial of job or entitlements, § 17.41

COOPERATIVES
Federal civil rights law,
    Housing discrimination prohibited, § 18.47
        Complaint, form, § 18.96

CORPORATE FRANCHISE TAX, STATE
    Generally, § 35.19
Activity required for tax, § 35.25
Apportionment of tax bases, § 35.35
    Business allocation percentage, § 35.36
    Investment allocation percentage, § 35.37
Calculation of tax, § 35.26
Capital base, tax on,
    Definitions, § 35.31
    Exemptions for small business, § 35.32
Capital structure, initial tax on, § 35.21
Checklist, § 35.39

INDEX

CORPORATE FRANCHISE TAX, STATE—Continued
Corporations subject to tax, § 35.23
Department of taxation and finance. Taxation and Finance Department, generally, this index
Exemptions, § 35.24
Federal taxation, compared, § 35.20
Fixed dollar minimum tax, § 35.34
Foreign corporations, § 35.22
Minimum taxable income base, § 35.33
Subsidiaries, items from, § 35.29
Subsidiary capital, defined, § 35.38
Tax on net income base, § 35.27
    Federal taxable income, subtractions from, § 35.28
Taxation and Finance Department, generally, this index

CORPORATIONS
Generally, § 1.1 et seq.
Bankruptcy,
    Chapter 7, discharge unavailable, § 9.205
Business combinations, § 1.81 et seq.
    Assets; sale, lease, exchange, or other disposition of, § 1.85
        Guarantee authorized by shareholders, § 1.87
        Mortgage or security interest in assets, § 1.86
    Checklist, § 1.93
        Transactional checklist, § 1.131
    Federal income tax aspects, § 1.91
    Fraud, § 1.89
    Insider trading, § 1.89
    Mergers and consolidations, § 1.82
        Domestic and foreign corporations, combination of, § 1.83
        Effect, § 1.84
        Procedure, § 1.83
        Shareholder authorization, § 1.83
        Short-form merger, § 1.83
    Ninety-percent subsidiaries, § 1.88
    Share exchanges, § 1.88
    Shareholder's right to receive payment for shares, § 1.90
    Summary, § 1.92
    Takeover bids, disclosure, § 1.89
Bylaws,
    Form, § 1.152
    Formation, § 1.22
    Procedural checklist, § 1.142
"C" corporations,
    Chart comparing New York entities, § 2.108
    Strategy, § 1.2
Capital structure, § 1.26 et seq.
    Authorized shares, § 1.27
    Checklist, § 1.36
    Consideration and payment for shares, § 1.30
    Convertible securities, § 1.33
    Corporate bonds, §§ 1.33, 1.34
    De facto corporation, § 1.34
    Federal income tax aspects, § 1.34
    Fractional shares, § 1.30
    Pass-through of income or loss, § 1.34
    Preferred shares in series, § 1.28
    Rights to purchase shares, § 1.31
    Scrip, § 1.30
    Stated capital, § 1.32
    Subscriptions for shares, § 1.29
    Summary, § 1.35
    Uncertificated shares, § 1.30

INDEX

CORPORATIONS—Continued
Certificate of incorporation,
  Amendment, § 1.72 et seq.
    Adversely affected rights, § 1.72
    Certificate of change, filing, § 1.76
    Checklist, § 1.80
    Class vote, § 1.74
    Contents, § 1.75
    Form, § 1.154
    Procedure, § 1.73
    Reorganization under act of congress, § 1.78
    Restated certificate of incorporation, § 1.77
    Summary, § 1.79
  Definitions, § 1.5
  Filing,
    Procedural checklist, § 1.141
  Filing fees, § 1.21
  Form, § 1.151
  Formation, §§ 1.7, 1.21
  Procedural checklist, § 1.139
    Filing, § 1.141
  Professional service corporations, § 1.122
Corporate Franchise Tax, State, generally, this index
Definitions, § 1.5
Directors, § 1.59 et seq.
  Business judgment rule, § 1.66
  Care, duty of, § 1.65
  Checklist, § 1.68
  Classification, § 1.59
  Contribution, right of, § 1.66
  Delegation of authority to committee, § 1.64
  Dissent, right to, § 1.66
  Due care, § 1.66
  Election, § 1.59
  Executive committee, § 1.64
  Fiduciary duties, § 1.65
  Indemnification, § 1.66
  Inspection of list of directors and officers, § 1.59
  Liability, § 1.66
  Loyalty, duty of, § 1.65
  Meetings, § 1.62
    Quorum and voting requirements, § 1.63
  Misconduct, action against directors and officers, § 1.66
  New directorships, § 1.60
  Removal, § 1.61
  Summary, § 1.67
  Vacancies, § 1.60
Dissolution, § 1.94 et seq.
  Checklist, § 1.110
    Transactional checklist, § 1.134
  Form, § 1.155
  Judicial, § 1.99
    Application for final order, § 1.104
    Attorney General's action, § 1.100
    Director's petition, § 1.101
    Discontinuance, § 1.104
    Hearing, § 1.104
    Injunctive relief, § 1.106
    Judgment, § 1.104
    Order to show cause, § 1.104
    Other circumstances, § 1.103
    Petition for dissolution, § 1.104

INDEX

CORPORATIONS—Continued
Dissolution—Continued
  Judicial—Continued
    Petition upon deadlock, § 1.103
    Preservation of assets, § 1.105
    Procedure, § 1.104
    Receiver, appointment, § 1.105
    Referee, § 1.104
    Shareholder's petition, § 1.102
    Venue, § 1.104
    Void transfers and judgments, § 1.106
  Liquidation distributions, § 1.107
    Federal income tax aspects, § 1.108
  Non-judicial,
    Authorization, § 1.96
    Certificate of dissolution, § 1.97
      Form, § 1.155
    Corporate continuity during winding-up, § 1.97
    Notice to creditors, § 1.98
    Petition to annul or suspend dissolution, § 1.95
    Winding-up corporation's affairs, § 1.97
  Summary, § 1.109
Distributions, § 1.37 et seq.
  Checklist, § 1.42
  Dividends, § 1.38
  Federal income tax aspects, § 1.40
  Purchase or redemption of shares, § 1.39
  Reacquired shares, § 1.39
  Redeemable shares, § 1.39
  Share distributions, § 1.38
  Summary, § 1.41
Domestic,
  Mergers and consolidations,
    Domestic and foreign corporations, combination of, § 1.83
  Share exchanges, § 1.88
Drafting checklist, § 1.149
Foreign, § 1.114 et seq.
  Application for authority, § 1.116
    Amendment, § 1.117
    Effect of filing, § 1.117
  Authorization to do business, § 1.115
  Checklist, § 1.121
  Fictitious name, § 1.115
  Indemnification of directors, insurance, § 1.66
  Mergers and consolidations,
    Domestic and foreign corporations, combination of, § 1.83
  Procedural checklist, § 1.148
    Reservation of corporate name, § 1.138
  Reservation of corporate name,
    Form, § 1.150
    Procedural checklist, § 1.138
  Service of process, unauthorized foreign corporations, § 1.19
  Share exchanges, § 1.88
  Summary, § 1.120
  Surrender of authority, § 1.118
  Termination of existence, § 1.119
  Violations, Attorney General action, § 1.115
Foreign corporations,
  Corporate franchise tax, state, § 35.22
Formation, § 1.6 et seq.
  Biennial statement, § 1.23
  Bylaws, § 1.22

INDEX

CORPORATIONS—Continued
Formation—Continued
  Certificate of incorporation, §§ 1.7, 1.21
  Checklist, § 1.25
    Transactional checklist, § 1.129
  Corporate name, § 1.13
    Assumed name certificate, § 1.13
    Form, § 1.150
    Reservation of name, § 1.14
  Corporate purposes, § 1.9
    Limitation of liability, § 1.10
    Piercing the corporate veil, § 1.10
    Powers, § 1.11
    Ultra vires defense, § 1.12
    Upholding and disregarding the corporate entity, § 1.10
  Corporate seal, § 1.8
  De facto corporation, § 1.21
  Fees, § 1.7
  Franchise tax, § 1.23
  Incorporators and promoters, § 1.20
  Notice, § 1.7
  Organization meeting, § 1.23
  Service of process, § 1.15
    Certificate of resignation of registered agent, § 1.18
    Records and certificates of Department of State, § 1.16
    Registered agent, designation, § 1.18
    Secretary of State as agent, statutory designation, § 1.17
    Unauthorized foreign corporations, § 1.19
  Summary, § 1.24
Mergers and consolidations, § 1.82
  Domestic and foreign corporations, combination of, § 1.83
  Effect, § 1.84
  Procedure, § 1.83
  Professional service corporations, § 1.122
  Shareholder authorization, § 1.83
  Short-form merger, § 1.83
Municipal Corporations, generally, this index
Officers, § 1.69 et seq.
  Authority, § 1.69
  Checklist, § 1.71
  Election and appointment, § 1.69
  Removal, § 1.69
  Summary, § 1.70
Overview, § 1.4
Procedural checklist, § 1.135 et seq.
  Bylaws, § 1.142
  Certificate of incorporation,
    Filing, § 1.141
    Mandatory and permissive provisions, § 1.139
  Close corporations, § 1.147
  Foreign corporations, § 1.148
  Incorporation, § 1.140
  Notices, § 1.136
  Organization meetings, § 1.143
  Reservation of corporate name, § 1.137
    Foreign corporations, § 1.138
  Share certificate, § 1.144
  Shareholder approval requirements, § 1.145
  Shareholder's right to receive payment for shares, § 1.146
Professional service corporations, § 1.122
  Checklist, § 1.124
  Corporate name, § 1.122

INDEX

CORPORATIONS—Continued
Professional service corporations—Continued
  Corporate name—Continued
    Form, § 1.150
  Death or disqualification of shareholders, corporate purchase of shares, § 1.122
  Foreign, § 1.125 et seq.
    Annual statement, § 1.125
    Application for authority to do business, § 1.125
    Checklist, § 1.127
    Licensing authority regulation of professions, § 1.125
    New York Business Corporation Law, applicability, § 1.125
    Summary, § 1.126
  Issuance of shares, § 1.122
  Limited liability companies, § 1.122
  Limited liability partnerships, § 1.122
  Mergers and consolidations, § 1.122
  New York Business Corporation Law, applicability, § 1.122
  Shareholders, directors, officers, and employees; qualification and disqualification, § 1.122
  Summary, § 1.123
  Transfer of shares, § 1.122
  Triennial statement, § 1.122
Receivers,
  Appointment, § 1.111
    Judicial dissolution, § 1.105
  Checklist, § 1.112
  Compensation, § 1.111
  Designation of depositories by court, § 1.111
  Final accounting, § 1.111
  Oath, § 1.111
  Omissions and defaults, § 1.111
  Powers and duties, § 1.111
  Removal, § 1.111
  Shareholders' meetings and agreements,
    Fiduciaries, receivers and pledgees, voting by, § 1.45
  Summary, § 1.112
  Vacancies, § 1.111
"S" corporations,
  Chart comparing New York entities, § 2.108
  Pass-through of income or loss, § 1.34
  Strategy, § 1.2
Scope, § 1.1
Shareholders' liabilities, § 1.56 et seq.
  Checklist, § 1.58
  Control of directors, § 1.56
  Summary, § 1.57
  Unpaid balance of subscription, § 1.56
  Wages due employees, § 1.56
Shareholders' meetings and agreements, § 1.43 et seq.
  Action without meeting, § 1.48
  Checklist, § 1.50
  Class voting, § 1.45
  Cumulative voting, § 1.45
  Fiduciaries, receivers and pledgees, voting by, § 1.45
  Notice, § 1.44
  Proxies, § 1.45
  Quorum requirement, § 1.46
  Shareholder voting agreements, § 1.47
  Special meeting for election of directors, § 1.43
  Summary, § 1.49
  Voting, § 1.45
  Voting trusts, § 1.47

INDEX

CORPORATIONS—Continued
Shareholders' rights, § 1.51 et seq.
    Checklist, § 1.55
    Inspection of books and records, § 1.53
    Preemptive rights, § 1.52
    Right to dissent and receive payment for shares, § 1.51
    Shareholders' derivative action, § 1.51
    Summary, § 1.54
Small Business, Purchase or Sale, generally, this index
Strategy, § 1.2
    Checklist, § 1.3
Subscription agreements,
    Fees, § 1.153
    Shareholders' liabilities for unpaid balance of subscription, § 1.56
    Subscriptions for shares, § 1.29
Tax Classification, generally, this index
Taxation,
    De facto corporation, § 1.34
    Federal income tax,
        Business combinations, § 1.91
        Capital structure, § 1.34
        Dissolution, liquidation distributions, § 1.108
        Distributions, § 1.40
    Franchise tax, § 1.23
    Organization tax, § 1.30
    Stock transfer tax, § 1.30
    Transfers of property to controlled corporation, § 1.34
Transactional checklist, § 1.128 et seq.
    Business combinations, § 1.131
    Dissolution, § 1.134
    Formation, § 1.129
    Liquidation, § 1.134
    Operation, § 1.130
    Repurchase of shares, § 1.133
    Spin-offs and split-offs, § 1.132

COUNTERCLAIMS AND CROSS-CLAIMS
Employment law, § 17.83
    Form, § 17.97
Mechanic's liens willfully exaggerated, § 10.75
    Defense and counterclaim, form, § 10.135
New York Landlord-Tenant Law, § 13.56
Personal injury cases, form, § 26.66

COUNTY COURTS
Appeals, § 37.126
    Appeals from justice courts or city courts, §§ 37.20, 37.93, 37.97
    Perfecting the appeal, § 38.55
    Stay pending appeal,
        Appeals to county court, § 38.54
        Notice of motion for stay of proceedings,
            Affirmation in support, form, § 37.132
            Form, § 37.130
        Order to show cause for stay of proceedings,
            Affirmation in support, form, § 37.132
            Form, § 37.131
Appellate division, civil,
    Appeals to,
        Civil case judgments and orders, § 37.16
        Civil cases from county court as intermediate appellate court, §§ 37.20, 37.126
Appellate division, criminal,
    Appeals to, § 38.4
Appellate term, appeals to in civil cases, § 37.126

INDEX

COUNTY COURTS—Continued
Change of venue,
    CPL § 170.15(3), § 38.58
    CPL § 255.20, § 38.58
    Original application, § 38.58
Constitutional basis, § 37.3
Costs on appeal to, § 37.98
Jurisdiction, § 37.126
Perfection of appeal from justice courts, § 37.96
Stay pending appeal,
    Appeals to county court, § 38.54
    Notice of motion for stay of proceedings,
        Affirmation in support, form, § 37.132
        Form, § 37.130
    Order to show cause for stay of proceedings,
        Affirmation in support, form, § 37.132
        Form, § 37.131

COURT EVALUATORS
Guardianships,
    Appointment, persons eligible for, § 22.25
    Compensation, § 22.27
    Counsel for incapacitated persons, appointment, § 22.28
    Duties, § 22.26
        Checklist, § 22.3(c)
    Education requirements, training, § 22.77
    Report,
        Checklists, § 22.91
        Forms, § 22.100
    Summary, § 22.29

COURT EXAMINERS
Guardianships, § 22.65
    Education requirements, training, § 22.78

COURT OF APPEALS
    Generally, § 39.1 et seq.
Admission of attorneys and licensing of foreign legal consultants, § 39.61
Certified questions from other courts, § 39.60
Civil appeals, § 39.3 et seq.
    Administrative proceedings, § 39.7
    Amicus curiae brief,
        Leave to appear, form, § 39.86
        Motion to file, § 39.34
    Appeal as of right, § 39.8 et seq.
        Appellate division orders or judgments, § 39.9
        CPLR 5601(b)(1), § 39.9
        CPLR 5601(c), § 39.9
        Direct involvement of substantial constitutional question, § 39.9
            Notice of appeal from order of appellate division, form, § 39.78
        Final judgment of court of original instance, § 39.10
            Notice of appeal from order of appellate division, form, § 39.77
        Judgment of court of original instance to review prior non-final determination of appellate division, § 39.11
            Notice of appeal from judgment of supreme court, form, § 39.81
        Order granting affirmation of new trial, § 39.9
            Notice of appeal from appellate division order, form, § 39.80
        Order granting hearing on stipulation for judgment absolute, § 39.9
            Notice of appeal from appellate division order, form, § 39.80
        Procedural checklist, § 39.64
        Time for taking appeal, § 39.20
            Notice of motion to dismiss appeal as untimely taken,
                  Affidavit in support, form, § 39.88

INDEX

COURT OF APPEALS—Continued
Civil appeals—Continued
  Appeal as of right—Continued
    Time for taking appeal—Continued
      Notice of motion to dismiss appeal as untimely taken—Continued
        Form, § 39.87
    Two judge dissent, § 39.9
      Notice of appeal from appellate division order, form, § 39.77
  Appeal by permission, § 39.12
    Final order of appellate division determining action, § 39.14
    Judgment of court of original instance to review prior non-final determination of appellate division, § 39.13
      Notice of appeal of judgment of supreme court, form, § 39.81
    Non-final order of appellate division in proceedings by or against public officers, § 39.15
    Procedural checklist, § 39.65
  Appealable paper, § 39.6
  Appeals from final determinations, § 39.7
  Appellant's brief, drafting checklist, § 39.75
  Cross appeals,
    Time for taking appeal, § 39.22
      Notice of motion to dismiss appeal as untimely taken,
        Affidavit in support, form, § 39.88
        Form, § 39.87
  Determination of appeal, § 39.31
  Expedited review pursuant to Rule 500.4,
    Procedural checklist, § 39.68
  Finality, § 39.4
  Forms, § 39.77 et seq.
  Harmless error, § 39.7
  Joinder of defendants,
    CPLR 5531 statement, form, § 39.89
  Jurisdiction,
    Drafting checklist, § 39.72
    Inquiry, § 39.27
    Statement, § 39.26
      Form, § 39.82
  Leave to appeal,
    Appellate division, civil appellate practice before, § 37.70
    Content, § 39.17
    Corporations, papers filed by, § 39.19
    Deadline for filing, § 39.19
    Filing fee, § 39.19
    Form, § 39.17
    Motions filed in appellate division, § 39.18
      Procedural checklist, § 39.67
    Motions filed in court of appeals, § 39.19
      Drafting checklist, § 39.73
      Leave to appear amicus curiae, form, § 39.86
      Notice of motion for leave to appeal from order of appellate division,
        Affidavit in support, form, § 39.84
        Form, § 39.83
      Notice of motion for reargument, form, § 39.85
    Moving papers, § 39.19
    Orders to show cause, § 39.19
    Procedural checklist, § 39.67
    Responding papers, § 39.19
    Return date, § 39.19
    Service of process, § 39.17
    Statistics, § 39.19
    Time for taking appeal, § 39.21
      Notice of motion to dismiss appeal as untimely taken,

INDEX

COURT OF APPEALS—Continued
Civil appeals—Continued
  Leave to appeal—Continued
    Time for taking appeal—Continued
      Notice of motion to dismiss appeal as untimely taken—Continued
        Affidavit in support, form, § 39.88
        Form, § 39.87
  Limited review, § 39.7
  Motions, § 39.32 et seq.
    Amicus curiae brief, motion to file, § 39.34
    Poor person relief, § 39.35
    Reconsideration, § 39.36
    Stay, § 39.33
  Non-appealable orders, § 39.5
  Non-reviewable matters, § 39.7
  Notice of appeal,
    Drafting checklist, § 39.71
    Form and content, § 39.25
    Order of appellate division,
      Final determination of action where constitutionality of statute involved, form, § 39.79
      Final determination of action where construction of constitution involved, form, § 39.78
      Final determination of action with two dissents on question of law, form, § 39.77
      Reversal granting new trial with stipulation for judgment absolute, form, § 39.80
    Prior non-final determination of appellate division, form, § 39.81
  Perfecting the appeal, § 39.28
    Appellant's papers, § 39.29
    Appendix method, § 39.29
    Calendar practice, § 39.29
    Filing fees, § 39.29
    Full record, § 39.29
    Oral argument, § 39.29
      Procedural checklist, § 39.69
    Respondent's papers, § 39.29
    Sua sponte merits consideration (SSM), § 39.30
    Time for filing, § 39.29
      Notice of motion to dismiss appeal as untimely taken,
        Affidavit in support, form, § 39.88
        Form, § 39.87
  Poor person relief, motion for, § 39.35
  Preservation of issue for appeal, § 39.7
  Reconsideration, § 39.36
  Remittitur, § 39.31
  Respondent's brief, drafting checklist, § 39.76
  Review of questions of law, §§ 37.3, 37.70
  Scope of review, § 39.7
    Administrative proceedings, § 39.7
    Appeals from final determinations, § 39.7
    Harmless error, § 39.7
    Limited review, § 39.7
    Non-reviewable matters, § 39.7
    Preservation of appeal, § 39.7
  Stays, § 39.33
    Stay of proceedings on appeal to, § 37.80
  Time for taking appeal, § 39.20 et seq.
    Appeal as of right, § 39.20
    Cross appeals, § 39.22
    Extensions of time, § 39.23
    Motions for leave to appeal, § 39.21
    Notice of motion to dismiss appeal as untimely taken,
      Affidavit in support, form, § 39.88

INDEX

COURT OF APPEALS—Continued
Civil appeals—Continued
    Time for taking appeal—Continued
        Notice of motion to dismiss appeal as untimely taken—Continued
            Form, § 39.87
        Omissions, § 39.24
Civil Court of New York City, from, § 37.121
Criminal appeals, § 39.37 et seq.
    Appeal by permission, § 39.44 et seq.
        Criminal leave application "CLA",
            Bail, continuation, § 39.48
            Continuation of bail, § 39.48
            Extensions of time, § 39.47
            Leave application to appellate division justice, § 39.47
                Procedural checklist, § 39.67
            Leave application to court of appeals judge, § 39.47
                Procedural checklist, § 39.66
            Reconsideration, time for seeking, § 39.47
            Stay of proceedings, § 39.48
            Time to seek leave to appeal, § 39.47
        Obligation of intermediate appellate court counsel, § 39.45
        Who may grant leave to appeal, § 39.46
    Appeals practice, § 39.49
    Appellant's brief, § 39.75
    Certiorari to U.S. Supreme Court, § 39.62
    Criminal action, defined, § 39.38
    Criminal Procedure Law, § 39.37
    Death penalty,
        Defendant, appeal by, § 39.40
        Prosecution, appeal by, § 39.41
        Scope of review, § 39.50
    Dismissal of appeal, § 39.55
    Disposition of appeal, § 39.51
    Drafting checklists, § 39.70 et seq.
    Expedited review pursuant to Rule 500.4,
        Procedural checklist, § 39.68
    Forms, § 39.77 et seq.
    Harmless error, § 39.50
    Indigent defendants, assignment of counsel, § 39.53
    Intermediate appellate courts, § 39.42
        Limitations on appealability, § 39.43
    Leave to appeal,
        Appellate division, civil,
            Post-disposition proceedings, § 37.70
        Drafting checklist, §§ 39.71, 39.74
        Extension of time, § 39.54
        Letter seeking leave to appeal, form, § 39.90
        Post-disposition proceedings,
            Notice of motion for reargument or leave to appeal to court of appeals, § 37.139
                Affirmation in support, form, § 37.140
        Procedural checklist, § 39.54
    Motions, § 39.52 et seq.
        Dismissal of appeal, § 39.55
        Extension of time to seek leave to appeal, § 39.54
        Poor person relief, § 39.53
        Reargument, § 39.57
        Withdrawal of appeal, § 39.56
    Non-reviewable matters, § 39.50
    Orders and judgments from which appeals may be taken, § 39.39
    Other proceedings, § 39.58 et seq.
    Poor person relief, § 39.53
    Preservation of issue for appeal, § 39.50

INDEX

COURT OF APPEALS—Continued
Criminal appeals—Continued
    Reargument, § 39.57
    Respondent's brief, drafting checklist, § 39.76
    Scope of review, § 39.50
        Death penalty cases, § 39.50
        Harmless error, § 39.50
        Non-reviewable matters, § 39.50
        Preservation of issue for appeal, § 39.50
    Withdrawal of appeal, § 39.56
Procedural checklists, § 39.63 et seq.
Review of determinations of commission on judicial conduct, § 39.59
Scope, § 39.1
Strategy, § 39.2

COURT OF CLAIMS
Appellate division, civil,
    Appeals to from civil case judgments and orders, § 37.17
    Applicability of CPLR to appeals, § 37.17
    Constitutional basis, § 37.3
    Governing practice, § 37.3
    Jurisdiction, § 37.17
    Notice of appeal, timing, § 37.17
Court of Claims Act, § 37.3
Eminent domain,
    Jurisdiction, §§ 14.48, 14.52
        Exclusive jurisdiction, § 14.53
        Filing, § 14.54
        Notice, § 14.54
        Vesting of title, § 14.55
    Just compensation, § 14.70
        Service of process, § 14.72
        Time to file claim, § 14.71
Notice of claim, § 26.41
Personal injury claims against state, § 26.41
Prisoners' rights, jurisdiction, § 18.29

COVENANTS
Non-competition, § 17.16
Restrictive, employee discharge severance agreements, § 17.16

CPLR
Appellate division, civil appellate practice before,
    Application of to appeals,
        City courts, from, § 37.103
        Civil Court of New York City, § 37.119
        Court of appeals,
            Appeals as of right,
                CPLR 5601(b)(1), § 39.9
                CPLR 5601(c), § 39.9
            Joinder of defendants,
                CPLR 5531 statement, form, § 39.89
        Court of claims, § 37.17
        District courts, from, § 37.111
        Family court, § 37.19
        Justice courts, from, § 37.94
        Surrogate's court, § 37.18
City courts,
    CPLR Article 55, applicability, § 37.103
Civil Court of New York City, CPLR applicability, § 37.119
Comparison with Uniform Justice Court Act, § 37.95
Court of appeals,
    Appeals as of right,

INDEX

CPLR—Continued
Court of appeals—Continued
  Appeals as of right—Continued
    CPLR 5601(b)(1), § 39.9
    CPLR 5601(c), § 39.9
  Joinder of defendants,
    CPLR 5531 statement, form, § 39.89
Court of claims, applicability of CPLR to appeals, § 37.17
CPLR 5704 ex parte order review, §§ 37.37, 37.89
CPLR Article 78 proceedings, § 37.87
District courts, applicability, § 37.111
Family court, applicability of CPLR to appeals, § 37.19
Justice courts,
  CPLR Article 55, applicability, § 37.94
Surrogate's court, applicability of CPLR to appeals, § 37.18

CREDIT
Consumer protection, § 7.1 et seq.
Reports,
  Agencies, § 7.48
  Complaints,
    Deceptive trade practices, § 7.60
    Fair credit reporting violations, § 7.60
  Consumer protection. resolutions, § 7.32
  Consumer rights, §§ 7.30, 7.31
  Damages for violations, § 7.48
  Employment law, denial of job or entitlements, § 17.42
  Lemon law, § 7.5
  Litigation, § 7.33
  Motor vehicle loans, § 7.5
  Motor vehicle sales, § 7.3

CREDITORS
Debtors and Creditors, generally, this index

CRIMINAL COURT OF NEW YORK CITY
Appeals, § 38.48
  Constitutional basis, § 37.3
  Kings, Queens, and Richmond county branches, § 38.50
  New York and Bronx county branches, § 38.49
  Stay pending appeal,
    Appeal from New York City criminal court to appellate term, § 38.54
    Notice of motion for stay of proceedings,
      Affirmation in support, form, § 37.132
      Form, § 37.130
    Order to show cause for stay of proceedings,
      Affirmation in support, form, § 37.132
      Form, § 37.131

CROSS-EXAMINATION
Adjudicatory proceedings, administrative law, § 4.16
Traffic offenses, speeding, § 33.68

CSRA
Elder law, § 23.39

DAMAGES
  Generally, § 30.1 et seq.
Answer,
  Defense of culpable conduct, form, § 30.50
  Defense of failure to use seat belt, form, § 30.51
  Strategy, § 30.3
Attorney fees, § 30.41 et seq.
  Agreements, § 30.43

INDEX

DAMAGES—Continued
Attorney fees—Continued
    Statutes, § 30.42
Bankruptcy, generally, this index
Bills of particulars, strategy, § 30.3
Breach of contract, § 30.19 et seq.
    Actual loss, § 30.20
    Anticipatory breach, § 30.23
    Building and construction, § 30.25
    Compensatory, § 30.19
    Contract price, § 30.20
    Damages within the contemplation of the parties, § 30.24
    Defective performance, § 30.22
    Delay in performance, § 30.21
    Difference in value rule, § 30.25
    Jury instructions, § 30.71
        Employment contract, § 30.72
    Loss of profits, § 30.24
    Punitive damages, inapplicable, § 30.34
    Quantum meruit, § 30.25
    Residential contract of sale, § 12.29
Burden of proof, § 30.5
Certificate of readiness, strategy, § 30.3
Collateral sources,
    Indemnification from collateral sources defense, form, § 30.52
    Jury instructions,
        Itemized verdict, § 30.68
Compensatory, § 30.6 et seq.
    Economic, § 30.7
    General, § 30.6
    Loss of consortium, § 30.15
        Wrongful death, inapplicable, § 30.15
    Non-economic, § 30.7
    Personal injury, § 30.7
        Actions based on property damage, § 30.9
        Aggravation of preexisting injury, § 30.11
            Jury instructions, § 30.64
        Fear of future economic loss, § 30.9
        Impairment of future earning ability, § 30.10
        Intentional infliction of emotional distress, § 30.9
        Loss of consortium, § 30.15
        Loss of earnings, § 30.10
            Jury instructions, § 30.62
        Loss of enjoyment of life, § 30.9
        Mental or emotional pain and suffering, § 30.9
        Mitigation and minimization of damages, § 30.28
        Physical pain and suffering, § 30.8
        Post-trauma neuroses, § 30.9
        Zone of danger actions, § 30.9
    Property damage, § 30.16 et seq.
        Jury instructions,
            With market value, § 30.69
            Without market value, § 30.69
        Personal property, § 30.18
        Real property, § 30.17
    Special, § 30.6
    Wrongful death, § 30.12
        Child, § 30.14
        Collateral relatives, § 30.14
        Conscious pain and suffering, § 30.13
            Jury instructions, § 30.67
        Damages sustained after death, § 30.14

INDEX

DAMAGES—Continued
Compensatory—Continued
  Wrongful death—Continued
    Damages sustained before death, § 30.13
    Interest, § 30.40
    Loss of consortium, inapplicable, § 30.15
    Parent, § 30.14
    "Pre-impact terror", § 30.13
    Spouse, § 30.14
    Survival statute, § 30.12
Complaint,
  Ad damnum clause, form, § 30.46
    Medical or dental malpractice action, § 30.47
    Municipal corporation, action against, § 30.47
  Demand for, § 17.82
  Motor vehicle accidents, form, § 30.48
  Strategy, § 30.3
Consequential,
  Eminent domain, just compensation, § 14.82
    Setoff, § 14.109
Contracts. Commercial Sales Contract, generally, this index
  Breach of contract, ante
Deceptive Practices Act, §§ 7.46, 7.47, 7.48
Direct,
  Eminent domain, just compensation, § 14.80
Employment law,
  Breach of contract, § 17.35
  Prima facie tort, § 17.31
Excessive, § 30.29
  Appellate division, civil,
    Scope of review, § 37.29
  Specific awards, § 30.30
Fair credit reporting violations, § 7.60
Forms, § 30.45 et seq.
Fraud, employment cases, § 17.27
Inability to convey property as partial defense, form, § 30.55
Inadequate, § 30.29
  Appellate division, civil,
    Scope of review, § 37.29
  Specific awards, § 30.30
Indemnification from collateral sources defense, form, § 30.52
Insurance,
  Duty to defend, breach, § 31.14
  Unfair claim settlement practices, § 31.17
Interest, § 30.40
  Notice of motion to amend verdict to add interest, form, § 30.56
    Affidavit in support, § 30.57
  Notice of motion to fix date from which interest is computed, form, § 30.58
    Affidavit in support, § 30.59
Interrogatories, strategy, § 30.3
Jury instructions, § 30.60 et seq.
  Breach of contract, § 30.71
    Employment contract, § 30.72
  Collateral sources, itemized verdict, § 30.68
  Personal injury,
    Aggravation of preexisting injury, § 30.64
    Loss of earnings, § 30.62
    Payment of income taxes, § 30.65
    Physical consequences of shock and fright, § 30.63
    Reduction to present value, § 30.66
    Shock and fright, § 30.63
    Subsequent injury, § 30.61

INDEX

DAMAGES—Continued
Jury instructions—Continued
    Property damage,
        With market value, § 30.70
        Without market value, § 30.69
    Wrongful death, conscious pain and suffering, § 30.67
Legal malpractice,
    Deceit, treble damages, § 28.24
Lemon law, §§ 7.12, 7.48, 7.56
Libel and slander, employment cases, § 17.25
Liquidated, § 30.39
    Penalties prohibited, § 30.39
Medical malpractice, §§ 26.58, 29.24
Medical or dental malpractice action,
    Complaint, ad damnum clause, form, § 30.47
    Nature and degree, strategy, § 29.4
    Request for supplemental relief, form, § 30.49
Minimization, § 30.26
    Contracts, § 30.27
    Personal injury, § 30.28
Mitigation, § 30.26
    Contracts, § 30.27
    Partial defense, form, § 30.53
    Personal injury, § 30.28
    Punitive, § 30.36
Motor Vehicle Retail Leasing Act, § 7.48
Municipal corporations,
    Request for supplemental relief, form, § 30.49
Nature of damages, § 30.5
New York Fair Credit Reporting Act, § 7.48
Nominal, § 30.37
Periodic payment of judgments, § 30.44
Personal injury, § 26.58
    Special damages, § 26.51
Punitive, § 30.31 et seq.
    Awards, § 30.35
    Breach of contract, inapplicable, § 30.34
    Intentional conduct, § 30.31
    Intentional torts, § 30.32
    Mitigation, § 30.36
    Negligence, § 30.33
    Products liability,
        Successor liability, § 27.28
    Reckless indifference to consequences, § 30.31
    Willful conduct, § 30.31
    Wrongful death, inapplicable, § 30.33
Scope, § 30.1
Statutory, § 30.38
Strategy, § 30.2 et seq.
    Answer, § 30.3
    Bills of particulars, § 30.3
    Certificate of readiness, § 30.3
    Complaint, § 30.3
    Interrogatories, § 30.3
    Pretrial, § 30.3
    Trial, § 30.4

DEATH PENALTY
Court of appeals,
    Defendant, appeal by, § 39.40
    Prosecution, appeal by, § 39.41
    Scope of review, § 39.50
Mental retardation,

INDEX

DEATH PENALTY—Continued
Mental retardation—Continued
    Appellate division, criminal, § 38.10

DEBT COLLECTION PROCEDURES ACT
Collection agencies, § 7.36

DEBT COLLECTORS
Collection Agencies, generally, this index

DEBTORS AND CREDITORS
Bankruptcy, generally, this index
Creditors,
    Commercial sales contract, third party interests, other creditors, § 5.56
    Corporations, nonjudicial dissolution,
        Notice to creditors, § 1.98
    Lawsuits against creditors, § 7.44
    Probate and estate administration,
        Claims against estate, § 25.40
        Petitioning for probate, § 25.15
        Postmortem planning,
            Disclaimers, creditor avoidance, § 24.70
Depositions,
    Subpoena duces tecum,
        Judgment debtor with restraining notice, form, § 8.50
Enforcement of Money Judgments, generally, this index
Fair Debt Collection Practices Act, § 7.3
Fraud, generally, this index
Lawsuits against creditors, § 7.44
Liens, generally, this index
Wills, provisions, § 24.10

DECEPTIVE PRACTICES ACT
Attorney fees, § 7.47
Broad application, § 7.46
Class actions, § 7.47
Damages, §§ 7.46, 7.47, 7.48
Injunctive relief, § 7.47
Limitation of actions, § 7.48
Provisions, § 7.45

DECEPTIVE TRADE PRACTICES
Complaint, § 7.65
    Attorney fees, § 7.62
    Defenses, § 7.53
    Fair credit reporting violations, § 7.60
    Motor vehicle leasing company, § 7.52
        Defenses, § 7.54
Consumer protection, § 7.2
Motor vehicle sales, § 7.3
    Attorney fees, § 7.7
Order to show cause,
    Preliminary injunction, § 7.63
    Temporary restraining order, § 7.63
Temporary restraining order and preliminary injunction,
    Affirmation in support, § 7.64

DECLARATORY RELIEF
Administrative law and proceedings,
    Rulemaking, declaratory rulings, § 4.51
Appellate division, civil,
    Disposition of appeal, § 37.65
Income tax, state,
    Judicial review, § 35.104

INDEX

DECLARATORY RELIEF—Continued
Income tax—Continued
    Petition for declaratory ruling, forms, § 35.135
Insurance, § 31.21
    Complaint by insurer for declaratory relief, forms, § 31.33
    Complaint by policyholder for declaratory relief and breach of contract, forms, § 31.32

DECREES
Judgments and Decrees, generally, this index

DEEDS
Bargain and sale deeds,
    Residential contract of sale, § 12.22
Full covenant and warrant deeds,
    Residential contract of sale, § 12.22
Mechanic's liens,
    Private improvements, priorities, § 10.31
Quit claim deeds,
    Residential contract of sale, § 12.22
Referee's deed,
    Mortgage foreclosure, § 11.51

DEFAMATION
Limitation of actions, § 17.77

DEFAULT JUDGMENTS
Appellate Division, civil,
    Aggrieved parties, defaulters, § 37.23
Enforcement of money judgments, § 8.4
    Affidavit of facts constituting claim, form, § 8.47
    Default and amount due, form, § 8.47
    Statement for judgment, form, § 8.47
Foreclosure, generally, this index
Real Property, generally, this index

DEFENSES
Absolute immunity,
    Federal civil rights law, § 18.31
    Police and prosecutorial misconduct, malicious prosecution, § 18.25
Affirmative Defenses, generally, this index
Damages,
    Culpable conduct, form, § 30.50
    Failure to use seat belt, form, § 30.51
    Indemnification from collateral sources, form, § 30.52
Federal civil rights law, § 18.30 et seq.
    Absolute immunity, § 18.31
    "Burford" abstention, § 18.36
    Collateral estoppel, § 18.37
    Eleventh Amendment, § 18.33
    Limitation of actions, § 18.38
    "Monell v. New York City Dept of Social Services", § 18.34
    "Pullman" abstention, § 18.36
    Qualified immunity, § 18.32
    Res judicata, § 18.37
    Respondeat superior doctrine, § 18.35
    "Younger" abstention, § 18.36
Fraudulent motor vehicle leasing cases, § 7.53
Holdover proceedings. Tenant Defenses, generally. Holdover Proceedings, this index
Medical malpractice, standard of care, § 29.17
Non-payment proceedings. Tenant Defenses, generally. Non-Payment Proceedings, this index
Odometer law, § 7.53
Products liability,
    Defective design, § 27.9

INDEX

DEFENSES—Continued
Products liability—Continued
    Failure to test, preemption defense, § 27.21
    Failure to warn, informed intermediary defense, § 27.15
    Preemption,
        Failure to test, § 27.21
        Private claims, § 27.49
Qualified immunity,
    Federal civil rights law, § 18.32
    Police and prosecutorial misconduct,
        Excessive force, § 18.21
        False arrest, § 18.22
        Malicious prosecution, § 18.25
Workers' compensation hearings, § 32.19

DEFINITIONS
Accessory apartments, § 16.120
Accessory uses, § 16.119
Action involving public petition and participation, § 18.80
Adoption, § 20.6
Advanced degree, § 19.24
Adversary proceedings, § 9.16
Affiliate, § 19.21
Agency, § 3.29
Aggrieved party, § 14.36
Air contaminant, § 15.21
Art, § 19.23
Authorized agency, § 20.86
Block busting, § 18.46
Bonds, § 1.5
Business, § 19.23
Capital, § 19.43
Capital asset, § 6.120
Certificate of incorporation, § 1.5
Child, § 19.11
Claim, § 9.36
Closing, § 12.22
Condemnees, § 14.99
Contract, § 3.22
Contractor, § 10.5
Contracts, § 5.4
Corporation, § 1.5
Course of dealing, § 5.21
Course of performance, § 5.21
Criminal action, § 39.38
Criminal proceeding, § 38.3
Defective, § 27.5
Director, § 1.5
Disinterested person, § 9.29
Doing business, § 19.21
Domestic corporation, § 1.5
Exclusionary zone, § 16.123
Executory contract, § 9.74
Extraordinary ability aliens, § 19.19
Facility, § 15.29
Family, § 16.122
Family farmer, § 9.212
Father, § 19.11
Final judgment, § 8.3
Fine arts, § 19.23
Foreign corporation, § 1.5
Foreign person, § 12.76
Good moral character, § 19.16

INDEX

DEFINITIONS—Continued
Hazardous substance, § 15.29
Hazardous substances, § 15.31
Hazardous waste, §§ 15.23, 15.31
Immediate relative, § 19.8
Insolvent, § 1.5
Interest, § 3.22
Interrogation, § 33.52
Invest, § 19.43
Judgments, § 8.3
Just compensation, § 14.18
Land use law, § 16.3
Legitimacy, § 19.8
Lemon law, § 7.19
Lessee, § 9.84
Local government, § 3.3
Managerial, § 19.21
Materialman, § 10.5
Mental Hygiene Law Article 81, § 22.9
Minimization of damages, § 30.26
Mitigation of damages, § 30.26
Mother, § 19.11
Municipal corporations, § 3.3
National interest, § 19.25
Navigable waters, § 15.15
Net assets, § 1.5
Nonconforming use, § 16.62
Office of corporation, § 1.5
Open meeting, § 3.28
Ordinary course of business, § 9.61
Organizational expenditure, § 1.34
Orphan, § 19.15
Outstanding, § 19.20
Parent, § 19.11
Permanent position, § 19.20
Point source, § 15.8
Political subdivision, § 3.3
Pollutant, § 15.8
Process, § 1.5
Profession, § 19.24
Property, § 8.19
Property of estate, § 9.49
Public accommodations, § 18.54
Public facility, § 18.57
Public use, benefit or purpose, § 14.15
Racial steering, § 18.46
Real property, § 14.8
Reasonable cause, § 33.4
Reasonable suspicion, § 33.5
Regional center, § 19.44
Release, § 15.29
Site plans, § 16.103
SLAPP suits, § 18.80
Small business, § 9.173
Small quantity generators, § 15.24
Solid waste, § 15.23
Special use permits, § 16.90
Start-up expenditure, § 1.34
Stated capital, § 1.5
Subsidiary, § 19.21
Substantial consummation, § 9.172
Surplus, § 1.5

INDEX

DEFINITIONS—Continued
Total amount realized, § 12.76
Trade name, § 6.19
Treasury shares, § 1.5
Unconscionable contract, § 5.12
Use variance, § 16.73
Used cars, § 7.11
Waste, § 15.23
Wetlands, § 15.15
Wrongful conception, § 29.11
Wrongful life, § 29.11

DENTAL MALPRACTICE
Damages,
    Complaint, ad damnum clause, form, § 30.47
    Request for supplemental relief, form, § 30.49
Expert witnesses, discovery, § 26.42
Medical malpractice, § 26.13

DEPARTMENT OF CONSUMER AFFAIRS
Consumer protection, powers and duties, § 7.2

DEPARTMENT OF TAXATION AND FINANCE
Taxation and Finance Department, generally, this index

DEPOSITIONS
Accusatory instruments. Supporting depositions, generally. Accusatory Instruments, this index
Demand for production of documents, § 26.43
Discrimination cases, § 17.72
Location, § 26.43
Medical malpractice,
    Medical literature, use for preparing for depositions, § 29.47
Personal injury cases, notice, § 26.43
Subpoena duces tecum,
    Judgment debtor with restraining notice, form, § 8.50
    Witness with restraining notice, form, § 8.51

DIRECTORS
Corporations, this index

DISABILITY BENEFITS LAW
    Generally, § 32.44
Claim filing, § 32.50
Conclusion, § 32.52
Employees,
    Benefits and contributions, § 32.47
    Eligibility, § 32.49
    Exempt employees, § 32.46
Employers' obligations, § 32.45
Pregnancy, § 32.51
Special fund for disability benefits, § 32.48

DISABILITY INSURANCE
Disability Benefits Law, generally, this index
Insurance, generally, this index
Social Security, generally, this index
Workers' Compensation, generally, this index

DISABLED PERSONS
Handicapped Persons, generally, this index

DISCHARGE PLANNING
Hospital patient rights, § 23.91

INDEX

DISCLAIMERS
Insurance, § 31.16
Postmortem planning, § 24.68
    Creditor avoidance, § 24.70
    Disclaimer trusts, § 24.69
    New York statutory requirements, § 24.71

DISCOS
License for sale of beer, wine and spirits, § 36.9

DISCOVERY
Adjudicatory proceedings,
    Administrative law, § 4.13
Discrimination cases,
    Document production, § 17.71
    Document request, § 17.72
Divorce cases, § 21.63
Eminent domain, pretaking discovery, § 14.42
Medical malpractice, § 29.64 et seq.
    Allied health provider records, § 29.70
    Autopsy report, § 29.72
    Billing records, § 29.68
    Form, § 26.68
    Hospital records, § 29.67
    Obtaining and identifying relevant records, § 29.65
    Pharmacy records, § 29.69
    Physician's records, § 29.66
    Pre-calendar conferences, § 29.30
    Workers' compensation, § 29.73
        Claim file, § 29.71
Motor vehicle accidents,
    Accident reports, form, § 26.70
    Insurance information, § 26.42
        Form, § 26.70
    Medical reports, form, § 26.68
    Witnesses, form, § 26.70
New York Landlord-Tenant Law, § 13.58
    Freedom of Information Law, § 13.60
    Notice to admit, § 13.59
Personal injury cases, § 26.42
    Medical reports, form, §§ 26.68, 26.70
Post-verdict discovery, enforcement of money judgments, § 8.2
Pretrial, § 33.31 et seq.
    Bills of particulars, § 33.35 et seq.
        Filing,
            Response time, § 33.37
            Time limits, § 33.36
        People's failure to comply with time limits, § 33.38
    Brady material, § 33.39 et seq.
        Prosecutor need not be aware of evidence, § 33.40
        Timely disclosure, § 33.41
    Demands to produce, § 33.35 et seq.
        Filing,
            Response time, § 33.37
            Time limits, § 33.36
        People's failure to comply with time limits, § 33.38
        Speeding ticket,
            Drafting checklist, § 33.97
            Form, § 33.101
            Procedural checklist, § 33.93
    Exculpatory evidence, § 33.39 et seq.
        Prosecutor need not be aware of evidence, § 33.40
        Timely disclosure, § 33.41

INDEX

DISCOVERY—Continued
Pretrial—Continued
    Simplified information, § 33.32
    Subpoenas, § 33.34
    Traffic offenses, § 33.33
Probate, administration or accounting proceedings, § 25.31
Products liability,
    Confidentiality orders or stipulations, § 27.38
    Design alternatives, § 27.37
    Effect of destruction of product upon plaintiff's ability to prove defect,
        Order compelling preservation or production, § 27.33
    Sealing court records, § 27.38
    Testing and safety design, § 27.37
Trial, speeding tickets, § 33.67

DISCRIMINATION
Age,
    Age Discrimination in Employment Act, § 18.59
        Antireprisal provisions, § 17.38
        Older Workers Benefit Protection Act amends ADEA, § 17.11
        Provisions of statute, § 17.37
Alienage, New York City Human Rights Law, § 17.49
Americans with Disabilities Act, § 17.43
Antireprisal provisions, § 17.59
Appeals, § 17.76
Attorney fees, § 17.75
Burden of proof, § 17.59
Citizenship status, New York City Human Rights Law, § 17.49
Class actions, §§ 17.59, 17.82
Collective bargaining protection, § 17.61
Complaint, form, § 17.89
Defenses, § 17.59
Depositions, § 17.72
Disparate impact cause of action, § 17.59
Document production, § 17.71
Document request, § 17.72
Employment, § 18.59 et seq.
    Age discrimination in Employment Act, § 18.59
    Alternate dispute resolution (ADR), § 17.7
    Equal Pay Act, § 18.59
    General provisions, § 18.60
    Handicapped persons, § 18.61
    Marital status, § 17.48
    Off duty conduct, § 17.47
    Persons with genetic disorders, § 18.62
    Title VII of Civil Rights Act of 1964, § 18.59
Equal Employment Opportunity Commission,
    Charge of discrimination,
        Affidavit, § 17.93
        Form, § 17.92
    Letter requesting dual-filed charge, form, § 17.94
    Letter requesting "Mohasco" waiver, form, § 17.88
Equal Pay Act, § 17.44
Federal civil rights law,
    42 U.S.C.A. Section 1981, § 18.17
    42 U.S.C.A. Section 1983, § 18.18
        Acting under color of state law, § 18.18
        Respondeat superior doctrine inapplicable, § 18.18
        State action, § 18.18
    42 U.S.C.A. Section 1985(3), § 18.19
    42 U.S.C.A. Section 1986, § 18.19
    Handicapped persons, prohibited, § 18.19
    Housing, § 18.39 et seq.

INDEX

DISCRIMINATION—Continued
Federal civil rights law—Continued
    Municipal corporations, applicability, § 18.17
    Rehabilitation Act, Section 504, § 18.19
Filing agency charges, §§ 17.66, 17.70
    Election of remedies, § 17.68
    Responses, § 17.67
Housing, § 18.39 et seq.
    Burden of proof, § 18.51
    Complaint, form, § 18.95
    Prima facie case, § 18.51
    Private housing, § 18.44 et seq.
        Cooperatives, § 18.47
        New York Human Rights Law, § 18.44
        Owners and lessors, § 18.45
        Real estate agents and brokers, § 18.46
        Remedies, § 18.48
            Actions in state and federal court, § 18.50
            Administrative proceedings, § 18.49
            New York City Commission on Human Rights, § 18.49
            New York State Division of Human Rights (SDHR), § 18.49
            Secretary of Housing and Urban Development, § 18.49
    Publicly assisted housing, § 18.40
        Complaint, form, § 18.95
        New York City Administrative Code, § 18.41
        New York Civil Rights Law, Section 18-a, § 18.41
        New York Human Rights Law, § 18.41
        Owners and lessors, § 18.41
            Complaint, form, § 18.95
        Real estate agents and brokers, § 18.42
        Remedies, § 18.43
Immigration Reform Control Act, § 17.49
Interrogatories, § 17.72
Jury instructions, § 17.74
Jury trials, § 17.82
Letter requesting administrative convenience dismissal, form, § 17.95
Limitation of actions, §§ 17.69, 17.77
Medical or psychological examination of plaintiff, § 17.72
National origin, § 17.49
    New York State Human Rights Law, § 17.49
New York City Human Rights Law, § 17.44
New York State Equal Pay Act, § 17.44
Pregnant workers, § 17.54
Prima facie case, § 17.59
Public accommodations and amusement, equal rights in places of, § 18.54
    General provisions, § 18.55
    Private clubs, § 18.56
Racial, § 17.49
    Employment law, § 17.49
    New York State Human Rights Law,
        Bona fide occupational qualification defense, § 17.49
Rehabilitation Act, § 17.43
Sexual orientation, § 17.58
Summary judgment, § 17.73
Trials, § 17.74
Voir dire, peremptory challenges, § 18.15
Workers' compensation, § 32.36

DISMISSAL OF ACTIONS
Accusatory instruments,
    Supporting depositions,
        Failure to serve, § 33.19
            Motion to dismiss,

INDEX

DISMISSAL OF ACTIONS—Continued
Accusatory instruments—Continued
  Supporting depositions—Continued
    Failure to serve—Continued
      Motion to dismiss—Continued
        Timeliness, § 33.21
          Writing requirement, § 33.20
        Not amendable defect, § 33.25
Motions,
  Holdover proceedings, § 13.48
  Non-payment proceedings, § 13.23

DISSENTERS' RIGHTS
Conversions/Mergers,
  Limited liability companies, § 2.42
  Limited partnerships, § 2.103
  Partnerships, § 2.70

DISSOLUTION
Limited liability companies, § 2.36
  Continuation of business after dissolution event, § 2.38
  Events, § 2.37
  Winding up, § 2.39
Limited partnerships, § 2.97
  Events, § 2.98
    Continuation of business after dissolution event, § 2.99
  Winding up, § 2.100
Partnerships, § 2.64
  Continuation of business after dissolution event, § 2.66
  Events, § 2.65
  Winding up, § 2.67

DISTRIBUTIONS
Retirement income from qualified plans, § 23.33

DISTRICT COURTS
Appeals, §§ 37.109 et seq., 38.47
  Appeal as of right, § 37.112
  Appeal by permission, § 37.112
  Bankruptcy,
    To court of appeals from district court, § 9.26
    To district court and bankruptcy appellate panel from bankruptcy court, § 9.25
  Costs on appeal, § 37.115
  Courts to which appeals are taken, § 37.110
  CPLR Article 55, applicability, § 37.111
  Perfecting the appeal, § 37.114
  Return on appeal, § 37.113
  Settlement of case, § 37.113
  Small claims review, § 37.116
  Stay pending appeal,
    Appeal from district court to appellate term, § 38.54
    Notice of motion for stay of proceedings,
      Affirmation in support, form, § 37.132
      Form, § 37.130
    Order to show cause for stay of proceedings,
      Affirmation in support, form, § 37.132
      Form, § 37.131

DIVORCE
Generally, § 21.1 et seq.
Abandonment, § 21.22
  Defenses, § 21.23
  Effect of separation agreement, § 21.24
Adultery as grounds, § 21.26

INDEX

DIVORCE—Continued
Adultery as grounds—Continued
    Defenses, § 21.27
    Effect of separation agreement, § 21.28
Alimony. Spousal support, generally, post
Analysis of case, §§ 21.1, 21.2
Case management rules, § 21.79
Child Support, generally, this index
Closing statement, § 21.80
  Filing, § 21.76
Complaints, § 26.36
  Drafting, § 21.82
  Filing, § 21.11
  Form, § 21.86
Consolidation of claims, § 21.17
Conversion ground for divorce, § 21.30
Cruel and inhuman treatment, § 21.20
  Defenses, § 21.21
Defendant's appearance, form, § 21.90
Disciplinary Rules, § 21.77
Disclosure on merits, § 21.64
Discovery orders, § 21.63
Distribution of property, §§ 21.7, 21.33 et seq.
  Classification of property, § 21.36
    Marital property, § 21.37
    Professional practices, § 21.39
    Separate property, §§ 21.40, 21.41
  Compensation for personal injuries, § 21.40
  Factors for consideration, § 21.44
  Identification of property, § 21.35
  Judgments, form, § 21.90
  Jurisdiction, § 21.34
  Ordered sale of home, § 21.44
    Tax considerations, § 21.45
  Pension plans, §§ 21.35, 21.38, 21.44
  Professional practices, §§ 21.39, 21.43
  Separate property, § 21.40
    Increase in value, § 21.41
  Tax considerations, § 21.44
  Title to marital residence, § 21.44
    Tax considerations, § 21.45
  Valuation dates, § 21.42
  Valuation methods, § 21.43
Dual divorce, § 21.31
Equitable distribution, § 21.33 et seq.
Estate planning, special situations, § 24.64
  Death during divorce proceedings, § 24.64
Expert witnesses, §§ 21.63, 21.79, 21.80
  Reports, §§ 21.63, 21.79
Fee agreement with client, § 21.76
  Disputes resolved by arbitration, §§ 21.76, 21.78
Financial disclosure by parties, § 21.63
Findings of fact and conclusions of law,
  Form, § 21.89
    Referee's report, § 21.91
Foreign judgment, distribution of property, § 21.7
Forms, § 21.84 et seq.
Full faith and credit, § 21.32
Grounds, § 21.18 et seq.
  Abandonment, § 21.22
    Defenses, § 21.23
    Effect of separation agreement, § 21.24

INDEX

DIVORCE—Continued
Grounds—Continued
    Adultery, § 21.26
        Defenses, § 21.27
        Effect of separation agreement, § 21.28
    Conversion, § 21.30
    Cruel and inhuman treatment, § 21.20
        Defenses, § 21.21
    Dual divorce, § 21.31
    Imprisonment, § 21.25
    Living apart pursuant to separation decree, §§ 21.29, 21.30
Joinder of claims, § 21.17
Joint trials, § 21.17
Judgments,
    Enforcement, §§ 21.72, 21.73
        Plenary action, § 21.73
    Form, § 21.90
        USC-113, § 21.67
Jurisdiction, § 21.3 et seq.
    In rem, § 21.13
    Long arm, § 21.12
    Personal, § 21.10 et seq.
    Quasi in rem, § 21.14
Jury trials, form, § 21.90
Maiden name resumed, form, § 21.90
Maintenance. Spousal support, generally, post
Matrimonial judgments, form, § 21.90
Modification of judgments, § 21.68
No-fault, § 21.19
Notice, filing, § 21.11
Preliminary conference, §§ 21.63, 21.79, 21.80
Referee's report,
    Findings of fact and conclusions of law, form, § 21.91
    Judgment entered upon, form, § 21.92
Request for judicial intervention, § 21.80
Residence requirements, § 21.4
Retainer agreements,
    Drafting checklist, § 21.81
    Fee arbitration, § 21.75
    Form, § 21.85
    Net worth statement, §§ 21.65, 21.79, 21.80
Schedule for discovery, § 21.79
Separation agreements, § 21.69
    Abandonment as grounds for divorce, effect, § 21.24
    Adultery as grounds for divorce, effect, § 21.28
    Judgments, form, § 21.90
Service of process, § 21.11
Spousal support, §§ 21.8, 21.44
    Arrears, defenses, § 21.74
    Earning capacity of parties, §§ 21.48, 21.49
    Effect of fault, § 21.48
    Factors for consideration, § 21.47
    Form USC-113, § 21.67
    Judgments,
        Enforcement, § 21.72
        Form, § 21.90
    Lifetime support, § 21.49
    Modification of judgments, § 21.68
        Change in circumstances, § 21.69
    Motions, § 21.79
    Net worth statement, § 21.65
    Payments fixed by agreement, § 21.50

INDEX

DIVORCE—Continued
Spousal support—Continued
    Predivorce standard of living, § 21.49
    Statement of agreement, § 21.66
    Tax considerations, § 21.51
    Terminating events, § 21.50
Statement of client's rights and responsibilities, § 21.76
    Form, § 21.85
Statement of net worth, form, § 21.87
Statement of proposed disposition, §§ 21.80, 21.83
    Form, § 21.88
Strategy, § 21.2
Summons, filing, § 21.11
Tax considerations, §§ 21.44, 21.45
Trial date, § 21.80
Uncontested, judgment, § 21.67
Venue, §§ 21.15, 21.16

DO NOT RESUSCITATE ORDERS
Health care decision making, § 23.112

DOCTORS
Physicians, generally, this index

DOCUMENTS
See Particular subject concerned

DOMESTIC RELATIONS
    Generally, § 21.1 et seq.
Alimony. Spousal Support, generally, this index
Child Custody, generally, this index
Child Support, generally, this index
Divorce, generally, this index
Domestic Violence, generally, this index
Marriages, generally, this index
Spousal Support, generally, this index

DOMESTIC VIOLENCE
Child custody cases, § 21.58

DOUBLE JEOPARDY
Accusatory instruments, supporting depositions,
    Re-filing of information upon dismissal of supporting deposition, § 33.24

DRUG STORES
License to sell beer and wine coolers, §§ 36.8, 36.10

DRUNK DRIVING
Miranda rights, custodial interrogation,
    Sobriety checkpoint stops non-custodial, § 33.51

DUE DILIGENCE
Due diligence investigation, § 6.13 et seq.
    Financial review, § 6.23
        Appraisers, § 6.28
        Asset value factor, § 6.29
        Audited statements, § 6.27
        Capitalized earnings method, § 6.29
        Cash flow method, § 6.29
        Compilation statements, § 6.27
        Financial statements, § 6.27
        Market value method, § 6.29
        Need for other professionals, § 6.28
        Records and reports,
            Buyer's records from seller's position, § 6.25

INDEX

DUE DILIGENCE—Continued
Due diligence investigation—Continued
  Financial review—Continued
    Records and reports—Continued
      Public records, § 6.26
      Seller's records from buyer's position, § 6.24
    Review statements, § 6.27
    Tax returns, § 6.30
    Valuation of business, § 6.29
  Legal review, § 6.14
    Assumed names, § 6.19
    Broker's fees, § 6.20
    Bylaws, § 6.15
    Certificate of good standing, § 6.15
    Certificate of incorporation, § 6.15
    Compliance with law, § 6.21
    Comprehensive Environmental Response, Compensation and Liability Act of 1980 (CERCLA), § 6.20
    Corporate names, § 6.19
    Customer lists and customer agreements, § 6.17
    Employment agreements, § 6.17
    Environmental issues, § 6.20
    Existing contracts, § 6.17
    Franchise agreements, § 6.17
    Good and marketable title, § 6.16
    Intellectual property rights, § 6.17
    Licenses, § 6.21
    Liens, § 6.18
    Lines of credit, § 6.17
    Litigation investigation, § 6.22
    Occupancy and use restrictions, § 6.20
    Organizational documents, § 6.15
    Ownership documents, § 6.16
    Pension and benefits contracts, § 6.17
    Permits, § 6.21
    Real estate, § 6.20
    Review of title, § 6.20
    Security interests, § 6.18
    Site inspection, § 6.20
    Supplier agreements, § 6.17
    Trade names, § 6.19
Non-corporate entities, § 2.105

DUE PROCESS
Administrative Law and Proceedings, generally, this index

DUNAWAY HEARINGS
Probable cause, § 33.27

DUTY OF GOOD FAITH AND FAIR DEALING
Insurance, § 31.17

DUTY TO DEFEND
  Generally, § 31.12
Breach of contract, § 31.14
Damages, breach of contract, § 31.14
Declaration excusing coverage, § 31.13
Disclaiming obligation to defend, § 31.13
Refusal to defend, § 31.13
Request for defense, responding to, § 31.13
Reservation of rights, §§ 31.13, 31.15

EASEMENTS
Eminent domain,

INDEX

EASEMENTS—Continued
  Eminent domain—Continued
    Just compensation, § 14.84
    Property rights subject to acquisition, § 14.9
  Real property, marketability of title,
    Driveway easements, effect, § 12.68
    Encroachments due to adverse possession, § 12.66

EISEP
  Home care coverage, § 23.87

ELDER LAW
  Generally, § 23.1 et seq.
  Consultation letter, forms, § 23.124
  Documentation letter, forms, § 23.123
  Ethical Considerations, this index
  Federal employees benefits, § 23.37
    Appeals, § 23.40
    Civil Service Retirement Act, § 23.39
    Federal employees retirement system, § 23.38
  Forms, § 23.122 et seq.
  Health care proxy statutory form, § 23.125
  Medicare, generally, this index
  Miscellaneous programs, § 23.119
    Elderly pharmaceutical insurance coverage program (EPIC), § 23.120
    Life line telephone service, § 23.121
  Railroad retirement benefits, § 23.36
  Retirement income from qualified plans, § 23.24
    Alienation and assignment, § 23.28
    Appeals, § 23.35
    Contribution limits, § 23.26
    Distributions, § 23.33
    Eligibility, vesting and accrual, § 23.25
    Employee Retirement Income Security Act (ERISA), § 23.24
    Payment of benefits, § 23.27
    Qualified domestic relations orders, § 23.30
    Spousal rights, § 23.29
      Waiver, § 23.31
    Taxation of contributions, § 23.32
    Termination or merger, § 23.34
    Waiver of spousal rights, § 23.31
  Scope, § 23.1
  Social security benefits, § 23.7
    Administrative and judicial appeals, § 23.15
    Calculation of benefits, § 23.10
    Insured status, § 23.9
    Overpayments and underpayments, § 23.14
    Quarters of coverage, § 23.8
    Reduction in benefits, earned income, § 23.13
    Representation by attorneys, § 23.16
    Retirement benefits, § 23.11
    Spouse, survivor and dependents benefits, § 23.12
  Strategy, § 23.2
  Supplemental security income for the elderly, § 23.17
    Administrative and judicial appeals, § 23.22
    Benefit calculation, § 23.20
    Categorical eligibility, § 23.18
    Financial eligibility, § 23.19
    Representation by attorneys, § 23.23
    Underpayments and overpayments, § 23.21
  Taxation, generally, this index
  Veterans' benefits, § 23.41

INDEX

ELDERLY PHARMACEUTICAL INSURANCE COVERAGE (EPIC)
Miscellaneous programs, elder law, § 23.120

ELECTRONIC COMMUNICATIONS PRIVACY ACT
  Generally, § 17.55

ELEVATORS
Public accommodations and amusement, equal rights in places of, § 18.54

EMINENT DOMAIN
  Generally, § 14.1 et seq.
Acquisition, § 14.47 et seq.
  Acquisition map, § 14.51
    Order to show cause, form, § 14.130
  Claim for damages, general form, § 14.133
  Immediate entry, § 14.67
    Order to show cause, form, § 14.129
  Judgment awarding compensation, form, § 14.134
  Jurisdiction, generally, post
  Limitation of actions, § 14.49
    Stages, § 14.50
  Notice of acquisition, § 14.66
  Summary, § 14.68
Appeals, § 14.2
Attorneys, role, § 14.2
Condemnation, § 14.20 et seq.
De facto taking, § 14.14
Exercise of power of eminent domain, § 14.3 et seq.
  Other public entities as condemnor, § 14.5
  Private entities, § 14.6
  State as condemnor, § 14.4
  Summary, § 14.19
Jurisdiction,
  Court of claims, §§ 14.48, 14.52
    Exclusive jurisdiction, § 14.53
    Filing, § 14.54
    Notice, § 14.54
    Vesting of title, § 14.55
  Supreme court, §§ 14.48, 14.56
    Answer by condemnee, § 14.63
      Defenses, § 14.64
    Answer, form, § 14.128
    Notice, § 14.61
      Acquisition, form, § 14.132
      Certification of names of reputed condemnees, § 14.62
      Pendency of proceedings, § 14.57
        Form, § 14.124
      Petition in proceedings, form, § 14.125
    Order, form, § 14.131
    Order of condemnation, § 14.65
    Petition in condemnation, § 14.58
      Content, § 14.59
      Non-governmental condemnors, content rules, § 14.60
    Petition in proceedings, form, § 14.126
      Petitioner exempt from compliance with Eminent Domain Procedure Law, § 14.127
    Vesting of title, § 14.65
Just compensation, §§ 14.18, 14.69 et seq.
  Abandonment of procedure by condemnor, § 14.111
  Additional costs and expenses, § 14.115
  Condemnor claiming no taking, finding contrary to claim, § 14.113
  Condemnor not legally authorized to acquire property, § 14.112
  Conflicting claims by condemnees, § 14.99 et seq.

INDEX

EMINENT DOMAIN—Continued
Just compensation—Continued
  Conflicting claims by condemnees—Continued
    Award, § 14.101
    Condemnor's offer, § 14.100
  Content of claim, § 14.76
  Court of claims, § 14.70
    Jurisdiction, ante
    Service of process, § 14.72
    Time to file claim, § 14.71
  Court's decision, § 14.114
  Entry of judgment, § 14.114
  Fixtures, § 14.91
    Compensable fixtures, § 14.92
    Valuation, § 14.93
  Going concern value, § 14.97
  "Highest and best use", § 14.78
  Incidental expenses, § 14.110
  Judgment awarding compensation, form, § 14.134
  Leasehold interests, §§ 14.94, 14.95
  Loss of business and goodwill, § 14.96
  Moving and relocation expenses, § 14.98
  Partial taking, § 14.82
    "Before and after" rule, § 14.82
    Consequential damages, § 14.82
  Payment pending appeal, § 14.116
  Proration of taxes, § 14.110
  Scope, § 14.77
  Setoff for indirect benefits, § 14.109
  Small claims proceedings, § 14.117
  Summary, § 14.118
  Supreme court, § 14.73
    Service of process, § 14.75
    Time to file claim, § 14.74
  Temporary taking, § 14.83
    Complaint by condemnee to establish value for temporary use, form, § 14.123
    Easements, § 14.84
  Total taking, § 14.79
    Direct damages, § 14.80
    Improvements, § 14.81
  Trial, § 14.102 et seq.
    Appraisals, filing and exchange of, § 14.104
    Expert witnesses, § 14.105
      Affidavit in support of motion for additional allowance to condemnee for expert witnesses, form, § 14.136
      Notice of motion for additional allowance to condemnee for expert witnesses, form, § 14.135
      Order granting additional allowance to condemnee for expert witnesses, form, § 14.137
    Interest, § 14.108
    Joint or consolidated trials, § 14.107
    Preference, § 14.103
    Viewing the property, § 14.106
  Valuation, § 14.85
    Cost approach, § 14.88
    Environmental contamination, effect, § 14.90
    Fixtures, § 14.93
    Going concern, § 14.97
    Income approach, § 14.87
    Leasehold interests, §§ 14.94, 14.95
    Market approach, § 14.86
    "Replacement cost less depreciation" approach, § 14.88

INDEX

EMINENT DOMAIN—Continued
Just compensation—Continued
    Valuation—Continued
        Specialty property, § 14.89
    Offer and negotiation, § 14.40 et seq.
        Advance payment, § 14.44
        Offer as payment in full, § 14.43
        Pretaking appraisals, § 14.41
        Pretaking discovery, § 14.42
        Summary, § 14.46
        Use and occupancy by condemnee after taking, § 14.45
Procedural checklist, § 14.119
Property rights subject to acquisition, § 14.7 et seq.
    Easements, § 14.9
    Excess property, § 14.13
    Leases, § 14.10
    Personal property, § 14.11
    Priority of taking, § 14.12
    Public property, § 14.12
    Real property, § 14.8
Public hearing, § 14.21
    Conduct of hearing, § 14.29
    Determination and findings, § 14.30
        Amendments for field conditions, § 14.33
        Interplay with SEQRA, § 14.32
        Judicial review, § 14.34
            Limitation of actions, § 14.37
            Persons entitled to review, § 14.36
            Prerequisite determination, § 14.35
            Scope of review, § 14.38
        Publication of synopsis, § 14.31
    Exemptions, § 14.22
        Alternate public hearing, § 14.25
        De minimus acquisition or emergency situation, § 14.26
        Mental Hygiene Law, section 41.34, § 14.27
        Overlap with issuance of certificate of environmental compatibility and public need, § 14.24
        Overlap with other governmental requirements, § 14.23
    Notice, § 14.28
    Record, § 14.29
    Summary, § 14.39
Public use, benefit or purpose, § 14.15 et seq.
    Demand on condemnor to file proceedings to determine need and location of public project with appellate division, form, § 14.120
    Incidental private benefit, § 14.17
    Judgment of appellate division rejecting determination and finding, form, § 14.122
    Particular uses, § 14.16
    Petition for review, form, § 14.121
Scope, § 14.1
Strategy, § 14.2
Use and occupancy by condemnee after taking, § 14.45

EMPLOYEE POLYGRAPH PROTECTION ACT
    Generally, § 17.52
Antireprisal provisions, § 17.38

EMPLOYEE RETIREMENT INCOME SECURITY ACT (ERISA)
Antireprisal provisions, § 17.38
Complaints, filing requirements, § 17.50
Elder law, retirement income from qualified plans, § 23.24
    Termination and merger, § 23.34
Limitation of actions, checklist, § 17.77
Pension plan protection, § 17.50

INDEX

EMPLOYERS
Disability Benefits Law,
    Employers' obligations, § 32.45
Social security disability cases, handling,
    Former employers,
        Evidence from, § 34.39
Workers' compensation,
    Attending doctor's report and carrier/employer billing form, § 32.56
    Employer's obligations and methods of coverage, § 32.12
    Employer's report of work-related accident/occupational disease, form, § 32.55
    Uninsured employers' fund, § 32.40

EMPLOYMENT LAW
Absenteeism, § 17.81
Affirmative defenses, § 17.83
Age discrimination,
    Provisions of statute, § 17.37
Alternative dispute resolution (ADR), § 17.1
    Negotiation, § 17.7
Answers to complaints, § 17.85
Anti-nepotism rules, § 17.48
Antireprisal provisions, § 17.38
Arbitration, § 17.9
Bankruptcy,
    Denial of job or entitlements, § 17.40
Battery, § 17.22
Benefits, § 17.81
Civil assault, § 17.21
Civil Rights Act, § 17.49
Civil service employees,
    Due process requirements, § 17.53
COBRA,
    Rights to health insurance, §§ 17.12, 17.46
Collective bargaining, § 17.53
Complaints,
    Answers, form, §§ 17.97, 17.99
    Drafting, § 17.83
    Jury trial demand, form, § 17.98
Contract of employment, §§ 17.33, 17.34
    Implied contracts, § 17.35
    Promissory estoppel, § 17.36
    Small business, purchase or sale,
        Due diligence investigation, legal review, § 6.17
Counterclaims, § 17.83
Denial of job or entitlements,
    Arrest record, § 17.39
    Credit reports, § 17.42
    Criminal record of employee, § 17.41
Discharge of employee, § 17.1
    Attorney fees, § 17.16
    Civil service employees, § 17.53
    Complaint, form, § 17.96
    Confidentiality, § 17.16
    Consulting agreement, § 17.16
    Contractual basis for job security, § 17.33
    Conversion charges, § 17.24
    Defamation, § 17.25
    Document review by attorney, § 17.19
    Exit incentives, waiver of rights, § 17.11
    False imprisonment, § 17.26
    Future cooperation, § 17.16
    Intentional infliction of emotional harm, § 17.28
    Intentional interference with contractual relations, § 17.29

INDEX

EMPLOYMENT LAW—Continued
Discharge of employee—Continued
    Leave pay, § 17.13
    Letter of reference, § 17.16
    Lump sum payments, § 17.13
    Malicious prosecution, § 17.26
    Negotiation, § 17.10
    Non-competition covenants, § 17.16
    Offsets against wages, § 17.13
    Outplacement services, § 17.16
    Personal property and perquisites, § 17.16
    Prima facie tort, § 17.31
    Prohibitions on re-applying for employment, § 17.16
    Rights under COBRA to health insurance, §§ 17.12, 17.46
    Salary continuation, § 17.13
    Severance packages, § 17.10
    Severance pay,
        Effect on benefits, § 17.15
        Releases and waivers, § 17.16
        Tax considerations, § 17.14
        Termination, § 17.13
    Unemployment insurance, § 17.16
    Wrongful discharge, § 17.32
Discrimination,
    Alienage or citizenship status, § 17.49
    Alternate dispute resolution (ADR), § 17.7
    Americans with Disabilities Act, § 17.43
    Antireprisal provisions, § 17.59
    Appeals, § 17.76
    Attorney fees, § 17.75
    Burden of proof, § 17.59
    Class actions, § 17.59
    Complaint, form, § 17.89
    Defenses, § 17.59
    Depositions, § 17.72
    Disparate impact cause of action, § 17.59
    Document production, § 17.71
    Document request, § 17.72
    Equal Employment Opportunity Commission,
        Charge of discrimination, form, §§ 17.92, 17.93
    Equal Pay Act, § 17.44
    Fetal protection policies, § 17.54
    Interrogatories, § 17.72
    Letter requesting administrative convenience dismissal, form, § 17.95
    Letter requesting dual-filed charge, form, § 17.94
    Limitation of actions, § 17.69
    Marital status, § 17.48
    Medical or psychological examination of plaintiff, § 17.72
    New York City Human Rights Law, §§ 17.43, 17.44, 17.49
    New York State Equal Pay Act, § 17.44
    New York State Human Rights Law, §§ 17.43, 17.49
    Off duty conduct, § 17.47
    Pre-trial preparation, § 17.70
    Pregnancy, § 17.54
    Prima facie case, § 17.59
    Rehabilitation Act, § 17.43
    Religion, § 17.56
    Sexual orientation, § 17.58
    Summary judgment, § 17.73
    Trials, § 17.74
    Unionization, § 17.61
Drug testing, § 17.55

INDEX

EMPLOYMENT LAW—Continued
Educational assistance, § 17.81
Electronic eavesdropping, § 17.55
Employment-at-will doctrine, § 17.33
    Limitations, § 17.34
Employment law, reduction in force, § 17.10
ERISA protection, § 17.50
Family and Medical Leave Act,
    Rights of employee, § 17.45
Family medical leave, § 17.81
Fetal protection policies, § 17.54
Fraudulent inducement, § 17.27
Glass ceiling review,
    Office of Federal Contract Compliance Programs, § 17.80
Handbooks, §§ 17.34, 17.81
Immigration Reform Control Act, § 17.49
Independent contractors,
    Determination, § 17.17
Intentional interference with contractual relations, § 17.29
Jury duty, § 17.81
Lawsuits,
    Client intake questionnaire, § 17.3
    Conflict of interest, § 17.4
    Conspiracy, § 17.23
    Determinations, § 17.18
    Document review, § 17.3
    Interview with client, §§ 17.2, 17.3
    Multiple representation, § 17.4
    Strategy, § 17.20
Management policies, handbooks, § 17.81
Mediation, § 17.8
Negligence, § 17.30
Negotiations, pre-litigation, § 17.6
Older Workers Benefit Protection Act, strict waiver requirements of rights, § 17.11
Pension plans, § 17.81
Personnel decisions, § 17.81
Plaintiff intake questionnaire, form, § 17.86
Polygraph protection, § 17.52
Privacy rights, § 17.55
Racial discrimination, § 17.49
Releases, form, § 17.87
Religious discrimination, § 17.56
Reporting violations, antireprisal provisions, § 17.38
Search and seizure, state employees, § 17.55
Settlement, pre-litigation, §§ 17.5, 17.6
Severance agreement, form, § 17.87
Sexual harassment, § 17.21
    Hostile work environment, § 17.57
    Intentional infliction of emotional harm, § 17.28
    Quid pro quo, § 17.57
Smoking policies, § 17.81
Taylor Law, § 17.53
Unemployment insurance, denial of benefits, § 17.60
Unfair labor practices, § 17.61
Unionization, § 17.61
Unsafe workplaces, § 17.62
Vacation policies, § 17.81
Wages and hours, §§ 17.63, 17.81
Whistleblower protection law, § 17.64
Worker Adjustment and Retraining Notification Act, § 17.51
Workers' compensation, § 17.65
Wrongful discharge, § 17.32

INDEX

ENERGY REORGANIZATION ACT
    Antireprisal provisions, § 17.38

ENFORCEMENT OF MONEY JUDGMENTS
    Generally, § 8.1 et seq.
    Actions on judgments, § 8.15
    Adverse claims, determination, § 8.45
    Amendment of judgment, § 8.14
    Arrest of judgment debtor, § 8.43
    Article 52 enforcement devices, § 8.24
        Arrest of judgment debtor, § 8.43
        Execution, generally, post
        Installment payment order,
            Application, § 8.36
            Nature and purpose, § 8.35
            Service, § 8.36
        Receiver, § 8.37
            Application, § 8.38
            Appointment, § 8.38
            Extension, § 8.38
        Restraining notices, generally, post
        Turnover orders for property or debts, § 8.39
            Garnishee, against, § 8.41
                Special proceedings, § 8.41
            Judgment debtor, against, § 8.40
    Assignment, § 8.12
    Breach of contract, interest, § 8.6
    Confession of judgment, § 8.4
        Affidavit of confession, form, § 8.48
    Contempt proceedings, § 8.42
        Affirmation order to show cause to punish judgment debtor or witness for contempt, form, § 8.56
        Restraining notices, § 8.27
        Subpoenas, § 8.23
    Correction of judgment, § 8.14
    Death of judgment debtor, § 8.13
    Default judgment, § 8.4
        Affidavit of facts constituting claim, form, § 8.47
        Default and amount due, form, § 8.47
        Statement for judgment, form, § 8.47
    Definitions, § 8.3
    Execution, § 8.28
        Fees, § 8.28
        Form, § 8.54
        Income execution, § 8.34
            Form, § 8.55
        Issuance, § 8.28
        Personal property, § 8.29
            Distribution of property, § 8.30
            Priority in proceeds, § 8.30
            Sale of property, § 8.30
        Real property, § 8.31
            Conveyance of title, § 8.33
            Distribution of proceeds, § 8.33
            Lien gap, § 8.31
            Notice of sale, § 8.32
    Failure to cure under stipulation, § 8.4
    Final judgment, § 8.3
    Foreign judgments,
        Federal court judgments, § 8.17
        Foreign country judgments, § 8.18
        Full faith and credit, § 8.16
        Sister-state judgments, § 8.16

INDEX

ENFORCEMENT OF MONEY JUDGMENTS—Continued
Foreign judgments—Continued
    Uniform Enforcement of Foreign Judgments Act, § 8.16
Form of judgment,
    Attorney fees, § 8.7
    Costs, § 8.7
    Disbursements, § 8.7
    Entry, § 8.8
    Fees, § 8.7
    Interest, § 8.6
    Judgment-roll, § 8.5
    Taxation of costs by clerk, § 8.7
    Transcript of judgment, § 8.9
Forms, § 8.46 et seq.
Installment payment order,
    Application, § 8.36
    Nature and purpose, § 8.35
    Service, § 8.36
Interest, § 8.6
Judgments after trial, § 8.4
Methods of obtaining judgment, § 8.4
Notice to judgment debtor, form, § 8.49
Post-verdict discovery, § 8.2
Preliminary investigations, § 8.2
Property, enforcement against,
    Definitions, § 8.19
    Disclosure of property, § 8.22
        Subpoenas, § 8.23
    Exemptions, § 8.20
    Garnishees, § 8.21
    Homestead exemption, § 8.20
    Property in possession of others, § 8.21
    Subpoenas, § 8.23
        Contempt proceedings, § 8.23
        Duces tecum, § 8.23
        Information subpoenas, § 8.23
            Form, § 8.52
        Testimonial examination, § 8.23
Protective orders, § 8.44
Receiver, extension, § 8.38
Res judicata, § 8.3
Restraining notices,
    Contempt proceedings, § 8.27
    Disobedience of, § 8.27
    Form, § 8.53
    Formal requirements, § 8.26
    Nature and use, § 8.25
    Service of, §§ 8.2, 8.27
Satisfaction of judgment, §§ 8.2, 8.11
Scope, § 8.1
Strategy, § 8.2
Subpoenas, § 8.2
    Subpoena duces tecum to take deposition of judgment debtor with restraining notice, form, § 8.50
    Subpoena duces tecum to take deposition of witness with restraining notice, form, § 8.51
Summary judgment, § 8.4
Turnover orders for property or debts, § 8.39
    Garnishee, against, § 8.41
        Special proceedings, § 8.41
    Judgment debtor, against, § 8.40
Vacatur, § 8.10

INDEX

ENVIRONMENTAL LAW
  Generally, § 15.1 et seq.
Above-ground storage tanks (AST),
  Federal law, § 15.26
  New York law, § 15.27
Air pollution control, § 15.19 et seq.
  Citizen suits, § 15.22
  Clean Air Act (CAA), § 15.19
    1990 CAA amendments, § 15.20
  Enforcement, § 15.22
  Injunctive relief, § 15.22
  National ambient air quality standards (NAAQS), § 15.19
  National emissions standards for hazardous air pollutants (NESHAPS), § 15.21
  New source performance standards (NSPS), § 15.19
  New York state requirements, § 15.21
Clean Water Act (CWA), § 15.8 et seq.
  Citizen suits, § 15.11
    Checklist, § 15.12
    Notice letter,
      Drafting checklist, § 15.35
        Resource Conservation and Recovery Act (RCRA), § 15.36
      Form, § 15.40
        Resource Conservation and Recovery Act (RCRA), § 15.41
  Complaint,
    Drafting checklist, § 15.37
    Form, § 15.42
  Enforcement, § 15.11
  Injunctive relief, § 15.11
  National pollutant discharge elimination system (NPDES), § 15.8
  Oil spills, § 15.10
    Complaint,
      Drafting checklist, § 15.39
      Form, § 15.44
  Point source, § 15.8
  State pollution discharge elimination system (SPDES), § 15.8
    "Anti-backsliding" provision, § 15.9
    Permit program, § 15.9
  Storm water discharges, § 15.10
Common law,
  Nuisance, § 15.32
    Complaint,
      Drafting checklist, § 15.38
      Form, § 15.43
    Injunctive relief, § 15.32
  Trespass, § 15.33
    Complaint,
      Drafting checklist, § 15.38
      Form, § 15.43
Hazardous waste regulation, § 15.23 et seq.
  Citizen suits, § 15.25
  Comprehensive Environmental Response, Compensation and Liability Act (CERCLA), § 15.25
  Enforcement, § 15.25
  Inactive hazardous waste sites, § 15.28 et seq.
    Comprehensive Environmental Response, Compensation and Liability Act (CERCLA), § 15.28
      Contribution, § 15.30
      Indemnification, § 15.30
      Innocent landowner exception, § 15.29
      Lender liability, § 15.30
      Section 107(a), § 15.29
      Strict liability, § 15.29

INDEX

ENVIRONMENTAL LAW—Continued
Hazardous waste regulation—Continued
    Inactive hazardous waste sites—Continued
        Comprehensive Environmental Response—Continued
            Third party defense, § 15.29
            Hazardous substance trust fund, § 15.28
            Interim remedial measures (IRMs), § 15.31
            New York Environmental Conservation Law (ECL), § 15.31
            Record of decision (ROD), § 15.31
            Remedial investigation and feasibility study (RI/FS), § 15.31
        Injunctive relief, § 15.25
        Materials recycling facilities (MRFs), § 15.23
        New York hazardous waste regulation, § 15.24
        New York State Environmental Conservation Law, § 15.23
        Resource Conservation and Recovery Act (RCRA), § 15.23
        Small quantity generators, § 15.24
        Treatment, storage and disposal facilities (TSDFs), § 15.24
    Petroleum storage tanks,
        Federal law, § 15.26
        Major onshore facilities (MOSFs), § 15.27
            Spill prevention control and countermeasure plan (SPCC plan), § 15.27
        New York law, § 15.27
        State Navigation Law, § 15.27
Regulatory takings, § 15.34
Scope, § 15.1
Solid waste regulation, § 15.23 et seq.
    Citizen suits, § 15.25
    Comprehensive Environmental Response, Compensation and Liability Act (CERCLA), § 15.25
    Enforcement, § 15.25
    Injunctive relief, § 15.25
    Materials recycling facilities (MRFs), § 15.23
    New York State Environmental Conservation Law, § 15.23
    Resource Conservation and Recovery Act (RCRA), § 15.23
State Environmental Quality Review Act (SEQRA), § 15.3 et seq.
    Checklist, § 15.7
    Determination of significance, § 15.4
    Environmental assessment form (EAF), § 15.4
        Long form, § 16.134
        Short form, § 16.133
    Environmental impact statements (EIS), §§ 15.4, 15.5
        Local land use law, § 16.52
    Findings statement, § 15.5
    Judicial review, § 15.6
    Limitation of actions, § 15.6
    Local land use law,
        Actions subject to SEQRA, § 16.53
            Building permits, § 16.54
            Rezoning, § 16.58
            Site plans, § 16.57
            Subdivisions, § 16.56
            Variances, § 16.55
        Environmental impact statements (EIS), § 16.52
    Rule of reason, § 15.6
    Type I actions, § 15.4
    Type II actions, § 15.4
Strategy, § 15.2
Underground storage tanks (UST),
    Federal law, § 15.26
    New York law, § 15.27
Wetlands protection, § 15.13 et seq.
    Federal scheme, § 15.15

INDEX

ENVIRONMENTAL LAW—Continued
Wetlands protection—Continued
    Freshwater wetlands, § 15.16
    New York Coastal Zone Management Program, § 15.15
    Penalties, § 15.18
    Permit procedure and criteria, § 15.17
    Strategy, checklist, § 15.14
    Tidal wetlands, § 15.16

EPIC
Elder law, miscellaneous programs, § 23.120

EQUAL EMPLOYMENT OPPORTUNITY COMMISSION
Charge of discrimination,
    Affidavit, form, § 17.93
    Form, § 17.92
    Letter requesting dual-filed charge, form, § 17.94
Filing charges, § 17.66
    Responses, § 17.67
Letter requesting "Mohasco" waiver, form, § 17.88
Right to sue letter, § 17.67

EQUAL PAY ACT
Antireprisal provisions, § 17.38
Employment law, prohibitions against discrimination, § 17.44

ERISA
Antireprisal provisions, § 17.38
Complaints, filing requirements, § 17.50
Limitation of actions, checklist, § 17.77
Pension plan protection, § 17.50

ESCROW
Personal injury,
    Retainer, escrow account, § 26.6
Private adoptions, § 20.2
Small business, purchase or sale,
    Structuring buyer's transaction, § 6.51
    Structuring seller's transaction, § 6.138

ESTATE ADMINISTRATION
Probate and Estate Administration, generally, this index

ESTATE PLANNING
    Generally, § 24.1 et seq.
Advance directives, § 24.90
    Health care proxies, § 24.91
Charitable bequests, § 24.32
Checklist, § 24.97
Client questionnaire, forms, § 24.99
Crummey powers,
    Life insurance trusts, planning with certain assets, § 24.36
    Notice, forms, § 24.101
Durable power of attorney, form, § 24.100
Ethical Considerations, this index
Forms, § 24.96 et seq.
Formula clauses, § 24.23
Health care proxies, § 24.91
Lifetime Planning, generally, this index
Marital deduction, utilizing, § 24.22
Planning with certain assets, § 24.33
    Business real property, § 24.42
    Closely held business interests, § 24.38
        Buy-sell agreements, § 24.39
        Liquidity issues, § 24.40

INDEX

ESTATE PLANNING—Continued
Planning with certain assets—Continued
    Closely held business interests—Continued
        Minority discounts, § 24.41
    Farms, § 24.42
    Installment obligations, § 24.43
    Life insurance, § 24.34
        Trusts, § 24.35
            Crummey powers, § 24.36
    Retirement benefits, § 24.37
Postmortem Planning, generally, this index
Powers of attorney, § 24.89
Sample information request letter, forms, § 24.98
Scope, § 24.1
Special situations,
    Divorce, § 24.64
        Death during divorce proceedings, § 24.65
    Multiple marriages, § 24.59
        Long term care, § 24.62
        Spousal rights, § 24.60
            Joint wills and contracts to make wills, § 24.61
    Non-citizen spouses, § 24.58
    Separation, § 24.63
    Terminally ill, § 24.56
        Self-cancelling installment notes, § 24.57
    Unmarried couples, § 24.66
Spousal conflicts letter, forms, § 24.102
Strategy, § 24.2
Taxes,
    Federal estate taxes, § 24.18
        Marital deduction, utilizing, § 24.22
        Rates, § 24.19
        Unified credit, utilizing, § 24.21
    State estate taxes,
        Rates, § 24.20
Unified credit, utilizing, § 24.21
Wills, generally, this index

ESTATE TAXES, FEDERAL
    Generally, § 24.18
Marital deduction, utilizing, § 24.22
Rates, § 24.19
Unified credit, utilizing, § 24.21

ESTATE TAXES, STATE
    Generally, § 24.20
Rates, § 24.20

ESTATES
Administration. Probate and Estate Administration, generally, this index
Federal Taxes. Estate Taxes, Federal, generally, this index
Planning. Estate Planning, generally, this index
Recoveries against estates,
    Medicaid, § 23.81
State Taxes. Estate Taxes, State, generally, this index

ESTOPPEL
Employment law, contracts, § 17.36
Legal malpractice defense, § 28.15

ETHICAL CONSIDERATIONS
Elder law, § 23.3
    Confidentiality, § 23.5
    Conflict of interest, § 23.4

INDEX

ETHICAL CONSIDERATIONS—Continued
Elder law—Continued
   Diminished capacity, § 23.6
   Identifying client, § 23.4
   Multiple representation, § 23.4
Estate planning, § 24.93
   Attorney/draftsman as fiduciary or beneficiary, § 24.95
   Multiple clients, § 24.94
   Putnam hearing, § 24.95
Municipal corporations, code of ethics, § 3.22
Personal injury cases,
   Skills of attorney, § 26.5
Putnam hearing,
   Estate planning, attorney/draftsman as fiduciary or beneficiary, § 24.95

EVIDENCE
   Generally, § 33.42 et seq.
Adjudicatory proceedings,
   Administrative law, § 4.15
Discrimination cases, § 17.74
Exculpatory evidence,
   Pretrial discovery, § 33.39 et seq.
     Prosecutor need not be aware of evidence, § 33.40
     Timely disclosure, § 33.41
Guardianships, hearing and order, § 22.33
Involuntary statements, § 33.57 et seq.
   Harmless error doctrine, § 33.59
   Huntley hearings, § 33.57
   Use to impeach prohibited, § 33.58
Miranda rights, § 33.48 et seq.
   Custodial interrogation,
     Interrogation defined, § 33.52
     Sobriety checkpoint stops non-custodial, § 33.51
     Stop and frisk not constituting, § 33.50
   Misdemeanor traffic offenses, § 33.49
   Pedigree exception, § 33.54
   Public safety exception, § 33.53
   Waiver,
     Following assertion of right to remain silent, § 33.55
Motion to suppress, § 33.43
   Appeal by the people, § 38.10
Personal injury trials, §§ 26.54, 26.55
Prior convictions, § 33.44 et seq.
   Criteria, § 33.46
   Defendant's presence at hearing, § 33.47
   Procedure, § 33.45
Products liability,
   Sufficiency, § 27.35
   Weight of evidence, § 27.35
Sandoval issues, § 33.44 et seq.
   Criteria, § 33.46
   Defendant's presence at hearing, § 33.47
   Procedure, § 33.45
Social security disability cases. Disability cases, generally. Social Security, this index
Sufficiency of evidence,
   Appellate division,
     Civil, § 38.65
     Criminal, scope of review, § 38.19
Weight of evidence,
   Appellate division, criminal,
     Scope of review, § 38.20

INDEX

EXCISE TAX
Alcoholic beverages, § 36.44

EXECUTORS
Commissions, waiving,
 Postmortem planning, § 24.79
Estate Planning, generally, this index
Probate and estate administration,
 Citation to show cause why executor should not account,
  Forms, § 25.65
 Compensation, § 25.46
 Declining to serve as, § 25.48
 Petition to judicially settle executor's account,
  Forms, § 25.64
Wills,
 Appointment provisions, § 24.15

EXHIBITS
Personal injury trials, § 26.54

EXPANDED IN-HOME SERVICES FOR THE ELDERLY PROGRAM (EISEP)
Home care coverage, § 23.87

EXPERT WITNESSES
Discrimination cases, § 17.74
Divorce cases, §§ 21.63, 21.79, 21.80
Eminent domain,
 Just compensation trial, § 14.105
  Affidavit in support of motion for additional allowance to condemnee for expert witnesses, form, § 14.136
  Notice of motion for additional allowance to condemnee for expert witnesses, form, § 14.135
  Order granting additional allowance to condemnee for expert witnesses, form, § 14.137
Legal malpractice cases, § 28.3
Medical malpractice, § 26.11
 Discovery, § 26.42
  Form, § 26.68
 Medical literature, § 29.43 et seq.
 Standard of care, § 29.16
Motor vehicle accidents, discovery, form, § 26.70
Personal injury cases,
 Discovery, § 26.42
  Form, § 26.68
Products liability,
 Causation, § 27.35
 "General acceptance" standard rejected, § 27.35
 "Helpfulness" standard, § 27.35

FAIR CREDIT REPORTING ACT
Consumer protection, § 7.31
Motor vehicle sales, § 7.3

FAIR DEBT COLLECTION PRACTICES ACT
Attorney fees, § 7.48
Collection agencies, §§ 7.3, 7.36
 Compliance, § 7.6
 Limitations, § 7.37
Complaint, attorney fees, § 7.62
False or misleading representations, §§ 7.39, 7.48
Limitation of actions, § 7.48
Motor vehicle sales, § 7.3
Prohibited activities, § 7.38

INDEX

FAIR LABOR STANDARDS ACT
Antireprisal provisions, § 17.38
Child labor, § 17.63
Claims under, § 17.63
Minimum wages, § 17.63
Overtime pay, § 17.63

FALSE ADVERTISING
Motor vehicle sales, § 7.3
    Attorney fees, § 7.7

FALSE CLAIMS ACT
Antireprisal provisions, § 17.38

FALSE IMPRISONMENT
Employment cases,
    Discharge of employee, § 17.26
Limitation of actions, § 17.77

FAMILY AND MEDICAL LEAVE ACT
Antireprisal provisions, § 17.38
Employment law, rights of employee, § 17.45

FAMILY COURT
Adoptions, jurisdiction, § 20.9
Appellate division, civil appellate practice before,
    Appeals as of right or by permission, § 37.19
    Appeals from criminal court transfer orders, § 37.19
    Appeals from various family court proceedings, § 37.19
    Appeals to appellate division from orders and judgments, generally, § 37.19
    Appellate counsel, advisements, § 37.19
    Applicability of CPLR to appeals, § 37.19
    Assignment of counsel, indigency, § 37.19
    Attorney fees on appeal, § 37.19
    Constitutional basis, § 37.3
    Family Court Act governing practice, § 37.3
    Filiation order, § 37.19
    Finality, § 37.19
    Jurisdiction, § 37.19
    Juvenile delinquency proceedings, § 37.19
    Law guardian program, § 37.8
    Law guardians, on appeal, § 37.19
    Papers on appeal, § 37.19
    Preferences in appeals, § 37.19
    Presentment agency, appeal by, § 37.19
    Stays of appeal, § 37.19
    Support proceedings, § 37.19
    Timeliness, notice, and service provisions for appeals, § 37.19
Change of venue,
    Criminal court to family court, § 38.8
    Family court to criminal court, § 38.8
Divorce, generally, this index
Stays,
    Appellate division, civil,
        Appeals to, § 37.19
    Notice of motion for stay of proceedings,
        Affirmation in support, form, § 37.132
        Form, § 37.130
    Order to show cause for stay of proceedings,
        Affirmation in support, form, § 37.132
        Form, § 37.131

FAMILY COURT ACT
Jurisdiction, § 21.7 et seq.

INDEX

FARMS
Estate planning with certain assets, § 24.42

FEDERAL EMPLOYEES RETIREMENT SYSTEM
Elder law, § 23.38

FEDERAL FALSE CLAIMS ACT
Qui tam provisions, § 17.64
Whistleblower protection, § 17.64

FEDERAL INSECTICIDE, FUNGICIDE AND RODENTICIDE ACT (FIFRA)
Products liability, preemption or private claims, § 27.47

FEDERAL MINE SAFETY AND HEALTH ACT
Antireprisal provisions, § 17.38

FEDERAL ODOMETER ACT
Motor vehicle sales, § 7.3

FEDERAL RAILROAD SAFETY ACT
Antireprisal provisions, § 17.38

FEDERAL RESERVE BOARD
Consumer protection, § 7.2

FEDERAL TRADE COMMISSION
Consumer protection, powers and duties, § 7.2

FEDERAL WATER POLLUTION CONTROL ACT
Antireprisal provisions, § 17.38

FEES
Alcoholic beverage control,
    Licenses,
        Application, form, § 36.73
        Retail licenses, § 36.42
            Schedule, form, § 36.73
    Permits, § 36.42
Attorney Fees, generally, this index
Bankruptcy,
    Chapter 7, § 9.179
    Professionals, employment of, fee applications, § 9.31
Broker's fees,
    Small business, purchase or sale,
        Due diligence investigation, legal review, § 6.20
Corporations,
    Filing fees, certificate of incorporation, § 1.21
    Formation, § 1.7
Enforcement of money judgments, § 8.7
    Execution, § 8.28
Fee disputes,
    Alternative dispute resolution (ADR), § 28.28 et seq.
    Arbitration,
        Legal malpractice cases, § 28.30
        Matrimonial cases, §§ 21.76, 21.78
Filing fees,
    Corporations, certificate of incorporation, § 1.21
    Perfecting the appeal, § 37.49
Medical malpractice, mandatory sliding-scale contingency fee, § 26.6

FERS
Elder law, § 23.38

FIDUCIARIES
Alternate or successor fiduciaries, will provisions, § 24.17
Attorney-client relationship, § 28.19

INDEX

FIDUCIARIES—Continued
Attorney/draftsman as,
    Ethical considerations, estate planning, § 24.95
Duties,
    Corporations, directors, § 1.65
Estate Planning, generally, this index
Guardianships, generally, this index
Powers, will provisions, § 24.16
Probate and estate administration,
    Duty to expeditiously seek probate, § 25.13
    Two or more fiduciaries in dispute, entitlement to assets, § 25.45
Trusts, generally, this index

FINDINGS OF COURT
Guardianships. Hearing and Order. Guardianships, this index

FIRST AMENDMENT
Federal civil rights law, § 18.26 et seq.
    Freedom of religion, § 18.28
        Refusal of medical treatment, § 18.28
    Freedom of speech, § 18.27

FORECLOSURE
    Generally, § 11.1 et seq.
Mechanic's Liens, generally, this index
Mortgages, § 11.1 et seq.
    Closing documents, § 11.51
    Commencement, § 11.16
        Lis pendens, § 11.17
        Notice of pendency of action, § 11.17
            Drafting checklist, § 11.58
    Complaints, § 11.20 et seq.
        Amendments, § 11.28
        Asserting defaults, § 11.24
        Drafting checklist, § 11.60
        Governmental entity, pleading with specificity, § 11.21
        Loan, note and mortgage, allegations regarding, § 11.22
        Motion to dismiss, § 11.36
        Parties, allegations regarding, § 11.21
        Pending action regarding mortgage debt, § 11.27
        References to pertinent terms of note and mortgage, § 11.23
        Reserving right to add advances made by plaintiff to indebtedness secured by mortgage, § 11.25
        Subordinate interest of defendants, allegations regarding, § 11.26
        Verified complaint for foreclosure,
            Commercial property, form, § 11.74
            Mixed property, form, § 11.74
            Multi-unit residential property, form, § 11.74
            Single family residence, form, § 11.73
    Defendant's response, § 11.35 et seq.
        Answer, § 11.37
        Defenses, § 11.37
        Motion to dismiss complaint, § 11.36
        Notice of appearance and waiver, § 11.38
    Deficiency judgment, § 11.52
    Drafting checklists, § 11.55 et seq.
    Foreclosure sale, § 11.47 et seq.
        Advertising sale, § 11.48
        Closing documents, § 11.51
        Conducting, § 11.49
        Deficiency judgment, § 11.52
        Eviction of tenants following sale, § 11.54
        Memorandum of sale,

INDEX

FORECLOSURE—Continued
Mortgages—Continued
  Foreclosure sale—Continued
    Memorandum of sale—Continued
      Drafting checklist, § 11.67
      Form, § 11.81
    Notice of sale, § 11.48
      Drafting checklist, § 11.66
      Form, § 11.80
    Referee's deed, § 11.51
    Referee's report of sale, § 11.51
    Surplus money proceedings, § 11.53
    Terms of sale, § 11.49
      Drafting checklist, § 11.67
      Form, § 11.81
    Vacating sale, § 11.50
    Writ of assistance, § 11.54
  Foreclosure title certificate,
    Pre-commencement procedure, § 11.13
    Strategy, § 11.4
  Forms, § 11.68 et seq.
  Judgment of foreclosure and sale, § 11.46
    Drafting checklist, § 11.65
    Form, § 11.79
  Necessary defendants,
    Determination, § 11.14
    United States as necessary defendant, § 11.15
  New York Mortgage Foreclosure Law, § 11.5
    Choice of remedies, § 11.6
    Foreclosure by advertisement, § 11.8
    Non-judicial foreclosure, § 11.8
    Partial foreclosure action, § 11.7
  Notice of acceleration,
    Drafting checklist, § 11.57
    Form, § 11.70
  Notice of default, § 11.11
    Drafting checklist, § 11.56
    Form, § 11.69
  Notice of pendency of action, § 11.17
    Drafting checklist, § 11.58
    Form, § 11.71
  Notice of sale, § 11.48
    Drafting checklist, § 11.66
  Obtaining judgment, § 11.39
    Motion for judgment, § 11.40
      Opposing motion, § 11.41
  Pre-commencement procedure, § 11.10
    Foreclosure title certificate, § 11.13
    Notice of acceleration, § 11.12
      Drafting checklist, § 11.57
    Notice of default, § 11.11
      Drafting checklists, § 11.56
  Priority rule, § 11.9
  Receivers, § 11.29 et seq.
    Appointment,
      Affidavit in support of motion for appointment of receiver, form, § 11.76
      Considerations in determining whether to seek appointment, § 11.30
      Drafting checklist, § 11.61
      Ex parte motion, § 11.31
        Affidavit in support, § 11.62
      Opposing appointment, § 11.33
      Order, form, § 11.75

INDEX

FORECLOSURE—Continued
Mortgages—Continued
  Receivers—Continued
    Compensation, § 11.32
    Discharging, § 11.34
    Double recovery theory, § 11.32
  Referee to compute, § 11.42
    Hearing, § 11.43
    Judgment of foreclosure and sale,
      Drafting checklist, § 11.65
      Form, § 11.79
    Motion to confirm referee's computation report and for judgment of foreclosure and sale, § 11.45
    Report of referee, § 11.44
  Referee's deed, § 11.51
  Referee's report of sale, § 11.51
  Scope, § 11.1
  Strategy,
    First review of loan documents, § 11.3
    Foreclosure title certificate, § 11.4
    Initial client interview, § 11.2
  Subordinate lienors, representing, § 11.9
  Summary judgment,
    Affidavit of regularity and in support of motion,
      Drafting checklist, § 11.64
      Form, § 11.78
    Notice of motion,
      Drafting checklist, § 11.63
      Form, § 11.77
  Summons, § 11.18
    Drafting checklist, § 11.59
    Form, § 11.72
    Venue, § 11.19
  Surplus money proceedings, § 11.53

FOREIGN INVESTORS REAL PROPERTY TAX ACT (FIRPTA)
Real property sale,
  Closing of title, disclosure, § 12.76

FORFEITURES
Appellate division. criminal,
  Appeal by the people, § 38.10

FORMATION
Limited Liability Companies, generally, this index
Limited Liability Partnerships, generally, this index
Limited Partnerships, generally, this index
Partnerships, generally, this index

FOSTER HOMES
Court intervention, § 20.88
Siblings placed together, § 20.124
Voluntary commitment, § 20.88

FRANCHISE TAX, STATE
Corporate Franchise Tax, State, generally, this index

FRANCHISES
Small business, purchase or sale,
  Asset sales for buyer, § 6.40
    Due diligence investigation, legal review, § 6.17

FRAUD
Affirmative defense, as, § 26.37
Bankruptcy,

INDEX

FRAUD—Continued
    Bankruptcy—Continued
        Avoiding powers,
            Constructive fraud, § 9.119
            Fraudulent conveyances, § 9.119
            Intentional fraud, § 9.119
            New York Fraudulent Conveyances Statute, §§ 9.113, 9.115
        Chapter 7,
            Exceptions to general discharge of debtor, § 9.205
        Statutory creditors committee,
            Fraudulent conveyance action against third party, § 9.45
Complaint, §§ 7.65, 26.36
Corporations, business combinations, § 1.89
Employment cases. fraudulent inducement, § 17.27
Income tax, state,
    Penalties, generally, this index
Motor vehicle leasing,
    Complaint, § 7.52
    Defenses, § 7.53
New York Fraudulent Conveyances Statute,
    Bankruptcy, avoiding powers, §§ 9.113, 9.115
Statute of Frauds, generally, this index

FREEDOM OF INFORMATION LAW
    Generally, § 17.55
Consumer protection cases, § 7.8
Local land use law, § 16.38
Municipal corporations, § 3.28
New York Landlord-Tenant Law,
    Discovery, § 13.60

FUNERALS
Expenses,
    Workers' compensation benefits,
        Death awards, § 32.31

GARAGES
Public accommodations and amusement, equal rights in places of, § 18.54

GENERAL PARTNERSHIPS
Partnerships, generally, this index

GENERATION SKIPPING TRANSFER TAXES
    Generally, § 24.24
Direct skips, § 24.26
Exemptions, § 24.30
Generation assignments, § 24.28
Multiple skips, § 24.29
Reverse QTIP, § 24.31
Taxable distributions, § 24.27
Taxable terminations, § 24.25

GIFT TAXES, FEDERAL
    Generally, § 24.18
Annual gift tax exclusion, § 24.49
    Crummey trusts, § 24.52
    Family limited partnerships, § 24.53
    Section 2503(c) trusts, § 24.50
    Uniform Transfers to Minor's Act accounts, § 24.51
Marital deduction, utilizing, § 24.22
Rates, § 24.19
Unified credit, utilizing, § 24.21

GIFT TAXES, STATE
    Generally, § 24.20

INDEX

GIFT TAXES, STATE—Continued
Rates, § 24.20

GLASS CEILING
Review by Office of Federal Contract Compliance Programs, § 17.80

GORR
Rulemaking,
    Administrative law, § 4.49

GOVERNOR'S OFFICE FOR REGULATORY REFORM (GORR)
Rulemaking,
    Administrative law, § 4.49

GRAND JURIES
Orders accepting or sealing grand jury reports,
    Appellate division, criminal, § 38.11
Subpoena of adoption records, § 20.128

GROCERY STORES
License to sell beer and wine coolers, § 36.8

GUARDIANS AD LITEM
Adoption proceedings, §§ 20.36, 20.43
Appointment, probate proceedings, § 25.23
Law Guardians, generally, this index

GUARDIANSHIPS
    Generally, § 22.1 et seq.
Accounts and Accounting, this index
Answers,
    Proceedings to recover property withheld, § 22.84
Appointment of guardian. Person to be appointed guardian, post
Bonds, § 22.42
Checklists, this index
Commission of guardian,
    Forms, § 22.103
    Issuance, § 22.43
Compensation of guardian, § 22.61
Court Evaluators, this index
Court examiners,
    Duties, § 22.65
    Education requirements,
        Training, § 22.78
Decree upon approving accounts, § 22.67
    Checklist, § 22.95
    Forms, § 22.106
Discharge. Removal, discharge and resignation, generally, post
Education requirements, § 22.75
    Compliance, § 22.79
    Court evaluators,
        Training, § 22.77
    Summary, § 22.80
    Training, § 22.76
Former law. Prior law, generally, post
Forms, § 22.97 et seq.
Hearing and order,
    Attorney fees, awarding to petitioner, § 22.39
    Bonds, § 22.42
    Commission of guardian,
        Issuance, § 22.43
    Dispositional alternatives, § 22.38
    Evidence, § 22.33
    Findings of court, § 22.34
        Personal needs, § 22.36

INDEX

GUARDIANSHIPS—Continued
Hearing and order—Continued
    Findings of court—Continued
        Property management, § 22.37
        Voluntary appointment, § 22.35
    Incapacitated persons, alleged,
        Presence at hearing, § 22.32
    Overview, § 22.30
    Person to be appointed guardian,
        Criteria for appointment, § 22.41
        Priority and criteria for appointment, § 22.41
        Requirements, § 22.40
    Procedure, § 22.31
    Protective arrangements, § 22.38
    Service of process, designation of clerk of court for, § 22.43
    Summary, § 22.44
Incapacitated persons,
    Counsel, appointment of, § 22.28
Interim guardians, § 22.72
Judgments,
    Checklists, § 22.92
    Forms,
        Order and judgment appointing guardian of person and property, § 22.101
Mental Hygiene Law Article 81, generally, this index
Nomination of guardian, § 22.40
Oath and designation of guardian, forms, § 22.102
Order and judgment appointing guardian of person and property, forms, § 22.101
Order to show cause, forms, § 22.98
Orders. Hearing and order, generally, ante
Petition, forms, § 22.99
Power to appoint guardian, § 22.11
    Elements, § 22.12
    Incapacity, § 22.13
    Jurisdiction, § 22.15
    Primary considerations, § 22.14
    Standing to commence proceeding, § 22.17
    Venue, § 22.16
Prior law, § 22.4
    Committees and conservators, role, § 22.5
    Matter of Grinker (Rose), impact, § 22.7
    Problems encountered, § 22.6
Proceeding to appoint guardian, § 22.19
    Notice, this index
    Petitions, § 22.23
    Summary, §§ 22.18, 22.24
Proceedings to recover property withheld, § 22.81
    Answer, § 22.84
    Decrees, § 22.86
    Grounds for inquiry, § 22.83
    Petition and supporting papers, § 22.82
        Checklists, § 22.96
        Forms, § 22.107
    Summary, § 22.87
    Trial, § 22.85
Provisional Remedies, this index
Removal, discharge and resignation, § 22.69
    Discharge or modification of powers, § 22.70
    Interim guardians, appointment, § 22.72
    Resignation or suspension of powers, § 22.71
    Standby guardians, appointment, § 22.73
    Successor guardians, appointment, § 22.72
    Summary, § 22.74

INDEX

GUARDIANSHIPS—Continued
Removal—Continued
    Vacancy in office, § 22.72
Reports, § 22.62
    Annual report, § 22.64
        Checklists, § 22.94
        Forms, § 22.105
    Decree upon approving accounts, § 22.67
    Examination of reports by court examiner, § 22.65
    Final reports, § 22.66
    Initial report, § 22.63
        Checklists, § 22.93
        Forms, § 22.104
    Intermediate reports, § 22.66
    Revised reports, § 22.65
    Sanctions, § 22.65
    Summary, § 22.68
Requirements, education, § 22.75
    Summary, § 22.80
    Training, § 22.76
Resignation. Removal, discharge and resignation, generally, ante
Role of guardian,
    Effect of appointment on incapacitated person, § 22.54
    Overview, § 22.45
    Petition for authorization to transfer property, § 22.49
        Considerations of court, § 22.51
        Granting petition, § 22.52
        Notice of application, § 22.50
    Powers and duties, § 22.46
        Personal needs, § 22.53
        Property management, § 22.47
    Substituted judgment doctrine, § 22.48
    Summary, § 22.55
Service of process, designation of clerk of court for, § 22.43
Standby guardians, § 22.73
Strategy, § 22.2
Successor guardians, § 22.72
Vacancy in office, § 22.72
Will provisions, § 24.14

GUILTY PLEAS
Accusatory instruments, supporting depositions,
    Guilty plea waiving defects, § 33.22
Appeal, waiver, § 38.8
Speedy trial, waiver of CPL § 30.300 motion, § 33.80

HABEAS CORPUS
Appellate division,
    Civil, § 37.88
    Criminal, § 38.8

HANDICAPPED PERSONS
Adoption of handicapped child, subsidized adoptions, § 20.113
Blind persons,
    Guide dogs,
        Discrimination in private housing prohibited, § 18.45
        Public accommodations and amusement, equal rights in places of, § 18.57
Employment discrimination prohibited, § 18.61
Federal civil rights law,
    Americans with Disabilities Act,
        Education, § 18.53
    Antireprisal provisions, § 17.38
    Discrimination prohibited, § 18.19

INDEX

HANDICAPPED PERSONS—Continued
Federal civil rights law—Continued
    Individuals with Disabilities Education Act (IDEA),
        Education, § 18.53
    Jurisdiction, § 18.5
    Public accommodations and amusement, equal rights in places of,
        Accompanied by guide dog, hearing dog or service dog, § 18.57

HEALTH CARE
Decision making, § 23.109
    Do not resuscitate orders, § 23.112
    Health care proxies, §§ 23.110, 24.91
        Statutory form, § 23.125
    Living Wills, generally, this index

HEALTH MAINTENANCE ORGANIZATIONS
Medical malpractice, standard of care, § 29.15

HEAP
Housing issues, elderly individuals, § 23.105

HEARINGS
Adoption, §§ 20.2, 20.36, 20.122
    Private, § 20.81
        Putative father, hearing on consent issue, § 20.76
Alcoholic beverage control,
    Five hundred foot rule, § 36.9
    Licenses, suspension,
        Administrative Procedures Act, § 36.2
        Notice of pleading and hearing, §§ 36.62, 36.64, 36.65
    New York State Liquor Authority, § 36.9
Bankruptcy,
    Adequate protection, § 9.59
    Automatic stay, obtaining relief, § 9.54
    Cash collateral, § 9.67
    Chapter 12 plan, § 9.225
    Postpetition financing, § 9.72
Corporations, judicial dissolution, § 1.104
Dunaway hearings, § 33.27
Eminent domain. Public Hearing, generally. Eminent Domain, this index
Enforcement matters, special issues in handling,
    Adjudicatory proceedings, administrative law, § 4.39
    Post-hearing issues,
        Adjudicatory proceedings, administrative law, § 4.40
Foreclosure,
    Mortgages, referee to compute, § 11.43
Guardianships, generally, this index
Huntley hearings, involuntary statements, § 33.57
Income tax, state,
    Audits and appeals, § 35.90
        Petitions to division of tax appeals, small claims hearings, § 35.96
Lemon law, arbitration, §§ 7.14, 7.15
Probable cause, § 33.27
Reconstruction hearing, § 38.40
Sandoval issues, defendant's presence at hearing, § 33.47
Social security disability cases. Disability cases, generally. Social Security, this index
Workers' Compensation, this index

HIV TESTS
Disclosure of results, restrictions, § 17.55

HOLDOVER PROCEEDINGS, § 13.35 et seq.
Burden of proof, § 13.62
Petition,

INDEX

HOLDOVER PROCEEDINGS, § 13.35 et seq.—Continued
Petition—Continued
  Amendment, § 13.62
  Answer, § 13.47
  Checklist, § 13.79
  Defects, § 13.44
  Dismiss, motion to, § 13.48
  Form and content, § 13.43
  Forms, § 13.84
  Notice of petition, § 13.41
    Defects, § 13.42
  Responding to, § 13.46
  Verification, § 13.45
    Attorney, form, § 13.88
    Corporate officer, form, § 13.86
    Defects, § 13.45
    Individual, form, § 13.85
    Partnership, form, § 13.87
Predicate notices, § 13.36 et seq.
  Defective notice, tenant defense, § 13.51
    Rent-regulated apartments, § 13.52
  Illegal use, § 13.38
  Month-to-month tenants, § 13.37
  Rent-controlled tenants, § 13.39
  Rent-stabilized tenants, § 13.40
Settlement stipulation,
  Checklist, § 13.81
  Tenant agrees to cure, form, § 13.92
  Tenant agrees to vacate premises, form, § 13.93
Stipulations, § 13.65
  Forms, § 13.92 et seq.
Tenant defenses, § 13.49 et seq.
  Acceptance of rent after expiration or termination of tenancy, § 13.50
  Defective predicate notice, § 13.51
    Rent-regulated apartments, § 13.52
  Equitable estoppel, § 13.54
  Succession rights to rent-regulated apartments, § 13.55
  Waiver, § 13.53
Warrant, stay, § 13.69

HOME CARE COVERAGE
Generally, § 23.84
Expanded in-home services for the elderly program (EISEP), § 23.87
Medicaid, § 23.86
Medicare, § 23.85
Private insurance, § 23.88

HOME ENERGY ASSISTANCE PROGRAM (HEAP)
Housing issues, elderly individuals, § 23.105

HOME HEALTH CARE
Medicare part A benefits, § 23.47

HOSPICE CARE
Medicare part A benefits, § 23.48

HOSPITAL PATIENT RIGHTS
  Generally, § 23.89
Bill of rights, § 23.90
Discharge planning, § 23.91

HOSPITALS
Medical malpractice
  See also Medical Malpractice, generally, this index

INDEX

HOSPITALS—Continued
Medical malpractice—Continued
    Hospital operations and medical negligence,
        Credentialling of physicians, § 29.32
        Departmentalization of services, § 29.34
        Quality assurance program, § 29.33
        Risk management program, § 29.33
    Hospital records, § 29.52
        Anesthesia record, § 29.57
        Consultation records, § 29.56
        Discharge summary, § 29.52
        Discovery, § 29.67
        Face sheet, § 29.52
        ICU/CCU records, § 29.62
        Informed consent forms, § 29.53
        Intake and output records, § 29.59
        Labor and delivery room records, § 29.61
        Medication records, § 29.58
        Nurse's notes, § 29.63
        Obstetric records, § 29.61
        Operative records, § 29.57
        Operative report, § 29.57
        Order sheets, § 29.55
        Pre-operative checklist, § 29.57
        Prenatal records, § 29.61
        Progress notes, § 29.54
        Radiographic records, § 29.60
        Recovery room record, § 29.57
    Regulatory standards, § 29.23
    Standard of care,
        Hospital's direct liability, § 29.13
        Hospital's respondeat-superior liability, § 29.12
Municipal, negligence claims, § 26.12
Records, motor vehicle accidents, § 26.22

HOTELS
Bankruptcy,
    Cash collateral, postpetition proceeds,
        Security interests in rents and hotel revenues, § 9.69
License for sale of beer, wine and spirits, §§ 36.9, 36.34
Public accommodations and amusement, equal rights in places of, § 18.54

HOUSING
Elderly individuals, § 23.99
    Community based services, § 23.108
    Home energy assistance program (HEAP), § 23.105
    Home equity loans, § 23.104
    Home repair assistance, § 23.103
    Life care retirement communities, § 23.107
    Real property taxation,
        Credits, § 23.101
        Exemptions, § 23.100
    Reverse mortgages, § 23.104
    Tax assistance loans, § 23.102
    Tenant protections, § 23.106

HOUSING AND COMMUNITY DEVELOPMENT ACT
Real property sale,
    Closing of title, disclosure,
        Lead paint hazards, § 12.80

HUMAN RIGHTS
Civil Rights, generally, this index
Discrimination, generally, this index

INDEX

HUMAN RIGHTS—Continued
New York City Human Rights Law, generally, this index
New York State Human Rights Law, generally, this index

HUNTLEY HEARINGS
Involuntary statements, § 33.57

IMMIGRATION
    Generally, § 19.1 et seq.
Adoption, foreign born children,
    Non-quota immigrant status, § 20.68
Application for permanent residency, § 19.51 et seq.
    Adjustment of status, § 19.57
        Administrative review, § 19.64
        Application process, § 19.61
        Checklist, § 19.65
        Completion of process, § 19.63
        Concurrent filing of petition and adjustment of status, § 19.62
        Discretionary factors, § 19.60
        General requirements, § 19.58
        Judicial review, § 19.64
        Section 245(i), § 19.59
        Special provisions, § 19.59
    Exclusionary grounds, § 19.52
        Adverse foreign policy concerns, § 19.52
        Criminal activity, § 19.52
        Health related grounds, § 19.52
        Security considerations, § 19.52
        Terrorist activities, § 19.52
    Immigrant visa processing, § 19.53
        Checklist, § 19.56
        Framework for processing system, § 19.54
        Public Law No. 103-317, § 19.55
        Special requirements, § 19.55
    Tactical considerations, § 19.66
        Flowchart, § 19.69
        Immigrant visa processing versus adjustment of status, § 19.68
        Nonimmigrant status as factor, § 19.67
Discrimination, Immigration Reform Control Act, § 17.49
Employment-based immigration, § 19.17 et seq.
    Fifth employment preference applicants,
        "Employment creation" visa, § 19.43
        Form I-526, § 19.43
        Immigrant investors, § 19.42 et seq.
        Petition procedures and requirements, § 19.43
        Pilot program, § 19.44
        Special immigrant investor programs, § 19.44
    First employment preference applicants, I-140 petition, § 19.29
    First employment preference applicants (priority workers), § 19.18
        Extraordinary ability aliens, § 19.19
        Managerial or executive intracompany transferees, § 19.21
        Outstanding professors and researchers, § 19.20
    Fourth employment preference applicants, § 19.40
        Form I-360, § 19.41
        Religious workers and ministers, § 19.41
        "Special immigrant" classification, § 19.41
    I-140 petition,
        Checklist, § 19.30
        Documentation, § 19.29
        Procedures, § 19.29
    Labor certification, § 19.31 et seq.
        Administrative appeals, § 19.39
        Approvals, § 19.37

INDEX

IMMIGRATION—Continued
Employment-based immigration—Continued
    Labor certification—Continued
        Board of Alien Labor Certification Appeals, § 19.33
        Business necessity, § 19.35
        Conflict of interest, § 19.33
        Denials, § 19.39
        Employment and training administration, § 19.32
        Job description, § 19.34
        Legal issues, § 19.33
        Notice of findings, § 19.38
        Procedures, § 19.32
        Recruitment, § 19.36
        "Sufficiently dissimilar" test, § 19.34
    Preference categories, § 19.5
    Priority workers, § 19.18
    Second employment preference applicants, § 19.22
        Advanced degree professionals, § 19.24
        Exceptional ability aliens, § 19.23
        I-140 petition, § 19.29
        National interest waiver, § 19.25
    Third employment preference applicants, § 19.26 et seq.
        I-140 petition, § 19.29
        Professionals, § 19.27
        Skilled workers, § 19.27
        Unskilled workers, § 19.28
Family-based immigration, § 19.7 et seq.
    Abused spouse and children, § 19.16
    Amerasians, § 19.15
        Adoption, § 19.15
    Burden of proof, § 19.10
    Documentation, § 19.10
    Family preference categories, § 19.9
    Family-sponsored preference categories, § 19.5
    Immediate relative categories, § 19.8
    Orphans, § 19.15
        Adoption, § 19.15
    Petition,
        Denial, appeal to board of immigration appeals, § 19.14
        I-130 petition, § 19.14
        Procedures and documentation, § 19.13
        Service lookout book, § 19.14
        "Stokes" interview, § 19.14
    Qualifying as relation, § 19.10
        "Child" issues, § 19.11
        "Marriage" issues, § 19.12
        "Parent" issues, § 19.11
Forms, § 19.75 et seq.
  I-130, § 19.76
  I-140, § 19.77
  I-485, § 19.78
  OF-230, § 19.79
"Green card", § 19.70 et seq.
    Citizenship through naturalization, § 19.70
    Conditional residence, § 19.71
        Immigrant investors, removal of condition, § 19.73
        Marriage cases, removal of condition, § 19.72
    Immigrant investors, removal of condition, § 19.73
    Immigration Marriage Fraud Amendment of 1986 (IMFA), § 19.72
    Marriage cases, removal of condition, § 19.72
    Marriage Fraud Act, § 19.72
    Returning resident immigrant, § 19.74

INDEX

IMMIGRATION—Continued
"Green card"—Continued
    Unconditional permanent residence, § 19.74
Immigration and Nationality Act of 1952, § 19.1
Immigration Marriage Fraud Amendments of 1986, § 19.8
Immigration Reform Control Act, § 17.49
Overview of U.S. immigration system, § 19.4 et seq.
    Foreign state chargeability, § 19.6
    Implementation, § 19.6
    Numerical limitations on immigrant selection, § 19.5
    "Quota allocation" system, §§ 19.5, 19.6
Scope, § 19.1
Special categories, § 19.45 et seq.
    Amnesty program, § 19.45
    Asylum, § 19.50
    Cancellation of removal, § 19.48
    "Continuous physical presence", § 19.48
    Diversity (lottery) program, § 19.46
    "Extreme hardship", § 19.48
    Legislatively created programs, § 19.49
    "Meaningfully interruptive standard", § 19.48
    Refugee status, § 19.50
    Registry, § 19.47
Strategy, § 19.2
    Flowchart, § 19.3

IMMIGRATION REFORM CONTROL ACT
Employment law, § 17.49

IMPEACHMENT
Defendant's pre-arrest silence, use prohibited, § 33.60
Involuntary statements, use prohibited, § 33.58

INCAPACITATED PERSONS
Counsel, appointment of, § 22.28
Guardians, appointment, § 22.13
    Effect, § 22.54

INCOME TAX, FEDERAL
Corporate franchise tax, state,
    Compared, § 35.20
    Tax on net income base, subtractions from federal taxable income, § 35.28
Divorce, § 21.45
Maintenance, § 21.51
Marital property distribution, § 21.45
Personal income tax,
    Computing federal adjusted gross income, § 35.5
    Computing federal taxable income, § 35.6
Residence trusts,
    Valuation of gifts,
        Lifetime planning, § 24.48
Spousal support, § 21.51

INCOME TAX, STATE
    Generally, § 35.1 et seq.
Application for extension of time for filing return, forms, § 35.129
    Application for additional extension of time to file for individuals, forms, § 35.130
Assessment of tax, § 35.108
    Checklist, § 35.120
    Deficiency assessment, § 35.110
    Jeopardy assessment, § 35.112
    Limitation of actions, § 35.111
    Summary assessment, § 35.109
Audits and appeals, § 35.85

INDEX

INCOME TAX, STATE—Continued
Audits and appeals—Continued
    Audit methods, § 35.86
    Checklist, § 35.98
    Conciliation and mediation services bureau, § 35.90
        Conciliation conferences, § 35.92
            Orders, § 35.93
            Requesting, § 35.91
    Petitions to division of tax appeals, § 35.94
        Referrals to bureau of conciliation and mediation services, § 35.95
        Small claims hearings, § 35.96
    Results of audit, § 35.89
    Summary, § 35.97
    Taxpayer bill of rights, § 35.87
    Taxpayer representation, § 35.88
Checklists, this index
Collection of tax, § 35.113
    Bankruptcy filing, § 35.119
    Checklist, § 35.120
    Installment payment agreements, § 35.117
    Levy or warrant, by, § 35.116
    Liens, § 35.114
        Duration, § 35.115
    Offer in compromise, § 35.118
Conciliation conference, request for, forms, § 35.136
Corporate Franchise Tax, State, generally, this index
Criminal tax provisions, § 35.121
    Returns,
        Failure to file, § 35.122
        False or fraudulent, § 35.123
            Aiding or assisting in, § 35.124
    Taxes,
        Failure to pay, § 35.125
        Failure to properly withhold, § 35.126
Department of taxation and finance. Taxation and Finance Department, generally, this index
Forms, § 35.127 et seq.
Fraud. Penalties, this index
Judicial review, § 35.99
    Appeal by Article 78 proceeding, § 35.100
        Burden of proof, § 35.103
        Initiation, § 35.102
        Taxes, payment of, § 35.101
    Appeal to N.Y. court of appeals, § 35.105
    Checklist, § 35.107
    Declaratory judgment actions, § 35.104
    Denied refund claims, § 35.62
    Summary, § 35.106
Limitation of Actions, this index
Notice of exception to tax tribunal, forms, § 35.131
Offer in compromise, forms, § 35.137
Penalties, this index
Personal income tax, § 35.4
    Adjusted gross income, New York, computing, § 35.8
    Checklist, § 35.18
    Domicile, § 35.16
    Federal adjusted gross income, computing, § 35.5
    Federal taxable income, computing, § 35.6
    Itemized deductions for married couples, § 35.11
    Minimum tax, New York, § 35.13
    Nonresident individuals, § 35.17
    Pension and disability distributions, exclusions, § 35.12

INDEX

INCOME TAX, STATE—Continued
Personal income tax—Continued
    Personal exemptions, New York, § 35.10
    Residency,
        Defined, § 35.14
        Non-residency, burden of proving, § 35.15
    Taxable income, New York,
        Computing, § 35.9
        Defined, § 35.7
Petitions, this index
Power of attorney to represent individual, forms, § 35.128
Residence trusts,
    Valuation of gifts,
        Lifetime planning, § 24.48
Returns, filing, § 35.51
    Checklist, § 35.63
    Extensions, § 35.54
    Forms, obtaining, § 35.55
    Recordkeeping, § 35.53
    Refunds,
        Claims for,
            Denied claims,
                Judicial review, § 35.62
            Federal changes, § 35.60
            Where to file, § 35.58
        Petitions for, § 35.61
        Special refund authority, § 35.59
    Refunds, claims for, § 35.56
    Time limitations, § 35.57
    Where to file, § 35.52
Scope, § 35.1
Statement of financial condition, forms, § 35.134
Strategy, § 35.2
    Checklist, § 35.3
Taxation and Finance Department, generally, this index

INDEMNIFICATION
Corporations, directors, § 1.66
    Corporate advances and court allowances. limitation, § 1.66
    Court award, by, § 1.66
    Insurance, § 1.66
        Foreign corporations, § 1.66
        Public policy, § 1.66
    Other than by court award, § 1.66
    Procedure, § 1.66
Damages, collateral sources defense, form, § 30.52
Legal malpractice cases, § 28.26
Motor Vehicle Accident Indemnification Corporation Act,
    Compensation for injuries, § 26.24
Partners, § 2.54
Small business, purchase or sale,
    Buyer's asset purchase agreement, drafting, § 6.62
    Buyer's stock purchase agreement, drafting, § 6.87
    Seller's asset sale agreement, drafting, § 6.149
    Seller's stock sale agreement, drafting, § 6.172

INDIAN CHILD WELFARE ACT
Adoption proceedings, § 20.69
Tribal court jurisdiction, child custody proceedings, § 20.50

INDIGENT PERSONS
Assignment of counsel,
    Adoption proceedings, § 20.93

INDEX

INDIGENT PERSONS—Continued
Assignment of counsel—Continued
  Appellate division,
    Civil, §§ 37.10, 37.48
    Criminal, § 38.16
  Family court, § 37.19
  Surrogate's court, § 37.18

INDIVIDUALS WITH DISABILITIES EDUCATION ACT (IDEA)
Federal civil rights law, education, § 18.53

INFORMANTS
News media, shield law, § 18.85

INFORMATION
Accusatory instruments, § 33.9
Prosecutor's information, § 33.11
  Appeal by the people, § 38.10
Reduction in count in indictment, appeal by the people, § 38.10
Simplified information, § 33.10
  Pretrial discovery, § 33.32
  Superseding information disallowed, § 33.23

INJUNCTIVE RELIEF
Bankruptcy, Chapter 11,
  Asbestos-related cases, channeling injunctions, § 9.171
Corporations, judicial dissolution, § 1.106
Deceptive Practices Act, § 7.47
Environmental law,
  Air pollution control, § 15.22
  Clean Water Act (CWA), § 15.11
Hazardous waste regulation, § 15.25
Local land use law, judicial review, § 16.50
Nuisance, § 15.32
Solid waste regulation, § 15.25
Temporary restraining orders,
  Deceptive trade practice case, § 7.63
    Affirmation in support, § 7.64
"Yellowstone" actions, § 13.70
  Obtaining injunction, § 13.71

INJURIES
Compensable injury, workers' compensation, § 32.13

INNS
Public accommodations and amusement, equal rights in places of, § 18.54

INQUIRIES
Guardianships,
  Proceedings to recover property withheld, grounds for inquiries, § 22.83

INSIDER TRADING
Corporations, business combinations, § 1.89

INSURANCE
  Generally, § 31.1 et seq.
Accidents, notice, § 31.10
Affirmative defenses asserted by insurer in coverage action, forms, § 31.35
Agents, § 31.7
Alien insurers, unauthorized,
  Bond or security, § 31.23
Ambiguous terms, § 31.9
Arbitration clauses, § 31.24
Bad faith refusal to settle, § 31.17
Bankruptcy,

INDEX

INSURANCE—Continued
Bankruptcy—Continued
    Retired employees' insurance benefits, § 9.87
        Modification, procedure, § 9.88
Bond or security, unauthorized alien insurers, § 31.23
Breach of contract, § 31.21
    Complaint by policyholder for declaratory relief and breach of contract, forms, § 31.32
Brokers, § 31.6
Burden of proof, § 31.27
Checklist, § 31.3
    Allegations, essential, § 31.31
Choice of law, § 31.25
Claims-made policies, § 31.8
Co-insurers, allocation of losses, § 31.30
Common speech test, policy interpretation, § 31.9
Complaint by insurer for rescission, forms, § 31.34
Complaint by policyholder for declaratory relief and breach of contract, forms, § 31.32
Contra proferentum rule of construction, § 31.9
Cooperation clause, duties under, § 31.11
Declaratory Relief, this index
Denying coverage, § 31.16
Disability insurance, ERISA protection, § 17.50
Disclaimer of coverage, § 31.16
Duty of good faith and fair dealing, § 31.17
Duty to Defend, generally, this index
Elderly pharmaceutical insurance coverage (EPIC),
    Miscellaneous programs, elder law, § 23.120
Employment law,
    COBRA, rights of employee to health insurance, §§ 17.12, 17.46
False claims, § 31.18
False information, § 31.18
Forms, § 31.32 et seq.
Health and life insurance, spousal support, § 21.57
Indemnification,
    Corporations, directors, § 1.66
    Insured, § 31.12
Insolvent insurers, § 31.28
Interpretation, § 31.9
Legal Malpractice Insurance, generally, this index
Life insurance,
    ERISA protection, § 17.50
    Estate planning with certain assets, § 24.34
        Trusts, § 24.35
            Crummey powers, § 24.36
Limitation of actions, § 31.26
Limits of policies, § 31.8
Liquidation orders, § 31.28
Long Term Care Insurance, generally, this index
Losses between co-insurers, allocation, § 31.30
Lost policies, § 31.20
Materiality, § 31.18
Mechanic's liens, extent of lien, § 10.10
Medical insurance,
    Adoption, birth mother, § 20.4
Misrepresentation, § 31.18
Motor Vehicle Insurance, generally, this index
Nature of insurance, § 31.8
New York law, sources, § 31.4
Non-waiver agreements, § 31.15
Notice, accident or occurrence, § 31.10
Occurrence-based policies, § 31.8
Pre-answer security, § 31.23

INDEX

INSURANCE—Continued
Private insurance, home care coverage, § 23.88
Reformation, § 31.19
Rescission of policies, § 31.18
    Complaint by insurer for, forms, § 31.34
Reservation of rights, § 31.15
Scope, § 31.1
Service of process, § 31.22
Strategy, § 31.2
Subrogation, § 31.29
Supplemental Medical Insurance (Medigap plans), generally, this index
Third parties involved in placement/administration of insurance contract, § 31.5
    Agents, § 31.7
Title insurance. Purchase and sale, generally. Real Property, this index
Unemployment insurance,
    Appeals, § 17.60
    Ban while receiving severance benefits, § 17.16
    Denial of benefits, § 17.60
Waiver, § 31.15
    Limitations of actions, § 31.26
Workers' compensation, § 32.41

INTELLECTUAL PROPERTY
Small business, purchase or sale,
    Due diligence investigation, legal review, § 6.17

INTENTIONAL INFLICTION OF EMOTIONAL HARM
Claims against debt collectors, §§ 7.35, 7.48
Employment cases,
    Discharge of employee, § 17.28
    Sexual harassment, § 17.28

INTENTIONAL INTERFERENCE WITH CONTRACTUAL RELATIONS
Employment cases, § 17.29

INTEREST
Damages, § 30.40
    Notice of motion to amend verdict to add interest, form, § 30.56
        Affidavit in support, § 30.57
    Notice of motion to fix date from which interest is computed, form, § 30.58
        Affidavit in support, § 30.59
Enforcement of money judgments, § 8.6
Income tax, state,
    Penalties, underpayment or overpayment of tax, § 35.83

INTERMEDIATE APPELLATE COURTS, § 38.46
Appeal as of right, § 38.52
Appeal by permission, § 38.53
Appellate Term, generally, this index
County Courts, generally, this index
CPL § 460.10(3), § 38.52
CPL § 460.50, § 38.54
CPL § 460.70(2), § 38.55
Criminal appeals, § 39.42
    Limitations on appealability, § 39.43
Determination of appeal, § 38.56
Judgments appealable, § 38.51
Local criminal courts, from, § 38.51
Orders, § 38.51
Perfecting the appeal, § 38.55
    CPL § 460.70(2), § 38.55
Sentences, § 38.51
Stay pending appeal, § 38.54
    Appeal from New York City criminal court to appellate term, § 38.54

INDEX

INTERMEDIATE APPELLATE COURTS, § 38.46—Continued
Stay pending appeal—Continued
    Appeal from village, town, city, or district courts to appellate term, § 38.54
    Appeals to county court, § 38.54
    CPL § 460.50, § 38.54
    Notice of motion for stay of proceedings,
        Affirmation in support, form, § 37.132
        Form, § 37.130
    Order to show cause for stay of proceedings,
        Affirmation in support, form, § 37.132
        Form, § 37.131
Transcribed proceedings, § 38.52
Untranscribed proceedings, § 38.52
    CPL § 460.10(3), § 38.52

INTERNATIONAL SAFE CONTAINER ACT
Antireprisal provisions, § 17.38

INTERROGATORIES
Damages, strategy, § 30.3
Discrimination cases, § 17.72
Objections, § 26.44
Personal injury cases, § 26.44

INTERSTATE COMMERCE COMMISSION
Consumer protection, § 7.2

INTERSTATE COMPACT ACT
Adoptions, § 20.3
Private adoptions, § 20.53

INTERVENTION
Adjudicatory proceedings, administrative law, § 4.20

INTESTATE SUCCESSION
Adopted children's rights, § 20.13
Estate Planning, generally, this index
Probate and Estate Administration, generally, this index

JUDGES
    See also particular court concerned
Absolute immunity, § 18.31
Appellate division, civil,
    Judiciary structure, § 37.3
Commission on judicial conduct,
    Review of determinations by court of appeals, § 39.59

JUDGMENTS AND DECREES
Appellate division, civil, § 37.38
Consent,
    Appellate division, civil, § 37.23
Enforcement of Money Judgments, generally, this index
Guardianships,
    Accounts, approving,
        Checklists, § 22.95
        Forms, § 22.106
    Checklists, § 22.92
        Order and judgment appointing guardian of person and property, forms, § 22.101
    Proceedings to recover property withheld, § 22.86
Intermediate appellate courts, appeals, § 38.51
Obtaining, § 11.39
    Motion for judgment, § 11.40
        Opposing motion, § 11.41

INDEX

JUDICIAL REVIEW
Administrative Law and Proceedings, this index
Appeals, generally, this index
Appellate Division, Civil Appellate Practice Before, generally, this index
Appellate Division, Criminal Appellate Practice Before, generally, this index
Appellate Term, generally, this index
Bankruptcy, generally, this index
City Courts, generally, this index
Civil Court of New York City, generally, this index
County Courts, generally, this index
Court of Appeals, generally, this index
Court of Claims, generally, this index
Criminal Court of New York City, generally, this index
Family Court, generally, this index
Income Tax, State, this index
Justice Courts, generally, this index
Local Criminal Courts, generally, this index
Supreme Court, generally, this index
Surrogate's Court, generally, this index
Town Courts, generally, this index
Village Courts, generally, this index

JURISDICTION
Accusatory instruments,
    Supporting depositions,
        Factual insufficiency not jurisdictional defect, § 33.22
Adoption proceedings, §§ 20.101, 20.102
Bankruptcy, § 9.18
    Retention of jurisdiction,
        Chapter 11 plan of reorganization, § 9.151
            Form, § 9.312
Change of venue. Venue, generally, this index
Civil rights, § 18.5
Court of appeals,
    Civil appeals,
        Jurisdictional inquiry, § 39.27
        Jurisdictional statement, § 39.26
Court of claims,
    Eminent domain, §§ 14.48, 14.52
        Exclusive jurisdiction, § 14.53
        Filing, § 14.54
        Notice, § 14.54
        Vesting of title, § 14.55
    Prisoners' rights, § 18.29
Eminent domain,
    Supreme court, §§ 14.48, 14.56
        Answer by condemnee, § 14.63
            Defenses, § 14.64
        Notice, § 14.61
        Notice of pendency, § 14.57
        Order of condemnation, § 14.65
        Petition in condemnation, § 14.58
            Content, § 14.59
            Non-governmental condemnors, content rules, § 14.60
        Vesting of title, § 14.65
Guardians, appointment, § 22.15
Matrimonial actions, § 21.10 et seq.
New York Landlord-Tenant Law, summary proceedings, § 13.5
Personal, lack of as defense in medical malpractice action, § 29.17
Primary jurisdiction,
    Judicial review, administrative law, § 4.73
Private adoptions, § 20.2
Probate and estate administration,

INDEX

JURISDICTION—Continued
Probate and estate administration—Continued
    Notice of objections, requirements to complete jurisdiction in contested probate, § 25.29
Subject matter,
    Appellate division, civil,
        Dismissal for lack of subject matter jurisdiction not appealable, § 37.37
    Court of appeals, jurisdictional inquiry, § 39.27
Subject matter jurisdiction,
    Article 78 proceedings,
        Judicial review, administrative law, § 4.84
Traffic offenses, speeding, § 33.68
Uniform Child Custody Jurisdiction Act, § 21.5

JURY DUTY
Employment law, handbooks, § 17.81
Jury Duty Act, antireprisal provisions, § 17.38

JURY INSTRUCTIONS
Damages, § 30.60 et seq.
    Breach of contract, § 30.71
        Employment contract, § 30.72
    Collateral sources, itemized verdict, § 30.68
    Personal injury,
        Aggravation of preexisting injury, § 30.64
        Loss of earnings, § 30.62
        Payment of income taxes, § 30.65
        Physical consequences of shock and fright, § 30.63
        Reduction to present value, § 30.66
        Shock and fright, § 30.63
    Property damage,
        With market value, § 30.70
        Without market value, § 30.69
    Subsequent injury, § 30.61
    Wrongful death, conscious pain and suffering, § 30.67
Discrimination cases, § 17.74

JURY TRIALS
Civil rights of jurors,
    New York Bill of Rights, § 18.15
Demand for, § 17.82
    Federal court, form, § 17.98
Discrimination cases, § 17.74
Divorce cases, form, § 21.90
Procedure. Trial, this index
Voir dire, peremptory challenges,
    Discrimination, § 18.15
    Personal injury cases, § 26.55

JUSTICE COURTS
Appeals from justice courts, § 37.92 et seq.
    Appeals as of right, § 37.95
    Appeals by permission, § 37.95
    Appellate term, § 37.93
    Appellate term, appeals to, § 37.97
    Costs on appeal, § 37.98
    County court, §§ 37.93, 37.97
    Courts to which appeals are taken, § 37.93
    CPLR Article 55, applicability, § 37.94
    Notice of appeal, § 37.96
    Perfecting the appeal, § 37.97
    Return on appeal, § 37.96
    Rule governance by administrative board, § 37.100
    Settlement of case, § 37.96
    Small claims review, § 37.99

INDEX

JUSTICE COURTS—Continued
Appeals from justice courts—Continued
    Taking the appeal, § 37.96
    Uniform Justice Court Act, § 37.92

JUVENILE DELINQUENCY
Family court,
    Appellate division, civil, appeals to, § 37.19

LABOR LAW
Child labor, § 17.63
Discrimination against employees for off duty conduct, § 17.47
Minimum wages, § 17.63
Overtime pay, § 17.63
Unpaid wages, § 17.63
Wage claims, § 17.63

LABOR-MANAGEMENT RELATIONSHIP ACT
Collective bargaining agreements,
    Enforcement, § 17.61

LABOR MANAGEMENT REPORTING AND DISCLOSURE ACT
Union elections, § 17.61

LACHES
Non-payment proceedings, as defense to, § 13.33

LANDLORD AND TENANT
New York Landlord-Tenant Law, generally, this index
Slip and fall cases,
    Complaint, § 26.58

LAW GUARDIANS
Appeals by, family court, § 37.19
Appellate division, civil, administrative powers, § 37.8

LAWSUITS
Actions, generally, this index

LEASES
Alcoholic beverage control, licenses,
    Lease for premises, §§ 36.2, 36.3
    Lease information, § 36.21
Bankruptcy,
    Executory contracts and unexpired leases, generally. Bankruptcy, this index
    Use, sale or lease of property,
        Appeals from order authorizing sale, § 9.64
        Chapter 13, § 9.244
        Sales free and clear of liens, § 9.63
Consumer Leasing Act, §§ 7.21 et seq., 7.48
Corporations,
    Assets; sale, lease, exchange, or other disposition of, § 1.85
        Guarantee authorized by shareholders, § 1.87
        Mortgage or security interest in assets, § 1.86
Eminent domain,
    Leasehold interests, § 14.94
        Valuation, § 14.95
    Property rights subject to acquisition, § 14.10
Motor Vehicle Sales, generally, this index
Motor vehicles, repossession, § 7.4

LEGAL MALPRACTICE
    Generally, § 28.1
Alternative dispute resolution (ADR), § 28.1
Answers, § 28.49
    Form, §§ 28.54, 28.55

INDEX

LEGAL MALPRACTICE—Continued
Arbitration,
    Retainer agreement provision, § 28.29
Compelled settlement doctrine, § 28.9
Complaints,
    Answers, § 28.49
        Form, §§ 28.54, 28.55
    Drafting, § 28.48
    Form, §§ 28.52, 28.53
Concealment, § 28.17
Conflicts of interest, §§ 28.20, 28.21
Contribution, § 28.26
Conversion of estate funds, § 28.22
Damages, § 28.3
    Actual, § 28.10
Deceit, treble damages, § 28.24
Defenses, §§ 28.2, 28.4
    Consistent positions, § 28.18
    Lack of foreseeability, § 28.16
    Lawyer's judgment rule, § 28.12
    Limitation of actions, §§ 28.1, 28.13
        Continuous representation tolling doctrine, § 28.14
        Estoppel doctrine, § 28.15
    Privity, §§ 28.1, 28.11
    Supervening act, § 28.16
Disqualification motions, § 28.21
Duty of care, § 28.3 et seq.
Erroneous advise, § 28.4
    Tax advise, § 28.5
Expert testimony, § 28.3
Fee disputes, §§ 28.1, 28.27 et seq.
    Alternative dispute resolution (ADR), § 28.28 et seq.
    Arbitration provision, § 28.30
    Statutory limitations, § 28.31
Fiduciary duty, § 28.19
Fraud, detection, § 28.7
Indemnity, § 28.26
Independent contractors, § 28.23
Insurance. Legal Malpractice Insurance, generally, this index
Lawyer's judgment rule, § 28.12
Limitation of actions, § 28.13 et seq.
Limited liability partnerships, § 28.25
Litigation, § 28.2
Misappropriation of client funds, § 28.22
Non-delegable duty of care, § 28.23
Precautions, § 28.2
Privity, §§ 28.1, 28.11
Proximate cause, §§ 28.3, 28.8
Retainer agreements, § 28.19
    Arbitration provisions, § 28.29
    Drafting, § 28.47
    Form, §§ 28.50, 28.51
Tax liability due to erroneous advise, § 28.5
Treble damages, § 28.24
Vicarious liability for partner's misdeeds, § 28.25
Withdrawal from case, § 28.6

LEGAL MALPRACTICE INSURANCE
    Generally, §§ 28.1, 28.2, 28.35 et seq.
Aggregate limits, § 28.39
Application, § 28.43
Bad faith, § 28.44
Cancellation, § 28.41

INDEX

LEGAL MALPRACTICE INSURANCE—Continued
Claim triggering coverage, § 28.37
"Claims made" policies, § 28.35
Deductibles, § 28.39
Dissolution of law firm, § 28.45
Exclusions, § 28.38
Innocent partner coverage, § 28.42
Limits, § 28.39
Non-renewal, § 28.41
Notice of occurrence, § 28.40
Occurrence coverage, § 28.35
Rescission, § 28.43
"Tail" coverage, § 28.36

LEGISLATORS
Absolute immunity, § 18.31

LEMON LAW
Generally, § 7.1 et seq.
Advantages of using, § 7.12
Appeals, § 7.48
Applications, § 7.10
Arbitration, §§ 7.3, 7.12, 7.48
    Appeals, §§ 7.16, 7.17
    Awards, § 7.15
    Burden of proof, § 7.15
    Hearing, §§ 7.14, 7.15
    Notice of petition to vacate award, § 7.50
    Petition to vacate award, § 7.51
    Procedure, § 7.13
Attorney fees, §§ 7.12, 7.48
Complaints, § 7.52
Credit reports, § 7.5
Damages, §§ 7.12, 7.48
Definitions, § 7.19
Document request, § 7.49
Enactment, § 7.9
Limitation of actions, § 7.48
Publications, § 7.18
Qualifications for protection under, §§ 7.10, 7.48
Rescission, notice of, § 7.56
Restitution, § 7.56
Revocation of acceptance, § 7.56
Settlement of claims, §§ 7.14, 7.48
    Stipulation, § 7.61
Used cars, § 7.9
    Definitions, § 7.11
    Warranties, § 7.48
Warranties, §§ 7.10, 7.11, 7.48

LIABILITY INSURANCE
Malpractice,
    Legal Malpractice Insurance, generally, this index

LIBEL AND SLANDER
Complaints, § 26.36
Damages, mitigation,
    Partial defense, form, § 30.54
Defenses, § 18.82
Employment cases, discharge of employee, § 17.25
First Amendment, freedom of speech, § 18.27
Miscellaneous civil rights and immunities, § 18.81

INDEX

LIBRARIES
Public accommodations and amusement, equal rights in places of, § 18.54

LICENSED REPRESENTATIVES
Workers' compensation, § 32.37
    Fees, § 32.38

LICENSES
Alcoholic Beverage Control, this index
Attorneys,
    Court of appeals, admission of attorneys and licensing of foreign legal consultants, § 39.61
Beer. Alcoholic Beverage Control, this index
Foreign professional service corporations,
    Licensing authority regulation of professions, § 1.125
Liquor. Alcoholic Beverage Control, generally, this index
Small business, purchase or sale,
    Due diligence investigation, legal review, § 6.21

LICENSING MATTERS
Adjudicatory proceedings. Administrative Law and Proceedings, this index

LIENS
Bankruptcy,
    Avoiding,
        Adversary proceedings to avoid liens and transfers, § 9.197
            Chapter 7, § 9.197
                Limitation of actions, § 9.198
            Limitation of actions, § 9.198
        Claims procedures, secured claims, § 9.101
            "Lien stripping", § 9.101
        Debtor's motion to avoid judicial lien or nonpossessory, nonpurchase-money security interest,
            Drafting checklist, § 9.301
            Procedural checklist, § 9.279
        Preferences, unavoidable statutory liens, exception, § 9.118
        Return of goods by debtor, exemptions, § 9.128
            Liens on exempt property, § 9.129
        Statutory liens, § 9.116
    Chapter 7, treatment of certain liens, § 9.199
    Return of goods by debtor, exemptions,
        Lien avoidance, § 9.128
        Liens on exempt property, § 9.129
    Secured claims,
        Avoidance of liens, § 9.101
        "Lien stripping", § 9.101
    Use, sale or lease of property,
        Sales free and clear of liens, § 9.63
Income tax, state,
    Collection of tax, duration, § 35.115
Mechanic's Liens, generally, this index
Medicaid, § 23.82
Motor vehicle repair shops, §§ 7.28, 7.29, 7.48
    Order to vacate, § 7.57
    Petition to vacate, § 7.58
        Affirmation in support, § 7.59
No-fault, § 26.49
Personal injury cases, § 26.49
Public assistance, § 26.49
Small business, purchase or sale,
    Due diligence investigation, legal review, § 6.18
Statutory liens,
    Bankruptcy, avoiding powers, § 9.116
Workers' compensation, §§ 26.49, 32.32

INDEX

LIFE INSURANCE
ERISA protection, § 17.50
Estate planning,
    Planning with certain assets, § 24.34
        Trusts, § 24.35
            Crummey powers, § 24.36
Insurance, this index

LIFETIME PLANNING
    Generally, § 24.44
Annual gift tax exclusion. Gift Taxes, Federal, generally, this index
Charitable lead trusts, § 24.55
Charitable remainder trusts, § 24.54
Valuation of gifts, § 24.45
    Grantor retained trusts, § 24.46
    Residence trusts, § 24.47
        Income tax considerations, § 24.48

LIMITATION OF ACTIONS
Affirmative defense, § 26.37
Bankruptcy,
    Adversary proceedings to avoid liens and transfers, § 9.198
    Avoiding powers, § 9.121
Breach of contract, § 17.77
Consumer Leasing Act, § 7.48
Deceptive Practices Act, § 7.48
Defamation, § 17.77
Discrimination cases, § 17.77
Eminent domain,
    Acquisition, § 14.49
        Stages, § 14.50
    Judicial review of public hearing determination and findings, § 14.37
Fair Debt Collection Practices Act, § 7.48
False imprisonment, § 17.77
Federal civil rights law, § 18.38
Income tax, state,
    Actions on taxpayer's returns, § 35.64
    Assessment and collection of tax, § 35.111
    Effect, § 35.66
    Exceptions, § 35.67
    Income tax assessment, general statutes for, § 35.65
    Prompt assessment, requests for, § 35.68
    Waiver, § 35.69
Insurance, § 31.26
Judicial review, administrative law, § 4.82
Legal malpractice, §§ 28.1, 28.13 et seq.
    Fee disputes, § 28.31
Lemon law, § 7.48
Local land use law, judicial review, § 16.43
Malicious prosecution, § 17.77
Medical malpractice, §§ 29.17, 29.26
New York Fair Credit Reporting Act, § 7.48
Personal injury cases, §§ 17.77, 26.32
Products liability, § 27.39
    Distributors' or sellers' liability,
        Physicians, § 27.25
Rehabilitation Act, § 17.77
State Environmental Quality Review Act (SEQRA), § 15.6
Torts, § 17.77
Wage claim, § 17.77
Whistleblower protection cases, § 17.77
Workers' compensation, § 17.77
    Hearings, § 32.18

INDEX

LIMITED LIABILITY COMPANIES
 Generally, §§ 2.14, 28.34
Assignment of Interests, this index
Chart comparing New York entities, § 2.108
Conversions/Mergers. Conversions, this index
Dissolution, this index
Due diligence considerations, § 2.105
Formation, § 2.16
 Articles of organization, § 2.17
  Forms, § 2.111
 Operating agreements, § 2.19
  Member-managed LLCs,
   Forms, § 2.112
  Other issues, § 2.20
 Publication, § 2.18
Governing law, § 2.15
Management, § 2.25
 Agency authority, § 2.32
 Delegation of responsibility, § 2.30
 Members versus managers, § 2.26
 Non-waivable requirements, § 2.29
 Standard of care, § 2.31
 Voting,
  Managers, § 2.28
  Members, § 2.27
Members, § 2.21
 Liability, § 2.23
 New members, admission, § 2.22
 One-member LLCs, § 2.24
Mergers. Conversions, this index
Partnerships, compared, § 2.10
 Flexibility, § 2.13
 Liability, § 2.12
 Tax implications, § 2.11
Professional limited liability companies, § 2.43
Professional service corporations, § 1.122
Securities laws issues, § 2.106
Summary, § 2.107
Tax Classification, generally, this index
Winding up, § 2.39

LIMITED LIABILITY PARTNERSHIPS
 Generally, §§ 2.72, 28.34
Chart comparing New York entities, § 2.108
Due diligence considerations, § 2.105
Formation/registration, § 2.75
 Certificate of registration, form, § 2.113
Governing law, § 2.73
Legal malpractice cases, § 28.25
Other issues, § 2.76
Partnerships, compared, § 2.74
Professional service corporations, § 1.122
Registration. Formation/registration, generally, ante
Securities laws issues, § 2.106
Summary, § 2.107
Tax Classification, generally, this index

LIMITED PARTNERSHIPS
 Generally, § 2.77
Assignment of Interests, this index
Certificate of limited partnership,
 Forms, § 2.114
Chart comparing New York entities, § 2.108

INDEX

LIMITED PARTNERSHIPS—Continued
Conversions%/mergers. Conversions, this index
Dissolution, this index
Due diligence considerations, § 2.105
Family limited partnerships, annual gift tax exclusion, § 24.53
Formation, § 2.79
    Agreement, § 2.82
        Forms, § 2.115
    Certificate of limited partnership, § 2.80
    Other issues, § 2.83
    Publication, § 2.81
Governing law, § 2.78
Management, § 2.88
    Agency authority, § 2.93
    Delegation of responsibility, § 2.91
    Standard of care, § 2.92
    Voting,
        General partners, § 2.89
        Limited partners, § 2.90
Professional organizations, § 2.104
Securities laws issues, § 2.106
Summary, § 2.107
Tax Classification, generally, this index

LIQUOR CONTROL
Alcoholic Beverage Control, generally, this index

LIVING WILLS
    Generally, § 24.92
Health care decision making, § 23.111
    Sample form, § 23.126

LOANS
Home equity loans, elderly individuals, § 23.104
Tax assistance loans, elderly individuals, § 23.102

LOCAL CRIMINAL COURTS
    Generally, § 33.1 et seq.
Accusatory instruments, § 33.8 et seq.
    Complaints, § 33.12
    Information, § 33.9
        Prosecutor's information, § 33.11
        Re-filing upon dismissal of supporting deposition not constituting double jeopardy, § 33.24
        Simplified information, § 33.10
            Pretrial discovery, § 33.32
            Superseding information disallowed, § 33.23
    Supporting depositions, § 33.13 et seq.
        Factual insufficiency not jurisdictional defect, § 33.22
        Guilty plea waiving defects, § 33.22
        Procedure, § 33.14
        Re-filing of information upon dismissal of supporting deposition, § 33.24
        Service of process,
            Dismissal for failure to serve, § 33.19
                Not amendable defect, § 33.25
            Motion to dismiss,
                Timeliness, § 33.21
                Writing requirement, § 33.20
            Request by attorney requiring service on counsel, § 33.18
            Requirements, § 33.15
            Timing, § 33.17
            Who must be served, § 33.16
    Verification, § 33.26
Appeals, intermediate appellate courts, § 38.46 et seq.

INDEX

LOCAL CRIMINAL COURTS—Continued
Appellate division, governance of term, § 38.57
CPL § 450.60, § 38.47
Overview of process, § 33.3
Police/citizen encounters, § 33.4 et seq.
    Arrest, § 33.4
    Common law inquiry, § 33.4
    Motor vehicle stops, § 33.5
        Parked cars, § 33.6
    Reasonable cause, defined, § 33.4
    Requests for information, § 33.4
    Stop, § 33.4
    Warrantless arrest, § 33.7
Scope, § 33.1
Strategy, § 33.2

LOCAL LAND USE LAW
    Generally, § 16.1 et seq.
Comprehensive plan, § 16.11 et seq.
    Judicial definition, § 16.12
    Preparation and adoption, § 16.14
    Protection of zoning from challenge, § 16.15
    Standard City Planning Enabling Act, § 16.11
    Standard State Zoning Enabling Act, § 16.11
    Statutory definition, § 16.13
    Summary, § 16.16
Definitions, § 16.3
Delegated authority, § 16.4
Enabling acts, § 16.5
    New York City, § 16.6
Home rule authority, § 16.7
    Flexibility, § 16.8
    Floating zone, § 16.9
Judicial review, § 16.42 et seq.
    Article 78 proceedings, §§ 16.43, 16.45
        Writ of certiorari, § 16.50
    Exhaustion of administrative remedies, § 16.49
    Injunctive relief, § 16.50
    Limitation of actions, § 16.43
    Procedures, § 16.43
    Remedies, § 16.50
    "Special damage" test, § 16.48
    Standard of review, § 16.44
        Constitutionality of statute, § 16.45
        Local legislature, § 16.45
        Planning board, § 16.47
        Zoning board of appeals, § 16.46
    Standing, § 16.48
    Summary, § 16.51
    Writ of certiorari, § 16.50
    Writ of mandamus, § 16.50
Local boards and practices, § 16.34 et seq.
    Conflicts of interest, § 16.40
    Freedom of Information Law, § 16.38
    Local legislature, role, § 16.35
    Open Meetings Law, § 16.39
    Planning boards, § 16.36
    Summary, § 16.41
    Zoning board of appeals, § 16.37
Local environmental review, § 16.52 et seq.
    Actions subject to SEQRA, § 16.53
        Building permits, § 16.54
        Rezoning, § 16.58

INDEX

LOCAL LAND USE LAW—Continued
Local environmental review—Continued
    Actions subject to SEQRA—Continued
        Site plans, § 16.57
        Subdivisions, § 16.56
            Approval, effect, § 16.98
        Variances, § 16.55
    Environmental impact statement (EIS), § 16.52
    Summary, § 16.59
Local process, § 16.27 et seq.
    Adoption, § 16.29
    Amendment, § 16.30
    Building regulations and permits, § 16.32
    Official map, § 16.31
    Site plan regulations, § 16.28
    Structure, § 16.28
    Subdivision regulations, § 16.28
    Summary, § 16.33
    Zoning ordinances, § 16.28
Scope, § 16.1
Site plans, § 16.103 et seq.
    Authority, delegation, § 16.103
    Definitions, § 16.103
    Local environmental review,
        Actions subject to SEQRA, §§ 16.57, 16.105
    Regulations, local process, § 16.28
    Responsible agency, § 16.104
        Conditions imposed, § 16.107
        Procedure, § 16.105
        Review standards, § 16.106
    Summary, § 16.108
Strategy, § 16.2
Subdivisions,
    Approval, § 16.96 et seq.
        Conditions, § 16.101
        Decisions, § 16.101
        Final plat, § 16.97
        Park land, § 16.100
        Preliminary plat or map, § 16.97
        Procedure, § 16.97
        Provision of essential services, § 16.99
        Recreational needs of residents, § 16.100
        SEQRA, effect, § 16.98
        Summary, § 16.102
    Local environmental review, actions subject to SEQRA, § 16.56
    Regulations, local process, § 16.28
Substantive limits, § 16.17 et seq.
    Commercial signs, § 16.25
    Delegation of authority, § 16.21
    Equal protection, § 16.20
    First amendment, § 16.25
    Free speech limitations, § 16.25
    Just compensation, § 16.22
    Legitimate public purpose, § 16.18
    Nonconforming uses, § 16.23
    Preemption by state and federal laws, § 16.24
    Procedural due process, § 16.19
    Regulatory takings, § 16.22
    Substantive due process, § 16.18
    Summary, § 16.26
    Ultra vires, § 16.21
    Vested rights, § 16.23

INDEX

LOCAL LAND USE LAW—Continued
Summary, § 16.10
Zoning, generally, this index

LODGING
Bankruptcy,
    Cash collateral, postpetition proceeds,
        Security interests in rents and hotel revenues, § 9.69
Hotels,
    License for sale of beer, wine and spirits, §§ 36.9, 36.34

LONG TERM CARE
Estate planning, special situations, multiple marriages, § 24.62

LONG TERM CARE INSURANCE
    Generally, § 23.63
Partnership for long term care/Robert Wood Johnson Program, § 23.66
Policy, choosing, § 23.67
Regulation under New York law, § 23.64
Relationship to Medicaid eligibility, § 23.65
Tax issues, § 23.68

LONGSHOREMEN'S AND HARBOR WORKERS' COMPENSATION ACT
Antireprisal provisions, § 17.38

MAINTENANCE
Bankruptcy preferences, exception, § 9.118
Income tax, federal, § 21.51
Spousal Support, generally, this index

MALICIOUS PROSECUTION
Employment cases, discharge of employee, § 17.26
Limitation of actions, § 17.77

MALT BEVERAGES
License to sell, § 36.9

MANAGEMENT
Limited Liability Companies, this index
Limited Partnerships, this index
Partnerships, this index

MANSION TAX
Real property sale,
    Closing of title, payment of taxes, § 12.83

MARRIAGES
Alimony. Spousal Support, generally, this index
Annulment of marriage,
    Distribution of property, § 21.7
    Judgments, form, § 21.90
Child Support, generally, this index
Divorce, generally, this index
"Heart balm" statute, § 18.74 et seq.
    Action for return of gifts made in contemplation of marriage, § 18.76
        Procedure, § 18.77
    Penalty for bringing action, § 18.75
Immigration, generally, this index
Maintenance. Spousal Support, generally, this index
Nullity of a void marriage, judgments, form, § 21.90
Spousal Support, generally, this index

MARSHALS
Appellate division, civil, administrative powers, § 37.12

INDEX

MECHANIC'S LIENS
    Generally, § 10.1 et seq.
    Affidavit for continuance, form, § 10.117
    Assignment, § 10.33
        Form, § 10.115
        Private improvements, notice of assignment, § 10.34
            Contents, § 10.35
            Extension of term, § 10.36
        Public improvements, § 10.37
            Assignment of moneys due or to become due under contract, form, § 10.116
            Form, § 10.114
    Bond to discharge liens,
        Action on bond, § 10.72
        Claim against bond, § 10.70
        Discharge of liens and notices of claims, § 10.73
            Affidavit for order fixing amount of bond, form, § 10.124
        Effect, § 10.68
        Notice of claim, § 10.71
        Requirements, § 10.69
    Building loan contracts,
        Checklist, § 10.60
        Filing, § 10.59
        Mortgages,
            Private improvements, priorities, § 10.28
    Creation,
        Consent or request of owner, § 10.7
        Elements, § 10.4 et seq.
        Improvements to real property, § 10.6
        Protected class, § 10.5
    Demand for terms of contract, form, § 10.111
    Discharge,
        Bond to discharge liens,
            Action on bond, § 10.72
            Affidavit for order fixing amount of bond, form, § 10.124
            Claim against bond, § 10.70
            Discharge of liens and notices of claims, § 10.73
            Effect, § 10.68
            Notice of claim, § 10.71
            Requirements, § 10.69
        Enforcement,
            Deposit of money or securities to discharge lien,
                Order, effect, § 10.86
                Preference over contractors, § 10.87
                Procedures, § 10.85
        Private improvements,
            Defective lien, § 10.48
                Petition to discharge, form, § 10.119
            Deposit of money with county clerk or court, § 10.49
            Expiration of term, § 10.43
            Failure to prosecute, § 10.45
            Judgment, § 10.47
            Satisfaction, § 10.42
            Termination of notice of pendency, § 10.44
            Undertaking, § 10.46
                Form, § 10.121
                Petition for order fixing amount, form, § 10.122
                Petition for order, form, § 10.120
        Public improvements,
            Deposit of money, § 10.53
            Expiration of lien, § 10.51
            Failure to prosecute, § 10.57
            Invalidity of lien, § 10.56

INDEX

MECHANIC'S LIENS—Continued
Discharge—Continued
  Public improvements—Continued
    Procedures, § 10.58
    Retention of credit, § 10.55
    Satisfaction of judgment, § 10.52
    Satisfaction of lien, § 10.50
    Undertaking, § 10.54
      Form, § 10.121
      Petition for order fixing amount, form, § 10.122
      Petition for order, form, § 10.120
  Sale of real property, § 10.65
Duration of lien,
  Private improvements,
    Notice of pendency, § 10.38
      Extensions, § 10.39
  Public improvements,
    Notice of pendency, § 10.40
      Extensions, § 10.41
Enforcement,
  Action to impress and enforce trust, § 10.147
  Affidavit in support of application to cancel notice of mechanic's lien for failure to commence action, form, § 10.130
  Affidavit in support of motion to determine if class action can be maintained, § 10.147
  Cancellation of bond, § 10.90
  Costs and disbursements, § 10.83
  Courts, § 10.77
    Courts not of record,
      Judgments and transcripts, § 10.82
      Proceedings upon return of summons, § 10.81
      Summons and complaint, § 10.80
    Courts of record,
      Necessary parties, § 10.79
      Procedures, § 10.78
  Deficiency judgments, § 10.89
  Delivery of property in lieu of money, § 10.88
  Deposit of money or securities to discharge lien,
    Acceptance of offer to pay money into court in discharge of mechanic's lien, form, § 10.138
    Offer to pay money into court in discharge of mechanic's lien, form, § 10.139
    Order, effect, § 10.86
    Preference over contractors, § 10.87
    Procedures, § 10.85
    Return of deposit, § 10.90
  Failure to establish lien, effect, § 10.84
  Foreclosure of mechanic's lien,
    Affidavit in support of motion to consolidate actions, form, § 10.136
    Complaint of contractor, form, § 10.134
    Judgment of foreclosure and sale, form, § 10.140
    Notice of motion to consolidate actions, form, § 10.137
  New parties, § 10.92
  Notice requiring lienor to commence action, form, § 10.129
  Public improvements, § 10.91
    Affidavit in support of application to cancel notice of mechanic's lien for failure to commence action, form, § 10.132
    Notice requiring lienor to commence action, form, § 10.131
  Vacating mechanic's lien, § 10.90
Extent of lien, § 10.8 et seq.
  Amount, § 10.11
  Breach of contract, § 10.12
  Insurance proceeds, § 10.10
  Loss of profits, § 10.12

INDEX

MECHANIC'S LIENS—Continued
Extent of lien—Continued
    Ownership interest at time of filing, § 10.8
    Sale of property, § 10.9
Forms, § 10.108 et seq.
Materialmen,
    Derivative rights, § 10.13
        Statutory protections, § 10.14
Nature of lien, § 10.3
New York Lien Law, § 10.4
Notice of lending, filing, § 10.99
Notice of lien,
    Amendment, § 10.19
        Correct name of owner of property, form, § 10.113
    Contents, § 10.16
    Filing, § 10.17
        Arbitration rights, effect, § 10.67
    General form, § 10.109
    Procedure, § 10.15
    Public improvements, § 10.22
        Filing notice of lien, § 10.23
        Form, § 10.110
    Service, § 10.18
Priorities,
    Private improvements,
        Assignments of contract rights, § 10.27
        Building loan mortgages, § 10.28
        Contracts of sale, § 10.29
        Deeds, § 10.31
        Parity of mechanic's liens, § 10.26
        Seller's mortgage, § 10.30
    Public improvements, § 10.32
Private improvements,
    Assignment,
        Notice of assignment, § 10.34
            Contents, § 10.35
            Extension of term, § 10.36
    Checklist, § 10.20
    Discharge,
        Defective lien, § 10.48
        Deposit of money with county clerk or court, § 10.49
        Expiration of term, § 10.43
        Failure to prosecute, § 10.45
        Judgment, § 10.47
        Satisfaction, § 10.42
        Termination of notice of pendency, § 10.44
        Undertaking, § 10.46
    Duration of lien,
        Notice of pendency, § 10.38
            Extensions, § 10.39
    Priorities,
        Assignments of contract rights, § 10.27
        Building loan mortgages, § 10.28
        Contracts of sale, § 10.29
        Deeds, § 10.31
        Parity of mechanic's liens, § 10.26
        Seller's mortgage, § 10.30
Procedural checklist, § 10.107
Protecting the owner,
    Itemized statement, § 10.74
        Affidavit in support of application to cancel mechanic's lien for failure to furnish itemized statement, form, § 10.128

INDEX

MECHANIC'S LIENS—Continued
Protecting the owner—Continued
    Itemized statement—Continued
        Demand, form, § 10.127
        Notice of application for order, form, § 10.126
        Petition for order, form, § 10.125
    Lien willfully exaggerated, § 10.75
        Defense and counterclaim, form, § 10.135
Public improvements,
    Affidavit for continuance, form, § 10.118
    Assignment, § 10.37
    Checklist, § 10.25
    Discharge,
        Deposit of money, § 10.53
        Expiration of lien, § 10.51
        Failure to prosecute, § 10.57
        Invalidity of lien, § 10.56
        Procedures, § 10.58
        Retention of credit, § 10.55
        Satisfaction of judgment, § 10.52
        Satisfaction of lien, § 10.50
        Undertaking, § 10.54
    Duration of lien,
        Notice of pendency, § 10.40
            Extensions, § 10.41
    Enforcement, § 10.91
        Affidavit in support of application to cancel notice of mechanic's lien for failure to commence action, form, § 10.132
        Notice requiring lienor to commence action, form, § 10.131
    Extent of lien, § 10.21
    Foreclosure of lien,
        Affidavit in support of motion for summary judgment, form, § 10.142
        Form, § 10.133
        Lien discharged and fund retained for public improvement, form, § 10.141
    Notice of completion and acceptance, § 10.24
        Form, § 10.112
    Notice of lien, § 10.22
        Filing, § 10.23
Repossession of materials not used, § 10.76
Scope, § 10.1
Strategy, § 10.2
Subcontractors,
    Derivative rights, § 10.13
        Statutory protections, § 10.14
Subordination of liens,
    Agreement with owner, § 10.61
        Postponement of judgments, § 10.62
    Approval by lienors of subordination to trust bond or note and mortgage, form, § 10.123
    Notices of lis pendens, § 10.64
    Subsequent mortgage, § 10.63
Trust funds,
    Action to enforce trust,
        Preferences, § 10.104
        Procedure, § 10.102
        Remedies, § 10.103
        Standing, § 10.102
    Beneficiaries, § 10.97
        Right to examine books or records, § 10.101
    Complaint by subcontractor to enforce trust against funds received by contractor or assignee, form, § 10.145
    Complaint by surety to have parties declared trustees of subcontract moneys and for accounting, form, § 10.146

INDEX

MECHANIC'S LIENS—Continued
Trust funds—Continued
    Contractors and subcontractors, § 10.96
    Creation, § 10.95
    Diversion of trust assets, § 10.98
    Misappropriation of trust funds, § 10.106
    Notice of lending, filing, § 10.99
    Purpose, § 10.94
    Record keeping obligations, § 10.100
    Relief after judgment on obligation constituting trust claim, § 10.105
    Verified statement from trustee,
        Demand for, form, § 10.143
        Petition for, form, § 10.144
Waiver, limitations, § 10.66

MEDIATION
Employment disputes, § 17.8
Personal injury cases, § 26.50

MEDICAID
    Generally, § 23.69
Administrative and judicial appeals, § 23.83
Covered services, § 23.70
Eligibility, basic requirements, § 23.71
Home care coverage, § 23.86
Hospital patient rights, discharge planning, § 23.91
Income, § 23.73
Liens, § 23.82
"Medically needy," surplus income program, § 23.72
Recoveries against estates, § 23.81
Resources, § 23.74
    Exempt resources, § 23.75
    Transfer, § 23.76
Spousal budgeting,
    Community spouse, protection of resources and income for, § 23.80
Surplus income program for the "medically needy", § 23.72
Taxpayer Relief Act of 1997, transfer of resources, § 23.76
Trusts,
    Treatment of trusts, § 23.77
        Self settled trusts, § 23.78
        Third party trusts, § 23.79

MEDICAL EVIDENCE
Disability Benefits Law, generally, this index
Medical Malpractice, generally, this index
Motor Vehicle Accidents, generally, this index
Personal Injury, generally, this index
Social Security, generally, this index
Workers' Compensation, generally, this index

MEDICAL MALPRACTICE
    Generally, § 29.1 et seq.
Certificate of merit, § 26.11
    Drafting checklist, § 29.79
    Form, § 29.83
Common law standards of care, §§ 29.10 et seq., 29.11
    Defenses, § 29.17
        Comparative negligence, § 29.17
        Informed consent, § 29.17
        Lack of personal jurisdiction, § 29.17
        Limitation of actions, § 29.17
    Expert witnesses, § 29.16
    Health maintenance organizations, § 29.15
    Hospital's direct liability, § 29.13

INDEX

MEDICAL MALPRACTICE—Continued
Common law standards of care—Continued
    Hospital's respondeat-superior liability, § 29.12
    Informed consent, § 29.14
        Battery as lack of consent, § 29.14
        Consent not required, § 29.14
        Defenses, § 29.17
        Forms, § 29.53
        Hospital records, § 29.53
        Implied consent, § 29.14
    Wrongful conception, § 29.11
    Wrongful life, § 29.11
Complaints,
    Answers, § 26.59
    Contents, § 26.58
    Demand for relief, § 26.36
Damages, §§ 26.58, 29.24
    Complaint, ad damnum clause, form, § 30.47
    Nature and degree, strategy, § 29.4
    Request for supplemental relief, form, § 30.49
Dental malpractice, § 26.13
    Expert witnesses, discovery, § 26.42
Discovery, §§ 29.64 et seq., 29.74
    Allied health provider records, § 29.70
    Autopsy report, § 29.72
    Billing records, § 29.68
    Hospital records, § 29.67
    Obtaining and identifying relevant records, § 29.65
    Pharmacy records, § 29.69
    Physician's records, § 29.66
    Pre-calendar conferences, § 29.30
    Workers' compensation, § 29.73
        Claim file, § 29.71
Drafting checklist, § 29.76 et seq.
Expert witnesses,
    Discovery, § 26.42
        Form, § 26.68
    Review of records, § 26.11
Filing, § 29.27 et seq.
    Certificate of merit, § 29.28
    Notice of medical malpractice action, § 29.29
    Pre-calendar conferences, § 29.30
Forms, § 29.80 et seq.
Hospital records, §§ 26.11, 29.52
    Anesthesia record, § 29.57
    Consultation records, § 29.56
    Discharge summary, § 29.52
    Discovery, § 29.67
    Face sheet, § 29.52
    ICU/CCU records, § 29.62
    Informed consent forms, § 29.53
    Intake and output records, § 29.59
    Labor and delivery room records, § 29.61
    Medication records, § 29.58
    Nurse's notes, § 29.63
    Obstetric records, § 29.61
    Operative records, § 29.57
    Operative report, § 29.57
    Order sheets, § 29.55
    Pre-operative checklist, § 29.57
    Prenatal records, § 29.61
    Progress notes, § 29.54

INDEX

MEDICAL MALPRACTICE—Continued
Hospital records—Continued
    Radiographic records, § 29.60
    Recovery room record, § 29.57
Hospitals,
    Claims against, § 26.12
    Hospital operations and medical negligence,
        Credentialling of physicians, § 29.32
        Departmentalization of services, § 29.34
        Quality assurance program, § 29.33
        Risk management program, § 29.33
    Standard of care,
        Hospital's direct liability, § 29.13
        Hospital's respondeat-superior liability, § 29.12
Investigation of case, §§ 26.9, 26.11
Limitation of actions, §§ 26.11, 29.26
Mandatory sliding-scale contingency fee, § 26.6
Medical literature, § 29.43 et seq.
    Computers, § 29.44
    Medical journals, § 29.45
    Medical libraries, § 29.44
    Obtaining, § 29.44
    Practice parameters and clinical practice guidelines, § 29.45
    Preparing for depositions, § 29.47
    Sources, § 29.45
    Textbooks, § 29.45
    Trial preparation, § 29.48
    Use of treatises in federal court, § 29.50
    Use of treatises in state court, § 29.49
    Use to evaluate case, § 29.46
Medical records, § 26.11
Order to show cause,
    Affirmation in support,
        Drafting checklist, § 29.78
        Form, § 29.82
    Drafting checklist, § 29.77
        Form, § 29.81
Periodic payment of large verdicts, § 29.31
Physical examination of plaintiff, § 26.42
Physicians,
    Records,
        Discovery, obtaining and identifying relevant records, § 29.66
        Evaluating and understanding medical records, § 29.51 et seq.
    Training and education, § 29.35 et seq.
        Board certification, § 29.40
        Continuing education, § 29.41
        Fellowships, § 29.39
        Internship, § 29.37
        Medical school, § 29.36
        Medical societies and associations, § 29.41
        National practitioner data bank, § 29.42
        PGY-I, § 29.37
        Re-certification, § 29.40
        Residency, § 29.38
Podiatric malpractice, § 26.13
    Expert witnesses, discovery, § 26.42
Procedure, § 29.25
Regulatory standards, § 29.18
    Blood banks, § 29.21
    Clinical laboratories, § 29.20
    Early intervention program, § 29.22
    Hospitals, § 29.23

INDEX

MEDICAL MALPRACTICE—Continued
Regulatory standards—Continued
    Nurse midwives, qualification, § 29.19
    Phenylketonuria testing, § 29.22
Scope, § 29.2
Standard of care, § 29.11
    Defenses, § 29.17
        Comparative negligence, § 29.17
        Informed consent, § 29.17
        Lack of personal jurisdiction, § 29.17
        Limitation of actions, § 29.17
    Expert witnesses, § 29.16
    Health maintenance organizations, § 29.15
    Hospital's direct liability, § 29.13
    Hospital's respondeat-superior liability, § 29.12
    Informed consent, § 29.14
        Battery as lack of consent, § 29.14
        Consent not required, § 29.14
        Defenses, § 29.17
        Forms, § 29.53
        Hospital records, § 29.53
        Implied consent, § 29.14
    Wrongful conception, § 29.11
    Wrongful life, § 29.11
Strategy, § 29.3 et seq.
    Damages, nature and degree, § 29.4
    Determination of presence or absence of medical malpractice, § 29.3
    Interviewing client, § 29.5 et seq.
        Current medical condition, § 29.8
        Disability policy applications, § 29.9
        History of current condition, § 29.6
        Miscellaneous, § 29.9
        Past litigation, § 29.9
        Past medical conditions, § 29.7
        Prior criminal convictions, § 29.9
        Social security applications, § 29.9
Trial preparation, § 29.75
Valuation of case, § 26.11
Venue, § 26.58

MEDICARE
    Generally, § 23.42
Administrative and judicial appeals. Appeals, this index
Eligibility and enrollment, § 23.43
Home care coverage, § 23.85
Hospital patient rights, discharge planning, § 23.91
Part A benefits, § 23.44
    Home health care, § 23.47
    Hospice care, § 23.48
    Hospital services, § 23.45
    Skilled nursing facilities, § 23.46
Part B supplementary medical insurance, § 23.49
    Assignment of claims, § 23.51
    Balance billing, limitations, § 23.52
    Deductibles and coinsurance, § 23.50
    Participating physicians, § 23.51
Supplemental Medical Insurance (Medigap Plans), generally, this index

MEDIGAP PLANS
Supplemental Medical Insurance (MEDIGAP Plans), generally, this index

MEETINGS
Bankruptcy,

INDEX

MEETINGS—Continued
Bankruptcy—Continued
    Meeting of creditors, § 9.37
        Scope of examination, § 9.38
Corporations, generally, this index
Municipal corporations, § 3.28
    Open Meetings Law, § 3.28
    Public meetings, § 3.28
Open Meetings Law,
    Definitions, § 3.28
    Local land use law, § 16.39
Shareholders' Meetings and Agreements, generally. Corporations, this index

MENTAL HYGIENE LAW ARTICLE 81
    Generally, § 22.1 et seq.
Definitions, § 22.9
Legislative purpose, § 22.8
Summary, § 22.10

MENTAL RETARDATION AND DEVELOPMENTALLY DISABLED PERSONS
Adoption proceedings, termination of parental rights, §§ 20.39, 20.101
Death penalty,
    Appellate division, criminal, § 38.10

MERGERS
Corporations. Business Combinations, generally. Corporations, this index
Limited liability companies. Conversions, generally, this index
Limited partnerships. Conversions, generally, this index
Partnerships. Conversions, generally, this index
Retirement income from qualified plans, § 23.34
Small business, purchase or sale,
    Tax issues,
        Buyer, for, § 6.45
        Seller, for,
            Stock purchases, § 6.133

MIDWIVES
Medical malpractice,
    Regulatory standards, nurse midwives, qualification, § 29.19

MIGRANT AND SEASONAL AGRICULTURAL WORKER PROTECTION ACT
Antireprisal provisions, § 17.38

MILITARY
Equipment and supplies, employment discrimination prohibited, § 18.60

MINORS
Employment, § 17.63

MIRANDA RIGHTS
Evidence, § 33.48 et seq.
    Custodial interrogation,
        Interrogation defined, § 33.52
        Sobriety checkpoint stops non-custodial, § 33.51
        Stop and frisk not constituting, § 33.50
    Pedigree exception, § 33.54
    Public safety exception, § 33.53
    Waiver,
        Following assertion of right to remain silent, § 33.55
        Following request for counsel, § 33.56
Misdemeanor traffic offenses, § 33.49

MISREPRESENTATION
Insurance, § 31.18

INDEX

MORTGAGES
Foreclosure, this index
Mechanic's liens,
    Private improvements, priorities,
        Building loan mortgages, § 10.28
        Seller's mortgage, § 10.30
    Subordination of liens, § 10.63
Real property,
    Residential contract of sale,
        Acceptable funds, § 12.16
        Assumption of existing mortgage, § 12.13
        Commitment date, § 12.15
        Mortgage contingency clause, § 12.15
        Purchase money mortgage, § 12.14
Reverse mortgages, elderly individuals, § 23.104

MOTELS
Bankruptcy,
    Cash collateral, postpetition proceeds,
        Security interests in rents and hotel revenues, § 9.69
Public accommodations and amusement, equal rights in places of, § 18.54

MOTIONS
Appellate division, criminal, § 38.36 et seq.
    Anders brief, § 38.38
    Assignment of new counsel, § 38.42
    Briefs, § 38.44
    Death or absence of defendant, § 38.41
    Dismissal, § 38.39
    Expanding the judgment roll, § 38.43
    Frivolous appeals, § 38.38
    Pro se supplemental brief, § 38.37
    Reconstruction hearing, § 38.40
    Summary reversal, § 38.40
    Withdrawal of appeal, § 38.45
Child support, § 21.79
Discrimination cases, § 17.74
Divorce, spousal support, § 21.79
Legal malpractice,
    Disqualification motions, § 28.21
Summary judgment, resale of repossessed motor vehicle, § 7.55

MOTOR VEHICLE ACCIDENT INDEMNIFICATION CORPORATION ACT
Compensation for injuries, § 26.24

MOTOR VEHICLE ACCIDENTS
Affidavits, notice of claim, § 26.25 et seq.
Arbitration, §§ 26.24, 26.30
Complaints,
    Answers, § 26.59
    Complaint and summons, form, § 26.65
    Damages, form, § 30.48
    Drafting, § 26.58
Damages,
    Complaint, form, § 30.48
    Defense of failure to use seat belt, form, § 30.51
Department of motor vehicles form MV104, §§ 26.20, 26.64
Discovery,
    Accident reports, form, §§ 26.68, 26.70
    Expert witnesses, form, § 26.70
    Insurance information, § 26.42
        Form, § 26.70
    Medical reports, § 26.42
        Form, § 26.68

INDEX

MOTOR VEHICLE ACCIDENTS—Continued
Discovery—Continued
    Witnesses, form, § 26.70
Hospital records, § 26.22
Insurance claims procedure, § 26.25 et seq.
    Filing notice of claim, § 26.26
        Affidavit, §§ 26.27, 26.28, 26.29
        Late claims, § 26.30
Medical records, § 26.22
Motor Vehicle Accident Indemnification Corporation Act,
    Compensation for injuries, § 26.24
No-Fault insurance provisions,
    Application for benefits, § 26.21
    Coverage, § 26.24
Notice,
    Accident or occurrance, § 31.10
    Insurance, § 31.10
    Notice of claim, affidavits, § 26.25 et seq.
Photographs, accident scene and vehicles, § 26.23
Physical examination of plaintiff, § 26.42
Police reports, § 26.18
    Insurance company information, § 26.24
Proof of negligence and serious injury, § 26.17
Records and reports,
    Accident reports, form, § 26.70
    Hospital records, § 26.22
    Medical, form, § 26.68
Summons, form, § 26.65
Uninsured and underinsured claims, § 26.24
    Procedures, § 26.25
    Set offs, § 26.24
    Stacking of coverage, § 26.24
Witness statements, § 26.19

MOTOR VEHICLE INSURANCE
Claims procedure for accidents, § 26.25
    Filing notice of claim, § 26.26
        Affidavit, §§ 26.27, 26.28, 26.29
        Late claims, § 26.30
No-Fault provisions,
    Application for benefits, § 26.21
    Coverage, § 26.24
Police reports, § 26.24
Uninsured and underinsured coverage, § 26.24
    Procedures, § 26.25
    Set offs, § 26.24
    Stacking, § 26.24

MOTOR VEHICLE REPAIR SHOP REGISTRATION ACT
Provisions, §§ 7.27, 7.48

MOTOR VEHICLE RETAIL INSTALLMENT SALES ACT
Provisions, §§ 7.23, 7.48

MOTOR VEHICLE RETAIL LEASING ACT
Attorney fees, § 7.22
Provisions, §§ 7.22, 7.48

MOTOR VEHICLE SALES
Collection agencies,
    Consumer protection, § 7.3
Consumer protection, § 7.1 et seq.
Credit reports, § 7.3
Deceptive trade practices, § 7.3

INDEX

MOTOR VEHICLE SALES—Continued
Deceptive trade practices—Continued
    Attorney fees, § 7.7
    Motor vehicle sales, § 7.3
Fair Credit Reporting Acts, § 7.3
Fair Debt Collection Practices Act, § 7.3
False advertising, § 7.3
    Attorney fees, § 7.7
Federal Odometer Act, § 7.3
Installment sales, § 7.48
Installment sales contract, § 7.3
Leasing,
    Cancellation, § 7.4
    Complaint for fraud, § 7.52
        Defenses, § 7.53
    Consumer Leasing Act, §§ 7.21, 7.48
    Consumer protection, §§ 7.1 et seq., 7.3
    Costs, § 7.19
    Defaults, § 7.20
    Lemon law, § 7.20
    Motor Vehicle Retail Leasing Act, §§ 7.22, 7.48
        Attorney fees, § 7.48
        Damages, § 7.48
    Repossession, §§ 7.3, 7.4
    Tax deductions, § 7.19
Repossession, §§ 7.3, 7.23 et seq.
    Answer to complaint, § 7.54
    Defenses, § 7.26
    Prevention, § 7.25
    Unreasonable resale, § 7.54
        Motion for summary judgment, § 7.55
    Voluntary, § 7.25
Retail Installment Sales Act, § 7.3
Secured transactions, § 7.3
Truth in Lending Act, § 7.3

MOTOR VEHICLE STOPS
Articulable reason to stop, § 33.5
Parked cars, § 33.6

MOTOR VEHICLES, DEFECTIVE
Accidents. Motor Vehicle Accidents, generally, this index
Insurance. Motor Vehicle Insurance, generally, this index
Lemon Law, generally, this index
Motor Vehicle Repair Shop Registration Act, provisions, §§ 7.27, 7.48
Motor Vehicle Retail Installment Sales Act, provisions, §§ 7.23, 7.48
Motor Vehicle Retail Leasing Act,
    Attorney fees, § 7.22
    Provisions, §§ 7.22, 7.48
Odometer law, defenses, § 7.53
Repair shops,
    Complaints, § 7.48
    Consumer rights, § 7.27
    Liens, §§ 7.28, 7.29, 7.48
        Affirmation in support of petition to vacate, § 7.59
        Order to vacate, § 7.57
        Petition to vacate, § 7.58
Sales. Motor Vehicle Sales, generally, this index
Stops,
    Articulable reason to stop, § 33.5
    Parked cars, § 33.6

INDEX

MUNICIPAL CORPORATIONS
    Generally, § 3.1 et seq.
Acquisition and disposition of property, § 3.16
Annexation, § 3.5
    Checklist, § 3.6
Article 78 proceedings, § 3.32
Business improvement districts, § 3.33
Challenges to governmental determinations, § 3.32
Codes of ethics, § 3.22
Consolidation, § 3.5
Contracts, § 3.24
    Breach, liability for, § 3.24
    Common law exceptions, § 3.25
    Competitive bidding, § 3.25
    "Professional services" exception, § 3.25
    Public works contracts, § 3.24
    Purchase contracts, § 3.24
Creation, § 3.4
Damages,
    Ad damnum clause, form, § 30.47
    Request for supplemental relief, form, § 30.49
Definitions, § 3.3
Dillon's rule, § 3.7
Dissolution, § 3.5
Drainage and refuse districts, § 3.33
Eminent domain, § 14.5
Federal civil rights law,
    42 U.S.C.A. Section 1981, applicability, § 18.17
    Defenses,
        "Monell v. New York City Dept of Social Services", § 18.34
Fire districts, § 3.33
Flood and shoreline erosion control districts, § 3.33
Foreclosure, mortgages,
    Complaints, pleading with specificity, § 11.21
Freedom of Information Law (FOIL), § 3.28
"General" law, § 3.7
Home rule power, § 3.2
    Legislative enactments, § 3.14
Hospitals, generally, this index
Hurricane protection districts, § 3.33
Immunity, waiver, § 3.30
Industrial development agencies (IDAs), § 3.34
Industrial revenue bonds, § 3.34
Legislative enactments,
    Constitutionality presumed, § 3.10
    Effective date, § 3.10
    Home rule power, § 3.14
    Local laws, § 3.14
    Ordinances, § 3.12
    Parking, rules and regulations, § 3.13
    Referendum requirements, § 3.15
    Resolutions, § 3.11
    Rules and regulations, § 3.13
    Traffic, rules and regulations, § 3.13
Meetings, § 3.28
Municipal finance, § 3.26
    Bonds and notes, § 3.27
    Borrowing, § 3.27
    Budget, § 3.26
    Revenue anticipation notes (RANs), § 3.27
    Tax anticipation notes (TANS), § 3.27
    Taxation, real property, § 3.26

INDEX

MUNICIPAL CORPORATIONS—Continued
Negligence, § 3.30
    Forms, § 3.36 et seq.
Notice of claim, § 26.39
    Examination of claimant, § 26.40
    Extensions, granting, § 26.40
    Service of process, § 26.40
    Statute, § 3.30
        Form, § 3.37
Officers and employees, § 3.17
    Collective bargaining, § 3.21
    Conflicts of interest, § 3.22
        Checklist, § 3.23
    Incompatible offices, § 3.18
    Public Officers Law, § 3.20
    Qualifications, § 3.18
    Removal, § 3.20
    Terms, § 3.19
Open Meetings Law, § 3.28
Personal injury claims, § 26.38
Personal property, acquisition and disposition, § 3.16
Powers, § 3.7
    "Balancing of public interests" test, § 3.8
    Governmental versus proprietary powers, § 3.8
    Police powers, § 3.9
Public authorities, § 3.35
Public meetings, § 3.28
Public Officers Law, § 3.28
Real property, acquisition and disposition, § 3.16
Records and reports,
    Access to public records, § 3.29
    Freedom of Information Law (FOIL), § 3.29
Scope, § 3.1
Sewer and water districts, § 3.33
Slip and fall cases, § 26.10
    Complaint, § 26.58
"Special" law, § 3.7
Special purpose units, § 3.33
    Industrial development agencies (IDAs), § 3.34
    Public authorities, § 3.35
Strategy, § 3.2
Summons and complaints,
    Filing and service, § 26.40
Taxpayers' actions, § 3.32
Tort claims against municipalities, § 3.30
    Checklist, § 3.31
    Form, § 3.38
    Verified complaint, form, § 3.38
Watershed protection districts, § 3.33
Wrongful death actions, § 3.30

NATIONAL LABOR RELATIONS ACT
Antireprisal provisions, § 17.38
Collective bargaining, protection against discrimination, § 17.61
Unfair labor practices, § 17.61

NATIONAL TRAFFIC AND MOTOR VEHICLE SAFETY ACT
Products liability,
    Preemption of private claims,
        Savings clause, § 27.45

NEGLIGENCE
Employment law, § 17.30

INDEX

NEGLIGENCE—Continued
Legal malpractice, § 28.3
Medical Malpractice, generally, this index

NEGOTIATIONS
Employment law, § 17.7
    Discharge of employee, § 17.10
    Pre-litigation, § 17.6

NEW YORK BUSINESS CORPORATION LAW
Corporations, generally, this index
Foreign professional service corporations, § 1.125
Professional service corporations, § 1.122

NEW YORK CITY COMMISSION ON HUMAN RIGHTS
Filing charges, § 17.66
    Election of remedies, § 17.68
    Responses, § 17.67

NEW YORK CITY CRIMINAL COURT
Criminal Court of New York City, generally, this index

NEW YORK CITY HUMAN RIGHTS LAW
Age discrimination provisions, § 17.37
Alienage or citizenship status, § 17.49
Antireprisal provisions, §§ 17.38, 17.59
Complaints, service of process, § 17.78
Disparate impact cause of action, § 17.59
Employment law,
    Prohibitions against discrimination, §§ 17.43, 17.44
        Marital status, § 17.48
Limitation of actions, discriminatory acts, § 17.69
Religious discrimination, § 17.56
Sexual harassment, § 17.57
Sexual orientation discrimination, § 17.58
Sick leave benefits for pregnant workers, § 17.54

NEW YORK CITY REAL PROPERTY TRANSFER TAX
Real property sale,
    Closing of title, payment of taxes, § 12.85

NEW YORK ENVIRONMENTAL CONSERVATION LAW (ECL)
Inactive hazardous waste sites, § 15.31

NEW YORK FAIR CREDIT REPORTING ACT
Attorney fees, §§ 7.48, 7.60
Complaint for violations, § 7.60
Consumer protection, § 7.31
Damages, § 7.48
Limitation of actions, § 7.48
Litigation, § 7.33

NEW YORK FRAUDULENT CONVEYANCES STATUTE
Bankruptcy, avoiding powers, § 9.115

NEW YORK LANDLORD-TENANT LAW
    Generally, § 13.1 et seq.
Article 7-A proceedings, § 13.72
Bankruptcy,
    Executory contracts and unexpired leases,
        Debtor as landlord/lessor, § 9.84
Bill of particulars, § 13.57
Checklists, § 13.77 et seq.
Counterclaims, § 13.56
Discovery, § 13.58
    Freedom of Information Law, § 13.60

INDEX

NEW YORK LANDLORD-TENANT LAW—Continued
Discovery—Continued
    Notice to admit, § 13.59
Essential allegations, checklist, § 13.77
Forms, § 13.82 et seq.
Holdover Proceedings, generally, this index
Judgment, § 13.67
Non-Payment Proceedings, generally, this index
Rent regulatory proceedings, § 13.73
    Major capital improvement rent increase (MCI), § 13.76
    Rent overcharge, § 13.74
    Service reduction, § 13.75
Scope, § 13.1
Slip and fall cases, § 26.10
Stipulations,
    Enforcement, § 13.66
    Holdover proceedings, § 13.65
        Tenant agrees to cure, form, § 13.92
        Tenant agrees to vacate premises, form, § 13.93
    Non-payment proceedings, § 13.64
        Settlement, form, § 13.90
        Settlement with final judgment, form, § 13.91
    Overview, § 13.63
    Vacatur, § 13.66
Strategy, § 13.2
    Checklists, § 13.3
Summary proceedings, § 13.4 et seq.
    Jurisdiction, § 13.5
    Posting of future rent and use and occupancy with court, § 13.61
    Real Property Actions and Proceedings Law, § 13.4
    Service of process, § 13.6
        Conspicuous place service, § 13.9
        New York City Civil Court "postcard" requirement, § 13.10
        Personal delivery, § 13.7
        Reasonable application standard, § 13.9
        Substituted service, § 13.8
    Venue, § 13.5
Trial,
    Adjournments, § 13.61
    Amendment of petition, § 13.62
    Burden of proof, § 13.62
Warrant, § 13.67
    Stay in holdover proceedings, § 13.69
    Stay in non-payment proceedings, § 13.68
"Yellowstone" actions, § 13.70
    Obtaining injunction, § 13.71

NEW YORK STATE DIVISION OF HUMAN RIGHTS
Client information sheet, form, §§ 17.90, 17.91
Complaint, form, § 17.89

NEW YORK STATE DIVISION OF HUMAN RIGHTS COMMISSION
Filing charges, § 17.66
    Election of remedies, § 17.68
    Responses, § 17.67

NEW YORK STATE ENVIRONMENTAL CONSERVATION LAW
Environmental Law, generally, this index
Hazardous waste regulation, § 15.23
Solid waste regulation, § 15.23

NEW YORK STATE EQUAL PAY ACT
Employment law, prohibitions against discrimination, § 17.44

INDEX

NEW YORK STATE HUMAN RIGHTS LAW
Antireprisal provisions, §§ 17.38, 17.59
Disparate impact cause of action, § 17.59
Employment law, prohibitions against discrimination, § 17.43
    Marital status, § 17.48
Limitation of actions, discriminatory acts, § 17.69
Provisions of statute, § 17.37
Racial discrimination, bona fide occupational qualification defense, § 17.49
Religious discrimination, § 17.56
Sexual harassment, § 17.57
Sick leave benefits for pregnant workers, § 17.54

NEW YORK STATE LIQUOR AUTHORITY
Full Board of Commissioners, § 36.6
Investigative powers, § 36.53
Jurisdiction, § 36.5 et seq.
License board, § 36.6
    Types of licenses, § 36.7 et seq.
Permits,
    Filing of penal bond, § 36.19
    Issuance, § 36.15 et seq.
Public hearings, five hundred foot rule, § 36.9
Rules and regulations, § 36.6 et seq.

NEW YORK STATE MISCELLANEOUS TAX BUREAU
Alcoholic beverages,
    Manufacturers to obtain clearance, § 36.12
    Wholesalers to obtain clearance, § 36.11

NEW YORK STATE REAL ESTATE TRANSFER TAX
Real property sale,
    Closing of title, payment of taxes, § 12.83

NON-CORPORATE ENTITIES
    Generally, § 2.1 et seq.
Checklist, § 2.109
Choice of entity, § 2.2
Due diligence considerations, § 2.105
Forms, § 2.110
Limited Liability Companies, generally, this index
Limited Liability Partnerships, generally, this index
Limited Partnerships, generally, this index
Partnerships, generally, this index
Strategy, choice of entity, § 2.2
Summary, § 2.107

NON-PAYMENT PROCEEDINGS
Burden of proof, § 13.62
New York Landlord-Tenant Law, § 13.11 et seq.
Petition,
    Amendment, § 13.62
    Answer, § 13.22
    Checklist, § 13.78
    Constructive eviction, § 13.24
        Tenant defenses, § 13.31
    Defects, § 13.18
    Dismiss, motion to, § 13.23
    Form and content, § 13.17
    Forms, § 13.83
    Notice of petition, § 13.13
        Contents, § 13.15
        Defects, § 13.16
        Form of notice, § 13.14
    Responding to, § 13.21

INDEX

NON-PAYMENT PROCEEDINGS—Continued
Petition—Continued
  Stay, motion to, § 13.24
  Tenant defenses, § 13.25 et seq.
    Actual eviction, § 13.30
    Constructive eviction, § 13.31
    Illegal rent, § 13.29
    Laches, § 13.33
    Multiple Dwelling Law, § 13.28
    No certificate of occupancy, § 13.28
    No landlord-tenant relationship, § 13.26
    No multiple dwelling registration, § 13.28
    Payment, § 13.34
    Rent-impairing violations, § 13.28
    Statutory noncompliance, § 13.28
    Tenant out of possession, § 13.27
    Warranty of habitability, § 13.32
  Verification, § 13.19
    Attorney, form, § 13.88
    Corporate officer, form, § 13.86
    Defects in verification, § 13.20
    Individual, form, § 13.85
    Partnership, form, § 13.87
Rent demand, § 13.12
Settlement stipulation,
  Checklist, § 13.80
  Final judgment, form, § 13.90
  Form, § 13.90
  Forms, § 13.90 et seq.
Stipulations, § 13.64
  Forms, § 13.90 et seq.
"Three-day notice", § 13.12
Warrant, stay, § 13.68

NONCONFORMING USE
Local land use law. Zoning, this index

NOTES
Self-cancelling installment notes,
  Estate planning, special situations, terminally ill, § 24.57

NOTICE
Administrative Law and Proceedings, this index
Adoption,
  Commencement of proceedings, notice to birth parents, § 20.100
  Notice of proposed adoption, § 20.32
    Exclusions, § 20.34
    Fathers' right to, § 20.35
  Termination of parental rights, extra-judicial surrender, § 20.94
Affidavits,
  Motor vehicle accident insurance, notice of claim, § 26.27 et seq.
Alcoholic beverage control,
  Licenses,
    Revocation,
      Notice of pleading, § 36.63
    Suspension,
      Notice of pleading and hearing, §§ 36.62, 36.64, 36.65
Appeal. Notice of Appeal, generally. Appellate Division, Civil Appellate Practice Before, this index
Arbitration,
  Lemon law, notice of petition to vacate award, § 7.50
  Mechanic's liens, filing notice of lien, effect, § 10.67
Attorney general,

INDEX

NOTICE—Continued
Attorney general—Continued
    Personal injury claim against state, notice of claim, § 26.41
Bankruptcy,
    Contested matters, notice of motion, form, § 9.307
    Examinations under Bankruptcy Rule 2004, § 9.40
    Notice of appearance, form, § 9.305
    U.S. trustee, notice of case, § 9.33
    Withdrawal of claims, notice, § 9.95
Civil rights,
    Public accommodations and amusement, equal rights in places of,
        Notice of commencement of action for discrimination, form, § 18.97
Clean Water Act (CWA),
    Citizen suits, notice letter,
        Drafting checklist, § 15.35
            Resource Conservation and Recovery Act (RCRA), § 15.36
        Form, § 15.40
            Resource Conservation and Recovery Act (RCRA), § 15.41
Commercial sales contract,
    Drafting checklists,
        Petition for order staying arbitration in dispute over contract for sale of goods,
            Notice of petition, § 5.61
        Plaintiff's notice of motion for summary judgment, § 5.59
            Affidavit in support by officer of plaintiff company, § 5.60
                Form, § 5.68
            Form, § 5.67
Corporations,
    Formation, § 1.7
    Procedural checklist, § 1.136
    Shareholders' meetings and agreements, § 1.44
Corporations, non-judicial dissolution,
    Notice to creditors, § 1.98
County clerks,
    Mechanic's liens, notice of lien, filing, § 10.17
Court of claims,
    Eminent domain, jurisdiction, § 14.54
    Notice of claim, § 26.41
Crummey notice,
    Forms, estate planning, § 24.101
Damages,
    Interest,
        Notice of motion to amend verdict to add interest, form, § 30.56
            Affidavit in support, § 30.57
        Notice of motion to fix date from which interest is computed, form, § 30.58
            Affidavit in support, § 30.59
Depositions, personal injury cases, § 26.43
Discovery,
    New York Landlord-Tenant Law, notice to admit, § 13.59
Divorce, filing, § 21.11
Eminent domain,
    Acquisition, notice, § 14.66
    Jurisdiction,
        Court of claims, § 14.54
        Supreme court, § 14.61
            Certification of names of reputed condemnees, § 14.62
            Notice of acquisition, form, § 14.132
            Notice of pendency of proceedings, § 14.57
                Form, § 14.124
            Notice of petition in proceedings, form, § 14.125
    Just compensation,
        Trial, expert witnesses,

INDEX

NOTICE—Continued
Eminent domain—Continued
  Just compensation—Continued
    Trial—Continued
      Notice of motion for additional allowance to condemnee for expert witnesses, form, § 14.135
  Public hearing, § 14.28
Enforcement of money judgments,
  Article 52 enforcement devices,
    Execution, real property, notice of sale, § 8.32
    Restraining notices,
      Contempt proceedings, § 8.27
      Disobedience of, § 8.27
      Form, § 8.53
      Formal requirements, § 8.26
      Nature and use, § 8.25
      Service of, § 8.27
  Contempt proceedings, restraining notices, § 8.27
  Execution, real property, notice of sale, § 8.32
  Notice to judgment debtor, form, § 8.49
  Subpoena duces tecum,
    Taking deposition of judgment debtor with restraining notice, form, § 8.50
    Taking deposition of witness with restraining notice, form, § 8.51
Expert witnesses,
  Eminent domain, just compensation trial,
    Notice of motion for additional allowance to condemnee for expert witnesses, form, § 14.135
Foreclosure, mortgages,
  Commencement, notice of pendency of action, § 11.17
    Drafting checklist, § 11.58
  Defendant's response, notice of appearance and waiver, § 11.38
  Foreclosure sale, notice of sale, § 11.48
    Drafting checklist, § 11.66
    Form, § 11.80
  Notice of acceleration, § 11.12
    Drafting checklist, § 11.57
    Form, § 11.70
  Notice of default, § 11.11
    Drafting checklist, § 11.56
    Form, § 11.69
  Notice of pendency of action, § 11.17
    Drafting checklist, § 11.58
    Form, § 11.71
  Summary judgment, notice of motion,
    Drafting checklist, § 11.63
    Form, § 11.77
Guardianships,
  Proceeding to appoint guardian,
    Persons entitled to, § 22.21
    Requirements, § 22.22
    Service, time and method of, § 22.20
  Role of guardian,
    Petition for authorization to transfer property,
      Notice of application, § 22.50
Holdover proceedings,
  Notice of petition, § 13.41
    Defects, § 13.42
  Predicate notices, § 13.36 et seq.
    Defective notice, tenant defense, § 13.51
      Rent-regulated apartments, § 13.52
    Illegal use, § 13.38
    Month-to-month tenants, § 13.37

INDEX

NOTICE—Continued
Holdover proceedings—Continued
    Predicate notices—Continued
        Rent-controlled tenants, § 13.39
        Rent-stabilized tenants, § 13.40
    Tenant defenses,
        Defective predicate notice, § 13.51
            Rent-regulated apartments, § 13.52
Immigration,
    Employment-based immigration, labor certification,
        Notice of findings, § 19.38
Income tax, state,
    Notice of exception to tax tribunal, forms, § 35.131
Insurance,
    Disclaimers, § 31.16
    Loss, § 31.10
Interest,
    Damages,
        Notice of motion to amend verdict to add interest, form, § 30.56
            Affidavit in support, § 30.57
        Notice of motion to fix date from which interest is computed, form, § 30.58
            Affidavit in support, § 30.59
Jurisdiction,
    Eminent domain,
        Court of claims, § 14.54
        Supreme court, § 14.61
            Notice of pendency, § 14.57
Legal malpractice insurance, notice of occurrence, § 28.40
Lemon law,
    Arbitration, notice of petition to vacate award, § 7.50
    Rescission, notice of, § 7.56
Limited liability companies, formation, § 2.18
Mechanic's liens,
    Assignment, private improvements,
        Notice of assignment, § 10.34
            Contents, § 10.35
    Bond to discharge liens,
        Discharge of liens and notices of claims, § 10.73
            Affidavit for order fixing amount of bond, form, § 10.124
        Notice of claim, § 10.71
    Discharge,
        Private improvements, termination of notice of pendency, § 10.44
    Duration of lien,
        Private improvements,
            Notice of pendency, § 10.38
                Extensions, § 10.39
        Public improvements,
            Notice of pendency, § 10.40
                Extensions, § 10.41
    Enforcement,
        Affidavit in support of application to cancel notice of mechanic's lien for failure to commence action, form, § 10.130
        Foreclosure of mechanic's lien,
            Notice of motion to consolidate actions, form, § 10.137
        Notice requiring lienor to commence action, form, § 10.129
        Public improvements,
            Affidavit in support of application to cancel notice of mechanic's lien for failure to commence action, form, § 10.132
            Notice requiring lienor to commence action, form, § 10.131
    Notice of lending, filing, § 10.99
    Notice of lien,
        Amendment, § 10.19

INDEX

NOTICE—Continued
Mechanic's liens—Continued
  Notice of lien—Continued
    Amendment—Continued
      Correct name of owner of property, form, § 10.113
    Contents, § 10.16
    Filing, § 10.17
      Arbitration rights, effect, § 10.67
    General form, § 10.109
    Procedure, § 10.15
    Public improvements, § 10.22
      Filing notice of lien, § 10.23
      Form, § 10.110
    Service, § 10.18
  Private improvements,
    Assignment,
      Notice of assignment, § 10.34
        Contents, § 10.35
        Extension of term, § 10.36
    Discharge, termination of notice of pendency, § 10.44
    Duration of lien,
      Notice of pendency, § 10.38
      Extensions, § 10.39
    Protecting the owner, itemized statement,
      Notice of application for order, form, § 10.126
  Public improvements,
    Duration of lien,
      Notice of pendency, § 10.40
        Extensions, § 10.41
    Enforcement,
      Affidavit in support of application to cancel notice of mechanic's lien for failure to commence action, form, § 10.132
      Notice requiring lienor to commence action, form, § 10.131
    Notice of completion and acceptance, § 10.24
      Form, § 10.112
    Notice of lien, § 10.22
      Filing, § 10.23
  Subordination of liens, notices of lis pendens, § 10.64
  Trust funds, notice of lending, filing, § 10.99
Medical malpractice,
  Filing, notice of medical malpractice action, § 29.29
Motor vehicle insurance,
  Claims procedure for accidents,
    Filing notice of claim, § 26.26
      Affidavit, §§ 26.27, 26.28, 26.29
      Late claims, § 26.30
Motor vehicle sales, repossession, § 7.26
Municipal corporations,
  Notice of claim, § 26.39
    Examination of claimant, § 26.40
    Extensions, granting, § 26.40
    Service of process, § 26.40
    Statute, § 3.30
      Form, § 3.37
New York Landlord-Tenant Law,
  Notice to admit, § 13.59
Non-payment proceedings,
  Notice of petition, § 13.13
    Contents, § 13.15
    Defects, § 13.16
    Form of notice, § 13.14
  "Three-day notice", § 13.12

INDEX

NOTICE—Continued
  Personal injury, depositions, § 26.43
  Probate and estate administration,
    Forms, § 25.58
    Notice of objections,
      Requirements to complete jurisdiction in contested probate, § 25.29
  Rent control,
    Holdover proceedings, predicate notices, § 13.39
  Rent stabilization,
    Holdover proceedings, predicate notices, § 13.40
  Resource Conservation and Recovery Act (RCRA),
    Clean Water Act (CWA),
      Citizen suits, notice letter,
        Drafting checklist, § 15.36
        Form, § 15.41
  Service of notice,
    Guardianships, proceeding to appoint guardian,
      Time and manner, § 22.20
  Service of process,
    Enforcement of money judgments,
      Article 52 enforcement devices, restraining notices, § 8.27
    Mechanic's liens, notice of lien, § 10.18
  Small business, purchase or sale,
    Buyer's asset purchase agreement, drafting, § 6.76
      Corporate name,
        Escrow agreement in lieu of UCC bulk sale notice, § 6.65
        Notice to customers and suppliers, § 6.64
        UCC bulk sale notices, § 6.65
      Escrow agreement in lieu of UCC bulk sale notice, § 6.65
      Notice to customers and suppliers, § 6.64
      UCC bulk sale notices, § 6.65
    Buyer's stock purchase agreement, drafting, § 6.96
    Post-contract and pre-closing, plant closing notice, § 6.101
    Seller's asset sale agreement, drafting, § 6.161
      Escrow agreement in lieu of UCC bulk sale notice, § 6.153
      Notice to customers and suppliers, § 6.151
      UCC bulk sale notices, § 6.153
    Seller's stock sale agreement, drafting, § 6.182
      Escrow agreement in lieu of UCC bulk sale notice, § 6.184
      Notice to customers and suppliers, § 6.176
      Plant closing notice, § 6.184
      UCC bulk sale notices, § 6.184
    UCC bulk sales,
      Buyer's asset purchase agreement, drafting,
        Corporate name, escrow agreement in lieu of UCC bulk sale notice, § 6.65
  Subpoena duces tecum,
    Enforcement of money judgments,
      To take deposition of judgment debtor with restraining notice, form, § 8.50
      To take deposition of witness with restraining notice, form, § 8.51
  Summary judgment, notice of motion,
    Mortgage foreclosure, drafting checklist, § 11.63
  Supreme court jurisdiction,
    Eminent domain, § 14.61
      Certification of names of reputed condemnees, § 14.62
      Notice of pendency, § 14.57
  Worker Adjustment and Retraining Notification Act,
    Plant closing notice, § 17.51
  Workers' compensation,
    Payment of compensation for disability has been stopped or modified, forms, § 32.58
    Posting notice of coverage, § 32.39
    Proof of claim for disability benefits, forms, § 32.59
    Right to compensation is controverted, forms, § 32.57

INDEX

NOTICE—Continued
Workers' compensation—Continued
    Total or partial rejection of claim for disability benefits, forms, § 32.60
Wrongful death, notice of claim, § 26.39

NUISANCE
Environmental law, § 15.32
Injunctive relief, § 15.32

NURSES
Medical malpractice,
    Hospital records, nurse's notes, § 29.63
    Regulatory standards, nurse midwives, qualification, § 29.19

NURSING HOMES
Resident's rights, § 23.92
    Admission to facility, § 23.93
    Bed hold policy, § 23.97
    Bill of rights, § 23.94
    Financial rights, § 23.95
    Remedies, violations of rights or improper treatment, § 23.98
    Transfer and discharge, § 23.96

OBJECTIONS
Probate and estate administration,
    Accounts, § 25.38
        Prosecuting, § 25.39
    Admission of will to probate, § 25.24
    Burden of proof, § 25.28
    Filing, timing, § 25.25
    Form, § 25.27
    Forms, § 25.60
    Notice of objections,
        Requirements to complete jurisdiction in contested probate, § 25.29

OCCUPATIONAL SAFETY AND HEALTH ACT
Antireprisal provisions, § 17.38
Violations, § 17.62

ODOMETER LAW
Defenses, § 7.53

OFFICE OF FEDERAL CONTRACT COMPLIANCE PROGRAMS
Affirmative action efforts review, § 17.80
Glass ceiling review, § 17.80

OFFICERS
Corporations, § 1.69 et seq.

OLDER WORKERS BENEFIT PROTECTION ACT
Age Discrimination Employment Act, strict waiver requirements of rights, § 17.11

OPEN MEETINGS LAW
Definitions, § 3.28
Local land use law, § 16.39
Municipal corporations, § 3.28

OPERATING AGREEMENTS
Limited liability companies,
    Formation, § 2.19
        Member-managed LLCs, forms, § 2.112

ORDERS. particular type of order concerned

ORPHANS
Adoption, alien orphans, § 20.25
Family-based immigration, § 19.15

INDEX

PACKAGE STORES
Credit provisions, § 36.44
Liquor licenses, §§ 36.8, 36.10, 36.36
200 foot rule, § 36.10

PARENT AND CHILD
Child Custody, generally, this index
Child Support, generally, this index
Divorce, generally, this index
Termination of relationship,
    Adoption proceedings, §§ 20.38, 20.39, 20.90 et seq., 20.101
Visitation rights,
    Adoption proceedings,
        Natural parents granted rights, § 20.123
        Siblings granted rights, § 20.124

PART A BENEFITS
Medicare, this index

PART B SUPPLEMENTARY MEDICAL INSURANCE
Medicare, this index

PARTNERS. particular type of partnership involved

PARTNERSHIP FOR LONG TERM CARE/ROBERT WOOD JOHNSON PROGRAM
Long term care insurance, § 23.66

PARTNERSHIPS
    Generally, § 2.44
Assignment of Interests, this index
Bankruptcy, chapter 7,
    Discharge unavailable, § 9.205
    General partners, liability, § 9.194
Chart comparing New York entities, § 2.108
Compared to limited liability partnerships, § 2.74
Dissolution, this index
Due diligence considerations, § 2.105
Family partnerships, assets protection, § 24.86
Formation, § 2.46
    Agreements, § 2.47
    Business certificates, § 2.48
    Other issues, § 2.50
    Publication, § 2.49
Governing law, § 2.45
Limited liability companies, compared, § 2.10
    Flexibility, § 2.13
    Liability, § 2.12
    Tax implications, § 2.11
Limited Liability Partnerships, generally, this index
Limited Partnerships, generally, this index
Management, § 2.55
    Agency authority, § 2.60
    Delegation of responsibility, § 2.58
    Non-waivable requirements, § 2.57
    Standard of care, § 2.59
    Voting, § 2.56
Professional organizations, § 2.71
Securities laws issues, § 2.106
Summary, § 2.107
Tax Classification, generally, this index
Winding up, § 2.67

PATENTS
Small business, purchase or sale,
    Asset sales, tax issues for buyer, § 6.40

INDEX

PENALTIES
Income tax, state, § 35.70
    Checklist, § 35.84
    Estimated taxes, underpayment, § 35.76
        Exceptions, § 35.77
    Filing, late, § 35.71
    Fraud, § 35.78
        Common cases, § 35.81
        Determination methods, specific, § 35.80
        Elements, § 35.79
        Proof, creative methods of, § 35.82
    Interest, underpayment or overpayment of tax, § 35.83
    Negligence, § 35.74
    Payment, late, § 35.72
    Reasonable cause, § 35.73
    Understatement, substantial, § 35.75

PENSIONS
Pension plans,
    Distribution pursuant to divorce, §§ 21.35, 21.38, 21.44
    Employment law, handbooks, § 17.81
    ERISA protection, § 17.50
    Severance pay, effect on, § 17.15
Small business, purchase or sale,
    Due diligence investigation, legal review,
        Pension and benefits contracts, § 6.17

PERMITS
Alcoholic Beverage Control, this index
Auctions, wine, § 36.44
Building permits,
    Local land use law, § 16.32
    State Environmental Quality Review Act (SEQRA), § 16.54
Bureau of Alcohol, Tobacco and Firearms,
    Manufacturing, importing or wholesaling of alcoholic beverages, §§ 36.4, 36.11
Clean Water Act (CWA),
    State pollution discharge elimination system (SPDES),
        Permit program, § 15.9
Small business, purchase or sale,
    Due diligence investigation, legal review, § 6.21
Special use permits, generally. Zoning, this index
State Environmental Quality Review Act (SEQRA), building permits, § 16.54
Wetlands protection, permit procedure and criteria, § 15.17

PERSONAL INJURY
    Generally, § 26.1
Affirmative defenses,
    Bills of particulars, § 26.60
Arbitration, § 26.50
Bills of particulars, §§ 26.46, 26.47
    Contents, § 26.60
    Form, §§ 26.67, 26.69
    Responses, § 26.61
Certificate of service, § 26.32
Chemical exposure, § 26.16
Client interview, § 26.3
Commencement by filing statute, §§ 26.32, 26.35
Complaints,
    Answers, §§ 26.37, 26.59
        Form, § 26.66
    Contents, § 26.58
    Demand for relief, § 26.36
    Filing, § 26.32

INDEX

PERSONAL INJURY—Continued
Complaints—Continued
    Service of process, § 26.36
        Form, § 26.65
Contingent fee, § 26.6
    Disbursement of proceeds, § 26.56
Counterclaims and cross-claims, form, § 26.66
Damages, § 26.58
    Lost wages, § 26.51
    Medical expenses, § 26.51
Depositions, notice, § 26.43
Discovery, § 26.42
    Medical reports, § 26.70
        Form, § 26.68
Document inspection, § 26.45
Dog bites, § 26.15
Expenses of case, § 26.8
Expert witnesses, discovery, § 26.42
    Form, § 26.68
Filing of summons and complaint,
    Index number and date of filing, § 26.32
Interrogatories, § 26.44
Investigation of case, §§ 26.3, 26.9
Liability, multiple theories, § 26.31
Liens, § 26.49
Limitation of actions, §§ 17.77, 26.32, 26.33
Mediation, § 26.50
Medical authorization, § 26.3
Motor Vehicle Accidents, generally, this index
Municipal corporations, claims against, § 26.38
Photograph of injury, § 26.3
Physical examination of plaintiff, § 26.42
Potential defendants, § 26.35
Previous injuries, § 26.3
Prior claims, § 26.3
Products Liability, generally, this index
Regional transit systems, claims against, § 26.38
Release after settlement, § 26.48
    Subrogation rights, § 26.49
Retainer,
    Agreement, form, § 26.62
    Escrow account, § 26.6
    Statement, § 26.7
        Form, § 26.63
Service of process, § 26.32
Settlement, §§ 26.2, 26.4, 26.48
    Closing statement, § 26.56
        Form, § 26.71
    Disbursement of proceeds, § 26.56
    Pre-trial conference, § 26.51
Skills of attorney, § 26.5
Slip and fall, § 26.10
    Complaint, § 26.58
Special damages, § 26.51
State, actions against, § 26.41
Statements to insurance company, § 26.3
Subpoenas,
    Duces tecum, § 26.53
    Fees, § 26.53
    Testimonial, § 26.53
Summons,
    Contents, § 26.36

INDEX

PERSONAL INJURY—Continued
Summons—Continued
    Filing, § 26.32
    Form, § 26.65
Tolling provisions, § 26.32
Trial,
    Bifurcation, § 26.52
    Evidence, §§ 26.54, 26.55
    Exhibits, § 26.54
    Jury selection, § 26.55
    Notebook, § 26.52
    Setting date, § 26.52
    Voir dire, § 26.55
Valuation of case, § 26.4
Venue, §§ 26.34, 26.58
Witnesses to injury, § 26.3
Workers' compensation, § 26.3

PERSONAL PRIVACY PROTECTION LAW
    Generally, § 17.55

PERSONAL PROPERTY
Bankruptcy,
    Executory contracts and unexpired personal property leases, § 9.85
Enforcement of money judgments,
    Article 52 enforcement devices,
        Execution, § 8.29
            Distribution of property, § 8.30
            Priority in proceeds, § 8.30
            Sale of property, § 8.30
Municipal corporations, acquisition and disposition, § 3.16
Wills, disposition provisions, § 24.9

PETITIONS
Guardianships,
    Checklists, § 22.90
    Forms, § 22.99
    Proceeding to appoint guardian, § 22.23
    Proceedings to recover property withheld, § 22.82
Income tax, state,
    Advisory opinion, for, forms, § 35.133
    Declaratory ruling, for, forms, § 35.135
    Division of tax appeals, to, forms, § 35.132
Lemon law, vacating arbitration award, § 7.51
Probate and Estate Administration, generally, this index

PHOTOGRAPHS
Motor vehicle accident scene and vehicles, § 26.23

PHYSICIANS
Assisted suicide, § 23.113
Cover letter to treating physician, § 34.76
Limitation of actions,
    Product liability, distributors' or sellers' liability, § 27.25
Medical Malpractice, generally, this index
Medical questionnaire for treating physician, forms, § 34.74
Participating physicians,
    Medicare part B supplementary medical insurance, § 23.51
Products liability,
    Distributors' or sellers' liability, § 27.25
Records and reports,
    Social security disability cases,
        Treating phyician's reports, § 34.37
Thank-you letter to treating physician, § 34.77

INDEX

PLANNING BOARDS
Local land use law, § 16.36

PLEA BARGAINING
    Generally, § 33.28
No penalty for asserting right to trial, § 33.30
Waiver of right to appeal, conditioning plea bargain on, § 33.29

POLICE
Inadequate training,
    Defenses,
        "Monell v. New York City Dept of Social Services", § 18.34
Police/citizen encounters, § 33.4 et seq.
Police misconduct, § 18.20 et seq.
    Excessive force, § 18.21
        Complaint, form, § 18.93
    False arrest, § 18.22
        Complaint, form, § 18.92
    False imprisonment, § 18.23
        Complaint, form, § 18.92
Reports,
    Motor vehicle accidents, § 26.18
        Insurance company information, § 26.24
Right to privacy, § 18.65

POOR PERSON RELIEF
Appellate division, criminal, § 38.16
Court of appeals,
    Civil appeals, § 39.35
    Criminal appeals, § 39.53

POSTMORTEM PLANNING
    Generally, § 24.67 et seq.
Alternate valuation date election, § 24.73
Commissions, waiving, § 24.79
Disclaimers, this index
Election to file joint return with decedent's spouse, § 24.78
Fiscal year of estate, choosing, § 24.77
Income and expenses, allocation, §§ 24.74, 24.76
    U.S. savings bonds, § 24.75
Partial QTIP election, § 24.72

POWERS OF APPOINTMENT
Will provisions, § 24.17

POWERS OF ATTORNEY
    Generally, § 24.89
Durable power of attorney,
    Real property sale, residential contract of sale, form, § 12.97
Durable power of attorney, form, § 24.100
Income tax, state,
    Representation of individuals, forms, § 35.128
Real property sale,
    Residential contract of sale, § 12.8
        Durable power of attorney,
            Form, § 12.97
        Power of attorney to take effect at later time,
            Form, § 12.98

PREEMPTION
Local land use law,
    Substantive limits, preemption by state and federal laws, § 16.24
    Zoning, public uses, implied preemption, § 16.128
Products liability,
    Defenses,

INDEX

PREEMPTION—Continued
Products liability—Continued
    Defenses—Continued
        Failure to test, § 27.21
    Private claims, § 27.42
        Checklist, § 27.51
        "Cipollone" decision, § 27.46
        Defenses, § 27.49
        Federal Insecticide, Fungicide and Rodenticide Act (FIFRA), § 27.47
        Limits on preemption, § 27.49
        Medical device amendments for FDA regulations, § 27.48
        National Traffic and Motor Vehicle Safety Act, § 27.45
        New rule, § 27.44
        Old rule, § 27.43
        Public Health Cigarette Labeling and Advertising Act of 1965, § 27.46
        Public Health Cigarette Smoking Act of 1969, § 27.46
        Savings clause, § 27.45
        Validity of safety standard or regulatory statute, § 27.50

PREGNANCY
Disability benefits law, § 32.51
Employment discrimination, prohibitions, § 17.54
Fetal protection policies, § 17.54

PREMISES LIABILITY
Complaint, § 26.58
Slip and fall, § 26.10

PRESUMPTIONS
Workers' compensation hearings, § 32.19

PRIOR CONVICTIONS
Criteria, § 33.46
Defendant's presence at hearing, § 33.47
Evidence, § 33.44 et seq.
Procedure, § 33.45

PRIVACY
Employment law, § 17.55
Expectation of privacy,
    Search and seizure, § 18.10
Invasion of privacy, § 18.63
Right to, § 18.63 et seq.
    Corrections officers, § 18.65
    Firefighters, § 18.65
    General provisions, § 18.64
    "Incidental use" exception, § 18.64
    "Newsworthy" exception, § 18.64
    Police officers, § 18.65
    Victims of sex offenses, § 18.66

PRIVILEGED INFORMATION
Employment law, discharge of employee, § 17.16

PROBATE AND ESTATE ADMINISTRATION
    Generally, § 25.1 et seq.
Administrators,
    Affidavit asking court to fix amount of bond, § 25.69
    Compensation, § 25.46
    Decree appointing, forms, § 25.68
Affidavits, this index
Attorney's fees, § 25.47
Avoidance of probate, § 24.80
    Revocable trusts, § 24.81
    Totten trusts, § 24.82

INDEX

PROBATE AND ESTATE ADMINISTRATION—Continued
Beneficiaries,
    Educational funds, obtaining, § 25.44
    Petitioning for probate, § 25.14
Citation in probate, form, § 25.54
    Affidavit of service, form, § 25.55
Citation that can be adopted for use in any proceeding, § 25.72
    Forms, § 25.72
Claimants against estate, representing, § 25.41
Claims against estate, proceeding when, § 25.43
Commencement of estate,
    Person dying with will, § 25.6
    Person dying without will, § 25.4
Completion, forcing estate administration, § 25.34
Concluding the estate,
    Decree based on filed receipts and releases, obtaining, § 25.36
    Formal judicial accounting, § 25.37
    Without accounting proceeding, § 25.35
Consent, forms, § 25.57
Creditors,
    Claims against estate, § 25.40
    Petitioning for probate, § 25.15
Decree granting probate, forms, § 25.61
Deposition affidavit of subscribing witness, forms, § 25.59
Discovery in probate, administration or accounting proceedings, § 25.31
Executors, this index
Fiduciaries,
    Duty to expeditiously seek probate, § 25.13
    Two or more fiduciaries in dispute, entitlement to assets, § 25.45
Forms, § 25.51 et seq.
Guardians ad litem, appointment, §§ 25.9, 25.23
Information gathering by attorney, § 25.17
Inheritance, renouncing, § 25.49
Jury trials, right to, § 25.30
Legal terms, § 25.2
Letters of administration, § 25.5
    Application for,
        Affidavit of mailing notice of,
            Forms, § 25.56
        Citation of parties, § 25.8
        Denial, § 25.10
        Documents required, § 25.7
        Revocation, § 25.10
    Limited letters, petition for, forms, § 25.67
    Person dying without will, § 25.32
    Petition for, forms, § 25.67
    Temporary administration, § 25.11
        Petition for, forms, § 25.67
Notice,
    Application for letters of administration, forms, § 25.71
    Forms, § 25.58
Objections, this index
Petitions for probate,
    Accompanying documents, § 25.19
    Contents, § 25.18
    Forms, § 25.52
    Persons in litigation with estate, § 25.16
Preliminary considerations, § 25.3
Procedures in estate administration, § 25.33
Property of estate, recovering, § 25.42
Receipt and release,
    Agreement concluding estate without accounting proceeding, forms, § 25.62

INDEX

PROBATE AND ESTATE ADMINISTRATION—Continued
Receipt and release—Continued
    Forms, § 25.63
Scope, § 25.1
Starting, delay in getting will admitted to probate, § 25.26
Taxes,
    Federal estate taxes, § 24.18
        Marital deduction, utilizing, § 24.22
        Rates, § 24.19
        Unified credit, utilizing, § 24.21
    State estate taxes,
        Rates, § 24.20
Trustees, declining to serve as, § 25.48
Venue, § 25.12
Waiver and consent, forms, § 25.57
Waiver of citation, renunciation of signer's claim to letters and consent to appointment of administrator, forms, § 25.70
Wills,
    Admission to probate,
        Delays in getting will admitted, starting estate administration, § 25.26
        Objections, filing, § 25.24
        Witnesses not available, § 25.22
    Construction, § 25.50
    Lost wills, requirements and procedure for proving, § 25.21
    Original wills,
        Inability to produce, § 25.20
        Lost wills, requirements and procedure for proving, § 25.21

PROCEDURAL DUE PROCESS
Administrative Law and Proceedings, generally, this index

PROCESS SERVERS
Liability, § 28.1

PRODUCTS LIABILITY
    Generally, § 27.1 et seq.
Answer, § 27.56
    Form, § 27.58
Bases of claim, § 27.4
Causation, § 27.34
    Expert witnesses, § 27.35
    Jury question, § 27.35
Chain of custody, § 26.14
Collateral estoppel, § 27.53
Complaint, § 27.55
    Form, § 27.57
Concert of action, § 27.52
Construction flaws, defective design flaws distinguished, § 27.6
Defective design, § 27.7
    Burden of proof, § 27.8
    Construction flaws distinguished, § 27.6
    Defenses, § 27.9
    Utility/risk balancing test, § 27.9
Design defect claim, § 26.31
Discovery,
    Confidentiality orders or stipulations, § 27.38
    Design alternatives, § 27.37
    Effect of destruction of product upon plaintiff's ability to prove defect,
        Order compelling preservation or production, § 27.33
    Sealing court records, § 27.38
    Testing and safety design, § 27.37
Distributors' or sellers' liability, § 27.22 et seq.
    Limitation of actions, § 27.25

INDEX

PRODUCTS LIABILITY—Continued
Distributors' or sellers' liability—Continued
    Medical care providers, § 27.25
    Physicians, § 27.25
    Sale as apart of ordinary business, § 27.23
    Service versus sales, § 27.24
Drafting checklist, § 27.55
Evidence,
    Causation, § 27.34
    Circumstantial evidence, § 27.34
    Effect of destruction of product upon plaintiff's ability to prove defect, § 27.33
    Other incidents, § 27.32
    Post-accident modification or repairs, § 27.31
    Sufficiency, § 27.35
    Weight of evidence, § 27.35
Expert witnesses,
    Causation, § 27.35
    "General acceptance" standard rejected, § 27.35
    "Helpfulness" standard, § 27.35
Failure to test, § 27.18 et seq.
    FDA approval, § 27.19
    Jury question, § 27.20
    Preemption defense, § 27.21
Failure to warn, § 27.10
    Adequacy of warnings, § 27.13
    Burden of proof, § 27.11
    Continuing duty to warn, § 27.13
    Duty to warn, § 27.12
        Unusually sensitive persons, § 27.16
    Informed intermediary defense, § 27.15
    Jury question, § 27.14
    Non-commercial cases, § 27.17
Failure to warn claim, § 26.31
Foreseeability, § 27.36
Historical overview, § 27.3
Imposing liability when manufacturer of fungible or generic food product is unknown, § 27.52
Intervening acts of negligence,
    Alteration of product after leaving hands of manufacturer, § 27.41
    Plaintiff's misuse of product, § 27.40
Investigation of case, §§ 26.9, 26.14
Limitation of actions, § 27.39
Manufacturer liability,
    Completed product, § 27.30
    Component parts, § 27.29
Manufacturing defect or mistake in manufacturing process, § 27.6
Market share liability, § 27.52
Physicians, distributors' or sellers' liability, § 27.25
Pleading checklist, § 27.56
Post-accident modification or repairs, admissibility, § 27.31
Preemption,
    Private claims, § 27.42
        Checklist, § 27.51
        "Cipollone" decision, § 27.46
        Defenses, § 27.49
        Federal Insecticide, Fungicide and Rodenticide Act (FIFRA), § 27.47
        Limits on preemption, § 27.49
        Medical device amendments for FDA regulations, § 27.48
        National Traffic and Motor Vehicle Safety Act, § 27.45
        New rule, § 27.44
        Old rule, § 27.43
        Public Health Cigarette Labeling and Advertising Act of 1965, § 27.46

INDEX

PRODUCTS LIABILITY—Continued
Preemption—Continued
    Private claims—Continued
        Public Health Cigarette Smoking Act of 1969, § 27.46
        Savings clause, § 27.45
        Validity of safety standard or regulatory statute, § 27.50
Proof of allegations checklist, § 27.54
Scope, § 27.1
Strategy, § 27.2
Successor liability, § 27.26 et seq.
    Burden of proof, § 27.27
    Continuity of enterprise, § 27.26
    "De facto merger", § 27.26
    Punitive damages, § 27.28
Theories of liability, § 27.5 et seq.
Workers' compensation claim, § 26.14

PROFESSIONAL LIMITED LIABILITY COMPANIES
    Generally, § 2.43

PROFESSIONAL ORGANIZATIONS
Limited partnerships, § 2.104
Partnerships, § 2.71

PROMISSORY NOTES
Small business, purchase or sale,
    Buyer's asset purchase agreement, drafting, § 6.57
    Buyer's stock purchase agreement, drafting, § 6.82
    Seller's asset sale agreement, drafting, § 6.167
    Structuring buyer's transaction, § 6.50
    Structuring seller's transaction, § 6.137

PROOF
Burden of Proof, generally, this index
Income tax, state,
    Penalties,
        Fraud,
            Creative methods of proof, § 35.82

PROPERTY
Bankruptcy, generally, this index
Business real property, estate planning with certain assets, § 24.42
Damages, generally, this index
Divorce, generally, this index
Easements, generally, this index
Eminent Domain, generally, this index
Enforcement of Money Judgments, generally, this index
Estate Planning, generally, this index
Foreign Investors Real Property Tax Act (FIRPTA),
    Closing of title, disclosure, § 12.26
Guardianships,
    Management,
        Hearing and order, findings of court, § 22.37
        Powers, § 22.47
    Role of guardian, generally. Guardianships, this index
Intellectual property,
    Small business, purchase or sale,
        Due diligence investigation, legal review, § 6.17
New York City real property transfer tax,
    Closing of title, payment of taxes, § 12.85
Personal Property, generally, this index
Probate and estate administration,
    Recovering, § 25.42
Real Property, generally, this index

INDEX

PROPERTY—Continued
Real Property Actions and Proceedings Law, summary proceedings, § 13.4
Real Property, Taxation, generally, this index
Real Property Transfer Gains Tax, generally, this index

PROSECUTORS
Absolute immunity, § 18.31
Appeals, appellate division, criminal, § 38.11
Brady material,
    Prosecutor need not be aware of evidence, § 33.40
    Timely disclosure, § 33.41
Criminal appeals, death penalty, § 39.41
Malicious prosecution,
    Employment cases, discharge of employee, § 17.26
    Limitation of actions, § 17.77
Plea bargaining, § 33.28 et seq.
Prosecutorial misconduct, § 18.20 et seq.
    Malicious prosecution, § 18.25

PROTECTIVE ORDERS
Enforcement of money judgments, § 8.44

PROVISIONAL REMEDIES
Guardianships, § 22.56
    Injunction and temporary restraining orders, § 22.58
    Notice of pendency, § 22.59
    Summary, § 22.60
    Temporary guardian, § 22.57

PROXIES
Health care proxies, §§ 23.110, 24.91
    Statutory form, § 23.125
Shareholders' meetings and agreements, § 1.45

PUBLIC AUTHORITIES LAW
Claims against regional transit systems, § 26.38

PUBLIC CONVEYANCES
Public accommodations and amusement, equal rights in places of, § 18.54

PUBLIC HALLS
Public accommodations and amusement, equal rights in places of, § 18.54

PUBLIC HEALTH CIGARETTE LABELING AND ADVERTISING ACT OF 1965
Products liability, preemption of private claims, § 27.46

PUBLIC HEALTH CIGARETTE SMOKING ACT OF 1969
Products liability, preemption of private claims, § 27.46

PUBLIC OFFICERS LAW
Municipal corporations, §§ 3.20, 3.28

PUBLICATION
Wills, execution requirements, § 24.6

QTIP
Partial QTIP election, postmortem planning, § 24.72
Reverse QTIP, generation skipping transfer taxes, § 24.31

QUALIFIED DOMESTIC RELATIONS ORDERS
Retirement income from qualified plans, § 23.30

RADAR
Traffic offenses. Speeding, generally. Traffic Offenses, this index

RAILROAD EMPLOYERS ACT
Antireprisal provisions, § 17.38

INDEX

RAILROAD RETIREMENT BENEFITS
Elder law, § 23.36

REAL ESTATE AGENTS AND BROKERS
Housing discrimination prohibited,
   "Block busting", § 18.46
   Private housing, § 18.46
   Publicly assisted housing, § 18.42
   "Racial steering", § 18.46

REAL PROPERTY
Bankruptcy, executory contracts and unexpired leases,
   Damages arising from allowed real property lease rejection, calculation, § 9.83
   Nonresidential real property leases, § 9.77
Business real property,
   Estate planning with certain assets, § 24.42
Compensatory damages, property damage, § 30.17
Eminent Domain, generally, this index
Enforcement of money judgments, definitions, § 8.19
Municipal corporations, acquisition and disposition by, § 3.16
Purchase and sale, § 12.1 et seq.
   Closing of title, § 12.72 et seq.
     Disclosure, § 12.75 et seq.
       Agricultural Foreign Investment Disclosure Act, § 12.81
       Cash payments receive by businesses in excess of $10,000, § 12.79
       Foreign Investors Real Property Tax Act (FIRPTA), § 12.76
       Form 1099-S federal requirement one to four family residence, § 12.77
         Checklist, § 12.78
       Housing and Community Development Act, § 12.80
       Lead paint hazards, § 12.80
       United States Real Property Interest (USRPI), § 12.76
     Filings, § 12.74
     New York state equalization and assessment form, § 12.91
     Other required forms and information, § 12.91
     Payment of taxes, § 12.82 et seq.
       Article 31-B, § 12.84
       Mansion Tax, § 12.83
       Method of payment, § 12.90
       Mortgage recording tax outside New York City, § 12.88
       Mortgage recording tax rate in New York City, § 12.89
       Mount Vernon, § 12.86
       New York City Real Property Transfer Tax, § 12.85
       New York State Real Estate Transfer Tax, § 12.83
       Real estate investment trusts (REIT), § 12.87
       Real Property Transfer Gains Tax, § 12.84
       Special additional mortgage tax, § 12.91
       Yonkers, § 12.86
     Recording fees, § 12.74
     Title company's checklist, § 12.73
   Condominium contract of sale, § 12.33
     Form, § 12.94
     Homeowner's associations, § 12.35
     Residential contract compared, § 12.34
   Contract of sale, § 12.4
     Delivery, § 12.5
     Form, § 12.93
     Preparation, § 12.5
     Recordation, § 12.6
     Statute of Frauds, § 12.4
   Cooperative apartment contract of sale, § 12.37
     Form, § 12.96
     Standard form, § 12.38
   Forms, § 12.92 et seq.

INDEX

REAL PROPERTY—Continued
Purchase and sale—Continued
    Marketability of title, § 12.64 et seq.
        Rendering title unmarketable, § 12.65
            Driveway easements, § 12.68
            Encroachments due to adverse possession, § 12.66
            Federal Navigational Servitude, § 12.71
            Land abutting bodies of water, § 12.71
            Other covenants and restrictions, § 12.69
            Party walls, § 12.67
            Reservations for public utilities, § 12.70
        Survey map, effect,
            Contract silent on matter of survey, § 12.59
            Contract subject to specific encroachments or facts show on specific survey, § 12.62
            Contract subject to state of facts accurate survey may show, § 12.60
            Contract subject to state of facts accurate survey may show provided same does not render title unmarketable, § 12.61
            Suggested clause, § 12.63
    New construction contract of sale, § 12.39
    Office, commercial and multi-family residential premises contract for sale, § 12.36
        Form, § 12.95
    Residential contract of sale, § 12.7 et seq.
        Apportionments, § 12.26
        "As is" clause, § 12.20
        Assignment, § 12.30
        Bargain and sale deeds, § 12.22
        Broker, § 12.31
        Closing, § 12.22
            Conditions, § 12.24
            Date and place, § 12.23
            "Time is of the essence" clause, § 12.23
        Condition of property, § 12.20
        Condominium contract compared, § 12.34
        Damages, § 12.29
        Deed transfer tax, § 12.25
        Defaults, § 12.29
        Fixtures, § 12.10
        Full covenant and warranty deeds, § 12.22
        Governmental violations and orders, § 12.18
        Insurable title, § 12.21
        Limitation of liability, § 12.28
        Marketable title, § 12.21
        Metes and bounds description, § 12.9
        Mortgage recording tax, § 12.25
        Parties, § 12.8
        Permitted exceptions, § 12.17
        Personal property, § 12.10
        Powers of attorney, § 12.8
            Durable power of attorney, form, § 12.97
            Power of attorney to take effect at later time, form, § 12.98
        Premises, § 12.9
        Purchase price and method of payment, § 12.11
            Acceptable funds, § 12.16
            Assumption of existing mortgage, § 12.13
            Commitment date, § 12.15
            Down payment, § 12.12
            Estoppel certificate, § 12.13
            Mortgage contingency clause, § 12.15
            Purchase money mortgage, § 12.14
        Quit claim deeds, § 12.22
        Remedies, § 12.29

INDEX

REAL PROPERTY—Continued
Purchase and sale—Continued
    Residential contract of sale—Continued
        Risk of loss, § 12.32
        Seller's inability to convey, § 12.28
        Seller's representations, § 12.19
        Title examination, § 12.28
        Unpaid taxes, allowance for, § 12.27
    Scope, § 12.1
    Strategy, § 12.2
        Pre-contract checklist, § 12.3
    Survey map, § 12.56 et seq.
        Marketability of title, effect, § 12.58
            Contract silent on matter of survey, § 12.59
            Contract subject to specific encroachments or facts show on specific survey, § 12.62
            Contract subject to state of facts accurate survey may show, § 12.60
            Contract subject to state of facts accurate survey may show provided same does not render title unmarketable, § 12.61
            Suggested clause, § 12.63
        What it may disclose, § 12.57
    Title examination,
        Deed requirements, Torrens system, § 12.53
        Deeds into an inter vivos trust, Torrens system, § 12.53
        Grantor/grantee index system, § 12.53
        Mortgages, Torrens system, § 12.53
        Objections to be disposed of prior to closing, § 12.54
            Checklist, § 12.55
        Torrens system, § 12.53
    Title insurance, § 12.40 et seq.
        Buyer's obligation, § 12.41
        Cost, § 12.43
        Duration, § 12.43
        Extended coverage policy, § 12.44
        Insurer's role, § 12.42
        Policies, § 12.45 et seq.
            American Land Title Policy form (ATLA), § 12.45
            Endorsements, § 12.51
            Exclusions, § 12.52
            Loan policy coverage, § 12.46
            New York modifications of loan policy, § 12.47
            New York modifications to owner's policy, § 12.49
            Owner's policy coverage, § 12.48
            Standard exceptions, § 12.50
        Standard coverage policy, § 12.44
Real Property Transfer Gains Tax, generally, this index
Sale of principal residence, tax issues, elderly individuals, § 23.117
Small business, purchase or sale,
  Due diligence investigation, legal review, § 6.20
Taxation. Real Property, Taxation, generally, this index
Wills, disposition provisions, § 24.11

REAL PROPERTY ACTIONS AND PROCEEDINGS LAW
Summary proceedings, § 13.4

REAL PROPERTY, TAXATION
Credits, housing issues, elderly individuals, § 23.101
Exemptions, housing issues, elderly individuals, § 23.100
Foreign Investors Real Property Tax Act, § 12.76
Municipal corporations, finance, § 3.26
Residential contract of sale,
  Deed transfer tax, § 12.25
  Mortgage recording tax, § 12.25

INDEX

REAL PROPERTY, TAXATION—Continued
Residential contract of sale—Continued
 Unpaid taxes, allowance for, § 12.27

REAL PROPERTY TRANSFER GAINS TAX
Real property sale,
 Closing of title, payment of taxes, § 12.84
Small business, purchase or sale,
 Post-contract and pre-closing, § 6.104

RECEIVERS
Corporations, this index

RECORDS AND REPORTS
Adoption,
 Home study report, § 20.114
 Medical records of natural parents, availability to child, § 20.129
 Recording placement of child, § 20.100
 Report of adoption, § 20.111
  Private adoption, § 20.74
 Sealing adoption records, § 20.125
  Constitutionality, § 20.126
  Good cause for unsealing records, § 20.127
   Religious identity crisis, § 20.130
 Subpoena of records by grand jury, § 20.128
 Termination of parental rights, recording of surrender, § 20.98
Agency information gathering, administrative law, § 4.64
Alcoholic beverage control,
 Licenses,
  Criminal record of applicant, § 36.4
  Reporting changes of facts, § 36.45 et seq.
 Manufacturing license, record keeping requirements, § 36.44
 Record-keeping requirements, § 36.44
 Wholesalers, record keeping requirements, § 36.44
Appellate division, civil,
 Matters dehors the record, § 37.28
  Notice of motion to strike,
   Affirmation in support, form, § 37.138
   Form, § 37.137
  Scope of review, § 37.28
 Perfecting the appeal,
  Agreed statement in lieu of record, § 37.51
  Full record, § 37.51
  Original record, § 37.51
Attorney fees,
 Fair credit reporting violations, § 7.62
 New York Fair Credit Reporting Act, §§ 7.48, 7.60
Bankruptcy,
 Chapter 7,
  Destruction or falsification of records,
   Exceptions to general discharge of debtor, § 9.205
  Surrender of property and records, § 9.192
 U.S. trustee,
  Record keeping, § 9.33
  Transmission of records, § 9.33
Child custody, expert witnesses' reports, § 21.79
Collection agencies,
 Complaints, fair credit reporting violations, § 7.62
Constitutionality, sealing adoption records, § 20.126
Consumer protection,
 Better Business Bureau reports, § 7.8
 Fair Credit Reporting Act, § 7.31
 New York Fair Credit Reporting Act, § 7.31

INDEX

RECORDS AND REPORTS—Continued
Corporations,
    Formation, service of process,
        Records and certificates of Department of State, § 1.16
    Shareholders' rights, inspection of books and records, § 1.53
Court of appeals,
    Perfecting the appeal, full record, § 39.29
Courts not of record,
    Mechanic's liens, enforcement,
        Complaints, § 10.80
        Judgments and transcripts, § 10.82
        Proceedings upon return of summons, § 10.81
        Summons and complaint, § 10.80
Courts of record,
    Mechanic's liens, enforcement,
        Necessary parties, § 10.79
        Procedures, § 10.78
Credit reports,
    Agencies, § 7.48
    Complaints,
        Deceptive trade practices, § 7.60
        Fair credit reporting violations, § 7.60
    Consumer protection, resolutions, § 7.32
    Consumer rights, §§ 7.30, 7.31
    Damages for violations, § 7.48
    Employment law, denial of job or entitlements, § 17.42
    Lemon law, § 7.5
    Litigation, § 7.33
    Motor vehicle loans, § 7.5
    Motor vehicle sales, § 7.3
Damages,
    Fair credit reporting violations, § 7.60
    New York Fair Credit Reporting Act, § 7.48
Deceptive trade practices,
    Fair credit reporting violations, complaint, § 7.60
Discovery,
    Medical malpractice,
        Allied health provider records, § 29.70
        Billing records, § 29.68
        Hospital records, § 29.67
        Obtaining and identifying relevant records, § 29.65
        Pharmacy records, § 29.69
        Physician's records, § 29.66
    Motor vehicle accidents,
        Accident reports, form, § 26.70
        Medical reports, form, § 26.68
    Personal injury cases,
        Medical reports, form, §§ 26.68, 26.70
    Products liability, sealing court records, § 27.38
Divorce,
    Expert reports, §§ 21.63, 21.79
    Referee's report,
        Findings of fact and conclusions of law, form, § 21.91
        Judgment entered upon, form, § 21.92
Eminent domain,
    Public hearings, § 14.29
Employment law,
    Denial of job or entitlements,
        Arrest record, § 17.39
        Credit reports, § 17.42
        Criminal record of employee, § 17.41
    Reporting violations, antireprisal provisions, § 17.38

INDEX

RECORDS AND REPORTS—Continued
Environmental law,
    Hazardous waste regulation,
        Inactive hazardous waste sites,
            Record of decision (ROD), § 15.31
Fair Credit Reporting Act,
    Consumer protection, § 7.31
    Motor vehicle sales, § 7.3
Grand juries, subpoena of adoption records, § 20.128
Guardianships. Reports, generally. Guardianships, this index
Medical Malpractice, this index
    Motor vehicle accidents, § 26.22
    Social security disability cases, handling, § 34.36
Income tax, state,
    Returns, filing, § 35.53
Labor Management Reporting and Disclosure Act,
    Union elections, § 17.61
Lemon law, credit reports, § 7.5
Limitation of actions, New York Fair Credit Reporting Act, § 7.48
Matters dehors the record,
    Appellate division, civil, § 37.28
        Notice of motion to strike,
            Affirmation in support, form, § 37.138
            Form, § 37.137
        Scope of review, § 37.28
Mechanic's liens,
    Enforcement,
        Courts not of record,
            Complaints, § 10.80
            Judgments and transcripts, § 10.82
            Proceedings upon return of summons, § 10.81
            Summons and complaint, § 10.80
        Courts of record,
            Necessary parties, § 10.79
            Procedures, § 10.78
    Trust funds,
        Beneficiaries, right to examine books or records, § 10.101
        Record keeping obligations, § 10.100
Medical malpractice,
    Expert review of records, § 26.11
    Hospital records, § 26.11
    Medical records, § 26.11
    Physicians' records,
        Discovery, obtaining and identifying relevant records, § 29.66
        Evaluating and understanding medical records, § 29.51 et seq.
Motor vehicle accidents,
    Discovery,
        Accident reports, form, §§ 26.68, 26.70
        Medical reports, § 26.42
            Form, § 26.68
    Police reports, § 26.18
        Insurance company information, § 26.24
Motor vehicle insurance, police reports, § 26.24
Motor vehicle sales,
    Credit reports, § 7.3
    Fair Credit Reporting Acts, § 7.3
Municipal corporations,
    Access to public records, § 3.29
    Freedom of Information Law (FOIL), § 3.29
New York Fair Credit Reporting Act,
    Attorney fees, §§ 7.48, 7.60
    Complaint for violations, § 7.60

INDEX

RECORDS AND REPORTS—Continued
New York Fair Credit Reporting Act—Continued
  Consumer protection, § 7.31
  Damages, § 7.48
  Limitation of actions, § 7.48
  Litigation, § 7.33
Perfecting the appeal,
  Agreed statement in lieu of record,
    Appellate division, civil, § 37.51
  Full record,
    Appellate division, civil, § 37.51
    Court of appeals, § 39.29
  Original record,
    Appellate division, civil, § 37.51
Personal injury,
  Discovery, medical reports, § 26.70
    Form, § 26.68
Physician's reports. Medical Malpractice, generally, this index
Police reports,
  Motor vehicle accidents, § 26.18
    Insurance company information, § 26.24
Products liability,
  Sealing court records, discovery, § 27.38
Public hearings, eminent domain, § 14.29
Referee's reports,
  Divorce cases, form, § 21.91
  Matrimonial judgment entered by court, form, § 21.92
Sealing court records,
  Products liability, discovery, § 27.38
Small business, purchase or sale,
  Due diligence investigation,
    Financial review,
      Buyer's records from seller's position, § 6.25
      Public records, § 6.26
      Seller's records from buyer's position, § 6.24
Social security disability cases,
  Medical records, requests for, forms, § 34.72
Social security disability cases, handling,
  Medical evidence, treating physicians' reports, § 34.37
Social security's records,
  Social security disability cases, handling, § 34.34

REFEREES
Reports,
  Divorce cases, form, § 21.91
  Matrimonial judgment entered by court, form, § 21.92

REFORMATION
Insurance, § 31.19

REHABILITATION ACT
Employment law, prohibitions against discrimination, § 17.43
Limitation of actions, § 17.77

RELEASES
Affirmative defense, § 26.37
Employment law, form, § 17.87
Personal injury settlement, § 26.48
Severance pay, § 17.16
Social security disability cases,
  Medical releases, forms, § 34.73

RELIGION
Employment discrimination, § 17.56

INDEX

REMEDIES
Nursing home resident's rights, violations of rights or improper treatment, § 23.98
Provisional Remedies, generally, this index
Workers' compensation, exclusive remedy doctrine, § 32.14
    Exceptions, § 32.14

RENT
Illegal,
    Non-Payment Proceedings, generally, this index
Rent control,
    Holdover proceedings, predicate notices, § 13.39
    Rent regulatory proceedings, § 13.73 et seq.
        Major capital improvement rent increase (MCI), § 13.76
        Rent overcharge, § 13.74
        Service reduction, § 13.75
Rent stabilization,
    Holdover proceedings, predicate notices, § 13.40
    Rent regulatory proceedings, § 13.73 et seq.
        Major capital improvement rent increase (MCI), § 13.76
        Rent overcharge, § 13.74
        Service reduction, § 13.75

REPOSSESSION
Leased motor vehicles, §§ 7.3, 7.4
Motor vehicle sales, § 7.3

RES JUDICATA
Adjudicatory proceedings, administrative law, § 4.25
Affirmative defense, § 26.37
Enforcement of money judgments, § 8.3
Federal civil rights law, defenses, § 18.37

RESCISSION
Lemon law, § 7.56

RESIDENCY REQUIREMENTS
Adoptive parents, § 20.51

RESOURCE CONSERVATION AND RECOVERY ACT (RCRA)
Clean Water Act (CWA),
    Citizen suits, notice letter,
        Drafting checklist, § 15.36
        Form, § 15.41
Hazardous waste regulation, § 15.23
Solid waste regulation, § 15.23
Underground storage tanks (UST), § 15.26

RESPONDEAT SUPERIOR
Federal civil rights law, § 18.35
    42 U.S.C.A. Section 1983, respondeat superior doctrine inapplicable, § 18.18
Hospital's liability for medical malpractice, § 29.12

RESTAURANTS
Alcoholic beverage control, § 36.2
Public accommodations and amusement, equal rights in places of, § 18.54
Wine license, § 36.9

RESTITUTION
Damages, generally, this index

RESTRAINING ORDERS
Bankruptcy, cash collateral, § 9.66
Temporary restraining orders,
    Deceptive trade practice case, § 7.63
        Affirmation in support, § 7.64

INDEX

RESTRICTIVE COVENANTS
Covenants, this index

RETAINER AGREEMENTS
Social security disability cases, § 34.33
    Concurrent benefits, forms, § 34.70

RETIREMENT BENEFITS
Estate planning with certain assets, § 24.37

RETIREMENT COMMUNITIES
Life care retirement communities,
    Housing issues, elderly individuals, § 23.107

RETIREMENT PLANS
ERISA protection, § 17.50

RIGHT TO COUNSEL
Adjudicatory proceedings, administrative law, § 4.14
Adoption,
    Private adoption,
        Independent counsel for birth mother, § 20.41
        Independent counsel for child, § 20.43
    Termination of parental rights, assigned counsel for indigent parents, § 20.93
Indigent defendants,
    Assignment of counsel,
        Adoption proceedings, § 20.93
        Appellate division,
            Civil, §§ 37.10, 37.48
            Criminal, § 38.16
        Court of appeals, § 39.53
        Family court, § 37.19
        Surrogate's court, § 37.18
Miranda rights, waiver, § 33.56

RIPENESS
Judicial review, administrative law, § 4.70

ROAD HOUSES
Public accommodations and amusement, equal rights in places of, § 18.54

RULEMAKING
Administrative Law and Proceedings, this index

SAFE DRINKING WATER ACT
Antireprisal provisions, § 17.38

SALE OF GOODS
Complaints, § 26.36

SANDOVAL ISSUES
Criteria, § 33.46
Defendant's presence at hearing, § 33.47
Evidence, § 33.44 et seq.
Procedure, § 33.45

SAPA
Role in licensing process,
    Adjudicatory proceedings, administrative law, § 4.29

SCHOOLS
Asbestos School Hazard Detection and Control Act, antireprisal provisions, § 17.38
Child support, private school education, § 21.55
Employment discrimination prohibited, § 18.60
Public accommodations and amusement, equal rights in places of, § 18.54

INDEX

SEARCH AND SEIZURE
Civil rights,
   New York Bill of Rights, § 18.9
      Civil liability, § 18.10
      Expectation of privacy, § 18.10
      Return of seized property, § 18.11
         Complaint, form, § 18.94
Employment law, state employees, § 17.55

SECRETARY OF STATE
Corporations, service of process,
   Secretary of State as agent, statutory designation, § 1.17

SECURITIES LAWS
Issues, § 2.106

SEPARATION
Spouses,
   Estate planning, special situations, § 24.63

SEQRA
State Environmental Quality Review Act (SEQRA), generally, this index

SERVICE OF PROCESS
Accusatory instruments,
   Supporting depositions,
      Dismissal for failure to serve, § 33.19
         Not amendable defect, § 33.25
      Motion to dismiss,
         Timeliness, § 33.21
         Writing requirement, § 33.20
      Request by attorney requiring service on counsel, § 33.18
      Requirements, § 33.15
      Timing, § 33.17
      Who must be served, § 33.16
Bankruptcy,
   Service demand, form, § 9.305
Civil complaints, § 17.78
Corporations,
   Formation, § 1.15
      Certificate of resignation of registered agent, § 1.18
      Records and certificates of Department of State, § 1.16
      Secretary of State as agent, statutory designation, § 1.17
      Unauthorized foreign corporations, § 1.19
Court of appeals,
   Civil appeals, leave to appeal, § 39.17
Eminent domain, just compensation,
   Court of claims, § 14.72
   Supreme court, § 14.75
Enforcement of money judgments,
   Article 52 enforcement devices,
      Installment payment order, § 8.36
      Restraining notices, § 8.27
Federal court actions, § 17.79
Guardianships, designation of clerk of court for, § 22.43
Insurance, § 31.22
Matrimonial actions, § 21.11
Mechanic's liens,
   Enforcement, service of answer on state or public corporation, § 10.93
   Notice of lien, § 10.18
Municipal corporations, actions against, § 26.40
Notice of appeal,
   Appellate division, civil, § 37.46
Personal injury lawsuits, § 26.32

INDEX

SERVICE OF PROCESS—Continued
Personal injury lawsuits—Continued
    Complaints, § 26.36
        Form, § 26.65
Summary proceedings,
    New York Landlord-Tenant Law, § 13.6
        Conspicuous place service, § 13.9
        New York City Civil Court "postcard" requirement, § 13.10
        Personal delivery, § 13.7
        Reasonable application standard, § 13.9
        Substituted service, § 13.8

SETTLEMENTS
Employment cases, § 17.5
Enforcement matters, special issues in handling,
    Adjudicatory proceedings, administrative law, § 4.38
Lemon law, §§ 7.14, 7.48
    Stipulation of settlement, § 7.61
Lump-sum settlements, workers' compensation benefits, § 32.32
Personal injury cases, §§ 26.2, 26.4, 26.48
    Closing statement, § 26.56
        Form, § 26.71
    Disbursement, § 26.56
    Pre-trial conference, § 26.51

SEVERANCE PAY
Effect on benefits, § 17.15
Releases and waivers, § 17.16
Tax considerations, § 17.14
Termination of pay, § 17.13

SEWER AND WATER DISTRICTS
Municipal corporations, special purpose units, § 3.33

SEXUAL HARASSMENT
Employment cases,
    Civil assault, § 17.21
        Intentional infliction of emotional harm, § 17.28
Hostile work environment, § 17.57
Quid pro quo, § 17.57

SIGNATURES
Wills, execution requirements, § 24.5

SKILLED NURSING FACILITIES
Medicare part A benefits, § 23.46

SMALL BUSINESS, PURCHASE OR SALE
    Generally, § 6.1 et seq.
Asset sales,
    Buyer's asset purchase agreement, drafting, post
Estate Planning, generally, this index
Probate and Estate Administration, generally, this index
Seller's asset sale agreement, Drafting, post
Tax issues,
    Buyer, for, § 6.32
        Allocation of purchase price, § 6.33
        Amortization, § 6.34
        Cash, § 6.38
        Covenants not to compete, § 6.36
        Depreciation of assets, § 6.34
        Franchises, § 6.40
        Good will, § 6.36
        Inventory, § 6.37
        Land, § 6.35

INDEX

SMALL BUSINESS, PURCHASE OR SALE—Continued
Asset sales—Continued
  Tax issues—Continued
    Buyer—Continued
      Residual method, § 6.33
      Supplies, § 6.39
      Tax Reform Act of 1986, § 6.33
      Trade names, § 6.40
      Trademarks, § 6.40
    Seller, for, § 6.117
      Allocation of sale price, § 6.118
      Amortization, § 6.119
      Capital gains and losses, § 6.120
      Consulting agreements, § 6.124
      Covenants not to compete, § 6.124
      Depreciation of assets, § 6.119
      Income to corporation, § 6.122
      Ordinary income, § 6.121
      Real property transfer gains tax, § 6.123
      Recapture, § 6.119
      Residual method, § 6.118
Buyer, representation of, § 6.2 et seq.
  Accountants, § 6.9
  Appraiser, § 6.9
  Attorney's role, §§ 6.3, 6.9
  Business broker, § 6.9
  Business consultant, § 6.9
  Confidentiality agreements, § 6.11
  Drafting the agreement, § 6.12
  Geographic location, § 6.8
  Investigating the business, § 6.6
  Letter of intent, § 6.10
  Nature and operation of business, § 6.7
  Negotiating team, § 6.9
  Non-disclosure agreements, § 6.11
  Stages of transaction, § 6.5
  Strategy, § 6.2
  Type of transaction, considerations, § 6.4
Buyer's asset purchase agreement, drafting, § 6.52 et seq.
  Assets and property to be conveyed, § 6.55
  Assumed name, § 6.63
  Closing, § 6.58
  Collateral documents, § 6.77
  Conditions precedent to,
    Purchaser's obligations, § 6.69
    Seller's obligations, § 6.70
  Conduct of business prior to closing, § 6.61
  Corporate name, § 6.63
    Covenant not to compete, § 6.67
    Escrow agreement in lieu of UCC bulk sale notice, § 6.65
    New York state bulk sales notification, § 6.66
    New York state sales tax, § 6.66
    Notice to customers and suppliers, § 6.64
    Severability clause, § 6.67
    UCC bulk sale notices, § 6.65
  Covenant not to compete, § 6.67
  Documents to be delivered to purchaser at closing, § 6.74
  Documents to be delivered to seller at closing, § 6.75
  Documents to be prepared or reviewed prior to closing, § 6.77
  Escrow agreement in lieu of UCC bulk sale notice, § 6.65
  Forms, § 6.187
  General provisions, § 6.76

INDEX

SMALL BUSINESS, PURCHASE OR SALE—Continued
Buyer's asset purchase agreement—Continued
    Identification of parties, § 6.53
    Indemnification, § 6.62
    Method of payment, § 6.57
    Miscellaneous agreements between buyer and seller, § 6.73
    Nature and survival of representations and warranties, § 6.71
    New York state bulk sales notification, § 6.66
    New York state sales tax, § 6.66
    Non-disclosure provisions, § 6.72
    Notice to customers and suppliers, § 6.64
    Notices, § 6.76
    Promissory notes, § 6.57
    Purchase price, § 6.57
    Real property, § 6.68
    Recitals, § 6.54
    Representations, warranties, and covenants of buyer, § 6.60
        Nature and survival of representations and warranties, § 6.71
    Representations, warranties, and covenants of seller, § 6.59
        Nature and survival of representations and warranties, § 6.71
    Retained assets of seller, § 6.56
    Severability, § 6.76
    Severability clause, § 6.67
    UCC bulk sale notices, § 6.65
Buyer's stock purchase agreement, drafting, § 6.78 et seq.
    Closing, § 6.83
        Conduct of business prior to, § 6.86
    Conditions precedent to purchaser's obligations, § 6.91
    Conditions precedent to seller's obligations, § 6.92
    Conduct of business prior to closing, § 6.86
    Covenant not to compete, § 6.88
    Documents to be delivered to purchaser at closing, § 6.94
    Documents to be delivered to seller at closing, § 6.95
    Documents to be prepared or reviewed prior to closing, § 6.97
    Escrow, shares placed in, § 6.82
    Forms, § 6.188
    General provisions, § 6.96
    Identification of parties, § 6.79
    Indemnification, § 6.87
    Method of payment, § 6.82
    Nature and survival of representations and warranties, § 6.93
    Nondisclosure provisions, § 6.90
    Notices, § 6.96
    Promissory notes of buyer, § 6.82
    Purchase price, § 6.82
    Real property, § 6.89
    Recitals, § 6.80
    Representations, warranties and covenants of buyer, § 6.85
        Nature and survival of representations and warranties, § 6.93
    Representations, warranties, and covenants of seller, nature and survival, § 6.93
    Sale of shares, § 6.81
    Severability, § 6.96
    Warranties and covenants of seller, § 6.84
Closing and post-closing, § 6.105
    Closing memorandum, § 6.105
Covenants not to compete,
    Asset sales,
        Tax issues,
            Buyer, for, § 6.36
            Seller, for, § 6.124
    Buyer's asset purchase agreement, drafting, § 6.67
        Corporate name, § 6.67

INDEX

SMALL BUSINESS, PURCHASE OR SALE—Continued
Covenants not to compete—Continued
    Buyer's stock purchase agreement, drafting, § 6.88
    Seller's asset sale agreement, drafting, § 6.152
    Seller's stock sale agreement, drafting, § 6.175
    Stock purchases,
        Tax issues,
            Seller, for, § 6.129
Due diligence investigation, § 6.13 et seq.
    Financial review, § 6.23
        Appraisers, § 6.28
        Asset value factor, § 6.29
        Audited statements, § 6.27
        Capitalized earnings method, § 6.29
        Cash flow method, § 6.29
        Compilation statements, § 6.27
        Financial statements, § 6.27
        Market value method, § 6.29
        Need for other professionals, § 6.28
        Records and reports,
            Buyer's records from seller's position, § 6.25
            Public records, § 6.26
            Seller's records from buyer's position, § 6.24
        Review statements, § 6.27
        Tax returns, § 6.30
        Valuation of business, § 6.29
    Legal review, § 6.14
        Assumed names, § 6.19
        Broker's fees, § 6.20
        Bylaws, § 6.15
        Certificate of good standing, § 6.15
        Certificate of incorporation, § 6.15
        Compliance with law, § 6.21
        Comprehensive Environmental Response, Compensation and Liability Act of 1980
            (CERCLA), § 6.20
        Corporate names, § 6.19
        Customer lists and customer agreements, § 6.17
        Employment agreements, § 6.17
        Environmental issues, § 6.20
        Existing contracts, § 6.17
        Franchise agreements, § 6.17
        Good and marketable title, § 6.16
        Intellectual property rights, § 6.17
        Licenses, § 6.21
        Liens, § 6.18
        Lines of credit, § 6.17
        Litigation investigation, § 6.22
        Occupancy and use restrictions, § 6.20
        Organizational documents, § 6.15
        Ownership documents, § 6.16
        Pension and benefits contracts, § 6.17
        Permits, § 6.21
        Real estate, § 6.20
        Review of title, § 6.20
        Security interests, § 6.18
        Site inspection, § 6.20
        Supplier agreements, § 6.17
        Trade names, § 6.19
Mergers,
    Tax issues for buyer, § 6.45
Post-contract and pre-closing, § 6.98 et seq.
    Certificate of good standing, § 6.103

INDEX

SMALL BUSINESS, PURCHASE OR SALE—Continued
Post-contract and pre-closing—Continued
    Corporate name,
        New York state bulk sales notification, § 6.100
        New York state sales tax, § 6.100
    Environmental searches and testing, § 6.102
    Plant closing notice, § 6.101
    Real property transfer gains tax, § 6.104
    UCC bulk sales, § 6.99
    Worker Adjustment and Retraining Notification Act (WARN), § 6.101
Scope, § 6.1
Seller, representation of, § 6.106 et seq.
    Accountants, § 6.112
    Attorney's role, § 6.107
    Business broker, § 6.112
    Confidentiality agreements, § 6.114
    Drafting the agreement, § 6.115
    General investigation, § 6.110
        Investigating the buyer, § 6.111
    Letter of intent, § 6.113
    Negotiation team, § 6.112
    Non-disclosure agreements, § 6.114
    Stages of transaction, § 6.109
    Strategy, § 6.106
    Type of transaction, considerations, § 6.108
Seller's asset sale agreement, drafting, § 6.139 et seq.
    Assets and property to be conveyed, § 6.142
    Closing, § 6.145
    Conditions precedent to purchaser's obligations, § 6.158
    Conditions precedent to seller's obligations, § 6.157
    Conduct of business prior to closing, § 6.148
    Consulting agreements, § 6.152
    Covenant not to compete, § 6.152
    Documents to be delivered to purchaser at closing, § 6.160
    Documents to be delivered to seller at closing, § 6.159
    Documents to be prepared or reviewed prior to closing, § 6.162
    Escrow agreement in lieu of UCC bulk sale notice, § 6.153
    Forms, § 6.187
    General provisions, § 6.161
    Identification of parties, § 6.140
    Indemnification, § 6.149
    Method of payment, § 6.144
    Nature and survival of representations and warranties, § 6.155
    New York state bulk sales notification, § 6.154
    New York state sales tax, § 6.154
    Non-disclosure provisions, § 6.156
    Notices, § 6.161
        Customers and suppliers, § 6.151
    Pre-closing covenants, § 6.147
    Promissory notes, § 6.144
    Real property, § 6.150
    Recitals, § 6.141
    Representations, warranties, and covenants of buyer, § 6.146
        Nature and survival of representations and warranties, § 6.155
    Representations, warranties, and covenants of seller, § 6.147
        Nature and survival of representations and warranties, § 6.155
    Retained assets of seller, § 6.143
    Sale price, § 6.144
    Severability clause, § 6.161
    UCC bulk sale notices, § 6.153
Seller's stock sale agreement, drafting, § 6.163 et seq.
    Closing, § 6.168

INDEX

SMALL BUSINESS, PURCHASE OR SALE—Continued
Seller's stock sale agreement—Continued
  Closing—Continued
    Conduct of business prior to, § 6.171
  Closing and post-closing, § 6.185
  Closing memorandum, §§ 6.184, 6.185
  Conditions precedent to purchaser's obligations, § 6.178
  Conditions precedent to seller's obligations, § 6.177
  Conduct of business prior to closing, § 6.171
  Consulting agreements, § 6.175
  Covenant not to compete, § 6.175
  Documents to be delivered to purchaser at closing, § 6.181
  Documents to be delivered to seller at closing, § 6.180
  Documents to be prepared or reviewed prior to closing, § 6.183
  Escrow agreement in lieu of UCC bulk sale notice, § 6.184
  Forms, § 6.188
  General provisions, § 6.182
  Identification of parties, § 6.164
  Indemnification, § 6.172
  Method of payment, § 6.167
  Nature and survival of representations and warranties, § 6.179
  New York state bulk sales notification, § 6.184
  New York state sales tax, § 6.184
  Non-disclosure provisions, § 6.174
  Notice to customers and suppliers, § 6.176
  Notices, § 6.182
  Plant closing notice, § 6.184
  Post-contract and pre-closing, § 6.184
  Pre-closing covenants, § 6.170
  Promissory notes of buyer, § 6.167
  Purchase price, § 6.167
  Real property, § 6.173
  Recitals, § 6.165
  Representations, warranties and covenants of buyer, § 6.169
    Nature and survival of representations and warranties, § 6.179
  Representations, warranties and covenants of seller, § 6.170
    Nature and survival of representations and warranties, § 6.179
  Sale of shares, § 6.166
  Severability clause, § 6.182
  UCC bulk sale notices, § 6.184
  Workers Adjustment and Retraining Notification Act (WARN), § 6.184
Stock purchases,
  Buyer's stock purchase agreement, drafting, ante
  Seller's stock sale agreement, drafting, ante
  Tax issues,
    Buyer, for, § 6.41 et seq.
      Corporate assets, basis of, § 6.43
      Election to treat stock purchase as asset sale, § 6.44
      Stock, basis of, § 6.42
    Seller, for, § 6.125 et seq.
      Capital gains and losses, § 6.126
      "Code section 1244 stock", § 6.130
      Collapsible corporation, § 6.132
      Consolidations, § 6.133
      Consulting agreements, § 6.129
      Covenants not to compete, § 6.129
      Exchanges, § 6.133
      Mergers, § 6.133
      No concern for income to corporate entity, § 6.127
      Real property transfer gains tax, § 6.128
      Small business stock, § 6.130
      Stock transfer tax, § 6.131

INDEX

SMALL BUSINESS, PURCHASE OR SALE—Continued
Structuring buyer's transaction, § 6.46 et seq.
  Assumption of seller's liabilities, § 6.48
  Escrow agreements, § 6.51
  Payment, § 6.47
  Promissory notes, § 6.50
  Security to seller, § 6.49
Structuring seller's transaction, § 6.134 et seq.
  Escrow agreements, § 6.138
  Payment, § 6.135
  Promissory notes, § 6.137
  Purchase price, § 6.135
  Security to seller, § 6.136
Tax issues,
  Buyer, for, § 6.31 et seq.
    Asset sales, § 6.32
      Allocation of purchase price, § 6.33
      Amortization, § 6.34
      Cash, § 6.38
      Covenants not to compete, § 6.36
      Depreciation of assets, § 6.34
      Franchises, § 6.40
      Good will, § 6.36
      Inventory, § 6.37
      Land, § 6.35
      Patents, § 6.40
      Residual method, § 6.33
      Supplies, § 6.39
      Tax Reform Act of 1986, § 6.33
      Trade names, § 6.40
      Trademarks, § 6.40
    Consolidations, § 6.45
    Exchanges, § 6.45
    Mergers, § 6.45
    Reorganization, § 6.45
    Stock purchases, § 6.41
      Corporate assets, basis of, § 6.43
      Election to treat stock purchase as asset sale, § 6.44
      Stock, basis of, § 6.42
  Seller, for, § 6.116 et seq.
    Asset sales, § 6.117
      Allocation of sale price, § 6.118
      Amortization, § 6.119
      Capital gains and losses, § 6.120
      Consulting agreements, § 6.124
      Covenants not to compete, § 6.124
      Depreciation of assets, § 6.119
      Income to corporation, § 6.122
      Ordinary income, § 6.121
      Real property transfer gains tax, § 6.123
      Recapture, § 6.119
      Residual method, § 6.118
    Capital gains, § 6.116
    Stock purchases, § 6.125 et seq.
      Capital gains and losses, § 6.126
      "Code section 1244 stock", § 6.130
      Collapsible corporation, § 6.132
      Consolidations, § 6.133
      Consulting agreements, § 6.129
      Covenants not to compete, § 6.129
      Exchanges, § 6.133
      Mergers, § 6.133

INDEX

SMALL BUSINESS, PURCHASE OR SALE—Continued
Tax issues—Continued
  Seller—Continued
    Stock purchases—Continued
      No concern for income to corporate entity, § 6.127
      Real property transfer gains tax, § 6.128
      Small business stock, § 6.130
      Stock transfer tax, § 6.131
UCC bulk sales, § 6.65
  Buyer's asset purchase agreement, drafting,
    Corporate name, § 6.65
      Escrow agreement in lieu of UCC bulk sale notice, § 6.65
  Post-contract and pre-closing, § 6.99

SMALL CLAIMS PROCEEDINGS
Appeals,
  City courts, § 37.108
  Civil court of New York City, § 37.125
  District courts, § 37.116
  Eminent domain, just compensation, § 14.117
  Justice courts, from,
    Appellate division, civil, § 37.99
Consumer protection, § 7.2

SOCIAL SECURITY
Disability cases,
  Appealing unfavorable decisions, § 34.55
    Strategic considerations, § 34.56
      Partially favorable decisions, § 34.57
  Appeals council review, request for,
    Forms, § 34.78
  Checklists, § 34.65
    Allegations checklist,
      Medical claims, § 34.66
      Psychiatric claims, § 34.67
  Claimant questionnaire, forms, § 34.68
  Cover letter to treating physician, forms, § 34.76
  Favorable decisions, implementing, § 34.49
    Attorneys' fees, collecting, § 34.52
      Fee agreements, § 34.54
        Maximum fee, form, § 34.71
      Fee applications, § 34.53
    Disability insurance benefits, collecting, § 34.50
    Supplemental security income, collecting, § 34.51
  Forms, § 34.68 et seq.
  Handling, § 34.31
    Evidence, § 34.38
      Family members, § 34.40
      Former co-workers and employers, § 34.39
      Medical evidence, § 34.35
        Hospital records, § 34.36
        Treating physicians' reports, § 34.37
    Favorable decisions, implementing, § 34.49
    Hearings,
      Conducting, § 34.44
        Medical advisors, § 34.46
        Testimony of claimant, § 34.45
        Vocational experts, § 34.47
      Post-hearing evidence and memoranda, § 34.48
      Preparing for, § 34.41
        Claimants, preparing, § 34.42
        Documents, § 34.43
        Witnesses, § 34.43

INDEX

SOCIAL SECURITY—Continued
Disability cases—Continued
  Handling—Continued
    Initial interview, § 34.32
    Retainer agreements, § 34.33
      Concurrent benefits, forms, § 34.70
      Forms, § 34.69
    Social security's records, § 34.34
  Law of disability, § 34.3
    Assessment of disability, sequential evaluation, § 34.8
      Impairments, listing, § 34.11
      Individualized assessment, dispensing with, § 34.14
      Other work, ability to do, § 34.13
      Past relevant work, ability to do, § 34.12
      Severity, § 34.10
      Substantial gainful activity, § 34.9
    Durational requirements, § 34.6
    Judicial definitions, § 34.5
    Statutory definition of disability, § 34.4
    Workers' compensation, comparison to, § 34.7
  Medical questionnaire for treating physician, forms, § 34.74
  Medical records, requests for, forms, § 34.72
  Medical releases, forms, § 34.73
  Psychiatric questionnaire, forms, § 34.75
  Reopening prior applications, § 34.58
  Reopening prior cases,
    Court decisions requiring reopening, § 34.63
    Denials of reopening, review of, § 34.62
    Disability insurance benefits, § 34.59
    Grants of reopening, review of, § 34.61
    Statutes and regulations requiring reopening, § 34.64
  Strategy, § 34.2
  Thank-you letter to treating physician, forms, § 34.77
  Workers' compensation, comparison to, § 34.7
Disability insurance benefits,
  Administrative procedure, § 34.23
    Administrative hearing, § 34.27
    Appeals council, § 34.28
    Application, § 34.24
    Federal district court, § 34.29
    Reconsideration, § 34.25
    Second circuit court of appeals, § 34.30
    Termination of benefits, § 34.26
  Collecting, § 34.50
  Financial considerations, § 34.15
    Assets, § 34.17
    Benefits, amount of, § 34.18
    Eligibility for SSI, § 34.21
    FICA withholding, § 34.20
    Income, § 34.16
    Retroactivity of benefits, § 34.22
  Reopening prior cases, § 34.59
Elder Law, generally, this index
Supplemental security income,
  Administrative procedure, § 34.23
    Administrative hearing, § 34.27
    Appeals council, § 34.28
    Application, § 34.24
    Federal district court, § 34.29
    Reconsideration, § 34.25
    Second circuit court of appeals, § 34.30
    Termination of benefits, § 34.26

INDEX

SOCIAL SECURITY—Continued
Supplemental security income—Continued
    Collecting, § 34.51
    Financial considerations, § 34.15
        Assets, § 34.17
        Benefits, amount of, § 34.18
        Eligibility for disability insurance benefits, § 34.21
        Financial need based, § 34.19
        Income, § 34.16
        Retroactivity of benefits, § 34.22
    Reopening prior cases, § 34.60

SOCIAL SERVICES LAW
Private placement adoptions, § 20.45

SOLID WASTE DISPOSAL ACT
Antireprisal provisions, § 17.38

SPECIAL DISABILITY FUND
Workers' compensation, wage replacement benefits, § 32.27

SPEEDY TRIAL
CPL § 30.20, § 33.71 et seq.
    Criteria, § 33.73
    Traffic infractions, § 33.72
CPL § 30.30, § 33.74 et seq.
    Appearance tickets, § 33.82
    Burden of proof, § 33.81
    Commencement of criminal action, § 33.82
    Excludable time, § 33.84 et seq.
        Adjournments, § 33.87
        Defective accusatory instruments, § 33.86
        Defendant's unavailability, effect, § 33.89
        Delays by court, § 33.88
        Motions, § 33.85
    Guilty pleas, waiver, § 33.80
    People's readiness rule, § 33.77
        Actual readiness, § 33.79
        Assertion of readiness, § 33.78
    Post readiness delay, § 33.90
    Uniform traffic tickets, § 33.83
    Vehicle and traffic law generally excluded, § 33.75
        Unless combined with felony, misdemeanor or violation, § 33.76
Guilty pleas,
    Waiver of CPL § 30.300 motion, § 33.80

SPOUSAL SUPPORT
    Generally, § 21.46
Arrears, defenses, § 21.74
Bankruptcy preferences, exception, § 9.118
Earning capacity of parties, §§ 21.48, 21.49
Effect of fault, § 21.48
Factors for consideration, § 21.47
Findings of fact and conclusions of law, form, § 21.89
Health and life insurance, § 21.57
Judgments,
    Enforcement, § 21.72
    Form, § 21.90
        USC-113, § 21.67
Jurisdiction, § 21.8
Lifetime support, § 21.49
Modification of judgments, § 21.68
    Change in circumstances, § 21.69
Motions, § 21.79

INDEX

SPOUSAL SUPPORT—Continued
Net worth statement, § 21.65
Payments fixed by agreement, § 21.50
Predivorce standard of living, § 21.49
Statement of agreement, § 21.66
Tax considerations, § 21.51
Terminating events, § 21.50

SPOUSES
Alimony. Spousal Support, generally, this index
Annulment of marriage,
    Distribution of property, § 21.7
    Judgments, form, § 21.90
Child Support, generally, this index
Conflicts letter, forms,
    Estate planning, § 24.102
Divorce, generally, this index
"Heart balm" statute, § 18.74 et seq.
    Action for return of gifts made in contemplation of marriage, § 18.76
        Procedure, § 18.77
    Penalty for bringing action, § 18.75
Immigration, generally, this index
Maintenance. Spousal Support, generally, this index
Non-citizen spouses, estate planning, special situations, § 24.58
Nullity of a void marriage, judgments, form, § 21.90
Rights,
    Multiple marriages, estate planning, special situations, § 24.60
Separation, estate planning, special situations, § 24.63
Spousal Support, generally, this index

STANDARD CITY PLANNING ENABLING ACT
Local land use law, comprehensive plan, § 16.11

STANDARD OF CARE
Limited liability companies, § 2.31
Limited partnerships, management, § 2.92
Medical Malpractice, generally, this index
Partnerships, management, § 2.59

STANDARD STATE ZONING ENABLING ACT
Local land use law, comprehensive plan, § 16.11

STANDARDS OF REVIEW
Adjudicatory proceedings. Administrative Law and Proceedings, this index

STANDING
Bankruptcy,
    Avoiding powers, § 9.121
    Subordination, § 9.107
Guardians, appointment, § 22.17
Judicial review, administrative law, § 4.69
Local land use law, judicial review, § 16.48

STATE ADMINISTRATIVE PROCEDURE ACT (SAPA)
Role in licensing process,
    Adjudicatory proceedings, administrative law, § 4.29

STATE ENVIRONMENTAL QUALITY REVIEW ACT (SEQRA)
Eminent domain, public hearing, determination and findings, § 14.32
Environmental Law, this index
Local land use law,
    Actions subject to SEQRA, § 16.53
        Building permits, § 16.54
        Rezoning, § 16.58
        Site plans, §§ 16.57, 16.105

INDEX

STATE ENVIRONMENTAL QUALITY REVIEW ACT (SEQRA)—Continued
Local land use law—Continued
  Actions subject to SEQRA—Continued
    Subdivisions, § 16.56
      Approval process, effect on, § 16.98
    Variances, § 16.55
    Environmental impact statement (EIS), § 16.52
Role in licensing process,
  Adjudicatory proceedings, administrative law, § 4.29

STATE INSURANCE FUND
Workers' compensation, § 32.42

STATE NAVIGATION LAW
Petroleum storage tanks, § 15.27

STATEMENTS
Child custody,
  Statement of agreement, § 21.66
  Statement of proposed disposition, § 21.83
  Visitation arrangements,
    Statement of agreement, § 21.66
Child support, statement of proposed disposition, § 21.83
Complaints, jurisdictional statement, § 17.82
Divorce,
  Closing statement, § 21.80
    Filing, § 21.76
  Retainer agreements,
    Net worth statement, §§ 21.65, 21.79, 21.80
  Spousal support,
    Net worth statement, § 21.65
    Statement of agreement, § 21.66
  Statement of client's rights and responsibilities, § 21.76
    Form, § 21.85
  Statement of net worth, form, § 21.87
  Statement of proposed disposition, §§ 21.80, 21.83
    Form, § 21.88
Involuntary statements, § 33.57 et seq.
  Harmless error doctrine, § 33.59
  Huntley hearings, § 33.57
  Use to impeach prohibited, § 33.58
Motor vehicle accidents, witness statements, § 26.19
Opening statements, discrimination cases, § 17.74
Personal injury,
  Retainer, § 26.7
    Form, § 26.63
  Settlement,
    Closing statement, § 26.56
      Form, § 26.71
  Statements to insurance company, § 26.3
Spousal support,
  Net worth statement, § 21.65
  Statement of agreement, § 21.66

STATUTE OF FRAUDS
Affirmative defense, § 26.37
Commercial Sales Contract, generally, this index
Real property, contract of sale, § 12.4

STATUTE OF LIMITATIONS
Limitation of Actions, generally, this index

STIPULATIONS
Alcoholic beverage control, retail licenses,

INDEX

STIPULATIONS—Continued
Alcoholic beverage control—Continued
    Holding Corporation Stipulation form, § 36.24
Child support, § 21.56
Holdover proceedings, § 13.65
    Forms, § 13.92 et seq.
Lemon law, settlement of claims, § 7.61
New York Landlord-Tenant Law, overview, § 13.63
Non-payment proceedings, § 13.64
    Forms, § 13.90 et seq.
Trade secrets,
    Discovery in products liability cases, confidentiality, § 27.38

STOCK
Severance pay, effect on, § 17.15

STOCK PURCHASES
Estate Planning, generally, this index
Probate and Estate Administration, generally, this index
Small Business, Purchase or Sale, this index

STORES
Public accommodations and amusement, equal rights in places of, § 18.54

SUBPOENAS
Adoption records by grand jury, § 20.128
Agency information gathering,
    Administrative law, § 4.63
Bankruptcy, examinations under Bankruptcy Rule 2004, § 9.41
Duces tecum,
    Enforcement of money judgments, § 8.2
        Property, enforcement against, § 8.23
        To take deposition of judgment debtor with restraining notice, form, § 8.50
        To take deposition of witness with restraining notice, form, § 8.51
Information subpoenas,
    Enforcement of money judgments, property against, § 8.23
    Form, § 8.52
Personal injury cases, § 26.53
Pretrial discovery, § 33.34
Testimonial examination,
    Enforcement of money judgments, property against, § 8.23

SUBROGATION
Insurance, § 31.29
Personal injury cases, release after settlement, § 26.49

SUBSTITUTED JUDGMENT DOCTRINE
Guardianships, role of guardian, § 22.48

SUICIDE
Physician assisted suicide, § 23.113

SUMMARY JUDGMENTS
Appellate division, civil,
    Disposition of appeal, § 37.65
Discrimination cases, § 17.73
Enforcement of money judgments, § 8.4
Mechanic's liens,
    Public improvements, foreclosure of lien,
        Affidavit in support of motion for summary judgment, form, § 10.142
Mortgage foreclosure,
    Affidavit of regularity and in support of motion, drafting checklist, § 11.64
    Notice of motion, drafting checklist, § 11.63
Resale of repossessed motor vehicle, § 7.55

INDEX

SUMMARY PROCEEDINGS
New York Landlord-Tenant Law, this index

SUMMONS
Divorce, filing, § 21.11
Mechanic's liens, enforcement,
    Courts not of record, § 10.80
        Proceedings upon return of summons, § 10.81
Mortgage foreclosure, § 11.18
    Drafting checklist, § 11.59
    Venue, § 11.19
Motor vehicle accidents, form, § 26.65
Municipal corporations, filing and service, § 26.40
Personal injury,
    Contents, § 26.36
    Filing, § 26.32
    Form, § 26.65
    Index number and date of filing, § 26.32

SUPPLEMENTAL MEDICAL INSURANCE (MEDIGAP PLANS)
    Generally, § 23.58
Criteria for choosing right plans, § 23.62
Federal and state regulation, § 23.60
Gaps in Medicare coverage, § 23.59
Ten standard plans, § 23.61

SUPREME COURT
Appeals, from,
    Notice of appeal, time limits, § 37.40
Appellate division, civil appellate practice before,
    Appeals to, § 37.16
    Lack of appellate jurisdiction, § 37.3
Appellate division, criminal appellate practice before,
    Appeals to, § 38.4
Eminent domain,
    Just compensation, § 14.73
        Service of process, § 14.75
        Time to file claim, § 14.74
Jurisdiction,
    Eminent domain, §§ 14.48, 14.56
        Answer by condemnee, § 14.63
            Defenses, § 14.64
            Notice, § 14.61
                Certification of names of reputed condemnees, § 14.62
                Notice of pendency, § 14.57
                      Form, § 14.124
                Notice of petition in proceedings, form, § 14.125
            Order of condemnation, § 14.65
            Petition in condemnation, § 14.58
                Content, § 14.59
                Non-governmental condemnors, content rules, § 14.60
            Vesting of title, § 14.65

SURFACE MINING CONTROL AND RECLAMATION ACT
Antireprisal provisions, § 17.38

SURROGATE'S COURT
Adoption, jurisdiction, § 20.9
Appeals by public administrator, § 37.18
Appellate division, civil appellate practice before,
    Appeals to appellate division from orders, decrees, and judgments, § 37.18
    Applicability of CPLR to appeals, § 37.18
    Assigned counsel on appeal, § 37.18
    Attorneys' fees on appeal, § 37.18

INDEX

SURROGATE'S COURT—Continued
Appellate division—Continued
    Constitutional basis, § 37.3
    Costs on appeal, § 37.18
    Counsel fees on appeal, § 37.18
    Governing practice, § 37.3
Assignment of counsel, § 37.18
Attorney fees, § 37.18
Costs on appeal, § 37.18
Courts of original jurisdiction from which appeals lie, § 37.15
Stays, § 37.18
    Notice of motion for stay of proceedings,
        Affirmation in support, form, § 37.132
        Form, § 37.130
    Order to show cause for stay of proceedings,
        Affirmation in support, form, § 37.132
        Form, § 37.131
Surrogate's Court Act, § 37.3
Time or time limits, civil appeals,
    Notice of appeal,
        Surrogate's court, appeal from, § 37.18

TAVERNS
Public accommodations and amusement, equal rights in places of, § 18.54

TAX CLASSIFICATION
    Generally, § 2.3
Corporate characteristics test,
    Former test, § 2.5
        Centralized management, § 2.9
        Continuity of life, § 2.7
        Free transferability of interests, § 2.8
        Limited liability, § 2.6
Simplification, eagerly awaited, § 2.4

TAX REFORM ACT OF 1986
Small business, purchase or sale,
    Asset sales, § 6.33

TAXATION
Alcoholic beverage control,
    Excise tax, § 36.44
    Licenses, tax bonds,
        Manufacturing, § 36.19
        Wholesale license, § 36.19
    Tax stamp, § 36.4
Bankruptcy, generally, this index
Corporations, generally, this index
Deductions,
    Additional standard deduction for the aged and blind, § 23.115
Divorce,
    Distribution of property, § 21.44
        Ordered sale of home, § 21.45
        Title to marital residence, § 21.45
    Spousal support, § 21.51
Elderly individuals, § 23.114
    Additional standard deduction for the aged and blind, § 23.115
    Incapacity, § 23.115
    Medical deductions, § 23.118
    Sale of principal residence, § 23.117
Employment law,
    Discharge of employee, severance pay, § 17.14
Excise tax, alcoholic beverages, § 36.44
Housing, elderly individuals, tax assistance loans, § 23.102

INDEX

TAXATION—Continued
Income tax, federal,
    Jury instructions on damages in personal injury cases, payment of income taxes, § 30.65
    Marital property distribution, § 21.45
Joint returns,
    Election to file with decedent's spouse, postmortem planning, § 24.78
Long term care insurance, § 23.68
Municipal Corporations, generally, this index
Real Property, Taxation, generally, this index
Retirement income from qualified plans, § 23.32
Small Business, Purchase or Sale, generally, this index
Tax stamp,
    Alcoholic beverage control, § 36.4
    Bureau of Alcohol, Tobacco and Firearms, § 36.4
Wills, provisions, § 24.10

TAXATION AND FINANCE DEPARTMENT
    Generally, § 35.40
Office of revenue and information management, § 35.43
Office of tax operations, § 35.44
    Audit division, § 35.45
    Division of tax appeals, § 35.49
    Office of tax enforcement, § 35.48
    Revenue opportunity division, § 35.47
    Tax compliance division, § 35.46
Office of the Counsel, role of, § 35.41
Summary, § 35.50
Taxpayer services division, § 35.42

TAXPAYER BILL OF RIGHTS
Income tax, state, § 35.87

TAXPAYER RELIEF ACT OF 1997
Medicaid, transfer of resources, § 23.76

TAYLOR LAW
Collective bargaining, protection against discrimination, § 17.61
Public Employment Relations Board, § 17.53

TELEPHONES
Life line telephone service,
    Miscellaneous programs,
        Elder law, § 23.121
Local land use law, zoning,
    Public uses, cellular transmission facilities, § 16.130

TEMPORARY RESTRAINING ORDERS
Injunctive Relief, this index

TENANTS
Housing issues, elderly individuals, § 23.106
New York Landlord-Tenant Law, generally, this index

TERMINATION
Retirement income from qualified plans, § 23.34

THEATERS
Public accommodations and amusement, equal rights in places of, § 18.54

TORTS
Limitation of actions, § 17.77
Nuisance, generally, this index

TOWN COURTS
Appeals, § 38.47
Justice Courts, generally, this index

INDEX

TOWN COURTS—Continued
Stay pending appeal,
    Appeal from town court to appellate term, § 38.54
    Notice of motion for stay of proceedings,
        Affirmation in support, form, § 37.132
        Form, § 37.130
    Order to show cause for stay of proceedings,
        Affirmation in support, form, § 37.132
        Form, § 37.131

TOXIC SUBSTANCES CONTROL ACT
Antireprisal provisions, § 17.38

TRADE NAMES
Small business, purchase or sale,
    Asset sales,
        Tax issues for buyer, § 6.40
        Due diligence investigation, legal review, § 6.19

TRADEMARKS
Small business, purchase or sale,
    Asset sales,
        Tax issues for buyer, § 6.40

TRAFFIC OFFENSES
Miranda warnings, § 33.49
Pretrial discovery, § 33.33
Speeding,
    Admissions, § 33.68
    Cross examination, § 33.68
    Discovery, demands to produce,
        Drafting checklist, § 33.97
        Form, § 33.101
        Procedural checklist, § 33.93
    Identification, § 33.68
    Jurisdiction, § 33.68
    Operation, § 33.68
    Pacing, § 33.68
    Radar, § 33.68
        Angle/cosine error, § 33.68
        Batching, § 33.68
        Certificates of calibration, § 33.68
        Jamming, § 33.68
        Moving mode, § 33.68
        Panning, § 33.68
        Scanning, § 33.68
        Shadowing, § 33.68
        Spurious readings, § 33.68
    Specific speed, § 33.68
    Supporting deposition, when not to request, § 33.69
    Trial, § 33.66
        Discovery, § 33.67
        Prima facie case, § 33.68
    Visual estimate of speed, § 33.68
Speedy trial, CPL § 30.30,
    Uniform traffic tickets, § 33.83
    Vehicle and traffic law generally excluded, § 33.75
        Unless combined with felony, misdemeanor or violation, § 33.76
Warrantless arrest, § 33.7

TRESPASS
Environmental law, § 15.33

INDEX

TRIAL
Bench trials, § 33.63
    Order of proceedings, § 33.65
Discrimination, § 17.74
Divorce,
    Joint trials, § 21.17
    Jury trials, form, § 21.90
    Trial date, § 21.80
Employment law, discrimination, § 17.74
Guardianships, proceedings to recover property withheld, § 22.85
Jury trials, § 33.63
    Discrimination, § 17.82
    Form,
        Divorce, § 21.90
        Employment law, § 17.98
        Federal court, § 17.98
    Order of proceedings, § 33.64
    Probate and estate administration, § 25.30
Modes of trial, § 33.63
Personal injury cases, § 26.52 et seq.
Procedures, § 33.62 et seq.
Speeding tickets, § 33.66
    Discovery, § 33.67
    Prima facie case, § 33.68
    Summary, § 33.70
    Supporting depositions, when not to request, § 33.69
Speedy Trial, generally, this index
Uniform trial court rules, case management rules, §§ 21.79, 21.80

TRUSTEES
Probate and estate administration, declining to serve as, § 25.48
Wills, appointment provisions, § 24.15

TRUSTS
Charitable lead trusts, lifetime planning, § 24.55
Charitable remainder trusts, lifetime planning, § 24.54
Crummey trusts,
    Annual gift tax exclusion, § 24.52
    Notice, estate planning, § 24.101
Disclaimer trusts, postmortem planning, § 24.69
Domestic trusts, asset protection, § 24.87
Foreign trusts, asset protection, § 24.88
Grantor retained trusts,
    Lifetime planning, valuation of gifts, § 24.46
Life insurance trusts,
    Crummey powers, estate planning with certain assets, § 24.36
    Estate planning, § 24.35
Maximum duration,
    Wills, provisions, § 24.17
Medicaid, this index
Real estate investment trusts (REIT),
    Real property sale, closing, payment of taxes, § 12.87
Residence trusts,
    Lifetime planning,
        Valuation of gifts, § 24.47
            Income tax considerations, § 24.48
Revocable trusts, probate avoidance, § 24.81
Section 2503(c) trusts, annual gift tax exclusion, § 24.50
Totten trusts, probate avoidance, § 24.82
Wills, provisions, § 24.13

TRUTH IN LENDING ACT
Consumer Leasing Act, § 7.21

INDEX

TRUTH IN LENDING ACT—Continued
Motor vehicle sales, § 7.3

UNEMPLOYMENT INSURANCE
Appeals, § 17.60
Ban while receiving severance benefits, § 17.16
Denial of benefits, § 17.60

UNIFORM ENFORCEMENT OF FOREIGN JUDGMENTS ACT
Enforcement of foreign money judgments, § 8.16

UNIFORM TRANSFERS TO MINORS ACT
Annual gift tax exclusion, § 24.51

UNIFORM TRIAL COURT RULES
Case management rules, §§ 21.79, 21.80

UNINSURED EMPLOYERS' FUND
Workers' compensation, § 32.40

UNIONS
Elections, Labor Management Reporting and Disclosure Act, § 17.61
Employment discrimination prohibited, § 18.60

UNIVERSITIES AND COLLEGES
Professors, immigration, § 19.20

UTILITIES
Bankruptcy, § 9.89
Public utilities,
    Employment discrimination prohibited, § 18.60
    Local land use law, zoning,
        Public uses, § 12.129
    Reservations for public utilities,
        Real property, marketability of title, effect, § 12.70

VENUE
Adoption proceedings, §§ 20.11, 20.87
    Private adoptions, § 20.2
Article 78 proceedings,
    Judicial review, administrative law, § 4.83
Bankruptcy, § 9.21
Change of venue,
    Appellate division, criminal, § 38.8
    County courts, original application, § 38.58
    Criminal court to family court, § 38.8
    Family court to criminal court, § 38.8
Corporations, judicial dissolution, § 1.104
Guardians, appointment, § 22.16
Matrimonial actions, §§ 21.15, 21.16
Medical malpractice cases, § 26.58
Mortgage foreclosure, § 11.19
New York Landlord-Tenant Law, summary proceedings, § 13.5
Personal injury cases, §§ 26.34, 26.58
Probate and estate administration, § 25.12

VETERANS' BENEFITS
Elder law, § 23.41

VICARIOUS LIABILITY
Legal malpractice, partner's misdeeds, § 28.25

VILLAGE COURTS
Appeals, § 38.47
Justice Courts, generally, this index
Stay pending appeal,

INDEX

VILLAGE COURTS—Continued
Stay pending appeal—Continued
    Appeal from village court to appellate term, § 38.54
    Notice of motion for stay of proceedings,
        Affirmation in support, form, § 37.132
        Form, § 37.130
    Order to show cause for stay of proceedings,
        Affirmation in support, form, § 37.132
        Form, § 37.131

VIOLENCE AGAINST WOMEN ACT
Federal civil rights law, education, § 18.53

VISITATION RIGHTS
Adoption proceedings,
    Natural parents granted rights, § 20.123
    Siblings granted rights, § 20.124
Divorce, generally, this index

VOIR DIRE
Peremptory challenges,
    Discrimination, § 18.15
    Personal injury trials, § 26.55

VOTING
Limited partnerships, management,
    General partners, § 2.89
    Limited partners, § 2.90
Partnerships, management, § 2.56
Shareholders' meetings and agreements, § 1.45

WAGES AND HOURS
Employee handbooks, § 17.81
Minimum wages, § 17.63
Overtime pay, § 17.63
Replacement wages,
    Benefits, generally. Workers' Compensation, this index
Wage claims,
    Attorney fees, § 17.63
    Limitation of actions, § 17.77
    Unpaid wages, § 17.63

WAIVER
Accusatory instruments,
    Supporting depositions, guilty plea waiving defects, § 33.22
Discrimination,
    Equal Employment Opportunity Commission, letter requesting "Mohasco" waiver, form, § 17.88
Employment law,
    Discharge of employee,
        Exit incentives, § 17.11
        Severance pay, releases and waivers, § 17.16
    Older Workers Benefit Protection Act, strict waiver requirements of rights, § 17.11
Income tax, state, limitation of actions, § 35.69
Insurance, § 31.15
    Limitations of actions, § 31.26
Private adoption, certification as qualified adoptive parents, § 20.56
Probate and estate administration, forms, § 25.57
Severance pay, § 17.16
Spousal rights, retirement income from qualified plans, § 23.31

WARRANTIES
Breach of,
    Complaints, § 7.52
        Defenses, § 7.53

INDEX

WARRANTIES—Continued
Commercial Sales Contract, generally, this index
Motor vehicles, lemon law, §§ 7.10, 7.11, 7.48
    Used cars, § 7.48
Small Business, Purchase or Sale, generally, this index

WARRANTLESS ARREST
Petty offenses, § 33.7
Police/citizen encounters, § 33.7
Traffic infractions, § 33.7

WARRANTY OF HABITABILITY
Non-payment proceedings, tenant defenses, § 13.32

WELFARE
ERISA protection, § 17.50

WETLANDS PROTECTION
Environmental Law, this index

WHISTLEBLOWER PROTECTION LAW
    Generally, § 17.64
Federal False Claims Act, § 17.64
Limitation of actions, § 17.77
Wrongful discharge of employee, § 17.32

WILLS
    Generally, § 24.3 et seq.
Accounting provisions, § 24.17
Affidavit proving correct copy of will, forms,
    Probate and estate administration, § 25.53
Contracts to make,
    Multiple marriages, spousal rights, § 24.61
Debt provisions, § 24.10
Execution requirements, § 24.4
    Publication, § 24.6
    Self-proving affidavits, § 24.8
    Signature, § 24.5
    Witnesses, § 24.7
Executors, appointment, § 24.15
Fiduciaries,
    Alternate or successor fiduciary provisions, § 24.17
    Powers, § 24.16
Guardianship provisions, § 24.14
Joint wills, multiple marriages, spousal rights, § 24.61
Living Wills, generally, this index
Minors provisions, § 24.17
Miscellaneous provisions, § 24.17
Personal property dispositions, § 24.9
Power of appointment provisions, § 24.17
Probate and estate administration, construction, § 25.50
Real property dispositions, § 24.11
Residuary estate provisions, § 24.12
Simultaneous death provisions, § 24.17
Spendthrift clause provisions, § 24.17
Tax provisions, § 24.10
Trustees, appointment, § 24.15
Trusts,
    Maximum duration provisions, § 24.17
    Provisions, § 24.13
"Wipeout clause" provisions, § 24.17

WINDING UP
Limited liability companies, § 2.39
Limited partnerships, § 2.100

INDEX

WINDING UP—Continued
Partnerships, § 2.67

WINE
Auction permit, §§ 36.17, 36.44
Drug stores, license to sell, §§ 36.8, 36.10
Grocery stores, license to sell, §§ 36.8, 36.10
Licenses to manufacture, § 36.12
Package stores, license to sell, §§ 36.8, 36.10

WITNESSES AND TESTIMONY
Attendance,
    Adjudicatory proceedings, administrative law, § 4.16
Expert Witnesses, generally, this index
Impeachment, generally, this index
Motor vehicle accidents, § 26.19
    Discovery, form, § 26.70
Personal injury cases, § 26.3
Probate and estate administration,
    Deposition affidavit of subscribing witness, forms, § 25.59
Social security disability cases, preparing for hearings, § 34.43
Wills,
    Execution requirements, § 24.7
    Unavailable witnesses, admission of will to probate, § 25.22

WORKER ADJUSTMENT AND RETRAINING NOTIFICATION ACT (WARN)
Plant closing notice, § 17.51
Small business, purchase or sale,
    Post-contract and pre-closing, § 6.101
    Seller's stock sale agreement, drafting, § 6.184

WORKERS' COMPENSATION
    Generally, §§ 17.65, 32.1 et seq.
Appeals, § 32.34
Appellate division, civil,
    Time for taking appeal, § 37.44
Attending doctor's report and carrier/employer billing form, § 32.56
Attorneys' fees, § 32.38
Benefits, § 32.21
    Assignments, § 32.32
    Death awards, § 32.30
        Funeral expenses, § 32.31
    Disability, classification of, § 32.22
    Facial disfigurement, § 32.29
    Liens, § 32.32
    Lump-sum settlements, § 32.32
    Medical benefits, § 32.28
    Wage replacement, § 32.23
        Industrially disabled, § 32.26
        Rehabilitation, § 32.25
        Schedule versus non-schedule awards, § 32.24
        Special disability fund, § 32.27
Board, § 32.11
    Decisions, orders and awards, review of, § 32.33
Checklists,
    Employee's counsel, § 32.4
    Employer's counsel, § 32.3
Claims, § 17.65
    Claim file, discovery, medical malpractice action, § 29.71
    Closed claims, reopening, § 32.35
    Compensation, for, forms, § 32.54
Compensable injury, § 32.13
Coverage,
    Methods of, § 32.12

INDEX

WORKERS' COMPENSATION—Continued
Coverage—Continued
    Posting notice of coverage, § 32.39
Decisions, orders and awards, board review of, § 32.33
Disability Benefits Law, generally, this index
Disability, classification of, § 32.22
Discovery,
    Medical malpractice action, § 29.73
        Claim file, § 29.71
Discrimination, § 32.36
Election to exclude certain unsalaried officers from coverage, § 32.41
Employee's counsel, § 32.4
Employer's counsel, § 32.3
Employer's obligations and methods of coverage, § 32.12
Employer's report of work-related accident/occupational disease, form, § 32.55
Exclusive remedy doctrine, § 32.14
    Exceptions, § 32.15
Federal laws and benefits, § 32.43
Forms, § 32.53 et seq.
Hearings, § 32.17
    Burden of proof, § 32.19
    Conciliation process, § 32.20
    Defenses, § 32.19
    Limitation of actions, § 32.18
    Pre-hearing conference, § 32.16
    Presumptions, § 32.19
Insurance policies, § 32.41
Introduction to law, § 32.5
    History and theory, § 32.6
        Constitutional amendment, § 32.8
        Statutory changes, § 32.10
        Workmen's Compensation Law of 1910, § 32.7
        Workmen's Compensation Law of 1914, § 32.9
Liens, § 26.49
Limitation of actions, § 17.77
Notice, this index
Personal injury cases, § 26.3
Posting, notice of coverage, § 32.39
Pre-hearing conference, § 32.16
Products liability action, § 26.14
Rehabilitation, benefits, wage replacement, § 32.25
Representatives, licensed, § 32.37
    Fees, § 32.38
Scope, § 32.1
Social security disability programs, comparison to, § 34.7
State insurance fund, § 32.42
Strategy, § 32.1
    Checklists, generally, ante
Uninsured employers' fund, § 32.40

"YELLOWSTONE" ACTIONS
New York Landlord-Tenant Law, § 13.70
    Obtaining injunction, § 13.71

ZONING
    Generally, § 16.60 et seq.
Area variance, § 16.82 et seq.
    Conditions imposed upon, § 16.89
    Minimum variance necessary, § 16.86
    Procedures, § 16.87
    Statutory balancing test, § 16.83
        Balancing factors, § 16.85
        Guiding principles from case law, § 16.84

INDEX

ZONING—Continued
Area variance—Continued
  Statutory balancing test—Continued
    Significant economic injury to individual compared to public purpose served by regulation, § 16.85
  Summary, § 16.88
As of right use, § 16.61
Comprehensive plan,
  Protection of zoning from challenge, § 16.15
  Standard State Zoning Enabling Act, § 16.11
Local Land Use Law, generally, this index
Nonconforming use,
  Abandonment, § 16.68
  Alteration or extension, § 16.65
  Amortization, § 16.69
  Application, § 16.62
  Changes, § 16.63
  Changes to another nonconforming use, § 16.66
  Definitions, § 16.62
  Procedures, § 16.71
  Reconstruction and restoration, § 16.64
  Summary, § 16.72
  Termination, § 16.67
  Transfer of ownership, § 16.70
Ordinances, local process, § 16.28
Overview, § 16.60
Particularized actions, § 16.109 et seq.
  Summary, § 16.117
Public uses,
  Implied preemption, § 16.128
  Public utilities, § 12.129
  Telephones, cellular transmission facilities, § 16.130
Public utilities, public uses, § 12.129
Rezoning, § 16.113
  Conditions, § 16.114
  Contract zoning, § 16.115
  Development agreements, § 16.116
  State Environmental Quality Review Act (SEQRA), § 16.58
  Summary, § 16.117
Special regulations, § 16.118 et seq.
  Accessory apartments, § 16.120
  Accessory uses, § 16.119
    Home offices, § 16.121
  Aesthetics, § 16.125
    Architectural review, § 16.126
    Design review board, § 16.126
    Historic preservation, § 16.127
    Landmark preservation commission, § 16.127
  Affordable housing, § 16.123
  Definition of family, § 16.122
  Exclusionary zoning, § 16.123
  Home offices, § 16.121
  Mobile homes, § 16.124
  Public uses, § 16.128
    Cellular transmission facilities, § 16.130
    Implied preemption, § 16.128
    Public utilities, § 16.129
    Religious uses, § 16.131
    "Superior sovereign" test, § 16.128
  Summary, § 16.132
Special use permits, § 16.90 et seq.
  Findings and determination of board, § 16.92

INDEX

ZONING—Continued
Special use permits—Continued
 Imposition and use of standards, § 16.91
 Limitations on imposition of conditions, § 16.93
 Procedure, § 16.94
 Summary, § 16.95
Spot zoning, § 16.110
 Challenge,
  Dismissal, § 16.111
  Successful challenge, § 16.112
 Summary, § 16.117
Standard State Zoning Enabling Act, comprehensive plan, § 16.11
State Environmental Quality Review Act (SEQRA), rezoning, § 16.58
Telephones, public uses,
 Cellular transmission facilities, § 16.130
Use variance, § 16.73 et seq.
 Conditions imposed upon, § 16.89
 Definitions, § 16.73
 Minimum variance needed, § 16.79
 Procedure, § 16.80
 Statutory standard, § 16.74
  Protection of essential neighborhood character, § 16.77
  Reasonable return, § 16.75
  Self-created hardship, § 16.78
  Unique hardship, § 16.76
 Summary, § 16.81
Zoning board of appeals,
 Appeals, § 16.37
 Judicial review, § 16.46

†

ZONING — Continued
  Special use permits — Continued
    Imposition and use of standards, § 16.91
    Limitation on imposition of conditions, § 16.91
    Procedure, § 16.94
    Summary, § 16.95
    Spot zoning, § 16.110
  Challenge
    Damaged party, 11
    Successful challenge, §§ 16.112
  Summary, § 16.140
  Standard State Zoning Enabling Act comprehensive plan, § 16.11
  State Environmental Quality Review Act (SEQRA), zoning, § 16.85
  Temporary public uses
    Similar transmission facilities, § 16.180
    Exceptions, § 16.75 et seq.
    Conditions imposed upon, § 16.38
    Definitions, § 16.72
    Minimum welfare standard, § 16.78
    Procedure, § 16.80
    Stallion standards, § 16.74
    Protection of essential neighborhood character, § 16.7
    Prospects resulting, 16.36
    Self-remediarianship, § 16.79
    Unique hardship, § 16.78
  Summary, § 16.97
  Zoning board of appeals
    Appeals, § 16.47
    Judicial review, 16.46

GENERAL PRACTICE IN NEW YORK

Volume 25

By

ROBERT L. OSTERTAG
HON. JAMES D. BENSON

Sections 38.1 to End
TABLES and INDEX

1999 Pocket Part

Insert this Pocket Part in back of Volume

ST. PAUL, MINN.
WEST GROUP
1999

GENERAL PRACTICE IN NEW YORK
FORMS ON DISK™

The **Forms on Disk**™ which accompany these volumes provide instant access to WordPerfect 5.1/5.2 versions of the forms included in *General Practice in New York*. These electronic forms will save you hours of time drafting legal documents. The electronic forms can be loaded into your word processing software and formatted to match the document style of your law firm. These electronic forms become templates for you to use over and over without having to retype them each time.

The forms in Volumes 20, 21, 22, 23, 24 and 25 that are included on the accompanying disks are marked with the following disk icon for easy identification.

COPYRIGHT © 1999
By
WEST GROUP

This is the 1999 Pocket Part to Volume 25 of

WEST'S NEW YORK PRACTICE SERIES

West's New York Practice Series

Vol. 1	Walker, et al., New York Limited Liability Companies and Partnerships: A Guide to Law and Practice
Vols. 2-4	Haig, et al., Commercial Litigation in New York State Courts
Vol. 5	Barker and Alexander, Evidence in New York State and Federal Courts
Vol. 6	Greenberg, Marcus, et al., New York Criminal Law
Vol. 7	Marks, et al., New York Pretrial Criminal Procedure
Vol. 8	Davies, Stecich, Gold, et al., New York Civil Appellate Practice
Vol. 9	Ginsberg, Weinberg, et al., Environmental Law and Regulation in New York
Vol. 10	Sobie, et al., New York Family Court Practice
Vols. 11-12	Scheinkman, et al., New York Law of Domestic Relation

Vol. 13	Taber, et al., Employment Litigation in New York
Vols. 14-16	Kreindler, Rodriguez, et al., New York Law of Torts
Vols. 17-19	Field, Moskin, et al., New York and Delaware Business Organizations: Choice, Formation, Operation, Financing and Acquisitions
Vols. 20-25	Ostertag, Benson, et al., General Practice in New York
Vol. 26	Borchers, Markell, et al., New York State Administrative Procedure and Practice
Vol. A	Borges, et al., Enforcing Judgments and Collecting Debts in New York
Vols. B-C	Bensel, Frank, McKeon, et al., Personal Injury Practice in New York
Vols. D-E	Preminger, et al., Trusts and Estates Practice in New York
Vols. F-G	Finkelstein and Ferrara, Landlord and Tenant Practice in New York

FOREWORD

Here is the first update to *General Practice in New York*, volume 25 of the New York Practice Series. The pocket part covers the significant changes in the applicable law from publication of the original volume until 1999. Many of the updates were prepared by one or more of the original chapter authors; others were editorially prepared in-house by West and are so indicated. With respect to chapters of the book not updated at all, West makes no representations with respect to the current status of ther material therein.

December 1999

COORDINATED RESEARCH IN NEW YORK FROM WEST

New York Practice 2d
David D. Siegel

Handling the DWI Case in New York
Peter Gerstenzang

New York Elder Law Practice
Vincent J. Russo and Marvin Rachlin

WEST'S McKINNEY'S FORMS

Civil Practice Law and Rules

Uniform Commercial Code

Business Corporation Law

Matrimonial and Family Law

Real Property Practice

Estates and Surrogate Practice

Criminal Procedure Law

Not-For-Profit Corporation Law

Tax Practice and Procedure

Local Government Forms

Selected Consolidated Law Forms

McKinney's Consolidated Laws of New York Annotated

West's New York Legal Update

New York Digest

New York Law Finder

PAMPHLETS

New York Civil Practice Law and Rules

New York Sentence Charts

Westlaw®

COORDINATED RESEARCH FROM WEST GROUP

WEST*Check*® and WESTMATE®

West CD–ROM Libraries™

To order any of these New York practice tools, call your West Group Representative or 1–800–328–9352.

> **NEED RESEARCH HELP?**
>
> **If you have research questions concerning Westlaw or West Group Publications, call West Group's Reference Attorneys at 1–800–733–2889.**

WESTLAW® ELECTRONIC RESEARCH GUIDE

Coordinating Legal Research with Westlaw

The *New York Practice Series* is an essential aid to legal research. Westlaw provides a vast, online library of over 8000 collections of documents and services that can supplement research begun in this publication, encompassing:

- Federal and state primary law (statutes, regulations, rules, and case law), including West's editorial enhancements, such as headnotes, Key Number classifications, annotations

- Secondary law resources (texts and treatises published by West Group and by other publishers, as well as law reviews)

- Legal news

- Directories of attorneys and experts

- Court records and filings

- Citators

Specialized topical subsets of these resources have been created for more than thirty areas of practice.

In addition to legal information, there are general news and reference databases and a broad array of specialized materials frequently useful in connection with legal matters, covering accounting, business, environment, ethics, finance, medicine, social and physical sciences.

This guide will focus on a few aspects of Westlaw use to supplement research begun in this publication, and will direct you to additional sources of assistance.

Databases

A database is a collection of documents with some features in common. It may contain statutes, court decisions, administrative materials, commentaries, news or other information. Each database has a unique identifier, used in many Westlaw commands to select a database of interest. For example, the database containing New York cases has the identifier NY-CS.

The Westlaw Directory is a comprehensive list of databases with information about each database, including the types of documents each contains. The first page of a standard or customized Westlaw Directory is displayed upon signing on to Westlaw, except when prior, saved re-

WESTLAW ELECTRONIC RESEARCH GUIDE

search is resumed. To access the Westlaw Directory at any time, enter DB.

Databases of potential interest in connection with your research include:

NY-AG	New York Attorney General Opinions
NYETH-EO	New York Ethics Opinions
NYETH-CS	Legal Ethics & Professional Responsibility - New York Cases
WLD-NY	West's Legal Directory - New York
LAWPRAC	The Legal Practice Database

For information as to currentness and search tips regarding any Westlaw database, enter the SCOPE command SC followed by the database identifier (e.g., SC NY-CS). It is not necessary to include the identifier to obtain scope information about the currently selected database.

Westlaw Highlights

Use of this publication may be supplemented through the Westlaw Bulletin (WLB), the Westlaw New York State Bulletin (WSB-NY) and various Topical Highlights. Highlights databases contain summaries of significant judicial, legislative and administrative developments and are updated daily; they are searchable both from an automatic list of recent documents and using general Westlaw search methods for documents accumulated over time. The full text of any judicial decision may be retrieved by entering FIND.

Consult the Westlaw Directory (enter DB) for a complete, current listing of highlights databases.

Retrieving a Specific Case

The FIND command can be used to quickly retrieve a case whose citation is known. For example:

FI 616 A.2d 1336

Updating Case Law Research

There are a variety of citator services on Westlaw for use in updating research.

KeyCite[SM] is an enhanced citator service that integrates all the case law on Westlaw. KeyCite provides direct and negative indirect history for any case within the scope of its coverage, citations to other decisions and secondary materials on Westlaw that have mentioned or discussed the cited case, and a complete integration with West Group's Key Number System so that you can track a legal issue explored in a case. KeyCite is as current as Westlaw and includes all cases on Westlaw, including unpublished opinions. To view the KeyCite history of a displayed case, enter the command KC. To view the KeyCite information for a selected case, simply enter a command in the following form:

KC 113 SCT 2786

To see a complete list of publications covered by KeyCite, enter the command KC PUBS. To ascertain the scope of coverage, enter the command SC KC. For the complete list of commands available enter KC CMDS.

Retrieving Statutes, Court Rules and Regulations

Annotated and unannotated versions of the New York statutes are searchable on Westlaw (identifiers NY-ST-ANN and NY-ST), as are New York court rules (NY-RULES) and New York Administrative Code (NY-ADC).

The United States Code and United States Code - Annotated are searchable databases on Westlaw (identifiers USC and USCA, respectively), as are federal court rules (US-RULES) and regulations (CFR).

In addition, the FIND command may be used to retrieve specific provisions by citation, obviating the need for database selection or search. To FIND a desired document, enter FI, followed by the citation of the desired document, using the full name of the publication, or one of the abbreviated styles recognized by Westlaw.

If Westlaw does not recognize the style you enter, you may enter one of the following, using US, NY, or any other state code in place of XX:

FI XX-ST	Displays templates for codified statutes
FI XX-LEGIS	Displays templates for legislation
FI XX-RULES	Displays templates for rules
FI XX-ORDERS	Displays templates for court orders

Alternatively, entering FI followed by the publication's full name or an accepted abbreviation will normally display templates, useful jump possibilities, or helpful information necessary to complete the FIND process. For example:

FI USCA	Displays templates for United States Code - Annotated
FI FRAP	Displays templates for Federal Rules of Appellate Procedure
FI FRCP	Displays templates for Federal Rules of Civil Procedure
FI FRCRP	Displays templates for Federal Rules of Criminal Procedure
FI FRE	Displays templates for Federal Rules of Evidence
FI CFR	Displays templates for Code of Federal Regulations
FI FR	Displays templates for Federal Register

To view the complete list of FINDable documents and associated prescribed forms, enter FI PUBS.

Updating Research in re Statutes, Rules and Regulations

When viewing a statute, rule or regulation on Westlaw after a search or FIND command, it is easy to update your research. A message will appear on the screen if relevant amendments, repeals or other new material are available through the UPDATE feature. Entering the UPDATE command will display such material.

Documents used to update New York statutes are also searchable in New York Legislative Service (NY-LEGIS). Those used to update rules are searchable in New York Orders (NY-ORDERS).

Documents used to update federal statutes, rules, and regulations are searchable in the United States Public Laws (US-PL), Federal Orders (US-ORDERS) and Federal Register (FR) databases, respectively.

When documents citing a statute, rule or regulation are of interest, Shepard's Citations on Westlaw may be of assistance. That service covers federal constitutional provisions, statutes and administrative provisions, and corresponding materials from many states. The command SH PUBS displays a directory of publications which may be Shepardized on Westlaw. Consult the Westlaw manual for more information about citator services.

Using Westlaw as a Citator

For research beyond the coverage of any citator service, go directly to the databases (cases, for example) containing citing documents and use standard Westlaw search techniques to retrieve documents citing specific constitutional provisions, statutes, standard jury instructions or other authorities.

Fortunately, the specific portion of a citation is often reasonably distinctive, such as 22:636.1, 301.65, 401(k), 12-21-5, 12052. When it is, a search on that specific portion alone may retrieve applicable documents without any substantial number of inapplicable ones (unless the number happens to be coincidentally popular in another context).

Similarly, if the citation involves more than one number, such as 42 U.S.C.A. §1201, a search containing both numbers (e.g., 42 +5 1201) is likely to produce mostly desired information, even though the component numbers are common.

If necessary, the search may be limited in several ways:

A. Switch from a general database to one containing mostly cases within the subject area of the cite being researched;

WESTLAW ELECTRONIC RESEARCH GUIDE

B. Use a connector (&, /S, /P, etc.) to narrow the search to documents including terms which are highly likely to accompany the correct citation in the context of the issue being researched;

C. Include other citation information in the query. Because of the variety of citation formats used in documents, this option should be used primarily where other options prove insufficient. Below are illustrative queries for any database containing New York cases:

>N.Y.Const.! Const.! Constitution /s 6 VI +3 3

will retrieve cases citing the New York State Constitution, Art. 6, §3; and

>"Criminal Procedure Law" CPL /s 30.30

will retrieve cases citing Criminal Procedure Law §30.30.

Alternative Retrieval Methods

WIN® (Westlaw Is Natural™) allows you to frame your issue in plain English to retrieve documents:

>Does new trial motion extend (toll) the time for filing (taking) appeal?

Alternatively, retrieval may be focused by use of the Terms and Connectors method:

>TO(30) /P DI(NEW +1 TRIAL /P EXTEND!
>EXTENSION TOLL! /P APPEAL)

In databases with Key Numbers, either of the above examples will identify Appeal and Error ⟶345.1 as a Key Number collecting headnotes relevant to this issue if there are pertinent cases.

Since the Key Numbers are affixed to points of law by trained specialists based on conceptual understanding of the case, relevant cases that were not retrieved by either of the language-dependent methods will often be found at a Key Number.

Similarly, citations in retrieved documents (to cases, statutes, rules, etc.) may suggest additional, fruitful research using other Westlaw databases (e.g., annotated statutes, rules) or services (e.g., citator services).

Key Number Search

Frequently, case law research rapidly converges on a few topics, headings and Key Numbers within West's Key Number System that are likely to contain relevant cases. These may be discovered from known, relevant reported cases from any jurisdiction; Library References in West publications; browsing in a digest; or browsing the Key Number System on Westlaw using the JUMP feature or the KEY command.

WESTLAW ELECTRONIC RESEARCH GUIDE

Once discovered, topics, subheadings or Key Numbers are useful as search terms (in databases containing reported cases) alone or with other search terms, to focus the search within a narrow range of potentially relevant material.

For example, to retrieve cases with at least one headnote classified to Appeal and Error ⚖︎345.1, sign on to a caselaw database and enter

> 30k345.1 [use with other search terms, if desired]

The topic name (Appeal and Error) is replaced by its numerical equivalent (30) and the ⚖︎ by the letter k. A list of topics and their numerical equivalents is in the Westlaw Reference Manual and is displayed in Westlaw when the KEY command is entered.

Using JUMP

Westlaw's JUMP feature allows you to move from one document to another or from one part of a document to another, then easily return to your original place, without losing your original result. Opportunities to move in this manner are marked in the text with a JUMP symbol (▶). Whenever you see the JUMP symbol, you may move to the place designated by the adjacent reference by using the Tab, arrow keys or mouse click to position the cursor on the JUMP symbol, then pressing Enter or clicking again with the mouse.

Within the text of a court opinion, JUMP arrows are adjacent to case cites and federal statute cites, and adjacent to parenthesized numbers marking discussions corresponding to headnotes.

On a screen containing the text of a headnote, the JUMP arrows allow movement to the corresponding discussion in the text of the opinion,

▶ (3)

and allow browsing West's Key Number System beginning at various heading levels:

- ▶ 30   APPEAL AND ERROR
- ▶ 30VII   Transfer of Cause
- ▶ 30VII(A)   Time of Taking Proceedings
- ▶ 30k343   Commencement of Period of Limitation
- ▶ 30k345.1 k.   Motion for new trial.

To return from a JUMP, enter GB (except for JUMPs between a headnote and the corresponding discussion in opinion, for which there is a matching number in parenthesis in both headnote and opinion). Returns from successive JUMPs (e.g., from case to cited case to case cited by cited case) without intervening returns may be accomplished by repeated entry of GB or by using the MAP command.

WESTLAW ELECTRONIC RESEARCH GUIDE

General Information

The information provided above illustrates some of the ways Westlaw can complement research using this publication. However, this brief overview illustrates only some of the power of Westlaw. The full range of Westlaw search techniques is available to support your research.

Please consult the Westlaw Reference Manual for additional information or assistance or call West's Reference Attorneys at 1-800-REF-ATTY (1-800-733-2889).

For information about subscribing to Westlaw, please call 1-800-328-9352.

SUMMARY OF CONTENTS

Volume 20

Chapter		Page
1.	Business Organizations: Corporations	2
2.	Non-corporate Entities	16
3.	Municipal Law	19
4.	Municipal Law	21
6.	Buying and Selling a Small Business	25

Volume 21

7.	Consumer Law	2
8.	Enforcement of Money Judgments	4
9.	Bankruptcy	5
11.	Mortgage Foreclosure	11
12.	Purchase and Sale of Real Estate	25

Volume 22

14.	Eminent Domain	2
15.	Environmental Law	5
16.	Land Use Law	8
17.	Employment Law	14
18.	Civil Rights Law	16
19.	Immigration and Nationality Law Permanent Residence Applications	39
20.	Adoptions	52

Volume 23

21.	Domestic Relations	2
22.	Guardianship	9
23.	Elder Law	21
24.	Estate Planning	30
25.	Probate and Estate Administration	37
26.	Personal Injury	51

Volume 24

28.	Legal Malpractice	2
29.	Medical Malpractice	20
30.	Damages	21

SUMMARY OF CONTENTS

Chapter	Page
31. Insurance	31
32. Workers' Compensation	34
33. Local Criminal Court Practice	39
34. Social Security Disability Cases	50
35. Income Tax	55
37. Civil Appellate Practice Before the Appellate Division and Other Intermediate Appellate Courts	58

Volume 25

38. Criminal Appellate Practice Before the Appellate Division and Other Intermediate Appellate Courts | 2
39. Civil and Criminal Appeals to the Court of Appeals | 4

Table of Statutes | 5
Table of Rules and Regulations | 15
Table of Cases | 17
Index | 31

WEST'S NEW YORK PRACTICE SERIES

General Practice in New York

Volume 25

Chapter 38

CRIMINAL APPELLATE PRACTICE BEFORE THE APPELLATE DIVISION AND OTHER INTERMEDIATE APPELLATE COURTS

(update prepared in-house)

Table of Sections

38.8   Appeals to the Appellate Division—Who May Appeal—Appeals by Defendant From Superior Courts—As of Right
38.26   ____ Disposition of Appeal—Reversal

Westlaw Electronic Research

See Westlaw Electronic Research Guide preceding the Summary of Contents.

---

§ 38.8 Appeals to the Appellate Division—Who May Appeal—Appeals by Defendant From Superior Courts—As of Right

PAGE 16:

[Add to end of note 20.]

20. *But see* People v. Hidalgo, 91 N.Y.2d 733, 675 N.Y.S.2d 327, 698 N.E.2d 46 (1998) (abrogating Leach; defendant could waive her right to appeal even though she was not informed of the length of her sentence, since she was advised of full range of sentencing options during plea colloquy, confirmed that she understood and confirmed that she had discussed waiver with counsel).

PAGE 17:

[Add to end of note 37.]

37. *But see* Matter of D.A.S., 951 S.W.2d 528 (Tex.App.1997) (attorney representing delinquent minor sought to file a brief in accord with Anders; court held that because a delinquency action is civil in nature and because a minor is under a legal disability and cannot appear in court except through a next friend, a guardian, or an attorney ad litem, such a brief is inappropriate).

PAGE 24:

[*In note 99, second CPL citation should be to CPL § 255.20(3).*]

§ 38.26 Appeals to the Appellate Division—Disposition of Appeal—Reversal

PAGE 103:

[*Add to end of note 7.*]

7. The lower court opinion in Rossey was reversed (89 N.Y.2d 970, 655 N.Y.S.2d 861, 678 N.E.2d 473 (1997)) because the lower court used an improper test for legal sufficiency. The proper standard is "whether the evidence, viewed in the light most favorable to the People, could lead a rational trier of fact to conclude that the elements of the crime had been proven beyond a reasonable doubt." 89 N.Y.2d at 971, 655 N.Y.S.2d at 861, 678 N.E.2d at 473.

Chapter 39

CIVIL AND CRIMINAL APPEALS TO THE COURT OF APPEALS

(update prepared in-house)

Table of Sections

39.4 Civil Appeals—Finality
39.5 ____ Non-appealable Orders
39.7 ____ Scope of Review

Westlaw Electronic Research

See Westlaw Electronic Research Guide preceding the Summary of Contents.

§ 39.4 Civil Appeals—Finality

PAGE 153:

[*In* note 14, updated citation is *Whitfield v. City of New York*, 90 N.Y.2d 777, 666 N.Y.S.2d 545, 689 N.E.2d 515 (1997).]

§ 39.5 Civil Appeals—Non-appealable Orders

PAGE 155:

[*In* note 4, updated citation is *Whitfield v. City of New York*, 90 N.Y.2d 777, 666 N.Y.S.2d 545, 689 N.E.2d 515 (1997).]

§ 39.7 Civil Appeals—Scope of Review

PAGE 156:

[*In* note 6, updated citation is *Papa v. Nassau County Dept. of Social Servs.*, 516 U.S. 1093, 116 S.Ct. 816, 133 L.Ed.2d 760 (1996).]

TABLE OF STATUTES

NEW YORK, MCKINNEY'S BANKING LAW

Sec.	This Pocket Part Sec.	Note
Art. 12–D	12.93	

NEW YORK, MCKINNEY'S BUSINESS CORPORATION LAW

Sec.	This Pocket Part Sec.	Note
104(a)	1.7	
104(c)	1.7	
104(d)	1.7	5
104(e)	1.7	
306(b)	1.83	18.2
511(a)(1)	1.38	16
511(a)(2)	1.38	16
609(a)	1.45	18
609(b)	1.114	8
609(i)	1.45	18
609(i)(1)	1.45	18
609(i)(2)	1.45	18
609(j)	1.45	18
613	1.22	
622(a)	1.52	3
622(b)	1.52	3
622(b)(1)	1.52	3
622(c)	1.52	3
623	1.83	18.2
713(b)	1.65	12
714(a)(2)	1.65	15
715(a)	1.69	1
718	1.69	1
901(b)(6)	1.83	1
901(b)(7)	1.83	1
901(c)	1.83	2
901(c)	1.83	18.2
903(a)(2)	1.83	6
903(b)	1.83	18.2
904–a(a)	1.83	18.2
904–a(a)(8)	1.83	18.2
904–a(b)	1.83	18.2
906(b)(3)	1.84	5
907(g)	1.83	18
913(c)(2)(A)	1.88	3
1308(a)(7)	1.119	1
1309(a)	1.117	8
1309–A	1.119	1
1309–A(b)	1.117	9
1315(a)	1.114	8
1315(b)	1.114	8
1315(c)	1.114	8
1318	1.114	11

NEW YORK, MCKINNEY'S CIVIL PRACTICE LAW AND RULES

Sec.	This Pocket Part Sec.	Note
Art. 12	22.8	4
3018	26.37	1
4504	22.2	9
4504	22.33	4
Art. 50–A	8.1	21
Art. 50–B	8.1	22
Art. 63	11.8o	
Art. 78	4.71	9
Art. 78	18.37	8
Art. 78	30.41	
7503(c)	31.24	5
8601	30.41	
8804(c)	35.102	

NEW YORK, MCKINNEY'S CIVIL RIGHTS LAW

Sec.	This Pocket Part Sec.	Note
40–c	18.19	8
40–c	18.55	7
44–a	18.60	5
47	18.57	1
50	18.64	10
50–a	18.65	
50–a	18.65	4.2
50–b	18.66	
51	18.64	10
79–i	18.86	
79–l	18.86a	

NEW YORK, MCKINNEY'S COUNTY LAW

Sec.	This Pocket Part Sec.	Note
215(11)	3.12	8

NEW YORK, MCKINNEY'S CRIMINAL PROCEDURE LAW

Sec.	This Pocket Part Sec.	Note
30.20	33.72	
30.20	33.72	1
30.30	33.75	
30.30	33.75	1
30.30(1)(a)	33.76	
30.30(1)(b)	33.76	
30.30(1)(c)	33.76	
60.45(2)(b)(i)	33.57	3.1

TABLE OF STATUTES

NEW YORK, MCKINNEY'S CRIMINAL PROCEDURE LAW

Sec.	This Pocket Part Sec.	Note
100.20	33.100	
100.20	33.101	
100.25	33.16	
100.25	33.33	
100.25	33.100	
100.25	33.101	
100.25(2)	33.14	3
100.25(2)	33.16	
100.25(2)	33.16	1
100.25(3)	33.14	
100.40	33.100	
100.45(4)	33.33	
140.10(1)	33.7	
140.10(3)	33.7	12
170.30	33.100	
170.35	33.100	
200.95(3)	33.36	3
Art. 240	33.33	
240.20	33.33	
240.20(1)	33.33	4
240.80(1)	33.36	3
240.20(1)(k)	33.33	
255.20(3)	38.8	

NEW YORK, MCKINNEY'S DEBTOR AND CREDITOR LAW

Sec.	This Pocket Part Sec.	Note
276–a	30.38	

NEW YORK, MCKINNEY'S DOMESTIC RELATIONS LAW

Sec.	This Pocket Part Sec.	Note
111	20.137	
111	20.138	
111(1)(d)	20.30	
111(1)(f)	20.145	
111(3)	20.137	
111(3)	20.139	
111–a	20.137	
111–a	20.139	
111–a	20.140	
111–a(1)	20.139	
112	20.2	
112	20.137	
112	20.138	
112	20.139	
112(2)(b)	20.138	
112(2)(b)	20.145	
112(3)	20.139	
112(3)	20.140	
112(3)	20.140	
113	20.138	
113	20.145	
114	20.138	
115	20.2	
115	20.133	

NEW YORK, MCKINNEY'S DOMESTIC RELATIONS LAW

Sec.	This Pocket Part Sec.	Note
115	20.136	
115	20.137	
115(d)	20.2	
115–b	20.134	
115–b	20.136	
115–b(3)	20.137	
115–c	20.134	
115–d	20.133	
115–d(6)	20.133	1
116	20.138	
236(B)(9)(a)	21.72	1
240(1)(b)	21.70	
240(1)(h)	21.70	3
240(1–b)(b)(1)	21.70	4
240(1–b)(f)	21.70	
240(2)(c)	21.70	7

NEW YORK, MCKINNEY'S EMINENT DOMAIN PROCEDURE LAW

Sec.	This Pocket Part Sec.	Note
402(B)(2)(b)	14.61	
701	14.88	

NEW YORK, MCKINNEY'S ESTATES, POWERS AND TRUSTS LAW

Sec.	This Pocket Part Sec.	Note
1–2.17	24.10	3
3–3.7(a)	24.12	2
7–1.17	24.12	2
7–6.5	24.17	1
7–6.21	24.51	2
11–1.1(b)(19)	24.17	2

NEW YORK, MCKINNEY'S EXECUTIVE LAW

Sec.	This Pocket Part Sec.	Note
130	12.99	
137	12.99	
292(21)	17.43	5.1
296(1)(a)	18.86	1
296(3)(a)	17.43	7
296(3)(b)	17.43	7.1
297(3)(c)	18.49	4
297(3)(c)	18.52	4
296(3–a)(g)	17.43	7.1

NEW YORK, MCKINNEY'S FAMILY COURT ACT

Sec.	This Pocket Part Sec.	Note
Art. 10	20.101	
262	20.136	

6

TABLE OF STATUTES

NEW YORK, MCKINNEY'S FAMILY COURT ACT

Sec.	This Pocket Part Sec.	Note
413(1)(f)	21.55	

NEW YORK, MCKINNEY'S GENERAL BUSINESS LAW

Sec.	This Pocket Part Sec.	Note
198–b	30.38	
380–b	7.31	6
380–j(f)(1)—(2)	7.31	5

NEW YORK, MCKINNEY'S GENERAL MUNICIPAL LAW

Sec.	This Pocket Part Sec.	Note
Art. 18	3.22	13

NEW YORK, MCKINNEY'S GENERAL OBLIGATIONS LAW

Sec.	This Pocket Part Sec.	Note
15–301(5)	12.23	1

NEW YORK, MCKINNEY'S INSURANCE LAW

Sec.	This Pocket Part Sec.	Note
3212	24.85	2.1
3216(d)(1)(K)	31.26	5
3229	23.68	4
3404	31.26	4
5102(a)	32.32	
5102(b)	32.32	
5104(a)	32.32	
5208(a)(1)(A)—(C)	26.27	1
5208(a)(2)(A)(i)—(iii)	26.28	2

NEW YORK, MCKINNEY'S JUDICIARY LAW

Sec.	This Pocket Part Sec.	Note
35	20.136	
487	28.24	2
487	28.24	5

NEW YORK, MCKINNEY'S LIMITED LIABILITY COMPANY LAW

Sec.	This Pocket Part Sec.	Note
202	2.16	5
206	2.18	1
206	2.18	2
206	2.18	3
206	2.18	4

NEW YORK, MCKINNEY'S LIMITED LIABILITY COMPANY LAW

Sec.	This Pocket Part Sec.	Note
211(a)	2.17	8
212	2.23	6
401(a)	2.26	3
408(a)	2.26	3
508(c)	2.23	8
701	2.37	
1001	1.83	18.1
1002(d)	1.83	18.2
1005	1.83	18.2

NEW YORK, MCKINNEY'S MENTAL HYGIENE LAW

Sec.	This Pocket Part Sec.	Note
Art. 33	22.13	6
Art. 33	22.53	5
Art. 81	22.8	4
Art. 81	22.8	9
Art. 81	22.13	6
Art. 81	22.15	7
Art. 81	22.28	18
Art. 81	22.38	
Art. 81	22.47	4
Art. 81	22.53	5
Art. 81	22.54	8
Art. 81	22.61	5
Art. 81	22.61	8
Art. 81	22.70	
Art. 81	30.41	
81.09(f)	22.27	1
81.16	22.38	
81.16(b)	22.38	
81.28	22.61	5.1
81.28(a)	22.61	5

NEW YORK, MCKINNEY'S NAVIGATION LAW

Sec.	This Pocket Part Sec.	Note
192	30.38	

NEW YORK, MCKINNEY'S PARTNERSHIP LAW

Sec.	This Pocket Part Sec.	Note
27	2.53	8
66	28.25	4

NEW YORK, MCKINNEY'S PENAL LAW

Sec.	This Pocket Part Sec.	Note
10.00(6)	33.7	11
125.15(1)	23.113	1

TABLE OF STATUTES

NEW YORK, MCKINNEY'S PERSONAL PROPERTY LAW

Sec.	This Pocket Part Sec.	Note
340(1)	7.26	8
403(2)(b)	7.25	7
403(2)(b)	7.26	3

NEW YORK, MCKINNEY'S PUBLIC HEALTH LAW

Sec.	This Pocket Part Sec.	Note
2803–c(3)(d)	23.95	

NEW YORK, MCKINNEY'S PUBLIC OFFICERS LAW

Sec.	This Pocket Part Sec.	Note
84 et seq.	30.41	

NEW YORK, MCKINNEY'S RACING, PARI–MUTUEL WAGERING AND BREEDING LAW

Sec.	This Pocket Part Sec.	Note
853	30.38	

NEW YORK, MCKINNEY'S REAL PROPERTY ACTIONS AND PROCEEDINGS LAW

Sec.	This Pocket Part Sec.	Note
Art. 13	11.8a	
Art. 13	11.8e	
Art. 13	11.8j	
Art. 13	11.8k	
Art. 13	11.8m	
Art. 13	11.8o	
Art. 13	11.8o	2
Art. 14	11.8b	
Art. 14	11.8c	
Art. 14	11.8d	
Art. 14	11.8e	
Art. 14	11.8f	
Art. 14	11.8j	
Art. 14	11.8k	
Art. 14	11.8m	
Art. 14	11.8n	
Art. 14	11.8o	
Art. 14	11.8o	2
Art. 14	11.8o	8
Art. 14 (former)	11.8a	
1401(1)	11.8b	1
1401(1)	11.8c	
1401(1)(A)	11.8c	1
1401(1)(B)	11.8c	2
1401(1)(C)	11.8c	3
1401(1)(D)	11.8c	4
1401(2)	11.8c	5

NEW YORK, MCKINNEY'S REAL PROPERTY ACTIONS AND PROCEEDINGS LAW

Sec.	This Pocket Part Sec.	Note
1402(1)	11.8e	1
1402(2)(A)	11.8e	2
1402(2)(B)	11.8e	3
1402(2)(C)	11.8c	4
1402(2)(D)	11.8e	5
1402(2)(E)	11.8e	6
1402(2)(F)	11.8e	7
1402(2)(G)	11.8e	8
1402(2)(H)	11.8e	9
1402(3)	11.8e	10
1403(1)	11.8d	1
1403(1)	11.8d	2
1403(1)	11.8d	4
1403(2)	11.8d	3
1403(4)	11.8d	5
1404(1)	11.8f	1
1404(2)	11.8f	2
1404(3)	11.8f	3
1404(4)	11.8f	4
1404(5)	11.8f	5
1404(6)	11.8f	6
1404(7)	11.8f	7
1404(8)	11.8f	8
1405(1)	11.8g	1
1405(1)	11.8g	5
1405(2)	11.8h	1
1405(3)	11.8h	2
1406(1)	11.8g	2
1406(2)	11.8g	3
1406(3)	11.8g	4
1408(1)	11.8i	1
1408(1)	11.8i	2
1408(2)	11.8i	3
1408(3)	11.8i	4
1408(4)	11.8i	5
1412(1)	11.8j	1
1412(1)	11.8j	2
1412(3)	11.8j	4
1413(1)	11.8k	1
1413(1)(A)	11.8k	3
1413(1)(B)	11.8k	4
1413(1)(C)	11.8k	5
1413(2)	11.8k	6
1414(1)	11.8l	1
1414(2)	11.8l	2
1414(3)	11.8l	3
1414(4)	11.8l	4
1415(1)	11.8l	5
1417	11.8k	4
1417(G)	11.8k	5
1418	11.8e	
1418(1)	11.8m	1
1418(3)	11.8m	3
1419	11.8e	
1419(2)	11.8m	4
1419(2)	11.8m	5
1420(1)	11.8n	2
1420(1)	11.8n	3
1420(2)	11.8n	4
1421	11.8e	

8

TABLE OF STATUTES

NEW YORK, MCKINNEY'S REAL PROPERTY ACTIONS AND PROCEEDINGS LAW

Sec.	This Pocket Part Sec.	Note
1421	11.80	
1421	11.80	1
1421(1)	11.80	2
1421(2)	11.80	3
1421(2)(B)(1)	11.80	4
1421(2)(B)(2)	11.80	5
1421(2)(B)(3)	11.80	6
1421(2)(B)(4)	11.80	7
1421(2)(B)(5)	11.80	8
1421(3)	11.80	9
1421(4)	11.80	10
1421(6)	11.80	11

NEW YORK, MCKINNEY'S REAL PROPERTY LAW

Sec.	This Pocket Part Sec.	Note
236	18.45	4.1
290 et seq.	12.74	
298	12.99	
299	12.99	
299(5)	12.99	
299–a	12.99	
300	12.99	
301	12.99	
301(1)	12.99	
301(7)	12.99	
301–a	12.99	
301–a(2)(a)	12.99	
301–a(2)(b)	12.99	
301–a(2)(c)	12.99	
303	12.99	
306	12.99	
307	12.99	5
307	12.99	7
308	12.99	
308	12.99	6
308	12.99	8
309–a	12.99	
309–a(2)	12.99	
310	12.99	
310(2)	12.99	
311	12.99	
311(1)	12.99	
311(2)	12.99	
311(3)	12.99	
311(4)	12.99	
312	12.99	
312(2)	12.99	
312(3)	12.99	
312(4)	12.99	
313	12.99	
314	12.99	
314–a	12.99	
318	12.99	

NEW YORK, MCKINNEY'S SOCIAL SERVICES LAW

Sec.	This Pocket Part Sec.	Note
104–b	26.49	2
104–b(2)	26.49	3
104–b(3)	26.49	4
111–h	21.70	
111–n	21.70	
374(6)	20.147	
374–a	20.137	
374–a	20.139	
378–a	20.2	
382	20.137	
382	20.139	
384	20.140	
384–b	20.101	
412	20.133	
412	20.137	
412	20.138	
412	20.139	

NEW YORK, MCKINNEY'S STATE ADMINISTRATIVE PROCEDURE ACT

Sec.	This Pocket Part Sec.	Note
Art. 2	4.50	4
Art. 3	4.11	2

NEW YORK, MCKINNEY'S SURROGATE'S COURT PROCEDURE ACT

Sec.	This Pocket Part Sec.	Note
407	20.136	
1725	20.134	
1725(1)	20.137	
2302(5)	37.18	
2302(6)	37.18	
2307	22.61	5.1
2307	25.46	
2307	25.47	
2307	25.47	2
2307(6)	25.46	
2307(6)	25.47	
2307–a	24.95	
2307–a	24.95	3
2307–a	25.46	
2307–a	25.47	
2307–a(1)	25.46	11
2307–a(1)	25.47	10
2307–a(2)	25.46	12
2307–a(2)	25.47	11
2307–a(5)	25.46	13
2307–a(5)	25.47	12
2307–a(6)	25.46	14
2307–a(6)	25.47	13
2309	22.61	5
2313	25.46	
2313	25.47	

TABLE OF STATUTES

NEW YORK, MCKINNEY'S TAX LAW

Sec.	This Pocket Part Sec.	Note
Art. 31	12.86a	
171.18–a	35.118	
208(1)	35.23	
208(9)(a)(1)	35.28	
210(1–c)	35.32	
605(b)	35.14	
612(b)(1)	35.8	2
612(b)(2)	35.8	3
612(b)(3)	35.8	4
612(b)(4)	35.8	5
612(b)(5)	35.8	6
631(a)(1)(C)	35.17	
685(d)	35.77	
955(f)	24.20	5
1147(c)	6.66	6
1230(b)	12.86	2
1449–aa	12.86a	
1449–aa et seq.	12.86a	1
1449–bb	12.86a	
1449–bb–3	12.86a	
1449–cc(4)	12.86a	
1449–dd	12.86a	
1449–ee	12.86a	
1449–ee(2)(j)	12.86a	
1449–ee(2)(k)	12.86a	
1449–ee(2)(*l*)	12.86a	
1449–ee(3)	12.86a	
1449–ff	12.86a	
1449–gg	12.86a	
1449–hh	12.86a	
1449–ii	12.86a	
1449–jj	12.86a	
1449–kk	12.86a	
1449–ll	12.86a	
1449–mm	12.86a	
1449–nn	12.86a	
1449–oo	12.86a	
2016	35.99	

NEW YORK, MCKINNEY'S TOWN LAW

Sec.	This Pocket Part Sec.	Note
65(3)	3.24	18

NEW YORK, MCKINNEY'S UNIFORM COMMERCIAL CODE

Sec.	This Pocket Part Sec.	Note
6–105	6.153	6
6–105	6.184	13
Art. 8	12.74	7
8–103	12.74	7
8–106	12.74	7
Art. 9	12.74	7
9–115	12.74	7
9–304(7)	12.74	7

NEW YORK, MCKINNEY'S WORKERS' COMPENSATION LAW

Sec.	This Pocket Part Sec.	Note
10	32.22	2
11	32.15	
21	32.19	
21(5)	32.19	8.1
28	32.28	

NEW YORK LAWS

Year	This Pocket Part Sec.	Note
1975, c. 412	12.99	
1989, c. 536	33.33	3
1997, c. 179	12.99	
1998, c. 231, § 2	11.8a	4
1998, c. 596	12.99	
1999, c. 7	20.2	

OFFICIAL COMPILATION OF CODES, RULES AND REGULATIONS OF THE STATE OF NEW YORK

Tit.	This Pocket Part Sec.	Note
6, § 617.7(d)	15.4	21
10, § 405.7(b)(4)	23.90	9
10, § 405.7(b)(6)	23.90	10
10, § 405.9(f)	23.93	2
10, § 415(c)(2)(ii)(b)	23.94	7
11, § 52.22(d)(6)(x)	23.88	2
11, § 52.22(d)(6)(x)(4)	23.88	4
11, § 65.11	26.21	2
12, § 325–1.23	32.28	
18, § 358–3.5	23.83	3
18, § 360–2.9	23.83	3
18, § 360–4.4(a)	23.74	1
18, § 360–4.4(b)	23.75	1
18, § 360–4.4(c)(1)(iii)(a)(2)	23.76	2
18, § 360–4.10(c)(1)(iii)	23.80	21
18, § 360–7.2	23.82	5
18, § 360–7.11(b)(5)	23.82	5
18, § 393.4(c)(3)	23.105	3
18, § 505.9(d)(6)(i)	23.97	5
18, § 505.9(d)(6)(iii)(a)	23.97	4
18, § 505.20(b)(3)(ii)	23.91	22
18, § 505.20(b)(3)(iii)	23.91	23
19, § 23–03(k)	12.85	2.1
20, § 1–2.5(c)	35.23	
20, § 132.17	35.17	
20, § 137.3	35.17	
20, § 2394.6	35.112	
20, § 2394.9	35.112	
22, § 130–1.1	28.24	5
22, § 202.42(d)	26.52	2
22, § 207.55(b)(2)	20.146	
22, § 207.55(b)(8)	20.147	
22, § 600.11(d)	37.51	
22, § 670.8(c)	37.51	
22, § 670.10(d)(2)	37.51	40
22, § 800.2(c)	35.99	

TABLE OF STATUTES

OFFICIAL COMPILATION OF CODES, RULES AND REGULATIONS OF THE STATE OF NEW YORK

Tit.	This Pocket Part Sec.	Note
22, § 800.13	37.19	
22, § 1000.4(a)(3)(iii)	37.51	17.1
22, § 1200.5	28.25	7.3
22, § 1200.31	28.18B	1
22, § 1400.6 (repealed)	21.76	
20, § 4000.3(a)	35.91	

UNITED STATES

UNITED STATES CONSTITUTION

Amend.	This Pocket Part Sec.	Note
1	18.27	7.2
1	18.28	
1	18.34	3
1	22.48	11
5	22.48	11
11	18.33	
11	18.33	3
14, § 5	18.28	2

UNITED STATES CODE ANNOTATED

5 U.S.C.A.—Government Organization and Employees

Sec.	This Pocket Part Sec.	Note
8336(a)	23.39	2
8336(b)	23.39	2
8336(f)	23.39	2
8341	23.39	4

8 U.S.C.A.—Aliens and Nationality

Sec.	This Pocket Part Sec.	Note
1101(b)(2)	19.11	12
1153(b)(2)(B)	19.25	1
1182(a)(10)	19.52	17
1183a(f)(1)	19.55	1
1183a(f)(2)	19.55	3
1183a(f)(5)	19.55	3
1227	19.52	
1228	19.52	19
1229	19.52	19
1255(i)	19.59	1

11 U.S.C.A.—Bankruptcy

Sec.	This Pocket Part Sec.	Note
106	9.18	2
Ch. 7	9.251	3
Ch. 11	9.3	4
Ch. 11	9.7	3
Ch. 12 (repealed)	9.1	

UNITED STATES CODE ANNOTATED

11 U.S.C.A.—Bankruptcy

Sec.	This Pocket Part Sec.	Note
Ch. 13	9.249	1
1322(c)(2)	9.249	1

15 U.S.C.A.—Commerce and Trade

Sec.	This Pocket Part Sec.	Note
1667d(c)	7.21	14
1681b	7.31	6
1681b(a)(3)(F)	7.31	6
1681b(b)(2)	7.31	6
1681c(b)	7.31	5

17 U.S.C.A.—Copyrights

Sec.	This Pocket Part Sec.	Note
302—304	6.40	1.1

25 U.S.C.A.—Indians

Sec.	This Pocket Part Sec.	Note
1901—1963	20.137	
1901—1963	20.139	

26 U.S.C.A.—Internal Revenue Code

Sec.	This Pocket Part Sec.	Note
1(h)	6.119	4
71(b)	21.51	1
101(a)(2)	24.34	5
179	6.34	
197	6.40	
213(d)(1)	23.68	7
351	1.34	
351(a)	1.34	
351(e)	1.34	
401(a)(17)	23.26	1
402(a)	23.32	1
642(c)(3)	24.54	6
721(a)	1.34	
721(b)	1.34	
1045	6.130	
1202	6.130	
1244	6.130	
1245	6.120	3
1250	6.119	
1250	6.120	3
1372	6.122	
1374	6.117	
2010	24.38	1
2033A	24.38	1
2034(a)(2)	24.40	9
2035(a)(2)	24.34	2
2035(a)(2)	24.35	2
2057	24.38	1
2522	24.32	6
2651(e)	24.28	3
7702B	23.118	7

TABLE OF STATUTES

UNITED STATES CODE ANNOTATED
38 U.S.C.A.—Veterans' Benefits

Sec.	This Pocket Part Sec.	Note
1710(b)(2)(A)	23.41	12
5904(d)(1)	23.41	19

42 U.S.C.A.—The Public Health and Welfare

Sec.	This Pocket Part Sec.	Note
426(a)	23.43	6
1320a–7b(a)	23.76	
1382(a)(1)(B)	23.19	10
1382(a)(2)(B)	23.19	11
1382(a)(3)(A)	23.19	11
1382(a)(3)(B)	23.19	10
1395i–3(a)	23.46	1
1395j	23.43	17
1395q(a)(2)(E)	23.43	14
1395ss(q)	23.60	7
1395ss(s)	23.60	7
1395–3(c)(6)(B)	23.95	3
1396p(c)	23.76	
1983	18.2	4
1983	18.2	4.1
1983	18.22	
1983	18.22	2
1983	18.31	2
1983	18.32	1
1983	18.32	6
1983	18.33	2
1983	18.34	2
1983	18.34	3
1983	18.34	4
1983	18.35	1
1983	18.35	2
1983	18.37	8
1983	18.38	
1983	18.38	1
1983	18.38	5
1983(3)	18.19	1
1985(3)	18.19	
1985(3)	18.19	8
1988(b)	18.19	
3601 et seq.	18.51	
12101 et seq.	18.19	

45 U.S.C.A.—Railroads

Sec.	This Pocket Part Sec.	Note
231a(c)	23.36	2

STATUTES AT LARGE

Year	This Pocket Part Sec.	Note
1990, P.L. 101–649, § 206(a)	19.21	10
1991, P.L. 102–232	19.25	1
1996, P.L. 104–208	19.50	6.1

STATUTES AT LARGE

Year	This Pocket Part Sec.	Note
1996, P.L. 104–317, § 309(c)	18.31	2
1997, P.L. 105–33, § 4734	22.48	11
1997, P.L. 105–54	19.41	
1998, P.L. 105–206	24.38	1

POPULAR NAME ACTS

CIVIL RIGHTS ACT OF 1964

Sec.	This Pocket Part Sec.	Note
Tit. VII	18.83	

COMPREHENSIVE ENVIRONMENTAL RESPONSE, COMPENSATION AND LIABILITY ACT

Sec.	This Pocket Part Sec.	Note
107(a)	15.30	7
113(g)	15.30	7

EDUCATION AMENDMENTS OF 1972

Sec.	This Pocket Part Sec.	Note
Tit. IX	18.53	

FEDERAL WATER POLLUTION CONTROL ACT

Sec.	This Pocket Part Sec.	Note
404	15.15	

HEALTH INSURANCE PORTABILITY AND ACCOUNTABILITY ACT

Sec.	This Pocket Part Sec.	Note
217	22.48	11

IMMIGRATION AND NATIONALITY ACT

Sec.	This Pocket Part Sec.	Note
101(b)(2)	19.11	12
121(a)	19.25	1
201(b)	19.12	
203(b)(2)(B)	19.25	1
212(a)(10)	19.52	17
213A(f)(1)	19.55	1
214A(f)(2)	19.55	3
214A(f)(5)	19.55	3
228	19.52	19
237	19.52	

TABLE OF STATUTES

IMMIGRATION AND NATIONALITY ACT

Sec.	This Pocket Part Sec.	Note
239	19.52	19

IMMIGRATION AND NATIONALITY ACT

Sec.	This Pocket Part Sec.	Note
245	19.59	
245(i)	19.59	
245(i)	19.59	1
302(b)(2)(D)	19.25	1

TABLE OF RULES AND REGULATIONS

DISCIPLINARY RULES OF THE NEW YORK CODE OF PROFESSIONAL RESPONSIBILITY

Sec.	This Pocket Part Sec.	Note
1–104	28.25	
1–104(A)	28.25	
1–104(C)	28.25	
1–104(D)	28.25	
6–102(A)	28.18B	
6–102(A)	28.18B	1

PROPOSED TREASURY REGULATIONS

Sec.	This Pocket Part Sec.	Note
301.6501(c)–1(f)	24.41	2

TREASURY REGULATIONS

Sec.	This Pocket Part Sec.	Note
1.351–1(c)(2)	1.34	
25.2518–2	24.68	4
25.2511–1(h)(4)	24.83	3
25.2702–5(b)(1)	24.48	
25.2702–5(c)(3)	24.47	3
25.2702–5(c)(9)	24.48	

CODE OF FEDERAL REGULATIONS

Tit.	This Pocket Part Sec.	Note
5, § 831.614	23.39	4
8, § 204.2(b)	19.12	12
8, § 204.2(c)	19.16	
8, § 204.2(d)(2)(i)	19.10	13
8, § 204.2(d)(2)(ii)	19.10	13
8, § 204.2(d)(2)(iii)	19.10	13
8, § 204.2(d)(2)(iii)	19.10	14
8, § 204.2(d)(4)	19.14	1
8, § 204.2(f)(ii)	19.11	13
8, § 208.4(a)(5)	19.50	6.3
8, § 208.30	19.50	6.2
8, § 213a.1	19.55	2
8, § 213a.2(c)	19.55	1
8, § 213a.2(c)	19.55	3

Tit.	Sec.	Note
20, § 216.60	23.36	2
20, § 404.900(a)	23.54	2
20, § 404.950(d)(1)	34.37	
20, § 404.950(d)(2)	34.37	
20, § 404.1450(d)(2)	34.37	
20, § 404.1527(d)(2)	34.37	
20, § 416.927(d)(2)	34.37	
20, § 416.1205	23.19	10
20, § 416.1205	23.19	11
20, § 416.1450(d)(1)	34.37	
20, § 416.1450(d)(2)	34.37	
38, § 3.1600	23.41	16
38, § 17.46	23.41	12
38, § 17.47	23.41	12
38, § 17.60	23.41	15
42, § 406.6(b)	23.43	6
42, § 406.10(a)	23.43	6
42, § 406.21(c)(3)	23.43	14
42, § 407.25(b)(1)	23.43	14
42, § 408.4(a)(1)	23.43	17
42, § 408.20(c)	23.43	17
42, § 409.33(c)	23.46	4
42, § 473.12(b)(2)(i)	23.56	10
42, § 473.12(b)(2)(ii)	23.56	11
42, § 483.10(b)(5)	23.95	5
42, § 483.102(b)(1)	23.93	14

FEDERAL REGISTER

Vol.	This Pocket Part Sec.	Note
56, p. 60897	19.25	2
56, p. 60900	19.25	2
62, p. 54346	19.55	1
62, p. 54346	19.55	2
62, p. 54346	19.55	3
63, p. 27193	19.55	4
63, p. 36040	15.15	10
63, p. 67135	19.43	8
63, p. 70313	19.4	2

PRIVATE LETTER RULINGS

PLR	This Pocket Part Sec.	Note
9751003	24.53	2
9842003	24.45	3

TABLE OF CASES

A

Abdelrazig v. Essence Communications, Inc., 225 A.D.2d 498, 639 N.Y.S.2d 811 (N.Y.A.D. 1 Dept.1996)—§ **18.64, n. 15.**
Ackerland, N.Y.L.J, 4/9/96, p. 27, col. 2 (Surr. Ct., N.Y. County)—§ **22.15, n. 7.**
Ackerman v. Price Waterhouse, 252 A.D.2d 179, 683 N.Y.S.2d 179 (N.Y.A.D. 1 Dept. 1998)—§ **28.13, n. 11.**
Acquisition of Real Property by Village of Marathon, Matter of, 174 Misc.2d 800, 666 N.Y.S.2d 365 (N.Y.Sup.1997)—§ **14.78, n. 1.**
Adam v. Cutner & Rathkopf, 238 A.D.2d 234, 656 N.Y.S.2d 753 (N.Y.A.D. 1 Dept. 1997)—§ **28.19, n. 1.**
Addo, N.Y.L.J., 9/30/97, p. 26, col. 4 (Sup. Ct., Bronx County)—§ **22.8, n. 4.**
Adelphi University v. Board of Regents of the State of N.Y., 229 A.D.2d 36, 652 N.Y.S.2d 837 (N.Y.A.D. 3 Dept.1997)—§ **4.71, n. 9.**
Affiliated Credit Adjustors, Inc. v. Carlucci & Legum, 139 A.D.2d 611, 527 N.Y.S.2d 426 (N.Y.A.D. 2 Dept.1988)—§ **28.10, n. 14.**
Aglira v. Julien & Schlesinger, P.C., 214 A.D.2d 178, 631 N.Y.S.2d 816 (N.Y.A.D. 1 Dept.1995)—§ **28.11, n. 4; § 28.26, n. 3.**
A.H. Harris & Sons Inc. v. Burke, Cavalier, Lindy and Engel P.C., 202 A.D.2d 929, 610 N.Y.S.2d 888 (N.Y.A.D. 3 Dept. 1994)—§ **28.12, n. 6.**
Ainbinder v. Chernis, 248 A.D.2d 337, 669 N.Y.S.2d 829 (N.Y.A.D. 2 Dept.1998)—§ **28.13, n. 15.**
Akzo Coatings, Inc. v. Aigner Corp., 30 F.3d 761 (7th Cir.1994)—§ **15.30, n. 7.**
Albany Sav. Bank, F.S.B. v. Caffry, Pontiff, Stewart, Rhodes & Judge, P.C., 95 A.D.2d 918, 463 N.Y.S.2d 896 (N.Y.A.D. 3 Dept.1983)—§ **28.14, n. 11.**
Albert v. Solimon, 252 A.D.2d 139, 684 N.Y.S.2d 375 (N.Y.A.D. 4 Dept.1998)—§ **18.57, n. 1.**
Albertsons, Inc. v. Kirkingburg, ___ U.S. ___, 119 S.Ct. 2162 (1999)—§ **18.19, n. 7.**
Alca Industries, Inc. v. Delaney, 686 N.Y.S.2d 356, 709 N.E.2d 97 (N.Y. 1999)—§ **4.50, n. 4.**
Alejandro, People v., 517 N.Y.S.2d 927, 511 N.E.2d 71 (N.Y.1987)—§ **33.10, n. 3.1.**
Allen, People v., N.Y.L.J., 7/29/94, p.25, Col.3 (North Hills Village Ct., Nassau Co.)—§ **33.33, n. 6.**
Altman, In re, 230 B.R. 6 (Bkrtcy.D.Conn. 1999)—§ **9.138, n. 1.**
Amateur Hockey Ass'n of the United States v. Parson, 244 A.D.2d 222, 664 N.Y.S.2d 919 (N.Y.A.D. 1 Dept.1997)—§ **28.13, n. 11.**
Amato v. City of Saratoga Springs, N.Y., 170 F.3d 311 (2nd Cir.1999)—§ **18.21, n. 3.**
Ansonia Associates Ltd. Partnership v. Ansonia Tenants' Coalition, Inc., 253 A.D.2d 706, 677 N.Y.S.2d 575 (N.Y.A.D. 1 Dept.1998)—§ **18.80, n. 2.**
Application of (see name of party)
Arecibo Community Health Care, Inc., In re, 233 B.R. 625 (D.Puerto Rico 1999)—§ **9.18, n. 2.**
Aria Contracting Corp. v. McGowan, 256 A.D.2d 1204, 684 N.Y.S.2d 93 (N.Y.A.D. 4 Dept.1998)—§ **4.15, n. 1; § 4.78, n. 7; § 4.81, n. 5.**
Arizin v. Covello, 175 Misc.2d 453, 669 N.Y.S.2d 189 (N.Y.Sup.1998)—§ **21.30, n. 4.**
Arnold O, In re, 256 A.D.2d 764, 681 N.Y.S.2d 627 (N.Y.A.D. 3 Dept.1998)—§ **22.61, n. 5.**
Atkins v. New York City, 143 F.3d 100 (2nd Cir.1998)—§ **18.21, n. 3.**
AT&T Communications of New York Inc. v. Public Service Com'n of the State of New York, 231 A.D.2d 155, 659 N.Y.S.2d 362 (N.Y.A.D. 3 Dept.1997)—§ **4.82, n. 9.**
Attie, People v., 131 Misc.2d 921, 502 N.Y.S.2d 342 (N.Y.City Ct.1986)—§ **33.72, n. 1; § 33.90A, n. 1.**
Ayala v. Speckard, 131 F.3d 62 (2nd Cir. 1997)—§ **18.13, n. 1.**
Ayala v. Speckard, 89 F.3d 91 (2nd Cir. 1996)—§ **18.13, n. 1.**

B

Baker v. Levitin, 211 A.D.2d 507, 622 N.Y.S.2d 8 (N.Y.A.D. 1 Dept.1995)—§ **28.11, n. 4.**
Ball, People v., 141 A.D.2d 743, 529 N.Y.S.2d 840 (N.Y.A.D. 2 Dept.1988)—§ **33.5, n. 9.**
Balsamo v. Chater, 142 F.3d 75 (2nd Cir. 1998)—§ **34.13; § 34.37.**

17

TABLE OF CASES

Bankers Trust Co. v. Cerrato, Sweeney, Cohn, Stahl & Vaccaro, 187 A.D.2d 384, 590 N.Y.S.2d 201 (N.Y.A.D. 1 Dept. 1992)—§ 28.25; § 28.25, n. 7.1.

Bapp v. Bowen, 802 F.2d 601 (2nd Cir. 1986)—§ 34.13.

Baron, Estate of, N.Y.L.J., 5/11/99, p.27, col.5 (Surr. Ct., New York County)—§ 22.70, n. 12.

Barrios–Paoli, Matter of, 173 Misc.2d 736, 662 N.Y.S.2d 388 (N.Y.Sup.1997)—§ 22.20, n. 5.

Barrios–Paoli, Application of, 173 Misc.2d 1032, 662 N.Y.S.2d 925 (N.Y.Sup. 1997)—§ 22.31, n. 14.1.

Bassim v. Halliday, 234 A.D.2d 628, 650 N.Y.S.2d 467 (N.Y.A.D. 3 Dept.1996)—§ 28.18A; § 28.18A, n. 5.

Beasley, In re Guardianship of, 234 A.D.2d 32, 650 N.Y.S.2d 170 (N.Y.A.D. 1 Dept. 1996)—§ 22.15, n. 6; § 22.16, n. 1, 8.

Bedford Affiliates v. Sills, 156 F.3d 416 (2nd Cir.1998)—§ 15.30, n. 7.

Benedek v. Heit, 139 A.D.2d 393, 531 N.Y.S.2d 266 (N.Y.A.D. 1 Dept.1988)—§ 28.11, n. 4.

Bernice B., In re Estate of, 179 Misc.2d 149, 683 N.Y.S.2d 713 (N.Y.Sur.1998)—§ 22.47.

Bernice B., Matter of Estate of, 176 Misc.2d 550, 672 N.Y.S.2d 994 (N.Y.Sur.1998)—§ 22.8, n. 9.

Bernstein v. Oppenheim & Co., P.C., 160 A.D.2d 428, 554 N.Y.S.2d 487 (N.Y.A.D. 1 Dept.1990)—§ 28.24, n. 3, 4.

Beshara v. Little, 215 A.D.2d 823, 626 N.Y.S.2d 310 (N.Y.A.D. 3 Dept.1995)—§ 28.24, n. 5.

Black v. Coughlin, 76 F.3d 72 (2nd Cir. 1996)—§ 18.38, n. 5.

Blake, People v., 154 Misc.2d 660, 585 N.Y.S.2d 993 (N.Y.City Crim.Ct.1992)—§ 33.75, n. 1.

Board of County Com'rs of Bryan County, Okl. v. Brown, 520 U.S. 397, 117 S.Ct. 1382, 137 L.Ed.2d 626 (1997)—§ 18.21; § 18.34, n. 3.

Board of Managers of the Ocean Club at Long Beach Condominium v. Mandel, 235 A.D.2d 382, 652 N.Y.S.2d 301 (N.Y.A.D. 2 Dept.1997)—§ 28.13, n. 11.

Boerne, City of v. Flores, 521 U.S. 507, 117 S.Ct. 2157, 138 L.Ed.2d 624 (1997)—§ 18.28, n. 2.

Bogan v. Scott–Harris, 523 U.S. 44, 118 S.Ct. 966, 140 L.Ed.2d 79 (1998)—§ 18.31, n. 4.

Boltz v. Town of Portland, 691 N.Y.S.2d 833 (N.Y.A.D. 4 Dept.1999)—§ 30.41, n. 1.1.

Bonnie Briar Syndicate, Inc., v. Town of Mamaroneck, 216 N.Y.L.J. 34 (1996) aff'd 242 A.D.2d 356, 661 N.Y.S.2d 1005 (2d Dep't 1997)—§ 16.22.

Bovi v. United Parcel Service, Inc., 992 F.Supp. 540 (E.D.N.Y.1997)—§ 28.13, n. 16.

Breard v. Greene, 523 U.S. 371, 118 S.Ct. 1352, 140 L.Ed.2d 529 (1998)—§ 18.18, n. 8.

Breen v. Garrison, 169 F.3d 152 (2nd Cir. 1999)—§ 18.25, n. 2.

Brockenshire, People v., 197 A.D.2d 921, 602 N.Y.S.2d 459 (N.Y.A.D. 4 Dept. 1993)—§ 33.47, n. 6.

Broome v. Biondi, 1997 WL 691421 (S.D.N.Y.1997)—§ 18.47, n. 2.1; § 18.50, n. 2.

Brown v. Apfel, 174 F.3d 59 (2nd Cir. 1999)—§ 34.11; § 34.29.

Brown v. Braun, 240 A.D.2d 663, 659 N.Y.S.2d 301 (N.Y.A.D. 2 Dept.1997)—§ 37.87, n. 3.

Brown v. City of Oneonta, N.Y., Police Dept., 106 F.3d 1125 (2nd Cir.1997)—§ 18.32, n. 2.

Brusco v. State, Div. of Housing and Community Renewal, 239 A.D.2d 210, 657 N.Y.S.2d 180 (N.Y.A.D. 1 Dept.1997)—§ 4.22, n. 1.

Brzonkala v. Virginia Polytechnic Institute and State University, 169 F.3d 820 (4th Cir.1999)—§ 18.53, n. 8.

Brzozowski v. Zio Italian Bistro, 178 Misc.2d 761, 680 N.Y.S.2d 806 (N.Y.Sup. 1998)—§ 28.13, n. 16.

Bubnis v. Apfel, 150 F.3d 177 (2nd Cir. 1998)—§ 34.7.

Buchanan v. Wing, 245 A.D.2d 634, 664 N.Y.S.2d 865 (N.Y.A.D. 3 Dept.1997)—§ 18.28; § 18.28, n. 12.

Budget Installment Corp., appellant, v. Levy, Ehrlich & Kronenberg, et al., respondents., 1999 WL 159197 (N.Y.A.D. 2 Dept.1999)—§ 28.13, n. 11.

Burnett v. Physician's Online, Inc., 99 F.3d 72 (2nd Cir.1996)—§ 18.36, n. 11.

Bystricky v. Bystricky, 177 Misc.2d 914, 677 N.Y.S.2d 443 (N.Y.Sup.1998)—§ 21.39, n. 14.

C

Cahill v. Rosa, 235 A.D.2d 534, 653 N.Y.S.2d 854 (N.Y.A.D. 2 Dept.1997)—§ 18.54, n. 4.

Cahill v. Rosa, 651 N.Y.S.2d 344, 674 N.E.2d 274 (N.Y.1996)—§ 18.54, n. 4.

Caiati v. Kimel Funding Corp., 154 A.D.2d 639, 546 N.Y.S.2d 877 (N.Y.A.D. 2 Dept. 1989)—§ 28.18A; § 28.18A, n. 1.

Camacho, People v., 664 N.Y.S.2d 578, 687 N.E.2d 396 (N.Y.1997)—§ 18.12, n. 2.

Campbell v. Louisiana, 523 U.S. 392, 118 S.Ct. 1419, 140 L.Ed.2d 551 (1998)—§ 18.15, n. 5.

TABLE OF CASES

Campbell v. Rogers & Wells, 218 A.D.2d 576, 631 N.Y.S.2d 6 (N.Y.A.D. 1 Dept. 1995)—§ **28.10, n. 5.**
Canale, People v., 240 A.D.2d 839, 658 N.Y.S.2d 715 (N.Y.A.D. 3 Dept.1997)— § **28.24, n. 10.**
Caruso v. Town of Oyster Bay, 172 Misc.2d 93, 656 N.Y.S.2d 809 (N.Y.Sup.1997)— § **16.19.**
Casella v. Equifax Credit Information Services, 56 F.3d 469 (2nd Cir.1995)— § **7.33.**
Cerio v. New York State Div. of Human Rights, 258 A.D.2d 873, 684 N.Y.S.2d 738 (N.Y.A.D. 4 Dept.1999)—§ **30.30, n. 14.2.**
Chenango Inc. v. County of Chenango, 256 A.D.2d 793, 681 N.Y.S.2d 640 (N.Y.A.D. 3 Dept.1998)—§ **15.32, n. 17.**
Chess, People v., 149 Misc.2d 430, 565 N.Y.S.2d 416 (N.Y.Just.Ct.1991)— § **33.32, n. 2; § 33.33, n. 2.**
Children's Village v. Greenburgh Eleven Teachers' Union Federation of Teachers, Local 1532, 258 A.D.2d 610, 685 N.Y.S.2d 754 (N.Y.A.D. 2 Dept.1999)— § **18.27, n. 7.2.**
Chrysler Financial Corp. v. De Luca, 256 A.D.2d 886, 681 N.Y.S.2d 855 (N.Y.A.D. 3 Dept.1998)—§ **30.22, n. 2.1.**
Cicorelli v. Capobianco, 89 A.D.2d 842, 90 A.D.2d 524, 453 N.Y.S.2d 21 (N.Y.A.D. 2 Dept.1982)—§ **28.18A; § 28.18A, n. 7.**
Ciotoli v. Goord, 256 A.D.2d 1192, 683 N.Y.S.2d 683 (N.Y.A.D. 4 Dept.1998)— § **4.78, n. 7.**
City of (see name of city)
Clarke's Estate, In re, 237 N.Y.S.2d 694, 188 N.E.2d 128 (N.Y.1962)—§ **28.19, n. 1.**
Coastal Broadway Associates v. Raphael, 246 A.D.2d 445, 668 N.Y.S.2d 586 (N.Y.A.D. 1 Dept.1998)—§ **28.13, n. 16.**
Cohen, People v., 131 Misc.2d 898, 502 N.Y.S.2d 123 (N.Y.City Ct.1986)— § **33.32, n. 2; § 33.33, n. 6.**
Colclough v. Interfaith Medical Center, 256 A.D.2d 497, 682 N.Y.S.2d 408 (N.Y.A.D. 2 Dept.1998)—§ **30.30, n. 15.6.**
Colorado & Eastern R. Co., United States v., 50 F.3d 1530 (10th Cir.1995)— § **15.30, n. 7.**
Colorado River Water Conservation Dist. v. United States, 424 U.S. 800, 96 S.Ct. 1236, 47 L.Ed.2d 483 (1976)—§ **18.36; § 18.36, n. 9.**
Commissioners of State Ins. Fund v. Liverpool Cent. School Dist. No. 1, 180 Misc.2d 501, 691 N.Y.S.2d 286 (N.Y.Sup. 1999)—§ **31.2, n. 3.**
Concha v. Local 1115 Employees Union Welfare Trust Fund, 216 A.D.2d 348, 628 N.Y.S.2d 172 (N.Y.A.D. 2 Dept. 1995)—§ **28.14, n. 17.**

Conti v. Polizzotto, 243 A.D.2d 672, 663 N.Y.S.2d 293 (N.Y.A.D. 2 Dept.1997)— § **28.11, n. 4.**
Cortes, People v., 590 N.Y.S.2d 9, 604 N.E.2d 71 (N.Y.1992)—§ **33.87.**
Countryman v. Schmitt, 176 Misc.2d 736, 673 N.Y.S.2d 521 (N.Y.Sup.1998)— § **16.18; § 16.125.**
County of (see name of county)
Covington v. City of New York, 171 F.3d 117 (2nd Cir.1999)—§ **18.22, n. 5; § 18.38, n. 3.1.**
Crawford v. New York City Health and Hosp. Corp., 257 A.D.2d 801, 683 N.Y.S.2d 652 (N.Y.A.D. 3 Dept.1999)— § **32.28.**
Cresswell v. Sullivan & Cromwell, 771 F.Supp. 580 (S.D.N.Y.1991)—§ **28.24, n. 2.**
Cricchio v. Pennisi, 660 N.Y.S.2d 679, 683 N.E.2d 301 (N.Y.1997)—§ **23.82, n. 2.**
Cruz v. Manhattan and Bronx Surface Transit Operating Authority, 259 A.D.2d 432, 687 N.Y.S.2d 350 (N.Y.A.D. 1 Dept. 1999)—§ **30.30, n. 26.2.**
Curtis v. Curtis, 237 A.D.2d 984, 654 N.Y.S.2d 538 (N.Y.A.D. 4 Dept.1997)— § **21.5, n. 6.**
CVC Capital Corp. v. Weil, Gotshal, Manges, 192 A.D.2d 324, 595 N.Y.S.2d 458 (N.Y.A.D. 1 Dept.1993)—§ **28.23, n. 4.**

D

Dabb v. NYNEX Corp., 691 N.Y.S.2d 840 (N.Y.A.D. 4 Dept.1999)—§ **30.9, n. 19.1.**
D'Accordo v. Spare Wheels and Car Shoppe of Sayville, 257 A.D.2d 966, 684 N.Y.S.2d 343 (N.Y.A.D. 3 Dept.1999)— § **32.19.**
Daily Gazette Co. v. City of Schenectady, 688 N.Y.S.2d 472, 710 N.E.2d 1072 (N.Y. 1999)—§ **18.65; § 18.65, n. 4.1.**
Daisy Pope, In re, N.Y.L.J., 1/12/99, p. 26, col. 2 (Sup. Ct., N.Y. County)—§ **22.61, n. 8.**
Dalhouse, People v., 240 A.D.2d 420, 658 N.Y.S.2d 408 (N.Y.A.D. 2 Dept.1997)— § **18.15, n. 9.**
D'Amico v. Commodities Exchange Inc., 235 A.D.2d 313, 652 N.Y.S.2d 294 (N.Y.A.D. 1 Dept.1997)—§ **18.54, n. 4.**
Dangler v. Town of Whitestown, 241 A.D.2d 290, 672 N.Y.S.2d 188 (N.Y.A.D. 4 Dept. 1998)—§ **30.9, n. 9.1.**
D.A.S., Matter of, 951 S.W.2d 528 (Tex. App.-Dallas 1997)—§ **38.8, n. 37.**
DaSilva v. Suozzi, English, Cianciulli & Peirez, P.C., 233 A.D.2d 172, 649 N.Y.S.2d 680 (N.Y.A.D. 1 Dept.1996)— § **28.12, n. 12.**
Davidson, People v., 653 N.Y.S.2d 254, 675 N.E.2d 1206 (N.Y.1996)—§ **18.12, n. 2.**

TABLE OF CASES

Dawn Joy Fashions, Inc. v. Commissioner of Labor of State of N.Y., 659 N.Y.S.2d 196, 681 N.E.2d 363 (N.Y.1997)—§ **4.77, n. 2.**

Deb–Jo Const., Inc. v. Westphal, 210 A.D.2d 951, 620 N.Y.S.2d 678 (N.Y.A.D. 4 Dept. 1994)—§ **28.12, n. 11.**

DeChirico v. Callahan, 134 F.3d 1177 (2nd Cir.1998)—§ **34.37.**

DeJesus v. DeJesus, 665 N.Y.S.2d 36, 687 N.E.2d 1319 (N.Y.1997)—§ **21.37, n. 1.**

Delta Resources, Inc., In re, 54 F.3d 722 (11th Cir.1995)—§ **9.102, n. 10.**

Desmond, Estate of v. Commissioner, T.C. Memo. 1999-76 (U.S.Tax Ct.1999)—§ **24.41, n. 2.**

Diaz v. Franco, 257 A.D.2d 449, 683 N.Y.S.2d 267 (N.Y.A.D. 1 Dept.1999)—§ **30.41, n. 9.1.**

DiBlasio v. City of New York, 102 F.3d 654 (2nd Cir.1996)—§ **18.25, n. 2.**

DiCecco, Matter of, 173 Misc.2d 692, 661 N.Y.S.2d 943 (N.Y.Sup.1997)—§ **22.48, n. 11.**

DiCecilia v. Early, 234 A.D.2d 335, 651 N.Y.S.2d 94 (N.Y.A.D. 2 Dept.1996)—§ **18.25, n. 2.**

Dillon v. Dean, 256 A.D.2d 436, 682 N.Y.S.2d 78 (N.Y.A.D. 2 Dept.1998)—§ **30.38, n. 11.**

Dirito v. Stanley, 203 A.D.2d 903, 611 N.Y.S.2d 65 (N.Y.A.D. 4 Dept.1994)—§ **28.10, n. 6.**

District of Columbia Court of Appeals v. Feldman, 460 U.S. 462, 103 S.Ct. 1303, 75 L.Ed.2d 206 (1983)—§ **18.36; § 18.36, n. 15.**

Doe v. Phillips, 81 F.3d 1204 (2nd Cir. 1996)—§ **18.31, n. 3.**

Donley, In re, 217 B.R. 1004 (Bkrtcy. S.D.Ohio 1998)—§ **9.251, n. 3.**

Dow Corning Corp., In re, 86 F.3d 482 (6th Cir.1996)—§ **9.19.**

Dowd v. Law Plan Hyatt Legal Services, 249 A.D.2d 503, 671 N.Y.S.2d 344 (N.Y.A.D. 2 Dept.1998)—§ **28.13, n. 11.**

Dresses for Less, Inc. v. Lenroth Realty Co., Inc., 688 N.Y.S.2d 50 (N.Y.A.D. 1 Dept. 1999)—§ **30.41, n. 8.1.**

Driscoll, Matter of, N.Y.L.J., 10/22/93, p.30, col.4 (Sup.Ct., Nassau County)—§ **23.76, n. 20.**

Dubroff, In re, 119 F.3d 75 (2nd Cir.1997)—§ **9.49, n. 1.**

E

Elghanian v. Eaton & Van Winkle, N.Y.L.J., June 24, 1997, p. 26, col. 5 (Sup. Ct., N.Y. Co.)—§ **28.13; § 28.13, n. 13.**

Elkins, Matter of, 248 A.D.2d 20, 680 N.Y.S.2d 5 (N.Y.A.D. 1 Dept.1998)—§ **28.19, n. 1.**

Ellis Center for Long Term Care v. DeBuono, 175 Misc.2d 443, 669 N.Y.S.2d 782 (N.Y.Sup.1998)—§ **4.77, n. 3.**

Elmer Q, In re, 250 A.D.2d 256, 681 N.Y.S.2d 637 (N.Y.A.D. 3 Dept.1998)—§ **22.28, n. 18.**

Enrico v. Russo, Garguilo & Fox, 1998 WL 178841 (E.D.N.Y.1998)—§ **28.13, n. 15.**

Envirodyne Industries, Inc., Matter of, 79 F.3d 579 (7th Cir.1996)—§ **9.107, n. 22.**

Erickson, People v., 156 A.D.2d 760, 549 N.Y.S.2d 182 (N.Y.A.D. 3 Dept.1989)—§ **33.38, n. 2.1.**

Ericson v. Syracuse University, 1999 WL 212684 (S.D.N.Y.1999)—§ **18.53, n. 8.**

Estabrook v. Chamberlain, 240 A.D. 899, 267 N.Y.S. 425 (N.Y.A.D. 2 Dept.1933)—§ **16.29, n. 7.**

Estate of (see name of party)

F

Faison, People v., 171 Misc.2d 68, 662 N.Y.S.2d 973 (N.Y.City Crim.Ct.1996)—§ **33.75, n. 1.**

FedPak Systems, Inc., Matter of, 80 F.3d 207 (7th Cir.1996)—§ **9.19, n. 6.**

Feeney v. City of New York, 255 A.D.2d 483, 680 N.Y.S.2d 646 (N.Y.A.D. 2 Dept. 1998)—§ **18.66, n. 3.1.**

Feggoudakis v. New York State Div. of Human Rights, 230 A.D.2d 739, 646 N.Y.S.2d 175 (N.Y.A.D. 2 Dept.1996)—§ **18.46, n. 5.1.**

Fiacco, People v., 146 Misc.2d 330, 549 N.Y.S.2d 901 (N.Y.City Ct.1989)—§ **33.72, n. 1; § 33.75, n. 1.**

Filicore v. Jossel, 173 Misc.2d 42, 660 N.Y.S.2d 786 (N.Y.Sup.1997)—§ **18.45, n. 4.1.**

Fine v. Berman, 238 A.D.2d 220, 657 N.Y.S.2d 6 (N.Y.A.D. 1 Dept.1997)—§ **18.51, n. 2.1.**

Fisher, People v., 167 Misc.2d 850, 635 N.Y.S.2d 1002 (N.Y.City Crim.Ct. 1995)—§ **33.72, n. 1; § 33.75, n. 1; § 33.90A, n. 1.**

Fleet Bank, Nat. Ass'n v. Burke, 160 F.3d 883 (2nd Cir.1998)—§ **18.36, n. 8.**

Flynn v. General Motors Acceptance Corp., 179 Misc.2d 555, 688 N.Y.S.2d 374 (N.Y.Sup.1998)—§ **30.44, n. 10.1.**

Forney v. Apfel, 524 U.S. 266, 118 S.Ct. 1984, 141 L.Ed.2d 269 (1998)—§ **34.30.**

Fort, People v., 145 A.D.2d 983, 536 N.Y.S.2d 621 (N.Y.A.D. 4 Dept.1988)—§ **33.5, n. 9.**

Foster v. Churchill, 642 N.Y.S.2d 583, 665 N.E.2d 153 (N.Y.1996)—§ **18.82, n. 5.**

Freitag v. New York Times, 687 N.Y.S.2d 809 (N.Y.A.D. 3 Dept.1999)—§ **32.19.**

TABLE OF CASES

G

Gambuti, In re Application of, 242 A.D.2d 431, 662 N.Y.S.2d 757 (N.Y.A.D. 1 Dept. 1997)—§ **22.38, n. 6.1.**
Gannett Co., Inc. v. Rochester City School Dist., 179 Misc.2d 502, 684 N.Y.S.2d 757 (N.Y.Sup.1998)—§ **30.41, n. 13.3.**
Gazzola Bldg. Corp. v. Shapiro, 181 A.D.2d 718, 580 N.Y.S.2d 477 (N.Y.A.D. 2 Dept. 1992)—§ **28.10, n. 5.**
GBJ Corp. v. Sequa Corp., 804 F.Supp. 564 (S.D.N.Y.1992)—§ **2.106, n. 10.**
Gedon v. University Medical Residents Services, P.C., 252 A.D.2d 744, 677 N.Y.S.2d 397 (N.Y.A.D. 3 Dept.1998)—§ **32.19.**
General Crushed Stone Co. v. State, 686 N.Y.S.2d 754, 709 N.E.2d 463 (N.Y. 1999)—§ **14.88.**
Gimbel v. Waldman, 193 Misc. 758, 84 N.Y.S.2d 888 (N.Y.Sup.1948)—§ **28.12, n. 6.**
Ginor, Estate of v. Landsberg, 960 F.Supp. 661 (S.D.N.Y.1996)—§ **28.3, n. 9.**
G.M. ex rel. R.F. v. New Britain Bd. of Educ., 173 F.3d 77 (2nd Cir.1999)—§ **18.53, n. 6.1.**
Goldsmith v. De Buono, 245 A.D.2d 627, 665 N.Y.S.2d 727 (N.Y.A.D. 3 Dept. 1997)—§ **4.21, n. 4; § 4.78, n. 7.**
Gold Star, Inc. v. Lloyds of London Ins. Underwriters, 113 F.3d 1229 (2nd Cir. 1997)—§ **31.6, n. 3.**
Golf v. New York State Dept. of Social Services, 674 N.Y.S.2d 600, 697 N.E.2d 555 (N.Y.1998)—§ **23.80, n. 13.**
Gomes, In re, 220 B.R. 84 (9th Cir.1998)—§ **9.209, n. 9.**
Gomez v. Feder, Connick & Goldstein, P.C., 687 N.Y.S.2d 679 (N.Y.A.D. 2 Dept. 1999)—§ **31.8, n. 6.**
Gonzalez v. Gordon, 233 A.D.2d 191, 649 N.Y.S.2d 701 (N.Y.A.D. 1 Dept.1996)—§ **28.24, n. 2.**
Gonzalez, People v., 168 Misc.2d 136, 645 N.Y.S.2d 978 (N.Y.Sup.App.Term 1996)—§ **33.75, n. 1; § 33.76; § 33.76, n. 1.**
Gonzalez v. Peterson, 177 Misc.2d 940, 678 N.Y.S.2d 855 (N.Y.Sup.App.Term 1998)—§ **37.28, n. 22.**
Grace v. Chenango County, 256 A.D.2d 890, 681 N.Y.S.2d 695 (N.Y.A.D. 3 Dept. 1998)—§ **30.41, n. 13.4.**
Grace PP, Matter of, 245 A.D.2d 824, 666 N.Y.S.2d 793 (N.Y.A.D. 3 Dept.1997)—§ **22.39, n. 4.1.**
Graf v. Foschio, 102 A.D.2d 891, 477 N.Y.S.2d 190 (N.Y.A.D. 2 Dept.1984)—§ **33.68, n. 14.**
Graham v. Henderson, 89 F.3d 75 (2nd Cir.1996)—§ **18.19, n. 1.**
Grand Jury Subpoenas Served on Nat. Broadcasting Co., Inc., In re, 178 Misc.2d 1052, 683 N.Y.S.2d 708 (N.Y.Sup.1998)—§ **18.85, n. 9.**
Gray v. Wallman & Kramer, 224 A.D.2d 275, 638 N.Y.S.2d 18 (N.Y.A.D. 1 Dept. 1996)—§ **28.14, n. 8.**
Greenwich v. Markhoff, 234 A.D.2d 112, 650 N.Y.S.2d 704 (N.Y.A.D. 1 Dept. 1996)—§ **28.3, n. 1.**
Griffin v. Coughlin, 649 N.Y.S.2d 903, 673 N.E.2d 98 (N.Y.1996)—§ **18.28, n. 3; § 18.29, n. 1.**
Grodin v. Liberty Cable, 244 A.D.2d 153, 664 N.Y.S.2d 276 (N.Y.A.D. 1 Dept. 1997)—§ **18.64, n. 10, 16.**
Grogan v. Garner, 498 U.S. 279, 111 S.Ct. 654, 112 L.Ed.2d 755 (1991)—§ **9.138, n. 1.**
Grucza v. Waste Stream Technology, 252 A.D.2d 901, 676 N.Y.S.2d 336 (N.Y.A.D. 3 Dept.1998)—§ **32.19.**
Grutman Katz Greene & Humphrey v. Goldman, 251 A.D.2d 7, 673 N.Y.S.2d 649 (N.Y.A.D. 1 Dept.1998)—§ **28.19, n. 1.**
Guardianship of (see name of party)
Guzman v. ARC XVI Inwood, Inc., 1999 WL 178786 (S.D.N.Y.1999)—§ **17.43, n. 6.1.**
Guzman v. Scully, 80 F.3d 772 (2nd Cir. 1996)—§ **18.13, n. 3.**

H

Hachamovitch v. DeBuono, 159 F.3d 687 (2nd Cir.1998)—§ **18.36, n. 6; § 18.37, n. 8.**
Hagerstown Fiber Ltd. Partnership, In re, 226 B.R. 353 (Bkrtcy.S.D.N.Y.1998)—§ **9.3, n. 4; § 9.7, n. 3.**
Hall & Co., Inc. v. Steiner and Mondore, 147 A.D.2d 225, 543 N.Y.S.2d 190 (N.Y.A.D. 3 Dept.1989)—§ **28.14, n. 4.**
Halsted v. Silberstein, 196 N.Y. 1, 89 N.E. 443 (N.Y.1909)—§ **28.13, n. 14.**
Harriet R., Matter of, 224 A.D.2d 625, 639 N.Y.S.2d 390 (N.Y.A.D. 2 Dept.1996)—§ **22.32, n. 9.**
Harris v. Moyer, 255 A.D.2d 890, 680 N.Y.S.2d 351 (N.Y.A.D. 4 Dept.1998)—§ **30.15, n. 8.1.**
Harris v. Village of Dobbs Ferry, 208 A.D. 853, 204 N.Y.S. 325 (N.Y.A.D. 2 Dept. 1924)—§ **16.12, n. 11.**
Harvey v. Brandt, 254 A.D.2d 718, 677 N.Y.S.2d 867 (N.Y.A.D. 4 Dept.1998)—§ **18.21, n. 3.**
Hashemi, In re, 104 F.3d 1122 (9th Cir. 1996)—§ **9.208.**
Hatfield v. 96-100 Prince St., Inc., 1997 WL 151502 (S.D.N.Y.1997)—§ **31.4, n. 4.**
Heck v. Humphrey, 512 U.S. 477, 114 S.Ct. 2364, 129 L.Ed.2d 383 (1994)—§ **18.38, n. 5.**
Hemphill v. Schott, 141 F.3d 412 (2nd Cir. 1998)—§ **18.32, n. 8; § 18.37, n. 1.**

TABLE OF CASES

Hidalgo, People v., 675 N.Y.S.2d 327, 698 N.E.2d 46 (N.Y.1998)—§ **38.8, n. 20.**
Hili v. Sciarrotta, 140 F.3d 210 (2nd Cir. 1998)—§ **18.31, n. 2.**
Hillard v. Clark, 254 A.D.2d 756, 677 N.Y.S.2d 857 (N.Y.A.D. 4 Dept.1998)—§ **18.84, n. 2.**
Hok Ming Chan, People v., 230 A.D.2d 165, 656 N.Y.S.2d 22 (N.Y.A.D. 1 Dept. 1997)—§ **18.12, n. 2.**
Holden, In re, 217 B.R. 161 (D.Vt.1997)—§ **9.109, n. 3.**
Hollman, People v., 581 N.Y.S.2d 619, 590 N.E.2d 204 (N.Y.1992)—§ **33.4; § 33.4, n. 9.**
Home Ins. Co. v. Liebman, Adolf & Charme, 257 A.D.2d 424, 683 N.Y.S.2d 519 (N.Y.A.D. 1 Dept.1999)—§ **28.9, n. 10.**
Horne v. Coughlin, 178 F.3d 603 (2nd Cir. 1999)—§ **18.32, n. 6.**
Howell, People v., 158 Misc.2d 653, 601 N.Y.S.2d 778 (N.Y.City Crim.Ct.1993)—§ **33.75, n. 1.**
Hubbard v. Samson Management Corp., 994 F.Supp. 187 (S.D.N.Y.1998)—§ **18.50, n. 2.1.**
Hyatt v. United States, 968 F.Supp. 96 (E.D.N.Y.1997)—§ **18.23, n. 7.**

I

Iannarone v. Gramer, 256 A.D.2d 443, 682 N.Y.S.2d 84 (N.Y.A.D. 2 Dept.1998)—§ **28.3, n. 1.**
Iazzetti v. City of New York, 256 A.D.2d 140, 681 N.Y.S.2d 507 (N.Y.A.D. 1 Dept. 1998)—§ **30.28, n. 3.1.**
Idaho v. Coeur d'Alene Tribe of Idaho, 521 U.S. 261, 117 S.Ct. 2028, 138 L.Ed.2d 438 (1997)—§ **18.33, n. 1.**
Iglesias v. Dazi, 253 A.D.2d 515, 677 N.Y.S.2d 158 (N.Y.A.D. 2 Dept.1998)—§ **15.33, n. 4.**
In re (see name of party)
Irons, People v., 137 Misc.2d 871, 523 N.Y.S.2d 731 (N.Y.City Crim.Ct.1987)—§ **33.76; § 33.76, n. 3.**
Isaacs v. Isaacs, 246 A.D.2d 428, 667 N.Y.S.2d 740 (N.Y.A.D. 1 Dept.1998)—§ **21.53, n. 1.**
Ivani Contracting Corp. v. City of New York, 103 F.3d 257 (2nd Cir.1997)—§ **18.38, n. 9.**

J

Johnson v. Berger, 193 A.D.2d 784, 598 N.Y.S.2d 270 (N.Y.A.D. 2 Dept.1993)—§ **28.11; § 28.11, n. 16; § 28.26, n. 3.**
Johnson v. Watkins, 101 F.3d 792 (2nd Cir.1996)—§ **18.37, n. 4.**

Jones v. New York State Division of Military and Naval Affairs, 166 F.3d 45 (2nd Cir.1999)—§ **18.33, n. 2.**
Jones v. Peacock, 183 A.D.2d 1039, 584 N.Y.S.2d 333 (N.Y.A.D. 3 Dept.1992)—§ **28.14, n. 17.**
Jones v. Reese, 227 A.D.2d 783, 642 N.Y.S.2d 378 (N.Y.A.D. 3 Dept.1996)—§ **21.55.**
Jorgensen v. Silverman, 224 A.D.2d 665, 638 N.Y.S.2d 482 (N.Y.A.D. 2 Dept. 1996)—§ **28.24, n. 6.**
Jorgenson v. B.F. Yenney Const. Co., Inc., 255 A.D.2d 1008, 679 N.Y.S.2d 775 (N.Y.A.D. 4 Dept.1998)—§ **30.9, n. 43.1.**
Juan C. v. Cortines, 657 N.Y.S.2d 581, 679 N.E.2d 1061 (N.Y.1997)—§ **18.37, n. 7.**

K

Kasiem H., Matter of, 230 A.D.2d 796, 646 N.Y.S.2d 541 (N.Y.A.D. 2 Dept.1996)—§ **20.30.**
Kassis v. Teacher's Ins. and Annuity Ass'n, 695 N.Y.S.2d 515, 717 N.E.2d 674 (N.Y. 1999)—§ **28.21, n. 6.**
Kathleen S., Matter of, N.Y.L.J., 4/30/98, p. 31, col. 6—§ **21.5, n. 1.**
Kauffman, Matter of, 99 A.D.2d 640, 471 N.Y.S.2d 719 (N.Y.A.D. 3 Dept.1984)—§ **28.25, n. 1.**
Kaufman & Kaufman v. Hoff, 213 A.D.2d 197, 624 N.Y.S.2d 107 (N.Y.A.D. 1 Dept. 1995)—§ **28.8, n. 2.**
Keller v. Lee, 152 F.3d 918 (2nd Cir.1998)—§ **28.13, n. 11.**
Kelly v. Cesarano, Haque & Khan, P.C., 178 Misc.2d 176, 678 N.Y.S.2d 708 (N.Y.Sup. 1998)—§ **28.13, n. 16.**
Kepenis v. Ro-Zap Enterprises, Inc., 179 Misc.2d 874, 686 N.Y.S.2d 248 (N.Y.Sup. 1998)—§ **30.38.**
Kiley, In re, 22 A.D.2d 527, 256 N.Y.S.2d 848 (N.Y.A.D. 1 Dept.1965)—§ **28.25, n. 1.**
Kim v. Kim, 170 Misc.2d 968, 652 N.Y.S.2d 694 (N.Y.Sup.1996)—§ **21.65, n. 4.**
Kinlock v. New York State and Local Employees' Retirement System, 237 A.D.2d 810, 655 N.Y.S.2d 457 (N.Y.A.D. 3 Dept. 1997)—§ **4.15, n. 1.**
Knapp v. County of Livingston, 175 Misc.2d 112, 667 N.Y.S.2d 662 (N.Y.Sup.1997)—§ **14.32, n. 2.**
Knowles v. Iowa, 525 U.S. 113, 119 S.Ct. 484, 142 L.Ed.2d 492 (1998)—§ **18.10, n. 12.**
Koppelman v. Liddle, O'Connor, Finkelstein & Robinson, 246 A.D.2d 365, 668 N.Y.S.2d 29 (N.Y.A.D. 1 Dept.1998)—§ **28.30, n. 2.**
Kornfein, Matter of, N.Y.L.J., 5/29/98, p. 31, col. 1 (Sup. Ct., Rockland County)—§ **22.13, n. 6; § 22.53, n. 5.**

TABLE OF CASES

Kotler v. State, 255 A.D.2d 429, 680 N.Y.S.2d 586 (N.Y.A.D. 2 Dept.1998)—§ 18.25, n. 5.
Koump v. Smith, 303 N.Y.S.2d 858, 250 N.E.2d 857 (N.Y.1969)—§ 26.42, n. 17.
Kurth v. Murphy, 255 A.D.2d 365, 679 N.Y.S.2d 690 (N.Y.A.D. 2 Dept.1998)—§ 30.9, n. 45.1.

L

Larson v. Albany Medical Center, 252 A.D.2d 936, 676 N.Y.S.2d 293 (N.Y.A.D. 3 Dept.1998)—§ 18.86, n. 1.
Lasser v. Rosa, 237 A.D.2d 361, 654 N.Y.S.2d 822 (N.Y.A.D. 2 Dept.1997)—§ 18.54, n. 4.
Lavanant v. General Acc. Ins. Co. of America, 164 A.D.2d 73, 561 N.Y.S.2d 164 (N.Y.A.D. 1 Dept.1990)—§ 28.11, n. 4.
Lazer Elec. Corp. v. Cecchi, 1997 WL 311925 (S.D.N.Y.1997)—§ 28.24, n. 10.
LeBlanc–Sternberg v. Fletcher, 143 F.3d 765 (2nd Cir.1998)—§ 18.19, n. 3.1.
Lee v. City of Rochester, 254 A.D.2d 790, 677 N.Y.S.2d 848 (N.Y.A.D. 4 Dept. 1998)—§ 37.2, n. 8.
Leon v. Martinez, 614 N.Y.S.2d 972, 638 N.E.2d 511 (N.Y.1994)—§ 28.19, n. 1.
Lepore v. City of New York, 258 A.D.2d 288, 685 N.Y.S.2d 52 (N.Y.A.D. 1 Dept. 1999)—§ 30.30, n. 14.1.
Leshowitz v. Conklin, 245 A.D.2d 343, 665 N.Y.S.2d 593 (N.Y.A.D. 2 Dept.1997)—§ 18.76, n. 5.
Levin v. Yeshiva University, 180 Misc.2d 829, 691 N.Y.S.2d 280 (N.Y.Sup.1999)—§ 18.45, n. 4.
Levine v. Lacher & Lovell–Taylor, 256 A.D.2d 147, 681 N.Y.S.2d 503 (N.Y.A.D. 1 Dept.1998)—§ 28.8, n. 2.
Liebert v. Gelbwaks, 234 A.D.2d 164, 651 N.Y.S.2d 307 (N.Y.A.D. 1 Dept.1996)—§ 28.24, n. 2.
Livingston, Estate of, N.Y.L.J., 6/7/99, p. 33, col. 6 (Sup. Ct., Queens County)—§ 22.61, n. 5.1.
Lopez v. Oquendo, 690 N.Y.S.2d 584 (N.Y.A.D. 1 Dept.1999)—§ 26.42, n. 17.
Lowe, Matter of, N.Y.L.J., 4/16/99, p. 36, col. 6 (Sup. Ct., Queens County)—§ 22.53, n. 5; § 22.54, n. 8.
Lowenschuss, In re, 67 F.3d 1394 (9th Cir. 1995)—§ 9.170, n. 2.
Lowth v. Town of Cheektowaga, 82 F.3d 563 (2nd Cir.1996)—§ 18.22, n. 4; § 18.25, n. 7.
Loyal Tire and Auto Center Inc. v. New York State Thruway Authority, 227 A.D.2d 82, 652 N.Y.S.2d 804 (N.Y.A.D. 3 Dept.1997)—§ 4.11, n. 2.
Luniewski v. Zeitlin, 188 A.D.2d 642, 591 N.Y.S.2d 524 (N.Y.A.D. 2 Dept.1992)—§ 28.10, n. 5.

M

MacFawn v. Kresler, 644 N.Y.S.2d 486, 666 N.E.2d 1359 (N.Y.1996)—§ 18.25, n. 2.
Maendel v. State, 178 Misc.2d 297, 679 N.Y.S.2d 537 (N.Y.Ct.Cl.1998)—§ 30.30, n. 15.1.
Maher, People v., 653 N.Y.S.2d 79, 675 N.E.2d 833 (N.Y.1996)—§ 18.12, n. 2.
Maier, Matter of, N.Y.L.J., 2/6/98, p. 28, col. 1 (Sup. Ct., Bronx County)—§ 22.17, n. 2.1; § 22.31, n. 10; § 22.35, n. 1.
Maisonaves v. Friedman, 255 A.D.2d 494, 680 N.Y.S.2d 619 (N.Y.A.D. 2 Dept. 1998)—§ 30.30, n. 15.3.
Majer v. Schmidt, 169 A.D.2d 501, 564 N.Y.S.2d 722 (N.Y.A.D. 1 Dept.1991)—§ 28.25, n. 4.
Majewski v. Broadalbin–Perth Cent. School Dist., 673 N.Y.S.2d 966, 696 N.E.2d 978 (N.Y.1998)—§ 32.15; § 32.15, n. 11.
Manna v. Ades, 237 A.D.2d 264, 655 N.Y.S.2d 412 (N.Y.A.D. 2 Dept.1997)—§ 28.24, n. 5.
Marine Bank v. Weaver, 455 U.S. 551, 102 S.Ct. 1220, 71 L.Ed.2d 409 (1982)—§ 2.106, n. 10.
Martin v. C.A. Productions Co., 203 N.Y.S.2d 845, 168 N.E.2d 666 (N.Y. 1960)—§ 32.15.
Martinez v. N.B.C., Inc., 49 F.Supp.2d 305 (S.D.N.Y.1999)—§ 18.83, n. 2.
Matisoff v. Dobi, 659 N.Y.S.2d 209, 681 N.E.2d 376 (N.Y.1997)—§ 21.30, n. 4.
Matter of (see name of party)
Matute, People v., 141 Misc.2d 988, 535 N.Y.S.2d 524 (N.Y.City Crim.Ct.1988)—§ 33.75, n. 1.
Maxwell v. N.W. Ayer, Inc., 159 Misc.2d 454, 605 N.Y.S.2d 174 (N.Y.Sup.1993)—§ 18.64, n. 1.
McGettrick, People v., 139 Misc.2d 403, 528 N.Y.S.2d 758 (N.Y.City Ct.1988)—§ 33.32, n. 2; § 33.33, n. 6.
McIntyre v. Manhattan Ford, Lincoln–Mercury, Inc., 256 A.D.2d 269, 682 N.Y.S.2d 167 (N.Y.A.D. 1 Dept.1998)—§ 30.9, n. 37; § 30.30, n. 26.4.
MCI Telecommunications Corp. v. Public Service Com'n of the State of N.Y., 231 A.D.2d 284, 659 N.Y.S.2d 563 (N.Y.A.D. 3 Dept.1997)—§ 4.82, n. 10.
McLane v. McLane, 209 A.D.2d 1001, 619 N.Y.S.2d 899 (N.Y.A.D. 4 Dept.1994)—§ 21.49, n. 6.
McMillian v. Monroe County, Ala., 520 U.S. 781, 117 S.Ct. 1734, 138 L.Ed.2d 1 (1997)—§ 18.34, n. 2.
Medvedev v. Wing, 249 A.D.2d 755, 671 N.Y.S.2d 806 (N.Y.A.D. 3 Dept.1998)—§ 18.28; § 18.28, n. 11.
Mercado v. Townsend, 225 A.D.2d 555, 638 N.Y.S.2d 762 (N.Y.A.D. 2 Dept.1996)—§ 18.70, n. 4.

TABLE OF CASES

Mergler v. Crystal Properties Associates, Ltd., 179 A.D.2d 177, 583 N.Y.S.2d 229 (N.Y.A.D. 1 Dept.1992)—§ 28.18B; § 28.18B, n. 2.
Merkert, Matter of, N.Y.L.J., 11/3/98, p. 30, col. 6 (Sup. Ct., Nassau County)—§ 22.69, n. 3.
Merson v. McNally, 665 N.Y.S.2d 605, 688 N.E.2d 479 (N.Y.1997)—§ 15.3, n. 3; § 15.4, n. 22; § 15.5, n. 1.
Michalek, People v., 138 Misc.2d 1, 521 N.Y.S.2d 609 (N.Y.City Crim.Ct.1987)—§ 33.75, n. 1.
Middle Market Financial Corp. v. D'Orazio, 1998 WL 397867 (S.D.N.Y.1998)—§ 28.13, n. 16.
Milbank, Tweed, Hadley & McCloy v. Boon, 13 F.3d 537 (2nd Cir.1994)—§ 28.26A; § 28.26A, n. 1.
Miller, In re, 252 A.D.2d 156, 684 N.Y.S.2d 368 (N.Y.A.D. 4 Dept.1998)—§ 18.28; § 18.28, n. 13.
Miller v. DeBuono, 666 N.Y.S.2d 548, 689 N.E.2d 518 (N.Y.1997)—§ 4.6, n. 3; § 4.7, n. 7; § 4.19; § 4.19, n. 3.
Miller v. Schwartz, 532 N.Y.S.2d 354, 528 N.E.2d 507 (N.Y.1988)—§ 33.32, n. 2; § 33.33; § 33.33, n. 1, 5.
M. M. v. E. M., 248 A.D.2d 109, 669 N.Y.S.2d 543 (N.Y.A.D. 1 Dept.1998)—§ 21.5, n. 1.
Monsky v. Moraghan, 127 F.3d 243 (2nd Cir.1997)—§ 18.18, n. 2.
Monterey, City of v. Del Monte Dunes at Monterey, Ltd., ___ U.S. ___, 119 S.Ct. 1624, 143 L.Ed.2d 882 (1999)—§ 18.2, n. 4, 4.1.
Montero v. Travis, 171 F.3d 757 (2nd Cir.1999)—§ 18.31, n. 5.
Moreau, Town of v. New York State Dept. of Environmental Conservation, 178 Misc.2d 56, 678 N.Y.S.2d 241 (N.Y.Sup.1998)—§ 15.24, n. 4.1.
Mount Vernon Fire Ins. Co. v. Jones, 1997 WL 37033 (E.D.N.Y.1997)—§ 31.6, n. 2.
Mrs. B. v. Milford Bd. of Educ., 103 F.3d 1114 (2nd Cir.1997)—§ 18.53, n. 5.
Munoz v. New York City Health and Hospitals Corp., 180 Misc.2d 527, 689 N.Y.S.2d 619 (N.Y.Sup.1999)—§ 30.44, n. 5.1.
Murphy v. United Parcel Service, Inc., ___ U.S. ___, 119 S.Ct. 2133 (1999)—§ 18.19, n. 7.
Muro, N.Y.L.J., 4/20/99, p. 30, col. 1 (Sup. Ct., Suffolk County)—§ 22.39, n. 3.
Myers v. County of Orange, 157 F.3d 66 (2nd Cir.1998)—§ 18.34.

N

Nabi v. Nabi, 242 A.D.2d 870, 662 N.Y.S.2d 906 (N.Y.A.D. 4 Dept.1997)—§ 21.5, n. 1.

Nate B. & Frances Spingold Foundation v. Wallin, Simon, Black and Co., 184 A.D.2d 464, 585 N.Y.S.2d 416 (N.Y.A.D. 1 Dept.1992)—§ 28.14, n. 11.
National Min. Ass'n v. United States Army Corps of Engineers, 145 F.3d 1399, 330 U.S.App.D.C. 329 (D.C.Cir.1998)—§ 15.15, n. 8.1.
Necker Pottick, Fox Run Woods Builders Corp. v. Duncan, 251 A.D.2d 333, 673 N.Y.S.2d 740 (N.Y.A.D. 2 Dept.1998)—§ 16.85.
New York Presbyterian Hospital (J.H.L.), Matter of, N.Y.L.J., 6/4/99, p. 33, col. 4 (Sup. Ct., Westchester County)—§ 22.13, n. 6; § 22.53, n. 5.
New York State Bar Ass'n v. Reno, 999 F.Supp. 710 (N.D.N.Y.1998)—§ 22.48, n. 11.
Niagara County Dept. of Social Services on Behalf of D.A.H. v. C.B., 234 A.D.2d 897, 651 N.Y.S.2d 785 (N.Y.A.D. 4 Dept.1996)—§ 21.55.
Ninth Ave. Remedial Group v. Allis Chalmers Corp., 974 F.Supp. 684 (N.D.Ind.1997)—§ 15.30, n. 7.
Noland, United States v., 517 U.S. 535, 116 S.Ct. 1524, 134 L.Ed.2d 748 (1996)—§ 9.107, n. 21.
Nowell, Estate of v. Commissioner, T.C. Memo. 1999-15 (U.S.Tax Ct.1999)—§ 24.45, n. 3.

O

O'Hara v. Bishop, 256 A.D.2d 983, 682 N.Y.S.2d 291 (N.Y.A.D. 3 Dept.1998)—§ 30.38, n. 9.
Ohio Agr. Commodity Depositors Fund v. Mahern, 517 U.S. 1130, 116 S.Ct. 1411, 134 L.Ed.2d 537 (1996)—§ 9.18.
Ormiston v. Nelson, 117 F.3d 69 (2nd Cir.1997)—§ 18.38, n. 1.
Osiecki v. Olympic Regional Development Authority, 256 A.D.2d 998, 682 N.Y.S.2d 312 (N.Y.A.D. 3 Dept.1998)—§ 30.30, n. 15.5.

P

Paccione v. Greenberg, 256 A.D.2d 559, 682 N.Y.S.2d 442 (N.Y.A.D. 2 Dept.1998)—§ 30.15, n. 14.1.
Pacesetter Communications Corp. v. Solin & Breindel, P.C., 150 A.D.2d 232, 541 N.Y.S.2d 404 (N.Y.A.D. 1 Dept.1989)—§ 28.3, n. 14; § 28.8, n. 2.
Padilla v. Style Management Co., Inc., 256 A.D.2d 27, 681 N.Y.S.2d 20 (N.Y.A.D. 1 Dept.1998)—§ 30.30, n. 15.4.
Pallette Stone Corp. v. State of New York Office of General Services, 245 A.D.2d

TABLE OF CASES

756, 665 N.Y.S.2d 457 (N.Y.A.D. 3 Dept. 1997)—§ 4.50, n. 4.
Panigeon v. Alliance Navigation Line, Inc., 1997 WL 473385 (S.D.N.Y.1997)—§ 28.13, n. 16.
Panossian v. Panossian, 201 A.D.2d 983, 607 N.Y.S.2d 840 (N.Y.A.D. 4 Dept. 1994)—§ 21.55.
Papa v. Nassau County Dept. of Social Services, 516 U.S. 1093, 116 S.Ct. 816, 133 L.Ed.2d 760 (1996)—§ 39.7, n. 6.
Parker v. Blauvelt Volunteer Fire Co., Inc., 690 N.Y.S.2d 478, 712 N.E.2d 647 (N.Y. 1999)—§ 18.37, n. 8.
Passino v. State, 689 N.Y.S.2d 258 (N.Y.A.D. 3 Dept.1999)—§ 18.21, n. 2.1.
Patel v. Cooper, 244 A.D.2d 265, 664 N.Y.S.2d 295 (N.Y.A.D. 1 Dept.1997)—§ 28.30, n. 2.
Pearson v. James, 105 F.3d 828 (2nd Cir. 1997)—§ 18.13, n. 1.
Pena, People v., 251 A.D.2d 26, 675 N.Y.S.2d 330 (N.Y.A.D. 1 Dept.1998)—§ 18.15, n. 9.
People v. ____(see opposing party)
Pepe, People v., 235 A.D.2d 221, 653 N.Y.S.2d 101 (N.Y.A.D. 1 Dept.1997)—§ 18.13, n. 1.
Perez v. Chater, 77 F.3d 41 (2nd Cir. 1996)—§ 34.29.
Peterson, People v., 151 A.D.2d 512, 542 N.Y.S.2d 301 (N.Y.A.D. 2 Dept.1989)—§ 33.47, n. 5.
Petty, In re, 256 A.D.2d 281, 682 N.Y.S.2d 183 (N.Y.A.D. 1 Dept.1998)—§ 22.27, n. 1.
Physicians' Reciprocal Insurers v. Keller, 243 A.D.2d 547, 665 N.Y.S.2d 515 (N.Y.A.D. 2 Dept.1997)—§ 31.11, n. 6.
Pilewski, People v., 173 Misc.2d 800, 660 N.Y.S.2d 525 (N.Y.Just.Ct.1997)—§ 20.147, n. 1; § 33.75, n. 1; § 33.90A, n. 1.
Pinal Creek Group v. Newmont Min. Corp., 118 F.3d 1298 (9th Cir.1997)—§ 15.30, n. 7.
Pirro & Monsell, P.C. v. Freddolino, 204 A.D.2d 613, 614 N.Y.S.2d 232 (N.Y.A.D. 2 Dept.1994)—§ 28.8, n. 2.
Plentino Realty, Ltd. v. Gitomer, 216 A.D.2d 87, 628 N.Y.S.2d 75 (N.Y.A.D. 1 Dept.1995)—§ 28.3, n. 1.
Pneumo Abex Corp. v. High Point, Thomasville and Denton R. Co., 142 F.3d 769 (4th Cir.1998)—§ 15.30, n. 7.
Pollack, Matter of, 142 A.D.2d 386, 536 N.Y.S.2d 437 (N.Y.A.D. 1 Dept.1989)—§ 28.25, n. 1.
Porcano v. Lehman, 255 A.D.2d 430, 680 N.Y.S.2d 590 (N.Y.A.D. 2 Dept.1998)—§ 30.30, n. 15.2.
Porter v. Saar, 688 N.Y.S.2d 137 (N.Y.A.D. 1 Dept.1999)—§ 30.10, n. 1.

Posner v. New York Law Pub. Co., 228 A.D.2d 318, 644 N.Y.S.2d 227 (N.Y.A.D. 1 Dept.1996)—§ 18.82, n. 1.
Posr v. Court Officer Shield No. 207, 180 F.3d 409 (2nd Cir.1999)—§ 18.22, n. 4; § 18.25, n. 2.
Prato v. Vigliotta, 253 A.D.2d 749, 677 N.Y.S.2d 380 (N.Y.A.D. 2 Dept.1998)—§ 15.33, n. 4.
Pregent, People v., 142 Misc.2d 344, 537 N.Y.S.2d 424 (N.Y.City Ct.1988)—§ 33.75, n. 1.
Price v. City of New York, 258 A.D.2d 635, 685 N.Y.S.2d 802 (N.Y.A.D. 2 Dept. 1999)—§ 30.28, n. 15.1.
Price, People v., 224 A.D.2d 1014, 637 N.Y.S.2d 536 (N.Y.A.D. 4 Dept.1996)—§ 33.57, n. 3.1.
Prudential Ins. Co. of America v. Dewey Ballantine, Bushby, Palmer & Wood, 170 A.D.2d 108, 573 N.Y.S.2d 981 (N.Y.A.D. 1 Dept.1991)—§ 28.9, n. 10.

Q

Quackenbush v. Allstate Ins. Co., 517 U.S. 706, 116 S.Ct. 1712, 135 L.Ed.2d 1 (1996)—§ 18.36, n. 6.

R

Raji v. Nejad, 256 A.D.2d 12, 680 N.Y.S.2d 520 (N.Y.A.D. 1 Dept.1998)—§ 18.76, n. 3.
Ramos, People v., 662 N.Y.S.2d 739, 685 N.E.2d 492 (N.Y.1997)—§ 18.13, n. 1; § 37.29, n. 44.
Redwing Carriers, Inc. v. Saraland Apartments, 94 F.3d 1489 (11th Cir.1996)—§ 15.30, n. 7.
Re, Estate of v. Kornstein Veisz & Wexler, 958 F.Supp. 907 (S.D.N.Y.1997)—§ 28.26A; § 28.26A, n. 3.
Reeves, In re, 221 B.R. 756 (Bkrtcy.C.D.Ill. 1998)—§ 9.249, n. 1.
Reeves v. Johnson Controls World Services, Inc., 140 F.3d 144 (2nd Cir.1998)—§ 17.43, n. 6.
Reorganized CF & I Fabricators of Utah, Inc., United States v., 518 U.S. 213, 116 S.Ct. 2106, 135 L.Ed.2d 506 (1996)—§ 9.107, n. 21.
Ricciuti v. N.Y.C. Transit Authority, 124 F.3d 123 (2nd Cir.1997)—§ 18.22, n. 4; § 18.25, n. 1, 7.
Richardson v. McKnight, 521 U.S. 399, 117 S.Ct. 2100, 138 L.Ed.2d 540 (1997)—§ 18.32, n. 1.
Rivet v. Regions Bank of Louisiana, 522 U.S. 470, 118 S.Ct. 921, 139 L.Ed.2d 912 (1998)—§ 18.37, n. 2.

TABLE OF CASES

Rodriguez v. 551 West 157th St. Owners Corp., 992 F.Supp. 385 (S.D.N.Y.1998)—§ 18.50, n. 2.1.
Rodriguez v. Fredericks, 213 A.D.2d 176, 623 N.Y.S.2d 241 (N.Y.A.D. 1 Dept. 1995)—§ 28.12, n. 6.
Rodriguez v. Weprin, 116 F.3d 62 (2nd Cir. 1997)—§ 18.31, n. 2.
Rogers v. Ettinger, 163 A.D.2d 257, 558 N.Y.S.2d 540 (N.Y.A.D. 1 Dept.1990)—§ 28.8, n. 2.
Romeo v. Schmidt, 244 A.D.2d 861, 668 N.Y.S.2d 113 (N.Y.A.D. 4 Dept.1997)—§ 28.13, n. 11.
Rooker v. Fidelity Trust Co., 263 U.S. 413, 44 S.Ct. 149, 68 L.Ed. 362 (1923)—§ 18.36; § 18.36, n. 13.
Rosa v. Callahan, 168 F.3d 72 (2nd Cir. 1999)—§ 34.13; § 34.37.
Rosario, United States v., 111 F.3d 293 (2nd Cir.1997)—§ 18.12, n. 2.
Ross & Cohen v. Kurtz Steel Corp., 237 A.D.2d 172, 654 N.Y.S.2d 375 (N.Y.A.D. 1 Dept.1997)—§ 28.24, n. 5.
Rubinberg v. Walker, 252 A.D.2d 466, 676 N.Y.S.2d 149 (N.Y.A.D. 1 Dept.1998)—§ 28.3, n. 2.
Ruffolo v. Garbarini & Scher, P.C., 239 A.D.2d 8, 668 N.Y.S.2d 169 (N.Y.A.D. 1 Dept.1998)—§ 28.13, n. 11.
Rye Citizens Committee v. Board of Trustees for Village of Port Chester, 249 A.D.2d 478, 671 N.Y.S.2d 528 (N.Y.A.D. 2 Dept.1998)—§ 16.111.

S

Sabel v. Insurance Co. of North America, 251 A.D.2d 645, 676 N.Y.S.2d 478 (N.Y.A.D. 2 Dept.1998)—§ 31.11, n. 3.
Sacramento, County of v. Lewis, 523 U.S. 833, 118 S.Ct. 1708, 140 L.Ed.2d 1043 (1998)—§ 18.32, n. 6.
Sage Realty Corp. v. Proskauer Rose Goetz & Mendelsohn L.L.P., 666 N.Y.S.2d 985, 689 N.E.2d 879 (N.Y.1997)—§ 28.19, n. 1.
Saglibene v. Baum, 246 A.D.2d 599, 668 N.Y.S.2d 39 (N.Y.A.D. 2 Dept.1998)—§ 16.121.
Sahid v. Chambers, 237 A.D.2d 175, 655 N.Y.S.2d 20 (N.Y.A.D. 1 Dept.1997)—§ 18.74, n. 1.
Salim v. Proulx, 93 F.3d 86 (2nd Cir. 1996)—§ 18.21, n. 3.
Sanders v. Rosen, 159 Misc.2d 563, 605 N.Y.S.2d 805 (N.Y.Sup.1993)—§ 28.10, n. 6.
SantaMarina v. Citrynell, 203 A.D.2d 57, 609 N.Y.S.2d 902 (N.Y.A.D. 1 Dept. 1994)—§ 28.26, n. 3.
Sassoonian v. City of New York, 178 Misc.2d 660, 679 N.Y.S.2d 803 (N.Y.Sup. 1998)—§ 30.40, n. 14.1.

Schenck v. Pro–Choice Network Of Western New York, 519 U.S. 357, 117 S.Ct. 855, 137 L.Ed.2d 1 (1997)—§ 18.19, n. 8.
Schlagler v. Phillips, 166 F.3d 439 (2nd Cir.1999)—§ 1, n. 4; § 18.36, n. 4.
Schlanger v. Flaton, 218 A.D.2d 597, 631 N.Y.S.2d 293 (N.Y.A.D. 1 Dept.1995)—§ 28.14, n. 8.
Schlosser, People v., 129 Misc.2d 690, 493 N.Y.S.2d 750 (N.Y.Dist.Ct.1985)—§ 33.16, n. 2.
Scotto v. Almenas, 143 F.3d 105 (2nd Cir. 1998)—§ 18.31, n. 5; § 18.35, n. 2.
S & D Petroleum Co., Inc. v. Tamsett, 144 A.D.2d 849, 534 N.Y.S.2d 800 (N.Y.A.D. 3 Dept.1988)—§ 28.3; § 28.3, n. 10.
Seidner, Matter of, N.Y.L.J., 10/8/97, p. 28, col. 4 (Sup. Ct., Nassau County)—§ 22.2, n. 9; § 22.33, n. 4.
Seminole Tribe of Florida v. Florida, 517 U.S. 44, 116 S.Ct. 1114, 134 L.Ed.2d 252 (1996)—§ 9.18; § 18.33, n. 1.
Sepulvado v. CSC Credit Services, Inc., 158 F.3d 890 (5th Cir.1998)—§ 7.31, n. 11.
Serhofer v. Groman & Wolf, P.C., 203 A.D.2d 354, 610 N.Y.S.2d 294 (N.Y.A.D. 2 Dept.1994)—§ 28.3; § 28.3, n. 12.
Shannon v. Gordon, 249 A.D.2d 291, 670 N.Y.S.2d 887 (N.Y.A.D. 2 Dept.1998)—§ 28.11, n. 4.
Shaughnessy v. Baron, 151 A.D.2d 561, 542 N.Y.S.2d 341 (N.Y.A.D. 2 Dept.1989)—§ 28.12, n. 11.
Shea & Gould, In re, 214 B.R. 739 (Bkrtcy. S.D.N.Y.1997)—§ 9.3, n. 4; § 9.7, n. 3.
Sherman v. Ansell, 207 A.D.2d 537, 616 N.Y.S.2d 90 (N.Y.A.D. 2 Dept.1994)—§ 28.30, n. 2.
Sherotov v. Capoccia, 161 A.D.2d 871, 555 N.Y.S.2d 918 (N.Y.A.D. 3 Dept.1990)—§ 28.11; § 28.11, n. 17.
Simplot, Estate of v. Commissioner, 112 T.C. No. 13 (U.S.Tax Ct.1999)—§ 24.41, n. 2.
Smith v. General Acc. Ins. Co., 674 N.Y.S.2d 267, 697 N.E.2d 168 (N.Y. 1998)—§ 31.17, n. 6.
Smith, People v., 227 A.D.2d 655, 641 N.Y.S.2d 905 (N.Y.A.D. 3 Dept.1996)—§ 1, n. 4; § 18.84, n. 4.
S.N.A. Nut Co., In re, 186 B.R. 98 (Bkrtcy. N.D.Ill.1995)—§ 9.62, n. 4.
Snell v. Apfel, 177 F.3d 128 (2nd Cir. 1999)—§ 34.28; § 34.37.
So v. Wing Tat Realty, Inc., 259 A.D.2d 373, 687 N.Y.S.2d 99 (N.Y.A.D. 1 Dept. 1999)—§ 30.30, n. 15.8.
Solomon, People v., 124 Misc.2d 33, 475 N.Y.S.2d 749 (N.Y.Dist.Ct.1984)—§ 33.75, n. 1.
Somerstein, United States v., 959 F.Supp. 592 (E.D.N.Y.1997)—§ 18.15, n. 7.
Soules v. United States Dept. of Housing and Urban Development, 967 F.2d 817 (2nd Cir.1992)—§ 18.51, n. 4.

TABLE OF CASES

Southmark Corp., In re, 163 F.3d 925 (5th Cir.1999)—§ **9.19, n. 4.**
Spencer v. Doe, 139 F.3d 107 (2nd Cir. 1998)—§ **18.33, n. 3.**
Spiegelman, People v., 142 Misc.2d 617, 537 N.Y.S.2d 964 (N.Y.Just.Ct.1989)—§ **33.16, n. 2.**
Stanski v. Ezersky, 210 A.D.2d 186, 621 N.Y.S.2d 18 (N.Y.A.D. 1 Dept.1994)—§ **28.23, n. 4.**
State v. ____(see opposing party)
State Div. of Human Rights on Complaint of McDermott v. Xerox Corp., 491 N.Y.S.2d 106, 480 N.E.2d 695 (N.Y. 1985)—§ **17.43, n. 6.**
Sternfeld v. Forcier, 248 A.D.2d 14, 679 N.Y.S.2d 219 (N.Y.A.D. 3 Dept.1998)—§ **30.28, n. 3.**
St. Luke's–Roosevelt Hosp. Center, In re, 691 N.Y.S.2d 414 (N.Y.A.D. 1 Dept. 1999)—§ **30.41.**
Storms v. Vargas, 256 A.D.2d 458, 682 N.Y.S.2d 404 (N.Y.A.D. 2 Dept.1998)—§ **30.30, n. 26.5.**
Straight, In re, 143 F.3d 1387 (10th Cir. 1998)—§ **9.18, n. 2.**
Straker v. Straker, 219 A.D.2d 707, 631 N.Y.S.2d 767 (N.Y.A.D. 2 Dept.1995)—§ **21.55.**
Stringfellow's of New York, Ltd. v. City of New York, 671 N.Y.S.2d 406, 694 N.E.2d 407 (N.Y.1998)—§ **16.25; § 18.27, n. 7.1.**
Sucese v. Kirsh, 199 A.D.2d 718, 606 N.Y.S.2d 60 (N.Y.A.D. 3 Dept.1993)—§ **28.11; § 28.11, n. 15.**
Summerville v. City of New York, 257 A.D.2d 566, 683 N.Y.S.2d 579 (N.Y.A.D. 2 Dept.1999)—§ **30.30, n. 26.1.**
Summit Solomon & Feldesman v. Matalon, 216 A.D.2d 91, 627 N.Y.S.2d 690 (N.Y.A.D. 1 Dept.1995)—§ **28.30, n. 2.**
Sunrise Plaza Associates, L.P. v. Town Bd. of Town of Babylon, 250 A.D.2d 690, 673 N.Y.S.2d 165 (N.Y.A.D. 2 Dept.1998)—§ **16.90.**
Super Value Inc., State v., 257 A.D.2d 708, 682 N.Y.S.2d 492 (N.Y.A.D. 3 Dept. 1999)—§ **30.38, n. 10.**
Susi v. Bermil Contracting Co., 256 A.D.2d 826, 681 N.Y.S.2d 676 (N.Y.A.D. 3 Dept. 1998)—§ **32.30, n. 8.**
Sutherland v. Glennon, 256 A.D.2d 984, 681 N.Y.S.2d 916 (N.Y.A.D. 3 Dept.1998)—§ **20.147, n. 13.2; § 30.41, n. 13.2.**
Sutton v. United Airlines, Inc., ___ U.S. ___, 119 S.Ct. 2139 (1999)—§ **18.19, n. 7.**
Svenska Finans Intern. BV v. Scolaro, Shulman, Cohen, Lawler & Burstein, P.C., 1999 WL 118313 (N.D.N.Y.1999)—§ **28.13, n. 16.**
SV Space Development Corp. v. Town of Babylon Zoning Bd. of Appeals, 256 A.D.2d 471, 682 N.Y.S.2d 95 (N.Y.A.D. 2 Dept.1998)—§ **16.46.**
Swift v. Choe, 242 A.D.2d 188, 674 N.Y.S.2d 17 (N.Y.A.D. 1 Dept.1998)—§ **28.18B; § 28.18B, n. 4; § 28.25, n. 7.4.**

T

Taffi, In re, 96 F.3d 1190 (9th Cir.1996)—§ **9.251.**
Tal–Spons Corp. v. Nurnberg, 213 A.D.2d 395, 623 N.Y.S.2d 604 (N.Y.A.D. 2 Dept. 1995)—§ **28.14, n. 11.**
Tankleff v. Senkowski, 135 F.3d 235 (2nd Cir.1998)—§ **18.15, n. 5.**
Tapia–Ortiz v. Doe, 171 F.3d 150 (2nd Cir. 1999)—§ **18.21; § 18.38, n. 3.**
Tate v. Estate of Dickens, 276 A.D. 94, 93 N.Y.S.2d 504 (N.Y.A.D. 3 Dept.1949)—§ **32.15.**
Tejada v. Apfel, 167 F.3d 770 (2nd Cir. 1999)—§ **34.13.**
Tekni–Plex, Inc. v. Meyner and Landis, 651 N.Y.S.2d 954, 674 N.E.2d 663 (N.Y. 1996)—§ **28.21, n. 6.**
10 Apartment Associates, Inc. v. New York State Div. of Housing and Community Renewal, 240 A.D.2d 585, 658 N.Y.S.2d 674 (N.Y.A.D. 2 Dept.1997)—§ **4.50, n. 4.**
Tenzer, Greenblatt, Fallon & Kaplan v. Ellenberg, 199 A.D.2d 45, 604 N.Y.S.2d 947 (N.Y.A.D. 1 Dept.1993)—§ **28.10, n. 13.**
Thomas v. Roach, 165 F.3d 137 (2nd Cir. 1999)—§ **18.19, n. 2; § 18.21, n. 3; § 18.34, n. 4.**
Thorpe, People v., 160 Misc.2d 558, 613 N.Y.S.2d 795 (N.Y.Sup.App.Term 1994)—§ **33.90A, n. 1.**
Thumser, People v., 148 Misc.2d 472, 567 N.Y.S.2d 571 (N.Y.Sup.App.Term 1990)—§ **33.16; § 33.16, n. 3.**
Tiara Motorcoach Corp., Matter of, 212 B.R. 133 (Bkrtcy.N.D.Ind.1997)—§ **9.62, n. 4.**
Ticketmaster Corp. v. Lidsky, 245 A.D.2d 142, 665 N.Y.S.2d 666 (N.Y.A.D. 1 Dept. 1997)—§ **28.24, n. 5.**
Till v. Paul Frederick Fox & Affiliates, 689 N.Y.S.2d 585 (N.Y.A.D. 4 Dept.1999)—§ **30.40, n. 14.2.**
Tissot v. Tissot, 243 A.D.2d 462, 662 N.Y.S.2d 599 (N.Y.A.D. 2 Dept.1997)—§ **21.22, n. 8.**
Titus, People v., 178 Misc.2d 687, 682 N.Y.S.2d 521 (N.Y.Sup.App.Term 1998)—§ **33.16, n. 3.**
Tormos v. Hammons, 259 A.D.2d 434, 687 N.Y.S.2d 336 (N.Y.A.D. 1 Dept.1999)—§ **30.41, n. 13.1.**
Torres v. City of New York, 259 A.D.2d 693, 686 N.Y.S.2d 847 (N.Y.A.D. 2 Dept. 1999)—§ **30.30, n. 26.3.**

TABLE OF CASES

Townes v. City of New York, 176 F.3d 138 (2nd Cir.1999)—§ 18.10; § 18.32, n. 3; § 18.34, n. 4.
Town of (see name of town)
Trear v. Sills, 82 Cal.Rptr.2d 281 (Cal.App. 4 Dist.1999)—§ 29.11, n. 5.
Tucker v. Outwater, 118 F.3d 930 (2nd Cir.1997)—§ 18.31, n. 2.
Tuckman v. Wachtel, 200 A.D.2d 507, 606 N.Y.S.2d 679 (N.Y.A.D. 1 Dept.1994)—§ 28.10, n. 5.
Tulloch v. Coughlin, 50 F.3d 114 (2nd Cir. 1995)—§ 18.31, n. 5.
Turner–Schraeter v. Brighton Travel Bureau, Inc., 258 A.D.2d 393, 685 N.Y.S.2d 692 (N.Y.A.D. 1 Dept.1999)—§ 30.39, n. 14.1.

U

Unadilla Silo Co. Inc. v. Ernst & Young, 234 A.D.2d 754, 651 N.Y.S.2d 216 (N.Y.A.D. 3 Dept.1996)—§ 28.13, n. 11.
United States v. ____(see opposing party)
United Technologies Corp. v. Browning–Ferris Industries, Inc., 33 F.3d 96 (1st Cir.1994)—§ 15.30, n. 7.
United Water New York, Inc. v. Public Service Com'n of State of N.Y., 252 A.D.2d 810, 676 N.Y.S.2d 709 (N.Y.A.D. 3 Dept. 1998)—§ 4.57, n. 4.
Uribe v. Merchants Bank of New York, 670 N.Y.S.2d 393, 693 N.E.2d 740 (N.Y. 1998)—§ 31.9, n. 6.

V

Vacco v. Quill, 521 U.S. 793, 117 S.Ct. 2293, 138 L.Ed.2d 834 (1997)—§ 23.113, n. 2.
Valley Falls, Village of v. Buchman, 179 Misc.2d 840, 686 N.Y.S.2d 693 (N.Y.Sup. 1999)—§ 14.61.
Vancol, People v., 166 Misc.2d 93, 631 N.Y.S.2d 996 (N.Y.Just.Ct.1995)—§ 33.72, n. 1; § 33.90A, n. 1.
Van Vlack v. Van Vlack, 233 A.D.2d 895, 649 N.Y.S.2d 255 (N.Y.A.D. 4 Dept. 1996)—§ 21.5, n. 1.
VDR Realty Corp. v. Mintz, 167 A.D.2d 986, 562 N.Y.S.2d 7 (N.Y.A.D. 4 Dept.1990)—§ 28.10, n. 15.
Velaire v. City of Schenectady, 235 A.D.2d 647, 651 N.Y.S.2d 735 (N.Y.A.D. 3 Dept. 1997)—§ 18.25, n. 5.
Village of (see name of village)
Vizcaino, Matter of, 19 I. & N. Dec. 644, Interim Decision (BIA) 3061 (BIA 1988)—§ 19.10.
Vogel v. Lyman, 246 A.D.2d 422, 668 N.Y.S.2d 162 (N.Y.A.D. 1 Dept.1998)—§ 28.11; § 28.11, n. 18; § 28.13, n. 11.

Volpe v. Canfield, 237 A.D.2d 282, 654 N.Y.S.2d 160 (N.Y.A.D. 2 Dept.1997)—§ 28.3, n. 1.
Vouniozos v. Helmsley–Spear, Inc., 257 A.D.2d 440, 683 N.Y.S.2d 512 (N.Y.A.D. 1 Dept.1999)—§ 30.30, n. 15.7.

W

Walker v. New York City, 694 N.Y.S.2d 2 (N.Y.A.D. 1 Dept.1999)—§ 30.41.
Wall Street Associates v. Brodsky, 257 A.D.2d 526, 684 N.Y.S.2d 244 (N.Y.A.D. 1 Dept.1999)—§ 28.3, n. 1.
Wal–Mart Stores Inc. v. Planning Bd. of Town of North Elba, 238 A.D.2d 93, 668 N.Y.S.2d 774 (N.Y.A.D. 3 Dept.1998)—§ 16.125.
Walter D. Peek Inc. v. Agee, 235 A.D.2d 790, 652 N.Y.S.2d 359 (N.Y.A.D. 3 Dept. 1997)—§ 28.18A; § 28.18A, n. 3.
Warner v. Orange County Dept. of Probation, 115 F.3d 1068 (2nd Cir.1996)—§ 18.28; § 18.28, n. 14; § 18.34, n. 3.
Warney v. McMahon Martine & Gallagher, 1996 WL 339997 (S.D.N.Y.1996)—§ 28.14, n. 8.
Washington v. Glucksberg, 521 U.S. 702, 117 S.Ct. 2258, 138 L.Ed.2d 772 (1997)—§ 23.113; § 23.113, n. 3.
Weed v. Meyers, 251 A.D.2d 1062, 674 N.Y.S.2d 242 (N.Y.A.D. 4 Dept.1998)—§ 30.9, n. 14.1.
Westfield, Village of v. Welch's, 170 F.3d 116 (2nd Cir.1999)—§ 18.36, n. 12.
Weyant v. Okst, 101 F.3d 845 (2nd Cir. 1996)—§ 18.22, n. 2.
White Trailer Corp., In re, 222 B.R. 322 (Bkrtcy.N.D.Ind.1998)—§ 9.19, n. 6.
Whitfield v. City of New York, 666 N.Y.S.2d 545, 689 N.E.2d 515 (N.Y.1997)—§ 39.4, n. 14; § 39.5, n. 4.
Whiting v. Incorporated Village of Old Brookville, 8 F.Supp.2d 202 (E.D.N.Y. 1998)—§ 18.55, n. 7; § 18.60, n. 5.
Wiggins, Matter of Estate of, 200 A.D.2d 813, 606 N.Y.S.2d 423 (N.Y.A.D. 3 Dept. 1994)—§ 25.47, n. 2.
Williams v. Hertzwig, 251 A.D.2d 655, 675 N.Y.S.2d 113 (N.Y.A.D. 2 Dept.1998)—§ 16.48.
Williams v. Key Service Corp., 257 A.D.2d 778, 684 N.Y.S.2d 19 (N.Y.A.D. 3 Dept. 1999)—§ 32.23, n. 4.
Willis, In re, 230 B.R. 619 (Bkrtcy. E.D.Okla.1999)—§ 9.18, n. 2.
Wilson v. Town of Mohawk, 246 A.D.2d 762, 668 N.Y.S.2d 62 (N.Y.A.D. 3 Dept. 1998)—§ 16.46.
Wilson v. Wilson, 244 A.D.2d 646, 663 N.Y.S.2d 710 (N.Y.A.D. 3 Dept.1997)—§ 21.5, n. 1.

TABLE OF CASES

Wisconsin Dept. of Corrections v. Schacht, 524 U.S. 381, 118 S.Ct. 2047, 141 L.Ed.2d 364 (1998)—§ 18.33, n. 5.1.
Wise, People v., 141 Misc.2d 409, 532 N.Y.S.2d 833 (N.Y.Dist.Ct.1988)—§ 33.75, n. 1.
Wohlers, People v., 138 A.D.2d 957, 526 N.Y.S.2d 290 (N.Y.A.D. 4 Dept.1988)—§ 33.5, n. 8.
Wooley, People v., 249 A.D.2d 46, 671 N.Y.S.2d 58 (N.Y.A.D. 1 Dept.1998)—§ 18.15, n. 9.
Wright, People v., 635 N.Y.S.2d 136, 658 N.E.2d 1009 (N.Y.1995)—§ 33.40; § 33.40, n. 0.1.

Y

Yancey v. Apfel, 145 F.3d 106 (2nd Cir. 1998)—§ 34.37.
Yonkers, City of, United States v., 96 F.3d 600 (2nd Cir.1996)—§ 18.33, n. 2.

Z

Zagorsky, People v., 73 Misc.2d 420, 341 N.Y.S.2d 791 (N.Y.Co.Ct.1973)—§ 33.72, n. 1; § 33.75, n. 1.
Zaref v. Berk & Michaels, P.C., 192 A.D.2d 346, 595 N.Y.S.2d 772 (N.Y.A.D. 1 Dept. 1993)—§ 28.14, n. 8.
Zaremba v. Zaremba, 222 A.D.2d 500, 635 N.Y.S.2d 532 (N.Y.A.D. 2 Dept.1995)—§ 21.55.
Zarin v. Reid & Priest, 184 A.D.2d 385, 585 N.Y.S.2d 379 (N.Y.A.D. 1 Dept.1992)—§ 28.10, n. 5, 11.
Zatz v. Moscovici, 258 A.D.2d 850, 686 N.Y.S.2d 167 (N.Y.A.D. 3 Dept.1999)—§ 32.15.
Zervakis v. Kyreakedes, 257 A.D.2d 619, 684 N.Y.S.2d 291 (N.Y.A.D. 2 Dept. 1999)—§ 30.39, n. 5.1.

INDEX

ACCUSATORY INSTRUMENTS
Supporting depositions
  Attorney affirmation in support of motion
    Updated form, § 33.100
  Notice of motion to dismiss for failure to serve a timely supporting deposition
    Attorney affirmation in support of motion
      Updated form, § 33.100

ADOPTION
Private
  Consent of legal parents
    Extra-judicial consent
      Form, § 20.136

AFFIDAVITS
Immigration visa, affidavits of support, § 19.55

CIVIL RIGHTS
Confidentiality of genetic test results, § 18.86a
Genetic tests, confidentiality of records, § 18.86a
Miscellaneous rights and immunities
  Genetic tests, confidentiality of records, § 18.86a

CONFIDENTIALITY
Genetic tests results, § 18.86a

CORPORATIONS
Authorized person, defined, § 1.5

DEFINITIONS
Authorized person, § 1.5

EVIDENCE
Real property conveyance, acknowledgment and proof, form, § 12.99

FORECLOSURE
Article 14, Real Property Actions and Proceedings Law
  Generally, §§ 11.8a et seq.
  Applicability, §§ 11.8b, 11.8c
  Commencement, § 11.8d
  Conducting sale, § 11.8i
  Conversion from non-judicial foreclosure to judicial foreclosure, § 11.8o
  Distribution of proceeds of non-judicial sale, § 11.8k

FORECLOSURE—Cont'd
Article 14—Cont'd
  Notice of sale
    Generally, §§ 11.8f et seq.
    Publication of notice of sale, § 11.8h
    Service of notice of sale, § 11.8g
  Power of sale deed, conveyance of property by, § 11.8j
  Purchase of index number and filing of notice of pendency, § 11.8d
  Receivership under Article 14, § 11.8n
  Report of non-judicial sale, § 11.8l
  Surplus money and deficiency judgment proceedings under Article 14, § 11.8m

GENETIC TESTS
Confidentiality of genetic test results, § 18.86a

IMMIGRATION
Affidavits of support, § 19.55
Application for permanent residency
  Immigrant visa processing
    Adjustment of status, affidavits of support, § 19.55
Forms
  OF-230, updated form, § 19.79

LEGAL MALPRACTICE
Damages
  Breach of fiduciary duty, § 28.26A
  Defenses, contributory fault and mitigation of damages, § 28.18A
Defenses
  Client responsibility, § 28.18A
  Contributory fault and mitigation of damages, § 28.18A
Release of malpractice claim, § 28.18B

LIMITATION OF ACTIONS
Municipal corporations, breach of contract, § 3.24

LOCAL CRIMINAL COURTS
Traffic infractions accompanied by misdemeanors or felonies, § 33.76

MUNICIPAL CORPORATIONS
Limitation of actions, breach of contract, § 3.24

NON-JUDICIAL FORECLOSURE
Commercial mortgages. Foreclosure, this index

INDEX

NOTICE OF INTENTION
Foreclosure, § 11.8e

NOTICE OF SALE
Foreclosure, this index

REAL PROPERTY
Foreclosure, this index
Purchase and sale
  Acknowledgment and proof of conveyance, form, § 12.99
  Closing of title
    Payment of taxes
      East Hampton, § 12.86a
      Peconic Bay region, § 12.86a

REAL PROPERTY—Cont'd
Purchase and sale—Cont'd
  Closing of title—Cont'd
    Payment of taxes—Cont'd
      Riverhead, § 12.86a
      Shelter Island, § 12.86a
      Southhampton, § 12.86a
      Southold, § 12.86a
      Suffolk County, § 12.86a
  Evidence and acknowledgment of conveyance, form, § 12.99

SPEEDY TRIAL
Traffic infractions, § 33.90A

TRAFFIC OFFENSES
Misdemeanors or felonies, traffic infractions accompanied by, § 33.76
Speedy trial right, § 33.90A